AMERICAN SONG

The Complete
Musical Theatre Companion

AMERICAN SONG

The Complete Musical Theatre Companion

SECOND EDITION, 1877–1995

VOLUME 2: T-Z AND INDEXES

KEN BLOOM

SCHIRMER BOOKS
An Imprint of Simon & Schuster Macmillan
New York

PRENTICE HALL INTERNATIONAL
London Mexico City New Delhi Singapore Sydney Toronto

Schirmer Books
An Imprint of Simon & Schuster Macmillan
1633 Broadway
New York, NY 10019

Library of Congress Catalog Card Number: 95–49840

Set ISBN: 0–02–870484–3
Volume 1: 0–02–864573–1
Volume 2: 0–02–864572–3

Printed in the United States of America

Printing Number
1 2 3 4 5 6 7 8 9 10

Library of Congress Cataloging-in-Publication Data

Bloom, Ken, 1949–
American song : the complete musical theatre companion / Ken Bloom. —2nd ed.
p. cm.
ISBN 0–02–864573–1 (v. 1). — ISBN 0–02–864572–3 (v. 2)
1. Musicals—United States—Bibliography. 2. Songs, English––United States—Indexes. I. Title.
ML128.M78B6 1996
782.1'4'0973—dc20 95–49840
CIP
MN

This paper meets the requirements of ANSI/NISO Z39.48–1992 (Permanence of Paper).

Introduction

Volume 2 includes three indexes to *American Song*. The first is a list of the people, both performers and technical personnel, involved. The second is a complete list of the songs of the American musical. The third index lists all shows' titles by year.

Please note that references are to record numbers, not page numbers. Whole words are alphabetized before combinations of words; punctuation is generally ignored. The abbreviation "inst." or "Dance" indicates an instrumental number and is not part of the song's name. Alternate titles or expanded titles are included in parentheses.

Because there are more than 70,000 songs in the song index, size limitations prohibited including the names of composers and lyricists with the song titles. While numerous songs appeared in more than one show, bear in mind that several different songs may share the same song title. When I could identify distinct songs with the same title in the same show, I have noted them as (1) or (2), but please understand that song titles with multiple record numbers may refer either to the same song in different shows or different songs sharing the same title. I tried to cross-reference songs as much as possible, but I may well have missed some songs that appeared in more than one show. Note, too, that programs may have referred to the same song with slightly different titles, so if you cannot find a song under a title you know, consult different variations.

The name index includes more than 27,000 people. However, each participant's function is listed separately; for example, there are separate index entries for George Abbott (Director), George Abbott (Librettist), and George Abbott (Producer). Companies and groups are listed where appropriate. All the personnel whose names appear in Volume 1 are listed. To make the index more user friendly, I listed entries like "Benny Goodman and His Orchestra" under "Goodman and His Orchestra, Benny."

I have tried as much as possible to refrain from tampering with the credited spelling of names. At different points in their careers actors, directors, writers, producers, and others use variants of their names. Each variation must be looked up to get a complete list of credits. For example, although "Al Goodman" and "Alfred Goodman" are the same person, entries appear under both forms depending on his program billing. Listings will be found for "Sam H. Harris" and also for "Sam Harris." Sometimes two people share the same name, for example, Ronald Graham and Ronny Graham. And take the example of company member Elizabeth Taylor, not the movie star! For people who have changed their names during their careers or used pseudonyms, I have cross-references in the index. For example "June Carroll" and "June Sillman" are cross-referenced.

Correct spelling of names is problematic because of the wide diversity in printed records and early programs. Lyricists' and composers' names were all checked, when possible, with ASCAP or BMI records. Other names were checked through a variety of sources. I feel secure that all spellings are correct ... with three possible exceptions: "Frank Saddler" appears an equal number of times as "Frank Sadler." "Jack Squire" also appears as "Jack Squires." And "Caroline Siedel" also appears as "Carol Siedle" and "Caroline Seidle." For these three names, I haven't been able to determine the correct spelling.

The chronological list of titles offers the reader the opportunity to gain a sense of the development of American musical theatre year by year. As noted in the Introduction to Volume 1, all Broadway, off-Broadway, and off-off-Broadway productions from 1877 to fall 1995 are included, together with all resident theatre productions of shows by major artists, shows that toured the country, shows that closed out-of-town, English and French productions of shows by major American songwriters, important revues, nightclub and vaudeville shows, touring shows, and straight plays with single

songs. When looking through the dates in this index you will notice dates like "00/00/1934." The zeros indicate that the exact opening date is not known; available records indicate only the year a particular show opened. Sometimes little is known except a year or maybe a month and a year. These shows turn up prior to the listings for January of each year.

KEN BLOOM
New York City
October 1995

Contents

T

4261 • T*TS D*AMOND

OPENED: 01/1977
Musical

Composer: Lee Pockriss
Lyricist: Steve Brown
Librettist: Mark Bramble

Notes: Produced at The Loft.

4262 • TABLE NUMBER SEVEN

Musical Unproduced

Composer: Charles Burr
Lyricist: Charles Burr

Source: SEPARATE TABLES (Play Terrance Rattigan)

Songs: Hum Along; I Could Still Try; I Met My Love; Not a Thing in the Papers Anymore!; Not of This World; Other People's Waltzes; Separate Tables; Small Talk; Up in My Room

4263 • TABOO REVUE

Notes: *See TIMOTHY GRAY'S TABOO REVUE.*

4264 • TAFFETAS, THE

OPENED: 04/09/1989 Theatre: Cherry Lane
Musical Off-Broadway: 165

Producer: James Shellenberger; Arthur Whitelaw
Director: Steve Harris

Choreographer: Tina Paul; **Costumes:** David Graden; **Lighting Designer:** Ken Billington; **Musical Director:** Rick Lewis; **Set Design:** Evelyn Sakash; **Vocal Arranger:** Rick Lewis

Songs: Achoo Cha-Cha (Gesundheit) (C/L: Michael Merlo; Patrick Welch); Allegheny Moon (C/L: Al Hoffman; Dick Manning); Around the World (C: Victor Young; L: Harold Adamson); Arriverderci Roma (C: R. Rascel; L: Giovanni; Carl Sigman); C-o-n-s- t-a-n-t-i-n-o-p-l-e (C/L: Harry Carlton); C'Est Si Bon (C: Henri Betti; L: Honeg; Jerry Seelen); Cry (C/L: Churchill Kohlman); Dedicated to the One I Love (C/L: Ralph Bass; Lowman Pauling); Happy Wanderer, The (Val-De Ri, Val-De Ra) (C: Friedrich Wilhelm Moeller; L: Antonia Ridge); Hot Canary, The (C: Peter Nero; L: Ray Gilbert); How Much Is That Doggy in the Window (C/L: Bob Merrill); I Cried (C/L: Unknown); I-M-4-U (C: Jose Melis; L: F. Marino); I'll Think of You (C/L: Clint Ballard Jr.; Noel Sherman); I'm Sorry (C/L: Dub Albritton; Bonnie Self); Johnny Angel (C/L: Lyn Duddy; Lee Pockriss); L-O-V-E (C/L: Milt Gabler; Bert Kaempfert); Little Darlin' (C/L: Maurice Williams); Lollipop (C/L: Julius Dixon; Beverly Ross); Love Is a Two-Way Street (C/L: J. Keller; Noel Sherman); Love Letters in the Sand (C: J. Fred Coots; L: Charles Kenny; Nick Kenny); Mockin' Bird Hill (C/L: Vaughn Horton); Mr. Lee (C/L: Heather Dixon; Helen Gathers; Emma Ruth Pought; Jannie Pought; Laura Webb); Mr. Sandman (C/L: Pat Ballard); Music! Music! Music! (C/L: Bernie Baum; Stephen Weiss); My Little Grass Shack (C/L: Bill Cogswell; Tommy Harrison; Johnny Noble); Nel Blue di Pinto di Blue (Volare) (C/L: Dominic Modugno; L: Migliani; Mitchell Parish); Old Cape Cod (C/L: Claire Rathrock; Milt Yakus; C: Allan Jeffrey; L: Alan Jeffrey); Oop Shoop (C/L: Joe Josea); Puppy Love (C/L: Paul Anka); Rag Mop (C/L: Deacon Anderson; Lee Wills); Ricochet (C: Larry Coleman; L: Joe Darion; Norman Gimbel); See the U.S.A. in Your Chevrolet (C/L: Leon Carr; Leo Corday); Sh-Boom (C/L: James Edwards; Carl Feaster; Claude Feaster; James Keyes; Floyd F. McRae); Sincerely (C/L: Alan Freed; Harvey Fuqua); Smile (C/L: Charlie Chaplin; Geoffrey Parsons; John Turner); Sweet Song of India (C/L: Clayton; Kaye); Tennessee Waltz (C/L: Pee Wee King; Red Stewart); Three Bells, The (C/L: Bert Reisfeld; Jean Villard); Tonight You Belong to Me (C: Lee David; L: Billy Rose); Tweedle Dee (C/L: Winfield Scott); Where the Boys Are (C/L: Howard Greenfield; Neil Sedaka); You Belong to Me (C/L: Pee Wee King; Chilton Price; Red Stewart); You, You, You (C: Lotar Olias; L: Robert Mellin; R. Olias); You're Just in Love (C/L: Irving Berlin)

Cast: Jody Abrahams; Karen Curlee; Melanie Mitchell; Tia Speros

Notes: No original songs in this show.

4265 • TAKE A BOW

OPENED: 06/15/1944 Theatre: Broadhurst
Revue Broadway: 12

Producer: Lou Walters
Director: Wally Wenger

Choreographer: Marjery Fielding; **Costumes:** Ben Wallace; **Musical Director:** Ray Kavanaugh; **Set Design:** Kaj Velden

Songs: Take a Bow (C: Ted Murry; L: Benny Davis)

Cast: Jay C. Flippen; Chico Marx; Pat Rooney; Gene Sheldon

4266 • TAKE A CHANCE (1923)

Notes: *See GINGER.*

4267 • TAKE A CHANCE (1932)

OPENED: 11/26/1932 Theatre: Apollo
Musical Broadway: 243

Composer: Nacio Herb Brown; Richard A. Whiting
Lyricist: B.G. DeSylva
Librettist: B.G. DeSylva; Laurence Schwab
Producer: B.G. DeSylva; Laurence Schwab
Director: Edgar MacGregor

Choreographer: Bobby Connolly; **Costumes:** Kiviette; Charles LeMaire; **Musical Director:** Max Meth; **Orchestrations:** Robert Russell Bennett; William Daly; Stephen Jones; Edward Powell; **Set Design:** Cleon Throckmorton; **Vocal Arranger:** Roger Edens

Songs: Charity; Eadie Was a Lady; Humpty-Dumpty [1]; I Got Religion (C: Vincent Youmans); I Want to Be with You [1] (C: Vincent Youmans); I'm Way Ahead of the Game [1]; Life of the Party, The; My Lover [2] (C: Vincent Youmans); Night, Hold Back the Dawn [1]; Oh How I Long to Belong to You (C: Vincent Youmans); Rise 'N' Shine [4] (C: Vincent Youmans); She's Nuts About Me; Should I Be Sweet (C: Vincent Youmans); So Do I (C: Vincent Youmans); Tickled Pink; Tonight Is Opening Night; Turn Out the Light; You're an Old Smoothie [3]

Cast: Josephine Dunn; Jack Haley; June Knight; Mitzi Mayfair; Ethel Merman; Oscar "Rags" Ragland; Sid Silvers; Jack Whiting; Douglas Wood

Notes: Titled HUMPTY DUMPTY during tryout. [1] Cut. [2] Cut. Music same as "Blue Bowery" from SMILES. [3] Also in London show NICE GOINGS ON. [4] Later interpolated into RISE AND SHINE (London).

4268 • TAKE FIVE

OPENED: 10/10/1957 Theatre: Upstairs at the Downstairs
Revue Nightclub

Librettist: Don Adams; Dee Caruso; Bill Levine; Steven Vinaver
Producer: Julius Monk
Director: Max Adrian; John Heawood

Vocal Arranger: Stan Keen

Songs: Cast Call (C/L: Stan Keen); Doing the Psycho- Neurotique (C/L: Ronny Graham); Gossiping Grapevine (C/L: Edward C. Redding); Gristedes (C: Jonathan Tunick; L: Steven Vinaver); Perfect Stranger (C/L: Bart Howard); Portofino [2] (C/L: Michael Brown); Pour Le Sport [1] (C/L: Stephen Sondheim); Pro Musica Antiqua, The (C: Jonathan Tunick; L: Steven Vinaver); Upstairs at the Downstairs Waltz (C/L: Bart Howard); Westport! (C: Philip Springer; L: Carolyn Leigh); Witchcraft (C/L: Michael Brown)

Cast: Jean Arnold; Ceil Cabot; Ronny Graham; Ellen Hanley; Gerry Matthews; **Pianist:** Gordon Connell; Stan Keen

Notes: [1] Written for unproduced show THE LAST RESORTS. [2] Also in DEMI-DOZEN.

4269 • TAKE IT FROM ME

OPENED: 03/31/1919 Theatre: 44th Street
Musical Broadway: 96

Composer: Will R. Anderson
Lyricist: Will B. Johnstone

Librettist: Will B. Johnstone
Producer: Joseph M. Gaites
Director: Fred A. Bishop; Joseph Gaites; Joseph C. Smith

Costumes: S. Zalud; **Musical Director:** George Trinkaus

Songs: Call of the Cozy Little Home, The; Camouflage; Explanations; From Then and Now [1]; Good, Bad, Beautiful Broadway; I Like to Linger in the Lingerie; It's Different Now [1]; Kiss, The; Movie Music; Opening Act I; Penny for Your Thoughts, A; Take It from Me; Tanglefoot, The; Tip Toe [1]; To Have and to Hold; Tomorrow; Vampire Dance (inst.); What Makes the Tired Businessman So Tired

Cast: Dorothy Betts; Fred Hillebrand; Ed Leech; Jack McGowan; Vera Michelena

Notes: [1] Out Washington, D.C. 12/22/18.

4270 • TAKE ME ALONG

OPENED: 10/22/1959 Theatre: Shubert
Musical Broadway: 448

Composer: Bob Merrill
Lyricist: Bob Merrill
Librettist: Robert Russell; Joseph Stein
Producer: David Merrick
Director: Peter Glenville

Source: AH, WILDERNESS! (Play: Eugene O'Neill); **Choreographer:** Onna White; **Costumes:** Miles White; **Dance Arranger:** Laurence Rosenthal; **Lighting Designer:** Jean Rosenthal; **Musical Director:** Lehman Engel; **Orchestrations:** Philip J. Lang; **Set Design:** Oliver Smith; **Vocal Arranger:** Lehman Engel

Songs: Beardsley Ballet (dance); But Yours; Company of Men, The [6]; Hurt They Write About, The [2]; I Get Embarrassed; I Would Die; If Jesus Don't Love You [3]; Knights on White Horses [3]; Little Green Snake; Marvelous Fire Machine [5]; Nine O'Clock; Oh Please; Parade, The [4]; Patience of a Saint [2]; Promise Me a Rose (A Slight Detail); Sid, Ol' Kid; Staying Young; Take Me Along; That Man's Wife [7]; That's How It Starts; Thinkin' Things [1]; Volunteer Fireman Picnic (For Sweet Charity) (The Only Pair I've Got); We're Home; Wint's Song (Pleasant Beach House)

Cast: Peter Conlow; James Cresson; Arlene Galonka; Jackie Gleason; Luke Halpin; Valerie Harper; Eileen Herlie; Susan Luckey; Una Merkel; Robert Morse; Zeme North; Walter Pidgeon; Gene Varrone

Notes: *See also AH! WILDERNESS.* [1] Not used. [2] Added to 1984 Off-Off-Broadway revival. [3] Added to 9/15/84 Goodspeed revival. [4] Same song as "Marvelous Fire Machine." [5] Added to 9/15/84 Goodspeed revival. Same song as "The Parade." [6] Added to Off-Off-Broadway and Goodspeed revivals. [7] Out Boston 9/7/59.

4271 • TAKE THE AIR

OPENED: 11/22/1927 Theatre: Waldorf
Musical Broadway: 208

Composer: Dave Stamper
Lyricist: Gene Buck
Librettist: Anne Caldwell
Producer: Gene Buck
Director: Alexander Leftwich

Choreographer: Ralph Reader; **Costumes:** Charles LeMaire; Cora MacGeachy; Lucille McCorder; **Lighting Designer:** Frank Detering; **Musical Director:** Charles Drury; **Set Design:** William Oden-Waller

Songs: All Aboard for Times Square; All I Want Is a Lullaby; Aviation Ballet; Carmela; Carmen Has Nothing on Me [1]; Ham and Eggs in the Morning (C: Con Conrad; Abner Silver; L: Al Dubin); Japanese Moon; Just Like a Wild, Wild, Rose; Maybe I'll Baby You; On a Pony for Two (C: James F. Hanley); Silver Wings; Take the Air; Tango Espagnol; We'd Rather Dance than Eat; We'll Have a New Home in the Morning (C/L: Gene Buck; J. Russel Robinson; Willard Robison); Wild and Wooly West, The

Cast: Greek Evans; Will Mahoney; Trini

Notes: [1] Also in ZIEGFELD MIDNIGHT FROLIC (6th Edition).

4272 • TAKING MY TURN

OPENED: 06/09/1983 Theatre: Entermedia
Revue Off-Broadway: 345

Composer: Gary William Friedman
Lyricist: Will Holt

Producer: Joanne Cummings; Sonny Fox; Anthony Kane; Arleen Kane; Maurice Levine; Richard Seader; Sally Sears
Director: Robert H. Livingston

Choreographer: Douglas Norwick; **Costumes:** Judith Dolan; **Lighting Designer:** David F. Segal; **Musical Director:** Barry Levitt; **Orchestrations:** Gary William Friedman; **Set Design:** Clarke Dunham; **Vocal Arranger:** Gary William Friedman

Songs: Do You Remember?; Fine for the Shape I'm In; Good Luck to You; I Am Not Old; I Like It; I Never Made Money from Music; In April; In the House; It Still Isn't Over; Janet Get Up; Kite, The; Pick More Daisies; Somebody Else; Sweet Longings; Taking Our Turn; This Is My Song; Two of Me; Vivaldi

Cast: Mace Barrett; Victor Griffin; Tiger Haynes; Cissy Houston; Marni Nixon; Sheila Smith; Ted Thurston; Margaret Whiting

4273 • TALENT 50

OPENED: 04/28/1950 Theatre: Guild
Revue Broadway: 1

Producer: Monroe B. Hack; Stage Managers Club
Director: Michael Ellis; Monroe Hack; George Hunter; David Jones; Ben Krany; Samuel Liff

Choreographer: Ted Cappy; Betty Lind; Patricia Newman; Vivian Smith; **Musical Director:** Herbert Kingsley

Songs: Big Top Parade (C: Jerry Bock; L: Larry Holofcener); Dear Old College Days (C: Jerry Bock; L: Fred Tobias); I Laughed at Spring (C: Don Gohman; L: Brown Furlow); Lil Ole Letter (C: Herbert Kingsley; L: Langston Hughes); New York Is Not a Town (C: Earl Cobb; L: John Morris); Outside Looking In (C/L: William Hunt); This Is Finale (C: Phil Kadison; L: Thomas B. Howell); Visions on Your Television Screen (C: Jerry Bock; L: Fred Tobias); We've Got a Date with Spring (C: Phil Kadison; L: Alice Hammerstein); We've Got Talent (C/L: William Hunt); When I Bounce Off to Bed (C: George Engles; L: Lowell Saloway); When We're Dancing (C/L: Elise Bretton; Sherman Edwards; Don Meyer)

Cast: Raimonda Arselli; Pat Carroll; Gene Kelley; Jay Lloyd; Janice Rule; Hiram Sherman; Swen Swenson

4274 • TALES OF PERICHOLE

Musical Unproduced

Composer: Jacques Offenbach
Lyricist: Ray Evans; Jay Livingston

Notes: No other information available.

4275 • TALES OF RIGO

OPENED: 05/30/1927 Theatre: Lyric
Play Broadway: 8

Composer: Ben Schwartz
Lyricist: Ben Schwartz
Author: Maurice V. Samuels
Producer: J. Oppenheimer
Director: Clarence Derwent

Source: UNKNOWN (Story: Hyman Adler); **Costumes:** Mahieu; **Set Design:** August Vimnera

Songs: I'll Tell You All Someday; In Romany; Little Princess; Rigo's Last Lullaby (C/L: Evelyn Adler); What Care We? (Song of Destiny); Zita

Cast: Hyman Adler; Madeline Grey; Mira Nirska; Warren Sterling

4276 • TALK ABOUT GIRLS

OPENED: 06/14/1927 Theatre: Waldorf
Musical Broadway: 15

Composer: Harold Orlob
Lyricist: Irving Caesar
Librettist: William Cary Duncan; Daniel Kussell
Producer: Sam H. Grisman; Harry Oshrin
Director: Daniel Kussell

Source: LIKE A KING (Play: John Hunter Booth); **Choreographer:** Sammy Lee

Songs: All the Time Is Loving Time; Come to Lower Falls; Home Town; In Central Park; In Twos; Lonely Girl, A; Love Birds [1]; Maybe I Will; Nineteen Twenty-Seven; One Boy's Enough for Me; Only Boy, The; Oo, How I Love You; Sex Appeal; Talk About Girls (C: Stephen Jones); That's My Man

Cast: William Frawley; Marilyn Killeen; Russell Mack; Jane Taylor; Andrew Tombes; Frances Upton

Notes: No program available. A reworking of SUZANNE. See that entry. [1] ASCAP only.

4277 • TALK OF NEW YORK, THE

OPENED: 12/03/1907 Theatre: Knickerbocker
Musical Broadway: 157

Composer: George M. Cohan
Lyricist: George M. Cohan
Librettist: George M. Cohan
Producer: George M. Cohan; Sam H. Harris
Director: George M. Cohan

Costumes: F. Richard Anderson; **Musical Director:** August Kleinecke; **Orchestrations:** Charles J. Gebest

Songs: Burning Up the Boulevard; Busy Little Broadway; Claremont; Drink with Me; Follow Your Uncle Dudley; Gee, Ain't I Glad I'm Home!; I Have a Longing for Long Acre Square [2]; I Want the World to Know I Love You; I Want You; Mr. Burns of New Rochelle; Put a Little Bet Down for Me; That's Some Love [1]; Under Any Old Flag at All; When a Fellow's on the Level with a Girl That's on the Square; When We Are M-A-Double-R-I-E-D

Cast: Jack Gardner; Emma Littlefield; Victor Moore; Gertrude Vanderbilt

Notes: [1] Out of town. Also in THE AMERICAN IDEA. [2] Sheet music only.

4278 • TALL STORY

OPENED: 01/29/1959 Theatre: Belasco
Play Broadway: 108

Composer: Ben G. Allen; Joe Hornsby; Jerry Teifer
Lyricist: Ben G. Allen; Joe Hornsby; Jerry Teifer
Author: Russel Crouse; Howard Lindsay
Producer: Emmett Rogers; Robert Weiner
Director: Herman Shumlin

Source: HOMECOMING GAME, THE (Novel: Howard Nemerov); **Arrangements:** Edward Thomas; **Costumes:** Noel Taylor; **Lighting Designer:** George Jenkins; **Set Design:** George Jenkins

Songs: That's My Daisy (C/L: Ben G. Allen; Mike Hansen; Joe Hornsby)

Cast: Mason Adams; John Astin; Marc Connelly; Hans Conreid; Robert Elston; Rex Everhart; Nina Wilson; Marian Winters; Robert Wright

Notes: No songs listed in program.

4279 • TALLULAH

OPENED: 10/30/1983 Theatre: West Side Arts Center
Musical Off-Broadway: 42

Composer: Arthur Siegel
Lyricist: Mae Richard
Librettist: Tony Lang
Producer: John Van Ness Philip; Mark deSolla Price; Leonard Soloway; David Susskind
Director: David Holdgrive

Choreographer: David Holdgrive; **Costumes:** John Falabella; **Lighting Designer:** Ken Billington; **Musical Director:** Bruce W. Coyle; **Set Design:** John Falabella; **Vocal Arranger:** Bruce W. Coyle

Songs: Darling; Don't Ever Book a Trip on the IRT; Home Sweet Home; I Can See Him Clearly; If Only He Were a Woman; I'm the Woman You Wanted; It's a Hit; It's in the Cards [1]; I've Got to Try Everything Once; Love Is on Its Knees; Party Is Where I Am, The; Stay Awhile; Tallulah; Talullahbaloo; When I Do a Dance for You; You Need a Lift!; You're You

Cast: Joel Craig; Helen Gallagher; Russell Nype

Notes: [1] Not used.

4280 • TAMBOURITA

OPENED: 1949
Musical Unproduced

Composer: Ernesto Lecuona
Lyricist: John Latouche
Librettist: Milton Herbert Gropper
Producer: Reginald Hammerstein

Notes: Apparently no score exists since Latouche's family destoryed his papers at his death.

4281 • TAN MANHATTAN

OPENED: 1941
Revue Closed out of town

Composer: Eubie Blake
Lyricist: Andy Razaf
Producer: Irvin C. Miller
Director: Irvin C. Miller

Choreographer: Addison Carey; Henry LeTang

Songs: Dixie Ann in Afghanistan; Dollar for a Dime; Down By the Railroad Track; Great Big Baby; Hep Cat, The; I'm Toein' the Line; Nickel for a Dime, A; Say Hello to the Folks Back Home; Shakin' Up the Folks Below; Sweet Magnolia Rose; Tan Manhattan; We Are Americans Too (C/L: Eubie Blake; Charles L. Cooke; Andy Razaf); With a Dream; Worry

Cast: Avon Long; Nina Mae McKinney; Flournoy Miller

Notes: Closed in Washington, D.C. No program available.

4282 • TAN TOWN TOPICS REVUE

OPENED: 1926
Revue

Producer: Cooper & Rector

Songs: Charleston Hound; I've Found a New Baby; Senorita Mine (C: Thomas "Fats" Waller; Clarence Williams; L: Eddie Rector; Spencer Williams)

Notes: No other information available.

4283 • TANGERINE

OPENED: 08/09/1921 Theatre: Casino
Revue Broadway: 337

Composer: Monte Carlo; Alma Sanders
Lyricist: Howard E. Johnson
Librettist: Guy Bolton
Producer: Carle Carlton
Director: Bert French; George Marion

Source: UNKNOWN (Play: Philip Bartholomae; Lawrence Langner); **Costumes:** Dorothy Armstrong; Mme. Francis; Pieter Meyer; **Musical Director:** Max Steiner; **Set Design:** P. Dodd Ackerman; Lee Simonson

Songs: Asbury Park (L: Monte Carlo); Baccanale Dance; Civilization; Dance Tangerine; Give Me Your Love [2] (L: Monte Carlo); Hallucination of Love [1] (L: Monte Carlo); Idle House [1] (L: Monte Carlo); In Our Mountain Bower; Isle of Tangerine; It's a Sunbeam [1] (L: Monte Carlo); It's Great to Be Married (and Lead a Single Life); It's Only Your Carriage That Counts; Knit, Knit, Knit [2] (L: Monte Carlo); Listen to Me [2]; Listen to the Raindrops (L: Monte Carlo); Lords of Creation [1] (C: Jean Schwartz); Love Is a Business; Man Is the Lord of It All (C: Jean Schwartz); Multiplied by Eight; Multiplied by Six [2] (L: Monte Carlo); Old Melodies; Point to Bear in Mind, The [2] (L: Monte Carlo); Sea of the Tropics Dance; She Was Very Dear to Me (C/L: Benjamin Hapgood Burt); South Sea Island Blues; Stolen Sweets [2] (C: Carle Carleton; Monte Carlo; Alma Sanders); Sweet Lady (C: Dave Zoob; L: Frank Crumit); There's a Sunbeam for Every Drop of Rain; Tropic Love [1] (L: Monte Carlo); Tropic Vamps; Variety Is the Spice of Life [2] (L: Monte Carlo); Voice at the End of the Line, The [1] (L: Monte Carlo); We'll Never Grow Old; You and I Atta Baby [3]

Cast: Joseph Cawthorn; Frank Crumit; John E. Hazzard; Allen Kearns; Jeanette MacDonald; Harry Puck; Julia Sanderson

Notes: [1] Out Asbury Park 8/1/21. [2] Out Atlantic City 2/21/21. [3] Johnson wrote a song of the same name for ATTA BABY the next year.

4284 • TANGLETOES

OPENED: 02/17/1925 Theatre: 39th St.
Play Broadway: 23

Author: Gertrude Purcell
Producer: Edmund Plohn
Director: Hubert Druce; Edwin Maxwell

Songs: Tangletoes (C: Vincent Rose; L: Gertrude Purcell)

Cast: Walker Ellis; Morgan Farley; Mildred MacLeod; Beatrice Nichols

4285 • TANTALIZING TOMMY

OPENED: 10/01/1912 Theatre: Criterion
Musical Broadway: 31

Composer: Hugo Felix
Lyricist: Adrian Ross

Librettist: Paul Gavault; Michael Morton
Producer: A.H. Woods
Director: George Marion

Source: LA PETITE CHOCOLATIERE (Play : Paul Gavault); **Musical Director:** Hans S. Linne; **Set Design:** Percy Anderson

Songs: Ballad of the Seigneur; Cupid's Car; Fairy Bells; I Am a Tom-Boy; Irish Stew; Just Like You; Oh, Go Away; Opening Chorus Act I; Opening Chorus Act II; Opening Chorus Act III; Song, The; Tandem, A; This and That and the Other; You Don't Know; Zizi

Cast: George Anderson; Elizabeth Brice; Harry Clarke; Peggy Forsyth; Madeline Harrison; John Park

4286 • TAP DANCE KID, THE

OPENED: 12/21/1983 Theatre: Broadhurst
Musical Broadway: 669

Composer: Henry Krieger
Lyricist: Robert Lorick
Librettist: Charles Blackwell
Producer: Evelyn Barron; Harvey J. Klaris; Michel Stuart; Stanley White
Director: Vivian Matalon

Source: NOBODY'S FAMILY IS GOING TO CHANGE (Novel: Louise Fitzhugh); **Choreographer:** Danny Daniels; **Musical Director:** Don Jones; **Orchestrations:** Harold Wheeler; **Set Design:** Michael Hotopp; Paul dePass; **Vocal Arranger:** Harold Wheeler

Songs: Another Day; Class Act; Crosstown; Daddy Says, Mama Says [1]; Dance If It Makes You Happy; Dancing Is Everything; Dipsey's Coming Over [1]; Dipsey's Vaudeville (inst.) [1]; Fabulous Feet; Four Strikes Against Me; I Could Get Used to Him; I Remember How It Was; Like Him; Lullabye; Man in the Moon; My Luck Is Changing; Someday; Something Better, Something More [1]; Tap Tap; They Never Hear What I Say; William's Song

Cast: Martine Allard; Hinton Battle; Barbara Montgomery; Alfonso Ribeiro; Alan Weeks; Hattie Winston; Samuel E. Wright

Notes: [1] Added for post-Broadway tour.

4287 • TARS AND SPARS

OPENED: 05/05/1944
Revue

Composer: Vernon Duke
Lyricist: Howard Dietz
Librettist: Howard Dietz
Producer: Max Liebman; U.S. Coast Guard
Director: Max Liebman

Choreographer: Gower Champion; Ted Gary

Songs: Apprentice Seaman; Arm in Arm; Civilian; Farewell for a While; Palm Beach; Silver Shield

Cast: Sid Caesar; Gower Champion; Victor Mature

Notes: This was the Coast Guard's equivilent to THIS IS THE ARMY, AT EASE, etc. The show played the Strand Theatre and then toured the country. No program available.

4288 • TATTERDEMALION

OPENED: 10/27/1985 Theatre: Douglas Fairbanks
Musical Off-Broadway: 25

Composer: Judd Woldin
Lyricist: Judd Woldin
Librettist: Judd Woldin
Producer: Eric Krebs
Director: Eric Krebs

Source: KING OF SCHNORRERS, THE (Novel: Israel Zangwill); **Choreographer:** Mary Jane Houdina; **Costumes:** Patricia Adshead; **Dance Arranger:** Peter Howard; **Lighting Designer:** Whitney Quesenbery; **Musical Director:** Edward G. Robinson; **Orchestrations:** Robert M. Freedman; Judd Woldin; **Set Design:** Ed Wittstein; **Vocal Arranger:** Peter Howard

Songs: Blood Lines; Chutzpah; Dead; Each of Us; I Have Not Lived in Vain; I'm Only a Woman (L: Susan Birkenhead); It's Over (L: Herb Martin); Leave the Thinking to Me (L: Susan Birkenhead); Murder; Ordinary Man, An (L: Susan Birkenhead); Ours; Petticoat Lane; Tell Me (L: Susan Birkenhead; Judd Woldin); Well Done, Da Costa (L: Susan Birkenhead)

Cast: Robert Blumenfeld; Suzanne Briar; Annie McGreevey; Jack Sevier; Tia Speros; K.C. Wilson; Ron Wisinski; Stuart Zagnit

Notes: *See also KING OF SCHNORRERS,* an earlier version of this show.

4289 • TATTERED TOM

OPENED: 1968
Musical Unproduced

Composer: Ralph Blane; Hugh Martin
Lyricist: Ralph Blane; Hugh Martin

Source: TATTERED TOM (Novel: Horatio Alger)

Songs: Don't Trust Anyone; Flame Water; He's a Fallen Angel; Heigh Ho for Mother (Heigh Ho for a Husband); How Do I Feel; I Love Your Vibrato; Kind of Girl I'd Like to Be, The; Melting Pot, The; New York; New York's Good Morning Song; One Good Friend's Enough; Tattered Tom; Tony Pastor's; 2 Is Company; Two's Company; Up to My Elbows; What's His Name; When I Join the Circus; Whenever I'm with You; Women Are Here to Stay

4290 • TATTLE TALES (1920)

OPENED: 1920
Musical Closed out of town

Composer: Archie Gottler
Lyricist: Howard Johnson
Librettist: Jimmy Hussey
Producer: Jimmy Hussey

Songs: I'm an Indian Assassin [1]; I'm Out on Strike for a Beautiful Girl [1]; In Watermelon Time; Lead Me to Laughter [1]; Life Without a Cigarette [1]; Rose of the Rotisserie [1] (C: James F. Hanley; L: Joe Goodwin; Jimmy Hussey); Star Eyes; Taps [1]; Tattle Tales; Those Mason-Dixon Blues [1]; Tip-Tip Tippy Canoe [1]; When the Statues Come to Life [1]; You've Got to Keep on Moving [1]

Cast: Joe Browning; Cliff Edwards; Jimmy Hussey; Rae Samuels; Jean Tennyson

Notes: Program from Detroit. Later revised as THE WHIRL OF THE TOWN and THE MIMIC WORLD OF 1921. [1] Sheet music only.

4291 • TATTLE TALES (1933)

OPENED: 06/01/1933 Theatre: Broadhurst
Revue Broadway: 28

Librettist: Nick Copeland; Frank Fay
Producer: Frank Fay
Director: Frank Fay; John Lonergan

Choreographer: Danny Dare; John Lonergan; LeRoy Prinz; **Costumes:** Elizabeth Zook; **Musical Director:** Arnold Johnson; **Orchestrations:** Howard Jackson; Edward Ward; **Set Design:** Martin

Songs: Another Case of the Blues (C: Richard Myers; L: Johnny Mercer); Breaking Up a Rhythm (C: Edward Ward; L: George Waggoner); Counting Sheep, Counting the Hours [2] (C: Louis Alter; L: Max Lief; Nathaniel Lief); Court of Louis XIV, The (C: Howard Jackson); First Spring Day, The (C: Howard Jackson; L: Edward Eliscu); Hang Up Your Hat on Broadway (C: Edward Ward; L: Grossman; Silverstein; George Waggoner); Harlem Lullaby (C/L: Margot Milhelm; Willard Robison); Hasta Manana (So This Is Havana) (C: Howard Jackson); Here We Are Together (C: Edward Ward; L: Frank Fay; William Walsh); I'll Take an Option on You (C: Ralph Rainger; L: Leo Robin); Jig Saw Jamboree (C: Eddie Bienbryer; L: William Walsh); Just a Sentimental Tune (C: Louis Alter; L: Max Lief; Nathaniel Lief); Percy with Perseverance (C: Edward Ward; L: George Waggoner); Sing American Tunes (1) (C: Harry Akst; L: Edward Eliscu); Sing American Tunes (2) [1] (C: Edward Ward; L: Frank Fay; William Walsh); You Got to Do Better Than That (C/L: Unknown)

Cast: Mary Barnett; Nick Copeland; Les Crane; Don Cumming; Dorothy Dell; Edith Evans; Frank Fay; William Hargrave; Ray Mayer; Lillian Reynolds; Barbara Stanwyck

Notes: [1] Out Wilkes-Barre 1933. [2] Not used.

4292 • TATTOOED COUNTESS, THE

OPENED: 04/03/1961 Theatre: Barbizon-Plaza
Musical Off-Broadway: 4

Composer: Coleman Dowell
Lyricist: Coleman Dowell
Librettist: Coleman Dowell
Producer: Robert D. Feldstein; Dick Randall
Director: Robert K. Adams

Source: TATTOOED COUNTESS, THE (Novel: Carl Van Vechten); **Choreographer:** Alex

Palermo; **Costumes:** Bill Hargate; **Dance Arranger:** David Hollister; **Musical Director:** Phil Fradkin; **Orchestrations:** David Hollister; **Set Design:** Robert Soule

Songs: Advice; Autumn; Brushing Stone, The; Dusters, Goggles and Hats; Fin de Sickle; Gossip; Got to Find My Way; High Up; Home Town Girl; How She Glows; I Can Take It; Je M'em Fiche; Opening, The; Rolling Stone; Tattooed Woman; That's Her Life; These Acres; Too Old for Love; Too Young; Waterworks Madrigal, The; Woman's Much Better Off Alone, A; You Take Paris

Cast: Travis Hudson; Irene Manning; Coe Norton; John Stewart

4293 • TATTOOED MAN, THE

OPENED: 02/18/1907 Theatre: Criterion
Musical Broadway: 59

Composer: Victor Herbert
Lyricist: Harry B. Smith
Librettist: A.N.C. Fowler; Harry B. Smith
Producer: Charles Dillingham
Director: Julian Mitchell

Costumes: Caroline Siedle; **Musical Director:** Arthur Weld; **Orchestrations:** Victor Herbert

Songs: Awfully Nice to Love One Girl [1]; Bedouin Chief; Boys Will Be Boys (and Girls Will Be Girls); Entrance of Arabs; Entrance of Shah; Floral Wedding, The; Hear My Song of Love (Serenade); I Say What I Mean and I Mean What I Say [1]; I'm Not So Particular Now [1]; It's Awfully Nice to Love One Girl; Kitten That Couldn't Be Good [1]; Land of Dreams, The; Legend of the Djin, The; Muezzins and Bayaderres; Never, Never Land [1]; Nobody Loves Me; Omar Khayyam; Opening Chorus; Oriental March (Entrance of Omar); Sleep Sublime and Perfect Poet [1]; Snake Charmer's Dance; Take Things Easy; There's Just One Girl I'd Like to Marry; Things We Are Not Supposed to Know; Watch the Professor; Wedding of the Lily and the Rose [1]

Cast: William P. Carleton; Gertie Carlisle; Harry Clarke; Frank Daniels; Sallie Fisher; Bessie Holbrook; May Vokes; Herbert Waterous

Notes: Complete song list not in program. Songs from vocal score. [1] ASCAP/Library of Congress only.

4294 • TAXI TALES

OPENED: 12/28/1978 Theatre: Century
Play Off-Broadway: 6

Author: Leonard Melfi
Producer: Joe Regan
Director: Edward Berkeley

Costumes: Hilary Rosenfeld; **Lighting Designer:** Arden Fingerhut; **Set Design:** Hugh Landwehr

Songs: Taxi (C/L: Jonathan Hogan)

Cast: Paula Christopher; Al Corley; Julie DeLaurier; Dolly Jonah; Ken Olin; Michael Strong

4295 • TEANECK TANZI: THE VENUS FLYTRAP

OPENED: 04/20/1983 Theatre: Nederlander
Musical Broadway: 2

Composer: Chris Monks
Lyricist: Claire Luckham
Librettist: Claire Luckham
Producer: Kenneth-Mark Productions; Stewart F. Lane; Charlene Nederlander; James M. Nederlander; Richard Vos
Director: Chris Bond

Cast: Caitlin Clarke; Clarence Felder; Deborah Harry; Andy Kaufman; Zora Rasmussen; Scott Renderer; Dana Vance; Thomas G. Waites

Notes: This show had two parts double cast, so there were two opening nights. Although the show closed opening night, there were two performances. No songs listed in program.

4296 • TED LEWIS FROLIC

OPENED: 1923
Revue Closed out of town

Composer: Milton Ager
Lyricist: Jack Yellen
Librettist: Bugs Baer; William K. Wells
Producer: Ted Lewis; Arthur Pearson
Director: Walter Wilson

Choreographer: Allan K. Foster; **Costumes:** Harry Collins; Mme. Francis; Hugh Willoughby; **Lighting Designer:** Fred Murray; **Musical Director:** Louis Gress; **Set Design:** Hugh Willoughby

Songs: Back Home; Beautiful Girls You Have the World at Your Feet; Beyond the Moonbeam Trail; Change Your Step; Oui, Oui, Monsieur; Paisley Shawl; See-No-Evil Eye; Struttin' School; They Weren't Any Better in the Good Old Days; Tick Tock (The Dresden Clock); Twinkle, Twinkle Little Star; We're Not as Bad as We're Painted

Cast: Ted Lewis

4297 TEDDY & ALICE

OPENED: 11/12/1987 Theatre: Minskoff
Musical Broadway: 77

Music Based On: John Philip Sousa
Composer: Richard Kapp
Lyricist: Hal Hackady
Librettist: Jerome Alden
Producer: Hinks Shimberg
Director: John Driver

Choreographer: Donald Saddler; **Costumes:** Theoni V. Aldredge; **Dance Arranger:** Gordon Lowry Harrell; **Lighting Designer:** Tharon Musser; **Musical Director:** Larry Blank; **Orchestrations:** Jim Tyler; **Set Design:** Robin Wagner; **Vocal Arranger:** Don Pippin

Songs: Battlelines; But Not Right Now; Can I Let Her Go?; Charge; Coming-Out Party, The; Election Eve; Fourth of July, The; He's Got to Go; Her Father's Daughter; House, The; Leg o' Mutton; Not Love; Nothing to Lose; Perfect for Each Other; Private Thoughts; She's Got to Go; Thunderer, The (inst.) (C: John Philip Sousa); Wave the Flag

Cast: Len Cariou; Beth Fowler; Nancy Hume; Nancy Opel; Gordon Stanley; Raymond Thorne; Christopher Wells; Karen Ziemba

Notes: Artistic consultant: Alan Jay Lerner.

4298 • TELEPHONE GIRL, THE

OPENED: 12/27/1897 Theatre: Casino
Musical Broadway: 104

Composer: Gustave Kerker
Librettist: Hugh Morton
Producer: George W. Lederer; George B. McLellan

Source: LA DEMOISELLE DU TELEPHONE (Musical: Maurice Desvallieres; Anthony Mass; Gaston Serpette)

Songs: Estelle; Keep Your Eye on Pretty Sarah; Telephone Girl, The

Cast: Charles Dickson; Clara Lipman; James F. MacDonald; Louis Mann; Sarah McVicker; Millicent Willson; Bessie Wynn

Notes: No program available.

4299 • TELL HER THE TRUTH

OPENED: 10/28/1932 Theatre: Cort
Musical Broadway: 11

Composer: Joseph Tunbridge; Jack Waller
Lyricist: Bert Lee; R.P. Weston
Librettist: Bert Lee; R.P. Weston
Producer: Tillie Leblang
Director: Morris Green; Henry Thomas

Source: NOTHING BUT THE TRUTH (Play: James Montgomery); **Source:** NOTHING BUT THE TRUTH (Novel: Frederic Isham); **Costumes:** Jay-Thorpe; **Musical Director:** Gene Salzer; **Set Design:** Teichner Studios

Songs: Happy the Day; Hoch, Caroline!; Horrortorio; Sing, Brothers!; Tell Her the Truth; That's Fine; Won't You Tell Me Why?

Cast: Hobart Cavanaugh; Edith Davis; Margaret Dumont; Lillian Emerson; William Frawley; Louise Kirtland; Lew Parker; John Sheehan Jr.; Andrew Tombes; Raymond Walburn; Thelma White

Notes: The source was used previously as the basis for the musical YES YES YVETTE.

4300 • TELL ME MORE

OPENED: 04/13/1925 Theatre: Winter Garden
Musical Broadway: 100

Composer: George Gershwin
Lyricist: B.G. DeSylva; Ira Gershwin
Librettist: Fred Thompson; William K. Wells
Producer: Alex A. Aarons
Director: John Harwood; Sammy Lee

Musical Director: Max Steiner

Songs: Baby! [1] [5]; Baby! [2] [6]; Finaletto, Act II Scene 1 (Kenneth Won the Yachting Race); Gushing (Gush, Gush, Gushing) [7] (L: Ira

Gershwin; Brian Hooker); Have You Heard [2] (L: Claude Hulburt); He-Man, The [1]; How Can I Win You Now? [4]; I'm Somethin' on Avenue A [1]; In Sardinia (Where the Delicatessen Flows) [4]; Kickin' the Clouds Away; Love, I Never Knew [2] (L: Desmond Carter); Love Is in the Air; Mr. and Mrs. Sipkin (Monty! Their Only Child); Murderous Monty (And Light-Fingered Jane) [3] (L: Desmond Carter); My Fair Lady (Lady Fair); Oh So La Me (C/L: Unknown); Once [1] (C: William Daly; L: Ira Gershwin); Poetry of Motion, The; Shop Girls and Mannikins; Tell Me More!; Three Times a Day; Ukulele Lorelei; When the Debbies Go By; Why Do I Love You?

Cast: Phyllis Cleveland; Alexander Gray; Emma Haig; Portland Hoffa; Lou Holtz; Esther Howard; Andrew Tombes

Notes: Out of town the show was titled MY FAIR LADY. [1] Cut prior to opening. [2] Added to London production 5/26/25. [3] Written for London production but not used. [4] Cut after opening. [5] Music originally used (with a Clifford Grey lyric) for "Sweetheart" written for the unproduced musical FLYING ISLAND and later in THE RAINBOW. [6] Added to London production 5/26/25. New music for this song (same lyric) written for London. [7] Hooker's participation uncertain. Not used. Also not used in ROSALIE.

4301 • TELL ME ON A SUNDAY

OPENED: 01/1980 Theatre: BBC
TV Musical

Composer: Andrew Lloyd Webber
Lyricist: Don Black

Musical Director: Harry Rabinowitz

Songs: Capped Teeth and Caesar Salad; Come Back with the Same Look in Your Eyes; I'm Very You, You're Very Me; It's Not the End of the World (If He's Younger); It's Not the End of the World (If He's Married); It's Not the End of the World (If I Lose Him); Let Me Finish; Let's Talk About You; Letter Home to England; Nothing Like You've Ever Known; Second Letter Home; Sheldon Bloom; Take That Look Off Your Face; Tell Me on a Sunday; You Made Me Think You Were in Love

Cast: Marti Webb

Notes: *See also SONG & DANCE.* This became the first act of that show.

4302 • TELLING THE TALE

OPENED: 08/31/1918 Theatre: Ambassadors'
Musical London: 90

Composer: Philip Braham
Lyricist: Douglas Hoare
Librettist: Sidney Blow; Douglas Hoare
Producer: Gerald Kirby; John Wyndham
Director: Sidney Blow

Source: OH, I SAY! (Play: Sidney Blow; Douglas Hoare); **Choreographer:** George Shurley; **Musical Director:** W. Vere Harker; **Set Design:** F. Bull; J. Hicks

Songs: Altogether Too Fond of You (C: Cole Porter; L: Melville Gideon; James Heard); Cocktail Time; Cook House Door, The; Queen of the South Sea Isles, The; Rin-tin-tin and Ninette

Cast: Marie Blanche; Douglas Blore; Edmee Dormeuil; Nancy Gibbs; Gerald Kirby; C. Dernier Warren

Notes: No program available.

4303 • TEMPEST IN A TEAPOT

OPENED: 11/17/1954
Musical 25

Composer: Ronald Lowden
Librettist: Richard Levinson; William Link
Producer: Robert Wickersham
Director: Chester R. Cooper

Choreographer: Walter F. Keenan; **Costumes:** Helen Stevenson West; **Incidental Music:** Al Boss; **Orchestrations:** Al Boss; **Set Design:** Robert Patterson

Songs: Boston Tea Party (inst.) (C: Allison Fleitas); Brazilian Interlude (C: Henning Ludlow; L: James McHugh); Coffee and Tea (C/L: Allison Fleitas); Gossip; If You'd Only Let Me (C/L: Allison Fleitas); I'm Through with You (C/L: Henning Ludlow); I've Changed My Mind; Loyalty (L: James McHugh); Meeting; Morality (C: Doun Bruce; L: James McHugh); Take a Look (C/L: Allison Fleitas); Toast, A; We've Got a Great Feeling (C: Henning Ludlow;

L: James McHugh); Where There's a Will (L: Thomas Scotes; Philip Struthers); Who's Boss in Boston (L: James McHugh); Wonderful You (C: Sydney Fisher; L: James McHugh)

Notes: Amateur show. Mask & Wig Club, University of Pennstylvania.

4304 • TEMPLE BELLES

OPENED: 03/20/1924
Musical

Composer: Richard Rodgers
Lyricist: Lorenz Hart
Librettist: Richard Rodgers
Producer: Park Avenue Synogogue
Director: Herbert Fields

Musical Director: Richard Rodgers

Songs: Bob-o-link (L: Dorothy Crowthers); Hermits, The [1]; Just a Little Lie [3]; Penny for Your Thoughts, A [2]

Notes: Amateur show. [1] Also in WINKLE TOWN, A DANISH YANKEE IN KING TUT'S COURT and DEAREST ENEMY. [2] Also in FLY WITH ME. [3] Also in YOU'LL NEVER KNOW and SAY IT WITH JAZZ.

4305 • TEMPORARY MRS. SMITH, THE

Notes: *See LOVELY ME.*

4306 • TEMPTATIONS

Notes: *See FOLIES BERGERE COMPANY.*

4307 • 10 DAYS TO BROADWAY

Notes: *See 13 DAYS TO BROADWAY.*

4308 • TEN FOR FIVE

OPENED: 1918
Musical

Composer: Henry Hanemann; Robert K. Lippmann
Lyricist: Oscar Hammerstein II; Henry Hanemann
Librettist: Oscar Hammerstein II
Producer: Columbia University War Show Committee
Director: Oscar Hammerstein II

Musical Director: Roy S. Webb

Notes: Amateur show.

4309 • TEN PERCENT REVUE

OPENED: 04/13/1988 Theatre: Susan Bloch
Revue Off-Broadway: 239

Composer: Tom Wilson Weinberg
Lyricist: Tom Wilson Weinberg
Producer: Laura Green
Director: Scott Green

Choreographer: Tee Scatuorchio; **Costumes:** Kevin-Robert; **Set Design:** Edwin Perez-Carrion

Songs: And the Supremes; Before Stonewall; Best Years of My Life; Flaunting It; Gay Name Game; High Risk for Afraids; Home; Homo Haven Fight Song; I'd Like to Be; If I Were; Not Allowed; Obituary; Personals; Safe Sex Slut; Threesome; Turkey Baster Baby; We're Everywhere; Wedding Song; Write a Letter

Cast: Lisa Bernstein; Valerie Hill; Trish Kane; Robert Tate; Timothy Williams

4310 • TEN-ISH, ANYONE?

Theatre: Downstairs at the Upstairs
Revue Nightclub

Songs: Daisy (C/L: G. Wood); Thor (C/L: Jack Holmes)

Cast: Jane Connell; Jack Fletcher

4311 • TENDERFOOT, THE

OPENED: 02/22/1904 Theatre: New York
Musical Broadway: 81

Composer: H.L. Heartz
Lyricist: Richard Carle
Librettist: Richard Carle
Producer: Dearborn Theatre Company
Director: Richard Carle

Songs: Adios; Dancing; Don't Forget You're Talking to a Lady (C: William Spink; L: Henry Blossom); Don't Mind Me; Fascinating Venus; Gay Lothario, A; I'm a Peaceable Party; Interrogative Child, The; Love Is Elusive [1];

Marriage Is a Lottery; Only a Kiss; Soldier of Fortune, A; Soldiery, The; Texas Rangers; Tortured Thomas Cat; Washing Song

Cast: Richard Carle; Helena Frederick; William Rock

Notes: [1] Also in MARY'S LAMB.

4312 • TENDERLOIN

OPENED: 10/17/1960 Theatre: 46th Street
Musical Broadway: 216

Composer: Jerry Bock
Lyricist: Sheldon Harnick
Librettist: George Abbott; Jerome Weidman
Producer: Robert E. Griffith; Harold Prince
Director: George Abbott

Source: TENDERLOIN (Novel: Samuel Hopkins Adams); **Choreographer:** Joe Layton; **Costumes:** Cecil Beaton; **Dance Arranger:** Jack Elliott; **Musical Director:** Harold Hastings; **Orchestrations:** Irwin Kostal; **Set Design:** Cecil Beaton

Songs: Army of the Just, The; Artificial Flowers; Bless This Land; Dear Friend; Dr. Brock; Finally [3]; First Things First [3]; Good Clean Fun; How the Money Changes Hands; I Wonder What It's Like [2]; Little Old New York; Lord of All Creation [3]; Lovely Laurie [1]; My Gentle Young Johnny; My Miss Mary; Nobody Cares [3]; Not Peace but a Sword [1]; Orgy Burlesque, The [1]; Picture of Happiness, The; Reform; Sea Shell [1]; Tenderloin Celebration, The; Tis Thy Beauty [1]; Tommy, Tommy; Trial, The; What's in It for You?

Cast: Ralph Dunn; Maurice Evans; Rex Everhart; Margery Gray; Ron Husmann; Eddie Phillips; Eileen Rodgers; Lee Theodore

Notes: [1] Not used. [2] Cut prior to opening. [3] Not in programs.

4313 • TERENCE

OPENED: 01/05/1904 Theatre: New York
Play Broadway: 56

Composer: Chauncey Olcott
Lyricist: Chauncey Olcott
Author: Mrs. Edmund Nash Morgan
Producer: Augustus Pitou
Director: Augustus Pitou

Source: UNKNOWN (Novel: Mrs. B.M. Croker); **Costumes:** H.A. Ogden; **Incidental Music:** Gustave Salzer; **Musical Director:** Clarence Rogerson

Songs: Girl I Used to Know, The; My Own Dear Irish Queen; My Sonny Boy; Terence; Tick, Tack, Toe

Cast: Harry Hanscombe; Adelaide Keim; Chauncey Olcott; Elizabeth Washburne; Amanda Wellington

4314 • TEXAS, LI'L DARLIN'

OPENED: 11/25/1949 Theatre: Mark Hellinger
Musical Broadway: 293

Composer: Robert Emmett Dolan
Lyricist: Johnny Mercer
Librettist: Sam Moore; John Whedon
Producer: Anthony Brady Farrell; Studio Productions
Director: Paul Crabtree

Choreographer: Al White Jr.; **Costumes:** Eleanor Goldsmith; **Lighting Designer:** Theodore Cooper; **Musical Director:** Will Irwin; **Orchestrations:** Robert Russell Bennett; **Set Design:** Theodore Cooper

Songs: Affable Balding Me; Big Movie Show in the Sky, The; Down in the Valley; Hootin' Owl Trail; Horseshoes Are Lucky; It's Great to Be Alive; Little Bit o' Country [1]; Love Me, Love My Dog; Month of Sundays, A; Our Family Tree [1]; Politics; Ride 'Em Cowboy; Square Dance (dance); Take a Crank Letter; Texas Li'l Darlin'; They Talk a Different Language (The Yodel Blues); Whichaway'd They Go; Whoopin' and a-Hollerin'

Cast: Kenny Delmar; Mary Hatcher; Danny Scholl; Loring Smith

Notes: [1] Out Westport 8/29/49.

4315 • THANK HEAVEN FOR THE HEATHEN

Notes: *See HEATHEN!*

4316 • THANK YOU, COLUMBUS!

OPENED: 11/15/1940 Theatre: Hollywood Playhouse
Musical Los Angeles

Composer: George Forrest; Robert Wright
Lyricist: George Forrest; Robert Wright
Librettist: Ben Barzman; Sol Barzman
Producer: Curt Bois; G.V. Gontard
Director: Curt Bois

Choreographer: Eddie Larkin; **Costumes:** Gerda Vanderneers; **Musical Director:** Leo Arnaud; **Orchestrations:** Leo Arnaud; **Set Design:** Gabriel Scognamillo; **Vocal Arranger:** Leo Arnaud

Songs: All's Well; Can You Can-Can; Dr. Clambake's Ballet; Dream for Sale; Empty Wigwam Blues; Genealogy of Daisy Belle, The; I Discover New Worlds; I Hear America Singing; I Never Had a Date Before; Make Way for Tomorrow; Manhattan's Automatons; Pilgrim's Chorus; Spinning Song; These Three; Thou Shalt Not Dance; Voice of Tomorrow, The; We Were Here First

Cast: Kenneth Stevens; Philip Van Zandt; Dave Willcock; Vivian Yarbo

4317 THAT CASEY GIRL

OPENED: 10/22/1923
Musical Closed out of town

Composer: Jean Schwartz
Lyricist: William Jerome
Librettist: George V. Hobart; Willard Mack

Songs: Casey Is a Wonderful Name; Ev'ry Day Is Mother's Day; I Love Rosie Casey; Please Come Again; Summer Days; When I Get in the Movies

Notes: Lyceum Theatre, Paterson, New Jersey.

4318 • THAT 5 A.M. JAZZ

OPENED: 10/19/1964 Theatre: Astor Place
Musical Off-Broadway: 94

Composer: Will Holt
Lyricist: Will Holt
Librettist: Will Holt
Producer: Muriel Morse; Jay Stanwyck
Director: Michael Kahn

Choreographer: Sandra Devlin; **Dance Arranger:** Ted Simons; **Lighting Designer:** Milton Drake; **Set Design:** Lloyd Burlingame; **Vocal Arranger:** Ted Simons

Songs: All-American Two-Step, The; Campaign Song; Gonna Get a Woman; Happy Daze Saloon, The; Nuevo Laredo; Some Sunday; Sweet Time; Those Were the Days

Cast: James Coco; Lester James; Ruth Jaroslow; Dolly Jonah

Notes: This was a bill of two one-act shows: THE FIRST and THAT 5 A.M. JAZZ. All songs were in part two.

4319 • THAT HAT!

OPENED: 09/23/1964 Theatre: Theatre Four
Musical Off-Broadway: 1

Composer: Cy Young
Lyricist: Cy Young
Librettist: Cy Young
Producer: Bonard Productions; Justin Sturn; Katherine Sturn
Director: Dania Krupska

Source: ITALIAN STRAW HAT, THE (Play: Eugene Labiche; Marc- Michel); **Choreographer:** Dania Krupska; **Costumes:** Bill Hargate; **Dance Arranger:** Gerald Alters; **Lighting Designer:** Patricia Collins; **Musical Director:** Gerald Alters; **Set Design:** Bill Hargate; **Vocal Arranger:** Gerald Alters

Songs: Apology, The; Do a Little Exercise; Draw Me a Circle; Exposition; Give Me a Pinch; I Love a Man; Interlude; Italian Straw Hat; It's All Off; Mad Ballet, The; My, It's Been Grand; My Husband; Pot of Myrtle, A; Sound of the Night; Sounds of the Day; Tete-a-tete, A; This World of Confusion; We Have Never Met

Cast: Carmen Alvarez; Merle Louise; Pierre Olaf; Joe Ross; Barbara Sharma; Elmarie Wendel

4320 • THAT'S A GOOD GIRL

OPENED: 06/05/1928 Theatre: London Hippodrome
Musical London: 363

Composer: Philip Charig; Joseph Meyer

Lyricist: Desmond Carter; Douglas Furber; Ira Gershwin
Librettist: Douglas Furber
Producer: Jack Buchanan; Moss Empires Ltd.; United Producing Corp.
Director: Jack Buchanan

Choreographer: Jack Buchanan; **Musical Director:** Leonard Hornsey; **Set Design:** F.L. Lyndhurst; Marc-Henri

Songs: Before We Were Married [1] (L: Ira Gershwin); Chirp- Chirp [2] (L: Ira Gershwin); Day After Day [1] (L: Ira Gershwin); Fancy Our Meeting (L: Douglas Furber); Finale Act I (L: Ira Gershwin); Hullo Hullo; Let Yourself Go! [3] (L: Ira Gershwin); Marching Song, A (L: Douglas Furber); One I'm Looking For, The (L: Douglas Furber; Ira Gershwin); Opening (What to Do) (L: Ira Gershwin); Parting Time (L: Douglas Furber); Sweet So-and-So [4] (L: Douglas Furber; Ira Gershwin); Tell Me Why (L: Desmond Carter); There I'd Settle Down [1] (L: Ira Gershwin); We've Got to Find William (L: Douglas Furber); Week End (L: Ira Gershwin); Whoopee (L: Ira Gershwin); Why Be Good? [1] (L: Ira Gershwin)

Cast: Jack Buchanan; Eight Tiller Girls, The; Dave Fitzgibbon; William Kendall; Elsie Randolph

Notes: [1] Not used. [2] Also in SHOOT THE WORKS. [3] Published music credits lyrics to Douglas Furber and Gershwin. [4] Gershwin's original lyric (written alone) was used in SWEET AND LOW.

4321 • THAT'S LIFE

OPENED: 1954

Composer: Ray Evans; Jay Livingston
Lyricist: Ray Evans; Jay Livingston

Songs: Chihuahua Choo-Choo [1]; Clink Clank Clunk; Livin' Lovin' Doll; That's Life; Why Am I in Love; You're So Right

Notes: No other information available. [1] Also in TV musical SATINS AND SPURS.

4322 • THAT'S MY BOY

OPENED: 11/1924
Play Closed out of town

Composer: Robert Simonds
Lyricist: Billy DuVal
Author: Karyl Norman; Edward A. Paulton
Producer: Joseph M. Gaites
Director: Lawrence Marston

Choreographer: Vaughn Godfrey; **Costumes:** Kiviette; **Musical Director:** Karyl Norman

Songs: In a World of Our Own; Me and the Boy Friend; Paris Rose; Play That Melody of Love; Somebody Like You (C: Walter Donaldson; L: Cliff Friend); Spain; Wonderful Mother

Cast: Betty Byron; Dan Marble; Karyl Norman; Helen Weir; Isabelle Winlocke

Notes: Program from Wilmington 11/3/24. Karyl Norman played both male and female rolse in this show.

4323 • THAT'S THE TICKET

OPENED: 09/27/1948
Musical Closed out of town

Composer: Harold Rome
Lyricist: Harold Rome
Librettist: Julius J. Epstein; Philip G. Epstein
Producer: Al Beckman; Joseph Kipness; John Pransky
Director: Jerome Robbins

Choreographer: Paul Godkin; **Costumes:** Miles White; **Lighting Designer:** Peggy Clark; **Musical Director:** Lehman Engel; **Orchestrations:** Robert Russell Bennett; **Set Design:** Oliver Smith; **Vocal Arranger:** Lehman Engel

Songs: Ballad of Marcia LaRue, The; Chivalry Reel; Cry, Baby [1]; Determined Woman, A; Dost Thou; Fair Sex, The; Gin Rummy Rhapsody; How Peaceful Is the Evening; I Shouldn't Love You; Looking for a Candidate; Money Song, The; Newsreel, The; Political Lady; Read All About It; Take Off the Coat [2]; We're Going Back; You Never Know What Hit You-When It's Love [2]

Cast: Rod Alexander; Kaye Ballard; Leif Erickson; Ralph Herz; George S. Irving; Edna Skinner; Loring Smith

Notes: [1] Later in ALIVE AND KICKING. [2] Later in BLESS YOU ALL.

4324 • THEBE

OPENED: 1906
Musical

Composer: Ben M. Jerome
Lyricist: I.L. Blumenstock
Librettist: I.L. Blumenstock

Songs: My Lotus Lady; My Sawdust Queen

Notes: No other information available.

4325 • THEDA BARA AND THE FRONTIER RABBI

OPENED: 01/09/1993
Musical Off-Off-Broadway

Composer: Bob Johnston
Lyricist: Jeff Hochhauser; Bob Johnston
Librettist: Jeff Hochhauser
Director: Lynne Taylor-Corbett

Songs: Arab Death; Bish Ne Ara; Bolt of Love; Faster and Faster; Frontier Rabbi; G.O.T.O.; It's Like a Movie; Ladies and Mateys of Hades, The; Lulu; Meddler, The; Only Dreamin'; Scene with the Grapes, The; Sermon, The; Thump Thump; Velcome to Shul

Cast: Jonathan Hadley; Robin Irwin; Jeanine LaManna; Ellen Margulies; Allen Lewis Rickman

4326 • THEIR WEDDING NIGHT

Notes: *See OH, I SAY.*

4327 • THEODORE AND CO.

OPENED: 09/19/1916 Theatre: Gaiety
Musical London: 503

Composer: Ivor Novello
Lyricist: Clifford Grey
Librettist: George Grossmith; H.M. Harwood
Producer: George Grossmith; Edward Laurillard
Director: Austen Hurgon

Source: THEODORE ET CIE (Play: Paul Gavault); **Choreographer:** Gwladys Dillon; **Costumes:** Lucille; Elspeth Phelps; Jules Poiret; **Musical Director:** Willie Redstone; **Set Design:** Alfred E. Craven; Joseph Harker; Phil Harker

Songs: All That I Want Is Somebody to Love Me [1] (C: Jerome Kern); Any Old Where; Candy Girls, The (L: Adrian Ross); Casino Music Hall, The (C: Jerome Kern); Ev'ry Little Girl Can Teach Me Something New (L: Adrian Ross); He's Going to Call on Baby Grand (L: Adrian Ross); I'll Make Myself at Home (L: Adrian Ross); I'm Getting Such a Big Girl Now (C: Philip Braham); Isn't There a Crowd Everywhere?; My Friend John; My Second Childhood (C: Philip Braham; L: Eric Blore; David Burnaby); That Come "Hither" Look [2] (C: Jerome Kern); 365 Days (C: Jerome Kern); Valse Saracenne (inst.); We Are Theodore & Company (L: Adrian Ross); We Can Jolly Along (C: Philip Braham; L: Eric Blore); What a Duke Should Be; You'd Better Not Wait for Him

Cast: Joyce Barbour; George Grossmith; Leslie Henson; Julia James; Madge Saunders

Notes: [1] Same music as "Can't You See I Mean You?" from 90 IN THE SHADE and as "Isn't It Great to Be Married" from VERY GOOD EDDIE. Grey revised M.E. Rourke's original lyric. [2] New lyric for "Those 'Come Hither' Eyes" from COUSIN LUCY.

4328 • THERE YOU ARE

OPENED: 05/16/1932 Theatre: George M. Cohan
Musical Broadway: 8

Composer: William Heagney
Lyricist: Tom Connell; William Heagney
Librettist: Carl Bartfeld
Producer: Hyman Adler
Director: Horace Sinclair

Choreographer: Vaughn Godfrey; **Costumes:** Bertha Beres; Eaves; **Musical Director:** Fred Hoff; **Orchestrations:** Irving Schloss; Roy Webb; **Set Design:** Carlo Studios

Songs: Aces Up; Carolina; Haunting Refrain; Just a Little Penthouse and You; Legend of the Mission Bells; Love Lives On; Love Potion, The; Lover's Holiday; More and More; Safe in Your Arms; Sounds of the Drum, The; There You Are; They All Love Me; Wings in the Morning

Cast: Hyman Adler; Robert Capron; Roy Cropper; Berta Donn; Joseph Lertora; Ilse Marvenga; O'Connor; Adrian Rosley

4329 • THERE'S A GIRL IN MY SOUP

OPENED: 10/18/1967 Theatre: Music Box
Play Broadway: 321

Author: Terence Frisby
Producer: Michael Codron; Saint-Subber
Director: Robert Chetwyn

Costumes: Stanley Simmons; **Lighting Designer:** Lloyd Burlingame; **Set Design:** Hutchinson Scott

Songs: Girl in My Soup (C/L: Norman Percival)

Cast: Erica Fitz; Rita Gam; George Hall; Jon Pertwee; Gig Young

4330 • THERE'S A HOLE IN MY SIDEWALK

Revue Closed out of town

Composer: Portia Nelson
Lyricist: Portia Nelson
Librettist: Portia Nelson
Director: David Rounds

Source: THERE'S A HOLE IN MY SIDEWALK (Book: Portia Nelson); **Lighting Designer:** Dan Boylan; **Musical Director:** Manford Abrahamson; **Set Design:** David Rounds

Songs: All the Ifs and Maybes; Decisions; Hole in My Sidewalk; How Wise of You to Wait; I Crowed What I Knowed; I Don't Smoke; In the Beginning; Into the Bright of Loving; It's a Dreary Day; Love Theme; Pieces; Try to Be My Age; What Foolish Creatures We Are; You Have Made a Fool of Me; You Say You Love Me

Cast: Carol Morley; David Rounds; John Seidman

4331 • THEY CAN'T GET YOU DOWN

OPENED: 12/1941
Musical Los Angeles

Composer: Jay Gorney
Lyricist: Edward Eliscu; Henry Myers
Librettist: Edward Eliscu; Henry Myers
Producer: Edward Eliscu; Jay Gorney; Jack Kirkland; Henry Myers; Dwight Deere Wiman

Choreographer: Danny Dare; **Costumes:** Georgia Anderson; **Set Design:** Frederick Stover; **Vocal Arranger:** Mort Werner; Leo Wolf

Songs: Ad Ripae Mildewensis Fluminis; Finaletto; It's No Fun Eating Alone; Love Can Settle Everything; Love in a Changing World; Mittel-Europa [1]; More Mittel-Europa; Musical Chairs; On the Banks of the Mildrew River; River to Dora Flora; Sir Pumphrey Mildew; Take Her My Boy [2]; They Can't Get You Down; Twenty-Five Bucks a Week; Twenty-One Bucks a Week; Unzer Amerika [2]; You're Only a Barefoot Boy

Cast: Gene Barry; Jan Clayton; Edward Emerson; Berni Gould; Jimmy Griffith; Eddie Johnson; Peggy Ryan; Julie Sherwin; Douglas Wood

Notes: [1] Also in LET FREEDOM SING. [2] ASCAP/Library of Congress only.

4332 • THEY DON'T MAKE 'EM LIKE THAT ANYMORE

OPENED: 06/06/1972 Theatre: Plaza 9 Music Hall
Revue Off-Broadway: 24

Composer: Hugh Martin
Lyricist: Timothy Gray; Hugh Martin
Producer: Timothy Gray; William Justus; Costas Omer
Director: Timothy Gray

Costumes: Stephen Chandler; E. Huntington Parker; **Lighting Designer:** Beverly Emmons; **Set Design:** Don Gordon

Songs: Architect, The; Buckle Down Winsocki [2] (C/L: Ralph Blane); Disraeli; Drama Quartet; Frank and Johnnies [3]; Get Me Out of Here [3]; Harvey; I Lost You; Invisible Man; Judy [3]; Once in Love with Amy [1] (C/L: Frank Loesser); Oscar; Paradise Lost [3]; Party's Over Now, The; Show Girl; Silence Is Golden; Something Tells Me; Sorry Wrong Valley; Sunset Boulevard; Swanislavsky; They Don't Make 'Em Like That Anymore; Victoria; What's His Name

Cast: Arthur Blake; Kevin Christopher; Dell Hanley; Clay Johns; Luba Lisa; Gene McCann; Phoebe Otis; Paris Todd

Notes: There may be some sketch titles in the song list as they weren't differentiated in the program. [1] From WHERE'S CHARLEY. [2] From BEST FOOT FORWARD. Though Ralph Blane wrote this song, he and Hugh Martin polished his version. [3] ASCAP/Library of Congress only.

4333 THEY LOVED A LASSIE

OPENED: 10/31/1909 Theatre: Whitney Opera House
Musical Chicago

Composer: Lyle Bloodgood
Librettist: George Arliss; Benjamin Hapgood Burt
Producer: B.C. Whitney
Director: Gus Sohlke

Cast: Charles E. Evans; Forrest Huff; Eugene Moulan; Alice Yorke

Notes: No songs listed in program.

4334 • THEY'RE PLAYING OUR SONG

OPENED: 02/11/1979 Theatre: Imperial
Musical Broadway: 1082

Composer: Marvin Hamlisch
Lyricist: Carole Bayer Sager
Librettist: Neil Simon
Producer: Emanuel Azenberg
Director: Robert Moore

Choreographer: Patricia Birch; **Costumes:** Ann Roth; **Lighting Designer:** Tharon Musser; **Musical Director:** Larry Blank; **Orchestrations:** Ralph Burns; Richard Hazard; Gene Page; **Set Design:** Douglas W. Schmidt

Songs: Fallin'; Fill in the Words; I Still Believe in Love; If He Really Knew Me; If We Give It Time [1]; I've Got Those One Foot Blues [1]; Just for Tonight; Right; They're Playing Our Song; When You're in My Arms; Workin' It Out

Cast: Lucie Arnaz; Robert Klein

Notes: [1] Cut prior to opening.

4335 • THIRD LITTLE SHOW, THE

OPENED: 06/01/1931 Theatre: Music Box
Revue Broadway: 136

Librettist: Marc Connelly; Noel Coward; Edward Eliscu; S.J. Perelman; Peter Spencer; Harry Wall
Producer: Tom Weatherly; Dwight Deere Wiman
Director: Alexander Leftwich

Choreographer: Dave Gould; **Costumes:** Raymond Sovey; **Musical Director:** Max Meth; **Orchestrations:** Howard Jackson; **Set Design:** Jo Mielziner

Songs: Africa Shrieks (C: Ned Lehac; L: Edward Eliscu); Any Little Fish [2] (C/L: Noel Coward); Cinema Lorelei (C: Ned Lehac; L: Edward Eliscu); Falling in Love (C: Henry Sullivan; L: Earle Crooker); Going, Going, Gone! (C: Henry Sullivan; L: Edward Eliscu); I'll Putcha Pitcha in the Papers (C: Michael Cleary; L: Max Lief; Nathaniel Lief); I've Lost My Heart (C: Morris Hamilton; L: Grace Henry); Le Five O'Clock (C: Will Irwin; L: Carl Randall); Little Geezer (C: Michael H. Cleary; L: Max Lief; Nathaniel Lief; Dave Oppenheim); Mad Dogs and Englishmen [1] (C/L: Noel Coward); Say the Word (C: Burton Lane; L: Harold Adamson); Sevilla (C: Ned Lehac; L: Edward Eliscu); There Are Fairies at the Bottom of My Garden (C: Liza Lehmann; L: Rose Fyleman); When Yuba Plays the Rumba on His Tuba (C/L: Herman Hupfeld); You Forgot Your Gloves (C: Ned Lehac; L: Edward Eliscu); You Might As Well Pretend (C: Morgan Lewis; L: Edward Eliscu; Ted Fetter)

Cast: Edward Arnold; Constance Carpenter; Dorothy Fitzgibbon; Sandra Gale; William Griffith; Beatrice Lillie; Gertrude McDonald; Jerry Norris; Walter O'Keefe; Carl Randall; Ernest Truex

Notes: [1] Originally in WORDS AND MUSIC. [2] Cut during tryout of this show. Originally in COCHRAN'S 1931 REVUE.

4336 • THIRTEEN CLOCKS

OPENED: 08/17/1953
Musical Closed out of town

Composer: Robert Gallico
Librettist: Frank Lowe

Source: THIRTEEN CLOCKS, THE (Story: James Thurber)

Notes: No program available.

4337 • 13 DAUGHTERS

OPENED: 03/02/1961 Theatre: 54th St.
Musical Broadway: 28

Composer: Eaton Magoon Jr.
Lyricist: Eaton Magoon Jr.
Librettist: Eaton Magoon Jr.; Leon Tolsatyan
Producer: Jack H. Silverman
Director: Billy Matthews

Choreographer: Rod Alexander; **Costumes:** Alvin Colt; **Dance Arranger:** Bob Atwood; **Lighting Designer:** George Jenkins; **Musical Director:** Pembroke Davenport; **Orchestrations:** Robert Russell Bennett; Joe Glover; **Set Design:** George Jenkins; **Vocal Arranger:** Pembroke Davenport

Songs: Alphabet Song; Calabash Cousins [1]; Cotillion, The; Daughter or Dowry [1]; Father and Son [2]; Goodbye Is Hard to Say [1]; Hiaka; Hoomalimali; House on the Hill; Ka Wahine Akamai; Kuli Kuli; Lei of Memories [1]; Let-a-Go Your Heart; Listen for the Rooster [2]; Long and Beautiful Life, A [1]; My Hawaii; My Pleasure; Never Without Your Love [2]; Nothing Man Cannot Do; Oriental Plan (C: Sherman Edwards; L: Sid Wayne); Paper of Gold; Puka Puka Pants; 13 Daughters; 13 Old Maids; Throw a Petal; Violets and Violins [2]; Wedding Processional [1]; When You Hear the Wind; You Fascinate Me So [2] (C: Cy Coleman; L: Carolyn Leigh); You Set My Heart to Music

Cast: Don Ameche; John Battles; Monica Boyar; Isabelle Farrell; Ed Kenney; Sylvia Syms; Richard Tone

Notes: [1] Written for Hawaiian production but dropped before Broadway. [2] Cut from score.

4338 • 13 DAYS TO BROADWAY

OPENED: 1985
Musical Unproduced

Composer: Cy Coleman
Lyricist: Barbara Fried
Librettist: Russell Baker
Director: Joe Layton

Costumes: Patricia Zipprodt; **Set Design:** Robin Wagner

Songs: You There in the Back Row

Notes: Workshopped but never produced. This show was known by many titles at one time or another. They include: 10 DAYS TO BROADWAY; BAKER'S BROADWAY; and SETS AND COSTUMES. This was a show based on the experiences of trying to bring HOME AGAIN, HOME AGAIN to the stage. The two shows shared some of the same songs.

4339 • THIS AND THAT

OPENED: 1919
Musical

Composer: C. Luckeyth Roberts
Lyricist: Alex Rogers
Librettist: Alex Rogers
Producer: C. Luckeyth Roberts; Alex Rogers
Director: Alex Rogers

Choreographer: Hazel Thompson Davis

Cast: Edna Brown; Lottie Harris; Ellis Stevens; Dink Stewart; Charley Woody

Notes: No other information available.

4340 • THIS IS THE ARMY

OPENED: 07/04/1942 Theatre: Broadway
Revue Broadway: 113

Composer: Irving Berlin
Lyricist: Irving Berlin
Producer: Uncle Sam
Director: Ezra Stone

Choreographer: Nelson Barclift; Robert Sydney; **Costumes:** John Koenig; **Musical Director:** Milton Rosenstock; **Set Design:** John Koenig

Songs: American Eagles; Army and the Shuberts Depend on You, The (Opening) [5]; Army's Made a Man Out of Me, The; Aryans Under the Skin; Fifth Army's Where My Heart Is, The [2]; How About a Cheer for the Navy?; I Get Along with the Aussies [6]; I Left My Heart at the Stage Door Canteen; I'm Getting Tired So I Can Sleep; Jap-German Sextette; Kick in the Pants, The [3]; Ladies of the Chorus; Mandy [1]; My British Buddy [3]; My Sergeant and I Are Buddies; Oh! How I Hate to Get Up in the Morning [7]; Oh to Be Home Again; Opening of Second Act [5]; Poor Little Me-I'm on KP [4]; Soldier's Dream, A; Some Dough for the Army Relief (Opening) [5];

That Russian Winter; That's What the Well Dressed Man in Harlem Will Wear; There Are No Wings on a Foxhole; This Is the Army, Mr. Jones; This Time (Is the Last Time); Ve Don't Like It [3]; What Are We Going to Do with All the Jeeps? [2]; What Does He Look Like?; With My Head in the Clouds

Cast: Irving Berlin; Stuart Churchill; Joe Cook Jr.; Burl Ives; Gary Merrill; Jules Oshins; Earl Oxford; Robert Shanley; Ezra Stone; Philip Truex

Notes: [1] Originally in YIP! YIP! YAPHANK! Also in ZIEGFELD FOLLIES OF 1919. [2] 1944 version-toured combat zones of Europe, Near East and Pacific. Added for that tour. [3] Overseas version of show toured England, Ireland and Scotland in 1943. Added for that tour. [4] Added for tour after Broadway. [5] Sheet music only. [6] 1945 tour. [7] Originally in YIP! YIP! YAPHANK!

4341 • THIS YEAR OF GRACE!

OPENED: 11/07/1928 Theatre: Selwyn
Musical Broadway: 158

Composer: Noel Coward
Lyricist: Noel Coward
Librettist: Noel Coward
Producer: Charles B. Cochran
Director: Frank Collins

Choreographer: Tilly Losch; Max Rivers; **Costumes:** G.E. Calthrop; Norman H. Hartnell; Idare; Christabel Russell; Doris Zinkeisen; **Musical Director:** Frank Tours; **Set Design:** G.E. Calthrop; Laverdet; Oliver Messel

Songs: Britannia Rules the Waves; Caballero; Chauve Souris; Dance Little Lady; English Lido; I Can't Think; I'm Mad About You; Lido Beach, The; Lilac Time; Little Women; Lorelei; Mary Make Believe; Mother's Complaint; Room with a View, A; Teach Me to Dance Like Grandma; Try to Learn to Love; Velasquez; Waiting in a Queue; World Weary

Cast: Noel Coward; Florence Desmond; Dick Francis; Madeline Gibson; Mimi Hayes; Queenie Leonard; Beatrice Lillie; Marc-Henri; Oliver Messel; Billy Milton; Muriel Montrose; Sonnie Ray

4342 • THOSE WERE THE DAYS

OPENED: 11/07/1990 Theatre: Edison
Revue Broadway: 130

Librettist: Zalmen Mlotek; Moishe Rosenfeld
Producer: Emanuel Azenberg; Moe Septee
Director: Eleanor Reissa

Choreographer: Eleanor Reissa; **Costumes:** Gail Cooper- Hecht; **Lighting Designer:** Tom Sturge; **Musical Director:** Zalmen Mlotek

Songs: Bei Mir Bist Du Schoen (To Me, You're Beautiful) (C: Sholom Secunda; L: Sammy Cahn; Saul Chaplin; Jacob Jacobs); Der Ayznban (The Train) (C/L: Traditional); Di Dinst (The Maid) (C/L: Traditional); Di Rod (The Circle) (C/L: M. Warshavsky); Figaro's Aria (C: Giochino Rossini; L: Robert Abelson; Moishe Rosenfeld); Halevay Volt Ikh Singl Geven (I Wish I Were Single Again) (C/L: Traditional; M. Younin); Hootsatsa (C/L: Finshl Kanapoff); Hudl Mitn Shtrudl (Hudl with the Shtrudl) (C/L: Aaron Lebedeff); In an Orem Shtibele (In a Poor Little House) (C/L: Traditional); Khazndl Oyf Shabes (A Cantor for the Sabbath), A (C/L: Traditional); Khosn — Kale Mazl Tov (Congratulations to the Bride and Groom) (C/L: Traditional); Litvak/ Galitsyaner (C/L: Hymie Jacobson); Lomir Loybn (Let Us Praise) (C/L: Traditional); Mamenyu Tayere (Dear Mama) (C: Traditional; L: Mani Leib); Mayn Alte Heym (C/L: Traditional); Motele (C/L: M. Gebirtig); My Yiddishe Mame (C: Lew Pollack; L: Jack Yellen); Oyfa Pripetshik (At the Fireplace) (C/L: M. Warshavsky); Palace of the Czar, The (C/L: Mel Tolkin); Papirosn (Cigarettes) (C/L: Bella Meisel; Herman Yablokoff); Rumania, Rumania (C/L: Aaron Lebedeff; Sholom Secunda); Saposhkelekh (The Boots) (C/L: Traditional); Sha Shtil (The Rabbi's Coming) (C/L: Traditional); Shabes, Shabes, Shabes (Welcome to the Sabbath) (C: Ben Yomen; L: Ben Bonus); Shloymele-Malkele (C: Joseph Rumshinsky); Shpil Gitar (Play Guitar) (C/L: Traditional); Those Were the Days (C/L: Gene Raskin); Ver Der Ershter Vet Lakhn (Who Will Laugh First?) (C/L: M. Gebirtig); Yiddish International Radio Hour (C: Traditional; L: Chana Mlotek); Yoshke Fort Avek (Yoshke's Going Away) (C/L: Traditional); Yosl Ber (C: Traditional; L: Itsik Manger); Yosl, Yosl (C: Samuel Steinberg; L: Nellie Casman)

Cast: Robert Abelson; Bruce Adler; Mina Bern; Eleanor Reissa; Lori Wilner

Notes: No original songs in this production.

4343 • THOUGHTS

OPENED: 03/19/1973 Theatre: Theatre de Lys
Revue Off-Broadway: 24

Composer: Lamar Alford
Lyricist: Lamar Alford; Jose Tapla; Megan Terry
Producer: Dallas Alinder; Seth Harrison; Arthur Whitelaw
Director: Michael Schultz

Costumes: Joseph Thomas; **Lighting Designer:** Ken Billington; **Set Design:** Stuart Wurtzel; **Vocal Arranger:** David Horowitz

Songs: Accepting the Tolls; Ain't That Something; At the Bottom of Your Heart; Bad Whitey; Blues Was a Pastime; Day Oh Day; Gone; I Can Do It to Myself; Jesus Is My Main Man; Many Men Like You [1]; Music in the Air; One of the Boys; Opening; Roofs [1]; Separate but Equal; Strange Fruit; Sunshine; Thoughts; Trying Hard; Walking in Strange New Places

Cast: Barbara Montgomery; Jeffrey Mylett; Howard Porter; Sarallen; E.H. Wright

Notes: [1] Cut after opening.

4344 • THREE AFTER THREE

Notes: *See WALK WITH MUSIC.*

4345 • THREE CHEERS

OPENED: 10/15/1928 Theatre: Globe
Musical Broadway: 210

Composer: Ray Henderson
Lyricist: B.G. DeSylva
Librettist: R.H. Burnside; Anne Caldwell
Producer: R.H. Burnside
Director: R.H. Burnside

Choreographer: David Bennett; Mary Read; **Set Design:** Raymond Sovey; Sheldon K. Viele

Songs: Americans Are Here, The; Because You're Beautiful; Bobby and Me; Bride Bells; Gee, It's Great to Be Alive; Happy Hoboes; It's an Old Spanish Custom (L: Lew Brown; B.G. DeSylva); Lady Luck (Smile on Me); Let's All Sing the Lard Song (C: Leslie Sarony; L: Anne Caldwell); Look Pleasant; Maybe This Is Love (L: Lew Brown; B.G. DeSylva); My Silver Tree (C: Raymond Hubbell; L: Anne Caldwell); Orange Blossom Home (C: Raymond Hubbell; L: Anne Caldwell); Pompanola (L: Lew Brown; B.G. DeSylva); Putting on the Ritz; Two Boys

Cast: Alan Edwards; Patsy Kelly; Will Rogers; Dorothy Stone

4346 • 3 FOR TONIGHT

OPENED: 04/06/1955 Theatre: Plymouth
Revue Broadway: 85

Composer: Walter Schumann
Lyricist: Robert Wells
Director: Gower Champion

Choreographer: Gower Champion; **Dance Arranger:** Nathan Scott; **Musical Director:** Richard Pribor; **Vocal Arranger:** Nathan Scott

Songs: All You Need Is a Song; Fly Bird

Cast: Harry Belafonte; Gower Champion; Marge Champion; Hiram Sherman

4347 • 3 FROM BROOKLYN

OPENED: 11/19/1992 Theatre: Helen Hayes
Revue Broadway: 9

Composer: Sandi Merle; Steve Michaels
Lyricist: Sandi Merle; Steve Michaels
Producer: Michael Frazier; Don Ravella; Larry Spellman
Director: Sal Richards

Lighting Designer: Phil Monat; **Musical Director:** Steve Michaels; **Set Design:** Charles E. McCarry

Cast: Bobby Alto; BQE Dancers; Roslyn Kind; Buddy Mantia; Sal Richards; Raymond Serra; Adrianne Tolsch

Notes: No songs listed in program.

4348 • THREE GRACES, THE

OPENED: 04/02/1906 Theatre: Chicago Opera House
Musical Chicago

Composer: Safford Watters
Lyricist: Harry B. Smith
Librettist: Harry B. Smith

Notes: No other information available.

4349 • 3 GUYS NAKED FROM THE WAIST DOWN

OPENED: 02/05/1985 Theatre: Minetta Lane
Musical Off-Broadway: 160

Composer: Michael Rupert
Lyricist: Jerry Colker
Librettist: Jerry Colker
Producer: James B. Freydberg; Max Weitzenhoffer; Stephen Wells
Director: Andrew Cadiff

Choreographer: Don Bondi; **Costumes:** Tom McKinley; **Lighting Designer:** Ken Billington; **Musical Director:** Henry Aronson; **Orchestrations:** Michael Starobin; **Set Design:** Clarke Dunham

Songs: Angry Guy; Don't Wanna Be No Superstar; Dreams of Heaven; Father Now, A; Hello Fellas; History of Stand-Up Comedy, The; I Don't Believe in Heroes Anymore; Kamikaze Kabaret; Lovely Day; Operator; Promise of Greatness; Screaming Clocks (The Dummies Song); Three Guys Naked from the Waist Down; What a Ride

Cast: Scott Bakula; Jerry Colker; John Kassir

4350 • THREE KISSES, THE

OPENED: 01/1921
Musical

Composer: Sigmund Romberg
Director: Hassard Short

Cast: Vivienne Segal

Notes: Closed in rehearsal before opening in Springfield, Mass.

4351 • THREE LIGHTS, THE

OPENED: 10/31/1911 Theatre: Bijou
Play Broadway: 7

Author: Charles T. Dazey; May Robson
Producer: L.S. Sire
Director: W.H. Post

Songs: Island of Roses and Love, The (C: Neil Moret; L: Earle C. Jones)

Cast: Edith Conrad; Paul Decker; May Robson; Jack Storey

4352 • THREE LITTLE GIRLS

OPENED: 04/14/1930 Theatre: Shubert
Musical Broadway: 104

Composer: Walter Kollo
Lyricist: Harry B. Smith
Librettist: Gertrude Purcell
Producer: Messrs. Shubert
Director: J.J. Shubert

Source: DREI ARME KLEINE MADELS (Musical: Herman Feiner; Bruno Hardt-Warden; Walter Kollo); **Costumes:** Ernest Schrapps; **Lighting Designer:** Marie Armstrong Hecht; **Musical Director:** Louis Kroll; **Set Design:** Watson Barratt

Songs: Annette; Cottage in the Country; Doll Song; Dream On; I'll Tell You; Letter Song; Love Comes Once in a Lifetime (C: Harry Perella; Harold Stern; L: Stella Unger); Love's Happy Dream; Prince Charming; Waltz with Me; Whistle While You Work, Boys

Cast: Margaret Adams; George Dobbs; Thelma Goodwin; Bettina Hall; Natalie Hall; Charles Hedley; Martha Lorber; Stephan Mills; Harry Puck; Raymond Walburn; Lorraine Weismar

4353 • THREE LITTLE LAMBS

OPENED: 12/25/1899 Theatre: Fifth Avenue
Musical Broadway: 49

Composer: E.W. Corliss
Librettist: R.A. Barnet
Producer: Edwin Knowles

Set Design: Ernest Gros; Henry E. Hoyt

Cast: Marie Cahill; William T. Carleton; Lillian Collins; Raymond Hitchcock; Clara Palmer; William E. Philp; Adele Ritchie

4354 • THREE LITTLE MAIDS (1903)

OPENED: 09/01/1903 Theatre: Daly's
Musical Broadway: 130

Composer: Paul Rubens
Lyricist: Paul Rubens
Librettist: Paul Rubens
Producer: George Edwardes; Charles Frohman

Musical Director: Frank E. Tours; **Set Design:** Hawes Craven; Joseph Harker

Songs: Algy's Simply Awfully Good at Algebra; Do I Like Love!; Do You Think That You Have Known Me Long Enought? (C: Walter Rubens; L: Percy Greenbank); Finale Act I (C: Howard Talbot; L: Percy Greenbank); Fishes in the Sea, The; Girl You Love, The; Girls, Girls, Girls; Golf; I'll Dream of You; I'm Only the Caddie (C: Walter Rubens; L: Percy Greenbank); Je Vous Adore; Love, You're a Wonderful Game; Me and the Post; Men; Miller's Daughter, The; My Little Girlie; Opening Chorus (C: Howard Talbot; L: Percy Greenbank); Opening Chorus Act II (C: Howard Talbot; L: Percy Greenbank); Opening Chorus Act III (C: Howard Talbot; L: Percy Greenbank); Real Town Lady, A; Sal; Something Sweet About Me; Suppose We Have a Breakdown (C: Howard Talbot; L: Percy Greenbank); That's a Very Different Thing; There Really Must Be Something Nice About Me; Three Little Maids; Town and Country Mouse, The; Wedding March; What Is a Maid to Do?

Cast: Madge Crichton; Maurice Farkoa; G.P. Huntley; Maggie May

Notes: No songs listed in program. Songs in vocal selection.

4355 • THREE LITTLE MAIDS (1930)

OPENED: 1930
Musical Unproduced

Composer: James P. Johnson
Producer: Shubert Brothers

Notes: No other information available.

4356 • THREE MILLION DOLLARS

Notes: *See THE WIFE HUNTERS.*

4357 • THREE MUSKETEERS, THE

OPENED: 03/13/1928 Theatre: Lyric
Musical Broadway: 319

Composer: Rudolf Friml
Lyricist: Clifford Grey; P.G. Wodehouse
Librettist: William Anthony McGuire
Producer: Florenz Ziegfeld
Director: William Anthony McGuire

Source: THREE MUSKETEERS, THE (Novel: Alexandre Dumas); **Choreographer:** Richard Boleslavsky; Albertina Rasch; **Costumes:** John W. Harkrider; **Musical Director:** Gus Salzer; **Orchestrations:** Hans Spialek; **Set Design:** Joseph Urban

Songs: Ahoy for a Sailor [1]; All for One and One for All; Ballet Romantique (inst.); Colonel and the Major, The; Danse Bohemienne (inst.); Day of the Fair [1]; Every Little While (L: Clifford Grey); Finalette; Gascony (L: Clifford Grey); Gossips; 'He' for Me, The (L: Clifford Grey); Heart of Mine (L: Clifford Grey); Kiss Before I Go, A (One Kiss) (L: Clifford Grey); Love Is the Sun (L: Clifford Grey); Low Moon [1]; Ma Belle (L: Clifford Grey); March of the Musketeers (L: P.G. Wodehouse); My Dreams (L: Clifford Grey); My Sword and I (L: Clifford Grey); Opening Chorus (L: Clifford Grey); Pages; Queen of My Heart (L: Clifford Grey); Queen's Aria [2]; Sabot Dance (inst.); Summertime; Vesper Bell; Welcome to the Queen; With Red Wine; You Walked By [1]; Your Eyes (L: P.G. Wodehouse)

Cast: Lester Allen; Clarence Derwent; Douglas Dumbrille; Harriet Hoctor; Dennis King; Reginald Owen; The Albertina Rasch Girls; Vivienne Segal; Tiller Girls, The

Notes: [1] Composed by Friml for the 1947 San Francisco revival. [2] ASCAP/Library of Congress only.

4358 • THREE POSTCARDS

OPENED: 05/14/1987 Theatre: Playwrights Horizons
Musical Off-Broadway: 22

Composer: Craig Carnelia
Lyricist: Craig Carnelia
Librettist: Craig Lucas
Producer: Playwrights Horizons
Director: Norman Rene

Choreographer: Linda Kostalik-Boussom; **Costumes:** Walter Hicklin; **Lighting Designer:** Debra Kletter; **Set Design:** Loy Arcenas

Songs: Cast of Thousands; I'm Standing in This Room; I've Been Watching You; Minute, A [1]; Opening; Picture in the Hall, The; See How the Sun Shines; She Was K.C.; Three Postcards; What the Song Should Say

Cast: Craig Carnelia; Jane Galloway; Brad O'Hare; Maureen Silliman; Karen Trott

Notes: [1] Added to 1994 revival.

4359 • THREE ROMEOS, THE

OPENED: 11/13/1911 Theatre: Globe
Musical Broadway: 56

Composer: Raymond Hubbell
Lyricist: R.H. Burnside
Librettist: R.H. Burnside
Producer: Dreyfuss-Fellner Co.
Director: R.H. Burnside

Songs: Along Broadway; Anabella Jerome; Between You and Me; Divorce; Education; He's Crazy; In the Spring It's Nice to Have Someone to Love; Lily and the Rose, The; Looking for a Girl Like You; Mary Ann; Matter of Experience, A; Molly Maguire; Moonlight; Off to the Matinee; Off to the Wedding; Oh, Fifth Avenue; Oh, Romeo!; Percy; She Didn't Seem to Care; Where's the Bridegroom?

Cast: Georgia Caine; William Danforth; Fritz Williams; Peggy Wood

Notes: No New York program available. Out-of-town program used.

4360 • THREE SHOWERS

OPENED: 04/05/1920 Theatre: Harris
Musical Broadway: 45

Composer: Turner Layton
Lyricist: Henry Creamer
Librettist: William Cary Duncan
Producer: Charles Coburn; Mrs. Charles Coburn
Director: Oscar Eagle

Choreographer: Edward P. Bower; **Costumes:** Irma Campbell; **Musical Director:** Ivan Rudisill; **Orchestrations:** Will Vodery; **Set Design:** Frank Gates; E.A. Morange

Songs: Always the Fault of the Men [1]; B Is the Note; Baby Lamb [1]; Dancing Tumble-Down [2]; He Raised Everybody's Rent but Kate's; How Wonderful You Are; If, and and But; I'll Have My Way; It Must Be Love; Love Me, Sweetheart Mine; Old Love Is the True Love, The; One of the Boys; Open Your Heart; Pussy Foot; Shower; There's a Way Out; Where Is the Love?; Work Chant; You May Be the World to Your Mother [1]

Cast: Paul Frawley; Andrew J. Lawlor Jr.; Anna Wheaton; Walter Wilson

Notes: [1] Out Baltimore 3/8/20. [2] Titled "Dancing Tumble- Tom" out Baltimore.

4361 • THREE SISTERS

OPENED: 04/09/1934 Theatre: Theatre Royal, Drury Lane
Musical London: 45

Composer: Jerome Kern
Lyricist: Oscar Hammerstein II
Librettist: Oscar Hammerstein II
Producer: H.M. Tennant
Director: Oscar Hammerstein II; Jerome Kern

Choreographer: Ralph Reader; **Costumes:** G.E. Calthrop; **Musical Director:** Charles Prentice; **Orchestrations:** Robert Russell Bennett; **Set Design:** G.E. Calthrop

Songs: Circus Queen [4]; Funny Old House; Gaiety Chorus Girls, The; Hand in Hand; Here It Comes [1]; I Won't Dance [3]; Impression of the Derby, An; Keep Smiling; Lonely Feet [2]; My Beautiful Circus Girl; Now That I Have Springtime; Roll On, Rolling Road; Somebody Wants to Go to Sleep; There's a Joy that Steals Upon You; Three Sisters Opening (Act Two); Welcome to the Bride; What Good Are Words?; What's in the Air Tonight?; You Are Doing Very Well

Cast: Adele Dixon; Dick Francis; Charlotte Greenwood; Gladys Henson; Stanley Holloway; Victoria Hopper; Esmond Knight; Eliot Makeham

Notes: [1] Cut. [2] Used later in film SWEET ADELINE. [3] Revised in 1935 with lyric by Dorothy Fields for film ROBERTA. [4] ASCAP/Library of Congress only.

4362 • THREE TO MAKE READY

OPENED: 03/07/1946 Theatre: Adelphi
Revue Broadway: 327

Composer: Morgan Lewis
Lyricist: Nancy Hamilton
Librettist: Nancy Hamilton
Producer: Stanley Gilkey; Barbara Payne
Director: John Murray Anderson

Choreographer: Robert Sidney; **Costumes:** Audre; **Musical Director:** Anthony Morelli; **Orchestrations:** Robert Russell Bennett; Charles L. Cooke; Elliot Jacoby; Walter Paul; Ted Royal; Hans Spialek; **Set Design:** Donald Oenslager; **Vocal Arranger:** Joe Moon

Songs: And Why Not I; Barnaby Beach; Furnished Bed [1]; If It's Love; It's a Nice Night for It; Kenosha Canoe Ballet; Lovely Lazy Kind of Day, A; Oh You're a Wonderful Person [2]; Old Soft Shoe, The; Rushing the Growler [1]; Tell Me the Story

Cast: Brenda Forbes; Arthur Godfrey; Gordon MacRae

Notes: [1] Out Boston 2/7/46. [2] Not in program.

4363 • THREE TO MAKE READY (MAGIC WITH MARY MARTIN)

OPENED: 03/29/1959 Theatre: NBC
TV Musical

Composer: Linda Melnick Rogers
Lyricist: Mary Rodgers

Musical Director: Thomas Scherman

Songs: Good Afternoon; I Took a Little Walk; It Takes Three to Make Music; Little Orchestra, The; May I Present; Middle of the Night, The; What Kind of Audience Are You?

Cast: Mary Martin; Dirk Sanders

4364 • THREE TWINS

OPENED: 06/15/1908 Theatre: Herald Square
Musical Broadway: 288

Composer: Karl Hoschna
Lyricist: Otto Harbach
Librettist: Charles Dickson
Producer: Joseph M. Gaites
Director: Gus Sohlke

Source: INCOQ (Play: Mrs. R. Pacheo); **Musical Director:** DeWitt C. Coolman

Songs: All My Girls [1] (L: Collin Davis); At a Reception; Begging [3]; Boo-Hoo Tee-Hee Ta Ha; Cuddle Up a Little Closer, Lovey Mine; Dear Little Game of Guessing [2]; Fifth Avenue Brigade, The; Gold to Make You a Queen [2]; Good Night, Sweetheart, Good Night; Hypnotic Kiss, The; I Nver Lose My Head [3]; In Cloudland [2]; It's Up to You to Do the Rest [3]; Little Girl Up There, The; Little Miss Up-to-Date; Over There; Specialist Am I [2]; Summer Pastimes; Three Twins [2]; We Belong to Old Broadway [2]; What's the Use [2]; When Woman, Lovely Woman, Gets Her Rights [2]; Yama Yama Man, The (Pajama Song) (L: Collin Davis); You Need No Crown of Gold to Make You a Queen [2]

Cast: Joseph Allen; Clifton Crawford; Bessie McCoy

Notes: [1] Out of town 10/18/08. [2] Not used. [3] Sheet music only.

4365 • THREE WALTZES

OPENED: 12/25/1937 Theatre: Majestic
Musical Broadway: 122

Composer: Oscar Straus
Lyricist: Clare Kummer
Librettist: Clare Kummer; Rowland Leigh
Producer: Messrs. Shubert
Director: Hassard Short

Source: DREI WALZER (Opera: Paul Knepler; Armin Robinson); **Choreographer:** Chester Hale; **Costumes:** Connie DePinna; **Musical Director:** Harold Levey; **Orchestrations:** Hilding Anderson; Conrad Salinger; Don Walker; **Set Design:** Watson Barratt

Songs: Ballet Rehearsal; Can-Can, The (Music Based On: Johann Strauss Sr.); Do You Recall? (Music Based On: Johann Strauss Sr.); History of Three Generations of Chorus Girls, The; I Sometimes Wonder; I'll Can-Can All Day (Music Based On: Johann Strauss Jr.); My Heart Controls My Head (Music Based On: Johann Strauss Sr.); Olden Days, The; Only One, The (Music Based On: Johann Strauss Jr.); Opening (Music Based On: Johann Strauss Sr.); Our Last Waltz Together; Paree (Music Based On: Johann Strauss

Jr.); Radetzky March; Scandal (Music Based On: Johann Strauss Jr.); Sextette (Music Based On: Johann Strauss Sr.); Springtime Is in the Air (Music Based On: Johann Strauss Sr.); Three Waltzes, The; To Live Is to Love (Music Based On: Johann Strauss Jr.); Vienna Gossip (Music Based On: Johann Strauss Sr.)

Cast: Glenn Anders; Ann Andrews; Charlie Arnt; John Barker; Michael Bartlett; Kitty Carlisle; Ruth Hammond; Jayne Manners; Harry Mestayer; Rosie Moran; Victor Morley; Marion Pierce; Ivy Scott; Louis Sorin; Marguerita Sylva

4366 • THREE WISHES FOR JAMIE

OPENED: 03/21/1952 Theatre: Mark Hellinger
Musical Broadway: 91

Composer: Ralph Blane
Lyricist: Ralph Blane
Librettist: Abe Burrows; Charles O'Neal
Producer: Albert Lewis; Arthur Lewis
Director: Abe Burrows

Source: THREE WISHES FOR JAMIE (Novel: Charles O'Neal); **Choreographer:** Ted Cappy; **Costumes:** Miles White; **Lighting Designer:** Feder; **Musical Director:** Joseph Littau; **Orchestrations:** Robert Russell Bennett; **Set Design:** George Jenkins; **Vocal Arranger:** William Ellfeldt

Songs: April Face; Army Mule Song, The; Expectant Father Dance (inst.) (C: Lee Pockriss); Girl That I Court in My Mind, The; Goin' on a Hayride; I'll Sing You a Song; It Must Be Spring; It's a Wishing World; Jamie's Responsibilities [1]; Kevin [2]; Love Has Nothing to Do with Looks (L: Charles Lederer); Magic Tree [2]; Maybe Is a Woman's Word [1]; My Heart's Darlin'; My Home's a Highway (Sunday Night Supper); Owen Roe [1]; People Talk Too Much [2]; Saint Patrick's Prayer [2]; Search, The [2]; Take Comfort [2]; 'Tis a Wonderful Thing in Nature [1]; Trottin' to the Fair; Wake, The; We're for Love; Wedding March, The; What Do I Know?; Woman's Work, A [2]

Cast: Peter Conlow; Anne Jeffreys; Charlotte Rae; John Raitt; Bert Wheeler

Notes: [1] Out San Francisco 7/30/51. [2] ASCAP/Library of Congress only.

4367 • THREE'S A CROWD

OPENED: 10/15/1930 Theatre: Selwyn
Revue Broadway: 272

Composer: Arthur Schwartz
Lyricist: Howard Dietz
Librettist: Fred Allen; Donald Blackwell; Howard Dietz; Corey Ford; Groucho Marx; William Miles; Laurence Schwab; Arthur Sheekman
Producer: Max Gordon
Director: Hassard Short

Choreographer: Albertina Rasch; **Costumes:** Kiviette; **Musical Director:** Nicholas Kempner; **Set Design:** Albert Johnson

Songs: All the King's Horses (C/L: Eddie Brandt; C: Alec Wilder); Body and Soul (C: John Green; L: Howard Dietz; Frank Eyton; Edward Heyman; Robert Sour); Forget All Your Books [3] (C: Burton Lane); Je T'Aime; Moment I Saw You, The [1]; Night After Night; Out in the Open Air [4] (C: Burton Lane); Practising Up on You (C: Philip Charig); Right at the Start of It; Something to Remember You By [2]; Talkative Toes (C: Vernon Duke); Yaller (C: Charles M. Schwab; L: Henry Myers)

Cast: Fred Allen; California Collegians, The; Tamara Geva; Portland Hoffa; Libby Holman; Margaret Lee; Earl Oxford; Amy Revere; Clifton Webb

Notes: Fred MacMurray was a member of The California Collegians. [1] In London show THE CO-OPTIMISTS OF 1930 with lyrics also credited to Greatrex Newman. [2] Music also used for "I Have No Words" from LITTLE TOMMY TUCKER. [3] Dietz rewrote Sam Lerner's original lyric. [4] Dietz rewrote Ted Pola's original lyric.

4368 • THREEPENNY OPERA, THE (1933)

OPENED: 04/13/1933 Theatre: Empire
Musical Broadway: 12

Composer: Kurt Weill
Lyrics Based On: Bertolt Brecht
Librettist: Gifford Cochran
Producer: Gifford Cochran; Jerrold Krimsky
Director: Frencesco von Mendelssohn

Source: BEGGAR'S OPERA, THE (Opera: John Gay); **Source:** DIE DREIGROSCHENOPER

(Musical: Bertolt Brecht; Kurt Weill); **English Lyrics:** Gifford Cochran; Jerrold Krimsky; **Musical Director:** Macklin Marrow; **Orchestrations:** Kurt Weill; **Set Design:** Caspar Neber; Cleon Throckmorton

Songs: Balled of the Easy Life, The; Cry from the Dungeon; Farewell Tango; First Finale; Jealousy Duet; Legend of Mackie Messer; Love Duet; Lucy's Song; Pirate Jenny; Poor Mrs. Peachum [1] (L: Yvette Guilbert); Second Finale; Soldier's Song, The; Song of the Aimlessness of Life; Tango Ballad; Testament; Third Finale; Wedding Song

Cast: Harry Belaver; Evelyn Beresford; Robert Chisholm; Marjorie Dille; Steffi Duna; Rex Evans; George Heller; Josephine Huston; Burgess Meredith; Herbert Rudlev; Rex Weber

Notes: *See also THE THREEPENNY OPERA 1954 and 1976 as well as 3 PENNY OPERA (1989).* [1] Written for Paris production.

4369 • THREEPENNY OPERA, THE (1954)

OPENED: 03/10/1954 Theatre: Theatre de Lys
Musical Off-Broadway: 2705

Composer: Kurt Weill
Lyrics Based On: Bertolt Brecht
Librettist: Marc Blitzstein
Producer: Carmen Capalbo; Stanley Chase
Director: Carmen Capalbo

Source: BEGGAR'S OPERA, THE (Opera: John Gay); **Source:** DIE DREIGROSCHENOPER (Musical: Bertolt Brecht; Kurt Weill); **English Lyrics:** Marc Blitzstein; **Musical Director:** Samuel Matlowsky; **Orchestrations:** Kurt Weill

Songs: Army Song; Ballad of Dependency; Ballad of Mack the Knife, The; Ballad of the Easy Life; Barbara Song; Bide-a-Wee in Soho, The; Call from the Grave; Death Message; How to Survive; Instead-of Song; Love Song; Morning Anthem; Mounted Messenger, The; Pirate Jenny; Polly's Song; Solomon Song; Tango-Ballad; Useless Song; Wedding Song; World Is Mean, The

Cast: Beatrice Arthur; John Astin; Joseph Beruh; Bernard Bogin; Paul Dooley; Lotte Lenya; Scott Merrill; Gerald Price; Charlotte Rae; Jo Sullivan; George Tyne; Martin Wolfson

Notes: The first run of this production played 94 performances. It then reopened on 9/30/55 for an additional 2,611 performances. *See also THE THREEPENNY OPERA 1933 and 1976 and 3 PENNY OPERA (1989).*

4370 • THREEPENNY OPERA, THE (1976)

OPENED: 05/01/1976 Theatre: Vivian Beaumont
Musical Off-Broadway: 306

Composer: Kurt Weill
Lyrics Based On: Bertolt Brecht
Librettist: Ralph Manheim; John Willett
Producer: N.Y. Shakespeare Festival; Joseph Papp
Director: Richard Foreman

Source: BEGGAR'S OPERA, THE (Opera: John Gay); **Source:** DIE DREIGROSCHENOPER (Musical: Bertolt Brecht; Kurt Weill); **English Lyrics:** Ralph Manheim; John Willett; **Costumes:** Theoni V. Aldredge; **Lighting Designer:** Pat Collins; **Musical Director:** Stanley Silverman; **Set Design:** Douglas W. Schmidt

Songs: Ballad in Which Macheath Begs All Men for Forgiveness; Ballad of Gracious Living; Ballad of Immoral Earnings; Ballad of Mac the Knife; Ballad of Sexual Obsession; Barbara Song; Call from the Grave; Cannon Song; First Threepenny Finale; Jealousy Duet; Liebeslied; "No They Can't" Song; Peachum's Morning Hymn; Pirate Jenny; Polly's Lied; Second Threepenny Finale; Solomon Song; Song of the Insufficiency of Human Endeavor; Third Threepenny Finale; Wedding Song for the Less Well-Off

Cast: C.K. Alexander; Tony Azito; Roy Brocksmith; Blair Brown; Ellen Greene; Raul Julia; Caroline Kava; Elizabeth Wilson; K.C. Wilson

Notes: No songs listed in program. *See also THE THREEPENNY OPERA 1933 and 1954* as well as *3 PENNY OPERA (1989).*

4371 • 3 PENNY OPERA, THE (1989)

OPENED: 11/05/1989 Theatre: Lunt-Fontanne
Musical Broadway: 65

Composer: Kurt Weill
Lyrics Based On: Bertolt Brecht
Librettist: Michael Feinstein

Producer: Jerome Hellman
Director: John Dexter

Source: BEGGAR'S OPERA, THE (Opera: John Gay); **English Lyrics:** Michael Feinstein; **Choreographer:** Peter Gennaro; **Costumes:** Jocelyn Herbert; **Lighting Designer:** Brian Nason; Andy Phillips; **Musical Director:** Julius Rudel; **Orchestrations:** Julius Rudel; Kurt Weill; **Set Design:** Jocelyn Herbert

Songs: Ballad of Living in Style; Ballad of Mack the Knife (Moritat); Ballad of the Prisoner of Sex; Barbara Song; Call from the Grave; Epitaph; First 3 Penny Finale; Jealousy Duet; Love Song; Lucy's Aria; March to the Gallows; Melodrama and Polly's Song; Peachum's Morning Hymn; Pimp's Ballad (Tango); Pirate Jenny; Second 3 Penny Finale; Soldiers' Song; Solomon Song; Song of Futility; Third 3 Penny Finale; Wedding Song; Why Can't They Song

Cast: Jeff Blumenkrantz; Georgia Brown; Kim Criswell; Suzanne Douglas; Ethyl Eichelberger; Alvin Epstein; Mitchell Greenberg; Larry Marshall; Maureen McGovern; Josh Mostel; Nancy Ringham; Philip Schechter; Sting; K.T. Sullivan

Notes: *See also THE THREEPENNY OPERA 1933, 1954 and 1976.*

4372 • THROUGH THE YEARS

OPENED: 01/28/1931 Theatre: Manhattan
Musical Broadway: 20

Composer: Vincent Youmans
Lyricist: Edward Heyman
Librettist: Brian Hooker
Producer: Vincent Youmans
Director: Edgar MacGregor

Source: SMILIN' THROUGH (Play: Jane Cowl; Langdon Martin); **Choreographer:** Jack Haskell; Max Scheck; **Costumes:** John Booth; **Musical Director:** William Daly; **Orchestrations:** Deems Taylor; **Set Design:** Ward & Harvey

Songs: An Invitation; Drums in My Heart; Finaletto Act II; He and I [2]; How Happy Is the Bride; I'll Come Back to You; Invitation, An [5]; It's Every Girl's Ambition [1]; Kathleen, Mine; Kinda Like You; Love Cannot Die [3]; My Heart Is Young [3]; Road to Home, The [4]; Through the Years; Trumpeter and the Lover, The; You're Everywhere; You're in Love [3]

Cast: Michael Bartlett; Gregory Gaye; Natalie Hall; Nick Long Jr.; Marsha Mason; Leone Neumann; Reginald Owen; Charles Winninger

Notes: Titled LOVE IS ALL in Washington, D.C. prior to New York. Titled SMILIN' THROUGH in Philadelphia 12/28/31. [1] Same music as "Daughters" cut from A NIGHT OUT. [2] Cut in rehearsal. [3] Cut during tryout. [4] Same music as "If I Told You" in WILDFLOWER, "Virginia" in RAINBOW and "Sweet Sugar Cane" in GREAT DAY. [5] ASCAP/Library of Congress only.

4373 • THUMBS UP! (1926)

OPENED: 1926
Musical Closed out of town

Composer: Jean Schwartz
Lyricist: George Marion Jr.

Songs: Boarding House Love Call; Cottage I Call Je T'Aime; Cute Peekin' Knees; Do a Duet; Fatal Blonde; Gentlemen of the Press; Guess-Yes; I'm a Little Movie Queen; Journey's End; Just a Little Extra; Ladies, The; Laugh at Love; Never Say Never; Reba; Saturday Night; Stares that Lead to Love; Studio Stamp; Thumbs Up

Notes: No program available. Information from ASCAP and Library of Congress.

4374 • THUMBS UP! (1934)

OPENED: 12/27/1934 Theatre: St. James
Revue Broadway: 156

Librettist: Alan Baxter; Ronald Jeans; Ballard Macdonald; H.I. Phillips; Charles Sherman
Producer: Eddie Dowling
Director: John Murray Anderson; Edward Clarke Lilley

Choreographer: Robert Alton; **Costumes:** Thomas Becher; James Morcon; Raoul Pene du Bois; James Reynolds; **Musical Director:** Gene Salzer; **Orchestrations:** David Raksin; Conrad Salinger; Hans Spialek; **Set Design:** Ted Weidhaus

Songs: Autumn in New York (C/L: Vernon Duke); Beautiful Night (C: James F. Hanley; L: Ballard Macdonald; Karl Stark); Catherine the Great

(C: Henry Sullivan); Color Blind (C: Henry Sullivan; L: Earle Crooker); Continental Honeymoon (C/L: James F. Hanley; L: Ballard Macdonald); Eileen Avourneen (C: Henry Sullivan; L: John Murray Anderson); Flamenco (C: Henry Sullivan; L: Earle Crooker); I've Gotta See a Man About His Daughter (C/L: James F. Hanley; Jean Herbert; Karl Stark); Jogging Along Thru the Park (C: James F. Hanley; L: Ballard Macdonald; Karl Stark); Lily Belle May June (C: Henry Sullivan; L: Earl Crooker); Merrily We Waltz Along (C: Henry Sullivan; L: Earle Crooker); Merry Widow Music without Words, The; Musical Chairs; My Arab Complex (C: James F. Hanley; L: Ballard Macdonald); My Girl's Gone Screwy Over Huey [1]; My Personal Rainbow (C/L: James F. Hanley; Arthur Swanstrom); Rehearsal Hall (C: Henry Sullivan); Ship's Concert, The (C: Henry Sullivan; L: Earle Crooker); Soldier of Love (C: Gerald Marks; L: Irving Caesar; Sammy Lerner); Tango Rhythm (C: Steve Child); Taste of the Sea, A (C: Henry Sullivan; L: Earle Crooker); Time and Tide; Torch Singer (What Do You Think My Heart Is Made Of?) (C: Henry Sullivan; L: Earle Crooker); Zing! Went the Strings of My Heart (C/L: James F. Hanley)

Cast: Margaret Adams; Sheila Barrett; Hugh Cameron; Bobby Clark; Jack Cole; Ray Dooley; Eddie Dowling; Paul Draper; Alice Dudley; John Fearnley; Eddie Garr; Eunice Healey; Rose King; Hal LeRoy; Irene McBride; Paul McCullough; J. Harold Murray; Barnett Parker; Pickens Sisters, The; Al Sexton; Billie Worth

Notes: Originally titled THE FATAL BLONDE. [1] Added after opening.

4375 • TICK-TACK-TOE

OPENED: 02/23/1920 Theatre: Princess
Revue Broadway: 32

Composer: Herman Timberg
Lyricist: Herman Timberg
Librettist: Herman Timberg
Producer: Herman Timberg

Costumes: Homer Conant; **Musical Director:** William A. Krauth; **Set Design:** Watson Barratt

Songs: Chinese-American Rag; Dardanella Blues, The (C: John S. Black; L: Fred Fisher); Double Order of Chicken, A; Girls, Girls, Girls; Hoppy Poppy Queen; I Fell in Love with You; My Manicure Maids; Take Me Back to Philadelphia, Pa.

Cast: Pearl Eaton; Jay Gould; Flo Lewis; Herman Timberg

Notes: No program available. Newspaper review at time said show had 23 numbers.

4376 • TICKETS PLEASE (1916)

OPENED: 04/03/1916
Musical Closed out of town

Composer: William B. Friedlander
Librettist: Will M. Hough

Notes: Played Wheeling, West Virginia at the Victoria Theater.

4377 • TICKETS PLEASE! (1950)

OPENED: 04/27/1950 Theatre: Coronet
Revue Broadway: 245

Composer: Lyn Duddy; Joan Edwards
Lyricist: Lyn Duddy; Joan Edwards
Librettist: Harry Herrmann; Ted Luce; Edmund Rice; Jack Roche
Producer: Arthur Klein
Director: Mervyn Nelson

Choreographer: Joan Mann; **Costumes:** Peggy Morrison; **Incidental Music:** Harold Hastings; Phil Ingalls; **Musical Director:** Phil Ingalls; **Orchestrations:** Ted Royal; **Set Design:** Ralph Alswang

Songs: Back at the Palace (C: Clay Warnick; L: Lucille Kallen; Mel Tolin); Darn It Baby, That's Love; Maha Roger (C: Clay Warnick; L: Lucille Kallen; Mel Tolin); Moment I Looked in Your Eyes, The; Restless; Tickets Please (C: Clay Warnick; L: Lucille Kallen; Mel Tolkin); Washington Square (C: Clay Warnick; L: Lucille Kallen; Mel Tolkin); You Can't Take It with You

Cast: Jack Albertson; Grace Hartman; Paul Hartman; Dorothy Jarnac; Larry Kert; Roger Price; Tommy Wonder

4378 • TICKLE ME

OPENED: 08/17/1920 Theatre: Selwyn
Musical Broadway: 207

Composer: Herbert Stothart
Lyricist: Oscar Hammerstein II; Otto Harbach
Librettist: Oscar Hammerstein II; Otto Harbach; Frank Mandel
Producer: Arthur Hammerstein
Director: William Collier

Choreographer: Bert French; **Costumes:** Charles LeMaire; **Musical Director:** Herbert Stothart; **Set Design:** Joseph Physioc

Songs: Bones [1]; Broadway Swell and Bowery Bum; Ceremony, The; Come Across [1]; Didja Ever See the Like? [1]; Famous You and Simple Me [1]; Finaletto Act I; I Don't Laugh at Love Any More; If a Wish Could Make It So; India Rubber [1]; Little Hindoo Man; Log of the Ship, The [1]; Perfect Lover, The; Safe in the Arms of Bill Hart; Sun Is Nigh, The; Tears of Love [1]; Temptation; Then Love Again; Tickle Me; Tragedy and Comedy [1]; Until You Say Goodbye; Valse du Salon; We've Got Something; You Never Know What a Kiss Can Mean [1]; You're the Type

Cast: Louise Allen; Vic Casmore; Allen Kearns; Frank Tinney; Marguerite Zender

Notes: [1] Cut.

4379 • TICKLES BY TUCHOLSKY

OPENED: 04/26/1976 Theatre: Theatre Four
Musical Off-Broadway: 16

Composer: Kurt Tucholsky
Lyricist: Kurt Tucholsky
Librettist: Kurt Tucholsky
Producer: Primavera Productions; Norman Stephens
Director: Moni Yakim

Costumes: A. Christina Giannini; **Lighting Designer:** Spencer Mosse; **Musical Director:** Wolfgang Knittel; **Set Design:** Don Jensen; **Vocal Arranger:** Wolfgang Knittel

Songs: Anna Louisa; Christmas Shopping; Come Avec!; Compromise Soft Shoe; Epilogue; Follow Schmidt; General! General!; German Evening; Heartbeat; How to Get Rich; I'm Out; It's Your Turn; King's Regiment; Lovers; Lullaby; Over the Trenches; Rising Expectations; Song of Indifference, The; Tickles; To You I Gave My All; Waiting; War Against War

Cast: Helen Gallagher; Jerry Jarrett; Joe Masiell; Joseph Neal; Jana Robbins

Notes: Translated and adapted by Louis Golden and Harold Poor.

4380 • TIGER RAG, THE

OPENED: 02/16/1961 Theatre: Cherry Lane
Musical Off-Broadway: 14

Composer: Kenneth Gaburo
Lyricist: Seyril Schochen
Librettist: Seyril Schochen
Producer: Lorin Ellington Price; Tira Productions
Director: Ella Gerber

Choreographer: Peter Conlow; **Costumes:** Bobb Nichols; **Lighting Designer:** Jules Fisher; **Musical Director:** Milton Seltzer; **Set Design:** Robert Soule

Songs: Apache; Cheerio, Old Boys; Flirtation Waltz; Flowery Waltz; Honeysuckle Vine; Irish Washerwoman's Lament; My Father Was a Peculiar Man; Razz-Me-Tazz-Jazz; Rhumba; Slewfoot Shuffle; Tango; Tiger Rag Blues; Travelling Song; We Were Born By Chance; What Is Good for Depression

Cast: Arthur Anderson; Nancy Andrews; Carlton Colyer; Brennan Moore; Patricia Roe

4381 • TIK TOK MAN OF OZ, THE

OPENED: 06/23/1913
Musical Closed out of town

Composer: Louis F. Gottschalk
Lyricist: L. Frank Baum
Librettist: L. Frank Baum
Producer: Oliver Morosco
Director: Frank Stammers

Source: TIK TOK MAN OF OZ, THE (Novel: L. Frank Baum); **Musical Director:** Victor Schertzinger; **Set Design:** Robert Brunton

Songs: Apple's the Cause of It All, An [1]; Army of Oogaboo, The; Ask the Flowers to Tell You; Clockwork Man, The; Dear Old Hank; Folly!; Gardeners' Chorus; I Think an Awful Lot of You; I Want to Be Somebody's Girlie [1] (C/L: Victor Schertzinger); I've Lost My Bow; Just for Fun; Magnet of Love, The [1]; March of the White and

Gold Imps; My Wonderful Dream Girl [2] (C: Victor Schertzinger; L: Oliver Morosco); Rainbow Bride [1]; Shaggy Man, The; So Do I!; Storm at Sea, A; Summer Rain; There's a Mate in This Big World for You; Waltz Scream, The [1]; Watch Me Close; When in Trouble Come to Papa [1]; Whirlwind, The; Work, Lads, Work!; You Remind Me of My Old Dad

Cast: Josie Intropodi; Thomas Meegan; Lenora Novasio; Adele Rowland; Joseph Whitehead; Fred Woodward

Notes: [1] Sheet music only. [2] Interpolated.

4382 • TILLIE'S NIGHTMARE

OPENED: 05/05/1910 Theatre: Herald Square
Musical Broadway: 77

Composer: A. Baldwin Sloane
Lyricist: Edgar Smith
Librettist: Edgar Smith
Producer: Lew Fields
Director: Ned Wayburn

Costumes: Melville Ellis; **Musical Director:** George A. Nichols; **Set Design:** John H. Young

Songs: Be-Bee; Come One Come All [1]; Dream Song [2]; Every Pretty Girl; Flight of the Air Ship; Good Little Kiddies [2]; Heaven Will Protect the Working Girl; Here's the Latest Thing [1]; Hustle Bustle [1]; I Want to Bring You a Ring (C/L: John Golden); If I Could Find Another Place Like That [2]; I'm Little Bo Peep [2]; I'm Tight [2]; In Paree [2]; It's Hard to Love Just One Girl All the Time [2]; It's the Dress That Makes the Girl [1]; Jazzbo the Jazz King [1]; Life Among the Roses [2]; Life Is Only What You Make It, After All; Little Girl Like You, A [2]; Mother Goose's School [2]; My Dainty Mermaid [2]; Old Gentlemen's Jazz [1]; On Broadway at Night [3]; Shipboard Frolics; Shopping; Shopping Glide, The; Spook Dance; There Goes Another One [3]; There He Goes; They're Off [2]; Tillie's Nightmare; We're the Noble Army [2]; Wedding Rehearsal, The; What I Could Do on the Stage; When I Struck New York [2]; White Light Lane

Cast: Octavia Broske; Marie Dressler; May Montford; Horace Newman; Lottie Uart

Notes: [1] Out Wilkes-Barre 1/21/20. [2] Out Chicago 1/2/10. [3] Out New York 10/16/11.

4383 • TIMBUKTU!

OPENED: 03/01/1978 Theatre: Mark Hellinger
Musical Broadway: 243

Music Based On: Alexander Borodin
Composer: George Forrest; Robert Wright
Lyricist: George Forrest; Robert Wright
Librettist: Luther Davis
Producer: Luther Davis
Director: Geoffrey Holder

Source: KISMET (Play: Edward Knoblock; Charles Lederer); **Source:** KISMET (Musical: Luther Davis; George Forrest; Robert Wright); **Choreographer:** Geoffrey Holder; **Costumes:** Geoffrey Holder; **Lighting Designer:** Ian Calderon; **Musical Director:** Charles H. Coleman; **Orchestrations:** Bill Brohn; **Set Design:** Tony Straiges

Songs: And This Is My Beloved [4]; Baubles, Bangles and Beads [4]; Fate [4]; Fly Away (The Kite Song) [1] (C: George Forrest; Robert Wright); Gesticulate [4]; Golden Land, Golden Life [3]; In the Beginning, Woman [3] (C: George Forrest; Robert Wright); Massa Marries Tonight (Nuptual Celebration), The (dance); My Magic Lamp [2]; Night of My Nights [4]; Power [1] (C: George Forrest; Robert Wright); Rahadlakum [3] (C: George Forrest; Robert Wright); Rhymes Have I [4]; Sands of Time [4]; Stranger in Paradise [4]; Zubbediya [4]

Cast: Ira Hawkins; Eartha Kitt; Eleanor McCoy; Melba Moore; Gilbert Price

Notes: Based on the musical KISMET. *See KISMET*. [1] Cut prior to opening. Not based on Borodin's music. [2] Cut from KISMET. [3] Not based on Borodin's music. [4] From KISMET.

4384 TIME FOR SINGING, A

OPENED: 05/21/1966 Theatre: Broadway
Musical Broadway: 41

Composer: John Morris
Lyricist: Gerald Freedman; John Morris
Librettist: Gerald Freedman; John Morris
Producer: Alexander H. Cohen
Director: Gerald Freedman

Source: HOW GREEN WAS MY VALLEY (Novel: Richard Llewellyn); **Choreographer:** Donald McKayle; **Costumes:** Theoni V. Aldredge;

Lighting Designer: Jean Rosenthal; **Musical Director:** Jay Blackton; **Orchestrations:** Don Walker; **Set Design:** Ming Cho Lee

Songs: And the Mountains Sing Back; Come You Men; Far From Home; Gone in Sorrow; Here Come Your Men; How Green Was My Valley; I Wonder If; I'm Always Wrong; I've Got Nothing to Give; Let Me Love You; Oh, How I Adore Your Name; Old Long John; Peace Come to Every Heart; Someone Must Try; Tell Her; That's What Young Ladies Do; There Is Beautiful You Are; Three Ships; Time for Singing, A; What a Good Day Is Saturday; What a Party; When He Looks at Me; When the Baby Comes; Why Would Anyone Want to Get Married

Cast: Ivor Emmanuel; Frank Griso; George Hearn; Elizabeth Hubbard; Laurence Naismith; Tessie O'Shea; Gene Rupert; Shani Wallis

4385 • TIME GOES BY

Notes: *See SARAFINA (1970).*

4386 • TIME REMEMBERED

OPENED: 11/12/1957 Theatre: Morosco
Play Broadway: 247

Composer: Vernon Duke
Lyricist: Vernon Duke
Author: Jean Anouilh
Translator: Patricia Noyes
Producer: Playwrights' Company, The; Milton Sperling
Director: Albert Marre

Costumes: Miles White; **Lighting Designer:** Feder; **Set Design:** Oliver Smith

Songs: Ages Ago; Time Remembered

Cast: Glenn Anders; Sig Arno; Richard Burton; Helen Hayes; Le Roi Operti; Susan Strasberg

4387 • TIME, THE PLACE AND THE GIRL, THE

OPENED: 08/05/1907 Theatre: Wallack
Musical Broadway: 32

Composer: Joseph E. Howard
Lyricist: Frank Adams; Will M. Hough
Librettist: Frank Adams; Will M. Hough
Producer: Mort H. Singer
Director: Ned Wayburn

Songs: Along Life's Highway [3] (L: G. Swarthart; I. Tressler); Blow the Smoke Away; Dixie, I Love You; Don't You Tell; First and Only [1]; I Don't Like Your Family; I Want a Thrill [3] (L: G. Swarthart; I. Tressler); It's Lonesome Tonight; Junior Miss (L: William B. Friedlander); Love Is a Will-O-the-Wisp (L: William B. Friedlander); Opening Chorus; Pop Step Melody [3] (L: I.R. Goodman); Someone Waiting for Me [3] (L: I.R. Goodman); That's What a Fellow Does When He's In Love [2] (L: Joseph E. Howard); Thursday Is My Jonah Day; Travelin' Man (L: William B. Friedlander); Uncle Sam's Best Girl [1]; Waning Honeymoon, The

Cast: Arthur Deagon; Florence Holbrook; Cecil Lean; Olive Vail

Notes: [1] Out New Bedford 9/28/07. [2] Out Wilkes-Barre 10/26/10. Written for THE FLOWER OF THE RANCH. [3] ASCAP/Library of Congress only.

4388 • TIMOTHY GRAY'S TABOO REVUE

OPENED: 1959 Theatre: Showplace, The
Musical Nightclub

Composer: Warren B. Meyers
Lyricist: Jerry De Bono; Timothy Gray
Producer: Robert Fletcher; Timothy Gray
Director: Timothy Gray

Choreographer: Robert Haddad; **Set Design:** Robert Fletcher

Songs: Come of Age (C: Dolores Clamen); Counter Melody [1] (C: Mary Rodgers; Jay Thompson; L: Marshall Barer); Cream of Mississippi (C: David Baker; L: Sheldon Harnick); Go Away (C: Dolores Clamen); Just Plain Will (C/L: Bill Angelos; Lan O'Kun); Kaleidoscope (C: Dolores Clamen); Kismet Quick (C: Dolores Clamen); Kite, The (C: Dolores Clamen); Lollipop (C/L: Lan O'Kun); Love on the Street (L: Robert A. Bernstein); Man, A (C: Dolores Clamen); Oscar (C/L: Ralph Blane; C: Hugh Martin; L: Timothy Gray); Part of Me (L: Robert A. Bernstein); Plea for Understanding, A (C: Hugh Martin; L: Timothy Gray); Revue Hoedown (C: Dolores

Clamen); This Way Out (C: Dolores Clamen); Triple Tango (C: Dolores Clamen); Two Graces, The (C: Dolores Clamen)

Cast: Don Crichton; Sheila Smith

Notes: [1] Also in FROM A TO Z.

4389 • TINSELTOWN

OPENED: 03/20/1981 Theatre: Shepard
Musical Los Angeles: 24

Composer: Mark Milner
Lyricist: Mark Milner
Librettist: John Vornaholt

Musical Director: Steven Applegate

Songs: Apartmento; Bozo Allegro; Buzz!!!; Commercials, Commercials; Hand Me Down My Dancin' Shoes; Life in the Theatre; SAG Card Blues; Screwing My Way to the Top; Showbiz Finale; This Could Be My Lucky Day; What About Today?; What's 3000 Miles?; Ya Gotta Have a Car

Cast: Diane Benedict; Lynda Lyons; David Pavlosky

Notes: No program available.

4390 • TINTYPES

OPENED: 04/17/1980 Theatre: John Golden
Revue Broadway: 230

Producer: Ivan Bloch; Richmond Crinkley; Royal Pardon Productions; Larry J. Silva; Eve Skina
Director: Gary Pearle

Choreographer: Mary Kyte; **Costumes:** Jess Goldstein; **Dance Arranger:** Mel Marvin; **Lighting Designer:** Paul Gallo; **Orchestrations:** John McKinney; **Set Design:** Tom Lynch; **Vocal Arranger:** Mel Marvin; John McKinney

Songs: America the Beautiful (C: Samuel Ward; L: Katherine Lee Bates); American Beauty (inst.) (C: Joseph F. Lamb); Ay, Lye, Luy, Lye (C/L: Traditional); Ballin' the Jack [1] (C: Chris Smith; L: Jim Burris); Berthena (inst.) (C: Scott Joplin); Bill Bailey, Won't You Please Come Home (C/L: Hughie Cannon); Bird in a Gilded Cage, A (C: Harry Von Tilzer; L: Arthur Lamb); Come Take a Trip in My Airship (C: Ren Shields; L: George Evans); Daisy Bell (C/L: Harry Dacre); El Capitan (inst.) (C: John Philip Sousa); Electricity (C: Karl Hoschna; L: Harry B. Smith); Elite Syncopation (C: Scott Joplin); Eugenia (inst.) (C: Scott Joplin); Fifty-Fifty (C: Chris Smith; L: James Burris); Hello, Ma Baby (C/L: Ida Emerson; Joseph E. Howard); Hot Time in the Old Town Tonight, A (C: Theodore M. Metz; L: Joe Hayden); I Don't Care (C: Jean Lenox; L: Harry O. Sutton); I Want What I Want When I Want It (C: Victor Herbert; L: Henry Blossom); Ida, Sweet As Apple Cider [1] (C/L: Eddie Leonard); If I Were on the Stage (Kiss Me Again) (C: Victor Herbert; L: Henry Blossom); I'll Take You Home Again, Kathleen (C: Thomas P. Westendorf); I'm Goin' to Live Anyhow, 'Til I Die (C/L: Shepard N. Edmonds); In My Merry Oldsmobile (C: Gus Edwards; L: Vincent J. Bryan); Iron Horse [1]; It's Delightful to Be Married (C: Vincent Scotto; L: Anna Held); Jonah Man (C/L: Alex Rogers); Kentucky Babe (C/L: Richard H. Buck; Adam Gelbel); Maiden with the Dreamy Eyes, The (C: Bob Cole; L: James Weldon Johnson); Meet Me in St. Louis, Louis (C: Kerry Mills; L: Andrew B. Sterling); Narcissus (inst.) (C: Ethelbert Nevin); Nobody (C: Bert Williams; L: Alex Rogers); Pastime Rag (inst.) (C: Artie Matthews); Ragtime Dance, The (inst.) (C: Scott Joplin); Ragtime Nightingale (inst.) (C: Joseph F. Lamb); She's Getting More Like the White Folks Every Day (C: Bert Williams; L: George Walker); Shine on Harvest Moon (C/L: Jack Norworth; L: Nora Bayes); Shortnin' Bread (C/L: Traditional); Smiles (C: Lee S. Roberts; L: J. Will Callahan); Solace (inst.) (C: Scott Joplin); Soldiers in the Park, The (C: Lionel Monckton; L: Harry Greenbank; Aubrey Hapwood); Sometimes I Feel Like a Motherless Child (C/L: Traditional); St. Louis Blues [1] (C/L: W.C. Handy); Stars and Stripes Forever (inst.) (C: John Philip Sousa); Streets of New York, The [1] (C: Victor Herbert; L: Henry Blossom); Strike Up the Band [1] (C: George Gershwin; L: Ira Gershwin); Ta-Ra-Ra-Boom-Dee-Ay! (C/L: Henry J. Sayers); Teddy De Roose (C: J. Fred Helf; L: Ed Moran); Then I'd Be Satisfied with Life (C/L: George M. Cohan); Toyland (C: Victor Herbert; L: Glen MacDonough); Wabash Cannonball (inst.) (C: Traditional); Wait for the Wagon (C/L: Traditional); Waltz Me Around Again, Willie (C: Ren Shields; L: Will D. Cobb); Wayfaring Stranger (C/L: Traditional); We Shall Not Be Moved (C/L: Traditional); What It Takes to

Make Me Love You-You've Got It (C: James Reese Europe; L: James Weldon Johnson); When It's All Goin' Out and Nothin' Comin' In (C: Bert Williams; L: George Walker); Yankee Doodle Boy, The (C/L: George M. Cohan); You're a Grand Old Flag (C/L: George M. Cohan)

Cast: Carolyn Mignini; Lynne Thigpen; Trey Wilson; Mary Catherine Wright; Jerry Zaks

Notes: No original songs in this show. Moved to Broadway 10/23/80 for an additional 93 performances. Run above is inclusive of both engagements. [1] Cut Washington prior to New York.

4391 • TINY TREE, THE

OPENED: 12/1975 Theatre: NBC
TV Musical

Composer: Johnny Marks
Lyricist: Johnny Marks

Songs: A Caroling We Go; I Heard the Bells on Christmas Day; (Jouyeux Noel, Buon Natale, Feliz Navidad) A Merry Merry Christmas to You; Joyous Christmas; Minuet for Clarinet; Tell It to a Turtle; To Love and Be Loved; When Autumn Comes

Voice: Buddy Ebsen; Roberta Flack

Notes: Ran five years on NBC.

4392 • TIP-TOES

OPENED: 12/28/1925 Theatre: Liberty
Musical Broadway: 194

Composer: George Gershwin; Ira Gershwin
Librettist: Guy Bolton; Fred Thompson
Producer: Alex A. Aarons; Vinton Freedley
Director: John Harwood

Choreographer: Sammy Lee; **Costumes:** Clare; Kiviette; **Musical Director:** William Daly; **Set Design:** John Young

Songs: Finale Act I; Gather Ye Rosebuds [4]; Harbor of Dreams [4]; Harlem River Chanty [4]; It's a Great Little World! [3]; Lady Luck; Life's Too Short to Be Blue [4]; Looking for a Boy; Nice Baby! (Come to Papa!); Nightie-Night; Our Little Captain; Sweet and Low-Down [2]; That Certain Feeling; These Charming People; Tip-Toes; Waiting for the Train (Florida); We [1]; Weaken a Bit [1]; When Do We Dance?

Cast: Robert Halliday; Allen Kearns; Jeanette MacDonald; Gertrude McDonald; Queenie Smith; Andrew Tombes; Harry Watson; **Pianist:** Victor Arden; Phil Ohman

Notes: [1] Not used. [2] Titled "Blow That Sweet and Low-Down" in London. [3] Sometimes titled "Give In" in London. [4] Cut prior to opening.

4393 • TIP TOP

OPENED: 10/05/1920 Theatre: Globe
Musical Broadway: 241

Composer: Ivan Caryll
Lyricist: Anne Caldwell
Librettist: R.H. Burnside
Producer: Charles Dillingham
Director: R.H. Burnside

Choreographer: Charles Mast; **Costumes:** O'Kane Conwell; Wilhelm; **Musical Director:** William E. MacQuinn

Songs: Beautiful Booby Prize; Cut Dance; Dance of the School Girls; Dance of the Valentines; Finders Is Keepers (and I Found You) [1] (C/L: Tom Brown; Jack Frost); Girl I've Never Met, The [1]; Girl Who Keeps Me Guessing; Give Me That Letter; Humming [1] (C: Ray Henderson; L: Louis Breau); I Don't Belong on a Farm (C: Arthur Swanstrom; L: Clark); I Want a Lily; I Want to See My Ida Hoe in Idaho (C: Bert Rule; L: Alex Sullivan); I'll Say I Love You [3] (C: Victor Jacobi; L: William Le Baron); In the Sea [3]; Keewa-Tak-A-Yaka-Holo (L: Louis Harrison); Lantern of Love, The [1]; Little Fairy in the Home; My Hortense [2]; Opening Chorus; She Knows It; Shoppers' Dance; Sweet Dreams; Tip Top; Wedding Bells (C/L: Benjamin Hapgood Burt); What Makes the Wild Waves Wild; When Shall We Meet Again (C: Richard A. Whiting; L: Raymond B. Egan); Wireless Heart, The [2] (C: Silvio Hein); Wonderful Girl- Wonderful Boy

Cast: Rosetta Duncan; Vivian Duncan; Pauline Hall; Oscar "Rags" Ragland; Helen Rich; Six Brown Brothers; Fred Stone; Violet Zell

Notes: [1] Sheet music only. [2] Out Washington, D.C. 4/16/22. [3] Out San Francisco 3/12/23.

4394 • 'TIS OF THEE

OPENED: 10/26/1940 Theatre: Maxine Elliott's
Revue Broadway: 1

Librettist: Sam Locke
Producer: Nat Lichtman
Director: Nat Lichtman

Choreographer: Esther Junger; **Musical Director:** Alex Saron; **Set Design:** Carl Kent

Songs: After Tonight (C: Al Moss; L: Alfred Hayes); Brooklyn Cantata (C: George Kleinsinger; L: Mike Stratton); Lady, The (C: Elsie Peters; L: Alfred Hayes); Lupe (C: Alex North; L: Alfred Hayes); Noises in the Street [1] (C: Richard Lewine; L: Peter Barry; David Greggory); Rhythm Is Red an' White an' Blue (C: Al Moss; L: David Greggory); Tis of Thee (C: Alex North; L: Alfred Hayes); Tomorrow (C: Alex North; L: Alfred Hayes); What's Mine Is Thine (C: Al Moss; L: Alfred Hayes); You've Got Something to Sing About (C: Al Moss; L: Alfred Hayes)

Cast: Esther Junger; George Lloyd; Mervyn Nelson

Notes: [1] Rewritten and put into MAKE MINE MANHATTAN.

4395 • TO BROADWAY WITH LOVE

OPENED: 04/21/1964
Revue N.Y. World's Fair: 97

Composer: Jerry Bock
Lyricist: Sheldon Harnick
Producer: Compass Fair; George Schaefer; Angus Wynne Jr.
Director: Morton Da Costa

Choreographer: Donald Saddler; **Costumes:** Freddy Wittop; **Lighting Designer:** Jean Rosenthal; **Musical Director:** Oscar Kosarin; **Orchestrations:** Philip J. Lang; **Set Design:** Peter Wolf

Songs: Beautiful Lady; 88 Rag, The (C: Colin Romoff; L: Martin Charnin); Mata Hari Mine; Popsicles in Paris; Remember Radio; To Broadway with Love

Cast: Carmen Alvarez; Kelly Brown; Patti Karr; Don Liberto; Rod Perry; Millie Slavin

Notes: Produced at the Texas Pavilion's Music Hall. This show was presented twice daily with two different casts.

4396 • TO LIVE ANOTHER SUMMER/ TO PASS ANOTHER WINTER

OPENED: 10/21/1971 Theatre: Helen Hayes
Revue Broadway: 173

Composer: Dov Seltzer
Lyricist: David Paulsen
Producer: Leonard Soloway
Director: Jonathan Karmon

Choreographer: Jonathan Karmon; **Costumes:** Lydia Pincus Gang; **Musical Director:** David Krivoshei; **Set Design:** Neil Peter Jampolis

Songs: Better Days; Boy with the Fiddle, The (C/L: Alexander Argov); Can You Hear My Voice? (C: Samuel Kraus; L: George Sherman); Don't Destroy the World; Give Me a Star (C: David Krivoshei); Give Shalom and Sabbath to Jerusalem; Grove of Eucalyptus, The (C: Naomi Shemer; L: George Sherman); Ha'am Haze; Hasidic Medley; I'm Alive (C: David Krivoshei); Mediteranee; Noah's Ark; Sacrifice, The; Son of Man (C/L: David Axelrod); Sorry We Won (C: David Krivoshei); To Live Another Summer to Pass Another Winter; What Are the Basic Things? (L: Lillian Burstein); When My Man Returns (C: George Moustaki)

Cast: Yona Atari; Aric Lavie; Rivka Raz

Notes: Lyrics translated by David Paulsen, Lillian Burstein, George Sherman.

4397 • TO THE WATER TOWER

OPENED: 04/03/1963 Theatre: Second City at Square East
Revue Off-Broadway: 210

Composer: Tom O'Horgan
Producer: Howard Alk; Bernard Sahlins; Paul Sills
Director: Paul Sills

Set Design: Ralph Alswang

Songs: Camp Let-Yourself-Go; Central Intelligence; How to Sell a Fall-Out Shelter; Khrushchev-Kennedy Press Conference; Looking for the

Action; Second City Theme Song; Truth About a Big Fish Story, The; Wordless Dentistry

Cast: Severn Darden; Paul Dooley; Andrew Duncan; Erin Martin; Paul Sand; Eugene Troobnick

Notes: These are songs and sketches. Scenes, dialogue and lyrics created by the company.

4398 • TO WHOM IT MAY CONCERN

OPENED: 12/16/1985 Theatre: St. Stephen's Church
Musical Off-Broadway: 106

Composer: Carol Hall
Lyricist: Carol Hall
Librettist: Carol Hall
Producer: Bedda Roses Company
Director: Geraldine Fitzgerald

Choreographer: Michael O'Flaherty; **Lighting Designer:** Christina Giannelli; **Musical Director:** Michael O'Flaherty; **Vocal Arranger:** Michael O'Flaherty

Songs: Ain't Love Easy; Ain't Nobody Got a Bed of Roses; Blessed Be God; Dancing Bear [1]; Holy God; I Believe in God [1]; I Only Miss the Feeling (Not the Man); In the Mirror's Reflection; Jenny Rebecca [2]; Kyrie [1]; Little Plastic Man [1]; Make a Joyful Noise; Miracles; My Sort of Ex-Boyfriend; Sandy; Skateboard Acrobats; To Whom It May Concern; Truly My Soul; Walk in Love; We Believe; We Were Friends; When I Consider the Heavens; Who Will Dance with the Blind Dancing Bear

Cast: Dylan Baker; Gretchen Cryer; Al DeCristo; Louise Edeiken; Becky Gelke; George Gerden; Carol Hall; William Hardy; Michael Hirsch; Kecia Lewis-Evans; Jennifer Naimo; Michael O'Flaherty; Guy Stroman; Tamara Tunie

Notes: [1] Cut out of town. [2] Not written for this show.

4399 • TOGETHER AGAIN FOR THE FIRST TIME

OPENED: 02/27/1989 Theatre: Kaufman
Revue Off-Broadway: 30

Composer: Frank Loesser
Lyricist: Frank Loesser
Additional Lyrics: Barry Kleinbort
Producer: Martin R. Kaurman
Director: Barry Kleinbort

Choreographer: Donald Saddler; **Costumes:** William Ivey Long; **Lighting Designer:** Ted Mather; **Musical Director:** Colin Romoff; **Set Design:** Philip Baldwin

Songs: Another Openin' Another Show [1] (C/L: Cole Porter); Anywhere I Wander [2]; Bushel and a Peck, A [3]; Can You Read My Mind [4] (C: John Williams; L: Leslie Bricusse); Can't You Just See Yourself [5] (C: Jule Styne; L: Sammy Cahn); Don't Let It Get You Down [6] (C: Burton Lane; L: E.Y. Harburg); Ev'ry Time [7] (C/L: Ralph Blane; Hugh Martin); Everything I've Got [8] (C: Richard Rodgers; L: Lorenz Hart); Family (C: Barry Kleinbort; L: Neil Kleinbort); Frank Loesser medley; Glamorous Life, The [9] (C/L: Stephen Sondheim); Heart [10] (C/L: Richard Adler; Jerry Ross); I Got Lost in His Arms [11] (C/L: Irving Berlin); I Love to Sing-A [12] (C: Harold Arlen; L: E.Y. Harburg); I Wish It So [13] (C/L: Marc Blitzstein); Inchworm [2]; I've Got a Crush on You [14] (C: George Gershwin; L: Ira Gershwin); Mack the Knife [15] (C: Kurt Weill; L: Marc Blitzstein); Mine [16] (C: George Gershwin; L: Ira Gershwin); One More Kiss [17] (C/L: Stephen Sondheim); Pack Up Your Sins [18] (C/L: Irving Berlin); Sing Something Simple [19] (C/L: Herman Hupfeld); There Is Nothin' Like a Dame [20] (C: Richard Rodgers; L: Oscar Hammerstein II); Thumbelina [2]; Travellin' Light [3]; What Is There to Say? [21] (C: Vernon Duke; L: E.Y. Harburg); What Was (C/L: Barry Kleinbort); What's Next (C/L: Barry Kleinbort); When I'm Not Near the Girl I Love [22] (C: Burton Lane; L: E.Y. Harburg); Wind Blows in My Window, The; Wonderful Copenhagen [2]; You Understand Me [23]

Cast: Emily Loesser; Jo Sullivan

Notes: [1] From KISS ME, KATE. [2] From the film HANS CHRISTIAN ANDERSEN. [3] From GUYS AND DOLLS. [4] From the film SUPERMAN. [5] From HIGH BUTTON SHOES. [6] From HOLD ON TO YOUR HATS. [7] From BEST FOOT FORWARD. [8] From BY JUPITER. [9] From A LITTLE NIGHT MUSIC. [10] From DAMN YANKEES. [11] From ANNIE GET YOUR GUN. [12] From the film THE SINGING

KID. [13] From JUNO. [14] From STRIKE UP THE BAND. [15] From THE THREEPENNY OPERA. [16] From LET 'EM EAT CAKE. [17] From FOLLIES. [18] From MUSIC BOX REVUE (SECOND EDITION). [19] From THE SECOND LITTLE SHOW. [20] From SOUTH PACIFIC. [21] From ZIEGFELD FOLLIES OF 1934. [22] From FINIAN'S RAINBOW. [23] From SENOR DISCRETION.

4400 • TOINETTE (1920)

Notes: *See ALWAYS YOU.*

4401 • 'TOINETTE (1961)

OPENED: 11/20/1961 Theatre: Theatre Marquee
Musical Off-Broadway: 31

Composer: Dede Meyer
Lyricist: Dede Meyer
Librettist: J.J. Rodale
Producer: Bickerstaff Productions
Director: Curt Conway

Source: LA MALADE IMAGINAIRE (Play: Moliere); **Choreographer:** Harry Wolever; **Costumes:** Joe Regan; **Lighting Designer:** Don Sussman; **Musical Director:** David Shire; **Set Design:** Stuart Bishop

Songs: Beat, Little Pulse; Bonjour; Come On Outside and Get Some Air; Dr. Iatro; Even a Doctor Can Make a Mistake; Father Speaks, A; Fly Away; Honest Honore; Lullaby, A; Madly in Love with You Am I; Rags; Recitative; Small Apartment; Someone to Count On; 'Toinette; Un, Deux, Trois; Why Shouldn't I?; You're the Most Impossible Person

Cast: Paul Dooley; Tom Ingham; Joelle Jones; Logan Ramsey; Bob Randall; Ellie Wood

4402 • TOLLER CRANSTON'S THE ICE SHOW

OPENED: 05/19/1977 Theatre: Palace
Revue Broadway: 60

Producer: Myrl A. Schreibman
Director: Myrl A. Schreibman

Choreographer: Brian Foley; **Costumes:** Miles White; **Lighting Designer:** D. Scott Linder; **Set Design:** Anthony Sabatino

Songs: Let's Hear It for Me [1]; Toller's Theme (inst.) (C: Joel Hirschhorn; Al Kasha)

Cast: Toller Cranston

Notes: Only original songs listed. [1] Written for this show.

4403 • TOM EYEN'S DIRTIEST MUSICAL

OPENED: 12/09/1975 Theatre: Truck and Warehouse
Musical Off-Broadway

Composer: Henry Krieger
Lyricist: Tom Eyen
Librettist: Tom Eyen

Songs: Angry Boogie; Attention; Can You See; Dirty; I Am Movin'; I Love You; I See You Everywhere; Looking for Something; One More Romance; Peace; Please Be Kind; Rainbow Shines; Smile; Would You Love Me More?

Cast: Hugh Allen; Nell Carter; Alison Fraser; Madeleine LeRoux; Michelle Shay; Ray Shell

Notes: No progam available.

4404 • TOM JONES (1907)

OPENED: 11/11/1907 Theatre: Astor
Musical Broadway: 55

Composer: Edward German
Lyricist: Charles H. Taylor
Librettist: Robert Courtneidge; A.M. Thompson
Producer: Henry W. Savage
Director: Robert Courtneidge; Edward German

Source: TOM JONES (Novel: Henry Fielding); **Costumes:** Mme. Herman; **Lighting Designer:** Joseph Wilson; **Musical Director:** Herman Perlet; **Set Design:** Walter Burridge

Songs: All for a Green Ribbon; As All the Maids [2]; Barley Mow, The; Beguile, Beguile, with Music Sweet; Benjamin Partridge a Person of Parts; Don't You Find the Weather Charming?; Dream O'Day Jill; Festina Lente [2]; For Aye, My Love; Gloss of Fashion; Hark! The Merry Marriage Bells; Here's a Paradox for Lovers; Hey Derry Down [2]; Hurry, Bustle!; I Wonder; If Love's Content; King Neptune; Let's Be Merry; Love

Maketh the Heart a Garden Fair; My Lady's Coach Has Been Attacked; On a January Morning (in Zummersetscheer); Person of Parts, A [2]; Scarlet Coat, A [2]; Today My Spinet; Uncle John Tappit; We Redcoat Soldiers Serve the King [1]; West Country Lad; Where Be My Daughter [2]; Which Is My Own True Self [2]; Wisdom Says "Festina Lente"; Wise Old Saws [2]; You Have a Pretty Wit [2]

Cast: John Bunny; Louise Gunning; William Norris; Gertrude Quinlan; Van Rensselaer Wheeler

Notes: [1] Added to post-London tour. [2] In original London version only.

4405 • TOM JONES (1969)

OPENED: 04/1969
Musical Closed out of town

Composer: Robert Archer
Lyricist: Peter Bergman; Joseph Mathewson
Librettist: Austin Pendleton
Producer: Extension Company, The
Director: Richard Michaels

Choreographer: Mary Fariday; **Lighting Designer:** Don Abrams; **Musical Director:** Herb Kaplan; **Orchestrations:** Arthur Rubinstein

Songs: Battle for the Western Name; Bright Moon Above; Bubble Bubble; Captain Jones; Charity; Get That Will; Homecoming Cantata; Infamy; Life Like That, A; She Was a Maid; Sunlight; Thank the Lord; Trunk Packing Song; Under the Allworthy Road; Waiting

4406 • TOM JONES (1976)

OPENED: 1976
Musical Closed out of town

Composer: Barbara Damashek
Lyricist: Larry Arrick; Barbara Damashek
Librettist: Larry Arrick

Source: TOM JONES (Novel: Henry Fielding)

Cast: James Naughton; Teri Ralston; Lea Richardson; Joy Smith

Notes: Closed Stamford, Conn. No program available.

4407 • TOM MOORE

OPENED: 08/31/1901 Theatre: Herald Square
Play Broadway

Composer: Andrew Mack
Lyricist: Andrew Mack
Author: Theodore Burt Sayre
Producer: Rich and Harris

Songs: My Love of Long Ago; Song Games

Cast: Myron Calice; Josephine Lovett; Andrew Mack; John Napier

4408 • TOM PIPER

OPENED: 07/14/1969
Musical Closed out of town

Composer: Edward Lasko
Lyricist: Edward Lasko
Librettist: Edward Lasko
Producer: Goodspeed Opera House
Director: Davey Marlin-Jones

Choreographer: Darwin Knight; **Costumes:** Evelyn Norton Anderson; **Lighting Designer:** John Sloat; **Musical Director:** Roy M. Rogosin; **Set Design:** Raymond T. Kurdt

Songs: Beautiful People; Before I'll Settle for Him; Chowder Ball; Civilization; Come with Me; Company Picnic; Dreams Have I; For the First Time; Give Me a Ship; Let Me Tell You About My House; My Tom; Obedience; Over and Over; Run Away; She Will Come Around; Ship Comin' In; Some Special Place for Me; That's the Way I Am; That's What a Woman Sees; Wedding Night

Cast: Dorothy Emmerson; Kathleen Freeman; Travis Hudson; Larry Kert; Peter Palmer

Notes: Goodspeed Opera House.

4409 • TOM SAWYER

OPENED: 11/21/1956 Theatre: CBS
TV Musical

Composer: Frank Luther
Lyricist: Frank Luther

Source: TOM SAWYER (Novel: Mark Twain); **Musical Director:** Ralph Norman Wilkinson

Songs: Aunt Polly's Prayer; Big Missouri, The; Girls Can't Lie; Have a Happy Holiday; He Wasn't a Bad Boy; I Gotta Whitewash; I Want to Go Home; In the Spring; It Ain't fer Me; McDougal's Cave; Missouri Meadowlark; My Friend Huckleberry Finn; My Love Has Gone Away; Please Make Up; Storm Come A' Risin'; That Lucky Boy Is Me; That's the Life for Me; There's a New Girl in Town; Time Has Come to Say Goodbye, The; We'll All Shout Together in the Mornin'; What Do You Kiss For?; Why Would You Want to Kiss Me?; You Can't Teach an Old Dog New Tricks

Cast: Rose Bampton; Jimmy Boyd; Clarence Cooper; Bennye Gatteye; John Sharpe; Song Spinners, The

Notes: Original TV musical.

4410 • TOM TAYLOR AS WOODY GUTHRIE

OPENED: 11/26/1979 Theatre: Cherry Lane
Musical Off-Broadway: 47

Composer: Woody Guthrie
Lyricist: Woody Guthrie
Librettist: George Boyd; Michael Diamond; Tom Taylor
Producer: Michael Diamond; Harold Leventhal
Director: George Boyd

Costumes: Robert Blackman; **Lighting Designer:** Daniel Adams; **Set Design:** Robert Blackman

Cast: Tom Taylor

Notes: No original songs in this one-man show.

4411 • TOM TOM

OPENED: 1903 Theatre: La Salle Chicago

Composer: Joseph E. Howard
Lyricist: Raymond W. Peck
Librettist: Raymond W. Peck

Notes: No other information available.

4412 • TOMFOOLERY

OPENED: 12/03/1981 Theatre: Top of the Gate
Revue Off-Broadway: 27

Composer: Tom Lehrer
Lyricist: Tom Lehrer
Producer: Cameron Mackintosh; Hinks Shimberg
Director: Mary Kyte; Gary Pearle

Costumes: Ann Emonts; **Lighting Designer:** Robert Jared; **Musical Director:** Eric Stern; **Set Design:** Tom Lynch; **Vocal Arranger:** John McKinney

Songs: Be Prepared; Bright College Days; Elements, The; Fight Fiercely, Harvard; Folk Song Army, The; Hunting Song; I Got It from Agnes; I Hold Your Hand in Mine; I Wanna Go Back to Dixie; In Old Mexico; Irish Ballad; Masochism Tango; My Home Town; National Brotherhood Week; New Math; Oedipus Rex; Old Dope Peddler, The; Poisoning Pigeons; Pollution; Send the Marines; She's My Girl; Silent E; So Long Mom; Vatican Rag, The; We Will All Go Together; Wernher von Braun; When You Are Old and Grey; Who's Next

Cast: Don Correia; MacIntyre Dixon; Joy Franz; Jonathan Hadary

Notes: No original songs in this show.

4413 • TOMMY

Notes: *See THE WHO'S TOMMY.*

4414 • TOMMY ROT

OPENED: 10/20/1902 Theatre: Mrs. Osborn's Playhouse
Musical Broadway: 39

Composer: Safford Waters
Lyricist: Safford Waters
Librettist: Joseph W. Herbert; Rupert Hughes; Kirke La Shelle; Paul West

Songs: Belle of Avenue A, The [1]; Every Dog Must Have His Day and Every Puss Her Afternoon; There's a Strange Fascination About the Stage

Cast: Evelyn Nesbitt; Fletcher Norton; Blanche Ring

Notes: No program available. [1] Interpolated.

4415 • TONGUE IN CHEEK (1949)

OPENED: 03/28/1949
Revue Closed out of town

Composer: Earl Brent
Lyricist: Earl Brent
Librettist: Charles Faber
Producer: Ross Hunter; Jacque Mapes
Director: Ross Hunter

Choreographer: Lester Horton; Bella Lewitzky; **Costumes:** Maria Donovan; **Musical Director:** John Lattimer; **Set Design:** Jacque Mapes; **Vocal Arranger:** Paul Owen

Songs: Autumn's in the Red Again; Body in the Trunk; Fabulous You; Girl in the Window (C/L: Ross Hunter); Heredity; House in the Country; I Call Him 'Al'; Jersey City Rhapsody; Move On (C/L: Buddy Pepper); Nice Little Day; Star without a Job (C: Earl Brent; Buddy Pepper; L: Ross Hunter); Tennessee (C/L: Buddy Pepper); World's Oldest Boy Violinist, The; You're Wonderful

Cast: Ross Hunter; Danny Scholl

4416 • TONGUE IN CHEEK (1958)

OPENED: 04/05/1958
Revue Closed out of town

Composer: Edward C. Redding
Lyricist: Edward C. Redding
Librettist: Earl Carroll; Edward Collins; Herbert Farjeon; Peg Harig; Jay Looney; Fred Rome
Producer: Frederick Burleigh

Choreographer: Robert Ragent; **Costumes:** Corinne Van Dame; **Dance Arranger:** James Reed Lawlor; **Musical Director:** James Reed Lawlor; **Set Design:** Barry Buchter; Robert Stanger; Tom Vawter; **Vocal Arranger:** James Reed Lawlor

Songs: Bad-Bad-Bad; Boy Meets Girl; Finale (C/L: James Reed Lawlor); Grapevine, The [1]; I Couldn't Be Happier [3] (C/L: Bud McCreery); I've Been to the Moon; Jefferson Davis Tyler's General Store [2]; Little Sambo; Love Was Dancing Beside Me; Mood Music (C/L: Portia Nelson); Opening; Since Memphis (C/L: Portia Nelson); Somebody's Got To; Too Many Men; Way of a Woman, The (C/L: Portia Nelson); We Who Are About to Die (C/L: Bud McCreery)

Cast: Joan Bails

Notes: [1] Also in TAKE FIVE as "Gossiping Grapevine." [2] Also in TAKE FIVE and FOUR BELOW STRIKES BACK. [3] Originally in SHOESTRING REVUE.

4417 • TONIGHT AT 8:30

Notes: *See FAMILY ALBUM, RED PEPPERS, SHADOW PLAY* and *WE WERE DANCING,* four musical one-acts that were part of the nine one-acts that comprised this show.

4418 • TONIGHT'S THE NIGHT (1914)

OPENED: 12/24/1914 Theatre: Shubert
Musical Broadway: 108

Composer: Paul Rubens
Lyricist: Percy Greenbank; Paul Rubens
Librettist: Fred Thompson
Producer: Messrs. Shubert
Director: Austen Hurgon

Source: LES DOMINOS ROSES (Play: Delacour; Hennequin); **Musical Director:** Frank Tours; **Set Design:** Brunskill; Alfred Craven; Joseph Harker; Phil Harker

Songs: Any Old Night (Is a Wonderful Night) [1] (C: Jerome Kern; Otto Motzan; L: Schuyler Greene; Harry B. Smith); I Could Love You If I Tried; I'm a Millionaire; Only Way, The; Pink and White; Play Me That Tune; Please Don't Flirt with Me; Round the Corner; Stars; They Didn't Believe Me [2] (C: Jerome Kern; L: Herbert Reynolds); To-night's the Night

Cast: James Blakeley; Fay Compton; Lauri De Frece; Maurice Farkoa; George Grossmith; Leslie Henson

Notes: No program available. Songs from English and American sheet music. [1] Added to English production. From NOBODY HOME. [2] Added to English production. From THE GIRL FROM UTAH.

4419 • TONIGHT'S THE NIGHT (1945)

OPENED: 12/24/1945 Theatre: Shubert
Musical Broadway: 108

Composer: Paul Rubens
Lyricist: Paul Rubens
Librettist: Fred Thompson
Producer: Messrs. Shubert
Director: Austen Hurgon

Songs: Any Old Night [2] (C: Jerome Kern; L: Otto Motzan); Boots and Shoes; Dancing Mad; I Could Love You If I Tried; I'd Like to Bring My Mother; I'm a Millionaire; Land and Water; Only Way, The; Pink and White; Round the Corner; Stars; They Didn't Believe Me [1] (C: Jerome Kern; L: Herbert Reynolds); Tonight's the Night; Too Particular; When the Boys Come Home to Tea; You Must Not Flirt with Me

Cast: Fay Compton; George Grossmith; Leslie Henson

Notes: [1] From THE GIRL FROM UTAH. Originally in NOBODY HOME with Schuyler Green and Harry B. Smith lyrics. [2] Originally in NOBODY HOME with Schuyler Green and Harry B. Smith lyrics. In London version only.

4420 • TOO MANY GIRLS

OPENED: 10/18/1939 Theatre: Imperial
Musical Broadway: 249

Composer: Richard Rodgers
Lyricist: Lorenz Hart
Librettist: George Marion Jr.
Producer: George Abbott
Director: George Abbott

Choreographer: Robert Alton; **Costumes:** Raoul Pene du Bois; **Lighting Designer:** Jo Mielziner; **Musical Director:** Harry Levant; **Orchestrations:** Hans Spialek; **Set Design:** Jo Mielziner; **Vocal Arranger:** Hugh Martin

Songs: 'Cause We Got Cake; Give It Back to the Indians; Heroes in the Fall (L: Richard Rodgers); Hunted Stag, The [1]; I Didn't Know What Time It Was; I Like to Recognize the Tune; Look Out; Love Never Went to College; My Prince (What a Prince!); Pottawatomie; She Could Shake the Maracas; Spic and Spanish; Sweethearts of the Team, The; Tempt Me Not; Too Many Girls; You're Nearer

Cast: Desi Arnaz; Eddie Bracken; Diosa Costello; Clyde Fillmore; Van Johnson; Richard Kollmar; Mildred Law; Hal LeRoy; Hans Robert; Mary Jane Walsh; Marcy Wescott

Notes: [1] Cut prior to opening.

4421 • TOOT SWEET

OPENED: 05/07/1919 Theatre: Princess
Revue Broadway: 45

Composer: Richard A. Whiting
Lyricist: Raymond B. Egan
Librettist: Everybody
Producer: Will Morrissey
Director: Will Morrissey

Musical Director: Hilding Anderson

Songs: America's Answer; Baby Vampire (C/L: Ray K. Moulton); Blightly Bound; Carolina; Charge of the Song Brigade; Dance de Nautica Americaine; Eyes of the Army; French Soldiers on Leave Dance; Give Him Back His Job; Je Ne Sais Pas; Just Around the Corner from Easy Street; L'Elefant Skeed; Madelon; One of the Ruins of France (C/L: Ray K. Moulton); Preliminary Skirmish; Rose of Verdun; Salvation Sal; Tout Suite; You'll Never Get a Whimper Out of Me (C/L: Will Morrissey)

Cast: May Boley; Elizabeth Brice; Lon Haskell; Will Morrissey; Sam Ward

Notes: Titled OVERSEAS REVUE in sheet music where Jack Mason was credited with direction and Elizabeth Brice was co-producer.

4422 • TOOT-TOOT!

OPENED: 03/11/1918 Theatre: Cohan
Musical Broadway: 40

Composer: Jerome Kern
Lyricist: Berton Braley
Librettist: Edgar Allen Woolf
Producer: Henry W. Savage
Director: Edward Rose; Edgar Allen Woolf

Source: EXCUSE ME (Play: Rupert Hughes); **Choreographer:** Robert Marks; **Costumes:** Faibsey; **Lighting Designer:** Joseph Wilson; **Musical Director:** Anton Heindl; **Set Design:** Clifford Pember

Songs: Every Girl in All America; Girlie; Good-Bye and Good Luck; Honey Moon Land; I Will Knit a Suit of Dreams (Teepee); If (There's Anything You Want); If You Only Care Enough

[1] (L: Berton Braley); Indian Fox Trot; It's Greek to Me; It's Immaterial to Me; Kan the Kaiser; Last Long Mile, The (C/L: Emil Breitenfeld); Let's Go; Quarrel and Part; Runaway Colts; Shower of Rice, A; Smoke; Toot-Toot!; When You Wake Up Dancing; Yankee Doodle on the Line [1] (L: Berton Braley); You're So Cute Soldier Boy (C: Anatole Freidland; L: Edgar Allen Woolf)

Cast: Louise Allen; Louise Groody; Florence Johns; William Kent; Flora Zabelle

Notes: [1] ASCAP/Library of Congress only.

4423 • TOP BANANA

OPENED: 11/01/1951 Theatre: Winter Garden
Musical Broadway: 350

Composer: Johnny Mercer
Lyricist: Johnny Mercer
Librettist: Hy Kraft
Producer: Mike Sloane; Paula Stone
Director: Jack Donahue

Choreographer: Ron Fletcher; **Costumes:** Alvin Colt; **Lighting Designer:** Jo Mielziner; **Musical Director:** Harold Hastings; **Orchestrations:** Don Walker; **Set Design:** Jo Mielziner; **Vocal Arranger:** Hugh Martin

Songs: Be My Guest; Dog Is a Man's Best Friend, A; Elevator Song (Go to the Rear of the Car Please); Girl of All Nations [1]; Hail to MacCracken's; Havin' a Ball [1]; I Fought Every Step of the Way; Man of the Year This Week, The; Meet Miss Blendo; My Home Is in My Shoes; Nobody Understands Me [1]; O.K. for T.V. (You're O.K. for T.V.); Only If You're in Love; Sans Souci; Senorita Diaz [1]; Slogan Song (You Gotta Have a Slogan); That's for Sure; Top Banana; Word a Day, A (Ambiguous Means I Love You); You're So Beautiful That —

Cast: Jack Albertson; Lindy Doherty; Herbie Faye; Joey Faye; Eddie Hanley; Judy Lynn; Rose Marie; Ted Morgan; Bob Scheerer; Phil Silvers

Notes: [1] ASCAP/Library of Congress only.

4424 • TOP-HOLE

OPENED: 09/01/1924 Theatre: Fulton
Musical Broadway: 104

Composer: Jay Gorney
Lyricist: Owen Murphy
Librettist: Eugene Conrad; George Dill; Gladys Unger
Producer: William Caryl
Director: David Bennett

Choreographer: David Bennett; Seymour Felix; **Musical Director:** William Daly

Songs: Cheerio! (C: Lewis E. Gensler; L: Ira Gershwin); Dance Your Way to Paradise; Every Silken Lady; Every Time the Clock Ticks [2]; Golfing (C: Robert Braine; L: Eugene Conrad); Imagine Me without My You (and You without Your Me) [3] (C: Lewis E. Gensler; L: Robert Russell Bennett; Ira Gershwin); Is It Any Wonder; Love Is a Sandman (C: Robert Braine; L: Eugene Conrad); Me and You [1]; Safe in Your Heart [1]; Stardust [1]; Then You Know That You're in Love (C/L: Jay Gorney; Owen Murphy; Harry Richman); There's Always Room for a Smile [1]; There's Music in an Irish Song; Top Hole [1]; We Ran Away from School; Whistle in the Rain [1] (C: J. Fred Coots; L: McElbert Moore); You Must Come Over Eyes

Cast: Ernest Glendinning; Clare Stratton

Notes: No New York program available. [1] Out Newark 4/28/24. [2] Out New Haven 8/28/23. [3] Not used.

4425 • TOP O' THE WORLD, THE

OPENED: 10/19/1907 Theatre: Majestic
Musical Broadway: 156

Composer: Anne Caldwell
Lyricist: James O'Dea
Librettist: Mark Swan
Producer: J.M. Allison
Director: Frank Smithson

Choreographer: Luigi Albertierri; William Rock

Songs: After All [1]; Aurora (from Aurora, Illinois); Busy Mr. Bee; Cupid and You and I (C/L: Manuel Klein); Doll Ballet (inst.) (C: Manuel Klein); Don't You Want to Be My Bow-Wow- Wow [2]; Eccentric Dance (inst.) (C: Manuel Klein); Entrance of Aurora [2]; Finale Act I; Finale Act II; Gold, Gold, Gold; Goodbye, Dinah; Hail to Aurora; Hand Me Out a Laugh; How'd You Like to Be My Bow-Wow-Wow?; Little Brown Hen; My Dolls; My

Shaggy Old Polar Bear; O'er the Snow; One Girl, The; Opening Chorus Act I (L: Joseph W. Herbert); Opening Chorus Act II (C: Manuel Klein); Perfectly Terrible [1]; Riddle- Ma-Ree; Sailing In a Sea-Going Hack (L: Joseph W. Herbert); Side By Side [1] (C: Manuel Klein); Tinymite (C: Manuel Klein); Where Fate Shall Guide; Why Don't You?; Yankee Doodle Yarns

Cast: Kathleen Clifford; Wellington Cross; Harry Fairleigh; Bessie Franklin; Anna Laughlin; George Monroe

Notes: [1] Out Kansas City 10/11/08. [2] Vocal score only.

4426 • TOP SPEED

OPENED: 12/25/1929 Theatre: 46th Street
Musical Broadway: 102

Composer: Harry Ruby
Lyricist: Bert Kalmar
Librettist: Guy Bolton; Bert Kalmar; Harry Ruby
Producer: Guy Bolton; Bert Kalmar; Harry Ruby
Director: John Harwood

Choreographer: John Boyle; LeRoy Prinz; **Costumes:** Kiviette; **Musical Director:** Ivan Rudisill; **Set Design:** Raymond Sovey

Songs: Dizzy Feet; Fireworks; Goodness Gracious [2]; Hot and Bothered; I'd Like to Be Liked; I'll Know and She'll Know [2]; In the Summer; Keep Your Undershirt On; Looking for the Lovelight in the Dark [2] (C: Joe Burke; L: Al Dubin); On the Border Line; Papers, The; Reaching for the Moon [2]; Sweeter Than You [1]; Try Dancing; We Want You; What Would I Care?; You Couldn't Blame Me for That

Cast: Lester Allen; Sunny Dale; Irene Delroy; Harland Dixon; Paul Frawley; Hermes Pan; Ginger Rogers

Notes: [1] Also in TWINKLE TWINKLE. [2] Sheet music only.

4427 • TOPICS OF 1923

OPENED: 11/20/1923 Theatre: Broadhurst
Revue Broadway: 143

Composer: Al Goodman; Jean Schwartz
Lyricist: Harold Atteridge
Librettist: Harold Atteridge; Harry Wagstaff Gribble
Producer: Messrs. Shubert
Director: J.C. Huffman

Choreographer: M. Francis Weldon; **Costumes:** Travis Banton; Erte; **Musical Director:** Al Goodman; **Set Design:** Watson Barratt

Songs: American Dancers; Doing the Apache; Flowers of Evil (Garden of Evil), The (C: Jean Schwartz); Good Queen Bess (C: Bert Grant; L: Tot Seymour); I'll Stand Beneath Your Window Tonight and Whistle [2] (C/L: Jerry Benson; Jimmy McHugh; George E. Price); In the Cottage of My Heart [1]; Jazz Wedding; Just Like a Diamond (C: Jean Schwartz); Legend of the Woodland, The; Lotus Flower; Love in a Haystack [1]; Minuette, A; Oedipus Rex a la Jazz; Oh, Alice (C: Bert Grant; L: Tot Seymour); On a Beautiful Evening (C: Jean Schwartz); Opening Ensemble; Queens of Long Ago; Ran Tin Tin; When You Love (C: Bert Grant; L: Tot Seymour); Yankee Doodle Oo-la-la, The

Cast: Alice Delysia; Jay Gould; Harry McNaughton; Nat Nazzarro Jr.; Jack Pearl; Ethel Shutta

Notes: [1] Sheet music only. [2] ASCAP/Library of Congress only. Listed under TOPICS OF 1922 by ASCAP.

4428 • TOPLITZKY OF NOTRE DAME

OPENED: 12/26/1946 Theatre: Century
Musical Broadway: 60

Composer: Sammy Fain
Lyricist: George Marion Jr.
Librettist: Jack Barnett; George Marion Jr.
Producer: William Cahn
Director: Jose Ruben

Choreographer: Robert Sidney; **Costumes:** Kenn Barr; **Musical Director:** Leon Leonardi; **Orchestrations:** Lewis Raymond; Menotti Salta; Allan Small; **Set Design:** Edward Gilbert; **Vocal Arranger:** Leon Leonardi

Songs: All-American Man; Baby Let's Face It; Common Sense; I Wanna Go to City College; Let Us Gather at the Goal Line; Love Is a Random Thing; McInerney's Farm [2]; Philadelphia

Feeling [1]; Slight Case of Ecstasy, A; Wolf Time; You Are My Downfall

Cast: J. Edward Bromberg; Warde Donovan; Walter Lang; Phyllis Lynne; Frank Marlowe; Estelle Sloan; Gus Van; Betty Jane Watson

Notes: [1] Out Chicago 9/29/7. [2] ASCAP/Library of Congress only.

4429 • TOPSY AND EVA

OPENED: 12/23/1924 Theatre: Sam H. Harris
Musical Broadway: 165

Composer: Rosetta Duncan; Vivian Duncan
Lyricist: Rosetta Duncan; Vivian Duncan
Librettist: Catherine Chisholm Cushing
Producer: Tom Wilkes
Director: Oscar Eagle

Source: UNCLE TOM'S CABIN (Novel: Harriet Beecher Stowe); **Choreographer:** Jack Holland; **Costumes:** Madam Keeler; **Musical Director:** Jerome Stewardson; **Set Design:** Dickson Morgan

Songs: Bird Dance; Cotton Time; Do-Re-Mi; Give Me Your Heart and Give Me Your Hand; Happy Go Lucky Days [3]; Heaven [1]; I Never Had a Mammy; In the Autumn [2]; Just for a Little While [3]; Kiss Me; Land of Long Ago, The; Lickin's [2]; Mariette; Moon Am Shinin'; Plantation Melodies; Rememb'ring; Sighin' [2]; Smiling Through My Tears [1]; Sweet Onion in Bermuda [1]; Ukulele Lady [1]; Um-Um-Da-Da; Uncle Tom's Cabin Blues; We'll Dance through Life Together [2]; Wedding Procession

Cast: Rosetta Duncan; Vivian Duncan; Harriet Hoctor; Basil Ruysdael; Frederick Santley

Notes: [1] Out Washington, D.C. 12/28/25. [2] Out San Francisco 7/8/23. [3] Out Newark 3/8/26.

4430 • TOREADOR, THE

OPENED: 01/06/1902 Theatre: Knickerbocker
Musical Broadway: 146

Composer: Lionel Monckton
Lyricist: Adrian Ross
Librettist: Harry Nichols; James T. Tanner
Producer: Nixon & Zimmerman
Director: Herbert Gresham

Musical Director: Louis F. Gottschalk

Songs: Archie; Blanks [1] (L: Percy Greenbank); Espana (C: Ivan Caryll); Everybody's Awfully Good to Me (C/L: Paul A. Rubens); Governor of Villaya, The (C: Ivan Caryll); Hall of Fame, The (C: John W. Bratton; L: Robb); Hear Me, Amelia (Finale Act I) (C: Ivan Caryll); Here They Come in Glittering Glory (C: Ivan Caryll); Husband and Wife [1]; If Ever I Marry (L: Percy Greenbank); I'm Romantic (I've Always Had a Passion); It Does Amuse Me So! [1] (L: Percy Greenbank); Keep Off the Grass (L: Leslie Mayne); Language of the Flowers, The (L: Percy Greenbank); Maud [1] (C: Unknown; L: Harry B. Smith); Moon, Moon (C/L: Nat D. Mann); My Toreador (C/L: Paul Rubens); My Zoo (C: Ivan Caryll; L: Percy Greenbank); Oh, Senor, Pray (C: Ivan Caryll; L: Percy Greenbank); Punch and Judy [1] (C: Ivan Caryll; L: Percy Greenbank); Ride in the Puff-Puff, A [1] (L: Percy Greenbank); Sir Archie [1] (L: George Grossmith Jr.); Toreador's Song (I'm the Glory and Pride of the Land of Spain) (C: Ivan Caryll); We're All of Us Lovely and Young (Chorus of Bridesmaids); When I Marry Amelia [1]; Where the Gigantic Ocean Atlantic (Opening Chorus) (C: Ivan Caryll); With All the Town in Bright Array (Opening Chorus Act II) (L: Percy Greenbank); Won't It Be a Lark (We're Dear Little Girls) (C: Ivan Caryll; L: Percy Greenbank)

Cast: Melville Ellis; Christie MacDonald; Maude Raymond; Maude Richie; Queenie Vassar; Francis Wilson

Notes: [1] London vocal score only.

4431 • TOUCH

OPENED: 11/08/1970 Theatre: Village Arena
Musical Off-Broadway: 422

Composer: Kenn Long
Lyricist: Kenn Long
Librettist: Kenn Long; Amy Saltz
Producer: Edith O'Hara; Two Arts Playhouse; Robert S. Weinstein
Director: Amy Saltz

Lighting Designer: Charles Lewis; **Musical Director:** Jim Crozier; David Rodman; **Set Design:** Robert Alexander Kates; Robert U. Taylor

Songs: Alphagenesis; City Song; Come to the Road; Confrontation Song; Declaration; Garden Song; Goodbyes; Guiness, Woman; Hasseltown; I Don't Care; Maxine!; Quiet Country; Reaching, Touching; Sitting in the Park; Susan's Song; Tripping; Watching; Windchild (C/L: Gary Graham)

Cast: Gerard S. Doff; Barbara Ellis; Kenn Long; Ava Rosenblum

4432 • TOUCH AND GO

OPENED: 10/13/1949 Theatre: Broadhurst
Revue Broadway: 176

Composer: Jay Gorney
Lyricist: Jean Kerr; Walter Kerr
Librettist: Jean Kerr; Walter Kerr
Producer: George Abbott
Director: Walter Kerr

Songs: American Primitive; Be a Mess; Broadway Love Song; Easy Does It; Funny Little Old World; Highbrow, Lowbrow; It'll Be All Right in a Hundred Years; Men of the Watermark; Miss Platt Selects Mate; Mister Brown, Miss Dupree; Opening for Everybody, An; This Had Better Be Love; Under the Sleeping Volcano; Wish Me Luck

Cast: Nancy Andrews; Peggy Cass; Nathaniel Frey; Helen Gallagher; George Hall; Pearl Lang; Jonathan Lucas; Kyle MacDonnell; Daniel Nagrin; Louis Nye; Dick Sykes

4433 • TOUR DE FOUR

OPENED: 06/18/1963 Theatre: Writers' Stage
Revue Off-Broadway: 16

Composer: Larry Alexander; John Aman; Jeanne Bargy; Albert Beach; Norman Brown; Coleman Cohen; Carl Crow; Gerry Donovan; Ed Fearon; Frank Gehrecke; Lee Holdridge; Jack Johnson; James Kason; Marty Kreiner; John McKellar; Dorothy Mendoza; Lance Mulcahy; Gratian Ouelette; Gary Popkin; Andrew Rosenthal; Peter Salamando; Arthur Siegel; Hugh Taliaferro; Rod Warren; Blair Weille; Edwin Weinberg; Bruce Williamson
Lyricist: Larry Alexander; John Aman; Jeanne Bargy; Albert Beach; Norman Brown; June Carroll; Coleman Cohen; Carl Crow; Gerry Donovan; Ed Fearon; Frank Gehrecke; Jack Johnson; James Kason; Marty Kreiner; John McKellar; Dorothy Mendoza; Lance Mulcahy; Gratian Ouelette; Gary Popkin; Andrew Rosenthal; Peter Salamando; Hugh Taliaferro; Rod Warren; Blair Weille; Edwin Weinberg; Bruce Williamson
Librettist: Larry Alexander; John Aman; Jeanne Bargy; Albert Beach; Norman Brown; Coleman Cohen; Carl Crow; Gerry Donovan; Ed Fearon; Frank Gehrecke; Jack Johnson; James Kason; Marty Kreiner; John McKellar; Dorothy Mendoza; Lance Mulcahy; Gratian Ouelette; Gary Popkin; Andrew Rosenthal; Peter Salamando; Hugh Taliaferro; Rod Warren; Blair Weille; Edwin Weinberg; Bruce Williamson
Producer: Susan Eden; Tom Eyen; Richard Everett Upton
Director: Tom Eyen

Costumes: Edward Charles; **Lighting Designer:** Gene Tunezi; **Musical Director:** Natalie Charlson

Songs: Baby John; Bus Stop; Call of the Wild; Cooperation; Cuckoo Song; D. and D. Rag; Fallout Shelter; Good Old Days; Hollywood Folk Song; Letters; Lyle's Wedding; Multi-Colored Bush; Rapid Reading Rachel; Six O'Clock; 1600 Pennsylvania Avenue; Small Town Girl; That Certain Look; Theatres; This Time Next Year; Tour de Four; Trio Con Brio; What I Want to Be; Whatever Happened; You Came from Outer Space; You Have . . .

Cast: Paul Blake; Carl Crow; Carol Fox; Lyle O'Hara

Notes: Composers, lyricists and writers were not differentiated. Some of these may be songs and some sketches.

4434 • TOURISTS, THE

OPENED: 08/25/1906 Theatre: Majestic
Musical Broadway: 132

Composer: Gustave Kerker
Lyricist: R.H. Burnside
Librettist: R.H. Burnside
Producer: Lee Shubert; Sam S. Shubert
Director: R.H. Burnside

Lighting Designer: George Morgan; **Musical Director:** Gustave Kerker; **Set Design:** George H. Williams

Songs: Dear Old Boston [2]; Dear Old Broadway; Different Girls; Entrance of the Rajah [3]; Game of Hearts, A; He's Gone; Here They Come; In Rang a Pang; It's Nice to Have a Sweetheart; Keep On Doing; Love Is a Wonderful Thing; Mary's Lamb; Natives; Oh, Mister Sun [1]; She Always Told the Truth; That's the Time; They Lived to Be Loved in Vain; We're the Gnomes; We're the Marriageable Daughters [3]; Wedding Procession [3]; When Love Dies [1]; When You Take a Trip; Which One Shall We Marry?; Wouldn't You Like to Know [1]

Cast: Grace LaRue; Vera Michelena; William Pruette; Julia Sanderson

Notes: [1] Sheet music only. [2] Out Boston 6/25/06. [3] Vocal selection only.

4435 • TOVARICH

OPENED: 03/18/1963 Theatre: Broadway
Musical Broadway: 264

Composer: Lee Pockriss
Lyricist: Anne Croswell
Librettist: David Shaw
Producer: Abel Farbman; Sylvia Harris
Director: Peter Glenville

Source: TOVARICH (Play: Jacques Deval; Robert E. Sherwood); **Choreographer:** Herbert Ross; **Costumes:** Motley; **Dance Arranger:** Dorothea Freitag; **Lighting Designer:** John Harvey; **Musical Director:** Stanley Lebowsky; **Orchestrations:** Philip J. Lang; **Set Design:** Rolf Gerard; **Vocal Arranger:** Stanley Lebowsky

Songs: All for You; Grand Polonaise (dance); I Go to Bed; I Know the Feeling; Introduction Tango (dance); It Used to Be; Kukla Katusha; Lullaby for a Princess [1]; Make a Friend; Managed; Nitchevo; No! No! No!; Only One, The; Opportunity [1]; Say You'll Stay; Small Cartel, A; Stuck with Each Other; That Face; Uh-Oh!; Wilkes-Barre, Pa.; You Love Me; You'll Make an Elegant Butler (C/L: Joan Javits; Phil Springer)

Cast: Jean Pierre Aumont; Margery Gray; George S. Irving; Michael Kermoyan; Vivien Leigh; Byron Mitchell; Alexander Scourby; Louise Troy; Gene Varrone

Notes: [1] Cut prior to opening.

4436 • TOWN CLOWN, THE

OPENED: 01/06/1924 Theatre: Illinois
Musical Chicago

Composer: Harry Ruby
Lyricist: Bert Kalmar
Librettist: Aaron Hoffman

Notes: Later revised into THE BELLE OF QUAKER TOWN and again into NO OTHER GIRL.

4437 • TOWN GOSSIP

OPENED: 1921
Revue Closed out of town

Composer: Harold Orlob
Lyricist: George E. Stoddard; Ned Wayburn
Librettist: George E. Stoddard; Ned Wayburn
Producer: Ned Wayburn
Director: Ned Wayburn

Costumes: Shirley Barker; Alice O'Neil; **Musical Director:** George A. Nichols

Songs: After We're Happily Married; Argentine; Burlesque Ballet; Catch As Catch Can; Contortion Dance; Family Jewels; Golden Evenings of Autumn Time; Golden Indian, The; Good Bye School Days; Historic Kisses; I Have Something Nice; Just Like the Sunshine; Lovely Lady Nicotine; Married Life; Meow Meow Meow; My Cave Man; Picture Any Girl Can Paint, A; Polo Dance; Put and Take Top, The; Rhythmic Rhapsodies on the Piano; Riding; Seven Syncopating Sirens; Sweet Yesterday; Take It from a Happy Married Man; Teaching the Baby to Walk; Town Gossip; Trombone Symphony; Wedding Rehearsal, The

Cast: Edythe Baker; Helen Broderick; John Dooley; Lillian Fitzgerald; Vinton Freedley; Grace Moore

4438 • TOWNSHIP FEVER

OPENED: 12/19/1990 Theatre: Majestic (Brooklyn)
Musical New York: 39

Composer: Mbongeni Ngema
Lyricist: Mbongeni Ngema
Librettist: Mbongeni Ngema
Producer: Brooklyn Academy of Music; Lincoln Center Theater
Director: Mbongeni Ngema

Arrangements: Mbongeni Ngema; **Choreographer:** Mbongeni Ngema; **Costumes:** Sarah Roberts; **Lighting Designer:** Mannie Manim; **Orchestrations:** Mbongeni Ngema; **Set Design:** Sarah Roberts

Songs: Amasendenduna (chant) (C/L: Traditional); Beautiful Little Mama; Blazing Like Fire; Corruption; Daveyton; Ekufikeni (C/L: Mbongeni Ngema; Isaiah Shembe); Freedom Charter (L: Unknown); Hear My Prayer; Hohihlahla Mandela (C/L: Mbongeni Ngema; Traditional); Intombenjani (C/L: Traditional); Isidudla (C/L: Mbongeni Ngema; Traditional); Izintombi Zomjolo; Lord Is My Shepherd (L: Traditional); Meleko; Mfoka Ngema; Mngani Wamina; Nduna Ngibolekinduku (The Zulu Warriors); Ngatheth Amacala; Ngobammakhosi; Oliver Tambo; Township Fever; U Mandela Uthayihlome; Ufil Ubotha (chant); Wasiqoqela Ndawonye (C/L: Mbongeni Ngema; Traditional); Xolisinhlizyo

Cast: Sindiswa Dlathu; John Lata; David Manqele; Brian Mazibuko; Themba Mbonani; Bheki Mqadi; Bhoyi Ngema; Clara Reyes; Mamthandi Zulu

4439 • TOYLAND

OPENED: 01/08/1908
Musical — Closed out of town

Composer: Hampton Durand; Harry L. Newton
Lyricist: Harry L. Newton

Source: UNKNOWN (Musical); **Musical Director:** Harry L. Newton

Songs: And Then She Winked Her Eye; Blowing Soap Bubbles; Bogie Ogie Man, The; By the Same Old Light Above; Finale Act I; Grand Review and Finale; I Want to Be a Soldier Boy in Blue; If You Love Me As I Love You; I'll Whistle and Wait for You; I'm a Crazy Jay on Circus Day; Jumpety Jump Family; King of the Imps Am I; Love Is the Same Everywhere; Mechanical Doll Dance, The; Rain, Rain Go Away; Snuggle Up Closer to Me; Stingy; Toy Song; Witch Dance

Cast: Augusta Belle; Billie Bordon; Florence Fields; Jules Held; James H. Stewart

Notes: Program of Cedar Rapids.

4440 • TRAINED NURSES, THE

OPENED: 1914
Musical

Composer: Leo Edwards
Lyricist: Blanche Merrill
Librettist: William Le Baron
Producer: Jesse Lasky

Musical Director: Marie Mosier

Songs: Come on a Whistle; Humpty Dumpty; I Can't Believe You Really Love Me; I Love to Quarrel with You; If You Don't Want Me [1] (C/L: Irving Berlin); It Can't Be True; Kiss, Kiss; Nurses Are We; Tango Tea; We've Had a Lovely Time, So Long, Good-Bye

Cast: Henry Bergman; Mae Bronte; George W. Callahan; Gladys Clark

Notes: Vaudeville musical. Program of 6/15/14. [1] Sheet music only.

4441 • TRAITORS, THE

OPENED: 03/1913 — Theatre: Lafayette
Musical — New York

Composer: Will Marion Cook
Producer: Negro Players

Notes: No other information available.

4442 • TRANSPOSED HEADS, THE

OPENED: 10/31/1986 — Theatre: Lincoln Center
Musical — Off-Broadway: 4

Composer: Elliot Goldenthal
Lyricist: Sidney Goldfarb
Librettist: Sidney Goldfarb; Julie Taymor
Director: Julie Taymor

Source: TRANSPOSED HEADS, THE (Novel: Thomas Mann); **Choreographer:** Swati Gupte Bhise; Company, The; Rajika Puri; Margo Sappington; Julie Taymor; **Conductor:** Joshua Rosenblum; **Costumes:** Carol Oditz; **Lighting Designer:** Marcia Madeira; **Musical Director:** Richard Martinez; **Set Design:** Alexander Okun

Cast: Yamil Borges; Scott Burkholder; Rajika Puri; Byron Utley

Notes: No songs listed in program.

4443 • TREASURE GIRL

OPENED: 11/08/1928 Theatre: Alvin
Musical Broadway: 69

Composer: George Gershwin
Lyricist: Ira Gershwin; Vincent Lawrence; Fred Thompson
Librettist: Alex A. Aarons; Vincent Lawrence
Producer: Alex A. Aarons; Vinton Freedley
Director: Bertram Harrison

Choreographer: Bobby Connolly; **Musical Director:** Alfred Newman

Songs: A-Hunting We Will Go; According to Mr. Grimes; Dead Men Tell No Tales [6]; Feeling I'm Falling; Finale Act I; Goodbye to the Old Love, Hello to the New [6]; Got a Rainbow; I Don't Think I'll Fall in Love Today; I Want to Marry a Marionette [6]; I've Got a Crush on You [3]; K-ra-zy for You; Oh, So Nice [5]; Place in the Country; Skull and Bones [4]; This Particular Party [2]; Treasure Island; What Are We Here For?; What Causes That?; Where's the Boy? Here's the Girl!

Cast: Walter Catlett; Peggy Conklin; Constance Cummings; Paul Frawley; Ferris Hartman; Mary Hay; Gertrude Lawrence; Beryl Wallace; Clifton Webb; **Pianist:** Victor Arden; Phil Ohman

Notes: [1] Added after opening. [2] Not used. [3] Also in STRIKE UP THE BAND (1930). [4] Music cut from concert piece AMERICAN IN PARIS. [5] Cut after opening. [6] Cut prior to opening.

4444 • TREASURE ISLAND (1973)

OPENED: 08/21/1973 Theatre: Town Hall
Musical Off-Broadway: 4

Composer: John Clifton
Lyricist: John Clifton
Librettist: Tom Tippett
Producer: N.Y. University's Town Hall; Performing Arts Repertory Theatre
Director: Evan Thompson

Source: TREASURE ISLAND (Novel: Robert Louis Stevenson); **Costumes:** Jennie Cleaver; **Set Design:** John Nelson

Songs: Gold; Honest Sailors; I'll Buy Me a Ship; Let's Be Friends; That's What I Would Do; Treasure Island; Yo-Ho

Cast: Joan Shepard; Bill Steele; Evan Thompson; Chester Thornhill

4445 • TREASURE ISLAND (1985)

Notes: *See PIECES OF EIGHT (1985).*

4446 • TREE GROWS IN BROOKLYN, A

OPENED: 04/19/1951 Theatre: Alvin
Musical Broadway: 267

Composer: Arthur Schwartz
Lyricist: Dorothy Fields
Librettist: George Abbott; Betty Smith
Producer: George Abbott
Director: George Abbott

Source: TREE GROWS IN BROOKLYN, A (Novel: Betty Smith); **Choreographer:** Herbert Ross; **Costumes:** Irene Sharaff; **Lighting Designer:** Jo Mielziner; **Musical Director:** Max Goberman; **Orchestrations:** Robert Russell Bennett; Joe Glover; **Set Design:** Jo Mielziner

Songs: Bride Wore Something Old, The [1]; Call on Your Neighbor [1]; Don't Be Afraid; Growing Pains; Halloween Ballet (dance); He Had Refinement; If You Haven't Got a Sweetheart; I'll Buy You a Star; I'm Like a New Broom; Is That My Prince?; Look Who's Dancing; Love Is the Reason; Make the Man Love Me; Mine 'til Monday; Oysters in July [1]; Payday; That's How It Goes; Tuscaloosa [2]

Cast: Shirley Booth; Nathaniel Frey; Johnny Johnston; Marcia Van Dyke

Notes: [1] Cut prior to opening. [2] Cut prior to opening. Same music as "Old Enough to Love" in BY THE BEAUTIFUL SEA.

4447 TREEMONISHA

OPENED: 10/21/1975 Theatre: Uris
Opera Broadway: 64

Composer: Scott Joplin
Lyricist: Scott Joplin
Librettist: Scott Joplin
Producer: Adela Holzer; Houston Grand Opera; Victor Lurie; James M. Nederlander
Director: Frank Corsaro

Choreographer: Louis Johnson; **Costumes:** Franco Colavecchia; **Lighting Designer:** Nananne Porcher; **Musical Director:** Gunther Schuller; **Orchestrations:** Scott Joplin; Gunther Schuller; **Set Design:** Franco Colavecchia

Songs: Abuse; Aunt Dinah Has Blowed de Horn; Bag of Luck, The; Confusion; Conjuror's Forgiven; Corn-Huskers, The; Frolic of the Bears; Going Home; Good Advice; I Want to See My Child; Real Slow Drag, A; Rescue, The; Sacred Tree, The; Superstition; Surprise; Treemonisha in Peril; Treemonisha's Bringing Up; Treemonisha's Return; Wasp Nest; We Will Rest Awhile; We Will Trust You as Our Leader; We're Goin' Around; When Villains Ramble Far and Near; Wreath, The; Wrong Is Never Right

Cast: Betty Allen; Carmen Balthrop; Kathleen Battle; Ben Harney; Kenneth Hicks; Cora Johnson; Lorna Myers; Edward Pierson; Curtis Rayam; Willard White

4448 • TRIAL HONEYMOON, A

OPENED: 1924 Theatre: La Salle
Musical Chicago

Composer: Harold Orlob
Lyricist: Harold Orlob
Librettist: Harold Orlob

Notes: No program available.

4449 • TRIALS OF OZ, THE

OPENED: 12/19/1972
Play Off-Broadway: 15

Composer: Mick Jagger; John Lennon; Buzzy Linhart; Yoko Ono
Lyricist: Mick Jagger; John Lennon; Buzzy Linhart; Yoko Ono
Author: Geoff Robertson
Producer: Friends of Van Wolf Prods.; Richard Scanga
Director: Jim Sharman

Costumes: Joseph G. Aulisi; **Lighting Designer:** Jules Fisher; **Set Design:** Mark Ravitz; **Vocal Arranger:** Bill Cunningham

Songs: Dirty Is the Funniest Thing I Know; Give Me Excess of It; God Save Us; If You Can't Join 'Em, Beat 'Em; Justice Game, The; Love's Still Growing, The; Masquerade Ball; Oranges and Lemons; Rupert Bear Song; Schoolboy Blues

Cast: Dallas Alinder; Greg Antonacci; Cliff DeYoung; Dan Leach; William Roerick

4450 • TRICKS

OPENED: 01/08/1973 Theatre: Alvin
Musical Broadway: 8

Composer: Jerry Blatt
Lyricist: Lonnie Burstein
Librettist: Lonnie Burstein; Jon Jory
Producer: Herman Levin
Director: Jon Jory

Source: LES FOURBERIES DE SCAPIN (Play: Moliere); **Source:** MONSIEUR SCAPIN (Play: Moliere); **Arrangements:** Peter Howard; **Choreographer:** Donald Saddler; **Costumes:** Miles White; **Dance Arranger:** Peter Howard; **Lighting Designer:** Martin Aronstein; **Musical Director:** David Frank; **Orchestrations:** Bert De Cocteau; **Set Design:** Oliver Smith

Songs: Anything Is Possible; Believe Me; Enter Hyacinthe; Gypsy Girl; Gypsy Love [1]; Hey, Say Anything [1]; How Sweetly Simple; Life Can Be Funny; Little Bit of Trouble on the Side, A [1]; Love or Money; Man of Spirit, A; Scapin; Somebody's Doin' Somebody All the Time; Sporting Man, A; Tricks; Trouble's a Ruler; Where Is Respect; Who Was I?; Wonderful! [1]

Cast: Rene Auberjonois; Walter Bobbie; Randy Herron; Ernestine Jackson; Carolyn Mignini; Joe Morton; Christopher Murney; Shezwae Powell; Tom Toner

Notes: [1] Out Detroit 11/25/72.

4451 • TRIP TO COONTOWN, A

OPENED: 04/04/1898 Theatre: Third Avenue
Musical Broadway: 8

Composer: Billy Johnson
Lyricist: Bob Cole

Songs: I Can Stand for Your Color, but Your Hair Won't Do [1]; I Must o' Been a Dreaming; If That's Society, Excuse Me [1]; Picking on a Chicken Bone

Cast: Camille Cassele; Bob Cole; Pauline Freeman; Billy Johnson

Notes: No program available. This show was based on a one-act mini-musical AT JOLLY COON-EY ISLAND which was part of BLACK PATTI'S TROUBADOURS (1896). [1] Added to 1901 edition.

4452 • TRIP TO JAPAN, A

OPENED: 09/04/1909 Theatre: Hippodrome
Musical Broadway: 447

Composer: Manuel Klein
Lyricist: R.H. Burnside; Manuel Klein
Librettist: R.H. Burnside
Producer: R.H. Burnside
Director: R.H. Burnside

Choreographer: Vincenzo Romeo; **Musical Director:** Manuel Klein; **Set Design:** Arthur Voegtlin

Songs: Ballet of Jewels, The; Every Girl Loves a Uniform; Fair Flower of Japan; Good Bye; I'm Goin' to Sea; Meet Me Where the Lanterns Glow; Opening Chorus; Our Navy's the Best in the World

Cast: Chief Ki Wi; E.A. Clark; W.H. Clark; Mabel Dwight; Nanette Flack; Harry Griffith; Marceline; Albertina Rasch

4453 • TRIP TO WASHINGTON, A

OPENED: 08/18/1913 Theatre: La Salle
Musical Chicago

Composer: Ben M. Jerome
Lyricist: Henry Blossom
Librettist: Henry Blossom
Producer: Harry Askin; Florenz Ziegfeld
Director: R.H. Burnside

Source: TEXAS STEER, A (Play: Charles H. Hoyt); **Musical Director:** Ben M. Jerome

Songs: Anybody Round Here Looking for a Scrap; Back in the Dear Old Days [1]; Best That I Can Do Is Try to Do the Best I Can, The; Chat-Chat-Chatter on the Telephone; Don't Go Too Fast Little Dearie; Every National Hymn Is Just a Rag-Time Tune; Give Us a Drink [1]; Good-Bye Forever; Good Morning; I Am a Lone-Star Girl; I Want Someone to Love; I Wonder Will You Forget [1]; It's the Uniform that Makes the Man; I've Always Been a Lucky Little Guy; Just a Kiss and Then Goodbye (C: Charles Miller; L: George V. Hobart); Just to Keep Peace in the Family; Nobody Cares; Off to Washington!; Scandal! Scandal!; Shame, Shame, Shame; There Is Something that I Like About You; Washington Squeeze, The; We Come from Maison de la Vere; You're the Only One for Me, Dear!

Cast: Mabella Baker; Rapley Holmes; Adele Rowler; Arthur Stanford; Katherine Stevenson; Harry Von Fossen

Notes: Songs also by Harry Williams according to the program but not credited individually. May have opened on August 24. [1] Sheet music only.

4454 • TRIXIE TRUE TEEN DETECTIVE

OPENED: 12/07/1980 Theatre: Theatre de Lys
Musical Off-Broadway: 94

Composer: Kelly Hamilton
Lyricist: Kelly Hamilton
Librettist: Kelly Hamilton
Producer: Joseph Butt; Doug Cole; Joe Novak; Spencer Tandy
Director: Bill Gile

Choreographer: Arthur Faria; **Costumes:** David Toser; **Dance Arranger:** Jimmy Roberts; **Lighting Designer:** Craig Miller; **Musical Director:** Robert Fisher; **Orchestrations:** Eddie Sauter; **Set Design:** Michael J. Hotopp; Paul de Pass; **Vocal Arranger:** Robert Fisher

Songs: In Cahoots; Juvenile Fiction; Katzenjammer Kinda Song, A; Most Popular and Most Likely to Succeed; Mr. and Mrs. Dick Dickerson; Mystery of the Moon, The; Rita from Argentina; Secret of the Tapping Shoes, The; This Is Indeed My Lucky Day; Trixie True Teen Detective!; Trixie's on the Case!; You Haven't Got Time for Love

Cast: Marianna Allen; Kathy Andrini; Alison Bevan; Keith Caldwell; Gene Lindsey; Jay Lowman; Keith Rice; Marilyn Sokol

4455 • TROISIEME AMBASSADEURS — SHOW OF 1928.

Notes: *See LA REVUE DES AMBASSADEURS.*

4456 • TROPICANA

OPENED: 05/29/1986
Musical Off-Off-Broadway

Composer: Robert Nassif
Lyricist: Peter Napolitano
Librettist: George Abbott

Notes: No program available.

4457 • TROUBLE IN TAHITI

Notes: *See ALL IN ONE.*

4458 • TROUBLES OF 1920

OPENED: 1921
Revue

Songs: I'm My Mama's Baby Boy (C: Louis Silvers; L: George Jessel; Roy Turk)

Notes: No other information available.

4459 • TRUCKLOAD

OPENED: 09/06/1975 Theatre: Lyceum
Musical Broadway

Composer: Louis St. Louis
Lyricist: Wes Harris
Librettist: Hugh Wheeler
Producer: Dick Clark; Adela Holzer; Shubert Organization
Director: Patricia Birch

Choreographer: Patricia Birch; **Costumes:** Carrie F. Robbins; **Lighting Designer:** John Gleason; **Orchestrations:** Michael Gibson; Bhen Lanzaroni; **Set Design:** Douglas W. Schmidt; **Vocal Arranger:** Carl Hall

Songs: Amelia's Theme; Bonnie's Song; Boogie Woogie Man; Cumbia/Wedding Party; Dragon Strikes Back; Find My Way Home; Hash House Habit; Hello Sunshine; I Guess Everything Will Turn Out All Right; Jesus Is My Main Man; Look at Us; Pour Out Your Soul; Rest Stop; Ricardo's Lament; Standing in this Phonebooth; Step-Mama; There's Nothing Like Music; Truckload

Cast: Deborah Allen; Cheryl Barnes; Donny Burks; Rene Enriquez; Ilene Graff; Sherry Mathis; Doug McKeon; Laurie Prange; Louis St. Louis; Kelly Ward

Notes: Closed in previews. Previews ended 9/11/75.

4460 • TRULY BLESSED

OPENED: 04/22/1990 Theatre: Longacre
Musical Broadway: 33

Composer: Queen Esther Marrow
Additional Music: Reginald Royal
Lyricist: Queen Esther Marrow
Additional Lyrics: Reginald Royal
Librettist: Queen Esther Marrow
Producer: Howard Hurst; Sophie Hurst; Philip Rose
Director: Robert Kalfin

Choreographer: Larry Vickers; **Costumes:** Andrew B. Marlay; **Lighting Designer:** Fred Kolo; **Orchestrations:** Joseph Joubert; **Set Design:** Fred Kolo

Songs: Battle Hymn of the Republic; Come on Children, Let's Sing; Didn't It Rain (C/L: Traditional); Even Me; Glory Hallelujah (C/L: Traditional); Happy Days Are Here Again (C: Milton Ager; L: Jack Yellen); He May Not Come When You Want Him; He's Got the Whole World in His Hands (C/L: Traditional); His Gift to Me; I Found the Answer; It's Amazing What God Can Do; I've Been 'Buked; Jesus Remembers When Others Forget; Lord, I'm Determined; Move on Up a Little Higher; Old Ship of Zion; On the Battlefield for My Lord; Precious Lord; Rusty Bell; Soon I Will Be Done; St. Louis Blues (C/L: W.C. Handy); Thank You for the Change in My Life; Truly Blessed; Wade in the Water (C/L: Traditional)

Cast: Lynette G. DuPre; Doug Eskew; Carl Hall; Queen Esther Marrow; Gwen Stewart

Notes: Songs not credited in program.

4461 • TRUTH ABOUT CINDERELLA, THE

OPENED: 1975
Musical Unproduced

Composer: Charles Strouse
Lyricist: David Rogers

Songs: Any Day's a Perfect Day for a Wedding; At Any Age at All; At the Palace; Big Night of the

Year, The; Clumsy Waltz, The; Find the Foot; Guilt; Help Stamp Out Dirt; New Kind of Girl; Princess for the Prince, A; Ready for You; Truth About Cinderella, The

Notes: No other information available.

4462 • TRUTH ABOUT RUTH, THE

OPENED: 07/1994 Theatre: Actors' Playhouse
Musical Off-Broadway

Composer: Brad Ellis
Lyricist: Peter Morris
Librettist: Peter Morris
Producer: Postage Stamp Xtravaganzas
Director: Phillip George

Choreographer: Phillip George; **Costumes:** Randy Carfagno; Gene Lauze; **Lighting Designer:** Mark Vogeley; **Musical Director:** Pete Blue; **Set Design:** B.T. Whitehill

Songs: Ballad of Mrs. Bluebeard, The; Bang!; Dear Ruth; Fabo Soap Jingle, The; Face the Fact; Hello! Hello!; Hit That High Note; Home Sweet Home; If I Were Beautiful; Love Nest; Low; Ruth's Hit Parade; Sermonette, The; This Is the Place to Be; Truth About Ruth; You're Unique

Cast: Ruth Fields; David Lowenstein

4463 • TRY IT, YOU'LL LIKE IT

OPENED: 03/14/1973 Theatre: Mayfair
Musical Off-Broadway: 87

Composer: Alexander Olshenetsky
Lyricist: Jacob Jacobs
Librettist: Jacob Jacobs; Max Zalotoff
Producer: Moishe Baruch
Director: Jacob Jacobs

Lighting Designer: Peter Xantho; **Musical Director:** Michael Richardone; **Set Design:** Peter Achilles; **Vocal Arranger:** Yasha Kreizberg

Songs: A Nier Tzeit; Du Zelbege Zah; Eibig Dein; Heint Viel eich Vu Tzi Zingen; Macht a Lehaim; Mirele; Oy Ses Git; Senior Citizens; Try It, You'll Like It; Ven Sis Du Lieve; Zal Shain Shulem Zine

Cast: Nellie Casman; Jaime Lewin; Thelma Mintz

4464 • TUMBLE INN

OPENED: 03/24/1919 Theatre: Selwyn
Musical Broadway: 128

Composer: Rudolf Friml
Lyricist: Otto Harbach
Librettist: Otto Harbach
Producer: Arthur Hammerstein
Director: Bertram Harrison

Choreographer: Bert French; **Musical Director:** Herbert Stothart

Songs: Gowns Soft and Clingy; I've Told My Love; Laugh, The; Limbo-Land; Little Chicken Fit for Old Broadway, A; Snuggle and Dream; Thoughts I Wrote on the Leaves of My Heart, The; Trousseau Ball, The; Trousseau Waltz; Valse au L'Air; Wedding Blues, The; Won't You Help Me Out?; You'll Do It All Over Again

Cast: Herbert Corthell; Johnny Ford; Peggy O'Neill; Charles Ruggles; Zelda Sears

4465 • TURN OF THE CENTURY, THE

OPENED: 1939 Theatre: Diamond Horseshoe
Musical Nightclub

Producer: Billy Rose
Director: John Murray Anderson

Choreographer: Lauretta Jefferson; **Costumes:** Raoul Pene du Bois; **Set Design:** Albert Johnson

Songs: Lady Known As Lulu (C/L: Unknown); Let's Dream Again (C: James F. Hanley; L: Jean Herbert; Billy Rose)

Cast: Harry Armstrong; Buddy Doyle; Emma Francis; Joseph E. Howard; Beatrice Kay; Frank Libuse; Della Lind; Elizabeth Murray; Tom Patricola; Fritzi Scheff; Noble Sissle and His Orchestra; Willie Solar

Notes: No songwriters credited in program. All songs not listed in program.

4466 • TURN TO THE RIGHT

OPENED: 08/08/1981 Theatre: Wilshire Los Angeles

Producer: Buddy Ebsen

Cast: Jan Clayton

Notes: No program available.

4467 • TURNABOUT! REVUES

OPENED: 07/1941
Revue Los Angeles

Composer: Forman Brown
Lyricist: Forman Brown

Songs: At the Drive In; Brunnhilde Rides Again; Catalog Woman; Claribel the Great; Doge's Dilemma, The; Faith, Hope and Charity; Fiji Fanny; Husband's Clock, The; I Didn't Know Where to Look; If You Can't Get in the Corners; If You Peek in My Gazebo; I'm Glad to See Your Back; Incident in Arch Street; It May Be Life; Janitor's Boy, The; Last Show, The; Linda and Her Londonderry Air; Little Fred; Lola's Saucepan; March of Rhyme; Mein Hertz; Melinda Matime; Mrs. Badger-Butts; Mrs. Pettibone's Chandelier; My New York Slip; Never Go Walking without Your Hat Pin; Please Sell No More Drink to My Father; Rat Catcher's Daughter; Ruined Maid, The; She Was Poor but Honest; Turnabout; Victory Garden; When a Lady Has a Piazza; Yashmack Song, The

Cast: Forman Brown; Bill Buck; Harry Burnett; Elsa Lanchester; Dorothy Newmann; Frances Osborne

Notes: From the Turnabout Theatre in Hollywood. Half of each show was a puppet show and the other half a live revue. The theatre finally closed in 1956 after 4,535 performances.

4468 • TUSCALOOSA'S CALLING ME . . . BUT I'M NOT GOING!

OPENED: 12/01/1975 Theatre: Top of the Gate
Revue Off-Broadway: 429

Composer: Hank Beebe
Lyricist: Bill Heyer
Librettist: Hank Beebe; Sam Dann; Bill Heyer
Producer: Arch Lustberg; Bruce Nelson; Jerry Schlossberg
Director: Gui Andrisano; James Hammerstein

Costumes: Rome Heyer; Charles E. Hoefler; **Lighting Designer:** Charles E. Hoefler; **Musical Director:** Jeremy Harris; **Set Design:** Charles E. Hoefler

Songs: Astrology; Backwards; Central Park on a Sunday Afternoon; Cold Cash; Delicatessen; Everything You Hate Is Right Here; Fugue for a Menage a Trois; Grafitti; I Dig Myself; New York '69; New York from the Air; Only Right Here in New York City; Poor; Things Were Out; Tuscaloosa's Calling Me but I'm Not Going

Cast: Len Gochman; Patti Perkins; Renny Temple

4469 • TWANG!

OPENED: 12/20/1965 Theatre: Shaftesbury
Musical London

Composer: Lionel Bart
Lyricist: Lionel Bart
Librettist: Lionel Bart; Harvey Orkin
Producer: John Bryan; Bernard Delfont
Director: Joan Littlewood; Burt Shevelove

Choreographer: Paddy Stone; **Costumes:** Oliver Messel; **Musical Director:** Gareth Davies; Kenneth Moule; **Set Design:** Oliver Messel

Songs: Dreamchild; Follow Your Leader; I'll Be Hanged; Make an Honest Woman of Me; Roger the Ugly; Sighs; To the Woods; Twang!!; Unseen Hands; Wanted; Welcome to Sherwood; What Makes a Star; Whose Little Girl Are You?; With Bells On; You Can't Catch Me

Cast: Kent Baker; Clive Barker; James Booth; Bernard Bresslaw; Frank Coda; George A. Cooper; Ronnie Corbett; Toni Eden; Howard Goorney; Bob Grant; Elric Hooper; Maxwell Shaw; Barbara Windsor

4470 • TWANGER

OPENED: 11/15/1972 Theatre: Van Dam
Musical Off-Broadway: 24

Composer: Ronnie Britton
Lyricist: Ronnie Britton
Librettist: Ronnie Britton
Producer: Wayne Clark
Director: Walter Ash

Costumes: Owen H. Goldstein; **Dance Arranger:** David Wahler; **Lighting Designer:** Peter

Anderson; **Musical Director:** Lee Gillespie; **Vocal Arranger:** Gordon Harrell

Songs: Big, Big Contest; But, I Love You; Five Minutes Ago; Forest of Silver; Francis' Feast; Frogs Perform, The; Garbage-Ella [1]; Have You Seen the Princess?; Impossibility; Magic Licorice; Normal, Normal, Normal; Obey, Abide; Phyllis Frog; Potion, A; Prologue; Sister and Brother, A; Sneaky, Creepy Fellows; Tiny Light; To Win a Prince; Twanger!; Wanna Get Married

Cast: Sue Renee Bernstein; Glen M. Castello; Charles Flanagan; George Heusinger; Andrea Noel; Charles Stuart

Notes: [1] Also in GREENWICH VILLAGE FOLLIES (1976).

4471 • 'TWAS THE NIGHT BEFORE CHRISTMAS

OPENED: 12/08/1974 Theatre: CBS
TV Musical

Composer: Maury Laws
Lyricist: Jules Bass

Songs: Christmas Chimes; Even a Miracle Needs a Hand; Give Your Heart a Try

Voice: George Gobel; Joel Grey; Tammy Grimes

4472 • TWENTIETH CENTURY GIRL, THE

OPENED: 1895 Theatre: Bijou
Musical Broadway

Composer: Ludwig Englander
Lyricist: Sydney Rosenfeld
Librettist: Sydney Rosenfeld

Notes: No other information available.

4473 • TWIDDLE-TWADDLE

OPENED: 01/11/1906 Theatre: Weber's Music Hall
Revue Broadway: 137

Composer: Maurice Levi
Lyricist: Edgar Smith
Librettist: Edgar Smith
Producer: Joseph Weber
Director: Al Holbrook

Musical Director: Maurice Levi

Songs: Butterflies of Fashion, The; Days of Forty-Nine, The; Days of My Boyhood; Hats; I Hope You'll Forgive These Tears; Little Bunch of Daisies, A; Looking for a Sure Thing [1]; My Syncopated Gypsy Maid; Next Summer in Old New York; Oh, Heigh-Ho!; Poor Little Red Papoose; Society Buds; Stories of the Stage [1]; 'Tis Dreadful! 'Tis Astonishing; 'Tis Hard to Be a Lady in a Case Like That; Venedig, Fair Venedig; When You've Pampered Your Adipose Tissue; You and the Girl You Love

Cast: Charles A. Bigelow; Marie Dressler; Trixie Friganza; Ernest Lambert; Bonnie Maginn; Joseph Weber

Notes: [1] Sheet music only.

4474 • TWIGS

OPENED: 11/14/1971 Theatre: Broadhurst
Play Broadway: 289

Author: George Furth
Producer: Frederick Brisson
Director: Michael Bennett

Costumes: Sara Brook; **Lighting Designer:** David F. Segal; **Set Design:** Peter Larkin

Songs: Hollywood and Vine (C: Stephen Sondheim; L: George Furth)

Cast: Conrad Bain; Mark Dawson; MacIntyre Dixon; A. Larry Haines; Simon Oakland; Sada Thompson

4475 TWILIGHT ALLEY

Notes: *See BEGGAR'S HOLIDAY.*

4476 • TWINKLE TWINKLE

OPENED: 11/16/1926 Theatre: Liberty
Musical Broadway: 167

Composer: Harry Archer
Lyricist: Harlan Thompson
Librettist: Harlan Thompson
Producer: Louis F. Werba
Director: Frank Craven

Choreographer: Julian Alfred; Harry Puck; **Costumes:** Charles LeMaire; **Musical Director:** Max Steiner; **Set Design:** P. Dodd Ackerman

Songs: Crime; Day Dreams [3] (C: Harry Ruby; L: Bert Kalmar); Find a Girl [2]; Get a Load of This; Hustle, Bustle; I Hate to Talk About Myself; Practically in Love with You [2]; Reuben; Sex Appeal [2]; Sunday Afternoon; Sweeter Than You [1] (C: Harry Ruby; L: Bert Kalmar); Twinkle Twinkle; We're on the Map (C: Harry Ruby; L: Bert Kalmar); When We're Bride and Groom; Whistle (C: Harry Ruby; L: Bert Kalmar); You Know I Know; You're the One [2]

Cast: Joe E. Brown; Alan Edwards; Joseph Lertora; Ona Munson; Florence Upton

Notes: [1] Also in TOP SPEED (1929). [2] Cut prior to opening. [3] Added after opening.

4477 • TWINKLING EYES

OPENED: 05/18/1919
Musical

Composer: Richard Rodgers
Lyricist: Richard Rodgers
Librettist: Myron D. Rosenthal; Harry Strong
Producer: Brooklyn YMHA
Director: Lorenz Hart

Songs: Advertise; Ali Baba; Asiatic Angels; Butterfly Love; Can It (L: Oscar Hammerstein II); Dearie; I'm So Shy; Japanese Jazz; Love Is Not in Vain; Love Me By Parcel Post (L: Mortimer W. Rodgers); Loving Cup; Now Listen; Out of a Job; Prisms, Plums and Prunes (L: Benjamin Kaye); There's Always Room for One More (L: Oscar Hammerstein II); Twinkling Eyes; Weaknesses (L: Oscar Hammerstein II); Wild Women's Wiles

Notes: Amateur show. Same songs as UP STAGE AND DOWN.

4478 • TWIRLY WHIRLY

OPENED: 09/11/1902 Theatre: Weber and Fields Music Hall
Musical Broadway: 244

Composer: William T. Francis
Lyricist: Edgar Smith
Librettist: Edgar Smith
Producer: Lew Fields; Joseph Weber
Director: Lew Fields; Julian Mitchell

Costumes: Will R. Barnes; **Set Design:** John Young

Songs: After Dinner; Big Pound Cake (C/L: John T. Kelly); Buena Senorita Am I, A; Bugaboo Man, The; Clog Dance; Come Down Ma Evening Star (C: John Stromberg; L: Robert B. Smith); Dream One Dream of Me (C: William T. Francis; John Stromberg; L: Edgar Smith); Etiquette (L: Robert B. Smith); Gay Old Seville; Geezer (C/L: Unknown); I Never Loved a Man As Much As That (L: Robert B. Smith); In Stage Land; Kit; Leader of Vanity Fair, The (L: Robert B. Smith); Little Widow Brown; Long Green, The (L: Robert B. Smith); Miss Pinchin's Boarding School; My Intimate Friend (L: Wilton Lackaye; Edgar Smith); Ping Pong (C: William T. Francis; John Stromberg; L: Robert B. Smith); Priscilla; Romeo; Sailing; Softly Stealing, Lanterns Gleaming; Strike Out McCracken; Susie Woosie; Vaudeville King, The; Ye Ho, for the Sailor's Life

Cast: Louise Allen; Mabel Barrison; Bessie Clayton; Willie Collier; Peter Dailey; Lew Fields; Bonnie Maginn; Lillian Russell; Fay Templeton; Joseph Weber

4479 • TWO BOUQUETS, THE

OPENED: 05/31/1938 Theatre: Windsor
Musical Broadway: 55

Lyricist: Eleanor Farjeon
Librettist: Eleanor Farjeon
Producer: Bela Blau; Marc Connelly
Director: Marc Connelly

Choreographer: Leslie French; Felicia Sorel; **Costumes:** Raoul Pene du Bois; **Musical Director:** Macklin Marrow; **Orchestrations:** Ernest Irving; **Set Design:** Robert Barnhart

Songs: Against the Storm; Ah, How Capricious; Albert Porter; Bashful Lover (C: C. Moulton); Courses of Nature, The; Dearest Miss Bell; Dearest Miss Flo; Fireworks, The; Fly Forth O Gentle Dove (C: M. Pinsuti); Git on de Boat, Chillun; Health to Dear Mama, A; Her Lilywhite Hand; How Can We Bring the Folks Round; I Wish I Was in Texas; I'll Tell Papa; Juanita; Kissing; Little Champagne for Papa, A; Man You

Love, The; Oh, the Regatta; Pretty Patty Moss; Rain Chorus; She Did the Fandango; She Loves Thee; Sweet Blossoms (C: M. Pinsuti); Toddy's the Drink for Me (C: Traditional); Varsovienne; What Can I Do?; When I Was but a Bounding Boy; White and the Pink, The; Yes or No; Young Girl and Young Man; Youth Who Sows, The

Cast: Jane Archer; Gabrielle Brune; Leo G. Carroll; Robert Chisholm; Alfred Drake; Leslie French; Enid Markey; Patricia Morison; Winston O'Keefe; Viola Roache; Robert Rounseville; John Tyers; Marcy Wescott; Joan Wetmore

Notes: The music was written by various uncredited Victorian composers.

4480 • 2 BY 5

OPENED: 10/18/1976 Theatre: Village Gate
Revue Off-Broadway: 57

Composer: John Kander
Lyricist: Fred Ebb
Producer: Judy Gordon; Jack Temchin
Director: Seth Glassman

Costumes: Dan Leigh; **Lighting Designer:** Martin Tudor; **Musical Director:** Joseph Clonick; **Set Design:** Dan Leigh

Songs: Among My Yesterdays [4]; Broadway, My Street [2]; Cabaret [1]; Class [9]; Home [2]; I Don't Remember You [4]; Isn't This Better [10]; Losers; Love Song (Sara Lee) [8]; Maybe This Time [13]; Me and My Baby [9]; Mein Herr [5]; Military Man; Money Song [5]; Mr. Cellophane [9]; My Own Best Friend [9]; New York, New York [6]; On Stage; Only Love [7]; Quiet Thing, A [3]; Razzle Dazzle [9]; Ring Them Bells [11]; Seeing Things [4]; Sign Here [3]; Sing Happy [3]; Ten Percent [12]; Why Can't I Speak [7]; Wilkommen [1]; World Goes Round, The [6]; Yes [2]

Cast: D'Jamin Bartlett; Kay Cummings; Daniel Fortus; Shirley Lemmon; Scott Stevensen

Notes: [1] From CABARET. [2] From 70 GIRLS 70. [3] From FLORA, THE RED MENACE. [4] From THE HAPPY TIME. [5] From the film CABARET. [6] From the film NEW YORK, NEW YORK. [7] From ZORBA. [8] From Kaye Ballard's nightclub act. [9] From CHICAGO. [10] From film FUNNY LADY. [11] From TV special LIZA WITH A "Z." [12] Cut from CHICAGO. [13] From Kaye Ballard's nightclub act. Also later put in film version of CABARET.

4481 • TWO BY TWO

OPENED: 11/10/1970 Theatre: Imperial
Musical Broadway: 343

Composer: Richard Rodgers
Lyricist: Martin Charnin
Librettist: Peter Stone
Producer: Richard Rodgers
Director: Joe Layton

Source: FLOWERING PEACH, THE (Play: Clifford Odets); **Costumes:** Fred Voelpel; **Dance Arranger:** Trude Rittman; **Lighting Designer:** John Gleason; **Musical Director:** Jay Blackton; **Orchestrations:** Eddie Sauter; **Set Design:** David Hays; **Vocal Arranger:** Trude Rittman

Songs: As Far As I'm Concerned [5]; Brother Department, The [1]; Covenant, The; Death of Me, The [3]; Ev'rything That's Gonna Be Has Been [3]; Forty Nights [3]; Getting Married to a Person [2]; Gitka's Song, The; Golden Ram, The; Hey Girlie; I Can't Complain [3]; I Do Not Know a Day I Did Not Love You; Ninety Again!; Old Man, An; Poppa Isn't Poppa Anymore [3]; Poppa Knows Best; Put Him Away; Something Doesn't Happen; Something, Somewhere; Two By Two; When It Dries; Why Me?; Without My Money [3]; You; You Couldn't Please Me More [4]; You Have Got to Have a Rudder on the Ark

Cast: Marilyn Cooper; Joan Copeland; Harry Goz; Madeline Kahn; Michael Karm; Danny Kaye; Tricia O'Neil; Walter Willison

Notes: [1] Same music as "As Far As I'm Concerned." Cut prior to opening. [2] Cut prior to opening. Music later used as "Mama Always Makes It Better" in I REMEMBER MAMA. [3] Cut prior to opening. [4] Cut prior to opening. Later in I REMEMBER MAMA. [5] Same music as "The Brother Department."

4482 • TWO FOR FUN

OPENED: 02/13/1961 Theatre: Madison Avenue Playhouse
Revue Off-Broadway: 34

Composer: Silvio Masciarelli; Lothar Perl
Librettist: Peter Good; Jack Woodford
Producer: Madison Productions
Director: Mata & Hari

Costumes: Freddy Wittop

Songs: Have Gun, Get Gold

Cast: Georgia Caine; May DeSousa; Claude Fleming; Mata & Hari

Notes: No program available.

4483 • TWO FOR THE SHOW

OPENED: 02/08/1940 Theatre: Booth
Revue Broadway: 124

Composer: Morgan Lewis
Lyricist: Nancy Hamilton
Librettist: Nancy Hamilton
Producer: Stanley Gilkey; Gertrude Macy
Director: John Murray Anderson; Joshua Logan

Choreographer: Robert Alton; **Costumes:** Raoul Pene du Bois; **Lighting Designer:** John Murray Anderson; **Musical Director:** Ray Kavanaugh; **Orchestrations:** Hans Spialek; Don Walker; **Set Design:** Raoul Pene du Bois; **Vocal Arranger:** Harold Cooke

Songs: All Girl Band, The; As Was and As Is [2]; At Last It's Love; Calypso Joe; Fool for Luck; House with a Little Red Barn, A; How High the Moon [2]; Teeter Totter Tessie [2]; That Terrible Tune; This Merry Christmas [1]; Where Do You Get Your Greens? [1]

Cast: Eve Arden; Alfred Drake; Brenda Forbes; Richard Haydn; Keenan Wynn

Notes: [1] Not in program. [2] Out White Plains 6/30/41.

4484 • TWO FOR TONIGHT

OPENED: 12/28/1939
Revue Off-Broadway: 30

Composer: Berenece Kazounoff
Lyricist: John Latouche
Librettist: Ralph Berton; Mitchell Hodges
Producer: Promenaders, The
Director: Max Scheck

Costumes: Doris Roberts; **Set Design:** Edwin Vandernoot

Songs: Blase; Blues (C: John Latouche); Call of the Wild (L: Sylvia Marks); Could You Use a New Friend? (C/L: Eugene Berton; Ralph Berton); Dancing Alone (C/L: Eugene Berton; Ralph Berton); Five O'Clock (C: Bernie Wayne; L: Ben Raleigh); Home Is Where You Hang Your Hat; Masquerade (C/L: Charles Herbert); Nursery (C/L: Charles Herbert); Personal Heaven (C/L: Eugene Berton; Ralph Berton); Slap on the Greasepaint; Windows (C/L: Eugene Berton; Ralph Berton)

Cast: Charlie Herbert; Grace Herbert; Billy Sands

4485 • TWO GENTLEMEN OF VERONA

OPENED: 07/27/1971 Theatre: St. James
Musical Broadway: 627

Composer: Galt MacDermot
Lyricist: John Guare
Librettist: John Guare; Mel Shapiro
Producer: N.Y. Shakespeare Festival; Joseph Papp
Director: Mel Shapiro

Source: TWO GENTLEMEN OF VERONA (Play: William Shakespeare); **Choreographer:** Jean Erdman; Dennis Nahat; **Costumes:** Theoni V. Aldredge; **Lighting Designer:** Lawrence Metzler; **Musical Director:** Harold Wheeler; **Set Design:** Ming Cho Lee

Songs: Bring All the Boys Back Home; Calla Lily Lady; Don't Have the Baby; Dragon Flight; Eglamour; Follow the Rainbow; Hot Lover; Howl [1]; I Am Not Interested in Love; I Love My Father; I'd Like to Be a Rose; Kidnapped; Land of Betrayal; Love Has Driven Me Sane; Love, Is That You?; Love Me; Love's Revenge; Mansion; Milkmaid; Night Letter; Pearls; Summer, Summer; Symphony; That's a Very Interesting Question; Thou, Julia, Thou Has Metamorphosed Me; Thou, Proteus, Thou Has Metamorphosed Me; Thurio's Samba; To Whom It May Concern Me; Two Gentlemen of Verona; What a Nice Idea; What Does a Lover Pack?; What's a Nice Girl Like Her; Where's North?; Who Is Sylvia? (L: William Shakespeare)

Cast: Jonelle Allen; John Bottoms; Diana Davila; Clifton Davis; Raul Julia

Notes: Moved from the Delacorte Theatre to the St. James on December 1, 1971 for an additional 614 performances. [1] Added to London production.

4486 • TWO HEARTS IN THREE-QUARTER TIME

OPENED: 07/08/1946
Musical Closed out of town

Composer: Robert Stolz
Lyricist: Dailey Paskman
Librettist: William A. Drake
Producer: Barrie O'Daniels
Director: James Westerfield

Source: DER VERLORENE WALTZER (Musical: Robert Gilbert; Paul Knepler; J.M. Welleminsky); **Source:** TWO HEARTS IN WALTZ TIME (ZWEI HERZEN IM DREIVIERTELTAKT) (Film: Walter Reisch; Franz Schulz); **Costumes:** Kate Drain Lawson; **Musical Director:** Ray Sinatra; **Set Design:** Norman Rock

Songs: Ballet (dance); Children of the Drama; Finaletto; Give Your Bride a Kiss; Lovely Little Sister; Old Vienna; Opening; Pain of Love's First Kiss, The; Tonight with You; Two Hearts in Waltz Time; Two Times Young and Twice in Love; Wasn't It Grand; What Does My Heart Keep Saying

Cast: Edit Angold; Kenny Baker; Patricia Bowman; Fred Brookins; Pamela Caveness; Chick Chandler; Paul Craik; Thomas Glynn; Alfred Hunter; Irene Manning; John Pelletti; Thayer Roberts; Alexis Rotov; Kirby Smith

Notes: From a program of the Greek Theatre, Los Angeles.

4487 • TWO HUSBANDS AND ONE WIFE

OPENED: 1916
Musical Closed out of town

Composer: Will Vodery
Lyricist: Frank Kennedy
Librettist: Frank Kennedy
Director: Hall Lane

Songs: Beautiful Band; Darkie's Serenade; Monterey; My Little Girl; Norway; Rag, Rag, Rag; Ragging Along; Tennessee; Virginia Rag; Wake Me Up with a Rag

Cast: Frank A. Burt; Girl Trust, The

Notes: A burlesque musical. Some of these songs were probably popular songs of the day uncredited.

4488 • TWO IF BY SEA!?

OPENED: 06/18/1971
Musical Closed out of town

Composer: Tony Hutchins
Lyricist: Priscilla B. Dewey
Librettist: Priscilla B. Dewey; Charles Werner Moore
Director: Charles Werner Moore

Choreographer: Ronald Johnston; **Dance Arranger:** Jeff Lass; **Lighting Designer:** Michael F. Hottois; **Set Design:** Jim Stewart; **Vocal Arranger:** John Nagy

Songs: Be More Aggressive; Follow Daddy (C: John Foster); How Are You Going to Start the American Revolution?; If By Sea; Lanterns; Law Breakers; Melt It Down; News, News; Off Limits (C: John Nagy); Paul Revere (C: John Nagy); People Who Live on Islands; Some Day Soon; Stamp Act; Tea Dance; Throw the Egg; Two If By Sea, I Think! (C: Paul Lass); We Stand for Moderation; Word, The; You'll Regret Your Stand

Cast: John Scoullar

Notes: Rhode Island program used.

4489 TWO IS COMPANY

OPENED: 09/22/1915 Theatre: Lyric
Musical Broadway: 29

Composer: Adolf Philipp
Lyricist: Edward A. Paulton; Adolf Philipp
Librettist: Edward A. Paulton; Adolf Philipp
Director: Adolf Philipp

Songs: Come with Me to Paree; Footman and the Maid, The; Free as Air; Free! Free!; I Prefer the Cat; If You But Knew What I Know; In the Land of Lorraine; La Belle Lulu; Lotus Land; Lure of the Waltz, The; Stamp Enclosed, A; Two Is Company; We Like to Whirl; You Loved Me Then

Cast: Georgia Caine; May DeSousa; Claude Fleming; Clarence Harvey; Ralph Nairn

Notes: No program available. Philipp credited the music to Jean Briquet and claimed the show was based on a play by Jean Herve. However, Briquet and Herve probably didn't exist. Paulton helped with the English language translations of book and lyrics.

4490 • TWO LITTLE BRIDES

OPENED: 04/23/1912 Theatre: Casino
Musical Broadway: 63

Composer: Gustave Kerker
Lyricist: Arthur Anderson; Harold Atteridge; James T. Powers
Librettist: Arthur Anderson; Harold Atteridge; James T. Powers
Producer: Messrs. Shubert
Director: J.C. Huffman; William J. Wilson

Source: SCHNEEGLOCKCHEN (Musical: Julius Wilhelm; A.M. Willner); **Musical Director:** Max Hershfeld

Songs: Are We Widows, Wives or What?; Buzz on Little Busy Bees!; Corsican, The; How Do You Do?; I Like All Girls; Kiss Me Again, Bebe; Meet Me at Eight in the Hall (The Letter Song); Oh! Be Careful [1]; Oh, Honorka; Opening Chorus; Snowdrops and the Spring; So Away with Sorrow; Somehow, Sometime, Somewhere (C/L: Louis A. Hirsch); Someone I Used to Know; Waiting for Me; Waltz without a Kiss, A (L: James T. Powers); What About It?

Cast: Flavia Arcaro; Frances Cameron; Leila Hughes; James T. Powers

Notes: [1] Sheet music only.

4491 • TWO LITTLE GIRLS IN BLUE

OPENED: 05/03/1921 Theatre: Cohan
Musical Broadway: 135

Composer: Paul Lannin; Vincent Youmans
Lyricist: Ira Gershwin [7]
Librettist: Fred Jackson
Producer: A.L. Erlanger
Director: Ned Wayburn

Choreographer: Ned Wayburn; **Costumes:** Shirley Barker; Iverson & Henneage; **Musical Director:** Charles Previn; **Orchestrations:** Stephen Jones; Paul Lannin; **Set Design:** H. Robert Law

Songs: Dolly (C: Vincent Youmans; L: Ira Gershwin; Schuyler Greene); Finale Act II (C: Vincent Youmans); Gypsy Trail, The (C: Paul Lannin; L: Irving Caesar); Happy Ending [2] (C: Paul Lannin); Here, Steward (C: Vincent Youmans); Honeymoon (When Will You Shine for Me?) (C: Paul Lannin); I'm Tickled Silly (Slapstick) (C: Paul Lannin); Just Like You (C: Paul Lannin); Little Bag of Tricks [2] (C: Paul Lannin); Make the Best of It [1] (C: Vincent Youmans); Mr. and Mrs. [4] (C: Vincent Youmans); Oh Me! Oh My! (Oh You) (C: Vincent Youmans); Orienta (C: Vincent Youmans; L: Irving Caesar; Schuyler Greene); Rice and Shoes [3] (C: Vincent Youmans; L: Ira Gershwin; Schuyler Green); She's Innocent; Silly Season, The (C: Vincent Youmans); Slapstick [1] (C: Paul Lannin); Somebody's Sunday [6] (C/L: Vernon Duke); Summertime [1] (C: Paul Lannin); There's Something About Me They Like (C: Vincent Youmans; L: Ira Gershwin; Fred Jackson); Two Little Girls in Blue (C: Vincent Youmans); Utopia [2] (C: Vincent Youmans); We're Off on a Wonderful Trip (C: Vincent Youmans); We're Off to India [8] (C: Vincent Youmans); When I'm with the Girls (C: Vincent Youmans); Who's Who with You [4] (C: Vincent Youmans); Win Some Winsome Girl [2] (C: Paul Lannin); Wonderful U.S.A. (Your Wonderful U.S.A.) (C: Paul Lannin); You Started Something (When You Came Along) [5] (C: Vincent Youmans)

Cast: Madeleine Fairbanks; Marion Fairbanks; Olin Howland; Emma Janvier; Julia Kelety; Evelyn Law; George Mack; Fred Santley; Oscar Shaw; Jack Tomson; Tommy Tomson

Notes: [1] Cut in rehearsal. [2] Cut in tryouts. [3] Called "Sweetest Girl" during tryouts. [4] Cut in tryouts. Previously in PICCADILLY TO BROADWAY. [5] Music used for "Waiting for You" from NO! NO! NANETTE! [6] Written for 1927 London version which closed out of town. [7]

Used pseudonym Arthur Francis. [8] Introduction music same as "The Silly Season." Chorus portion same music as "Win Some Winsome Girl."

4492 • TWO LOTS IN THE BRONX

OPENED: 11/1913 Theatre: Adolf Philipp
Musical Broadway

Composer: Adolf Philipp
Lyricist: Edward Paulton; Adolf Philipp
Librettist: Edward Paulton; Adolf Philipp
Producer: Oliver Morosco

Songs: Here's to Us; I'm Fond of You-You're Fond of Me; It's Simply My Smile; Money Makes the World Go 'Round; My Darling Wife; Robbers Everywhere; Tell Me That You Love Me; 2 Lots in the Bronx

Cast: Emil Berla; Adolf Philipp; Marie Serina; Grete von Mayhof

Notes: Paulton helped with the English language lyrics and libretto.

4493 • TWO MEN AND A GIRL

OPENED: 02/13/1911
Musical Closed out of town

Composer: Julian Edwards
Lyricist: Charles J. Campbell; Ralph M. Skinner
Librettist: Charles J. Campbell; Ralph M. Skinner
Producer: Lee Shubert; Sam S. Shubert
Director: William J. Wilson

Songs: Herman, Let's Dance That Beautiful Waltz (C: Ted Snyder; L: Irving Berlin); Wishing (C: Ted Snyder; L: Irving Berlin)

Cast: Ralph Austin; Fred Bailey

Notes: No program available. Clipping from Detroit 2/15/11 used. This was a revision of THE MOTOR GIRL. See also under that title.

4494 • TWO MUCH

OPENED: 1967 Theatre: Madeira Club
Musical Nightclub

Author: Don Brockett; William Dyer; Joanne Pasquinelli

Cast: John Paul Hudson; Don Parks; Lily Tomlin

Notes: Provincetown, Massachusetts revue.

4495 • TWO ON AN ISLAND

OPENED: 01/25/1940 Theatre: Broadhurst
Play Broadway: 96

Author: Elmer Rice
Producer: Playwrights' Company, The
Director: Elmer Rice

Incidental Music: Kurt Weill; **Set Design:** Jo Mielziner

Cast: Luther Adler; Howard Da Silva; Betty Field; Martin Ritt; Robert Williams

4496 • TWO ON THE AISLE

OPENED: 07/19/1951 Theatre: Mark Hellinger
Revue Broadway: 279

Composer: Jule Styne
Lyricist: Betty Comden; Adolph Green
Librettist: Betty Comden; Adolph Green
Producer: Arthur Lesser
Director: Abe Burrows

Choreographer: Ted Cappy; **Costumes:** Joan Personette; **Dance Arranger:** Genevieve Pitot; **Lighting Designer:** Howard Bay; **Musical Director:** Herbert Greene; **Orchestrations:** Philip J. Lang; **Set Design:** Howard Bay

Songs: Catch Our Act at the Met (Vaudeville Ain't Dead); Clown, The; Everlasting; Give a Little, Get a Little; Here She Comes Now (East River Hoedown); Hold Me-Hold Me-Hold Me; How Will He Know?; If You Hadn't but You Did; Show Train; So Far, So Good [1]; There Never Was a Baby Like My Baby; Triangle (sketch)

Cast: Dolores Gray; Bert Lahr; Colette Marchand; Elliott Reid

Notes: [1] Cut prior to opening. Music from "Give Me a Song with a Beautiful Melody" from film IT'S A GREAT FEELING.

4497 • TWO ROSES, THE

OPENED: 11/21/1904 Theatre: Broadway
Musical Broadway: 29

Composer: Ludwig Englander
Lyricist: Stanislaus Stange
Librettist: Stanislaus Stange
Producer: Charles B. Dillingham
Director: Fred G. Latham

Source: SHE STOOPS TO CONQUER (Play: Oliver Goldsmith); **Choreographer:** A.M. Holbrook; **Costumes:** Mme. Seidle; **Musical Director:** John Lund; **Set Design:** Emens & Unitt

Songs: Airy Mary; Appearances Are Deceitful; Battle on the Tiles, The; Ding Dong, Ding Dong (Finale Act I); Fairest of Roses [1]; Jack in the Box; Just Three Words; Love's Misgivings; Making of a Woman, The; Remarkable Doctor, A; Rose Marie; Simple Dimple, A; Sing Hey, Sing Ho (Opening Chorus Act II); Smile and Be Merry; Spirit of Mischief, The; There's Not a Thing I Wouldn't Do; 'Tis the Hour (Opening Chorus); What May a Lovesick Maiden Do; What's a Kiss; Why?

Cast: Josephine Bartlett; Louis Harrison; Louise LeBaron; Fritzi Scheff

Notes: No songs listed in program. [1] Vocal score only.

4498 • TWO WEEKS WITH PAY

OPENED: 06/24/1940
Revue Closed out of town

Librettist: Peter Barry; David Greggory; Charles Sherman
Producer: Olneys, The

Choreographer: Gene Kelly; **Costumes:** Marion Herwood; **Set Design:** Lawrence L. Goldwasser; **Vocal Arranger:** Harold Cooke

Songs: All That and Heaven Too (C: Richard Lewine; L: Peter Barry; David Greggory); As Long as You're Along (C: Baldwin Bergersen; L: David Greggory); Dear Horse (C: Richard Lewine; L: Ted Fetter); Five Cent Piece (C: Richard Lewine; L: Ted Fetter); Hey Gal (C: Will Irwin; L: Peter Barry); I Would Rather Be (C: Baldwin Bergersen; L: Peter Barry; David Greggory); Jig Is Up, The (C: Richard Lewine; L: Ted Fetter); June, Moon, Spoon (C/L: Herman Hupfeld); Just Another Page in Your Diary [2] (C/L: Cole Porter); Noises in the Street (C: Richard Lewine; L: Peter Barry; David Greggory); Now That I Know You [1] (C: Richard Rodgers; L: Lorenz Hart); Once Upon a Morning (sketch) (C: Eyck Van Goetz); Praised Be Moses (C: Charles Marvin; L: William Borden); Secret Snow (C: Baldwin Bergersen; L: Peter Barry; David Greggory); Will You Love Me on Monday Morning (C: Harold Arlen; L: Ira Gershwin; E.Y. Harburg); With You with Me (C: John Green; L: Johnny Mercer)

Cast: Remo Bufano's Puppets; Eugene Hari; Pat Harrington; Bill Johnson; Ruth Mata; Marie Nash; Earl Oxford; Hiram Sherman

Notes: [1] Same music as original deleted I'D RATHER BE RIGHT title song. [2] Cut from LEAVE IT TO ME!

4499 • TWO'S COMPANY

OPENED: 12/15/1952 Theatre: Alvin
Revue Broadway: 91

Composer: Vernon Duke
Lyricist: Ogden Nash
Librettist: Peter DeVries; Charles Sherman
Producer: Michael Ellis; James Russo
Director: Jules Dassin

Choreographer: Jerome Robbins; **Costumes:** Miles White; **Musical Director:** Milton Rosenstock; **Orchestrations:** Clare Grundman; Don Walker; **Set Design:** Ralph Alswang

Songs: Baby Couldn't Dance; Esther (L: Sammy Cahn); Good Little Girls [2] (L: Sammy Cahn); Haunted Hot Spot; I Think You're Pretty Too [1]; It Just Occurred to Me (L: Sammy Cahn); Just Like a Man [4]; Man's Home, A (C/L: Sheldon Harnick); Merry Minuet [3] (C/L: Sheldon Harnick); Out of the Clear Blue Sky; Purple Rose; Roll Along, Sadie; Roundabout [4]; Theatre Is a Lady, The; Turn Me Loose on Broadway

Cast: David Burns; Bill Callahan; Bette Davis; Ellen Hanley; Peter Kelley; Tina Louise; Deborah Remsen; Hiram Sherman

Notes: Production under the supervision of John Murray Anderson. [1] Out Pittsburgh 1/10/52. [2] Out Detroit 10/19/52, later in THE LITTLEST REVUE. Originally written for and cut from the film APRIL IN PARIS. [3] Cut. Later used in JOHN MURRAY ANDERSON'S ALMANAC. [4] Originally in SWEET BYE AND BYE.

4500 • TZIGANE, THE

OPENED: 05/16/1895 Musical

Theatre: Abbey's Broadway

Composer: Reginald De Koven
Lyricist: Harry B. Smith
Librettist: Harry B. Smith
Producer: Abbey; Grau; Schoeffel
Director: Max Freeman

Costumes: Mme. Seidle; **Musical Director:** Paul Steindorff; **Set Design:** Henry E. Hoyt

Cast: Jefferson De Angelis; Joseph Herbert; Clare Lane; Lillian Russell; Frederic Solomon; Hubert Wilke

Notes: No songs listed in program.

U

4501 • UBANGI CLUB FOLLIES (1935)

OPENED: 1935 Theatre: Ubangi Club Nightclub
Revue

Composer: Andy Razaf
Lyricist: Andy Razaf
Producer: Leonard Harper

Songs: At the Reefer Smoker's Ball (C: Mildred Bailey; Andy Razaf); You Broke It Up (When You Said Dixie) (C: Duke Yellman)

Cast: Gladys Bentley; Billie Daniels; Velma Middleton

Notes: No program available. The Ubangi Club occupied the same space as the uptown Connie's Inn.

4502 • UBANGI CLUB FOLLIES (1941)

OPENED: 1941 Theatre: Ubangi Club Nightclub
Revue

Composer: Paul Denniker
Lyricist: Andy Razaf

Songs: Get Rhythm in Your Feet; I Guess We're Gonna Get Along

Cast: Bunny Briggs; Erskine Hawkins' 'Bama State Coll.; Velma Middleton

Notes: No program available.

4503 • UBANGI CLUB REVUES

Theatre: Ubangi Club Nightclub
Revue

Composer: Eubie Blake
Lyricist: Andy Razaf

Songs: Boogie Woogie Bunga Boo; Conga Tap, The; Cradle of Rhythm (C: Paul Denniker); Harlem's a Garden; I'm Percy Pinchill of Harlem; Jungle Rhythm Roundup (C: Paul Denniker); Native Son, A; Red, A; Snooty, The; Sweep No More My Lady; To Arms (Dear One, Divine) (C: Paul Denniker)

Notes: Songs from various undated Ubangi Club revues.

4504 • ULYSSES AFRICANUS

OPENED: 1945
Unproduced

Composer: Kurt Weill
Lyricist: Maxwell Anderson

Source: ULYSSES AFRICANUS (Novel: Henry Stillwell Edwards)

Songs: Big Mole [1]; Lady, You Drop Yo Feminine Wiles; Little Tin God, The [2]; Lost in the Stars [1]; Stay Well [1]; Trouble Man [1]; When I Was a Pickaninny; White Folks

Cast: Paul Robeson

Notes: Songs written for this show ended up in LOST IN THE STARS. [1] Later in LOST IN THE STARS. [2] Later in LOST IN THE STARS with lyric changed to "Little Grey House."

4505 • UMBRELLAS OF CHERBOURG, THE

OPENED: 01/02/1979 Theatre: Public
Musical Off-Broadway: 36

Composer: Michel Legrand
Lyricist: Charles Burr; Sheldon Harnick
Librettist: Charles Burr; Sheldon Harnick
Producer: N.Y. Shakespeare Festival; Joseph Papp
Director: Andrei Serban

Source: LES PARAPLUIES DE CHERBOURG (Film: Jacques Demy; Michel Legrand); French Lyrics: Jacques Demy; Michel Legrand; French Libretto: Charles Burr; Jacques Demy; **Choreographer:** Dorothy Danner; **Costumes:**

Jane Greenwood; **Dance Arranger:** Steven Margoshes; **Lighting Designer:** Ian Calderon; **Musical Director:** Steven Margoshes; **Orchestrations:** Michel Legrand; Steven Margoshes; **Set Design:** Michael H. Yeargan; **Vocal Arranger:** Michel Legrand; Steven Margoshes

Cast: Stephen Bogardus; Laurence Guittard; Marc Jordan; Dean Pitchford; Maureen Silliman

Notes: Same songs as in movie. English translation by Sheldon Harnick in association with Charles Burr.

4506 • UMPIRE, THE

OPENED: 12/02/1905 Theatre: La Salle
Musical Chicago

Composer: Joseph E. Howard
Lyricist: Frank R. Adams; Will M. Hough
Librettist: Frank R. Adams; Will M. Hough
Producer: Mort Singer
Director: Arthur Sanders; Gus Sohlke

Songs: Big Banshee, The; Clorinda Jackson; Cross Your Heart; Drums of the Fore and Aft (L: Rudyard Kipling); I Want a Girl Like You; Let's Take a Trolley Ride; Opening Chorus; Quarterback, The; Sun That Shines on Dixieland, The; Umpire Is a Most Unhappy Man, The; You Look Awful Good to Father

Cast: Florence Holbrook; Cecil Lean; Olive Vail

4507 • UNCLE TOM'S CABIN

OPENED: 01/27/1902
Musical

Composer: Jerome Kern
Librettist: Rosewell G. Thompson
Producer: Newark Yacht Club

Songs: I Never Do a Thing Like That; Ma Blossom; Marcella; Mighty Svengali Legree, The; Opening Chorus Act II; Song of the Sheriffs; Things Have Changed from Then to Now; When Rogers Come to Town; Yo! Ho! When You're in the Chorus

Cast: Daniel Blakeman; Charles P. Gillan; Rosewell G. Thompson; Gus Troxler; Nicholas J. Tynan

Notes: Amateur show.

4508 • UNDER COVER

OPENED: 09/14/1903 Theatre: Murray Hill
Play Broadway: 90

Composer: George Braham
Lyricist: Edward Harrigan
Author: Edward Harrigan
Producer: Liebler & Company

Musical Director: George Braham

Songs: Coon Will Follow a Band, A; Fringe of Society, The; Limerick's Running Yet; Lulu's Honeymoon; Oh, What's the Use; When Mamie Sweet Mamie's a Bride

Cast: Dan Collyer; Jane Elton; Edward Harrigan; Elizabeth King

4509 • UNDER MANY FLAGS

OPENED: 05/31/1912 Theatre: Hippodrome
Musical Broadway: 445

Composer: Manuel Klein
Lyricist: Manuel Klein
Librettist: Carroll Fleming
Producer: Messrs. Shubert
Director: Carroll Fleming

Choreographer: William J. Wilson; **Musical Director:** Manuel Klein; **Set Design:** Arthur Voegtlin

Songs: Dear Old White House, The; Every Nation Has a Flower; Fishing; Flowers of the Nations Ballet; For Universal Peace; Home Is Where the Heart Is (Home Sweet Home); March of the Dragon; Once a Fisherman Went to Sea; Pretty Little Maiden on the Screen; Scotland Forever; Sweetheart Let's Go a Walking; Temple Bells; 'Tis Summer; Tulips with Your Color So Bright; Youngsters of the Navy

Cast: Elsie Baird; Leonard Kirtley; Albert Pellaton; Edith Singleton; Harry Truax

4510 • UNDER THE COUNTER

OPENED: 10/03/1947 Theatre: Shubert
Musical Broadway: 27

Composer: Manning Sherwin
Lyricist: Harold Purcell
Librettist: Arthur Macrae
Producer: Lee Ephraim; Messrs. Shubert
Director: Jack Hurlbert

Choreographer: John Gregory; Jack Hurlbert; **Musical Director:** Harry Levant; **Set Design:** Clifford Pember

Songs: Ai Yi Yi; Everywhere; Let's Get Back to Glamour; Moment I Saw You, The; No-one's Tried to Kiss Me

Cast: Cicely Courtneidge; Wilfred Hyde-White

4511 • UNDER THE RED GLOBE

OPENED: 02/18/1897 Theatre: Weber & Fields Broadway Music Hall
Musical Broadway

Composer: John Stromberg
Librettist: Joseph Herbert

Cast: Lew Fields; Joseph Weber

Notes: No program available. A burlesque on UNDER THE RED ROBE.

4512 • UNDERWORLD

OPENED: 1960
Musical Unproduced

Composer: Jerome Moross
Lyricist: John Hollander; Lester Judson
Librettist: Moss Hart

Songs: Beer and Flowers (L: John Hollander); Cream of Society, The; It's Almost Time Now; I've Even Been in Love; Love Me (L: John Hollander); Paddy Boy; Prologue; That Extra Bit

Notes: Hollander wrote the lyrics which were polished and added to by Judson.

4513 • UNDINE

OPENED: 11/20/1911 Theatre: Winter Garden
Musical Broadway

Composer: Manuel Klein
Lyricist: Manuel Klein
Librettist: Manuel Klein

Notes: A one-act musical.

4514 • UNFAIR TO GOLIATH

OPENED: 01/25/1970 Theatre: Cherry Lane
Musical Off-Broadway: 73

Composer: Menachem Zur
Lyricist: Herbert Appleman
Librettist: Ephaim Kishon
Producer: Alexander Beck; Edward Schreiber
Director: Herbert Appleman; Ephaim Kishon

Costumes: Pamela Scofield; **Lighting Designer:** C. Murawski; **Musical Director:** Menachem Zur; **Set Design:** C. Murawski

Songs: Danger of Peace Is Over, The; Famous Rabbi, The; In the Reign of Chaim; Parking Meter Like Me, A; Rooster and the Hen, The; Sabra, The; Song of Sallah Shabeti, The; What Abraham Lincoln Once Said; What Kind of Baby; When Moses Spake to Goldstein

Cast: Hugh Alexander; Jim Brochu; Guy Devlin; Corinne Kason; Laura May Lewis

4515 • UNFINISHED SONG, AN

OPENED: 02/10/1991 Theatre: Provincetown Playhouse
Musical Off-Broadway: 25

Composer: James J. Mellon
Lyricist: James J. Mellon
Librettist: James J. Mellon
Producer: Cheryl L. Fluehr; Starbuck Productions, Ltd.
Director: Simon Levy

Arrangements: Lawrence Yurman; **Costumes:** Jeffrey Ullman; **Lighting Designer:** Robert M. Wierzel; **Musical Director:** Mark Mitchell; **Set Design:** Scott Bradley

Songs: As I Say Goodbye; Balance the Plate; Being Left Out; Blonde Haired Babies; Crossing Boundaries; Frying Pan, The; Hobby Horses; How Could I Let You Leave Me; Is That Love; Keeping Score with Myself [1]; New Hampshire Nights; Remember the Ocean [1]; Things We've Collected; Tightrope [1]; Unfinished Song, An; We Were Here

Cast: Aloysius Gigl; Joanna Glushak; Robert Lambert; Ken Land; Beth Leavel

Notes: [1] Added to 2/1/95 revival in Boston.

4516 • UNSINKABLE MOLLY BROWN, THE

OPENED: 11/03/1960 Theatre: Winter Garden
Musical Broadway: 532

Composer: Meredith Willson
Lyricist: Meredith Willson
Librettist: Robert Morris
Producer: Dore Schary; Theatre Guild, The
Director: Dore Schary

Choreographer: Peter Gennaro; **Costumes:** Miles White; **Dance Arranger:** Sol Berkowitz; **Lighting Designer:** Peggy Clark; **Musical Director:** Herbert Greene; **Orchestrations:** Don Walker; **Set Design:** Oliver Smith; **Vocal Arranger:** Herbert Greene

Songs: Ambassador's Polka, The [1]; Another Big Strike [1]; Are You Sure?; Beautiful People of Denver; Belly Up to the Bar, Boys; Bon Jour (The Language Song); Chick-a-pen; Colorado, My Home [2]; Denver Police, The; Dolce Far Niente; Extra! Extra! [1]; Happy Birthday, Mrs. J.J. Brown; I Ain't Down Yet; I May Never Fall in Love with You; If I Knew; I'll Never Say No; I've Already Started In; Keep-a-Hoppin'; Leadville Johnny Brown; My Old Brass Bed; One Day at a Time [1]; Read the Label (Don't Take My Word for It Neighbor) (Get Away You Bother Me) [1]; Tomorrow [3]; Up Where the Joke's Goin' On [1]; Up Where the People Are (dance)

Cast: Tammy Grimes; Jack Harrold; Christopher Hewett; Edith Meiser; Harve Presnell; Cameron Prud'homme; Joseph Sirola

Notes: [1] Cut prior to opening. [2] Cut after opening and added to film version. [3] Cut prior to opening. Also cut from THE MUSIC MAN.

4517 • UNSUNG COLE

OPENED: 09/04/1977 Theatre: Circle Repertory
Revue Off-Broadway: 78

Composer: Cole Porter
Lyricist: Cole Porter
Producer: Circle Repertory Company
Director: Norman L. Berman

Choreographer: Dennis Grimaldi; **Costumes:** Carol Oditz; **Lighting Designer:** Arden Fingerhut; **Musical Director:** Leon Odenz; **Set Design:** Peter Harvey; **Vocal Arranger:** Norman L. Berman

Songs: Abracadabra [11]; After You, Who? [15]; Almiro [7] (L: Cole Porter; Rene Pujol); Dancin' to a Jungle Drum [9]; Down in the Depths [6]; Farming [2]; Friendship [18]; Give Me the Land [10]; Goodbye Little Dream, Goodbye [6]; Great Indoors, The [3]; I Happen to Like New York [3]; If Ever Married I'm [17]; I'm Getting Myself Ready for You [3]; I've Got Some Unfinished Business with You [2]; Just Another Page in Your Diary [12]; Kate the Great [16]; Lady Needs a Rest, A [2]; Lost Liberty Blues [7]; Love for Sale [3]; Nobody's Chasing Me [13]; Olga [8]; Ours [6]; Pick Me Up and Lay Me Down [1]; Poor Young Millionaire [5]; Queen of Terre Haute, The [4]; Red, Hot and Blue! [6]; Sing to Me Guitar [11]; Swingin' the Jinx Away [14]; Take Me Back to Manhattan [3]; Tale of an Oyster, The [4]; Thank You So Much Mrs. Lowsborough- Goodby; That's Why I Love You [4]; When the Hen Stops Laying [12]; Why Don't We Try Staying Home [4]

Cast: Gene Lindsey; Mary Louise; Maureen Moore; Anita Morris; John Sloman

Notes: No original songs in this show. [1] From STARDUST. [2] From LET'S FACE IT. [3] From THE NEW YORKERS. [4] From FIFTY MILLION FRENCHMEN. [5] Written in the 30's and used in the film AT LONG, LAST LOVE. [6] From RED, HOT AND BLUE! [7] From LA REVUE DES AMBASSADEURS. [8] From MAYFAIR AND MONTMARTRE. [9] From SEVEN LIVELY ARTS. [10] From SILK STOCKINGS. [11] From MEXICAN HAYRIDE. [12] From LEAVE IT TO ME! [13] From OUT OF THIS WORLD. [14] From BORN TO SWING. [15] From GAY DIVORCE. [16] From ANYTHING GOES. [17] From KISS ME, KATE. [18] From DUBARRY WAS A LADY. [19] From LA REVUE DES AMBASSADEURS. French lyrics by Rene Pujol.

4518 • UP AGAINST IT

OPENED: 12/04/1989 Theatre: Public
Musical Off-Broadway: 16

Composer: Todd Rundgren
Lyricist: Todd Rundgren
Librettist: Tom Ross
Producer: N.Y. Shakespeare Festival
Director: Kenneth Elliott

Source: UP AGAINST IT (Film: Joe Orton); **Choreographer:** Jennifer Muller; **Costumes:** John Glaser; **Lighting Designer:** Vivien Leone; **Musical Director:** Tom Fay; **Orchestrations:** Doug Katsaros; **Set Design:** B.T. Whitehill; **Vocal Arranger:** Todd Rundgren

Songs: Entropy; From Hunger; If I Have to Be Alone; Life Is a Drag; Lilly's Address; Love in Disguise; Male and Twenty-One; Maybe I'm Better Off; Parallel Lines; Smell of Money, The; Up Against It; When Worlds Collide; You'll Thank Me in the End

Cast: Roger Bart; Philip Casnoff; Toni Dibuono; Alison Fraser; Mari Nelson; Dan Tubb

4519 • UP AND DOING

OPENED: 04/17/1940 Theatre: Saville
Revue London: 503

Composer: Richard Rodgers
Lyricist: Lorenz Hart
Librettist: Graham John
Producer: F. Firth Shepard

Songs: Falling in Love with Love [1]; Sing for Your Supper [1]; This Can't Be Love [1]

Cast: Patricia Burke; Binnie Hale; Leslie Henson; Stanley Holloway; Enid Lowe; Graham Payn; Cyril Ritchard

Notes: No program available. Two runs of 171 and 332 performances. [1] From THE BOYS FROM SYRACUSE.

4520 • UP AND DOWN

OPENED: 1922
Musical

Composer: J. Homer Tutt; Salem Tutt Whitney
Lyricist: J. Homer Tutt; Salem Tutt Whitney
Librettist: J. Homer Tutt; Salem Tutt Whitney
Producer: J. Homer Tutt; Salem Tutt Whitney

Songs: Backbiting Me; Male Vamps; Rock Me, Daddy; We Want to Booze; When You're Crazy Over Daddy

Cast: Blanche Calloway; Jennie Dancey; Alonzo Fenderson; Alberta Jones; Margaret Simms; Henry Thomson; J. Homer Tutt; Salem Tutt Whitney

Notes: No other information available.

4521 • UP AND DOWN BROADWAY

OPENED: 07/18/1910 Theatre: Casino
Musical Broadway: 72

Composer: Jean Schwartz
Lyricist: William Jerome
Librettist: Edgar Smith
Producer: Lee Shubert; Sam S. Shubert
Director: William J. Wilson

Costumes: Melville Ellis

Songs: Chinatown, My Chinatown; Chocolate Soldier [2]; Come Down to Earth, My Dearie; Dope Fiend, The (C: Melville Ellis); 1861 [2]; Everybody Is Bagpipe Crazy [1]; Ghost of Kelly, The; Go On Your Mission [2]; Have a Smile with Momus [2]; I Am Melpomene [2]; I Want a Lot of Girlies, Girlies (I Want a Whole Lot of Girls); I'm Always Happy when I'm Sad [1]; I'm the Lily; Kellerman Girlie, The [1]; Mary Ann; Military Glide, The; My Operatic Samson [1]; New York Isn't Such a Bad Old Town [1]; Oh, That Beautiful Rag (C: Ted Snyder; L: Irving Berlin); Pretty Little Girl Inside, The; Soldier's Life Is Grand, A [1]; Spanish Fandango Rag, The (Dreamy Fandango Tune) [2]; Sweet Italian Love [1] (C: Ted Snyder; L: Irving Berlin); There Must Be a Girl in the Moon [1]; Throw Up Your Hands [1]; Ticket Speculator, The [2]; When Sist' Tetrazin' Met Cousin Carus [2]; Where Are Your Actors [1]

Cast: Adelaide and Hughes; Irving Berlin; Emma Carus; Eddie Foy Sr.; Ernest Hare; Oscar Shaw; Ted Snyder; Lenore Ulric; Anna Wheaton

Notes: [1] Sheet music only. [2] Out Washington, D.C. 10/9/10.

4522 • UP EDEN

OPENED: 11/27/1968 Theatre: Jan Hus Playhouse
Musical Off-Broadway: 8

Composer: Robert Rosenblum
Lyricist: Robert Rosenblum; Howard Schuman

Librettist: Robert Rosenblum; Howard Schuman
Producer: Jack Farren; Evan William Mandel
Director: John Bishop

Source: COSI FAN TUTTE (Opera: Wolfgang Amadeus Mozart); **Choreographer:** Patricia Birch; **Costumes:** Gordon Micunis; **Lighting Designer:** Louise Guthman; **Musical Director:** Wally Harper; **Orchestrations:** Wally Harper; Richard Hurwitz; **Set Design:** Gordon Micunis; **Vocal Arranger:** Jack Lee

Songs: Hannibal's Comin'; Haven't You Wondered; Homesick; Let Me Show You the World; Little More Like You, A; Mowla, The; No More Edens; Nothing Ever Happens Till 2 A.M.; Passin' Through; Playboy's Work Is Never Done, A; Remember Me Smiling; Virgin of Velez-Jermano, The; Was That Me Talking?; Will, The; Wishy Washy Woman

Cast: Robert Balaban; Blythe Danner; Deborah Deeble; George S. Irving; Patti Karr; Denny Shearer

4523 • UP FROM PARADISE

OPENED: 06/14/1977
Musical — Closed out of town

Composer: Stanley Silverman
Lyricist: Arthur Miller
Librettist: Arthur Miller

2:Source: CREATION OF THE WORLD AND OTHER BUSINESS, THE (Play: Arthur Miller); **Musical Director:** Gary Adams

Songs: Adorable; All Love, All Love; As Good As Paradise; Creation of Eve, The; God's Curse; Hallelujah; How Fine It Is to Name Things; I Can See the Lord in the Garden Now; If Something Leads to Good, Can It Be Bad?; I'm Lonely; I'm Me; In the Center of Your Mind Keep the Lord; It's Just Like I Was You; Lamentation; Loneliness Song, The; Mother of Mankind, The; Nothing's Left of God; Terrible Feeling, A; When Eve Is Alone

Cast: Walter Bobbie; David Patrick Kelly; Austin Pendleton; Patti Perkins; Harris Poor; Paul Ukena

Notes: No program available. Presented as part of the Kennedy Center Musical Theatre Lab.

4524 • UP IN CENTRAL PARK

OPENED: 01/27/1945 — Theatre: Century
Musical — Broadway: 504

Composer: Sigmund Romberg
Lyricist: Dorothy Fields
Librettist: Dorothy Fields; Herbert Fields
Producer: Michael Todd
Director: John Kennedy

Choreographer: Lew Kessler; Helen Tamiris; **Costumes:** Grace Houston; Ernest Schrapps; **Lighting Designer:** Howard Bay; **Musical Director:** Max Meth; **Orchestrations:** Don Walker; **Set Design:** Howard Bay

Songs: April Snow; Big Back Yard, The; Birds and the Bees, The; Boss Tweed; Carousel in the Park; Close As Pages in a Book; Currier and Ives; Fireman's Bride, The; It Doesn't Cost You Anything to Dream; Maypole Dance (inst.); Opening Scene III; Opening Scene V; Rip Van Winkle; Up from the Gutter; When She Walks in the Room; When the Party Gives a Party; You Can't Get Over the Wall

Cast: Noah Beery Sr.; Betty Bruce; Maureen Burke; Maureen Cannon; Wilbur Evans; Charles Irwin; Daniel Nagrin; Paul Reed; Guy Standing Jr.; Rowan Tudor

4525 • UP IN LIGHTS

OPENED: 08/01/1954
Musical — Closed out of town

Composer: William Angelas; Lan O'Kun
Librettist: William Dixon; William Levine

Notes: No other information available. Produced at Syracuse University.

4526 • UP IN MABEL'S ROOM

OPENED: 01/15/1919 — Theatre: Eltinge
Play — Broadway: 229

Author: Wilson Collison; Otto Harbach
Producer: A.H. Woods
Director: Bertram Harrison

Songs: Up in Mabel's Room (C: Abner Silver; L: Alex Gerber)

Cast: John Cumberland; Hazel Dawn; Enid Markey

Notes: This song may not have been in the play but just inspired by it.

4527 • UP IN THE AIR, BOYS

OPENED: 11/29/1974 Theatre: Hartley House
Musical Off-Off-Broadway

Composer: Robert Dahdah
Lyricist: Mary Boylan; Robert Dahdah
Librettist: Mary Boylan; Robert Dahdah
Director: Robert Dahdah

Choreographer: Robert Durkin; **Costumes:** Gene Calvin; **Musical Director:** Robert Marks

Songs: Apache Dance; Do the Heavenental; Don't Make Me Dance; Dreams Don't Mean a Thing; How Could I Forget; Laughing Daffodil; Musical Me; Reach; Top Spot; Up in the Air, Boys; Voodoo Night in Hotchkiss Corners; When Marie Antoinette Learned to Pet; You Never Change

Cast: Margaret Benczak; Peggylee Brennan; Dennis Deal; Tom Offt

4528 • UP IN THE CLOUDS

OPENED: 01/02/1922 Theatre: Lyric
Musical Broadway: 89

Composer: Tom Johnstone
Lyricist: Will B. Johnstone
Librettist: Will B. Johnstone
Producer: Joseph M. Gaites
Director: Lawrence Marston

Choreographer: Allan K. Foster; Vaughn Godfrey; Max Scheck; **Musical Director:** Hilding Anderson

Songs: At the Fountain; Ballet of Wealth; Betsy Ross; Birth of American Fantasy Dance; Friends; Girl I Marry, The; Happiness; How Dry I Am; I See Your Face; It's a Great Life If You Don't Weaken; Jean; Last Girl Is the Best Girl, The; Look-a-Look; Movie Lesson, The; Nobody Knows; Passing of Six Months; Rum-Tum-Tiddle; Up in the Clouds; Wonderful Something

Cast: "Skeets" Gallagher; Grace Moore; June Roberts; Hal Van Rensellaer; Max Welty

4529 • UP SHE GOES

OPENED: 11/06/1922 Theatre: Playhouse
Musical Broadway: 252

Composer: Harry Tierney
Lyricist: Joseph McCarthy
Librettist: Frank Craven
Producer: William A. Brady
Director: Frank Craven; Bert French

Source: TOO MANY COOKS (Play: Frank Craven); **Choreographer:** Bert French; **Orchestrations:** Frank Barry

Songs: Bob About a Bit; Journey's End; Lady Luck Smile on Me; Let's Kiss and Make Up; Nearing the Day; Opening Act II; Roof Tree; Settle Down, Travel Round; Strike, The; Takes a Heap of Love; Tyup; Up She Goes; Up with the Stars; Visitors, The; We'll Do the Riviera

Cast: Helen Bolton; Donald Brian; Gloria Foy; "Skeets" Gallagher; Frederick Graham

4530 • UP STAGE AND DOWN

OPENED: 03/08/1917
Musical

Composer: Richard Rodgers
Lyricist: Richard Rodgers
Librettist: Myron D. Rosenthal
Producer: Infants Relief Society
Director: Harry A. Goldberg

Choreographer: Sydney Oberfelder

Songs: Advertise; Ali Baba; Asiatic Angles; Butterfly Love; Can It (L: Oscar Hammerstein II); Dearie; I'm So Shy; Japanese Jazz; Love Is Not in Vain; Love Me By Parcel Post (L: Mortimer W. Rodgers); Loving Cup; Now Listen; Out of a Job; Prisms, Plums and Prunes (L: Benjamin Kaye); There's Always Room for One More (L: Oscar Hammerstein II); Twinkling Eyes; Weaknesses (L: Oscar Hammerstein II); Wild Women's Wiles

Notes: Amateur production. Reopened as TWINKLING EYES 5/18/19. See that entry.

4531 • UP TO DATE

OPENED: 05/15/1893 Theatre: Palmer's
Musical Broadway

Composer: Carl Pfleuger
Lyricist: R.A. Barnet
Librettist: R.A. Barnet

Notes: No program available.

4532 • UPS-A-DAISY

OPENED: 10/08/1928 Theatre: Shubert
Musical Broadway: 320

Composer: Lewis E. Gensler
Lyricist: Robert A. Simon
Librettist: Clifford Grey; Robert A. Simon
Producer: Lewis E. Gensler
Director: Edgar MacGregor

Source: DER HOCHTOURIST (Play: Kurt Kraatz); **Choreographer:** Earl Lindsay; **Costumes:** Kiviette; **Musical Director:** Gene Salzer; **Orchestrations:** Frank Black; **Set Design:** John Wenger

Songs: Desire Under the Alps; Give Us a Tune [1]; Great Little Guy; Hot; I Can't Believe It's True [2]; I've Got a Baby; Oh, How Happy We'll Be (L: Clifford Grey; Robert A. Simon); Oh-How-I-Miss-You Blues (L: Clifford Grey; Robert A. Simon); Opening Chorus; Sweet One; Sweetest of the Roses; Tell Me Who You Are; Ups-a-Daisy; Will You Remember? Will You Forget? (L: Clifford Grey; Robert A. Simon)

Cast: Luella Gear; Bob Hope; William Kent; Roy Royston; Marie Saxon

Notes: [1] Out Newark 10/01/28. [2] Cut.

4533 • UPSTAIRS AT O'NEAL'S

OPENED: 10/28/1982 Theatre: O'Neal's
Revue Nightclub: 308

Producer: Martin Charnin; Michael O'Neal; Patrick O'Neal
Director: Martin Charnin

Choreographer: Ed Love; **Costumes:** Zoran; **Dance Arranger:** David Krane; **Lighting Designer:** Ray Recht; **Musical Director:** David Krane; **Set Design:** Ray Recht; **Vocal Arranger:** David Krane

Songs: All I Can Do Is Cry (C/L: Michael Abbott; Sarah Weeks); Ballad of Cy and Beatrice, The (C: Paul Trueblood; L: Jim Morgan); Boy, Do We Need It Now [1] (C/L: Charles Strouse); Cancun (C/L: John Forster; Michael Leeds); Cover Girls (C/L: Seth Friedman; L: David Crane; Marta Kauffman); Feet, The (C/L: Seth Friedman; L: David Crane; Marta Kauffman); I Furnished My One Room Apartment (C: Stephen Hoffman; L: Michael Mooney); Little H and Little G (C/L: Ronald Melrose); Mommas' Turn (C/L: Douglas Bernstein; Denis Markell); Signed, Peeled, Delivered (C/L: Ronald Melrose); Soap Operettas (C/L: Seth Friedman; L: David Crane; Marta Kauffman); Soldier and the Washer-woman, The (C/L: Ronald Melrose); Something (C/L: Douglas Bernstein; Denis Markell); Stools (C/L: Martin Charnin); Talkin' Morosco Blues (C: Willie Nininger; L: Murray Horwitz); Upstairs at O'Neal's (C/L: Martin Charnin); We'll Be Right Back After This Message (C/L: Douglas Bernstein; Denis Markell)

Cast: Douglas Bernstein; Randall Edwards; Bebe Neuwirth; Michon Peacock; Richard Ryder; Sarah Weeks; **Pianist:** Paul Ford; David Krane

Notes: [1] Written for the film THAT'S ENTERTAINMENT PART 2.

4534 • UPTOWN . . . IT'S HOT!

OPENED: 01/29/1986 Theatre: Lunt-Fontanne
Revue Broadway: 24

Librettist: Marion Ramsey; Jeffrey V. Thompson
Producer: Larry Magid; Allen Spivak
Director: Maurice Hines

Choreographer: Maurice Hines; **Costumes:** Ellen Lee; **Dance Arranger:** Thom Bridwell; Frank Owens; **Lighting Designer:** Marc B. Weiss; **Musical Director:** Frank Owens; **Set Design:** Tom McPhillips

Songs: A-Tisket A-Tasket (C: Van Alexander; L: Ella Fitzgerald); Ain't Too Proud to Beg (C/L: Eddie Holland; Norman Whitfield); Amazing Grace (C/L: Traditional); Be My Baby (C/L: Jeff Barry; Ellie Greenwich; Phil Spector); Blueberry Hill (C/L: Al Lewis; Vincent Rose; Larry Stock); Body and Soul (C: Johnny Green; L: Howard Dietz; Frank Eyton; Edward Heyman; Robert Sour); Cotton Club Stomp (inst.) (C: Duke Ellington); Dancin' in the

Streets (C/L: Marvin Gaye; Ivy Hunter; William Stevenson); Daybreak Express (inst.) (C: Duke Ellington); Diga Diga Doo (C: Jimmy McHugh; L: Dorothy Fields); Dinah (C: Harry Akst; L: Lewis F. Muir; Joseph Young); Do I Do (C/L: Stevie Wonder); Don't Mess with Bill (C/L: Smokey Robinson); Express (C/L: B.T. Express); Higher Ground (C/L: Stevie Wonder); His Eye Is on the Sparrow (C/L: Traditional); Ill Wind (C: Harold Arlen; L: Ted Koehler); Jim Jam Jumpin' (C: Cab Calloway); Johnny B. Goode (C/L: Chuck Berry); Jumpin' at the Woodside (inst.) (C: Count Basie); Just a Closer Walk with Thee (C/L: Traditional); Keep on Running (C/L: Stevie Wonder); Lady Be Good (C: George Gershwin; L: Ira Gershwin); Let's Get Together (inst.) (C: Chick Webb); 1999 (C/L: Prince); Old Landmark (C/L: M.A. Brunner); Proud Mary (C/L: John Fogarty); Stop in the Name of Love (C/L: Lamont Dozier; Brian Holland; Eddie Holland); Stormy Weather (C: Harold Arlen; L: Ted Koehler); Superstition (C/L: Stevie Wonder); Swing That Music (C: Louis Armstrong; L: H. Gerlach); Tap Along with Me (inst.) (C: Frank Owens); Tutti Frutti (C/L: Richard Penniman); When Your Lover Has Gone (C/L: E.A. Swan); Why Do Fools Fall in Love (C/L: Frankie Lymon); Will You Still Love Me Tomorrow (C/L: Gerry Goffin; Carole King); You Send Me (C/L: Sam Cooke)

Cast: Alisa Gyse; Lawrence Hamilton; Maurice Hines; Tommi Johnson; Marion Ramsey; Jeffrey V. Thompson

Notes: No original songs in this show.

4535 • URBAN BLIGHT

OPENED: 06/19/1988 Theatre: Manhattan Theatre Club
Revue Off-Broadway: 12

Composer: David Shire
Lyricist: Richard Maltby Jr.
Librettist: John Augustine; John Bishop; Christopher Durang; Jules Feiffer; Larry Fishburne; Charles Fuller; Nancy Giles; A.R. Gurney; E. Katherine Kerr; Richard Maltby Jr.; David Mamet; Terrence McNally; Arthur Miller; Shel Silverstein; Ted Tally; Wendy Wasserstein; Richard Wesley; George C. Wolfe
Producer: Manhattan Theater Club
Director: Richard Maltby Jr.; John Tillinger

Choreographer: Charles Randolph-Wright; **Conductor:** Michael Skloff; **Costumes:** C.L. Hundley; **Lighting Designer:** Natasha Katz; **Set Design:** Heidi Landesman

Songs: Aerobicantata; Bill of Fare; Don't Fall for the Lights; Life Story [1]; Miss Byrd [1]; Self-Portrait (C/L: Edward Kleban); There

Cast: Larry Fishburne; Nancy Giles; E. Katherine Kerr; Oliver Platt; Faith Prince; Rex Robbins; John Rubinstein

Notes: [1] Later in CLOSER THAN EVER.

4536 • UTOPIA!

OPENED: 05/06/1963 Theatre: Folksbiene
Musical Off-Broadway: 11

Composer: William Klenosky
Lyricist: William Klenosky
Librettist: William Klenosky
Producer: William Klenosky
Director: Cecil Reddick

Choreographer: Melinda Taintor; **Costumes:** Edith Arin; **Dance Arranger:** Stephen Lawrence; **Lighting Designer:** Gary Zeller; **Musical Director:** Stephen Lawrence; **Set Design:** Gary Zeller; **Vocal Arranger:** Stephen Lawrence

Songs: All You Need Is a Little Love; April in Siberia; Ballad of Utopia, The; Hooligan's Hop; I Can't Pretend; I Work for Pravda; Masses Are Asses, The; National Anthem of Utopia, The; Tax Collector's Soliloquy, The; Utopia Ballet; We've Got a Feeling in Our Bones; What Am I Hangin' Around For?; Why Are We Here?; You Gotta Have a Destination; You've Got the Devil in Your Eyes

Cast: Ray Gilbert; Lewis Pierce; Guje Seastrom; Vilma Vacarra

4537 • UTTER GLORY OF MORRISSEY HALL, THE

OPENED: 05/13/1979 Theatre: Mark Hellinger
Musical Broadway: 1

Composer: Clark Gesner
Lyricist: Clark Gesner
Librettist: Clark Gesner; Nagle Jackson

Producer: H. Ridgely Bullock; Albert W. Selden; Arthur Whitelaw
Director: Nagle Jackson

Choreographer: Buddy Schwab; **Costumes:** David Graden; **Dance Arranger:** Allen Cohen; **Lighting Designer:** Howard Bay; **Musical Director:** John Lesko; **Orchestrations:** Jay Blackton; Russell Warner; **Set Design:** Howard Bay

Songs: Dance of Resignation (dance); Duet; Elizabeth's Song; Ending, The; Give Me That Key; Interlude and Gallop; Letter, The; Like a Rock [1]; Lost; Morning; Oh, Sun; Promenade; Proud, Erstwhile, Upright, Fair; Reflection; See the Blue; War, The; Way Back When; Whose Little Bird Are You [1]; You Will Know When the Time Has Come; You Would Say

Cast: Marilyn Copkey; Taina Elg; Laurie Franks; Celeste Holm; Polly Pen; Mary Saunders

Notes: [1] Out Philadelphia 11/25/77.

V

4538 • VAGABOND HERO, A

Notes: *See THE WHITE FLAME.*

4539 • VAGABOND KING, THE

OPENED: 09/21/1925 Theatre: Casino
Musical Broadway: 511

Composer: Rudolf Friml
Lyricist: Brian Hooker
Librettist: Brian Hooker; Russell Janney; William H. Post
Producer: Russell Janney
Director: Max Figman

Source: IF I WERE KING (Play: Justin Huntley McCarthy); **Choreographer:** Julian Alfred; **Costumes:** James Reynolds; **Musical Director:** Anton Heindl; **Orchestrations:** Anton Heindl; **Set Design:** James Reynolds; **Vocal Arranger:** Anton Heindl

Songs: Ballet; Drinking Song; Finale Second Act; Finale Ultimo; Finaletto Act II; Huguette Waltz; Hunting; Lady Mary's Song to Taberie [2] (L: Russell Janney); Love for Sale; Love Me Tonight; Love Song of a Thief, The [2] (L: Russell Janney); Love That Cannot Be [2] (L: Russell Janney); Merry Gallows, The [2] (L: Russell Janney); Nocturne; Only a Rose; Opening Act IV — Scene 1; Opening Act IV — Scene 2; Scotch Archer's Song; Serenade; Some Day; Song of the Vagabonds; Te Deum Laudamus! [1]; Tomorrow; Vagabond King; Victory March, The [1]

Cast: Herbert Corthell; Max Figman; Dennis King; Carolyn Thomson

Notes: [1] Not in program. [2] Written for 1954 revival.

4540 • VALENTINE'S DAY

Theatre: Manhattan Theatre Club
Musical Off-Broadway

Composer: Saul Naishtat
Lyricist: Ron Cowen
Librettist: Ron Cowen
Director: Seth Glassman

Costumes: Richard Westby-Gibson; **Lighting Designer:** Sari Weisman; **Musical Director:** Thomas Babbitt

Songs: Arizona; Biarritz and Bali; Get Up; His and Hers; How Do I Get Out of This; Mr. What's-His-Name; My Father Took Me Dancing; My Room and Me; People Have to Change; People Shouldn't Change; Sandpaper; Something for Nothing; Traveling Memories; Valentine's Day; Wonderful Dreams

Cast: Jeanne Arnold; Jerry Jarrett; Alice Playten; Chip Zien

4541 • VALMOUTH

OPENED: 10/06/1960 Theatre: York Playhouse
Musical Off-Broadway: 14

Composer: Sandy Wilson
Lyricist: Sandy Wilson
Librettist: Sandy Wilson
Producer: Gene Andrewski; Barbara Griner; Morton Segal
Director: Vida Hope

Source: VALMOUTH (Novel: Ronald Firbank); **Choreographer:** Harry Naughton; **Conductor:** Jack Lee; **Costumes:** Tony Walton; **Musical Director:** Julian Stein; **Orchestrations:** Julian Stein; **Set Design:** Tony Walton

Songs: All the Girls Were Pretty; Big Best Shoes; Cathedral of Clemenza, The; Cry of the Peacock; I Loved a Man; I Will Miss You; Just Once More; Lady of the Manor; Little Girl Baby; Magic Fingers; Mustapha; My Talking Day; Niri-Esther; Only a Passing Phase; Pinpipi's Sob of Love; Valmouth; What Do I Want with Love?; What Then Can Make Him Come So Slow? [1]; Where the Trees Are Green with Parrots

Cast: William Beck; Philippa Bevans; Constance Carpenter; Anne Francine; Gail Jones; Gene Rupert; Elly Stone; Alfred Toigo

Notes: [1] Added to BBC radio version.

4542 • VAMP, THE

OPENED: 11/10/1955 Theatre: Winter Garden
Musical Broadway: 60

Composer: John Mundy
Lyricist: John Latouche
Librettist: John Latouche; Sam Locke
Producer: Alexander Carson; Martin Cohen; Oscar Lerman
Director: David Alexander

Choreographer: Robert Alton; **Costumes:** Raoul Pene du Bois; **Musical Director:** Milton Rosenstock; **Orchestrations:** James Mundy; **Set Design:** Raoul Pene du Bois; **Vocal Arranger:** Milton Rosenstock

Songs: Delilah's Dilemma; Fan Club Chant; Flickers, The; Four Little Misfits; Have You Met Delilah?; I'm Everybody's Baby; Impossible She, The; I've Always Loved You; Keep Your Nose to the Grindstone; Little Miss Dracula [1]; Mr. Right [1]; Ragtime Romeo; Samson and Delilah; Spiel, The; That's Where a Man Fits In; Vamps, The; Who Needs Love? [1]; Why Does It Have to Be You?; Yeemy Yeemy; You're Colossal

Cast: David Atkinson; Carol Channing; Will Geer; Patricia Hammerlee; Jack Harrold; Paul Lipson; Matt Mattox; Bibi Osterwald; Steve Reeves; Robert Rippy; Jack Waldron

Notes: Titled DELILAH in out-of-town ads. [1] Out Washington, D.C. 10/18/55.

4543 • VAMP TILL READY

OPENED: 11/22/1955
Revue

Composer: Ronald Lowden
Lyricist: Richard Levinson; William Link
Librettist: Carl Leswing; Richard Levinson; William Link
Producer: Robert Wickersham
Director: Chet Cooper; Robert Wickersham

Choreographer: Walter F. Keenan; **Costumes:** Marjorie Kellberg; **Orchestrations:** Al Boss; Frank Juele; **Set Design:** Marjorie Kellberg; **Vocal Arranger:** Bruce Montgomery; Clay Warnick

Songs: Ballad of Sheriff Dunlap (C: Al Ross); Be a Vamp (C: Henning Ludlow); Charlie Chaplin Dance (inst.); Diggin' Up Dirt; Finale; I'm Great; Keep Your Dreams; Mostes' to Say the Least, The (C: Al Ross; L: Charles Roth); Party (L: T.J. Scotes); Perils of Paulette, The; Screen Test (inst.); Since You Said You're Mine; Spread Some Joy Around (L: Charles Roth); Vive Paulette (C: Henning Ludlow)

Cast: Robert M. Jaffe; Eli Subin; Alfred Toigo

Notes: Amateur show. Mask & Wig Club, University of Pennsylvania.

4544 • VANDERBILT CUP, THE

OPENED: 01/16/1906 Theatre: Broadway
Musical Broadway: 143

Composer: Robert Hood Bowers
Lyricist: Raymond W. Peck
Librettist: Sydney Rosenfeld
Producer: Liebler and Company

Songs: Dear Old Farm; Down the Mississippi [2]; Fatal Curse of Beauty; I Can't Help Thinking of You [1] (C: Ernest R. Ball; L: Maurice J. Stonehill); If You Were I and I Were You; If You Were Lost to Me [2]; Lament of the Crusty Dames, The; Let Me Be Your House Boat Beau; Light in Girlish Eyes, The; Little Chauffeur, The; Looking for a Happy Man [1]; Love's Wireless Telephone [1]; Man with an Axe to Grind, A [2]; Ride to the Course, The [1]; So I've Been Told; Somewhere in the World (There's a Little Girl for Me); Toy Broadway, The; Vanderbilt Cup Gallop; Wine, Women and Song

Cast: Aubrey Boucicault; Charles Dow Clark; Grace Gaylor Clark; Otis Harlan; Elsie Janis; Kate Mayhew

Notes: [1] Out Cedar Rapids 11/16/06. [2] Sheet music only.

4545 • VANDERBILT REVUE, THE

OPENED: 11/03/1930 Theatre: Vanderbilt
Revue Broadway: 13

Composer: Jimmy McHugh
Lyricist: Dorothy Fields
Librettist: Arthur Burns; James Coghlan; Edwin Gilbert; Sig Herzig; Ellis Jones; Kenyon Nicholson

Producer: Lyle D. Andrews; Lew Fields
Director: Lew Fields; Theodore Hammerstein

Choreographer: Jack Haskell; John E. Lonergan; **Costumes:** Robert Stevenson; **Musical Director:** Gus Salzer; **Set Design:** Ward & Harvey

Songs: Better Not Try It (C: Michael Cleary; L: Herb Magidson; Ned Washington); Blue Again; Button Up Your Heart; Cut In; Ex-Gigolo (C: Mario Braggiotti; L: E.Y. Harburg); Half Way to Heaven (C: Mario Braggiotti; L: David Sidney); I Give Myself Away (C: Jacques Fray; L: Edward Eliscu); I'm from Granada (C: Mario Braggiotti; L: David Sidney); I'm Plenty That Way Too [1] (C: Jacques Fray; L: E.Y. Harburg); Jackdaw of Rhiems, The (sketch) (C: Edward Horan); Lady of the Fan (C: Jacques Fray; L: Mario Braggiotti); Please Don't Take My Boop-a-Doop Away [1] (C: Sammy Timberg; L: Sammy Lerner); Then Came the War (C/L: Ben Black); What's My Man Gonna Be Like? (C/L: Cole Porter); You're the Better Half of Me

Cast: Charles Barnes; Francesca Braggiotti; Mario Braggiotti; Jean Carpenter; Dorothy Dixon; Jacques Fray; Evelyn Hoey; Tonia Ingre; Richard Lane; Olga Markoff; Lulu McConnell; Joe Penner; Gus Schilling; Teddy Walters; Franker Woods

Notes: [1] Out Newark 10/20/30.

4546 • VEILS

OPENED: 03/13/1928
Musical — Closed out of town

Librettist: Donald Heywood

Notes: No program available.

4547 • VELVET LADY, THE

OPENED: 02/03/1919 — Theatre: New Amsterdam
Musical — Broadway: 136

Composer: Victor Herbert
Lyricist: Henry Blossom
Librettist: Henry Blossom; Fred Jackson
Producer: Klaw & Erlanger
Director: Edgar MacGregor; Julian Mitchell

Source: FULL HOUSE, A (Play: Fred Jackson); **Musical Director:** Frederic Stahlberg; **Orchestrations:** Victor Herbert

Songs: Any Time New York Goes Dry [1]; Bubbles; Come Be My Wife; Dancing at the Wedding; Fair Honeymoon Shine On; I've Danced to Beat the Band; Life and Love; Little Girl and Boy; Logic; Merry Wedding Bells; Policeology [1]; Scandal; Spooky- Ookum; There's Nothing Too Fine for the Finest; Throwing the Bull; Tonight's the Night; Velvet Lady [2]; Way Down in Yucatan; Wedding Bells; What a Position for Me

Cast: Eddie Dowling; Fay Marbe; Georgia O'Ramey; Jed Prouty; Ernest Torrence

Notes: *See also SHE TOOK A CHANCE.* [1] Out Philadelphia 12/23/18. [2] ASCAP/Library of Congress.

4548 • VENETIAN GLASS NEPHEW, THE

OPENED: 02/23/1931 — Theatre: Vanderbilt
Musical — Broadway: 8

Composer: Eugene Bonner
Lyricist: Eugene Bonner
Librettist: Ruth Hale
Producer: Walter Greenough
Director: Walter Greenough

Costumes: Brooks; **Musical Director:** Leon Barzin; **Set Design:** Edgar Bohlman; Sointu Syrjala

Cast: Lee Burgess; Gage Clarke; George Houston; Raymond Huntley; Dodd Mehan; Mary Silviera; Edgar Stehli; Louis Yaeckel

4549 • VENETIAN ROMANCE, A

OPENED: 05/02/1904 — Theatre: Knickerbocker
Musical — Broadway: 31

Composer: Frederic Colt Wright
Librettist: Cornelia Osgood Taylor
Producer: Frank Perley Opera Company
Director: Al Holbrook

Songs: But Our Charms Do Not Stop Quite There

Cast: Harry MacDonough; Ignacio Martinetti

4550 • VENUS IN SILK

OPENED: 10/01/1935
Musical — Closed out of town

Composer: Robert Stolz
Lyricist: Lester O'Keefe
Librettist: Lester O'Keefe; Laurence Schwab
Producer: Laurence Schwab
Director: Zeke Colvan

Source: VENUS IN SEIDE (Musical: Alfred Grunwald; Ludwig Herzer); **Choreographer:** William Holbrook; **Costumes:** Kay Morrison; **Musical Director:** George Hirst; **Orchestrations:** George Hirst; Hans Spialek; Robert Stolz; **Set Design:** Raymond Sovey; **Vocal Arranger:** George Hirst

Songs: Baby, Play with Me; Czardas; Dance, Oh, Lonely Gypsy Maid [1]; Drag 'Em Out Dragoons; Ducky; Eyes That Are Smiling; Flame of Love; Hail, the Falcon; I Ask Not Who You Are; If I Were a Bandit; Just for You; Musical Scene; Opening; Play in Native Fashion [1]; Slave Song and Dance [1]; Sweetly I Spoke; This Life Will Roll Along; Waltz Continental; Waltz That Is Fashioned for Love, A [1]; Welcome, Happy Groom [1]; You Are the One; Zingra

Cast: Florenz Ames; Audrey Christie; Jack Cole; Alice Dudley; Gilbert Lamb; Nancy McCord; J. Harold Murray

Notes: Program Pittsburgh 10/1/35 and Washington, D.C. used. Also known as BELOVED ROGUE. [1] Added to Muny Opera (St. Louis) revival 1948.

4551 • VENUS, 1906

OPENED: 04/17/1906 Theatre: Empire
Revue London

Composer: Jerome Kern
Lyricist: George Grossmith Jr.

Songs: Leader of the Labour Party, The; Won't You Buy a Little Canoe

Notes: Part of a longer music hall bill.

4552 • VENUS ON BROADWAY

OPENED: 10/01/1917 Theatre: Palais Royal
Revue

Composer: A. Baldwin Sloane
Director: John Murray Anderson

Notes: No other information available.

4553 • VERA VIOLETTA

OPENED: 11/20/1911 Theatre: Winter Garden
Musical Broadway: 112

Composer: Edmund Eysler
Lyricist: Harold Atteridge
Librettist: Harold Atteridge; Leonard Liebling
Producer: Winter Garden Company

Source: VERA VIOLETTA (Musical: Edmund Eysler; Leo Stein); **Musical Director:** Samuel Lehman

Songs: Angeline from the Opera Comique (C: Louis A. Hirsch; L: Melville Gideon); Cave Man, The; Come and Dance (C: Louis A. Hirsch; L: Melville Gideon); Come Back to Me; Fifty-Seven Ways to Win a Man; Gaby Glide, The (C: Louis A. Hirsch; L: Harry Pilcer); I Want Something New to Play With; I Wonder If It's True; I've Heard That Before (C: Louis A. Hirsch; L: Melville Gideon); My Lou; Olga from the Volga; Paree, Gay Paree; Rum Tum Tiddle (C: Jean Schwartz; L: Edward Madden); That Haunting Melody (C/L: George M. Cohan); Vera Violetta; When You Hear Love's Hello [1] (C: Louis A. Hirsch; L: Harold Atteridge; E. Ray Goetz)

Cast: Barney Bernard; Gaby Deslys; Melville Ellis; Ernest Hare; Al Jolson; Annette Kellerman; Stella Mayhew; Billie Taylor; Mae West

Notes: [1] ASCAP/Library of Congress only.

4554 • VERONIQUE

OPENED: 10/30/1905 Theatre: Broadway
Musical Broadway: 81

Composer: Andre Messager
Lyricist: Lillian Eldee; Percy Greenbank
Librettist: Henry Hamilton
Producer: Klaw & Erlanger
Director: Marcus Mayer

Source: VERONIQUE (Musical: G. Duval; Andre Messager; Albert Vanloo); **Set Design:** Ernest Gros

Songs: Ah, Well, We'll Try to Be Precise; Ah, You? Oh! Strange Situation [2]; As Along the Street We Wander; At Weddings as a General Rule; Between Us All Is O'er; Bloom of the Apple Tree, The; Come Drink a Toast to Man and Wife;

Come One and All, Haste to the Ball; Farewell, I Go, It Must Be So; Flowers of Springtime, Sweetly Scented (Opening Chorus); Garden of Love, The; Hush! Hush! She's Meditating; I Thank You for Your Welcome; I've Got a Little Hubby Now [1]; Life Is Short, My Dear Friends; Little Goose, A [2]; Now My Little Story's Ended; Now the Carriages All Are Waiting; Now Then, Where Is the Blushing Bride?; Oh, Strange Situation; Oh, What a Dainty Profession; One Day, 'Neath an Apple Tree Laden [2]; Out in the Breezy Morning Air; Please, Sir, We Want If We May; Sweet Lisette, So People Say; Swing Song, The (You Are Laughing); Take Estelle, and Veronique; Trot Here and There, Take Care, Take Care; When Not Engaged in Fighting; While I Am Waiting; You're a Charming Little Maiden

Cast: Kitty Gordon; Valli Valli; Ruth Vincent

Notes: [1] Out Boston 1/29/06. [2] British vocal score only.

4555 • VERY GOOD EDDIE

OPENED: 12/23/1915 Theatre: Princess
Musical Broadway: 341

Composer: Jerome Kern
Lyricist: Schuyler Greene; Herbert Reynolds
Librettist: Philip Bartholomae; Guy Bolton
Producer: F. Ray Comstock; Elisabeth Marbury
Director: Frank McCormack

Source: OVER-NIGHT (Play: Philip Bartholomae); **Choreographer:** David Bennett; **Costumes:** Melville Ellis; Finchley; **Musical Director:** Max Hirschfeld; **Orchestrations:** Frank Sadler; **Set Design:** Elsie De Wolfe

Songs: Alone at Last (L: Herbert Reynolds); Alone with You (All Alone) [1] (C: Cole Porter; L: Melville Gideon); Babes in the Wood (L: Schuyler Greene; Jerome Kern); Buffo Dance (inst.); Dance Trio (inst.); Fashion Show, The; Hands Up [3]; I'd Like to Have a Million in the Bank (L: Herbert Reynolds); If I Find the Girl (L: John E. Hazzard; Herbert Reynolds); Isn't It Great to Be Married [4] (L: Schuyler Greene); I've Got to Dance [3] (L: Schuyler Greene); Nodding Roses (L: Schuyler Greene; Herbert Reynolds); Oceans of Love [3]; Old Bill Baker (Undertaker) [2] (L: Ring Lardner); Old Boy Neutral [6] (L: Schuyler Greene); On the Shore at Le Lei Wi [5] (C: Henry Kailimai; Jerome Kern; L: Herbert Reynolds); Same Old Game, The; Some Sort of Somebody (All the Time) [7] (L: Elsie Janis); Triangle, The (scene) [9] (L: Guy Bolton); We're on Our Way (L: Schuyler Greene); Wedding Bells Are Calling Me [8] (L: Harry B. Smith); When You Wear a 13 Collar (L: Schuyler Greene)

Cast: Alice Dovey; John E. Hazzard; Ada Lewis; Helen Raymond; Oscar Shaw; Ernest Truex

Notes: [1] Added to London production. [2] Written for ZIEGFELD FOLLIES of 1915. Added after opening. [3] Cut prior to opening. [4] Same music as "Can't You See I Mean You" from 90 IN THE SHADE and "All That I Want Is Somebody to Love Me" from 90 IN THE SHADE. [5] Kern wrote verse. Kailimai wrote chorus. From MISS INFORMATION. [6] Same music as "A Little Love" from MISS INFORMATION. [7] From MISS INFORMATION. [8] From NOBODY HOME. [9] In 90 IN THE SHADE. Published in the VERY GOOD EDDIE score, might not have been in production.

4556 • VERY LITTLE FAUST AND MUCH MARGUERITE

OPENED: 08/30/1897 Theatre: Hammerstein's Olympia
Musical Broadway: 24

Composer: Fred J. Eustis; Florimond Herve
Lyricist: Richard F. Carroll
Additional Lyrics: Clement King
Librettist: Richard F. Carroll

Cast: Florence Bell; John Belton; Richard F. Carroll; Beatrice Hamilton

Notes: No program available.

4557 • VERY WARM FOR MAY

OPENED: 11/17/1939 Theatre: Alvin
Musical Broadway: 59

Composer: Jerome Kern
Lyricist: Oscar Hammerstein II
Librettist: Oscar Hammerstein II
Producer: Max Gordon
Director: Oscar Hammerstein II; Vincente Minnelli

Choreographer: Harry Losee; Albertina Rasch; **Costumes:** Vincente Minnelli; **Musical Director:** Robert Emmett Dolan; **Orchestrations:** Robert Russell Bennett; **Set Design:** Vincente Minnelli; **Vocal Arranger:** Ralph Blane; Hugh Martin

Songs: All in Fun; All the Things You Are; Audition; Ballet Peculaire (inst.); Deer and the Park Avenue Lady, The; Heaven in My Arms (Music in My Heart); High Up in Harlem [1]; In Other Words, Seventeen; In the Heart of the Dark; L'Histoire de Madame de la Tour; May Tells All; Me and the Role and You [1]; Schottische Scena; Stop Dance (inst.); Strange Case of Adam Standish, The; That Lucky Fellow [2]; That Lucky Lady [2]

Cast: June Allyson; Eve Arden; Maxine Barat; Helena Bliss; Donald Brian; Andre Charise; Sally Craven; Kate Friedlich; Avon Long; Don Loper; Grace McDonald; Frances Mercer; Richard Quine; Hollace Shaw; Hiram Sherman; Max Showalter; Ralph Stuart; Vera- Ellen; Jack Whiting; Billie Worth

Notes: [1] Cut prior to opening. [2] Same music.

4558 • VIA GALACTICA

OPENED: 11/28/1972 Theatre: Uris
Musical Broadway: 7

Composer: Galt MacDermot
Lyricist: Christopher Gore
Librettist: Christopher Gore; Judith Ross
Producer: George W. George; Nat Shapiro; Barnard S. Strauss
Director: Peter Hall

Costumes: John Bury; **Lighting Designer:** Lloyd Burlingame; **Musical Director:** Joyce Brown; **Orchestrations:** Danny Hurd; Bhen Lanzaroni; Horace Ott; **Set Design:** John Bury; **Vocal Arranger:** Joyce Brown

Songs: All My Good Mornings; Children of the Sun; Cross On Over; Dance the Dark Away!; Different; Finale Act I; Four Hundred Girls Ago; Gospel of Gabriel Finn; Great Forever Wagon, The; Helen of Troy; Home [1]; Hush; Ilmar's Tomb; Isaac's Equation; Lady Isn't Looking; Life Wins; New Jerusalem; Other Side of the Sky, The; Oysters; Shall We Friend; Take Your Hat Off; Terre Haute High; Up [1]; Via Galactica; We Are One; Worm Gene, The

Cast: Jacqueline Britt; Irene Cara; Ralph Carter; Melanie Chartoff; Keene Curtis; James Dybas; Raul Julia; Virginia Vestoff

Notes: [1] Cut prior to opening.

4559 • VICEROY, THE

OPENED: 04/09/1900 Theatre: Knickerbocker
Musical Broadway: 28

Composer: Victor Herbert
Lyricist: Harry B. Smith
Librettist: Harry B. Smith
Producer: Bostonians, The; Klaw & Erlanger
Director: William H. Fitzgerald

Musical Director: Samuel L. Studley; **Orchestrations:** Victor Herbert

Songs: All Men Have Their Troubles; By This Sweet Token; Eyes of Black and Eyes of Blue; Finale Act I; Hear Me; I See By Your Smile; I'm the Leader of Society; In a Smuggler's Cave; Just for Today; Love May Come, Love May Go; 'Neath the Blue Neapolitan Sky; On My Nuptial Day; One Fellow's Joy Is Another Fellow's Woe; Robin and the Rose, The; Sailor's Life, A; Since I Am Queen of the Carnival; So They Say; That's My Idea of Love; Thy Subjects Are We; Tivolini; Viceroy; We Come to the Lively Market Square; We'll Catch You at Last, Tivolini!; With Military Pomp

Cast: Henry Clay Barnabee; Helen Bertram; Grace Cameron; Henry Miller; Frank Rushworth; Marcia Van Dresser

4560 • VICTOR/VICTORIA

OPENED: 10/25/1995 Theatre: Marquis
Musical Broadway

Composer: Henry Mancini
Lyricist: Leslie Bricusse
Librettist: Blake Edwards
Producer: Tony Adams; Blake Edwards; Polygram Diversified Ent.
Director: Blake Edwards

Source: VICTOR/VICTORIA (Film: Blake Edwards); **Costumes:** Willa Kim; **Incidental Music:** David Krane; **Lighting Designer:** Peggy Eisenhauer; Jules Fisher; **Musical Director:** Ian Fraser; **Orchestrations:** Billy Byers; **Set Design:** Robin Wagner; **Vocal Arranger:** Ian Fraser

Songs: Almost a Love Song; Apache; Attitude; Chicago, Illinois [1]; Crazy World [1]; I Know Where I'm Going [2]; If I Were a Man; I've No Idea Where I'm Going (The Victoria Variations); King's Dilemma; Le Jazz Hot [1]; Living in the Shadows (C: Frank Wildhorn); Louis Says [2] (C: Frank Wildhorn); Paris By Night; Paris Makes Me Horny; Someone Else [2]; Tango, The; This Is Not Going to Change My Life [2]; Trust Me (C: Frank Wildhorn); Victor/Victoria; Victoria Variations [2]; You & Me [1]; You'd Be Surprised [2]

Cast: Julie Andrews; Michael Cripe; Hillel Gitter; Adam Heller; Gregory Jbara; Michael Nouri; Tony Roberts; Richard B. Shull; Rachel York

Notes: Still running as of publication. Wildhorn and Bricusse wrote six songs for this show of which three were accepted. [1] From score of previous film version. [2] Cut.

4561 • VICTORY CANTEEN

OPENED: 1971
Revue Los Angeles

Composer: Richard M. Sherman
Lyricist: Robert B. Sherman

Songs: Axe the Axis Polka; Doughnuts; Happy Tomorrows; Hawks!; (They Just Can't Ration) L-O-V-E; Lafayette, We're Here!; Let's Go Native; Loose Lips (Sink Ships); My Window Full of Stars; Smoke 'Em Up, Smoke 'Em Up!; South Sea Island Rhapsody; Va-Va-Va-Vee (for Victory); Victory Canteen; We Two (Someday)

Notes: No other information available.

4562 • VICTORY GIRL, THE

OPENED: 11/16/1918
Musical Closed out of town

Composer: Silvio Hein
Lyricist: Philip Barholomae
Librettist: Lynn Cowan; Alex Sullivan

Notes: A revision of GIRL O' MINE.

4563 • VIENNA LIFE

OPENED: 01/23/1901 Theatre: Broadway
Musical Broadway: 35

Composer: Johann Strauss
Lyricist: Glen MacDonough
Librettist: Glen MacDonough

Source: WIENER BLUT (Musical: Victor Leon; Leo Stein; Johann Strauss)

Cast: William Blaisdell; Charles H. Drew; Raymond Hitchcock; Ethel Jackson; Julia Raymond; Amelia Stone; Maude Thomas

Notes: No other information available.

4564 • VILLAGE BLACKSMITH, THE

OPENED: 12/29/1912 Theatre: Lambs' Club
Musical Broadway

Composer: Victor Herbert
Librettist: George V. Hobart

Notes: A one-act musical presented at the Lambs' Club.

4565 • VINCENT YOUMANS' BALLET REVUE

OPENED: 01/27/1944
Revue Closed out of town

Composer: Ernesto Lecuona; Vincent Youmans
Lyricist: Gladys Shelley; Maria Shelton
Librettist: Eric Tatch

Choreographer: Leonide Massine; **Costumes:** John N. Booth Jr.; **Set Design:** Woodman Thompson

Songs: Black Rhapsody (C: Ernesto Lecuona)

Cast: Mason Adams; Glenn Anders; June MacLaren; Herbert Ross; Deems Taylor

Notes: Closed in Baltimore.

4566 • VINTAGE '60

OPENED: 09/12/1960 Theatre: Brooks Atkinson
Revue Broadway: 8

Librettist: Maxwell Grant; Alan Jeffreys; Jack Wilson
Producer: Zev Bufman; David Merrick
Director: Michael Ross

Choreographer: Jonathan Lucas; **Costumes:** Fred Voelpel; **Musical Director:** Gershon Kingsley; **Orchestrations:** Allyn Ferguson; Robert Ginzler; Gershon Kingsley; John Lesko; John Mandel; Peter Matz; Sid Ramin; **Set Design:** Fred Voelpel

Songs: Afraid of Love (C/L: Alice Clark; David Morton); All American (C: David Baker; L: Sheldon Harnick); Do It in Two (C/L: Alan Jeffreys; Jack Wilson); Down in the Streets (C/L: Tommy Garlock; Alan Jeffreys); Dublin Town (C/L: Fred Ebb; Lee Goldsmith; Paul Klein); Forget Me (C: David Baker; L: Sheldon Harnick); Isms (C: David Baker; L: Sheldon Harnick); Time Is Now, The (C: Mark Bucci; L: David Rogers)

Cast: Bert Convy; Fay De Witt; Barbara Heller; Michele Lee; Dick Patterson

4567 • VIOLINS OVER BROADWAY

Revue — Theatre: Diamond Horseshoe Nightclub

Producer: Billy Rose
Director: John Murray Anderson

Choreographer: Esther Junger; **Costumes:** Thomas Becher; **Lighting Designer:** John Murray Anderson; **Musical Director:** Harold Sandler; **Orchestrations:** Gleb Yellin; **Set Design:** Herman Rosse; **Vocal Arranger:** Maurice Levine

Songs: Violins Over Broadway (C/L: Unknown)

Notes: No program available.

4568 • VIRGINIA (1923)

Notes: *See CAROLINE.*

4569 • VIRGINIA (1937)

OPENED: 09/02/1937 — Theatre: Center
Musical — Broadway: 60

Composer: Arthur Schwartz
Lyricist: Albert Sillman
Librettist: Owen Davis; Laurence Stallings
Producer: Center Theatre, The
Director: Leon Leonidoff; Edward Clarke Lilley

Choreographer: Florence Rogge; **Costumes:** Irene Sharaff; **Musical Director:** John McManus; **Orchestrations:** Hans Spialek; Will Vodery; Phil Wall; **Set Design:** Lee Simonson

Songs: Fee-Fie-Fo-Fum; Good and Lucky; Goodbye, Jonah; If You Were Someone Else; I'll Be Sittin' in de Lap o' de Lord; It's Our Duty to the King; Meet Me at the Fair; My Bridal Gown (L: Laurence Stallings; Al Stillman); My Heart Is Dancing; Old Flame Never Dies, An (L: Laurence Stallings; Al Stillman); Send One Angel Down; Virginia; We Had to Rehearse; You and I Know (L: Laurence Stallings; Al Stillman)

Cast: Avis Andrews; Mona Barrie; Bertha Belmore; Anne Booth; Patricia Bowman; Nigel Bruce; John W. Bubbles; Ford L. Buck; Ronald Graham; Lansing Hatfield; Dennis Hoey; Nora Kaye; Gene Lockhart; Billy Redfield; Gordon Richards; Valia Valentinoff

4570 • VISIONS OF 1969

OPENED: 1919
Musical

Composer: Neil Moret
Lyricist: Harry Williams
Librettist: Jack Lait
Producer: Winnie Baldwin; Percy Bronson

Notes: Vaudeville musical.

4571 • VIVA AMIGOS

OPENED: 1944
Revue

Composer: Ted Murry
Lyricist: Benny Davis

Songs: Brazilian Can-Can; Dancing to the Rhythm of Love; Viva Amigos; You Bring the Scotch and I'll Bring the Soda

Notes: No other information available. Information from ASCAP/Library of Congress.

4572 • VIVA O'BRIEN

OPENED: 10/09/1941 — Theatre: Majestic
Musical — Broadway: 20

Composer: Maria Grever
Lyricist: Raymond Leveen
Librettist: Eleanor Wells; William K. Wells

Producer: Hickey, Hale & Robinson
Director: Robert Milton; William K. Wells

Choreographer: Chester Hale; **Costumes:** John N. Booth Jr.; **Musical Director:** Ray Kavanaugh; **Orchestrations:** Charles L. Cooke; **Set Design:** Clark Robinson; **Vocal Arranger:** Leonard dePaur

Songs: Broken Hearted Romeo; Carinito; Don Jose O'Brien; El Matador Terrifico; How Long?; Matador Dance; Mexican Bad Men; Mood of the Moment; Mozambamba; Our Song; Rain Ballet; Ritual Dance; Sailors, The; To Prove My Love; Wrap Me in Your Serape; Yucatana

Cast: Ruth Clayton; Victoria Cordova; Marie Nash

4573 • VIVE LA FEMME

OPENED: 1924

Songs: Chili Bom Bom (C: Walter Donaldson; L: Cliff Friend)

Notes: No other information available.

4574 • VOGUES AND VANITIES

Notes: *See PICCADILLY TO BROADWAY.*

4575 • VOGUES OF 1924

OPENED: 03/27/1924 Theatre: Shubert
Revue Broadway: 114

Composer: Herbert Stothart
Lyricist: Clifford Grey
Librettist: Fred Thompson
Producer: Messrs. Shubert
Director: Alexander Leftwich; Frank Smithson

Choreographer: David Bennett; **Costumes:** Charles LeMaire; **Musical Director:** Alfred Newman; **Set Design:** Watson Barratt

Songs: Belle of the Ball, The; Belle of Today, The; Dressing; Eldorado; Hee-Bee Jee-Bees [1] (C: Jay Gorney; Herbert Stothart); Hush, Look Away; Katinka; Laugh and Play; Legend of the Shirt, The; Medicos; Pierrot; Rain; Spielman, The; Star of Destiny; Three Little Maids; When the Piper Plays

Cast: Fred Allen; May Boley; J. Harold Murray; Odette Myrtil; Jimmy Savo

Notes: [1] Sheet music only.

4576 • VOICE OF MCCONNELL, THE

OPENED: 12/25/1918 Theatre: Manhattan Opera House
Play Broadway: 30

Composer: George M. Cohan
Lyricist: George M. Cohan
Author: George M. Cohan
Producer: George M. Cohan; Sam H. Harris
Director: George M. Cohan; Sam Forrest

Songs: I'm True to Them All, and They're Just as True to Me [1]; Ireland, Land of My Dreams; That Tumble Down Shack in Athlone (C: Monte Carlo; Alma Sanders; L: Richard W. Pascoe); When I Look Into Your Eyes Mavourneen; You Can't Deny You're Irish

Cast: Roy Cochrane; Edna Leslie; Chauncey Olcott; Arthur Shields

Notes: [1] ASCAP/Library of Congress only.

W

4577 • W.C.

OPENED: 1971
Musical Closed out of town

Composer: Al Carmines
Lyricist: Al Carmines
Librettist: Sam Locke; Milton Sperling
Producer: Shelly Gross; Lee Guber
Director: Richard Altman

Source: W.C. FIELDS, HIS FOLLIES AND FORTUNES (Book: Robert Lewis Taylor); **Choreographer:** Bob Herget; **Costumes:** Sara Brook; **Dance Arranger:** John Berkman; **Lighting Designer:** Lester Tapper; **Musical Director:** Susan Romann; **Orchestrations:** Carlyle Hall; **Set Design:** Peter Larkin

Songs: Being a Pal; Bring on the Booze; Chickadee Girls, The; Dummy Juggler [2]; Fifty Years of Making People Laugh; Greatest Comic of Them All, The; I Knew It All the Time; I'll Follow My Star; I'll Still Be Here; I'm a Two Way Woman [1]; I'm Through with Men; Love Can Get Your Down; Never Give a Sucker an Even Break; Never Trust Anyone Under Three; Old Days, The; Philadelphia 1890; Serenade; There's a Little Boy in Every Man; Where Is This Man? [1]; Why Do Women Always Choose the Wrong Man?; You Come First After Me; You Could; You've Gotta Leave Them Laughing

Cast: Jack Bittner; Essie Borden; Virginia Martin; Bernadette Peters; Barry Preston; Mickey Rooney; Rudy Tronto

Notes: [1] Not in program. [2] Cut.

4578 • WAC MUSICAL

OPENED: 1944
Revue

Songs: WAC Hymn, The (C/L: Frank Loesser)

Notes: Title unknown. No other informatin available.

4579 • WAIT A MINIM!

OPENED: 03/07/1966 Theatre: John Golden
Revue Broadway: 457

Composer: Jeremy Taylor
Lyricist: Jeremy Taylor
Producer: Frank Productions
Director: Leon Gluckman

Choreographer: Kendrew Lascelles; Frank Staff; **Costumes:** Heather MacDonald-Rouse; **Lighting Designer:** Leon Gluckman; Frank Rembach; **Musical Director:** Andrew Tracey; **Set Design:** Frank Rembach

Songs: Ag Pleez Deddy [2]; Ajade Papa; Amasalela; Aria; Ayama; Ballad of the Southern Suburbs [1]; Black-White Calypso; Bold Logger, The [1]; Butter Milk Soldier (Johnny Soldier); Celeste Aida (C: Giuseppe Verdi); Cingoma Chakabaruka; Confession [1]; Cool; Crow, The [2]; Cruel Youth, The [1]; Die Meistertrinker (Deutsches Weinlied . . . Watschplattltanz); Dingere Dingale; Dirty Old Town; Foyo; Hammer Song; Hoe Ry Die Boere; Hush Little Baby [1]; I Came Home [1]; I Gave My Love a Cherry; I Know Where I'm Going; Izicatulo Gumboot Dance; Jikel Emaweni; Jo'burg Talking Blues [1]; Kapurapura Kupika; Last Summer; Latirette, Le Roi a Fait Battre Tambour; Little Sir Hugh [1]; London Talking Blues; Love Life of a Gondolier, The; Marabi Dance Song (Chuzi Mama/Gwabi Gwabi); Mgeniso WaMgodo WaShambini [2]; Ndinosara Nani? (With Whom Shall I Stay?); North of the Popo; On Guard; Opening Knight; Out of Focus; Over the Hills; Piece of Ground, A; Red Red Rose; Samandoza-we!; Single Girl [1]; Sir Oswald Sodde; Skalo-Zwi; Strangest Dream, The [1]; Subuhi Sana; Table Bay; This Is South Africa; This Is the Land; This Is Worth Fighting For; Tour de France; Transkei Xha Xha [2]; Vive La Difference; Wee Copper o' Fife, The

Cast: Sarah Atkinson; Kendrew Lascelles; Michel Martel; April Olrich; Nigel Pegram; Andrew Tracey; Paul Tracey; Dana Valery

Notes: [1] Cut from South African production prior to Broadway. [2] Cut from London version prior to Broadway.

4580 • WAIT FOR ME WORLD

Musical Unproduced

Composer: John Kander
Lyricist: Fred Ebb

Notes: No other information available.

4581 • WAKE UP AND DREAM

OPENED: 12/30/1929 Theatre: Selwyn
Musical Broadway: 127

Composer: Cole Porter
Lyricist: Cole Porter
Librettist: John Hastings Turner
Producer: Charles B. Cochran
Director: Frank Collins

Choreographer: Jack Buchanan; Tilly Losch; Max Rivers; **Costumes:** Paul Colin; Marc-Henri; Oliver Messel; Ada Peacock; **Set Design:** Paul Colin; Oliver Messel; Ada Peacock

Songs: After All, I'm Only a Schoolgirl; Agua Sincopada Tango (inst.); Banjo that Man Joe Plays, The; Dance of the Crinoline Ladies; Dance of the Ragamuffins; Entrance of Emigrants [7]; Extra Man, The [9]; Fancy Our Meeting (C: Philip Charig; Joseph Meyer; L: Douglas Furber); I Dream of a Girl in a Shawl [3]; I Loved Him but He Didn't Love Me [6]; I Want to Be Raided By You [6]; I'm a Gigolo; I've Got a Crush on You; Lady I Love, The [1]; Let's Do It, Let's Fall in Love [5]; Looking at You; More Incredible Happenings (C/L: Ronald Jeans); My Louisa [2]; Night Club Opening [6]; Operatic Pills; She's Such a Comfort to Me [10] (C: Arthur Schwartz; L: Douglas Furber; Max Lief; Nathaniel Lief; Donovan Parsons); Tale of an Oyster [8]; Wait Until It's Bedtime [6]; Wake Up and Dream; What Is This Called Love?; Which [4]; Why Wouldn't I Do? (C/L: Ivor Novello; L: Desmond Carter)

Cast: Toni Birkmeyer; Sonnie Hale; Tilly Losch; Jessie Matthews; Georges Metaxa; William Stephens

Notes: [1] Cut prior to London opening (3/27/29). [2] Cut prior to London opening (3/27/29). Not used in NYMPH ERRANT. Cut also from THE NEW YORKERS (1930). [3] Originally in HITCHY-KOO OF 1922 as "My Spanish Shawl." [4] Not used in PARIS. [5] Not in New York production. [6] Originally in PARIS. [7] Cut from FIFTY MILLION FRENCHMEN. [8] Not used. Also not used in the 9:15 REVUE and THE NEW YORKERS (1930). [9] Cut prior to London opening. Also cut from FIFTY MILLION FRENCHMEN. [10] Originally in THE HOUSE THAT JACK BUILT (1929).

4582 • WAKE UP, DARLING

OPENED: 05/02/1956 Theatre: Ethel Barrymore
Play Broadway: 5

Author: Alec Gottlieb
Producer: Richard Cook; Gordon W. Pollock; Lee Segall
Director: Ezra Stone

Costumes: Guy Kent; **Lighting Designer:** David Ballou; **Set Design:** David Ballou

Songs: Li'l Ol' You and Li'l Ol' Me (C: Jule Styne; L: Leo Robin)

Cast: Barbara Britton; Kay Medford; Barry Nelson; Russell Nype; Richard B. Shull; Paula Trueman

4583 • WALK A LITTLE FASTER

OPENED: 12/07/1932 Theatre: St. James
Revue Broadway: 121

Composer: Vernon Duke
Lyricist: E.Y. Harburg
Librettist: Robert McGunigle; S.J. Perelman
Producer: Courtney Burr
Director: Monty Woolley

Choreographer: Albertina Rasch; **Costumes:** Kiviette; **Musical Director:** Nicholas Kempner; **Orchestrations:** Robert Russell Bennett; Conrad Salinger; **Set Design:** Boris Aronson

Songs: April in Paris; End of a Perfect Night; Frisco Fanny (C: Henry Sullivan; L: Earle Crooker); (Manhattan's the) Loneliest Isle [1]; Mayfair (C: William Waliter; L: Rowland Leigh); Off Again, On Again; Penny for Your Thoughts, A; So Nonchalant (L: E.Y. Harburg; Charles Tobias); Speaking of Love; That's Life; Time and Tide;

Unaccustomed As I Am; Where Have We Met Before?

Cast: Charles Burr; Bobby Clark; Dave Fitzgibbon; Dorothy Fitzgibbon; Sue Hicks; Evelyn Hoey; John Hundley; Beatrice Lillie; Paul McCullough; Jerry Norris; Penny Singleton

Notes: [1] Cut.

4584 • WALK DOWN MAH STREET!

OPENED: 06/12/1968 Theatre: Players
Musical Off-Broadway: 135

Composer: Norman Curtis
Lyricist: Patricia Taylor Curtis
Librettist: Patricia Taylor Curtis
Producer: Audience Associates, Inc.
Director: Patricia Taylor Curtis

Choreographer: Patricia Taylor Curtis; **Costumes:** Bob Rogers; **Dance Arranger:** Norman Curtis; **Lighting Designer:** Bruce D. Bassman; **Set Design:** Jack Logan; **Vocal Arranger:** Norman Curtis

Songs: Basic Black; Clean Up Your Own Backyard; Don't Have to Take It Any More; Flower Child; For Four Hundred Years; If You Want to Get Ahead; I'm Just a Statistic; Just One More Time; Lonely Girl; Someday, If We Grow Up; Teeny Bopper; Walk Down My Street; Walk, Lordy, Walk; Want to Get Retarded?; We're Today; What Shadows We Are

Cast: Denise Delapenha; Freddy Diaz; Lorraine Feather; Kenneth Frett; Vaughan Martinez; Gene Rounds

Notes: Special Material: James Taylor, Cagriel Levenson and Next Stage Theatre Co.

4585 • WALK TALL

OPENED: 07/12/1954
Revue Closed out of town

Composer: Dean Fuller; Albert W. Selden; Ralph Strain
Lyricist: Marshall Barer; Valerie Bettis; Billings Brown
Librettist: Bud Burtson; William Engvick; Arnold B. Horwitt
Producer: Fred Miller; Martha Miller
Director: George Englund

Choreographer: Ray Harrison; **Costumes:** Robert Fletcher; **Musical Director:** Peter Matz; **Set Design:** Emanuel Gerard

Songs: Get Married Shyrlee [1] (C: Albert Selden; L: Burt Shevelove); I'll Dance You; Yesterday I Loved You

Cast: Jane Dulo; William Dwyer; June Ericson; Paul Hartman; Pat Stanley

Notes: No program available. [1] Also in SMALL WONDER and A MONTH OF SUNDAYS (1951).

4586 • WALK WITH MUSIC

OPENED: 06/04/1940 Theatre: Ethel Barrymore
Musical Broadway: 55

Composer: Hoagy Carmichael
Lyricist: Johnny Mercer
Librettist: Guy Bolton; Parke Levy; Alan Lipscott
Producer: Ruth Selwyn; Messrs. Shubert
Director: R.H. Burnside

Source: UNKNOWN (Play: Stephen Powys); **Choreographer:** Anton Dolin; Herbert Harper; **Costumes:** Tom Lee; **Musical Director:** Joseph Littau; **Orchestrations:** Arden Cornwell; Joe Dubin; Hans Spialek; Fred Van Epps; Don Walker; Clay Warnick; **Set Design:** Watson Barratt; **Vocal Arranger:** Hugh Martin

Songs: Amazing What Love Can Do [1]; Break It Up Cinderella [3]; Darn Clever These Chinese [1]; Even If I Say It Myself; Everything Happens to Me; Friend of the Family; Give, Baby, Give [2] (C: Irving Gellers; Otis Spencer; L: Gladys Shelley); Greetings, Gates; Happy New Year to You [1]; How Nice for Me; I Like Love [2] (C/L: Hugh Martin); I Walk with Music; Love Song [1]; Newsy Bluesies [1]; Ooh! What You Said; Put Music in the Barn [1]; Rhumba Jumps!, The; Smile for the Press; Today I Am a Glamour Girl; Wait Till You See Me in the Morning [4]; Way Back in 1939 A.D.; We're Off the Wagon [1]; What'll They Think of Next?

Cast: Kitty Carlisle; Stepin Fetchit; Mitzi Green; Art Jarrett; Betty Lawford; Marty May; Frances Williams

Notes: Titled THREE AFTER THREE out of town

when it was based on a play by Guy Bolton. [1] Out Philadelphia 12/25/39. [2] Out Detroit 1940. [3] Revised as "Break It Now, Buck Private" in AT EASE! [4] Revised and put into AT EASE!

4587 • WALKING DELEGATE, THE

Notes: *See THE KOREANS.*

4588 • WALKING HAPPY

OPENED: 11/26/1966 Theatre: Lunt-Fontanne
Musical Broadway: 161

Composer: Jimmy Van Heusen
Lyricist: Sammy Cahn
Librettist: Ketti Frings; Roger O. Hirson
Producer: Cy Feuer; Ernest Martin
Director: Cy Feuer

Source: HOBSON'S CHOICE (Play: Harold Brighouse); **Choreographer:** Danny Daniels; **Costumes:** Robert Fletcher; **Dance Arranger:** Ed Scott; **Lighting Designer:** Robert Randolph; **Musical Director:** Herbert Grossman; **Orchestrations:** Larry Wilcox; **Set Design:** Robert Randolph; **Vocal Arranger:** Herbert Grossman

Songs: Be Joyful [1]; Circle This Day on the Calendar [2]; Clog and Grog (dance); How D'Ya Talk to a Girl; I Don't Think I'm in Love; I Should've Said [2]; If I Be Your Best Chance; If Me No If — But Me No But [5]; I'll Make a Man of the Man; It Might As Well Be Her; Joyful Thing, A; Love Will Find a Way — They Say [3]; Man Has Got to Wear the Pants, The [5]; Most Girls [3]; Must You Go [3]; People Who Are Nice (No More Mr. Nice); Policeman's Whistle, A [5]; Such a Sociable Sort; There's No Love Like [3]; Think of Something Else; To Keep the Chill Off the Bones [3]; Touch a Hair of His Head [3]; Use Your Noggin; Very Close to Wonderful [2]; Walking Happy [4]; What Makes It Happen; When Willie Waltzes with Me [5]; Where Was I; Wouldn't It Break Your Heart? [5]; You're Right, You're Right

Cast: Chad Black; Gordon Dilworth; George Rose; Louise Troy; Gretchen Van Aken; Norman Wisdom

Notes: [1] Not in programs. [2] Out Detroit 10/25/66. [3] ASCAP only. [4] Written for unproduced Fred Astaire film. [5] Not used.

4589 • WALL STREET GIRL, THE

OPENED: 04/15/1912 Theatre: Cohan
Musical Broadway: 56

Composer: Karl Hoschna
Lyricist: Benjamin Hapgood Burt
Librettist: Margaret Mayo; Edgar Selwyn
Producer: Frederic McKay
Director: Charles Winninger

Choreographer: Gus Sohlke; **Musical Director:** William Lorraine

Songs: Chicken Pie [1]; Deedle-Dee-Dum, The (C: Silvio Hein); Every Day [1] (C/L: Daniels; Jones); Finale; Finale Act II (C: Nat D. Ayer; L: A. Seymour Brown); Finale Act III (C: Karl Hoschna; L: Benjamin Hapgood Burt); Finnegan [2] (C: Nat D. Ayer; L: A. Seymour Brown); Georgia Land [2] (C: Harry Carroll; L: Arthur Fields); I Can Drink (C/L: Benjamin Hapgood Burt); I Never Knew (C: Henry I. Marshall; L: Stanley Murphy); I Should Have Been Born a Boy (C: Nat D. Ayer; L: A. Seymour Brown); I Want a Regular Man; If You Only Will [1] (C/L: Benjamin Hapgood Burt); In Old Wall Street [2]; Indian Rag, The [3] (C: Nat D. Ayer; L: A. Seymour Brown); Love Is a Peculiarity (C: Al Piantadosi; L: Joseph McCarthy); Medley of College Songs; Moving Pictures [1]; My Irish Girl [2] (C: Henriette-Blanke Blacher; L: Alfred Bryan); On the Quiet; Opening Chorus; Opening Chorus Act II (C/L: Benjamin Hapgood Burt); Spoony Land (C: M.J. Fitzpatrick; L: Edward Madden); That Baboon Baby Dance [2] (C: Joe Cooper; L: Dave Oppenheim); Under the Love Tree [1] (C: Bert Grant; L: A. Seymour Brown); Walk This Way (C: Fred Fisher; L: Grant Clarke); Whistle It (C: Jean Schwartz; L: Alfred Bryan; Grant Clarke); You're Exactly My Style of Girl [2] (C: Hector McCarthy; L: Arthur Denvir); You're Some Girl (C: Nat D. Ayer; L: A. Seymour Brown)

Cast: Wellington Cross; Blanche Ring; Will Rogers; Charles Winninger

Notes: [1] Out Washington, D.C. 5/1/12. [2] Sheet music only. [3] Also in BING BOYS ON BROADWAY.

4590 • WALTZ DREAM, A

OPENED: 01/27/1908 Theatre: Broadway
Musical Broadway: 111

Composer: Oscar Straus
Lyricist: Joseph W. Herbert
Librettist: Joseph W. Herbert
Producer: Inter-State Amusement Co.
Director: Herbert Gresham

Source: EIN WALZERLRAUM (Musical: Felix Dormann; Leopold Jacobson; Oscar Straus); **Costumes:** F. Richard Anderson; **Set Design:** Homer Emens

Songs: Come Join in the Waltz [3]; Country Lass and a Courtly Dame, A [2]; Family's Ancient Tree, The; Finale Act II; Finale Act III; Gay Lothario, The [2] (C: Jerome Kern; L: C.H. Bovill); Hail, We Hope It's a Male [3]; Husband's Love, A; I Love and the World Is Mine (C: Charles Gilbert Spross; L: Florence Earle Coates); I'd Much Rather Stay at Home (C: Jerome Kern; L: C.H. Bovill); Just Because You Love [2] (C/L: Arthur Weld); Kissing Time; Lesson in Love, A; Life Is Love and Laughter; Love Cannot Be Bought; Love's Roundelay [2]; Love's Thoughts (C/L: Florence Duncan); Oh Joy, Let Our Song of Gladness Be Heard on Ever Side; Opening Chorus; Piccolo; Prater, The [1] (C: Ivan Caryll); Soldier Stole Her Heart, A; Sweetest Maid of All; Trumpets Blare, The; Two Is Plenty; Vienna (C: Jerome Kern; L: Adrian Ross); Wedding March and Hymn; When the Song of Love Is Heard (C: Arthur Weld)

Cast: Charles A. Bigelow; Sophie Brandt; Magda Dahl; Harry Fairleigh; Joseph W. Herbert; Edward Johnson; Josie Sadler

Notes: An English version of the original Straus songs was written by Grace Isabel Colbron and published by the Continental Publishing Company but I don't believe they were ever used on stage. [1] Out 2/15/09. [2] Sheet music only. [3] Added for revival Muny Opera, St. Louis 1938.

4591 • WALTZ OF THE STORK

OPENED: 01/05/1982 Theatre: Century
Musical Broadway: 146

Composer: Melvin Van Peebles
Lyricist: Melvin Van Peebles
Librettist: Melvin Van Peebles
Producer: Melvin Van Peebles
Director: Melvin Van Peebles

Costumes: Bernard Johnson; **Lighting Designer:** Shirley Prendergast; **Musical Director:** Bob Carten; **Set Design:** Kert Lundell

Songs: And I Love You; Apple Sketching, The; Mother's Prayer; My Love Belongs to You; One Hundred and Fifteen; Play It As It Lays; Shoulders to Lean On; Tender Understanding (C/L: Mark Burkan; Ted Hayes); There; Weddings and Funerals (C/L: Mark Burken; Ted Hayes)

Cast: Bob Carten; C.J. Critt; Mario Van Peebles; Melvin Van Peebles

4592 • WALTZ OF THE TOREADORS

Musical Unproduced

Composer: Harold Rome
Lyricist: Harold Rome

Source: WALTZ OF THE TOREADORS, THE (Play: Jean Anouilh)

Notes: No other information available.

4593 • WALTZ WAS BORN IN VIENNA

OPENED: 04/25/1936
Musical

Composer: Frederick Loewe
Lyricist: Earle Crooker
Librettist: Earle Crooker
Director: Donald Brian

Cast: Donald Brian

Notes: A musical skit that was part of THE LAMBS SPRING GAMBOL at the Waldorf-Astoria Hotel. There were no songs identified. See under that name for additional credits.

4594 • WALTZES FROM VIENNA

Notes: *See THE GREAT WALTZ (1934).*

4595 • WANTED

OPENED: 01/19/1972 Theatre: Cherry Lane
Musical Off-Broadway: 79

Composer: Al Carmines
Lyricist: Al Carmines
Librettist: David Epstein
Producer: Arthur D. Zinberg
Director: Lawrence Kornfeld

Costumes: Linda Giese; **Lighting Designer:** Roger Morgan; **Musical Director:** Susan Romann; **Set Design:** Paul Zalon

Songs: As I'm Growing Older; Guns Are Fun; I Am the Man; I Do the Best I Can (L: Al Carmines; David Epstein); I Want to Blow Up the World; I Want to Ride with You (L: Al Carmines; David Epstein); Indian Benefit Ball, The; It's Love; Jailhouse Blues; Lord Is My Light, The (L: Al Carmines; David Epstein); Outlaw Man; Parasol Lady; Wahoo!; Where Have You Been Up to Now?; Whispering to You; Who's on Our Side? (L: Al Carmines; David Epstein); You Do This

Cast: Reathel Bean; Frank Coppola; June Gable; Lee Guilliatt; John Kuhner; Peter Lombard

4596 • WANTED — A WIFE

OPENED: 1917
Musical

Composer: Walter L. Rosemont
Lyricist: Darl MacBoyle
Librettist: Alan Brooks
Producer: George Choos

Costumes: Edyth Bloodgood; **Set Design:** P. Dodd Ackerman

Songs: I Am Longing, My Dearie, for You; If You Ever Want to Do Some Lovin'; Oh! I'll Be Good

Cast: Frank Harrington; Al Hinton; Charlotte Taylor

Notes: A one-act vaudeville musical in Philadelphia.

4597 • WAR BUBBLES

OPENED: 05/16/1898 Theatre: Hammerstein's Olympia
Musical Broadway: 26

Composer: Oscar Hammerstein I
Lyricist: Oscar Hammerstein I
Librettist: Oscar Hammerstein I
Producer: Oscar Hammerstein I

Cast: Allene Crater; Oscar Figman; Lucy Nelson

Notes: No program available.

4598 • WAR-TIME WEDDING OR, IN MEXICO IN 1847, A

OPENED: 1896
Musical Closed out of town

Composer: Oscar Weil
Librettist: C.T. Dazey; Oscar Weil
Producer: Bostonians

Musical Director: S.L. Studley

Cast: Henry Clay Barnabee; Eugene Cowles; William H. MacDonald; Alice Nielsen

Notes: No other information available.

4599 • WARS OF THE WORLD

OPENED: 09/05/1914 Theatre: Hippodrome
Musical Broadway: 229

Composer: Manuel Klein
Lyricist: Manuel Klein
Librettist: John P. Wilson
Producer: Messrs. Shubert
Director: William J. Wilson

Costumes: Max & Mahieu; Frances M. Ziebarth; **Set Design:** Arthur Voegtlin

Songs: Baby Eyes; In Siam; Under a Gay Sombrero; When You Come Home Again, Johnny; You're Just the One I've Waited For

Cast: John Gibson; Lawrence Grant; Marceline; John P. Wilson

Notes: No program available.

4600 • WASHINGTON SQUARE

OPENED: 01/23/1947
Play Closed out of town

Author: Augustus Goetz; Ruth Goodman Goetz
Producer: Oscar Serlin
Director: Jack Minster

Source: WASHINGTON SQUARE (Novel: Henry James); **Lighting Designer:** Donald Oenslager; **Set Design:** Donald Oenslager

Songs: Comme Tu Es Different (C/L: Dorothie Bigelow)

Cast: Peter Cookson; John Halliday; Barbara Leeds

Notes: Opened in New Haven. The play was overhauled (only Peter Cookson and the authors survived) and reopened as THE HEIRESS.

4601 • WATCH ON THE RHINE

OPENED: 01/03/1980 Theatre: John Golden
Play Broadway: 36

Author: Lillian Hellman
Producer: Spencer H. Berlin; Marc Howard; John F. Kennedy Center; Long Wharf Theatre; Lester Osterman
Director: Arvin Brown

Costumes: Bill Walker; **Lighting Designer:** Ronald Wallace; **Set Design:** John Jensen

Songs: Soldier's Song (C/L: Thomas Fay)

Cast: Joyce Ebert; Jill Eikenberry; George Hearn; Mark McLaughlin; Jan Miner; Bobby Scott; Monica Snowden; Harris Yulin

4602 • WATCH OUT ANGEL

OPENED: 04/03/1945
Musical Closed out of town

Composer: Josef Myrow
Lyricist: Eddie De Lange
Librettist: David Alison; Isabel Dawn
Producer: David Alison
Director: Harry Howell

Choreographer: Aida Broadhust; **Costumes:** Martingale; **Musical Director:** Charles Hathaway; **Set Design:** Richard Jackson

Songs: Co-op-hooray-shun; Don't You Believe It; Everybody Wants to Get into the Act; Five A.M. Ballet; Half a Dream to Go; I Love You but Good (L: Eddie De Lange; Jerry Seelen); It's a Great Life If You Weaken; Joyride; Out of My Mind; Publicity; Short and Sweet; That Does It [1] (L: Eddie De Lange; Jerry Seelen); To Be Young; Watch Out, Angel! (L: Eddie De Lange; Jerry Seelen); What's New in New York; Where Is the Boss

Cast: Lester Allen; Carol Haney; Marilyn Hare; Donald Kerr; Lucien Littlefield; Eden Nicholas; Jim Nolan

Notes: Program of San Francisco 4/3/45. [1] Not used.

4603 • WATCH YOUR STEP

OPENED: 12/08/1914 Theatre: New Amsterdam
Musical Broadway: 175

Composer: Irving Berlin
Lyricist: Irving Berlin
Librettist: Harry B. Smith
Producer: Charles B. Dillingham
Director: R.H. Burnside

Source: ROUND THE CLOCK (Play: Augustin Daly); **Costumes:** Helen Dryden; Lucille; **Musical Director:** DeWitt Coolman; **Set Design:** Helen Dryden

Songs: Chatter Chatter; Come to the Land of the Argentine [1]; Homeward Bound [1]; I Hate You [1]; I Love to Have the Boys Around Me; I'm a Dancing Teacher Now; I've Gotta Go Back to Texas [1]; Lead Me to Love [1] (C: Ted Snyder); Let's Go Around the Town; Lock Me in Your Harem and Throw Away the Key [1]; Look at Them Doing It!; Metropolitan Nights; Minstrel Parade, The; Move Over; Office Hours; Old Operas in a New Way (Opera Medley); Settle Down in a One-Horse Town; Show Us How to Do the Fox Trot; Simple Melody; Syncopated Walk, The; They Always Follow Me Around; Watch Your Step [1]; What Is Love?; When I Discovered You (C/L: Irving Berlin; E. Ray Goetz); When It's Night Time in Dixie Land [1]

Cast: Elizabeth Brice; Irene Castle; Vernon Castle; Sallie Fisher; Justine Johnstone; Harry Kelly; Charles King; Elizabeth Murray; Frank Tinney

Notes: [1] Not in program. [2] Vocal score only.

4604 • WATER'S FINE, THE

OPENED: 1919
Musical

Composer: Ted Snyder
Lyricist: Sam M. Lewis; Joe Young

Songs: Boys Are Like Wonderful Toys; I'm in Love with You; In the Land of Go to Bed Early; Jazzin' the Alphabet; Shadows Always Make Me Blue; Way to Win a Girl, The; With a Little Bit of Cider Inside of Ida, Ida Was Full of Ideas

Notes: No other information available.

4605 • WAY TO KENMARE, THE

OPENED: 01/13/1906
Play Closed out of town

Composer: Andrew Mack
Lyricist: Andrew Mack

Songs: Dan, My Darlin Dan; Legend of the Maguires, The; Rose of Kenmare, The; She Just Suits Me

Cast: Albert Andrews; George W. Deyo; Josephine Lovett; Andrew Mack

Notes: Out Cedar Rapids. No writing credits in program.

4606 • WAYWARD WAY, THE

OPENED: 09/03/1953
Musical Closed out of town

Composer: Lorne Huycke
Lyricist: Bill Howe

Source: DRUNKARD, THE (Play: W.H. Smith)

Notes: No program available. Opened at the Hollywood Theatre Mart.

4607 • WE DID IT BEFORE

Notes: See BANJO EYES.

4608 • WE SHOULD WORRY

OPENED: 10/26/1917
Musical Closed out of town

Composer A. Baldwin Sloane
Lyricist: Henry Blossom
Librettist: Henry Blossom

Source: UNKNOWN (Play: Charles Hoyt)

Notes: Atlantic City.

4609 • WE TAKE THE TOWN

OPENED: 02/17/1962
Musical Closed out of town

Composer: Harold Karr
Lyricist: Matt Dubey
Librettist: Felice Bauer; Matt Dubey
Producer: Stuart Ostrow
Director: Alex Segal

Source: VIVA VILLA! (Film: Ben Hecht); **Choreographer:** Donald Saddler; **Costumes:** Motley; **Dance Arranger:** Mordecai Sheinkman; **Lighting Designer:** Tharon Musser; **Musical Director:** Colin Romoff; **Orchestrations:** Robert Russell Bennett; Hershy Kay; **Set Design:** Peter Larkin; **Vocal Arranger:** Colin Romoff

Songs: Beautiful People; Good Old Porfirio Diaz; How Does the Wine Taste?; I Don't Know How to Talk to a Lady; I Marry You; I've Got a Girl; Jesus [1]; Killing [1]; Mister Madero and Friend; Ode to a Friend; Only Girl, The; Pleadle-Eadle; Please Don't Despise Me; Poncho the Bull; Poncho's Thoughts (Little Man); Silverware; Viva Villa; We Take the Town; Wedded Man, A

Cast: Carmen Alvarez; Romney Brent; John Cullum; Mike Kellin; Robert Preston; Lester Rawlins; Kathleen Widdoes

Notes: [1] Out New Haven 2/17/62.

4610 • WE WERE DANCING

OPENED: 12/24/1936 Theatre: National
Play Broadway: 113

Author: Noel Coward
Producer: John C. Wilson
Director: Noel Coward

Musical Director: John McManus; **Set Design:** G.E. Calthrop

Songs: We Were Dancing (C/L: Noel Coward)

Cast: Joyce Carey; Noel Coward; Gertrude Lawrence; Moya Nugent; Edward Underdown; Alan Webb

Notes: Part of TONIGHT AT 8:30.

4611 • WE'D RATHER SWITCH

OPENED: 05/02/1969 Theatre: Mermaid
Revue Off-Broadway

Composer: Larry Crane
Lyricist: Larry Crane
Librettist: Walter Berger
Producer: Mario Manzini
Director: Robert Spelly

Choreographer: Robert Spelly; **Lighting Designer:** Donald L. Brooks; **Musical Director:** Rikki Dawn; **Set Design:** Frank Wakula

Songs: Golden Gang, The; Greatest Show on Earth; I'm Going Down the River and Have Myself a Darn Good Cry; Let's All Sing; Let's Do It All Over Again; Make Me Over; Man Is Good for Something After All, A; Man Isn't Old, A; Mod Man of Manhattan; On the Pier; Strangest Show on Earth, The; Stud Shows Us; Villains Aren't Bad Anymore; We'd Rather Switch

Cast: Robert Speller

4612 • WE'LL MEET AGAIN

Notes: *See SMILING THROUGH.*

4613 • WEBER & FIELDS JUBILEE

Revue Broadway

Songs: Island of Roses and Love, The (C: Neil Moret; L: Earle C. Jones)

Cast: Lillian Russell

Notes: No other information available.

4614 • WEDDING DAY, THE

OPENED: 04/08/1897 Theatre: Casino
Musical Broadway: 36

Composer: Julian Edwards
Lyricist: Stanislaus Stange
Librettist: Stanislaus Stange
Producer: Frank Murray
Director: Richard Barker

Costumes: Mme. Siedle; **Musical Director:** Julian Edwards; **Set Design:** Ernest Albert; Walter Burridge

Songs: At Last I Find in You; Come My Dearest; Confiding Woman; Days of Long Ago; Gaily Marches the Soldier; General Has Relented, The; He Never Said a Word; How I Danced Away; I Am a Simple Norman Maid; It Is Really to Good to Be True; Ladies, I Am Sorry; Life Is but Short at Best; Love's Prescription; Maid and the Officer, The; Mermaid and the Whale, The; Mon General; Nation's Pride, A; Planchette, Planchette; Rogue Lies Hid in the Wine, A; Rose Marie; Soldiers of the Parliment; This Is the Hour; Through the Years; Tomtit and the Nightingale, The; Vivandiers; Wise Little Maid, The; Woman's Tact, A

Cast: Jefferson De Angelis; Della Fox; Tom Greene; Lillian Russell

Notes: No songs listed in program. Songs from vocal score.

4615 • WEDDING OF IPHIGENIA, THE

OPENED: 12/16/1971 Theatre: Public
Musical Off-Broadway: 139

Composer: Peter Link
Lyricist: Gretchen Cryer; Doug Dyer; Peter Link
Author: Euripides
Producer: N.Y. Shakespeare Festival; Joseph Papp
Director: Gerald Freedman

Source: IPHIGENIA (Play: Euripides)

Songs: All Greece; All Hail the King; And Now; Can't Stand in the Way of My Country; Come Let Us Dance; Crown Us with the Truth; Gate Tender; How Can I Tell My Joy?; I Was First to Call You Father; I Wonder; Last Night in a Dream; Lead Me Now; Line Is Unbroken, The; Oh, What Bridal Song; On a Ship with Fifty Oars; Only Stone; Opening; Ride on to Highest Destiny; They Sing My Marriage Song at Home; This New Land; To Greece I Gave This Body of Mine; Unhappiness Remembering; What Has Your Tongue to Tell?; Who Will Lay Hands?; Your Turn Has Come

Cast: Nell Carter; Leata Galloway; Marta Heflin; Lynda Lee Lawley; Marion Ramsey

4616 • WEDDING TRIP, THE

OPENED: 12/25/1911 Theatre: Broadway
Musical Broadway: 48

Composer: Reginald De Koven
Lyricist: Harry B. Smith
Librettist: Fred De Gresac
Producer: Lee Shubert; Sam S. Shubert
Director: William J. Wilson

Songs: Ah, At Last; Awakened Love; Bivouac Song; Curfew Bell Has Sounded, The; Family Council, The; Flirtation; Fond Love [2]; Gentlemanly Brigand, The; Gypsy Kiss; Hail the Wedding Pair; Here Is the Tunic of a Soldier; Interrupted Love Song, The; Le Beau Sabreur; Lesson in Love, A; Little Bride, A; Love Waltz [2]; Marie [1]; Miraculous Cure, The; Modern Banditti, The; Opening Ensemble; Sea Shell Telephone, The; Soldier's Song [1]; Sweet Sixteen

Cast: Charles Angelo; Arthur Cordero; Grace Emmons; Dorothy Jardon; George Madison; Edward Martindel; Dorothy Morton; Christine Nielson

Notes: [1] Sheet music only. [2] ASCAP/Library of Congress.

4617 • WEE BIT O' SCOTCH, A

OPENED: 1970
Musical Unproduced

Composer: Harold Rome
Lyricist: Harold Rome
Librettist: Jerome Chodorov

Source: ENGAGED (Play: W.S. Gilbert)

Songs: As the Case May Be; Belinda's Love Song; Engaged; Farewell, My Life's True Love; Happy Hindu Waltz; I Am Losing My Little Wren; I Hate Her; I Intend to End It All; I Shall Be Happy; I Shall Not Let Money Get in My Way; Marriage; Name the Lady; Two Little Kittens; Wee Bit o' Scotch, A; What Am I?; You Are the Tree

4618 • WEEKEND

OPENED: 10/24/1983 Theatre: Theater at St. Peter's
Musical Off-Broadway: 8

Composer: Roger Lax
Lyricist: Roger Lax
Librettist: Roger Lax
Producer: Mae Richard
Director: David H. Bell

Choreographer: David H. Bell; **Costumes:** Sally Lesser; **Lighting Designer:** Toni Goldin; **Musical Director:** Clay Fullum; **Orchestrations:** Robby Merkin; **Set Design:** Ursula Belden

Cast: Louise Edeiken; Gregg Edelman; Justin Ross; Carole-Ann Scott

4619 • WELCOME TO THE CLUB

OPENED: 04/13/1989 Theatre: Music Box
Musical Broadway: 12

Composer: Cy Coleman
Lyricist: Cy Coleman; A.E. Hotchner
Librettist: A.E. Hotchner
Producer: Cy Coleman; A.E. Hotchner; William H. Kessler Jr.; Michael M. Weatherly
Director: Peter Mark Schifter

Choreographer: Patricia Birch; **Costumes:** William Ivey Long; **Lighting Designer:** Tharon Musser; **Musical Director:** David Pogue; **Orchestrations:** Doug Katsaros; **Set Design:** David Jenkins; **Vocal Arranger:** Cy Coleman; David Pogue

Songs: At My Side; Bachelors [1]; Boom Chicka Boom [1]; By Dawn's Early Light [1]; Chickabees [1]; Combat Pay [1]; Guilty; Holidays; Honeymoon Is Over, The [1]; I Get Tired [1]; In the Name of Love; It Wouldn't Be You; It's Love! It's Love!; King of the Mound [1]; Late Bloomer [1]; Let 'Em Rot [1]; Love Behind Bars; Man of the People [1]; Meyer Chickerman; Miami Beach; Mother-in-Law; Mrs. Meltzer Wants the Money Now!; No Croissants [1]; Pal Is a Pal, A [1]; Pay the Lawyer; Peace of Mind [1]; Piece of Cake, A; Place Called Alimony Jail, A; Rap-Up, The (Alimony Rap) [1]; Rio; Single [1]; Southern Comfort; That's a Woman; To Live Again [1]; Trouble with You, The; Two of Us, The; Welcome to the Club [1]

Cast: Jodi Benson; Bill Buell; Sally Mayes; Marcia Mitzman; Avery Schreiber; Marilyn Sokol; Scott Waara; Scott Wentworth; Terri White; Samuel E. Wright

Notes: Titled LET 'EM ROT out of town. [1] Not used.

4620 • WELL OF ROMANCE, THE

OPENED: 11/07/1930 Theatre: Craig
Musical Broadway: 8

Composer: H. Maurice Jacquet
Lyricist: Preston Sturges
Librettist: Preston Sturges
Producer: G.W. McGregor
Director: J.H. Benrimo

Choreographer: Leon Leonidoff; Florence Rogge; **Musical Director:** H. Maurice Jacquet; **Set Design:** Frank Gates; E.A. Morange

Songs: At Lovetime; Be Oh So Careful Ann; Cow's Divertissement [2]; Fare Thee Well; For You and For Me; German Country Dance [2]; Hail the King; How Can You Tell?; I Want to Be Loved By an Expert [2]; I'll Never Complain; Intermezzo [2]; Mazourka [2]; Melancholy Lady [1]; Moon's Shining Cool, The [2]; My Dream of Dreams; One Night; Rhapsody of Love; Serenade; Since You're Alone; Well of Romance, The

Cast: Lina Abarbanell; Laine Blaire; Max Figman; Howard Marsh; Tommy Monroe; Louis Sorin; Norma Terris

Notes: [1] Sheet music only. [2] Not in programs.

4621 • WELL, WELL, WELL

OPENED: 12/1928
Musical

Composer: Muriel Pollock; Arthur Schwartz
Lyricist: Max Lief; Nathaniel Lief
Librettist: Harold Atteridge; Montague Glass; Jules Eckert Goodman
Producer: Independent Prod. Company
Director: Lew Morton

Choreographer: John Boyle; Dave Gould; **Musical Director:** Harold Stern; **Set Design:** Watson Barratt

Songs: Dancing in the Moonlight; Have Pity, Sheriff; I'll Always Remember; Me 'n You; Night Life; Not Even You; Oh What a Man; Pep Up, Step Up; We Love to Go to Work; We'll Get Along; When He's Near

Cast: Virginia Barratt; Noel Francis; Fred Lightner; Jack Pearl; Jack Waterous

Notes: Program from Washington, D.C. 12/25/28. This show became PLEASURE BOUND. See that entry.

4622 • WE'RE ALL DRESSED UP AND WE DON'T KNOW HUERTO GO

OPENED: 05/22/1914
Play

Composer: Cole Porter
Lyricist: Cole Porter
Producer: Members Yale Drama Assn.

Songs: Cincinnati

Cast: Johnfritz Achelis; Lawrence Cornwell; Hay Langenheim; Phelps Newberry; Newbold Noyes; Cole Porter; Monty Woolley

Notes: Score lost except for "Cincinnati." Performed at Hotel Gibson, Cincinnati.

4623 • WE'RE CIVILIZED?

OPENED: 11/08/1962 Theatre: Jan Hus House
Musical Off-Broadway: 22

Composer: Ray Haney
Lyricist: Alfred Aiken
Librettist: Alfred Aiken
Producer: Rendell Productions
Director: Martin B. Cohen

Choreographer: Bhaskar; **Costumes:** Sonia Lowenstein; **Dance Arranger:** Michael Leonard; **Lighting Designer:** Roger Morgan; **Musical Director:** Michael Leonard; **Set Design:** Jack H. Cornwell; **Vocal Arranger:** Michael Leonard

Songs: Bad If He Does, Worse If He Don't; Brewing the Love Potion; Diversion; Everything Is Wonderful; Fertility Dance; I Like; J.B. Pictures, Inc.; Knife Dance; Lullaby Wind; Me Atahualpa; Mother Nature; Muted (C: Michael Leonard); No Place to Go; Procession; Snake Dance; Stretto; Too Old; We're Civilized; Welcome Home; Witch Song; Yankee Stay; You Can Hang Your Hat Here; You're Like

Cast: Bhaskar; Karen Black; Sally DeMay; John McLeod; Marty Ross

4624 • WEST POINT CADET, THE

OPENED: 09/30/1904 Theatre: Princess
Musical Broadway: 4

Composer: A.M. Norden
Lyricist: A.M. Norden
Librettist: A.M. Norden
Producer: Nathaniel Roth

Source: LE NOUVEAU REGIMENT (Musical: Antoine Banes; Albert Barre; Henri Bernard; E. Martin); **Musical Director:** Jose Vandenberg

Cast: Edward Abeles; Della Fox; Joseph W. Herbert; Richie Ling; Clara Palmer

Notes: No songs listed in program.

4625 • WEST SIDE STORY

OPENED: 09/26/1957 Theatre: Winter Garden
Musical Broadway: 732

Composer: Leonard Bernstein
Lyricist: Stephen Sondheim
Librettist: Arthur Laurents
Producer: Robert E. Griffith; Harold Prince
Director: Jerome Robbins

Choreographer: Peter Gennaro; Jerome Robbins; **Dance Arranger:** Betty Walberg; **Lighting Designer:** Jean Rosenthal; **Musical Director:** Max Goberman; **Orchestrations:** Leonard Bernstein; Irwin Kostal; Sid Ramin; **Set Design:** Oliver Smith

Songs: America; Boy Like That, A; Cool; Dance at the Gym, The (dance); Gee, Officer Krupke; I Feel Pretty; I Have a Love; Jet Song; Kids Ain't (Like Everybody Else) [1]; Maria; Mix! [1]; My Greatest Day! [1]; One Hand, One Heart; Prologue (dance); Rumble, The (dance); Something's Coming; Somewhere; This Turf Is Ours [1]; Tonight; Up to the Moon [1]

Cast: Tommy Abbott; Lee Becker; William Bramley; Mickey Calin; Martin Charnin; Marilyn Cooper; Wilma Curley; Grover Dale; Al De Sio; Reri Grist; Carmen Guiterrez; John Harkins; Arch Johnson; Larry Kert; Carol Lawrence; Ken Le Roy; Tony Mordente; Liane Plane; Chita Rivera; Eddie Roll; Lynn Ross; Jaime Sanchez; Art Smith; Elizabeth Taylor; David Winters

Notes: Returned for an additional 249 performances on 4/27/60. The run above does not include these extra performances. [1] Cut prior to opening.

4626 • WET AND DRY

OPENED: 1920
Musical Chicago

Composer: Jean C. Havez
Lyricist: Jean C. Havez
Producer: Max Dill; William C. Kolb

Songs: Beautiful Garden of Day Dreams; Everybody in the Town Is Sober Since My Cellar Went Dry; I'm Glad He's Irish; Let's Pretend; Love's Bouquet; Pickaninny Sam

Notes: No other information available.

4627 • WET PAINT

OPENED: 04/12/1965 Theatre: Renata
Revue Off-Broadway: 16

Librettist: Pierre Berton; Leslie H. Carter; Tony Geiss; Stanley Handleman; Herbert Hartig; Bob Hilliard; Dolly Jonah; Lois Balk Korey; Marc London; Paul Lynde; Pat McCormick; Judith Milan; David Panich; Bob Rosenblum; Paul Sand; Howard Schulman
Producer: Lee Reynolds; Isobel Robins
Director: Michael Ross

Choreographer: Rudy Tronto; **Costumes:** Mostoller; **Dance Arranger:** Gerald Alters; **Lighting Designer:** David Moon; **Musical Director:** Gerald Alters; **Set Design:** David Moon; **Vocal Arranger:** Gerald Alters

Songs: Canary (C: Stan Davis; L: Giles O'Connor); Cantata (C: Gerald Alters; L: Herbert Hartig); Concert Encore (C/L: Sheldon Harnick); Cream in My Coffee (C: Ed Scott; L: Anne Croswell); I Know He'll Understand (C/L: Johnny Myers); Love Affair (C: Bob Kessler; L: Martin Charnin); Neville (C/L: Tony Geiss); Puns (C: Gerald Alters; L: Herbert Hartig); Showstopper (C/L: Johnny Myers); These Things I Know Are True (C/L: Jennifer Konecky); Unrequited Love March [1] (C/L: Ronny Graham)

Cast: Gene Allen; Hank Garrett; Linda Lavin; Bill McCutcheon; Isobel Robins; Paul Sand

Notes: [1] Later added to NEW FACES OF 1968.

4628 • WHAT A DAY FOR A MIRACLE

Notes: *See THE CHILDREN'S CRUSADE.*

4629 • WHAT A KILLING

OPENED: 03/27/1961 Theatre: Folksbiene
Musical Off-Broadway: 1

Composer: George Harwell
Lyricist: Joan Anenia; George Harwell
Librettist: Fred Herbert
Producer: Jack Collins
Director: Gene Montefiore

Source: UNKNOWN (Story: Jack Waldron); **Choreographer:** Bob Hamilton; **Costumes:** Hugh Whitfield; **Dance Arranger:** Andrew Lesko; **Lighting Designer:** Robert Wightman; **Musical Director:** Andrew Lesko; **Orchestrations:** Andrew Lesko; **Set Design:** Robert Wightman

Songs: Chicago That I Knew, The; Customer Is Always Right; Face the Facts; Fools Come and Fools Go; Here I Come; I'm a Positive Guy; Laughing Out Loud; Lennie; Look at What It's Done; Nobody Cheats Big Mike; Oh, How I Love You; Out of Luck with Luck; Pride in My Work; Race, The; Rag, a Bone, a Hank of Hair, A; Rockette's Dance; Troubled Lady; What a Killing

Cast: Chanin Hale; Paul Hartman; Barney Martin; Lou Wills Jr.

4630 • WHAT DOES THE PUBLIC WANT?

Musical

Composer: Barney Gerard
Lyricist: Barney Gerard
Librettist: Barney Gerard
Director: Barney Gerard

Songs: I Wonder Why They Stare at Me; It Would Be Nice; It's Great Sport Just the Same; I've Got No Use for Opera When There's Ragtime; Red Riding Hood (C/L: Jeff T. Branen); Salvation Tess (C/L: B. Brown; Barney Gerard); San Francisco Fair (C/L: B. Brown; Barney Gerard); Up and Down (C/L: B. Brown; Barney Gerard); Virginia Rose (C/L: B. Brown; Barney Gerard); We're the Famous Impresarios (C/L: B. Brown; Barney Gerard); What Does the Public Want?; When I'm Dancing with Peg o' My Heart

Cast: Gertrude Hayes; Sam Sidman

Notes: Burlesque musical in Toledo.

4631 • WHAT EVER HAPPENED TO GEORGIE TAPPS?

OPENED: 08/12/1980 Theatre: Westwood Playhouse
Revue Los Angeles

Cast: Georgie Tapps

Notes: No program available.

4632 • WHAT IS LOVE?

OPENED: 07/02/1917
Musical Closed out of town

Composer: Joseph E. Howard

Notes: Closed at the National Theatre, Washington, D.C. No other information available.

4633 • WHAT MAKES SAMMY RUN?

OPENED: 02/27/1964 Theatre: 54th St.
Musical Broadway: 541

Composer: Ervin Drake
Lyricist: Ervin Drake
Librettist: Budd Schulberg; Stuart Schulberg
Producer: Joseph Cates
Director: Abe Burrows

Source: WHAT MAKES SAMMY RUN? (Novel: Budd Schulberg); **Choreographer:** Matt Mattox; **Costumes:** Noel Taylor; **Dance Arranger:** Arnold Goland; **Lighting Designer:** Helen Pond; Herbert Senn; **Musical Director:** Lehman Engel; **Orchestrations:** Don Walker; **Set Design:** Helen Pond; Herbert Senn; **Vocal Arranger:** Lehman Engel

Songs: Bachelor Gal [1]; Friendliest Thing, The; I Feel Humble; I See Something; Kiss Me No Kisses; Lites-Camera-Platitude; Maybe Some Other Time; Monsoon (dance); My Hometown; New Boy, A [1]; New Pair of Shoes, A; Paint a Rainbow; Room Without Windows, A; Some Days Everything Goes Wrong; Something to Live For; Sweetie [1]; Tender Spot, A; Warm Spot in My Heart, A [2]; Wedding of the Year, The; You Can Trust Me; You Help Me; You're No Good

Cast: Robert Alda; George Coe; Graciela Daniele; Arny Freeman; Sally Ann Howes; Steve Lawrence; Bernice Massi; Barry Newman; Ralph Stanley

Notes: [1] Out Philadelphia 1/64. [2] ASCAP/Library of Congress only.

4634 • WHAT NEXT?

OPENED: 06/24/1917
Musical Closed out of town

Composer: Harry Tierney
Lyricist: Alfred Bryan
Librettist: Elmer Harris; Oliver Morosco
Producer: Oliver Morosco
Director: Fred A. Bishop

Set Design: Robert McQuinn

Songs: Angie's Patriotic Rally; Chasing the Squirrel; Cleopatra; Fame, Fame, Fame; For One Sweet Day; Get a Girl to Lead the Army; Hello Girlie; I Want a Good Girl (and I Want Her Bad); I Want You to Want Me with You; If You'll Be a Soldier, I'll Be a Red Cross Nurse; I've Got a Vegetable Garden (Garden of Liberty) (Vegetable Song); Just to Keep Expenses Down; Keep on the Right Hand Side of Father; Keep Your Eye on Little Mary Brown; Rescue, The; Routine Exercise, The; Seminary Girl, The; Send Me Back My Husband, You've Had Him Long Enough; We Do the Best That We Can; When a Pretty Peeping Ankle Peeps at You

Cast: Eva Fallon; Blanche Ring; Charles Winninger; Fannie Yantis

Notes: Program from Los Angeles 6/24/17. [1] Not in program.

4635 • WHAT'S A NICE COUNTRY LIKE YOU DOING IN A STATE LIKE THIS?

OPENED: 04/19/1973 Theatre: Upstage at Jimmy's
Revue Off-Broadway: 477

Composer: Cary Hoffman
Lyricist: Ira Gasman
Director: Miriam Fond

Choreographer: Miriam Fond; **Costumes:** Danny Morgan; **Lighting Designer:** Richard Delahanty; **Musical Director:** Arnold Gross; **Orchestrations:** Hurbert Arnold; **Set Design:** Bill Puzo

Songs: America, You're Looking Good [1]; Bar, The; Bedroom, The; But I Love New York; Carlos, Juan and Miguel [1]; Changing Partners; Chicago; Church and State [1]; Come On, Daisy; Crime in the Streets; Daniel Boone; Dow Jones; Everybody Ought to Have a Gun; Farewell [1]; Farewell First Amendment; Fill 'Er Up [1]; Get Out of Here [1]; Girl of My Dreams [1]; Hallelujah; Hollywood; How'm I Doing? [1]; I Found the Girl of My Dreams on Broadway; I Just Pressed Button A [1]; I Like Me; I Like New York; I'm in Love With . . .; I'm Not Myself Anymore; I'm Not Taking a Chance on Love [1]; It's a Political-Satirical Revue; It's Getting Better; Johannesburg; Keeping the Peace; Kissinger und Kleindienst und Klein; Last One of the Boys, The [1]; Liberal's Lament; Liberation Tango [1]; Love Story; Mafia; Male Chauvinist Pig of Myself; Massage a Trois; Mugger's Work Is Never Done, A; Nicaragua [1]; Nuclear Winter [1]; On a Scale of One to Ten; People Are Like Porcupines; Primary Tango; Right Place at the Right Time, The; Rise and Fall of the American Empire Waltz, The; Runaways [1]; San Francisco; Street People; Take Us Back King George; Terrorist Trio [1]; Test Tube Baby; They Aren't There [1]; Things I Used to Know; Threesome; Trial of the Century; Update; Vasectomy; Watergate Suite; What the Hell [1]; What's a Nice Country Like You; Whatever Happened to the Communist Menace; Why Do I Keep Going to the Theatre?; Why Johnny?; You're Dull Johnny

Cast: Betty Buckley; Sam Freed; Bill LaVallee; Priscilla Lopez; Barry Michlin

Notes: Some sources list run as 477 performances. [1] Added for revival of 7/31/85.

4636 • WHAT'S GOING ON

OPENED: 1915
Musical

Songs: Girl You Left Behind (C: Jean Schwartz; L: William Jerome)

Notes: No other information available.

4637 • WHAT'S IN A NAME?

OPENED: 03/19/1920 Theatre: Maxine Elliott's
Musical Broadway: 87

Composer: Milton Ager
Lyricist: John Murray Anderson; Anna Wynne O'Ryan [2]; Jack Yellen
Librettist: John Murray Anderson
Producer: John Murray Anderson

Choreographer: Michio Ito; **Costumes:** Robert E. Locher; Kay Turner; **Musical Director:** Augustus Barratt; **Orchestrations:** Maurice DePackh; Arthur Lange; **Set Design:** James Reynolds

Songs: In Fair Japan; In the Year of Fifty-Fifty [1]; Jewels of Pandora, The; My Bridal Veil; Rap-Tap-a-Tap; Strike; That Reminiscent Melody; Theatrical Blues, The; Valley of Dreams, The; What's in a Name? (Love Is Always Love); Without Kissing Love Isn't Love; Young Man's Fancy, A (Music Box Song)

Cast: James J. Corbett; Marie Gaspar; Billy B. Van; Herb Williams

Notes: [1] Sheet music only. [2] Not credited copyright records.

4638 • WHAT'S THE ODDS?

Notes: *See HONEYDEW.*

4639 • WHAT'S THE RUSH

OPENED: 1954

Composer: Charles Strouse
Lyricist: Lee Adams

Songs: Conversation; Happy Hollywood; Heart of a Girl, The; Let's Fly Away; Right Kind of Love (from the Wrong Kind of Guy); Romantic Night; Sphinx Won't Tell, The; Tame Me; To Get Us All Together; What's the Rush; When You Grow Up

Notes: No other information available. Might have been produced at Green Mansions resort.

4640 • WHAT'S UP?

OPENED: 11/11/1943 Theatre: National
Revue Broadway: 63

Composer: Frederick Loewe
Lyricist: Alan Jay Lerner
Librettist: Alan Jay Lerner; Arthur Pierson
Producer: Mark Warnow
Director: George Balanchine; Robert H. Gordon

Choreographer: George Balanchine; **Costumes:** Grace Huston; **Musical Director:** Will Irwin; **Orchestrations:** Van Cleave; **Set Design:** Boris Aronson; **Vocal Arranger:** Bobby Tucker

Songs: From the Chimney to the Cellar; Girl is Like a Book, A; How Fly Times; Ill-Tempered Clavichord, The; Joshua; Miss Langley's School for Girls; My Last Love; Three Girls in a Boat; You Wash and I'll Dry; You've Got a Hold on Me

Cast: Larry Douglas; Lynn Gardner; Rodney McLennan; Jimmy Savo

4641 • WHEN CLAUDIA SMILES (1913)

OPENED: 04/13/1913 Theatre: Illinois
Musical Chicago

Composer: Jean Schwartz
Lyricist: William Jerome
Librettist: Leo Ditrichstein

Notes: This show was revised for Broadway the following year. *See also WHEN CLAUDIA SMILES (1914).*

4642 • WHEN CLAUDIA SMILES (1914)

OPENED: 02/02/1914 Theatre: 39th St.
Play Broadway: 56

Composer: Jean Schwartz
Lyricist: Anne Caldwell
Author: Anne Caldwell
Producer: Frederic McKay
Director: Charles Winninger

Source: WHEN CLAUDIA SMILES (Musical: Leo Ditrichstein; William Jerome; Jean Schwartz)

Songs: Boys All Fall for Me, The [1]; Boys, Boys, Boys; Dear Old Dinah (C: Henry Marshall; L: Stanley Murphy); Everybody Sometime Must Love Someone (C: Dave Stamper; L: Gene Buck); Flower Garden Ball, The (L: William Jerome); Grand Old Life; He's a Dear Old Pet [2] (L: William Jerome); If They'd Only Move Old Ireland Over Here; I've Got Everything I Want but You; Let Us Dance the Boston [1] (C/L: George A. Spink); Ssh! You'll Waken Mr. Doyle (C: John Golden; L: Jerome Kern; E.W. Rogers); Why Is the Ocean So Near the Shore? (C: Clarence Jones; L: Arthur Weinberg); You're My Boy

Cast: Harry Conor; Blanche Ring; Charles Winninger

Notes: *See also WHEN CLAUDIA SMILES (1913)*, an earlier version of this show. [1] Out Albany 12/29/13. [2] Sheet music only.

4643 • WHEN DO THE WORDS COME TRUE

OPENED: 1971
Musical — Closed out of town

Composer: John Meyer
Lyricist: John Meyer
Librettist: John Meyer
Producer: Madeline Gilford; Gerard Oestreicher
Director: Edward Earle

Choreographer: Patti Karr; **Lighting Designer:** Don Yopp; **Musical Director:** Richard J. Leonard; **Orchestrations:** Richard J. Leonard; **Set Design:** Louis John Dezserian; **Vocal Arranger:** Richard J. Leonard

Songs: After the Holidays; Be Good to Her; But Now; Cable Car; Colder By the Hour (C: Jacques Urbont); First Thing About You, The; From Where I Stand; His Room; I'm All Yours; See You in San Diego; When Do the Word Come True; World Outside, The

Cast: David Brooks; Gloria De Haven; Jamie Donnelly; Edward Earle; Bill Gerber; Patti Karr

Notes: Closed at Bucks County Playhouse, Pennsylvania.

4644 • WHEN DREAMS COME TRUE

OPENED: 08/18/1913 — Theatre: Lyric
Musical — Broadway: 64

Composer: Silvio Hein
Lyricist: Philip Bartholomae
Librettist: Philip Bartholomae
Producer: Philip Bartholomae
Director: Frank Smithson

Choreographer: Joseph Santley

Songs: America; Beautiful Bounding Sea [2]; Boy with the Violin, The; Come Along to the Movies; Come On, All Together [2]; Dear World; Dream Waltz; Giddy Up, Giddy Up, Dearie; It's Great to Be a Wonderful Detective; Laughing Water Ripple; Love Is Such a Funny Little Feeling; Love with a Capital L [3]; Minnie, Ha Ha; O.K. Two Step; There Ain't No Harm in What You Do; Town That Grows Where the Hudson Flows, The; Waltz Aviation [3]; Wedding Rehearsal; When Dreams Come True (C: Silvio Hein; Roy Webb); When the Clock Strikes One; Who's the Little Girl?; Y-O-U, Dear, Y-O-U; You're Here and I'm Here [1] (C: Jerome Kern; L: Harry B. Smith)

Cast: Joseph Santley; Amelia Summerville; May Vokes; Anna Wheaton

Notes: [1] Originally in THE LAUGHING HUSBAND. [2] Out Chicago 4/3/13. [3] Out San Antonio.

4645 • WHEN HELL FREEZES OVER I'LL SKATE

OPENED: 07/22/1983
Revue — Closed out of town

Composer: Cleavant Derricks; Clinton Derricks-Carroll
Lyricist: Linda Michelle Baron; Cleavant Derricks; Clinton Derricks-Carroll
Producer: Cocoanut Grove Playhouse; Florida Arts Council
Director: Vinnette Carroll

Choreographer: Michele Simmons; **Costumes:** William Schroder; **Dance Arranger:** George Broderick; **Lighting Designer:** Pat Simmons; **Musical Director:** George Broderick; **Orchestrations:** George Broderick; **Set Design:**

William Schroder; **Vocal Arranger:** Cleavant Derricks

Songs: Cleo's Theme; Diet; Elijah Rock; Gather to the Water; Harlem Beat; I Wanna Get to You; I'm Going Through a Change; Just Dissatisfied; Liza Jane; Lord, Hear Your Child A-Callin'; Lost in the Wilderness; Medley of Negro Spirituals; Not in the Mood for Blues; Survive; Travellin'; You Can't Get By Me

Cast: Lynne Clifton-Allen; Nora Cole; Sheila Ellis; Jamil K. Garland; L. Michael Gray; Trina Thomas

4646 • WHEN JOHNNY COMES MARCHING HOME

OPENED: 12/16/1902 Theatre: New York
Musical Broadway: 71

Composer: Julian Edwards
Lyricist: Stanislaus Stange
Librettist: Stanislaus Stange
Producer: Whitney Opera Company
Director: A.M. Holbrook

Costumes: Caroline Seidle; **Musical Director:** William E. MacQuinn

Songs: Ariella [3]; But They Didn't; Did He, No He Didn't [2]; Drums, The; Fairyland; Flag of My Country; Good Day, Yankees!; I Could Waltz on Forever; I Was Quite Upset [3]; I'm So Upset [2]; Just Marry the Man and Be Merry; Katie, My Southern Rose; Love's Night [1]; My Honeysuckle Girl [4]; My Own United States; Of the Stars and Stripes I Am Dreaming [2]; Ootsey Tootsey [2]; Opening Chorus; Sing, Sing, Darkies, Sing; Sir Frog and Mistress Toad [3]; Spring, Sweet Spring; Swanee River, The; 'Twas Down in the Garden of Eden; What's in a Name [3]; When Our Lips In Kisses Met; While You're Thinking; Who Knows?; Years Touch Not the Heart

Cast: Thelma Fair; Julia Gifford; Maude Lambert; Homer Lind; Albert McGuckin; William G. Stewart

Notes: [1] May be "Love's Light." [2] Cut out of town. [3] Sheet music only. [4] Also referred to as "My Honeysuckle Gal."

4647 • WHEN LOVE IS YOUNG

OPENED: 10/28/1913 Theatre: Cort
Musical Chicago

Composer: William Schroeder
Lyricist: William Cary Duncan
Librettist: Rida Johnson Young

Cast: Joe Hyams; Leila McIntyre

Notes: A sequel to THE GIRL OF MY DREAMS.

4648 • WHEN SUMMER COMES

OPENED: 02/15/1925
Musical Closed out of town

Composer: A. Baldwin Sloane
Lyricist: Jack Arnold
Librettist: Jack Arnold
Producer: Theodore J. Hammerstein; Jerome Quinn
Director: Walter Wilson

Choreographer: Raymond Midgley; **Musical Director:** Albert Hurley

Songs: Business Man, A; Carry Me Back; Geography; I Had a Sweet, Sweet Mamma (C/L: Ruby Cowan); I've Lost My Head Over You (C/L: Asher; Razoff); I'm Lonesome for Someone Like You; Lonesome; Main Street; Papa; Peaches; Ring, Ring, Ring; Virginia Clay; Voodoo Hagamin & Hamid; Wedding Ring; What Am I Going to Say; When Summer Comes; When Summer Comes; Whoa!; You're in Love

Cast: James Barton; Nellie Fillmore; Jack McGowan; Ray Raymond

Notes: Poli's Theatre, Washington, D.C. and Easton, Pa. 2/14/25.

4649 • WHEN SWEET SIXTEEN

OPENED: 09/14/1911 Theatre: Daly's
Musical Broadway: 12

Composer: Victor Herbert
Lyricist: George V. Hobart
Librettist: George V. Hobart
Producer: Everall & Wallach Company
Director: R.H. Burnside; George V. Hobart

Musical Director: Louis F. Gottschalk; **Orchestrations:** Victor Herbert; **Set Design:** Bernard MacDonald

Songs: Dear Old Fairyland; Fairies' Revel; Frolic of the Fairies [1]; Golden Long Ago, The; Ha! Ha!

Ha! [1]; Has Cupid Laid in Wait for You; Hearts Are Trumps; Honey Love; I Love to Read the Papers in the Morning [1]; I Want to Be a Wild, WIld Rose (The Wild Rose); I'm Not a Bit Superstitious [1]; In Fairyland; In So-So Society [1]; In the Golden Long Ago; Island of Sweet Sixteen [1]; It's Always Going to Be that Way; Lanciers (Finale Ultimo) [1]; Laughs; Little Fifi; Mah Honey Love; Man's a Man for A' That, A; Mary Drew [1]; My Toast to You; Oh! Mary You're Contrary [1]; Oh, the Things They Put in the Papers Now-a- Days [1]; Oh, Those Boys!; Opening; People Will Talk, You Know; Pourquoi?; (There's None So Sweet As) Rosalind; Since Papa Becomes a Billionaire [1]; That's Boys Your Boys [1]; There Once Was a Princess; There's Money in Graft (There's a Raft of Money in Graft! Graft! Graft!); They Follow Me Everywhere; While the Big Old World Rolls Round [1]; Wild Rose, The

Cast: Josie Intropodi; William Norris; Roy Purviance

Notes: [1] ASCAP/Library of Congress only.

4650 • WHEN WE WERE FORTY-ONE

OPENED: 06/12/1905 Theatre: New York Roof
Musical Broadway: 66

Composer: Gus Edwards
Lyricist: Robert B. Smith
Librettist: Robert B. Smith
Director: Edward E. Rice

Choreographer: Gertrude Hoffman; Joseph Smith; **Musical Director:** Robert Hood Bowers

Songs: Advantage of a College Education, The; Brother Masons (C: Gertrude Hoffman; L: Vincent Bryan); Goddess of Rector's, The; I Am a Regular Romeo; Kindly Pass the Chloroform Along (C: Gertrude Hoffman; L: Vincent Bryan); Maiden of the Wild and Woolly West [2]; Man That Leads the Band Leads the Army, The; Meet Me Under the Wysteria; Simple Simon [2]; Sweet Kitty Kellairs [1]; Up and Down the Boardwalk; Write to Marian the Maid

Cast: Harry Bulger; Emma Carus; LaBelle Dazie; Elsie Janis; John McVeigh; Harry Meehan; Charles H. Prince

Notes: A parody of WHEN WE WERE TWENTY-ONE. Sometimes referred to as WHEN WE ARE FORTY-ONE. [1] A parody on the play SWEET KITTY BELLAIRS. [2] ASCAP/Library of Congress only.

4651 • WHEN YOU SMILE

OPENED: 10/25/1925 Theatre: National
Musical Broadway: 49

Composer: Tom Johnstone
Lyricist: Phil Cook
Librettist: Jack Alicoate; Tom Johnstone
Producer: James P. Beury
Director: Oscar Eagle

Choreographer: Raymond Midgley; **Musical Director:** F. Wheeler Wadsworth

Songs: All Work and No Play; Buy an Extra; Gee, We Get Along; June; Keep Building Your Castles; Keep Them Guessing; Let's Dance and Make Up; Let's Have a Good Time; Naughty Eyes; Oh, What a Girl; One Little Girl; She Loves Me; Spanish Moon; When You Smile; Wonderful Rhythm; Wonderful Yesterday

Cast: Imogene Coca; Phil Cook; Carol Joyce; Philip Lord; Ray Raymond; Jack Whiting

4652 • WHERE'S CHARLEY?

OPENED: 10/11/1948 Theatre: St. James
Musical Broadway: 792

Composer: Frank Loesser
Lyricist: Frank Loesser
Librettist: George Abbott
Producer: Cy Feuer; Ernest H. Martin; Gwen Rickard
Director: George Abbott

Source: CHARLEY'S AUNT (Play: Brandon Thomas); **Choreographer:** George Balanchine; Fred Danielli; **Costumes:** David Ffolkes; **Musical Director:** Max Goberman; **Orchestrations:** Philip J. Lang; Ted Royal; Hans Spialek; **Set Design:** David Ffolkes; **Vocal Arranger:** Garry Dolin

Songs: Argument, The [1]; At the Red Rose Cotillion; Bee, The [1]; Better Get Out of Here; Don't Introduce Me to That Angel [2]; Gossips, The; Lovelier Than Ever; Make a Miracle; My Darling, My Darling; New Ashmolean Marching

Society and Students Conservatory Band, The; Once in Love with Amy; Pernambuco; Saunter Away [1]; Serenade with Asides; Train That Brought You to Town, The [1]; Where's Charley?; Woman in His Room, A; Years Before Us, The; Your Own College Band [1]

Cast: Ray Bolger; Paul England; Jane Lawrence; Allyn Ann McLerie; Doretta Morrow; Byron Palmer

Notes: [1] Cut prior to opening. [2] Cut prior to opening. Later in stage version of HANS CHRISTIAN ANDERSEN (titled HANS ANDERSEN) under the name "Jenny Kissed Me."

4653 • WHERE'S MAMIE?

Notes: *See FIRST LADY SUITE.*

4654 • WHIRL OF NEW YORK, THE

OPENED: 06/13/1921 Theatre: Winter Garden
Musical Broadway: 124

Composer: Al Goodman; Lew Pollack
Lyricist: Sidney D. Mitchell; Lew Morton; Edgar Smith
Librettist: Lew Morton; Edgar Smith
Producer: J.J. Shubert; Lee Shubert
Director: Lew Morton

Source: BELLE OF NEW YORK, THE (Musical: Leo Edwards; Gustave Kerker); **Choreographer:** Allan K. Foster; **Musical Director:** Al Goodman; **Set Design:** Watson Barratt

Songs: Belle of New York, The; Chain Dance; Chinese New Year's Ballet; Cora Angelique (Musical Comedy Queen) (The Queen of Musical Comedy) (C: Lew Pollack; L: Sidney D. Mitchell); Dance, Dance, Dance; Dancing Fools; Follow On; From Far Cohoes; Gee, I Wish I Had a Girl; I Do So There!; I Know That I'm in Love (C: Lew Pollack; L: Sidney D. Mitchell); Just One Good Time; La Belle Parisienne; Little Baby; Mandalay; Molly, Molly; Molly on the Trolley; Opening Chorus; Pastry Cooks, The [2]; Purity Brigadiers, The; Spirit of the Chinese Vase, The; Take Her Down to Coney and Give Her the Air [1] (C/L: Lew Pollack; Ed Rose; Richard A. Whiting); Teach Me How to Kiss; Tiffin, Tiffin; When We Are Married; Whistling

Cast: Mlle. Adelaide; Charles Dale; Louis Mann; J. Harold Murray; John T. Murray; Joe Smith

Notes: [1] Added after opening. [2] Out Boston 10/26/21.

4655 • WHIRL OF SOCIETY, THE

OPENED: 03/05/1912 Theatre: Winter Garden
Musical Broadway: 136

Composer: Louis A. Hirsch
Lyricist: Harold Atteridge
Librettist: Harrison Rhodes
Producer: Winter Garden Company

Choreographer: William J. Wilson; **Costumes:** Melville Ellis; **Musical Director:** Samuel Lehman; **Set Design:** H. Robert Law

Songs: Billy Ballou (C/L: Will Hardy); Billy's Melody [1] (C: Joe Cooper; L: L. Wolfe Gilbert); Blow on Your Piccolo; Cinderella Waltz [1]; Come Back to Me; Cotillion, The; Fol-De-Rol-Dol-Doi (C: Jean Schwartz; L: Edward Madden); Four O'Clock Tea; Gaby Glide, The [1] (C: Louis A. Hirsch; L: Harry Pilcer); Ghost of the Violin [5] (C: Ted Snyder; L: Bert Kalmar); Hard Luck in Society [1]; Here Comes the Bride [5]; Hitchy-Koo [5] (C: Lewis F. Muir; L: Maurice Abrahams; L. Wolfe Gilbert); How Do You Do, Miss Ragtime (C/L: Louis A. Hirsch); How Do You Know?; Hypnotizing Man; I Want Something New to Play With; I Want to Be in Dixie [4] (C: Ted Snyder; L: Irving Berlin); I'm Going Back to Dixie; I'm Saving My Kisses; Lead Me to That Beautiful Band [5]; Meet Me in Peacock Alley [5]; My Sumuran Girl (C: Louis A. Hirsch; L: Al Jolson); Oh, Mister Dream Man [1]; On the Mississippi [3] (C: Harry Carroll; Arthur Fields; L: Ballard Macdonald); Opening Chorus; Oriental Rose [1] (C/L: Louis A. Hirsch); Ragtime Sextette [2] (C/L: Irving Berlin; Music Based On: Gaetano Donizetti); Ragtime Soldier Man [5] (C/L: Irving Berlin); Row, Row, Row [5] (C: James V. Monaco; L: William Jerome); Snap Your Fingers [1] (C: Harry Von Tilzer; L: William Jerome); That Society Bear [1] (C/L: Irving Berlin); Villain Still Pursued Her, The (C: Harry Von Tilzer; L: William Jerome); Which Shall I Choose

Cast: Barney Bernard; Gaby Deslys; Melville Ellis; Ernest Hare; Al Jolson; Stella Mayhew; Blossom Seeley; Billie Taylor; George White

Notes: Part one was titled THE WHIRL OF SOCIETY, part two titled A NIGHT WITH THE PIERROTS, part three titled THE CAPTIVE (pantomime). [1] Sheet music only. [2] Parody of "Chi Mi Frena" from LUCIA DI LAMMERMOOR by Donizetti. Also in HANKY-PANKY as "Lucia Sextette Burlesqe." [3] Also in HANKY-PANKY. [4] Also in HULLO, RAGTIME. [5] Not in programs.

4656 • WHIRL OF THE TOWN, THE

OPENED: 1921
Musical Closed out of town

Songs: Any Night on Old Broadway (L: Harold Atteridge); How'd You Like to Put Your Head Upon My Pillow (C: Jean Schwartz; L: Alfred Bryan); Trial of Shimmy Mae, The

Cast: Georgie Price; Mae West

Notes: *See TATTLE TALES*, an earlier version of this show. *See also THE MIMIC WORLD OF 1921*, a later version.

4657 • WHIRL OF THE WORLD, THE

OPENED: 01/10/1914 Theatre: Winter Garden
Revue Broadway: 161

Composer: Sigmund Romberg
Lyricist: Harold Atteridge
Librettist: Harold Atteridge
Producer: Winter Garden Company
Director: William J. Wilson

Costumes: Melville Ellis

Songs: All Aboard; Amber Club, The; American Maxixe, The; Broadway in Paree, A (C/L: Henry Lehman); College Boy, A; Come On In the Dancing's Fine; Dance Eccentric [1]; Dance Extraordinaire [1]; Dance of the Fortune Wheel, The; Dancing Romeo, A; Early Hours of the Morn; Everybody Means It When They Say Good-Bye; Good-Bye, London Town; Hallo! Little Miss U.S.A. (C/L: Harry Gifford; Fred Godfrey); How Do You Do-Good Bye; I'll Come Back to You; Life's a Dress Parade; Lovely Trip, A; My Cleopatra Girl; Noble Cause of Art, The; Nobody Was in Love with Me; Oh, Allah; Pavlova Gavotte, The; Ragtime Arabian Nights [2]; Ragtime Pinafore (C/L: Henry Lehman); Twentieth Century Rag (C/L: Henry Lehman); Visit, The; We Forgot the Number of the House; What'll; Whirl of the Opera, The; Whirl of the World, The; Why Don't You Get a Girl Like Me

Cast: Roszika Dolly; Bernard Granville; Ralph Herz; Eugene Howard; Willie Howard; Walter C. Kelly; Lillian Lorraine

Notes: [1] Sheet music only. [2] One source credited the song to Henry Lehman

4658 • WHIRL-I-GIG

OPENED: 09/21/1899 Theatre: Weber & Fields' Music Hall
Musical Broadway: 264

Composer: John Stromberg
Lyricist: Harry B. Smith
Librettist: Edgar Smith
Producer: Lew Fields; Joseph Weber

Cast: Peter F. Dailey; Lew Fields; John T. Kelly; Bonnie Maginn; Charles J. Ross; Lillian Russell; David Warfield; Joseph Weber

Notes: This evening included THE GIRL FROM MARTIN'S (a burlesque of THE GIRL FROM MAXIM'S), SAPOLIO (a burlesque of SAPPHO) and THE OTHER WAY (a burlesque of THE ONLY WAY).

4659 • WHISPERS ON THE WIND

OPENED: 06/03/1970 Theatre: Theatre de Lys
Musical Off-Broadway: 9

Composer: Lor Crane
Lyricist: John B. Kuntz
Librettist: John B. Kuntz
Producer: Mitchell Fink; Bruce W. Paltrow
Director: Burt Brinckerhoff

Costumes: Joseph G. Aulisi; **Lighting Designer:** David F. Segal; **Musical Director:** Jack Holmes; **Orchestrations:** Arthur Rubenstein; **Set Design:** David F. Segal

Songs: Apples and Raisins; Carmen Vincenzo; Children's Games; Children's Sake, The [1]; Down the Fields [1]; In the Mind's Eye [1]; Is There a City?; It Won't Be Long; Midwestern Summer;

Miss Cadwallader; Neighbors; Prove I'm Really Here; Strawberries; Then in the Middle [1]; Things Are Going Nicely; Upstairs- Downstairs; Very First Girl, The [1]; Welcome, Little One; Whispers on the Wind; Why and Because

Cast: R.G. Brown; David Cryer; Nancy Dussault; Patrick Fox; Mary Louise Wilson

Notes: [1] Cut prior to opening.

4660 • WHISTLING WIZARD AND THE SULTAN OF TUFFET, THE

OPENED: 10/17/1973 Theatre: Bil Baird
Musical Off-Broadway: 36

Composer: Bil Baird; Alan Stern
Lyricist: Bil Baird; Alan Stern
Librettist: Alan Stern
Producer: American Puppet Arts Coun.; Bil Baird
Director: Frank Sullivan; Lee Theodore

Source: WHISTLING WIZARD, THE (Television Program: Bil Baird); **Lighting Designer:** Peggy Clark; **Musical Director:** Alvy West

Puppeteer: Peter Baird; Olga Felgemacher; Jonathan E. Freeman; John O'Malley; Sean O'Malley; Bill Tost; Byron Whiting

Notes: Based on the classic TV series.

4661 • WHITE BIRDS

OPENED: 05/31/1927 Theatre: His Majesty's
Revue London: 63

Composer: George W. Meyer
Lyricist: George W. Meyer
Librettist: Lew Leslie
Producer: Lew Leslie

Arrangements: Will Vodery; **Costumes:** Val St. Cyr; **Musical Director:** Jones; **Set Design:** John Bull

Songs: Cuddle Up; Da Da Da (The Da Da Strain); Flower of Spain; I've Got a Wonderful Girl; Sing a Little Love Song; What's to Become of the Children (C/L: Noel Coward)

Cast: Florence Brady; Maurice Chevalier; Jose Collins; Anton Dolin; Maisie Gay; Edward Lowry; Billy Mayerl; Carl Randall; Ninette de Valois

Notes: No program available.

4662 • WHITE CAT, THE

OPENED: 11/02/1905 Theatre: New Amsterdam
Musical Broadway: 46

Composer: Ludwig Englander
Lyricist: Harry B. Smith
Librettist: Harry B. Smith
Producer: Klaw & Erlanger
Director: Herbert Gresham; Ned Wayburn

Source: WHITE CAT, THE (Musical: Arthur Collins; J. Hickory Wood); **Musical Director:** Frederic Solomon; **Set Design:** Ernest D'Auban

Songs: Antonio (C: Jean Schwartz; L: William Jerome); Catland; Cherries Ripe; Court Is Like a Chessboard, A; Dance Noveau (C: Frederic Solomon); Down the Line with Arabella (C: Jean Schwartz; L: William Jerome); Get the Money (C: Jean Schwartz; L: William Jerome); Girls and Boys; Golden Net, The; Goodbye, Maggie Doyle (C: Jean Schwartz; L: William Jerome); Graft; Henny Klein (C: Jean Schwartz; L: William Jerome); Highland Mary (C: Jean Schwartz; L: William Jerome); Kisses [1] (C: Jean Schwartz; L: William Jerome); Let the Trumpets Sound; Meet Me on the Fence Tonight (C: Jean Schwartz; L: William Jerome); My Lady of Japan (C: Jean Schwartz; L: William Jerome); Penang-Ourang- Outang, The (C/L: Philip Braham); Sailing Away; Where Broadway Meets Fifth Avenue (C/L: Keith; John Kemble); Year and a Day, A

Cast: Edgar Atchinson-Ely; Herbert Corthell; William T. Hodge; Maude Lambert; Helen Lathrop

Notes: [1] Sheet music only.

4663 • WHITE CHRYSANTHEMUM, THE

OPENED: 08/31/1905 Theatre: Criterion
Musical London: 179

Composer: Howard Talbot
Lyricist: Arthur Anderson
Librettist: Arthur Anderson; Leedham Bantock
Producer: Frank Curzon
Director: Austen Hurgon

Costumes: Karl; **Musical Director:** Howard Talbot; **Set Design:** W.T. Hemsley

Songs: Bill's a Liar (C: Jerome Kern; L: Paul West); Butterfly and the Flower, The; I Just Couldn't Do Without You (C: Jerome Kern; L: Paul West); Latest News, The; Love of a Maid of a Man, The; Mammy's Pickaninny; O Wandering Breeze; Only Pebble on the Beach, The; You Can't Please Everybody Always

Cast: Rutland Barrington; Marie George; Lawrence Grossmith; Isabel Jay; Gracie Leigh; Henry A. Lytton; R. Morand

Notes: No program available.

4664 • WHITE EAGLE, THE

OPENED: 12/26/1927 Theatre: Casino
Musical Broadway: 48

Composer: Rudolf Friml
Lyricist: Brian Hooker
Librettist: Brian Hooker; W.H. Post
Producer: Russell Janney
Director: Richard Boleslavsky

Source: SQUAW MAN, THE (Play: Edwin Milton Royle)

Songs: Alone (My Lover); Bad Man Number; Dance, Dance, Dance; Gather the Rose; Give Me One Hour [1]; Home for You, A; Hymn to the Sun [1]; Indian Ceremonial Music [1]; Indian Lullaby; Interlude [1]; My Heaven with You; Regimental Song; Silver Wing [1]; Smile, Darn You, Smile; Thunder Dance [1]; Winona

Cast: Lawrence D'Orsay; Blanche Fleming; Forrest Huff; Marion Keeler; Allan Prior; Fred Tilden

Notes: [1] ASCAP/Library of Congress only.

4665 • WHITE FLAME, THE

OPENED: 1939
Musical Unproduced

Composer: Vernon Duke
Lyricist: Charles O. Locke

Songs: Bend Your Knee and Tie My Shoe; Bonjour Goodbye; Dance of the Waitresses; I Cling to You; Lisette; Shadow of Love (L: Ted Fetter; Charles O. Locke); Sport of Kings, The

4666 • WHITE HEN, THE

OPENED: 02/16/1907 Theatre: Casino
Musical Broadway: 94

Composer: Gustave Kerker
Lyricist: Paul West
Librettist: Roderic C. Penfield
Producer: Lee Shubert; Sam S. Shubert
Director: J.C. Huffman; Julian Mitchell

Songs: At Last We're Alone, Dear; Edelweiss [1]; Everything Is Higher Nowadays; Fishing; Follow, Follow, Follow; Hands Off [1]; I'm Married Now; Keep Cool; Man Is Only a Man, A; Mountain Maids; Nothing More — Excepting You [1]; Prima Donna, The; Printemps; Smile; Swartz and Weiss [1]; That's Why the Danube Was Blue; Thrush and the Star, The; Very Well Then; Waiting for the Ride

Cast: Lotta Faust; Louise Gunning; Ralph Herz; Louis Mann

Notes: Also known as THE GIRL FROM VIENNA. [1] Sheet music only.

4667 • WHITE HORSE INN

OPENED: 10/01/1936 Theatre: Center
Musical Broadway: 223

Composer: Ralph Benatzky
Lyricist: Irving Caesar
Librettist: David Freedman; Harry Graham
Producer: Laurence Rivers
Director: Erik Charell

Source: IM WEISSEN ROSSL (Operetta: Erik Charell; Robert Gilbert; Hans Muller); **Source:** UNKNOWN (Play: Oskar Blumenthal; Gustave Kadelburg); **Choreographer:** Max Rivers; **Costumes:** Irene Sharaff; **Musical Director:** Victor Baravalle; **Orchestrations:** Hans Spialek; **Set Design:** Ernest Stern

Songs: Alpine Symphony (inst.) (C: Adam Gelbtrunk); Arrival of Steamboat; Arrival of Tourists; Blue Eyes (C: Robert Stolz); Cowshed Rhapsody [2] (C: Adam Gelbtrunk); Good-Bye, Au Revoir, Auf Wiedersehen [1] (C: Eric Coates); High Up in the Hills; I Cannot Live Without

Your Love; I Would Love to Have You Love Me (C: Gerald Marks; L: Irving Caesar; Sammy Lerner); In a Little Swiss Chalet (C: Will Irwin; L: Norman Zeno); Leave It to Katrina (C: Jara Benes); Market Day in the Village; Rain Finale; Serenade to the Emperor; Spade Ballet; Waltz of Love, The (C: Richard Fall); We Prize Most the Things We Miss; Welcome to the Landing Stage; White Horse Inn; White Sails [2] (C: Vivian Ellis)

Cast: Kitty Carlisle; Alfred Drake; William Gaxton; Frederick Graham; Robert Halliday; Billy House; Arnold Korff; Melissa Mason; Oscar "Rags" Ragland; Carol Stone; Buster West

Notes: [1] Adapted from Coates' "Knightsbridge March." [2] ASCAP/Library of Congress only.

4668 • WHITE LIGHTS

OPENED: 10/11/1927 Theatre: Ritz
Musical Broadway: 31

Composer: J. Fred Coots
Lyricist: Al Dubin
Librettist: Leo Donnelly; Paul Gerard Smith
Producer: James LaPenna

Choreographer: Walter Brooks; Ray Perez; **Musical Director:** T.L. Jones; **Orchestrations:** Louis Katzman

Songs: Beautiful Show Girls [1]; Better Times Are Coming (C: Jimmie Steiger; L: Dolph Singer); Deceiving Blue Bird; Don't Throw Me Down; Eyeful of You; I'll Keep on Dreaming of You (C: J. Fred Coots; Walter S. Roele); Romany Rover; Sitting in the Sun [1]; Some Other Day; Tappin' the Toe; We Are the Girls in the Chorus; White Lights

Cast: Sam Ash; Rosalie Claire; Leo Donnelly; Florence Parker; Tammany Young

Notes: Titled MITZI originally. [1] Out Stamford 08/12/27.

4669 • WHITE LILACS

OPENED: 09/10/1928 Theatre: Shubert
Musical Broadway: 138

Music Based On: Frederic Chopin
Composer: Karl Hajos
Lyricist: J. Keirn Brennan
Librettist: Harry B. Smith
Producer: Messrs. Shubert
Director: George Marion

Source: CHOPIN (Musical: Istvan Bertha; Jeno Farago); **Choreographer:** Vaughn Godfrey; **Musical Director:** Pierre de Reeder; **Set Design:** Rollo Wayne

Songs: Adorable You (C: Maurie Rubens; L: David Goldberg); Don't Go Too Far Girls; Far Away and Long Ago; I Love Love; I Love You and I Adore You; Know When to Smile; Melodies Within My Heart; Music Call, The; Our Castle of Love (C: Sammy Timberg); Star in the Twilight; White Lilacs; Words, Music, Cash

Cast: DeWolf Hopper; Odette Myrtil; Guy Robertson

Notes: Later known as THE CHARMER.

4670 • WHITE PLUME, THE

OPENED: 12/26/1939
Musical Closed out of town

Composer: Samuel D. Pokrass
Lyricist: Charles O. Locke
Librettist: Charles O. Locke
Producer: Messrs. Shubert
Director: George Houston; Charles O. Locke

Source: CYRANO DE BERGERAC (Play: Edmond Rostand); **Choreographer:** Natalie Kamarova; **Costumes:** Ernest Schrapps; **Set Design:** Watson Barratt

Songs: Ballade of the Duel; Bonjour Goodbye (C: Vernon Duke); Cyrano; Dance of the Waitresses (C: Vernon Duke); I Cling to You (C: Vernon Duke); Letter Duet; Lisette; Little Musketeer; Mamselle; Men of Jaloux; Minuette; My Nose; Pavanne; Play's the Thing, The; Shadow of Love (C: Vernon Duke; L: Ted Fetter; Charles O. Locke); Song of the Balcony; Song of the Gascon Cadets; Sweets to the Sweet; Tell Me of Love; What My Lips Can Never Say; World Is Young, The

Cast: Robert Chisholm; Hal Forde; Truman Gaige; George Houston; Eric Mattson; Ruby Mercer; Cornel Wilde

Notes: This show was first produced in 11/4/32 as CYRANO DE BERGERAC. It was retitled

ROXANNE before closing. Seven years later the Shuberts gave it another go as THE WHITE PLUME. This production later changed its name to A VAGABOND HERO, but it too closed before coming to New York.

4671 • WHITE SISTER, THE (1909)

OPENED: 09/27/1909 Theatre: Daly's
Play Broadway: 48

Composer: William Furst
Author: Marion Crawford; Walter Hackett
Director: Hugh Ford

Source: WHITE SISTER, THE (Novel: Marion Crawford); **Musical Director:** George Wiseman; **Set Design:** Frank Gates; E.A. Morange

Cast: Viola Allen; William Farnum; James O'Neill

Notes: No songs listed in program.

4672 • WHITE SISTER, THE (1927)

OPENED: 05/17/1927 Theatre: Wallack's
Musical Broadway: 7

Composer: Clement Giglio
Lyricist: Clement Giglio
Librettist: Clement Giglio

Source: WHITE SISTER, THE (Novel: Marion Crawford); **Musical Director:** Chavalier Lovreiglo

Cast: Josie Jones; Eugene Scudder

Notes: No songs listed in program. Produced in Italian on 14th St. the previous year. It was such a success it was reopened uptown for one week in English.

4673 • WHO CARES?

OPENED: 07/08/1930 Theatre: 46th Street
Revue Broadway: 30

Composer: Percy Wenrich
Lyricist: Harry Clarke
Librettist: John Cantwell; Edward Clarke Lilley; Bertrand Robinson; Kenneth Webb
Producer: Satirists Inc.
Director: Edward Clarke Lilley; George Vivian

Choreographer: William Holbrook; **Musical Director:** Irvi ng Schloss; **Set Design:** Cirker & Robbins

Songs: Believe It or Not; Broadway; Dance of the Fan; Dixieland; Heldites, The; Hunt, The; Make My Bed Down in Dixieland; Opening Number; Sun Up; Tennis; Who Cares?

Cast: Florenz Ames; John Cherry; Margaret Dale; Arthur Hartley; William Holbrook; Don Lanning; Peggy O'Neill; Olive Olsen; Robert Pitkin; Ralph Riggs; Marjorie Seltzer; Templeton Brothers

4674 • WHO IS WHO

OPENED: 02/07/1898 Theatre: Third Avenue
Musical Broadway: 8

Composer: Joe Kelly; Charles A. Mason

Cast: Blanche Boyer; Joe Kelly; Charles A. Mason; Georgia Tompkins

Notes: No program available.

4675 • WHO TO LOVE

Notes: *See CRY FOR US ALL.*

4676 • WHO'S TOMMY, THE

OPENED: 04/22/1993 Theatre: St. James
Musical Broadway: 900

Composer: Peter Townshend
Additional Music: John Entwistle; Keith Moon
Lyricist: Peter Townshend
Additional Lyrics: John Entwistle; Keith Moon
Librettist: Des McAnuff; Peter Townshend
Producer: Dodger Productions; Kardana Productions; Pace Theatrical Group
Director: Des McAnuff

Source: TOMMY (Opera: Peter Townshend); **Choreographer:** Wayne Cilento; **Costumes:** David C. Woolard; **Lighting Designer:** Chris Parry; **Musical Director:** Joseph Church; **Orchestrations:** Steve Margoshes; **Set Design:** John Arnone

Songs: Acid Queen; Amazing Journey; Captain Walker; Christmas; Cousin Kevin; Do You Think It's Alright; Eyesight to the Blind; Fiddle About; Go to the Mirror; I Believe My Own Eyes; I'm Free; It's a Boy; Listening to You; Miracle Cure; Pinball Wizard; Sally Simpson; See Me, Feel Me; Sensation; Smash the Mirror; Sparks; There's a

Doctor; Tommy Can You Hear Me; Tommy's Holiday Camp; Twenty-One; We're Not Going to Take It; We've Won; Welcome

Cast: Anthony Barrile; Maria Calabrese; Michael Cerveris; Paul Kandel; Marcia Mitzman; Buddy Smith

4677 • WHO'S WHO

OPENED: 03/01/1938 Theatre: Hudson
Revue Broadway: 23

Librettist: Everett Marcy; Leonard Sillman
Producer: Elsa Maxwell
Director: Leonard Sillman

Costumes: Billy Livingston; **Musical Director:** Earl Busby; **Orchestrations:** Richard DuPage; **Set Design:** Mercedes

Songs: Croupier (C: Baldwin Bergersen; L: June Sillman); Dusky Debutante (C: Baldwin Bergersen; L: June Sillman); Girl with the Paint on Her Face, The (C/L: Irvin Graham); I Dance Alone (C/L: James Shelton); I Must Have a Dinner Coat (C/L: James Shelton); I Must Waltz (C: Baldwin Bergersen; L: Irvin Graham); If You Want a Kiss [1] (C: Paul McGrane; L: June Sillman); Intoxication Dance (inst.) (C: Jaroslav Jezek); It's You I Want (C: Paul McGrane; L: Al Stillman); Let Down Your Hair with a Bang (C: Baldwin Bergersen; L: June Sillman); Rinka Tinka Man (C: Lew Kessler; L: June Sillman); Skiing at Saks (C/L: Irvin Graham); Sunday Morning in June (C: Paul McGrane; L: Neville Fleeson); Train Time (C: Baldwin Bergersen; L: June Sillman); Who's Who (C: Baldwin Bergersen; L: June Sillman)

Cast: Joseph Beale; Jack Blair; June Blair; Imogene Coca; Lotte Goslar; Michael Loring; Chet O'Brien; Mort O'Brien; Oscar "Rags" Ragland; Edna Russell; James Shelton; June Sillman; Leone Sousa; Mildred Todd; Sonny Tufts; Johnnie Tunsill

Notes: [1] Sheet music only.

4678 • WHO'S WHO, BABY?

OPENED: 01/29/1968 Theatre: Players
Musical Off-Broadway: 16

Composer: Johnny Brandon
Lyricist: Johnny Brandon
Librettist: Gerald Frank
Producer: Edmund J. Ferdinand; Charlotte Schiff
Director: Marvin Gordon

Source: WHO'S WHO (Play: Guy Bolton; P.G. Wodehouse); **Choreographer:** Marvin Gordon; **Costumes:** Alan Kimmel; **Dance Arranger:** Leslie Harley; Clark McClellan; **Lighting Designer:** John Beaumont; **Musical Director:** Leslie Harley; **Orchestrations:** Clark McClellan; **Set Design:** Alan Kimmel

Songs: Come-Along-a-Me, Babe; Drums; Feminine-inity; How Do You Stop Loving Someone?; Island of Happiness; Me; Nobody to Cry To; Nothin's Gonna Change; Syncopatin'; That'll Be the Day; That's What's Happening, Baby; There Aren't Many Ladies in the Mile End Road; Voodoo

Cast: Frank Andre; Erik Howell; Gloria Kaye; Jacqueline Mayro

4679 • WHO'S WHOM?

OPENED: 02/04/1971
Revue

Composer: Ronald Lowden
Lyricist: Stephen de Baum
Librettist: Howard Jaffe; Mark Mancini; Sandy Schussel; Frederick Swartz
Producer: Stephen Goff; Stephen de Baum
Director: Bruce Montgomery

Arrangements: Roy Straiges; **Choreographer:** Walter Keenan; **Costumes:** Stephen Goff; Stephen de Baum; **Musical Director:** William Lessig; **Set Design:** Stephen Goff; Stephen de Baum

Songs: Billy the Kid; Cocktails with Conservatives; Fantasy (C/L: Laurence Tarica); Give 'Em Hell (C: Thomas Wilson); H.M.S. Goldilocks or the Lass That Loved a Mailman (C: Bruce Montgomery); Hemlines; It's Good to Have God on Your Side (C: Roy Straiges); Lib & Let Live; Pusher, The (C: Roy Straiges); Where Are the Rich Little Poor Little Children? (C/L: Thomas Wilson); Who's Whom? (C: Seth Kane)

Cast: Bob Myer; Billy Rosenberg; Laurence Tarica

Notes: Amateur show. Mask & Wig Club, University of Pennsylvania.

4680 • WHOLE DAMN FAMILY, THE

Notes: *See LIFTING THE LID.*

4681 • WHOOP-DE-DOO

OPENED: 09/24/1903 Theatre: Weber & Fields Music Hall
Musical Broadway: 151

Composer: William T. Francis
Lyricist: Edgar Smith
Librettist: Edgar Smith
Producer: Lew Fields; Joseph Weber
Director: Ben Teal

Set Design: John H. Young

Songs: Big Indian Chief (C: J. Rosamond Johnson; L: Bob Cole); Down By the Ocean Strand; Flowers of Dixieland, The (C: J. Rosamond Johnson; L: Bob Cole; Edgar Smith); Good Old U.S.A., The; Hoch! Hoch! Hoch!; If I Were an Actress; In Dreamland (L: Abeles); Looney Park; Maid of Timbuctoo (C: J. Rosamond Johnson; L: Bob Cole); My Goo-Goo Queen; On the Boulevard (C: A.M. Norden); Papa Wouldn't Care for That [1]; Paris on a Moonlight Night; Ragtime in Europe

Cast: Eva Allen; Marie Christie; Peter F. Dailey; Carter De Haven; Helen Du Heron; Lew Fields; John T. Kelly; Al Lewis; Jane Mandeville; Louis Mann; Maud Morris; Lillian Russell; Evie Stetson; Joe Weber

Notes: Second part of the show was called CATHERINE. [1] Out of town only.

4682 • WHOOP-UP

OPENED: 11/22/1958 Theatre: Shubert
Musical Broadway: 56

Composer: Moose Charlap
Lyricist: Norman Gimbel
Librettist: Dan Cushman; Cy Feuer; Ernest H. Martin
Producer: Cy Feuer; Ernest H. Martin
Director: Cy Feuer

Source: STAY AWAY, JOE (Story: Dan Cushman); **Choreographer:** Onna White; **Costumes:** Anna Hill Johnstone; **Dance Arranger:** Peter Matz; **Lighting Designer:** Jo Mielziner; **Musical Director:** Stanley Lebowsky; **Orchestrations:** Philip J. Lang; **Set Design:** Jo Mielziner

Songs: Best of What This Country's Got; Caress Me, Possess Me Perfume; Chief Rocky Boy; Flattery; Girl in His Arms, The; Glenda's Place; I Wash My Hands; I'm on My Way [1]; Love Eyes; Men; Montana; Never Before; Nobody Throw Those Bull; Quarrel-tet; She or Her; Sorry for Myself; 'Til the Big Fat Moon Falls Down; What I Mean to Say; When the Tall Man Talks

Cast: Paul Ford; Susan Johnson; Julienne Marie; Danny Meehan; Estelle Parsons; Sylvia Syms; Ralph Young

Notes: [1] Cut.

4683 • WHOOPEE

OPENED: 12/04/1928 Theatre: New Amsterdam
Musical Broadway: 407

Composer: Walter Donaldson
Lyricist: Gus Kahn
Librettist: William Anthony McGuire
Producer: Florenz Ziegfeld
Director: William Anthony McGuire

Source: NERVOUS WRECK, THE (Play: Owen Davis); **Choreographer:** Seymour Felix; Tamara Geva; **Costumes:** John Harkrider; **Musical Director:** Gus Salzer; **Set Design:** Joseph Urban

Songs: Automobile Horn Song [1] (C/L: Bennett; Carlton; Clarence Gaskill; Henry Tobias); Come West, Little Girl, Come West; Ever Since the Movies Learned to Talk [1] (C/L: Unknown); Girl Friend of a Boy Friend of Mine, A; Go Get 'Im; Gypsy Joe; Hallowe'en Whoopee Ball; Here's to the Girl of My Heart; Hungry Women [1] (C: Milton Ager; L: Jack Yellen); I Faw Down and Go Boom [1] (C/L: James Brockman; Leonard Stevens); I'll Still Belong to You (C: Nacio Herb Brown; L: Edward Eliscu); I'm Bringing a Red, Red Rose; It's a Beautiful Day Today; Love Me or Leave Me [2]; Makin' Whoopee; My Baby Just Cares for Me; My Blackbirds Are Bluebirds Now [1] (C: Cliff Friend; L: Irving Caesar); Song of the Setting Sun; Stetson; Taps; Until You Get Somebody Else; Where the Sunset Meets the Sea (Gypsy Song)

Cast: Josephine Adair; Bob Borger; Eddie Cantor; Spencer Charters; Ruth Etting; Fran Frey; Tamara Geva; Jack Gifford; Gladys Glad; George Olsen's Orchestra; Bob Rice; Jack Shaw; Ethel Shutta; Frances Upton

Notes: Closed for summer vacation after 253

performances. Reopened 8/5/1929 for 155 more. [1] Interpolated. [2] Also in SIMPLE SIMON.

4684 • WHY I LOVE NEW YORK

OPENED: 10/10/1975 Theatre: Judson Poets'
Musical Off-Off-Broadway

Composer: Al Carmines
Lyricist: Al Carmines
Librettist: Al Carmines
Director: Leonard Peters

Costumes: Carol Oditz; **Lighting Designer:** Todd Lichtenstein; **Set Design:** Irving Cuomo

Songs: 8th Avenue; Hard-On; How Do You Love a City?; I'm Gonna Be a Star; Loneliness Trio; Love Comes in the Strangest Ways; Micritza Violetta Doanne; New York Is My Home; New York Love Is So Hard; Now and Then; Ordinary Woman; Pearl; Rags; Staten Island Barcarole; What Ever Happened to You?; Why Does Everybody in the City Put You Down; Woman Needs Approval, A

Cast: Essie Borden; Lee Guilliatt; Philip Owens; Margaret Wright

4685 • WHY THE CHICKEN?

Play

Author: John McGrath
Producer: Michael Codron
Director: Lionel Bart

Songs: Why the Chicken? (C/L: Lionel Bart)

Cast: Peter Craze; Terence Stamp

Notes: No other information available. Closed out-of-town-London.

4686 • WHY WORRY?

OPENED: 08/23/1918 Theatre: Harris
Play Broadway: 27

Composer: Blanche Merrill
Lyricist: Blanche Merrill
Producer: A.H. Woods
Director: George Marion

Songs: I'm an Indian; I'm Bad

Cast: Fanny Brice; Charles Dale; Harry Goodwin; Irving Kaufman; Jack Sharkey; George Sidney; Joe Smith

Notes: No songs listed in program.

4687 • WIFE HUNTERS,THE

OPENED: 11/02/1911 Theatre: Herald Square
Musical Broadway: 36

Composer: Malvin Franklin; Anatole Friedland
Lyricist: Malvin F. Franklin; David Kemper
Librettist: Edgar Allen Woolf
Producer: Lew Fields
Director: Ned Wayburn

Choreographer: Ned Wayburn; **Musical Director:** Lee Orean Smith

Songs: All Life Is Full of Pleasure [1] (C: Anatole Friedland); Bill of Fare [1] (C: Anatole Friedland); Casey Jones [2] (C: Anatole Friedland); Down at Mammy Jinny's [1] (C: Anatole Friedland); Faint Heart Ne'er Won Fair Lady [1] (C: Anatole Friedland); Folette (C: Anatole Friedland); Girls, Girls, Keep Your Figure (C: Anatole Friedland); Honeyland; In Your Arms; Leonara (C: Anatole Friedland); Let's Take Him Home in Triumph; Little Dancing Jumping Jigger (C: Anatole Friedland); Love Waves (C: Anatole Friedland); Mammy Jinny; My Grammar Book [1] (C: Anatole Friedland); My Havana Maid (C: Anatole Friedland); On the Avenue; P.S. I Love You [1]; Pas de Seul; Picnic Club, The; Recitative; Swinging with Someone [1] (C: Anatole Friedland); Waltz of the Wild, The; Wave Crest Waltz, The

Cast: Dorothy Brenner; Emma Carus; Arthur Conrad; Edith Decker

Notes: Titled THREE MILLION DOLLARS out of town prior to New York. [1] Cut out of town. [2] Cut out of town. The famous song "Casey Jones" by T. Lawrence Seibert and Eddie Newton was written in 1909.

4688 • WIFE TAMERS, THE

OPENED: 08/08/1910
Musical Closed out of town

Composer: Robert Hood Bowers
Lyricist: Clarence Harvey; Oliver Herford

Source: FLORIST SHOP, THE (Play: Oliver Herford)

Songs: Flannigan; I'm Looking for a Certain Little Boy [1]

Cast: Gertrude Bryan; Florence Reid; Lionel Walsh

Notes: From Atlantic City program. [1] Interpolated.

4689 • WILD AND WONDERFUL

OPENED: 12/07/1971 Theatre: Lyceum
Musical Broadway: 1

Composer: Bob Goodman
Lyricist: Bob Goodman
Librettist: Phil Phillips
Producer: Rick Hobard; Raymonde Weil
Director: Burry Fredrik

Choreographer: Ronn Forella; **Costumes:** Frank Thompson; **Dance Arranger:** Tom Janusz; **Lighting Designer:** Neil Peter Jampolis; **Musical Director:** Tom Janusz; **Orchestrations:** Luther Henderson; **Set Design:** Stephen Hendrickson; **Vocal Arranger:** Tom Janusz

Songs: Chances; Come a Little Closer; Desmond's Dilemma; Different Kind of World, A; Fallen Angels; I Spy; Is This My Town; Jenny; Little Bits and Pieces; Moment Is Now; My First Moment; Petty Crime; She Should Have Me; Something Wonderful Can Happen; Wait for Me; Wild and Wonderful; You Can Reach the Sun

Cast: Robert Burr; Laura McDuffie; Ann Reinking; Larry Small; Ted Thurston; Walter Willison

4690 • WILD MEN

OPENED: 05/06/1993 Theatre: Westside
Musical Off-Broadway: 59

Composer: Mark Nutter
Lyricist: Mark Nutter
Librettist: Peter Burns; Mark Nutter; Rob Riley; Tom Wolfe
Producer: James D. Stern
Director: Rob Riley

Choreographer: Jim Corti; **Costumes:** John Paoletti; **Lighting Designer:** Geoffrey Bushor; **Musical Director:** Lisa Yeargan; **Set Design:** Mary Griswold

Songs: Come Away; Get Pissed; It's You; Lookit Those Stars; My Friend, My Father; Now I Am a Man; Ooh, That's Hot; True Value; 'Un' Song, The; We're Wild Men; What Stuart Has Planted; Wimmins

Cast: Peter Burns; David Lewman; Joe Liss; Rob Riley; George Wendt

4691 • WILD ROSE, THE (1902)

OPENED: 05/05/1902 Theatre: Knickerbocker
Musical Broadway: 136

Composer: Ludwig Englander
Lyricist: George V. Hobart
Librettist: Harry B. Smith
Producer: George W. Lederer
Director: George W. Lederer

Choreographer: Adolph Newberger; **Costumes:** Mme. Siedle; **Set Design:** D. Frank Dodge

Songs: Cupid Is the Captain; I Sing a Little Tenor (C: Harry Linton; L: John Gilroy); Love's Young Dream; My Little Gypsy Maid [1] (C: Will Marion Cook; L: Cecil Mack; Harry B. Smith); Nancy Brown (C/L: Clifton Crawford); Soldier's Story, The; They Were All Doing the Same (C/L: Ren Shields)

Cast: Irene Bentley; Marie Cahill; Marguerite Clark; Eddie Foy Sr.; Albert Hart; Junie McCree; Evelyn Nesbitt

Notes: No songs listed in program. [1] Some sources erroneously credit the lyrics to Paul Lawrence Dunbar.

4692 • WILD ROSE, THE (1926)

OPENED: 10/20/1926 Theatre: Martin Beck
Musical Broadway: 62

Composer: Rudolf Friml
Lyricist: Oscar Hammerstein II; Otto Harbach
Librettist: Oscar Hammerstein II; Otto Harbach
Producer: Arthur Hammerstein
Director: William J. Wilson

Choreographer: Busby Berkeley; **Costumes:** Mark Mooring; **Musical Director:** Herbert Stothart; **Set Design:** Joseph Urban

Songs: Brown Eyes; Coronation, The; Dramatico Musical Scene; How Can You Keep Your Mind

on Business? [1]; I'm the Extra Man; It Was Fate; Lady of the Rose; L'Heure D'Or (One Golden Hour) [2] (L: Otto Harbach; J.B. Kantor); Love Me, Don't You?; Lovely Lady; Opening Act II; Revolution Festival; Riviera; Rumble, Rumble, Rumble [1]; That's Why I Love You [1]; We'll Have a Kingdom; Wild Rose; Won't You Come Across?

Cast: Nana Bryant; William Collier; Inez Courtney; Jerome Daley; Desiree Ellinger; Joseph Macaulay; Fuller Mellish; Len Menace; Joseph Santley; Gus Shy

Notes: [1] Out Philadelphia 10/20/26. [2] French lyrics by J.B. Kantor.

4693 • WILDCAT

OPENED: 12/16/1960 Theatre: Alvin
Musical Broadway: 171

Composer: Cy Coleman
Lyricist: Carolyn Leigh
Librettist: N. Richard Nash
Producer: Michael Kidd; N. Richard Nash
Director: Michael Kidd

Choreographer: Michael Kidd; **Costumes:** Alvin Colt; **Dance Arranger:** John Morris; **Lighting Designer:** Charles Elson; **Musical Director:** John Morris; **Orchestrations:** Robert Ginzler; Sid Ramin; **Set Design:** Peter Larkin; **Vocal Arranger:** John Morris

Songs: Ain't It Sad [1]; Angelina [1]; (We Keep) Bouncing Back for More [2]; Corduroy Road; Day I Do, The [1]; El Sombrero; Foller It Through [1]; Give a Little Whistle (and I'll Be There); Hey, Look Me Over; I Got My Man [1]; I Hear (Oil); I Like the Ladies [1]; Joe Dynamite's Dentistry Song [1]; Little What-If, Little Could-Be [1]; Once Day We Dance; Tall Hope; That's What I Want for Janie [3]; Thinkability [4]; Tippy Tippy Toes; We Have So Much in Common [1]; What Takes My Fancy; Wildcat [3]; You're a Liar; You're Far Away from Home [1]; You've Come Home

Cast: Keith Andes; Lucille Ball; Clifford David; Edith King; Al Lanti; Paula Stewart; Swen Swenson; Don Tomkins

Notes: [1] Cut prior to opening. [2] Cut prior to opening. Later in HELLZAPOPPIN 1976. [3] Cut after opening. [4] Cut prior to opening. Music later used for "We're Heading for a Wedding" in THE WILL ROGERS FOLLIES.

4694 • WILDFLOWER

OPENED: 02/07/1923 Theatre: Casino
Musical Broadway: 477

Composer: Vincent Youmans
Lyricist: Oscar Hammerstein II; Otto Harbach
Librettist: Oscar Hammerstein II; Otto Harbach
Producer: Arthur Hammerstein
Director: Oscar Eagle

Choreographer: David Bennett; **Costumes:** Charles LeMaire; **Musical Director:** Herbert Stothart; **Orchestrations:** Robert Russell Bennett; **Set Design:** Frank Gates; E.A. Morange

Songs: April Blossoms (C: Herbert Stothart); Bambalina; Best Dance I've Had Tonight, The; Como Camel Corps, The [4]; 'Course I Will; Everything Is All Right [1]; Finale Act I; Finale Act II; Finale Act III; Friends Who Understand [1]; Girl from Casimo (C: Herbert Stothart); Good-Bye, Little Rose-Bud (C: Herbert Stothart); I Can Always Find Another Partner; If I Told You [3]; If Your Name Had Been LaRocca [4]; I'll Collaborate with You (C: Herbert Stothart); Iloveyouiloveyouiloveyou; Some Like to Hunt (C: Herbert Stothart); Spring Is Here [4]; True Love Will Never Grow Cold [1]; Wild-Flower; World's Worst Woman, The (C: Herbert Stothart); You Can Never Blame a Girl for Dreaming [2]

Cast: Evelyn Cavanagh; Jerome Daley; Edith Day; James Doyle; Esther Howard; Olin Howland; Charles Judels; Guy Robertson

Notes: [1] Cut. [2] Added after opening. [3] Cut after opening. Music used as "Virginia" in RAINBOW. [4] Added to 1926 London production.

4695 • WILL ROGERS FOLLIES, THE

OPENED: 05/01/1991 Theatre: Palace
Musical Broadway: 963

Composer: Cy Coleman
Lyricist: Betty Comden; Adolph Green
Librettist: Peter Stone
Producer: Pierre Cosette; Sam Crothers; Stewart F.

Lane; James M. Nederlander; Martin Richards; Max Weitzenhoffer
Director: Tommy Tune

Choreographer: Tommy Tune; **Costumes:** Willa Kim; **Dance Arranger:** Cy Coleman; **Lighting Designer:** Jules Fisher; **Musical Director:** Eric Stern; **Orchestrations:** Bill Byers; **Set Design:** Tony Walton; **Vocal Arranger:** Cy Coleman

Songs: Big Time, The [2]; Favorite Son; Give a Man Enough Rope; I Got You; It's a Boy!; Let's Go Flying; Look Around; Marry Me Now; My Big Mistake; My Unknown Someone; Never Met a Man I Didn't Like; No Man Left for Me; Presents for Mr. Rogers; So Long Pa; We're Heading for a Wedding [3]; Will-a-Mania; Without You

Cast: Bonnie Brackney; Tom Brackney; Vince Bruce; Keith Carradine; Dee Hoty; Cady Huffman; Dick Latessa; Gregory Peck[1]; Paul Ukena Jr.

Notes: [1] Voice on tape only. [2] Melody from an unproduced musical version of "The Wonderful O." [3] Same music as "Thinkability" cut from WILDCAT.

4696 • WILL THE MILK TRAIN RUN TONIGHT?

OPENED: 01/09/1964 Theatre: New Bowery
Musical Off-Broadway: 8

Composer: Alyn Heim
Lyricist: Malcolm I. LaPrade
Librettist: Malcolm I. LaPrade
Producer: Jon Baisch
Director: Jon Baisch

Source: UNKNOWN (Play: Hugh Neville); **Choreographer:** Lynne Fippinger; **Costumes:** Joe Crosby; **Lighting Designer:** Joseph Kreisel; **Set Design:** Gene Czernicki

Songs: Age of Miracles; Bitter Tears; Comes the Dawn; Dearer to Me; Fall of Valor, The; Heroism; Hickory, Dickory; Honeymoon Choo-Choo; I'll Walk Alone; Nature's Serenade; No Sacrifice; Paper Matches; Prudence, Have Faith; Remember Him; Slip of a Girl, A; So Much to Be Thankful For; This Decadent Age; Three Cowards Craven; To Dream or Not to Dream; Vengeance; Villainy

Cast: Barbara Cole; Fred Jackson; Peter Lombard; Naomi Riseman

4697 • WILLIAMS & WALKER

OPENED: 03/09/1986 Theatre: American Place
Musical Off-Broadway: 77

Librettist: Vincent D. Smith
Producer: Woodie King; New Federal Theatre
Director: Shauneille Perry

Choreographer: Lenwood Sloan; **Costumes:** Judy Dearing; **Lighting Designer:** Marc D. Malamud; **Musical Director:** Ron Metcalf; **Set Design:** Marc D. Malamud

Songs: Bon Bon Buddy (C: Will Marion Cook; L: Alex Rogers); Chocolate Drop (inst.) (C: Will Marion Cook); Constantly (C: Bert Williams; L: Barris; Smith); Everybody Wants to See the Baby (C: Bob Cole; L: James Weldon Johnson); I May Be Crazy but I Ain't No Fool (C/L: Alex Rogers); I'd Rather Have Nothin' All the Time Than Somethin' for a Little While (C: Bert Williams; L: John B. Lowitz); I'm a Jonah Man (C/L: Alex Rogers); Magnetic Rag (inst.) (C: Scott Joplin); Nobody (C: Bert Williams; L: Alex Rogers); Original Rag (inst.) (C: Scott Joplin); Save Your Money John (C/L: Les Copeland; Alex Rogers); Somebody Stole My Gal (C/L: Leo Wood)

Cast: Vondie Curtis-Hall; Ben Harney; Joe Marshall; Ron Metcalf

Notes: No original songs in this show.

4698 • WILLIE THE WEEPER

Notes: *See BALLET BALLADS.*

4699 • WILLOW PLATE, THE

OPENED: 1924
Play

Composer: Victor Herbert
Producer: Tony Sarg
Director: Tony Sarg

Songs: Chang, the Lover (inst.); Kongshee, the Mandarin's Daughter (inst.); Little Gardenhouse, The (inst.); Mandarin's Garden, The (inst.); Wedding Procession, A (inst.)

Notes: A puppet show.

4700 • WILSON MIZNER PROJECT

Musical

Songs: Life in Venetia (C/L: Stephen Sondheim)

Notes: Unfinished. No other information available.

4701 • WIND IN THE WILLOWS

OPENED: 12/19/1985 Theatre: Nederlander
Musical Broadway: 4

Composer: William Perry
Lyricist: Robert McGough; William Perry
Librettist: Jane Iredale
Producer: Liniva Productions, Inc.; RLM Productions, Inc.
Director: Tony Stevens

Source: WIND IN THE WILLOWS, THE (Novel: Kenneth Grahame); **Choreographer:** Margery Beddow; **Costumes:** Freddy Wittop; **Lighting Designer:** Craig Miller; **Musical Director:** Robert Rogers; **Orchestrations:** William D. Brohn; **Set Design:** Sam Kirkpatrick; **Vocal Arranger:** Robert Rogers

Songs: Brief Encounter; Come What May; Day You Came Into My Life, The; Evil Weasel; Follow Your Instinct; Gasoline Can-Can, The; I'd Be Attracted; Mediterranean; Messing About in Boats; Moving Up in the World; S-S-Something Comes Over Me; That's What Friends Are For; When Springtime Comes to My River; Where Am I Now?; Wind in the Willows, The; World Is Waiting for Me, The; You'll Love It in Jail

Cast: Irving Barnes; P.J. Benjamin; David Carroll; Donna Drake; John Jellison; Nathan Lane; Vicki Lewis; Jackie Lowe; Nora Mae Lyng; Scott Waara

4702 • WINDY CITY (1946)

OPENED: 04/18/1946
Musical Closed out of town

Composer: Walter Jurmann
Lyricist: Paul Francis Webster
Librettist: Philip Yordan
Producer: Harry Brandt; Richard Kollmar
Director: Edward Rivaux

Choreographer: Katherine Dunham; **Costumes:** Rose Bogdanoff; **Dance Arranger:** Dorothea Freitag; **Lighting Designer:** Jo Mielziner; **Musical Director:** Charles Sanford; **Orchestrations:** Don Walker; **Set Design:** Jo Mielziner; **Vocal Arranger:** Clay Warnick

Songs: Don't Ever Run Away from Love; Gambler's Lullaby; Gentleman of the Old School [1]; Harry Is Only Physical [1]; It's the Better Me; It's Time I Had a Break; Lucky Duck [1]; Out on a Limb; (As the Wind Bloweth) There Goeth I; Where Do We Go from Here

Cast: John Conte; Susan Miller; Al Shean; Betty Jane Smith; Loring Smith; Frances Williams

Notes: [1] ASCAP/Library of Congress only.

4703 • WINDY CITY (1985)

OPENED: 09/18/1985
Musical Closed out of town

Composer: Tony Macaulay
Lyricist: Dick Vosburgh
Librettist: Dick Vosburgh
Director: David H. Bell

Source: FRONT PAGE, THE (Play: Ben Hecht; Charles MacArthur); **Arrangements:** Kevin Stites; **Choreographer:** David H. Bell; **Costumes:** Guy Geoly; **Lighting Designer:** Jeff Davis; **Orchestrations:** David Siegel; **Set Design:** Michael Anania

Songs: Bensinger's Poem; Born Reporter; Circles 'Round Us; Day I Quit This Rag, The; Hey Hallelujah! [1]; I Can Talk to You; Just Imagine It; Long Night Again Tonight [1]; Mollie Has Her Say; Natalie; No One Walks Out on Me [1]; Perfect Casting [1]; Pressroom Pasa Doble; Round in Circles; Saturday [1]; Stamp! Stamp! Stamp!; Ten Years from Now; Times We Had, The; Wait Till I Get You on Your Own; Waltz for Mollie — Never Even Touched Me; Water Under the Bridge; Windy City

Cast: Pamela Clifford; MacIntyre Dixon; Tony Gilbert; Ronald Holgate; Judy Kaye; Jack Kopye; Jack Kyrieleison; Gary Sandy; Alan Sues

Notes: Paper Mill Playhouse, Millburn, N.J. Produced in London, 7/20/1982 for 250 performances at the Victoria Palace Theatre. [1] Used in original British production only.

4704 • WINE, WOMEN AND SONG (0000)

Revue

Composer: Carl Schilling
Lyricist: Edward Corbett
Librettist: Edward Corbett
Producer: John W. Isham; George Paxton

Costumes: Madame Thompson; **Set Design:** Frank Gates; E.A. Morange

Songs: Along the Old Canal; Fastest Man in New York; Girls of the Midnight Matinee; I Sail the Airy Blue; Imprisoned; It Fills Me with Distress; Maidens Aquatic; Maybe You Think I Did; Old Rip Was a Flip; Pop, Pop, Pop; Rah-Rah-Rah; Tale of a Decent Married Hen; Wedding Bells Won't Ring Tonight; Whip-poor-wills

Notes: No other information available.

4705 • WINE, WOMEN AND SONG (1898)

OPENED: 09/19/1898 Theatre: Grand Opera House
Musical Broadway: 8

Composer: Carl Schilling
Librettist: Edward Corbett
Director: George Paxton

Set Design: Frank E. Gates; Edward A. Morange

Cast: James Horan; Robert Quigley; Ruth Robinson

Notes: No program available.

4706 • WINGED VICTORY

OPENED: 11/20/1943 Theatre: 44th Street
Play Broadway: 212

Composer: David Rose
Lyricist: David Rose
Author: Moss Hart
Producer: U.S. Army Air Forces
Director: Moss Hart

Choreographer: Leonard dePaur; **Costumes:** Howard Shoup; **Lighting Designer:** Abe Feder; **Orchestrations:** David Rose; **Set Design:** Harry Horner; **Vocal Arranger:** Leonard dePaur

Songs: Army Air Corps Song (C/L: Robert Crawford); My Dream Book of Memories; Winged Victory; You're So Nice to Remember [1] (L: Leo Robin)

Cast: Whitney Bissell; Philip Bourneuf; Red Buttons; Peter Lind Hayes; Karl Malden; Kevin McCarthy; Edward McMahon; Gary Merrill; Ray Middleton; Barry Nelson; Edmond O'Brien; George Reeves

Notes: [1] Cut prior to opening.

4707 • WINGS (1975)

OPENED: 03/16/1975 Theatre: Eastside Playhouse
Musical Off-Broadway: 9

Composer: Robert McLaughlin; Peter Ryan
Lyricist: Robert McLaughlin; Peter Ryan
Librettist: Robert McLaughlin; Peter Ryan
Producer: Stephen Weill
Director: Robert McLaughlin

Source: BIRDS, THE (Play: Aristophanes); **Choreographer:** Nora Christiansen; **Costumes:** Shadow; **Lighting Designer:** Karl Eigsti; **Musical Director:** Larry Hochman; **Orchestrations:** Bill Brohn; **Set Design:** Karl Eigsti; **Vocal Arranger:** Bill Brohn

Songs: Call of the Birds; Comfort for the Taking; Finale; First I Propose; Great Immortals, The; How Great It Is to Be a Bird; Human Species, The; Iris the Fleet; O Sacrilege; Our Goose Is Cooked [1]; Rah Tah Tah Tio Beep Doo Doo; Take to the Air; Time to Find Something to Do; Wall Song, The; Wings; You'll Regret It!

Cast: Peter Jurasik; David Kolatch; James Howard Laurence; Stuart Pankin; Jay E. Raphael; Jerry Sroka

Notes: [1] Not in program.

4708 • WINGS (1993)

OPENED: 03/09/1993 Theatre: Public
Musical Off-Broadway: 47

Composer: Jeffrey Lunden
Lyricist: Arthur Perlman
Librettist: Arthur Perlman
Director: Michael Maggio

Source: WINGS (Play: Arthur Kopit); **Costumes:** Birgit Rattenborg; **Lighting Designer:** Robert Christen; **Musical Director:** Bradley Vieth; **Set Design:** Linda Buchanan

Cast: William Brown; Rita Gardner; Ora Jones; Ross Lehman; Hollis Resnik; Linda Stephens

Notes: No songs listed in program.

4709 • WINKLE TOWN

OPENED: 1922
Musical Unproduced

Composer: Richard Rodgers
Lyricist: Lorenz Hart
Librettist: Herbert Fields; Oscar Hammerstein II

Songs: Baby Wants to Dance; Comfort Me; Congratulations; Darling Will Not Grow Older [3]; Hermits, The (What Do All the Hermits Do in Springtime?) [2]; Hollyhocks of Hollywood, The; I Know You're Too Wonderful for Me; I Want a Man [4]; If I Were King [6]; I'll Always Be an Optimist; Manhattan [7]; Old Enough to Love [1]; One a Day; Since I Remember You; Three Musketeers, The [5]; We Came, We Saw, We Made 'Em!

Notes: [1] Later in DEAREST ENEMY. [2] Later in A DANISH YANKEE IN KING TUT'S COURT, TEMPLE BELLES and DEAREST ENEMY. [3] Sung in counterpoint to SILVER THREADS AMONG THE GOLD. Later in BAD HABITS OF 1925. [4] Lyrics revised for LIDO LADY and AMERICA'S SWEETHEART. [5] Later in THE GARRICK GAIETIES (1926) and in that show's 1930 touring production. [6] Later in IF I WERE KING, A DANISH YANKEE IN KING TUT'S COURT and BAD HABITS OF 1925. [7] Later in THE GARRICK GAIETIES with somewhat revised lyrics.

4710 • WINNIE THE POOH

OPENED: 10/29/1972 Theatre: Bil Baird
Musical Off-Broadway: 44

Composer: Jack Brooks
Lyricist: Jack Brooks; A.A. Milne
Librettist: A.J. Russell
Producer: Amer. Puppet Arts Council
Director: Lee Theodore

Source: WINNIE THE POOH (Story: A.A. Milne); **Musical Director:** Alvy West; **Vocal Arranger:** Alvy West

Songs: Bear Likes Honey, A; Birthdays Are Fun; Cottleston Pie; How Sweet to Be a Cloud; Poor Little Trigger; Sing Ho for the Life of a Bear; Spring Is Spring; They've All Got Tails but Me; Tiddley Pom; Vespers

Puppeteer: Bil Baird; Peter Baird; Pady Blackwood; Olga Felgemacher; Carl Harms; Frank Sullivan; William Tost; Byron Whiting

Notes: Song list from 1960 Television special.

4711 • WINNING MISS, A

OPENED: 11/21/1908 Theatre: Garden
Musical Chicago

Composer: William F. Peters
Lyricist: Harold Atteridge
Librettist: Harold Atteridge

Songs: I Love You for Keeps

Notes: No other information available.

4712 • WINSOME WIDOW, A

OPENED: 04/11/1912 Theatre: Moulin Rouge
Musical Broadway: 172

Composer: Raymond Hubbell
Producer: Florenz Ziegfeld
Director: Julian Mitchell

Source: TRIP TO CHINATOWN, A (Musical: Charles H. Hoyt)

Songs: Be My Little Baby Bumble Bee (C: Henry Marshall; L: Stanley Murphy); Call Me Flo (C/L: John Golden; Jerome Kern); Could You Love a Girl Like Me? (L: Robert B. Smith); Fascinating Girl; Frisco, The; I Never Knew What Eyes Could Do Till Yours Looked Into Mine (C: Henry Marshall; L: Stanley Murphy); I Take After Dad; Pousse Cafe; Purity Brigade March; Skate Boy, The; Songs of Yesterday; String a Ring of Roses 'Round Your Rosie (C: Jean Schwartz; L: William Jerome); Teach Me Everything You Know; They Mean More; Toodle-oodle-oodle on Your Piccolo (C/L: Griffin; Murtagh); When I Waltz with You

[1] (C: Albert Gumble; L: Alfred Bryan); You're a Regular Girl

Cast: Elizabeth Brice; Jack Clifford; Kathleen Clifford; Dolly Sisters, The; Leon Errol; Harry Kelly; Charles King; Charles J. Ross; Frank Tinney; Mae West

Notes: [1] Sheet music only.

4713 • WINSOME WINNIE

OPENED: 12/01/1903 Theatre: Casino
Musical Broadway: 56

Composer: Gustave Kerker
Lyricist: Frederick Ranken
Librettist: Frederick Ranken
Producer: Nixon & Zimmerman; Sam S. Shubert

Songs: Cities I Love (C: Edward Jakobowski); Englishman, The (C: Edward Jakobowski; L: Harry Paulton); Everything Is Big in Chicago; Finale Act II; Heroes; Hola; I Don't Remember That; I Love You Only; In the Good Old Days; Jenny (C: Edward Jakobowski; L: Harry Paulton); Loud Let the Bugle Sound; Maid and the Miller, The; Miss Walker of Kalamazoo (C: Edward Jacobowski; L: Harry Paulton); Montenegrin Patrol (C: Edward Jacobowski; L: Harry Paulton); Oh Maiden; Oh, The Paying Guests (C: Edward Jakobowski; L: Harry Paulton); Rose, Rose, Rose (C/L: Dick Temple); Sing Song Lee; There's a Yacht Come In; They're Looking for Me; Two Little Doves; Winsome Winnie

Cast: Paula Edwardes; Jobyna Howland; Joseph Miron; Helen Redmond; Julia Sanderson; Dick Temple

4714 • WINTER GARDEN VAUDEVILLE SHOW

OPENED: 1911 Theatre: Winter Garden
Revue Broadway

Producer: Messrs. Shubert

Songs: Sombrero Land (C: Irving Berlin; L: E. Ray Goetz; Ted Snyder)

Cast: Dolly Jardon

Notes: No program available.

4715 • WINTER'S TALE, THE

OPENED: 07/20/1958
Play

Composer: Marc Blitzstein
Author: William Shakespeare
Producer: American Shakespeare Fest.; John Houseman
Director: John Houseman; Jack Landau

Choreographer: George Balanchine; **Incidental Music:** Marc Blitzstein

Songs: Shepherd's Song (When Daffodils Begin to Peer) (L: William Shakespeare); Song of the Glove (L: Ben Jonson); Vendor's Song (Lawn as White as Driven Snow) (L: William Shakespeare)

Cast: John Colicos; Richard Easton; Will Geer; Ellis Rabb; Hiram Sherman; Inga Swenson; Nancy Wickwire

Notes: Produced at the American Shakespeare Festival, Stratford, Conn.

4716 • WISE CHILD, A

Musical

Composer: William Schroeder
Lyricist: Rida Johnson Young
Librettist: Rida Johnson Young
Producer: Charles Dillingham
Director: Fred G. Latham

Costumes: Mme. Francis; **Set Design:** Frank Gates; E.A. Morange

Songs: Baby Blue; My Dear Old Daddie; Oh Joy; Roses Say You Will, The

Cast: Vivienne Segal

Notes: No other information available.

4717 • WISE GUY, THE

OPENED: 1899
Musical Broadway

Composer: George M. Cohan
Lyricist: George M. Cohan

Songs: Dear Little Girly Girly; Hannah's a Hummer; My Babe from Boston Town; P.S. Mr. Johnson Sends His Regards; San Francisco Sadie; Telephone Me, Baby; To Boston on Business; Who Says a Coon Can't Love

4718 • WISH YOU WERE HERE

OPENED: 06/25/1952 Theatre: Imperial
Musical Broadway: 598

Composer: Harold Rome
Lyricist: Harold Rome
Librettist: Arthur Kober; Joshua Logan
Producer: Leland Hayward; Joshua Logan
Director: Joshua Logan

Source: HAVING WONDERFUL TIME (Play: Arthur Kober); **Choreographer:** Joshua Logan; **Costumes:** Robert Mackintosh; **Dance Arranger:** Trude Rittman; **Lighting Designer:** Jo Mielziner; **Musical Director:** Jay Blackton; **Orchestrations:** Don Walker; **Set Design:** Jo Mielziner; **Vocal Arranger:** Trude Rittman

Songs: Ain't Nature Grand [1]; Bright College Days; Camp Karefree; Certain Individuals; Could Be; Don Jose of Far Rockaway; Everybody Loves Everybody; Flattery; Glimpse of Love [1]; Goodbye Love [2]; Investigation [1]; Mix and Mingle; Relax; Shopping Around; Social Director; Summer Afternoon; There's Nothing Nicer Than People [3]; They Won't Know Me; Tripping the Light Fantastic; Where Did the Night Go?; Who Could Eat Now [1]; Wish You Were Here

Cast: Sidney Armus; Larry Blyden; Sheila Bond; Jack Cassidy; Florence Henderson; Patricia Marand; Phyllis Newman; John Perkins; Sammy Smith; Tom Tryon; Paul Valentine

Notes: Swimmers trained by Eleanor Holm Rose. [1] Cut prior to opening. [2] Cut after opening. [3] Added after opening.

4719 • WISHING WELL, THE

OPENED: 1929
Musical

Composer: Harold Garstin
Lyricist: Peter Cawthorne
Librettist: Peter Cawthorne
Producer: MacFarland Productions
Director: Peter Cawthorne

Choreographer: Marion Morgan; **Costumes:** Marion Morgan

Songs: Birdie and Ferdie; Dance of Love; Dogs; Follow Your Heart to Fairyland; Happiest Girl in the World, The; Hark to the Sound of the Horn; Healer Am I of All Sorrow, The; I Cannot Speak; I Love You; I Think I'll Go Back to Bed; Legend of the Wishing Well, The; Let's Get a Move On; Love of Mine; Peeping Tom of Coventry; Sawney Pott, the Idiot; Simple Simon; Thank God for the Homeland; This Lovely Night in June; Time for Dreams, A; Whoops-a-Daisy

Cast: Harriet Bennet; Reginald Dandy

Notes: No other information available.

4720 • WITHIN THE LOOP

OPENED: 1915
Musical

Composer: Harry Carroll
Lyricist: Ballard Macdonald

Songs: College Inn Rag, The (L: Coleman Goetz; Ballard Macdonald); Drip, Drip, Drip, Went the Waterfall; I'll Cling to You; Irish Heart, An; My Lady of the Lake; Same Little Girl; Thou Art Mine (L: Coleman Goetz; Ballard Macdonald); You Wake Up in the Morning in Chicago (L: Coleman Goetz; Ballard Macdonald)

Notes: No other information available. Possibly a Chicago show.

4721 • WITHOUT THE LAW

OPENED: 11/21/1912 Theatre: Weber and Fields Music Hall
Musical Broadway

Composer A. Baldwin Sloane
Lyricist: E. Ray Goetz
Librettist: Edgar Smith

Notes: One-act musical. The second half of ROLY POLY.

4722 • WIZ, THE

OPENED: 01/05/1975 Theatre: Majestic
Musical Broadway: 1672

Composer: Charlie Smalls
Lyricist: Charlie Smalls
Librettist: William F. Brown
Producer: Ken Harper
Director: Geoffrey Holder; Gilbert Moses

Source: WONDERFUL WIZARD OF OZ, THE (Novel: L. Frank Baum); **Choreographer:** George Faison; **Costumes:** Geoffrey Holder; **Dance Arranger:** Timothy Graphenreed; **Lighting Designer:** Tharon Musser; **Musical Director:** Charles H. Coleman; Tania Leon; **Orchestrations:** Harold Wheeler; **Set Design:** Tom H. John; **Vocal Arranger:** Charles H. Coleman

Songs: Be a Lion; Ease on Down the Road; Emerald City Ballet (inst.) (C: George Faison; Timothy Graphenreed); Everybody Rejoice (Brand New Day) (C/L: Luther Vandross); Feeling We Once Had, The; Funky Monkeys; Girl Don't Cry [1]; He's the Wizard; Home; I Was Born on the Day Before Yesterday; If You Believe (Believe in Yourself); Kalidah Battle; Lion's Dream; Mean Old Lion; No Bad News; Rested Body Is a Rested Mind, A; Slide Some Oil to Me; So You Wanted to Meet the Wizard; Soon As I Get Home; Tornado Ballet (C: Timothy Graphenreed); What Would I Do If I Could Feel; Which Witch [1]; Who Do You Think You Are?; Y'All Got It!; You Can't Win [1]

Cast: Hinton Battle; Danny Beard; Dee Dee Bridgewater; Andre De Shields; Pi Douglass; Tiger Haynes; Mabel King; Esther Marrow; Stephanie Mills; Ted Ross; Clarice Taylor; Carl Earl Weaver; Ralph Wilcox

Notes: [1] Cut prior to opening.

4723 • WIZARD OF OZ, THE

OPENED: 01/21/1903 Theatre: Majestic
Musical Broadway: 293

Composer: A. Baldwin Sloane; Paul Tietjens
Lyricist: L. Frank Baum
Librettist: L. Frank Baum
Producer: Fred R. Hamlin
Director: Julian Mitchell

Source: WONDERFUL WIZARD OF OZ, THE (Novel: L. Frank Baum); **Costumes:** W.W. Denislow; Mrs. Edward Siedle; **Musical Director:** Charles Zimmerman; **Set Design:** Walter Burridge; Fred Gibson; John Young

Songs: Alas for a Man without Brains (C: Paul Tietjens); All Aboard for Sunny Kansas (C/L: Unknown); Ball of All Nations (C: A. Baldwin Sloane; L: Edgar Smith); Carrie Barry (C: A. Baldwin Sloane; L: Glen MacDonough); Connemara Christening (C: A. Baldwin Sloane; L: Edgar Smith); Different Ways of Making Love, The [1] (C: Paul Tietjens); Guardians of the Gate, The [1] (C: Paul Tietjens); Honey Is Sweet (C: Henry Blossom; L: George Spink); How'd You Like to Like a Girl Like Me? [1] (C: Joseph S. Nathan; L: Felix F. Feist); Hurrah for Baffin's Bay [2] (C: Theodore F. Morse; L: Vincent Bryan); I Love Only One Girl in the Wide, Wide World (C: Gus Edwards; L: Will D. Cobb); I'll Be Your Honey in the Springtime [1] (C/L: Harry Freeman); In Michigan (C: A. Baldwin Sloane; L: Glen MacDonough); It Happens Every Day [1] (C: Paul Tietjens); It's Lovely to Love a Lovely Girl [1] (C: Seymour Furth; L: Edward P. Moran); Just a Simple Girl from the Prairie [1] (C: Paul Tietjens); Life in Kansas (C: Paul Tietjens); Love Is Love [1] (C: Paul Tietjens); Must You (C/L: Unknown); Niccolo's Piccolo (C: A. Baldwin Sloane; L: Glen MacDonough); On a Pay Night Evening (C: Schlinker; L: Paul West); Phantom Patrol (C: Paul Tietjens); Poppy Chorus (C: Paul Tietjens); Rosalie (C: Gus Edwards; L: Will D. Cobb); Sammy [2] (C: Edward Hutchinson; L: James O'Dea); She Really Didn't Mind the Thing at All [1] (C: Paul Tietjens); She's My Native Land (C: A. Baldwin Sloane; L: Glen MacDonough); Spanish Bolero (C: A. Baldwin Sloane; L: Edgar Smith); Star of My Native Land (C: A. Baldwin Sloane; L: Edgar Smith); That Is Love (C/L: Maurice Steinberg); That's Where She Sits All Day (C/L: Unknown); Things That We Don't Learn at School (C: A. Baldwin Sloane); Traveler and the Pie, The (C: Paul Tietjens); Wee Highland Mon (C: A. Baldwin Sloane; L: Edgar Smith); When the Circus Comes to Town (C: Bob Adams; L: James O'Dea); When We Get What's Coming to Us [1] (C: Paul Tietjens); When You Love, Love, Love (C: Paul Tietjens); Witch Behind the Man, The (C: Albert; L: Louis Weslyn)

Cast: Grace Kimball; Anna Laughlin; Dave Montgomery; Fred Stone; Bessie Wynn

Notes: This Majestic Theatre was built by the Shuberts on Columbus Circle and opened with this production. The theatre can be seen briefly in the film IT SHOULD HAPPEN TO YOU." [1] Sheet music only. [2] Added after opening.

4724 • WIZARD OF THE NILE, THE

OPENED: 11/21/1895 Theatre: Casino
Musical Broadway

Composer: Victor Herbert
Lyricist: Harry B. Smith
Librettist: Harry B. Smith
Producer: Arthur F. Clark; Kirke La Shelle

Costumes: Mme. Seidle; **Musical Director:** Frank Palma; **Set Design:** Ernest Albert

Songs: Am I a Wizard; Bang, Bang, the Most Harmonious Sound; Cheer for the Kibosh, A; Cleopatra's Aria; Echo Song, The; Father Nile, Keep Us in Thy Care; Finale Act III; Gaze on This Face; I Adore Thee; I Am the Ruler; I Envy the Bird; I Have Been A-Maying; If I Were a King; In Dreamland; Incantation; I've Appeared Before Crowned Heads; Know Ye the Sound; Lancers; List to Our Matin Serenade; My Angeline; My Love Awaits; Nature's Song Is But a Dream; On Cleopatra's Wedding Day; Oriental March; Pure and White As the Lotus; Song of the Optimist; Star Light, Star Bright (Starlight Waltz); Stonecutters' Song (Work Away with a Song, My Boys); Strew the Way with Flor'rets Blooming; That's One Thing a Wizard Can Do; There's One Thing a Wizard Can Do; To the Pyramid; What Is Love?; When the Bugles Are Calling

Cast: Walter Allen; Frank Daniels; Dorothy Morton; Mary Palmer; Helen Redmond; Louise Royce

Notes: No songs listed in program. Songs from vocal score.

4725 • WOGGLE BUG, THE

OPENED: 06/20/1905
Musical Closed out of town

Composer: Frederic Chapin
Lyricist: L. Frank Baum
Librettist: L. Frank Baum

Source: WOGGLE BUG BOOK, THE (Story: L. Frank Baum)

Songs: Doll and the Jumping Jack, The; Equine Paradox; Hobgoblins; Household Brigade, The; I'll Get Another Place; Mr. H.M. Woggle-Bug, T.E.; Patty Cake, Baker Man; Soldiers; Sweet Matilda; There's a Lady-Bug A'Waitin'; To the Victor Belongs the Spoils (Chewing Gum Song)

Cast: Helen Allyn; Phoebe Coyne; Blanche Deyo; Hal Godfred; Mabel Hite; Fred Mace

Notes: No program available. Produced in Chicago.

4726 • WOMAN HATERS, THE

OPENED: 10/07/1912 Theatre: Astor
Musical Broadway: 32

Composer: Edmund Eysler
Lyricist: George V. Hobart
Librettist: George V. Hobart
Producer: A.H. Woods
Director: George Marion

Source: DIE FRAULEIN FRESSEN (Play: Carl Lindau; Leo Stein)

Songs: Come On Over Here [1] (C: Walter Kollo; L: George V. Hobart; Jerome Kern); Dance the Polka; He Will Take Me to His Heart (L: M.E. Rourke); It Was Marie; Little Girl Come Back to Me (L: M.E. Rourke)

Cast: Sallie Fisher; Joseph Santley

Notes: No songs listed in program. [1] Also in THE DOLL GIRL.

4727 • WOMAN OF THE YEAR

OPENED: 03/29/1981 Theatre: Palace
Musical Broadway: 770

Composer: John Kander
Lyricist: Fred Ebb
Librettist: Peter Stone
Producer: Lawrence Kasha; David S. Landay; Stewart F. Lane; James M. Nederlander; Carole J. Shorenstein; Warner Theatre Productions
Director: Robert Moore

Source: WOMAN OF THE YEAR, THE (Film: Michael Kanin; Ring Lardner Jr.); **Choreographer:** Tony Charmoli; **Costumes:** Theoni V. Aldredge; **Dance Arranger:** Ronald Melrose; **Lighting Designer:** Marilyn Rennagel; **Musical Director:** Donald Pippin; **Orchestrations:** Michael Gibson; **Set Design:** Tony Walton; **Vocal Arranger:** Donald Pippin

Songs: Grass Is Always Greener, The; Happy in the Morning; I Told You So; I Wrote the Book; It Isn't Working; Man About Town [1]; Nothing Personal [1]; One of the Boys; Open the Window [3]; Poker Game, The; See You in the Funny Papers; Shut Up Gerald; So What Else Is New?; Sometimes a Day Goes By; Table Talk; That's the Way It Is [1]; Two of Us, The; We're Gonna Work It Out; Who Would Have Dreamed [2]; Woman of the Year (1); Woman of the Year (2) [3]; You're Right You're Right

Cast: Lauren Bacall; Helon Blount; Roderick Cook; Marilyn Cooper; Rex Everhart; Grace Keagy; Jamie Ross

Notes: [1] Cut prior to opening. [2] Cut prior to opening then added when Raquel Welch succeeded Lauren Bacall. [3] Added for national tour after Broadway.

4728 • WOMAN-KING, THE

OPENED: 1893
Musical — Closed out of town

Composer: Ludwig Englander

Source: RAINMAKER OF SYRIA, THE (Musical: Rudolf Aronson)

Notes: Newark 11/20/1893. No other information available.

4729 • WOMB, THE

OPENED: 11/22/1986
Musical

Composer: John Pike
Additional Music: Christina Dougherty; Joseph M. Santi
Lyricist: John Pike
Librettist: John Pike
Producer: Naomi Grabel; Harold Wolpert
Director: John Pike

Costumes: Astrid Sosa; **Lighting Designer:** Ed Wilcox; **Set Design:** Ed Wilcox

Songs: Here in the Womb; Julie's Song; One More, One Less; Through the Door

Cast: Bobbi Block; Wier Harman; Lee S. Wind

Notes: Performed at the Annenberg Center Studio Theatre, Philadelphia.

4730 • WONDER BAR, THE

OPENED: 03/17/1931 — Theatre: Nora Bayes
Musical — Broadway: 86

Composer: Robert Katscher
Lyricist: Irving Caesar
Librettist: Irving Caesar; Aben Kandel
Producer: Morris Gest; Messrs. Shubert
Director: William Mollison

Source: WUNDERBAR (Musical: Karl Farkas; Geza Herczeg); **Choreographer:** John Pierce; Albertina Rasch; **Costumes:** Charles LeMaire; **Musical Director:** Louis Silver; **Set Design:** Watson Barratt

Songs: Dance We All Do for Al, The [2]; Dying Flamingo, The [2]; Elizabeth; Ev'ry Day Can't Be a Sunday [3] (C/L: Al Jolson); Good Evening, Friends; I'm Falling in Love; Lenox Avenue [3] (C/L: Irving Caesar; Al Jolson; Joseph Meyer); Ma Mere [1] (C: Harry Warren; L: Irving Caesar; Al Jolson); Oh, Donna Clara (C: J. Petersburski; L: Beda; Irving Caesar); Something Seems to Tell Me [3]

Cast: Carol Chilton; Signorina Medea Columbara; Doris Groday; Al Jolson; Patsy Kelly; Wanda Lyon; Rex O'Malley; Al Segal; Vernon Steele; Maceo Thomas; Arthur Treacher; Trini

Notes: [1] Also in SWEET AND LOW. [2] Out Detroit 12/6/31. [3] Sheet music only.

4731 • WONDER YEARS, THE

OPENED: 05/25/1988 — Theatre: Top of the Gate
Musical — Off-Broadway: 23

Composer: David Levy
Lyricist: David Levy
Librettist: David Holdgrive; Terry LaBolt; David Levy; Steve Liebman
Producer: Dwight Frye; Russ Thacker
Director: David Holdgrive

Choreographer: David Holdgrive; **Costumes:** Richard Schurkamp; **Lighting Designer:** Ken Billington; **Musical Director:** Keith Thompson; **Set Design:** Nancy Thun

Songs: Another Elementary School; Baby Boom Babies; First Love; Flowers from the Sixties; Gimme Get Me I Want It; Girl Most Likely, The; Me Suite, The; Monarch Notes; Pushing Thirty; Takin' Him Home to Meet Mom; Teach Me How to Fast Dance; Through You; Wonder Years, The

Cast: Adam Bryant; Meghan Duffy; Louisa Flaningam; Kathy Morath; Alan Osburn; Lenny Wolpe

Notes: No songs listed in program.

4732 • WONDERFUL LIFE, A

Musical Closed out of town

Composer: Joe Raposo
Lyricist: Sheldon Harnick
Librettist: Sheldon Harnick
Director: Brent Wagner

Source: IT'S A WONDERFUL LIFE (Film: Frank Capra; Frances Goodrich; Albert Hackett); **Choreographer:** Tim Millett; **Conductor:** Bradley Bloom; **Lighting Designer:** Ken Yunker; **Musical Director:** Jerry DePuit; **Orchestrations:** Jerry DePuit; **Set Design:** David Leugs

Songs: Can You Find Me a House; Christmas Gifts; First Class All the Way; Good Night; I Couldn't Be with Anyone but You; If I Had a Wish; In a State; Linguine; Mystery, A; Not What I Expected; On to Pittsburgh; One of the Lucky Ones; Opening: Prayer; Panic at the Building and Loan; Precious Little; Ruth; Show Me a Suitcase; "Unborn" Sequence; Welcome a Hero; Wings; Wonderful Life, A

Cast: Mark E. Doerr; Andrew E. Lippa; Connie Sa Loutos; Edward J. Smit; Beth Spencer; Paul Winberg

Notes: Program of the Power Center of the Performing Arts used.

4733 • WONDERFUL NIGHT, A

OPENED: 10/31/1929 Theatre: Majestic
Musical Broadway: 125

Composer: Johann Strauss
Lyricist: Fanny Todd Mitchell
Librettist: Fanny Todd Mitchell
Producer: Messrs. Shubert
Director: Jose Ruben

Source: LE REVEILLON (Story); **Costumes:** Orry Kelly; Ernest Schrapps; **Set Design:** Watson Barratt; Herbert Moore

Cast: Hal Forde; Cary Grant[1]; Robert Irving; Joseph Letora; Solly Ward

Songs: Chacun a Son Gout; Girls Must Live; Letter Song; Two in Love

Notes: The story was also the basis for DIE FLEDERMAUS. Songs not listed in program. [1] Billed as Archie Leach.

4734 • WONDERFUL TOWN

OPENED: 02/25/1953 Theatre: Winter Garden
Musical Broadway: 559

Composer: Leonard Bernstein
Lyricist: Betty Comden; Adolph Green
Librettist: Jerome Chodorov; Joseph Fields
Producer: Robert Fryer
Director: George Abbott

Source: MY SISTER EILEEN (Play: Jerome Chodorov; Joseph Fields); **Source:** MY SISTER EILEEN (Story: Ruth McKenney); **Choreographer:** Donald Saddler; **Costumes:** Mainbocher; Raoul Pene du Bois; **Lighting Designer:** Peggy Clark; **Musical Director:** Lehman Engel; **Orchestrations:** Don Walker; **Set Design:** Raoul Pene du Bois

Songs: Ballet at the Village Vortex (dance); Christopher Street; Conga!; Conquering New York (dance) [4]; Conversation Piece (Nice Talk, Nice People); It's Love; Lallapalooza [3]; Let It Come Down [2]; Little Bit in Love, A; My Darlin' Eileen; Ohio; One Hundred Easy Ways; Pass the Football; Quiet Girl, A; Self- Expression [1]; Story of My Life, The [2]; Swing!; What a Waste; Wrong Note Rag

Cast: Edith Adams; Cris Alexander; Jordan Bentley; Dort Clark; Warren Galjour; George Gaynes; Dody Goodman; Henry Lascoe; Rosalind Russell

Notes: [1] Out New Haven 1/19/53. [2] Cut prior to opening. [3] Out New Haven 1/19/53. Same song as "Hallapalooza" cut from PETER PAN (1950). [4] Lyric cut prior to opening.

4735 • WONDERLAND

OPENED: 10/24/1905 Theatre: Majestic
Musical Broadway: 73

Composer: Victor Herbert
Lyricist: Glen MacDonough
Librettist: Glen MacDonough
Producer: Julian Mitchell
Director: Julian Mitchell

Source: DANCING PRINCESS, THE (Story: Brothers Grimm); **Musical Director:** Carl Styx; **Orchestrations:** Victor Herbert; **Set Design:** E.G. Unitt; John Young

Songs: Barbarian Dance; Broadway Favorites; Companions of the Blade; Crew of the Peek-a-Boo, The; Eccentric Dance; From You I'll Never Part (C: Helen M. Trigg; L: Walter H. Faulkner); Hallowe'en [3]; How to Tell a Fairy Tale [1]; Hunting of the Cook, The; I and Myself and Me (L: Vincent Bryan); It's Hard to Be a Hero [2]; Jografree; Knave of Hearts, The [1]; Little Black Sheep [1]; Love's Golden Day; Minuet; Nature Class, The; Nineteen Princesses Song [2]; No Show Tonight; Only One, The; Opening Chorus Act II [1]; Oriental Dance [2]; Ossified Man, The; Popular Pauline; Tale of a Music Box Shop (Tale of a Song Box Shop); That's Why They Say I'm Crazy [1]; Until We Meet Again; Voice for It, The; When Perrico Plays; With Frame, Two Forty Nine [1]; Woman's First Thought Is a Man, A [1]; Your Heart, If You Please [1]

Cast: Sam Chip; Bessie Clayton; James Cook; Eva Davenport; Lotta Faust; James Smith; Bessie Wynn

Notes: Titled ALICE AND THE EIGHT PRINCESSES out of town. [1] Sheet music only. [2] ASCAP/Library of Congress only. [3] Vocal score only.

4736 • WONDERLAND IN CONCERT

OPENED: 12/27/1978 Theatre: Public
Musical Off-Broadway: 3

Composer: Elizabeth Swados
Lyricist: Elizabeth Swados
Librettist: Elizabeth Swados
Producer: N.Y. Shakespeare Festival; Joseph Papp
Director: Elizabeth Swados

Source: ALICE'S ADVENTURES IN WONDERLAND (Novel: Lewis Carroll); **Source:** THROUGH THE LOOKING GLASS (Novel: Lewis Carroll); **Lighting Designer:** Jennifer Tipton

Cast: Karen Evans; Gloria Hodes; Rodney Hudson; Paul Kreppel; Joan MacIntosh; Jim McConaughty; William Parry; JoAnna Peled; Meryl Streep

Notes: *See also ALICE IN CONCERT*, a revision of this show.

4737 • WONDERWORLD

OPENED: 04/07/1964 Theatre: Amphitheatre-on-the-lake
Revue N.Y. World's Fair

Composer: Jule Styne
Lyricist: Stanley Styne
Producer: Meyer Davis
Director: Leon Leonidoff

Choreographer: Michael Kidd; **Costumes:** Alvin Colt; **Lighting Designer:** Jules Fisher; **Dance Arranger:** Peter Howard; **Orchestrations:** Meyer Davis; **Set Design:** Richard Rychtarik; Don Shirley

Songs: Age of Rock-Rock of Ages; Alfa Romeo; Coco Palm Tree Island; Good Old Fashioned Get Together; Happy Days; Independence Day Parade; Meet the Press; Welcome; Woman's Place; (The Wonder of It All) Wonderworld; Your Isle

Cast: Chita Rivera; Gretchen Wyler

4738 • WOODLAND

OPENED: 11/21/1904 Theatre: New York
Musical Broadway: 83

Composer: Gustav Luders
Lyricist: Frank Pixley
Librettist: Frank Pixley
Producer: Henry W. Savage
Director: George Marion

Choreographer: Sam Marion; **Costumes:** Archie Gunn; **Lighting Designer:** Joe Wilson; **Musical Director:** Gustav Luders; **Set Design:** Walter Burridge; Edward La Moss

Songs: At Night, At Night; Bird and the Bottle, The [2]; Bye-Bye Baby; Cheer Boys, Cheer; Clear the Way; Dainty Little Ingenue; Execution of Prince Eagle [3]; Firefly, The [2]; If You Love Me, Lindy; Keep on Smiling; Message of Spring, The;

No Bird Ever Flew So High He Didn't Have to Light (C: Harry Bulger; L: Will D. Cobb); Old Blue Jay, The [3]; Prince Eagle's Entrance; Romance of a Bachelor Bird, The; Society; Some Day When My Dreams Come True; Tale of a Turtle Dove, The; They'll Have to Go; Time Is Flying; Valley of Hokus-Po, The; When Duty Calls; When the Heart Is Light; Will You Be My Little Bride [1]; You Never Can Tell Till You Try

Cast: Harry Bulger; Emma Carus; Helen Hale; Ida Brooks Hunt

Notes: [1] Out Boston 4/24/05. [2] Sheet music only. [3] Vocal score only.

4739 • WOODY GUTHRIE

Notes: *See TOM TAYLOR AS WOODY GUTHRIE.*

4740 • WOODY GUTHRIE'S AMERICAN SONG

OPENED: 07/31/1991
Revue Closed out of town

Composer: Woody Guthrie
Lyricist: Woody Guthrie
Librettist: Woody Guthrie
Adaptation: Peter Glazer
Producer: Goodspeed Opera House
Director: Peter Glazer

Choreographer: Jennifer Martin; **Costumes:** Baker S. Smith; Mindy Wolfe; **Lighting Designer:** David Noling; **Musical Director:** Malcolm Ruhl; **Orchestrations:** Jeff Waxman; **Set Design:** Philipp Jung; **Vocal Arranger:** Jeff Waxman

Songs: Ain't Gonna Be Treated This Way; Better World; Bound for Glory; Deportee (Plane Wreck at Los Gatos); Do Re Mi; Dust Bowl Refugee; Dust Storm Disaster; End of My Line; Grand Coulee Dam; Hard, Ain't It Hard; Hard Travelin'; I Don't Feel at Home on the Bowery No More; Lonesome Valley; New York Town; Nine Hundred Miles; Oklahoma Hills; Pastures of Plenty; Sinking of the Reuben James, The; Talkin' Subway; This Land Is Your Land; Union Maid; Worried Man

Cast: Jane Gillman; Brian Gunter; Ora Jones; Susan Moniz; John Reeger; Malcolm Ruhl; L.J. Slavin; Christopher Walz

Notes: No songs written for this show.

4741 • WOOF, WOOF

OPENED: 12/25/1929 Theatre: Royale
Musical Broadway: 45

Composer: Edward Pola
Lyricist: Eddie Brandt
Librettist: Estelle Hunt; Sam Summers; Cyrus Wood
Producer: William Demarest; Bernard Lohmuller
Director: William Caryl

Choreographer: Dan Healy; Leonide Massine; **Costumes:** Mabel Johnston; **Orchestrations:** Ken Macomber; **Set Designer:** Clark Robinson

Songs: Fair Weather; Girl Like You, A; I Like It; I Mean What I Say; I'll Take Care of You; Lay Your Bets; Satanic Strut; Shh!; That Certain Thing; Topple Down; Why Didn't You Tell Me; Won't I Do?; You're All the World to Me

Cast: Louise Brown; Eddie Nelson; Al Sexton; Jack Squires

4742 • WORDS AND MUSIC (1917)

OPENED: 11/24/1917 Theatre: Fulton
Revue Broadway: 24

Composer: E. Ray Goetz
Lyricist: E. Ray Goetz
Librettist: Raymond Hitchcock
Producer: E. Ray Goetz; Raymond Hitchcock
Director: Leon Errol

Songs: Brickerty-Brackety — Tootsies; Call On Rag Doll (C: Willy White); Camouflaging (C: Jean Schwartz); Christmastide Love (C: Willy White); Dance of the Dolls; Everything Looks Rosy and Bright; First Nighters; Ginger; I May Stay Away a Little Longer; If You Hadn't Answered No (C: Harry Ruby; L: Bert Kalmar; Edgar Leslie); It's All Right If You Love (One Another) (C: Harry Ruby; L: Edgar Leslie); Ladies, The; Lady Romance; March of the Enchantress; My Broadway Butterfly (C: Willy White); New York, What's Become of You?; Nonsense; Oriental Prelude; Stop Your Camouflaging with Me (C: Jean Schwartz); They'll Be Whistling It All Over Town (C: Jean Schwartz); Wait Till the Silver Moon Rolls By; Walk Down the Avenue with Me; While We Go Marching Along [1]

Cast: Edna Aug; Elizabeth Brice; Richard Carle; Wellington Cross; Marion Davies; Gordon Dooley; William Ray

Notes: [1] Sheet music only.

4743 • WORDS AND MUSIC (1974)

OPENED: 04/16/1974 Theatre: John Golden
Revue Broadway: 127

Composer: Jule Styne
Lyricist: Sammy Cahn
Librettist: Sammy Cahn
Producer: Alexander H. Cohen; Harvey Granat
Director: Jerry Adler

Lighting Designer: Marc B. Weiss; **Musical Director:** Richard J. Leonard; **Set Design:** Robert Randolph

Songs: All the Way [5] (C: James Van Heusen); Be My Love [6] (C: Nicholas Brodszky); Call Me Irresponsible [7] (C: James Van Heusen); Christmas Waltz, The; Come Fly with Me (C: James Van Heusen); Day By Day (C: Axel Stordahl; Paul Weston); Everybody Has the Right to Be Wrong [1] (C: James Van Heusen); Five Minutes More [8]; High Hopes [10] (C: James Van Heusen); I Fall in Love Too Easily [11]; I Guess I'll Hang My Tears Out to Dry [9]; I Only Miss Him When I Think of Him [1] (C: James Van Heusen); I Should Care [12] (C: Axel Stordahl; Paul Weston); I'll Never Stop Loving You [14] (C: Nicholas Brodszky); I'll Walk Alone [15]; It's Been a Long, Long Time; It's Magic [17]; I've Heard That Song Before [16]; Let It Snow! Let It Snow! Let It Snow!; Love and Marriage [4] (C: James Van Heusen); My Kind of Town [18] (C: James Van Heusen); Papa, Won't You Dance with Me [3]; Please Be Kind (C: Saul Chaplin); Pocket Full of Miracles [19] (C: James Van Heusen); Put 'Em in a Box [17]; Rhythm Is Our Business (C: Saul Chaplin; Jimmy Lunceford); Saturday Night (Is the Loneliest Night in the Week); Second Time Around, The [20] (C: James Van Heusen); Shake Your Head from Side to Side (C: Bob Gerow); Teach Me Tonight (C: Gene DePaul); (Love Is) The Tender Trap [21] (C: James Van Heusen); Things We Did Last Summer, The; Thoroughly Modern Millie [22] (C: James Van Heusen); Three Coins in the Fountain [23]; Time After Time [24]; Touch of Class, A [25] (C: George Barrie); Until the Real Thing Comes Along (C/L: Sammy Cahn; Saul Chaplin; L.E. Freeman); Walking Happy [2] (C: James Van Heusen); Wonder Why [13] (C: Nicholas Brodszky); You'll Never Know Where You're Going Till You Get There [26]; You're My Girl [3]

Cast: Sammy Cahn; Kelly Garrett; Shirley Lemmon; Jon Peck

Notes: Sammy Cahn sings his own songs and discusses his career. No original songs in this show. Produced in London as THE SAMMY CAHN SONGBOOK. [1] From SKYSCRAPER. [2] From WALKING HAPPY. [3] From HIGH BUTTON SHOES. [4] From TV musical OUR TOWN. [5] From film THE JOKER IS WILD. [6] From film THE TOAST OF NEW ORLEANS. [7] From film PAPA'S DELICATE CONDITION. [8] From film THE SWEETHEART OF SIGMA CHI. [9] From GLAD TO SEE YA. [10] From film A HOLE IN THE HEAD. [11] From film ANCHORS AWEIGH. [12] From film THRILL OF ROMANCE. [13] From film RICH, YOUNG AND PRETTY. [14] From film LOVE ME OR LEAVE ME. [15] From film THREE CHEERS FOR THE BOYS. [16] From film YOUTH ON PARADE. [17] From film ROMANCE ON THE HIGH SEAS. [18] From film ROBIN AND THE SEVEN HOODS. [19] From film POCKETFUL OF MIRACLES. [20] From film HIGH TIME. [21] From film THE TENDER TRAP. [22] From film THOROUGHLY MODERN MILLIE. [23] From film THREE COINS IN THE FOUNTAIN. [24] From film IT HAPPENED IN BROOKLYN. [25] From film A TOUCH OF CLASS. [26] From film CINDERELLA JONES.

4744 • WORKING

OPENED: 05/14/1978 Theatre: 46th Street
Revue Broadway: 25

Librettist: Stephen Schwartz
Producer: Stephen R. Friedman; Irwin Meyer
Director: Stephen Schwartz

Source: Working (Book: Studs Terkel); **Choreographer:** Onna White; **Costumes:** Marjorie Slaiman; **Dance Arranger:** Michele Brourman; **Lighting Designer:** Ken Billington; **Musical Director:** Stephen Reinhardt; **Orchestrations:** Kirk Nurock; **Set Design:** David Mitchell; **Vocal Arranger:** Stephen Reinhardt

Songs: All the Livelong Day (I Hear America Singing) [2] (C/L: Stephen Schwartz; L: Walt Whitman); America Dreaming [1] (C/L: James Taylor); Brother Trucker (C/L: James Taylor); Cleanin' Women (C/L: Micki Grant); Fathers and

Sons (C/L: Stephen Schwartz); Husbands and Wives Dance (C/L: Michele Brourman); If I Could've Been (C/L: Micki Grant); It's an Art (C/L: Stephen Schwartz); Joe (C/L: Craig Carnelia); Just a Housewife (C/L: Craig Carnelia); Lovin' Al (C/L: Micki Grant); Mason, The (C/L: Craig Carnelia); Millwork (C/L: Stephen Schwartz; C: Michele Brourman); Neat to Be a Newsboy (C/L: Stephen Schwartz); Nightskate (C/L: Stephen Schwartz; C: Michele Brourman); Nobody Goes Out Anymore [1] (C/L: Craig Carnelia); Nobody Tells Me How (C: Mary Rodgers; L: Susan Birkenhead); Something to Point To (C/L: Craig Carnelia); Treasure Island Trio Dance (inst.) (C: Michele Brourman); Un Mejor Dia Vendra (C: James Taylor; L: Graciela Daniele; Matt Landers); Working Girl's Apache (dance) [1] (C: Michele Brourman)

Cast: Susan Bigelow; Steven Boockvor; Rex Everhart; Arny Freeman; Bob Gunton; David Patrick Kelly; Matt Landers; Bobo Lewis; Patti LuPone; Matthew McGrath; Lenora Nemetz; David Langston Smyrl; Lynne Thigpen

Notes: [1] Out Chicago 1/78. [2] Lyrics based on poem by Walt Whitman.

4745 • WORLD OF BLACK AND WHITE, THE

Notes: *See A REEL AMERICAN HERO.*

4746 • WORLD OF JULES FEIFFER, THE

OPENED: 07/02/1962
Revue Closed out of town

Composer: Stephen Sondheim
Lyricist: Stephen Sondheim
Librettist: Jules Feiffer
Producer: Lewis Allen; Harry Rigby
Director: Mike Nichols

Set Designer: Don J. Remacle; **Lighting Designer:** Richard Drew; **Musical Director:** Robert Colston

Songs: Truly Content

Cast: Ronny Graham; Dorothy Loudon; Paul Sand

Notes: Part of this show was a one-act version of the story "Passionella." Jerry Bock and Sheldon Harnick also musicalized this story as part of THE APPLE TREE.

4747 • WORLD OF PLEASURE, A (1915)

OPENED: 10/14/1915 Theatre: Winter Garden
Musical Broadway: 116

Composer: Sigmund Romberg
Lyricist: Harold Atteridge
Librettist: Harold Atteridge
Producer: Winter Garden Company
Director: J.C. Huffman

Choreographer: Theodore Kosloff; Jack Mason; **Costumes:** Mrs. J.J. Shubert; **Musical Director:** Oscar Radin

Songs: At the Toy Shop; Dance of the Midnight Sons, The (inst.); Dance of the Squareheads (inst.); Dancing Festival, The; Danse Excentrique (inst.); Doll Dance, The (inst.); Down in Catty Corner; Employment Agency, The; Fascination; Fifth Avenue; Flights of Fancy; Girl of the Fan, The; Girlies Are Out of My Life; Good Fellows Club, The; Greatest Battle-Song of All, The (L: Harold Atteridge; Jack Wilson); I Could Go Home to a Girlie Like You; I Played My Concertina; I'll Make You Like the Town; In Arabia; In the War Against Men; Japanese Ballet; Jigaree, The; Mark Anthony; Mechanical Soldiers; Melting Pot, The; Miss Innovation; Polo Rag (inst.); Ragtime Carnival; Ragtime Pipes of Pan, The; Rosey-Posey; Shopping [1]; Syncopation (C/L: J. Leubrie Hill); Take Me Home with You; Wop Cabaret, The (C/L: John Golden)

Cast: Clifton Crawford; Sahari Djeli; Kitty Gordon; Sydney Greenstreet; Lou Holtz; Stella Mayhew

Notes: [1] Vocal score only.

4748 • WORLD OF PLEASURE (1925)

OPENED: 1925

Composer: George David Weist [1]
Lyricist: Mack Gordon; Anton F. Scibilia

Songs: Cinderella; Make Up Your Mind; Midsummer Night's Dream

Notes: No other information available. [1] Later known as George David Weiss.

4749 • WORLD OF SUZIE WONG, THE

OPENED: 10/14/1958 Theatre: Broadhurst
Play Broadway: 508

Author: Paul Osborn
Producer: Mansfield Productions; David Merrick; Seven Arts Productions, Inc
Director: Joshua Logan

Source: WORLD OF SUZIE WONG, THE (Novel: Richard Mason); **Costumes:** Dorothy Jenkins; **Lighting Designer:** Jo Mielziner; **Set Design:** Jo Mielziner

Songs: Ding Dong Song, The [2] (C/L: Lionel Bart; L: Yao Ming); How Can You Forget [1] (C: Richard Rodgers; L: Lorenz Hart)

Cast: Sarah Marshall; France Nuyen; Ron Randell; William Shatner; Kathleen Widdoes

Notes: [1] Originally in FOOLS FOR SCANDAL. [2] Only in London production.

4750 • WORLD'S MY OYSTER, THE

OPENED: 07/31/1956 Theatre: Actors' Playhouse
Musical Off-Broadway: 40

Composer: Lorenzo Fuller; Carley Mills
Lyricist: Lorenzo Fuller; Carley Mills
Librettist: Lorenzo Fuller; Carley Mills
Producer: Actors' Playhouse
Director: Jed Duane

Choreographer: Walter Hicks; Louis Johnson; **Costumes:** Lew Smith; **Set Design:** Henry Buckmaster

Songs: Devil Is a Man You Know, The; Finer Things of Life, The; Footprints in the Sand; Friendship Ain't No One Way Street; I Set My Heart on One Love; I Wouldn't Bother You About So Much; Just Before I Go to Sleep; Merchandise; Moola Makes the Hula Feel Much Cooler; Quiet Little Royal Household; Rich Enough to Be Rude; Shoeshine; Thing Like This, A; This Is the Life for Me; World in a Jug, The

Cast: Lorenzo Fuller; Dolores Harper; Butterfly McQueen

4751 • WRONG MR. PRESIDENT, THE

OPENED: 1913
Musical

Composer: Trevor Corwell; Russell Smith
Lyricist: J. Homer Tutt; Salem Tutt Whitney
Librettist: J. Homer Tutt; Salem Tutt Whitney
Producer: J. Homer Tutt; Salem Tutt Whitney

Musical Director: Clarence G. Wilson

Songs: All I Ask Is to Forget You; Come Out; For Honor; Have Patience, Don't Worry; Hesitation Waltz; Intruder, The; Just a Pickaninny All Dressed Up (C/L: Lewis T. Thomas); Love You Can't Forget, The; My Heart for You Pines Away (C: Russell Smith; L: Noble Sissle); Romance Espanola; Smart Set Tango; Tourists Are We; Tutt's Todalo (C/L: Lewis T. Thomas); We Welcome Thee; What You Need Is Ginger Springs; When Your Country Calls to Arms; Ye Olde Quadrille (inst.)

Cast: Greensbury Holmes; Frank Jackson; Alfred Strauder; J. Homer Tutt; Salem Tutt Whitney

Notes: No other information available.

4752 • WRONG NUMBER, THE

Notes: *See OH, WHAT A GIRL!*

Y

4753 • YANKEE CIRCUS ON MARS, A

OPENED: 04/12/1905 Theatre: Hippodrome
Musical Broadway: 120

Composer: Jean Schwartz
Lyricist: Manuel Klein; Jean Schwartz; Harry Williams
Librettist: George V. Hobart
Producer: Elmer S. Dundy; Frederick W. Thompson
Director: Edward P. Temple

Choreographer: Sam Marion; Vincente Romeo; **Costumes:** Alfredo Edel; **Musical Director:** Manuel Klein; **Set Design:** Arthur Voegtlin

Songs: Animal King, The (C: Manuel Klein; L: George V. Hobart); Aurora Borealis (L: George V. Hobart); Bogie Man, The (L: Harry Williams); Ensemble (C: Manuel Klein; L: George V. Hobart); Entrance of Messenger from Mars (C: Manuel Klein); Entrance of Soubrette (C: Manuel Klein); Entrance of Yankee Circus (C: Manuel Klein); Get a Horse (L: Harry Williams); Grand Ensemble of Martians (C: Manuel Klein; L: George V. Hobart); Hey! Rube! (L: Stanley Crawford; Harry Williams); Hold Your Horses (L: Harry Williams); Milkmaids' Chorus (L: Manuel Klein; Harry Williams); Opening Chorus (C: Manuel Klein); Reuben Tell Your Mandy (L: Harry Williams)

Cast: James Cherry; Felix Haney; Albert Hart; Vernon Lee; Bessie McCoy; Olive North; Rio Brothers, The; Florence Sinnot; Ty Bell Sisters, The

Notes: "Dance of the Hours" from LA GIOCONDA, directed by Vincenzo Romeo was the second part of the bill. ANDERSONVILLE OR A STORY OF WILSON'S RAIDERS was the third part of the bill. This had a book by Carroll Fleming and mechanical effects by John E Corrigan. ANDERSONVILLE was replaced by THE ROMANCE OF A HINDO PRINCESS in October of 1905. It also had a book by Carroll Fleming and starred James Cherry, Florence Sinnot and Vernon Lee who are all listed above.

4754 • YANKEE CONSUL, THE

OPENED: 02/22/1904 Theatre: Broadway
Musical Broadway: 115

Composer: Alfred G. Robyn
Lyricist: Henry Blossom
Librettist: Henry Blossom
Producer: Henry W. Savage
Director: George Marion

Costumes: Will R. Barnes; **Musical Director:** Frank N. Darling; **Set Design:** Walter Burridge; Edward La Moss

Songs: Ain't It Funny What a Difference Just a Few Hours Make; Con-Con-Con [1]; Cupid Has Found My Heart; Gossips' Chorus; Hammers Will Go Rap, Rap, Rap, The; Hark, While I Sing to Thee! [1]; Hola!; I'd Like to Be a Soldier; In Old New York; In the Days of Old; Mermaid and the Lobster, The [1]; Mosquito and the Midge, The; My San Domingo Maid; Nine [1]; Tell Me [1]; Viva the Gay Fiesta; We Come from Proud Castilian Blood; We Were Taught to Walk Demurely; When the Goblins Are at Play [1]

Cast: William Danforth; Eva Davenport; John E. Hazzard; Raymond Hitchcock; Flora Zabelle

Notes: [1] Sheet music only.

4755 • YANKEE DOODLE SCOUTS

Musical

Composer: Gus Edwards
Lyricist: Will D. Cobb
Librettist: Thomas J. Gray
Producer: Gus Edwards
Director: Gus Edwards

Cast: Hattie Kneitel

Notes: A vaudeville musical. No other information available.

4756 • YANKEE DRUMMERS, THE

OPENED: 01/19/1908
Musical Closed out of town

Songs: Because I'm Married Now; Honey Boy; I'd Like to Know Your Address and Your Name; In the Land of the Buffalo; In Those Boyhood Days; Insanity; Keep on Smiling; Little Bit of Everything, A; Little Bit of Now and Then; Old Fashioned Buggy Ride, An; School Days; There's Only Moon Beams; Uncle Bill

Cast: Lyman Twins; Patti Rosa; Clarence A. Sterling; Myrtle Thompson

Notes: Program of Cedar Rapids. Only cast credits in program. These may not be original songs.

4757 • YANKEE GIRL, THE

OPENED: 12/10/1910 Theatre: Herald Square
Musical Broadway: 92

Composer: Silvio Hein
Lyricist: George V. Hobart
Librettist: George V. Hobart
Producer: Lew Fields
Director: Ned Wayburn

Songs: All, All Alone; Clap Hands [2] (C: Seymour Furth; L: Will A. Heelan); Hands Up [2] (C: J. Fred Helf; L: Arthur J. Lamb); I'll Make a Ring Around Rosie; In 1999 [1]; I've Got Rings on My Fingers or Mumbo-Jumbo-Jijjiboo-J. O'Shay [3] (C: Maurice Scott; L: F.J. Barnes; R.P. Weston); Let's Make Love Among the Roses [2] (C: Jean Schwartz; L: William Jerome); Lousiana Lizabeth; Maid of Sevilla; Nora Malone Call Me By Phone (C: Albert Von Tilzer; L: Junie McCree); Pretty Polly [2]; Tell It to Sweeney (C: Harry Von Tilzer; L: Will Dillon); That Hypnotizing Rag (C/L: C.F. Zittel); Top of the Morning, The; Where's Mama?; Whoop Daddy Ooden Dooden Day; Yankee Girl, The

Cast: Harry Gilfoil; William Halliday; Dorothy Jardon; Blanche Ring; Charles Winninger

Notes: [1] Out prior to New York. [2] Sheet music only. [3] Also in THE MIDNIGHT SONS.

4758 • YANKEE MANDARIN, THE

OPENED: 1909
Musical

Composer: Reginald De Koven
Lyricist: Edward Paulton
Librettist: Edward Paulton
Producer: F. Ray Comstock; Morris Gest

Songs: Back to New York; Dot and Carry One; Gipsy of Poughkeepsie; I Must Have a Picture of That; If I Had a Chance Like That; Oh Papa; Pocket Telephone, The; Sea Siren, The; Something Tells Me; Song of the Clock; Song of the Lantern; Sun Gold; True Blue American Boy; Two Dummies, The; Willow Pattern Plate, The

Notes: No other information available.

4759 • YANKEE PRINCE, THE

OPENED: 04/20/1908 Theatre: Knickerbocker
Musical Broadway: 28

Composer: George M. Cohan
Lyricist: George M. Cohan
Librettist: George M. Cohan
Producer: George M. Cohan; Sam H. Harris
Director: George M. Cohan

Musical Director: Charles J. Gebest; **Orchestrations:** Charles J. Gebest

Songs: A-B-C's of the U.S.A., The; American Idea, The [1]; Cohan's Rag Babe; Come on Down Town; Dancing Ceremony, The [1]; From the Land of Dreams; I Say, Flo; I'm Awfully Strong for You; I'm Going to Marry a Nobleman; M-O-N-E-Y; Nothing New Beneath the Sun [1]; Showing the Yankees London Town; Soldiers of the King; Song of the King, A; Think It Over Carefully; Tommy Atkins, You're All Right; Villains in the Play; Yankee Doodle's Come to Town; Yankee Prince March & Two-Step, The (inst.) [2]; Yankee Prince Waltz (inst.) (C: Charles J. Gebest)

Cast: George M. Cohan; Helen Cohan; Jerry Cohan; Josie Cohan; Donald Crisp; Jack Gardner; Tom Lewis

Notes: [1] Out Washington D.C. 9/20/09. [2] Sheet music only.

4760 • YANKEE PRINCESS, THE

OPENED: 10/02/1922 Theatre: Knickerbocker
Musical Broadway: 80

Composer: Emmerich Kalman
Lyricist: B.G. DeSylva
Librettist: William Le Baron
Producer: A.L. Erlanger
Director: Fred G. Latham; Julian Mitchell

Source: DIE BAJADERE (Musical: Julius Brammer; Alfred Gruenwald; Emmerich Kalman); **Costumes:** Wilhelm; **Lighting Designer:** Tony Greshoff; **Musical Director:** William Daly

Songs: Can It Be That I'm in Love?; Eyes So Dark and Luring; Forbidden Fruit; Friendship; Husband's Only a Husband, A; I Still Can Dream; I'll Dance My Way Into Your Heart; In the Starlight; Lotus Flower; Love the Wife of Your Neighbor; My Bajadere; Roses, Lovely Roses; Stars of the Stage; Waltz Was Made for Lovers, The

Cast: Thorpe Bates; John T. Murray; Vivian Oakland; Vivienne Segal

4761 • YANKEE REGENT, THE

OPENED: 09/17/1907
Musical Closed out of town

Composer: Ben M. Jerome
Lyricist: Chas. Adelman; Irving B. Lee
Librettist: Chas. Adelman; Irving B. Lee
Producer: H.H. Frazee

Musical Director: Ben M. Jerome

Songs: Army and Navy, The; Childhood Days; Clock in the Tower, The; Dancing Sal; Entrance of Regent; Finale Act II; Here's Looking at You; Heyday; I'm Growing Wary; Indigent Aristocrat, An; Land of the Wiener and the Wurst, The; Lilies in the Pond Are not for Me, The (L: Irving B. Lee); Mary Jane; Military, The; Opening Chorus; Proposal, The; Suppose

Cast: Elsie Baird; Thomas Burton; Osborne Clemson; Toby Lyons; Bertha Shalek; Fred Walton

Notes: Program of Cedar Rapids.

4762 • YANKEE TOURIST, A

OPENED: 08/12/1907 Theatre: Astor
Musical Broadway: 103

Composer: Alfred G. Robyn
Lyricist: Wallace Irwin
Librettist: Richard Harding Davis
Producer: Henry W. Savage
Director: George Marion

Source: GALLOPER, THE (Play: Richard Harding Davis); **Musical Director:** John McGhie

Songs: Alabama [1]; And the World Goes On Just the Same [1] (C: Harry O. Sutton; L: Jean Lenox); Broadway Means Home to Me [1]; By the Side of the Zuyder Zee [1] (C: Bennett Scott; L: A.J. Mills); Come and Have a Smile with Me; Come in Out of the Wet [1]; Finale Act II [2]; Gee! Ain't It H — to Be Rich [1]; Glad Hand Girl, The [2]; Golden Sails; Greek Dance; Irish Lads; It's Always Nice Weather Indoors or Oh! Oh! Oh! Says Rosie [1] (C: S.R. Henry; L: Arthur J. Lamb); Longshoreman's Chanty; Love Me Enough to Remember [1]; My Volo Maid [1]; Night Before To-morow, The [2]; Opening Chorus; Opening Chorus Act III [2]; Rainbow; Saracen Song March; So Long Bill (Take Care O' Yourself) [1] (C: Alfred G. Robyn; L: Wallace Irwin); So What's the Use [1] (C/L: Edward Montagu); Steward's Song; Teddy Girl, The; Underneath a Parasol with You [1] (C/L: John B. "Swifty" Lowitz); Wal, I Swan! (Ebenezer Frye) [1] (C/L: Benjamin Hapgood Burt); What's the Use?; When a Girl Is Born to Be a Lady; When You Done Gone Broke [1]; Wouldn't You Like to Have Me for a Sweetheart?; Yankee Millionaire

Cast: Wallace Beery; Herbert Cawthorne; Eva Fallon; Raymond Hitchcock; Harry West; Flora Zabelle

Notes: [1] Sheet music only. [2] Vocal score only.

4763 • YEAH MAN

OPENED: 05/26/1932 Theatre: Park Lane
Revue Broadway: 2

Composer: Ken Macomber; Charles Weinberg; Al Wilson
Lyricist: Ken Macomber; Charles Weinberg; Al Wilson
Librettist: Billy Mills; Leigh Whipper
Producer: Walter Campbell; Jesse Wank
Director: Walter Campbell

Choreographer: Marcus Slayter; **Musical Director:** Billy Butler; **Orchestrations:** Billy Butler; Lorenzo Caldwell; Charles Cooke

Songs: At the Barbecue; Baby, I Could Do It for You; Come to Harlem; Crazy Idea of Love; Dancin' Fool; Give Me Your Love; Gotta Get de Boat Loaded; I'm Always Happy When I'm in Your Arms; I've Got What It Takes; Mississippi Joys; Qualifications (C/L: Porter Grainger); Shady Dan; Shake Your Music; Spell of Those Harlem Nights; That's Religion (C/L: Porter Grainger)

Cast: Rose Henderson; Melodee Four, The; Billy Mills; Mantan Moreland; Eddie Rector; Marcus Slayter; Leigh Whipper; Lily Yuen

4764 • YEARLING, THE

OPENED: 12/10/1965 Theatre: Alvin
Musical Broadway: 3

Composer: Michael Leonard
Lyricist: Herbert Martin
Librettist: Herbert Martin; Lore Noto
Producer: Lore Noto
Director: Lloyd Richards

Source: YEARLING, THE (Novel: Marjorie Kinnan Rawlings); **Choreographer:** Ralph Beaumont; **Costumes:** Ed Wittstein; **Dance Arranger:** David Baker; **Lighting Designer:** Jules Fisher; **Musical Director:** Julian Stein; **Orchestrations:** Larry Wilcox; **Set Design:** Ed Wittstein; **Vocal Arranger:** Julian Stein

Songs: Ain't He a Joy?; Bear Hunt; Boy Talk; Do What the Good Book Says [1]; Everything Beautiful; Everything in the World I Love; Fluttermill Song [1]; Growing Up Is Learning How to Say Goodbye [2]; I Love This Child [2]; I Love You [3]; I Need a Friend [3]; I'd Kick Up My Heels [3]; I'm All Smiles; In That Clearing [4]; Judgement Day [1]; Kind of a Man a Woman Needs, The; Let Him Kick Up His Heels; Little Girl [1]; Lonely Clearing; Moonshine [3]; My Pa [1]; My Prayers Have Come True [3]; Nothing More; One Promise; Planting Fever [4]; Shoot the Pig [3]; Slewfoot [3]; Some Day I'm Gonna Fly; Spring Is a New Beginning [2]; Startin' Over [3]; Teach Me How to Dance [2]; What a Happy Day; What Can I Name Him [1]; Why Did I Choose You?; You're Everything in the World I Love [4]

Cast: Carmen Alvarez; Gordon B. Clarke; Tom Fleetwood; David Hartman; Carmen Mathews; Steve Sanders; David Wayne; Dolores Wilson

Notes: [1] Cut prior to opening. [2] In CBS Radio version. [3] Added to 1985 revival in Atlanta. [4] Out Philadelphia 11/65.

4765 • YELLOW MASK, THE

OPENED: 02/08/1928 Theatre: Carlton
Musical London: 218

Composer: Vernon Duke
Lyricist: Desmond Carter
Producer: Laddie Cliff; Julian Wylie
Director: Laddie Cliff

Choreographer: Max Rivers; **Set Designer:** Joseph and Phil Harker; Marc Henri; Hugh Gee

Songs: Bacon and the Egg, The; Blowing the Blues Away (L: Eric Little); Chinese Ballet (inst.); Chinese March (inst.); Deep Sea; Half a Kiss (L: Eric Little); I Love You So; I Still Believe in You (L: Desmond Carter; Vernon Duke); I'm Wonderful; March (inst.); Opening Chorus Act One; Some Sort of Something (L: Vernon Duke; Eric Little); Walking on Air; Yellow Mask; You Do, I Don't

Cast: Phyllis Dare; Leslie Henson; Bobby Howes

Notes: No program available.

4766 • YES, YES, YVETTE

OPENED: 10/03/1927 Theatre: Sam H. Harris
Musical Broadway: 40

Lyricist: Irving Caesar
Librettist: William Cary Duncan; James Montgomery
Producer: H.H. Frazee

Source: NOTHING BUT THE TRUTH (Play: Frederic S. Isham); **Choreographer:** Sammy Lee; **Costumes:** Milgrim; **Musical Director:** Ben M. Jerome

Songs: Do You Love As I Love? (C: Joseph Meyer); Finale Act I; Finale Act II; For Days and Days (I Love You, I Do) [1] (C: Phil Charig); Good Morning [1] (C: Irving Caesar); How'd You Like To? (C: Stephen Jones); I'm a Little Bit Fonder of You [1] (C: Irving Caesar); My Lady (C: Ben

Jerome; L: Frank Crumit); Opening Act II; Opening Act III; Opening Chorus; Pack Up Your Blues and Smile (C: Peter De Rose; Albert Von Tilzer; L: Jo Trent); Sing, Dance and Smile (C: Philip Charig; Ben Jerome); Six O'Clock (C: Philip Charig); Two of Us, The [1]; What Kind of Boy; Woe Is Me; Yes, Yes, Yvette (C: Philip Charig); You or Nobody! (C: Irving Caesar); You're So Nice to Me

Cast: Jeanette MacDonald; Jack Whiting; Charles Winninger

Notes: [1] Sheet music only.

4767 • YESTERDAY

OPENED: 03/10/1919
Musical — Closed out of town

Composer: Reginald De Koven
Lyricist: Glen MacDonough
Librettist: Glen MacDonough
Producer: Messrs. Shubert

Songs: Bebe; Clown, The; It Isn't the Same in the Daylight; It's Paris Everywhere; Man's Forever, A; Montebanks, The (inst.); My Yesterday; Phantom Rose

4768 • YESTERDAY IS OVER

Play

Author: Mady Christians
Composer: Bill Roscoe
Lyricist: Mady Christians
Director: Margot Lewitin

Songs: The Banco Number; I'm in the Market for a Dream; Oh How I loved Him; Sawing a Woman in Half; Yesterday Is Over

Cast: Elizabeth Franz; Margot Lewitin; Lucille Patton; **Pianist:** David Tice

4769 • YIDDLE WITH A FIDDLE

OPENED: 10/28/1990 — Theatre: Town Hall
Musical — Off-Broadway: 55

Composer: Abraham Ellstein
Lyricist: Isaiah Sheffer
Librettist: Isaiah Sheffer
Producer: Raymond Ariel; Lawrence Toppall
Director: Ran Avni

Source: YITL MIDN FIDL (Film: Joseph Green); **Choreographer:** Helen Butleroff; **Costumes:** Karen Hummel; **Lighting Designer:** Robert Bessoir; **Musical Director:** Lanny Meyers; **Orchestrations:** Lanny Meyers; **Set Design:** Jeffrey Schneider

Songs: Badchen's Verses; Come Gather 'Round; Hard As a Nail; Help Is on the Way!; How Can the Cat Cross the Water?; If You Wanna Dance; I'll Sing; Man to Man; Music, It's a Necessity; New Rhythm; Oh Mama, Am I in Love; Only for a Moment; Stay Home Here with Me; Take It from the Top; To Tell the Truth; Travelling First Class Style; Warsaw!; We'll Sing; Wedding Bulgar Dance (inst.); Yiddle with a Fiddle

Cast: Mitchell Greenberg; Emily Loesser; Patricia Ben Peterson; Steve Sterner

4770 • YIP! YIP! YAPHANK!

OPENED: 08/19/1918 — Theatre: Century
Revue — Broadway: 32

Composer: Irving Berlin
Lyricist: Irving Berlin

Songs: Bevo [4]; Ding Dong [6]; Dream on Little Soldier Boy (L: Jean Havez); God Bless America [1]; Hello, Hello, Hello; I Can Always Find a Little Sunshine in the Y.M.C.A.; Mandy [5]; Oh! How I Hate to Get Up in the Morning [7]; Poor Little Me, I'm on K.P. [2]; Ragtime Razor Brigade; We're on Our Way to France; What a Difference a Uniform Will Make [3]

Cast: 350 Soldiers; William Bauman; Irving Berlin; Dan Healy; Sammy Lee; Benny Leonard

Notes: [1] Written as finale but cut. [2] Also known as "Kitchen Police." [3] Also known as "Ever Since I Put on a Uniform." [4] Also in ZIEGFELD FOLLIES OF 1919. [5] Also in ZIEGFELD FOLLIES OF 1919 and THIS IS THE ARMY (1942). [6] Also in THE CANARY. [7] Also in ZIEGFELD FOLLIES OF 1918 and THIS IS THE ARMY.

4771 • YO-SAN

Notes: *See CHERRY BLOSSOMS.*

4772 • YOKEL BOY

OPENED: 07/06/1939 — Theatre: Majestic
Musical — Broadway: 208

Composer: Sam H. Stept
Lyricist: Lew Brown; Charles Tobias
Librettist: Lew Brown
Producer: Lew Brown
Director: Lew Brown

Choreographer: Gene Snyder; **Costumes:** Frances Feist; **Musical Director:** Al Goodman; **Set Design:** Walter Jagermann

Songs: 'Baby Wampus' Stars, The [2]; Beer Barrel Polka [1] (C: Jaromir Vejvoda; L: Lew Brown); Boy Named Lem, A; Catherine the Great; Comes Love; For the Sake of Lexington; Hollywood and Vine [2]; I Can't Afford to Dream; I Know I'm Nobody; If I Feel This Way Tomorrow [2] (C: Ray Henderson; L: Lew Brown); It's Me Again; Let's Make Memories Tonight; Ship Has Sailed, The; Time for Jukin' (C: Walter Kent); Uncle Sam's Lullaby; When the Berry Blossoms Bloom [2]

Cast: Charles Althoff; Judy Canova; Dixie Dunbar; Buddy Ebsen; Lew Hearn; Jackie Heller; Ralph Holmes; Lois January; Mark Plant; Ralph Riggs; Phil Silvers

Notes: [1] Added after opening. [2] Out Washington, D.C. 12/30/40.

4773 • YOSHE KALB

OPENED: 10/22/1972
Musical Off-Broadway: 95

Composer: Maurice Rauch
Lyricist: Isaac Dogim
Librettist: David Licht
Producer: S. Ehrenfeld & Assoc.; Jewish Nostalgic Prods.; Harry Rothpearl
Director: David Licht

Source: YOSHE KALB (Story: Isaac Bashevis Singer); **Choreographer:** Lillian Shapero; **Costumes:** Sylvia Friedlander; **Lighting Designer:** Tom Meleck; **Musical Director:** Renee Solomon; **Set Design:** Jorday Barry

Songs: Badchen; Bwis Jolem Tanz; Chosen Doime le Meilech & Rikodle; Ein Koloheinu; Malkele's Song; Rosh Hashono; Song of Joy; Three Good Deeds, The; Trio; Tsivye's Song; Wedding Dance; Wedding Procession

Cast: Jacob Ben-Ami; Isaac Dogim; David Ellis; Miriam Kessyn; David Opatoshu; Warren Pincus; Ruth Vool

4774 • YOU BET YOUR ASSETS

OPENED: 01/25/1979
Revue

Composer: Roy Straiges
Lyricist: Stephen de Baum
Librettist: Robert Brown; Louis Day; Sam Domsky; Paul Provenza; Stephen de Baum
Producer: Donald Fisher
Director: Bruce Montgomery

Arrangements: Bruce Montgomery; Roy Straiges; **Choreographer:** Bruce Montgomery; Robert Wilson; **Musical Director:** William Lessig; **Set Design:** Douglas Cohen; Peter Saylor

Songs: At the Casino (L: Robert Wilson; Stephen de Baum); Das Telefunken (C: Bruce Montgomery); Dow Jones Disco, The (inst.); Endangered Species, An; Fugue for Thought (C: Bruce Montgomery); Humility; Love Affair, A; Martini Rock, The; Standing Ovulation, A (C: Mark Cornfield; Murray Indick; L: Paul Provenza); Ticker Tape Caper (inst.); You Bet Your Assets

Cast: Ron Alper; Joe Fillip; Dan Helming

Notes: Amateur show. Mask & Wig Club, University of Pennsylvania.

4775 • YOU COULD BE HOME NOW

OPENED: 10/11/1992 Theatre: Public
Play Off-Broadway: 25

Composer: Tom Judson
Lyricist: Tom Judson
Author: Ann Magnuson
Producer: N.Y. Shakespeare Festival; Women's Project & Prods.
Director: David Schweizer

Choreographer: William Fleet Lively; Jerry Mitchell; **Costumes:** Pilar Limosner; **Incidental Music:** Tom Judson; **Lighting Designer:** Heather Carson; **Set Design:** Bill Clarke

Songs: Folk Song (C/L: Ann Magnuson); West Virginia's Home to Me (C/L: Lyell B. Clay)

Cast: Ann Magnuson

4776 • YOU KNEW ME AL

Musical

Composer: Burton Hamilton
Lyricist: William A. Halloran Jr.

Songs: Bring Back that Yama Dance to Me; Garden of Love for Two; I Want the Boys Around Me (C: Burton Hamilton; Sid Marion); I'm Going Back to Mobile, Alabam'; Let Me Have a Little Corner of Your Heart (C/L: Leon De Costa); My Heart Belongs to the U.S.A.; My Little Loving Baby Mine (C: William A. Halloran Jr.)

Notes: No other information available.

4777 • YOU NEVER KNOW

OPENED: 09/21/1938 Theatre: Winter Garden
Musical Broadway: 78

Composer: Cole Porter
Lyricist: Cole Porter
Librettist: Rowland Leigh
Producer: John Shubert; Messrs. Shubert
Director: Rowland Leigh

Source: BEI KERZENLICHT (Musical: Karl Farkas); **Source:** CANDLE LIGHT (Play: Siegfried Geyer; Robert Katscher); **Choreographer:** Robert Alton; **Costumes:** Brooks; Jenkins; Charles LeMaire; Veronica; Wilma; **Musical Director:** John McManus; Menotti Salta; **Orchestrations:** Claude Austin; Maurice DePackh; Max Hoffmann; Hans Spialek; Don Walker; **Set Design:** Watson Barratt; Albert Johnson

Songs: At Long Last Love; Au Revoir, Cher Baron; By Candlelight (1) [1]; By Candlelight (2) (C: Robert Katscher; L: Rowland Leigh); Cafe Society Set, The [2]; Don't Let It Get You Down [4]; For No Rhyme or Reason; From Alpha to Omega; Gendarmes (C: Robert Katscher; L: Rowland Leigh); Good Evening, Princesse; Ha, Ha, Ha [1]; I Am Gaston; I'll Black His Eyes [2]; I'm Back in Circulation [1]; I'm Going in for Love [1]; I'm Yours [2]; It's No Laughing Matter [1]; Ladies Room (C: Alex Fogarty; L: Edwin Gilbert); Let's Put It to Music (C: Alex Fogarty; L: Edwin Gilbert); Maria; No (You Can't Have My Heart) (C/L: Dana Suesse); One Step Ahead of Love [3]; Opening Act II; Take Yourself a Trip (C: Alex Fogarty; L: Edwin Gilbert); They Learn About Women from Me; Waiters, The [2]; What a Priceless Pleasure [5]; What Is That Tune?; What Shall I Do? (L: Rowland Leigh; Cole Porter); Yes, Yes, Yes; You Never Know

Cast: Debonairs, The; Truman Gaige; Don Harden; Grace Hartman; Paul Hartman; Libby Holman; Charles Kemper; Jean Morehead; Rex O'Malley; June Preisser; Roger Stearns; Lupe Velez; Clifton Webb; Toby Wing

Notes: [1] Not used. [2] Out New Haven 3/3/38. [3] Out Washington, D.C. 3/21/38. [4] Not used in film BREAK THE NEWS. [5] Cut.

4778 • YOU SAID IT

OPENED: 01/19/1931 Theatre: 46th Street
Musical Broadway: 192

Composer: Harold Arlen
Lyricist: Jack Yellen
Librettist: Sid Silvers; Jack Yellen
Producer: Lou Holtz; Jack Yellen
Director: John Harwood

Choreographer: Danny Dare; **Costumes:** Kiviette; **Musical Director:** Louis Gress; **Orchestrations:** Howard Jackson; **Set Design:** Donald Oenslager; **Vocal Arranger:** Charles Henderson

Songs: Alma Mater [2]; Beatin' the Blues [2]; Best Part College Days [2]; Bright and Early [2]; Ha-Ha-Ha (Gang Song) [1] (L: Ted Koehler); If He Really Loves Me; It's Different with Me; Learn to Croon; Sweet and Hot; Tell Me with a Love Song [1] (L: Ted Koehler); They Learn About Women from Me; What Do We Care?; What'd We Come to College For?; While You Are Young; You Said It; You'll Do

Cast: Benny Baker; Peggy Bernier; Hughie Clarke; Oscar Grogan; George Haggarty; Lou Holtz; Mary Lawlor; Lyda Roberti; Slate Brothers; Stanley Smith

Notes: Special music effects: Fred Waring. [1] Not used. [2] ASCAP/Library of Congress only.

4779 • YOU TAKE IT

Musical

Composer: Dennis E. Connell
Lyricist: Dennis E. Connell

Choreographer: Estelle Murray; **Musical Director:** Elizabeth Bogan

Songs: Any Place Would Be Paradise (C/L: Joseph Vance)

Cast: James K. Young

Notes: No other information available.

4780 • YOU'D BE SURPRISED

OPENED: 1920
Musical

Composer: Richard Rodgers
Lyricist: Lorenz Hart
Librettist: Milton Bender
Producer: Akron Club
Director: Milton Bender

Musical Director: Richard Rodgers

Songs: Aphrodite; Boomerang, The; Breath of Spring, A; China; College Baby (L: Robert A. Simon); Don't Love Me Like Othello [2]; Flying the Blimp [3]; I Hate to Talk About Myself [3]; Kid, I Love You; Little Girl, Little Boy [3]; Mary, Queen of Scots [1] (L: Herbert Fields); My World of Romance; Poor Fish; Princess of the Willow Tree (L: Milton G. Bender); Spain; That Boy of Mine (L: Oscar Hammerstein II); When We Are Married (L: Milton G. Bender); You Don't Have to Be a Toreado

Cast: Dorothy Fields

Notes: Amateur production. The Hart lyrics may have been written in collaboration with Milton Bender. [1] Also in POOR LITTLE RITZ GIRL and JAZZ A LA CARTE. [2] Also in FLY WITH ME. [3] ASCAP/Library of Congress only.

4781 • YOU'LL NEVER KNOW

OPENED: 04/20/1921
Musical

Composer: Richard Rodgers
Lyricist: Lorenz Hart
Librettist: Herman Axelrod; Henry William Hanemann
Producer: Columbia University Players
Director: Herman Axelrod; Oscar Hammerstein II; Henry William Hanemann

Choreographer: Herbert Fields; **Musical Director:** Richard Rodgers; **Set Design:** Joseph Physioc

Songs: Chorus Girl Blues [2]; Don't Think That We're the Chorus of the Show [3]; I'm Broke; Jumping Jack; Just a Little Lie; Law [3]; Let Me Drink in Your Eyes [1]; Mr. Director [3]; Something Like Me [4]; Virtue Wins the Day; Watch Yourself [5]; We Take Only the Bets [3]; When I Go on the Stage; Will You Forgive Me?; You'll Never Know; Your Lullaby

Notes: Amateur production. [1] Also in POOR LITTLE RITZ GIRL. [2] Also in SAY IT WITH JAZZ and SAY MAMA. [3] ASCAP/Library of Congress only. [4] ASCAP/Library of Congress only. Also in SAY IT WITH JAZZ. [5] Also in SAY MAMA.

4782 • YOU'LL SEE STARS

OPENED: 12/29/1942 Theatre: Maxine Elliott's
Musical Broadway: 4

Composer: Leo Edwards
Lyricist: Herman Timberg
Librettist: Herman Timberg
Producer: Dave Kramer
Director: Dave Kramer; Herman Timberg

Choreographer: Eric Victor; **Dance Arranger:** Adam Carroll; Bernard Weissman; **Musical Director:** Charles Sanford; **Orchestrations:** Adam Carroll; Bernard Weissman; **Set Design:** Perry Watkins; **Vocal Arranger:** Adam Carroll; Bernard Weissman

Songs: All You Have to Do Is Stand There; America; Betcha I Make Good; Dancing on a Rainbow; Future Stars; It Could Happen, It's Possible; Jelly Beans at Walgreens; Readin', Writin' and 'Rhythmatic; Silvery Moon; Swinging the Bhumba; Time and Time Again; What a Pretty Baby Are You

Cast: Jackie Green; Jackie Michaels; Alan Ray; Arnold Stang; Eric Victor

4783 • YOU'RE A GOOD MAN, CHARLIE BROWN

OPENED: 03/07/1967 Theatre: Theatre 80 St. Marks
Musical Off-Broadway: 1597

Composer: Clark Gesner
Lyricist: Clark Gesner
Librettist: John Gordon [1]

Producer: Gene Persson; Arthur Whitelaw
Director: Joseph Hardy

Source: PEANUTS (Comic Strip: Charles M. Schulz); **Costumes:** Alan Kimmel; **Lighting Designer:** Jules Fisher; **Musical Director:** Joseph Raposo; **Set Design:** Alan Kimmel; **Vocal Arranger:** Joseph Raposo

Songs: Book Report; Dr. Lucy (The Doctor Is In); Happiness; Kite; Little Known Facts; My Blanket and Me; Schroeder; Snoopy; Suppertime; T.E.A.M. (The Baseball Game); You're a Good Man, Charlie Brown

Cast: Bob Balaban; Gary Burghoff; Bill Hinnant; Skip Hinnant; Karen Johnson; Reva Rose

Notes: [1] John Gordon is a pseudonym for the staff and cast of this show.

4784 • YOU'RE IN LOVE

OPENED: 02/06/1917 Theatre: Casino
Musical Broadway: 167

Composer: Rudolf Friml
Lyricist: Edward Clark; Otto Harbach
Librettist: Edward Clark; Otto Harbach
Producer: Arthur Hammerstein
Director: Edward Clark

Choreographer: Robert Marks

Songs: Be Sure It's Light; Boola Boo (L: Otto Harbach); Buck Up; Dance of the Rose, The [1]; He Will Understand; I'm Only Dreaming; Keep Off the Grass; Love-Land (L: Otto Harbach); Married Life; Mignonette (inst.); Musical Snore, The; Opening; Pretty Lips of Velvet [1]; Snatched from the Cradle; Suck Up [2]; That's the Only Place Where Our Flag Shall Fly; Things That They Must Not Do; We'll Drift Along (Opening Chorus Act II); What's the Use of Being Lonesome [1]; Year Is a Long Long Time, A; You're in Love

Cast: Carl McCullough; Clarence Nordstrom; May Thompson

Notes: [1] Out Shubert Theatre 12/17/16. [2] ASCAP/Library of Congress only.

4785 • YOUNG ABE LINCOLN

OPENED: 04/25/1961 Theatre: Eugene O'Neill
Musical Broadway: 93

Composer: Victor Ziskin
Lyricist: Joan Javits; Arnold Sundgaard
Librettist: John Allen; Richard N. Bernstein
Producer: Arthur Shimkin
Director: Jay Harnick

Choreographer: Rhoda Levine; **Costumes:** Fred Voelpel; **Lighting Designer:** Fred Voelpel; **Musical Director:** Victor Ziskin; **Set Design:** Fred Voelpel

Songs: Captain Lincoln March, The; Cheer Up!; Don't P-P-Point Them Guns at Me; Frontier Politics; I Want to Be a Little Frog in a Little Pond; Run, Indian, Run; Same Old Me, The; Someone You Know; Vote for Lincoln; Welcome Home Again; You Can Dance

Cast: Lou Cutell; Judy Foster; Joan Kibrig; Dan Resin; Darrell Sandeen

Notes: Opened Off-Broadway at the York Playhouse 4/3/61 for 18 performances. Moved to Broadway for 27 performances, then reopened at the York for 48 more performances.

4786 • YOUNGER MAN, OLDER WOMAN

OPENED: 10/10/1995 Theatre: Beacon
Musical New York: 28

Composer: Douglas Knyght-Smith; Playe Scott
Lyricist: Douglas Knyght-Smith; Playe Scott
Librettist: Doug Smith; Helen Smith

Songs: Baby I'm Ready Now (C/L: Millie Jackson; Doulgas Knyght-Smith; Playe Scott); Don't Wanna B N Luv; I Wish It Would Rain Down (C/L: Phil Collins); Living with a Stranger; People in My Head (C/L: Millie Jackson; Douglas Knyght-Smith; Playe Scott); Someday We'll All Be Free (C/L: Donny Hathaway); Taking My Life Back (C/L: Millie Jackson; Jolyon Skinner); Weight of Love, The (C/L: Millie Jackson; Reynaldo Rey); When a Woman Makes Up Her Mind; You Gonna Miss Me; Young Man, Older Woman (C/L: Millie Jackson; Jolyon Skinner)

Cast: Keisha Jackson; Millie Jackson; Douglas Knyght; Kenneth "Chocolate Thunder" Montague; Reynaldo Rey

Notes: This show toured the country. No program available.

4787 • YOUNG TURK, THE

OPENED: 01/31/1910 Theatre: New York
Musical Broadway: 32

Composer: Max Hoffmann
Lyricist: Harry Williams
Librettist: Aaron Hoffman
Producer: Klaw & Erlanger
Director: Herbert Gresham

Choreographer: Jack Mason

Songs: At Arrowhead Inn; Chauffeur, The; Did You Ever Hear That in Turkey?; I Thought I Wanted Opera; I'll Be Happy Too; Opening Act II; Parisian Glide; Proposals; Sword Is My Sweetheart True, The; Those Dear Old Wedding Bells [1]; Under the Oriental Moon

Cast: Fred Bowers; Mae Murray; Max Rogers

Notes: [1] Sheet music only.

4788 • YOUR ARMS TOO SHORT TO BOX WITH GOD

OPENED: 12/22/1976 Theatre: Lyceum
Revue Broadway: 149

Composer: Alex Bradford; Micki Grant
Lyricist: Alex Bradford; Micki Grant
Librettist: Vinnette Carroll
Producer: Frankie Hewitt; Tom Mallow
Director: Vinnette Carroll

Source: GOSPEL ACCORDING TO ST. MATTHEW, THE (Book); **Choreographer:** Talley Beatty; **Costumes:** William Schroder; **Dance Arranger:** H.B. Barnum; **Lighting Designer:** Gilbert V. Hemsley Jr.; Richard Winkler; **Musical Director:** George Broderick; Michael Powell; **Orchestrations:** H.B. Barnum; **Set Design:** William Schroder; **Vocal Arranger:** Chapman Roberts

Songs: As Long As I Live; Band, The; Be Careful Whom You Kiss (C/L: Alex Bradford); Beatitudes; Can't No Grave Hold My Body Down (C/L: Alex Bradford); Come on Down; Didn't I Tell You (C/L: Alex Bradford); Do You Know Jesus; Everybody Has His Own Way (C/L: Alex Bradford); Give Us Barabbas; He's a Wonder; I Know I Have to Leave Here; I Love You So Much Jesus (C/L: Alex Bradford); It Was Alone; It's Too Late; Judas Dance (inst.) (C: H.B. Barnum); Just a Little Bit of Jesus Goes a Long Way; See How They Done My Lord (C/L: Alex Bradford); Something Is Wrong in Jerusalem; There's a Stranger in Town (C/L: Alex Bradford); Trial; We Are the Priests and Elders (C/L: Alex Bradford); We're Gonna Have a Good Time; When the Power Comes; Your Arms Too Short to Box with God (C/L: Alex Bradford)

Cast: Salome Bey; Clinton Derricks-Carroll; Delores Hall; Hector Jaime Mercado

4789 • YOUR OWN THING

OPENED: 01/13/1968 Theatre: Orpheum
Musical Off-Broadway: 937

Composer: Danny Apolinar; Hal Hester
Lyricist: Danny Apolinar; Hal Hester
Librettist: Donald Driver
Producer: Zev Bufman; Dorothy Love
Director: Donald Driver

Source: TWELFTH NIGHT (Play: William Shakespeare); **Costumes:** Albert Wolsky; **Dance Arranger:** Charles Schneider; **Lighting Designer:** Tom Skelton; **Musical Director:** Charles Schneider; **Orchestrations:** Hayward Morris; **Set Design:** Robert Guerra

Songs: Apocalypse Fugue; Baby! Baby! (Somethin's Happ'nin'); Be Gentle; Come Away; Death; Do Your Own Thing; Don't Leave Me; Flowers, The; Hunca Munca; I'm Me! (I'm Not Afraid); I'm on My Way to the Top; Let It Be [1]; Middle Years, The; No One's Perfect, Dear; Now Generation, The; She Never Told Her Love; What Do I Know?; When You're Young and In Love

Cast: Danny Apolinar; Imogene Bliss; Igors Gavon; John Kuhner; Tom Ligon; Marian Mercer; Leland Palmer; Russ Thacker; Michael Valenti

Notes: [1] Added for tour 5/69.

4790 • YOURS, ANNE

OPENED: 10/13/1985 Theatre: Playhouse 91
Musical Off-Broadway: 57

Composer: Michael Cohen
Lyricist: Enid Futterman
Librettist: Enid Futterman
Producer: John Flaxman
Director: Arthur Masella

Source: ANNE FRANK: THE DIARY OF A YOUNG GIRL (Book: Anne Frank); **Source:**

DIARY OF ANNE FRANK, THE (Play: Frances Goodrich; Albert Hackett); **Choreographer:** Helena Andreyko; **Costumes:** Judith Dolan; **Lighting Designer:** Beverly Emmons; **Musical Director:** Dan Strickland; **Orchestrations:** James Stenborg; **Set Design:** Franco Colavecchia

Songs: Dear Kitty: I Am a Woman; Dear Kitty: I Am Longing; Dear Kitty: I Am Thirteen Years Old; Dear Kitty: I Have a Nicer Side; Dear Kitty: I Still Believe; Dear Kitty: In the Night; Dear Kitty: It's a Dangerous Adventure; Dear Kitty: It's a New Year; Dear Kitty: My Sweet Secret; Dear Kitty: We Live with Fear; First Chanukah Night, The; For the Children; Hollywood; I Remember; I Think Myself Out; I'm Not a Jew; My Wife; Nightmare; Ordinary Day, An; Prologue; Schlal; She Doesn't Understand Me; Something to Get Up For; They Don't Have To; We're Here; When We Are Free; Writer, A

Cast: Betty Aberlin; Trini Alvarado; David Cady; Merwin Goldsmith; George Guidall; Hal Robinson; Ann Talman; Dana Zeller- Alexis

4791 • YOURS, EVER YOURS

Notes: *See EVER YOURS.*

4792 • YOURS IS MY HEART

OPENED: 09/05/1946 Theatre: Shubert
Musical Broadway: 36

Composer: Franz Lehar
Lyricist: Ira Cobb; Karl Farkas; Harry Graham
Librettist: Ira Cobb; Karl Farkas; Harry Graham
Producer: Arthur Spitz
Director: Theodore Bache; Monroe Manning

Source: DAS LAND DES LACHELNS (Musical: Ludwig Herzer; Franz Lehar; Fritz Lohner-Beda); **Choreographer:** Henry Shwarze; **Costumes:** H.A. Condell; **Lighting Designer:** Milton Lowe; **Musical Director:** George Schick; **Set Design:** H.A. Condell

Songs: Beneath the Window of My Love [1]; Chinese Ceremony; Chinese Melody; Chingo-Pingo; Cup of China Tea, A; Free As the Air; Goodbye, Paree; I Love You, You Love Me [1]; Love, What Has Given You This Magic Power?; Ma Petite Cherie (The Land of Smiles); Men of China; Paris Sings Again (C: Paul Durant); Patiently Smiling; Sad at Heart Am I [1]; Upon a Moonlight Night in May; Wedding Ceremony; You Are My Heart's Delight [1]; Yours Is My Heart Alone; Zig, Zig, Zig [1]

Cast: Stella Andreva; Alexander D'Arcy; Fred Keating; Richard Tauber; Sammy White

Notes: [1] In original London (LAND OF SMILES) or German productions.

4793 • YOURS TRULY

OPENED: 01/25/1927 Theatre: Shubert
Musical Broadway: 127

Composer: Raymond Hubbell
Lyricist: Anne Caldwell
Librettist: Clyde North
Producer: Gene Buck
Director: Paul Dickey

Choreographer: Ralph Reader; **Costumes:** Mabel E. Johnston; **Musical Director:** Raymond Hubbell; **Set Design:** Joseph Urban

Songs: Dawn of Dreams; Don't Shake My Tree; Fearfully, Frightful Love [1]; Follow the Guide; Googly, Googly, Goos; Gunman, The [1]; High Yaller; I Want a Pal; Jade; Look at the World and Smile; Lotus Flower, The; Mary Has a Little Fair; Mayfair; Open Door Club; Quit Kiddin'; Shuffling Bill; Somebody Else; Yours Truly

Cast: Irene Dunne; Leon Errol; Jack Squires; Tiller Girls, The

Notes: [1] Sheet music only.

4794 • YVETTE

OPENED: 08/10/1916 Theatre: 39th St.
Musical Broadway: 4

Composer: Frederick Herendeen
Lyricist: Frederick Herendeen
Librettist: Benjamin Thorpe Gilbert
Producer: Paul Benedek
Director: M. Ring

Musical Director: Arthur Gutman; **Orchestrations:** Arthur Gutman

Songs: American Beauties; Galloping Major; I Love You So; I Want All the Boys; Just One More Kiss;

Love Holds Sway; Love's Serenade; Modern Melody, A; Opening Chorus; Silly Ass; Since I Met You; Some Girls; Someone Just Like You; St. Cyr March; Summer Night; Tick-Tick; Wimmens; Wonderful Kiss

Cast: Chapine; Rose La Harte; Rena Parker; Eugene Redding

Notes: Interpolated songs by Hanley and Jackson not credited in program.

4795 • YVONNE

OPENED: 05/22/1926 Theatre: Daly's
Musical London: 280

Composer: Vernon Duke
Lyricist: Percy Greenbank
Librettist: Percy Greenbank
Producer: George Edwardes
Director: Herbert Mason

Source: USCHI (Musical: Jean Gilbert; Leon Kastner; Alfred Moller); **Choreographer:** Fred A. Leslie; **Costumes:** De Veville; **Musical Director:** Arthur Wood

Songs: All Men Are the Same; Billing and Cooing (C: Jean Gilbert; Brother and Sister (C: Rex Kerwell; L: Percy Greenbank); Charming Weather (Opening); Day Dreams; Don't Forget the Waiter; Finale Act I (C: Jean Gilbert); Finale Act II (Jean Gilbert); I Love the Charleston (C: Edmund Eysler); It's Nicer to Be Naughty; Lucky; Magic of the Moon, The; One of the Things I Don't Profess to Know (C: Arthur Wood); Oom Ta-ra-ra (C: Marc Anthony); Opening Act II (C: Jean Gilbert); Teach Me to Dance (C: Marc Anthony; L: Harry Graham); Temperament (C: Jean Gilbert); Wake Up (C: Jean Gilbert); We Always Disagree; Yvonne (L: Jean Gilbert)

Cast: Mark Lester; Hal Sherman; Ivy Tresmand

Notes: No program available.

Z

4796 • ZAPATA

OPENED: 09/17/1980
Musical — Closed out of town

Composer: Perry Botkin Jr.; Harry Nilsson
Lyricist: Perry Botkin Jr.; Harry Nilsson
Librettist: Allan Katz
Producer: Goodspeed Opera House
Director: Bert Convy

Source: UNKNOWN (Play: Rafael Bunuel); **Choreographer:** Dan Siretta; **Costumes:** David Toser; **Dance Arranger:** Russell Warner; **Lighting Designer:** Peter M. Ehrnhardt; **Musical Director:** Lynn Crigler; **Orchestrations:** Bill Stafford; **Set Design:** John Jensen

Songs: Bedsprings; Big White Horse; Fiesta; I Got It; Mexico City; Mi Amigo; Nice Girls; Stand By Me; These Are the Brave; This Means War; Up the Revolution

Cast: Shawn Elliott; Pierre Epstein; Gary Gage; Larry Gelman; Stephen Hanan; Richard Karron; Bobbi Jo Lathan; Reni Santoni; Norman Snow

Notes: Goodspeed Opera House.

4797 • ZAZA

OPENED: 1899 — Theatre: Weber & Fields' Music Hall
Musical — Broadway

Composer: John Stromberg
Lyricist: Edgar Smith
Librettist: Edgar Smith
Producer: Lew Fields; Joseph Weber

Cast: Lew Fields; Joseph Weber

Notes: No program available.

4798 • ZENDA

OPENED: 08/05/1963
Musical — Closed out of town

Composer: Vernon Duke
Lyricist: Martin Charnin
Librettist: Everett Freeman
Producer: Edwin Lester; San Francisco Civic Light Opera
Director: George Schaefer

Source: PRISONER OF ZENDA, THE (Novel: Anthony Hope); **Choreographer:** Jack Cole; **Costumes:** Miles White; **Dance Arranger:** Harper MacKay; **Lighting Designer:** Klaus Holm; **Musical Director:** Pembroke Davenport; **Orchestrations:** Irwin Kostal; **Set Design:** Harry Horner; **Vocal Arranger:** Irwin Kostal

Songs: Alive at Last; Alone at Night (L: Leonard Adelson); Announcement/Rehearsal (inst.); Artists (L: Sid Kuller); Athena (L: Unknown); Athena's Dance (inst.); Bird That Never Learned to Fly, A; Born at Last; Bounce; Breakfast for Two; Business or Pleasure; Charming Waltz (inst.); Come to Me; Command Performance (L: Unknown); Count the Stars (L: Leonard Adelson); Elusive Mr. Rassendyl, The (L: Leonard Adelson; Sid Kuller); Enchanting Girls [1] (L: Sid Kuller); Festive March (inst.); Flavia (inst.); For the Common Good of Mankind (L: Unknown); Gift for Each Day of the Week, A (L: Leonard Adelson); Gift of Love, A; Gift of Time, A (L: Leonard Adelson); Girls (L: Unknown); Girls and Rassendyl (L: Unknown); Happy Horns and Merry Bells (L: Leonard Adelson; Sid Kuller); He Wouldn't Dare; Hello!, Must Do a Show, Goodbye! (L: Leonard Adelson; Sid Kuller); Here and There; I Won't Stand in Your Way; I Wonder What He Meant By That (L: Leonard Adelson); I'll Marry a Soldier; Introducing Mr. Rassendyl (inst.); It Does Not (L: Leonard Adelson); It's a Quaint Little Custom (L: Leonard Adelson); Kings and Cabbages; Let Her Not Be Beautiful; Love Is the Worst Possible Thing; Loveless You and Hateful Me (L: Sid Kuller); Magic Music (inst.); Man Loves Me, The; Mazurka, The (inst.); Montage Poster (inst.); Morning You Were Born, The; My Heart Has Come a Tumbling Down; My Royal Majesty (L: Leonard Adelson; Martin Charnin); My Son in Law the King (L: Unknown); National Anthem; Never Let Them Know What's

Going On (L: Unknown); Night Is Filled with Wonderful Sounds, The; No Ifs! No Ands! No Buts!; No More Love; Now the World Begins Again (L: Leonard Adelson); Old Friend (L: Leonard Adelson); On My Own (L: Unknown); One Night Ago (L: Unknown); Organization (L: Leonard Adelson); Our Usual Place (L: Unknown); Patroness of Art (L: Sid Kuller); Pull a Rabbit Out of the Hat (L: Leonard Adelson); Queen Mother's Crossover (inst.); Royal Confession, A (L: Sid Kuller); Segue to Palace (inst.); Sign on the Dotted Line (L: Leonard Adelson); Something New (L: Leonard Adelson); Thanks to Love (L: Leonard Adelson; Sid Kuller); That Man Loves Me (L: Unknown); That Was Then, Mr. Rassendyl; That's the Way It Goes (L: Unknown); There Are Girls (L: Leonard Adelson); There Is Nothing Like a Wedding; There's Nothing Wrong with Marriage; There's Room for Her; Too Beautiful Tonight (L: Unknown); Tour de Force (L: Sid Kuller); Train Music (inst.); Trust In Me (L: Leonard Adelson); Turlututu (L: Vernon Duke); Verdi Duo (inst.); Vernon Duccini (inst.); Waltz Fantasy (inst.); We; We Just Might (L: Leonard Adelson); Wedding March (inst.); What Does One Do?; When Athena Dances (inst.); When You Stop and Think; Whole Lot of Happy, A; Why Not?; Wine Is Mine, The (L: Leonard Adelson); Words, Words, Words! [1] (L: Sid Kuller); Yesterday's Forgotten; You Are All That's Beautiful (L: Unknown); You Took My Breath Away (L: Unknown); You're Not at All Like You; You're Not Old Enough (L: Leonard Adelson); Zarape (Antoinette's Dance) (inst.); Zenda (L: Leonard Adelson)

Cast: Alfred Drake; Truman Gaige; Earl Hammond; Carmen Mathews; Chita Rivera; Anne Rogers

Notes: [1] Same music.

4799 • ZIEGFELD A NIGHT AT THE FOLLIES

OPENED: 1991

Musical — Closed out of town

Librettist: Dallett Norris
Producer: Troika Organization, The
Director: Joe Leonardo

Arrangements: John Mezzio; David Siegel; **Choreographer:** Kathryn Kendall; **Costumes:** Nanzi Adzima; Theoni V. Aldredge; **Lighting Designer:** Charles Houghton; **Musical Director:** John Mezzio; **Orchestrations:** John Mezzio; David Siegel; **Set Design:** Jeffrey Schneider

Songs: Destination Broadway (C: Bryon Sommers; L: David Zippel); Do the New York (C: Ben Oakland; L: J.P. Murray; Barry Trivers); Easy to Love (C/L: Cole Porter); Find Me a Primitive Man (C/L: Cole Porter); Girl for Each Month of the Year A (C: Louis A. Hirsch; L: Channing Pollock; Rennold Wolf); Girl on the Magazine Cover, The (C/L: Irving Berlin); Harlem Waltz, The (C: Walter Kent; L: Richard Jerome); Hat Song, The (C: Maurice Levi; L: Harry B. Smith); I Only Have Eyes for You (C: Harry Warren; L: Al Dubin); If You Knew Susie (C: Joseph Meyer; L: B.G. DeSylva); It's Only a Paper Moon (C: Harold Arlen; L: E.Y. "Yip" Harburg; Billy Rose); Lost Liberty Blues (C/L: Cole Porter); Meet Me Tonight in Dreamland (C: Leo Friedman; L: Beth Slater Whitson); Most Gentlemen Don't Like Love (C/L: Cole Porter); My Baby Just Cares for Me (C: Gus Kahn; L: Walter Donaldson); My Old Flame (C: Arthur Johnson; L: Sam Coslow); Object of My Affection, The (C/L: Jimmy Grier; Coy Poe; Pinky Tomlin); Oh, You Beautiful Doll (C: Nat D. Ayer; L: A. Seymour Brown); Poor Butterfly (C: John L. Golden; L: Raymond Hubbell); Pretty Girl Is Like a Melody, A (C/L: Irving Berlin); Shaking the Blues Away (C/L: Irving Berlin); So Long! Oo-Long (C: Harry Ruby; L: Harry Kalmar); Stairway to the Stars (C: Matt Malneck; Frank Signorelli; L: Mitchell Parish); Taking a Chance on Love (C: Vernon Duke; L: Ted Fetter; John Latouche); They All Need a Little Hot-Cha (C: Ray Henderson; L: Lew Brown); Too Marvelous for Words (C: Richard A. Whiting; L: Johnny Mercer); Toy Trumpet, The (C: Raymond Scott; L: Sidney D. Mitchell; Lew Pollack); What'll I Do (C/L: Irving Berlin); Who? (C: Jerome Kern; L: Oscar Hammerstein II; Otto Harbach); You Cannot Make Your Shimmy Shake on Tea (C/L: Irving Berlin; Rennold Wolf); You Stepped Out of a Dream (C: Nacio Herb Brown; L: Gus Kahn)

Cast: Carole Cianelli; Bruce C. Ewing; Paul Finocchiaro; A.J. Graham; Karlah Hamilton; Catherine Hart; David Nehls; Kathy Reid; Michael Lee Scott; Michael Shiles; Judy A. Walstrum

Notes: This show toured the country with sets and costumes from the British show ZIEGFELD.

4800 • ZIEGFELD AMERICAN REVUE OF 1926.

Notes: *See NO FOOLIN'.*

4801 • ZIEGFELD FOLLIES OF 1907

OPENED: 07/08/1907 Theatre: Jardin de Paris
Revue Broadway: 70

Librettist: Harry B. Smith
Producer: Florenz Ziegfeld
Director: Herbert Gresham

Choreographer: Julian Mitchell; **Costumes:** Mme. Freisinger; W.H. Matthews; **Set Design:** John H. Young

Songs: Alabama Sam [3]; Band Box Girl, The (C: Seymour Furth; L: Edgar Selden); Bridget Salome [2]; Budweiser's a Friend of Mine (C: Seymour Furth; L: Vincent Bryan); Bye, Bye Dear Old Broadway (C: Gus Edwards; L: Will D. Cobb); Cigarette [4] (C: Gertrude Hoffman; L: Vincent Bryan); Come and Float Me Freddie Dear (C: E. Ray Goetz; L: Vincent Bryan); Come Down Salomy Jane [5] (C: E. Ray Goetz; L: Vincent Bryan); Fencing Girls, The [1]; Foolish Song, A [1]; Gibson Bathing Girls, The (C: Alfred Solman; L: Paul West); Handle Me with Care (C: Jean Schwartz; L: William Jerome); Heart Breaker, The [3]; I Don't Want an Auto (C: Seymour Furth; L: William Jerome); I Think I Oughtn't Auto Any More (C: E. Ray Goetz; L: William Jerome); I Want to Be a Drummer Boy (C: Silvio Hein; L: Matt Woodward); If We Knew What the Milkman Knows [5] (C: E. Ray Goetz; L: Vincent Bryan); Imaginary Man, The [3]; In the Surf; Jiu Jitsu Waltz; Little of Everything, A [3]; Man Who Built the Subway, The [4] (C: Gertrude Hoffman; L: Vincent Bryan); Miss Ginger of Jamaica (C/L: Billy Gaston); Oh Marie [1]; On the Grand Old Sands [3] (C: Gus Edwards; L: Will D. Cobb); Pocahontas (C: Seymour Furth; L: Edgar Selden); Re-Incarnation (C: E. Ray Goetz; L: Vincent Bryan); That's How We Met the Girl [5] (C: E. Ray Goetz; L: Vincent Bryan); They All Look Alike to Mary [2]; Whistle If You Want Me Dear [3]

Cast: Nora Bayes; George Bickel; Helen Broderick; Emma Carus; Mlle. Dazie; Grace LaRue; Dave Lewis; Charles J. Ross; Marion Sunshine; Florence Tempest; Prince Tokio; Harry Watson Jr.

Notes: [1] Out Boston 9/30/07. [2] Out of town 11/4/07. [3] Out Kansas City 10/4/08. [4] Not in programs. [5] ASCAP only.

4802 • ZIEGFELD FOLLIES OF 1908

OPENED: 06/15/1908 Theatre: Jardin de Paris
Revue Broadway: 120

Composer: Maurice Levi
Lyricist: Harry B. Smith
Librettist: Harry B. Smith
Producer: Florenz Ziegfeld
Director: Herbert Gresham

Choreographer: Julian Mitchell; **Costumes:** Alfredo Edel; Mme. Freisinger; Hafleigh; W.H. Matthews; **Lighting Designer:** Tony Greshoff; **Musical Director:** Frederic Solomon; **Set Design:** John H. Young

Songs: As You Walk Down the Strand [2]; Be Good [2]; Big Hats, The (Hat Song); Duchess of Table D'Hote; Follow the Flag [4]; Girls I Left Behind, The [4]; I Wonder If They're All True to Me [3]; International Merry Widow, The; Let's Get the Umpire's Goat [1] (C/L: Nora Bayes; Jack Norworth); Mosquito Song; Nell Brinkley Girl, The; Nothing Ever Ever Ever Hardly Ever Troubles Me (C: Albert Von Tilzer; L: Jack Norworth); Over on the Jersey Side [4] (C/L: Jack Norworth); Rajah of Broadway, The; Sextette [6]; Shine on Harvest Moon [5] (C/L: Jack Norworth; C: Nora Bayes); Since Mother Was a Girl (C: Albert Von Tilzer; L: Jack Norworth); Sing Me a Come All Ye (Like My Daddy Sang to Me) [4] (C/L: Jack Norworth; C: Nora Bayes); Society [2]; Song of the Navy [2]; Take Me 'Round in a Taxicab (C: Melville Gideon; L: Edgar Selden); That's All [2]; Titles; Wax Works [6]; When the Girl You Love Is Loving You (C: Jean Schwartz; L: William Jerome); You Will Have to Sing an Irish Song (C: Albert Von Tilzer; L: Jack Norworth)

Cast: Nora Bayes; Barney Bernard; George Bickel; Mlle. Dazie; Arthur Deagon; Rosie Green; Lee Harrison; Grace LaRue; Grace Leigh; Mae Murray; Jack Norworth; William Powers; Billie Reeves; William C. Schrode; Gertrude Vanderbilt; Florence Walton; Harry Watson; Lucy Weston

Notes: [1] Also in ZIEGFELD FOLLIES OF 1909. Some sources only credit Norworth alone. Out

Boston 4/26/09. [2] Not in programs. [3] Out Boston 4/26/09. [4] Out Boston 1/11/08. [5] Also in MISS INNOCENCE. [6] Sheet music only.

4803 • ZIEGFELD FOLLIES OF 1909

OPENED: 06/14/1909 Theatre: Jardin de Paris
Revue Broadway: 64

Composer: Maurice Levi
Lyricist: Harry B. Smith
Librettist: Harry B. Smith
Producer: Florenz Ziegfeld
Director: Herbert Gresham; Julian Mitchell

Choreographer: Julian Mitchell; **Costumes:** Alfredo Edel; W.H. Matthews; **Musical Director:** Frederic Solomon; **Set Design:** John H. Young

Songs: And the World Keeps Rolling Along; Bathing Girls, The; Blarney (C/L: Nora Bayes; Jack Norworth); By the Light of the Silvery Moon (C: Gus Edwards; L: Edward Madden); Christy Girl, The; Come On and Play Ball with Me (C: Gus Edwards; L: Edward Madden); Dance de Maitre de Ballet; Dance of the Parisian Twist, The; Dance of the Widow Mexetexa (C: Lewis F. Muir); Dear Old Father [2] (C/L: Nora Bayes; Jack Norworth); Falling Stars (C/L: Nora Bayes; Jack Norworth); Go As Far As You Like; Greatest Navy in the World, The; Hindoo Honey; I Don't Care (C: Harry O. Sutton; L: Jean Lenox); I Wish I Was a Boy and I Wish I Was a Girl [1] (C/L: Nora Bayes; Jack Norworth); I'm After Madame Tetrazzini's Job (C/L: Gus Edwards); It's Nothing but a Bubble; Let's Get the Umpire's Goat [5] (C/L: Nora Bayes; Jack Norworth); Linger Longer, Lingerie; Love in the Springtime [4]; Mad Opera House (C/L: Nora Bayes; Jack Norworth); Madame Venus (Take a Tip from Venus); Moving Day in Jungle Town (C: Nat D. Ayer; L: A. Seymour Brown); My Cousin Carus [3] (C: Gus Edwards; L: Edward Madden); Play That Fandango Rag (C: Lewis F. Muir; L: E. Ray Goetz); Roosevelt of Germany; Rulers of the Earth; Sextette; That Aero-Naughty Girl [6]; Up! Up! Up! in My Aeroplane (C: Gus Edwards; L: Edward Madden); What Every Woman Knows

Cast: Nora Bayes; William Bonelli; Bessie Clayton; Arthur Deagon; Harry Kelly; Lillian Lorraine; Mae Murray; Jack Norworth; Eva Tanguay; Sophie Tucker; Gertrude Vanderbilt; Annabelle Whitford

Notes: [1] Also called "I'm Glad, I'm Glad." [2] Also called "Poor Old Dad." [3] From MISS INNOCENCE. [4] Not in program. [5] Cut from ZIEGFELD FOLLIES OF 1908. [6] Sheet music only.

4804 • ZIEGFELD FOLLIES OF 1910

OPENED: 06/20/1910 Theatre: Jardin de Paris
Revue Broadway: 88

Composer: Gus Edwards
Lyricist: Harry B. Smith
Librettist: Harry B. Smith
Producer: Florenz Ziegfeld
Director: Julian Mitchell

Costumes: Crage; W.H. Matthews; **Musical Director:** Frank Darling; **Set Design:** Ernest Albert; John H. Young

Songs: Believe Me [1]; Chicken Thief Man, The; Cock of the Walk, The; Come Along Mandy; Constantly [1] (C: Bert Williams; L: James Henry Burris; Chris Smith); Cuban Glide, The [7]; Dance of the Grizzly Bear, The (C: George Botsford; L: Irving Berlin); Don't Take a Girl Down to Coney (L: Will D. Cobb); Fandango Rag [4] (C: Lewis F. Muir; L: E. Ray Goetz); Franco American Rag [7] (C/L: Unknown); Good Bye Becky Cohen [8] (C/L: Irving Berlin); I Love It Rag [7] (C: Harry Von Tilzer; L: Addison Burkhardt); I Thought He Was a Business Man [7]; I'll Get You Yet (C: Von Tilzer; L: Addison Burkhardt); I'll Lend You Everything I've Got Except My Wife [5] (C: Harry Von Tilzer; L: Jean C. Havez); I'm in Love with You [7]; In the Evening [1]; Kidland (L: Will D. Cobb); Late Hours [5]; Look Me Over Carefully and Tell Me Will I Do (L: Will D. Cobb); Lovie Joe (C: Joe Jordan; L: Will Marion Cook); Ma Blushin' Rosie [9] (C: John Stromberg; L: Edgar Smith); Mister Earth and His Comet Love (The Comet and the Earth); My Yiddish Colleen [7] (L: Edward Madden); Nix on the Glow-Worm, Lena! [6] (C: Harry Carroll; L: Ballard Macdonald); Nobody [5] (C: Bert Williams; L: Alex Rogers); Our American Colleges; Pensacola Mooch, The (C: Ford Dabney; L: Will Marion Cook); Play That Barbershop Chord [5] (C: Lewis F. Muir; L: William Tracey); Rosalie [10] (C: Gus Edwards; L: Will D. Cobb); Rosey Posey [7]; Sadie Salome Go Home [5] (C/L: Irving Berlin; Edgar Leslie); Sweet Kitty Bellairs; Swing Me High, Swing Me Low (C: Victor Hollander;

L: Ballard Macdonald); Telephone Your Riffky Issey [2]; That Horrible Hobble Skirt [5]; That Minor Strain [5] (C: Ford Dabney; L: Cecil Mack); Vision of Salome (inst.) [11] (C: Archibald. Joyce); Waltzing Lieutenant, The; What Has Become of the Girls I Used to Know (C: Gus Edwards); Woman's Dream, A; Yankiana Rag [3] (C: Ludwig Englander); You're Gwine to Get Something What You Don't Have [5] (C: Harry Von Tilzer; L: Jean Havez)

Cast: George Bickel; Fanny Brice; Lillian Lorraine; Vera Maxwell; Bobby North; Billie Reeves; Grace Tyson; Harry Watson; Bert Williams

Notes: [1] Out Nebraska 5/23/10. [2] Out Boston 2/20/11. [3] From MISS INNOCENCE. [4] From ZIEGFELD FOLLIES OF 1909. [5] Not in programs. [6] Titled "Nix on the Concertina Lena" in some programs. In program of 8/22/10 it was credited to Ball and Macdonald. ASCAP credits this song to Edwards and Smith. The sheet music credits to as above. [7] Added after opening. [8] May not be by Berlin. [9] Not in programs. From FIDDLE DEE DEE. [10] Added after opening. From THE WIZARD OF OZ. [11] Sheet music only.

4805 • ZIEGFELD FOLLIES OF 1911

OPENED: 06/26/1911 Theatre: Jardin de Paris
Revue Broadway: 80

Composer: Raymond Hubbell; Maurice Levi
Lyricist: George V. Hobart
Librettist: George V. Hobart
Producer: Florenz Ziegfeld
Director: Julian Mitchell

Choreographer: Jack Mason; Gus Sohlke; **Costumes:** W.H. Matthews; **Set Design:** Ernest Albert; Unitt & Wickes

Songs: Bumble Bee [5] (C: James B. Blyer; L: Donnelly; Jean Havez); Cakewalk (inst.) [3] (C: Raymond Hubbell); Doggone That Chili Man [1] (C/L: Irving Berlin); Ephraham Played Upon the Piano [1] (C: Irving Berlin; L: Vincent Bryan); Girl in Pink, The (C: Raymond Hubbell); How Would You Like to Be My Pony? [3] (C: Raymond Hubbell); I'm a Crazy Daffydill (C: Jerome Kern; L: Bessie McCoy); Imitation Rag, The; It Was Me [3] (C: Seymour Furth; L: George W. Day); My Beautiful Lady [4] (C: Ivan Caryll; L: C.M.S. McLellan); New York (You're the Best Town in Europe) (C: Raymond Hubbell; L: Raymond W. Peck); Pots and Pans [3] (C: Jean Schwartz; L: Charles Grapewin); Take Care, Little Girl, Take Care (C: Raymond Hubbell); Texas Tommy Swing (C/L: Sid Brown; Val Harris); That's Harmony [3] (C: Bert Williams; L: Grant Clarke); Turkey Gobbler's Ball [6] (C: James B. Blyer; L: Donnelly; Jean Havez); Whippoorwill (Never Again for Me) [3] (C: James Blyler; L: Fagan); Widow Wood, The (C: Maurice Levi; L: Channing Pollock; Rennold Wolf); Woodman, Woodman, Spare That Tree [1] (C: Irving Berlin; L: Vincent Bryan); You've Built a Fire Down in My Heart [2] (C/L: Irving Berlin)

Cast: Fanny Brice; Dolly Sisters, The; Leon Errol; Lillian Lorraine; Bessie McCoy; Harry Watson; George White; Bert Williams

Notes: [1] Originally in JARDIN DE PARIS. [2] Originally in JARDIN DE PARIS. Also in THE FASCINATING WIDOW. [3] Not in program. [4] Not in program. Also in THE PINK LADY. [5] This is not "Be My Little Baby Bumble Bee" by Henry Marshall and Stanley Murphy. [6] Sheet music only.

4806 • ZIEGFELD FOLLIES OF 1912

OPENED: 10/21/1912 Theatre: Moulin Rouge
Revue Broadway: 88

Composer: Raymond Hubbell
Lyricist: Harry B. Smith
Librettist: Harry B. Smith
Producer: Florenz Ziegfeld
Director: Julian Mitchell

Costumes: Callot; **Musical Director:** Frank Darling; **Orchestrations:** Frank Saddler; **Set Design:** Ernest Albert

Songs: Beautiful, Beautiful Girl (L: John E. Hazzard); Blackberryin' To-day (C/L: Bert Williams); Borrow from Me [1]; Broadway Glide, The (C: Bert Grant; L: A. Seymour Brown); Coffee Mother Used to Make, The [1]; Daddy Has a Sweetheart and Mother Is Her Name [2] (C: Dave Stamper; L: Gene Buck); Dingle, Dingle, Dingle [1] (C: Con Conrad; Jay Whidden; L: Joe Young); Dip, Dip, Dip; Down in Dear Old New Orleans (C: Con Conrad; Jay Whidden; L: Joe Young); Good Night Nurse [1] (C: W. Raymond Walker; L: Thomas J. Gray); Good Old Circus Band; Hurry, Little Children; I Ain't No Fool [1];

I Should Worry [1]; In a Pretty Little Cottage; In a Pretty Little White House of Our Own (C: Leo Edwards; L: Blanche Merrill); Little Bit of Everything, A (C/L: Irving Berlin); Louisiana; Million, The; Mother Doesn't Know; My Landlady [1]; My Little Lady Bug [1]; Romantic Girl; Row, Row, Row (C: James V. Monaco; L: William Jerome); Society Circus Parade (C: Dave Stamper; L: Gene Buck); Society Circus Parade (inst.); Some Boy [2] (C: Dave Stamper; L: Gene Buck); Stage Door Number; That Shakespearian Rag [3] (C: Dave Stamper; L: Gene Buck; Herman Ruby); That Wonderful Tune [4] (C: Jean Schwartz; L: Grant Clarke); There's One in a Million Like You (C: Jean Schwartz; L: Grant Clarke); When You Meet Them on Broadway [1]; Yodel Song; You Gotta Keep Movin' and Dance (You Gotta Keep A' Going); You Might As Well Stay on Broadway; You Should Have Most Everything [1]; You're a Great Big, Blue-Eyed Baby Boy [1] (C/L: A. Seymour Brown); You're on the Right Road [1]

Cast: Elizabeth Brice; Leon Errol; Bernard Granville; Lillian Lorraine; Rae Samuels; Harry Watson; Bert Williams

Notes: [1] Out Philadelphia 10/7/12. [2] Not in programs. [3] Out Philadelphia 10/7/12. *See PASSING SHOW OF 1915* for "The Shakespeare Rag." [4] Sheet music only.

4807 • ZIEGFELD FOLLIES OF 1913

OPENED: 06/16/1913 Theatre: New Amsterdam
Revue Broadway: 96

Composer: Raymond Hubbell
Lyricist: George V. Hobart
Librettist: George V. Hobart
Producer: Florenz Ziegfeld
Director: Julian Mitchell

Costumes: Schneider & Anderson; **Lighting Designer:** Frank Detering; **Musical Director:** Frank Darling; **Set Design:** Ernest Albert; Frank Gates; E.A. Morange; John H. Young

Songs: Bye and Bye You Will Miss Me [1] (C: Dave Stamper; L: Gene Buck); Cupid's Dart (C: Louis Dannenberg); Dance Classiceccentrique; Everybody Sometime Must Love Somebody (C: Dave Stamper; L: Gene Buck); Going There; Good-Bye My Tango [4]; He's So Good (C: Dave Stamper; L: Gene Buck); Hello, Honey; I Can Live without You [3] (C: Dave Stamper; L: Gene Buck); If a Table at Rector's Could Talk (L: Will D. Cobb); In the Cradle of Love [2] (C/L: J. Leubrie Hill); Isle D'Amour (C: Leo Edwards; L: Earl Carroll); Just You and I and the Moon (C: Dave Stamper; L: Gene Buck); Katie Rooney; Little Love, a Little Kiss, A [1] (C: Leo Silesu; L: Nilson Fysher; Adrian Ross); New York, What's the Matter with You?; On Her Veranda [4] (C: Ethel Ponce; L: Phil L. Ponce); Panama; Peg O' My Heart [1] (C: Fred Fisher; L: Alfred Bryan); Ragtime Suffragette, The; Rebecca of Sunnybook Farm [3] (C: Albert Gumble; L: A. Seymour Brown); Sleep Time, My Honey; Tangoitis Dance; Turkish Trotteshness; Without You (C: Dave Stamper; L: Gene Buck); You Must Have Experience; You're Never Too Old to Love [1] (C: Albert Gumble; L: Alfred Bryan; William Jerome); You're Some Girl

Cast: Elizabeth Brice; Leon Errol; Ann Pennington; Frank Tinney; Nat Wills

Notes: [1] Out Boston 10/20/13. [2] Out Indianapolis 1/19/14. [3] Not in program. [4] Sheet music only.

4808 • ZIEGFELD FOLLIES OF 1914

OPENED: 06/01/1914 Theatre: New Amsterdam
Revue Broadway: 112

Composer: Raymond Hubbell; Dave Stamper
Lyricist: Gene Buck
Librettist: George V. Hobart
Producer: Florenz Ziegfeld
Director: Leon Errol

Costumes: Cora MacGeachy; **Musical Director:** Frank Darling; **Set Design:** William H. Matthews

Songs: At the Ball [5] (C/L: J. Leubrie Hill); Baby Love [3] (C: Harry Von Tilzer; L: Paul Cunningham; George Whiting); Be Careful What You Do; Because I Can't Tango; Darktown Poker Club [2]; Futurist Girl, The (C: Dave Stamper); Good Night (C: Dave Stamper); Goodnight Mirster Hurdy-Gurdy Man; If You Dance Dear, I Know a Cabaret [4] (C: Raymond Hubbell; L: George V. Hobart); I'm a Statesman [3]; I'm Cured [3] (C: Bert Williams; L: Jean Havez); I've Got Him Now! (C: Dave Stamper); Keep Your Love for Me (Save Your Love for Me) [1] (C: Raymond Hubbell); Lone Star Girl, The; Man Who Wrote "The Vampire" Must Have Known

My Wife [2] (C: Bert Williams; L: Gene Buck; Earle C. Jones); My Little Pet Chicken (L: George V. Hobart); Neptune's Daughter [2] (C: Jean Schwartz; L: Grant Clarke); Night Life in Old Manhattan; Nobody Seems to Know; Nothing to Wear (C: Dave Stamper); Nut Sundae, A; Prunella Mine (C: Dave Stamper); Put Your Lovin' Arms Around Me, Dearie [2]; Rock Me in the Cradle of Love (C/L: J. Leubrie Hill); Tango Brazilian Dreams; Tangorilla; There's Something in the Air in Springtime (C: Dave Stamper); Underneath the Japanese Moon [1] (C: Walter Gustave Haenschen); When the Ragtime Army Goes Away to War (C/L: A. Seymour Brown); Wonderful Garden of Love [2] (C: Dave Stamper)

Cast: Arthur Deagon; Leon Errol; Rita Gould; Kay Laurell; Vera Michelena; Ann Pennington; Gertrude Vanderbilt; Bert Williams; Ed Wynn

Notes: [1] Added after opening. [2] Not in program. [3] ASCAP/Library of Congress only. [4] Sheet music only. [5] Originally in MY FRIEND FROM KENTUCKY.

4809 • ZIEGFELD FOLLIES OF 1915

OPENED: 06/21/1915 Theatre: New Amsterdam
Revue Broadway: 104

Composer: Louis A. Hirsch; Dave Stamper
Lyricist: Channing Pollock; Dave Stamper; Rennold Wolf
Librettist: Gene Buck; Channing Pollock; Rennold Wolf
Producer: Florenz Ziegfeld
Director: Leon Errol; Julian Mitchell

Costumes: Lady Duff-Gordon; **Musical Director:** Frank Darling; **Set Design:** Joseph Urban

Songs: Arabia My Land of Sweet Romance [1] (C: J. Frederick Hanley; L: Bernard Granville); Bird of a Chicken, The (dance); Bowling [1]; Every-body Dance [1] (C: Dave Stamper; L: Gene Buck); Girl for Each Month in the Year, A; Hello, Frisco! (I Called You Up to Say Hello) (C: Louis A. Hirsch; L: Gene Buck); Hold Me in Your Loving Arms (C: Louis A. Hirsch; L: Gene Buck); I Can't Do Without Girls; I Love to Be Loved [1] (C: Dave Stamper; L: Gene Buck); If the Girlies Could Be Soldiers [1] (C: Dave Stamper; L: Gene Buck); I'll Be a Santa Claus to You (C: Louis A. Hirsch; L: Gene Buck); I'm a Nurse for Aching Hearts [2] (C: Louis A. Hirsch; L: Gene Buck); I'm Neutral; In the Evening; Marie Odile (C: Louis A. Hirsch; L: Channing Pollock; Rennold Wolf); Midnight Frolic Glide (C: Dave Stamper; Will Vodery); My Little Submarine [1] (C: Dave Stamper; L: Louis A. Hirsch); My Radium Girl (C: Louis A. Hirsch; L: Gene Buck); My Zebra Lady Fair; Oriental Love; They're in the Junk Pile Now [1] (C: Dave Stamper; L: Gene Buck); Trilby [1] (C: Dave Stamper; L: Gene Buck); Twenty Years Ago; Under the Sea [2]; We'll Build a Little Home in the U.S.A. (C: Charles Elbert; L: Ward Wesley); Zebra Girl [2] (C: Dave Stamper; L: Gene Buck)

Cast: Ina Claire; Leon Errol; W.C. Fields; Bernard Granville; Justine Johnstone; Kay Laurell; Mae Murray; Ann Pennington; Carl Randall; Olive Thomas; George White; Bert Williams; Ed Wynn

Notes: [1] Sheet music only. [2] Not in programs.

4810 • ZIEGFELD FOLLIES OF 1916

OPENED: 06/12/1916 Theatre: New Amsterdam
Revue Broadway: 104

Composer: Louis A. Hirsch
Lyricist: Gene Buck
Librettist: Gene Buck; George V. Hobart
Producer: Florenz Ziegfeld
Director: Ned Wayburn

Costumes: Lady Duff-Gordon; Cora MacGeachy; Alice O'Neil; **Musical Director:** Frank Darling; **Set Design:** Joseph Urban

Songs: Ain't It Funny What a Difference a Few Drinks Make [3] (C: Jerome Kern); Beautiful Island of Girls [4]; Dying Swan, The [5] (C: Leo Edwards; L: Blanche Merrill); Goodbye, Dear Old Bachelor Days; Hat, The [5] (C: Leo Edwards; L: Blanche Merrill); Have a Heart [3] (C: Jerome Kern); I Left Her on the Beach at Honolulu; I Want That Star [3] (L: George V. Hobart); In Florida Among the Palms [2] (C/L: Irving Berlin); I've Said Goodbye to Broadway (C: Dave Stamper); I've Saved All My Lovin' for You (C: Dave Stamper); Midnight Frolic Rag, The [3]; My Lady of the Nile (1) [1]; My Lady of the Nile (2) (C: Jerome Kern); Nijinksy [3] (C: Dave Stamper); Six Little Wives of the King; Somnambulistic Tune (C: Dave Stamper); Stop and Go; There's Ragtime in the Air (C: Dave

Stamper); Walking the Dog [1] (C: Eubie Blake; L: Noble Sissle); When the Lights Are Low [3] (C: Jerome Kern)

Cast: Don Barclay; Fanny Brice; Ina Claire; Marion Davies; W.C. Fields; Bernard Granville; Emma Haig; Sam Hardy; Justine Johnstone; Allyn King; Ann Pennington; Tot Qualters; Carl Randall; William Rock; Lilyan Tashman; Frances White; Bert Williams

Notes: Fanny Brice songs not identified in program but written by Blanche Merrill. [1] Not used. [2] Added after opening. [3] Cut after opening. [4] Music adapted from Lehar's GYPSY LOVE. [5] Not in programs. Sung by Brice.

4811 • ZIEGFELD FOLLIES OF 1917

OPENED: 06/12/1917 Theatre: New Amsterdam
Revue Broadway: 111

Composer: Raymond Hubbell; Dave Stamper
Lyricist: Gene Buck
Librettist: Gene Buck; George V. Hobart
Producer Florenz Ziegfeld
Director: Ned Wayburn

Costumes: Lady Duff-Gordon; **Musical Director:** Frank Darling; **Set Design:** Joseph Urban

Songs: Auto Girls Song [1] (C: Raymond Hubbell); Beautiful Garden of Girls (C: Raymond Hubbell); Beautiful Girl, Goodbye (C: Dave Stamper); Can't You Hear Your Country Calling: The Spirit Calling (C: Victor Herbert); Chu, Chin, Chow (C: Dave Stamper); Egyptian [4] (C: Leo Edwards; L: Blanche Merrill); Hello, My Dearie! (C: Dave Stamper); Home Sweet Home (C/L: Ring Lardner); I Ain't Married No More [3] (C: Les Copeland; L: Rennold Wolf); I'll Be Somewhere in France (C: Raymond Hubbell); I'm So Happy (C: Turner Layton; L: Henry Creamer); Jealous Moon; Just Because You're You (Because You Are Just You) [2] (C: Jerome Kern); Just You and Me (C: Dave Stamper); Modern Maiden's Prayer, The (C: James F. Hanley; L: Ballard Macdonald); My Arabian Maid (C: Raymond Hubbell); Potato Bug, The [4] (C: Dave Stamper); Same Old Moon [4] (C: Dave Stamper); Spirit of the Garden (scene) (C: Victor Herbert); That's the Kind of Baby for Me, The (C: Jack Egan; L: Alfred Harriman); Unhappy (C: Turner Layton; L: Henry Creamer); Ziegfeld Follies Rag (C: Dave Stamper)

Cast: Fanny Brice; Walter Catlett; Dorothy Dickson; W.C. Fields; Irving Fisher; Peggy Hopkins; Carl Hyson; Allyn King; Lilyan Tashman; Bert Williams

Notes: [1] Sheet music only. [2] Originally in THE DOLL GIRL as "When Three Is Company" with lyrics by M.E. Rourke. [3] Out Philadelphia 11/5/17. [4] Not in program.

4812 • ZIEGFELD FOLLIES OF 1918

OPENED: 06/18/1918 Theatre: New Amsterdam
Revue Broadway: 151

Composer: Louis A. Hirsch; Dave Stamper
Lyricist: Gene Buck
Librettist: Gene Buck; Rennold Wolf
Producer: Florenz Ziegfeld
Director: Ned Wayburn

Costumes: Croydon; Lady Duff-Gordon; Lucille; Schneider- Anderson; **Lighting Designer:** Ben Beerwald; **Musical Director:** Frank Darling; **Set Design:** Joseph Urban

Songs: Any Old Time at All (C: Louis A. Hirsch); Blue Devils of France (C/L: Irving Berlin); But After the Ball Was Over! (Then He Made Up for Lost Time) [1] (C/L: B.G. DeSylva; Arthur Jackson); Come on Papa [1] (C: Harry Ruby; L: Edgar Leslie); Dream, A (scene) (C: Victor Herbert); Garden of My Dreams, The (C: Louis A. Hirsch; Dave Stamper); I Want to Learn to Jazz Dance (C: Dave Stamper); If She Means What I Think She Means [1] (C: Arthur Jackson; L: B.G. DeSylva); I'm Gonna Pin My Medal on the Girl I Left Behind (C/L: Irving Berlin); I'm Making a Study of Beautiful Girls (and I'm Still in My A.B.C.'s) [1] (C/L: Eddie Cantor; Jack Glogau; Al Piantadosi); In Old Versailles (C: Louis A. Hirsch); Mine Was a Marriage of Convenience (C: Louis A. Hirsch); Oh How I Hate to Get Up in the Morning [4] (C/L: Irving Berlin); Poor Little Me; Save Your Money, John [2] (C: Eubie Blake; L: Noble Sissle); Starlight (C: Dave Stamper); Tackin' 'Em Down [1] (C: Albert Gumble; L: B.G. DeSylva); We Are the Follies [1]; We're Busy Building Boats (Ship Building Song) (C: Louis A. Hirsch); When I Hear a Syncopated Tune (C: Louis A. Hirsch); When I'm Looking at You (C: Dave Stamper); Would You Rather Be a Soldier with a Eagle on Your Shoulder or a Private with a Chicken on Your Knee? [3] (C: Archie Gottler; L: Sidney D. Mitchell)

Cast: Eddie Cantor; Frank Carter; Dolores; Fairbanks Twins, The; W.C. Fields; Joe Frisco; Harry Kelly; Allyn King; Kay Laurell; Lillian Lorraine; Marilyn Miller; Ann Pennington

Notes: [1] Sheet music only. [2] Not in program, however sheet music credits Les Copeland and Alex Rogers and places the song in the FOLLIES OF 1919. [3] Not in program. [4] Added three months after opening. Used in YIP! YIP! YAPHANK!

4813 • ZIEGFELD FOLLIES OF 1919

OPENED: 06/16/1919 Theatre: New Amsterdam
Revue Broadway: 171

Composer: Irving Berlin
Lyricist: Irving Berlin
Librettist: Gene Buck; Dave Stamper; Rennold Wolf
Producer: Florenz Ziegfeld
Director: Ned Wayburn

Choreographer: Ned Wayburn; **Costumes:** Lady Duff-Gordon; Mme. Francis; Lucille; Cora MacGeachy; Alice O'Neil; **Lighting Designer:** Ben Beewald; **Musical Director:** Frank Darling; **Orchestrations:** Stephen Jones; **Set Design:** Joseph Urban

Songs: Bevo [2]; Bring Back Those Wonderful Days [4] (C/L: Nat Vincent; Darl MacBoyle); Checkers [4] (C: Paul Rubens; L: Billy Curtis); Circus Ballet, The (inst.) (C: Victor Herbert); Everybody Wants a Key to My Cellar [4] (L: Billy Baskette; Ed Rose); Follies Minstrel, The [5]; Follies Salad, The (C: Dave Stamper; L: Gene Buck); Goodbye Sunshine Hello Moon [7] (C: Dave Stamper; L: Gene Buck); Harem Life; How Ya' Gonna Keep 'Em Down on the Farm (After They've Seen Paree)? [4] (C: Walter Donaldson; L: Sam M. Lewis; Joe Young); I'd Rather See a Minstrel Show; I'm Sorry I Ain't Got It If I Had It You Could Have It Blues [4] (C: Ted Snyder; L: Sam M. Lewis; Joe Young); I'm the Guy Who Guards the Harem; I've Got My Captain Working for Me Now [4]; Look Out for the Bolsheviki Man [1]; Mandy [6]; My Baby's Arms (C: Harry Tierney; L: Joseph McCarthy); My Orchard of Girls [1]; My Tambourine Girl; Near Future, The; Oh, How She Can Sing [4] (C/L: Joe Schenck; Gus Van; Jack Yellen); Oh! The Last Rose of Summer [4] (C: Harry Ruby; L: Eddie Cantor; Manuel Ponce); Popular Pests, The (C: Dave Stamper; L: Gene Buck); Pretty Girl Is Like a Melody, A; Prohibition; Save Your Money, John [1] (C: Les Copeland; L: Alex Rogers); Shimmy Town (C: Dave Stamper; L: Gene Buck); Skadatin-Dee [4] (C/L: Joe Schenck; Gus Van); Somebody [4] (C: James F. Hanley; L: Ballard Macdonald); Sweet Kisses [1] (C: Albert Von Tilzer; L: Lew Brown; Eddie Buzzell); Sweet Sixteen [5] (C: Dave Stamper; L: Gene Buck); Syncopated Cocktail, A; Tulip Time (C: Dave Stamper; L: Gene Buck); We Made the Doughnuts Over There; When the Moon Shines on the Moonshine (C: Robert Hood Bowers; L: Francis DeWitt); When They're Old Enough to Know Better It's Better to Leave Them Alone [4] (C: Harry Ruby; L: Sam M. Lewis; Joe Young); Willie or Will He Not [4] (C: Maurice Abrahams; L: Sam M. Lewis; Joe Young); World Has Gone Shimmy Mad, The [7] (C: Dave Stamper; L: Gene Buck); You Cannot Make Your Shimmy Shake on Tea (L: Irving Berlin; Rennold Wolf); You Don't Need the Wine to Have a Wonderful Time [4] (C: Harry Akst; L: Howard Rogers); You'd Be Surprised [3]

Cast: Delyle Alda; Eddie Cantor; Johnny Dooley; Ray Dooley; Eddie Dowling; Fairbanks Twins, The; Mary Hay; Marilyn Miller; Joe Schenck; John Steel; Gus Van; Bert Williams

Notes: [1] Sheet music only. [2] Sheet music only. Previously in YIP! YIP! YAPHANK! and THIS IS THE ARMY. [3] Added after opening. Later in SHUBERT GAIETIES and OH! WHAT A GIRL. [4] Not in programs. [5] Added after opening. [6] Previously in YIP! YIP! YAPHANK! and THIS IS THE ARMY. [7] ASCAP/Library of Congress only.

4814 • ZIEGFELD FOLLIES OF 1920

OPENED: 06/22/1920 Theatre: New Amsterdam
Revue Broadway: 123

Composer: Irving Berlin
Lyricist: Irving Berlin
Producer: Florenz Ziegfeld
Director: Edward Royce

Costumes: Lady Duff-Gordon; Alice O'Neil; **Musical Director:** Frank Tours; **Orchestrations:** Maurice DePackh; Charles Grant; Victor Herbert; Stephen Jones; Frank Saddler; **Set Design:** Joseph Urban

Songs: All She'd Say Was 'Um Hum' [5] (C/L: Mac Emery; Joe Schenck; Gus Van; King Zany); Any Place Would Be Wonderful with You (C: Dave Stamper; L: Gene Buck); Bells; Chiffon Fantasie [6]; Chinese Fireworks; Come Along; Creation Scene (inst.) (C: Victor Herbert); Dancing School-Her First Lesson, The (scene) (C: Victor Herbert); Every Blossom I See Reminds Me of You (scene) [4] (C: Victor Herbert); Everybody Tells It to Sweeney [4] (C: George Fairman; L: Sidney D. Mitchell); Girls of My Dreams; Hold Me [2] (C/L: Ben Black; Art Hickman); I Found a Baby on My Doorstep [4] (C/L: Unknown); I Live in Turkey; I Was a Florodora Baby (C: Harry Carroll; L: Ballard Macdonald); I'm a Vamp from East Broadway (C/L: Irving Berlin; Bert Kalmar; Harry Ruby); I'm an Indian [5] (C: Leo Edwards; L: Blanche Merrill); It's the Smart Little Feller Who Stocked Up His Cellar, That's Getting the Beautiful Girls [5] (C: Milton Ager; L: Grant Clarke); Leg of Nations, The; Little Follies Theatre-During Intermission (sketch); Love Boat, The (C: Victor Herbert; L: Gene Buck); Mary and Doug (C: Dave Stamper; L: Gene Buck); My Home Town Is a One-Horse Town [4] (C: Abner Silver; L: Alex Gerber); My Midnight Frolic Girl [2] (C/L: Ben Black; Art Hickman); On Fifth Avenue-The Ziegfeld Follies Sextette; Opening; So Hard to Keep When They're Beautiful [1] (C: Harry Tierney; L: Joseph McCarthy); Sunshine and Shadows (C: Dave Stamper; L: Gene Buck); Syncopated Vamp, The; Tell Me Little Gypsy; Two Rubes [3] (C/L: Unknown); When the Right One Comes Along (C: Victor Herbert; L: Gene Buck); Where Do Mosquitos Go? [1] (C: Harry Tierney; L: Joseph McCarthy)

Cast: Delyle Alda; Fanny Brice; Jack Donahue; Ray Dooley; Mary Eaton; W.C. Fields; Bernard Granville; Art Hickman's Orchestra; Charles Mack; George Moran; Carl Randall; Jess Reed; Joe Schenck; John Steel; Gus Van; Charles Winninger

Notes: [1] Cut after opening. [2] Added after opening. [3] Added for tour. [4] Sheet music only. [5] Not in program. [6] ASCAP/Library of Congress only.

4815 • ZIEGFELD FOLLIES OF 1921

OPENED: 06/21/1921 Theatre: Globe
Revue Broadway: 119

Librettist: Gene Buck; B.G. DeSylva; Rudolf Friml; Victor Herbert; Willard Mack; Channing Pollock; Ralph Spence
Producer: Florenz Ziegfeld
Director: George Marion

Costumes: James Reynolds; **Musical Director:** Frank Tours; **Orchestrations:** Maurice DePackh; Stephen Jones; **Set Design:** Joseph Urban

Songs: Ain't Nature Grand? [1] (C: Irving Berlin; L: Billy Rose; Ben Ryan); Allay Up (C: James F. Hanley; L: Ballard Macdonald); Birthday of the Dauphin, The (scene) (C: Victor Herbert); Bring Back My Blushing Rose (C: Rudolf Friml; L: Gene Buck); Championship of the World, The [6] (C: Victor Herbert); Come Back to Our Alley Sally (C: Dave Stamper; L: Gene Buck); Every Time I Hear a Band Play (C: Rudolf Friml; L: Gene Buck); Four Little Girls with a Future and Four Little Girls with a Past (C: Rudolf Friml; L: B.G. DeSylva); I Can't Resist Them When They're Beautiful [1]; I Hold Her Hand and She Holds Mine [1] (C: Irving Bibo; L: Billy Rose; Ben Ryan); If Plymouth Rock Had Landed on the Pilgrims Instead of the Pilgrims Landing on the Rock [2] (C: Dave Stamper; L: Channing Pollock); I'm a Hieland Lassie [3] (C: Leo Edwards; L: Blanche Merrill); In Khorossan (C: Victor Herbert; L: Gene Buck); In My Tippy Canoe [1] (C/L: Fred Fisher); In That Little Irish Home Sweet Home [6] (C: Harry Von Tilzer; L: William Jerome); In the Old Town Hall [1] (C: Ed G. Nelson; L: Howard Johnson; Harry Pease); Legend of the Cyclamen Tree, The (The Legend of the Golden Tree) (C: Victor Herbert; L: Gene Buck); My Man (C: Maurice Yvain; L: Channing Pollock); Now I Know (C: James V. Monaco; L: Grant Clarke); O'Reilly [1] (C: Ed G. Nelson; Elsie White; L: Harry Pease); Our Home Town (C: Harry Carroll; L: Ballard Macdonald); Princess of My Dreams, The (C: Victor Herbert; L: Gene Buck); Raggedy Rag (C: Dave Stamper; L: Gene Buck); Rosemary (C: Dave Stamper; L: B.G. DeSylva); Roses in the Garden [1] (C: Rudolf Friml; L: Brian Hooker); Sally, Won't You Come Back (Come Back to Our Alley, Sally?) [3] (C: Dave Stamper; L: Gene Buck); Scotch Lassie (C: Leo Edwards; L: Blanche Merrill); Second-Hand Rose (C: James F. Hanley; L: Grant Clarke); So This Is Venice [6] (C: Harry Warren; L: Edgar Leslie); Some Day the Sun Will Shine [5] (C: James V. Monaco; L: Grant Clarke); Strut Miss Lizzy (C: Turner Layton; L: Henry Creamer); Two Lovely Lying Eyes [1] (C: Rudolf

Friml; L: Gene Buck); Wang-Wang Blues [1] (C: Henry Busse; Buster Johnson; Gustave Mueller; L: Leo Wood); What a World This Would Be [1] (C: Dave Stamper; L: B.G. DeSylva); You Must Come Over (C: Jerome Kern; L: B.G. DeSylva)

Cast: Fanny Brice; John Clarke; Ray Dooley; Mary Eaton; W.C. Fields; Raymond Hitchcock; Mary Lewis; Vera Michelena; Mary Milburn; Florence O'Denishawn; Joe Schenck

Notes: [1] Sheet music only. [2] Also titled "If the Plymouth Rock Had Landed on the Pilgrims." [3] Not in program. [4] Brian Hooker sometimes cocredited with lyrics in some sources, but not ASCAP. [5] Sheet music only. ASCAP credits this song to James F. Hanley and Grant Clarke. [6] ASCAP/Library of Congress.

4816 • ZIEGFELD FOLLIES OF 1922

OPENED: 06/05/1922 Theatre: New Amsterdam
Revue Broadway: 426

Composer: Louis A. Hirsch
Lyricist: Gene Buck
Librettist: Gene Buck; Ring Lardner; Ralph Spence
Producer: Florenz Ziegfeld
Director: Ned Wayburn

Choreographer: Michel Fokine; John Tiller; Ned Wayburn; **Costumes:** Ada Fields; Cora MacGeachy; Alice O'Neil; James Reynolds; **Musical Director:** Oscar Radin; **Set Design:** Joseph Urban

Songs: Bally-Burlesk [7]; Blunderland; Bring on the Girls [8] (C: Dave Stamper); Come Along (C: Turner Layton; L: Henry Creamer); Dreams for Sale [7] (C: James F. Hanley; L: Herbert Reynolds); Ensemble Finale (C: Louis A. Hirsch; Dave Stamper); Everybody's Making It Now [7] (C/L: Jimmy Duffy); Fairylands (scene) [7] (C: Victor Herbert); Farijandis (scene) (C: Victor Herbert); Flappers [7] (C: Dave Stamper); Four Well Known Dames and a Guy (Song Scene) [7] (C: Raymond Hubbell); Hello, Hello, Hello (C: Dave Stamper); I Don't Know What I'd Do Without You [2]; I Don't Want to Be in Dixie [2] (C: Louis A. Hirsch; Dave Stamper); I'm Satisfied [7]; It's Getting Dark on Old Broadway (C: Dave Stamper); Kiss in the Dark, A [4] (C: Victor Herbert; L: B.G. DeSylva); Lace Land (scene) [1] (C: Victor Herbert); List'ning on Some Radio (C: Dave Stamper); Marches (inst.) (C: Victor Herbert); Mr. Gallagher and Mr. Shean (C/L: Ed Gallagher; Al Shean); My Melody [3]; My Rambler Rose (C: Louis A. Hirsch; Dave Stamper); 'Neath the South Sea Moon (C: Louis A. Hirsch; Dave Stamper); Nobody but You [7] (C: Louis A. Hirsch; Dave Stamper); Oh Gee! Oh Gosh! Oh Golly! I'm in Love [2] (C: Ernest Breuer; L: Chic Johnson; Ole Olsen); Pep It Up (C: Dave Stamper); Sing a Song of Sunshine [5]; Sing a Swanee Song [7] (C: Louis Breau; L: Nat Sanders); Sitting in a Corner [1]; Some Sweet Day (C: Louis A. Hirsch; Dave Stamper); Songs I Can't Forget (C: Louis A. Hirsch); Sunny South [7] (C: Louis A. Hirsch); Throw Me a Kiss [6] (C: Louis A. Hirsch; Dave Stamper; Maurice Yvain); Weaving My Dreams (C: Victor Herbert)

Cast: Mary Eaton; Ed Gallagher; Gilda Gray; Chic Johnson; Evelyn Law; Charles LeMaire; Lulu McConnell; Ole Olsen; Will Rogers; Al Shean; Tiller Girls

Notes: [1] Out Newark 5/5/24. [2] Sheet music only. [3] Added after opening. [4] Originally in ORANGE BLOSSOMS. [5] Not in programs. [6] Yvain not credited in some programs. [7] Cut after opening. [8] ASCAP credits this to Victor Herbert.

4817 • ZIEGFELD FOLLIES OF 1923

OPENED: 10/20/1923 Theatre: New Amsterdam
Revue Broadway: 233

Composer: Dave Stamper
Lyricist: Gene Buck
Librettist: Florenz Ziegfeld
Director: Ned Wayburn

Costumes: Erte; Evlyn McHorter; Alice O'Neil; James Reynolds; **Musical Director:** Oscar Radin; **Set Design:** Joseph Urban

Songs: As Long As He Loves Me [1] (C: James F. Hanley; L: Lew Brown); Bebe [1] (C: Abner Silver; L: Sam Coslow); Broadway Indians; Cane Dance [2]; Chansonette [4] (C: Rudolf Friml; L: Irving Caesar; Dailey Paskman; Sigmund Spaeth); Dancing Mad [7] (C: Leo Edwards; L: Blanche Merrill); Everlovin' Bee [2]; Fencing (C: Victor Herbert); Fool, The (C: Lee David; L: Benton Ley); Glorifying the Girls; Good Night [7]; Harlequin's Doll (C: Gabriel Daray); I Must Go to Moscow [3] (C: Ernest Breuer; L: Mort Dixon;

Leon Flatow); I Want 'em Wild, Weak, Warm and Willing [8] (C/L: Eddie Cantor; Sam Coslow); I Wonder How They Get That Way [7]; I'd Love to Waltz Through Life with You (C: Victor Herbert); If I Can't Get the Sweetie I Want I Pity the Sweetie I Get [1] (C: Jean Schwartz; L: Sam M. Lewis; Joe Young); I'm a Manicurist [7] (C/L: Blanche Merrill); I'm Bugs Over You [7]; Kayo Tortoni; Lady Fair [7] (C: Rudolf Friml); Lady of the Lantern [3] (C: Victor Herbert); Legend of the Drums (C: Victor Herbert); Little Old New York (C: Victor Herbert); Lonesome Cinderella [1] (C: James F. Hanley; L: Lew Brown); Maid of Gold (C: Rudolf Friml); Mammy [7] (C: Walter Donaldson; L: Sam M. Lewis; Joe Young); Mary Rose (C: Maurice Yvain); Moonlight Ballet (inst.) [6] (C: Victor Herbert); Oh! Gee, Oh! Gosh, Oh! Golly, I'm in Love [5] (C: Ernest Breuer; L: Chic Johnson; Ole Olsen); Red Light Annie [3]; Russian Art [6] (C: Leo Edwards; L: Blanche Merrill); Shake Your Feet; So This Is Venice [3] (C: Harry Warren; L: Grant Clarke; Edgar Leslie); Springtime [6]; Steady Eddie [3]; Swanee River Blues [7]; Sweet Alice [1] (C/L: Frank Crumit); Take Those Lips Away (C: Harry Tierney; L: Joseph McCarthy); That Old Fashioned Garden of Mine [7] (C: Victor Herbert); That Society Budd (I'm a Society Bud) [7] (C: Harry Ruby; L: Bert Kalmar); Wedding Scene [7] (C: Victor Herbert); What Thrills Can There Be (L: Harry Ruskin); Why Did I Buy That Morris Chair for Morris? [8] (C/L: Bert Kalmar; Murray Kissen; Harry Ruby); You Gotta Yes 'Em to Know Them [3] (C/L: Blanche Merrill; Dave Stamper); Your Eyes Have Told Me That You Love Me [8]

Cast: Lina Basquette; Fanny Brice; Eddie Cantor; Harland Dixon; Lew Hearn; Brooke Johns; Tom Lewis; Hap Ward; Bert Wheeler; Betty Wheeler; Paul Whiteman and His Orchestra; Imogene Wilson

Notes: [1] Sheet music only. [2] Out Newark 2/23/25. [3] Not in program. [4] Not in program. Music later became "Donkey Serenade." [5] Not in program. Also in ZIEGFELD FOLLIES OF 1922. [6] Added after opening. [7] Cut after opening. [8] ASCAP/Library of Congress only.

4818 • ZIEGFELD FOLLIES OF 1924

OPENED: 06/24/1924 Theatre: New Amsterdam
Revue Broadway: 401

Composer: Harry Tierney
Lyricist: Joseph McCarthy
Librettist: William Anthony McGuire; Will Rogers
Producer: Florenz Ziegfeld
Director: Julian Mitchell

Costumes: Erte; Charles LeMaire; Miss McWhorter; James Reynolds; **Musical Director:** Victor Baravalle; **Orchestrations:** Fred Barry; Robert Russell Bennett; Raymond Hubbell; Stephen Jones; Harold Sandford; **Set Design:** Gates & Morange; Ludwig Kainer; H. Robert Law; Joseph Urban; John Wenger

Songs: Absinthe Frappe [2] (C: Victor Herbert; L: Glen MacDonough); Adoring You; All Pepped Up; Big Glass Cage, A; Biminy (C: Dave Stamper; L: Gene Buck); Ever Lovin' Bee [4] (C: Dave Stamper; L: Gene Buck); Fine Feathers Make Fine Birds [5]; Follow the Swallow [5] (C: Ray Henderson; L: Mort Dixon; Billy Rose); Garden — The Beauty Contest, A (C: Victor Herbert; Harry Tierney); Great Wide Open Spaces, The (C: Dave Stamper; L: Gene Buck); Gypsy Love Song (C: Victor Herbert); I Believe You [6] (C: Dave Stamper; L: Gene Buck); I Can't Do the Sum [1] (C: Victor Herbert; L: Glen MacDonough); If I Were on the Stage (Kiss Me Again) [3] (C: Victor Herbert; L: Henry Blossom); London Empire Girls (C: Dave Stamper); Lonely Little Melody (C: Dave Stamper; L: Gene Buck); March of the Toys [1] (C: Victor Herbert; L: Glen MacDonough); Mirage Dance, The (inst.) [4] (C: Borel Clerc; Laurent Halet); Montmartre (C: Raymond Hubbell; L: Gene Buck); Night in June, A (C: Raymond Hubbell; L: Gene Buck); Old Town Band, The; Pearl of the East (scene) (C: Raymond Hubbell); Plot, The (scene) (C: Raymond Hubbell; L: Gene Buck); Rose of My Heart (C: Albert Sirmay; L: Gene Buck); Tiller Girls Dance (inst.) (C: Victor Herbert); Toyland [1] (C: Victor Herbert; L: Glen MacDonough); You're My Happy Ending (C: James F. Hanley; L: Gene Buck)

Cast: Ray Dooley; W.C. Fields; Irving Fisher; Lupino Lane; Evelyn Law; Tom Lewis; George Olsen; Ann Pennington; James Reynolds; Will Rogers; Vivienne Segal; Tiller Girls

Notes: The number of performances includes the run of ZIEGFELD FOLLIES OF 1925 since it was basically a continuation of the 1924 edition. [1] Originally in BABES IN TOYLAND. [2] Originally in IT HAPPENED IN NORDLAND. [3] Originally

in MLLE. MODISTE. [4] Added for Fall Edition and kept for ZIEGFELD FOLLIES OF 1925. [5] Not in program. [6] ASCAP list only.

4819 • ZIEGFELD FOLLIES OF 1925

OPENED: 03/10/1925 Theatre: New Amsterdam
Revue Broadway: 223

Lyricist: Gene Buck
Librettist: W.C. Fields; J.P. McEvoy; Will Rogers
Producer: Florenz Ziegfeld
Director: Julian Mitchell

Costumes: Ben Ali Haggin; John Held Jr.; **Musical Director:** Victor Baravalle; **Orchestrations:** Fred Barry; Robert Russell Bennett; Stephen Jones; Harold Sandford; **Set Design:** Norman Bel Geddes; Gates & Morange; Ludwig Kainer; H. Robert Law; John Wenger

Songs: Bertie (C: Sigmund Romberg; L: Clifford Grey); Eddie, Be Good [2] (C: Dave Stamper); Ever Lovin' Bee [1] (C: Dave Stamper); Everybody Knows What Jazz Is (C: Werner Janssen); Home Again [2] (C: Raymond Hubbell); I'd Like to Be a Gardener in a Garden of Girls [2] (C: Raymond Hubbell); I'd Like to Corral a Gal (C: Raymond Hubbell); In the Shade of the Alamo [2] (C: Raymond Hubbell); Pearl of the East (scene) (C: Raymond Hubbell); Settle Down in a Little Town (C: Werner Janssen); Syncopating Baby (Syncopating Sadie) [2] (C: Dave Stamper); Titina (C: Leo Daniderff); Toddle Along (C: Werner Janssen); Tondelayo (C: Dave Stamper; L: Gene Buck; Jack Osterman); When Nathan Was Married to Rose of Washington Square [3] (C: Dave Stamper)

Cast: Ray Dooley; Peggy Fears; W.C. Fields; Al Oches; Will Rogers; Ethel Shutta; Tiller Girls, The

Notes: The 1925 FOLLIES is a continuation of the 1924 FOLLIES with additional cast, sketches and songs. This edition played 135 performances. The Summer Edition followed 7/6/25 for 88 performances. [1] Also in ZIEGFELD FOLLIES OF 1924. [2] Added for summer edition as was Ethel Shutta. [3] Not in programs.

4820 • ZIEGFELD FOLLIES OF 1926

Notes: *See NO FOOLIN'*. This was tour name of that show.

4821 • ZIEGFELD FOLLIES OF 1927

OPENED: 08/16/1927 Theatre: New Amsterdam
Revue Broadway: 167

Composer: Irving Berlin
Lyricist: Irving Berlin
Librettist: Harold Atteridge; Eddie Cantor
Producer: Florenz Ziegfeld
Director: Zeke Colvan

Choreographer: Sammy Lee; Albertina Rasch; **Costumes:** John Harkrider; **Musical Director:** Frank Tours; **Orchestrations:** Ferde Grofe; Arthur Gutman; Louis Katzman; Paul Lannin; Frank Tours; Roy Webb; **Set Design:** Joseph Urban

Songs: Ev'rybody Loves My Girl [1] (C: Maurice Abrahams; L: Sam M. Lewis; Joe Young); I Want to Be Glorified; It All Belongs to Me; (Hooray, Hooray) It's Ray-Ray-Raining [1] (C: Al Sherman; L: Howard Johnson; Charles Tobias); It's Up to the Band; Jimmy; Jungle Jingle; Learn to Sing a Love Song; My Blue Heaven [2] (C: Walter Donaldson; L: George Whiting); My New York [2]; My Old Girl Is My New Girl Now; Now We Are Glorified [4]; Ooh, Maybe It's You; Rainbow of Girls; Ribbons and Bows; Shaking the Blues Away; She Don't Wanna [1] (C: Milton Ager; L: Jack Yellen); Tickling the Ivories; What Makes Me Love You? [1]; You Gotta Have 'IT' [3]

Cast: Franklin Baur; Brox Sisters, The; Eddie Cantor; Irene Delroy; Ruth Etting; Dan Healy; Claire Luce; Harry McNaughton; Frances Upton

Notes: [1] Sheet music only. [2] Not in program. [3] Not in program. A Berlin re-write of a song by Eddie Cantor. [4] Added after opening.

4822 • ZIEGFELD FOLLIES OF 1930

OPENED: 1930
Revue

Songs: You'll Give In (C: James F. Hanley; L: Joseph McCarthy)

Notes: No other information available. This song may have been written for an unproduced edition of the Follies or might have been interpolated into a touring production of a previous edition.

4823 • ZIEGFELD FOLLIES OF 1931

OPENED: 07/01/1931 Theatre: Ziegfeld
Revue Broadway: 165

Composer: Harry Revel
Lyricist: Mack Gordon
Librettist: Gene Buck; Mark Hellinger; J.P. Murray
Producer: Florenz Ziegfeld
Director: Edward Clarke Lilley

Choreographer: Bobby Connolly; Albertina Rasch; **Costumes:** John Harkrider; **Musical Director:** Victor Baravalle; **Orchestrations:** Maurice DePackh; Howard Jackson; Joe Jordan; Will Vodery; **Set Design:** Joseph Urban

Songs: Bring on the Follies' Girls (C: Dave Stamper; L: Gene Buck); Broadway Reverie (C: Dave Stamper; L: Gene Buck); Changing of the Guards (C: Ben Oakland; L: J.P. Murray; Barry Trivers); Cigarettes, Cigars (C: Harry Revel; L: Mack Gordon); Clinching the Sale (C: Ben Oakland; L: J.P. Murray; Barry Trivers); Dance (C: Harry Revel; L: Mack Gordon); Doin' the New York (C: Ben Oakland; L: J.P. Murray; Barry Trivers); Fandango Dance [2] (C: Dimitri Tiomkin); Half Caste Woman (C/L: Noel Coward); Help Yourself to Happiness (C: Harry Revel; L: Mack Gordon; Harry Richman); Here We Are in Love [1] (C: Ben Oakland; L: J.P. Murray; Barry Trivers); Illusion in White (C: Dimitri Tiomkin); I'm Good for Nothing but Love (C: Bernard Maltin; L: Ballard); I'm with You (C/L: Walter Donaldson); Legend of the Islands (C/L: Powell; Stevens); Leonard Stokes and Hal LeRoy (scene) (C: Dave Stamper); Let's K'nock K'nees [5] (C: Harry Revel; L: Mack Gordon); Mailu [4] (C: Jay Gorney; L: E.Y. Harburg); Picture Bride, The (scene) (C: Hugo Riesenfeld; Dave Stamper); Pink Lady Waltz (inst.) (C: Ivan Caryll); Rhythm of the Day [6] (C: Ben Oakland; L: J.P. Murray; Barry Trivers); Shine on Harvest Moon [3] (C/L: Jack Norworth; L: Nora Bayes); Tom-Tom Dance (C: Dimitri Tiomkin); Victim of the Talkies (C: Ben Oakland; L: J.P. Murray; Barry Trivers); Waltz (C: Dave Stamper); Was I? (C: Chick Endor; L: Charles Farrell); Who Paid the Rent for Mrs. Rip Van Winkle When Rip Van Winkle Went Away (C: Fred Fisher; L: Alfred Bryan); (I'm) Wrapped Up in You (C: Ben Oakland; L: J.P. Murray; Barry Trivers); You Made Me Love You (C: James V. Monaco; L: Joseph McCarthy); Your Sunny Southern Smile (C: Harry Revel; L: Mack Gordon)

Cast: Faith Bacon; Edith Borden; Frank Britton; Milt Britton; John Bubbles; Ford Buck; Arthur Campbell; Albert Carroll; Collette Sisters, The; Dorothy Dell; Ruth Etting; Gladys Glad; Cliff Hall; Hal LeRoy; Mitzi Mayfair; Helen Morgan; Pearl Osgood; Earl Oxford; Jack Pearl; Reri; Harry Richman

Notes: [1] Sheet music only. [2] This is the name of a song not just a dance number. [3] Originally in ZIEGFELD FOLLIES OF 1908. [4] Hugo Riesenfeld also credited with music by ASCAP. [5] Not used. Later used in film THE GAY DIVORCEE. [6] ASCAP/Library of Congress only.

4824 • ZIEGFELD FOLLIES OF 1934

OPENED: 01/04/1934 Theatre: New Amsterdam
Revue Broadway: 182

Composer: Vernon Duke
Lyricist: E.Y. Harburg
Librettist: Fred Allen; David Freedman; Ballard Macdonald; H.I. Phillips; Harry Turgend
Producer: Billie Burke; Messrs. Shubert
Director: John Murray Anderson; Bobby Connolly; Edward Clarke Lilley

Choreographer: Robert Alton; Bobby Connolly; **Costumes:** Kiviette; Charles LeMaire; Billy Livingston; Russell Patterson; Raoul Pene du Bois; **Lighting Designer:** John Murray Anderson; **Musical Director:** John McManus; **Set Design:** Watson Barratt; Albert Johnson

Songs: Careful with My Heart (C: Samuel Pokrass); Countess Dubinsky (C: Joseph Meyer; L: Ballard Macdonald; Billy Rose); Follies Chorale Ensemble (C: Samuel Pokrass); Goo-Goo Da Da (Goo Goo G'Da) [5] (C: Ernest Breuer; L: Billy Frisch; Raymond Leveen; Frank Loesser); Green Eyes (C: Robert Emmett Dolan); House Is Haunted, The (By the Echo of Your Last Goodbye) [3] (C: Basil Adlam; L: Billy Rose); I Like the Likes of You; Just a Barefoot Boy (A'Whistlin' to His Dog) [3] (C: James F. Hanley; L: Chris Taylor); Last Roundup, The (C/L: Billy Hill); Moon About Town (C: Dana Suesse); Poor Fellow [4] (C/L: Ben Oakland); Rain in My Heart [4] (C: Louis Alter; L: Arthur Swanstrom); Rose of Washington Square [1] (C: James F. Hanley; L: Ballard Macdonald); Sarah, the Sunshine Girl (C: Joseph Meyer; L: Ballard Macdonald; Billy Rose); Shim Sham [4] (C: Louis Alter; L: Arthur

Swanstrom); Sidewalk in Paris, A [7] (C: Arthur Swanstrom); (It's) Smart to Be Smart [4]; Soul Saving Sadie (C: Joseph Meyer; L: Ballard Macdonald; Billy Rose); Stop that Clock [4]; Suddenly (L: E.Y. Harburg; Billy Rose); That's Where We Come In (C: Samuel Pokrass); Then I'll Be Tired of You [2] (C: Arthur Schwartz); This Is Not a Song (L: E.Y. Harburg; E. Hartman); Time Is a Gypsy (C: Richard Myers; L: E.Y. Harburg); To the Beat of My Heart (C: Samuel Pokrass); Wagon Wheels (C: Peter De Rose; L: Billy Hill); Water Under the Bridge; What Is There to Say?; Why Am I Blue [6] (C: Peter De Rose; L: Billy Hill); Winter Wonderland (C/L: Felix Bernard; Dick Smith); You Oughta Be in Pictures [3] (C: Dana Suesse; L: Edward Heyman)

Cast: Eve Arden; Judith Barron; Betzi Beaton; Fanny Brice; Patricia Browman; Jacques Cartier; Robert Cummings; Buddy Ebsen; Vilma Ebsen; Jane Froman; Eugene Howard; Willie Howard; Ina Ray Hutton; Vivian Janis; Everett Marshall; Victor Morley; Cherry Preisser; June Preisser; Don Ross; Oliver Wakefield

Notes: [1] Interpolated. Originally in ZIEGFELD FOLLIES OF 1920 and ZIEGFELD MIDNIGHT FROLIC OF 1919. Added after opening. [2] Not in program. [3] Added after opening. [4] Out Boston 11/13/33. [5] Out Detroit 12/4/33. [6] Out Detroit 11/25/34. [7] Titled "Fifth Avenue — A Sidewalk in Paris" by ASCAP.

4825 • ZIEGFELD FOLLIES OF 1936

OPENED: 01/30/1936 Theatre: Winter Garden
Revue Broadway: 115

Composer: Vernon Duke
Lyricist: Ira Gershwin
Librettist: David Freedman
Producer: Billie Burke; Messrs. Shubert
Director: John Murray Anderson; Edward Clarke Lilley

Choreographer: Robert Alton; George Balanchine; **Costumes:** Vincente Minnelli; **Musical Director:** John McManus; **Orchestrations:** Robert Russell Bennett; Conrad Salinger; Hans Spialek; Don Walker; **Set Design:** Vincente Minnelli

Songs: Announcement for Broadway Gold Melody Diggers of 42nd Street [1]; Are You Havin' Any Fun [4] (C: Sammy Fain; L: Jack Yellen); Ballad of Baby Face McGinty (Who Bit Off More Than He Could Chew), The [3]; Better Half Knows Better, The [1]; Dancing to the Score; Does a Duck Love Water? [3]; Economic Situation, The (Aren't You Wonderful); Fancy! Fancy!; Five A.M.; Gazooka, The; He Hasn't a Thing Except Me; Hot Number [1]; I Can't Get Started; I Used to Be Above Love [1]; I'm Sharing My Wealth [1]; Island in the West Indies; It's a Different World; Knife-Thrower's Wife, The [3]; Last of the Cabbies, The [3]; Maharanee; Midnight Blue [2] (C: Joseph Burke; L: Edgar Leslie); Modernistic Moe (L: Ira Gershwin; Billy Rose); My Red-Letter Day; Oh, Bring Back the Ballet Again [1]; Please Send My Daddy Back Home [3]; Ridin' the Rails (C: Harold Spina; L: Edward Heyman); Save Your Yesses [1]; Sentimental Weather; Sunday Tan [1]; That Moment of Moments; Time Marches On!; Trailer for the 1936 Broadway Gold Melody Diggers; Why Save for That Rainy Day? [1]; Wishing Tree of Harlem [1]; Words Without Music; You Don't Love Right [2] (C: Vee Lawnhurst; L: Tot Seymour)

Cast: Eve Arden; Josephine Baker; Fanny Brice; Hugh Cameron; Judy Canova; George Church; Bobby Clark; Cass Daley; Ruth Fisher; Alex Harrison; Harriet Hoctor; Bob Hope; John Hoysradt; Stan Kavanaugh; Gypsy Rose Lee; Duke McHale; Rodney McLennan; Nicholas Brothers, The; Gertrude Niesen; Hugh O'Connell; Jane Pickens; Cherry Preisser; June Preisser; Ben Yost Varsity Eight

Notes: The cast listed is for the second edition which opened 9/14/36 and was titled NEW ZIEGFELD FOLLIES OF 1936-1937. The number of performances above is for both editions. [1] Not used. [2] Added to second edition. [3] Cut prior to opening. [4] Added to second edition. Later in GEORGE WHITE'S SCANDALS OF 1939.

4826 • ZIEGFELD FOLLIES OF 1943

OPENED: 04/01/1943 Theatre: Winter Garden
Revue Broadway: 553

Composer: Ray Henderson
Lyricist: Jack Yellen
Producer: Messrs. Shubert
Director: John Murray Anderson; Arthur Pierson; Fred de Cordova

Choreographer: Robert Alton; **Costumes:** Miles White; **Musical Director:** John McManus;

Orchestrations: Don Walker; **Set Design:** Watson Barratt

Songs: Advertising Song, The [1] (C/L: Harold Rome); Back to the Farm (C: Dan White; L: Bud Burtson); Come Up and Have a Cup of Coffee; Hep, Hot and Solid Sweet [4]; Hindoo Serenade; Hold That Smile; Love Songs Are Made in the Night; Micromaniac (C/L: Harold Rome); (There Are) New Roses Every Summer; Saga of Carmen, The (Carmen Was); Sue Ryan (C: Dan White; L: Bud Burtson); Swing Your Lady Mister Hemingway; Thirty-Five Summers Ago; This Is It; Under My Umbrella [2] (C: Vernon Duke; L: Howard Dietz); Wedding of a Solid Sender, The (dance) (C: Baldwin Bergersen); You're Dreamlike [3] (C: Vernon Duke; L: Howard Dietz)

Cast: Christine Ayers; Bil Baird; Cora Baird; Milton Berle; Eric Blore; Imogene Carpenter; Jack Cole; Nadine Gae; Ilona Massey; Jack McCauley; Sue Ryan; Arthur Treacher; Tommy Wonder

Notes: [1] Added after opening. [2] Not used. Also not used in DANCING IN THE STREETS. [3] Not used. Also not used in SADIE THOMPSON. [4] ASCAP/Library of Congress only.

4827 • ZIEGFELD FOLLIES OF 1956

OPENED: 04/16/1956
Revue — Closed out of town

Librettist: Ronny Graham; Arnold B. Horwitt; Stanley Prager; David Rogers
Producer: James W. Gardiner; Richard Kollmar
Director: Christopher Hewett

Choreographer: Jack Cole; **Costumes:** Raoul Pene du Bois; **Dance Arranger:** Hal Schaefer; **Lighting Designer:** Peggy Clark; **Musical Director:** Anton Coppola; **Orchestrations:** George Bassman; Albert Sendry; **Set Design:** Raoul Pene du Bois; **Vocal Arranger:** Hugh Martin

Songs: Ballad of Herman Schlepps, The (C: Albert Hague; L: Arnold B. Horwitt); Don't Knock It (C/L: Herbert Baker); Downtown (C: Charles Strouse; L: Lee Adams); Faster Than Sound [1] (C/L: Ralph Blane; Hugh Martin); Finale; Go Bravely On (C/L: Sydney Shaw); Lady Is Indisposed, The (C: Cy Coleman; L: Joseph McCarthy Jr.); Miser's Serenade, The (C: Marvin Fisher; Jack Val; L: Fred Patrick; Claude Reese); Night the Lion Broke Loose, The (C: Milton De Lugg; L: Chuck Sweeney); Noises in the Theatre (C: Richard Lewine; L: Arnold B. Horwitt); Opening Number; Runaway (C: Alton Rinker; L: Floyd Huddleston); Small Winner (C: Albert Hague; L: Arnold B. Horwitt); Thing About Willie, The (C: Alton Rinker; L: Floyd Huddleston); What It Was Was Love (C: Albert Hague; L: Arnold B. Horwitt); When Papa Would Waltz (C: Jerry Bock; L: Larry Holofcener); Whip, The (C: Jerry Bock; L: Larry Holofcener)

Cast: Tallulah Bankhead; Mae Barnes; David Burns; Joan Diener; Timothy Gray; Carol Haney; Larry Kert; Preshy Marker; Matt Mattox; Elliott Reid

Notes: Irving Berlin also listed in program but not for a specific song. [1] Later in HIGH SPIRITS.

4828 • ZIEGFELD FOLLIES OF 1957

OPENED: 03/01/1957 — Theatre: Winter Garden
Revue — Broadway: 123

Librettist: Maxwell Grant; Coleman Jacoby; Alan Jeffreys; David Rogers; Arnie Rosen
Producer: Charles Conaway; Mark Kroll
Director: John Kennedy

Choreographer: Frank Wagner; **Costumes:** Raoul Pene du Bois; **Dance Arranger:** Rene Weigert; **Lighting Designer:** Paul Morrison; **Musical Director:** Max Meth; **Orchestrations:** Robert Russell Bennett; Joe Glover; Bob Noelmeter; Bill Stegmeyer; **Set Design:** Raoul Pene du Bois; **Vocal Arranger:** Earl Rogers

Songs: Better Than Ever [3] (C: Richard Myers; L: Jack Lawrence); Bring on the Girls (C: Richard Myers; L: Jack Lawrence); Don't Tell a Soul [2] (C: Colin Romoff; L: David Rogers); (That) Element of Doubt (C: Sammy Fain; L: Howard Dietz); Finale (C: Richard Myers; L: Jack Lawrence); Follies Nocturne [2] (C/L: Bernie Wayne); Golden Anniversary [2] (C: Richard Myers; L: Jack Lawrence); Hazards of the Profession [2] (C: Dean Fuller; L: Marshall Barer); Honorable Mambo (C: Dean Fuller; L: Marshall Barer); I Don't Wanna Rock (C: Colin Romoff; L: David Rogers); If You Got Music (C: Colin Romoff; L: David Rogers); Intoxication (C: Dean Fuller; L: Marshall Barer); Lover in Me, The (C: Philip Springer; L: Carolyn Leigh); Make Me

(C/L: Uhpio Minucci; Larry Spier; Tony Velona); Mangoes (C/L: Dee Libbey); Miss Follies (C: Colin Romoff; L: David Rogers); Miss Follies of 192 . . . (C/L: Herman Hupfeld); Music for Madame (C: Richard Myers; L: Jack Lawrence); My Late, Late Lady (C: Dean Fuller; L: Marshall Barer); Producer's Office [2] (C: Richard Myers; L: Jack Lawrence); Salesmanship (C: Philip Springer; L: Carolyn Leigh); Stay on the Subject [1] (C: Dean Fuller; L: Marshall Barer); Time Magazine [1] (C/L: Maxwell Grant; Alan Jeffreys; Jack Wilson); Two a Day on the Milky Way (C: Dean Fuller; L: Marshall Barer)

Cast: Billy De Wolfe; Harold Lang; Carol Lawrence; Beatrice Lillie; Jane Morgan

Notes: [1] Cut prior to opening. [2] Out D.C. 2/18/57. [3] ASCAP/Library of Congress only.

4829 • ZIEGFELD FOLLIES (1958)

OPENED: 09/30/1957
Revue — Closed out of town

Lyricist: David Rogers
Librettist: Eddie Davis; Coleman Jacoby; Loney Lewis; David Rogers; Arnie Rosen; Ira Wallach
Producer: Charles Conaway; Mark Kroll
Director: Mervyn Nelson

Choreographer: Bob Copsey; **Costumes:** Raoul Pene du Bois; **Lighting Designer:** Louis Popiel; **Musical Director:** Ray O'Brien; **Orchestrations:** Joe Sherman; **Set Design:** Raoul Pene du Bois

Songs: Be Bop Lullaby (C: Ralph Strain; L: Marshall Barer); Happiest Millionaires, The (C: Paul Klein; L: Fred Ebb); Honorable Mambo (C: Marshal Rosen; L: Coleman Jacoby); It's Silk, Feel It (C: Dean Fuller; L: Marshall Barer); Lonesome Is As Lonesome Does (C/L: Joe Sherman; Noel Sherman); Miss Follies (C: Colin Romoff); One More Samba (C: Gerald Alters); Parade Is Passing Me By, The (C/L: Joe Sherman; Noel Sherman); Play, Mr. Bailey (C/L: Biff Jones; Chuck Meyer); Pretty Girl Is Like a Melody, A [1] (C/L: Irving Berlin); Somebody's Keeping Score (C: Sammy Fain; L: Jackie Barnett); When Papa Would Waltz (C: Jerry Bock; L: Larry Holofcener); Ziegfeld Show, A (C: Otis Clements)

Cast: Sara Aman; Jobee Ayers; Kaye Ballard; Lord Buckley; Bob Copsey; Richard Curry; Paul Gilbert; Patrice Helene; Lew Herbert; Jan Howard; Kitty Lester; Loney Lewis; Micki Marlo; Jimmy Roma

Notes: Program of Hanna Theatre, Cleveland, Ohio. [1] From ZIEGFELD FOLLIES OF 1919.

4830 • ZIEGFELD GIRL, THE

OPENED: 01/23/1989 — Theatre: New Ziegfeld
Musical — Off-Off-Broadway: 16

Composer: Christopher Berg
Lyricist: Jordan Tinsley
Librettist: Michael Proft; Jordan Tinsley
Producer: Shoestring Follies Prod.
Director: Jordan Tinsley

Source: WHEN SHE WAS BAD (Play: H. Owen Barrie); **Arrangements:** Christopher Berg; **Choreographer:** Jordan Tinsley; **Musical Director:** Christopher Berg

Songs: Argument, The (C/L: Tom Judson); Bon Jour! (C/L: Tom Judson); Butcher, the Baker, the Candlestick Maker, The; Chocolate Covered Future [1]; Dressing Room, A [1]; Feathers; Follow Your Heart; I Don't Want to Be Hurt Again [1]; I'm a Lady!; Love in the Smoking Car; Love Is Around the Corner; Miss May; Satin, Cigarettes and Warm Brandy; Singin' the Red Hot Blues; Southern Charm [1]; Star in Heaven's Firmament, A; That Winter Was a Spring; The End [1]; Trip to Paris, A; What You're Gonna Do for Me; Why Don't We Move to Philadelphia (C/L: Tom Judson); Ziegfeld Girl, The

Cast: Joann Bright; Marla Cahan; Paul Hoffman; Ellen Mittenthal; Myka Ryan; Hans Tester; Jordan Tinsley; Victoria Trost; Michael Walsh; Michael Wilkinson

Notes: [1] Cut.

4831 • ZIEGFELD GIRLS OF 1920

OPENED: 03/08/1920 — Theatre: New Amsterdam Roof
Revue — Broadway: 78

Composer: Dave Stamper
Lyricist: Gene Buck
Producer: Florenz Ziegfeld
Director: Ned Wayburn

Costumes: Marie Cook; Alice O'Neil; **Musical Director:** George A. Nichols; **Set Design:** Joseph Urban

Songs: Emancipation Day; Every Telephone (Telephone Song); I'm Crazy About Somebody; Metropolitan Ladies [1] (C/L: Irving Berlin); My Man [2] (C: Maurice Yvain; L: Channing Pollock); My Rosary of Melodies [1]; Orchard of Girls (L: Rennold Wolf); We Are the Maids of the Merry Merry; When Grandpa Was a Boy; Where Are the Plays of Yesterday; Winter Beaches, The; Wonderful Girl; You Know What I Mean

Cast: Fanny Brice; W.C. Fields; John Price Jones; Allyn King; Lillian Lorraine

Notes: This show also known as ZIEGFELD'S NINE O'CLOCK REVUE. [1] Also in ZIEGFELD 9 O'CLOCK FROLIC (9TH EDITION). [2] Also in ZIEGFELD FOLLIES OF 1921, ZIEGFELD 9 O'CLOCK FROLIC (9TH EDITION) and ZIEGFELD MIDNIGHT FROLIC (2ND 1929 EDITION). James F. Hanley and Gene Buck might have had something to do with the Americanizing of this song, they're credited by ASCAP.

4832 • ZIEGFELD MIDNIGHT FROLIC (UNKNOWN EDITION)

Theatre: New Amsterdam Roof

Revue — Broadway

Composer: Dave Stamper
Lyricist: Gene Buck
Producer: Florenz Ziegfeld

Songs: Bachelor's Dream, The; I Love to Raise the Dickens; Pharoah's Daughter

Notes: No other information available.

4833 • ZIEGFELD MIDNIGHT FROLIC (1ST EDITION)

OPENED: 03/1915 — Theatre: New Amsterdam Roof

Revue — Broadway

Composer: Louis A. Hirsch; Dave Stamper
Lyricist: Gene Buck
Producer: Florenz Ziegfeld
Director: Ned Wayburn

Costumes: Cora MacGeachy; **Lighting Designer:** Tony Greshoff; **Musical Director:** George A. Nichols; **Set Design:** Joseph Urban

Songs: Gee I Only Wish I Could Make My Dreams Come True [1] (C: Dave Stamper); Girl from My Home Town, The (C: Dave Stamper); Humpty Dumpty Drag (C: Dave Stamper); I Want Someone to Make a Fuss Over Me; I'm Sober; Jungle Ball (C: Dave Stamper); My Midnight Girl; My Spooky Girl; My Tango Girl; My Ziegfeld Midnight Girl [1] (C: Dave Stamper); Red, White and Blue; Scaddle-de-Mooch [2] (C/L: Cecil Mack; Chris Smith)

Cast: Bernard Granville; Muriel Hudson; Charles Purcell

Notes: Also titled NOTHING BUT GIRLS. [1] ASCAP/Library of Congress lists only. [2] Sheet music only. This may have been in the second 1915 edition.

4834 • ZIEGFELD MIDNIGHT FROLIC (2ND EDITION)

OPENED: 09/1915 — Theatre: New Amsterdam Roof

Revue — Broadway

Composer: Dave Stamper
Lyricist: Gene Buck
Producer: Florenz Ziegfeld
Director: Leon Errol

Costumes: Cora MacGeachy; **Musical Director:** George A. Nichols; **Set Design:** Joseph Urban

Songs: Bathing; Come Along; Hold Me in Your Loving Arms [1]; I Love to Be Loved; In Grandma's Day They Never Did the Fox Trot; Yankee Doodle Patriotic Tune

Cast: Sybil Carmen; Allyn King; Sue Loring; Will Rogers; Dave Stamper

Notes: Also titled JUST GIRLS (2nd of series). [1] Added after opening.

4835 • ZIEGFELD MIDNIGHT FROLIC (1916)

OPENED: 1916

Revue — Broadway

Composer: Dave Stamper
Lyricist: Gene Buck
Producer: Florenz Ziegfeld

Songs: Don't You Wish You Were a Kid Again; Every Girl Is Fishing; Indian Fox Trot Ball; Luana Lou; My American Beauty Girl (The Melting Pot); When He Comes Back to Me; Will-of-the-Wisp

Notes: No program available. Information from ASCAP and Library of Congress.

4836 • ZIEGFELD MIDNIGHT FROLIC (5TH EDITION)

OPENED: 07/27/1917 Theatre: New Amsterdam Roof
Revue Broadway

Composer: Dave Stamper
Lyricist: Gene Buck
Producer: Florenz Ziegfeld
Director: Ned Wayburn

Costumes: Marie Cook; Cora MacGeachy; **Musical Director:** George A. Nichols; **Set Design:** Alice O'Neil; Joseph Urban

Songs: B-R-O-A-D-W-A-Y; Flag of Our Land; Just Girls; Midnight Zeppo, The; Mississippi; Mons. France and Miss America; My Little Belgian Maid; Sweetie Mine; They're Getting Shorter All the Time; When I Hear That Jazz Band Play

Cast: Jack McGowan; Ann Pennington; William Rock; Dorothy St. Claire; Frances White

Notes: Also titled ZIEGFELD NEW 11:30 MIDNIGHT FROLIC.

4837 • ZIEGFELD MIDNIGHT FROLIC (6TH EDITION)

OPENED: 1917 Theatre: New Amsterdam Roof
Revue Broadway

Composer: Dave Stamper
Lyricist: Gene Buck
Producer: Florenz Ziegfeld
Director: Ned Wayburn

Costumes: Marie Cook; Alice O'Neil; **Musical Director:** George A. Nichols

Songs: Carmen Has Nothing on Me [2]; Cutey (C/L: Leslie Stuart); Every Girl Is Doing Her Bit; Gozinto; I'm Looking for the Great White Way (I'm Looking for Old Broadway); Long, Long Ago; My Tiger Rose (C: Gene Buck); Uncle Sam Is Santa Claus to the World; We Are Going on Our Honeymoon; We Are the Bright Lights of Broadway [1]

Notes: [1] Also in 7TH EDITION. [2] Also in TAKE THE AIR. [3] Not in programs.

4838 • ZIEGFELD MIDNIGHT FROLIC (7TH EDITION)

OPENED: 1918 Theatre: New Amsterdam Roof
Revue Broadway

Composer: Dave Stamper
Lyricist: Gene Buck
Producer: Florenz Ziegfeld
Director: Ned Wayburn

Musical Director: George A. Nichols; **Set Design:** Joseph Urban

Songs: Becky Is Back at the Ballet [1] (C: Leo Edwards; L: Blanche Merrill); Egyptian [1] (C: Leo Edwards; L: Blanche Merrill); Here Come the Yanks; Motor Girl, The; Spring Drive, The; Swinging Along; Syncopated Frolic, A; Tackin' 'Em Down [4] (C: Albert Gumble; L: B.G. DeSylva); Try a Ring, Dear!; Victory; We Are the Bright Lights of Broadway [2]; What Do I Care [3] (C: Walter Donaldson; L: Roy Turk); You'll Find Old Dixieland in France [5] (C: George W. Meyer; L: Grant Clarke)

Cast: Gladys Buckeridge; Lillian Lorraine; Bee Palmer; Bert Williams

Notes: [1] Added after opening for the two weeks that Fanny Brice joined this show. [2] Also in the ZIEGFELD MIDNIGHT FROLIC (6th Edition). [3] ASCAP/Library of Congress only. [4] Also in ZIEGFELD FOLLIES OF 1918. [5] May be in the next 1918 edition. Sheet music only. The song was sung by Bert Williams.

4839 • ZIEGFELD MIDNIGHT FROLIC OF 1918 (B)

OPENED: 1918 Theatre: New Amsterdam Roof
Revue Broadway

Composer: Dave Stamper
Lyricist: Gene Buck
Producer: Florenz Ziegfeld
Director: Leon Errol

Songs: Beautiful Girl; Cane Song; Carmen; I'm Looking for Old Broadway; My Little Belgian Maid; Springtime; Sweetie Mine; Swinging Along; They're Getting Shorter All the Time; When I Hear That Jazz Band Play

Notes: No other information available except sheet music.

4840 • ZIEGFELD MIDNIGHT FROLIC (2ND 1919 EDITION)

OPENED: 10/02/1919 Theatre: New Amsterdam Roof
Revue Broadway: 171

Composer: Dave Stamper
Lyricist: Gene Buck
Producer: Florenz Ziegfeld

Songs: Baby (C: Egbert Van Alstyne; L: Gus Kahn); By Pigeon Post; I Long to Linger Longer Dearie; I Love the River and You; I'll See You in C-U-B-A [2] (C/L: Irving Berlin); It's Nobody's Business but My Own (C: Marshall Walker; L: Will Skidmore); Lonesome Alimony Blues [1] (C: James F. Hanley; L: William Tracey); Rose of Washington Square (C: James F. Hanley; L: Ballard Macdonald); Shanghai; Tipperary Mary

Cast: Fanny Brice; W.C. Fields; Allyn King; Ted Lewis; Chic Sale; Frances White

Notes: No program available. Also known as ZIEGFELD NEW 11:30 MIDNIGHT FROLIC SHOW. [1] ASCAP/Library of Congress only. [2] Also in ZIEGFELD MIDNIGHT FROLIC OF 1920 (? Edition).

4841 • ZIEGFELD MIDNIGHT FROLIC (SECOND 1919 EDITION)

OPENED: 1919 Theatre: New Amsterdam Roof
Revue Broadway

Composer: Dave Stamper
Lyricist: Gene Buck
Producer: Florenz Ziegfeld

Songs: Colonial Days; Early to Bed and To Rise Never Made Anyone Wise (C: Abner Silver; L: Alex Gerber); Shanghai; You're a Perfect Jewel to Me

Cast: Eddie Cantor

Notes: The existence of this revue is uncertain but the sheet music seems to indicate it's another edition in 1919.

4842 • ZIEGFELD MIDNIGHT FROLIC OF 1920 (? EDITION)

OPENED: 03/15/1920 Theatre: Ziegfeld Danse de Follies
Revue Broadway: 148

Composer: Dave Stamper
Lyricist: Gene Buck
Producer: Florenz Ziegfeld

Songs: All the Boys Love Mary [3] (C/L: Joe Schenck; Andrew B. Sterling; Gus Van); Beautiful Birds; Colonial Days [1]; I'll See You in C-U-B-A [2] (C/L: Irving Berlin); Rockaway Mary [1] (C: Henry Piani; Sam H. Stept; L: Ballard Macdonald); Rose of Washington Square (C: James F. Hanley; L: Ballard Macdonald); World Is Going Shimmy Mad, The

Cast: Fanny Brice; W.C. Fields; John Price Jones; Allyn King; Lillian Lorraine; Carl Randall

Notes: [1] ASCAP/Library of Congress only. [2] Also in ZIEGFELD MIDNIGHT FROLIC (2ND 1919 EDITION). [3] Sheet music only.

4843 • ZIEGFELD MIDNIGHT FROLIC (11TH EDITION)

OPENED: 02/09/1921 Theatre: Ziegfeld Danse de Follies
Revue Broadway: 29

Composer: Dave Stamper
Lyricist: Gene Buck
Producer: Florenz Ziegfeld
Director: Edward Royce

Songs: Commerce, The; Compere, The; Gondolier (L: Ballard Macdonald); I'm Gonna Do It If I

Like It; Love is Like a Mushroom; Lovelight; Metropolitan Handicap, The; Pretty Faces; Puff, Puff, Puff; Rose of My Heart (C: Albert Sirmay); Summertime; Ten Fingers of Syncopation; World Goes Bobbing Up and Down; Ziegfeld Dollies, The

Cast: Fairbanks Twins, The; Herbert Hoey

Notes: This might have also been titled ZIEGFELD 9 O'CLOCK FROLIC, as most of the Midnight Frolics were. Also titled ZIEGFELD'S NEW MIDNIGHT FROLIC.

4844 • ZIEGFELD MIDNIGHT FROLIC (16TH EDITION)

OPENED: 11/17/1921 Theatre: New Amsterdam Roof
Revue Broadway: 123

Composer: Dave Stamper
Lyricist: Gene Buck
Producer: Florenz Ziegfeld
Director: Leon Errol

Costumes: Howard Greer; Cora MacGeachy; **Musical Director:** Gus Salzer; **Set Design:** Joseph Urban

Songs: Bouncing All Over Town; Come On, Let's Go; Dancing Shoes; Honey-Bunch [1]; Let Me Whirl to an Old Refrain; Lovelight; Masks; Sally Slide, The; Swinging Along; Violet Ray

Cast: Leon Errol; Gloria Foy; Alexander Grey; Aubrey L. Lyles; Flournoy Miller; Carl Randall; Will Rogers; Muriel Stryker

Notes: [1] ASCAP/Library of Congress only.

4845 • ZIEGFELD MIDNIGHT FROLIC (2ND 1928 EDITION)

OPENED: 12/28/1928
Revue Broadway

Producer: Florenz Ziegfeld

Cast: Eddie Cantor; Helen Morgan; Paul Whiteman and His Orchestra

Notes: No other information available.

4846 • ZIEGFELD MIDNIGHT FROLIC (1ST 1929 EDITION)

OPENED: 01/07/1929
Revue Broadway

Producer: Florenz Ziegfeld
Director: Seymour Felix

Costumes: John W. Harkrider; Charles LeMaire; **Set Design:** Joseph Urban

Songs: Reminiscing (C: Walter Donaldson; L: Edgar Leslie)

Cast: Paul Whiteman and His Orchestra

Notes: This consisted of songs from prior Ziegfeld shows.

4847 • ZIEGFELD MIDNIGHT FROLIC (2ND 1929 EDITION)

OPENED: 02/06/1929
Revue Broadway

Composer: Jimmy McHugh
Lyricist: Dorothy Fields
Producer: Florenz Ziegfeld

Choreographer: Sammy Lee; **Costumes:** John W. Harkrider; Charles LeMaire; **Set Design:** Joseph Urban

Songs: Looking for Love; My Man [1] (C: Maurice Yvain; L: Channing Pollock); Squeaky Shoes; What a Whalen of a Difference Just a Few Lights Make

Cast: Paul Gregory; Helen Morgan; Lillian Roth; Paul Whiteman

Notes: [1] Also in ZIEGFELD FOLLIES OF 1921, ZIEGFELD GIRLS OF 1920, and ZIEGFELD 9 O'CLOCK FROLIC (9TH EDITION).

4848 • ZIEGFELD MIDNIGHT FROLIC (SECOND 1929 EDITION)

OPENED: 1929
Revue Broadway

Composer: Jimmy McHugh
Lyricist: Dorothy Fields
Producer: Florenz Ziegfeld

Songs: Because I Love Nice Things; I Can't Wait; Raisin' the Roof

Notes: No other information available.

4849 • ZIEGFELD MIDNIGHT FROLIC (? EDITION)

Revue Broadway

Composer: Dave Stamper
Lyricist: Gene Buck
Producer: Florenz Ziegfeld
Director: Ned Wayburn

Set Design: Joseph Urban

Songs: Bachelor's Dream, The; I Love to Raise the Dickens; Pharoah's Daughter; When My Sweetie Comes Back to Me

Cast: Hal Hixon; Lillian Lorraine; Bee Palmer

4850 • ZIEGFELD NEW 11:30 MIDNIGHT FROLIC

Notes: All Midnight Frolics are under ZIEGFELD MIDNIGHT FROLIC even if they were titled ZIEGFELD NEW 11:30 MIDNIGHT FROLIC.

4851 • ZIEGFELD 9 O'CLOCK FROLIC OF 1918

OPENED: 1918
Revue Broadway

Composer: Dave Stamper
Lyricist: Gene Buck
Producer: Florenz Ziegfeld
Director: Ned Wayburn

Costumes: Alice O'Neil; **Musical Director:** George A. Nichols; **Orchestrations:** Stephen Jones; **Set Design:** Joseph Urban

Songs: Acrobatic Rag, The; After the First of July; And She Went Home in a Barrel; I Love to Linger with You; Let Me Shimmy and I'm Satisfied; Tipperary Mary; When My Sweetie Comes Back to Me; Won't You Play the Game?; Yiddishe Wampire, A (C/L: Blanche Merrill)

Cast: Delyle Alda; Fanny Brice; Lillian Leitzell; Lillian Lorraine; Bee Palmer; George Price; Bert Williams

4852 • ZIEGFELD 9 O'CLOCK FROLIC (9TH EDITION)

OPENED: 08/02/1920
Revue Broadway

Composer: Dave Stamper
Lyricist: Gene Buck
Producer: Florenz Ziegfeld

Costumes: Marie Cook; Alice O'Neil; **Orchestrations:** Stephen Jones; **Set Design:** Joseph Urban

Songs: Beautiful Birds; Metropolitan Ladies [1] (C/L: Irving Berlin); My Man [2] (C: Maurice Yvain; L: Channing Pollock); My Rosary of Melodies [1]

Cast: Eddie Cantor; Billy Dove; John Price Jones; Gladys Loftus

Notes: [1] Also in ZIEGFELD GIRLS OF 1920. [2] Also in ZIEGFELD FOLLIES OF 1921, ZIEGFELD GIRLS OF 1920 and ZIEGFELD MIDNIGHT FROLIC (2ND 1929 EDITION).

4853 • ZIEGFELD 9 O'CLOCK FROLIC OF 1921 (3RD EDITION)

OPENED: 02/08/1921 Theatre: Ziegfeld Danse de Follies
Revue Broadway: 29

Composer: Harry Carroll
Lyricist: Ballard Macdonald
Producer: Florenz Ziegfeld
Director: Edward Royce

Musical Director: Max Hoffmann; **Orchestrations:** Al Dalby

Songs: Face to Face; Gondolier (C: Dave Stamper); Icy Switzerland; I'm Gonna Do It If I Like It (C: Harry Akst; L: Irving Berlin); Little Love Mill,

The; Little Red Book (C: Dave Stamper); Love Nests in France; Painted Butterfly; Two Quick Quackers (C/L: Herman Hupfeld); When Sunday Comes Around; Ziegfeld Paper Dollies

Cast: Fairbanks Twins, The; Princess White Deer; Oscar Shaw; Anna Wheaton

4854 • ZIEGFELD PALM BEACH NIGHTS

Notes: *See NO FOOLIN'.*

4855 • ZIEGFELD'S NEW MIDNIGHT FROLIC

Notes: *See ZIEGFELD MIDNIGHT FROLIC (11th Edition).*

4856 • ZIEGFELD'S NEW MIDNIGHT FROLIC

Notes: *See ZIEGFELD MIDNIGHT FROLIC (16th Edition).*

4857 • ZIEGFELD'S NINE O'CLOCK REVUE.

Notes: *See ZIEGFELD GIRLS OF 1920.*

4858 • ZIG ZAG

OPENED: 09/1922
Revue Closed out of town

Composer: Milton Ager
Lyricist: Jack Yellen
Producer: Arthur Pearson
Director: Arthur Pearson

Choreographer: Larry Ceballos

Songs: Cartoon Town; Harry Masters, Jack Craft and Company (C: J. Fred Coots; L: Irving Caesar); Jingle Bells; (We Are the Girls in the Chorus) Please Tell Me Who Looks Good to You; Steppin' School; When the Autumn Leaves Are Falling [1] (C: Dave Stamper; L: Gene Buck); Zig Zag

Cast: Cecil Lean; Cleo Mayfield

Notes: [1] Not in programs.

4859 • ZIG ZAG ALLEY

OPENED: 1902
Musical Closed out of town

Composer: James Gorman
Lyricist: James Gorman
Librettist: James Gorman
Producer: W.E. Flack; Walter Floyd
Director: James Gorman

Incidental Music: Karl Weixelbaum

Songs: Belles of Zig-Zag Alley; Dreaming on the Ohio; Girl with the Banjo Eyes, The; Is It Love?; Kitty Kitty; Off for Atlantic City; Pinky Panky Poo; Queen of the Alley; Sally in Our Alley (C/L: Henry Carey); Southern Nightingale, The; We Are Four Actors; When I'm an Alderman

Cast: Ella Shields; Happy Zarrow; Jolly Zeb

Notes: Closed in Chicago.

4860 • ZIP GOES A MILLION

OPENED: 1920
Musical Closed out of town

Composer: Jerome Kern
Lyricist: B.G. DeSylva
Librettist: Guy Bolton
Producer: F. Ray Comstock; Morris Gest
Director: Oscar Eagle

Source: BREWSTER'S MILLIONS (Play: Byron Ongley; Winchell Smith); **Source:** BREWSTER'S MILLIONS (Novel: George Barr McCutcheon); **Choreographer:** Julian Mitchell; **Orchestrations:** Maurice DePackh; Frank Saddler

Songs: Bill [2]; Business of Our Own, A; Forget-Me-Not; Furnished for Monty; Give a Little Thought to Me; Hail to Monty; It's a Bother to Be a Man; Language of Love; Little Backyard Band, The; Look for the Silver Lining [1]; Man Around the House, A; Mandolin and the Man, The; Producers; Telephone Girls; When You're Smiling (What a Smile Can Do); Whip-Poor-Will [1]; You Tell 'Em

Cast: Marie Carroll; Harry Fox

Notes: [1] Later in SALLY. [2] Different lyrics than the Hammerstein/Wodehouse "Bill."

4861 • ZOOT SUIT

OPENED: 03/25/1979 Theatre: Winter Garden
Play Broadway: 41

Composer: Lalo Guerrero
Lyricist: Lalo Guerrero
Author: Luis Valdez
Producer: Center Theatre Group; Gordon Davidson; Shubert Organization
Director: Luis Valdez

Choreographer: Patricia Birch; **Costumes:** Peter J. Hall; **Dance Arranger:** Dan Kuramoto; **Lighting Designer:** Dawn Chiang; **Orchestrations:** Dan Kuramoto; **Set Design:** Thomas A. Walsh; **Vocal Arranger:** Dan Kuramoto; Daniel Valdez

Songs: Los Chuchos Suaves; Vamos a Bailar; Zoot Suit Theme (inst.) (C: Daniel Valdez)

Cast: Charles Aidman; Roberta Delgado Esparza; Abel Franco; Karen Hensel; Edward James Olmos; Lupe Ontiveros; Tony Plana; Daniel Valdez

4862 • ZORBA

OPENED: 11/17/1968 Theatre: Imperial
Musical Broadway: 305

Composer: John Kander
Lyricist: Fred Ebb
Librettist: Joseph Stein
Producer: Harold Prince
Director: Harold Prince

Source: ZORBA THE GREEK (Novel: Nikos Kazantzakis); **Choreographer:** Ron Field; **Costumes:** Patricia Zipprodt; **Dance Arranger:** Dorothea Freitag; **Lighting Designer:** Richard Pilbrow; **Musical Director:** Harold Hastings; **Orchestrations:** Don Walker; **Set Design:** Boris Aronson

Songs: Bells (Sousta) (dance); Bend of the Road, The [4]; Better Than Nothing [2]; Bouboulina [1]; Butterfly, The; Crow, The; First Time, The; Goodbye, Canavaro; Grandpapa; Happy Birthday; I Am Free; I Have a Friend [2]; Life Is; Mine Celebration (dance); No Boom Boom; Only Love; That's a Beginning [5]; Top of the Hill, The [4]; Vive la Difference; Why Can't I Speak?; Woman [3]; Y'assou

Cast: Carmen Alvarez; Herschel Bernardi; John Cunningham; Al De Sio; Maria Karnilova; James Luisi; Lorraine Serabian

Notes: [1] Added for tour. [2] Cut prior to opening. [3] Added to revival. [4] Same music. [5] Added for tour. Contains "Why Can't I Speak?"

4863 • ZULU AND THE ZAYDA, THE

OPENED: 11/10/1965 Theatre: Cort
Play Broadway: 179

Composer: Harold Rome
Lyricist: Harold Rome
Librettist: Theodore Mann; Dore Schary
Author: Howard Da Silva
Director: Dore Schary

Source: ZULU AND THE ZAYDA, THE (Story: Dan Jacobson); **Costumes:** Frank Thompson; **Lighting Designer:** Jean Eckart; William Eckart; **Musical Director:** Michael Spivakowsky; **Orchestrations:** Meyer Kupferman; **Set Design:** Jean Eckart; William Eckart

Songs: Biggest Men Stumble, The [2]; Cold, Cold Room; Crocodile Wife; Eagle Soliloquy; How Cold, Cold, Cold (An Empty Room); It's Good to Be Alive; Like the Breeze Blows; May Your Heart Stay Young (L'Chayim); Oisgetzaychnet (Out of This World); Rivers of Tears; Some Things (1); Some Things (2) [1]; Tkambuza (Zulu Hunting Song); Water Wears Down the Stone, The; Yi, Yi, Yi (Aye, Aye, Aye) [1]; Zulu Love Song (Wait for Me)

Cast: Ossie Davis; Louis Gossett; Yaphet Kotto; Joe Silver; Menasha Skulnik

Notes: [1] Cut prior to opening. [2] ASCAP/Library of Congress.

Name Index

A

Aaron, Paul *(Director)* 2618, 3824, 3900
Aarons, Alex A. *(Composer)* 246, 2465
Aarons, Alex A. *(Librettist)* 4443
Aarons, Alex A. *(Lyricist)* 246
Aarons, Alex A. *(Producer)* 1419, 1528, 1800, 1859, 1879, 1929, 2363, 2376, 3157, 3243, 3319, 3379, 3993, 4118, 4300, 4392, 4443
Aarons, Alfred E. *(Composer)* 734, 1003, 1547, 1910, 2343, 2863, 3029
Aarons, Alfred E. *(Producer)* 1003, 1547, 1910, 2374, 2714, 2863, 2899, 3063, 3319
Aarons, Ruth Hughes *(Lyricist)* 2168, 4015, 4191
Aaronson's Commanders, Irving *(Cast)* 3382
Aarseth, Art *(Composer)* 3256
Abaldo, Joseph *(Cast)* 2146
Abarbanell, Lina *(Cast)* 1309, 1756, 2603, 2667, 2903, 2926, 3978, 4187, 4620
Abbate, Charles *(Composer)* 2749
Abbate, Charles *(Lyricist)* 2749
Abbey *(Producer)* 4500
Abbott *(Costumes)* 1869
Abbott *(Set Design)* 1869
Abbott, Allen *(Lyricist)* 1244
Abbott, Annie *(Cast)* 4172
Abbott, Bud *(Cast)* 4174
Abbott, Bud *(Librettist)* 1038
Abbott, Charles *(Cast)* 1445
Abbott, Charles *(Choreographer)* 4102
Abbott, Charles *(Director)* 4102
Abbott, Eleanor *(Set Design)* 1096
Abbott, Gardner *(Cast)* 1866, 1868
Abbott, George *(Author)* 297, 2449
Abbott, George *(Director)* 32, 161, 304, 323, 372, 404, 514, 619, 957, 1158, 1227, 1273, 1280, 1310, 1382, 1422, 1672, 1886, 2014, 2258, 2311, 2582, 2797, 3015, 3097, 3113, 3278, 3283, 3288, 3351, 3353, 4312, 4420, 4446, 4652, 4734
Abbott, George *(Librettist)* 161, 323, 514, 957, 1280, 1310, 1382, 1886, 2456, 3015, 3113, 3283, 3351, 3353, 4312, 4446, 4456, 4652
Abbott, George *(Producer)* 304, 323, 372, 514, 2582, 3353, 4420, 4432, 4446
Abbott, Joan *(Cast)* 1492, 2300, 3639
Abbott, Joseph LeGrange *(Cast)* 1624
Abbott, Judith *(Producer)* 32
Abbott, Marion *(Cast)* 1538
Abbott, Merriel
See also Abbott Dancers.
Abbott, Merriel *(Choreographer)* 787, 1275, 4025
Abbott, Michael *(Composer)* 3181, 4533
Abbott, Michael *(Librettist)* 3181
Abbott, Michael *(Lyricist)* 3181, 4533
Abbott, Michael *(Orchestrations)* 2646
Abbott, Rita *(Cast)* 3028
Abbott, Tommy *(Cast)* 4625
Abbott Dancers
See also Merriel Abbott.
Abbott Dancers, The *(Cast)* 1491
Abbott-Dunning Inc. *(Producer)* 2311
Abboud, Mona *(Cast)* 1648
Abdallah, Leigh *(Choreographer)* 518
Abdallah's Arabs *(Cast)* 1631
Abdillah, Shion *(Cast)* 730
Abdulov, Alexander *(Cast)* 2269
Abel, Chele *(Choreographer)* 2219
Abel, Ron *(Arrangements)* 2651
Abel, Ron *(Composer)* 4171
Abel, Ron *(Dance Arranger)* 450
Abel, Ron *(Lyricist)* 4171
Abel, Ron *(Musical Director)* 450
Abel, Ron *(Vocal Arranger)* 450
Abel, Walter *(Cast)* 1187, 2821
Abeles *(Lyricist)* 4681
Abeles, Edward *(Cast)* 1593, 4624
Abelson, Robert *(Cast)* 4342
Abelson, Robert *(Lyricist)* 4342
Abene, Michael *(Dance Arranger)* 2578
Abene, Michael *(Orchestrations)* 2578
Aber, Arline *(Cast)* 4023
Aber, Charline *(Cast)* 4023
Aberlin, Betty *(Cast)* 54, 1438, 2074, 2279, 4790
Abernathy, Lee Roy *(Composer)* 4030
Abernathy, Lee Roy *(Lyricist)* 4030
Abernathy, Pat *(Composer)* 226
Able, Will B. *(Cast)* 348, 798, 1841
Abraham, F. Murray *(Cast)* 2435
Abraham, Pal *(Author)* 277
Abraham, Paul *(Composer)* 277
Abrahams, Jody *(Cast)* 4264
Abrahams, Maurice *(Composer)* 965, 2939, 3259, 3399, 3525, 4813, 4821
Abrahams, Maurice *(Lyricist)* 3399, 4655
Abrahamsen, Dan *(Lighting Designer)* 1450
Abrahamson, Eric *(Composer)* 2039
Abrahamson, Eric *(Lyricist)* 2039
Abrahamson, Manford *(Dance Arranger)* 1092
Abrahamson, Manford *(Musical Director)* 4330
Abrams, Don *(Lighting Designer)* 4405
Abrams, Larry *(Producer)* 3059

Abrams, Steve *(Producer)* 4145
Abramson, Charles H. *(Producer)* 82, 3314
Abravanel, Maurice *(Musical Director)* 1284, 2344, 2386, 3301, 3691, 4169
Abravanel, Wayne *(Musical Director)* 2197
Acaro, Flavia *(Cast)* 742, 2684
Accooe, Will *(Composer)* 352
Accooe, Will *(Lyricist)* 352
Accooe, William *(Composer)* 2465
Accurso, Aron *(Cast)* 143
Ace, Goodman *(Librettist)* 1397
Achelis, Johnfritz *(Cast)* 4622
Achilles, Peter *(Set Design)* 3669, 4463
Ackel *(Lyricist)* 2419
Acker, Mitch *(Lighting Designer)* 2759
Ackerman, Dorine *(Costumes)* 348
Ackerman, Loni *(Cast)* 1038, 1478, 3456, 4038, 4145
Ackerman, P. Dodd *(Lighting Designer)* 2601
Ackerman, P. Dodd *(Set Design)* 381, 648, 670, 717, 765, 931, 1088, 1215, 1285, 1345, 1378, 1424, 1513, 1529, 1584, 1722, 1839, 1847, 1852, 1980, 2271, 2516, 2527, 2574, 2601, 2827, 2833, 3042, 3063, 3168, 3184, 3369, 3535, 3613, 3737, 4001, 4283, 4476, 4596
Ackerman, Robert Allan *(Director)* 2146, 2437
Ackland, Joss *(Cast)* 2240
Acosta, Elizabeth *(Cast)* 949
Acres, Harry *(Composer)* 4765, 4795
Acting Company, The *(Producer)* 693
Actman, Irving *(Composer)* 398, 850, 1126, 1414, 1415, 1989, 2105, 3410, 4191
Actman, Irving *(Lyricist)* 1989
Actman, Irving *(Musical Director)* 95, 1567, 1706, 4015
Actor-Managers, The *(Producer)* 1656
Actors Studio, Inc. *(Producer)* 477
Actors' Playhouse *(Producer)* 4750
Actors-Managers Inc., The *(Producer)* 1657
Acuff, Roy *(Composer)* 655
Acuff, Roy *(Lyricist)* 655
Ada-May *(Cast)* 791
Adair, Eddie *(Composer)* 1541
Adair, Eddie *(Director)* 1541
Adair, Eddie *(Lyricist)* 1541
Adair, Frank *(Cast)* 2761
Adair, Janet *(Cast)* 487, 1643, 3404, 3405
Adair, Jean *(Cast)* 933, 3002
Adair, John *(Cast)* 919
Adair, Josephine *(Cast)* 4683
Adair, Josephine *(Lyricist)* 1689
Adair, Patricia *(Cast)* 854, 856
Adair, Tom *(Cast)* 3121
Adair, Tom *(Lyricist)* 95, 3453
Adair, Yvonne *(Cast)* 1475, 2439, 4180
Adam, Noelle *(Cast)* 3187
Adams, Becky *(Cast)* 3601
Adams, Bob *(Cast)* 186
Adams, Bob *(Composer)* 830, 1908, 1910, 4723
Adams, Bob *(Lyricist)* 830, 1316, 1910
Adams, Clifford *(Lyricist)* 1136
Adams, Daniel *(Lighting Designer)* 4410
Adams, David *(Lighting Designer)* 3814
Adams, Dianne *(Vocal Arranger)* 4139
Adams, Dick *(Composer)* 1296
Adams, Dick *(Lyricist)* 1296
Adams, Don *(Librettist)* 4268
Adams, Edith *(Cast)* 616, 759, 2484, 4734
Adams, Edward B. *(Choreographer)* 1459
Adams, Emily *(Cast)* 2124, 2220
Adams, Frank *(Librettist)* 1307, 1563, 1593, 1967, 2155, 2408, 3579, 4185, 4387
Adams, Frank *(Lyricist)* 1307, 1563, 1593, 1967, 2155, 2408, 3579, 4185, 4387
Adams, Frank R. *(Author)* 2926, 3580
Adams, Frank R. *(Librettist)* 1606, 1801, 1908, 2926, 4506
Adams, Frank R. *(Lyricist)* 1316, 1606, 1801, 1908, 2512, 2901, 2926, 4506
Adams, Franklin P. *(Lyricist)* 1357, 2559
Adams, Gary *(Musical Director)* 4523
Adams, J.B. *(Cast)* 155, 275
Adams, Lee *(Librettist)* 36, 2288
Adams, Lee *(Lyricist)* 36, 57, 64, 167, 534, 550, 602, 607, 673, 1306, 1393, 1601, 1828, 1873, 2047, 2163, 2554, 2758, 2804, 3549, 3940, 3941, 3942, 4135, 4639, 4827
Adams, Leslie *(Cast)* 207
Adams, Margaret *(Cast)* 117, 2252, 4352, 4374
Adams, Mary *(Cast)* 203, 1836
Adams, Mason *(Cast)* 4278, 4565
Adams, Maude *(Cast)* 2329, 3450
Adams, Neile *(Cast)* 223
Adams, Nick *(Cast)* 3047, 3519
Adams, Pamela *(Cast)* 840
Adams, Robert K. *(Director)* 4292
Adams, Robert K. *(Producer)* 1435
Adams, Roger *(Composer)* 596
Adams, Roger *(Dance Arranger)* 145, 367, 596, 957, 1760, 2106, 2713, 2777, 2797, 3113, 3288, 3687, 4180
Adams, Roger *(Lyricist)* 3453
Adams, Roger J. *(Librettist)* 1469
Adams, Roger J. *(Lyricist)* 1469
Adams, Samuel Hopkins *(Author)* 4312
Adams, Stanley *(Lyricist)* 166, 417, 2397, 3018, 3907, 3955
Adams, Tony *(Producer)* 4560
Adamski, Johann *(Cast)* 214
Adamson, Harold *(Lyricist)* 190, 206, 297, 1136, 1207, 1251, 1879, 3249, 3993, 4023, 4025, 4180, 4197, 4264, 4335
Adano, Ernie *(Cast)* 4157
Adderley, Nat *(Cast)* 2692
Adderley Jr., Nat *(Composer)* 1637
Adderley Jr., Nat *(Lyricist)* 1637
Addinsell, Richard *(Composer)* 55, 392, 702, 818, 1618, 2227, 3186, 3940
Addison, John *(Composer)* 920
Addison, John *(Lyricist)* 920
Ade, George *(Author)* 2430, 4017
Ade, George *(Librettist)* 772, 1230, 1870, 3154, 3268, 3437, 3943, 4201
Ade, George *(Lyricist)* 1230, 3268, 3437, 3943, 4201
Adelaide, La Petite *(Cast)* 246, 1316, 2116, 2291, 2398, 2842
Adelaide, Mlle. *(Cast)* 4654
Adelaide, Petite *(Cast)* 470
Adelaide and Hughes *(Cast)* 2939, 3087, 3395, 4521
Adelman, Chas. *(Librettist)* 4761
Adelman, Chas. *(Lyricist)* 4761

Adelson, Leonard *(Librettist)* 2925
Adelson, Leonard *(Lyricist)* 90, 1716, 2246, 2925, 3383, 3558, 4798
Ades, Hawley *(Orchestrations)* 3100
Adiarte, Patrick *(Cast)* 658, 1315
Adkins, Walter *(Cast)* 4251
Adlam, Basil *(Composer)* 4824
Adler, Bernard *(Composer)* 2840
Adler, Bruce *(Cast)* 400, 921, 1609, 2352, 3231, 3722, 4342
Adler, Bruce *(Lyricist)* 573, 1609
Adler, Celia *(Cast)* 1299
Adler, Christopher *(Lyricist)* 1865, 2196, 3936
Adler, David *(Cast)* 2108
Adler, Elsa *(Cast)* 2264
Adler, Evelyn *(Composer)* 4275
Adler, Evelyn *(Lyricist)* 4275
Adler, Felix *(Cast)* 3865
Adler, Gil *(Producer)* 1166
Adler, H. *(Composer)* 1267
Adler, H. *(Lyricist)* 1267
Adler, Hyman *(Author)* 4275
Adler, Hyman *(Cast)* 4275, 4328
Adler, Hyman *(Producer)* 4328
Adler, Jacob *(Cast)* 1639
Adler, Jerry *(Director)* 1621, 1841, 1842, 2539, 3076, 3517, 4743
Adler, Jerry *(Producer)* 1094
Adler, Julius *(Cast)* 2352
Adler, Larry *(Cast)* 787, 1322, 2301, 4023
Adler, Lou *(Producer)* 3742
Adler, Luther *(Cast)* 1299, 2228, 4495
Adler, Luther *(Director)* 1299
Adler, Marion *(Cast)* 1702
Adler, Marion *(Composer)* 1702
Adler, Marion *(Lyricist)* 1702
Adler, Peter Herman *(Musical Director)* 1085
Adler, Richard *(Composer)* 957, 1507, 2227, 2355, 2550, 2965, 3015, 3227, 3273, 3351, 3984, 4399
Adler, Richard *(Lyricist)* 957, 1507, 2227, 2355, 2550, 2965, 3227, 3273, 3351, 3984, 4399
Adler, Richard *(Producer)* 3015, 3273, 3702, 3984
Adler, Stella *(Director)* 3536
Adler, William *(Costumes)* 4250
Adnopoz, David *(Cast)* 945
Adolphus, Theodore *(Choreographer)* 82, 1476, 2479, 3823
Adrian *(Costumes)* 223, 623, 1250, 2686, 3008
Adrian *(Set Design)* 2686
Adrian, Gilbert *(Costumes)* 1484, 1691, 3007, 3144
Adrian, Henry *(Director)* 1539
Adrian, Henry *(Producer)* 1539
Adrian, Iris *(Cast)* 1979, 3131
Adrian, Louis *(Musical Director)* 2234, 2327, 3453
Adrian, Max *(Cast)* 630
Adrian, Max *(Director)* 4268
Adshead, Patricia *(Costumes)* 1903, 2146, 2320, 4288
Adzima, Nancy *(Costumes)* 2332
Adzima, Nanzi *(Costumes)* 4799
Aeromaniacs, The *(Cast)* 3121
Aerseth, Arthur E. *(Composer)* 1629
Agee, James *(Lyricist)* 2633
Agee, John *(Cast)* 3533
Ager, Milton *(Composer)* 393, 418, 487, 712, 1395, 1919, 2135, 2706, 3005, 3175, 3428, 3648, 4197, 4296, 4460, 4637, 4683, 4814, 4821, 4858
Aghayan, Ray *(Costumes)* 167, 2590
Aghayan, Ray *(Director)* 2969
Aghayan, Ray *(Librettist)* 2969
Aghayan, Ray *(Producer)* 2969
Agnese, Rita *(Cast)* 1326
Agnolucci, Mario *(Musical Director)* 2605, 4085
Agombar, Elizabeth *(Costumes)* 129
Agostini, Lucio *(Orchestrations)* 3485
Agoust, Emile *(Choreographer)* 2825
Agoust Family, The *(Cast)* 4130
Agress, Ted *(Cast)* 3928
Ahern, Will *(Cast)* 2709, 3980
Aherne, Brian *(Cast)* 1007
Ahlberg, Irene *(Cast)* 1135, 1136
Ahlert, Fred E. *(Cast)* 3153
Ahlert, Fred E. *(Composer)* 39, 428, 2161, 2308, 2939, 3726
Ahlert, Fred E. *(Lyricist)* 2308
Ahrens, Lynn *(Librettist)* 754, 2646, 3285
Ahrens, Lynn *(Lyricist)* 754, 2646, 3039, 3285
Ahronheim, Albert *(Musical Director)* 1149
Ahronheim, Albert *(Vocal Arranger)* 1149
Aibel, Douglas *(Director)* 1739
Aidman, Charles *(Cast)* 4111, 4861
Aidman, Charles *(Librettist)* 4111
Aidman, Charles *(Lyricist)* 4111
Aiello, Frank *(Cast)* 2153
Aiken, Alfred *(Librettist)* 4623
Aiken, Alfred *(Lyricist)* 4623
Aiken, D.M. *(Set Design)* 3230
Ailes, Roger *(Composer)* 2962
Ailes, Roger *(Lyricist)* 2962
Ailes, Roger *(Producer)* 2146, 2962, 3557
Ailey, Alvin *(Choreographer)* 2368, 2775
Ailey, Alvin *(Director)* 2203
Ailey American Dance Theatre, Alvin *(Cast)* 2775
Ails, Roscoe *(Cast)* 423
Aimes, Paul *(Costumes)* 3533
Aingell, Gene *(Set Design)* 3752
Ainsley, Paul *(Cast)* 2212
Ainslie, Scott *(Cast)* 900
Ainsworth, Alyn *(Orchestrations)* 1741
Airaldi, Remo *(Cast)* 3937
Aitken, G. *(Composer)* 2498
Aitken, Iaian *(Set Design)* 1079
Aitken, J. *(Cast)* 874
Akerlind, Christopher *(Lighting Designer)* 1232, 3227
Akers, Andra *(Cast)* 3444
Akers, Hattie *(Cast)* 1479
Akers, Karen *(Cast)* 1649, 3171
Ako *(Cast)* 2861
Akron Club *(Producer)* 3296, 3848, 4780
Akst, Harry *(Composer)* 26, 202, 432, 478, 622, 665, 1293, 1813, 2373, 2587, 3120, 3144, 3444, 3709, 4291, 4534, 4813, 4853
Akst, Harry *(Lyricist)* 2227
Akst, Harry *(Orchestrations)* 3006, 3007
Alan, Charles *(Director)* 3647
Alan, Charles *(Lyricist)* 3647

Alban, Manny *(Orchestrations)* 1273
Albani, Olga *(Cast)* 3117
Albee, Edward *(Librettist)* 521
Albeniz *(Composer)* 1342
Alberg, Mildred Freed *(Producer)* 1742
Alberghetti, Anna Maria *(Cast)* 44, 347, 656
Alberni, Luis *(Cast)* 1020, 2371, 3063
Albert *(Composer)* 4723
Albert, Eddie *(Cast)* 499, 514, 2894, 3696
Albert, Ernest *(Set Design)* 113, 185, 350, 357, 377, 396, 476, 559, 591, 666, 976, 1095, 1295, 1356, 1458, 1459, 1543, 1712, 1746, 1758, 1881, 2101, 2117, 2123, 2145, 2181, 2184, 2213, 2465, 2506, 2534, 2667, 2715, 2722, 2725, 2974, 3129, 3494, 3570, 3581, 3773, 3977, 4181, 4219, 4247, 4614, 4724, 4804, 4805, 4806, 4807
Albert, Nelson *(Cast)* 743
Alberte, Charles S. *(Lyricist)* 3737
Albertieri, M. *(Choreographer)* 2374
Albertieri, Signor *(Choreographer)* 1285
Albertierri, Luigi *(Choreographer)* 4425
Albertino, Chateau *(Composer)* 4154
Albertino, Chateau *(Lyricist)* 4154
Albertson, Coit *(Cast)* 960
Albertson, Frank *(Cast)* 3895
Albertson, Jack *(Cast)* 84, 1040, 2397, 2653, 2809, 4152, 4377, 4423
Albertson, Lillian *(Director)* 1944
Albery, Donald *(Producer)* 455, 1277, 1644, 2240, 3271
Albini, Felix *(Author)* 307, 2538, 2668
Albini, Felix *(Composer)* 307, 2538, 2668
Albrecht, Gretchen *(Cast)* 2565
Albrecht, Johanna *(Cast)* 4002
Albright, Frank *(Conductor)* 345
Albritton, Dub *(Composer)* 4264
Albritton, Dub *(Lyricist)* 4264
Albro, Arthur *(Cast)* 1712, 2567
Alchourron, Rodolfo *(Dance Arranger)* 975
Alchourron, Rodolfo *(Vocal Arranger)* 975
Alcorn, Mlle. *(Cast)* 3405
Alcott, Louisa May *(Author)* 2219, 2550
Alcover *(Cast)* 2753
Alda, Alan *(Cast)* 170, 615, 991, 1389
Alda, Alan *(Librettist)* 991
Alda, Delyle *(Cast)* 465, 4033, 4813, 4814, 4851
Alda, Robert *(Cast)* 1706, 4633
Alden, Betty *(Cast)* 3866
Alden, Donald *(Librettist)* 2841
Alden, Hazel *(Cast)* 165
Alden, Jane *(Cast)* 1492
Alden, Jerome *(Librettist)* 4297
Alder, Elsie *(Cast)* 2907
Aldredge, Theoni V. *(Costumes)* 54, 150, 154, 155, 160, 162, 273, 278, 287, 305, 406, 459, 721, 722, 746, 807, 1103, 1159, 1359, 1660, 1890, 1990, 2048, 2064, 2106, 2360, 2677, 2820, 2983, 3000, 3018, 3075, 3094, 3305, 3338, 3718, 3862, 4013, 4028, 4067, 4151, 4297, 4370, 4384, 4485, 4727, 4799
Aldredge, Thomas *(Cast)* 3094
Aldredge, Tom *(Cast)* 2143, 3411, 3702, 4151
Aldrich, Charles T. *(Cast)* 736, 1208, 2184
Aldrich, David *(Composer)* 1635
Aldrich, Janet *(Cast)* 2654, 3568
Aldrich, Richard *(Producer)* 3457
Alegretti, Theodore *(Cast)* 1862
Aleichem, Sholom *(Author)* 400, 1265
Alers, Yassmin *(Cast)* 535
Alessandrini, Gerard *(Cast)* 1348
Alessandrini, Gerard *(Composer)* 1038, 1348, 1349, 1350
Alessandrini, Gerard *(Director)* 1348, 1349, 1350
Alessandrini, Gerard *(Lyricist)* 1038, 1348, 1349, 1350
Aletter, Frank *(Cast)* 363
Aletter, W. *(Composer)* 3753
Alevy, Maurice *(Director)* 1046
Alevy, Maurice *(Librettist)* 1046
Alex, Joe *(Cast)* 2753
Alexander, Adinah *(Cast)* 3181
Alexander, Alice *(Producer)* 3713
Alexander, Arthur *(Cast)* 803
Alexander, Brooks *(Musical Director)* 344
Alexander, Brooks *(Vocal Arranger)* 344
Alexander, C.K. *(Cast)* 181, 4370
Alexander, Calvin *(Composer)* 4
Alexander, Calvin *(Lyricist)* 4
Alexander, Cheryl *(Cast)* 3136, 3169
Alexander, Cris *(Cast)* 98, 3278, 4734
Alexander, David *(Director)* 1791, 2556, 4542
Alexander, Gus *(Cast)* 3028
Alexander, Hugh *(Cast)* 4514
Alexander, Hy *(Librettist)* 2105
Alexander, Irene *(Lyricist)* 3457
Alexander, Jace *(Cast)* 212
Alexander, Janet *(Cast)* 933
Alexander, Jason *(Cast)* 2205, 2822, 3448, 3718
Alexander, Jason *(Librettist)* 2205
Alexander, Jeff *(Composer)* 732
Alexander, John *(Cast)* 3097
Alexander, Katherine *(Cast)* 2613
Alexander, Larry *(Composer)* 4433
Alexander, Larry *(Librettist)* 4433
Alexander, Larry *(Lyricist)* 973, 2279, 4433
Alexander, Melville *(Lyricist)* 136, 697, 904, 1292, 2387
Alexander, Melville *(Producer)* 2387
Alexander, Newton *(Cast)* 1460, 1461
Alexander, Rod *(Cast)* 1679, 1933, 2137, 2837, 4323
Alexander, Rod *(Choreographer)* 177, 520, 3934, 4337
Alexander, Sharon *(Costumes)* 3905
Alexander, Sheryn *(Lyricist)* 2288
Alexander, Van *(Composer)* 4534
Alf, Johnny *(Composer)* 2245
Alf, Johnny *(Lyricist)* 2245
Alfonso, Gerald *(Musical Director)* 3264
Alfonso, Gerald *(Orchestrations)* 3264
Alford, Lamar *(Cast)* 1595
Alford, Lamar *(Composer)* 4343
Alford, Lamar *(Lyricist)* 4343
Alford, Larry *(Director)* 2208
Alfred, Julian *(Choreographer)* 136, 336, 780, 1552, 2119, 2363, 2377, 2461, 2666, 2691, 2710, 2834, 3043, 3177, 3237, 3295, 3319, 3540, 3617, 3866, 3868, 4037, 4248, 4476, 4539
Alfred, Julian *(Director)* 1584, 1882, 1921, 2446, 2601, 2834, 2922, 3213, 3222, 3478, 4001

Alfred, William *(Author)* 935, 942
Alfred, William *(Librettist)* 935
Alfred, William *(Lyricist)* 935, 942
Alfred, William *(Producer)* 942
Alger, Horatio *(Author)* 4289
Alger, Joseph *(Librettist)* 3104
Ali, George *(Cast)* 591
Aliabeck *(Composer)* 710
Aliabieff *(Composer)* 710
Alicoate, Jack *(Librettist)* 4651
Alinder, Dallas *(Cast)* 4449
Alinder, Dallas *(Producer)* 4343
Alison, David *(Librettist)* 4602
Alison, David *(Producer)* 4602
Alk, Howard *(Producer)* 4397
Allan, Dennis *(Orchestrations)* 3195
Allan, Dorothy *(Cast)* 2161, 2162
Allan, Lewis *(Librettist)* 2948
Allan, Lewis *(Lyricist)* 467, 2175, 2447, 2653, 3226
Allard, Martine *(Cast)* 4286
Allard, Michel *(Cast)* 1834
Allbritton, Dub *(Composer)* 3793
Allbritton, Dub *(Lyricist)* 3793
Allen, Amelia *(Cast)* 2605
Allen, Beatrice *(Cast)* 2351
Allen, Ben G. *(Composer)* 4278
Allen, Ben G. *(Lyricist)* 4278
Allen, Betty *(Cast)* 1109, 1494, 4447
Allen, Billie *(Cast)* 2513
Allen, Charles *(Producer)* 338
Allen, Cliff *(Cast)* 1342, 3103, 3104
Allen, Cliff *(Composer)* 3103
Allen, Clifford *(Cast)* 1729
Allen, Debbie *(Cast)* 52
Allen, Debbie *(Choreographer)* 661
Allen, Deborah *(Cast)* 3656, 4459
Allen, Dennis *(Cast)* 2018
Allen, Diane *(Costumes)* 1940
Allen, Edgar *(Cast)* 3365
Allen, Edward *(Cast)* 1916
Allen, Elizabeth *(Cast)* 1060, 1456, 3761, 3931
Allen, Eva *(Cast)* 4681
Allen, Fred *(Cast)* 2545, 3405, 3532, 4367, 4575
Allen, Fred *(Librettist)* 4367, 4824
Allen, G. Brandon *(Cast)* 2993
Allen, Gaelle *(Costumes)* 299
Allen, Gene *(Cast)* 4627
Allen, Gene *(Composer)* 406
Allen, Gene *(Lyricist)* 406
Allen, George *(Composer)* 1370
Allen, Georgia *(Cast)* 3684
Allen, Gracie
See Burns and Allen.
Allen, Harry *(Cast)* 3580
Allen, Hugh *(Cast)* 4403
Allen, Irvin *(Cast)* 434
Allen, Irving *(Cast)* 692
Allen, Jay *(Librettist)* 2047
Allen, Jay Presson *(Librettist)* 499, 3624
Allen, John *(Librettist)* 4785
Allen, Jonelle *(Cast)* 1478, 2001, 4485
Allen, Joseph *(Cast)* 3786, 4364
Allen, Josephine *(Cast)* 677, 2041
Allen, Laurette *(Cast)* 1751
Allen, Lee *(Cast)* 169
Allen, Lester *(Cast)* 1312, 1483, 1484, 1485, 1486, 2902, 3352, 3409, 3907, 4357, 4426, 4602
Allen, Lester *(Composer)* 1460
Allen, Lewis *(Librettist)* 2815
Allen, Lewis *(Producer)* 52, 150, 154, 414, 2468, 4746
Allen, Lewis M. *(Producer)* 2047
Allen, Louise *(Cast)* 102, 1368, 1516, 4378, 4422, 4478
Allen, Lynne Clifton *(Cast)* 1099
Allen, Mana *(Cast)* 3227, 3306
Allen, Margit *(Lighting Designer)* 871
Allen, Marianna *(Cast)* 4454
Allen, Marty *(Cast)* 2479
Allen, Mord *(Lyricist)* 295
Allen, Nita *(Cast)* 1835
Allen, Norma Bradley *(Author)* 3631
Allen, Norman *(Cast)* 1721
Allen, Peter *(Cast)* 2437, 4089
Allen, Peter *(Composer)* 146, 1298, 2437, 2677
Allen, Peter *(Lyricist)* 1298, 2437
Allen, Philip Richard *(Cast)* 3198
Allen, Rae *(Cast)* 957, 1116, 3274
Allen, Ralph *(Librettist)* 1970
Allen, Ralph *(Lyricist)* 1970
Allen, Ralph G. *(Librettist)* 1038, 4197
Allen, Raymond *(Cast)* 1974
Allen, Redge *(Producer)* 1734
Allen, Robert *(Composer)* 1941, 3287
Allen, Robert *(Lyricist)* 3287
Allen, Robert Lee *(Cast)* 3011
Allen, Ross *(Conductor)* 3643
Allen, Ross *(Musical Director)* 3643
Allen, Sandra *(Cast)* 4217
Allen, Scott *(Cast)* 746, 2318
Allen, Searl *(Composer)* 1340
Allen, Seth *(Cast)* 2877, 2953
Allen, Steve *(Composer)* 42, 362, 4090
Allen, Steve *(Lyricist)* 42, 362, 4090
Allen, Ted *(Librettist)* 757
Allen, Thomas S. *(Composer)* 2745
Allen, Vera *(Cast)* 216, 904, 1654, 1656, 3955
Allen, Viola *(Cast)* 4671
Allen, Vivienne *(Cast)* 4143
Allen, Walter *(Cast)* 1661, 2156, 4724
Allen, Woody *(Author)* 3516
Allen, Woody *(Cast)* 3516
Allen, Woody *(Librettist)* 1408, 1648, 3186
Allen Jr., Joseph *(Cast)* 2729
Allen-Hodgdon *(Producer)* 1721
Allers, Franz *(Musical Director)* 530, 623, 1742, 1748, 2838, 3035, 3038, 3347, 3509
Allinson, Michael *(Cast)* 62, 2617
Allison, Bernie *(Cast)* 3806
Allison, Bessie *(Cast)* 1020
Allison, Fran *(Cast)* 3496
Allison, Fred *(Lighting Designer)* 2599
Allison, J.M. *(Producer)* 4425
Allison, Karl *(Producer)* 1082, 1873

Allison, Patti *(Cast)* 135, 1997
Alloway, Jackie *(Cast)* 1841
Alloway, Jacqueline *(Cast)* 1478
Alloy, Al *(Lighting Designer)* 4214
Allvine, Glendon *(Author)* 2348
Allyn, Helen *(Cast)* 4725
Allyson, June *(Cast)* 372, 3990, 4557
Almagor, Dan *(Librettist)* 2075
Almberg, John *(Cast)* 1172
Almy, Brooks *(Cast)* 690, 1161
Aloha Maids, The *(Cast)* 1840
Aloni, Yona *(Choreographer)* 3669
Alonzo, Alicia *(Cast)* 1670, 4142
Alper, Ron *(Cast)* 4774
Alper, Steven M. *(Composer)* 3181
Alper, Steven M. (Incidental Music) 1509
Alper, Steven M. *(Musical Director)* 1509, 2229
Alper, Steven M. *(Orchestrations)* 3181
Alperin, Yankele *(Cast)* 3670, 3781
Alperin, Yankele *(Director)* 2866
Alperin, Yankele *(Lyricist)* 2866
Alpert, Larry *(Cast)* 268, 2449
Alphin, Charles *(Composer)* 4007
Alphin, Charles *(Librettist)* 4007
Alphin, Charles *(Lyricist)* 4007
Alpin, Charles *(Composer)* 4184
Alpin, Charles *(Librettist)* 4184
Alpin, Charles *(Lyricist)* 4184
Alson, Johnny *(Cast)* 3871
Alsop, Peter *(Producer)* 1813
Alston, Barbara *(Cast)* 40
Alstone, Alex *(Lyricist)* 1834
Alswang, Ralph *(Lighting Designer)* 220, 221, 911, 1567, 3321, 3452, 4018
Alswang, Ralph *(Set Design)* 673, 911, 1567, 3321, 3452, 4018, 4377, 4397, 4499
Alter, Louis *(Cast)* 3153
Alter, Louis *(Composer)* 2, 124, 288, 418, 667, 703, 1128, 1132, 1134, 1932, 3382, 3444, 3840, 4043, 4235, 4291, 4824
Alterman, Michael *(Musical Director)* 2618
Alterman, Michael *(Orchestrations)* 2618
Alters, Gerald *(Composer)* 1233, 2288, 4627, 4829
Alters, Gerald *(Dance Arranger)* 1237, 1745, 2227, 4319, 4627
Alters, Gerald *(Musical Director)* 1892, 4319, 4627
Alters, Gerald *(Orchestrations)* 534
Alters, Gerald *(Pianist)* 1892
Alters, Gerald *(Vocal Arranger)* 4319, 4627
Altfeld, Vivien *(Choreographer)* 1754
Althoff, Charles *(Cast)* 4772
Altman, A. Arthur *(Producer)* 843
Altman, Arthur *(Composer)* 4193
Altman, Arthur *(Lyricist)* 4193
Altman, H. *(Lyricist)* 907
Altman, Jean *(Producer)* 843
Altman, Richard *(Director)* 722, 4577
Altman, Ruth *(Cast)* 507, 2636
Altmann, Adolf *(Author)* 3771
Alto, Bobby *(Cast)* 4347
Alton, Robert *(Cast)* 4050
Alton, Robert *(Choreographer)* 163, 173, 383, 397, 417, 420, 601, 901, 971, 1109, 1140, 1791, 1894, 1932, 1973, 2400, 2432, 2460, 2475, 2797, 3292, 3353, 3359, 3365, 3955, 4086, 4174, 4374, 4420, 4483, 4542, 4777, 4824, 4825, 4826
Alvarado, Trini *(Cast)* 3806, 4019, 4790
Alvarez, Anita *(Cast)* 1278, 1475, 2653
Alvarez, Carmen *(Cast)* 170, 1018, 2484, 2583, 4319, 4395, 4609, 4764, 4862
Alvarez Band, Fernando *(Cast)* 858
Alvarez Orchestra, Fernando *(Cast)* 854, 856, 857
Alverez, Marie *(Cast)* 3605
Amado, Jorge *(Author)* 3838
Aman, John *(Cast)* 1761
Aman, John *(Composer)* 4433
Aman, John *(Librettist)* 4433
Aman, John *(Lyricist)* 4433
Aman, Sara *(Cast)* 4829
Amaro, Richard *(Cast)* 975
AMAS Musical Theatre *(Producer)* 1702
AMAS Repertory Theatre *(Producer)* 1816, 4192
Ambassadors, The *(Cast)* 2818
Amber, Lili *(Composer)* 3669
Amber, Lili *(Lyricist)* 3669
Ambient, Mark *(Librettist)* 178
Ambler, William *(Cast)* 283
Amdrus, Sam *(Lighting Designer)* 3278
Ameche, Don *(Cast)* 1614, 1846, 2207, 2267, 3972, 4337
Amend, Karle O. *(Set Design)* 86, 1131, 1710, 2302, 2457, 3168, 3965, 4021, 4249
Amendolia, Don *(Cast)* 785, 1161
American Allied Arts *(Producer)* 1182
American Ent. Enterprises *(Producer)* 251
American League for a free Palestine *(Producer)* 1299
American Legion *(Producer)* 3683
American Musical Theatre Festival *(Producer)* 171, 2970, 3628
American National Theatre and Academy
See ANTA.
American Place Theatre *(Producer)* 2236, 2290, 4167
American Producing Company *(Producer)* 2639
American Puppet Arts Council
See also Bil Baird and Arthur Cantor.
American Puppet Arts Council *(Producer)* 56, 997, 3449, 3498, 4660, 4710
American Repertory Theatre *(Producer)* 4147
American Revue Theatre *(Producer)* 2259
American Shakespeare Fest. *(Producer)* 2859, 4715
Amer. Theatre and Academy *(Producer)* 3631
American Theatre Wing, The *(Producer)* 2175, 2653
American Viennese Group *(Producer)* 3698
American Youth Theatre *(Producer)* 3226
Ames, Ed *(Cast)* 134, 928
Ames, Elliot *(Musical Director)* 3654
Ames, Florenz *(Cast)* 138, 183, 1678, 2068, 2378, 2444, 3225, 3995, 4010, 4550, 4673
Ames, Florenz *(Choreographer)* 3995
Ames, Percy *(Cast)* 1417, 1579, 3710, 4059
Ames, Roger *(Composer)* 2766
Amoretti *(Lyricist)* 2859
Amos, Herbert *(Cast)* 3945

Amos, Keith *(Orchestrations)* 1616
Amos, Keith Lorenzo *(Cast)* 105
Amos, Kevin *(Musical Director)* 3429
Amram, David *(Composer)* 1775
Amram, David *(Lyricist)* 1775
Amron, Jacob *(Producer)* 1949, 1950
Amsterdam, Morey *(Cast)* 1040, 1898
Amsterdam, Morey *(Director)* 1898
Amsterdam, Morey *(Librettist)* 1898
Amstrong and His Orchestra, Louis *(Cast)* 889
Amundsen, Monte *(Cast)* 615, 2268
Amus Producing Company *(Producer)* 1458
Anania, John *(Cast)* 2523, 3526
Anania, Martin *(Set Design)* 3364
Anania, Michael *(Set Design)* 81, 690, 2861, 3708, 3851, 4703
Anarchestra *(Cast)* 655
Anchel, David *(Cast)* 2784
Anchutina, Leda *(Cast)* 1670
Ander, Alex *(Composer)* 459
Ander, Alex *(Lyricist)* 459
Anders, Darlene *(Cast)* 3577
Anders, Glenn *(Cast)* 2274, 3319, 4365, 4386, 4565
Anders, Karen *(Cast)* 90, 2737, 3126
Andersen, Christine *(Cast)* 2451
Andersen, D.R. *(Librettist)* 426
Andersen, Hans Christian *(Author)* 3164
Anderson *(Composer)* 2419
Anderson *(Lyricist)* 2419
Anderson, Adrienne *(Composer)* 1298
Anderson, Adrienne *(Lyricist)* 1298
Anderson, Alfred *(Librettist)* 645
Anderson, Andy *(Choreographer)* 3919
Anderson, Anita *(Cast)* 2076
Anderson, Arthur *(Author)* 1526
Anderson, Arthur *(Cast)* 4380
Anderson, Arthur *(Librettist)* 4490, 4663
Anderson, Arthur *(Lyricist)* 758, 1526, 2761, 2825, 4490, 4663
Anderson, Christine *(Cast)* 3211
Anderson, Clint *(Cast)* 1370
Anderson, Craig *(Director)* 2578
Anderson, Craig *(Producer)* 1732
Anderson, David *(Cast)* 92
Anderson, Deacon *(Composer)* 4264
Anderson, Deacon *(Lyricist)* 4264
Anderson, Del *(Cast)* 3113
Anderson, Dennis *(Author)* 669
Anderson, Ed *(Lyricist)* 2259
Anderson, Eddie *(Cast)* 2640
Anderson, Elman *(Musical Director)* 1002, 2949, 3939
Anderson, Elman *(Orchestrations)* 1134, 2689, 2737, 3020, 3126, 3939
Anderson, Elna *(Cast)* 3914
Anderson, Evelyn Norton *(Costumes)* 1837, 2219, 4408
Anderson, F. Richard *(Costumes)* 115, 252, 256, 405, 527, 749, 1199, 1271, 1356, 1375, 1388, 1403, 2029, 2465, 2481, 2534, 2723, 2844, 2907, 3494, 3745, 3977, 4130, 4236, 4277, 4590
Anderson, G.M. *(Producer)* 236, 1404, 1911, 2059, 2274, 4113
Anderson, Gary *(Orchestrations)* 534, 1164
Anderson, George *(Cast)* 2623, 4285
Anderson, Georgia *(Costumes)* 1415, 4331
Anderson, Hilding *(Composer)* 1562, 1563, 3618
Anderson, Hilding *(Musical Director)* 577, 735, 1384, 1587, 1685, 1801, 2595, 2950, 3087, 3252, 3915, 4053, 4179, 4248, 4421, 4528
Anderson, Hilding *(Orchestrations)* 2, 70, 378, 1307, 1525, 1685, 1738, 2351, 3069, 3096, 4206, 4365
Anderson, Hilding *(Vocal Arranger)* 2595
Anderson, Ingrid *(Cast)* 2611
Anderson, Ivy *(Cast)* 875, 885, 886, 2259
Anderson, John Murray *(Director)* 70, 173, 397, 417, 420, 662, 1013, 1284, 1685, 1686, 1687, 1688, 1689, 1690, 1811, 1827, 2180, 2227, 2258, 2400, 2460, 3005, 3009, 3100, 3107, 3166, 3292, 3975, 4117, 4214, 4362, 4374, 4465, 4483, 4552, 4567, 4824, 4825, 4826
Anderson, John Murray *(Librettist)* 1685, 1687, 1689, 3005, 4637
Anderson, John Murray *(Lighting Designer)* 173, 397, 1811, 2460, 3100, 3975, 4483, 4567, 4824
Anderson, John Murray *(Lyricist)* 1685, 1686, 1687, 1688, 1689, 1690, 1691, 2180, 2227, 3005, 4374, 4637
Anderson, John Murray *(Producer)* 1687, 3005, 4637
Anderson, Jonathan *(Composer)* 1736
Anderson, Jonathan *(Lyricist)* 1736
Anderson, Jonathan *(Musical Director)* 1736, 2235
Anderson, Jonathan *(Vocal Arranger)* 2235
Anderson, Judith *(Cast)* 499, 818
Anderson, Keith *(Costumes)* 2805
Anderson, Keith *(Set Design)* 2805
Anderson, Leona *(Cast)* 1968
Anderson, Leroy *(Composer)* 1614, 4137
Anderson, Leroy *(Conductor)* 1231
Anderson, Leroy *(Orchestrations)* 1614
Anderson, M.C. *(Producer)* 3504
Anderson, Maxwell *(Author)* 1171, 1893
Anderson, Maxwell *(Librettist)* 752, 1893, 2030, 2344, 2591, 2653
Anderson, Maxwell *(Lyricist)* 369, 752, 1120, 1893, 2030, 2344, 2591, 4504
Anderson, Percy *(Choreographer)* 2802
Anderson, Percy *(Costumes)* 165, 727, 758, 906, 1030, 1470, 1905, 2184, 2502, 2836, 2937, 3092, 3583, 4017
Anderson, Percy *(Set Design)* 4285
Anderson, Peter *(Lighting Designer)* 2783, 4470
Anderson, R. Alex *(Composer)* 92
Anderson, R. Alex *(Librettist)* 92
Anderson, R. Alex *(Lyricist)* 92
Anderson, Robert *(Librettist)* 961
Anderson, Sue *(Musical Director)* 2766, 3377
Anderson, Telford *(Librettist)* 646
Anderson, Wayne *(Cast)* 1004
Anderson, Will R. *(Composer)* 470, 1569, 2576, 2624, 3976, 4269
Anderson, Will R. *(Lyricist)* 470, 1569, 2576, 2624, 3976
Andersson, Benny *(Composer)* 721
Andes, Keith *(Cast)* 1933, 2680, 4693
Anditzer, Charles J. *(Composer)* 2701
Andre *(Costumes)* 3615, 4243
Andre, Frank *(Cast)* 4678

Andreas, Otto *(Cast)* 1413
Andreas, Otto *(Composer)* 1413
Andreopoulos, Dennis *(Composer)* 1713
Andreopoulos, Dennis *(Lyricist)* 1713
Andres, Barbara *(Cast)* 259, 1077, 3123, 3702, 3743
Andreva, Stella *(Cast)* 4792
Andrews, Adora *(Cast)* 2569
Andrews, Albert *(Cast)* 4605
Andrews, Andrew *(Cast)* 3947
Andrews, Ann *(Cast)* 4365
Andrews, Avis *(Cast)* 883, 884, 3365, 3704, 4021, 4569
Andrews, Bart *(Librettist)* 164
Andrews, Billy *(Cast)* 14
Andrews, Caroline *(Cast)* 4218
Andrews, Charles *(Librettist)* 1281
Andrews, Christine *(Costumes)* 3164
Andrews, Doug *(Cast)* 412
Andrews, Dusty *(Cast)* 290
Andrews, Ernest *(Cast)* 3814
Andrews, Frank *(Cast)* 2390
Andrews, George Lee *(Cast)* 825, 2536, 2820, 3080, 3279, 3377, 3464, 3485, 4145
Andrews, Herbert *(Costumes)* 4256
Andrews, Herbert *(Set Design)* 2447, 4256
Andrews, Jack *(Orchestrations)* 825, 1611, 2217, 2965, 4022
Andrews, Jennifer Lee *(Cast)* 2654
Andrews, Jerome *(Cast)* 4166
Andrews, Jerome *(Choreographer)* 4166
Andrews, Julie *(Cast)* 507, 623, 759, 1893, 3038, 4067, 4560
Andrews, Linda *(Cast)* 2583
Andrews, Lois *(Cast)* 1494
Andrews, Lyle D. *(Producer)* 834, 2382, 2833, 3042, 3436, 4545
Andrews, Maidie *(Cast)* 841, 3885
Andrews, Maxene *(Cast)* 3330
Andrews, Nancy *(Cast)* 520, 751, 1898, 2268, 2523, 2664, 3509, 4380, 4432
Andrews, Nancy *(Lyricist)* 520
Andrews, Patty *(Cast)* 3330
Andrewski, Gene *(Producer)* 4541
Andreyko, Helena *(Choreographer)* 4790
Andrini, Kathy *(Cast)* 695, 4454
Andrisano, Gui *(Director)* 3690, 4468
Anenia, Joan *(Lyricist)* 4629
Anes, Don *(Lyricist)* 4110
Angel, Barry *(Cast)* 299
Angel, Morris *(Costumes)* 292, 972, 2392
Angel & Co., Morris *(Costumes)* 3139
Angela, June *(Cast)* 3944
Angelas, William *(Composer)* 4525
Angeles, Aimee *(Cast)* 737, 3753
Angeles Sisters, The *(Cast)* 2041
Angelescu, Jackie *(Cast)* 3306
Angeli, Vincent *(Cast)* 2839
Angelo, Charles *(Cast)* 4212, 4616
Angelo, Judy Hart *(Composer)* 3555
Angelo, Judy Hart *(Lyricist)* 3555
Angelo, Waldo *(Costumes)* 3966
Angelos, Bill *(Composer)* 4388
Angelos, Bill *(Lyricist)* 4388
Angelos, William *(Composer)* 3615
Angelos, William *(Lyricist)* 3615
Angelus, Muriel *(Cast)* 514, 1140, 4214
Angles, Bert *(Choreographer)* 3025
Angold, Edit *(Cast)* 4486
Anhalt & Bachelder *(Producer)* 717
Animals, The *(Cast)* 974
Aniston, John *(Cast)* 2522
Anka, Paul *(Composer)* 2356, 4264
Anka, Paul *(Lyricist)* 2356, 4264
Anker, Charlotte *(Librettist)* 3305
Anker, Charlotte *(Lyricist)* 3305
Annals, Michael *(Costumes)* 1848, 2954
Annals, Michael *(Set Design)* 1848, 2954
Anne, Jean *(Cast)* 3530
Anne, Jean *(Costumes)* 3530
Anne, Jean *(Librettist)* 3530
Anne, Jean *(Lyricist)* 3530
Anonymous *(Composer)* 2203
Anonymous *(Lyricist)* 2633, 2859
Anouilh, Jean *(Author)* 172, 2411, 2674, 2678, 3355, 3377, 4386, 4592
Ansell, John *(Musical Director)* 334, 611, 3569
Anson, G.W. *(Cast)* 2365
Anstey, F. *(Author)* 1360
Anstey, F. *(Composer)* 3301
ANTA *(Producer)* 2702
Antelme, Leopold *(Composer)* 3940
Anthony, Earle C. *(Librettist)* 3423
Anthony, Earle C. *(Lyricist)* 3423
Anthony, Edward *(Librettist)* 1624
Anthony, Edward *(Lyricist)* 1624
Anthony, Emmett *(Cast)* 43
Anthony, Eugene J. *(Cast)* 2542
Anthony, John D. *(Cast)* 838
Anthony, Joseph *(Director)* 521, 1119, 2217, 2411, 2961, 3294, 3493
Anthony, Marc *(Composer)* 2843, 4154, 4795
Anthony, Michael *(Cast)* 1498
Anthony, Norman *(Librettist)* 289
Anthony, Norman *(Producer)* 289
Anthony, Philip *(Cast)* 580
Anthony, Ralph *(Cast)* 1412
Anthony, Sal *(Costumes)* 855, 1567
Antier, Benjamin *(Author)* 1193
Antonacci, Greg *(Cast)* 963, 4449
Antonacci, Greg *(Composer)* 963
Antonacci, Greg *(Librettist)* 963
Antonacci, Greg *(Lyricist)* 963
Antone *(Composer)* 510
Antonia *(Composer)* 3309
Antonia *(Lyricist)* 3309
Antonini, Alfredo *(Musical Director)* 759
Antoon, A.J. *(Director)* 1620, 3000, 3718, 4076
Anzell, Hy *(Cast)* 1597, 2544
APJAC International *(Producer)* 946
Aplon, Boris *(Cast)* 2422
Apolinar, Danny *(Cast)* 4789
Apolinar, Danny *(Composer)* 4789
Apolinar, Danny *(Lyricist)* 692, 4789
Apollo Leisure Group *(Producer)* 846

Apollo Quartet, The *(Cast)* 1493
Apollo Theatre *(Producer)* 2908
Apollon, Diane *(Cast)* 512
Apostoleris, Lee *(Producer)* 2796
Appell, Don *(Librettist)* 2864
Applebaum, Stan *(Orchestrations)* 3643
Applebaum, Stanley *(Orchestrations)* 534
Applegate, Steven *(Musical Director)* 4389
Appleman, Herbert *(Director)* 4514
Appleman, Herbert *(Lyricist)* 4514
Appleton, Jack *(Lyricist)* 3729
April *(Cast)* 2432, 3713
Arbuckle, Maclyn *(Cast)* 2830
Arcaro, Flavia *(Cast)* 1013, 1522, 1784, 1975, 2524, 2723, 3134, 3681, 4104, 4187, 4490
Arcenas, Loy *(Set Design)* 240, 595, 3285, 4358
Arch Productions *(Producer)* 2351
Archangelsky, Alexei *(Composer)* 710
Archangelsky, Alexei *(Lyricist)* 710
Archer, Cheryl *(Cast)* 2615
Archer, Donald *(Cast)* 3030
Archer, Harry
See also Harry Archer's Orchestra.
Archer, Harry *(Author)* 1814
Archer, Harry *(Composer)* 1191, 1814, 2271, 2296, 2516, 2833, 3042, 3369, 4235, 4476
Archer, Harry *(Lyricist)* 2296
Archer, Harry *(Musical Director)* 3946
Archer, Jane *(Cast)* 4479
Archer, John *(Cast)* 999
Archer, Julie *(Lighting Designer)* 1636
Archer, Nicholas *(Arrangements)* 793
Archer, Nicholas *(Dance Arranger)* 147
Archer, Nicholas *(Musical Director)* 36, 147
Archer, Robert *(Composer)* 4405
Archer's Orchestra, Harry
See also Harry Archer.
Archer's Orchestra, Harry *(Cast)* 1267
Archibald, William *(Cast)* 3292
Archibald, William *(Choreographer)* 937
Archibald, William *(Director)* 937
Archibald, William *(Librettist)* 651, 937, 3764
Archibald, William *(Lyricist)* 651, 937, 3764
Ard, Ken *(Cast)* 4031
Ard, Kenneth *(Cast)* 678
Ardao, David *(Cast)* 2242, 3600
Ardath, Fred *(Cast)* 117
Ardell, Franklyn *(Cast)* 1882, 2292, 4241
Ardelli, Roberto *(Cast)* 1020
Arden, Eve *(Cast)* 2453, 3365, 4152, 4483, 4557, 4824, 4825
Arden, Helene *(Cast)* 1710
Arden, Mary *(Cast)* 831
Arden, Toni *(Cast)* 857, 858, 864
Arden, Vic *(Producer)* 4118
Arden, Victor *(Composer)* 1819
Arden, Victor *(Lyricist)* 1819
Arden, Victor *(Pianist)* 1419, 1494, 2376, 3243, 4392, 4443
Arena Managers Association *(Producer)* 2078
Arena Stage *(Producer)* 2579
Arenal, Julie *(Choreographer)* 10, 482, 2153, 4205
Arenal, Julie *(Director)* 2153
Arenberg, Lee *(Cast)* 655
Arenel, Julie *(Choreographer)* 1717
Arent, Arthur *(Author)* 2175
Arent, Arthur *(Librettist)* 3501
Argent, Rod *(Composer)* 3695
Argent, Rod *(Lyricist)* 3695
Argentinita *(Cast)* 2140
Argov, Alexander *(Composer)* 4396
Argov, Alexander *(Lyricist)* 4396
Ariel, Raymond *(Producer)* 3781, 4769
Arin, Edith *(Costumes)* 4536
Aristides, John *(Cast)* 1959
Aristophanes *(Author)* 1406, 1745, 2659, 3418, 4707
Aristotle Productions *(Producer)* 1797
Arkell, Reginald *(Composer)* 702
Arkell, Reginald *(Librettist)* 475, 2323
Arkell, Reginald *(Lyricist)* 475, 2323
Arkin, Alan *(Cast)* 1190
Arkin, Alan *(Director)* 2925
Arkin, Juki *(Cast)* 2864
Arkin, Michael *(Cast)* 2852
Arlen, Harold *(Cast)* 3153
Arlen, Harold *(Composer)* 125, 213, 389, 432, 462, 478, 570, 781, 876, 877, 878, 879, 880, 885, 1135, 1137, 1385, 1481, 1672, 1763, 1813, 1856, 1973, 2000, 2190, 2294, 2475, 2611, 3018, 3172, 3175, 3178, 3181, 3709, 3837, 3905, 3955, 4048, 4123, 4131, 4259, 4399, 4498, 4534, 4778, 4799
Arlen, Harold *(Lyricist)* 781, 2000
Arlen, Jerry *(Composer)* 879
Arlen, Jerry *(Lyricist)* 879
Arlen, Jerry *(Musical Director)* 2000, 2707, 3837
Arlen, Robert *(Choreographer)* 3863
Arlen, Steve *(Cast)* 935, 1369
Arlington, Paul *(Costumes)* 97, 1129, 1345, 1531, 3406
Arliss, George *(Librettist)* 4333
Armbruster, Robert *(Composer)* 584
Armbruster, Robert *(Musical Director)* 584
Armbruster, Robert *(Orchestrations)* 584
Arment, Gwen *(Cast)* 1412
Armida *(Cast)* 557, 3170
Armin, Walter *(Cast)* 680, 1109, 2432
Armistead, Horace *(Set Design)* 183, 3691
Armitage, Richard *(Producer)* 2798
Armont, Paul *(Author)* 1391, 1992
Armour *(Composer)* 3381
Arms, Russell *(Cast)* 4230
Armstrong *(Composer)* 3981
Armstrong, Adrienne *(Cast)* 2735
Armstrong, Dorothy *(Costumes)* 208, 4283
Armstrong, Harry *(Cast)* 3153, 4465
Armstrong, Henry *(Composer)* 890
Armstrong, Henry *(Lyricist)* 890
Armstrong, Lil *(Composer)* 1713
Armstrong, Lil *(Lyricist)* 1713
Armstrong, Louis *(Cast)* 2561, 2588, 4256
Armstrong, Louis *(Composer)* 432, 3840, 4534
Armstrong, Louis *(Lyricist)* 3840
Armstrong, Paul *(Author)* 381
Armstrong, Peter *(Lighting Designer)* 3228
Armstrong, Vanessa Bell *(Cast)* 1073
Armstrong, Will M. *(Cast)* 3582

Armstrong, Will Steven *(Lighting Designer)* 656, 2048, 2053, 2097, 2355, 4190
Armstrong, Will Steven *(Set Design)* 656, 2048, 2053, 2097, 2355, 3551, 4190
Armus, Sidney *(Cast)* 4718
Arnaud, Leo *(Musical Director)* 4316
Arnaud, Leo *(Orchestrations)* 4316
Arnaud, Leo *(Vocal Arranger)* 4316
Arnaud, Yvonne *(Cast)* 1554
Arnaz, Desi *(Cast)* 4420
Arnaz, Lucie *(Cast)* 4334
Arndt, Dennis *(Cast)* 282
Arndt, Felix *(Composer)* 2291
Arne, Thomas *(Composer)* 3450
Arnell, France *(Cast)* 2362
Arney, Randall *(Producer)* 4074
Arnheim, Gus *(Composer)* 544, 2747
Arnheim, Gus *(Lyricist)* 544
Arno, Peter *(Author)* 3131
Arno, Peter *(Costumes)* 3005, 3131
Arno, Peter *(Librettist)* 1856, 3005, 3946
Arno, Peter *(Producer)* 1856
Arno, Peter *(Set Design)* 1856
Arno, Sig *(Cast)* 1681, 2838, 4075, 4386
Arnold, Anne S. *(Costumes)* 4149
Arnold, Barry *(Librettist)* 3752
Arnold, Barry *(Lighting Designer)* 576, 583, 941, 1581, 2110, 2242, 3600, 4022
Arnold, Barry *(Set Design)* 583, 3559
Arnold, Edward *(Cast)* 2194, 4335
Arnold, Franz *(Author)* 1534
Arnold, Helen *(Cast)* 1481
Arnold, Hurbert *(Orchestrations)* 4635
Arnold, Jack *(Librettist)* 4648
Arnold, Jack *(Lyricist)* 4648
Arnold, Jean *(Author)* 3564
Arnold, Jean *(Cast)* 1023, 2804, 4268
Arnold, Jeanne *(Cast)* 798, 1764, 4540
Arnold, Ken *(Musical Director)* 2303
Arnold, Lucille *(Cast)* 202
Arnold, Malcolm *(Lyricist)* 1201
Arnold, Marshal *(Cast)* 2303
Arnold, Maurice *(Musical Director)* 362
Arnold, Maurice *(Vocal Arranger)* 362
Arnold, Phyl *(Cast)* 1333, 2467
Arnold, Robert S. *(Composer)* 4030
Arnold, Robert S. *(Lyricist)* 4030
Arnold, Seth *(Cast)* 183
Arnold, Stanley *(Composer)* 1898
Arnold, Stanley *(Lyricist)* 1898
Arnold, Tom *(Producer)* 972, 1467, 2682
Arnone, John *(Costumes)* 2784
Arnone, John *(Set Design)* 373, 2784, 3010, 4129, 4676
Arnst, Bobbe *(Cast)* 2, 1690, 2872, 3766, 3796, 3980
Arnt, Charlie *(Cast)* 4365
Aroeste, Joel *(Cast)* 114
Arons, Ellyn *(Cast)* 4136
Aronson, Boris *(Costumes)* 612
Aronson, Boris *(Set Design)* 610, 612, 832, 933, 1061, 1265, 1294, 1329, 1571, 1711, 2536, 2615, 2948, 3340, 3813, 4237, 4583, 4640, 4862
Aronson, Frances *(Lighting Designer)* 109, 992, 1872, 2177, 2746, 3010, 3368, 3666
Aronson, Henry *(Dance Arranger)* 2012, 3576, 4139
Aronson, Henry *(Musical Director)* 143, 1276, 2012, 4139, 4349
Aronson, Rudolf *(Author)* 4728
Aronstein, Martin *(Lighting Designer)* 40, 101, 302, 406, 578, 766, 956, 1045, 1074, 1158, 1478, 1660, 1848, 2014, 2043, 2075, 2368, 2785, 2918, 2953, 2954, 2958, 3000, 3018, 3075, 3389, 3516, 3603, 3825, 4029, 4196, 4450
Arrabal, Fernando *(Author)* 237
Arrant *(Composer)* 3297
Arrant *(Lyricist)* 3297
Arrick, Larry *(Librettist)* 4406
Arrick, Larry *(Lyricist)* 4406
Arrighi, Luciana *(Set Design)* 2047
Arrnunziato, John *(Producer)* 2759
Arselli, Raimonda *(Cast)* 4273
Arsenault, Darlene *(Cast)* 2521
Arthur, Art *(Librettist)* 1930
Arthur, Beatrice *(Cast)* 1265, 2713, 2910, 2965, 3899, 3941, 4369
Arthur, Carol *(Cast)* 1891
Arthur, Daniel V. *(Director)* 2254
Arthur, Daniel V. *(Producer)* 511, 2254, 2765, 2782, 2951, 3073, 3177, 3308, 3372
Arthur, Frederick *(Author)* 1551
Arthur, George *(Lyricist)* 3322
Arthur, George K. *(Librettist)* 3605
Arthur, Gus *(Cast)* 3316
Arthur, Helen *(Cast)* 1654
Arthur, Helen-Jean *(Cast)* 3874
Arthur, Henry *(Cast)* 3713
Arthur, Jean *(Cast)* 901, 1383, 3452
Arthur, Ken *(Cast)* 1371
Arthur, Lee *(Librettist)* 522, 2029
Arthur, Paul *(Cast)* 2548
Arthur, Robert Alan *(Librettist)* 2355
Arthur Film Prods., Michael *(Producer)* 369
Arthurs, George *(Composer)* 1067, 1783, 3322
Arthurs, George *(Lyricist)* 248, 356, 1067, 1783, 2385, 2854, 3996
Artigas, Michelle *(Cast)* 595
Artists Prod. Corp. *(Producer)* 560
Artman, George *(Producer)* 600
Arvold, Mason *(Lighting Designer)* 59
Asaf, George *(Lyricist)* 964, 1852, 3259
Asaf, Michele *(Choreographer)* 535, 4139
Asbury, Claudia *(Choreographer)* 695
Asbury, Cleve *(Cast)* 1776
Asche, Oscar *(Librettist)* 758, 2802
Asche, Oscar *(Lyricist)* 758, 2802
Ascher, Leo *(Composer)* 1334, 3592
Ascher, Leo *(Librettist)* 1334
Aschinger, Brian *(Director)* 1903
Aschziger, Lowell B. *(Lighting Designer)* 1595
Ash, Randl *(Cast)* 3346
Ash, Sam *(Cast)* 796, 1026, 1065, 1944, 1962, 2005, 2939, 3258, 3405, 3995, 4054, 4668
Ash, Sam *(Composer)* 1026
Ash, Sam *(Lyricist)* 1026

Ash, Samuel *(Cast)* 2292
Ash, Walter *(Director)* 4470
Ashburn, Carroll *(Cast)* 514
Asher *(Composer)* 4648
Asher *(Lyricist)* 4648
Asher, Frances *(Cast)* 2648
Ashland, Camila *(Cast)* 2928
Ashley, Barbara *(Cast)* 283, 3326
Ashley, Christopher *(Director)* 992
Ashley, Clayton *(Librettist)* 2397
Ashley, Elizabeth *(Cast)* 2435
Ashley, J.W. *(Director)* 1248
Ashley, Mary Ellen *(Cast)* 1108, 1279, 2012
Ashley, Minnie *(Cast)* 906, 1682
Ashlyn *(Composer)* 3562
Ashlynd, Denise *(Cast)* 139
Ashman, Howard *(Director)* 1591, 2544, 4020
Ashman, Howard *(Librettist)* 245, 1591, 2544, 3666, 4020
Ashman, Howard *(Lyricist)* 245, 330, 1038, 1104, 1591, 2038, 2544, 4020
Ashton, Colleen *(Cast)* 958
Ashton, Frederick *(Choreographer)* 1366
Ashton, Linda *(Librettist)* 1107
Ashton, Linda *(Lyricist)* 1438
Ashwood, Michael *(Librettist)* 3528
Ashwood, Michael *(Producer)* 3528
Askam, Perry *(Cast)* 3385
Askin, Harry
See also Askin-Singer Co.
Askin, Harry *(Producer)* 2326, 4103, 4453
Askin-Singer Co.
See also Harry Askin and Mort Singer.
Askin-Singer Co. *(Producer)* 1563
Asro, Alexander *(Cast)* 2432
Assaly, Edmund *(Musical Director)* 83
Assante, Armand *(Cast)* 482
Associated Artists, Inc. *(Producer)* 3388
Associated Theatre Design *(Lighting Designer)* 251
Association of St. Louis, Municipal Theatre *(Producer)* 1476
Astaire, Adele *(Cast)* 17, 168, 294, 582, 1345, 1419, 2376, 2614, 3333, 3402, 4023
Astaire, Fred *(Cast)* 17, 168, 294, 582, 1345, 1419, 1453, 2376, 2403, 2614, 3333, 3402, 3833, 4023
Astaire, Fred *(Choreographer)* 4212
Astin, John *(Cast)* 4278, 4369
Astley, Blanche *(Cast)* 770
Astley, Edward *(Cast)* 3901
Astley, Edward *(Librettist)* 3901
Astley, Susan *(Director)* 3901
Astley, Susan *(Librettist)* 3901
Astor, Suzanne *(Cast)* 3111, 3112
Astroba, Marie *(Cast)* 4227
Atari, Yona *(Cast)* 4396
Atchinson-Ely, Edgar *(Cast)* 511, 2358, 2668, 2722, 2917, 2990, 3985, 4662
Atchison, David *(Lighting Designer)* 60, 1927
Ates, Nejla *(Cast)* 1242
Ates, Rosco *(Cast)* 3860
Atherton, Daisy *(Cast)* 2275
Atherton, Effie *(Cast)* 704
Atherton, William *(Cast)* 1999
Atkins, Boyd *(Composer)* 1813, 3840
Atkins, Boyd *(Lyricist)* 1813, 3840
Atkins, Charles *(Cast)* 1474
Atkins, Cholly *(Choreographer)* 432
Atkins, Joe *(Lighting Designer)* 460
Atkins, Roy *(Cast)* 876, 877, 3709
Atkinson, Betty *(Cast)* 2085
Atkinson, Clare *(Cast)* 1206
Atkinson, David *(Cast)* 71, 190, 223, 743, 1548, 2750, 4542
Atkinson, Don *(Cast)* 2618
Atkinson, Peggy *(Cast)* 1229
Atkinson, Sarah *(Cast)* 4579
Atlantic Overtures *(Producer)* 730
Attaway, Ruth *(Cast)* 2994
Atteridge, Harold *(Composer)* 1735
Atteridge, Harold *(Librettist)* 199, 201, 351, 391, 487, 764, 910, 965, 969, 1065, 1096, 1267, 1460, 1461, 1462, 1678, 1693, 1767, 1923, 2135, 2419, 2490, 2494, 2538, 2696, 2706, 2857, 2939, 3148, 3149, 3395, 3396, 3397, 3399, 3400, 3401, 3402, 3403, 3404, 3405, 3406, 3407, 3523, 3737, 3778, 3958, 3985, 4010, 4427, 4490, 4553, 4621, 4657, 4711, 4747, 4821
Atteridge, Harold *(Lyricist)* 199, 351, 473, 487, 551, 558, 764, 827, 910, 917, 965, 969, 1065, 1096, 1270, 1327, 1335, 1460, 1550, 1693, 1735, 1767, 1963, 2135, 2419, 2494, 2538, 2667, 2696, 2706, 2732, 2757, 2870, 2939, 3313, 3333, 3395, 3396, 3397, 3399, 3400, 3401, 3402, 3403, 3404, 3405, 3406, 3407, 3424, 3523, 3701, 3737, 3778, 3799, 3827, 3958, 3985, 4010, 4427, 4490, 4553, 4655, 4656, 4657, 4711, 4747
Attfield, Howard *(Cast)* 846
Attfield, Kitty *(Cast)* 466
Attie, Paulette *(Cast)* 3876
Attles, Joe *(Cast)* 2225
Attles, Joseph *(Cast)* 441, 576, 2203
Atwell, Lester *(Author)* 1310
Atwell, Rick *(Cast)* 2375
Atwell, Rick *(Choreographer)* 3838, 4171
Atwell, Rick *(Composer)* 4171
Atwell, Rick *(Director)* 3838, 4171
Atwell, Rick *(Lyricist)* 4171
Atwell, Roy *(Cast)* 93, 123, 124, 168, 1285, 1819, 1966, 2406, 2424, 2532, 2765, 2869, 2951, 3005, 3250, 4177
Atwell, Roy *(Lyricist)* 75, 93
Atwill, Lionel *(Cast)* 1281
Atwood, Bob *(Dance Arranger)* 941, 4337
Atwood, Bob *(Musical Director)* 941
Atwood, Robert *(Dance Arranger)* 3801
Auberjonois, Rene *(Cast)* 394, 775, 798, 4450
Aubert, Jane *(Cast)* 1461
Aubert, Jeanne *(Cast)* 111, 289, 2423, 2813, 3584
Aubrey, Monte *(Musical Director)* 679
Auden, W.H. *(Librettist)* 3441
Auden, W.H. *(Lyricist)* 3441
Audience Associates, Inc. *(Producer)* 4584
Audran, E. *(Author)* 1650
Audran, Edmond *(Author)* 2365
Audran, Edmond *(Composer)* 526, 2365
Audre *(Costumes)* 183, 2551, 4362
Audy, Robert *(Choreographer)* 2913

Audy, Robert *(Director)* 2913
Auer, Mischa *(Cast)* 2379, 2629, 2838
Auerbach, Arnold *(Cast)* 3460
Auerbach, Arnold *(Librettist)* 7, 454, 620, 1880, 2137
Auerbach, Arnold *(Lyricist)* 1957
Auerbach, Boris *(Cast)* 3336
Aug, Edna *(Cast)* 1543, 4742
Augard, Amy *(Cast)* 2524
Augarde, Adrienne *(Cast)* 1114, 3098
Augins, Charles *(Choreographer)* 1296
Augins, Charles *(Director)* 1296
Augustine, John *(Librettist)* 4535
Aulicino, Armand *(Librettist)* 3938
Aulicino, Armand *(Lyricist)* 3938
Aulisi, Joseph G. *(Costumes)* 518, 1222, 2134, 2754, 3636, 3741, 4449, 4659
Ault, Helen *(Cast)* 4234
Ault, Natalie *(Cast)* 824, 1247, 1565, 1663
Aumont, Jean Pierre *(Cast)* 4435
Aunt Jemima
See also Tess Gardella.
Auracher, Harry *(Composer)* 1404, 2261, 3423
Auracher, Harry *(Lyricist)* 1404
Auracher, Harry *(Musical Director)* 1404
Austen, Jane *(Author)* 1290
Austen, Phyllis *(Cast)* 3605
Austin, Beth *(Cast)* 3305
Austin, Bethe B. *(Cast)* 2065
Austin, Clara *(Cast)* 2122
Austin, Claude *(Orchestrations)* 4777
Austin, Elizabeth *(Cast)* 1108, 1797
Austin, Ivy *(Cast)* 3643
Austin, Ivy *(Voice)* 56
Austin, Jennie *(Cast)* 2122
Austin, John W. *(Cast)* 818
Austin, Leslie *(Cast)* 3314
Austin, Lyn *(Producer)* 868, 1064
Austin, Pamela *(Cast)* 2364
Austin, Ralph *(Cast)* 1975, 4493
Austin, S. *(Composer)* 1296
Austin, S. *(Lyricist)* 1296
Austin-Moore, George *(Cast)* 3747
Authors Producing Co., The *(Producer)* 1434
Autry, Herman *(Composer)* 39
Avedisian, Paul *(Cast)* 1903
Aveling, Charles *(Cast)* 1593
Aveling, Claude *(Lyricist)* 351, 1537
Averell, Robert *(Cast)* 1554
Averyt, Bennet *(Set Design)* 4244
Avian, Bob *(Choreographer)* 287, 2905, 4067, 4217
Avian, Bob *(Producer)* 1103
Avilla, Manuel *(Set Design)* 3380
Avnet, Brian *(Producer)* 3903
Avni, Ran *(Director)* 2354, 4769
Avon Comedy Four *(Cast)* 3403
Awan, Adrian *(Lighting Designer)* 1711
Axe, Ronald *(Librettist)* 427, 1648
Axelrod, David *(Composer)* 3111, 4396
Axelrod, David *(Librettist)* 108, 1648, 3077, 3111, 3112
Axelrod, David *(Lyricist)* 108, 427, 1648, 3111, 3112, 4396
Axelrod, George *(Author)* 3894
Axelrod, George *(Librettist)* 63, 943, 4018
Axelrod, Herman *(Director)* 4781
Axelrod, Herman *(Librettist)* 4781
Axelrod, Herman A. *(Librettist)* 1956
Axelrod, Herman A. *(Lyricist)* 1956
Axlerod, David *(Librettist)* 2935, 3484
Axlerod, David *(Lyricist)* 2935
Axt, William P. *(Musical Director)* 2340, 3775
Axtell, Barry *(Set Design)* 275, 3211
Axton, Hoyt *(Composer)* 3739
Axton, Hoyt *(Lyricist)* 3739
Axton, Max Boren *(Composer)* 3739
Axton, Max Boren *(Lyricist)* 3739
Ayer, Ethan *(Lyricist)* 3195
Ayer, Nat D. *(Composer)* 605, 662, 1151, 2448, 2892, 3134, 3681, 3827, 3996, 4589, 4799, 4803
Ayers, Bo *(Musical Director)* 2689
Ayers, Christine *(Cast)* 2397, 4826
Ayers, Jobee *(Cast)* 4829
Ayers, Lemuel *(Costumes)* 2327, 2331, 3035, 3326, 3351, 4123
Ayers, Lemuel *(Lighting Designer)* 462
Ayers, Lemuel *(Producer)* 2331, 3326
Ayers, Lemuel *(Set Design)* 462, 2137, 2327, 2331, 3035, 3263, 3326, 3351, 4075, 4123
Ayers, Mitchell *(Vocal Arranger)* 2750
Ayler, Ethel *(Cast)* 2190, 2355
Aylesworth, Arthur *(Cast)* 2262
Aylesworth, John *(Librettist)* 1120
Aylesworth, John *(Lyricist)* 1120
Aylward, Tony *(Cast)* 871
Aylwin, Jean *(Cast)* 3322
Ayr, Michael *(Cast)* 1669
Ayres, Bob *(Musical Director)* 2611
Ayres, Mitchell *(Musical Director)* 190, 2750
Ayres, Mitchell *(Vocal Arranger)* 189
Azenberg, Emanuel *(Producer)* 39, 40, 1325, 1620, 1633, 2205, 4062, 4210, 4334, 4342
Azenberg, Karen *(Choreographer)* 3601
Azenberg, Karen *(Director)* 3601
Azenzer, Arthur *(Musical Director)* 2043
Azito, Tony *(Cast)* 1638, 1755, 4370
Aznavour, Charles *(Composer)* 2245, 2558
Aznavour, Charles *(Lyricist)* 2245

B

B and M Productions *(Producer)* 1766
B.F. Concerts *(Producer)* 922
B.T. Express *(Composer)* 4534
B.T. Express *(Lyricist)* 4534
BMC Productions *(Producer)* 4205
BQE Dancers *(Cast)* 4347
Baba *(Costumes)* 128
Babatunde, Obba *(Cast)* 1103, 2173, 2513, 3690
Babb, Kevin *(Cast)* 828
Babb, Roger *(Cast)* 1715
Babbitt, Thomas *(Musical Director)* 4540
Babcock, Donald *(Cast)* 4186

Babcock, F.R. *(Composer)* 246
Babcock, F.R. *(Lyricist)* 246
Babcock, Jeannean *(Lighting Designer)* 1347
Babette *(Cast)* 3213
Babson, Edith *(Cast)* 1267
Bacall, Lauren *(Cast)* 167, 4727
Bach, Ernest *(Author)* 1534
Bach, Johann Sebastian *(Composer)* 964, 2913
Bach, William *(Cast)* 2995
Bacharach, Burt *(Composer)* 261, 3275, 3603, 4193
Bache, Theodore *(Director)* 4792
Bacher, William *(Producer)* 3899
Backar, Sol *(Cast)* 1358
Backus, Jim *(Voice)* 2980
Backus, Richard *(Cast)* 546
Baclanova, Olga *(Cast)* 3002
Bacon, Faith *(Cast)* 1135, 4823
Bacon, Frank *(Cast)* 763
Bacon, Gaspar *(Composer)* 814
Bacon, Gaspar *(Lyricist)* 814
Bacon, Gerald *(Producer)* 3593
Bacon, Glen *(Composer)* 70
Bacon, Glen *(Dance Arranger)* 70
Badale, Andy *(Composer)* 2164
Badale, Andy *(Lyricist)* 2164
Baddeley, Hermione *(Cast)* 634, 792, 842, 4154
Badloni, Rudolfo *(Cast)* 3168
Baer, Abel *(Composer)* 393, 710, 1643, 2380, 3018
Baer, Abel *(Lyricist)* 3018
Baer, Bugs *(Cast)* 3179
Baer, Bugs *(Librettist)* 1484, 1847, 4296
Baer, Cynthia *(Director)* 3217
Baer, Cynthia *(Producer)* 2522, 2664
Baer, Max *(Cast)* 1879
Baerwitz, Samuel *(Producer)* 1779
Baffa, Emil *(Musical Director)* 1938
Bafunno, Anthony *(Composer)* 4056
Bafunno, Antonio *(Musical Director)* 606, 1154, 3443
Bagby, George *(Composer)* 1281
Bagby, George *(Librettist)* 1281
Bagdasian, Harry M. *(Director)* 1004
Bagdasian, Harry M. *(Producer)* 528, 1004, 1155, 3165, 3329
Bagg, Helen *(Librettist)* 1550
Bagley, Albert *(Lyricist)* 513
Bagley, Ben *(Director)* 1018, 3186, 3890, 3940, 3941, 4047
Bagley, Ben *(Producer)* 392, 1018, 3940, 3941, 3942
Bagley, Eleanor *(Cast)* 3914
Bagneris, Vernel *(Additional Lyrics)* 4127
Bagneris, Vernel *(Cast)* 1425, 3297
Bagneris, Vernel *(Composer)* 1425
Bagneris, Vernel *(Director)* 1425, 3297, 4127
Bagneris, Vernel *(Librettist)* 1425
Bagneris, Vernel *(Lyricist)* 1425, 4127
Bagwell, Marsha *(Cast)* 695, 1997, 2861
Bahler, Mark *(Musical Director)* 107
Bahler, Tom *(Composer)* 107, 2689, 3126
Bahler, Tom *(Lyricist)* 107, 2689, 3126
Baier, Frank *(Cast)* 3136
Bailey, Adrian *(Cast)* 4031, 4091
Bailey, Alan *(Composer)* 4030
Bailey, Alan *(Director)* 3641, 4030
Bailey, Alan *(Lyricist)* 4030
Bailey, Bill *(Cast)* 885, 897, 4256
Bailey, Bob *(Composer)* 2520
Bailey, Dennis *(Cast)* 1108, 1665, 1797, 2427, 3600, 3817
Bailey, Frankie *(Cast)* 436, 1515, 1927
Bailey, Fred *(Cast)* 4493
Bailey, Hillary *(Cast)* 3688
Bailey, Jeff *(Lyricist)* 2168, 2629
Bailey, Jeff *(Producer)* 2948
Bailey, Maureen *(Cast)* 1567
Bailey, Mildred *(Composer)* 4501
Bailey, Pearl *(Cast)* 183, 454, 2000, 4061, 4123
Bailey, Robin *(Cast)* 2201
Bailey and Schwartz Prods. *(Producer)* 2643
Bails, Joan *(Cast)* 4416
Bain, Conrad *(Cast)* 630, 4005, 4474
Bainbridge, John *(Cast)* 225
Baines, Pearl *(Cast)* 725
Bainter, Fay *(Cast)* 1142, 1187, 2328, 3776
Baio, Joey *(Cast)* 2011
Baird, Bil
See also Bil Baird Marionettes and American Puppet Arts Council.
Baird, Bil *(Author)* 4660
Baird, Bil *(Cast)* 50, 4826
Baird, Bil *(Composer)* 3440, 4660
Baird, Bil *(Lyricist)* 4660
Baird, Bil *(Producer)* 56, 3449, 3498, 4660
Baird, Bil *(Puppeteer)* 192, 193, 997, 2726, 3091, 4710
Baird, Bil *(Set Design)* 56, 3449
Baird, Bil *(Voice)* 56
Baird, Cora *(Cast)* 4826
Baird, Cora *(Puppeteer)* 192, 193, 2726, 3091
Baird, Elsie *(Cast)* 4509, 4761
Baird, Ethel *(Cast)* 466
Baird, John *(Director)* 2610
Baird, John F. *(Director)* 1862
Baird, Peter (Puppeteer) 56, 997, 3449, 3498, 4660, 4710
Baird, Stewart *(Cast)* 326, 2145, 3658, 4258
Baird, Stewart *(Director)* 637
Baird, Stewart *(Librettist)* 637
Baird, Stewart *(Lyricist)* 637
Baird, Tom *(Composer)* 716
Baird Marionettes, Bil
See also Bil Baird.
Baird Marionettes, Bil *(Cast)* 2234
Baird Marionettes, Bil & Cora *(Cast)* 1815
Baird Marionettes, Bil and Cora *(Cast)* 192, 193
Baird's Marionettes, Bil *(Cast)* 1300
Baisch, Jon *(Director)* 4696
Baisch, Jon *(Producer)* 4696
Bakeffi, S. *(Author)* 1506
Baker, Alice *(Lyricist)* 369
Baker, Belle *(Cast)* 376
Baker, Benny *(Cast)* 2187, 2453, 4778
Baker, Benny *(Librettist)* 3933
Baker, Bertilla *(Cast)* 2970
Baker, Bonnie *(Cast)* 1109
Baker, Carroll *(Cast)* 820
Baker, Darrin *(Cast)* 4217

Baker, David *(Composer)* 823, 868, 1047, 2168, 2227, 2288, 2804, 3473, 3940, 3941, 4028, 4153, 4388, 4566
Baker, David *(Dance Arranger)* 134, 823, 1061, 1310, 3577, 3702, 4764
Baker, David *(Producer)* 1047
Baker, Dylan *(Cast)* 4398
Baker, Edythe *(Cast)* 391, 1831, 1923, 2135, 3291, 4437
Baker, Evelyn *(Composer)* 470, 675, 1043
Baker, Gale *(Cast)* 2969
Baker, Herbert *(Composer)* 4827
Baker, Herbert *(Librettist)* 3499
Baker, Herbert *(Lyricist)* 1817, 4827
Baker, Jack *(Choreographer)* 1884
Baker, Jennifer *(Cast)* 4160
Baker, Joe Don *(Cast)* 477
Baker, Joseph *(Arrangements)* 3667
Baker, Josephine *(Cast)* 740, 4825
Baker, Kenny *(Cast)* 3301, 4486
Baker, Kent *(Cast)* 4469
Baker, Lenny *(Cast)* 2058, 3370
Baker, Mabel *(Cast)* 2978
Baker, Mabella *(Cast)* 527, 4453
Baker, Marilyn Cantor *(Producer)* 2657
Baker, Mildred *(Cast)* 3857
Baker, Paul *(Composer)* 226
Baker, Phil *(Cast)* 201, 203, 418, 622, 1395, 3008, 3149, 3406, 3523, 3594
Baker, Phil *(Composer)* 565, 1687, 3149, 3523
Baker, Phil *(Lyricist)* 3149
Baker, R. Melville *(Librettist)* 1374, 1573
Baker, R. Melville *(Lyricist)* 639
Baker, R.M. *(Librettist)* 2902
Baker, R.M. *(Lyricist)* 2902
Baker, Raymond *(Cast)* 2152
Baker, Rita *(Director)* 778
Baker, Robert M. *(Librettist)* 639
Baker, Robert M. *(Lyricist)* 639
Baker, Robert Michael *(Cast)* 549
Baker, Robert N. *(Lyricist)* 3033
Baker, Russell *(Librettist)* 1955, 4338
Baker, Sam *(Cast)* 3093
Baker, Scott *(Cast)* 2783
Baker, Susan *(Cast)* 4160
Baker, Theodore *(Lyricist)* 1589
Baker, Word *(Director)* 496, 1245, 2074, 2418, 3209
Baker-Bergen, Stuart *(Cast)* 54
Bakst, Leon *(Costumes)* 165, 2802
Bakst, Leon *(Set Design)* 396
Bakula, Scott *(Cast)* 2171, 2754, 3760, 4349
Bal, Jeanne *(Cast)* 1456
Balaban, Bob *(Cast)* 4783
Balaban, Bob *(Director)* 1575
Balaban, Cherry *(Composer)* 2288
Balaban, Cherry *(Lyricist)* 2288
Balaban, Robert *(Cast)* 4522
Balanchine, George *(Choreographer)* 247, 514, 612, 791, 911, 1101, 2061, 2379, 2597, 2859, 2909, 2985, 3283, 3767, 4075, 4640, 4652, 4715, 4825
Balanchine, George *(Director)* 612, 4640
Balding, Ivor David *(Producer)* 2663
Baldomero, Brian R. *(Cast)* 2905
Baldoni, Gail *(Costumes)* 760
Baldwin, Alec *(Cast)* 3884
Baldwin, Brooks *(Cast)* 693
Baldwin, Clive *(Cast)* 2235, 2436
Baldwin, George *(Cast)* 433
Baldwin, George *(Librettist)* 433
Baldwin, Islish *(Composer)* 1978
Baldwin, Islish *(Lyricist)* 1978
Baldwin, James *(Author)* 105, 477
Baldwin, John *(Composer)* 3739
Baldwin, John *(Lyricist)* 3739
Baldwin, Philip *(Set Design)* 4399
Baldwin, Tallmadge *(Cast)* 4103
Baldwin, Winnie *(Cast)* 2818
Baldwin, Winnie *(Producer)* 4570
Baleff, Ariel *(Costumes)* 1892
Baleff, Ariel *(Set Design)* 1892
Balemar Productions *(Producer)* 3902
Balfe, M.W. *(Composer)* 1897
Balfe, Michael *(Composer)* 1710
Balfour, William *(Cast)* 3219
Balieff, Nikita *(Cast)* 710, 839
Balin, Edmund *(Choreographer)* 600, 1047, 2288
Balk, H. Wesley *(Director)* 2001
Ball, Ernest R. *(Composer)* 310, 591, 1751, 1803, 1897, 2154, 231 0, 2498, 2662, 2990, 3642, 3753, 3827, 3910, 3981, 4544
Ball, George *(Cast)* 2578
Ball, Jonathan *(Cast)* 2416
Ball, Lucille *(Cast)* 4693
Ball, Michael *(Cast)* 211
Ball, Samuel C. *(Costumes)* 3711
Ball, Samuel C. *(Set Design)* 3711
Ball, Thomas *(Composer)* 4240
Ball, Thomas *(Producer)* 4240
Ballantine, Carl *(Cast)* 2965
Ballantine, Paul *(Composer)* 2140
Ballard *(Lyricist)* 4823
Ballard, Beverly *(Cast)* 2018
Ballard, Bob *(Orchestrations)* 2095, 2096
Ballard, Clint *(Composer)* 3111
Ballard, Clinton *(Composer)* 280
Ballard, F.D. *(Composer)* 3455
Ballard, F.D. *(Lyricist)* 3455
Ballard, Hank *(Composer)* 3739
Ballard, Hank *(Lyricist)* 3739
Ballard, Kay *(Cast)* 2925, 3925
Ballard, Kaye *(Author)* 1873
Ballard, Kaye *(Cast)* 322, 656, 759, 1018, 1600, 1873, 2294, 3524, 3696, 3788, 4323, 4829
Ballard, Kaye *(Composer)* 2294
Ballard, Kaye *(Lyricist)* 1873, 2294
Ballard, Lucinda *(Costumes)* 85, 117, 153, 657, 1456, 1670, 1749, 1894, 2144, 2615, 2817, 3036, 3972, 3989, 4095, 4143, 4169
Ballard, Pat *(Composer)* 3645, 4170, 4264
Ballard, Pat *(Lyricist)* 3645, 4170, 4264
Ballard Jr., Clint *(Composer)* 3671, 3925, 4264
Ballard Jr., Clint *(Lyricist)* 4264

Ballard Jr., Clint *(Orchestrations)* 3671
Ballard Jr., Clint *(Vocal Arranger)* 3671
Ballet Concepts *(Producer)* 4172
Ballou, David *(Costumes)* 3938
Ballou, David *(Lighting Designer)* 4582
Ballou, David *(Set Design)* 2664, 3619, 3938, 4582
Balmain, Pierre *(Costumes)* 1762
Balsam, Martin *(Cast)* 2464, 3210
Balthrop, Carmen *(Cast)* 4447
Balzar, George *(Librettist)* 180
Bamboschek, Giuseppe *(Musical Director)* 3219
Bambrelli, Maria *(Cast)* 2115
Bamford, George *(Composer)* 1978
Bamford, George *(Lyricist)* 1978
Bampton, Rose *(Cast)* 4409
Bancroft, Anne *(Cast)* 2073
Bancroft, George *(Cast)* 765
Bane, Paula *(Cast)* 620, 3893
Banes, Antoine *(Author)* 4624
Bangs, Charles Kendrick *(Lyricist)* 2724
Bangs, John Kendrick *(Author)* 2005
Bangs, John Kendrick *(Librettist)* 2399
Bangs, John Kendrick *(Lyricist)* 2399
Bankey, Chris *(Orchestrations)* 36
Bankey, Christopher *(Orchestrations)* 1813, 2208, 2790
Bankhead, Tallulah *(Cast)* 1416, 2510, 4059, 4827
Banks, Ada *(Cast)* 2979
Banks, Ernie *(Cast)* 1073
Banks, Larry *(Composer)* 3695
Banks, Larry *(Lyricist)* 3695
Banks, Leslie *(Cast)* 2591, 3451, 4207
Banner, John *(Cast)* 1413, 1681
Bannister, Albert *(Director)* 3457, 3596
Bannister, Albert *(Producer)* 3596, 3860
Bannister, Frank *(Lyricist)* 1836
Banome, Nino *(Lyricist)* 1436
Bantock, Leedham *(Author)* 1526
Bantock, Leedham *(Composer)* 906
Bantock, Leedham *(Librettist)* 353, 4663
Banton, Travis *(Costumes)* 910, 1250, 1577, 4427
Bantry, Bryan *(Producer)* 1873
Baral, Vicki *(Lighting Designer)* 2470
Baral, Vicki *(Set Design)* 2470, 2702, 3643
Barand, Robert *(Cast)* 3970
Baranov, Alvin B. *(Producer)* 1884, 4199
Baranova, Irina *(Cast)* 1336
Baranski, Christine *(Cast)* 829, 3142
Barasch, Norman *(Author)* 3874
Barat, Maxine *(Cast)* 4557
Baravalle, Victor *(Musical Director)* 25, 78, 126, 376, 582, 672, 773, 827, 841, 1551, 1625, 2816, 3014, 3144, 3146, 3699, 3735, 3949, 4150, 4667, 4818, 4819, 4823
Barbary Coast Prod. *(Producer)* 302
Barbeau, Adrienne *(Cast)* 1664, 4124
Barber, Ada Lytton *(Cast)* 1795
Barber, Bernie *(Composer)* 3614
Barber, Bernie *(Lyricist)* 3614
Barber, Ellen *(Cast)* 1418
Barber, Vivian *(Cast)* 1514
Barbier *(Costumes)* 201, 3150, 4170
Barbosa *(Costumes)* 3139
Barbour, Dave *(Composer)* 3428
Barbour, Joyce *(Cast)* 1202, 2238, 2570, 2788, 3556, 3634, 4010, 4118, 4327
Barbour, Nina *(Cast)* 1183
Barcelo, Randy *(Costumes)* 550, 1116, 1236, 2212, 2687, 2790, 2992, 3159, 3169, 3873, 3903
Barcelo, Randy *(Set Design)* 2790
Barclay, Don *(Cast)* 125, 1587, 2827, 3170, 3252, 4810
Barclay, Jered *(Choreographer)* 3902
Barclay, Jered *(Director)* 3902
Barclay, John *(Cast)* 689
Barclay, William *(Set Design)* 1589, 3667, 3724
Barclift, Nelson *(Cast)* 2057
Barclift, Nelson *(Choreographer)* 189, 2057, 4340
Bard, Robert *(Cast)* 3104
Bardaretto, Burrell *(Cast)* 1629
Barde, Andre *(Author)* 25, 2637
Barde, Andre *(Librettist)* 1309
Barefield, Eddie *(Musical Director)* 898
Barefield, Edward *(Orchestrations)* 242
Barer, Marshall *(Librettist)* 3288
Barer, Marshall *(Lyricist)* 1408, 1818, 1873, 2246, 2357, 2535, 2663, 3108, 3286, 3288, 3524, 3551, 3889, 4388, 4585, 4828, 4829
Bargy, Jeanne *(Composer)* 1697, 4433
Bargy, Jeanne *(Dance Arranger)* 1697
Bargy, Jeanne *(Librettist)* 4433
Bargy, Jeanne *(Lyricist)* 1697, 4433
Bargy, Jeanne *(Vocal Arranger)* 1697
Barholomae, Philip *(Lyricist)* 4562
Bari, Charles *(Cast)* 1258
Barie, B.J. *(Cast)* 3668
Barilum, Trudy *(Costumes)* 1347
Baring-Gould, Sabine *(Lyricist)* 3259
Barkan, M. *(Composer)* 4193
Barkan, M. *(Lyricist)* 4193
Barkdull, Leo *(Librettist)* 2114
Barker, Albert *(Librettist)* 2817
Barker, Clive *(Cast)* 4469
Barker, Edith *(Cast)* 191, 1445
Barker, Howard *(Costumes)* 249, 2522
Barker, Howard *(Producer)* 2522, 2664
Barker, Howard *(Set Design)* 2522
Barker, Jack *(Cast)* 799, 3184, 3819
Barker, Jean *(Cast)* 3544
Barker, John *(Cast)* 294, 1339, 2602, 3352, 4365
Barker, Marguerite Abbott *(Producer)* 1244
Barker, Richard *(Director)* 45, 476, 618, 727, 995, 1030, 1305, 1473, 1720, 2233, 2502, 2548, 2733, 3582, 4125, 4614
Barker, Ronnie *(Cast)* 3630
Barker, Shirley *(Costumes)* 1587, 1847, 2378, 2519, 4437, 4491
Barker, Shirley *(Set Design)* 1685
Barker, William *(Cast)* 2111
Barklie, Lance *(Librettist)* 348
Barklie, Lance *(Producer)* 348
Barlow, Anna Marie *(Librettist)* 101, 1727
Barlow, Howard *(Musical Director)* 1654, 1655
Barmark, Ira *(Librettist)* 1369

Barnabee, Henry Clay *(Cast)* 2345, 2697, 3570, 3736, 3881, 4559, 4598
Barnard, Armand *(Librettist)* 2782
Barnes *(Costumes)* 998
Barnes, Billy *(Cast)* 412, 3447
Barnes, Billy *(Composer)* 316, 407, 408, 410, 411, 412, 413, 450, 1341, 2080, 2969, 3447, 3499, 4057
Barnes, Billy *(Librettist)* 2969
Barnes, Billy *(Lyricist)* 316, 407, 408, 410, 411, 412, 413, 450, 2080, 2969, 3447, 3499, 4057
Barnes, Billy *(Musical Director)* 411, 413
Barnes, Billy *(Producer)* 413
Barnes, Binnie *(Cast)* 2547
Barnes, Charles *(Cast)* 4545
Barnes, Charles *(Composer)* 3594
Barnes, Charles *(Lyricist)* 3594
Barnes, Cheryl *(Cast)* 4459
Barnes, Eric *(Arrangements)* 3004
Barnes, Eric *(Musical Director)* 3004
Barnes, Eric *(Orchestrations)* 3004
Barnes, F.J. *(Lyricist)* 2858, 4757
Barnes, Gregg *(Costumes)* 3346, 4193
Barnes, Harry *(Choreographer)* 3228
Barnes, Irving *(Cast)* 1385, 4701
Barnes, Johnny *(Cast)* 1109
Barnes, Mae *(Cast)* 108, 603, 1989, 3660, 4827
Barnes, Marjorie *(Cast)* 1671, 2284
Barnes, May *(Cast)* 1050
Barnes, Paul *(Lighting Designer)* 1993
Barnes, Paul *(Set Design)* 1993, 2313
Barnes, T. Roy *(Cast)* 3333, 3672
Barnes, Terry *(Cast)* 2285
Barnes, Theo *(Cast)* 755
Barnes, Theo *(Costumes)* 755
Barnes, Tom *(Set Design)* 1412
Barnes, Wade *(Composer)* 3630
Barnes, Wade *(Librettist)* 3630
Barnes, Wade *(Lyricist)* 3630
Barnes, Will R. *(Composer)* 336
Barnes, Will R. *(Costumes)* 175, 185, 378, 712, 968, 1095, 1118, 1176, 1208, 1264, 1459, 1525, 1631, 1753, 1758, 1868, 1925, 1926, 2041, 2385, 2917, 2919, 2938, 3081, 3268, 3337, 3578, 3626, 3732, 3951, 4201, 4478, 4754
Barnes, Will R. *(Lyricist)* 336
Barnes, William C. *(Cast)* 255
Barnes, William C. *(Lyricist)* 255
Barnet, R.A. *(Director)* 761
Barnet, R.A. *(Librettist)* 306, 761, 1213, 2181, 2902, 2906, 3047, 3951, 4353, 4531
Barnet, R.A. *(Lyricist)* 306, 761, 2906, 3047, 4531
Barnett, Eileen *(Cast)* 2969, 3641
Barnett, Jack *(Composer)* 1120
Barnett, Jack *(Librettist)* 4428
Barnett, Jack *(Lyricist)* 1120
Barnett, Jackie *(Composer)* 1120
Barnett, Jackie *(Lyricist)* 1120, 4829
Barnett, Mary *(Cast)* 4291
Barnett, Mary *(Choreographer)* 4147
Barnett, Randy *(Musical Director)* 602
Barnett, Rose *(Cast)* 3951
Barnett, Stanley *(Producer)* 1380
Barnett, Zoe *(Cast)* 60, 2854, 3681
Barney, Alice *(Librettist)* 2943
Barney, Ariel *(Producer)* 2502
Barnhart, Robert *(Set Design)* 3457, 4479
Barnum, H.B. *(Composer)* 4788
Barnum, H.B. *(Dance Arranger)* 593, 4788
Barnum, H.B. *(Orchestrations)* 52, 593, 4788
Barnum, H.B. *(Vocal Arranger)* 52
Baron, Art *(Cast)* 4076
Baron, Christy *(Cast)* 3227
Baron, Evalyn *(Cast)* 394, 1256, 1897, 2049, 3631, 3644, 3858
Baron, Linda Michelle *(Lyricist)* 4645
Baron, Marie *(Cast)* 1079
Baron, Maurice *(Orchestrations)* 3639
Baron, Sandy *(Cast)* 1471
Barone, John *(Cast)* 3463
Barovick, Fred *(Orchestrations)* 137
Barr, Edna *(Cast)* 2640
Barr, George *(Librettist)* 627
Barr, Kenn *(Costumes)* 1571, 2751, 2940, 3947, 4428
Barr, Michael *(Composer)* 1107
Barr, Richard *(Producer)* 72, 1662, 2678, 4233
Barraclough, Sydney *(Cast)* 2506
Barrat, Maxine *(Cast)* 3292
Barratt, Augustus *(Composer)* 1240, 1519, 1544, 1852, 2180, 2546, 3031, 3402, 3618
Barratt, Augustus *(Lyricist)* 1240, 1544, 1852, 2180, 2816, 3618
Barratt, Augustus *(Musical Director)* 1565, 1780, 1852, 2056, 2399, 2524, 2546, 2603, 3031, 3618, 3978, 4219, 4637
Barratt, Virginia *(Cast)* 4621
Barratt, Watson *(Costumes)* 1506
Barratt, Watson *(Librettist)* 199
Barratt, Watson *(Lighting Designer)* 1506
Barratt, Watson *(Set Design)* 110, 138, 184, 199, 200, 201, 202, 203, 204, 324, 391, 463, 487, 495, 659, 718, 764, 771, 814, 905, 948, 969, 1033, 1096, 1207, 1219, 1384, 1460, 1461, 1462, 1506, 1557, 1678, 1693, 1799, 1836, 1992, 2115, 2135, 2293, 2384, 2396, 2397, 2419, 2540, 2546, 2595, 2602, 2622, 2628, 2637, 2706, 2747, 2757, 2789, 2808, 2816, 2843, 2870, 2939, 2947, 3011, 3012, 3056, 3064, 3084, 3148, 3149, 3150, 3152, 3170, 3258, 3310, 3402, 3403, 3405, 3406, 3407, 3410, 3523, 3573, 3586, 3680, 3778, 3974, 3985, 4010, 4025, 4121, 4170, 4188, 4213, 4352, 4365, 4375, 4427, 4575, 4586, 4621, 4654, 4670, 4730, 4733, 4777, 4824, 4826
Barre *(Author)* 3237
Barre, Albert *(Author)* 4624
Barre, Gabriel *(Cast)* 147, 1353, 3456, 3695, 4139
Barre, Gabriel *(Director)* 1969, 2224, 3377
Barre, Stella *(Cast)* 3122
Barreca, Chris *(Set Design)* 789
Barrett, Alan *(Costumes)* 2047
Barrett, Brent *(Cast)* 589, 784, 3544
Barrett, Christopher *(Cast)* 16
Barrett, Gene *(Cast)* 1269, 3669
Barrett, James Lee *(Author)* 3928
Barrett, James Lee *(Librettist)* 3928
Barrett, Joe *(Cast)* 508, 1172
Barrett, John *(Cast)* 2124

Barrett, Leslie *(Cast)* 3059
Barrett, Lester *(Lyricist)* 1430
Barrett, Mace *(Cast)* 1567, 4272
Barrett, Nancy *(Cast)* 3482
Barrett, Sheila *(Cast)* 1693, 4374
Barrett, William E. *(Author)* 2583
Barrett Jr., Oscar *(Producer)* 3213
Barri, Bebe *(Choreographer)* 2972
Barri, Maud Lillian *(Cast)* 2502
Barrie, Alexandra *(Cast)* 459
Barrie, Ann *(Cast)* 3822
Barrie, Barbara *(Cast)* 262, 832, 1977, 2859, 3871
Barrie, George *(Composer)* 4743
Barrie, Gracie *(Cast)* 1493, 3955, 4177
Barrie, H. Owen *(Author)* 4830
Barrie, James *(Author)* 2680
Barrie, James M. *(Author)* 2329, 3439, 3450, 3451, 3453, 3454, 3472, 3779
Barrie, James M. *(Composer)* 3450
Barrie, James M. *(Librettist)* 3452, 3453
Barrie, James M. *(Lyricist)* 3450
Barrie, Leslie *(Cast)* 163
Barrie, Mona *(Cast)* 4569
Barrile, Anthony *(Cast)* 4676
Barrillet, Pierre *(Author)* 98
Barrington, Rutland *(Cast)* 4663
Barrington, Rutland *(Lyricist)* 906
Barris *(Lyricist)* 4697
Barris, Harry *(Composer)* 1425
Barris, Harry *(Lyricist)* 1425
Barrison, Mabel *(Cast)* 250, 472, 1054, 1316, 2408, 2649, 3566, 4478
Barron, David *(Cast)* 451, 1258, 2654, 3864
Barron, Evelyn *(Producer)* 4286
Barron, Judith *(Cast)* 4824
Barron, P.J. *(Librettist)* 353
Barrosa, A.E. *(Set Design)* 703
Barrow, Bernard *(Director)* 4124
Barrow, P.J. *(Lyricist)* 353
Barrow, Patrick *(Composer)* 3828
Barrow, Patrick *(Lyricist)* 3828
Barrow, Ting *(Lighting Designer)* 3111
Barrows, Fred *(Cast)* 696
Barrows, Richard *(Cast)* 1085, 2658
Barrows, William *(Cast)* 263
Barruschee, Leo *(Choreographer)* 396
Barry, Carolyne *(Director)* 2046
Barry, Frank *(Orchestrations)* 670, 2308, 2380, 2461, 3719, 3946, 4529
Barry, Fred *(Orchestrations)* 4818, 4819
Barry, Gene *(Cast)* 454, 1577, 1748, 2360, 3767, 4114, 4331
Barry, Jeff *(Composer)* 1383, 2427, 3739, 4193, 4534
Barry, Jeff *(Lyricist)* 1383, 2427, 3739, 4193, 4534
Barry, Jimmie *(Cast)* 3323
Barry, John *(Composer)* 2539, 2568
Barry, Jorday *(Set Design)* 4773
Barry, Julian *(Librettist)* 2196
Barry, Katie *(Cast)* 2716
Barry, Leonard *(Cast)* 1502
Barry, Michael *(Cast)* 1657
Barry, Mrs. Jimmy *(Cast)* 3323
Barry, Peter *(Librettist)* 4498
Barry, Peter *(Lyricist)* 2707, 3698, 4394, 4498
Barry, Philip *(Author)* 1762, 3468
Barry, Robert *(Lighting Designer)* 759
Barry, Rod *(Cast)* 3112
Barry, Rodd *(Cast)* 3111
Barry, Suzanne *(Cast)* 2011
Barry Sisters *(Cast)* 862
Barrymore, Ethel *(Cast)* 17, 2855, 4230
Barrymore, John *(Cast)* 515, 3686, 4185
Barrymore, Lionel *(Cast)* 2403
Barsky, Barbara *(Cast)* 871
Barsony, Rosy *(Cast)* 277
Barstow, Edith *(Choreographer)* 3715
Barstow, Richard *(Choreographer)* 304, 3107
Barstow, Richard *(Director)* 3715
Bart, Lionel *(Cast)* 2572
Bart, Lionel *(Composer)* 455, 874, 1089, 1277, 2368, 2572, 2682, 3271, 4469, 4685, 4749
Bart, Lionel *(Director)* 455, 4685
Bart, Lionel *(Librettist)* 455, 3271, 4469
Bart, Lionel *(Lyricist)* 455, 874, 1089, 1277, 2368, 2563, 2572, 2682, 3271, 4469, 4685, 4749
Bart, Roger *(Cast)* 4518
Barte, Leon *(Cast)* 4166
Bartel, Paul *(Librettist)* 1149
Bartel, Paul *(Screenwriter)* 1149
Bartels, Louis John *(Cast)* 1297
Bartes, John *(Cast)* 1047
Bartfeld, Carl *(Librettist)* 4328
Barth, Gene *(Costumes)* 2887
Barth, Lee *(Lyricist)* 3155
Bartholomae, Donald *(Librettist)* 4167
Bartholomae, Philip *(Author)* 2342, 4283, 4555
Bartholomae, Philip *(Librettist)* 1557, 1685, 2342, 2884, 3300, 3333, 4555, 4644
Bartholomae, Philip *(Lyricist)* 1557, 1685, 2884, 3300, 3333, 4644
Bartholomae, Philip *(Producer)* 2884, 4644
Bartlett, D'Jamin *(Cast)* 482, 1581, 2536, 4114, 4480
Bartlett, Harry *(Cast)* 3026
Bartlett, Josephine *(Cast)* 2697, 4497
Bartlett, Lisbeth *(Cast)* 264
Bartlett, Michael *(Cast)* 1329, 4365, 4372
Bartley, Dallas *(Composer)* 1296
Bartley, Dallas *(Lyricist)* 1296
Bartley, Nailbro *(Author)* 1796
Barto, Betty Lou *(Cast)* 206
Barton, Dewey *(Cast)* 1840
Barton, Earl *(Choreographer)* 2742
Barton, Fred *(Cast)* 1348
Barton, Fred *(Musical Director)* 1348, 2022
Barton, James *(Cast)* 397, 532, 1033, 2419, 3179, 3347, 3403, 3407, 3778, 3984, 4235, 4648
Barton, Julien *(Director)* 938
Barton, Mary *(Cast)* 2085
Barton, Steve *(Cast)* 3464, 3682
Barton, William *(Lyricist)* 1392
Bartow, Arthur *(Cast)* 2584, 3876
Bartsch, Michael *(Cast)* 1701
Barty, Billy *(Cast)* 1730

Baruch, Hugo *(Costumes)* 742
Baruch, Hugo *(Set Design)* 3092
Baruch, Moishe *(Producer)* 3669, 4463
Baruch, Steven *(Producer)* 992, 4031, 4076
Barzell, Wolfe *(Cast)* 4191
Barzin, Leon *(Musical Director)* 4548
Barzman, Ben *(Librettist)* 2809, 4316
Barzman, Sol *(Librettist)* 2809, 4316
Basie, Count *(Composer)* 4534
Basile, Frank *(Producer)* 2852
Baskcomb, A.W. *(Cast)* 1454, 2788
Baskerville, Priscilla *(Cast)* 1291, 4091
Baskette, Billy *(Composer)* 3401
Baskette, Billy *(Lyricist)* 4813
Baskette, Jimmie *(Cast)* 443, 1980, 1984
Basotina, James *(Cast)* 3938
Basquette, Lina *(Cast)* 4817
Bass, Emory *(Cast)* 2659, 3427, 3897
Bass, George Houston *(Lyricist)* 3001
Bass, Jules *(Director)* 928
Bass, Jules *(Lyricist)* 928, 2941, 3833, 4471
Bass, Jules *(Producer)* 928, 2941
Bass, Paul *(Cast)* 2690, 3054
Bass, R. *(Composer)* 4193
Bass, R. *(Lyricist)* 4193
Bass, Ralph *(Composer)* 4264
Bass, Ralph *(Lyricist)* 4264
Basse, Eli *(Librettist)* 4180
Bassett, John A. *(Librettist)* 2249
Bassett, John A. *(Lyricist)* 2249
Bassett, Peter *(Cast)* 3432
Bassman, Bruce D. *(Lighting Designer)* 4584
Bassman, George *(Composer)* 2809
Bassman, George *(Musical Director)* 2975
Bassman, George *(Orchestrations)* 59, 1706, 2809, 4827
Bataille, Henri *(Lyricist)* 4240
Batchelder, William H. *(Lighting Designer)* 1075
Batchelor, Ruth *(Lyricist)* 3619
Batchelor, W.H. *(Composer)* 45, 175, 1466
Batchelor, William H. *(Musical Director)* 1374
Bateman, Edgar *(Lyricist)* 3857
Bateman, James *(Lyricist)* 932
Bateman, R. *(Composer)* 4193
Bateman, R. *(Lyricist)* 4193
Bates, Blanche *(Cast)* 1502
Bates, Charles *(Cast)* 1646
Bates, Charles *(Lyricist)* 2135
Bates, Edna *(Cast)* 2184
Bates, Jerome Preston *(Cast)* 2239
Bates, Katherine Lee *(Lyricist)* 4390
Bates, Kathy *(Cast)* 3010
Bates, Lulu *(Cast)* 420, 1237, 1300, 3113
Bates, Peg Leg *(Cast)* 445, 886
Bates, Sally *(Cast)* 2739
Bates, Thorpe *(Cast)* 1610, 4760
Batie, Franklyn *(Cast)* 391, 1462
Batt, Bryan *(Cast)* 4217
Batt, Mike *(Lyricist)* 3464
Batten, Tom *(Cast)* 3279
Batterberry, Michael *(Director)* 1370
Batterberry, Michael *(Producer)* 1370
Battie, Franklyn *(Cast)* 3401
Battis, Emery *(Cast)* 951, 3195
Battista, Lloyd *(Cast)* 1377, 2320
Battista, Miriam *(Cast)* 1342, 1979
Battista, Miriam *(Librettist)* 4015
Battista, Miriam *(Lyricist)* 4015
Battle, Edwin *(Cast)* 1099, 2970
Battle, Hinton *(Cast)* 2905, 3932, 4091, 4286, 4722
Battle, Joseph *(Cast)* 303
Battle, Kathleen *(Cast)* 4447
Battles, George *(Cast)* 2302
Battles, John *(Cast)* 85, 3278, 4337
Bauduc, Ray *(Composer)* 964
Bauer, Felice *(Librettist)* 4609
Bauer, George *(Arrangements)* 382
Bauer, George *(Composer)* 4153
Bauer, George *(Dance Arranger)* 4153
Bauer, George *(Librettist)* 4153
Bauer, George *(Lyricist)* 4153
Bauer, George *(Musical Director)* 382, 2439, 4153
Bauer, George (Pianist) 2439
Bauer, George *(Vocal Arranger)* 4153
Bauer, Julius *(Author)* 2732
Baughan, Terry *(Cast)* 809
Baughman, Renee *(Cast)* 746
Baum, Bernie *(Composer)* 4264
Baum, Bernie *(Lyricist)* 4264
Baum, Gene *(Lighting Designer)* 177
Baum, Joanne *(Cast)* 3811
Baum, L. Frank *(Author)* 4381, 4722, 4723, 4725
Baum, L. Frank *(Librettist)* 4381, 4723, 4725
Baum, L. Frank *(Lyricist)* 4381, 4723, 4725
Baum, Marilyn *(Director)* 3034
Baum, Susan J. *(Cast)* 2055
Baum, Vicki *(Author)* 223, 1649
Bauman, John *(Musical Director)* 3824
Bauman, William *(Cast)* 4770
Baur, Franklin *(Cast)* 4821
Bautier, Michele *(Cast)* 4137
Bavaar, Tony *(Cast)* 3347
Bavan, Yolande *(Cast)* 756, 1809, 2236, 2433, 3824, 4035
Bawtree, Michael *(Director)* 599
Baxley, Barbara *(Cast)* 3918
Baxt, George *(Librettist)* 2554
Baxter, Alan *(Librettist)* 622, 2475, 3365, 4374
Baxter, George *(Cast)* 2595
Baxter, Gladys *(Cast)* 948, 3573
Baxter, Rebecca *(Cast)* 2199
Baxter, Skippy *(Cast)* 4143
Baxtresser, Suzanne *(Cast)* 1715
Bay, Howard *(Costumes)* 1959, 2727
Bay, Howard *(Director)* 206
Bay, Howard *(Lighting Designer)* 935, 1300, 1336, 1577, 1730, 1959, 2679, 2727, 2748, 2864, 3016, 3612, 3831, 4496, 4524, 4537
Bay, Howard *(Set Design)* 206, 653, 901, 935, 1300, 1336, 1577, 1730, 1959, 2175, 2234, 2510, 2679, 2727, 2748, 2755, 2850, 2864, 3016, 3180, 3301, 3536, 3612, 3831, 4058, 4117, 4496, 4524, 4537
Bayer, Carole
See also Carole Bayer Sager.

Bayer, Carole *(Lyricist)* 1497
Bayer, Gary *(Cast)* 1914
Bayes, Edna *(Cast)* 1961
Bayes, Nora *(Cast)* 805, 1847, 2232, 2373, 2528, 2696, 3623, 3751, 3755, 4033, 4801, 4802, 4803
Bayes, Nora *(Composer)* 2232, 2373, 2528, 2587, 2696, 2892, 3222, 3755, 4206, 4802, 4803
Bayes, Nora *(Lyricist)* 2373, 2528, 2892, 3222, 3623, 3755, 4390, 4802, 4803, 4823
Bayes, Nora *(Producer)* 1847, 2373
Bayes, Sammy *(Cast)* 2958
Bayes, Sammy *(Choreographer)* 634, 1809, 3653, 3927
Bayfield, St. Clair *(Cast)* 3567
Bayha, Charles *(Composer)* 545
Bayha, Charles *(Lyricist)* 545, 3962
Baylis, John *(Cast)* 227, 937, 2988
Bayliss, Gene *(Choreographer)* 1727, 1918
Baynes, Eustace *(Lyricist)* 954
Baynes, Sydney *(Composer)* 2004
Baynes, Sydney *(Musical Director)* 1333, 2004, 2467
Bayntun, Amelia *(Cast)* 455
Bayton, Ida *(Cast)* 1457
Beaber, Jack *(Choreographer)* 71
Beach, Albert *(Composer)* 4433
Beach, Albert *(Librettist)* 4433
Beach, Albert *(Lyricist)* 4433
Beach, Gary *(Cast)* 330, 583, 602, 753, 1077, 2146, 2422, 2949, 4022, 4062
Beach, Lillian *(Cast)* 2795
Beach, Rex *(Author)* 381
Beachner, Louis *(Cast)* 1497
Beadle, Spofford J. *(Producer)* 2472
Beagle, Peter S. *(Author)* 1276
Beal, John *(Cast)* 406, 1092, 2234
Beal, John *(Director)* 3107
Beale, Joseph *(Cast)* 4677
Beall, Diana *(Cast)* 453
Beam One, Ltd. *(Producer)* 3181
Bean, J.W. *(Cast)* 538
Bean, Orson
See also Orson Bean Productions.
Bean, Orson *(Cast)* 2106, 2227, 3097, 4190
Bean, Reathel *(Cast)* 394, 624, 1426, 2478, 2630, 3227, 3418, 3661, 4030, 4595
Bean Productions, Orson
See also Orson Bean.
Bean Productions, Orson *(Producer)* 1958
Beane *(Composer)* 4255
Beane, George A. *(Cast)* 2675, 3999
Beane, Reginald *(Cast)* 4191
Beane, Reginald *(Vocal Arranger)* 2712
Bear, Emily *(Cast)* 2197
Beard, Danny *(Cast)* 4722
Beard, Mark *(Set Design)* 2038
Bearden, Romare *(Set Design)* 3628
Beaton, Betzi *(Cast)* 1342, 4824
Beaton, Cecil *(Costumes)* 798, 1007, 3038, 3837, 4312
Beaton, Cecil *(Set Design)* 798, 3837, 4312
Beatts, Anne *(Librettist)* 1512, 2427
Beatty, Colin *(Cast)* 2096
Beatty, Ethel *(Cast)* 576, 1198, 3599
Beatty, John Lee *(Set Design)* 253, 942, 1268, 2152, 2555, 2578, 3671, 4076, 4162
Beatty, Roberta *(Cast)* 582, 3735, 4188
Beatty, Talley *(Cast)* 4117
Beatty, Talley *(Choreographer)* 52, 181, 279, 415, 593, 1319, 4788
Beau *(Cast)* 154
Beaubian, Susan *(Cast)* 1970
Beauchamp, Guy *(Librettist)* 814
Beaudet, Louise *(Cast)* 2179
Beaumont, Adrian *(Cast)* 730
Beaumont, John *(Lighting Designer)* 4678
Beaumont, John Henry *(Set Design)* 1395
Beaumont, Lucy *(Cast)* 758
Beaumont, Nellie *(Cast)* 677, 2343, 2714, 3604
Beaumont, Nelly *(Cast)* 2041
Beaumont, Ralph *(Cast)* 629
Beaumont, Ralph *(Choreographer)* 249, 3788, 3837, 4764
Beaumont, Rose *(Cast)* 677, 2714, 3604
Beaumont, Sascha *(Cast)* 1483
Beauvais, Jeanne *(Cast)* 2511
Beban, George *(Cast)* 8, 115, 1243, 1526, 1927, 2951, 3073
Bebee, Irving *(Cast)* 1312
Becaud, Gilbert *(Composer)* 1427, 3792
Becham, Larl *(Cast)* 3814
Becham, Larl *(Choreographer)* 3814
Becher, J.C. *(Set Design)* 1801
Becher, Thomas *(Costumes)* 98, 420, 673, 2227, 2460, 3107, 3108, 3110, 4374, 4567
Beck, Alexander *(Producer)* 4514
Beck, Arthur *(Orchestrations)* 3288
Beck, Bill *(Musical Director)* 973
Beck, Billy *(Lyricist)* 565
Beck, Francis *(Cast)* 2661
Beck, Jean Waldo *(Cast)* 1139
Beck, Lisa *(Set Design)* 562
Beck, Martin *(Producer)* 1197, 2666
Beck, Stu *(Cast)* 3714
Beck, Vincent *(Cast)* 90
Beck, William *(Cast)* 4541
Beck, William *(Composer)* 405
Beck, William *(Lyricist)* 405
Becke, Eve *(Cast)* 4159
Becker, Gerry *(Cast)* 4074
Becker, Lee
See also Lee Theodore
Becker, Lee *(Cast)* 4625
Becker, Randy *(Lighting Designer)* 2735
Becker, Thomas *(Costumes)* 817
Becker, Will H. *(Composer)* 2710
Becker, Will H. *(Lyricist)* 2710
Becker, William *(Composer)* 1531
Becker, William *(Lyricist)* 1531
Becker Bros. Studios *(Set Design)* 1423
Beckerman, Mara *(Cast)* 705
Becket, Rose *(Choreographer)* 2592
Beckett, Hal *(Dance Arranger)* 4006
Beckett, Hal *(Orchestrations)* 4006
Beckett, Hal *(Vocal Arranger)* 4006
Beckett, Samuel *(Librettist)* 3233
Beckham, Willard *(Cast)* 4062

Beckham, Willard *(Composer)* 2643
Beckham, Willard *(Librettist)* 2643
Beckham, Willard *(Lyricist)* 2643
Beckhard, Richard *(Cast)* 2175
Beckman, Al *(Producer)* 4323
Beckman, Irving *(Producer)* 268
Beckman, Roberta *(Composer)* 932
Becknell, Howard *(Lighting Designer)* 1081, 2388, 4173
Becknell, Howard *(Set Design)* 1081, 4173
Beckwith, Geraldine *(Costumes)* 796
Beckworth, Reginald *(Librettist)* 2168
Becton, Sheldon *(Composer)* 2239
Becton, Sheldon *(Lyricist)* 2239
Beda *(Lyricist)* 4730
Bedda Roses Company *(Producer)* 4398
Beddow, Margery *(Choreographer)* 4701
Bedella, Phyllis *(Cast)* 3213
Bedford, Brian *(Cast)* 134, 2260
Bedford-Lloyd, John *(Cast)* 3544
Bedini, Jean *(Librettist)* 3426
Bedsow, Len *(Producer)* 4090
Beebe, Hank *(Composer)* 1842, 2388, 4468
Beebe, Hank *(Librettist)* 1842, 4468
Beebe, Hank *(Lyricist)* 2388
Beebe, Harold *(Musical Director)* 2067
Beebe, Irving *(Cast)* 25, 130, 2756, 3466, 4241
Beecher, Janet *(Cast)* 3613
Beecher, Robert I. *(Lyricist)* 2793
Beecher, Sylvia *(Cast)* 3898
Beechman, Laurie *(Cast)* 150, 789, 2242
Beekman, Jack *(Producer)* 2551
Beer, Alice *(Costumes)* 1651
Beerbohm, Max *(Author)* 1761
Beere, Donald C. *(Composer)* 6
Beers, Francine *(Cast)* 942
Beerwald, Ben *(Lighting Designer)* 2907, 3727, 4812
Beery, Leigh *(Cast)* 496, 1739, 2565, 3734, 4002
Beery, Wallace *(Cast)* 4762
Beery Sr., Noah *(Cast)* 4524
Beeson, Jack *(Composer)* 643
Beeson, Larry *(Composer)* 1136
Beethoven, Ludwig *(Music Based On)* 3014
Beewald, Ben *(Lighting Designer)* 4813
Begley, Edward *(Cast)* 3675
Behar, Joy *(Cast)* 826
Behman, L.C. *(Producer)* 1640
Behn, Noel *(Producer)* 1194
Behrman, S.N. *(Author)* 1660, 2450, 3880
Behrman, S.N. *(Librettist)* 1242, 3880
Beigel, Victor *(Composer)* 934
Beiner, Arthur L. *(Composer)* 3617
Beiner, Arthur L. *(Lyricist)* 3617
Beisner, M. Eliot *(Cast)* 3227
Bekins, Richard *(Cast)* 1762
Bel Geddes, Edith Lutyens *(Costumes)* 1062, 2306
Bel Geddes, Norman *(Costumes)* 1196, 2161, 2162
Bel Geddes, Norman *(Lighting Designer)* 1196, 1322
Bel Geddes, Norman *(Set Design)* 685, 827, 1196, 1272, 1297, 1322, 2161, 2162, 2376, 3312, 4819
Belafonte, Harry *(Cast)* 1389, 2227, 4346
Belafonte, Harry *(Composer)* 2227
Belafonte, Harry *(Lyricist)* 2227
Belanger, Michael *(Cast)* 3606
Belasco, David *(Author)* 2309, 2340, 3532, 4066
Belasco, David *(Director)* 2309, 4066
Belasco, David *(Lyricist)* 4066
Belasco, David *(Producer)* 2309, 4066
Belasco, Grace *(Cast)* 2500, 4125
Belasco, Jacques *(Composer)* 1539
Belasco, Jacques *(Orchestrations)* 1539
Belasco, Jacques *(Vocal Arranger)* 1539
Belasco, Leon *(Cast)* 1760, 3972
Belaver, Harry *(Cast)* 4368
Belden, Ursula *(Set Design)* 2049, 3631, 4618
Belew, Bill *(Costumes)* 272, 427
Belfer, Harold *(Choreographer)* 1680
Belgrader, Andrei *(Director)* 2945, 3853
Belgrader, Andrei *(Librettist)* 3853
Belknap, Allen R. *(Director)* 3539
Bell, Charles W. *(Librettist)* 977, 1174, 3369
Bell, David H. *(Choreographer)* 690, 4618, 4703
Bell, David H. *(Director)* 690, 1172, 4618, 4703
Bell, Digby *(Cast)* 694, 2982, 3625
Bell, Florence *(Cast)* 4556
Bell, Ida *(Costumes)* 567
Bell, James *(Cast)* 2311
Bell, Laura Jones *(Cast)* 3625
Bell, Laura Joyce *(Cast)* 4103
Bell, Marie *(Cast)* 449
Bell, Marion *(Cast)* 530, 1085
Bell, Marjorie *(Cast)* 2504
Bell, Richard *(Producer)* 576
Bell, S.N. *(Composer)* 4193
Bell, S.N. *(Lyricist)* 4193
Bellamy, Claxson *(Author)* 1193
Bellamy, Claxson *(Librettist)* 1193
Bellamy, Claxson *(Lyricist)* 1193
Bellamy, Franklyn *(Cast)* 822
Bellamy, Ned *(Cast)* 655
Belland, B. *(Composer)* 4193
Belland, B. *(Lyricist)* 4193
Belland, Bruce *(Librettist)* 3629
Belland, Bruce *(Lyricist)* 3629
Bellaver, Harry *(Cast)* 153
Belle, Augusta *(Cast)* 4439
Belledna, Alex *(Composer)* 3297
Belledna, Alex *(Librettist)* 3361
Bellenda, Alex *(Composer)* 478
Bellesen, Pearl *(Costumes)* 3901
Bellesen, Pearl *(Set Design)* 3901
Bellew, Cosmo *(Cast)* 1014
Belling, Andy *(Lyricist)* 1159
Bellini, Cal *(Cast)* 1848
Bellote, Pete *(Composer)* 3739
Bellote, Pete *(Lyricist)* 3739
Bellson, Louis *(Composer)* 3543
Bellwood, Peter *(Librettist)* 1441
Belmont, Grace *(Cast)* 1543, 2343, 2906, 3883
Belmonte, Vicki *(Cast)* 3211
Belmore, Bertha *(Cast)* 601, 4569
Belson, Jerry *(Screenwriter)* 4020
Belson, Susan *(Cast)* 1478

Belt, Madeline *(Cast)* 1989, 2034
Belton, John *(Cast)* 4556
Belushi, John *(Cast)* 3077
Belushi, John *(Librettist)* 3076
Belzer, Rick *(Lighting Designer)* 172, 1732, 2759
Ben-Ami, Jacob *(Cast)* 4773
Ben-Ari, Neal *(Cast)* 721
Ben-Zali, Daniel *(Cast)* 3015
Benatzky, Ralph *(Author)* 795, 2610, 2808
Benatzky, Ralph *(Composer)* 659, 795, 2419, 2610, 2808, 4667
Benatzky, Ralph *(Lyricist)* 2808
Benavente, Jacinto *(Author)* 3412
Benavente, Joseph *(Musical Director)* 138
Benbow, William M. *(Cast)* 4112
Benbow, William M. *(Producer)* 4112
Benchley, Nathaniel *(Librettist)* 4039
Benchley, Robert *(Cast)* 3008
Benchley, Robert *(Librettist)* 1357
Benczak, Margaret *(Cast)* 4527
Benda, G.K. *(Costumes)* 133, 702, 704
Bendel, Henri *(Costumes)* 2216
Bendell, Alfred *(Musical Director)* 3237
Bender, Milton *(Director)* 3130, 4780
Bender, Milton *(Librettist)* 4780
Bender, Milton G. *(Composer)* 3296
Bender, Milton G. *(Director)* 3296
Bender, Milton G. *(Lyricist)* 4780
Bendix *(Composer)* 3981
Bendix, Charles *(Composer)* 2952
Bendix, Max *(Choreographer)* 102
Bendix, Max *(Composer)* 742
Bendix, Max *(Musical Director)* 670, 3537, 4119
Bendix, Theodore *(Composer)* 830
Bendix, Theodore *(Musical Director)* 4012
Beneboch, Julian *(Musical Director)* 2407
Beneby, Lehman *(Cast)* 10, 4055
Benedek, Paul *(Producer)* 4794
Benedict, Diane *(Cast)* 4389
Benedict, Gail *(Cast)* 1075
Benes, Jara *(Composer)* 702, 4667
Benet, Laura *(Librettist)* 2653
Benet, Stephen Vincent *(Author)* 2229, 3888
Benham, Earl *(Cast)* 801, 803, 1154
Beniades, Ted *(Cast)* 1354, 4028
Benjamin, Bennie *(Composer)* 3695
Benjamin, Bennie *(Lyricist)* 3695
Benjamin, Carla *(Cast)* 922
Benjamin, Fred *(Choreographer)* 4089
Benjamin, Joseph *(Librettist)* 3725
Benjamin, P.J. *(Cast)* 143, 699, 2289, 3838, 4091, 4701
Benjamin School for Girls *(Producer)* 738, 2102, 3595
Bennet, Harriet *(Cast)* 4719
Bennett *(Composer)* 4683
Bennett *(Lyricist)* 4683
Bennett, Alan *(Cast)* 384
Bennett, Alan *(Librettist)* 384
Bennett, Arnold *(Author)* 989
Bennett, Bernie *(Composer)* 4260
Bennett, Bernie *(Lyricist)* 4260
Bennett, David *(Arrangements)* 132
Bennett, David *(Choreographer)* 21, 133, 381, 930, 994, 1011, 1096, 1128, 1131, 1132, 1308, 1588, 1603, 1829, 1911, 2174, 2264, 2387, 2430, 2570, 2628, 2638, 2686, 2739, 2757, 2972, 3063, 3193, 3207, 3246, 3254, 3508, 3538, 3623, 3712, 3772, 4012, 4212, 4345, 4424, 4555, 4575, 4694
Bennett, David *(Director)* 380, 2739, 2960, 4424
Bennett, Evelyn *(Cast)* 1617
Bennett, Florence *(Cast)* 116
Bennett, George J. *(Lyricist)* 1694
Bennett, Harry Gordon *(Set Design)* 966, 3336
Bennett, Joan *(Cast)* 2267
Bennett, Johnstone *(Cast)* 1259
Bennett, Jordan *(Cast)* 949
Bennett, Joseph *(Composer)* 3178
Bennett, Joseph *(Lyricist)* 3178
Bennett, Keith Robert *(Cast)* 1890
Bennett, Leo *(Composer)* 2358
Bennett, Mark *(Composer)* 2037, 2488
Bennett, Mark *(Lyricist)* 2488
Bennett, Matthew *(Cast)* 838, 2046
Bennett, Meg *(Cast)* 1664
Bennett, Michael *(Cast)* 269, 4190
Bennett, Michael *(Choreographer)* 287, 746, 798, 832, 1103, 1329, 1846, 2248, 3603, 3869
Bennett, Michael *(Director)* 287, 746, 1103, 1329, 3852, 3869, 4474
Bennett, Michael *(Librettist)* 3869
Bennett, Michael *(Producer)* 287, 1103
Bennett, Milton *(Composer)* 3695
Bennett, Milton *(Lyricist)* 3695
Bennett, Richard *(Cast)* 1267
Bennett, Robert Russell *(Composer)* 372, 1283, 1932, 3583
Bennett, Robert Russell *(Dance Arranger)* 3703
Bennett, Robert Russell *(Incidental Music)* 1749
Bennett, Robert Russell *(Lyricist)* 3703, 4424
Bennett, Robert Russell *(Orchestrations)* 44, 82, 85, 111, 134, 153, 163, 189, 216, 294, 363, 462, 466, 512, 603, 623, 653, 672, 759, 773, 901, 930, 961, 1109, 1202, 1225, 1278, 1315, 1322, 1342, 1453, 1493, 1528, 1534, 1564, 1662, 1679, 1689, 1745, 1800, 1811, 1879, 1932, 1979, 2103, 2115, 2137, 2187, 2201, 2252, 2268, 2312, 2331, 2423, 2475, 2479, 2569, 2595, 2597, 2638, 2691, 2777, 2786, 2847, 3014, 3038, 3113, 3214, 3225, 3263, 3274, 3291, 3326, 3359, 3365, 3379, 3386, 3505, 3622, 3674, 3687, 3699, 3703, 3735, 3743, 3772, 3850, 3949, 3993, 4001, 4058, 4077, 4095, 4096, 4150, 4212, 4234, 4267, 4314, 4323, 4337, 4361, 4362, 4366, 4446, 4557, 4583, 4609, 4694, 4818, 4819, 4825, 4828
Bennett, Robert Russell *(Vocal Arranger)* 3703
Bennett, Russell
See also Robert Russell Bennett.
Bennett, Sid *(Lighting Designer)* 3932
Bennett, Stanley *(Musical Director)* 691, 981
Bennett, Stanley *(Vocal Arranger)* 691
Bennett, Terry *(Set Design)* 564
Bennett, Thomas *(Choreographer)* 1866
Bennett, Virgil *(Choreographer)* 3877
Bennett, Virgil *(Director)* 1550, 1556
Bennett, Wilda *(Cast)* 168, 1210, 1527, 2666, 3006, 3304, 3727

Bennett Sisters *(Lyricist)* 487
Bennington, Whitney *(Musical Director)* 2986
Bennison, Louis *(Cast)* 1026
Benny, Jack *(Cast)* 536, 1135, 1395, 1416, 1678, 3153
Benrimo *(Author)* 718
Benrimo *(Director)* 93, 473, 1530, 1629, 1735, 2620, 3087, 3193, 3256, 3865
Benrimo, J.H. *(Director)* 2390, 3424, 4620
Benskin, Sammy *(Conductor)* 766
Benskin, Sammy *(Dance Arranger)* 415
Benskin, Sammy *(Musical Director)* 279, 415
Benskin, Sammy *(Orchestrations)* 279
Benskin, Sammy *(Vocal Arranger)* 415
Benson, Ada *(Composer)* 39
Benson, Ada *(Lyricist)* 39
Benson, Cindy *(Cast)* 1149
Benson, Jerry *(Composer)* 4427
Benson, Jerry *(Lyricist)* 4427
Benson, Jodi *(Cast)* 921, 4020, 4619
Benson, Marion J. *(Cast)* 540
Benson, Robby *(Cast)* 3780
Benson, Sally *(Author)* 2805
Benson, Sally *(Librettist)* 2817, 3895
Bent, Marion *(Cast)* 994, 2601, 3717, 3911
Benthall, Michael *(Director)* 798, 2075
Bentham, M.S. *(Musical Director)* 1292
Bentley, Earlene *(Cast)* 730
Bentley, Gladys *(Cast)* 3782, 4501
Bentley, Irene *(Cast)* 350, 356, 666, 1535, 2181, 2869, 4181, 4691
Bentley, Jordan *(Cast)* 4734
Bentley, Mary Denise *(Cast)* 1350
Bentley, W.H. *(Cast)* 3658
Bentley, W.H. *(Director)* 3658
Bentley, William H. *(Cast)* 1535
Benton, Fremont *(Cast)* 1553
Benton, Kirsten *(Cast)* 2651
Benton, Nicholas *(Producer)* 3818
Benton, Robert *(Librettist)* 2163, 3233
Bents, Kevin *(Composer)* 1232
Benzell, Mimi *(Cast)* 2864
Benzinger, Suzy *(Costumes)* 36, 2905
Berc, Shelley *(Librettist)* 3853
Berens, Susan *(Cast)* 2084, 2096
Bereny, Henry *(Author)* 2495
Bereny, Henry *(Composer)* 1538, 2495
Beres, Bertha *(Costumes)* 4328
Beresford, Evelyn *(Cast)* 4368
Beresovsky, S. *(Composer)* 1609
Beretta, Joanne *(Cast)* 788, 809
Berezowsky, Sol *(Composer)* 2421
Berg, Barry *(Librettist)* 3019
Berg, Christopher *(Arrangements)* 4830
Berg, Christopher *(Composer)* 260, 4830
Berg, Christopher *(Musical Director)* 4830
Berg, Gertrude *(Author)* 2925
Berg, Harold *(Producer)* 4021
Berg, Jimmy *(Cast)* 1413
Berg, Leon *(Composer)* 513
Berg, Lynn *(Cast)* 2433
Berg, Richard *(Librettist)* 1969
Berg, Sallie *(Cast)* 2863
Berg, Tony *(Dance Arranger)* 1262
Berg, Tony *(Vocal Arranger)* 1262
Berge, Irenee *(Composer)* 303
Bergen, Edgar *(Cast)* 2406
Bergen, Jerry *(Cast)* 3810
Bergen, Nella *(Cast)* 527, 698, 1388
Bergen, Polly *(Cast)* 1290, 2227
Berger, Jessie Ira *(Lighting Designer)* 3202
Berger, Keith *(Cast)* 562
Berger, Keith *(Composer)* 562
Berger, Keith *(Librettist)* 562
Berger, Keith *(Lyricist)* 562
Berger, Richard *(Producer)* 1476
Berger, Stephen *(Cast)* 1510, 1832, 2992, 3178
Berger, Ted *(Librettist)* 3939
Berger, Ted *(Lyricist)* 3939
Berger, Walter *(Librettist)* 4611
Bergeron, George *(Costumes)* 3561
Bergersen, Baldwin *(Composer)* 70, 84, 621, 651, 937, 3178, 3226, 3764, 4018, 4498, 4677, 4826
Bergersen, Baldwin *(Musical Director)* 937
Bergerson, Baldwin *(Composer)* 2168
Berghof, Herbert *(Cast)* 2894
Berghof, Herbert *(Director)* 1062, 1413, 3698
Bergman, Alan *(Lyricist)* 287, 1298, 2079, 4060
Bergman, Ben *(Composer)* 1532
Bergman, Caryl *(Cast)* 4234
Bergman, Henry *(Cast)* 1518, 2863, 3363, 4045, 4440
Bergman, Ingmar *(Author)* 2536, 3456
Bergman, Marilyn *(Lyricist)* 287, 1298, 2079, 4060
Bergman, Peter *(Lyricist)* 4405
Bergman, Sandahl *(Cast)* 964, 1511
Bergman Studios *(Set Design)* 376
Bergner, Elisabeth *(Director)* 3335
Beri, Maude Lillian *(Cast)* 1650
Berk, Phyllis *(Cast)* 1609
Berkeley, Busby *(Cast)* 3556
Berkeley, Busby *(Choreographer)* 834, 1113, 1134, 1617, 1935, 2140, 2380, 3150, 3172, 3523, 3556, 3650, 4170, 4235, 4240, 4692
Berkeley, Busby *(Director)* 1113, 1577, 4170
Berkeley, Busby *(Producer)* 4170
Berkeley, Edward *(Director)* 1985, 3817, 4294
Berkman, Jesse *(Composer)* 1880
Berkman, Jesse *(Lyricist)* 1880
Berkman, John *(Composer)* 1329
Berkman, John *(Dance Arranger)* 823, 1329, 1662, 1841, 2217, 3506, 4029, 4196, 4577
Berkman, John *(Musical Director)* 1841, 2874
Berkman, John *(Vocal Arranger)* 2874
Berkowitz, Judith *(Costumes)* 1958
Berkowitz, Sol *(Cast)* 2958
Berkowitz, Sol *(Composer)* 2887, 3210, 3940, 3942
Berkowitz, Sol *(Dance Arranger)* 4516
Berkowitz, Sol *(Lyricist)* 3940
Berkshire Boys' Choir *(Cast)* 2775
Berkson, Michael *(Cast)* 3956
Berla, Emil *(Cast)* 4492
Berle, Milton *(Cast)* 1137, 1397, 2653, 3153, 3822, 4117, 4152, 4826

Berle, Milton *(Composer)* 924, 1415, 1892
Berle, Milton *(Lyricist)* 924, 3822, 3926
Berle, Milton *(Producer)* 3895
Berlin, Irving *(Cast)* 1399, 3006, 3153, 4340, 4521, 4770
Berlin, Irving *(Composer)* 25, 60, 79, 94, 149, 153, 207, 376, 545, 619, 627, 683, 789, 799, 805, 959, 1042, 1208, 1225, 1247, 1298, 1327, 1398, 1399, 1416, 1488, 1501, 1519, 1598, 1685, 1686, 1738, 1793, 1813, 1920, 1927, 2184, 2205, 2261, 2294, 2301, 2363, 2525, 2597, 2894, 2983, 3006, 3007, 3008, 3009, 3031, 3079, 3096, 3175, 3258, 3395, 3412, 3627, 3658, 3665, 3791, 3827, 3917, 3926, 3946, 3962, 4045, 4131, 4144, 4148, 4153, 4154, 4158, 4159, 4206, 4264, 4340, 4399, 4440, 4603, 4655, 4714, 4770, 4799, 4804, 4805, 4806, 4810, 4812, 4813, 4814, 4815, 4821, 4829, 4831, 4840, 4842, 4852
Berlin, Irving *(Librettist)* 1225
Berlin, Irving *(Lyricist)* 25, 60, 79, 94, 149, 153, 179, 207, 376, 511, 545, 619, 627, 683, 789, 799, 805, 959, 1042, 1208, 1225, 1247, 1298, 1327, 1398, 1399, 1416, 1488, 1501, 1523, 1550, 1598, 1685, 1686, 1738, 1793, 1813, 1920, 1927, 2184, 2205, 2232, 2294, 2301, 2363, 2525, 2597, 2894, 2983, 3006, 3007, 3008, 3009, 3031, 3079, 3096, 3175, 3258, 3395, 3412, 3627, 3658, 3665, 3791, 3827, 3917, 3926, 3946, 3962, 4045, 4131, 4144, 4148, 4153, 4154, 4158, 4159, 4206, 4264, 4340, 4399, 4440, 4493, 4521, 4603, 4655, 4770, 4799, 4804, 4805, 4806, 4810, 4812, 4813, 4814, 4821, 4829, 4831, 4840, 4842, 4852, 4853
Berlin, Irving *(Producer)* 2894
Berlin, Spencer H. *(Producer)* 4601
Berlind, Roger *(Producer)* 154, 393, 450, 775, 1262, 2205, 3015, 3175, 3411, 3702, 3718, 4091
Berlind, Roger S. *(Producer)* 3171
Berliner, Rudolf *(Musical Director)* 1746
Berlinger, Warren *(Cast)* 550
Berman, David *(Cast)* 3908
Berman, M. *(Costumes)* 972
Berman, Marjorie *(Cast)* 3631
Berman, Norman L. (Additional Music) 4176
Berman, Norman L. *(Director)* 4517
Berman, Norman L. *(Musical Director)* 4176
Berman, Norman L. *(Orchestrations)* 4176
Berman, Norman L. *(Vocal Arranger)* 2320, 4176, 4517
Berman, Shelley *(Cast)* 1237, 1567
Berman and Sons, Max *(Costumes)* 408
Bern, Mina *(Cast)* 2356, 2421, 4342
Bernal, Barry K. *(Cast)* 2905
Bernard, Ada *(Cast)* 618, 2343
Bernard, Barney *(Cast)* 506, 2358, 4553, 4655, 4802
Bernard, Ben *(Director)* 439
Bernard, Ben *(Lyricist)* 439
Bernard, Ben *(Producer)* 439
Bernard, Billy *(Lyricist)* 3241
Bernard, Felix *(Composer)* 25, 3955, 4824
Bernard, Felix *(Lyricist)* 4824
Bernard, Francis *(Cast)* 3490
Bernard, Henri *(Author)* 4624
Bernard, Loraine *(Cast)* 1521
Bernard, Lygia *(Costumes)* 2275
Bernard, Mitchell *(Lyricist)* 747
Bernard, Nan *(Cast)* 4120
Bernard, Olive P. *(Set Design)* 2040
Bernard, Peter *(Composer)* 377
Bernard, Peter *(Lyricist)* 377
Bernard, Sam *(Cast)* 68, 208, 350, 351, 666, 683, 976, 1523, 1537, 1578, 1793, 1926, 2725, 3006, 3085, 3489, 3710, 3753, 3976
Bernard, Sam *(Director)* 364
Bernard, Sam *(Librettist)* 364, 3144
Bernard, Tristan *(Author)* 2025, 2497
Bernard Jr., Sam *(Lyricist)* 364
Bernardi, Herschel *(Cast)* 269, 4862
Bernauer, Rudolf *(Author)* 1561, 2469, 2794, 4121
Bernauer, Rudolph *(Author)* 742
Bernhard, Arnold *(Producer)* 1776
Bernie, Al *(Cast)* 242, 622, 855
Bernie, Ben *(Cast)* 1859, 2739
Bernie, Ben *(Composer)* 393, 3905
Bernie, Ben *(Lyricist)* 3905
Bernier, Buddy *(Composer)* 1296
Bernier, Buddy *(Lyricist)* 1296, 3647
Bernier, Peggy *(Cast)* 4778
Berns, Bert *(Composer)* 3695
Berns, Bert *(Lyricist)* 3695
Bernstein, Aline *(Cast)* 1655
Bernstein, Aline *(Costumes)* 1652, 1653, 1654, 1655, 1656, 1657, 2510, 3691
Bernstein, Aline *(Set Design)* 1652, 1654, 1655, 1656, 1657
Bernstein, B. *(Cast)* 907
Bernstein, Douglas *(Cast)* 262, 2790, 3960, 4533
Bernstein, Douglas *(Composer)* 262, 3181, 3960, 4533
Bernstein, Douglas *(Librettist)* 262, 1832, 3181, 3960
Bernstein, Douglas *(Lyricist)* 262, 3181, 3960, 4533
Bernstein, Elmer *(Composer)* 2010, 2014, 2820
Bernstein, Elmer *(Incidental Music)* 3453
Bernstein, Ira *(Producer)* 1497, 1611, 3175
Bernstein, Leonard *(Composer)* 72, 599, 630, 1214, 1294, 2205, 2411, 2677, 2775, 3018, 3278, 3452, 3967, 4004, 4008, 4625, 4734
Bernstein, Leonard *(Incidental Music)* 2411
Bernstein, Leonard *(Lyricist)* 72, 599, 630, 1294, 2411, 2677, 2775, 3278, 3452
Bernstein, Leonard
See also The Revuers
Bernstein, Leonard *(Orchestrations)* 630, 3278, 4625
Bernstein, Lisa *(Cast)* 4309
Bernstein, Richard N. *(Librettist)* 4785
Bernstein, Robert A. *(Librettist)* 90
Bernstein, Robert A. *(Lyricist)* 4388
Bernstein, Rube *(Librettist)* 1532
Bernstein, Sid *(Producer)* 2248, 2440
Bernstein, Stanley *(Producer)* 2440
Bernstein, Sue Renee *(Cast)* 4470
Berr, Georges *(Author)* 2808, 3251, 3494
Berra, Mabel *(Cast)* 1197
Berri, Beth *(Cast)* 2180, 2308
Berri, Maude Lillian *(Cast)* 2035, 4201
Berrington & Berrington *(Cast)* 986
Berry, Ada *(Cast)* 3202
Berry, Chu *(Composer)* 887
Berry, Chu *(Lyricist)* 887
Berry, Chuck *(Composer)* 3739, 4534

Berry, Chuck *(Lyricist)* 3739, 4534
Berry, Eliza *(Cast)* 2704
Berry, Eric *(Cast)* 507, 3506
Berry, Gabriel *(Costumes)* 494
Berry, John *(Cast)* 2175
Berry, John *(Director)* 273
Berry, Ken *(Cast)* 407, 408, 410, 411, 413
Berry, Leigh *(Cast)* 946, 3479
Berry, Lillian *(Cast)* 1088
Berry, Lydia *(Cast)* 3701
Berry, Mary Sue *(Cast)* 623
Berry, Scott *(Orchestrations)* 2074
Berry, W.H. *(Cast)* 1534, 1610, 3583
Berry Brothers *(Cast)* 847, 3639
Berry Brothers, The *(Cast)* 443, 883, 887, 3704, 3709
Berryhill, Robert *(Composer)* 3695
Berryhill, Robert *(Lyricist)* 3695
Berskon, Michael *(Cast)* 1736
Bert, Florence *(Cast)* 1923
Bertal-Maubon *(Lyricist)* 3617
Berte, Emil *(Author)* 3012
Berte, Emil *(Composer)* 3012
Berte, Heinrich *(Author)* 3776
Berte, Heinrich *(Composer)* 3776
Berte, Heinrich *(Music Based On)* 463
Bertelsen, Paul *(Lighting Designer)* 3816
Bertelsen, Paul *(Set Design)* 3816
Bertha, Istvan *(Author)* 4669
Berthald, Barron *(Cast)* 3732
Berthe, Mme. *(Costumes)* 1874
Berthel, Louise *(Cast)* 340
Bertin, Albert *(Musical Director)* 1462
Bertish, Suzanne *(Cast)* 2474
Berton, Charles *(Composer)* 2944
Berton, Charles *(Musical Director)* 1182, 2944
Berton, Charles *(Orchestrations)* 1182
Berton, Eugene *(Composer)* 4484
Berton, Eugene *(Librettist)* 2595
Berton, Eugene *(Lyricist)* 4484
Berton, Eugene L. *(Composer)* 720
Berton, Pierre *(Librettist)* 4627
Berton, Ralph *(Composer)* 4484
Berton, Ralph *(Librettist)* 4484
Berton, Ralph *(Lyricist)* 4484
Bertoncini, G. *(Composer)* 1370
Bertram, Helen *(Cast)* 1515, 2500, 4559
Beruh, Joseph *(Cast)* 4369
Beruh, Joseph *(Producer)* 547, 825, 1184, 1595, 2339, 2687, 3159, 3602
Besch, Betty Ann *(Producer)* 1999
Besier, Rudolf *(Author)* 3734
Besoyan, Rick *(Cast)* 1883
Besoyan, Rick *(Composer)* 249, 1883, 2522, 4186
Besoyan, Rick *(Director)* 249, 2522, 4186
Besoyan, Rick *(Librettist)* 249, 2522, 4186
Besoyan, Rick *(Lyricist)* 249, 1883, 2522, 4186
Besser, Joe *(Cast)* 2103, 3409, 4086
Bessinger *(Composer)* 1460
Bessoir, Bob *(Lighting Designer)* 1279
Bessoir, Robert *(Lighting Designer)* 3926, 4769
Bessy, Maurice *(Author)* 2318
Best, Dolly *(Cast)* 1404
Best, Edna *(Cast)* 4207
Best, Monique *(Cast)* 3769
Best, Paul *(Cast)* 3767
Besterman, Brian *(Orchestrations)* 4255
Besterman, Douglas *(Musical Director)* 4229
Besterman, Douglas *(Orchestrations)* 1509, 2185, 2229, 3306
Besterman, Douglas *(Vocal Arranger)* 4229
Bestor, Vernon *(Musical Director)* 3677
Beswick, Harry *(Lyricist)* 2469
Betancourt, Jeffrey
See also Jeffrey Betancourt Prods.
Bethel, MacSlator *(Composer)* 1867
Bethel, Pepsi *(Choreographer)* 1425, 4127
Bethune, Zina *(Cast)* 2550, 2961
Betie, Franklyn *(Producer)* 1462
Betmar *(Producer)* 338
Better Company, The *(Producer)* 2171
Bettger, Lyle *(Cast)* 2615
Betti, Henri *(Composer)* 1326, 2356, 4264
Bettinelli, Angelo *(Composer)* 364
Bettinson, Rob *(Director)* 580
Bettis, John *(Lyricist)* 2651, 4229
Bettis, Valerie *(Cast)* 454, 1679, 2137
Bettis, Valerie *(Choreographer)* 341, 1577, 3551
Bettis, Valerie *(Lyricist)* 4585
Betts, Dorothy *(Cast)* 4269
Betts, Jack *(Cast)* 33, 1294, 1697
Beule, Carol H. *(Costumes)* 2231
Beury, James P. *(Producer)* 2071, 4651
Bevan, Alison *(Cast)* 1510, 4454
Bevan, Frank *(Costumes)* 2344, 3703
Bevans, Philippa *(Cast)* 2313, 3038, 3816, 4155, 4541
Beverley, Trazana *(Cast)* 1344
Bey, Andy *(Cast)* 2784
Bey, Salome *(Cast)* 1116, 2618, 4788
Beyer, Herman *(Director)* 2567
Bhaskar *(Cast)* 4623
Bhaskar *(Choreographer)* 4623
Bhise, Swati Gupte *(Choreographer)* 4442
Bhumibol *(Composer)* 2850
Bhumibol *(Lyricist)* 2850
Bialik, C.N. *(Lyricist)* 1609
Bianco, Joe *(Lyricist)* 1201
Bibb, Leon *(Cast)* 3831
Bibevran, Mimert *(Choreographer)* 2156
Bibo, Irving *(Composer)* 1131, 1343, 3369, 4815
Bibo, Irving *(Lyricist)* 25, 200, 1343, 1687, 2446, 2461, 4100
Bicat, Nick *(Composer)* 2346
Bichel, Ken *(Cast)* 2058
Bichel, Ken *(Musical Director)* 482
Bichel, Kenneth *(Orchestrations)* 3169
Bickel, George *(Cast)* 558, 771, 1335, 1482, 1712, 3369, 3977, 4801, 4802, 4804
Bickell, Ross *(Cast)* 3598
Bickerstaff Productions *(Producer)* 4401
Biddle, Nicholas *(Composer)* 2842
Biddle, Nicholas *(Lyricist)* 2851
Bidgood, James *(Costumes)* 1878
Bieber, Ethel *(Lyricist)* 1974
Biedermann, Edouard *(Set Design)* 2286

Bieff-Herrera *(Costumes)* 1249
Bienbryer, Eddie *(Composer)* 4291
Bienstock, Miriam *(Producer)* 4176
Bierbower, Neil *(Set Design)* 1377
Bierman, Emil *(Composer)* 3129
Biern, Harvey *(Composer)* 2039
Biern, Natalie *(Lyricist)* 2039
Big Rosie *(Cast)* 2258
Bigard, Barney *(Composer)* 4091
Bigard, Barney *(Lyricist)* 4091
Bigelow, Charles A. *(Cast)* 88, 1188, 1213, 1392, 1540, 1881, 2500, 2506, 2722, 2892, 3363, 3387, 4473, 4590
Bigelow, Dorothie *(Cast)* 3865
Bigelow, Dorothie *(Composer)* 4600
Bigelow, Dorothie *(Lyricist)* 4600
Bigelow, Joe *(Librettist)* 1112
Bigelow, Robert *(Composer)* 2135
Bigelow, Roger *(Cast)* 2660
Bigelow, Susan *(Cast)* 1038, 2142, 3201, 4744
Biggers, Earl Derr *(Librettist)* 3868
Biggers, Earl Derr *(Lyricist)* 3868
Bigley, Isabel *(Cast)* 1706, 2797
Bigtree, Norma *(Cast)* 941
Bikel, Theodore *(Cast)* 615, 2313, 2411, 3551, 4095
Bilhaud, Paul *(Author)* 3363
Bilik, Jerry *(Composer)* 3840
Bilik, Jerry *(Director)* 3840
Bilik, Jerry *(Librettist)* 3840
Bilik, Jerry *(Lyricist)* 3840
Billig, M. *(Composer)* 1957
Billig, Robert *(Conductor)* 373, 1638, 2320, 3088
Billig, Robert *(Musical Director)* 273, 374, 1873, 2442, 2544, 3992
Billig, Robert *(Vocal Arranger)* 374, 1638, 2544
Billings, James *(Cast)* 2839
Billings, Jef *(Set Design)* 2969
Billington, Ken *(Lighting Designer)* 36, 107, 146, 154, 155, 478, 593, 869, 1038, 1068, 1146, 1186, 1372, 1671, 1699, 1762, 2204, 2420, 2521, 2607, 2677, 2689, 2805, 2846, 3279, 3444, 3565, 3628, 3637, 3682, 3743, 3792, 3936, 3967, 4003, 4034, 4035, 4136, 4137, 4233, 4264, 4279, 4343, 4349, 4731, 4744
Billone, Joseph *(Director)* 198
Billy Rose Foundation
See also Rose, Billy
Billy Rose Foundation *(Producer)* 2260
Bilowit, Ira J. *(Librettist)* 3224
Bilowit, Ira J. *(Lyricist)* 3224
Bilowit, Ira J. *(Producer)* 3224
Bimonte, David *(Lyricist)* 3615
Binder, Jay *(Director)* 1797
Bindley, Florence *(Cast)* 361, 1520
Bindley, Florence *(Composer)* 1520
Bindley, Florence *(Lyricist)* 1520
Bingham, Amelia *(Cast)* 977, 1806
Bingham, Bob *(Cast)* 2212
Bingham, G. Clifton *(Composer)* 1897
Bingham, G. Clifton *(Lyricist)* 1897
Bingham, Marie *(Cast)* 2029
Bingham, Susan Hulsman *(Composer)* 2918
Binkley, Howard *(Lighting Designer)* 4229
Binkley, Howell *(Lighting Designer)* 2198, 2333, 3456
Binney, Constance *(Cast)* 4241
Binotto, Paul *(Cast)* 3227
Biondi, Remo *(Composer)* 3444
Birbari, Elizabeth *(Costumes)* 382, 2483
Birch, Billy *(Cast)* 1913
Birch, Pat *(Director)* 2065
Birch, Patricia *(Cast)* 1354
Birch, Patricia *(Choreographer)* 119, 147, 1037, 1164, 1222, 1512, 1664, 1755, 1985, 2536, 2801, 3015, 3330, 3340, 3643, 3668, 3792, 4027, 4334, 4459, 4522, 4619, 4861
Birch, Patricia *(Director)* 114, 119, 1164, 2241, 3643, 3668, 4027, 4459
Birch, Reginald *(Costumes)* 571
Birchard, Ralph *(Lyricist)* 96
Bird, Cora *(Cast)* 2222
Bird, Dorothy *(Cast)* 4166
Bird, John *(Cast)* 1195
Bird, John *(Composer)* 1195
Bird, John *(Director)* 1857
Bird, John *(Librettist)* 1857
Bird, John *(Lyricist)* 1195, 1857
Bird, Richard *(Director)* 3756
Birinski, Leo *(Author)* 2830
Birkenhead, Susan *(Lyricist)* 4, 2200, 2320, 2578, 2598, 3485, 3961, 4288, 4744
Birkin, Andrew *(Librettist)* 3454
Birkmeyer, Toni *(Cast)* 4581
Birmingham, Barbara *(Lyricist)* 932
Birn, David *(Set Design)* 1232
Birnkrant, Arthur *(Librettist)* 997
Birse *(Cast)* 710
Bisaccia, Bob *(Producer)* 426
Bishir, Jane *(Librettist)* 67
Bisholo, Solomzi *(Cast)* 209
Bishop, Adelaide *(Cast)* 1539
Bishop, Al *(Composer)* 3992
Bishop, Bill *(Cast)* 1222
Bishop, Carole
See also Kelly Bishop.
Bishop, Carole *(Cast)* 746, 3603, 3636
Bishop, David *(Arrangements)* 789
Bishop, David *(Composer)* 99, 2541, 3463
Bishop, David *(Librettist)* 789
Bishop, David *(Lyricist)* 99
Bishop, David *(Musical Director)* 99, 166, 2565
Bishop, David *(Vocal Arranger)* 166
Bishop, Fred *(Cast)* 1412
Bishop, Fred A. *(Director)* 4269, 4634
Bishop, Frederick *(Director)* 531
Bishop, Frederick A. *(Choreographer)* 531, 1183
Bishop, George *(Cast)* 1544
Bishop, John *(Author)* 1669
Bishop, John *(Director)* 597, 2219, 4522
Bishop, John *(Librettist)* 1172, 4535
Bishop, John *(Lyricist)* 1172
Bishop, Kelly
See also Carole Bishop.
Bishop, Kelly *(Cast)* 692, 3476
Bishop, Marilyn *(Cast)* 1750
Bishop, Randy *(Composer)* 3690

Bishop, Randy *(Lyricist)* 3690
Bishop, Sir Henry Rowley *(Composer)* 1425
Bishop, Stuart *(Librettist)* 2169, 3920, 4243
Bishop, Stuart *(Producer)* 3920
Bishop, Stuart *(Set Design)* 4401
Bishop, Thom *(Composer)* 494
Bishop, Thom *(Librettist)* 494
Bishop, Thom *(Lyricist)* 494
Bissell, Gene *(Composer)* 2913
Bissell, Gene *(Lyricist)* 2913
Bissell, Gene P. *(Composer)* 3112
Bissell, Gene P. *(Lyricist)* 3112
Bissell, Marian *(Librettist)* 3845
Bissell, Richard *(Author)* 3351
Bissell, Richard *(Librettist)* 3351, 3845
Bissell, Whitney *(Cast)* 55, 4706
Bissing *(Producer)* 1504
Bissing, H. *(Lighting Designer)* 1403
Bisson, Alexandre *(Author)* 1347, 3146
Bittan, Roy *(Musical Director)* 1769
Bittner, Jack *(Cast)* 31, 599, 3835, 4155, 4577
Bittner, Julius *(Orchestrations)* 1680
Bixby, Frank *(Cast)* 1501
Bixby, Johnathan *(Costumes)* 2198
Bizet, Georges *(Author)* 653
Bizet, Georges *(Composer)* 653
Bjornson, Maria *(Costumes)* 211
Bjornson, Maria *(Set Design)* 211, 3464
Blacher, Henriette-Blanke *(Composer)* 4589
Black, Ben *(Composer)* 2088, 4545, 4814
Black, Ben *(Lyricist)* 2088, 4545, 4814
Black, Chad *(Cast)* 4588
Black, David *(Director)* 4114
Black, David *(Producer)* 1139, 1256, 1478, 2659, 3824
Black, Don *(Librettist)* 4217
Black, Don *(Lyricist)* 211, 299, 2539, 2820, 3930, 4068, 4138, 4217, 4301
Black, Frank *(Composer)* 1112, 2045
Black, Frank *(Orchestrations)* 4532
Black, John S. *(Composer)* 4375
Black, Johnny *(Composer)* 1686
Black, Johnny S. *(Composer)* 25
Black, Karen *(Cast)* 2297, 4623
Black, Malcolm *(Director)* 3491
Black, Max *(Cast)* 1439
Black, Robert *(Cast)* 1439
Black, Valerie *(Cast)* 3321
Black Patti Troubadours *(Producer)* 982
Black-Brown, Shirley *(Cast)* 166, 2427
Blackbirds Productions *(Producer)* 3704
Blackburn, Charles *(Cast)* 3469
Blackburn, Charles *(Costumes)* 491, 3469, 3542
Blackburn, Clarice *(Cast)* 2268
Blackburn, Mary *(Costumes)* 1266
Blackburn, Ticia *(Costumes)* 4205
Blackfriars' Guild *(Producer)* 2661
Blackhurst, Klea *(Cast)* 3641
Blackman, Charles *(Musical Director)* 4237
Blackman, Jack *(Lighting Designer)* 2278, 2306, 2657
Blackman, Jack *(Set Design)* 2278, 2306, 2657
Blackman, Robert *(Costumes)* 282, 4410
Blackman, Robert *(Set Design)* 4410
Blackman, Teddy *(Director)* 1772
Blackmer, Sidney *(Cast)* 2967, 4043
Blackmon, Ted *(Producer)* 1772
Blackmon, Teddy *(Director)* 1981, 1982
Blackmore, Peter *(Author)* 3816
Blackston, Phyllis *(Choreographer)* 3756
Blackstone, Nan *(Cast)* 1448, 3172
Blackton, Jack *(Cast)* 1770, 2284
Blackton, Jay
See also Jacob Schwartzdorf.
Blackton, Jay *(Composer)* 4035
Blackton, Jay *(Dance Arranger)* 3234
Blackton, Jay *(Musical Director)* 134, 153, 223, 603, 619, 751, 1478, 1564, 1616, 1760, 2064, 2137, 2449, 2894, 2898, 2983, 3108, 3234, 3263, 3687, 3702, 3931, 4214, 4384, 4481, 4718
Blackton, Jay *(Orchestrations)* 4537
Blackton, Jay *(Vocal Arranger)* 603, 1478, 1564, 2064, 2983, 3234, 3687, 3931
Blackwell, Carlyle *(Cast)* 1718, 3975
Blackwell, Charles *(Librettist)* 4286
Blackwell, Charles *(Producer)* 40
Blackwell, Donald *(Librettist)* 2105, 3861, 4367
Blackwell, Otis *(Composer)* 3695, 3739
Blackwell, Otis *(Lyricist)* 3695, 3739
Blackwell, Robert *(Composer)* 3695
Blackwell, Robert *(Lyricist)* 3695
Blackwood, Pady *(Puppeteer)* 997, 4710
Blaine, Martin *(Producer)* 2167
Blaine, Rose *(Cast)* 851
Blaine, Vivian *(Cast)* 853, 1190, 1706, 3845
Blair, Barbara *(Cast)* 1492
Blair, Frank *(Cast)* 476
Blair, Jack *(Cast)* 3104, 4677
Blair, Jimmy *(Cast)* 2167
Blair, Joyce *(Cast)* 299
Blair, June *(Cast)* 3104, 4677
Blair, Milton *(Cast)* 96
Blair, Milton J. *(Lyricist)* 96
Blair, Nicholas *(Librettist)* 3375
Blair, Pamela *(Cast)* 374, 746, 1082, 1915, 2318, 3666, 4196
Blair, Richard *(Cast)* 272, 366, 1091, 1436, 1438, 2279
Blair, Tony *(Cast)* 117
Blaire, Laine *(Cast)* 608, 4620
Blaisdell, William *(Cast)* 311, 4563
Blake, Ann-Marie *(Cast)* 2689
Blake, Arthur *(Cast)* 4332
Blake, Bob *(Cast)* 2085
Blake, Curtis *(Cast)* 3987
Blake, Eubie
See also Eubie Blake and His Orchestra
Blake, Eubie *(Cast)* 740, 1984, 3963, 3966
Blake, Eubie *(Composer)* 133, 318, 393, 432, 443, 740, 792, 1052, 1063, 1174, 1198, 1328, 1765, 1917, 1989, 2151, 2570, 2856, 3020, 3144, 3512, 3905, 3963, 3965, 3966, 4154, 4253, 4281, 4503, 4810, 4812
Blake, Eubie *(Director)* 740
Blake, Eubie *(Librettist)* 498
Blake, Eubie *(Lyricist)* 3144, 4281
Blake, Eubie *(Musical Director)* 443, 740, 3963, 3965, 3993

Blake, George *(Lyricist)* 532, 3810
Blake, Harold *(Cast)* 113
Blake, J.W. *(Lyricist)* 3968
Blake, Josh *(Cast)* 2033, 3644
Blake, Paul *(Cast)* 4433
Blake, Richard *(Cast)* 544, 1509
Blake, Richard H. *(Cast)* 3576
Blake, Sydney *(Cast)* 1249
Blake, Winfield *(Cast)* 3585
Blake and His Orchestra, Eubie
See also Eubie Blake.
Blake and His Orchestra, Eubie *(Cast)* 3993
Blakeley, James *(Cast)* 1569, 4418
Blakeley, Jane *(Cast)* 2498
Blakely, Bidda *(Cast)* 3986
Blakely, Milton *(Cast)* 1934
Blakely, Ronee *(Cast)* 4216
Blakely, Ronee *(Composer)* 2435
Blakely, Ronee *(Lyricist)* 2435
Blakeman, Daniel *(Cast)* 4507
Blakemore, Michael *(Director)* 775
Blakeslee, Suzanne *(Cast)* 430, 1349, 1350
Blanc, Mel *(Voice)* 57
Blanche, Marie *(Cast)* 4302
Bland, James A. *(Composer)* 2415
Bland, James A. *(Lyricist)* 2415
Blane, Barbara *(Cast)* 1950
Blane, Ralph *(Cast)* 966, 1973, 2597, 3104
Blane, Ralph *(Composer)* 372, 1628, 2805, 3175, 3630, 4289, 4332, 4366, 4388, 4399, 4827
Blane, Ralph *(Librettist)* 3630
Blane, Ralph *(Lyricist)* 372, 1385, 1628, 2805, 3175, 3630, 4289, 4332, 4366, 4388, 4399, 4827
Blane, Ralph *(Vocal Arranger)* 612, 1109, 2597, 4142, 4557
Blane, Sue *(Costumes)* 3742
Blaney, Charles E. *(Author)* 2973
Blaney, Charles E. *(Librettist)* 263, 509, 1902
Blaney, Charles E. *(Lyricist)* 1259
Blaney, Charles E. *(Producer)* 263, 1051, 1259, 1902
Blaney, Harry Clay *(Cast)* 509
Blaney, Norah *(Librettist)* 133, 702
Blank, Dorothy Ann *(Author)* 4035
Blank, Larry *(Musical Director)* 808, 869, 3305, 4297, 4334
Blank, Larry *(Orchestrations)* 593
Blank, Larry *(Vocal Arranger)* 808, 869, 3305
Blank, Lawrence J. *(Dance Arranger)* 337
Blank, Lawrence J. *(Musical Director)* 337, 1634
Blankfort, Henry *(Librettist)* 2809
Blankfort, Michael *(Librettist)* 3365
Blankfort, Michael *(Lyricist)* 3365
Blankman, Howard *(Composer)* 600, 842
Blankman, Howard *(Lyricist)* 600, 842
Blatt, Beth *(Cast)* 2416
Blatt, Jerry *(Composer)* 1786, 4450
Blatt, Jerry *(Librettist)* 1786
Blatt, Jerry *(Lyricist)* 1786
Blau, Bela *(Producer)* 4479
Blau, Eric *(Director)* 793, 2017
Blau, Eric *(Librettist)* 793, 1079, 2017, 3932
Blau, Eric *(Lyricist)* 793, 1079, 2017, 2188
Blau, Renee *(Producer)* 573, 2754
Blaufoix, Paul *(Director)* 37
Blaufuss, Walter *(Composer)* 1823, 3246
Blausen, Whitney *(Costumes)* 4004
Blausen, Whitney *(Set Design)* 3939
Blauvelt, Lillian *(Cast)* 1095
Blazer, Judy *(Cast)* 690, 1822, 2185
Blechman, Marcus *(Cast)* 3699
Bleckner, Jeff *(Director)* 4151
Bledsoe, Jules *(Cast)* 110, 1020, 1876, 3949
Bleezarde, Gloria *(Cast)* 62, 3112, 3124
Bleichman, Rudolf *(Author)* 4188
Blethen, Joseph *(Librettist)* 47
Blethen, Joseph *(Lyricist)* 47
Bleyer, Archie *(Musical Director)* 197, 323, 372, 1140, 2809
Bleyer, Archie *(Orchestrations)* 2809, 3523
Blindt, N.D. *(Musical Director)* 325
Blinhorn, Joseph *(Producer)* 3571
Blinn, Holbrook *(Cast)* 1114, 1502
Blinn, Holbrook *(Director)* 1114, 1502
Bliss, Helena *(Cast)* 1711, 2837, 4075, 4557
Bliss, Imogene *(Cast)* 4789
Bliss, Janet *(Cast)* 2784
Blitz, R.D. *(Cast)* 4157
Blitzstein, Marc *(Author)* 951
Blitzstein, Marc *(Cast)* 919
Blitzstein, Marc *(Composer)* 919, 951, 979, 1448, 2257, 2268, 2447, 2653, 2859, 3180, 3365, 3691, 3696, 4152, 4399, 4715
Blitzstein, Marc *(English Lyrics)* 4369
Blitzstein, Marc *(Incidental Music)* 979, 2257, 2859, 4715
Blitzstein, Marc *(Librettist)* 919, 3180, 3501, 3691, 3696, 4369
Blitzstein, Marc *(Lyricist)* 369, 919, 951, 979, 2268, 2447, 2653, 3180, 3365, 3691, 3696, 3840, 4152, 4399
Blitzstein, Marc *(Musical Director)* 919
Blitzstein, Marc *(Orchestrations)* 919, 2268, 3691, 3696
Bloch, Ivan *(Producer)* 253, 2283, 4390
Block, Bobbi *(Cast)* 4729
Block, Chad *(Cast)* 3564
Block, Frederic *(Composer)* 3600
Block, Frederic *(Lyricist)* 3600
Block, Frederic *(Producer)* 3600
Block, Hal *(Librettist)* 4086
Block, Jesse *(Cast)* 1397
Block, Larry *(Cast)* 829, 1915, 3937
Block, Will J. *(Producer)* 1469, 2286
Block Amusement Co., Will J. *(Producer)* 830
Blodget, Alden S. *(Director)* 3386
Blodget, Alden S. *(Producer)* 3386
Blodget, Carol *(Cast)* 3571
Blon, F.V. *(Composer)* 2952
Blondeau, Henri *(Author)* 3372
Blood Company *(Composer)* 459
Blood Company *(Lyricist)* 459
Bloodgood *(Composer)* 3384
Bloodgood *(Costumes)* 349
Bloodgood, Edyth *(Costumes)* 4596
Bloodgood, Linda *(Composer)* 2186
Bloodgood, Linda *(Musical Director)* 2186
Bloodgood, Lyle *(Composer)* 4333
Bloom, Bradley *(Conductor)* 4732

Bloom, Ken *(Director)* 528, 1155, 3165, 3997
Bloom, Ken *(Librettist)* 2541, 3997
Bloom, Ken *(Lighting Designer)* 3997
Bloom, Ken *(Producer)* 528, 1155, 3165, 3329, 3997
Bloom, Ken *(Set Design)* 3997
Bloom, Leo *(Cast)* 2876
Bloom, Rube *(Composer)* 420, 446, 447, 882, 888, 3705, 4137
Bloomfield, Harry *(Producer)* 3536
Bloomfield, Maggie *(Lyricist)* 4
Bloomgarden, Kermit *(Producer)* 162, 933, 1456, 2106, 2146, 2411, 2961, 3016, 3210
Bloomingdale, Alfred *(Producer)* 84, 1889
Blore, Douglas *(Cast)* 4302
Blore, Eric *(Cast)* 138, 1113, 1453, 1856, 1859, 2277, 2526, 4826
Blore, Eric *(Lyricist)* 133, 702, 4327
Blossom, Henry *(Author)* 1961
Blossom, Henry *(Composer)* 4723
Blossom, Henry *(Librettist)* 68, 126, 307, 1162, 1335, 1578, 2723, 2915, 3304, 3567, 3590, 3675, 3921, 4017, 4453, 4547, 4608, 4754
Blossom, Henry *(Lyricist)* 68, 126, 307, 683, 1162, 1335, 1578, 2025, 2723, 2906, 2915, 3304, 3567, 3590, 3675, 3685, 3820, 3921, 4017, 4311, 4390, 4453, 4547, 4608, 4754, 4818
Blossom, Roberts *(Cast)* 3309
Blount, Helon *(Cast)* 941, 1060, 1319, 1329, 2961, 3067, 3619, 3725, 4727
Blount Jr., Roy *(Librettist)* 1038
Blow, Sidney *(Author)* 4302
Blow, Sidney *(Director)* 4302
Blow, Sidney *(Librettist)* 3237, 4302
Blue, Ben *(Cast)* 1494
Blue, Peggie *(Cast)* 166, 2754
Blue, Pete *(Musical Director)* 4462
Bluestone, Henry *(Composer)* 1415
Blum, Joel *(Cast)* 1120, 1146
Blum, Robert *(Author)* 2808
Blumberg, David A. *(Producer)* 1832
Blume, Norman A. *(Cast)* 2760
Blumenfeld, Robert *(Cast)* 4288
Blumenkrantz, Jeff *(Cast)* 4371
Blumenstock, I.L. *(Librettist)* 4324
Blumenstock, I.L. *(Lyricist)* 4324
Blumenthal, A.C. *(Producer)* 3014
Blumenthal, Oskar *(Author)* 4667
Bluth *(Director)* 1093
Bluth, Fred *(Librettist)* 1093
Bluth, Fred *(Lyricist)* 1093
Blyden, Larry *(Cast)* 170, 1315, 1373, 1406, 2178, 3273, 4718
Blyer, James B. *(Composer)* 4805
Blyler, James *(Composer)* 2857, 4805
Blythe *(Costumes)* 1251
Boak, Mike *(Set Design)* 2477
Boardman, Chris *(Orchestrations)* 695
Bobbie, Walter *(Cast)* 1093, 1380, 4450, 4523
Bobby, Anne Marie *(Cast)* 119, 171, 4020
Bobley, Peter *(Producer)* 1289
Boccaccio, Giovanni *(Author)* 482, 1017, 2931
Bock *(Lyricist)* 4247
Bock, Jerry *(Composer)* 160, 170, 270, 390, 483, 635, 673, 1190, 1265, 1280, 1471, 1848, 2205, 2246, 2589, 2726, 2804, 2987, 3018, 3097, 3780, 3890, 3918, 4260, 4273, 4312, 4395, 4827, 4829
Bock, Jerry *(Incidental Music)* 1471
Bock, Jerry *(Librettist)* 170
Bock, Jerry *(Lyricist)* 2677, 2987
Bock, W.E. *(Composer)* 1535
Bodanzky, Robert *(Author)* 93, 307, 902, 967, 1199, 1455, 1712, 2334, 2947, 4010
Bodenheim, Maxwell *(Librettist)* 1244
Boder, Lada *(Cast)* 4217
Bodo, Yakov *(Cast)* 2866
Bodry, Penelope *(Cast)* 1053, 1216
Boesky, Billy *(Composer)* 1232
Boesky, Billy *(Librettist)* 1232
Boesky, Billy *(Lyricist)* 1232
Bogaev, Paul *(Conductor)* 4217
Bogaev, Paul *(Musical Director)* 211, 721, 4138
Bogan, Elizabeth *(Musical Director)* 4779
Bogard, Michael *(Lighting Designer)* 4129
Bogardus, Janet *(Choreographer)* 1291
Bogardus, Stephen *(Cast)* 1161, 1234, 1258, 2746, 4505
Bogart, Andrew *(Cast)* 1521
Bogart, Humphrey *(Cast)* 2060
Bogart, Neil *(Producer)* 1289
Bogart, Paul *(Director)* 1200, 1744, 3496
Bogdanoff, Rose *(Costumes)* 2748, 4702
Boggs, Gail *(Cast)* 2648, 2962
Bogin, Abba *(Dance Arranger)* 3725
Bogin, Abba *(Musical Director)* 157, 1273, 1698, 2994, 3110
Bogin, Abba *(Orchestrations)* 157, 461
Bogin, Abba *(Vocal Arranger)* 157, 3696, 3725
Bogin, Bernard *(Cast)* 4369
Bogok, Gusti *(Cast)* 2440
Bohannon, M.T. *(Cast)* 3348
Bohemians, The *(Producer)* 1685, 1686, 1688, 1689, 1691, 1692, 1693
Bohlman, Edgar *(Set Design)* 4548
Bohmler, Craig *(Composer)* 1702
Bohmler, Craig *(Lyricist)* 1702
Bohmler, Craig *(Musical Director)* 1702
Bohmler, Craig *(Orchestrations)* 1702
Bohmler, Craig *(Vocal Arranger)* 1702
Bohnen, Roman *(Cast)* 2228
Bohner, Aloys *(Costumes)* 3737
Bois, Curt *(Cast)* 3536
Bois, Curt *(Director)* 4316
Bois, Curt *(Producer)* 4316
Bojar, Alvin *(Producer)* 3018
Boland, Clay *(Composer)* 18, 750, 1885, 3150, 3870, 3914
Boland, Clay *(Director)* 1885
Boland, Clay *(Lyricist)* 18, 898, 3150
Boland, Clay *(Orchestrations)* 18, 750
Boland, Clay *(Vocal Arranger)* 18, 750
Boland, Mary *(Cast)* 1225, 2252
Boland Jr., Clay *(Lyricist)* 18
Bolasni, Saul *(Costumes)* 911
Bolcom, William *(Composer)* 1122
Bold, Richard *(Cast)* 1134, 1460, 1461, 1485, 1486, 1487
Boldi, J.B. *(Composer)* 1569

Bolen, Virginia *(Cast)* 3986
Bolender, Todd *(Cast)* 1384
Bolender, Todd *(Choreographer)* 935, 2357
Boles, John *(Cast)* 804, 2342, 3301, 3399
Boles, Steve *(Cast)* 2250
Boleslavsky, Richard *(Choreographer)* 1235, 4357
Boleslavsky, Richard *(Director)* 1235, 2981, 3829, 4664
Boleslavsky, Richard *(Producer)* 2981
Boley, May *(Cast)* 694, 1111, 1355, 1923, 2040, 2252, 2695, 2793, 2888, 3252, 3396, 3580, 3754, 3770, 3994, 4037, 4421, 4575
Bolger, Ray *(Cast)* 64, 601, 823, 1492, 1800, 2301, 2401, 2475, 3148, 3283, 3639, 4652
Bolin, Shannon *(Cast)* 957, 1600, 3602, 4186
Bolles, Reginald F. *(Cast)* 761
Bolm, Adolph *(Choreographer)* 2900
Bologna, Joseph *(Librettist)* 2016
Bolton, Betty *(Cast)* 700
Bolton, Guy *(Author)* 161, 2467, 3535, 4207, 4678
Bolton, Guy *(Librettist)* 145, 161, 163, 292, 466, 921, 953, 1203, 1297, 1336, 1527, 1528, 1784, 1931, 1992, 2187, 2340, 2376, 2430, 2900, 2907, 3163, 3177, 3193, 3230, 3243, 3245, 3250, 3532, 3569, 3659, 3719, 3727, 3766, 3775, 3819, 3924, 3980, 4001, 4283, 4392, 4426, 4555, 4586, 4860
Bolton, Guy *(Lyricist)* 3177, 3230, 3866, 4555
Bolton, Guy *(Producer)* 4426
Bolton, Helen *(Cast)* 1966, 3508, 4529
Bolton, John Keene *(Cast)* 760
Bonard Prods. *(Producer)* 322
Bonard Productions *(Producer)* 3815, 4319
Bond *(Composer)* 3981
Bond, Chris *(Director)* 4295
Bond, Christopher *(Author)* 4233
Bond, Fred *(Cast)* 1246, 1553
Bond, Frederic *(Cast)* 4044
Bond, Helen *(Cast)* 1588
Bond, Lillian *(Cast)* 2636
Bond, Robert *(Composer)* 3076
Bond, Robin *(Composer)* 574
Bond, Rudy *(Cast)* 2106, 2965
Bond, Sheila *(Cast)* 84, 204, 2707, 4169, 4718
Bond, Sudie *(Cast)* 1958, 2297, 3890
Bond, William *(Cast)* 255
Bondi, Don *(Choreographer)* 4349
Bondor, Rebecca *(Puppeteer)* 56, 3449
Bonelle, Richard *(Cast)* 2657
Bonelli, William *(Cast)* 1522, 2869, 4803
Bonfiglio, G. *(Cast)* 4113
Bonfils, Helen *(Producer)* 3338
Bonham, John *(Composer)* 3739
Bonham, John *(Lyricist)* 3739
Bonheur, Jacqueline *(Cast)* 186
Boni, John *(Librettist)* 2913
Boni, John *(Lyricist)* 3077
Boniface Jr., George *(Cast)* 734, 2714
Boniface Jr., George C. *(Cast)* 2673, 2733
Bonita *(Cast)* 30, 3665
Bonita Amusement Co. *(Producer)* 3665
Bonnelli, Sem *(Author)* 2211
Bonner, Eugene *(Composer)* 4548
Bonner, Eugene *(Lyricist)* 4548
Bono, Sonny *(Composer)* 3739
Bono, Sonny *(Lyricist)* 3739
Bontemps, Arna *(Librettist)* 4123
Bonus, Ben *(Cast)* 2421
Bonus, Ben *(Composer)* 2356
Bonus, Ben *(Lyricist)* 2356, 4342
Boockvor, Steven *(Cast)* 4744
Booke, Sorrell *(Cast)* 2236, 2954
Booker, George *(Cast)* 4253
Bookman, Kirk *(Lighting Designer)* 2065, 2285, 3987
Boone, Debby *(Cast)* 3888
Boone, Jobriath *(Composer)* 2877
Boone, Jobriath *(Lyricist)* 2877
Boone, Michael Kelly *(Cast)* 143
Boone, Pat *(Lyricist)* 3261
Boone, Steve *(Composer)* 3739
Boone, Steve *(Lyricist)* 3739
Booth
See also John N. Booth Jr., John Booth and John Newton Booth.
Booth *(Costumes)* 1267, 1529
Booth *(Set Design)* 1267
Booth, Anne *(Cast)* 4569
Booth, James *(Cast)* 42, 1277, 4469
Booth, James *(Librettist)* 42
Booth, James *(Lyricist)* 42
Booth, John *(Costumes)* 711, 2005, 2444, 3978, 4372
Booth, John Hunter *(Author)* 4226, 4276
Booth, John Newton
See also Booth, John N. Booth Jr., and John Booth.
Booth, John Newton *(Costumes)* 740
Booth, Randy *(Musical Director)* 2643
Booth, Shirley *(Cast)* 603, 1948, 2268, 2583, 2653, 4446
Booth, Webster *(Cast)* 2323
Booth, John N. Jr.
See also Booth, John Booth, and John Newton Booth.
Booth Jr., John N. *(Costumes)* 82, 670, 3822, 4565, 4572
Borde, Albert *(Producer)* 1336
Borde, Percival *(Choreographer)* 2719
Borden, Bill *(Composer)* 1370
Borden, Bill *(Lyricist)* 1370
Borden, Eddie *(Cast)* 1947, 3173
Borden, Edith *(Cast)* 4823
Borden, Essie *(Cast)* 624, 755, 1229, 1426, 2124, 2220, 2243, 2579, 3418, 4577, 4684
Borden, Eugene *(Cast)* 1391
Borden, Laverne *(Cast)* 1974
Borden, William *(Lyricist)* 4498
Bordon, Bert *(Cast)* 1484
Bordon, Billie *(Cast)* 4439
Bordoni, Irene *(Cast)* 17, 208, 558, 1391, 1670, 1919, 1920, 2526, 2597, 2891, 3079, 3382
Boretz, Allen *(Lyricist)* 1448, 4235
Borger, Bob *(Cast)* 4683
Borges, Yamil *(Cast)* 3792, 4442
Borget, Arnold *(Composer)* 1978
Borget, Arnold *(Lyricist)* 1978
Bories, Merton *(Lyricist)* 3512
Boring, Jack A. *(Composer)* 1261
Boris, Ruthanna *(Cast)* 1973, 4166

Boris, Ruthanna *(Choreographer)* 2234
Bormann, James *(Cast)* 2661
Bormet, Garry *(Director)* 2783
Bormet, Garry *(Librettist)* 2783
Bormet, Garry *(Lyricist)* 2783
Borne, Hal *(Composer)* 59, 673, 1892, 2259, 3683
Borne, Hal *(Lyricist)* 3683
Borne, Hal *(Orchestrations)* 2259
Borne, Hal *(Vocal Arranger)* 2259
Borodin, A. *(Composer)* 1963
Borodin, Alexander *(Music Based On)* 2327, 4383
Boros, Ferike *(Cast)* 1098
Boros, Frank J. *(Costumes)* 916, 2472, 3830, 3909
Boros, Frank J. *(Set Design)* 916, 2472, 3830, 3909
Borow, Rena Berkowicz *(Librettist)* 4082
Borowitz, Katherine *(Cast)* 2440
Borts, Joanne *(Cast)* 1609
Bosco, Philip *(Cast)* 345, 932, 1076, 2028, 3309
Bosen, Harry *(Costumes)* 3380
Bosley, Tom *(Cast)* 330, 1158, 1280, 3210
Boss, Al *(Incidental Music)* 1604, 4303
Boss, Al *(Orchestrations)* 18, 750, 1604, 4303, 4543
Boss, Al *(Vocal Arranger)* 18, 1604
Bostock, Claude W. *(Librettist)* 1502
Boston, Steve *(Composer)* 1637
Boston, Steve *(Lyricist)* 1637
Boston Cadet Corps *(Producer)* 2902
Bostonians *(Producer)* 2345, 4032, 4598
Bostonians, The *(Producer)* 2697, 4559
Bostwick, Barry *(Cast)* 807, 1664, 2001, 3142, 3733, 4089
Bosveld, Alice *(Cast)* 2124
Boswell, William *(Composer)* 2069
Boswell, William *(Musical Director)* 2069
Boswell, William *(Vocal Arranger)* 2069
Bosworth, Patricia *(Cast)* 3984
Botari, Michael *(Costumes)* 3576
Botari, Michael *(Set Design)* 3576
Botemps, Arna *(Author)* 4123
Botkin Jr., Perry *(Arrangements)* 928
Botkin Jr., Perry *(Composer)* 4796
Botkin Jr., Perry *(Lyricist)* 4796
Botkin Jr., Perry *(Musical Director)* 928
Botsford, George *(Composer)* 1531, 4804
Bottari, Michael *(Costumes)* 4146
Botto, Louis *(Composer)* 3186
Botto, Louis *(Librettist)* 3108
Botto, Louis *(Lyricist)* 272, 1107, 1363, 3186, 3890
Bottomley, Roland *(Cast)* 1453, 3344
Bottoms, John *(Cast)* 963, 1086, 2877, 4485
Botwin, Shirley *(Composer)* 2876
Boublil, Alain *(Librettist)* 2442, 2905
Boublil, Alain *(Lyricist)* 2905
Boucher, Dolores *(Cast)* 3
Boucicault, Aubrey *(Cast)* 1994, 2326, 2673, 4544
Boucicault, Aubrey *(Composer)* 1994
Boucicault, Aubrey *(Lyricist)* 1994
Boucicault, Dion *(Author)* 191, 298, 4173
Boucicault, Dion G. *(Director)* 2871
Boucree, Gladys *(Cast)* 4254
Boudreau, Robin *(Cast)* 109
Boudreaux, Darleen *(Cast)* 1075
Bougla, Charles *(Cast)* 449, 641, 982
Boulanger, Daniel *(Author)* 2318
Boulden, Alice *(Cast)* 1275
Boulton, Milo *(Cast)* 1846
Bourchier, Arthur *(Producer)* 1805
Bouret, Grace *(Lyricist)* 318
Bourne, Matthew *(Choreographer)* 730
Bourneuf, Philip *(Cast)* 1286, 2894, 3292, 4706
Bousard, Joe *(Cast)* 3571
Bousard, Joe *(Musical Director)* 3527
Boutelje, Phil *(Composer)* 831
Bouton, Mabel *(Cast)* 3199
Boutsikaris, Dennis *(Cast)* 1418
Bouvier, Adine *(Cast)* 906
Bouvier, Yvonne *(Cast)* 4174
Bova, Joe *(Cast)* 3288
Bova, Joseph *(Cast)* 825, 1359, 1991
Bovill, C.H. *(Librettist)* 3213
Bovill, C.H. *(Lyricist)* 396, 1318, 1454, 1569, 2498, 3213, 3433, 4590
Bowab, John *(Producer)* 1273, 2681, 3876
Bowan, Sybil *(Cast)* 1127
Bowden, Charles *(Producer)* 72
Bowden, Jonny *(Musical Director)* 140, 1161, 2852
Bowden, Jonny *(Vocal Arranger)* 1161
Bowen, Paul H. *(Lighting Designer)* 1750
Bowen, Paul H. *(Set Design)* 1750
Bowen, Thomas *(Lighting Designer)* 1377
Bower, Edward *(Choreographer)* 1404
Bower, Edward P. *(Choreographer)* 4360
Bower, Joy *(Orchestrations)* 3110
Bowers, Bobby *(Cast)* 508
Bowers, Charles B. *(Cast)* 3566
Bowers, Charles H. *(Cast)* 457, 947, 1535
Bowers, Clent *(Cast)* 1289, 1776
Bowers, Fred *(Cast)* 4787
Bowers, Frederick *(Composer)* 2316
Bowers, Frederick V. *(Cast)* 811
Bowers, Frederick V. *(Composer)* 811, 4130
Bowers, Kenneth *(Cast)* 372
Bowers, Kenny *(Cast)* 153, 1577
Bowers, Robert Hood *(Composer)* 219, 326, 545, 617, 687, 1142, 1144, 1327, 2025, 2126, 2574, 2695, 2770, 3236, 3681, 3771, 3977, 4115, 4119, 4544, 4688, 4813
Bowers, Robert Hood *(Lyricist)* 2574
Bowers, Robert Hood *(Musical Director)* 75, 1230, 2025, 2574, 2695, 2900, 3236, 3304, 3771, 3977, 4158, 4650
Bowers, Robert Hood *(Orchestrations)* 2040
Bowers, Teresa *(Cast)* 1496
Bowes, Major Edward *(Producer)* 638
Bowie, David *(Composer)* 3739
Bowie, David *(Lyricist)* 3739
Bowie, John *(Cast)* 3983
Bowie, Pat *(Cast)* 4074
Bowler, Walter S. *(Cast)* 1866
Bowles, Anthony *(Musical Director)* 920
Bowman, Laura *(Cast)* 3904
Bowman, Patricia *(Cast)* 622, 3639, 4486, 4569
Bowman, Rob *(Dance Arranger)* 690
Bowman, Rob *(Musical Director)* 690, 1172
Bowman Productions *(Producer)* 1045

Bowron, Lloyd *(Musical Director)* 4239
Boxer, Walter *(Producer)* 3565
Boxwill, James *(Cast)* 444, 4253
Boyar, Monica *(Cast)* 4337
Boyd, Elisse *(Composer)* 3110, 3484
Boyd, Elisse *(Lyricist)* 3107, 3108, 3110, 3484
Boyd, George *(Director)* 4410
Boyd, George *(Librettist)* 4410
Boyd, Gregory *(Director)* 2198, 4229
Boyd, Gregory *(Librettist)* 4229
Boyd, Gregory *(Lyricist)* 4229
Boyd, Jimmy *(Cast)* 4409
Boyd, Julianne *(Director)* 4, 533, 1198, 2283, 3305
Boyd, Julie *(Cast)* 172
Boyd, Mae *(Cast)* 552
Boyd, Tom *(Cast)* 4197
Boyd-Jones, Ernest *(Lyricist)* 1313
Boyer, Blanche *(Cast)* 4674
Boyer, Jean *(Lyricist)* 2467
Boyer, Lucienne *(Cast)* 839, 2095
Boyer, Rika *(Cast)* 2095
Boyington, Kathryn *(Composer)* 4030
Boyington, Kathryn *(Lyricist)* 4030
Boylan, Arthur *(Cast)* 671
Boylan, Dan *(Lighting Designer)* 4330
Boylan, Malcolm *(Librettist)* 1046
Boylan, Mary *(Cast)* 459
Boylan, Mary *(Composer)* 459
Boylan, Mary *(Librettist)* 941, 4527
Boylan, Mary *(Lyricist)* 459, 4527
Boylan, Rose *(Cast)* 671
Boyle, Betty *(Cast)* 985
Boyle, Francis J. *(Cast)* 4046
Boyle, Jack *(Cast)* 3400
Boyle, John *(Cast)* 2884
Boyle, John *(Choreographer)* 125, 495, 670, 1215, 2709, 3179, 3342, 3489, 3523, 4178, 4426, 4621
Boyle, Johnny *(Cast)* 3946
Boyle, Johnny *(Choreographer)* 3946
Boyle, Pierre *(Lyricist)* 839
Boys of Camp Merritt, The *(Producer)* 1624
Boyt, John *(Costumes)* 1299
Bozeman, Beverley *(Cast)* 2554
Bozyk, Reizl *(Cast)* 3781
Bracey, Sidney *(Cast)* 3777
Bracken, Eddie *(Cast)* 339, 3934, 4420
Bracken, Eddie *(Producer)* 339
Bracket, Rose *(Choreographer)* 1080
Brackett, Charles *(Author)* 3972
Brackett, Charles *(Screenwriter)* 4217
Brackett, Raymond O. *(Producer)* 1121
Brackman, Jacob *(Lyricist)* 2318
Brackney, Bonnie *(Cast)* 4695
Brackney, Tom *(Cast)* 4695
Bradbury, George *(Cast)* 538
Bradbury, James *(Cast)* 94
Bradbury, Lane *(Cast)* 1709
Bradbury, Ray *(Author)* 973
Bradbury, Ray *(Librettist)* 973
Bradbury, Ray *(Lyricist)* 973
Bradbury, William B. *(Composer)* 3020
Bradbury, William B. *(Lyricist)* 3020
Braddon, Mary Elizabeth *(Author)* 2375
Braden, John *(Composer)* 1086
Braden, John *(Lyricist)* 1086
Bradfield, W, Kiyus *(Cast)* 2131
Bradford, Alberta *(Cast)* 1072
Bradford, Alex *(Cast)* 1072
Bradford, Alex *(Composer)* 4788
Bradford, Alex *(Lyricist)* 4788
Bradford, Benjamin *(Librettist)* 916
Bradford, Benjamin *(Lyricist)* 916
Bradford, Billy *(Cast)* 792
Bradford, Don *(Cast)* 2069
Bradford, Geoff *(Composer)* 4171
Bradford, Geoff *(Lyricist)* 4171
Bradford, Johnny *(Lyricist)* 1326
Bradford, Percy *(Lyricist)* 2845
Bradford, Perry *(Composer)* 2672
Bradford, Perry *(Lyricist)* 2302, 2672
Bradford, Roark *(Librettist)* 2225
Bradford, Roark *(Lyricist)* 2225
Bradley, Arthur *(Choreographer)* 1342
Bradley, Bruce Vernon *(Cast)* 328
Bradley, Buddy *(Choreographer)* 1202, 1763, 3139
Bradley, Charles *(Author)* 3689
Bradley, Frank *(Cast)* 2532
Bradley, Jeanette *(Cast)* 2540
Bradley, Oscar *(Musical Director)* 82, 288, 324, 1027, 1145, 2384, 3719, 3766, 3980, 4188
Bradley, Scott *(Set Design)* 4515
Bradley, Vi *(Composer)* 3683
Bradley, Vi *(Lyricist)* 3683
Bradley, Virginia *(Cast)* 2641
Bradstreet, Anne *(Lyricist)* 2633
Brady, Alice *(Cast)* 276, 2614, 3248
Brady, Fay *(Cast)* 3861
Brady, Florence *(Cast)* 4661
Brady, Helen *(Cast)* 985
Brady, James Edmund *(Costumes)* 83
Brady, James Edward *(Costumes)* 2100
Brady, Leo *(Director)* 2028
Brady, Leo *(Librettist)* 821, 901, 2641
Brady, Leo *(Lyricist)* 821, 2641
Brady, Patrick *(Conductor)* 3908
Brady, Patrick Scott *(Cast)* 784
Brady, Patrick Scott *(Musical Director)* 784
Brady, Patrick Scott *(Vocal Arranger)* 784
Brady, Scott *(Cast)* 1029
Brady, William *(Producer)* 65, 1975, 3867
Brady, William A. *(Producer)* 235, 340, 814, 1342, 1519, 1573, 2342, 2545, 2711, 3248, 4529
Brady, William S. *(Librettist)* 3978
Brady, William S. *(Lyricist)* 3978
Brady Jr., William A. *(Producer)* 3861
Bragdon, Guy *(Director)* 1121, 2972
Bragdon, Guy *(Librettist)* 1121
Bragdon, Helen *(Lyricist)* 90
Bragg, Melvyn *(Author)* 1903
Bragg, Melvyn *(Librettist)* 1903
Bragg, Melvyn *(Lyricist)* 1903
Braggins, Nellie *(Cast)* 1896

Braggiotti, Francesca *(Cast)* 4545
Braggiotti, Mario *(Cast)* 4545
Braggiotti, Mario *(Composer)* 4545
Braggiotti, Mario *(Lyricist)* 4545
Bragiotti, S. Herbert *(Cast)* 3680
Braham, Dave *(Composer)* 114, 1776, 2428, 3266
Braham, Dave *(Incidental Music)* 4239
Braham, Dave *(Lyricist)* 114
Braham, George *(Composer)* 4508
Braham, George *(Musical Director)* 4508
Braham, George F. *(Composer)* 516
Braham, George F. *(Lyricist)* 516
Braham, Harry *(Cast)* 3883
Braham, Harry *(Composer)* 1148
Braham, Harry *(Musical Director)* 687, 1148, 1501
Braham, Horace *(Cast)* 993
Braham, John *(Composer)* 476
Braham, John *(Lyricist)* 476
Braham, John J. *(Composer)* 175
Braham, John J. *(Musical Director)* 175, 2779, 3828, 3887
Braham, Lionel *(Cast)* 2802
Braham, Philip *(Composer)* 133, 700, 702, 1569, 2570, 2972, 4154, 4302, 4327, 4662
Braham, Philip *(Lyricist)* 605, 702, 2972, 4154, 4662
Braham, Philip *(Musical Director)* 133, 704, 2570
Brahms, Johannes *(Composer)* 1589
Braine, Robert *(Composer)* 4424
Brainin, Jerome *(Composer)* 4131
Brainin, Jerome *(Lyricist)* 4131
Brainsfather, Bruce *(Librettist)* 377
Braithwaite, Clara *(Cast)* 3857
Braley, Berton *(Composer)* 1132
Braley, Berton *(Lyricist)* 1132, 4422
Brambell, Wilfred *(Cast)* 2304
Bramble, Mark *(Director)* 1253
Bramble, Mark *(Librettist)* 305, 1171, 1253, 1359, 1660, 3208, 3485, 4261
Bramley, William *(Cast)* 4625
Brammel, David *(Cast)* 1079
Brammer, Julius *(Author)* 905, 1113, 1530, 2424, 3051, 4760
Brammer, Julius *(Librettist)* 771, 1113
Brammer, Julius *(Lyricist)* 393
Branch, Billy *(Cast)* 4174
Branch, Gretchen *(Cast)* 27, 444
Branch, James *(Cast)* 2393
Branch, Nick *(Composer)* 1201
Branch, Susan *(Costumes)* 1832
Brand, David *(Cast)* 3568
Brand, Georgiana *(Cast)* 3495
Brand, Gibby *(Cast)* 669, 2289, 2993, 3411, 3666
Brand, John *(Cast)* 762
Brand, John E. *(Cast)* 727
Brand, Max *(Author)* 1027
Brand, Oscar *(Composer)* 1158, 2018, 2248
Brand, Oscar *(Lyricist)* 1158, 2018, 2248
Brand, Phoebe *(Cast)* 2228
Brandeaux, Pal'mere *(Choreographer)* 203, 1836, 2238, 3168, 3573
Brandeaux, Pal'mere *(Director)* 242, 398
Brandeaux, Pal'mere *(Producer)* 242, 849
Brandell, William *(Director)* 1397
Brander, Arthur *(Composer)* 1655, 3898
Brander, Arthur *(Lyricist)* 3898
Brandfon, Joe *(Composer)* 1722
Brandfon, Joe *(Lyricist)* 1722
Brandl, Johann *(Composer)* 2824
Brando, Marlon *(Cast)* 1299
Brandon, Charles A. *(Costumes)* 3224
Brandon, Charles A. *(Lighting Designer)* 3224
Brandon, Charles A. *(Set Design)* 3204, 3224
Brandon, Joclyn *(Author)* 1551
Brandon, John *(Composer)* 3752
Brandon, John *(Lyricist)* 3752
Brandon, Johnny *(Cast)* 2608
Brandon, Johnny *(Composer)* 415, 766, 1816, 2616, 3427, 3932, 4192, 4678
Brandon, Johnny *(Librettist)* 2616, 4192
Brandon, Johnny *(Lyricist)* 415, 766, 1198, 1816, 2616, 3427, 3932, 4192, 4678
Brandt, Denise *(Cast)* 2098
Brandt, Eddie *(Composer)* 4367
Brandt, Eddie *(Lyricist)* 4367, 4741
Brandt, Harry *(Producer)* 4702
Brandt, Jerry *(Producer)* 1637
Brandt, Mike *(Composer)* 1216
Brandt, Mike *(Lyricist)* 1216
Brandt, Sophie *(Cast)* 4590
Brandt Sisters *(Cast)* 1782
Brandywine Orchestra, Nat *(Cast)* 849
Brandzel, Robert *(Musical Director)* 3711
Brandzel, Robert *(Orchestrations)* 3711
Brandzel, Robert *(Vocal Arranger)* 3711
Branen, Jeff T. *(Composer)* 295, 4630
Branen, Jeff T. *(Lyricist)* 295, 830, 3073, 3396, 4181, 4630
Brantley, Marion *(Cast)* 4253
Brasington, Alan *(Cast)* 2820, 3909
Brass, Stacey Lynn *(Cast)* 3757
Brassard, Gail *(Costumes)* 3227, 4136
Brasser, Victoria *(Cast)* 2674
Braswell, Adrienne *(Cast)* 914
Braswell, Adrienne *(Composer)* 914
Braswell, Adrienne *(Librettist)* 914
Braswell, Adrienne *(Lyricist)* 914
Braswell, Charles *(Cast)* 832, 3815
Braswell, John *(Director)* 300, 654
Braswell, John *(Lyricist)* 300
Bratt, J. *(Lyricist)* 2421
Bratton, John W. *(Composer)* 591, 702, 719, 737, 1464, 1925, 2261, 2465, 2722, 2990, 3134, 3229, 3422, 3753, 3856, 3857, 3882, 3951, 4130, 4430
Bratton, John W. *(Lyricist)* 702, 3753
Braun, Eugene *(Lighting Designer)* 2023, 2024, 2098, 2099, 4143
Braun, Gene *(Lighting Designer)* 4180
Braun, Ralph *(Cast)* 2784
Braunstein, Alan *(Cast)* 2212, 3456
Braunstein, Lester *(Producer)* 1205
Braxton, Brenda *(Cast)* 4031
Bray, Bonnie *(Cast)* 1781
Bray, David *(Cast)* 1781
Brayfield, Doug *(Lyricist)* 1159
Brayton, Jude *(Librettist)* 37

Brayton, Jude *(Lyricist)* 37
Breau, Louis *(Composer)* 2857, 2972, 4816
Breau, Louis *(Lyricist)* 4393
Breaux, Marc *(Cast)* 309, 1029, 2484
Breaux, Marc *(Choreographer)* 1061, 2626, 2874, 4034
Brecher, Irving *(Author)* 2805
Brecht, Bertolt *(Author)* 1214, 4368, 4369, 4370
Brecht, Bertolt *(Librettist)* 1755
Brecht, Bertolt *(Lyricist)* 369, 1755, 3840
Brecht, Bertolt *(Lyrics Based On)* 4368, 4369, 4370, 4371
Bredin, Patricia *(Cast)* 1386, 1887
Bredschneider, Willie *(Composer)* 1561
Bredschneider, Willy *(Author)* 2794
Bredt, James *(Composer)* 1761
Breen, Grace *(Cast)* 1162
Breen, Harry *(Lyricist)* 1560
Breen, Jerry *(Lyricist)* 2512
Breen, Margaret *(Cast)* 1113
Breen, Nellie *(Cast)* 1027, 1513
Breen, Robert *(Director)* 1385
Breffort, Alexandre *(Author)* 2150
Bregman, Buddy *(Musical Director)* 3800
Breier, Edward F. *(Composer)* 1626, 3552
Breier, Edward F. *(Lyricist)* 1626, 3552
Breitenbach, Robert *(Librettist)* 1608
Breitenfeld, Emil *(Composer)* 4422
Breitenfeld, Emil *(Lyricist)* 4422
Brel, Jacques *(Composer)* 2188, 3338
Brel, Jacques *(Lyricist)* 2188, 3338
Bremseth, Lloyd *(Cast)* 2332
Brendel, El *(Cast)* 1923, 2870
Brennan, A. St. John *(Lyricist)* 1743
Brennan, Eileen *(Cast)* 908, 1828, 2522, 4186
Brennan, Frederick Hazlett *(Librettist)* 2679
Brennan, J. Keirn *(Additional Lyrics)* 718
Brennan, J. Keirn *(Composer)* 1026
Brennan, J. Keirn *(Librettist)* 3150
Brennan, J. Keirn *(Lyricist)* 202, 495, 551, 718, 1026, 1461, 1462, 1751, 1803, 2310, 2636, 2662, 3012, 3150, 3238, 3415, 3642, 3680, 4189, 4669
Brennan, James *(Cast)* 2250
Brennan, James *(Lyricist)* 3443
Brennan, James A. *(Composer)* 487
Brennan, James A. *(Lyricist)* 487
Brennan, Jay
See also Savoy & Brennan
Brennan, Jay *(Cast)* 201, 1281, 1686, 1780
Brennan, Jimmy *(Cast)* 3743
Brennan, Maureen *(Cast)* 2235, 4137
Brennan, Nan *(Cast)* 4206
Brennan, Nora *(Choreographer)* 3076
Brennan, Peggylee *(Cast)* 4527
Brennan, Tom *(Director)* 71
Brenner, Dorothy *(Cast)* 4687
Brenner, Janet *(Producer)* 784
Brenner, Ruth *(Costumes)* 2545
Brenner, S.M. *(Librettist)* 1521
Brenner, S.M. *(Lyricist)* 1521
Brent, Earl *(Composer)* 4047, 4415
Brent, Earl *(Lyricist)* 544, 4047, 4415
Brent, Romney *(Cast)* 1446, 1447, 2459, 2545, 4609
Brent, Romney *(Director)* 2379, 3214
Brent, Romney *(Librettist)* 3214
Brentano, Felix *(Director)* 2985, 3767
Brentano, Felix *(Producer)* 2985
Brentano, Lowell *(Author)* 4105
Brentano, Lowell *(Librettist)* 1670
Bresbey, Eugene W. *(Author)* 3050
Bresler, Jerry *(Composer)* 1296, 4114
Bresler, Jerry *(Lyricist)* 1296
Breslin, Tom *(Cast)* 3019
Breslin, Tommy *(Cast)* 1010, 2305, 3846, 3900
Bresslaw, Bernard *(Cast)* 4469
Brest, Arthur G. *(Director)* 4009
Brett, Jason *(Producer)* 2470
Brett, Simon *(Librettist)* 3930
Bretton, Elise *(Composer)* 4273
Bretton, Elise *(Lyricist)* 4273
Bretton, Elise *(Vocal Arranger)* 1813, 3897, 4252
Breuer, Ernest *(Composer)* 4816, 4817, 4824
Breuer, Kurt *(Author)* 3012
Breuer, Lee *(Director)* 1636
Breuer, Lee *(Librettist)* 1636
Breuer, Lee *(Lyricist)* 1636
Breuler, Robert *(Cast)* 4074
Brevis, Skip *(Dance Arranger)* 338
Brevis, Skip *(Musical Director)* 338
Brevis, Skip *(Vocal Arranger)* 338
Brewer, Robert *(Director)* 962
Brewerton, Henry R. *(Librettist)* 6
Brewerton, Henry R. *(Lyricist)* 6
Brewster, Townsend *(Author)* 3522
Brian, Antony *(Cast)* 841
Brian, Donald *(Cast)* 354, 579, 910, 1067, 1356, 1527, 1544, 1851, 2517, 2761, 2836, 3153, 3996, 4258, 4529, 4557, 4593
Brian, Donald *(Composer)* 2761, 3996
Brian, Donald *(Director)* 4593
Brian, Donald *(Lyricist)* 2761, 3996
Briant, Roy *(Cast)* 2274
Briants, The *(Cast)* 1973
Briar, Suzanne *(Cast)* 4288
Brice, Carol *(Cast)* 1474, 1662, 3837
Brice, Elizabeth *(Cast)* 598, 2232, 2900, 2914, 2966, 3085, 4017, 4044, 4285, 4421, 4603, 4712, 4742, 4806, 4807
Brice, Elizabeth *(Composer)* 4017
Brice, Elizabeth *(Lyricist)* 4017
Brice, Fanny *(Cast)* 418, 1281, 1944, 1963, 3009, 4235, 4686, 4804, 4805, 4810, 4811, 4814, 4815, 4817, 4824, 4825, 4831, 4840, 4842, 4851
Brice, Fanny *(Costumes)* 418
Brice, Fanny *(Librettist)* 1944
Brice, Fanny *(Lyricist)* 3926
Brice, Fanny *(Producer)* 568
Brice, Lew *(Cast)* 123, 124, 418, 2696, 3396, 3397, 4148
Brice, Monte *(Lyricist)* 3717
Brick, Eva *(Cast)* 1733
Brickell, Beth *(Cast)* 1674
Brickhill, Joan *(Choreographer)* 2805
Brickhill-Burke Prods. *(Producer)* 2805
Bricklayers, The *(Cast)* 3121
Bricklin, Jonathan *(Cast)* 319

Brickman, Marshall *(Librettist)* 2913, 4167
Bricusse, Leslie *(Composer)* 3454, 3482, 3731, 3846, 4160
Bricusse, Leslie *(Librettist)* 2198, 3731, 3846, 4160
Bricusse, Leslie *(Lyricist)* 2198, 3454, 3482, 3731, 3846, 3878, 3879, 4160, 4399, 4560
Bridge, Andrew *(Lighting Designer)* 211, 1296, 3464, 4217
Bridge Theatre Prod. Co. *(Producer)* 564
Bridges, Kenneth *(Cast)* 1634
Bridges, Mark *(Costumes)* 1732
Bridgewater, Dee Dee *(Cast)* 3175, 4722
Bridwell, Thom *(Composer)* 2908
Bridwell, Thom *(Dance Arranger)* 2908, 4534
Bridwell, Thom *(Musical Director)* 2908
Bridwell, Thom *(Vocal Arranger)* 2908
Bridwell, Thomas *(Musical Director)* 3932
Brigate, Edward *(Composer)* 3739
Brigate, Edward *(Lyricist)* 3739
Brigati, E. *(Composer)* 4193
Brigati, E. *(Lyricist)* 4193
Brigel, Stockton *(Cast)* 2279
Briggs, Bunny *(Cast)* 432, 4502
Briggs, Casey *(Cast)* 1172
Briggs, Clare *(Librettist)* 199
Briggs, John R. *(Composer)* 3517
Briggs, John R. *(Lyricist)* 3517
Briggs, Matt *(Cast)* 462, 2311
Briggs, Rita *(Lyricist)* 3908
Briggs, Tom *(Librettist)* 4146
Brigham, Constance *(Cast)* 72
Brighouse, Harold *(Author)* 4588
Bright, Joann *(Cast)* 4830
Bright, Joe *(Cast)* 1499
Bright, Joe *(Librettist)* 1499
Bright, Richard S. *(Producer)* 1914
Brightman, Sarah *(Cast)* 3464
Brightman, Stanley *(Author)* 2972
Brighton, Hilda *(Lyricist)* 702
Brill, E.S. *(Composer)* 1318
Brill, E.S. *(Lyricist)* 1318
Brill, Fran *(Cast)* 3684
Brill, Klaus *(Cast)* 3698
Brill, Leighton K. *(Librettist)* 288
Brill, Leighton K. *(Lyricist)* 288
Brill, Marty *(Cast)* 171
Brill, Marty *(Lyricist)* 615
Brinckerhoff, Burt *(Cast)* 2297
Brinckerhoff, Burt *(Director)* 4659
Brindley, Madge *(Cast)* 635
Brink, Robert *(Director)* 1092
Brinkley, Grace *(Cast)* 1323, 1693, 1856, 3225
Briquet, Jean *(Composer)* 20, 1565
Brisebois, Danielle *(Cast)* 150
Brisker, Yankl *(Lyricist)* 1609
Brisson, Carl *(Cast)* 1352
Brisson, Frederick *(Producer)* 798, 957, 958, 1471, 2260, 3113, 3351, 4038, 4474
Brit, Browley *(Composer)* 1296
Brit, Browley *(Lyricist)* 1296
Brita, Inga *(Cast)* 2091
Britt, Jacqueline *(Cast)* 2775, 2874, 4558
Britt, Kelly *(Cast)* 3752
Brittan, Robert *(Lyricist)* 3656
Britton, Barbara *(Cast)* 4582
Britton, Dorothy *(Cast)* 1135
Britton, Florence *(Cast)* 3596
Britton, Frank *(Cast)* 4823
Britton, Jeff *(Producer)* 426, 535, 669, 1974, 2231, 2785, 2801
Britton, John *(Producer)* 692
Britton, Milt *(Cast)* 4823
Britton, Pamela *(Cast)* 530
Britton, Ronnie *(Composer)* 1508, 1695, 1978, 4470
Britton, Ronnie *(Director)* 1695
Britton, Ronnie *(Librettist)* 1508, 1695, 4470
Britton, Ronnie *(Lyricist)* 1508, 1695, 1978, 4470
Britz, John R. *(Musical Director)* 543
Bro, Judith *(Cast)* 2285
Broad, Jay *(Director)* 3684
Broad, Jay *(Librettist)* 3517, 3684
Broadbent, Aida *(Choreographer)* 1711
Broadhurst, George *(Author)* 1014, 1519
Broadhurst, George *(Librettist)* 1118, 1519, 1794, 2383
Broadhurst, George *(Lyricist)* 1118, 1519, 1794, 2383
Broadhurst, George *(Producer)* 1118, 1794, 2383
Broadhust, Aida *(Choreographer)* 4602
Broadway Productions *(Producer)* 3380
Brochu, Jim *(Cast)* 4514
Brock, Heinie *(Cast)* 2085, 2088
Brockbank, Harrison *(Composer)* 1502
Brockbank, Harrison *(Lyricist)* 1502
Brockett, Don *(Author)* 4494
Brockman, James *(Composer)* 805, 2261, 4683
Brockman, James *(Lyricist)* 2261, 4683
Brockmeier, William *(Cast)* 1508
Brocksmith, Roy *(Cast)* 4252, 4370
Broderick, George *(Dance Arranger)* 4645
Broderick, George *(Musical Director)* 1970, 4645, 4788
Broderick, George *(Orchestrations)* 4645
Broderick, George *(Vocal Arranger)* 1970
Broderick, Helen *(Cast)* 48, 207, 294, 1137, 1272, 1563, 3144, 3254, 3466, 3478, 3617, 4437, 4801
Broderick, James *(Cast)* 2680
Broderick, William *(Cast)* 1260
Brodszky, Nicholas *(Composer)* 2458, 4743
Brodszky, Nicholas *(Incidental Music)* 2458
Brody, Lee *(Cast)* 3946, 4166
Brody, Lee *(Composer)* 1342, 4152
Brody, Lee *(Librettist)* 4174
Brody, Lee *(Lyricist)* 1342, 4152
Brody, Leo *(Producer)* 2580
Brody, Max *(Author)* 2761
Brody, Miksa *(Author)* 4258
Brody, Miska *(Author)* 2907
Broecker, Tom *(Costumes)* 1291
Brohn, Bill *(Composer)* 485
Brohn, Bill *(Musical Director)* 3201
Brohn, Bill *(Orchestrations)* 669, 1638, 2318, 2332, 2433, 2754, 2877, 3743, 3876, 4383, 4707
Brohn, Bill *(Vocal Arranger)* 3619, 4707
Brohn, William D. *(Musical Director)* 3908
Brohn, William D. *(Orchestrations)* 496, 921, 2205, 2905, 3544, 3682, 3862, 4701
Brohn, William David *(Orchestrations)* 589

Broich, Madame *(Costumes)* 377
Brokaw, Mark *(Director)* 240
Bromberg, J. Edward *(Cast)* 2450, 4428
Bromfield, Valri *(Cast)* 1575
Bron, Eleanor *(Cast)* 1195
Bronell, Barbara *(Cast)* 2492
Bronfman, Edgar M. *(Producer)* 535, 4252
Bronfman Jr., Edgar *(Producer)* 546
Bronson, Edna *(Cast)* 1295
Bronson, Percy *(Cast)* 2347, 2383
Bronson, Percy *(Producer)* 4570
Bronte, Mae *(Cast)* 4440
Brook, Peter *(Director)* 2000, 2150, 3445
Brook, Sara *(Costumes)* 181, 2043, 2278, 2941, 3427, 4474, 4577
Brooke, Clifford *(Director)* 465, 680, 1011, 1142, 1281, 1580, 1794, 2387
Brooke, J. Clifford *(Director)* 1266, 1557, 2684, 3043
Brooke, J. Clifford *(Librettist)* 2684
Brooke, John *(Cast)* 3168
Brooke, Walter *(Cast)* 225
Brooke, William *(Librettist)* 2069
Brooker, Gary *(Composer)* 3739
Brooker, Gary *(Lyricist)* 3739
Brookfield, Charles H.E. *(Librettist)* 356
Brookins, Fred *(Cast)* 4486
Brooklyn Academy of Music *(Producer)* 4438
Brooklyn YMHA *(Producer)* 4477
Brooks *(Costumes)* 567, 689, 2034, 2071, 3069, 3243, 3860, 3907, 4548, 4777
Brooks, Alan *(Librettist)* 4596
Brooks, Alfred *(Composer)* 3224
Brooks, Arthur D. *(Costumes)* 968, 1867
Brooks, Arthur D. *(Set Design)* 1867
Brooks, Charles *(Choreographer)* 2976
Brooks, David *(Cast)* 462, 530, 1880, 2983, 3389, 3831, 3947, 4643
Brooks, David *(Director)* 72, 298
Brooks, David Allen *(Cast)* 3198
Brooks, Donald *(Costumes)* 127, 652, 958, 1049, 1227, 1310, 2874, 3020, 3187, 3274, 3603
Brooks, Donald L. *(Lighting Designer)* 4611
Brooks, Donald L. *(Set Design)* 1304
Brooks, Dudley *(Musical Director)* 4199
Brooks, Eleanor *(Cast)* 1118
Brooks, Florence *(Cast)* 3417
Brooks, Georgia *(Cast)* 1118
Brooks, Harry *(Composer)* 39, 432, 1980, 3020, 4033
Brooks, Irving *(Cast)* 2407
Brooks, Jack *(Composer)* 4710
Brooks, Jack *(Lyricist)* 4710
Brooks, Jeff *(Cast)* 3142
Brooks, Juanita *(Cast)* 4127
Brooks, Lawrence *(Cast)* 596, 3064, 3725, 4075
Brooks, Leon *(Cast)* 676
Brooks, Louis *(Costumes)* 972
Brooks, Marion *(Cast)* 1192
Brooks, Marion *(Director)* 1192
Brooks, Marion *(Librettist)* 1192
Brooks, Marion A. *(Librettist)* 3358
Brooks, Marjorie *(Cast)* 133, 3139
Brooks, Matt *(Librettist)* 1397, 1494, 1930, 1931
Brooks, Mel *(Cast)* 1389
Brooks, Mel *(Librettist)* 64, 943, 3107, 3286, 3934
Brooks, Phyllis *(Cast)* 3359
Brooks, Shelton *(Cast)* 567, 1058, 3513
Brooks, Shelton *(Composer)* 1813, 3297, 4197
Brooks, Shelton *(Lyricist)* 1813, 3297, 4197
Brooks, Tyler *(Cast)* 136
Brooks, Walter *(Choreographer)* 1174, 1270, 1335, 1747, 2309, 3533, 4668
Brooks, Walter *(Director)* 1308, 1513, 1587, 1747, 2516, 2557, 2807, 3042, 3252, 3511, 3963, 3965
Brooks, Walter *(Producer)* 2807
Broome, John *(Choreographer)* 4160
Broomfeld & Greeley *(Cast)* 2640
Broones, Martin *(Composer)* 46, 1780, 3391, 3796
Broones, Martin *(Lyricist)* 3796
Brophy, Edmund *(Producer)* 4243
Broske, Octavia *(Cast)* 3251, 4382
Brosset, Colette *(Cast)* 2364
Brosset, Colette *(Choreographer)* 2362, 2364
Brosten, Harve *(Producer)* 3272, 3760
Brothers, Bowman *(Lyricist)* 2996
Brothers, Carla *(Cast)* 2239
Brothers, Howard *(Composer)* 3405
Brothers, Howard *(Lyricist)* 3405
Brotherson, Eric *(Cast)* 383, 1475, 3036, 3526
Brougham, St. John *(Composer)* 2509
Broughton, Philip *(Composer)* 1191, 3172
Broun, Heywood *(Cast)* 3783, 3946
Broun, Heywood *(Librettist)* 3946
Broun, Heywood *(Producer)* 3946
Broun, Heywood Hale *(Cast)* 3874
Brourman, Michele *(Composer)* 1804, 4744
Brourman, Michele *(Dance Arranger)* 4744
Brourman, Michele *(Lyricist)* 4744
Brower, Jay *(Musical Director)* 945
Brower, Jay *(Orchestrations)* 945, 1408
Browman, Patricia *(Cast)* 4824
Brown, A. Seymour *(Cast)* 2481
Brown, A. Seymour *(Composer)* 257, 736, 1901, 4806, 4808
Brown, A. Seymour *(Librettist)* 21, 1692
Brown, A. Seymour *(Lyricist)* 21, 257, 608, 662, 736, 1151, 1901, 2448, 2696, 2782, 2892, 3134, 3681, 4589, 4799, 4803, 4806, 4807, 4808
Brown, Ada *(Cast)* 567, 2817
Brown, Agnes *(Cast)* 3736
Brown, Agnes Cain *(Cast)* 3774
Brown, Al W. *(Composer)* 1582, 1963, 2538, 2732, 3396
Brown, Al W. *(Lyricist)* 1582
Brown, Albert W. *(Composer)* 3396
Brown, Alex *(Lyricist)* 1713
Brown, Alice *(Cast)* 2009, 4182
Brown, Aline *(Cast)* 1056
Brown, Allan *(Producer)* 164
Brown, Ann Wiggins *(Cast)* 1416
Brown, Anne *(Cast)* 3541
Brown, Anthony *(Director)* 2225
Brown, Arvin *(Director)* 951, 4601
Brown, B. *(Composer)* 4630
Brown, B. *(Lyricist)* 4630

Brown, Babe *(Cast)* 1906
Brown, Barry *(Producer)* 2360, 3787
Brown, Barry M. *(Producer)* 3515
Brown, Bessie *(Cast)* 676
Brown, Bill *(Cast)* 128
Brown, Billings *(Lyricist)* 4585
Brown, Billy *(Cast)* 4183
Brown, Blaine *(Cast)* 676
Brown, Blair *(Cast)* 4370
Brown, Bob *(Puppeteer)* 2726
Brown, Calvin *(Librettist)* 3849
Brown, Candy *(Cast)* 723
Brown, Charles *(Lyricist)* 2922
Brown, Charles D. *(Cast)* 587, 3365
Brown, Charles D. *(Lyricist)* 2485
Brown, Charles H. *(Lyricist)* 2485, 3981
Brown, Claudia *(Costumes)* 1169
Brown, Daisy *(Cast)* 3041
Brown, Daniel *(Cast)* 314, 1959
Brown, Dave *(Composer)* 1256
Brown, Dave *(Orchestrations)* 140
Brown, David *(Cast)* 4149
Brown, David *(Producer)* 227
Brown, Dewey *(Cast)* 1773, 1981, 2561
Brown, Domer C. *(Composer)* 552
Brown, Earl *(Vocal Arranger)* 16, 2969
Brown, Eddy *(Composer)* 3754
Brown, Edna *(Cast)* 4339
Brown, Esther *(Cast)* 3599
Brown, Fleta Ian *(Lyricist)* 1802
Brown, Fleta Ian *(Composer)* 4094
Brown, Flo *(Cast)* 554, 2034
Brown, Forman *(Cast)* 4467
Brown, Forman *(Composer)* 4467
Brown, Forman *(Lyricist)* 1415, 1680, 1681, 1959, 2838, 3013, 3772, 4467
Brown, Gaye *(Cast)* 874
Brown, George *(Lyricist)* 1415, 2077
Brown, George R. *(Lyricist)* 398, 1415
Brown, Georgia *(Cast)* 42, 652, 3271, 3792, 4371
Brown, Gerard *(Author)* 2239
Brown, Grace *(Costumes)* 4047
Brown, Harry *(Cast)* 3881
Brown, Harry *(Composer)* 2990
Brown, Harry *(Lyricist)* 2990
Brown, Helen *(Cast)* 3480
Brown, Honey *(Cast)* 2302
Brown, Ian *(Cast)* 4173
Brown, Ida *(Cast)* 43, 254
Brown, Jack *(Lighting Designer)* 367
Brown, Jack *(Set Design)* 415, 1809
Brown, James *(Composer)* 3695, 3739, 4193
Brown, James *(Lyricist)* 3695, 3739, 4193
Brown, Jason *(Cast)* 2658
Brown, Jason Robert *(Arrangements)* 3125, 3456
Brown, Jason Robert *(Musical Director)* 3125, 3456
Brown, Jason Robert *(Orchestrations)* 2224, 3125
Brown, Jean *(Cast)* 3821
Brown, Jeffrey *(Cast)* 2039
Brown, Jessie *(Cast)* 581
Brown, Joe David *(Author)* 3364
Brown, Joe E. *(Cast)* 381, 642, 911, 2214, 4476
Brown, Johnny *(Cast)* 1601
Brown, Joyce *(Musical Director)* 52, 278, 3610, 4558
Brown, Joyce *(Vocal Arranger)* 1289, 3656, 4558
Brown, Ka-Ron *(Cast)* 3830
Brown, Kay *(Cast)* 837
Brown, Kelly *(Cast)* 722, 1614, 4395
Brown, Kid *(Cast)* 2984
Brown, Kid *(Producer)* 2984
Brown, Kitty *(Cast)* 981
Brown, L. Russell *(Composer)* 2235, 4197
Brown, L. Russell *(Lyricist)* 2235, 4197
Brown, L. Slade *(Producer)* 64, 534, 607, 1993, 2248, 2898, 3788, 4002
Brown, Leroy *(Cast)* 3022
Brown, Leroy *(Composer)* 3022
Brown, Leroy *(Lyricist)* 3022
Brown, Lester *(Cast)* 1563
Brown, Lester *(Director)* 909, 2944
Brown, Lew *(Cast)* 3153
Brown, Lew *(Composer)* 391, 2189, 2308, 3376, 3926
Brown, Lew *(Director)* 622, 4177, 4772
Brown, Lew *(Librettist)* 622, 924, 1323, 1492, 1979, 4177, 4772
Brown, Lew *(Lyricist)* 202, 391, 393, 573, 622, 665, 1215, 1293, 1323, 1339, 1460, 1486, 1488, 1489, 1490, 1491, 1492, 1628, 1688, 1692, 1813, 1919, 1929, 1979, 2066, 2111, 2189, 2308, 2467, 2489, 2706, 2734, 2857, 3020, 3297, 3376, 3489, 3535, 3926, 3969, 3973, 4177, 4253, 4345, 4772, 4799, 4813, 4817
Brown, Lew *(Producer)* 622, 4177, 4772
Brown, Lewis *(Costumes)* 2218, 3001
Brown, Lottie *(Cast)* 2021
Brown, Louise *(Cast)* 642, 2382, 3650, 4741
Brown, Lydia *(Cast)* 489
Brown, Mae *(Cast)* 981
Brown, Mae *(Choreographer)* 981
Brown, Mae *(Composer)* 981
Brown, Mae *(Librettist)* 981
Brown, Mae *(Lyricist)* 981
Brown, Marjorie *(Cast)* 1871
Brown, Mark A. *(Lyricist)* 1055
Brown, Martin *(Cast)* 2966
Brown, Martin *(Librettist)* 3382
Brown, Martin *(Lyricist)* 2334
Brown, Martin G. *(Lyricist)* 2825
Brown, Max *(Producer)* 1029, 1634, 2874
Brown, Max J. *(Producer)* 594, 2583
Brown, Maxine *(Cast)* 2950
Brown, Michael *(Composer)* 272, 427, 943, 1023, 1045, 1049, 1107, 1362, 1363, 2294, 2554, 2988, 3107, 3108, 3889, 4268
Brown, Michael *(Director)* 1045, 2988
Brown, Michael *(Librettist)* 1045, 2988
Brown, Michael *(Lyricist)* 272, 427, 943, 1023, 1045, 1049, 1107, 1362, 1363, 2000, 2294, 2554, 2988, 3107, 3108, 3889, 4268
Brown, Michael *(Producer)* 2630
Brown, Nacio Herb *(Composer)* 393, 487, 544, 1138, 1943, 1944, 1946, 3139, 3992, 4267, 4683, 4799
Brown, Nacio Herb *(Lyricist)* 1298

Brown, Norman *(Composer)* 4433
Brown, Norman *(Librettist)* 4433
Brown, Norman *(Lyricist)* 4433
Brown, Patrika *(Lighting Designer)* 482, 1498, 1769
Brown, Pendleton *(Cast)* 4089
Brown, Peter *(Composer)* 3739
Brown, Peter *(Lyricist)* 3739
Brown, R.A. *(Composer)* 2481
Brown, R.A. *(Lyricist)* 2481
Brown, R.G. *(Cast)* 1436, 1438, 2279, 3110, 4659
Brown, R.G. *(Librettist)* 1436, 3110
Brown, Ralph *(Cast)* 432
Brown, Raymond *(Composer)* 1148
Brown, Raymond *(Lyricist)* 1148
Brown, Rita *(Costumes)* 3066
Brown, Robert *(Librettist)* 4774
Brown, Robert F. *(Librettist)* 750
Brown, Ronnie *(Cast)* 2039
Brown, Roo *(Cast)* 4
Brown, Rose *(Cast)* 1987
Brown, Russ *(Cast)* 957, 1323
Brown, Ruth *(Cast)* 105, 432, 4127
Brown, Sherman *(Producer)* 2264
Brown, Sid *(Composer)* 4805
Brown, Sid *(Lyricist)* 4805
Brown, Steve *(English Lyrics)* 4176
Brown, Steve *(Librettist)* 1897
Brown, Steve *(Lyricist)* 669, 840, 1249, 1897, 4261
Brown, Susan *(Cast)* 3807
Brown, Tom *(Cast)* 1208, 2979
Brown, Tom *(Composer)* 1154, 4393
Brown, Tom *(Lyricist)* 4393
Brown, Troy *(Cast)* 4256
Brown, Vanessa *(Cast)* 3894
Brown, W. *(Librettist)* 4242
Brown, W. *(Lyricist)* 4242
Brown, W.P. *(Musical Director)* 3049
Brown, Warwick *(Set Design)* 3286
Brown, Will P. *(Composer)* 1540
Brown, Will P. *(Lyricist)* 1540
Brown, William *(Cast)* 4708
Brown, William *(Lyricist)* 1049
Brown, William F. *(Composer)* 3889
Brown, William F. *(Librettist)* 272, 427, 550, 1049, 2018, 3112, 3479, 4722
Brown, William F. *(Lyricist)* 427, 3479, 3889
Brown, William P. *(Composer)* 1301
Brown, William P. *(Lyricist)* 1301
Brown, Zoe *(Costumes)* 3902
Brown Jr., J. Terry *(Producer)* 71
Brown Jr., Oscar *(Cast)* 2245
Brown Jr., Oscar *(Composer)* 578, 2245, 2306
Brown Jr., Oscar *(Director)* 578
Brown Jr., Oscar *(Librettist)* 578, 2245, 2306
Brown Jr., Oscar *(Lyricist)* 578, 2245, 2306
Browne *(Composer)* 246
Browne *(Lyricist)* 246
Browne, Bothwell *(Cast)* 2893
Browne, Bothwell *(Choreographer)* 2893
Browne, Bothwell *(Costumes)* 2893
Browne, Irene *(Cast)* 841, 1564
Browne, J. Albert *(Musical Director)* 929, 3712
Browne, L.A. *(Librettist)* 3593
Browne, Leslie *(Cast)* 3682
Browne, Lester *(Cast)* 1292
Browne, Lester *(Director)* 1292
Browne, Lewis Allen *(Librettist)* 3344, 3580
Browne, Porter Emerson *(Librettist)* 1559
Browne, Richard *(Cast)* 4035
Browne, Roscoe Lee *(Cast)* 3060
Browne, Simon *(Cast)* 456
Browne, Tyrone *(Cast)* 3522
Browne, Walter *(Author)* 1210
Browne, Walter *(Librettist)* 2929
Browne, Walter *(Lyricist)* 2929
Browne, William Maynadier *(Librettist)* 4103
Browne, Winifred *(Cast)* 2334
Browning, Billy *(Cast)* 3025
Browning, Connie *(Cast)* 2571
Browning, Ivan Harold *(Cast)* 740
Browning, Joe *(Cast)* 4290
Browning, Kirk *(Director)* 3287
Browning, Robert *(Cast)* 4102
Browning, Susan *(Cast)* 394, 832, 1049, 1634, 2219, 3927
Brownlee, Frank *(Director)* 2778
Brownlow, Wallace *(Cast)* 2632
Brox Sisters, The *(Cast)* 799, 3006, 3008, 3009, 4821
Bruant, Aristide *(Composer)* 3386
Brubeck, Dave *(Composer)* 2611
Bruce, Allan *(Cast)* 1676
Bruce, Betty *(Cast)* 857, 1889, 2458, 4058, 4524
Bruce, Carol *(Cast)* 95, 1060, 1846, 2458, 2597, 3121, 3138
Bruce, Dan *(Cast)* 1563
Bruce, Doun *(Composer)* 4303
Bruce, Eddie *(Cast)* 4021
Bruce, Jack *(Composer)* 3739
Bruce, Jack *(Lyricist)* 3739
Bruce, Judy *(Cast)* 194
Bruce, Michael *(Composer)* 3739
Bruce, Michael *(Lyricist)* 3739
Bruce, Nigel *(Cast)* 2348, 4154, 4569
Bruce, Shelley *(Cast)* 150, 556, 2578
Bruce, Thomas
See also Tom Jones.
Bruce, Vince *(Cast)* 4695
Bruce, Virginia *(Cast)* 111, 4023
Bruck, Arnold *(Producer)* 2754
Bruder, Patsy *(Cast)* 2556
Brugger, George *(Cast)* 3537
Brugiere, Emil *(Composer)* 308
Bruhns, Arthur *(Composer)* 906
Brumage, Bruce H. *(Costumes)* 2783
Brumley, Albert E. *(Composer)* 4030
Brumley, Albert E. *(Lyricist)* 4030
Brumm, Carol *(Cast)* 1883
Brummel, Barbara *(Cast)* 3557
Brummel, David *(Cast)* 1510
Brummel, Harry S. *(Cast)* 3270
Brummel, Harry S. *(Composer)* 3270
Brummel, Harry S. *(Lyricist)* 3270
Brun, George L. *(Composer)* 4201
Brunce, David *(Cast)* 114

Brune, Gabrielle *(Cast)* 4479
Brune, Paul *(Costumes)* 3380
Brune, Phebe *(Cast)* 4077
Bruneau, Ralph *(Cast)* 1077
Brunetti, Ted *(Cast)* 240
Brunner, M.A. *(Composer)* 4534
Brunner, M.A. *(Lyricist)* 4534
Brunner, Roslyn *(Costumes)* 3667
Bruno, Albert *(Cast)* 2788
Bruno, Jean *(Cast)* 2590
Bruns, Philip *(Cast)* 461, 3889
Brunskill *(Set Design)* 4418
Brunton, John *(Lighting Designer)* 3006
Brunton, Robert *(Set Design)* 3562, 4381
Brush, Bob *(Composer)* 1289
Brusie, Judson D. *(Librettist)* 2062, 2576
Brusie, Judson D. *(Lyricist)* 2576
Bruskin, Perry *(Cast)* 3226
Bruskin, Perry *(Director)* 3226
Bruskin, Perry *(Producer)* 1740
Brustein, Robert *(Librettist)* 3937
Bryan *(Composer)* 1327
Bryan *(Lyricist)* 736, 2493, 3747
Bryan, Al *(Lyricist)* 965
Bryan, Alfred *(Composer)* 1247, 3827, 3926
Bryan, Alfred *(Lyricist)* 208, 351, 405, 684, 822, 965, 1065, 1154, 1174, 1247, 1334, 1626, 1784, 1799, 1823, 1951, 1963, 1992, 1998, 2336, 2706, 2856, 2939, 2974, 3018, 3020, 3149, 3403, 3404, 3429, 3432, 3926, 3962, 3985, 4589, 4634, 4656, 4712, 4807, 4823
Bryan, C.D.B. *(Librettist)* 3530
Bryan, Frank *(Composer)* 2481
Bryan, Frank *(Lyricist)* 2481
Bryan, Gertrude *(Cast)* 2495, 3433, 4001, 4688
Bryan, John *(Producer)* 4469
Bryan, Vincent *(Composer)* 1327
Bryan, Vincent *(Librettist)* 2724, 3545
Bryan, Vincent *(Lyricist)* 48, 954, 1118, 1243, 1307, 1327, 1472, 1526, 1569, 1845, 2111, 2335, 2800, 2974, 3191, 3268, 3313, 3387, 3545, 3626, 3745, 3773, 3855, 3856, 3857, 4014, 4650, 4723, 4735, 4801, 4805
Bryan, Vincent J. *(Lyricist)* 4390
Bryan, Wayne *(Cast)* 112, 3743
Bryan, Wayne *(Director)* 1262
Bryant, Adam *(Cast)* 4731
Bryant, Anita *(Cast)* 1261
Bryant, Ben *(Cast)* 280, 1736
Bryant, Boudleaux *(Composer)* 3739
Bryant, Boudleaux *(Lyricist)* 3739
Bryant, David C. *(Director)* 80, 3471
Bryant, Felice *(Composer)* 3739
Bryant, Felice *(Lyricist)* 3739
Bryant, Francis *(Author)* 21
Bryant, Francis *(Composer)* 2675
Bryant, Francis *(Lyricist)* 2675
Bryant, George *(Composer)* 1995
Bryant, Gerald *(Lyricist)* 2168
Bryant, Glenn *(Cast)* 653
Bryant, Hugh *(Cast)* 920
Bryant, Katie *(Cast)* 1421
Bryant, Marie *(Cast)* 341, 2259
Bryant, Nana *(Cast)* 834, 1110, 4692
Bryant, Willie *(Cast)* 467, 2712
Bryce, Peter C. *(Director)* 870
Brydon, Eugene *(Director)* 2103
Bryer, Vera *(Cast)* 1855, 2392
Bryggman, Larry *(Cast)* 2918
Bryk, Hugo *(Musical Director)* 2317
Brymer *(Costumes)* 3002
Brymn, J. Tim *(Composer)* 9, 434
Brymn, James *(Composer)* 2044
Brymn, James *(Lyricist)* 2044
Brymn, James T. *(Composer)* 1758, 1909, 2029, 3358
Brymn, Tim *(Composer)* 1050, 3614
Brymn, Tim *(Lyricist)* 1050
Brymn, Tim *(Musical Director)* 2557, 3614
Bryne, Barbara *(Cast)* 1787
Brynner, Yul *(Cast)* 1959, 2312, 2655
Bryon, Lord *(Lyricist)* 2633
Bryson, Arthur *(Cast)* 925, 1989
Bua, Gene *(Cast)* 729
Bubbles, John *(Cast)* 3541, 4823
Bubbles, John W.
See also Buck & Bubbles.
Bubbles, John W. *(Cast)* 4569
Bucalossi, Ernest *(Composer)* 1537
Bucci, Mark *(Composer)* 19, 3110, 4566
Bucci, Mark *(Lyricist)* 19, 3110
Bucci, Mark *(Orchestrations)* 3110
Buchanan, Jack *(Cast)* 133, 383, 702, 4320
Buchanan, Jack *(Choreographer)* 702, 4320, 4581
Buchanan, Jack *(Director)* 702, 4320
Buchanan, Jack *(Producer)* 4320
Buchanan, Linda *(Set Design)* 158, 4708
Buchanan, Thompson *(Author)* 2649
Buchbinder, Bernhard *(Author)* 1522
Buchen, Walter *(Cast)* 96
Buchen, Walter *(Lyricist)* 96
Buchholz, Fred *(Lighting Designer)* 1402, 2787, 3608
Buchholz, Fred *(Set Design)* 1402
Buchner, Georg *(Author)* 979
Buchs, Sherri *(Costumes)* 3202
Buchter, Barry *(Set Design)* 4416
Buck, Bill *(Cast)* 4467
Buck, Dennis *(Composer)* 3302
Buck, Ford *(Cast)* 3541, 4823
Buck, Ford L.
See also Buck & Bubbles.
Buck, Ford L. *(Cast)* 4569
Buck, Gene *(Composer)* 4271, 4837
Buck, Gene *(Librettist)* 3179, 4809, 4810, 4811, 4812, 4813, 4815, 4816, 4823
Buck, Gene *(Lyricist)* 152, 335, 993, 1124, 1154, 2126, 2446, 2570, 3179, 4206, 4271, 4642, 4806, 4807, 4808, 4809, 4810, 4811, 4812, 4813, 4814, 4815, 4816, 4817, 4818, 4819, 4823, 4831, 4832, 4833, 4834, 4835, 4836, 4837, 4838, 4839, 4840, 4841, 4842, 4843, 4844, 4849, 4851, 4852, 4858
Buck, Gene *(Producer)* 4271, 4793
Buck, Pearl S. *(Librettist)* 751
Buck, Randy *(Librettist)* 3568
Buck, Richard H. *(Composer)* 4390

Buck, Richard H. *(Lyricist)* 4390
Buck, Susan Hum *(Costumes)* 963
Buck & Bubbles
See also John W. Bubbles and Ford Buck.
Buck & Bubbles *(Cast)* 443, 1983, 3657
Buck Jr., Fred C. *(Vocal Arranger)* 1839
Buckeridge, Gladys *(Cast)* 4838
Buckhantz, Allan A. *(Director)* 1766
Buckley, Betty *(Cast)* 280, 661, 678, 3070, 3897, 4635
Buckley, Candy *(Cast)* 3456
Buckley, Dennis *(Cast)* 2212
Buckley, Emerson *(Musical Director)* 1474
Buckley, Hal *(Cast)* 3890
Buckley, John *(Producer)* 346
Buckley, Lord *(Cast)* 4829
Buckley, May *(Cast)* 1806
Buckley, Ralph *(Cast)* 3606
Buckley, Ralph *(Librettist)* 3557
Buckley, Robert A. *(Producer)* 209
Buckmaster, Henry *(Set Design)* 4750
Buckner, Martin *(Choreographer)* 528
Bucks County Playhouse *(Producer)* 2169
Bucksey, Colin *(Director)* 682
Budd, Julie *(Cast)* 3311
Buele, Carol H. *(Costumes)* 1412
Buell, Bill *(Cast)* 4619
Buell, Mabel *(Set Design)* 447, 2613, 3511, 3860
Buell, Mabel A. *(Set Design)* 444, 563, 1270, 4204
Buell, William *(Cast)* 922
Bufano, Remo *(Cast)* 1244
Bufano, Rocco *(Director)* 1977
Bufano, Rocco *(Lyricist)* 1977
Bufano's Puppets, Remo *(Cast)* 4498
Buffalo Bills, The *(Cast)* 3016
Buffaloe, Katherine *(Cast)* 2250
Buffano, Jules *(Cast)* 860, 862
Buffano, Jules *(Composer)* 1120
Buffano, Jules *(Lyricist)* 1120
Bufman, Zev *(Producer)* 578, 1289, 2208, 2218, 2242, 3136, 3231, 3428, 4019, 4566, 4789
Buhrer, Suzanne *(Cast)* 3318
Buhrer, Suzanne *(Composer)* 2294, 3318
Buhrer, Suzanne *(Librettist)* 3318
Buhrer, Suzanne *(Lyricist)* 2294, 3318
Bulger, Harry *(Cast)* 215, 604, 804, 2324, 2964, 3154, 4650, 4738
Bulger, Harry *(Composer)* 215, 604, 2724, 4738
Bulger, Harry *(Librettist)* 604
Bulger, Harry *(Lyricist)* 215, 604
Bulger, Harry *(Producer)* 215
Bull, D. Thomas *(Composer)* 3450
Bull, F. *(Set Design)* 4302
Bull, John *(Librettist)* 4154
Bull, John *(Set Design)* 4661
Bull, Peter *(Cast)* 3482
Bullins, Ed *(Librettist)* 4162
Bullock, Donna *(Cast)* 2241, 3544
Bullock, H. Ridgely *(Producer)* 4537
Bullock, Lou *(Cast)* 624
Bullock, Ridgely *(Producer)* 828
Bullock, Turner *(Librettist)* 3365, 3986
Bullock, Walter *(Librettist)* 1679
Bullock, Walter *(Lyricist)* 1679
Bulmash, Jay S. *(Producer)* 3760
Buloff, Joseph *(Cast)* 1269, 3263
Buloff, Joseph *(Director)* 1269
Bumpass, Rodger *(Cast)* 3076
Bunce, Alan *(Cast)* 868
Bunch, Jack *(Director)* 302
Bundsmann, Anton *(Director)* 3104
Bundy, Laura *(Cast)* 3811
Bunin, Shmuel *(Director)* 2811
Bunker, Ralph *(Cast)* 1565, 3481
Bunn, Alfred *(Author)* 1710
Bunn, Alfred *(Lyricist)* 1897
Bunnage, Avis *(Cast)* 874
Bunny, John *(Cast)* 235, 1148, 1318, 3265, 4404
Bunson, Bertha M. *(Cast)* 3480
Bunt, George *(Choreographer)* 1108, 2026, 2231, 2375, 3688
Bunuel, Rafael *(Author)* 4796
Bunyan, Vashti *(Composer)* 1736
Bunyan, Vashti *(Lyricist)* 1736
Buono, Victor *(Cast)* 2742
Burbridge, Edward *(Set Design)* 578, 1592, 2218, 2415, 2719, 3001, 3690, 3840
Burch, Cassie *(Cast)* 813
Burch, Edwin *(Composer)* 2206, 2761
Burch, Edwin *(Lyricist)* 2206
Burch, Fred *(Librettist)* 119
Burch, Fred *(Lyricist)* 119
Burch, Shelly *(Cast)* 3171
Burdick, David *(Cast)* 674
Burdon, Albert *(Cast)* 1202
Burdon, Eric *(Composer)* 3695
Burdon, Eric *(Lyricist)* 3695
Burge, Gregg *(Cast)* 4068, 4091
Burge, Gregg *(Choreographer)* 838
Burger, John *(Composer)* 2162
Burger, Lt. Fairfax *(Cast)* 1972
Burgess, Anthony *(Librettist)* 946
Burgess, Anthony *(Lyricist)* 946
Burgess, Dorothy *(Cast)* 608
Burgess, Gelett *(Lyricist)* 3611
Burgess, Granville *(Librettist)* 838
Burgess, Grover *(Cast)* 2228
Burgess, Kendall *(Composer)* 3084
Burgess, Lee *(Cast)* 4548
Burghoff, Gary *(Cast)* 4783
Burgie, Irving *(Composer)* 279
Burgie, Irving *(Librettist)* 279
Burgie, Irving *(Lyricist)* 279
Burgoyne, Ollie *(Cast)* 2942
Burk, Bobby *(Lyricist)* 364
Burkan, Mark *(Composer)* 4591
Burkan, Mark *(Lyricist)* 4591
Burke, Albert *(Cast)* 1267
Burke, Billie *(Cast)* 100, 152, 2206, 2624, 2871, 3768
Burke, Billie *(Producer)* 4824, 4825
Burke, Charles *(Cast)* 2694
Burke, Charles A. *(Cast)* 4125
Burke, Deirdre *(Costumes)* 3926
Burke, Dorothea *(Choreographer)* 1110

Burke, Joe *(Composer)* 417, 1134, 2460, 4426
Burke, Johnny *(Cast)* 1823
Burke, Johnny *(Composer)* 1076, 1255, 4255
Burke, Johnny *(Lyricist)* 657, 1076, 1255, 1296, 3091, 4255
Burke, Joseph *(Composer)* 173, 1134, 4825
Burke, Joseph A. *(Composer)* 3958
Burke, Louis *(Director)* 2805
Burke, Marie *(Cast)* 1680, 3307
Burke, Maureen *(Cast)* 4524
Burke, Melville *(Director)* 1215
Burke, Patricia *(Cast)* 1763, 3756, 4519
Burke, Sonny *(Composer)* 59, 3905
Burke, Thomas *(Lyricist)* 1871
Burke, Tom *(Composer)* 1780
Burke, Willi *(Cast)* 3279
Burke, Wilma *(Cast)* 932
Burken, Mark *(Composer)* 4591
Burken, Mark *(Lyricist)* 4591
Burker, Maidie *(Cast)* 822
Burkhardt, Addison *(Composer)* 8, 1609
Burkhardt, Addison *(Librettist)* 2596, 3293, 3805, 4247
Burkhardt, Addison *(Lyricist)* 8, 248, 470, 830, 1593, 1609, 2408, 2596, 2869, 2892, 3387, 3746, 3805, 4094, 4247, 4804
Burkhardt, Gerry *(Cast)* 921
Burkholder, Scott *(Cast)* 4442
Burks, Donnie *(Cast)* 415
Burks, Donny *(Cast)* 4459
Burks, Hattie *(Cast)* 1026, 1911, 2216
Burleigh, Frederick *(Producer)* 382, 2483, 4416
Burlingame, Lloyd *(Lighting Designer)* 280, 2563, 3491, 3863, 4329, 4558
Burlingame, Lloyd *(Set Design)* 1727, 2297, 2563, 3491, 3863, 4318
Burmester, Leo *(Cast)* 2442, 3643
Burnaby, David *(Lyricist)* 4327
Burnaby, Davy *(Cast)* 700
Burnaby, Davy *(Composer)* 700
Burnaby, Davy *(Lyricist)* 700
Burnand, Francis C. *(Librettist)* 727
Burnell, Buster *(Choreographer)* 3264
Burnell, Helen *(Cast)* 2004
Burnett, Carol *(Cast)* 1227, 3288
Burnett, Frances Hodgson *(Author)* 3862
Burnett, Francis Hodgson *(Author)* 1255
Burnett, Harry *(Cast)* 4467
Burnett, Howard J. *(Producer)* 583
Burnett, Martha *(Cast)* 848
Burnette, Brevard *(Cast)* 290
Burney, Steve *(Cast)* 1256
Burnier, Jeannine *(Cast)* 407
Burns, Annelu *(Lyricist)* 1972
Burns, Arthur *(Librettist)* 2726, 4545
Burns, Catherine *(Cast)* 3309
Burns, David *(Cast)* 59, 404, 520, 673, 1061, 1225, 1422, 1811, 1828, 2626, 2653, 2707, 2729, 3016, 3036, 3214, 3326, 3535, 3563, 4499, 4827
Burns, George
See also Burns and Allen.
Burns, George E. *(Producer)* 1924
Burns, Helen *(Cast)* 3818
Burns, Jack *(Librettist)* 3454
Burns, Jeanne *(Composer)* 879
Burns, Jeanne *(Lyricist)* 879
Burns, Peter *(Cast)* 4690
Burns, Peter *(Librettist)* 4690
Burns, Ralph *(Composer)* 964
Burns, Ralph *(Orchestrations)* 16, 393, 521, 534, 723, 868, 964, 989, 1060, 1227, 1420, 1601, 1842, 1991, 2097, 2106, 2523, 2874, 3187, 3273, 3473, 3506, 3524, 3564, 3925, 4060, 4180, 4238, 4334
Burns, Robert *(Lyricist)* 1897, 3450
Burns, Sandy *(Cast)* 4231
Burns, Sandy *(Librettist)* 4231
Burns, Sandy *(Producer)* 4231
Burns and Allen *(Cast)* 3153
Burnside, Molly *(Cast)* 266
Burnside, R.H. *(Cast)* 425
Burnside, R.H. *(Director)* 126, 246, 335, 355, 378, 396, 712, 735, 736, 773, 930, 968, 1178, 1208, 1243, 1395, 1524, 1534, 1535, 1536, 1631, 1667, 1753, 1768, 1866, 1867, 1868, 1901, 1932, 2139, 2184, 2394, 2399, 2403, 2666, 2848, 2917, 3052, 3144, 3486, 3681, 3790, 3883, 4025, 4044, 4054, 4113, 4150, 4158, 4178, 4345, 4359, 4393, 4434, 4452, 4453, 4586, 4603, 4649
Burnside, R.H. *(Librettist)* 286, 378, 396, 588, 712, 736, 968, 1208, 1246, 1534, 1631, 1753, 1869, 1901, 2139, 2184, 2897, 3052, 3486, 3883, 4054, 4113, 4150, 4345, 4359, 4393, 4434, 4452
Burnside, R.H. *(Lyricist)* 248, 378, 396, 968, 1208, 1246, 1534, 1631, 1753, 1867, 1868, 1901, 2184, 2897, 3486, 3883, 4054, 4359, 4434, 4452
Burnside, R.H. *(Musical Director)* 1524
Burnside, R.H. *(Producer)* 286, 1246, 1464, 1534, 4113, 4345, 4452
Burnson, George *(Cast)* 2085, 2841
Burr, Charles *(Cast)* 4583
Burr, Charles *(Composer)* 1770, 3280, 4262
Burr, Charles *(French Libretto)* 4505
Burr, Charles *(Librettist)* 4505
Burr, Charles *(Lyricist)* 1770, 1959, 3280, 4262, 4505
Burr, Courtney *(Producer)* 1775, 3874, 3894, 4583
Burr, Donald *(Cast)* 1814, 2747, 3931
Burr, Henry *(Composer)* 560
Burr, Henry *(Lyricist)* 560
Burr, Robert *(Cast)* 269, 3468, 4689
Burrell, Deborah *(Cast)* 1103, 2173
Burrell, John *(Director)* 3452
Burrell, Pamela *(Cast)* 3682, 4176
Burrell, Teresa *(Cast)* 1970, 2283, 3628
Burrell, Terry *(Cast)* 4255
Burrell-Cleveland, Deborah *(Cast)* 1890
Burress, William *(Cast)* 2543, 3122, 3529, 4119
Burridge, Walter *(Set Design)* 906, 1433, 2117, 2233, 2315, 2515, 2592, 2723, 2724, 2836, 3437, 3943, 4201, 4404, 4614, 4723, 4738, 4754
Burris, James *(Cast)* 434, 1087, 1909
Burris, James *(Lyricist)* 1909, 4390
Burris, James Henry *(Lyricist)* 1544, 4804
Burris, Jim *(Cast)* 254, 984
Burris, Jim *(Composer)* 146
Burris, Jim *(Lyricist)* 146, 4390

Burroughs, Don *(Cast)* 1391, 3026
Burrow, David *(Cast)* 3802
Burrows, Abe *(Director)* 629, 1290, 1760, 2019, 3845, 4366, 4496, 4633
Burrows, Abe *(Librettist)* 629, 1290, 1706, 1842, 2019, 3845, 3972, 4366
Burrows, Ann *(Costumes)* 1378
Burrows, Joe *(Librettist)* 3133
Burrows, Joe *(Lyricist)* 1121
Burstein, Lillian *(Lyricist)* 4396
Burstein, Lonnie *(Librettist)* 1786, 4450
Burstein, Lonnie *(Lyricist)* 1786, 4450
Burstein, Mike *(Cast)* 2811
Burstein, Pesach *(Cast)* 2811, 3669
Burstein, Pesach *(Director)* 3669
Burstein, Pesach *(Librettist)* 3669
Burstyn, Mike *(Cast)* 36
Burt, Benj. Hapgood *(Composer)* 75, 379
Burt, Benj. Hapgood *(Lyricist)* 93, 246, 335, 379, 606, 627, 675
Burt, Benjamin H. *(Lyricist)* 425
Burt, Benjamin Hapggod *(Composer)* 2765
Burt, Benjamin Hapgood *(Composer)* 712, 772, 1518, 1553, 1566, 1901, 2892, 2906, 2951, 3229, 3753, 3882, 4283, 4393, 4589, 4762
Burt, Benjamin Hapgood *(Librettist)* 425, 1312, 2922, 4333
Burt, Benjamin Hapgood *(Lyricist)* 75, 379, 712, 1312, 1518, 1553, 1901, 2184, 2671, 2765, 2892, 2922, 2951, 3229, 3753, 3857, 3882, 4283, 4393, 4589, 4762
Burt, Flo *(Cast)* 764
Burt, Frank A. *(Cast)* 4487
Burt, Frederic *(Cast)* 4066
Burt, Harriet *(Cast)* 2056, 2213
Burt, Laura *(Cast)* 976
Burt, Sadie *(Cast)* 3396
Burt, Willie *(Costumes)* 874, 2572
Burton, Brenda *(Costumes)* 2676
Burton, Donald *(Cast)* 3598
Burton, Ebbie *(Cast)* 986
Burton, Eugene *(Composer)* 2032, 3410
Burton, Eugene *(Lyricist)* 2032, 3410
Burton, Frederick *(Cast)* 1020
Burton, Hal *(Lyricist)* 3891
Burton, Irving *(Cast)* 757
Burton, Jenny *(Cast)* 3724
Burton, Kate *(Cast)* 1077
Burton, Kenneth *(Composer)* 637, 1678, 3382
Burton, Miriam *(Cast)* 2000
Burton, Nat *(Lyricist)* 3018, 4027
Burton, Richard *(Cast)* 623, 4386
Burton, Robert *(Cast)* 1342, 4166
Burton, Thomas *(Cast)* 4761
Burton, Val *(Composer)* 1947, 3173
Burton, Val *(Lyricist)* 1947, 3173
Burtson, Bud *(Librettist)* 4585
Burtson, Bud *(Lyricist)* 673, 2397, 4826
Burwell, Cliff *(Composer)* 4137
Bury, John *(Costumes)* 3780, 4558
Bury, John *(Lighting Designer)* 2196, 3259
Bury, John *(Set Design)* 1277, 2196, 3259, 3780, 4558
Busby, Earl *(Musical Director)* 163, 1528, 2637, 3379, 4677
Busby, Georgia *(Cast)* 4239
Busby, Michelle *(Cast)* 2521
Busch, Charles *(Author)* 3606
Busch, Charles *(Cast)* 3606
Busch, Lou *(Orchestrations)* 127
Busch, Mae *(Cast)* 3332
Bushar, George *(Producer)* 814
Bushe Company *(Producer)* 3725
Bushkin, Joe *(Composer)* 4255
Bushman, Francis X. *(Cast)* 3626
Bushor, Geoffrey *(Lighting Designer)* 4690
Busia, Akosua *(Cast)* 3001
Busley, Jessie *(Cast)* 1680
Busling, Elfreda *(Cast)* 639
Busse, Henry *(Composer)* 4815
Bussert, Anna *(Cast)* 1455
Bussert, Meg *(Cast)* 3600, 3908
Bussert, Victoria *(Director)* 1510
Bussins, Jack *(Composer)* 314
Bussins, Jack *(Librettist)* 314
Bussins, Jack *(Lyricist)* 314
Bustle, Jonathan *(Cast)* 99
Butcher, George *(Dance Arranger)* 105
Buterbaugh, Keith *(Cast)* 2674
Butler, A.F. *(Cast)* 1560
Butler, Artie *(Musical Director)* 845
Butler, Bill *(Costumes)* 580
Butler, Billy *(Musical Director)* 467, 1984, 4763
Butler, Billy *(Orchestrations)* 4763
Butler, Bruce *(Cast)* 2272
Butler, Buddy *(Lighting Designer)* 2719
Butler, Daws *(Voice)* 2092, 2093
Butler, Edward L. *(Producer)* 1152
Butler, Gregory *(Cast)* 1630, 4055
Butler, James *(Choreographer)* 322
Butler, John *(Choreographer)* 1237, 1742, 2556
Butler, Mark Anthony *(Cast)* 3806
Butler, Michael *(Producer)* 1717, 3690
Butler, Nellie *(Cast)* 4165
Butler, Paul Lindsay *(Lighting Designer)* 916, 4251
Butler, Ralph *(Lyricist)* 2798
Butler, Rhoda *(Cast)* 808, 1249
Butler, Rick *(Lighting Designer)* 696
Butler, Rick *(Set Design)* 696
Butler Jr., Sam *(Cast)* 1636
Butleroff, Helen *(Choreographer)* 1092, 2197, 4769
Butt, Alfred *(Producer)* 3398
Butt, Billy *(Lyricist)* 2689, 3637
Butt, Dan *(Lighting Designer)* 790, 1047
Butt, Jennifer *(Cast)* 2442
Butt, Joseph *(Producer)* 1813, 4454
Butterfield, Everett *(Director)* 728
Butterworth, Charles *(Cast)* 86, 123, 901, 1322, 1617, 4234
Butterworth, Michael *(Author)* 2646
Buttkay, Akos *(Author)* 3537
Button, Dick *(Cast)* 1742
Button, Dick *(Choreographer)* 2097
Button, Dick *(Director)* 2097
Button, Dick *(Producer)* 1062, 2097
Button, Jeanne *(Costumes)* 112, 496, 1383, 1406, 1500, 3209, 3733, 3876, 3960

Buttons, Red *(Cast)* 304, 1744, 1930, 4706
Buttons, Red *(Voice)* 3793
Buttram, Jan *(Cast)* 1249
Buzzell, Eddie *(Cast)* 1027, 1516, 1617, 3185, 4249
Buzzell, Eddie *(Librettist)* 2382
Buzzell, Eddie *(Lyricist)* 4813
Buzzi, Ruth *(Cast)* 249, 272, 1438, 4238
Bybell, Patricia *(Cast)* 85
Byck, Dann *(Producer)* 166
Byers, Bill *(Musical Director)* 499
Byers, Bill *(Orchestrations)* 322, 547, 695, 746, 1068, 1298, 1699, 3126, 3444, 3846, 4020, 4695
Byers, Billy *(Orchestrations)* 775, 1633, 4560
Byers, Ralph *(Cast)* 3456
Byng, Douglas *(Cast)* 791, 792, 1877, 3291, 4154
Byrd, Anthony D. *(Cast)* 982
Byrd, Debra *(Cast)* 1713
Byrd, Joe *(Cast)* 14, 435
Byrd, Joseph *(Cast)* 27
Byrd, Sam *(Producer)* 2225
Byrde, Edye *(Cast)* 4162
Byrne, Barbara *(Cast)* 2143, 4210
Byrne, Beatrice *(Choreographer)* 1972
Byrne, C.A. *(Librettist)* 2157
Byrne, C.A. *(Lyricist)* 2157
Byrne, Charles Alfred *(Librettist)* 2156
Byrne, Charles Wilson *(Librettist)* 3199
Byrne, Gaylea *(Cast)* 71
Byrne, Gypsy *(Cast)* 2271
Byrne, J. Edmund *(Producer)* 3860
Byrne, John *(Set Design)* 2988
Byrne, Kiki *(Costumes)* 4160
Byrnes, James *(Composer)* 3222
Byrnes, James *(Musical Director)* 3222
Byrns, Harold *(Orchestrations)* 999
Byron, Arthur *(Cast)* 2202, 3917
Byron, Ben B. *(Cast)* 540
Byron, Bert *(Cast)* 538
Byron, Betty *(Cast)* 4322
Byron, George *(Cast)* 2077, 3104
Byron, Helen *(Cast)* 3065
Byron-Kirk, Keith *(Cast)* 494

C

C.T.A. *(Lyricist)* 123
CHS Productions *(Producer)* 2416, 3178
CSC Repertory *(Producer)* 3853
Cabell, Robert W. *(Composer)* 3561
Cabell, Robert W. *(Librettist)* 3561
Cabell, Robert W. *(Lyricist)* 3561
Cabot, Ceil *(Cast)* 1023, 1107, 3484, 3889, 4065, 4268
Cabot, Tony *(Musical Director)* 961
Caccia, Roger *(Cast)* 2364
Cacoyannis, Michael *(Director)* 2659
Cacoyannis, Michael *(Translator)* 2659
Cadby, Peter *(Composer)* 4153
Cadby, Peter *(Lyricist)* 4153
Caddick, David *(Musical Director)* 3464, 4138, 4217
Caddick, Edward *(Cast)* 455, 1277
Cadenhead, Ian *(Lighting Designer)* 1017
Caderette, Christine *(Musical Director)* 533
Cadiff, Andrew *(Director)* 572, 2702, 4349
Cadiff, Andrew *(Librettist)* 572
Cadman, Ethel *(Cast)* 178, 822
Cady, David *(Cast)* 4790
Caesar, Adolph *(Cast)* 1671
Caesar, Arthur *(Librettist)* 1690
Caesar, Irving *(Cast)* 1396
Caesar, Irving *(Composer)* 1396, 1481, 2706, 2818, 3036, 3721, 4212, 4730, 4766
Caesar, Irving *(Librettist)* 376, 969, 1396, 1492, 1690, 2112, 2567, 3036, 3179, 3907, 4730
Caesar, Irving *(Lyricist)* 124, 146, 292, 376, 381, 393, 465, 487, 545, 638, 702, 773, 969, 1026, 1120, 1179, 1193, 1396, 1432, 1481, 1491, 1626, 1688, 1689, 1690, 1691, 1859, 1920, 1923, 2112, 2180, 2336, 2363, 2385, 2387, 2567, 2594, 2606, 2706, 2757, 2813, 2818, 3020, 3036, 3140, 3144, 3157, 3170, 3172, 3179, 3184, 3249, 3319, 3443, 3500, 3532, 3540, 3639, 3662, 3721, 3762, 3953, 3985, 4104, 4212, 4235, 4249, 4276, 4374, 4491, 4667, 4683, 4730, 4766, 4817, 4858
Caesar, Irving *(Producer)* 3036
Caesar, Jimmy *(Cast)* 92
Caesar, Robert *(Cast)* 600
Caesar, Sid *(Cast)* 2523, 2707, 4287
Caffey, Marion J. *(Cast)* 2790
Cagney, James *(Cast)* 1656, 1657, 3508
Cagney, James *(Choreographer)* 1656
Cagney, James *(Voice)* 281
Cahan, Abraham *(Author)* 3722
Cahan, Marla *(Cast)* 4830
Cahill, Alfred *(Cast)* 1613
Cahill, James *(Cast)* 775
Cahill, Marie *(Cast)* 511, 1213, 1599, 2160, 2254, 2274, 2765, 2827, 2938, 2951, 3073, 3131, 3177, 3308, 3820, 4130, 4353, 4691
Cahill, Marie *(Composer)* 2765
Cahill, Marie *(Lyricist)* 2765
Cahill, Paul *(Cast)* 941
Cahill, William *(Lyricist)* 2765
Cahn, Cathy *(Cast)* 4034
Cahn, Sammy *(Cast)* 4743
Cahn, Sammy *(Composer)* 1813, 4743
Cahn, Sammy *(Librettist)* 4743
Cahn, Sammy *(Lyricist)* 51, 172, 432, 486, 664, 820, 889, 1577, 1658, 1659, 1813, 1886, 1982, 2076, 2183, 2205, 2443, 2554, 2583, 2737, 3160, 3324, 3683, 3832, 3844, 4013, 4342, 4399, 4499, 4588, 4743
Cahn, William *(Producer)* 4428
Caillavet, G. *(Author)* 2624
Cain, John E. *(Cast)* 45, 537, 540
Cain, Sibol *(Cast)* 653
Cain, Viola *(Cast)* 3308
Caine, Georgia *(Cast)* 20, 317, 1123, 1375, 2533, 2592, 2668, 2844, 2889, 2966, 3218, 3437, 3710, 3750, 3820, 3943, 4023, 4359, 4482, 4489
Caine, William *(Lyricist)* 356
Caird, John *(Director)* 730, 2442
Caird, John *(Librettist)* 730

Caird, Laurence *(Cast)* 2131
Caisons, Currie *(Cast)* 2984
Calabrese, Maria *(Cast)* 4676
Calbes, Eleanor A. *(Cast)* 2626
Calder, Crane *(Vocal Arranger)* 341, 1679, 3509, 3895
Calderon, Ian *(Lighting Designer)* 546, 2017, 2415, 2472, 4151, 4383, 4505
Calduel, Lorenzo *(Orchestrations)* 740
Calduel, Lorenzo *(Vocal Arranger)* 740
Caldwell, Anne *(Author)* 736, 2919, 4642
Caldwell, Anne *(Cast)* 4223
Caldwell, Anne *(Composer)* 246, 3882, 4044, 4425
Caldwell, Anne *(Librettist)* 582, 736, 930, 1588, 1625, 1922, 2184, 2385, 2394, 2691, 2919, 2921, 3146, 3254, 3537, 3923, 4150, 4248, 4271, 4345
Caldwell, Anne *(Lyricist)* 396, 582, 611, 627, 736, 765, 773, 930, 1588, 1625, 1780, 1922, 2184, 2372, 2385, 2394, 2518, 2691, 2919, 2921, 3146, 3249, 3254, 3431, 3537, 3819, 3923, 4150, 4248, 4345, 4393, 4642, 4793
Caldwell, Ben *(Librettist)* 2932
Caldwell, Gladys *(Cast)* 1536
Caldwell, Gloria *(Composer)* 3695
Caldwell, Gloria *(Lyricist)* 3695
Caldwell, Keith *(Cast)* 4454
Caldwell, Lorenzo *(Musical Director)* 4253
Caldwell, Lorenzo *(Orchestrations)* 4253, 4763
Caldwell, Neal *(Cast)* 1448
Caldwell, Orville R. *(Cast)* 2802
Caldwell, Zoe *(Cast)* 807
Cale, Bennett *(Cast)* 4139
Calhoun, Charles *(Composer)* 3695
Calhoun, Charles *(Lyricist)* 3695
Calhoun, Jeff *(Choreographer)* 373, 589
Calhoun, Jeff *(Director)* 589
Calhoun, Rory *(Producer)* 362
Calice, Myron *(Cast)* 4407
California Collegians, The *(Cast)* 3735, 4367
California State College at Fullerton *(Producer)* 973
Californians, The *(Cast)* 662
Calin, Mickey *(Cast)* 4191, 4625
Calkin, Philip *(Composer)* 2757
Calkins, Florence *(Librettist)* 1874
Calkins, Michael *(Cast)* 2616
Call, John *(Cast)* 2910, 3482
Callahan, Bill *(Cast)* 206, 620, 4499
Callahan, George *(Cast)* 2340
Callahan, George W. *(Cast)* 1743, 4440
Callahan, J. Will *(Lyricist)* 3402, 4390
Callahan, Marie *(Cast)* 75, 1944, 3117
Callan, Christopher *(Cast)* 843, 2969
Callan, Michael *(Cast)* 171
Callaway, Bill *(Cast)* 2965
Callaway, Joe *(Cast)* 279
Callaway, Liz *(Cast)* 253, 572, 2783, 2905
Callaway, Thomas *(Cast)* 1104
Callen, Chris *(Cast)* 3576
Callen, Michael *(Composer)* 3198
Callen, Michael *(Lyricist)* 3198
Callish, Betty *(Cast)* 3812
Callot *(Costumes)* 4806
Calloway, Blanche *(Cast)* 4520
Calloway, Cab *(Cast)* 898, 1980, 2553, 3153
Calloway, Cab *(Composer)* 883, 887, 896, 4137, 4534
Calloway, Cab *(Lyricist)* 877, 883, 887, 896
Calloway, Chris *(Cast)* 2195
Calloway, Harriet *(Cast)* 2337
Calloway, Northern J. *(Cast)* 2801
Calloway and His Orchestra, Cab *(Cast)* 876, 877, 879, 883, 884, 887, 888, 896, 3709
Calthrop, G.E. *(Costumes)* 841, 1855, 3885, 4341, 4361
Calthrop, G.E. *(Set Design)* 429, 841, 1238, 3597, 3678, 3885, 3906, 4341, 4361, 4610
Calthrop, Gladys E. *(Costumes)* 3339
Calthrop, Gladys E. *(Set Design)* 3339
Calvert, Bob *(Cast)* 3507
Calvert, Robert *(Cast)* 164
Calvi, Gerard *(Composer)* 2362, 2364
Calvi, Gerard *(Lyricist)* 2364
Calvi, Gerard *(Orchestrations)* 2362, 2364
Calvin, Gene *(Costumes)* 4527
Calvin, Henry *(Cast)* 1748, 2327
Camarata, Toots *(Orchestrations)* 341
Camarata, Tutti *(Musical Director)* 4155
Cambridge, Ed *(Director)* 279
Cambridge, Godfrey *(Cast)* 2016
Cameron, Bill *(Cast)* 2089, 2090
Cameron, Cecil *(Cast)* 1114
Cameron, Frances *(Cast)* 1295, 1911, 2454, 2574, 2836, 4063, 4490
Cameron, Grace *(Cast)* 2724, 3486, 3488, 4559
Cameron, Hugh *(Cast)* 208, 289, 628, 680, 1109, 3006, 3384, 3980, 4077, 4374, 4825
Cameron, Kay *(Musical Director)* 4146
Cameron, Kay *(Vocal Arranger)* 4146
Cameron, Madeline *(Cast)* 376, 1339, 1916
Cameron, Rudolph *(Cast)* 4001
Cameron, Suzan *(Cast)* 874
Cameron, William *(Cast)* 48, 113, 357, 1351, 2209, 2213, 2724, 2895, 3129, 3486, 3566
Cameron, Yukona *(Cast)* 3861
Cameron Sisters, The *(Cast)* 4037
Camilo, Michael *(Composer)* 146
Camilo, Michael *(Lyricist)* 146
Cammeyer, A.D. *(Composer)* 1537, 2844
Cammeyer, Alfred D. *(Composer)* 3803
Camp, Hamilton *(Cast)* 52
Camp, Richard *(Librettist)* 1038
Camp, Shep *(Composer)* 1722
Campanella, Frank *(Cast)* 3210, 4005
Campanella, Joseph *(Cast)* 1991
Campanella, Philip *(Musical Director)* 3598
Campanella, Philip *(Orchestrations)* 4175
Campanile, Festa *(Librettist)* 3798
Campbell *(Costumes)* 2246
Campbell *(Lyricist)* 2793
Campbell, Alan *(Cast)* 4217
Campbell, Alan *(Orchestrations)* 2573
Campbell, Arthur *(Cast)* 1020, 1971, 3069, 4823
Campbell, Bill *(Costumes)* 2080, 2443
Campbell, Charles *(Cast)* 1072
Campbell, Charles J. *(Librettist)* 1910, 2966, 4493
Campbell, Charles J. *(Lyricist)* 1458, 1910, 2966, 4493

Campbell, Chris *(Cast)* 793
Campbell, Colin *(Cast)* 1733, 3219
Campbell, Craig *(Cast)* 1285
Campbell, David *(Librettist)* 1970
Campbell, David *(Lyricist)* 1970
Campbell, Donald F. *(Cast)* 1155
Campbell, Edna *(Cast)* 3804
Campbell, Eric *(Cast)* 3537
Campbell, Frank *(Composer)* 1897
Campbell, Frank *(Lyricist)* 1897
Campbell, George *(Librettist)* 3538
Campbell, Graeme *(Cast)* 3485
Campbell, Irma *(Costumes)* 4360
Campbell, James *(Lyricist)* 1135, 1136
Campbell, Jermaine *(Cast)* 3668
Campbell, Larry *(Cast)* 1282, 4168
Campbell, Manzie *(Cast)* 1421
Campbell, Margaret *(Cast)* 1534
Campbell, Muriel *(Cast)* 536
Campbell, Norman *(Composer)* 148
Campbell, Norman *(Lyricist)* 148
Campbell, Patton *(Composer)* 72
Campbell, Patton *(Costumes)* 32, 64, 837, 1616, 1676, 2727, 3612
Campbell, Paul *(Composer)* 2203
Campbell, Paul *(Lyricist)* 2203
Campbell, Sande *(Arrangements)* 944
Campbell, Sande *(Musical Director)* 944, 1770, 2731, 2962
Campbell, Sande *(Orchestrations)* 944
Campbell, Sande *(Vocal Arranger)* 1770
Campbell, Stu *(Cast)* 4047
Campbell, Stuart *(Producer)* 4047
Campbell, Tisha *(Cast)* 3668
Campbell, Walter *(Director)* 4763
Campbell, Walter *(Producer)* 3054, 4763
Campbell's Continentals, Roy *(Cast)* 3955
Campodonico, James *(Composer)* 3004
Campodonico, James *(Lyricist)* 3004
Campone, Marv *(Lyricist)* 426
Camuti Jr., Louis *(Cast)* 2641
Canadian National Musical Theatre *(Producer)* 148
Canary, David *(Cast)* 915, 1878
Canary, Thomas *(Producer)* 113, 1599, 2116, 2842
Canciani, Christian *(Cast)* 1236
Candee Jr., Charles E. *(Musical Director)* 375
Canemaker, John *(Cast)* 3491
Caney, R. *(Cast)* 4014
Caney, R. *(Set Design)* 2964
Canfield, Doris *(Cast)* 1267
Canfield, Eugene *(Cast)* 1259
Canning, James *(Cast)* 1664
Cannon, Alice *(Cast)* 31, 2731
Cannon, Hughie *(Composer)* 2990, 4390
Cannon, Hughie *(Lyricist)* 2990, 4390
Cannon, Maureen *(Cast)* 372, 1718, 4524
Canova, Judy *(Cast)* 622, 4772, 4825
Cansinos, The *(Cast)* 370
Cantin, Jim *(Musical Director)* 2477
Cantor, Arthur *(Producer)* 2006, 2204, 2726, 3615
Cantor, Eddie *(Cast)* 297, 545, 1416, 2308, 2403, 2706, 2857, 4683, 4812, 4813, 4817, 4821, 4841, 4845, 4852
Cantor, Eddie *(Composer)* 2308, 2706, 2857, 4812, 4817
Cantor, Eddie *(Librettist)* 1126, 3172, 4821
Cantor, Eddie *(Lyricist)* 2308, 2706, 2857, 4812, 4813, 4817
Cantor, Eddie *(Producer)* 3091
Cantor, Lew *(Producer)* 4208
Cantor, Marilyn *(Cast)* 4047
Cantor, Robin *(Cast)* 4168
Cantril, Ken *(Cast)* 600
Cantwell, John *(Librettist)* 4673
Canyon Productions *(Producer)* 2368
Cap and Bells, Inc. *(Producer)* 80, 3471
Capalbo, Carmen *(Director)* 4369
Capalbo, Carmen *(Producer)* 4369
Cape, Vandy *(Cast)* 1342
Cape Playhouse, The *(Producer)* 637
Capehart, Charles *(Producer)* 728
Capel, J.M. *(Composer)* 2844
Capella & Patricia *(Cast)* 848
Capers, Virginia *(Cast)* 3656
Capillupo, Rinaldo *(Director)* 1924
Capital Cities/ABC *(Producer)* 3411
Capital Cities/ABC Inc. *(Producer)* 3285
Capitol Theatre *(Producer)* 638
Capizzi, Leonard *(Composer)* 3695
Capizzi, Leonard *(Lyricist)* 3695
Caples, Martha *(Composer)* 2294, 3103, 3104, 3292
Caples, Martha *(Lyricist)* 2294
Caplin, Gertrude *(Producer)* 4005
Capone, Clifford *(Costumes)* 753, 2172, 3565, 4062
Capote, Truman *(Author)* 521, 1662
Capote, Truman *(Librettist)* 2000
Capote, Truman *(Lyricist)* 2000
Capp, Al *(Author)* 2484
Capps, Al *(Musical Director)* 57
Capps, Kendall *(Cast)* 1691
Cappy, Ted *(Choreographer)* 2928, 4273, 4366, 4496
Capra, Frank *(Author)* 4732
Caprin, Sandra *(Cast)* 2332
Caprin, Sandra *(Choreographer)* 2332
Capron, Robert *(Cast)* 4328
Cara, Irene *(Cast)* 1637, 2801, 4558
Carby, Fanny *(Cast)* 3259
Card, Jack *(Cast)* 362
Card, Jack *(Choreographer)* 362
Card, Virginia *(Cast)* 2841
Carden, Carl *(Cast)* 214
Carder, Tom *(Cast)* 2242
Cardin, Pierre *(Producer)* 2269
Cardoze, F.T. *(Lyricist)* 248
Carew, Lisa *(Cast)* 2198
Carey, A.J. *(Composer)* 969
Carey, Addison *(Choreographer)* 498, 567, 4281
Carey, Addison *(Director)* 1876, 2337
Carey, Addison *(Librettist)* 1876
Carey, David *(Cast)* 1269, 3669, 3781
Carey, David *(Producer)* 3781
Carey, Denis *(Director)* 1386
Carey, Frank *(Cast)* 3599
Carey, Henry *(Composer)* 3450, 3820, 4859
Carey, Henry *(Lyricist)* 3450, 3820, 4859
Carey, Joyce *(Cast)* 1238, 3678, 3906, 4610

Carey, Macdonald *(Cast)* 2386
Carey, Michael *(Composer)* 1501
Carey, Michael *(Lyricist)* 1501
Carey, Robert *(Cast)* 3606
Carfagno, Randy *(Costumes)* 4462
Carine, Martha *(Cast)* 767
Cariou, Len *(Cast)* 167, 958, 2536, 4233, 4297
Carl, George *(Cast)* 1326
Carl, Joseph *(Set Design)* 972
Carlbach, Schlomo *(Composer)* 1609
Carle, Cynthia *(Cast)* 2152
Carle, Richard *(Cast)* 21, 560, 804, 1066, 1213, 1220, 1538, 1682, 2116, 2261, 2374, 2398, 2695, 2714, 2770, 2793, 3131, 3177, 4161, 4218, 4311, 4742
Carle, Richard *(Choreographer)* 2040
Carle, Richard *(Composer)* 121, 506, 2261, 2695, 2770, 4115, 4161
Carle, Richard *(Director)* 2040, 2261, 2695, 4311
Carle, Richard *(Librettist)* 506, 2040, 2261, 2695, 2714, 2770, 2793, 4115, 4161, 4311
Carle, Richard *(Lyricist)* 506, 560, 2040, 2261, 2374, 2529, 2695, 2714, 2770, 2793, 4115, 4161, 4311
Carle, Richard *(Producer)* 2695, 2770, 2793, 4115
Carle, Virginia *(Cast)* 3803
Carleton, Arthur *(Cast)* 1206
Carleton, Carle *(Composer)* 4283
Carleton, Claire *(Cast)* 536
Carleton, W.P. *(Cast)* 3566
Carleton, W.T. *(Cast)* 1178, 2803, 2914, 3575
Carleton, Will *(Librettist)* 141, 2222
Carleton, Will *(Lyricist)* 141, 2222
Carleton, William *(Cast)* 2399
Carleton, William *(Librettist)* 668
Carleton, William P. *(Cast)* 4293
Carleton, William T. *(Cast)* 1576, 4353
Carleton Jr., Wm. P. *(Cast)* 2716
Carlin, Tony *(Cast)* 1739
Carlini, John *(Orchestrations)* 4076
Carlisle, Gertie *(Cast)* 2543, 3422, 4293
Carlisle, Kevin *(Choreographer)* 1729
Carlisle, Kitty *(Cast)* 689, 1933, 4365, 4586, 4667
Carlisle, Louise *(Cast)* 1165
Carlo, Monte *(Composer)* 606, 728, 1132, 1174, 2005, 2595, 3580, 4283, 4576
Carlo, Monte *(Lyricist)* 606, 728, 1132, 1174, 2005, 2595, 3069, 3252, 3580, 4283
Carlo Studios *(Set Design)* 4328
Carlos, Laurie *(Cast)* 1344
Carlson, Deborah *(Cast)* 198, 2968
Carlson, Richard *(Cast)* 621, 4142
Carlson, Violet *(Cast)* 3680, 4188, 4234
Carlton *(Composer)* 4683
Carlton *(Lyricist)* 4683
Carlton, Bob *(Director)* 2654, 3695
Carlton, Bob *(Librettist)* 3695
Carlton, Carle *(Composer)* 230, 2371, 3369
Carlton, Carle *(Director)* 2371, 3369
Carlton, Carle *(Lyricist)* 2371
Carlton, Carle *(Producer)* 2371, 3369, 4283
Carlton, Carle *(Set Design)* 2371
Carlton, Graeme *(Choreographer)* 3490
Carlton, Harry *(Composer)* 4264
Carlton, Harry *(Lyricist)* 605, 4264
Carlton, Sidney *(Librettist)* 2938
Carlton, Will *(Director)* 3951
Carlton, William *(Lyricist)* 2062
Carlysle, Lynn *(Cast)* 3338
Carmel, Kate *(Costumes)* 788, 3162
Carmel, Kate *(Set Design)* 788
Carmello, Carolee *(Cast)* 198, 992, 1822
Carmen, Sybil *(Cast)* 4834
Carmeron, Grace *(Cast)* 2505
Carmichael, Bill *(Cast)* 1348
Carmichael, Hoagy *(Composer)* 39, 59, 213, 3444, 3955, 4137, 4586
Carmichael, Patricia *(Director)* 3565, 3764
Carminati, Tullio *(Cast)* 1670, 3014
Carmines, Al *(Cast)* 755, 1229, 1958, 2110, 2220
Carmines, Al *(Composer)* 624, 755, 1229, 1426, 1958, 2110, 2124, 2220, 2243, 2478, 2579, 3418, 3602, 4577, 4595, 4684
Carmines, Al *(Director)* 1229, 2220
Carmines, Al *(Librettist)* 624, 755, 1229, 1426, 2220, 2243, 2478, 2579, 4684
Carmines, Al *(Lyricist)* 624, 755, 1229, 1426, 2124, 2220, 2243, 2478, 2579, 3418, 4577, 4595, 4684
Carmines, Al *(Musical Director)* 2220, 3418, 3602
Carmines, Al *(Orchestrations)* 2579
Carmines, Al *(Pianist)* 3418
Carmines, Al *(Vocal Arranger)* 2579
Carmody, John *(Cast)* 1795
Carnahan, Kirsti *(Cast)* 2333
Carnegie, Hattie *(Costumes)* 2386, 3243, 3335
Carnelia, Craig *(Cast)* 4358
Carnelia, Craig *(Composer)* 1038, 2152, 3181, 4358, 4744
Carnelia, Craig *(Lyricist)* 1038, 2152, 3181, 4358, 4744
Carnes, Kathleen *(Cast)* 153
Carney, Alan *(Cast)* 1242
Carney, Art *(Cast)* 192, 193
Carney, George *(Cast)* 1618
Carney, Grace *(Cast)* 135, 1076, 3059
Carney, Harry *(Composer)* 875, 885, 895, 4091
Carnovsky, Morris *(Cast)* 1237, 2228, 2450, 2859
Carol, Hope *(Cast)* 3002
Carol, Jacqueline *(Cast)* 1695
Carothers, A.J. *(Librettist)* 589
Carousel Group, Inc. *(Producer)* 2692
Carpenter, Carleton *(Cast)* 2227
Carpenter, Constance *(Cast)* 133, 702, 703, 834, 1763, 3011, 3243, 4335, 4541
Carpenter, E.J. *(Librettist)* 3025
Carpenter, Edward Childs *(Author)* 763
Carpenter, Edward Childs *(Librettist)* 2002, 2813
Carpenter, Edward Childs *(Lyricist)* 763
Carpenter, Francis *(Cast)* 2257
Carpenter, Freddie *(Choreographer)* 972
Carpenter, Frederick *(Cast)* 1333
Carpenter, Imogene *(Cast)* 4826
Carpenter, J.E. *(Composer)* 1897
Carpenter, J.E. *(Lyricist)* 1897
Carpenter, Jean *(Cast)* 4545
Carpenter, John A. *(Librettist)* 2508

Carpenter, John A. *(Lyricist)* 2508
Carpenter, Larry *(Director)* 3598, 4139
Carpenter, Larry *(Producer)* 33
Carpenter, Thelma *(Cast)* 145, 2137, 2817, 3966
Carr, Alexander *(Cast)* 1464, 1728, 2596
Carr, Allan *(Producer)* 2360
Carr, Charmian *(Cast)* 1200
Carr, F. Osmond *(Composer)* 1905, 2131
Carr, George *(Cast)* 1466
Carr, George H. *(Cast)* 2316
Carr, Henry *(Director)* 1887
Carr, Jack *(Cast)* 27, 653
Carr, Jack *(Librettist)* 345
Carr, Jimmie *(Musical Director)* 2296
Carr, Kenneth *(Cast)* 3636
Carr, Lawrence *(Producer)* 603, 1273, 1991, 2713, 3687, 3913, 4238
Carr, Leon *(Composer)* 3863, 4264
Carr, Leon *(Lyricist)* 4264
Carr, Michael *(Additional Music)* 2572
Carr, Tottie *(Cast)* 1445
Carra, Lawrence *(Director)* 825, 2339, 4191
Carra, Lawrence *(Librettist)* 825
Carra, Lawrence *(Producer)* 2339
Carradine, John *(Cast)* 1422
Carradine, Keith *(Cast)* 1372, 4695
Carrafa, John *(Choreographer)* 647
Carras, Nicholas *(Orchestrations)* 1766
Carre, Albert *(Author)* 1347
Carre fils, Michel *(Author)* 25
Carrere, Fernando *(Set Design)* 2091
Carrick, Hartley *(Lyricist)* 758
Carrillo, Leo *(Cast)* 1228
Carrington, Katherine *(Cast)* 1196, 1225, 1448, 3014
Carrington, Will *(Cast)* 434
Carrol, W.F. *(Librettist)* 3348
Carroll, Adam *(Dance Arranger)* 4782
Carroll, Adam *(Orchestrations)* 4782
Carroll, Adam *(Pianist)* 138, 2545
Carroll, Adam *(Vocal Arranger)* 4782
Carroll, Albert *(Cast)* 125, 1357, 1448, 1651, 1652, 1653, 1654, 1655, 1656, 1657, 4823
Carroll, Albert *(Choreographer)* 1357, 1652, 1653
Carroll, Albert *(Composer)* 1651
Carroll, Albert *(Dance Arranger)* 1651
Carroll, Albert *(Librettist)* 621
Carroll, Albert *(Lyricist)* 1651, 1652, 1654, 1655, 1657
Carroll, Barbara *(Cast)* 2797
Carroll, Bob *(Cast)* 3577, 3683
Carroll, Carroll *(Librettist)* 1448
Carroll, Carroll *(Lyricist)* 720
Carroll, Chris *(Cast)* 3557
Carroll, Danny *(Cast)* 249, 287, 1359, 1478, 3186
Carroll, David *(Cast)* 721, 1649, 2359, 4701
Carroll, David-James *(Cast)* 2785, 3231, 3743, 3888, 4114
Carroll, Diahann *(Cast)* 2000, 3187
Carroll, Earl *(Composer)* 628, 1129, 1130, 2939, 3395, 3562, 3662, 3812, 4037
Carroll, Earl *(Director)* 1126, 1127, 1128, 1130, 1131, 1132, 1134, 1135, 1136, 1137, 1138, 1312, 3002
Carroll, Earl *(Librettist)* 1130, 1138, 2619, 3002, 4416
Carroll, Earl *(Lyricist)* 60, 351, 628, 1129, 1130, 1138, 1309, 2619, 2939, 3332, 3395, 3562, 3662, 3812, 3827, 4037, 4807
Carroll, Earl *(Producer)* 1125, 1126, 1127, 1128, 1129, 1130, 1131, 1132, 1134, 1135, 1136, 1137, 1138, 1281, 1312, 2020, 3002
Carroll, Eddie *(Cast)* 2436
Carroll, Georgia *(Cast)* 2597
Carroll, Gladys *(Costumes)* 4152
Carroll, Harry *(Cast)* 2696
Carroll, Harry *(Composer)* 351, 448, 965, 1209, 1270, 1486, 1694, 1738, 1777, 1778, 1920, 1963, 2494, 2696, 3246, 3354, 3397, 4589, 4655, 4720, 4804, 4814, 4815, 4853
Carroll, Harry *(Lyricist)* 448, 1209
Carroll, Harry *(Producer)* 3246
Carroll, Helena *(Cast)* 3482
Carroll, Irving *(Musical Director)* 268
Carroll, James *(Costumes)* 858
Carroll, Jane *(Cast)* 2430
Carroll, Joan *(Cast)* 3359
Carroll, John *(Cast)* 2742
Carroll, June
See also June Sillman.
Carroll, June *(Cast)* 817, 3107
Carroll, June *(Librettist)* 2103, 3105
Carroll, June *(Lyricist)* 679, 817, 1878, 2103, 2294, 2772, 3105, 3107, 3108, 3110, 3111, 3112, 3178, 3320, 3880, 3890, 3941, 4433
Carroll, Lambert *(Librettist)* 1207
Carroll, Leo G. *(Cast)* 2786, 4100, 4479
Carroll, Lewis *(Author)* 52, 54, 55, 56, 57, 58, 593, 4736
Carroll, Lewis *(Lyricist)* 55
Carroll, Marie *(Cast)* 3043, 3230, 4860
Carroll, Nancy *(Cast)* 391, 910, 3072
Carroll, Pat *(Cast)* 673, 2742, 4273
Carroll, Pauline *(Composer)* 448
Carroll, Pauline *(Lyricist)* 448
Carroll, R.F. *(Lyricist)* 539
Carroll, Richard *(Cast)* 47, 976, 3049, 3199
Carroll, Richard *(Composer)* 3022
Carroll, Richard *(Director)* 541, 1912, 3025
Carroll, Richard *(Lyricist)* 47, 3022
Carroll, Richard F. *(Author)* 2326
Carroll, Richard F. *(Cast)* 523, 2350, 4556
Carroll, Richard F. *(Director)* 3022
Carroll, Richard F. *(Librettist)* 4556
Carroll, Richard F. *(Lyricist)* 4556
Carroll, Richard F. *(Producer)* 2518
Carroll, Robert *(Cast)* 3013
Carroll, Ronn *(Cast)* 373, 921, 2346, 2542, 3517, 3718
Carroll, Sidney *(Librettist)* 2772, 3108
Carroll, Vinnette *(Director)* 52, 1072, 4645, 4788
Carroll, Vinnette *(Librettist)* 52, 593, 4788
Carry, Louis *(Cast)* 2737
Carson, Alexander *(Producer)* 4542
Carson, Doris *(Cast)* 672, 2636, 3283, 4179
Carson, Heather *(Lighting Designer)* 1509, 4775
Carson, Irwin *(Composer)* 3714
Carson, Jack *(Cast)* 1204
Carson, James B. *(Cast)* 292, 1308
Carson, Jean *(Cast)* 2608
Carson, Jeannie *(Cast)* 461, 1815, 2550, 3630

Carson, Mindy *(Cast)* 483
Carson, Sue *(Cast)* 865, 1341
Carson, Susan Dawn *(Cast)* 4055, 4217
Carten, Bob *(Cast)* 4591
Carten, Bob *(Musical Director)* 4591
Carten, Kenneth *(Cast)* 3885
Carter *(Librettist)* 1995
Carter *(Lyricist)* 1995
Carter, Alice E. *(Costumes)* 2908
Carter, Benjamin *(Cast)* 344
Carter, Claire *(Lighting Designer)* 2988
Carter, Desmond *(Composer)* 2376
Carter, Desmond *(Librettist)* 1110, 2323, 2547
Carter, Desmond *(Lyricist)* 700, 791, 834, 921, 1338, 1680, 1681, 1756, 1855, 2004, 2323, 2376, 2547, 3430, 3569, 4027, 4207, 4212, 4300, 4320, 4581, 4765
Carter, Dixie *(Cast)* 2838, 3902
Carter, Frank *(Cast)* 3868, 4812
Carter, Frank *(Composer)* 3333
Carter, Genna *(Cast)* 366
Carter, Jack *(Cast)* 649, 2987
Carter, Janis *(Cast)* 1109
Carter, Joey *(Cast)* 3110
Carter, Joey *(Librettist)* 3110
Carter, Joey *(Lyricist)* 3110
Carter, Lavada *(Cast)* 3965
Carter, Leslie H. *(Librettist)* 4627
Carter, Lincoln J. *(Producer)* 1185
Carter, Louise *(Cast)* 2826
Carter, Nell *(Cast)* 39, 314, 1116, 2898, 4089, 4403, 4615
Carter, Ralph *(Cast)* 1116, 2290, 3656, 4558
Carter, Robert Peyton *(Cast)* 2383
Carter, Rosanna *(Cast)* 2133
Carter, Sidney *(Lyricist)* 220
Carter, Stanley *(Lyricist)* 2389
Carter, Terry *(Cast)* 2355, 2994
Carter, Vicki *(Musical Director)* 1198, 2027
Carter-Waddell, Joan *(Cast)* 1874
Carthay, Dan *(Cast)* 1136, 2300
Carthe, Dan *(Choreographer)* 3409
Cartier, Deidre *(Costumes)* 461, 1761
Cartier, Jacques *(Cast)* 1603, 4824
Cartier, Jeanne *(Cast)* 3865
Cartwright, Charles *(Director)* 2819
Cartwright, Peggy *(Cast)* 125
Carty Jr., Edward M. *(Lighting Designer)* 4149
Carucci, Frank *(Director)* 843
Carus, Emma *(Cast)* 1021, 1505, 1728, 2324, 2803, 2851, 4521, 4650, 4687, 4738, 4801
Caruso, Dee *(Librettist)* 272, 427, 1049, 1648, 3186, 4153, 4268
Caruso, Fran *(Costumes)* 1978
Carver, Brent *(Cast)* 2333
Carvill, Rosemary *(Costumes)* 1386
Carwell, T.L. *(Composer)* 987
Cary, Addison *(Choreographer)* 497
Cary, Claiborne *(Cast)* 73, 198, 339, 4028
Caryl, William *(Director)* 2540, 4240, 4741
Caryl, William *(Producer)* 4424
Caryll, Fred *(Librettist)* 3434
Caryll, Fred *(Lyricist)* 3434
Caryll, Ivan *(Author)* 351, 3322, 4115
Caryll, Ivan *(Composer)* 351, 627, 719, 736, 770, 1114, 1123, 1313, 1527, 1537, 1540, 1569, 1992, 2184, 2336, 2374, 2497, 2498, 2500, 2760, 2844, 3020, 3092, 3098, 3251, 3313, 3322, 3362, 3494, 3803, 3948, 3976, 3999, 4115, 4393, 4430, 4590, 4805, 4823
Caryll, Ivan *(Musical Director)* 1114, 3098
Caryll, Ivan *(Orchestrations)* 2336
Casale, Glenn *(Director)* 2651
Casanave, Carolyn *(Cast)* 140, 583
Cascio, Gigi *(Lighting Designer)* 679
Cascone, Michael *(Cast)* 2630
Case, Allen *(Cast)* 649, 1729, 3288, 3696
Case, Mary *(Puppeteer)* 56, 3449
Case, Ronald *(Costumes)* 3576, 4146
Case, Ronald *(Set Design)* 3576
Case, Russ *(Musical Director)* 3490
Case, Russ *(Orchestrations)* 3490
Casella, Martin *(Librettist)* 3364
Casella, Matt *(Director)* 3364
Casey, Charles E. *(Composer)* 3220
Casey, Charles E. *(Lyricist)* 3220
Casey, Dorothy *(Cast)* 2253
Casey, Gene *(Composer)* 2026, 3318
Casey, Gene *(Librettist)* 3318
Casey, Gene *(Lyricist)* 2026, 3318
Casey, Gene *(Orchestrations)* 3318
Casey, Jan *(Composer)* 2026
Casey, Jan *(Librettist)* 2026
Casey, Kenneth *(Composer)* 3905
Casey, Kenneth *(Lyricist)* 3905
Casey, Michael *(Costumes)* 107, 1638, 2737
Casey, Warren *(Composer)* 1664
Casey, Warren *(Librettist)* 1664
Casey, Warren *(Lyricist)* 1664
Cash, Estelle *(Cast)* 254
Cash, Nat *(Choreographer)* 1328, 1989, 3361
Cash, Rosalind *(Cast)* 1592
Casher, Izidor *(Cast)* 3336
Casher, Jennie *(Cast)* 3336
Cashman, Edward *(Composer)* 821, 2641
Cashman, Edward *(Dance Arranger)* 345
Cashman, Edward *(Lyricist)* 821
Cashman, Edward *(Musical Director)* 345
Cashone, Regina *(Cast)* 4168
Casler, Richard *(Lighting Designer)* 161, 937, 3684
Casler, Richard *(Set Design)* 937
Casman, Nellie *(Cast)* 4463
Casman, Nellie *(Composer)* 1279
Casman, Nellie *(Lyricist)* 1279, 4342
Casmore, Vic *(Cast)* 4378
Casmore, Victor *(Cast)* 2747, 3170
Casnoff, Philip *(Cast)* 496, 721, 2269, 2320, 3944, 4518
Cason, Barbara *(Cast)* 272, 427, 3235
Cass, Byrle *(Director)* 1918
Cass, Carol *(Cast)* 2177
Cass, Lee *(Cast)* 71, 1698, 1993, 2961
Cass, Peggy *(Cast)* 98, 4432
Cass, Ronald *(Composer)* 392, 3890
Cass, Ronnie *(Composer)* 3186
Cass, Ronnie *(Lyricist)* 3186

Cassel, Walter *(Cast)* 1670, 2458, 4142
Cassele, Camille *(Cast)* 4451
Cassidy, David *(Cast)* 1273
Cassidy, Jack *(Cast)* 59, 189, 1227, 1389, 2163, 2681, 2910, 3831, 3913, 3918, 4018, 4117, 4718
Cassidy, Jack *(Voice)* 2980
Cassidy, Martin J. *(Cast)* 3725
Cassidy, Patrick *(Cast)* 212, 2427, 2766
Cassidy, Tim *(Cast)* 3126
Cassin, S.B. *(Librettist)* 185, 434
Cassin, S.B. *(Lyricist)* 434
Cassini, Igor *(Producer)* 4180
Cassini, Oleg *(Costumes)* 206, 820
Casson, Jill *(Costumes)* 3139
Casson, Reginald *(Composer)* 703
Cast, The *(Cast)* 3076
Cast, The *(Composer)* 1166
Cast, The *(Librettist)* 3077, 3557
Cast, The *(Lyricist)* 1166
Castaneda, David *(Lighting Designer)* 1055
Castang, Veronica *(Cast)* 785, 2146
Castel-Bert, E. *(Set Design)* 3585
Castel-Bert, Mme. *(Costumes)* 1095, 1458, 1900, 3093
Castellino, Bill *(Choreographer)* 1804, 2237
Castellino, Bill *(Director)* 1804
Castello, Glen M. *(Cast)* 4470
Castillo *(Costumes)* 1614, 2137
Castle, Diana *(Cast)* 2852
Castle, Gene *(Cast)* 1478, 1990
Castle, Gene *(Choreographer)* 2650
Castle, Irene *(Cast)* 2900, 4219, 4603
Castle, John *(Cast)* 1497
Castle, Nick *(Choreographer)* 1811, 2246, 2259
Castle, Nick *(Director)* 2259
Castle, Roy *(Cast)* 58, 3482
Castle, Vernon *(Cast)* 8, 1526, 1845, 2394, 2858, 2869, 3265, 4203, 4219, 4603
Castle, William
See also Dodge and Castle.
Castle, William *(Set Design)* 2569, 2691, 4250
Castle, William E. *(Set Design)* 2972
Castling, Harry *(Composer)* 1544
Castling, Harry *(Lyricist)* 1544
Casto, Jean *(Cast)* 660, 3353
Casucci, Leonello *(Composer)* 393
Catalina Prod. Group Ltd. *(Producer)* 3318
Catanese, Charles *(Producer)* 2022
Catenhusen, Ernest *(Musical Director)* 1030
Cates, Joseph *(Producer)* 1441, 1848, 4111, 4633
Cathcart, Minnie *(Cast)* 205
Cathon, William C. *(Musical Director)* 4149
Catlett, Mary Jo *(Cast)* 1045, 1249, 1828, 2026, 2659, 3517
Catlett, Walter *(Cast)* 1011, 1335, 2376, 2403, 2546, 2638, 3719, 3819, 4037, 4443, 4811
Catlett, Walter *(Librettist)* 3007
Catlin, George *(Cast)* 2111
Cato, Bob *(Producer)* 1498
Cato, Minto *(Cast)* 443, 1476, 2225
Caton, Edward *(Choreographer)* 3091, 3813
Cauble, Rebekah *(Cast)* 3252
Caulfield, Joan *(Cast)* 323
Caully, Zachary *(Cast)* 3170
Caumont, Mlle. *(Cast)* 30
Cavaliere, F. *(Composer)* 4193
Cavaliere, F. *(Lyricist)* 4193
Cavaliere, Felix *(Composer)* 3739
Cavaliere, Felix *(Lyricist)* 3739
Cavan, Jack *(Musical Director)* 3380
Cavanagh, Evelyn *(Cast)* 4694
Cavanagh, Maura *(Lyricist)* 922
Cavanagh, Paul *(Cast)* 2392
Cavanass, J.M. *(Lyricist)* 3840
Cavanaugh, Alice *(Cast)* 1314
Cavanaugh, Evelyn *(Cast)* 1529
Cavanaugh, Hobart *(Cast)* 2148, 4299
Cavanaugh, Ray *(Musical Director)* 1934
Cavanaugh, Stan *(Cast)* 2460
Cavander, Kenneth *(Librettist)* 482
Cavander, Kenneth *(Lyricist)* 482
Caveness, Pamela *(Cast)* 4486
Caverly, Frank *(Cast)* 1531
Cavett, Dick *(Cast)* 945, 1389
Cawthorn, Joseph *(Cast)* 468, 627, 1388, 1403, 1544, 1566, 1723, 2025, 2403, 2534, 2964, 3658, 3994, 4017, 4212, 4219, 4258, 4283
Cawthorn, Joseph *(Lyricist)* 2025, 4219, 4258
Cawthorne, Herbert *(Cast)* 2159, 2745, 2974, 3566, 4762
Cawthorne, Herbert *(Composer)* 3999
Cawthorne, Herbert *(Lyricist)* 3999
Cawthorne, Joseph *(Cast)* 1355, 3784
Cawthorne, Peter *(Director)* 4719
Cawthorne, Peter *(Librettist)* 4719
Cawthorne, Peter *(Lyricist)* 4719
Caymmi, Dorival *(Composer)* 4131
Ceballos, Larry *(Choreographer)* 123, 124, 391, 848, 1272, 1534, 1689, 1690, 1691, 1692, 2180, 2843, 2950, 3185, 4208, 4227, 4249, 4858
Ceballos, Larry *(Director)* 3426
Ceballos, Larry *(Producer)* 848
Ceballos, Rene *(Cast)* 678, 964, 975
Cecil, Lawrence *(Cast)* 1235
Cecil, Sylvia *(Cast)* 3339
Cedar, Ivan *(Producer)* 2255
Cedar, Larry *(Cast)* 2969
Ceeley, Leonard *(Cast)* 1414, 2569, 2747, 3170
Cele, Thomas *(Cast)* 209
Celeste, Marie *(Cast)* 3828
Celeste, Olive *(Cast)* 3673
Celian, Charles *(Producer)* 3876
Cellier, Alfred *(Composer)* 1080
Centaur Productions *(Lighting Designer)* 2451
Center Theatre Group *(Producer)* 2617, 2796, 4861
Center Theatre, The *(Producer)* 4569
Cerabone, Raymond *(Cast)* 4102
Cerlian, Mme. Louis *(Costumes)* 3048
Cernovich, Nicola *(Lighting Designer)* 1958
Cerow, Vincent *(Producer)* 3983
Cerruti, Debra *(Cast)* 3165
Cervallo *(Choreographer)* 1071
Cerveris, Michael *(Cast)* 4676
Cesana, Otto *(Orchestrations)* 3639
Cesario, Michael J. *(Costumes)* 3019

Chadal, Georges *(Cast)* 1743
Chadman, Christopher *(Cast)* 723, 964, 3506, 3741
Chadman, Christopher *(Choreographer)* 2307, 2820
Chadwick, Cyril *(Cast)* 1197, 3011
Chadwick, George Whitefield *(Composer)* 1210
Chadwick, Ida May *(Cast)* 3369
Chaflin, Paul *(Costumes)* 2900
Chaikin, Shami *(Cast)* 1715
Chakraband, B. *(Composer)* 2850
Chakraband, B. *(Lyricist)* 2850
Chalfonte, Lucille *(Cast)* 1688
Chaliapine, Lydia *(Cast)* 839
Chalif, Louis *(Choreographer)* 3219
Challis, William *(Orchestrations)* 1384
Chalmers, Anthony *(Lyricist)* 3940
Chalmers, Cary *(Set Design)* 2759
Chalmers, H. Hilbert *(Librettist)* 1752
Chalmers, Thomas *(Cast)* 1196
Chalzel, Leo *(Cast)* 1352, 1973
Chamber, Peter *(Cast)* 294
Chamberlain, Douglas *(Cast)* 3066
Chamberlain, Richard *(Cast)* 521
Chamberlin, Ida Hoyt *(Composer)* 1182
Chamberlin, Ida Hoyt *(Librettist)* 1182
Chamberlin, Ida Hoyt *(Lyricist)* 1182
Chamberlin, Ida Hoyt *(Set Design)* 1182
Chamberlin, Kevin *(Cast)* 4030
Chamberlyn, A.H. *(Producer)* 613, 1021, 2959, 3047, 3566
Chambers, David *(Director)* 1684, 1914
Chambers, Ernest *(Librettist)* 1107, 1878, 3954
Chambers, Ernest A. *(Lyricist)* 427
Chambers, H. Kellett *(Librettist)* 375
Chambers, Howard *(Cast)* 310
Chambers, Marilyn *(Cast)* 2426
Chambers, Peter *(Cast)* 672
Chambers, Ralph *(Cast)* 619
Chambers, Ralph W. *(Cast)* 536
Chambers, Robert *(Producer)* 2522, 2664
Chambers, Robert W. *(Author)* 2145
Chambers, Robert W. *(Librettist)* 2145
Chambers, Robert W. *(Lyricist)* 2145
Chambers-Ketchum, Annie *(Lyricist)* 3020
Chaminade *(Composer)* 77
Chaminade *(Lyricist)* 77
Champagne, Michael *(Director)* 430
Champagne, Michael *(Lyricist)* 430
Champion, Gower *(Cast)* 2379, 4174, 4287, 4346
Champion, Gower *(Choreographer)* 550, 607, 656, 1359, 1764, 1828, 2050, 2439, 2660, 2705, 3741, 4018, 4196, 4287, 4346
Champion, Gower *(Director)* 550, 607, 656, 1359, 1764, 1828, 2050, 2660, 3564, 3741, 4196, 4346
Champion, Marge *(Cast)* 1205, 1298, 4346
Chan, Don *(Arrangements)* 4251
Chan, Eric *(Cast)* 3944
Chance, Anna *(Cast)* 1641
Chandler, Anna *(Cast)* 1337
Chandler, Byron *(Producer)* 375, 2929
Chandler, Chick *(Cast)* 4486
Chandler, Evelyn *(Cast)* 2086
Chandler, Helen *(Cast)* 2396
Chandler, Richard *(Author)* 1383
Chandler, Richard *(Producer)* 681
Chandler, Stan *(Cast)* 1353
Chandler, Stephen *(Costumes)* 4332
Chandler, Wilfred *(Lyricist)* 1066
Chaney, Jan *(Cast)* 3543
Chaney, Lon *(Cast)* 432
Chaney, Stewart *(Costumes)* 1679, 2379, 3104, 3916
Chaney, Stewart *(Lighting Designer)* 1679
Chaney, Stewart *(Set Design)* 842, 1101, 1679, 2255, 2311, 2379, 2400, 2985, 3104, 3895, 3916, 4180, 4214
Channing, Carol *(Cast)* 658, 1389, 1475, 1828, 2072, 2439, 2590, 3180, 3954, 4230, 4542
Chansky, Dorothy *(Cast)* 4172
Chansky, Dorothy *(Librettist)* 564
Chansky, Dorothy *(Lyricist)* 564
Chansky, Dorothy *(Producer)* 564
Chapel, C.M. *(Composer)* 2286, 4094
Chapin, Carl *(Cast)* 3986
Chapin, Eleanor *(Choreographer)* 4157
Chapin, Frederic *(Composer)* 1351, 2694, 3738, 4725
Chapin, Frederic *(Librettist)* 2694
Chapin, Frederic *(Lyricist)* 2694
Chapin, Fredric *(Composer)* 4161
Chapin, Harry *(Cast)* 3159
Chapin, Harry *(Composer)* 900, 2470, 3159
Chapin, Harry *(Lyricist)* 900, 2470, 3159
Chapin, Sandy *(Composer)* 2470
Chapin, Sandy *(Lyricist)* 2470
Chapin, Stephen *(Cast)* 3159
Chapin, Stephen *(Dance Arranger)* 2470
Chapin, Stephen *(Musical Director)* 2470, 3159
Chapin, Stephen *(Vocal Arranger)* 2470
Chapin, Tom *(Cast)* 3159
Chapin, Tom *(Dance Arranger)* 2470
Chapin, Tom *(Musical Director)* 900
Chapin, Tom *(Orchestrations)* 2470
Chapin, Tom *(Vocal Arranger)* 2470
Chapine *(Cast)* 2867, 3776, 4794
Chaplin, Charlie *(Composer)* 4264
Chaplin, Charlie *(Lyricist)* 4264
Chaplin, Saul *(Composer)* 432, 490, 889, 1658, 1659, 1813, 1982, 4743
Chaplin, Saul *(Lyricist)* 1813, 4342, 4743
Chaplin, Sydney *(Cast)* 363, 1420, 4190
Chapman, David *(Costumes)* 2426, 3684, 4089
Chapman, David *(Lighting Designer)* 2426, 4124
Chapman, David *(Set Design)* 840, 1289, 1713, 2231, 2426, 2433, 2687, 3018, 3075, 3517, 3684, 4124
Chapman, Edwin *(Cast)* 2500
Chapman, Elmer B. *(Musical Director)* 3877
Chapman, Frank *(Cast)* 3168
Chapman, Gary *(Cast)* 393, 4003
Chapman, J.S. (Additional Music) 761
Chapman, Michael *(Director)* 1348
Chapman, Stella *(Cast)* 129
Chapman, Topsy *(Cast)* 1425, 3297
Chapman, Topsy *(Vocal Arranger)* 1425
Chapman, William *(Cast)* 177, 630, 1698
Chappell, Delos *(Producer)* 818
Chappell, George S. *(Librettist)* 824

Chappell, George S. *(Lyricist)* 824
Chappell, Helen *(Cast)* 2153
Chappell, Vickie *(Cast)* 2784
Chappelle, Chappie *(Cast)* 1019
Chappelle, Chappy *(Cast)* 2009, 4198
Chappelle, Frederic *(Composer)* 2571, 3500
Charell, Erik *(Author)* 4667
Charell, Erik *(Director)* 4256, 4667
Charell, Erik *(Librettist)* 4256
Charell, Erik *(Producer)* 4256
Charig, Phil *(Composer)* 1395, 1397, 1690, 2392, 3255, 3861, 4766
Charig, Phil *(Lyricist)* 1397
Charig, Philip *(Composer)* 86, 123, 204, 673, 1215, 1336, 1892, 2246, 2277, 3168, 3352, 3532, 3946, 4235, 4320, 4367, 4581, 4766
Charioteers, The *(Cast)* 1840
Charise, Andre *(Cast)* 3699, 4557
Charisse, Zan *(Cast)* 915
Charkham, David *(Cast)* 635
Charlap, Moose *(Composer)* 58, 786, 837, 1298, 2205, 2304, 2313, 3453, 3940, 4682
Charlap, Moose *(Lyricist)* 58
Charles, Edward *(Costumes)* 4433
Charles, Hughie *(Composer)* 4027
Charles, Hughie *(Lyricist)* 4027
Charles, Jacques *(Lyricist)* 1176, 3905
Charles, Keith *(Cast)* 681
Charles, Lee *(Cast)* 2556
Charles, Milton *(Composer)* 200
Charles, Ray
See also Ray Charles Choir.
Charles, Ray *(Vocal Arranger)* 3428
Charles, Robert *(Choreographer)* 2661
Charles, Vicki
See also Vicki Cummings.
Charles, Walter *(Cast)* 211, 754, 2360, 2766
Charles Choir, Ray
See also Ray Charles.
Charles Choir, Ray *(Cast)* 2182
Charlip, Remy *(Choreographer)* 2236
Charlip, Remy *(Costumes)* 2236
Charlip, Remy *(Set Design)* 2236
Charlot, Andre *(Director)* 133
Charlot, Andre *(Producer)* 703, 3521, 3827
Charlotte *(Cast)* 396
Charlson, Natalie *(Dance Arranger)* 1727
Charlson, Natalie *(Musical Director)* 249, 4433
Charlton, Richard *(Producer)* 920
Charmoli, Tony *(Choreographer)* 58, 145, 1119, 1326, 2313, 4727
Charmoli, Tony *(Producer)* 1257
Charnas, Fran *(Choreographer)* 74
Charnas, Fran *(Director)* 74
Charnas, Fran *(Librettist)* 74
Charney, Jordan *(Cast)* 1736
Charney, Suzanne *(Cast)* 108
Charnin, Martin *(Cast)* 1567, 4625
Charnin, Martin *(Composer)* 1233, 3181, 4533
Charnin, Martin *(Director)* 150, 154, 155, 262, 278, 299, 1289, 2230, 3018, 3075, 3181, 4136, 4533
Charnin, Martin *(Librettist)* 1233, 3181
Charnin, Martin *(Lyricist)* 150, 154, 155, 278, 602, 1233, 1257, 1289, 1370, 1991, 2064, 2288, 2368, 2777, 3018, 3181, 3484, 3615, 3889, 4048, 4395, 4481, 4533, 4627, 4798
Charnin, Martin *(Producer)* 4533
Charnin, Sasha *(Cast)* 2230, 3181
Charsky, Boris *(Producer)* 796
Charters, Spencer *(Cast)* 1368, 4683
Chartoff, Melanie *(Cast)* 2633, 4558
Chase, Arlene *(Cast)* 2430
Chase, Chaz *(Cast)* 288, 1889, 3822
Chase, Chevy *(Cast)* 3077
Chase, Chevy *(Librettist)* 3076
Chase, Colin *(Cast)* 1404
Chase, Ilka *(Cast)* 759, 2301, 3699
Chase, Lloyd *(Composer)* 796
Chase, Lloyd *(Librettist)* 796
Chase, Lloyd *(Lyricist)* 796
Chase, Mary *(Author)* 2993, 3846
Chase, Pauline *(Cast)* 3322
Chase, Stanley *(Producer)* 1385, 4369
Chase, William P. *(Composer)* 2665
Chase, William P. *(Lyricist)* 2665
Chasemore, Arthur *(Costumes)* 476
Chasen, Dave *(Cast)* 1275, 1932
Chasin, Susan *(Cast)* 2124
Chastain, Don *(Cast)* 2163, 2992, 3187
Chatelaine, Stella *(Cast)* 1647
Chatrian *(Author)* 1401
Chatterton, Ruth *(Cast)* 2691
Chatto, Tom *(Cast)* 1277
Chaucer, Geoffrey *(Author)* 634, 1500
Chaykin, Maury *(Cast)* 2429
Cheek, Jean *(Cast)* 105
Chekhov, Anton *(Author)* 1620
Chelsea Productions *(Producer)* 2180
Chelsea Theatre Center *(Producer)* 599, 1037, 1684, 1897, 4176
Chelsi, Laurence *(Cast)* 3920
Chenault, Cory *(Costumes)* 3004
Chenault, Lawrence *(Cast)* 1499
Cheney, Ed *(Cast)* 2423
Cheng, Kam *(Cast)* 2905
Chermayeff, S. *(Costumes)* 703
Chermayeff, S. *(Set Design)* 703
Chernis, Jay *(Composer)* 2169
Cherpakov, Gary *(Composer)* 2676, 3239
Cherpakov, Gary *(Lyricist)* 2676, 3239
Cherry, James *(Cast)* 3745, 3751, 4753
Cherry, John *(Cast)* 4227, 4673
Cherry, Paul *(Librettist)* 3389
Cherry, Paul *(Lyricist)* 3389
Chesnutt, Jim *(Set Design)* 3239
Chester, Alfred "Slick" *(Cast)* 2720
Chester, Eddie *(Cast)* 202
Chetwyn, Robert *(Director)* 4329
Chevalier, Louis *(Cast)* 2552
Chevalier, Maurice *(Cast)* 1396, 4661
Chew, Christopher *(Cast)* 3306
Chew, Ray *(Composer)* 1637
Chew, Ray *(Lyricist)* 1637

Chiang, Dawn *(Lighting Designer)* 4861
Chiari, Walter *(Cast)* 1456
Chiasson, Gilles *(Cast)* 1804
Chicago Federal Theatre *(Producer)* 4254
Chicas, Roy *(Cast)* 535
Chief Iron Shell *(Cast)* 2413
Chief Ki Wi *(Cast)* 4452
Chiffarelli, Albert *(Orchestrations)* 2298
Chihara, Paul *(Composer)* 3944
Chijo, Antonio Torroella *(Composer)* 3755, 4206
Child, Alan
See also Lawrence Langner.
Child, Alan *(Librettist)* 689
Child, Marilyn *(Cast)* 1229, 3111
Child, Steve *(Composer)* 4374
Children of Eden, Ltd. *(Producer)* 730
Childs, Jennifer *(Cast)* 264
Childs, Reginald *(Musical Director)* 1267
Chilton, Carol *(Cast)* 4730
Chilvers, Hugh *(Cast)* 1682, 1851, 3176
Chilvers, Thomas *(Composer)* 2515
Chiment, Marie Anne *(Costumes)* 2846
Chimola, George *(Lyricist)* 1689
Ching, William *(Cast)* 85
Chinn, Lori Tan *(Cast)* 282
Chip, Sam *(Cast)* **4735**
Chipmonck *(Lighting Designer)* 3742
Chisholm, Hazel *(Composer)* 2476
Chisholm, Robert *(Cast)* 1603, 1894, 2636, 3390, 4368, 4479, 4670
Chivot *(Author)* 1650
Chivot, Henri *(Author)* 1305
Chocolateers, The *(Cast)* 467, 886
Choder, Jill *(Cast)* 482, 1842
Chodorov, Jerome *(Author)* 2267, 4734
Chodorov, Jerome *(Director)* 751
Chodorov, Jerome *(Librettist)* 59, 1119, 1548, 2053, 3273, 3563, 4617, 4734
Chodosh, Richard *(Composer)* 3186
Chodosh, Richard B. *(Composer)* 4173
Choos, George *(Producer)* 1223, 1839, 2503, 2972, 4596
Chopin, Frederic *(Music Based On)* 745, 3536, 4669
Choraleers, The *(Cast)* 1423
Chorpenning, Ruth *(Cast)* 1448
Chotin, Andre *(Set Design)* 1244
Choyce, Root *(Lighting Designer)* 914
Chris, Marilyn *(Cast)* 2422
Chrisdie, Charles *(Costumes)* 1395
Chrisman, Richard *(Cast)* 2703
Chrispijn, Rob *(Lyricist)* 1865
Christen, Robert *(Lighting Designer)* 158, 4074, 4708
Christenberry Jr., Charles W. *(Director)* 1918
Christians, Mady *(Author)* 4768
Christians, Mady *(Composer)* 4768
Christians, Mady *(Lyricist)* 4768
Christians, William *(Costumes)* 159
Christiansen, Nora *(Choreographer)* 4707
Christianson, Bob *(Musical Director)* 251
Christianson, Bob *(Orchestrations)* 251
Christie, Audrey *(Cast)* 297, 1112, 1879, 2061, 2709, 3907, 4550
Christie, Frank M. *(Cast)* 542
Christie, George Stuart *(Cast)* 1098
Christie, Irene *(Cast)* 117
Christie, Ken *(Vocal Arranger)* 117
Christie, Marice *(Cast)* 3573
Christie, Marie *(Cast)* 4681
Christine, Henri *(Author)* 3466
Christine, Henri *(Composer)* 2356, 3079, 3466, 3467
Christine, Lily *(Cast)* 2850, 4180
Christine, Marilyn *(Choreographer)* 2104
Christine, Mrs. *(Composer)* 998
Christine, P.H. *(Composer)* 377, 1066, 2385, 3177, 3387
Christmas, David *(Cast)* 956, 1591
Christmas, Eric *(Cast)* 3818
Christofferson, Nancy *(Costumes)* 3418
Christopher, Don *(Lyricist)* 2599
Christopher, Gavin *(Composer)* 1298
Christopher, Gavin *(Lyricist)* 1298
Christopher, Kevin *(Cast)* 4332
Christopher, Paula *(Cast)* 4294
Christopher, Tony *(Composer)* 1159
Christopher, Tony *(Librettist)* 1159
Christopher, Tony *(Lyricist)* 1159
Christy, Chandler *(Cast)* 1460
Christy, Harold *(Lyricist)* 3032
Christy, Lew *(Cast)* 102
Chryst, Gary *(Cast)* 146
Church, George *(Cast)* 4825
Church, Harden *(Composer)* 680
Church, Jordan *(Cast)* 2676
Church, Joseph *(Composer)* 1201
Church, Joseph *(Musical Director)* 674, 1201, 4676
Church, Sandra *(Cast)* 1709
Church, Stanley *(Cast)* 278
Churchill, Benton *(Cast)* 2121
Churchill, Caryl *(Author)* 785, 3884
Churchill, E.P. *(Producer)* 1556
Churchill, Frank *(Author)* 4035
Churchill, Frank *(Composer)* 4035
Churchill, Stuart *(Cast)* 4340
Chute, B.J. *(Author)* 1698
Cianelli, Carole *(Cast)* 4799
Ciannelli, Eduardo *(Cast)* 97, 3772
Ciccone, Sandra *(Cast)* 2521
Ciesla, Diane *(Cast)* 760
Cilento, Wayne *(Cast)* 393, 746, 964, 3444
Cilento, Wayne *(Choreographer)* 140, 253, 2208, 3548, 4676
Cina, John *(Musical Director)* 2375
Cina, John *(Vocal Arranger)* 2375
Cindy Lou *(Cast)* 155
Cindy Pritzker, Inc. *(Producer)* 3992
Cinko, Paula *(Cast)* 3619
Cioffi, Charles *(Cast)* 496
Circle Production Co. *(Producer)* 2826
Circle Repertory Company *(Producer)* 1268, 1346, 4517
Circle Repertory Theatre *(Producer)* 3034
Circle in the Square *(Producer)* 147, 788, 1222, 4109
Cirker & Robbins *(Set Design)* 288, 423, 1251, 2636, 4673
Cissel, Chuck *(Cast)* 746
Citadel Theatre *(Producer)* 3485
City Center, The *(Producer)* 148, 3018

Ciucicini, Signor *(Lyricist)* 3567
Claflin, Rick *(Lighting Designer)* 2776
Claghorn, Senator
See also Kenny Delmar.
Claghorn, Senator *(Cast)* 1899
Claire, Helen *(Cast)* 4214
Claire, Ina *(Cast)* 1327, 2261, 2390, 3618, 4809, 4810
Claire, Marion *(Cast)* 1680
Claire, Rosalie *(Cast)* 4668
Claire, Stella *(Cast)* 194
Clamen, Dolores *(Composer)* 4388
Clancy, Elizabeth Hope *(Costumes)* 3853
Clapton, Eric *(Composer)* 3739
Clapton, Eric *(Lyricist)* 3739
Clare *(Costumes)* 4392
Clare, Henry *(Lyricist)* 3523
Clare, Johnne *(Cast)* 1267
Clare, Joseph *(Set Design)* 1576
Clare, Sidney *(Composer)* 3770
Clare, Sidney *(Lyricist)* 1137, 1692, 2857, 2870, 3020, 3249
Claret, Gaston *(Composer)* 839
Claribol *(Composer)* 77
Claribol *(Lyricist)* 77
Clark *(Lyricist)* 4393
Clark, Alexander *(Cast)* 132, 354, 1021, 1580, 1613, 2374, 2914, 2922, 3078, 3082, 3590, 3681, 3805, 4236
Clark, Alexander *(Librettist)* 3290
Clark, Alice *(Composer)* 4566
Clark, Alice *(Lyricist)* 4566
Clark, Arthur F. *(Producer)* 4724
Clark, Bessie *(Cast)* 1499
Clark, Bobby
See also Clark & McCullough.
Clark, Bobby *(Cast)* 206, 1856, 2234, 2402, 2403, 2847, 3426, 3659, 4131, 4174, 4179, 4374, 4583, 4825
Clark, Bobby *(Director)* 2850
Clark, Bobby *(Librettist)* 2850
Clark, Bryan *(Cast)* 1914
Clark, Buddy *(Cast)* 532
Clark, Capt. Anson *(Cast)* 1972
Clark, Charles Dow *(Cast)* 1360, 4544
Clark, Cheryl *(Cast)* 723
Clark, Cumberland *(Composer)* 605
Clark, Cumberland *(Lyricist)* 605
Clark, Dick
See also Dick Clark Inc.
Clark, Dick *(Producer)* 4459
Clark, Dort *(Cast)* 363, 1749, 4734
Clark, E.A. *(Cast)* 4452
Clark, Eddie *(Choreographer)* 1003
Clark, Edward *(Director)* 1335, 1424, 1551, 3258, 4784
Clark, Edward *(Librettist)* 765, 1424, 1551, 1961, 2527, 3258, 3369, 4784
Clark, Edward *(Lyricist)* 765, 1424, 1551, 2527, 3258, 3332, 4784
Clark, Edwin A. *(Cast)* 4046
Clark, Eva *(Cast)* 2768, 3323, 3662, 3842, 4211
Clark, Fred *(Cast)* 3761
Clark, Fred *(Choreographer)* 2457
Clark, Fred *(Director)* 2457
Clark, Gilbert *(Costumes)* 2180
Clark, Gladys *(Cast)* 4045, 4148, 4440
Clark, Grace Gaylor *(Cast)* 4544
Clark, Grant *(Lyricist)* 1058
Clark, Helen *(Cast)* 2363
Clark, Hilda *(Cast)* 1896, 3582
Clark, James Nisbet *(Cast)* 793
Clark, James Nisbet *(Lighting Designer)* 2188
Clark, John F. *(Cast)* 2991
Clark, Keith *(Cast)* 1137
Clark, Kenneth *(Composer)* 2481
Clark, Kenneth *(Lyricist)* 2481
Clark, Kenneth S. *(Composer)* 2481, 3134, 3710, 4026, 4094
Clark, Kenneth S. *(Lyricist)* 2481, 3134, 3710, 4094
Clark, Lillion *(Cast)* 1352
Clark, Marguerite *(Cast)* 336, 350, 1768, 2317, 2724, 2982, 3129, 3486, 4691
Clark, Norman *(Librettist)* 3861
Clark, Peggy *(Costumes)* 1546, 2175
Clark, Peggy *(Lighting Designer)* 56, 95, 98, 189, 269, 341, 363, 411, 607, 649, 657, 943, 989, 1119, 1315, 1369, 1564, 1886, 2217, 2234, 2268, 2327, 2615, 2680, 2987, 3019, 3108, 3188, 3347, 3371, 3453, 3498, 3509, 3815, 3845, 3954, 4323, 4516, 4660, 4734, 4827
Clark, Peggy *(Set Design)* 943
Clark, Rudy *(Composer)* 3695
Clark, Rudy *(Lyricist)* 3695
Clark, Thais *(Cast)* 3297
Clark, Tony *(Cast)* 1229
Clark, W.H. *(Cast)* 1351, 2126, 2139, 3504, 4452
Clark, Wayne *(Producer)* 1508, 4470
Clark & McCullough
See also Bobby Clark and Paul McCullough.
Clark & McCullough *(Cast)* 3007, 3009
Clark Bros. *(Cast)* 1423
Clarke *(Composer)* 3322
Clarke, Alex *(Cast)* 4222
Clarke, Alexander *(Cast)* 2159, 2500
Clarke, Bert *(Composer)* 1342
Clarke, Bert *(Lyricist)* 1342
Clarke, Bill *(Set Design)* 4775
Clarke, Caitlin *(Cast)* 4295
Clarke, Charlene *(Cast)* 2521
Clarke, Corson *(Cast)* 1523
Clarke, Della *(Cast)* 2008
Clarke, Edwin A. *(Cast)* 3093
Clarke, Gage *(Cast)* 4548
Clarke, George *(Composer)* 1342
Clarke, George *(Lyricist)* 1342
Clarke, Gordon *(Cast)* 3986
Clarke, Gordon B. *(Cast)* 4764
Clarke, Grant *(Composer)* 3737
Clarke, Grant *(Lyricist)* 432, 478, 487, 558, 805, 1058, 1154, 1334, 1735, 1763, 2462, 2923, 3031, 3525, 3737, 3827, 3973, 4033, 4589, 4805, 4806, 4808, 4814, 4815, 4817, 4838
Clarke, Harry *(Cast)* 735, 1033, 1558, 1882, 2331, 2455, 3580, 4206, 4285, 4293
Clarke, Harry *(Composer)* 2373
Clarke, Harry *(Librettist)* 184, 2540, 2747, 4025
Clarke, Harry *(Lyricist)* 627, 2174, 2373, 2402, 2405, 2747, 4673

Clarke, Henry *(Librettist)* 3573
Clarke, Henry Corson *(Cast)* 2986
Clarke, Hope *(Cast)* 1072, 1699
Clarke, Hope *(Choreographer)* 2200
Clarke, Hughie *(Cast)* 4778
Clarke, John *(Cast)* 2937, 3011, 4815
Clarke, John Lee *(Lyricist)* 2990
Clarke, Kenneth S. *(Composer)* 1526
Clarke, Kenneth S. *(Lyricist)* 1526
Clarke, Lawrence *(Author)* 82
Clarke, Lulu Belle *(Cast)* 183
Clarke, M. *(Cast)* 1332
Clarke, Sadie *(Composer)* 515
Clarke, Sadie *(Lyricist)* 515
Clarke, Stephen *(Cast)* 2435
Clarke, Urana *(Lyricist)* 637
Clarke, W.H. *(Cast)* 3093
Clarke, Wilfred *(Cast)* 3803, 3828
Clarkson, Grady *(Cast)* 840
Clarkson, Joan *(Cast)* 791, 792
Clary, Patricia *(Cast)* 2763, 4120
Clary, Robert *(Cast)* 190, 1815, 3107, 3899
Clary, Wilton *(Cast)* 309
Claudet, Frances *(Choreographer)* 2091, 2092, 2093
Claudet, Frances *(Director)* 2083, 2089, 2090
Clavell, James *(Author)* 3944
Clavell, James *(Producer)* 3944
Clay, Cassius *(Cast)* 578
Clay, Charles *(Cast)* 3756
Clay, Lyell B. *(Composer)* 4775
Clay, Lyell B. *(Lyricist)* 4775
Clayburgh, Jill *(Cast)* 2260, 3506, 3780
Claypoole, Edward B. *(Lyricist)* 3085
Claypoole, Milton E. *(Cast)* 1632
Clayton *(Composer)* 4264
Clayton *(Lyricist)* 4264
Clayton, Bessie *(Cast)* 356, 370, 436, 677, 1264, 1900, 1926, 1927, 2041, 2160, 2835, 3396, 3755, 4478, 4735, 4803
Clayton, Gilbert *(Choreographer)* 2670
Clayton, Herbert *(Author)* 203
Clayton, Herbert *(Cast)* 3777
Clayton, Herbert *(Producer)* 2547
Clayton, Jan *(Cast)* 660, 4331, 4466
Clayton, Lawrence *(Cast)* 1890, 2250, 3757
Clayton, Lou
See also Clayton, Jackson, & Durante.
Clayton, Lou *(Cast)* 1823, 3131, 3402, 3953, 3958
Clayton, Ruth *(Cast)* 4572
Clayton Concerts Ltd., Barry *(Producer)* 846
Clayton, Jackson & Durante
See also Lou Clayton, Eddie Jackson, and Jimmy Durante.
Clayton, Jackson & Durante *(Cast)* 1396
Cleale, Lewis *(Cast)* 4255
Cleary, Michael *(Composer)* 1134, 1136, 1874, 1949, 1950, 3409, 4335, 4545
Cleary, Michael H. *(Composer)* 2105, 3860, 3946, 4335
Cleave, Van *(Orchestrations)* 4640
Cleaveland, Del *(Composer)* 3861
Cleaver, Jennie *(Costumes)* 3802, 4444
Clef Club Orchestra *(Cast)* 1726
Clemens, Gertrude *(Cast)* 3254
Clement, Clay *(Cast)* 3170
Clement, Frank *(Lyricist)* 1313
Clement, Joan *(Cast)* 3924
Clement, Laura *(Cast)* 526
Clemente, Aixa *(Cast)* 4168
Clemente, Rene *(Cast)* 678
Clements, Dudley *(Cast)* 680, 1856, 2444, 2479, 3225, 3822, 4075, 4179
Clements, Hal *(Cast)* 349
Clements, Jehan *(Cast)* 1978
Clements, Jehan *(Composer)* 1978
Clements, Jehan *(Lyricist)* 1978
Clements, Otis *(Composer)* 4829
Clements, Otis *(Lyricist)* 2148
Clemons, LeRoy *(Librettist)* 465
Clemson, Osborne *(Cast)* 4761
Clenn, Gregory *(Costumes)* 2272
Clerc, Borel *(Composer)* 4818
Clerk, Clive *(Cast)* 746
Cleve, Van *(Orchestrations)* 3916
Cleveland, John *(Librettist)* 3107
Cleveland, John *(Lyricist)* 924
Cleveland, Luther *(Lyricist)* 924
Cleveland, Phyllis *(Cast)* 773, 799, 4226, 4300
Clevenger, JoAnn *(Costumes)* 1425, 3297, 4127
Clewes, Jack *(Cast)* 1333
Cliff, Bobbie *(Cast)* 1267
Cliff, Laddie *(Cast)* 1327, 2389
Cliff, Laddie *(Choreographer)* 704, 3569
Cliff, Laddie *(Director)* 503, 4765
Cliff, Laddie *(Lyricist)* 702
Cliff, Laddie *(Producer)* 503, 4765
Cliff, Lora Lee *(Cast)* 760
Clifford, Alice *(Cast)* 2343
Clifford, Bessie *(Cast)* 2857, 3096
Clifford, Jack *(Cast)* 1582, 4712
Clifford, Kathleen *(Cast)* 355, 1226, 4425, 4712
Clifford, Marie *(Cast)* 1975
Clifford, Pamela *(Cast)* 4703
Clifford, William H. *(Librettist)* 2454, 3072
Clifford, William H. *(Lyricist)* 3072
Clift, Montgomery *(Cast)* 2252
Clifton, Bernard *(Cast)* 3583
Clifton, John *(Cast)* 4157
Clifton, John *(Composer)* 1164, 2677, 2731, 3619, 4444
Clifton, John *(Lyricist)* 1164, 2731, 4444
Clifton, John *(Musical Director)* 426, 3802
Clifton, John *(Orchestrations)* 1797, 2677
Clifton, William *(Cast)* 3134, 3652
Clifton-Allen, Lynne *(Cast)* 593, 4645
Cline, Edward *(Director)* 2400
Clinger, Bijou *(Cast)* 564
Clinton, Helen *(Cast)* 2013
Clive, Vincent *(Cast)* 292
Clonick, Joseph *(Musical Director)* 4480
Close, Del *(Cast)* 3094, 3484
Close, Glenn *(Cast)* 305, 2607, 3702, 4217
Clough, Arthur *(Cast)* 2886
Clough, Peter H. *(Director)* 3463
Clow, James *(Cast)* 460

Clugston, Glen *(Musical Director)* 227, 3925
Clugston, Glen *(Orchestrations)* 227
Clugston, Glen *(Vocal Arranger)* 3925
Clurman, Harold *(Director)* 3505
Clurman, Harold *(Producer)* 2450
Clute, Chester *(Cast)* 3130
Clutsam, G.A. *(Orchestrations)* 1680
Clyburn, Rose *(Cast)* 3987
Clyde, June *(Cast)* 297, 1973
Coates, Dorothy Love *(Composer)* 3987
Coates, Dorothy Love *(Lyricist)* 3987
Coates, Eric *(Choreographer)* 703
Coates, Eric *(Composer)* 4667
Coates, Florence Earle *(Lyricist)* 4590
Coates, Norman *(Lighting Designer)* 3136, 3576
Cobb, Earl *(Composer)* 4273
Cobb, George L. *(Composer)* 1888, 2696
Cobb, Ira *(Librettist)* 4792
Cobb, Ira *(Lyricist)* 4792
Cobb, Irvin *(Librettist)* 1417
Cobb, John S. *(Producer)* 90
Cobb, Lee J. *(Cast)* 2228
Cobb, Will D. *(Composer)* 3999
Cobb, Will D. *(Lyricist)* 8, 326, 511, 1391, 1434, 1464, 1526, 1703, 1704, 1900, 1910, 1919, 1998, 2803, 2835, 2858, 2885, 2974, 2990, 3322, 3387, 3855, 4079, 4181, 4209, 4390, 4723, 4738, 4755, 4801, 4804, 4807
Cobb Jr., Henry Ives *(Set Design)* 1784, 2532
Cobey, Louis *(Composer)* 3140
Coburn, Charles *(Cast)* 377, 563, 1235
Coburn, Charles *(Producer)* 1235, 4360
Coburn, D.L. *(Author)* 2230
Coburn, Mrs. Charles *(Cast)* 377, 563, 1235
Coburn, Mrs. Charles *(Producer)* 4360
Coburn, Richard *(Composer)* 1120
Coburn, Richard *(Lyricist)* 1120, 3246
Coca, Imogene *(Cast)* 70, 621, 1322, 1342, 1448, 3103, 3104, 3279, 3800, 3946, 4166, 4651, 4677
Coccia, Aurelia *(Choreographer)* 350
Coccia, Aurelio *(Choreographer)* 3348
Cochran, C.B. *(Producer)* 453, 1153
Cochran, Charles *(Producer)* 2462, 2788
Cochran, Charles B. *(Producer)* 700, 841, 1202, 1338, 1763, 3214, 3291, 3467, 3597, 4154, 4341, 4581
Cochran, Dorcas *(Lyricist)* 1138
Cochran, Gifford (English Lyrics) 4368
Cochran, Gifford *(Librettist)* 4368
Cochran, Gifford *(Producer)* 4368
Cochrane, James *(Costumes)* 3495
Cochrane, Jeannetta *(Costumes)* 346
Cochrane, June *(Cast)* 834, 1446, 1529
Cochrane, Roy *(Cast)* 4576
Cochren, Felix E. *(Costumes)* 105
Cochren, Felix E. *(Set Design)* 2133
Coco, James *(Cast)* 546, 991, 1864, 2553, 4318
Coco, Jim *(Cast)* 2511
Cocoanut Grove Playhouse *(Producer)* 4645
Cocteau, Jean *(Set Design)* 2611
Coda, Alfred *(Cast)* 2393
Coda, Frank *(Cast)* 4469
Codron, Michael *(Producer)* 4329, 4685
Coe, Fred *(Producer)* 1497, 2313, 3324
Coe, George *(Cast)* 832, 1232, 2713, 2935, 3279, 4633
Coe, John *(Cast)* 2236, 2368
Coe, Peter *(Director)* 3271, 3482, 4002
Coes, G. *(Composer)* 476
Coffin, Frederick *(Cast)* 1591, 3000, 4019
Coffin, Gene *(Costumes)* 3816
Coffin, Maurice *(Musical Director)* 1989
Coggin, Barbara *(Cast)* 164, 3671
Coghill, Nevill *(Librettist)* 634
Coghill, Nevill *(Lyricist)* 634
Coghlan, James *(Librettist)* 3861, 4545
Coghlan, Rosalind *(Cast)* 1501
Cogley, Edward F. *(Composer)* 405
Cogley, Edward F. *(Lyricist)* 405
Cogswell, Bill *(Composer)* 4264
Cogswell, Bill *(Lyricist)* 4264
Cohan, Cora *(Choreographer)* 459
Cohan, George M. *(Author)* 403, 1271, 2730, 4576
Cohan, George M. *(Cast)* 1399, 1480, 1640, 1826, 1968, 2068, 2517, 2525, 2829, 3153, 3809, 4759
Cohan, George M. *(Choreographer)* 805
Cohan, George M. *(Composer)* 115, 403, 800, 801, 803, 804, 805, 964, 1271, 1356, 1478, 1480, 1527, 1640, 1826, 1968, 1988, 2415, 2493, 2517, 2525, 2533, 2730, 2829, 2964, 2975, 3018, 3020, 3153, 3723, 3791, 3809, 4277, 4390, 4553, 4576, 4717, 4759
Cohan, George M. *(Director)* 115, 800, 803, 804, 805, 1271, 1356, 1399, 1480, 2517, 2525, 2533, 2730, 3809, 4277, 4576, 4759
Cohan, George M. *(Librettist)* 115, 403, 800, 801, 803, 804, 805, 1356, 1480, 1640, 1826, 1968, 2517, 2525, 2533, 2730, 2829, 3723, 3809, 4277, 4759
Cohan, George M. *(Lyricist)* 115, 403, 800, 801, 803, 804, 805, 964, 1271, 1356, 1478, 1480, 1527, 1640, 1826, 1968, 1988, 2415, 2493, 2517, 2525, 2533, 2730, 2829, 2964, 2975, 3018, 3020, 3153, 3723, 3791, 3809, 4277, 4390, 4553, 4576, 4717, 4759
Cohan, George M. *(Producer)* 115, 335, 403, 800, 801, 802, 803, 804, 805, 1271, 1360, 1598, 1803, 1826, 2525, 2533, 2730, 2767, 2829, 3218, 3529, 3685, 3791, 4277, 4576, 4759
Cohan, Helen *(Cast)* 1480, 1640, 1968, 2517, 2525, 3809, 4759
Cohan, Jerry *(Cast)* 1480, 1640, 1968, 2517, 2525, 3809, 4759
Cohan, John C. *(Producer)* 2551
Cohan, Josephine *(Cast)* 3749
Cohan, Josie *(Cast)* 1640, 3809, 4759
Cohen, Alexander *(Producer)* 1841
Cohen, Alexander H. *(Director)* 826
Cohen, Alexander H. *(Producer)* 220, 221, 270, 532, 826, 1000, 1012, 1621, 1842, 2064, 2072, 2705, 3226, 3564, 3798, 4384, 4743
Cohen, Allen *(Composer)* 3557
Cohen, Allen *(Dance Arranger)* 4537
Cohen, Allen *(Lyricist)* 3557
Cohen, Coleman *(Composer)* 4433
Cohen, Coleman *(Librettist)* 4433
Cohen, Coleman *(Lyricist)* 4433
Cohen, Darren R. *(Musical Director)* 3227

Cohen, David *(Composer)* 459
Cohen, Douglas *(Set Design)* 4774
Cohen, Douglas J. *(Composer)* 1510
Cohen, Douglas J. *(Librettist)* 1510
Cohen, Douglas J. *(Lyricist)* 1510
Cohen, Douglas J. *(Vocal Arranger)* 1510
Cohen, Hanoch *(Composer)* 2421
Cohen, Harold *(Composer)* 2397
Cohen, Harry R. *(Composer)* 1795
Cohen, Jay *(Producer)* 166
Cohen, Jay J. *(Producer)* 2133
Cohen, Joyce *(Cast)* 1037
Cohen, Julie *(Cast)* 455
Cohen, Lawrence D. *(Librettist)* 661
Cohen, Margery *(Cast)* 369, 599, 4145
Cohen, Martin *(Producer)* 4542
Cohen, Martin B. *(Director)* 4623
Cohen, Martin B. *(Producer)* 751
Cohen, Michael *(Composer)* 1438, 2913, 3112, 4790
Cohen, Michael *(Dance Arranger)* 2913
Cohen, Michael *(Musical Director)* 366
Cohen, Michael *(Orchestrations)* 2913
Cohen, Michael (Pianist) 366, 1436, 2279, 2913
Cohen, Michael *(Vocal Arranger)* 2913
Cohen, N.D. *(Cast)* 1624
Cohen, Phil *(Composer)* 1126
Cohen, Robert *(Lyricist)* 387
Cohen, S.A. *(Lighting Designer)* 1637
Cohen, Sol *(Composer)* 2943
Cohen, Steve *(Orchestrations)* 4107
Cohen, Ze-eva *(Choreographer)* 2918
Cohenour, Patti *(Cast)* 394, 1068, 2359, 3070, 3464
Cohn, Al *(Orchestrations)* 3018, 3656, 4091
Cohn, Max *(Costumes)* 1513
Cohn, Sam *(Producer)* 1354
Coile, Bob *(Lyricist)* 2493
Coini, Jacques *(Director)* 824, 1743, 3081
Coit-Wright, Fredrick *(Composer)* 1518
Cokas, Nicholas *(Cast)* 1804
Cokayne, A.H. *(Musical Director)* 2222
Coke, Peter *(Author)* 3900
Colavecchia, Franco *(Costumes)* 4447
Colavecchia, Franco *(Set Design)* 4447, 4790
Colbin, Rod *(Cast)* 2664
Colby, Archie *(Librettist)* 1533
Colby, Jack *(Cast)* 288
Colby, Marion *(Cast)* 2809, 3351
Colby, Michael *(Librettist)* 705, 1757, 2647, 2993, 3201
Colby, Michael *(Lyricist)* 705, 1757, 2647, 2993, 3201
Colby, Robert *(Composer)* 1727
Colby, Robert *(Lyricist)* 1727
Coldrey, Jeff *(Composer)* 296
Coldrey, Jeff *(Lyricist)* 296
Cole *(Composer)* 1076
Cole, Barbara *(Cast)* 4696
Cole, Barbara *(Choreographer)* 2641
Cole, Beatrice *(Author)* 2629
Cole, Bob *(Cast)* 633, 3676, 3945, 4451
Cole, Bob *(Composer)* 982, 2029, 2035, 2044, 2111, 2325, 2765, 2892, 2951, 3073, 3945, 4390, 4697
Cole, Bob *(Librettist)* 3676, 3945
Cole, Bob *(Lyricist)* 217, 352, 633, 982, 1188, 1535, 1537, 2035, 2044, 2111, 2123, 2493, 2506, 2805, 2892, 2964, 2974, 3073, 3676, 3820, 3945, 3999, 4014, 4451, 4681
Cole, Bob *(Producer)* 633
Cole, Charles W. *(Cast)* 1274
Cole, Christopher *(Set Design)* 3178
Cole, Cosy *(Cast)* 653
Cole, Doris *(Producer)* 467
Cole, Doug *(Producer)* 4454
Cole, Jack
See also Jack Cole and His Dancers.
Cole, Jack *(Cast)* 59, 680, 2786, 4374, 4550, 4826
Cole, Jack *(Choreographer)* 59, 84, 657, 1076, 1373, 1422, 2190, 2295, 2327, 2679, 2727, 2777, 4058, 4798, 4827
Cole, Jack *(Director)* 1076, 2295
Cole, Kay *(Cast)* 746, 3277, 3651, 3903, 4034
Cole, Kay *(Choreographer)* 456, 1737
Cole, Kay *(Librettist)* 456
Cole, Lester *(Cast)* 3436
Cole, Louis *(Cast)* 500
Cole, Nat "King" *(Composer)* 39
Cole, Nat "King" *(Lyricist)* 39
Cole, Nora *(Cast)* 2968, 4645
Cole and His Dancers, Jack
See also Jack Cole.
Cole and His Dancers, Jack *(Cast)* 397
Coleman, Charles *(Cast)* 478
Coleman, Charles H. *(Dance Arranger)* 1762
Coleman, Charles H. *(Musical Director)* 4383, 4722
Coleman, Charles H. *(Vocal Arranger)* 4722
Coleman, Cy *(Composer)* 229, 305, 327, 775, 1023, 1038, 1097, 1168, 1648, 1708, 1842, 1955, 2058, 2227, 2294, 2297, 2473, 2523, 2804, 3279, 3428, 3869, 3936, 4167, 4238, 4337, 4338, 4619, 4693, 4695, 4827
Coleman, Cy *(Dance Arranger)* 1955, 2058, 3869, 4695
Coleman, Cy *(Librettist)* 2473
Coleman, Cy *(Lyricist)* 4619
Coleman, Cy *(Producer)* 305, 4619
Coleman, Cy *(Vocal Arranger)* 305, 775, 1955, 2058, 4619, 4695
Coleman, Dan *(Cast)* 2314
Coleman, David *(Composer)* 1120
Coleman, David *(Lyricist)* 1120
Coleman, Don *(Lighting Designer)* 484, 4244
Coleman, Ed Lea *(Cast)* 2113
Coleman, Gladys *(Cast)* 1602
Coleman, Hamilton *(Composer)* 4092
Coleman, Hamilton *(Director)* 4092
Coleman, Hamilton *(Librettist)* 4092
Coleman, Hamilton *(Lyricist)* 4092
Coleman, Herbert *(Cast)* 2591
Coleman, Jim *(Musical Director)* 3734
Coleman, Jim *(Vocal Arranger)* 3734
Coleman, Larry *(Cast)* 4220
Coleman, Larry *(Composer)* 4264
Coleman, Lillian *(Cast)* 246, 3578, 3747
Coleman, Marilyn B. *(Cast)* 40
Coleman, Shepard *(Musical Director)* 1828, 1846, 3259, 4186
Coleman, Shepard *(Vocal Arranger)* 1828, 1846
Coleman, Ted *(Composer)* 263

Coleman, Ted *(Musical Director)* 2071
Coleman, Warren *(Cast)* 3541, 4256
Coles, Charles "Honi" *(Cast)* 3060
Coles, Honi *(Cast)* 3705
Colesano, Mark *(Cast)* 635
Colette *(Author)* 807, 809, 1511, 3010
Coley, Dottie *(Cast)* 4220
Coley, Thomas *(Cast)* 4256
Colicos, John *(Cast)* 2859, 4715
Coligan, James *(Producer)* 1754
Colin, Jean *(Cast)* 1855
Colin, Paul *(Costumes)* 4581
Colin, Paul *(Set Design)* 4581
Colker, Jerry *(Cast)* 4349
Colker, Jerry *(Librettist)* 2702, 4349
Colker, Jerry *(Lyricist)* 2702, 4349
Collett, Jeannette *(Choreographer)* 720
Collette Sisters, The *(Cast)* 1135, 4823
Collier, John *(Author)* 1200
Collier, William *(Author)* 3508, 4249
Collier, William *(Cast)* 1360, 1399, 1826, 4692
Collier, William *(Director)* 317, 687, 1129, 3048, 3144, 3189, 3917, 4249, 4378
Collier, William *(Librettist)* 1129, 3144
Collier, Willie *(Cast)* 1927, 2827, 3006, 4478
Collier, Willie *(Director)* 3006
Collier, Willie *(Librettist)* 3006
Colligan, Billy *(Lyricist)* 487
Collinge, Patricia *(Cast)* 1210, 2510
Collingham, Malcolm *(Cast)* 2682
Collings, Nancy *(Lighting Designer)* 3601
Collins, "Chink" *(Cast)* 2561
Collins, A.M. *(Librettist)* 140
Collins, Arthur *(Author)* 1975, 2035, 2964, 2974, 4014, 4662
Collins, Charles *(Cast)* 2479, 3415, 3721, 3850, 3860, 3927, 4025, 4159
Collins, Charles *(Composer)* 2498, 4027
Collins, Charles *(Librettist)* 3293
Collins, Charles *(Lyricist)* 2498, 4027
Collins, Courtenay *(Cast)* 1149
Collins, Dorothy *(Cast)* 1329
Collins, Ed *(Lyricist)* 2483
Collins, Edward *(Librettist)* 4416
Collins, Frank *(Director)* 25, 791, 792, 1202, 3291, 4341, 4581
Collins, George Eaton *(Cast)* 3774
Collins, Harry *(Composer)* 3025
Collins, Harry *(Costumes)* 1424, 1580, 3245, 3866, 4296
Collins, Jack *(Producer)* 4629
Collins, James *(Cast)* 539
Collins, Janet *(Cast)* 3326
Collins, Jose *(Cast)* 93, 3397, 4228, 4661
Collins, Ken *(Dance Arranger)* 2235
Collins, Ken *(Musical Director)* 491, 3469
Collins, Lillian *(Cast)* 4353
Collins, Madeline *(Cast)* 3078
Collins, Melville *(Cast)* 3585
Collins, Melville S. *(Composer)* 457
Collins, Melville S. *(Lyricist)* 457
Collins, Michael *(Musical Director)* 453
Collins, Pat *(Lighting Designer)* 112, 169, 253, 1172, 2318, 2555, 3364, 4370
Collins, Patricia *(Lighting Designer)* 4319
Collins, Phil *(Composer)* 4786
Collins, Phil *(Lyricist)* 4786
Collins, Ray *(Cast)* 1903
Collins, Rise *(Cast)* 1344
Collins, Russell *(Cast)* 2228, 2464
Collins, Sam *(Cast)* 1881
Collins, Stephen *(Cast)* 682, 2953, 4067
Collins, Stephen *(Librettist)* 3076
Collins, Tom *(Director)* 2868
Collins, Una *(Costumes)* 3259
Collinson, Frank *(Musical Director)* 1763
Collison, Wilson *(Author)* 4526
Collodi, Carlo *(Author)* 3495, 3496, 3497, 3498, 3499
Collyer, Dan *(Cast)* 4508
Colonna, Jerry *(Cast)* 3496
Colson, C. David *(Cast)* 2418, 3610
Colson, Kevin *(Cast)* 211, 730
Colson, Osborne *(Cast)* 2087
Colston, Percy *(Cast)* 2690
Colston, Robert *(Arrangements)* 3479
Colston, Robert *(Cast)* 272, 1359
Colston, Robert *(Musical Director)* 3479, 3764, 4746
Colston, Robert (Pianist) 427, 1049, 1363
Colt, Alvin *(Costumes)* 189, 280, 304, 547, 751, 826, 868, 1029, 1242, 1290, 1600, 1611, 1698, 1706, 1842, 1846, 1860, 2411, 2484, 2554, 2556, 2590, 2965, 3013, 3278, 3473, 3505, 3801, 3845, 4060, 4196, 4337, 4423, 4693, 4737
Colt, Alvin *(Set Design)* 939, 3013
Colt, Ethel Barrymore *(Cast)* 1329, 1492
Coltellacci, Giulio *(Set Design)* 3798
Coltellacci, Guilio *(Costumes)* 3798
Colton, Chevi *(Cast)* 1660, 3215
Colton, Evans *(Cast)* 3461
Colton, Jacque Lynn *(Cast)* 2110, 2478
Colton, Sammy *(Lyricist)* 1982
Columbara, Signorina Medea *(Cast)* 4730
Columbia Concerts Corp. *(Producer)* 3441
Columbia Pictures Stage Pr. *(Producer)* 2820
Columbia University Players *(Producer)* 1956, 3284, 3419, 4781
Columbia University War Show Comm. *(Producer)* 4308
Columbo, A.C. *(Orchestrations)* 1686
Columbus, Charles *(Cast)* 1384, 1836
Colvan, Zeke *(Cast)* 1835, 3401
Colvan, Zeke *(Director)* 3409, 3823, 3949, 3953, 3980, 4550, 4821
Colvig, Helen *(Costumes)* 2084, 2093, 2094, 2095, 2096
Colyer, Carlton *(Cast)* 4380
Comber, Bobbie *(Cast)* 1610, 2004
Comden, Betty
See also the Revuers.
Comden, Betty *(Cast)* 3278
Comden, Betty *(Librettist)* 167, 363, 404, 490, 599, 1068, 1227, 3278, 3279, 3992, 4008, 4190, 4496
Comden, Betty *(Lyricist)* 363, 404, 490, 599, 1038, 1061, 1068, 1227, 1729, 2073, 2076, 2205, 2452, 2590, 2677, 3278, 3279, 3452, 3453, 3845, 3992, 4008, 4167, 4190, 4496, 4695, 4734

Comden, Betty *(Screenwriter)* 3992
Comedian's Guild *(Producer)* 3173
Comelli *(Costumes)* 334, 902, 1561, 2974, 3156, 3663
Comelli, A. *(Costumes)* 4187
Comfort, Vaughn *(Cast)* 801, 803
Comor, Henry *(Cast)* 2278
Comor, Henry *(Director)* 2278
Comor, Henry *(Librettist)* 2278
Comor, Henry *(Lyricist)* 2633
Company, The *(Choreographer)* 4442
Company, The *(Librettist)* 3997
Compass Fair *(Producer)* 4395
Complex IV *(Producer)* 2925
Compton, Betty *(Cast)* 123, 827, 1272, 1419, 1929, 3243
Compton, Fay *(Cast)* 4418, 4419
Compton, Francis *(Cast)* 2275
Compton, Frank *(Lyricist)* 675
Comstock, F. Ray *(Director)* 1246
Comstock, F. Ray *(Producer)* 25, 165, 295, 336, 684, 710, 758, 1246, 1588, 1975, 2340, 2430, 2698, 2802, 2979, 3193, 3230, 3245, 3250, 3535, 3775, 4555, 4758, 4860
Comstock, Frances *(Cast)* 3292
Conant, Homer *(Costumes)* 208, 764, 1065, 2794, 2856, 3333, 3865, 3958, 3985, 4056, 4375
Conant, Homer *(Set Design)* 764, 2794, 2856
Conaway, Charles *(Producer)* 4828, 4829
Conaway, Jeff *(Cast)* 3136
Conaway, Joe *(Producer)* 2027
Condell, H.A. *(Costumes)* 4792
Condell, H.A. *(Set Design)* 309, 4792
Conderman, Susan *(Cast)* 1978
Condon, Dennis *(Lighting Designer)* 2436
Condon, Eva *(Cast)* 1894
Condon, Kate *(Cast)* 3560, 3736
Condon, Kate *(Composer)* 1178
Condos, Frank *(Cast)* 1135
Condos, Harry *(Cast)* 1135
Condray, Peggy *(Cast)* 919
Cone, Tom *(Author)* 1872
Conforti, Gino *(Cast)* 1369, 2727, 3612, 3918, 4028
Conforti, Robert *(Cast)* 821
Conforti, Tom *(Producer)* 3905
Conforti, Tony *(Producer)* 2759
Confrey, Zez *(Composer)* 3261
Congdon, James *(Cast)* 253
Congreve, William *(Author)* 2607
Conkey, Thomas *(Cast)* 371, 3323
Conklin, Bill *(Librettist)* 3217
Conklin, Bill *(Lyricist)* 597, 3217
Conklin, John *(Costumes)* 1786, 3702, 3835
Conklin, John *(Set Design)* 808, 945, 1017, 1786, 2590, 3195, 3468, 3702, 3835
Conklin, Peggy *(Cast)* 2545, 4443
Conkwright, Anna *(Costumes)* 1555
Conlee, John Ellison *(Cast)* 2038
Conley, Larry *(Composer)* 1241
Conley, Matt *(Cast)* 2017
Conley, Robert *(Choreographer)* 3939
Conley, Robert *(Set Design)* 239
Conley, Shannon *(Cast)* 1232
Conlow, Peter *(Cast)* 108, 4270, 4366
Conlow, Peter *(Choreographer)* 4380
Conlow, Peter *(Director)* 73
Conmee, Marie *(Cast)* 2682
Conn, Harry *(Librettist)* 1492
Conn, Irving *(Composer)* 3008
Connaughton, Kevin *(Lighting Designer)* 4106
Connell, Dennis E. *(Composer)* 4779
Connell, Dennis E. *(Lyricist)* 4779
Connell, Gordon *(Cast)* 394, 1107, 1828, 2033, 2659, 3484, 4190
Connell, Gordon *(Composer)* 2294
Connell, Gordon *(Lyricist)* 2294
Connell, Gordon *(Musical Director)* 3615
Connell, Gordon *(Pianist)* 1023, 4268
Connell, Jane *(Cast)* 921, 1012, 1023, 1081, 1093, 1094, 1354, 2659, 2713, 2798, 3108, 3186, 3484, 3615, 3788, 4310
Connell, Tom *(Lyricist)* 4328
Connelli, Regina *(Cast)* 1560
Connelly, David *(Cast)* 4074
Connelly, Edward *(Cast)* 252
Connelly, Marc *(Author)* 647
Connelly, Marc *(Cast)* 4278
Connelly, Marc *(Director)* 1357, 3699, 4479
Connelly, Marc *(Librettist)* 102, 216, 317, 1357, 1819, 2020, 2402, 3783, 3861, 4335
Connelly, Marc *(Lyricist)* 102, 317, 1901, 2698
Connelly, Marc *(Producer)* 3546, 4479
Connelly, Reg *(Composer)* 4027
Connelly, Reg *(Lyricist)* 1135, 1136, 4027
Conner, Bruce *(Cast)* 1897
Conners, Jack *(Choreographer)* 3137
Connolly, Bobby *(Choreographer)* 111, 289, 1027, 1145, 1323, 1339, 1387, 1419, 1628, 1879, 1965, 1979, 2253, 2342, 2813, 3117, 3796, 3953, 4118, 4267, 4443, 4823, 4824
Connolly, Bobby *(Director)* 2366, 3584, 4087, 4824
Connolly, Bobby *(Producer)* 289, 3584, 4087
Connolly, Don *(Cast)* 680
Connolly, Edward J. *(Cast)* 228
Connolly, Joseph *(Composer)* 1873
Connolly, Joseph *(Lyricist)* 1873
Connolly, Marc *(Author)* 80, 317
Connolly, Patrick *(Composer)* 3695
Connolly, Patrick *(Lyricist)* 3695
Connor, Joseph *(Composer)* 2148
Connor, Joseph *(Lyricist)* 2148
Connor, Maureen *(Costumes)* 2746
Connor, Peggy *(Composer)* 702
Connor, Peggy *(Lyricist)* 2570
Connor, Zoe *(Cast)* 3752
Connors, Barry *(Author)* 3415
Connors, Barry *(Librettist)* 3415
Connors, Edgar *(Cast)* 2942
Connors, Frankie *(Cast)* 851
Connors, Jack *(Choreographer)* 1182, 1314, 2112
Connors, Kevin *(Composer)* 3568
Connors, Kevin *(Director)* 3568
Connors, Kevin *(Lyricist)* 3568
Connors & Bennett *(Set Design)* 3130
Conoly, Joseph *(Composer)* 3022

Conoly, Joseph *(Lyricist)* 3022
Conoly, Joseph *(Producer)* 3022
Conor, Harry *(Cast)* 457, 472, 694, 1226, 1240, 1522, 1543, 2390, 2649, 2760, 3308, 4165, 4642
Conor, Harry *(Composer)* 436
Conor, Harry *(Lyricist)* 436
Conrad, Art *(Composer)* 1223
Conrad, Art *(Lyricist)* 1223
Conrad, Arthur *(Cast)* 1824, 4687
Conrad, Arthur *(Choreographer)* 1824
Conrad, Con *(Composer)* 103, 123, 124, 200, 381, 391, 487, 545, 827, 1154, 1689, 2302, 2342, 2467, 2818, 2856, 2857, 2950, 3032, 4033, 4271, 4806
Conrad, Con *(Director)* 2302
Conrad, Con *(Lyricist)* 487, 545, 827, 1689, 2302, 2342, 2818, 2856, 3770, 4033
Conrad, Con *(Producer)* 2302
Conrad, Constance *(Composer)* 2580
Conrad, Eddie *(Cast)* 1460
Conrad, Eddie *(Composer)* 3717
Conrad, Eddie *(Lyricist)* 1693, 3148, 3717
Conrad, Edith *(Cast)* 4351
Conrad, Eugene *(Librettist)* 557, 1127, 1135, 2400, 3380, 3822, 4424
Conrad, Eugene *(Lyricist)* 557, 4424
Conradt, Mark *(Librettist)* 1676
Conreid, Hans *(Cast)* 1257, 3900, 4278
Conried, Hans *(Cast)* 629, 928
Conrow, Jonathan *(Producer)* 3020
Conroy, Frances *(Cast)* 1575
Conroy, Frank *(Cast)* 1560, 2510, 3768
Conroy, Pat *(Author)* 838
Consentino, Nicholas *(Author)* 2946
Conte, John *(Cast)* 85, 2837, 4702
Continental Music Halls *(Producer)* 431
Continentals, The *(Cast)* 216
Continer, Anthony *(Set Design)* 27
Contreras, Ray *(Cast)* 1053, 2970, 3806
Contrucci, Lance *(Librettist)* 3076
Converse, C.C. *(Composer)* 2046
Converse, C.C. *(Lyricist)* 2046
Converse, Frank *(Cast)* 1999
Converse, Harry E. *(Producer)* 1515
Convy, Bert *(Cast)* 322, 411, 610, 1265, 2958, 3210, 4566
Convy, Bert *(Director)* 4796
Conway, Bert *(Cast)* 3180
Conway, Curt *(Cast)* 3180, 3226
Conway, Curt *(Director)* 4237, 4401
Conway, Daniel *(Set Design)* 1915
Conway, Gary *(Cast)* 1750
Conway, Gordon *(Costumes)* 703, 706, 3583
Conway, Lizzie *(Cast)* 3270
Conway, Shirl *(Cast)* 3509
Conwell, O'Kane *(Costumes)* 136, 1536, 1922, 3146, 4393
Conwit, Phil *(Lyricist)* 3986
Coogan, Jack *(Lyricist)* 1063
Coogan, Joe *(Librettist)* 932
Cook, Barbara *(Cast)* 630, 1300, 1456, 1662, 1744, 3016, 3509, 3918, 4060
Cook, Carole *(Cast)* 1359, 2011
Cook, Cecil *(Composer)* 1537
Cook, Charles Emerson *(Director)* 3774
Cook, Charles Emerson *(Librettist)* 3774
Cook, Charles Emerson *(Lyricist)* 1394, 1397, 3673, 3774
Cook, Christopher *(Cast)* 752
Cook, Gregory *(Cast)* 1695
Cook, Harold *(Cast)* 1973
Cook, Hartwell *(Choreographer)* 2942
Cook, Howard *(Musical Director)* 1502
Cook, James *(Cast)* 4735
Cook, Jill *(Cast)* 964, 1665, 3444, 3548
Cook, Joe *(Additional Dialogue)* 1932
Cook, Joe *(Cast)* 1129, 1130, 1275, 1396, 1726, 1921, 1932, 2020, 2161, 2162, 3426, 3648
Cook, Joe *(Librettist)* 1275, 4035
Cook, Joe *(Lyricist)* 4035
Cook, Joe *(Producer)* 1932
Cook, John H. *(Composer)* 2111
Cook, Judy *(Costumes)* 2076
Cook, Louise *(Cast)* 1772
Cook, Marie *(Costumes)* 683, 3538, 3652, 4831, 4836, 4837, 4852
Cook, Olga *(Cast)* 463, 3407, 4209
Cook, Patrick *(Librettist)* 647
Cook, Patrick *(Lyricist)* 647
Cook, Peter *(Cast)* 384, 1621
Cook, Peter *(Librettist)* 384, 1621
Cook, Peter *(Lyricist)* 1621
Cook, Peter *(Producer)* 1195
Cook, Phil *(Cast)* 4651
Cook, Phil *(Composer)* 3511
Cook, Phil *(Librettist)* 3511
Cook, Phil *(Lyricist)* 1533, 2927, 3511, 4651
Cook, Ray *(Musical Director)* 2196, 3967
Cook, Ray *(Vocal Arranger)* 2949
Cook, Richard *(Producer)* 4582
Cook, Roderick *(Cast)* 1564, 2295, 3235, 4727
Cook, Roderick *(Director)* 3235
Cook, Roderick *(Librettist)* 3196
Cook, Roderick *(Lyricist)* 4134
Cook, Victor Trent *(Cast)* 3757, 4031
Cook, Virginia *(Composer)* 4030
Cook, Virginia *(Lyricist)* 4030
Cook, W.A. *(Cast)* 449
Cook, Will A. *(Cast)* 641, 982, 1050, 2127
Cook, Will A. *(Librettist)* 2127
Cook, Will Marion *(Composer)* 9, 295, 511, 633, 783, 988, 1535, 2111, 2127, 2210, 2254, 2990, 3089, 3129, 4088, 4098, 4441, 4691, 4697
Cook, Will Marion *(Lyricist)* 26, 511, 2127, 2881, 2990, 3089, 3129, 4804
Cook, Will Marion *(Musical Director)* 295, 783
Cook, Will Marion *(Orchestrations)* 9
Cook, Will Marion *(Producer)* 3089
Cook Jr., Elisha *(Cast)* 1831
Cook Jr., Joe *(Cast)* 557, 4340
Cooke, Charles *(Orchestrations)* 3813, 3907, 4763
Cooke, Charles L. *(Composer)* 3985, 4281
Cooke, Charles L. *(Lyricist)* 4281
Cooke, Charles L. *(Musical Director)* 567
Cooke, Charles L. *(Orchestrations)* 70, 341, 507, 567, 612, 1336, 1748, 1987, 2748, 3966, 4086, 4362, 4572

Cooke, Charles L. *(Vocal Arranger)* 2379
Cooke, Edmund Vance *(Composer)* 998
Cooke, Emerson *(Librettist)* 2350
Cooke, Harold *(Vocal Arranger)* 4483, 4498
Cooke, Leonard *(Lyricist)* 632
Cooke, Malcolm *(Producer)* 2754
Cooke, Rose *(Cast)* 472
Cooke, Sam *(Composer)* 4534
Cooke, Sam *(Lyricist)* 4534
Cooksey, Curtis *(Cast)* 1036
Cookson, Peter *(Cast)* 629, 4600
Cookson, Peter *(Producer)* 840
Cool, Walter *(Composer)* 2661
Cool, Walter *(Director)* 2393, 2661
Cool, Walter *(Librettist)* 2661
Cool, Walter *(Lyricist)* 2661
Cooley, Dennis *(Cast)* 2164
Cooley, Eddie *(Composer)* 3428
Cooley, Eddie *(Lyricist)* 3428
Cooley, Lee *(Director)* 2551
Cooley, Lee *(Librettist)* 2551
Coolidge, Philip *(Cast)* 3989
Coolman, DeWitt *(Composer)* 1151
Coolman, DeWitt *(Lyricist)* 1151
Coolman, DeWitt *(Musical Director)* 60, 3332, 3755, 4603
Coolman, DeWitt C. *(Musical Director)* 1151, 4364
Coombs, Frank T. *(Cast)* 2962
Coombs, J. Parker *(Cast)* 236, 3093
Coombs, J.P. *(Cast)* 3504
Coombs, Kristi *(Cast)* 2754
Cooms, Robert *(Composer)* 1897
Cooms, Robert *(Lyricist)* 1897
Cooney, Kevin *(Cast)* 373
Cooney, Warren *(Lyricist)* 467
Coons, Cheri *(Lyricist)* 3461
Cooper, Adrienne *(Cast)* 4082
Cooper, Alice *(Composer)* 3739
Cooper, Alice *(Lyricist)* 3739
Cooper, Ashley *(Cast)* 3993
Cooper, Bob *(Cast)* 420
Cooper, Chester R. *(Director)* 1604, 4303
Cooper, Chet *(Director)* 4543
Cooper, Chet *(Producer)* 4093
Cooper, Christopher *(Cast)* 282
Cooper, Chuck *(Cast)* 105, 240
Cooper, Clarence *(Cast)* 4409
Cooper, Dick *(Cast)* 2092, 2094, 2095
Cooper, Dulcie *(Cast)* 2175
Cooper, Edward *(Composer)* 700
Cooper, Frank Kemble *(Cast)* 3328
Cooper, Fred *(Lyricist)* 1342
Cooper, George *(Composer)* 1897
Cooper, George *(Lyricist)* 1897
Cooper, George A. *(Cast)* 4469
Cooper, Harry *(Cast)* 1738, 3081, 3525
Cooper, Harry *(Composer)* 1738
Cooper, Hy *(Librettist)* 1539
Cooper, Irving *(Producer)* 290, 488
Cooper, James E. *(Librettist)* 2912
Cooper, Jane *(Cast)* 1493
Cooper, Joe *(Composer)* 505, 1400, 1738, 2696, 4589, 4655
Cooper, Judith *(Costumes)* 2001
Cooper, Lillian Kemble *(Cast)* 1921
Cooper, Lou *(Cast)* 2373
Cooper, Lou *(Composer)* 2447, 3226
Cooper, Lou *(Musical Director)* 2447, 3226
Cooper, Mabel *(Cast)* 116
Cooper, Marilyn *(Cast)* 287, 1427, 1709, 1729, 2048, 2651, 3088, 3456, 4481, 4625, 4727
Cooper, Maurice *(Cast)* 4254
Cooper, Max *(Producer)* 826
Cooper, Melville *(Cast)* 649, 1284, 1711, 2252, 2464, 2547, 2705, 3291
Cooper, Melville *(Director)* 1817
Cooper, Neil *(Costumes)* 1508
Cooper, Opal *(Cast)* 984
Cooper, Pamela *(Lighting Designer)* 2427
Cooper, Patricia *(Author)* 3631
Cooper, Peggy *(Cast)* 2368
Cooper, Randi *(Cast)* 2676
Cooper, Robert M. *(Director)* 576
Cooper, Robert M. *(Producer)* 576
Cooper, Roy *(Cast)* 634
Cooper, Sara Lou *(Cast)* 1697
Cooper, Susan *(Author)* 1372
Cooper, Susan *(Lyricist)* 1372
Cooper, Theodore *(Lighting Designer)* 4314
Cooper, Theodore *(Set Design)* 4314
Cooper, Tod *(Musical Director)* 2195
Cooper, Violet Kemble *(Cast)* 3974
Cooper & Rector *(Producer)* 4282
Cooper-Cliffe, H. *(Cast)* 3219
Cooper-Hecht, Gail *(Costumes)* 2420, 3811, 4342
Cooper-Hecht, Gail *(Lighting Designer)* 2012
Cooperman, Alvin *(Librettist)* 786
Cooperman, Alvin *(Lyricist)* 786
Coopersmith, Jerome *(Librettist)* 170, 278, 1168, 2777, 3498
Coote, Henry *(Cast)* 371
Coote, Robert *(Cast)* 58, 3038
Coots, J. Fred *(Composer)* 200, 201, 208, 274, 320, 551, 667, 885, 886, 887, 1033, 1300, 1460, 1461, 1693, 1829, 1939, 2135, 2263, 2273, 2669, 2789, 2843, 3020, 3148, 3175, 3721, 3821, 3833, 4000, 4087, 4104, 4249, 4264, 4424, 4668, 4858
Coots, J. Fred *(Lyricist)* 883, 884, 897
Copani, Peter *(Composer)* 1282, 4168
Copani, Peter *(Director)* 4168
Copani, Peter *(Librettist)* 1282, 4168
Copani, Peter *(Lyricist)* 1282, 4168
Cope, Foster *(Orchestrations)* 2083, 2089, 2090, 2092, 2093, 2094
Copeland, A.A. *(Cast)* 1995
Copeland, Arnold *(Composer)* 4047
Copeland, Arnold *(Lyricist)* 4047
Copeland, Carolyn Rossi *(Director)* 1509
Copeland, Carolyn Rossi *(Producer)* 2224
Copeland, Joan *(Cast)* 4060, 4481
Copeland, Les *(Composer)* 1531, 4697, 4811, 4813
Copeland, Les *(Lyricist)* 4697
Copeland, Nick *(Cast)* 4291
Copeland, Nick *(Librettist)* 4291

Copkey, Marilyn *(Cast)* 4537
Copland, Aaron *(Composer)* 3441
Copley, Johnathan *(Librettist)* 2426
Coppe, Carlo *(Choreographer)* 45
Coppel, Alec *(Author)* 3234
Coppicus, F.C. *(Producer)* 2567, 3441
Coppin, Grace *(Cast)* 1286
Copping, C.S. *(Orchestrations)* 584
Coppola, Anton *(Musical Director)* 507, 519, 2556, 3107, 3798, 3972, 4827
Coppola, Anton *(Vocal Arranger)* 519
Coppola, Frank *(Cast)* 4595
Copsey, Bob *(Cast)* 4829
Copsey, Bob *(Choreographer)* 4829
Coral, Tito *(Cast)* 1979
Corato, Lou *(Cast)* 3697
Corbet, Frank *(Cast)* 994
Corbett, Edward *(Librettist)* 4704, 4705
Corbett, Edward *(Lyricist)* 4704
Corbett, James J. *(Cast)* 1065, 4637
Corbett, Leonora *(Cast)* 3390
Corbett, Michael *(Cast)* 2783
Corbett, Ronnie *(Cast)* 4469
Corbin, Ramilles *(Cast)* 730
Corbin, Roso *(Costumes)* 1341
Corby, Mabelina *(Composer)* 575
Corday, Leo *(Composer)* 4264
Corday, Leo *(Lyricist)* 4264
Corden, Henry *(Voice)* 57
Corden, Julia *(Cast)* 3732
Corder, Leeta *(Cast)* 1513
Cordero, Arthur *(Cast)* 4616
Cordettes, The *(Cast)* 197
Cordner, Blaine *(Cast)* 1839
Cordova, Victoria *(Cast)* 189, 4572
Corey, Herb *(Lyricist)* 1697
Corey, Irwin *(Cast)* 1300, 1748, 1811, 3140
Corey, Madison *(Producer)* 102, 1663
Corey, Wendell *(Cast)* 2175, 2187
Corin *(Lyricist)* 1520
Corin, Joel P. *(Composer)* 1318, 4012
Cork, J. Frank *(Musical Director)* 2601, 2789, 3860
Corkill, Cathy *(Cast)* 832
Corlett, Irene *(Cast)* 601
Corley, Al *(Cast)* 4294
Corley, Nick *(Cast)* 754, 2230
Corley, Pat *(Cast)* 477
Corliss, E.W. *(Composer)* 2906, 3951, 4353
Corliss, Edward W. *(Composer)* 306, 761, 3047, 3951
Corliss, William *(Cast)* 104
Cormack, Rennie *(Composer)* 543
Corman, Paul *(Cast)* 4172
Corman, Roger *(Author)* 2544
Corn, Belmont *(Set Design)* 1957
Corneal, Joran *(Cast)* 838
Corneille, Rosaline *(Cast)* 1333
Cornell, Katharine *(Cast)* 1007, 1294
Cornell, Katharine *(Producer)* 1294
Cornett, Ewel *(Composer)* 1781
Cornett, Ewel *(Director)* 1781
Cornfield, Mark *(Composer)* 4774
Cornwall, Ardon *(Orchestrations)* 4256
Cornwell, Arden *(Orchestrations)* 4586
Cornwell, Eric *(Lighting Designer)* 430, 3249
Cornwell, Jack H. *(Set Design)* 2322, 3217, 4623
Cornwell, Lawrence *(Cast)* 4622
Corona, Sandra *(Composer)* 3103
Correia, Don *(Cast)* 1298, 3444, 3499, 3992, 4412
Corrigan, Nancy *(Cast)* 1916
Corrigan, William *(Director)* 2550
Corrin, George *(Lighting Designer)* 2339
Corrine *(Cast)* 734, 2481, 3746
Corrod, Vinny *(Cast)* 1742
Corry, James *(Costumes)* 2177
Corsaro, Frank *(Director)* 2173, 4447
Cort, Harry *(Producer)* 1173
Cort, Harry L. *(Librettist)* 735, 1587, 2214, 2270, 2491, 3915
Cort, Harry L. *(Lyricist)* 735, 2214, 2270, 2491
Cort, Harry L. *(Producer)* 82, 1378, 3533
Cort, Irene *(Cast)* 3528
Cort, John *(Producer)* 47, 118, 735, 1266, 1308, 1309, 1580, 1587, 1707, 2214, 2270, 2491, 2774, 2931, 3590, 3754, 3776, 3915, 4226
Cortelyou, Winthrop *(Composer)* 2330, 3692
Cortez, Billy *(Cast)* 290
Corthell, Herbert *(Cast)* 78, 110, 201, 276, 628, 910, 929, 1270, 1433, 1519, 1524, 3396, 3729, 3866, 4178, 4464, 4539, 4662
Corti, Jean *(Composer)* 2188
Corti, Jim *(Cast)* 158, 599
Corti, Jim *(Choreographer)* 4690
Cortner, Jack *(Orchestrations)* 3564
Corto, Diana *(Cast)* 1848
Corwell, T.L. *(Cast)* 3062
Corwell, T.L. *(Composer)* 2792
Corwell, Taylor L. *(Composer)* 2013, 3040
Corwell, Trevor *(Composer)* 4751
Corwin, Norman *(Librettist)* 2653
Corwin, Norman *(Lyricist)* 3226
Cory, Kenneth *(Cast)* 314
Cosette, Pierre *(Producer)* 4695
Cosler, Charles *(Set Design)* 908
Coslow, Sam *(Composer)* 794, 1381, 1638, 2593, 3756, 4817
Coslow, Sam *(Lyricist)* 200, 487, 794, 1343, 1381, 2593, 2987, 3406, 3756, 4240, 4799, 4817
Cossart, Ernest *(Cast)* 971, 1569, 1680
Costa, Bill *(Musical Director)* 1697
Costa, Bill *(Orchestrations)* 1697
Costa-Greenspon, Muriel *(Cast)* 2017
Costello, Bartley *(Lyricist)* 694, 1907, 2662
Costello, Bartley C. *(Lyricist)* 310
Costello, Diosa *(Cast)* 4420
Costello, Dolores *(Cast)* 1485, 1487
Costello, Helene *(Cast)* 1487
Costello, John *(Cast)* 283
Costello, Julian *(Cast)* 2013, 3241
Costello, Lou *(Cast)* 4174
Costello, Lou *(Librettist)* 1038
Costello, Shirley *(Choreographer)* 2482
Costello, Ward *(Cast)* 2411
Coster, Nicholas *(Cast)* 3217
Coster, Nicolas *(Cast)* 2185

Costigan, James *(Cast)* 322
Costigan, James *(Librettist)* 322
Costigan, James *(Lyricist)* 322
Costigan, Ken *(Director)* 3939
Costigan, Ken *(Producer)* 3939
Costing, Stephen *(Cast)* 451, 3864
Cota, Keith *(Cast)* 1761
Cothran, Robert *(Set Design)* 1970
Cotsirilos, Stephanie *(Cast)* 169, 1684
Cotten, Joseph *(Cast)* 979, 2257
Cottle, Mitzi *(Composer)* 2483
Cottle, Mitzi *(Lyricist)* 2483
Cotton, Robert F. *(Cast)* 2117
Cotton Club, The *(Producer)* 875
Cottrell, Bessie *(Cast)* 3446
Coudray, Peggy *(Cast)* 2108, 3986
Coudy, Doug *(Director)* 854, 855, 857, 859, 860, 864, 865
Coudy, Douglas *(Choreographer)* 1734, 1948
Coudy, Douglas *(Director)* 851, 853, 856, 858, 861, 862
Coughlin, Bruce *(Musical Director)* 2152
Coughlin, Bruce *(Orchestrations)* 158, 992, 2152, 2651
Coullet, Rhonda *(Cast)* 2992, 3733
Coulon, F. *(Lyricist)* 3148
Coulouris, George *(Cast)* 490, 2257
Coulter, Ned *(Cast)* 3908
Counsel, John *(Director)* 1644
Counsell, Elizabeth *(Cast)* 2196
Coupe-Frankel, Diane *(Choreographer)* 2388
Cournoyer, Jerry *(Arrangements)* 2611
Courtenay, William *(Cast)* 2698
Courtland, Jerome *(Cast)* 1300, 4180
Courtleigh, William *(Cast)* 2765
Courtneidge, Charles *(Cast)* 1333
Courtneidge, Cicely *(Cast)* 1467, 2004, 2467, 4510
Courtneidge, Robert *(Director)* 4404
Courtneidge, Robert *(Librettist)* 246, 954, 4404
Courtney, Alex *(Cast)* 247
Courtney, C.C. *(Cast)* 1139, 3824
Courtney, C.C. *(Composer)* 1139, 3824
Courtney, C.C. *(Director)* 1139
Courtney, C.C. *(Librettist)* 1139, 3824
Courtney, C.C. *(Lyricist)* 1139, 3824
Courtney, Florence *(Cast)* 1176
Courtney, Inez *(Cast)* 111, 1628, 1932, 3532, 4050, 4118, 4240, 4692
Courtney, Margaret *(Author)* 2201
Courtney, Ragan *(Cast)* 1139
Courtney, Ragan *(Composer)* 1139
Courtney, Ragan *(Librettist)* 1139
Courtney, Ragan *(Lyricist)* 1139
Courtney Sisters *(Cast)* 1124
Courts, Randy *(Composer)* 1509, 2185, 2229, 2241
Courts, Randy *(Lyricist)* 1509, 2185, 2229, 2241
Cousins, Derek *(Set Design)* 634
Covan and Florence *(Cast)* 1057
Coventry, Gerald *(Director)* 737, 3176, 3228
Coventry, Gerard *(Director)* 3488, 3805
Cover, A.D. *(Cast)* 674
Cover, Frankie *(Cast)* 1383
Coverdale, Minerva *(Cast)* 1835
Coverly, Robert *(Composer)* 311
Covert, Earl *(Cast)* 3415
Covington, Robert *(Cast)* 1632
Cowan, Edie *(Choreographer)* 2544
Cowan, Irv *(Producer)* 3428
Cowan, Jerome *(Cast)* 207, 3801, 3845
Cowan, Lynn *(Librettist)* 4562
Cowan, Marge *(Producer)* 3428
Cowan, Rubey *(Lyricist)* 1922
Cowan, Ruby *(Composer)* 2457, 4648
Cowan, Ruby *(Lyricist)* 2457, 4648
Cowan, Stanley *(Composer)* 2085, 2086, 2087
Cowan, Stanley *(Lyricist)* 2085, 2086, 2087
Coward, Noel *(Author)* 1238, 1787, 1891, 3678, 3906, 4610
Coward, Noel *(Cast)* 134, 1238, 2570, 3597, 3678, 3906, 4341, 4610
Coward, Noel *(Composer)* 133, 146, 429, 702, 841, 1238, 1564, 2570, 3018, 3020, 3196, 3235, 3339, 3597, 3678, 3815, 3885, 3906, 4335, 4341, 4610, 4661, 4823
Coward, Noel *(Director)* 429, 841, 1238, 1891, 3339, 3597, 3678, 3815, 3885, 3906, 4610
Coward, Noel *(Librettist)* 429, 841, 2570, 3005, 3339, 3815, 3885, 4335, 4341
Coward, Noel *(Lyricist)* 133, 146, 429, 702, 841, 1238, 1564, 2570, 3018, 3020, 3196, 3235, 3339, 3597, 3678, 3815, 3885, 3906, 4335, 4341, 4610, 4661, 4823
Coward, Noel *(Producer)* 3597
Cowart, Sheri *(Cast)* 695
Cowen, Ron *(Librettist)* 4540
Cowen, Ron *(Lyricist)* 4540
Cowl, Jane *(Author)* 4372
Cowl, Jane *(Cast)* 1434
Cowles, Albert *(Librettist)* 2380
Cowles, Chandler *(Cast)* 620, 4018
Cowles, Eugene *(Cast)* 252, 511, 2345, 2765, 3570, 3773, 3881, 3994, 4598
Cox, Baby *(Cast)* 1980
Cox, Catherine *(Cast)* 253, 2171, 3015, 3299, 3661, 3909, 4055
Cox, Christopher *(Composer)* 459
Cox, Christopher *(Lyricist)* 459
Cox, Eddie *(Cast)* 2494
Cox, Eddie *(Composer)* 3399
Cox, Eddie *(Lyricist)* 3399
Cox, Eugene *(Set Design)* 4092
Cox, Gertrude "Baby" *(Cast)* 2034
Cox, Hazel *(Cast)* 2893
Cox, Ida *(Composer)* 146, 478
Cox, Ida *(Lyricist)* 146, 478
Cox, Jimmy *(Composer)* 478
Cox, Jimmy *(Lyricist)* 478
Cox, Palmer *(Costumes)* 571
Cox, Palmer *(Librettist)* 571
Cox, Richard *(Cast)* 54, 3515
Cox, Ronny *(Cast)* 1955
Cox, Tony *(Arrangements)* 949
Cox, Veanne *(Cast)* 3076, 3960, 4020
Cox, Wally *(Cast)* 961, 1815
Cox, Wally *(Librettist)* 961
Cox, William *(Dance Arranger)* 135, 3015
Cox, William *(Musical Director)* 135, 1427
Cox, William *(Vocal Arranger)* 3015

Coxon, Eric *(Cast)* 475
Coyero, Monica *(Cast)* 2115
Coyle, Bruce W. *(Musical Director)* 3600, 4279
Coyle, Bruce W. *(Vocal Arranger)* 4279
Coyne, Joe *(Cast)* 2123
Coyne, Joseph *(Cast)* 1627, 3052, 3092, 3154, 3753, 4044, 4130
Coyne, Phoebe *(Cast)* 4725
Crabbe, Buster *(Cast)* 3100
Crabtree, Don *(Cast)* 374, 1029, 1237, 1359, 3294
Crabtree, Howard *(Cast)* 2022
Crabtree, Howard *(Costumes)* 2022
Crabtree, Paul *(Director)* 4314
Cracraft, Tom Adrian *(Set Design)* 1871, 3907
Craddock & Shandney *(Cast)* 500
Crage *(Costumes)* 4804
Craig, Bradford *(Choreographer)* 1993
Craig, Casey *(Cast)* 4022
Craig, David *(Librettist)* 868
Craig, David *(Lyricist)* 868, 943, 2168, 3473, 4153
Craig, David *(Vocal Arranger)* 1734
Craig, Dick *(Cast)* 2023, 2024
Craig, Helen *(Cast)* 3104
Craig, Joel *(Cast)* 4279
Craig, Richard *(Cast)* 2098, 2099
Craig, Virginia *(Cast)* 2583
Craig, Walter *(Lyricist)* 637
Craig, William *(Lyricist)* 3382
Craig Jr., Richy *(Cast)* 1874
Craig Jr., Richy *(Librettist)* 1874
Craik, Paul *(Cast)* 4486
Crain, Stephen *(Cast)* 3517
Cramer, Augustus *(Cast)* 2938
Crandall, Charles D. *(Lyricist)* 114
Crandall, Courtney *(Composer)* 1862
Crandall, Victoria *(Producer)* 2219
Crandell, Elizabeth *(Cast)* 3011
Crane, A. Wilbur *(Costumes)* 591, 2722
Crane, Bettymae *(Cast)* 1840
Crane, Beverly *(Cast)* 1840
Crane, David *(Librettist)* 4, 198, 2197, 3448
Crane, David *(Lyricist)* 4, 198, 2197, 3448, 4533
Crane, Harold *(Cast)* 3575, 4206
Crane, Irving *(Lyricist)* 3986
Crane, Larry *(Composer)* 4611
Crane, Larry *(Lyricist)* 4611
Crane, Les *(Cast)* 4291
Crane, Lor *(Composer)* 4659
Crane, Thurston *(Cast)* 3674
Crane, Virginia *(Cast)* 3255
Cranko, John *(Director)* 920
Cranko, John *(Lyricist)* 920
Cranston, Deborah *(Cast)* 455
Cranston, Toller *(Cast)* 4402
Cranton, Hal *(Author)* 596
Crashaw, Richard *(Lyricist)* 2633
Crater, Allene *(Cast)* 45, 2184, 2502, 2906, 3675, 4597
Crave, Warren *(Lighting Designer)* 991
Craven, Alfred *(Set Design)* 4418
Craven, Alfred E. *(Set Design)* 4327
Craven, Frank *(Author)* 4529
Craven, Frank *(Cast)* 1536, 1598
Craven, Frank *(Director)* 4476, 4529
Craven, Frank *(Librettist)* 1536, 4529
Craven, Frank *(Lyricist)* 1360, 1536, 1588, 3146, 3372
Craven, Hawes *(Set Design)* 3098, 3625, 4354
Craven, Richard *(Librettist)* 427
Craven, Richard *(Lyricist)* 1370
Craven, Sally *(Cast)* 4557
Craven, Sydney *(Cast)* 1606
Craver, Mark *(Composer)* 3261
Craver, Mark *(Lyricist)* 3261
Craver, Mike *(Arrangements)* 4030
Craver, Mike *(Cast)* 3261, 3641
Craver, Mike *(Composer)* 3261, 3641, 4030
Craver, Mike *(Librettist)* 3261, 3641
Craver, Mike *(Lyricist)* 3261, 3641, 4030
Craver, Mike *(Musical Director)* 4030
Crawford, Ann *(Musical Director)* 1903
Crawford, Boyd *(Cast)* 4256
Crawford, Cheryl *(Librettist)* 1300
Crawford, Cheryl *(Producer)* 530, 681, 807, 1383, 1571, 1928, 2007, 2201, 2615, 3301, 3347, 3691, 3696
Crawford, Clifton *(Cast)* 30, 1240, 1374, 1852, 2056, 2213, 2964, 3031, 3048, 3424, 3618, 3867, 4364, 4747
Crawford, Clifton *(Composer)* 627, 639, 1240, 1573, 1852, 2465, 2906, 2964, 3031, 3047, 3048, 3400, 3424, 3618, 4691
Crawford, Clifton *(Librettist)* 2056, 3867
Crawford, Clifton *(Lyricist)* 627, 639, 1240, 1573, 1852, 2056, 2465, 2964, 3031, 3047, 3048, 3400, 3424, 3618, 3867, 4691
Crawford, Clifton *(Producer)* 2056
Crawford, Douglas *(Producer)* 2563
Crawford, Ellen *(Cast)* 1059
Crawford, Gary *(Librettist)* 1159
Crawford, Jayne *(Cast)* 1938
Crawford, Kathryn *(Cast)* 2222, 3131
Crawford, Lew *(Choreographer)* 439, 2720
Crawford, Marion *(Author)* 4671, 4672
Crawford, Michael *(Additional Music)* 1159
Crawford, Michael *(Cast)* 1159, 3464
Crawford, Mimi *(Cast)* 3634
Crawford, Neil *(Producer)* 1644
Crawford, Robert *(Composer)* 4706
Crawford, Robert *(Lyricist)* 4706
Crawford, Stanley *(Lyricist)* 4753
Crawley, Sayre *(Cast)* 55
Cray, Richard *(Cast)* 747
Crayon *(Set Design)* 1898
Craze, Peter *(Cast)* 4685
Creamer, Henry *(Cast)* 4182
Creamer, Henry *(Composer)* 432, 1965, 2009, 4037
Creamer, Henry *(Director)* 1019
Creamer, Henry *(Librettist)* 4182
Creamer, Henry *(Lyricist)* 2, 432, 513, 563, 724, 1019, 1128, 1132, 1334, 1460, 1468, 1965, 2009, 2135, 2302, 2757, 2796, 3020, 3297, 3337, 3840, 3985, 4054, 4104, 4182, 4360, 4811, 4815, 4816
Creamer, Henry S. *(Lyricist)* 511, 1087
Crean, Richard *(Musical Director)* 1202
Creatore, Luigi *(Composer)* 825, 2230, 2681, 4022
Creatore, Luigi *(Librettist)* 825, 2230, 2681

Creatore, Luigi *(Lyricist)* 2230, 2681, 4022
Creedon, Richard *(Author)* 4035
Creek, Luther *(Cast)* 4016
Creeley, Leonard *(Cast)* 324, 3063
Creighton, Georgia *(Cast)* 2674, 3439
Creighton, Maude *(Cast)* 2714
Cremieux, Octave *(Composer)* 1569
Crescy, Elsie *(Cast)* 1562
Cresson, James *(Cast)* 1310, 4270
Cresson, James *(Producer)* 723
Crewe, Bob *(Composer)* 722
Crewe, Bob *(Lyricist)* 722
Crews, Laura Hope *(Cast)* 1850, 2819
Cribari, Donna *(Composer)* 3539
Cribari, Donna *(Dance Arranger)* 3539
Cribari, Donna *(Musical Director)* 3539
Cribari, Donna *(Vocal Arranger)* 3539
Crichton, Don *(Cast)* 1227, 4388
Crichton, Kyle *(Librettist)* 3365
Crichton, Kyle *(Lyricist)* 3365
Crichton, Madge *(Cast)* 3052, 4354
Crigler, Lynn *(Dance Arranger)* 2026
Crigler, Lynn *(Musical Director)* 915, 1665, 1997, 2026, 2319, 2542, 2578, 3671, 3928, 4796
Crimmens and Bryant Barbour *(Producer)* 1215
Crimmins, Agnes *(Author)* 3917
Crimmins & Smith *(Lighting Designer)* 793
Crinkley, Richmond *(Producer)* 3787, 4390
Crip, Big Time *(Cast)* 1773
Cripe, Michael *(Cast)* 4560
Cripps, H.A. *(Director)* 698, 1090, 1165, 3360
Criscuolo, Louis *(Cast)* 2043
Crisp, Donald *(Cast)* 2525, 4759
Criswell, Kim *(Cast)* 4137, 4371
Criterion Theatre Orchestra *(Cast)* 2403
Critt, C.J. *(Cast)* 4591
Crivello, Anthony *(Cast)* 2333, 2442, 3136
Crivello, Mary Lou *(Choreographer)* 843
Crofoot, Gayle *(Cast)* 16
Crofoot, Leonard John *(Cast)* 305, 658, 1511, 1699, 2578
Crofoot, Ron *(Cast)* 181
Croft, Annie *(Cast)* 792
Croft, David *(Lyricist)* 1313
Croft, Peter *(Lyricist)* 1313
Croft, Walter *(Cast)* 2148
Croker, Mrs. B.M. *(Author)* 4313
Croker Jr., Sam *(Producer)* 2520
Cromer, Harold *(Cast)* 1109
Crompton, Nanci *(Cast)* 2227
Cromwell, J.T. *(Cast)* 3346
Cromwell, John *(Director)* 1593, 2342, 3248
Cromwell, Keith *(Cast)* 2022
Cromwell, Richard *(Set Design)* 2573
Cronyn, Hume *(Author)* 1372
Cronyn, Hume *(Cast)* 1372
Cronyn, Hume *(Lyricist)* 1372
Crook, James *(Composer)* 3450
Crook, John *(Composer)* 1675, 3779
Crook, John *(Lyricist)* 2871
Crooker, Earl *(Lyricist)* 4374
Crooker, Earle *(Cast)* 1858
Crooker, Earle *(Composer)* 2105
Crooker, Earle *(Librettist)* 1670, 3823, 4593
Crooker, Earle *(Lyricist)* 1670, 1747, 2401, 2479, 2540, 2545, 3290, 3823, 4335, 4374, 4583, 4593
Crooks, Richard *(Cast)* 2405
Cropper, Roy *(Cast)* 4328
Crosby, B.J. *(Cast)* 4031
Crosby, Bing *(Cast)* 51, 1615, 1893
Crosby, Bing *(Composer)* 4137
Crosby, Bob *(Composer)* 964
Crosby, Don *(Cast)* 3601
Crosby, James *(Cast)* 982
Crosby, Joe *(Costumes)* 4696
Crosby, Kathryn *(Cast)* 1615, 4146
Crosby, Kim *(Cast)* 1496, 2143, 2208
Crosby, Mary Frances *(Cast)* 1615
Crosby, Phoebe *(Cast)* 1121
Crosby, Vivian *(Librettist)* 1971
Croshaw, James *(Costumes)* 2611
Crosley, Harry *(Choreographer)* 2140
Crosman, Grace *(Choreographer)* 1972
Cross, Archie *(Cast)* 2720
Cross, Beverly *(Librettist)* 1721, 1741, 2240
Cross, Murphy *(Cast)* 576
Cross, Sam *(Cast)* 691, 3807
Cross, Tillie *(Cast)* 2984
Cross, Wellington *(Cast)* 1588, 2270, 3087, 3184, 3237, 3396, 4425, 4589, 4742
Crosse, Margaret *(Lyricist)* 2996
Croswell, Anne *(Librettist)* 1194, 2075
Croswell, Anne *(Lyricist)* 838, 1194, 2075, 4435, 4627
Crothers, Rachael *(Author)* 1221, 1803
Crothers, Rachael *(Director)* 1221
Crothers, Rachael *(Lyricist)* 1221
Crothers, Sam *(Producer)* 1649, 3792, 4695
Crothers, Scatman *(Voice)* 57
Crouch, Andre *(Composer)* 3987
Crouch, Andre *(Lyricist)* 3987
Crouch, Michael *(Cast)* 3239
Crouse, Lindsay *(Cast)* 3000
Crouse, Russel *(Author)* 4180, 4278
Crouse, Russel *(Librettist)* 163, 619, 1440, 1683, 1760, 1932, 1973, 2983, 3674, 4095
Crow, Carl *(Cast)* 4433
Crow, Carl *(Composer)* 4433
Crow, Carl *(Librettist)* 4433
Crow, Carl *(Lyricist)* 4433
Crow, Laura *(Costumes)* 1268, 1669
Crowley, Anne *(Cast)* 3895
Crowley, Mart *(Cast)* 932
Crowther, Eunice *(Choreographer)* 1467
Crowther, Jack *(Cast)* 1319
Crowthers, Dorothy *(Librettist)* 978, 2193, 3847
Crowthers, Dorothy *(Lyricist)* 978, 4304
Crox, Elvia *(Cast)* 2156
Croydon *(Costumes)* 4812
Crozier, Emmet *(Librettist)* 3086
Crozier, George *(Orchestrations)* 796
Crozier, Jim *(Musical Director)* 4431
Cruise, Julie *(Cast)* 3695
Crumb, Ann *(Cast)* 147, 211, 2442

Crumit, Frank *(Cast)* 380, 1686, 3144, 4283
Crumit, Frank *(Composer)* 3144, 4817
Crumit, Frank *(Lyricist)* 3144, 3622, 4283, 4766, 4817
Crump, Owen *(Director)* 3683
Crusar, Don *(Composer)* 1304
Crutchfield, Buddy *(Cast)* 2737
Cryer, David *(Cast)* 181, 823, 2674, 2775, 3209, 3542, 4173, 4659
Cryer, David *(Producer)* 3209
Cryer, Gretchen *(Cast)* 474, 2074, 2523, 3294, 4398
Cryer, Gretchen *(Composer)* 1737, 2074
Cryer, Gretchen *(Director)* 1169
Cryer, Gretchen *(Librettist)* 1169, 2074, 2418, 3209, 3927
Cryer, Gretchen *(Lyricist)* 496, 1169, 1737, 2074, 2418, 3209, 3927, 4615
Crystal, Raphael *(Composer)* 2354
Crystal, Raphael *(Musical Director)* 2354
Crystal, Raphael *(Orchestrations)* 2354
Crystall, Jeanne *(Cast)* 2090
Csaszar, Lou Ann *(Cast)* 2737
Cuadro Productions *(Producer)* 3286
Cuccioli, Robert *(Cast)* 131, 2198
Cuervo, Alma *(Cast)* 682, 2152, 3631
Cukor, George *(Cast)* 1026
Culbertson, Sandy *(Cast)* 2097
Culkin, Joan *(Costumes)* 1371
Cullen, Countee *(Librettist)* 4123
Cullen, David *(Orchestrations)* 211, 678, 730, 3464, 3944, 4068, 4138, 4217
Cullen, Michael *(Cast)* 2704
Cullinan, Ralph *(Librettist)* 648
Cullman, Joan *(Producer)* 652, 1149, 3299, 3718
Cullum, John *(Cast)* 134, 623, 1369, 2199, 3274, 3279, 3928, 4609
Cullum, John *(Director)* 3671
Culver, Dick *(Cast)* 1754
Cumberland, John *(Cast)* 3481, 4526
Cumby, Billy *(Cast)* 2942, 3528
Cumming, Don *(Cast)* 4291
Cumming, Howard T. *(Cast)* 2287
Cumming, Richard *(Musical Director)* 35, 3938
Cummings, Agnes *(Cast)* 1155
Cummings, Constance *(Cast)* 4443
Cummings, Gretel *(Cast)* 1958
Cummings, Joanne *(Producer)* 4272
Cummings, Kay *(Cast)* 4480
Cummings, Robert *(Cast)* 1137, 4824
Cummings, Roy *(Cast)* 3406
Cummings, Vicki *(Cast)* 966, 1856, 3138, 3314, 4214
Cunningham, Arthur *(Cast)* 734, 2358
Cunningham, Beau *(Cast)* 283
Cunningham, Bill *(Dance Arranger)* 3636
Cunningham, Bill *(Musical Director)* 1002
Cunningham, Bill *(Vocal Arranger)* 4449
Cunningham, Billy *(Dance Arranger)* 2451
Cunningham, Billy *(Musical Director)* 2451
Cunningham, Billy *(Vocal Arranger)* 2451
Cunningham, Cecil *(Cast)* 1267, 3775
Cunningham, Charles *(Cast)* 3349
Cunningham, Davis *(Cast)* 4142
Cunningham, George *(Choreographer)* 1836, 1944
Cunningham, George *(Director)* 3349
Cunningham, Jo Ann *(Cast)* 3249
Cunningham, John *(Cast)* 147, 491, 832, 945, 1797, 2599, 3195, 3491, 4862
Cunningham, Joy *(Cast)* 914
Cunningham, Joy *(Librettist)* 914
Cunningham, Margo *(Cast)* 2682
Cunningham, Paul *(Lyricist)* 1687, 4808
Cunningham, Robert *(Cast)* 2937
Cunningham, Scott *(Cast)* 3937
Cunnningham, Arthur *(Cast)* 340
Cuomo, Irving *(Set Design)* 4684
Cuomo, Jimmy *(Set Design)* 2968
Cupero, Edward V. *(Composer)* 3545
Cupero, Edward V. *(Musical Director)* 3545
Curcio, Armando *(Author)* 1354
Curiale, James *(Composer)* 4171
Curiale, James *(Lyricist)* 4171
Curiel, Gonzalo *(Composer)* 1840
Curlee, Karen *(Cast)* 4264
Curley, George *(Cast)* 1245
Curley, George *(Lighting Designer)* 2935, 3186
Curley, Wilma *(Cast)* 4625
Curley Company, The *(Producer)* 941
Curnock, Richard *(Cast)* 3756
Curran, Frank *(Cast)* 3312
Curran, Gerard *(Cast)* 114
Curran, Homer *(Author)* 4075
Curran, Homer *(Librettist)* 2679
Curran, Homer *(Producer)* 2679
Curran, Keith *(Cast)* 2283, 2305, 2790, 2968
Curran, Michael *(Cast)* 139
Currie *(Producer)* 1118, 2383
Currie, Donal *(Producer)* 4243
Currie, Richard *(Lighting Designer)* 2037, 2488
Currier, Terrence *(Cast)* 2199
Curry, J. Dan *(Cast)* 3318
Curry, John *(Cast)* 3598
Curry, Richard *(Cast)* 4829
Curry, Steve *(Cast)* 1717
Curry, Tim *(Cast)* 3039, 3742
Curry, Virgil *(Cast)* 128, 157, 1436, 4243
Curti *(Composer)* 3981
Curtin, Jane *(Cast)* 3565
Curtin, Jane *(Librettist)* 3565
Curtis, Ann *(Costumes)* 2798
Curtis, Billy *(Lyricist)* 1241, 4813
Curtis, Donna *(Cast)* 2375
Curtis, Francis I. *(Producer)* 3914
Curtis, June *(Producer)* 2754
Curtis, Keene *(Cast)* 273, 807, 3780, 4558
Curtis, Mann *(Lyricist)* 2227
Curtis, Norman *(Composer)* 4584
Curtis, Norman *(Dance Arranger)* 4584
Curtis, Norman *(Vocal Arranger)* 4584
Curtis, Patricia Taylor *(Choreographer)* 4584
Curtis, Patricia Taylor *(Director)* 4584
Curtis, Patricia Taylor *(Librettist)* 4584
Curtis, Patricia Taylor *(Lyricist)* 4584
Curtis-Hall, Vondie *(Cast)* 1103, 2852, 4697
Curty, Gene *(Composer)* 2472

Curty, Gene *(Librettist)* 2472
Curty, Gene *(Lyricist)* 2472
Curzon, Frank *(Librettist)* 276
Curzon, Frank *(Producer)* 4663
Curzon, George *(Cast)* 635, 2486
Cushing, Bartley *(Director)* 2155
Cushing, C.C.S. *(Librettist)* 3839
Cushing, C.C.S. *(Lyricist)* 3839
Cushing, Catherine Chisholm *(Author)* 2206, 2412
Cushing, Catherine Chisholm *(Librettist)* 385, 1580, 2412, 2756, 4429
Cushing, Catherine Chisholm *(Lyricist)* 102, 385, 1580, 2412
Cushing, J.D. *(Composer)* 4047
Cushing, Tom *(Librettist)* 3325
Cushman, Dan *(Author)* 4682
Cushman, Dan *(Librettist)* 4682
Cushman, Nancy *(Cast)* 1010
Cusseaux, Zulema *(Dance Arranger)* 2195
Cutell, Lou *(Cast)* 4785
Cutler, Ben *(Cast)* 1286
Cutler, Robert F. *(Producer)* 3292
Cutter, Murray *(Orchestrations)* 2258
Cutting, Ernest *(Musical Director)* 1529, 3042, 3849
Cutts, Patricia *(Cast)* 2295
Cuvillier, Charles *(Author)* 2486
Cuvillier, Charles *(Composer)* 25, 1309, 2486
Cypher, Jon *(Cast)* 759, 798, 2727, 3564, 3612, 3931
Cypkin, Diane *(Cast)* 400, 2866
Cyrus, Jim *(Cast)* 164, 3557
Czajka, Mariusz *(Cast)* 2846
Czaroulch *(Composer)* 710
Czaroulch *(Lyricist)* 710
Czernicki, Gene *(Set Design)* 4696
Czettel, Ladislas *(Costumes)* 1817, 2948, 3767
Czinner, Paul *(Producer)* 3335

D

Dabdoub, Jack *(Cast)* 177, 753, 1092, 2012, 2565, 2573
Dabney, Ford *(Composer)* 2111, 3193, 3660, 4253, 4804
Dabney, Ford *(Lyricist)* 2415
Dabney, Ford T. *(Composer)* 1909
Dabney, Sheila *(Cast)* 54
Daboll, W.S. *(Cast)* 1193
Da Costa, Morton *(Director)* 2681, 3016, 3020, 3188, 3509, 3837, 3956, 4395
Da Costa, Morton *(Librettist)* 3720, 3837
Da Costa, Morton *(Lyricist)* 3720
Dacre, Harry *(Composer)* 662, 3989, 4109, 4390
Dacre, Harry *(Lyricist)* 662, 3989, 4109, 4390
Daffodil Productions *(Producer)* 4102
Dagand, Henry *(Lyricist)* 1836
Daggett, Robert *(Producer)* 2560
Dagmar *(Cast)* 98
Dagnall, E. *(Cast)* 3092
Dahdah, Robert *(Composer)* 941, 4527
Dahdah, Robert *(Director)* 941, 4527
Dahdah, Robert *(Librettist)* 941, 4527
Dahdah, Robert *(Lyricist)* 941, 4527
Dahl, Gail *(Lighting Designer)* 319
Dahl, Magda *(Cast)* 4590
Dahlia, Helen *(Cast)* 1923
Dailey, Dan *(Cast)* 4142
Dailey, Peter *(Cast)* 2123, 4478
Dailey, Peter F. *(Cast)* 677, 688, 1925, 2041, 2493, 2835, 3560, 4658, 4681
Dailey, Robert *(Cast)* 1531
Daily, Pat *(Producer)* 1589
Dalby, Al *(Orchestrations)* 4853
Dalby, Alfred *(Musical Director)* 2040
Dalby, Alfred *(Orchestrations)* 2040, 3006, 3007, 3973
Dalby, Alfred *(Vocal Arranger)* 2446
D'Alby, Pierre *(Costumes)* 1075
Dale, Billy *(Cast)* 2749
Dale, Charles
See also Smith & Dale.
Dale, Charles *(Cast)* 17, 532, 1132, 3264, 3968, 4204, 4654, 4686
Dale, Chester *(Choreographer)* 138
Dale, Cynthia *(Cast)* 3066
Dale, Fern *(Cast)* 1337
Dale, Glen *(Cast)* 1027
Dale, Grover *(Cast)* 98, 1233, 1698, 1721, 2484, 3815, 4019, 4625
Dale, Grover *(Choreographer)* 406, 2320, 2687, 2702, 2925, 3280, 3869
Dale, Grover *(Director)* 2320, 2687
Dale, Harry *(Cast)* 3093, 4113
Dale, Jack *(Composer)* 1337
Dale, Jack *(Lyricist)* 1337
Dale, James E. *(Orchestrations)* 1120
Dale, Janet *(Cast)* 2474
Dale, Jim *(Cast)* 305, 3598
Dale, Karen Lynn *(Cast)* 3544
Dale, Margaret *(Cast)* 2386, 3766, 4673
Dale, Mary *(Cast)* 2992
Dale, Maryon *(Cast)* 364
Dale, Sunny *(Cast)* 4426
Dale, Violet *(Cast)* 2695
Daley, Cass *(Cast)* 4825
Daley, George *(Producer)* 2925
Daley, Jerome *(Cast)* 4692, 4694
Daley, John W. *(Musical Director)* 1887
Daley, Mary Pat *(Librettist)* 932
Dall, Evelyn *(Cast)* 3365
Dallas, Lorna *(Cast)* 2169
Dallas, Walter *(Director)* 2932
Dallavo, John *(Lyricist)* 1251
Dallin, Jacques *(Dance Arranger)* 924
Dallin, Jacques *(Orchestrations)* 924
Dallin, Jacques *(Vocal Arranger)* 924
Dalton, Doris *(Cast)* 3895
Dalton, Dorothy *(Cast)* 165
Daly, Ambrose *(Cast)* 2502
Daly, Arnold *(Cast)* 515, 1535
Daly, Arnold *(Costumes)* 1250
Daly, Arnold *(Director)* 515
Daly, Augustin
See also Augustin Daly Musical Co.

Daly, Augustin *(Author)* 4603
Daly, Augustin *(Director)* 1470, 3803
Daly, Augustin *(Producer)* 770, 906, 1429, 1470, 3803
Daly, Bill *(Musical Director)* 4235
Daly, Dan *(Cast)* 357, 613, 2181, 2398, 2824, 2842, 3129, 3784
Daly, Joseph M. *(Composer)* 545
Daly, Lucy *(Cast)* 1646, 1798, 3205
Daly, Nellie *(Cast)* 2035
Daly, Orlando *(Cast)* 3079
Daly, Robert *(Cast)* 115
Daly, Thomas *(Cast)* 3154
Daly, William *(Composer)* 745, 1129, 1208, 1345, 2112, 2180, 2336, 3323, 3649, 3866, 4300
Daly, William *(Musical Director)* 168, 1129, 1345, 1487, 1488, 1489, 1490, 2444, 3243, 3923, 3953, 4178, 4372, 4392, 4424, 4760
Daly, William *(Orchestrations)* 3225, 3243, 3379, 4267
Daly, William Harrigan *(Orchestrations)* 787
Daly, William J. *(Musical Director)* 379
Daly Musical Co., Augustin
See also Augustin Daly.
Daly Musical Co., Augustin *(Producer)* 3828
Dam, H.J. *(Librettist)* 3948
Dam, H.J.W. *(Librettist)* 3625
Damashek, Barbara *(Composer)* 3631, 4406
Damashek, Barbara *(Director)* 3631
Damashek, Barbara *(Librettist)* 3631
Damashek, Barbara *(Lyricist)* 3631, 4406
D'Amboise, Charlotte *(Cast)* 661, 2205, 4068
d'Amboise, Christopher *(Cast)* 4068
D'Amboise, Jacques *(Cast)* 1933, 3934
D'Amboise, Jacques *(Choreographer)* 3763
D'Ambricourt, Adrienne *(Cast)* 1391
Damerel, George *(Cast)* 1801
Damita, Lily *(Cast)* 1481, 4087
D'Amore, L'Alba *(Lyricist)* 1285
Damon, Cathryn *(Cast)* 823, 1237, 1310, 1373, 3863, 3956
Damon, Stuart *(Cast)* 842, 1060, 1408, 2150
Damone, Vic *(Cast)* 974, 4155
Damrosch, Walter *(Composer)* 1083
Dana, Barbara *(Cast)* 1190
Dana, Bill *(Librettist)* 1023, 3484
Dana, Bill *(Voice)* 57
Dana, Dick "Gabby" *(Cast)* 2850
Dana, F. Mitchell *(Lighting Designer)* 908, 2245, 2305, 2654
Dana, Frederick *(Composer)* 1627
Danby, Charles *(Cast)* 2398
Dance *(Composer)* 737
Dance *(Lyricist)* 737
Dance, George *(Director)* 2398
Dance, George *(Librettist)* 737, 1540, 2374, 2398
Dance, George *(Lyricist)* 737, 2374
Danceny, Robert *(Author)* 511
Dancer, Earl *(Director)* 26, 435, 2640, 2881
Dancer, Earl *(Librettist)* 2881
Dancer, Earl *(Lyricist)* 2881
Dancer, Earl *(Producer)* 26, 435, 2881
Dancey, Jennie *(Cast)* 4520
Dancey, John *(Choreographer)* 2720
Dancing Duchess Company *(Producer)* 968
d'Ancona, Miranda *(Producer)* 101
d'Ancourt, Grenet *(Author)* 3362
Dancrey, Anne *(Cast)* 3396
Dancy, John *(Choreographer)* 1499
Dancy, Virginia *(Set Design)* 2776
Dandora Associates *(Costumes)* 4106
Dandridge, Dorothy *(Cast)* 2259, 4256
Dandridge, Etta *(Cast)* 4256
Dandridge, Vivian *(Cast)* 4256
Dandridge Sisters, The *(Cast)* 887
Dandy, Jess *(Cast)* 2745, 3096
Dandy, Jess *(Lyricist)* 2745
Dandy, Reginald *(Cast)* 4719
Dane, Clemence *(Author)* 589
Dane, Clemence *(Director)* 818
Dane, Clemence *(Librettist)* 818
Dane, Clemence *(Lyricist)* 818
Dane, Rita *(Cast)* 3537
Danford, Andrea *(Cast)* 74
Danforth, Will *(Cast)* 1768, 2101
Danforth, William *(Cast)* 20, 104, 824, 1016, 1335, 1538, 1565, 2317, 2528, 2698, 2906, 2974, 4359, 4754
D'Angelo, Beverly *(Cast)* 3741
Dangerfield, Fred *(Set Design)* 175
Dangerfield, Frederick *(Set Design)* 45, 2733
Dangler, Anita *(Cast)* 790
Daniderff, Leo *(Composer)* 3617, 4819
Daniele, Graciela *(Cast)* 723, 1329, 3603, 4633
Daniele, Graciela *(Choreographer)* 54, 112, 756, 975, 1633, 1822, 1914, 3070, 3285, 3718, 4019
Daniele, Graciela *(Director)* 756, 975, 1822, 3285, 4019
Daniele, Graciela *(Librettist)* 756, 975
Daniele, Graciela *(Lyricist)* 4744
Danielle, Marlene *(Cast)* 2544
Danielle, Martha *(Cast)* 3702
Danielli, Fred *(Choreographer)* 4652
Daniels *(Composer)* 4589
Daniels *(Lyricist)* 4589
Daniels, Bebe *(Cast)* 1939
Daniels, Billie *(Cast)* 4501
Daniels, Billy *(Cast)* 1601, 2817
Daniels, Danny *(Cast)* 372, 404, 2707, 4169
Daniels, Danny *(Choreographer)* 64, 154, 1369, 1891, 1892, 1990, 2064, 2617, 3940, 4286, 4588
Daniels, Danny *(Director)* 2617
Daniels, David *(Cast)* 298, 3491, 3509
Daniels, Frank *(Cast)* 104, 353, 2101, 2906, 3229, 3755, 3882, 4293, 4724
Daniels, Frank *(Producer)* 104
Daniels, Jeff *(Cast)* 1268
Daniels, M.W. *(Composer)* 306, 3951
Daniels, Marc *(Director)* 868, 3473
Daniels, Sharon *(Cast)* 451, 3864
Daniels, Stan *(Composer)* 392, 3890, 4038
Daniels, Stan *(Lyricist)* 392, 3890, 4038
Daniels, Walker *(Cast)* 1500
Daniels, William *(Cast)* 3274, 3897
Danilova, Alexandra *(Cast)* 1680, 3234, 4075
Danko, Harold *(Composer)* 2784
Danks, H.P. *(Composer)* 1897
Danks, H.P. *(Lyricist)* 1897

Dann, Larry *(Cast)* 456, 874
Dann, Roger *(Cast)* 3756
Dann, Sam *(Librettist)* 4468
Dannenberg, Louis *(Composer)* 4807
Danner, Blythe *(Cast)* 594, 2777, 3468, 4522
Danner, Braden *(Cast)* 2442, 4138
Danner, Dorothy *(Choreographer)* 4505
Danner, Dorothy *(Director)* 3864
Dano, Royal *(Cast)* 1278
Dansicker, Michael *(Composer)* 3277
Dansicker, Michael *(Dance Arranger)* 3277
Dansicker, Michael *(Musical Director)* 74
Dansicker, Michael *(Orchestrations)* 74
Dansicker, Michael *(Vocal Arranger)* 3277
D'Antalffy, Desdit *(Orchestrations)* 3639
Dante, Nicholas *(Librettist)* 746
Dante, Ron *(Composer)* 406
Dante, Ron *(Lyricist)* 406
Dante, Ron *(Producer)* 39
D'Antonakis, Fleury *(Cast)* 1060
Dantuono, Mike *(Cast)* 4244
Danyliw, Annastasia *(Cast)* 2521
Danziger, Harry Lee *(Musical Director)* 1618
Da Pron, Louis *(Choreographer)* 2496
D'Aquuila, Kenny *(Cast)* 556
Daray, Gabriel *(Composer)* 4817
Darcel, Denise *(Cast)* 3381
D'Arcy, Alexander *(Cast)* 4792
D'Arcy, Bette *(Cast)* 1470
Darcy, Jacques *(Costumes)* 3005
D'Arcy, Mary *(Cast)* 262, 3992, 4210
Darcy, Maurice *(Cast)* 2101, 2711
D'Arcy, Pattie *(Cast)* 1402
Darcy, Pattie *(Cast)* 338, 2427
D'Arcy, Richard *(Choreographer)* 3954
Darden, Severn *(Cast)* 4397
Dare, Ada *(Cast)* 357, 1576, 1599
Dare, Danny *(Cast)* 132, 1297
Dare, Danny *(Choreographer)* 1980, 2545, 4234, 4235, 4291, 4331, 4778
Dare, Danny *(Director)* 1395, 1949, 1950, 1951, 2809
Dare, Danny *(Librettist)* 2809
Dare, Dorothy *(Cast)* 111, 787, 1856, 4177
Dare, Phyllis *(Cast)* 2467, 4765
Dare, Violet *(Cast)* 1307
Dare, Zena *(Cast)* 650
Daresford Prod. Company *(Producer)* 1248
Darewski, Herman *(Composer)* 208, 377, 1153, 1430, 1763, 1963, 2571, 3663, 3710, 3779, 4017
Darewski, Hermann E. *(Composer)* 3259
Darewski, Max *(Composer)* 396, 1208, 1733, 1805
Darewski, Max *(Lyricist)* 1588
Darian, Anita *(Cast)* 1648, 3696, 3938
Darion, Joe *(Librettist)* 2811, 3934
Darion, Joe *(Lyricist)* 50, 2106, 2727, 2811, 3226, 3934, 4264
D'Arle, Yvonne *(Cast)* 905
Darling, Candy *(Cast)* 3671
Darling, Clifton *(Cast)* 247
Darling, Denver *(Composer)* 1296
Darling, Denver *(Lyricist)* 1296
Darling, Eddie *(Producer)* 1811
Darling, Frank *(Musical Director)* 2770, 4804, 4806, 4807, 4808, 4809, 4810, 4811, 4812, 4813
Darling, Frank N. *(Musical Director)* 4754
Darling, James *(Director)* 1544, 2770
Darling, Jean *(Cast)* 660, 2751
Darling, Robert E. *(Lighting Designer)* 157
Darling, Robert E. *(Set Design)* 157
Darmon, Leonie *(Cast)* 2029
D'Armond, Frank *(Composer)* 3822
D'Armond, Isabel *(Cast)* 1563
d'Arnell, Nydia *(Cast)* 1603
D'Arnell, Nydia *(Cast)* 1756
Darnell, Robert *(Cast)* 2043
Darnley, Herbert *(Composer)* 2986
Darnley, Herbert *(Librettist)* 2986
Darrah, James *(Cast)* 1146
Darrieux, Danielle *(Cast)* 101
Darrow, Harry *(Set Design)* 1785
Darrow, Harry Silverglat *(Lighting Designer)* 3688
Darrow, Harry Silverglat *(Set Design)* 3688
Darrow, Jason *(Lyricist)* 1427
Darrow, Richard *(Cast)* 2051
D'Arville, Camille *(Cast)* 355, 995, 2673
d'Arville, Camille *(Cast)* 3834
D'Arville, Camille *(Producer)* 2673
Darvis, Charlie *(Composer)* 478
Darvis, Charlie *(Lyricist)* 478
Darway, Chris *(Composer)* 4171
Darway, Chris *(Lyricist)* 4171
Dash, Irwin *(Composer)* 4197
Dash, Irwin *(Lyricist)* 4197
Dash, Julian *(Composer)* 3018
Da Silva, Howard *(Adaptation)* 3280
Da Silva, Howard *(Author)* 4863
Da Silva, Howard *(Cast)* 55, 919, 1091, 1280, 2027, 2357, 2653, 3263, 3897, 3947, 4495
Da Silva, Howard *(Director)* 31, 3280, 3831
Dassin, Jules *(Director)* 2106, 2679, 4499
Dassin, Jules *(Librettist)* 2106
D'Auban, Ernest *(Choreographer)* 2035, 2964, 2974
D'Auban, Ernest *(Director)* 1975
D'Auban, Ernest *(Set Design)* 4662
D'Auban, John *(Choreographer)* 205
Daugherty, Doc *(Composer)* 432
Dave and Tressie *(Cast)* 3512
Davenport *(Composer)* 2162
Davenport *(Lyricist)* 2162
Davenport, David *(Lyricist)* 3484
Davenport, Eva *(Cast)* 1078, 1392, 1783, 2548, 3363, 3790, 4735, 4754
Davenport, Harry *(Cast)* 357, 968, 1021, 1537, 1543, 2117, 2160, 2326, 2465, 3784, 3839
Davenport, Johnny *(Composer)* 3428
Davenport, Johnny *(Lyricist)* 3428
Davenport, Marie *(Cast)* 1078
Davenport, Millie *(Costumes)* 1235
Davenport, Pembroke *(Composer)* 70, 1091, 2458
Davenport, Pembroke *(Lyricist)* 2458
Davenport, Pembroke *(Musical Director)* 31, 177, 651, 1791, 2053, 2295, 2331, 2357, 2582, 2748, 3046, 3280, 3326, 3371, 3947, 4337, 4798

Davenport, Pembroke *(Orchestrations)* 1091
Davenport, Pembroke *(Vocal Arranger)* 70, 177, 1843, 2053, 2295, 2331, 2357, 2748, 3046, 3371, 4086, 4337
Davey, Leon *(Set Design)* 346
David, Clifford *(Cast)* 134, 2248, 3195, 3274, 3897, 4693
David, Daniel *(Cast)* 778
David, Frank *(Composer)* 1259
David, George *(Producer)* 2168
David, Hal *(Lyricist)* 261, 518, 3275, 3603, 4193
David, Jim *(Cast)* 373
David, Jim *(Producer)* 261
David, Keith *(Cast)* 2200, 2359
David, Larry *(Composer)* 2429
David, Lee *(Composer)* 875, 1690, 3150, 3342, 4264, 4817
David, Lee *(Lyricist)* 875, 885, 886
David, Linda *(Cast)* 1695
David, Mack *(Composer)* 1040
David, Mack *(Lyricist)* 166, 532, 1040, 2925, 4091
David, Worton *(Composer)* 1067, 1544, 1588, 2385, 3144, 3193, 3996, 4154
David, Worton *(Librettist)* 25
David, Worton *(Lyricist)* 1067, 3322
Davidson, Gordon *(Director)* 2775
Davidson, Gordon *(Producer)* 4861
Davidson, Jan *(Composer)* 1037
Davidson, Jan *(Lyricist)* 1037
Davidson, John *(Cast)* 1373, 3571, 4146
Davidson, Lorraine *(Cast)* 2451
Davidson, Mark *(Orchestrations)* 2084, 2096
Davidson, Michael *(Lighting Designer)* 1500
Davidson, W.B. *(Cast)* 2264
Davidson, Walter *(Composer)* 1454
Davidson, Walter *(Lyricist)* 1454
Davies, Andrew *(Librettist)* 626, 1256
Davies, Andrew *(Lyricist)* 1256
Davies, Brian *(Cast)* 1422, 4095
Davies, Gareth *(Musical Director)* 2047, 4469
Davies, Griffith *(Cast)* 874, 2572
Davies, Irving *(Choreographer)* 1467, 2196, 2240
Davies, Lillian *(Cast)* 2293
Davies, Marie Thompson *(Author)* 2816
Davies, Marie Thompson *(Librettist)* 2816
Davies, Marion *(Cast)* 379, 1154, 2900, 3230, 4158, 4742, 4810
Davies, Ray *(Composer)* 1161
Davies, Ray *(Lyricist)* 1161
Davies, Spencer *(Set Design)* 407, 410
Davies, Valentine *(Author)* 1860
Davies, Victor *(Composer)* 2521
Davies, Victor *(Lyricist)* 2521
Davila, Diana *(Cast)* 1959, 4485
Davis, A.E. Sidney *(Lyricist)* 3710
Davis, Al *(Producer)* 2557
Davis, Allan *(Director)* 2297
Davis, Barbara *(Cast)* 4220
Davis, Benny *(Composer)* 883, 884, 897, 898, 1771, 1825
Davis, Benny *(Lyricist)* 123, 202, 321, 487, 847, 867, 886, 887, 1126, 1771, 1825, 3144, 3145, 3401, 3721, 4087, 4104, 4265, 4571
Davis, Bessie McCoy
See also Bessie McCoy.
Davis, Bessie McCoy *(Cast)* 371, 1685, 2960
Davis, Bette *(Cast)* 2898, 4499
Davis, Bill *(Composer)* 1296
Davis, Bill *(Lyricist)* 1296
Davis, Bill C. *(Librettist)* 3227
Davis, Bill C. *(Lyricist)* 3227
Davis, Blevins *(Lyricist)* 3703
Davis, Blevins *(Producer)* 3703
Davis, Boyd *(Cast)* 2808
Davis, Brad *(Cast)* 3198
Davis, Bruce Anthony *(Cast)* 393
Davis, Buster *(Composer)* 1056, 1063, 3440, 4153
Davis, Buster *(Dance Arranger)* 3743
Davis, Buster *(Librettist)* 1063
Davis, Buster *(Lyricist)* 1063, 4153
Davis, Buster *(Musical Director)* 989, 1056, 1063, 1729, 1762, 2227, 3473, 3524, 3743, 4062, 4180
Davis, Buster *(Vocal Arranger)* 363, 989, 1061, 1063, 1227, 1290, 1420, 1721, 1729, 1742, 1762, 2227, 2583, 2590, 3524, 4019, 4020, 4060
Davis, Carlos *(Librettist)* 3555
Davis, Carlos *(Producer)* 3555
Davis, Charles *(Choreographer)* 567, 740, 3963
Davis, Charles *(Director)* 1876, 2337, 3660
Davis, Charley *(Choreographer)* 2690
Davis, Charlie *(Musical Director)* 1950
Davis, Cherry *(Cast)* 2664, 2887, 3920
Davis, Clifton *(Cast)* 952, 2018, 4485
Davis, Clive *(Producer)* 2152
Davis, Colin *(Lyricist)* 1562
Davis, Collin *(Librettist)* 548, 2108, 2635
Davis, Collin *(Lyricist)* 531, 548, 1054, 1308, 1316, 1593, 1835, 2108, 2600, 2635, 3618, 4071, 4247, 4364
Davis, Diane *(Cast)* 849
Davis, Dru *(Choreographer)* 3126
Davis, Eddie *(Librettist)* 1336, 1494, 1577, 1931, 4829
Davis, Edith *(Cast)* 4299
Davis, Edward H. *(Producer)* 1676, 1970
Davis, Frank *(Cast)* 1404
Davis, Frank T. *(Director)* 1241
Davis, Gerald *(Costumes)* 3827
Davis, Gerald A. *(Producer)* 2993, 3606
Davis, Hal *(Cast)* 3306, 3600
Davis, Hal *(Composer)* 3739
Davis, Hal *(Lyricist)* 3739
Davis, Hazel *(Choreographer)* 4254
Davis, Hazel Thompson *(Choreographer)* 4339
Davis, Hubert *(Costumes)* 1013
Davis, Inez *(Cast)* 4231
Davis, Janette *(Cast)* 197
Davis, Jeff *(Lighting Designer)* 690, 708, 1797, 2616, 3544, 3708, 3711, 4703
Davis, Jessie Bartlett *(Cast)* 3570, 3881
Davis, Jimmie *(Musical Director)* 2034
Davis, Jimmy *(Composer)* 478, 4030
Davis, Jimmy *(Lyricist)* 478, 4030
Davis, Joan *(Choreographer)* 650
Davis, Joe *(Composer)* 1495, 3707
Davis, Joe *(Lighting Designer)* 2150
Davis, Joe *(Lyricist)* 3707
Davis, Joe *(Producer)* 415

Davis, John *(Composer)* 1637
Davis, John *(Lyricist)* 1637
Davis, John H.P. *(Producer)* 3668
Davis, Johnny *(Cast)* 396
Davis, Keith *(Cast)* 166, 3279
Davis, Kevin *(Cast)* 1636
Davis, Laird *(Lighting Designer)* 1681
Davis, Larry *(Musical Director)* 2429
Davis, Lindsay *(Costumes)* 2651, 2674
Davis, Lindsay W. *(Costumes)* 131, 1298, 2441, 2861, 3070, 3598, 3708
Davis, Lou *(Lyricist)* 3443
Davis, Luther *(Author)* 4383
Davis, Luther *(Composer)* 924
Davis, Luther *(Librettist)* 223, 1649, 2327, 3107, 4383
Davis, Luther *(Producer)* 4383
Davis, Mac *(Composer)* 3018
Davis, Mac *(Lyricist)* 3018
Davis, Mary Bond *(Cast)* 2046, 2200
Davis, Maureen *(Cast)* 2143
Davis, Meyer *(Orchestrations)* 4737
Davis, Meyer *(Producer)* 4737
Davis, Michael *(Cast)* 547, 826, 1012, 2011, 3490, 3526, 3644
Davis, Myra *(Cast)* 4161
Davis, N. Newnham *(Author)* 3052
Davis, Nancy *(Cast)* 2655
Davis, Neva *(Cast)* 2321
Davis, Ossie *(Author)* 3610
Davis, Ossie *(Cast)* 279, 2190, 4863
Davis, Ossie *(Librettist)* 3610
Davis, Ossie *(Producer)* 279
Davis, Owen *(Author)* 224, 2008, 2382, 4118, 4683
Davis, Owen *(Librettist)* 563, 768, 939, 2485, 3345, 4118, 4569
Davis, Owen *(Lyricist)* 2485
Davis, Paul E. *(Director)* 2887
Davis, Paul E. *(Producer)* 2887
Davis, Philip *(Cast)* 874
Davis, Pike
See also The Pike Davis Orchestra.
Davis, Pike *(Cast)* 567
Davis, Pike *(Musical Director)* 3704
Davis, Ray C. *(Cast)* 299, 1619
Davis, Richard Harding *(Author)* 1433, 1536, 4762
Davis, Richard Harding *(Librettist)* 4762
Davis, Robert *(Cast)* 981
Davis, Rodger *(Cast)* 418
Davis, Sheila Kay *(Cast)* 2544
Davis, Sid *(Librettist)* 2913
Davis, Stan *(Composer)* 4627
Davis, Sylvia *(Cast)* 3059
Davis, Virgil *(Musical Director)* 92
Davis, Virgil *(Orchestrations)* 92
Davis, Wayne *(Composer)* 3991
Davis, Wayne *(Lyricist)* 3991
Davis, Whitlock *(Cast)* 3030
Davis & Carey *(Choreographer)* 2034, 3965
Davis Jr., Sammy *(Cast)* 861, 1601, 2987
Davis Jr., Sammy (Voice) 57
Davis Orchestra, The Pike
See also Pike Davis
Davis Orchestra, The Pike *(Cast)* 444
Davis Sr., Sammy *(Cast)* 2987
Davison, Lesley *(Composer)* 272, 427, 1049, 1107, 1438, 2288, 3479, 3889
Davison, Lesley *(Lyricist)* 272, 427, 1049, 1107, 1438, 2288, 3479, 3889
Davison, Robert *(Director)* 3654
Davison, Robert *(Set Design)* 189, 999, 1299
Dawn, Elinor *(Cast)* 3184
Dawn, Gloria *(Cast)* 2569
Dawn, Hazel *(Cast)* 683, 1016, 1678, 2298, 2497, 3144, 3494, 4526
Dawn, Isabel *(Cast)* 1795
Dawn, Isabel *(Librettist)* 4602
Dawn, Nicola *(Cast)* 846
Dawn, Rikki *(Musical Director)* 4611
Dawn Jr., Hazel *(Cast)* 3064
Dawson *(Composer)* 2754
Dawson *(Lyricist)* 2754
Dawson, Curt *(Cast)* 33
Dawson, Frederick *(Costumes)* 972
Dawson, Gregory *(Librettist)* 1676
Dawson, Mark *(Cast)* 145, 601, 1280, 1679, 2797, 3564, 4474
Dawson, Mark *(Set Design)* 396
Dawson, Milton *(Cast)* 4218
Dawson, Robert Fletcher *(Cast)* 1885
Dawson, Suzanne *(Cast)* 708, 2416
Day, Anne Reynolds *(Choreographer)* 1155, 3165, 3329
Day, Connie *(Cast)* 2925
Day, Edith *(Cast)* 1334, 2148, 3312, 3537, 4694
Day, Frederick *(Lyricist)* 1845, 2358, 3322
Day, George *(Cast)* 449
Day, George W. *(Lyricist)* 4805
Day, Holman *(Author)* 94
Day, Juliette *(Cast)* 977, 2070, 3727, 3915
Day, June *(Cast)* 568
Day, Louis *(Librettist)* 4774
Day, Marie *(Costumes)* 148
Day, Mary *(Choreographer)* 821
Day, Mary Louise *(Cast)* 571
Daye, Margaret *(Costumes)* 3130
Daylida, Stewart *(Cast)* 1159
Dayton, Danny *(Director)* 2742
Dayton, Helena Smith *(Librettist)* 199
Dazey, C.T. *(Librettist)* 4598
Dazey, Charles T. *(Author)* 391, 2034, 4351
Dazian *(Costumes)* 1193, 1295, 2025, 2698, 2889, 2900, 2936, 4165
Dazian *(Set Design)* 1481
Dazie, LaBelle *(Cast)* 4650
Dazie, Mlle. *(Cast)* 2358, 2696, 4801, 4802
DeAcutis, William *(Cast)* 3198
de Alarcon, Pedro *(Author)* 3699
DeAnda, Peter *(Cast)* 2001
DeAngelis, Jefferson *(Cast)* 336, 1178
De Angelis, Jefferson *(Cast)* 77, 618, 1243, 1305, 1464, 1521, 2233, 2548, 3401, 3423, 3790, 4054, 4500, 4614
De Angelis, Jefferson *(Director)* 1521
De Angelis, Jefferson *(Producer)* 3790
De Angelis Opera Company, Jefferson *(Producer)* 1521, 2233

de Baum, Stephen *(Composer)* 4093
de Baum, Stephen *(Costumes)* 4679
de Baum, Stephen *(Librettist)* 4093, 4774
de Baum, Stephen *(Lyricist)* 4093, 4679, 4774
de Baum, Stephen *(Producer)* 4679
de Baum, Stephen *(Set Design)* 4679
de Bear, Archibald *(Producer)* 3634
DeBecker, Nesta *(Cast)* 310
de Benedictis, Richard *(Dance Arranger)* 269, 1060, 1227
de Benedictis, Richard (Pianist) 1648
De Bere, Elsie *(Cast)* 3673
de Boer, Ed *(Set Design)* 1865
De Bono, Jerry *(Lyricist)* 4388
de Botton, Yvette *(Cast)* 3463
de Broca, Philippe *(Author)* 2318
de Brugada, Philippe *(Cast)* 1695
de Caillaux, Pierre *(Composer)* 703
de Caillaux, Pierre *(Orchestrations)* 703
de Caillavet, A. *(Author)* 1066
DeCardi, Laura *(Cast)* 2768
De Carlo, Yvonne *(Cast)* 1329
de Cervantes, Miguel *(Author)* 2727, 3829
De Cocteau, Bert *(Orchestrations)* 4450
de Cordoba, Pedro *(Cast)* 1904, 3177, 3812
de Cordova, Fred *(Director)* 4826
deCordova, Fred *(Director)* 383
De Cormier, Robert *(Musical Director)* 1745, 4061
De Cormier, Robert *(Vocal Arranger)* 1745, 2618, 3294
DeCosta, Harry *(Composer)* 2308
DeCosta, Harry *(Lyricist)* 2308, 3297
De Costa, Leon *(Composer)* 458, 1270, 2107, 2351, 2613, 3344, 4776
De Costa, Leon *(Librettist)* 458, 2351
De Costa, Leon *(Lyricist)* 458, 1270, 2351, 2613, 3344, 4776
De Costa, Leon *(Producer)* 3344
De Costa, Viola *(Cast)* 2717
DeCottons *(Author)* 613
de Courville, Albert *(Director)* 3500
de Courville, Albert *(Librettist)* 2571, 3500, 3649, 3663
de Courville, Albert *(Lyricist)* 2571, 3663
de Courville, Albert *(Producer)* 2571, 3500, 3649, 3663
de Croisset, Francois *(Author)* 3312
DeCristo, Al *(Cast)* 3463, 3792, 4398
De Falla, Manuel *(Composer)* 1112
DeFaria, Walt *(Producer)* 499
DeFelice, Harold *(Producer)* 1038
de Feure, George *(Set Design)* 3827
de Filippo, Eduardo *(Author)* 1354
DeFlers, R. *(Author)* 2624
de Fleurs *(Author)* 1066
DeFore, Don *(Cast)* 3647
De Frece, Lauri *(Cast)* 4418
DeFrece, Lauri *(Cast)* 2509
de Freitas, Lois *(Cast)* 1883
de Freitas, Lois *(Librettist)* 1883
DeGaston, Gallie *(Cast)* 554
De Gaston, Zudora *(Cast)* 981
de Gerald, Guy *(Costumes)* 1333
De Gerald, Guy *(Costumes)* 133, 2004, 2467
De Gerald, Guy *(Set Design)* 133
DeGerde, Oliver *(Composer)* 377
DeGerde, Oliver *(Lyricist)* 377
de Gray, Sidney *(Cast)* 2938
De Gresac, Fred *(Author)* 3312
De Gresac, Fred *(Librettist)* 1183, 1308, 3312, 3613, 4250, 4616
De Gresac, Fred *(Lyricist)* 3613, 4250
De Grey, Sydney *(Cast)* 2986
De Grey, Sydney *(Cast)* 2986
de Groot, Myra *(Cast)* 3890
de Guzman, Jossie *(Cast)* 652, 1439, 2648, 3806
de Hartog, Jan *(Author)* 2050
De Haven, Carter *(Cast)* 60, 1147, 1212, 1553, 1738, 1911, 2885, 3396, 3626, 4681
De Haven, Carter *(Director)* 1553
De Haven, Carter *(Librettist)* 1942
De Haven, Carter *(Lyricist)* 1212, 2978
De Haven, Carter *(Producer)* 1946
De Haven, Charles *(Cast)* 4063
De Haven, Gloria *(Cast)* 1786, 2975, 3899, 4643
De Haven, Rose *(Cast)* 1147
De Haven, Rose *(Composer)* 1147
de Jari, M. *(Cast)* 1131
de Jari, M. *(Composer)* 1132
de Jari, M. *(Lyricist)* 1132
DeJesus, Luchi *(Orchestrations)* 2742
De Karlo, Sergio *(Cast)* 2458
De Karlo, Sergio *(Composer)* 4110
De Karlo, Sergio *(Lyricist)* 4110
DeKnight, Jimmy *(Composer)* 3739
DeKnight, Jimmy *(Lyricist)* 3739
de Knight, Rene *(Vocal Arranger)* 2817
De Koven, Reginald *(Composer)* 49, 336, 559, 934, 1260, 1375, 1570, 1602, 1768, 1849, 1896, 2209, 2345, 2506, 2697, 2725, 2733, 3363, 3621, 3673, 3732, 3736, 4187, 4500, 4616, 4758, 4767
De Koven, Roger *(Cast)* 1196, 2411, 4176
de la Fontaine, Gerald *(Cast)* 4256
De Lange, Eddie *(Lyricist)* 445, 850, 851, 1808, 3914, 4091, 4256, 4602
de Lange, Louis *(Librettist)* 833, 2515, 2963, 3550, 4236
de la Passardiere, Guy *(Producer)* 3551
de la Pena, George *(Cast)* 756, 3682
de Lappe, Gemze *(Choreographer)* 793
de Lappe, Gemze *(Cast)* 1635, 2268, 3473
DeLaurier, Julie *(Cast)* 4294
de Lavallade, Carmen *(Cast)* 1406, 1991
de Lavallade, Carmen *(Choreographer)* 1406
De Laurentis, Semina *(Cast)* 1426, 1785, 2243, 2579, 3211
De Leo, Don *(Cast)* 404
de Leon, Jack *(Producer)* 129
DeLeon, Michael *(Cast)* 4096
DeLeon, Noel *(Cast)* 4096
De Leon, Walter *(Composer)* 545
De Leon, Walter *(Librettist)* 1033, 1058, 1839, 3655
DeLiagre, Alfred *(Producer)* 1600
DeLiagre Jr., Alfred *(Producer)* 2355, 3457
de Lima, C.A. *(Director)* 2527
de Lima, C.A. *(Librettist)* 2407
De Lisle, Rouget *(Composer)* 4023
De Lisle, Rouget *(Lyricist)* 4023
De Lon, Jack *(Cast)* 108, 1237, 2201

DeLong, George *(Librettist)* 308
DeLong, George *(Lyricist)* 308
DeLorenzo, Michael *(Cast)* 4171
de Lorme, Pauline *(Cast)* 2528
de los Reyes, Imelda *(Cast)* 535
de Luce, Virginia *(Cast)* 722, 3107
De Lugg, Milton *(Composer)* 2231, 3444, 4827
De Luise, Dom *(Cast)* 71, 157, 190, 1727, 4186
De Lyons, Frank *(Cast)* 3945
del Valle, Peter *(Director)* 2630
del Valle, Peter *(Librettist)* 2630
del Valle, Peter *(Lyricist)* 2630
de Mailly, Diane *(Producer)* 2764, 4216
DeMain, John *(Musical Director)* 3088
De Maio, Tommy *(Producer)* 3561
DeMar, Carrie *(Cast)* 1374, 2408, 2711, 3867
DeMar, Fleurette *(Cast)* 3384, 3867
DeMarco, Antonio *(Cast)* 1528, 1979
DeMarco, Antonio *(Choreographer)* 1778
DeMarco, Renee *(Cast)* 1528, 1979
De Maria, Paul *(Producer)* 2946
De Maris, Merrill *(Author)* 4035
De Martin, Imelda *(Cast)* 127, 1567, 1709, 2201
De Martini, Henri *(Composer)* 3535
DeMattis *(Cast)* 2241
de Mattis, Ray *(Cast)* 1164, 1172
DeMay, Sally *(Cast)* 4623
De Medico, Michael *(Cast)* 2051
De Mert, Lucille *(Composer)* 1009
De Mert, Lucille *(Lyricist)* 1009
De Meuil, Francois *(Producer)* 2152
de Mille, Agnes *(Choreographer)* 85, 462, 530, 660, 823, 1475, 1548, 1614, 1973, 2268, 2355, 3214, 3263, 3294, 3301, 3347, 4256
de Mille, Agnes *(Director)* 85, 823, 3326
DeMille, Cecil *(Librettist)* 617
DeMille, Cecil B. *(Cast)* 1806
DeMille, Cecil B. *(Director)* 2126
DeMille, Cecil B. *(Librettist)* 219, 1472, 2126
DeMille, Vincent *(Librettist)* 1472
De Molas, Nicolas *(Costumes)* 2504
DeMonde, Dolores *(Cast)* 203
de Mora, Robert *(Costumes)* 790, 2416, 2427
de Mora, Robert *(Set Design)* 790
de Nerval, Gerard *(Lyricist)* 220
DeNormandie, Robert L. *(Producer)* 3714
DeNovellis, A. *(Musical Director)* 307, 405, 559, 666, 727, 742, 1080, 1375, 1458, 2209, 2671, 2885, 3053, 3729, 4098
DeNovellis, Antonio *(Musical Director)* 3732
De Noyer, Edward *(Cast)* 3068
de Orellana, I.A. *(Musical Director)* 3467
DePackh, Maurice *(Composer)* 1582
DePackh, Maurice *(Musical Director)* 2734
DePackh, Maurice *(Orchestrations)* 2, 317, 577, 685, 787, 930, 931, 1176, 1225, 1481, 1487, 1488, 1489, 1490, 1491, 1529, 1827, 1839, 1920, 2180, 2253, 2342, 2927, 3006, 3008, 3009, 3069, 4085, 4249, 4637, 4777, 4814, 4815, 4823, 4860
de Paris, Adele *(Costumes)* 1610
de Pass, Paul *(Set Design)* 2114, 3557, 4454
dePass, Paul *(Costumes)* 251, 3557
dePass, Paul *(Lighting Designer)* 778
dePass, Paul *(Set Design)* 251, 2171, 3231, 4286
DePaul, Gene *(Composer)* 90, 2484, 3888, 4743
DePaul, Gene *(Vocal Arranger)* 1879
dePaur, Leonard *(Choreographer)* 4706
dePaur, Leonard *(Vocal Arranger)* 4572, 4706
De Pena, Valerie *(Cast)* 3004
DePinna, Connie *(Costumes)* 2252, 4365
DePuit, Jerry *(Musical Director)* 1347, 4732
DePuit, Jerry *(Orchestrations)* 1347, 4732
De Rankie, Sylvia "Cuddles" *(Cast)* 1556
de Reeder, Pierre *(Musical Director)* 2070, 2610, 2947, 4170, 4669
De Rose, Peter *(Composer)* 297, 587, 903, 1134, 1138, 1411, 2077, 2161, 3297, 3523, 4137, 4766, 4824
de Rothschild, Robert *(Producer)* 747
De Russo, Bobby *(Cast)* 2243
de Saint-Exupery, Antoine *(Author)* 2539
DeSalvo, Anne *(Cast)* 1575, 1591
DeSantis, John *(Lighting Designer)* 550
de Segouzac, Daisy *(Composer)* 3849
de Segouziac, Daisy
See also Daisy Segovia who is probably the same person.
DeSio, Al *(Cast)* 3612
de Sousa, May *(Cast)* 694
De Shields, Andre *(Cast)* 39, 1713, 2195, 2283, 3636, 4137, 4722
De Shields, Andre *(Composer)* 1713
De Shields, Andre *(Director)* 1713
De Shields, Andre *(Librettist)* 1713
De Shields, Andre *(Lyricist)* 1713
d'Esposito, Salve *(Composer)* 2227
De Sio, Al *(Cast)* 3788, 3918, 4625, 4862
DeSousa, May *(Cast)* 1593, 2469, 4012, 4161, 4482, 4489
DeSylva, B.G. *(Author)* 2597
DeSylva, B.G. *(Composer)* 391, 487, 1335, 2070, 3985, 4812
DeSylva, B.G. *(Librettist)* 1109, 1323, 1339, 1628, 1929, 2960, 3359, 3622, 4267, 4815
DeSylva, B.G. *(Lyricist)* 123, 202, 391, 393, 487, 560, 642, 1215, 1323, 1339, 1391, 1425, 1460, 1485, 1486, 1487, 1488, 1489, 1490, 1491, 1626, 1628, 1686, 1873, 1929, 2070, 2204, 2363, 2467, 2526, 2606, 2734, 2960, 3009, 3018, 3020, 3060, 3139, 3144, 3184, 3249, 3297, 3312, 3404, 3443, 3451, 3569, 3622, 3819, 3985, 4104, 4241, 4267, 4300, 4345, 4760, 4799, 4812, 4815, 4816, 4838, 4860
DeSylva, B.G. *(Producer)* 1109, 2597, 3359, 4267
de Valois, Ninette *(Cast)* 4661
De Veuille *(Costumes)* 4795
DeVito, Karen *(Cast)* 3476
DeVivo, Walter *(Composer)* 2849
DeVivo, Walter *(Lyricist)* 2849
DeVoie, Bessie *(Cast)* 2974
DeVore, Jesse *(Cast)* 344
DeVore, Jesse *(Producer)* 344
De Vol, Gordon *(Cast)* 1511
DeVries, Jon *(Cast)* 282
DeVries, Michael *(Cast)* 2416
DeVries, Peter *(Librettist)* 3107, 3111, 3112, 4499

DeVries, Peter *(Lyricist)* 3107
DeWalbe, F. *(Costumes)* 1230
DeWitt *(Composer)* 604
De Witt, Fay *(Cast)* 1300, 3178, 3381, 3940, 3942, 4566
DeWitt, Francis *(Librettist)* 3236
DeWitt, Francis *(Lyricist)* 545, 1144, 2261, 2564, 3236, 4813
De Witt, Josie *(Cast)* 215
De Witte, Daisy *(Cast)* 3842
DeWolf, Ward *(Cast)* 2385De Wolfe, Billy *(Cast)* 1389, 2227, 4828
De Wolfe, Elsie *(Set Design)* 3193, 4555
De Wolfe, Mme. *(Costumes)* 1900
DeYoung, Cliff *(Cast)* 4151, 4449
de Zulueta, Pedro *(Composer)* 2761
Deacon, Richard *(Cast)* 1040
Deagle, Tessie *(Cast)* 516
Deagon, Arthur *(Cast)* 1083, 1901, 2315, 2533, 3437, 3772, 4387, 4802, 4803, 4808
Deagrave, Charles *(Cast)* 284
Deaker, Thomas *(Cast)* 1995
Deal, Bordon *(Author)* 2248
Deal, Dennis *(Cast)* 4527
Deal, Dennis *(Choreographer)* 3178
Deal, Dennis *(Composer)* 3178
Deal, Dennis *(Director)* 3178
Deal, Dennis *(Librettist)* 3178
Deal, Dennis *(Lyricist)* 3178
Deal, Dennis *(Orchestrations)* 3178
Deal, Dennis *(Vocal Arranger)* 3178
Dean, Basil *(Director)* 3451, 4207
Dean, Eddie *(Cast)* 3512
Dean, Eddie *(Lyricist)* 4260
Dean, Gerri *(Cast)* 2796, 3825
Dean, Hazel *(Cast)* 1343
Dean, J. *(Composer)* 1713
Dean, J. *(Lyricist)* 1713
Dean, Laura *(Cast)* 674, 1077, 1258, 3448
Dean, Norman *(Composer)* 239
Dean, Norman *(Librettist)* 239
Dean, Norman *(Lyricist)* 239
Dean, Norman *(Orchestrations)* 239
Dean, Rita *(Cast)* 4046
Dean, Virginia L. *(Producer)* 2735
Deane, Barbara *(Cast)* 1454
Deane, Berna *(Cast)* 324, 2602
Deane, Michael Howell *(Cast)* 2372
Deane, Sydney *(Cast)* 1313, 2343, 3049
Dearborn Theatre Company *(Producer)* 4311
Dearborn Theatre Management *(Producer)* 1351
Dearing, Judy *(Costumes)* 1099, 1344, 2007, 2237, 2908, 2932, 3285, 3599, 3840, 4255, 4697
Deas, Lawrence *(Choreographer)* 691, 3963
Deasy, Mary *(Author)* 2958
Deaves, Ada *(Cast)* 45, 4161
Debenham, Cecily *(Cast)* 2509
Debenham, Cicely *(Cast)* 1733
Debenham & Freebody *(Costumes)* 292
Debin, David *(Lyricist)* 3636
Debonaires, The *(Cast)* 2458
Debonairs, The *(Cast)* 383, 4777
Decareau, Dick *(Cast)* 2674
Decker, Edith *(Cast)* 1783, 3771, 4687
Decker, Gertrude *(Cast)* 4092
Decker, John *(Set Design)* 1244
Decker, Lindsey *(Set Design)* 1609
Decker, Paul *(Cast)* 1565, 4351
Decks, Barbara *(Cast)* 2608
Dedrickson, Tracy *(Lighting Designer)* 2022
Dee, Pauline *(Cast)* 2005, 3069
Dee, Sandra *(Composer)* 4193
Dee, Sandra *(Lyricist)* 4193
Dee, Sylvia *(Composer)* 3695
Dee, Sylvia *(Lyricist)* 304, 3261, 3695
Deeble, Deborah *(Cast)* 4522
Deedee *(Cast)* 3860
Deegan, John Michael *(Lighting Designer)* 3568, 4246
Deel, Sandra *(Cast)* 4096
Deems, Mickey *(Cast)* 59, 2288, 2523, 3788
Deep River Boys *(Cast)* 4256
Deerin, Oliver *(Lyricist)* 2180
Deering, Jane *(Cast)* 1140
Deering, Olive *(Cast)* 1196, 3180
Dees, Billy *(Composer)* 3695
Dees, Billy *(Lyricist)* 3695
Dekker, Albert *(Cast)* 2228
Dekker, Thomas *(Author)* 3939
Dekker, Thomas *(Lyricist)* 3450
Del Bondio, J.H. *(Producer)* 1670
Del Bondio, John H. *(Producer)* 1874
Del Duca Jr., Lennie *(Cast)* 2759
Del Rossi, Angelo *(Producer)* 3734, 3851
Delacour *(Author)* 4418
Delafield, Anne *(Cast)* 3451
Delahanty, Richard *(Lighting Designer)* 4635
Delamater, A.G. *(Producer)* 3033
Delamater, G. *(Director)* 1098
Delaney, Edward *(Set Design)* 972, 1467
Delaney, William M. *(Lyricist)* 114
Delapenha, Denise *(Cast)* 4584
Delerue, Georges *(Composer)* 1865
Delettre, Jean *(Composer)* 839, 4137
Delf, Harry *(Cast)* 804, 1132, 1685, 2216, 2854, 3652, 4208
Delf, Harry *(Composer)* 4053, 4208
Delf, Harry *(Librettist)* 4053, 4208
Delf, Harry *(Lyricist)* 4053, 4208
Delfont, Bernard *(Producer)* 1619, 1621, 2682, 3482, 4469
Dell, Claudia *(Cast)* 1460
Dell, Dorothy *(Cast)* 4291, 4823
Dell, Gabriel *(Cast)* 145, 162, 237, 1354, 1892
Dell, Marlene *(Cast)* 788
Dell'Isola, Salvatore *(Musical Director)* 85, 145, 1315, 2797, 3505, 4096
Delmar, Elaine *(Cast)* 2204
Delmar, Ethel *(Cast)* 3652
Delmar, Harry *(Director)* 1336
Delmar, Harry *(Producer)* 1779
Delmar, Kenny
See also Senator Claghorn.
Delmar, Kenny *(Cast)* 4314
Delmet, Paul *(Composer)* 3386
Delroy, Irene *(Cast)* 1339, 1404, 1689, 1691, 1859, 3783, 4426, 4821

Delsener, Ron *(Producer)* 1512, 2558
Delta Rhythm Boys *(Cast)* 497, 2817
Delu, Dahl *(Lighting Designer)* 2618
Delysia, Alice *(Cast)* 25, 910, 2788, 3583, 4154, 4427
Demarest, Frances *(Cast)* 473, 1424, 1530, 1578, 1593, 1712, 2424, 2667, 3397, 3399, 3400
Demarest, Margaret *(Cast)* 116
Demarest, William *(Cast)* 1126, 1136, 3973
Demarest, William *(Producer)* 4741
Demas, Carole *(Cast)* 1664, 2018, 2958, 3763
Demetriou, Claude *(Composer)* 1296
Demetriou, Claude *(Lyricist)* 1296
Demick, Ken *(Lighting Designer)* 4047
Demidoff, Alexander *(Choreographer)* 910
Deming, Will J. *(Cast)* 1584
Demmher, Edward *(Lighting Designer)* 378
Dempsey *(Composer)* 938
Dempsey *(Lyricist)* 938
Dempsey, Jerome *(Cast)* 1406, 3070
Dempsey, Mark *(Cast)* 2777, 3233
Dempster, Robert *(Cast)* 3730
Dempster, Roger *(Cast)* 2317
Demy, Jacques *(Author)* 4505
Demy, Jacques (French Libretto) 4505
Demy, Jacques (French Lyrics) 4505
Denaker, Susan *(Cast)* 456
Denby, Edwin (Adaptation) 3441
Denby, Edwin *(Choreographer)* 2344
Denby, Edwin *(Lyricist)* 3441
Dench, Judi *(Cast)* 1619
Denee, Charles *(Composer)* 1021, 2543
Denere, Billy *(Cast)* 917
Denes, Oskar *(Cast)* 277
Denham, George W. *(Cast)* 250
Denise, Patricia *(Cast)* 3
Denislow, W.W. *(Costumes)* 4723
Denison, Robert G. *(Cast)* 840
Dennam, Barry *(Cast)* 3186
Dennehy, Dennis *(Choreographer)* 696, 705, 2420, 2472, 2993, 4246
Dennen, Barry *(Cast)* 2212
Denney, Nicholas *(Cast)* 2572
Denni, Gwynne *(Lyricist)* 1756
Denni, Lucien *(Composer)* 1756, 3617
Dennigan, Gib *(Librettist)* 2584
Denniker, Paul *(Composer)* 725, 1981, 3707, 3782, 4502, 4503
Denniker, Paul *(Lyricist)* 3707
Denning, Frank *(Orchestrations)* 2397
Denning, Nancy *(Cast)* 2332
Denning, Nancy Ann *(Cast)* 518
Dennis, Carol *(Cast)* 2932, 3724
Dennis, Inez *(Cast)* 1057, 2942
Dennis, Inez *(Composer)* 1057
Dennis, Inez *(Director)* 4231
Dennis, Patrick *(Author)* 2523, 2713
Dennis, Patrick *(Librettist)* 1622
Dennis, Robert *(Composer)* 1370
Dennis, Robert *(Orchestrations)* 1977
Dennis, Ronald *(Cast)* 746
Dennis, Sandy *(Cast)* 160
Denniston, Leslie *(Cast)* 869, 1762
Denny, Christopher *(Dance Arranger)* 33
Denny, Dodo *(Cast)* 348
Denny, George *(Cast)* 3714
Denny, Harry *(Cast)* 1343
Denny, Harry *(Composer)* 1343
Denny, Harry *(Lyricist)* 1343
Denny, Reginald *(Cast)* 3403
Denslow, W.W. *(Librettist)* 3422
Denslow, W.W. *(Set Design)* 3422
Denton, Clara J. *(Lyricist)* 3631
Denton, Jimmy *(Composer)* 3178
Denton, Jimmy *(Lyricist)* 3178
Denver Theatre Center *(Producer)* 3631
Denvir, Arthur *(Lyricist)* 4589
Denys, Marguerite *(Cast)* 132
Depp, Harry *(Cast)* 1230, 2025, 2497
Deppe, Lois *(Cast)* 1251, 1667, 1836
Derain, Andre *(Costumes)* 792
Derain, Andre *(Set Design)* 792
Derbas, Frank *(Choreographer)* 1194
Derbil, Albert *(Cast)* 385
Derefinko, Rod *(Musical Director)* 681, 2674
Derosa, Rob *(Cast)* 1418
Derr, Richard *(Cast)* 3509
Derricks, Cleavant *(Cast)* 52, 393, 593, 1103, 3757
Derricks, Cleavant *(Composer)* 4645
Derricks, Cleavant *(Lyricist)* 4645
Derricks, Cleavant *(Vocal Arranger)* 593, 1103, 4645
Derricks-Carroll, Clinton *(Cast)* 52, 4788
Derricks-Carroll, Clinton *(Composer)* 4645
Derricks-Carroll, Clinton *(Lyricist)* 4645
Derro, John *(Costumes)* 4018
Derwent, Clarence *(Cast)* 1711, 2396, 2655, 4357
Derwent, Clarence *(Director)* 4275
Derx, Hallam B. *(Lighting Designer)* 3539
Deshe, A. *(Producer)* 2147
Designers Circle *(Set Design)* 3427
Deslys, Gaby *(Cast)* 351, 1963, 2538, 3098, 3701, 3779, 4158, 4553, 4655
Desmond, Dan *(Cast)* 1406
Desmond, Denny *(Cast)* 673
Desmond, Ferral *(Cast)* 2711
Desmond, Florence *(Cast)* 703, 792, 2103, 4341
Desmond, Johnny *(Cast)* 98, 3845, 4155
Desmond, Mary *(Cast)* 77
Despo *(Cast)* 2106, 2536
Despotovich, Nada *(Cast)* 1915
Desrocher, Tom *(Cast)* 3169
Destazio, Brian *(Cast)* 1959
Desvallieres, Maurice *(Author)* 4298
Detering, Frank *(Lighting Designer)* 902, 1199, 4271, 4807
Detling, Rose *(Cast)* 2486
Detric *(Lighting Designer)* 4198
Detweiler, Lowell *(Costumes)* 2953
Detweiler, Lowell *(Set Design)* 4139
Deuth, Celeste *(Cast)* 834
Deutsch, Adolph *(Musical Director)* 1856, 2258
Deutsch, Adolph *(Orchestrations)* 207, 2258, 3379
Deutsch, Helen *(Author)* 656
Deutsch, Helen *(Lyricist)* 2182

Deutsch, Nicholas *(Orchestrations)* 3235
Deval, Jacques *(Author)* 2753, 4435
Deval, Jacques *(Librettist)* 2753
Deval, Jacques *(Lyricist)* 369, 2753
Devane, William *(Cast)* 1383
Devere, William *(Cast)* 998
Devere, William *(Composer)* 436, 998
Devere, William *(Lyricist)* 436
Devin, Richard *(Lighting Designer)* 35, 2332, 3195
Devin, Richard *(Set Design)* 2332
Devine, Elizabeth *(Cast)* 1897
Devine, Erick *(Cast)* 2542
Devine, Jeanne *(Cast)* 3491
Devine, Jerry *(Cast)* 2814
Devine, Jerry *(Librettist)* 127
Devine, Jerry *(Producer)* 127
Devine, Loretta *(Cast)* 393, 550, 828, 1103, 1638, 2692, 2908
Devlin, Guy *(Cast)* 4514
Devlin, John *(Cast)* 406
Devlin, Sandra *(Choreographer)* 1974, 3491, 4318
Devlin, Sandra *(Director)* 366, 1438, 2279
Dew, Edward *(Cast)* 2103
Dewey, Earle S. *(Cast)* 2238
Dewey, Frances *(Cast)* 3103, 3946
Dewey, Priscilla B. *(Librettist)* 4488
Dewey, Priscilla B. *(Lyricist)* 4488
Dexter, Joan *(Cast)* 2447
Dexter, John *(Director)* 1060, 3299, 4371
Dexter, Rose *(Cast)* 3104
Dexter, Van *(Cast)* 790
Deykarhanova, Mesdames *(Cast)* 710
Deyle, John *(Cast)* 3764
Deyo, Blanche *(Cast)* 75, 767, 2835, 2848, 2902, 4044, 4725
Deyo, George W. *(Cast)* 4605
Dezina, Kate *(Cast)* 2132
Dezserian, Louis John *(Set Design)* 4643
Dhery, Robert *(Cast)* 2364
Dhery, Robert *(Director)* 2362, 2364
Dhery, Robert *(Librettist)* 2362, 2364
Dhery, Robert *(Lyricist)* 2364
Di Giovanni, Paul *(Cast)* 932
Di Leone, Leon *(Lighting Designer)* 1903
DiGiovanni, Paul *(Lyricist)* 932
DiLuca, Dino *(Cast)* 2000
Diamini, Khumbuzle *(Cast)* 3836
Diamini, Ntomb'khona *(Cast)* 3836
Diamond, Eddie *(Choreographer)* 3173
Diamond, Eddie *(Director)* 1947, 3173
Diamond, I.A.L. *(Author)* 3603, 4196
Diamond, I.A.L. *(Librettist)* 59
Diamond, I.A.L. *(Lyricist)* 673, 1892, 2246
Diamond, Jack *(Cast)* 2331
Diamond, Michael *(Librettist)* 4410
Diamond, Michael *(Producer)* 4410
Diamond, Neil *(Composer)* 964
Diamond, Neil *(Lyricist)* 964
Diard, Fatimah *(Cast)* 2345
Diard, William *(Cast)* 2977
Dias, Susan *(Lyricist)* 4244
Diaz, Freddy *(Cast)* 4584
Diaz, Nancy *(Cast)* 4172
Dibuono, Toni *(Cast)* 4518
Dick, Paul *(Composer)* 2055
Dick, Paul *(Lyricist)* 2055
Dick Clark Inc.
  See also Dick Clark.
Dick Clark Inc. *(Producer)* 3739
Dickens, Charles *(Author)* 752, 753, 754, 828, 869, 2474, 2980, 2982, 3070, 3143, 3271, 3481, 3482, 4155
Dickens, Matthew *(Cast)* 4217
Dickinson, Emily *(Lyricist)* 2124
Dicker, Dorothy *(Producer)* 974
Dickerson, Dudley *(Cast)* 2561
Dickerson, Glenda *(Director)* 3690
Dickerson, Jennie *(Cast)* 1565
Dickerson, Jenny *(Cast)* 3582
Dickerson Orchestra, Carroll *(Cast)* 3707
Dickey, Annamary *(Cast)* 85, 1476, 1948, 3703, 3823
Dickey, Paul *(Director)* 3772, 4793
Dickey, Paul *(Librettist)* 2891
Dickson, Charles *(Author)* 531
Dickson, Charles *(Cast)* 2824, 2842, 4298
Dickson, Charles *(Librettist)* 531, 1629, 3256, 4364
Dickson, Charles *(Lyricist)* 1629
Dickson, Dorothy *(Cast)* 17, 334, 611, 650, 1557, 2412, 3740, 3791, 4159, 4811
Didjah, Belle *(Cast)* 1710
Diehl, Crandall *(Cast)* 3696
Diehl, Otto F. *(Lighting Designer)* 142
Diem, Charles J. *(Cast)* 1902
Diener, Joan *(Cast)* 223, 935, 1959, 2327, 2357, 2727, 3612, 4018, 4827
Dietrichstein, Leo
  See also Leo Ditrichstein.
Dietz, Carl *(Cast)* 2567
Dietz, Howard *(Director)* 1322, 3699
Dietz, Howard *(Librettist)* 216, 294, 383, 971, 1322, 1357, 2545, 2827, 3540, 3699, 3813, 4287, 4367
Dietz, Howard *(Lyricist)* 213, 216, 294, 347, 383, 432, 844, 971, 1011, 1322, 1338, 1357, 1448, 1456, 1657, 1763, 1855, 1971, 2137, 2187, 2201, 2246, 2301, 2545, 2653, 2743, 2827, 2989, 3020, 3243, 3540, 3699, 3709, 3813, 3861, 3905, 3955, 4159, 4287, 4367, 4534, 4826, 4828
Dietz, Susan *(Producer)* 2702
Diffen, Ray *(Costumes)* 1959, 2617
Diggs, Dudley *(Cast)* 971
Diggs, Dudley *(Lyricist)* 1446
Dill, George *(Librettist)* 4424
Dill, Max *(Cast)* 3520, 3531
Dill, Max *(Producer)* 3425, 3520, 3531, 4626
Dill, Max M. *(Cast)* 2062, 2576, 3349, 3425
Dill, Max M. *(Director)* 2576
Dill, Max M. *(Producer)* 2062, 2576
Dill, Mollie *(Cast)* 3945
Dille, David *(Costumes)* 338, 3724
Dille, Marjorie *(Cast)* 110, 4368
Dillea, Herbert *(Musical Director)* 187
Dilley, Dorothy *(Cast)* 2342, 3236
Dillingham, Charles *(Cast)* 4039

Dillingham, Charles *(Producer)* 168, 252, 378, 379, 736, 930, 1151, 1175, 1208, 1230, 1555, 1625, 1723, 1753, 1901, 2184, 2638, 2666, 2671, 2891, 2915, 3103, 3254, 3268, 3295, 3332, 3451, 3567, 3675, 3768, 3923, 4017, 4150, 4158, 4212, 4293, 4393, 4716
Dillingham, Charles B. *(Producer)* 396, 582, 627, 632, 683, 773, 1536, 1631, 2025, 2394, 2614, 2885, 2900, 3144, 3146, 3229, 3617, 3721, 3882, 3924, 3968, 4497, 4603
Dillon, Denny *(Cast)* 1775, 3060
Dillon, Gwladys *(Choreographer)* 4327
Dillon, Harry *(Composer)* 2025
Dillon, J.J. *(Composer)* 3220
Dillon, J.J. *(Lyricist)* 3220
Dillon, Mia *(Cast)* 1787
Dillon, Richard *(Cast)* 1163
Dillon, Will *(Composer)* 543
Dillon, Will *(Lyricist)* 543, 1613, 4757
Dillon, William *(Lyricist)* 4197
Dilworth, Gordon *(Cast)* 3038, 4214, 4588
Dilworth, Hugh *(Cast)* 2190
Dimitrov, Olga *(Costumes)* 3846
Dinehart, Allan *(Cast)* 3768
Dinehart, Allan *(Director)* 123, 124, 2827
Dingenary, Gene *(Producer)* 101, 4173
Dingle, Charles *(Cast)* 2894
Dingle, Tom *(Cast)* 1826, 2601, 3433, 4208
Dinroe, Dorothy *(Cast)* 344
Dinroe, Dorothy A. *(Composer)* 3522
DioGuardi, Joseph *(Producer)* 2754
Dippel, Andreas *(Producer)* 2619
Dishy, Bob *(Cast)* 1047, 1310, 1408
Disipio, Fred *(Producer)* 3739
Dissell, Betty *(Cast)* 80
Ditrichstein, Leo *(Author)* 179, 4642
Ditrichstein, Leo *(Cast)* 179, 1594, 4125
Ditrichstein, Leo *(Librettist)* 1888, 4641
Ditsch, James *(Cast)* 643
Dittman, Dean *(Cast)* 3279, 3696
Dix, Beulah Marie *(Author)* 1096, 3730
Dix, Frank *(Author)* 1975
Dix, Lillian *(Cast)* 998, 2996
Dix, Richard *(Cast)* 2059
Dix, Tommy *(Cast)* 372
Dixey, Henry E. *(Cast)* 586, 758, 1465, 3887
Dixey, Henry E. *(Director)* 3887
Dixey, Henry E. *(Librettist)* 3887
Dixie Nightingales *(Cast)* 1772
Dixon, Adele *(Cast)* 346, 383, 3168, 4361
Dixon, Dorothy *(Cast)* 1492, 2960, 4545
Dixon, Ed *(Cast)* 599, 949, 2320, 4136
Dixon, Gale *(Cast)* 798
Dixon, Harland
Part of team of Dodge & Dixon.
Dixon, Harland *(Cast)* 627, 965, 1625, 2308, 2403, 2734, 3243, 3650, 4426, 4817
Dixon, Harland *(Choreographer)* 703
Dixon, Harold *(Cast)* 3166
Dixon, Harry *(Cast)* 1492
Dixon, Heather *(Composer)* 4264
Dixon, Heather *(Lyricist)* 4264
Dixon, Jean *(Cast)* 2265
Dixon, Jerry *(Cast)* 1296, 3285
Dixon, Julius *(Composer)* 4264
Dixon, Julius *(Lyricist)* 4264
Dixon, Lee *(Cast)* 1814, 1894, 3138, 3263
Dixon, MacIntyre *(Cast)* 679, 2072, 2663, 3330, 4412, 4474, 4703
Dixon, Mildred *(Cast)* 892
Dixon, Mort *(Lyricist)* 418, 1359, 1813, 2423, 4235, 4817, 4818
Dixon, Roy *(Librettist)* 4227
Dixon, Roy *(Lyricist)* 4227
Dixon, Will *(Cast)* 1479, 2791
Dixon, William *(Librettist)* 4525
Djeli, Sahari *(Cast)* 4747
Dlathu, Sindiswa *(Cast)* 4438
D'Lugoff, Art *(Producer)* 3297, 3987
D'Lugoff, Burt *(Producer)* 3297, 3987
D'Lugoff, Burt Charles *(Producer)* 2306
Dlugos, Gregory J. *(Musical Director)* 2420
Doane, Frank *(Cast)* 830, 1529, 1743, 1994, 3251, 3466, 3924
Doane, Melanie *(Cast)* 580
Dobbins, Tim *(Puppeteer)* 56, 3449
Dobbs, George *(Cast)* 4352
Dobbs, George *(Choreographer)* 3148
Dobos, Viola *(Cast)* 2140
Dobson, James *(Cast)* 2175
Dobson, West *(Producer)* 2372
Docherty, Peter *(Set Design)* 3967
Dockery, Leslie *(Choreographer)* 338
Dockery, Leslie *(Director)* 2272
Docket, Larry *(Cast)* 3359
Dockstader, Lew *(Cast)* 2710, 3545, 4054
Dockstader, Lew *(Director)* 3545
Dockstader, Lew *(Producer)* 3545
Doctor, Rubin *(Composer)* 1609
Doctor, Rubin *(Lyricist)* 1609
Doda, Dan *(Director)* 806
Dodd, Clare *(Cast)* 4023
Dodd, John *(Lighting Designer)* 2134
Dodd, Johnny *(Lighting Designer)* 4011
Dodd, Malcolm *(Cast)* 2164
Dodd, Rory *(Cast)* 3741
Dodds, Malcolm *(Vocal Arranger)* 4091
Dodds and the Tunedrops, Malcolm *(Cast)* 898
Dodge, Anna Bacon *(Composer)* 364
Dodge, D. Frank
See also Dodge & Castle.
Dodge, D. Frank *(Set Design)* 113, 175, 350, 357, 457, 523, 559, 561, 737, 976, 1021, 1243, 1392, 1469, 1540, 2116, 2123, 2179, 2347, 2398, 2695, 2725, 3129, 3732, 3790, 3820, 3856, 3951, 4098, 4236, 4250, 4691
Dodge, Jerry *(Cast)* 1478, 1828, 2660, 3294, 3835
Dodge, Jerry *(Director)* 3876
Dodge, Marcia Milgrom *(Choreographer)* 494, 784, 2477, 2542, 3227
Dodge, Marcia Milgrom *(Director)* 3227
Dodge, Mary Mapes *(Source Author)* 1742
Dodge & Castle
See also D. Frank Dodge and William Castle.
Dodge & Castle *(Set Design)* 1626, 2373, 3048

Dodger Productions *(Producer)* 394, 1402, 1636, 3862, 4676
Dodger Productions, Inc. *(Producer)* 3608
Dods, Marcus *(Musical Director)* 455, 2682
Dodson, A.E. *(Director)* 3948
Dodson, Colleen *(Cast)* 2783
Dody, Dan *(Choreographer)* 185, 1032, 1457
Dody, Dan *(Composer)* 1032
Dody, Dan *(Lyricist)* 1032
Dody, Sam *(Cast)* 1824
Dody, Sam *(Librettist)* 1824
Doe, Joe *(Librettist)* 3417
Doemland, Ann *(Cast)* 2124
Doermann, Felix *(Author)* 1334
Doermann, Felix *(Librettist)* 1309, 1334
Doerr, Mark E. *(Cast)* 4732
Doerr, Mary *(Cast)* 303
Doff, Gerard S. *(Cast)* 4431
Dogim, Isaac *(Cast)* 4773
Dogim, Isaac *(Lyricist)* 4773
Dohanos, Peter *(Lighting Designer)* 1194
Dohanos, Peter *(Set Design)* 1194, 2551
Dohanos, Stevan *(Set Design)* 4047
Doherty, Lindy *(Cast)* 4423
Dolan, Gerald *(Composer)* 966
Dolan, Judith *(Costumes)* 1038, 2242, 2822, 3456, 4272, 4790
Dolan, Robert Emmett *(Composer)* 1373, 3584, 4314, 4824
Dolan, Robert Emmett *(Musical Director)* 44, 798, 1352, 1973, 2268, 2597, 2786, 4557
Dolan, Robert Emmett *(Vocal Arranger)* 1322
Dolgoy, Sholem *(Lighting Designer)* 1120
Dolin, Anton *(Cast)* 703, 2140, 3893, 4661
Dolin, Anton *(Choreographer)* 1128, 4586
Dolin, Garry *(Vocal Arranger)* 4652
Dolin, Gerald *(Composer)* 1945, 4021
Dolin, Gerald *(Lyricist)* 1945
Dolin, Gerald *(Musical Director)* 4021
Doll, Roy *(Composer)* 1134
Doll, Roy *(Lyricist)* 1134
Dollar, William *(Choreographer)* 1670
Dolloff, William *(Producer)* 1971
Dolly, Edward *(Choreographer)* 1805, 2788, 3467
Dolly, Edward *(Director)* 2788, 3467
Dolly, Helen *(Cast)* 4231
Dolly, Roszika *(Cast)* 1151, 1904, 2469, 2825, 4657
Dolly, Yancsi *(Cast)* 1151, 1904, 1963, 2696, 2825
Dolly Sisters
See also Roszika Dolly and Yansci Dolly.
Dolly Sisters *(Choreographer)* 3467
Dolly Sisters, The *(Cast)* 1690, 4712, 4805
Dolman, Richard *(Cast)* 1855, 2392
Dolores *(Cast)* 910, 4812
Domino, Antoine "Fats" *(Composer)* 3739
Domino, Antoine "Fats" *(Lyricist)* 3739
Domsky, Sam *(Librettist)* 4774
Don, Robin *(Set Design)* 299
DonHowe, Gwyda *(Cast)* 550, 1797, 3763
Donaggio, Pino *(Composer)* 4193
Donaggio, Pino *(Lyricist)* 4193
Donaghey, Frederick *(Librettist)* 1524, 2596
Donaghey, Frederick *(Lyricist)* 2596
Donaghy, Harry *(Composer)* 1722
Donaghy, Harry *(Lyricist)* 1722
Donahue, Gus *(Orchestrations)* 2084
Donahue, Jack *(Cast)* 136, 317, 2855, 2927, 3766, 3907, 4087, 4212, 4814
Donahue, Jack *(Choreographer)* 180, 277, 1251, 2234, 2540, 2987, 3907
Donahue, Jack *(Composer)* 1267
Donahue, Jack *(Director)* 2234, 2987, 3801, 3893, 4423
Donahue, Jack *(Librettist)* 3584, 4087
Donahue, Jack *(Lyricist)* 1267
Donahue, James *(Cast)* 2284
Donahue Sales Corporation *(Producer)* 2988
Donald, Donald K. *(Producer)* 432, 3643
Donaldson, Arthur *(Cast)* 3578, 4236
Donaldson, John *(Cast)* 3314
Donaldson, Norma *(Cast)* 3619
Donaldson, Walter *(Composer)* 123, 391, 393, 487, 1084, 1154, 1395, 1638, 2342, 2385, 2706, 3018, 3020, 3175, 3405, 3717, 3783, 3973, 3980, 3985, 3989, 4023, 4037, 4249, 4322, 4573, 4683, 4813, 4817, 4821, 4823, 4838, 4846
Donaldson, Walter *(Lyricist)* 1395, 1638, 3175, 3783, 3980, 3989, 4023, 4037, 4799, 4823
Donaldson, Wharton *(Cast)* 4093
Donath, Ludwig *(Cast)* 3918
Dondlinger, Mary Jo *(Lighting Designer)* 147, 809, 1510, 1630, 1737
Donegan, Francis X. *(Cast)* 1529
Donehue, Vincent J. *(Cast)* 2202
Donehue, Vincent J. *(Director)* 2201, 4095
Donen, Stanley *(Cast)* 323, 372, 3353
Donen, Stanley *(Director)* 3682
Doner, Kitty *(Cast)* 969, 3737, 3985
Doner, Ted *(Cast)* 771, 969, 1944, 2135
Donizetti, Gaetano *(Author)* 3197
Donizetti, Gaetano (Music Based On) 3197, 4655
Donklin, Willis P. *(Cast)* 1957
Donlevy, Brian *(Cast)* 1916, 2475, 3650
Donley, Robert *(Cast)* 3671
Donlin, Mike *(Cast)* 687
Donn, Berta *(Cast)* 4328
Donnelly *(Lyricist)* 4805
Donnelly, Arthur *(Cast)* 2857
Donnelly, Candice *(Costumes)* 2945
Donnelly, Dorothy *(Director)* 3540
Donnelly, Dorothy *(Librettist)* 463, 1240, 1309, 1831, 3056, 3063, 3540, 4188
Donnelly, Dorothy *(Lyricist)* 463, 1831, 3020, 3056, 3063, 3540, 4188
Donnelly, Elsie *(Cast)* 1833
Donnelly, Harry *(Composer)* 1120
Donnelly, Harry *(Lyricist)* 1120
Donnelly, Jamie *(Cast)* 1478, 3742, 3743, 4643
Donnelly, Ken *(Librettist)* 3019
Donnelly, Leo *(Cast)* 913, 4668
Donnelly, Leo *(Librettist)* 3701, 4668
Donnelly, Leo *(Lyricist)* 3701
Donnelly, Ruth *(Cast)* 208, 1598
Donner, Vyvyan *(Costumes)* 1027

Donnet, Mary *(Cast)* 2049
Donnolly, Candice *(Costumes)* 3853
D'Onofrio, Benny *(Cast)* 2521
D'Onofrio, Rip *(Cast)* 985
Donovan, Gerry *(Composer)* 4433
Donovan, Gerry *(Librettist)* 4433
Donovan, Gerry *(Lyricist)* 4433
Donovan, Joe *(Choreographer)* 3651
Donovan, Joe *(Director)* 3651
Donovan, King *(Cast)* 2057
Donovan, Linda *(Cast)* 1380
Donovan, Maria *(Costumes)* 4415
Donovan, Nancy *(Cast)* 2610
Donovan, Walter *(Composer)* 3589
Donovan, Warde *(Cast)* 853, 3837, 4428
Dooley, Gordon *(Cast)* 1134, 1488, 4742
Dooley, John *(Cast)* 4437
Dooley, John *(Composer)* 1924
Dooley, John *(Librettist)* 1924
Dooley, John *(Lyricist)* 1924
Dooley, Johnny *(Cast)* 1486, 1552, 2264, 2298, 2491, 3401, 3478, 4813
Dooley, Paul *(Cast)* 1091, 1233, 4369, 4397, 4401
Dooley, Ray *(Cast)* 582, 827, 1134, 1920, 3144, 3179, 3968, 4374, 4813, 4814, 4815, 4818, 4819
Dooley, Sean *(Cast)* 3125
Doolittle, James A. *(Producer)* 3954
Doran, Johnny *(Cast)* 1222
Doran, Mr. *(Cast)* 1743
Dore, Daniel *(Composer)* 224
Dore, Daniel *(Lyricist)* 224
Dore, Daniel *(Musical Director)* 1910, 2538
Dore, Demaris *(Cast)* 3556
Dore, Lynn *(Cast)* 3172
Dorff, Steve *(Arrangements)* 2651
Dorff, Steve *(Composer)* 2651
Dorfman, Andrew *(Musical Director)* 3739
Dorfman, Nat *(Librettist)* 444, 447, 787, 2140, 3705
Dorfman, Robert *(Cast)* 109, 3198
Dorfmunder, Dieter *(Lyricist)* 154
Dorman, Edna *(Cast)* 2795
Dormann, Felix *(Author)* 3771, 4590
Dormeuil, Edmee *(Cast)* 4302
Dormont, Frances *(Costumes)* 4047
Dorn, Margaret *(Composer)* 459
Doro, Marie *(Cast)* 405, 1537, 2952
Doro, Marie *(Composer)* 2498
Doro, Marie *(Lyricist)* 2498
Dorothy, Isabelle *(Cast)* 2571
Dorr, Dorothy *(Cast)* 3805
D'Orsay, Fifi *(Cast)* 1329
D'Orsay, Lawrence *(Cast)* 60, 205, 351, 2892, 3737, 3985, 4664
Dorsell, Sabry *(Cast)* 188
Dorsett, Flora *(Cast)* 2771
Dorsey, Abner *(Cast)* 1366
Dorsey, Frances *(Cast)* 2083
Dorsey, Jimmy *(Cast)* 1207, 1528
Dorsey, Kent *(Lighting Designer)* 4193
Dorsey, Tommy *(Cast)* 1207
Dorsey, Tommy *(Composer)* 1825
Dorsey, Tommy *(Lyricist)* 1825
Dorsey, Will *(Composer)* 2984
D'Orso, Wisa *(Cast)* 2288, 2983, 3204
Dossert, Frank *(Composer)* 4012
Dossett, John *(Cast)* 1377, 1822
Dotrice, Roy *(Cast)* 1787
Dotson, Deborah *(Cast)* 2993
Doty, Charles *(Librettist)* 4044
Doty, Dan *(Director)* 513
Doty, David *(Cast)* 373
Doucet, Catherine *(Cast)* 3415
Doucette, David *(Costumes)* 2482
Dougall, Bernard *(Lyricist)* 2204, 3735
Dougherty, Byrd *(Composer)* 2959, 2978
Dougherty, Byrd *(Musical Director)* 782
Dougherty, Christina *(Additional Music)* 4729
Dougherty, Dan *(Composer)* 700
Dougherty, Dennis *(Set Design)* 1977
Dougherty, George *(Composer)* 1523
Dougherty, George Byrd *(Composer)* 1523
Dougherty, J.P. *(Cast)* 1785, 3169, 3757, 3873
Dougherty, Joseph *(Librettist)* 3039
Douglas, Bob *(Cast)* 601
Douglas, C. Noel *(Lyricist)* 2990
Douglas, C.N. *(Lyricist)* 694
Douglas, Charles Noel *(Librettist)* 15
Douglas, Charles Noel *(Lyricist)* 15, 250, 1532, 3753, 3857
Douglas, Fred *(Cast)* 2111
Douglas, George *(Cast)* 3158
Douglas, Gilbert *(Cast)* 2059
Douglas, Jerry *(Librettist)* 3763
Douglas, Jerry *(Lyricist)* 3763
Douglas, Kirk *(Cast)* 1089
Douglas, Larry *(Cast)* 1860, 2312, 4640
Douglas, Louis *(Choreographer)* 26
Douglas, Malcolm *(Composer)* 571
Douglas, Melvyn *(Cast)* 1416, 2268, 2450
Douglas, Melvyn *(Producer)* 620
Douglas, Milton *(Cast)* 2813
Douglas, Noel *(Lyricist)* 3753
Douglas, Suzanne *(Cast)* 4371
Douglas, Wade *(Set Design)* 1009
Douglas, Walter *(Cast)* 1513
Douglas, Warren *(Librettist)* 362
Douglas, Warren *(Lyricist)* 362
Douglas, William *(Cast)* 2023
Douglass, Jane *(Composer)* 348
Douglass, Jane *(Dance Arranger)* 348
Douglass, Jane *(Musical Director)* 348
Douglass, Jane *(Vocal Arranger)* 348
Douglass, Louis *(Cast)* 3089
Douglass, Louis *(Director)* 3528
Douglass, Louis *(Lyricist)* 3528
Douglass, Pi *(Cast)* 1497, 3871, 4722
Douglass, Stephen *(Cast)* 957, 1600, 2705, 3294, 3801
Douthitt, Wilfred *(Cast)* 2486
Douthitt, Wilfred *(Lyricist)* 2486
Dova, Ben *(Cast)* 4174
Dova, Nina *(Cast)* 2052
Dove, Billy *(Cast)* 4852

Dove, Julius *(Set Design)* 97
Dovey, Alice *(Cast)* 1735, 3193, 3265, 3362, 3494, 3579, 3627, 4185, 4203, 4555
Dovey, Ethel *(Cast)* 88
Dow, Susan *(Cast)* 3555
Dowd, M'el *(Cast)* 623
Dowdy, Helen *(Cast)* 2994, 3541
Dowe, Julius *(Set Design)* 3081
Dowell, Coleman *(Composer)* 34, 4292
Dowell, Coleman *(Librettist)* 4292
Dowell, Coleman *(Lyricist)* 4292
Dowell, Edgar *(Composer)* 1876, 3514
Dowell, Edgar *(Lyricist)* 1876
Dowell, J. Edgar *(Composer)* 1658
Dowell, J. Edgar *(Lyricist)* 1658
Dowling, Doris *(Cast)* 323
Dowling, Eddie *(Cast)* 1965, 3153, 3821, 3968, 4374, 4547, 4813
Dowling, Eddie *(Composer)* 1965
Dowling, Eddie *(Director)* 717, 2504, 3321
Dowling, Eddie *(Librettist)* 1965, 3821, 3968
Dowling, Eddie *(Lyricist)* 1965, 3968
Dowling, Eddie *(Producer)* 717, 2504, 3321, 4374
Dowling, Edward *(Cast)* 79
Dowling, Edward *(Producer)* 79
Dowling, Edward Duryea *(Director)* 383, 1763, 1840, 2301, 4086, 4174
Dowling, Edward Duryea *(Librettist)* 4174
Dowling, Edward Duryea *(Lighting Designer)* 4086
Dowling, M.L. *(Costumes)* 1392, 1540
Dowling, Vincent *(Librettist)* 451
Downey, Morton *(Cast)* 173, 1215, 1416, 2366, 2460, 4178
Downie, Barbara *(Cast)* 283
Downing, David *(Cast)* 1592, 1671, 3522
Downs, Johnny *(Cast)* 180, 1930, 4177
Downs, Michael E. *(Set Design)* 1832, 2237
Downs, Sarah *(Cast)* 1757
Downs, Stephen *(Composer)* 1262
Downs, Stephen *(Librettist)* 1262
Downs, Stephen *(Lyricist)* 1262
Downs Jr., Edward R. *(Producer)* 3015
Doyle, Arthur Conan *(Author)* 270
Doyle, Buddy *(Cast)* 4465
Doyle, David *(Cast)* 1860
Doyle, David *(Director)* 339
Doyle, James *(Cast)* 627, 965, 3252, 4694
Doyle, Ted *(Cast)* 821
Doyle, William *(Musical Director)* 4193
Doyle & Dixon *(Cast)* 558, 683, 1963, 4158
Dozer, David *(Librettist)* 3527
Dozier, Lamont *(Composer)* 146, 3739, 4193, 4534
Dozier, Lamont *(Lyricist)* 146, 3739, 4193, 4534
Dozzel, Master *(Cast)* 1192
Drabble, Richard *(Cast)* 456
Drabinsky, Garth H. *(Producer)* 550
Drake, Alfred (Adaptation) 3280
Drake, Alfred *(Cast)* 23, 31, 247, 341, 1435, 1511, 2295, 2327, 2331, 3263, 3280, 3292, 3989, 4166, 4479, 4483, 4667, 4798
Drake, Alfred *(Director)* 911, 1091, 2464, 2563
Drake, Alfred *(Librettist)* 1091, 2464, 3798
Drake, David *(Cast)* 3346
Drake, Donna *(Cast)* 484, 746, 4701
Drake, Ervin *(Composer)* 204, 1848, 4091, 4633
Drake, Ervin *(Librettist)* 1848
Drake, Ervin *(Lyricist)* 204, 1848, 3905, 4091, 4633
Drake, Milton *(Composer)* 478, 2060
Drake, Milton *(Lighting Designer)* 4318
Drake, Milton *(Lyricist)* 478, 2060, 3374
Drake, Ronald *(Cast)* 461, 4244
Drake, William A. *(Librettist)* 4486
Drakeley, Ray *(Cast)* 23
Draper, Alexander *(Cast)* 3853
Draper, Kate *(Cast)* 1000
Draper, Paul *(Cast)* 1416, 2406, 2504, 3594, 4374
Draper, Paul *(Choreographer)* 1474
Drayton, Mary *(Cast)* 3647
Drayton, Otto *(Librettist)* 3692
Drayton, Thaddius *(Cast)* 2557
Drean, Robert *(Director)* 1347
Dregely, Gabriel *(Author)* 2526
Dreiser, Theodore *(Author)* 3831
Drescher, Otto *(Orchestrations)* 1343
Dreskin, William *(Composer)* 3448
Dresselhuys, Lorraine Manville *(Producer)* 3703
Dresser, Forrest J. *(Cast)* 1868
Dresser, Louise *(Cast)* 8, 558, 632, 1526, 1569, 1613, 1784, 1826, 2782, 3740
Dresser, Richard *(Author)* 1915
Dressler, Eric *(Cast)* 1215
Dressler, Marie *(Cast)* 77, 506, 683, 969, 1728, 1881, 1994, 2316, 2324, 2398, 2673, 2725, 2904, 3404, 3755, 4125, 4382, 4473
Dressler, Marie *(Costumes)* 77
Dressler, Marie *(Director)* 77
Dressler, Marie *(Librettist)* 77
Drew, Bernard *(Librettist)* 2275
Drew, Bill *(Cast)* 3439
Drew, Charles H. *(Cast)* 4563
Drew, Doris (Voice) 57
Drew, George *(Costumes)* 3059
Drew, Georgie *(Costumes)* 1834
Drew, John *(Cast)* 17
Drew, Louise *(Cast)* 17, 2624
Drew, Maurice *(Cast)* 3910
Drew, Richard *(Lighting Designer)* 4746
Drexler, Rosalyn *(Librettist)* 1958
Drexler, Rosalyn *(Lyricist)* 1958
Dreyer, Bob *(Cast)* 1883
Dreyer, Dave *(Composer)* 393, 1404, 1643, 3020, 3149
Dreyer, Dave *(Lyricist)* 1404
Dreyfuss, Henry *(Costumes)* 2739
Dreyfuss, Henry *(Director)* 839
Dreyfuss, Henry *(Lighting Designer)* 3946
Dreyfuss, Henry *(Set Design)* 672, 715, 1275, 1440, 1929, 2739, 3946, 4177
Dreyfuss-Fellner Co. *(Producer)* 4359
Drischell, Ralph *(Cast)* 3671
Driscoll, Clara *(Librettist)* 2848
Drivas, Robert *(Cast)* 1294
Drivas, Robert *(Director)* 546, 2435, 3428

Driver, Donald *(Choreographer)* 3231
Driver, Donald *(Director)* 547, 2218, 3231, 4789
Driver, Donald *(Librettist)* 3231, 4789
Driver, Donald *(Lyricist)* 3231
Driver, John *(Cast)* 3330, 3858
Driver, John *(Composer)* 3711, 3858
Driver, John *(Director)* 729, 3858, 3909, 4297
Driver, John *(Librettist)* 729, 3711, 3858, 3944
Driver, John *(Lyricist)* 3711, 3858, 3944
Drix, Walter *(Composer)* 1413
Drotos, Ron *(Arrangements)* 4255
Drowne, Edwin S. *(Cast)* 1274
Druce, Hubert *(Director)* 4284
Druce, Olga *(Cast)* 2946
Drum, Leonard *(Cast)* 2288, 3215, 4107
Drummond, David K. *(Producer)* 4246
Drummond, Jack *(Cast)* 2664
Drummond, Nolan *(Costumes)* 337
Drury, Charles *(Musical Director)* 418, 1460, 1486, 1494, 3091, 4271
Drury, Hazel *(Cast)* 1603
Drury, Ian *(Lyricist)* 3884
Dryden, Helen *(Costumes)* 4603
Dryden, Helen *(Set Design)* 4603
Dryer, Jay *(Orchestrations)* 2018
Dryer, Jerome Jay *(Orchestrations)* 1059
Dryer, Jerome Jay *(Vocal Arranger)* 1059
Du Clos, Danielle *(Cast)* 211
Du Clos, Deanna *(Cast)* 211
Du Heron, Helen *(Cast)* 4681
Du Shon, Jean *(Cast)* 478
DuBois, Geraldine *(Cast)* 856
DuBois, Jeannette *(Cast)* 1601
duBois, Raul Pene
See Pene du Bois, Raoul.
DuBois, William *(Author)* 2060
DuMont, William *(Cast)* 489
DuMouchel, Michael *(Set Design)* 3004
DuPage, Richard *(Orchestrations)* 4677
DuPre, Lynette G. *(Cast)* 4460
DuVal, Billy *(Lyricist)* 4322
Duane, Jed *(Director)* 4750
Dubberley, Robert E. *(Producer)* 1255
Dubens, A. *(Costumes)* 1610
Duberman, Martin *(Librettist)* 4089
Dubey, Matt *(Librettist)* 4029, 4609
Dubey, Matt *(Lyricist)* 860, 1760, 3108, 4029, 4609
Dubin, Al *(Lyricist)* 397, 543, 702, 1359, 1687, 2301, 2400, 2662, 2772, 3018, 3020, 3916, 3958, 4131, 4174, 4197, 4235, 4271, 4426, 4668, 4799
Dubin, Charles S. *(Director)* 1933
Dubin, Joe *(Orchestrations)* 4586
Dubinsky, Barney *(Cast)* 3480
Dubinsky, Barney *(Producer)* 3480
Dubinsky, M.M. *(Cast)* 3480
Dubinsky, M.M. *(Producer)* 3480
Duchin, Eddie *(Cast)* 3153
Duckworth, Dortha *(Cast)* 1310, 1698, 3271
Duddy, Lyn *(Composer)* 197, 858, 4193, 4264, 4377
Duddy, Lyn *(Lyricist)* 197, 858, 859, 4114, 4193, 4264, 4377
Dudley, Alice *(Cast)* 680, 4374, 4550
Dudley, Bide *(Librettist)* 608, 815, 2780, 3222, 4194
Dudley, Bide *(Lyricist)* 815, 2549, 2780, 3222, 4194
Dudley, Bide *(Producer)* 4194
Dudley, Bronson *(Cast)* 4166
Dudley, Ethel *(Cast)* 2524
Dudley, Grace *(Cast)* 1537
Dudley, John *(Set Design)* 3207
Dudley, Mrs. S.H. *(Cast)* 1909
Dudley, S.H. *(Cast)* 1087, 1909
Dudley, S.H. *(Director)* 1909
Dudley, S.H. *(Lyricist)* 434
Dudley, S.H. *(Producer)* 986, 1087
Dudley, Sherman H. *(Cast)* 434
Dudley, Sherman H. *(Librettist)* 434
Dudley, Sherman H. *(Producer)* 434
Duer, Fred *(Set Design)* 450
Dufault, Buddy *(Orchestrations)* 817
Duff, J.C. *(Director)* 906, 2361
Duff, J.C. *(Producer)* 767
Duff, Michael *(Composer)* 3461
Duff-Gordon, Lady *(Costumes)* 4809, 4810, 4811, 4812, 4813, 4814
Duffield, Blanche *(Cast)* 307
Duffrey, J.H. *(Cast)* 3771
Duffy, Anna Nichols *(Author)* 4120
Duffy, Anna Nichols *(Lyricist)* 4120
Duffy, Gordon *(Composer)* 1766
Duffy, Henry *(Producer)* 46, 2479, 3013, 3415
Duffy, Herbert *(Cast)* 1036
Duffy, James *(Lyricist)* 1538
Duffy, Jimmy *(Composer)* 2296, 4816
Duffy, Jimmy *(Librettist)* 2296
Duffy, Jimmy *(Lyricist)* 2296, 4816
Duffy, John *(Composer)* 1977
Duffy, John *(Lyricist)* 1977
Duffy, John *(Orchestrations)* 1977
Duffy, Meghan *(Cast)* 4731
Duffy, William *(Producer)* 2296
Duggan, Louis *(Composer)* 1632
Duggan, Thomas *(Cast)* 3973
Duggan, Thomas *(Librettist)* 3973
Dukas, Paul *(Composer)* 193
Duke, Bill *(Cast)* 40
Duke, Edward *(Cast)* 3429
Duke, Irving Milton *(Set Design)* 2069
Duke, Milton *(Costumes)* 4102
Duke, Milton *(Lighting Designer)* 4102
Duke, Milton *(Set Design)* 4102
Duke, Patty *(Cast)* 3287
Duke, Robert *(Librettist)* 2103
Duke, Stuart *(Lighting Designer)* 549, 838, 2224, 2651, 4055
Duke, Vernon
See also Vernon Dukelsky.
Duke, Vernon *(Composer)* 125, 213, 297, 478, 503, 612, 664, 924, 971, 1035, 1048, 1448, 1792, 1818, 2077, 2161, 2187, 2293, 2301, 2379, 2554, 3074, 3307, 3383, 3493, 3813, 3946, 3955, 4237, 4287, 4367, 4374, 4386, 4399, 4491, 4499, 4583, 4665, 4670, 4765, 4795, 4798, 4799, 4824, 4825, 4826

Duke, Vernon *(Lyricist)* 478, 612, 924, 3493, 4374, 4386, 4491, 4765, 4798
Duke, Vernon *(Orchestrations)* 2187, 3813
Duke, Vernon *(Vocal Arranger)* 3813, 4237
Dukelsky, Vernon
See also Vernon Duke.
Dukelsky, Vladimir *(Composer)* 3955
Dukes, Ashley *(Author)* 2731
Dukes, David *(Cast)* 2607
Dulac, Edward *(Costumes)* 3467
Dulac, Edward *(Set Design)* 3467
Dulchin, Edwin *(Librettist)* 2674
Dulchin, Edwin *(Lyricist)* 2633, 2674
Dulin, Michael *(Set Design)* 1508
Dull, Harry *(Lyricist)* 1340
Dull, Harry *(Producer)* 1340
Dullea, Keir *(Cast)* 594
Dulo, Jane *(Cast)* 180, 4585
Dumakude, Thuli *(Cast)* 1719
Dumakude, Thuli *(Choreographer)* 1719
Dumakude, Thuli *(Vocal Arranger)* 1719
Dumaresq, William *(Librettist)* 2033, 2153
Dumaresq, William *(Lyricist)* 2033, 2153
Dumas, Alexandre *(Author)* 168, 3047, 4357
du Maurier, George *(Author)* 4230
du Maurier, Gerald *(Author)* 4229
Dumbells, The *(Cast)* 388
Dumbrille, Douglas *(Cast)* 3584, 3586, 4357
Dumke, Ralph *(Cast)* 2985, 3813
Dumont, Frank *(Librettist)* 3028
Dumont, Frank *(Lyricist)* 3024
Dumont, Margaret *(Cast)* 142, 799, 1368, 1584, 2479, 4299
Dumont, Marie *(Cast)* 349
Dumrose, Boyd *(Lighting Designer)* 3988
Dumrose, Boyd *(Set Design)* 3988
Duna, Steffi *(Cast)* 4368
Dunaway, Faye *(Cast)* 942
Dunbar, Dixie *(Cast)* 2475, 4772
Dunbar, Paul Laurence *(Librettist)* 633, 783, 2210
Dunbar, Paul Laurence *(Lyricist)* 783, 1803, 2111, 2210, 2662
Duncan, A. Clark *(Set Design)* 3318
Duncan, Andrew *(Cast)* 4397
Duncan, Augustin *(Cast)* 2504
Duncan, Augustin *(Director)* 827
Duncan, Doris *(Cast)* 1314, 3349
Duncan, Florence *(Composer)* 4590
Duncan, Florence *(Lyricist)* 4590
Duncan, Harold *(Composer)* 3104
Duncan, Ina *(Cast)* 4198
Duncan, Isadora *(Cast)* 1470
Duncan, Jessica *(Cast)* 1466
Duncan, Laura *(Cast)* 2175, 3885
Duncan, Rosetta
See also Duncan Sisters.
Duncan, Rosetta *(Cast)* 1065, 4393, 4429
Duncan, Rosetta *(Composer)* 4429
Duncan, Rosetta *(Lyricist)* 4429
Duncan, Sandy *(Cast)* 634, 1298, 3499
Duncan, Stuart *(Producer)* 825, 1595, 4022
Duncan, Todd *(Cast)* 612, 2591, 3541, 4207
Duncan, Vivian
See also Duncan Sisters.
Duncan, Vivian *(Cast)* 1065, 4393, 4429
Duncan, Vivian *(Composer)* 4429
Duncan, Vivian *(Lyricist)* 4429
Duncan, William Cary *(Composer)* 1432, 2112
Duncan, William Cary *(Librettist)* 468, 640, 1266, 1911, 2112, 2273, 2291, 2768, 2927, 2943, 3580, 3613, 3692, 3770, 3791, 4213, 4218, 4226, 4276, 4360, 4766
Duncan, William Cary *(Lyricist)* 468, 1266, 1733, 1911, 2112, 2273, 2291, 2623, 2768, 3249, 3613, 3770, 3791, 4213, 4218, 4226, 4647
Duncan Sisters
See also Rosetta Duncan and Vivian Duncan.
Duncan Sisters, The *(Cast)* 3923
Dundes, Alan *(Composer)* 4041
Dundy, Elmer S. *(Producer)* 4046, 4753
Dunham, By *(Lyricist)* 4204
Dunham, Clarke *(Lighting Designer)* 2018, 2801
Dunham, Clarke *(Set Design)* 171, 576, 1186, 1699, 2018, 2420, 2801, 4272, 4349
Dunham, David *(Director)* 2051
Dunham, Joan *(Producer)* 708
Dunham, Katherine *(Cast)* 612, 651
Dunham, Katherine *(Choreographer)* 467, 651, 3427, 4702
Dunham, Ronald *(Cast)* 52
Dunham Dancers, Katherine *(Cast)* 467
Dunkel, Eugene *(Set Design)* 1286, 1342, 1546, 3082
Dunkle, Nancy *(Cast)* 932
Dunlay, William *(Cast)* 2181
Dunlay, Willie *(Cast)* 1550
Dunleavy, Timothy *(Costumes)* 2555
Dunlop, Geoffrey (Translator) 979
Dunn, Arthur *(Cast)* 1213, 2029, 2518
Dunn, Cesar *(Author)* 1368
Dunn, Edward *(Lyricist)* 583
Dunn, Edward Delaney *(Author)* 3472
Dunn, Edward Delaney *(Librettist)* 659, 1033, 2419
Dunn, Edward Delaney *(Lyricist)* 659, 2419, 3472, 3680
Dunn, Elaine *(Cast)* 673, 2227
Dunn, Griffin *(Cast)* 829
Dunn, Jack *(Cast)* 673
Dunn, James *(Cast)* 2975, 3359
Dunn, James *(Producer)* 1754
Dunn, Josephine *(Cast)* 4267
Dunn, Kathy *(Cast)* 4095
Dunn, Mrs. Edward Delaney *(Lyricist)* 3472
Dunn, Ralph *(Cast)* 3351, 3898, 4312
Dunn, Vera *(Cast)* 163
Dunne, Irene *(Cast)* 773, 780, 1121, 2637, 3924, 4249, 4793
Dunne, John W. *(Producer)* 782
Dunne, Stephan *(Cast)* 3539
Dunning, Philip *(Author)* 2311
Dunning, Philip *(Director)* 387
Dunning, Philip *(Librettist)* 387
Dunning, Philip *(Lyricist)* 387
Dunnock, Mildred *(Cast)* 807, 937, 2655
Dunsmore, John *(Cast)* 1650, 1710
Dunsmore, John H. *(Composer)* 3627

Dunsmore, John H. *(Lyricist)* 3627
Dunstedter, Eddie *(Composer)* 7, 3444
Dupont, Jacques *(Costumes)* 2362
Dupont, Jacques *(Set Design)* 2362
Dupont, Paul *(Costumes)* 23
du Pont, David *(Cast)* 4093
du Pont, Paul *(Costumes)* 1815, 2228, 2447, 3301
duPont, Paul *(Costumes)* 3841
Dupree, Frank *(Librettist)* 1722
Dupree, Frank *(Lyricist)* 263, 1722
Dupree, Minnie *(Cast)* 3730
Dupuis, Marie *(Cast)* 2902
Dupuy, Diane Lynn *(Director)* 2521
Duquette, Tony *(Costumes)* 623
Durand, Edouard *(Cast)* 1391
Durand, Hampton *(Composer)* 1550, 4439
Durand, Hampton *(Lyricist)* 1550
Durand, Hampton *(Musical Director)* 1550
Durang, Christopher *(Author)* 1914
Durang, Christopher *(Cast)* 4067
Durang, Christopher *(Librettist)* 4535
Durang, Christopher *(Lyricist)* 1914
Durant, Jack *(Cast)* 1136, 3353
Durant, Paul *(Composer)* 4792
Durante, Jimmy
See also Clayton, Jackson, & Durante.
Durante, Jimmy *(Cast)* 58, 848, 858, 860, 862, 2258, 2301, 3131, 3674, 3953, 4142, 4177
Durante, Jimmy *(Composer)* 1120, 3131, 3953
Durante, Jimmy *(Lyricist)* 1120, 3131, 3953
Durden, Tommy *(Composer)* 3739
Durden, Tommy *(Lyricist)* 3739
Durfee, Duke *(Set Design)* 2658
Durfus, Christine *(Cast)* 4092
Durham, Christopher *(Cast)* 3708
Durkee, Norman (Incidental Music) 282
Durkin, James *(Director)* 4226
Durkin, Robert *(Choreographer)* 4527
Durning, Charles *(Cast)* 1094, 3551
Durrant, Hugh *(Costumes)* 846
Durso, Michael *(Composer)* 855
Durso Band, Michael *(Cast)* 862
Durso Band, Mike *(Cast)* 858
Durso Orchestra, Michael *(Cast)* 854, 855, 856, 857, 859, 860, 861, 863
Duru *(Author)* 1650
Duru, Alfred *(Author)* 1305
Duryea, Dan *(Cast)* 2510
Dusenbury, Karen *(Costumes)* 562
du Souchet, H.A. *(Librettist)* 3332
Dussault, Nancy *(Cast)* 31, 269, 1056, 1061, 1091, 1363, 2563, 2578, 3280, 4659
Dussell, Daniel *(Director)* 1516
Dutton, Carolyn *(Vocal Arranger)* 54
Duval *(Author)* 4115
Duval, G. *(Author)* 4554
Duval, Georges *(Author)* 2524
Duval, Jose *(Cast)* 3938
Dux, Francis *(Cast)* 2887
Dvonch, Frederick *(Musical Director)* 183, 1060, 1290, 2312, 3801, 4095
Dvorsky, George *(Cast)* 2754, 3411
Dweir, Irv *(Musical Director)* 2941
Dweir, Irv *(Orchestrations)* 2941
Dwight, Mabel *(Cast)* 4452
Dwyer, John *(Set Design)* 3137
Dwyer, Richard *(Cast)* 2083, 2084, 2091
Dwyer, W. *(Lyricist)* 1370
Dwyer, William *(Cast)* 4585
Dyall, Valentine *(Cast)* 1857
Dyas, James *(Director)* 3874
Dybas, James *(Cast)* 1060, 3340, 4558
Dyer, Doug *(Cast)* 459
Dyer, Doug *(Composer)* 459
Dyer, Doug *(Librettist)* 459
Dyer, Doug *(Lyricist)* 459, 4615
Dyer, Doug *(Set Design)* 459
Dyer, Sammy *(Choreographer)* 4254
Dyer, Sharon *(Cast)* 3066
Dyer, William *(Author)* 4494
Dyer, William *(Composer)* 272, 1408, 2219, 2288
Dyer, William *(Librettist)* 2219
Dyer, William *(Lyricist)* 2219
Dylan, Bob *(Composer)* 3739
Dylan, Bob *(Lyricist)* 3739
Dymond, Lou *(Composer)* 3434
Dymond, Lou *(Musical Director)* 3434
Dymow, Ossip *(Author)* 563
Dymow, Ossip *(Director)* 563
Dyrenforth, David *(Lyricist)* 3296
Dyrenforth, James *(Lyricist)* 418, 503, 1582, 3168
Dyson, Erika *(Costumes)* 1349, 1350
Dyson, Hal *(Composer)* 2263, 4010
Dyson, Hal *(Lyricist)* 4010
Dyson, Hal *(Musical Director)* 371, 1549
Dyson, Ronald *(Cast)* 1717
Dyville, Jack *(Choreographer)* 2968
Dzigan, Shimon *(Cast)* 2421
Dzigan, Shimon *(Director)* 2421

E

EPI Productions *(Producer)* 2805
Eagan, Daisy *(Cast)* 3862
Eagan, Michael *(Set Design)* 1762
Eageard, Jeanette *(Cast)* 1553
Eagels, Jeanne *(Cast)* 2261, 2871, 3480
Eager, Edward *(Librettist)* 1091, 1474, 1761, 2464
Eager, Edward *(Lyricist)* 23, 320, 1091, 1101, 1474, 1761, 1933, 2464, 3798, 3989
Eagle, Oscar *(Director)* 142, 799, 1182, 1935, 2005, 2216, 2276, 2494, 2549, 2756, 2816, 3580, 3611, 4063, 4360, 4429, 4651, 4694, 4860
Earl, Louise *(Cast)* 538, 542
Earl, Mary *(Composer)* 4054
Earl, Maud *(Cast)* 349, 2717
Earle, Charles *(Cast)* 1078
Earle, Dorothy *(Cast)* 3877
Earle, Edward *(Cast)* 699, 3019, 4643
Earle, Edward *(Choreographer)* 1017, 4243

Earle, Edward *(Composer)* 1017
Earle, Edward *(Dance Arranger)* 4243
Earle, Edward *(Director)* 4643
Earle, Florence *(Cast)* 2567
Earle, Fred *(Composer)* 675
Earle, Fred *(Lyricist)* 675
Earle, Harry *(Cast)* 1213
Earle, Ronald Hamilton *(Cast)* 1707
Earle, Virginia *(Cast)* 350, 666, 770, 1543, 1599, 2116, 2123, 2398, 2481, 3129, 3883
Earley, Candice *(Cast)* 2114
Earley, J.B. *(Composer)* 806
Early, Dan *(Director)* 3167
Easen, Otto *(Cast)* 4006
Easley, Holmes *(Set Design)* 705
East, Ed *(Composer)* 3407
East, Ed *(Lyricist)* 3407
Easterbrook, Randall *(Cast)* 3019
Eastham, Dickinson and Richard Eastham are the same person.
Eastham, Dickinson *(Cast)* 4096
Eastham, Richard *(Cast)* 1815
Eastman, Gretchen *(Cast)* 2145, 3729
Eastman, Joan *(Cast)* 1974
Eastman, Nikki *(Set Design)* 1834
Eastman, Virginia *(Cast)* 3434
Eastmond, Barry *(Musical Director)* 2133
Easton, Jack (Conductor) 4028
Easton, Jack *(Musical Director)* 400
Easton, Richard *(Cast)* 3818, 4715
Easton, Sidney *(Cast)* 2021
Easton, Sidney *(Composer)* 3709
Easton, Sidney *(Lyricist)* 3709
Eastright, Bob *(Librettist)* 1880
Eastwood, Gini *(Cast)* 1769
Eaton, Bob *(Author)* 2440
Eaton, Bob *(Director)* 2440
Eaton, Charles *(Cast)* 3451
Eaton, Doris *(Cast)* 1215, 1943, 3185
Eaton, Mary *(Cast)* 1297, 2308, 2638, 3333, 4814, 4815, 4816
Eaton, Pearl *(Cast)* 1131, 3924, 4375
Eaton, Sally *(Cast)* 1717
Eaton Associates *(Producer)* 3527
Eaves *(Costumes)* 1251, 1710, 3082, 4328
Ebb, Fred *(Composer)* 3615, 4566
Ebb, Fred *(Librettist)* 723, 2958, 3900
Ebb, Fred *(Lyricist)* 16, 131, 392, 610, 723, 826, 1038, 1310, 1408, 1585, 1605, 1764, 1770, 1787, 2333, 2558, 2677, 2958, 3615, 3718, 3900, 4480, 4566, 4580, 4727, 4829, 4862
Eben, Al *(Cast)* 3501
Eberhard, Deac *(Orchestrations)* 855, 864
Eberhard, Eliot G. *(Orchestrations)* 858
Eberhard, Eliot G. "Deac" *(Orchestrations)* 857
Eberhard, Leslie *(Composer)* 1873, 2294
Eberhard, Leslie *(Librettist)* 2235
Eberhard, Leslie *(Lyricist)* 1873, 2294
Ebersole, Christine *(Cast)* 1684, 1776
Ebert, Franz *(Cast)* 1608
Ebert, Joyce *(Cast)* 951, 4601
Ebony Jo-Ann *(Cast)* 1236
Ebsen, Buddy *(Cast)* 1322, 4772, 4824
Ebsen, Buddy *(Producer)* 4466
Ebsen, Buddy (Voice) 4391
Ebsen, Vilma *(Cast)* 383, 1322, 4824
Eburne, Maude *(Cast)* 1667, 2605
Eck, Marsha Louis *(Set Design)* 1222, 2925
Eckart, Jean *(Costumes)* 759, 957, 1280, 3288, 3696
Eckart, Jean *(Lighting Designer)* 32, 483, 868, 1227, 1280, 1745, 2449, 2484, 3097, 3918, 4863
Eckart, Jean *(Producer)* 3288
Eckart, Jean *(Set Design)* 32, 162, 483, 759, 868, 957, 1158, 1227, 1273, 1280, 1310, 1600, 1729, 1745, 1860, 2449, 2484, 2556, 2643, 2681, 2713, 2965, 3097, 3288, 3696, 3876, 3918, 4863
Eckart, William *(Costumes)* 759, 957, 1280, 3288, 3696
Eckart, William *(Lighting Designer)* 32, 483, 868, 1227, 1280, 1745, 2449, 2484, 3097, 3918, 4863
Eckart, William *(Producer)* 3288
Eckart, William *(Set Design)* 32, 162, 483, 759, 868, 957, 1158, 1227, 1273, 1280, 1310, 1600, 1729, 1745, 1860, 2449, 2484, 2556, 2643, 2681, 2713, 2965, 3097, 3288, 3696, 3876, 3918, 4863
Eckhart, Lois *(Cast)* 1493
Eckley, Dan *(Choreographer)* 1814, 2447, 2748
Eckstein, George *(Producer)* 408, 411
Eckstein, William *(Composer)* 1154
Ecton, Robert *(Cast)* 488, 3704
Eda-Young, Barbara *(Cast)* 3309
Eddinger, Lawrence *(Cast)* 2967, 3618
Eddington, Paul *(Cast)* 2240
Eddleman, Jack *(Cast)* 1092, 1676, 3234
Eddy, David *(Lyricist)* 227
Eddy, Eddie *(Set Design)* 2207
Ede, George *(Cast)* 2607, 3468
Edegran, Lars *(Arrangements)* 1425
Edegran, Lars *(Orchestrations)* 3297
Edegran, Lars *(Vocal Arranger)* 1425
Edeiken, Louise *(Cast)* 1496, 4398, 4618
Edeken, Louise *(Cast)* 2372
Edel, Alfredo *(Costumes)* 286, 1318, 3093, 3753, 4046, 4113, 4753, 4802, 4803
Edell, Ruth *(Cast)* 4021
Edelman, Gregg *(Cast)* 147, 775, 1496, 3411, 4618
Edelman, Herbert *(Cast)* 269, 1842
Edelshtat, David *(Lyricist)* 1609
Eden, Sidney *(Producer)* 3925
Eden, Susan *(Producer)* 4433
Eden, Toni *(Cast)* 4469
Edens, Roger *(Cast)* 1528
Edens, Roger *(Composer)* 3992
Edens, Roger *(Vocal Arranger)* 4267
Eder, Linda *(Cast)* 2198, 4229
Ederle, Gertrude *(Cast)* 173
Edgar, David *(Author)* 2474
Edgar, Kate *(Musical Director)* 3695
Edgerton, Sandy *(Cast)* 450
Edgewood Productions, Inc. *(Producer)* 3991
Edington, May *(Author)* 3048
Ediss, Connie *(Cast)* 178, 1526, 1561, 1613, 3098, 3948
Edlin, Teddy *(Cast)* 2788

Edmead, Wendy *(Cast)* 107, 678, 3456
Edmond, Grace *(Cast)* 1532, 3251
Edmonds, Charles *(Composer)* 1687
Edmonds, Louis *(Cast)* 630, 1017, 1194, 3788
Edmonds, Shepard N. *(Composer)* 4390
Edmonds, Shepard N. *(Lyricist)* 4390
Edmonton Jounal *(Producer)* 3485
Edmunds, Kate *(Set Design)* 699, 4216
Edouin, Willie *(Cast)* 1313, 1537
Edouin, Willie *(Director)* 1313
Edson, Eda *(Director)* 1337
Edvina, Louise *(Cast)* 1805
Edward, Carlo *(Musical Director)* 1016
Edward, Felix *(Director)* 2376
Edward Spector Prod. Inc. *(Producer)* 3874
Edwardes, Felix *(Producer)* 2389
Edwardes, George *(Author)* 3322
Edwardes, George *(Director)* 1429
Edwardes, George *(Producer)* 1114, 1537, 3098, 4354, 4795
Edwardes, Kathleen *(Cast)* 2747
Edwardes, Paula *(Cast)* 1021, 2181, 3581, 3951, 4713
Edwards, Alan *(Cast)* 2376, 2829, 3540, 3980, 4033, 4345, 4476
Edwards, Ben *(Lighting Designer)* 1383, 2450
Edwards, Ben *(Set Design)* 747, 1383, 3610
Edwards, Blake *(Author)* 4560
Edwards, Blake *(Director)* 4560
Edwards, Blake *(Librettist)* 4560
Edwards, Blake *(Producer)* 4560
Edwards, Bobby *(Cast)* 2456
Edwards, Bobby *(Composer)* 1244
Edwards, Bobby *(Lyricist)* 1244
Edwards, Brandt *(Cast)* 746
Edwards, Bucky *(Cast)* 985
Edwards, Carlo *(Musical Director)* 1218
Edwards, Cliff *(Cast)* 1493, 2376, 2403, 2405, 2870, 4212, 4290
Edwards, Cliff *(Composer)* 2376, 4212
Edwards, Cliff *(Lyricist)* 2376, 4212
Edwards, Cuddles *(Cast)* 1703
Edwards, David *(Cast)* 430
Edwards, Frank *(Cast)* 1004
Edwards, Gail *(Cast)* 337
Edwards, Gail *(Composer)* 337
Edwards, Gail *(Librettist)* 337
Edwards, Gail *(Lyricist)* 337
Edwards, George *(Lyricist)* 1308
Edwards, Glynn *(Cast)* 1277
Edwards, Gus *(Cast)* 2493, 2781, 3153
Edwards, Gus *(Composer)* 8, 470, 522, 557, 1243, 1391, 1434, 1703, 1704, 1900, 1910, 1919, 1925, 1998, 2096, 2493, 2747, 2781, 2803, 2826, 2892, 2974, 2990, 3327, 3387, 3397, 3855, 3856, 3857, 4079, 4181, 4209, 4390, 4650, 4723, 4755, 4801, 4803, 4804
Edwards, Gus *(Director)* 1703, 4755
Edwards, Gus *(Librettist)* 1703, 1704
Edwards, Gus *(Lyricist)* 2096, 2493, 2781, 2892, 3999, 4803
Edwards, Gus *(Producer)* 557, 2781, 3327, 3855, 4755
Edwards, Henry Stillwell *(Author)* 4504
Edwards, Jack *(Cast)* 1447
Edwards, James *(Composer)* 3739, 4264
Edwards, James *(Lyricist)* 3739, 4264
Edwards, Joan *(Composer)* 197, 858, 859, 4377
Edwards, Joan *(Lyricist)* 197, 858, 4377
Edwards, John *(Lyricist)* 3381
Edwards, Julian *(Composer)* 355, 523, 1071, 1401, 1458, 1521, 1523, 1594, 1910, 2233, 2632, 2673, 2899, 2929, 2966, 3585, 4493, 4614, 4646
Edwards, Julian *(Director)* 1458
Edwards, Julian *(Librettist)* 2673
Edwards, Julian *(Musical Director)* 2673, 4614
Edwards, Leo *(Composer)* 326, 419, 473, 522, 539, 773, 1998, 2696, 2834, 2856, 3009, 3399, 3969, 4440, 4782, 4806, 4807, 4810, 4811, 4814, 4815, 4817, 4838
Edwards, Leo *(Lyricist)* 2696, 3009, 3926, 4654
Edwards, Lotta *(Cast)* 538
Edwards, Marcelle *(Cast)* 1137
Edwards, Michael *(Composer)* 4137
Edwards, Michele *(Costumes)* 624, 2243
Edwards, Nazig *(Cast)* 3239
Edwards, Paula *(Cast)* 2361
Edwards, Randall *(Cast)* 4533
Edwards, Richard *(Cast)* 1337
Edwards, Robert W. *(Composer)* 3384
Edwards, Robert W. *(Musical Director)* 3384
Edwards, S. *(Composer)* 4193
Edwards, S. *(Lyricist)* 4193
Edwards, Sam *(Cast)* 3865
Edwards, Samuel *(Cast)* 2350
Edwards, Sherman *(Composer)* 3897, 4273, 4337
Edwards, Sherman *(Lyricist)* 3897, 4273
Edwards, Snitz *(Cast)* 436, 1888, 2543
Edwards, Tom *(Librettist)* 474
Edwards, Zelda *(Cast)* 3157
Edwards and Edwards *(Cast)* 3804
Edwin, David *(Librettist)* 2771
Efron, Marshall *(Cast)* 3000
Egan, Jack *(Composer)* 4811
Egan, John *(Composer)* 1221, 3540
Egan, Raymond B. *(Lyricist)* 46, 324, 393, 709, 1127, 1689, 1935, 2574, 2856, 2946, 3404, 3430, 3783, 3842, 4393, 4421
Egan, Robert *(Director)* 282
Egan, Susan *(Cast)* 330
Egbert, June *(Cast)* 2602
Egen, Von *(Composer)* 364
Eggerth, Marta *(Cast)* 808, 1894, 3536
Eggett, Charles *(Composer)* 3332
Eglevsky, Andre *(Cast)* 1670
Egnos, Bertha *(Composer)* 2147
Egnos, Bertha *(Director)* 2147
Egnos, Bertha *(Librettist)* 2147
Ehlert, Matt *(Lighting Designer)* 2416
Ehman, Don *(Lighting Designer)* 4030
Ehrenfeld & Assoc., S. *(Producer)* 4773
Ehrenreich, Jake *(Cast)* 2237
Ehrhardt, Bess *(Cast)* 2086
Ehrhardt, Peter M. *(Lighting Designer)* 915, 2026, 2578, 3671
Ehrle, John *(Cast)* 1275

Ehrlich, Sam *(Lyricist)* 1517
Ehrnhardt, Peter M. *(Lighting Designer)* 4796
Eich, Stephen *(Producer)* 4074
Eichel, Paul *(Cast)* 1063
Eichelberger, Ethyl *(Cast)* 4371
Eidman, Earl *(Lighting Designer)* 2220, 2243, 2478
Eidman, Earl *(Set Design)* 2220, 2243
Eigenberg, Julie *(Composer)* 146
Eigenberg, Julie *(Lyricist)* 146
Eiger, Walter *(Orchestrations)* 3234, 3813
Eight Tiller Girls, The *(Cast)* 4320
Eigsti, Karl *(Lighting Designer)* 1664, 4707
Eigsti, Karl *(Set Design)* 105, 1198, 1402, 1669, 1999, 2242, 2290, 3276, 4707
Eikenberry, Jill *(Cast)* 3305, 3817, 4601
Eilber, Janet *(Cast)* 2539, 4252
Eilers, Jim Paul *(Producer)* 3161
Einedshofer, Jules *(Composer)* 396, 1901
Einhorn, Abe *(Author)* 32
Einhorn, Frederick *(Cast)* 2197
Einhorn, Susan *(Director)* 674, 2049
Eisele, Lou *(Costumes)* 1336, 1539, 2098, 2397, 3064
Eisenberg, Emanuel *(Librettist)* 3501
Eisenberg, Emanuel *(Lyricist)* 3365
Eisenberg, Lawrence B. *(Librettist)* 3527
Eisenberg, Lee *(Librettist)* 1038
Eisenhauer, Peggy *(Lighting Designer)* 373, 754, 975, 1149, 1822, 4560
Eisfeldt and Anhalt *(Producer)* 3917
Eisler, Chuck *(Set Design)* 4157
Eisler, Paul *(Composer)* 2532
Eisner, Joseph *(Lighting Designer)* 2139
Eissing, Cecile *(Cast)* 2179
Elaine, Mabel *(Cast)* 1799, 3677
Elaine, Mildred *(Cast)* 2834
Elbert, Charles *(Composer)* 4809
Eldee, Lillian *(Lyricist)* 4554
Elder, Eldon *(Costumes)* 33
Elder, Eldon *(Lighting Designer)* 72, 1548, 2811, 2958
Elder, Eldon *(Set Design)* 33, 72, 1548, 2958, 3015, 3473, 3934
Eldridge, Florence *(Cast)* 121
Electric Comedy Four *(Composer)* 2485
Electric Comedy Four *(Lyricist)* 2485
Eley, Valerie K. *(Cast)* 3724
Elg, Taina *(Cast)* 2583, 3171, 4537
Elias, Al *(Composer)* 2164
Elias, Al *(Lyricist)* 2164
Elias, Charmaine *(Cast)* 2164
Elias, Tom *(Cast)* 778
Elice, Eric *(Choreographer)* 2787
Elinore, Kate *(Cast)* 3030
Elinson, Izzy *(Librettist)* 297
Eliot, Drew *(Cast)* 589
Eliot, T.S. *(Author)* 678
Eliot, T.S. *(Lyricist)* 678
Eliran, Ron *(Cast)* 1075, 3167
Eliran, Ron *(Composer)* 1075, 3167
Eliran, Ron *(Lyricist)* 1075, 3167
Eliscu, Edward *(Librettist)* 298, 1384, 2748, 2809, 4152, 4331, 4335
Eliscu, Edward *(Lyricist)* 298, 324, 418, 1007, 1113, 1207, 1384, 1448, 1667, 1873, 2382, 2447, 2540, 2685, 2747, 2748, 2809, 2810, 2827, 3005, 3018, 3020, 3172, 3249, 4152, 4170, 4235, 4291, 4331, 4335, 4545, 4683
Eliscu, Edward *(Producer)* 4331
Elisha, Rina *(Choreographer)* 2007
Elisha, Rina *(Director)* 2007
Elizondo, J.F. *(Author)* 2407
Eljas, Anders *(Dance Arranger)* 721
Eljas, Anders *(Orchestrations)* 661, 721
Eljas, Anders *(Vocal Arranger)* 721
Elkins, Flora *(Cast)* 3571
Elkins, Hillard *(Producer)* 820, 1601, 3780
Elkins, Robert *(Musical Director)* 1781
Ellen, David *(Cast)* 3781
Ellen, Sandy *(Cast)* 1094
Ellenburg, Eric *(Cast)* 2243
Eller, Carol *(Choreographer)* 255
Eller, Celia *(Costumes)* 74
Ellerton *(Composer)* 3259
Ellerton *(Lyricist)* 3259
Ellfeldt, William *(Vocal Arranger)* 4366
Elliman, Yvonne *(Cast)* 2212
Ellinger, Desiree *(Cast)* 718, 2330, 4692
Ellington, Duke
See also Duke Ellington and His Orchestra.
Ellington, Duke *(Composer)* 146, 315, 341, 432, 437, 741, 875, 885, 886, 893, 895, 1980, 2259, 3020, 3175, 3551, 3628, 3709, 3905, 4091, 4137, 4235, 4534
Ellington, Duke *(Lyricist)* 432, 2259, 3628, 3905, 4091
Ellington, Duke *(Orchestrations)* 2259
Ellington, Mercedes *(Cast)* 1842, 3159, 4091
Ellington, Mercedes *(Choreographer)* 2250
Ellington, Mercer *(Composer)* 2259
Ellington, Mercer *(Musical Director)* 4091
Ellington Orchestra, Duke *(Cast)* 892
Ellington and His Orchestra, Duke
See also Duke Ellington.
Ellington and His Orchestra, Duke *(Cast)* 437, 442, 875, 878, 885, 886, 893, 894, 895, 2259, 3953
Elliot, Ann *(Costumes)* 1934
Elliot, Arthur *(Librettist)* 377
Elliot, J. Arthur *(Producer)* 314
Elliot, Marc *(Composer)* 1638
Elliot, Marc *(Lyricist)* 1638
Elliot, Mariana *(Costumes)* 2288
Elliot, Patricia *(Cast)* 599
Elliot, Robert *(Librettist)* 3479
Elliot, Shawn *(Cast)* 2188
Elliot, Stephen *(Cast)* 1497
Elliot, Sumner Locke *(Librettist)* 2227
Elliot, William *(Cast)* 1218
Elliot, William *(Producer)* 684, 758, 1218, 1588, 2340, 3230, 3245, 3250
Elliott, Beth *(Cast)* 1460
Elliott, Bill *(Orchestrations)* 1804
Elliott, Don *(Composer)* 322
Elliott, Don (Conductor) 322
Elliott, Don *(Musical Director)* 1261
Elliott, Donald *(Producer)* 1695
Elliott, Jack *(Dance Arranger)* 1280, 2983, 4312

Elliott, Jack *(Lyricist)* 2165, 3683
Elliott, Jack *(Orchestrations)* 786
Elliott, James W. *(Producer)* 670
Elliott, Kenneth *(Director)* 3606, 4518
Elliott, Kenneth *(Lyricist)* 3606
Elliott, Kenneth *(Producer)* 3606
Elliott, Mariana *(Lighting Designer)* 2288
Elliott, Patricia *(Cast)* 2536
Elliott, Paul *(Producer)* 580
Elliott, Robert *(Librettist)* 272
Elliott, Shawn *(Cast)* 775, 4796
Elliott, Sumner Locke *(Librettist)* 2313
Elliott, Verne *(Director)* 2413
Elliott, William *(Composer)* 774, 3197
Elliott, William (Conductor) 2359
Elliott, William *(Producer)* 2698
Elliott, Zo *(Composer)* 3259
Ellis, Anita *(Cast)* 1315
Ellis, Antonia *(Cast)* 2702
Ellis, Barbara *(Cast)* 4431
Ellis, Brad *(Cast)* 1350
Ellis, Brad *(Composer)* 4462
Ellis, Brad *(Musical Director)* 1350
Ellis, C.J. *(Lyricist)* 2970
Ellis, Charles T. *(Cast)* 668
Ellis, Charles T. *(Composer)* 668
Ellis, Charles T. *(Librettist)* 668
Ellis, Charles T. *(Lyricist)* 668
Ellis, Chris *(Lighting Designer)* 2798
Ellis, David *(Cast)* 4773
Ellis, Edith *(Librettist)* 2623
Ellis, Evelyn *(Cast)* 467
Ellis, Gene *(Librettist)* 1884
Ellis, Harold *(Librettist)* 470
Ellis, James *(Cast)* 3056
Ellis, John *(Cast)* 2841
Ellis, Larry *(Cast)* 1380
Ellis, Leigh *(Cast)* 611
Ellis, Mary *(Cast)* 715, 972, 3772
Ellis, Maurice *(Cast)* 1987
Ellis, Melville *(Cast)* 965, 1403, 1464, 1963, 2891, 3313, 3747, 3999, 4430, 4553, 4655
Ellis, Melville *(Composer)* 8, 737, 934, 2825, 2869, 3220, 3730, 3747, 4154, 4521
Ellis, Melville *(Costumes)* 60, 68, 75, 276, 351, 353, 558, 965, 1218, 1522, 1578, 1613, 1793, 1963, 2232, 2317, 2334, 2358, 2696, 2732, 2825, 2854, 2858, 3237, 3265, 3396, 3397, 3424, 3701, 3865, 4382, 4521, 4555, 4655, 4657
Ellis, Melville *(Dance Arranger)* 965, 3397
Ellis, Melville *(Lyricist)* 737, 3220
Ellis, Michael *(Director)* 4273
Ellis, Michael *(Producer)* 911, 4499
Ellis, Perry *(Costumes)* 3181
Ellis, Philip *(Orchestrations)* 27
Ellis, Philip *(Vocal Arranger)* 1840
Ellis, Ray *(Dance Arranger)* 3863
Ellis, Ray *(Orchestrations)* 1227
Ellis, Ray *(Vocal Arranger)* 3863
Ellis, Rina *(Cast)* 3669
Ellis, Scott *(Cast)* 1897, 3718
Ellis, Scott *(Director)* 131
Ellis, Sheila *(Cast)* 1103, 4645
Ellis, Toni *(Cast)* 444
Ellis, Vivian *(Composer)* 129, 453, 605, 700, 791, 834, 1333, 2004, 2547, 2976, 4207, 4667
Ellis, Vivian *(Lyricist)* 129, 791, 2976, 4207
Ellis, Walker *(Cast)* 4284
Ellison, Ben *(Lyricist)* 2640
Ellison, Bob *(Librettist)* 2072
Ellison, Sydney *(Director)* 205, 1522, 2486, 3031, 3092, 3156
Ellmore Sisters *(Cast)* 2991
Ellsler, Effie *(Cast)* 1517
Ellsner, Joseph *(Lighting Designer)* 396, 1901
Ellstein, Abe *(Composer)* 423, 1279
Ellstein, Abe *(Lyricist)* 1279
Ellstein, Abe *(Musical Director)* 423
Ellstein, Abe *(Orchestrations)* 423
Ellstein, Abraham *(Composer)* 1609, 1679, 2751, 3670, 4769
Ellstein, Abraham *(Lyricist)* 3670
Ellstein, Abraham *(Musical Director)* 2751
Ellstein, Abraham *(Orchestrations)* 2751
Ellsworth, Eugene *(Composer)* 3073
Ellsworth, Eugene *(Lyricist)* 3073
Ellsworth, Olin *(Composer)* 314
Ellsworth, Olin *(Librettist)* 314
Ellsworth, Olin *(Lyricist)* 314
Ellsworth, Ursula *(Cast)* 2639
Elm City Four, The *(Cast)* 1491
Elmer, George *(Producer)* 944
Elmo, Monte *(Cast)* 1388
Elmore, Steve *(Cast)* 832, 956, 1184, 3075, 3476, 4019
Elmslie, Kenward *(Author)* 774
Elmslie, Kenward *(Librettist)* 1662, 2565
Elmslie, Kenward *(Lyricist)* 237, 392, 774, 1362, 1662, 2554, 2565, 2678
Elsass, Jeff *(Cast)* 1757
Elsie, Lily *(Cast)* 475
Elsner, Edward *(Director)* 375, 2330, 2967, 3898, 4218
Elsner, Edward *(Producer)* 2330
Elsner, Joseph *(Lighting Designer)* 1208, 1753
Elsom, Isobel *(Cast)* 30
Elson, Anita *(Cast)* 1805
Elson, Charles *(Lighting Designer)* 1290, 2364, 3691, 4693
Elston, Robert *(Cast)* 4111, 4278
Eltinge, Julian *(Cast)* 800, 913, 929, 1177, 1247, 1947, 2986, 3166, 3173
Eltinge, Julian *(Costumes)* 929
Eltinge, Julian *(Lyricist)* 929, 3425
Elton, Jane *(Cast)* 4508
Elton, William *(Orchestrations)* 3018
Elward, James *(Lyricist)* 932
Elwell *(Set Design)* 1814
Elwin, Maurice *(Lyricist)* 2798
Elzy, Ruby *(Cast)* 1251, 2225, 3541
Embs, Lisa *(Cast)* 2555
Emden, H. *(Set Design)* 2974
Emden, Henry *(Set Design)* 2964
Emens, Homer
See also Emens & Unitt.

Emens, Homer *(Cast)* 1030
Emens, Homer *(Set Design)* 178, 250, 252, 379, 736, 749, 815, 1026, 1030, 1071, 1230, 1538, 1555, 1901, 2025, 2184, 2394, 2915, 3220, 3268, 3488, 3562, 3658, 3675, 3774, 3996, 4219, 4258, 4590
Emens, Homer F. *(Set Design)* 618, 1301
Emens & Unitt
See also Homes Emens and E.G. Unitt.
Emens & Unitt *(Set Design)* 2671, 4497
Emer, Michael *(Composer)* 67, 1834
Emerick, George H. *(Librettist)* 187
Emerson, Edward *(Cast)* 4331
Emerson, Gordon *(Orchestrations)* 73
Emerson, Hope *(Cast)* 4025, 4169
Emerson, Ida *(Composer)* 4390
Emerson, Ida *(Lyricist)* 4390
Emerson, John *(Author)* 715, 4043
Emerson, John *(Cast)* 472, 2403
Emerson, John *(Director)* 715, 929, 4043
Emerson, John *(Librettist)* 3172, 3349
Emerson, Lillian *(Cast)* 3850, 4299
Emery, Curtis W. *(Producer)* 2476
Emery, Edward *(Cast)* 1387
Emery, Edward T. *(Director)* 2587
Emery, Edwin T. *(Director)* 351, 1722, 3203
Emery, Edwin T. *(Producer)* 68
Emery, Lin *(Set Design)* 2288
Emery, Mac *(Composer)* 4814
Emery, Mac *(Lyricist)* 4814
Emery, Rick *(Cast)* 3201
Emhardt, Robert *(Cast)* 3894
Emmanuel, Ivor *(Cast)* 4384
Emmerich, Robert *(Composer)* 1296
Emmerich, Robert *(Lyricist)* 1296
Emmerson, Dorothy *(Cast)* 4408
Emmett, Dan *(Composer)* 2415, 3989
Emmett, Dan *(Lyricist)* 2415, 3989
Emmett, Robert *(Librettist)* 658, 974, 3275, 3427
Emmons, Beverly *(Lighting Designer)* 756, 1000, 1077, 1099, 1890, 2237, 2474, 2646, 3077, 3411, 3690, 3876, 4332, 4790
Emmons, Grace *(Cast)* 4616
Emmons, Sadie *(Cast)* 104
Emney, Fred *(Cast)* 1454
Emonts, Ann *(Costumes)* 572, 828, 829, 3231, 3548, 4412
Empery, Arthur Guy *(Cast)* 3341
Empery, Arthur Guy *(Composer)* 3341
Empery, Arthur Guy *(Lyricist)* 3341
Empire Producing Company *(Producer)* 2336
Empire State Institute *(Producer)* 3643
Emsden, H. *(Cast)* 4014
En Yu Tan, Victor *(Lighting Designer)* 533, 2049, 2132, 2429, 2692, 3164, 3276
Encompass the Music Theatre *(Producer)* 1171
Encore A Partnership *(Producer)* 4127
Endor, Chick *(Composer)* 792, 4823
Endor, Chick *(Lyricist)* 792, 4212
Engel, George *(Composer)* 2168
Engel, Georgia *(Cast)* 944
Engel, Lehman *(Composer)* 1871, 2464, 2815, 2948
Engel, Lehman *(Librettist)* 3880
Engel, Lehman *(Musical Director)* 59, 269, 322, 454, 620, 1029, 1061, 1242, 1614, 2048, 2190, 2228, 2362, 2464, 2484, 2504, 2940, 3913, 4270, 4323, 4633, 4734
Engel, Lehman *(Orchestrations)* 2464
Engel, Lehman *(Vocal Arranger)* 59, 269, 454, 1029, 2048, 2504, 2940, 3913, 4270, 4323, 4633
Engel, Lew *(Cast)* 263
Engelberger, Willy *(Composer)* 1691
Engelsman, Ralph G. *(Librettist)* 3296
Engelsman, Ralph G. *(Lyricist)* 3296
Engeran, Virgil *(Composer)* 3202
Engeran, Virgil *(Librettist)* 3202
Engeran, Virgil *(Lyricist)* 3202
Engeran, Virgil *(Producer)* 3202
England, Paul *(Cast)* 4652
Englander, Ludwig *(Author)* 995, 4181
Englander, Ludwig *(Composer)* 350, 613, 618, 666, 995, 1464, 1465, 1535, 1720, 2117, 2213, 2502, 2665, 2671, 2725, 2892, 2936, 3129, 3229, 3394, 3710, 3784, 3820, 3896, 4181, 4472, 4497, 4662, 4691, 4728, 4804
Englander, Ludwig *(Musical Director)* 4181
Englander, Otto *(Author)* 4035
Engle, Dale *(Set Design)* 3697
Engles, George *(Composer)* 4273
English, Anna *(Cast)* 3983
English, Donna *(Cast)* 112, 1439, 1510, 2416, 3811
English, Ellia *(Cast)* 1713
English, Genora *(Cast)* 3986, 4253
English, Granville *(Lyricist)* 3310
English, S. *(Composer)* 4193
English, S. *(Lyricist)* 4193
Englund, George *(Director)* 4585
Engquist, Richard *(Librettist)* 2354
Engquist, Richard *(Lyricist)* 1171, 2513
Engvick, William *(Librettist)* 4585
Engvick, William *(Lyricist)* 1049, 1744, 3286, 3496
Enico, Joe *(Cast)* 909
Enriquez, Rene *(Cast)* 4459
Ensign, Herman Lee *(Librettist)* 3176
Enten, Boni *(Cast)* 2164, 2579, 3233, 3742
Enters, Warren *(Director)* 482, 3204
Entertainment Group, The *(Producer)* 2437
Entratter, Jack *(Producer)* 857, 858
Entwistle, John (Additional Lyrics) 4676
Entwistle, John (Additional Music) 4676
Envel *(Author)* 2619
Epailly, Jules *(Cast)* 1197, 1979
Ephraim, Lee *(Producer)* 466, 4510
Ephron, Henry *(Author)* 1205
Ephron, Henry *(Director)* 1205
Ephron, Henry *(Lyricist)* 1205
Ephron, Phoebe *(Author)* 1205
Ephron, Phoebe *(Lyricist)* 1205
Eplet, F. *(Composer)* 2131
Eppel, Asar *(Author)* 2012
Epps, Sheldon *(Director)* 478, 2250
Epps, Sheldon *(Librettist)* 478
Epstein, Alvin *(Cast)* 1406, 1408, 3187, 4371
Epstein, Dasha *(Producer)* 39, 992, 3760, 4062
Epstein, David *(Librettist)* 4595
Epstein, David *(Lyricist)* 4595

Epstein, I.L. *(Dance Arranger)* 3495
Epstein, I.L. *(Vocal Arranger)* 3495
Epstein, Julius J. *(Author)* 663, 3843
Epstein, Julius J. *(Librettist)* 2057, 3843, 4323
Epstein, L.I. *(Musical Director)* 2257
Epstein, Philip G. *(Author)* 663, 3843
Epstein, Philip G. *(Librettist)* 2057, 4323
Epstein, Pierre *(Cast)* 282, 1190, 1591, 3497, 3602, 4796
Equity Players *(Producer)* 1221
Erckmann *(Author)* 1401
Ercole, Joe *(Composer)* 2285
Ercole, Joe *(Orchestrations)* 2285
Erdman, Ernie *(Composer)* 487, 3404
Erdman, Ernie *(Lyricist)* 487, 3404
Erdman, Jean *(Cast)* 790
Erdman, Jean *(Choreographer)* 4485
Erdman, Jean *(Director)* 790
Erdman, Jean *(Librettist)* 790
Erickson, Leif *(Cast)* 1894, 3493, 4323
Ericson, June *(Cast)* 1362, 3286, 4065, 4585
Erlanger, A.L.
See also Erlanger Prods., Klaw & Erlanger and Klaw & Erlanger Opera Co.
Erlanger, A.L. *(Producer)* 527, 571, 605, 1399, 1643, 1756, 1965, 2181, 4491, 4760
Erlanger, Alene *(Librettist)* 2739
Erlanger Prods.
See also A.L. Erlanger, Klaw & Erlanger, Klaw & Erlanger Opera Co.
Erlanger Productions *(Producer)* 4043
Erlich, Sam *(Lyricist)* 1824, 1900
Ernie, Val *(Musical Director)* 1889
Ernotte, Andre *(Director)* 829, 1589, 3667, 4216
Ernst, Leila *(Cast)* 2103, 3353
Ernster, Mary *(Cast)* 158
Ernstoff, Jeffrey *(Composer)* 1146
Ernstoff, Jeffrey *(Lyricist)* 1146
Errico, Melissa *(Cast)* 147
Errol, Leon *(Cast)* 425, 683, 959, 1281, 1647, 1919, 1920, 2403, 2594, 3819, 4712, 4793, 4805, 4806, 4807, 4808, 4809, 4844
Errol, Leon *(Choreographer)* 78
Errol, Leon *(Composer)* 1117, 1647
Errol, Leon *(Director)* 468, 683, 1919, 1920, 3593, 4033, 4742, 4808, 4809, 4834, 4839, 4844
Errol, Leon *(Librettist)* 1117, 1647
Errol, Leon *(Lyricist)* 1117, 1647
Errolle, Martha *(Cast)* 2234, 3390
Ershova *(Cast)* 710
Ersi, Elsa *(Cast)* 568
Erskine, Howard *(Producer)* 160
Erte *(Costumes)* 201, 910, 1146, 1485, 1486, 1487, 1488, 1489, 1490, 1491, 2734, 3150, 4427, 4817, 4818
Erte *(Set Design)* 1146, 2364
Ertegun, Ahmet *(Producer)* 3636
Erwin, Ralph *(Composer)* 2382
Erwin, Stuart *(Cast)* 1679, 3153
Escudero, Vicente *(Orchestrations)* 839
Eskew, Doug *(Cast)* 1296, 4460
Eskew, Jack *(Orchestrations)* 3126
Eskow, Jerome *(Director)* 615, 1319, 3224
Eskow, Jerome *(Librettist)* 1319
Esmond, Annie *(Cast)* 2891
Esmond, Jill *(Cast)* 3597
Esparza, Roberta Delgado *(Cast)* 4861
Espero, Sidonie *(Cast)* 2698
Espinosa, Kelland *(Choreographer)* 3156, 3583
Esposito, Giancarlo *(Cast)* 1073, 2898, 3869
Esposito, Larry *(Musical Director)* 1377
Esposito, Larry *(Vocal Arranger)* 1377
Esposito, Laurence J. *(Musical Director)* 2783
Esposito, Mark *(Cast)* 2416
Essen, Viola *(Cast)* 1948
Essex, Francis *(Lyricist)* 392, 3186
Essler, Fred *(Cast)* 1413
Estabrook, Howard *(Cast)* 2891
Estey, Carol *(Cast)* 181, 1116, 2785
Estey, Robert *(Dance Arranger)* 4102
Estey, Robert *(Musical Director)* 2657, 4102
Estey, Robert *(Vocal Arranger)* 2657, 4102
Estey, Suellen *(Cast)* 597, 825, 1435, 3871, 4022
Estin, Amelia *(Cast)* 1004
Estrin, Melvyn J. *(Producer)* 2242
Esudero, Vicente *(Cast)* 839
Etchison, Gregory *(Set Design)* 1347
Etheridge, Dorothy *(Cast)* 3013
Etra, Will *(Composer)* 3076
Etting, Ruth *(Cast)* 3172, 3980, 4683, 4821, 4823
Ettinger, Daniel *(Set Design)* 3346
Ettlinger, Don *(Librettist)* 101
Eugene, Max C. *(Composer)* 1123, 2986
Eugene Productions *(Producer)* 2207
Eugster, Carl *(Composer)* 2042
Eugster, Carl *(Lyricist)* 2042
Euklewitz, Abel *(Producer)* 3983
Eula, Joe *(Costumes)* 1637
Eureka *(Cast)* 2037, 2488
Euripides *(Author)* 4615
Europe, James Reese *(Composer)* 434, 2025, 2493, 2964, 3193, 3676, 3945, 3963, 4390
Europe, James Reese *(Lyricist)* 434, 1198, 2025, 2493, 2964
Eustis, Fred *(Musical Director)* 561
Eustis, Fred J. (Arrangements) 3228
Eustis, Fred J. *(Composer)* 476, 3228, 4556
Eustis, Fred J. *(Musical Director)* 3228
Eustis, Frederick *(Composer)* 2963
Eustis, Frederick J. *(Composer)* 625, 976, 2543
Eustis, Frederick J. *(Musical Director)* 976
Evanko, Ed *(Cast)* 634, 2618, 3702
Evans, Al *(Musical Director)* 1286, 1546
Evans, Alan *(Cast)* 2451
Evans, Albert *(Composer)* 3178, 3346
Evans, Albert *(Lyricist)* 2861, 3178
Evans, Albert *(Orchestrations)* 3178
Evans, Albert *(Vocal Arranger)* 3178
Evans, Alfred *(Musical Director)* 3410
Evans, Barbara *(Cast)* 194
Evans, Bobby *(Cast)* 447
Evans, Bruce Balfour *(Lyricist)* 2401
Evans, Charles *(Cast)* 3392, 3943
Evans, Charles *(Set Design)* 413

Evans, Charles E. *(Cast)* 4333
Evans, Craig *(Lighting Designer)* 1258, 1591, 2544, 3125
Evans, David (Arrangements) 81
Evans, David *(Composer)* 4, 424
Evans, David *(Librettist)* 424
Evans, David *(Musical Director)* 81, 1510, 1822, 1832
Evans, David *(Vocal Arranger)* 1510, 1832
Evans, Dell *(Cast)* 2455
Evans, Dickie *(Cast)* 1002
Evans, Don *(Librettist)* 2692
Evans, Don *(Lyricist)* 2692
Evans, Don *(Musical Director)* 3970
Evans, Edith *(Cast)* 4152, 4291
Evans, Frank *(Lyricist)* 260
Evans, Freida *(Costumes)* 4157
Evans, Frieda *(Set Design)* 2067
Evans, G. Douglas *(Cast)* 834
Evans, George *(Cast)* 800, 801
Evans, George *(Composer)* 662, 1021
Evans, George *(Lyricist)* 4390
Evans, George "Honey Boy" *(Cast)* 803
Evans, George "Honey Boy" *(Composer)* 1226, 1686, 2978
Evans, George "Honey Boy" *(Lyricist)* 1226, 1686
Evans, Greek *(Cast)* 1182, 3012, 4077, 4271
Evans, Gwyllum *(Cast)* 4244
Evans, Harry *(Librettist)* 2105
Evans, Harvey *(Cast)* 155, 162, 1329, 1478, 3902
Evans, Helena *(Librettist)* 1756
Evans, Helena *(Lyricist)* 1756
Evans, Karen *(Cast)* 1053, 3162, 3806, 4736
Evans, Margie *(Cast)* 202, 1462
Evans, Maurice *(Cast)* 277, 4312
Evans, Maurice *(Producer)* 3188
Evans, Peter *(Cast)* 3339
Evans, Ray *(Composer)* 3182, 3841, 4197, 4321
Evans, Ray *(Lyricist)* 2057, 2449, 3182, 3234, 3841, 4197, 4274, 4321
Evans, Raymond *(Cast)* 2611
Evans, Rex *(Cast)* 700, 1475, 3064, 4368
Evans, Rex *(Composer)* 700
Evans, Sandy *(Cast)* 861
Evans, Sticks *(Musical Director)* 3983
Evans, Thomas *(Choreographer)* 998
Evans, Tudor *(Cast)* 3339
Evans, W.J. *(Set Design)* 2482
Evans, Warwick *(Cast)* 460
Evans, Wilbur *(Cast)* 603, 2847, 4524
Evans, William Kendall *(Lyricist)* 115
Evelyn, John *(Cast)* 429
Evelyn, Judith *(Cast)* 3335
Everage, Kenneth *(Costumes)* 2006
Everall & Wallach Company *(Producer)* 4649
Everard, George *(Composer)* 2986
Everest, John *(Lyricist)* 1035
Everett, Frances *(Cast)* 4253
Everett, Paul *(Lighting Designer)* 1201, 1897
Everett, Tanya *(Cast)* 1265
Everett, Timmy *(Cast)* 2556, 3696
Everhard, Eliot G. *(Orchestrations)* 860
Everhart, Rex *(Cast)* 259, 1955, 3188, 3644, 4013, 4278, 4312, 4727, 4744
Everly, Jack *(Musical Director)* 1633
Everly, Phil *(Composer)* 3739
Everly, Phil *(Lyricist)* 3739
Everson, Patricia Ann *(Cast)* 3987
Everton, Paul *(Cast)* 834
Everybody *(Librettist)* 4421
Evett, Benjamin *(Cast)* 3937
Ewell, Lois *(Cast)* 2836
Ewell, Tom *(Cast)* 3138, 3894, 4018, 4214
Ewing, Bruce C. *(Cast)* 4799
Ewing, Marjorie *(Producer)* 137
Ewing, Max *(Composer)* 1652, 1655, 1656, 1657
Ewing, Max *(Lyricist)* 1656, 1657
Ewing, Sherman *(Producer)* 137
Excell, E.O. *(Composer)* 3261
Excell, E.O. *(Lyricist)* 3261
Extension Company, The *(Producer)* 4405
Eyck, Ten *(Costumes)* 1352
Eyen, Tom *(Director)* 2307, 3636, 4433
Eyen, Tom *(Librettist)* 1103, 2307, 3636, 4403
Eyen, Tom *(Lyricist)* 1103, 2307, 4403
Eyen, Tom *(Producer)* 4433
Eysler, Edmund *(Author)* 473, 2424, 2603, 4553
Eysler, Edmund *(Composer)* 473, 2262, 2424, 2603, 4553, 4726, 4795
Eysler, Edward *(Author)* 2262
Eysler, Edward *(Lyricist)* 3753
Eythe, William *(Cast)* 2439, 2464, 3326
Eythe, William *(Director)* 520
Eythe, William *(Producer)* 2439
Eyton, Frank *(Librettist)* 4174
Eyton, Frank *(Lyricist)* 432, 1618, 3139, 3905, 4367, 4534
Ezell, John *(Set Design)* 1439

F

F.W. Woolworth Company *(Producer)* 2988
F.W.M. Producing Group *(Producer)* 4068
FPC *(Producer)* 2018
Faber, Charles *(Librettist)* 4415
Faber, Ron *(Cast)* 1064, 2646
Fabian, Robert *(Producer)* 1256
Fabiani, Joel *(Cast)* 2607
Fabray, Nanette *(Cast)* 58, 183, 225, 1886, 2187, 2453, 2615, 2705, 2809, 2983, 3036
Fabrizi, Aldo *(Cast)* 3798
Factora, Marshall *(Cast)* 114
Faded Glory *(Costumes)* 843
Fagan *(Lyricist)* 4805
Fagan, Barney *(Cast)* 3968
Fagan, Barney *(Choreographer)* 2722
Fagan, Barney *(Composer)* 191, 604, 1897
Fagan, Barney *(Lyricist)* 191, 1897
Fagan, Garth *(Choreographer)* 3628
Fagan, Garth *(Director)* 3628
Fagan, J.B. *(Librettist)* 129
Fagan, Joan *(Cast)* 1076

Fagan, Scott *(Composer)* 4089
Fagan, Scott *(Lyricist)* 4089
Fagerbakke, Bill *(Cast)* 262
Fagin, Gary S. *(Orchestrations)* 3175
Faibsey *(Costumes)* 2900, 3230, 3400, 3737, 4422
Fain, Sammy *(Author)* 616
Fain, Sammy *(Cast)* 447
Fain, Sammy *(Composer)* 59, 145, 190, 447, 512, 616, 673, 710, 751, 1034, 1207, 1300, 1494, 1813, 1840, 2234, 2246, 2772, 2850, 3046, 3166, 3178, 3356, 3404, 3713, 3739, 3789, 3916, 4010, 4060, 4086, 4137, 4428, 4825, 4828, 4829
Fair, Thelma *(Cast)* 2986, 4646
Fairbanks, Ethel *(Cast)* 77
Fairbanks, Gladys *(Cast)* 3686
Fairbanks, Madeleine *(Cast)* 86, 1747, 1780, 2818, 4491
Fairbanks, Marion *(Cast)* 1643, 4491
Fairbanks, Nola *(Cast)* 2023, 2024, 2099, 3151
Fairbanks Jr., Douglas *(Cast)* 635, 1243
Fairbanks Twins, The *(Cast)* 1489, 3007, 3243, 4812, 4813, 4843, 4853
Fairbrother, Sydney *(Cast)* 333, 1454
Fairchild, Charlotte *(Cast)* 3439
Fairchild, Edgar *(Cast)* 622, 931
Fairchild, Edgar *(Composer)* 2105, 2396, 3130
Fairleigh, Harry *(Cast)* 3753, 4425, 4590
Fairman, George *(Composer)* 4814
Faison, George *(Cast)* 3610
Faison, George *(Choreographer)* 166, 789, 1072, 2949, 3991, 4004, 4722
Faison, George *(Composer)* 3991, 4722
Faison, George *(Director)* 166, 789, 3991, 4004
Faison, George *(Librettist)* 166, 789, 3991
Faison, George *(Lyricist)* 166, 3991
Faison, Sandy *(Cast)* 150, 699, 2152
Falabella, John *(Costumes)* 426, 900, 1797, 3444, 4279
Falabella, John *(Set Design)* 426, 478, 900, 1797, 2177, 3444, 4279
Falana, Lola *(Cast)* 108, 1063
Falco, Anthony *(Cast)* 3126
Falconer, Helen *(Cast)* 736, 2184
Falconer, Sheila *(Choreographer)* 3429
Falk, Eleanor *(Cast)* 4242
Falk, Henri *(Author)* 3079
Falk, Lee *(Librettist)* 1754
Falk, Willy *(Cast)* 2754, 2905
Falkenburg, Jinx *(Cast)* 1931
Fall, Leo *(Author)* 1067, 1555, 2249, 2469, 2666, 3996
Fall, Leo *(Composer)* 1066, 1067, 1197, 1555, 2249, 2469, 2666, 3778, 3996
Fall, Richard *(Composer)* 710, 1067, 4667
Fallon, Eva *(Cast)* 256, 1003, 1151, 1975, 2603, 2854, 2929, 3590, 3613, 4056, 4187, 4634, 4762
Fallon, Larry *(Dance Arranger)* 692
Fallon, Larry *(Musical Director)* 3428
Fallon, Larry *(Orchestrations)* 692, 1809, 3869
Fallon, Larry *(Vocal Arranger)* 692
Falls, Arlene *(Costumes)* 2159, 2347, 3068
Falls, Charles B. *(Set Design)* 1685
Falls, Robert *(Director)* 494
Famous People Players *(Producer)* 2521
Fanale, Susan *(Cast)* 1757
Fanchon, Miss *(Choreographer)* 2085
Fanchon, Miss *(Costumes)* 3842
Fanchon, Miss *(Director)* 2085, 2086, 2087
Fanchon & Marco
See also Miss Fanchon and Marco.
Fanchon & Marco *(Cast)* 3842, 4211
Fanchon & Marco *(Composer)* 3842, 4211
Fanchon & Marco *(Director)* 4211
Fanchon & Marco *(Librettist)* 4211
Fanchon & Marco *(Lyricist)* 3842, 4211
Fanchon & Marco *(Producer)* 3842, 4128, 4211
Fanchonetti, Marie *(Cast)* 1565
Fancy, Richard *(Cast)* 3992
Fantasy Factory, The *(Producer)* 1450, 2776
Faraday, P. Michael *(Director)* 1554
Faraday, P. Michael *(Producer)* 1554
Farago, Geza *(Costumes)* 4154
Farago, Geza *(Set Design)* 4154
Farago, Jeno *(Author)* 2622, 4669
Farber, Mitch *(Orchestrations)* 3126
Farber, Sandy *(Producer)* 249, 1380, 4186
Farbman, Abel *(Producer)* 4435
Farer, Ronnie *(Cast)* 674
Fargue, Annie *(Producer)* 3739
Faria, Arthur *(Cast)* 1497, 4196
Faria, Arthur *(Choreographer)* 547, 583, 4162, 4454
Faria, Arthur *(Director)* 583, 4162
Faria, Scott *(Director)* 1159
Fariday, Mary *(Choreographer)* 4405
Farina, Marilyn *(Cast)* 3211
Faris, Alexander *(Musical Director)* 299, 3756
Faris, Alexander *(Vocal Arranger)* 299
Farjeon, Eleanor *(Librettist)* 4479
Farjeon, Eleanor *(Lyricist)* 4479
Farjeon, Herbert *(Librettist)* 2227, 2483, 4153, 4416
Farjeon, Herbert *(Lyricist)* 3107, 4153
Farkas, Carl *(Author)* 3756
Farkas, Jonathan *(Producer)* 3718
Farkas, Karl *(Author)* 4730, 4777
Farkas, Karl *(Director)* 2755
Farkas, Karl *(Librettist)* 2755, 4792
Farkas, Karl *(Lyricist)* 2755, 4792
Farkoa, Maurice *(Cast)* 1095, 2825, 2891, 4354, 4418
Farleigh, Harry *(Cast)* 3820
Farley, Alice *(Costumes)* 2970
Farley, Edward *(Composer)* 393, 1813
Farley, Edward *(Lyricist)* 393
Farley, J.J. *(Cast)* 1636
Farley, Morgan *(Cast)* 4284
Farnham, Hilda *(Costumes)* 691
Farnum, Dustin *(Cast)* 3759
Farnum, Franklyn *(Cast)* 1606
Farnum, Hilda *(Costumes)* 1876
Farnum, William *(Cast)* 4671
Farr, Kimberly *(Cast)* 572, 1762, 2953, 2962, 3925
Farr, Lowell *(Musical Director)* 3215
Farrar, Tony *(Cast)* 3105
Farrell, Anthony B. *(Producer)* 67, 1791
Farrell, Anthony Brady *(Producer)* 145, 183, 4314
Farrell, Charles *(Cast)* 4207

Farrell, Charles *(Lyricist)* 4823
Farrell, Genevieve *(Lyricist)* 574
Farrell, Isabelle *(Cast)* 4243, 4337
Farrell, Kevin *(Musical Director)* 550
Farrell, Peter *(Cast)* 2153
Farrell, W.H. *(Composer)* 3953
Farrell, W.H. *(Lyricist)* 3953
Farrell, William H. *(Composer)* 1120
Farrell, William H. *(Lyricist)* 1120
Farren, Jack *(Producer)* 4522
Farrington, Frank *(Cast)* 1553
Farrow, Mia *(Cast)* 3454
Farwell, Tommy *(Cast)* 304
Fashion Productions *(Producer)* 1250
Fasman, Barry *(Composer)* 1298
Fasman, Barry *(Lyricist)* 1298
Fassell, Otto *(Cast)* 3639
Fata, Wesley *(Choreographer)* 2945, 3136, 3169, 3873
Fatone, Charles *(Costumes)* 1018
Faulkner, Rex *(Cast)* 1337
Faulkner, Virginia *(Librettist)* 70
Faulkner, Virginia *(Lyricist)* 70
Faulkner, Walter H. *(Lyricist)* 4735
Faun, Florence *(Cast)* 3130
Faussett, Hudson *(Director)* 3810
Faussett, Hudson *(Producer)* 3810
Faust, Allen *(Orchestrations)* 3126
Faust, Lotta *(Cast)* 666, 1526, 2465, 2858, 2869, 4666, 4735
Faversham, William *(Cast)* 3974
Faversham, William *(Director)* 3974
Fawcett, George *(Cast)* 1501
Fay, Elfie *(Cast)* 349
Fay, Frank *(Cast)* 199, 1378, 1557, 1779, 2104, 2214, 3258, 3402, 3662, 4291
Fay, Frank *(Composer)* 2104
Fay, Frank *(Director)* 1378, 4291
Fay, Frank *(Librettist)* 1378, 2104, 4291
Fay, Frank *(Lyricist)* 2104, 4291
Fay, Frank *(Producer)* 4291
Fay, Gus *(Cast)* 116, 332, 2107
Fay, Meagen *(Cast)* 2065
Fay, Patricia *(Cast)* 991
Fay, Sally *(Composer)* 3181
Fay, Sally *(Lyricist)* 3181
Fay, Thomas *(Arrangements)* 951
Fay, Thomas *(Composer)* 4601
Fay, Thomas *(Dance Arranger)* 4019
Fay, Thomas *(Lyricist)* 4601
Fay, Thomas *(Musical Director)* 951, 4109
Fay, Tom (Arrangements) 4027
Fay, Tom *(Dance Arranger)* 1699, 2702, 2822, 3718
Fay, Tom *(Musical Director)* 2702, 4027, 4518
Fay, Vivian *(Cast)* 1481, 2813
Faye, Alice *(Cast)* 1492
Faye, Francis *(Cast)* 204
Faye, Herbie *(Cast)* 4423
Faye, Joey *(Cast)* 84, 98, 843, 1112, 1699, 1842, 1886, 2523, 2653, 2657, 3900, 3990, 4180, 4423
Fazakas, Franz *(Puppeteer)* 2726
Fazan, Eleanor *(Choreographer)* 194, 1644
Fazan, Eleanor *(Director)* 1644
Fazioli, Billy *(Composer)* 1154
Fearnley, John *(Cast)* 4374
Fearnley, John *(Director)* 4153
Fearnley, John *(Producer)* 2680
Fearon, Ed *(Composer)* 4433
Fearon, Ed *(Librettist)* 4433
Fearon, Ed *(Lyricist)* 2279, 4433
Fears, Peggy *(Cast)* 1784, 3179, 3796, 4819
Fears, Peggy *(Producer)* 3014
Feaster, Carl *(Composer)* 3739, 4264
Feaster, Carl *(Lyricist)* 3739, 4264
Feaster, Claude *(Composer)* 4264
Feaster, Claude *(Lyricist)* 4264
Feather, Lorraine *(Cast)* 4584
Fechheimer, Richard *(Lyricist)* 627, 1175
Fechheimer, Richard B. *(Cast)* 1632
Fechheimer, Richard B. *(Librettist)* 1632
Fechheimer, Richard B. *(Lyricist)* 1632
Fechner, Dianina *(Cast)* 710
Feder *(Lighting Designer)* 223, 477, 507, 622, 623, 652, 1063, 1366, 1614, 1634, 1698, 1931, 3038, 3104, 3274, 3495, 3899, 4366, 4386
Feder *(Set Design)* 477, 507
Feder, Abe *(Lighting Designer)* 4706
Federal Theatre Project *(Producer)* 1337
Fedor, Marck Adrian *(Producer)* 3311
Fehlhaber, Fred R. *(Producer)* 161
Feiffer, Jules *(Author)* 170
Feiffer, Jules *(Librettist)* 2611, 3233, 4535, 4746
Feiffer, Jules *(Lyricist)* 2611
Feigay, Paul *(Producer)* 404, 490, 1062, 1742, 2097, 3278
Feigenbaum, Ziske *(Composer)* 1609
Fein, Lupin *(Composer)* 875, 885
Fein, Lupin *(Lyricist)* 885, 2540
Feiner, Harry *(Set Design)* 760
Feiner, Herman *(Author)* 4352
Feingold, Michael *(Lyricist)* 369
Feinstein, Michael (English Lyrics) 4371
Feinstein, Michael *(Librettist)* 4371
Feirce, Louis *(Cast)* 2008
Feist, Felix F. *(Lyricist)* 1318, 1520, 4012, 4723
Feist, Frances *(Costumes)* 447, 4772
Fekaris, Dino *(Composer)* 3739
Fekaris, Dino *(Lyricist)* 3739
Feld, Eliot *(Cast)* 3831
Feld, Kenneth *(Producer)* 3840
Felder, Clarence *(Cast)* 3684, 4295
Feldkamp, Walter *(Composer)* 3103
Feldman, Al *(Composer)* 887
Feldman, Al *(Lyricist)* 887
Feldman, Dick *(Director)* 192
Feldman, Jack *(Composer)* 829, 2022, 2677
Feldman, Jack *(Librettist)* 846
Feldman, Jack *(Lyricist)* 829, 846, 2022, 2677
Feldman, Peter *(Cast)* 1056
Feldon, Barbara *(Cast)* 944
Feldshuh, Tovah *(Cast)* 518, 946, 1832, 3743, 3838, 4167
Feldstein, Robert D. *(Producer)* 2876, 3988, 4292
Felgemacher, Olga *(Puppeteer)* 56, 997, 3449, 3498, 4660, 4710

Felix, Edmund *(Costumes)* 139
Felix, Hugo *(Author)* 2667
Felix, Hugo *(Composer)* 2412, 2667, 2756, 3431, 3534, 3537, 3618, 3829, 4248, 4285
Felix, Hugo *(Lyricist)* 3829
Felix, Seymour *(Choreographer)* 200, 391, 1461, 1780, 1831, 1916, 2135, 3084, 3407, 3436, 3766, 3980, 4010, 4177, 4208, 4424, 4683
Felix, Seymour *(Director)* 1267, 1831, 4846
Feller, Sid *(Musical Director)* 928
Fellini, Federico *(Author)* 1189, 2368, 3171, 4238
Fellows, Don *(Cast)* 1471
Fellows, Edith *(Cast)* 2595
Femia, Tommy *(Cast)* 2022
Fender, Harry *(Cast)* 2594
Fenderson, Alonzo *(Cast)* 291, 980, 984, 1050, 1960, 2013, 2942, 4520
Fenholt, Jeff *(Cast)* 2212
Fenn, Frederick *(Librettist)* 1554
Fenn, Jean *(Cast)* 1369
Fenning, Stephen *(Cast)* 4034
Fenstock, Belle *(Composer)* 417, 3140
Fenton, Frank *(Cast)* 3219
Fenton, Mabel *(Cast)* 1505, 1900, 4044
Fenwick, Herbert *(Cast)* 1610
Fenwick, Irene *(Cast)* 94
Fenwick, John *(Dance Arranger)* 1255
Fenwick, John (Music Adaptation) 1255
Fenwick, John *(Musical Director)* 148
Fenwick, John *(Orchestrations)* 148, 1255, 3818
Fenwick, John *(Vocal Arranger)* 1255
Feranda, Fredda *(Orchestrations)* 27
Ferber, Edna *(Author)* 3787, 3837, 3949
Ferden, Dennis *(Cast)* 3539
Ferdinand, Edmund J. *(Producer)* 4678
Ferdos *(Librettist)* 1995
Ferdos *(Lyricist)* 1995
Ferguson, Allyn *(Orchestrations)* 786, 4566
Ferguson, Elsie *(Cast)* 1537, 2885
Ferguson, Lester *(Cast)* 2910
Ferguson, Lorena *(Cast)* 421
Ferguson, Robert V. *(Cast)* 2662
Ferland, Danielle *(Cast)* 2143, 3368, 3377
Fernandez, Bijou *(Cast)* 2068
Fernandez, Jose *(Librettist)* 1164, 1236
Ferrante, Elena *(Cast)* 3169
Ferrari, Gustave *(Musical Director)* 758
Ferrat, Jean *(Composer)* 1865
Ferrat, Jean *(Lyricist)* 1865
Ferre, Cliff *(Choreographer)* 3683
Ferrer, Jose *(Cast)* 1564, 4073
Ferrer, Jose *(Director)* 652, 2268, 3234
Ferrer, Jose *(Librettist)* 3234, 4073
Ferrer, Richard *(Set Design)* 3653
Ferris *(Composer)* 4093
Ferris *(Lyricist)* 4093
Ferris, Chet *(Costumes)* 1348
Festa, James *(Cast)* 1004
Fetchit, Stepin *(Cast)* 4586
Fetter, Ted *(Cast)* 1448, 2252
Fetter, Ted *(Lyricist)* 173, 397, 557, 612, 1191, 1286, 1546, 2460, 2707, 2940, 3082, 3861, 3914, 3955, 4335, 4498, 4665, 4670, 4799
Fetzko, Donald C. *(Producer)* 1046
Feuer, Cy *(Director)* 2064, 2523, 3972, 4013, 4588, 4682
Feuer, Cy *(Librettist)* 4682
Feuer, Cy *(Producer)* 16, 507, 629, 1706, 2019, 2523, 3972, 4013, 4588, 4652, 4682
Feuer, Howard *(Producer)* 4019
Feuer, Jed *(Composer)* 1149
Feuer, Jed *(Vocal Arranger)* 1149
Fevrier, Henri *(Composer)* 165
Feydeau, Georges *(Author)* 1538, 1993, 3156
Feyder, Jacques *(Author)* 657
Ffolkes, David *(Costumes)* 95, 530, 1300, 3895, 4015, 4652
Ffolkes, David *(Set Design)* 4652
Fiander, Lewis *(Cast)* 2047
Fibich, Felix *(Choreographer)* 2866, 3670, 3781
Fichandler, Zelda *(Producer)* 2579
Fickett, Homer *(Librettist)* 3104
Fidler, Samuel *(Musical Director)* 1397
Fieg, Jonathan *(Cast)* 3806
Fieger, Addy *(Composer)* 692, 1010
Field, Alice *(Producer)* 140
Field, B. Eugene *(Director)* 489
Field, Betty *(Cast)* 4495
Field, Billy *(Composer)* 1298
Field, Billy *(Lyricist)* 1298
Field, Daniel Thomas *(Set Design)* 3764
Field, Grace *(Cast)* 2528, 2931, 3679
Field, Leonard *(Producer)* 3563
Field, Robin *(Cast)* 4102
Field, Ron *(Choreographer)* 167, 610, 615, 1298, 2318, 3210, 3644, 4862
Field, Ron *(Director)* 167, 1298, 2318, 3499
Field, Sylvia *(Cast)* 3324
Fielding, Harold *(Producer)* 1616, 1721, 1741
Fielding, Henry *(Author)* 2563, 4404, 4406
Fielding, Jerry *(Arrangements)* 1326
Fielding, Marjery *(Choreographer)* 3594, 3975, 4117, 4265
Fielding, Marjery *(Composer)* 3594
Fielding, Marjery *(Director)* 3375
Fielding, Marjery *(Lyricist)* 3594
Fielding, May *(Cast)* 762
Fields, Ada *(Costumes)* 1484, 3443, 3723, 4816
Fields, Al *(Cast)* 3133
Fields, Arthur *(Composer)* 1738, 4655
Fields, Arthur *(Lyricist)* 3401, 3589, 4589
Fields, Benny *(Cast)* 1693
Fields, Bertha A. *(Costumes)* 2264
Fields, Chip *(Cast)* 1073
Fields, Clare *(Cast)* 3181
Fields, Dolly *(Cast)* 1457
Fields, Dorothy *(Cast)* 738, 3153, 3595, 3639, 3848, 4780
Fields, Dorothy *(Librettist)* 153, 183, 603, 2453, 2847, 3687, 4058, 4524
Fields, Dorothy *(Lyricist)* 39, 183, 393, 432, 441, 442, 603, 787, 892, 893, 894, 895, 1168, 1827, 1928, 2140, 2204, 2267, 2294, 2297, 2372, 2772, 3428, 3639, 3687, 3704, 3709, 3869, 3905, 3946, 3993, 4142, 4152, 4197, 4238, 4446, 4524, 4534, 4545, 4847, 4848

Fields, Florence *(Cast)* 4439
Fields, Frank *(Composer)* 3938
Fields, Frank *(Orchestrations)* 3938
Fields, Herbert
See also Herbert Richard Lorenz.
Fields, Herbert *(Cast)* 2574
Fields, Herbert *(Choreographer)* 1321, 1446, 1447, 4781
Fields, Herbert *(Director)* 978, 2102, 2193, 3595, 3848, 4058, 4304
Fields, Herbert *(Librettist)* 111, 153, 183, 603, 711, 834, 978, 1013, 1109, 1272, 1447, 1529, 1827, 1916, 1944, 2453, 2847, 3131, 3379, 3436, 3556, 3687, 4058, 4524, 4709
Fields, Herbert *(Lyricist)* 978, 3538, 3595, 4780
Fields, Herbert *(Producer)* 3359
Fields, Joe *(Cast)* 40, 1672
Fields, Joseph *(Author)* 2267, 4734
Fields, Joseph *(Librettist)* 1315, 1475, 1548, 2653, 4734
Fields, Joseph *(Producer)* 1315
Fields, Lew *(Cast)* 8, 60, 182, 258, 301, 465, 677, 940, 1217, 1264, 1526, 1827, 1845, 1900, 1926, 1927, 2041, 2160, 2574, 2814, 2900, 3265, 3303, 3632, 3639, 3755, 4033, 4148, 4203, 4478, 4511, 4658, 4681, 4797
Fields, Lew *(Director)* 1689, 1690, 1916, 4478, 4545
Fields, Lew *(Librettist)* 1690, 2574, 3538
Fields, Lew *(Producer)* 8, 60, 182, 301, 677, 711, 834, 940, 1188, 1217, 1264, 1526, 1529, 1578, 1738, 1827, 1845, 1916, 1926, 1927, 2160, 2232, 2262, 2814, 2858, 2869, 3096, 3265, 3303, 3436, 3525, 3538, 3556, 3575, 3632, 3773, 4033, 4203, 4206, 4228, 4382, 4478, 4545, 4658, 4681, 4687, 4757, 4797
Fields, Nat *(Cast)* 2232
Fields, Nelson *(Costumes)* 2573
Fields, Richard *(Producer)* 3927
Fields, Ronnie *(Choreographer)* 3725
Fields, Ruth *(Cast)* 4462
Fields, Sol *(Director)* 3384
Fields, W.C. *(Cast)* 288, 827, 1134, 1485, 1731, 2403, 3540, 4809, 4810, 4811, 4812, 4814, 4815, 4818, 4819, 4831, 4840, 4842
Fields, W.C. *(Librettist)* 1134, 1485, 4819
Fier, Newman *(Composer)* 1395
Fier, Newman *(Lyricist)* 1395
Fierstein, Harvey *(Cast)* 1304
Fierstein, Harvey *(Librettist)* 1304, 2360, 2437
Fierstein, Harvey *(Lyricist)* 1304
Fifth Avenue Productions *(Producer)* 154, 1636
Figman, Max *(Cast)* 523, 1110, 1599, 2309, 3117, 4539, 4620
Figman, Max *(Director)* 3673, 4539
Figman, Max *(Librettist)* 47
Figman, Oscar *(Cast)* 1259, 1308, 2293, 2489, 3431, 4597
Fillip, Joe *(Cast)* 4774
Fillmore, Clyde *(Cast)* 1225, 4420
Fillmore, Nellie *(Cast)* 4648
Fillmore, Russell *(Cast)* 3415
Fillmore, Russell *(Director)* 2479, 3415
Fimberg, Hal *(Librettist)* 3, 2259
Fimberg, Hal *(Lyricist)* 2259
Finch, R. Thomas *(Set Design)* 1978
Finchley *(Costumes)* 2148, 2569, 4555
Finck, Henry *(Cast)* 697
Finck, Herman *(Composer)* 186, 1176, 1544, 1845, 2891, 3020, 3096, 3259, 3397, 3398
Finck, Herman *(Lyricist)* 3259
Findlay, Agnes *(Cast)* 235, 2716, 3363
Findlay, Diane *(Cast)* 825, 4022
Findlay, Hal *(Musical Director)* 2640
Findlay, Thomas *(Cast)* 4066
Findley, Danielle *(Cast)* 154
Fine, Laura *(Director)* 760
Fine, Sylvia *(Composer)* 2453, 4166
Fine, Sylvia *(Lyricist)* 2453, 4166
Finger, Leonard *(Producer)* 583
Finger, Thelma *(Producer)* 4005
Fingerhut, Arden *(Lighting Designer)* 54, 474, 1684, 1715, 1787, 2877, 3277, 4294, 4517
Fingleton, Anthony *(Producer)* 3555
Fink, Mitchell *(Producer)* 4659
Finkbinder, T.G. *(Cast)* 1155
Finkel, Alicia *(Costumes)* 2375
Finkel, Alicia *(Set Design)* 2375
Finkel, Barry *(Cast)* 198, 2654
Finkel, Barry *(Choreographer)* 2654
Finkel, Elliot *(Composer)* 1279
Finkel, Elliot *(Musical Director)* 3669
Finkel, Fyvush *(Cast)* 1279
Finkelstein, Norman *(Lighting Designer)* 4243
Finkelstein, Richard *(Set Design)* 114
Finkle, David *(Composer)* 3181
Finkle, David *(Lyricist)* 2043, 2075, 2279, 2913, 3181, 3479
Finklehoffe, Fred *(Librettist)* 1879
Finklehoffe, Fred F. *(Author)* 2805
Finklehoffe, Fred F. *(Director)* 145
Finklehoffe, Fred F. *(Librettist)* 447
Finklehoffe, Fred F. *(Producer)* 145, 1205
Finletter, Gretchen *(Librettist)* 1448
Finley, Grace *(Cast)* 148
Finley, Pat *(Cast)* 1697
Finn, Robyn *(Cast)* 2578
Finn, Terry *(Cast)* 2822
Finn, William *(Composer)* 109, 1234, 2132, 2746, 3757
Finn, William *(Librettist)* 1234, 2132, 2746, 3757
Finn, William *(Lyricist)* 109, 975, 1234, 2132, 2746, 3757
Finn Productions, Jeffrey *(Producer)* 4016
Finner, Leigh *(Cast)* 2784
Finnerty, Mary Sue *(Cast)* 3743
Finney, Mary *(Cast)* 1290, 1760
Finocchiaro, Paul *(Cast)* 4799
Fiocca, Richard *(Musical Director)* 1450
Fiocca, Richard *(Orchestrations)* 1450
Fiocca, Richard *(Vocal Arranger)* 1450
Fiordellsi, Angelina *(Cast)* 1785
Fiore, Roland *(Musical Director)* 3064
Fiorentino, Imero *(Lighting Designer)* 3159
Fiorini, Lando *(Cast)* 3798
Fiorito, Ted *(Composer)* 393, 3962
Fiorito, Ted *(Lyricist)* 487, 3962
Fippinger, Lynne *(Choreographer)* 4696
Firbank, Ronald *(Author)* 4541

First, Harry *(Cast)* 1531
First All Children's Th. *(Producer)* 3164
First Durante Tour Company *(Producer)* 1120
Firth, Shephard *(Librettist)* 2389
Firth, Tazeena *(Costumes)* 1211
Firth, Tazeena *(Set Design)* 1068, 1211
Fischer, Clifford C. *(Producer)* 822, 3121, 3594
Fischer, Robert *(Cast)* 1680
Fischer, Robert C. *(Cast)* 2786, 4234
Fischer, William S. *(Composer)* 2332
Fischoff, George *(Composer)* 1497, 3571, 3851
Fish, Donald *(Cast)* 2676
Fishback, Cliff *(Composer)* 226
Fishback, John *(Lighting Designer)* 3557
Fishback, John *(Producer)* 3557
Fishbein, Zenon *(Musical Director)* 2178
Fishburne, Larry *(Cast)* 4535
Fishburne, Larry *(Librettist)* 4535
Fisher, Al *(Choreographer)* 1971
Fisher, Alex *(Cast)* 4177
Fisher, Alfred *(Cast)* 2119
Fisher, Alice *(Cast)* 830, 1417, 3488, 4148
Fisher, Bruce *(Composer)* 3739
Fisher, Bruce *(Lyricist)* 3739
Fisher, Bud *(Author)* 3021, 3024, 3026, 3028
Fisher, Bud *(Librettist)* 3021
Fisher, Carrie *(Cast)* 682
Fisher, Donald *(Producer)* 4774
Fisher, Doris *(Composer)* 1773, 1951
Fisher, Doris *(Lyricist)* 1773
Fisher, Fred *(Composer)* 39, 89, 351, 393, 822, 917, 965, 1065, 1246, 1773, 1963, 2336, 2706, 2826, 2857, 3086, 3429, 3432, 3926, 3980, 4589, 4807, 4815, 4823
Fisher, Fred *(Lyricist)* 25, 39, 393, 917, 965, 1154, 1773, 2706, 2857, 3086, 3926, 4375, 4815
Fisher, Gary *(Lyricist)* 3901
Fisher, Grace *(Cast)* 2112, 2619
Fisher, Ham *(Author)* 3025
Fisher, Ham *(Librettist)* 2653
Fisher, Harrison *(Cast)* 1399
Fisher, Harrison *(Dance Arranger)* 280
Fisher, Harrison *(Musical Director)* 280, 564, 4172
Fisher, Harrison *(Orchestrations)* 1435
Fisher, Harry *(Cast)* 8, 2160, 2358, 2428, 2858
Fisher, Harry S. *(Cast)* 1902
Fisher, Irving *(Cast)* 683, 805, 959, 1533, 2373, 2637, 3179, 3819, 3962, 4811, 4818
Fisher, Irving *(Lyricist)* 2373, 2587
Fisher, Irving (Pianist) 3133
Fisher, J.W. *(Producer)* 652
Fisher, John C. *(Director)* 3976
Fisher, John C. *(Producer)* 246, 248, 1016, 1313, 1579, 2716, 2803, 3588, 3976
Fisher, Jules *(Lighting Designer)* 71, 162, 298, 373, 393, 424, 594, 634, 723, 754, 756, 964, 1018, 1060, 1195, 1319, 1427, 1441, 1596, 1649, 1697, 1717, 1721, 1727, 1761, 1822, 1841, 1864, 1891, 1974, 2200, 2212, 2360, 2437, 2558, 2568, 2617, 2659, 2728, 2874, 2925, 3039, 3217, 3338, 3482, 3506, 3602, 3636, 3644, 3725, 3739, 3741, 3788, 3869, 3903, 4019, 4068, 4089, 4111, 4380, 4449, 4560, 4695, 4737, 4764, 4783
Fisher, Jules *(Producer)* 964, 975, 3718, 3739
Fisher, Linda *(Costumes)* 262, 482, 1372, 2290, 3195
Fisher, Lola *(Cast)* 1623
Fisher, M. Anthony *(Producer)* 394, 2143
Fisher, Madelyn *(Cast)* 3025
Fisher, Marvin *(Composer)* 4827
Fisher, Marvin *(Lyricist)* 4153
Fisher, Mary *(Costumes)* 292
Fisher, Mary L. *(Lyricist)* 474
Fisher, Max *(Musical Director)* 3173
Fisher, Nelle *(Cast)* 2707, 3947
Fisher, Nelle *(Choreographer)* 3664, 3810
Fisher, Rick *(Lighting Designer)* 3884
Fisher, Robert *(Musical Director)* 4454
Fisher, Robert *(Vocal Arranger)* 4454
Fisher, Ruth *(Cast)* 4825
Fisher, Sallie *(Cast)* 405, 744, 1199, 1801, 2347, 2923, 3579, 3882, 4185, 4293, 4603, 4726
Fisher, Snow *(Cast)* 26
Fisher, Susie *(Cast)* 2493
Fisher, Sydney *(Composer)* 4303
Fisher, William Arms *(Composer)* 1813
Fisher, William Arms *(Lyricist)* 1813
Fisher Theatre Foundation *(Producer)* 699, 1897, 2783
Fisher and His Orchestra, Max *(Cast)* 1947
Fiske, George *(Cast)* 2159
Fiske, Robert *(Cast)* 3048
Fistos, John *(Cast)* 1740
Fitch, Bob *(Cast)* 937
Fitch, Clyde *(Author)* 324, 325, 472, 642, 643, 1897, 2494, 3056
Fitch, Clyde *(Director)* 472
Fitch, George *(Lyricist)* 637
Fitch, Robert *(Cast)* 150, 798, 1059, 2590, 2660, 2887, 3603
Fite, Mark *(Cast)* 778
Fitt, Tom *(Vocal Arranger)* 74
Fitts, Dudley *(Author)* 1636
Fitz *(Composer)* 3566
Fitz *(Lyricist)* 3566
Fitz, Erica *(Cast)* 4329
FitzPatrick, Eileen *(Cast)* 99
Fitzgerald, Ara *(Choreographer)* 1589, 2648
Fitzgerald, Aubrey *(Lyricist)* 1537
Fitzgerald, Ella *(Composer)* 887
Fitzgerald, Ella *(Lyricist)* 887, 4534
Fitzgerald, F. Scott *(Author)* 1451
Fitzgerald, Geraldine *(Cast)* 951, 4175
Fitzgerald, Geraldine *(Director)* 4398
Fitzgerald, Geraldine *(Librettist)* 951, 4175
Fitzgerald, Kathy *(Cast)* 4255
Fitzgerald, Lillian *(Cast)* 125, 467, 1773, 2835, 4437
Fitzgerald, Robert *(Author)* 1636
Fitzgerald, William H. *(Director)* 4559
Fitzgerald Jr., Louis *(Cast)* 934
Fitzgerald Jr., Louis *(Librettist)* 934
Fitzgibbon, Bert *(Composer)* 4094
Fitzgibbon, Bert *(Lyricist)* 4094
Fitzgibbon, Dave *(Cast)* 2467, 4320, 4583
Fitzgibbon, David E. *(Director)* 1880
Fitzgibbon, Dorothy *(Cast)* 3849, 4335, 4583

Fitzhugh, Ellen *(Additional Lyrics)* 146
Fitzhugh, Ellen *(Cast)* 2703
Fitzhugh, Ellen *(Lyricist)* 1038, 1186, 1699, 1861, 1872, 3364
Fitzhugh, Ida *(Cast)* 1183, 1305
Fitzhugh, Louise *(Author)* 4286
Fitzhugh, Venita *(Cast)* 1544, 2761
Fitziu, Anna *(Cast)* 308
Fitziu, Anna *(Lyricist)* 3137
Fitzpatrick, Allen *(Cast)* 2185
Fitzpatrick, Any *(Cast)* 2521
Fitzpatrick, Colleen *(Cast)* 3411
Fitzpatrick, Jim *(Cast)* 760
Fitzpatrick, M.J. *(Composer)* 4589
Fitzpatrick, Margaret *(Cast)* 1445
Fitzsimmons, Robert *(Cast)* 3871
Five Blind Boys of Alabama *(Cast)* 1636
Flack, Nanette *(Cast)* 286, 378, 1631, 1831, 2407, 3192, 4452
Flack, Roberta (Voice) 4391
Flack, W.E. *(Producer)* 4859
Flagg, Fannie *(Cast)* 1750, 2279
Flagg, Fannie *(Librettist)* 2279
Flagg, James Montgomery *(Librettist)* 199
Flaherty, Hugh *(Choreographer)* 1912
Flaherty, Stephen *(Composer)* 2646, 3039, 3285
Flaherty, Stephen *(Musical Director)* 3960
Flaiano, Ennio *(Author)* 3171, 4238
Flanagan, Bud *(Cast)* 1763
Flanagan, Bud *(Composer)* 4027
Flanagan, Bud *(Lyricist)* 4027
Flanagan, Charles *(Cast)* 4470
Flanders, Michael *(Cast)* 220, 221
Flanders, Michael *(Lyricist)* 220, 221
Flanders, Richard *(Cast)* 1347
Flaningam, Louisa *(Cast)* 143, 2289, 2346, 2579, 3517, 4731
Flash, Serge *(Cast)* 2077
Flatow, Leon *(Composer)* 3401
Flatow, Leon *(Lyricist)* 4817
Flatt, Ernest *(Choreographer)* 223, 1227, 2163, 2590, 4197
Flatt, Ernest O. *(Choreographer)* 1970
Flatt, Ernest O. *(Director)* 1120, 1970
Flaxman, John *(Producer)* 3871, 4790
Fleeson, Neville *(Composer)* 3005
Fleeson, Neville *(Lyricist)* 608, 1516, 1961, 3005, 4050, 4677
Fleetwood, Tom *(Cast)* 4764
Fleishman, Philip *(Composer)* 3802
Fleitas, Allison *(Composer)* 1604, 4303
Fleitas, Allison *(Lyricist)* 1604, 4303
Fleming, Blanche *(Cast)* 1447, 4664
Fleming, Carroll *(Author)* 3998
Fleming, Carroll *(Director)* 188, 4509
Fleming, Carroll *(Librettist)* 188, 3504, 4509
Fleming, Carroll *(Lyricist)* 3998
Fleming, Claude *(Cast)* 4482, 4489
Fleming, Conn *(Librettist)* 3671, 4252
Fleming, Conn *(Lyricist)* 3671
Fleming, Eugene *(Cast)* 1890, 4255
Fleming, Fred *(Musical Director)* 385, 1656, 1657, 4208
Fleming, Peggy *(Cast)* 2094
Flesh, Ed *(Set Design)* 600
Fless, Scott *(Cast)* 1732
Fletcher, Allen *(Director)* 255
Fletcher, Bramwell *(Cast)* 2396, 2680
Fletcher, Charles *(Cast)* 1593
Fletcher, Dusty *(Cast)* 1251
Fletcher, George *(Composer)* 1340, 2771
Fletcher, George *(Lyricist)* 2771
Fletcher, Jack *(Cast)* 127, 367, 1023, 1049, 1094, 1362, 1841, 2590, 2659, 3497, 4065, 4153, 4156, 4197, 4310
Fletcher, Joe *(Composer)* 1343
Fletcher, Joe *(Lyricist)* 1343
Fletcher, Juanita *(Cast)* 977, 1882, 2527
Fletcher, Percy *(Musical Director)* 292
Fletcher, Percy *(Orchestrations)* 758
Fletcher, Percy E. *(Composer)* 2802
Fletcher, Robert *(Costumes)* 935, 1237, 1294, 1373, 1727, 1745, 1891, 2019, 2168, 2357, 2523, 3210, 3273, 4585, 4588
Fletcher, Robert *(Producer)* 1891, 4388
Fletcher, Robert *(Set Design)* 1891, 4388
Fletcher, Ron *(Choreographer)* 315, 4423
Fletcher, Susann *(Cast)* 1633, 2205
Flett, Sharon *(Cast)* 3066
Flick, Pat *(Cast)* 760
Flick, Pat C. *(Librettist)* 512
Flick, Patsy *(Cast)* 622
Flicker, Theodore J. *(Director)* 2067, 3094
Flicker, Theodore J. *(Librettist)* 3094
Flicker, Theodore J. *(Producer)* 2067
Flickinger, Brad *(Orchestrations)* 1630
Flink, Stanley *(Producer)* 3818
Flinn, Brook *(Composer)* 2039
Flinn, Denny Martin *(Cast)* 302, 3956, 4196
Flinn, Denny Martin *(Choreographer)* 4002
Flinn, Dylan *(Lyricist)* 2039
Flint, Shelby *(Cast)* 499
Flippen, Jay C. *(Cast)* 1678, 1831, 2263, 2653, 3342, 3861, 4265
Flood, Peter *(Producer)* 3927
Florell, Walter *(Costumes)* 341, 2985
Florell, Walter *(Director)* 848
Florelle *(Cast)* 2753
Florence, Kathryn *(Cast)* 3952
Florenz, Paul *(Choreographer)* 4021
Florenz & Alvarez *(Cast)* 1950
Florida Arts Council *(Producer)* 4645
Florida Atlantic University *(Producer)* 2027
Flovie, Mlle. *(Librettist)* 3203
Flower, Belle *(Cast)* 2275
Flower, Chris *(Set Design)* 3629
Flowers, Martha *(Cast)* 1385
Flowerton, Consuelo *(Cast)* 1110, 2444, 2813
Floyd, Gene *(Cast)* 2094
Floyd, Walter *(Producer)* 4859
Fludd III, Quitman *(Cast)* 1164, 3279
Fludd III, Quitman D. *(Cast)* 1063
Fluehr, Cheryl L. *(Producer)* 4515
Fluty, Rex *(Set Design)* 2027

Flynn, Elinor *(Cast)* 1342
Flynn, Jimmy *(Lyricist)* 3614
Flynn, John *(Composer)* 3322
Flynn, John H. *(Composer)* 2835, 2858
Flynn, Kitty *(Cast)* 1531, 3821
Flynn, Marie *(Cast)* 697, 1519, 1606, 2854, 3344, 3866
Flynn, Maryellen *(Producer)* 908
Flynn, Susan *(Cast)* 484, 549
Flynn, Terrance *(Cast)* 647
Fodor, Joleen *(Cast)* 249, 1676
Foerster, Frederick H. *(Composer)* 6
Fogarty, Alex *(Composer)* 3103, 3104, 4777
Fogarty, Alexander *(Composer)* 637
Fogarty, John *(Composer)* 4534
Fogarty, John *(Lyricist)* 4534
Fogarty, John C. *(Composer)* 3739
Fogarty, John C. *(Lyricist)* 3739
Fokine, Michel *(Cast)* 3153
Fokine, Michel *(Choreographer)* 165, 1656, 4816
Folden, Lewis *(Set Design)* 2704
Foldes, Lew *(Cast)* 660
Foley, Brian *(Choreographer)* 4402
Foley, Ellen *(Composer)* 2427
Foley, Ellen *(Lyricist)* 2427
Foley, John *(Cast)* 3608
Foley, John *(Composer)* 3608
Foley, John *(Lyricist)* 3608
Foley, John *(Musical Director)* 4030
Foley Jr., Daniel G. *(Composer)* 1604
Foley Jr., Daniel G. *(Lyricist)* 18, 1604
Folger Theatre Group *(Producer)* 699
Follis, Dorothy *(Cast)* 1962
Follmann Jr., Joseph F. *(Musical Director)* 18, 750, 1885
Folmer, Wallace Walter *(Cast)* 3647
Folsom, Bobby *(Cast)* 1131
Fond, Miriam *(Choreographer)* 871, 4635
Fond, Miriam *(Director)* 871, 4635
Fonda, Henry *(Cast)* 1471, 2060, 3103
Fonda, Jane *(Cast)* 2144
Fong, Joseph *(Cast)* 595
Fonson *(Author)* 94
Fontaine, Gene *(Cast)* 4021
Fontaine, Joel *(Set Design)* 2354
Fontaine, Robert L. *(Author)* 1764
Fontana, Georges *(Cast)* 3975
Fontanne, Lynn *(Cast)* 1416, 2121, 3328
Food Industries, The *(Producer)* 2175
Foote, Don *(Costumes)* 227
Foote, Gene *(Cast)* 723, 3506
Foote, Gene *(Choreographer)* 3561
Foote, Gene *(Director)* 3561
Foote, Horton *(Librettist)* 1616
Foote, Jay *(Composer)* 128, 1049
Foran, William *(Cast)* 2311
Foray, June *(Voice)* 2015
Forbes, Barbara *(Costumes)* 549, 2199
Forbes, Brenda *(Author)* 3764
Forbes, Brenda *(Cast)* 989, 3292, 4362, 4483
Forbes, Donna Liggitt *(Cast)* 2043, 4022
Forbes, Edward *(Cast)* 1871
Forbes, Elliot *(Composer)* 1231
Forbes, Esther *(Author)* 823
Forbes, Grace *(Cast)* 2492
Forbes, Hazel *(Cast)* 3980
Forbes, Kathryn *(Author)* 2064
Forbes, Ralph *(Cast)* 2691
Forbes-Robinson, Beatrice *(Cast)* 2952
Forcen, Ida *(Cast)* 982
Forchion, Raymond George *(Cast)* 2027
Ford, Anna *(Cast)* 2254
Ford, Chip *(Cast)* 3928
Ford, Constance *(Cast)* 3845
Ford, Corey *(Librettist)* 1322, 1932, 4367
Ford, David *(Cast)* 3897
Ford, Frank *(Producer)* 3931
Ford, George *(Producer)* 1013
Ford, Harry *(Director)* 1013
Ford, Helen *(Cast)* 97, 711, 1013, 1345, 1516, 1670, 1819, 3185, 3436, 4248
Ford, Henry *(Cast)* 475
Ford, Hugh *(Director)* 1501, 4671
Ford, Inez *(Cast)* 1922
Ford, Joan *(Lyricist)* 1614
Ford, Joe Taylor *(Librettist)* 2415
Ford, John *(Director)* 1076
Ford, Johnny *(Cast)* 4464
Ford, Johnny *(Choreographer)* 2277
Ford, Lena Guilbert *(Lyricist)* 3259
Ford, Nancy *(Additional Music)* 1439
Ford, Nancy *(Arrangements)* 1169, 1439
Ford, Nancy *(Composer)* 944, 1169, 1737, 2074, 2418, 3209, 3927
Ford, Nancy *(Lyricist)* 1737
Ford, Nancy *(Orchestrations)* 2074
Ford, Nancy *(Vocal Arranger)* 3209
Ford, Paul *(Cast)* 2267, 3097, 4682
Ford, Paul (Pianist) 4533
Ford, Phyllis *(Cast)* 3810
Ford, Rodney *(Costumes)* 2654
Ford, Rodney *(Set Design)* 2654, 3695
Ford, Ruth *(Cast)* 979, 1662, 1775, 4256
Ford, Steven *(Musical Director)* 1073
Ford, Tom *(Composer)* 1131, 1132, 3172
Ford, Tom *(Lyricist)* 1131, 1132
Ford, Vesta *(Cast)* 985
Ford, Walter *(Lyricist)* 1925, 3951, 4130
Ford, Wrena *(Composer)* 477
Ford's Theatre Society *(Producer)* 3318, 4162
Forde, Hal *(Cast)* 20, 207, 787, 1493, 1530, 1780, 1962, 2005, 2402, 2567, 2696, 2927, 3230, 3236, 4670, 4733
Forde, Hal *(Director)* 3290
Forde, Larry *(Director)* 1637, 3261
Forde, Stanley *(Cast)* 2363, 2373, 2730, 3420, 3580, 3581
Fordin, Wolff *(Costumes)* 331
Forella, Ronn *(Cast)* 1990
Forella, Ronn *(Choreographer)* 692, 4689
Foreman, Richard *(Director)* 1064, 4370
Foreman, Richard *(Lyricist)* 1064
Foreman, Richard *(Set Design)* 1064
Fores, J.F. *(Cast)* 3797
Forestieri, Lou *(Orchestrations)* 562
Forestieri, Marcel *(Cast)* 534

Foresythe, Reginald *(Composer)* 885
Forgy, Ann *(Cast)* 2573
Forkins, Marty *(Producer)* 567, 1984
Forman, Lou *(Musical Director)* 3121, 3594
Forman, Norman *(Producer)* 2322
Formead, William *(Producer)* 2332
Formilli, C. *(Set Design)* 2964
Fornes, Maria Irene *(Librettist)* 3602
Fornes, Maria Irene *(Lyricist)* 3602
Forrest, Almyra *(Cast)* 1515
Forrest, Chet
See also George Forrest.
Forrest, Chet *(Composer)* 1415
Forrest, Chet *(Lyricist)* 1415, 1680, 1681
Forrest, George
See also Chet Forrest.
Forrest, George *(Author)* 4383
Forrest, George *(Composer)* 161, 223, 649, 848, 849, 1119, 1649, 2295, 2327, 3683, 4073, 4075, 4117, 4316, 4383
Forrest, George *(Director)* 1711
Forrest, George *(Librettist)* 649
Forrest, George *(Lyricist)* 161, 223, 649, 848, 849, 1119, 1649, 1711, 2295, 2327, 2679, 3683, 4073, 4075, 4117, 4316, 4383
Forrest, June *(Cast)* 2161, 2162
Forrest, Maude *(Cast)* 2996
Forrest, Robert *(Composer)* 3368
Forrest, Sam *(Director)* 1360, 1961, 2537, 2767, 2829, 3063, 3791, 4576
Forrest, Steve *(Cast)* 483
Forrester, B.E. *(Producer)* 361, 1520, 3519
Forrester, Lynne *(Cast)* 2306
Forsey, Jeanette *(Cast)* 80
Forster, John *(Composer)* 3565, 4533
Forster, John *(Lyricist)* 1099, 2142, 3565, 4533
Forster, Margaret *(Author)* 1497
Forster, Margaret *(Screenwriter)* 1497
Forston, Don *(Cast)* 3461
Forsyth, Jerold R. *(Lighting Designer)* 264
Forsyth, Peggy *(Cast)* 4285
Forsythe, Henderson *(Cast)* 374
Fort, Sylvill *(Choreographer)* 1122
Fort Worth Frontier Centennial *(Producer)* 662
Forte, Mozelle *(Costumes)* 279
Fortenberry, Philip *(Cast)* 1349
Forteppe, Bob *(Author)* 831
Fortesque, George *(Cast)* 2524
Fortesque, George K. *(Cast)* 3828
Fortier, Bob *(Cast)* 2797
Fortier, Daniel *(Cast)* 3202
Fortis, John *(Composer)* 1782, 2098, 2099
Fortis, John *(Lyricist)* 2098, 2099
Fortune, John *(Cast)* 1195
Fortus, Daniel *(Cast)* 1002, 2874, 2925, 2969, 4480
Forwood, Luke *(Composer)* 675
Foss, Harlan *(Cast)* 2839
Fosse, Bob *(Cast)* 961, 2707
Fosse, Bob *(Choreographer)* 363, 393, 723, 837, 957, 964, 2019, 2523, 2558, 3113, 3351, 3506, 3526, 3687, 4238
Fosse, Bob *(Director)* 393, 723, 837, 964, 2523, 2558, 3506, 3526, 3687, 4238
Fosse, Bob *(Librettist)* 393, 723, 3506
Foster *(Composer)* 2454
Foster *(Lyricist)* 2454
Foster, Allan K.
See also Foster Girls, Allan K.
Foster, Allan K. *(Choreographer)* 487, 764, 771, 1016, 1065, 1334, 1345, 1404, 1530, 1557, 1723, 1823, 2020, 2108, 2258, 2384, 2419, 2665, 2684, 2706, 2747, 2794, 2816, 2939, 3051, 3087, 3400, 3401, 3403, 3405, 3406, 3434, 3677, 3737, 3778, 3821, 3958, 3962, 4063, 4121, 4296, 4528, 4654
Foster, Allan K. *(Director)* 2870, 3649, 4104
Foster, Allan K. *(Producer)* 2034
Foster, Allen *(Orchestrations)* 1011
Foster, Charles *(Cast)* 3337
Foster, Claiborne *(Author)* 423
Foster, Gae *(Choreographer)* 1840, 3100, 4006
Foster, Gae *(Director)* 4006
Foster, George *(Choreographer)* 2080, 2482
Foster, J.D. *(Incidental Music)* 264
Foster, J.D. *(Musical Director)* 264
Foster, John *(Composer)* 4488
Foster, Judy *(Cast)* 4785
Foster, Margaret *(Composer)* 2876
Foster, Margaret *(Musical Director)* 2876
Foster, Norman *(Cast)* 2265
Foster, Oliver *(Cast)* 488
Foster, Peg *(Musical Director)* 2664
Foster, Phoebe *(Cast)* 763, 1517
Foster, Stephen *(Composer)* 1897, 2415, 3989, 4149
Foster, Stephen *(Lyricist)* 110, 1897, 2415, 3989, 4149
Foster, Stephen (Music Based On) 110
Foster & Marino *(Producer)* 14
Foster Girls, Allan K.
See also Foster, Allan K.
Foster Girls, Allen K. *(Cast)* 3150
Fote, Dee Dee *(Costumes)* 337
Fountain, Clarence *(Cast)* 1636
Fountain, William *(Cast)* 739, 980
Fountaine, William *(Cast)* 567
Four Bruises, The *(Cast)* 4143
Four Esquires *(Cast)* 855
Four Flash Devils *(Cast)* 3965
Four Lads, The *(Cast)* 4155
Four Mills Brothers
See also Mills Brothers.
Four Mills Brothers *(Cast)* 1986
4 Step Brothers, The *(Cast)* 886
Foursome, The *(Cast)* 1528
Fowler, A.N.C. *(Librettist)* 4293
Fowler, Beth *(Cast)* 253, 330, 1496, 2536, 2643, 2766, 3555, 4297
Fowler, Edwin *(Cast)* 2717
Fowler, Gene *(Author)* 1672, 2217
Fowler, Gertrude *(Cast)* 1795
Fowler, Lemuel *(Composer)* 3963
Fowler, Lemuel *(Lyricist)* 3963
Fowler, Scott *(Cast)* 36, 3682
Fowler, Wally *(Composer)* 4030
Fowler, Wally *(Lyricist)* 4030
Fowles, Glenys *(Cast)* 2839

Fownes, Henry *(Producer)* 1848
Fox, Carol *(Cast)* 4433
Fox, Chester *(Producer)* 3169, 3873
Fox, Della *(Cast)* 1305, 2515, 2548, 3360, 3744, 4614, 4624
Fox, Dorothy *(Cast)* 3365, 3990
Fox, Ed *(Producer)* 1658
Fox, Edna *(Vocal Arranger)* 2453
Fox, Elizabeth *(Cast)* 2455
Fox, Fontaine *(Librettist)* 199
Fox, Frederick *(Lighting Designer)* 3874, 3894
Fox, Frederick *(Set Design)* 23, 1815, 2395, 2707, 2751, 3314, 3841, 3874, 3894, 3947
Fox, George *(Cast)* 2902
Fox, Harry *(Cast)* 1332, 1488, 1963, 2696, 3246, 3395, 3783, 4158, 4860
Fox, Herschel *(Cast)* 2421
Fox, James *(Set Design)* 1458
Fox, Janet *(Cast)* 1342, 1894, 3931
Fox, Jay *(Choreographer)* 1450
Fox, Kevin *(Cast)* 1969
Fox, Lou *(Composer)* 1658
Fox, Lou *(Lyricist)* 1658
Fox, Manheim *(Producer)* 4091
Fox, Maxine *(Producer)* 1664, 3330
Fox, Nancy *(Cast)* 3888
Fox, Patrick *(Cast)* 459, 4659
Fox, Patrick *(Composer)* 459
Fox, Patrick *(Lyricist)* 459
Fox, Patrick *(Musical Director)* 459
Fox, Rick *(Musical Director)* 460, 1079
Fox, Sonny *(Producer)* 4272
Fox, William *(Cast)* 3974
Fox, William *(Producer)* 1531
Fox Theatricals *(Producer)* 2198
Foy, Bryan *(Composer)* 2363
Foy, Cathy *(Cast)* 4076
Foy, Edwin *(Cast)* 4181
Foy, Gloria *(Cast)* 381, 771, 4050, 4529, 4844
Foy, Ken *(Set Design)* 533, 535
Foy, Kenneth *(Set Design)* 3548, 3722, 4136
Foy Jr., Eddie *(Cast)* 216, 672, 1076, 1395, 1577, 2975, 3182, 3273, 3314, 3351, 3721, 3801, 3953, 4023
Foy Sr., Eddie *(Cast)* 175, 476, 1123, 1994, 2974, 2978, 3228, 3313, 3332, 3488, 4521, 4691
Foyer, Bernie *(Producer)* 3895
Fracht, J. Albert *(Librettist)* 227
Fraction, Edward *(Cast)* 4254
Fradkin, Phil *(Musical Director)* 4292
Fradrich, James *(Composer)* 3201
Fradrich, James *(Librettist)* 3201
Fradrich, James *(Musical Director)* 1508
Fradrich, James *(Orchestrations)* 2776
Fradrich, James *(Vocal Arranger)* 1508
Fradrich, Jim *(Musical Director)* 1412
Fradrich, Jim *(Orchestrations)* 1412
Fradrich, Jim *(Vocal Arranger)* 1412
Fram, Joel *(Musical Director)* 2224
Frame, Grazina *(Cast)* 455
Franbau, Ella *(Cast)* 1657
France, Millard *(Set Design)* 2455
France, Richard *(Cast)* 603, 1567
France, Wesley *(Lighting Designer)* 209
Francell, Jacqueline *(Cast)* 2323
Frances, Arlene *(Cast)* 2653
Franceschina, John *(Musical Director)* 708, 2114
Franceschina, John *(Vocal Arranger)* 314
Franchi, Sergio *(Cast)* 1060
Francillion *(Costumes)* 3924
Francine, Anne *(Cast)* 550, 603, 2653, 2898, 4035, 4541
Francioli, Signor *(Choreographer)* 357, 2116
Franciosa, Massimo *(Librettist)* 3798
Francis, Adele *(Cast)* 2895
Francis, Alfred *(Composer)* 2619
Francis, Allan *(Producer)* 1762
Francis, Arlene *(Cast)* 979, 2060
Francis, Arthur
See also Ira Gershwin.
Francis, Dick *(Cast)* 277, 4341, 4361
Francis, Dorothy *(Cast)* 930, 2622, 4212
Francis, Emma *(Cast)* 4465
Francis, Helen *(Cast)* 524
Francis, James *(Director)* 1274
Francis, Mamie *(Cast)* 2413
Francis, May *(Cast)* 1114
Francis, Mme. *(Costumes)* 152, 396, 2667, 2923, 4195, 4283, 4296, 4716, 4813
Francis, Noel *(Cast)* 4621
Francis, W.T. *(Composer)* 675, 954, 1067, 1569, 1927, 2515, 3753, 3856, 3857, 3951
Francis, W.T. *(Lyricist)* 3857
Francis, W.T. *(Musical Director)* 1067, 1569, 2341, 3092, 3322
Francis, William *(Cast)* 1590
Francis, William T. *(Composer)* 675, 1318, 3790, 4478, 4681
Francis, William T. *(Musical Director)* 675, 3790, 3857
Francisco, William *(Choreographer)* 3925
Francisco, William *(Composer)* 3835
Francisco, William *(Director)* 3763, 3835, 3925
Franck, Nelly *(Cast)* 1413
Franck, Nelly *(Composer)* 3698
Francks, Don *(Cast)* 2304
Franco, Abel *(Cast)* 4861
Franco, Ramon *(Cast)* 4205
Frandsen, Erik *(Cast)* 4076
Frandsen, Erik *(Composer)* 4076
Frandsen, Erik *(Librettist)* 4076
Frandsen, Erik *(Lyricist)* 4076
Frangipane, Ronald *(Orchestrations)* 406
Frank, Allen *(Cast)* 3495
Frank, Anne *(Author)* 4790
Frank, Arthur *(Musical Director)* 2169
Frank, Ben *(Cast)* 2321
Frank, Benno D. *(Director)* 3439
Frank, David *(Musical Director)* 3902, 4450
Frank, David *(Orchestrations)* 3902
Frank, Dottie *(Cast)* 3111
Frank, Doug *(Composer)* 2754
Frank, Doug *(Lyricist)* 2754
Frank, Erle *(Costumes)* 3185

Frank, Gerald *(Librettist)* 4678
Frank, Gerri-Ann *(Cast)* 1269, 2356
Frank, Judy *(Cast)* 3209
Frank, Larry *(Composer)* 1380
Frank, Larry *(Librettist)* 1380
Frank, Larry *(Lyricist)* 1380
Frank, Melvin *(Author)* 652
Frank, Melvin *(Librettist)* 2301, 2484
Frank, Melvin *(Producer)* 2484
Frank, Paul *(Author)* 2594
Frank, Ruella *(Choreographer)* 729
Frank, Sherman *(Musical Director)* 837, 3493, 3551
Frank, Willie *(Producer)* 2168
Frank, Yasha *(Director)* 1744, 3495
Frank, Yasha *(Librettist)* 1744, 3495, 3496
Frank Productions *(Producer)* 634, 1698, 3016, 3526, 4579
Frankel, Gene *(Director)* 3159
Frankel, Jerry *(Producer)* 2198
Frankel, Kenneth *(Director)* 753, 4109
Frankel, Leo *(Cast)* 340
Frankel, Richard *(Producer)* 573, 992, 4031, 4076
Frankel, Scott *(Musical Director)* 4067
Franken, Steve *(Cast)* 408
Franklin, Barbara *(Cast)* 3818
Franklin, Bessie *(Cast)* 2966, 4425
Franklin, Bonnie *(Cast)* 167, 752, 1093
Franklin, Edgar S. *(Author)* 2527
Franklin, Frederic *(Cast)* 4075
Franklin, Harold B. *(Producer)* 839, 841, 3699
Franklin, Hazel *(Cast)* 2089
Franklin, Irene *(Cast)* 1687, 1735, 3313, 3401, 4203, 4234
Franklin, Irene *(Lyricist)* 2816, 4203, 4234
Franklin, J.E. *(Librettist)* 3599
Franklin, J.E. *(Lyricist)* 3599
Franklin, Judy *(Cast)* 752
Franklin, Malvin *(Composer)* 1014, 4687
Franklin, Malvin *(Lyricist)* 1014
Franklin, Malvin *(Musical Director)* 1014
Franklin, Malvin F. *(Composer)* 60, 1911, 2574, 4033
Franklin, Malvin F. *(Lyricist)* 4687
Franklin, Malvin M. *(Composer)* 2486, 2574, 4033
Franklin, Nat *(Cast)* 1647
Franklin, Tony *(Cast)* 1053, 1103
Franklin, William *(Cast)* 651, 4254
Franklyn, Beth *(Cast)* 3910
Franklyn, Blanche *(Lyricist)* 1404
Franks, Danny *(Lighting Designer)* 658
Franks, Dobbs *(Musical Director)* 2322
Franks, Laurie *(Cast)* 1435, 4232, 4537
Fransworth, Scott *(Librettist)* 1884
Franz, Al *(Cast)* 319
Franz, Elizabeth *(Cast)* 4768
Franz, Joy *(Cast)* 212, 2049, 2143, 2988, 3019, 4412
Franzell, Carlotta *(Cast)* 653
Fraser, Alec *(Cast)* 2514
Fraser, Alex *(Cast)* 3663
Fraser, Alison *(Cast)* 338, 2746, 3760, 3862, 4403, 4518
Fraser, Ann *(Cast)* 1648
Fraser, George *(Composer)* 1887
Fraser, Ian *(Dance Arranger)* 3846
Fraser, Ian *(Musical Director)* 695, 3454, 3482, 4560
Fraser, Ian *(Orchestrations)* 4160
Fraser, Ian *(Vocal Arranger)* 3482, 3846, 4560
Fraser, J.A. *(Librettist)* 3298
Fraser, Jane *(Cast)* 3353
Fraser, Jean *(Lyricist)* 1134
Fraser, Ronald *(Cast)* 2362
Fraser, Sally *(Cast)* 752
Fraser-Simpson, Harold *(Composer)* 2698, 3634
Fratantoni, Diane *(Cast)* 275
Fratti, Mario *(Librettist)* 3171
Frawley, James *(Cast)* 162
Frawley, Mark *(Cast)* 3239
Frawley, Paul *(Cast)* 638, 815, 1819, 1856, 2336, 2734, 3006, 3222, 4212, 4360, 4426, 4443
Frawley, T. Daniel *(Director)* 3562
Frawley, William *(Cast)* 608, 1859, 2709, 2833, 3924, 4087, 4276, 4299
Fray, Jacques *(Cast)* 4545
Fray, Jacques *(Composer)* 3172, 4545
Frazee, H.H. *(Director)* 3048, 3184
Frazee, H.H. *(Producer)* 1746, 2145, 2261, 2667, 2670, 3048, 3184, 4761, 4766
Frazee, Jane
See also Frazee Sisters.
Frazee, Jane *(Cast)* 2460
Frazee, Marion *(Costumes)* 2789
Frazee Sisters, The
See also Jane Frazee.
Frazee Sisters, The *(Cast)* 417, 420
Frazier, Grenoldo *(Cast)* 2932
Frazier, Grenoldo *(Composer)* 2932
Frazier, Grenoldo *(Lyricist)* 2932
Frazier, Michael *(Producer)* 1186, 1425, 1699, 1865, 2702, 4347
Fredena Productions *(Producer)* 1596
Frederic, Helen *(Cast)* 3586
Frederick, Helena *(Cast)* 4311
Frederick, Jean *(Lyricist)* 200
Frederick, Lee *(Cast)* 117
Frederick, Pauline *(Cast)* 2160, 3588, 3745
Fredericks, Charles *(Cast)* 3013
Fredericks, Chester *(Cast)* 1461, 4209
Fredericks, Rita *(Producer)* 482
Fredericks, William *(Cast)* 2055
Frederickson, Carl *(Composer)* 2115
Fredhoven, Hans (Pianist) 3290
Fredhoven, John *(Musical Director)* 1670
Fredrik, Burry *(Director)* 1017, 4689
Fredrik, Burry *(Producer)* 3565, 3787
Free Space Ltd. *(Producer)* 2968
Freeborn, Cassius *(Cast)* 3384
Freeborn, Cassius *(Composer)* 1907, 2717, 3910
Freeborn, Cassius *(Musical Director)* 1922, 2485, 3910
Freed, Alan *(Composer)* 4264
Freed, Alan *(Lyricist)* 4264
Freed, Arthur *(Composer)* 69, 196, 544, 1298, 1777, 1942, 1944, 1946, 3349
Freed, Arthur *(Lyricist)* 69, 196, 393, 544, 1638, 1777, 1942, 1944, 1946, 2215, 3349, 3973, 3992
Freed, Cathy *(Cast)* 2092
Freed, Ralph *(Lyricist)* 3175, 3374

Freed, Sam *(Cast)* 4635
Freedley, Vinton *(Cast)* 977, 1174, 1345, 2897, 3319, 4437
Freedley, Vinton *(Composer)* 1863
Freedley, Vinton *(Director)* 3379
Freedley, Vinton *(Producer)* 163, 612, 971, 1419, 1528, 1679, 1683, 1800, 1859, 1929, 2187, 2376, 2432, 2453, 3243, 3379, 3674, 3993, 4118, 4392, 4443
Freedley Jr., Vinton *(Cast)* 4039
Freedman, Betty *(Librettist)* 3527
Freedman, Danny *(Cast)* 1695
Freedman, David *(Librettist)* 376, 418, 2475, 3955, 4235, 4667, 4824, 4825
Freedman, Gerald *(Choreographer)* 1439
Freedman, Gerald *(Director)* 112, 693, 807, 1439, 1456, 1660, 2726, 3733, 3825, 4089, 4384, 4615
Freedman, Gerald *(Librettist)* 2097, 4384
Freedman, Gerald *(Lyricist)* 2097, 4384
Freedman, Louis *(Librettist)* 343
Freedman, Max *(Composer)* 3739
Freedman, Max *(Lyricist)* 3739
Freedman, Melvin H. *(Librettist)* 3697
Freedman, Melvin H. *(Lyricist)* 3697
Freedman, Robert M. *(Orchestrations)* 550, 952, 1914, 2689, 2898, 3088, 3656, 4288
Freeman, Arny *(Cast)* 1991, 2975, 3000, 3175, 4633, 4744
Freeman, Bud
See also Bud Freeman's Summa Cum Laude Band.
Freeman, Bud *(Author)* 339
Freeman, Bud *(Librettist)* 339
Freeman, Bud *(Lyricist)* 339
Freeman, Charles K. *(Director)* 4075
Freeman, Charles K. *(Librettist)* 616
Freeman, Damita Jo *(Cast)* 3515
Freeman, Everett *(Librettist)* 4798
Freeman, Gladys *(Cast)* 4220
Freeman, Grace *(Cast)* 906, 3759
Freeman, H. Lawrence *(Composer)* 645, 3358
Freeman, Harry *(Composer)* 4723
Freeman, Harry *(Lyricist)* 4723
Freeman, Howard *(Cast)* 1991, 2344
Freeman, Jay *(Musical Director)* 4006
Freeman, Jonathan E. *(Cast)* 3498
Freeman, Jonathan E. *(Puppeteer)* 4660
Freeman, K. Todd *(Producer)* 4074
Freeman, Kathleen *(Cast)* 2057, 4408
Freeman, L.E. *(Composer)* 1813, 4743
Freeman, L.E. *(Lyricist)* 1813, 4743
Freeman, Louis *(Librettist)* 2352
Freeman, Max *(Cast)* 1193, 1553, 3784
Freeman, Max *(Director)* 457, 559, 639, 734, 1594, 1896, 2179, 2326, 2507, 2632, 2673, 2963, 3732, 3784, 4236, 4500
Freeman, Max *(Librettist)* 2507
Freeman, Morgan *(Cast)* 166, 1636
Freeman, Pauline *(Cast)* 4451
Freeman, Stan *(Composer)* 2053, 2626
Freeman, Stan *(Lyricist)* 2053, 2626
Freeman, Steven *(Musical Director)* 3202
Freeman, Stu *(Cast)* 1769
Freeman, Vera *(Cast)* 3467
Freeman, Virginia *(Choreographer)* 143, 699
Freeman Jr., Al *(Cast)* 477, 1671, 2306, 2583
Freeman's Summa Cum Laude Band, Bud
See also Bud Freeman.
Freeman's Summa Cum Laude, Bud *(Cast)* 4256
Frees, Paul *(Cast)* 928, 3833
Freidland, Anatole *(Composer)* 4422
Freiman, L. *(Author)* 3669
Freirson, Andrea *(Cast)* 3285
Freisinger, Mme. *(Costumes)* 379, 1469, 2159, 3078, 3519, 4801, 4802
Freitag, Dorothea (Arrangements) 3656
Freitag, Dorothea *(Cast)* 3900
Freitag, Dorothea *(Composer)* 722, 2772
Freitag, Dorothea *(Dance Arranger)* 1012, 1441, 1892, 2075, 2318, 2772, 2804, 4435, 4702, 4862
Freitag, Dorothea *(Musical Director)* 722, 840, 2772, 2918, 3186, 3940
Freitag, Dorothea *(Orchestrations)* 722, 3940
Freitag, Dorothea (Pianist) 1892, 2439, 3186
Freitag, Dorothea *(Vocal Arranger)* 2439, 2772, 3186
Freitas, Richard *(Composer)* 1046
Freitas, Richard *(Musical Director)* 1046
Freitas, Richard *(Orchestrations)* 1046
Fremont, Rob *(Composer)* 3476
Fremont, Rob *(Librettist)* 3476
French, Adelaide *(Librettist)* 3344
French, Arthur *(Cast)* 40, 1592, 2719
French, Bert *(Choreographer)* 385, 465, 728, 1174, 1580, 1794, 2216, 2276, 2494, 2549, 2569, 2698, 2756, 3006, 4378, 4464, 4529
French, Bert *(Costumes)* 3712
French, Bert *(Director)* 560, 1582, 1819, 1961, 4283, 4529
French, Charles K. *(Cast)* 2029
French, Harold *(Cast)* 2467
French, Hugh *(Cast)* 3885
French, Jack *(Musical Director)* 2558, 3936
French, Larry *(Cast)* 2703
French, Leslie *(Cast)* 4479
French, Leslie *(Choreographer)* 4479
French, Pauline *(Cast)* 1851
French, Percy *(Cast)* 1013
French, Rick *(Lyricist)* 95
French, T.R. *(Producer)* 1576
Freschi, Bob *(Cast)* 1955
Fresco, Al *(Cast)* 3361
Fresnay, Pierre *(Cast)* 841, 3216
Frett, Kenneth *(Cast)* 4584
Freund, Julius *(Author)* 3627
Frey, Blanche *(Cast)* 1457
Frey, Fran *(Cast)* 4683
Frey, Fran *(Orchestrations)* 3381
Frey, Fran *(Vocal Arranger)* 3381
Frey, Hugo *(Composer)* 1173, 1308, 3313
Frey, Hugo *(Musical Director)* 88, 1593, 2835
Frey, Leonard *(Cast)* 790, 2568
Frey, Nathaniel *(Cast)* 957, 1158, 1280, 1614, 3918, 4432, 4446
Freydberg, James B. *(Producer)* 253, 4349
Freyer, Frederick *(Composer)* 647
Freyer, Frederick *(Vocal Arranger)* 647
Freyman, Evelyn *(Producer)* 1734

Friberg, Carl *(Composer)* 3112
Frick, Mr. *(Cast)* 2083, 2084
Frick and Frack *(Cast)* 2085, 2086, 2088, 2089, 2090
Friebus, Florida *(Cast)* 55
Friebus, Florida *(Librettist)* 55
Friebus, Theodore *(Cast)* 3560
Fried, Barbara *(Lyricist)* 1955, 4338
Fried, Kenneth *(Composer)* 1836
Fried, Kenneth *(Lyricist)* 1836
Fried, Martin *(Musical Director)* 637
Fried, Walter *(Producer)* 2450
Friedberg, Billy *(Librettist)* 2554
Friedberg, William *(Librettist)* 23, 743, 1815, 2837, 3841
Friedland, Anatol *(Composer)* 2858
Friedland, Anatole *(Composer)* 558, 904, 1065, 1292, 1334, 3446, 4687
Friedlander, Sylvia *(Costumes)* 4773
Friedlander, William B. *(Choreographer)* 1404
Friedlander, William B. *(Composer)* 1343, 1404, 2238, 2706, 2818, 2950, 3083, 3508, 4376
Friedlander, William B. *(Director)* 2238, 2818, 2950, 3168, 3489, 4100
Friedlander, William B. *(Librettist)* 2818
Friedlander, William B. *(Lyricist)* 1343, 1404, 2238, 2706, 2818, 2950, 3508, 4387
Friedlander, William B. *(Producer)* 2238, 3489, 3508, 4100
Friedlich, Kate *(Cast)* 4018, 4557
Friedman, Alan *(Composer)* 1233, 1436, 1438, 2279, 3484
Friedman, Alan *(Lyricist)* 1436, 1438, 2279
Friedman, Allan Jay *(Composer)* 3908
Friedman, Arthur *(Cast)* 283
Friedman, Bruce Jay *(Author)* 2965
Friedman, Bruce Jay *(Librettist)* 2965
Friedman, Charles *(Director)* 653, 2225, 3035, 3501, 3990, 4169
Friedman, Charles *(Librettist)* 3035, 3501, 3990
Friedman, Charles *(Lyricist)* 3035, 3501
Friedman, Charles *(Producer)* 3800
Friedman, David *(Librettist)* 2402
Friedman, David *(Musical Director)* 172, 508, 1591, 2242, 2283, 2539, 3838
Friedman, David *(Orchestrations)* 1786
Friedman, David *(Vocal Arranger)* 330, 508, 1591, 2539, 3838
Friedman, Gary William *(Author)* 4216
Friedman, Gary William *(Composer)* 535, 669, 1714, 2422, 2801, 3515, 4216, 4272
Friedman, Gary William *(Dance Arranger)* 2801
Friedman, Gary William *(Orchestrations)* 2801, 4216, 4272
Friedman, Gary William *(Vocal Arranger)* 535, 2801, 3515, 4216, 4272
Friedman, Joel Phillip *(Composer)* 3448
Friedman, Kim *(Director)* 2953
Friedman, Leo *(Composer)* 3581, 4799
Friedman, Lewis *(Producer)* 2470, 2852
Friedman, Louis *(Lyricist)* 2419
Friedman, Martin *(Lighting Designer)* 2633
Friedman, Peter *(Cast)* 2607
Friedman, Samuel J. *(Producer)* 2110
Friedman, Seth *(Composer)* 3448, 4533
Friedman, Seth *(Librettist)* 3448
Friedman, Seth *(Lyricist)* 3448, 4533
Friedman, Stephen R. *(Producer)* 150, 1955, 4744
Friedman, Susan *(Cast)* 2354
Friedman, Tracy *(Choreographer)* 2470, 2852
Friedman, Tracy *(Director)* 2852
Frieman, Max *(Director)* 2515
Friend, Cliff *(Composer)* 297, 391, 487, 1136, 1481, 1491, 2066, 2857, 3489, 3532, 3623, 4607, 4683
Friend, Cliff *(Lyricist)* 391, 487, 1136, 1491, 1643, 1689, 2857, 3623, 3907, 4322, 4573
Friend, John Edward *(Costumes)* 1885
Friend, John Edward *(Set Design)* 1885
Friend, William *(Cast)* 1646
Friends of Van Wolf Prods. *(Producer)* 4449
Fries, Catherine *(Cast)* 1059
Friesen, Dick (Arrangements) 2095
Friesen, Dick *(Composer)* 2084, 2092, 2093, 2094, 2095, 2096
Friesen, Dick *(Lyricist)* 2084, 2092, 2093, 2094, 2095, 2096
Friesen, Dick *(Orchestrations)* 2084, 2092
Friesen, John *(Orchestrations)* 2096
Friganza, Trixie *(Cast)* 115, 350, 628, 694, 2365, 2851, 3005, 3087, 3313, 3395, 4247, 4473
Frilling, Ednor *(Cast)* 1267
Friml, Rudolf *(Composer)* 102, 152, 234, 288, 385, 468, 765, 1033, 1285, 1442, 1580, 1888, 2121, 2264, 2292, 2340, 2549, 2636, 3011, 3020, 3172, 3179, 3424, 3772, 4063, 4357, 4464, 4539, 4664, 4692, 4784, 4815, 4817
Friml, Rudolf *(Librettist)* 4815
Friml, William *(Composer)* 1754, 2234
Frings, Ketti *(Author)* 135
Frings, Ketti *(Librettist)* 135, 4588
Friquet, Jules *(Musical Director)* 1902
Frisby, Terence *(Author)* 4329
Frisch, Billy *(Composer)* 1065
Frisch, Billy *(Lyricist)* 1065, 4824
Frisco, Joe *(Cast)* 1134, 1395, 4812
Frisco, Joe *(Librettist)* 1134
Fritzke, Michael *(Cast)* 2356
Froehlich, Rico *(Cast)* 108, 223, 519, 2961, 3696
Frohman, Charles *(Producer)* 100, 178, 205, 675, 719, 954, 1066, 1067, 1318, 1454, 1537, 1538, 1543, 1544, 1559, 1569, 1806, 1905, 2131, 2206, 2329, 2341, 2424, 2498, 2526, 2624, 2761, 2871, 2889, 2952, 3049, 3079, 3092, 3322, 3658, 3710, 3753, 3779, 3857, 3948, 3996, 4219, 4258, 4354
Frohman, Daniel *(Producer)* 515, 2315
Frolich, Otto *(Musical Director)* 1834
Froman, Jane *(Cast)* 204, 2301, 4824
Froman, Jay *(Cast)* 1754
Frondale, Pierre *(Librettist)* 165
Frontiere, Dominic *(Orchestrations)* 3428
Frontiere, Georgia *(Producer)* 3428
Froos, Sylvia *(Cast)* 1462
Frost, Jack *(Composer)* 2298, 4393
Frost, Jack *(Lyricist)* 560, 4197, 4393
Frost, Russell *(Cast)* 1556
Frost, Sue *(Producer)* 595, 1997, 2289

Frost, Thomas *(Lyricist)* 2824
Frothingham, George *(Cast)* 3570, 3736, 3881
Frothingham, George B. *(Cast)* 1768, 2697
Fry, Alex *(Composer)* 1062
Fry, Christopher *(Author)* 1294
Fry, Stephen *(Librettist)* 2798
Frye, Dwight *(Cast)* 4001
Frye, Dwight *(Producer)* 4731
Frye, Edward *(Cast)* 4253
Fryer, Robert *(Producer)* 603, 723, 1068, 1991, 2713, 2822, 3687, 3837, 3913, 4233, 4238, 4734
Fuchs, Isadore *(Author)* 3625
Fuchs, Leo *(Cast)* 343
Fuchs, Peter *(Musical Director)* 1974
Fuchs, Peter *(Vocal Arranger)* 1974
Fuerst, Jim *(Lyricist)* 3110
Fujii, Timm *(Cast)* 3340
Fuller, Charles *(Librettist)* 4535
Fuller, Dean *(Composer)* 943, 1734, 2168, 2246, 3108, 3286, 3524, 4029, 4585, 4828, 4829
Fuller, Dean *(Dance Arranger)* 2680
Fuller, Dean *(Librettist)* 3288, 4029
Fuller, Dean *(Lyricist)* 3286
Fuller, Dean *(Vocal Arranger)* 1734, 4029
Fuller, Edward *(Cast)* 3986
Fuller, Frances *(Cast)* 1850, 2060
Fuller, James *(Composer)* 3695
Fuller, James *(Lyricist)* 3695
Fuller, Jerry *(Composer)* 3695
Fuller, Jerry *(Lyricist)* 3695
Fuller, Larry *(Choreographer)* 461, 1068, 1211, 1638, 1837, 2152, 2198, 2822, 3279, 4233
Fuller, Larry *(Director)* 1638, 1837, 2598
Fuller, Lorenzo *(Cast)* 1278, 2331, 4750
Fuller, Lorenzo *(Composer)* 2580, 4102, 4750
Fuller, Lorenzo *(Dance Arranger)* 2580
Fuller, Lorenzo *(Librettist)* 4750
Fuller, Lorenzo *(Lyricist)* 4102, 4750
Fuller, Lorenzo *(Musical Director)* 2580
Fuller, Lorenzo *(Vocal Arranger)* 2580
Fuller, Molly *(Cast)* 1599
Fuller, Paul *(Musical Director)* 2896
Fuller, Paul Fairfax *(Composer)* 2896
Fuller, Paul Fairfax *(Librettist)* 2896
Fuller, Paul Fairfax *(Lyricist)* 2896
Fuller, Penny *(Cast)* 167, 3702
Fullerton, Joyce *(Cast)* 1201
Fullum, Clay *(Dance Arranger)* 3780
Fullum, Clay *(Musical Director)* 583, 599, 1809, 1914, 2134, 2418, 4618
Fullum, Clay *(Orchestrations)* 2418
Fullum, Clay *(Vocal Arranger)* 599
Fulton, Maude *(Cast)* 632, 1417, 2779, 3313, 3738
Funking, Bob *(Producer)* 2231
Fuqua, Harvey *(Composer)* 4264
Fuqua, Harvey *(Lyricist)* 4264
Fuqua, V.C. *(Lighting Designer)* 2663, 3551
Furber, Douglas *(Author)* 2972
Furber, Douglas *(Cast)* 133, 702
Furber, Douglas *(Librettist)* 1333, 2004, 2798, 3139, 4320
Furber, Douglas *(Lyricist)* 25, 133, 292, 702, 704, 1333, 2004, 2570, 2798, 3139, 3532, 3924, 4320, 4581
Furlow, Brown *(Composer)* 2560
Furlow, Brown *(Lyricist)* 2560, 4273
Furman, Ariel *(Cast)* 2811
Furman, John *(Cast)* 1871
Furse, Roger *(Costumes)* 3482
Furst, William *(Composer)* 1305, 2156, 2548, 3199, 4671
Furth, George *(Author)* 4474
Furth, George *(Cast)* 1363
Furth, George *(Librettist)* 16, 832, 2822
Furth, George *(Lyricist)* 4474
Furth, Seymour *(Composer)* 539, 1464, 1523, 2498, 2869, 2996, 3085, 3203, 3313, 3387, 3417, 3753, 4094, 4104, 4723, 4757, 4801, 4805
Furth, Seymour *(Lyricist)* 3085
Futrelle, Virginia *(Cast)* 378
Futterman, Enid *(Librettist)* 3544, 4790
Futterman, Enid *(Lyricist)* 3544, 4790
Fyfe, Jim *(Cast)* 2437, 3598
Fyffe, Will *(Cast)* 1137
Fyleman, Rose *(Lyricist)* 4335
Fysher, Nilson *(Lyricist)* 4807

G

Gabel, Martin *(Cast)* 270, 979, 2257
Gabel, Martin *(Librettist)* 4141
Gaberman, Alexander *(Cast)* 3456
Gabhardt, George *(Lighting Designer)* 1299
Gable, Christopher *(Cast)* 1619
Gable, June *(Cast)* 829, 1002, 2375, 3080, 3195, 4595
Gable, Martin *(Cast)* 4141
Gabler, Milt *(Composer)* 1296, 4264
Gabler, Milt *(Lyricist)* 1296, 4264
Gabor, Eva *(Cast)* 3816
Gabriel, Master *(Cast)* 591, 2461, 2534, 4242
Gabrielle, Caryl *(Librettist)* 1010
Gabrielle, Caryl *(Lyricist)* 1010
Gabrielson, Frank *(Librettist)* 2105, 2475, 3365
Gabrielson, Frank *(Lyricist)* 1710
Gabrilov, Alexander *(Choreographer)* 1691
Gaburo, Kenneth *(Composer)* 4380
Gaby, Frank *(Cast)* 200, 551, 1461, 1462, 3133
Gaby, Frank *(Producer)* 1462
Gae, Nadine *(Cast)* 3292, 4826
Gaebler, Mary *(Cast)* 753
Gage, Gary *(Cast)* 1093, 4062, 4796
Gage, Lila *(Cast)* 616
Gagel, Frederick *(Composer)* 1661, 2963
Gagliano, Frank *(Author)* 3370
Gagliano, Frank *(Lyricist)* 3370
Gagnon, Roland *(Musical Director)* 1755, 4004
Gaige, Crosby *(Producer)* 1187, 1196, 2060
Gaige, Truman *(Cast)* 110, 948, 1119, 1511, 3011, 3837, 4670, 4777, 4798
Gail, Janet *(Cast)* 2682
Gaillard, Francis *(Cast)* 526

Gaines, David *(Musical Director)* 3181
Gaines, Frederick *(Librettist)* 2001
Gaines, Frederick *(Lyricist)* 2001
Gaines, Lee *(Lyricist)* 2259, 4091
Gaines, Muriel *(Cast)* 467
Gaines, Sam *(Cast)* 3041
Gaites, Joseph *(Director)* 4269
Gaites, Joseph M. *(Producer)* 531, 1088, 1183, 1558, 2291, 2623, 3613, 4269, 4322, 4364, 4528
Gaither, David S. *(Set Design)* 2423
Gaither, Gant *(Producer)* 3899
Gal, Riki *(Cast)* 1075
Galantich, Tom *(Cast)* 2674
Galarno, Bill *(Librettist)* 1347
Galde, Anthony *(Cast)* 3576
Gale, Edwin *(Lyricist)* 2402
Gale, Jack *(Orchestrations)* 314, 2598
Gale, Nita *(Cast)* 27
Gale, Sandra *(Cast)* 4335
Gale Quadruplets, The *(Cast)* 1323, 1492
Galjour, Warren *(Cast)* 4734
Gallagher, David *(Composer)* 2022
Gallagher, Dick *(Composer)* 1785
Gallagher, Dick *(Librettist)* 2022
Gallagher, Dick *(Lyricist)* 1785, 2022
Gallagher, Ed *(Cast)* 1432, 3771, 4816
Gallagher, Ed *(Composer)* 4816
Gallagher, Ed *(Lyricist)* 4816
Gallagher, Edward *(Cast)* 1404, 2112
Gallagher, Helen *(Cast)* 404, 530, 935, 1791, 1886, 2049, 2705, 2877, 2928, 3543, 3893, 4238, 4279, 4379, 4432
Gallagher, Jennifer *(Set Design)* 1740
Gallagher, Larry *(Director)* 338
Gallagher, Larry *(Librettist)* 338
Gallagher, Laura *(Cast)* 2076
Gallagher, Micky *(Composer)* 3884
Gallagher, Peter *(Cast)* 1068
Gallagher, Richard "Skeets" *(Cast)* 2638
Gallagher, Skeets *(Cast)* 773, 1884, 1939, 2691, 2757, 3434, 4528, 4529
Gallardo, Edward *(Librettist)* 3456
Gallaudet, John *(Cast)* 1440, 1856
Gallegher, John *(Librettist)* 1108
Gallegher, John *(Lyricist)* 1108
Gallegly, David *(Cast)* 508
Gallen, Judy *(Set Design)* 2945
Gallico, Paul *(Author)* 656, 2989, 3287
Gallico, Paul *(Librettist)* 2909
Gallico, Robert *(Composer)* 4336
Galligan, David *(Director)* 450
Gallimore, Catherine *(Cast)* 202
Gallin, Sandy *(Producer)* 695
Gallis, Paul *(Set Design)* 949
Gallo, Paul *(Lighting Designer)* 212, 775, 829, 921, 1418, 2359, 3070, 4020, 4390
Galloway, Jane *(Cast)* 4358
Galloway, Leata *(Cast)* 2033, 3741, 4089, 4615
Galloway, Louise *(Cast)* 1852, 2639, 3655
Gallup, Sammy *(Lyricist)* 67, 2227
Galonka, Arlene *(Cast)* 4270
Galster, Robert *(Set Design)* 817
Galvin, Gene *(Costumes)* 3239
Gam, Rita *(Cast)* 4329
Gamache, Laurie *(Cast)* 589, 3682
Gambarelli, Maria *(Cast)* 858
Gammon, James *(Cast)* 2468
Gampel, Chris *(Cast)* 1294
Ganeau, Wilda *(Cast)* 293
Gang, Lydia Pincus *(Costumes)* 4396
Gangi, Jamie Dawn *(Cast)* 3461
Gannaway, Lynne *(Choreographer)* 426, 2285
Gannaway, Lynne *(Director)* 4176
Ganne, Louis *(Author)* 1743
Ganne, Louis *(Composer)* 466
Ganne, M. Louis *(Composer)* 1743
Gannon, Kim *(Lyricist)* 3895
Gannon, Paul *(Cast)* 2085, 2086, 2087, 2089, 2091
Ganon, David *(Director)* 2488
Ganor, Warwick *(Cast)* 3176
Gant, H.C. *(Librettist)* 1541
Gant, Rosemary *(Lighting Designer)* 1435
Gantry, Don *(Cast)* 1184
Gantvoort, Carl *(Cast)* 2546
Garber, Victor *(Cast)* 212, 3852, 4233
Garde, Betty *(Cast)* 32, 3263, 4043
Gardella, Tess *(Cast)* 1484, 2504, 3949
Gardenia, Vincent *(Cast)* 287
Gardenier, Ed *(Lyricist)* 3745, 3747, 3748, 3749, 3855
Gardes, George *(Cast)* 1915
Gardiner, Frank *(Cast)* 1121, 1466
Gardiner, James W. *(Producer)* 180, 3509, 4827
Gardiner, Reginald *(Cast)* 216, 3955
Gardiner, Reginald *(Librettist)* 216
Gardner, Aaron *(Producer)* 1878
Gardner, Ann *(Cast)* 634
Gardner, Brenda *(Cast)* 3059
Gardner, Gary *(Librettist)* 2783
Gardner, Gary *(Lyricist)* 2783
Gardner, Helene *(Cast)* 4212
Gardner, Henry D. *(Cast)* 1274
Gardner, Herb *(Librettist)* 3299
Gardner, Herb *(Lyricist)* 3299
Gardner, Hy *(Producer)* 1880
Gardner, Jack *(Cast)* 356, 742, 1318, 2667, 4277, 4759
Gardner, Lynn *(Cast)* 4640
Gardner, Nat *(Composer)* 1982
Gardner, Rick *(Cast)* 2114
Gardner, Rita *(Cast)* 1237, 1245, 2578, 3161, 4244, 4708
Gardner, Robert *(Composer)* 4093
Gardner, Robert *(Lyricist)* 4093
Gardner, Sam *(Cast)* 1479, 3040
Gardner, William H. *(Lyricist)* 2415
Gardner, Worth *(Composer)* 35
Gardner, Worth *(Director)* 3987
Garey, James R. *(Director)* 263, 1902
Garfein, Jack *(Director)* 1571, 3984
Garfield, David *(Cast)* 1736
Garfield, John *(Cast)* 2228, 4152
Garfinkle, Louis *(Librettist)* 2925
Gargan, Edward *(Cast)* 1225
Gari, Brian *(Composer)* 2420
Gari, Brian *(Lyricist)* 2420

Gari, Janet *(Composer)* 2657
Garin, Michael *(Cast)* 4076
Garin, Michael *(Composer)* 3076, 4076
Garin, Michael *(Librettist)* 4076
Garin, Michael *(Lyricist)* 3076, 4076
Garinei, Pietro *(Director)* 3798
Garinei, Pietro *(Librettist)* 3798
Garinei, Pietro *(Lyricist)* 3798
Garing, A.J. *(Musical Director)* 378, 1208, 1753
Garland, Jamil K. *(Cast)* 4645
Garland, Joe *(Composer)* 3018
Garland, Nicholas *(Director)* 1195
Garland, Patricia *(Cast)* 746
Garland, Robert *(Librettist)* 621
Garlid, Karl *(Cast)* 2124
Garlock, Tommy *(Composer)* 4566
Garlock, Tommy *(Lyricist)* 4153, 4566
Garn, Jack *(Choreographer)* 293
Garn, Jack *(Director)* 293
Garner, Jay *(Cast)* 374, 1161, 1634, 2319, 2360, 3684
Garner, Josie *(Costumes)* 4251
Garnett, Chip *(Cast)* 2539
Garnett, David *(Author)* 211
Garon, Jay *(Producer)* 33
Garr, Eddie *(Cast)* 2405, 2467, 4177, 4374
Garr, Stanton *(Cast)* 3004
Garrambone, Joe *(Cast)* 4168
Garreau, Claude *(Vocal Arranger)* 3966
Garrett, Betty *(Cast)* 339, 620, 2187, 2400, 2447, 2653, 2805, 3226, 4058, 4111
Garrett, Bob *(Composer)* 4171
Garrett, Bob *(Lyricist)* 4171
Garrett, Hank *(Cast)* 4627
Garrett, Joy *(Cast)* 1498
Garrett, Kelly *(Cast)* 2962, 3159, 4743
Garrett, Russell *(Cast)* 3346
Garrick, Beulah *(Cast)* 869, 2268
Garrick, David *(Author)* 1071
Garrick, John *(Cast)* 2540
Garrick, Kathy *(Cast)* 450
Garringer, Nelson *(Lyricist)* 3479
Garrison, David *(Cast)* 1000, 1597, 1914, 4034
Garrison, Sean *(Cast)* 1727, 1990
Garsia, Marston *(Cast)* 1610
Garson, M. *(Composer)* 4193
Garson, Toby *(Lyricist)* 2657
Garstin, Harold *(Composer)* 4719
Garth, Caswell *(Author)* 1680
Garth, Caswell *(Librettist)* 2547
Gartlan, Anne *(Cast)* 564
Gartlan, George H. *(Composer)* 2763, 2779, 4120
Gartlan, George H. *(Lyricist)* 2763
Garvie, Eddie *(Cast)* 1247, 1248, 1569, 2491, 2567, 3581, 4025
Garvie, Edward *(Cast)* 1925, 2695
Garwood, Patti *(Musical Director)* 3461
Gary, Harold *(Cast)* 2106, 2449
Gary, Romain *(Author)* 3792
Gary, Ted *(Cast)* 4142
Gary, Ted *(Choreographer)* 4287
Garza, Ronald *(Cast)* 4138
Garza, Troy *(Choreographer)* 1371, 1637
Gascoine, Jill *(Cast)* 3454
Gaskill, Clarence *(Composer)* 883, 896, 1131, 1378, 2296, 4683
Gaskill, Clarence *(Lyricist)* 437, 883, 896, 1131, 1378, 1460, 2296, 4683
Gasman, Ira *(Librettist)* 2473
Gasman, Ira *(Lyricist)* 2473, 4167, 4635
Gaspar, Marie *(Cast)* 4637
Gaspard, Ray *(Producer)* 2049
Gaspard, Raymond L. *(Producer)* 3901
Gasper, Eddie *(Cast)* 2523, 3526
Gasper, Eddie *(Choreographer)* 1273
Gass, Kyle *(Composer)* 655
Gaston, Billy *(Composer)* 246, 697, 2576, 3685, 4801
Gaston, Billy *(Lyricist)* 246, 697, 2576, 3685, 4801
Gaston, Ken *(Producer)* 181, 1809
Gaston, Lydia *(Cast)* 3682
Gaston, Penny *(Cast)* 3939
Gaston, William *(Lyricist)* 1780
Gatchell Jr., R. Tyler *(Producer)* 131
Gates, Aaron *(Producer)* 4183
Gates, Charles *(Cast)* 2492
Gates, Frank
See also Gates & Morange.
Gates, Frank *(Set Design)* 185, 376, 577, 749, 815, 1501, 1625, 1667, 2515, 2768, 2819, 2884, 3519, 3650, 3772, 3865, 3868, 4234, 4360, 4620, 4671, 4694, 4704, 4716, 4807
Gates, Frank E. *(Set Design)* 1243, 2326, 3228, 3774, 4705
Gates, Larry *(Cast)* 1200
Gates, Lewis *(Lyricist)* 4094
Gates, Terry *(Set Design)* 4003
Gates & Morange
See also Frank E. Gates and E.A. Morange.
Gates & Morange *(Set Design)* 3073, 3675, 4818, 4819
Gateson, Marjorie *(Cast)* 458, 1345, 1784, 2378, 2497, 2519, 2527, 2546, 2614, 3236, 3345, 4241
Gathers, Helen *(Composer)* 4264
Gathers, Helen *(Lyricist)* 4264
Gatteye, Bennye *(Cast)* 4409
Gatti, A. & S. *(Producer)* 719
Gattinguer, Robert *(Composer)* 3827
Gatts, George M. *(Producer)* 452
Gaudin, Kevin *(Cast)* 2735
Gaughan, Jack *(Musical Director)* 1171
Gaumont, Irving *(Producer)* 3966
Gaus, Robert T. *(Producer)* 2611
Gauthier, Katherine *(Cast)* 1657
Gautier, Dick *(Cast)* 607
Gavault, Paul *(Author)* 613, 4285, 4327
Gavault, Paul *(Librettist)* 4285
Gavon, Igors *(Cast)* 1216, 3020, 3427, 3564, 4196, 4789
Gawthorne, Peter *(Cast)* 3583
Gaxton, William *(Cast)* 69, 163, 834, 1272, 1948, 2402, 2432, 2444, 2597, 2888, 3007, 3091, 3225, 3371, 4667
Gay *(Composer)* 2454
Gay *(Lyricist)* 2454
Gay, Alden *(Cast)* 1013
Gay, Byron *(Composer)* 69, 1687, 1819, 1966, 3246
Gay, Byron *(Lyricist)* 1687, 1819, 3246

Gay, John *(Author)* 341, 4368, 4369, 4370, 4371
Gay, John *(Lyricist)* 1589
Gay, Maisie *(Cast)* 704, 791, 2570, 3500, 4258, 4661
Gay, Noel *(Composer)* 2148, 2798, 4027
Gay, Noel *(Lyricist)* 2148, 2798
Gaye, Gregory *(Cast)* 4372
Gaye, Marvin *(Composer)* 4534
Gaye, Marvin *(Lyricist)* 4534
Gaylord, Al E. *(Musical Director)* 1271
Gaynes, Edmund *(Cast)* 2579, 3696
Gaynes, George
See also George Jongeyans.
Gaynes, George *(Cast)* 616, 1122, 3696, 4734
Gaynor, Charles *(Composer)* 382, 2148, 2168, 2439, 2483, 3954, 4230
Gaynor, Charles *(Director)* 3954
Gaynor, Charles *(Librettist)* 382, 2168, 2439, 2483, 3954
Gaynor, Charles *(Lyricist)* 382, 2148, 2168, 2439, 2483, 3954, 4153, 4230
Gaynor, Jane *(Producer)* 39
Gaynor, Janet *(Cast)* 1775
Gaynor, Mitzi *(Cast)* 2234
Gaze, Hal *(Composer)* 2341
Gaze, Hal *(Lyricist)* 2341
GeBauer, Judy *(Librettist)* 3688
Gear, Florence *(Cast)* 939
Gear, Luella *(Cast)* 901, 924, 1453, 2475, 2620, 3064, 3283, 3310, 3540, 3622, 4174, 4532
Geary, Arthur *(Cast)* 2747
Geary, Joyce *(Lyricist)* 90
Gebest, Charles *(Composer)* 604
Gebest, Charles J. *(Composer)* 335, 3685, 4759
Gebest, Charles J. *(Musical Director)* 335, 804, 805, 1640, 1826, 2533, 2767, 2829, 3218, 3685, 3809, 4759
Gebest, Charles J. *(Orchestrations)* 115, 1271, 2517, 3809, 4277, 4759
Gebirtig, M. *(Composer)* 4342
Gebirtig, M. *(Lyricist)* 4342
Gebirtig, Mordechai *(Composer)* 2356
Gebirtig, Mordechai *(Lyricist)* 2356
Gee, George *(Cast)* 2323
Gee, Hugh *(Set Designer)* 4765
Gee, Kevin John *(Cast)* 595
Gee, Lottie *(Cast)* 740, 3676, 3963
Geer, Kevin *(Cast)* 1304
Geer, Shippen *(Lyricist)* 1370
Geer, Shippen *(Producer)* 1370
Geer, Will *(Cast)* 919, 1977, 2653, 2859, 3294, 3990, 4542, 4715
Geffen, David *(Producer)* 678, 2544
Geffen Records *(Producer)* 1103
Gehman, Richard *(Lyricist)* 600
Gehrecke, Frank *(Composer)* 4433
Gehrecke, Frank *(Director)* 1697
Gehrecke, Frank *(Librettist)* 1697, 4433
Gehrecke, Frank *(Lyricist)* 1697, 4433
Gehrue, Mayme *(Cast)* 666, 2324
Geidt, Jeremy *(Cast)* 1195, 1406
Geiger *(Composer)* 2419
Geiger *(Lyricist)* 2419
Geise, Sugar *(Cast)* 1938
Geiss, Tony *(Composer)* 4627
Geiss, Tony *(Librettist)* 3479, 4627
Geiss, Tony *(Lyricist)* 2913, 3112, 4627
Geissmann, Bob *(Set Design)* 4047
Geist, Lisa *(Cast)* 1159
Geistinger, Marie *(Cast)* 3896
Gelb, Philip *(Set Design)* 2476
Gelbart, Larry *(Librettist)* 775, 837, 1422, 3046
Gelbel, Adam *(Composer)* 4390
Gelbel, Adam *(Lyricist)* 4390
Gelber, Stanley Jay *(Composer)* 2599
Gelbert, Franklin *(Producer)* 2439
Gelbtrunk, Adam *(Composer)* 4667
Geld, Gary *(Composer)* 135, 3610, 3928
Gelfand, Carol *(Cast)* 832
Gelfer, Steven *(Cast)* 678
Gelfman, Sam W. *(Producer)* 2067
Gelke, Becky *(Cast)* 4398
Geller, Bruce *(Librettist)* 71, 2556
Geller, Bruce *(Lyricist)* 71, 2556, 3889
Geller, Helen *(Cast)* 3641
Gellers, Irving *(Composer)* 4586
Gelman, Larry *(Cast)* 4796
Gemignani, Paul *(Composer)* 2607
Gemignani, Paul *(Musical Director)* 212, 754, 921, 1038, 1068, 1184, 1699, 2143, 2205, 2822, 3015, 3279, 3340, 3411, 3718, 4020, 4210, 4233
Gemignani, Paul *(Orchestrations)* 1038
Gene *(Costumes)* 876
Genee, Adeline *(Cast)* 256, 4094
Genee, Richard *(Author)* 689, 3150, 3151
Genevieve *(Cast)* 3841
Gennaro, Liza *(Choreographer)* 2766
Gennaro, Peter *(Cast)* 183, 363, 1706, 3351, 3563
Gennaro, Peter *(Choreographer)* 150, 155, 269, 299, 652, 1280, 2217, 2643, 2983, 3299, 3899, 4371, 4516, 4625
Genni, Gwynne *(Lyricist)* 3617
Geno, Alton *(Choreographer)* 778
Genovese, Gen *(Author)* 596
Genovese, Gen *(Librettist)* 596
Genovese, Gen *(Lyricist)* 596
Genovese, Gen *(Producer)* 596
Gensler, Lewis *(Composer)* 317
Gensler, Lewis E. *(Composer)* 289, 317, 391, 393, 642, 1357, 1440, 1689, 1923, 3622, 3623, 4424, 4532
Gensler, Lewis E. *(Producer)* 289, 1275, 1440, 4532
Genteel, Grace *(Cast)* 4191
Gentile, Pietro *(Cast)* 1950
Gentry, Derek *(Cast)* 3227
Gentry, Minnie *(Cast)* 40
Genus, Karl *(Director)* 3543
Geoffreys, Stephen *(Cast)* 2033
Geoly, Guy *(Costumes)* 3734, 4703
George, Andre *(Cast)* 2735
George, Betty *(Cast)* 145
George, Bob *(Orchestrations)* 2074
George, Charles *(Composer)* 1584, 2492
George, Charles *(Costumes)* 2492
George, Charles *(Director)* 2492
George, Charles *(Librettist)* 1584, 2492

George, Charles *(Lyricist)* 1584, 2492
George, Charles *(Set Design)* 2492
George, Don *(Composer)* 1840, 4091
George, Don *(Lyricist)* 146, 4091
George, George W. *(Producer)* 160, 367, 4558
George, Gladys *(Cast)* 3068
George, Hal *(Costumes)* 3988
George, Johnny *(Director)* 1754
George, Joseph *(Lighting Designer)* 457, 1469
George, Marie *(Cast)* 2117, 3784, 4181, 4663
George, Phillip *(Choreographer)* 4462
George, Phillip *(Director)* 1349, 2022, 4462
George, Susan *(Cast)* 1089
George, Yvonne *(Cast)* 3148
George Street Playhouse *(Producer)* 3306
Gerald, Jack *(Composer)* 2447
Gerald, John *(Composer)* 2162
Gerald Wexler Presents Inc. *(Producer)* 3987
Gerard, Alfred *(Cast)* 433
Gerard, Barbara *(Costumes)* 1201
Gerard, Barney *(Composer)* 4630
Gerard, Barney *(Director)* 4630
Gerard, Barney *(Librettist)* 1332, 4630
Gerard, Barney *(Lyricist)* 1332, 4630
Gerard, Danny *(Cast)* 1234, 2142
Gerard, Emanuel *(Set Design)* 4585
Gerard, Gil *(Producer)* 105
Gerard, Rolf *(Costumes)* 2150
Gerard, Rolf *(Set Design)* 2150, 4435
Gerard, Teddie *(Cast)* 2570
Gerard, Will *(Cast)* 2754
Gerber, Alex *(Lyricist)* 815, 1685, 2684, 2706, 3407, 3538, 4033, 4526, 4814, 4841
Gerber, Bill *(Cast)* 3075, 4643
Gerber, Ella *(Director)* 4380
Gerber, Jay *(Cast)* 2011
Gerbidon, Marcel *(Author)* 1391, 1992
Gerden, George *(Cast)* 4398
Gere, Richard *(Cast)* 4089
Gereghty, Bob *(Composer)* 1136
Gerety, Peter *(Cast)* 2229
Gering, Marion *(Director)* 2751
Gering, Marion *(Producer)* 2751
Gerlach, H. *(Lyricist)* 4534
Gerlach, Robert *(Composer)* 4062
Gerlach, Robert *(Librettist)* 4062
Gerlach, Robert *(Lyricist)* 4062
Germain, Stuart *(Cast)* 259
German, Edward *(Composer)* 3588, 4404
German, Edward *(Director)* 4404
German, Edward *(Lyricist)* 1178
Germann, Greg *(Cast)* 212
Gerow, Bob *(Composer)* 4743
Gerrard, Alfred *(Cast)* 3921
Gerrits, Paul *(Cast)* 3002
Gershe, Leonard *(Author)* 594
Gershe, Leonard *(Librettist)* 1029, 1734
Gershe, Leonard *(Lyricist)* 1734, 1892
Gershman, Caryl Ginsburg *(Musical Director)* 139
Gershovsky, Yaron *(Vocal Arranger)* 775, 4076
Gershwin, Arthur *(Composer)* 2397
Gershwin, Frances *(Cast)* 2366, 2827
Gershwin, George *(Author)* 4179
Gershwin, George *(Cast)* 3153
Gershwin, George *(Composer)* 123, 445, 447, 465, 487, 545, 560, 638, 877, 921, 969, 977, 1026, 1154, 1324, 1325, 1345, 1391, 1419, 1483, 1484, 1485, 1486, 1487, 1489, 1528, 1626, 1638, 1689, 1726, 1763, 1873, 1920, 2363, 2373, 2376, 2385, 2444, 2450, 2526, 2587, 2872, 2960, 3018, 3020, 3060, 3127, 3144, 3172, 3175, 3225, 3243, 3323, 3379, 3400, 3443, 3478, 3541, 3569, 3640, 3649, 3704, 3705, 3709, 3766, 3905, 3953, 3955, 3985, 3989, 4033, 4077, 4104, 4178, 4179, 4241, 4248, 4300, 4390, 4392, 4399, 4443, 4534
Gershwin, George *(Orchestrations)* 3541
Gershwin, Ira *(Author)* 4179
Gershwin, Ira *(Composer)* 4392
Gershwin, Ira *(Librettist)* 1284, 2475
Gershwin, Ira *(Lyricist)* 123, 213, 317, 369, 418, 642, 745, 877, 921, 977, 1026, 1283, 1284, 1298, 1325, 1345, 1419, 1448, 1485, 1528, 1638, 1689, 1726, 1763, 2204, 2372, 2373, 2376, 2386, 2444, 2450, 2475, 2526, 2653, 2872, 2927, 3018, 3020, 3060, 3127, 3144, 3157, 3172, 3175, 3225, 3243, 3249, 3379, 3390, 3478, 3500, 3541, 3569, 3709, 3766, 3905, 3946, 3953, 3955, 3989, 4043, 4152, 4178, 4179, 4235, 4248, 4300, 4320, 4390, 4399, 4424, 4443, 4491, 4498, 4534, 4825
Gerson, Hal *(Director)* 2439
Gerson, Joe *(Set Design)* 2511
Gerson, Karen *(Costumes)* 564, 1092, 1737, 3864
Gerstad, John *(Cast)* 823
Gerstad, John *(Director)* 3894
Gersten, Berta *(Cast)* 4090
Gerstenberger, Emil *(Composer)* 2371
Gerstenberger, Emil *(Orchestrations)* 138, 200, 201, 577, 1013, 1460, 2594, 3117, 3407, 3523, 4121, 4188
Gerut, Rosalie *(Cast)* 3937, 4082
Gerut, Rosalie *(Composer)* 4082
Gerwig, David *(Conductor)* 3507
Gesman, Charles *(Costumes)* 2135
Gesner, Clark *(Composer)* 143, 272, 427, 3111, 3112, 3479, 4537, 4783
Gesner, Clark *(Librettist)* 143, 4537
Gesner, Clark *(Lyricist)* 143, 272, 427, 3111, 3112, 3479, 4537, 4783
Gest, Morris *(Director)* 558
Gest, Morris *(Producer)* 25, 165, 336, 684, 710, 758, 1975, 2340, 2396, 2430, 2698, 2802, 2960, 3245, 3535, 3775, 4730, 4758, 4860
Gestenberger, Emil *(Orchestrations)* 3179
Geto, Al *(Librettist)* 3226
Gets, Malcolm *(Cast)* 1822, 2766
Getter, Philip M. *(Producer)* 900
Getz, Charles *(Set Design)* 571
Getz, Mara *(Cast)* 2702
Geva, Tamara *(Cast)* 1322, 3283, 4367, 4683
Geva, Tamara *(Choreographer)* 4683
Gewandter, Holly *(Composer)* 573
Gewandter, Holly *(Lyricist)* 573
Geyer, Siegfried *(Author)* 3756, 4777
Geyra, Ellida *(Choreographer)* 2178
Gherpakov, Gary *(Lyricist)* 3239

Ghoshal, Kurnar *(Cast)* 1603
Ghostley, Alice *(Cast)* 52, 72, 759, 1047, 1474, 2556, 2611, 3107, 3831, 3913
Giacosa, Giuseppe *(Librettist)* 2359
Giagni, D.J. *(Choreographer)* 171, 212, 1776, 3448
Giamatti, Bartlett *(Cast)* 945
Giampa, W.J. *(Set Design)* 1450
Gianfrancesco, Edward T. *(Set Design)* 1258, 1591, 2544
Gianiotis, Anna *(Cast)* 3539
Giannelli, Christina *(Lighting Designer)* 4398
Giannini, A. Christina *(Costumes)* 1171, 4172, 4379
Gianono, Joe *(Orchestrations)* 674
Gianono, Joseph *(Orchestrations)* 146, 1149, 2208
Giasco, Kitty *(Cast)* 1824
Gibb, Barry *(Composer)* 3739
Gibb, Barry *(Lyricist)* 3739
Gibb, Maurice *(Composer)* 3739
Gibb, Maurice *(Lyricist)* 3739
Gibb, Robin *(Composer)* 3739
Gibb, Robin *(Lyricist)* 3739
Gibberson, Bill *(Cast)* 1815
Gibbings, Jim *(Lighting Designer)* 3841
Gibbons, Carroll *(Composer)* 418
Gibbs, Georgia *(Cast)* 2653
Gibbs, Lloyd *(Cast)* 4088
Gibbs, Nancy *(Cast)* 4302
Gibbs, Sheila *(Cast)* 3285
Gibney, Susan *(Cast)* 1232
Gibson, B.G. *(Cast)* 3903
Gibson, Corine *(Cast)* 986
Gibson, Fred *(Set Design)* 4723
Gibson, Joanne *(Cast)* 1249
Gibson, Joe *(Composer)* 2856
Gibson, Joe *(Lyricist)* 2856
Gibson, John *(Cast)* 4599
Gibson, Judy *(Cast)* 3741, 3876
Gibson, Julie *(Cast)* 242
Gibson, Madeline *(Cast)* 4341
Gibson, Michael *(Dance Arranger)* 2146
Gibson, Michael *(Orchestrations)* 146, 535, 757, 1146, 1164, 1172, 1510, 1638, 2333, 2689, 2702, 2737, 2805, 3060, 3126, 3305, 3330, 3577, 3718, 3792, 4459, 4727
Gibson, Michael *(Vocal Arranger)* 1510, 2146, 2728
Gibson, Tanya *(Cast)* 432
Gibson, Virginia *(Cast)* 1681, 1760
Gibson, William *(Author)* 3869
Gibson, William *(Librettist)* 1601, 3643
Gibson, William *(Lyricist)* 3643
Gideon, I.E. *(Producer)* 1995
Gideon, Melville *(Cast)* 3310
Gideon, Melville *(Composer)* 208, 336, 511, 1153, 1327, 1523, 1613, 1801, 2892, 3213, 3310, 3701, 3827, 4802
Gideon, Melville *(Lyricist)* 201, 377, 1523, 4302, 4553, 4555
Gideon, Melville *(Producer)* 3310
Gideon, Melville T. *(Composer)* 3061
Gideon, Steve *(Cast)* 3178
Giehse, Theodore *(Director)* 3441
Giehse, Therese *(Cast)* 3441
Gielgud, Sir John *(Narrator)* 3454
Gierasch, Stefan *(Cast)* 4095
Giersberg, Max *(Author)* 82
Giese, Linda *(Costumes)* 4595
Gifford, Harry *(Composer)* 336, 2334, 3755, 4206, 4657
Gifford, Harry *(Lyricist)* 2334, 3755, 4206, 4657
Gifford, Jack *(Cast)* 4683
Gifford, Julia *(Cast)* 1248, 4646
Giftos, Elaine *(Cast)* 3112
Gigl, Aloysius *(Cast)* 4515
Giglio, Clement *(Composer)* 4672
Giglio, Clement *(Librettist)* 4672
Giglio, Clement *(Lyricist)* 4672
Gignoux, Regis *(Author)* 2669
Gilb, Melinda *(Cast)* 261, 3992, 4193
Gilb, Melinda *(Librettist)* 4193
Gilbert, Alan *(Cast)* 4096
Gilbert, Barbara *(Cast)* 3124
Gilbert, Benjamin Thorpe *(Librettist)* 4794
Gilbert, Bert *(Cast)* 2701
Gilbert, Billy *(Cast)* 596, 1711, 2182
Gilbert, Billy *(Librettist)* 596
Gilbert, Craig P. *(Librettist)* 1862
Gilbert, Edward *(Costumes)* 3105
Gilbert, Edward *(Lighting Designer)* 1204
Gilbert, Edward *(Set Design)* 67, 70, 1204, 1930, 2098, 2099, 2103, 3105, 3335, 4166, 4428
Gilbert, Edwin *(Librettist)* 3104, 4545
Gilbert, Edwin *(Lyricist)* 3103, 3104, 4777
Gilbert, Franklin *(Producer)* 2680
Gilbert, Fred *(Composer)* 1301
Gilbert, Fred *(Lyricist)* 1301
Gilbert, George *(Producer)* 1290, 2987
Gilbert, Gloria *(Cast)* 289, 1423, 4174
Gilbert, H. *(Author)* 2610
Gilbert, Hy *(Lyricist)* 3851
Gilbert, James *(Composer)* 1644
Gilbert, James *(Lyricist)* 1644
Gilbert, Jean *(Author)* 12, 1554, 2293, 2384, 2923, 3529, 4795
Gilbert, Jean *(Composer)* 184, 965, 1534, 1554, 2293, 2384, 2385, 2747, 2922, 2923, 3237, 3529, 3627, 3680, 4170, 4795
Gilbert, Jean *(Lyricist)* 4795
Gilbert, John *(Composer)* 2747
Gilbert, John D. *(Librettist)* 3228
Gilbert, John D. *(Lyricist)* 3228
Gilbert, L. Wolfe *(Lyricist)* 433, 558, 710, 1065, 1334, 1400, 1531, 2415, 2486, 3018, 3259, 3614, 3995, 4655
Gilbert, Lisa *(Cast)* 3002
Gilbert, Lorenz *(Cast)* 1624
Gilbert, Lou *(Cast)* 1122, 2319
Gilbert, Maud *(Cast)* 175
Gilbert, Melvin B. *(Choreographer)* 761
Gilbert, Mercedes *(Cast)* 488
Gilbert, Olive *(Cast)* 650, 972
Gilbert, Paul *(Cast)* 2742, 4829
Gilbert, Ray *(Cast)* 4536
Gilbert, Ray *(Lyricist)* 4264
Gilbert, Robert *(Author)* 2610, 4486, 4667
Gilbert, Tony *(Cast)* 4703
Gilbert, W.S. *(Author)* 345, 1948, 2817, 2861, 4617
Gilbert, W.S. *(Librettist)* 1905, 1987, 4254

Gilbert, W.S. *(Lyricist)* 1905, 1987, 2348, 2977, 3280, 4254
Gilbert, W.S. *(Music Based On)* 2817
Gilbert, Willie *(Librettist)* 1991, 2019
Gilder, Vanessa K. *(Cast)* 3522
Gile, Bill *(Director)* 2877, 3080, 4454
Gile, William *(Director)* 2026
Giler, Bernie *(Author)* 1539
Giles, Anthony *(Librettist)* 3197
Giles, Anthony *(Lyricist)* 3197
Giles, Nancy *(Cast)* 2790, 4535
Giles, Nancy *(Librettist)* 4535
Gilfether, Daniel *(Cast)* 1445, 3759, 4239
Gilfoil, Harry *(Cast)* 2465, 4165, 4181, 4757
Gilford, Jack *(Cast)* 59, 610, 1422, 2809, 3286, 3288, 3761
Gilford, Madeline *(Producer)* 4643
Gilk, Hirsh *(Lyricist)* 1740
Gilkey, Stanley *(Producer)* 3292, 4362, 4483
Gill, Brenden *(Librettist)* 2357
Gill, Gus *(Librettist)* 3024
Gill, Michael *(Producer)* 784
Gill, Ray *(Cast)* 583
Gill, William *(Cast)* 3856
Gill, William *(Librettist)* 3887
Gill, William *(Set Design)* 3047
Gillan, Charles P. *(Cast)* 4507
Gillen, Frank *(Composer)* 1223
Gillen, Frank *(Lyricist)* 1223
Gillespie, Arthur *(Composer)* 2286
Gillespie, Arthur *(Librettist)* 1173, 3877
Gillespie, Arthur *(Lyricist)* 1054, 1212, 1316, 2793, 3877
Gillespie, Christina *(Cast)* 71, 1194
Gillespie, Conor *(Cast)* 2229
Gillespie, Frank M. *(Choreographer)* 463, 659
Gillespie, Frank M. *(Director)* 1667
Gillespie, H.L. *(Producer)* 2532
Gillespie, Haven *(Lyricist)* 885, 1137, 1939, 3020, 3175, 3833
Gillespie, Lee *(Dance Arranger)* 1978
Gillespie, Lee *(Musical Director)* 1978, 4470
Gillespie, Marion *(Lyricist)* 293, 377
Gillespie, Robert *(Director)* 1256
Gillespie, T. *(Cast)* 1604
Gillespie, Tinker *(Cast)* 1010
Gillette, Anita *(Cast)* 64, 656, 2217, 2304, 2983, 3497, 3810
Gillette, Bobby *(Cast)* 3946
Gillette, Priscilla *(Cast)* 1600, 3326, 3691
Gillette, Ruth *(Cast)* 1460
Gillette, Viola *(Cast)* 1518, 1975
Gillette, William *(Author)* 1270
Gilliam, Michael *(Lighting Designer)* 450
Gilliam, Philip *(Lighting Designer)* 4220
Gilliam, Philip *(Set Design)* 4022, 4220
Gillian, Allie *(Cast)* 2520
Gilligan, Helen *(Cast)* 4179
Gilliland, Helen *(Cast)* 3680
Gilliland, Jane *(Producer)* 4173
Gillingwater, Claude *(Cast)* 509, 1555, 2915
Gillins, Bobby *(Cast)* 1421
Gillins, George *(Composer)* 1421
Gillman, Jane *(Cast)* 4740
Gillmore, Ruth *(Cast)* 1357
Gillsepie, Arthur *(Librettist)* 2635
Gillsepie, Arthur *(Lyricist)* 2635
Gilman, D. *(Costumes)* 3580
Gilman, Eliot *(Orchestrations)* 2785
Gilman, Mabel *(Cast)* 2117, 3784
Gilman, Mabelle *(Cast)* 666, 2917
Gilman, Mme. *(Costumes)* 2557, 2601
Gilman, Sondra *(Producer)* 4091
Gilmore, Douglas *(Author)* 1939
Gilmore, Margalo *(Cast)* 3453, 3815
Gilmore, Mary *(Cast)* 1538
Gilmore, Paul *(Cast)* 224, 515
Gilmore, Paul *(Director)* 3192
Gilmore, W.H. *(Director)* 1391, 2526, 2757, 3079, 3323, 3382, 3466, 3472
Gilmour, David *(Composer)* 3739
Gilpin, Charles *(Cast)* 645, 2520
Gilpin, Charles *(Composer)* 525, 2490
Gilpin, Charles *(Lyricist)* 525, 2490
Gilpin, Charles A. *(Cast)* 2044
Gilrod, Louis *(Lyricist)* 573, 1609
Gilroy, Frank *(Author)* 139, 1510
Gilroy, John *(Cast)* 2592
Gilroy, John *(Librettist)* 2851
Gilroy, John *(Lyricist)* 470, 2465, 2851, 4691
Gimbel, Norman *(Composer)* 863, 4193
Gimbel, Norman *(Lyricist)* 837, 863, 3940, 3941, 4193, 4264, 4682
Gimble, Harriet *(Cast)* 1686
Gimpel, Erica *(Cast)* 119
Gindi, Roger Alan *(Producer)* 2171
Gingold, Hermione *(Cast)* 1119, 1290, 1408, 2168, 2227, 2536, 4153
Gingold, Hermione *(Librettist)* 2168, 2483, 4153
Gingold, Hermione *(Lyricist)* 2168, 2227, 4153
Ginnes, Abram S. *(Librettist)* 2449
Ginzler, Robert *(Orchestrations)* 64, 519, 607, 837, 1076, 1237, 1567, 1709, 2019, 2150, 3210, 3234, 4566, 4693
Ginzler, Robert *(Vocal Arranger)* 837
Gioe, Salvatore *(Musical Director)* 817
Giono, Jean *(Author)* 273
Giordano, Frank *(Cast)* 1498
Giordano, Gus *(Choreographer)* 3925
Giovanni *(Lyricist)* 4264
Giovannini, Sandro *(Director)* 3798
Giovannini, Sandro *(Librettist)* 3798
Giovannini, Sandro *(Lyricist)* 3798
Giradot, Etienne *(Cast)* 2827
Girard, Dixie *(Cast)* 396
Girard, Eddie *(Cast)* 2181
Girard, Harry *(Composer)* 47
Girard, Teddy *(Cast)* 1153
Giraudoux, Jean *(Author)* 1012
Girdler, Deb G. *(Cast)* 3306
Girio, Cesar *(Costumes)* 3144
Girl Friends, The *(Cast)* 1950
Girl Trust, The *(Cast)* 4487
Girlando, Paul J. *(Composer)* 1710
Girls from the Follies, The *(Cast)* 806
Girolami, Peter *(Set Design)* 2611

Giroux, Germaine *(Cast)* 4105
Girvin, T. Galen *(Cast)* 3539
Gish, Lillian *(Cast)* 161, 3020
Gisondi, John *(Lighting Designer)* 33
Gittens, Hugh *(Director)* 3814
Gitter, Chaim *(Lighting Designer)* 3654
Gitter, Hillel *(Cast)* 4560
Gittler, Barbara *(Producer)* 2195
Givot, George *(Cast)* 125, 223, 1061, 1126, 2847, 3153, 3379
Gizienski, George *(Lighting Designer)* 1262
Gizienski, George *(Set Design)* 1262
Glad, Gladys *(Cast)* 3766, 4683, 4823
Glade, Carol *(Cast)* 249
Glade, Coe *(Cast)* 3639
Gladke, Peter *(Cast)* 190
Gladstein, Renee *(Costumes)* 3781
Glaser, C.J.M. *(Composer)* 3977
Glaser, C.J.M. *(Musical Director)* 3977
Glaser, John *(Costumes)* 4518
Glaser, Lulu *(Cast)* 727, 947, 1030, 1071, 1292, 1522, 1720, 2282, 2502, 2566, 2671, 2835, 2885, 2886, 2914, 3566, 4236
Glaser, Lulu *(Composer)* 1292
Glaser, Michael *(Cast)* 594
Glaser and Company, Lulu *(Producer)* 4236
Glass, George *(Musical Director)* 1647
Glass, Montague *(Librettist)* 2407, 4621
Glassman, Seth *(Director)* 4480, 4540
Glassman, Stephen *(Librettist)* 406
Glave, Jeffrey *(Set Design)* 2388
Glawson, Carol *(Lighting Designer)* 2573
Glazener, Janet *(Musical Director)* 2208, 3277
Glazer, Benjamin *(Lyricist)* 2487
Glazer, Peter *(Adaptation)* 4740
Glazer, Peter *(Director)* 4740
Glazier, Marie *(Cast)* 2518
Gleason, Helen *(Cast)* 1384, 3152
Gleason, Jackie *(Cast)* 95, 204, 1336, 4270
Gleason, James *(Cast)* 42, 2403, 3562
Gleason, James *(Librettist)* 3648
Gleason, Joanna *(Cast)* 2058, 2143, 3142
Gleason, John *(Lighting Designer)* 135, 1380, 2362, 2590, 3309, 3330, 3468, 3515, 3787, 4459, 4481
Gleason, Thomas *(Cast)* 603
Gleason, William *(Librettist)* 843
Gleason, William *(Lyricist)* 843
Glecker, Robert *(Cast)* 1979
Gleeson, Colette *(Cast)* 1741
Glendenning, John *(Cast)* 1553
Glendinning, Ernest *(Cast)* 1517, 2070, 2537, 2922, 2950, 4085, 4424
Glendinning, Jessie *(Cast)* 2613
Glenn, "Happy" Julius *(Cast)* 641
Glenn, Julius *(Cast)* 2127
Glenn, Nettie *(Cast)* 3945
Glenn-Smith, Michael *(Cast)* 681, 3469
Glenville, Peter *(Director)* 4270, 4435
Glenville, Shaun *(Cast)* 3472
Glick, Ben *(Set Design)* 1514
Glickman, Stanley A. *(Producer)* 74
Glickman, Will *(Librettist)* 59, 483, 743, 2267, 2439, 2837, 2987, 3509
Glines, John *(Composer)* 1590
Glines, John *(Director)* 4157
Glines, John *(Librettist)* 1590
Glines, John *(Lyricist)* 1590
Glines, John *(Producer)* 2022
Glines, The *(Producer)* 2022
Glist, Alan *(Producer)* 3926
Glist, Kathi *(Producer)* 3926
Glitter, Jimmy *(Composer)* 2580
Glogau, Jack *(Composer)* 60, 2189, 4812
Glogau, Jack *(Lyricist)* 4812
Glopen, Joe *(Cast)* 4107
Glosser, Daniel *(Musical Director)* 1346
Glover, Beth *(Cast)* 484, 3568
Glover, Corey *(Cast)* 1232
Glover, Cyd *(Cast)* 432
Glover, Ernest *(Set Design)* 2841
Glover, J.M. *(Composer)* 2035, 2964, 4014
Glover, J.M. *(Lyricist)* 2964
Glover, Joe *(Orchestrations)* 98, 177, 180, 1091, 1336, 2103, 2554, 2556, 3108, 3234, 3371, 3813, 4337, 4446, 4828
Glover, John *(Cast)* 3871
Glover, Ralph *(Cast)* 711, 3131
Glover, Rita *(Set Design)* 2496
Glover, S. *(Composer)* 1897
Glover, S. *(Lyricist)* 1897
Glover, Savion *(Cast)* 432, 2200
Glover, William *(Cast)* 2650
Glover, William *(Director)* 2650
Glover, William *(Librettist)* 2650
Gloves, W.F. *(Arrangements)* 45
Gluck, J. *(Composer)* 4193
Gluck, J. *(Lyricist)* 4193
Gluck, M. Senia *(Choreographer)* 1131, 2330
Gluck, Marvin A. *(Author)* 2578
Gluck, Wally *(Producer)* 1722
Gluckman, Leon *(Director)* 4579
Gluckman, Leon *(Lighting Designer)* 4579
Glushak, Joanna *(Cast)* 2470, 4515
Glynn, Carlin *(Cast)* 374
Glynn, Thomas *(Cast)* 4486
Gobel, George *(Cast)* 2449
Gobel, George *(Voice)* 4471
Goberman, Max *(Musical Director)* 404, 2563, 2864, 3278, 4446, 4625, 4652
Gochman, Len *(Cast)* 1010, 4468
Gockel, Fred *(Cast)* 239
Godard, Charles *(Composer)* 364
Godard, Flora *(Costumes)* 2547
Goddard, Charles W. *(Librettist)* 2891
Goddard, Gary *(Composer)* 1159
Goddard, Gary *(Lyricist)* 1159
Goddard, Malcolm *(Choreographer)* 3445
Goddard, Mark *(Cast)* 16
Goddard, Willoughby *(Cast)* 3271
Godfred, Hal *(Cast)* 4725
Godfrey *(Lyricist)* 4154
Godfrey, Arthur *(Cast)* 197, 4362

Godfrey, Arthur E. *(Musical Director)* 2976
Godfrey, Fred *(Composer)* 4657
Godfrey, Fred *(Lyricist)* 4657
Godfrey, Jeff *(Composer)* 3397
Godfrey, Jeff *(Lyricist)* 965
Godfrey, Lynnie *(Cast)* 1198
Godfrey, Mostyn *(Cast)* 1610
Godfrey, Roy *(Cast)* 1386
Godfrey, Vaughn *(Choreographer)* 1710, 2071, 4322, 4328, 4528, 4669
Godkin, Paul *(Cast)* 283, 1670, 1886, 4142
Godkin, Paul *(Choreographer)* 283, 4323
Godowsky, Leopold *(Composer)* 4033
Godreau, Miguel *(Cast)* 1012
Godreau, Miguel *(Choreographer)* 3830
Godreau, Miguel *(Director)* 3830
Godwin, Howard *(Composer)* 662, 1415
Goëckner, Anton *(Musical Director)* 982
Goehr, Rudolph *(Orchestrations)* 1748
Goehring, George *(Composer)* 2375, 3695
Goehring, George *(Lyricist)* 3695
Goering, Hal *(Composer)* 393
Goetz, Augustus *(Author)* 4600
Goetz, Coleman *(Lyricist)* 965, 1084, 4720
Goetz, E. Ray *(Composer)* 60, 208, 470, 913, 954, 1391, 1464, 1735, 1919, 1920, 1927, 2456, 2526, 3052, 3079, 3096, 3191, 3313, 3382, 3525, 4044, 4148, 4206, 4603, 4742, 4801
Goetz, E. Ray *(Director)* 3131
Goetz, E. Ray *(Librettist)* 1920
Goetz, E. Ray *(Lyricist)* 60, 201, 208, 336, 802, 910, 913, 960, 1063, 1153, 1247, 1391, 1464, 1485, 1486, 1613, 1626, 1735, 1738, 1835, 1845, 1919, 1920, 1927, 2262, 2456, 2526, 2782, 2892, 3052, 3079, 3096, 3175, 3382, 3466, 3478, 3525, 3575, 3715, 3716, 3737, 3755, 4033, 4044, 4148, 4206, 4553, 4603, 4714, 4721, 4742, 4803, 4804
Goetz, E. Ray *(Producer)* 208, 1272, 1335, 1391, 3079, 3131, 3382, 3478, 4742
Goetz, Ruth Goodman *(Author)* 4600
Goetzl, Anselm *(Composer)* 165, 3770, 3791, 4066
Goetzl, Anselm *(Musical Director)* 2486
Goetzl, Anselm *(Producer)* 3770
Goff, Charles *(Cast)* 3682
Goff, Jerry *(Cast)* 4179
Goff, Stephen *(Costumes)* 4679
Goff, Stephen *(Producer)* 4679
Goff, Stephen *(Set Design)* 4093, 4679
Goffin, Gerry *(Composer)* 3739, 4193, 4534
Goffin, Gerry *(Lyricist)* 3739, 4193, 4534
Goggie *(Costumes)* 2709
Goggin, Dan *(Cast)* 1770
Goggin, Dan *(Choreographer)* 275
Goggin, Dan *(Composer)* 275, 546, 1770, 2435, 3211
Goggin, Dan *(Director)* 275, 3211
Goggin, Dan *(Librettist)* 275, 3211
Goggin, Dan *(Lyricist)* 275, 3211
Goggin, Victoria *(Cast)* 3671
Gogotsky, N. *(Composer)* 464
Gohl, James F. *(Set Design)* 1500
Gohman, Don *(Composer)* 101, 4273
Going, John *(Director)* 1079, 2565
Goland, Arnold *(Dance Arranger)* 249, 1864, 4186, 4633
Goland, Arnold *(Orchestrations)* 249, 1380, 2522, 4186
Goland, Arnold *(Vocal Arranger)* 249, 4186
Gold, Al *(Cast)* 3946
Gold, Annabelle *(Cast)* 3505
Gold, Belle *(Cast)* 1519
Gold, David *(Cast)* 1094
Gold, David *(Musical Director)* 874
Gold, Ernest *(Composer)* 2075, 3261
Gold, Joe *(Composer)* 2856
Gold, W. *(Composer)* 4193
Gold, W. *(Lyricist)* 4193
Gold, Zisha *(Cast)* 2811
Goldberg, David *(Lyricist)* 1657, 4669
Goldberg, Diana *(Cast)* 3559
Goldberg, Harry *(Producer)* 926, 927
Goldberg, Harry A. *(Director)* 4530
Goldberg, Jack *(Producer)* 3614
Goldberg, Jerry *(Composer)* 1873
Goldberg, Jerry *(Lyricist)* 1873
Goldberg, Jerry *(Musical Director)* 2925, 3988
Goldberg, Jerry *(Vocal Arranger)* 2925
Goldberg, Leonard *(Producer)* 181
Goldberg, Leonard J. *(Producer)* 1809
Goldberg, Rube *(Librettist)* 199, 3005, 3810, 4047
Goldberg, Rube *(Lyricist)* 1689
Goldberg, Russell *(Cast)* 484
Goldblatt, Hanan *(Cast)* 1075
Goldblum, Jeff *(Cast)* 2949
Goldby, Derek *(Director)* 1848
Golden, Annie *(Cast)* 212, 2427, 3076
Golden, E. *(Composer)* 1688
Golden, E. *(Lyricist)* 1688
Golden, Edward *(Composer)* 2349
Golden, Edward *(Librettist)* 2349
Golden, Edward *(Lyricist)* 2349
Golden, Ernie *(Composer)* 203, 1134, 1687
Golden, Ernie *(Lyricist)* 203, 1134
Golden, Grace *(Cast)* 311
Golden, John *(Composer)* 632, 782, 960, 1009, 1151, 1360, 1588, 2025, 2254, 2904, 3332, 3372, 3737, 4017, 4219, 4258, 4382, 4642, 4712, 4747
Golden, John *(Librettist)* 782, 1360, 1588
Golden, John *(Lyricist)* 396, 632, 712, 736, 782, 1151, 1208, 1360, 1538, 1566, 1588, 1901, 2025, 2254, 2891, 2904, 3332, 3737, 4258, 4382, 4712, 4747
Golden, John *(Producer)* 1009
Golden, John L. *(Composer)* 1430, 1455, 4799
Golden, John L. *(Lyricist)* 396, 1455
Golden, Lee *(Cast)* 2654
Golden, Ray *(Composer)* 59, 1892, 2246, 2742, 2962
Golden, Ray *(Director)* 1892, 2246, 2962
Golden, Ray *(Librettist)* 2742, 2809, 3255
Golden, Ray *(Lyricist)* 59, 673, 1892, 2246, 2259, 2742, 2962, 3255
Golden, Ray *(Producer)* 59, 2246
Golden, Richard *(Cast)* 1355
Golden Glow Unlimited, Ltd. *(Producer)* 2704
Goldenberg, Billy *(Composer)* 287, 973, 1298
Goldenberg, Billy *(Dance Arranger)* 2449

Goldenberg, William *(Composer)* 2279
Goldenberg, William *(Dance Arranger)* 1846, 1891, 3294
Goldenthal, Elliot *(Composer)* 4442
Goldfaden, Abraham *(Composer)* 1279
Goldfaden, Abraham *(Lyricist)* 1279
Goldfarb, Sidney *(Librettist)* 4442
Goldfarb, Sidney *(Lyricist)* 4442
Goldin, Al *(Producer)* 820
Goldin, Toni *(Lighting Designer)* 3239, 4618
Golding, Samuel R. *(Librettist)* 563
Goldman, Byron *(Producer)* 594, 1634, 2205, 2874
Goldman, Donald H. *(Producer)* 2731
Goldman, Harold *(Composer)* 1448
Goldman, Harold *(Librettist)* 4152
Goldman, Harold *(Lyricist)* 1448, 3103
Goldman, James *(Librettist)* 1200, 1237, 1329
Goldman, James *(Lyricist)* 1237
Goldman, Jerry *(Librettist)* 1233, 3484
Goldman, Kathleen *(Librettist)* 4152
Goldman, Louis S. *(Producer)* 461
Goldman, Robert *(Lyricist)* 1290
Goldman, Sherwin M. *(Producer)* 1609, 3088
Goldman, William *(Librettist)* 1237
Goldman, William *(Lyricist)* 1237
Goldmark, Leo *(Author)* 995
Goldmark, Leo *(Librettist)* 3896
Goldmark, Leo *(Lyricist)* 3896
Goldner, Charles *(Cast)* 1548
Goldner, Charles *(Director)* 346
Goldner, George *(Composer)* 166
Goldner, George *(Lyricist)* 166
Goldoni, Carlo *(Author)* 225, 2464, 2910, 4244
Goldsmith, Abe *(Librettist)* 1233, 3484
Goldsmith, Beatrice *(Lyricist)* 3226
Goldsmith, C. Gerald *(Producer)* 935
Goldsmith, Eleanor *(Costumes)* 1278, 2137, 2629, 4314
Goldsmith, George *(Author)* 1783
Goldsmith, Lee *(Composer)* 4566
Goldsmith, Lee *(Librettist)* 3902, 3925
Goldsmith, Lee *(Lyricist)* 1408, 3902, 3925, 4566
Goldsmith, Merwin *(Cast)* 36, 171, 198, 2359, 3666, 3702, 4790
Goldsmith, Oliver *(Author)* 2650, 3215, 3302, 4497
Goldsmith, Ted *(Composer)* 1342
Goldsmith, Ted *(Lyricist)* 1342
Goldstein, Hy *(Cast)* 3501
Goldstein, Jerome *(Dance Arranger)* 268
Goldstein, Jerome *(Vocal Arranger)* 268
Goldstein, Jess *(Costumes)* 595, 699, 784, 2766, 3277, 4390
Goldstein, Joel *(Producer)* 105
Goldstein, Jonathan *(Cast)* 1232
Goldstein, Nat *(Composer)* 2363
Goldstein, Nat *(Lyricist)* 2363
Goldstein, Owen H. *(Costumes)* 4470
Goldstein, Ted *(Set Design)* 624
Goldstone, Bob *(Arrangements)* 573
Goldstone, Bob *(Dance Arranger)* 1092
Goldstone, Bob *(Musical Director)* 573, 647, 843, 1092, 3817
Goldstone, Bob *(Orchestrations)* 1092, 1739
Goldstone, Bob *(Vocal Arranger)* 1092
Goldstone, Nat *(Producer)* 462
Goldstone, Robert *(Dance Arranger)* 3764
Goldstone, Robert *(Vocal Arranger)* 3764
Goldsworthy, John *(Cast)* 3865
Goldwasser, Lawrence L. *(Set Design)* 1862, 2610, 4174, 4498
Golladlay, Nancy *(Lighting Designer)* 1978
Golman, Daniel A. *(Producer)* 1059
Goloboff, Mim *(Cast)* 1757
Golomb, Sheldon *(Cast)* 2322
Golonka, Arlene *(Cast)* 3612
Golub, Solomon *(Composer)* 1279
Golub, Solomon *(Lyricist)* 1279
Gomez *(Cast)* 2105
Gomez, Vincente *(Cast)* 7
Gomez and Winona *(Cast)* 662
Gon, Zamira *(Choreographer)* 1299
Gondra, Arthur *(Librettist)* 4110
Gontard, G.V. *(Producer)* 4316
Gonzalez, Ernesto *(Cast)* 3711
Gonzalez, Raoul *(Composer)* 2288, 2580
Gonzalez, Raoul *(Lyricist)* 2288
Good, Jack *(Cast)* 796, 1225, 1414, 1836
Good, Peter *(Librettist)* 4482
Goodacre, Ralph *(Set Design)* 3173
Goodall, Howard *(Composer)* 1903
Goodchild, Tim *(Set Design)* 456, 1296
Goode, Herbert *(Composer)* 3946
Goode, Herbert *(Lyricist)* 3946
Goode, Jack *(Cast)* 1711
Goode, Mort *(Lyricist)* 2260
Goode, Richard *(Cast)* 3871
Goodelle, Niela *(Cast)* 2105
Goodfriend, Oscar *(Musical Director)* 3357
Goodhall, Elizabeth *(Cast)* 93, 4133
Goodhart, Al *(Composer)* 544
Goodhart, William *(Author)* 1471
Goodhart, William *(Lyricist)* 1471
Goodhue, Willis Maxwell *(Librettist)* 625
Goodhue, Willis Maxwell *(Lyricist)* 625
Goodings, Sally *(Cast)* 878
Goodjohn, Arlouine *(Cast)* 283
Goodman, Al *(Cast)* 3153
Goodman, Al *(Composer)* 201, 659, 905, 969, 1033, 1460, 2384, 2419, 2489, 2832, 3148, 3405, 4010, 4427, 4654
Goodman, Al *(Incidental Music)* 3404
Goodman, Al *(Musical Director)* 216, 294, 622, 771, 910, 969, 1096, 1322, 1323, 1339, 1894, 1931, 2135, 2475, 2622, 2870, 3011, 3117, 3131, 3407, 3584, 4427, 4654, 4772
Goodman, Al *(Orchestrations)* 2135, 3117
Goodman, Alfred *(Composer)* 199, 659, 1033, 1460, 3084
Goodman, Alfred *(Musical Director)* 391, 487, 718, 1481, 1492, 1628, 1979, 2813, 3179, 3405, 3406, 3586, 3778, 3921, 3985, 4104, 4142, 4177
Goodman, Alfred *(Orchestrations)* 199, 441, 4142
Goodman, Arthur *(Librettist)* 227
Goodman, Aubrey *(Composer)* 4041
Goodman, Aubrey *(Librettist)* 4041
Goodman, Aubrey *(Lyricist)* 4041

Goodman, Benny
See also Benny Goodman Sextette and Benny Goodman's Orchestra.
Goodman, Benny *(Cast)* 1528, 2402, 3893, 4256
Goodman, Benny *(Composer)* 146, 432, 4137, 4256
Goodman, Bill *(Cast)* 2676
Goodman, Bob *(Composer)* 4689
Goodman, Bob *(Lyricist)* 4689
Goodman, Charles *(Composer)* 4030
Goodman, Charles *(Lyricist)* 4030
Goodman, Dody *(Cast)* 1362, 2590, 2898, 3366, 3940, 3941, 4047, 4734
Goodman, Doug *(Producer)* 166
Goodman, Douglas F. *(Producer)* 4
Goodman, Frank *(Composer)* 2587
Goodman, Frank *(Lyricist)* 2587
Goodman, I.R. *(Lyricist)* 4387
Goodman, John *(Cast)* 394
Goodman, Jules Eckert *(Librettist)* 4621
Goodman, Kenneth Sawyer *(Author)* 1797
Goodman, Lee *(Cast)* 657, 961, 2898, 4038
Goodman, Lee *(Librettist)* 961
Goodman, Paul *(Librettist)* 2236
Goodman, Paul *(Lyricist)* 2236
Goodman, Philip *(Producer)* 1011, 1297, 3540, 3650, 3659
Goodman, Susan *(Cast)* 2442
Goodman, Susan *(Composer)* 2039
Goodman, Tommy *(Dance Arranger)* 3972
Goodman, Tommy *(Orchestrations)* 2554
Goodman Sextette, Benny
See also Benny Goodman and Benny Goodman's Orchestra.
Goodman Sextette, Benny *(Cast)* 4256
Goodman Theater *(Producer)* 158
Goodman Theatre *(Producer)* 494
Goodman's Orchestra, Benny
See also Benny Goodman and Benny Goodman Sextette.
Goodman's Orchestra, Benny *(Cast)* 1387
Goodmanson, Tim *(Set Design)* 484
Goodrich, Ace *(Cast)* 4141
Goodrich, Ace *(Choreographer)* 4141
Goodrich, Ace *(Composer)* 4141
Goodrich, Ace *(Librettist)* 4141
Goodrich, Ace *(Lyricist)* 4141
Goodrich, Bruce *(Set Design)* 3926
Goodrich, D. Parsons *(Musical Director)* 1568
Goodrich, Edna *(Cast)* 2715, 3805
Goodrich, Frances *(Author)* 1207, 3142, 4732, 4790
Goodrich, Francis *(Author)* 3888
Goodrow, Garry *(Cast)* 3077
Goodsight, Larry *(Lyricist)* 3601
Goodspeed Opera House *(Producer)* 198, 544, 595, 647, 838, 915, 1276, 1496, 1630, 1665, 1804, 1969, 1997, 2026, 2230, 2289, 2542, 2578, 2993, 3667, 3671, 4055, 4136, 4255, 4408, 4740, 4796
Goodwin, Bill *(Set Design)* 2080
Goodwin, Doug *(Musical Director)* 1615
Goodwin, Harry *(Cast)* 4686
Goodwin, J. Cheever *(Author)* 3689
Goodwin, J. Cheever *(Librettist)* 45, 175, 995, 1030, 1090, 1305, 1518, 1576, 2361, 2592, 2936, 3199, 3360, 4014
Goodwin, J. Cheever *(Lyricist)* 613, 934, 1090, 1188, 1305, 2361, 2936, 2974, 3744, 3745, 4014
Goodwin, Joe *(Composer)* 1532
Goodwin, Joe *(Lyricist)* 879, 1391, 1686, 1963, 2214, 2448, 2706, 3137, 3500, 3958, 4290
Goodwin, John *(Composer)* 319
Goodwin, John *(Librettist)* 319, 3103
Goodwin, John *(Lyricist)* 319
Goodwin, Thelma *(Cast)* 4352
Goodwin, Theodore *(Lyricist)* 1654
Goolden, Richard *(Cast)* 1857
Goorney, Howard *(Cast)* 4469
Goralik, Mordecai *(Set Design)* 3984
Gorbea, Carlos *(Composer)* 696
Gorbea, Carlos *(Librettist)* 696
Gorbea, Carlos *(Lyricist)* 696
Gorcey, Bernard *(Cast)* 97, 718, 4077
Gordon, Al
See also Al Gordon's Dogs.
Gordon, Alex *(Librettist)* 1864
Gordon, Alvin J. *(Cast)* 1957
Gordon, Arthur *(Composer)* 1974
Gordon, Barry H. *(Musical Director)* 3019
Gordon, Ben *(Lyricist)* 715
Gordon, Bert *(Cast)* 1931
Gordon, Bert *(Composer)* 2168
Gordon, Bob *(Orchestrations)* 2083, 2092, 2093
Gordon, Bruce *(Cast)* 3210
Gordon, Charles *(Producer)* 568
Gordon, Dan *(Dance Arranger)* 1924
Gordon, David *(Choreographer)* 3937
Gordon, David *(Director)* 3937
Gordon, David P. *(Set Design)* 264
Gordon, Don *(Set Design)* 4332
Gordon, Everett *(Musical Director)* 1596
Gordon, Gloria *(Cast)* 831
Gordon, Hayes *(Cast)* 4018
Gordon, Irving *(Composer)* 4131
Gordon, Irving *(Lyricist)* 4131
Gordon, John *(Librettist)* 4783
Gordon, Jon *(Arrangements)* 2735
Gordon, Jon *(Cast)* 4076
Gordon, Judith *(Producer)* 1914
Gordon, Judy *(Producer)* 305, 1890, 4480
Gordon, Katherine *(Cast)* 1640
Gordon, Kitty *(Cast)* 88, 1183, 1523, 2358, 2387, 3092, 4554, 4747
Gordon, Lady Duff *(Costumes)* 2900
Gordon, Lawrence *(Producer)* 4019, 4020
Gordon, Leon *(Librettist)* 465
Gordon, Mack *(Librettist)* 4177
Gordon, Mack *(Lyricist)* 244, 478, 1207, 1251, 1298, 1302, 1395, 2747, 2808, 3175, 3249, 3343, 3639, 4023, 4025, 4748, 4823
Gordon, Margaret *(Cast)* 3450
Gordon, Marie *(Composer)* 2168, 2288, 3110
Gordon, Mark *(Librettist)* 1581
Gordon, Marvin *(Choreographer)* 766, 1596, 4678
Gordon, Marvin *(Director)* 766, 2657, 4678
Gordon, Marvin *(Librettist)* 4172
Gordon, Marvin *(Lyricist)* 4172

Gordon, Mary Turner *(Cast)* 94
Gordon, Max *(Producer)* 121, 294, 672, 1204, 1284, 1322, 1395, 1680, 1850, 1948, 2252, 3390, 3735, 3990, 4214, 4367, 4557
Gordon, Michael *(Director)* 2680
Gordon, Peggy *(Cast)* 1595
Gordon, Peggy *(Composer)* 1595
Gordon, Rita *(Cast)* 508
Gordon, Robert H. *(Director)* 7, 59, 84, 620, 2137, 2748, 3986, 4640
Gordon, Roy *(Cast)* 3584
Gordon, Ruth *(Cast)* 2628
Gordon, Steve *(Author)* 198
Gordon, Taylor *(Cast)* 3946
Gordon, Tom *(Cast)* 2762
Gordon, Waxey *(Producer)* 4177
Gordon, William *(Cast)* 617
Gordon, Withald *(Set Design)* 208
Gordon's Dogs, Al *(Cast)* 1973
Gordon-Lennox *(Producer)* 2709
Gordon-North Amus. Rev. Co. *(Producer)* 2834
Gordy, Berry *(Composer)* 3739
Gordy, Berry *(Lyricist)* 3739
Gore, Christopher *(Librettist)* 3088, 4558
Gore, Christopher *(Lyricist)* 229, 3088, 4558
Gore, Jim *(Lighting Designer)* 2522
Gore, Michael *(Composer)* 661, 1236
Goreau, Laurraine *(Author)* 2692
Gorey, Cecil *(Producer)* 916
Gorey, Edward *(Author)* 1635
Gorey, Edward *(Lyricist)* 1635
Gorey, Edward *(Set Design)* 1635
Gorham, George H. *(Librettist)* 690
Gorham, George H. *(Lyricist)* 690
Gorham, Mel *(Cast)* 696
Goring *(Composer)* 77
Goring *(Lyricist)* 77
Gorman, Bob *(Cast)* 1441, 4190
Gorman, F. *(Composer)* 4193
Gorman, F. *(Lyricist)* 4193
Gorman, George *(Director)* 538, 3026
Gorman, James *(Choreographer)* 800, 805, 1826, 2525, 3423, 3685
Gorman, James *(Composer)* 4859
Gorman, James *(Director)* 591, 1646, 3809, 4859
Gorman, James *(Librettist)* 4859
Gorman, James *(Lyricist)* 4859
Gorman, Pat *(Costumes)* 3539
Gorman, Pat *(Set Design)* 3539
Gorman, Robert *(Cast)* 3498
Gorman, Ross *(Composer)* 3175
Gorme, Eydie *(Cast)* 1611
Gormley, Robert *(Cast)* 345
Gorney, Jay *(Composer)* 12, 125, 317, 475, 648, 969, 1126, 1131, 1135, 1448, 1477, 1609, 1690, 1780, 1811, 1971, 2020, 2308, 2447, 2748, 2809, 2810, 2823, 2827, 2888, 2933, 3018, 3406, 3946, 4152, 4249, 4331, 4424, 4432, 4575, 4823
Gorney, Jay *(Librettist)* 2748, 2888
Gorney, Jay *(Lyricist)* 648, 4424
Gorney, Jay *(Musical Director)* 125, 1971, 2020, 2888, 3714
Gorney, Jay *(Producer)* 4331
Gorniak, Edyta *(Cast)* 2846
Gorodetsky *(Cast)* 710
Gorsey, Renee *(Cast)* 3527
Gorshin, Frank *(Cast)* 2217
Gorski, Virginia *(Cast)* 2582
Goslar, Lotte *(Cast)* 3441, 3698, 4677
Goslar, Lotte *(Choreographer)* 3698
Gosnell, Evelyn *(Cast)* 3079
Goss, Bick *(Choreographer)* 597, 708, 753, 916, 2051, 3527, 3571, 3932
Goss, Robert *(Cast)* 2838
Gossett, Louis *(Cast)* 108, 1601, 4863
Gotsford, George *(Composer)* 1531
Gottesfeld, Charles *(Librettist)* 3036
Gottler, Archie *(Composer)* 545, 965, 3705, 4290, 4812
Gottler, Archie *(Lyricist)* 3335
Gottler, Jerome *(Composer)* 3335
Gottlieb, Alec *(Author)* 4582
Gottlieb, Morton *(Producer)* 98, 1190, 3338
Gottlieb, S. *(Composer)* 4193
Gottlieb, S. *(Lyricist)* 4193
Gottschalk, Ferdinand *(Cast)* 1535, 2211
Gottschalk, Louis *(Composer)* 761
Gottschalk, Louis F. *(Composer)* 47, 2465, 4381
Gottschalk, Louis F. *(Musical Director)* 104, 767, 1095, 1712, 2836, 2844, 2923, 3265, 3673, 3681, 4430, 4649
Gotwald, David *(Lighting Designer)* 2565
Gough, Lloyd *(Cast)* 3180
Gough, Philip *(Set Design)* 703
Gould, Berni *(Cast)* 2447, 4331
Gould, Billy *(Lyricist)* 3562
Gould, Chuck *(Composer)* 1423
Gould, Chuck *(Lyricist)* 1423
Gould, Dave *(Choreographer)* 1275, 1440, 1657, 1839, 1843, 1874, 3861, 3990, 4335, 4621
Gould, Dave *(Director)* 1415, 1938, 3933
Gould, Dave *(Librettist)* 1311
Gould, Edith Kelly *(Cast)* 3500
Gould, Ellen *(Composer)* 573
Gould, Ellen *(Librettist)* 573
Gould, Ellen *(Lyricist)* 573
Gould, Elliott *(Cast)* 1094, 2048
Gould, Gordon *(Cast)* 4176
Gould, Harold *(Cast)* 1999
Gould, Heywood *(Librettist)* 1380
Gould, Howard *(Cast)* 27
Gould, Jay *(Cast)* 560, 685, 3511, 4375, 4427
Gould, Morton *(Composer)* 183, 404, 1189, 2161, 2205, 4061
Gould, Morton *(Orchestrations)* 183, 2447
Gould, Morton *(Pianist)* 818
Gould, Peter David *(Set Design)* 2440
Gould, Rita *(Cast)* 4808
Gould, William *(Cast)* 4098
Gould, William *(Composer)* 3805
Goulet, Robert *(Cast)* 623, 1764
Goulston, Andre *(Producer)* 1158
Gouraud, Jack *(Composer)* 3129
Gouraud, Jackson *(Composer)* 2498
Gouraud, Powers *(Composer)* 1461

Gouraud, Powers *(Lyricist)* 1461
Gourlay, John *(Cast)* 1392
Gout, Alan *(Musical Director)* 2474
Govatos, Marguerite *(Costumes)* 985
Govatos, Marguerite *(Set Design)* 985
Govern, Alonzo *(Lyricist)* 2720
Gowers, Patrick *(Composer)* 1195, 1857
Gowers, Patrick *(Lyricist)* 1195
Goyen, William *(Librettist)* 35
Goyen, William *(Lyricist)* 35
Goyle, Jack *(Cast)* 1343
Goz, Harry *(Cast)* 171, 721, 4481
Graae, Jason *(Cast)* 1258, 1353, 1832, 2283, 3272, 3960, 4137
Grabel, Naomi *(Producer)* 4729
Grable, Betty *(Cast)* 362, 1109, 1416
Grace, Michael *(Composer)* 2227
Grace, Michael L. *(Librettist)* 4034
Grace, Timothy *(Cast)* 2817
Grace, Wayne *(Cast)* 732
Grace Costumes *(Costumes)* 2294
Grad, Peter *(Producer)* 2043
Grade, Lord *(Producer)* 2822, 4138
Graden, David *(Costumes)* 456, 1591, 4034, 4264, 4537
Graden, David *(Set Design)* 4034
Grady, Don *(Composer)* 1159
Grady, Don *(Musical Director)* 1159
Grady, Lotte *(Cast)* 645
Grady, Lottie *(Cast)* 2044, 2840, 2979, 3979
Grady, Thomas J. *(Director)* 2303
Grady, Tom *(Composer)* 541
Grael, Barry *(Cast)* 2052
Grael, Barry Alan *(Cast)* 4173
Grael, Barry Alan *(Librettist)* 2052, 4173
Grael, Barry Alan *(Lyricist)* 3186, 4173
Graf, Herbert *(Director)* 1817
Graf, James M. *(Producer)* 3069
Graff, George *(Lyricist)* 1751
Graff, Grace *(Cast)* 3255
Graff, Ilene *(Cast)* 2058, 4459
Graff, Kurt *(Cast)* 3255
Graff, Randy *(Cast)* 4, 775, 1161, 2305, 2442
Graff, Todd *(Cast)* 119, 253
Graff Jr., George *(Lyricist)* 310, 2154, 3642, 3910
Grafton, Gerald *(Composer)* 3098
Grafton, Gerald *(Lyricist)* 3098
Grafton, Gloria *(Cast)* 2258, 2311, 3861
Grafton, Portia *(Cast)* 3584
Graham, A.J. *(Cast)* 4799
Graham, Boyd *(Cast)* 2477
Graham, Boyd *(Librettist)* 2477
Graham, Boyd *(Lyricist)* 1149, 2477
Graham, Deborah *(Cast)* 3760, 4034
Graham, Fred *(Cast)* 2497
Graham, Frederick *(Cast)* 2594, 4529, 4667
Graham, Gary *(Composer)* 4431
Graham, Gary *(Lyricist)* 4431
Graham, H. Gordon *(Director)* 3986
Graham, Harry *(Author)* 4010
Graham, Harry *(Composer)* 2392
Graham, Harry *(Librettist)* 2509, 4010, 4258, 4667, 4792
Graham, Harry *(Lyricist)* 466, 1121, 1618, 2293, 2384, 2392, 2509, 2698, 2798, 4258, 4792, 4795
Graham, Hedley Gordon *(Director)* 3255
Graham, Irvin *(Composer)* 63, 70, 621, 924, 943, 2772, 3104, 3108, 4677
Graham, Irvin *(Librettist)* 3104
Graham, Irvin *(Lyricist)* 63, 70, 621, 924, 943, 2772, 3108, 4677
Graham, John McDougal *(Librettist)* 4039
Graham, June *(Choreographer)* 2680
Graham, Larry *(Lyricist)* 1713
Graham, Martha
See also Martha Graham and Her Dance Group.
Graham, Mose *(Cast)* 4112
Graham, R.E. *(Cast)* 1313, 2836
Graham, Rachael *(Cast)* 2805
Graham, Richard *(Cast)* 3837
Graham, Robert *(Composer)* 3103
Graham, Ronald
Not the same as Ronny Graham.
Graham, Ronald *(Cast)* 514, 601, 1101, 1109, 1476, 2379, 4569
Graham, Ronny
Not the same as Ronald Graham.
Graham, Ronny *(Cast)* 108, 154, 2168, 2230, 3107, 3111, 4060, 4268, 4746
Graham, Ronny *(Choreographer)* 3111
Graham, Ronny *(Composer)* 679, 1363, 1648, 2168, 2772, 3107, 3110, 3111, 3112, 3941, 4268, 4627
Graham, Ronny *(Director)* 1648, 2935, 3111
Graham, Ronny *(Librettist)* 2168, 2772, 3107, 3110, 3111, 3112, 3181, 4827
Graham, Ronny *(Lyricist)* 519, 679, 1363, 1648, 2168, 2772, 3107, 3110, 3111, 3112, 3484, 3941, 4268, 4627
Graham, Ronny *(Producer)* 1648
Graham, Stephen *(Producer)* 2468
Graham, William *(Cast)* 2522
Graham and Her Dance Group, Martha *(Cast)* 3639
Graham-Dent, Nellie *(Cast)* 2549
Graham-Geraci, Phillip *(Producer)* 2630
Grahame, Kenneth *(Author)* 4701
Grahame, Sheilah *(Cast)* 3291
Grainer, Ron *(Composer)* 3734
Grainger, Percy *(Composer)* 1989
Grainger, Porter *(Cast)* 2645
Grainger, Porter *(Composer)* 39, 432, 567, 1251, 1499, 1960, 1984, 2645, 3808, 4763
Grainger, Porter *(Librettist)* 2645
Grainger, Porter *(Lyricist)* 39, 432, 567, 1251, 1499, 1960, 1984, 2645, 4763
Grammer, Sidney *(Cast)* 841
Grammis, Adam *(Choreographer)* 1082
Granat, Frank *(Producer)* 160, 367
Granat, Harvey *(Producer)* 4743
Granat, Louis *(Cast)* 2842
Granat, Richard *(Cast)* 1990
Granata, Dona *(Costumes)* 3311, 4004
Grand, Murray *(Composer)* 722, 1362, 1370, 1622, 3107, 3108, 3110, 3111, 3112, 3178, 3286, 4153
Grand, Murray *(Librettist)* 4153

Grand, Murray *(Lyricist)* 1362, 1370, 1622, 3107, 3108, 3110, 3111, 3112, 3178, 4153
Grand, Murray *(Musical Director)* 1362
Grand, Murray *(Pianist)* 1362, 4065
Grande, George *(Lyricist)* 3103
Grandee, George *(Composer)* 3415
Grandy, Fred *(Librettist)* 3565
Graneto, Madeline Ann *(Costumes)* 302, 1262, 3318
Granger, Dick *(Costumes)* 3186
Granger, Farley *(Cast)* 1290
Granger, Maude *(Cast)* 1537
Granger, Michael *(Cast)* 1265
Granger, Porter *(Composer)* 14
Granger, Porter *(Librettist)* 14
Granger, Porter *(Lyricist)* 14
Granger, Stewart *(Cast)* 4207
Granichstaedten, Bruno *(Author)* 1805, 3771
Granichstaedten, Bruno *(Composer)* 1805, 3771
Granier *(Costumes)* 710
Granlund, Nils Thor *(Producer)* 1938
Grant, Arthur R. *(Composer)* 2662
Grant, Bert *(Composer)* 149, 257, 764, 1626, 1735, 3525, 3985, 4148, 4427, 4589, 4806
Grant, Bert *(Lyricist)* 149, 3926
Grant, Bob *(Cast)* 455, 4469
Grant, Cary
See also Archie Leach.
Grant, Cary *(Cast)* 3168, 4733
Grant, Charles *(Orchestrations)* 2, 2574, 3006, 3007, 3008, 3179, 4814
Grant, Charles N. *(Composer)* 543, 1588, 3332, 3658
Grant, Coley *(Cast)* 633
Grant, E.S. *(Cast)* 526
Grant, Earl *(Cast)* 865
Grant, Edward *(Lyricist)* 587
Grant, Faye *(Cast)* 3992
Grant, Henry *(Cast)* 3676
Grant, Ian *(Lyricist)* 1763
Grant, J. Lloyd *(Producer)* 576
Grant, John O. *(Cast)* 1833
Grant, John O. *(Composer)* 1833
Grant, John O. *(Lyricist)* 1833
Grant, Lawrence *(Cast)* 4599
Grant, Lisa Ann *(Cast)* 119
Grant, Martin *(Set Design)* 846
Grant, Mary *(Cast)* 345
Grant, Mary *(Costumes)* 2115, 2755, 2847, 3536
Grant, Matthew *(Set Design)* 2573
Grant, Maxwell *(Composer)* 4828
Grant, Maxwell *(Librettist)* 4566, 4828
Grant, Maxwell *(Lyricist)* 4828
Grant, Micki *(Cast)* 1072, 1319
Grant, Micki *(Composer)* 52, 1072, 2173, 3599, 4744, 4788
Grant, Micki *(Librettist)* 2173
Grant, Micki *(Lyricist)* 52, 1072, 2173, 3599, 4744, 4788
Grant, Pauline *(Choreographer)* 346, 2608
Grant, Richard *(Librettist)* 4098
Grant, Richard *(Lyricist)* 4098
Grant, Sean *(Cast)* 535, 3576, 4138
Grant, Sidney *(Composer)* 3562
Grant, Sidney *(Lyricist)* 3562
Grant, Sterling *(Cast)* 691
Grant, Sydney *(Cast)* 571, 1314, 2549, 2732, 2929, 3395, 3396, 3562, 3915, 4037
Granville, Bernard *(Cast)* 670, 965, 1129, 1378, 1587, 1966, 1971, 2494, 2596, 2960, 3397, 4657, 4806, 4809, 4810, 4814, 4833
Granville, Bernard *(Lyricist)* 4809
Granville, Charlotte *(Cast)* 3866
Granville, Homer *(Cast)* 1537
Granville, Joseph *(Cast)* 1894
Granville, Taylor *(Cast)* 2863, 3422
Grapewin, Charles *(Composer)* 561
Grapewin, Charles *(Librettist)* 69
Grapewin, Charles *(Lyricist)* 4805
Grapewin, Charley *(Director)* 399
Graphenreed, Timothy *(Arrangements)* 3932
Graphenreed, Timothy *(Composer)* 166, 4722
Graphenreed, Timothy *(Dance Arranger)* 119, 789, 828, 2427, 2949, 4722
Graphenreed, Timothy *(Librettist)* 166
Graphenreed, Timothy *(Lyricist)* 166
Graphenreed, Timothy *(Musical Director)* 119
Graphenreed, Timothy *(Orchestrations)* 119, 3932
Graphenreed, Timothy *(Vocal Arranger)* 119
Grasso, Arthur *(Producer)* 991
Grattan, Harry *(Choreographer)* 3098
Grattan, Harry *(Librettist)* 1919, 3827
Grattan, Jack *(Cast)* 3451
Grau *(Producer)* 4500
Graubart, Judy *(Cast)* 2913
Grauman, Sid *(Producer)* 497
Graves, Eileen *(Cast)* 3605
Graves, Ernest *(Cast)* 4191
Graves, George *(Cast)* 2524
Graves, Peter *(Cast)* 650, 972
Graves, Rupert *(Musical Director)* 3829, 4056
Graves, Yolanda *(Cast)* 1970
Gravitte, Debbie Shapiro *(Cast)* 36
Gray, Alexander *(Cast)* 2225, 2843, 3084, 4300
Gray, Carl C. *(Composer)* 149
Gray, Carl C. *(Musical Director)* 149, 2238
Gray, Charles *(Producer)* 2651
Gray, Clifford *(Librettist)* 2976
Gray, Clifford *(Lyricist)* 2976, 3086
Gray, Dolly *(Cast)* 538
Gray, Dolores *(Cast)* 180, 657, 1029, 1415, 3893, 3931, 4237, 4496
Gray, Eden *(Cast)* 1283
Gray, Gilda *(Cast)* 1823, 3166, 3962, 3975, 4033, 4816
Gray, Harold *(Author)* 150, 154, 155
Gray, Helen *(Cast)* 3172, 3735, 3861
Gray, Jack
See Timothy Gray.
Gray, John *(Cast)* 414
Gray, John *(Composer)* 414
Gray, John *(Director)* 414
Gray, John *(Librettist)* 414
Gray, John *(Lyricist)* 414
Gray, Julia *(Cast)* 1185
Gray, Kevin *(Cast)* 757, 2346
Gray, Kristen *(Cast)* 3873

Gray, L. Michael *(Cast)* 4645
Gray, Lawrence *(Cast)* 2423
Gray, Len *(Lyricist)* 500
Gray, Margery *(Cast)* 4312, 4435
Gray, Margery *(Voice)* 56, 3498
Gray, Oliver *(Cast)* 2295
Gray, Patricia *(Librettist)* 2553
Gray, Ralph *(Musical Director)* 3270
Gray, Roger *(Choreographer)* 1458
Gray, Roger *(Librettist)* 3086, 3137
Gray, Roger *(Lyricist)* 1780, 2403
Gray, Rudolf *(Cast)* 14
Gray, Scott *(Costumes)* 1644
Gray, T.J. *(Librettist)* 3006
Gray, Thomas *(Librettist)* 3087
Gray, Thomas *(Lyricist)* 3087
Gray, Thomas J. *(Librettist)* 560, 1686, 4195, 4755
Gray, Thomas J. *(Lyricist)* 909, 1911, 3087, 4195, 4806
Gray, Timothy *(Cast)* 4827
Gray, Timothy *(Composer)* 1891, 2148, 3302
Gray, Timothy *(Director)* 4332, 4388
Gray, Timothy *(Librettist)* 1891, 3302
Gray, Timothy *(Lyricist)* 1891, 2148, 2608, 2705, 3302, 4332, 4388
Gray, Timothy *(Producer)* 4332, 4388
Gray, Timothy *(Vocal Arranger)* 1891
Gray, William *(Director)* 3270
Gray, William *(Producer)* 3270
Grayhorn, Joseph *(Composer)* 2067
Grayhorn, Joseph *(Lyricist)* 2067
Grayhorn, Joseph *(Producer)* 2067
Grayson, Lee *(Orchestrations)* 2074
Grayson Jr., Milton B. *(Cast)* 2372
Graziano, Stephen *(Composer)* 2477
Greaza, Walter N. *(Cast)* 3335
Grec, George *(Producer)* 1785
Greco, Lois *(Cast)* 3539
Gredy, Pierre *(Author)* 98
Greeley, Aurora *(Cast)* 554
Green, Adolph
See also The Revuers.
Green, Adolph *(Cast)* 490, 3278
Green, Adolph *(Librettist)* 167, 363, 404, 490, 599, 1068, 1227, 3278, 3279, 3992, 4008, 4190, 4496
Green, Adolph *(Lyricist)* 363, 404, 490, 599, 1038, 1061, 1068, 1227, 1729, 2073, 2076, 2205, 2452, 2590, 2677, 3278, 3279, 3452, 3453, 3845, 3992, 4008, 4167, 4190, 4496, 4695, 4734
Green, Adolph *(Screenwriter)* 3992
Green, Adoph *(Lyricist)* 3453
Green, Amanda *(Cast)* 2197, 3926
Green, Bernard *(Composer)* 3622
Green, Bernard *(Lyricist)* 3622
Green, Billy *(Cast)* 3605
Green, Bud *(Composer)* 3926, 3962
Green, Bud *(Lyricist)* 418, 1425, 1460, 2141, 2587, 3382, 3907, 3926, 3962, 4240
Green, Burton *(Cast)* 1735, 3401, 4203
Green, Burton *(Composer)* 2816, 4203
Green, Cliff *(Cast)* 813
Green, Cora *(Cast)* 1772, 3614, 4182
Green, Daisy *(Cast)* 1313
Green, Dennis *(Librettist)* 1104
Green, Dennis *(Lyricist)* 1591, 1714
Green, Doe Doe *(Cast)* 1960
Green, Eddie *(Cast)* 439, 1987
Green, Eddie *(Composer)* 2796, 3297
Green, Eddie *(Librettist)* 439, 1980
Green, Eddie *(Lyricist)* 2796, 3297
Green, Eugene *(Cast)* 643
Green, Gerald *(Author)* 4060
Green, H.F. *(Cast)* 3113
Green, H.J. *(Composer)* 1535
Green, Howard J. *(Librettist)* 1446
Green, J. Ed *(Cast)* 645, 982, 3797
Green, J. Ed *(Director)* 645, 2044, 3358
Green, J. Ed *(Librettist)* 645
Green, J. Ed *(Producer)* 645, 2044, 3358, 3797
Green, Jack *(Composer)* 1486
Green, Jackie *(Cast)* 4782
Green, Jane *(Cast)* 1691, 2857
Green, John *(Cast)* 982, 3153
Green, John *(Composer)* 323, 1856, 3905, 4152, 4367, 4498
Green, John *(Musical Director)* 4152
Green, Johnny *(Composer)* 418, 432, 1879, 2772, 3002, 3980, 4159, 4534
Green, Johnny *(Musical Director)* 601, 1879
Green, Johnny *(Vocal Arranger)* 601
Green, Joseph *(Cast)* 361
Green, Joseph *(Screenwriter)* 4769
Green, Laura *(Producer)* 4309
Green, Laurence *(Cast)* 2467
Green, Marion *(Cast)* 152, 1110, 2068, 2937
Green, Martyn *(Cast)* 634, 2977, 3496, 3913, 4155
Green, Martyn *(Director)* 2977
Green, Martyn *(Librettist)* 2977
Green, Milton *(Vocal Arranger)* 483
Green, Mitzi *(Cast)* 247, 404, 2447, 4586
Green, Morris *(Director)* 1110, 1275, 4299
Green, Morris *(Producer)* 1110, 1275, 1440, 1690, 2112, 3185, 3648
Green, Norma *(Cast)* 3180
Green, Paul *(Author)* 2573
Green, Paul *(Librettist)* 2228
Green, Paul *(Lyricist)* 369, 2228
Green, Phil *(Composer)* 2608
Green, Phil *(Orchestrations)* 2608
Green, R. *(Cast)* 1604
Green, Robert *(Lighting Designer)* 3067
Green, Robert *(Set Design)* 3067
Green, Rosie *(Cast)* 4802
Green, Ruby *(Cast)* 1385
Green, Sarah *(Cast)* 449, 641
Green, Schuyler *(Lyricist)* 1607, 4491
Green, Scott *(Director)* 4309
Green, Sylvan *(Composer)* 3605
Green, Teddy *(Cast)* 989
Green, Wayne *(Musical Director)* 3164
Green & Blyer *(Cast)* 684
Green Jr., Isaac *(Librettist)* 2595
Green and Roberta, Tim *(Cast)* 1421

Greenbank, Harry *(Composer)* 1429
Greenbank, Harry *(Lyricist)* 205, 770, 1429, 1470, 1682, 2938, 3803, 3828, 3999, 4390
Greenbank, Percy *(Author)* 4115
Greenbank, Percy *(Composer)* 30, 1470
Greenbank, Percy *(Librettist)* 4795
Greenbank, Percy *(Lyricist)* 30, 178, 353, 470, 767, 906, 1123, 1537, 1538, 1544, 1561, 1626, 2293, 2524, 2844, 3049, 3052, 3098, 3313, 3322, 3618, 3976, 4115, 4354, 4418, 4430, 4554, 4795
Greenbaum, Hyman *(Musical Director)* 3214
Greenberg, Edward *(Director)* 2838
Greenberg, Edwin *(Composer)* 3490
Greenberg, Edwin *(Librettist)* 3490
Greenberg, Edwin *(Lyricist)* 3490
Greenberg, Mitchell *(Cast)* 2142, 2754, 4371, 4769
Greenberg, Rob *(Director)* 1232
Greenberg, Rocky *(Cast)* 3162
Greenberg, Steven A. *(Producer)* 2172
Greenblatt, Kenneth D. *(Producer)* 1649, 1699, 2360, 3171
Greenblatt, Nat *(Librettist)* 62
Greenblatt, Nat *(Producer)* 62
Greenburg, Dan *(Author)* 2016
Greenburg, Dan *(Librettist)* 3233
Greene, Alan *(Composer)* 159, 2580
Greene, Alan *(Lyricist)* 159, 2580
Greene, Bradford *(Composer)* 3713
Greene, Clay M. *(Librettist)* 476, 2117, 2548, 3689, 3976
Greene, Clay M. *(Lyricist)* 235, 476, 687, 3689
Greene, Ellen *(Cast)* 2539, 2544, 3636, 4370
Greene, Evie *(Cast)* 1114
Greene, Frank *(Cast)* 3772
Greene, H.C. *(Director)* 2271
Greene, H.C. *(Librettist)* 2271
Greene, H.C. *(Producer)* 2271
Greene, Harrison *(Cast)* 1206
Greene, Herbert *(Musical Director)* 162, 1456, 2961, 3016, 3210, 4496, 4516
Greene, Herbert *(Producer)* 3016, 3210
Greene, Herbert *(Vocal Arranger)* 162, 363, 1456, 1706, 1748, 3016, 3210, 3837, 3972, 4018, 4516
Greene, Herman *(Cast)* 4254
Greene, I.M. *(Composer)* 1179
Greene, James *(Cast)* 1086
Greene, Jo *(Composer)* 1296
Greene, Jo *(Lyricist)* 1296
Greene, Lyn *(Cast)* 212
Greene, Marge *(Director)* 2388
Greene, Marge *(Librettist)* 2388
Greene, Marion *(Cast)* 3778
Greene, Milton *(Composer)* 2246
Greene, Milton *(Dance Arranger)* 3204
Greene, Milton *(Lyricist)* 2246
Greene, Milton *(Musical Director)* 483, 673, 1265, 1408, 2246, 3204, 3780
Greene, Milton *(Orchestrations)* 2246
Greene, Milton *(Vocal Arranger)* 1265, 1408, 3204, 3780
Greene, Ruby *(Cast)* 1251
Greene, Schuyler *(Lyricist)* 543, 913, 1559, 1588, 1784, 2309, 2373, 2587, 2696, 3184, 3193, 3658, 4418, 4491, 4555
Greene, Tom *(Cast)* 4614
Greener, Dorothy *(Cast)* 1596, 2246, 3664, 3940, 3941, 3942
Greenfield, Debra *(Cast)* 562, 2759
Greenfield, George T. *(Cast)* 1867
Greenfield, H. *(Composer)* 4193
Greenfield, H. *(Lyricist)* 4193
Greenfield, Howard *(Composer)* 4264
Greenfield, Howard *(Lyricist)* 4264
Greenfield, Lillian *(Costumes)* 3662
Greenfield, T. *(Set Design)* 2488
Greenhalgh, Edward *(Cast)* 1373
Greenhouse, Joel *(Librettist)* 1785
Greenhut, Andrew *(Lighting Designer)* 1002
Greenhut, Andrew *(Set Design)* 1002
Greenleaf, Augusta *(Cast)* 3675
Greenleaf, Mace *(Cast)* 1157
Greenough, Walter *(Director)* 4548
Greenough, Walter *(Producer)* 4548
Greenspon, Muriel *(Cast)* 3215
Greenstein, Michael *(Director)* 3670, 3781
Greenstreet, Sydney *(Cast)* 2377, 2669, 2686, 3652, 3735, 4747
Greentrack Entertainment *(Producer)* 3178
Greenville Company, The *(Producer)* 3217
Greenwald, Joseph *(Cast)* 1352
Greenwald, Robert *(Director)* 2796
Greenwald, Tom *(Librettist)* 2224
Greenwald, Tom *(Lyricist)* 2224
Greenwich, Ellie *(Cast)* 2427
Greenwich, Ellie *(Composer)* 2427, 3739, 4193, 4534
Greenwich, Ellie *(Lyricist)* 2427, 3739, 4193, 4534
Greenwich Musical Guild *(Producer)* 3605
Greenwich Village Players *(Producer)* 2203
Greenwich Villagers, *(Producer)* 293
Greenwood, Barrett *(Cast)* 2533, 3677
Greenwood, Charlotte *(Cast)* 1780, 2446, 2461, 2489, 2732, 3007, 3326, 3395, 3396, 3562, 3796, 4037, 4361
Greenwood, Jane *(Costumes)* 1955, 1999, 2075, 2359, 3411, 3577, 3900, 4505
Greenwood, Joan *(Cast)* 2313
Greenwood, Lottie *(Cast)* 3748
Greenwood, Michael *(Cast)* 3227
Greer, Howard *(Costumes)* 1688, 1689, 1944, 2180, 4844
Greer, Howard *(Set Design)* 1688
Greer, Jean *(Cast)* 3654
Greer, Jesse *(Composer)* 567, 771, 1128, 1132, 1134, 1778, 1779, 3342, 3796, 3849, 3907, 3973
Gregg, Bud (Pianist) 3914
Gregg, Hubert *(Composer)* 4027
Gregg, Hubert *(Lyricist)* 4027
Gregg, Jess *(Librettist)* 915
Gregg, Mitchell *(Cast)* 3187
Gregg, Norma *(Composer)* 2
Gregg, Norma *(Lyricist)* 2
Greggory, David *(Librettist)* 1413, 4498
Greggory, David *(Lyricist)* 2707, 3698, 4394, 4498
Gregorio, Rose *(Cast)* 2218
Gregory, Dave *(Librettist)* 1987
Gregory, David *(Librettist)* 3501
Gregory, David *(Lyricist)* 2162, 2167, 2447

Gregory, Don *(Producer)* 869
Gregory, Elsie *(Cast)* 503
Gregory, Fred *(Cast)* 396
Gregory, Gilbert *(Cast)* 1515, 2159, 3047
Gregory, Gillian *(Choreographer)* 2798
Gregory, Helen *(Arrangements)* 2038
Gregory, Helen *(Musical Director)* 2038
Gregory, Helen *(Orchestrations)* 2038
Gregory, James *(Composer)* 4171
Gregory, James *(Dance Arranger)* 4171
Gregory, James *(Lyricist)* 4171
Gregory, James *(Orchestrations)* 4171
Gregory, John *(Choreographer)* 4510
Gregory, Johnny *(Orchestrations)* 194
Gregory, Paul *(Cast)* 1603, 4023, 4847
Gregory, Paul *(Producer)* 1341, 3493
Gregory, Virginia *(Cast)* 3469
Gregson, Richard *(Producer)* 946
Greig, Robert *(Cast)* 3157
Greiner, Seth *(Orchestrations)* 2928
Grennan, Sean *(Librettist)* 3461
Grenville, Claire *(Cast)* 3652
Gresham, Edith *(Cast)* 1384
Gresham, Gloria *(Costumes)* 3956
Gresham, Herbert *(Cast)* 770, 1470, 3999
Gresham, Herbert *(Director)* 186, 405, 902, 1199, 1228, 1388, 1403, 1650, 1731, 2035, 2123, 2363, 2465, 2481, 2493, 2497, 2534, 2697, 2830, 2844, 2907, 2964, 2974, 3053, 3251, 3319, 3422, 3494, 3627, 3652, 3727, 3746, 3747, 3749, 3882, 3977, 4094, 4430, 4590, 4662, 4787, 4801, 4802, 4803
Gresham, Kike *(Cast)* 1421
Gresham, Marion *(Cast)* 1421
Greshoff, Tony *(Lighting Designer)* 21, 136, 740, 1552, 3443, 3652, 4248, 4760, 4802, 4833
Gress, Louis *(Musical Director)* 545, 931, 2380, 2706, 2856, 3314, 3489, 4296, 4778
Gretchaninoff *(Composer)* 710
Grever, Maria *(Composer)* 166, 4572
Grew, William A. *(Author)* 2207
Grew, William A. *(Director)* 1132, 2207
Grew, William A. *(Librettist)* 1131, 1132, 1312
Grey, Alan *(Composer)* 4137
Grey, Alexander *(Cast)* 4844
Grey, Betty *(Cast)* 3587
Grey, Clifford *(Librettist)* 577, 2378, 2757, 2789, 3310, 4213, 4532
Grey, Clifford *(Lyricist)* 152, 200, 201, 465, 466, 568, 1324, 1460, 1461, 1678, 1756, 1916, 1992, 2263, 2293, 2336, 2378, 2519, 2594, 2669, 2757, 2789, 2843, 2976, 3020, 3086, 3148, 3156, 3157, 3163, 3249, 3310, 3323, 3467, 3649, 3819, 4010, 4023, 4213, 4327, 4357, 4532, 4575, 4819
Grey, Elaine *(Cast)* 538
Grey, Frank *(Composer)* 538, 1747, 2545, 2780
Grey, Frank H. *(Composer)* 537, 540, 2780, 4194
Grey, Frank H. *(Musical Director)* 2780, 4194
Grey, H. *(Composer)* 478
Grey, H. *(Lyricist)* 478
Grey, Joel *(Cast)* 610, 1478, 1634, 1660, 2182, 2246, 2554
Grey, Joel (Voice) 4471
Grey, Madeline *(Cast)* 540, 2238, 2271, 4275
Grey, Oscar *(Director)* 2780
Gribble, Harry Wagstaff *(Author)* 2395
Gribble, Harry Wagstaff *(Director)* 199, 200, 720, 1971, 2255, 2395
Gribble, Harry Wagstaff *(Librettist)* 199, 910, 1971, 2263, 2808, 4427
Gribble, Henry Wagstaff *(Librettist)* 201, 3466
Grieg, Edvard *(Composer)* 3487
Grieg, Edvard *(Music Based On)* 4075
Grier, David Alan *(Cast)* 1289
Grier, Jimmy
See also Jimmy Grier's Orchestra.
Grier, Jimmy *(Composer)* 1813, 4799
Grier, Jimmy *(Lyricist)* 1813, 4799
Grier, Rosey *(Cast)* 1389
Grier's Orchestra, Jimmy
See also Jimmy Grier.
Grier's Orchestra, Jimmy *(Cast)* 1311
Grifasi, Joe *(Cast)* 3070, 3197
Griffen, Joyce *(Cast)* 3814
Griffen, Norman *(Cast)* 3157
Griffen, R.L. *(Producer)* 2902
Griffies, Ethel *(Cast)* 2894
Griffin *(Composer)* 4712
Griffin *(Lyricist)* 4712
Griffin, Brent *(Costumes)* 114
Griffin, E.J. *(Lyricist)* 3332
Griffin, Gerald *(Composer)* 452
Griffin, Gerald *(Lyricist)* 452
Griffin, Norman *(Cast)* 611
Griffin, Paul *(Orchestrations)* 3276
Griffin, Paul *(Vocal Arranger)* 3276
Griffin, Peter *(Cast)* 2642
Griffin, Rodney *(Choreographer)* 1903
Griffin, Sean *(Cast)* 951
Griffin, Victor *(Cast)* 1329, 4272
Griffis, William *(Cast)* 935, 1860, 2217, 3702
Griffith, Andy *(Cast)* 1029, 3188
Griffith, Eleanor *(Cast)* 3538, 4105
Griffith, Harry *(Cast)* 4452
Griffith, Harry L. *(Cast)* 617
Griffith, Herbert *(Orchestrations)* 1680
Griffith, Jimmy *(Cast)* 4331
Griffith, Peter *(Cast)* 4169
Griffith, Robert E. *(Producer)* 957, 1280, 2417, 3113, 3351, 4312, 4625
Griffith, Viola *(Cast)* 1460
Griffith, William *(Cast)* 711, 4335
Griffith, William *(Librettist)* 3103
Griffith, William M. *(Cast)* 1447
Griffiths, Frederick R. *(Director)* 18
Griffiths, Frederick R. *(Librettist)* 18
Griffiths, Frederick Richard *(Cast)* 1885
Griffiths, Horald *(Cast)* 459
Griffiths, Horald *(Composer)* 459
Griffiths, Horald *(Lyricist)* 459
Griffiths, May *(Cast)* 2524
Grignon, Monica *(Cast)* 1978
Grimaldi, Dennis *(Choreographer)* 4517
Grimaldi, Dennis *(Producer)* 155, 1890

Grimball, Elizabeth B. *(Director)* 2739
Grimes, Rollin *(Cast)* 953
Grimes, Scott *(Cast)* 695
Grimes, Tammy *(Cast)* 98, 499, 1359, 1427, 1507, 1891, 1933, 2554, 2674, 3020, 4216, 4516
Grimes, Tammy *(Voice)* 4471
Grimm, Brothers *(Author)* 1727, 4106, 4735
Grimwood, Herbert *(Cast)* 2802
Griner, Barbara *(Producer)* 4541
Grinnage, Jack *(Cast)* 407, 410, 413
Grisham, Walter *(Director)* 2168
Grisman, Sam H. *(Director)* 2009
Grisman, Sam H. *(Producer)* 919, 1352, 4276
Grismer, Joseph R. *(Director)* 235
Grismer, Joseph R. *(Producer)* 235
Griso, Frank *(Cast)* 4384
Grist, Reri *(Cast)* 309, 4625
Griswold, Mary *(Set Design)* 4690
Grizzard, George *(Cast)* 3196
Groberg, Susan *(Choreographer)* 3997
Groday, Doris *(Cast)* 1387, 4730
Grodin, Charles *(Director)* 1974
Grodin, Charles *(Librettist)* 1974
Grodin, Charles *(Lyricist)* 1974
Groenendaal, Cris *(Cast)* 2766, 3411, 3464, 4210, 4233
Groener, Harry *(Cast)* 678, 921, 1776, 2152, 3231
Grofe, Ferde *(Composer)* 3639
Grofe, Ferde *(Orchestrations)* 444, 447, 787, 3639, 4821
Grogan, Oscar *(Cast)* 4778
Grollner, Jerry *(Lighting Designer)* 2969
Gromelski, Brad *(Producer)* 3539
Grona, Van *(Choreographer)* 1539
Groneman, Sammy *(Author)* 2075
Groniec, Katarzyna *(Cast)* 2846
Groody, Helen *(Cast)* 1378, 1582
Groody, Louise *(Cast)* 17, 186, 1266, 1625, 1916, 3146, 3184, 3295, 4422
Grooney, E. *(Musical Director)* 617
Grooney, Ernest G. *(Musical Director)* 370, 2126
Gropman, David *(Set Design)* 414, 3175
Gropper, Milton Herbert *(Librettist)* 4280
Gros, Ernest *(Set Design)* 113, 618, 675, 749, 1067, 1090, 1165, 1543, 1905, 2029, 2117, 2233, 2309, 2548, 2624, 2723, 2952, 3144, 3450, 3745, 3751, 3753, 3857, 3948, 4066, 4353, 4554
Gros, Ernest M. *(Set Design)* 357, 527, 770, 3360, 3582
Grose, Robert Paine *(Set Design)* 991
Gross, Arnie *(Arrangements)* 3561
Gross, Arnold *(Dance Arranger)* 2785, 2822, 2925, 4197
Gross, Arnold *(Musical Director)* 1010, 2284, 2785, 4635
Gross, Arnold *(Orchestrations)* 829
Gross, Arnold *(Vocal Arranger)* 2785
Gross, Charles *(Vocal Arranger)* 1878
Gross, Edward *(Producer)* 4123
Gross, Michael *(Cast)* 3468
Gross, Milt *(Librettist)* 2809
Gross, Shelly
See also Guber & Gross Productions.
Gross, Shelly *(Producer)* 534, 1837, 2590, 3427, 3931, 4577
Gross Associates, Lee *(Producer)* 146
Grosser, Maurice *(Librettist)* 1366
Grossman *(Lyricist)* 4291
Grossman, Allen *(Producer)* 1082
Grossman, Bernard *(Lyricist)* 2446, 2489, 2832
Grossman, Bill *(Choreographer)* 962
Grossman, Hal *(Producer)* 4090
Grossman, Herbert *(Composer)* 1136
Grossman, Herbert *(Musical Director)* 101, 935, 1094, 2568, 3731, 4588
Grossman, Herbert *(Vocal Arranger)* 101, 1094, 2568, 4588
Grossman, Larry *(Composer)* 1038, 1068, 1146, 1186, 1634, 1699, 2874, 3186, 3364, 3637, 4034
Grossman, Larry *(Lyricist)* 1038, 3186, 3516
Grossman, Larry *(Vocal Arranger)* 146
Grossman, Shirley *(Composer)* 3530
Grossman, Shirley *(Lyricist)* 3530
Grossmith, Edward *(Lyricist)* 913
Grossmith, George *(Author)* 3157, 4115
Grossmith, George *(Cast)* 334, 611, 1318, 1561, 2392, 2808, 3583, 3584, 3857, 4327, 4418, 4419
Grossmith, George *(Director)* 611
Grossmith, George *(Librettist)* 334, 611, 1067, 3156, 3157, 3569, 4327, 4551
Grossmith, George *(Lyricist)* 334, 611, 1067, 1318, 2498, 3322, 3494, 4115
Grossmith, George *(Producer)* 334, 611, 3569, 4327
Grossmith, Lawrence *(Cast)* 672, 2620, 3193, 3974, 4663
Grossmith, Lawrence *(Lyricist)* 3193
Grossmith Jr., George *(Cast)* 3098, 3948
Grossmith Jr., George *(Librettist)* 3433
Grossmith Jr., George *(Lyricist)* 1569, 3098, 3313, 4115, 4430
Group Theatre *(Producer)* 2228
Grout, James *(Cast)* 1721
Grouya, Ted *(Composer)* 2259
Grove, Betty Ann *(Cast)* 1478, 2064
Grover, Kit *(Set Design)* 3329
Grover, Stanley *(Cast)* 2449, 2651, 2983, 3123
Gruber, Franz *(Composer)* 3259
Grubman, Patty *(Producer)* 2318
Grudeff, Marian *(Composer)* 270, 1841
Grudeff, Marian *(Librettist)* 1107
Grudeff, Marian *(Lyricist)* 270, 1841
Gruenbaum, Fritz *(Author)* 12
Gruenberg, Louis *(Composer)* 3754
Gruenewald, Tom *(Director)* 2731
Gruenwald, Alfred *(Author)* 1113, 4760
Gruenwald, Alfred *(Librettist)* 1113, 2985
Gruenwald, Tom *(Director)* 3527
Grunbaum, Alfred *(Author)* 2334
Grunbaum, Fritz *(Author)* 1067, 2886, 3839
Grundman, Clare *(Orchestrations)* 1094, 2439, 3473, 3954, 4499
Grundmann, Tim *(Composer)* 528, 1004, 1155, 3165, 3329, 3997
Grundmann, Tim *(Dance Arranger)* 528, 1155, 3329, 3997
Grundmann, Tim *(Librettist)* 528, 1004, 1155, 3165, 3329, 3997

Grundmann, Tim *(Lyricist)* 528, 1004, 1155, 3165, 3329, 3997
Grundmann, Tim *(Musical Director)* 528, 1004, 1155, 3165, 3329, 3997
Grundmann, Tim *(Orchestrations)* 528, 1004, 1155, 3165, 3329, 3997
Grundmann, Tim *(Pianist)* 528
Grundmann, Tim *(Producer)* 3997
Grundmann, Tim *(Vocal Arranger)* 528, 1004, 1155, 3165, 3329, 3997
Grundy, Will *(Cast)* 1909
Grunwald, Alfred *(Author)* 277, 475, 905, 1530, 2424, 3051, 4550
Grunwald, Alfred *(Librettist)* 771
Gryning, Heather Hope *(Cast)* 544
Guardino, Harry *(Cast)* 162
Guare, John *(Author)* 1999, 2945
Guare, John *(Composer)* 1999, 2945
Guare, John *(Librettist)* 1214, 4485
Guare, John *(Lyricist)* 1999, 2945, 4091, 4485
Guber, Lee
See also Guber & Gross Productions.
Guber, Lee *(Producer)* 534, 1745, 1837, 2590, 3427, 3644, 3931, 4577
Guber & Gross Productions
See also Lee Guber and Shelly Gross.
Guber & Gross Productions *(Producer)* 3936
Gudrun, Elna *(Cast)* 2843
Guerin *(Author)* 3433
Guerite, Laura *(Cast)* 1553, 2986
Guerra, Robert *(Lighting Designer)* 2584
Guerra, Robert *(Set Design)* 107, 2584, 2737, 4789
Guerrero, Danny *(Cast)* 1770
Guerrero, Lalo *(Composer)* 4861
Guerrero, Lalo *(Lyricist)* 4861
Guess, Alvaleta *(Cast)* 240, 4255
Guest, Chrisopher *(Composer)* 3077
Guest, Christopher *(Cast)* 3077
Guest, Christopher *(Composer)* 3077
Guest, Christopher *(Librettist)* 3076
Guest, Christopher *(Orchestrations)* 3077
Guest, Christopher *(Vocal Arranger)* 3077
Guest, Clifford *(Cast)* 2850
Guetary, Georges *(Cast)* 183, 453, 3543
Guggenheimer, Elinor *(Librettist)* 3548
Guggenheimer, Elinor *(Lyricist)* 3548
Guida, Mlle. *(Choreographer)* 758
Guidall, George *(Cast)* 3559, 4790
Guilbert, Ann *(Cast)* 255, 408, 411
Guilbert, Warburton *(Composer)* 1342, 3103
Guilbert, Yvette *(Composer)* 3386
Guilbert, Yvette *(Lyricist)* 3386, 4368
Guilford, Nanette *(Cast)* 680
Guilford, Willor *(Cast)* 3528
Guillatt, Lee *(Cast)* 2220
Guillaume, Robert *(Cast)* 169, 1319, 2355, 3018
Guillemaud, Marcel *(Author)* 3251, 3494
Guillen, Nicolas *(Lyricist)* 2395
Guilliatt, Lee *(Cast)* 624, 755, 1229, 1426, 2110, 2124, 2243, 2579, 4595, 4684
Guinan, Texas *(Cast)* 1975, 3342
Guion, David W. *(Composer)* 805
Guiterrez, Carmen *(Cast)* 4625
Guitry, Sacha *(Lyricist)* 3079
Guittard, Laurence *(Cast)* 1427, 2536, 2617, 3743, 4505
Gulfport, Billy *(Cast)* 4183
Gullan, Campbell *(Director)* 3481
Gulon, Jack *(Composer)* 1334
Gumble, Albert *(Composer)* 257, 965, 1404, 2696, 2981, 3677, 3977, 3985, 4712, 4807, 4812, 4838
Gumble, Albert *(Lyricist)* 2981
Gunderson, Steve *(Cast)* 261, 4193
Gunderson, Steve *(Librettist)* 4193
Gunderson, Steve *(Musical Director)* 261
Gunderson, Steve *(Orchestrations)* 261
Gunderson, Steve *(Vocal Arranger)* 261, 4193
Gunn, Archie *(Costumes)* 457, 2209, 2286, 2695, 2724, 4046, 4738
Gunn, Billy *(Cast)* 1838
Gunn, John *(Director)* 1905
Gunning, Louise *(Cast)* 118, 276, 694, 998, 2632, 2745, 2982, 3229, 3750, 4404, 4666
Gunter, Brian *(Cast)* 4740
Gunther, Archibald Clavering *(Author)* 3685
Gunther, John *(Author)* 2137
Gunther, William *(Musical Director)* 2421
Gunton, Bob *(Cast)* 394, 1015, 1211, 2318, 3671, 3792, 4744
Gurney, A.R. *(Librettist)* 4535
Guske, Bill *(Choreographer)* 549, 840, 2235
Guske, Bill *(Director)* 549, 2235
Gusman, Samuel *(Producer)* 1019
Gustafson, Karen *(Musical Director)* 2106, 2318, 2433, 2728, 3075, 3619, 3763, 3956
Gustafson, Karen *(Vocal Arranger)* 2106, 3763, 3956
Guster, Al *(Cast)* 2259
Guterson, Waldemar *(Musical Director)* 1415
Guthman, Louise *(Lighting Designer)* 4522
Guthrie, David *(Costumes)* 1045
Guthrie, David *(Set Design)* 1045, 2785
Guthrie, Tyrone *(Director)* 630
Guthrie, Woody *(Cast)* 2175
Guthrie, Woody *(Composer)* 2175, 3840, 4410, 4740
Guthrie, Woody *(Librettist)* 4740
Guthrie, Woody *(Lyricist)* 2175, 3840, 4410, 4740
Gutierrez, Gerald *(Director)* 942, 2643
Gutman, Arthur *(Composer)* 1250, 2825
Gutman, Arthur *(Musical Director)* 1847, 4794
Gutman, Arthur *(Orchestrations)* 557, 1847, 3007, 4794, 4821
Gutman, Arthur H. *(Composer)* 1212, 3466, 4227
Gutman, Arthur H. *(Musical Director)* 2270, 4227
Gutman, Arthur H. *(Orchestrations)* 4227
Guy, Edna *(Cast)* 1251
Guy, Jasmine *(Cast)* 338, 2427
Guy, Rosa *(Author)* 3285
Guyll, Judy *(Cast)* 1697
Guys, Sheila *(Cast)* 2817
Guyves, Noel *(Composer)* 3954
Guyves, Noel *(Lyricist)* 3954
Guzzone, Paul *(Composer)* 3076
Gwenn, Edmund *(Cast)* 1534, 1855

Gwillim, Jack *(Cast)* 181
Gwin, Byrne *(Cast)* 3224
Gwynne, Fred *(Cast)* 135, 1860, 2150, 2553, 2953
Gwyther, Geoffrey *(Cast)* 466, 3307
Gwyther, Geoffrey *(Composer)* 3719
Gwyther, Geoffrey *(Lyricist)* 702, 3719
Gyarmathy, Michel *(Costumes)* 1326
Gyarmathy, Michel *(Producer)* 1326
Gyarmathy, Michel *(Set Design)* 1326
Gyde, Courier *(Composer)* 1213
Gyngell, Paul *(Cast)* 661
Gynt, Kaj *(Librettist)* 3660
Gyse, Alisa *(Cast)* 4534

H

H.M. Tennent *(Producer)* 66
Haack, Morton *(Costumes)* 2707
Haagensen, Erik *(Librettist)* 1276, 2012, 3221
Haagensen, Erik *(Lyricist)* 1276, 2012, 3221, 4004
Haakon, Paul *(Cast)* 117, 216, 689, 1973, 2402, 2847, 3011, 3683, 3955, 4110
Haakon, Paul *(Choreographer)* 2847, 3683, 4110
Haas, Helen A. *(Costumes)* 1378
Haas, Holly *(Set Design)* 3209
Haas, Hugo *(Cast)* 2679
Haase, Oscar *(Composer)* 2701
Haatainen, Christina *(Costumes)* 3752
Habbema, Eddy *(Director)* 949
Haber, Carl *(Director)* 562
Haber, John L. *(Director)* 1037, 1402
Haber, John L. *(Librettist)* 1402
Haber, John L. *(Producer)* 1402
Haber, Louis *(Composer)* 447, 3705
Haberman, Linda *(Choreographer)* 424, 2230
Hack, Moe *(Lighting Designer)* 2175
Hack, Monroe *(Director)* 4273
Hack, Monroe B. *(Director)* 467
Hack, Monroe B. *(Producer)* 4273
Hackady, Hal *(Composer)* 456, 3516
Hackady, Hal *(Librettist)* 90, 3708
Hackady, Hal *(Lyricist)* 90, 101, 456, 1146, 1634, 2874, 3111, 3112, 3637, 3708, 4034, 4297
Hacker, Linda *(Set Design)* 198, 1804, 1873, 3034
Hacker, Phil M. *(Lyricist)* 331
Hacker, Seymour *(Producer)* 2220
Hacket, George *(Arrangements)* 2094
Hackett, Albert *(Author)* 1207, 3142, 3888, 4732, 4790
Hackett, Buddy *(Cast)* 2053
Hackett, George *(Arrangements)* 2092, 2093
Hackett, George *(Musical Director)* 2083, 2091, 2092, 2093, 2094, 2095
Hackett, George *(Orchestrations)* 2085, 2089, 2090, 2092
Hackett, Hal *(Cast)* 490
Hackett, Jeanne *(Costumes)* 1779
Hackett, Jeanne *(Lyricist)* 1779
Hackett, Joan *(Cast)* 3389
Hackett, Lester *(Producer)* 600
Hackett, Raymond *(Cast)* 423
Hackett, Ron *(Cast)* 2572
Hackett, W. Broderick *(Set Design)* 2910
Hackett, Walter *(Author)* 4671
Hackforth, Norman *(Composer)* 703, 2168, 2227
Hackforth, Norman *(Lyricist)* 2168, 2227
Hackman, Gene *(Cast)* 160
Hackney, John C. *(Composer)* 1604
Hadary, Jonathan *(Cast)* 212, 829, 1591, 4412
Haddad, Robert *(Choreographer)* 2977, 3186, 4388
Haddon, Peter *(Cast)* 704
Haddow, Jeffrey *(Cast)* 3858
Haddow, Jeffrey *(Composer)* 3858
Haddow, Jeffrey *(Librettist)* 3858
Haddow, Jeffrey *(Lyricist)* 3858
Hadjidakis, Manos *(Composer)* 2106
Hadley, Bob *(Producer)* 239
Hadley, Henry *(Composer)* 3073, 3147
Hadley, Henry *(Musical Director)* 3147
Hadley, Jonathan *(Cast)* 3568, 4325
Haenschen, Walter *(Orchestrations)* 3179
Haenschen, Walter Gustave *(Composer)* 1654, 4808
Haffner, Karl *(Author)* 689
Hafleigh *(Costumes)* 4802
Hafner, Julia J. *(Cast)* 788
Hafner, Tom *(Cast)* 3555
Hagan, Aaron *(Arrangements)* 2065
Hagan, Aaron *(Musical Director)* 2065, 2241
Hagan, Howard *(Cast)* 319, 3697
Hageman, Maurice *(Librettist)* 1459
Hagen, Earle *(Composer)* 1713
Hagen, Gay *(Cast)* 3318
Hagen, John Milton *(Composer)* 293
Hagen, John Milton *(Lyricist)* 293
Hager, Clyde *(Cast)* 2300
Hager, Frederick W. *(Composer)* 2964
Hager, Louis Busch *(Producer)* 1402, 1636, 3429, 3608
Hagerman, Maurice *(Librettist)* 1758
Hagerman, Maurice *(Lyricist)* 1758
Hagerty, Julie *(Cast)* 2945
Haggard, Stephen *(Cast)* 818
Haggart, Bob *(Composer)* 964, 4255
Haggart, Bobby *(Orchestrations)* 1336
Haggarty, George *(Cast)* 4778
Haggin, Ben Ali *(Costumes)* 3768, 4819
Haggins, Jon *(Costumes)* 3522
Haggott, John *(Director)* 1284
Haggott, John *(Librettist)* 1284
Hagler, Stan *(Lyricist)* 90
Hagman, Larry *(Cast)* 3094
Hague, Aaron *(Musical Director)* 533
Hague, Aaron *(Orchestrations)* 533
Hague, Albert *(Composer)* 615, 961, 1273, 1306, 1567, 1832, 2015, 2168, 2898, 3123, 3509, 3687, 3694, 4827
Hague, Albert *(Dance Arranger)* 2898
Hague, Albert *(Vocal Arranger)* 2898
Haig, Emma *(Cast)* 1920, 3006, 3323, 4300, 4810
Haig, Peter *(Cast)* 2918
Haigh, Kenneth *(Cast)* 2682
Haight, Reba *(Cast)* 222
Haight Jr., George *(Librettist)* 3086

Haile, Evans *(Musical Director)* 3864
Haimsohn, George *(Librettist)* 956
Haimsohn, George *(Lyricist)* 956
Hain, William *(Cast)* 1110, 3735
Hainert, Henry *(Cast)* 2762
Haines, A. Larry *(Cast)* 1471, 3603, 4474
Haines, H.E. *(Composer)* 246
Haines, Herbert E. *(Composer)* 333, 675, 1043
Haines, Jim *(Lyricist)* 757
Haines, Louis *(Cast)* 1388
Haines, Will E. *(Composer)* 1066, 3820
Haines, Will E. *(Lyricist)* 3820
Hairston, William *(Librettist)* 2203
Hajos, Karl *(Composer)* 110, 3078, 4669
Hajos, Karl *(Music Adaptation)* 110
Hajos, Karl *(Musical Director)* 4226
Hajos, Karl *(Orchestrations)* 110, 4226
Hajos, Mitzi *(Cast)* 1849, 2358, 3537, 3621, 3839
Hakesworth, Jenny *(Librettist)* 1253
Haldane, Harry *(Lyricist)* 2042
Haldane, Harry M. *(Composer)* 1766
Haldeman, Ed *(Librettist)* 3683
Hale, Alan *(Cast)* 2574
Hale, Binnie *(Cast)* 2976, 4519
Hale, Bobby *(Cast)* 396
Hale, Chanin *(Cast)* 4629
Hale, Charles *(Cast)* 1196
Hale, Chester *(Cast)* 3006, 3431
Hale, Chester
See also Chester Hale Girls.
Hale, Chester *(Choreographer)* 1384, 1693, 1694, 1779, 1780, 2005, 2078, 2140, 2504, 2628, 2691, 2947, 3002, 3012, 3150, 3431, 3680, 4365, 4572
Hale, Creighton *(Cast)* 977
Hale, Diana *(Cast)* 92
Hale, George *(Choreographer)* 1528, 3225, 3379, 3674, 4179
Hale, George *(Director)* 63, 3966
Hale, George *(Lyricist)* 1411
Hale, George *(Producer)* 1411, 1931, 2379
Hale, Georgie *(Cast)* 608, 1690, 2706
Hale, Georgie *(Choreographer)* 1136, 1800, 3131
Hale, Georgie *(Director)* 1800
Hale, Georgie *(Producer)* 1825
Hale, Helen *(Cast)* 3437, 4738
Hale, John *(Cast)* 1135, 1137
Hale, Louise Closser *(Cast)* 1221, 3382, 3799
Hale, Richard *(Cast)* 165
Hale, Ruth *(Librettist)* 4548
Hale, Sonnie *(Cast)* 1202, 3291, 4581
Hale, Tom *(Arrangements)* 914
Hale, Walter *(Cast)* 3050
Hale Girls, Chester
See also Chester Hale.
Hale Girls, Chester *(Cast)* 3150
Haleloke *(Cast)* 197
Halet, Laurent *(Composer)* 4818
Halevy, Ludovic *(Author)* 653, 2507
Haley, Jack *(Cast)* 1339, 1387, 1396, 1460, 1461, 1894, 2137, 3783, 4267
Haley Sisters, The *(Cast)* 1911
Haliday, Bryant *(Producer)* 2772
Hall, Adelaide *(Cast)* 441, 567, 880, 1028, 2190, 2608, 3808, 4207
Hall, Adrian *(Director)* 35, 3725
Hall, Annette *(Cast)* 2559
Hall, Bettina *(Cast)* 163, 672, 2545, 2808, 4352
Hall, Cameron *(Cast)* 814
Hall, Carl *(Cast)* 4460
Hall, Carl *(Vocal Arranger)* 4459
Hall, Carlyle *(Orchestrations)* 823, 935, 1730, 4577
Hall, Carol *(Cast)* 4398
Hall, Carol *(Composer)* 4, 373, 374, 1389, 1630, 4398
Hall, Carol *(Librettist)* 4, 4398
Hall, Carol *(Lyricist)* 4, 373, 374, 1389, 1630, 3364, 4398
Hall, Charles Edward *(Cast)* 3637
Hall, Cliff *(Cast)* 1860, 3379, 4823
Hall, Cliff *(Lyricist)* 3241
Hall, Davis *(Director)* 1702
Hall, Delores *(Cast)* 374, 1116, 2134, 2372, 3159, 3871, 4788
Hall, Donald *(Cast)* 954
Hall, Dorothy *(Cast)* 1323, 4100
Hall, George *(Cast)* 44, 620, 759, 809, 1023, 1194, 2439, 3914, 4329, 4432
Hall, George *(Librettist)* 3914
Hall, Glenn *(Cast)* 2340, 2385, 2670
Hall, Grayson *(Cast)* 1755, 4190
Hall, Gus *(Cast)* 449
Hall, Harrison *(Producer)* 3168
Hall, Howard *(Lyricist)* 510
Hall, Jessie Mae *(Cast)* 938
Hall, John *(Cast)* 2285
Hall, John *(Composer)* 2954
Hall, John T. *(Composer)* 3626
Hall, Josephine *(Cast)* 41, 734, 1540, 2302, 2343, 2374, 2714, 2863, 3790
Hall, Juanita *(Cast)* 1315, 2000, 2750, 4096, 4123
Hall, Kate *(Cast)* 447
Hall, Laura Nelson *(Cast)* 1210
Hall, Lewis *(Composer)* 114
Hall, Lisa *(Cast)* 2055
Hall, Margaret *(Cast)* 1891
Hall, Marie *(Cast)* 1703
Hall, Mollie *(Cast)* 264
Hall, Natalie *(Cast)* 277, 2348, 3011, 3014, 4352, 4372
Hall, Owen *(Author)* 351, 3976
Hall, Owen *(Librettist)* 205, 351, 1313, 1429, 1470, 1537, 1682, 2498, 2803, 3882
Hall, Owen *(Lyricist)* 2498, 3882
Hall, Pamela *(Cast)* 1012
Hall, Pauline *(Cast)* 1193, 4393
Hall, Peter *(Director)* 2196, 4558
Hall, Peter J. *(Costumes)* 4861
Hall, Phil *(Musical Director)* 3517, 3708
Hall, Phil *(Vocal Arranger)* 3517
Hall, Porter *(Cast)* 536
Hall, Ralston *(Cast)* 2229
Hall, Ronnie *(Cast)* 3124
Hall, Steve *(Cast)* 2759
Hall, Steven F. *(Cast)* 809

Hall, Teddy *(Composer)* 532
Hall, Teddy *(Lyricist)* 532, 1840
Hall, Terry *(Composer)* 3739
Hall, Terry *(Lyricist)* 3739
Hall, Thurston *(Cast)* 1391, 1784, 3304
Hall, William D. *(Librettist)* 3797
Hall Johnson Choir *(Cast)* 467
Hall Jr., Barrie Lee *(Orchestrations)* 3628
Hallam, Basil *(Cast)* 3398
Hallelujah Quartette *(Cast)* 2640
Hallem, Henry *(Cast)* 1473
Haller, Herman *(Author)* 659
Haller, Tobias *(Cast)* 1635
Halley, Sharon *(Choreographer)* 1171, 2651
Halley Jr., Ben *(Cast)* 1914
Hallick, Ned *(Lighting Designer)* 426, 3123
Halliday, Andy *(Cast)* 3606
Halliday, Buzz *(Cast)* 1567, 3204, 3615
Halliday, Francis *(Cast)* 2972
Halliday, Heller *(Cast)* 3453
Halliday, Hildegarde *(Cast)* 1446, 1447, 1448, 3064, 3103
Halliday, John *(Cast)* 1144, 4105, 4600
Halliday, Richard *(Producer)* 2201, 3453, 4095
Halliday, Robert *(Cast)* 1027, 3011, 3117, 3584, 4392, 4667
Halliday, Will *(Cast)* 3348
Halliday, William *(Cast)* 4757
Halligan, William *(Director)* 79, 3796
Halligan, William *(Producer)* 79
Hallor, Edith *(Cast)* 2430
Halloran Jr., William A. *(Composer)* 4776
Halloran Jr., William A. *(Lyricist)* 4776
Hallow, John *(Cast)* 3126
Hally, Martha *(Costumes)* 140
Halperin, Nan *(Cast)* 2516, 2706, 4104
Halpern, Jeff *(Musical Director)* 992
Halpin, Helen *(Cast)* 673
Halpin, Luke *(Cast)* 4270
Halstead, Edgar *(Cast)* 1230
Halston *(Costumes)* 16
Halt, Spaulding *(Lyricist)* 720
Halvertson, Lynn *(Cast)* 3561
Hambitzer, Charles *(Composer)* 2623, 3692
Hamblen, Bernard *(Composer)* 717
Hambleton, John *(Costumes)* 2061, 2068, 2225, 2821, 3990, 4142
Hambleton, T. Edward *(Producer)* 2958, 3288
Hamblin, Bernard *(Composer)* 3481
Hamblin, Bernard *(Lyricist)* 3481
Hamburger, Jay *(Lyricist)* 1595
Hamerman, Marc *(Producer)* 2055
Hamill, Harriet *(Cast)* 266
Hamill, Katherine *(Cast)* 4179
Hamill, Mark *(Cast)* 1776
Hamill, Stuart *(Librettist)* 303
Hamilton, Al *(Costumes)* 1880
Hamilton, Al *(Set Design)* 1880
Hamilton, Beatrice *(Cast)* 4556
Hamilton, Bob *(Choreographer)* 2246, 3801, 4629
Hamilton, Burton *(Composer)* 4776
Hamilton, Caroline *(Cast)* 3570
Hamilton, Christian *(Librettist)* 2617
Hamilton, Cosmo *(Author)* 675, 3481, 3974
Hamilton, Cosmo *(Librettist)* 333, 356, 675, 1043, 1309, 2025, 4133
Hamilton, Gertrude *(Cast)* 2698
Hamilton, Gloria *(Cast)* 2439
Hamilton, Grace *(Cast)* 199, 4121
Hamilton, Hale *(Author)* 1009
Hamilton, Hale *(Cast)* 1009
Hamilton, Hamtree *(Cast)* 2540
Hamilton, Harry *(Lyricist)* 1429
Hamilton, Henry *(Librettist)* 1114, 2524, 3857, 4554
Hamilton, Henry *(Lyricist)* 1114, 1429, 1454
Hamilton, Holly *(Cast)* 3814
Hamilton, James *(Cast)* 2780
Hamilton, James *(Set Design)* 1637
Hamilton, John F. *(Cast)* 3224
Hamilton, Karlah *(Cast)* 4799
Hamilton, Kelly *(Composer)* 962, 4454
Hamilton, Kelly *(Librettist)* 962, 4454
Hamilton, Kelly *(Lyricist)* 962, 4454
Hamilton, Laura *(Cast)* 1228, 3222, 3396, 3652
Hamilton, Lawrence *(Cast)* 3724, 4534
Hamilton, Les *(Cast)* 2086
Hamilton, Margaret *(Cast)* 823, 1614, 2496, 3287
Hamilton, Marion *(Cast)* 792
Hamilton, Morris *(Composer)* 1128, 1132, 1134, 2545, 4335
Hamilton, Nancy *(Cast)* 3103, 3292
Hamilton, Nancy *(Composer)* 2294
Hamilton, Nancy *(Librettist)* 3103, 3292, 4362, 4483
Hamilton, Nancy *(Lyricist)* 2294, 3103, 3104, 3292, 3453, 4362, 4483
Hamilton, Ord *(Composer)* 203, 3020
Hamilton, Ord *(Lyricist)* 203
Hamilton, Patrick *(Cast)* 1732
Hamilton, Peter *(Choreographer)* 339, 2168, 2339
Hamilton, Roger *(Cast)* 3506
Hamilton, Spike *(Cast)* 2850
Hamilton, Thomas *(Cast)* 207
Hamilton, W. Franklin *(Set Design)* 2159
Hamilton, William *(Cast)* 402, 1080
Hamlin, Fred R. *(Producer)* 250, 2160, 4723
Hamlin, Stephen *(Lighting Designer)* 945
Hamlisch, Marvin *(Composer)* 427, 746, 1436, 1437, 1633, 2038, 2196, 3181, 3936, 4019, 4020, 4334
Hamlisch, Marvin *(Dance Arranger)* 1611, 1846, 2874
Hammel, T.A. *(Composer)* 3022
Hammel, T.A. *(Lyricist)* 3022
Hammer, Jack *(Composer)* 3695, 3739
Hammer, Jack *(Lyricist)* 3695, 3739
Hammer, Mark *(Cast)* 3000
Hammer, Robert *(Vocal Arranger)* 1924
Hammerlee, Patricia *(Cast)* 3107, 3899, 4542
Hammerschlag, Peter *(Librettist)* 1413
Hammerstein, Alice *(Lyricist)* 4273
Hammerstein, Arthur *(Director)* 97
Hammerstein, Arthur *(Lyricist)* 4056
Hammerstein, Arthur *(Producer)* 97, 288, 468, 953, 1424, 1603, 1617, 1888, 2216, 2292, 2636, 2708, 2768,

3532, 3772, 4056, 4063, 4077, 4234, 4378, 4464, 4692, 4694, 4784
Hammerstein, Elaine *(Cast)* 1888
Hammerstein, James *(Director)* 4146, 4468
Hammerstein, Reginald *(Director)* 277, 288, 1603, 1617, 4234
Hammerstein, Reginald *(Producer)* 145, 4280
Hammerstein, Stella *(Cast)* 1210
Hammerstein, Theodore *(Director)* 3907, 3946, 4545
Hammerstein, Theodore *(Producer)* 606
Hammerstein, Theodore J. *(Producer)* 4648
Hammerstein I, Oscar *(Composer)* 2995, 3609, 3834, 4242, 4597
Hammerstein I, Oscar *(Librettist)* 2995, 3609, 3834, 4597
Hammerstein I, Oscar *(Lyricist)* 2995, 3609, 3834, 4242, 4597
Hammerstein I, Oscar *(Producer)* 2157, 2365, 2995, 3081, 3609, 3834, 4242, 4597
Hammerstein II, Oscar *(Cast)* 1956, 3284, 3419
Hammerstein II, Oscar *(Director)* 277, 1145, 1387, 1440, 2348, 3014, 3117, 3650, 3949, 4214, 4308, 4361, 4557, 4781
Hammerstein II, Oscar *(Librettist)* 85, 97, 277, 653, 660, 759, 953, 1027, 1145, 1315, 1387, 1440, 1476, 1603, 1617, 1956, 2216, 2312, 2768, 2797, 3014, 3117, 3263, 3505, 3623, 3650, 3772, 3949, 4077, 4096, 4212, 4214, 4234, 4308, 4361, 4378, 4557, 4692, 4694, 4709
Hammerstein II, Oscar *(Lyricist)* 85, 97, 117, 277, 288, 555, 653, 660, 759, 930, 953, 1027, 1040, 1145, 1315, 1321, 1387, 1424, 1476, 1603, 1733, 1749, 1788, 1840, 1956, 1984, 2193, 2204, 2205, 2216, 2312, 2372, 2611, 2653, 2708, 2768, 2786, 2797, 3014, 3018, 3020, 3117, 3150, 3175, 3249, 3261, 3263, 3505, 3623, 3650, 3772, 3783, 3847, 3936, 3949, 4077, 4096, 4146, 4212, 4214, 4234, 4308, 4361, 4378, 4399, 4477, 4530, 4557, 4692, 4694, 4780, 4799
Hammerstein II, Oscar *(Producer)* 153, 1315, 1749, 2312, 2797, 3505, 4095, 4096
Hammett, Dashiell *(Author)* 3142
Hammond, Andrew *(Cast)* 2970
Hammond, Blair *(Choreographer)* 1347
Hammond, Earl *(Cast)* 2268, 4798
Hammond, Paul *(Cast)* 831
Hammond, Percy *(Cast)* 1523
Hammond, Ruth *(Cast)* 4365
Hammond, Thomas *(Producer)* 2464, 2948, 3439
Hammond, Virginia *(Cast)* 2729
Hamp, Charles *(Cast)* 1632
Hampden, Walter *(Cast)* 1623
Hample, Stuart *(Librettist)* 3871
Hampshire, Susan *(Cast)* 1089
Hampton, Christopher *(Librettist)* 4217
Hampton, Christopher *(Lyricist)* 4217
Hampton, Dawn *(Cast)* 1697
Hampton, Ethel *(Cast)* 3283
Hampton, Hope *(Cast)* 1834, 3063
Hampton, Mark *(Librettist)* 1813
Hampton, Max *(Librettist)* 1766
Hampton, Pete *(Cast)* 2111
Hampton, Stewart *(Cast)* 471
Hanafin, Hope *(Costumes)* 1509
Hanaford, Edwin *(Librettist)* 1909
Hanan, Stephen *(Cast)* 678, 4796
Hancock, Carolyn *(Costumes)* 1446, 1447
Hancock, Carolyn *(Set Design)* 1446, 1447
Hancock, Louis *(Musical Director)* 4220
Hancock, Sheila *(Cast)* 1857
Hand, Carl *(Lyricist)* 3417
Hand, David Hale *(Lighting Designer)* 2910
Hand, Margot *(Cast)* 4173
Handleman, Stanley *(Librettist)* 4627
Handley, Alan *(Cast)* 1286, 3103
Handley, Alan *(Composer)* 4230
Handley, Alan *(Director)* 58, 4230
Handley, Alan *(Lyricist)* 4230
Handley, Alan *(Producer)* 58, 4230
Handman, Lou *(Composer)* 879, 1154, 1643, 3149
Handman, Lou *(Lyricist)* 3149, 4193
Hands, Divers *(Composer)* 3440
Hands, Divers *(Lyricist)* 3440
Hands, Terry *(Director)* 661
Hands, Terry *(Lighting Designer)* 661
Handy, John *(Orchestrations)* 2080
Handy, Lucille *(Cast)* 3089
Handy, W.C. *(Additional Music)* 552
Handy, W.C. *(Cast)* 887
Handy, W.C. *(Composer)* 432, 441, 662, 691, 1813, 3704, 3840, 3962, 4390, 4460
Handy, W.C. *(Lyricist)* 432, 441, 662, 691, 1813, 3704, 3840, 3962, 4390, 4460
Hanegan, Ernest *(Lyricist)* 3820
Hanemann, H.W. *(Librettist)* 3172
Hanemann, Henry *(Composer)* 4308
Hanemann, Henry *(Lyricist)* 4308
Hanemann, Henry William *(Director)* 4781
Hanemann, Henry William *(Librettist)* 4781
Haness, Abigale *(Cast)* 3742
Haney, Carol *(Cast)* 3351, 4602, 4827
Haney, Carol *(Choreographer)* 519, 1315, 1420, 3918
Haney, Felix *(Cast)* 188, 1388, 4046, 4753
Haney, Ray *(Composer)* 4623
Hanford, Charles *(Costumes)* 1056
Hanford, Ed *(Librettist)* 2853
Hanford, Ed *(Lyricist)* 2853
Hanighen, Bernard *(Composer)* 478
Hanighen, Bernard *(Lyricist)* 2655
Hankerson, Barry *(Producer)* 1073
Hanley, Dell *(Cast)* 4332
Hanley, Eddie *(Cast)* 4423
Hanley, Ellen *(Cast)* 153, 304, 1280, 1290, 4268, 4499
Hanley, J. Frederick *(Composer)* 4809
Hanley, James F. *(Composer)* 123, 391, 545, 638, 1250, 1391, 1460, 1484, 1486, 1686, 1756, 1911, 1965, 2135, 2214, 2296, 2446, 2461, 2564, 2706, 2757, 3009, 3179, 3455, 3500, 3622, 3737, 3840, 3968, 4104, 4271, 4290, 4374, 4465, 4811, 4813, 4815, 4816, 4817, 4818, 4822, 4824, 4840, 4842
Hanley, James F. *(Librettist)* 3179
Hanley, James F. *(Lyricist)* 1250, 1486, 1965, 2296, 3179, 3455, 3737, 4104, 4374
Hanley, M.W. *(Director)* 2428
Hanley, Matt *(Cast)* 2407

Hanley, Matthew *(Cast)* 2886
Hanlon, Bert *(Cast)* 1267
Hanlon, Bert *(Composer)* 1267, 1992
Hanlon, Bert *(Librettist)* 3861
Hanlon, Bert *(Lyricist)* 1267, 1919
Hanlon, Harry *(Cast)* 1563
Hanlon Jr., George *(Librettist)* 574
Hanlon Jr., George *(Lyricist)* 574
Hann, Walter *(Set Design)* 333, 2524
Hanna, William A. *(Set Design)* 584
Hannan, Walter F. *(Lyricist)* 4163
Hanneford, Poodles *(Cast)* 771, 2258
Hanneford Family *(Cast)* 1631
Hanneford Family, The *(Cast)* 1753
Hanning, Geraldine *(Cast)* 3697
Hansberry, Lorraine *(Author)* 3656
Hansberry, Lorraine *(Director)* 2306
Hanscombe, Harry *(Cast)* 4313
Hansen, Judith *(Cast)* 3606
Hansen, Kim *(Cast)* 2521
Hansen, Mike *(Composer)* 4278
Hansen, Mike *(Lyricist)* 4278
Hansen, Steve *(Puppeteer)* 56, 3449
Hanson, Dave *(Librettist)* 3076
Hanson, Dorothy *(Cast)* 1153
Hanson, Gladys *(Cast)* 2206, 2802
Hanson, Grace *(Cast)* 537
Happ, William *(Librettist)* 2560
Happy Medium Theatre *(Producer)* 1081
Hapwood, Aubrey *(Lyricist)* 4390
Harary, Nettie *(Cast)* 3501
Harbach, Otto *(Author)* 4526
Harbach, Otto *(Composer)* 2549
Harbach, Otto *(Librettist)* 381, 468, 672, 929, 930, 1027, 1088, 1247, 1248, 1285, 1352, 1476, 1598, 1603, 1617, 1888, 2180, 2216, 2264, 2292, 2308, 2342, 2425, 2549, 2638, 2667, 2767, 2927, 3170, 3184, 3218, 3254, 3735, 3772, 4077, 4212, 4228, 4378, 4464, 4692, 4694, 4784
Harbach, Otto *(Lyricist)* 288, 381, 468, 497, 531, 672, 903, 930, 1027, 1088, 1247, 1248, 1285, 1352, 1476, 1558, 1598, 1603, 1617, 1788, 1888, 2180, 2204, 2216, 2292, 2340, 2342, 2372, 2425, 2549, 2638, 2667, 2767, 2806, 3020, 3170, 3184, 3218, 3249, 3254, 3475, 3735, 3772, 4077, 4212, 4228, 4364, 4378, 4464, 4692, 4694, 4784, 4799
Harbert, James *(Composer)* 2080
Harbert, James *(Lyricist)* 2080
Harbert, James *(Orchestrations)* 2080
Harbert, Jim *(Composer)* 2080
Harbert, Jim *(Lyricist)* 2080
Harbord, Carl *(Cast)* 841
Harburg, E.Y. *(Author)* 2234
Harburg, E.Y. *(Composer)* 418
Harburg, E.Y. *(Director)* 462, 1300
Harburg, E.Y. *(Librettist)* 1278, 1300, 2190, 2234, 2475
Harburg, E.Y. *(Lyricist)* 12, 125, 213, 289, 418, 462, 467, 732, 839, 989, 1126, 1135, 1278, 1298, 1300, 1448, 1609, 1672, 1674, 1745, 1763, 1931, 1973, 2076, 2190, 2204, 2234, 2294, 2372, 2475, 3018, 3103, 3940, 3946, 3955, 3980, 4152, 4159, 4399, 4498, 4545, 4583, 4823, 4824
Harburg, E.Y. "Yip" *(Lyricist)* 4799
Harcourt, William J. *(Cast)* 3567
Hardeen, Theo *(Cast)* 1840
Harden, Don *(Cast)* 2105, 4777
Harding *(Composer)* 2493
Harding *(Lyricist)* 2493
Harding, John *(Musical Director)* 2029
Harding, May *(Cast)* 1537
Hards, Ira *(Director)* 780, 2569, 2686, 3623, 4204
Hardt-Warden, Bruno *(Author)* 4010, 4352
Hardwick, Cheryl *(Composer)* 4, 944, 1575
Hardwick, Cheryl *(Dance Arranger)* 1737
Hardwick, Cheryl *(Musical Director)* 1737
Hardwick, Cheryl *(Orchestrations)* 1737
Hardwick, Cheryl *(Vocal Arranger)* 1737
Hardwick, Mark *(Arrangements)* 4030
Hardwick, Mark *(Cast)* 3261, 3608
Hardwick, Mark *(Composer)* 3261, 3608, 3641, 4030
Hardwick, Mark *(Librettist)* 3261, 3641
Hardwick, Mark *(Lyricist)* 3608, 3641, 4030
Hardwicke, Catherine *(Set Design)* 655
Hardy, Jim *(Lighting Designer)* 2051
Hardy, Joseph *(Cast)* 1383
Hardy, Joseph *(Director)* 1511, 3516, 4173, 4783
Hardy, Mark *(Cast)* 2250
Hardy, Patricia *(Cast)* 3815
Hardy, Sam *(Cast)* 627, 3590, 3727, 4810
Hardy, Sam B. *(Cast)* 2309
Hardy, Stephani *(Cast)* 3181
Hardy, Thomas *(Author)* 962
Hardy, Will *(Composer)* 4655
Hardy, Will *(Lyricist)* 4655
Hardy, William *(Cast)* 198, 4398
Hare, Betty *(Cast)* 3214, 3339
Hare, David *(Librettist)* 2346
Hare, Ernest *(Cast)* 1783, 3395, 3399, 3424, 3701, 3958, 4521, 4553, 4655
Hare, Lumsden *(Cast)* 2206
Hare, Marilyn *(Cast)* 4602
Hare, Robertson *(Cast)* 3139
Haresfoot Club *(Producer)* 96
Haresfoot Club, The *(Producer)* 390
Harewood, Dorian *(Cast)* 518, 2898
Harford, W. *(Set Design)* 719, 2514
Hargate, Bill *(Costumes)* 2928, 4292, 4319
Hargate, Bill *(Set Design)* 127, 4319
Hargate, William *(Costumes)* 1047
Hargrave, Roy *(Cast)* 4105
Hargrave, Roy *(Director)* 2187
Hargrave, William *(Cast)* 3822, 4291
Hargreaves, Reginald *(Librettist)* 700
Hargreaves, William *(Composer)* 353
Hargreaves, William *(Lyricist)* 353
Hargreeves, William *(Composer)* 1148
Hargreeves, William *(Lyricist)* 1148
Hari, Eugene *(Cast)* 4498
Hari, Otto *(Cast)* 4166
Harig, Peg *(Librettist)* 4416
Harig, Peg *(Lyricist)* 2483
Haring, Forrest C. *(Producer)* 1874
Hariton, Gerry *(Lighting Designer)* 2470
Hariton, Gerry *(Set Design)* 2470, 2702, 3643

Harker, Joseph *(Set Design)* 165, 277, 292, 334, 466, 758, 2389, 2392, 2524, 2802, 2844, 3098, 3139, 3625, 4327, 4354, 4418, 4765
Harker, Phil *(Set Design)* 165, 277, 292, 334, 466, 758, 2389, 2392, 2802, 3098, 3139, 4327, 4418, 4765
Harker, W. Vere *(Musical Director)* 4302
Harkins, Evelyn *(Cast)* 4092
Harkins, John *(Cast)* 4625
Harkins, Mary Thomasine *(Costumes)* 81
Harkleroad, Mary *(Cast)* 2028
Harkrider, John *(Costumes)* 2453, 3014, 3179, 3719, 3949, 3953, 4023, 4683, 4821, 4823
Harkrider, John W. *(Costumes)* 4357, 4846, 4847
Harlan, Otis *(Cast)* 436, 559, 561, 968, 998, 1095, 1327, 1543, 2495, 3177, 3433, 4130, 4544
Harlan, Otis *(Composer)* 436
Harlan, Otis *(Lyricist)* 436
Harlan, Scott *(Cast)* 1161
Harland, Robert *(Cast)* 1185
Harlekyn U.S.A. Company *(Producer)* 1865
Harlem Producing Company *(Producer)* 1499
Harlem Productions *(Producer)* 2645
Harley, John F. *(Director)* 1466
Harley, John F. *(Lyricist)* 476, 1466
Harley, Leslie *(Dance Arranger)* 4678
Harley, Leslie *(Musical Director)* 4678
Harley, Margot *(Cast)* 1194
Harley, Margot *(Producer)* 942, 3733
Harling, W. Frank *(Composer)* 1020, 3849
Harling, W. Frank *(Lyricist)* 3849
Harling, W. Franke *(Composer)* 1244, 1780, 1819, 2987
Harlon, Beatrice *(Cast)* 2303
Harlowe, Beatrice *(Cast)* 539
Harman, Barry *(Director)* 3272, 3760
Harman, Barry *(Librettist)* 3272, 3760
Harman, Barry *(Lyricist)* 3272, 3760
Harman, Paul *(Cast)* 3926
Harman, Wier *(Cast)* 4729
Harmon, April *(Cast)* 2467
Harmon, Erv *(Cast)* 1709
Harmon, Jane *(Producer)* 209
Harmon, Johnny *(Cast)* 766
Harmon, Keith *(Cast)* 643
Harmon, Lucille *(Cast)* 3842
Harmon, Peggy *(Lyricist)* 1589
Harmon, Steve *(Cast)* 2657
Harms, Carl *(Lighting Designer)* 3449
Harms, Carl *(Puppeteer)* 997, 4710
Harney, Ben *(Cast)* 518, 572, 1103, 4447, 4697
Harney, Ben *(Composer)* 2796
Harney, Ben *(Lyricist)* 2796
Harnick, Jay *(Director)* 2197, 2231, 4785
Harnick, Sheldon *(Additional Lyrics)* 98, 949, 3913
Harnick, Sheldon *(Composer)* 1092, 1892, 2227, 2246, 2288, 2554, 2611, 2677, 2804, 3107, 3941, 4499, 4627
Harnick, Sheldon *(Librettist)* 170, 643, 1092, 3107, 3941, 4505, 4732
Harnick, Sheldon *(Lyricist)* 56, 160, 170, 192, 270, 483, 635, 643, 753, 1092, 1190, 1265, 1280, 1389, 1848, 1892, 2205, 2227, 2246, 2288, 2554, 2589, 2611, 2726, 2804, 2839, 3018, 3097, 3107, 3498, 3543, 3702, 3780, 3918, 3940, 3941, 4028, 4312, 4388, 4395, 4499, 4505, 4566, 4627, 4732
Harnick, Sheldon *(Voice)* 56
Harnley, Leslie *(Composer)* 1370
Harnley, Leslie *(Dance Arranger)* 3427
Harnley, Leslie *(Musical Director)* 1370
Harp, William *(Set Design)* 2560
Harper, Billy *(Cast)* 2520
Harper, Dolores *(Cast)* 2000, 4750
Harper, Don *(Orchestrations)* 2689
Harper, Helen *(Cast)* 1906
Harper, Herbert *(Choreographer)* 4586
Harper, Jessica *(Cast)* 1064
Harper, Ken *(Producer)* 4722
Harper, Leonard *(Director)* 1980
Harper, Leonard *(Producer)* 725, 1986, 2561, 3707, 3782, 4501
Harper, Richard *(Lighting Designer)* 1282
Harper, Richard *(Set Design)* 1282
Harper, Robert Alan *(Set Design)* 3600
Harper, Valerie *(Cast)* 1585, 4190, 4270
Harper, Ves *(Costumes)* 2203
Harper, Ves *(Lighting Designer)* 2203
Harper, Wally *(Additional Music)* 1649
Harper, Wally *(Arrangements)* 544
Harper, Wally *(Composer)* 1298, 2148, 2171, 2754, 3876
Harper, Wally *(Dance Arranger)* 373, 832, 1000, 2584, 3018, 3039, 3060, 3088, 4038, 4114
Harper, Wally *(Musical Director)* 1000, 1660, 3171, 4002, 4522
Harper, Wally *(Orchestrations)* 544, 2584, 4522
Harper, Wally *(Vocal Arranger)* 373, 1000
Harper, William *(Orchestrations)* 2766
Harper and Blanks *(Cast)* 3512
Harra, Henrietta *(Costumes)* 2395
Harrell, Gordon *(Dance Arranger)* 2134, 2360, 2542, 3682
Harrell, Gordon *(Orchestrations)* 2134
Harrell, Gordon *(Vocal Arranger)* 4470
Harrell, Gordon Lowry *(Dance Arranger)* 393, 964, 1146, 1842, 4297
Harrell, Gordon Lowry *(Musical Director)* 775, 964, 3169, 3741, 3873, 3903
Harrell, Gordon Lowry *(Vocal Arranger)* 393, 964, 3741, 3903
Harrigan, Edward *(Author)* 4508
Harrigan, Edward *(Cast)* 2428, 3266, 4508
Harrigan, Edward *(Composer)* 114, 516
Harrigan, Edward *(Librettist)* 2428, 3266
Harrigan, Edward *(Lyricist)* 114, 516, 1776, 3266, 4508
Harrigan, James *(Cast)* 215
Harrigan, Mary *(Cast)* 345
Harriman, Alfred *(Lyricist)* 4811
Harriman, P. Chelsea *(Costumes)* 3600
Harrington, Bobby *(Cast)* 187
Harrington, Delphi *(Cast)* 272
Harrington, Frank *(Cast)* 4596
Harrington, Giles *(Cast)* 3068
Harrington, Hamtree *(Cast)* 207, 447, 691, 1058, 3614, 4182
Harrington, Helen *(Cast)* 3622
Harrington, Laura *(Librettist)* 2766

Harrington, Laura *(Lyricist)* 2766
Harrington, Pat *(Cast)* 619, 1204, 3359, 4131, 4498
Harrington, Robert *(Cast)* 3453
Harris, Al *(Orchestrations)* 3046
Harris, Albert *(Director)* 2674, 4137
Harris, Albert *(Librettist)* 2674
Harris, Ann *(Composer)* 4011
Harris, Ann *(Lyricist)* 4011
Harris, Arthur *(Orchestrations)* 1045, 2689, 2737
Harris, Barbara *(Cast)* 170, 1122, 3274
Harris, Ben *(Composer)* 2009
Harris, Ben *(Lyricist)* 2009
Harris, Bud *(Composer)* 621, 1342, 3104
Harris, Charlene *(Cast)* 593
Harris, Charles *(Cast)* 1401
Harris, Charles K. *(Composer)* 3926, 3949
Harris, Charles K. *(Lyricist)* 2247, 3926, 3949
Harris, Clifford *(Lyricist)* 333, 675, 1208, 1538, 1588, 2498, 2698, 3827, 3882
Harris, Daniel *(Cast)* 1352
Harris, Diane *(Lyricist)* 4108
Harris, Diane David *(Lyricist)* 2998
Harris, Donald *(Set Design)* 2796
Harris, Donny *(Cast)* 206
Harris, Elmer *(Librettist)* 2832, 3562, 4037, 4634
Harris, Eva *(Cast)* 2984
Harris, Frank *(Author)* 1256
Harris, Frederic *(Dance Arranger)* 4011
Harris, Frederic *(Vocal Arranger)* 4011
Harris, Gary *(Lighting Designer)* 2908
Harris, Hazel *(Cast)* 203
Harris, Henry B. *(Producer)* 1, 1327, 1835, 3618, 4012
Harris, Holly *(Cast)* 2615
Harris, Howard *(Composer)* 1402
Harris, Howard *(Dance Arranger)* 1402
Harris, Howard *(Librettist)* 1898
Harris, Howard *(Musical Director)* 1402
Harris, Howard *(Vocal Arranger)* 1402
Harris, James Berton *(Costumes)* 35, 3653
Harris, Jayne Anne *(Cast)* 4011
Harris, Jayne Anne *(Choreographer)* 4011
Harris, Jeannie *(Cast)* 1619
Harris, Jed *(Director)* 933
Harris, Jeff *(Composer)* 157
Harris, Jeff *(Librettist)* 157
Harris, Jeff *(Lyricist)* 157
Harris, Jeremiah *(Producer)* 1159
Harris, Jeremy *(Musical Director)* 1108, 4468
Harris, Jeremy *(Vocal Arranger)* 1108
Harris, Jimmy *(Composer)* 3178
Harris, Jimmy *(Lyricist)* 3178
Harris, Joseph *(Producer)* 1068, 1273, 2726, 3944
Harris, Joseph P. *(Producer)* 1497, 1611, 2713, 3175, 4238
Harris, Julian *(Cast)* 1592
Harris, Julie *(Cast)* 2411, 4013
Harris, Lawrence *(Lyricist)* 621, 1342, 3104
Harris, Lew *(Orchestrations)* 1494
Harris, Lionel *(Composer)* 392
Harris, Lottie *(Cast)* 4339
Harris, Lulu Belle *(Cast)* 4011
Harris, Lulu Belle *(Choreographer)* 4011
Harris, Margaret *(Musical Director)* 105
Harris, Mrs. Henry B. *(Producer)* 4050
Harris, Niki *(Cast)* 1000
Harris, Paul *(Cast)* 1385
Harris, Phil *(Cast)* 3153
Harris, Ralph *(Cast)* 3361
Harris, Robert *(Cast)* 2582
Harris, Robert H. *(Cast)* 1373
Harris, Rosemary *(Cast)* 1787, 3787
Harris, Sam *(Composer)* 337
Harris, Sam *(Librettist)* 337
Harris, Sam *(Lyricist)* 337
Harris, Sam *(Producer)* 115, 121, 802, 1480, 1598, 1803, 1826, 1961, 2068, 2252, 2517, 2537, 3529, 4105
Harris, Sam H. *(Director)* 3009
Harris, Sam H. *(Producer)* 142, 207, 335, 536, 800, 801, 803, 804, 805, 1225, 1271, 1360, 1395, 1399, 1968, 2194, 2265, 2386, 2444, 2525, 2729, 2730, 2821, 3007, 3008, 3009, 3225, 3685, 3791, 4277, 4576, 4759
Harris, Scott *(Director)* 36, 2229
Harris, Steve *(Director)* 4264
Harris, Sylvia *(Producer)* 4435
Harris, Timmy *(Lighting Designer)* 2284
Harris, Tom *(Cast)* 1664, 4184
Harris, Val *(Composer)* 4805
Harris, Val *(Lyricist)* 4805
Harris, Wes *(Lyricist)* 4459
Harris, William *(Producer)* 1142, 1627
Harris Jr., William *(Librettist)* 4012
Harris Jr., William *(Lyricist)* 4012
Harris Jr., William *(Producer)* 2121
Harrison, Alex *(Cast)* 4825
Harrison, Bertram *(Director)* 381, 1584, 1819, 1904, 3849, 3850, 3860, 3993, 4443, 4464, 4526
Harrison, Gregory *(Cast)* 3364
Harrison, Gregory *(Producer)* 450
Harrison, Lee *(Cast)* 1926, 2123, 3744, 3745, 3747, 3750, 4094, 4802
Harrison, Lee *(Producer)* 3681
Harrison, Llewellyn *(Lighting Designer)* 3901
Harrison, Llewellyn *(Set Design)* 1073
Harrison, Louis *(Cast)* 627, 1246, 1505, 1576, 1728, 1793, 2209, 2324, 2481, 2592, 2666, 3053, 4125, 4497
Harrison, Louis *(Director)* 2675
Harrison, Louis *(Librettist)* 559, 2156, 2865
Harrison, Louis *(Lyricist)* 559, 976, 1026, 1246, 2184, 4393
Harrison, Louis B. *(Cast)* 252, 1602
Harrison, Madeline *(Cast)* 4285
Harrison, Muriel *(Cast)* 2366
Harrison, Paul Carter *(Author)* 1671
Harrison, Peter *(Set Design)* 2229, 4030
Harrison, Ray *(Cast)* 3278, 3326, 3947
Harrison, Ray *(Choreographer)* 1408, 2522, 3217, 3543, 4186, 4585
Harrison, Ray *(Director)* 2522
Harrison, Rex *(Cast)* 3038
Harrison, Ruth *(Cast)* 4177
Harrison, Seth *(Producer)* 4343
Harrison, Stafford *(Composer)* 3690
Harrison, Stafford *(Librettist)* 3690

Harrison, Stafford *(Lyricist)* 3690
Harrison, Stanley *(Cast)* 203
Harrison, Tommy *(Composer)* 4264
Harrison, Tommy *(Lyricist)* 4264
Harrity, Roy *(Cast)* 427
Harrod, James *(Cast)* 2486
Harrold, Jack *(Cast)* 4516, 4542
Harrold, Orville *(Cast)* 355, 1935, 3081
Harrold, Patti *(Cast)* 1582, 1935
Harron, Donald *(Librettist)* 148
Harron, Donald *(Lyricist)* 148
Harrow, Bruce *(Costumes)* 1809
Harry, Deborah *(Cast)* 4295
Harry, Jackee *(Cast)* 1038
Hart, Albert *(Cast)* 457, 527, 666, 734, 1388, 1535, 1975, 2710, 2835, 4098, 4691, 4753
Hart, Bruce *(Librettist)* 1648
Hart, Bruce *(Lyricist)* 1389
Hart, Catherine *(Cast)* 4799
Hart, Charles *(Cast)* 3147
Hart, Charles *(Lyricist)* 211, 3464
Hart, Charlotte *(Cast)* 3357
Hart, Chas. *(Cast)* 822
Hart, Chas. T. *(Cast)* 3270
Hart, Dolores *(Cast)* 3103
Hart, Elizabeth *(Cast)* 1909
Hart, Florence *(Cast)* 2552
Hart, Jack *(Choreographer)* 1964
Hart, John C. *(Cast)* 2694
Hart, Joseph *(Cast)* 1374, 2711
Hart, Joseph *(Composer)* 1374
Hart, Joseph *(Director)* 1197
Hart, Joseph *(Librettist)* 1573, 2711, 3867
Hart, Joseph *(Lyricist)* 1374, 2711, 3867
Hart, Joseph *(Producer)* 3867
Hart, Lily *(Cast)* 2694
Hart, Linda *(Cast)* 2555
Hart, Lorenz
See also Herbert Richard Lorenz.
Hart, Lorenz *(Cast)* 3419
Hart, Lorenz *(Director)* 265, 4477
Hart, Lorenz *(Librettist)* 247, 601, 1321, 2061, 3283
Hart, Lorenz *(Lyricist)* 66, 85, 111, 146, 243, 247, 265, 376, 418, 420, 514, 601, 703, 711, 791, 834, 978, 1013, 1202, 1267, 1298, 1321, 1446, 1447, 1448, 1529, 1724, 1725, 1763, 1800, 1819, 1894, 1944, 2031, 2032, 2061, 2068, 2102, 2193, 2258, 2263, 2382, 2389, 2459, 2467, 2574, 2677, 2772, 2909, 3018, 3020, 3172, 3175, 3283, 3291, 3353, 3419, 3428, 3436, 3518, 3521, 3538, 3546, 3556, 3634, 3743, 3847, 3848, 3924, 3955, 3980, 3989, 4059, 4118, 4235, 4304, 4399, 4420, 4498, 4519, 4709, 4749, 4780, 4781
Hart, Lori *(Cast)* 4255
Hart, Mark *(Cast)* 1531
Hart, Melissa *(Cast)* 1497, 2027
Hart, Moss *(Author)* 121, 1597, 1681, 1741, 2729, 2821, 2822, 3931, 4706
Hart, Moss *(Director)* 623, 2894, 3038, 4706
Hart, Moss *(Librettist)* 207, 1225, 1680, 2068, 2130, 2137, 2238, 2252, 2386, 2653, 3893, 3955, 4512
Hart, Moss *(Producer)* 623, 2894, 3990
Hart, Rose *(Cast)* 1535
Hart, Stan *(Librettist)* 2663, 2737
Hart, Stan *(Lyricist)* 2663
Hart, Stanley *(Librettist)* 3126
Hart, Teddy *(Cast)* 514, 2032, 3301
Hart, Thomas *(Arrangements)* 914
Hart, Thomas A. *(Director)* 1462, 3150
Hart, Tommy *(Cast)* 214
Hart, Tony *(Cast)* 399
Hart, Vivian *(Cast)* 1131, 2371, 3978, 4178
Hart, Walter *(Librettist)* 3947
Hart Jr., John N. *(Producer)* 3305
Hart Jr., Tony *(Cast)* 3154
Hart Operating Co. *(Producer)* 1833
Harte, Rose *(Lyricist)* 2483
Harte Jr., Stan *(Composer)* 2433
Harte Jr., Stan *(Director)* 2433
Harte Jr., Stan *(Librettist)* 2433
Hartford, Huntington *(Producer)* 2246, 3816
Hartford, Lucia *(Cast)* 3856
Hartig, Cecile *(Composer)* 2819
Hartig, Herb *(Composer)* 392
Hartig, Herb *(Librettist)* 392, 3186
Hartig, Herb *(Lyricist)* 392, 1233
Hartig, Herbert *(Librettist)* 1363, 1648, 2231, 2288, 2804, 3204, 4627
Hartig, Herbert *(Lyricist)* 2231, 2288, 4627
Hartke, Rev. Gilbert V. *(Director)* 821, 932, 2641
Hartke, Rev. Gilbert V. *(Librettist)* 932
Hartley, Arthur *(Cast)* 2489, 4673
Hartley, Richard *(Dance Arranger)* 3742
Hartley, Richard *(Vocal Arranger)* 3742
Hartman, David *(Cast)* 1828, 4764
Hartman, E. *(Lyricist)* 4824
Hartman, Elizabeth *(Cast)* 1205
Hartman, Ferris *(Cast)* 2365, 4443
Hartman, Grace *(Cast)* 67, 137, 289, 3674, 4377, 4777
Hartman, Grace *(Librettist)* 67
Hartman, Paul *(Cast)* 67, 137, 289, 3324, 3674, 4377, 4585, 4629, 4777
Hartman, Paul *(Librettist)* 67, 137
Hartmann, Tonette *(Cast)* 1004, 1155
Hartnell, Norman *(Costumes)* 3139
Hartnell, Norman H. *(Costumes)* 4341
Hartwell, Peter *(Costumes)* 3884
Hartwell, Peter *(Set Design)* 3884
Hartwig, Mrs. Walter *(Producer)* 2275
Harty, Tom *(Cast)* 289
Harvey, Clarence *(Cast)* 2363, 3951, 4489
Harvey, Clarence *(Lyricist)* 4688
Harvey, Georgette *(Cast)* 439, 3541
Harvey, J. *(Composer)* 4193
Harvey, J. *(Lyricist)* 1370, 4193
Harvey, J. Clarence *(Librettist)* 1464
Harvey, John *(Lighting Designer)* 820, 1991, 2295, 3294, 4435
Harvey, Lillian *(Cast)* 2159
Harvey, Michael *(Producer)* 1289, 1662, 1755
Harvey, Morris *(Cast)* 704, 1733
Harvey, Morris *(Librettist)* 1733
Harvey, Paul *(Cast)* 4105

Harvey, Peter *(Costumes)* 956, 1974, 2663, 3389
Harvey, Peter *(Set Design)* 956, 1216, 1974, 2284, 2663, 2935, 3389, 3615, 3902, 4167, 4517
Harvey, Richard *(Cast)* 283
Harvey, Robert *(Cast)* 2225
Harvey, Roslyn *(Lyricist)* 2447, 3226
Harvey, Walter H.
See also Ward & Harvey.
Harvey, Walter H. *(Set Design)* 3613
Harwell, George *(Composer)* 4629
Harwell, George *(Lyricist)* 4629
Harwood, H.M. *(Librettist)* 4327
Harwood, James *(Cast)* 1697
Harwood, Jill *(Cast)* 3764
Harwood, John *(Director)* 466, 931, 1297, 1529, 1992, 2180, 2392, 2613, 3243, 3307, 3532, 3659, 3719, 4300, 4392, 4426, 4778
Harwood, Ronald *(Librettist)* 1619
Hasbrook, Ethelberta *(Lyricist)* 1747
Hascall, Lon *(Cast)* 2298, 3403
Hasen, Irwin *(Librettist)* 3810
Haskell, Charles *(Cast)* 86
Haskell, David *(Cast)* 1595
Haskell, Jack *(Cast)* 2983
Haskell, Jack *(Choreographer)* 201, 568, 611, 711, 1297, 1529, 1929, 3310, 3532, 3611, 4050, 4077, 4372, 4545
Haskell, Jimmie *(Orchestrations)* 3515
Haskell, Jimmie *(Vocal Arranger)* 3515
Haskell, Lon *(Cast)* 4421
Haskins, James *(Cast)* 2754
Hasomeris, Nick *(Cast)* 4016
Hassall, Christopher *(Librettist)* 650
Hassall, Christopher *(Lyricist)* 972
Hassell, George *(Cast)* 203, 324, 711, 948, 1530, 1626, 1735, 1827, 2620, 2788, 3310, 3402, 3406, 3407, 3799, 4188
Hassert, Bernard *(Costumes)* 3173
Hassler, Simon *(Musical Director)* 2428
Hastings, Basil Macdonald *(Librettist)* 3663
Hastings, Frederick *(Cast)* 77
Hastings, Hal *(Musical Director)* 270, 610, 1329, 1422, 1507, 2368, 2550, 3113, 3288, 3351
Hastings, Harold *(Dance Arranger)* 1010
Hastings, Harold *(Incidental Music)* 4377
Hastings, Harold *(Musical Director)* 161, 657, 832, 957, 1280, 1310, 2163, 2536, 3871, 3918, 4312, 4423, 4862
Hastings, Harold *(Vocal Arranger)* 1010
Hastings, J.B. *(Musical Director)* 1153, 2788, 3291, 4154
Hastings, John *(Lighting Designer)* 198, 2171
Hastings, Lew *(Librettist)* 1340
Hasting's, Sue
See also Sue Hasting's Marionettes.
Hastings, Tom *(Cast)* 2069
Hastings' Marionettes, Sue *(Cast)* 125, 216, 1973
Hasty Pudding Club *(Producer)* 1231, 4039
Hatch, Eric *(Author)* 3055
Hatch, Frank *(Director)* 1881
Hatch, James *(Composer)* 1319
Hatch, James *(Librettist)* 1319
Hatch, James *(Lyricist)* 1319
Hatch, Joel *(Cast)* 155
Hatch, Riley *(Cast)* 830
Hatch, Tony *(Composer)* 626, 4193
Hatch, Tony *(Lyricist)* 626, 4193
Hatcher, James *(Director)* 1750
Hatcher, James *(Producer)* 1750
Hatcher, Mary *(Cast)* 4314
Hatcher, Tom *(Cast)* 2144
Hateley, Linzi *(Cast)* 661
Hatfield, Lansing *(Cast)* 3813, 4569
Hatfield, Mark *(Cast)* 456
Hathaway, Charles *(Musical Director)* 4602
Hathaway, Donny *(Composer)* 4786
Hathaway, Donny *(Lyricist)* 4786
Hathaway, Gus *(Cast)* 3165
Hatten, Tom *(Cast)* 408
Hatvany, Lila *(Author)* 3152
Hauer, Mary Elizabeth *(Librettist)* 2784
Hauer, Mary Elizabeth *(Lyricist)* 2784
Hauerbach, Otto
See Otto Harbach.
Hauptman, William *(Librettist)* 394
Hauptmann, Elisabeth *(Author)* 1755
Hauser, Franklin *(Composer)* 3219
Hauser, Kim *(Cast)* 544, 3718
Havel, Arthur *(Cast)* 2271
Havel, Morton *(Cast)* 2271
Havel, Tommy *(Cast)* 2271
Havens, Patricia *(Costumes)* 1862
Havens, Richie *(Producer)* 3814
Haverstick, Madame *(Costumes)* 764
Havez, Jean *(Librettist)* 3701
Havez, Jean *(Lyricist)* 538, 1703, 1704, 3327, 3701, 4770, 4804, 4805, 4808
Havez, Jean C. *(Composer)* 4626
Havez, Jean C. *(Librettist)* 3842
Havez, Jean C. *(Lyricist)* 1531, 4626, 4804
Havez, Lou *(Lyricist)* 3397
Havoc, June *(Cast)* 1352, 1397, 2847, 2859, 2975, 3353, 3813
Havoc, June *(Director)* 3788
Hawkes, Albert *(Lighting Designer)* 1654
Hawkins, Erskine
See Erskine Hawkins and His Band and Erskine Hawkins' `Bama State Coll.
Hawkins, Ira *(Cast)* 1970, 3792, 4162, 4383
Hawkins, John *(Composer)* 634
Hawkins, John *(Orchestrations)* 634
Hawkins, John *(Set Design)* 711
Hawkins, June *(Cast)* 653, 4123
Hawkins, Lynette *(Cast)* 3991
Hawkins, Michael *(Cast)* 2599
Hawkins, Rick *(Librettist)* 2651
Hawkins, Stanley *(Cast)* 1118, 2399, 3951
Hawkins, Tom *(Composer)* 1978
Hawkins, Tom *(Lyricist)* 1978
Hawkins, Walter *(Composer)* 3987
Hawkins, Walter *(Lyricist)* 3987
Hawkins, Wood *(Cast)* 3605
Hawkins Jr., John *(Costumes)* 834
Hawkins Jr., John *(Set Design)* 834

Hawkins and His Band, Erskine *(Cast)* 1773
Hawkins' 'Bama State Coll., Erskine *(Cast)* 4502
Hawley, Andros *(Composer)* 2986
Hawley, Colette *(Cast)* 240
Hawley, Ida *(Cast)* 2383
Hawley, Monte *(Cast)* 488
Hawley, William *(Set Design)* 2238
Hawley, William R. *(Cast)* 236
Haworth, Jill *(Cast)* 610
Hawthorne, Jim *(Cast)* 4096
Hawthorne, Lillian *(Cast)* 3228
Hawthorne, Nathaniel *(Author)* 1258
Hawtrey, Charles *(Director)* 1153
Hay, Ian *(Librettist)* 1502
Hay, Mary *(Cast)* 2756, 2768, 3819, 4212, 4443, 4813
Hay, Richard *(Set Design)* 255
Hay, Richard L. *(Set Design)* 143
Hayden *(Costumes)* 434, 1759
Hayden, Carl *(Cast)* 1712
Hayden, Cissie *(Choreographer)* 1867
Hayden, Frank *(Costumes)* 540, 541, 1459
Hayden, Joe *(Lyricist)* 662, 1425, 2415, 2796, 4390
Hayden, John *(Director)* 383, 2253
Hayden, John *(Lyricist)* 1858
Hayden, Larry *(Choreographer)* 1897
Hayden, Naura *(Cast)* 314
Hayden-Clarendon, J. *(Lyricist)* 1602
Haydn, Richard *(Cast)* 2313, 3885, 4483
Haydon, Julie *(Cast)* 3321
Hayes, Alfred *(Composer)* 1840
Hayes, Alfred *(Lyricist)* 1840, 2175, 3226, 4394
Hayes, Bill *(Cast)* 1423, 2550, 2797
Hayes, Bobby *(Cast)* 1773
Hayes, Carleton *(Musical Director)* 2742
Hayes, Charles *(Cast)* 325
Hayes, Christopher *(Cast)* 1624
Hayes, Dermot *(Set Design)* 2474
Hayes, Georgia *(Cast)* 1836
Hayes, Gertrude *(Cast)* 1332, 4630
Hayes, Grace *(Cast)* 288, 2540, 2843, 3649
Hayes, H.R. *(Author)* 996
Hayes, H.R. *(Lyricist)* 996
Hayes, Helen *(Cast)* 1416, 1749, 3096, 3265, 3779, 4203, 4386
Hayes, Lorey *(Cast)* 2133
Hayes, Maggie *(Cast)* 3493
Hayes, Mimi *(Cast)* 4341
Hayes, Peter Lind *(Cast)* 1811, 4706
Hayes, Peter Lind *(Composer)* 3444
Hayes, Peter Lind *(Lyricist)* 7
Hayes, Richard *(Cast)* 322, 2388, 3094
Hayes, Scott *(Librettist)* 3080
Hayes, Scott *(Lyricist)* 3080
Hayes, Ted *(Composer)* 4591
Hayes, Ted *(Lyricist)* 4591
Hayman, Al *(Producer)* 1905, 2131, 3948
Hayman, Edward *(Lyricist)* 3172
Hayman, Keith *(Musical Director)* 4016
Hayman, Lillian *(Cast)* 1063, 1729, 3900
Hayman, Richard *(Musical Director)* 2551
Hayman, Richard *(Vocal Arranger)* 2551
Haynes, Tiger *(Cast)* 550, 828, 1227, 3108, 4272, 4722
Haynes, Virginia Ellen *(Cast)* 2661
Hays, David *(Lighting Designer)* 534, 1094, 1237, 3187, 4028
Hays, David *(Set Design)* 1094, 1237, 1616, 3187, 3515, 4481
Hays, Kathryn *(Cast)* 1369, 1990
Hays, Rex David *(Cast)* 2318
Hayseed Productions *(Producer)* 3323
Hayton, Lennie *(Musical Director)* 2183
Hayward, Ina *(Cast)* 1250, 1824
Hayward, Leland *(Producer)* 619, 1709, 1990, 2983, 4095, 4096, 4718
Hayward, Thomas Tibbet *(Cast)* 3151
Hayward-Jones, Michael *(Cast)* 843
Haywood, Billie *(Cast)* 3103, 3104
Haywood, Matilda A. *(Cast)* 3840
Haywood, Nancy *(Cast)* 322
Hazard, Dick *(Orchestrations)* 2084, 2096, 4020
Hazard, Richard *(Orchestrations)* 4334
Hazel, Rupert *(Lyricist)* 3500
Hazell, Hy *(Cast)* 3526
Hazelton, George C. *(Author)* 3341
Hazelton, George C. *(Librettist)* 165
Hazelton, Jack *(Set Design)* 1940
Hazelwood, Lee *(Composer)* 4193
Hazelwood, Lee *(Lyricist)* 4193
Hazin, Rosalie *(Lyricist)* 2483
Hazzard, Jack *(Cast)* 3946
Hazzard, John *(Cast)* 1688, 1707, 2005
Hazzard, John E. *(Cast)* 606, 689, 1111, 1151, 1345, 1527, 1569, 2040, 2363, 2486, 2907, 2996, 3146, 3295, 3681, 4283, 4555, 4754
Hazzard, John E. *(Librettist)* 1031, 1588, 2005
Hazzard, John E. *(Lyricist)* 1031, 1318, 1569, 1588, 2990, 2996, 3384, 4555, 4806
Hazzell, George *(Cast)* 3405
Head, Cloyd *(Librettist)* 174
Head, Cloyd *(Lyricist)* 174
Headley, George L. *(Cast)* 1539
Headley, H.B. *(Lyricist)* 702
Heagney, William *(Composer)* 4328
Heagney, William *(Lyricist)* 4328
Heal, Joan *(Cast)* 1644
Heald, Louise *(Lyricist)* 310
Heale, Timothy *(Lighting Designer)* 2147
Healey, Eunice *(Cast)* 1528, 1931, 2423, 4374
Healey Jr., John *(Cast)* 3329
Healy, Betty *(Cast)* 1131
Healy, Dan *(Cast)* 376, 1617, 3511, 4248, 4770, 4821
Healy, Dan *(Choreographer)* 4741
Healy, Dan *(Director)* 437, 880, 3709
Healy, Dan *(Producer)* 878, 880, 892, 3709
Healy, Frances *(Cast)* 3342
Healy, Joseph *(Composer)* 516
Healy, Joseph *(Lyricist)* 516
Healy, Martin *(Cast)* 2485
Healy, Mary *(Cast)* 189, 901, 966
Healy, Robert *(Librettist)* 214
Healy, Ted *(Cast)* 418, 1131, 1440, 3149, 3150
Healy, Ted *(Composer)* 3149

Healy, Ted *(Director)* 876
Healy, Ted *(Lyricist)* 3149
Healy, Ted *(Producer)* 570, 876
Heaney, Ned Joyce *(Librettist)* 1944
Heard, James *(Lyricist)* 377, 4302
Hearn, George *(Cast)* 747, 1068, 2064, 2360, 2805, 3485, 4217, 4384, 4601
Hearn, Lew *(Cast)* 30, 787, 966, 2108, 2135, 2380, 2706, 2856, 3086, 3087, 3665, 4228, 4772, 4817
Hearn, Lew *(Librettist)* 3086
Hearn, Sam *(Cast)* 1617, 1691, 2818, 4104
Hearshen, Ira *(Orchestrations)* 2142
Heartstrong Prod. *(Producer)* 337
Heartz, H.L. *(Composer)* 506, 2040, 2770, 2906, 3047, 3951, 4311
Heath *(Cast)* 3677
Heath, Bobby *(Lyricist)* 2892
Heath, E.P. *(Librettist)* 3839
Heath, E.P. *(Lyricist)* 3839
Heath, Frankie *(Cast)* 1947, 3173
Heath, Hy *(Composer)* 1296
Heath, Hy *(Lyricist)* 1296
Heath, Sigrid *(Cast)* 2633
Heath, Thomas *(Cast)* 2119
Heath, Thomas K. *(Cast)* 1731, 1799
Heath, Tom
See also McIntyre & Heath.
Heath, Tom *(Cast)* 110
Heather, Lea *(Director)* 4016
Heather Brothers, The *(Composer)* 2654, 4016
Heather Brothers, The *(Librettist)* 2654, 4016
Heather Brothers, The *(Lyricist)* 2654, 4016
Heatherton, Joey *(Cast)* 4095
Heatherton, Ray *(Cast)* 247, 1448
Heawood, John *(Choreographer)* 507, 4153, 4155
Heawood, John *(Director)* 1023, 1362, 4268
Hebert, Gail *(Cast)* 1371
Hebert, Omar *(Composer)* 3579, 3877
Hebert, Omar *(Lyricist)* 3579
Hecht, Ben *(Author)* 1299, 1672, 1791, 3279, 4609, 4703
Hecht, Ben *(Librettist)* 1244, 1416, 1791, 2258, 3893
Hecht, Harold *(Cast)* 1656
Hecht, Harold *(Choreographer)* 2032, 2640
Hecht, Harold *(Director)* 3986
Hecht, Harold *(Producer)* 2032
Hecht, Herbert *(Musical Director)* 1837
Hecht, Joshua *(Cast)* 2169
Hecht, Marie Armstrong *(Lighting Designer)* 4352
Hecht, Paul *(Cast)* 2877, 3780, 3897
Heckart, Eileen *(Cast)* 594, 1237, 2144
Heckert, M. *(Director)* 434
Heckert, M.L. *(Director)* 185, 1459, 1758, 1759
Heckroth, H. *(Set Designer)* 2323
Hector, Frank *(Cast)* 1733
Hedges, Elven E. *(Lyricist)* 537
Hedley, Charles *(Cast)* 4352
Hedley, H.B. *(Composer)* 2389
Hedwig, Ula *(Lyricist)* 1713
Heelan, Will *(Lyricist)* 1523, 2493, 2964, 2996, 3085, 3313, 4094
Heelan, Will A. *(Lyricist)* 1188, 3073, 4757
Heeley, Desmond *(Costumes)* 946, 2305
Heeley, Desmond *(Set Design)* 2305
Heffernan, John *(Cast)* 2954, 3610
Heffernan, T. *(Lyricist)* 3882
Heflin, Evan *(Cast)* 2981
Heflin, Marta *(Cast)* 3824, 4089, 4615
Hegira, Anne *(Cast)* 2368
Heider, Fred *(Lyricist)* 3810
Heifner, Jack *(Librettist)* 3010, 4019
Heifner, Jack *(Lyricist)* 3010
Heikin, Nancy *(Librettist)* 3197
Heikin, Nancy *(Lyricist)* 3197
Heilbron, Adelaide *(Author)* 4059
Heilemann, Charles *(Set Design)* 4047
Heilweil, David *(Producer)* 3664
Heim, Alyn *(Composer)* 4696
Hein, Ed *(Composer)* 943
Hein, Ed *(Lyricist)* 943
Hein, Silvio *(Composer)* 75, 93, 335, 379, 405, 425, 465, 511, 1142, 1218, 1308, 1424, 1536, 1588, 1607, 1794, 2029, 2254, 2506, 2587, 2708, 2765, 2782, 2878, 2884, 2951, 2996, 3073, 3300, 3332, 3372, 4054, 4200, 4393, 4562, 4589, 4644, 4757, 4801
Hein, Silvio *(Musical Director)* 425, 511, 1972, 2765, 2951, 3372, 3701
Hein, Silvio *(Orchestrations)* 1911
Heindl, Anton *(Musical Director)* 142, 902, 1388, 1536, 1602, 1900, 2254, 2567, 2723, 3006, 3369, 4054, 4422, 4539
Heindl, Anton *(Orchestrations)* 4539
Heindl, Anton *(Vocal Arranger)* 4539
Heinemann, Eda *(Cast)* 183
Heinfling, Martin *(Producer)* 154, 3644
Heinman, Henry *(Set Design)* 2500
Heinmiller, Glenn *(Lighting Designer)* 74
Heis, Helena *(Cast)* 1978
Heisler, Jack *(Choreographer)* 1692, 1747
Heit, Sally-Jane *(Cast)* 287
Helbig, Herbert *(Orchestrations)* 3235
Helburn, Theresa *(Librettist)* 1871
Held, Anna *(Cast)* 1334, 1881, 2365, 2715, 2892, 3363, 3387, 3392
Held, Anna *(Lyricist)* 1334, 3387, 4390
Held, Dan *(Cast)* 2243
Held, Jules *(Cast)* 4439
Held, Ludwig *(Composer)* 205
Held, Wilbur *(Lyricist)* 2706
Held Jr., John *(Costumes)* 124, 827, 4819
Held Jr., John *(Set Design)* 123, 124
Helen Jackson Girls, The *(Cast)* 1137
Helene, Patrice *(Cast)* 4829
Helf, J. Fred *(Composer)* 246, 248, 2493, 2964, 3052, 4390, 4757
Helf, J. Fred *(Lyricist)* 248
Helfman, Max *(Composer)* 1609
Heller, Adam *(Cast)* 2354, 4560
Heller, Barbara *(Cast)* 4566
Heller, Buck *(Choreographer)* 2177, 2616
Heller, Buck *(Director)* 2616
Heller, George *(Cast)* 1657, 4368
Heller, Jackie *(Cast)* 4772

Heller, Jayne *(Cast)* 3505
Heller, Randee *(Cast)* 2043
Heller, Richard *(Composer)* 4041
Heller, Richard *(Librettist)* 4041
Heller, Richard *(Lyricist)* 4041
Hellerman, Fred *(Composer)* 3112
Hellinger, Mark *(Cast)* 3153
Hellinger, Mark *(Librettist)* 1979, 4823
Hellman, Jerome *(Producer)* 4371
Hellman, Lillian *(Adaptation)* 2411
Hellman, Lillian *(Author)* 2510, 3691, 4601
Hellman, Lillian *(Librettist)* 630, 2653
Hellman, Lillian *(Lyricist)* 630
Helm, Mornay D. *(Orchestrations)* 1686
Helm, Thomas *(Conductor)* 2798
Helm, Thomas *(Musical Director)* 1298
Helm, Tom *(Musical Director)* 2861
Helming, Dan *(Cast)* 4774
Helmond, Katherine *(Cast)* 1999
Helms, Edwin I. *(Composer)* 3611
Helmsley, Estelle *(Cast)* 2994
Helmsley, W. *(Set Design)* 3092
Helpmann, Robert *(Cast)* 808, 4159
Helpmann, Robert *(Librettist)* 1809
Helward, Dale *(Cast)* 942
Heming, Percy *(Cast)* 3569
Heming, Violet *(Cast)* 1318, 2211
Hemion, Dwight *(Director)* 3454
Hemion, Dwight *(Producer)* 3454
Hemmer, Carl *(Choreographer)* 86, 1013, 1121, 2669
Hemmer, Carl *(Director)* 86
Hemphill, A. Marcus *(Author)* 2133
Hemphill, Barry *(Cast)* 344
Hemsley, Sherman *(Cast)* 3610
Hemsley, W.T. *(Set Design)* 4663
Hemsley, Winston De Witt *(Cast)* 597, 1729, 3741, 4003
Hemsley Jr., Gilbert V. *(Lighting Designer)* 808, 828, 946, 2058, 2260, 2775, 3088, 4197, 4788
Hendee, Harold *(Cast)* 2613
Henderson, Al *(Librettist)* 4110
Henderson, Charles *(Cast)* 1971
Henderson, Charles *(Composer)* 3645, 4170
Henderson, Charles *(Lyricist)* 3131, 3645, 4170
Henderson, Charles *(Vocal Arranger)* 2258, 4778
Henderson, David *(Producer)* 45
Henderson, F.A. *(Cast)* 761
Henderson, Fletcher
See also Fletcher Henderson and His Orchestra.
Henderson, Fletcher *(Musical Director)* 925, 926
Henderson, Fletcher *(Orchestrations)* 4256
Henderson, Florence *(Cast)* 1242, 1564, 1681, 2550, 4718
Henderson, Isabel *(Cast)* 1710
Henderson, John *(Cast)* 554
Henderson, Katherine *(Cast)* 500
Henderson, L.D. *(Cast)* 2721
Henderson, Luther *(Composer)* 2200
Henderson, Luther *(Dance Arranger)* 432, 519, 1222, 1289, 1315, 1420, 1611, 1729, 2053, 2195, 2513, 3610, 4162
Henderson, Luther *(Incidental Music)* 1063
Henderson, Luther *(Music Adaptation)* 2200
Henderson, Luther *(Musical Director)* 2692
Henderson, Luther *(Orchestrations)* 341, 432, 1061, 1063, 1222, 1289, 1762, 1991, 2195, 2200, 2513, 3280, 3610, 3743, 4003, 4038, 4162, 4689
Henderson, Luther *(Vocal Arranger)* 432, 1222, 2195, 2513, 3610, 3743, 4162
Henderson, Marcia *(Cast)* 3452
Henderson, Ray *(Cast)* 3153
Henderson, Ray *(Composer)* 202, 391, 393, 1215, 1323, 1339, 1425, 1488, 1489, 1490, 1491, 1492, 1493, 1628, 1688, 1813, 1929, 1979, 2467, 2734, 3020, 3241, 3297, 3850, 3936, 4152, 4177, 4345, 4393, 4772, 4799, 4818, 4826
Henderson, Ray *(Dance Arranger)* 410
Henderson, Ray *(Director)* 4177
Henderson, Ray *(Librettist)* 1979, 4177
Henderson, Ray *(Musical Director)* 408, 410, 4163
Henderson, Ray *(Producer)* 3850, 4177
Henderson, Ray *(Vocal Arranger)* 410
Henderson, Rose *(Cast)* 4763
Henderson, Slim *(Cast)* 500
Henderson, W.C. *(Composer)* 3024
Henderson and His Orchestra, Fletcher
See also Fletcher Henderson.
Henderson and His Orchestra, Fletcher *(Cast)* 925
Hendra, Tony *(Director)* 3077
Hendra, Tony *(Librettist)* 3077, 4029
Hendra, Tony *(Lyricist)* 3077
Hendra, Tony *(Orchestrations)* 3077
Hendra, Tony *(Producer)* 3077
Hendra, Tony *(Vocal Arranger)* 3077
Hendricks, Jon *(Cast)* 1710
Hendricks, Jon *(Composer)* 1296, 3178
Hendricks, Jon *(Lyricist)* 1296, 3178
Hendrickson, Hugh *(Cast)* 2089
Hendrickson, Ned *(Producer)* 348
Hendrickson, Stephen *(Set Design)* 4689
Hendry, Tom *(Lyricist)* 1064
Heneker, David *(Composer)* 194, 1721, 2240, 3429
Heneker, David *(Librettist)* 2150
Heneker, David *(Lyricist)* 194, 1721, 2150, 2240, 3429
Henie, Sonja *(Librettist)* 2024
Henie, Sonja *(Producer)* 1782, 2023, 2098, 2099, 2161, 2162, 4143
Henkins, Hezekiah *(Composer)* 3297
Henkins, Hezekiah *(Lyricist)* 3297
Henley, Bob *(Librettist)* 3916
Hennequin *(Author)* 4418
Hennequin, Maurice *(Author)* 68, 1527, 2824, 3254, 3363, 3784, 4213
Henner, Marilu *(Cast)* 3330
Hennes, Tom *(Lighting Designer)* 3311
Henning, Doug *(Cast)* 2687, 2820
Henning, Leo *(Cast)* 539
Henning, Magnus *(Composer)* 3441
Henning, Magnus *(Musical Director)* 3441
Henning, Pat *(Cast)* 3287
Hennings, John E. *(Cast)* 1121
Henri, F. *(Composer)* 560
Henrikson, Eve *(Costumes)* 239
Henrique, Luis *(Composer)* 2245

Henrique, Luis *(Lyricist)* 2245
Henry, B.C. *(Composer)* 306
Henry, Chad *(Composer)* 140
Henry, Chad *(Lyricist)* 140
Henry, Donna Jean *(Cast)* 2483
Henry, Eleanor *(Cast)* 1882, 2489
Henry, Grace *(Librettist)* 1863
Henry, Grace *(Lyricist)* 1128, 1132, 1134, 1281, 2545, 4335
Henry, John *(Choreographer)* 3752
Henry, Judith *(Producer)* 105
Henry, Leonard *(Composer)* 702
Henry, Marc *(Librettist)* 4154
Henry, O. *(Author)* 1306, 1507, 1508, 1509, 3221
Henry, O. *(Librettist)* 2559
Henry, Peggie *(Cast)* 4220
Henry, S.R. *(Composer)* 2527, 4762
Henry, Suzanne *(Cast)* 2764
Henry B. Harris Estate *(Producer)* 2486
Hensel, Christopher *(Cast)* 3202
Hensel, Karen *(Cast)* 4861
Henshaw, Hal *(Set Design)* 1644
Henshaw, John E. *(Cast)* 308, 639, 2725
Henske, Judy *(Cast)* 1596
Henson, Gladys *(Cast)* 3885, 4361
Henson, Leslie *(Cast)* 129, 334, 2389, 3139, 3156, 3569, 4327, 4418, 4419, 4519, 4765
Henson, Leslie *(Director)* 844, 3139
Henson, Leslie *(Producer)* 346, 3139
Hepburn, Katharine *(Cast)* 798
Herbert, A.J. *(Cast)* 1858, 2446
Herbert, A.P. *(Librettist)* 453
Herbert, A.P. *(Lyricist)* 453, 1763
Herbert, Charles *(Composer)* 4484
Herbert, Charles *(Lyricist)* 4484
Herbert, Charlie *(Cast)* 3255, 4484
Herbert, Evelyn *(Cast)* 1962, 2622, 2813, 3056, 3117, 3584, 3586, 4150
Herbert, Fred *(Librettist)* 4629
Herbert, Fred *(Producer)* 1076
Herbert, Gene *(Composer)* 532
Herbert, Gene *(Lyricist)* 532
Herbert, Grace *(Cast)* 3255, 4484
Herbert, H.E. *(Cast)* 2871
Herbert, Jean *(Composer)* 4374
Herbert, Jean *(Lyricist)* 1126, 1989, 4374, 4465
Herbert, Jocelyn *(Costumes)* 4371
Herbert, Jocelyn *(Set Design)* 4371
Herbert, Joseph *(Cast)* 1355, 2507, 2592, 3732, 4500
Herbert, Joseph *(Director)* 2317
Herbert, Joseph *(Librettist)* 4511
Herbert, Joseph W. *(Author)* 1962
Herbert, Joseph W. *(Cast)* 8, 45, 335, 379, 1540, 2160, 2506, 2715, 2848, 2886, 3237, 3313, 3820, 3994, 4590, 4624
Herbert, Joseph W. *(Composer)* 3193
Herbert, Joseph W. *(Director)* 1351, 2538, 2668, 2715, 3673, 3679, 4194
Herbert, Joseph W. *(Librettist)* 8, 336, 1111, 1246, 1613, 1962, 1963, 2538, 2668, 2715, 2956, 3313, 4044, 4194, 4414, 4590
Herbert, Joseph W. *(Lyricist)* 8, 93, 195, 336, 1111, 1962, 2668, 2715, 2855, 2886, 2938, 4044, 4425, 4590
Herbert, Lew *(Cast)* 4829
Herbert, Lillian *(Cast)* 1462
Herbert, Victor *(Author)* 251, 3773
Herbert, Victor *(Composer)* 48, 104, 136, 250, 251, 252, 638, 683, 763, 947, 1016, 1095, 1096, 1098, 1111, 1162, 1183, 1355, 1394, 1397, 1552, 1599, 1711, 1851, 2101, 2160, 2370, 2394, 2404, 2465, 2481, 2534, 2670, 2855, 2882, 2885, 2900, 2915, 3043, 3081, 3122, 3172, 3265, 3304, 3312, 3319, 3567, 3570, 3590, 3675, 3704, 3773, 3783, 3819, 3881, 3994, 4010, 4017, 4070, 4250, 4293, 4390, 4547, 4559, 4564, 4649, 4699, 4724, 4735, 4811, 4812, 4813, 4814, 4815, 4816, 4817, 4818
Herbert, Victor *(Librettist)* 4815
Herbert, Victor *(Music Based On)* 1711
Herbert, Victor *(Orchestrations)* 1016, 1111, 1183, 2670, 2885, 2915, 3081, 3304, 3312, 3590, 3675, 3773, 4250, 4293, 4547, 4559, 4649, 4735, 4814
Herberth, Hans *(Cast)* 1413
Herbold, Lisa *(Cast)* 2488
Herbst, Jeffrey *(Cast)* 690
Herbstritt, Larry *(Arrangements)* 2651
Herczeg, Geza *(Author)* 4730
Herczeg, Geza *(Librettist)* 2985
Herczeq, Franz *(Author)* 3974
Hereford, Kathryn *(Cast)* 3721, 4023
Herendeen, Fred *(Librettist)* 3069, 3314
Herendeen, Fred *(Lyricist)* 1920, 2774, 3314
Herendeen, Frederick *(Composer)* 4794
Herendeen, Frederick *(Librettist)* 82, 1560, 3605
Herendeen, Frederick *(Lyricist)* 82, 1173, 3605, 4794
Herford, Beatrice *(Cast)* 2456
Herford, Oliver *(Author)* 4688
Herford, Oliver *(Librettist)* 2603
Herford, Oliver *(Lyricist)* 2603, 4688
Herget, Bob *(Cast)* 3664
Herget, Bob *(Choreographer)* 624, 842, 1237, 1435, 3956, 4060, 4577
Heritage Project, Inc., The *(Producer)* 1903
Herk, I.H. *(Director)* 1032
Herk, I.H. *(Producer)* 1032
Herko, Fred *(Cast)* 1958
Herlein, Lillian *(Cast)* 3773
Herlie, Eileen *(Cast)* 64, 4270
Herman, Al *(Cast)* 1947, 3173
Herman, Danny *(Choreographer)* 158
Herman, George *(Cast)* 930
Herman, George *(Composer)* 2028
Herman, George *(Librettist)* 2028
Herman, George *(Lyricist)* 2028
Herman, Harold *(Librettist)* 1539
Herman, Jerry *(Composer)* 367, 1000, 1012, 1408, 1660, 1828, 2052, 2208, 2360, 2660, 2664, 2713, 2864, 3018, 3161, 3366, 3840, 3942
Herman, Jerry *(Director)* 2052, 3161, 3366
Herman, Jerry *(Lyricist)* 367, 1000, 1012, 1408, 1660, 1828, 2052, 2208, 2360, 2660, 2664, 2713, 2864, 3018, 3161, 3366, 3840, 3942
Herman, John *(Producer)* 1991
Herman, Mme. *(Costumes)* 4404

Herman, Oscar *(Cast)* 1267
Herman, Oscar *(Composer)* 1267
Herman, Oscar *(Lyricist)* 1267
Herman, Otto *(Composer)* 2912
Herman & Gantvoort *(Producer)* 3978
Herman Oppenheimer Co. *(Producer)* 2868
Hermann, Mme. *(Costumes)* 2836
Hermione *(Cast)* 3858
Hermit Club of Cleveland *(Producer)* 1866, 1867, 1868
Hern, Bernie *(Lyricist)* 4260
Hernandez, Juan *(Cast)* 880, 1251, 4256
Hernandez, Philip *(Cast)* 2333
Hernandez, Rafael *(Composer)* 3440
Hernandez Brothers, The *(Cast)* 1979
Herndon, Ann *(Cast)* 2385
Herndon, Richard *(Producer)* 123, 648, 2827, 3431
Herndon, Richard G. *(Producer)* 364, 2527, 3662
Herndon Corp, The *(Producer)* 2385
Herne, Julie *(Cast)* 1148
Heron, Eddie *(Cast)* 3774
Herr, Michael *(Author)* 1053
Herrera, John *(Cast)* 2470, 3070
Herrick, Landon *(Librettist)* 1448
Herrick, Robert *(Lyricist)* 2633
Herriman, Horation N. *(Cast)* 1866, 1867, 1868
Herriman, Horation N. *(Librettist)* 1867
Herriman, Horation N. *(Lyricist)* 1867
Herrman, Edward *(Cast)* 3468
Herrmann, Bernard *(Composer)* 125, 752, 2319
Herrmann, Bernard *(Musical Director)* 752
Herrmann, Harry *(Librettist)* 4377
Herrmann, Keith *(Composer)* 3305, 3601, 3760
Herrmann, Keith *(Dance Arranger)* 3601, 3760
Herrmann, Keith *(Musical Director)* 682
Herrmann, Keith *(Vocal Arranger)* 3305, 3601, 3760
Herron, Randy *(Cast)* 4450
Herrup, Leo *(Cast)* 1624
Herscher, Lou *(Composer)* 715
Hersey, David *(Lighting Designer)* 299, 678, 721, 730, 1211, 2442, 2474, 2822, 2905, 4138
Hershberg, Herman *(Cast)* 1472
Hershey, Don *(Director)* 4180
Hershfeld, Max *(Musical Director)* 4490
Hershfield, Harry *(Librettist)* 199
Hershkowitz, J. *(Lyricist)* 560
Herson, Frank *(Cast)* 1051
Herson, Frank *(Composer)* 1051
Herson, Frank *(Lyricist)* 1051
Hertsens, Marc *(Choreographer)* 2928
Herve, Florimond *(Composer)* 4556
Herve, Paul *(Author)* 1565
Herver, John *(Cast)* 507
Herwood, Marion *(Costumes)* 4498
Herz, Ralph *(Cast)* 97, 697, 1088, 1629, 1735, 2566, 2665, 2667, 2885, 2901, 2939, 3799, 4094, 4323, 4657, 4666
Herz, Ralph *(Producer)* 1629, 3256
Herz, Renee Semes *(Producer)* 164
Herzer, Ludwig *(Author)* 3573, 4792
Herzer, Ludwig *(Lyricist)* 4550
Herzig, Sig *(Librettist)* 190, 289, 462, 2750, 3946, 4545
Herzog Jr., Arthur *(Composer)* 3905
Herzog Jr., Arthur *(Lyricist)* 266, 3905
Hess, Bob *(Conductor)* 3490
Hess, Cliff *(Composer)* 805, 1735, 3717, 3911, 4148
Hess, Cliff *(Lyricist)* 994, 1686, 3717
Hess, Nancy *(Cast)* 2205
Hess, Rodger *(Producer)* 3548
Hess, Roger *(Producer)* 1232
Hester, Hal *(Composer)* 916, 4789
Hester, Hal *(Lyricist)* 916, 4789
Hester, Hal *(Musical Director)* 916
Heuberger, Richard *(Composer)* 3308
Heuett, E.J. *(Costumes)* 2829
Heuman, Barbara *(Cast)* 4062
Heusinger, George *(Cast)* 4470
Heuvel, Jacques *(Musical Director)* 1554, 2509
Hevner, Suzanne *(Cast)* 275
Hewaley, Joseph H. *(Cast)* 516
Hewer, John *(Cast)* 3429
Hewett, Christopher *(Cast)* 31, 1290, 2295, 3015, 3956, 4516
Hewett, Christopher *(Director)* 90, 1408, 1435, 3302, 3427, 3941, 4827
Hewett, Peggy *(Cast)* 1000, 3272, 3757
Hewett, Petty *(Cast)* 109
Hewison, Robert *(Composer)* 1736
Hewison, Robert *(Lyricist)* 1736
Hewitt, Alan *(Cast)* 619
Hewitt, Frankie *(Producer)* 1427, 4162, 4788
Hewitt, Georgiana *(Cast)* 1014
Hewitt, Mary E. *(Composer)* 1897
Hewitt, Mary E. *(Lyricist)* 1897
Hewitt, Sean *(Cast)* 1079
Heyblum, I. *(Librettist)* 2421
Heydt, Louis Jean *(Cast)* 1749, 3168
Heyer, Bill *(Librettist)* 1842, 4468
Heyer, Bill *(Lyricist)* 1842, 4468
Heyer, Rome *(Costumes)* 4468
Heyer, Rosemarie *(Cast)* 1761
Heyer, Rosemary *(Costumes)* 2584
Heyman, Barton *(Cast)* 1184
Heyman, Edward *(Author)* 226
Heyman, Edward *(Composer)* 680, 3728
Heyman, Edward *(Lyricist)* 3, 226, 418, 432, 680, 1137, 1813, 1856, 2772, 3002, 3103, 3104, 3249, 3381, 3728, 3905, 3919, 4159, 4163, 4367, 4372, 4534, 4824, 4825
Heyman, Edward *(Producer)* 3
Heymann, Henry *(Costumes)* 1474
Heyward, Dorothy *(Author)* 2238, 2712, 3541
Heyward, DuBose *(Author)* 2712, 3541
Heyward, DuBose *(Librettist)* 3541
Heyward, DuBose *(Lyricist)* 2712, 3018, 3541
Heywood, Billie *(Cast)* 1342
Heywood, Chester D. *(Librettist)* 1447
Heywood, Donald *(Cast)* 1499
Heywood, Donald *(Composer)* 26, 27, 435, 439, 471, 498, 500, 816, 1499, 1514, 1989, 2021, 2736, 2881, 3200
Heywood, Donald *(Director)* 435, 1514
Heywood, Donald *(Librettist)* 26, 27, 435, 1514, 4546
Heywood, Donald *(Lyricist)* 26, 27, 435, 439, 471, 500, 1499, 1514, 1989, 2881
Heywood, Donald *(Musical Director)* 27, 435

Hezer, Ludwig *(Author)* 1384
Hi-Hatters, The *(Cast)* 2259
Hiatt, Jessie *(Cast)* 3158
Hibbert, Edward *(Cast)* 3598
Hibbert, Geoffrey *(Cast)* 346, 507
Hibiscus Productions *(Producer)* 4011
Hickey, Bill *(Cast)* 134
Hickey, Ed *(Cast)* 376
Hickey, John *(Lighting Designer)* 338
Hickey, John *(Musical Director)* 3730
Hickey, John *(Set Design)* 338
Hickey, William *(Cast)* 1018
Hickey Jr., John *(Producer)* 2296
Hickey, Hale & Robinson *(Producer)* 4572
Hicklin, Margery *(Cast)* 3569
Hicklin, Walter *(Costumes)* 2477, 4358
Hickman, Alfred *(Director)* 2527
Hickman, Annie *(Costumes)* 2970
Hickman, Art
See also Art Hickman's Orchestra.
Hickman, Art *(Composer)* 4814
Hickman, Art *(Lyricist)* 4814
Hickman, Charles *(Director)* 2608
Hickman, George *(Composer)* 3103
Hickman, George *(Lyricist)* 3103
Hickman, Leo *(Composer)* 1296
Hickman, Leo *(Lyricist)* 1296
Hickman's Orchestra, Art
See also Art Hickman.
Hickman's Orchestra, Art *(Cast)* 4814
Hickok, John *(Cast)* 789, 2065
Hicks, Bill *(Cast)* 1037
Hicks, Charles K. *(Musical Director)* 3026
Hicks, J. *(Set Design)* 4302
Hicks, James *(Cast)* 552
Hicks, Juanita *(Cast)* 552
Hicks, Julian *(Set Design)* 4014
Hicks, Kenneth *(Cast)* 4447
Hicks, Marva *(Cast)* 4127
Hicks, Munson *(Cast)* 482
Hicks, Munson *(Director)* 251, 2289
Hicks, Russell *(Cast)* 82
Hicks, Seymour *(Author)* 675, 1188, 2991
Hicks, Seymour *(Cast)* 333, 719, 1454, 3948
Hicks, Seymour *(Director)* 333, 1454
Hicks, Seymour *(Librettist)* 333, 675, 719, 1043, 1123, 1454, 2509, 3803
Hicks, Seymour *(Musical Director)* 719
Hicks, Seymour *(Producer)* 2509
Hicks, Sue *(Cast)* 4583
Hicks, Walter *(Choreographer)* 4750
Hicks and Brooks *(Set Design)* 2974
Hidalgo, Allen *(Cast)* 1236
Hide, Eugene *(Set Design)* 2630
Hidey, Hal *(Musical Director)* 339, 407
Hidey, Hal *(Orchestrations)* 339
Hidlay, William *(Cast)* 2511
Hidlay, William *(Choreographer)* 2511
Higgens, Joel *(Cast)* 135
Higginbotham, Irene *(Composer)* 498
Higgins, Billy *(Cast)* 899
Higgins, Colin *(Author)* 1775
Higgins, Douglas *(Set Design)* 2607
Higgins, Joel *(Cast)* 3928
Higgins, John Michael *(Cast)* 3076
Higgins, Michael *(Cast)* 2411
Higgins, Peter *(Cast)* 1387
Higgins, Steven *(Lyricist)* 2039
High John Prods. *(Producer)* 578
Highley, Ronald *(Cast)* 643
Hight, Pearl *(Cast)* 3254
Hightower, Robert *(Cast)* 601
Higlen, David *(Cast)* 564
Hiken, Gerald *(Cast)* 747, 1047, 3094, 4176, 4229
Hiken, Nat *(Librettist)* 95, 2554, 2653
Hiken, Nat *(Lyricist)* 95
Hilb, Emil *(Composer)* 2249
Hildebrand, Fred *(Cast)* 2490, 4209
Hilder *(Cast)* 1181
Hilditch, Doris *(Cast)* 325
Hilferty, Susan *(Costumes)* 1161
Hill, Alex *(Composer)* 3782
Hill, Alex *(Lyricist)* 3782
Hill, Alexander *(Composer)* 432, 2034
Hill, Alexander *(Lyricist)* 2034
Hill, Annabelle *(Cast)* 2331
Hill, Arthur *(Cast)* 4060
Hill, Bette Cerf *(Producer)* 4074
Hill, Billy *(Composer)* 3596, 4824
Hill, Billy *(Lyricist)* 3457, 3596, 4824
Hill, Bobby *(Cast)* 1072
Hill, Craig *(Cast)* 752
Hill, Dule *(Cast)* 2542
Hill, Erin *(Cast)* 1969
Hill, Errol *(Author)* 2719
Hill, Errol *(Lyricist)* 2719
Hill, George B. *(Cast)* 96
Hill, George B. *(Lyricist)* 96
Hill, George Roy *(Director)* 1698, 1846
Hill, Graham *(Author)* 1783
Hill, Gus *(Producer)* 537, 538, 539, 540, 541, 542, 3021, 3022, 3026, 3028, 3030
Hill, Homer *(Set Design)* 4047
Hill, J. Leubrie *(Cast)* 295, 984, 2979, 3041, 3797
Hill, J. Leubrie *(Composer)* 295, 983, 984, 2979, 3041, 3399, 4747, 4807, 4808
Hill, J. Leubrie *(Director)* 984
Hill, J. Leubrie *(Librettist)* 3041
Hill, J. Leubrie *(Lyricist)* 983, 984, 1835, 2111, 2979, 3041, 3399, 4747, 4807, 4808
Hill, J. Leubrie *(Producer)* 983, 984, 3041
Hill, Jack *(Librettist)* 1880
Hill, Jack *(Lyricist)* 1880
Hill, James *(Cast)* 2111
Hill, Joe *(Composer)* 1609
Hill, Joe *(Lyricist)* 1609
Hill, John-Edward *(Producer)* 3448
Hill, Ken *(Cast)* 874
Hill, Ken *(Librettist)* 3462
Hill, Ken *(Lyricist)* 3462

Hill, Leitha *(Cast)* 876, 877, 880, 3709
Hill, Ralston *(Cast)* 2415, 4173
Hill, Richard *(Composer)* 634
Hill, Richard *(Orchestrations)* 634
Hill, Ruby *(Cast)* 4123
Hill, Teddy
See also Teddy Hill Orchestra.
Hill, Teddy *(Musical Director)* 897
Hill, Valerie *(Cast)* 4309
Hill Orchestra, Teddy
See also Teddy Hill.
Hill Orchestra, Teddy *(Cast)* 3782
Hillbrandt, James *(Cast)* 282
Hillebrand, Fred *(Cast)* 4269
Hillebrand, Fred *(Composer)* 2406
Hillebrand, Fred *(Lyricist)* 2406
Hiller, J. Sebastian *(Composer)* 830, 4026
Hiller, J.S. *(Lyricist)* 185
Hiller, J.S. *(Musical Director)* 3360
Hiller, John S. *(Musical Director)* 1165
Hiller, John Sebastian *(Composer)* 830
Hiller, John Sebastian *(Musical Director)* 3488
Hiller, Rose *(Cast)* 455
Hilliam, B.C. *(Author)* 325
Hilliam, B.C. *(Composer)* 325, 579, 1175, 3317
Hilliam, B.C. *(Librettist)* 3593
Hilliam, B.C. *(Lyricist)* 325, 579, 3317, 3593
Hilliam, B.C. *(Musical Director)* 579
Hilliard, Bob *(Composer)* 854
Hilliard, Bob *(Librettist)* 4627
Hilliard, Bob *(Lyricist)* 137, 854, 856, 857, 861, 862, 1791, 2076, 2850, 3683, 4193
Hilliard, Mack *(Producer)* 3434
Hilliard, Mark *(Producer)* 1368
Hillias, Peg *(Cast)* 3452
Hillman *(Composer)* 1627
Hillman *(Lyricist)* 1627
Hillman, B. *(Cast)* 3062
Hillman, George *(Cast)* 941
Hillman, Gerald Paul *(Lyricist)* 3688
Hillman, Gerald Paul *(Producer)* 3688
Hillman, Nancy Tribush *(Director)* 3688
Hills, Alice *(Cast)* 2532
Hilton, James *(Author)* 3913
Hilton, James *(Librettist)* 3913
Hilton, James *(Lyricist)* 3913
Himber, Richard *(Composer)* 1899
Himber, Richard *(Lyricist)* 1899
Himber, Richard *(Producer)* 1899
Himber Orchestra, Richard *(Cast)* 1899
Hindman, James *(Cast)* 789
Hinds, Ernie *(Cast)* 985
Hinds, Ernie *(Set Design)* 985
Hindus, Milton *(Lyricist)* 3698
Hines, Altona *(Cast)* 1366
Hines, Babe *(Cast)* 90, 98, 961
Hines, Earl
See also Earl Hines Orchestra.
Hines, Elizabeth *(Cast)* 2263, 2533, 2601, 2757, 2931, 3218, 3868
Hines, Gregory *(Cast)* 828, 1198, 2200, 2415, 4091
Hines, Gregory *(Choreographer)* 2200
Hines, Jack *(Lyricist)* 3405
Hines, Jackson *(Cast)* 2340
Hines, John *(Cast)* 3855
Hines, Johnny *(Cast)* 2270
Hines, Maurice *(Cast)* 534, 1198, 4534
Hines, Maurice *(Choreographer)* 3840, 4534
Hines, Maurice *(Director)* 4534
Hines, Nat C. *(Cast)* 1836
Hines, Patrick *(Cast)* 946, 1985
Hines Orchestra, Earl *(Cast)* 725
Hingle, Pat *(Cast)* 477, 1571, 3871
Hinkle, Velma *(Cast)* 1556
Hinkley, Brett *(Cast)* 655
Hinnant, Bill *(Cast)* 73, 945, 1107, 1380, 1590, 2617, 3479, 4041, 4783
Hinnant, Skip *(Cast)* 4783
Hinton, Al *(Cast)* 4596
Hipkens, Robert *(Cast)* 4076
Hipkens, Robert *(Composer)* 4076
Hipkens, Robert *(Librettist)* 4076
Hipkens, Robert *(Lyricist)* 4076
Hipp, Paul *(Cast)* 580
Hippen, Lynn *(Cast)* 251
Hirsch, Hugo *(Author)* 2567
Hirsch, Hugo *(Composer)* 2567
Hirsch, John *(Costumes)* 941
Hirsch, John *(Lyricist)* 1064
Hirsch, Ken *(Composer)* 952
Hirsch, Louis *(Composer)* 1613, 1663
Hirsch, Louis A. *(Composer)* 186, 258, 381, 822, 1464, 1523, 1598, 1663, 1688, 1689, 1793, 2334, 2538, 2767, 2854, 2869, 2892, 2926, 3045, 3085, 3218, 3250, 3395, 3652, 3701, 3868, 4094, 4490, 4553, 4655, 4799, 4809, 4810, 4812, 4816, 4833
Hirsch, Louis A. *(Lyricist)* 186, 3395, 4490, 4655, 4809
Hirsch, Michael *(Cast)* 4398
Hirsch, Walter *(Composer)* 487
Hirsch, Walter *(Lyricist)* 393, 487, 1658
Hirschfeld, Abe *(Producer)* 3576
Hirschfeld, Al *(Librettist)* 4237
Hirschfeld, Max *(Musical Director)* 250, 694, 1543, 1555, 1582, 1588, 1962, 2160, 2213, 2534, 2670, 2886, 3078, 3193, 3230, 3245, 3675, 4555
Hirschfeld, Susan *(Costumes)* 2993, 4139
Hirschhorn, Joel *(Composer)* 869, 3888, 4402
Hirschhorn, Joel *(Librettist)* 869
Hirschhorn, Joel *(Lyricist)* 869, 3888
Hirschhorn, Naomi Caryl *(Cast)* 4111
Hirschhorn, Naomi Caryl *(Composer)* 4111
Hirschhorn, Robert *(Musical Director)* 2049
Hirschman, Herbert *(Director)* 939
Hirsh, George *(Cast)* 2164
Hirson, Roger O. *(Librettist)* 3506, 4588
Hirst, George *(Composer)* 1176
Hirst, George *(Lyricist)* 2747
Hirst, George *(Musical Director)* 799, 1414, 1476, 1948, 2747, 3823, 4550
Hirst, George *(Orchestrations)* 4550

Hirst, George *(Vocal Arranger)* 4550
Hiss, Anthony *(Author)* 1402
Hitchcock, Raymond *(Cast)* 335, 352, 379, 586, 1148, 1433, 1780, 1919, 1920, 1921, 1922, 1923, 2277, 2315, 2730, 3662, 3685, 4187, 4353, 4563, 4754, 4762, 4815
Hitchcock, Raymond *(Librettist)* 4742
Hitchcock, Raymond *(Producer)* 1335, 1920, 1921, 1922, 4742
Hite, Mabel *(Cast)* 687, 1518, 2826, 4725
Hite, Mabel *(Composer)* 687
Hite, Mabel *(Lyricist)* 687
Hixon, Hal *(Cast)* 684, 4849
Hlela, Betty-Boo *(Cast)* 2147
Hlophe, Bongani *(Cast)* 209
Hoadley, Helen *(Cast)* 1863
Hoagland, Carleton *(Producer)* 3717
Hoare, Douglas *(Author)* 4302
Hoare, Douglas *(Librettist)* 3237, 4302
Hoare, Douglas *(Lyricist)* 4302
Hoare, Ken *(Additional Material)* 1857
Hoban, Stella *(Cast)* 3400
Hoban et Jeanne *(Costumes)* 2467
Hobard, Rick *(Producer)* 3763, 4689
Hobart, George V. *(Author)* 69, 399, 1014, 1218, 2176, 2274, 2710, 2878, 2990, 2996
Hobart, George V. *(Director)* 1218, 2461, 4085, 4649
Hobart, George V. *(Librettist)* 29, 69, 88, 228, 258, 511, 559, 579, 632, 830, 1430, 1566, 1688, 1731, 1921, 1925, 2209, 2324, 2336, 2408, 2461, 2835, 2863, 2865, 2878, 2882, 2895, 2904, 2951, 3006, 3007, 3090, 3332, 3529, 3820, 4085, 4317, 4564, 4649, 4726, 4753, 4757, 4805, 4807, 4808, 4810, 4811
Hobart, George V. *(Lyricist)* 29, 88, 126, 228, 258, 354, 465, 511, 559, 830, 1151, 1430, 1728, 2209, 2324, 2336, 2835, 2863, 2865, 2878, 2951, 2964, 2996, 3090, 3122, 3129, 3265, 3529, 3746, 3747, 3749, 3820, 4026, 4070, 4085, 4453, 4649, 4691, 4726, 4753, 4757, 4805, 4807, 4808, 4810
Hobart, Rose *(Cast)* 2060
Hobbs, Jack *(Cast)* 334
Hobbs, Robert *(Cast)* 133, 2140
Hobson, I.M. *(Cast)* 109, 958
Hochhauser, Jeff *(Librettist)* 4325
Hochhauser, Jeff *(Lyricist)* 4325
Hochman, Larry *(Composer)* 3202
Hochman, Larry *(Dance Arranger)* 3202
Hochman, Larry *(Musical Director)* 1059, 3666, 4707
Hochman, Larry *(Orchestrations)* 2420
Hochman, Larry *(Vocal Arranger)* 1059, 3202, 3666
Hockwald, Arthur *(Producer)* 4184
Hoctor, Harriet *(Cast)* 2, 1137, 1932, 3953, 3980, 4357, 4429, 4825
Hoctor, Harriet *(Choreographer)* 1932
Hodapp, Ann *(Cast)* 1256, 1590
Hoder, Mark *(Musical Director)* 42
Hodes, Gloria *(Cast)* 788, 4736
Hodge, William T. *(Cast)* 1095, 4662
Hodges, Ann *(Cast)* 3187
Hodges, Eddie *(Cast)* 3016
Hodges, Elijah *(Cast)* 1385
Hodges, John *(Lyricist)* 1026
Hodges, John King *(Librettist)* 1863
Hodges, John King *(Lyricist)* 1863
Hodges, Johnnie *(Composer)* 4091
Hodges, Johnnie *(Lyricist)* 4091
Hodges, Johnny *(Composer)* 895
Hodges, Joy *(Cast)* 1101, 2068, 2219, 3091
Hodges, Mitchell *(Librettist)* 4484
Hodges, Raymond *(Composer)* 1026
Hodgkins, Gene *(Composer)* 697
Hodgkins, Gene *(Lyricist)* 697
Hodgkinson, Guy *(Set Design)* 874, 2572
Hodgson, Red *(Composer)* 393
Hodgson, Red *(Lyricist)* 393, 1813
Hodley, Henry *(Composer)* 2855
Hodshire, Allan *(Director)* 1697
Hodshire, Allan *(Producer)* 1697
Hoebee, Mark S. *(Choreographer)* 3461
Hoefler, Charles E. *(Costumes)* 4468
Hoefler, Charles E. *(Lighting Designer)* 2173, 4468
Hoefler, Charles E. *(Set Design)* 2173, 4468
Hoey, Bill *(Cast)* 3392
Hoey, Dennis *(Cast)* 2293, 4569
Hoey, Evelyn *(Cast)* 1272, 2366, 4545, 4583
Hoey, Herbert *(Cast)* 4843
Hoey, William F. *(Cast)* 1301
Hoff, Edwin H. *(Cast)* 2345
Hoff, Fred *(Musical Director)* 659, 728, 1710, 1819, 2112, 2739, 3207, 4328
Hoff, Louise *(Cast)* 1408, 2910
Hoff, Louise *(Composer)* 4153
Hoff, Louise *(Lyricist)* 4153
Hoff, Robin *(Cast)* 1427
Hoffa, Portland *(Cast)* 4300, 4367
Hoffenstein, Samuel *(Librettist)* 1453
Hoffert, Paul *(Composer)* 1500
Hoffert, Paul *(Orchestrations)* 1500
Hoffman, Aaron *(Librettist)* 349, 358, 1531, 2314, 2448, 3134, 3185, 3519, 3520, 3531, 3748, 3855, 4436, 4787
Hoffman, Aaron *(Lyricist)* 2299
Hoffman, Aaron S. *(Lyricist)* 248, 3073
Hoffman, Al *(Composer)* 544, 4264
Hoffman, Al *(Lyricist)* 4264
Hoffman, Armin *(Pianist)* 412
Hoffman, Avi *(Cast)* 1609, 3722, 4082
Hoffman, Avi *(Director)* 4082
Hoffman, Avi Ber *(Cast)* 1279
Hoffman, Bena *(Choreographer)* 3590
Hoffman, Bill *(Librettist)* 2357
Hoffman, Bill *(Set Design)* 131
Hoffman, Cary *(Composer)* 4635
Hoffman, Dustin *(Cast)* 2218
Hoffman, E.A. *(Composer)* 3631
Hoffman, E.A. *(Lyricist)* 3631
Hoffman, Ferdi *(Cast)* 1284
Hoffman, G. Wayne *(Cast)* 1732
Hoffman, Gertrude
See also Gertrude Hoffman Girls.
Hoffman, Gertrude *(Cast)* 558, 959, 1829, 1968, 2209, 3387, 3609
Hoffman, Gertrude *(Choreographer)* 201, 2800, 2951, 3148, 3149, 3409, 4650

Hoffman, Gertrude *(Composer)* 2724, 3387, 4650, 4801
Hoffman, Miriam *(Librettist)* 4082
Hoffman, Paul *(Cast)* 4830
Hoffman, Pauline *(Cast)* 376
Hoffman, Philip *(Cast)* 2143, 2152, 4229
Hoffman, Stephen *(Composer)* 4533
Hoffman Girls, The Gertrude
See also Gertrude Hoffman.
Hoffman Girls, The Gertrude *(Cast)* 3148
Hoffmann, Max *(Cast)* 1573
Hoffmann, Max *(Composer)* 558, 1118, 1829, 2209, 2800, 3154, 3387, 3746, 3747, 3748, 3749, 4787
Hoffmann, Max *(Lyricist)* 558, 1829, 3387, 3746, 3749
Hoffmann, Max *(Musical Director)* 558, 683, 2851, 3149, 3154, 3907, 4853
Hoffmann, Max *(Orchestrations)* 4777
Hoffmann Jr., Max *(Cast)* 288, 1461, 3623, 3907, 4178, 4234
Hofsiss, Jack *(Director)* 595
Hogan, Ernest *(Cast)* 633, 783, 3337
Hogan, Ernest *(Composer)* 2675, 3337, 3797
Hogan, Ernest *(Director)* 3337
Hogan, Ernest *(Lyricist)* 2675
Hogan, Ernest *(Producer)* 2210
Hogan, Jonathan *(Cast)* 1268
Hogan, Jonathan *(Composer)* 1268, 4294
Hogan, Jonathan *(Lyricist)* 1268, 4294
Hogya, Giles *(Lighting Designer)* 3688
Hoh, Richard Charles *(Cast)* 249
Hohengarten, Carl *(Orchestrations)* 2928
Holamon, Ken *(Set Design)* 2285
Holbrook, A.M. *(Cast)* 947, 1594, 2502
Holbrook, A.M. *(Choreographer)* 1555, 4497
Holbrook, A.M. *(Director)* 308, 947, 1602, 1707, 2880, 2885, 2886, 2915, 3199, 4181, 4646
Holbrook, Al *(Cast)* 2507
Holbrook, Al *(Choreographer)* 307, 742, 1151
Holbrook, Al *(Director)* 252, 1071, 1095, 1417, 1525, 1570, 2119, 2448, 2566, 2936, 3229, 3423, 4473, 4549
Holbrook, Alice *(Cast)* 727, 2350
Holbrook, Bessie *(Cast)* 4293
Holbrook, Florence *(Cast)* 531, 1525, 2155, 4094, 4387, 4506
Holbrook, Florence *(Composer)* 531
Holbrook, Hal *(Cast)* 1062
Holbrook, Harry *(Cast)* 2271
Holbrook, William *(Cast)* 2, 1448, 1919, 3086, 4673
Holbrook, William *(Choreographer)* 1207, 1231, 3005, 3144, 3721, 4039, 4550, 4673
Holbrook, William R. *(Choreographer)* 324
Holcomb, Willard *(Librettist)* 2800, 3357
Holcombe, Gary *(Cast)* 4149
Holden, John *(Director)* 4005
Holden, Molly *(Cast)* 932
Holden, Richard *(Lyricist)* 3698
Holden, William *(Cast)* 2628
Holder, Christopher *(Cast)* 1940
Holder, Don *(Lighting Designer)* 647
Holder, Donald *(Costumes)* 2674
Holder, Donald *(Lighting Designer)* 240, 2199
Holder, Geoffrey *(Cast)* 134, 2000
Holder, Geoffrey *(Choreographer)* 4383
Holder, Geoffrey *(Costumes)* 4383, 4722
Holder, Geoffrey *(Director)* 4383, 4722
Holder, Ray *(Dance Arranger)* 299
Holdgrive, David *(Choreographer)* 139, 1079, 2565, 4279, 4731
Holdgrive, David *(Director)* 139, 4279, 4731
Holdgrive, David *(Librettist)* 4731
Holdridge, Lee *(Arrangements)* 4093
Holdridge, Lee *(Composer)* 2142, 2279, 4433
Holdridge, Lee *(Dance Arranger)* 1158, 2248
Holgate, Danny *(Composer)* 576
Holgate, Danny *(Dance Arranger)* 952, 1198, 1816, 4192
Holgate, Danny *(Musical Director)* 576, 1072, 1816, 3653
Holgate, Danny *(Orchestrations)* 2173, 3653
Holgate, Danny *(Vocal Arranger)* 952, 1072
Holgate, Ron *(Cast)* 474, 1660, 1924, 1974, 3019
Holgate, Ronald *(Cast)* 1422, 3897, 4703
Holiday, Bob *(Cast)* 1280, 2163
Holiday, Hope *(Cast)* 177
Holiday, Joy *(Cast)* 1638
Holiday, Ron *(Cast)* 1638
Holiner, Mann *(Librettist)* 444
Holiner, Mann *(Lyricist)* 138, 444, 495, 1461, 1874, 2140, 2637, 3680, 3704
Holland, Anthony *(Cast)* 1406
Holland, Brian *(Composer)* 146, 3739, 4193, 4534
Holland, Brian *(Lyricist)* 146, 3739, 4193, 4534
Holland, Charles *(Producer)* 1876
Holland, Eddie *(Composer)* 146, 3739, 4193, 4534
Holland, Eddie *(Lyricist)* 146, 3739, 4193, 4534
Holland, George *(Cast)* 3504, 4113
Holland, Jack *(Cast)* 1979
Holland, Jack *(Choreographer)* 4429
Holland, Joseph *(Cast)* 2257, 4256
Holland, Maurice *(Cast)* 1241, 2112
Holland, Robert *(Cast)* 1085
Hollander, Emile *(Musical Director)* 2413
Hollander, Frederick *(Composer)* 3444
Hollander, Irma *(Composer)* 3036
Hollander, Irma *(Lyricist)* 3036
Hollander, Joe *(Composer)* 116, 332
Hollander, Joe *(Lyricist)* 116, 2122
Hollander, John *(Lyricist)* 4512
Hollander, Victor *(Composer)* 697, 2922, 4804
Holler, Dick *(Composer)* 3018
Holler, Dick *(Lyricist)* 3018
Hollerith Jr., Charles *(Producer)* 127, 3162
Holley, Patty *(Cast)* 2646, 3628
Holliday, Billie *(Composer)* 3905
Holliday, Billie *(Lyricist)* 3905
Holliday, David *(Cast)* 798, 3015, 3444
Holliday, Harry *(Cast)* 2906
Holliday, Jennifer *(Cast)* 1103, 3991
Holliday, Judy
See also The Revuers.
Holliday, Judy *(Cast)* 363, 1991
Holliday, Judy *(Lyricist)* 1750
Holliday, Robert *(Cast)* 2112
Hollins, Hilda *(Cast)* 2673
Hollins, M.H. *(Composer)* 2059

Hollins, Mabel H. *(Lyricist)* 1
Hollins, Maud *(Cast)* 2233, 2673
Hollis, Tommy *(Cast)* 3368
Hollister, David *(Composer)* 1233, 2288
Hollister, David *(Dance Arranger)* 4292
Hollister, David *(Orchestrations)* 2887, 4292
Hollmann, Erica *(Costumes)* 2285
Holloway, Joan *(Cast)* 3800, 3913
Holloway, Stanley *(Cast)* 842, 844, 1089, 3038, 3156, 4361, 4519
Holloway, Sterling *(Cast)* 1446, 1447, 1448, 2032
Holloway, Sterling *(Librettist)* 1448
Hollywood, Daniel *(Producer)* 3097
Hollywood Alliance *(Producer)* 2809
Holm, Celeste *(Cast)* 462, 2144, 2182, 3263, 4191, 4537
Holm, Eleanor *(Cast)* 173, 417, 3100
Holm, Hanya *(Choreographer)* 161, 283, 623, 751, 1600, 2331, 2464, 2948, 3035, 3038, 3326, 3496, 3696, 4048
Holm, Hanya *(Director)* 4048
Holm, John Cecil *(Author)* 297, 2449
Holm, John Cecil *(Librettist)* 372, 971
Holm, Klaus *(Lighting Designer)* 842, 1076, 1600, 2554, 2556, 3473, 4798
Holm, Klaus *(Set Design)* 2554
Holman, Bill *(Orchestrations)* 3428
Holman, Libby *(Cast)* 1446, 2545, 2827, 3086, 3650, 3699, 4367, 4777
Holmes, Ben *(Cast)* 1461
Holmes, Ben *(Director)* 1836
Holmes, Greenberg *(Cast)* 1906
Holmes, Greensbury *(Cast)* 4751
Holmes, J. Merrill *(Cast)* 1036
Holmes, Jack *(Composer)* 392, 597, 679, 1049, 1107, 1408, 3110, 3217, 3889, 3890, 4310
Holmes, Jack *(Conductor)* 1380
Holmes, Jack *(Dance Arranger)* 1380, 1408, 2522, 3110
Holmes, Jack *(Librettist)* 392, 597
Holmes, Jack *(Lyricist)* 392, 679, 1049, 1107, 1408, 3110, 3889, 3890, 4310
Holmes, Jack *(Musical Director)* 3217, 4173, 4659
Holmes, Jack *(Pianist)* 392
Holmes, Jack *(Vocal Arranger)* 2522, 4173
Holmes, Jerry *(Cast)* 2011
Holmes, Leroy *(Composer)* 2072
Holmes, Leroy *(Musical Director)* 2072
Holmes, Lucy *(Cast)* 1347
Holmes, Michael *(Musical Director)* 319
Holmes, Michael *(Orchestrations)* 319
Holmes, Ralph *(Cast)* 4772
Holmes, Rapley *(Cast)* 4453
Holmes, Roy *(Lighting Designer)* 2809
Holmes, Rupert *(Composer)* 3070
Holmes, Rupert *(Librettist)* 3070
Holmes, Rupert *(Lyricist)* 3070
Holmes, Rupert *(Orchestrations)* 3070
Holmes, Scott *(Cast)* 1038, 2204, 3718
Holmes, Taylor *(Cast)* 1756, 1992, 2068, 2858, 3850, 4064
Holmes, Vernon *(Musical Director)* 392
Holmes, Violet *(Choreographer)* 107, 2689, 2737, 3126, 3637, 3638
Holmes a Court, Peter *(Producer)* 1232
Holofcener, Larry *(Composer)* 2987, 3186
Holofcener, Larry *(Lyricist)* 673, 2246, 2987, 3186, 3890, 4260, 4273, 4827, 4829
Holpit, Penny *(Set Design)* 3960
Holse, Glenn *(Set Design)* 411
Holst, Edouard *(Composer)* 3176
Holt, Calvin *(Cast)* 673
Holt, Fritz *(Director)* 3444
Holt, Fritz *(Producer)* 2360, 2677, 3515, 3787
Holt, Henry *(Cast)* 1523
Holt, Shannon *(Cast)* 655
Holt, Stella *(Producer)* 70, 71
Holt, Vivian *(Cast)* 1799
Holt, Will *(Author)* 4216
Holt, Will *(Cast)* 2246, 3970
Holt, Will *(Composer)* 33, 3970, 4318
Holt, Will *(Librettist)* 823, 2796, 3330, 3515, 3970, 4216, 4318
Holt, Will *(Lyricist)* 33, 823, 2801, 3015, 3338, 3515, 3970, 4216, 4272, 4318
Holter, Bill *(Cast)* 3530
Holter, Bob *(Composer)* 1677
Holton, Robert *(Composer)* 1878
Holtz, Lou *(Cast)* 622, 1396, 1482, 1483, 2734, 3153, 3416, 3594, 4300, 4747, 4778
Holtz, Lou *(Director)* 1396
Holtz, Lou *(Producer)* 4778
Holtz Sr., Gregory *(Cast)* 2239
Holtzman, Jonathan *(Composer)* 1372, 1669
Holtzman, Jonathan *(Lyricist)* 1372, 1669
Holtzman, Jonathan *(Musical Director)* 1372
Holtzman, Jonathan *(Orchestrations)* 1372
Holtzman, Willy *(Librettist)* 2007
Holtzman, Willy *(Lyricist)* 451
Holzer, Adela *(Producer)* 518, 1116, 3169, 3873, 4447, 4459
Holzer, Jane *(Cast)* 1637
Holzer, Peter *(Producer)* 1116
Holzman, Winnie *(Librettist)* 424
Holzman, Winnie *(Lyricist)* 4, 424
Home, Cyril Morton *(Composer)* 2763
Home, Cyril Morton *(Lyricist)* 2763
Home Town Quartet, The *(Cast)* 1507
Homer *(Author)* 1816, 1959
Honan, Mark *(Cast)* 533, 760
Honeg *(Lyricist)* 4264
Honey, George *(Cast)* 1392
Hong, Arabella *(Cast)* 1315
Honrath, Donald *(Composer)* 3103
Hood, Basil *(Librettist)* 1178, 1392, 1473, 2514, 2836, 3588, 3777
Hood, Basil *(Lyricist)* 356, 902, 1473, 1569, 3588
Hood, Janet *(Dance Arranger)* 1371
Hood, Janet *(Musical Director)* 1371
Hood, Janet *(Vocal Arranger)* 1371
Hood, Noel *(Cast)* 325
Hood, Thomas *(Lyricist)* 2633
Hook, James *(Composer)* 3450
Hook, Nina Warner *(Librettist)* 2168, 4153
Hooker, Brian *(Librettist)* 3219, 3323, 4372, 4539, 4664

Hooker, Brian *(Lyricist)* 710, 1235, 2264, 2756, 3020, 3219, 3323, 3649, 4300, 4539, 4664, 4815
Hooker, Michael S. *(Lighting Designer)* 3925
Hooks, Robert *(Cast)* 1729
Hooper, Claire *(Cast)* 1836
Hooper, Elric *(Cast)* 4469
Hooper, Lewis *(Choreographer)* 2383
Hooper, Lewis *(Director)* 830, 1313
Hoover, J. *(Composer)* 4193
Hoover, J. *(Lyricist)* 4193
Hope, Anthony *(Author)* 3586, 3595, 4798
Hope, Bob *(Cast)* 289, 3153, 3674, 3735, 3850, 3968, 4023, 4532, 4825
Hope, Dorothy *(Cast)* 3451
Hope, Edward *(Author)* 3919
Hope, Edward *(Librettist)* 1447
Hope, Maidie *(Cast)* 3213
Hope, Peggy *(Cast)* 1687, 2888
Hope, Vida *(Director)* 507, 4541
Hopkins, Anthony *(Composer)* 3761
Hopkins, Anthony *(Director)* 1623
Hopkins, Anthony *(Lyricist)* 3761
Hopkins, Anthony *(Producer)* 1623
Hopkins, Arthur *(Author)* 587
Hopkins, Arthur *(Director)* 587, 1020, 1517, 2211, 3686
Hopkins, Arthur *(Lyricist)* 3686
Hopkins, Arthur *(Producer)* 587, 1020, 1517, 2211
Hopkins, Bruce *(Cast)* 1426
Hopkins, Bruce *(Director)* 1785
Hopkins, Kaitlin *(Cast)* 2229
Hopkins, Ken *(Orchestrations)* 2850
Hopkins, Kenyon *(Musical Director)* 3287
Hopkins, Linda *(Cast)* 432, 2134, 2796, 3610
Hopkins, May *(Cast)* 77
Hopkins, Miriam *(Cast)* 1215, 2516
Hopkins, Peggy *(Cast)* 4811
Hoppenstein, Reuben *(Producer)* 1079
Hopper, DeWolf *(Cast)* 340, 698, 1090, 1165, 1208, 1264, 1768, 1926, 1975, 2403, 2469, 2724, 2782, 2982, 3360, 3401, 3486, 3639, 4033, 4054, 4669
Hopper, DeWolf *(Producer)* 2982, 4054
Hopper, Edna Wallace *(Cast)* 8, 749, 1090, 1271, 1313, 1557, 2261, 3976
Hopper, Irma *(Composer)* 3849
Hopper, Irma *(Lyricist)* 3849
Hopper, Victoria *(Cast)* 4361
Hopwood, Aubrey *(Lyricist)* 1313, 3803
Hopwood, Avery *(Author)* 2526, 3079, 3812, 3860
Hopwood, Avery *(Librettist)* 2070, 2254, 4064
Hopwood, Avery *(Lyricist)* 719, 2254, 4064
Horan, Edward *(Composer)* 3500, 4545
Horan, Edward A. *(Composer)* 82
Horan, James *(Cast)* 4705
Horchow, Roger *(Producer)* 921
Hord, Parker *(Librettist)* 4200
Horen, Michael *(Set Design)* 1761
Horn, Barbara Lee *(Producer)* 3956
Horn, Frank *(Cast)* 3170
Horne, C. Morton *(Cast)* 2760
Horne, Lena *(Cast)* 447, 854, 880, 882, 2190
Horne, Marie *(Composer)* 353
Horne, William *(Cast)* 1817
Horner, Carrie *(Cast)* 2064
Horner, Chuck *(Librettist)* 2657
Horner, Harry *(Costumes)* 2202, 3647
Horner, Harry *(Lighting Designer)* 1791
Horner, Harry *(Set Design)* 297, 1791, 2202, 2386, 2453, 3046, 3138, 3647, 3698, 4131, 4706, 4798
Horner, Louise *(Cast)* 510
Horner, Paul *(Composer)* 3428
Horner, Richard *(Producer)* 2965, 3743
Hornez, Andre *(Lyricist)* 2356
Hornsbee, Leonard *(Musical Director)* 1561
Hornsby, Joe *(Composer)* 4278
Hornsby, Joe *(Lyricist)* 4278
Hornsey, Leonard *(Musical Director)* 184, 351, 1534, 1855, 3573, 4320
Hornung, Richard *(Costumes)* 3136
Horovitz, Israel *(Author)* 2954
Horovitz, Israel *(Lyricist)* 2954
Horowitz, Charles *(Librettist)* 3030
Horowitz, David *(Vocal Arranger)* 4343
Horowitz, Herschel *(Composer)* 3530
Horowitz, Jimmy *(Composer)* 2759
Horowitz, Jimmy *(Lyricist)* 2759
Horowitz, Jimmy *(Orchestrations)* 2759
Horowitz, Jimmy *(Vocal Arranger)* 2759
Horton, Edward Everett *(Cast)* 1119, 2837
Horton, John *(Cast)* 171, 4109
Horton, Josiah T.S. *(Librettist)* 3471
Horton, Lester *(Choreographer)* 3947, 4415
Horton, Robert *(Cast)* 3294
Horton, Ron *(Cast)* 4220
Horton, Vaughn *(Composer)* 1296, 4264
Horton, Vaughn *(Lyricist)* 1296, 4264
Horvath, Jan *(Cast)* 3125, 3464
Horwitt, Arnold *(Librettist)* 2422
Horwitt, Arnold *(Lyricist)* 2422
Horwitt, Arnold B. *(Librettist)* 620, 1567, 2137, 2707, 4585, 4827
Horwitt, Arnold B. *(Lyricist)* 180, 1567, 2707, 3501, 3509, 4827
Horwitz, Charles *(Librettist)* 2316
Horwitz, Charles *(Lyricist)* 2316
Horwitz, Murray *(Director)* 1713
Horwitz, Murray *(Librettist)* 1713
Horwitz, Murray *(Lyricist)* 39, 4533
Hosbein, James *(Cast)* 871
Hoschna, Karl *(Composer)* 15, 361, 531, 1088, 1151, 1247, 1558, 2261, 2291, 2667, 3475, 3574, 3977, 4364, 4390, 4589
Hoschna, Karl *(Orchestrations)* 559
Hoschna, Karl L. *(Composer)* 1532
Hoshour, Robert *(Cast)* 3760
Hosier, Beverly *(Cast)* 2439
Hoskins, Ray *(Cast)* 2572
Hosmer *(Cast)* 1181
Hosmer, Lucius *(Composer)* 2350, 3774
Hossack, Grant *(Musical Director)* 2240
Hotchner, A.E. *(Librettist)* 4619
Hotchner, A.E. *(Lyricist)* 4619
Hotchner, A.E. *(Producer)* 4619

Hotopp, Michael *(Costumes)* 3280
Hotopp, Michael *(Lighting Designer)* 944
Hotopp, Michael *(Set Design)* 944, 3280, 4286
Hotopp, Michael J. *(Costumes)* 251
Hotopp, Michael J. *(Lighting Designer)* 31, 778
Hotopp, Michael J. *(Set Design)* 31, 251, 2114, 2171, 3231, 4454
Hott, Jordan *(Producer)* 956, 4029
Hottois, Michael F. *(Lighting Designer)* 4488
Hoty, Dee *(Cast)* 373, 775, 2578, 3448, 4695
Houck, Ted *(Cast)* 3764
Houdina, Mary Jane *(Cast)* 1329
Houdina, Mary Jane *(Choreographer)* 2142, 4288
Houdini, Harry *(Cast)* 712, 1208
Hough, Will M. *(Librettist)* 1307, 1524, 1563, 1593, 1606, 1801, 1908, 1966, 1967, 2155, 2408, 3083, 3508, 3579, 4185, 4376, 4387, 4506
Hough, Will M. *(Lyricist)* 1307, 1316, 1563, 1593, 1801, 1908, 1966, 1967, 2155, 2408, 2512, 2575, 2901, 2922, 3508, 3579, 4185, 4387, 4506
Houghton, Charles *(Lighting Designer)* 4799
Houghton, Norris *(Producer)* 3288
Hould-Ward, Ann *(Costumes)* 1776, 2143, 2230, 2283, 2643, 3448
Hould-Ward, Anne *(Costumes)* 330, 4210
Housam, Robert *(Author)* 1517
House, Billy *(Cast)* 3002, 4667
House, Billy *(Composer)* 2637
House, Eric *(Cast)* 3066
House, Estelle *(Cast)* 149
House, Ron *(Cast)* 1166
Houseman, A.E. *(Lyricist)* 2633
Houseman, John *(Director)* 1366, 2655, 4715
Houseman, John *(Producer)* 919, 942, 979, 2257, 2859, 3733, 4715
Housman, Laurence *(Author)* 738
Houston, Cissy *(Cast)* 4272
Houston, Elizabeth *(Cast)* 2105
Houston, Ethel Dufre *(Cast)* 307, 4250
Houston, George *(Cast)* 680, 711, 948, 1281, 2813, 3219, 4548, 4670
Houston, George *(Director)* 4670
Houston, George *(Librettist)* 2841
Houston, George *(Lyricist)* 2841
Houston, Grace *(Costumes)* 620, 1941, 2024, 4524
Houston Grand Opera *(Producer)* 4447
Hoven, Louise *(Cast)* 518
Hovenden, Peggy *(Cast)* 1342
Howard, Ada *(Cast)* 2896
Howard, Alan *(Cast)* 2322
Howard, Andree *(Choreographer)* 325
Howard, Bart *(Composer)* 943, 1107, 1370, 2227, 3484, 4268
Howard, Bart *(Lyricist)* 943, 1107, 1370, 2227, 3484, 4268
Howard, Bruce *(Cast)* 1366
Howard, Charles *(Cast)* 2122
Howard, Charlotte *(Cast)* 2682
Howard, Cindi *(Cast)* 2965
Howard, Don *(Cast)* 1126
Howard, Elizabeth *(Composer)* 459
Howard, Esther *(Cast)* 3117, 4212, 4300, 4694
Howard, Eugene *(Cast)* 289, 1489, 1490, 1491, 1492, 1493, 1494, 3395, 3399, 3402, 3405, 3958, 4657, 4824
Howard, Eugene *(Lyricist)* 3404
Howard, Florence *(Cast)* 1806
Howard, Frederick *(Cast)* 2623
Howard, Frederick *(Librettist)* 2402
Howard, Garland *(Cast)* 691, 981
Howard, Garland *(Choreographer)* 981
Howard, Garland *(Composer)* 981
Howard, Garland *(Librettist)* 691, 981
Howard, Garland *(Lyricist)* 981
Howard, George *(Cast)* 3753
Howard, George Bronson *(Librettist)* 558
Howard, George W. *(Cast)* 3887
Howard, Gus *(Cast)* 1145, 3823
Howard, Jack *(Cast)* 117
Howard, Jan *(Cast)* 4829
Howard, Jerry *(Cast)* 2097
Howard, Joe (Joseph E.)
See also Joseph E. Howard Amusement Co.
Howard, Joe *(Composer)* 1967, 3579, 3949
Howard, Joe *(Lyricist)* 3949
Howard, Joe *(Producer)* 24
Howard, John *(Cast)* 1791
Howard, Joseph E. *(Cast)* 1054, 1316, 1560, 2155, 2408, 3975, 4465
Howard, Joseph E. *(Composer)* 472, 548, 733, 1054, 1263, 1307, 1316, 1405, 1560, 1563, 1593, 1606, 1897, 1908, 2108, 2155, 2247, 2408, 2512, 2600, 2635, 2649, 2901, 3057, 3367, 4071, 4185, 4247, 4387, 4390, 4411, 4506, 4632
Howard, Joseph E. *(Director)* 1593, 1908
Howard, Joseph E. *(Librettist)* 1054, 1316
Howard, Joseph E. *(Lyricist)* 472, 1054, 1263, 1316, 1405, 1563, 1593, 1606, 1897, 1908, 2408, 2600, 2649, 2740, 4387, 4390
Howard, Joseph E. *(Producer)* 1593
Howard, Ken *(Cast)* 3603, 3869, 3897, 4004
Howard, Madeline *(Cast)* 1218
Howard, Marc *(Producer)* 4601
Howard, May *(Cast)* 2842
Howard, Mel *(Producer)* 432
Howard, Michael *(Director)* 3215
Howard, Noel *(Costumes)* 1296
Howard, Olin *(Cast)* 2489
Howard, Peter *(Arrangements)* 4450
Howard, Peter *(Dance Arranger)* 150, 154, 181, 656, 723, 921, 1660, 1828, 1848, 1860, 2014, 2048, 2368, 2874, 3731, 3897, 4190, 4252, 4255, 4288, 4450, 4737
Howard, Peter *(Musical Director)* 150, 154, 253, 305, 826, 958, 1776, 1848, 2014, 2142, 2204, 2422, 3564, 3897, 4252
Howard, Peter *(Producer)* 3845
Howard, Peter *(Vocal Arranger)* 2014, 3731, 4288
Howard, Richard *(Translator)* 237
Howard, Shafter *(Composer)* 1912
Howard, Shafter *(Librettist)* 1912
Howard, Shafter *(Lyricist)* 1912
Howard, Shemp *(Cast)* 3409
Howard, Sidney *(Author)* 2961
Howard, Sidney *(Librettist)* 2655
Howard, Sonny *(Cast)* 863

Howard, Tom *(Cast)* 1440, 1689, 1691, 2300, 3648, 4023
Howard, Tom *(Librettist)* 1058, 1692
Howard, William *(Musical Director)* 2587
Howard, Willie *(Cast)* 289, 924, 1489, 1490, 1491, 1492, 1493, 1494, 1528, 2506, 3036, 3395, 3399, 3402, 3405, 3410, 3594, 3958, 4010, 4657, 4824
Howard, Willie *(Lyricist)* 3404
Howard Amusement Co., Joseph E. See also Joe (Joseph E.) Howard.
Howard Amusement Co., Joseph E. *(Producer)* 1316
Howarth, Anthony *(Lyricist)* 4041
Howden, Philip *(Set Design)* 1454, 4765
Howe, Bill *(Lyricist)* 4606
Howe, Bob *(Choreographer)* 3967
Howe, E.T. *(Musical Director)* 2517
Howe, George *(Cast)* 700
Howe, Julia Ward *(Lyricist)* 2203, 3020
Howe, Junius *(Producer)* 2963
Howe, Margaret *(Cast)* 2682
Howe, Michael *(Musical Director)* 3318
Howe, William *(Composer)* 3940
Howell, Erik *(Cast)* 4678
Howell, Harry *(Director)* 4602
Howell, Lottice *(Cast)* 1020
Howell, Rita *(Cast)* 1924
Howell, Thomas *(Lyricist)* 95
Howell, Thomas B. *(Lyricist)* 4273
Hower, Frank *(Vocal Arranger)* 1839
Howerd, Frankie *(Cast)* 635
Howes, Basil *(Cast)* 792, 2366, 2976
Howes, Bobby *(Cast)* 66, 475, 2976, 4765
Howes, Sally Ann *(Cast)* 1507, 2355, 4633
Howland, Beth *(Cast)* 832, 1891
Howland, Jason *(Vocal Arranger)* 2198
Howland, Jobyna *(Cast)* 17, 1335, 1613, 1731, 2282, 2844, 2904, 3395, 3799, 4713
Howland, Katherine *(Cast)* 48
Howland, Olin *(Cast)* 340, 2276, 3323, 3923, 4491, 4694
Howland, Olin *(Choreographer)* 1448
Howse, Lola *(Cast)* 2451
Hoy, Toots *(Cast)* 1821
Hoyer, Roy *(Cast)* 138, 4150
Hoylen, Tony *(Cast)* 2852
Hoysradt, John *(Cast)* 3325, 4825
Hoyt, Charles *(Author)* 3392, 4608
Hoyt, Charles *(Librettist)* 3392
Hoyt, Charles H. *(Author)* 4165, 4453, 4712
Hoyt, Charles H. *(Composer)* 436, 998
Hoyt, Charles H. *(Director)* 998, 4165
Hoyt, Charles H. *(Librettist)* 436, 998
Hoyt, Charles H. *(Lyricist)* 436, 4165
Hoyt, Charles H. *(Producer)* 436, 998, 4165
Hoyt, Grace *(Cast)* 934
Hoyt, Harry *(Lyricist)* 811
Hoyt, Henry E. *(Set Design)* 175, 476, 559, 727, 770, 906, 1193, 1213, 1470, 1576, 1594, 2156, 2507, 2725, 2936, 3732, 4353, 4500
Hoyt, Howard *(Producer)* 145, 4180
Hoyt, Lon *(Cast)* 3739
Hoyt, Peggy *(Costumes)* 780
Hruba, Vera *(Cast)* 2078
Hsiung, S.I. *(Author)* 2396
Hsiung, S.I. *(Director)* 2396
Huara, Helba *(Cast)* 3149
Hubbard, Bruce *(Cast)* 2648
Hubbard, Elizabeth *(Cast)* 2064, 2563, 4384
Hubbell, Raymond *(Composer)* 8, 41, 126, 246, 256, 378, 396, 712, 824, 993, 1177, 1208, 1228, 1243, 1525, 1534, 1588, 1631, 1753, 1780, 1901, 1920, 2232, 2328, 2347, 2716, 2723, 2848, 2858, 2897, 2919, 2921, 3096, 3144, 3617, 3685, 3805, 3977, 4054, 4085, 4345, 4359, 4712, 4793, 4805, 4806, 4807, 4808, 4811, 4816, 4818, 4819
Hubbell, Raymond *(Lyricist)* 4799
Hubbell, Raymond *(Musical Director)* 396, 712, 1228, 1901, 3617, 4793
Hubbell, Raymond *(Orchestrations)* 4818
Huber, Lon *(Cast)* 3318
Huber, Paul *(Cast)* 3131, 3584
Huber Marionettes, The *(Cast)* 589
Hubert, Hugh *(Cast)* 3533
Hubert, Hugh W. *(Composer)* 1457
Hubert, Hugh W. *(Lyricist)* 1457
Hubert, Janet L. *(Cast)* 678
Hubert, Rene *(Costumes)* 650, 2622, 2838
Huddleston, David *(Cast)* 1289
Huddleston, Floyd *(Lyricist)* 3683, 3966, 4827
Hudgins, Johnny *(Cast)* 441, 1989, 2462
Hudson, Charles *(Cast)* 159, 1676, 2284
Hudson, Helen *(Cast)* 1486, 1487
Hudson, Joe *(Composer)* 4171
Hudson, Joe *(Lyricist)* 4171
Hudson, John Paul *(Cast)* 4494
Hudson, Muriel *(Cast)* 4833
Hudson, Rodney *(Cast)* 54, 109, 1053, 4736
Hudson, Rodney Scott *(Cast)* 789
Hudson, Travis *(Cast)* 547, 915, 1500, 1660, 3110, 3551, 4292, 4408
Hudson, Walter *(Cast)* 647, 1785
Hudson, Will *(Composer)* 445, 4137
Hudson, Will *(Lyricist)* 2161
Hudson Guild Theatre *(Producer)* 962
Hudson Productions Co. *(Producer)* 1584
Huey, Richard *(Cast)* 462, 3990
Huff, Carrie *(Cast)* 4198
Huff, Forrest *(Cast)* 351, 487, 561, 1578, 1731, 2390, 2825, 3776, 3985, 4333, 4664
Huff, L. *(Composer)* 4193
Huff, L. *(Lyricist)* 4193
Huffine, Charles *(Orchestrations)* 341, 620
Huffman, Cady *(Cast)* 393, 2199, 4695
Huffman, J.C. *(Director)* 75, 202, 391, 463, 487, 545, 764, 771, 905, 910, 965, 969, 1065, 1096, 1111, 1218, 1240, 1461, 1526, 1613, 1678, 1693, 1923, 2262, 2281, 2282, 2293, 2334, 2358, 2419, 2602, 2628, 2649, 2684, 2696, 2706, 2732, 2747, 2843, 2869, 2884, 2914, 2939, 3051, 3056, 3063, 3085, 3096, 3148, 3170, 3237, 3333, 3397, 3399, 3400, 3401, 3402, 3403, 3404, 3405, 3406, 3407, 3424, 3586, 3680, 3730, 3737, 3778, 3958, 3962, 3985, 4121, 4188, 4427, 4490, 4666, 4747
Huffman, J.C. *(Librettist)* 248
Huffman, J.C. *(Producer)* 3586
Huffman, Mike *(Musical Director)* 1279

Hughes, Allen Lee *(Lighting Designer)* 140, 595, 1004, 3001, 3285, 3631, 4127
Hughes, Barnard *(Cast)* 499, 1186, 1620, 3000
Hughes, Dickson *(Cast)* 4232
Hughes, Dickson *(Composer)* 1408
Hughes, Dickson *(Librettist)* 4232
Hughes, Dickson *(Lyricist)* 1408, 4232
Hughes, Felix *(Cast)* 1866
Hughes, J.J. *(Choreographer)* 2371
Hughes, John *(Choreographer)* 1513
Hughes, Langston *(Author)* 2513, 3001
Hughes, Langston *(Composer)* 2203
Hughes, Langston *(Librettist)* 309, 2203, 2259, 2653, 3315, 3983
Hughes, Langston *(Lyricist)* 309, 369, 2203, 2275, 3001, 3315, 3983, 4169, 4273
Hughes, Leila *(Cast)* 2701, 2922, 3053, 3672, 4490
Hughes, Michael *(Composer)* 1023
Hughes, Revella *(Cast)* 290, 488, 1989, 3808
Hughes, Rhetta *(Cast)* 105
Hughes, Richard B. *(Lighting Designer)* 348
Hughes, Richard B. *(Set Design)* 348
Hughes, Rosamond *(Composer)* 1026
Hughes, Rupert *(Author)* 4422
Hughes, Rupert *(Librettist)* 311, 1226, 4414
Hugill, J. Randall *(Choreographer)* 1630
Hugill, J. Randall *(Director)* 1630
Hugo, Victor *(Author)* 2037, 2442, 3208
Huhn, Bruno *(Composer)* 1502
Huhn, Bruno *(Lyricist)* 1502
Hulbert, Claude *(Cast)* 3569
Hulbert, Jack *(Cast)* 1333, 2467, 2509
Hulbert, Jack *(Choreographer)* 1333, 2392
Hulbert, Jack *(Director)* 1333, 1467, 2004, 2467
Hulbert, Jack *(Producer)* 475, 1333, 2467
Hulburt, Claude *(Lyricist)* 4300
Hulett, Otto *(Cast)* 1448
Hull, Henry *(Cast)* 2121
Hull, Katherine *(Choreographer)* 2426
Hull, Shelley *(Cast)* 100, 763
Hull, Warren *(Cast)* 3648
Humans, Maria *(Costumes)* 924
Humason, Sally *(Librettist)* 1448, 3914
Hume, Edward *(Cast)* 1316
Hume, Michael J. *(Cast)* 1201
Hume, Nancy *(Cast)* 4297
Humes, Bibi *(Cast)* 3668
Hummel, Karen *(Costumes)* 2354, 4769
Hummel, Mark *(Dance Arranger)* 1146, 1298, 1633, 2208, 2437, 2820, 3637
Hummel, Mark *(Musical Director)* 534, 1289
Hummel, Mark *(Vocal Arranger)* 534
Humphrey, Cavada *(Cast)* 206, 4191
Humphrey, Doris
See also Doris Humphrey Group.
Humphrey, Doris *(Choreographer)* 3989
Humphrey, Doris *(Director)* 309
Humphrey, James Luther *(Director)* 810
Humphrey, Jay *(Cast)* 2095
Humphrey Group, Doris
See also Doris Humphrey.
Humphrey Group, Doris *(Cast)* 125
Humphreys, Joseph *(Director)* 1090
Humphries, Barry *(Author)* 2006
Humphries, Barry *(Cast)* 2006, 2682, 3271
Humphries, Barry *(Composer)* 2006
Humphries, Barry *(Director)* 2006
Humphries, Barry *(Lyricist)* 2006
Humphries, Ernest J. *(Set Design)* 292
Hundley, C.L. *(Costumes)* 4535
Hundley, John *(Cast)* 4118, 4583
Hungerford, Edward *(Librettist)* 3647
Hungerford, Edward *(Producer)* 3647
Hunnewell, Clyde *(Cast)* 1357
Hunt, Allen *(Director)* 3318
Hunt, Carl *(Director)* 385
Hunt, Carl *(Producer)* 385
Hunt, Don *(Composer)* 3922
Hunt, Don *(Lyricist)* 3922
Hunt, Dorothy *(Set Design)* 1244
Hunt, E. Howard *(Librettist)* 328
Hunt, Edward A. *(Musical Director)* 4166
Hunt, Estelle *(Librettist)* 4741
Hunt, Grady *(Costumes)* 410
Hunt, Ida Brooks *(Cast)* 48, 742, 4738
Hunt, Leigh *(Lyricist)* 2633
Hunt, Linda *(Cast)* 1186
Hunt, Lois *(Cast)* 596
Hunt, Pamela *(Choreographer)* 2416
Hunt, Pamela *(Director)* 2416
Hunt, Peter *(Director)* 1497, 1634, 3897
Hunt, Peter *(Lighting Designer)* 1122, 1786, 3196, 3835
Hunt, William *(Composer)* 4273
Hunt, William *(Lyricist)* 4273
Hunt, William E. *(Director)* 2372, 4220
Hunter, Alberta *(Cast)* 691, 897, 1981, 2712
Hunter, Alberta *(Composer)* 478
Hunter, Alberta *(Lyricist)* 478
Hunter, Alfred *(Cast)* 4486
Hunter, Alison McLellan *(Costumes)* 1207, 1219, 2540
Hunter, Anne *(Cast)* 1546
Hunter, Barbara *(Cast)* 3082
Hunter, Charles A. *(Librettist)* 3358
Hunter, Chas. A. *(Lyricist)* 3676
Hunter, Eddie *(Cast)* 444, 2009, 3054
Hunter, Eddie *(Librettist)* 2009, 3054
Hunter, Frank *(Librettist)* 3847
Hunter, Frank *(Lyricist)* 2193, 3847
Hunter, George *(Director)* 4273
Hunter, Glenn *(Cast)* 4118
Hunter, Ian McLellan *(Librettist)* 1373
Hunter, Ivy *(Composer)* 4534
Hunter, Ivy *(Lyricist)* 4534
Hunter, James *(Cast)* 1391
Hunter, JoAnn M. *(Cast)* 2905, 3944
Hunter, Kevin *(Cast)* 2055
Hunter, Kim *(Cast)* 2230
Hunter, Louise *(Cast)* 1603
Hunter, Mary *(Director)* 283, 651, 1679, 2948
Hunter, Nina *(Cast)* 2009

Hunter, Robert *(Musical Director)* 658, 3954
Hunter, Robert *(Orchestrations)* 3954
Hunter, Ross *(Cast)* 4415
Hunter, Ross *(Composer)* 4415
Hunter, Ross *(Director)* 4415
Hunter, Ross *(Lyricist)* 4415
Hunter, Ross *(Producer)* 4415
Hunter, Tab *(Cast)* 1742
Hunter, Timothy *(Lighting Designer)* 3346, 4031
Hunter, Walt *(Cast)* 4216
Hunting, John *(Cast)* 1340
Hunting, Lew *(Cast)* 1340
Hunting, Mollie *(Cast)* 1340
Hunting, Tony *(Cast)* 1340
Huntley, Fred *(Cast)* 3588
Huntley, G.P. *(Cast)* 1453, 1922, 2341, 3431, 4354
Huntley, Raymond *(Cast)* 4548
Hup, Irving *(Composer)* 2857
Hup, Irving *(Lyricist)* 2857
Hupfeld, Herman *(Cast)* 3153
Hupfeld, Herman *(Composer)* 2, 203, 961, 1207, 1219, 1481, 1763, 1874, 2545, 2843, 3002, 3172, 3409, 3861, 3955, 4335, 4399, 4498, 4828, 4853
Hupfeld, Herman *(Lyricist)* 2, 203, 961, 1207, 1219, 1481, 1763, 1874, 2545, 2843, 3002, 3172, 3409, 3861, 3955, 4335, 4399, 4498, 4828, 4853
Hurd, Danny *(Orchestrations)* 4558
Hurd, Earl *(Author)* 4035
Hurdle, Lawrence *(Director)* 3105
Hurgon, Austen *(Director)* 2341, 2760, 4017, 4327, 4418, 4419, 4663
Hurgon, Austen *(Librettist)* 1197, 2889
Hurgon, Austen *(Lyricist)* 1197
Hurgon, Austen *(Producer)* 1610
Hurlbert, Jack *(Cast)* 2004
Hurlbert, Jack *(Choreographer)* 4510
Hurlbert, Jack *(Director)* 4510
Hurlbert, Jack *(Producer)* 2004
Hurlburt, Jack *(Cast)* 605
Hurlburt, William J. *(Librettist)* 2528
Hurlbut, Gladys *(Librettist)* 1894
Hurley, Albert *(Musical Director)* 4648
Hurley, Arthur *(Director)* 1027, 1283
Hurley, Brian *(Cast)* 2992
Hurley, Edwin *(Librettist)* 1989
Hurley, Laurel *(Cast)* 3151
Hurok, Sol *(Producer)* 2775
Hurry, Leslie *(Costumes)* 2682
Hurst, David *(Cast)* 623
Hurst, Fannie *(Author)* 1496
Hurst, Gregory S. *(Director)* 2199, 3932
Hurst, Howard *(Producer)* 4460
Hurst, James *(Cast)* 278
Hurst, Sophie *(Producer)* 4460
Hurston, Zora Neale *(Author)* 3001
Hurt, Marybeth *(Cast)* 2607, 2953
Hurt, William *(Cast)* 1268, 1669
Hurtig, Joe *(Director)* 1457, 1824, 2720
Hurtig, Joe *(Producer)* 1457, 2223, 2720
Hurtig, Jules *(Director)* 2122, 2800
Hurtig, Jules *(Producer)* 2122, 2281
Hurtig & Seamon *(Producer)* 2111, 3337
Hurwit, Lawrence *(Composer)* 3902
Hurwitz, Deborah *(Dance Arranger)* 484
Hurwitz, Deborah *(Musical Director)* 484
Hurwitz, Deborah *(Orchestrations)* 484
Hurwitz, Richard *(Orchestrations)* 4522
Husmann, Ron *(Cast)* 64, 1280, 2584, 2626, 4312
Hussar, E. *(Composer)* 2684
Hussey, James *(Cast)* 3400
Hussey, James *(Lyricist)* 2870
Hussey, Jimmy *(Cast)* 376, 3617, 4290
Hussey, Jimmy *(Librettist)* 4290
Hussey, Jimmy *(Lyricist)* 4290
Hussey, Jimmy *(Producer)* 4290
Huston, Grace *(Costumes)* 4640
Huston, Jon *(Orchestrations)* 4089
Huston, Josephine *(Cast)* 1137, 2475, 3379, 4368
Huston, Philip *(Cast)* 1546
Huston, Walter *(Cast)* 2344
Hutch, Willie *(Composer)* 3739
Hutch, Willie *(Lyricist)* 3739
Hutcheson, David *(Cast)* 1387
Hutchins, Emory *(Cast)* 3657
Hutchins, Emory *(Producer)* 1288
Hutchins, Harriet *(Cast)* 2300
Hutchins, Tony *(Composer)* 4488
Hutchinson, E.S. *(Composer)* 560
Hutchinson, E.S. *(Lyricist)* 3026
Hutchinson, E.S.S. *(Lyricist)* 3021
Hutchinson, Ed *(Choreographer)* 473, 2602, 3024
Hutchinson, Ed *(Composer)* 3155
Hutchinson, Edward *(Choreographer)* 537, 538, 1557, 2587, 3026, 3865
Hutchinson, Edward *(Composer)* 2303, 3026, 4723
Hutchinson, Edward *(Director)* 540
Hutchinson, Edward *(Lyricist)* 540, 3203
Hutchinson, Edward *(Producer)* 3203
Hutchinson, Georgia *(Cast)* 813
Hutchinson, Josephine *(Cast)* 55
Hutchinson, Kathryn *(Cast)* 2025
Hutchinson, Leslie *(Pianist)* 791, 3291
Hutchinson, Mark Michael *(Cast)* 460
Hutchinson, Mary *(Cast)* 1971
Hutson, Eric *(Cast)* 2798
Hutton, Betty *(Cast)* 3359, 3841
Hutton, Bill *(Cast)* 450, 1262, 2242
Hutton, C.A. *(Cast)* 251
Hutton, Ina Ray *(Cast)* 2813, 4824
Huycke, Lorne *(Composer)* 4606
Hwarng, Wern-Ying *(Costumes)* 2046
Hyams, Barry *(Cast)* 2813
Hyams, Joe *(Cast)* 4647
Hyams, John *(Cast)* 350, 968, 1558, 2374, 3045, 3488
Hyatt, Maggie *(Composer)* 459
Hyde, Bruce *(Cast)* 634
Hyde, James *(Producer)* 2991
Hyde, R.N. *(Costumes)* 1162
Hyde, Raymond Newton *(Costumes)* 102
Hyde, Victor *(Choreographer)* 1964
Hyde-White, Wilfred *(Cast)* 4510
Hydes, Watty *(Composer)* 1078

Hydes, Watty *(Musical Director)* 178, 2675, 3229, 3882, 3999
Hyer, June *(Cast)* 2664
Hyers, Frank *(Cast)* 3359
Hyland, Al *(Lyricist)* 1964
Hyland, Lily *(Composer)* 1652, 1653, 1654, 1656, 1657
Hyland, Lily *(Incidental Music)* 1653
Hylands, Fred *(Composer)* 331
Hylands, Fred *(Musical Director)* 331
Hylands, Scott *(Cast)* 42
Hyldorf, Joan *(Cast)* 2099
Hylton, Jack *(Producer)* 3798
Hylton Sisters, The *(Cast)* 4174
Hyman, Dick *(Orchestrations)* 4197
Hyman, Earle *(Cast)* 2236, 3188
Hyman, Fracaswell *(Cast)* 1201
Hyman, Jack *(Composer)* 2476
Hyman, Jack *(Lyricist)* 2476
Hyman, Joseph *(Producer)* 2707
Hyman, Larry *(Choreographer)* 450
Hyman, Mac *(Author)* 3188
Hyman, Phyllis *(Cast)* 4091
Hyman, Robert *(Cast)* 2242
Hyman, Sarah Ellis *(Author)* 3898
Hymer, John B. *(Author)* 1142, 2872
Hymes *(Choreographer)* 349
Hymes, Phil *(Lighting Designer)* 2551
Hynd, Ghrett *(Costumes)* 1636
Hynes, John *(Cast)* 1220
Hyperion Productions *(Producer)* 3654
Hyslop, Jeff *(Cast)* 148
Hyson, Carl *(Cast)* 17, 685, 1557, 2412, 2960, 3740, 3791, 4811
Hyson, Carl *(Choreographer)* 3569
Hytner, Nicholas *(Director)* 2905

I

I, Robert *(Lyricist)* 1713
Ianni, Richard *(Cast)* 2055
Ibert, Jacques *(Composer)* 2178
Ibrahim, El Tahra *(Cast)* 2735
Idare *(Costumes)* 4341
Idare & Cie *(Costumes)* 2392
Idare & Co. *(Costumes)* 1610
Ide, Bernard *(Lyricist)* 1884
Ide, Letitia *(Cast)* 125
Ide, Richard *(Cast)* 2556
Ideal Extravaganza Company *(Producer)* 476
Idoine, Christopher M. *(Set Design)* 83
Ihmsen, Josephine *(Composer)* 2454
Ihmsen, Josephine *(Lyricist)* 2454
Ikeda, Thomas *(Cast)* 2861
Illica, Luigi *(Librettist)* 2359
Illmann, Margaret *(Cast)* 3682
Immerman, Connie *(Producer)* 1980, 1981
Immerman, George *(Producer)* 1980
Immerman, Joseph *(Producer)* 2904
Imperato, Carlo *(Cast)* 3806
Improvisation, The *(Producer)* 2069
Independent Prod. Company *(Producer)* 4621
Indick, Murray *(Composer)* 4774
Infants Relief Society *(Producer)* 4530
Ing, Alvin *(Cast)* 3340, 4002
Inga, Laura *(Costumes)* 1757
Ingalls, James F. *(Lighting Designer)* 494, 2033
Ingalls, Phil *(Incidental Music)* 4377
Ingalls, Phil *(Musical Director)* 137, 4377
Inge, William *(Author)* 716, 1990, 3925
Ingham, Barrie *(Cast)* 869
Ingham, Tom *(Cast)* 4401
Inghram, Rose *(Cast)* 3536
Ingle, Doug *(Composer)* 3261
Ingle, Doug *(Lyricist)* 3261
Ingle, John *(Cast)* 2630
Inglesi, Ricky *(Cast)* 2084, 2094, 2096
Inglett, Donald *(Costumes)* 3889
Ingraham, Herbert *(Composer)* 470, 3977
Ingraham, Herbert *(Lyricist)* 470, 3977
Ingraham, Roy *(Composer)* 1311, 1938
Ingram, Michael *(Cast)* 2229, 3555, 3838
Ingram, Rex *(Cast)* 612, 2355, 3990, 4123
Ingram, Tad *(Cast)* 3682
Ingre, Tonia *(Cast)* 4545
Inkijinoff *(Cast)* 2753
Inman, Billy *(Cast)* 1964
Innerarity, Memrie *(Cast)* 788, 1813
Institute of Musical Art *(Producer)* 978, 2193, 3847
Institutional Radio Choir *(Cast)* 1636
Insull, Sigrid *(Costumes)* 809, 4244
Inter-State Amusement Co. *(Producer)* 4590
Inter-Theatre Arts, Inc. *(Producer)* 720
Interludes *(Producer)* 2100
International Artistic Prods., Inc. *(Producer)* 2356
Intropidi, Josephine *(Cast)* 947
Intropodi, Ethel *(Cast)* 2669, 2914, 3746
Intropodi, Josie *(Cast)* 1220, 1266, 1375, 1851, 2291, 2424, 2461, 2665, 2914, 2931, 3746, 4161, 4236, 4381, 4649
Investors Production Co. *(Producer)* 2278
Ionesco, Eugene *(Additional Materal)* 1857
Ionesco, Eugene *(Author)* 2017, 2146
Irby, Iva *(Cast)* 2448
Iredale, Jane *(Librettist)* 4701
Iredale, Martin *(Cast)* 2509
Ireland, Joe *(Cast)* 4220
Irizarry, Vincent *(Cast)* 2440
Irvin, Rea *(Set Design)* 199
Irvine, Mabel *(Cast)* 2326
Irving, Ernest *(Musical Director)* 792
Irving, Ernest *(Orchestrations)* 4479
Irving, George S. *(Cast)* 161, 519, 825, 869, 1475, 1933, 2064, 2150, 2563, 2797, 2798, 3221, 3263, 3602, 3934, 4038, 4323, 4435, 4522
Irving, George S. (Voice) 56, 3449
Irving, Isabel *(Cast)* 2778
Irving, John *(Cast)* 1194
Irving, Laurence *(Costumes)* 4207
Irving, Laurence *(Set Design)* 4207
Irving, Margaret *(Cast)* 1027, 4174
Irving, Robert *(Cast)* 4733

Irving, Washington *(Author)* 239, 2100, 2344, 3720, 4015
Irwin, Bill *(Cast)* 1298
Irwin, Charles *(Cast)* 2, 3086, 4524
Irwin, Flo *(Cast)* 1465, 1582
Irwin, Fred *(Librettist)* 116
Irwin, Fred *(Producer)* 116
Irwin, Marc *(Conductor)* 2992
Irwin, May *(Cast)* 8, 352, 934, 1357, 1501, 2675, 2990, 2996, 3189, 3917, 3999
Irwin, May *(Composer)* 2990, 2996
Irwin, May *(Lyricist)* 2990
Irwin, May *(Producer)* 2996, 3999
Irwin, Robin *(Cast)* 4325
Irwin, Virginia *(Director)* 2076
Irwin, Virginia *(Librettist)* 2076
Irwin, Wallace *(Librettist)* 1083
Irwin, Wallace *(Lyricist)* 1083, 1318, 1417, 4762
Irwin, Will *(Composer)* 70, 1127, 1342, 1657, 1874, 3105, 3365, 3409, 3543, 3638, 3955, 3990, 4086, 4235, 4335, 4498, 4667
Irwin, Will *(Librettist)* 2655
Irwin, Will *(Lyricist)* 3638
Irwin, Will *(Musical Director)* 180, 1336, 2103, 2554, 3543, 3638, 4314, 4640
Irwin, Will *(Vocal Arranger)* 3638
Iscove, Rob *(Choreographer)* 869
Iscove, Rob *(Director)* 869
Isen, Richard *(Composer)* 1276
Isham, Frederic *(Author)* 4299, 4766
Isham, Frederic *(Librettist)* 2180
Isham, John W. *(Producer)* 4704
Ishee, Suzanne *(Cast)* 2654
Isherwood, Christopher *(Author)* 610
Ishii, Leslie *(Cast)* 3944
Island Stage *(Producer)* 2076
Isley, B. *(Composer)* 4193
Isley, B. *(Lyricist)* 4193
Isley, O. *(Composer)* 4193
Isley, O. *(Lyricist)* 4193
Isley, R. *(Composer)* 4193
Isley, R. *(Lyricist)* 4193
Isquith, Louis *(Director)* 2845
Isquith, Louis *(Producer)* 2845
Israel, Neil *(Director)* 3370
Israel, Robert *(Set Design)* 3937
Israel, William *(Lyricist)* 387
Issa, Paul *(Lyricist)* 3636
Ito, Michio *(Choreographer)* 718, 1689, 3662, 4637
Ito, Teiji *(Composer)* 790
Ivanek, Zeljko *(Cast)* 785
Ivanoff, Alexander *(Lyricist)* 3686
Ivanoff, Alexandra *(Dance Arranger)* 788
Ivanoff, Alexandra *(Musical Director)* 788
Ivanoff, Alexandra *(Vocal Arranger)* 788
Iverson & Henneage *(Costumes)* 2376, 4491
Ives, Burl *(Cast)* 514, 3497, 3794, 3989, 4340
Ives, Charles *(Composer)* 1589
Ivey, Dana *(Cast)* 4210
Ivey, Judith *(Cast)* 1575
Ivey, Scott K. *(Cast)* 4055
Ivins, Perry *(Director)* 266
Ivins, Perry *(Lyricist)* 266
Ivor-Szinngey, Stephen *(Librettist)* 3791

J

J.D. Steele Singers, The *(Cast)* 1636
Jabara, Paul *(Cast)* 1717, 3636
Jabara, Paul *(Composer)* 1298, 3636
Jabara, Paul *(Librettist)* 3636
Jabara, Paul *(Lyricist)* 1298, 3636
Jablons, Karen *(Cast)* 99, 181, 2132
Jablonski, Carl *(Choreographer)* 808
Jablonski, Peter *(Lyricist)* 4137
Jac-Lewis *(Costumes)* 2610
Jack, Angel *(Cast)* 4011
Jack, Angel *(Costumes)* 4011
Jack, Angel *(Set Design)* 4011
Jack, Burt M. *(Cast)* 2771
Jackel, Paul *(Cast)* 81, 1509
Jackman, Hope *(Cast)* 1619, 3271
Jackness, Andrew *(Set Design)* 829
Jacks, Susan *(Cast)* 4172
Jackson *(Costumes)* 998
Jackson, "Poppa" Charlie *(Composer)* 3001
Jackson, "Poppa" Charlie *(Lyricist)* 3001
Jackson, Al *(Librettist)* 1533
Jackson, Alfred *(Librettist)* 3489
Jackson, Arthur *(Composer)* 3399, 4812
Jackson, Arthur *(Lyricist)* 545, 1345, 1482, 1483, 1484, 1873, 1911, 2363, 2376, 3399, 4812
Jackson, Brady *(Cast)* 444
Jackson, Brian *(Costumes)* 1255
Jackson, Brian *(Set Design)* 1255
Jackson, Byron *(Cast)* 2077
Jackson, C. *(Composer)* 1319
Jackson, C. *(Librettist)* 1319
Jackson, C. *(Lyricist)* 1319
Jackson, Charlie *(Composer)* 3297
Jackson, Charlie *(Lyricist)* 3297
Jackson, Danny *(Composer)* 819
Jackson, Danny *(Librettist)* 819
Jackson, Danny *(Lyricist)* 819
Jackson, David *(Cast)* 1649
Jackson, Donald *(Cast)* 2094
Jackson, Eddie
See also Clayton, Jackson, & Durante.
Jackson, Eddie *(Cast)* 848, 858, 860, 3131, 3953
Jackson, Emma *(Cast)* 291, 980, 1906
Jackson, Ernestine *(Cast)* 572, 3656, 3661, 4450
Jackson, Ethel *(Cast)* 470, 1994, 2543, 2836, 4563
Jackson, Eugene *(Cast)* 2415
Jackson, Frank *(Cast)* 1479, 3040, 4751
Jackson, Frank *(Director)* 815
Jackson, Fred *(Author)* 3921, 4547
Jackson, Fred *(Cast)* 4696
Jackson, Fred *(Librettist)* 1345, 2363, 3307, 4491, 4547
Jackson, Fred *(Lyricist)* 4491
Jackson, Gary *(Composer)* 146, 1638, 3739
Jackson, Gary *(Lyricist)* 146, 1638, 3739

Jackson, Glenda *(Cast)* 3445
Jackson, Helen
See Helen Jackson Girls.
Jackson, Howard *(Composer)* 4291
Jackson, Howard *(Orchestrations)* 1492, 4291, 4335, 4778, 4823
Jackson, J.W. *(Choreographer)* 292
Jackson, Jerry *(Choreographer)* 3888
Jackson, Jo *(Cast)* 344
Jackson, Jo *(Librettist)* 344
Jackson, Joe *(Cast)* 117, 959, 1631, 2696
Jackson, Keisha *(Cast)* 4786
Jackson, Laura Mae *(Lighting Designer)* 3280
Jackson, Lemuel *(Cast)* 1050
Jackson, Leonard *(Cast)* 2290
Jackson, Margaret *(Cast)* 4184
Jackson, Marlene *(Cast)* 2091
Jackson, Melinda *(Cast)* 2735
Jackson, Millie *(Cast)* 4786
Jackson, Millie *(Composer)* 4786
Jackson, Millie *(Lyricist)* 4786
Jackson, Nagle *(Cast)* 272, 427
Jackson, Nagle *(Director)* 83, 2305, 4537
Jackson, Nagle *(Librettist)* 83, 4537
Jackson, Papa Charlie *(Composer)* 26, 3709
Jackson, Papa Charlie *(Lyricist)* 26, 3709
Jackson, R. *(Composer)* 4242
Jackson, Richard *(Lighting Designer)* 2104
Jackson, Richard *(Set Design)* 941, 2104, 4602
Jackson, Robert *(Cast)* 828, 3656
Jackson, Shirley *(Cast)* 344
Jackson, Tod *(Choreographer)* 13, 1045, 2785
Jackson, Tod *(Director)* 2785
Jackson, Tony *(Composer)* 3400
Jackson, Zaidee *(Cast)* 3660
Jackson Jr., Joe *(Cast)* 2077
Jackson Jr., Oliver *(Cast)* 4076
Jacob, Bill *(Composer)* 2217
Jacob, Bill *(Lyricist)* 2217
Jacob, Jackie *(Cast)* 2356
Jacob, Jackie *(Lyricist)* 2356
Jacob, Norman *(Cast)* 1304
Jacob, Patti *(Composer)* 2217
Jacob, Patti *(Lyricist)* 1261, 2217
Jacob, Steven *(Cast)* 1732
Jacobi, Georgio *(Dance Arranger)* 45
Jacobi, Lou *(Cast)* 1227, 3273
Jacobi, Paula *(Author)* 19
Jacobi, Victor *(Author)* 2761, 4258
Jacobi, Victor *(Composer)* 168, 364, 1723, 2614, 2761, 3658, 4258, 4393
Jacobowski, Edward
See Edward Jakobowski.
Jacobs, Al *(Composer)* 1953
Jacobs, Al *(Lyricist)* 1953
Jacobs, Hal *(Set Design)* 3161
Jacobs, Harvey *(Author)* 1075
Jacobs, Harvey *(Librettist)* 107, 1075
Jacobs, Iona *(Cast)* 1556
Jacobs, Ira *(Musical Director)* 1130, 3511
Jacobs, Jacob *(Cast)* 343, 3559
Jacobs, Jacob *(Director)* 3559, 4463
Jacobs, Jacob *(Librettist)* 4463
Jacobs, Jacob *(Lyricist)* 343, 1609, 3559, 4342, 4463
Jacobs, Jacob *(Producer)* 343, 3559
Jacobs, Jim *(Composer)* 1664
Jacobs, Jim *(Librettist)* 1664
Jacobs, Jim *(Lyricist)* 1664
Jacobs, Louis *(Librettist)* 3947
Jacobs, Pat *(Composer)* 2039
Jacobs, Pat *(Lyricist)* 2039
Jacobs, Paul *(Cast)* 3077
Jacobs, Paul *(Composer)* 3077
Jacobs, Paul *(Musical Director)* 3077
Jacobs, Sally *(Set Design)* 3445
Jacobs, Sander *(Producer)* 1649
Jacobs, Will *(Cast)* 2962
Jacobson *(Author)* 967
Jacobson, Dan *(Author)* 4863
Jacobson, Helen *(Producer)* 1319
Jacobson, Henrietta *(Cast)* 2352, 3900
Jacobson, Henrietta *(Choreographer)* 2352, 3559
Jacobson, Henrietta *(Set Design)* 2352
Jacobson, Hy *(Lyricist)* 268
Jacobson, Hymie *(Composer)* 4342
Jacobson, Hymie *(Lyricist)* 4342
Jacobson, Irving *(Cast)* 1190, 2352, 2727, 3612
Jacobson, John *(Composer)* 2784
Jacobson, John *(Musical Director)* 2784
Jacobson, Kenneth *(Composer)* 1990, 3956
Jacobson, Leopold *(Author)* 742, 2293, 4590
Jacobus, Robert *(Lighting Designer)* 4047
Jacoby, Coleman *(Librettist)* 3524, 4828, 4829
Jacoby, Coleman *(Lyricist)* 4829
Jacoby, Elliot *(Orchestrations)* 1898, 3091, 3278, 4362
Jacoby, Mark *(Cast)* 3734
Jacoby, Scott *(Cast)* 732, 1611
Jacquemot, Ray *(Cast)* 1085
Jacquet, H. Maurice *(Composer)* 3978, 4620
Jacquet, H. Maurice *(Musical Director)* 4620
Jaffe, George *(Additional Lyrics)* 2275
Jaffe, Howard *(Composer)* 4093
Jaffe, Howard *(Librettist)* 4679
Jaffe, Howard *(Lyricist)* 4093
Jaffe, Joan *(Cast)* 696
Jaffe, Moe *(Composer)* 18
Jaffe, Moe *(Librettist)* 3150
Jaffe, Moe *(Lyricist)* 18, 551, 750, 2540, 3150, 3523
Jaffe, Robert M. *(Cast)* 4543
Jaffe, Sam *(Cast)* 1196, 1396, 2194, 2653
Jaffe, Sam *(Librettist)* 1446
Jaffee, Lynne *(Cast)* 3501
Jagermann, Walter *(Set Design)* 1493, 4256, 4772
Jagger, Mick *(Composer)* 3739, 4449
Jagger, Mick *(Lyricist)* 3739, 4449
Jahan, Marine *(Cast)* 484
Jaime *(Author)* 4115
Jaimes, Ray *(Orchestrations)* 3234
Jaimes, Raymond *(Orchestrations)* 2449
Jakobowski, Edward *(Author)* 1193, 3625
Jakobowski, Edward *(Composer)* 1030, 1193, 3625, 4713
Jakobs, Ned *(Producer)* 2005

Jakubovic, Jaroslav *(Musical Director)* 3167
Jamal, Sati *(Cast)* 1671
Jamerson, Thomas *(Cast)* 2839
James, Alex *(Composer)* 1132
James, Alex *(Lyricist)* 1132
James, Arthur *(Composer)* 1919
James, Arthur *(Lyricist)* 1919
James, Bob *(Composer)* 3871
James, Byron *(Cast)* 2302
James, Carolyne *(Cast)* 643
James, Dan *(Author)* 462
James, David *(Costumes)* 3010
James, Don *(Composer)* 2082, 2482
James, Don *(Lyricist)* 2082, 2482
James, Don *(Musical Director)* 757
James, Don *(Orchestrations)* 2482
James, Dorothea *(Cast)* 3584
James, Ethel *(Cast)* 2984
James, Graham *(Cast)* 455
James, Hal *(Producer)* 823, 1729, 2727, 3280
James, Harry *(Composer)* 509, 4091
James, Harry *(Lyricist)* 4091
James, Harry *(Musical Director)* 2378, 2446, 2461, 4037
James, Henry *(Author)* 101, 4600
James, Henry *(Composer)* 3562
James, Henry *(Lyricist)* 3562
James, Hilary *(Cast)* 1804
James, Ida *(Cast)* 2817
James, Jessica *(Cast)* 556, 4180
James, Julia *(Cast)* 4327
James, Lester *(Cast)* 3366, 4318
James, Miller *(Cast)* 2263
James, Olga *(Cast)* 2987
James, Paul *(Lyricist)* 1134, 1275, 1448, 2545, 3172, 3849
James, Philip *(Musical Director)* 3043
James, Polly *(Cast)* 1721, 2047
James, Ray *(Cast)* 2522
James, Ray *(Choreographer)* 1924
James, Rian *(Author)* 1359
James, Stephanie Renee *(Cast)* 3724
James, Stephen *(Cast)* 1000, 1684, 3175
James, Ted *(Librettist)* 3479
James, Toni-Leslie *(Costumes)* 756, 789, 1822, 2200
James-Mark *(Orchestrations)* 3195
Jameson, House *(Cast)* 3097
Jameson, Joyce *(Cast)* 407, 408, 410, 411, 412, 413, 1341
Jamison, Betsy *(Cast)* 2177
Jamison, Judith *(Cast)* 2775, 4091
Jamison, Marshall *(Director)* 603
Jampolis, Neil Peter *(Lighting Designer)* 259, 432, 1164, 1775, 1955, 2142, 3318, 3752, 3763, 3846, 3956, 4162, 4689
Jampolis, Neil Peter *(Set Design)* 1139, 1353, 2142, 2474, 3485, 3661, 3846, 4396
Janas, Mark *(Composer)* 2573
Janas, Mark *(Lyricist)* 2573
Janas, Mark *(Musical Director)* 2573
Jane, Mary *(Cast)* 2216
Janes, Alan *(Librettist)* 580
Janet Sisters, The *(Cast)* 560
Jani, Robert F. *(Director)* 2689, 3126
Jani, Robert F. *(Producer)* 107, 2689, 2737, 3126, 3637, 4035
Janik, Ada *(Dance Arranger)* 3019
Janik, Ada *(Orchestrations)* 3019
Janik, Ada *(Vocal Arranger)* 3019
Janine *(Costumes)* 3827
Janis, Beverly *(Cast)* 2275
Janis, Conrad *(Cast)* 1204, 2246
Janis, Elsie *(Cast)* 683, 1175, 1176, 1230, 2025, 2394, 2891, 3398, 4017, 4544, 4650
Janis, Elsie *(Composer)* 1176, 3332, 3617
Janis, Elsie *(Director)* 1175, 3103
Janis, Elsie *(Librettist)* 1175, 3617
Janis, Elsie *(Lyricist)* 683, 1175, 1176, 2891, 3332, 3617, 4017, 4555
Janis, Vivian *(Cast)* 4824
Jankel, Chas *(Composer)* 3884
Jankowski, Steven *(Composer)* 1377
Jannath, Heba *(Lyricist)* 1989
Janney, Allison *(Cast)* 1169
Janney, Leon *(Cast)* 2304, 3365, 3526
Janney, Russell *(Librettist)* 3219, 4539
Janney, Russell *(Lyricist)* 3219, 4539
Janney, Russell *(Producer)* 2756, 3219, 3829, 4539, 4664
Janowski, Robert *(Cast)* 2846
Jans, Harry
See also Jans & Whelan.
Jans, Harry *(Cast)* 2140, 2636
Jans & Whelan
See also Harry Jans and Harold Whelan.
Jans & Whalen *(Cast)* 1693
Jansen, Marie *(Cast)* 2824
Jansen, Robert *(Cast)* 3682
Janssen, Werner *(Composer)* 495, 1780, 2378, 2446, 2461, 2519, 2564, 2605, 2637, 3137, 4819
Jansson, A.L. *(Lyricist)* 2159
January, Lois *(Cast)* 4772
Janus, Billy *(Composer)* 487
Janus, Billy *(Lyricist)* 487
Janusz, Tom *(Dance Arranger)* 4689
Janusz, Tom *(Musical Director)* 1216, 4689
Janusz, Tom *(Orchestrations)* 1216
Janusz, Tom *(Vocal Arranger)* 4689
Janvier, Emma *(Cast)* 102, 1271, 2592, 2793, 2892, 3176, 4115, 4491
Janvier, Marcel *(Author)* 904
Jarboe, Richard *(Composer)* 1732
Jarboe, Richard *(Librettist)* 1732
Jarboe, Richard *(Lyricist)* 1732
Jardon, Dolly *(Cast)* 4714
Jardon, Dorothy *(Cast)* 968, 1295, 2358, 2826, 3362, 3525, 3701, 4616, 4757
Jardon, Dorothy *(Composer)* 545
Jardon, Dorothy *(Lyricist)* 545
Jared, Robert *(Lighting Designer)* 4216, 4412
Jarick Prods. Ltd. *(Producer)* 2354
Jarnac, Dorothy *(Cast)* 1811, 2554, 4377
Jarnagin, Jerry *(Composer)* 4234
Jarno, Georges *(Composer)* 1522
Jaroslow, Ruth *(Cast)* 2236, 2965, 4318
Jarratt, Howard *(Cast)* 3035

Jarrett, Art *(Cast)* 1979, 4586
Jarrett, Arthur *(Cast)* 3220
Jarrett, Daniel *(Cast)* 1157, 3220
Jarrett, Jerry *(Cast)* 2195, 2231, 2422, 4379, 4540
Jarvis, Graham *(Cast)* 2953, 3742
Jarvis, Scott *(Cast)* 2433
Jarvis, Sidney *(Cast)* 1851, 2025
Jasien, Deborah *(Set Design)* 2199
Jason, Michael *(Cast)* 2212
Jason, Mitchell *(Cast)* 1227, 1649, 2231, 4038
Jason, Will *(Composer)* 1947, 3173
Jason, Will *(Lyricist)* 1947, 3173
Jatim, Arthur *(Author)* 831
Javits, Joan *(Composer)* 4435
Javits, Joan *(Lyricist)* 1993, 3966, 4435, 4785
Javits, Marion *(Producer)* 1736
Jaxson, Frankie *(Cast)* 3528
Jay, Isabel *(Cast)* 4663
Jay-Thorpe *(Costumes)* 3860, 4299
Jaycox, Martin *(Cast)* 1636
Jayne, Estelle *(Cast)* 1493
Jayson, Paul *(Cast)* 1341
Jbara, Gregory *(Cast)* 1785, 3598, 4560
Jeanmaire *(Cast)* 1548
Jeans, Ronald *(Composer)* 605, 4581
Jeans, Ronald *(Director)* 703
Jeans, Ronald *(Librettist)* 605, 703, 704, 792, 1128, 1338, 2004, 2467, 2483, 2570, 3005, 3291, 4374
Jeans, Ronald *(Lyricist)* 133, 702, 1448, 2570, 4581
Jebe, Halfdau *(Producer)* 1117
Jecko, Timothy *(Cast)* 3908
Jefferson, C.B. *(Producer)* 571
Jefferson, Lauretta *(Choreographer)* 420, 2187, 2460, 4465
Jefferson, William *(Composer)* 352
Jefferson, William *(Lyricist)* 352
Jeffrey, Alan *(Lyricist)* 4264
Jeffrey, Allan *(Composer)* 4264
Jeffrey, Clare *(Costumes)* 3818
Jeffrey, Howard *(Choreographer)* 786, 1497
Jeffrey Betancourt Prods. *(Producer)* 3311
Jeffreys, Alan *(Composer)* 4153, 4566, 4828
Jeffreys, Alan *(Librettist)* 4566, 4828
Jeffreys, Alan *(Lyricist)* 4153, 4566, 4828
Jeffreys, Anne *(Cast)* 1415, 2837, 3064, 4169, 4366
Jeffries, Herb *(Cast)* 2259
Jeffries, Jay *(Lyricist)* 1346, 4137
Jeffries, Will *(Cast)* 2783
Jellison, John *(Cast)* 212, 2440, 4701
Jenbach, Bela *(Author)* 473, 1121, 2486, 2509, 2538, 2668
Jenkins *(Costumes)* 163, 2376, 3314, 4777
Jenkins, Allen *(Cast)* 4058
Jenkins, Daniel *(Cast)* 2229
Jenkins, Daniel H. *(Cast)* 394
Jenkins, David *(Set Design)* 140, 474, 573, 951, 2648, 3555, 3743, 4137, 4619
Jenkins, Dorothy *(Costumes)* 4749
Jenkins, Frank *(Cast)* 2791
Jenkins, George *(Choreographer)* 2847
Jenkins, George *(Lighting Designer)* 84, 145, 180, 1205, 1471, 2750, 3801, 4278, 4337
Jenkins, George *(Set Design)* 84, 145, 180, 190, 1140, 1205, 1471, 2201, 2591, 2750, 2817, 3371, 3801, 4278, 4337, 4366
Jenkins, Gordon *(Composer)* 95, 478, 2677
Jenkins, Gordon *(Lyricist)* 2677, 3992
Jenkins, Gordon *(Musical Director)* 3955
Jenkins, Gordon *(Orchestrations)* 95, 3428, 3955
Jenkins, Gordon *(Vocal Arranger)* 95
Jenkins, John *(Cast)* 945
Jenkins, Joseph *(Arrangements)* 2028
Jenkins, Sharon *(Choreographer)* 35
Jenkins, W.E.C. *(Cast)* 1202
Jenks, Mrs. Donald F. *(Cast)* 1972
Jenks Jr., Almet F. *(Director)* 3547
Jenks Jr., Almet F. *(Librettist)* 3547
Jenn, Myvanwy *(Cast)* 2064
Jennings, Don *(Musical Director)* 287, 652, 1406
Jennings, John *(Composer)* 3725
Jennings, John *(Lyricist)* 3725
Jennings, Ken *(Cast)* 754, 1649, 2542, 2790, 4233
Jennings, Mary *(Choreographer)* 587
Jennings, P. O'Malley *(Cast)* 617
Jens, Alaric *(Composer)* 1059
Jens, Alaric *(Lyricist)* 1059
Jens, Salome *(Cast)* 2075, 4005
Jensbach, Bela *(Author)* 3727
Jensen, Carol-Leigh *(Cast)* 3067
Jensen, Don *(Costumes)* 2017, 2616
Jensen, Don *(Set Design)* 692, 2017, 2616, 3568, 4379
Jensen, Donald *(Costumes)* 793
Jensen, Donald *(Set Design)* 793
Jensen, John *(Set Design)* 946, 4601, 4796
Jensen, Rick *(Musical Director)* 2305
Jergens, Adele *(Cast)* 1109, 2432
Jerome, Ben *(Composer)* 1524, 1535, 1793, 2029, 2869, 2922, 3622, 4766
Jerome, Ben *(Lyricist)* 2974
Jerome, Ben M. *(Composer)* 248, 2159, 2596, 2851, 2869, 2978, 3745, 3786, 4324, 4453, 4761
Jerome, Ben M. *(Musical Director)* 2922, 2966, 2978, 3786, 4453, 4761, 4766
Jerome, Helen *(Author)* 1290
Jerome, Jerome K. *(Author)* 3652
Jerome, Jerome K. *(Composer)* 2056
Jerome, M.K. *(Composer)* 714, 2194, 3683
Jerome, Richard *(Lyricist)* 4799
Jerome, Timothy *(Cast)* 809, 1649, 2169, 2798, 2949, 3456, 3565
Jerome, William *(Author)* 2991, 4642
Jerome, William *(Composer)* 3951
Jerome, William *(Lyricist)* 115, 379, 685, 688, 712, 737, 800, 910, 1151, 1188, 1208, 1247, 1403, 1579, 1731, 1735, 1868, 1901, 1910, 1926, 1927, 1963, 2119, 2209, 2481, 2498, 2566, 2892, 2956, 2964, 2974, 2991, 3031, 3259, 3313, 3332, 3488, 3525, 3537, 3560, 3685, 3710, 3882, 3977, 4014, 4130, 4148, 4181, 4317, 4521, 4636, 4641, 4642, 4655, 4662, 4712, 4757, 4801, 4802, 4806, 4807, 4815
Jerry, Philip *(Cast)* 975
Jessel, George *(Cast)* 431, 504, 1396, 1416, 1889, 2194, 3406, 3962, 4235

Jessel, George *(Composer)* 504
Jessel, George *(Costumes)* 504
Jessel, George *(Librettist)* 504, 1889
Jessel, George *(Lyricist)* 504, 4458
Jessel, George *(Producer)* 1819
Jessel, George *(Set Design)* 504
Jessel, Leon *(Composer)* 710
Jessel, Ray *(Composer)* 3890
Jessel, Ray *(Lyricist)* 3890
Jessel, Raymond *(Composer)* 270, 392, 1107, 1841
Jessel, Raymond *(Lyricist)* 270, 392, 1107, 1841, 2064
Jessop, George H. *(Librettist)* 3049, 3912
Jessop, George H. *(Lyricist)* 3049
Jessup, Stanley *(Cast)* 3170
Jessye, Eva *(Vocal Arranger)* 1366, 3541
Jeter, Michael *(Cast)* 54, 1164, 1649
Jethro, Phil *(Cast)* 2212
Jewell, Clara Alene *(Cast)* 3176
Jewell, Violet *(Cast)* 2465
Jewett, John *(Librettist)* 2168
Jewett, Tom *(Set Design)* 2275
Jewish Nostalgic Prods. *(Producer)* 400, 1269, 4773
Jewish Repertory Theater *(Producer)* 2354
Jezek, Jaroslav *(Composer)* 4677
Jiler, John *(Librettist)* 240
Jiler, John *(Lyricist)* 240
Jillian, Ann *(Cast)* 4197
Jillson, Joyce *(Cast)* 3731
Jines, Henry *(Cast)* 552
Joannest, Gerard *(Composer)* 2188
Jochim, Keith *(Cast)* 31, 1164, 3280
Jockin, H. DeSilva *(Composer)* 1722
Jockin, H. DeSilva *(Lyricist)* 1722
Jockin, Henry *(Composer)* 1722
Jockin, Henry *(Lyricist)* 1722
Joffe, Bob *(Lyricist)* 567
Johanis, Rudolf *(Composer)* 3432
Johann, Cameron *(Cast)* 3171
Johanson, Jane *(Cast)* 1120
Johanson, Robert *(Choreographer)* 2861, 3734
Johanson, Robert *(Composer)* 81
Johanson, Robert *(Director)* 81, 2861, 3734, 3851
Johanson, Robert *(Lyricist)* 81
Johansson, Don *(Choreographer)* 2764
John, Elton *(Composer)* 3739
John, Elton *(Lyricist)* 3739
John, Graham *(Librettist)* 466, 4519
John, Graham *(Lyricist)* 466, 605, 1733, 1780, 1805, 2392, 3721, 4170
John, Mary W. *(Producer)* 1010
John, Michael *(Cast)* 3702
John, Tom H. *(Set Design)* 1298, 1380, 1478, 2754, 3428, 3871, 3956, 4722
John F. Kennedy Center *(Producer)* 699, 808, 958, 1186, 1959, 2260, 2435, 2702, 2775, 3231, 3631, 3643, 4601
Johnakins, Leslie *(Composer)* 432
Johns, Al *(Composer)* 295, 2979, 2990
Johns, Al *(Lyricist)* 2979
Johns, Barter *(Musical Director)* 3948
Johns, Brooke *(Cast)* 827, 2180, 3489, 4817
Johns, Clay *(Cast)* 4332
Johns, Florence *(Cast)* 4422
Johns, Glynis *(Cast)* 172, 2536
Johns, Kenneth *(Librettist)* 1710
Johns, Kurt *(Cast)* 721
Johns, Martin *(Set Design)* 2798
Johnson *(Composer)* 2111
Johnson, A. David *(Cast)* 528, 1155, 3165, 3329, 3997
Johnson, Adel *(Cast)* 3041
Johnson, Alan *(Choreographer)* 146, 278, 1289, 2437, 3936, 4038
Johnson, Alan *(Director)* 146, 3936
Johnson, Alan *(Musical Director)* 1291
Johnson, Albert *(Lighting Designer)* 125, 924, 1539
Johnson, Albert *(Producer)* 117
Johnson, Albert *(Set Design)* 117, 125, 173, 207, 294, 383, 397, 417, 420, 662, 924, 1225, 1494, 1539, 1670, 1680, 2225, 2258, 2413, 2432, 2444, 2475, 3036, 3381, 3699, 3966, 3989, 4367, 4465, 4777, 4824
Johnson, Alice *(Cast)* 2515
Johnson, Allie *(Cast)* 1421
Johnson, Arch *(Cast)* 4625
Johnson, Arnold *(Composer)* 1126, 1858, 2401, 4137
Johnson, Arnold *(Director)* 2401
Johnson, Arnold *(Musical Director)* 4291
Johnson, Arte *(Cast)* 3941
Johnson, Arthur *(Composer)* 4799
Johnson, Arthur *(Vocal Arranger)* 3009
Johnson, Bayn *(Cast)* 941
Johnson, Ben *(Cast)* 1218
Johnson, Benny *(Choreographer)* 4253
Johnson, Bernard *(Choreographer)* 1816
Johnson, Bernard *(Costumes)* 40, 166, 576, 952, 1074, 1198, 1592, 1816, 2513, 2719, 3656, 3932, 4591
Johnson, Bill *(Cast)* 297, 999, 4058, 4498
Johnson, Bill *(Choreographer)* 645
Johnson, Billy *(Cast)* 4451
Johnson, Billy *(Composer)* 217, 2964, 3999, 4451
Johnson, Billy *(Lyricist)* 2029, 2325, 2964
Johnson, Bobby *(Cast)* 3104
Johnson, Buddy *(Composer)* 1495
Johnson, Buddy *(Lyricist)* 1495
Johnson, Buster *(Composer)* 4815
Johnson, Cameron *(Set Design)* 1887
Johnson, Carroll *(Cast)* 3545
Johnson, Charlie *(Composer)* 39
Johnson, Charlie *(Lyricist)* 39
Johnson, Charles
See Charles Johnson's Orchestra.
Johnson, Chic *(Cast)* 1423, 1840, 2400, 3380, 3381, 4086, 4816
Johnson, Chic *(Composer)* 1423
Johnson, Chic *(Director)* 1423
Johnson, Chic *(Librettist)* 1840, 2400, 3381, 4086
Johnson, Chic *(Lyricist)* 1423, 3381, 4816, 4817
Johnson, Chic *(Producer)* 901, 1840, 2400, 3381, 4174
Johnson, Choo Choo *(Cast)* 1140
Johnson, Christine *(Cast)* 660
Johnson, Cora *(Cast)* 4447
Johnson, Danny *(Set Design)* 520
Johnson, Doug *(Director)* 3608
Johnson, Doug *(Set Design)* 3608

Johnson, Eddie *(Cast)* 4331
Johnson, Edward *(Cast)* 4590
Johnson, Eleanor *(Cast)* 2984
Johnson, Ethel *(Cast)* 1351, 3675, 4218
Johnson, Freddie *(Choreographer)* 2645
Johnson, Freddie *(Composer)* 14, 2645
Johnson, Freddie *(Director)* 14
Johnson, Freddie *(Librettist)* 14, 2645
Johnson, Freddie *(Lyricist)* 14, 2645
Johnson, George C. *(Librettist)* 11
Johnson, George C. *(Lyricist)* 11
Johnson, Grace *(Cast)* 1387
Johnson, Grace *(Librettist)* 2709
Johnson, Greer *(Author)* 2994
Johnson, Greer *(Lyricist)* 2994
Johnson, Haven *(Composer)* 3103
Johnson, Haven *(Lyricist)* 3103
Johnson, Howard *(Cast)* 136
Johnson, Howard *(Composer)* 1065
Johnson, Howard *(Lyricist)* 230, 557, 965, 1065, 1334, 1686, 2371, 3020, 3030, 3369, 4290, 4815, 4821
Johnson, Howard *(Musical Director)* 3082
Johnson, Howard E. *(Composer)* 3369
Johnson, Howard E. *(Lyricist)* 4209, 4283
Johnson, J. Rosamond *(Cast)* 633, 2712, 3153, 3541, 3676, 3945
Johnson, J. Rosamond *(Composer)* 9, 352, 822, 982, 1188, 1535, 1537, 1835, 2035, 2044, 2111, 2123, 2493, 2506, 2528, 2805, 2892, 2908, 2964, 2974, 2979, 3073, 3676, 3820, 3945, 4014, 4681
Johnson, J. Rosamond *(Librettist)* 633
Johnson, J. Rosamond *(Lyricist)* 567, 633, 982, 1251, 2044, 2111, 2765, 3073
Johnson, J. Rosamond *(Vocal Arranger)* 443, 447
Johnson, Jack *(Composer)* 3890, 4433
Johnson, Jack *(Librettist)* 4433
Johnson, Jack *(Lyricist)* 3890, 4433
Johnson, James Arthur *(Cast)* 4171
Johnson, James C. *(Composer)* 2, 26, 567, 691, 879, 1028, 3807
Johnson, James C. *(Lyricist)* 26, 39, 567, 691, 3807
Johnson, James P. *(Cast)* 899, 983, 2302
Johnson, James P. *(Composer)* 2, 532, 724, 899, 1105, 1128, 1132, 1135, 1468, 1668, 1772, 1986, 2302, 2337, 2338, 2807, 2845, 2942, 3089, 3315, 3512, 3528, 3657, 3808, 3964, 4198, 4199, 4355
Johnson, James P. *(Lyricist)* 2942
Johnson, James P. *(Musical Director)* 2302, 2845, 3089, 3512
Johnson, James Weldon *(Composer)* 3073, 3820
Johnson, James Weldon *(Lyricist)* 9, 352, 2035, 2123, 2506, 2528, 2908, 2951, 3073, 3820, 3945, 4014, 4390, 4697
Johnson, Jeff *(Cast)* 107, 3873
Johnson, John *(Musical Director)* 2654
Johnson, Julie *(Cast)* 992, 3946
Johnson, Julie Lea *(Cast)* 1804
Johnson, June *(Cast)* 1423
Johnson, Karen *(Cast)* 4783
Johnson, Laurie *(Composer)* 2563
Johnson, Lawrence E. *(Author)* 3860
Johnson, Lee *(Composer)* 141, 2062
Johnson, Louis *(Choreographer)* 496, 991, 1592, 2195, 2908, 3126, 3610, 4447, 4750
Johnson, Louis *(Composer)* 2908
Johnson, Louis *(Dance Arranger)* 2908
Johnson, Louis *(Director)* 2195, 2908
Johnson, Louis *(Set Design)* 2908
Johnson, Louis *(Vocal Arranger)* 2908
Johnson, Mae *(Cast)* 884, 886, 887, 3709
Johnson, Marion Page *(Librettist)* 1447
Johnson, Mary *(Cast)* 1883, 4220
Johnson, Mary *(Librettist)* 1883
Johnson, Mary Lea *(Producer)* 1068, 1649, 1699, 2790, 3792, 4233
Johnson, Myra *(Cast)* 2337
Johnson, Naomi *(Cast)* 203
Johnson, Nora *(Author)* 1846
Johnson, Nunnally *(Author)* 3390
Johnson, Nunnally *(Librettist)* 1846, 3390, 3946
Johnson, Orrin *(Cast)* 2605
Johnson, Oscar
See also Shipstads and Johnson.
Johnson, Oscar *(Cast)* 2088
Johnson, Oscar *(Producer)* 2083, 2086, 2087, 2088, 2089, 2090, 2091, 2092, 2093, 2094
Johnson, Philander *(Lyricist)* 2336
Johnson, Scott *(Lighting Designer)* 963
Johnson, Scott *(Set Design)* 669, 963
Johnson, Stretch *(Cast)* 3104
Johnson, Susan *(Cast)* 596, 649, 1076, 2961, 3234, 4682
Johnson, Sy *(Dance Arranger)* 432
Johnson, Sy *(Orchestrations)* 432, 478
Johnson, Sy *(Vocal Arranger)* 432
Johnson, Taborah *(Cast)* 4129
Johnson, Tina *(Cast)* 474, 1262, 2283
Johnson, Tommi *(Cast)* 4534
Johnson, Van *(Cast)* 820, 3104, 3353, 3487, 4420
Johnson, Virginia *(Costumes)* 4192
Johnson, Walter *(Cast)* 202
Johnson, William *(Cast)* 3505
Johnson, Winnie *(Cast)* 3104
Johnson Jr., Mel *(Cast)* 393, 2616, 3661, 3718
Johnson Orchestra, Charles *(Cast)* 2337
Johnson's Syncopaters, Jimmy *(Cast)* 1288
Johnson-White, Carolyn *(Cast)* 1636
Johnsrud, Harold *(Director)* 125
Johnsrud, Harold *(Librettist)* 3365
Johnston, Alice *(Cast)* 476
Johnston, Arthur *(Composer)* 1058, 1763, 2462, 3248, 4255
Johnston, Audre *(Cast)* 1727
Johnston, Ben *(Composer)* 654
Johnston, Bob *(Composer)* 4325
Johnston, Bob *(Lyricist)* 4325
Johnston, Donald *(Dance Arranger)* 550, 869, 1359, 2231, 2754, 3305
Johnston, Donald *(Incidental Music)* 593, 869
Johnston, Donald *(Musical Director)* 593, 2474
Johnston, Donald *(Orchestrations)* 2754
Johnston, Donald *(Vocal Arranger)* 2231
Johnston, Gail *(Cast)* 2069, 4173
Johnston, Jane A. *(Cast)* 1697

Johnston, Johnny *(Cast)* 4446
Johnston, Justine *(Cast)* 135, 1329, 1842, 2798, 2925
Johnston, Keith *(Cast)* 240
Johnston, Mabel *(Costumes)* 142, 1134, 1643, 1667, 2829, 2950, 3009, 4208
Johnston, Mabel E. *(Costumes)* 931, 2516, 3420, 3617, 4741, 4793
Johnston, Romain *(Costumes)* 2052
Johnston, Romain *(Set Design)* 2052, 2339
Johnston, Ronald *(Choreographer)* 4488
Johnston, Roy *(Cast)* 1085
Johnstone, Alex *(Lyricist)* 3672
Johnstone, Alexander *(Composer)* 375, 1266, 4218
Johnstone, Alexander *(Producer)* 4218
Johnstone, Alick *(Set Design)* 650, 972
Johnstone, Anna Hill *(Costumes)* 2591, 3984, 4682
Johnstone, Arthur *(Orchestrations)* 1827
Johnstone, Arthur *(Vocal Arranger)* 2, 799, 3008
Johnstone, Fannie *(Cast)* 1313
Johnstone, Gordon *(Composer)* 1722
Johnstone, Gordon *(Lyricist)* 1722
Johnstone, Johnny *(Cast)* 851
Johnstone, Justine *(Cast)* 3230, 3333, 4028, 4603, 4809, 4810
Johnstone, Tom *(Cast)* 2194
Johnstone, Tom *(Composer)* 1404, 1533, 2071, 2903, 2927, 3511, 4528, 4651
Johnstone, Tom *(Librettist)* 4651
Johnstone, Tom *(Lyricist)* 1404
Johnstone, Walter *(Set Design)* 3092
Johnstone, Will *(Librettist)* 3672
Johnstone, Will *(Lyricist)* 2903
Johnstone, Will B. *(Librettist)* 2071, 4269, 4528
Johnstone, Will B. *(Lyricist)* 375, 1191, 2071, 3172, 4269, 4528
Jolandrea Music Inc. *(Producer)* 2426
Jolley, Nick *(Cast)* 564
Jolly, Edward *(Composer)* 248
Jolly, Russ *(Cast)* 580
Jolson, Al *(Cast)* 391, 487, 965, 1931, 1963, 2358, 2403, 2710, 3737, 3985, 4553, 4655, 4730
Jolson, Al *(Composer)* 393, 487, 1963, 3020, 3404, 3985, 4730
Jolson, Al *(Lyricist)* 391, 487, 822, 3149, 3985, 4235, 4655, 4730
Jolson, Al *(Producer)* 1931
Jolson, Harry *(Cast)* 3701
Jon Silverman Assoc. Ltd. *(Producer)* 3643
Jon-Lee *(Producer)* 2016
Jonah, Dolly *(Cast)* 3970, 4294, 4318
Jonah, Dolly *(Librettist)* 3970, 4627
Jonas, Joanne *(Cast)* 1595
Jonas, Nita *(Lyricist)* 1727
Jonay, Roberta *(Cast)* 85
Jones *(Composer)* 4589
Jones *(Lyricist)* 4589
Jones *(Musical Director)* 4661
Jones, A.L. *(Producer)* 520, 1690, 2112, 3185, 3648
Jones, Alberta *(Cast)* 4520
Jones, Alexander *(Costumes)* 1871, 4253
Jones, Allan *(Cast)* 110, 324, 948, 2187
Jones, Arthur *(Composer)* 596, 3605
Jones, Arthur *(Lyricist)* 3605
Jones, Arthur *(Musical Director)* 429
Jones, Biff *(Composer)* 4829
Jones, Biff *(Lyricist)* 4829
Jones, Bobby *(Composer)* 3396, 3399
Jones, Bobby *(Lyricist)* 1154, 3396, 3399, 4206
Jones, Broadway *(Cast)* 443, 4198
Jones, Charles *(Choreographer)* 2335
Jones, Charles *(Director)* 4201
Jones, Charles H. *(Director)* 2286, 2315, 2716
Jones, Charlotte *(Cast)* 1676, 2014, 3788
Jones, Cherry *(Cast)* 282
Jones, Chuck *(Director)* 2015
Jones, Chuck *(Producer)* 2015
Jones, Clarence *(Composer)* 4642
Jones, Clark *(Director)* 2072, 3800
Jones, Cliff *(Composer)* 3741
Jones, Cliff *(Librettist)* 3741
Jones, Cliff *(Lyricist)* 3741
Jones, Dave *(Cast)* 3283
Jones, Davey *(Cast)* 3861
Jones, David *(Cast)* 3271
Jones, David *(Director)* 4273
Jones, Dean *(Cast)* 832, 1674, 2142
Jones, Disley *(Set Design)* 2240
Jones, Don *(Librettist)* 4055
Jones, Don *(Musical Director)* 572, 3909, 4286
Jones, Don *(Orchestrations)* 2783, 3909
Jones, Don *(Vocal Arranger)* 3909
Jones, Donald G. *(Dance Arranger)* 2968
Jones, Donald G. *(Musical Director)* 2968
Jones, Donald G. *(Vocal Arranger)* 2968
Jones, Dorothy *(Cast)* 637
Jones, Earle C. *(Lyricist)* 9, 2232, 2879, 2996, 3387, 3693, 4351, 4613, 4808
Jones, Eddie *(Vocal Arranger)* 2259
Jones, Edward *(Composer)* 3827
Jones, Elinor *(Librettist)* 807
Jones, Ellis *(Librettist)* 4545
Jones, Frederick *(Set Design)* 642
Jones, Gail *(Cast)* 4541
Jones, Gattison *(Cast)* 138
Jones, Glen *(Cast)* 3991
Jones, Guy *(Composer)* 1454
Jones, Guy *(Lyricist)* 3213
Jones, Irving *(Composer)* 2714
Jones, Irving *(Lyricist)* 2714
Jones, Isham *(Composer)* 605, 3402, 4154
Jones, Isham *(Lyricist)* 605, 4154
Jones, Jeffrey *(Cast)* 785
Jones, Joe *(Cast)* 2451
Jones, Joelle *(Cast)* 4401
Jones, John Price *(Cast)* 2020, 2382, 3252, 3295, 3508, 3796, 4831, 4842, 4852
Jones, Johnnie *(Set Design)* 2110
Jones, Jonathan Howard *(Cast)* 2055
Jones, Josie *(Cast)* 4672
Jones, Judd *(Cast)* 3204
Jones, Kevin *(Lighting Designer)* 562
Jones, Lauren *(Cast)* 40

Jones, Leilani *(Cast)* 1699
Jones, Leslie Julian *(Cast)* 3877
Jones, Leslie Julian *(Composer)* 4027, 4153
Jones, Leslie Julian *(Lyricist)* 4027, 4153
Jones, Lyman *(Cast)* 3539
Jones, Olive *(Cast)* 689
Jones, Ora *(Cast)* 4708, 4740
Jones, Pattie Darcy *(Cast)* 4031
Jones, Quincy *(Composer)* 3126
Jones, Quincy *(Musical Director)* 1385
Jones, Quincy *(Orchestrations)* 3126
Jones, Reed *(Cast)* 107, 146, 678, 3517
Jones, Richard *(Composer)* 1342
Jones, Richard *(Lyricist)* 1342
Jones, Rick *(Composer)* 626
Jones, Rick *(Lyricist)* 626
Jones, Robert *(Author)* 2623
Jones, Robert *(Costumes)* 558
Jones, Robert Earl *(Cast)* 1636, 3001
Jones, Robert Edmond *(Costumes)* 1624, 2655
Jones, Robert Edmond *(Lighting Designer)* 971, 1817, 2655, 2981
Jones, Robert Edmond *(Set Design)* 971, 1623, 1624, 1817, 2187, 2211, 2655, 2967, 2981, 3639, 3686
Jones, Robert Owen *(Cast)* 643
Jones, Robin *(Librettist)* 4041
Jones, Shirley *(Cast)* 1389, 2681
Jones, Shrimp *(Musical Director)* 2462
Jones, Sidney *(Composer)* 205, 1429, 1470, 1544, 1682, 2317, 2803, 3049, 3828
Jones, Simon *(Cast)* 3598
Jones, Sissieretta *(Cast)* 641, 982, 2127
Jones, Stephen *(Composer)* 642, 2263, 2302, 2757, 3540, 4276, 4766
Jones, Stephen *(Lyricist)* 642
Jones, Stephen *(Orchestrations)* 2, 317, 545, 582, 1154, 1625, 1667, 1827, 1916, 1921, 1948, 2180, 2376, 2378, 3006, 3007, 3008, 3009, 4249, 4267, 4491, 4813, 4814, 4815, 4818, 4819, 4851, 4852
Jones, Steve *(Orchestrations)* 3179
Jones, Steven *(Costumes)* 3272, 3760
Jones, T.C. *(Cast)* 2772, 3108
Jones, T.L. *(Musical Director)* 4668
Jones, Thomas *(Composer)* 1637
Jones, Thomas *(Lyricist)* 1637
Jones, Tom *(Cast)* 1245, 1701, 3542
Jones, Tom *(Director)* 681
Jones, Tom *(Librettist)* 681, 808, 809, 1245, 1363, 1439, 1701, 2050, 2288, 3469
Jones, Tom *(Lyricist)* 491, 681, 807, 808, 809, 1023, 1245, 1362, 1363, 1364, 1439, 1701, 2050, 2244, 2288, 3294, 3469, 3479, 3484, 3542, 3940
Jones, Tom *(Musical Director)* 622, 1207, 1448, 1493, 1836, 3409
Jones, Trevor *(Lyricist)* 3605
Jones, Walker *(Cast)* 3853
Jones, Walter *(Cast)* 75, 694, 1516, 2398, 2725, 2835, 2902, 3154, 3237
Jones, Walton *(Director)* 3175
Jones, Walton *(Librettist)* 3175
Jones III, Frederick *(Costumes)* 2180
Jones III, Frederick *(Set Design)* 2180
Jones Jr., George *(Cast)* 2225
Jongerius, Gerard *(Set Design)* 1865
Jongeyans, George
See also George Gaynes.
Jongeyans, George *(Cast)* 3326
Jons, Joelle *(Cast)* 298
Jonsen, Tommy *(Choreographer)* 3825
Jonson, Ben *(Author)* 1373
Jonson, Ben *(Lyricist)* 4715
Jonson, Bill *(Dance Arranger)* 911
Joplin, Scott *(Composer)* 573, 4196, 4390, 4447, 4697
Joplin, Scott *(Librettist)* 4447
Joplin, Scott *(Lyricist)* 4447
Joplin, Scott *(Orchestrations)* 4447
Jordan, Bert *(Cast)* 4150
Jordan, Chas. *(Cast)* 3480
Jordan, Clarence *(Author)* 900
Jordan, Dale *(Lighting Designer)* 1169
Jordan, Dorothy *(Cast)* 1447
Jordan, G. Adam *(Director)* 157
Jordan, Glenn *(Director)* 4141
Jordan, Hal *(Composer)* 3763
Jordan, Joe *(Composer)* 295, 567, 1019, 1251, 2044, 2721, 3797, 4182, 4804
Jordan, Joe *(Lyricist)* 295, 500, 567
Jordan, Joe *(Musical Director)* 1251, 4182
Jordan, Joe *(Orchestrations)* 444, 567, 4823
Jordan, Joseph *(Orchestrations)* 3860
Jordan, Jules *(Cast)* 2814
Jordan, Leslie *(Cast)* 2046
Jordan, Leslie *(Librettist)* 2046
Jordan, Louis *(Composer)* 1296
Jordan, Louis *(Lyricist)* 1296
Jordan, Marc *(Cast)* 170, 652, 695, 825, 989, 1775, 2523, 3015, 4062, 4114, 4505
Jordan, Richard *(Cast)* 1471
Jordon, Dale F. *(Lighting Designer)* 3463
Jordon, Dale F. *(Set Design)* 3463
Jory, Jon *(Director)* 4450
Jory, Jon *(Librettist)* 4450
Josea, Joe *(Composer)* 4264
Josea, Joe *(Lyricist)* 4264
Joseloff, Stanley *(Lyricist)* 417, 662
Joseph *(Costumes)* 3974
Joseph, Bob *(Composer)* 3557
Joseph, Bob *(Lyricist)* 3557
Joseph, Edmund *(Composer)* 3533
Joseph, Edmund *(Librettist)* 2640, 3533
Joseph, Edmund *(Lyricist)* 3533
Joseph, Irving *(Musical Director)* 2218
Joseph, Jackie *(Cast)* 410, 411, 412, 1257
Joseph, Peter *(Composer)* 298
Joseph, Peter *(Costumes)* 2248
Joseph, Robert L. *(Producer)* 3035
Joslyn, Allyn *(Cast)* 1283
Joslyn, Betsy *(Cast)* 1068, 2542, 4233
Jossey, William *(Cast)* 1185
Jossey, William *(Composer)* 1185
Jossey, William *(Director)* 1185
Jossey, William *(Librettist)* 1185

Jossey, William *(Lyricist)* 1185
Jouannest, Gerard *(Composer)* 2188
Joubert, Joseph *(Orchestrations)* 4460
Jourge *(Costumes)* 1938
Jowitt, John *(Composer)* 4153
Jowitt, John *(Lyricist)* 2168, 4153
Joy *(Costumes)* 945
Joy, Bernie *(Lighting Designer)* 3920
Joy, James Leonard *(Set Design)* 1099, 1496, 1665, 2250, 2542, 4146
Joy, Leonard John *(Set Design)* 2230
Joy, Nicholas *(Cast)* 3014
Joy, Robert *(Cast)* 1787
Joy, Signa *(Cast)* 518
Joyce, Archibald *(Lyricist)* 3562
Joyce, Archibald. *(Composer)* 4804
Joyce, Baby *(Cast)* 2720
Joyce, Carol *(Cast)* 584, 1971, 4651
Joyce, Elaine *(Cast)* 4196
Joyce, Emmett *(Cast)* 715
Joyce, Frances *(Cast)* 1126
Joyce, James *(Author)* 790
Joyce, Joe *(Cast)* 3346
Joyce, Paddy *(Cast)* 1277
Joyce, Peggy Hopkins *(Cast)* 1129
Joyce, Phyllis *(Cast)* 1733
Joyce, Yootha *(Cast)* 2572
Joyner, B.B. *(Cast)* 3904
Jozefowicz, Janusz *(Cast)* 2846
Jozefowicz, Janusz *(Choreographer)* 2846
Jozefowicz, Janusz *(Director)* 2846
Jozefowicz, Janusz *(Librettist)* 2846
Jozwick, Jim *(Set Design)* 2289
Jscherey & Hully *(Cast)* 202
Jubilee Singers, The *(Cast)* 1836, 1980
Judd, Carl *(Cast)* 3537
Judd, Charles *(Costumes)* 703, 3139
Judd, Rebecca *(Cast)* 3862
Jude, Patrick *(Cast)* 699, 1637, 1715, 2759, 3136
Jude, Patrick *(Vocal Arranger)* 2759
Judels, Charles *(Cast)* 1345, 2343, 2595, 2832, 3265, 4694
Judels, Charles *(Director)* 202, 1460, 1461, 2843, 3149
Judels, May *(Director)* 4143
Judge, Arline *(Cast)* 3861
Judge, Count Wellington *(Cast)* 2147
Judge, Ian *(Director)* 3429
Judge, Jack *(Composer)* 736, 965, 3020, 3259
Judge, Jack *(Lyricist)* 3020, 3259
Judge, Jane *(Cast)* 2876
Judge, Peter *(Costumes)* 700
Judson, Alice *(Cast)* 559, 698, 2524
Judson, Lester *(Composer)* 722
Judson, Lester *(Librettist)* 722
Judson, Lester *(Lyricist)* 722, 4512
Judson, Tom *(Composer)* 4775, 4830
Judson, Tom *(Incidental Music)* 4775
Judson, Tom *(Lyricist)* 4775, 4830
Judson Poets' Theatre *(Producer)* 1958, 2110
Judy, James *(Cast)* 171, 674, 1510
Juele, Frank *(Musical Director)* 1604
Juele, Frank *(Orchestrations)* 4543
Juielle, Don *(Musical Director)* 4249
Jujamcyn Productions *(Producer)* 652, 3175
Jujamcyn Theaters *(Producer)* 589, 775, 1649, 2143, 3862, 4031
Juke, Guy *(Additional Dialogue)* 264
Jule, Charles *(Composer)* 3258
Jule, Charles *(Librettist)* 2511
Julia, Raul *(Cast)* 2319, 3171, 3370, 4370, 4485, 4558
Julian, Doris *(Librettist)* 315
Julian, Doris *(Producer)* 315
Julian-Jones, Leslie *(Lyricist)* 3108
Juliana *(Cast)* 3069
Juliano, Frank *(Cast)* 3539
Julien, Jay *(Producer)* 2173
Jullis Productions *(Producer)* 3938
Jun, Rose Marie (Voice) 56
June, Roma *(Cast)* 4053
Jung, Philipp *(Set Design)* 424, 784, 2674, 2677, 4740
Junge, Alexa *(Librettist)* 4136
Junge, Alexa *(Lyricist)* 4136
Junger, Esther *(Cast)* 2475, 3365, 4394
Junger, Esther *(Choreographer)* 4117, 4394, 4567
Junior, John *(Cast)* 1501, 3189
Junker, Hans *(Cast)* 3896
Juracek, Judy *(Set Design)* 99
Jurasik, Peter *(Cast)* 4707
Jurist, Irma *(Composer)* 1892, 3664, 4018
Jurist, Irma *(Dance Arranger)* 1930
Jurist, Irma (Pianist) 2175
Jurman, Karl (Conductor) 2470
Jurman, Karl *(Musical Director)* 373
Jurmann, Walter *(Composer)* 464, 4702
Jurmann, Walter *(Producer)* 2259
Jury, Paul *(Musical Director)* 580
Justice, Jimmy *(Composer)* 3830
Justice, Jimmy *(Lyricist)* 3830
Justice, Jimmy *(Musical Director)* 3830
Justus, William *(Producer)* 4332

K

Kabler, James *(Producer)* 2754
Kaczorowski, Peter *(Lighting Designer)* 573, 3937, 4076
Kadelburg, Gustave *(Author)* 4667
Kadison, Luba *(Librettist)* 1269
Kadison, Luba *(Lyricist)* 1269
Kadison, Phil *(Composer)* 4273
Kadison, Philip *(Composer)* 95
Kadogo, Aku *(Cast)* 1344
Kadokawa, Haruki *(Producer)* 3944
Kaempfert, Bert *(Composer)* 4264
Kaempfert, Bert *(Lyricist)* 4264
Kagan, Richard *(Producer)* 1633, 4019
Kagan, Richard M. *(Producer)* 4020
Kahal, Irving *(Lyricist)* 173, 512, 662, 1126, 1207, 1343, 1813, 2413, 2772, 3356, 3523, 3713, 3789, 4086
Kahan, Judy *(Cast)* 2536, 3565
Kahan, Judy *(Librettist)* 3565
Kahl, Leona *(Librettist)* 1244

Kahn, Grace LeRoy
See also Grace LeRoy.
Kahn, Grace LeRoy *(Composer)* 2158, 2261
Kahn, Gus *(Composer)* 487, 3985, 4799
Kahn, Gus *(Lyricist)* 123, 393, 544, 921, 965, 1026, 1626, 1629, 1689, 1823, 1935, 2158, 2204, 2261, 2274, 2342, 2706, 3018, 3020, 3246, 3249, 3400, 3405, 3430, 3650, 3842, 3953, 3980, 3985, 3989, 3992, 4683, 4799, 4840
Kahn, Herman *(Composer)* 452
Kahn, Herman *(Lyricist)* 452
Kahn, Madeline *(Cast)* 366, 2279, 2913, 3112, 3279, 3602, 4481
Kahn, Marvin *(Composer)* 855, 864, 865
Kahn, Michael *(Director)* 1383, 1864, 4318
Kahn, Mme. *(Costumes)* 1852, 3051
Kahn, Roger Wolfe *(Composer)* 124, 1859, 3172
Kahn, Stanley *(Director)* 2089
Kahn, Stanley D. *(Cast)* 2090
Kahn, Stanley D. *(Choreographer)* 2091
Kahn, Stanley D. *(Director)* 2083
Kahn, Sy *(Composer)* 4055
Kahn, Sy *(Lyricist)* 4055
Kahn, Theodore *(Set Design)* 567, 4198
Kahn Jr., E.J. *(Author)* 1776
Kailimai, Henry *(Composer)* 2891, 4555
Kainer, Ludwig *(Set Design)* 4818, 4819
Kaitz, Emily *(Composer)* 914
Kaitz, Emily *(Lyricist)* 914
Kalbuss, F. *(Author)* 2540
Kalcheim, Lee *(Librettist)* 2043
Kaldenberg, Keith *(Cast)* 2961
Kalegi, Sylvia *(Costumes)* 3527
Kales, Arthur F. *(Librettist)* 3423
Kales, Arthur F. *(Lyricist)* 3423
Kalfin, Robert *(Director)* 599, 1276, 1755, 1897, 2012, 4176, 4460
Kalfin, Robert *(Librettist)* 1897
Kaliban, Bob *(Cast)* 367, 837, 1648
Kalich, Jacob *(Cast)* 2352, 3336
Kalich, Jacob *(Director)* 2352, 3336
Kalich, Jacob *(Librettist)* 2352, 3336
Kalich, Jacob *(Producer)* 423
Kalil-Ogly *(Cast)* 3170
Kalioujny, Alexandre *(Cast)* 1548
Kalish, Larry *(Producer)* 2173
Kaliz, Armand *(Cast)* 2025, 2328, 4080, 4104
Kaliz, Armand *(Composer)* 4080
Kaliz, Armand *(Lyricist)* 4104
Kaliz, Armand *(Producer)* 4104
Kallaghan, Kathie *(Choreographer)* 1346
Kallan, Randi *(Cast)* 4102
Kallen, Lucille *(Author)* 2578
Kallen, Lucille *(Librettist)* 4153
Kallen, Lucille *(Lyricist)* 4377
Kallini, Joseph *(Cast)* 2432
Kallman, Dick *(Cast)* 3895
Kalman, Emmerich *(Author)* 1113, 1455, 1852, 2509, 2907, 3727, 3839, 4760
Kalman, Emmerich *(Composer)* 771, 905, 1113, 1121, 1455, 1603, 1788, 1852, 2509, 2755, 2907, 2909, 3020, 3385, 3727, 3839, 4760
Kalmanov, H. *(Librettist)* 3559
Kalmar, Bert *(Author)* 2467
Kalmar, Bert *(Cast)* 79, 581, 1396, 2485
Kalmar, Bert *(Composer)* 2392, 4814, 4817
Kalmar, Bert *(Librettist)* 1396, 1889, 1935, 1944, 3009, 3659, 3924, 4426
Kalmar, Bert *(Lyricist)* 142, 176, 358, 545, 581, 930, 1297, 1368, 1617, 1686, 1688, 1691, 1819, 1873, 1889, 1944, 2373, 2392, 2638, 2696, 2706, 2857, 3020, 3144, 3185, 3293, 3399, 3583, 3617, 3659, 3695, 3827, 3926, 4033, 4249, 4426, 4436, 4476, 4655, 4742, 4814, 4817
Kalmar, Bert *(Producer)* 4426
Kalmar, Harry *(Lyricist)* 4799
Kalmar Jr., Bert *(Composer)* 943
Kalmar Jr., Bert *(Lyricist)* 943
Kaly Dancers, Chandra *(Cast)* 849
Kaman, Michael *(Composer)* 3690
Kamaroff, George *(Composer)* 2397
Kamarova, Mlle. *(Costumes)* 3410
Kamarova, Natalie *(Choreographer)* 204, 2397, 4670
Kamen, Michael *(Composer)* 3690
Kamen, Michael *(Lyricist)* 3690
Kamen, Michael *(Musical Director)* 3690
Kami, Virginia *(Cast)* 3174
Kaminsky, Helen *(Lyricist)* 2476
Kamlot, Robert *(Producer)* 1194
Kamnetz, Eddie *(Composer)* 3241
Kanapoff, Finshl *(Composer)* 4342
Kanapoff, Finshl *(Lyricist)* 4342
Kandel, Aben *(Librettist)* 4730
Kandel, Paul *(Cast)* 3162, 4676
Kander, John *(Composer)* 16, 131, 610, 723, 826, 1038, 1237, 1310, 1585, 1605, 1764, 1787, 2333, 2558, 2677, 3110, 3718, 3900, 4480, 4580, 4727, 4862
Kander, John *(Dance Arranger)* 1709, 2150
Kander, John *(Incidental Music)* 3097
Kane, Anthony *(Producer)* 4272
Kane, Arleen *(Producer)* 4272
Kane, Donna *(Cast)* 2805
Kane, Edward *(Cast)* 4142
Kane, Francis *(Cast)* 4076
Kane, Gail *(Cast)* 2662
Kane, Helen *(Cast)* 1617, 3149, 3907
Kane, Lyda *(Cast)* 537
Kane, Seth *(Composer)* 4679
Kane, Sonny *(Lyricist)* 2168
Kane, Trish *(Cast)* 4309
Kane, Whitford *(Cast)* 1651
Kane Triplets, The *(Cast)* 1993
Kanfer, Stefan *(Composer)* 2067
Kanfer, Stefan *(Librettist)* 2067
Kanfer, Stefan *(Lyricist)* 2067
Kanin, Fay *(Author)* 1699
Kanin, Fay *(Librettist)* 1456, 1699
Kanin, Garson *(Author)* 820, 1061
Kanin, Garson *(Director)* 820, 1061, 1420, 4152
Kanin, Garson *(Librettist)* 1061
Kanin, Michael *(Author)* 4727
Kanin, Michael *(Librettist)* 1456
Kanin, Myer *(Set Design)* 439
Kann, Manny *(Cast)* 214

Kanoa, Kapule *(Composer)* 422
Kantor, J.B. *(Lyricist)* 4692
Kantor, Karen *(Producer)* 74
Kantrowitz, Jason *(Lighting Designer)* 705, 1146, 2993, 4139
Kaper, Bronislau *(Composer)* 3536
Kaplan, Henry *(Director)* 3338
Kaplan, Herb *(Composer)* 2677
Kaplan, Herb *(Musical Director)* 4405
Kaplan, Herbert *(Musical Director)* 1164, 1797, 2332, 2677, 3195
Kaplan, Herbert *(Orchestrations)* 3195
Kaplan, Herbert *(Vocal Arranger)* 1164, 1797, 2332
Kaplan, Isabel deWitt *(Lyricist)* 2724
Kaplan, Mary Jo *(Cast)* 300
Kaplan, Sol *(Composer)* 298, 400, 1007, 2685, 3947
Kaplan, Sol *(Incidental Music)* 1007
Kaplan, Sol *(Orchestrations)* 298
Kaplan, Steve *(Lyricist)* 3714
Kaplin, Henry *(Director)* 160
Kapon, Michael B. *(Producer)* 3733
Kapp, David *(Producer)* 1076
Kapp, Richard *(Composer)* 4297
Kapton *(Costumes)* 1695
Kaptzan, Kyra *(Composer)* 4171
Kaptzan, Kyra *(Lyricist)* 4171
Karabanova *(Cast)* 710
Karachentsev, Nikolai *(Cast)* 2269
Karam, Eddie *(Musical Director)* 3499
Karaty, Tommy *(Cast)* 766
Karbi, Ras *(Composer)* 3690
Karbi, Ras *(Lyricist)* 3690
Kardana Productions *(Producer)* 4676
Karel, Charles *(Cast)* 1828
Karel, Chuck *(Cast)* 708
Karel, William Chuck *(Cast)* 1108
Karin, Tia *(Cast)* 3366
Karkalits, Patti *(Cast)* 3505
Karl *(Costumes)* 4663
Karlin, Fred *(Orchestrations)* 2958
Karlin, Fred *(Vocal Arranger)* 2958
Karlin, Miriam *(Cast)* 1277
Karliss, Gregory V. *(Cast)* 3651
Karloff, Boris *(Cast)* 2411, 3452
Karloff, Boris *(Narrator)* 2015
Karlton, Sylvia *(Cast)* 85
Karm, Michael *(Cast)* 4481
Karmer, Les *(Lyricist)* 3810
Karmon, Jonathan *(Choreographer)* 1075, 4396
Karmon, Jonathan *(Director)* 1075, 4396
Karlinoff, Maria
See also Maria Karnilova.
Karnilova, Maria *(Cast)* 519, 534, 620, 1265, 1511, 1709, 2288, 2894, 4142, 4862
Karpilovsky, Murray *(Musical Director)* 4141
Karr, Harold *(Composer)* 860, 1760, 3108, 4609
Karr, Patti *(Cast)* 550, 1045, 1637, 2007, 2583, 2659, 2941, 3019, 4395, 4522, 4643
Karr, Patti *(Choreographer)* 4643
Karron, Richard *(Cast)* 4796
Karson, Nat *(Costumes)* 1987, 2458
Karson, Nat *(Director)* 2458, 3091, 4237
Karson, Nat *(Producer)* 283, 1889, 3091, 4237
Karson, Nat *(Set Design)* 622, 1889, 1987, 2458, 3091
Karweis, Oscar *(Cast)* 3767
Kasdin, Karin *(Librettist)* 4107
Kasha, Al *(Composer)* 869, 4402
Kasha, Al *(Director)* 3888
Kasha, Al *(Librettist)* 869, 3888
Kasha, Al *(Lyricist)* 869, 3888
Kasha, Al *(Producer)* 3888
Kasha, Lawrence *(Director)* 269, 2626
Kasha, Lawrence *(Producer)* 167, 2134, 2965, 3366, 3869, 3918, 4727
Kasher, Charles *(Producer)* 937
Kashman, Betty *(Cast)* 2946
Kasia *(Costumes)* 467
Kason, Corinne *(Cast)* 2284, 4514
Kason, James *(Composer)* 4433
Kason, James *(Librettist)* 4433
Kason, James *(Lyricist)* 4433
Kasper, Edwin H. *(Cast)* 458
Kass, Alan *(Cast)* 314
Kass, Jerome *(Author)* 287
Kass, Jerome *(Librettist)* 287
Kassir, John *(Cast)* 4349
Kastner, Leon *(Author)* 4795
Kastner, Peter *(Cast)* 3653
Kasznar, Kurt *(Cast)* 134, 1196, 3899, 4095
Kasznar, Kurt *(Director)* 924
Kasznar, Kurt *(Lyricist)* 924
Kasznar, Kurt *(Producer)* 924
Kates, Robert Alexander *(Set Design)* 4431
Katis, Merry Lynn *(Choreographer)* 2146
Katsaros, Doug *(Composer)* 4, 1038, 1171, 2171, 2283
Katsaros, Doug *(Dance Arranger)* 2283, 3741
Katsaros, Doug *(Orchestrations)* 4, 1171, 2283, 4518, 4619
Katsaros, Doug *(Vocal Arranger)* 1171, 2283
Katscher, Robert *(Author)* 4777
Katscher, Robert *(Composer)* 4730, 4777
Katselas, Milton *(Director)* 594
Katydid Productions *(Producer)* 3067
Katz, Allan *(Librettist)* 4076, 4796
Katz, Bill *(Lyricist)* 4091
Katz, Fred *(Musical Director)* 1742
Katz, Madame *(Costumes)* 2122
Katz, Natasha *(Lighting Designer)* 330, 784, 1159, 1700, 1970, 3198, 3261, 3944, 4146, 4535
Katz, Norman *(Orchestrations)* 932
Katz, Peter S. *(Producer)* 160
Katz, Raymond *(Producer)* 695
Katzan, Olga *(Cast)* 3481
Katzell, William R. *(Producer)* 59, 1278, 2439
Katzman, Drew *(Producer)* 491, 3542
Katzman, Lou *(Orchestrations)* 497
Katzman, Louis *(Orchestrations)* 2, 2818, 3168, 4668, 4821
Kauffman, Marta *(Librettist)* 4, 198, 2197, 3448
Kauffman, Marta *(Lyricist)* 4, 198, 2197, 3448, 4533
Kauffmann, Chris *(Cast)* 3165
Kauffmann, Christian *(Cast)* 2437

Kaufman, Alvin *(Composer)* 364
Kaufman, Andy *(Cast)* 4295
Kaufman, Bill *(Composer)* 2913
Kaufman, Bill *(Librettist)* 1436, 2279
Kaufman, Don *(Producer)* 2925
Kaufman, Eric *(Cast)* 1997, 2356
Kaufman, George S. *(Author)* 80, 121, 317, 536, 1597, 2265, 2729, 2821, 2822, 3787, 3931, 4179
Kaufman, George S. *(Composer)* 2265
Kaufman, George S. *(Director)* 536, 1225, 1357, 1706, 1948, 2068, 2265, 2444, 2729, 2821, 3225, 3390, 3563, 3761
Kaufman, George S. *(Librettist)* 142, 294, 317, 799, 1322, 1357, 1819, 1948, 2068, 2402, 2444, 2653, 3225, 3390, 3783, 3893, 3972, 4178
Kaufman, George S. *(Lyricist)* 317, 1948, 2265, 3783
Kaufman, George S. *(Producer)* 3990
Kaufman, Hank *(Producer)* 369
Kaufman, Harry *(Producer)* 4166
Kaufman, Irving *(Cast)* 4169, 4686
Kaufman, Martin R. *(Producer)* 2294
Kaufman, Mildred *(Lyricist)* 364
Kaufman, S. Jay *(Librettist)* 2301, 4174
Kaufman, S. Jay *(Producer)* 3783
Kaur, Vidya *(Cast)* 3688
Kaurman, Martin R. *(Producer)* 4399
Kautzenbach, Arthur *(Musical Director)* 1162, 2390
Kava, Caroline *(Cast)* 1169, 4370
Kavan, Albia *(Cast)* 4166
Kavanaugh, Ray *(Musical Director)* 70, 787, 1126, 1127, 1134, 1135, 1136, 1137, 2115, 2479, 3002, 3104, 3292, 4265, 4483, 4572
Kavanaugh, Stan *(Cast)* 4825
Kay, Arthur *(Dance Arranger)* 4117
Kay, Arthur *(Musical Director)* 1681, 1711, 1944, 2679, 4075
Kay, Arthur *(Orchestrations)* 223, 1711, 2327, 4075, 4117
Kay, Arthur *(Vocal Arranger)* 1711, 2085, 2327, 4075, 4117
Kay, Beatrice *(Cast)* 2748, 3605, 4465
Kay, Harry B. *(Cast)* 3028
Kay, Hershy *(Orchestrations)* 305, 341, 615, 630, 652, 693, 746, 798, 1094, 1211, 1600, 1745, 2075, 2234, 2268, 2304, 2556, 2617, 2864, 3015, 3020, 3278, 3279, 3288, 3294, 3452, 3696, 3831, 3947, 4004, 4609
Kay, Kathy *(Cast)* 2095
Kay, Megan *(Cast)* 1216
Kay, Susan *(Composer)* 1216
Kay, Susan *(Lyricist)* 1216
Kayden, Mildred *(Composer)* 944, 2146, 3370, 4162
Kayden, Mildred *(Dance Arranger)* 2146
Kayden, Mildred *(Lyricist)* 2146, 4162
Kayden, Mildred *(Vocal Arranger)* 2146
Kaye *(Composer)* 4264
Kaye *(Lyricist)* 4264
Kaye, A.P. *(Cast)* 814
Kaye, Alma *(Cast)* 3989
Kaye, Anne *(Cast)* 1786, 3209
Kaye, Benjamin *(Lyricist)* 4477, 4530
Kaye, Benjamin M. *(Librettist)* 1446, 1447, 1448
Kaye, Benjamin M. *(Lyricist)* 1446
Kaye, Buddy *(Composer)* 1898
Kaye, Buddy *(Lyricist)* 1898
Kaye, Danny *(Cast)* 2386, 2401, 2453, 3454, 3499, 4166, 4481
Kaye, Fred *(Cast)* 675, 1429
Kaye, Gloria *(Cast)* 4678
Kaye, Jim *(Lyricist)* 90
Kaye, Judy *(Cast)* 1597, 2598, 2949, 3231, 3279, 3377, 3464, 4703
Kaye, Kaplan *(Cast)* 455
Kaye, Lila *(Cast)* 1741
Kaye, Nora *(Cast)* 1670, 4142, 4569
Kaye, Paul *(Cast)* 1506
Kaye, Robert *(Cast)* 1310, 2681
Kaye, Stubby *(Cast)* 1699, 1706, 1744, 2484, 3496
Kaye, Tom *(Producer)* 2754
Kaye, Toni *(Choreographer)* 1120
Kaye, William *(Librettist)* 3491
Kaye, William *(Lyricist)* 3491
Kays, Alan *(Cast)* 2839
Kazan, Elia *(Cast)* 2228
Kazan, Elia *(Director)* 2175, 2615, 3301
Kazan, Lainie *(Cast)* 1420, 1745, 2339, 3039
Kazantzakis, Nikos *(Author)* 4862
Kazounoff, Berenece *(Composer)* 2105, 2540, 3501, 3698, 4484
Keagy, Grace *(Cast)* 496, 652, 1634, 1660, 3019, 4727
Keal, Anita *(Cast)* 4102
Kealy, Kenny *(Cast)* 837
Kean, Betty *(Cast)* 145, 859, 1415, 1481
Kean, Jane *(Cast)* 145, 859, 1140, 1415, 1539
Kean, Norman *(Producer)* 482, 550, 602, 1075
Keane, George *(Cast)* 530, 3894
Keane, Robert Emmett *(Cast)* 110, 1911
Kearney, Tyrone *(Cast)* 3283
Kearns, Allen *(Cast)* 376, 815, 1419, 1528, 1827, 1859, 2378, 2516, 2519, 2818, 2884, 4283, 4378, 4392
Kearns, Thomas F. *(Cast)* 2938
Keating, Barry *(Composer)* 4139
Keating, Barry *(Librettist)* 4139
Keating, Barry *(Lyricist)* 4139
Keating, Fred *(Cast)* 3005, 3172, 4792
Keaton, Diane *(Cast)* 1717, 3516
Keats, Mildred *(Cast)* 3508
Keck, John William *(Set Design)* 3126, 4035
Keefe, John *(Composer)* 3998
Keefe, John *(Lyricist)* 3998
Keel, Howard *(Cast)* 101, 3837
Keeler, Kate *(Costumes)* 2667
Keeler, Madam *(Costumes)* 3045, 4429
Keeler, Marion *(Cast)* 4664
Keeler, Mme. *(Costumes)* 2454
Keeler, Ruby *(Cast)* 608, 2638, 3723, 3953, 3968
Keeling, Deborah *(Cast)* 2272
Keen, Stan *(Composer)* 4268
Keen, Stan *(Lyricist)* 4268
Keen, Stan (Pianist) 1023, 1362, 4268
Keen, Stan *(Producer)* 4065
Keen, Stan *(Vocal Arranger)* 1023, 4268

Keenan, Walter *(Choreographer)* 18, 750, 4093, 4679
Keenan, Walter F. *(Choreographer)* 1604, 1885, 4303, 4543
Keene *(Composer)* 4255
Keene, Dick *(Cast)* 3352, 4118
Keene, Elizabeth *(Cast)* 2768
Keene, Lew *(Cast)* 3513
Keene, Margaret *(Cast)* 2768
Keene, Richard *(Cast)* 1831, 3006
Keener, Suzanne *(Cast)* 3431
Keeth, Trevor *(Cast)* 112
Kehr, Don *(Cast)* 119, 2033
Keifert *(Orchestrations)* 4227
Keiffer, Lester *(Composer)* 2986
Keightley, Cyril *(Cast)* 2624
Keil, Mary *(Producer)* 4139
Keim, Adelaide *(Cast)* 4313
Keir, Andrew *(Cast)* 2682
Keitel, Harvey *(Cast)* 2468
Keith *(Composer)* 1246, 4662
Keith *(Lyricist)* 1246, 4662
Keith, A.L. *(Composer)* 3079
Keith, A.L. *(Lyricist)* 3079
Keith, B.F. *(Producer)* 1703
Keith, David *(Cast)* 3671
Keith, Ian *(Cast)* 3974
Keith, Isham *(Cast)* 1286
Keith, Kenneth *(Composer)* 4104
Keith, Kenneth *(Lyricist)* 953
Keith, Laurence *(Cast)* 1891
Keith, Lester *(Composer)* 1433, 2716
Kelety, Julia *(Cast)* 97, 1722, 2056, 4491
Kelk, Jackie *(Cast)* 2797
Kellaher, Ed *(Librettist)* 13
Kellam *(Set Design)* 3562
Kellaway, Cecil *(Cast)* 1698
Kellberg, Marjorie *(Costumes)* 4543
Kellberg, Marjorie *(Set Design)* 4543
Keller, J. *(Composer)* 4264
Keller, J. *(Lyricist)* 4264
Keller, Jeff *(Cast)* 754, 3448
Keller, Sheldon *(Author)* 652
Kellerman, Annette *(Cast)* 149, 2919, 2921, 4553
Kellerman, Annette *(Director)* 149
Kellerman, Sally *(Cast)* 521
Kellerman Girls, The *(Cast)* 149
Kellermann, Susan *(Cast)* 2945
Kellette, John William *(Composer)* 3402
Kellette, John William *(Lyricist)* 3402
Kelley, Barry *(Cast)* 3263
Kelley, Clarence *(Composer)* 890
Kelley, Clarence *(Lyricist)* 890
Kelley, Gene *(Cast)* 4273
Kelley, Janey *(Cast)* 319
Kelley, Louise *(Cast)* 2587, 2814, 3304
Kelley, Peter *(Cast)* 4499
Kellin, Mike *(Cast)* 1955, 2450, 3505, 4609
Kellin, Orange *(Arrangements)* 1425
Kellin, Orange *(Musical Director)* 1425
Kellin, Orange *(Orchestrations)* 3297
Kellogg, Christine *(Cast)* 450
Kellogg, Lynn *(Cast)* 1717
Kellogg, Marjorie *(Costumes)* 1684
Kellogg, Marjorie *(Set Design)* 374, 1684, 3825, 4109
Kellogg, Marjorie Bradley *(Set Design)* 1172
Kellogg, Peter *(Librettist)* 147
Kellogg, Peter *(Lyricist)* 147
Kellogg, Shirley *(Cast)* 3663
Kelly *(Composer)* 436
Kelly *(Lyricist)* 436, 515
Kelly, Al *(Cast)* 3410
Kelly, Alice *(Cast)* 3205
Kelly, Brian *(Cast)* 2360
Kelly, Constance *(Librettist)* 4153
Kelly, David Patrick *(Cast)* 1086, 2440, 3903, 4523, 4744
Kelly, David Paul *(Cast)* 2152
Kelly, Frank *(Cast)* 2515
Kelly, Frank *(Librettist)* 3346
Kelly, Frank *(Lyricist)* 3346
Kelly, Fred *(Cast)* 2275
Kelly, Fred *(Choreographer)* 2275, 4237
Kelly, Frederic N. *(Choreographer)* 3064
Kelly, Gene *(Cast)* 2183, 2432, 3292, 3353
Kelly, Gene *(Choreographer)* 372, 3166, 4498
Kelly, Gene *(Director)* 786, 1315, 2183
Kelly, Gene *(Producer)* 2183
Kelly, George *(Director)* 2
Kelly, George *(Librettist)* 2
Kelly, Georgia *(Cast)* 3820
Kelly, Glen *(Composer)* 2861
Kelly, Glen *(Dance Arranger)* 330, 754, 3708
Kelly, Glen *(Incidental Music)* 754
Kelly, Gregory *(Cast)* 3855
Kelly, Harry *(Cast)* 199, 405, 1003, 1543, 1910, 1912, 2343, 2534, 2856, 2900, 3258, 3319, 4603, 4712, 4803, 4812
Kelly, Horace L. *(Director)* 4149
Kelly, Jean *(Cast)* 2143
Kelly, Joe *(Cast)* 4674
Kelly, Joe *(Composer)* 4674
Kelly, John T. *(Cast)* 421, 677, 687, 1926, 1927, 2041, 4658, 4681
Kelly, John T. *(Composer)* 2116, 4478
Kelly, John T. *(Lyricist)* 4478
Kelly, Kate *(Cast)* 1346
Kelly, Kitty *(Cast)* 2768, 3069
Kelly, Martha *(Costumes)* 1377
Kelly, Moiya *(Cast)* 2608
Kelly, Nell *(Cast)* 4170
Kelly, Orry *(Costumes)* 1491, 1533, 1722, 3170, 3342, 3954, 4733
Kelly, Pat *(Cast)* 1337
Kelly, Patsy *(Cast)* 1126, 1135, 1137, 1322, 1779, 4345, 4730
Kelly, Paul *(Cast)* 3172
Kelly, Paula *(Cast)* 52, 3454
Kelly, Perry J. *(Producer)* 3045
Kelly, Ritamarie *(Cast)* 1785
Kelly, Sean *(Librettist)* 1038, 3077
Kelly, Sean *(Lyricist)* 3077
Kelly, Tom *(Composer)* 687
Kelly, Walter C. *(Cast)* 1667, 3229, 3958, 4657

Kelsey, Carlton *(Composer)* 4010
Kelsey, Carlton *(Musical Director)* 1747, 3342, 4010
Kelsey, Karl F. *(Musical Director)* 2763
Kelso, Louis *(Cast)* 1469, 3994
Kelso, Maym *(Cast)* 1469, 2040
Kelton, Gene *(Cast)* 287
Kelton, Pert *(Cast)* 1110, 1297, 1698, 3016, 3138, 4212
Kelton, Pert *(Composer)* 4212
Kelton, Pert *(Lyricist)* 4212
Kemble, John *(Composer)* 1246, 4662
Kemble, John *(Lyricist)* 1246, 1433, 2716, 2986, 4662
Kemmerling, Michael *(Cast)* 1201
Kemp, Bobby *(Cast)* 982
Kemp, Emme *(Lyricist)* 576
Kemp, Ethel *(Lyricist)* 576
Kemp, Henry *(Cast)* 2976
Kemp, Mae *(Cast)* 3200
Kemper, Charles *(Cast)* 4777
Kemper, Dave *(Lyricist)* 295
Kemper, David *(Lyricist)* 3357, 4687
Kempinski, Thomas *(Cast)* 455
Kempner, Nicholas *(Composer)* 3540, 4170
Kempner, Nicholas *(Musical Director)* 86, 1667, 3184, 4367, 4583
Kempson, Voigt *(Choreographer)* 922
Kempson, Voigt *(Director)* 922
Kenbrovin, Jean *(Composer)* 3402
Kenbrovin, Jean *(Lyricist)* 3402
Kendall, Don *(Composer)* 2281
Kendall, Henry *(Cast)* 703, 704, 3079
Kendall, Kathryn *(Choreographer)* 4799
Kendall, Kuy *(Cast)* 1962
Kendall, Kuy *(Choreographer)* 1378, 1962, 3962
Kendall, Lottie *(Cast)* 4007
Kendall, Pat *(Cast)* 4154
Kendall, Tom *(Cast)* 4007
Kendall, William *(Cast)* 383, 4320
Kendirck, D. Polly *(Costumes)* 2224
Kendis, James *(Composer)* 8, 1518, 1963, 4010
Kendis, James *(Lyricist)* 8, 2263, 4010
Kendrick, Rexford *(Cast)* 2145
Kener, David *(Cast)* 4082
Kenneally, Nina *(Producer)* 209
Kennedy *(Composer)* 2493
Kennedy *(Lyricist)* 2493
Kennedy, Arthur *(Cast)* 933
Kennedy, Bob *(Cast)* 1539, 2275
Kennedy, Cheryl *(Cast)* 2240
Kennedy, Clayton *(Choreographer)* 2286
Kennedy, Francis *(Cast)* 132, 353, 2155, 3679
Kennedy, Frank *(Librettist)* 3203, 4487
Kennedy, Frank *(Lyricist)* 592, 4487
Kennedy, Harold J. *(Director)* 1884
Kennedy, James *(Lyricist)* 3605
Kennedy, Jay *(Orchestrations)* 3126
Kennedy, Jimmy *(Composer)* 4027, 4109
Kennedy, Jimmy *(Lyricist)* 4027
Kennedy, John *(Director)* 137, 204, 2847, 4524, 4828
Kennedy, John *(Producer)* 616, 2928
Kennedy, Madge *(Cast)* 1472, 3540
Kennedy, Matt *(Librettist)* 3137
Kennedy, Mimi *(Cast)* 1985
Kennedy, Sandy *(Cast)* 2312
Kennedy, Tara *(Cast)* 2064
Kennedy, Zona *(Cast)* 239
Kennedy-Fox, Dorothy *(Cast)* 1342, 3103
Kennel, Louis *(Costumes)* 1046
Kennel, Louis *(Lighting Designer)* 1046
Kennel, Louis *(Set Design)* 1046, 1235, 2946
Kennel & Entwhistle *(Set Design)* 2380
Kenneny, A. *(Librettist)* 4106
Kenneny, A. *(Lyricist)* 4106
Kenneny, C.E. *(Composer)* 4106
Kenneny, C.E. *(Director)* 4106
Kenneny, C.E. *(Librettist)* 4106
Kenneny, C.E. *(Lyricist)* 4106
Kenneny, C.E. *(Orchestrations)* 4106
Kenner, Chris *(Composer)* 3739
Kenner, Chris *(Lyricist)* 3739
Kenneth-John Productions *(Producer)* 253, 1038, 2208, 3718
Kenneth-Mark Productions *(Producer)* 3060, 4295
Kennett, Karl *(Lyricist)* 1038
Kenney, Doug *(Lyricist)* 3077
Kenney, Ed *(Cast)* 1315, 4337
Kenney, James C. *(Cast)* 392
Kenney, Kay *(Author)* 1939
Kenney, Kay *(Librettist)* 110, 2947
Kenney, Kay *(Lyricist)* 2947
Kennon, Skip *(Cast)* 1872
Kennon, Skip *(Composer)* 451, 1258, 1861, 1872
Kennon, Skip *(Lyricist)* 451, 1258
Kennon, Skip *(Musical Director)* 451, 3557
Kenny, Charles *(Lyricist)* 364, 3409, 3907, 4264
Kenny, Gerard *(Composer)* 3055
Kenny, Nick *(Lyricist)* 4091, 4264
Kenny, Sean *(Costumes)* 2563, 3271
Kenny, Sean *(Lighting Designer)* 786, 2563, 3731, 4160
Kenny, Sean *(Set Design)* 455, 786, 2682, 3271, 3482, 3731, 4160
Kenny, Walter *(Director)* 2896
Keno, Joe *(Cast)* 1796, 3855
Kent, Arthur *(Composer)* 3261
Kent, Billy *(Cast)* 228, 349
Kent, Carl *(Composer)* 924
Kent, Carl *(Lyricist)* 924
Kent, Carl *(Set Design)* 4394
Kent, Charlotte *(Composer)* 924, 943, 1136, 2105, 2545, 4235
Kent, Charlotte *(Librettist)* 3986
Kent, Charlotte *(Lyricist)* 924, 943, 1136, 2105, 2294, 2545, 4235
Kent, Eleanor *(Cast)* 1707
Kent, Gordon *(Composer)* 3688
Kent, Gordon *(Orchestrations)* 3688
Kent, Gordon *(Vocal Arranger)* 3688
Kent, Guy *(Costumes)* 1204, 2313, 2449, 4582
Kent, Jeff *(Composer)* 2427
Kent, Jeff *(Lyricist)* 2427
Kent, Lennie *(Cast)* 1718
Kent, Lucille *(Cast)* 1703

Kent, Stapleton *(Cast)* 1506
Kent, Walter *(Composer)* 2060, 2447, 3018, 3895, 4027, 4772, 4799
Kent, Walter *(Lyricist)* 2060
Kent, William *(Cast)* 228, 1419, 1528, 2373, 2540, 2972, 3508, 3772, 4056, 4422, 4532
Kenton, Stan *(Arrangements)* 2611
Kenton, Stan *(Composer)* 2611
Kenwright, Bill *(Director)* 460
Kenwright, Bill *(Producer)* 460
Kenyon, Doris *(Cast)* 3590
Kenyon, Laura *(Cast)* 1172
Kenyon, Neal *(Choreographer)* 956, 1380, 4173
Kenyon, Neal *(Director)* 956, 1380, 4029
Keough, William *(Cast)* 1640, 1968
Keough, William C. *(Cast)* 1867
Kerby, Paul *(Lyricist)* 3767
Kercheval, Ken *(Cast)* 369, 1864
Kerker, Gustave *(Author)* 4654
Kerker, Gustave *(Composer)* 8, 113, 357, 405, 457, 588, 982, 1246, 1543, 2116, 2326, 2383, 2398, 2500, 2725, 2952, 4044, 4054, 4298, 4434, 4490, 4666, 4713
Kerker, Gustave *(Musical Director)* 457, 1599, 2116, 2398, 2500, 4434
Kerker, Gustave *(Orchestrations)* 737
Kerko, Mark S. *(Director)* 3004
Kermoyan, Michael *(Cast)* 161, 649, 3831, 4060, 4435
Kern, Jerome *(Cast)* 2812, 3153
Kern, Jerome *(Composer)* 100, 246, 248, 333, 334, 393, 466, 497, 555, 582, 611, 627, 672, 675, 706, 773, 913, 930, 954, 1011, 1043, 1066, 1067, 1123, 1151, 1152, 1188, 1228, 1246, 1298, 1318, 1455, 1464, 1476, 1519, 1523, 1538, 1544, 1559, 1569, 1588, 1613, 1625, 1784, 1796, 1845, 1888, 1922, 1928, 1984, 2204, 2294, 2317, 2334, 2341, 2358, 2372, 2385, 2392, 2424, 2430, 2469, 2498, 2528, 2620, 2638, 2653, 2712, 2761, 2772, 2806, 2812, 2871, 2891, 2900, 2907, 2922, 2952, 2986, 3014, 3018, 3020, 3052, 3146, 3175, 3177, 3193, 3230, 3237, 3245, 3250, 3259, 3308, 3313, 3322, 3398, 3450, 3451, 3529, 3627, 3679, 3710, 3721, 3727, 3735, 3740, 3768, 3779, 3819, 3923, 3949, 3976, 3996, 4001, 4115, 4150, 4212, 4219, 4234, 4327, 4361, 4418, 4419, 4422, 4507, 4551, 4555, 4557, 4590, 4644, 4663, 4712, 4799, 4805, 4810, 4811, 4815, 4860
Kern, Jerome *(Director)* 4361
Kern, Jerome *(Lyricist)* 333, 675, 913, 1066, 1123, 1246, 1464, 1784, 1796, 2498, 2761, 2986, 3230, 3313, 3322, 3529, 3710, 3976, 3996, 4001, 4551, 4555, 4642, 4712, 4726
Kern, Jerome D. *(Composer)* 1538
Kern, Teddy *(Choreographer)* 2776
Kernan *(Composer)* 4093
Kernan *(Lyricist)* 4093
Kernan, David *(Cast)* 3967
Kernan, David *(Director)* 2204
Kernell, William B. *(Composer)* 627, 1175, 1632, 1831
Kerner, Mme. *(Costumes)* 1309, 1580
Kerner, Norberto *(Cast)* 3059
Kerner, R. *(Costumes)* 1308
Kerns, Linda *(Cast)* 4030
Keroul *(Author)* 3237
Kerper, Mitch *(Vocal Arranger)* 1637
Kerr, C. Herbert *(Composer)* 2505
Kerr, C. Herbert *(Musical Director)* 1264
Kerr, C.H. *(Composer)* 331
Kerr, C.H. *(Librettist)* 968
Kerr, C.H. *(Lyricist)* 968
Kerr, Clarence Vincent *(Librettist)* 1866, 1868
Kerr, Darwin *(Cast)* 1520
Kerr, Donald *(Cast)* 568, 1687, 4211, 4602
Kerr, E. Katherine *(Cast)* 785, 4535
Kerr, E. Katherine *(Librettist)* 4535
Kerr, Elizabeth *(Cast)* 837
Kerr, Geoffrey *(Librettist)* 3172
Kerr, Harry D. *(Lyricist)* 1795
Kerr, Herbert *(Musical Director)* 118, 2854
Kerr, Janet *(Choreographer)* 491, 3469, 3542
Kerr, Jean *(Librettist)* 1614, 2227, 2417, 4432
Kerr, Jean *(Lyricist)* 1614, 4432
Kerr, Walter *(Director)* 1614, 3989, 4432
Kerr, Walter *(Librettist)* 901, 1614, 3989, 4432
Kerr, Walter *(Lyricist)* 1614, 4432
Kerrigan, J.M. *(Cast)* 2020
Kerry, Addison *(Director)* 1984
Kert, A. *(Composer)* 4193
Kert, A. *(Lyricist)* 4193
Kert, Larry *(Cast)* 521, 692, 1237, 2227, 2231, 2368, 3018, 3020, 3644, 3722, 4377, 4408, 4625, 4827
Kerwell, Rex *(Composer)* 4795
Kerwin, Susie *(Costumes)* 470
Kerwin, Terry *(Cast)* 4034
Kerz, Leo *(Lighting Designer)* 1918, 2115, 2595
Kerz, Leo *(Set Design)* 1918
Kesler, Lew *(Composer)* 90
Kesler, Lew *(Director)* 90, 3914
Kesner, John *(Composer)* 3889
Kessler, Bob *(Composer)* 1370, 2288, 3484, 4627
Kessler, Jody *(Costumes)* 3925
Kessler, Lew *(Choreographer)* 4058, 4524
Kessler, Lew *(Composer)* 90, 3086, 4677
Kessler, Lew *(Director)* 1711
Kessler, Merle *(Author)* 3817
Kessler, Merle *(Librettist)* 3817
Kessler, Merle *(Lyricist)* 3817
Kessler, Michael *(Cast)* 2735
Kessler, Michael *(Choreographer)* 2735
Kessler, Michael *(Composer)* 2703, 2735
Kessler, Michael *(Director)* 2735
Kessler, Michael *(Lyricist)* 2703, 2735
Kessler, Robert *(Composer)* 1233, 2288, 3215, 3615
Kessler, Zale *(Cast)* 1441
Kessler Jr., William H. *(Producer)* 4137, 4619
Kessner, Rose *(Cast)* 3024
Kessyn, Miriam *(Cast)* 4773
Ketchum, Dave *(Cast)* 410
Kett, J. Ward *(Cast)* 2552
Kett, J. Ward *(Composer)* 2552
Kett, J. Ward *(Librettist)* 2552
Kett, J. Ward *(Lyricist)* 2552
Ketterer, Cynthia *(Costumes)* 2641
Keubler, Charles *(Orchestrations)* 11
Kevin-Robert *(Costumes)* 4309

Key, Francis Scott *(Lyricist)* 117, 1897, 3739
Key, Tom *(Cast)* 900
Key, Tom *(Librettist)* 900
Keyava, Stan *(Composer)* 1884
Keyava, Stan *(Musical Director)* 1884
Keyes, Bert *(Composer)* 593
Keyes, Bert *(Orchestrations)* 593
Keyes, Daniel *(Author)* 699
Keyes, Daniel *(Cast)* 751, 1974, 2578, 3653
Keyes, Evelyn *(Cast)* 2302
Keyes, George *(Cast)* 2413
Keyes, James *(Composer)* 3739, 4264
Keyes, James *(Lyricist)* 3739, 4264
Keys, Nelson *(Lyricist)* 1733
Khalaf, Ramzi *(Cast)* 647, 4107
Khumalo, Leleti *(Cast)* 3836
Khuzwayo, Mhlathi *(Cast)* 3836
Kiam, Omar *(Costumes)* 2981
Kibbee, Roland *(Librettist)* 1959
Kibby, William *(Lighting Designer)* 255
Kibrig, Joan *(Cast)* 4785
Kidd, Johnny *(Composer)* 3695
Kidd, Johnny *(Lyricist)* 3695
Kidd, Kathleen *(Cast)* 1657
Kidd, Michael *(Cast)* 3563, 3647
Kidd, Michael *(Choreographer)* 183, 521, 629, 1029, 1278, 1706, 1860, 1930, 2484, 2615, 3563, 3780, 4013, 4190, 4693, 4737
Kidd, Michael *(Director)* 367, 946, 1029, 1633, 2484, 3780, 4190, 4693
Kidd, Michael *(Producer)* 2484, 4693
Kidder, Edward *(Author)* 3998
Kidder, Edward E. *(Author)* 1148
Kiefert, Carl *(Composer)* 284
Kiefert, Carl *(Orchestrations)* 1962
Kiehl, William *(Cast)* 2992
Kiepura, Jan *(Cast)* 1416, 3536
Kilbride, Percy *(Cast)* 1672
Kilburn, Terry *(Director)* 2057
Kiley, Richard *(Cast)* 753, 1848, 2053, 2327, 2727, 2940, 3187, 3612, 3687
Kilgallen, Dorothy *(Librettist)* 1101
Kilgore, Robert *(Orchestrations)* 2441
Kilgour, Garfield *(Lyricist)* 733
Kilgour, Joseph *(Cast)* 94
Killalea, J. Edward *(Lyricist)* 1803
Killeen, Marilyn *(Cast)* 4276
Killian, Scott *(Composer)* 2441
Killian, Scott *(Lyricist)* 2441
Killian, Scott *(Orchestrations)* 2441
Killian, Victor *(Cast)* 536
Kilpatrick, James *(Cast)* 3317
Kilpatrick, Joan *(Costumes)* 2220
Kilroy & Britton *(Producer)* 917
Kilty, Jack *(Cast)* 2161, 2162, 4143
Kilty, Jerome *(Author)* 1007
Kilty, Jerome *(Director)* 1007
Kim, Randy *(Cast)* 2290
Kim, Willa *(Costumes)* 180, 589, 695, 964, 1112, 1354, 1634, 2260, 2437, 2659, 3309, 3602, 4068, 4091, 4560, 4695
Kim, Willa *(Set Design)* 1122
Kim Loo Sisters, The *(Cast)* 1494
Kimball, Grace *(Cast)* 4723
Kimball, John *(Producer)* 2651
Kimball, Steve *(Producer)* 3817
Kimborough, Emily *(Author)* 3320
Kimbrough, Charles *(Cast)* 83, 832, 1787, 2607, 3299, 4210
Kimbrough, Mary Jane *(Cast)* 83
Kimmel, Alan *(Costumes)* 4678, 4783
Kimmel, Alan *(Set Design)* 2416, 2962, 4678, 4783
Kimmins, Ken *(Cast)* 1346
Kimmins, Kenneth *(Cast)* 1273
Kinch, Myra *(Choreographer)* 2610
Kind, Roslyn *(Cast)* 4347
Kindl, Ruth *(Cast)* 382
Kindley, Jeff *(Author)* 2152
Kindley, Jeffrey *(Librettist)* 2152
King, Alexander *(Librettist)* 2948
King, Allyn *(Cast)* 2950, 4208, 4810, 4811, 4812, 4831, 4834, 4840, 4842
King, Beula *(Author)* 3860
King, Billy *(Cast)* 676, 1838
King, Billy *(Librettist)* 1838
King, Billy *(Producer)* 676, 1838
King, Calvin *(Choreographer)* 1632
King, Carlton *(Cast)* 1220
King, Carole *(Composer)* 3668, 3739, 4193, 4534
King, Carole *(Lyricist)* 3739, 4193, 4534
King, Carrie *(Cast)* 731, 980, 2013
King, Charles *(Cast)* 397, 685, 1484, 1626, 1916, 2174, 2298, 2533, 2869, 3131, 3179, 3396, 3556, 3860, 3975, 4017, 4050, 4603, 4712
King, Charles *(Composer)* 4017
King, Charles *(Lyricist)* 4017
King, Clement *(Additional Lyrics)* 4556
King, Cory *(Cast)* 838
King, Denis *(Composer)* 3598
King, Dennis *(Cast)* 44, 1384, 2061, 3457, 3772, 3913, 3916, 4357, 4539
King, Dennis *(Producer)* 3916
King, Donna *(Cast)* 678
King, Ed *(Composer)* 1159
King, Edith *(Cast)* 1384, 3048, 3837, 4693
King, Elizabeth *(Cast)* 4508
King, Everett *(Producer)* 942
King, Hattie *(Cast)* 2720
King, Jack *(Composer)* 733
King, Jane *(Cast)* 2446
King, John *(Cast)* 801, 803
King, John Michael *(Cast)* 161, 652, 1786, 2563, 3038
King, Larry L. *(Author)* 374
King, Larry L. *(Librettist)* 373, 374
King, Lawrence *(Costumes)* 599
King, Lawrence *(Set Design)* 599
King, Mabel *(Cast)* 1074, 2173, 4722
King, Mary *(Cast)* 2446
King, Mazie *(Cast)* 3348
King, Michael *(Cast)* 2797
King, Michael *(Puppeteer)* 2726
King, Mollie *(Cast)* 465, 1626, 3396

King, Nellie *(Cast)* 1626, 3237
King, Patsy *(Cast)* 1337
King, Pee Wee *(Composer)* 4264
King, Pee Wee *(Lyricist)* 4264
King, Peggy *(Cast)* 1742, 2182
King, Pete *(Musical Director)* 3487
King, Pete *(Vocal Arranger)* 1879
King, Peter *(Lighting Designer)* 4130
King, Robert A. *(Composer)* 638, 3989
King, Robert A. *(Lyricist)* 3989
King, Rose *(Cast)* 2, 1889, 4374
King, Rufus *(Librettist)* 3002
King, Rufus F. *(Cast)* 2287, 3378
King, Sidney *(Composer)* 2455
King, Sidney *(Lyricist)* 2455
King, Stephen *(Author)* 661
King, Stoddard *(Lyricist)* 3259
King, Walter Woolf *(Cast)* 2786
King, Wayne *(Composer)* 200
King, William *(Director)* 985
King, Wilson *(Lighting Designer)* 922
King, Woodie *(Producer)* 4697
King & King *(Cast)* 202
King Jr., Woodie *(Producer)* 1344, 3599
King Sisters, The *(Cast)* 2214
Kingsburry, Lillian *(Cast)* 1283
Kingsbury, George A. *(Producer)* 1274
Kingsford, Walter *(Cast)* 4075
Kingsley, Evelyn *(Cast)* 1269
Kingsley, Gershon *(Dance Arranger)* 1194, 2322, 3615
Kingsley, Gershon *(Musical Director)* 615, 1319, 1993, 2075, 2364, 4566
Kingsley, Gershon *(Orchestrations)* 1194, 1319, 1676, 1974, 1993, 4566
Kingsley, Gershon *(Vocal Arranger)* 615, 1194, 1319, 2075, 3615
Kingsley, Herbert *(Composer)* 3212, 4273
Kingsley, Herbert *(Musical Director)* 4273
Kinkin, Ethel *(Cast)* 524
Kinkman, Tamara *(Set Design)* 1903
Kinney, Ray *(Cast)* 1840
Kinney, Sharon *(Choreographer)* 2132
Kinoy, Ernest *(Librettist)* 269, 1503, 1611, 3497
Kinsely, Dan *(Lighting Designer)* 2354
Kinser-Lau, Patrick *(Cast)* 3340
Kinsey, Bennett *(Cast)* 1002
Kinsey, Tony *(Composer)* 1195
Kinsey, Tony *(Lyricist)* 1195
Kinsley, Dorothy *(Author)* 3888
Kinsley, Herbert *(Composer)* 467
Kinzy, Rebecca *(Cast)* 4112
Kipling, Rudyard *(Author)* 647, 2283, 2970
Kipling, Rudyard *(Lyricist)* 1502, 4506
Kipness, Joseph *(Producer)* 167, 1886, 2053, 2058, 2134, 2318, 2362, 2364, 3299, 3741, 3869, 3947, 4323
Kirby *(Lyricist)* 3941
Kirby, Gerald *(Cast)* 4302
Kirby, Gerald *(Producer)* 4302
Kirby, John Mason *(Producer)* 4062
Kirby, Johnny *(Cast)* 2496
Kirby, Langford *(Cast)* 3092
Kirby, Maurice B. *(Lyricist)* 1455
Kirby, Maurice Brown *(Librettist)* 1455
Kirby, Maurice Brown *(Lyricist)* 1455
Kirchner, Raphael *(Costumes)* 683
Kirk, Andy
See also Andy Kirk and His Clouds of Joy.
Kirk, Andy *(Composer)* 432, 890
Kirk, Andy *(Lyricist)* 890
Kirk, Deanna *(Composer)* 1232
Kirk, Deanna *(Lyricist)* 1232
Kirk, George *(Cast)* 1322, 3170, 3699
Kirk, Jody *(Cast)* 1754
Kirk, Joe *(Cast)* 1938
Kirk, Lisa *(Cast)* 85, 1955, 2331, 2660
Kirk, William *(Lyricist)* 2495
Kirk and His Clouds of Joy, Andy
See also Andy Kirk.
Kirk and His Clouds of Joy, Andy *(Cast)* 890
Kirkbride, Bradford *(Cast)* 4194
Kirke, Hazel *(Cast)* 2145, 2262, 3258, 3729, 3755
Kirkeby, Ed *(Lyricist)* 39
Kirkland *(Composer)* 432
Kirkland *(Lyricist)* 432
Kirkland, Jack *(Producer)* 1352, 4331
Kirkland, Leroy *(Composer)* 3178
Kirkland, Leroy *(Lyricist)* 3178
Kirkpatrick, John *(Director)* 2275
Kirkpatrick, Sam *(Costumes)* 3088
Kirkpatrick, Sam *(Set Design)* 3088, 4701
Kirkpatrick, Sidney *(Cast)* 646, 3904
Kirksbride, Bradford *(Cast)* 3593
Kirkwood, James *(Cast)* 961
Kirkwood, James *(Librettist)* 746, 961
Kirkwood, Kathleen *(Director)* 303
Kirkwood, Kathleen *(Lighting Designer)* 303
Kirkwood, Kathleen *(Producer)* 303
Kirs, William F. *(Composer)* 123
Kirsch, Carolyn *(Cast)* 746
Kirschner, Jan *(Lyricist)* 3076
Kirsh, Bob *(Cast)* 2038
Kirsten, Dorothy *(Cast)* 1670, 1681
Kirtland, Louise *(Cast)* 2479, 2813, 3907, 4299
Kirtley, Leonard *(Cast)* 4509
Kirwin, Terry *(Cast)* 2643
Kisco, Charley *(Composer)* 3933
Kiser, Terry *(Cast)* 2953, 3370, 3927
Kishon, Ephaim *(Director)* 4514
Kishon, Ephaim *(Librettist)* 2421, 4514
Kissen, Murray *(Composer)* 4817
Kissen, Murray *(Lyricist)* 4817
Kitsopoulos, Constantine *(Conductor)* 3628
Kitsopoulos, Constantine *(Musical Director)* 949
Kitt, Eartha *(Cast)* 916, 2994, 3107, 3427, 3934, 4383
Kiviette *(Costumes)* 294, 383, 441, 642, 672, 740, 971, 1011, 1225, 1339, 1387, 1419, 1481, 1528, 1628, 1800, 1856, 1859, 1929, 2187, 2298, 2376, 2382, 2444, 2475, 2939, 2972, 3144, 3172, 3222, 3735, 3946, 3973, 3993, 4118, 4177, 4267, 4322, 4367, 4392, 4426, 4532, 4583, 4778, 4824
Klages, Raymond *(Lyricist)* 567, 771, 1128, 1132, 1134, 1136, 1778, 3821, 3849

Klain, Margery *(Producer)* 992
Klapis, Ralph *(Cast)* 643
Klaris, Harvey J. *(Producer)* 785, 3171, 4286
Klassen, Ben *(Cast)* 4006
Klausen, Ray *(Set Design)* 826
Klausner, Brachah *(Costumes)* 1358
Klausner, Terri *(Cast)* 1589, 1737, 2470, 4091
Klaussner, Josh *(Composer)* 1232
Klaussner, Josh *(Lyricist)* 1232
Klavan, Walter *(Cast)* 3845
Klaw, Joseph
See also Klaw & Erlanger.
Klaw, Joseph *(Producer)* 4053
Klaw, Marc *(Producer)* 527, 571, 2181
Klaw, Marcus
See also Klaw & Erlanger and Klaw & Erlanger Opera Co.
Klaw, Marcus *(Producer)* 1026
Klaw & Erlanger
See also A.L. Erlanger, Erlanger Prods., Klaw & Erlanger Opera Co., Marcus Klaw and Joseph Klaw.
Klaw & Erlanger *(Producer)* 186, 256, 405, 749, 902, 1199, 1228, 1356, 1388, 1403, 1527, 1650, 1731, 2029, 2035, 2119, 2123, 2465, 2481, 2493, 2497, 2534, 2566, 2723, 2830, 2907, 2964, 2974, 3251, 3328, 3362, 3422, 3494, 3652, 3727, 3744, 3745, 3747, 3749, 3751, 3921, 3977, 4014, 4547, 4554, 4559, 4662, 4787
Klaw & Erlanger Opera Co. *(Producer)* 1375
Kleban, Ed *(Composer)* 2677
Kleban, Ed *(Lyricist)* 2677
Kleban, Edward *(Composer)* 4535
Kleban, Edward *(Lyricist)* 746, 4535
Kleiman, Harlan P. *(Producer)* 1786
Klein, A. Edward *(Lighting Designer)* 2393
Klein, A. Edward *(Set Design)* 2393
Klein, A.A. *(Cast)* 1316
Klein, Alan *(Composer)* 874
Klein, Alan *(Lyricist)* 874
Klein, Albert *(Librettist)* 1829
Klein, Alfred *(Cast)* 1165
Klein, Allen Edward *(Lighting Designer)* 2661
Klein, Allen Edward *(Set Design)* 2661
Klein, Amanda *(Costumes)* 10
Klein, Arthur *(Producer)* 4377
Klein, Charles *(Author)* 1434
Klein, Charles *(Librettist)* 698, 913, 1165, 2824, 2982, 3673, 3790
Klein, Charles *(Lyricist)* 698, 1165
Klein, Hermann *(Lyricist)* 2982
Klein, John *(Orchestrations)* 3813
Klein, Joseph *(Musical Director)* 3330
Klein, Joy *(Producer)* 2598
Klein, Lou *(Lyricist)* 1963
Klein, Manuel *(Composer)* 106, 188, 236, 719, 1041, 1535, 1557, 1875, 1882, 1975, 2139, 2174, 2724, 2982, 3093, 3486, 3504, 3642, 4046, 4113, 4425, 4452, 4509, 4513, 4599, 4753
Klein, Manuel *(Librettist)* 236, 3093, 4513
Klein, Manuel *(Lyricist)* 106, 188, 236, 1557, 2139, 2724, 3093, 3504, 3642, 4046, 4113, 4425, 4452, 4509, 4513, 4599, 4753
Klein, Manuel *(Musical Director)* 1031, 1975, 2139, 2982, 4113, 4452, 4509, 4753
Klein, Maurice *(Composer)* 3663
Klein, Maxine *(Director)* 518, 2332
Klein, Maxine *(Librettist)* 518, 2332
Klein, Maxine *(Lyricist)* 2332
Klein, Paul *(Composer)* 1408, 2958, 4566, 4829
Klein, Paul *(Lyricist)* 4566
Klein, Randy *(Composer)* 2177
Klein, Randy *(Dance Arranger)* 2177
Klein, Randy *(Orchestrations)* 2177
Klein, Randy *(Vocal Arranger)* 2177
Klein, Robert *(Cast)* 170, 2954, 3112, 4334
Klein, Robert *(Librettist)* 3112
Klein, Sally *(Cast)* 2822
Kleinbort, Barry *(Additional Lyrics)* 4399
Kleinbort, Barry *(Composer)* 139, 2294, 3587, 4399
Kleinbort, Barry *(Director)* 2294, 4399
Kleinbort, Barry *(Librettist)* 139, 3587
Kleinbort, Barry *(Lyricist)* 139, 2294, 3587, 4399
Kleinbort, Neil *(Lyricist)* 4399
Kleinecke, August *(Musical Director)* 115, 568, 2262, 2405, 2406, 2665, 2858, 2884, 2919, 3137, 4206, 4277
Kleinman, Sy *(Composer)* 673, 2246
Kleinman, Sy *(Lyricist)* 673, 2246
Kleinman, Sy *(Producer)* 673
Kleinschmitt, Carl *(Librettist)* 544
Kleinsinger, George *(Composer)* 50, 1416, 3226, 3934, 4394
Kleinsinger, George *(Orchestrations)* 3934
Klemperer, Werner *(Cast)* 3577
Klenner, John *(Orchestrations)* 266
Klenosky, William *(Composer)* 4536
Klenosky, William *(Librettist)* 4536
Klenosky, William *(Lyricist)* 4536
Klenosky, William *(Producer)* 4536
Kletter, Debra *(Lighting Designer)* 4358
Kletter, Debra J. *(Lighting Designer)* 2477, 2764
Klimczewska, Violetta *(Cast)* 2846
Kline, Kevin *(Cast)* 962, 3279
Kline, Marvin *(Director)* 92
Kline, Norman *(Lyricist)* 3112
Klotz, Florence *(Costumes)* 546, 775, 1068, 1205, 1329, 1699, 1775, 2163, 2208, 2333, 2435, 2536, 3097, 3279, 3340, 3428, 3644, 3792, 3967
Kluger, Bruce *(Librettist)* 2285
Kluger, Bruce *(Lyricist)* 2285
Kluger, Bruce *(Producer)* 2285
Klugman, Jack *(Cast)* 1709
Klugman, Kate *(Cast)* 2784
Knaiz, Judy *(Cast)* 1436
Knapheis, M. *(Lyricist)* 1609
Knapp, Dorothy *(Cast)* 1129, 1132, 1134, 1281, 1387
Knapp, Eleanor *(Cast)* 2727
Knapp, Marjorie *(Cast)* 4131
Knapp, Sarah *(Cast)* 1509, 3181
Knauer, Max *(Musical Director)* 2917
Knee, Allan *(Librettist)* 2420
Kneebone, Tom *(Cast)* 3818
Kneeland, Richard *(Cast)* 1010
Kneitel, Hattie *(Cast)* 4755

Knepler, Paul *(Author)* 1110, 4365, 4486
Knepper, Trent *(Cast)* 2028
Knick Knacks Inc. *(Producer)* 3137
Knickerbocker Productions *(Producer)* 1091
Knight, Bill *(Musical Director)* 1754
Knight, Darwin *(Choreographer)* 1500, 3067, 4408
Knight, Darwin *(Director)* 1770, 3249, 3619
Knight, Darwin *(Librettist)* 3249
Knight, Dorothy *(Cast)* 1502
Knight, Ed *(Cast)* 2548
Knight, Esmond *(Cast)* 4361
Knight, Frederick *(Cast)* 1316
Knight, Fuzzy *(Cast)* 1859, 3086
Knight, Hilda *(Cast)* 1481, 3314
Knight, June *(Cast)* 1577, 1979, 2252, 3335, 4267
Knight, Michael *(Composer)* 1216
Knight, Michael *(Lyricist)* 1216
Knight, Patricia *(Cast)* 3860
Knight, Percival *(Cast)* 126, 178, 1031, 1067, 1502, 1588, 2341, 2761, 3618
Knight, Percival *(Composer)* 377
Knight, Percival *(Director)* 126, 377
Knight, Percival *(Librettist)* 1031, 1502
Knight, Percival *(Lyricist)* 126, 377, 1031, 1502, 1523, 2317
Knight, Peter *(Orchestrations)* 1741
Knight, Raymond *(Cast)* 2739
Knight, Raymond *(Librettist)* 216
Knight, Raymond *(Lyricist)* 2479
Knight, Willa *(Cast)* 92
Knight, William *(Lighting Designer)* 1742
Knight Sisters, The *(Cast)* 1494
Knittel, Wolfgang *(Musical Director)* 2017, 3370, 4379
Knittel, Wolfgang *(Orchestrations)* 2188
Knittel, Wolfgang *(Vocal Arranger)* 2017, 4379
Knoblauh, M.T. *(Director)* 1508
Knoblock *(Author)* 2327
Knoblock, Edward *(Author)* 4100, 4383
Knoblock, Edward *(Librettist)* 1618
Knoblock, Edward *(Lyricist)* 3310
Knopf, Edwin H. *(Lyricist)* 4037
Knotts, Don *(Cast)* 3188
Knowles, Edwin *(Producer)* 4353
Knowles, Mark *(Choreographer)* 2046
Knowles, Michael *(Cast)* 1702
Knowles, Michael D. *(Cast)* 4168
Knowles, R.G. *(Cast)* 3213
Knowles, R.G. *(Composer)* 3229
Knowles, R.G. *(Lyricist)* 3229
Knowlton, Arthur *(Orchestrations)* 2034
Knox, Collie *(Lyricist)* 133, 3307
Knox, Linda *(Lighting Designer)* 2076
Knox, Teddy *(Cast)* 3500
Knox-Johnston, John *(Cast)* 2076
Knudson, Kurt *(Cast)* 2643
Knull, Chuck *(Librettist)* 3539
Knull, Chuck *(Lyricist)* 3539
Knyght, Douglas *(Cast)* 4768
Knyght-Smith, Douglas *(Composer)* 4786
Knyght-Smith, Douglas *(Lyricist)* 4786
Knyght-Smith, Doulgas *(Composer)* 4786
Knyght-Smith, Doulgas *(Lyricist)* 4786
Kobart, Ruth *(Cast)* 1422, 2019, 2750, 3505
Kober, Arthur *(Author)* 4718
Kober, Arthur *(Librettist)* 4152, 4718
Kobin, Bob *(Lyricist)* 4260
Kobler, John *(Author)* 112
Koch, George *(Composer)* 1412
Koch, Howard W. *(Author)* 663
Kochan, Tom *(Composer)* 3606
Kochan, Tom *(Incidental Music)* 3606
Kochno, Boris *(Choreographer)* 791
Kociolek, Ted *(Composer)* 10
Kociolek, Ted *(Librettist)* 10
Kociolek, Ted *(Musical Director)* 2250, 3851
Koeck, Karl *(Set Design)* 152
Koehbi, Kevin *(Cast)* 1159
Koehler, Ted *(Composer)* 1135
Koehler, Ted *(Lyricist)* 39, 389, 432, 478, 570, 876, 877, 878, 879, 880, 882, 885, 888, 1137, 1385, 1813, 1856, 3018, 3172, 3709, 3850, 4197, 4259, 4534, 4778
Koenig *(Composer)* 3981
Koenig, John *(Costumes)* 3353, 4340
Koenig, John *(Set Design)* 4340
Koenig, Tommy *(Cast)* 3076
Koerner, Spider John *(Composer)* 3608
Koerner, Spider John *(Lyricist)* 3608
Koff, Charles *(Orchestrations)* 497
Kogel, George *(Producer)* 4028
Kohan, Alan *(Composer)* 3615
Kohan, Alan *(Lyricist)* 3615
Kohan, Buz *(Lyricist)* 3936
Kohlman, Churchill *(Composer)* 4264
Kohlman, Churchill *(Lyricist)* 4264
Kohlsaat, Caroline *(Composer)* 1609
Kohn, Edwin E. *(Producer)* 2613
Kohner, Joy *(Cast)* 3167
Kolarik, Jack *(Orchestrations)* 255
Kolatch, David *(Cast)* 4707
Kolb, C. William *(Cast)* 2062, 2576, 3349, 3520, 3531
Kolb, C. William *(Director)* 2576
Kolb, C. William *(Producer)* 2062, 2576, 3520, 3531
Kolb, Clarence *(Producer)* 3425
Kolb, Mina *(Cast)* 1974
Kolb, William *(Cast)* 3425
Kolb, William C. *(Producer)* 4626
Kolborne Jr., William S. *(Librettist)* 1797
Kolborne Jr., William S. *(Lyricist)* 1797
Kolezke, Peter *(Lighting Designer)* 2441
Kolinksi, Joseph *(Cast)* 451
Kolinski, Joseph *(Cast)* 754, 1897, 2033, 2703, 3463
Kolitz, Zvi *(Producer)* 2075, 2811
Kollmar, Richard *(Cast)* 1140, 2344, 4420
Kollmar, Richard *(Director)* 1101
Kollmar, Richard *(Lyricist)* 924
Kollmar, Richard *(Producer)* 180, 483, 1101, 1140, 3509, 4702, 4827
Kollo, Walter *(Author)* 2794, 4121, 4352
Kollo, Walter *(Composer)* 710, 1066, 1561, 2282, 3382, 3472, 4121, 4352, 4726
Kolmes, Matthew *(Cast)* 3668
Kolo, Fred *(Lighting Designer)* 1276, 4460

Kolo, Fred *(Set Design)* 1276, 4460
Koloc, Bonnie *(Cast)* 2033
Kolodner, Arnie *(Cast)* 3606
Komack *(Composer)* 2754
Komack *(Lyricist)* 2754
Komack, Jimmie *(Cast)* 3524, 4005
Komack, Jimmy *(Cast)* 957
Komisarjevskaia *(Cast)* 710
Komisarjevsky, Theodore *(Costumes)* 1805
Komisarjevsky, Theodore *(Director)* 1805, 3699
Komisarjevsky, Theodore *(Set Design)* 1805
Komolova, Valentina *(Costumes)* 2269
Kondolf, George *(Producer)* 3255
Konecky, Isobel Robins *(Producer)* 699
Konecky, Jennifer *(Composer)* 4627
Konecky, Jennifer *(Lyricist)* 4627
Konrardy, Nancy *(Costumes)* 3076
Kook, Edward F. *(Producer)* 2618
Kookoolis, Joseph Martinez *(Composer)* 4089
Koontz, Porter *(Cast)* 1004
Kopit, Arthur *(Author)* 1186, 4708
Kopit, Arthur *(Librettist)* 3171, 3465
Kopp, Norma *(Cast)* 2101
Kopp, William G. *(Composer)* 3220
Kopp, William G. *(Lyricist)* 3220
Koppell, Al *(Lyricist)* 1989
Kopyc, Frank W. *(Cast)* 3539
Kopye, Jack *(Cast)* 4703
Korbich, Eddie *(Cast)* 212, 1149, 2230, 2416
Koreto, Paul *(Librettist)* 1436, 2279
Koreto, Paul *(Lyricist)* 2913
Korey, Alexandra *(Cast)* 109, 451, 1258
Korey, Alix *(Cast)* 36, 2185, 3757
Korey, Lois *(Librettist)* 1363
Korey, Lois Balk *(Librettist)* 4627
Korf, Gene R. *(Producer)* 131
Korff, Arnold *(Cast)* 4667
Korie, Michael *(Lyricist)* 451
Korman, Jess J. *(Composer)* 2067
Korman, Jess J. *(Lyricist)* 2067
Kornblum, I.B. *(Composer)* 465, 733, 3057
Kornblum, I.B. *(Lyricist)* 733
Kornfeld, Lawrence *(Director)* 1958, 2110, 2236, 2579, 3418, 3602, 4595
Kornfeld, Robert *(Librettist)* 3697
Kornfeld, Robert *(Lyricist)* 3697
Korngold, Erich Wolfgang *(Composer)* 225, 1817, 3767
Korngold, Erich Wolfgang *(Music Adaptation)* 1681
Korngold, Erich Wolfgang *(Musical Director)* 1817, 3767
Korngold, Erich Wolfgang *(Orchestrations)* 1680
Koroll, Gary *(Composer)* 2321
Koron, Barry *(Musical Director)* 2993
Korthaze, Richard *(Cast)* 723, 964, 3506
Kortlander, Max *(Composer)* 3402, 3535
Kosarin, Michael *(Dance Arranger)* 992, 2643, 2790
Kosarin, Michael *(Musical Director)* 330, 2790, 3862
Kosarin, Michael *(Vocal Arranger)* 2790, 3862
Kosarin, Oscar *(Musical Director)* 634, 1764, 3389, 3900, 4060, 4395
Kosarin, Oscar *(Orchestrations)* 3234, 3389
Kosarin, Oscar *(Vocal Arranger)* 1764, 3900
Kosary, Emma *(Cast)* 184
Koski, Hilary *(Composer)* 146
Koski, Hilary *(Lyricist)* 146
Kosloff, Alexis *(Choreographer)* 758, 1460, 2622, 4212
Kosloff, Theodore *(Choreographer)* 3395, 3399, 3865, 4747
Koslow, Pamela *(Producer)* 2200
Kosta, Tessa *(Cast)* 17, 659, 758, 2412, 2830, 3580, 3593, 3778, 3791, 4077
Kostal, Irwin *(Arrangements)* 1815, 3841
Kostal, Irwin *(Musical Director)* 1742
Kostal, Irwin *(Orchestrations)* 23, 299, 869, 1280, 1369, 1422, 1511, 1742, 2355, 2850, 3702, 3815, 3888, 4312, 4625, 4798
Kostal, Irwin *(Vocal Arranger)* 4798
Kostalik-Boussom, Linda *(Choreographer)* 4358
Kostelanetz, Andre *(Vocal Arranger)* 1322
Koster & Bial *(Producer)* 1466
Kostka, Karol *(Cast)* 2977
Kotai, Ralph *(Set Design)* 661
Kotchetovsky *(Choreographer)* 3407
Kotchoff, Ted *(Director)* 2682
Kotite, Tony *(Director)* 1149
Kotlowitz, Dan *(Lighting Designer)* 2372
Kotto, Yaphet *(Cast)* 4863
Kourkoulos, Nikos *(Cast)* 2106
Kovachy, Ed *(Cast)* 3714
Kowal, James *(Dance Arranger)* 975
Kowal, James *(Musical Director)* 975
Kowal, James *(Vocal Arranger)* 975
Kowal, Marsha *(Costumes)* 2470
Kowalski, George W. *(Cast)* 1632
Kozak, Greg *(Cast)* 2521
Kraatz, Kurt *(Author)* 2914, 3529, 4532
Kraber, Gerrit Tony *(Cast)* 2228
Kraber, Tony *(Cast)* 1546
Krachmalnick, Samuel *(Musical Director)* 630, 649, 1766
Krachmalnick, Samuel *(Vocal Arranger)* 1766
Kraft, Beatrice *(Cast)* 2837
Kraft, Helen *(Author)* 3304
Kraft, Hy *(Author)* 615, 1979
Kraft, Hy *(Librettist)* 615, 4152, 4423
Kraft, Hy *(Lyricist)* 4152
Kraft, Randy *(Pianist)* 3914
Kragen, Ken *(Producer)* 2470
Krakeur, Richard W. *(Director)* 709
Krakeur, Richard W. *(Producer)* 2757
Krakeur II, Jacques *(Composer)* 1952
Krakeur II, Jacques *(Lyricist)* 1952
Krakowski, Jane *(Cast)* 1649, 4138
Krall, Heidi *(Cast)* 961
Kramer, Alex *(Composer)* 1296
Kramer, Alex *(Lyricist)* 1296
Kramer, Allan *(Producer)* 407
Kramer, Arthur *(Lyricist)* 3501
Kramer, Dave *(Director)* 4782
Kramer, Dave *(Producer)* 4782
Kramer, Joel *(Cast)* 669
Kramer, Larry *(Author)* 3198
Kramer, Leo *(Librettist)* 3810
Kramer, Les *(Lyricist)* 3810

Kramer, Terry Allen *(Producer)* 1635, 2058, 2798, 3142, 4197
Krancer, Elliot *(Lighting Designer)* 4153
Krane, David *(Composer)* 1120
Krane, David *(Dance Arranger)* 652, 808, 1120, 1970, 2333, 4533
Krane, David *(Incidental Music)* 4560
Krane, David *(Musical Director)* 2633, 4533
Krane, David *(Orchestrations)* 131, 1665
Krane, David *(Pianist)* 4533
Krane, David *(Vocal Arranger)* 1120, 4533
Kranth, William *(Musical Director)* 1337
Krany, Ben *(Director)* 4273
Krasny, Diana *(Producer)* 162
Krass, Michael *(Costumes)* 2038, 2646
Kratzinger, Ernest *(Musical Director)* 2085, 2086, 2087, 2088
Kraus, Philip *(Cast)* 3927
Kraus, Samuel *(Composer)* 4396
Krause, Albert *(Musical Director)* 256, 1613, 4236
Krause, Jay *(Set Design)* 2246
Krause, Marc *(Cast)* 1609
Kraushaar, Arnold A. *(Set Design)* 2377
Krauss, Marvin A. *(Producer)* 2360, 2820, 3644
Krausz, Diane F. *(Producer)* 1832
Krausz, Michael *(Composer)* 1044
Krausz, Rob *(Librettist)* 1832
Krauth, William A. *(Musical Director)* 4375
Kravat, Jerry *(Producer)* 2790
Krawford, Gary *(Cast)* 1079, 1158
Krebs, Cela *(Cast)* 3314
Krebs, Eric *(Director)* 4288
Krebs, Eric *(Producer)* 549, 1279, 1719, 2320, 2654, 3722, 4288
Kreck, Karl *(Composer)* 2
Kreck, Karl *(Lyricist)* 2
Kreffert, Charles *(Orchestrations)* 728
Kreiner, Marty *(Composer)* 4433
Kreiner, Marty *(Librettist)* 4433
Kreiner, Marty *(Lyricist)* 4433
Kreis, Robert *(Composer)* 328
Kreis, Robert *(Lyricist)* 328
Kreisel, Betty *(Costumes)* 2742
Kreisel, Joseph *(Lighting Designer)* 4696
Kreisler, Fritz *(Composer)* 168, 3698, 3703
Kreisler, Fritz *(Lyricist)* 3698
Kreizberg, Yasha *(Vocal Arranger)* 4463
Kren, Jean *(Author)* 1925
Krenn, L. *(Author)* 4181
Krenz, Frank *(Costumes)* 4027, 4076
Kreppel, Paul *(Cast)* 1832, 4736
Kresley, Ed *(Composer)* 2279, 2913
Kress, Helmy *(Orchestrations)* 207
Kressin, Lianne *(Cast)* 3557
Kressyn, Miriam *(Cast)* 343, 400, 1269
Kretzmer, Herbert *(Lyricist)* 2442
Kreuder, Peter *(Composer)* 3441
Krick, Cynthia *(Costumes)* 1781
Krieger, Henry *(Composer)* 1103, 1253, 3034, 4286, 4403
Krieger, Henry *(Lyricist)* 1253
Krimsky, Jerrold *(English Lyrics)* 4368
Krimsky, Jerrold *(Producer)* 3003, 3082, 4368
Krimsky, John *(Producer)* 920, 1286, 1546, 3003, 3082
Krimsley, John *(Producer)* 1195
Kristen, Ilene *(Cast)* 1510, 2790
Kristen, Karen *(Choreographer)* 3527
Kristofer, Lou *(Choreographer)* 3439
Kristofferson, Kris *(Cast)* 2241
Kristofferson, Kris *(Composer)* 914
Kristofferson, Kris *(Lyricist)* 914
Kristy, Carol *(Cast)* 2650, 2962
Krivoshei, David *(Composer)* 4396
Krivoshei, David *(Musical Director)* 1075, 4396
Kroeger, Berry *(Cast)* 3913
Kroeger, Perry Arthur *(Composer)* 4171
Kroeger, Perry Arthur *(Librettist)* 3873
Kroeger, Perry Arthur *(Lyricist)* 3873, 4171
Kroeger, Perry Arthur *(Set Design)* 4107
Krofft, Marty *(Director)* 2443
Krofft, Marty *(Producer)* 2443
Krofft, Sid *(Cast)* 3380
Krofft, Sid *(Director)* 2443
Krofft, Sid *(Producer)* 2443
Krogstad, Bob *(Orchestrations)* 2689
Kroll, Bernice *(Composer)* 3664
Kroll, Louis *(Musical Director)* 2419, 2619, 3580, 4352
Kroll, Louis *(Orchestrations)* 3580
Kroll, Mark *(Producer)* 4828, 4829
Kroll, William *(Composer)* 2193, 3847
Kroll, William *(Musical Director)* 2193
Krone, Gerard *(Producer)* 3491
Kronenberger, Louis J. *(Author)* 2674
Krones, Fred R. *(Producer)* 478
Krones, Michael *(Lighting Designer)* 626
Krones, Michael *(Set Design)* 626
Kronyack, Nick *(Lighting Designer)* 965, 3397
Kroopf, Milton *(Librettist)* 1321
Kroschell, Joan *(Cast)* 1761
Krueger, Martin *(Lighting Designer)* 45
Kruger, George *(Musical Director)* 293
Kruger, Jerrie *(Cast)* 1938
Krumgold, Sigmund *(Composer)* 978
Krumgold, Sigmund *(Lyricist)* 2193
Krummer, Roy *(Composer)* 1342
Krupa, Gene *(Cast)* 1528
Krupa, Gene *(Composer)* 3444
Krupska, Dania *(Cast)* 629
Krupska, Dania *(Choreographer)* 649, 1745, 1848, 2012, 2961, 3702, 3798, 3895, 3941, 4319
Krupska, Dania *(Director)* 4319
Krusader, Goldie *(Cast)* 1703
Kruschen, Jack *(Cast)* 2048
Kruse, Werner *(Composer)* 3441
Krushin, Jeff *(Composer)* 1159
Kubala, Michael *(Cast)* 146, 921, 2205, 2754
Kuchiki, Sashi *(Cast)* 2080
Kuczewski, Ed *(Cast)* 1450, 2776
Kuczewski, Ed *(Librettist)* 1450, 2776
Kughn, Richard *(Producer)* 2142
Kuhlman, Ron *(Cast)* 746
Kuhn, Judy *(Cast)* 721, 2442, 2766, 3070, 3644

Kuhn, Katherine *(Costumes)* 204, 1948, 2023, 2024, 2099, 2103
Kuhn, Walt *(Choreographer)* 2827
Kuhner, John *(Cast)* 4595, 4789
Kuller, Doris *(Producer)* 3370
Kuller, Sid *(Director)* 2259
Kuller, Sid *(Librettist)* 2259, 2809, 3255
Kuller, Sid *(Lyricist)* 59, 2259, 3255, 4091, 4798
Kulok, Peter T. *(Producer)* 949
Kulp, Nancy *(Cast)* 4230
Kulukundis, Eddie *(Producer)* 682
Kummer, Clare *(Author)* 1623, 1850, 2967
Kummer, Clare *(Composer)* 152, 737, 744, 1537, 1555, 1623, 1850, 1963, 2347, 2498, 2967, 3177, 3191, 3753, 3882
Kummer, Clare *(Director)* 2967
Kummer, Clare *(Librettist)* 152, 2666, 3295, 3308, 4365
Kummer, Clare *(Lyricist)* 152, 737, 744, 1537, 1555, 1623, 1850, 1963, 2347, 2498, 2666, 2967, 3177, 3191, 3295, 3308, 3753, 3882, 4365
Kummer, Frederic Arnold *(Author)* 2255
Kummer, Frederic Arnold *(Librettist)* 2684, 3043
Kummer, Frederic Arnold *(Lyricist)* 2684, 3043
Kummer, Marjorie *(Cast)* 2967
Kuney, Scott *(Orchestrations)* 534
Kunneke, Edward *(Author)* 659
Kunneke, Edward *(Composer)* 659, 2622, 2789
Kuntz, John *(Lyricist)* 2375
Kuntz, John B. *(Librettist)* 4659
Kuntz, John B. *(Lyricist)* 4659
Kupferberg, Tuli *(Composer)* 3309
Kupferberg, Tuli *(Lyricist)* 3309
Kupferman, Meyer *(Composer)* 2236
Kupferman, Meyer *(Orchestrations)* 4863
Kupperman, Alvin *(Cast)* 2874
Kuramoto, Dan *(Dance Arranger)* 4861
Kuramoto, Dan *(Orchestrations)* 4861
Kuramoto, Dan *(Vocal Arranger)* 4861
Kurdt, Raymond T. *(Set Design)* 2026, 4408
Kurlan, David *(Cast)* 3151
Kurland, Jeffrey *(Costumes)* 3364
Kurnitz, Harry *(Librettist)* 1564
Kurnitz, Julie *(Cast)* 1229, 1426, 1635, 2110, 2220, 2243, 2478, 2579, 2874, 3201, 3418
Kurowski, Ron *(Cast)* 3601
Kurth, Juliette *(Cast)* 2704
Kurtz, Manny *(Lyricist)* 4091
Kurtz, Swoosie *(Cast)* 1914, 3852
Kurz, Fredrich *(Producer)* 661
Kurz, Leo *(Set Design)* 3524
Kushner, Gordon *(Musical Director)* 3818
Kushner, Gordon *(Orchestrations)* 3818
Kushner, James *(Cast)* 2746
Kusmiak, Eugene *(Musical Director)* 2655
Kussack, Manny *(Cast)* 214
Kussel, Maurice L. *(Choreographer)* 622
Kussell, Daniel *(Director)* 1516, 4276
Kussell, Daniel *(Librettist)* 931, 1516, 3489, 4276
Kussell, Daniel *(Producer)* 1516
Kutrzeba, Joseph S. *(Producer)* 2472
Kyme *(Cast)* 1970
Kyrieleison, Jack *(Cast)* 4703
Kyte, Mary *(Choreographer)* 109, 602, 1591, 4020, 4390
Kyte, Mary *(Director)* 109, 4412

L

L.A. Civic Light Opera *(Producer)* 223, 1119, 1681, 2679
La Chanze *(Cast)* 3285
La Forge, Eleanor *(Cast)* 1924
La Fosse, Robert *(Cast)* 2205
La Harte, Rose *(Cast)* 188, 3093, 4046, 4794
La Mama *(Producer)* 654
La Marchina, Robert *(Musical Director)* 1119
La Moss, Edward *(Set Design)* 4738, 4754
La Motta, Johnny *(Cast)* 1590
La Penner, James *(Producer)* 4249
La Petite Marguerite
See also Mlle. Marguerite.
La Petite Marguerite *(Cast)* 2857
La Redd, Cora *(Cast)* 691, 878, 896, 2845, 3709
La Reviere, Lucien *(Lyricist)* 364
La Rosa, Julius *(Cast)* 197
La Rue, Jack *(Cast)* 1036
La Salle Theatre Co. *(Producer)* 3786
La Shelle, Kirke *(Librettist)* 104, 3585, 4414
La Shelle, Kirke *(Lyricist)* 3585
La Shelle, Kirke *(Producer)* 2101, 2906, 4724
La Torjada *(Cast)* 2374
La Varre, Madelon *(Cast)* 684, 2856
LaBenz IV, Joe *(Cast)* 3668
LaBolt, Terry *(Librettist)* 4731
LaBourdette, Katie *(Cast)* 2436, 2969
LaChiusa, Michael John *(Composer)* 756, 1291, 1822, 3456
LaChiusa, Michael John *(Librettist)* 1291, 1822
LaChiusa, Michael John *(Lyricist)* 756, 1291, 1822, 3456
LaFaille, Michel *(Director)* 1865
LaFerla, Sandro *(Set Design)* 1897
LaGranna, Louis *(Cast)* 1836
LaManna, Jeanine *(Cast)* 4325
LaMar, Albert *(Cast)* 4242
LaMarr, Moses *(Cast)* 1385
LaMoss, Edward *(Set Design)* 3437
LaMott, Nancy *(Cast)* 2171
LaPenna, James *(Producer)* 4668
LaPrade, Malcolm I. *(Librettist)* 4696
LaPrade, Malcolm I. *(Lyricist)* 4696
LaRocco, Rob *(Composer)* 2171
LaRocco, Rob *(Musical Director)* 2171
LaRue, Grace *(Cast)* 375, 470, 1009, 1693, 1919, 2668, 2929, 3007, 4434, 4801, 4802
LaRue, Grace *(Lyricist)* 1009
LaSalle, Eriq *(Cast)* 2239
LaTour, George *(Producer)* 3232
LaVallee, Bill *(Cast)* 4635

LaVine, W. Robert *(Costumes)* 2681
LaZarre, Jerry *(Cast)* 3505
Labiche, Eugene *(Author)* 693, 2178, 4319
Labor Stage *(Producer)* 3315
Labor Stage, Inc. *(Producer)* 3501
Lacey, Florence *(Cast)* 1171, 1660
Lacey, Franklin *(Author)* 3016
Lackaye, Wilton *(Author)* 3248
Lackaye, Wilton *(Cast)* 425
Lackaye, Wilton *(Lyricist)* 4478
Lackey, Herndon *(Cast)* 1350, 2333
Lacy, Harry *(Cast)* 762
Lacy, Jerry *(Cast)* 3516
Lacy, Margo *(Cast)* 2055
Lacy, Tom *(Cast)* 3939
Laczko, Brian *(Set Design)* 4055
Ladd, Hank *(Cast)* 95
Ladd, Hank *(Librettist)* 137
Ladd, Johnny *(Cast)* 1644
Laddie, Ltd. *(Costumes)* 2392
Ladies Garment Workers Union *(Producer)* 3315
Ladysmith Black Mambazo *(Cast)* 4074
Ladysmith Black Mambazo *(Composer)* 4074
Ladysmith Black Mambazo *(Lyricist)* 4074
Laemmle, Carla *(Cast)* 3174
Lafevre, Jean *(Cast)* 2364
Lagerwall, Berit *(Cast)* 1775
Lagomarsino, Ron *(Director)* 3039
Lahr, Bert *(Cast)* 1109, 1323, 1373, 1395, 1481, 1493, 1567, 1779, 1929, 1979, 2475, 3893, 3955, 4152, 4496
Lahr, John *(Librettist)* 1038
Laibson, Michael David *(Cast)* 2069
Laidlaw, Betty Morse *(Composer)* 3150
Laidlaw, Betty Morse *(Lyricist)* 3150
Laine, Cleo *(Cast)* 1857, 3070
Laird, Marvin *(Composer)* 1741, 1997, 3811
Laird, Marvin *(Dance Arranger)* 521, 547, 1146, 1497, 1764, 3231, 3299, 3637, 4013
Laird, Marvin *(Lyricist)* 1741
Laird, Marvin *(Musical Director)* 547, 3231, 3811
Laird, Marvin *(Vocal Arranger)* 547, 3231
Laird, Roso *(Cast)* 4092
Lait, Jack *(Author)* 89, 3032
Lait, Jack *(Librettist)* 3032, 3796, 4104, 4570
Lait, Jack *(Lyricist)* 4104
Lake, Harriette *(Cast)* 111
Lake, M.L. *(Musical Director)* 2795
Lake, M.L. *(Orchestrations)* 3723
Lake, Mike *(Orchestrations)* 2829
Lakier, Gail *(Lyricist)* 2147
Lalor, Edward *(Cast)* 3495
Lalor, Frank *(Cast)* 228, 256, 292, 632, 1188, 1629, 1911, 2145, 2637, 2986, 3256, 3362, 3466, 3494, 3560, 3574, 3951, 4158, 4226, 4227
Lamare, Marguerite *(Cast)* 2387
Lamas, Fernando *(Cast)* 1760
Lamb *(Lyricist)* 811
Lamb, Arthur *(Lyricist)* 4390
Lamb, Arthur J. *(Librettist)* 1295
Lamb, Arthur J. *(Lyricist)* 103, 248, 1295, 2214, 2286, 2415, 4094, 4757, 4762
Lamb, Don *(Lighting Designer)* 272, 1049
Lamb, Gil *(Cast)* 1931, 3900, 4015
Lamb, Gilbert *(Cast)* 4550
Lamb, Joseph F. *(Composer)* 4390
Lamb, Myrna *(Librettist)* 169, 2918
Lamb, Myrna *(Lyricist)* 169, 2918
Lamb, Ruth *(Costumes)* 2853
Lamb, Wendy *(Librettist)* 2250
Lamb, Wendy *(Lyricist)* 2250
Lamb's Theater Company *(Producer)* 1509, 2224, 2229, 4030
Lambelet, Napoleon *(Composer)* 1470
Lambelet, Napoleon *(Lyricist)* 1470
Lambert, Eddie *(Cast)* 1947, 3173, 3174, 3385
Lambert, Eddie *(Composer)* 787
Lambert, Eddie *(Lyricist)* 787, 3173
Lambert, Eddie *(Producer)* 1947
Lambert, Edward J. *(Cast)* 3822, 4021
Lambert, Edward J. *(Composer)* 1945, 4021
Lambert, Edward J. *(Librettist)* 966, 4021
Lambert, Edward J. *(Lyricist)* 966, 1945, 4021
Lambert, Ernest *(Cast)* 48, 1537, 1707, 1783, 2300, 2665, 3322, 3681, 4033, 4473
Lambert, Happy *(Cast)* 802
Lambert, Happy Jack *(Cast)* 1753
Lambert, Hugh *(Choreographer)* 2019, 3273
Lambert, John *(Cast)* 4150
Lambert, Juliet *(Cast)* 2805, 3411
Lambert, Mark *(Cast)* 2536
Lambert, Maude *(Cast)* 246, 2481, 2576, 4646, 4662
Lambert, Richard *(Cast)* 1226
Lambert, Robert *(Cast)* 4515
Lambert, Sammy *(Producer)* 67, 1930, 3895
Lamberti, Professor *(Cast)* 4131
Lamberts, Heath *(Cast)* 330
Lambrinos, Ted *(Cast)* 1081
Lambriuos, Vassili *(Director)* 1878
Lammar, Lew *(Cast)* 3979
Lammers, Paul *(Director)* 2554, 2560, 3940
Lamont, Frederick *(Cast)* 1862
Lamont, Jennie *(Cast)* 2662
Lamont, Jenny *(Cast)* 2154
Lamont, Louis *(Lighting Designer)* 3387
Lamont, Michael *(Cast)* 1060
Lamont, Robin *(Cast)* 1595
Lamonthe, Wano *(Cast)* 1806
Lamos, Mark *(Cast)* 946
Lamos, Mark *(Director)* 2766
Lampe, J. Bodewalt *(Orchestrations)* 1962, 3403
Lampe, J. Dell *(Musical Director)* 2300
Lampe, J. Dell *(Orchestrations)* 2706, 3677
Lampell, Millard *(Lyricist)* 4018
Lampert, Diane *(Lyricist)* 2319
Lampert, Rachel *(Choreographer)* 2877
Lamphier & Buhler *(Set Design)* 604
Lampl, Carl *(Composer)* 1898
Lampl, Carl *(Lyricist)* 1898
Lamprey, Peggy Hagen *(Cast)* 3653

Lan-Fang, Mei *(Costumes)* 2396
Lancaster, Lucie *(Cast)* 269, 1564, 3900
Lanchester, Elsa *(Cast)* 1815, 4467
Land, Ken *(Cast)* 3908, 4515
Landau, Irving *(Orchestrations)* 3813
Landau, Jack *(Director)* 98, 2859, 4715
Landau, Lucy *(Cast)* 1194
Landau, Natasha *(Costumes)* 1609
Landay, David S. *(Librettist)* 3888
Landay, David S. *(Producer)* 3888, 4727
Lander, Jeff *(Cast)* 3682
Lander, Judy *(Cast)* 369
Landers, Matt *(Cast)* 4744
Landers, Matt *(Lyricist)* 4744
Landers, Minnie *(Cast)* 2156
Landesman, Fran *(Lyricist)* 2928, 3094
Landesman, Heidi *(Producer)* 394, 2143, 3862
Landesman, Heidi *(Set Design)* 119, 394, 2429, 2787, 3682, 3862, 4031, 4535
Landesman, Jay *(Author)* 3094
Landesman, Jay *(Librettist)* 2928, 3094
Landesman, Rocco *(Producer)* 394, 2143
Landfield, Timothy *(Cast)* 1161
Landis, Carole *(Cast)* 2397
Landis, Erol K.C. *(Cast)* 114
Landis, Jesse Royce *(Cast)* 129
Landis, Jessie Royce *(Cast)* 2821
Landis, Jessie Royce *(Director)* 2629
Landis, Monty *(Cast)* 3612
Landis, Sam *(Producer)* 2320
Landolff of Paris *(Costumes)* 1743
Landon *(Costumes)* 1869
Landon *(Set Design)* 1869
Landon, Margaret *(Author)* 2312
Landow, Irving *(Vocal Arranger)* 3536
Landron, Jack *(Cast)* 2043
Landrum, Kenny *(Musical Director)* 2759
Landry, Paul *(Lighting Designer)* 2483
Landwehr, Hugh *(Set Design)* 4294
Landwehr, Michael *(Librettist)* 456
Lane, Abbe *(Cast)* 928, 3234
Lane, Burton *(Composer)* 125, 203, 652, 1136, 1278, 1300, 1931, 2234, 2267, 2400, 3175, 3274, 3444, 3993, 4335, 4367, 4399
Lane, Burton *(Lyricist)* 2400
Lane, Charles *(Cast)* 2779
Lane, Clara *(Cast)* 175
Lane, Clare *(Cast)* 4500
Lane, Diane *(Cast)* 3806
Lane, Hall *(Director)* 4487
Lane, John *(Producer)* 2275
Lane, Lupino *(Cast)* 25, 1805, 3521, 4818
Lane, Marjorie *(Cast)* 2533
Lane, Nancy *(Cast)* 746
Lane, Nathan *(Cast)* 2598, 2820, 4701
Lane, Ralph *(Orchestrations)* 2397
Lane, Richard *(Cast)* 4545
Lane, Rosemary *(Cast)* 372
Lane, Stewart F. *(Producer)* 690, 1149, 1633, 2360, 4295, 4695, 4727
Lane, Ziggy *(Cast)* 4141
Lang, Andrew *(Author)* 1871
Lang, Barbara *(Cast)* 162, 1068, 2536, 3733, 3763, 4038
Lang, Clifford *(Composer)* 2476
Lang, Clifford *(Lyricist)* 2476
Lang, Eric *(Cast)* 2728
Lang, Gertrude *(Cast)* 1722, 3012
Lang, Harold *(Cast)* 1018, 2048, 2331, 2582, 2705, 2985, 3913, 4828
Lang, Henry *(Cast)* 395
Lang, Howard *(Cast)* 1144, 2194
Lang, Jeanie *(Cast)* 288
Lang, Lise *(Cast)* 2754
Lang, Pearl *(Cast)* 660, 4432
Lang, Peter *(Cast)* 947, 1720, 3570
Lang, Philip J. *(Orchestrations)* 101, 150, 153, 167, 181, 183, 190, 302, 304, 367, 534, 616, 623, 629, 656, 699, 751, 861, 862, 946, 1012, 1029, 1242, 1359, 1478, 1614, 1660, 1828, 1886, 1990, 2014, 2050, 2053, 2064, 2190, 2201, 2295, 2357, 2447, 2484, 2590, 2626, 2660, 2681, 2689, 2705, 2713, 2737, 2750, 2983, 3020, 3038, 3113, 3126, 3234, 3299, 3427, 3428, 3509, 3526, 3543, 3687, 3731, 3763, 3837, 3913, 3956, 4035, 4190, 4196, 4270, 4395, 4435, 4496, 4652, 4682
Lang, Philip J. *(Vocal Arranger)* 616, 3476
Lang, Stephen *(Cast)* 33
Lang, Tony *(Librettist)* 871, 2416, 4279
Lang, Tony *(Lyricist)* 871, 2416
Lang, Walter *(Cast)* 4428
Langdon, Dorothy *(Cast)* 3251
Langdon, Gwynn *(Librettist)* 3605
Langdon, Harry *(Cast)* 2214
Langdon, J. Jewett *(Cast)* 945
Lange, Arthur *(Composer)* 1334, 3396
Lange, Arthur *(Musical Director)* 1965
Lange, Arthur *(Orchestrations)* 1134, 1250, 1819, 1965, 2527, 3712, 4637
Lange, Johnny *(Composer)* 1296
Lange, Johnny *(Lyricist)* 1296
Lange, Juliette *(Cast)* 2559
Langenheim, Hay *(Cast)* 4622
Langford, Edward *(Cast)* 986
Langford, Frances *(Cast)* 1856, 3153
Langford, Gordon *(Orchestrations)* 4160
Langley, Gary *(Costumes)* 4168
Langley, Gary *(Lighting Designer)* 4168
Langley, Gary *(Set Design)* 4168
Langlois, Sylvain *(Cast)* 3883
Langner, Christine *(Cast)* 678
Langner, Lawrence
See also Alan Child.
Langner, Lawrence *(Author)* 183, 4283
Langner, Ruth *(Lyricist)* 2202
Langstaff, A.M. *(Musical Director)* 3422
Langworthy, David *(Producer)* 4193
Langworthy, Norma *(Producer)* 4193
Lankston, John *(Cast)* 1420
Lannin, Paul *(Composer)* 2, 568, 1345, 2387, 4491
Lannin, Paul *(Lyricist)* 2
Lannin, Paul *(Musical Director)* 1667, 1859, 1916, 2376

Lannin, Paul *(Orchestrations)* 1916, 3157, 3650, 4023, 4491, 4821
Lanning, Don *(Cast)* 4673
Lanning, Jerry *(Cast)* 147, 302, 369, 1040, 2713, 3368, 3902
Lannon, David *(Lyricist)* 4039
Lanouette *(Costumes)* 762
Lansbury, Angela *(Cast)* 162, 1012, 2713, 3564, 4233
Lansbury, Edgar *(Producer)* 547, 825, 1184, 1595, 2583, 2687, 3159, 3602
Lansing, Charlotte *(Cast)* 1145
Lantern Productions *(Producer)* 3476
Lanti, Al *(Cast)* 4693
Lantz, Robert *(Producer)* 2295, 3094
Lantzy, Tom *(Cast)* 4172
Lanyer, Charles *(Cast)* 54
Lanzaroni, Bhen *(Musical Director)* 2018
Lanzaroni, Bhen *(Orchestrations)* 2018, 4459, 4558
Lapine, James *(Director)* 1234, 2143, 2746, 3411, 4210
Lapine, James *(Librettist)* 1234, 2143, 3411, 4210
Larabee, Louise *(Cast)* 4028
Laraia, Frank *(Producer)* 1785
Lardner, Ring *(Author)* 2265
Lardner, Ring *(Composer)* 4811
Lardner, Ring *(Librettist)* 1357, 2265, 3172, 4816
Lardner, Ring *(Lyricist)* 2265, 4023, 4555, 4811
Lardner Jr., Ring *(Author)* 4727
Lardner Jr., Ring *(Librettist)* 1373
Larimer, Bob *(Composer)* 593
Larimer, Bob *(Librettist)* 593
Larimer, Bob *(Lyricist)* 593
Larimer, Robert *(Composer)* 2322
Larimer, Robert *(Lyricist)* 2322
Larkey, Joan *(Lighting Designer)* 2731, 2941
Larkey, Joan *(Set Design)* 2731, 3824
Larkin, Eddie *(Choreographer)* 4316
Larkin, Peter *(Set Design)* 259, 393, 546, 547, 964, 1077, 1290, 1614, 1698, 1955, 3108, 3188, 3210, 3453, 3718, 3913, 4474, 4577, 4609, 4693
Larkins, Ellis *(Cast)* 3551
Larned, Mel *(Cast)* 3941
Larner, Elizabeth *(Cast)* 2798
Larrimore, Francine *(Cast)* 4063
Larrimore, Martha *(Cast)* 1600
Larry, Sheldon *(Director)* 1082
Larsen, Carl *(Librettist)* 3527
Larsen, Liz *(Cast)* 1732, 3708
Larsen, William *(Cast)* 1012, 1245, 3491
Larson, Bev *(Cast)* 2049
Larson, Dennis *(Cast)* 499
Larson, G. *(Composer)* 4193
Larson, G. *(Lyricist)* 4193
Larson, Liz *(Cast)* 4139
Larson, Peter *(Cast)* 3555
Larson, Peter *(Composer)* 572
Larson, Peter *(Dance Arranger)* 1059, 3060
Larson, Peter *(Lyricist)* 572
Larson, Peter *(Orchestrations)* 3555, 4062
Larson, Rick *(Cast)* 669
Lascelles, Kendrew *(Cast)* 4579
Lascelles, Kendrew *(Choreographer)* 4579
Lascelles, Kendrew *(Composer)* 3690
Lascelles, Kendrew *(Librettist)* 3690
Lascelles, Kendrew *(Lyricist)* 3690
Lasco, Morry *(Composer)* 1296
Lasco, Morry *(Lyricist)* 1296
Lascoe, Henry *(Cast)* 656, 2975, 3761, 3972, 4734
Lasha, Joseph *(Lyricist)* 3357
Lasher, Albert C. *(Producer)* 1081
Laska, Edward *(Composer)* 224, 246, 515, 1088, 1123
Laska, Edward *(Lyricist)* 224, 246, 1088, 1123, 2372, 3710
Lasker, Harvey *(Director)* 3264
Lasker, Harvey *(Librettist)* 3264
Lasker, Harvey *(Lyricist)* 3264
Lasker, Harvey *(Producer)* 3264
Laskey, Charles *(Cast)* 2061, 2597
Lasko, Edward *(Composer)* 4408
Lasko, Edward *(Librettist)* 4408
Lasko, Edward *(Lyricist)* 4408
Lasky, Jesse *(Lyricist)* 2826
Lasky, Jesse *(Producer)* 1, 326, 1124, 1327, 1835, 2126, 4440
Lasky, Jesse L. *(Producer)* 617, 4045
Lass, Jeff *(Dance Arranger)* 4488
Lass, Paul *(Composer)* 4488
Lassar, Al *(Musical Director)* 977
Lasser, Brian *(Composer)* 583, 2783, 3181
Lasser, Brian *(Director)* 2783
Lasser, Brian *(Lyricist)* 2783
Lasser, Louise *(Cast)* 1846
Lassie Company *(Producer)* 2412
Laszlo, Miklos Nikolaus *(Author)* 3918
Lata, John *(Cast)* 4438
Latell, Blanche *(Cast)* 3254
Latessa, Dick *(Cast)* 109, 1038, 1104, 1329, 3469, 3491, 3644, 4695
Latessa, Richard *(Cast)* 2887
Latham, Bradley *(Cast)* 2689
Latham, Cynthia *(Cast)* 3687
Latham, Fred G. *(Director)* 168, 252, 582, 627, 632, 659, 1033, 1151, 1162, 1183, 1230, 1285, 1555, 1723, 1851, 2622, 2670, 2915, 3084, 3146, 3295, 3304, 3567, 3590, 3675, 3685, 3923, 4001, 4010, 4250, 4258, 4497, 4716, 4760
Latham, Stacy *(Cast)* 2689
Lathan, Bobbi Jo *(Cast)* 4796
Lathram, Elizabeth *(Cast)* 729
Lathrop, Alton *(Cast)* 1671
Lathrop, Helen *(Cast)* 4662
Latimer, William *(Cast)* 643
Latouche, John *(Adaptation)* 3441
Latouche, John *(Author)* 3003
Latouche, John *(Cast)* 3441
Latouche, John *(Composer)* 924, 4484
Latouche, John *(Librettist)* 341, 1600, 4542
Latouche, John *(Lyricist)* 34, 283, 297, 315, 341, 599, 612, 630, 924, 1600, 1754, 1873, 2077, 2294, 2379, 2554, 2948, 3003, 3212, 3441, 3501, 3536, 3551, 3703, 3986, 4280, 4484, 4542, 4799
Latta, Richard *(Lighting Designer)* 3178

Lattimer, John *(Musical Director)* 4415
Lattimer, John *(Vocal Arranger)* 3493
Lauber, Liza *(Cast)* 119
Lauchaume, Aime *(Composer)* 934, 2465, 3566
Lauchaume, Aime *(Musical Director)* 2465
Lauder, Harry *(Cast)* 1829
Lauder, Willie *(Cast)* 1829
Lauderdale, Jim *(Cast)* 900
Laufer, Murray *(Set Design)* 148, 3818
Laughlin, Alvin *(Director)* 1967
Laughlin, Anna *(Cast)* 350, 1558, 1912, 2710, 3129, 4425, 4723
Laughlin, Jane *(Cast)* 190
Laughlin, Sharon *(Cast)* 2918
Laun, Louis *(Librettist)* 4018
Laurell, Kay *(Cast)* 4808, 4809, 4812
Lauren, Lilyan *(Cast)* 3130
Laurence, James Howard *(Cast)* 4707
Laurence, Jeanne *(Costumes)* 3622
Laurence, Larry
See also Enzo Stuarti.
Laurence, Larry *(Cast)* 189
Laurence, Paula *(Cast)* 1112, 1744, 2255, 2464, 3301, 3986, 4058
Laurence, Vincent *(Author)* 2121
Laurens, Marie *(Cast)* 2842
Laurents, Arthur *(Author)* 1060, 1184, 2144
Laurents, Arthur *(Cast)* 2479
Laurents, Arthur *(Director)* 162, 424, 1184, 2048, 2144, 2360, 2677, 3142
Laurents, Arthur *(Librettist)* 162, 1060, 1709, 1729, 2677, 3142, 4625
Laurents, Arthur *(Lyricist)* 2677
Laurie, Joe *(Cast)* 3333
Laurie Jr., Joe *(Cast)* 3511
Laurier, Jay *(Cast)* 3467
Laurillard, Edward *(Producer)* 4327
Lautner, Joe *(Cast)* 2339
Lauze, Gene *(Costumes)* 4462
Lavalle, Pat *(Cast)* 1104
Lavella, Gertrude *(Cast)* 539
Lavendero, Leo S. *(Director)* 4041
Laver, James *(Librettist)* 4174
Laverdet *(Set Design)* 700, 703, 2570, 3827, 4341
Laverty, Johnny *(Cast)* 817
Laverty, W.A. *(Cast)* 727
Lavie, Aric *(Cast)* 4396
Lavin, Julian C. *(Lighting Designer)* 1640
Lavin, Linda *(Cast)* 1237, 1370, 1438, 1993, 2163, 2663, 4627
Lavine, Audrey *(Cast)* 451, 1813
Lavine, W. Robert *(Costumes)* 2217
Lavino, Edwin M. *(Librettist)* 525
Law, Alex *(Orchestrations)* 2092, 2093
Law, Evelyn *(Cast)* 376, 2594, 4491, 4816, 4818
Law, H. Robert *(Set Design)* 60, 472, 712, 968, 1631, 1735, 1829, 1868, 1920, 2148, 2174, 2276, 2298, 2351, 2363, 2587, 2696, 2869, 2893, 2931, 3538, 3618, 3737, 4012, 4491, 4655, 4818, 4819
Law, Jenny Lou *(Cast)* 382, 1363, 2168, 2439
Law, Mildred *(Cast)* 4420
Lawford, Betty *(Cast)* 4586
Lawford, Ernest *(Cast)* 2624, 3450
Lawford, Peter *(Cast)* 3800
Lawler, Anderson *(Producer)* 1679
Lawless, Sue *(Cast)* 3939
Lawless, Sue *(Director)* 484, 708, 944, 2114, 3548, 3722
Lawless, Tommy *(Set Design)* 2089
Lawley, Lynda Lee *(Cast)* 4615
Lawlor, C.B. *(Composer)* 3968
Lawlor, Frank *(Cast)* 102, 1274
Lawlor, James Reed *(Composer)* 3664, 4416
Lawlor, James Reed *(Dance Arranger)* 3664, 4416
Lawlor, James Reed *(Lyricist)* 4416
Lawlor, James Reed *(Musical Director)* 3067, 3664, 4416
Lawlor, James Reed *(Orchestrations)* 3067
Lawlor, James Reed *(Vocal Arranger)* 4416
Lawlor, Mary *(Cast)* 931, 1628, 1827, 3184, 3622, 3723, 4778
Lawlor Jr., Andrew *(Cast)* 1013
Lawlor Jr., Andrew J. *(Cast)* 4360
Lawn, Sand *(Dance Arranger)* 2651
Lawn, Sand *(Musical Director)* 1258, 3249
Lawn, Sand *(Vocal Arranger)* 3249
Lawner, Mordecai *(Cast)* 3644
Lawnhurst, Vee *(Composer)* 4204, 4825
Lawrence, Alfred S. *(Composer)* 2334
Lawrence, Alfred S. *(Lyricist)* 2334
Lawrence, Bert *(Librettist)* 2809
Lawrence, Beth *(Composer)* 2754
Lawrence, Beth *(Lyricist)* 2754
Lawrence, Bob *(Cast)* 417, 2258, 4214
Lawrence, Carol *(Cast)* 3107, 3837, 3913, 4190, 4625, 4828
Lawrence, Charles *(Cast)* 488, 3069, 3172
Lawrence, Clara *(Cast)* 1565
Lawrence, David *(Cast)* 3365
Lawrence, David *(Orchestrations)* 1832
Lawrence, Donald *(Composer)* 3987
Lawrence, Donald *(Lyricist)* 3987
Lawrence, Donald *(Musical Director)* 3987
Lawrence, Eddie *(Cast)* 363, 3931
Lawrence, Eddie *(Librettist)* 2304
Lawrence, Eddie *(Lyricist)* 2304
Lawrence, Elliot *(Composer)* 1205, 2368
Lawrence, Elliot *(Musical Director)* 170, 607, 1497, 1601, 1611, 1860, 2019, 4196
Lawrence, Elliot *(Orchestrations)* 3018, 3564
Lawrence, Elliot *(Vocal Arranger)* 170, 1497, 1611, 1860, 4196
Lawrence, Elliott *(Composer)* 2452
Lawrence, Francis *(Composer)* 1231
Lawrence, Gertrude *(Cast)* 133, 702, 1238, 2140, 2312, 2386, 2570, 3214, 3243, 3597, 3678, 3906, 4443, 4610
Lawrence, Jack *(Composer)* 924, 2053
Lawrence, Jack *(Lyricist)* 911, 924, 2053, 3816, 4828
Lawrence, Jane *(Cast)* 4652
Lawrence, Jerome *(Author)* 2713
Lawrence, Jerome *(Librettist)* 1012, 2582, 2713, 3913
Lawrence, Jerome *(Lyricist)* 1048, 3913

Lawrence, Lawrence Shubert *(Producer)* 2947
Lawrence, Lionel *(Director)* 2717
Lawrence, Madge *(Cast)* 3384
Lawrence, Mal Z. *(Cast)* 3456
Lawrence, Mark *(Composer)* 4018
Lawrence, Mark *(Lyricist)* 4018, 4153
Lawrence, Pauline *(Costumes)* 2475
Lawrence, Peter *(Producer)* 3452, 3934
Lawrence, Reginald *(Librettist)* 3326
Lawrence, Stephanie *(Cast)* 460
Lawrence, Stephen *(Composer)* 4, 1389, 2279, 2913, 3186
Lawrence, Stephen *(Dance Arranger)* 4536
Lawrence, Stephen *(Musical Director)* 1389, 3209, 4536
Lawrence, Stephen *(Orchestrations)* 1676
Lawrence, Stephen *(Vocal Arranger)* 3209, 4536
Lawrence, Steve *(Cast)* 1611, 4633
Lawrence, Vincent *(Author)* 3335
Lawrence, Vincent *(Librettist)* 1747, 4443
Lawrence, Vincent *(Lyricist)* 4443
Lawrence, Walter *(Cast)* 132, 1613, 2454
Lawrence, Walter *(Director)* 132
Lawrence, Walter *(Producer)* 2454
Lawrence, Walter A. *(Lyricist)* 4201
Lawrence, Walter N. *(Producer)* 2779
Lawrie, Ted *(Cast)* 283
Laws, Maury *(Composer)* 928, 2941, 3833, 4471
Lawson, Claude *(Cast)* 488
Lawson, Daniel *(Costumes)* 2250
Lawson, Denis *(Cast)* 2654
Lawson, Kate Drain *(Costumes)* 1366, 1448, 2348, 2809, 4486
Lawson, Kate Drain *(Set Design)* 1448
Lawson, Lee *(Cast)* 32, 1990
Lawson, Mark *(Set Design)* 378, 712, 1631
Lawson, Roger *(Cast)* 251, 1053
Lawson, Stephen R. *(Cast)* 1406
Lawton, Thais *(Cast)* 670
Lax, Roger *(Composer)* 4618
Lax, Roger *(Librettist)* 4618
Lax, Roger *(Lyricist)* 4618
Lay, Dilys *(Cast)* 507
Laye, Evalyn *(Cast)* 3467
Laye, Evelyn *(Cast)* 383, 429, 466
Laye, Gilbert *(Director)* 3049
Layton, Joe *(Choreographer)* 305, 658, 1012, 1094, 1478, 1616, 1698, 3187, 3275, 3288, 3485, 3515, 3739, 3815, 3931, 4095, 4312
Layton, Joe *(Director)* 134, 305, 534, 658, 1012, 1094, 1478, 1564, 1616, 1776, 2553, 3187, 3275, 3485, 3515, 3739, 3931, 4338, 4481
Layton, Joe *(Producer)* 658
Layton, Turner *(Cast)* 4182
Layton, Turner *(Composer)* 432, 563, 1334, 2796, 3297, 3808, 3840, 3985, 4054, 4104, 4182, 4360, 4811, 4815, 4816
Layton, Turner *(Lyricist)* 432, 4037
Lazar, Alice *(Cast)* 1964
Lazarus, Emma *(Lyricist)* 2894
Lazarus, Frank *(Cast)* 1000
Lazarus, Frank *(Composer)* 1000
Lazarus, Milton *(Librettist)* 1681, 2838, 3946, 4075
Lazarus, Paul *(Director)* 3448
Lazarus, Sidney *(Librettist)* 1058
Lazzo, Josephine *(Cast)* 1995
Le Baron, William *(Author)* 2059
Le Baron, William *(Librettist)* 168, 1151, 1723, 1835, 1851, 2614, 2950, 4440, 4760
Le Baron, William *(Lyricist)* 1, 168, 326, 1151, 1723, 1851, 2059, 2614, 3672, 4393
Le Breton, Flora *(Cast)* 672, 3556, 3995
Le Comte & Fisher *(Producer)* 2492
Le Fevre, Guy *(Cast)* 30
Le Fre, Albert *(Cast)* 3213
Le Galliene, Eva *(Director)* 55
Le Galliene, Eva *(Librettist)* 55
Le Gallienne, Eva *(Cast)* 1175, 2487, 3787
Le Gallienne, Richard *(Lyricist)* 1163, 3642
Le Grant, Dave *(Cast)* 1884
Le Hay, John *(Cast)* 3777
Le Mack, Tom *(Composer)* 1627
Le Roy, Gloria *(Cast)* 204, 348, 3956
Le Roy, Ken *(Cast)* 98, 2048, 4625
Le Roy, Maude *(Cast)* 2895
Le Seyeux, Jean *(Costumes)* 1138
Le Seyeux, Jean *(Director)* 3121
Le Seyeux, Jean *(Set Design)* 1138
Le Soir, Jack *(Composer)* 1134
Le Soir, Jack *(Lyricist)* 1134
LeBaron, Louise *(Cast)* 4497
LeBrunn, Leo *(Composer)* 2506
LeBrunn, Leo *(Lyricist)* 2506
LeClercq, Charles *(Cast)* 762
LeClerq, Arthur *(Composer)* 4027
LeClerq, Arthur *(Lyricist)* 4027
LeFrak, Francine *(Producer)* 3060, 3171
LeFranc, Mr. *(Choreographer)* 205
LeGon, Jeni *(Cast)* 435
LeGrady, T. *(Composer)* 1370
LeMaire, Charles *(Cast)* 4816
LeMaire, Charles *(Costumes)* 26, 111, 200, 288, 317, 376, 381, 444, 545, 568, 799, 953, 1131, 1135, 1136, 1145, 1175, 1176, 1275, 1281, 1297, 1323, 1481, 1490, 1491, 1492, 1493, 1643, 1691, 1780, 1827, 1839, 1979, 2567, 2628, 2636, 2691, 2768, 2813, 3005, 3008, 3063, 3117, 3131, 3157, 3225, 3407, 3431, 3540, 3584, 3650, 3659, 3721, 3772, 3796, 3850, 3946, 4001, 4177, 4179, 4234, 4249, 4267, 4271, 4378, 4476, 4575, 4694, 4730, 4777, 4818, 4824, 4846, 4847
LeMaire, Charles *(Set Design)* 231
LeMaire, George *(Cast)* 545, 1460, 1484, 1560
LeMaire, George *(Librettist)* 545
LeMaire, Rufus *(Producer)* 381, 545, 1819, 2757, 3796
LeMassena, William *(Cast)* 1222, 3687
LeMoyne, W.J. *(Cast)* 2361
LeNoire, Rosetta *(Cast)* 477, 1029, 1081, 1987, 2053, 2653, 2748, 3787, 4090
LePue, Maurice *(Cast)* 1836
LeRoux, Madeleine *(Cast)* 4403
LeRoy, Grace
See also Grace LeRoy Kahn.

LeRoy, Grace *(Composer)* 965
LeRoy, Hal *(Cast)* 901, 1395, 1440, 4177, 4374, 4420, 4823
LeRoy, Hal *(Choreographer)* 239
LeRoy, Hal *(Director)* 239
LeSoir, George *(Cast)* 4256
LeTang, Henry *(Choreographer)* 432, 1198, 3932, 3966, 4091, 4137, 4192, 4281
LeTang, Henry *(Director)* 4192
LeVan, Harry S. *(Cast)* 2853
Lea, Barbara *(Cast)* 3671
Leach, Archie
See also Cary Grant.
Leach, Archie *(Cast)* 1603
Leach, Dan *(Cast)* 4449
Leach, Marjory *(Cast)* 2135
Leach, Nicole *(Cast)* 535
Leach, Wilford *(Director)* 654, 2033, 2359, 3070
Leach, Wilford *(Librettist)* 654
Leachman, Cloris *(Cast)* 2450
Leacock, Philip *(Director)* 1674
Leaf, Paul *(Director)* 56, 3449
League, Janet *(Cast)* 1344, 3522
Leahy, Jill *(Cast)* 2641
Leahy, Joe *(Musical Director)* 2182
Leake, Damien *(Cast)* 1978
Leaman, Lou *(Composer)* 3354
Leamon, Eddie *(Cast)* 540
Lean, Cecil *(Cast)* 86, 473, 480, 531, 577, 1207, 1525, 2135, 2155, 2587, 2732, 2900, 4094, 4387, 4506, 4858
Lean, Cecil *(Composer)* 473
Lean, Cecil *(Lyricist)* 473, 531, 2587, 4094
Leanca, Alexander *(Composer)* 810
Leanca, Miron *(Lyricist)* 810
Lear, Evelyn *(Cast)* 3696
Leary, Helen *(Librettist)* 364
Leary, Nolan *(Librettist)* 364
Leary, Thomas C. *(Cast)* 4187
Leasor, James *(Librettist)* 2584
Leath, Ron *(Cast)* 3067
Leavel, Beth *(Cast)* 549, 4515
Leavitt, A. Douglas *(Librettist)* 1875
Leavitt, Abe *(Librettist)* 332
Leavitt, Abe *(Lyricist)* 332
Leavitt, Douglas *(Librettist)* 1882, 2174
Leavitt, Douglass *(Cast)* 1461
Leavitt, Philip *(Librettist)* 1321
Leavitt/Fox/Mages *(Producer)* 992
Lebedeff, Aaron *(Composer)* 573, 1609, 2356, 4342
Lebedeff, Aaron *(Lyricist)* 573, 1609, 2356, 4342
Leblang, Tillie *(Producer)* 1110, 4299
Lebowsky, Stan *(Composer)* 272, 427
Lebowsky, Stanley *(Cast)* 3175
Lebowsky, Stanley *(Composer)* 1441, 2689, 3479, 3637
Lebowsky, Stanley *(Dance Arranger)* 3992
Lebowsky, Stanley *(Musical Director)* 16, 181, 521, 678, 723, 1237, 1721, 1955, 2057, 2150, 2798, 3175, 3506, 4435, 4682
Lebowsky, Stanley *(Vocal Arranger)* 181, 521, 1441, 1955, 2150, 3992, 4435
Lebret, J.F. *(Producer)* 12
Lecesne, James *(Librettist)* 1638
Lechine, David *(Director)* 3703
Lecocq, Charles *(Author)* 1576, 2507
Lecocq, Charles *(Composer)* 1576, 2507
Lecuona, Ernesto *(Composer)* 4280, 4565
Lederer, Charles *(Author)* 4383
Lederer, Charles *(Librettist)* 2327
Lederer, Charles *(Lyricist)* 4366
Lederer, Charles *(Producer)* 2327
Lederer, George *(Composer)* 830
Lederer, George *(Director)* 1746, 2667, 2851, 3352
Lederer, George *(Librettist)* 3352
Lederer, George *(Producer)* 1746, 2261, 2667, 2851, 3352
Lederer, George W. *(Director)* 113, 136, 350, 357, 694, 697, 976, 1552, 2116, 2209, 2213, 2398, 2665, 2725, 3129, 3820, 4098, 4691
Lederer, George W. *(Librettist)* 2398
Lederer, George W. *(Producer)* 113, 136, 350, 357, 457, 666, 697, 976, 1552, 1599, 2116, 2117, 2209, 2213, 2710, 2725, 2842, 3129, 3784, 3820, 4098, 4181, 4298, 4691
Lederer, Suzanne *(Cast)* 259, 951
Leduc, Bob *(Cast)* 2096
Leduc Brothers *(Cast)* 2090
Lee, Alfred *(Composer)* 1897
Lee, Alfred *(Lyricist)* 1897
Lee, Allen *(Cast)* 692
Lee, Auriol *(Director)* 703
Lee, Baayork *(Cast)* 746, 2312, 3603, 3869
Lee, Baayork *(Choreographer)* 2049
Lee, Beatrice *(Cast)* 3184, 4100
Lee, Bert *(Composer)* 133, 1208, 2528
Lee, Bert *(Librettist)* 133, 702, 1855, 2547, 4299
Lee, Bert *(Lyricist)* 1208, 1544, 1916, 2528, 2833, 3084, 3117, 3259, 4299
Lee, Bobby *(Choreographer)* 314
Lee, Brenda *(Composer)* 3793
Lee, Brenda *(Lyricist)* 3793
Lee, Bryan *(Composer)* 2930
Lee, C.Y. *(Author)* 1315
Lee, Canada *(Cast)* 2712
Lee, Darren *(Cast)* 3456
Lee, Eileen *(Lyricist)* 2930
Lee, Ellen *(Costumes)* 4534
Lee, Eugene *(Set Design)* 35, 282, 1116, 1427, 1512, 2172, 2539, 2822, 3198, 4233
Lee, Franne *(Costumes)* 484, 1149, 1234, 1427, 1512, 2542, 2607, 2949, 3739, 4171, 4233
Lee, Franne *(Set Design)* 1116, 4171
Lee, Grace *(Cast)* 1404
Lee, Gypsy Rose *(Author)* 1709
Lee, Gypsy Rose *(Cast)* 1979, 2813, 4131, 4825
Lee, Heather *(Cast)* 2651
Lee, Helen *(Cast)* 1623
Lee, Irving *(Cast)* 3711, 3741
Lee, Irving B. *(Librettist)* 4761
Lee, Irving B. *(Lyricist)* 4761
Lee, Jack (Conductor) 1273, 4541
Lee, Jack *(Dance Arranger)* 1273
Lee, Jack *(Musical Director)* 406, 1354, 1380, 1649, 2306, 2584, 3060, 3876, 4114

Lee, Jack *(Orchestrations)* 1354
Lee, Jack *(Vocal Arranger)* 1380, 2306, 4114, 4522
Lee, Jean Marie *(Producer)* 2584
Lee, Joshua *(Choreographer)* 3321
Lee, Joshua *(Composer)* 3321
Lee, Joy *(Cast)* 3001
Lee, Kathryn *(Cast)* 85, 206
Lee, Lester *(Composer)* 67, 1779, 2296, 2379, 3121, 4131
Lee, Lester *(Lyricist)* 67, 1779, 2296, 2379, 3121
Lee, Lila *(Cast)* 3975
Lee, Lillian *(Cast)* 75
Lee, Lora *(Composer)* 1296
Lee, Lora *(Lyricist)* 1296
Lee, Mabel *(Cast)* 2853
Lee, Margaret *(Cast)* 1225, 1339, 3699, 4367
Lee, Marguerite *(Cast)* 3022
Lee, Marvin *(Lyricist)* 2232
Lee, Max *(Set Design)* 1130
Lee, Michele *(Cast)* 519, 3869, 4566
Lee, Ming Cho *(Set Design)* 135, 155, 406, 1344, 1660, 1864, 2368, 2568, 3000, 3825, 4384, 4485
Lee, Onike *(Cast)* 3814
Lee, Peggy *(Cast)* 855, 3428
Lee, Peggy *(Composer)* 3428
Lee, Peggy *(Librettist)* 3428
Lee, Peggy *(Lyricist)* 3428
Lee, Peter *(Composer)* 92
Lee, Peter *(Librettist)* 92
Lee, Peter *(Lyricist)* 92
Lee, Pinky *(Cast)* 2551
Lee, Rastus *(Cast)* 1838
Lee, Robert E. *(Author)* 2713
Lee, Robert E. *(Librettist)* 1012, 2582, 2713, 3913
Lee, Robert E. *(Lyricist)* 1048, 3913
Lee, Robert J. *(Set Design)* 4047
Lee, Robin *(Cast)* 2077
Lee, Sam *(Cast)* 801, 3523
Lee, Sammy *(Cast)* 1285, 1297, 4770
Lee, Sammy *(Choreographer)* 274, 317, 376, 418, 642, 799, 1129, 1130, 1285, 1516, 1859, 2376, 2382, 2527, 2768, 3008, 3184, 3243, 3420, 3622, 3659, 3719, 3949, 3993, 4276, 4392, 4766, 4821, 4847
Lee, Sammy *(Director)* 4241, 4300
Lee, Sammy *(Producer)* 931
Lee, Sondra *(Cast)* 1828, 3453, 3496, 3696
Lee, Sondra *(Director)* 1216
Lee, Spencer *(Composer)* 1296
Lee, Spencer *(Lyricist)* 1296
Lee, Stan *(Cast)* 803
Lee, Stephen *(Cast)* 3598
Lee, Thelma *(Cast)* 557
Lee, Tom *(Costumes)* 1879, 2597, 4586
Lee, Tom *(Set Design)* 1879, 2597
Lee, Valerie *(Cast)* 1860
Lee, Vernon *(Cast)* 4753
Lee, Vernon H. *(Cast)* 1535
Lee, Will *(Cast)* 2228
Lee, Willard *(Cast)* 1473
Lee, William *(Lyricist)* 336
Lee and Lee *(Cast)* 3804
Leech, Al *(Cast)* 1573
Leech, Al *(Lyricist)* 1752
Leech, Ed *(Cast)* 4269
Leech, Kitty *(Costumes)* 1589
Leedom, Edna *(Cast)* 2628
Leeds, Barbara *(Cast)* 4600
Leeds, Michael *(Choreographer)* 1832, 1997, 3960
Leeds, Michael *(Composer)* 4533
Leeds, Michael *(Director)* 1832, 1997, 3960, 4255
Leeds, Michael *(Librettist)* 4255
Leeds, Michael *(Lyricist)* 3181, 4533
Leeds, Nancy *(Lyricist)* 1676
Leeds, Peter *(Cast)* 4197
Leeds, Phil *(Cast)* 298, 629, 751, 943, 1993, 2043, 2447, 2705, 2750, 3210, 3226, 3761, 4028, 4090
Leeman, George *(Orchestrations)* 1336
Leete, Richard *(Cast)* 2124
Leffler, Ben *(Lighting Designer)* 1314
Leffler-Bratton Co. *(Producer)* 2448, 3134
Lefour, Andre *(Director)* 2753
Leftwich, Alexander *(Director)* 201, 391, 711, 796, 834, 1250, 1528, 1827, 1874, 1916, 2545, 2814, 3172, 3314, 3556, 3648, 4010, 4083, 4118, 4179, 4235, 4271, 4335, 4575
Legrand, Michel *(Author)* 4505
Legrand, Michel *(Composer)* 518, 753, 4505
Legrand, Michel *(French Lyrics)* 4505
Legrand, Michel *(Orchestrations)* 518, 4505
Legrand, Michel *(Vocal Arranger)* 4505
Legras, Jacques *(Cast)* 2364
Lehac, Ned *(Composer)* 418, 1448, 2460, 3172, 3226, 3986, 4235, 4335
Lehar, Franz *(Author)* 902, 1199, 1712, 2701, 2732, 2836, 2837, 2838, 2947, 3573, 4792
Lehar, Franz *(Composer)* 93, 702, 902, 1199, 1384, 1550, 1712, 2701, 2732, 2835, 2836, 2837, 2838, 2839, 2947, 3018, 3020, 3573, 4133, 4228, 4792
Lehew, Stephen *(Cast)* 451, 3743
Lehl, Philip *(Cast)* 2038
Lehman, Al *(Costumes)* 2339, 3863
Lehman, Alfred *(Costumes)* 1596
Lehman, Henry *(Composer)* 4657
Lehman, Henry *(Lyricist)* 4657
Lehman, Jeanne *(Cast)* 2703, 2993
Lehman, John *(Musical Director)* 2285
Lehman, John *(Vocal Arranger)* 2285
Lehman, Kenny *(Composer)* 1637
Lehman, Kenny *(Lyricist)* 1637
Lehman, Kenny *(Musical Director)* 1637
Lehman, Kenny *(Vocal Arranger)* 1637
Lehman, Liza *(Composer)* 3882
Lehman, Paul *(Producer)* 1081
Lehman, Ross *(Cast)* 4708
Lehman, Samuel *(Composer)* 3357
Lehman, Samuel *(Musical Director)* 3395, 4553, 4655
Lehman, Susan *(Director)* 1346
Lehmann, Jo Anna *(Cast)* 556
Lehmann, Jo Anna *(Choreographer)* 556
Lehmann, Liza *(Composer)* 3882, 4335
Lehmann, Maurice *(Producer)* 3769

Lehr, Fred *(Cast)* 2853
Lehr, Wilson *(Librettist)* 1507, 2550
Lehrer, Tom *(Composer)* 4412
Lehrer, Tom *(Lyricist)* 4412
Lehue, John *(Director)* 322
Leib, Dick *(Dance Arranger)* 3019
Leib, Dick *(Orchestrations)* 3019
Leib, Dick *(Vocal Arranger)* 3019
Leib, Mani *(Lyricist)* 4342
Leib, Russell *(Librettist)* 2785
Leibell, Richard *(Cast)* 4232
Leiber, Jerry *(Composer)* 964, 3428, 3739, 4031
Leiber, Jerry *(Lyricist)* 599, 964, 1214, 3428, 3739, 4031
Leibman, Harriet *(Costumes)* 2020
Leibman, Ron *(Cast)* 3197
Leigh *(Composer)* 710, 1318
Leigh *(Lyricist)* 710
Leigh, Carol *(Cast)* 603
Leigh, Carolyn *(Librettist)* 2072
Leigh, Carolyn *(Lyricist)* 614, 743, 1023, 1097, 1189, 1298, 1451, 1648, 1708, 1815, 1842, 2010, 2014, 2072, 2205, 2294, 2523, 2688, 2804, 2837, 3453, 3485, 3637, 3940, 4019, 4061, 4268, 4337, 4693, 4828
Leigh, Dan *(Costumes)* 4480
Leigh, Dan *(Lighting Designer)* 164
Leigh, Dan *(Set Design)* 164, 337, 4480
Leigh, Fred W. *(Composer)* 4027
Leigh, Fred W. *(Lyricist)* 675, 2858, 4027
Leigh, Grace *(Cast)* 4802
Leigh, Gracie *(Cast)* 4663
Leigh, Jaime *(Cast)* 1496
Leigh, Lesley *(Cast)* 4113
Leigh, Leslie *(Cast)* 617
Leigh, Lisle *(Cast)* 1907
Leigh, Mary *(Cast)* 2366
Leigh, Mitch *(Composer)* 36, 172, 757, 935, 1730, 1959, 2727, 3612, 3838, 3844
Leigh, Mitch *(Producer)* 935
Leigh, Paul *(Lyricist)* 3208
Leigh, Rowland *(Author)* 1506
Leigh, Rowland *(Director)* 1110, 1414, 1506, 3064, 4777
Leigh, Rowland *(Librettist)* 1110, 1414, 2610, 3011, 3064, 3152, 4365, 4777
Leigh, Rowland *(Lyricist)* 700, 702, 703, 791, 797, 1110, 1414, 1506, 2610, 3011, 3064, 3152, 4583, 4777
Leigh, Vivien *(Cast)* 4435
Leigh, Walter *(Composer)* 4153
Leigh, Walter *(Librettist)* 4153
Leight, Warren *(Librettist)* 2790
Leight, Warren *(Lyricist)* 2790
Leighton, Dot *(Cast)* 1532
Leighton, Isabel *(Librettist)* 2293, 2818, 3532
Leighton, Mauri *(Cast)* 898
Leighton, Rose *(Cast)* 1080, 1576
Leisek, Liz *(Cast)* 3561
Leiser, Henri *(Producer)* 2395
Leiserowitz, Jacob *(Composer)* 1609
Leisten, Annette *(Lyricist)* 251
Leitheed, Mike *(Cast)* 3606
Leitzell, Lillian *(Cast)* 4851
Leland, Dawn *(Cast)* 3997
Lellon, Charles A. *(Director)* 2749
Lelong, Lucien *(Costumes)* 702
Lemac, Linda *(Choreographer)* 107, 2689, 2737, 3126, 3637
Leman, Harry N. *(Musical Director)* 1678
Lemarque, Francis *(Composer)* 3107
Lemarque, Francis *(Lyricist)* 3107
Lembeck, Harvey *(Cast)* 3473
Lembeck, Michael *(Cast)* 140
Lemberg, Stephen H. *(Composer)* 2195
Lemberg, Stephen H. *(Librettist)* 2195
Lemberg, Stephen H. *(Lyricist)* 2195
Lemberg, Steve *(Composer)* 1713
Lemberg, Steve *(Lyricist)* 1713
Lemming, Geo. A. *(Cast)* 1562
Lemmon, Shirley *(Cast)* 4480, 4743
Lemonier, Tom *(Composer)* 295, 2111, 3753, 3797
Lemos, Murray *(Composer)* 2164
Lemos, Murray *(Lyricist)* 2164
Lenert, Marguerite *(Cast)* 35
Lengsfelder, Hans *(Composer)* 4091
Lengsfelder, Hans *(Lyricist)* 3905, 4091
Lengson, Jose *(Costumes)* 1146, 3637
Lengyil, Melchoir *(Librettist)* 3829
Lenn, Robert *(Cast)* 153, 283
Lenn, Robert *(Musical Director)* 4243
Lennart, Isobel *(Librettist)* 1420
Lennon, John *(Author)* 3903
Lennon, John *(Composer)* 3739, 3903, 3936, 4193, 4449
Lennon, John *(Librettist)* 3233
Lennon, John *(Lyricist)* 3739, 3903, 3936, 4193, 4449
Lennon, Rusell *(Cast)* 2448
Lennox, Annie *(Composer)* 1713
Lennox, Fred *(Cast)* 2695, 3582
Lennox, Gilbert *(Librettist)* 346
Lennox, Jane *(Cast)* 604
Lennox, Vera *(Cast)* 1618, 3569
Lennox, William *(Librettist)* 1270
Lenoir, Jean *(Composer)* 839
Lenoir, Jean *(Lyricist)* 839
Lenox, Adriane *(Cast)* 338
Lenox, Jean *(Composer)* 4390
Lenox, Jean *(Lyricist)* 1148, 1246, 4762, 4803
Lenya, Lotte *(Cast)* 610, 1196, 1284, 2678, 4369
Lenzberg, Jules *(Musical Director)* 3168
Leo, Frank *(Composer)* 1783, 3882
Leo, Frank *(Lyricist)* 1783, 3882
Leogrande, Ernest *(Librettist)* 3527
Leon, Daisy *(Cast)* 3423
Leon, Felix (Adaptation) 3280
Leon, Frederic A. *(Director)* 284
Leon, Geoff *(Lyricist)* 583
Leon, Harry *(Composer)* 3820
Leon, Harry *(Lyricist)* 3820
Leon, Joseph *(Cast)* 2235, 2838
Leon, Lillian *(Cast)* 1515
Leon, Tania *(Conductor)* 2033
Leon, Tania *(Musical Director)* 4722
Leon, Victor *(Author)* 1555, 1852, 2701, 2836, 2837, 2838, 3308, 4563

Leonard, Benny *(Cast)* 1923, 4770
Leonard, Billie *(Cast)* 292, 680, 1534
Leonard, Charles *(Librettist)* 2259
Leonard, Eddie *(Cast)* 800, 2481, 3166, 3754, 4098
Leonard, Eddie *(Composer)* 4390
Leonard, Eddie *(Director)* 977
Leonard, Eddie *(Lyricist)* 3754, 4390
Leonard, Eddie *(Producer)* 977
Leonard, Jack *(Cast)* 3738
Leonard, John F. *(Cast)* 3348
Leonard, Leon *(Cast)* 1308
Leonard, Lu *(Cast)* 519, 1094, 1456, 1745
Leonard, Michael *(Composer)* 2016, 3551, 4623, 4764
Leonard, Michael *(Dance Arranger)* 4623
Leonard, Michael *(Musical Director)* 4623
Leonard, Michael *(Orchestrations)* 1664
Leonard, Michael *(Vocal Arranger)* 4623
Leonard, Parker *(Cast)* 340
Leonard, Patrick A. *(Producer)* 680
Leonard, Queenie *(Cast)* 752, 3214, 4341
Leonard, Richard J. *(Musical Director)* 956, 1761, 4643, 4743
Leonard, Richard J. *(Orchestrations)* 1761, 4643
Leonard, Richard J. *(Vocal Arranger)* 956, 4643
Leonard, Robert Z. *(Producer)* 3421
Leonard, Roger *(Cast)* 1010
Leonard, Susanne *(Cast)* 113
Leonard, Suzanne *(Cast)* 3625
Leonardi, Leon *(Musical Director)* 462, 905, 2496, 4123, 4428
Leonardi, Leon *(Vocal Arranger)* 4123, 4428
Leonardo, Joe *(Director)* 3461, 4799
Leonardo, Joseph *(Director)* 1597, 2171
Leonardo, Joseph *(Librettist)* 1377, 1597
Leonardos, Urylee *(Cast)* 415
Leone, Henry *(Cast)* 2518
Leone, John *(Cast)* 240, 533
Leone, Vivien *(Lighting Designer)* 1740, 4518
Leong, Terry *(Costumes)* 3125
Leong, Terry *(Set Design)* 3125
Leonidoff, Leon *(Choreographer)* 3172, 4620
Leonidoff, Leon *(Director)* 117, 177, 1843, 2161, 2162, 3989, 4569, 4737
Leonora, Lily *(Choreographer)* 377
Lepane Amusement Co. *(Producer)* 1795
Lepere, William H. *(Librettist)* 2179
Leporaka, Zoya *(Choreographer)* 3224
Lerch, Stuart *(Cast)* 3329
Lerman, April *(Cast)* 3668
Lerman, Oscar *(Producer)* 4542
Lerman, Oscar S. *(Producer)* 751
Lerman, Rhonda *(Author)* 1169
Lerman, Rhonda *(Librettist)* 1169
Lerner, Alan Jay *(Cast)* 4039
Lerner, Alan Jay *(Composer)* 1231, 2611, 4039
Lerner, Alan Jay *(Director)* 958
Lerner, Alan Jay *(Librettist)* 530, 623, 652, 798, 958, 999, 1231, 1511, 2479, 2568, 2615, 3018, 3038, 3274, 3347, 4004, 4640
Lerner, Alan Jay *(Lyricist)* 369, 530, 623, 652, 798, 958, 999, 1231, 1511, 2401, 2568, 2615, 3018, 3038, 3055, 3274, 3347, 4004, 4039, 4640
Lerner, Alan Jay *(Producer)* 623, 3274
Lerner, Alan Jay *(Screenwriter)* 1511
Lerner, Gene *(Librettist)* 369
Lerner, Gene *(Lyricist)* 369
Lerner, Gene *(Producer)* 369
Lerner, Sam *(Lyricist)* 1930, 3036
Lerner, Sammy *(Composer)* 3036
Lerner, Sammy *(Lyricist)* 203, 431, 3036, 4374, 4545, 4667
Leroux, Gaston *(Author)* 3462, 3463, 3464, 3465
Leroux, Xaver *(Composer)* 3148
Leroux, Xaver *(Lyricist)* 3148
Leroy, Nat *(Librettist)* 539, 541
Lertora, Joseph *(Cast)* 4328, 4476
Les Quat' Jeudis *(Cast)* 3954
Lesan, David *(Cast)* 3365
Lesan, David *(Librettist)* 2105, 3365, 3986
Leser, Tina *(Costumes)* 3390
Leska, Elene *(Cast)* 4064
Lesker, Lorraine *(Producer)* 4015
Lesko, Andrew *(Dance Arranger)* 4629
Lesko, Andrew *(Musical Director)* 4629
Lesko, Andrew *(Orchestrations)* 4629
Lesko, John *(Musical Director)* 842, 1359, 1435, 1730, 1842, 2050, 2201, 2681, 3018, 3020, 4013, 4038, 4244, 4537
Lesko, John *(Orchestrations)* 4566
Lesko, John *(Vocal Arranger)* 1359, 2681, 3018
Leslee, Ray *(Composer)* 240, 4129
Leslee, Ray *(Lyricist)* 240
Leslee, Ray *(Musical Director)* 4129
Lesley, Charlotte *(Cast)* 2485
Leslie, Bert *(Cast)* 3087, 3322
Leslie, Diane *(Composer)* 843
Leslie, Doree *(Cast)* 3980
Leslie, Earl *(Cast)* 2135
Leslie, Eddie *(Cast)* 364
Leslie, Edgar *(Composer)* 4804
Leslie, Edgar *(Lyricist)* 173, 379, 417, 418, 487, 558, 965, 1613, 1813, 2373, 2460, 3175, 3293, 3399, 3525, 3705, 3737, 3827, 3840, 3977, 4235, 4742, 4804, 4812, 4815, 4817, 4825, 4846
Leslie, Edna *(Cast)* 4576
Leslie, Fred *(Cast)* 133, 4249
Leslie, Fred *(Choreographer)* 334, 466, 4795
Leslie, Fred A. *(Cast)* 3649
Leslie, Fred A. *(Choreographer)* 2976
Leslie, Henry *(Composer)* 1065
Leslie, Henry *(Lyricist)* 1065
Leslie, Lew *(Choreographer)* 787, 3783
Leslie, Lew *(Director)* 441, 443, 444, 447, 787, 1058, 2140, 3704, 3705
Leslie, Lew *(Librettist)* 444, 447, 787, 1058, 2140, 3705, 4661
Leslie, Lew *(Producer)* 441, 443, 445, 447, 787, 1058, 2140, 2462, 3513, 3514, 3704, 4661
Leslie, Lew *(Vocal Arranger)* 445
Leslie, Michael *(Cast)* 2970, 3169
Leslie, Norma *(Cast)* 132

Leslie, Sylvia *(Cast)* 841
Leslie-Smith, Kenneth *(Composer)* 4207
Lessac, Arthur *(Vocal Arranger)* 3989
Lesser, Arthur *(Producer)* 95, 2362, 4496
Lesser, Sally *(Costumes)* 2544, 4618
Lesser, Sally I. *(Costumes)* 3695
Lessey, George A. *(Cast)* 3220
Lessig, William *(Musical Director)* 4093, 4679, 4774
Lessing, Edith Maida *(Lyricist)* 1738
Lessing, Madge *(Cast)* 976, 1228, 2116, 2181, 2543, 2936
Lessner, George *(Composer)* 2985, 4015
Lessner, George *(Orchestrations)* 2985, 3152, 4015
Lester, Alfred *(Cast)* 1153
Lester, Edwin *(Producer)* 223, 1119, 1369, 1511, 1681, 1711, 2234, 2327, 3453, 4075, 4798
Lester, Florence *(Cast)* 1163
Lester, Hugh *(Lighting Designer)* 699
Lester, Jerry *(Cast)* 323, 1138, 1950, 2187
Lester, Kitty *(Cast)* 4829
Lester, Mark *(Cast)* 466, 4795
Lester, Noble Lee *(Composer)* 2239
Lester, Noble Lee *(Lyricist)* 2239
Lester Ltd. *(Costumes)* 787
Leswing, Carl *(Director)* 4093
Leswing, Carl *(Librettist)* 4543
Leterrier, Eugene *(Author)* 1576, 1720
Letora, Joseph *(Cast)* 728, 4733
Lett, Robert *(Cast)* 2025
Letters, Will *(Composer)* 2232
Letters, Will *(Lyricist)* 2232
Leugs, David *(Set Design)* 4732
Levans, Daniel *(Choreographer)* 533
Levant, Harry *(Musical Director)* 189, 514, 1539, 2068, 2140, 2847, 3036, 3353, 4420, 4510
Levant, Lila *(Librettist)* 4102
Levant, Lila *(Lyricist)* 4102
Levant, Oscar *(Cast)* 587
Levant, Oscar *(Composer)* 3721
Levant, Oscar *(Musical Director)* 121
Leve, Sam *(Librettist)* 615
Leve, Sam *(Set Design)* 615
Leve, Samuel *(Lighting Designer)* 596
Leve, Samuel *(Set Design)* 323, 596, 2257
Leveen, Raymond *(Lyricist)* 4572, 4824
Leveilee, Claude *(Composer)* 1596
Levene, Sam *(Cast)* 615, 1706, 2449, 3577, 3787
Levenson, Jeanine *(Dance Arranger)* 3862
Levenson, Jeanine *(Musical Director)* 595
Levenson, Keith *(Arrangements)* 533
Levenson, Keith *(Librettist)* 4136
Levenson, Keith *(Lyricist)* 4136
Levenson, Keith *(Musical Director)* 155
Levenson, Keith *(Orchestrations)* 155, 595
Levenson, Lew *(Lyricist)* 1855, 2545
Leventhal, Harold *(Producer)* 4410
Leventhal, Jules J. *(Producer)* 1506
Leveridge, Lynn Ann *(Cast)* 4244
Levering, Nancy *(Producer)* 101
Levey, Ethel *(Cast)* 1480, 1584, 1640, 2517, 2755, 3085, 3809, 4214
Levey, Harold *(Composer)* 1691, 1692, 1796, 2628, 2686, 3655
Levey, Harold *(Musical Director)* 924, 1796, 2628, 2686, 4365
Levey, Harold A. *(Composer)* 780, 2377, 2691
Levey, Harold A. *(Musical Director)* 780, 2691
Levi, Maurice *(Additional Music)* 215
Levi, Maurice *(Composer)* 1327, 1881, 3744, 3745, 3751, 4094, 4473, 4799, 4802, 4803, 4805
Levi, Maurice *(Musical Director)* 3744, 4473
Levi, Richard *(Choreographer)* 747
Levin, Chaim *(Cast)* 2866
Levin, Charles *(Cast)* 1406, 3937
Levin, Herman *(Producer)* 454, 490, 620, 1475, 1564, 2626, 3038, 4450
Levin, Ira *(Author)* 3188
Levin, Ira *(Librettist)* 1094
Levin, Ira *(Lyricist)* 1094
Levin, Maurice L. *(Lyricist)* 1957
Levin, Sylvan *(Musical Director)* 1548
Levine, Bill *(Librettist)* 272, 427, 1049, 4268
Levine, David *(Composer)* 147
Levine, Irwin *(Composer)* 2235, 4197
Levine, Irwin *(Lyricist)* 2235, 4197
Levine, Joseph E. *(Producer)* 2304
Levine, Louis *(Composer)* 3605
Levine, Maurice *(Musical Director)* 596, 868, 1300, 2591, 2680, 3934
Levine, Maurice *(Producer)* 4272
Levine, Maurice *(Vocal Arranger)* 652, 868, 1300, 4567
Levine, Rhoda *(Choreographer)* 1662, 1857, 1977, 2067, 2563, 2599, 4785
Levine, Sam *(Producer)* 2051
Levine, Susan *(Cast)* 3601
Levine, Wally *(Musical Director)* 2052
Levine, William *(Librettist)* 1648, 4525
Levinsky, Walt *(Dance Arranger)* 482
Levinsky, Walt *(Orchestrations)* 482, 2231
Levinsky, Walt *(Vocal Arranger)* 482
Levinson, Fred *(Producer)* 3444
Levinson, J.J. *(Producer)* 2330
Levinson, Leonard *(Lyricist)* 1944, 1946
Levinson, Leonard I. *(Librettist)* 2985
Levinson, Leonard Louis *(Librettist)* 3703
Levinson, Richard *(Composer)* 3076
Levinson, Richard *(Librettist)* 2820, 4303, 4543
Levinson, Richard *(Lyricist)* 3076, 4543
Levinson, Sam *(Cast)* 863
Levister, Alonzo *(Composer)* 3112
Levister, Alonzo *(Orchestrations)* 2306
Levit, Ben *(Director)* 109, 264, 1872
Levitas, Willard *(Producer)* 1200, 3273
Levitch, Sula *(Composer)* 4260
Levitt, Barry *(Musical Director)* 4255, 4272
Levitt, Barry *(Orchestrations)* 4255
Levitt, Barry *(Vocal Arranger)* 4255
Levy, Abe *(Producer)* 3357
Levy, Abraham *(Producer)* 2549
Levy, Al *(Cast)* 3501
Levy, Arnold H. *(Producer)* 2375

Levy, Benn W. *(Librettist)* 1202
Levy, Bert *(Cast)* 1208
Levy, Charles *(Orchestrations)* 4254
Levy, Dan *(Arrangements)* 760
Levy, Dan *(Composer)* 760
Levy, Dan *(Lyricist)* 760
Levy, David *(Composer)* 1873, 2294, 4731
Levy, David *(Librettist)* 2235, 4731
Levy, David *(Lyricist)* 1873, 2294, 4731
Levy, Eric *(Librettist)* 1216
Levy, Franklin R. *(Producer)* 450, 1262
Levy, Hank *(Musical Director)* 2372, 3463
Levy, J.H. *(Producer)* 435
Levy, Jacques *(Director)* 259, 1077, 1609
Levy, Jacques *(Librettist)* 259, 3233, 3553
Levy, Jacques *(Lyricist)* 259, 573, 1236, 1609, 3553
Levy, Ned *(Arrangements)* 1304
Levy, Ned *(Cast)* 1304
Levy, Newman *(Librettist)* 1447, 1448, 2300, 3103
Levy, Newman *(Lyricist)* 1448
Levy, Parke *(Librettist)* 2301, 3713, 4586
Levy, Ralph *(Director)* 752
Levy, Ralph *(Producer)* 752
Levy, Simon *(Director)* 4515
Levy, Ted *(Cast)* 432
Levy, Ted L. *(Cast)* 789
Levy, Ted L. *(Choreographer)* 2200
Lewin, Jaime *(Cast)* 4463
Lewin, John *(Librettist)* 461
Lewin, John *(Lyricist)* 461, 2633
Lewine, Richard *(Composer)* 557, 1191, 1286, 1342, 1546, 1567, 2707, 3003, 3082, 3914, 4394, 4498, 4827
Lewine, Richard *(Lyricist)* 1191, 1342
Lewine, Richard *(Musical Director)* 1231
Lewine, Richard *(Producer)* 44, 759, 974, 2267, 2583, 3275, 3497
Lewis *(Composer)* 1215
Lewis, Ada *(Cast)* 968, 1065, 1246, 1327, 1403, 1625, 1728, 1927, 1963, 2491, 3146, 3265, 3750, 4044, 4203, 4222, 4555
Lewis, Al *(Cast)* 1061, 1758, 4681
Lewis, Al *(Composer)* 393, 1127, 1491, 4534
Lewis, Al *(Lyricist)* 24, 393, 1127, 1491, 3739, 4534
Lewis, Albert *(Director)* 297, 612, 2194, 4105
Lewis, Albert *(Producer)* 297, 612, 4105, 4366
Lewis, Andy *(Composer)* 248
Lewis, Arthur *(Producer)* 4366
Lewis, Bobo *(Cast)* 2288, 2804, 3161, 4744
Lewis, Brenda *(Cast)* 615, 1548, 3691
Lewis, Carol Jean *(Cast)* 4167
Lewis, Charles *(Lighting Designer)* 4431
Lewis, Daniel *(Choreographer)* 3088
Lewis, Dave *(Cast)* 1054, 1469, 2869, 2904, 3786, 4801
Lewis, Dave *(Composer)* 830
Lewis, Dave *(Lyricist)* 830
Lewis, Flo *(Cast)* 391, 4375
Lewis, Frederick *(Cast)* 2666
Lewis, Frederick G. *(Cast)* 818
Lewis, Gillian *(Cast)* 1386
Lewis, Harold *(Composer)* 1314, 2709
Lewis, Harold *(Musical Director)* 1314
Lewis, Henry *(Cast)* 1065, 1404, 1531, 3962
Lewis, Henry *(Composer)* 1334, 1404
Lewis, Henry *(Lyricist)* 1065, 1334, 1404
Lewis, Jenifer *(Cast)* 1055, 2171, 3739
Lewis, Jenifer *(Composer)* 1055
Lewis, Jenifer *(Librettist)* 1055
Lewis, Jenifer *(Lyricist)* 1055
Lewis, Jerry *(Cast)* 853, 857, 1842
Lewis, Jim *(Librettist)* 756, 975
Lewis, Joe *(Costumes)* 849
Lewis, Joe E. *(Cast)* 847, 851, 859, 864, 2379, 3713
Lewis, John *(Composer)* 2611, 2692
Lewis, John Richard *(Musical Director)* 3661
Lewis, John Richard *(Vocal Arranger)* 3661
Lewis, Joseph *(Costumes)* 345, 821, 2028
Lewis, Laura May *(Cast)* 4514
Lewis, Loney *(Cast)* 4829
Lewis, Loney *(Librettist)* 4829
Lewis, Marcia *(Cast)* 589, 1590, 3644, 3792
Lewis, Marjo *(Lyricist)* 575
Lewis, Mary *(Cast)* 4815
Lewis, Mary Jane *(Choreographer)* 2086, 2087, 2091
Lewis, Mary Jane *(Director)* 2083, 2089, 2090
Lewis, Mattie *(Cast)* 2013
Lewis, Michael *(Cast)* 3274
Lewis, Michael J. *(Composer)* 946
Lewis, Morgan *(Composer)* 2294, 3103, 3292, 3453, 3861, 4335, 4362, 4483
Lewis, Morgan *(Director)* 1286, 3082
Lewis, Morgan *(Lyricist)* 2294
Lewis, Mort *(Librettist)* 2301, 3104
Lewis, Preston *(Cast)* 2896
Lewis, Rick *(Musical Director)* 4264
Lewis, Rick *(Vocal Arranger)* 4264
Lewis, Robert *(Cast)* 2228
Lewis, Robert *(Director)* 530, 1373, 1775, 2190, 2355, 3274, 3691, 3696
Lewis, Ron *(Choreographer)* 16, 2558
Lewis, Sam M. *(Cast)* 1824, 3495
Lewis, Sam M. *(Composer)* 123, 3926
Lewis, Sam M. *(Librettist)* 1824
Lewis, Sam M. *(Lyricist)* 26, 391, 393, 428, 505, 830, 1127, 1247, 1334, 1405, 1626, 1813, 1840, 1904, 2194, 2308, 2358, 2380, 2382, 2939, 3018, 3031, 3120, 3401, 3709, 3737, 3926, 3985, 4148, 4257, 4604, 4813, 4817, 4821
Lewis, Sinclair *(Author)* 1172, 1441
Lewis, St. John *(Set Design)* 1728, 2324, 2725
Lewis, Stephen *(Author)* 2572
Lewis, Stephen *(Librettist)* 2572
Lewis, Steve J. *(Composer)* 3297
Lewis, Steve J. *(Lyricist)* 3297
Lewis, Sylvia *(Choreographer)* 408
Lewis, Ted *(Cast)* 202, 856, 1685, 1687, 3796, 4296, 4840
Lewis, Ted *(Composer)* 202, 3407
Lewis, Ted *(Lyricist)* 202, 1685, 3407
Lewis, Ted *(Producer)* 4296
Lewis, Tom *(Cast)* 1819, 1888, 1900, 2517, 2525, 2931, 2939, 3401, 3712, 3958, 4219, 4759, 4817, 4818

Lewis, Vicki *(Cast)* 140, 494, 583, 1092, 4034, 4171, 4701
Lewis, Walter *(Set Design)* 26
Lewis, Walter H. *(Composer)* 1220
Lewis, William J. *(Composer)* 4104
Lewis & MacCoughtry *(Set Design)* 1505, 2675
Lewis Jr., Alde *(Cast)* 393
Lewis Jr., J.C. *(Composer)* 3933
Lewis Jr., J.C. *(Lyricist)* 3933
Lewis and Gordon *(Producer)* 2194
Lewis-Evans, Kecia *(Cast)* 3285, 4398
Lewisohn, Irene *(Cast)* 1654
Lewitin, Margot *(Cast)* 4768
Lewitin, Margot *(Director)* 4768
Lewitzky, Bella *(Choreographer)* 4415
Lewman, David *(Cast)* 4690
Ley, Benton *(Lyricist)* 1690, 4817
Leybourne, George *(Composer)* 1897
Leybourne, George *(Lyricist)* 1897
Leyden, Jimmy *(Orchestrations)* 520
Leyden, Jimmy *(Vocal Arranger)* 520
Leyden, Leo *(Cast)* 2798
Leyden, Norman *(Orchestrations)* 1864
Leys, Bryan D. *(Librettist)* 3004
Leyton, Drue *(Cast)* 1871
Liandre, Lil *(Choreographer)* 2653
Libbey, Dee *(Composer)* 4828
Libbey, Dee *(Lyricist)* 4828
Libby, J. Aldrich *(Cast)* 2157
Libertini, Richard *(Cast)* 679, 2663
Liberto, Don *(Cast)* 2339, 2582, 4395
Liberto, Don *(Choreographer)* 2103
Libin, Paul *(Producer)* 298, 2220
Libowitsky, Hervig *(Set Design)* 2142
Librandi, Geraldine *(Cast)* 81
Libuse, Frank *(Cast)* 2400, 4465
Lichine, David *(Choreographer)* 323, 3536
Licht, David *(Director)* 4773
Licht, David *(Librettist)* 4773
Lichtefeld, Michael *(Choreographer)* 1258, 2185, 3862
Lichtenstein, Todd *(Lighting Designer)* 4684
Lichtman, Nat *(Director)* 4394
Lichtman, Nat *(Producer)* 4394
Lieb, Dick *(Orchestrations)* 1146
Lieb, Francis *(Cast)* 1707, 4161
Lieb, Francis *(Producer)* 2062
Lieb, Francis K. *(Cast)* 617
Lieb, Gil *(Vocal Arranger)* 74
Lieb, Lora *(Cast)* 326
Lieberman, Maurice *(Librettist)* 3847
Lieberson, Goddard *(Composer)* 1342
Liebert, Dick *(Composer)* 532
Liebgold, Leon *(Cast)* 2356, 3781
Liebler & Company *(Producer)* 1501, 2760, 2819, 4544, 4508
Liebling, Howard *(Lyricist)* 427, 1436, 1437, 3479
Liebling, Leonard *(Librettist)* 118, 1522, 4553
Liebling, Leonard *(Lyricist)* 118, 1522
Liebman, Harriet *(Costumes)* 2789
Liebman, Max *(Composer)* 2453
Liebman, Max *(Director)* 23, 1815, 1933, 2707, 3841, 4166, 4287
Liebman, Max *(Librettist)* 2105, 3841, 4166
Liebman, Max *(Lyricist)* 2140, 2453
Liebman, Max *(Producer)* 23, 743, 1815, 1933, 2837, 3841, 3947, 4287
Liebman, Steve *(Librettist)* 4731
Lieder, Rose *(Cast)* 1286
Liederman, Susan *(Producer)* 4074
Lief, Arthur *(Musical Director)* 298
Lief, Max *(Lyricist)* 1136, 1657, 1693, 1855, 1874, 2105, 2637, 3409, 3523, 3849, 3946, 4291, 4335, 4581, 4621
Lief, Nathaniel *(Lyricist)* 1136, 1657, 1693, 1855, 1874, 2105, 2637, 3409, 3523, 3849, 3946, 4291, 4335, 4581, 4621
Liepman, Joan *(Lighting Designer)* 4145
Lieurance, Thurlow *(Composer)* 3840
Liff, Samuel *(Director)* 4273
Lifshey, Oscar *(Musical Director)* 1221
Lifshitz, Max *(Musical Director)* 1695
Light, James *(Cast)* 421
Lightfoot, J.E. *(Cast)* 9
Lightfoot, James *(Cast)* 1909
Lightner, Fred *(Cast)* 4621
Lightner, Winnie *(Cast)* 1460, 1461, 1485, 1486, 1487, 1779
Ligon, Tom *(Cast)* 4789
Lilley, Edward Clarke *(Director)* 145, 814, 948, 1127, 1231, 1323, 1539, 1856, 1979, 2140, 2413, 2709, 3292, 3584, 3955, 4039, 4374, 4569, 4673, 4823, 4824, 4825
Lilley, Edward Clarke *(Librettist)* 4673
Lilley, Joseph *(Vocal Arranger)* 1931
Lilley, Joseph J. *(Composer)* 3444
Lilley, Joseph J. *(Musical Director)* 1893
Lillian, Isodore *(Composer)* 1609
Lillian, Isodore *(Lyricist)* 1609
Lilliard, James A. *(Cast)* 500
Lillie, Beatrice *(Cast)* 133, 216, 702, 703, 1763, 1891, 2137, 3254, 3521, 3885, 3893, 3924, 3955, 4335, 4341, 4583, 4828
Lillie, Muriel *(Composer)* 702, 1733
Lillis Jr., Joseph H. *(Producer)* 843
Lilly, Andrea *(Costumes)* 4003
Lilo *(Cast)* 629, 3551
Lim, Debbie *(Cast)* 2521
Lime Trio, The *(Cast)* 662
Limon, Jose *(Cast)* 125, 207, 3767
Limon, Jose *(Choreographer)* 1880, 3735
Limosner, Pilar *(Costumes)* 4775
Lincke, Paul *(Composer)* 1526, 2858, 4094, 4228
Lincke, Paul *(Lyricist)* 1526, 2858
Lincoln, Harry J. *(Composer)* 1443
Lincoln Center Theater *(Producer)* 756, 3001, 3039, 3468, 3836, 4438
Lind, Betty *(Choreographer)* 4273
Lind, Christina *(Cast)* 153, 3990
Lind, Della *(Cast)* 3975, 4174, 4465
Lind, Homer *(Cast)* 1515, 4646
Lind, Oona *(Cast)* 562
Lindau, Carl *(Author)* 2262, 2495, 2603, 4181, 4726

Linden, Hal *(Cast)* 1158, 2106, 2617, 3780, 3800, 4060
Linder, D. Scott *(Lighting Designer)* 4402
Linder, Helen *(Cast)* 1608
Linder, Jack *(Producer)* 1036, 4204
Linder, Mark *(Author)* 4204
Linderman, Ed *(Additional Music)* 4062
Linderman, Ed *(Cast)* 549
Linderman, Ed *(Musical Director)* 2146
Lindholm, Robert *(Cast)* 622
Lindley, Donald *(Lyricist)* 1131
Lindon, Michael *(Lyricist)* 2388
Lindsay, Carl *(Author)* 132
Lindsay, Earl *(Choreographer)* 202, 288, 1177, 1460, 1678, 2298, 2636, 2789, 3344, 3968, 3973, 4532
Lindsay, Earl *(Composer)* 1678
Lindsay, Earl *(Director)* 3344
Lindsay, Howard *(Author)* 3919, 4180, 4278
Lindsay, Howard *(Cast)* 759, 1357
Lindsay, Howard *(Director)* 163, 1357, 1453, 1973, 3674, 3919
Lindsay, Howard *(Librettist)* 163, 619, 1683, 1760, 1973, 2983, 3674, 4095
Lindsay, John *(Composer)* 60
Lindsay, Robert *(Cast)* 2798
Lindsay, Walter C. *(Producer)* 1562
Lindsay-Hogg, Michael *(Director)* 3198
Lindsey, Gene *(Cast)* 518, 1596, 4454, 4517
Lindsey, Kathleen *(Producer)* 3136
Lindsey, Mort *(Orchestrations)* 269
Lindsey, Robert Nassif *(Additional Dialogue)* 1969
Lindsey, Robert Nassif *(Composer)* 1969, 3306
Lindsey, Robert Nassif *(Librettist)* 3306
Lindsey, Robert Nassif *(Lyricist)* 1969, 3306
Lindup, David *(Orchestrations)* 4160
Lines, Harry *(Set Design)* 2195
Ling, Richie *(Cast)* 252, 308, 1154, 1594, 2507, 3768, 3994, 4624
Ling, Ritchie *(Cast)* 1521
Lingard, William *(Composer)* 1897
Lingard, William *(Lyricist)* 1897
Lingard, William Horace *(Lyricist)* 3989
Linhart, Buzzy *(Composer)* 4449
Linhart, Buzzy *(Lyricist)* 4449
Liniva Productions, Inc. *(Producer)* 4701
Link, Harry *(Composer)* 39, 478, 1813
Link, Harry *(Lyricist)* 478
Link, Peter *(Cast)* 3824
Link, Peter *(Composer)* 1139, 1620, 2318, 2659, 3000, 3724, 3824, 4615
Link, Peter *(Librettist)* 3824
Link, Peter *(Lyricist)* 2659, 3000, 3724, 3824, 4615
Link, William *(Librettist)* 2820, 4303, 4543
Link, William *(Lyricist)* 4543
Linkey, Henry *(Cast)* 2694
Linley, Betty *(Cast)* 3596
Linn, Bambi *(Cast)* 660, 1679, 2048, 2837
Linn, Ben *(Librettist)* 3203
Linn, Diana *(Cast)* 2267
Linn, John *(Cast)* 3446
Linn, Margaret *(Cast)* 1999
Linn, Ralph *(Cast)* 660, 2484, 2797
Linn, Ralph *(Choreographer)* 2910
Linn, Ray *(Composer)* 2084, 2096
Linn, Ray *(Lyricist)* 2084, 2096
Linn, Ray *(Vocal Arranger)* 2084, 2096
Linn Jr., Ray *(Vocal Arranger)* 2092, 2094, 2095
Linn-Baker, Mark *(Cast)* 54, 1015, 1077, 2787
Linne, Hans *(Composer)* 2710
Linne, Hans *(Musical Director)* 2710
Linne, Hans S. *(Composer)* 8, 2261
Linne, Hans S. *(Musical Director)* 2261, 2667, 4285
Linnit & Dunfee *(Producer)* 1386
Linsenmann, George W. *(Composer)* 427
Linthicum, Lotta *(Cast)* 4050
Linti, Arnoldo *(Cast)* 3639
Linton, Bill *(Cast)* 62
Linton, Harry *(Author)* 3068
Linton, Harry *(Composer)* 2465, 4691
Linton, W. *(Composer)* 4193
Linton, W. *(Lyricist)* 4193
Linz *(Composer)* 2162
Linz *(Lyricist)* 2162
Linzberg, Julius *(Musical Director)* 1482
Lion, Margo *(Producer)* 2200
Lion Theatre Company *(Producer)* 3010
Lionel Productions *(Producer)* 3898
Liotta, Jerome *(Lighting Designer)* 2067
Lipman, Clara *(Cast)* 1540, 4298
Lipner, Nancy *(Cast)* 3764
Lippa, Andrew *(Composer)* 2224
Lippa, Andrew *(Dance Arranger)* 1630
Lippa, Andrew *(Librettist)* 2224
Lippa, Andrew *(Orchestrations)* 1630
Lippa, Andrew E. *(Cast)* 4732
Lippen, Renee *(Cast)* 3564
Lipper, Arthur *(Producer)* 3822
Lipper Productions *(Producer)* 3987
Lippman, Sidney *(Composer)* 304
Lippmann, Arthur *(Lyricist)* 1207
Lippmann, Robert *(Composer)* 1956
Lippmann, Robert K. *(Composer)* 4308
Lipscott, Alan *(Librettist)* 2301, 3713, 4586
Lipson, Ann K. *(Composer)* 3654
Lipson, Ann K. *(Lyricist)* 3654
Lipson, Arthur *(Cast)* 2262, 3740
Lipson, Paul *(Cast)* 657, 4542
Lipton *(Composer)* 246
Lipton *(Lyricist)* 246
Lipton, Celia *(Cast)* 2227, 2680
Lipton, Dan *(Composer)* 2528, 3193
Lipton, Dan *(Lyricist)* 2528, 3827
Lipton, George *(Cast)* 153
Lipton, Holly T. *(Cast)* 3167
Lipton, James *(Librettist)* 2887, 3210, 3931
Lipton, James *(Lyricist)* 327, 2887, 3210, 3931
Lipton, Richard *(Producer)* 1229
Lisa, Luba *(Cast)* 656, 1841, 2053, 4332
Lisanby, Charles *(Costumes)* 71
Lisanby, Charles *(Set Design)* 71, 2689, 3637
Liss, Joe *(Cast)* 4690

Lissauer, John *(Orchestrations)* 1770
Lissauer, Robert *(Producer)* 1770
Lister, Lance *(Cast)* 3291
Lister, Laurie *(Director)* 194
Liston, Dave *(Cast)* 2013
Lisz, Gary *(Costumes)* 908
Litel, John B. *(Cast)* 2148
Lithgow, John *(Cast)* 4109
Litomy, Leslie *(Cast)* 3082, 3990
Litomy, Leslie *(Vocal Arranger)* 1286
Litt, Jim *(Musical Director)* 922
Littau, Frank *(Composer)* 1481
Littau, Frank *(Lyricist)* 1481
Littau, Joseph *(Musical Director)* 653, 660, 2615, 3152, 3895, 4366, 4586
Litten, Jim *(Cast)* 2472, 3743
Little, Cleavon *(Cast)* 2218, 3610
Little, Eric *(Lyricist)* 605, 4765, 4795
Little, George A. *(Composer)* 879, 3405
Little, George A. *(Lyricist)* 567, 879, 3405
Little, J. *(Composer)* 3953
Little, Little Jack *(Composer)* 3375
Little Billie *(Cast)* 804
Little Billy *(Cast)* 2
Little Jr., Bascom *(Composer)* 1342
Little Prince Productions *(Producer)* 2539
Little Theatre Playes *(Producer)* 524
Littlefield, Carl *(Choreographer)* 1941
Littlefield, Carl *(Director)* 1941
Littlefield, Catherine *(Choreographer)* 117, 924, 1284, 1336, 1423, 1931, 2023, 2024, 2098, 2099, 2161, 2162, 4143
Littlefield, Catherine *(Director)* 1782, 2023, 2024, 2098, 2099, 4143
Littlefield, Emma *(Cast)* 1746, 4277
Littlefield, James *(Lyricist)* 1782
Littlefield, Lucien *(Cast)* 4602
Littler, Emile *(Lyricist)* 3756
Littler, Emile *(Producer)* 3756
Littlewood, Joan *(Director)* 874, 1277, 2572, 3259, 4469
Littlewood, Joan *(Librettist)* 3259
Liturgy of the Roman Mass *(Lyricist)* 2775
Litvinoff, Si *(Producer)* 2047
Litwack, Ned C. *(Producer)* 1811
Litwin, Burton L. *(Producer)* 4091, 4137
Litz, Katherine *(Cast)* 283, 2243
Litz, Katherine *(Choreographer)* 283, 2243
Lively, DeLee *(Cast)* 4031
Lively, William Fleet *(Choreographer)* 1997, 2674, 4775
Lively and Yiddish Co., The *(Producer)* 2421
Livent (U.S.) Inc. *(Producer)* 2333
Liveright *(Producer)* 1283
Liverpool, Charles *(Cast)* 646
Livings, George *(Cast)* 643
Livingston, Billy *(Costumes)* 63, 67, 622, 853, 854, 856, 857, 858, 859, 860, 864, 865, 1476, 2023, 2024, 2098, 2400, 2475, 3138, 3365, 3907, 4058, 4677, 4824
Livingston, Fudd *(Orchestrations)* 612, 1827
Livingston, Jay *(Composer)* 2057, 2449, 3182, 3234, 3841, 4197, 4321
Livingston, Jay *(Lyricist)* 2057, 2449, 3182, 3234, 3841, 4197, 4274, 4321
Livingston, Jerry *(Composer)* 532, 1040, 1716, 1951, 2182, 2925, 3558
Livingston, Jerry *(Lyricist)* 1040
Livingston, Johnny *(Cast)* 641
Livingston, Robert H. *(Director)* 1279, 2018, 2801, 3871, 4272
Livingston, Robert H. *(Librettist)* 1279
Llewellyn, Dorothy *(Cast)* 637
Llewellyn, Richard *(Author)* 4384
Lloyd, Bernard *(Cast)* 2240
Lloyd, Christopher *(Cast)* 1755
Lloyd, Evans *(Composer)* 295, 830, 4181
Lloyd, Evans *(Lyricist)* 295
Lloyd, Florence *(Cast)* 2131
Lloyd, George *(Cast)* 3292, 4394
Lloyd, Henry *(Composer)* 364
Lloyd, Jack *(Cast)* 185
Lloyd, Jack *(Lyricist)* 2148
Lloyd, Jay *(Cast)* 4273
Lloyd, John Robert *(Lighting Designer)* 90
Lloyd, John Robert *(Set Design)* 90
Lloyd, Kevin *(Cast)* 3111
Lloyd, Norman *(Cast)* 2257
Lloyd, Norman *(Director)* 1600
Lloyd, Pat *(Cast)* 1257
Lloyd, Violet *(Cast)* 3213
Lloyd Webber, Andrew *(Composer)* 211, 678, 1211, 2212, 2242, 3464, 4068, 4138, 4217, 4301
Lloyd Webber, Andrew *(Librettist)* 211, 3464
Lloyd Webber, Andrew *(Orchestrations)* 211, 678, 1211, 2212, 3464, 4068, 4138, 4217
Lloyd-King, Richard *(Cast)* 730
Loane, Mary *(Cast)* 3931
Lobato, Eber *(Composer)* 2356
Lobato, Eber *(Lyricist)* 2356
Lobban, Lynn *(Cast)* 3631
Lobel, Adrianne *(Set Design)* 2320, 3060, 3411
Loblov, Bela *(Musical Director)* 266
Lobos, Alan *(Cast)* 239
Local 840, U.A.W. *(Producer)* 985
Locatelli, Basillio *(Author)* 825
Locher, Robert E. *(Costumes)* 1686, 2180, 4637
Locher, Robert E. *(Set Design)* 1686
Lochner, Robert E. *(Set Design)* 2788
Locke, Charles *(Lyricist)* 3290
Locke, Charles O. *(Director)* 4670
Locke, Charles O. *(Librettist)* 948, 4670
Locke, Charles O. *(Lyricist)* 948, 1836, 4665, 4670
Locke, Edward *(Author)* 1098
Locke, Edward *(Cast)* 3050
Locke, Edward *(Librettist)* 2602
Locke, Edward *(Lyricist)* 1098
Locke, R. *(Lyricist)* 670
Locke, Ralph *(Cast)* 125, 3248
Locke, Sam *(Librettist)* 2447, 3226, 4394, 4542, 4577
Locke, Shamus *(Producer)* 649
Locke, W.J. *(Author)* 2952
Locker, Robert E. *(Costumes)* 2788, 3005

Lockhart, Calvin *(Cast)* 3690
Lockhart, Gene *(Cast)* 584, 2940, 3727, 4569
Lockhart, Gene *(Composer)* 584
Lockhart, Gene *(Director)* 584
Lockhart, Gene *(Librettist)* 584
Lockhart, Gene *(Lyricist)* 584
Lockhart, Helen *(Cast)* 2271
Lockhart, Warren *(Librettist)* 4034
Lockhart, Warren L. *(Producer)* 499
Lockheart, Paula *(Composer)* 4076
Lockheart, Paula *(Librettist)* 4076
Lockheart, Paula *(Lyricist)* 4076
Lockin, Danny *(Cast)* 2958
Locknay, Clement *(Composer)* 1078
Lockway, Gertrude *(Cast)* 283
Lockwood, Ruth Mary *(Cast)* 2174
Lodeizen, Hans *(Lyricist)* 1865
Loden, Barbara *(Cast)* 1358
Lodge, Henry Cabot *(Composer)* 3005
Lodge, John *(Cast)* 3152
Lodge, Thomas *(Lyricist)* 2633
Lodin, Jeff *(Musical Director)* 3555
Lodin, Jeff *(Vocal Arranger)* 3555
Loeb, John Jacob *(Composer)* 2750, 3002
Loeb, John Jacob *(Librettist)* 3371
Loeb, John Jacob *(Lyricist)* 177, 2750, 3371
Loeb, Philip *(Cast)* 294, 711, 1322, 1447, 1448, 2265, 2444, 2504, 2827, 3990
Loeb, Philip *(Director)* 1446, 1447, 1448, 2748, 3365, 3893, 4256
Loebell, Marc *(Cast)* 1655, 1657
Loebell, Marc *(Lyricist)* 1653, 1655, 1656, 1657
Loesser, Emily *(Cast)* 4399, 4769
Loesser, Frank
See also Frank Productions.
Loesser, Frank *(Author)* 1741
Loesser, Frank *(Composer)* 7, 1698, 1706, 1741, 1880, 2019, 2961, 3261, 3262, 3444, 3460, 3526, 3875, 4009, 4332, 4399, 4578, 4652
Loesser, Frank *(Librettist)* 1698, 2961, 3526, 3875
Loesser, Frank *(Lyricist)* 7, 39, 1698, 1706, 1741, 1880, 1937, 2019, 2076, 2105, 2400, 2961, 3178, 3261, 3262, 3444, 3460, 3526, 3875, 4009, 4332, 4399, 4578, 4652, 4824
Loesser, Lynn *(Producer)* 649, 2961
Loew, Steve *(Lighting Designer)* 1695
Loewe, Frederick *(Composer)* 530, 623, 999, 1511, 1670, 2479, 3018, 3038, 3290, 3347, 3457, 3823, 4593, 4640
Loewe, Frederick *(Lyricist)* 2105, 2611
Loewe, Frederick *(Pianist)* 3290
Loewe, Frederick *(Producer)* 623
Loewy, Peter J. *(Director)* 4107
Loften, Amy *(Cast)* 4184
Loftus, Cecilia *(Cast)* 1095, 2821
Loftus, Cissie *(Composer)* 352, 3999
Loftus, Cissie *(Lyricist)* 352, 3999
Loftus, Gladys *(Cast)* 4852
Logan, Ella *(Cast)* 622, 1278, 1416, 1494, 1879, 3307, 4086
Logan, Frederic Knight *(Composer)* 2662
Logan, Frederic Knight *(Incidental Music)* 2662
Logan, Frederic Knight *(Lyricist)* 2662
Logan, Jack *(Set Design)* 2633, 4584
Logan, Jenny *(Cast)* 846
Logan, Joshua *(Choreographer)* 4096, 4718
Logan, Joshua *(Director)* 64, 153, 601, 716, 1242, 1749, 1894, 1990, 2027, 2061, 2344, 2583, 2898, 2983, 4096, 4142, 4483, 4718, 4749
Logan, Joshua *(Librettist)* 1242, 1894, 2027, 2898, 4718
Logan, Joshua *(Lyricist)* 2027
Logan, Joshua *(Producer)* 1242, 4096, 4718
Logan, Marjorie *(Cast)* 1979
Logan, Michael *(Cast)* 3482
Logan, Stacey *(Cast)* 330
Logan, Stanley *(Cast)* 2526
Logan, Stanley *(Director)* 1113, 3012
Logan, Tom *(Cast)* 434
Logue, Christopher *(Composer)* 1195
Logue, Christopher *(Lyricist)* 1195
Logue, Spain *(Cast)* 169
Loguillon, Lisa *(Cast)* 756
Lohmuller, Bernard *(Producer)* 4741
Lohmuller, Bernard *(Set Design)* 1126
Lohmuller and Phillips *(Lighting Designer)* 2950
Lohner-Beda, Fritz *(Author)* 277, 1384, 3573, 4792
Lois, Edith *(Lyricist)* 637
Lollos, John *(Director)* 2599
Lollos, John *(Librettist)* 2599
Lollos, John *(Lyricist)* 2599
Lomakina *(Cast)* 710
Loman, Hal *(Cast)* 1892, 2987
Loman, Jules *(Lyricist)* 2255, 3442
Loman, Michael *(Librettist)* 2542, 2578
Lomax, Bess *(Lyricist)* 2246
Lombard, Michael *(Cast)* 3142
Lombard, Peter *(Cast)* 3564, 4595, 4696
Lombardi, Frank *(Cast)* 3411
Lombardi, Linda *(Set Design)* 3905
Lombardo, Carmen *(Composer)* 177, 1481, 2750, 3371
Lombardo, Carmen *(Librettist)* 3371
Lombardo, Carmen *(Lyricist)* 2750
Lombardo, Carmen *(Producer)* 3371
Lombardo, Guy *(Producer)* 177, 190, 2750
London, Becky *(Cast)* 3606
London, Gene *(Costumes)* 785
London, Marc *(Cast)* 3863
London, Marc *(Librettist)* 4627
Lonergan, John *(Choreographer)* 637, 3735, 4291
Lonergan, John *(Director)* 4291
Lonergan, John E. *(Choreographer)* 680, 4545
Lonergan, Lenore *(Cast)* 59, 1734, 3563
Lonergan, Lester *(Director)* 1144
Lonergan Jr., Lester *(Cast)* 2175
Long *(Composer)* 3259
Long *(Lyricist)* 3259
Long, Avon *(Cast)* 341, 435, 576, 651, 880, 1074, 1319, 1474, 1476, 2275, 2817, 2898, 2994, 3707, 3782, 3966, 4281, 4557
Long, J.P. *(Lyricist)* 3193
Long, Johnny Lee *(Cast)* 439, 1989
Long, Johnny Lee *(Librettist)* 1989

Long, Kenn *(Cast)* 4431
Long, Kenn *(Composer)* 4431
Long, Kenn *(Librettist)* 4431
Long, Kenn *(Lyricist)* 4431
Long, Lois *(Composer)* 924
Long, Lois *(Lyricist)* 924
Long, Ray *(Cast)* 3914
Long, Shorty *(Cast)* 2961
Long, Sumner Arthur *(Author)* 3097
Long, Tamara *(Cast)* 956, 2590
Long, Walter *(Cast)* 512, 1336
Long, William Ivey *(Costumes)* 119, 212, 544, 754, 921, 1186, 1873, 2307, 2702, 3171, 3175, 4020, 4031, 4399, 4619
Long Jr., Nick *(Cast)* 324, 1338, 2342, 2569, 2597, 2990, 3850, 3924, 4170, 4226, 4372
Long Wharf Theatre *(Producer)* 4109, 4601
Longbottom, Robert *(Choreographer)* 3346
Longbottom, Robert *(Director)* 3346
Longpre, Guy *(Cast)* 2097
Longstaffe, Ernest *(Musical Director)* 1610
Longstreet, Stephen *(Author)* 1886
Longstreet, Stephen *(Librettist)* 1886
Lonner, Mara *(Costumes)* 562
Lonsdale, Frederick *(Author)* 2698
Lonsdale, Frederick *(Librettist)* 276, 379, 2293, 2317, 2384, 2392, 2698, 2937
Lonsdale, Harold *(Composer)* 2341, 3322
Loomis, Frederick *(Cast)* 1185
Loomis, Joe *(Cast)* 981
Loomis Sisters, The *(Cast)* 1481, 1492
Looney, Jay *(Librettist)* 4416
Loos, Anita *(Author)* 715, 1475, 1749, 1750, 4043
Loos, Anita *(Director)* 4043
Loos, Anita *(Librettist)* 98, 1475, 1596, 1750, 3172, 3349
Loper, Don *(Cast)* 3292, 4557
Loper, Don *(Costumes)* 847
Loper, Don *(Director)* 847
Lopez, Jess *(Cast)* 214
Lopez, Lilian *(Lyricist)* 576
Lopez, Paul *(Costumes)* 2482
Lopez, Perry N. *(Composer)* 722
Lopez, Priscilla *(Cast)* 521, 746, 1000, 2659, 3197, 4635
Lopez, Vincent *(Cast)* 2601
Lopez, Vincent *(Musical Director)* 3100
Lopez and His Orchestra, Vincent *(Cast)* 1690, 3717
Loquasto, Santo *(Costumes)* 109, 693, 1633, 1649, 3838
Loquasto, Santo *(Set Design)* 109, 496, 693, 952, 1633, 2318, 2435, 3838, 3992, 4151
Lor, Denise *(Cast)* 3811
Loraine, Oscar *(Musical Director)* 2298
Lorber, Martha *(Cast)* 4352
Lord, Arthur *(Lyricist)* 1946
Lord, Frederick *(Cast)* 3157
Lord, Frederick *(Choreographer)* 1855
Lord, Helen *(Cast)* 2906
Lord, Mindret *(Librettist)* 3103, 3104
Lord, Philip *(Cast)* 1387, 1856, 2747, 4651
Lord, Philip *(Librettist)* 1447
Lord, Robert *(Lyricist)* 1944, 1946
Lord, Sylvia *(Cast)* 679
Loredo, Armando *(Composer)* 3495
Loredo, Armando *(Lyricist)* 3495
Lorenz, Fred *(Cast)* 3698
Lorenz, Herbert Richard
See also Herbert Fields, Richard Rodgers and Lorenz Hart.
Lorenz, Herbert Richard *(Author)* 2814
Lorenz, Herbert Richard *(Composer)* 2814
Lorenz, Herbert Richard *(Lyricist)* 2814
Lorenz, Mort *(Cast)* 2335
Loretta, Dee *(Cast)* 2216
Lorette, Mariette *(Choreographer)* 396, 1901
Lorick, Robert *(Lyricist)* 546, 1770, 4286
Lorin, Will *(Composer)* 2167, 3874
Loring, Ernest *(Choreographer)* 1681
Loring, Estelle *(Cast)* 2940
Loring, Eugene *(Choreographer)* 596, 653, 3972
Loring, Eugene *(Director)* 596
Loring, Michael *(Cast)* 3990, 4677
Loring, Sue *(Cast)* 4834
Lorne, Marion *(Cast)* 961
Lorraine, Betty *(Cast)* 861
Lorraine, Lillian *(Cast)* 468, 2494, 2892, 3222, 3332, 4657, 4803, 4804, 4805, 4806, 4812, 4831, 4838, 4842, 4849, 4851
Lorraine, Roy *(Cast)* 2514
Lorraine, Ted *(Cast)* 473, 2419, 2816, 2856, 2966, 3333, 3962
Lorraine, William *(Composer)* 1274, 2454, 3437, 3560
Lorraine, William *(Musical Director)* 2454, 3045, 4589
Lorraine and Walton *(Cast)* 684
Lortel, Lucille *(Producer)* 3615
Lorwin, Liza *(Producer)* 1636
Los Angeles Civic Light Opera *(Producer)* 1369
Losch, Tilly *(Cast)* 294, 4581
Losch, Tilly *(Choreographer)* 429, 1440, 4341, 4581
Losee, Harry *(Choreographer)* 216, 2300, 4557
Lotito, Mark *(Cast)* 2229
Lott, Lawrence *(Cast)* 3198
Lotti, Antonio *(Composer)* 1589
Loud, David *(Dance Arranger)* 131
Loud, David *(Musical Director)* 131, 3368
Loudon, Dorothy *(Cast)* 150, 154, 287, 826, 1273, 2208, 2568, 3196, 3210, 4746
Loughrane, Basil *(Cast)* 2351
Loughrey, J.B. *(Lyricist)* 954, 1569
Louiguy *(Composer)* 2356
Louis, Jean *(Costumes)* 3493
Louis, Murray *(Choreographer)* 2441
Louis, Murray *(Director)* 2441
Louise, Mary *(Cast)* 483, 1319, 4192, 4517
Louise, Merle *(Cast)* 705, 832, 2143, 2333, 2360, 4233, 4319
Louise, Tina *(Cast)* 1227, 2227, 4499
Louys, Pierre *(Author)* 165
Love, Clarence *(Musical Director)* 1248
Love, Darlene *(Cast)* 661, 2427
Love, Dorothy *(Director)* 692
Love, Dorothy *(Librettist)* 692

Love, Dorothy *(Producer)* 692, 4789
Love, Ed *(Choreographer)* 4533
Love, Edmond *(Cast)* 4066
Love, Edmund G. *(Author)* 4190
Love, Edward *(Cast)* 682
Love, Edward *(Choreographer)* 4
Love, Kermit *(Costumes)* 1286, 3301
Love, Mike *(Composer)* 3695, 3739
Love, Mike *(Lyricist)* 3695, 3739
Love and Let Love Company *(Producer)* 2599
Lovejoy, Alec *(Cast)* 2881
Lovejoy, Alex *(Cast)* 2640
Lovelace, Henrietta *(Cast)* 2225
Loveland, Carl *(Lyricist)* 1443
Lovelass, Henrietta *(Cast)* 14
Loveless, David *(Costumes)* 261
Lovell, Katherine H. *(Costumes)* 712
Lovelle, Louise *(Cast)* 2034
Lovett, Josephine *(Cast)* 4407, 4605
Lovett, Marcus *(Cast)* 2442
Lovitt, Shifee *(Cast)* 4172
Lovreiglo, Chavalier *(Musical Director)* 4672
Low, Betty *(Cast)* 2887
Low, Colin *(Set Design)* 1062
Lowden, Ronald *(Composer)* 4093, 4303, 4543, 4679
Lowe, Allen *(Librettist)* 1021, 2159, 2286, 2868
Lowe, Allen *(Lyricist)* 1021, 2286, 2868
Lowe, Charles *(Producer)* 3954
Lowe, David *(Producer)* 2629
Lowe, Enid *(Cast)* 4519
Lowe, Frank *(Librettist)* 4336
Lowe, Gwen Hiller *(Cast)* 556
Lowe, Gwen Hiller *(Choreographer)* 556
Lowe, Jackie *(Cast)* 4701
Lowe, John *(Cast)* 1551
Lowe, John V. *(Cast)* 1250
Lowe, John V. *(Choreographer)* 1250
Lowe, Milton *(Lighting Designer)* 4792
Lowe, Mundell *(Orchestrations)* 2084, 2095, 2096
Lowe, Ralph *(Cast)* 3810
Lowe, Ruth *(Composer)* 3175
Lowe, Ruth *(Lyricist)* 3175
Lowe, Sammy *(Musical Director)* 2164
Lowell, Helen *(Cast)* 3679
Lowenstein, David *(Cast)* 2022, 4462
Lowenstein, David *(Choreographer)* 2022
Lowenstein, Sonia *(Costumes)* 3215, 3491, 4623
Lowenstein, Sonia *(Set Design)* 1924
Lowery, Robert J. *(Composer)* 1216
Lowery, Robert J. *(Lyricist)* 1216
Lowitz, John *(Lyricist)* 295
Lowitz, John B. *(Composer)* 2996
Lowitz, John B. *(Lyricist)* 2671, 3085, 4697
Lowitz, John B. "Swifty" *(Composer)* 4762
Lowitz, John B. "Swifty" *(Lyricist)* 4762
Lowman, Jay *(Cast)* 4454
Lowman, Sarah *(Cast)* 1897
Lowrie, Jeannette *(Cast)* 1388, 2871
Lowry, Edward *(Cast)* 4661
Lowry, Terence *(Composer)* 736
Lowry, Terence *(Lyricist)* 736
LuPone, Patti *(Cast)* 109, 273, 1211, 4744
LuPone, Robert *(Cast)* 746, 2420, 2440, 2687, 2874, 3088, 3196, 4252
Luard, Nicholas *(Producer)* 1195
Lubell, Lily *(Cast)* 1651, 1657
Lubin, Harry *(Composer)* 3995
Lubin, Harry *(Musical Director)* 3995
Lubliner, Sheldon R. *(Producer)* 4114
Luboff, Norman *(Arrangements)* 928
Luboff, Norman *(Musical Director)* 928, 2267
Luboff Choir, Norman *(Cast)* 928
Lubovitch, Lar *(Choreographer)* 2143, 3682
Lubritzky, David *(Choreographer)* 3336
Lucas, Craig *(Cast)* 2764, 3928
Lucas, Craig *(Librettist)* 4358
Lucas, David *(Musical Director)* 1612
Lucas, George *(Author)* 4135
Lucas, Jamilah *(Cast)* 3936
Lucas, Jeanne *(Cast)* 3542
Lucas, Jonathan *(Cast)* 1600, 4432
Lucas, Jonathan *(Choreographer)* 128, 759, 1290, 3890, 4566
Lucas, Jonathan *(Director)* 128, 1436, 3890
Lucas, Marie *(Arrangements)* 1821
Lucas, Marie *(Composer)* 1821
Lucas, Mitzy *(Cast)* 2413
Lucas, Nick *(Cast)* 3953
Lucas, Philip *(Cast)* 2011
Lucas, R. Scott *(Producer)* 1249
Lucas, Roxie *(Cast)* 1776, 3364
Lucas, Sam *(Cast)* 3676
Luce, Claire *(Cast)* 1011, 1338, 1453, 3009, 4821
Luce, Claire Booth *(Cast)* 3179
Luce, Ted *(Librettist)* 67, 137, 4377
Luce, William *(Librettist)* 3851
Lucey, Leola *(Cast)* 3729
Lucille *(Costumes)* 2148, 2509, 3256, 3618, 3663, 3740, 4327, 4603, 4812, 4813
Luckey, Susan *(Cast)* 4270
Luckham, Claire *(Librettist)* 4295
Luckham, Claire *(Lyricist)* 4295
Luckinbill, Laurence *(Cast)* 1977
Luckstone, Harry *(Cast)* 4218
Lucy Productions Corp. *(Producer)* 2692
Luders, Gustav *(Composer)* 586, 604, 1230, 1650, 1707, 2315, 2715, 2745, 3268, 3578, 3943, 4046, 4064, 4738
Luders, Gustav *(Musical Director)* 604, 3578, 4738
Ludlow, Ben *(Orchestrations)* 620, 1286, 1546
Ludlow, Henning *(Composer)* 1604, 4303, 4543
Ludlow, Henning *(Lyricist)* 1604, 4303
Ludlow, Patrick *(Cast)* 429
Ludlow Jr., Ben *(Orchestrations)* 2464
Ludlum, Edward *(Director)* 2321
Ludlum, John Plumer *(Set Design)* 3605
Ludwig, Arthur *(Cast)* 3772
Ludwig, Ken *(Librettist)* 921
Ludwig, the Wonder Horse *(Cast)* 2640
Luescher, Mark A.
See also Werba & Luescher.

Luescher, Mark A. *(Producer)* 2528, 2886, 4119
Luetters, Ray *(Cast)* 1903
Luftig, Hal *(Producer)* 261
Lugg, William *(Cast)* 1454
Lugosi, Bela *(Cast)* 3002
Luigs, Jim *(Librettist)* 992
Luigs, Jim *(Lyricist)* 992
Luisi, James *(Cast)* 1060, 4238, 4862
Lukas, Paul *(Cast)* 619
Luke, Keye *(Cast)* 1315
Luker, Rebecca *(Cast)* 3464, 3862
Lum, Alvin *(Cast)* 757, 775, 3201
Lumet, Baruch *(Cast)* 1196
Lumet, Sidney *(Cast)* 1196, 1299
Lumet, Sidney *(Director)* 1742, 2975, 3210
Lumet, Sidney *(Producer)* 2975
Luna, Barbara *(Cast)* 4096
Lunceford, Jimmy *(Composer)* 432, 4743
Lunceford and His Orchestra, Jimmy *(Cast)* 880, 882
Lund, Alan *(Choreographer)* 148, 1255, 3818
Lund, Alan *(Director)* 148, 1255
Lund, Art *(Cast)* 521, 1076, 2961, 3224, 4090
Lund, Blanche *(Choreographer)* 3818
Lund, Erika *(Cast)* 3
Lund, Hettice *(Cast)* 3777
Lund, John *(Cast)* 1140, 3105
Lund, John *(Composer)* 68
Lund, John *(Librettist)* 3105
Lund, John *(Lyricist)* 3105
Lund, John *(Musical Director)* 68, 252, 2915, 3567, 4497
Lundborg, Arne *(Set Design)* 2105
Lundell, Kert *(Set Design)* 40, 518, 1074, 1596, 3159, 4089, 4591
Lundell, Kurt *(Set Design)* 3741, 4004
Lunden, Jeffrey *(Composer)* 158, 4708
Lundy, Pat *(Cast)* 2616
Luner, Fritz *(Librettist)* 1043
Luner, Fritz *(Lyricist)* 1043
Luneska, Gene *(Cast)* 1430
Lupino, Barry *(Cast)* 3737
Lupino, Stanley *(Cast)* 3084, 3163, 3467
Lurenz, Betty *(Costumes)* 2436
Lurie, Carol *(Cast)* 1068
Lurie, Victor *(Producer)* 4447
Lusby, Ruby *(Lyricist)* 3155
Lusby, Vernon *(Cast)* 3294
Lusby, Vernon *(Choreographer)* 392, 681, 1018
Lusby, Vernon *(Director)* 392
Lusk, Milton *(Composer)* 968, 1868, 1869, 1870
Lusk, Milton W. *(Composer)* 115, 1867, 4115
Lussier, Laura *(Cast)* 1391
Lussier, R. Robert *(Lighting Designer)* 344
Lussier, R. Robert *(Producer)* 3939
Lustberg, Arch *(Cast)* 3530
Lustberg, Arch *(Director)* 3530
Lustberg, Arch *(Producer)* 1072, 3530, 4468
Lustig, Alexander *(Additional Music)* 3670
Lustig, Alexander *(Composer)* 2866
Lustig, I. *(Composer)* 2421
Luther, Frank *(Composer)* 4409
Luther, Frank *(Librettist)* 204
Luther, Frank *(Lyricist)* 4409
Luther, Harry H. *(Lyricist)* 2902
Lutken, David M. *(Cast)* 1969
Lutkus III, Frank Charles *(Cast)* 544
Luttrell, Helen *(Cast)* 929
Lutvak, Steven *(Composer)* 1740
Lutvak, Steven *(Incidental Music)* 1740
Lutvak, Steven *(Lyricist)* 1740
Lutyens, Edith *(Costumes)* 933
Lutz, Meyer *(Composer)* 175, 1537
Lux, Lillian *(Cast)* 2811, 3669
Luz, Franc *(Cast)* 2544
Lydecker, George *(Cast)* 1538, 2730, 3193, 3308, 3748
Lydercker, George *(Cast)* 2407
Lydiard, Robert *(Cast)* 164
Lyding, George *(Musical Director)* 1803
Lyle, Jack *(Cast)* 1759
Lyles, Aubrey L. *(Cast)* 697, 988, 1488, 1667, 1678, 2302, 3089, 3660, 3808, 3963, 4198, 4844
Lyles, Aubrey L. *(Composer)* 813
Lyles, Aubrey L. *(Director)* 3660
Lyles, Aubrey L. *(Librettist)* 813, 988, 1960, 2044, 2302, 2721, 3089, 3337, 3808, 3963
Lyles, Aubrey L. *(Lyricist)* 813, 2044
Lyles, Aubrey L. *(Producer)* 813, 1960
Lylleton, Trevor *(Composer)* 1000
Lyman, Abe
  See also Abe Lyman Orchestra and Abe Lyman and His Californians.
Lyman, Abe *(Composer)* 544, 3149
Lyman, Abe *(Lyricist)* 544
Lyman, Abe *(Musical Director)* 1951
Lyman, Dorothy *(Director)* 908
Lyman, Tommy *(Composer)* 452
Lyman, Tommy *(Lyricist)* 452
Lyman Orchestra, Abe
  See also Abe Lyman and Abe Lyman and His Californians.
Lyman Orchestra, Abe *(Cast)* 851
Lyman Twins *(Cast)* 4756
Lyman and His Californians, Abe
  See also Abe Lyman and Abe Lyman Orchestra.
Lyman and His Californians, Abe *(Cast)* 2460
Lymon, Frankie *(Composer)* 166, 3739, 4534
Lymon, Frankie *(Lyricist)* 166, 3739, 4534
Lynch, Hal *(Cast)* 4111
Lynch, Louise Teddy *(Cast)* 3103
Lynch, Michael *(Cast)* 2205
Lynch, Teddy *(Cast)* 1342
Lynch, Thomas *(Set Design)* 146, 3039
Lynch, Tom *(Set Design)* 1164, 4390, 4412
Lynch Jr., Kenneth *(Cast)* 1924
Lynd, Helen *(Cast)* 1136, 2105, 3650, 4209
Lyndal, Percy *(Cast)* 531
Lynde, Janice *(Cast)* 3368
Lynde, Paul *(Cast)* 607, 817, 1047, 3107, 3800
Lynde, Paul *(Director)* 3108
Lynde, Paul *(Librettist)* 3107, 3108, 3110, 4627

Lyndeck, Edmund *(Cast)* 190, 1068, 2143, 2820, 2928, 3897, 4233
Lyndhurst, F.L. *(Set Design)* 475, 1333, 2547, 3583, 4320
Lyndon, Richard *(Cast)* 846
Lyne, Felice *(Cast)* 1743
Lyng, Nora Mae *(Cast)* 1348, 3708, 4701
Lynley, Carol *(Cast)* 2267
Lynn, Amber *(Cast)* 392
Lynn, Bambi *(Cast)* 1933, 3263
Lynn, Eleanor *(Cast)* 4256
Lynn, Jonathan *(Director)* 2949
Lynn, Joyce *(Cast)* 239
Lynn, Judanna *(Costumes)* 2658
Lynn, Judy *(Cast)* 4423
Lynn, Lee *(Costumes)* 3814
Lynn, Mara *(Cast)* 483
Lynn-Thomas, Derrick *(Producer)* 3664
Lynne, Carol *(Cast)* 1782, 3388, 4143
Lynne, Gillian *(Choreographer)* 211, 678, 2014, 3464, 3482, 3731
Lynne, Phyllis *(Cast)* 4428
Lynton, Everett *(Composer)* 605
Lynton, Everett *(Lyricist)* 605
Lyon, Annabelle *(Cast)* 1670
Lyon, Ben *(Cast)* 1939
Lyon, Marisa *(Cast)* 1695
Lyon, Milton *(Director)* 1815
Lyon, Sue *(Cast)* 3410
Lyon, Wanda *(Cast)* 2121, 3489, 3921, 4730
Lyons, Colette *(Cast)* 1494
Lyons, Jeff *(Cast)* 1349, 1350
Lyons, Joe *(Cast)* 1691, 3648
Lyons, Lynda *(Cast)* 4389
Lyons, Toby *(Cast)* 4761
Lyons, Warren *(Cast)* 3338
Lyons, Warren *(Producer)* 1999
Lysinger, Pat *(Cast)* 4252
Lytell, Bert *(Cast)* 2386
Lytell, W.H. *(Librettist)* 1466
Lythgow, David *(Cast)* 284, 2986
Lytton, Henry A. *(Cast)* 4663
Lytton Jr., Henry *(Cast)* 1128

M

M & P Enterprises *(Producer)* 430
M Square Entertainment *(Producer)* 747
M Square Productions *(Producer)* 140
M&M American Dance Theatre *(Producer)* 2735
M2 Entertainment Inc *(Producer)* 478
MCA *(Producer)* 2212
MCA/Universal *(Producer)* 373, 3682
MCB Company *(Producer)* 2114
MGM Grand *(Producer)* 1159
MSO Productions *(Producer)* 99
Ma, Jason *(Cast)* 2861, 3576, 3944
Mabley, Jackie "Moms" *(Cast)* 439, 1251, 4256
MacArthur *(Composer)* 3981
MacArthur, C.E. *(Musical Director)* 1558
MacArthur, Charles *(Author)* 3279, 4703
MacArthur, Charles *(Librettist)* 1416, 2258
MacArthur, Claude *(Musical Director)* 3821
MacArthur, Claude *(Orchestrations)* 2271, 2336
MacArthur, Claude E. *(Composer)* 1424
MacArthur, James *(Cast)* 2144
MacAvoy, Dan *(Cast)* 29, 2715
MacBoyle, Darl *(Cast)* 1327
MacBoyle, Darl *(Lyricist)* 93, 1208, 1266, 1852, 2503, 2564, 3500, 3808, 4596, 4813
MacCloy, June *(Cast)* 1979
MacColl, James *(Cast)* 216, 2475, 3536
MacConnell, H.T. *(Composer)* 2465
MacConnell, Harry T. *(Composer)* 350, 666
MacCunn, Hamish *(Musical Director)* 2514
MacDermot, Galt *(Composer)* 1116, 1717, 2033, 2153, 2172, 2290, 2945, 4147, 4151, 4167, 4205, 4485, 4558
MacDermot, Galt *(Musical Director)* 1717, 2033, 2172, 4147
MacDermot, Galt *(Orchestrations)* 2033
MacDermot, Galt *(Vocal Arranger)* 2290
MacDevitt, Brian *(Lighting Designer)* 1291
MacDonagh, Donagh *(Librettist)* 1748
MacDonagh, Donagh *(Lyricist)* 1748
MacDonald, Agnes *(Lyricist)* 1652
MacDonald, Bernard *(Set Design)* 4649
MacDonald, Brian *(Choreographer)* 2681
MacDonald, Cathy *(Musical Director)* 300
MacDonald, Cathy *(Vocal Arranger)* 300
MacDonald, Charles *(Cast)* 3679
MacDonald, Christie *(Cast)* 356, 613, 727, 1030, 1188, 1720, 1925, 2532, 2725, 2848, 2889, 3575, 3585, 3943, 4103, 4119, 4250, 4430
MacDonald, Harry *(Cast)* 3372
MacDonald, James F. *(Cast)* 4298
MacDonald, James F. *(Choreographer)* 4201
MacDonald, Jeanette *(Cast)* 138, 495, 577, 638, 1244, 2686, 4213, 4283, 4392, 4766
MacDonald, Jet *(Cast)* 341, 1930
MacDonald, W.H. *(Cast)* 734, 2697
MacDonald, William H. *(Cast)* 4598
MacDonald & Sullivan *(Producer)* 308
MacDonald-Rouse, Heather *(Costumes)* 4579
MacDonnell, Kyle *(Cast)* 2707, 4432
MacDonough, Donald *(Author)* 1748
MacDonough, Glen *(Author)* 251, 3147, 3773
MacDonough, Glen *(Librettist)* 48, 208, 250, 352, 749, 902, 1177, 1199, 1228, 1599, 1613, 1845, 1919, 1920, 1922, 2160, 2232, 2328, 2830, 2858, 3096, 3129, 3466, 3627, 3773, 3999, 4203, 4563, 4735, 4767
MacDonough, Glen *(Lyricist)* 48, 126, 250, 251, 749, 824, 902, 1177, 1199, 1228, 1599, 1919, 1920, 1922, 2160, 2232, 2328, 2830, 2858, 3478, 3627, 3773, 4203, 4390, 4563, 4723, 4735, 4767, 4818
MacDonough, Harry *(Cast)* 405, 995, 1375, 1570, 2233, 2500, 2670, 3422, 3581, 3882, 4549
MacDonough, Harry *(Composer)* 2500
MacDonough Jr., Harry *(Cast)* 2334

MacFarland Productions *(Producer)* 4719
MacFarlane, George *(Cast)* 336, 340, 1518, 2469, 2854, 2907, 4121
MacFarlane, George *(Producer)* 3655
MacFarlane, George A. *(Cast)* 1295
MacGeachy, Cora *(Costumes)* 188, 378, 683, 764, 804, 1016, 1486, 1491, 1738, 1826, 1900, 1927, 2574, 2706, 2829, 2900, 3006, 3087, 3144, 3404, 3443, 3525, 3538, 3623, 3723, 3755, 3985, 4271, 4808, 4810, 4813, 4816, 4833, 4834, 4836, 4844
MacGill, Moyna *(Cast)* 507
MacGrath, Leueen *(Librettist)* 3972
MacGregor, Donald *(Composer)* 1392
MacGregor, Edgar *(Director)* 21, 608, 642, 971, 1109, 1126, 1134, 1136, 1137, 1174, 1339, 1419, 1482, 1516, 1527, 1814, 1931, 1965, 1979, 2214, 2298, 2328, 2380, 2382, 2453, 2595, 2597, 2601, 3036, 3078, 3323, 3359, 3622, 3921, 3968, 4241, 4248, 4267, 4372, 4532, 4547
MacGregor, Edgar *(Producer)* 977, 4248
MacGregor, Frank *(Director)* 1628
MacGregor, Mary Kay *(Costumes)* 528, 3165
MacIntosh, Joan *(Cast)* 1053, 4736
MacKay, Bruce *(Cast)* 1848
MacKay, Harper *(Dance Arranger)* 4798
MacKay, Harper *(Orchestrations)* 1119
MacKay, Harper *(Vocal Arranger)* 1119
MacKaye, Hazel *(Cast)* 2778
MacKaye, Percy *(Author)* 2778
MacKenzie, Alice *(Cast)* 2005
MacKenzie, Arthur *(Producer)* 3448
MacKenzie, Donald *(Cast)* 4105
MacKenzie, Gisele *(Cast)* 3182
MacKenzie, Philip *(Cast)* 840
MacLaine, Shirley *(Cast)* 3936
MacLaren, June *(Cast)* 4565
MacLarty, Scott *(Composer)* 564
MacLeish, Archibald *(Cast)* 2287, 3378
MacLeish, Archibald *(Lyricist)* 2653
MacLeish, Elizabeth *(Set Design)* 2147
MacLeod, Charles *(Lighting Designer)* 143
MacLeod, Mildred *(Cast)* 4284
MacMahon, Aline *(Cast)* 1651, 1652, 1653
MacMillan, Louis *(Director)* 3920, 4243
MacMiller Jr., Hugh *(Costumes)* 18
MacMiller Jr., Hugh *(Set Design)* 18
MacMurdo, Judy *(Cast)* 3619
MacMurrough, Dermont *(Composer)* 2662
MacMurray, Fred
See The California Collegians.
MacNaughton, Tom *(Cast)* 1228, 4119, 4228, 4250
MacQuinn, William *(Musical Director)* 2394, 2904, 4017
MacQuinn, William E. *(Musical Director)* 8, 2632, 3585, 4393, 4646
MacRae, Gordon *(Cast)* 1507, 4362
MacRae, Heather *(Cast)* 1234
MacShane, Anita *(Producer)* 593
MacSweeney, J.P. *(Cast)* 1515
MacVae, Cynthia *(Cast)* 3254
MacVeigh, Earle *(Cast)* 2786, 3823
MacWatters, Virginia *(Cast)* 2751, 2985, 3767
Macaire, Robert *(Author)* 1193
Macarthy, Henry *(Composer)* 3020
Macaulay, Joseph *(Cast)* 689, 1196, 1225, 1577, 1670, 1711, 2068, 2330, 2602, 2636, 2686, 2947, 3699, 3953, 4028, 4117, 4692
Macaulay, Tony *(Composer)* 4703
Macbeth, Robert *(Director)* 3276
Macdonald, Ballard *(Librettist)* 231, 293, 1267, 1777, 1989, 2972, 3342, 3796, 4374, 4824
Macdonald, Ballard *(Lyricist)* 231, 351, 391, 545, 638, 710, 1343, 1460, 1484, 1486, 1487, 1493, 1738, 1777, 1779, 1911, 1963, 2214, 2274, 2446, 2461, 2564, 2601, 2858, 2972, 3179, 3342, 3395, 3500, 3663, 3737, 3770, 3796, 3840, 4235, 4240, 4249, 4374, 4655, 4720, 4804, 4811, 4813, 4814, 4815, 4824, 4840, 4842, 4843, 4853
Macdonald, Billy *(Lyricist)* 419
Macdonald, Donald *(Cast)* 102, 1735, 1784, 2180, 2385, 2387, 2931, 3679
Macdonald, W.H. *(Cast)* 2345
Mace, Fred *(Cast)* 4725
Macfarlane, George *(Cast)* 2639
Macguire, R. Reid *(Set Design)* 1129
Machiz, Herbert *(Director)* 237, 842, 1498
Macho, Carole *(Choreographer)* 932
Macia, Luis *(Cast)* 1304
Macintyre, Marguerite *(Cast)* 155
Mack, Adrian *(Composer)* 1337, 4128
Mack, Andrew *(Cast)* 191, 3575, 4407, 4605
Mack, Andrew *(Composer)* 191, 3575, 4407, 4605
Mack, Andrew *(Lyricist)* 191, 3575, 4407, 4605
Mack, Billy *(Cast)* 1337
Mack, Cecil
See also Cecil Mack Choir and Cecil Mack's Southland Choir.
Mack, Cecil *(Cast)* 3808
Mack, Cecil *(Composer)* 2415, 2942, 4833
Mack, Cecil *(Director)* 4253
Mack, Cecil *(Librettist)* 3705, 4253
Mack, Cecil *(Lyricist)* 2111, 2765, 2942, 3808, 4253, 4691, 4804, 4833
Mack, Cecil *(Vocal Arranger)* 3705
Mack, Charles *(Cast)* 1128, 1132, 4814
Mack, Ernie *(Cast)* 1795
Mack, George *(Cast)* 735, 4491
Mack, George C. *(Lyricist)* 1629, 3256
Mack, George E. *(Cast)* 163, 1935, 2432, 2444, 2716, 3225, 3658, 3883, 4258
Mack, Georgie *(Cast)* 2587, 2782, 3519
Mack, Gill *(Cast)* 2056
Mack, Lavinia *(Cast)* 3660
Mack, Ollie *(Cast)* 187
Mack, Ollie *(Director)* 187
Mack, Russell *(Cast)* 97, 1368, 3042, 3434, 4276
Mack, Russell *(Director)* 3410
Mack, Stan *(Author)* 3666
Mack, W.H. *(Cast)* 1515
Mack, Wilbur *(Cast)* 2631, 3589
Mack, Willard *(Author)* 543
Mack, Willard *(Director)* 568
Mack, Willard *(Librettist)* 4317, 4815

Mack, William B. *(Cast)* 1434
Mack, Willie *(Cast)* 2853
Mack Choir, Cecil
See also Cecil Mack and Cecil Mack's Southland Singers.
Mack Choir, Cecil *(Cast)* 443, 444, 3704, 3705
Mack's Southland Choir
See Cecil Mack and Cecil Mack Choir.
Mack's Southland Singers, Cecil *(Cast)* 488
Mackay, Edward *(Cast)* 1210
Mackay, Wm. Wellington *(Librettist)* 415
Mackay Production Co. *(Producer)* 3672
Mackaye, Dorothy *(Cast)* 3772, 4077
Mackeben, Theo *(Orchestrations)* 1110
Mackenberg, Charles *(Orchestrations)* 4141
Mackenzie, Len *(Composer)* 3175
Mackenzie, Len *(Lyricist)* 3175
Mackenzie, Will *(Cast)* 1721, 2958, 3000, 3018
Mackey, Bill *(Cast)* 1959
Mackey, Percival *(Orchestrations)* 3139
Mackie, Bob *(Costumes)* 373, 407, 2590, 2969, 3515
Mackie, Bob *(Librettist)* 2969
Mackie, Bob *(Producer)* 2969
Mackintosh, Cameron *(Producer)* 678, 1296, 2442, 2544, 2905, 3464, 4068, 4412
Mackintosh, Robert *(Costumes)* 507, 594, 1184, 1273, 1993, 2014, 2415, 2713, 2898, 2987, 3931, 3972, 4114, 4718
Mackintosh, Woods *(Set Design)* 3806
Macklin, Albert *(Cast)* 1077
Macklin, Clara *(Cast)* 2274
Maclagan, T. *(Composer)* 3989
Macloon, Louis *(Producer)* 1944
Macnichol, Lizzie *(Cast)* 2326, 3732
Macomber, Ken *(Arrangements)* 3528
Macomber, Ken *(Composer)* 4763
Macomber, Ken *(Lyricist)* 4763
Macomber, Ken *(Musical Director)* 444
Macomber, Ken *(Orchestrations)* 441, 443, 444, 447, 787, 4741
Macrae, Arthur *(Librettist)* 2227, 2483, 4510
Macrae, Arthur *(Lyricist)* 392, 2227, 3186, 3940
Mactayne, C.S. *(Librettist)* 4194
Macy, Bill *(Cast)* 3233
Macy, Gertrude *(Producer)* 3292, 4483
Madden, Danny *(Cast)* 3724
Madden, Danny *(Vocal Arranger)* 3724
Madden, Donald *(Cast)* 1290
Madden, Edward *(Composer)* 1523, 3926
Madden, Edward *(Librettist)* 598
Madden, Edward *(Lighting Designer)* 2027
Madden, Edward *(Lyricist)* 371, 598, 675, 913, 1247, 1318, 1523, 1613, 1704, 1793, 2215, 2358, 2495, 2576, 2826, 2869, 2892, 2978, 3073, 3327, 3519, 3737, 3748, 4553, 4589, 4655, 4803, 4804
Madden, Edward J. *(Lyricist)* 2858
Madden, George *(Conductor)* 985
Madden, Harry *(Author)* 2311
Madden, Jeanne *(Cast)* 2344
Madden, Sharon *(Cast)* 1346
Maddern, Merle *(Cast)* 1221
Maddern, Richard *(Composer)* 476
Maddock & Hart *(Producer)* 3207
Maddox, Web *(Lyricist)* 805
Maddux, Frances *(Cast)* 1874
Maddux, James *(Cast)* 1781
Madeira, Marcia *(Lighting Designer)* 785, 2648, 2754, 3060, 3171, 3598, 4442
Madera, J. *(Composer)* 4193
Madera, J. *(Lyricist)* 4193
Madero, Ralph *(Lighting Designer)* 2173
Madigan, Betty *(Cast)* 4155
Madison, Coressa *(Cast)* 3657
Madison, Ellen *(Producer)* 135
Madison, George *(Cast)* 4616
Madison Productions *(Producer)* 4482
Madison Square Garden *(Producer)* 754
Maeder, Fred G. *(Librettist)* 644
Maganini, Margaretta *(Costumes)* 1590
Magee, Patrick *(Cast)* 3445
Magee, Sherry *(Musical Director)* 1874
Mages, Libby Adler *(Producer)* 1059
Maggart, Brandon *(Cast)* 108, 167, 1841, 1842, 2072, 2590, 3019, 3111, 3112, 3299, 3548, 3615, 4167
Maggio, Michael *(Director)* 158, 4708
Maggio, Ross *(Arrangements)* 1337
Magid, Karen *(Cast)* 3539
Magid, Larry *(Producer)* 4534
Magidson, Herb *(Composer)* 1134
Magidson, Herb *(Lyricist)* 1134, 1481, 1494, 2850, 4083, 4545
Magidson, Herbert *(Lyricist)* 1481
Maginn, Bonnie *(Cast)* 1264, 1881, 1926, 2974, 4473, 4478, 4658
Magito, Suria *(Arrangements)* 972
Magnes, Alex *(Musical Director)* 3130
Magness, Marilyn *(Choreographer)* 2689
Magnusen, Michael *(Cast)* 1262
Magnuson, Ann *(Author)* 4775
Magnuson, Ann *(Cast)* 4775
Magnuson, Ann *(Composer)* 4775
Magnuson, Ann *(Lyricist)* 4775
Magoon Jr., Eaton *(Composer)* 1809, 4337
Magoon Jr., Eaton *(Librettist)* 1809, 4337
Magoon Jr., Eaton *(Lyricist)* 1809, 4337
Maguire, Fred *(Cast)* 1610
Maguire, George F. *(Cast)* 4244
Maguire, Michael *(Cast)* 2442
Maguire, Sylvester *(Librettist)* 3748
Mahaffey, Valerie *(Cast)* 1256
Mahan, Kevin *(Lighting Designer)* 3641
Mahard, Fran *(Set Design)* 3714
Maher, Joseph *(Cast)* 3787, 4109
Maher, William Michael *(Director)* 1412
Mahieu
See also Max & Mahieu.
Mahieu *(Costumes)* 984, 1343, 1718, 1840, 1984, 2071, 2302, 2330, 2587, 3342, 4198, 4275
Mahieu, Hilaire *(Costumes)* 2455
Mahin, John Lee *(Author)* 647

Mahlangu, Lorraine *(Cast)* 1719
Mahler, Fritz *(Musical Director)* 3703
Mahoney, Bill *(Composer)* 3067
Mahoney, Bill *(Librettist)* 3067
Mahoney, Bill *(Lyricist)* 3067
Mahoney, Francis X. *(Cast)* 3949
Mahoney, Jack *(Lyricist)* 3259, 3425
Mahoney, Jack F. *(Lyricist)* 1138, 1208
Mahoney, Jim *(Composer)* 3941
Mahoney, Jim *(Lyricist)* 3941
Mahoney, Paul *(Cast)* 4093
Mahoney, Will *(Cast)* 1126, 1136, 1487, 4271
Mahoney, Will *(Lyricist)* 1136, 3405
Mahy, Daune *(Cast)* 4149
Mailman, Bruce *(Producer)* 300, 1229
Main, Marjorie *(Cast)* 3014
Mainbocher *(Costumes)* 3301, 4095, 4734
Maine, Bruno *(Set Design)* 2023, 2024, 2099, 4143
Mainstage Productions *(Producer)* 3272
Mais, Michele *(Cast)* 3792
Maisano, Joel *(Musical Director)* 2676
Maisell, Joe *(Cast)* 1012
Maison Blum *(Costumes)* 3618
Maison Ross *(Costumes)* 292
Maitland, Arthur *(Cast)* 3910
Maitland, Joan *(Librettist)* 455
Maitland, Ruth *(Cast)* 2976
Maizee, Alice *(Cast)* 1224
Majeroni, Giorgio *(Cast)* 355
Majeski, Bill *(Librettist)* 3111
Majilton, A.H. *(Choreographer)* 1153
Major, Charles *(Author)* 2671
Makalif, Edmund *(Cast)* 149
Makas, Anthony *(Musical Director)* 2977
Makas, Maxine *(Cast)* 2977
Makeham, Eliot *(Cast)* 4361
Mako *(Cast)* 3340
Malamet, Marsha *(Composer)* 1104
Malamud, Marc D. *(Lighting Designer)* 4697
Malamud, Marc D. *(Set Design)* 4697
Malas, Spiro *(Cast)* 2229
Malbin, Elaine *(Cast)* 3035, 3371
Malcles, Denis *(Set Design)* 3761
Malden, Karl *(Cast)* 4706
Maletsky, Sophie *(Cast)* 2037
Malie, T. *(Lyricist)* 3953
Malie, Thomas *(Lyricist)* 1689
Malina, Luba *(Cast)* 2629, 2847
Malina, Robert *(Producer)* 40
Malina, Stuart *(Dance Arranger)* 3601
Malina, Stuart *(Musical Director)* 3601
Malina, Stuart *(Vocal Arranger)* 3601
Mallet, David *(Lyricist)* 3450
Malley, Sean *(Cast)* 3498
Mallin, Glen *(Lyricist)* 1370
Mallory, Victoria *(Cast)* 1329, 2536
Mallow, Tom *(Producer)* 4788
Malloy, Francetta *(Cast)* 125
Malneck, Matt *(Composer)* 3178, 3428, 4137, 4799
Malneck, Matty *(Composer)* 3444
Malo, Gina *(Cast)* 1440
Malone, Geraldine *(Cast)* 1388
Malone, J.A.E. *(Director)* 1067, 1544, 1569, 2131, 2524, 2698, 3618, 3857, 4219
Malone, J.A.E. *(Producer)* 30, 611, 3569
Malone, J.A.E. *(Set Design)* 770
Malone, Mike *(Choreographer)* 952, 3690
Malone, Ray *(Cast)* 853
Malone, William H. *(Cast)* 2455
Maloney, Maureen *(Cast)* 669, 2069
Maloney, Russell *(Librettist)* 4015
Maloney, Russell *(Lyricist)* 4015
Malotte, Albert Hay *(Composer)* 2857
Malroy, Jack *(Composer)* 1154
Malroy, Jack *(Lyricist)* 1154
Maltby Jr., Richard *(Additional Lyrics)* 4068
Maltby Jr., Richard *(Choreographer)* 2555
Maltby Jr., Richard *(Director)* 253, 784, 1737, 2555, 4068, 4145, 4175, 4535
Maltby Jr., Richard *(Librettist)* 945, 951, 2905, 3111, 4535
Maltby Jr., Richard *(Lyricist)* 39, 253, 784, 945, 1298, 1648, 2011, 2617, 2905, 3112, 3142, 3835, 4145, 4535
Maltin, Bernard *(Composer)* 290, 1134, 4823
Maltin, Bernard *(Lyricist)* 290
Malvin, Arthur *(Composer)* 4197
Malvin, Arthur *(Lyricist)* 4197
Malvin, Arthur *(Vocal Arranger)* 4197
Malvina, Madame *(Choreographer)* 749
Mama Hare's Tree *(Producer)* 1978
Mame Productions *(Producer)* 815
Mamet, David *(Librettist)* 4535
Mamlet, Alexandra *(Choreographer)* 3495
Mamoulian, Rouben *(Director)* 183, 660, 2591, 3263, 3541, 3813, 4123
Mamoulian, Rouben *(Librettist)* 183, 3813
Mana Lucca *(Cast)* 3153
Mana-Zucca *(Composer)* 1446
Manasseri, Michael *(Cast)* 140
Manatt, Fred *(Cast)* 1494
Manatt, Frederick *(Director)* 78
Manchester, George *(Librettist)* 3856
Manchester, Joe *(Librettist)* 3863
Manchester, Joe *(Producer)* 3863
Manchester, Melissa *(Arrangements)* 2065
Manchester, Melissa *(Composer)* 964, 2065, 2677
Manchester, Melissa *(Lyricist)* 964, 2065
Mancini, Al *(Cast)* 42, 2067
Mancini, Henry *(Composer)* 2611, 4560
Mancini, Mark *(Librettist)* 4679
Mandan, Robert *(Cast)* 167, 2702
Mandel, Evan William *(Producer)* 4522
Mandel, Frank *(Author)* 1827, 3184, 3304
Mandel, Frank *(Director)* 3117
Mandel, Frank *(Librettist)* 642, 1021, 1027, 1145, 2216, 2587, 2767, 2786, 2903, 3048, 3117, 3184, 3218, 3623, 4241, 4378
Mandel, Frank *(Lyricist)* 1027, 3117
Mandel, Frank *(Producer)* 111, 642, 1027, 1145, 1283, 1339, 1387, 1628, 3117

Mandel, Howard *(Set Design)* 3498
Mandel, Jeff *(Composer)* 3076
Mandel, Jeff *(Lyricist)* 3076
Mandel, John *(Orchestrations)* 3126, 4566
Mandel, Johnny *(Orchestrations)* 3428
Mandel, Mel *(Composer)* 3059
Mandel, Mel *(Librettist)* 3059
Mandel, Mel *(Lyricist)* 31, 865, 1089, 1435, 2199, 3059
Mandel, Tom *(Composer)* 300
Mandel, Tom *(Lyricist)* 300
Mandel, Tom *(Musical Director)* 300
Mandel, Tom *(Vocal Arranger)* 300
Mandell, Michael *(Cast)* 754, 3757
Mandells, The *(Cast)* 1689
Mandeville, Frank A. *(Incidental Music)* 1157
Mandeville, Jane *(Cast)* 4681
Manetto, Corinna *(Cast)* 2553
Manfredi, Harry *(Composer)* 3517
Manfredi, Harry *(Lyricist)* 3517
Manfredi, Nino *(Cast)* 3798
Mangan, Thomas *(Set Design)* 1114
Manger, Itsik *(Author)* 4082
Manger, Itsik *(Lyricist)* 1609, 4082, 4342
Manhattan Punch Line *(Producer)* 1915
Manhattan Rhythm Kings *(Cast)* 921
Manhattan Theater Club *(Producer)* 39, 262, 1700, 1737, 2555, 3277, 3666, 4067, 4535
Manhatters Company *(Producer)* 2739
Manheim, Mannie *(Author)* 1204
Manheim, Martha *(Composer)* 1204
Manheim, Martha *(Lyricist)* 1204
Manheim, Ralph (English Lyrics) 4370
Manheim, Ralph *(Librettist)* 4370
Manhoff, William *(Librettist)* 3046
Manilow, Barry *(Arrangements)* 846
Manilow, Barry *(Cast)* 845
Manilow, Barry *(Composer)* 146, 845, 846, 2677
Manilow, Barry *(Librettist)* 846
Manilow, Barry *(Lyricist)* 2677
Manilow, Barry *(Orchestrations)* 846
Manim, Mannie *(Lighting Designer)* 3836, 4438
Mankiewicz, Herman J. *(Director)* 3783
Mankiewicz, Herman J. *(Librettist)* 1692, 3419, 3783
Mankiewicz, Herman J. *(Lyricist)* 3419
Mankiewicz, Herman J. *(Producer)* 3783
Mankiewicz, Joseph *(Author)* 167
Mankiewicz, Tom *(Librettist)* 1497
Mankowitz, Wolf *(Librettist)* 3482
Mann, Abby *(Librettist)* 2275
Mann, Barry *(Composer)* 964
Mann, Barry *(Lyricist)* 964
Mann, Ben *(Lyricist)* 1934
Mann, Daniel *(Director)* 3347
Mann, Dave *(Composer)* 856, 857, 861, 862
Mann, David *(Orchestrations)* 137
Mann, Delbert *(Director)* 3324
Mann, Edward *(Producer)* 105
Mann, Erika *(Librettist)* 3441
Mann, Erika *(Lyricist)* 3441
Mann, Gabi *(Cast)* 1056
Mann, George *(Cast)* 1840
Mann, Heinrich *(Author)* 3551
Mann, J. Patrick
See also Patrick Mann.
Mann, J. Patrick *(Set Design)* 1201
Mann, Joan *(Choreographer)* 4377
Mann, Johnny *(Composer)* 1978
Mann, Johnny *(Lyricist)* 1978
Mann, June *(Cast)* 1494, 3975
Mann, Klaus *(Librettist)* 3441
Mann, Klaus *(Lyricist)* 3441
Mann, Louis *(Cast)* 4298, 4654, 4666, 4681
Mann, Louise *(Vocal Arranger)* 2140
Mann, Michael *(Cast)* 1842
Mann, Nat D. *(Composer)* 47, 246, 4201, 4430
Mann, Nat D. *(Lyricist)* 246, 4430
Mann, Patrick *(Set Design)* 4192
Mann, Patrick
See also J. Patrick Mann.
Mann, Paul *(Cast)* 2167
Mann, Paul *(Composer)* 1840
Mann, Peanuts *(Cast)* 2850
Mann, Sam *(Cast)* 3225
Mann, Sylvia *(Cast)* 766
Mann, Terrence *(Cast)* 212, 330, 2442, 3644
Mann, Terrence V. *(Cast)* 305, 678
Mann, Theodore *(Director)* 147, 1222, 4028
Mann, Theodore *(Librettist)* 4863
Mann, Theodore *(Producer)* 2220, 4028
Mann, Thomas *(Author)* 4442
Mann, Thomas *(Cast)* 1533
Mann, W.D. *(Director)* 1301
Manna, Charles *(Cast)* 4153
Manna, Charles *(Librettist)* 4153
Manne, Joe *(Lyricist)* 3402
Mannering, Gwen *(Cast)* 3157
Manners, Ginger *(Cast)* 3990
Manners, J. Hartley *(Author)* 3427, 3429, 3431, 3432
Manners, J. Hartley *(Director)* 3328, 3431, 3432
Manners, J. Hartley *(Librettist)* 1502, 1523, 3431, 3575
Manners, Jayne *(Cast)* 532, 601, 4365
Manners, Zeke *(Composer)* 1303
Manners, Zeke *(Lyricist)* 1303
Mannes, Marya *(Librettist)* 961
Manning, Charles *(Lyricist)* 3333
Manning, Dan *(Cast)* 4030
Manning, Dick *(Composer)* 1269, 2551, 4027, 4264
Manning, Dick *(Lyricist)* 1269, 2551, 4027, 4264
Manning, Frankie *(Choreographer)* 432
Manning, Hallie *(Cast)* 3369
Manning, Hope *(Cast)* 1476
Manning, Irene *(Cast)* 999, 2313, 4292, 4486
Manning, Jack *(Cast)* 1060
Manning, James H. *(Cast)* 1968
Manning, Jane *(Producer)* 1581
Manning, Laura *(Cast)* 159
Manning, Laura *(Composer)* 159
Manning, Laura *(Lyricist)* 159
Manning, Maybelle *(Costumes)* 3968
Manning, Monroe *(Director)* 4792

Manning, Ruth *(Cast)* 2925
Manning, Sylvia *(Choreographer)* 1871
Mannings, Allan *(Librettist)* 2554
Manocherian, Jennifer *(Producer)* 3960
Manocherian, Jennifer R. *(Producer)* 1832
Manoff, Dinah *(Cast)* 2427
Manola, Marion *(Cast)* 1401
Manqele, David *(Cast)* 4438
Mansfield, Laurie *(Producer)* 580
Mansfield, Scott *(Composer)* 2426
Mansfield, Scott *(Director)* 2426
Mansfield, Scott *(Librettist)* 2426
Mansfield, Scott *(Lyricist)* 2426
Mansfield, Scott *(Producer)* 4145
Mansfield Productions *(Producer)* 4749
Manson, Alan *(Cast)* 620
Manson, Bevan *(Arrangements)* 4082
Mansur, Byrd *(Cast)* 4147
Mansur, Susan *(Cast)* 3811
Mantell, June *(Cast)* 2709
Mantia, Buddy *(Cast)* 4347
Mantovani *(Musical Director)* 129, 3339
Manulis, John Bard *(Director)* 1669
Manulis, Martin *(Director)* 1112
Manulis, Martin E. *(Cast)* 1957
Manuscript Prods. *(Producer)* 253
Manville, Lorraine *(Cast)* 3511
Manzano, Sonia *(Cast)* 1595
Manzini, Mario *(Producer)* 4611
Mao, Freddy *(Cast)* 3340
Mapes, Jacque *(Producer)* 4415
Mapes, Jacque *(Set Design)* 4415
Maple, Audrey *(Cast)* 1285, 1629, 1851, 3084
Marand, Patricia *(Cast)* 2163, 4718
Marascalco, John *(Composer)* 3695
Marascalco, John *(Lyricist)* 3695
Marba, Joseph S. *(Cast)* 929
Marbe, Fay *(Cast)* 910, 2567, 2684, 4547
Marble, Anna *(Composer)* 3073
Marble, Anna *(Lyricist)* 3073
Marble, Carolyn *(Cast)* 3643
Marble, Dan *(Cast)* 4322
Marbury, Elisabeth *(Producer)* 1557, 2620, 3193, 3849, 3865, 4555
Marc, Peter *(Cast)* 450
Marc Henri *(Set Design)* 3291
Marc-Henri *(Cast)* 4341
Marc-Henri *(Costumes)* 4581
Marc-Henri *(Set Design)* 133, 700, 703, 704, 791, 1610, 2570, 3827, 4320, 4765
Marc-Michel *(Author)* 2178, 4319
Marceline *(Cast)* 188, 236, 378, 3093, 4046, 4113, 4452, 4599
March, Bill *(Cast)* 1508
March, David L. *(Producer)* 1255
March, Fredric *(Cast)* 121, 752, 2653, 2814
March, Ursula *(Cast)* 2454
Marchand, Colette *(Cast)* 4496
Marchand, Susan *(Cast)* 1635
Marchante, Marion *(Cast)* 3170
Marchetti, Filiberto *(Choreographer)* 175
Marchetti, H. *(Choreographer)* 2938
Marco
  See also Fanchon & Marco.
Marco *(Director)* 4128
Marco, Maria *(Cast)* 2407
Marco, Sano *(Composer)* 2580
Marcone, Lance *(Cast)* 1695
Marcovicci, Andrea *(Cast)* 695, 3088
Marcus, A.B. *(Producer)* 2749
Marcus, D. Frank *(Composer)* 290, 488
Marcus, D. Frank *(Librettist)* 290, 488
Marcus, D. Frank *(Lyricist)* 290, 488
Marcus, Daniel *(Cast)* 1702
Marcus, Linda *(Lyricist)* 328
Marcus, Madame *(Costumes)* 792
Marcus, Ruth *(Cast)* 2321
Marcus, Sol *(Composer)* 3695
Marcus, Sol *(Lyricist)* 3695
Marcy, Everett *(Librettist)* 70, 3104, 4677
Marcy, Everett *(Lyricist)* 621, 3103, 3104
Marcy, George *(Cast)* 406, 2554
Marden, Ben *(Producer)* 3726
Mardirosian, Tom *(Cast)* 3039
Marek, Mary Ann *(Cast)* 2356
Marek, Rochelle *(Cast)* 4157
Maresch, Harold *(Producer)* 3046
Margetson, Arthur *(Cast)* 189, 3390
Margo, Philip F. *(Composer)* 2785
Margo, Philip F. *(Lyricist)* 2785
Margolies, Abe *(Producer)* 2075, 2440
Margoshes, Steve *(Dance Arranger)* 2953, 3651
Margoshes, Steve *(Musical Director)* 2953, 3651
Margoshes, Steve *(Orchestrations)* 4031, 4676
Margoshes, Steve *(Vocal Arranger)* 2953, 3651
Margoshes, Steven *(Composer)* 1236
Margoshes, Steven *(Dance Arranger)* 1737, 4505
Margoshes, Steven *(Musical Director)* 1236, 2754, 4505
Margoshes, Steven *(Orchestrations)* 171, 394, 583, 753, 1236, 1737, 2643, 2754, 3944, 4505
Margoshes, Steven *(Vocal Arranger)* 583, 753, 1737, 2754, 4505
Margosian, Linda *(Costumes)* 99
Marguerite, Mlle.
  See also La Petite Marguerite.
Marguerite, Mlle. *(Cast)* 1962
Margulies, David *(Cast)* 3577
Margulies, Ellen *(Cast)* 4325
Mari, Floria *(Cast)* 2322
Maricle, Marijane *(Cast)* 607
Marie, Julienne *(Cast)* 699, 1060, 1373, 4682
Marie, Rose *(Cast)* 4423
Marik, Carol *(Choreographer)* 2783
Marineau, Barbara *(Cast)* 430
Mariners, The *(Cast)* 197
Marino, F. *(Lyricist)* 4264
Marion, David *(Choreographer)* 4064
Marion, Frank *(Choreographer)* 2896
Marion, George *(Cast)* 48, 1663, 2506, 3363

Marion, George *(Choreographer)* 1162
Marion, George *(Director)* 48, 94, 102, 118, 138, 208, 495, 511, 613, 1016, 1026, 1148, 1210, 1247, 1327, 1433, 1455, 1663, 1712, 1796, 1849, 1881, 2506, 2532, 2701, 2724, 2755, 2826, 2836, 2923, 2931, 2982, 3085, 3298, 3437, 3478, 3537, 3578, 3613, 3771, 3839, 3943, 4119, 4185, 4187, 4228, 4283, 4285, 4669, 4686, 4726, 4738, 4754, 4762, 4815
Marion, George *(Librettist)* 2755
Marion, George *(Lyricist)* 2755
Marion, George F. *(Director)* 1563
Marion, Sam *(Cast)* 1627
Marion, Sam *(Choreographer)* 1118, 1881, 3805, 4738, 4753
Marion, Samuel *(Choreographer)* 2733
Marion, Sid *(Composer)* 4776
Marion Jr., George *(Librettist)* 84, 177, 323, 1140, 4420, 4428
Marion Jr., George *(Lyricist)* 39, 84, 323, 1140, 4373, 4428
Marischka, Ernst *(Author)* 1680, 1805
Marjoroni, George *(Cast)* 2966
Mark, Donald *(Cast)* 4172
Mark, F.W. *(Lyricist)* 3779
Mark, Michael *(Cast)* 900, 2058
Markam, Genevieve *(Cast)* 953
Marke, Fay *(Cast)* 2387
Markell, Denis *(Composer)* 262, 3181, 3960, 4533
Markell, Denis *(Librettist)* 262, 3181, 3960
Markell, Denis *(Lyricist)* 262, 3181, 3960, 4533
Marker, Preshy *(Cast)* 1422, 4827
Markert, Russell *(Choreographer)* 142, 1481, 1490, 1493, 1827, 1856, 2271, 2296, 3639, 3850
Markert, Russell *(Director)* 2077
Markert, Russell *(Producer)* 1679
Markey, Enid *(Cast)* 98, 458, 1749, 2994, 4479, 4526
Markham, Dewey "Pigmeat" *(Cast)* 439, 447, 1989
Markham, Dewey "Pigmeat" *(Librettist)* 1989
Markham, Shelly *(Composer)* 251
Markham, Shelly *(Musical Director)* 597
Markinson, Martin *(Producer)* 1890
Markoe, Gerald *(Composer)* 1757
Markoe, Gerald Jay *(Composer)* 705, 2647
Markoff, Olga *(Cast)* 1836, 4545
Markova, Alicia *(Cast)* 3893
Marks, Alfred *(Cast)* 3526
Marks, Charles *(Producer)* 2040
Marks, Clarence *(Cast)* 803
Marks, Clarence *(Lyricist)* 2601
Marks, Clarence *(Musical Director)* 554
Marks, Dennis *(Lyricist)* 1233, 3484
Marks, Frank *(Orchestrations)* 3046
Marks, Gerald *(Composer)* 431, 1127, 1658, 1892, 1930, 3036, 4374, 4667
Marks, Hugo *(Musical Director)* 1606
Marks, J. *(Additional Lyrics)* 2611
Marks, J. *(Cast)* 2611
Marks, J. *(Choreographer)* 2611
Marks, J. *(Director)* 2611
Marks, J. *(Librettist)* 2611
Marks, J. *(Lighting Designer)* 2611
Marks, J. *(Lyricist)* 2611
Marks, Joe *(Cast)* 1889
Marks, Joe E. *(Cast)* 462, 1310, 2106, 3452, 3453
Marks, Johnny *(Composer)* 281, 3793, 3794, 3795, 4391
Marks, Johnny *(Lyricist)* 281, 3793, 3794, 3795, 4391
Marks, Larry B. *(Librettist)* 1837
Marks, Laurence *(Librettist)* 3046
Marks, Maurice *(Librettist)* 3648, 3822
Marks, Maurice E. *(Lyricist)* 335
Marks, Robert *(Arrangements)* 2676
Marks, Robert *(Choreographer)* 97, 1424, 2214, 2853, 3740, 4218, 4422, 4784
Marks, Robert *(Dance Arranger)* 3239
Marks, Robert *(Director)* 2270, 2491
Marks, Robert *(Musical Director)* 3239, 4527
Marks, Robert *(Vocal Arranger)* 2676, 3239
Marks, Robert A. *(Director)* 4007
Marks, Sylvia *(Lyricist)* 3226, 4484
Marks, Walter *(Composer)* 269, 484, 547, 1363, 1585, 1611, 2627, 3479, 3497
Marks, Walter *(Librettist)* 484
Marks, Walter *(Lyricist)* 269, 484, 547, 1363, 1585, 1611, 2627, 3479, 3497
Marksman Jr., D.M. *(Screenwriter)* 4217
Markush, Fred *(Composer)* 4137
Marlatt, William F. *(Set Design)* 2167
Marlay, Andrew B. *(Costumes)* 1496, 3249, 4176, 4460
Marlin-Jones, Davey *(Director)* 4408
Marlo, Micki *(Cast)* 4829
Marlow, Brian *(Librettist)* 568
Marlow, Mary *(Cast)* 1889
Marlowe, Alan *(Musical Director)* 1786
Marlowe, Christopher *(Lyricist)* 3909
Marlowe, Frank *(Cast)* 4428
Marlowe, Gloria *(Cast)* 3509
Marlowe, Harry *(Composer)* 3322
Marlowe, Jack *(Librettist)* 2742
Marlowe, James *(Cast)* 4185
Marlowe, James C. *(Cast)* 246, 1271, 4053
Marlowe, Marion *(Cast)* 197, 4095
Marlowe, Marlon *(Cast)* 227
Marlowe, Theresa *(Cast)* 3606
Marlowe, Vivian *(Cast)* 3236
Maronek, James *(Set Design)* 1059
Maronek, James E. *(Set Design)* 3925
Marquard, Rube *(Cast)* 4195
Marquez, Gabriel Garcia *(Author)* 756
Marquis, Don *(Author)* 3934
Marquis, Marjorie *(Cast)* 1235
Marr, Richard *(Cast)* 159
Marracci, Livia *(Cast)* 2140
Marre, Albert *(Choreographer)* 1959
Marre, Albert *(Director)* 223, 757, 935, 1730, 1959, 2327, 2357, 2727, 2864, 3913, 4386
Marre, Albert *(Librettist)* 1959
Marre, Albert *(Producer)* 2357
Marre, Gilbert *(Orchestrations)* 172

Marren, Howard *(Composer)* 1496, 2598, 3377, 3544
Marrow, Esther *(Cast)* 166, 2692, 3991, 4722
Marrow, Macklin *(Musical Director)* 4368, 4479
Marrow, Queen Esther *(Cast)* 1172, 4460
Marrow, Queen Esther *(Composer)* 4460
Marrow, Queen Esther *(Librettist)* 4460
Marrow, Queen Esther *(Lyricist)* 4460
Mars, Anthony *(Author)* 1553
Mars, Antony *(Author)* 3784
Mars, Antony *(Librettist)* 1212
Mars Bonfire *(Composer)* 3695
Mars Bonfire *(Lyricist)* 3695
Marsden, Frank *(Set Design)* 1356
Marsden, Richard *(Set Design)* 1576
Marsh, Diane *(Choreographer)* 63
Marsh, Howard *(Cast)* 463, 718, 1663, 1686, 3949, 4188, 4620
Marsh, John *(Author)* 1257
Marsh, Mary *(Cast)* 2739
Marsh, Roy K. *(Composer)* 2856
Marsh, Roy K. *(Lyricist)* 2856
Marsh, Vera *(Cast)* 111, 1145, 1387, 3365
Marshall, Amelia *(Cast)* 1776
Marshall, Armina *(Author)* 183
Marshall, Austin *(Cast)* 2068
Marshall, Boots *(Choreographer)* 1499
Marshall, Boyd *(Cast)* 1796, 2377
Marshall, Capt. Robert *(Author)* 138
Marshall, Donna *(Cast)* 602
Marshall, E.G. *(Cast)* 933, 2553, 3075
Marshall, Eric *(Cast)* 791
Marshall, Ethel *(Cast)* 1479, 2791, 2792
Marshall, Everett *(Cast)* 622, 662, 1492, 2813, 3100, 4824
Marshall, George *(Cast)* 3409
Marshall, George Preston *(Producer)* 3356
Marshall, Henry *(Composer)* 3384, 4642, 4712
Marshall, Henry *(Librettist)* 3384
Marshall, Henry *(Lyricist)* 3384
Marshall, Henry I. *(Composer)* 2667, 4017, 4589
Marshall, Iris *(Cast)* 512
Marshall, James R. *(Cast)* 4227
Marshall, Jay *(Cast)* 2615
Marshall, Joe *(Cast)* 4697
Marshall, Kathleen *(Choreographer)* 4255
Marshall, Ken *(Cast)* 259
Marshall, Larry *(Cast)* 393, 550, 828, 2134, 2648, 2775, 2953, 3231, 3628, 3741, 4147, 4371
Marshall, Madeline *(Cast)* 2157
Marshall, Mort *(Cast)* 1475, 1709, 2523, 3497, 3526, 4018, 4029
Marshall, Pat *(Cast)* 1782, 2987
Marshall, Patricia *(Cast)* 999
Marshall, Peter L. *(Cast)* 4013
Marshall, Red *(Cast)* 70, 2850
Marshall, Rob *(Cast)* 146, 3070
Marshall, Rob *(Choreographer)* 2333, 3456
Marshall, Sarah *(Cast)* 4749
Marshe, Vera *(Cast)* 289
Marsicano, Mary *(Costumes)* 696
Marsolais, Ken *(Producer)* 1589, 2415
Marston, Lawrence *(Director)* 1722, 2490, 2814, 4322, 4528
Marston, Richard *(Set Design)* 1030, 1305, 2123, 2493, 2500, 2502, 4125
Martel, Janece *(Cast)* 3669
Martel, Michel *(Cast)* 4579
Martel, Tom *(Cast)* 1769
Martel, Tom *(Composer)* 1769
Martel, Tom *(Lyricist)* 1769
Martel, William *(Cast)* 227
Martell, Fred *(Cast)* 2023
Martell, Karla *(Author)* 225
Martell, Philip *(Musical Director)* 1386, 2608
Martelle, Thomas *(Cast)* 1248
Martens, George *(Musical Director)* 1187
Martens, Mme. *(Costumes)* 1080
Marti Band, Frank *(Cast)* 862
Marti Orchestra, Frank *(Cast)* 847, 849, 855, 859, 860, 861, 863
Martin *(Set Design)* 4291
Martin, Andrea *(Cast)* 3039
Martin, Angel *(Cast)* 4168
Martin, Angela *(Cast)* 1478
Martin, Ann-Ngaire *(Cast)* 3277
Martin, Barbara *(Cast)* 2097
Martin, Barney *(Cast)* 190, 723, 2651, 4629
Martin, Bernard *(Lyricist)* 488
Martin, Bob *(Vocal Arranger)* 1886
Martin, Daisy *(Cast)* 1087
Martin, David *(Composer)* 3983
Martin, David *(Orchestrations)* 3983
Martin, Dean *(Cast)* 853, 857
Martin, Denis *(Cast)* 3339
Martin, Dolores *(Cast)* 1278
Martin, E. *(Author)* 4624
Martin, Ellen *(Cast)* 2988
Martin, Elliot *(Producer)* 1776, 3097
Martin, Erin *(Cast)* 4397
Martin, Ernest *(Producer)* 507, 629, 1706, 2019, 2523, 3972, 4013, 4588
Martin, Ernest H. *(Librettist)* 4682
Martin, Ernest H. *(Producer)* 16, 4652, 4682
Martin, Ethel *(Choreographer)* 693, 3871, 4145
Martin, Evelyn *(Cast)* 3369
Martin, Frank *(Director)* 1377
Martin, Fred *(Producer)* 2580
Martin, George N. *(Cast)* 3070
Martin, Helen *(Cast)* 3610
Martin, Herb *(Lyricist)* 2320, 4288
Martin, Herbert *(Librettist)* 4764
Martin, Herbert *(Lyricist)* 2016, 3551, 4764
Martin, Hugh *(Cast)* 1973, 2597, 4174
Martin, Hugh *(Composer)* 372, 1628, 1742, 1891, 2148, 2535, 2582, 2608, 2705, 2805, 3175, 4289, 4332, 4388, 4399, 4586, 4827
Martin, Hugh *(Librettist)* 1891
Martin, Hugh *(Lyricist)* 372, 1628, 1742, 1891, 2148, 2582, 2608, 2705, 2805, 3175, 4289, 4332, 4399, 4586, 4827

Martin, Hugh *(Vocal Arranger)* 206, 304, 612, 1109, 1475, 1791, 1811, 1879, 1891, 1973, 2582, 2590, 2597, 2705, 2805, 4142, 4174, 4420, 4423, 4557, 4586, 4827
Martin, Jack *(Orchestrations)* 2339
Martin, Janet *(Cast)* 3721
Martin, Jay *(Cast)* 2098
Martin, Jeff *(Director)* 1348
Martin, Jennifer *(Choreographer)* 4740
Martin, John J. *(Cast)* 3126
Martin, Kristina *(Cast)* 1940
Martin, Langdon *(Author)* 4372
Martin, Leila *(Cast)* 237, 1194, 3464, 3469, 3491, 3780
Martin, Luke *(Cast)* 3759
Martin, Marion *(Cast)* 3104
Martin, Mary *(Cast)* 971, 2050, 2201, 2432, 2655, 3138, 3301, 3339, 3453, 4095, 4096, 4363
Martin, Mel *(Lyricist)* 1834
Martin, Millicent *(Cast)* 507, 2318, 2910, 3967
Martin, Norman *(Composer)* 1408, 2294
Martin, Norman *(Lyricist)* 1408, 2294
Martin, Norman L. *(Composer)* 392, 673, 1408, 1770, 2925, 3615
Martin, Norman L. *(Librettist)* 3900
Martin, Norman L. *(Lyricist)* 673, 1408, 2925
Martin, Owen *(Cast)* 3263
Martin, Paul *(Director)* 2476
Martin, Perry *(Composer)* 1423
Martin, Perry *(Lyricist)* 1423
Martin, Randal *(Librettist)* 1262
Martin, Randal *(Lyricist)* 1262
Martin, Ron *(Cast)* 3876
Martin, Ruth *(Lyricist)* 3151
Martin, Sara *(Cast)* 500
Martin, Scott *(Cast)* 3587
Martin, Stephen G. *(Producer)* 1038
Martin, Ted *(Cast)* 3684
Martin, Thomas *(Lyricist)* 3151
Martin, Thomas *(Musical Director)* 3151
Martin, Virginia *(Cast)* 597, 649, 652, 2019, 2523, 3108, 4577
Martin, Vivian *(Cast)* 2281
Martin, William *(Director)* 696, 916, 2472
Martindel, Edward *(Cast)* 1162, 1626, 2494, 2848, 3081, 3613, 3943, 4616
Martinetti, Ignacio *(Cast)* 356, 559, 1526, 1888, 2675, 2803, 2826, 2865, 3252, 4549
Martinez, J. Preston *(Composer)* 4030
Martinez, J. Preston *(Lyricist)* 4030
Martinez, Richard *(Musical Director)* 4442
Martinez, Vaughan *(Cast)* 4584
Martingale *(Costumes)* 4602
Martino, Mark *(Cast)* 2305
Martinot, Sadie *(Cast)* 4165
Martins, Peter *(Choreographer)* 4068
Marton, Ferenc *(Author)* 3583, 3584
Martone, Marco *(Director)* 159
Martos, Ferenc *(Author)* 2761, 2907, 4228, 4258
Martos Orchestra, Frank *(Cast)* 865
Martyn, Greg *(Cast)* 2440
Martyn, Kathlene *(Cast)* 2376
Marulli, Renato *(Cast)* 2521
Marvell, Holt *(Composer)* 478
Marvell, Holt *(Lyricist)* 478, 1813
Marvenga, Ilse *(Cast)* 4188, 4328
Marvey, Gene *(Cast)* 117
Marvin, Charles *(Composer)* 4498
Marvin, Charles S. *(Composer)* 1370
Marvin, Charles S. *(Lyricist)* 1370
Marvin, Jack *(Cast)* 938
Marvin, Johnny *(Cast)* 1965
Marvin, Mel *(Composer)* 1172, 1418, 1684, 1914, 3939
Marvin, Mel *(Dance Arranger)* 167, 825, 1809, 4390
Marvin, Mel *(Orchestrations)* 1684
Marvin, Mel *(Vocal Arranger)* 825, 1684, 1809, 4390
Marwig, Carl *(Choreographer)* 457, 559, 571, 1505, 1896, 2117, 2181, 2725, 2865, 3856
Marx, Arthur *(Author)* 1204
Marx, Arthur *(Librettist)* 2874
Marx, Chico *(Cast)* 142, 2071, 4265
Marx, Groucho *(Cast)* 142, 2071
Marx, Groucho *(Librettist)* 2653, 4367
Marx, Harpo *(Cast)* 142, 2071
Marx, Irene *(Composer)* 1204
Marx, Irene *(Lyricist)* 1204
Marx, Robert *(Librettist)* 2874
Marx, Zeppo *(Cast)* 142, 2071
Marx Brothers
See Chico Marx, Groucho Marx, Harpo Marx and Zeppo Marx.
Marx Brothers, The *(Cast)* 799
Mary Fisher Productions *(Producer)* 2283
Maryan, Charles *(Director)* 4244
Marzoff, Les *(Set Design)* 4199
Marzullo, Steve *(Musical Director)* 3285, 3364
Marzullo, Steve *(Vocal Arranger)* 3364
Maschwitz, Eric *(Librettist)* 346, 2483, 2608, 3756
Maschwitz, Eric *(Lyricist)* 346, 3756, 4027
Masciarelli, Silvio *(Composer)* 4482
Mascolo, Joseph *(Cast)* 1837, 3309
Masekela, Hugh *(Composer)* 3836
Masekela, Hugh *(Dance Arranger)* 3836
Masekela, Hugh *(Lyricist)* 3836
Masekela, Hugh *(Vocal Arranger)* 3836
Masella, Arthur *(Director)* 4790
Masella, Arthur *(Librettist)* 1038
Masella, Joni *(Cast)* 2208
Masiell, Joe *(Cast)* 766, 1045, 1637, 2017, 2433, 2785, 3197, 3876, 4379
Maslansky, Harris *(Producer)* 2152
Maslow, Sophie *(Choreographer)* 400, 1269, 3831, 3938
Mason, Billy *(Cast)* 3714
Mason, Carmeron *(Cast)* 746
Mason, Charles A. *(Cast)* 4674
Mason, Charles A. *(Composer)* 4674
Mason, Charles A. *(Lyricist)* 3985
Mason, Dan *(Cast)* 1459, 2543
Mason, Dan *(Director)* 2543
Mason, Della *(Cast)* 3052
Mason, Herbert *(Director)* 2570, 4795

Mason, Jack *(Choreographer)* 75, 351, 545, 684, 805, 815, 905, 965, 1118, 1240, 1247, 1334, 1531, 1566, 1626, 1735, 1852, 2122, 2135, 2384, 2419, 2495, 2546, 2574, 2642, 2696, 2829, 2854, 2856, 2884, 3056, 3369, 3397, 3399, 3402, 3424, 3681, 3985, 4017, 4148, 4194, 4258, 4747, 4787, 4805
Mason, Jack *(Director)* 231, 433, 1531, 2857, 4253
Mason, Jane *(Cast)* 837
Mason, Jason *(Cast)* 444
Mason, John *(Cast)* 497, 1019, 1401, 1876, 1984
Mason, John *(Librettist)* 1876
Mason, Karen *(Cast)* 131, 583, 1804, 2783
Mason, Marlyn *(Cast)* 408, 413, 1990, 2014
Mason, Marsha *(Cast)* 1620, 4372
Mason, Marshall W. *(Director)* 1268, 1669
Mason, Melissa *(Cast)* 4667
Mason, Nan *(Composer)* 2737
Mason, Nan *(Lyricist)* 2689, 2737
Mason, Pauline *(Cast)* 1965
Mason, Reginald *(Cast)* 3432
Mason, Richard *(Author)* 4749
Mason, Richard G. *(Librettist)* 2178
Mason, Richard G. *(Set Design)* 2178
Mason, Snippy *(Cast)* 2557
Mason, T.E. *(Costumes)* 1229
Mason, T.E. *(Set Design)* 1229
Mason, Virginia *(Choreographer)* 1887, 4160
Mason & Shaw *(Cast)* 3133
Masquers, The *(Producer)* 1940
Mass, Anthony *(Cast)* 4298
Massee, Michael *(Costumes)* 3476
Massee, Michael *(Set Design)* 1346, 2573, 3476
Massey, Daniel *(Cast)* 1511, 3918
Massey, Ilona *(Cast)* 4826
Massi, Bernice *(Cast)* 339, 2284, 3187, 3577, 4633
Massine, Leonide *(Cast)* 792, 4154
Massine, Leonide *(Choreographer)* 792, 1817, 4154, 4565, 4741
Mast, Charles *(Choreographer)* 4393
Mast, Charles *(Director)* 1173
Masteroff, Joe *(Librettist)* 610, 1496, 3377, 3900, 3918
Masteroff, Joe *(Lyricist)* 1496, 3377
Masters, Edgar Lee *(Author)* 4111
Masters, Frankie *(Composer)* 4255
Masters, Grace *(Cast)* 3133
Masterson, Carroll *(Producer)* 269, 339, 1408, 3110
Masterson, Danny *(Cast)* 1092
Masterson, Harris *(Producer)* 269, 339, 1408, 3110
Masterson, Kathleen *(Librettist)* 99, 3463
Masterson, Kathleen *(Lyricist)* 99, 3463
Masterson, Peter *(Director)* 373, 374
Masterson, Peter *(Librettist)* 373, 374
Mastin, Will *(Cast)* 2987
Mastin Trio, Will *(Cast)* 861
Mastrantonio, Mary Elizabeth *(Cast)* 2033, 2346, 3231
Mastrocola, Frank *(Cast)* 3718, 4138
Masullo, Tony *(Choreographer)* 4172
Mata, Meta *(Cast)* 4166
Mata, Ruth *(Cast)* 4498
Mata & Hari *(Cast)* 2400, 4482
Mata & Hari *(Director)* 4482
Matalon, Vivian *(Director)* 4286
Matalon, Zack *(Cast)* 2150
Mataresse, Tony *(Composer)* 3530
Matesky, Jared *(Cast)* 4172
Mather, Sydney *(Cast)* 3537
Mather, Ted *(Lighting Designer)* 4399
Matheson, Barbara *(Costumes)* 3714
Mathews, Bert *(Cast)* 2238
Mathews, Carmen *(Cast)* 101, 869, 911, 1012, 1742, 2075, 3172, 4764, 4798
Mathews, Frances Aymar *(Author)* 3050
Mathews, George *(Cast)* 134, 1061
Mathews, J. Sherrie *(Cast)* 215, 604
Mathews, J. Sherrie *(Composer)* 215, 604
Mathews, J. Sherrie *(Librettist)* 604
Mathews, J. Sherrie *(Lyricist)* 215, 604, 3154
Mathews, Jimmy *(Cast)* 4197
Mathewson, Joseph *(Lyricist)* 4405
Mathieson, Greg *(Composer)* 3636
Mathieson, Greg *(Lyricist)* 3636
Mathieson, Muir *(Musical Director)* 2323
Mathis, Sherry *(Cast)* 2536, 3015, 4459
Mathis, Stanley Wayne *(Cast)* 1099
Mathison, A.E. *(Costumes)* 2645
Mathues, Craig *(Cast)* 1494
Mathven, Jennetta *(Cast)* 4133
Matlock, Norman *(Cast)* 2290, 4147
Matlovsky, Sam *(Musical Director)* 2304
Matlovsky, Samuel *(Composer)* 3286
Matlovsky, Samuel *(Musical Director)* 3224
Matlovsky, Samuel *(Orchestrations)* 747, 3224
Matlowsky, Samuel *(Musical Director)* 4369
Matons, Bill *(Choreographer)* 3647
Matray, Ernst *(Choreographer)* 3, 3381
Matray, Ernst *(Director)* 3
Matray, Ernst *(Librettist)* 3
Matray, Ernst *(Producer)* 3, 2323
Matray, Maria *(Choreographer)* 3, 3381
Matray, Maria *(Director)* 3
Matray, Maria *(Producer)* 3
Matson, Vera *(Composer)* 3739
Matson, Vera *(Lyricist)* 3739
Matsusaka, Tom *(Cast)* 3598
Matteson, Ruth *(Cast)* 2985, 3292
Mattfeld, Julius *(Composer)* 1244
Matthai, Konrad *(Producer)* 1478
Matthau, Walter *(Cast)* 2464
Matthew, Dana *(Producer)* 2046
Matthews, Adelaide *(Author)* 2281
Matthews, Adelaide *(Cast)* 2310
Matthews, Adelaide *(Lyricist)* 2281
Matthews, Artie *(Composer)* 4390
Matthews, Babe *(Cast)* 435
Matthews, Billy *(Director)* 339, 4337
Matthews, Brian *(Cast)* 869
Matthews, Edward *(Cast)* 1366, 1763, 3541
Matthews, Gerry *(Cast)* 427, 1023, 1049, 1107, 1362, 3274, 3484, 4065, 4268
Matthews, Hale *(Producer)* 1635, 1762

Matthews, Inez *(Cast)* 2591
Matthews, Jessie *(Cast)* 133, 1128, 1202, 3291, 4581
Matthews, Jon *(Cast)* 3806
Matthews, Julian *(Producer)* 215
Matthews, Junius *(Cast)* 1651, 1657
Matthews, Karen *(Costumes)* 1872
Matthews, Lester *(Cast)* 2392
Matthews, Robert *(Cast)* 793
Matthews, Roger *(Cast)* 3963
Matthews, Tom *(Cast)* 4011
Matthews, W. *(Costumes)* 1285
Matthews, W.H. *(Costumes)* 1357, 2670, 2691, 2756, 4801, 4802, 4803, 4804, 4805
Matthews, William H. *(Costumes)* 378, 712, 1134, 1208, 1281, 1378, 1552, 1900, 1901, 2922, 3978, 4012
Matthews, William H. *(Set Design)* 4808
Matthews, William Henry *(Costumes)* 683, 1016, 3525, 4247
Matthews Jr., William Henry *(Costumes)* 1524
Mattioli, Louis *(Librettist)* 4146
Mattison, Johnny *(Choreographer)* 3860
Mattox, Matt *(Cast)* 2679, 3288, 3496, 3845, 4542, 4827
Mattox, Matt *(Choreographer)* 2201, 2551, 3493, 3845, 4633
Mattson, Eric *(Cast)* 660, 4670
Mature, Victor *(Cast)* 2386, 4287
Matz, Peter *(Arrangements)* 3275
Matz, Peter *(Dance Arranger)* 98, 2190, 3187, 3286, 3815, 4682
Matz, Peter *(Musical Director)* 3187, 3275, 3286, 3815, 4585
Matz, Peter *(Orchestrations)* 147, 339, 373, 1649, 1729, 3126, 4566
Matz, Peter *(Vocal Arranger)* 98, 3286
Matz, Theodore A. *(Composer)* 3297
Matz, Theodore A. *(Lyricist)* 3297
Matzanauer, Adrienne *(Cast)* 2475
Maubourg, Jeanne *(Cast)* 2486
Mauceri, John *(Musical Director)* 4068
Maugham, Dora *(Cast)* 1275
Maugham, Somerset *(Author)* 1144
Maul, Betty *(Cast)* 1104
Maule, Brad *(Cast)* 2969
Maultsby, Carl *(Dance Arranger)* 2173
Maultsby, Carl *(Vocal Arranger)* 1816, 4192
Maurer, Michael *(Director)* 2142, 3752
Maurer, Michael *(Librettist)* 3752
Maurette, Marcelle *(Author)* 161
Maurice, Albert *(Composer)* 3856
Maurice, Marcus *(Cast)* 3568
Maurice, May *(Cast)* 2008
Maury, Richard *(Director)* 3110
Maury, Richard *(Librettist)* 2246, 3108, 3110, 3941
Maury, Richard *(Lyricist)* 3108, 3110
Mavin Productions *(Producer)* 1059
Mawin Productions *(Producer)* 3965
Max & Mahieu
See also Mahieu.
Max & Mahieu *(Costumes)* 335, 3308, 4250, 4599
Maxcellas, The *(Cast)* 3822
Maxim, John *(Cast)* 2362
Maxmen, Mimi *(Costumes)* 1279, 3722
Maxmen, Mimi *(Set Design)* 1279
Maxson, Bob *(Choreographer)* 2084, 2096
Maxson, Bob *(Director)* 2084, 2096
Maxson, Helen *(Choreographer)* 2084, 2095, 2096
Maxson, Helen *(Director)* 2084, 2096
Maxson, Ruby *(Cast)* 2088
Maxwell, Arthur *(Cast)* 63, 2439, 2797
Maxwell, Chris *(Choreographer)* 3134
Maxwell, Edwin *(Director)* 4284
Maxwell, Elsa *(Composer)* 665
Maxwell, Elsa *(Producer)* 4677
Maxwell, Frank *(Cast)* 2680
Maxwell, Marilyn *(Cast)* 3091
Maxwell, Michael *(Producer)* 626
Maxwell, Mitchell *(Director)* 140, 747
Maxwell, Mitchell *(Producer)* 140, 478, 747
Maxwell, Vera *(Cast)* 4804
Maxwell, Vera *(Choreographer)* 968
Maxwell, William *(Cast)* 1646
May, Ada *(Cast)* 791, 3719
May, Billy *(Orchestrations)* 3428
May, Bobby *(Cast)* 4006
May, Deborah *(Cast)* 1402
May, Earl C. *(Cast)* 4076
May, Edna *(Cast)* 357, 675, 1543, 2788, 3092, 3834, 3857
May, Florence *(Cast)* 2291
May, Helen *(Cast)* 3446
May, Jane *(Cast)* 675
May, Maggie *(Cast)* 4354
May, Marty *(Cast)* 153, 372, 1423, 2401, 3381, 4586
May, Olive *(Cast)* 3388
May, Val *(Director)* 2240
May, William *(Producer)* 2754
Maye, Edythe *(Cast)* 1944
Mayehoff, Eddie *(Cast)* 3703
Mayer, Don *(Lyricist)* 3942
Mayer, Edwin Justus *(Author)* 1283, 1284
Mayer, Edwin Justus *(Librettist)* 1284
Mayer, George *(Set Design)* 1435
Mayer, Hy *(Costumes)* 1210, 4064
Mayer, Jeremy *(Cast)* 3318
Mayer, Jo *(Lighting Designer)* 2968, 3167
Mayer, Joseph *(Composer)* 2392, 3946, 4249
Mayer, Marcus *(Director)* 4554
Mayer, Michael *(Director)* 2038
Mayer, Ray *(Cast)* 297, 4152, 4291
Mayer, Timothy S. *(Librettist)* 3060
Mayerl, Billy *(Cast)* 4661
Mayerl, Billy *(Composer)* 702
Mayers, Lloyd *(Dance Arranger)* 4091
Mayers, Lloyd *(Vocal Arranger)* 4091
Mayerson, Frederic H. *(Producer)* 2143, 3862, 4031
Mayes, Sally *(Cast)* 784, 992, 4619
Mayfair, Mitzi *(Cast)* 622, 3955, 4267, 4823
Mayfair Productions *(Producer)* 1939
Mayfield, Cleo *(Cast)* 86, 473, 480, 577, 2135, 2587, 2732, 2900, 4858

Mayfield, Julian *(Cast)* 2591
Mayfield, Kathryn *(Cast)* 3104, 3415, 3860
Mayfield, Menlo *(Librettist)* 293
Mayfield, Menlo *(Lyricist)* 293
Mayfield, Percy *(Composer)* 1713
Mayfield, Percy *(Lyricist)* 1713
Mayhall, Jerry *(Arrangements)* 2077
Mayhew, Billy *(Composer)* 39
Mayhew, Billy *(Lyricist)* 39
Mayhew, Kate *(Cast)* 4544
Mayhew, Stella *(Cast)* 830, 1403, 1836, 1916, 2232, 2358, 2371, 2481, 2722, 4553, 4655, 4747
Mayhood, Orville *(Musical Director)* 2387
Mayhood, Orville L. *(Lyricist)* 3738
Maynard, Charles A. *(Director)* 2825, 3569
Maynard, Dorothy *(Cast)* 385, 3319
Maynard, Edwin *(Cast)* 1563
Maynard, Ruth *(Cast)* 3271
Mayne, Frank *(Cast)* 3323
Mayne, Leslie *(Lyricist)* 2844, 3098, 3313, 3322, 3803, 4115, 4430
Mayo, Don *(Cast)* 1510
Mayo, Fred *(Composer)* 1626
Mayo, Harry *(Cast)* 953
Mayo, Joan *(Costumes)* 2633
Mayo, Margaret *(Author)* 1904, 3534, 3740
Mayo, Margaret *(Librettist)* 3534, 3740, 4589
Mayo, Margaret *(Lyricist)* 3534
Mayo, Sam *(Composer)* 1763
Mayo, Sam *(Lyricist)* 1763
Mayon, John *(Cast)* 2498
Mayro, Jacqueline *(Cast)* 181, 766, 1709, 2278, 4678
Mayson, Edward *(Composer)* 3248
Mazel Musicals *(Producer)* 3926
Mazibuko, Brian *(Cast)* 4438
Mazier, Eddie *(Cast)* 3545
Mazin, Stan *(Choreographer)* 1262
Mazursky, Paul *(Cast)* 3940
Mazursky, Paul *(Director)* 2288
Mazzeo, Roger *(Cast)* 240
Mazzie, Marin *(Cast)* 3411
Mbonani, Themba *(Cast)* 4438
McAfee, Don *(Composer)* 1676
McAliece, F.J. *(Lighting Designer)* 722
McAlister, David *(Cast)* 3429
McAllen, Kathleen Rowe *(Cast)* 158
McAllister, Blue *(Cast)* 444, 3704
McAloney, Michael *(Producer)* 3846
McAnuff, Des *(Composer)* 1015, 2429
McAnuff, Des *(Director)* 394, 1015, 2429, 4676
McAnuff, Des *(Librettist)* 1015, 2429, 4676
McAnuff, Des *(Lyricist)* 1015, 2429
McAnuff, Des *(Vocal Arranger)* 1015
McArdle, Andrea *(Cast)* 150, 4138, 4146
McArdle, John *(Cast)* 1561
McArt, Jan *(Cast)* 190
McArt, Jan *(Producer)* 3576
McArthur, Edwin *(Composer)* 3720
McArthur, Edwin *(Musical Director)* 616
McArthur, Neil *(Orchestrations)* 1296
McAteer, Kathryn *(Cast)* 2142, 2790
McAuliffe, Jason *(Cast)* 1346
McAuliffe, Jason *(Composer)* 1346
McAuliffe, Jerry *(Cast)* 3423
McAvoy, Dan *(Cast)* 830, 2974, 3820
McAvoy, Dan *(Composer)* 2974
McAvoy, J.P. *(Author)* 3953
McBain, Allison *(Cast)* 2620
McBride, Edith Ethel *(Cast)* 1526
McBride, Irene *(Cast)* 2068, 4374
McBride, Ora *(Cast)* 2977
McBroom, Amanda *(Composer)* 4, 1804
McBroom, Amanda *(Librettist)* 1804
McBroom, Amanda *(Lyricist)* 4, 1804
McCabe, James *(Orchestrations)* 1962
McCabe, James C. *(Orchestrations)* 3403
McCall, Janet *(Cast)* 793
McCall, Marti *(Composer)* 1713
McCall, Marti *(Lyricist)* 1713
McCall, Nancy *(Cast)* 1813
McCallion, Joseph *(Cast)* 1014
McCamm, James *(Lighting Designer)* 3683
McCamm, James *(Set Design)* 3683
McCandless, Stanley *(Lighting Designer)* 3703
McCane, Mabel *(Cast)* 1560, 1562, 3866
McCane, Mabel *(Lyricist)* 548
McCann, Elizabeth I. *(Producer)* 2474
McCann, Elizabeth Ireland *(Producer)* 3142
McCann, Gene *(Cast)* 4332
McCann, Geraldine *(Cast)* 4125
McCarroll, Earl *(Cast)* 81
McCarroll, Earl *(Librettist)* 81
McCarroll, Ernest *(Cast)* 4220
McCarron, Charles *(Composer)* 3297
McCarron, Charles *(Lyricist)* 965, 1063, 3297, 3737
McCarron, Charles A. *(Composer)* 370
McCarron, Charles A. *(Lyricist)* 370
McCarry, Charles E. *(Set Design)* 1969, 2046, 2224, 4347
McCarter Theatre Company *(Producer)* 2305
McCarthy, Bob *(Lighting Designer)* 1269
McCarthy, Charles *(Cast)* 1283
McCarthy, Dorothy *(Cast)* 2382
McCarthy, Hector *(Composer)* 4589
McCarthy, Jeff *(Cast)* 533, 4020
McCarthy, Joe *(Lyricist)* 1963
McCarthy, Joseph *(Composer)* 4153
McCarthy, Joseph *(Lyricist)* 25, 89, 501, 560, 685, 931, 965, 1065, 1208, 1334, 1501, 1582, 1873, 1963, 2148, 2308, 3100, 3246, 3396, 3719, 3737, 3791, 4529, 4589, 4813, 4814, 4817, 4818, 4822, 4823
McCarthy, Justin Huntley *(Author)* 2670, 3219, 4539
McCarthy, Justin Huntley *(Librettist)* 2670
McCarthy, Justin Huntley *(Lyricist)* 2670
McCarthy, Kevin *(Cast)* 3841, 4706
McCarthy, Lawrence *(Librettist)* 2394
McCarthy, Margaret *(Cast)* 2382
McCarthy, Mary *(Cast)* 4015
McCarthy, Tom *(Cast)* 264
McCarthy, W.J. *(Cast)* 2258

McCarthy, William *(Cast)* 689, 3924
McCarthy Jr., Joseph *(Lyricist)* 2227, 4827
McCarthy Sisters, The *(Cast)* 1489
McCartney, Ellen *(Costumes)* 240
McCartney, Mary *(Librettist)* 164
McCartney, Paul *(Author)* 3903
McCartney, Paul *(Composer)* 3739, 4193
McCartney, Paul *(Librettist)* 3903
McCartney, Paul *(Lyricist)* 3739, 3903, 4193
McCarty, Ernest *(Composer)* 2051
McCarty, Ernest *(Lyricist)* 2051
McCarty, Mary *(Cast)* 454, 723, 1329, 2894, 4018
McCarty, Mary *(Composer)* 2294
McCarty, Mary *(Lyricist)* 2294
McCarty, Michael *(Cast)* 2318
McCarver, Bamboo *(Cast)* 2845
McCary, Ernest *(Orchestrations)* 2051
McCauley, Jack *(Cast)* 1440, 1475, 1874, 1886, 3409, 3955, 4174, 4826
McCauley, John *(Cast)* 1916
McCauley, Judith *(Cast)* 2219
McChesney, Ernest *(Cast)* 3767
McClain, Florence *(Additional Lyrics)* 1821
McClain, Florence *(Additional Music)* 1821
McClain, Florence *(Cast)* 2113
McClain, George *(Cast)* 1479, 1909
McClain, Marcia *(Cast)* 426, 1086
McClain, Saundra *(Cast)* 828
McClanahan, Rue *(Cast)* 2218
McClaskie, Alden *(Cast)* 3028
McCleary, Michael *(Composer)* 1134
McCleary, R.C. *(Set Design)* 719, 1454, 2964, 2974, 4014
McCleery, R.C. *(Musical Director)* 1610
McClellan, Clark *(Dance Arranger)* 4678
McClellan, Clark *(Musical Director)* 766, 2616
McClellan, Clark *(Orchestrations)* 415, 766, 4678
McClellan, Clark *(Vocal Arranger)* 415, 2616
McClellan, George B. *(Producer)* 976
McClellan, Jack *(Librettist)* 2380
McClelland, Kay *(Cast)* 775, 2143
McClelland, Keith *(Orchestrations)* 941
McClendon, Afi *(Cast)* 3285
McClendon, Rue *(Cast)* 1020
McClennahan, Charles *(Set Design)* 1425
McClennon, George *(Cast)* 3200, 3965
McClintic, Guthrie *(Director)* 2712, 2994
McClintic, Guthrie *(Producer)* 1007, 2712
McCloud *(Composer)* 655
McCloud *(Lyricist)* 655
McClure, Bob *(Cast)* 2357
McClure, Edna *(Cast)* 308
McColl, Mitzi *(Cast)* 4230
McCollin, A.W.F. *(Cast)* 402
McComas, Carroll *(Cast)* 3422
McComb, Malcolm *(Lyricist)* 1874, 4235
McConaughty, Jim *(Cast)* 4736
McConnell *(Composer)* 1925
McConnell *(Lyricist)* 1925
McConnell, Lula *(Cast)* 3407
McConnell, Lulu *(Cast)* 289, 931, 3436, 3538, 4033, 4545, 4816
McConnell, Ty *(Cast)* 840, 1012, 1249, 2633, 3602
McConrad, Guthrie *(Director)* 557
McCord, Nancy *(Cast)* 82, 324, 2786, 4550
McCorder, Lucille *(Costumes)* 4271
McCorkle, David *(Cast)* 2220
McCormack, Danny *(Cast)* 3025, 3026
McCormack, Frank *(Director)* 110, 2888, 3147, 4148, 4555
McCormick, Andrew A. *(Producer)* 1896
McCormick, Dolly *(Cast)* 1980
McCormick, Frank *(Director)* 2489
McCormick, Michael *(Cast)* 705, 2333, 3853
McCormick, Myron *(Cast)* 3188, 4096
McCormick, Pat *(Librettist)* 4627
McCormick, Pearl *(Cast)* 3361
McCormick, Robert *(Cast)* 2654, 3695
McCourt, Sean *(Cast)* 1969
McCown, Ellen *(Cast)* 1698
McCoy, Bessie
See also Bessie McCoy Davis.
McCoy, Bessie *(Cast)* 1151, 2715, 2900, 4115, 4364, 4753, 4805
McCoy, Bessie *(Lyricist)* 4805
McCoy, Eleanor *(Cast)* 4383
McCoy, Frank *(Director)* 1275, 1440
McCoy, Joe *(Composer)* 3428
McCoy, Joe *(Lyricist)* 3428
McCoy, Kerry *(Musical Director)* 2436
McCoy, Michael *(Composer)* 1232
McCoy, Nellie *(Cast)* 2715, 3977
McCoy, R. *(Composer)* 1296
McCoy, R. *(Lyricist)* 1296
McCracken, Joan *(Cast)* 404, 462, 596, 961, 2797, 3263
McCrane, Paul *(Cast)* 1053
McCree, Junie *(Cast)* 228, 246, 1563, 1728, 1746, 2710, 2851, 3883, 4098, 4222, 4691
McCree, Junie *(Composer)* 3313
McCree, Junie *(Librettist)* 1746, 2710, 3026
McCree, Junie *(Lyricist)* 246, 1120, 1746, 2261, 2667, 2710, 3313, 4757
McCreery, Bud *(Cast)* 3940
McCreery, Bud *(Composer)* 272, 1023, 1049, 1362, 1363, 2554, 2804, 3186, 3484, 3615, 3940, 3941, 3942, 4047, 4416
McCreery, Bud *(Librettist)* 2554, 2804
McCreery, Bud *(Lyricist)* 272, 1023, 1049, 1362, 1363, 2554, 2804, 3186, 3484, 3615, 3940, 3941, 3942, 4047, 4416
McCreery, Bud *(Producer)* 4156
McCreery, Bud *(Vocal Arranger)* 2804
McCullers, Carson *(Author)* 1222
McCullers, Carson *(Librettist)* 1222
McCulloh, Barbara *(Cast)* 2354
McCullough, Carl *(Cast)* 628, 2119, 4784
McCullough, Paul
See also Clark & McCullough.
McCullough, Paul *(Cast)* 1856, 2403, 3426, 3659, 4179, 4374, 4583

McCutcheon, Bill *(Cast)* 825, 1648, 2018, 3108, 3186, 3942, 4627
McCutcheon, George Barr *(Author)* 4860
McCutcheon, John T. *(Costumes)* 4201
McCutcheon, Wallace *(Cast)* 1131, 1199, 1569, 1849, 3621, 3681, 4017
McCutcheon, Wallace *(Choreographer)* 968
McDaniel *(Composer)* 432
McDaniel *(Lyricist)* 432
McDaniel, John *(Dance Arranger)* 589
McDaniel, John *(Musical Director)* 589
McDaniel, John *(Vocal Arranger)* 589
McDaniel, Keith *(Cast)* 2427
McDaniel, William Foster *(Arrangements)* 1099
McDaniel, William Foster *(Musical Director)* 1099
McDermott, Keith *(Cast)* 1775
McDermott, Michelle *(Cast)* 2676
McDermott, W.J. *(Cast)* 1758
McDevitt, Bob *(Producer)* 280
McDonald, Bill *(Choreographer)* 62
McDonald, Gertrude *(Cast)* 1419, 3254, 4335, 4392
McDonald, Grace *(Cast)* 3292, 4557
McDonald, James *(Composer)* 4062
McDonald, James *(Librettist)* 4062
McDonald, James *(Lyricist)* 4062
McDonald, Joe *(Composer)* 3739
McDonald, Joe *(Lyricist)* 3739
McDonald, Marie *(Cast)* 1565
McDonald, Ray *(Cast)* 247, 3390
McDonald, Sadie *(Cast)* 3228
McDonald, Tanny *(Cast)* 2229
McDonald, W.H. *(Cast)* 3570, 3881
McDonough, Glen *(Author)* 2795
McDonough, Harry *(Cast)* 175
McDowall, Roddy *(Cast)* 623, 928, 3188
McDowell, Bob *(Arrangements)* 2416
McDowell, Bob *(Musical Director)* 2416
McDowell, John *(Cast)* 202
McDuffie, Laura *(Cast)* 4689
McElhinay, Rick *(Cast)* 2320
McElroy, Jackie *(Cast)* 3505
McElroy, Michael *(Cast)* 1890
McElwaine, James *(Musical Director)* 2441
McElwaine, James *(Orchestrations)* 1589, 2441, 4139
McEnroe, Robert E. *(Librettist)* 1076
McEvoy, J.P. *(Librettist)* 86, 123, 125, 827, 3179, 4142, 4819
McEvoy, J.P. *(Lyricist)* 123, 124, 827
McEwen, Odetta *(Cast)* 1046
McEwen, Walter *(Cast)* 3948
McFadden *(Composer)* 2133
McFadden *(Lyricist)* 2133
McFarland, C.K. *(Cast)* 914
McFarland, C.K. *(Librettist)* 914
McGail, Paul *(Cast)* 782
McGarity, Jerry *(Cast)* 992
McGarrahan, Jerry *(Musical Director)* 1957
McGee, Corliss *(Set Design)* 2032
McGee, Richard Dwight *(Costumes)* 3329
McGee, Rusty *(Composer)* 3853
McGee, Rusty *(Lyricist)* 3853
McGee, Truly *(Choreographer)* 1987, 3121
McGee, Truly *(Director)* 1934
McGhee, Brownie *(Cast)* 3983
McGhee, John *(Musical Director)* 2698
McGhie, John *(Musical Director)* 48, 276, 968, 1111, 2145, 2292, 2430, 2502, 2532, 2701, 2724, 3177, 3773, 3943, 4250, 4762
McGibeney, Donald *(Composer)* 3768
McGill, Alma *(Cast)* 3357
McGill, Bruce *(Cast)* 3060
McGill, Everett *(Cast)* 3764
McGillin, Howard *(Cast)* 2359, 3070
McGinley, Phyllis *(Lyricist)* 3178, 4018
McGinn, Frank *(Cast)* 3230
McGinn, Walter *(Cast)* 1864
McGinness, Joe *(Author)* 3871
McGiveney *(Cast)* 3629
McGiveney, Michael *(Librettist)* 3629
McGiver, John *(Cast)* 1674
McGlennon, George *(Cast)* 1983
McGonigal, William *(Director)* 516
McGough, Robert *(Lyricist)* 4701
McGourty, Patricia *(Costumes)* 394, 669, 1015, 1077, 1402, 3555, 3608, 4022
McGovern, Dennis *(Cast)* 1635
McGovern, Maureen *(Cast)* 4019, 4371
McGowan, Jack *(Cast)* 1485, 2268, 2494, 2767, 3723, 4269, 4648, 4836
McGowan, Jack *(Director)* 4177
McGowan, Jack *(Librettist)* 1137, 1800, 3850, 4177, 4240
McGowan, Jack *(Producer)* 3850
McGowan, Jane *(Cast)* 2085
McGowan, John *(Author)* 1215, 3993
McGowan, John *(Director)* 3379
McGowan, John *(Librettist)* 921, 1323, 1528, 1929, 3005
McGrane, Don *(Orchestrations)* 3166
McGrane, Paul *(Composer)* 2099, 4143, 4677
McGrane, Paul *(Conductor)* 507
McGrath, George *(Cast)* 1064, 3418
McGrath, John *(Author)* 4685
McGrath, Mark *(Cast)* 1092
McGrath, Matthew *(Cast)* 4744
McGrath, Michael *(Cast)* 4255
McGrath, Paul *(Cast)* 3816
McGrath, Thomas *(Cast)* 3450
McGraw, Martha *(Cast)* 3450
McGraw, William *(Cast)* 1085
McGreevey, Annie *(Cast)* 2687, 2949, 4288
McGregor, Dion *(Lyricist)* 1107
McGregor, G.W. *(Producer)* 4620
McGroder, Carol *(Producer)* 1581
McGroder, Jack *(Costumes)* 319
McGroder, Jack *(Set Design)* 319
McGuckin, Albert *(Cast)* 4646
McGuinn, Roger *(Composer)* 3695
McGuinn, Roger *(Lyricist)* 3695
McGuire, Biff *(Additional Dialogue)* 3630
McGuire, Biff *(Cast)* 339, 961, 1766, 2234, 3630, 4096
McGuire, Dorothy *(Cast)* 4256

McGuire, Paul C. *(Set Design)* 2928
McGuire, William Anthony *(Director)* 376, 1404, 3721, 3766, 4023, 4357, 4683
McGuire, William Anthony *(Librettist)* 376, 1404, 1667, 2308, 2872, 3721, 3766, 3953, 4023, 4357, 4683, 4818
McGuire III, John Thomas *(Cast)* 2658
McGunigle, Brian *(Librettist)* 3714
McGunigle, Robert *(Librettist)* 4583
McGurn, Ned *(Choreographer)* 1137, 2068, 2444, 3002, 3104, 3990
McHale, Duke *(Cast)* 247, 3584, 4825
McHorter, Evlyn *(Costumes)* 3511, 4817
McHugh, Augustin *(Librettist)* 1875, 1882, 2174
McHugh, Burke *(Cast)* 1697
McHugh, David *(Composer)* 1282
McHugh, Frank *(Cast)* 993, 1215, 3953
McHugh, James *(Lyricist)* 4303
McHugh, Jimmy *(Cast)* 3153, 3639
McHugh, Jimmy *(Composer)* 39, 206, 432, 441, 442, 487, 787, 892, 893, 894, 895, 1460, 1827, 2140, 2301, 3018, 3444, 3639, 3704, 3709, 3905, 3946, 3993, 4010, 4131, 4174, 4180, 4197, 4427, 4534, 4545, 4847, 4848
McHugh, Jimmy *(Lyricist)* 4427
McIlmoyle, Jean *(Cast)* 1466
McIlvane, Thomas *(Costumes)* 1640
McInerney, Bernie *(Cast)* 942
McIntosh, Hattie *(Cast)* 2111, 2979, 4088
McIntyre, Dianne *(Choreographer)* 1161, 1671, 3001
McIntyre, Frank *(Cast)* 495, 1691, 3251, 3622, 3775, 4001, 4213
McIntyre, Gerry *(Cast)* 549, 3285
McIntyre, Jack *(Cast)* 3604
McIntyre, James
See also McIntyre & Heath.
McIntyre, James *(Cast)* 110, 1731, 1799, 3677
McIntyre, John *(Cast)* 2119
McIntyre, Leila *(Cast)* 968, 1558, 2493, 2964, 3045, 4647
McIntyre, Molly *(Cast)* 1221
McIntyre & Heath
See also Tom Heath and James McIntyre.
McIntyre & Heath *(Cast)* 1823, 3958
McIver, Ray *(Librettist)* 1592
McIver, Ray *(Lyricist)* 1592
McKay, Frederic *(Producer)* 543, 4589, 4642
McKay, Kay *(Cast)* 203, 2808
McKay, Neil *(Choreographer)* 2147
McKay, Windsor *(Author)* 2534
McKaye, Dorothea *(Cast)* 3868
McKayle, Donald *(Choreographer)* 1063, 1601, 2075, 2306, 3656, 4091, 4384
McKayle, Donald *(Director)* 1063, 2415, 3656
McKean, Verd *(Arrangements)* 1883
McKean, Verd *(Musical Director)* 1883
McKechnie, Donna *(Cast)* 155, 746, 832, 944, 1158, 2072, 3018, 3603, 4146
McKee *(Producer)* 998
McKee, Frank *(Producer)* 48, 1521, 1925, 4130, 4165
McKee, Jeanellen *(Producer)* 2288
McKee, John *(Cast)* 1520
McKee, John *(Director)* 2377, 2564, 2605, 3868
McKee, Julia *(Director)* 2446
McKee, Lonette *(Cast)* 1289
McKee, Tom *(Lyricist)* 242
McKeever, Jacquelyn *(Cast)* 649, 3234
McKellar, John *(Composer)* 4433
McKellar, John *(Librettist)* 2305, 4433
McKellar, John *(Lyricist)* 2305, 4433
McKenna, Boots *(Choreographer)* 1127, 1414, 2397, 3822
McKenna, J.P. *(Composer)* 2996
McKenna, J.P. *(Lyricist)* 2996
McKenna, Kenneth *(Cast)* 2821
McKenna, Philip C. *(Producer)* 3918
McKenna, Virginia *(Cast)* 3454
McKenna, William *(Lyricist)* 3729
McKenna, William C. *(Lyricist)* 2232
McKenna, William J. *(Composer)* 592
McKennan, Arnett *(Lyricist)* 814
McKenney, John *(Musical Director)* 1418
McKenney, Ruth *(Author)* 4734
McKenzie, Alice *(Cast)* 3978
McKenzie, Branice *(Cast)* 3905
McKenzie, Branice *(Composer)* 3905
McKenzie, Branice *(Lyricist)* 3905
McKenzie, Herbert *(Cast)* 929
McKenzie, Julia *(Cast)* 2682, 3967
McKenzie, Julia *(Director)* 4067
McKeon, Doug *(Cast)* 4459
McKeon, Joseph H. *(Lyricist)* 2825
McKernon, John *(Lighting Designer)* 1425
McKie, Shirley *(Cast)* 344
McKinley, Mary *(Costumes)* 1010, 2297, 2962
McKinley, Philip William *(Cast)* 2861
McKinley, Philip William *(Director)* 3708
McKinley, Tom *(Costumes)* 4349
McKinney, John *(Composer)* 3010
McKinney, John *(Dance Arranger)* 1776, 2993
McKinney, John *(Librettist)* 1897
McKinney, John *(Orchestrations)* 705, 1776, 1897, 3368, 4390
McKinney, John *(Vocal Arranger)* 198, 1776, 4390, 4412
McKinney, Julian Jean *(Cast)* 1876
McKinney, Nina Mae *(Cast)* 289, 882, 4281
McKinney, Tom *(Cast)* 1092
McKinnon, Fred *(Lighting Designer)* 1815
McKinnon, Rik *(Cast)* 2092, 2094, 2095
McKneely, Joey *(Choreographer)* 4031
McKnight, Thomas *(Composer)* 1448
McKnight, Thomas *(Lyricist)* 1448
McKnight, Tom *(Additional Dialogue)* 1840
McKnight, Tom *(Librettist)* 4174
McKuen, Rod *(Cast)* 499
McKuen, Rod *(Composer)* 499
McKuen, Rod *(Lyricist)* 499
McLain, John *(Lighting Designer)* 114, 496, 1609, 2970, 2992, 3169, 3873, 3908, 4109, 4171
McLane, Derek *(Set Design)* 1291, 1822
McLane, Lorenzo *(Cast)* 471
McLaren, Ivor *(Cast)* 2004

McLaren, Jack *(Librettist)* 388
McLaughlin, Andra *(Cast)* 2083
McLaughlin, Don *(Cast)* 2413
McLaughlin, Edith *(Costumes)* 1337
McLaughlin, Gene *(Cast)* 2413
McLaughlin, Mark *(Cast)* 4601
McLaughlin, Robert *(Composer)* 4707
McLaughlin, Robert *(Director)* 4707
McLaughlin, Robert *(Librettist)* 4707
McLaughlin, Robert *(Lyricist)* 4707
McLean, Don *(Composer)* 3739
McLean, Don *(Lyricist)* 3739
McLean, Ross *(Cast)* 1492
McLellan, C.M.S. *(Librettist)* 186, 2497, 2760, 3092, 3251, 3494
McLellan, C.M.S. *(Lyricist)* 186, 2497, 2760, 3092, 3251, 3494, 4805
McLellan, E.G. *(Composer)* 954
McLellan, E.G. *(Lyricist)* 954
McLellan, George B. *(Producer)* 4298
McLellan, Harry *(Composer)* 3689
McLellan, Robert *(Cast)* 378
McLennan, Oliver *(Cast)* 3766
McLennan, Rod *(Cast)* 3038
McLennan, Rodney *(Cast)* 4640, 4825
McLeod, Callum *(Composer)* 3208
McLeod, Debbie *(Cast)* 251
McLeod, John *(Cast)* 4623
McLeod, Lane *(Cast)* 1176
McLerie, Allyn *(Cast)* 2894
McLerie, Allyn Ann *(Cast)* 322, 490, 616, 4652
McLiam, John *(Author)* 3984
McLure, James *(Cast)* 3010
McLusky, Graham *(Lighting Designer)* 580
McMahon, Edward *(Cast)* 4706
McMahon, Horace *(Cast)* 3845
McMahon, Jere *(Cast)* 3893
McMahon, Jere *(Choreographer)* 2483
McMahon, Jere *(Lyricist)* 2483
McMahon, Jim *(Cast)* 3476
McManus, George *(Author)* 537, 538, 539, 540, 541, 542, 2448, 3134, 3357
McManus, John *(Composer)* 2174, 2401
McManus, John *(Lyricist)* 2174
McManus, John *(Musical Director)* 512, 901, 1113, 1176, 1238, 1387, 1882, 2342, 2400, 2423, 3678, 3822, 3885, 3906, 4174, 4569, 4610, 4777, 4824, 4825, 4826
McManus, John L. *(Composer)* 2174
McManus, John L. *(Dance Arranger)* 3796
McManus, John L. *(Musical Director)* 1779, 2174, 2757, 3796
McManus, John L. *(Orchestrations)* 3796
McManus, John L. *(Vocal Arranger)* 3796
McManus, May *(Cast)* 1218
McManus, Thomas *(Musical Director)* 1396
McMartin, John *(Cast)* 837, 1329, 1762, 2522, 2607, 2877, 3526, 4238
McMillan, Kenneth *(Cast)* 249
McNair, Barbara *(Cast)* 483
McNally, John J. *(Librettist)* 1318, 1403, 1627, 2035, 2119, 2123, 2481, 2493, 2566, 2964, 2974, 3744, 3745, 3746, 3747, 3749, 3750, 3751, 4014, 4130
McNally, Leonard *(Lyricist)* 3450
McNally, Terrence *(Author)* 546
McNally, Terrence *(Librettist)* 2333, 3718, 4535
McNally, Walter *(Cast)* 1121
McNamara, Maureen *(Cast)* 36, 1262
McNamara, Rosemary *(Cast)* 3631
McNaughton, Charles *(Cast)* 377, 1066, 3051, 3481, 3511
McNaughton, Harry *(Cast)* 622, 910, 3172, 3236, 3407, 3489, 4427, 4821
McNaughton, Stephen *(Cast)* 708
McNaughton, Steve *(Cast)* 2242
McNaughton, Tom *(Cast)* 3537
McNaughton, Tom *(Composer)* 2684
McNaughton, Tom *(Lyricist)* 2684
McNeely, Anna *(Cast)* 678
McNeil, Claudia *(Cast)* 1848, 3983
McNeil, Dan *(Cast)* 1549
McNeil, Lonnie *(Cast)* 576, 1198
McNeil, Neil *(Cast)* 2493
McNeil, Nell *(Cast)* 2938
McNight, Sharon *(Cast)* 4139
McNulty, Dorothy *(Cast)* 4010, 4249
McNulty, Frank *(Composer)* 2483
McNutt, Eileen *(Cast)* 2124
McPherran, Florence *(Composer)* 1518
McPherson, Don *(Cast)* 2097
McPherson, R.C. *(Lyricist)* 9, 295, 434, 2029, 2990
McPhillips, Tom *(Set Design)* 3991, 4534
McQueen, Armelia *(Cast)* 39, 1298, 1776
McQueen, Butterfly *(Cast)* 227, 4256, 4750
McQueen, Robert *(Costumes)* 1208
McQuiggan, John A. *(Producer)* 424, 1977
McQuinn, Robert *(Costumes)* 378, 396, 712, 1901, 4158
McQuinn, Robert *(Set Design)* 628, 4158, 4634
McRae *(Composer)* 3188
McRae *(Lyricist)* 3188
McRae, Bruce *(Cast)* 2526
McRae, Floyd F. *(Composer)* 3739, 4264
McRae, Floyd F. *(Lyricist)* 3739, 4264
McRae, Heather *(Cast)* 1864
McRae, Tom *(Librettist)* 2912
McRitchie, Greig *(Orchestrations)* 2083, 2084, 2092, 2093, 2094, 2095, 2096
McRoberts, Briony *(Cast)* 3454
McRoberts, Pat *(Cast)* 3125
McSweeney, J.P. *(Cast)* 1316
McVeigh, John *(Cast)* 2035, 4650
McVicker, Sarah *(Cast)* 4298
McWhinney, Michael *(Composer)* 392, 3111, 3186
McWhinney, Michael *(Librettist)* 1107, 3111
McWhinney, Michael *(Lyricist)* 62, 128, 366, 392, 1107, 1438, 1770, 2279, 2913, 3110, 3111, 3112, 3124, 3186
McWhinney, Michael *(Producer)* 128
McWhorter, Miss *(Costumes)* 4818
McWilliams, Caroline *(Cast)* 482
Mead, Shepherd *(Author)* 2019
Meade *(Composer)* 1869
Meade *(Costumes)* 1869

Meade *(Set Design)* 1869
Meade, Ada *(Cast)* 3658
Meade, Norman *(Composer)* 3739
Meade, Norman *(Lyricist)* 3739
Meade, Tom *(Cast)* 537
Meade, Tommy *(Cast)* 543
Meader, George *(Cast)* 672, 2255
Meadows, Hunt *(Cast)* 3997
Meadows, Kristen *(Cast)* 1256
Meadows, Michael *(Set Design)* 1816
Meara, Anne *(Cast)* 1999, 2804
Meara, Anne *(Librettist)* 4
Mears, DeAnn *(Cast)* 1017
Mears, Elizabeth *(Cast)* 2253
Mears, John Henry *(Librettist)* 2960
Mears, John Henry *(Lyricist)* 560, 685, 2960
Mears, John Henry *(Producer)* 2253
Mears, Stannard *(Author)* 1831
Meat Loaf *(Cast)* 2953, 3651, 3741, 3742
Medford, Don *(Producer)* 1754
Medford, Kay *(Cast)* 90, 607, 1420, 2227, 4582
Medley, Cassandra *(Librettist)* 4
Medoff, Mark *(Author)* 2704
Medoff, Mark *(Lyricist)* 2704
Mee, Kirk *(Director)* 973
Meech, Cliff *(Lyricist)* 2122
Meech, George J. *(Cast)* 2761
Meegan, Patrick *(Composer)* 533
Meegan, Thomas *(Cast)* 4381
Meehan, Aileen *(Cast)* 3185
Meehan, Danny *(Cast)* 1420, 1427, 4028, 4682
Meehan, Harry *(Cast)* 117, 1286, 3003, 3082, 4650
Meehan, John *(Director)* 1484, 3185, 3723
Meehan, Thomas *(Librettist)* 36, 150, 154, 155, 2064, 3181
Meehan, Thomas *(Lyricist)* 2662
Meehan Jr., John *(Librettist)* 1817, 3767
Meek, Donald *(Cast)* 1598, 2537, 2981, 3063, 3207
Meek, Joe *(Composer)* 3695
Meek, Joe *(Lyricist)* 3695
Meek, Kate *(Cast)* 2624
Meeker, George *(Cast)* 2253
Meeker, Jesse *(Dance Arranger)* 619
Meers, Paul *(Cast)* 3709
Megley, Macklin *(Director)* 1352
Megrue, Roi Cooper *(Author)* 126
Megrue, Roi Cooper *(Librettist)* 126
Mehan, Dodd *(Cast)* 4548
Mehler, Jack *(Lighting Designer)* 2038
Mehr, Rachel *(Costumes)* 2322
Meier, Ron *(Cast)* 3561
Meighan, Thomas *(Cast)* 41, 425
Meilhac, Henri *(Author)* 653, 2507
Meisel, Bella *(Composer)* 4342
Meisel, Bella *(Lyricist)* 4342
Meiser, Edith *(Cast)* 1446, 1447, 1448, 2453, 3436, 4516
Meiser, Edith *(Librettist)* 1446
Meiser, Edith *(Lyricist)* 1446
Meisner, Sanford *(Cast)* 1446, 2228
Meiss, Edwin *(Librettist)* 3104
Meister, Norman *(Cast)* 337
Meit, Marvin R. *(Producer)* 140, 747
Mekka, Eddie *(Cast)* 2472
Melanie *(Composer)* 13
Melanie *(Lyricist)* 13
Melchior, Lauritz *(Cast)* 177
Mele, Rande *(Cast)* 2704
Meleck, Tom *(Lighting Designer)* 400, 4773
Melfi, Leonard *(Author)* 4294
Melfi, Leonard *(Librettist)* 781, 3233
Melford, Austin *(Cast)* 3156
Melford, Austin *(Librettist)* 700, 3310
Melford, Austin *(Lyricist)* 3310
Melford, Jack *(Cast)* 2976
Melford, Quentin *(Author)* 2972
Melin, Frank *(Director)* 3822
Melis, Jose *(Composer)* 4264
Mell, Marisa *(Cast)* 2777
Mellin, Robert *(Lyricist)* 4264
Mellish, Fuller *(Cast)* 3056, 4692
Mellish, Harold *(Cast)* 3436
Mellish, Mary *(Cast)* 3078
Mellish Jr., Fuller *(Cast)* 3436, 3556
Mello, Al *(Dance Arranger)* 2626
Mellon, Edward *(Musical Director)* 1632
Mellon, Edward *(Vocal Arranger)* 1632
Mellon, James J. *(Choreographer)* 1279
Mellon, James J. *(Composer)* 4515
Mellon, James J. *(Librettist)* 4515
Mellon, James J. *(Lyricist)* 4515
Mellor, Tom *(Composer)* 2334, 3755, 4206
Mellor, Tom *(Lyricist)* 2334, 3755, 4206
Mellow, Stephen *(Producer)* 2018
Melnick, Daniel *(Producer)* 2304
Melnick, Linda Rodgers *(Composer)* 4363
Melnick, Marjorie *(Director)* 564
Melnotte, Violet *(Producer)* 2570
Melodee Four, The *(Cast)* 4763
Melrose, Ron *(Dance Arranger)* 16
Melrose, Ronald *(Composer)* 1371, 4533
Melrose, Ronald *(Dance Arranger)* 146, 2754, 3444, 4727
Melrose, Ronald *(Lyricist)* 4533
Melrose, Ronald *(Musical Director)* 146, 4034
Melrose, Ronald *(Orchestrations)* 4034
Melrose, Walter *(Composer)* 478, 2200
Melrose, Walter *(Lyricist)* 478, 1063
Melso, Chino *(Cast)* 4205
Melson, Joe *(Composer)* 3695
Melson, Joe *(Lyricist)* 3695
Meltzer, Robert *(Lyricist)* 2748
Melville, Alan *(Librettist)* 2168, 3107
Melville, Alan *(Lyricist)* 1408, 1467, 2168, 2227, 3107, 4153
Melville, Emile *(Cast)* 3432
Melville, Herman *(Author)* 406
Melville, Rose *(Cast)* 604, 3998
Melville, Rose *(Composer)* 3998
Melville, Rose *(Lyricist)* 3998

Melville, Winnie *(Cast)* 3583
Melvin, Murray *(Cast)* 3259
Members Yale Drama Assn.
See also Yale University Dramatic Assn.
Members Yale Drama Assn. *(Producer)* 4622
Members of the 385th Inf. *(Producer)* 214
Menace, Len *(Cast)* 4692
Menchell, Ivan *(Librettist)* 4027
Menchen, Joseph *(Lighting Designer)* 1459, 3585, 3951
Menchen, Joseph C. *(Lighting Designer)* 737
Mencher, Murray *(Composer)* 1127
Mendelsohn, David *(Orchestrations)* 2610
Mendelson, Gary *(Cast)* 3601
Mendelssohn, Felix *(Music Based On)* 4256
Mendoza, David *(Musical Director)* 2023, 2024, 2098, 2099, 2161, 2162, 4143
Mendoza, Dorothy *(Composer)* 4433
Mendoza, Dorothy *(Librettist)* 4433
Mendoza, Dorothy *(Lyricist)* 4433
Mendum, Georgia Drew *(Cast)* 1563, 2922
Menefee, Pete *(Costumes)* 2796, 3637
Menendez, Brad *(Cast)* 1757
Menken, Alan *(Composer)* 171, 245, 330, 754, 1038, 1591, 2038, 2171, 2307, 2544, 3448, 3557, 3666
Menken, Alan *(Director)* 3666
Menken, Alan *(Lyricist)* 3557, 3666
Menkes *(Costumes)* 3034
Mennefee, Pete *(Costumes)* 3936
Mensoff, Richard *(Lighting Designer)* 2913
Mentel, Jim *(Composer)* 3076
Mentel, Jim *(Lyricist)* 3076
Menten, Dale F. *(Composer)* 2001
Menten, Dale F. *(Lyricist)* 2001
Menten, Dale F. *(Musical Director)* 2001
Menzies, Angus *(Cast)* 3885
Meorz, Otto C.A. *(Orchestrations)* 968
Meranus, Norman *(Composer)* 2511
Meranus, Norman *(Lyricist)* 2511
Mercado, Hector *(Cast)* 2775
Mercado, Hector Jaime *(Cast)* 678, 1063, 3830, 4788
Mercardo, Ralph *(Producer)* 2356
Mercedes *(Set Design)* 621, 4677
Mercer, Beryl *(Cast)* 1357
Mercer, Frances *(Cast)* 4557
Mercer, Johnny *(Composer)* 3178, 3837, 4423
Mercer, Johnny *(Lyricist)* 125, 146, 213, 446, 447, 478, 964, 1359, 1373, 1385, 1448, 1619, 2204, 2484, 2611, 3175, 3178, 3352, 3385, 3428, 3705, 3837, 3840, 3888, 3905, 4091, 4123, 4131, 4291, 4314, 4423, 4498, 4586, 4799
Mercer, Mabel *(Cast)* 1318
Mercer, Marian *(Cast)* 128, 1436, 1993, 3110, 3111, 3195, 3603, 4789
Mercer, Ruby *(Cast)* 1352, 4670
Mercer, Will *(Composer)* 4098
Mercer, Will *(Lyricist)* 4098
Mercier, G.W. *(Costumes)* 674, 1700
Mercier, G.W. *(Set Design)* 674, 1700, 1739
Mercier, Rene *(Composer)* 1343, 4240
Mercouri, Melina *(Cast)* 2106, 2659
Mercury Theatre *(Producer)* 189, 919
Meredith, Burgess *(Cast)* 55, 1416, 1748, 2306, 3919, 4368
Meredith, Burgess *(Director)* 477, 1748, 2450
Meredith, Lee *(Cast)* 3019
Meredith, Morley *(Cast)* 751
Merimee, Prosper *(Author)* 653
Merkel, Una *(Cast)* 4270
Merkerson, S. Epatha *(Cast)* 166, 1099
Merkin, Robby *(Dance Arranger)* 2852
Merkin, Robby *(Orchestrations)* 474, 690, 1161, 1873, 2544, 2598, 2852, 4618
Merkin, Robby *(Vocal Arranger)* 474, 2852
Merkyl, John *(Cast)* 1014, 2387, 3323
Merle, Margaret *(Cast)* 3172
Merle, Sandi *(Composer)* 4347
Merle, Sandi *(Lyricist)* 4347
Merley, Heinz *(Author)* 3012
Merlin, F.S. *(Librettist)* 568
Merlin, Frank *(Cast)* 3874
Merlin, Frank *(Producer)* 4253
Merlin, Frank S. *(Director)* 670, 4021
Merlin, Joanna *(Cast)* 1265, 3927
Merlin, Ving *(Musical Director)* 84, 2397
Merlin, Ving *(Orchestrations)* 2397
Merlo, Michael *(Composer)* 4264
Merlo, Michael *(Lyricist)* 4264
Merman, Ethel *(Cast)* 153, 163, 619, 1109, 1416, 1492, 1528, 1709, 1760, 3359, 3674, 4058, 4142, 4267
Merman, Ethel *(Voice)* 3793
Merola, Gaetano *(Composer)* 93
Merola, Gaetano *(Musical Director)* 1285, 1530, 3051, 3081, 4133
Merriam, Eve *(Author)* 2134
Merriam, Eve *(Librettist)* 788
Merriam, Eve *(Lyricist)* 2134
Merrick, David *(Producer)* 34, 273, 521, 656, 1029, 1061, 1242, 1359, 1373, 1709, 1764, 1828, 1990, 2014, 2048, 2050, 2150, 2190, 2297, 2364, 2660, 2777, 3259, 3271, 3294, 3445, 3482, 3516, 3603, 3731, 3761, 4160, 4190, 4196, 4270, 4566, 4749
Merrick, Mike *(Producer)* 869
Merrick, Walt *(Composer)* 1296
Merrick, Walt *(Lyricist)* 1296
Merrigal, Alice *(Costumes)* 2393, 2661
Merrill, Blanche *(Composer)* 815, 3009, 3617, 4686, 4817, 4851
Merrill, Blanche *(Lyricist)* 70, 473, 815, 1704, 1944, 1946, 2180, 2696, 3009, 3345, 3399, 3617, 4440, 4686, 4806, 4810, 4811, 4814, 4815, 4817, 4838, 4851
Merrill, Bob *(Composer)* 521, 656, 1645, 1739, 1828, 1846, 1873, 3113, 3577, 4196, 4264, 4270
Merrill, Bob *(Librettist)* 1645, 1739, 3564, 3577
Merrill, Bob *(Lyricist)* 521, 656, 974, 1420, 1645, 1739, 1828, 1846, 1873, 2076, 2980, 3113, 3564, 3577, 3682, 4196, 4264, 4270
Merrill, Gary *(Cast)* 4340, 4706
Merrill, Howard *(Producer)* 3234
Merrill, Louis G. *(Composer)* 1624

Merrill, Marcia Lee *(Choreographer)* 345
Merrill, Paul *(Cast)* 564
Merrill, Scott *(Cast)* 4369
Merriman, Leo *(Musical Director)* 1758, 2328, 2335
Merritt, Theresa *(Cast)* 1222, 1616, 3001, 3321
Merson, Billy *(Composer)* 1963
Merson, Billy *(Lyricist)* 1963
Merson, Marc *(Producer)* 134
Mertz, Paul *(Vocal Arranger)* 1839
Merzvinsky, Edward *(Producer)* 1164
Meskill, Jack *(Composer)* 1136
Meskill, Jack *(Lyricist)* 1136
Messager, Andre *(Author)* 2524, 4554
Messager, Andre *(Composer)* 2524, 2937, 3079, 4554
Messel, Oliver *(Cast)* 4341
Messel, Oliver *(Costumes)* 791, 1511, 2000, 4469, 4581
Messel, Oliver *(Set Design)* 791, 2000, 4341, 4469, 4581
Messick, Don *(Voice)* 57
Mestayer, Harry *(Cast)* 3011, 4365
Metaxa, Georges *(Cast)* 503, 672, 1805, 3699, 4581
Metcalf, Ron *(Cast)* 4697
Metcalf, Ron *(Musical Director)* 4697
Metcalf, Ronald P. *(Musical Director)* 3724
Metcalf, Steven *(Composer)* 1093
Metcalf, Steven *(Musical Director)* 1093
Metcalfe, Edward *(Cast)* 2071
Metezl, Lothar *(Lyricist)* 3698
Meth, Max *(Musical Director)* 202, 203, 204, 206, 289, 341, 612, 971, 1101, 1342, 1577, 1679, 1693, 1799, 2187, 2432, 2453, 3170, 3365, 3850, 3899, 3990, 4267, 4335, 4524, 4828
Metheny, Russell *(Set Design)* 528, 1004, 1155, 2651, 3165
Methot, Mayo *(Cast)* 1667, 4083
Methven, Florence *(Composer)* 377
Metropolitan Stage Prods. *(Producer)* 2222
Metz, Janet *(Cast)* 1234
Metz, Theodore *(Composer)* 2796
Metz, Theodore M. *(Composer)* 662, 1425, 2415, 4390
Metzl, Beatrice *(Lyricist)* 2751
Metzl, Ervine *(Set Design)* 4047
Metzl, Lothar *(Librettist)* 1413
Metzl, Lothar *(Lyricist)* 2751, 3036, 3698
Metzler, Lawrence *(Lighting Designer)* 2375, 4485
Meyer, Adolf *(Producer)* 606
Meyer, Charles *(Cast)* 1078
Meyer, Chuck *(Composer)* 4829
Meyer, Chuck *(Lyricist)* 4829
Meyer, Dede *(Composer)* 3920, 4157, 4401
Meyer, Dede *(Lyricist)* 3920, 4157, 4401
Meyer, Dede *(Producer)* 3920
Meyer, Deed *(Composer)* 1347
Meyer, Deed *(Lyricist)* 1347
Meyer, Don *(Composer)* 4273
Meyer, Don *(Lyricist)* 4273
Meyer, Donna *(Costumes)* 962
Meyer, George *(Composer)* 3031, 4033
Meyer, George W. *(Composer)* 959, 1058, 1334, 1405, 1626, 1763, 2448, 2462, 2856, 3018, 3175, 3737, 3827, 4033, 4661, 4838
Meyer, George W. *(Lyricist)* 2462, 4661
Meyer, Henry *(Lyricist)* 4249
Meyer, Henry *(Producer)* 3907
Meyer, Irwin *(Producer)* 150, 1955, 4744
Meyer, John *(Composer)* 1436, 1648, 3484, 3890, 4643
Meyer, John *(Librettist)* 1363, 4643
Meyer, John *(Lyricist)* 1436, 1648, 2279, 2913, 3484, 3890, 4643
Meyer, Joseph *(Composer)* 124, 292, 391, 487, 702, 1296, 1460, 1859, 1923, 2112, 2238, 2277, 2382, 2392, 2972, 3020, 3103, 3104, 3149, 3444, 3662, 3953, 3966, 4235, 4249, 4320, 4581, 4730, 4766, 4799, 4824
Meyer, Joseph *(Lyricist)* 1296, 4730
Meyer, Joseph *(Orchestrations)* 2636
Meyer, Leo *(Composer)* 3926
Meyer, Leo *(Costumes)* 3302
Meyer, Leo *(Set Design)* 3302
Meyer, Leo W. *(Composer)* 3926
Meyer, Leo W. *(Lyricist)* 3926
Meyer, Paul *(Musical Director)* 2393
Meyer, Pieter *(Costumes)* 208, 4283
Meyer, Richard *(Composer)* 2976
Meyer, Sol *(Lyricist)* 2077, 2078
Meyer, Stan *(Set Design)* 330
Meyerhoff, Tom O. *(Producer)* 2852
Meyerovitch, D. *(Composer)* 1609
Meyerovitch, D. *(Lyricist)* 1609
Meyerowitz, David *(Composer)* 1279
Meyerowitz, David *(Lyricist)* 1279
Meyerowitz, Jan *(Composer)* 309
Meyers, Bubsy *(Composer)* 1296
Meyers, Bubsy *(Lyricist)* 1296
Meyers, Lanny *(Arrangements)* 3926
Meyers, Lanny *(Composer)* 1736, 3926
Meyers, Lanny *(Dance Arranger)* 1974, 3217
Meyers, Lanny *(Librettist)* 4167
Meyers, Lanny *(Lyricist)* 1736, 3926
Meyers, Lanny *(Musical Director)* 3722, 3926, 4167, 4769
Meyers, Lanny *(Orchestrations)* 3112, 3217, 4769
Meyers, Lanny *(Vocal Arranger)* 3217
Meyers, Nicholas *(Arrangements)* 793
Meyers, Nicholas *(Composer)* 169, 793
Meyers, Timothy *(Cast)* 1664
Meyers, Warren B. *(Composer)* 4388
Meyers, Zeke *(Lyricist)* 465, 733, 3057
Mezzio, John *(Arrangements)* 4799
Mezzio, John *(Musical Director)* 4799
Mezzio, John *(Orchestrations)* 4799
Mgt. III Prods. *(Producer)* 634
Mhlongo, Ndaba *(Conductor)* 3836
Michael, Margaret *(Librettist)* 1270
Michael, Patricia *(Cast)* 3429
Michael, Paul *(Cast)* 3988
Michaelis, Lisa *(Cast)* 3136
Michaelis, Robert *(Cast)* 1610
Michaels, Bert *(Cast)* 2660, 3564
Michaels, Bert *(Choreographer)* 1730, 2433
Michaels, Edwin *(Cast)* 3495
Michaels, Frankie *(Cast)* 2713

Michaels, Gloria *(Cast)* 2511
Michaels, Jackie *(Cast)* 4782
Michaels, Jerryn *(Lighting Designer)* 1508
Michaels, Laura *(Cast)* 2962
Michaels, Lorne *(Librettist)* 1512
Michaels, Lorne *(Producer)* 1512
Michaels, Patricia *(Librettist)* 2754
Michaels, Richard *(Director)* 4405
Michaels, Sidney *(Author)* 1730
Michaels, Sidney *(Librettist)* 367, 1634, 1730
Michaels, Sidney *(Lyricist)* 367, 1730
Michaels, Steve *(Composer)* 4347
Michaels, Steve *(Lyricist)* 4347
Michaels, Steve *(Musical Director)* 4347
Michel, Henry *(Cast)* 4096
Michel, Scott *(Author)* 4005
Michel, Werner *(Composer)* 1413, 3698
Michel, Werner *(Librettist)* 1413
Michel, Werner *(Lyricist)* 3036, 3698
Michele, Linda *(Cast)* 2742
Michelena, Kate *(Cast)* 1682
Michelena, Vera *(Cast)* 1308, 1417, 1519, 1555, 1570, 1967, 2490, 2605, 2832, 3087, 4269, 4434, 4808, 4815
Michell, Keith *(Cast)* 129, 2150
Michelle, Melanie *(Cast)* 1978
Michener, James A. *(Author)* 3851, 4096
Michi *(Costumes)* 861, 862, 1918
Michlin, Barry *(Cast)* 4635
Michon, Joe *(Cast)* 3172
Michon, Pete *(Cast)* 3172
Micunis, Gordon *(Costumes)* 4522
Micunis, Gordon *(Set Design)* 1837, 2219, 4522
Middleton, George *(Librettist)* 3532
Middleton, Ray *(Cast)* 117, 153, 752, 1899, 2344, 2615, 2727, 3612, 3735, 4706
Middleton, Raymond *(Cast)* 1494
Middleton, Velma *(Cast)* 497, 4501, 4502
Midgley, Fanny *(Cast)* 1388
Midgley, Raymond *(Choreographer)* 948, 1533, 2749, 2827, 3580, 3680, 4648, 4651
Miele, Elizabeth *(Lyricist)* 1918
Miele, Elizabeth *(Producer)* 1918
Mielziner, Jo *(Lighting Designer)* 64, 153, 304, 514, 629, 651, 751, 961, 1242, 1278, 1284, 1497, 1706, 1709, 1749, 1760, 2312, 2411, 2583, 2777, 2797, 2898, 2940, 2961, 2983, 3234, 3353, 3505, 3897, 3972, 4015, 4169, 4420, 4423, 4446, 4682, 4702, 4718, 4749
Mielziner, Jo *(Producer)* 1760
Mielziner, Jo *(Set Design)* 64, 85, 153, 273, 304, 372, 514, 601, 603, 629, 651, 660, 689, 751, 961, 1242, 1278, 1284, 1453, 1497, 1706, 1709, 1749, 1760, 1874, 1894, 1948, 2061, 2252, 2312, 2344, 2411, 2504, 2545, 2583, 2618, 2777, 2797, 2821, 2898, 2940, 2961, 2983, 3225, 3234, 3283, 3353, 3505, 3861, 3897, 3972, 3990, 4015, 4096, 4142, 4169, 4235, 4335, 4420, 4423, 4446, 4495, 4682, 4702, 4718, 4749
Mieszkuc, Ruth *(Producer)* 4127
Migenes, Julia *(Cast)* 1265
Migliani *(Lyricist)* 4137, 4264
Mignini, Carolyn *(Cast)* 4390, 4450
Mikesell, Emily *(Cast)* 3641
Miklaszewska, Agata *(Librettist)* 2846
Miklaszewska, Agata *(Lyricist)* 2846
Miklaszewska, Maryna *(Librettist)* 2846
Miklaszewska, Maryna *(Lyricist)* 2846
Milan, Joe *(Choreographer)* 157
Milan, Judith *(Librettist)* 4627
Milazzo, Ann Marie *(Arrangements)* 1700
Milazzo, Ann Marie *(Cast)* 2237
Milazzo, Ann Marie *(Musical Director)* 1700
Milbank, Stephen *(Dance Arranger)* 1739
Milbank, Stephen (Incidental Music) 1739
Milbank, Stephen *(Musical Director)* 1739
Milbank, Stephen *(Vocal Arranger)* 1739
Milbro Productions *(Producer)* 3718
Milburn, Ann *(Cast)* 1533, 2490, 4010
Milburn, Mary *(Cast)* 1461, 1552, 2491, 2927, 3921, 4249, 4815
Milch, David H. *(Choreographer)* 264
Milchan, Arnon *(Producer)* 2173
Miles, Bernard *(Librettist)* 2563
Miles, Dean *(Cast)* 4110
Miles, Sara *(Cast)* 146
Miles, Sherman *(Composer)* 4153
Miles, Sylvia *(Cast)* 2172
Miles, Sylvia *(Librettist)* 2172
Miles, Sylvia *(Lyricist)* 2172
Miles, William *(Director)* 3916
Miles, William *(Librettist)* 3861, 4367
Miley, Bubber *(Cast)* 4235
Miley, Bubber *(Composer)* 432, 875, 885, 895, 4235
Milford, Jim *(Producer)* 534
Milford, Kim *(Cast)* 2555, 3741, 3742, 4216
Milford, Penelope *(Cast)* 3928
Milgrim *(Costumes)* 2342, 3556, 4766
Milgrim, Lynn *(Cast)* 3370
Milhelm, Margot *(Composer)* 4291
Milhelm, Margot *(Lyricist)* 4291
Milholland, Bruce *(Author)* 3279
Milikin, Paul *(Cast)* 3544
Militello, Anne *(Lighting Designer)* 3661, 4082
Militello, Anne E. *(Lighting Designer)* 2468
Milk, Ed *(Librettist)* 1880
Millar, Gertie *(Cast)* 3098
Millaud, Albert *(Author)* 2824
Millay, Edna St. Vincent *(Lyricist)* 1648
Mille, Antoinette *(Cast)* 4251
Mille, E.P. *(Cast)* 3480
Miller *(Composer)* 3382
Miller *(Lyricist)* 3382
Miller, Albert G. *(Librettist)* 2496
Miller, Albert G. *(Lyricist)* 2168, 2496
Miller, Alex *(Composer)* 933
Miller, Alex *(Lyricist)* 933
Miller, Alice Duer *(Author)* 706, 2263, 2691, 3735
Miller, Alice Duer *(Lyricist)* 706
Miller, Amy *(Cast)* 1059
Miller, Ann *(Cast)* 1494, 4197
Miller, Arthur *(Author)* 933, 3157, 4523
Miller, Arthur *(Librettist)* 3157, 4523, 4535

Miller, Arthur *(Lyricist)* 4523
Miller, Barbara *(Set Design)* 2599
Miller, Beth *(Cast)* 3388
Miller, Bill *(Cast)* 3742
Miller, Bill *(Choreographer)* 3124
Miller, Bob *(Cast)* 2052
Miller, Bob *(Librettist)* 3217
Miller, Bob *(Lyricist)* 597, 3217
Miller, Buzz *(Cast)* 177, 519, 2797, 3351, 3687
Miller, Buzz *(Choreographer)* 793, 4216
Miller, Carlton *(Cast)* 3461
Miller, Cathy *(Cast)* 2095
Miller, Charles *(Composer)* 4453
Miller, Charles *(Orchestrations)* 378, 577, 2809
Miller, Court *(Cast)* 1289
Miller, Craig *(Lighting Designer)* 305, 1665, 2283, 2542, 3760, 4027, 4454, 4701
Miller, Edward *(Cast)* 249
Miller, Edward A. *(Producer)* 4249
Miller, Elinor *(Cast)* 3938
Miller, Everett *(Composer)* 1448
Miller, Flournoy *(Cast)* 443, 697, 988, 1488, 1667, 1678, 3660, 3808, 3966, 4198, 4281, 4844
Miller, Flournoy *(Director)* 1668, 3660
Miller, Flournoy *(Librettist)* 443, 988, 3808, 3963, 3966
Miller, Flournoy *(Producer)* 1668
Miller, Flournoy E. *(Cast)* 813, 1192, 1960, 2302, 3089, 3963, 3965
Miller, Flournoy E. *(Librettist)* 813, 1192, 1960, 2302, 2721, 2807, 3089, 3337, 3965, 4199
Miller, Flournoy E. *(Lyricist)* 813, 1198, 1917, 2151, 2338, 2807, 4199
Miller, Flournoy E. *(Producer)* 813, 1960
Miller, Fred *(Producer)* 4585
Miller, Gilbert *(Producer)* 1203, 2937, 3382
Miller, Gladys *(Cast)* 2148
Miller, Glenn *(Cast)* 1528
Miller, Glenn *(Composer)* 4137
Miller, Gregory *(Cast)* 2133
Miller, Harry *(Composer)* 1897
Miller, Harry *(Lyricist)* 1897
Miller, Helen *(Composer)* 2134
Miller, Helen *(Vocal Arranger)* 2134
Miller, Henry *(Cast)* 4559
Miller, Henry *(Director)* 2154, 3910
Miller, Henry *(Producer)* 2691, 2778
Miller, Hugh *(Cast)* 2747, 3481
Miller, Irvin C. *(Cast)* 43, 489, 552, 553, 554, 813, 1050, 2557, 2984
Miller, Irvin C. *(Director)* 489, 554, 3614, 4281
Miller, Irvin C. *(Librettist)* 43, 471, 489, 552, 553, 554, 1050, 2557, 2984, 3614
Miller, Irvin C. *(Lyricist)* 471, 2984
Miller, Irvin C. *(Producer)* 43, 471, 489, 498, 552, 553, 554, 739, 813, 1028, 1050, 2151, 2984, 3614, 4281
Miller, J.E. *(Cast)* 2763
Miller, James M. *(Costumes)* 778
Miller, Jenia *(Costumes)* 1604
Miller, Jim *(Cast)* 2056
Miller, John *(Cast)* 2058
Miller, John *(Composer)* 6
Miller, John *(Musical Director)* 2058
Miller, Jonathan *(Cast)* 384
Miller, Jonathan *(Librettist)* 384
Miller, Joseph E. *(Lyricist)* 3052
Miller, Karen D. *(Costumes)* 2132
Miller, Lawrence *(Set Design)* 785, 3171
Miller, Margot *(Costumes)* 3167
Miller, Marilyn *(Cast)* 207, 1240, 3397, 3399, 3451, 3766, 3819, 3958, 4023, 4212, 4812, 4813
Miller, Marilyn *(Producer)* 1342
Miller, Marilyn Suzanne *(Librettist)* 1512, 1575
Miller, Marilyn Suzanne *(Lyricist)* 1575
Miller, Martha *(Producer)* 4585
Miller, Midge *(Cast)* 2296
Miller, Midge *(Choreographer)* 1989
Miller, Midgie *(Cast)* 3533
Miller, Mitch *(Producer)* 1864
Miller, Patsy Ruth *(Librettist)* 3013
Miller, Paul *(Lighting Designer)* 275
Miller, Paula *(Cast)* 2228
Miller, Quintard *(Cast)* 553
Miller, Quintard *(Director)* 553
Miller, Quintard *(Librettist)* 1057
Miller, Quintard *(Producer)* 1057
Miller, Ray *(Cast)* 2258
Miller, Ray *(Composer)* 1154
Miller, Rev. Earl F. *(Cast)* 1636
Miller, Richard A. *(Set Design)* 1072
Miller, Robert *(Set Design)* 1049
Miller, Robert Strong *(Costumes)* 1969, 3601
Miller, Robin *(Librettist)* 956, 3429
Miller, Robin *(Lyricist)* 722, 956
Miller, Roger *(Composer)* 394
Miller, Roger *(Lyricist)* 394
Miller, Ron *(Librettist)* 952
Miller, Ron *(Lyricist)* 716, 952, 3485
Miller, Ronald *(Librettist)* 3734
Miller, Ronald *(Lyricist)* 3734
Miller, Sharron *(Cast)* 1770
Miller, Shelley *(Lyricist)* 1389
Miller, Sidney *(Cast)* 3846
Miller, Sidney *(Lyricist)* 2259
Miller, Skedge *(Cast)* 3920
Miller, Stanley *(Composer)* 2401
Miller, Susan *(Cast)* 323, 1138, 4702
Miller, Taps *(Cast)* 447, 3965
Miller, Timothy *(Costumes)* 169
Miller, Tod *(Cast)* 4124
Miller, Walter C. *(Director)* 499
Miller, William Henry *(Director)* 2662
Miller, William P. *(Producer)* 155
Miller, Woods *(Cast)* 216, 1136, 2300, 3002
Miller, Wynne *(Cast)* 600
Miller & Mantan *(Cast)* 882
Miller Brothers, The *(Cast)* 2034
Miller-Moffatt *(Lighting Designer)* 2219
Millership, Florrie *(Cast)* 1332
Millership, Lillian *(Cast)* 1332
Millett, Tim *(Choreographer)* 4732

Millham, Margot *(Composer)* 1932
Millham, Margot *(Lyricist)* 1932
Millhollin, James *(Cast)* 3837
Milligan, Tuck *(Cast)* 916
Millikin, Robert *(Cast)* 2944
Millington, Gertrude *(Cast)* 3679
Millocker, Carl *(Composer)* 340, 1110
Mills, A.J. *(Lyricist)* 4762
Mills, Annette *(Lyricist)* 1840
Mills, Bertha *(Cast)* 2040
Mills, Billy *(Cast)* 26, 4763
Mills, Billy *(Librettist)* 4763
Mills, C. Richard *(Set Design)* 3599
Mills, Carley *(Composer)* 3914, 4750
Mills, Carley *(Librettist)* 4750
Mills, Carley *(Lyricist)* 90, 969, 3914, 4750
Mills, Carley *(Vocal Arranger)* 2453
Mills, Eleanor *(Cast)* 166
Mills, F.A. *(Composer)* 1247
Mills, Florence *(Cast)* 1058, 1666, 2148, 2462, 3513
Mills, George *(Cast)* 3286
Mills, Grant *(Cast)* 2821
Mills, Harry *(Cast)* 526
Mills, Irving *(Cast)* 2972
Mills, Irving *(Composer)* 437, 883, 885, 896, 4091, 4137
Mills, Irving *(Lyricist)* 437, 445, 875, 881, 883, 885, 886, 896, 1125, 3018, 3020, 4091
Mills, Jerry *(Cast)* 2044, 2302, 2840
Mills, Jerry *(Director)* 646, 2127
Mills, Jim *(Cast)* 2511
Mills, John *(Cast)* 1619
Mills, Kerry *(Composer)* 662, 1246, 1247, 1535, 2415, 2805, 3905, 4390
Mills, Kerry *(Lyricist)* 2805, 3905
Mills, Maude *(Cast)* 925
Mills, Richard M. *(Producer)* 1619
Mills, Shirley *(Cast)* 1257
Mills, Stephan *(Cast)* 4352
Mills, Stephanie *(Cast)* 4722
Mills Brothers
See also Four Mills Brothers.
Mills Brothers *(Cast)* 3153
Millstein, Jack *(Producer)* 956
Millward, Jessie *(Cast)* 1553
Milne, A.A. *(Author)* 4710
Milne, A.A. *(Lyricist)* 3634, 4710
Milner, Mark *(Composer)* 4389
Milner, Mark *(Lyricist)* 4389
Milner, Ron *(Director)* 1073
Milner, Ron *(Librettist)* 1073
Milner & Gehard *(Producer)* 1332
Milton, Billy *(Cast)* 1342, 4341
Milton, Burt *(Lyricist)* 1539
Milton, Frank *(Producer)* 1775
Milton, Katie *(Cast)* 3979
Milton, Robert *(Author)* 706
Milton, Robert *(Director)* 763, 913, 2020, 2121, 2385, 2891, 3177, 3219, 3230, 3245, 3246, 3250, 3436, 3775, 3812, 3866, 4572
Milton, Robert *(Producer)* 706, 1187
Milton, Robert *(Set Design)* 3250
Milward, Jo *(Author)* 2476
Milwaukee Repertory Theatre *(Producer)* 83
Minami, Roger *(Cast)* 16
Mindell, Fanin *(Costumes)* 3686
Mineo, John *(Cast)* 964, 975, 3299, 3330, 3506, 4196
Mineo, John *(Choreographer)* 337
Mineo, John *(Director)* 337
Mineo, Sal *(Cast)* 44
Miner, Jan *(Cast)* 1017, 1383, 4601
Miner, Raynard *(Composer)* 146, 1638
Miner, Raynard *(Lyricist)* 146, 1638
Miner, Renard *(Composer)* 3739
Miner, Renard *(Lyricist)* 3739
Miner, Worthington *(Director)* 1850, 2060, 3283, 3699
Minevitch, Borrah *(Cast)* 1617, 4235
Ming, Yao *(Lyricist)* 4749
Minick, Wendell *(Producer)* 3764
Mink, Gary *(Cast)* 2037
Mink, Louise *(Cast)* 4185
Minkoff, Fran *(Lyricist)* 3112
Minkovsky *(Composer)* 1609
Minkowski, Giack *(Composer)* 4032
Minkus, Barbara *(Cast)* 427, 1158
Minnelli, Liza *(Cast)* 16, 974, 1310, 2558, 3718
Minnelli, Vincente *(Costumes)* 216, 443, 1110, 1135, 1136, 1137, 3955, 4557, 4825
Minnelli, Vincente *(Director)* 216, 2777, 3955, 4557
Minnelli, Vincente *(Librettist)* 961
Minnelli, Vincente *(Set Design)* 216, 1110, 1136, 1137, 1973, 3955, 4557, 4825
Minoff, Tammy *(Cast)* 1633
Minskoff, Jerome *(Producer)* 393, 958, 1730, 1842, 2754
Minskoff, Maggie *(Producer)* 1842, 2598
Minster, Jack *(Director)* 4600
Minter, Mary Miles
See Miss Minter.
Minter, Miss *(Cast)* 3025
Minton Jr., David M. *(Composer)* 4037
Minturn, Harry *(Director)* 4254
Mintz, Eli *(Cast)* 2218, 2925
Mintz, Thelma *(Cast)* 4463
Mintzer, Bill *(Lighting Designer)* 2195
Mintzer, Helen *(Producer)* 1785
Mintzer, William *(Lighting Designer)* 166, 1198, 1216, 1590, 1914, 2579, 3656
Minucci, Uhpio *(Composer)* 4828
Minucci, Uhpio *(Lyricist)* 4828
Minzey, Frank *(Composer)* 3998
Minzey, Frank *(Lyricist)* 3998
Mio, Tesore *(Cast)* 680
Miracle Expressions, Inc. *(Producer)* 2784
Miranda, Carmen *(Cast)* 4086, 4174
Miranda, Evan *(Cast)* 3806
Miranda, Sylvia *(Cast)* 1282
Mirande, Yves *(Author)* 468, 3295
Miron, J.C. *(Cast)* 1030, 1720, 3585
Miron, Joseph *(Cast)* 1417, 2335, 4713
Miron, Joseph C. *(Cast)* 694, 727, 1458, 1521
Mironchik, James *(Musical Director)* 4082

Mironchik, Jim *(Musical Director)* 3561
Mirvish, David *(Producer)* 580, 3846
Mirvish, Edwin *(Producer)* 3846
Misita, Michael *(Cast)* 1329
Miss Faun *(Cast)* 2294
Missimi, Dominic *(Choreographer)* 1701
Missimi, Dominic *(Director)* 1701
Missimi, Nancy *(Costumes)* 1701, 3461
Mistinguett *(Cast)* 2135
Mistretta, Sal *(Cast)* 3279
Mitch Leigh Company, The *(Producer)* 757
Mitchell, Abbie *(Cast)* 295, 2510, 3089, 3358, 3541
Mitchell, Abbie *(Librettist)* 3089
Mitchell, Adrian *(Adaptation)* 3445
Mitchell, Arthur *(Cast)* 3196
Mitchell, Barbara *(Cast)* 3615
Mitchell, Billy *(Producer)* 2942
Mitchell, Brian *(Cast)* 2702
Mitchell, Brian *(Composer)* 2702
Mitchell, Bryon *(Cast)* 937
Mitchell, Byron *(Cast)* 4435
Mitchell, Cameron *(Cast)* 2202
Mitchell, David *(Set Design)* 36, 150, 154, 169, 305, 534, 807, 958, 1159, 1372, 1776, 1890, 2058, 2064, 2360, 2437, 3577, 3628, 4744
Mitchell, Doris *(Cast)* 1566, 2059
Mitchell, Fanny Todd *(Librettist)* 138, 495, 3012, 4733
Mitchell, Fanny Todd *(Lyricist)* 4733
Mitchell, Frank *(Cast)* 1136
Mitchell, Georges *(Author)* 1743
Mitchell, Georges *(Librettist)* 1743
Mitchell, Grant *(Author)* 3349
Mitchell, Howard Johnstone *(Librettist)* 2901
Mitchell, James *(Cast)* 404, 530, 656, 2556, 2660
Mitchell, Jerry *(Choreographer)* 4775
Mitchell, John Cameron *(Cast)* 1822, 3862
Mitchell, Joni *(Composer)* 3739
Mitchell, Joni *(Lyricist)* 3739
Mitchell, Joseph *(Author)* 269
Mitchell, Julian *(Choreographer)* 186, 208, 740, 827, 902, 1199, 1228, 1527, 1796, 2497, 2567, 2830, 2907, 2927, 3251, 3323, 3494, 3585, 3627, 3723, 3727, 3921, 3977, 4212, 4226, 4258, 4801, 4802, 4803, 4860
Mitchell, Julian *(Director)* 8, 175, 215, 250, 256, 425, 468, 740, 953, 993, 1264, 1355, 1360, 1526, 1543, 1643, 1849, 1900, 1919, 1926, 2041, 2101, 2160, 2328, 2767, 2835, 2892, 2960, 3218, 3387, 3443, 3500, 3585, 3652, 3775, 3791, 3994, 4053, 4094, 4293, 4478, 4547, 4666, 4712, 4723, 4735, 4760, 4803, 4804, 4805, 4806, 4807, 4809, 4818, 4819
Mitchell, Julian *(Producer)* 250, 2160, 4735
Mitchell, Kitty *(Cast)* 2963
Mitchell, Lauren *(Cast)* 154, 2143
Mitchell, Loften *(Librettist)* 576
Mitchell, Loften *(Lyricist)* 576
Mitchell, Margaret *(Author)* 1616
Mitchell, Mark *(Musical Director)* 494, 4515
Mitchell, Mary-Jennifer *(Cast)* 3077
Mitchell, Mel *(Lyricist)* 855, 864
Mitchell, Melanie *(Cast)* 4264
Mitchell, Millard *(Cast)* 2629
Mitchell, Norma *(Librettist)* 1692
Mitchell, Robert *(Orchestrations)* 2573
Mitchell, Robert *(Set Design)* 757
Mitchell, Robert D. *(Set Design)* 172
Mitchell, Ruth *(Cast)* 1921
Mitchell, Ruth *(Producer)* 2163, 2536
Mitchell, Sidney D. *(Lyricist)* 1687, 1847, 1920, 2856, 4033, 4104, 4654, 4799, 4812, 4814
Mitchell, Thomas *(Cast)* 1791, 2309, 3686
Mitchell, Thomas *(Director)* 216, 622, 1939, 4059
Mitchell, Vontress *(Cast)* 3937
Mitchell & Durant *(Cast)* 1491
Mitgang, Norman *(Librettist)* 486
Mitgang, Norman *(Lyricist)* 485
Mittenthal, Ellen *(Cast)* 4830
Mittoo, Jackie *(Composer)* 3690
Mittoo, Jackie *(Lyricist)* 3690
Mitzi *(Cast)* 2377, 2669, 2686, 3084
Mitzman, Marcia *(Cast)* 721, 4619, 4676
Mixon, Tom *(Cast)* 600, 1837, 2052, 2288
Mizner, Wilson *(Librettist)* 822
Mizzy, Vic *(Composer)* 447, 524, 4006
Mlotek, Chana *(Lyricist)* 4342
Mlotek, Chane *(Lyricist)* 1609
Mlotek, Zalmen *(Additional Music)* 3937
Mlotek, Zalmen *(Dance Arranger)* 1609
Mlotek, Zalmen *(Librettist)* 4342
Mlotek, Zalmen *(Lyricist)* 573, 1609
Mlotek, Zalmen *(Musical Director)* 1609, 3937, 4342
Mlotek, Zalmen *(Vocal Arranger)* 1609
Mobley, Mary Ann *(Cast)* 3210
Mobley, Ross *(Musical Director)* 380, 1584
Modick, Murray *(Cast)* 3501
Modugno, Domenic *(Composer)* 4137
Modugno, Dominic *(Composer)* 4264
Modugno, Dominic *(Lyricist)* 4264
Moehl, Robert *(Composer)* 2676
Moeller, Friedrich Wilhelm *(Composer)* 4264
Moffat, John *(Lighting Designer)* 600
Moffatt, Harold *(Cast)* 3225
Moffett, D.W. *(Cast)* 3198
Mofletti, Duke *(Composer)* 497
Mofletti, Duke *(Lyricist)* 497
Mohr, Joseph *(Lyricist)* 3259
Moir, Ronald *(Cast)* 80
Moise, Solo *(Cast)* 2866
Moiseiwitsch, Tanya *(Costumes)* 453
Moiseiwitsch, Tanya *(Set Design)* 453
Mokae, Zakes *(Cast)* 4074
Molaskey, Jessica *(Cast)* 158
Moliere *(Author)* 127, 649, 1091, 2877, 3853, 3956, 4401, 4450
Molina, Alex *(Cast)* 2578
Molinaro, Thom *(Cast)* 1056
Molineaux, Constance *(Cast)* 3910
Moll, Billy *(Composer)* 1965
Moll, Billy *(Lyricist)* 1965
Moll, William *(Lyricist)* 2238
Mollenhauer, E.R. *(Musical Director)* 762

Moller, Alfred *(Author)* 4795
Mollison, Clifford *(Cast)* 1855
Mollison, William *(Director)* 1207, 2547, 2808, 3216, 4730
Mollison, William *(Producer)* 3216, 3583
Molloy, J.L. *(Composer)* 1897
Molloy, J.L. *(Lyricist)* 1897
Molloy, Molly *(Cast)* 791
Molly, Michael *(Set Design)* 4172
Molnar, Ferenc *(Author)* 660, 2487, 2614, 2705
Molyneux, Edward *(Costumes)* 2570
Momand, Pop *(Author)* 2303
Moms Company *(Producer)* 2932
Monaco, James *(Composer)* 1813
Monaco, James V. *(Composer)* 25, 418, 487, 1334, 1738, 1779, 1873, 1963, 3259, 3396, 3737, 4033, 4255, 4655, 4806, 4815, 4823
Monaco, James V. *(Lyricist)* 25
Monagas, Lionel *(Cast)* 2690, 2720, 2881
Monahan, Dick *(Cast)* 1889
Monaster, Nate *(Librettist)* 4060
Monat, Phil *(Lighting Designer)* 131, 1589, 1739, 1969, 2046, 2852, 2861, 3667, 3722, 3724, 4347
Monckton, Lionel *(Author)* 3322, 4115
Monckton, Lionel *(Composer)* 178, 351, 767, 770, 906, 1470, 1538, 1569, 1626, 1682, 1994, 2341, 2844, 3020, 3098, 3313, 3322, 3618, 3803, 3828, 3948, 3999, 4115, 4390, 4430
Monckton, Lionel *(Lyricist)* 178, 1569, 3322, 3618, 3803, 4115
Monehan, Joseph *(Cast)* 2497
Monferdini, Carole *(Cast)* 788
Monica, Corbett *(Cast)* 32
Moniz, Susan *(Cast)* 4740
Monk, Debra *(Cast)* 212, 3142, 3261, 3608
Monk, Debra *(Composer)* 3261, 3608
Monk, Debra *(Librettist)* 3261
Monk, Debra *(Lyricist)* 3261, 3608
Monk, Isabell *(Cast)* 1636
Monk, Julius *(Director)* 272, 1049, 1107, 1363, 3479, 4156
Monk, Julius *(Producer)* 272, 427, 1023, 1049, 1107, 1362, 1363, 1364, 3484, 4065, 4156, 4268
Monk, Robby *(Lighting Designer)* 3548, 4176
Monk, Terence *(Cast)* 1616, 3763
Monkhouse, Gladys *(Costumes)* 378, 712, 1208, 3923
Monkhouse, Harry *(Cast)* 1429
Monkman, Dorothy *(Cast)* 3213
Monkman, Phyllis *(Cast)* 704, 2389, 3156, 4159
Monks, Chris *(Composer)* 4295
Monks Jr., John *(Librettist)* 447, 1879
Monnot, Marguerite *(Author)* 2150
Monnot, Marguerite *(Composer)* 2150
Monroe, Bruce *(Set Design)* 314
Monroe, Dale *(Cast)* 722
Monroe, George *(Cast)* 60, 902, 1919, 2858, 2869, 3096, 3397, 3399, 3958, 4206, 4425
Monroe, George W. *(Cast)* 2995
Monroe, Lucy *(Cast)* 117, 1839, 3219, 3532
Monroe, Tommy *(Cast)* 4620
Montagne, Louise *(Cast)* 3228
Montagu, Edward *(Composer)* 4762
Montagu, Edward *(Lyricist)* 4762
Montague, Edward *(Lyricist)* 3581
Montague, J. *(Lyricist)* 675
Montague, J.J. *(Composer)* 954
Montague, J.J. *(Lyricist)* 954
Montague, James *(Lyricist)* 2793
Montague, James R. *(Lyricist)* 2793
Montague, Kenneth "Chocolate Thunder" *(Cast)* 4786
Montalban, Ricardo *(Cast)* 58, 2190, 3899
Montano, Robert *(Cast)* 139
Monte, Barbara *(Cast)* 406
Monte Carlo Girls, The *(Cast)* 61
Montefiore, Gene *(Director)* 4629
Montel, Michael *(Director)* 1665, 2100
Monterey, Carlotta *(Cast)* 1250
Montero, Gus *(Dance Arranger)* 2472
Montero, Gus *(Vocal Arranger)* 2472
Montevecchi, Liliane *(Cast)* 1638, 1649, 3171
Montford, May *(Cast)* 4382
Montgomery, Andre *(Cast)* 3181
Montgomery, Barbara *(Cast)* 2133, 4286, 4343
Montgomery, Bruce *(Arrangements)* 4774
Montgomery, Bruce *(Choreographer)* 4774
Montgomery, Bruce *(Composer)* 127, 4679, 4774
Montgomery, Bruce *(Director)* 4679, 4774
Montgomery, Bruce *(Lyricist)* 127
Montgomery, Bruce *(Vocal Arranger)* 4543
Montgomery, Dave *(Cast)* 736, 1543, 2394, 3268, 3675, 4723
Montgomery, Dick *(Cast)* 653
Montgomery, Douglass *(Cast)* 3168
Montgomery, Frank *(Cast)* 1821, 2113
Montgomery, Frank *(Choreographer)* 2009, 3200, 3657
Montgomery, Frank *(Composer)* 1821, 2113, 3022
Montgomery, Frank *(Dance Arranger)* 1821
Montgomery, Frank *(Director)* 1983
Montgomery, Frank *(Librettist)* 2113
Montgomery, Frank *(Lyricist)* 1821, 2113, 3022
Montgomery, Frank *(Musical Director)* 3022
Montgomery, Frank *(Producer)* 1821, 2113
Montgomery, Garth *(Composer)* 3175
Montgomery, Garth *(Lyricist)* 3175
Montgomery, I.M. *(Author)* 148
Montgomery, James *(Author)* 1598, 2148, 3246, 4299
Montgomery, James *(Director)* 1598
Montgomery, James *(Librettist)* 773, 1582, 2148, 3246, 4766
Montgomery, Janice Lynn *(Cast)* 3825
Montgomery, John *(Choreographer)* 2633
Montgomery, Louis *(Cast)* 4242
Montgomery, Mabel *(Cast)* 4125
Montgomery, Richard *(Set Design)* 4147
Montgomery, Robert *(Cast)* 266
Montgomery, Robert *(Librettist)* 1684
Montgomery, Robert *(Lighting Designer)* 1255
Montgomery, Robert *(Lyricist)* 1684
Montgomery, Ron *(Lighting Designer)* 1079
Montgomery, Ronald *(Lighting Designer)* 148
Montgomery, William *(Cast)* 1738, 3525

Monti, Mili *(Cast)* 2504
Montresor, Beni *(Costumes)* 1060
Montresor, Beni *(Set Design)* 1060, 3644
Montrose, Helen *(Cast)* 3712
Montrose, Muriel *(Cast)* 2467, 4341
Moody, David *(Cast)* 578
Moon, David *(Lighting Designer)* 4627
Moon, David *(Set Design)* 4627
Moon, Edna *(Cast)* 3821
Moon, Joe *(Vocal Arranger)* 4362
Moon, Keith *(Additional Lyrics)* 4676
Moon, Keith *(Additional Music)* 4676
Moon, Marjorie *(Producer)* 2133
Mooney, Hal *(Musical Director)* 2588
Mooney, Michael *(Lyricist)* 4533
Mooney, Robert *(Cast)* 760
Moor, James *(Choreographer)* 3110
Moore *(Composer)* 2133
Moore *(Lyricist)* 2133
Moore, Ada *(Cast)* 2000
Moore, Al *(Cast)* 3704
Moore, Allen *(Vocal Arranger)* 4055
Moore, Brennan *(Cast)* 4380
Moore, Carroll *(Author)* 3874
Moore, Charles H. *(Cast)* 9
Moore, Charles Werner *(Director)* 4488
Moore, Charles Werner *(Librettist)* 4488
Moore, Charlotte *(Cast)* 2607, 2805
Moore, Constance *(Cast)* 601
Moore, Dana *(Cast)* 975
Moore, Dennie *(Cast)* 1145, 1672, 2504, 3850
Moore, Donald C. *(Cast)* 3764
Moore, Dudley *(Cast)* 384, 1621
Moore, Dudley *(Composer)* 384, 1621
Moore, Dudley *(Librettist)* 384, 1621
Moore, Dudley *(Lyricist)* 384, 1621
Moore, Elsie *(Cast)* 1560
Moore, Fleecie *(Composer)* 1296
Moore, Fleecie *(Lyricist)* 1296
Moore, Florence *(Cast)* 17, 202, 1691, 1738, 1826, 2140, 3006, 3008, 3400, 3409, 3525
Moore, Frank F. *(Cast)* 2834
Moore, Garry *(Narrator)* 2975
Moore, George Austin *(Cast)* 558, 1403, 1650, 1920, 3749
Moore, George Leon *(Cast)* 2532
Moore, Gladys *(Cast)* 2858
Moore, Grace *(Cast)* 1110, 1922, 3008, 3009, 4437, 4528
Moore, Herbert *(Set Design)* 136, 4248, 4733
Moore, J.C. *(Composer)* 3631
Moore, J.C. *(Lyricist)* 3631
Moore, James *(Cast)* 1192, 2451
Moore, James *(Choreographer)* 3111
Moore, John *(Cast)* 2348
Moore, John H. *(Composer)* 666
Moore, John H. *(Lyricist)* 666
Moore, John J. *(Lighting Designer)* 2016
Moore, John J. *(Set Design)* 2728
Moore, Joseph *(Vocal Arranger)* 3543
Moore, Judith *(Cast)* 2654
Moore, Julian *(Librettist)* 2150
Moore, Julian *(Lyricist)* 2150
Moore, Karen *(Cast)* 1709
Moore, Kenny *(Composer)* 1713
Moore, Kenny *(Lyricist)* 1713
Moore, Larry *(Orchestrations)* 139
Moore, Laura *(Cast)* 1473
Moore, Marshall *(Director)* 4014
Moore, Mary Tyler *(Cast)* 521, 1040
Moore, Maureen *(Cast)* 314, 602, 1059, 1291, 4517
Moore, Mavor *(Composer)* 3110
Moore, Mavor *(Librettist)* 1255
Moore, Mavor *(Lyricist)* 1255, 3110
Moore, McElbert *(Composer)* 2780
Moore, McElbert *(Librettist)* 12, 1747, 2780, 3511
Moore, McElbert *(Lyricist)* 274, 1033, 1747, 1829, 2135, 2780, 3148, 4000, 4104, 4424
Moore, Melba *(Cast)* 1717, 2133, 3610, 4383
Moore, Melton *(Cast)* 3365
Moore, Monette *(Cast)* 1322, 2645
Moore, Monica *(Cast)* 601, 2595
Moore, Napier *(Librettist)* 2105
Moore, Pauline *(Cast)* 2309, 3002
Moore, Percival *(Composer)* 515
Moore, Percival *(Lyricist)* 515
Moore, Phil *(Composer)* 2748
Moore, Phil *(Musical Director)* 4003
Moore, Phil *(Orchestrations)* 4003
Moore, Raymond *(Producer)* 621
Moore, Richard *(Lighting Designer)* 4232
Moore, Richard *(Set Design)* 4232
Moore, Robert *(Director)* 345, 2590, 3603, 4334, 4727
Moore, Sam *(Librettist)* 4314
Moore, Stanley *(Set Design)* 129, 1644
Moore, Thomas *(Lyricist)* 2633
Moore, Tim *(Cast)* 439, 441, 445, 447, 1251, 2645, 3705
Moore, Tom *(Director)* 1664, 3330
Moore, Tom *(Set Design)* 2037
Moore, Tony *(Cast)* 2737
Moore, Victor *(Cast)* 86, 163, 1356, 1419, 1746, 1800, 1929, 1948, 2402, 2432, 2444, 2597, 3091, 3225, 3243, 3584, 4277
Moore, William *(Orchestrations)* 2271
Moore & Megley *(Producer)* 2927
Moorehead, Agnes *(Cast)* 58, 1511, 3493
Moorehead, Jean *(Cast)* 2400
Mooring, Mark *(Costumes)* 317, 1013, 1027, 1603, 1617, 1691, 1916, 3436, 4077, 4692
Mooser, George *(Director)* 3425
Mopsy *(Costumes)* 2018
Morales, Mark *(Cast)* 107
Moran, Alan *(Composer)* 2023, 2024
Moran, E.P. *(Lyricist)* 1963, 2111, 2299, 3387, 3753
Moran, Ed *(Lyricist)* 805, 4104, 4390
Moran, Edward P. *(Lyricist)* 2498, 2996, 3313, 4094, 4723
Moran, George *(Cast)* 1128, 1132, 4814
Moran, Lois *(Cast)* 2444, 3225
Moran, Rosie *(Cast)* 3860, 4365

Moran & Mack *(Cast)* 1690, 3179
Morand, R. *(Cast)* 4663
Morando, Estelle *(Librettist)* 3907
Morange, E.A.
See also Gates & Marange.
Morange, E.A. *(Set Design)* 185, 376, 577, 749, 815, 1243, 1501, 1625, 1667, 2768, 2819, 2884, 3228, 3519, 3650, 3772, 3774, 3865, 3868, 4234, 4360, 4620, 4671, 4694, 4704, 4716, 4807
Morange, Edward A. *(Set Design)* 2326, 4705
Moras, Alan *(Musical Director)* 1814
Morath, Kathryn *(Cast)* 54
Morath, Kathy *(Cast)* 3142, 3221, 3600, 4731
Moray, Stella *(Cast)* 346
Morcon, James *(Costumes)* 4374
Mordecai, David *(Conductor)* 2447
Mordecai, James *(Cast)* 3986, 4253
Mordente, Lisa *(Cast)* 2759, 3515
Mordente, Tony *(Cast)* 2484, 4625
Mordente, Tony *(Choreographer)* 1864
Morder, Georgio *(Composer)* 3739
Morder, Georgio *(Lyricist)* 3739
Mordhorst, Gunda *(Cast)* 791
Mordkin, Michael *(Choreographer)* 3699
More, Julian *(Librettist)* 194, 1644, 2949, 3792
More, Julian *(Lyricist)* 194, 1644, 2949, 3792
Morea, Robert *(Cast)* 4157
Morehead, Jean *(Cast)* 4777
Morehouse, Harold *(Producer)* 2640
Moreland, Mantan *(Cast)* 439, 441, 443, 3965, 3993, 4763
Morell, Peter *(Director)* 27
Morelli, Anthony *(Musical Director)* 4362
Morelli, Toni *(Musical Director)* 4117
Moreno, Rita *(Cast)* 1441
Morenzic, Leon *(Cast)* 4147
Morenzie, Leon *(Cast)* 793
Mores, Mariano *(Composer)* 2356
Moret, Neil *(Composer)* 685, 1531, 1927, 2747, 2960, 3297, 4351, 4570, 4613
Moret, Neil *(Lyricist)* 1531, 1927, 3297
Moretty, C.R. *(Composer)* 1678
Morey, Larry *(Author)* 4035
Morey, Larry *(Composer)* 2083, 2089, 2090, 2091
Morey, Larry *(Lyricist)* 2083, 2089, 2090, 2091, 4035
Morgan, Agnes *(Cast)* 1651, 1653, 1655, 1657
Morgan, Agnes *(Director)* 1651, 1653, 1654, 1655, 1656, 1657, 1871
Morgan, Agnes *(Librettist)* 1652, 1653, 1654, 1655, 1656, 1657, 2732
Morgan, Agnes *(Lyricist)* 1652, 1653, 1654, 1655, 1656, 1657, 1871
Morgan, Al *(Librettist)* 3234
Morgan, Carey *(Composer)* 1063, 1176, 1687, 2700
Morgan, Cass *(Cast)* 1402, 1737, 2346, 2359, 3608
Morgan, Cass *(Composer)* 3608
Morgan, Cass *(Lyricist)* 3608
Morgan, Claudia *(Cast)* 2729
Morgan, Danny *(Costumes)* 1770, 3764, 4635
Morgan, Denise *(Cast)* 838
Morgan, Dickson *(Director)* 3072
Morgan, Dickson *(Set Design)* 4429
Morgan, Elizabeth *(Cast)* 1176
Morgan, Frank *(Cast)* 294, 1283, 1847, 1874, 3048, 3740, 3766
Morgan, Gary *(Cast)* 2318
Morgan, George *(Lighting Designer)* 4434
Morgan, Helen *(Cast)* 123, 1488, 2459, 3949, 4234, 4823, 4845, 4847
Morgan, Henry *(Librettist)* 59
Morgan, J.L. *(Composer)* 1063
Morgan, James *(Set Design)* 147, 451, 549, 809, 1092, 1510, 1630, 1737, 2565, 3202, 3864, 4027
Morgan, Jane *(Cast)* 4828
Morgan, Jim *(Lyricist)* 4533
Morgan, L. *(Producer)* 292
Morgan, Marion *(Choreographer)* 4719
Morgan, Marion *(Costumes)* 4719
Morgan, Merlin *(Composer)* 2698
Morgan, Merlin *(Lyricist)* 379
Morgan, Miles *(Lighting Designer)* 2168
Morgan, Mme. *(Costumes)* 1984
Morgan, Mrs. Edmund Nash *(Author)* 4313
Morgan, Priscilla *(Cast)* 2474
Morgan, Ralph *(Cast)* 2121
Morgan, Robert *(Lighting Designer)* 547
Morgan, Roger *(Lighting Designer)* 807, 825, 900, 1222, 1512, 1635, 2064, 2172, 2236, 2290, 2539, 2798, 3418, 4114, 4167, 4595, 4623
Morgan, Roger *(Set Design)* 1116
Morgan, Russ *(Composer)* 4137
Morgan, Stuart
See Stuart Morgan Dancers.
Morgan, Ted *(Cast)* 4423
Morgan, W. Aston *(Composer)* 553
Morgan, Wallace *(Author)* 1318
Morgan, William T. *(Cast)* 2310
Morgan Dancers, Stuart *(Cast)* 1889
Morgan Jr., Charles S. *(Choreographer)* 2390, 4250
Morganstern, C. William *(Producer)* 3342
Morgenstern, Christopher *(Lyricist)* 1589
Morgenstern, Sam *(Dance Arranger)* 3215
Morgenstern, Sam *(Orchestrations)* 3215
Morgenstern, Sam *(Vocal Arranger)* 3215
Moriarty, George *(Lyricist)* 545
Moriarty, Michael *(Producer)* 4003
Morick, Jeanine *(Cast)* 674
Morin, Terry *(Composer)* 2580
Morinelli, Patricia *(Producer)* 1638
Morison, Patricia *(Cast)* 84, 2331, 4479
Moritz, Al *(Composer)* 467
Moritz, Al *(Lyricist)* 467
Morley, Al *(Producer)* 407, 413
Morley, Angela *(Orchestrations)* 695, 1619
Morley, Carol *(Cast)* 128, 1436, 3548, 4029, 4330
Morley, Jay *(Costumes)* 2234
Morley, Karen *(Cast)* 298
Morley, Ruth *(Costumes)* 4, 171, 615, 747, 1864, 2173, 3908, 4167
Morley, Victor *(Cast)* 1123, 1663, 2619, 2813, 3043, 3177, 4115, 4365, 4824

Morley, Victor *(Director)* 3069
Morne, Maryland *(Cast)* 2121
Morningstar, Carter *(Costumes)* 339
Morningstar, Carter *(Lighting Designer)* 339, 3941
Morningstar, Carter *(Set Design)* 339, 3941
Morosco, Leslie *(Producer)* 2564
Morosco, Oliver *(Director)* 628, 2605, 4037
Morosco, Oliver *(Librettist)* 628, 2461, 2832, 2955, 3562, 4037, 4634
Morosco, Oliver *(Lyricist)* 2605, 2955, 4381
Morosco, Oliver *(Producer)* 233, 422, 628, 763, 2378, 2446, 2461, 2489, 2519, 2605, 2832, 2955, 3432, 3562, 3812, 4037, 4381, 4492, 4634
Moross, Jerome *(Composer)* 283, 1474, 1600, 1873, 2294, 3365, 4512
Moross, Jerome *(Librettist)* 1474
Moross, Jerome *(Orchestrations)* 1600, 3365
Morreale, Enrico *(Musical Director)* 1071, 2936
Morrell, Don *(Cast)* 1836
Morris, Anita *(Cast)* 1955, 2687, 3171, 3636, 3869, 4517
Morris, Bobby *(Cast)* 3410
Morris, Chester *(Cast)* 2967
Morris, David *(Cast)* 1275, 3283, 4142
Morris, Edward *(Pianist)* 366, 2279
Morris, Edward *(Producer)* 2913
Morris, Edwin H. *(Producer)* 3940
Morris, Garrett *(Cast)* 40, 1081, 1729, 2075, 3309
Morris, Gary *(Cast)* 2359
Morris, George *(Director)* 1514
Morris, George *(Librettist)* 1514
Morris, George *(Lyricist)* 1514
Morris, Hayward *(Orchestrations)* 4789
Morris, Howard *(Cast)* 44, 1475
Morris, I.N. *(Librettist)* 2779
Morris, Janet S. *(Costumes)* 143
Morris, Jeremiah *(Director)* 2043
Morris, Jeremiah *(Librettist)* 2043
Morris, Joe *(Cast)* 2631
Morris, John *(Arrangements)* 635
Morris, John *(Composer)* 2097, 4384
Morris, John *(Dance Arranger)* 64, 270, 363, 607, 868, 1290, 1567, 1742, 2355, 2568, 3159, 3473, 3505, 3931, 4693
Morris, John *(Incidental Music)* 2660
Morris, John *(Librettist)* 4384
Morris, John *(Lyricist)* 2097, 4273, 4384
Morris, John *(Musical Director)* 64, 635, 2097, 2553, 4693
Morris, John *(Orchestrations)* 3075
Morris, John *(Pianist)* 1047
Morris, John *(Vocal Arranger)* 1991, 4693
Morris, June *(Choreographer)* 4163
Morris, Kenny *(Cast)* 1377
Morris, Kenny *(Lyricist)* 1377
Morris, Lynne *(Choreographer)* 2962
Morris, Mary *(Cast)* 2476
Morris, Maud *(Cast)* 4681
Morris, McKay *(Cast)* 121, 165
Morris, Mickey *(Cast)* 2655
Morris, Mildred *(Cast)* 3450
Morris, Nat *(Cast)* 1116
Morris, Peter *(Cast)* 2022
Morris, Peter *(Librettist)* 2022, 4462
Morris, Peter *(Lyricist)* 2022, 4462
Morris, Phil *(Producer)* 2271
Morris, Ramsey *(Librettist)* 2675
Morris, Richard *(Director)* 1369
Morris, Richard *(Librettist)* 1369, 1605
Morris, Robert *(Librettist)* 4516
Morris, Seymour *(Lyricist)* 637
Morris, Thomas *(Composer)* 1687
Morris, William *(Set Design)* 302
Morris, William E. *(Cast)* 4105
Morris, William E. *(Director)* 3995
Morris Jr., William *(Director)* 1411
Morrisey, Bob *(Cast)* 171, 2146, 3643
Morrisey, J. *(Composer)* 1957
Morrison, Alex *(Cast)* 3406
Morrison, Ann *(Cast)* 1589, 2822, 3429
Morrison, Dorothy *(Cast)* 4021
Morrison, Ethel *(Cast)* 1235
Morrison, Florence *(Cast)* 2373, 3623
Morrison, Kay *(Costumes)* 2786, 4550
Morrison, Lee *(Director)* 1014, 3605
Morrison, Lee *(Producer)* 1014
Morrison, Paul *(Costumes)* 4153
Morrison, Paul *(Lighting Designer)* 249, 630, 920, 1766, 2144, 3094, 3984, 4005, 4186, 4828
Morrison, Paul *(Set Design)* 249, 3094, 4005
Morrison, Peggy *(Costumes)* 4377
Morrison, Priestley *(Director)* 1098
Morrison, Priestly *(Director)* 1135, 1177, 1345
Morrison, Sam *(Composer)* 4204
Morrison, Van *(Composer)* 3695
Morrison, Van *(Lyricist)* 3695
Morrison, Wayne *(Composer)* 1637
Morrison, Wayne *(Lyricist)* 1637
Morrison, William *(Cast)* 119
Morrison Jr., Charles T. *(Set Design)* 4163
Morrissey *(Composer)* 1963
Morrissey *(Lyricist)* 1963
Morrissey, Paul *(Director)* 2728
Morrissey, Will *(Cast)* 598, 2296, 4421
Morrissey, Will *(Composer)* 78, 598, 2296, 2397, 3133, 3399, 3410, 3533, 3891, 4421
Morrissey, Will *(Director)* 598, 1989, 3133, 3533, 4421
Morrissey, Will *(Librettist)* 78, 598, 1989, 2296, 3133, 3533, 3822
Morrissey, Will *(Lyricist)* 78, 443, 598, 1328, 1989, 2296, 2397, 3133, 3399, 3410, 3533, 3822, 4421
Morrissey, Will *(Producer)* 398, 598, 1328, 3133, 4421
Morrow, Doretta *(Cast)* 23, 1933, 2312, 2327, 3947, 4652
Morrow, Helen *(Cast)* 1871
Morrow, Karen *(Cast)* 1597, 1662, 2053, 2072, 2075, 2248, 3018, 3871, 3988
Morrow, Macklin *(Musical Director)* 818
Morrow, Milo *(Costumes)* 2918, 3825
Morrow, Rob *(Cast)* 747
Morscher, Sepp *(Musical Director)* 1020
Morse, Barry *(Director)* 3818

Morse, Carl F. *(Cast)* 1868
Morse, Harry M. *(Cast)* 800
Morse, John A. *(Cast)* 3329
Morse, John A. *(Lyricist)* 2039
Morse, John P. *(Cast)* 1556
Morse, Josephine *(Cast)* 1707
Morse, Muriel *(Producer)* 4318
Morse, Richard *(Cast)* 73
Morse, Robert *(Cast)* 1389, 2019, 3845, 4038, 4196, 4270
Morse, Robert G. *(Composer)* 3047
Morse, Robin *(Cast)* 534
Morse, Stacy *(Costumes)* 2970
Morse, Theodore *(Composer)* 246, 675, 1907, 2576, 2826, 2974, 3030, 3519
Morse, Theodore *(Director)* 2954
Morse, Theodore F. *(Composer)* 2974, 3073, 4723
Morse, Tilda *(Choreographer)* 1370
Morse, Woolson *(Composer)* 1090, 2592, 3360
Morse, Woolson *(Librettist)* 762
Morsell, Fred *(Cast)* 3059
Mortimer, Charles *(Composer)* 4171
Mortimer, Charles *(Lyricist)* 4171
Mortimer, Jeannie *(Cast)* 300
Mortimer, Nellie *(Cast)* 402
Mortiz, Dave *(Composer)* 4171
Mortiz, Dave *(Lyricist)* 4171
Morton, Brooks *(Cast)* 1848, 3725
Morton, Clara *(Cast)* 399, 522
Morton, David *(Composer)* 4566
Morton, David *(Lyricist)* 4566
Morton, Dorothy *(Cast)* 175, 1682, 3199, 4616, 4724
Morton, Edna *(Cast)* 3041
Morton, Edward *(Librettist)* 3828
Morton, Emma *(Cast)* 2113
Morton, Fred *(Composer)* 1120
Morton, Fred *(Lyricist)* 1120
Morton, Frederic *(Author)* 3780
Morton, George "Shadow" *(Composer)* 2427
Morton, George "Shadow" *(Lyricist)* 2427
Morton, Gregory *(Cast)* 1119
Morton, Harry K. *(Cast)* 332, 905, 2605, 2622, 3532, 4170
Morton, Harry K. *(Composer)* 905
Morton, Hugh *(Librettist)* 113, 357, 1543, 1579, 2116, 4298
Morton, Hugh *(Lyricist)* 357, 982, 1543, 1579, 4044
Morton, Hughie *(Musical Director)* 2457
Morton, James C. *(Cast)* 558, 1935, 2834, 3434
Morton, James J. *(Cast)* 1835, 2826
Morton, Jelly Roll *(Music Based On)* 2200
Morton, Joe *(Cast)* 1970, 3231, 3564, 3656, 3824, 4450
Morton, Kate *(Cast)* 399, 522
Morton, Lew *(Choreographer)* 2107, 3372
Morton, Lew *(Director)* 684, 718, 2602, 2637, 2856, 3012, 3150, 3523, 3573, 4621, 4654
Morton, Lew *(Librettist)* 4654
Morton, Lew *(Lyricist)* 4654
Morton, Lewis *(Choreographer)* 2254
Morton, Lewis *(Director)* 2293, 2893, 3163, 3701, 3981
Morton, Mark *(Set Design)* 2993
Morton, Martha *(Cast)* 1134
Morton, Michael *(Librettist)* 4285
Morton, Moe *(Producer)* 3933
Morton, Paul *(Cast)* 399, 522
Morton, Richard *(Composer)* 3229
Morton, Richard *(Lyricist)* 3229
Morton, Sam *(Cast)* 399, 522
Morton, Tommy *(Cast)* 2439, 2554
Morton, William K. *(Cast)* 4248
Morton, Winn *(Costumes)* 190, 1158, 2097, 2657, 2750, 3112, 3371, 3928, 4029
Morton, Winn *(Set Design)* 3112
Mosby, Marion *(Cast)* 178, 2494
Mosconi, Charles *(Choreographer)* 431, 3290
Moscowitz, Jennie *(Cast)* 4083
Mosel, Tad *(Librettist)* 2664
Moseley, Peggy *(Cast)* 1492, 1493
Moser, Barbara *(Cast)* 2464
Moser, Margo *(Cast)* 1730
Moses, Burke *(Cast)* 330
Moses, Gilbert *(Director)* 40, 4004, 4722
Moses, Harry *(Producer)* 1366
Moses & Hamilton *(Set Design)* 1313, 2803
Mosher, Sue *(Cast)* 261
Mosher, Susan *(Cast)* 4193
Mosier, Enid *(Cast)* 2000
Mosier, Marie *(Musical Director)* 4440
Mosiman, Marnie *(Cast)* 3764
Moss *(Composer)* 3747
Moss, Al *(Composer)* 2167, 4394
Moss, Anguss *(Lighting Designer)* 314
Moss, Arnold *(Cast)* 23, 1329
Moss, Earl *(Arrangements)* 2077
Moss, Herbert M. *(Producer)* 1744, 3496
Moss, Jeffrey *(Composer)* 1082
Moss, Jeffrey *(Librettist)* 1082
Moss, Jeffrey *(Lyricist)* 1082
Moss, Jeffrey B. *(Costumes)* 400, 1269
Moss, Jeffrey B. *(Director)* 2790
Moss, Jeffrey B. *(Set Design)* 400, 1269
Moss, Jo *(Cast)* 1951
Moss, Joe *(Producer)* 1949, 1950
Moss, Kathi *(Cast)* 1664
Moss, Kurt *(Composer)* 3530
Moss, Larry *(Cast)* 2913
Moss, Lawrence John *(Cast)* 4038
Moss, Paul *(Producer)* 1657
Moss, Paula *(Cast)* 1344
Moss, Paula *(Choreographer)* 1344
Moss Empires Ltd. *(Producer)* 4320
Moss and Fry *(Cast)* 1404
Mosse, Spencer *(Lighting Designer)* 1249, 1439, 3653, 4379
Mosser, Jack *(Additional Music)* 3381
Mosser, Jack *(Costumes)* 3381
Most, Earle *(Orchestrations)* 3639
Mostel, Josh *(Cast)* 3039, 4167, 4371
Mostel, Joshua *(Cast)* 2877
Mostel, Kate *(Cast)* 3299
Mostel, Zero *(Cast)* 341, 1265, 1422, 2653, 3286

Mostel, Zero *(Librettist)* 2653
Mostoller *(Costumes)* 4627
Mostyn, Hadden *(Cast)* 995
Moten, Etta *(Cast)* 1251
Mothersbaugh, Mark *(Composer)* 3739
Mothersbaugh, Mark *(Lyricist)* 3739
Motion Pictures Artists Co. *(Producer)* 4152
Motley *(Costumes)* 270, 367, 629, 651, 1748, 2355, 2464, 2894, 2961, 3294, 3347, 3452, 3453, 3813, 3934, 4096, 4155, 4435, 4609
Motley *(Set Design)* 1748
Motown *(Producer)* 952
Motteaux, Peter Anthony *(Lyricist)* 2633
Motts, Robert *(Producer)* 3979
Motzan, Otto *(Composer)* 1266, 2696, 2922, 3193, 3400, 3401, 3958, 4418
Motzan, Otto *(Lyricist)* 3400, 4419
Mouezy-Eon *(Librettist)* 3769
Moulan, Eugene *(Cast)* 4333
Moulan, Frank *(Cast)* 178, 902, 1228, 1650, 1851, 2035, 2276, 2527, 3593, 3627, 3996, 4201
Moule, Kenneth *(Musical Director)* 4469
Moulton, C. *(Composer)* 4479
Moulton, Harold *(Cast)* 55
Moulton, Ray K. *(Composer)* 4421
Moulton, Ray K. *(Lyricist)* 4421
Mountain, Vince *(Set Design)* 2198
Mourning, Inez *(Choreographer)* 2436
Moustaki, George *(Composer)* 4396
Moveing Day Company *(Producer)* 4198
Mowatt, Anna Cora *(Author)* 1249
Mowbray, Alan *(Cast)* 1190
Mowell, Shelley *(Composer)* 3664, 3940, 3942
Mowry, Greg *(Cast)* 4138
Moyen *(Costumes)* 3524
Moyer, Edythe *(Cast)* 1728
Moylan, Mary Ellen *(Cast)* 3841
Mozart, Wolfgang Amadeus *(Author)* 4522
Mozart, Wolfgang Amadeus *(Composer)* 221
Mqadi, Bheki *(Cast)* 209, 4438
Msomi, Mandla *(Cast)* 1719
Msomi, Welcome *(Composer)* 1719
Msomi, Welcome *(Director)* 1719
Msomi, Welcome *(Librettist)* 1719
Msomi, Welcome *(Lyricist)* 1719
Mucci, David *(Cast)* 580
Muchison, Kenneth M. *(Composer)* 824
Mudie, Alan *(Cast)* 178
Mudie, Leonard *(Cast)* 1144
Mueller, Gustave *(Composer)* 4815
Mueller, Karl *(Cast)* 1413
Mueller, Mark *(Librettist)* 595
Mueller, Mark *(Lyricist)* 595
Mueller, Zizi *(Musical Director)* 654
Mueltzer *(Costumes)* 1712
Muenz, Richard *(Cast)* 721, 784, 3577, 4004
Muffatti, S. Todd *(Set Design)* 973
Muhammed Ali
See Cassius Clay.
Muhsam, Erich *(Librettist)* 3441
Muhsam, Erich *(Lyricist)* 3441
Muir, Gavin *(Cast)* 715
Muir, Lewis F. *(Composer)* 433, 558, 1531, 2415, 3259, 4655, 4803, 4804
Muir, Lewis F. *(Lyricist)* 4534
Muir, William *(Director)* 2946
Mulaney, Jan *(Composer)* 2289
Mulcahy, Lance *(Composer)* 1978, 2305, 3389, 3890, 3909, 4246, 4433
Mulcahy, Lance *(Librettist)* 4433
Mulcahy, Lance *(Lyricist)* 1978, 3890, 4433
Mulgrew, J.P. *(Librettist)* 538
Mulgrew, James P. *(Librettist)* 2303
Mulgrew, John P. *(Librettist)* 537, 540
Mulhern, Michael *(Cast)* 2861
Mullally, W.S. *(Arrangements)* 1913
Mullaly, Harry G. *(Musical Director)* 2952
Mulle, Ida *(Cast)* 571
Mullen *(Composer)* 2493
Mullen, Charles E. *(Composer)* 917
Mullen, J.B. *(Composer)* 2481
Mullen, J.B. *(Lyricist)* 2481
Mullen, Joseph *(Costumes)* 266
Mullen, Joseph *(Set Design)* 266
Muller, Ernst *(Composer)* 3600
Muller, Ernst *(Lyricist)* 3600
Muller, Hans *(Author)* 4667
Muller, Jennifer *(Choreographer)* 1015, 1236, 4518
Muller, Romeo *(Author)* 2941
Muller, Romeo *(Librettist)* 928, 2941
Muller-Norden, Alfred *(Composer)* 1188
Muller-Norden, Alfred *(Lyricist)* 1188
Mulligan, Charles *(Producer)* 1314
Mulligan, Gerry *(Composer)* 1750
Mulligan, Ralph *(Costumes)* 1962, 3006, 3007, 3008, 3770
Mulligan, Richard *(Cast)* 1205
Mulligan, Robert J. *(Cast)* 3353
Mullins, Melinda *(Cast)* 3884
Mulvey, Ben *(Cast)* 953
Mumford, Ethel Watts *(Lyricist)* 1009
Munce, Howard *(Librettist)* 4047
Mundin, Herbert *(Cast)* 133, 702, 1128, 2392
Mundy, James *(Orchestrations)* 4542
Mundy, John *(Composer)* 2464, 3989, 4542
Mundy, Meg *(Cast)* 1680, 1973, 3468
Munford, Gordon *(Musical Director)* 239
Muni, Paul *(Cast)* 223
Munier, Leon *(Lighting Designer)* 3059
Munier, Leon *(Set Design)* 3059
Munnik, Rob *(Lighting Designer)* 1865
Munoz, Rodney *(Costumes)* 2065
Munro, BIll *(Composer)* 1685
Munroe, Walter *(Cast)* 3219, 3536
Munsel, Patrice *(Cast)* 2838, 3020, 4155
Munshin, Jules *(Cast)* 7, 454, 620, 1456, 3954
Munson, Eddie *(Composer)* 3754
Munson, Ona *(Cast)* 1482, 1929, 1932, 2734, 4476
Muntz, Elsie *(Composer)* 3827
Munz, Louis G. *(Composer)* 3073
Mura, Corinna *(Cast)* 2847

Murawski, C. *(Lighting Designer)* 840, 4514
Murawski, C. *(Set Design)* 1612, 3928, 4514
Mure, Glenn *(Cast)* 922
Murfitt, Mary *(Cast)* 3261
Murfitt, Mary *(Librettist)* 3261
Murger, Henri *(Author)* 2359
Murin, David *(Costumes)* 424, 474, 478, 533, 690, 1172, 1258, 1635
Murney, Christopher *(Cast)* 4450
Murphy, Brian *(Cast)* 3259
Murphy, C.W. *(Composer)* 246, 1148, 1544, 2232, 2528, 2858, 3193
Murphy, C.W. *(Lyricist)* 1148, 1544, 2232, 2528, 3144
Murphy, Danny *(Cast)* 3158
Murphy, Donna *(Cast)* 1377, 1822, 3070, 3411, 3598, 3960, 4076
Murphy, Edward *(Choreographer)* 3912
Murphy, Frank "Rags" *(Composer)* 2349
Murphy, Frank "Rags" *(Librettist)* 2349
Murphy, Frank "Rags" *(Lyricist)* 2349
Murphy, George *(Cast)* 3225, 3735, 3946
Murphy, George *(Director)* 2496
Murphy, George P. *(Cast)* 2448
Murphy, Jeanette *(Cast)* 449
Murphy, John Daly *(Cast)* 1368, 1501, 3866
Murphy, Judy *(Cast)* 2124
Murphy, Lyle *(Composer)* 2084
Murphy, Lyle *(Lyricist)* 2084
Murphy, Lyle *(Orchestrations)* 2084, 2093, 2095, 2096
Murphy, Owen *(Composer)* 1131, 2870, 3648, 3655, 3677, 4104, 4424
Murphy, Owen *(Librettist)* 3655
Murphy, Owen *(Lyricist)* 317, 1131, 1440, 1690, 1691, 1692, 1780, 1932, 2020, 2308, 2870, 3648, 3655, 3677, 4104, 4424
Murphy, Pixie *(Cast)* 2608
Murphy, Ralph *(Lyricist)* 1314
Murphy, Reggie *(Cast)* 531
Murphy, Rosemary *(Cast)* 160
Murphy, Stanley *(Composer)* 1501
Murphy, Stanley *(Lyricist)* 1501, 2667, 2922, 3396, 4017, 4589, 4642, 4712
Murphy, William *(Cast)* 750
Murphy III, William *(Producer)* 3539
Murray, Alan *(Choreographer)* 388
Murray, Alfred *(Librettist)* 2844
Murray, Alfred *(Lyricist)* 1313
Murray, Art *(Librettist)* 4
Murray, Braham *(Choreographer)* 1736
Murray, Braham *(Director)* 1619, 1736
Murray, Brian *(Director)* 1787
Murray, Carl *(Cast)* 4220
Murray, Charles *(Cast)* 2884
Murray, Charles A. *(Librettist)* 4215
Murray, Chas. A. *(Cast)* 187
Murray, Don *(Cast)* 4029
Murray, Edgar *(Cast)* 4247
Murray, Elizabeth *(Cast)* 804, 1212, 1629, 1888, 2601, 2667, 2671, 4465, 4603
Murray, Estelle *(Choreographer)* 4779
Murray, Frank *(Producer)* 4614
Murray, Fred *(Lighting Designer)* 4296
Murray, George *(Librettist)* 728
Murray, J. Harold *(Cast)* 642, 659, 670, 735, 1145, 1225, 2706, 2857, 3404, 3719, 4121, 4374, 4550, 4575, 4654
Murray, J.K. *(Cast)* 175, 2673
Murray, J.P. *(Librettist)* 4823
Murray, J.P. *(Lyricist)* 1932, 4799, 4823
Murray, J.S. *(Director)* 1910
Murray, Jack *(Composer)* 1722
Murray, Jack *(Librettist)* 3986
Murray, Jack *(Lyricist)* 1722
Murray, James *(Cast)* 1910
Murray, Jan *(Cast)* 3013
Murray, John *(Composer)* 4152
Murray, John *(Director)* 4152
Murray, John *(Lyricist)* 124, 4152
Murray, John T. *(Cast)* 764, 3174, 3399, 3958, 4133, 4654, 4760
Murray, Kathleen *(Cast)* 2339
Murray, Ken *(Cast)* 1127, 2459
Murray, Lyn *(Vocal Arranger)* 1278, 2453, 3359, 4256
Murray, Mae *(Cast)* 256, 1849, 2025, 2884, 3153, 3421, 3975, 4787, 4802, 4803, 4809
Murray, Mary *(Cast)* 3172
Murray, Mary Gordon *(Cast)* 4, 474, 2346, 3517
Murray, Michael *(Cast)* 2661
Murray, Pat *(Cast)* 214
Murray, Paul *(Producer)* 1333, 2467
Murray, Peg *(Cast)* 162, 610, 1184, 1709, 3918, 4060
Murray, S. Barkley *(Cast)* 251
Murray, Ted *(Composer)* 847
Murray, Wynn *(Cast)* 70, 117, 247, 514, 2379
Murray Singers, The, Lyn *(Cast)* 1278
Murril, Herbert *(Composer)* 3441
Murry, Jules *(Director)* 224
Murry, Jules *(Producer)* 939
Murry, Ted *(Composer)* 24, 867, 3145, 4265, 4571
Murtagh *(Composer)* 4712
Murtagh *(Lyricist)* 4712
Muse, Clarence *(Composer)* 3840
Muse, Clarence *(Lyricist)* 3840
Musel, Bob *(Composer)* 2653
Musel, Bob *(Lyricist)* 2653
Music Maker, Inc. *(Orchestrations)* 2727
Music Maker, Inc. *(Vocal Arranger)* 2727
Music Makers, Inc. *(Dance Arranger)* 2727
Music Theatre of Lincoln Center *(Producer)* 2838
Music Theater Workshop *(Producer)* 451, 1092, 3864
Musical Theater Works *(Producer)* 10, 3811
Musicworks Inc. *(Orchestrations)* 2007
Musky, Jane *(Set Design)* 3136
Musser, Tharon *(Lighting Designer)* 16, 160, 167, 287, 461, 521, 746, 1103, 1273, 1294, 1310, 1329, 1359, 1601, 1620, 1633, 1729, 1860, 2208, 2304, 2536, 2660, 2681, 2713, 2796, 2820, 2949, 2965, 3175, 3210, 3288, 3340, 3862, 3934, 4004, 4067, 4297, 4334, 4609, 4619, 4722
Muzio, Gloria *(Director)* 573
Myer, Bob *(Cast)* 4679
Myerberg, Michael *(Producer)* 309, 2655

Myers, Damar *(Costumes)* 1884
Myers, Edward *(Costumes)* 3490
Myers, Edward *(Librettist)* 2748
Myers, Edward *(Lyricist)* 2748
Myers, Henry *(Author)* 732
Myers, Henry *(Composer)* 732
Myers, Henry *(Librettist)* 732, 1617, 1711, 1745, 4331
Myers, Henry *(Lyricist)* 303, 1448, 1477, 2447, 2545, 2809, 2810, 2823, 2933, 3005, 3130, 4249, 4331, 4367
Myers, Henry *(Producer)* 4331
Myers, Joanna *(Cast)* 4102
Myers, John Bernard *(Producer)* 1498
Myers, Johnny *(Composer)* 2580, 4627
Myers, Johnny *(Lyricist)* 4627
Myers, Lorna *(Cast)* 4447
Myers, Louise *(Cast)* 1961
Myers, Margot *(Cast)* 1357
Myers, Nancy *(Cast)* 427
Myers, Pamela *(Cast)* 832, 3871
Myers, Peter *(Composer)* 392, 2168
Myers, Peter *(Librettist)* 2168
Myers, Peter *(Lyricist)* 392, 2168, 3186, 3890
Myers, Richard *(Composer)* 86, 125, 577, 605, 1137, 1448, 1691, 1839, 1856, 2976, 3002, 3172, 3352, 3816, 4170, 4291, 4824, 4828
Myers, Stan *(Orchestrations)* 2089
Myers, Stanley *(Composer)* 1195
Myers, Stanley *(Lyricist)* 392, 1195
Myers, Stanley *(Musical Director)* 1644
Mylett, Jeffrey *(Cast)* 1595, 4343
Myrow, Josef *(Composer)* 851, 1125, 1298, 1808, 4602
Myrtil, Odette *(Cast)* 551, 672, 2622, 2680, 3837, 4575, 4669
Myrtil, Odette *(Costumes)* 2496
Mysels, George *(Lyricist)* 1046
Mysteria, Princess *(Cast)* 471

N

N.E.T.W.O.R.K. *(Producer)* 916
N.I.M. and A. Co. *(Producer)* 4007
N.N.N. Company *(Producer)* 275
N.Y. City Center *(Producer)* 1474
N.Y. Shakespeare Festival *(Producer)* 54, 169, 282, 459, 655, 746, 1015, 1053, 1055, 1344, 1575, 1715, 2033, 2237, 2239, 2359, 2429, 2441, 2648, 2877, 2918, 2953, 3000, 3197, 3198, 3276, 3456, 3757, 3806, 3825, 3830, 4151, 4370, 4485, 4505, 4518, 4615, 4736, 4775
N.Y. State Theatre Inst. *(Producer)* 114
N.Y. University's Town Hall *(Producer)* 4444
N.Y. World's Fair Co *(Producer)* 117
Nabel, Bill *(Cast)* 36
Nabokov, Vladimir *(Author)* 2568
Nadeau, Nicky *(Set Design)* 544, 2443
Nadel, Arlene *(Cast)* 3684
Nadel, E.K. *(Producer)* 2298
Nadler, Arch *(Producer)* 593
Nadler, Mark *(Cast)* 3641, 3926
Nador, Mihaly *(Author)* 2622
Nadoud, Serge *(Cast)* 2753
Nagle, Jeri *(Choreographer)* 2028
Nagler, A.N. *(Author)* 3703
Nagrin, Daniel *(Cast)* 153, 3226, 3509, 4432, 4524
Nagy, John *(Composer)* 4488
Nagy, John *(Vocal Arranger)* 4488
Nahat, Dennis *(Choreographer)* 2260, 4485
Naify, Marshall *(Producer)* 2001
Naimo, Jennifer *(Cast)* 3377, 4398
Nainby, Robert *(Cast)* 3098
Nairn, Ralph *(Cast)* 4489
Naishtat, Saul *(Composer)* 4540
Naismith, Laurence *(Cast)* 406, 1860, 4384
Najimy, Kathy *(Director)* 261
Najimy, Kathy *(Producer)* 261
Naldi, Nita *(Cast)* 3402, 3975
Namanworth, Phillip *(Lyricist)* 1279
Namara, Madame *(Cast)* 93
Namara, Marguerite *(Cast)* 3152
Namuth, Harold *(Composer)* 1957
Nankwill, Guy *(Lyricist)* 4104
Napier, John *(Cast)* 4407
Napier, John *(Costumes)* 678, 2474, 4138
Napier, John *(Set Design)* 678, 730, 2442, 2474, 2905, 4138, 4217
Napier, Nina *(Cast)* 2292
Napoli, Jeanne *(Composer)* 2754
Napoli, Jeanne *(Lyricist)* 2754
Napolitano, Peter *(Lyricist)* 4456
Nappo, Carmen *(Composer)* 1934
Nardo, Eric *(Composer)* 1250
Narmore, Eugene *(Composer)* 1637
Narmore, Eugene *(Lyricist)* 1637
Nash, Florence *(Cast)* 48, 2889
Nash, George *(Cast)* 1434
Nash, John *(Director)* 523, 2345
Nash, Marie *(Cast)* 924, 2068, 4498, 4572
Nash, Mary *(Cast)* 1570
Nash, N. Richard *(Author)* 1571
Nash, N. Richard *(Librettist)* 1764, 3294, 3838, 4693
Nash, N. Richard *(Lyricist)* 3838
Nash, N. Richard *(Producer)* 4693
Nash, Ogden *(Librettist)* 1874, 3301
Nash, Ogden *(Lyricist)* 192, 193, 369, 1792, 1874, 2554, 3075, 3301, 3449, 4237, 4499
Nash, Robert *(Cast)* 2809
Nash, Ron *(Director)* 1732, 2055
Nason, Brian *(Lighting Designer)* 4371
Nassau, Paul *(Composer)* 1158, 1233, 1766, 2248, 3108
Nassau, Paul *(Lyricist)* 1158, 1233, 1766, 2248, 3108, 3112
Nassif, Robert *(Composer)* 4456
Nassif-Lindsey, Robert
See Lindsay, Robert Nassif.
Nathan, Adele Gutman *(Author)* 2348
Nathan, Caspar *(Lyricist)* 3402
Nathan, Joseph *(Composer)* 688, 3384
Nathan, Joseph *(Lyricist)* 3384
Nathan, Joseph S. *(Composer)* 1520, 4723
Nathan, L & H *(Costumes)* 972, 3139

Nathan, Robert *(Author)* 2237, 3544
Nathan, Stephen *(Cast)* 1595
Nathan Jr., Alfred *(Composer)* 2739, 3783
National CIO War Prods. *(Producer)* 2748
Nations, Curt *(Set Design)* 1766
Natwick, Mildred *(Cast)* 1294, 3900, 4142
Naudain, May *(Cast)* 1526
Naughton, Amanda *(Cast)* 2038, 3377, 3757
Naughton, Bill *(Author)* 2297
Naughton, Harry *(Choreographer)* 4541
Naughton, James *(Cast)* 775, 2058, 4406
Naumkin, Yuri *(Cast)* 2269
Navarre, Jay *(Composer)* 673, 2246
Navarro, Jesus *(Cast)* 2407
Navasio, Lenora *(Cast)* 1360
Navon, Ruthi *(Cast)* 1075
Naylor, Ian *(Cast)* 2451
Naylor, Ian *(Choreographer)* 2451
Nayor, Ed *(Director)* 62
Nayor, Ed *(Librettist)* 62
Nazareth, Ernesto *(Composer)* 3397
Nazhad, Eric *(Producer)* 3690
Nazzarro, Nat *(Producer)* 1983, 3657
Nazzarro Jr., Nat *(Cast)* 969, 3069, 3137, 3397, 3405, 3406, 4427
Neal, Joseph *(Cast)* 169, 793, 4379
Neal, Joseph *(Librettist)* 1560
Neal, Joseph *(Lyricist)* 1560
Neal, Kathleen *(Cast)* 540
Neale, Grant *(Cast)* 2488
Nealy *(Musical Director)* 4220
Nealy, Milton Craig *(Cast)* 1296, 3285
Nease, Byron *(Cast)* 430
Neber, Caspar *(Set Design)* 4368
Nedbal, Oscar *(Composer)* 3424
Nederlander, Charlene *(Producer)* 3142, 4295
Nederlander, Gladys *(Producer)* 1633
Nederlander, James M. *(Producer)* 547, 695, 958, 975, 1068, 1633, 1660, 1699, 2360, 2437, 2798, 2820, 3142, 3171, 3299, 3682, 3869, 4295, 4447, 4695, 4727
Nederlander, Joseph Z. *(Producer)* 2142
Nederlander Organization *(Producer)* 1645, 3936
Neeley, Ted *(Cast)* 3903
Neenan, Audrie *(Cast)* 942
Neff, Clad *(Musical Director)* 2771
Neff, Hildegarde *(Cast)* 3972
Neff, Morty *(Lyricist)* 1046
Negro Ensemble Company *(Producer)* 1592, 1671, 2272, 2719
Negro Players *(Producer)* 4441
Negulesco, Dusky *(Lyricist)* 3383
Nehls, David *(Cast)* 4799
Neiburg, Al J. *(Lyricist)* 1951
Neidlinger, W.H. *(Composer)* 4236
Neil, Fred *(Composer)* 3739
Neil, Fred *(Lyricist)* 3739
Neil, Grace *(Cast)* 3952
Neil, Julian *(Director)* 1201
Neil, Roger *(Cast)* 3858
Neil, Roger *(Dance Arranger)* 3688
Neil, Roger *(Musical Director)* 3688
Neil, Roger *(Vocal Arranger)* 3858
Neill, Jeffrey K. *(Choreographer)* 159, 164, 3697
Neill, Jeffrey K. *(Director)* 164, 3697
Neilson, Alice *(Cast)* 1355, 3881
Neilson, Evelyn *(Cast)* 325
Neilson, Francis *(Librettist)* 2370, 3570
Neiman, Harold *(Musical Director)* 200
Nell Jr., Edward *(Cast)* 3117
Nelligan, Kate *(Cast)* 3884
Nelova, Dorissa *(Cast)* 289
Nelson, Arvid *(Lighting Designer)* 408
Nelson, Barry *(Cast)* 16, 1273, 4582, 4706
Nelson, Bob *(Cast)* 199
Nelson, Bruce *(Producer)* 4468
Nelson, Ed G. *(Composer)* 567, 1626, 4815
Nelson, Ed G. *(Lyricist)* 567
Nelson, Eddie *(Cast)* 1152, 4741
Nelson, Edgar *(Cast)* 94
Nelson, Gail *(Cast)* 602, 3018, 4002
Nelson, Gene *(Cast)* 1329, 1341, 2439, 3018
Nelson, Gene *(Choreographer)* 1341
Nelson, Gene *(Director)* 1341
Nelson, Joan Marie *(Cast)* 821
Nelson, John *(Set Design)* 3802, 4444
Nelson, John L. *(Composer)* 815
Nelson, John L. *(Lyricist)* 815
Nelson, Keith *(Lighting Designer)* 459
Nelson, Kenneth *(Cast)* 1245, 2288, 2626, 3161, 3788, 3835, 3895
Nelson, Lee Mark *(Cast)* 589
Nelson, Lucy *(Cast)* 4597
Nelson, Mari *(Cast)* 4518
Nelson, Mervyn *(Cast)* 2748, 3105, 4394
Nelson, Mervyn *(Director)* 943, 1834, 3863, 4377, 4829
Nelson, Mervyn *(Producer)* 943
Nelson, Nan-Lynn *(Cast)* 3806
Nelson, Novella *(Cast)* 1977, 3610
Nelson, Ozzie
See Ozzie Nelson and His Orchestra.
Nelson, Portia *(Author)* 4330
Nelson, Portia *(Cast)* 273, 1600
Nelson, Portia *(Composer)* 90, 1023, 4153, 4330, 4416
Nelson, Portia *(Librettist)* 4330
Nelson, Portia *(Lyricist)* 90, 1023, 4153, 4330, 4416
Nelson, Ralph *(Director)* 44, 759, 2267
Nelson, Ralph *(Producer)* 2583
Nelson, Richard *(Librettist)* 721
Nelson, Richard *(Lighting Designer)* 572, 674, 682, 692, 789, 826, 1015, 1093, 1298, 1776, 1924, 2143, 2320, 2687, 2702, 3204, 3231, 3305, 3448, 3695, 4038, 4210, 4255
Nelson, Richard *(Set Design)* 4002
Nelson, Rick *(Cast)* 3275
Nelson, Rowland *(Cast)* 1957
Nelson, Rudolph *(Author)* 2886
Nelson, Rudolph *(Composer)* 2886
Nelson, Steve *(Lyricist)* 3793
Nelson and His Orch., Ozzie *(Cast)* 397
Nemerov, Howard *(Author)* 4278
Nemetz, Lee *(Director)* 3938

Nemetz, Lenora *(Cast)* 109, 4114, 4744
Nemiroff, Robert *(Librettist)* 3656
Nemiroff, Robert *(Producer)* 3656
Nemiroff, Robert B. *(Producer)* 2306
Nemo, Henry *(Composer)* 2653
Nemo, Henry *(Lyricist)* 886, 2653, 4091
Neofitou, Andreane *(Costumes)* 2442, 2905
Neptune, Peter *(Cast)* 2427
Nero, Peter *(Composer)* 4264
Nesbit, Wilbur *(Librettist)* 1558
Nesbit, William D. *(Lyricist)* 3437
Nesbitt, Cathleen *(Cast)* 1257, 3038
Nesbitt, Evelyn *(Cast)* 1535, 4414, 4691
Nesbitt, Miriam *(Cast)* 3267
Nesby, Ann *(Cast)* 3987
Nestler, L.A. *(Lighting Designer)* 1267
Nestor, Pat *(Cast)* 2246
Netsky, Hankus *(Composer)* 3937
Netsky, Hankus *(Orchestrations)* 3937
Neubach, Ernst *(Author)* 184, 2747
Neubauer, Nicholas *(Producer)* 3136
Neuberger, Jan *(Cast)* 198, 690, 708, 3221
Neuburger, Ad *(Choreographer)* 1469
Neufeld, Peter *(Producer)* 131
Neuman, Joan *(Cast)* 1450
Neumann, Dorothy *(Costumes)* 939
Neumann, Elizabeth *(Cast)* 1413
Neumann, Leone *(Cast)* 4372
Neuwirth, Bebe *(Cast)* 4533
Never or Now Company, The *(Producer)* 674
Neville, Frank *(Cast)* 1556
Neville, Harry *(Cast)* 2497
Neville, Hugh *(Author)* 4696
Neville, John *(Cast)* 2568
Neville-Andrews, John *(Cast)* 1166
Neville-Andrews, John *(Vocal Arranger)* 1166
Nevin, Arthur *(Composer)* 666
Nevin, Ethelbert *(Composer)* 4390
Nevins, Frances *(Cast)* 3946
New Day Productions *(Producer)* 2283
New Era Productions *(Producer)* 20, 2433
New Federal Theatre *(Producer)* 3544, 4697
New Opera Company, The *(Producer)* 1817, 3767
New Playwrights' Theatre *(Producer)* 528, 1004, 1155, 3165, 3329, 3997
New Princess Company *(Producer)* 1056
New Seekers *(Cast)* 1389
New Stock Company *(Producer)* 248
New Theatre Oxford *(Producer)* 194
New World Theatre *(Producer)* 3249
New York Football Jets, The *(Cast)* 3273
Newark Yacht Club *(Producer)* 4507
Neway, Patricia *(Cast)* 2958, 4095
Newberger, Ad *(Choreographer)* 2040, 2793, 4115
Newberger, Adolph *(Choreographer)* 2695, 4691
Newberry, Barbara *(Cast)* 376, 1617, 1800, 2540, 3352, 3379, 3953
Newberry, Barbara *(Choreographer)* 1453
Newberry, Cammann *(Composer)* 814
Newberry, Phelps *(Cast)* 4622
Newbold, Robinson *(Cast)* 1110
Newburger, David *(Composer)* 2558
Newburger, David *(Librettist)* 4124
Newburger, David *(Lyricist)* 4124
Newcomb, Jessamine *(Cast)* 3472
Newcombe, Blanche *(Cast)* 537, 3025
Newdahl, Clifford *(Cast)* 3573
Newell, Erika *(Cast)* 114
Newell, Norman *(Composer)* 2148
Newell, Norman *(Lyricist)* 2148
Newley, Anthony *(Cast)* 695, 920, 3731, 4160
Newley, Anthony *(Composer)* 695, 3454, 3731, 4160
Newley, Anthony *(Director)* 3731, 4160
Newley, Anthony *(Librettist)* 695, 3731, 4160
Newley, Anthony *(Lyricist)* 695, 3454, 3731, 4160
Newman, Alfred *(Composer)* 2112, 2180, 3444
Newman, Alfred *(Musical Director)* 111, 930, 1033, 1419, 1483, 1484, 1689, 1690, 1691, 1692, 1800, 2330, 3185, 3659, 4118, 4443, 4575
Newman, Andrew Hill *(Cast)* 2651
Newman, Barry *(Cast)* 4633
Newman, Charles *(Librettist)* 591
Newman, Charles *(Lyricist)* 497, 1127
Newman, David *(Librettist)* 2163, 2473, 3233
Newman, Del *(Arrangements)* 460
Newman, Greatrex *(Librettist)* 844, 1534, 2976, 3310
Newman, Greatrex *(Lyricist)* 844, 1534, 2389, 2976, 3310
Newman, Horace *(Cast)* 4382
Newman, Irving *(Composer)* 3002
Newman, Irving *(Lyricist)* 3002
Newman, Lionel *(Composer)* 3002
Newman, Lionel *(Lyricist)* 3002
Newman, Lionel *(Musical Director)* 1138
Newman, Molly *(Librettist)* 3631
Newman, Patricia *(Choreographer)* 4273
Newman, Paul *(Cast)* 3324
Newman, Peter *(Cast)* 3688
Newman, Phyllis *(Cast)* 1290, 2011, 2052, 2677, 3273, 3526, 4190, 4191, 4718
Newman, Phyllis *(Choreographer)* 3161
Newman, Phyllis *(Director)* 4167
Newman, Phyllis *(Librettist)* 2677
Newman, Phyllis *(Lyricist)* 2677
Newman, Randy *(Composer)* 2787, 2852
Newman, Randy *(Lyricist)* 2787, 2852
Newman, Ronnie *(Cast)* 4176
Newman, Stephen D. *(Cast)* 3702
Newmann, Dorothy *(Cast)* 4467
Newmar, Julie *(Cast)* 3972
Newsome, Betty *(Composer)* 3695
Newsome, Betty *(Lyricist)* 3695
Newton, Eddie *(Composer)* 3989
Newton, Harry L. *(Composer)* 4439
Newton, Harry L. *(Lyricist)* 4439
Newton, Harry L. *(Musical Director)* 4439
Newton, John *(Cast)* 3902
Newton-Brown, Michael *(Lighting Designer)* 1371
Ney, Frederick *(Composer)* 924
Ney, Richard *(Composer)* 3543
Ney, Richard *(Librettist)* 3543

Ney, Richard *(Lyricist)* 3543
Neyman, Al *(Producer)* 205
Ngema, Bhoyi *(Cast)* 209, 4438
Ngema, Mbongeni *(Arrangements)* 4438
Ngema, Mbongeni *(Author)* 209
Ngema, Mbongeni *(Choreographer)* 4438
Ngema, Mbongeni *(Composer)* 3836, 4438
Ngema, Mbongeni *(Dance Arranger)* 3836
Ngema, Mbongeni *(Director)* 209, 3836, 4438
Ngema, Mbongeni *(Librettist)* 3836, 4438
Ngema, Mbongeni *(Lyricist)* 3836, 4438
Ngema, Mbongeni *(Orchestrations)* 4438
Ngema, Mbongeni *(Vocal Arranger)* 3836
Ngema, Nhlanhla *(Cast)* 3836
Nhlanhla, Thandekile *(Cast)* 3836
Niblo, Fred *(Cast)* 3749
Niblo, Fred *(Producer)* 3809
Nicander, Edwin *(Cast)* 1623
Nicastro, Michelle *(Cast)* 2820
Nice, Emily *(Cast)* 1833
Nice, Nellie *(Cast)* 1833
Nicholas, Anna *(Cast)* 846
Nicholas, Eden *(Cast)* 4602
Nicholas, Fayard
See also The Nicholas Brothers.
Nicholas, Fayard *(Cast)* 247, 4123
Nicholas, Fayard *(Choreographer)* 432
Nicholas, Harold
See also The Nicholas Brothers.
Nicholas, Harold *(Cast)* 247, 1385, 4123
Nicholas Brothers, The
See also Fayard Nicholas and Harold Nicholas.
Nicholas Brothers, The *(Cast)* 446, 859, 875, 876, 877, 884, 885, 887, 4825
Nicholes, Bud *(Lighting Designer)* 3161
Nicholls, Allan *(Cast)* 3903
Nicholls, Horatio *(Composer)* 200
Nichols, Alberta *(Composer)* 138, 444, 1461, 1874, 2140, 3680, 3704
Nichols, Anne *(Author)* 1751, 2281, 2763
Nichols, Anne *(Cast)* 2310
Nichols, Anne *(Librettist)* 1751, 2489, 2605
Nichols, Anne *(Lyricist)* 2763
Nichols, Anne *(Producer)* 3922
Nichols, Barbara *(Cast)* 2246, 2449
Nichols, Beatrice *(Cast)* 4284
Nichols, Beverely *(Composer)* 791
Nichols, Beverely *(Librettist)* 791
Nichols, Beverely *(Lyricist)* 791
Nichols, Billy *(Composer)* 4167
Nichols, Billy *(Lyricist)* 4167
Nichols, Bobb *(Costumes)* 4380
Nichols, George *(Composer)* 3998
Nichols, George A. *(Composer)* 768, 2642
Nichols, George A. *(Lyricist)* 768
Nichols, George A. *(Musical Director)* 1927, 2642, 2990, 3723, 4195, 4382, 4437, 4831, 4833, 4834, 4836, 4837, 4838, 4851
Nichols, Harry *(Librettist)* 3803, 4430
Nichols, Joy *(Cast)* 1567
Nichols, Mike *(Director)* 170, 3624, 4129, 4746
Nichols, Mike *(Producer)* 52, 150, 414
Nichols, Nichelle *(Cast)* 2306
Nichols, Peter *(Author)* 3598
Nichols, Peter *(Lyricist)* 3598
Nichols, Peter *(Screenwriter)* 1497
Nichols, Red
See Red Nichols Orchestra.
Nichols III, George *(Producer)* 4018
Nichols Orchestra, Red *(Cast)* 1528, 4179
Nicholson, John *(Cast)* 2802
Nicholson, John *(Director)* 2108
Nicholson, Kenyon *(Author)* 3138
Nicholson, Kenyon *(Librettist)* 4545
Nicholson, Paul *(Cast)* 2358
Nicholson, William *(Costumes)* 4154
Nicholson, William *(Set Design)* 4154
Nichtern, Claire *(Producer)* 298, 2218
Nick and Arnold *(Producer)* 817
Nickelodeon Family Classics *(Producer)* 754
Nickerson, Charles *(Cast)* 2113
Nickerson, Dawn *(Cast)* 3725
Nickerson, Denise *(Cast)* 2568
Nicodemus *(Cast)* 2597, 4256
Nicol, Lesslie *(Cast)* 2731
Nicol, Megg *(Cast)* 456
Nicola, James *(Director)* 1104
Nicolai *(Author)* 2841
Nicoll, Charles *(Choreographer)* 2876
Nido, Estaban Rio
See Stephen Sondheim.
Nieburg, Al *(Lyricist)* 432
Niederhorn, Joe *(Cast)* 2094
Niehaus, Lennie *(Arrangements)* 2611
Nielsen, Alice *(Cast)* 2340, 3994, 4598
Nielsen Opera Company, Alice *(Producer)* 3994
Nielson, Christine *(Cast)* 276, 1738, 4616
Nieman, Harry *(Musical Director)* 201, 1461
Niemeyer, Joseph *(Cast)* 1606
Niesen, Gertrude *(Cast)* 622, 1336, 3409, 4825
Nightingale, Bill *(Cast)* 3539
Nigro, Robert *(Director)* 2152, 2542
Nikardi Productions *(Producer)* 1046
Nikko Producing Company *(Producer)* 3963
Nikolais, Alwin *(Choreographer)* 2441
Nikolais, Alwin *(Director)* 2441
Nikolais, Alwin *(Lighting Designer)* 2441
Nikolais, Alwin *(Set Design)* 2441
Niles, Barbara *(Cast)* 518, 1104
Niles, Marion *(Cast)* 1539
Niles, Mary Ann *(Cast)* 961, 2275, 2496, 4047
Niles, Mary Ann *(Choreographer)* 4047
Nilley, Florence *(Cast)* 1661
Nilo *(Costumes)* 1107, 1697, 3161, 3366
Nilsen, Harry *(Cast)* 1606
Nilsson, Harry *(Composer)* 4796
Nilsson, Harry *(Lyricist)* 4796
Nilsson, Walter *(Cast)* 1840
Nimura, Yeichi *(Choreographer)* 2655
Nininger, Willie *(Composer)* 4533

Nip, Tom *(Choreographer)* 1275
Nirska *(Cast)* 1423
Nirska, Mira *(Cast)* 4275
Nisbet, Lindy *(Cast)* 1262, 3318
Nishimura, Deborah *(Cast)* 3318
Nissen, Greta *(Cast)* 1877, 3179
Nissen, Naomi *(Cast)* 99
Nissenson, Gloria *(Lyricist)* 1382, 3576
Nita, Marta *(Choreographer)* 4110
Nitke, Maurice *(Composer)* 1283, 2211, 3686
Nitke, Maurice *(Lyricist)* 2211
Nitke, Maurice *(Musical Director)* 3686
Niven, Kip *(Cast)* 155, 3142
Niven, Sally *(Cast)* 3209
Nixon, Marni *(Cast)* 2183, 4272
Nixon, Nanette *(Cast)* 2116, 2842
Nixon & Zimmerman *(Producer)* 737, 1535, 2485, 2844, 2880, 3765, 3805, 4430, 4713
Noah, Mordecai *(Author)* 669
Nobel, Michael *(Cast)* 3557
Noble, Dennis *(Cast)* 1680
Noble, Johnny *(Composer)* 4264
Noble, Johnny *(Lyricist)* 4264
Noble, Ray *(Composer)* 1135, 1136
Noble, Trisha *(Cast)* 2072
Nocciolino, Albert *(Producer)* 2470, 2852
Nodin, Gerald *(Cast)* 429
Noel, Andrea *(Cast)* 4470
Noel, M. *(Cast)* 1610
Noel, Tom *(Cast)* 2731
Noelmeter, Bob *(Orchestrations)* 4828
Nohl, Joseph *(Composer)* 154
Nolan, Jim *(Cast)* 4602
Nolan, Kathy *(Cast)* 3453
Nolan, Lloyd *(Cast)* 125
Nolan, Peter *(Composer)* 1448
Noland, Nancy *(Cast)* 3104
Nolen, Timothy *(Cast)* 949, 1699, 3377
Noles, Hatty *(Cast)* 981
Nolfi, Ed *(Choreographer)* 302
Nolin, Denise *(Cast)* 3178
Noling, David *(Lighting Designer)* 4740
Noll, Edward *(Choreographer)* 137
Nolte, Carolyn *(Cast)* 1491, 4177
Noman, Pierre *(Lyricist)* 2162
Nones, Walter *(Composer)* 924
Nones, Walter *(Lyricist)* 924
Nonziato, Fran *(Choreographer)* 345
Noodles, Harry *(Lighting Designer)* 2455
Noon, Paisley *(Choreographer)* 3133
Noonan, John Ford *(Author)* 908
Noonan, Roger *(Cast)* 3202
Noone, James *(Set Design)* 2065, 3368, 3811
Noone, Peter *(Cast)* 635, 3497
Norden, A.M. *(Composer)* 4624, 4681
Norden, A.M. *(Librettist)* 4624
Norden, A.M. *(Lyricist)* 4624
Norden, Dennis *(Author)* 652
Nordstrom, Clarence *(Cast)* 827, 931, 1076, 1691, 2264, 2344, 2373, 2619, 3207, 3246, 3622, 3877, 4784
Nordstrom, Frances *(Librettist)* 3006, 3007, 4050
Nordstrom, Frances *(Lyricist)* 1250, 4033
Nordstrom, Marie *(Cast)* 1557, 3401, 4240
Nordstrom, Marie *(Costumes)* 1250
Norfleet, Cecilia *(Cast)* 3869
Norlin, Lloyd *(Composer)* 2804, 3941
Norman *(Composer)* 3926
Norman *(Lyricist)* 3926
Norman, Carl *(Pianist)* 427, 1049, *1107*, 3484
Norman, Carl *(Producer)* 3889
Norman, Christine *(Cast)* 3432
Norman, Frank *(Librettist)* 874, 1277
Norman, Henry *(Cast)* 1118, 1994, 2733
Norman, Henry *(Lyricist)* 1392
Norman, Henry "Bootsie" *(Musical Director)* 2659
Norman, Jay *(Choreographer)* 280, 3711
Norman, John *(Cast)* 2442
Norman, Karyl *(Author)* 4322
Norman, Karyl *(Cast)* 2380, 4322
Norman, Karyl *(Musical Director)* 4322
Norman, Marsha *(Cast)* 3104
Norman, Marsha *(Librettist)* 3682, 3862
Norman, Marsha *(Lyricist)* 3682, 3862
Norman, Monty *(Composer)* 194, 2949
Norman, Monty *(Librettist)* 2949
Norman, Monty *(Lyricist)* 194, 2150
Norman, Pierre *(Composer)* 1813
Norris, Arthur *(Musical Director)* 1718, 1918
Norris, Arthur *(Vocal Arranger)* 1918
Norris, Christopher *(Cast)* 3863
Norris, Dallett *(Librettist)* 4799
Norris, Dorothy *(Choreographer)* 1972
Norris, Ethel *(Cast)* 418, 1667, 2747
Norris, Frank *(Cast)* 2336
Norris, James *(Cast)* 1448, 1971
Norris, Jerry *(Cast)* 1874, 2238, 4235, 4335, 4583
Norris, Lee *(Composer)* 673
Norris, Lee *(Dance Arranger)* 658
Norris, Lee *(Lyricist)* 673
Norris, Lee *(Orchestrations)* 2043
Norris, William *(Cast)* 186, 250, 767, 834, 906, 2317, 2408, 2424, 2794, 2922, 3199, 4404, 4649
Norris, William *(Director)* 3033
Norris, William *(Producer)* 3033
North, Alex *(Composer)* 146, 1880, 3226, 4394
North, Bobby *(Cast)* 1455, 1735, 1738, 2826, 3525, 4804
North, Clyde *(Director)* 1780
North, Clyde *(Librettist)* 4793
North, John Ringling *(Composer)* 3715, 3716
North, John Ringling *(Producer)* 3715
North, Olive *(Cast)* 4046, 4753
North, Sheree *(Cast)* 1791, 2048
North, Zeme *(Cast)* 4270
North Shore Music Theater *(Producer)* 2651
Northcote, Freda *(Cast)* 296
Northen, Michael *(Lighting Designer)* 362
Northrop, Theodore *(Composer)* 47
Northrup, Theodore *(Composer)* 47, 2675
Northrup, Theodore *(Lyricist)* 2675
Northrup, Theodore H. *(Composer)* 1157

Northrup, Theodore H. *(Lyricist)* 1157
Norton, Coe *(Cast)* 4292
Norton, Edgar *(Cast)* 511, 2695, 3085, 3578
Norton, Fletcher *(Cast)* 1003, 1910, 2119, 2715, 3134, 4414
Norton, Frederick *(Composer)* 333, 758, 2701
Norton, Frederick *(Lyricist)* 333, 758, 2701
Norton, George *(Composer)* 1535
Norton, Jack *(Cast)* 1131
Norton, Mary *(Author)* 499
Norton, May *(Cast)* 749
Norton, Richard *(Producer)* 1149
Norton, Ruby *(Cast)* 1285, 1308, 1424, 3207
Norton and Margot, Harold *(Cast)* 897
Nortzar Productions *(Producer)* 1425
Norvo, Jimmy *(Cast)* 3500
Norvo, Red *(Cast)* 3893
Norwick, Douglas *(Choreographer)* 474, 556, 3666, 4272
Norworth, Jack *(Cast)* 8, 2232, 2528, 3222, 3755, 3779, 4802, 4803
Norworth, Jack *(Composer)* 2232, 2528, 2892, 3222, 3755, 4206, 4390, 4802, 4803, 4823
Norworth, Jack *(Librettist)* 3222
Norworth, Jack *(Lyricist)* 8, 1038, 2232, 2528, 2892, 3222, 3755, 4206, 4390, 4802, 4803, 4823
Norworth, Jack *(Producer)* 3222
Noto, Lore *(Librettist)* 4764
Noto, Lore *(Producer)* 1245, 4764
Noto, Tony *(Cast)* 4041
Nouri, Michael *(Cast)* 3088, 4560
Nova, Marta *(Cast)* 1244
Novak, Joe *(Producer)* 4454
Novasio, Lenora *(Cast)* 3434, 4381
Novello, Don *(Cast)* 1512
Novello, Don *(Librettist)* 1512
Novello, Ivor *(Cast)* 650, 972
Novello, Ivor *(Composer)* 133, 582, 650, 702, 703, 791, 972, 1467, 1610, 2004, 2570, 3020, 3259, 3924, 4154, 4327, 4581
Novello, Ivor *(Librettist)* 972, 1467
Novello, Ivor *(Lyricist)* 650, 702, 4581
Novis, Donald *(Cast)* 2258, 2636
Novotna, Jarmila *(Cast)* 1742, 1817
Novy, Nita *(Cast)* 1775
Nowak, Christopher *(Set Design)* 1872, 3608
Noyes, Newbold *(Cast)* 2287, 3378, 4622
Noyes, Patricia *(Translator)* 4386
Noyes, Thomas *(Producer)* 868
Nudelman, M. *(Librettist)* 2421
Nugent, Elliott *(Producer)* 3894
Nugent, Frank *(Author)* 1076
Nugent, Kitty *(Cast)* 2904
Nugent, Maude *(Composer)* 688, 1188
Nugent, Maude *(Lyricist)* 688
Nugent, Moya *(Cast)* 841, 1238, 3214, 3339, 3678, 3885, 3906, 4610
Nugent, Nelle *(Producer)* 2474
Nugent, Reita *(Cast)* 2976
Nunn, Trevor *(Director)* 211, 678, 721, 2442, 2474, 4138, 4217
Nunn, Trevor *(Lyricist)* 678
Nunn, Wayne *(Cast)* 1560
Nunsense Theatrical Co. *(Producer)* 3211
Nurock, Kirk *(Arrangements)* 2970
Nurock, Kirk *(Composer)* 2970
Nurock, Kirk *(Musical Director)* 3927
Nurock, Kirk *(Orchestrations)* 3824, 4744
Nurock, Kirk *(Vocal Arranger)* 251, 2970, 3927
Nurok, Robert *(Musical Director)* 3415
Nusbaum, Jane C. *(Producer)* 1729
Nussbaum, Joseph *(Orchestrations)* 2258, 3342
Nussbaum, Mike *(Director)* 1059
Nutter, Eileen *(Librettist)* 2034
Nutter, Mark *(Composer)* 4690
Nutter, Mark *(Librettist)* 4690
Nutter, Mark *(Lyricist)* 4690
Nuyen, France *(Cast)* 4749
Nyberg, David *(Orchestrations)* 275
Nye, April Ann *(Composer)* 4030
Nye, April Ann *(Lyricist)* 4030
Nye, Bill *(Librettist)* 4125
Nye, Carrie *(Cast)* 945, 1721
Nye, Louis *(Cast)* 2137, 4432
Nygh, Anna *(Choreographer)* 1166
Nyitray, Emil *(Author)* 2818, 3184
Nyitray, Emil *(Librettist)* 3048
Nyman, Betty Anne *(Cast)* 153, 851
Nype, Russell *(Cast)* 619, 1614, 2375, 3691, 4279, 4582

O

O'Brian, Hugh *(Cast)* 1257
O'Brien, Chester *(Choreographer)* 1342
O'Brien, Chet *(Cast)* 4677
O'Brien, Edmond *(Cast)* 4706
O'Brien, Eileen *(Cast)* 99
O'Brien, Gypsy *(Cast)* 1144, 2059
O'Brien, Jack *(Director)* 3088
O'Brien, Jack *(Librettist)* 3871
O'Brien, Jack *(Lyricist)* 3871
O'Brien, John J. *(Lyricist)* 543
O'Brien, Margaret *(Cast)* 2550
O'Brien, Marietta *(Cast)* 202
O'Brien, Michael Miguel *(Cast)* 3874
O'Brien, Mort *(Cast)* 4677
O'Brien, Ray *(Musical Director)* 4829
O'Brien, Richard *(Composer)* 3742
O'Brien, Richard *(Librettist)* 3742
O'Brien, Richard *(Lyricist)* 3742
O'Brien, Ritz *(Cast)* 3742
O'Brien, Sylvia *(Cast)* 1010
O'Brien, Timothy *(Costumes)* 1211
O'Brien, Timothy *(Set Design)* 1068, 1211
O'Brien, Virginia (*Cast*) 2020, 2301, 2492, 3434, 3723
O'Casey, Sean *(Author)* 2268, 3612
O'Casey, Sean *(Librettist)* 3612
O'Casey, Sean *(Lyricist)* 3612
O'Connell, Hugh *(Cast)* 1225, 4825

O'Connell, Maggie *(Cast)* 3544
O'Connor *(Cast)* 4328
O'Connor, Brian Brucker *(Cast)* 3076
O'Connor, Brian Brucker *(Lyricist)* 3076
O'Connor, Daniel *(Director)* 319
O'Connor, Daniel *(Librettist)* 319
O'Connor, Donald *(Cast)* 534, 3273, 3846
O'Connor, Giles *(Lyricist)* 4627
O'Connor, Richard *(Choreographer)* 1509
O'Connor, Robert *(Cast)* 2486
O'Connor, Shamus *(Composer)* 3479
O'Curran, Charles *(Choreographer)* 3841
O'Curran, Charles *(Director)* 4199
O'Daniels, Barrie *(Director)* 1414, 3152
O'Daniels, Barrie *(Producer)* 4486
O'Day, Alice *(Cast)* 3467
O'Day, Nell *(Cast)* 1275, 3292
O'Dea, James *(Cast)* 3225
O'Dea, James *(Composer)* 2518
O'Dea, James *(Lyricist)* 246, 736, 1246, 1518, 1646, 2394, 2481, 2675, 3882, 4044, 4425, 4723
O'Dea, June *(Cast)* 403, 1859, 2238, 3622
O'Dea, Sunnie *(Cast)* 289, 1127, 2453, 2653
O'Denishawn, Florence *(Cast)* 1920, 1921, 1922, 3008, 3768, 4815
O'Donnell, Charlie *(Composer)* 2892
O'Donnell, George *(Cast)* 3582
O'Donoghue, Michael *(Librettist)* 1512
O'Flaherty, Michael *(Cast)* 1169, 1897, 4398
O'Flaherty, Michael *(Choreographer)* 4398
O'Flaherty, Michael *(Musical Director)* 1169, 1897, 4136, 4398
O'Flaherty, Michael *(Orchestrations)* 1630
O'Flaherty, Michael *(Vocal Arranger)* 4398
O'Gorman, Michael *(Cast)* 4020
O'Grady, Dan *(Cast)* 450
O'Hanlon, James *(Author)* 616
O'Hara, Brian *(Cast)* 4011
O'Hara, Brian *(Director)* 4011
O'Hara, Brian *(Librettist)* 4011
O'Hara, Edith *(Producer)* 508, 4431
O'Hara, Fiske *(Cast)* 1051, 1751, 1907, 2186, 2207, 2310, 2763, 2973, 3968, 4120
O'Hara, Fiske *(Composer)* 1051, 2207, 2973
O'Hara, Fiske *(Lyricist)* 1051, 1907, 2186, 2207, 2310, 2763, 2973, 4120
O'Hara, Geoffrey *(Composer)* 1722, 1774, 3591
O'Hara, Geoffrey *(Lyricist)* 1722
O'Hara, Helen *(Cast)* 3103
O'Hara, Jenny *(Cast)* 1273, 1736
O'Hara, Jill *(Cast)* 1478, 1736, 3603, 3788
O'Hara, John *(Author)* 3353
O'Hara, John *(Librettist)* 3353
O'Hara, Joseph *(Cast)* 1896
O'Hara, Lyle *(Cast)* 4433
O'Hara, Maureen *(Cast)* 751
O'Hara, Paige *(Cast)* 1508
O'Hare, Brad *(Cast)* 4358
O'Hare, Michael *(Cast)* 4019
O'Hay, Irving *(Narrator)* 2413
O'Hearn, Patricia *(Cast)* 2519
O'Hearn, Robert *(Set Design)* 2168
O'Horgan, Tom *(Composer)* 3169, 3873, 4397
O'Horgan, Tom *(Director)* 1116, 1717, 2134, 2212, 2970, 2992, 3169, 3873, 3903
O'Horgan, Tom *(Librettist)* 2970, 2992, 3903
O'Horgan, Tom *(Producer)* 2134
O'Kane, Mrs. *(Costumes)* 102
O'Keefe, James *(Composer)* 2373
O'Keefe, James *(Lyricist)* 2373
O'Keefe, Lester *(Cast)* 1483
O'Keefe, Lester *(Librettist)* 4550
O'Keefe, Lester *(Lyricist)* 4550
O'Keefe, Walter *(Cast)* 4237, 4335
O'Keefe, Walter *(Lyricist)* 2271, 3584
O'Keefe, Winston *(Cast)* 4479
O'Kun, Lan *(Composer)* 2553, 4388, 4525
O'Kun, Lan *(Librettist)* 2553
O'Kun, Lan *(Lyricist)* 2553, 4388
O'Leary, Chris *(Lighting Designer)* 2676
O'Leary, Chris *(Set Design)* 2676
O'Madigan, Isabel *(Cast)* 3866
O'Malley, John *(Cast)* 3498
O'Malley, John *(Puppeteer)* 4660
O'Malley, Muriel *(Cast)* 85
O'Malley, Rex *(Cast)* 1219, 2655, 2729, 3699, 4730, 4777
O'Malley, Sean *(Puppeteer)* 4660
O'Malley, Tom *(Librettist)* 348
O'Malley, Tom *(Lyricist)* 348
O'Mara, Terry *(Cast)* 1364
O'Neal, Charles *(Author)* 4366
O'Neal, Charles *(Librettist)* 4366
O'Neal, Cynthia *(Costumes)* 4129
O'Neal, Frederick *(Cast)* 279, 2000, 2395
O'Neal, Harry *(Cast)* 202
O'Neal, Michael *(Producer)* 4533
O'Neal, Patrick *(Producer)* 4533
O'Neal, William *(Cast)* 153, 1027, 3117, 3946, 4214
O'Neal, Zelma *(Cast)* 1339, 1440, 1628, 3139
O'Neil, Alice *(Costumes)* 1484, 1643, 2802, 2907, 3006, 3218, 3652, 3727, 3791, 3819, 4001, 4437, 4810, 4813, 4814, 4816, 4817, 4831, 4837, 4851, 4852
O'Neil, Alice *(Set Design)* 4836
O'Neil, Bobby *(Cast)* 4194
O'Neil, J.R. *(Choreographer)* 3192
O'Neil, Nance *(Cast)* 17, 3412
O'Neil, Nellie *(Cast)* 509, 998, 1259
O'Neil, Tricia *(Cast)* 4481
O'Neil, William J. *(Director)* 1882
O'Neil & Greenwald *(Producer)* 3512
O'Neill, Con *(Cast)* 460
O'Neill, Dick *(Cast)* 4013
O'Neill, Eugene *(Author)* 34, 1105, 3113, 4270
O'Neill, Frank *(Librettist)* 1918
O'Neill, Henry *(Cast)* 2060
O'Neill, James *(Cast)* 3031, 4671
O'Neill, Peggy *(Cast)* 4464, 4673
O'Neill, Standish *(Producer)* 2946
O'Neill, Terrence *(Costumes)* 944
O'Neill, Thomas *(Set Design)* 1884

O'Ramey, Georgia *(Cast)* 186, 953, 965, 2180, 2576, 2907, 3184, 3319, 3659, 4547
O'Rourke, Eugene *(Cast)* 1579, 2315, 3744
O'Rourke, Leo *(Musical Director)* 938
O'Rourke, P.J. *(Lyricist)* 3077
O'Ryan, Anna Wynne *(Librettist)* 2276
O'Ryan, Anna Wynne *(Lyricist)* 4637
O'Shaughnessy, John *(Director)* 4015
O'Shea, Helen *(Cast)* 994
O'Shea, Milo *(Cast)* 951, 1012, 1741, 2805
O'Shea, Sally *(Choreographer)* 4106
O'Shea, Tessie *(Cast)* 547, 1564, 2388, 4062, 4384
O'Shea, Tessie *(Composer)* 2388
O'Shea, Tessie *(Lyricist)* 2388
O'Steen, Michael *(Cast)* 1236, 2805
O'Sullivan, Denie *(Cast)* 3912
O'Sullivan, Denis *(Cast)* 2502
O'Sullivan, Maureen *(Cast)* 2297, 3097
O'Sullivan, Michael *(Cast)* 2163, 2599
O'Toole, Annette *(Cast)* 845
Oak, Dawna *(Costumes)* 3641
Oaker, Jane *(Cast)* 913, 1971
Oakes, Betty *(Cast)* 159, 3831, 3920
Oakes, Gary *(Cast)* 3939
Oakland, Ben *(Composer)* 124, 478, 881, 1932, 3374, 4137, 4799, 4823, 4824
Oakland, Ben *(Lyricist)* 478, 1932, 4824
Oakland, Simon *(Cast)* 4474
Oakland, Vivian *(Cast)* 684, 1551, 2856, 3333, 4760
Oakland, Will *(Cast)* 803
Oakley, Silvers *(Cast)* 4046
Oakley, Slivers *(Cast)* 286
Oatman, Rev. Johnson *(Composer)* 3261
Oatman, Rev. Johnson *(Lyricist)* 3261
Ober, Ruth Boyd *(Cast)* 2407
Ober, Ruth Boyd *(Librettist)* 2407
Ober, Ruth Boyd *(Lyricist)* 2407
Oberfelder, Sydney *(Choreographer)* 265, 4530
Oches, Al *(Cast)* 4819
Ockenfels, Emily L. *(Costumes)* 198
Ockerhauser, Karl F. *(Librettist)* 6
Ockerhauser, Karl F. *(Lyricist)* 6
Ockrent, Michael *(Director)* 921
Ockrent, Mike *(Director)* 754, 2798
Ockrent, Mike *(Librettist)* 754, 2798
Odell, Maude *(Cast)* 1530, 2495, 2624, 3193, 3372, 3433, 3466
Oden-Waller, William *(Set Design)* 512, 1489, 1491, 2265, 2734, 4043, 4083, 4105, 4218, 4271
Odenz, Leon *(Dance Arranger)* 1435, 2776
Odenz, Leon *(Musical Director)* 2776, 4517
Odenz, Leon *(Orchestrations)* 2776
Odenz, Leon *(Vocal Arranger)* 2776
Odets, Clifford *(Author)* 1601, 4481
Odets, Clifford *(Librettist)* 1601
Oditz, Carol *(Costumes)* 1418, 1813, 2152, 3517, 4162, 4442, 4517, 4684
Odle, Dwight Richard *(Costumes)* 973
Oenslager, Donald *(Lighting Designer)* 137, 2629, 3386, 3390, 3493, 4600
Oenslager, Donald *(Set Design)* 111, 121, 137, 163, 1007, 1145, 1339, 1387, 1413, 1528, 1628, 1718, 1800, 1939, 2068, 2228, 2464, 2629, 2729, 3117, 3386, 3390, 3493, 3674, 3993, 4059, 4362, 4600, 4778
Oesterman, Phil *(Director)* 952, 2451
Oesterman, Phil *(Librettist)* 2451
Oesterman, Phillip *(Director)* 3125
Oesterreicher, Rudolph *(Author)* 2293
Oestreicher, Gerard *(Producer)* 2357, 2864, 4643
Offenbach, Jacques *(Author)* 1817, 2357
Offenbach, Jacques *(Composer)* 1439, 1745, 1763, 2464, 4274
Offenbach, Jacques *(Music Based On)* 1817, 1818, 2357, 2493, 2622
Office Two-One Inc. *(Producer)* 1633
Officer, Phillip *(Cast)* 4136
Offner, Mortimer *(Director)* 2809
Offner, Mortimer *(Librettist)* 2809
Offt, Tom *(Cast)* 4527
Ogden, Angela *(Cast)* 2329
Ogden, H.A. *(Costumes)* 1157, 4239, 4313
Ogerman, Claus *(Composer)* 2260
Ogerman, Claus *(Orchestrations)* 2260
Oh, Soon-Teck *(Cast)* 3340
Ohman, Phil *(Composer)* 1819
Ohman, Phil *(Lyricist)* 1819
Ohman, Phil *(Pianist)* 1419, 1800, 2376, 3243, 4392, 4443
Ohman, Phil *(Producer)* 4118
Ohringer, Jane *(Cast)* 1211
Oirich, Steven *(Musical Director)* 3548
Oirich, Steven *(Orchestrations)* 3448
Okazaki, Alan *(Set Design)* 4193
Oken, Stuart *(Producer)* 2470
Okie, William *(Author)* 225
Okie, William *(Lyricist)* 225
Okonkowski, Georg *(Author)* 1554, 2922, 2923, 3529, 3627
Okun, Alexander *(Set Design)* 1236, 3792, 4442
Olaf, Pierre *(Cast)* 656, 2364, 4319
Olcott, Charles *(Cast)* 2373
Olcott, Chauncey *(Cast)* 310, 1157, 1163, 1445, 1803, 2154, 2662, 2875, 3220, 3267, 3642, 3759, 3910, 4239, 4313, 4576
Olcott, Chauncey *(Composer)* 310, 516, 1157, 1163, 1445, 2154, 2662, 2875, 3220, 3267, 3642, 3759, 3910, 4239, 4313
Olcott, Chauncey *(Lyricist)* 310, 516, 1157, 1163, 1445, 2154, 2662, 2875, 3220, 3267, 3642, 3759, 3910, 4239, 4313
Olcott, Nick *(Cast)* 1004
Olcott, Rita *(Author)* 3642
Oldfield, Emmett *(Cast)* 2475
Oldfield, Mike *(Composer)* 3739
Oleksa *(Costumes)* 2764
Olias, Lotar *(Composer)* 4264
Olias, R. *(Lyricist)* 4264
Olim, Dorothy *(Producer)* 3491
Olin, Ken *(Cast)* 4294
Oliphant, Tom *(Cast)* 3714

Oliver, Barrie *(Cast)* 700, 3131, 3605
Oliver, Barrie *(Choreographer)* 700
Oliver, Barrie *(Librettist)* 3605
Oliver, Don *(Cast)* 344
Oliver, Edna May *(Cast)* 1723, 3043, 3230, 3949, 4178
Oliver, Ike *(Cast)* 1316
Oliver, Joseph "King" *(Composer)* 1063
Oliver, King *(Composer)* 2200, 3840
Oliver, King *(Lyricist)* 3840
Oliver, Rochelle *(Cast)* 1184
Oliver, Roland *(Librettist)* 1343, 1629, 3256
Oliver, Roland *(Lyricist)* 1629, 3256
Oliver, Stephen *(Composer)* 2474
Oliver, Stephen *(Lyricist)* 2474
Oliver, Sy *(Musical Director)* 108
Oliver, Sy *(Orchestrations)* 3110, 3234
Oliver, Thelma *(Cast)* 766, 1319, 4238
Olivier, Laurence *(Cast)* 3597
Olman, Abe *(Composer)* 1334, 2856
Olmos, Edward James *(Cast)* 4861
Olneys, The *(Producer)* 1814, 4498
Olon, John *(Director)* 4246
Olrich, April *(Cast)* 4579
Olsen, Bob (Set *Design)* 3814
Olsen, George
See also George Olsen and His Orchestra/ Olsen's Orchestra.
Olsen, George *(Cast)* 2308, 4818
Olsen, Harry B. *(Composer)* 37, 1629, 3256
Olsen, Harry B. *(Musical Director)* 37, 3256
Olsen, Irene *(Cast)* 953, 1733
Olsen, J.C. *(Cast)* 1423
Olsen, Morry *(Composer)* 3314
Olsen, Morry *(Lyricist)* 3314
Olsen, Ole *(Cast)* 1423, 1840, 2400, 3380, 3381, 4086, 4816
Olsen, Ole *(Composer)* 1423
Olsen, Ole *(Director)* 1423
Olsen, Ole *(Librettist)* 1840, 2400, 3381, 4086
Olsen, Ole *(Lyricist)* 1423, 3381, 4816, 4817
Olsen, Ole *(Producer)* 901, 1840, 2400, 3381, 4174
Olsen, Olive *(Cast)* 1136, 2808, 4673
Olsen, Robert *(Cast)* 4030
Olsen and His Orchestra/Olsen's Orchestra, George
See also George Olsen.
Olsen and His Orchestra, George *(Cast)* 1628
Olsen's Orchestra, George *(Cast)* 4683
Olshanetsky, Alexander *(Composer)* 573, 1279, 1609
Olshanetsky, Alexander *(Lyricist)* 573, 1609
Olshenetsky, Alexander *(Composer)* 4463
Olson, Marcus *(Cast)* 212, 3411
Olson, Nancy *(Cast)* 3874
Olson, Scott *(Lyricist)* 3894
Olsson, Jack *(Composer)* 345
Olsson, Jack *(Lyricist)* 345
Olvis, William *(Cast)* 649, 3035
Omer, Costas *(Producer)* 4332
Omeron, Guen *(Cast)* 3151
Omeron, Gueneth *(Cast)* 2841
Ongley, Byron *(Author)* 577, 4860
Ongley, Byron *(Director)* 1520
Ono, Yoko *(Composer)* 3125, 4449
Ono, Yoko *(Librettist)* 3125
Ono, Yoko *(Lyricist)* 3125, 4449
Onrubia, Cynthia *(Cast)* 678
Ontiveros, Lupe *(Cast)* 4861
Onuki, Haru *(Cast)* 396
Opalach, Dorothy *(Musical Director)* 669
Opatoshu, David *(Cast)* 223, 400, 519, 3972, 4773
Opatoshu, David *(Director)* 400
Opatoshu, David *(Librettist)* 400
Opel, Nancy *(Cast)* 2038, 3448, 4210, 4297
Open Window, The *(Composer)* 3233
Open Window, The *(Lyricist)* 3233
Operti, Albert *(Set Design)* 2543
Operti, Le Roi *(Cast)* 919, 1343, 2610, 2729, 4386
Ophir, Shai K. *(Cast)* 1358
Ophir, Shai K. *(Director)* 1358
Ophir, Shai K. *(Librettist)* 1358
Ophir, Shai K. *(Lyricist)* 1358
Oppenheim, Dave *(Composer)* 1952
Oppenheim, Dave *(Lyricist)* 567, 1738, 1938, 1949, 1950, 1952, 1953, 1963, 3375, 4335, 4589
Oppenheim, David *(Lyricist)* 1311
Oppenheim, E. Phillips *(Librettist)* 1153
Oppenheim, James *(Lyricist)* 1609
Oppenheimer, Alan *(Cast)* 4217
Oppenheimer, George S. *(Librettist)* 961, 2739
Oppenheimer, George S. *(Lyricist)* 2739
Oppenheimer, J. *(Producer)* 4275
Opper, Frederick Burr *(Author)* 1758, 1759
Opsahl, Jason *(Cast)* 3708
Oram, Harold L. *(Producer)* 344
Orange *(Costumes)* 2884
Orange, Fredi *(Cast)* 3814
Orbach, Jerry *(Cast)* 656, 723, 1245, 1359, 3603
Orbach, Ron *(Cast)* 2470
Orbison, Roy *(Composer)* 3695
Orbison, Roy *(Lyricist)* 3695
Orchard, Julian *(Cast)* 3482
Orczy, Baroness *(Author)* 3491
Ordonneau, Maurice *(Author)* 1994, 2365, 2667, 2723
Ordynski, Richard *(Director)* 1309
Orefice, Frank *(Librettist)* 242
Orenstein, Larry *(Composer)* 732
Orezzoli, Hector *(Costumes)* 432
Orezzoli, Hector (Set *Design)* 432
Orfaly, Alexander *(Cast)* 3711
Original Dixieland Jass Band *(Composer)* 3297
Orkin, Harvey *(Librettist)* 4469
Orlando, Phil *(Vocal Arranger)* 1924
Orlob, Harold *(Composer)* 1, 144, 246, 248, 638, 1307, 1513, 1718, 1801, 1920, 2270, 2491, 2774, 2901, 3052, 3087, 3207, 3395, 3579, 3672, 4226, 4276, 4437, 4448
Orlob, Harold *(Librettist)* 2270, 2709, 4448
Orlob, Harold *(Lyricist)* 1307, 1593, 1718, 2270, 2709, 2901, 3395, 4448
Orlob, Harold *(Producer)* 1513, 1718
Orloff, Penny *(Cast)* 1068
Orlova, Gay *(Cast)* 3002

Orme, Gordon *(Cast)* 3103
Ormes, Alberta *(Cast)* 1909
Ormiston, George *(Cast)* 3111
Ormont, Dave *(Lyricist)* 673
Ormont, David *(Lyricist)* 1892
Ormston, George *(Set Design)* 796
Ornadel, Cyril *(Composer)* 1313, 3482
Ornbo, Robert *(Lighting Designer)* 832, 2047
Orr, Ann *(Cast)* 1531, 3923
Orr, Clifford *(Lyricist)* 3005
Orr, Forrest *(Cast)* 3674
Orr, Mary *(Author)* 167
Orr, William P. *(Producer)* 2328
Ortega, Eva *(Cast)* 3885
Ortega, Kenny *(Choreographer)* 2754
Ortega, Kenny *(Director)* 2754
Orth, Louise *(Cast)* 1919
Ortmann, Will *(Additional Music)* 718
Ortmann, Will *(Composer)* 718, 1935, 1944, 3430, 3783, 4189
Ortmann, Will *(Lyricist)* 1944
Orton, Chip *(Lyricist)* 1638
Orton, Joe *(Screenwriter)* 4518
Ory, Kid *(Composer)* 3297
Osato, Sono *(Cast)* 283, 3278, 3286, 3301
Osborn, Hubert *(Author)* 1916
Osborn, Paul *(Author)* 4749
Osborn, Paul *(Librettist)* 1990
Osborne, Frances *(Cast)* 4467
Osborne, Loraine *(Cast)* 1535
Osborne, Nat *(Composer)* 231, 1407, 1517, 1824, 2274
Osborne, Nat *(Librettist)* 231
Osborne, Vivienne *(Cast)* 3974
Osburn, Alan *(Cast)* 4731
Osburne, Oran *(Cast)* 1029
Oscar, Brad *(Cast)* 2198
Oscar, Gail *(Cast)* 871
Oscar, Henry *(Cast)* 4207
Osgood, Pearl *(Cast)* 1323, 4823
Oshins, Jules *(Cast)* 4340
Oshrin, Harry *(Producer)* 4276
Oshrin, Sidney S. *(Producer)* 2052
Osser, Glenn *(Arrangements)* 1744
Osser, Glenn *(Musical Director)* 1744, 2522, 3496
Osser, Glenn *(Orchestrations)* 1146, 1864, 3126
Osterman, Jack *(Cast)* 202, 3148, 3409, 4021
Osterman, Jack *(Lyricist)* 202, 4819
Osterman, Lester *(Producer)* 630, 1227, 1891, 2965, 2987, 3299, 3741, 3743, 3780, 3845, 4060, 4601
Ostermann, Curt *(Lighting Designer)* 962, 1496, 1997, 3764
Osterwald, Bibi *(Cast)* 108, 1237, 1507, 1600, 3914, 3989, 4156, 4542
Ostranger, A.A. *(Set Design)* 1112
Ostrov, Dmitri *(Director)* 1710
Ostrov, Dmitri *(Producer)* 1710
Ostrow, Stuart *(Director)* 1860, 4252
Ostrow, Stuart *(Producer)* 119, 170, 1214, 1860, 2949, 3506, 3897, 4252, 4609
Otero, Emma *(Cast)* 1414
Otis, Elita Proctor *(Cast)* 2770, 3613
Otis, Phoebe *(Cast)* 4332
Ott, Horace *(Dance Arranger)* 1116
Ott, Horace *(Orchestrations)* 1116, 4558
Ott, Horace *(Vocal Arranger)* 1116
Ott, Joseph *(Cast)* 559, 2865
Ott, Matthew *(Cast)* 1213
Ott, Matthew *(Librettist)* 2934
Ott, Matthew *(Lyricist)* 2934
Ott, Phil *(Composer)* 2934
Ott, Phil *(Librettist)* 1964
Ott, Phil *(Producer)* 1964
Ott & Wallin *(Producer)* 2934
Otto, Arthur *(Cast)* 361
Otto, Ernest *(Cast)* 361
Otto, Frank *(Cast)* 2265
Otto, Liz *(Cast)* 2051
Otvos, A. Dorian *(Composer)* 2972, 3369
Otvos, A. Dorian *(Librettist)* 622, 1493, 1692, 3172
Oudin, Eugene *(Cast)* 1080
Ouelette, Gratian *(Composer)* 4433
Ouelette, Gratian *(Librettist)* 4433
Ouelette, Gratian *(Lyricist)* 4433
Oumansky, Alexander *(Choreographer)* 2413, 3008
Oursler, Fulton *(Author)* 4105
Ousley, Robert *(Cast)* 4233
Ouspenskaya, Maria *(Cast)* 2211
Outcault, R.E. *(Author)* 591
Ouzounian, Richard *(Director)* 426
Ouzounian, Richard *(Lyricist)* 426
Overholt, Miles *(Librettist)* 2454
Overman, Lynne *(Cast)* 1961, 1979, 2281, 4213
Overstreet, Benton *(Composer)* 4231
Overstreet, William *(Composer)* 1838
Overstreet, William Benton *(Additional Music)* 1499
Overton, Frank *(Cast)* 4191
Overton, Jane *(Cast)* 1013
Owen, Alun *(Librettist)* 2682
Owen, Delos *(Composer)* 4240
Owen, Delos *(Librettist)* 4240
Owen, Garry *(Cast)* 2896
Owen, Guy *(Cast)* 4143
Owen, Hayden *(Musical Director)* 1098
Owen, J. Edwin *(Librettist)* 3316
Owen, John *(Director)* 4041
Owen, John *(Librettist)* 4041
Owen, Margaret *(Cast)* 1098
Owen, Nancy *(Cast)* 4149
Owen, Paul *(Vocal Arranger)* 4415
Owen, Reginald *(Cast)* 4357, 4372
Owen, Wallace *(Cast)* 2274
Owens, Daniel *(Librettist)* 2513
Owens, Flo *(Cast)* 395
Owens, Frank *(Composer)* 3905, 4171, 4534
Owens, Frank *(Dance Arranger)* 3905, 4171, 4534
Owens, Frank *(Lyricist)* 3905, 4171
Owens, Frank *(Musical Director)* 3905, 4534
Owens, Frank *(Orchestrations)* 4171
Owens, Frank *(Vocal Arranger)* 3905
Owens, Frederick B. *(Cast)* 4031

Owens, Hugh *(Composer)* 2528
Owens, Hugh *(Lyricist)* 2528
Owens, Philip *(Cast)* 1229, 4684
Owens, Rochelle *(Librettist)* 2290
Owens, Rochelle *(Lyricist)* 2290
Owsley, Tim *(Cast)* 3904, 3979
Owsley, Tim *(Librettist)* 3904
Owsley, Tim *(Lyricist)* 1421
Owsley, Tim *(Producer)* 1421
Oxford, Earl *(Cast)* 2105, 2475, 3365, 4340, 4367, 4498, 4823
Oxford Ltd, The *(Producer)* 2788
Oxley, Leonard *(Musical Director)* 2513
Oyra, Jan *(Cast)* 202
Oyra, Jan *(Choreographer)* 202

P

P.G.J. Productions *(Producer)* 679
PACE Theatrical Group *(Producer)* 2198
PQU Productions, Inc. *(Producer)* 3601
Paaz, Nira *(Cast)* 1358
Pace, Atkin *(Set Design)* 2283
Pace, Jean *(Cast)* 2245
Pace, Jean *(Costumes)* 578
Pace, Jean *(Director)* 578
Pace, Michael *(Cast)* 3739
Pace Theatrical Group *(Producer)* 4676
Pacheo, Mrs. R. *(Author)* 4364
Pack, Lorenzo *(Composer)* 890
Pack, Lorenzo *(Lyricist)* 890
Pack, The *(Producer)* 2427
Packer, Jerry *(Vocal Arranger)* 2449
Packer, Nedda *(Cast)* 1706
Packey, Anna *(Cast)* 3041
Paddison, Gordon *(Cast)* 474
Padgett, Billy *(Cast)* 3708
Padilla, Jose *(Composer)* 1678, 2526, 4033
Padron, Aurelio *(Cast)* 1164
Padula, Edward *(Director)* 999, 2248
Padula, Edward *(Librettist)* 2248
Padula, Edward *(Producer)* 64, 269, 607, 1072, 2248, 3389, 3684
Page, Carolann *(Cast)* 1291
Page, Gene *(Orchestrations)* 4334
Page, Geraldine *(Cast)* 546, 2468, 3338
Page, John Patrick *(Composer)* 3739
Page, John Patrick *(Lyricist)* 3739
Page, Ken *(Cast)* 39, 678, 730
Page, Lucille *(Cast)* 1136, 1782
Page, Rita *(Cast)* 2547
Page, Robert *(Orchestrations)* 2219
Page, Robert *(Vocal Arranger)* 2219
Page, Ruth *(Cast)* 3007
Page, Ruth *(Choreographer)* 3013
Page, Stan *(Cast)* 1359, 1660, 3526
Pagent, Robert *(Cast)* 660
Paget, Daniel *(Musical Director)* 2599
Paget, Dennis *(Producer)* 2440
Paget, Ffoliott *(Cast)* 3189
Pagnol, Marcel *(Author)* 273, 1242
Pahl, Mel *(Composer)* 23, 1933
Pahl, Mel *(Dance Arranger)* 2850
Pahl, Mel *(Vocal Arranger)* 2235, 2850
Paige, Janis *(Cast)* 1860, 3351
Paige, Patricia L. *(Choreographer)* 1702
Paine, Albert Bigelow *(Lyricist)* 2938
Painter, Eleanor *(Cast)* 728, 1580, 2419, 2486, 3163
Painter, Walter *(Choreographer)* 775
Paintor, Eleanor *(Cast)* 3590
Paisley, Tom *(Composer)* 1770
Paisley, Tom *(Lyricist)* 1770
Paisner, Dina *(Cast)* 3835
Paiva, Jararaca *(Composer)* 1138
Paiva, Vincente *(Composer)* 1138
Pakledinaz, Marty *(Costumes)* 2133
Palance, Jack *(Cast)* 58
Palermo, Alex *(Choreographer)* 227, 2887, 2988, 4292
Palermo, Alex *(Director)* 227
Paley, Herman *(Composer)* 8, 1518
Paley, Herman *(Lyricist)* 3827
Paley, Joel *(Director)* 3811
Paley, Joel *(Librettist)* 3811
Paley, Joel *(Lyricist)* 3811
Paley, Lou *(Lyricist)* 638, 1154, 1528, 2363, 2376, 2385
Palings, W. *(Librettist)* 770
Palkowsky, Dan *(Dance Arranger)* 2784
Palkowsky, Dan *(Vocal Arranger)* 2784
Pallavicini, V. *(Composer)* 4193
Pallavicini, V. *(Lyricist)* 4193
Palling, L. *(Composer)* 4193
Palling, L. *(Lyricist)* 4193
Palma, Frank *(Musical Director)* 1351, 1417, 2101, 4115, 4724
Palmer, A.M. *(Producer)* 4125
Palmer, Adele *(Costumes)* 1681
Palmer, Audrey *(Cast)* 1109
Palmer, Bee *(Cast)* 4838, 4849, 4851
Palmer, Byron *(Cast)* 4652
Palmer, Cathryn Rowe *(Cast)* 1524
Palmer, Clara *(Cast)* 470, 511, 1003, 1213, 1360, 1783, 2317, 2936, 2951, 3237, 3865, 4353, 4624
Palmer, Elizabeth *(Costumes)* 3631
Palmer, Elizabeth P. *(Costumes)* 1897
Palmer, Hattie *(Cast)* 2868
Palmer, Inda *(Cast)* 1520
Palmer, Jack *(Composer)* 393, 432, 1813, 1953, 3297
Palmer, Jack *(Lyricist)* 393, 432, 1813, 1953, 3297
Palmer, Jeree *(Cast)* 3905
Palmer, Jeree *(Composer)* 3905
Palmer, Jeree *(Lyricist)* 3905
Palmer, Leland *(Cast)* 2248, 3506, 3526, 4789
Palmer, Mary *(Cast)* 4724
Palmer, Minnie *(Cast)* 3028, 3856
Palmer, Peter *(Cast)* 2484, 2590, 4408
Palmer, Toni *(Cast)* 1277

Palmer, Winthrop *(Author)* 2887
Palmer, Winthrop *(Producer)* 2887
Palsson's Supper Club *(Producer)* 430
Paltrow, Bruce W. *(Producer)* 4659
Palumbo, Gene *(Composer)* 1638
Palumbo, Gene *(Musical Director)* 1638
Palumbo, Gene *(Vocal Arranger)* 1638
Pan, Hermes *(Cast)* 1747, 4426
Pan, Hermes *(Choreographer)* 206
Panama, Norman *(Librettist)* 2301, 2484
Panama, Norman *(Producer)* 2484
Panaro, Hugh *(Cast)* 3682
Panetta, George *(Author)* 2322
Panetta, George *(Librettist)* 2322
Pangborn, Franklin *(Cast)* 4230
Panich, David *(Librettist)* 1233, 2288, 4627
Panis, Reuben *(Costumes)* 2294
Pankey, Anna Cook *(Cast)* 3797
Pankin, Stuart *(Cast)* 4707
Panko, Tom *(Choreographer)* 1611, 3204
Panko, Tom *(Director)* 1002
Pankow, John *(Cast)* 3884
Pantages, Rodney *(Producer)* 2640
Paoletti, John *(Costumes)* 4690
Pape, Joan *(Cast)* 1914
Paper Mill Playhouse *(Producer)* 3851
Papez & Zwack *(Cast)* 2086
Papp, Joseph *(Director)* 54, 169, 2918
Papp, Joseph *(Producer)* 54, 282, 459, 746, 1015, 1053, 1344, 1575, 1715, 2033, 2074, 2239, 2359, 2429, 2648, 2877, 2918, 2953, 3000, 3070, 3198, 3276, 3806, 3825, 3830, 3884, 4151, 4370, 4485, 4505, 4615, 4736
Papp Yiddish Theater, Joseph *(Producer)* 4082
Pappas, Evan *(Cast)* 1120, 3039
Pappas, Theodore *(Choreographer)* 829, 1038, 1872, 3368
Pappas, Theodore *(Director)* 3368
Pappen, Delmar *(Cast)* 2396
Paragon Park Prods. *(Producer)* 573
Parallel Productions *(Producer)* 1216
Paramount Pictures *(Producer)* 1649
Paramount Theatre Prods. *(Producer)* 3060
Pardo, Eddie *(Cast)* 2490
Parell, Nancy *(Cast)* 3479
Parent, Gail *(Composer)* 3112
Parent, Gail *(Librettist)* 2590, 3111, 3112
Parent, Gail *(Lyricist)* 3112
Parent, Nicole *(Cast)* 2364
Parenteau, Zoel *(Composer)* 102, 1335, 2309
Parenteau, Zoel J. *(Composer)* 1901
Paret, Frank *(Musical Director)* 1626
Parichy, Dennis *(Lighting Designer)* 374, 942, 1669, 2152, 2440
Paris, Judith *(Choreographer)* 874
Paris, Norman *(Musical Director)* 2988
Paris, Norman *(Orchestrations)* 1045, 4191
Parise, Tony *(Choreographer)* 275, 3346
Parise, Tony *(Director)* 275
Parisette, Mildred *(Cast)* 2813
Parish, Mitchell *(Lyricist)* 445, 447, 710, 839, 881, 1138, 1813, 1939, 2077, 2161, 2178, 3020, 3354, 3950, 4091, 4137, 4264, 4799
Park, John *(Cast)* 118, 830, 1469, 1962, 2335, 2770, 2844, 3437, 3786, 4285
Park, John B. *(Cast)* 132
Park, Michael *(Cast)* 1822, 4031
Park, Phil *(Lyricist)* 4027
Park, R. Vincent *(Librettist)* 3136
Park, R. Vincent *(Producer)* 3136
Park Avenue Synogogue *(Producer)* 4304
Parker, Barnett *(Cast)* 910, 4374
Parker, Dell *(Cast)* 512
Parker, Dorothy *(Author)* 1861
Parker, Dorothy *(Cast)* 1218
Parker, Dorothy *(Librettist)* 1357, 3946
Parker, Dorothy *(Lyricist)* 630, 2633, 3783
Parker, E. Huntington *(Costumes)* 4332
Parker, Flora *(Cast)* 60, 1212, 1523, 1911, 2974, 3626
Parker, Florence *(Cast)* 4668
Parker, Frank *(Cast)* 197, 1336
Parker, George D. *(Author)* 2613
Parker, George D. *(Director)* 2976
Parker, Harry Doel *(Librettist)* 4223
Parker, Howard *(Choreographer)* 2737, 3126
Parker, Jimmie *(Cast)* 553
Parker, Lem B. *(Librettist)* 631, 917
Parker, Lem B. *(Lyricist)* 917
Parker, Lew *(Cast)* 127, 145, 180, 1397, 1528, 3823, 4299
Parker, Loria *(Cast)* 139
Parker, Lotta *(Cast)* 2524
Parker, Lou *(Cast)* 2709
Parker, Louis N. *(Author)* 2756
Parker, Rena *(Cast)* 4794
Parker, Robert *(Cast)* 2937
Parker, Ross *(Cast)* 2364
Parker, Ross *(Composer)* 4027
Parker, Ross *(English Lyrics)* 2364
Parker, Ross *(Lyricist)* 4027
Parker, Roxann *(Cast)* 1262, 3318
Parker, Stewart *(Author)* 4109
Parker, Stewart *(Lyricist)* 4109
Parker, Walter Coleman *(Librettist)* 2631
Parker Jr., R. *(Composer)* 1298
Parker Jr., R. *(Lyricist)* 1298
Parks, Bernice *(Cast)* 341, 3947, 4117
Parks, Beverly *(Costumes)* 2692
Parks, Don *(Cast)* 4494
Parks, Don *(Librettist)* 2219, 2288
Parks, Don *(Lyricist)* 272, 1408, 2219
Parks, Hildy *(Producer)* 1000, 2064
Parks, John *(Choreographer)* 2513
Parks, Larry *(Cast)* 339
Parks, Melvin *(Cast)* 3103, 3104
Parks, Michael *(Cast)* 1709
Parks, Robert *(Cast)* 2483
Parks, Trina *(Cast)* 692
Parlato, Dennis *(Cast)* 1785, 1822
Parnell, Jack *(Conductor)* 3454
Parnis, Molly *(Composer)* 72

Parr, Albert *(Cast)* 2697, 3073, 3883
Parr-Davies, Harry *(Composer)* 4027
Parrinello, Richard *(Musical Director)* 3888, 4029
Parrish, Elizabeth *(Cast)* 2360, 2522, 3195, 3725
Parrish, Robert *(Cast)* 1987
Parry, Chris *(Lighting Designer)* 4676
Parry, Frederick *(Director)* 2951
Parry, Sally E. *(Producer)* 3697
Parry, William *(Cast)* 212, 1053, 1510, 1630, 2142, 2346, 3411, 3903, 4736
Parry, William *(Director)* 2374
Parson, William *(Musical Director)* 1987, 4018, 4058
Parson, William *(Vocal Arranger)* 4058
Parsons, Chauncey *(Cast)* 202
Parsons, Donovan *(Lyricist)* 700, 702, 792, 2004, 2789, 2843, 4581
Parsons, Estelle *(Cast)* 237, 339, 1171, 1760, 3484, 4682
Parsons, Geoffrey *(Composer)* 4264
Parsons, Geoffrey *(Lyricist)* 4264
Parsons, George *(Cast)* 1271, 2525
Parsons, Jennifer *(Cast)* 3631
Parsons, Joseph *(Cast)* 1631
Partington, Jeanne *(Costumes)* 3940
Parva, Cynthia *(Cast)* 3548
Pascal, Fran *(Librettist)* 1478
Pascal, John *(Librettist)* 1478
Pascal, Milton *(Composer)* 1397
Pascal, Milton *(Lyricist)* 95, 204, 673, 1207, 1336, 1397, 1892, 2105, 2246, 2396
Pascaud, Mme. *(Costumes)* 208
Pascoe, Richard W. *(Lyricist)* 4576
Pasekoff, Marilyn *(Cast)* 518, 1349, 3600
Paskman, Dailey *(Composer)* 710
Paskman, Dailey *(Lyricist)* 710, 2121, 4486, 4817
Pasquinelli, Joanne *(Author)* 4494
Passman, Ray *(Composer)* 2580
Passman, Ray *(Lyricist)* 2580
Patch, William *(Cast)* 382
Patch, William Moore *(Producer)* 1882, 2174, 4248
Patek, Patrick J. *(Producer)* 131
Paterson, Vincent *(Choreographer)* 2333
Patinkin, Mandy *(Cast)* 1211, 2346, 2429, 3862, 4210
Paton, Alan *(Author)* 2591
Patrelle, Francis *(Choreographer)* 3565
Patrick, Dennis *(Cast)* 1837
Patrick, Fred *(Lyricist)* 4827
Patrick, John *(Author)* 347, 2626
Patrick, John *(Librettist)* 2626
Patrick, Lee *(Cast)* 423, 2265
Patrick, Nigel *(Cast)* 1205
Patrick, Robert *(Author)* 3034
Patrick, Robert *(Lyricist)* 3034
Patricola, Tom *(Cast)* 1486, 1487, 1488, 1489, 1490, 1932, 2460, 4465
Patricola Jr., Tom *(Cast)* 3264
Patron, Elias *(Cast)* 1269
Patston, Doris *(Cast)* 324, 1384, 2293, 2628, 4025
Patten, Caymichael *(Director)* 3661
Patterson, Chuck *(Cast)* 2692
Patterson, Dianthia *(Cast)* 2059
Patterson, Dick *(Cast)* 410, 1227, 4020, 4566
Patterson, Elizabeth *(Cast)* 1850
Patterson, Helen *(Cast)* 2271
Patterson, James *(Composer)* 1964
Patterson, Lorna *(Cast)* 140
Patterson, Neva *(Cast)* 3841, 3894
Patterson, Raymond *(Cast)* 2992, 3169, 3739
Patterson, Robert *(Set Design)* 1604, 4303
Patterson, Russell *(Costumes)* 289, 1342, 1440, 1932, 4824
Patterson, Russell *(Musical Director)* 643
Patterson, Russell *(Producer)* 289, 3810
Patterson, Russell *(Set Design)* 289, 1342, 1493, 1932
Patterson, Ruth Cleary *(Composer)* 3810
Patterson, Ruth Cleary *(Musical Director)* 3810
Patterson, Stark *(Cast)* 711
Patterson, Vaughn *(Set Design)* 2197
Patton, Lucille *(Cast)* 169, 2368, 4768
Patton, Mal *(Cast)* 4184
Patton, Will *(Cast)* 2468
Paul, Agnes *(Cast)* 1220, 1720
Paul, Alan *(Cast)* 1664
Paul, Betty *(Cast)* 2680
Paul, Bobby *(Composer)* 3722
Paul, Cedar *(Librettist)* 2202
Paul, Eden *(Librettist)* 2202
Paul, Gene *(Lyricist)* 702
Paul, Tina *(Cast)* 975
Paul, Tina *(Choreographer)* 975, 1739, 3142, 4264
Paul, Walter *(Orchestrations)* 180, 1336, 2103, 4123, 4362
Paulee, Mona *(Cast)* 2664, 2961
Paulette, Larry *(Cast)* 2451
Pauley, Pat *(Cast)* 2097
Pauling, Lowman *(Composer)* 4264
Pauling, Lowman *(Lyricist)* 4264
Paull, Harry *(Cast)* 904
Paull, Morgan *(Cast)* 3111
Paulsen, David *(Lyricist)* 4396
Paulson, Kay *(Cast)* 512
Paulton, Edward *(Author)* 1193, 2336
Paulton, Edward *(Director)* 1078
Paulton, Edward *(Librettist)* 20, 517, 955, 1078, 1193, 1301, 1875, 2495, 2867, 3071, 3627, 4200, 4492, 4758
Paulton, Edward *(Lyricist)* 20, 465, 517, 1193, 1301, 1308, 1875, 1882, 2174, 2495, 2587, 2867, 3627, 4200, 4492, 4758
Paulton, Edward A. *(Author)* 4322
Paulton, Edward A. *(Composer)* 2495
Paulton, Edward A. *(Librettist)* 233, 717, 1565, 2387, 2665, 2854, 3051, 3052, 3581, 4489
Paulton, Edward A. *(Lyricist)* 233, 717, 1041, 1565, 2495, 2665, 2854, 3051, 3581, 3855, 4489
Paulton, Harry *(Cast)* 1080
Paulton, Harry *(Director)* 1193
Paulton, Harry *(Librettist)* 1078, 1301
Paulton, Harry *(Lyricist)* 1301, 4713
Paulton, Jack *(Cast)* 1626
Pavell, Barbara *(Cast)* 3920

Pavlosky, David *(Cast)* 4389
Pavlowa, Anna *(Cast)* 396
Pawk, Michele *(Cast)* 1822
Pawle, Lennox *(Cast)* 1538, 2756, 2937, 3980
Pawley, Edward *(Cast)* 2476
Paxton, George *(Director)* 4705
Paxton, George *(Producer)* 4704
Paxton, Glenn *(Composer)* 1290
Paxton, John *(Librettist)* 1674
Payan, Genaro *(Cast)* 3714
Payn, Graham *(Cast)* 3339, 4519
Payne, Barbara *(Producer)* 4362
Payne, Benny *(Composer)* 887
Payne, Benny *(Lyricist)* 887
Payne, Edmund *(Cast)* 3098
Payne, Eric A. *(Cast)* 2239
Payne, Freda *(Cast)* 952
Payne, Jim *(Director)* 2968, 3202
Payne, Jim *(Producer)* 2285, 3202
Payne, Jimmy *(Choreographer)* 3528
Payne, John Howard *(Composer)* 1897
Payne, John Howard *(Lyricist)* 1425, 1897
Payne, Leon *(Composer)* 655
Payne, Leon *(Lyricist)* 655
Payne, Virginia *(Cast)* 1227
Paynter, Lynn *(Cast)* 3181
Payton, Dave *(Composer)* 3904, 4183
Payton, Dave *(Director)* 4183
Payton, Dave *(Lyricist)* 3904
Payton, Lew *(Cast)* 740
Payton, Lew *(Librettist)* 740
Payton-Wright, Pamela *(Cast)* 35, 2218
Peabody, Christopher *(Lighting Designer)* 3697
Peabody, Ray *(Composer)* 1556
Peachena *(Cast)* 2451
Peacock, Ada *(Costumes)* 1965, 4581
Peacock, Ada *(Set Design)* 4581
Peacock, Bertram *(Cast)* 463, 2005
Peacock, Michon *(Cast)* 4533
Pearce, Alice *(Cast)* 868, 1475, 2227, 2582, 3105, 3278, 3815, 4018, 4156
Pearce, Alice *(Producer)* 2811
Pearce, Marion *(Cast)* 3104
Pearce, Nayan *(Cast)* 202, 2300, 3735
Pearce, Philip *(Librettist)* 255
Pearce, Vera *(Cast)* 203
Pearl, Irwin *(Cast)* 2874
Pearl, Jack *(Cast)* 202, 969, 1899, 1923, 2140, 3148, 3153, 3379, 3523, 4427, 4621, 4823
Pearl, Larry *(Director)* 214
Pearl, Larry *(Librettist)* 214
Pearle, Gary *(Director)* 4390, 4412
Pearlman, Nan *(Producer)* 1082
Pearlman, Stephen *(Cast)* 171, 2368
Pearlmutter, Ben *(Orchestrations)* 2928
Pearsall, Harold *(Cast)* 214
Pearson, Arthur *(Director)* 4858
Pearson, Arthur *(Producer)* 4296, 4858
Pearson, David P. *(Costumes)* 2372
Pearson, Dunn *(Orchestrations)* 105
Pearson, Molly *(Cast)* 2396
Pearson, Pauletta *(Cast)* 1402, 1816, 3909
Pearson, Sybille *(Librettist)* 253
Pearson Brothers, The *(Cast)* 2366
Pearsons, Lyle *(Cast)* 2332
Pease, Harry *(Lyricist)* 1626, 4815
Peaslee, Richard *(Composer)* 482, 3445
Peaslee, Richard *(Orchestrations)* 482
Peaslee, Richard *(Vocal Arranger)* 482
Peck, Elcie *(Cast)* 2371
Peck, Gregory *(Cast)* 4695
Peck, Jon *(Cast)* 4743
Peck, Raymond W. *(Librettist)* 132, 670, 1292, 3367, 3712, 3771, 4411
Peck, Raymond W. *(Lyricist)* 132, 670, 2025, 3367, 3712, 3771, 4411, 4544, 4805
Peck Jr., Charles *(Librettist)* 2368
Peck Jr., Charles *(Producer)* 2368
Peck Jr., Charles K. *(Librettist)* 520, 751
Pedi, Tom *(Cast)* 1706, 2322
Peerce, Jan *(Cast)* 2422, 3153, 3639
Pegram, Nigel *(Cast)* 4579
Peipers, David H. *(Producer)* 2735, 3181
Peiro Brothers, The *(Cast)* 2850
Pekin Stock Company *(Producer)* 646, 2721, 3979
Peldon, Courtney *(Cast)* 2805
Peled, JoAnna *(Cast)* 3162, 4736
Pelish, Thelma *(Cast)* 2864, 3351
Pelissier, Antony *(Cast)* 3885
Pell, Arthur *(Musical Director)* 4185
Pell, Peter *(Producer)* 722
Pell, Stephen *(Cast)* 2037
Pellaton, Albert *(Cast)* 2701, 4509
Pelletier, Gilles *(Cast)* 3338
Pelletti, John *(Cast)* 4486
Peltz & Carson *(Set Design)* 3256
Peluso, Tom *(Composer)* 439
Pelzig, Daniel *(Choreographer)* 198, 3598, 4136
Pember, Clifford *(Librettist)* 648
Pember, Clifford *(Set Design)* 468, 953, 1144, 1502, 1527, 2328, 3245, 3921, 4422, 4510
Pember, Clifford F. *(Set Design)* 4085
Pemberton, Max *(Librettist)* 822
Pen, Polly *(Cast)* 4537
Pen, Polly *(Composer)* 1589
Pen, Polly *(Lyricist)* 1589
Pence, Ann-Carol *(Musical Director)* 1804
Pendarvis, Leon *(Orchestrations)* 3428
Pendleton, Austin *(Cast)* 945, 1265, 2418, 4523
Pendleton, Austin *(Director)* 171, 3927
Pendleton, Austin *(Librettist)* 171, 496, 4405
Pendleton, E.H. *(Composer)* 1535
Pendleton, E.H. *(Lyricist)* 1535
Pendleton, Nat *(Cast)* 3079
Pene du Bois, Henri *(Costumes)* 1448
Pene du Bois, Raoul *(Costumes)* 59, 173, 180, 363, 397, 417, 420, 619, 653, 662, 808, 974, 989, 1063, 1109, 1284, 1709, 1811, 1841, 1931, 1973, 2258, 2413, 2432, 2439, 2460, 2475, 2680, 2705, 2994, 3016, 3100, 3166, 3292, 3338, 3359, 3509, 3690, 3763, 3788, 3975, 4086, 4186,

4197, 4374, 4420, 4465, 4479, 4483, 4542, 4734, 4824, 4827, 4828, 4829
Pene du Bois, Raoul *(Lighting Designer)* 2439
Pene du Bois, Raoul *(Set Design)* 59, 363, 619, 974, 1063, 1109, 1811, 1841, 1931, 2227, 2439, 2460, 2680, 2705, 2994, 3100, 3107, 3166, 3292, 3338, 3359, 3509, 3763, 3788, 3975, 4086, 4186, 4197, 4483, 4542, 4734, 4827, 4828, 4829
Peneman, Richard *(Composer)* 3739
Peneman, Richard *(Lyricist)* 3739
Penfield, Roderic C. *(Librettist)* 2399, 4666
Penman, Lea *(Cast)* 153
Penn *(Composer)* 3566
Penn *(Lyricist)* 3566
Penn, Arthur *(Composer)* 2493
Penn, Arthur *(Director)* 1601, 2313
Penn, Arthur *(Lyricist)* 2493
Penn, Arthur A. *(Composer)* 3673
Penn, Arthur A. *(Lyricist)* 165, 3673
Penn, Bill *(Director)* 600, 1081, 2804, 3124, 3615, 3988
Penn, Ed *(Cast)* 1837, 3067
Penn, Edward *(Cast)* 4102
Penn, Jacqueline *(Vocal Arranger)* 4089
Penn, Les *(Cast)* 3224
Penn, Nina *(Cast)* 2020
Penn, Robert *(Cast)* 759, 2464, 3347
Penn, William *(Composer)* 3817
Penn, William H. *(Composer)* 2906, 2964, 3820
Penn, William H. *(Lyricist)* 2906, 2959, 2964
Penna, Philip Della *(Musical Director)* 3273
Pennec, Henri *(Cast)* 2364
Penner, Joe *(Cast)* 1145, 4545
Penniman, Richard *(Composer)* 4534
Penniman, Richard *(Lyricist)* 4534
Pennington, Ann *(Cast)* 662, 1207, 1482, 1483, 1484, 1489, 1490, 2180, 2900, 3131, 3529, 4807, 4808, 4809, 4810, 4812, 4818, 4836
Pennyfeather, James *(Lighting Designer)* 45
Pentecost, George *(Cast)* 4167
Penzer, William *(Composer)* 302
Penzer, William *(Librettist)* 302
Penzer, William *(Lyricist)* 302
Penzner, Seymour *(Cast)* 2784
Peoples Performing Company *(Producer)* 1282, 4168
Peple, Edward *(Author)* 3622
Peple, Edward *(Librettist)* 697
Peple, Edward *(Lyricist)* 697
Peppard, George *(Cast)* 1571
Pepper, Buddy *(Composer)* 2294, 4415
Pepper, Buddy *(Lyricist)* 2294, 4415
Pepper, Harry *(Author)* 1384
Peppiatt, Charles *(Librettist)* 1120
Peppiatt, Frank *(Librettist)* 1120
Peppiatt, Frank *(Lyricist)* 1120
PepsiCo Summerfare *(Producer)* 496
PepsiCo Summerfare '83 *(Producer)* 2992, 3908
Peralta, Craig *(Cast)* 3888
Percassi, Don *(Cast)* 746
Percival, Norman *(Composer)* 4329
Percival, Norman *(Lyricist)* 4329
Percival, Walter *(Cast)* 824, 1199, 1417, 1458, 1602, 2383, 2723, 2915, 3882
Percy, W.S. *(Cast)* 2701
Perea, Carol *(Cast)* 3264
Perella, Harry *(Composer)* 4352
Perelman, S.J. *(Librettist)* 44, 2653, 3301, 4237, 4335, 4583
Perenchio, Jerrold *(Producer)* 2142
Peress, Maurice *(Dance Arranger)* 3628
Peress, Maurice *(Musical Director)* 2775, 3628
Peress, Maurice *(Orchestrations)* 3628
Peress, Maurice *(Vocal Arranger)* 3628
Peretti, Hugo *(Composer)* 825, 2230, 2681, 4022
Peretti, Hugo *(Librettist)* 825, 2230, 2681
Peretti, Hugo *(Lyricist)* 2230, 2681, 4022
Perez, Luis *(Cast)* 36, 756, 975, 2205
Perez, Ray *(Choreographer)* 2005, 3655, 4668
Perez, Raymond B. *(Choreographer)* 2490
Perez-Carrion, Edwin *(Set Design)* 4309
Performing Arts Rep. Th. *(Producer)* 4444
Performing Arts Repertory T *(Producer)* 3802
Pergament, Lola *(Librettist)* 3215
Pergament, Lola *(Lyricist)* 3215
Perkins, Alberta *(Cast)* 691
Perkins, Anthony *(Cast)* 1200, 1698
Perkins, Bobbie *(Cast)* 376, 1916
Perkins, Carrie *(Cast)* 1661
Perkins, Edward P. *(Director)* 1726
Perkins, Edward P. *(Lyricist)* 1726
Perkins, Edward P. *(Producer)* 1726
Perkins, Frank *(Composer)* 1813, 3950, 4137
Perkins, Frank *(Orchestrations)* 3683
Perkins, Frank *(Vocal Arranger)* 3683
Perkins, Fred *(Musical Director)* 1295
Perkins, John *(Cast)* 4718
Perkins, Kenneth *(Author)* 2595
Perkins, Ollie *(Cast)* 3807
Perkins, Patti *(Cast)* 840, 1739, 2787, 3909, 4468, 4523
Perkins, Ray *(Composer)* 560, 568, 1693, 2174, 2857, 3144, 3401, 3402, 3419, 3538, 3849, 4105
Perkins, Ray *(Lyricist)* 560, 2174, 3144, 4105
Perkins, Rita *(Cast)* 2826
Perkins, W. *(Set Design)* 3625
Perkinson, Coleridge-Taylor *(Composer)* 1592, 1671, 2719
Perkinson, Coleridge-Taylor *(Dance Arranger)* 406
Perkinson, Coleridge-Taylor *(Musical Director)* 2173
Perkinson, Coleridge-Taylor *(Orchestrations)* 534
Perkis, Susan *(Librettist)* 2043
Perl, Lothar *(Arrangements)* 2841
Perl, Lothar *(Composer)* 4482
Perleno, Hilda *(Cast)* 488
Perlet, Herman *(Composer)* 1392, 1925, 2157, 2506, 2714, 2895, 2938, 3348, 4125, 4130
Perlet, Herman *(Lyricist)* 3348
Perlet, Herman *(Musical Director)* 355, 737, 1355, 1473, 1518, 1768, 2179, 2506, 2715, 2848, 2938, 4404
Perley, Frank L. *(Producer)* 694
Perley, William *(Cast)* 2007
Perley Opera Company *(Producer)* 1518

Perley Opera Company, Frank *(Producer)* 4549
Perlino, Hilda *(Cast)* 1989
Perlman, Arthur *(Librettist)* 158, 4708
Perlman, Arthur *(Lyricist)* 158, 4708
Perlman, Max *(Composer)* 2356
Perlman, Max *(Lyricist)* 2356
Perlmutter *(Composer)* 907
Perlmutter, Arnold *(Composer)* 1609
Perlmutter, Arnold *(Lyricist)* 1609
Perr, Harvey *(Librettist)* 3902
Perrault, Charles *(Author)* 759
Perren, Frederick J. *(Composer)* 3739
Perren, Frederick J. *(Lyricist)* 3739
Perri, Valerie *(Cast)* 3277
Perrin *(Composer)* 1627
Perrin *(Lyricist)* 1627
Perrin, Adrian S. *(Choreographer)* 584, 3192
Perrin, Adrian S. *(Director)* 3192
Perrin, Margaret *(Composer)* 272
Perrin, Nat *(Librettist)* 2640
Perrin, Sam *(Librettist)* 180
Perrin, Sidney *(Composer)* 813
Perrin, Sidney L. *(Composer)* 719
Perrin, Sidney L. *(Lyricist)* 719
Perrin, Sydney L. *(Composer)* 719
Perrin, Sydney L. *(Lyricist)* 719
Perrineau, Harold *(Cast)* 240
Perrineau Jr., Harold *(Cast)* 1236
Perry, Alan D. *(Producer)* 261
Perry, Barbara *(Cast)* 1748, 2103
Perry, E. Martin *(Musical Director)* 2764
Perry, Elaine *(Cast)* 3180
Perry, Irene *(Cast)* 618
Perry, Jaime *(Cast)* 2239
Perry, John Bennett *(Cast)* 280, 2941, 2962
Perry, Karen *(Costumes)* 2239
Perry, Katheryn *(Cast)* 444, 888
Perry, Keith *(Cast)* 3364
Perry, Lynnette *(Cast)* 747, 1649, 3125
Perry, Marsha *(Cast)* 166
Perry, Robert E. *(Director)* 1930
Perry, Robert E. *(Producer)* 1892
Perry, Rod *(Cast)* 952, 3111, 3112, 4395
Perry, Sara *(Cast)* 1806
Perry, Shauneille *(Director)* 3599, 4697
Perry, Shauneille *(Librettist)* 952
Perry, Steve *(Cast)* 2278
Perry, Steven *(Set Design)* 4082
Perry, William *(Cast)* 843
Perry, William *(Composer)* 4701
Perry, William *(Lyricist)* 4701
Perry/Wood Company *(Producer)* 27
Perryman, Al *(Choreographer)* 105
Perschk, Max *(Composer)* 4228
Pershing, D'Vaughn *(Musical Director)* 3742
Persoff, Nehemiah *(Cast)* 3452
Personette, Joan *(Costumes)* 1840, 4006, 4496
Persson, Gene *(Director)* 3653
Persson, Gene *(Producer)* 4034, 4783
Persson, Ruby *(Cast)* 3653
Pertwee, Jon *(Cast)* 4329
Pertwee, Michael *(Librettist)* 814
Perugini, Sidmund *(Cast)* 2179
Peskanov, Alexander *(Composer)* 456
Peter, Fred *(Pianist)* 214
Peter, Rene *(Author)* 511, 3079
Peters, Bernadette *(Cast)* 941, 956, 1478, 1633, 2143, 2368, 2660, 3439, 4068, 4210, 4577
Peters, Beth *(Cast)* 2650
Peters, Brandon *(Cast)* 1283
Peters, Brock *(Cast)* 483, 2355
Peters, Burt *(Composer)* 2232
Peters, Clarke *(Librettist)* 1296
Peters, Elsie *(Composer)* 4394
Peters, Joan *(Costumes)* 2970
Peters, Lauri *(Cast)* 1290, 4095
Peters, Leonard *(Director)* 1418, 4684
Peters, Mason *(Producer)* 1515
Peters, Michael *(Cast)* 406, 3610, 4003
Peters, Michael *(Choreographer)* 828, 1103, 2427
Peters, Michael *(Director)* 2427
Peters, N. *(Cast)* 1604
Peters, Paul *(Librettist)* 3365
Peters, Paul *(Lyricist)* 3365
Peters, Roger *(Producer)* 1787
Peters, Shannon Reyshard *(Cast)* 535
Peters, Stephanie *(Composer)* 3688
Peters, Stephanie *(Lyricist)* 3688
Peters, W.H. *(Composer)* 3399
Peters, William F. *(Composer)* 934, 1767, 2145, 2893, 3399, 3820, 3866, 4711
Peters, William Frederick *(Composer)* 2793, 3033, 3613
Petersburski, J. *(Composer)* 4730
Peterson, Aleigh *(Choreographer)* 3966
Peterson, Don *(Composer)* 2288
Peterson, Eric *(Cast)* 414
Peterson, Eric *(Composer)* 414
Peterson, Eric *(Lyricist)* 414
Peterson, Erika *(Cast)* 1222
Peterson, Kurt *(Cast)* 273, 599, 1012, 1329
Peterson, Lenka *(Cast)* 3631
Peterson, Margorie *(Cast)* 1131
Peterson, Mary *(Costumes)* 275
Peterson, Nora *(Choreographer)* 3476, 3817
Peterson, Patricia Ben *(Cast)* 4769
Pether, Henry E. *(Composer)* 675, 1544, 3268
Petherbridge, Edward *(Cast)* 2474
Petina, Irra *(Cast)* 161, 630, 1918, 2679, 4075
Petit, Charles *(Author)* 711
Petrayer, Sophia *(Cast)* 1531
Petricoff, Elaine *(Cast)* 1770, 3711
Petrides, Avra *(Lyricist)* 459
Petrie, Dan *(Director)* 4155
Petrie, Daniel *(Director)* 2958
Petrie, George *(Cast)* 1546
Petrie, H.W. *(Composer)* 1301
Petrillo, Stephen *(Lighting Designer)* 760
Petro, Michael *(Cast)* 2243
Petroff, Boris *(Director)* 831
Petroff, Boris *(Producer)* 831

Petrova, Olga *(Cast)* 3618
Petrow, Mischa *(Set Design)* 1166
Petsche, Bruce *(Composer)* 1108
Pettengill, George B. *(Cast)* 1866
Petti, Emile *(Musical Director)* 63
Pettiford, Valerie *(Cast)* 393, 1699
Pettiford, Valerie *(Choreographer)* 2372
Pettit, James J. *(Cast)* 1868
Pettit, Gemmel and Tocher, Guyvers, Potterton, *(Costumes)* 1610
Petite Adelaide
See La Petite Adelaide.
Petite Marguerite
See La Petite Marguerite.
Petty, Ross *(Cast)* 2177
Pevney, Joseph *(Cast)* 2228
Pevney, Joseph C. *(Director)* 2447
Peyer, Miriam *(Cast)* 524
Peyton, Bruce *(Librettist)* 1258
Peyton, Caroline *(Cast)* 2033, 2359
Pezza, Francis *(Set Design)* 3654
Pezza, Mariner James *(Producer)* 4106
Pezza, Mariner James *(Set Design)* 4106
Pfeiffer, Jack *(Musical Director)* 1423, 2161, 2162
Pfleuger, Carl *(Composer)* 4531
Phace, Hapi *(Cast)* 2037
Phalen, Robert *(Cast)* 3309
Phase Three Productions *(Producer)* 944
Phelps, Eleanor *(Cast)* 3082
Phelps, Elspeth *(Costumes)* 2900, 4327
Phelps, Jack *(Composer)* 1957
Phelps, Lyon *(Lyricist)* 1062
Phelps, Maud *(Cast)* 2771
Phelps, William *(Cast)* 1871
Phelps Twins *(Cast)* 1126
Phi Opera Company *(Producer)* 870
Philbin, Jack *(Producer)* 3287
Philbrick, Will *(Cast)* 60, 3219, 3357, 3400, 4064
Philbrick, Will *(Director)* 331
Philip, John Van Ness *(Producer)* 4279
Philip, William *(Cast)* 1905
Philip R Productions *(Producer)* 3619
Philipi, Michael *(Set Design)* 494
Philipp, Adolf *(Author)* 88, 1409, 1565, 2336, 2854
Philipp, Adolf *(Cast)* 233, 1409, 4492
Philipp, Adolf *(Composer)* 20, 88, 233, 1409, 2854, 2867, 4489, 4492
Philipp, Adolf *(Director)* 4489
Philipp, Adolf *(Librettist)* 20, 233, 1409, 1565, 2854, 2867, 4489, 4492
Philipp, Adolf *(Lyricist)* 1409, 1565, 2854, 4489, 4492
Philipp, Karen *(Cast)* 729
Philippe-Gerard *(Composer)* 1865
Philips, Mardi *(Costumes)* 1970, 2289, 4137
Philips, Nancie *(Cast)* 3111
Philips, Tim *(Lighting Designer)* 2133
Phillips, Andy *(Lighting Designer)* 3299, 4371
Phillips, Arlene *(Choreographer)* 4138
Phillips, Arte *(Cast)* 3637
Phillips, Bob *(Set Design)* 3249, 3601
Phillips, Dorothy *(Costumes)* 1887
Phillips, Eddie *(Cast)* 658, 957, 1706, 2940, 3113, 4312
Phillips, Edna *(Cast)* 1157
Phillips, Ethan *(Cast)* 3039
Phillips, Fred *(Lyricist)* 1131
Phillips, H.I. *(Librettist)* 1513, 2475, 2850, 3946, 4374, 4824
Phillips, H.I. *(Lyricist)* 1513
Phillips, Irving *(Librettist)* 2042, 3801
Phillips, John *(Composer)* 2728
Phillips, John *(Librettist)* 2728
Phillips, John *(Lyricist)* 2728
Phillips, Joseph A. *(Cast)* 1351
Phillips, Mary Bracken *(Cast)* 1045, 1169, 1985, 2043, 2289, 2584, 2775
Phillips, Mary Bracken *(Composer)* 2289
Phillips, Mary Bracken *(Librettist)* 533, 2289, 2846
Phillips, Mary Bracken *(Lyricist)* 533, 2289, 2846
Phillips, Murray *(Producer)* 1747
Phillips, Peter *(Musical Director)* 3000
Phillips, Phil *(Librettist)* 4689
Phillips, Sian *(Cast)* 3429
Phillips, Stanley *(Director)* 991
Phillips, Steve *(Producer)* 373
Phillips, Will *(Cast)* 2385
Phillpotts, Eden *(Author)* 911
Philp, James *(Composer)* 1470
Philp, William E. *(Cast)* 4353
Phipps, Brian *(Cast)* 3544
Phoenix Theatre *(Producer)* 1600, 1985, 2554, 2556, 2607, 3473, 3565, 3831
Physioc, Joseph *(Set Design)* 191, 350, 1065, 1154, 1355, 1627, 2216, 2780, 3176, 3434, 3732, 3740, 3994, 4130, 4378, 4781
Piaf, Edith *(Composer)* 166, 2558
Piaf, Edith *(Lyricist)* 2356
Piani, Harry M. *(Composer)* 3395
Piani, Henry *(Composer)* 4842
Piantadosi, Al *(Composer)* 501, 1065, 2587, 3018, 3020, 3977, 4589, 4812
Piantadosi, Al *(Lyricist)* 2587, 4812
Piantadosi, Lou *(Composer)* 1501
Piazza, Marguerite *(Cast)* 1748
Picard, Andre *(Author)* 2309
Pichler, Maria *(Cast)* 1413
Pickard, Alma *(Cast)* 1911
Pickens, Jane *(Cast)* 3691, 4825
Pickens Sisters, The *(Cast)* 4374
Pickert, Willis *(Cast)* 571
Pickett, Bobby *(Composer)* 3695
Pickett, Bobby *(Lyricist)* 3695
Pickford, Jack
See Ethel Smith.
Pickford, Lotte
See Lotte Smith
Pickford, Mary
See Miss Pickford and Gladys Smith.
Pickford, Miss *(Cast)* 3025
Picon, Molly *(Cast)* 423, 2016, 2352, 2864, 3153, 3336

Picon, Molly *(Composer)* 3336
Picon, Molly *(Lyricist)* 1279
Picture, Kay *(Cast)* 2300, 2432
Pidgeon, Walter *(Cast)* 3617, 4059, 4270
Piech, Jennifer *(Cast)* 2654
Pierantozzi, Victor *(Cast)* 4243
Pierce, Betty *(Cast)* 2174
Pierce, Billy *(Choreographer)* 1202, 1722, 4043
Pierce, Charlie *(Composer)* 3962
Pierce, Charlie *(Lyricist)* 3962
Pierce, Frank *(Cast)* 1224
Pierce, Jo Carol *(Librettist)* 264
Pierce, Jo Carol *(Lyricist)* 264
Pierce, John *(Choreographer)* 966, 1546, 1862, 2808, 4730
Pierce, Lewis *(Cast)* 4536
Pierce, Marion *(Cast)* 4365
Pierce, Wendell *(Cast)* 3628
Pierce, Wesley *(Cast)* 203
Pierlot, Francis *(Cast)* 294, 2344
Pierlot, Frank *(Cast)* 2771
Pierpont, J.S. *(Composer)* 3175
Pierpont, J.S. *(Lyricist)* 3175
Pierre, Christopher *(Cast)* 2908
Pierre, Jacques *(Producer)* 1177
Pierre, Mabelle *(Cast)* 1248
Pierre, Olivier *(Cast)* 1256
Pierro, Christina *(Cast)* 328
Pierson, Arthur *(Director)* 4826
Pierson, Arthur *(Librettist)* 3290, 4640
Pierson, Edward *(Cast)* 4447
Pierson, Harold *(Cast)* 4238
Pierson, Rita *(Cast)* 2025
Pierson, Thomas *(Musical Director)* 518, 946, 1116
Pierson, Thomas *(Orchestrations)* 599, 3927
Pierson, William *(Cast)* 4022
Piffi, Henry *(Librettist)* 3
Piggot, J.W. *(Librettist)* 2341
Piggot, J.W. *(Lyricist)* 2341
Pigliavento, Debra *(Choreographer)* 2737
Pigliavento, Michele *(Cast)* 2372
Pigott, Colin *(Set Design)* 2204
Pigott, J.W. *(Author)* 2341
Pike, John *(Composer)* 4729
Pike, John *(Director)* 4729
Pike, John *(Librettist)* 4729
Pike, John *(Lyricist)* 4729
Pilbrow, Richard *(Lighting Designer)* 589, 3780, 3927, 4252, 4862
Pilbrow, Richard *(Producer)* 1619
Pilcer, Harry *(Cast)* 263, 351, 1307, 1801, 1835, 1963, 2538, 3500, 4158
Pilcer, Harry *(Choreographer)* 1472
Pilcer, Harry *(Lyricist)* 2538, 4553, 4655
Pilgrim, Chris *(Composer)* 1865
Piller, Heinar *(Director)* 3066
Pils, Jacques *(Cast)* 3756
Pinaud, Lena *(Cast)* 909
Pinchot, Rosamond *(Cast)* 1196
Pincus, Henry *(Producer)* 2717
Pincus, Warren *(Cast)* 4773
Pincus, Warren *(Producer)* 2993
Pine, Lester *(Librettist)* 2246
Pinelli, Tullio *(Author)* 3171, 4238
Pinero, Arthur Wing *(Author)* 100, 2871
Pinero, Arthur Wing *(Lyricist)* 2871
Pinero, Miguel *(Author)* 4205
Pink, Wal *(Librettist)* 2571, 3500, 3663
Pink, Wal *(Lyricist)* 3663
Pinkard, Fred *(Cast)* 2075
Pinkard, Maceo *(Composer)* 489, 554, 2204, 2557, 3361, 3905, 3962, 4104
Pinkard, Maceo *(Lyricist)* 2557, 3361, 3905
Pinkard, Maceo *(Producer)* 3361
Pinkham, Richard *(Librettist)* 3916
Pinkins, Tonya *(Cast)* 2200
Pinkney, Mikell *(Director)* 2133
Pinkney, Scott *(Lighting Designer)* 2704
Pinsuti, M. *(Composer)* 4479
Pinto, Cola *(Cast)* 2114
Pinza, Ezio *(Cast)* 1242, 4096
Piontek, Michael *(Cast)* 1997
Pip *(Author)* 208
Piper, John *(Set Design)* 920
Piper Jr., Ralph *(Composer)* 2239
Piper Jr., Ralph *(Lyricist)* 2239
Pippin, Don *(Composer)* 669, 840, 2688, 2689, 3637
Pippin, Don *(Musical Director)* 1146, 3637, 3869
Pippin, Don *(Vocal Arranger)* 840, 1146, 2713, 3869, 4297
Pippin, Donald *(Arrangements)* 3682
Pippin, Donald *(Composer)* 1249, 2737
Pippin, Donald *(Dance Arranger)* 145, 1249
Pippin, Donald *(Musical Director)* 167, 367, 746, 1012, 1373, 2360, 2660, 2713, 2737, 3126, 3271, 3294, 3682, 4727
Pippin, Donald *(Orchestrations)* 1002, 1093
Pippin, Donald *(Vocal Arranger)* 167, 367, 550, 746, 1002, 1012, 1249, 1373, 1660, 2360, 2660, 4727
Piquet, Rolf *(Composer)* 3443
Pirkle, Mac *(Director)* 4055
Pirkle, Mac *(Librettist)* 4055
Piron, A.J. *(Composer)* 1063, 3297
Piron, A.J. *(Lyricist)* 1063, 3297
Pirosh, Robert *(Librettist)* 3893
Piscariello, Frederick A. *(Composer)* 722
Piscariello, Frederick A. *(Lyricist)* 722
Pistone, Charles *(Cast)* 647, 1510
Pitchford, Dean *(Cast)* 3817, 4505
Pitchford, Dean *(Lyricist)* 661, 1236
Pitilli, Lawrence *(Composer)* 1282
Pitkin, Robert *(Cast)* 1278, 1888, 3345, 4673
Pitkin, William *(Costumes)* 597, 825
Pitkin, William *(Set Design)* 597, 825, 837, 1010, 1474, 2144
Pitot, Genevieve *(Dance Arranger)* 483, 619, 629, 842, 1029, 1094, 1564, 1679, 2137, 2331, 2357, 2484, 2556, 2864, 3837, 3913, 4090, 4496
Pitou, Augustus *(Author)* 1445, 3267, 3759, 4239
Pitou, Augustus *(Director)* 1445, 3267, 3759, 4239, 4313

Pitou, Augustus *(Producer)* 1157, 1163, 1907, 2662, 2763, 3220, 3267, 3642, 4120, 4313
Pitou Jr., Augustus *(Director)* 2186
Pitou Jr., Augustus *(Producer)* 2186, 2310
Pitou Sr., Augustus *(Author)* 2186, 2310
Pitou Sr., Augustus *(Director)* 2310
Pitt, Charles D. *(Director)* 4227
Pitts, Tom *(Composer)* 2856
Pitts, Tom *(Lyricist)* 2856
Pitts. Civic Light Opera *(Producer)* 2651
Pixley, Frank *(Librettist)* 586, 1313, 1650, 1707, 2315, 2745, 3578, 4738
Pixley, Frank *(Lyricist)* 586, 1650, 1707, 2315, 2745, 3578, 4738
Pixley, Gus *(Cast)* 187, 250
Pizzolla, Astor *(Composer)* 975
Placzek, Ron *(Set Design)* 556, 3311
Plain Jane Incorporated *(Producer)* 3511
Plaisted, T.S. *(Set Design)* 1193
Plamstierna-Weiss, Gunilla *(Costumes)* 3445
Plana, Tony *(Cast)* 4861
Plane, Liane *(Cast)* 4625
Planquette, Robert *(Author)* 3372
Planquette, Robert *(Composer)* 102, 3372
Plant, Mark *(Cast)* 4772
Plate, Jennie *(Cast)* 1499
Platt, Edward *(Cast)* 3234
Platt, George Foster *(Director)* 2779
Platt, Howard *(Cast)* 1169
Platt, Livingston *(Costumes)* 1935
Platt, Livingston *(Set Design)* 2, 1935, 2121, 2342, 3185, 3248, 3849
Platt, Marc *(Cast)* 323, 2252, 2379, 2680, 3263
Platt, Maxwell *(Director)* 293
Platt, Oliver *(Cast)* 2945, 4535
Platt, William *(Cast)* 263
Platzman, Eugene *(Composer)* 710
Platzman, Eugene *(Lyricist)* 710
Plautus *(Author)* 514, 1422
Players Club of Columbia U. *(Producer)* 1724, 1725
Players Ring, The *(Producer)* 2057
Playfair, Arthur *(Cast)* 1554
Playfair, Nigel *(Producer)* 325
Playhouse Square Center *(Producer)* 1636
Playkill Productions, Inc. *(Producer)* 1348
Playten, Alice *(Cast)* 1291, 1828, 1846, 3077, 3271, 3602, 4540
Playwrights Horizons *(Producer)* 109, 212, 829, 1234, 1872, 2185, 2746, 3368, 4210, 4358
Playwrights' Company, The *(Producer)* 2268, 2344, 2591, 4169, 4386, 4495
Plaza Theatre *(Producer)* 2643
Pleasence, Donald *(Cast)* 1089
Pleininger, Carl *(Composer)* 1608
Pleis, Jack *(Composer)* 2168
Plimmer, Harry *(Cast)* 3481
Plimpton, Martha *(Cast)* 119
Plimpton, Shelley *(Cast)* 1717, 3162
Plohn, Edmund *(Producer)* 4284
Ploner, George *(Lyricist)* 272
Plotnick, Jack *(Cast)* 3926
Plowman, Cory *(Cast)* 810
Plowman, Justin *(Cast)* 810
Plowman, Pat *(Author)* 810
Plowman, Travis *(Cast)* 810
Plumer, Lincoln *(Cast)* 3529
Plummer, Amanda *(Cast)* 54, 2468
Plummer, Christopher *(Cast)* 946, 1620, 2411
Plummer, H. Joseph *(Cast)* 821
Plunkett, Blanche *(Cast)* 1720
Plunkett, Charles *(Cast)* 976
Plunkett, M.W. *(Producer)* 388
Plunkett, Maryann *(Cast)* 81, 2798
Plunkett, Paul *(Cast)* 1561
Pober, Leon *(Composer)* 339
Pockriss, Lee *(Composer)* 614, 838, 1194, 1451, 4193, 4260, 4261, 4264, 4366, 4435
Pockriss, Lee *(Lyricist)* 4193, 4264
Poddany, Eugene *(Musical Director)* 2015
Poddubiuk, Christina *(Costumes)* 1120
Podell, Jules *(Producer)* 857, 858, 863
Podell, Rick *(Cast)* 597, 2579, 2962
Poe, Aileen *(Cast)* 1227, 2684, 3538, 3898
Poe, Coy *(Composer)* 1813, 4799
Poe, Coy *(Lyricist)* 1813, 4799
Pogany, Willy *(Costumes)* 2684, 2900
Pogany, Willy *(Set Design)* 2005, 2666, 2684, 3622
Pogue, David *(Musical Director)* 4619
Pogue, David *(Vocal Arranger)* 4619
Pohl, Richard *(Author)* 2538, 2668
Poindexter, H.R. *(Lighting Designer)* 1616, 3015
Pointing, Audrey *(Cast)* 429
Points, Ruth *(Costumes)* 2483
Poiret, Jean *(Author)* 2360, 3624
Poiret, Jules *(Costumes)* 4327
Poiret, Paul *(Costumes)* 25, 208, 582, 1712, 3312
Poiret, Paul *(Set Design)* 25, 582
Pokrass, Dmitiri *(Composer)* 1740
Pokrass, Samuel *(Composer)* 948, 3409, 4824
Pokrass, Samuel D. *(Composer)* 4670
Pola, Edward *(Composer)* 4741
Polacheck, Charles *(Cast)* 3180
Polacheck, Charles *(Director)* 1085
Polachek, Leon *(Musical Director)* 399
Polakov, Lester *(Costumes)* 924, 3698
Polakov, Lester *(Set Design)* 620
Polanco, Iraida *(Cast)* 696
Poland, Albert *(Producer)* 300, 3209, 4074
Polcsa, Juliet *(Costumes)* 2846, 2852
Poldine, Leo *(Librettist)* 1448
Polechek, Leon *(Musical Director)* 433
Polen, Linda *(Cast)* 626
Polenz, Robert *(Cast)* 169, 729
Poleo, Dom *(Lighting Designer)* 1878
Polk, Gordon *(Cast)* 1760
Polk, Jeffrey *(Cast)* 1159
Polk, Oscar *(Cast)* 536, 1225, 4256
Polla, W.C. *(Composer)* 1646
Polla, William *(Composer)* 2857
Polla, William C. *(Composer)* 2481

Pollack, Channing *(Librettist)* 3685
Pollack, Lew *(Composer)* 497, 2311, 2637, 2857, 2870, 3020, 3402, 3404, 4235, 4342, 4654
Pollack, Lew *(Lyricist)* 2637, 2857, 4654, 4799
Pollack and His Orchestra, Ben *(Cast)* 1827
Pollard, Daphne *(Cast)* 1689, 2978, 3399
Pollard, Dave *(Librettist)* 390
Pollard, May *(Cast)* 132, 2762
Pollard, Michael J. *(Cast)* 607, 1190
Pollard, William K. *(Librettist)* 2762
Pollard, William K. *(Producer)* 2762
Pollard, Willie *(Cast)* 2454
Pollock, Alan *(Cast)* 2206
Pollock, Bert *(Lyricist)* 2483
Pollock, Channing *(Author)* 1187, 1849, 2981
Pollock, Channing *(Librettist)* 335, 1327, 1663, 1849, 3031, 4809, 4815
Pollock, Channing *(Lyricist)* 1425, 1663, 1849, 3031, 3685, 3905, 4799, 4805, 4809, 4815, 4831, 4847, 4852
Pollock, Frank *(Cast)* 527, 1083, 1743, 3729
Pollock, Gordon W. *(Producer)* 4582
Pollock, Milt *(Cast)* 2986
Pollock, Muriel *(Composer)* 2180, 3103, 3104, 3523, 3728, 4621
Pollock, Muriel *(Lyricist)* 3728
Pollock Productions *(Producer)* 2021
Polygram Diversified Ent. *(Producer)* 4560
Pomahac, Bruce *(Composer)* 2027
Pomahac, Bruce *(Musical Director)* 2805
Pomahac, Bruce *(Orchestrations)* 942, 2565, 4146
Pomahac, Bruce *(Vocal Arranger)* 2565, 2805
Pomerantz, John J. *(Producer)* 1699
Pompeii, James *(Cast)* 1697
Pomus, Doc *(Composer)* 3695
Pomus, Doc *(Lyricist)* 3695
Ponazecki, Joe *(Cast)* 1265, 2319, 3874
Ponce *(Composer)* 1688
Ponce *(Lyricist)* 1688
Ponce, Ethel *(Composer)* 4807
Ponce, Manuel *(Lyricist)* 4813
Ponce, Phil *(Lyricist)* 700
Ponce, Phil L. *(Lyricist)* 4807
Pond, Helen *(Lighting Designer)* 2235, 3215, 4633
Pond, Helen *(Set Design)* 369, 1676, 2235, 3196, 3215, 3235, 3920, 4028, 4633
Pons, Helene *(Costumes)* 247, 1874, 3386, 3647, 3761, 3815, 3861
Pool, John *(Producer)* 410
Poole, Alice Maude *(Cast)* 2986
Poole, John Clayton *(Costumes)* 2640
Poole, Roy *(Cast)* 3897
Poole, Wakefield *(Choreographer)* 2584
Poole, Wakefield *(Director)* 2584
Poor, Harris *(Cast)* 4523
Popcorn Productions *(Producer)* 1108
Pope, Peggy *(Cast)* 2319
Pope, Robert *(Cast)* 4123
Pope, Stephanie *(Cast)* 789
Popiel, Louis *(Lighting Designer)* 4829
Popkin, Gary *(Composer)* 4433
Popkin, Gary *(Librettist)* 4433
Popkin, Gary *(Lyricist)* 4433
Popp, Andre *(Orchestrations)* 2150
Popp, Bill *(Arrangements)* 2611
Popp, Carolyn *(Cast)* 1903
Poppen, Detmar *(Cast)* 1973, 3699
Pops and Louie *(Cast)* 880
Porcasi, Paul *(Cast)* 2216
Porcelain, Syd *(Author)* 524
Porcher, Nananne *(Lighting Designer)* 181, 3564, 3734, 3830, 4447
Poretta, Frank *(Cast)* 1119, 2838
Poretta, Matthew *(Cast)* 3411
Porgina, Ludmilla *(Cast)* 2269
Porocopio, Rennie *(Costumes)* 600
Porte, Pierre *(Composer)* 1638
Porteous, Cameron *(Set Design)* 1120
Porter, Brent J. *(Costumes)* 164
Porter, Cathy *(Cast)* 2237
Porter, Cole *(Cast)* 870, 3547, 4622
Porter, Cole *(Composer)* 44, 130, 146, 163, 189, 201, 579, 629, 870, 875, 885, 969, 1018, 1109, 1153, 1203, 1272, 1453, 1638, 1683, 1690, 1735, 1762, 1873, 1877, 1921, 1923, 2252, 2287, 2294, 2331, 2366, 2432, 2453, 2611, 2677, 2729, 2788, 2847, 2891, 3020, 3131, 3156, 3172, 3196, 3214, 3216, 3235, 3291, 3325, 3326, 3359, 3378, 3382, 3467, 3547, 3674, 3865, 3893, 3972, 4058, 4132, 4207, 4302, 4399, 4498, 4517, 4545, 4555, 4581, 4622, 4777, 4799
Porter, Cole *(Director)* 130
Porter, Cole *(Librettist)* 3378, 3547, 3865
Porter, Cole *(Lyricist)* 44, 130, 146, 163, 189, 208, 579, 629, 870, 875, 885, 969, 1018, 1109, 1153, 1203, 1272, 1453, 1638, 1683, 1690, 1735, 1762, 1873, 1877, 1921, 1923, 2252, 2287, 2294, 2331, 2366, 2432, 2453, 2611, 2677, 2729, 2788, 2847, 3020, 3131, 3172, 3214, 3216, 3259, 3291, 3325, 3326, 3359, 3378, 3382, 3467, 3547, 3674, 3865, 3893, 3972, 4058, 4132, 4207, 4399, 4498, 4517, 4545, 4581, 4622, 4777, 4799
Porter, Don *(Cast)* 160
Porter, Ellis *(Costumes)* 2380
Porter, Howard *(Cast)* 1671, 3564, 4343
Porter, Hugh *(Musical Director)* 2203
Porter, Mike *(Set Design)* 682
Porter, Paul *(Cast)* 587
Porter, Paul *(Director)* 3137
Porter, Paul *(Librettist)* 3137
Porter, Paul *(Lyricist)* 3137
Porter, Stan *(Cast)* 400, 1269
Portfolio Productions *(Producer)* 3469
Portfolio Studios *(Producer)* 3542
Portnoff, Mischa *(Composer)* 1748
Portnoff, Mischa *(Dance Arranger)* 454
Portnoff, Wesley *(Composer)* 1748
Portnoff, Wesley *(Dance Arranger)* 454
Portnoy, Gary *(Composer)* 2754, 3555
Portnoy, Gary *(Lyricist)* 2754, 3555
Porto, Gary *(Lighting Designer)* 3476
Poser, Linda *(Cast)* 869
Posin, Katheryn *(Choreographer)* 3824

Posluns, Leah *(Producer)* 1079
Posnak, Charles *(Composer)* 364
Posner, Kenneth *(Lighting Designer)* 2229, 3811
Posner, Lee *(Librettist)* 439
Post, August *(Lyricist)* 3686
Post, Douglas *(Composer)* 3667
Post, Douglas *(Librettist)* 3667
Post, Douglas *(Lyricist)* 3667
Post, J. *(Composer)* 4193
Post, J. *(Lyricist)* 4193
Post, W. *(Composer)* 1342
Post, W.H. *(Author)* 4249
Post, W.H. *(Director)* 60, 2574, 4053, 4351
Post, W.H. *(Librettist)* 4664
Post, William H. *(Director)* 1270, 1472
Post, William H. *(Librettist)* 354, 2264, 3729, 4539
Postage Stamp Xtravaganzas *(Producer)* 4462
Postell, Steve *(Composer)* 1232
Postell, Steve *(Musical Director)* 1232
Poston, Tom *(Cast)* 837
Pot, Pan and Skillet *(Cast)* 2259
Pothier, Charles *(Lyricist)* 4240
Potok, Chaim *(Author)* 747
Potter, Chandler *(Set Design)* 2483
Potter, Clare *(Costumes)* 3894
Potter, Edward *(Cast)* 1342
Potter, H.C. *(Director)* 649, 1219
Potter, Henry C. *(Cast)* 3325
Potter, Jane *(Cast)* 4030
Potter, L.S. *(Composer)* 3828
Potter, L.S. *(Lyricist)* 3828
Potter, Maude *(Cast)* 3877
Potter, Paul *(Author)* 3866
Potter, Paul *(Librettist)* 1312, 3626, 3857, 4125
Potter, Paul *(Lyricist)* 1312, 1318
Potter, Paul M. *(Librettist)* 2732
Potter, Paul M. *(Lyricist)* 2732
Potter, S. *(Composer)* 1429
Pottle, Sam *(Cast)* 4041
Pottle, Sam *(Composer)* 73, 108, 427, 1049, 1648, 2935, 3111, 3112, 4041
Pottle, Sam *(Dance Arranger)* 2935
Pottle, Sam *(Librettist)* 3111
Pottle, Sam *(Lyricist)* 3111
Pottle, Sam *(Musical Director)* 2663, 2935
Pottle, Sam *(Pianist)* 4041
Pottle, Sam *(Producer)* 3186
Pottle, Sam *(Vocal Arranger)* 2935
Potts, David *(Set Design)* 3932, 4205
Potts, Nancy *(Costumes)* 52, 942, 1059, 1662, 1717, 1977, 2368, 3468, 3651, 3871, 3991
Pought, Emma Ruth *(Composer)* 4264
Pought, Emma Ruth *(Lyricist)* 4264
Pought, Jannie *(Composer)* 4264
Pought, Jannie *(Lyricist)* 4264
Pound, Courtice *(Composer)* 758
Pound, Courtice *(Lyricist)* 758
Pounds, Courtice *(Cast)* 719
Pounds, Louie *(Cast)* 2514
Pounds, Toots *(Cast)* 3157
Pourcel, F. *(Composer)* 4193
Pourcel, F. *(Lyricist)* 4193
Powell *(Composer)* 4823
Powell *(Lyricist)* 4823
Powell, Addison *(Cast)* 3577
Powell, Anthony *(Costumes)* 4217
Powell, Dawn *(Librettist)* 2379
Powell, Dick *(Cast)* 2371
Powell, Eddie *(Orchestrations)* 207
Powell, Edgar *(Composer)* 291
Powell, Edgar *(Lyricist)* 291
Powell, Edward *(Orchestrations)* 680, 1322, 1672, 2444, 3002, 4267
Powell, Edward B. *(Orchestrations)* 1137
Powell, Eleanor *(Cast)* 216, 1275, 1339, 1481, 1979, 3310
Powell, Felix *(Composer)* 964, 1852, 1919, 3259
Powell, Gary *(Arrangements)* 914
Powell, Jack *(Cast)* 1932, 2423
Powell, Jane *(Cast)* 1257, 3800
Powell, Janet *(Cast)* 3651
Powell, Jerry *(Composer)* 62, 128, 366, 1120, 1637, 2913, 3111, 3112, 3124
Powell, Jerry *(Lyricist)* 1120, 1637, 3111
Powell, Lovelady *(Cast)* 1990, 3725
Powell, Michael *(Author)* 3682
Powell, Michael *(Musical Director)* 4788
Powell, Shezwae *(Cast)* 730, 4450
Power, Chosei Funahara *(Composer)* 3739
Power, Chosei Funahara *(Lyricist)* 3739
Power, Udana *(Cast)* 1616
Power Productions *(Producer)* 705
Power Sr., Tyrone *(Cast)* 758
Powers, Amy *(Lyricist)* 760
Powers, Arthur Augustus *(Lyricist)* 1392
Powers, Augustus *(Lyricist)* 1392
Powers, George *(Cast)* 1913, 4007
Powers, Georgia *(Cast)* 2361
Powers, James T. *(Author)* 2378
Powers, James T. *(Cast)* 470, 770, 1783, 2213, 2519, 2803, 2844, 3588, 3828, 3834, 4490
Powers, James T. *(Librettist)* 1783, 2519, 4490
Powers, James T. *(Lyricist)* 1783, 2519, 4490
Powers, John *(Orchestrations)* 92
Powers, John R. *(Author)* 1059
Powers, John R. *(Librettist)* 1059
Powers, Leona *(Cast)* 3713
Powers, Manila *(Cast)* 202, 3680
Powers, Margot *(Cast)* 2057
Powers, Neva Rae *(Cast)* 2318, 2616
Powers, T. *(Composer)* 4193
Powers, T. *(Lyricist)* 4193
Powers, Tom *(Cast)* 2605, 3230
Powers, Tony *(Composer)* 2427
Powers, Tony *(Lyricist)* 2427
Powers, W.H. *(Cast)* 2494
Powers, William *(Cast)* 4802
Powys, Stephen *(Author)* 4586
Poynter, Edward *(Cast)* 1368
Prager, Stanley *(Cast)* 3351

Prager, Stanley *(Director)* 519, 2449, 2874, 3273, 3286, 3900
Prager, Stanley *(Librettist)* 4827
Prange, Laurie *(Cast)* 4459
Pransky, John *(Producer)* 268, 4323
Prather, Tom Ross *(Director)* 3067
Pratt, Alvin Ronn *(Cast)* 1671
Pratt, Charles E. *(Composer)* 1897
Pratt, Charles E. *(Lyricist)* 1897
Pratt, John *(Costumes)* 1370, 2582, 4254
Pratt, Ron *(Set Design)* 3752
Pratt, Thomas Charles *(Costumes)* 2104
Praxis Group *(Producer)* 1377
Preble, Ed *(Librettist)* 2423
Precarious Productions *(Producer)* 3970
Preisser, Cherry *(Cast)* 4824, 4825
Preisser, June *(Cast)* 901, 4777, 4824, 4825
Premice, Josephine *(Cast)* 576, 2190, 3524
Premus, Judy *(Cast)* 3926
Prendergast, Shirley *(Lighting Designer)* 105, 1073, 2513, 4591
Prentice, Amelia *(Cast)* 549
Prentice, Charles *(Composer)* 702
Prentice, Charles *(Musical Director)* 277, 475, 650, 791, 972, 2392, 4361
Prentice, Charles *(Orchestrations)* 841, 972
Prentice, Keith *(Cast)* 3815
Presburg, Jacques *(Composer)* 3258
Presburg, Jacques *(Orchestrations)* 3258
Presbury, Eugene *(Director)* 2824
Presnell, Harve *(Cast)* 154, 155, 1674, 4516
Press, Brian *(Cast)* 330
Press, Jacques *(Lyricist)* 1937
Press, Richard *(Producer)* 166
Pressburger, Emeric *(Author)* 3682
Pressel, Marc *(Musical Director)* 2212
Pressley, Brenda *(Cast)* 131
Pressman, Aaron *(Musical Director)* 3495
Pressman, Kenneth *(Lyricist)* 2633
Preston, Barry *(Cast)* 576, 4577
Preston, Billy *(Composer)* 3739
Preston, Billy *(Lyricist)* 3739
Preston, J. David *(Librettist)* 1231
Preston, Morgan *(Librettist)* 1231
Preston, Rob *(Lyricist)* 3908
Preston, Robert *(Cast)* 367, 2050, 2660, 3016, 3577, 4609
Preston, Robert W. *(Composer)* 1978
Preston, Robert W. *(Lyricist)* 1978
Preston, Robert W. *(Musical Director)* 1581, 4145
Preston, Tony *(Librettist)* 3814
Preston-Smith, Roger *(Choreographer)* 3764
Previn, Andre *(Composer)* 798, 1619
Previn, Charles *(Musical Director)* 186, 1527, 1686, 2180, 2363, 2684, 2907, 3157, 3225, 3538, 3727, 4491
Prewitt, Arrington *(Lyricist)* 47
Pribor, Richard *(Dance Arranger)* 2705
Pribor, Richard *(Musical Director)* 1341, 4346
Priborsky, Richard *(Musical Director)* 1257
Price, Allan *(Cast)* 3650
Price, Alonzo *(Cast)* 3532, 3951
Price, Alonzo *(Director)* 606, 1533, 2768, 3978, 4056, 4209
Price, Alonzo *(Librettist)* 606, 3978, 4056
Price, Alonzo *(Lyricist)* 3978, 4056
Price, Chilton *(Composer)* 4264
Price, Chilton *(Lyricist)* 4264
Price, Don *(Choreographer)* 2284, 2759
Price, Don *(Director)* 2284, 2759
Price, Edwin *(Director)* 3828
Price, George *(Cast)* 764, 1703, 4851
Price, George E. *(Composer)* 4427
Price, George E. *(Lyricist)* 4104, 4427
Price, Georgie *(Cast)* 1395, 1396, 4083, 4104, 4656
Price, Georgie *(Composer)* 4083
Price, Gerald *(Cast)* 1242, 2178, 4369
Price, Gilbert *(Cast)* 1119, 1319, 2203, 3159, 3602, 3731, 4002, 4004, 4383
Price, Henry *(Cast)* 2839
Price, John *(Cast)* 2795
Price, Lonny *(Cast)* 171, 1120, 2822, 3644
Price, Lonny *(Director)* 838
Price, Lonny *(Lyricist)* 1120
Price, Lorin *(Producer)* 1478
Price, Lorin E. *(Producer)* 3869, 3956
Price, Lorin Ellington *(Producer)* 4380
Price, Mark deSolla *(Producer)* 4279
Price, Mme. Helene *(Costumes)* 1014
Price, Paul B. *(Cast)* 3217
Price, Roger *(Cast)* 4377
Price, Roger *(Librettist)* 3107
Price, Tim Rose *(Lyricist)* 2346
Price, Tom *(Composer)* 1298
Price, Tom *(Lyricist)* 1298
Price, Vincent *(Cast)* 989
Pride, Malcolm *(Costumes)* 1619
Pride, Malcolm *(Set Design)* 1619
Priest, Janet *(Cast)* 2485, 2695, 3855
Priestley, J.B. *(Author)* 1618
Priestley, J.B. *(Librettist)* 1618
Prima, Louis *(Composer)* 146, 964
Primary Stages *(Producer)* 2065
Primavera Productions *(Producer)* 3522, 4379
Primont, Marian *(Cast)* 1897
Primrose, Joe *(Composer)* 445
Primrose, Joe *(Lyricist)* 445
Primrose Sisters *(Cast)* 1824
Primus, Barry *(Cast)* 1064
Prince *(Composer)* 4534
Prince *(Lyricist)* 4534
Prince, Charles *(Cast)* 354, 1728, 2324, 3423, 4185
Prince, Charles A. *(Musical Director)* 3063
Prince, Charles H. *(Cast)* 1505, 2865, 4650
Prince, Daisy *(Cast)* 3456
Prince, Faith *(Cast)* 1234, 1665, 2205, 2643, 3142, 4535
Prince, Graham *(Composer)* 432
Prince, Graham *(Lyricist)* 432
Prince, Harold *(Director)* 270, 610, 832, 1038, 1068, 1186, 1211, 1237, 1329, 1699, 2163, 2333, 2536, 2607, 2822, 3279, 3340, 3456, 3464, 3702, 3792, 3918, 4233, 4862

Prince, Harold *(Producer)* 610, 832, 957, 1265, 1280, 1310, 1329, 1422, 1699, 2163, 2417, 2536, 2822, 3113, 3340, 3351, 3918, 3967, 4312, 4625, 4862
Prince, Hughie *(Composer)* 1539, 3739
Prince, Hughie *(Lyricist)* 1539
Prince, Jack *(Cast)* 1029
Prince, Robert *(Composer)* 4060
Prince, Robert *(Dance Arranger)* 1721, 1990, 4060
Prince, Robert *(Orchestrations)* 1227
Prince, William *(Conductor)* 2027
Prince-Joseph, Bruce *(Musical Director)* 2910
Princess White Deer *(Cast)* 4853
Princess White Durrah *(Cast)* 1421
Pringle, Marjorie *(Cast)* 815, 1549
Printemps, Yvonne *(Cast)* 841, 3216
Prinz, Eddie *(Choreographer)* 1138, 3173
Prinz, Eddie *(Director)* 1947, 3173
Prinz, LeRoy *(Choreographer)* 1126, 1135, 1281, 1462, 1667, 1799, 3978, 4291, 4426
Prinz, LeRoy *(Director)* 2640, 3683
Prior, Allan *(Cast)* 1667, 2293, 2622, 3407, 4664
Prior, Thomas W. *(Lyricist)* 331
Priscilla, Victor *(Lyricist)* 621
Pritchard, John *(Composer)* 3186
Pritchard, Mark *(Set Design)* 874, 2572
Pritchard, Ted *(Cast)* 1092, 3018
Pritchett, James *(Cast)* 3815
Pritchett, John *(Composer)* 392
Pritchett, John *(Lyricist)* 392
Pritchett, Liz *(Cast)* 1766
Probst, Gerry *(Cast)* 3104
Probst, Robert *(Musical Director)* 1467
Prochaska, Bobby *(Cast)* 580
Prochnik, Bruce *(Cast)* 3271
Proctor, Catherine *(Cast)* 1144
Proctor, David *(Cast)* 3693
Proctor, Ethelyn *(Cast)* 1479
Proctor, Phil *(Composer)* 3076
Proctor, Phil *(Lyricist)* 3076
Proctor, Philip *(Cast)* 127
Proctor, Warren *(Cast)* 3472
Producers Associates *(Producer)* 1414
Producers Circle *(Producer)* 229
Producers Circle 2, The *(Producer)* 3279
Producers Circle Co. *(Producer)* 3792
Proett, Daniel *(Set Design)* 3076
Proft, Michael *(Librettist)* 4830
Program Devlopment Co. *(Producer)* 4127
Proia, Alexandre *(Cast)* 756
Prokofiev, Serge *(Composer)* 192
Prokofiev, Serge *(Music Based On)* 3449
Promenaders, The *(Producer)* 4484
Prophet Company, The *(Producer)* 3568
Proser, Monte *(Producer)* 850, 1811, 1886
Prosper and Maret *(Cast)* 1460
Prosser, Julie *(Cast)* 2027
Prostak, Edward *(Cast)* 2689
Proud, Peter *(Set Design)* 362
Prouty, Jed *(Cast)* 78, 1566, 2291, 2907, 3304, 3866, 4054, 4058, 4547
Provenza, Paul *(Librettist)* 4774
Provenza, Paul *(Lyricist)* 4774
Provenza, Rosario *(Set Design)* 2932
Provost, William *(Composer)* 924
Prucell, Charles *(Cast)* 1309
Prud'homme, Cameron *(Cast)* 603, 3113, 4516
Prudhomme Prod. Ltd. *(Producer)* 105
Pruette, William *(Cast)* 48, 737, 742, 1088, 1783, 2665, 2671, 2915, 3053, 3679, 3732, 4434
Prunczik, Karen *(Cast)* 1359
Pruneau, Phillip *(Librettist)* 4090
Prussian, E.D. *(Composer)* 1535
Pruyn, William *(Dance Arranger)* 3840
Pruyn, William *(Vocal Arranger)* 3840
Pryce, Jonathan *(Cast)* 2905
Prymus, Ken *(Cast)* 2250, 3628
Pryor, Arthur *(Composer)* 3268
Pryor, Marjorie *(Cast)* 2131
Pryor, Roger *(Cast)* 4178
Pryor, Roger *(Librettist)* 1856
Psacharopoulos, Nikos *(Director)* 945, 3195
Ptaszynski, Andre *(Producer)* 3695
Public Players, Inc. *(Producer)* 319
Puccini, Giacomo *(Author)* 595
Puccini, Giacomo *(Composer)* 2359, 3079
Puck, Eva *(Cast)* 1529, 1689, 1823, 2148, 2814, 3949
Puck, Harry *(Cast)* 2569, 2637, 2669, 2833, 3042, 4240, 4283, 4352
Puck, Harry *(Choreographer)* 2637, 2833, 4476
Puehringer, F. *(Composer)* 2895
Puerner, Charles *(Musical Director)* 1576
Puerto Rican Travelling Th. *(Producer)* 696
Pugh, E.E. *(Cast)* 14
Pugh, Ed *(Cast)* 26
Pugh, Ted *(Cast)* 708, 1786
Puig, Manuel *(Author)* 2333
Pujol, Rene *(French Lyrics)* 2366
Pujol, Rene *(Lyricist)* 4517
Pulen, Sim *(Cast)* 1388
Pulitzer, Walter *(Composer)* 2624
Pulitzer, Walter *(Lyricist)* 2624
Pullman, Kate *(Cast)* 3754
Pully, B.S. *(Cast)* 1706
Purcell, Charles *(Cast)* 1013, 1602, 2253, 2684, 2794, 2939, 3051, 3254, 3538, 3562, 3712, 3770, 3907, 4833
Purcell, Gertrude *(Author)* 4284
Purcell, Gertrude *(Cast)* 2816
Purcell, Gertrude *(Librettist)* 2277, 2490, 2637, 2669, 4352
Purcell, Gertrude *(Lyricist)* 4284
Purcell, Harold *(Lyricist)* 4510
Purcell, Jack *(Cast)* 859
Purcell, John H. *(Cast)* 2126
Purchese, Donald *(Musical Director)* 1857
Purdham, David *(Cast)* 2539
Purdom, Ralph *(Cast)* 73, 2750, 3371
Purdy, Richard *(Cast)* 629
Puri, Rajika *(Cast)* 4442
Puri, Rajika *(Choreographer)* 4442
Purinton, Jock *(Lighting Designer)* 92

Purinton, Jock *(Set Design)* 92
Purnell, Carrie *(Cast)* 552
Pursley, David *(Cast)* 1229
Purviance, Roy *(Cast)* 3045, 4649
Purvis, James *(Cast)* 2795
Pusey, Charles A. *(Cast)* 1213
Pusilo, Robert *(Costumes)* 344, 840
Puzo, Bill *(Set Design)* 4635
Pysher, Ernie *(Cast)* 3159

Q

Qrezzoli, Hector *(Director)* 432
Quackenbush, Karyn *(Cast)* 789, 1630
Quadri, Therese *(Cast)* 3597
Quality Amusement Company *(Producer)* 254
Qualters, Tot *(Cast)* 684, 736, 2706, 2856, 2857, 3866, 4810
Quaney, Barbara *(Cast)* 2067, 2935
Quartermaine, Leon *(Cast)* 3779
Quartet Productions *(Producer)* 3835
Quayle, Anna *(Cast)* 4160
Quayle, Anthony *(Cast)* 1294
Quayle, Anthony *(Director)* 1294
Quesenbery, Whitney *(Lighting Designer)* 1719, 4288
Questel, Mae *(Cast)* 269
Quick, George *(Cast)* 2838
Quick, Louise *(Cast)* 1273
Quick, Louise *(Choreographer)* 2426
Quigley, Erin *(Costumes)* 4074
Quigley, Herb *(Orchestrations)* 4256
Quigley, Jack *(Dance Arranger)* 302
Quigley, Jack *(Vocal Arranger)* 302
Quigley, Martin *(Librettist)* 2928
Quigley, Robert *(Cast)* 4705
Quillan, Joe *(Librettist)* 297
Quilley, Dennis *(Cast)* 129, 1644
Quilter, Roger *(Composer)* 4154
Quin, Mike *(Librettist)* 2809
Quine, Richard *(Cast)* 4557
Quinlan, Dan *(Cast)* 1823, 3677
Quinlan, Gertrude *(Cast)* 1845, 2315, 4201, 4404
Quinlan, John *(Cast)* 2666
Quinn, Aidan *(Cast)* 2468
Quinn, Anthony *(Cast)* 2450
Quinn, Colleen *(Cast)* 533
Quinn, Florence *(Cast)* 2716
Quinn, James *(Composer)* 1059
Quinn, James *(Lyricist)* 1059
Quinn, Jerome *(Producer)* 4648
Quinn, Marie *(Cast)* 2310
Quinn, Michael *(Cast)* 3113
Quinn, Patricia *(Cast)* 477, 2207
Quinn, Patrick *(Cast)* 1597
Quinson, Gustave *(Author)* 468
Quintero, Jose *(Director)* 1427, 3551
Quintero, Jose *(Librettist)* 1427
Quinton, Dolores *(Producer)* 2754
Quinton, Everett *(Cast)* 2037, 2488
Quinton, Everett *(Costumes)* 2037
Quinton, Everett *(Director)* 2037
Quinton, Everett *(Librettist)* 2037, 2488
Quinton, Everett *(Lyricist)* 2037, 2488
Quixano, Dave *(Cast)* 2587
Quong, Rose *(Cast)* 1315

R

RLM Productions, Inc. *(Producer)* 4701
Rabb, Ellis *(Cast)* 2859, 3787, 4715
Rabb, Ellis *(Director)* 1662, 3468, 3787
Rabe, David *(Cast)* 4151
Rabe, David *(Lyricist)* 4151
Rabinowitz, Harry *(Musical Director)* 4301
Rabiroff, Jacques *(Musical Director)* 2379, 3916
Rachael, Anne *(Cast)* 3824
Racheff, James *(Librettist)* 10
Racheff, James *(Lyricist)* 10
Rachel Productions *(Producer)* 3831
Rachmaninoff, Sergei *(Music Based On)* 161
Rackerby, Donald *(Cast)* 80
Rackmil, Gladys *(Producer)* 1645, 2435, 2677, 3444, 3515
Racolin, Alexander E. *(Producer)* 2110
Racolin, Dina *(Producer)* 2110
Radaelli *(Cast)* 2140
Radcliffe, Carrie *(Cast)* 2675
Radford, Dave *(Lyricist)* 3737
Radford, Robert *(Cast)* 3992
Radin, Al *(Musical Director)* 2843
Radin, Oscar *(Musical Director)* 463, 684, 764, 1065, 1111, 1343, 1522, 1920, 1929, 2358, 2373, 2666, 2668, 2696, 2732, 2825, 2856, 3246, 3397, 3399, 3400, 3401, 3403, 3525, 3680, 3958, 4747, 4816, 4817
Radin, Oscar *(Orchestrations)* 965, 2282, 2378, 2519, 2684, 3006, 3395, 3403, 3650, 3737
Radio City Mu. Hall *(Producer)* 107
Radio City Music Hall *(Producer)* 2737, 3126, 3638, 4035
Radio City Music Hall Prod. *(Producer)* 1298
Radio City Music Hall Prods *(Producer)* 1146, 1638
Radio Rogues, The *(Cast)* 1840
Radner, Gilda *(Cast)* 1512
Radner, Gilda *(Librettist)* 1512
Radner, Gilda *(Lyricist)* 1512
Rado, James (Cast) 1717, 1736
Rado, James *(Composer)* 3651
Rado, James *(Librettist)* 1717, 3651
Rado, James *(Lyricist)* 1717, 3651
Rado, James *(Producer)* 3651
Rado, Ted *(Librettist)* 3651
Rado, Ted *(Producer)* 3651
Radomski, James *(Composer)* 932
Radomski, James *(Lyricist)* 932
Radomski, Jim *(Cast)* 932
Radomski, Jim *(Composer)* 932
Radomski, Jim *(Lyricist)* 932
Radomsky, Saul *(Set Design)* 2949

Rae, Charlotte *(Cast)* 2484, 2554, 2954, 3482, 3497, 3564, 4366, 4369
Rae, Florence *(Cast)* 2083
Rae, Olive *(Cast)* 2514
Rae, Phyllis *(Cast)* 3924
Rael, Elsa *(Lyricist)* 2633
Raft, Dick *(Cast)* 3403
Raft, George *(Cast)* 773, 1416, 3342, 3403
Rafter, Adele *(Cast)* 2697
Rafter, Frank *(Set Design)* 175, 284, 1213, 1392, 1540, 2500, 2543, 2938, 2986
Ragent, Robert *(Choreographer)* 4416
Raggio, Lisa *(Cast)* 1637
Ragland, Oscar "Rags" *(Cast)* 930, 2184, 2978, 3131, 3172, 3359, 4150, 4267, 4393, 4667, 4677
Ragni, Gerome *(Cast)* 1717, 1736
Ragni, Gerome *(Librettist)* 1116, 1717
Ragni, Gerome *(Lyricist)* 1116, 1717
Rago, Jerry *(Cast)* 2573
Ragotzy, Jack *(Director)* 2322
Ragusa, Michele *(Cast)* 3926
Rahn, Muriel *(Cast)* 309, 818, 3807, 4256
Rahn, Patsy *(Cast)* 2618
Raiff, Stan *(Producer)* 705
Raiken, Larry *(Cast)* 3722, 3926
Railey, Thomas *(Librettist)* 513
Railey, Thomas *(Lyricist)* 3065, 3268
Raine, Lola *(Cast)* 1693, 3649
Rainer, Louise *(Cast)* 1506
Raineri, Orestes *(Set Design)* 3995
Raines, John *(Librettist)* 2720
Raines, Quinton *(Director)* 314
Raines, Ron *(Cast)* 451, 808
Rainey, Joel *(Musical Director)* 496
Rainey, Ma *(Composer)* 3297
Rainey, Ma *(Lyricist)* 3297
Rainger, Frank *(Choreographer)* 628
Rainger, Frank *(Director)* 3621
Rainger, Frank M. *(Director)* 2222
Rainger, Ralph *(Cast)* 931
Rainger, Ralph *(Composer)* 2032, 2545, 3138, 3172, 4291
Rainger, Ralph *(Lyricist)* 1638
Rainger, Ralph *(Pianist)* 138, 2545
Rains, Claude *(Cast)* 3287
Raisa *(Composer)* 819
Raisa *(Librettist)* 819
Raisa *(Lyricist)* 819
Raison, Milton *(Producer)* 3946
Raiter, Frank *(Cast)* 3227
Raitt, James *(Arrangements)* 1353, 3346
Raitt, James *(Composer)* 4137
Raitt, James *(Dance Arranger)* 2420, 2805
Raitt, James *(Musical Director)* 1353, 3346, 4137
Raitt, James *(Orchestrations)* 3346, 4137
Raitt, James *(Vocal Arranger)* 2420, 4137
Raitt, John *(Cast)* 657, 660, 2248, 2679, 2742, 3020, 3182, 3351, 4366
Raker, Lorin *(Cast)* 3623
Rakov, Theresa *(Cast)* 1660
Raksin, David *(Composer)* 2103
Raksin, David *(Orchestrations)* 216, 2809, 3104, 3365, 4374
Raleigh, Ben *(Composer)* 4193
Raleigh, Ben *(Lyricist)* 4193, 4484
Raleigh, Cecil *(Librettist)* 2500, 4219
Raleigh, Cecil *(Lyricist)* 2500
Raleigh, R. *(Composer)* 4193
Raleigh, R. *(Lyricist)* 4193
Raleigh, Sir Walter *(Lyricist)* 2633
Raleigh, Stuart W. *(Musical Director)* 1439
Raley, Wade *(Cast)* 3668
Rall, Tommy *(Cast)* 615, 619, 935, 2268, 2582, 2864, 2894, 4018
Ralph, Cecil *(Author)* 1806
Ralph, Harry B. *(Lyricist)* 2923
Ralph, Jessie *(Cast)* 215, 1904
Ralph, Julia *(Cast)* 1356, 1911
Ralph, Sheryl Lee *(Cast)* 1103, 3690
Ralston, Alfred *(Dance Arranger)* 3259
Ralston, Alfred *(Vocal Arranger)* 3259
Ralston, Curt *(Cast)* 164
Ralston, Teri *(Cast)* 273, 832, 1955, 2536, 2651, 4406
Rambeau, Edward *(Cast)* 1809
Rambeau, Marjorie *(Cast)* 3812
Rambo, David *(Composer)* 2022
Rambo, David *(Lyricist)* 2022
Ramer, Jack *(Librettist)* 2051
Ramer, Jack *(Lyricist)* 2051
Ramin, Jordan *(Composer)* 2584
Ramin, Sid *(Composer)* 32
Ramin, Sid *(Lyricist)* 32
Ramin, Sid *(Orchestrations)* 837, 1422, 1567, 1709, 2048, 2205, 2355, 3682, 4004, 4020, 4090, 4566, 4625, 4693
Ramin, Sid *(Vocal Arranger)* 837, 2584
Ramirez, Ramiro *(Composer)* 3830
Ramirez, Ramiro *(Librettist)* 3830
Ramirez, Ramiro *(Lyricist)* 3830
Ramirez, Ray *(Cast)* 2580
Ramirez, Roger *(Composer)* 478
Ramirez, Roger *(Lyricist)* 478
Rampino, Lewis D. *(Costumes)* 1439, 3015
Ramsay, Remak *(Cast)* 1736, 2260, 2626, 3142
Ramsey, Gordon *(Cast)* 652, 2114
Ramsey, John *(Producer)* 2332
Ramsey, Kevin *(Cast)* 432, 1296, 2250, 4127
Ramsey, Logan *(Cast)* 4401
Ramsey, Marion *(Cast)* 1198, 1699, 2775, 2898, 3636, 3739, 4089, 4534, 4615
Ramsey, Marion *(Librettist)* 4534
Ramsey, Stanley *(Cast)* 576
Ramsey, Van Broughton *(Costumes)* 871
Ramsey, Will *(Cast)* 434
Rand, Lionel *(Orchestrations)* 4131
Rand, Sally *(Cast)* 662, 2460, 2636
Randall, Andre *(Cast)* 1137
Randall, Bob *(Cast)* 4401
Randall, Bob *(Librettist)* 2687
Randall, Carl *(Cast)* 17, 905, 924, 1688, 2403, 2540, 2855, 3009, 3245, 3379, 4085, 4213, 4335, 4661, 4809, 4810, 4814, 4842, 4844

Randall, Carl *(Choreographer)* 17, 905, 924, 1266, 1309, 1453, 1688, 1847, 1889, 2105, 2344, 2597, 3009, 3410, 4085, 4142, 4214
Randall, Carl *(Director)* 1718, 2403
Randall, Carl *(Lyricist)* 684, 2105, 4335
Randall, Dick *(Producer)* 4292
Randall, Fred *(Cast)* 2097
Randall, Jack *(Cast)* 1867
Randall, Nellie *(Cast)* 542
Randall, Sharon *(Cast)* 1884
Randall, Tony *(Cast)* 2553, 3234
Randall Sisters, The *(Cast)* 1847
Randell, Ron *(Cast)* 3734, 4749
Randie, Doug *(Orchestrations)* 1255
Randole, Leo *(Librettist)* 680
Randolph, A.P. *(Composer)* 3179
Randolph, A.P. *(Lyricist)* 3179
Randolph, Anne *(Cast)* 1750
Randolph, Bob *(Lyricist)* 4110
Randolph, Elsie *(Cast)* 844, 4320
Randolph, Forbes *(Director)* 2115
Randolph, Forbes *(Librettist)* 1251, 2115
Randolph, Forbes *(Lyricist)* 2115
Randolph, Forbes *(Producer)* 1251, 2115
Randolph, Jack *(Cast)* 361
Randolph, James *(Cast)* 1385
Randolph, Jimmy *(Cast)* 279
Randolph, Mimi *(Cast)* 71, 2219
Randolph, Robert *(Costumes)* 3888
Randolph, Robert *(Lighting Designer)* 519, 1184, 1373, 1420, 1611, 1842, 1846, 2019, 2163, 2523, 3526, 3900, 3931, 4013, 4060, 4090, 4238, 4588
Randolph, Robert *(Set Design)* 160, 161, 167, 181, 519, 607, 1184, 1373, 1420, 1611, 1621, 1842, 1846, 2016, 2019, 2163, 2523, 3526, 3888, 3900, 3931, 4013, 4060, 4090, 4114, 4238, 4588, 4743
Randolph, Virgil *(Producer)* 3712
Randolph-Wright, Charles *(Choreographer)* 4535
Randolph-Wright, Charles *(Composer)* 1055
Randolph-Wright, Charles *(Director)* 1055
Randolph-Wright, Charles *(Librettist)* 1055
Randolph-Wright, Charles *(Lyricist)* 1055
Raniello, John *(Composer)* 2968
Raniello, John *(Lyricist)* 2968
Ranken, Frederick *(Librettist)* 694, 1515, 1768, 2213, 3073, 4032, 4187, 4713
Ranken, Frederick *(Lyricist)* 694, 1515, 1768, 2213, 3073, 3753, 4032, 4187, 4713
Ranken, Frederick M. *(Librettist)* 104
Rankin, Phyllis *(Cast)* 1579, 3784
Rankin Jr., Arthur *(Director)* 928
Rankin Jr., Arthur *(Librettist)* 928
Rankin Jr., Arthur *(Producer)* 928, 2941
Ransome, John *(Cast)* 2040, 3578
Ransome, John W. *(Cast)* 3433, 4222
Rapee, Erno *(Musical Director)* 2412, 3639
Raphael, Arthur *(Librettist)* 1692
Raphael, Gerrianne *(Cast)* 1194, 1370, 2318, 3899
Raphael, Jay E. *(Cast)* 4707
Raphaelson, Samson *(Author)* 2194
Raposo, Joe *(Composer)* 56, 2542, 2677, 3643, 3988, 4732
Raposo, Joe *(Lyricist)* 2542, 2677
Raposo, Joe *(Musical Director)* 1676
Raposo, Joe *(Orchestrations)* 1676, 3988
Raposo, Joseph *(Musical Director)* 4783
Raposo, Joseph *(Vocal Arranger)* 4783
Rapp, Anthony *(Cast)* 2539
Rapp, Philip *(Director)* 4117
Rapp, Philip *(Librettist)* 4117
Rappaport, Barbara *(Cast)* 1004, 1155, 3165, 3329
Rapposelli, Michael *(Cast)* 3873
Raquello, Edward *(Cast)* 4023
Rascel, R. *(Composer)* 4264
Rasch, Albertina *(Cast)* 286, 2139, 4452
Rasch, Albertina *(Choreographer)* 294, 512, 672, 1207, 1225, 1322, 1680, 2252, 2386, 2423, 2540, 2638, 2755, 3063, 3352, 3584, 3719, 3953, 4087, 4131, 4357, 4367, 4557, 4583, 4730, 4821, 4823
Rasch Girls, The Albertina *(Cast)* 4357
Rasche, David *(Cast)* 3852
Rasey, Adelle *(Cast)* 278
Rasimi, Mme. B. *(Costumes)* 1922
Raskin, Gene *(Composer)* 4342
Raskin, Gene *(Lyricist)* 4342
Raskin, Harry *(Lyricist)* 1780
Raskin, Kenny *(Cast)* 330
Raskin, Ruby *(Orchestrations)* 2496, 3381
Raskin, Ruby *(Vocal Arranger)* 3381
Rasmuson, Judy *(Lighting Designer)* 150, 753, 2230, 2289
Rasmussen, Zora *(Cast)* 2427, 2555, 4295
Rassen, Robin *(Choreographer)* 3654
Rastelli, Bob *(Cast)* 3507
Ratcliffe, Samuel D. *(Cast)* 2043
Rath Brothers, The *(Cast)* 2960
Rathbone, Basil *(Cast)* 44, 752, 1742, 4155, 4230
Rathbun, Gil *(Cast)* 821
Rathburn, Roger *(Cast)* 729
Rathrock, Claire *(Composer)* 4264
Rathrock, Claire *(Lyricist)* 4264
Ratliff, Joseph *(Cast)* 3736
Ratliff, Joseph M. *(Cast)* 3675
Ratnikoff, Larisa *(Costumes)* 264
Rattenborg, Birgit *(Costumes)* 4708
Rattigan, Terence *(Author)* 1564
Rattigan, Terrance *(Author)* 4262
Rau, Santha Rama *(Librettist)* 4048
Rauber, Francois *(Lyricist)* 2188
Rauch, Fred *(Composer)* 3178
Rauch, Fred *(Lyricist)* 3178
Rauch, Maurice *(Composer)* 4773
Raucher, Gary *(Cast)* 2874
Rauh, Stanley E. *(Librettist)* 1132
Ravel, Maurice *(Music Based On)* 1110
Ravella, Don *(Producer)* 4347
Ravenscroft, Thurl *(Voice)* 2015
Ravinett, Ted *(Producer)* 963
Ravitz, Mark *(Set Design)* 3739, 4449
Rawlings, Herbert *(Cast)* 166

Rawlings, Marjorie Kinnan *(Author)* 4764
Rawlings Jr., Herbert Lee *(Cast)* 2908
Rawlins, Lester *(Cast)* 4609
Rawlins, W.H. *(Cast)* 25, 3948
Rawlston, Zelma *(Cast)* 1123
Rawson, Denys *(Musical Director)* 1619
Rawson, Ron *(Producer)* 4153
Rawson, Ronald *(Producer)* 1047
Rawson, Ruth *(Director)* 1047
Rawtenburg, Gene *(Orchestrations)* 1624
Ray, Alan *(Cast)* 4782
Ray, Anje *(Cast)* 344
Ray, Arthur *(Cast)* 3945
Ray, Connie *(Cast)* 4030
Ray, Connie *(Librettist)* 4030
Ray, Ed *(Lyricist)* 2834
Ray, Gene Anthony *(Cast)* 661
Ray, Joey *(Cast)* 1134, 3861
Ray, Johnny *(Cast)* 2314
Ray, Kathryn *(Cast)* 1131, 2366
Ray, Leslie Ann *(Cast)* 135
Ray, Lois *(Cast)* 864
Ray, Naomi *(Cast)* 3002
Ray, Nicholas *(Director)* 341
Ray, Phil *(Composer)* 1148
Ray, Phil *(Lyricist)* 1148
Ray, Scot *(Choreographer)* 4149
Ray, Sonnie *(Cast)* 4341
Ray, William *(Cast)* 4742
Ray Waves Prods. *(Producer)* 3901
Rayam, Curtis *(Cast)* 4447
Raye, Carol *(Cast)* 490
Raye, Don *(Lyricist)* 90, 3739
Raye, Martha *(Cast)* 622, 1837, 1931
Raye, Michael *(Composer)* 2239
Raye, Michael *(Lyricist)* 2239
Rayes, Billy *(Cast)* 1494
Raymaker, Norrice *(Cast)* 3364
Raymond, Al *(Cast)* 1531
Raymond, Charles *(Cast)* 2299
Raymond, Dorothy *(Cast)* 2194
Raymond, Guy *(Cast)* 3841
Raymond, Harry *(Lyricist)* 1535
Raymond, Helen *(Cast)* 163, 1110, 1539, 2115, 3016, 3596, 3823, 3907, 4555
Raymond, Julia *(Cast)* 4563
Raymond, Lewis *(Orchestrations)* 4428
Raymond, Maude *(Cast)* 1464, 1566, 2209, 2978, 3701, 3750, 4044, 4430
Raymond, Melville *(Cast)* 2879
Raymond, Melville *(Director)* 591
Raymond, Melville *(Librettist)* 591
Raymond, Melville *(Producer)* 9
Raymond, Melville B. *(Producer)* 2722
Raymond, Ray *(Cast)* 465, 631, 917, 3921, 4648, 4651
Raymond, Ray *(Lyricist)* 631
Raymond, William *(Cast)* 2871, 3567
Raymond Jr., Frederick *(Cast)* 2527
Rayner, Minnie *(Cast)* 650
Raynes, J.A. *(Composer)* 2576, 3437, 3520
Raynor, Minnie *(Cast)* 972
Rayson, Benjamin *(Cast)* 1755
Raywin, Hal *(Director)* 1727
Raywin, Hal *(Producer)* 1727
Raywood, Keith *(Set Design)* 3198
Raz, Rivka *(Cast)* 1075, 4396
Razaf, Andy *(Cast)* 926, 927
Razaf, Andy *(Composer)* 927, 1986, 3396, 3707, 3782, 4281, 4501
Razaf, Andy *(Librettist)* 498
Razaf, Andy *(Lyricist)* 26, 39, 146, 432, 443, 478, 498, 725, 885, 927, 1028, 1198, 1328, 1495, 1772, 1980, 1981, 1986, 2223, 2302, 2337, 2561, 3018, 3020, 3297, 3396, 3514, 3707, 3782, 4281, 4501, 4502, 4503
Razoff *(Composer)* 4648
Razoff *(Lyricist)* 4648
Rea, Kitty *(Cast)* 1104
Rea, Lawrence *(Cast)* 4119
Rea, Oliver *(Producer)* 2268
Read, David *(Lighting Designer)* 3445
Read, John B. *(Lighting Designer)* 1619
Read, Mary *(Choreographer)* 2569, 3605, 3721, 3924, 4345
Read, P. *(Composer)* 2367
Reade, Janet *(Cast)* 288
Reader, Ralph *(Choreographer)* 202, 266, 718, 791, 1693, 2547, 2888, 3149, 4213, 4271, 4361, 4793
Readinger, Jeanne *(Cast)* 4174
Readinger, Jo *(Cast)* 4174
Really Useful Company, The *(Producer)* 678, 3464, 4217
Reamer, Robert Adams *(Set Design)* 2709
Reams, Lee Roy *(Cast)* 167, 1359, 2590, 3548
Reaney, James *(Cast)* 1230, 1555, 2394
Reaney, James C. *(Cast)* 3229
Reardon, Casper *(Cast)* 2061
Reardon, E.H. *(Cast)* 2662
Reardon, Frank *(Lyricist)* 3801
Reardon, Greg *(Librettist)* 3654
Reardon, Greg *(Lyricist)* 3654
Reardon, John *(Cast)* 808, 1061, 3108
Reaves-Phillips, Sandra *(Cast)* 1425
Recasner, Ron *(Cast)* 1406
Recht, Ray *(Lighting Designer)* 4533
Recht, Ray *(Set Design)* 4, 262, 4533
Recht, Raymond C. *(Set Design)* 2007
Rechzeit, Jack *(Cast)* 1269, 3559
Rector, Drury *(Cast)* 3981
Rector, Eddie *(Cast)* 498, 1960, 1989, 3704, 4763
Rector, Eddie *(Choreographer)* 1989, 2845
Rector, Eddie *(Lyricist)* 4282
Rector, Grace *(Cast)* 4182
Rector, Henry *(Cast)* 1499
Rector, Julia *(Director)* 3904
Red, Buryl *(Orchestrations)* 1959
Red Barn Theatre *(Producer)* 2560
Red Clay Ramblers, The *(Cast)* 2468
Redcott, Eileen *(Cast)* 3583
Redd, Veronica *(Cast)* 344
Reddick, Cecil *(Director)* 4536

Reddie, J. Milton *(Lyricist)* 4253
Reddin, Keith *(Cast)* 1915
Redding, Earl *(Cast)* 3024
Redding, Edward C. *(Composer)* 722, 1363, 1892, 4268, 4416
Redding, Edward C. *(Lyricist)* 722, 1363, 1892, 4268, 4416
Redding, Edward C. *(Pianist)* 4156
Redding, Eugene *(Cast)* 1551, 4794
Redding, Otis *(Composer)* 146, 3695, 3739, 4193
Redding, Otis *(Lyricist)* 146, 3695, 3739, 4193
Reddon, Nancy *(Cast)* 2069
Redfarn, Roger *(Director)* 846
Redfield, Adam *(Cast)* 4252
Redfield, Billy *(Cast)* 4569
Redfield, Harry C. *(Musical Director)* 1722
Redfield, Henry *(Orchestrations)* 3907
Redfield, Liza *(Musical Director)* 112, 169, 699, 1194, 1222, 2231, 2887, 2918, 4090
Redfield, Liza *(Orchestrations)* 2918
Redfield, Liza *(Vocal Arranger)* 4090
Redfield, William *(Cast)* 134, 304, 1116, 3326
Redfield, William *(Orchestrations)* 3580, 4206
Redfield, William M. *(Orchestrations)* 606
Redford, Harry *(Composer)* 1208
Redford, Harry *(Lyricist)* 1208
Redford, Jeff *(Cast)* 2650
Redford, William *(Cast)* 2300
Redgrave, Lynn *(Cast)* 1842
Redgrave, Michael *(Cast)* 635, 1089, 3800
Redlin, Richard *(Producer)* 4193
Redman, Don *(Cast)* 2000
Redman, Scott *(Director)* 4172
Redman Orchestra, Don *(Cast)* 1986
Redman and His Orchestra, Don *(Cast)* 1772
Redmond, Helen *(Cast)* 104, 2101, 4713, 4724
Redmond, John *(Composer)* 875, 885, 886
Redmond, John *(Lyricist)* 875, 4091
Redmond, Marge *(Cast)* 3473
Redmond, Rita *(Cast)* 2834
Redpath, Olive *(Cast)* 2963
Redstone, Willie *(Author)* 3157
Redstone, Willie *(Musical Director)* 3156, 4327
Redwine, Skip *(Composer)* 1380
Redwine, Skip *(Dance Arranger)* 1018
Redwine, Skip *(Librettist)* 1380
Redwine, Skip *(Lyricist)* 1380
Redwine, Skip *(Musical Director)* 1018, 3788
Redwine, Skip *(Vocal Arranger)* 1018
Ree, Max *(Costumes)* 3009
Reece, Kathryn *(Cast)* 1182, 1235
Reed *(Composer)* 3297
Reed *(Lyricist)* 3297
Reed, Alaina *(Cast)* 4, 1198, 2132, 3903
Reed, Alan *(Cast)* 2653
Reed, Alfred *(Orchestrations)* 63
Reed, Alyson *(Cast)* 302, 958, 1597, 1638, 2754, 3231
Reed, Bobby *(Cast)* 508, 2488
Reed, Carl *(Producer)* 1935, 3849
Reed, Dave *(Composer)* 1925
Reed, Dave *(Lyricist)* 1925, 3981
Reed, Florence *(Cast)* 758, 1144
Reed, Harry *(Cast)* 3337
Reed, Jess *(Cast)* 4814
Reed, Jessie *(Cast)* 3402
Reed, Jozella *(Cast)* 3636
Reed, Lou *(Composer)* 3739
Reed, Lou *(Lyricist)* 3739
Reed, Luther *(Author)* 1009
Reed, Mabel *(Cast)* 3417
Reed, Maggi-Meg *(Cast)* 3169
Reed, Mark *(Author)* 3457
Reed, Michael *(Composer)* 2148
Reed, Michael *(Lyricist)* 2148
Reed, Michael *(Musical Director)* 1741
Reed, Michael *(Orchestrations)* 1256, 1741
Reed, Napoleon *(Cast)* 653
Reed, Nat *(Composer)* 567
Reed, Nat *(Lyricist)* 567
Reed, Paul *(Cast)* 657, 1706, 1860, 2019, 3016, 3603, 4524
Reed, Pauline *(Costumes)* 2111
Reed, Roland *(Cast)* 526
Reed, Samuel *(Cast)* 2025
Reed, Stuart *(Librettist)* 947
Reed, Vivian *(Cast)* 576, 1890, 2173
Reed, William L. *(Composer)* 1887
Reed Jr., Dave *(Composer)* 675, 1537, 2261, 2675, 3313, 4014, 4130
Reed Jr., Dave *(Lyricist)* 310, 591, 675, 1537, 2261, 2675, 3313, 3753, 4014, 4130
Reeder, George *(Cast)* 134, 2484
Reeder, James *(Cast)* 3318
Reeger, John *(Cast)* 1439, 4740
Reehling, Joyce *(Cast)* 1268
Reeker, Cecelia *(Composer)* 725
Rees, Roger *(Cast)* 2474
Rees, Vernon *(Cast)* 2682
Reese, Bob *(Producer)* 411
Reese, Claude *(Lyricist)* 4827
Reese, Della *(Cast)* 2415
Reese, Oliver *(Cast)* 1462
Reeves, Al *(Composer)* 3982
Reeves, Al *(Director)* 3982
Reeves, Al *(Librettist)* 3982
Reeves, Al *(Lyricist)* 3982
Reeves, Billie *(Cast)* 4802, 4804
Reeves, Cheryl *(Cast)* 2037
Reeves, D.W. *(Composer)* 938
Reeves, D.W. *(Lyricist)* 938
Reeves, George *(Cast)* 4706
Reeves, Peter *(Lyricist)* 949, 4138
Reeves, Steve *(Cast)* 4542
Reeves-Smith, H. *(Cast)* 1680, 3432
Refregier, Anton *(Set Design)* 3441
Refugee Artists Group, The *(Producer)* 1413
Regal, Henry *(Cast)* 1154
Regan, J.D. *(Lighting Designer)* 344
Regan, Jay *(Cast)* 3973

Regan, Joe *(Costumes)* 4401
Regan, Joe *(Producer)* 4294
Regan, Patti *(Cast)* 410, 412, 413, 1341, 3186
Regan, Sylvia *(Author)* 1269
Regan, Sylvia *(Librettist)* 1679, 2751
Regan, Walter *(Cast)* 765, 2148
Regay, Pearl *(Cast)* 638, 1027, 1485, 3772
Rego, Luis *(Author)* 2058
Rehan, Ada *(Cast)* 762
Reich, Adina *(Set Design)* 3670, 3781
Reich, Herbert *(Librettist)* 2288
Reich, Holly *(Cast)* 1155
Reicher, Frank *(Director)* 2487, 4077
Reichert, Heinz *(Author)* 463, 1680, 2886
Reichner, Bickley *(Composer)* 2772
Reichner, Bickley *(Lyricist)* 1885, 2772, 3103, 3104, 3870
Reichner, S. Bickley *(Lyricist)* 18
Reid, Alexander *(Costumes)* 661
Reid, Carl Benton *(Cast)* 2510
Reid, Elliott *(Cast)* 1408, 4496, 4827
Reid, Florence *(Cast)* 1455, 4688
Reid, Hal *(Librettist)* 1520
Reid, Hugh L. *(Set Design)* 284
Reid, Hugh Logan *(Set Design)* 1429, 2500
Reid, James Allen *(Composer)* 2876
Reid, James Allen *(Director)* 2876
Reid, James Allen *(Librettist)* 2876
Reid, James Allen *(Lyricist)* 2876
Reid, James Allen *(Producer)* 2876
Reid, John *(Costumes)* 2055
Reid, Kathy *(Cast)* 4799
Reid, Keith *(Composer)* 3739
Reid, Keith *(Lyricist)* 3739
Reid, M.W. *(Cast)* 1149
Reid, Stephen O. *(Producer)* 2477
Reiff, Linda *(Choreographer)* 3164
Reigert, Peter *(Cast)* 682
Reilley, Victor *(Cast)* 3286
Reilly, C. *(Author)* 3481
Reilly, Charles Nelson *(Cast)* 1233, 1828, 2019, 3161, 3366, 4013
Reilly, Frank C. *(Producer)* 3481
Reilly, Jacqueline *(Cast)* 164
Reilly, William *(Choreographer)* 83
Reillys, Five *(Cast)* 1973
Reimherr, George *(Cast)* 3078
Rein, Martin *(Producer)* 4137
Reina *(Set Design)* 914
Reina, Mark *(Cast)* 3936
Reine *(Costumes)* 1989
Reiner, Carl *(Author)* 1190, 4038
Reiner, Carl *(Cast)* 59, 2137, 3563
Reiner, Ethel Linder *(Producer)* 630
Reinhardt, Gottfried *(Librettist)* 1817, 3536, 3767
Reinhardt, Heinrich *(Author)* 3613, 4119
Reinhardt, Heinrich *(Composer)* 3613, 4119
Reinhardt, Max *(Director)* 225, 1196
Reinhardt, Max *(Librettist)* 3767
Reinhardt, Stephen *(Choreographer)* 825
Reinhardt, Stephen *(Dance Arranger)* 1581
Reinhardt, Stephen *(Musical Director)* 2687, 4744
Reinhardt, Stephen *(Orchestrations)* 1581
Reinhardt, Stephen *(Vocal Arranger)* 1581, 4744
Reinking, Ann *(Cast)* 146, 964, 1634, 3330, 4689
Reinking, Ann *(Choreographer)* 1169
Reisch, Michele *(Costumes)* 705
Reisch, Walter *(Author)* 3972, 4486
Reisch, Walter *(Lyricist)* 3946
Reisen, A. *(Composer)* 1279
Reisen, A. *(Lyricist)* 1279
Reisenfeld, Hugo *(Composer)* 380
Reisenfeld, Hugo *(Musical Director)* 1199
Reisfeld, Bert *(Composer)* 4264
Reisfeld, Bert *(Lyricist)* 4264
Reisig, Theodore *(Set Design)* 1218, 2986, 3081
Reisig-Dove *(Set Design)* 1285
Reisman, Jane *(Lighting Designer)* 127, 432, 1353, 2134
Reisman, Joe *(Dance Arranger)* 2443
Reisman, Joe *(Musical Director)* 2443
Reisman, Joe *(Orchestrations)* 2443
Reisman, Joe *(Vocal Arranger)* 2443
Reisman's Orchestra, Leo *(Cast)* 1625
Reismueller, Ross *(Musical Director)* 1959
Reisner, C. Francis *(Lyricist)* 3401
Reiss, Martin *(Lighting Designer)* 3110
Reiss, Martin *(Set Design)* 3110
Reissa, Eleanor *(Cast)* 3697, 3722, 4082, 4342
Reissa, Eleanor *(Choreographer)* 4082, 4342
Reissa, Eleanor *(Director)* 4342
Reissa, Eleanor *(Lyricist)* 1609
Reiter, Tom *(Costumes)* 1510
Reiter, Val *(Cast)* 1282
Reitman, Ivan *(Director)* 2820
Reitman, Ivan *(Producer)* 2687, 2820
Reizner, June *(Composer)* 272, 1049, 1364, 2913, 3479
Reizner, June *(Lyricist)* 272, 1049, 1364, 2913, 3479
Relkin, Edwin A. *(Producer)* 3336
Relyea, Marjorie *(Cast)* 284, 1313
Remacle, Don J. *(Set Designer)* 4746
Remaily, Robin *(Composer)* 3309
Remaily, Robin *(Lyricist)* 3309
Rembach, Frank *(Lighting Designer)* 4579
Rembach, Frank *(Set Design)* 4579
Remick, Lee *(Cast)* 162
Remlinger, William *(Lighting Designer)* 3753
Remos, Susanne *(Choreographer)* 3226
Remsen, Deborah *(Cast)* 4499
Remus, Jorie *(Cast)* 1878
Renard, Jules *(Author)* 3760
Renaud, Andre *(Cast)* 1137
Renaud, Andre *(Composer)* 1137
Renaud, William *(Cast)* 3369
Renault, Paul *(Cast)* 1500
Rendell Productions *(Producer)* 4623
Renderer, Scott *(Cast)* 4295
Rene, Leon
See also Leon Rene's Lucky Day Band.
Rene, Leon *(Composer)* 2640, 3840
Rene, Leon *(Lyricist)* 3840

Rene, Nikki *(Cast)* 1890, 3285
Rene, Norman *(Director)* 2477, 2764, 4358
Rene, Otis *(Composer)* 2259, 2640, 3840
Rene, Otis *(Lyricist)* 3840
Rene's Lucky Day Band, Leon *(Cast)* 2640
Rene's Lucky Day Orchestra, Leon
See also Leon Rene.
Rengier, John *(Librettist)* 600
Rengier, John *(Lyricist)* 600
Renie *(Costumes)* 2083
Rennagel, Marilyn *(Lighting Designer)* 544, 1059, 1082, 2643, 3302, 4727
Rennie, James *(Cast)* 3002
Rennie, Malcolm *(Cast)* 1619
Reno, Don *(Composer)* 4030
Reno, Don *(Lyricist)* 4030
Renyi, Aladar *(Author)* 4228
Renyi, Aladar *(Composer)* 4228
Repertory Theatre of Lincoln Center *(Producer)* 3309
Requa, Roy *(Costumes)* 3009
Reri *(Cast)* 4823
Reseen, Robin *(Choreographer)* 1412, 3202
Resin, Dan *(Cast)* 2941, 4785
Resnick, Michael *(Lyricist)* 2498
Resnik, Hollis *(Cast)* 494, 4708
Resnik, Holly *(Cast)* 158
Resnik, Muriel *(Author)* 160
Resta, Francis E. *(Composer)* 6
Reveaux, Edward *(Director)* 67, 180, 3664
Revel, Billy *(Cast)* 1127
Revel, Harry *(Composer)* 180, 244, 478, 703, 1207, 1251, 1395, 2747, 2808, 3444, 3639, 4025, 4823
Revel, Harry *(Lyricist)* 3172
Revel, Harry *(Music Based On)* 180
Revere, Amy *(Cast)* 4367
Revil, Rudi *(Composer)* 924
Revill, Clive *(Cast)* 2150, 3271, 3499, 3931
Reville Ltd. *(Costumes)* 1202
Revson, Iris *(Cast)* 107
Revuers, The
See also Leonard Bernstein, Betty Comden, Adolph Green and Judy Holliday.
Revuers, The *(Composer)* 3036
Revuers, The *(Lyricist)* 3036
Rexford, Eben E. *(Composer)* 1897
Rexford, Eben E. *(Lyricist)* 1897
Rey, Billy *(Cast)* 3011
Rey, Reynaldo *(Cast)* 4786
Rey, Reynaldo *(Composer)* 4786
Rey, Reynaldo *(Lyricist)* 4786
Reyde, Gwendolyn *(Cast)* 1987
Reyes, Clara *(Cast)* 4438
Reyes, Raul *(Choreographer)* 4110
Reyes, Riva *(Cast)* 1836
Reynolds, Alan S. *(Cast)* 2027
Reynolds, Charlotte *(Cast)* 423
Reynolds, Clarke *(Producer)* 362
Reynolds, Dorothy *(Cast)* 1386
Reynolds, Dorothy *(Librettist)* 1386, 3818
Reynolds, Dorothy *(Lyricist)* 1386, 3818
Reynolds, E.R. *(Producer)* 698
Reynolds, Ellis *(Composer)* 432
Reynolds, Gertrude *(Cast)* 2350
Reynolds, Herbert
See also M.E. Rourke.
Reynolds, Herbert *(Lyricist)* 473, 1544, 1607, 1784, 1965, 2204, 2372, 2620, 2843, 2907, 3020, 3177, 3193, 3230, 3424, 3740, 4104, 4150, 4418, 4419, 4555, 4816
Reynolds, James *(Cast)* 4818
Reynolds, James *(Costumes)* 1011, 1013, 1272, 1690, 2258, 2475, 2638, 2788, 3009, 3219, 3254, 3617, 3829, 4212, 4235, 4374, 4539, 4815, 4816, 4817, 4818
Reynolds, James *(Set Design)* 773, 818, 930, 1690, 2638, 2788, 3009, 3219, 3254, 3829, 4212, 4539, 4637
Reynolds, Joseph *(Cast)* 2543
Reynolds, Lee *(Producer)* 4627
Reynolds, Lillian *(Cast)* 4291
Reynolds, Lucille *(Cast)* 2552
Reynolds, Mary *(Arrangements)* 914
Reynolds, Paul B. *(Producer)* 1590
Reynolds, Quentin *(Cast)* 1299
Reynolds, T. *(Director)* 2889
Reynolds, Thomas *(Director)* 178, 3322, 3996
Reynolds, Thomas L. *(Director)* 1538
Reynolds, Tim *(Librettist)* 3418
Reynolds, Tom *(Director)* 3157
Reynolds, Tom *(Producer)* 3156
Reynolds Sisters, The *(Cast)* 1800
Rezlit, Albert *(Composer)* 2465
Rhapsody in Black, Inc. *(Producer)* 3705
Rheams, Grace *(Cast)* 1556
Rhian, Geff *(Costumes)* 2735
Rhodes, Betty *(Cast)* 339
Rhodes, Burt *(Musical Director)* 194
Rhodes, Burt *(Orchestrations)* 4160
Rhodes, Erik *(Cast)* 629, 961, 1453, 1879, 2190, 3934, 4237
Rhodes, Evan H. *(Author)* 3576
Rhodes, Harrison *(Author)* 718
Rhodes, Harrison *(Librettist)* 3799, 4655
Rhodes, Joseph *(Producer)* 2284
Rhodes, Nancy *(Director)* 1171
Rhodes, Robert *(Cast)* 3192
Rhodes, William *(Cast)* 263
Rhys, Robert *(Cast)* 2260
Rhythmettes, The *(Cast)* 4256
Riabouchinska, Tania *(Cast)* 3536
Rialto Theatre Orchestra *(Cast)* 2403
Riano, Rene *(Cast)* 1691
Riashentsev, Uri *(Lyricist)* 4176
Ribaud, Joe *(Composer)* 2856
Ribaud, Joe *(Lyricist)* 2856
Ribeiro, Alfonso *(Cast)* 4286
Riberto, Vel *(Costumes)* 2195
Ribnikov, Alexis *(Composer)* 2269
Ricard, Amy *(Cast)* 250, 2779
Ricardel, Molly *(Author)* 2060
Ricardo, R.M. *(Cast)* 1913
Ricciardelli, John *(Producer)* 2754
Rice, Adnia *(Cast)* 2523

Rice, Andy *(Director)* 86
Rice, Andy *(Librettist)* 1483, 1485, 1778, 3796
Rice, Blanche *(Cast)* 2836
Rice, Bob *(Cast)* 4683
Rice, E.E. *(Composer)* 830, 1392, 2543
Rice, Edmund *(Librettist)* 4377
Rice, Edward E. *(Composer)* 1213, 2938, 2986, 3887
Rice, Edward E. *(Director)* 2500, 4650
Rice, Edward E. *(Producer)* 284, 783, 1392, 1540, 1994, 2316, 2500, 2938, 2986, 3887, 3951
Rice, Elmer *(Author)* 1097, 1933, 4013, 4495
Rice, Elmer *(Director)* 4495
Rice, Elmer *(Librettist)* 4169
Rice, Elmer *(Lyricist)* 4169
Rice, Fanny *(Cast)* 222
Rice, Felix *(Composer)* 1966
Rice, Florence D. *(Cast)* 2265
Rice, Gitz *(Cast)* 1502, 3137
Rice, Gitz *(Composer)* 208, 1502, 1551, 2698, 3137, 3328, 3593
Rice, Gitz *(Lyricist)* 1502, 3328
Rice, J. Clifford *(Cast)* 1836
Rice, John C. *(Cast)* 1301
Rice, Keith *(Cast)* 4454
Rice, Lillian *(Cast)* 2394
Rice, Michael *(Conductor)* 1785
Rice, Michael *(Dance Arranger)* 1638
Rice, Michael *(Musical Director)* 275, 1785, 3211
Rice, Michael *(Orchestrations)* 275
Rice, Peter *(Costumes)* 101, 3429, 3482
Rice, Peter *(Set Design)* 101, 3429
Rice, Sam *(Composer)* 2693
Rice, Sam *(Lyricist)* 2693
Rice, Sarah *(Cast)* 4233
Rice, Susan *(Librettist)* 1630
Rice, Tim *(Lyricist)* 330, 721, 1211, 2212, 2242
Rice Jr., Andy *(Cast)* 288
Rice and Prevost *(Cast)* 800
Rich, Buddy *(Cast)* 3255
Rich, Charles T. *(Producer)* 1627
Rich, Charlie *(Composer)* 3608
Rich, Charlie *(Lyricist)* 3608
Rich, Chuck *(Composer)* 914
Rich, Chuck *(Lyricist)* 914
Rich, Doris *(Cast)* 3687
Rich, Freddie
See Freddie Rich and His Orchestra.
Rich, Helen *(Cast)* 4393
Rich, Irene *(Cast)* 206
Rich, James *(Cast)* 2555
Rich, John *(Director)* 1040
Rich, Max *(Composer)* 1481, 2300
Rich, Max *(Lyricist)* 1481
Rich, Nancy *(Cast)* 2968
Rich, Ron *(Cast)* 578
Rich, Sylvan *(Composer)* 72
Rich, Tony *(Cast)* 74
Rich, Vinnie *(Composer)* 4171
Rich, Vinnie *(Lyricist)* 4171
Rich and Harris *(Producer)* 191, 4407
Rich and His Orchestra, Freddie *(Cast)* 2459
Richard, Emily *(Cast)* 2474
Richard, Gene *(Choreographer)* 265
Richard, Mae *(Lyricist)* 944, 4279
Richard, Mae *(Producer)* 4618
Richard, Thomas *(Cast)* 2886
Richardone, Michael *(Musical Director)* 4463
Richards, Al *(Cast)* 443
Richards, Al *(Choreographer)* 443, 444, 1251
Richards, Carol *(Cast)* 2496
Richards, Don *(Lyricist)* 2288
Richards, Donald *(Cast)* 95, 1278
Richards, Evan *(Cast)* 869
Richards, George *(Cast)* 1259
Richards, Gordon *(Cast)* 4569
Richards, Houston *(Cast)* 163
Richards, Jess *(Cast)* 2633, 3019, 3688
Richards, Jess *(Vocal Arranger)* 74
Richards, Jim *(Cast)* 2968
Richards, Keith *(Composer)* 3739
Richards, Keith *(Lyricist)* 3739
Richards, Lloyd *(Director)* 2053, 4764
Richards, Martin *(Producer)* 1068, 1649, 1699, 2360, 2790, 4233, 4695
Richards, Marty *(Producer)* 3792
Richards, Reve *(Costumes)* 2630, 2776
Richards, Sal *(Cast)* 4347
Richards, Sal *(Director)* 4347
Richards, Thomas D. *(Cast)* 1292
Richardson, Barbara *(Cast)* 1371
Richardson, Claibe *(Composer)* 392, 942, 1049, 1362, 1662, 2565, 2611, 2678, 3468, 3479, 3484, 3787, 3940
Richardson, Claibe *(Lyricist)* 3468, 3479, 3484, 3787
Richardson, George T. *(Librettist)* 2543
Richardson, Ian *(Cast)* 3445
Richardson, Jane *(Cast)* 3775
Richardson, Jazzlips *(Cast)* 443, 1980
Richardson, Jim *(Cast)* 225
Richardson, Lea *(Cast)* 4406
Richardson, Lea *(Musical Director)* 952
Richardson, Robert E. *(Producer)* 415, 2616
Richardson, Ron *(Cast)* 394
Richardson, Walter *(Cast)* 27, 435, 1499, 2111
Richel, George *(Cast)* 2800
Richert, Wanda *(Cast)* 1359
Richett, Edward *(Composer)* 1655
Richie, Adele *(Cast)* 613, 737, 2324, 4044
Richie, Maude *(Cast)* 4430
Richler, Mordecai *(Author)* 171
Richler, Mordecai *(Librettist)* 171
Richman, Arthur *(Author)* 2789
Richman, Harry *(Cast)* 1395, 1416, 1481, 1489, 1490, 1825, 2140, 3121, 3153, 3623, 3850, 4823
Richman, Harry *(Composer)* 3020, 3297, 3623, 4424
Richman, Harry *(Lyricist)* 3443, 3623, 4424, 4823
Richmond, Elizabeth *(Cast)* 4136
Richmond, June *(Cast)* 180, 887
Richmond, Wynn *(Cast)* 1733
Richter, Carolyn *(Cast)* 1754
Richter, Carolyn *(Librettist)* 280

Richter, Carolyn *(Lyricist)* 280
Richter, Joseph *(Musical Director)* 2804
Richter, Joseph *(Vocal Arranger)* 2804
Richter, Will *(Cast)* 227
Rickabaugh, Clive *(Set Design)* 4254
Rickard, Dick *(Author)* 4035
Rickard, Earl *(Cast)* 3649
Rickard, Gwen *(Producer)* 4652
Rickenback, Don *(Arrangements)* 2076
Rickenback, Don *(Cast)* 2076
Rickenback, Don *(Musical Director)* 2076
Ricker, Benjamin F. *(Director)* 750
Ricketts, Bob *(Additional Music)* 1499
Ricketts, Bob *(Composer)* 1960
Ricketts, Bob *(Lyricist)* 1960
Ricketts, Robert W. *(Orchestrations)* 3022
Ricketts, Tom *(Director)* 2986
Rickey, Al *(Musical Director)* 90
Rickman, Allen Lewis *(Cast)* 4325
Rickman, Carl *(Librettist)* 567
Riddell, Richard *(Lighting Designer)* 394, 4147
Riddle, George *(Cast)* 1581
Riddle, Nelson *(Arrangements)* 3841
Riddle, Nelson *(Cast)* 3324
Riddle, Nelson *(Musical Director)* 3324
Riddle, Richard *(Composer)* 915
Riddle, Richard *(Lyricist)* 915
Rideamus, Edward *(Author)* 659
Ridge, Antonia *(Lyricist)* 4264
Ridge, John David *(Costumes)* 869, 3370
Ridges, Stanley *(Cast)* 425, 993, 1174, 3729, 3819
Ridiculous Theatrical Co. *(Producer)* 2037
Rieffel, Lisa *(Cast)* 3643
Riegel, Eden *(Cast)* 4107
Riehl, Bob *(Cast)* 239
Riemueller, Ross *(Musical Director)* 1511
Riesenfeld, Hugo *(Composer)* 2830, 4823
Riesenfeld, Hugo *(Musical Director)* 2403, 2830, 3627
Rieser, Terry *(Choreographer)* 1797, 2289
Riffle, Miles *(Cast)* 214
Rigby, Harry *(Producer)* 808, 1635, 1721, 1729, 2058, 2705, 4197, 4746
Rigdon, Kevin *(Set Design)* 4074
Rigg, Diana *(Cast)* 808
Riggs, Lynn *(Author)* 3263
Riggs, Ralph *(Cast)* 1183, 1476, 2444, 2597, 3137, 3225, 3263, 3365, 3590, 3955, 4673, 4772
Riggs, Ralph *(Choreographer)* 2351, 3236
Riggs, Ralph *(Costumes)* 1183
Riggs, Stanley *(Cast)* 495
Riggs, T. Lawrason *(Librettist)* 3378, 3865
Rigsby, Gordon *(Director)* 3273
Riha, Bobby *(Cast)* 2183
Riley *(Cast)* 3142
Riley, Betsy *(Musical Director)* 114
Riley, Eric *(Cast)* 3285
Riley, James *(Set Design)* 4038
Riley, Larry *(Cast)* 1038, 1099, 1402, 3909
Riley, Lary *(Cast)* 550
Riley, Michael *(Composer)* 393, 1813
Riley, Michael *(Lyricist)* 393
Riley, Rob *(Cast)* 4690
Riley, Rob *(Director)* 4690
Riley, Rob *(Librettist)* 4690
Riley, Sid *(Musical Director)* 2253
Riley, Thomas W. *(Producer)* 356
Rimsky-Korsakov *(Music Based On)* 23
Rinal *(Cast)* 471
Rinehimer, John *(Conductor)* 3136
Rinehimer, John *(Dance Arranger)* 3136
Rinehimer, John *(Orchestrations)* 3136
Rinehimer, John *(Vocal Arranger)* 3136
Ring, Blanche *(Cast)* 8, 17, 457, 543, 560, 1021, 1226, 1464, 1910, 1912, 2005, 2209, 2213, 2835, 2858, 3153, 3166, 3403, 3713, 3882, 4179, 4414, 4589, 4634, 4642, 4757
Ring, M. *(Director)* 4794
Ring, Michael *(Choreographer)* 1624
Ringgold, Jennie *(Cast)* 2044
Ringham, Nancy *(Cast)* 1169, 4371
Ringle, Dave *(Composer)* 1343, 3989
Ringle, Dave *(Lyricist)* 1343, 3989
Ringwald, Roy *(Vocal Arranger)* 3100
Rinker, Al *(Composer)* 3683
Rinker, Alton *(Composer)* 4827
Rinker, Kenneth *(Choreographer)* 4252
Rio Brothers, The *(Cast)* 4753
Rios, Augie *(Cast)* 3837
Ripley, Alice *(Cast)* 4217
Ripley, Constance *(Costumes)* 125, 294, 672, 1322, 1672, 3365, 3674, 3699
Ripley, Madame *(Costumes)* 2986
Ripley, Patricia *(Cast)* 2617
Ripple, Pacie *(Cast)* 3117
Rippy, Robert *(Cast)* 4542
Riscoe, Arthur *(Lyricist)* 3500
Riseman, Naomi *(Cast)* 4696
Riser, P. *(Composer)* 1713
Riser, P. *(Lyricist)* 1713
Rising, Lawrence *(Author)* 1904
Riskin, Irving *(Orchestrations)* 2397
Risque, W.H. *(Author)* 3976
Risque, W.H. *(Librettist)* 3098
Risque, W.H. *(Lyricist)* 3098, 3976
Riss, Sheldon *(Producer)* 3668
Ritchard, Cyril *(Cast)* 44, 844, 974, 1745, 2182, 2313, 2389, 3020, 3453, 3617, 3634, 3731, 4196, 4519
Ritchard, Cyril *(Director)* 1745, 2227
Ritchie, Adele *(Cast)* 68, 1030, 1243, 1246, 1579, 2733, 3049, 4353
Ritchie, Bill *(Cast)* 185
Ritchie, Robert G. *(Producer)* 1879
Riter, Joseph *(Producer)* 102
Ritholz Associates *(Set Design)* 2804
Ritman, William *(Costumes)* 3810
Ritman, William *(Lighting Designer)* 1354, 2322, 3810
Ritman, William *(Set Design)* 1047, 1354, 3186, 3305, 3516, 3810
Ritt, Martin *(Cast)* 3180, 4495
Ritter, Tex *(Cast)* 4163

Ritter, Thelma *(Cast)* 3113
Rittman, Trude *(Composer)* 2582, 3453
Rittman, Trude *(Dance Arranger)* 85, 101, 223, 623, 660, 751, 989, 1242, 1475, 1511, 1548, 1616, 1991, 2201, 2312, 2582, 2681, 3020, 3038, 3452, 3453, 4481, 4718
Rittman, Trude *(Incidental Music)* 3453
Rittman, Trude *(Vocal Arranger)* 623, 751, 823, 1616, 2201, 3274, 3347, 3452, 4095, 4481, 4718
Ritz Brothers, The *(Cast)* 1312
Ritzer, Jeremy *(Producer)* 4019
Riva, William *(Set Design)* 3664, 3940
Rivaux, Edward *(Director)* 4702
Rivera, Chita *(Cast)* 269, 534, 607, 723, 1369, 2208, 2333, 2820, 2987, 3718, 3899, 3941, 4625, 4737, 4798
Rivera, Jose M. *(Costumes)* 4107
Rivera, Martin *(Cast)* 2630
Rivera, Martin *(Choreographer)* 2776
Rivera, Walter *(Cast)* 3903
Rivers, Cecil *(Cast)* 554, 1050, 2034
Rivers, H. Fletcher *(Choreographer)* 215, 434, 1540
Rivers, J. *(Composer)* 4193
Rivers, J. *(Lyricist)* 4193
Rivers, Joan *(Librettist)* 1436
Rivers, Laurence *(Producer)* 4667
Rivers, Max *(Choreographer)* 792, 2389, 2976, 3291, 4154, 4341, 4581, 4667, 4765
Rivers, Professor *(Composer)* 1759
Riverside Shakespeare Co. *(Producer)* 760
Rivkin, Allen *(Librettist)* 4152
Rivoli Theatre Orchestra *(Cast)* 2403
Rizzio, R.H. *(Lighting Designer)* 159
Rizzo, Michael *(Set Design)* 708
Roach, Tanis *(Cast)* 528, 1004, 1155, 3165, 3329, 3997
Roache, Viola *(Cast)* 1734, 4479
Roane, Frank *(Cast)* 2591
Robards, Jason *(Cast)* 4048
Robb *(Lyricist)* 4430
Robb, Frank *(Musical Director)* 2292
Robbie, Seymour *(Director)* 193
Robbins, Billy *(Composer)* 214
Robbins, Billy *(Pianist)* 214
Robbins, Carrie *(Costumes)* 147, 3643, 4205
Robbins, Carrie F. *(Costumes)* 1164, 1256, 1289, 1664, 1755, 2583, 2877, 2925, 3330, 4459
Robbins, Cindy *(Cast)* 1766
Robbins, David *(Composer)* 655
Robbins, David *(Musical Director)* 655
Robbins, Everett *(Lyricist)* 39
Robbins, Gale *(Cast)* 3
Robbins, Gil *(Cast)* 2898, 2941, 3653
Robbins, Jana *(Cast)* 809, 4379
Robbins, Jana *(Vocal Arranger)* 74
Robbins, Jane Marla *(Cast)* 2954
Robbins, Jerome *(Cast)* 1670, 4142, 4166
Robbins, Jerome *(Choreographer)* 363, 404, 619, 1265, 1709, 1886, 2205, 2312, 2582, 2894, 3278, 3453, 4499, 4625
Robbins, Jerome *(Director)* 363, 1214, 1265, 1420, 1709, 2205, 2582, 3351, 3453, 4323, 4625
Robbins, Norman *(Librettist)* 760
Robbins, R.N. *(Set Design)* 3898
Robbins, Rex *(Cast)* 1049, 1364, 2617, 3479, 3889, 4535
Robbins, Tim *(Author)* 655
Robbins, Tim *(Composer)* 655
Robbins, Tim *(Director)* 655
Robbins, Tim *(Lyricist)* 655
Robbins, Tom *(Cast)* 2205, 2283
Robe, Harold *(Lyricist)* 1502, 3397
Robe, Harry *(Composer)* 965
Roberson, Ken *(Choreographer)* 240
Roberson, Rudy *(Cast)* 2648
Robert, Hans *(Cast)* 1519, 4420
Robert Fox, Ltd. *(Producer)* 721
Roberti, Lyda *(Cast)* 3379, 3735, 4778
Roberts *(Composer)* 1963
Roberts *(Lyricist)* 1963
Roberts, Allan *(Composer)* 67, 4131
Roberts, Allan *(Lyricist)* 67, 2255, 3442, 4131
Roberts, Andy *(Composer)* 682
Roberts, Andy *(Lyricist)* 682
Roberts, Annie *(Cast)* 3912
Roberts, Anthony *(Cast)* 2014, 3516
Roberts, Arthur *(Cast)* 3467
Roberts, Ben *(Librettist)* 1101, 2187
Roberts, C. Luckeyth *(Composer)* 254, 487, 980, 1587, 2690, 3054, 3062, 3915, 4339
Roberts, C. Luckeyth *(Director)* 3054
Roberts, C. Luckeyth *(Musical Director)* 980
Roberts, C. Luckeyth *(Producer)* 4339
Roberts, Chapman *(Cast)* 2618, 3824
Roberts, Chapman *(Musical Director)* 240, 478
Roberts, Chapman *(Vocal Arranger)* 240, 478, 576, 1198, 1296, 4788
Roberts, Darcie *(Cast)* 589
Roberts, Donald *(Cast)* 3912
Roberts, Doris *(Costumes)* 4484
Roberts, Edna *(Cast)* 1224
Roberts, Eric *(Cast)* 2504
Roberts, Howard *(Musical Director)* 828, 2415
Roberts, Howard *(Orchestrations)* 2415
Roberts, Howard A. *(Musical Director)* 1813, 3656
Roberts, Howard A. *(Vocal Arranger)* 3656
Roberts, J.H. *(Cast)* 703, 3634
Roberts, James *(Set Design)* 762
Roberts, Jeremy *(Musical Director)* 2198
Roberts, Jeremy *(Orchestrations)* 4229
Roberts, Jimmy *(Composer)* 2171
Roberts, Jimmy *(Dance Arranger)* 1591, 4454
Roberts, Jimmy *(Musical Director)* 474
Roberts, Joan *(Cast)* 180, 1814, 2755, 3263, 4214
Roberts, John *(Producer)* 3108
Roberts, June *(Cast)* 4528
Roberts, Kathryn B. *(Cast)* 1206
Roberts, Lee S. *(Composer)* 3402, 4390
Roberts, Les *(Composer)* 1436
Roberts, Les *(Librettist)* 1436
Roberts, Les *(Lyricist)* 1436
Roberts, Luckeyth
See C. Luckeyth Roberts.

Roberts, Nelson *(Producer)* 1912
Roberts, Pernell *(Cast)* 1616, 2777
Roberts, R.A. *(Cast)* 1465, 1627
Roberts, R.A. *(Director)* 1627, 1925
Roberts, R.A. *(Lyricist)* 3065
Roberts, R.A. *(Producer)* 3065
Roberts, Rachel *(Cast)* 2682
Roberts, Ralph *(Cast)* 2411, 3157, 3214, 3890
Roberts, Ralph *(Lyricist)* 1569, 2341, 3322
Roberts, Rhoda *(Lyricist)* 1990, 3956
Roberts, Roy *(Cast)* 657
Roberts, Ruth *(Lighting Designer)* 1256, 1873, 2598, 4205
Roberts, Sarah *(Costumes)* 3836, 4438
Roberts, Sarah *(Set Design)* 3836, 4438
Roberts, Thayer *(Cast)* 4486
Roberts, Tony *(Cast)* 4196, 4560
Robertson, Alene *(Cast)* 155
Robertson, Geoff *(Author)* 4449
Robertson, Guy *(Cast)* 82, 771, 953, 1680, 2628, 2747, 3170, 3443, 3713, 3823, 3868, 4077, 4170, 4669, 4694
Robertson, Guy *(Lyricist)* 2747
Robertson, J. Robbie *(Composer)* 3739
Robertson, J. Robbie *(Lyricist)* 3739
Robertson, Jane *(Cast)* 3636
Robertson, Liz *(Cast)* 958, 2204
Robertson, Patrick *(Set Design)* 1386
Robertson, R.A. *(Lyricist)* 1159
Robertson, Ronnie *(Cast)* 2097, 3287
Robertson, Ross *(Cast)* 2492
Robertson, Scott *(Cast)* 262
Robertson, Will *(Director)* 4193
Robertson, Will *(Producer)* 4193
Robertston, Warren *(Cast)* 1046
Robeson, Paul *(Cast)* 2225, 4504
Robey, Ken *(Producer)* 1898
Robi, Armand *(Composer)* 1314
Robi, Armand *(Director)* 1314
Robi, Armand *(Librettist)* 1314
Robin, Gil *(Composer)* 964
Robin, Jean-Claude *(Costumes)* 1713
Robin, Leo *(Additional Lyrics)* 2976
Robin, Leo *(Composer)* 1916
Robin, Leo *(Lyricist)* 2, 86, 393, 464, 577, 605, 663, 1475, 1548, 1691, 1839, 1916, 2076, 2253, 2277, 2367, 2372, 2392, 2590, 2976, 3020, 3138, 3249, 3683, 3800, 3946, 4291, 4582, 4706
Robin, Sid *(Composer)* 1296
Robin, Sid *(Lyricist)* 1296
Robins, Edward H. *(Cast)* 2432, 2444, 3225
Robins, Isobel *(Cast)* 4627
Robins, Isobel *(Producer)* 4627
Robins, J.J. *(Lyricist)* 3103
Robins, Kenneth *(Librettist)* 2441
Robins, Kenneth *(Lyricist)* 2441
Robinson, A. *(Lyricist)* 3946
Robinson, Adelaide *(Cast)* 340
Robinson, Andre *(Cast)* 3814
Robinson, Ann *(Cast)* 2817
Robinson, Anna *(Cast)* 1392
Robinson, Armin *(Author)* 2610, 4365
Robinson, Bartlett *(Cast)* 3082
Robinson, Bertrand *(Director)* 3713
Robinson, Bertrand *(Librettist)* 4673
Robinson, Bill *(Cast)* 70, 441, 444, 445, 497, 567, 883, 1416, 1984, 1987, 2817, 3153
Robinson, Bill "Bojangles" *(Cast)* 888
Robinson, Blondie *(Cast)* 1821
Robinson, Cardew *(Cast)* 3630
Robinson, Charles *(Author)* 3138
Robinson, Charles *(Cast)* 2853
Robinson, Charles *(Director)* 2853
Robinson, Charles *(Librettist)* 2853
Robinson, Charles *(Lyricist)* 2853
Robinson, Charles *(Producer)* 2853
Robinson, Cheryl *(Cast)* 1616
Robinson, Christine *(Costumes)* 2204
Robinson, Clarence *(Cast)* 2302, 3709
Robinson, Clarence *(Choreographer)* 883, 897, 2302
Robinson, Clarence *(Director)* 875, 883
Robinson, Clark *(Lighting Designer)* 418, 1779, 2423
Robinson, Clark *(Set Design)* 557, 568, 1013, 1127, 1691, 1692, 1779, 1780, 2300, 3005, 3006, 3007, 3008, 3009, 3172, 3431, 3436, 3735, 3850, 4572, 4741
Robinson, David *(Composer)* 1298
Robinson, David *(Costumes)* 3568
Robinson, David *(Lyricist)* 1298
Robinson, Doug *(Cast)* 382
Robinson, Earl *(Composer)* 467, 1674, 1840, 2175, 2447, 3831, 3986
Robinson, Earl *(Librettist)* 3831
Robinson, Earl *(Lyricist)* 1840
Robinson, Edward G. *(Cast)* 1283
Robinson, Edward G. *(Musical Director)* 3944, 4288
Robinson, Florence *(Cast)* 1491, 1806
Robinson, Hal *(Cast)* 4790
Robinson, J. Russel *(Composer)* 481, 565, 1129, 2308, 2706, 2856, 3513, 4271
Robinson, J. Russel *(Lyricist)* 2706, 2856, 3953, 4271
Robinson, Jack (Director) 1337
Robinson, Jack *(Librettist)* 1337
Robinson, Lilla Cayley *(Lyricist)* 1526
Robinson, Mabel *(Choreographer)* 2173, 2692
Robinson, Martin P. *(Cast)* 2544
Robinson, Meghan *(Cast)* 3606
Robinson, Muriel *(Composer)* 3557
Robinson, Muriel *(Lyricist)* 3557
Robinson, Phyllis *(Lyricist)* 935
Robinson, Richard *(Composer)* 2913
Robinson, Richard *(Lyricist)* 2913
Robinson, Roberta *(Cast)* 294
Robinson, Roger *(Cast)* 105, 2852
Robinson, Ruth *(Cast)* 4705
Robinson, Smokey *(Composer)* 4534
Robinson, Smokey *(Lyricist)* 4534
Robinson, Walter *(Cast)* 3450
Robinson, Wayne *(Arrangements)* 928
Robinson, Wayne *(Orchestrations)* 2443
Robinson, William *(Composer)* 166
Robinson, William *(Lyricist)* 166

Robinson Jr., Andre *(Director)* 2239
Robinson-Wayne, Beatrice *(Cast)* 1366
Robison, Willard *(Composer)* 478, 1448, 4271, 4291
Robison, Willard *(Lyricist)* 478, 1448, 4271, 4291
Robledo, Julian *(Composer)* 1687
Robson, Eleanor *(Cast)* 2819
Robson, Maud *(Cast)* 1429
Robson, May *(Author)* 4351
Robson, May *(Cast)* 405, 2160, 2844, 3693, 4351
Robson, Robert *(Cast)* 3829
Robson, T.F. *(Lyricist)* 3268
Roby, Fred *(Cast)* 1326
Robyn, Alfred *(Composer)* 307
Robyn, Alfred G. *(Composer)* 68, 307, 1578, 2179, 3065, 3268, 3562, 3581, 4754, 4762
Rocco, James *(Cast)* 2861
Roche, Eugene *(Cast)* 3863
Roche, Jack *(Librettist)* 4377
Roche, Mary *(Cast)* 3893
Roche, Tudi *(Cast)* 3555
Rochelle, Lisa *(Cast)* 2925
Rochester, W.F. *(Cast)* 104
Rock, Norman *(Set Design)* 4486
Rock, William *(Cast)* 632, 1417, 1526, 1919, 2456, 2793, 3313, 3738, 3973, 4161, 4311, 4810, 4836
Rock, William *(Choreographer)* 632, 1151, 1230, 3085, 3313, 4425
Rock, William *(Producer)* 3973
Rockets, The *(Cast)* 2259
Rockettes, The *(Cast)* 1146, 1298, 1638, 2689, 3637
Rockwell, Doc *(Cast)* 1693
Rockwell, Doctor *(Cast)* 2460, 3639
Rockwell, George "Doc" *(Cast)* 1483
Rockwell, Maude *(Cast)* 1531, 3982
Rockwell, Penny *(Librettist)* 1785
Rodale, J.J. *(Librettist)* 4157, 4401
Rodale, J.J. *(Producer)* 4157
Rodd, Marcia *(Cast)* 302, 2049, 2599, 3217, 3927
Rodd, Marcia *(Voice)* 3498
Rodden, Dan *(Librettist)* 932
Rode, Alfred *(Cast)* 125
Roden, Illa *(Cast)* 1413
Roder, Milan *(Composer)* 1313
Roder, Milan *(Musical Director)* 815, 1250, 2756
Roder, Milan *(Orchestrations)* 1250
Roderick, William *(Cast)* 1925
Rodgers, Bob *(Cast)* 407, 411, 412, 413
Rodgers, Bob *(Director)* 407, 408, 410, 411, 412, 413, 1341
Rodgers, Bob *(Librettist)* 407, 408, 410, 411, 412, 413, 1341
Rodgers, Bob *(Lyricist)* 1341
Rodgers, Chev *(Cast)* 757
Rodgers, Douglas Fletcher *(Cast)* 3509
Rodgers, Eileen *(Cast)* 722, 1047, 1280, 2304, 4312
Rodgers, Gladys *(Lyricist)* 2302
Rodgers, Howard Emmett *(Librettist)* 709
Rodgers, Mary *(Composer)* 51, 912, 997, 1257, 1389, 1408, 1991, 2663, 2677, 3288, 3498, 3967, 4388, 4744
Rodgers, Mary *(Librettist)* 912
Rodgers, Mary *(Lyricist)* 912, 997, 4363
Rodgers, Mortimer W. *(Lyricist)* 4477, 4530
Rodgers, Richard
See also Herbert Richard Lorenz.
Rodgers, Richard *(Cast)* 3153
Rodgers, Richard *(Composer)* 66, 85, 111, 134, 146, 247, 265, 372, 376, 418, 420, 514, 601, 660, 703, 711, 738, 759, 791, 792, 834, 978, 1013, 1040, 1060, 1202, 1267, 1298, 1315, 1321, 1446, 1447, 1448, 1529, 1724, 1725, 1749, 1763, 1800, 1894, 1944, 2031, 2032, 2061, 2064, 2068, 2102, 2193, 2205, 2258, 2263, 2312, 2382, 2389, 2459, 2467, 2574, 2611, 2677, 2772, 2797, 3018, 3020, 3128, 3172, 3175, 3187, 3261, 3263, 3274, 3283, 3291, 3296, 3353, 3428, 3436, 3505, 3518, 3521, 3538, 3546, 3556, 3595, 3634, 3702, 3743, 3847, 3848, 3924, 3936, 3955, 3967, 3980, 3989, 4059, 4095, 4096, 4118, 4146, 4235, 4304, 4399, 4420, 4477, 4481, 4498, 4519, 4530, 4709, 4749, 4780, 4781
Rodgers, Richard *(Director)* 2193
Rodgers, Richard *(Librettist)* 247, 601, 978, 2061, 2102, 2193, 3283, 4304
Rodgers, Richard *(Lyricist)* 134, 372, 978, 1321, 1725, 2102, 3128, 3187, 3296, 4095, 4146, 4420, 4477, 4530
Rodgers, Richard *(Musical Director)* 265, 978, 1013, 1321, 1446, 2102, 3595, 4304, 4780, 4781
Rodgers, Richard *(Producer)* 153, 372, 601, 1060, 1315, 1749, 2312, 2797, 3187, 3505, 4095, 4096, 4481
Rodgers, Robert *(Orchestrations)* 2877
Rodgers, Rod *(Choreographer)* 3599
Rodgers, Shev *(Cast)* 1500, 3612
Rodges, Stanley *(Cast)* 2768
Rodman, David *(Musical Director)* 4431
Rodney, Jean *(Producer)* 4256
Rodriguez, Burt *(Cast)* 2472
Rodriguez, Charlie J. *(Cast)* 2962
Rodriguez, Domingo *(Lighting Designer)* 3490
Rodriguez, Domingo *(Set Design)* 3490
Rodriguez, G.H. Matos *(Composer)* 1638
Roe, Patricia *(Cast)* 1990, 4380
Roeder, Chas W. *(Costumes)* 3697
Roele, Walter S. *(Composer)* 4668
Roelker, Edward *(Set Design)* 378
Roemheld, Heinz *(Composer)* 4137
Roerick, William *(Cast)* 1762, 4449
Roesner, George *(Librettist)* 3011
Roff, Rev. Joseph *(Composer)* 2393
Roffman, Frederick *(Dance Arranger)* 164
Roffman, Frederick *(Musical Director)* 164
Roffman, Frederick *(Vocal Arranger)* 164
Roger, Alan *(Orchestrations)* 1741
Roger, Victor *(Author)* 1994, 3784
Roger, Victor *(Composer)* 1994
Rogers, Alex *(Cast)* 9, 254, 295, 984, 2979
Rogers, Alex *(Composer)* 2111, 2127, 2690, 4390, 4697
Rogers, Alex *(Director)* 9, 3054, 4339
Rogers, Alex *(Librettist)* 9, 254, 295, 984, 2690, 2979, 4339
Rogers, Alex *(Lyricist)* 9, 254, 295, 1587, 2111, 2127, 2690, 2979, 3054, 3915, 4088, 4339, 4390, 4697, 4804, 4813
Rogers, Alex *(Producer)* 4339
Rogers, Alexander *(Cast)* 2111

Rogers, Ann *(Cast)* 1733
Rogers, Anne *(Cast)* 4798
Rogers, Ben *(Cast)* 2028
Rogers, Bob *(Costumes)* 4584
Rogers, Buddy *(Cast)* 1979
Rogers, Buddy *(Director)* 1604
Rogers, Cynthia *(Cast)* 1286, 1448
Rogers, David *(Cast)* 1236
Rogers, David *(Librettist)* 699, 2168, 4827, 4828, 4829
Rogers, David *(Lyricist)* 602, 699, 2168, 2288, 3110, 4461, 4566, 4828, 4829
Rogers, Dick *(Composer)* 1539
Rogers, Dick *(Lyricist)* 1539, 1713
Rogers, Don Loring *(Cast)* 1782
Rogers, Doug *(Choreographer)* 2016, 3159, 4124
Rogers, E.W. *(Lyricist)* 4642
Rogers, Earl *(Vocal Arranger)* 4828
Rogers, Ed *(Composer)* 2991
Rogers, Ed *(Lyricist)* 2991
Rogers, Emmett *(Producer)* 3188, 4278
Rogers, Eric *(Orchestrations)* 3271, 3482
Rogers, Ferne *(Cast)* 3677
Rogers, Frederick *(Cast)* 1316
Rogers, Ginger *(Cast)* 1528, 3493, 4426
Rogers, Gus *(Cast)* 3744, 3745, 3746, 3747, 3748, 3749, 3750, 3751
Rogers, Gus *(Producer)* 3748
Rogers, Hilda *(Cast)* 2690, 3054
Rogers, Howard *(Lyricist)* 4813
Rogers, Howard E. *(Lyricist)* 2856
Rogers, Howard Emmett *(Director)* 2636
Rogers, Howard Emmett *(Librettist)* 684, 2636, 2856
Rogers, Jaime *(Cast)* 1601
Rogers, Jaime *(Choreographer)* 1158
Rogers, James D. *(Cast)* 345
Rogers, Jay *(Cast)* 2022
Rogers, Jay *(Composer)* 1506
Rogers, Jay *(Lyricist)* 1506
Rogers, Jo Jean *(Cast)* 2597
Rogers, John P. *(Cast)* 801, 803
Rogers, Lavinia *(Cast)* 254, 295
Rogers, Louis T. *(Producer)* 3241
Rogers, Marshall *(Cast)* 2881
Rogers, Max *(Cast)* 1738, 3525, 3744, 3745, 3746, 3747, 3748, 3749, 3750, 3751, 4787
Rogers, Max *(Producer)* 3748
Rogers, Mickie *(Cast)* 3264
Rogers, Paul *(Cast)* 1864
Rogers, Phyllis *(Cast)* 2597
Rogers, Ralph *(Cast)* 1833
Rogers, Ric *(Lighting Designer)* 2239
Rogers, Robert *(Arrangements)* 1590, 3111
Rogers, Robert *(Dance Arranger)* 2898
Rogers, Robert *(Musical Director)* 1590, 3111, 3491, 4701
Rogers, Robert *(Orchestrations)* 1590
Rogers, Robert *(Vocal Arranger)* 4701
Rogers, Shoshanna *(Cast)* 1500
Rogers, Stanley *(Cast)* 1462
Rogers, Vivien *(Cast)* 3031
Rogers, Will *(Cast)* 792, 1735, 2403, 3087, 4345, 4589, 4816, 4818, 4819, 4834, 4844
Rogers, Will *(Librettist)* 4818, 4819
Rogerson, Bob *(Cast)* 1349
Rogerson, Clarence *(Musical Director)* 353, 1783, 1912, 2745, 4313
Rogge, Florence *(Choreographer)* 4569, 4620
Rogness, Peter *(Set Design)* 261, 3561
Rogoff, Renee *(Cast)* 2483
Rogosin, Roy *(Musical Director)* 3643
Rogosin, Roy M. *(Composer)* 3629
Rogosin, Roy M. *(Director)* 3629
Rogosin, Roy M. *(Librettist)* 3629
Rogosin, Roy M. *(Musical Director)* 4408
Rohrer, Andy *(Cast)* 3653
Roland, Steve *(Cast)* 3294, 3889
Rolfe, Wendy A. *(Costumes)* 1232
Rolfing, Tom *(Cast)* 1377
Rolin, Judi *(Cast)* 58
Roll, Eddie *(Cast)* 4090, 4625
Roll, Edward *(Choreographer)* 3612
Rolle, Esther *(Cast)* 1074, 1592, 2719
Roller, Olga *(Cast)* 2665
Rollins, Jack *(Composer)* 3793
Rollins, Jack *(Producer)* 3112
Rollins, Pierce *(Lyricist)* 3530
Rollins, Rowena *(Cast)* 597, 843
Rollins, Sherwood *(Composer)* 1231
Rollins, Sherwood *(Lyricist)* 1231
Rollit, George *(Lyricist)* 3976
Rollnick, William D. *(Producer)* 757
Rolph, Marti *(Cast)* 1329, 3817
Rolt, Bernard *(Composer)* 719, 954, 1537, 2724, 2964, 3313
Rolt, Bernard *(Lyricist)* 719, 954, 1537, 3313
Roma, Caro *(Cast)* 2848
Roma, Caro *(Composer)* 2415
Roma, Jimmy *(Cast)* 4829
Romagnoli, Joe *(Cast)* 3548
Romaguera, Joaquin *(Cast)* 2674, 4233
Romaine, George *(Cast)* 335
Romaine, Margaret *(Cast)* 2854
Romaine, W.L. *(Cast)* 2724, 3486
Roman, Bob *(Cast)* 1017
Roman, Lawrence *(Author)* 3338
Roman, Martin *(Composer)* 1358
Roman, Paul Reid *(Cast)* 1729
Romann, Susan *(Cast)* 1249
Romann, Susan *(Conductor)* 3602
Romann, Susan *(Musical Director)* 1249, 2579, 4577, 4595
Romano, Cathi *(Cast)* 2580
Romano, Jane *(Cast)* 483
Romano, Tom *(Lyricist)* 3810
Romanoff, Prince Michael *(Cast)* 3850
Romay, Lina *(Cast)* 2850
Romberg, Sigmund *(Cast)* 3153
Romberg, Sigmund *(Composer)* 152, 200, 201, 463, 473, 480, 487, 718, 910, 965, 969, 1027, 1065, 1096, 1145, 1334, 1335, 1352, 1530, 1548, 1735, 1852, 2135,

2384, 2594, 2601, 2602, 2684, 2696, 2757, 2786, 2794, 2813, 2816, 2939, 3018, 3020, 3051, 3056, 3063, 3064, 3117, 3170, 3253, 3333, 3397, 3400, 3401, 3402, 3403, 3406, 3407, 3538, 3586, 3737, 3766, 3769, 3778, 3799, 3958, 3985, 4121, 4188, 4214, 4350, 4524, 4657, 4747, 4819
Romberg, Sigmund *(Producer)* 2601, 2684
Rome, Fred *(Librettist)* 4416
Rome, Harold *(Composer)* 5, 59, 454, 620, 1029, 1242, 1616, 1763, 2048, 2130, 2447, 2504, 2653, 2718, 2850, 3018, 3074, 3178, 3501, 3563, 3761, 3990, 4009, 4099, 4131, 4141, 4174, 4323, 4592, 4617, 4718, 4826, 4863
Rome, Harold *(Incidental Music)* 3761
Rome, Harold *(Librettist)* 3990
Rome, Harold *(Lyricist)* 5, 59, 454, 620, 1029, 1242, 1616, 1763, 2048, 2130, 2362, 2447, 2504, 2653, 2718, 2850, 3018, 3074, 3178, 3501, 3563, 3761, 3986, 3990, 4009, 4099, 4131, 4141, 4174, 4323, 4592, 4617, 4718, 4826, 4863
Romeo, John *(Cast)* 114
Romeo, Max *(Composer)* 3690
Romeo, Max *(Lyricist)* 3690
Romeo, Signor *(Choreographer)* 3570
Romeo, Vincente *(Choreographer)* 4753
Romeo, Vincenzo *(Cast)* 286
Romeo, Vincenzo *(Choreographer)* 3093, 4046, 4452
Romeo, Vincenzo *(Director)* 286
Romeo Jr., Vincent *(Cast)* 3093
Romer, Leila *(Cast)* 4046
Romero, Alex *(Choreographer)* 1760, 3524
Romero, Cesar *(Cast)* 4043, 4170
Romero, Miguel *(Set Design)* 2953
Romilli, G. *(Composer)* 1281
Romilli, G. *(Lyricist)* 1281
Romoff, Colin *(Composer)* 4395, 4828, 4829
Romoff, Colin *(Dance Arranger)* 2965
Romoff, Colin *(Musical Director)* 1227, 2355, 2777, 2965, 3577, 4399, 4609
Romoff, Colin *(Pianist)* 3845
Romoff, Colin *(Vocal Arranger)* 2777, 2965, 3577, 4609
Romoff, Wood *(Cast)* 2838, 3918
Romoff, Woody *(Cast)* 3526
Romshinsky, Joseph *(Composer)* 573
Ron, Shoshana *(Cast)* 2421
Ronald, Landon *(Composer)* 3976
Rondell, Gloria *(Cast)* 3104
Ronell, Ann *(Composer)* 478, 901, 933, 2841, 3946
Ronell, Ann *(Lyricist)* 478, 901, 933, 2841, 3946
Ronn, E. *(Lyricist)* 3617
Ronstadt, Linda *(Cast)* 2359
Rooney *(Composer)* 1318
Rooney, Katie *(Cast)* 3024
Rooney, Mickey *(Cast)* 2975, 3496, 3833, 4197, 4577
Rooney, Mickey *(Composer)* 2259, 4197
Rooney, Mickey *(Lyricist)* 4197
Rooney, Mickey *(Voice)* 3793
Rooney, Pat *(Cast)* 994, 1395, 1505, 2403, 2601, 2851, 2865, 2964, 3166, 3717, 3745, 3751, 3911, 4265
Rooney, Pat *(Choreographer)* 3748
Rooney, Pat *(Director)* 994, 3717, 3911
Rooney, Sherry *(Cast)* 2235
Rooney, Wallace *(Cast)* 3441
Rooney III, Pat *(Cast)* 994
Rooney Sr., Pat *(Cast)* 1706
Roos, Casper *(Cast)* 181, 1060, 2142, 2874, 3928
Roos, Delmar *(Cast)* 3490
Roos, Joanna *(Librettist)* 2948
Roos, Patricia *(Cast)* 946
Roos, William *(Librettist)* 206, 911, 2850
Root, Lynn *(Librettist)* 612
Roovray, Verna *(Lyricist)* 3248
Ropes, Bradford *(Author)* 1359
Rork, Samuel E. *(Producer)* 1274, 3574
Rosa, Dennis *(Choreographer)* 3544, 3908
Rosa, Dennis *(Director)* 808, 3544, 3908
Rosa, Dennis *(Librettist)* 3544
Rosa, Patti *(Cast)* 4756
Rosaire, Robert *(Cast)* 396
Rosalie *(Cast)* 922
Rosato, Mary Lou *(Cast)* 693, 3733
Roscoe, Bill *(Composer)* 4768
Roscoe, Bill *(Lyricist)* 4768
Rose, Alice *(Cast)* 2995
Rose, Billy *(Composer)* 418, 2311, 3926
Rose, Billy *(Director)* 418
Rose, Billy *(Librettist)* 2653, 3100
Rose, Billy *(Lyricist)* 39, 173, 393, 397, 417, 418, 419, 420, 662, 702, 1126, 1667, 1672, 1779, 1873, 2204, 2413, 2460, 2706, 3018, 3020, 3100, 3149, 3166, 3179, 3249, 3342, 3796, 3926, 3975, 3980, 4235, 4264, 4465, 4799, 4815, 4818, 4824, 4825
Rose, Billy *(Producer)* 173, 397, 417, 418, 653, 662, 1267, 1672, 2258, 2413, 2460, 3166, 3893, 3975, 4235, 4465, 4567
Rose, Charles J. *(Cast)* 677
Rose, Charlie *(Cast)* 2113
Rose, David *(Composer)* 3683, 4706
Rose, David *(Lighting Designer)* 914
Rose, David *(Lyricist)* 4706
Rose, David *(Musical Director)* 3683
Rose, David *(Orchestrations)* 4706
Rose, Ed *(Composer)* 4654
Rose, Ed *(Lyricist)* 830, 1334, 1573, 4654, 4813
Rose, Edward *(Author)* 452
Rose, Edward *(Director)* 349, 361, 4422
Rose, Edward *(Producer)* 2543
Rose, Fred *(Composer)* 3404
Rose, Fred *(Lyricist)* 3404
Rose, George *(Cast)* 634, 798, 958, 2553, 3070, 4588
Rose, Gilberg *(Costumes)* 1244
Rose, Helen *(Costumes)* 2085, 2086, 2087, 2088, 2089, 2090, 2091
Rose, Howard *(Producer)* 4137
Rose, Jack *(Cast)* 3407
Rose, Jack *(Composer)* 924
Rose, Jack *(Lyricist)* 924
Rose, Jerry *(Choreographer)* 1781
Rose, Julian *(Cast)* 2119
Rose, L. Arthur *(Librettist)* 2798
Rose, L. Arthur *(Lyricist)* 2798

Rose, Lew *(Cast)* 3232
Rose, Lew *(Director)* 3232
Rose, Lew *(Librettist)* 3232
Rose, Lew *(Lyricist)* 3232
Rose, Louisa *(Librettist)* 300
Rose, Louisa *(Lyricist)* 300
Rose, Margot *(Cast)* 2074
Rose, Michael *(Musical Director)* 1256
Rose, Morris *(Producer)* 465
Rose, Patrick *(Cast)* 426
Rose, Patrick *(Composer)* 426
Rose, Philip *(Director)* 105, 135, 828, 3059, 3610
Rose, Philip *(Librettist)* 105, 828, 3610, 3928
Rose, Philip *(Producer)* 135, 519, 615, 3610, 3928, 4460
Rose, Ralph *(Director)* 567
Rose, Reva *(Cast)* 4783
Rose, S. Lee *(Choreographer)* 2780
Rose, Sam *(Choreographer)* 2, 290, 1929
Rose, Stephen *(Composer)* 164
Rose, Susan R. *(Producer)* 2242
Rose, Vincent *(Composer)* 487, 1120, 1126, 1136, 3246, 3739, 3985, 4284, 4534
Rose, Vincent *(Lyricist)* 1120, 1417, 4534
Rose Marie *(Cast)* 1040, 3153, 4117
Rosebach, Sophie *(Set Design)* 2739
Rosebrook, Leon *(Composer)* 3973
Rosebrook, Leon *(Musical Director)* 1513, 2371, 2519, 3973, 4213
Rosebrook, Leon *(Orchestrations)* 3973
Rosegarten, Rory *(Producer)* 2420
Roseleigh, Jack *(Director)* 1795
Roselle, William *(Cast)* 834, 1502, 1523
Rosemont, Norman *(Producer)* 1094
Rosemont, Walter L. *(Composer)* 2503, 2972, 4596
Rosemont, Walter L. *(Dance Arranger)* 2972
Rosemont, Walter L. *(Vocal Arranger)* 2972
Rosen, Arnie *(Librettist)* 4828, 4829
Rosen, Arnold *(Librettist)* 3524
Rosen, Burt *(Producer)* 1089
Rosen, Louis *(Composer)* 494
Rosen, Louis *(Librettist)* 494
Rosen, Louis *(Lyricist)* 494
Rosen, Marshal *(Composer)* 4829
Rosen, Sam *(Lyricist)* 90
Rosenbaum, Edward *(Producer)* 2780
Rosenberg, Billy *(Cast)* 4679
Rosenberg, Irene *(Librettist)* 3305
Rosenberg, Irene *(Lyricist)* 3305
Rosenberg, J.B. *(Librettist)* 3105
Rosenberg, J.B. *(Lyricist)* 3105
Rosenberg, Jan *(Musical Director)* 705, 3080
Rosenberg, Victor I. *(Producer)* 2643
Rosenblat, Barbara *(Cast)* 2646
Rosenblatt, Marcell *(Cast)* 3227
Rosenbloom, Jonathan *(Lighting Designer)* 1757
Rosenbloom, Jonathan *(Set Design)* 1757
Rosenblum, Ava *(Cast)* 4431
Rosenblum, Bob *(Librettist)* 4627
Rosenblum, Joshua *(Conductor)* 4442
Rosenblum, Robert *(Composer)* 4522
Rosenblum, Robert *(Librettist)* 4522
Rosenblum, Robert *(Lyricist)* 4522
Rosenburg, Sophie *(Costumes)* 1250
Rosener, George *(Author)* 4100
Rosener, George *(Director)* 2300, 3011
Rosener, George *(Librettist)* 199, 2300
Rosenfeld, Carl *(Director)* 1608
Rosenfeld, Carl *(Producer)* 1608
Rosenfeld, Grace *(Producer)* 3966
Rosenfeld, Hilary *(Costumes)* 1053, 1985, 2648, 2787, 3806, 4294
Rosenfeld, Lois F. *(Producer)* 305, 3992
Rosenfeld, M.H. *(Composer)* 2952
Rosenfeld, Moishe *(Librettist)* 4342
Rosenfeld, Moishe *(Lyricist)* 573, 1609, 4342
Rosenfeld, Moishe *(Producer)* 1609
Rosenfeld, Stephen *(Director)* 3557
Rosenfeld, Stephen *(Librettist)* 3557
Rosenfeld, Sydney *(Composer)* 4046, 4222
Rosenfeld, Sydney *(Librettist)* 526, 976, 1464, 1728, 1746, 1975, 2261, 2324, 2914, 2917, 3308, 3394, 3753, 3776, 4046, 4222, 4472, 4544
Rosenfeld, Sydney *(Lyricist)* 526, 1464, 1505, 1746, 1975, 2324, 2914, 2917, 3308, 3753, 3776, 4046, 4222, 4472
Rosenfeld, Sydney *(Producer)* 2324
Rosenfeld, Theodore *(Producer)* 1608
Rosenfield, Maurice *(Producer)* 305, 3992
Rosenstock, Milton *(Composer)* 3075
Rosenstock, Milton *(Musical Director)* 304, 363, 629, 823, 943, 1278, 1420, 1475, 1709, 1886, 1990, 1991, 2217, 2583, 2590, 2705, 3846, 4160, 4190, 4340, 4499, 4542
Rosenstock, Milton *(Vocal Arranger)* 1990, 2217, 4542
Rosenthal, Andrew *(Composer)* 4433
Rosenthal, Andrew *(Librettist)* 4433
Rosenthal, Andrew *(Lyricist)* 4433
Rosenthal, Chayele *(Cast)* 3559
Rosenthal, Harry *(Cast)* 2265
Rosenthal, Harry *(Composer)* 292, 3532, 3614, 3762
Rosenthal, Harry *(Musical Director)* 1396
Rosenthal, Jack *(Author)* 299
Rosenthal, Jack *(Librettist)* 299
Rosenthal, Jean *(Lighting Designer)* 170, 270, 322, 610, 837, 1007, 1012, 1029, 1265, 1383, 1422, 1456, 1764, 1828, 1990, 2000, 2050, 2106, 2190, 2201, 3687, 3767, 3837, 4095, 4270, 4384, 4395, 4625
Rosenthal, Jean *(Set Design)* 322, 837, 1383
Rosenthal, Laurence *(Composer)* 3931
Rosenthal, Laurence *(Dance Arranger)* 1076, 1614, 3016, 4270
Rosenthal, Leo *(Producer)* 2754
Rosenthal, Myron D. *(Librettist)* 4477, 4530
Rosenthal, Nancy *(Producer)* 1775
Roset, Val *(Choreographer)* 1539
Rosey, George *(Composer)* 2286
Rosey, George *(Librettist)* 2286
Rosey, Joseph *(Lyricist)* 3856, 3857
Rosing, Vladimir *(Director)* 1681
Rosko *(Cast)* 119
Rosley, Adrian *(Cast)* 4023, 4328
Rosner, Paul *(Lyricist)* 3890, 3940

Rosoff, Charles *(Composer)* 1138, 2253, 2392
Ross, Adrian *(Author)* 1384, 4115
Ross, Adrian *(Librettist)* 2131
Ross, Adrian *(Lyricist)* 284, 351, 379, 659, 767, 770, 902, 906, 1067, 1114, 1153, 1470, 1537, 1544, 1561, 1569, 1626, 1682, 1783, 2131, 2317, 2761, 2836, 2844, 2937, 3098, 3313, 3322, 3618, 3828, 3857, 3948, 3996, 3999, 4115, 4285, 4327, 4430, 4590, 4807
Ross, Al *(Composer)* 4543
Ross, Alan *(Cast)* 943
Ross, Allan *(Cast)* 1781
Ross, Allie *(Musical Director)* 26, 441
Ross, Annie *(Cast)* 920
Ross, Arthur *(Librettist)* 2809
Ross, Beverly *(Composer)* 4264
Ross, Beverly *(Lyricist)* 4264
Ross, Budd *(Cast)* 2895
Ross, Charles *(Cast)* 1900
Ross, Charles J. *(Cast)* 1264, 2041, 2603, 2835, 4044, 4658, 4712, 4801
Ross, Clarke *(Producer)* 3252
Ross, David *(Director)* 2178
Ross, David *(Producer)* 2178
Ross, Diana *(Cast)* 1389
Ross, Diane *(Choreographer)* 345
Ross, Don *(Cast)* 4824
Ross, Don *(Librettist)* 204
Ross, Don *(Producer)* 204
Ross, Eliza *(Cast)* 62
Ross, Eliza *(Librettist)* 1648
Ross, Hank *(Musical Director)* 2320
Ross, Herbert *(Cast)* 341, 3947, 4565
Ross, Herbert *(Choreographer)* 98, 162, 170, 483, 1060, 1456, 2000, 2048, 2304, 3274, 4435, 4446
Ross, Herbert *(Director)* 2304
Ross, Howard *(Cast)* 652, 3469, 4004
Ross, Howard *(Composer)* 3020
Ross, Howard *(Lyricist)* 3020
Ross, Hugh *(Musical Director)* 283, 1600
Ross, Jack *(Director)* 4106
Ross, Jamie *(Cast)* 181, 272, 427, 1045, 2199, 2563, 3235, 3439, 4727
Ross, Jerry *(Cast)* 1101
Ross, Jerry *(Composer)* 957, 2227, 3351, 4399
Ross, Jerry *(Lyricist)* 957, 2227, 3351, 4399
Ross, Joe *(Cast)* 98, 483, 937, 1511, 4319
Ross, Jonathan *(Cast)* 3485
Ross, Judith *(Librettist)* 4558
Ross, Justin *(Cast)* 1371, 1637, 2953, 3181, 4618
Ross, King *(Orchestrations)* 3946
Ross, Lynn *(Cast)* 4625
Ross, Mae *(Cast)* 2089
Ross, Marilyn *(Cast)* 1300
Ross, Martin *(Cast)* 2026, 2584
Ross, Marty *(Cast)* 4623
Ross, Michael *(Director)* 1993, 4566, 4627
Ross, Robert *(Cast)* 4142
Ross, Robert *(Director)* 901, 1546, 2817
Ross, Roy *(Cast)* 1109
Ross, Sandra *(Lighting Designer)* 2272
Ross, Shirley *(Cast)* 1894
Ross, Stanley Stephen *(Composer)* 695
Ross, Stanley Stephen *(Librettist)* 695
Ross, Stanley Stephen *(Lyricist)* 695
Ross, Stephen *(Lighting Designer)* 3066
Ross, Stuart *(Choreographer)* 674, 1353, 1813
Ross, Stuart *(Director)* 1353, 1813
Ross, Stuart *(Librettist)* 1353, 1813, 4139
Ross, Ted *(Cast)* 578, 952, 3610, 3656, 4722
Ross, Tom *(Librettist)* 4518
Ross, William *(Producer)* 1740
Rosse, Frederick *(Composer)* 2317, 3882
Rosse, Frederick *(Lyricist)* 3882
Rosse, Herman *(Set Design)* 1672, 1827, 4567
Rossen, Debbie *(Cast)* 2521
Rossetti, Christina *(Author)* 1589
Rossetti, Christina *(Lyricist)* 1589, 2633
Rossi, Tony *(Cast)* 2676
Rossini, Giochino *(Composer)* 4342
Rossini, Giochino *(Music Based On)* 225
Rossiter, Len *(Cast)* 1386
Rossiter, P.T. *(Producer)* 3236
Rossiter, Will *(Arrangements)* 2552
Rost, Leo *(Librettist)* 2759
Rost, Leo *(Lyricist)* 2759
Rostand, Edmond *(Author)* 945, 946, 947, 948, 949, 1245, 4073, 4670
Rosten, Leo *(Author)* 1158, 2422
Roston, Karen *(Costumes)* 1512, 2142, 2195
Rotante, Ted *(Choreographer)* 2992
Rotenberg, David *(Director)* 3136
Rotenberg, David *(Librettist)* 3136
Roter, Ted *(Cast)* 2321
Roter, Ted *(Librettist)* 2321
Roth, Ann *(Costumes)* 374, 1194, 1441, 2053, 3516, 3564, 3610, 3787, 3869, 3992, 4334
Roth, Charles *(Lyricist)* 4543
Roth, Daryl *(Producer)* 261, 784, 992, 3142
Roth, Don *(Librettist)* 2834
Roth, Jack *(Cast)* 860, 862
Roth, Lillian *(Cast)* 1134, 1136, 2048, 3342, 3900, 4847
Roth, Lillian *(Composer)* 1134
Roth, Lillian *(Lyricist)* 1134
Roth, Michael *(Musical Director)* 1015
Roth, Michael *(Vocal Arranger)* 1015
Roth, Michael S. *(Musical Director)* 2787
Roth, Michael S. *(Vocal Arranger)* 2787
Roth, Murray *(Lyricist)* 1685, 1686, 2706, 3400
Roth, Nat *(Producer)* 618, 2515, 2548
Roth, Nathaniel *(Producer)* 4624
Roth, Robert Jess *(Director)* 330
Roth, Wolfgang *(Set Design)* 3543, 4176
Rothafel, Samuel "Roxy" *(Producer)* 3639
Rothlein, Arlene *(Choreographer)* 3418
Rothman, Bernard *(Producer)* 3499
Rothpearl, Harry *(Producer)* 400, 1269, 4773
Rothweiler Jr., Larry N. *(Musical Director)* 4107
Rotondaro, Stephen *(Costumes)* 3178
Rotondi, Michael G. *(Cast)* 139

Rotov, Alexis *(Cast)* 4486
Rott, Bernard *(Composer)* 1579
Roudenko, Lubov *(Cast)* 153
Roullier, Ron *(Composer)* 3697
Roulston, Allison *(Lyricist)* 128, 1049
Roundabout Theater Company *(Producer)* 572, 3598, 4175
Rounds, David *(Cast)* 273, 1373, 1872, 2935, 3780, 4330
Rounds, David *(Director)* 4330
Rounds, David *(Set Design)* 4330
Rounds, Gene *(Cast)* 4584
Rounseville, Robert *(Cast)* 247, 630, 1894, 2344, 2727, 3612, 3647, 4479
Rourke, M.E.
See also Herbert Reynolds.
Rourke, M.E. *(Librettist)* 506
Rourke, M.E. *(Lyricist)* 121, 506, 954, 1066, 1067, 1151, 1152, 1246, 1455, 1464, 1519, 1538, 1569, 1613, 1888, 2282, 2317, 2341, 2358, 2469, 2498, 2761, 2793, 2952, 3177, 3322, 3679, 3710, 3996, 4115, 4219, 4726
Rousseau, Emil *(Cast)* 4092
Roussimoff, Ari *(Cast)* 2356
Roussin, Andre *(Author)* 3338
Routledge, Patricia *(Cast)* 134, 989, 2617, 3846, 4004
Roven, Glen *(Composer)* 4, 1638
Roven, Glen *(Dance Arranger)* 1082
Roven, Glen *(Lyricist)* 1638
Roven, Glen *(Musical Director)* 4197
Rovin, Robert *(Cast)* 366, 2913, 3551
Rowan, James *(Cast)* 3840
Rowe, Caryl *(Cast)* 407
Rowe, Eleanor *(Cast)* 2814
Rowe, Hansford *(Cast)* 2026, 2346, 3992
Rowe, Josephine V. *(Lyricist)* 2662
Rowland, Adele *(Cast)* 17, 1318, 1793, 1852, 2040, 2119, 2292, 2334, 2385, 2695, 2793, 3193, 3304, 3672, 4115, 4381
Rowland, Betty *(Composer)* 1637
Rowland, Betty *(Lyricist)* 1637
Rowland, Julia *(Cast)* 917
Rowland, Rowena *(Cast)* 3410
Rowland, Steve *(Cast)* 2053
Rowland, William *(Cast)* 1502
Rowland & Clifford Amus. Co *(Producer)* 3316
Rowlands, Gena *(Cast)* 63
Rowler, Adele *(Cast)* 4453
Rowles, Polly *(Cast)* 3187, 4114
Rowley, Bill *(Cast)* 3708
Rowley, Eddie *(Cast)* 77
Rowley, J. Henry *(Costumes)* 1459, 1900
Rowser, Bertin *(Composer)* 535
Rowser, Bertin *(Director)* 535
Rowser, Bertin *(Lyricist)* 535
Rox, John *(Composer)* 70, 1342, 2227, 3108
Rox, John *(Lyricist)* 70, 1342, 2168, 2227, 3108
Roxolo, Conrado N. *(Author)* 1046
Roy, Lillian *(Composer)* 632
Roy, Neil *(Cast)* 2238
Roy, Sheila *(Cast)* 790
Roy, Vernon *(Lyricist)* 675, 954, 3753
Roy, William *(Cast)* 262, 272
Roy, William *(Composer)* 272, 427, 1049, 1107, 1363, 2357, 2680, 3110, 3439, 3484, 3889, 4134
Roy, William *(Librettist)* 3439
Roy, William *(Lyricist)* 272, 1107, 1363, 2680, 3439, 3484, 3889
Roy, William *(Musical Director)* 262, 272, 427, 3889
Roy, William *(Orchestrations)* 1049
Roy, William *(Pianist)* 1049, 1107, 3484, 3889
Roy, William *(Vocal Arranger)* 272, 1049, 1107, 1363, 3889
Royal, Charles *(Cast)* 3005
Royal, Mathew J. *(Librettist)* 235
Royal, Reginald *(Additional Lyrics)* 4460
Royal, Reginald *(Additional Music)* 4460
Royal, Reginald *(Musical Director)* 1296
Royal, Ted *(Orchestrations)* 90, 153, 180, 189, 206, 483, 507, 530, 1045, 1109, 1300, 1494, 1539, 1706, 1760, 1930, 2000, 2103, 2187, 2227, 2453, 2479, 2707, 2817, 2940, 2987, 3036, 3091, 3107, 3108, 3110, 3278, 3347, 3801, 3895, 4015, 4018, 4058, 4123, 4362, 4377, 4652
Royal, Ted *(Vocal Arranger)* 1539
Royal Pardon Productions *(Producer)* 4390
Royce, Edward *(Choreographer)* 333, 683, 1066, 1454, 2614, 3819
Royce, Edward *(Director)* 152, 168, 379, 627, 684, 685, 765, 815, 1598, 1625, 1784, 2070, 2148, 2308, 2336, 2340, 2412, 2424, 2430, 2594, 2614, 2761, 2829, 3230, 3245, 3250, 3312, 3740, 3819, 3924, 4814, 4843, 4853
Royce, Edward *(Librettist)* 3246
Royce, Edward *(Lyricist)* 3246
Royce, Edward *(Producer)* 577, 765, 3312
Royce, Jack *(Lyricist)* 390
Royce, Louise *(Cast)* 4724
Royce, Shirley *(Cast)* 764
Royce, Stanley *(Composer)* 3238
Royce, William *(Director)* 1966
Royce Jr., E.W. *(Choreographer)* 2514
Roye, Dorothy *(Cast)* 711
Roye, Ruth *(Cast)* 3589
Royle, Edwin Milton *(Author)* 4664
Royle, Edwin Milton *(Director)* 2765
Royle, Edwin Milton *(Librettist)* 2765, 2951
Royle, Edwin Milton *(Lyricist)* 2951
Roynton, Helen *(Cast)* 734
Royon *(Composer)* 1869
Royston, Roy *(Cast)* 791, 2263, 3431, 4025, 4532
Rozario, Bob *(Musical Director)* 2969
Rozario, Bob *(Orchestrations)* 2969
Rozovsky, M. *(Composer)* 4176
Rozovsky, Mark *(Author)* 4176
Rubel, Reverand Hines *(Composer)* 3104
Ruben, Aaron *(Director)* 1567
Ruben, Jose *(Cast)* 672, 3680
Ruben, Jose *(Director)* 82, 324, 672, 1352, 2786, 4428, 4733
Rubens, Bernice *(Author)* 2065
Rubens, Hugo *(Composer)* 2255
Rubens, Maurie *(Composer)* 201, 202, 545, 551, 1113,

1460, 1461, 1462, 1678, 1693, 1836, 2293, 2637, 2669, 2747, 2789, 2843, 3012, 3084, 3148, 3150, 3523, 3680, 4010, 4669
Rubens, Maurie *(Musical Director)* 2540
Rubens, Paul *(Author)* 3052
Rubens, Paul *(Composer)* 30, 276, 379, 470, 906, 954, 1188, 1313, 1391, 1472, 1526, 1537, 1538, 1544, 1561, 1666, 2495, 2526, 2761, 2889, 2901, 3052, 3079, 3259, 3313, 3387, 3828, 3856, 3857, 4219, 4354, 4418, 4419, 4430, 4813
Rubens, Paul *(Librettist)* 2889, 4219, 4354
Rubens, Paul *(Lyricist)* 30, 276, 379, 470, 954, 1188, 1313, 1391, 1537, 1538, 2761, 2889, 2901, 3052, 3259, 3313, 3387, 3856, 3857, 4219, 4354, 4418, 4419, 4430
Rubens, Paul A. *(Composer)* 1537, 2844, 4430
Rubens, Paul A. *(Lyricist)* 2844, 3857, 4219, 4430
Rubens, Walter *(Composer)* 4354
Rubenstein, Arthur *(Orchestrations)* 4659
Rubenstein, Arthur B. *(Composer)* 496, 1634
Rubenstein, Barbara *(Cast)* 576
Rubenstein, Carol *(Lighting Designer)* 3209
Rubenstein, Marty *(Vocal Arranger)* 2804
Rubenstein, Steve *(Producer)* 963
Rubin, Arthur *(Cast)* 2295
Rubin, Arthur *(Producer)* 36, 695, 975, 2437
Rubin, Benny *(Cast)* 1722
Rubin, Benny *(Choreographer)* 1722
Rubin, Charles *(Librettist)* 109
Rubin, Cyma *(Producer)* 1063
Rubin, Pedro *(Cast)* 3719
Rubin, Ruth *(Composer)* 1609
Rubin, Ruth *(Lyricist)* 1609
Rubin, Steven *(Set Design)* 1732, 3760
Rubinek, Saul *(Cast)* 2429
Rubins, Josh *(Composer)* 572
Rubins, Josh *(Librettist)* 572
Rubins, Josh *(Lyricist)* 572
Rubinstein, Arthur *(Musical Director)* 1441
Rubinstein, Arthur *(Orchestrations)* 2599, 4405
Rubinstein, Arthur B. *(Incidental Music)* 1634
Rubinstein, Arthur B. *(Musical Director)* 1634
Rubinstein, John *(Cast)* 3506, 4535
Rubinstein, Ruth *(Cast)* 3501
Ruby, Cyrus *(Lyricist)* 3248
Ruby, Harry *(Author)* 2467
Ruby, Harry *(Cast)* 79, 1396
Ruby, Harry *(Composer)* 142, 176, 358, 545, 1297, 1368, 1617, 1686, 1688, 1691, 1819, 1873, 1889, 1944, 2373, 2392, 2638, 2706, 2857, 3020, 3144, 3185, 3583, 3617, 3659, 3695, 3926, 4033, 4249, 4426, 4436, 4476, 4742, 4799, 4812, 4813, 4814, 4817
Ruby, Harry *(Librettist)* 1396, 1889, 1935, 1944, 3009, 3659, 3924, 4426
Ruby, Harry *(Lyricist)* 95, 930, 2392, 2638, 4814, 4817
Ruby, Harry *(Producer)* 4426
Ruby, Herman *(Lyricist)* 1643, 2857, 3248, 4806
Rubykate Inc. *(Producer)* 3653
Rudas, Anna *(Choreographer)* 1326
Rudas, Tibor *(Choreographer)* 1326
Rudd, Gertrude *(Cast)* 3026
Rudel, Julius *(Musical Director)* 2839, 4371
Rudel, Julius *(Orchestrations)* 4371
Rudel, Rickie *(Cast)* 821, 2641
Rudetsky, Seth *(Vocal Arranger)* 3004
Rudie, Evelyn *(Choreographer)* 2321
Rudie, Evelyn *(Lyricist)* 2321
Rudie, Evelyn *(Musical Director)* 2321
Rudin, Scott *(Producer)* 3411
Rudisill, Ivan *(Musical Director)* 598, 642, 680, 2276, 2528, 2636, 3508, 3622, 4241, 4360, 4426
Rudlev, Herbert *(Cast)* 4368
Rudnick, Max *(Producer)* 439, 1989
Rudolph, Jerome *(Producer)* 1727
Rudolph, Walter *(Musical Director)* 2089
Rudolph, Walter J. *(Arrangements)* 2090
Rudolph, Walter J. *(Musical Director)* 2090
Ruff, Alton *(Choreographer)* 2969
Ruffelle, Frances *(Cast)* 730, 2442
Ruffin, Clovis *(Costumes)* 2294
Ruffin, Eric *(Cast)* 2197
Ruffini, Giovanni *(Author)* 3197
Ruffo, Titta *(Cast)* 3639
Rugel, Yvette *(Cast)* 1482, 3401
Ruggles, Charles *(Cast)* 628, 2972, 3402, 3622, 3866, 4118, 4464
Ruggles, Charlie *(Cast)* 2479, 3287, 3650
Ruhl, Malcolm *(Cast)* 4740
Ruhl, Malcolm *(Musical Director)* 4740
Ruhl, Pat *(Cast)* 1107
Ruisinger, Thomas *(Cast)* 2689, 2737
Ruivivar, Francis *(Cast)* 2241, 3411, 3944
Ruiz, Randy *(Cast)* 3806
Rule, Arthur *(Musical Director)* 3139
Rule, Bert *(Composer)* 1026, 4393
Rule, Bert *(Lyricist)* 1026
Rule, Bert L. *(Composer)* 1963
Rule, Charles *(Cast)* 98, 273, 1634, 3702
Rule, James *(Composer)* 2662
Rule, Janice *(Cast)* 1745, 4273
Rumble, Andy *(Arrangements)* 846
Rumble, Andy *(Musical Director)* 846
Rumble, Andy *(Orchestrations)* 846
Rumbold, Hugh *(Composer)* 675
Rummler, Tom *(Cast)* 73, 945
Rumshinsky, J.M. *(Composer)* 1208
Rumshinsky, Joseph *(Composer)* 1609, 2356, 3995, 4342
Rumshinsky, Murray *(Composer)* 3559
Rumshinsky, Murray *(Musical Director)* 3559
Rumshisky, J.M. *(Composer)* 1639
Rumshisky, J.M. *(Lyricist)* 1639
Runanin, Boris *(Choreographer)* 1567, 3473, 3505
Rundback *(Composer)* 2341
Rundgren, Todd *(Composer)* 4518
Rundgren, Todd *(Lyricist)* 4518
Rundgren, Todd *(Vocal Arranger)* 4518
Runitch, Emma *(Cast)* 839
Runner, Joseph L. *(Producer)* 1412
Runolfsson, Anne *(Cast)* 949

Runowska, Iwona *(Cast)* 2846
Runyon, Damon *(Author)* 1706
Ruocco, John *(Choreographer)* 2038
Rupert, Gene *(Cast)* 4384, 4541
Rupert, Michael *(Cast)* 158, 1234, 1262, 1764, 2702, 2746, 3909, 4067
Rupert, Michael *(Composer)* 2702, 4349
Rupnik, Kevin *(Costumes)* 2598
Rupnik, Kevin *(Set Design)* 112, 2598
Ruprecht, David *(Cast)* 3444
Rush, Charles E. *(Lighting Designer)* 3007, 3008
Rush, Deborah *(Cast)* 54, 963, 1787, 2787, 2877
Rush, Jo Anna *(Cast)* 3311
Rush, Madge *(Cast)* 2587
Rushakoff, Sidney *(Set Design)* 2057
Rushworth, Frank *(Cast)* 2126, 4559
Rusk, James *(Composer)* 1436, 1648, 2913
Rusk, James *(Lyricist)* 1436, 1648, 2913
Rusk, Jim *(Composer)* 1770
Rusk, Jim *(Lyricist)* 1770
Ruska, Dani *(Producer)* 562
Ruskay, Everett *(Lyricist)* 2779
Ruskin, Coby *(Cast)* 3180, 3986
Ruskin, Harry *(Director)* 3005
Ruskin, Harry *(Librettist)* 288, 1874, 3005
Ruskin, Harry *(Lyricist)* 288, 1691, 3005, 3409, 3796, 4817
Ruskin, Robert *(Librettist)* 3172
Ruslander, Daniel *(Cast)* 3530
Ruslander, Daniel *(Lyricist)* 3530
Ruslander, Daniel *(Musical Director)* 3530
Ruslander, Danny *(Cast)* 2028
Ruslander, Danny *(Composer)* 932
Ruslander, Danny *(Musical Director)* 932
Russell, A.J. *(Librettist)* 56, 192, 193, 519, 3287, 3449, 4710
Russell, Benee *(Composer)* 1126
Russell, Benee *(Lyricist)* 1126
Russell, Bill *(Composer)* 90
Russell, Bill *(Librettist)* 1371, 3346
Russell, Bill *(Lyricist)* 1371, 3346
Russell, Bob *(Composer)* 853, 4193
Russell, Bob *(Lyricist)* 70, 853, 3947, 4091, 4193, 4196
Russell, Burt *(Composer)* 3739
Russell, Burt *(Lyricist)* 3739
Russell, Christabel *(Costumes)* 4341
Russell, Connie *(Cast)* 847
Russell, David *(Cast)* 3928
Russell, Diana *(Cast)* 2611
Russell, Dorothy *(Cast)* 2868
Russell, Eddie *(Cast)* 396
Russell, Edna *(Cast)* 4677
Russell, Evelyn *(Cast)* 1047
Russell, Flora Bonfanti *(Cast)* 1902, 2222
Russell, Forbesy *(Cast)* 2007
Russell, Gilbert *(Cast)* 1948, 2115
Russell, Henry *(Composer)* 3314
Russell, Henry *(Lyricist)* 3314
Russell, Herbert *(Cast)* 1154
Russell, Howell *(Costumes)* 45, 175
Russell, Irene *(Cast)* 2004
Russell, Jack *(Cast)* 1046, 2837, 3151
Russell, James *(Cast)* 1902, 4242
Russell, James *(Composer)* 1902
Russell, James *(Lyricist)* 1902
Russell, Jessica *(Cast)* 653
Russell, Jim *(Choreographer)* 722, 1697, 2772
Russell, Joe *(Cast)* 3022
Russell, John *(Cast)* 828, 1902, 4242
Russell, John Patton *(Author)* 575
Russell, Kennedy *(Musical Director)* 466, 3649
Russell, Lillian *(Cast)* 113, 1080, 1264, 1576, 1594, 1926, 1927, 2370, 2399, 2507, 3022, 3625, 4478, 4500, 4613, 4614, 4658, 4681
Russell, Maude *(Cast)* 435, 2302, 2561
Russell, Milly *(Costumes)* 1450
Russell, Robert *(Librettist)* 1310, 4022, 4270
Russell, Rosalind *(Cast)* 1448, 4734
Russell, Sam *(Cast)* 4231
Russell, W. *(Lyricist)* 545
Russell, Willy *(Composer)* 460
Russell, Willy *(Librettist)* 460
Russell, Willy *(Lyricist)* 460
Russo, Dan *(Composer)* 487
Russo, Dan *(Lyricist)* 487
Russo, James *(Cast)* 1546
Russo, James *(Producer)* 911, 4499
Russo, James Vincent *(Director)* 616, 2928
Russotto, Leo *(Orchestrations)* 1396
Russotto, Leo *(Vocal Arranger)* 1396
Ruthchild, Mac *(Composer)* 3926
Ruthchild, Mac *(Lyricist)* 3926
Rutherford *(Composer)* 3188
Rutherford *(Lyricist)* 3188
Rutherford, Tom *(Cast)* 3104
Rutledge, Gertrude *(Cast)* 187
Ruysdael, Basil *(Cast)* 1182, 4429
Ryack, Rita *(Costumes)* 2033, 2468, 3060
Ryall, David *(Cast)* 2196
Ryan, Ben *(Composer)* 1120
Ryan, Ben *(Lyricist)* 1120, 4815
Ryan, Benny *(Lyricist)* 1919
Ryan, Chilton *(Lyricist)* 1370
Ryan, Coletta *(Cast)* 1485, 1856
Ryan, D.D. *(Costumes)* 832
Ryan, E.H. *(Set Design)* 292
Ryan, Elsa *(Cast)* 1650, 2399
Ryan, Gus *(Lyricist)* 2506
Ryan, Irene *(Cast)* 3506
Ryan, J. Keith *(Cast)* 3548
Ryan, Mary *(Cast)* 1351
Ryan, Myka *(Cast)* 4830
Ryan, Peggy *(Cast)* 2809, 4331
Ryan, Peggy *(Choreographer)* 92
Ryan, Peter *(Composer)* 4707
Ryan, Peter *(Librettist)* 4707
Ryan, Peter *(Lyricist)* 4707
Ryan, Robert *(Cast)* 2983
Ryan, Sam J. *(Cast)* 2517

Ryan, Sue *(Cast)* 2397, 4826
Ryan, T.E. *(Set Design)* 2844
Ryan, Theodore S. *(Cast)* 3325
Ryan, Thomas M. *(Set Design)* 3461
Ryan, Walter *(Cast)* 1582
Ryan, William J. *(Set Design)* 382
Rychtarik, Richard *(Costumes)* 177
Rychtarik, Richard *(Set Design)* 177, 4737
Rydell, Charles *(Cast)* 3863
Ryder, Alfred *(Cast)* 3180
Ryder, Donald *(Set Design)* 279
Ryder, Philip *(Cast)* 3995
Ryder, Ric *(Cast)* 3169, 3873
Ryder, Richard *(Cast)* 1684, 3476, 3661, 4533
Rye, Frank *(Director)* 3361
Ryley, Charles *(Cast)* 1429
Ryley, J.H. *(Cast)* 402
Ryley, Thomas *(Producer)* 1313
Ryley, Thomas W. *(Producer)* 1417, 1579, 2803, 3433, 3626
Ryman, Add *(Cast)* 1913
Ryman, Add *(Librettist)* 1913
Rynharrt, Shryl *(Cast)* 319
Ryskind, Morrie *(Author)* 536
Ryskind, Morrie *(Composer)* 1357
Ryskind, Morrie *(Librettist)* 142, 1357, 1396, 1440, 1446, 2444, 2597, 2827, 3086, 3225, 4179
Ryskind, Morrie *(Lyricist)* 123, 536, 1357, 2827, 3086, 3623

S

Sa Loutos, Connie *(Cast)* 4732
Sabatino, Anthony *(Set Design)* 4402
Sabbar, Demetrius *(Cast)* 214
Sabel, Josephine *(Cast)* 3025, 3030, 3254, 3968
Sabel, Josie *(Cast)* 3609
Sabel, Shelly *(Lighting Designer)* 4016
Sabin, David *(Cast)* 496, 681, 1427, 1441, 2199, 2218, 2898, 3015, 3209
Sabinson, Lee *(Producer)* 1278
Sablon, Jean *(Cast)* 4174
Sac. Air Service Command *(Producer)* 226
Sacha, Ken *(Cast)* 1298
Sachelli, Robert *(Choreographer)* 1004
Sacher, Toby *(Composer)* 3226
Sachs, C. Colby *(Musical Director)* 1757
Sachs, Chuck *(Cast)* 1757
Sachs, Danny *(Composer)* 1873
Sachs, Danny *(Lyricist)* 1873
Sachs, Dorothy *(Lyricist)* 447, 3105
Sachs, Norman *(Composer)* 31, 922, 1089, 1435, 2199, 3059
Sachs, Norman *(Librettist)* 3059
Sachs, Norman *(Lyricist)* 3059
Sackeroff, David *(Lighting Designer)* 508, 2146
Sackeroff, David *(Set Design)* 508, 2146
Sackler, Howard *(Additional Materal)* 1857
Sacks, Dorothy *(Lyricist)* 3705
Sacks, Mike *(Cast)* 2749
Sacre Monte Gypsies *(Cast)* 839
Saddler, Donald *(Cast)* 454, 961
Saddler, Donald *(Choreographer)* 1609, 1660, 1762, 1842, 2227, 2578, 2864, 2898, 2958, 3000, 3733, 3743, 3846, 3913, 4090, 4297, 4395, 4399, 4450, 4609, 4734
Saddler, Donald *(Director)* 369, 1382
Saddler, Frank *(Orchestrations)* 126, 256, 378, 559, 805, 965, 968, 1154, 1483, 1598, 1784, 1920, 1922, 2070, 2232, 2430, 2620, 2723, 2858, 2919, 3087, 3146, 3193, 3230, 3237, 3245, 3395, 3488, 3679, 3737, 3923, 4158, 4203, 4555, 4806, 4814, 4860
Sadler, Bill *(Cast)* 2440
Sadler, Frank
See Frank Saddler.
Sadler, Josie *(Cast)* 559, 1627, 2232, 2938, 3437, 3976, 4222, 4590
Sadusk, Maureen *(Cast)* 3197
Safan, Craig *(Composer)* 595
Safan, Craig *(Librettist)* 595
Saffran, Christina *(Cast)* 146, 3126
Sagall, Solomon *(Producer)* 2075, 2811
Sagan, Leontine *(Director)* 650, 972
Sage, C. Russell *(Cast)* 2996
Sager *(Composer)* 4181
Sager, Carole Bayer
See also Carole Bayer.
Sager, Carole Bayer *(Composer)* 964
Sager, Carole Bayer *(Lyricist)* 146, 964, 2677, 4334
Sager, Charles *(Cast)* 2721
Sager, Charles S. *(Director)* 2721
Sagittarius Ent. *(Producer)* 546
Sagittarius Productions *(Producer)* 4089
Sahl, Mort *(Cast)* 826
Sahlins, Bernard *(Producer)* 4397
Saidenberg, Ted *(Musical Director)* 3427
Saidenberg, Ted *(Vocal Arranger)* 3427
Saidenberg, Theodore *(Musical Director)* 1864, 2617, 2626, 3274
Saidenberg, Theodore *(Vocal Arranger)* 1864
Saidy, Fred *(Author)* 2234
Saidy, Fred *(Librettist)* 462, 1278, 1300, 1745, 2190, 2234
Saint, David *(Director)* 1236
Saint, Eva Marie *(Cast)* 3324
Saint-Amand *(Author)* 1193
Saint-Saens, Camille *(Music Based On)* 1119
Saint-Subber *(Producer)* 1511, 2000, 2331, 3326, 4329
Sainthill, Loudon *(Costumes)* 634, 1721
Sainthill, Loudon *(Set Design)* 1721
Saitta, Paul *(Lighting Designer)* 2887
Sakash, Evelyn *(Set Design)* 10, 1997, 3181, 4264
Saki, Marion *(Cast)* 4050, 4249
Saks, Gene *(Cast)* 2910
Saks, Gene *(Director)* 1190, 1471, 1721, 1955, 2058, 2713, 2965, 3577, 3644
Salamando, Peter *(Composer)* 4433
Salamando, Peter *(Librettist)* 1648, 4433
Salamando, Peter *(Lyricist)* 4433

Salami, A. *(Composer)* 710
Salami, A. *(Lyricist)* 710
Salata, Gregory *(Cast)* 4172
Sale, Chic *(Cast)* 1460, 1461, 1462, 1836, 2939, 4840
Sale, Chic *(Producer)* 1462
Sale, Virginia *(Librettist)* 2483
Salerno, Mary Jo *(Cast)* 4035
Sales, Soupy *(Cast)* 1841
Salinger, Conrad *(Orchestrations)* 125, 622, 1342, 1493, 1856, 2258, 3365, 3850, 4365, 4374, 4583, 4825
Salisbury, Fran *(Cast)* 1816, 3690
Salisbury, Frances *(Cast)* 3599
Salisbury, Jean *(Cast)* 2518
Sallert, Ulla *(Cast)* 367
Salmon, Scott *(Choreographer)* 1146, 2360, 2953, 3637
Salmon, Scott *(Director)* 1146, 3637
Salonga, Lea *(Cast)* 2905
Salonis, Clarke *(Cast)* 2243
Saloway, Lowell *(Lyricist)* 4273
Salsberg, Gerry *(Cast)* 3066
Salt, Waldo *(Librettist)* 997, 3831
Salt, Waldo *(Lyricist)* 3831
Salt and Pepper *(Cast)* 1460
Salta, Menotti *(Musical Director)* 4777
Salta, Menotti *(Orchestrations)* 4123, 4428
Saltz, Amy *(Director)* 4431
Saltz, Amy *(Librettist)* 4431
Saltzman, Mark *(Lyricist)* 4
Saltzman, Simon L. *(Producer)* 3370
Salvador, Dom *(Dance Arranger)* 3838
Salvatore, John *(Cast)* 3346
Salvio, Robert *(Cast)* 406
Salzer, Eugene *(Composer)* 1174
Salzer, Eugene *(Musical Director)* 465, 1174, 1961, 2448, 2494, 3866
Salzer, Gene *(Musical Director)* 123, 124, 247, 1109, 1272, 1275, 1440, 1453, 1932, 2061, 2105, 2264, 2827, 3005, 3283, 3359, 3623, 3924, 4299, 4374, 4532
Salzer, Gus *(Cast)* 4234
Salzer, Gus *(Musical Director)* 152, 1011, 1088, 1163, 1183, 1297, 1318, 1378, 1455, 1537, 1544, 1598, 1784, 2148, 2214, 2291, 2491, 2527, 2545, 2594, 2638, 2722, 3103, 3220, 3254, 3312, 3431, 3533, 3721, 3753, 3819, 3861, 4212, 4234, 4357, 4545, 4683, 4844
Salzer, Gustave *(Incidental Music)* 4313
Salzer, Gustave *(Musical Director)* 531, 1066, 1110, 1309, 3590, 3613
Sam, Long Tack *(Cast)* 378
Samish, Adrian *(Composer)* 1836
Samish, Adrian *(Lyricist)* 1836
Sammler, B.J. *(Lighting Designer)* 1072
Samoiloff, Adrian *(Costumes)* 1153
Samoiloff, Adrian *(Set Design)* 1153
Sampson, Edgar *(Composer)* 146, 432, 4137
Sampson, Roy *(Cast)* 1619
Sampson, William *(Cast)* 2029
Sams, Jeffrey D. *(Cast)* 1296
Samuel, Harold *(Composer)* 719
Samuel, Peter *(Cast)* 2766
Samuels, Arthur *(Composer)* 1357, 3540
Samuels, Arthur H. *(Composer)* 3783
Samuels, D.S. *(Musical Director)* 2649
Samuels, Lesser *(Librettist)* 1698
Samuels, Lucille *(Costumes)* 2396
Samuels, Maurice V. *(Author)* 4275
Samuels, Rae *(Cast)* 4290, 4806
Samuels, Walter G. *(Composer)* 3086
Samuelson, Rich *(Cast)* 2580
San, Dan *(Lyricist)* 1053
San Francisco Civic Light Opera *(Producer)* 1369, 4798
San Juan, Olga *(Cast)* 847, 3347
Sanacino, Ernest *(Director)* 1940
Sanchez, Dorian *(Choreographer)* 846
Sanchez, Fernando *(Costumes)* 2260
Sanchez, Jaime *(Cast)* 4625
Sanchez, Jaime *(Director)* 4205
Sand, Paul *(Cast)* 1993, 2663, 4397, 4627, 4746
Sand, Paul *(Librettist)* 4627
Sandberg, Steve *(Dance Arranger)* 756
Sandberg, Steve *(Musical Director)* 756
Sande, Margaret *(Cast)* 2068, 4159
Sandeen, Darrell *(Cast)* 4785
Sanders, Alma *(Composer)* 606, 728, 1132, 1174, 2005, 2595, 3069, 3252, 3580, 4283, 4576
Sanders, Alma *(Lyricist)* 606, 728, 2595, 3580
Sanders, Arthur *(Director)* 1562, 4506
Sanders, Dirk *(Cast)* 4363
Sanders, Donna *(Cast)* 3889
Sanders, Fred *(Cast)* 580
Sanders, George *(Cast)* 841
Sanders, Honey *(Cast)* 1158, 3920
Sanders, Jay *(Cast)* 1575
Sanders, Jay O. *(Cast)* 2132
Sanders, Marta *(Cast)* 374
Sanders, Nat *(Lyricist)* 4816
Sanders, Steve *(Cast)* 4764
Sanderson, Julia *(Cast)* 178, 627, 954, 1243, 1544, 1922, 2341, 3153, 3658, 3996, 4219, 4258, 4283, 4434, 4713
Sanderson, Kristen *(Director)* 1291
Sandford, Harold *(Orchestrations)* 4818, 4819
Sandifur, Virginia *(Cast)* 708, 1329, 3444, 3743, 3926, 4029
Sandler, Harold *(Musical Director)* 4567
Sandler, Peretz *(Composer)* 3781
Sandler, Peretz *(Lyricist)* 3781
Sandor, Gluck *(Choreographer)* 1136, 1137, 3501
Sandrich Jr., Mark *(Composer)* 367
Sandrow, Nahma *(Librettist)* 2354
Sands, Billy *(Cast)* 4484
Sands, Christofer *(Cast)* 1940
Sands, Diana *(Cast)* 157, 477, 1389
Sands, Donna *(Cast)* 1093
Sands, Dorothy *(Cast)* 823, 1652, 1655, 1656
Sands, Dorothy *(Lyricist)* 1655
Sandy, Gary *(Cast)* 915, 3925, 4703
Sanford, Bobby *(Director)* 1953
Sanford, Bobby *(Producer)* 1953, 3950
Sanford, Charles *(Musical Director)* 23, 743, 1112, 1815, 1933, 2523, 2707, 2817, 3390, 3813, 3841, 4702, 4782
Sanford, Henry L. *(Composer)* 1866
Sanford, Isabel *(Cast)* 1674

Sanford, Louis *(Cast)* 1459
Sanford, Ralph *(Cast)* 1874
Sanford, Robert *(Choreographer)* 3314
Sanger, Eugene *(Director)* 2071
Sangor, Ben *(Producer)* 2893
Sankey, Tom *(Composer)* 1612
Sankey, Tom *(Librettist)* 1612
Sankey, Tom *(Lyricist)* 1612
Sankowich, Lee D. *(Director)* 3711
Sannuto, John *(Choreographer)* 1757
Sansonia, Michael *(Composer)* 3076
Sansonia, Michael *(Lyricist)* 3076
Santamaria, Mongo *(Composer)* 2245
Santamaria, Mongo *(Lyricist)* 2245
Santell, Marie *(Cast)* 1878, 2660, 3651
Santen, Kathy *(Librettist)* 3461
Santi, Joseph M. *(Additional Music)* 4729
Santiago, Manuel *(Cast)* 3276
Santiago, Saundra *(Cast)* 756, 4019
Santley, Charles *(Composer)* 4239
Santley, Charles *(Lyricist)* 4239
Santley, Fred *(Cast)* 804, 805, 1747, 2330, 2351, 3791, 4491
Santley, Frederick *(Cast)* 3137, 4429
Santley, Joseph *(Author)* 421
Santley, Joseph *(Cast)* 75, 379, 421, 1723, 2254, 2277, 2638, 2782, 2789, 3006, 3008, 3096, 3250, 3923, 4158, 4644, 4692, 4726
Santley, Joseph *(Choreographer)* 4644
Santley, Joseph *(Composer)* 421, 994, 3020, 3717
Santley, Joseph *(Director)* 2277, 2789
Santley, Joseph *(Librettist)* 75, 2277
Santley, Joseph *(Lyricist)* 421, 3911
Santley, Joseph *(Producer)* 2277
Santley, Ralph *(Cast)* 3988
Santly, Henry W. *(Composer)* 2308
Santly, Henry W. *(Lyricist)* 2308
Santly, Lester A. *(Lyricist)* 39
Santoni, Reni *(Cast)* 4796
Santoro, Michael *(Cast)* 3198
Santra, Henry J. *(Cast)* 1388
Sapara, Henry *(Cast)* 3022
Saperstein, Jerry *(Producer)* 3905
Sapin, Louis *(Author)* 952
Sappington, Margo *(Cast)* 3233, 3603
Sappington, Margo *(Choreographer)* 259, 1077, 3233, 3517, 4442
Sarallen *(Cast)* 4343
Sarandon, Chris *(Cast)* 3142, 3780
Sarandon, Christopher *(Cast)* 682
Sarandon, Susan *(Cast)* 908
Sardou *(Author)* 1114
Sarg, Tony *(Director)* 4699
Sarg, Tony *(Producer)* 4699
Sarg's Marionettes, Tony *(Cast)* 4150
Sargent, Alvin *(Author)* 3364
Sargent, George *(Choreographer)* 720
Sargent, Jean *(Cast)* 1225, 1322
Sargent, Joe *(Cast)* 3286
Sargent, Mary *(Cast)* 3860
Sargent, Winthrop *(Composer)* 125
Sarnoff, Dorothy *(Cast)* 2312, 2679, 3035, 3767
Sarnoff, Rosita *(Producer)* 4, 3162, 3661
Sarofeen, Anne *(Cast)* 1769
Saron, Alex *(Musical Director)* 4394
Saron, Alexander *(Musical Director)* 1871
Saron, Alexander *(Orchestrations)* 1871
Sarony, Leslie *(Composer)* 4345
Saroyan, Lucy *(Cast)* 2051
Saroyan, William *(Author)* 2033
Sarron, Bernard *(Costumes)* 455
Sartre, Jean-Paul *(Author)* 2295
Saslavsky, N.L. *(Composer)* 1279
Saslavsky, N.L. *(Lyricist)* 1279
Sasso, Dick *(Director)* 1108
Sater, Alex *(Musical Director)* 3352
Satirists Inc. *(Producer)* 4673
Satlin, Stan *(Composer)* 729
Satlin, Stan *(Lyricist)* 729
Sato, Isao *(Cast)* 3340
Sattin, Lonnie *(Cast)* 483
Satuloff, Robert *(Lyricist)* 1172, 1418
Sauber, Harry *(Director)* 3173
Sauber, Harry *(Librettist)* 3173
Sauer, Bernard *(Cast)* 3669
Saulpaugh, Edwin *(Director)* 3822
Saulter, Dotty *(Cast)* 2275
Saulter, Joe *(Cast)* 2058
Saunders, Brenda Fountain *(Vocal Arranger)* 2692
Saunders, Gertrude *(Cast)* 489, 899, 1050, 2557, 3963, 4183
Saunders, John *(Director)* 1568
Saunders, John *(Librettist)* 1568
Saunders, John *(Lyricist)* 1568
Saunders, John Monk *(Author)* 3168
Saunders, John Monk *(Librettist)* 3168
Saunders, Madge *(Cast)* 4327
Saunders, Marilyn *(Cast)* 825, 832, 4022
Saunders, Mary *(Cast)* 451, 1508, 4537
Saunders, Merl *(Dance Arranger)* 578
Saunders, Merl *(Musical Director)* 578
Saunders, Merl *(Vocal Arranger)* 578
Sauter, Eddie *(Orchestrations)* 170, 693, 1373, 1497, 1846, 2163, 2284, 2368, 2568, 2864, 2925, 3602, 3897, 4252, 4454, 4481
Sauter, Joe *(Librettist)* 766
Savage, Archie *(Cast)* 4096
Savage, Blane *(Cast)* 964
Savage, Henry *(Producer)* 94, 2315
Savage, Henry W. *(Producer)* 780, 1148, 1210, 1433, 1455, 1784, 1796, 2377, 2495, 2569, 2603, 2686, 2724, 2836, 3437, 3537, 3578, 3839, 3868, 3943, 4064, 4187, 4201, 4404, 4422, 4738, 4754, 4762
Savage, John *(Cast)* 181, 1540, 3876
Savage, Lesley *(Producer)* 3019
Savage, Steele *(Costumes)* 680
Savage, Steele *(Set Design)* 680
Savage, Tom *(Composer)* 3019
Savage, Tom *(Librettist)* 3019
Savage, Tom *(Lyricist)* 3019

Saver, Jeffrey *(Arrangements)* 198
Saver, Jeffrey *(Dance Arranger)* 198
Saver, Jeffrey *(Musical Director)* 198, 2646
Savile, Edith *(Cast)* 2976
Saville, Nina *(Cast)* 3693
Savin, M. *(Composer)* 2527
Savin, M. *(Orchestrations)* 2527
Savin, Ron Lee *(Cast)* 1509, 4171
Savino, Domenico *(Dance Arranger)* 4086
Savino, Domenico *(Orchestrations)* 297, 612, 1126, 1135, 1136, 1281, 2379, 4086
Savino, Domenico *(Vocal Arranger)* 2379
Saviola, Camille *(Cast)* 140, 3171
Savo, Jimmy *(Author)* 2551
Savo, Jimmy *(Cast)* 514, 1135, 3005, 3153, 3365, 4178, 4575, 4640
Savo, Nina *(Author)* 3788
Savoy, Bert
See also Savoy & Brennan.
Savoy, Bert *(Cast)* 1686
Savoy & Brennan
See also Bert Savoy and Jay Brennan.
Savoy & Brennan *(Cast)* 1688, 2855, 2900
Savoy Lindy Hoppers *(Cast)* 435
Savoy Producing Cooperative *(Producer)* 3434
Sawyer, Charles Carroll *(Lyricist)* 3259
Sawyer, Connie *(Cast)* 817
Sawyer, Donald *(Cast)* 1847
Sawyer, Ivy *(Cast)* 379, 1723, 2277, 2789, 3006, 3008, 3250, 3923
Sawyer, Mary Pat *(Choreographer)* 255
Sawyer, Michael *(Librettist)* 1002
Sawyer, Mike *(Librettist)* 766, 3427
Saxe, Phil *(Cast)* 3617
Saxe, Phil *(Musical Director)* 822
Saxe, Templar *(Cast)* 470, 904, 1123, 1188, 2374, 4201
Saxon, David *(Composer)* 520
Saxon, Don *(Producer)* 2925
Saxon, Luther *(Cast)* 653
Saxon, Marie *(Cast)* 2833, 2972, 3659, 4532
Sayag, Edmond *(Producer)* 1411, 2366
Sayer *(Composer)* 3073
Sayers, Henry J. *(Composer)* 1627, 4390
Sayers, Henry J. *(Lyricist)* 4390
Saylor, Peter *(Set Design)* 4774
Sayre, Theodore Burt *(Author)* 1157, 1163, 3220, 4407
Scaasi, Arnold *(Costumes)* 1622
Scaife, Marvin *(Cast)* 4039
Scalici, Jack *(Cast)* 793
Scanga, Richard *(Producer)* 4449
Scanlan, Dick *(Cast)* 3346
Scanlan, James *(Director)* 526
Scanlan, Robert *(Director)* 4147
Scanlon, Walter *(Cast)* 97, 452, 1162, 4056
Scarborough, George *(Author)* 4066
Scarbrough, Jan *(Composer)* 2704
Scarbrough, Jan *(Lyricist)* 2704
Scardino, Don *(Cast)* 135, 1082, 1581, 1737, 2074, 3389
Scardino, Don *(Director)* 1915
Scardino, Don *(Orchestrations)* 2074
Scardino, Donald *(Cast)* 2318
Scarpelli, Glenn *(Cast)* 4171
Scarritt, Leigh *(Cast)* 2969
Scarsborough, George *(Lyricist)* 4066
Scatamacchia, Charlie *(Cast)* 2968
Scatuorchio, Tee *(Choreographer)* 4309
Schaaf, George *(Lighting Designer)* 2666
Schacher, Richard A. *(Musical Director)* 2007
Schacher, Richard A. *(Vocal Arranger)* 2007
Schaefer, David *(Composer)* 1873
Schaefer, David *(Lyricist)* 1873
Schaefer, George *(Director)* 483, 1507, 4798
Schaefer, George *(Producer)* 1507, 4395
Schaefer, Hal *(Dance Arranger)* 1373, 1422, 3788, 4827
Schaefer, Hal *(Orchestrations)* 1373
Schaefer, Will *(Orchestrations)* 4114
Schaeffer, Carl *(Producer)* 1383
Schaetzlein, Larry *(Composer)* 3405
Schaetzlein, Larry *(Lyricist)* 3405
Schafer, Jerry *(Lyricist)* 362
Schafer, Milton *(Composer)* 519, 1094
Schafer, Natalie *(Cast)* 635, 715, 2386, 2396, 3761
Schafer, Scott *(Cast)* 3643
Schaffer, Lawrence *(Set Design)* 3066
Schaffer, Mary *(Composer)* 3605
Schaffer, Mary *(Lyricist)* 3605
Schaffner, Walter *(Set Design)* 3252
Schak, John *(Director)* 491
Schak, John *(Producer)* 491, 3542
Schall, David *(Cast)* 3697
Schalow, Betty *(Cast)* 2089
Schanzer, Rudolf *(Author)* 1538, 1561, 2384, 2495, 2666, 2794, 3084, 4121
Schanzer, Rudolf *(Librettist)* 1044
Schanzer, Rudolf *(Lyricist)* 1044
Schapiro, Herb *(Librettist)* 535
Schapiro, Herb *(Lyricist)* 535
Scharer, Jonathan *(Producer)* 1349, 1350, 1371, 3346
Scharf, Walter *(Arrangements)* 974
Scharf, Walter *(Musical Director)* 974
Scharfman, Nitra *(Composer)* 2472
Scharfman, Nitra *(Librettist)* 2472
Scharfman, Nitra *(Lyricist)* 2472
Scharnberg, Kim *(Orchestrations)* 2198
Schary, Dore *(Director)* 4516, 4863
Schary, Dore *(Librettist)* 159, 4863
Schary, Dore *(Producer)* 4516
Schary Productions, Dore *(Producer)* 159
Schasny, John *(Composer)* 2039
Schechter, David *(Author)* 1740
Schechter, David *(Cast)* 1715, 1740, 3162, 3806
Schechter, David *(Composer)* 1740
Schechter, David *(Director)* 1740
Schechter, David *(Lyricist)* 1740
Schechter, Philip *(Cast)* 4371
Schechtman, Richie *(Cast)* 3075
Schechtman, Saul *(Dance Arranger)* 1233
Schechtman, Saul *(Musical Director)* 98, 656, 1233
Schechtman, Saul *(Vocal Arranger)* 656, 1233

Scheck, Max *(Choreographer)* 709, 1014, 1992, 2293, 2622, 3157, 3407, 3472, 3586, 3770, 3849, 4188, 4209, 4372, 4528
Scheck, Max *(Director)* 364, 4484
Schecter, David *(Cast)* 1053
Schecter, Lee *(Librettist)* 3075
Scheeder, Louis W. *(Director)* 699
Scheeder, Louis W. *(Producer)* 1038
Scheerer, Bob *(Cast)* 507, 961, 2439, 4423
Scheff, Fritzi *(Cast)* 252, 1111, 2623, 2915, 3562, 3567, 4465, 4497
Scheidt, Scott *(Lighting Designer)* 3080
Schenck, Eliot *(Musical Director)* 377
Schenck, Joe *(Cast)* 683, 959, 2900, 3144, 4813, 4814, 4815
Schenck, Joe *(Composer)* 4813, 4814, 4842
Schenck, Joe *(Lyricist)* 3144, 4813, 4814, 4842
Schenck, Leopold *(Composer)* 976
Schenck, Mary *(Costumes)* 4117
Schenck, Mary Percy *(Costumes)* 1948
Schenker, Joel *(Producer)* 989
Schenker, Joel W. *(Producer)* 2618
Scherer, John *(Cast)* 2372
Scherman, Thomas *(Musical Director)* 4363
Schermasser, Dick *(Vocal Arranger)* 74
Schertler, Nancy *(Lighting Designer)* 1234
Schertzinger, Victor *(Composer)* 3444, 4381
Schertzinger, Victor *(Lyricist)* 1309, 4381
Schertzinger, Victor *(Musical Director)* 4381
Scheuer, Charles *(Librettist)* 943
Scheuer, Steven H. *(Producer)* 3210
Schick, George *(Musical Director)* 4792
Schickele, Peter
See The Open Window.
Schielke, Joanna *(Lighting Designer)* 2784, 3297
Schiera, Thom *(Librettist)* 1164
Schierhorn, Paul *(Composer)* 3136
Schierhorn, Paul *(Dance Arranger)* 3136
Schierhorn, Paul *(Librettist)* 3136
Schierhorn, Paul *(Lyricist)* 3136
Schierhorn, Paul *(Vocal Arranger)* 3136, 3175
Schiff, Charlotte *(Producer)* 4678
Schiff, Dan *(Cast)* 2654
Schiff, Larry *(Composer)* 3539
Schiff, Larry *(Librettist)* 3539
Schiff, Larry *(Lyricist)* 3539
Schifter, Peter Mark *(Director)* 4619
Schildkraut, Joseph *(Cast)* 55, 1283, 2487
Schiller, George *(Cast)* 102, 2493
Schiller, Joel *(Set Design)* 1341
Schiller, Miriam *(Choreographer)* 1773, 4253
Schilling, Carl *(Composer)* 4704, 4705
Schilling, Carl *(Musical Director)* 800
Schilling, Gus *(Cast)* 1323, 4545
Schimmel, John *(Cast)* 3608
Schindler, Paul *(Composer)* 830, 1469, 2159, 2286, 3129
Schindler, Paul *(Musical Director)* 830, 1308, 1469, 1738, 2159, 2286, 2347, 3047
Schirmer, Gus *(Cast)* 3103
Schirmer Jr., Gus *(Director)* 1734
Schirmer Jr., Gus *(Lyricist)* 924
Schisgal, Murray *(Author)* 2218, 2598
Schisgal, Murray *(Librettist)* 2925
Schissler, Jeffrey *(Lighting Designer)* 451, 1092, 1785, 2100, 2294, 3864
Schissler, Jeffrey *(Set Design)* 2294, 3261
Schlamme, Martha *(Cast)* 2777, 2941
Schlegel, Jeanne *(Cast)* 1347
Schlein, Hap *(Librettist)* 1436, 2785
Schlesinger, John *(Director)* 2047
Schlesinger, Sarah *(Lyricist)* 3277
Schlinker *(Composer)* 4723
Schlissel, Jack *(Producer)* 1660
Schlitt, Robert *(Librettist)* 3788
Schloss, Irving *(Musical Director)* 2293, 2808, 4673
Schloss, Irving *(Orchestrations)* 4328
Schloss, Sybille *(Cast)* 3441
Schlossberg, Jerry *(Producer)* 1441, 4468
Schmeed Trio *(Cast)* 1815
Schmid *(Composer)* 938
Schmid *(Lyricist)* 938
Schmidt, Douglas W. *(Set Design)* 52, 695, 1015, 1161, 1664, 3309, 3330, 3733, 3806, 4019, 4020, 4334, 4370, 4459
Schmidt, Harvey *(Cast)* 1701, 3542
Schmidt, Harvey *(Composer)* 491, 681, 807, 808, 809, 1023, 1245, 1362, 1364, 1701, 2050, 2244, 3294, 3469, 3479, 3484, 3542, 3940
Schmidt, Harvey *(Director)* 3469
Schmidt, Harvey *(Lyricist)* 1023, 3940
Schmidt, Harvey *(Musical Director)* 807
Schmidt, Harvey *(Pianist)* 3542
Schmidt, Jack *(Cast)* 4062
Schmied, Wally *(Composer)* 3178
Schmied, Wally *(Lyricist)* 3178
Schmitt, Virginia *(Cast)* 1750
Schnabel, Stefan *(Cast)* 2257, 3509
Schneider, Alan *(Director)* 461, 2368
Schneider, C.N. *(Composer)* 248
Schneider, Charles *(Dance Arranger)* 4789
Schneider, Charles *(Musical Director)* 3196, 4789
Schneider, Charles *(Vocal Arranger)* 3196
Schneider, Frank *(Lighting Designer)* 3009
Schneider, Jana *(Cast)* 3070
Schneider, Jeffrey *(Set Design)* 4769, 4799
Schneider & Anderson *(Costumes)* 1026, 1251, 2698, 2830, 4807
Schneider-Anderson *(Costumes)* 685, 4812
Schnitzer, Ignaz *(Author)* 3776
Schnitzler, Arthur *(Author)* 1439, 1456, 1822, 3760, 3763
Schochen, Seyril *(Librettist)* 4380
Schochen, Seyril *(Lyricist)* 4380
Schocket, Steve *(Cast)* 2970
Schoeffel *(Producer)* 4500
Schoeffler, Paul *(Cast)* 949
Schoenfeld, Mae *(Cast)* 2352
Schoenfield, A. *(Author)* 2922
Scholl, Danny *(Cast)* 620, 4314, 4415
Scholl, Jack *(Composer)* 1481
Scholl, Jack *(Librettist)* 2300

Scholl, Jack *(Lyricist)* 714, 1328, 1481, 1989, 2300, 3683
Scholl, John Jay *(Producer)* 1174
Scholtz, Christa *(Costumes)* 2539
Schon, Bonnie *(Cast)* 3644
Schon, Kenneth *(Cast)* 3035, 3151
Schonberg, Claude-Michel *(Composer)* 2442, 2905
Schonberg, Claude-Michel *(Librettist)* 2442, 2905
Schonberger, John *(Composer)* 1120
Schonberger, John *(Lyricist)* 1120
Schonfeld, Alfred *(Author)* 2923, 3529
Schooler, Dave *(Musical Director)* 1843
Schooley, Edgar I. *(Choreographer)* 2455
Schoonmaker, Charles *(Costumes)* 3544
Schoonover, Meredith *(Cast)* 2641
Schoop, Trudi *(Choreographer)* 3046
Schorr, Anschel *(Lyricist)* 1609
Schorr, Eric *(Composer)* 2022
Schorr, Moshe *(Librettist)* 3781
Schorr, William *(Director)* 462
Schottenfeld, Barbara *(Composer)* 674, 2049
Schottenfeld, Barbara *(Librettist)* 674, 2049
Schottenfeld, Barbara *(Lyricist)* 674, 2049
Schottenfeld, Barbara *(Orchestrations)* 2049
Schrader, Frederick E. *(Librettist)* 222
Schrader, Frederick F. *(Lyricist)* 307
Schrager, Rudolph *(Musical Director)* 2032
Schramm Twins *(Cast)* 2090
Schrank, Joseph *(Librettist)* 2504, 3893
Schrapps, E.R. *(Costumes)* 2622, 2628, 2843
Schrapps, Ernest *(Costumes)* 110, 199, 200, 202, 203, 718, 948, 1219, 1462, 1693, 1799, 1831, 2540, 2637, 2747, 2947, 3011, 3148, 3149, 3150, 3152, 3407, 3409, 3523, 3680, 4025, 4104, 4352, 4524, 4670, 4733
Schrapps, Ernest R. *(Costumes)* 324
Schreiber, Avery *(Cast)* 4619
Schreiber, Avery *(Director)* 2016
Schreiber, Edward *(Producer)* 4514
Schreibman, Myrl A. *(Director)* 4402
Schreibman, Myrl A. *(Producer)* 4402
Schreibman, Paul P. *(Producer)* 1884, 4199
Schrode, William C. *(Cast)* 4802
Schroder, William *(Costumes)* 593, 2565, 4645, 4788
Schroder, William *(Set Design)* 593, 4645, 4788
Schroeder, Aaron *(Producer)* 249
Schroeder, Charles *(Composer)* 4030
Schroeder, Charles *(Lyricist)* 4030
Schroeder, William *(Composer)* 387, 640, 1911, 2282, 2390, 2537, 4647, 4716
Schroeder, William *(Musical Director)* 1175
Schuba, Trixi *(Cast)* 2084
Schubert, Franz *(Music Based On)* 463
Schue, Peter A. *(Set Design)* 3202
Schulberg, B.P. *(Producer)* 2751
Schulberg, Budd *(Author)* 3875, 4633
Schulberg, Budd *(Librettist)* 3875, 4633
Schulberg, Stuart *(Librettist)* 4633
Schuller, Gunther *(Musical Director)* 4447
Schuller, Gunther *(Orchestrations)* 4447
Schulman, Arnold *(Librettist)* 2201
Schulman, Howard *(Librettist)* 4627
Schulman, Susan H. *(Director)* 451, 1258, 1873, 2185, 3862
Schultz, Dwight *(Cast)* 1418
Schultz, Michael *(Director)* 3001, 4343
Schultz, Michael A. *(Director)* 1592, 3309
Schultze, Charles *(Author)* 1374
Schulz, Charles M. *(Author)* 4034, 4783
Schulz, Franz *(Author)* 4486
Schuman, Edward L. *(Producer)* 209
Schuman, Howard *(Librettist)* 682, 4522
Schuman, Howard *(Lyricist)* 4522
Schumann, Robert *(Music Based On)* 1815, 2358
Schumann, Walter *(Composer)* 4346
Schumann-Heink, Madame *(Cast)* 2632
Schumer, Leo *(Composer)* 59, 1892, 3664
Schupf, John *(Composer)* 4093
Schurkamp, Richard *(Costumes)* 4731
Schussel, Sandy *(Librettist)* 4679
Schuster, Alan J. *(Producer)* 140, 478, 747
Schutt, Arthur *(Orchestrations)* 1322
Schutz, Herb *(Dance Arranger)* 673
Schutz, Herbert *(Vocal Arranger)* 3664
Schwab, Buddy *(Cast)* 1706
Schwab, Buddy *(Choreographer)* 1233, 1841, 4537
Schwab, Buddy *(Director)* 3484
Schwab, Charles *(Composer)* 3103
Schwab, Charles M. *(Composer)* 303, 1448, 3130, 4367
Schwab, Laurence *(Director)* 3117
Schwab, Laurence *(Librettist)* 642, 1339, 1387, 1628, 2348, 3117, 3138, 3622, 4241, 4267, 4367, 4550
Schwab, Laurence *(Lyricist)* 3117
Schwab, Laurence *(Producer)* 111, 642, 1027, 1145, 1283, 1339, 1387, 1516, 1628, 2786, 3117, 3138, 4241, 4267, 4550
Schwab, Sophie *(Cast)* 305, 2320
Schwantes, Leland *(Cast)* 2785, 3000, 3020
Schwartz, Abe *(Composer)* 1279, 1609
Schwartz, Abe *(Lyricist)* 1279, 1609
Schwartz, Arthur *(Cast)* 3153
Schwartz, Arthur *(Composer)* 117, 213, 216, 294, 347, 383, 536, 603, 663, 844, 1322, 1338, 1456, 1617, 1654, 1657, 1763, 1855, 1893, 2004, 2137, 2201, 2545, 2547, 2743, 2989, 3020, 3086, 3130, 3139, 3143, 3178, 3390, 3444, 3584, 3680, 3699, 3709, 3861, 3919, 3955, 4142, 4159, 4367, 4446, 4569, 4581, 4621, 4824
Schwartz, Arthur *(Lyricist)* 603, 3139, 3143
Schwartz, Arthur *(Producer)* 2137
Schwartz, Ben *(Composer)* 4275
Schwartz, Ben *(Lyricist)* 4275
Schwartz, Bob *(Director)* 1590
Schwartz, Bonnie Nelson *(Producer)* 2204
Schwartz, Bruce *(Composer)* 485
Schwartz, Fred *(Composer)* 3350
Schwartz, Fred *(Musical Director)* 2351
Schwartz, Frederick *(Musical Director)* 77
Schwartz, Gwen Gibson *(Lyricist)* 3530
Schwartz, Jean *(Author)* 4642
Schwartz, Jean *(Cast)* 3153
Schwartz, Jean *(Composer)* 47, 115, 152, 199, 228, 274,

379, 558, 561, 684, 688, 737, 797, 800, 910, 1033, 1151, 1188, 1247, 1403, 1414, 1506, 1579, 1731, 1735, 1799, 1823, 1826, 1868, 1901, 1904, 1910, 1926, 1927, 1963, 2119, 2135, 2209, 2481, 2498, 2566, 2706, 2856, 2857, 2870, 2892, 2923, 2939, 2956, 2964, 2974, 2990, 2991, 3031, 3072, 3149, 3250, 3313, 3332, 3345, 3396, 3399, 3402, 3403, 3404, 3406, 3407, 3488, 3525, 3537, 3560, 3710, 3827, 3866, 3882, 3962, 3977, 3985, 4014, 4181, 4213, 4283, 4317, 4373, 4427, 4521, 4553, 4589, 4636, 4641, 4642, 4655, 4656, 4662, 4712, 4742, 4753, 4757, 4801, 4802, 4805, 4806, 4808, 4817
Schwartz, Jean *(Lyricist)* 3402, 3951, 4753
Schwartz, Jerome J. *(Librettist)* 1993
Schwartz, Leybele *(Composer)* 2356
Schwartz, Leybele *(Lyricist)* 2356
Schwartz, Nat *(Lyricist)* 879
Schwartz, Noel *(Choreographer)* 2731
Schwartz, Paul *(Musical Director)* 661
Schwartz, Paul *(Orchestrations)* 2012
Schwartz, Phil *(Composer)* 1550, 2667, 3399, 3737
Schwartz, Phil *(Lyricist)* 2696
Schwartz, Sidney *(Composer)* 3530
Schwartz, Stephen *(Composer)* 273, 594, 730, 1595, 2687, 3448, 3506, 3507, 4167, 4744
Schwartz, Stephen *(Director)* 4744
Schwartz, Stephen *(Librettist)* 4744
Schwartz, Stephen *(Lyricist)* 273, 594, 730, 1595, 2687, 2775, 3506, 3507, 3644, 4167, 4744
Schwartz, Stephen *(Vocal Arranger)* 1595
Schwartz, Suzanne J. *(Producer)* 253, 3960
Schwartz, Yevgeny *(Author)* 1092
Schwartzdorf, Jacob
See Jay Blackton.
Schwary, Oscar *(Cast)* 822
Schwarz, Vera *(Cast)* 3639
Schwarzwald, Milton *(Composer)* 317, 1309, 1678, 1966, 2927
Schwarzwald, Milton *(Musical Director)* 2, 317
Schwarzwald, Milton E. *(Musical Director)* 2927
Schwei, Barbara *(Librettist)* 3075
Schweid, Carole *(Cast)* 729, 746
Schweikert, Ernest G. *(Composer)* 3801
Schweizer, David *(Director)* 4775
Schwerin, Doris *(Composer)* 2284
Schwinn, Ron *(Cast)* 723, 1359
Schwinn, Tom *(Set Design)* 166
Sciandra, Gian *(Producer)* 237
Scibila, Anton F. *(Producer)* 3342
Scibilia, Anton *(Lyricist)* 1302
Scibilia, Anton F. *(Lyricist)* 4748
Scimmel, John *(Composer)* 3608
Scimmel, John *(Lyricist)* 3608
Scofield, Al *(Composer)* 532
Scofield, Pamela *(Costumes)* 4030, 4514
Scognamillo, Gabriel *(Set Design)* 4316
Scola, Ettore *(Director)* 3411
Scooler, Svee *(Cast)* 1715
Scordino, Bruno C. *(Set Design)* 159
Scotes, T.J. *(Lyricist)* 4543
Scotes, Thomas *(Lyricist)* 4303
Scotia Productions *(Producer)* 1676
Scott *(Composer)* 3259
Scott *(Lyricist)* 1246, 3259
Scott, Adrian *(Author)* 1674
Scott, Alan *(Cast)* 2426
Scott, Barbara Ann *(Cast)* 1941
Scott, Bennett *(Composer)* 4762
Scott, Bobby *(Cast)* 4601
Scott, Bonnie *(Cast)* 2019
Scott, Bruce *(Cast)* 278, 3876
Scott, Bryan *(Librettist)* 4193
Scott, Bryan *(Producer)* 4193
Scott, Campbell *(Cast)* 1787
Scott, Carole-Ann *(Cast)* 1092, 4618
Scott, Christopher *(Cast)* 2197
Scott, Clement *(Lyricist)* 3736
Scott, Cyril *(Cast)* 770, 969, 1313, 1579, 2803, 3803, 3976
Scott, Cyril *(Choreographer)* 703
Scott, Cyril *(Director)* 2803, 3588
Scott, Donald *(Cast)* 1887
Scott, E.T. *(Cast)* 263
Scott, Ed *(Composer)* 90, 4627
Scott, Ed *(Dance Arranger)* 4588
Scott, Eddie *(Composer)* 1415
Scott, Edward *(Cast)* 3157
Scott, Edward *(Composer)* 2246
Scott, Fred *(Cast)* 1938
Scott, Gayton *(Cast)* 139
Scott, Hazel *(Cast)* 3594, 3990
Scott, Helena *(Cast)* 177, 298, 2797
Scott, Hutchinson *(Set Design)* 4329
Scott, Ivy *(Cast)* 3699, 4075, 4365
Scott, James *(Costumes)* 1739
Scott, James *(Producer)* 1589
Scott, Jessye *(Cast)* 897
Scott, Joel *(Librettist)* 2426
Scott, Johnnie *(Composer)* 95
Scott, Kenneth *(Cast)* 1729
Scott, Kenyon *(Composer)* 3192
Scott, Kenyon *(Librettist)* 3192
Scott, Kenyon *(Lyricist)* 3192
Scott, Lee *(Choreographer)* 1766
Scott, Leroy *(Author)* 3189
Scott, Luke *(Cast)* 1479
Scott, Mabel *(Cast)* 497, 3782
Scott, Maurice *(Composer)* 2858, 3857, 4757
Scott, Michael Lee *(Cast)* 4799
Scott, Molly *(Cast)* 155
Scott, Nathan *(Dance Arranger)* 4346
Scott, Nathan *(Vocal Arranger)* 4346
Scott, Noel *(Librettist)* 3649
Scott, Oz *(Director)* 1344, 2692
Scott, Phil *(Cast)* 444
Scott, Playe *(Composer)* 4786
Scott, Playe *(Lyricist)* 4786
Scott, Raymond *(Composer)* 445, 2161, 2655, 2850, 4799
Scott, Raymond *(Lyricist)* 2850
Scott, Raymond *(Orchestrations)* 2655
Scott, Ted *(Vocal Arranger)* 2479

Scott, Thomas *(Cast)* 803
Scott, Timothy *(Cast)* 678
Scott, Vincent *(Lyricist)* 2467
Scott, Winfield *(Composer)* 4264
Scott, Winfield *(Lyricist)* 4264
Scott, Zanzele *(Cast)* 2272
Scott & Raynor *(Producer)* 2771
Scott III, Henry E. *(Set Design)* 2188
Scott Sisters, The *(Cast)* 1491
Scotti, Vito *(Cast)* 3495
Scotto, Vincent *(Composer)* 3387, 3617, 4390
Scotto, Vincent *(Lyricist)* 3617
Scoullar, John *(Cast)* 922, 4488
Scourby, Alexander *(Cast)* 4435
Scribner Choir, Norman *(Cast)* 2775
Scriven, George *(Composer)* 2046
Scriven, George *(Lyricist)* 2046
Scruggs, Sharon *(Cast)* 778, 1172
Scudder, Eugene *(Cast)* 4672
Scudder, Rose *(Cast)* 556
Scudder, William M. *(Lyricist)* 1862
Scurlock, Jerry *(Cast)* 3908
Seabolt, Frank *(Cast)* 283
Seabrooke, Christopher *(Producer)* 2805
Seabrooke, Thomas Q. *(Cast)* 354, 737, 1661, 2156, 2848, 3673, 3784, 4222
Seabury, William *(Choreographer)* 2818, 3007
Seader, Richard *(Producer)* 4272
Seagram, Wilfred *(Cast)* 1460
Seal, Elizabeth *(Cast)* 2150
Sealby, Mabel *(Cast)* 30
Seale, Douglas *(Cast)* 2375
Seale, Douglas *(Director)* 2375
Seale, Douglas *(Librettist)* 2375
Sealey, Carol B. *(Lighting Designer)* 1171
Seamon, Edward *(Cast)* 1669
Sears, Lucille *(Cast)* 2639
Sears, Sally *(Producer)* 3522, 4272
Sears, Ted *(Author)* 4035
Sears, Zelda *(Author)* 2639, 3655
Sears, Zelda *(Cast)* 2569, 3085, 4464
Sears, Zelda *(Librettist)* 780, 2377, 2569, 2686
Sears, Zelda *(Lyricist)* 780, 2377, 2569, 2686, 3184, 3249, 3655
Seary, Kim *(Cast)* 3901
Seary, Kim *(Composer)* 3901
Seary, Kim *(Librettist)* 3901
Seary, Kim *(Lyricist)* 3901
Seastrom, Guje *(Cast)* 4536
Seaton, George *(Author)* 1860
Seaton, Violet *(Cast)* 1707
Seawell, Brockman *(Producer)* 3631
Sebastian, John *(Composer)* 2218, 3739
Sebastian, John *(Lyricist)* 2218, 3739
Sebastian, Mark *(Composer)* 3739
Sebastian, Mark *(Lyricist)* 3739
Sebesky, Don *(Composer)* 3576
Sebesky, Don *(Orchestrations)* 3428
Sebree, Charles *(Author)* 2994
Sebree, Charles *(Lyricist)* 2994
Secombe, Harry *(Cast)* 3482
Second Stage, The *(Producer)* 2132
Secter, David *(Librettist)* 1500
Secter, David *(Lyricist)* 1500
Secter, David *(Producer)* 1500
Secunda, Sholom *(Composer)* 268, 343, 1609, 2352, 2356, 4342
Secunda, Sholom *(Lyricist)* 1609, 2352, 2356, 4342
Secunda, Sholom *(Musical Director)* 343
Sedaka, Neil *(Composer)* 4193, 4264
Sedaka, Neil *(Lyricist)* 4193, 4264
Sedley, Harry *(Director)* 2455
Sedley, Harry *(Librettist)* 2455
Sedley, Roy *(Cast)* 1979
Seegar, Sara *(Cast)* 1194
Seelen, Jerry *(Composer)* 2379, 3121
Seelen, Jerry *(Lyricist)* 2379, 3121, 4131, 4264, 4602
Seeley, Blossom *(Cast)* 697, 1042, 1693, 1845, 2696, 3087, 4158, 4195, 4655
Seeley, Inez *(Cast)* 1989
Seff, Richard *(Librettist)* 4114
Segal, Al *(Cast)* 4730
Segal, Al *(Composer)* 376
Segal, Alex *(Director)* 4609
Segal, David F. *(Lighting Designer)* 415, 693, 1010, 1161, 2001, 2418, 2737, 3233, 3370, 3733, 3838, 4272, 4474, 4659
Segal, David F. *(Set Design)* 2001, 3370, 4659
Segal, Erich *(Librettist)* 3988
Segal, Erich *(Lyricist)* 2075, 3988
Segal, George *(Cast)* 2357
Segal, Kathrin King *(Cast)* 3469, 3542
Segal, Morton *(Producer)* 4541
Segal, Vivienne *(Cast)* 17, 21, 473, 670, 1027, 1312, 1679, 2061, 2549, 2653, 2855, 2900, 3013, 3051, 3153, 3245, 3353, 4350, 4357, 4716, 4760, 4818
Segall, Bernardo *(Composer)* 1770
Segall, Bernardo *(Lyricist)* 1770
Segall, Lee *(Producer)* 4582
Segalla, Irene *(Costumes)* 2392
Segasture, Jack *(Producer)* 3524
Seger, Richard *(Set Design)* 594, 4062
Segovia, Claudio *(Costumes)* 432
Segovia, Claudio *(Director)* 432
Segovia, Claudio *(Set Design)* 432
Segovia, Daisy
See Daisy de Segouzac.
Segovia, Yolanda *(Musical Director)* 1103, 3444
Segue Productions *(Producer)* 708
Seguin, Tillie *(Cast)* 2127
Seibert, T. Lawrence *(Lyricist)* 3989
Seidel, Virginia *(Cast)* 1597
Seidelman, Arthur A. *(Director)* 406
Seidenman Jr., Sidney *(Musical Director)* 821
Seidle, C.F./Caroline/Mme.
See also under Siedle.
Seidle, C.F. *(Costumes)* 3585
Seidle, Caroline *(Costumes)* 2101, 2324, 3052, 3387, 3488, 3790, 3805, 4646
Seidle, Mme. *(Costumes)* 2885, 3129, 4497, 4500, 4724

Seidman, Amy *(Lyricist)* 2320
Seidman, John *(Cast)* 4330
Seigal, Maxwell *(Lyricist)* 3889
Seiger, Marvin *(Author)* 339
Seitz, Dran *(Cast)* 1242, 1745
Seitz, George B. *(Producer)* 2363
Seitz, Tani *(Cast)* 1242, 3094
Seitz, W. Thomas *(Costumes)* 4173
Selbert, Marianne *(Choreographer)* 3637
Selden, Albert *(Composer)* 98, 2940, 4018, 4585
Selden, Albert *(Lyricist)* 98, 4018
Selden, Albert *(Producer)* 98, 483, 1567, 2550
Selden, Albert W. *(Composer)* 4585
Selden, Albert W. *(Producer)* 31, 823, 828, 1729, 1730, 2727, 3612, 4537
Selden, Edgar *(Composer)* 697
Selden, Edgar *(Lyricist)* 697, 1526, 3061, 4801, 4802
Seldes, Gilbert *(Librettist)* 4256
Seldes, Marian *(Cast)* 154
Self, Bonnie *(Composer)* 4264
Self, Bonnie *(Lyricist)* 4264
Sell, Janie *(Cast)* 599, 1591, 2026, 2913, 3330, 3666
Sell, Janie *(Choreographer)* 262, 3277
Sells, Edward *(Cast)* 1796
Selten, Morton *(Cast)* 2329
Seltzer, David *(Producer)* 2659
Seltzer, Dov *(Composer)* 2811, 4396
Seltzer, Dov *(Musical Director)* 2811
Seltzer, Dov *(Orchestrations)* 2811
Seltzer, Gary *(Lighting Designer)* 3034
Seltzer, Jerry *(Producer)* 3752
Seltzer, Marjorie *(Cast)* 4673
Seltzer, Milton *(Musical Director)* 73, 461, 4380
Selwyn, Arch *(Producer)* 133, 429, 579, 702, 715, 839, 841, 3699, 3740, 4033
Selwyn, Edgar *(Director)* 468, 1157
Selwyn, Edgar *(Librettist)* 1011, 4589
Selwyn, Edgar *(Producer)* 133, 579, 3740, 4033, 4178, 4179
Selwyn, Ruth *(Producer)* 3172, 4586
Selwyn and Co. *(Producer)* 126
Selwyns, The *(Producer)* 4085
Semans, William H. *(Producer)* 2001
Semos, Murray *(Librettist)* 2584
Senaille, J.B. *(Composer)* 1865
Sendak, Maurice *(Author)* 3668
Sendak, Maurice *(Costumes)* 3668
Sendak, Maurice *(Librettist)* 3668
Sendak, Maurice *(Lyricist)* 3668
Sendak, Maurice *(Set Design)* 3668
Sendholm, Ruth *(Cast)* 225
Sendry, Albert *(Orchestrations)* 223, 3108, 3453, 3493, 4827
Senesh, Hannah *(Author)* 1740
Senesh, Hannah *(Lyricist)* 1740
Senior, Raimond D. *(Costumes)* 18
Senior, Raimond D. *(Director)* 18
Senior, Raimond D. *(Librettist)* 18
Senior, Raimond D. *(Set Design)* 18
Senior, Susanna *(Cast)* 2228
Senn, Herbert *(Lighting Designer)* 2235, 3215, 4633
Senn, Herbert *(Set Design)* 369, 1676, 2235, 3020, 3196, 3215, 3235, 3920, 4028, 4633
Senna, Charles *(Cast)* 2020
Sennes, Frank *(Producer)* 2742
Sennett, Dorothy *(Composer)* 932
Sennett, Dorothy *(Lyricist)* 932
Sennett, Mack *(Cast)* 515, 737, 2915, 3488
Senske, Rebecca *(Costumes)* 3987
Sepia Guild Players *(Producer)* 444
Seplow, Evan *(Cast)* 534
Seppe, Christopher *(Cast)* 705, 3080
Seppe, Christopher *(Composer)* 3080
Seppe, Christopher *(Lyricist)* 3080
Septee, Moe *(Producer)* 576, 4342
Serabian, Lorraine *(Cast)* 3863, 4862
Serban, Andrei *(Director)* 4505
Sereda, John *(Composer)* 3901
Sereda, John *(Lyricist)* 3901
Sereda, John *(Musical Director)* 3901
Sergava, Katherine *(Cast)* 3263
Sergides, Miguel *(Cast)* 2153
Serina, Marie *(Cast)* 4492
Serko, David *(Cast)* 139
Serlin, Oscar *(Producer)* 4600
Serova, Madame *(Choreographer)* 3009
Serpette, Gaston *(Author)* 4298
Serra, Hal *(Musical Director)* 692
Serra, Raymond *(Cast)* 2437, 2759, 4347
Serrano, Charlie *(Cast)* 2242
Serrano, Nestor *(Cast)* 1038
Serrano, Vincent *(Cast)* 3719
Serrecchia, Michael *(Cast)* 746
Servais, Yvan *(Cast)* 2937
Sesma, Thom *(Cast)* 3142
Sessa, Jay *(Producer)* 4220
Seton, Bruce *(Cast)* 325
Setterberg, Carl *(Set Design)* 4047
Seuss, Dr. *(Librettist)* 2015
Seuss, Dr. *(Lyricist)* 2015
Seuss, Dr. *(Producer)* 2015
Sevec, Christine *(Cast)* 4193
Seven Arts Productions, Inc *(Producer)* 4749
764 Californians *(Producer)* 3046
Sevier, Jack *(Cast)* 564, 4288
Sevra, Robert *(Cast)* 2630, 4244
Sevran, Pascal *(Lyricist)* 1638
Sewell, Cissie *(Cast)* 2761
Sewell, Danny *(Cast)* 2375, 3271
Sexton, Al *(Cast)* 764, 1839, 1965, 4050, 4249, 4374, 4741
Seyler, Clifford *(Lyricist)* 702, 3310
Seymour, Anne *(Cast)* 97, 1874, 3150
Seymour, Caroline *(Cast)* 1787
Seymour, Dan *(Cast)* 3255
Seymour, Dan *(Producer)* 4163
Seymour, James *(Author)* 1359
Seymour, Jane *(Cast)* 1187, 2060
Seymour, John *(Cast)* 1013, 1235
Seymour, John D. *(Cast)* 4234
Seymour, Madeline *(Cast)* 1561

Seymour, Paul *(Cast)* 3501
Seymour, Tot *(Lyricist)* 2135, 4204, 4427, 4825
Seymour, W.H. *(Cast)* 402
Seymour, William *(Director)* 191, 2624, 4103
Seymoure, Norma *(Cast)* 574
Shactman, Murray *(Cast)* 1978
Shade, Lillian *(Cast)* 1137
Shadow *(Costumes)* 4707
Shafer, George *(Producer)* 1415
Shafer, Hal *(Set Design)* 4153
Shafer, Jerry *(Producer)* 362
Shafer, June *(Cast)* 2032
Shafer, Robert *(Cast)* 957, 1973, 3955, 4075
Shaffer, Henry *(Costumes)* 3997
Shaffer, Paul *(Cast)* 1512
Shaffer, Paul *(Composer)* 1512
Shaffer, Paul *(Librettist)* 1512
Shaffer, Victoria *(Costumes)* 1073
Shaffer, Wilhelm *(Choreographer)* 3298
Shaffer, William *(Orchestrations)* 2800
Shaffner, Walter *(Set Design)* 606
Shafman, Arthur *(Producer)* 3909
Shaiman, Marc *(Cast)* 1713
Shaiman, Marc *(Composer)* 1638, 1713, 2555
Shaiman, Marc *(Librettist)* 2555
Shaiman, Marc *(Lyricist)* 1638, 1713, 2555
Shaiman, Marc *(Musical Director)* 1713, 2555
Shaiman, Marc *(Orchestrations)* 1713
Shaiman, Marc *(Vocal Arranger)* 1713, 2427, 2555
Shakespeare, William *(Author)* 249, 514, 1104, 2244, 2257, 2599, 2841, 2859, 3000, 3015, 3231, 3539, 3741, 3876, 4256, 4485, 4715, 4789
Shakespeare, William *(Lyricist)* 1616, 1897, 2257, 2859, 3280, 4129, 4246, 4485, 4715
Shakespeare, William *(Lyrics Based On)* 3909
Shale, Betty *(Cast)* 841
Shale, Dorothy *(Cast)* 292
Shalek, Bertha *(Cast)* 4761
Shaler, Eleanor *(Cast)* 2366, 2739, 3005, 3379
Shalhoub, Tony *(Cast)* 2945
Shalom Yiddish Musical Comedy Theatre *(Producer)* 2866, 3670
Shane, Diana *(Cast)* 821
Shange, Ntozake *(Author)* 1344
Shange, Ntozake *(Lyricist)* 1344
Shanina, Yelena *(Cast)* 2269
Shank, Richard C. *(Director)* 348
Shanks, Alec *(Director)* 2364
Shanley, Robert *(Cast)* 1670, 4142, 4340
Shannon *(Producer)* 3222
Shannon, Effie *(Cast)* 1617, 2202
Shannon, Frank *(Cast)* 2528
Shannon, Harry T. *(Cast)* 2238, 3379
Shannon, James Royce *(Composer)* 3910
Shannon, James Royce *(Lyricist)* 3910
Shannon, Kitty *(Costumes)* 3291
Shannon, Peggy *(Cast)* 2476
Shannon, Walter *(Cast)* 2917
Shanstrom, David *(Director)* 3571
Shapero, Lillian *(Choreographer)* 4773
Shapiro, Dan *(Composer)* 1397
Shapiro, Dan *(Lyricist)* 145, 204, 673, 1336, 1397, 2246, 2850, 3178
Shapiro, Danny *(Composer)* 2379
Shapiro, Danny *(Lyricist)* 1892, 2379
Shapiro, Debbie *(Cast)* 478, 2205, 3444, 4114, 4252
Shapiro, Irwin *(Producer)* 467
Shapiro, Mel *(Director)* 1999, 2290, 3846, 4485
Shapiro, Mel *(Librettist)* 4485
Shapiro, Nat *(Producer)* 4558
Shapiro, Richard *(Producer)* 2001
Shapiro, Ted *(Cast)* 1333
Shapiro, Ted *(Composer)* 1333, 1825
Shapiro, Ted *(Lyricist)* 1825
Shapiro, Ted *(Pianist)* 1889
Sharaff, Irene *(Costumes)* 70, 121, 207, 297, 404, 512, 514, 601, 603, 630, 901, 961, 1061, 1315, 1413, 1420, 1564, 1680, 1729, 1760, 2068, 2201, 2252, 2268, 2312, 2386, 2475, 2679, 2777, 2797, 2850, 3283, 3365, 3913, 4131, 4174, 4214, 4238, 4446, 4569, 4667
Sharaff, Irene *(Set Design)* 55
Sharkey, Jack *(Cast)* 4686
Sharkey, Jack *(Librettist)* 3112
Sharkey the Seal *(Cast)* 1894
Sharma, Barbara *(Cast)* 450, 823, 1729, 1848, 3526, 4238, 4319
Sharman, Jim *(Director)* 3742, 4449
Sharon, Ula *(Cast)* 4077
Sharp, Adelaide *(Cast)* 2966
Sharp, Bobby *(Lyricist)* 477
Sharp, Jeffrey Day *(Producer)* 1073
Sharp, John Marshall *(Cast)* 3682
Sharp, Michael *(Costumes)* 1108
Sharp, Michael *(Set Design)* 1108, 1813
Sharpe, Albert *(Cast)* 1278
Sharpe, Ernest *(Cast)* 1874
Sharpe, John *(Cast)* 2523, 4409
Sharples, Richard *(Costumes)* 730
Sharrock, Ian *(Cast)* 3454
Shatner, William *(Cast)* 4749
Shattuck, Truly *(Cast)* 1188, 1480, 2254, 2383, 2517, 3387
Shaughnessy, Michael *(Cast)* 854
Shaughnessy, Mickey *(Cast)* 2304
Shavel, L.W. *(Set Design)* 1401
Shavelson, Melville *(Librettist)* 2217
Shaver, Bob *(Cast)* 3108
Shaw, Al *(Cast)* 1297, 3523
Shaw, Bernard *(Author)* 134
Shaw, Bill *(Composer)* 1415
Shaw, Bob *(Set Design)* 2033, 2359, 2646, 3070
Shaw, Carr *(Choreographer)* 3912
Shaw, David *(Librettist)* 3324, 3687, 3800, 4435
Shaw, Deborah *(Costumes)* 2440
Shaw, George Bernard *(Author)* 451, 742, 1848, 3038
Shaw, Hollace *(Cast)* 4557
Shaw, Howard *(Author)* 519
Shaw, Jack *(Cast)* 4683
Shaw, Kendall *(Set Design)* 1498

Shaw, Leon *(Cast)* 190, 1635
Shaw, Maxwell *(Cast)* 4469
Shaw, Neeka *(Cast)* 443, 691, 1019, 1251
Shaw, Oscar *(Cast)* 425, 993, 1011, 1207, 1297, 1323, 1625, 1723, 2430, 2460, 2872, 3009, 3243, 3295, 3457, 3596, 3775, 4491, 4521, 4555, 4853
Shaw, Reta *(Cast)* 1475, 3351
Shaw, Robert *(Cast)* 1441
Shaw, Robert *(Musical Director)* 2401
Shaw, Robert *(Vocal Arranger)* 653
Shaw, Sydney *(Composer)* 3112, 4827
Shaw, Sydney *(Lyricist)* 3112, 4827
Shaw, Ted *(Costumes)* 851
Shaw, Wini *(Cast)* 3166
Shaw and Lee *(Cast)* 1643
Shawhan, April *(Cast)* 616, 1914, 2219, 2918, 3000, 3330, 3702
Shawn, Allan *(Musical Director)* 2877
Shawn, Dick *(Cast)* 1474, 1730, 1955, 2073, 2075, 3020
Shawn, Michael *(Cast)* 3603
Shawn, Michael *(Choreographer)* 3305, 3724, 4029
Shawn, Michael *(Director)* 3311, 3724
Shawn, Peter *(Cast)* 3318
Shawn, Ted *(Choreographer)* 1235
Shawn Dancers, Ted *(Cast)* 3647
Shay, Michelle *(Cast)* 4403
Shay, Paula *(Cast)* 3048
Shay, Rita *(Cast)* 600
Shayne, Alan *(Cast)* 1194
Shea, Frank W. *(Director)* 2947
Shea, Jeanne *(Cast)* 937
Shea, Jere *(Cast)* 3411
Shea, John *(Cast)* 1186
Shea, Sandra *(Cast)* 2611
Shea, Steve *(Librettist)* 3714
Shea, William *(Cast)* 2311
Shealy, George *(Set Design)* 4047
Shean, Al *(Cast)* 376, 1295, 1432, 1908, 2112, 2155, 3014, 3590, 3771, 4702, 4816
Shean, Al *(Composer)* 4816
Shean, Al *(Lyricist)* 4816
Shearer, Denny *(Cast)* 658, 4522
Shearer, Toni *(Composer)* 2962
Shearman, Alan *(Cast)* 1166
Shearman, Alan *(Vocal Arranger)* 1166
Shearon, James K. *(Costumes)* 2001
Sheck, Max *(Cast)* 2835
Shecter, Ben *(Set Design)* 3439
Sheehan, Jack *(Cast)* 324, 1207, 1352, 2293, 2628, 3170
Sheehan, John *(Cast)* 111, 568, 1628, 2154, 3185, 3842
Sheehan, Joseph *(Cast)* 2733, 3570
Sheehan, Mike *(Cast)* 1037
Sheehan, W.T. *(Cast)* 4120
Sheehan Jr., John *(Cast)* 4299
Sheekman, Arthur *(Composer)* 3849
Sheekman, Arthur *(Librettist)* 4367
Sheer, William *(Producer)* 3246
Sheesley, John M. *(Producer)* 2455
Sheets, Walter *(Dance Arranger)* 1341
Sheets, Walter *(Vocal Arranger)* 1341
Sheffer, Isaiah *(Composer)* 3926
Sheffer, Isaiah *(Librettist)* 3722, 3926, 4769
Sheffer, Isaiah *(Lyricist)* 3722, 3926, 4769
Sheffer, Jonathan *(Composer)* 146, 1038, 1597, 2038, 2171
Sheffield, Ann *(Set Design)* 838
Sheffield, Buddy *(Composer)* 778
Sheffield, Buddy *(Librettist)* 778
Sheffield, Buddy *(Lyricist)* 778
Sheffield, David *(Librettist)* 778
Sheffield, Dick *(Cast)* 778
Sheffrey, Donald *(Musical Director)* 255
Sheffrey, Donald *(Orchestrations)* 255
Sheidy, William *(Composer)* 1362
Sheidy, William *(Lyricist)* 1362
Sheinkman, Mordecai *(Composer)* 237
Sheinkman, Mordecai *(Dance Arranger)* 4609
Sheintsiss, Oleg *(Set Design)* 2269
Shelby, Lillian *(Cast)* 3702
Sheldon, Edward *(Author)* 3063, 3064
Sheldon, Gene *(Cast)* 3594, 4237, 4265
Sheldon, Sidney *(Librettist)* 1101, 2187, 3687
Shell, Ray *(Cast)* 730, 4403
Shellenberger, James *(Producer)* 4264
Shelley, Carole *(Cast)* 194, 1082, 3196
Shelley, Frances *(Cast)* 3069, 3172
Shelley, Gladys *(Cast)* 2946
Shelley, Gladys *(Composer)* 2772
Shelley, Gladys *(Librettist)* 1112, 1814
Shelley, Gladys *(Lyricist)* 1112, 1596, 2772, 3810, 4565, 4586
Shelley, Herbert *(Composer)* 3828
Shelley, Herbert *(Lyricist)* 3828
Shelley, Joshua *(Cast)* 1880, 2067, 2464, 2707, 3473
Shelley, Joshua *(Director)* 280, 3983
Shelley, Mary *(Author)* 1382
Shelley, Paul *(Arrangements)* 865
Shelley, Paul *(Cast)* 865
Shelley, Paul *(Orchestrations)* 2397
Shelly, Howard M. *(Librettist)* 331
Shelly, Norman *(Cast)* 3452, 3453, 3603
Shelly, Robert *(Producer)* 1002
Shelton, Bob *(Cast)* 420
Shelton, Hall *(Producer)* 2595
Shelton, James *(Cast)* 90, 3103, 4166, 4677
Shelton, James *(Composer)* 90, 961, 1342, 2458, 2994, 3103, 3914, 4166, 4677
Shelton, James *(Director)* 961
Shelton, James *(Librettist)* 90, 961, 3914
Shelton, James *(Lyricist)* 90, 961, 1342, 2458, 2994, 3103, 3914, 4166, 4677
Shelton, Maria *(Lyricist)* 4565
Shelton, Reid *(Cast)* 150, 634, 2731, 3038, 3259, 4004
Shelton, Tommy *(Cast)* 2413
Shembe, Isaiah *(Composer)* 4438
Shembe, Isaiah *(Lyricist)* 4438
Shemer, Naomi *(Composer)* 4396
Shepard, Constance *(Composer)* 2780
Shepard, Joan *(Cast)* 3571, 3802, 4444

Shepard, Joan *(Composer)* 3802
Shepard, Joan *(Librettist)* 3802
Shepard, Karen *(Cast)* 2750
Shepard, Kiki *(Cast)* 166
Shepard, Sam *(Author)* 2468, 3309
Shepard, Sam *(Composer)* 3309
Shepard, Sam *(Director)* 2468
Shepard, Sam *(Librettist)* 3233
Shepard, Sam *(Lyricist)* 3309
Shephard, F. Firth *(Producer)* 3139, 4519
Shepherd, Jean *(Librettist)* 3110
Shepherd, Leonard *(Cast)* 3220
Shepley, Michael *(Producer)* 1418
Sheppard, Drey *(Lyricist)* 2279, 2913
Sheppard, Madelyn *(Composer)* 1972, 2276
Sheppard Jr., John R. *(Producer)* 341
Sher, Gloria *(Producer)* 3928
Sher, Gloria Hope *(Producer)* 2133
Sher, Louis K. *(Producer)* 3928
Shere, Michael *(Lighting Designer)* 2443
Sheridan, Edith *(Cast)* 3103
Sheridan, Eileen *(Cast)* 263
Sheridan, Kenneth *(Composer)* 2222
Sheridan, Liz *(Cast)* 278, 1364, 1590, 1755, 2043, 3479, 4062
Sheridan, Maura *(Lighting Designer)* 261
Sheridan, Richard Brinsley *(Author)* 71, 2057, 2399
Sheridan, Richard Brinsley *(Lyricist)* 2633
Sheridan, Wayne *(Librettist)* 1412
Sheridan, Wayne *(Lyricist)* 1412
Sherin, Edwin *(Director)* 3702
Sherman, Al *(Composer)* 393, 1127, 1491, 3406, 4821
Sherman, Al *(Lyricist)* 393, 1127, 1460, 1491
Sherman, Allan *(Lyricist)* 1832
Sherman, Allen *(Librettist)* 1273
Sherman, Allen *(Lyricist)* 1273
Sherman, Arthur *(Director)* 2172
Sherman, Arthur *(Librettist)* 3204
Sherman, Arthur *(Lyricist)* 3204
Sherman, Charles *(Director)* 490
Sherman, Charles *(Librettist)* 70, 95, 1322, 1415, 3893, 4174, 4374, 4498, 4499
Sherman, Garry *(Composer)* 105, 828
Sherman, Garry *(Orchestrations)* 105, 828, 1427, 3610
Sherman, Garry *(Vocal Arranger)* 105, 828, 3610
Sherman, George *(Lyricist)* 4396
Sherman, Hal *(Cast)* 1840, 4795
Sherman, Hiram *(Cast)* 194, 919, 1205, 2014, 2257, 2859, 3990, 4273, 4346, 4498, 4499, 4557, 4715
Sherman, Jimmy *(Composer)* 478
Sherman, Jimmy *(Lyricist)* 478
Sherman, Joe *(Composer)* 2275, 4829
Sherman, Joe *(Lyricist)* 4829
Sherman, Joe *(Orchestrations)* 4829
Sherman, Kim D. *(Composer)* 2441
Sherman, Kim D. *(Lyricist)* 2441
Sherman, Kim D. *(Orchestrations)* 2441
Sherman, Lee *(Choreographer)* 673, 2707, 3091
Sherman, Lee *(Lyricist)* 4260
Sherman, Loren *(Costumes)* 2852
Sherman, Loren *(Set Design)* 212, 572, 1149, 2852, 3448, 3598, 3944
Sherman, Milt *(Dance Arranger)* 2750, 3371
Sherman, Noel *(Composer)* 4264, 4829
Sherman, Noel *(Lyricist)* 4264, 4829
Sherman, Richard M. *(Composer)* 589, 1615, 3330, 4561
Sherman, Richard M. *(Lyricist)* 589, 1615, 3330
Sherman, Robert B. *(Composer)* 589, 1615, 3330
Sherman, Robert B. *(Lyricist)* 589, 1615, 3330, 4561
Sherman-Fowler, B. *(Composer)* 934
Sherri, Andre *(Costumes)* 231
Sherri, Andre *(Librettist)* 231
Sherrin, Ned *(Cast)* 3967
Sherrin, Ned *(Director)* 3967
Sherrin, Ned *(Librettist)* 3967
Sherwin, Jeannette *(Cast)* 2526
Sherwin, Julie *(Cast)* 4331
Sherwin, Manning *(Composer)* 266, 418, 1207, 2827, 3172, 4027, 4510
Sherwood, Blanche *(Cast)* 3154
Sherwood, Gail *(Cast)* 3683
Sherwood, Madeleine *(Cast)* 933, 1060, 2144
Sherwood, Ray *(Lyricist)* 1963
Sherwood, Robert E. *(Author)* 958, 4435
Sherwood, Robert E. *(Librettist)* 2894
Sherwood, Robert E. *(Lyricist)* 1357
Sherwood, Robert E. *(Producer)* 2894
Sherwood, Roberta *(Cast)* 2975
Sherwood, Toba *(Cast)* 2372
Sherwood, Walter *(Set Design)* 458
Shevelove, Bert *(Producer)* 193
Shevelove, Burt *(Director)* 635, 1406, 1729, 1762, 2940, 3743, 4018, 4038, 4469
Shevelove, Burt *(Librettist)* 635, 1406, 1422, 1762, 2940
Shevelove, Burt *(Lyricist)* 1762, 2940, 4018, 4585
Shevelove, Burt *(Producer)* 192
Shiebler, Howard *(Librettist)* 1493
Shield, Harvey *(Composer)* 1732
Shield, Harvey *(Librettist)* 1732
Shield, Harvey *(Lyricist)* 1732
Shields, Arthur *(Cast)* 4576
Shields, Ella *(Cast)* 4859
Shields, Maud *(Lyricist)* 470
Shields, Ren *(Composer)* 8, 1910, 2885, 4390, 4691
Shields, Ren *(Lyricist)* 8, 662, 1021, 2978, 2996, 4691
Shields, Robert *(Cast)* 547
Shields, Roy *(Musical Director)* 1244
Shields, Thomas *(Cast)* 2730
Shiffman, Jan Frederick *(Cast)* 528, 1155, 3165, 3329, 3997
Shiles, Michael *(Cast)* 4799
Shilkret, Nathaniel *(Musical Director)* 3386
Shimberg, Hinks *(Producer)* 4139, 4297, 4412
Shimerman, Armin *(Cast)* 2064
Shimkin, Arthur *(Producer)* 4785
Shimoda, Yuki *(Cast)* 3340
Shimono, Sab *(Cast)* 302, 2713, 3340, 3711
Shine, John L. *(Librettist)* 3776
Shipley, John *(Set Design)* 3629
Shipman, Helen *(Cast)* 1794, 2351, 2476, 2564, 2960, 3342, 3369, 3406, 3737

Shipman, Samuel *(Author)* 1142, 2595, 2872
Shipp, J.A. *(Cast)* 9, 295, 2111, 4088
Shipp, J.A. *(Composer)* 981
Shipp, J.A. *(Director)* 9, 2111
Shipp, J.A. *(Librettist)* 9, 295, 981, 2111, 2979, 3200
Shipp, J.A. *(Lyricist)* 9, 981, 2979
Shipp, Jesse A. *(Cast)* 3200
Shipp, Jesse A. *(Librettist)* 2520, 2942, 4088
Shipstad, Bob *(Director)* 2092, 2093, 2094
Shipstad, Bob *(Producer)* 2084, 2095, 2096
Shipstad, Eddie *(Producer)* 2083, 2086, 2087, 2088, 2089, 2090, 2091, 2092, 2093, 2094
Shipstad, Roy *(Cast)* 2088, 2089
Shipstad, Roy *(Producer)* 2083, 2086, 2087, 2088, 2089, 2090, 2091, 2092, 2093, 2094
Shipstads & Johnson
See also Bob Shipstad, Roy Shipstad and Oscar Johnson.
Shipstads & Johnson *(Producer)* 2085
Shire, David *(Composer)* 253, 784, 1298, 1648, 2011,2617, 3112, 3835, 4145, 4535
Shire, David *(Dance Arranger)* 832, 1648, 2617, 3835
Shire, David *(Librettist)* 3111
Shire, David *(Lyricist)* 784, 4145
Shire, David *(Musical Director)* 1648, 4401
Shire, David *(Orchestrations)* 3835
Shire, David *(Pianist)* 1648
Shire, David *(Vocal Arranger)* 1648, 2617, 3835
Shire, David L. *(Composer)* 945
Shirley, Bill *(Cast)* 3, 1681, 2168, 3381
Shirley, Don *(Set Design)* 4737
Shiryayev, Vladimir *(Cast)* 2269
Shlefer, Mack *(Conductor)* 2584
Shlenker, Sidney *(Producer)* 942, 4019
Shlenker, Sidney L. *(Producer)* 1068, 4020
Shlinker, Sidney *(Producer)* 1164
Shmulewitz, Solomon *(Composer)* 1609
Shmulewitz, Solomon *(Lyricist)* 1609
Shoctor, Joseph *(Producer)* 406
Shoemaker, Ann *(Cast)* 1721, 4100
Shoemaker, Richard *(Set Design)* 3111
Shoestring Follies Prod. *(Producer)* 4830
Shore, Allen M. *(Producer)* 1890, 1970
Shore, Howard *(Musical Director)* 1512
Shore, Lois *(Cast)* 1655
Shore, Ted *(Costumes)* 4117
Shore, Viola Brothers *(Librettist)* 1342, 3103
Shore, Viola Brothers *(Lyricist)* 3103
Shorenstein, Carole J. *(Producer)* 4727
Short, Bernice *(Cast)* 3709
Short, Frank Lea *(Director)* 1624
Short, Gloria *(Cast)* 1423
Short, Harry *(Cast)* 2717, 4007
Short, Hassard *(Cast)* 375, 1142
Short, Hassard *(Costumes)* 17, 960
Short, Hassard *(Director)* 17, 207, 294, 297, 383, 653, 960, 1225, 1384, 1680, 1691, 1692, 1847, 1962, 1987, 2252, 2386, 2638, 2691, 2707, 2755, 2847, 2850, 2855, 3006, 3007, 3008, 3013, 3147, 3254, 3735, 3770, 3893, 3895, 4058, 4131, 4212, 4213, 4350, 4365, 4367
Short, Hassard *(Lighting Designer)* 121, 207, 297, 653, 1225, 1413, 1680, 2252, 2386, 2707, 2847, 2850, 3013, 3035, 4058, 4131
Short, Hassard *(Lyricist)* 1142
Short, Hassard *(Producer)* 1780, 4159, 4213
Short, Hassard *(Set Design)* 1962
Short, John *(Cast)* 394
Short, Martin *(Cast)* 1633
Shorter, James *(Composer)* 4
Shorter, James *(Lyricist)* 4
Shoup, Howard *(Costumes)* 3014, 3683, 4706
Showalter, Elma *(Composer)* 2168
Showalter, Max *(Cast)* 1662, 2707, 4557
Showalter, Max *(Composer)* 1776, 2168, 2496
Showalter, Max *(Lyricist)* 2168, 3940
Showell, Jill *(Cast)* 2278
Showell, Jill *(Librettist)* 2278
Shriner, Herb *(Cast)* 2137
Shubert, Eddie *(Cast)* 3409
Shubert, J.J.
See also Messrs. Shubert and Shubert Brothers.
Shubert, J.J. *(Director)* 201, 1852, 2263, 3170, 4352
Shubert, J.J. *(Producer)* 8, 274, 324, 391, 480, 487, 764, 771, 905, 969, 1065, 1096, 1240, 1414, 1557, 1823, 1923, 1992, 2397, 2419, 2816, 2857, 2939, 3258, 3333, 3403, 3404, 3405, 3406, 3407, 3472, 3586, 3778, 3962, 3985, 4113, 4133, 4654
Shubert, John *(Director)* 1932
Shubert, John *(Librettist)* 3011
Shubert, John *(Lyricist)* 3011
Shubert, John *(Producer)* 4777
Shubert, Joseph *(Cast)* 2028
Shubert, Lee
See also Messrs. Shubert and Shubert Brothers.
Shubert, Lee *(Producer)* 125, 274, 276, 353, 391, 480, 487, 764, 771, 905, 969, 1041, 1065, 1096, 1111, 1240, 1464, 1522, 1523, 1526, 1557, 1570, 1613, 1618, 1768, 1783, 1793, 1823, 1923, 1992, 2282, 2317, 2334, 2419, 2745, 2816, 2848, 2857, 2869, 2914, 2939, 2978, 3052, 3085, 3258, 3265, 3313, 3333, 3403, 3404, 3405, 3406, 3407, 3472, 3486, 3560, 3586, 3730, 3778, 3962, 3974, 3985, 4044, 4113, 4133, 4434, 4493, 4521, 4616, 4654, 4666
Shubert, Messrs.
See also J.J. Shubert and Lee Shubert.
Shubert, Messrs. *(Producer)* 75, 93, 106, 110, 138, 184, 188, 199, 200, 201, 202, 203, 216, 236, 340, 351, 355, 383, 463, 470, 473, 495, 558, 659, 684, 718, 901, 910, 948, 1033, 1042, 1113, 1207, 1334, 1384, 1460, 1461, 1462, 1506, 1530, 1551, 1561, 1626, 1678, 1735, 1831, 1836, 1840, 1852, 1932, 1973, 2135, 2139, 2281, 2293, 2301, 2358, 2384, 2399, 2400, 2490, 2540, 2546, 2574, 2602, 2610, 2620, 2622, 2628, 2637, 2649, 2668, 2669, 2732, 2747, 2789, 2794, 2808, 2825, 2843, 2854, 2856, 2870, 3011, 3012, 3032, 3051, 3056, 3064, 3084, 3148, 3149, 3150, 3152, 3163, 3170, 3237, 3345, 3402, 3409, 3410, 3424, 3504, 3523, 3573, 3677, 3679, 3680, 3799, 3821, 3955, 4010, 4025, 4059, 4086, 4117, 4121, 4166, 4174, 4188, 4352, 4365, 4418, 4419, 4427, 4490, 4509, 4510, 4575, 4586, 4599, 4669, 4670, 4714, 4730, 4733, 4767, 4777, 4824, 4825, 4826

Shubert, Mrs. J.J. *(Costumes)* 3399, 4747
Shubert, Sam S. *(Librettist)* 1243
Shubert, Sam S. *(Producer)* 8, 276, 353, 737, 1041, 1111, 1123, 1178, 1243, 1464, 1522, 1523, 1526, 1535, 1570, 1613, 1768, 1783, 1793, 2282, 2317, 2334, 2745, 2848, 2869, 2914, 2978, 3052, 3085, 3265, 3313, 3486, 3560, 3730, 3805, 4044, 4434, 4493, 4521, 4616, 4666, 4713
Shubert Brothers
See also J.J. Shubert and Lee Shubert.
Shubert Brothers *(Producer)* 4355
Shubert Jr., J.J. *(Composer)* 3148
Shubert Organization *(Producer)* 16, 39, 393, 678, 1103, 1776, 2033, 2474, 2544, 2558, 3159, 3577, 4068, 4210, 4459, 4861
Shubert Organization, The *(Producer)* 721, 775, 2205, 3285, 3411, 3792, 4129
Shuck, John *(Cast)* 3164
Shull, Richard B. *(Cast)* 36, 1402, 1634, 2874, 3080, 3231, 4560, 4582
Shulman, A. *(Librettist)* 2421
Shulman, Arnold *(Author)* 1611
Shulman, Max *(Author)* 304
Shulman, Max *(Librettist)* 67, 304, 2014
Shulman, Michael *(Cast)* 212
Shuman, Earl *(Lyricist)* 3863
Shuman, Francis K. *(Composer)* 3442
Shuman, Mort *(Cast)* 2188
Shuman, Mort *(Composer)* 2017, 3695
Shuman, Mort *(Lyricist)* 2188, 3695
Shuman, Mort *(Musical Director)* 2188
Shumlin, Herman *(Director)* 2510, 4278
Shumlin, Herman *(Producer)* 2510
Shurley, George *(Choreographer)* 3827, 4302
Shuster, Joe *(Author)* 2163
Shuster, Rosie *(Librettist)* 1512
Shutta, Ethel *(Cast)* 1329, 2201, 2594, 2757, 3036, 3405, 4427, 4683, 4819
Shwarze, Henry *(Choreographer)* 4792
Shy, Gus *(Cast)* 111, 1176, 1628, 2569, 3117, 4050, 4240, 4692
Shyre, Paul *(Director)* 33
Shyre, Paul *(Librettist)* 33, 2055
Sibanda, Seth *(Cast)* 1719
Sibley, Harper *(Producer)* 2754
Sica, Joy Lynne *(Cast)* 1233
Sicangco, Eduardo *(Costumes)* 992, 1146, 1702, 3628
Sicangco, Eduardo *(Set Design)* 992, 1146, 1638, 1702
Sicari, Joseph R. *(Cast)* 825, 956
Sicari, Sal *(Musical Director)* 2055
Sidman, Sam *(Cast)* 2271, 4630
Sidney, Carl *(Costumes)* 2105
Sidney, David *(Lyricist)* 4545
Sidney, George *(Cast)* 592, 3153, 3246, 4686
Sidney, George *(Lyricist)* 3129
Sidney, Robert *(Choreographer)* 95, 961, 4362, 4428
Sidney, Susanne *(Cast)* 2267
Sidney, Sylvia *(Cast)* 1190
Sidon, Herbert *(Costumes)* 1644
Sieber, Christopher *(Cast)* 3227
Siebert, Charles *(Cast)* 807
Sieczynski *(Composer)* 3020
Sieczynski, Rudolf *(Composer)* 3540
Siedel, Mme. *(Costumes)* 618
Siedle *(Costumes)* 2507
Siedle, C.F. *(Costumes)* 1165, 3820
Siedle, Caroline *(Costumes)* 8, 250, 559, 639, 666, 737, 1071, 4181, 4293
Siedle, Edward *(Librettist)* 1458
Siedle, Mme./C.F./Caroline/Mme.
See also under Seidle.
Siedle, Mme. *(Costumes)* 113, 350, 357, 976, 1543, 1896, 2116, 2345, 2398, 2733, 2824, 3176, 3570, 4098, 4614, 4691
Siedle, Mrs. Edward *(Costumes)* 4723
Siegal, Al *(Producer)* 851
Siegal, Don *(Composer)* 3557
Siegal, Don *(Lyricist)* 3557
Siegal, Michael *(Composer)* 2578
Siegel, Arthur *(Cast)* 2294, 2629
Siegel, Arthur *(Composer)* 679, 817, 871, 943, 2168, 2294, 2416, 2629, 2772, 2998, 3107, 3108, 3110, 3111, 3112, 3178, 3186, 3204, 3320, 3619, 3880, 3890, 3941, 4108, 4279, 4433
Siegel, Arthur *(Lyricist)* 3112
Siegel, Arthur *(Musical Director)* 679, 3890
Siegel, Arthur *(Pianist)* 1873
Siegel, Arthur *(Producer)* 3890
Siegel, Arthur *(Vocal Arranger)* 3890
Siegel, David *(Arrangements)* 4799
Siegel, David *(Orchestrations)* 1701, 3461, 4703, 4799
Siegel, Jerry *(Author)* 2163
Siegel, Joel *(Librettist)* 1289
Siegel, June *(Lyricist)* 4, 2007
Siegel, Larry *(Librettist)* 2663
Siegel, Larry *(Lyricist)* 2663
Siegel, Larry *(Set Design)* 1958
Siegel, M. *(Composer)* 376
Siegel, Mark *(Cast)* 518
Siegel, Maxwell Edward *(Lyricist)* 1049
Siegel, William *(Librettist)* 3670
Sieger, Charles *(Musical Director)* 1831
Siegle, Gloria *(Cast)* 2483
Siegle, Gloria *(Composer)* 2483
Siegler, Robert *(Director)* 1612
Siegmeister, Elie *(Composer)* 3989
Siegmeister, Elie *(Dance Arranger)* 657, 2295
Siegmeister, Elie *(Musical Director)* 3989
Siegmeister, Elie *(Orchestrations)* 3989
Siegmeister, Elie *(Vocal Arranger)* 657, 4015
Siegrist, Topsy *(Cast)* 1526
Siems, Bobby *(Composer)* 2555
Siepi, Cesare *(Cast)* 519, 652
Sievier, Bruce *(Lyricist)* 3020
Siff, Andrew *(Producer)* 1237
Siff, Ira *(Cast)* 755, 1229, 1426, 1715, 2220, 2243, 2579
Siff, Ira *(Costumes)* 2220, 2243, 2478
Siggins, Jeff *(Cast)* 3551
Sigler, Maurice *(Lyricist)* 3822
Sigman, Carl *(Composer)* 137, 857
Sigman, Carl *(Lyricist)* 4264
Sigman, H.E. *(Musical Director)* 917

Signore, Don *(Director)* 1282
Signorelli, Frank *(Composer)* 4137, 4799
Silber, Arthur *(Producer)* 2640
Silberman, David *(Producer)* 3204
Silberman, Joel *(Cast)* 3476
Silberman, Joel *(Dance Arranger)* 3668
Silberman, Joel *(Musical Director)* 13, 2199, 3476, 3576, 3668
Silberman, Joel *(Vocal Arranger)* 3576, 3668
Silen, Hal *(Producer)* 3752
Silesu, Leo *(Composer)* 4807
Siletti, Mario *(Cast)* 2522
Silliman, Maureen *(Cast)* 2026, 2064, 4358, 4505
Sillman, Albert *(Lyricist)* 4569
Sillman, June
See also June Carroll.
Sillman, June *(Cast)* 621, 2032, 4677
Sillman, June *(Lyricist)* 70, 621, 1342, 3103, 3104, 4677
Sillman, June *(Producer)* 3105
Sillman, Leonard *(Cast)* 1342, 2032, 2827, 3103, 3105, 3532
Sillman, Leonard *(Composer)* 2032
Sillman, Leonard *(Director)* 70, 621, 1342, 2772, 3104, 3110, 3111, 3112, 4677
Sillman, Leonard *(Librettist)* 621, 3104, 4677
Sillman, Leonard *(Lyricist)* 2032
Sillman, Leonard *(Producer)* 70, 817, 1748, 2103, 2772, 2994, 3104, 3107, 3108, 3880
Sills, Beverly *(Cast)* 2839
Sills, Paul *(Director)* 1122, 4397
Sills, Paul *(Producer)* 4397
Sills, Stephanie *(Producer)* 1216
Silva, Larry J. *(Producer)* 4390
Silva, Mario *(Musical Director)* 796
Silva, Nino *(Musical Director)* 991
Silver, Abner *(Composer)* 447, 487, 567, 815, 1126, 1127, 1134, 1491, 1685, 2060, 2706, 2772, 3404, 4104, 4271, 4526, 4814, 4817, 4841
Silver, Abner *(Lyricist)* 487, 1126, 1127, 1134, 1491, 2060, 2706, 2772, 3404, 4083
Silver, Frank *(Lyricist)* 3008
Silver, Fred *(Composer)* 2114, 2294, 3479
Silver, Fred *(Lyricist)* 2114, 2294
Silver, Frederick *(Arrangements)* 3479
Silver, Frederick *(Musical Director)* 3479
Silver, Joan Micklin *(Director)* 4, 2787
Silver, Joan Micklin *(Librettist)* 2787
Silver, Joe *(Cast)* 1709, 2164, 2437, 3215, 3846, 4863
Silver, Johnny *(Cast)* 1706, 2841
Silver, Louis *(Composer)* 538
Silver, Louis *(Musical Director)* 4730
Silver, Maxwell *(Composer)* 1573
Silver, Morris S. *(Librettist)* 1147
Silver, Morris S. *(Lyricist)* 1147
Silver, Raphael *(Producer)* 2787
Silver, Stuart *(Cast)* 4172
Silvera, Richard *(Cast)* 4096
Silverglat, Harry *(Set Design)* 1371, 3167
Silverheels *(Cast)* 421
Silverman, Jack H. *(Producer)* 4337
Silverman, Jeffrey *(Cast)* 556, 3311
Silverman, Jeffrey *(Composer)* 556, 3311
Silverman, Jeffrey *(Producer)* 556
Silverman, Jon D. *(Producer)* 3448
Silverman, Stanley *(Composer)* 1064, 4523
Silverman, Stanley *(Lyricist)* 1064
Silverman, Stanley *(Musical Director)* 1064, 4370
Silverman, Stanley *(Orchestrations)* 1064
Silverman, Treva *(Librettist)* 128, 272, 1436, 3111, 3852
Silverman, Treva *(Lyricist)* 3186
Silvernail, Clarke *(Director)* 1839
Silvers, Frank *(Composer)* 1381
Silvers, Frank *(Lyricist)* 1381
Silvers, Louis *(Composer)* 79, 487, 1395, 1626, 1686, 2215, 2606, 3397, 3421, 4458
Silvers, Louis *(Lyricist)* 3421
Silvers, Louis *(Musical Director)* 208, 1395, 3258, 3333
Silvers, Phil *(Cast)* 1061, 1886, 4423, 4772
Silvers, Phil *(Librettist)* 1886
Silvers, Sid *(Cast)* 1879, 3149, 4267
Silvers, Sid *(Composer)* 3108
Silvers, Sid *(Librettist)* 1879, 4778
Silvers, Sid *(Lyricist)* 565, 3108, 3149, 3523
Silverstein *(Lyricist)* 4291
Silverstein, Shel *(Composer)* 1389
Silverstein, Shel *(Librettist)* 4535
Silverstein, Shel *(Lyricist)* 1389
Silvestri, Martin *(Musical Director)* 1635
Silvestri, Martin *(Orchestrations)* 2242
Silviera, Mary *(Cast)* 4548
Siman, Barbara *(Choreographer)* 2658, 2790
Siman, Barbara *(Director)* 2658
Simington, William *(Cast)* 1730
Simmonds, Stanley *(Cast)* 2217, 2484, 2660, 2681, 3279
Simmons, "Red" *(Cast)* 2561
Simmons, Albert *(Librettist)* 58
Simmons, Andrew *(Librettist)* 3076
Simmons, B.J. *(Costumes)* 292
Simmons, Bartlett *(Cast)* 1460, 2423, 2475, 3012, 3849
Simmons, Bonnie *(Cast)* 678
Simmons, Chandra *(Cast)* 2272
Simmons, Danny *(Cast)* 539
Simmons, Elsie *(Librettist)* 58
Simmons, Elsie *(Lyricist)* 58
Simmons, Gene *(Composer)* 3739
Simmons, Gene *(Lyricist)* 3739
Simmons, J.K. *(Cast)* 992, 1172, 2241
Simmons, Kay *(Cast)* 202
Simmons, Matty *(Librettist)* 3076
Simmons, Michael *(Librettist)* 3076
Simmons, Michael *(Producer)* 3076
Simmons, Michele *(Choreographer)* 4645
Simmons, Pat *(Lighting Designer)* 73, 4645
Simmons, Philip *(Cast)* 3157
Simmons, Pousseau *(Lyricist)* 553
Simmons, Roscoe "Red" *(Cast)* 1514
Simmons, Rosseau *(Composer)* 3297
Simmons, Rosseau *(Lyricist)* 3297
Simmons, Stanley *(Costumes)* 90, 823, 1216, 3204, 3743, 4038, 4145, 4329
Simmons, Ted *(Composer)* 4172

Simmons Jr., Roscoe *(Choreographer)* 2942
Simms, Hilda *(Cast)* 2395
Simms, Lu Ann *(Cast)* 197
Simms, Margaret *(Cast)* 498, 1050, 1980, 2557, 4520
Simon, Adam *(Author)* 655
Simon, Alfred *(Composer)* 1342
Simon, D. Bernard *(Lyricist)* 2458
Simon, Danny *(Director)* 673
Simon, Danny *(Librettist)* 673, 1892, 2246
Simon, Herb *(Cast)* 1595
Simon, Ilona *(Composer)* 716
Simon, Ilona *(Lyricist)* 716
Simon, John *(Composer)* 272
Simon, John *(Dance Arranger)* 3739
Simon, John *(Orchestrations)* 3739
Simon, John *(Vocal Arranger)* 3739
Simon, Louis *(Cast)* 2291
Simon, Louis *(Costumes)* 1448
Simon, Louis *(Librettist)* 608, 1448
Simon, Lucy *(Composer)* 4, 3553, 3862
Simon, Max *(Librettist)* 2330
Simon, Neil *(Author)* 1620, 3864
Simon, Neil *(Librettist)* 23, 673, 743, 1325, 1633, 1815, 1892, 2246, 2523, 2837, 3603, 4238, 4334
Simon, Neil *(Lyricist)* 1620
Simon, Neil *(Screenwriter)* 1633
Simon, Owen *(Cast)* 2028
Simon, Paul *(Composer)* 3739
Simon, Paul *(Lyricist)* 2775, 3739
Simon, Robert *(Cast)* 3180
Simon, Robert A. *(Composer)* 1932, 3926
Simon, Robert A. *(Librettist)* 4532
Simon, Robert A. *(Lyricist)* 265, 689, 978, 1440, 1654, 1932, 3926, 4532, 4780
Simon Sisters, The *(Puppeteer)* 997
Simonds, Robert *(Composer)* 4322
Simons, Seymour *(Composer)* 1176, 1847
Simons, Seymour *(Lyricist)* 1176, 1847
Simons, Seymour B. *(Composer)* 2373
Simons, Seymour B. *(Lyricist)* 2373
Simons, Ted *(Composer)* 3548
Simons, Ted *(Dance Arranger)* 4318
Simons, Ted *(Musical Director)* 127, 1585, 3112, 3835
Simons, Ted *(Vocal Arranger)* 4318
Simonson, Eric *(Director)* 4074
Simonson, Lee *(Costumes)* 2487
Simonson, Lee *(Set Design)* 2487, 3365, 4283, 4569
Simonson, S. *(Musical Director)* 526
Simonson, Timothy *(Cast)* 2239
Simpson, B. *(Composer)* 3608
Simpson, B. *(Lyricist)* 3608
Simpson, Bland *(Cast)* 1037
Simpson, Bland *(Composer)* 1037, 1985
Simpson, Bland *(Lyricist)* 1037, 1985
Simpson, Carole *(Cast)* 1195
Simpson, Charles *(Cast)* 3047
Simpson, Cheridah *(Cast)* 1301
Simpson, Donald *(Cast)* 1887
Simpson, Harold *(Author)* 325
Simpson, Harold *(Librettist)* 605, 1733
Simpson, Marty *(Cast)* 4229
Simpson, Michael *(Composer)* 3380
Simpson, Michael *(Lyricist)* 3380
Simpson, N.F. *(Additional Materal)* 1857
Simpson, Nora *(Composer)* 3380
Simpson, Nora *(Lyricist)* 3380
Simpson, Rick *(Cast)* 1037
Simpson, Robert *(Choreographer)* 2027
Simpson, Robert *(Director)* 4022
Sims, George R. *(Author)* 1975
Sims, George R. *(Librettist)* 2500
Sims, George R. *(Lyricist)* 2500
Sims, John *(Cast)* 3993
Sinatra, Frank *(Cast)* 3324
Sinatra, Ray *(Musical Director)* 4486
Sinatra, Ray *(Orchestrations)* 971
Sinatra, Raymond *(Musical Director)* 297, 4131
Sinatra, Raymond *(Orchestrations)* 4131
Sinatra, Raymond *(Vocal Arranger)* 4131
Sinclair, Andrew *(Additional Materal)* 1857
Sinclair, Arthur *(Cast)* 2258
Sinclair, Charles *(Cast)* 3520
Sinclair, Charles *(Director)* 1013, 1532, 2384, 2631, 3520, 3915
Sinclair, Charles *(Producer)* 904
Sinclair, Horace *(Director)* 4328
Sinclair, Hugh *(Cast)* 702, 1618
Sinclair, Robert *(Director)* 247
Sinclair, Robert B. *(Director)* 1204
Sinclair, Vera *(Cast)* 1561
Sindler, Merrill *(Costumes)* 73
Sindler, Merrill *(Set Design)* 73
Singer, Andre *(Composer)* 3698
Singer, David *(Producer)* 1785
Singer, Dolph *(Lyricist)* 4204, 4668
Singer, Isaac Bashevis *(Author)* 3937, 4773
Singer, Lou *(Composer)* 7
Singer, Louis J. *(Producer)* 3321
Singer, Marion *(Cast)* 1356
Singer, Mort
See also The Askin-Singer Company.
Singer, Mort *(Producer)* 4506
Singer, Mort H. *(Producer)* 1307, 1472, 1525, 4185, 4387
Singer, Reuben *(Cast)* 1227
Singer, Ron *(Pianist)* 4041
Singer Midgets, The *(Cast)* 2300
Singleton, C. *(Composer)* 1296
Singleton, C. *(Lyricist)* 1296
Singleton, Edith *(Cast)* 4509
Singleton, Penny *(Cast)* 1874, 4583
Sinn, Minnie *(Cast)* 1640
Sinnot, Florence *(Cast)* 4753
Sircom, Arthur *(Director)* 3138, 3816
Sire, L.S. *(Producer)* 3693, 4351
Sire, Messrs. *(Producer)* 1505, 2917
Sire Bros. *(Producer)* 354, 1728, 4222
Siretta, Dan *(Cast)* 798, 1094, 3815
Siretta, Dan *(Choreographer)* 1099, 1427, 1665, 2568, 3671, 3926, 4107, 4796
Siretta, Dan *(Director)* 1099, 3926

Sirlin, Jerome *(Set Design)* 2185, 2333, 4229
Sirmay, Albert *(Composer)* 292, 1561, 2392, 3584, 3721, 4818, 4843
Sirola, Joseph *(Cast)* 1611, 4516
Sislian, Nicole *(Cast)* 2676
Sissle, Noble *(Cast)* 740, 3963, 3965, 3966
Sissle, Noble *(Composer)* 740, 3144
Sissle, Noble *(Director)* 740
Sissle, Noble *(Librettist)* 740
Sissle, Noble *(Lyricist)* 133, 393, 740, 792, 1052, 1174, 1198, 1765, 2570, 2856, 3020, 3144, 3512, 3905, 3963, 3964, 3965, 3966, 4154, 4751, 4810, 4812
Sissle, Noble *(Musical Director)* 3975
Sissle and His Orchestra, Noble *(Cast)* 3166, 4465
Sissle's Orchestra, Noble *(Cast)* 3975
Sissons, Narelle *(Set Design)* 3227
Sister Mary Francis P.C. *(Librettist)* 2393
Sister Mary Francis P.C. *(Lyricist)* 2393
Sisters and Brothers, The *(Cast)* 1389
Sisti, Michelan *(Cast)* 3643
Sivuca *(Cast)* 2245
Sivuca *(Composer)* 2245
Sivuca *(Lyricist)* 2245
Six Brown Brothers *(Cast)* 736, 4393
6 Spirits of Rhythm *(Cast)* 216
Sizemore, Art *(Composer)* 567
Skala, Lilia *(Cast)* 619
Skardon, Steve *(Cast)* 1004
Skatula, Kathryn *(Cast)* 2969
Skelly, Hal *(Cast)* 17, 381, 587, 993, 1266, 1552, 2107, 2403, 2768, 2813, 3146, 3312
Skelly, J.P. *(Composer)* 1897
Skelly, J.P. *(Lyricist)* 1897
Skelton, Geoffrey *(Translator)* 3445
Skelton, Red *(Voice)* 3795
Skelton, Richard "Red" *(Cast)* 1476
Skelton, Thomas *(Lighting Designer)* 369, 518, 798, 823, 958, 1511, 2218, 2435, 2626, 3020, 3428, 3610, 3840, 3871, 3928, 3991
Skelton, Thomas R. *(Lighting Designer)* 747
Skelton, Tom *(Lighting Designer)* 3577, 3888, 4789
Skerrett Jr., H.H. *(Lyricist)* 231
Skidmore, Katherine *(Cast)* 1241
Skidmore, Will *(Lyricist)* 4840
Skiles, Steve *(Cast)* 3209
Skina, Eve *(Producer)* 4390
Skinner *(Lyricist)* 2793
Skinner, Cornelia Otis *(Cast)* 3386
Skinner, Cornelia Otis *(Librettist)* 3386
Skinner, Edna *(Cast)* 4323
Skinner, Frank *(Orchestrations)* 1667
Skinner, Jolyon *(Composer)* 4786
Skinner, Jolyon *(Lyricist)* 4786
Skinner, Laurie Dawn *(Cast)* 1637
Skinner, Otis *(Cast)* 3829
Skinner, Ralph *(Librettist)* 1910, 2966
Skinner, Ralph *(Lyricist)* 1910, 2966
Skinner, Ralph M. *(Librettist)* 4493
Skinner, Ralph M. *(Lyricist)* 4493
Skinner, Randy *(Choreographer)* 36, 4146
Skinner, Randy *(Director)* 4146
Skinner, Richard *(Producer)* 1734, 3816
Skipper, William *(Choreographer)* 90, 3914
Skipworth, Alison *(Cast)* 138, 3849
Sklar, Daniel *(Cast)* 99
Sklar, George *(Librettist)* 3365
Sklar, George *(Lyricist)* 3365
Sklar, Roberta *(Director)* 1786
Skloff, Michael *(Arrangements)* 198
Skloff, Michael *(Composer)* 4, 198, 1055, 2197, 3448
Skloff, Michael *(Conductor)* 4535
Skloff, Michael *(Dance Arranger)* 198, 2230
Skloff, Michael *(Lyricist)* 1055
Skloff, Michael *(Musical Director)* 4, 1055, 3448
Skloff, Michael *(Vocal Arranger)* 3448
Skobel, Ron *(Cast)* 2022
Skolsky, Sidney *(Lyricist)* 3953
Skouras Theatres *(Producer)* 2175
Skulnick, Menasha *(Composer)* 1609
Skulnick, Menasha *(Lyricist)* 1609
Skulnik, Menasha *(Cast)* 2357, 4863
Sky, Don *(Choreographer)* 348
Slade, Julian *(Composer)* 1386, 3818
Slade, Julian *(Librettist)* 3818
Slade, Julian *(Lyricist)* 1386, 3818
Slade, Stuart *(Set Design)* 4243
Slaiman, Marjorie *(Costumes)* 1914, 2579, 4744
Slate, Henry *(Cast)* 4096
Slate Brothers *(Cast)* 1136, 4778
Slater, B.J. *(Cast)* 2026
Slater, Bob *(Composer)* 719
Slater, Bob *(Lyricist)* 719
Slater, Christian *(Cast)* 2820
Slater, George M. *(Lyricist)* 719
Slater, Mary Jo *(Producer)* 4145
Slaughter, Walter *(Author)* 1188, 2991
Slaughter, Walter *(Composer)* 1392, 1473, 2514, 2529
Slaughter, William *(Composer)* 476
Slavin, John *(Cast)* 41, 307, 683, 1270, 1599, 2116, 2347, 2465, 2632, 2695, 2716, 4012, 4125
Slavin, John C. *(Cast)* 523, 2029, 2515, 3994
Slavin, John C. *(Choreographer)* 2515
Slavin, L.J. *(Cast)* 4740
Slavin, Mildred *(Cast)* 3505
Slavin, Millie *(Cast)* 3603, 4395
Slawson, Dana *(Composer)* 3410
Slawson, Dana *(Lyricist)* 3410
Slay, Frank C. *(Composer)* 722
Slay, Frank C. *(Lyricist)* 722
Slayter, Marcus *(Cast)* 4763
Slayter, Marcus *(Choreographer)* 4763
Slayter, Marcus *(Composer)* 1057
Slayter, Marcus *(Producer)* 1057
Slezak, Walter *(Cast)* 1242, 1261, 2061, 2786, 2808, 3014, 3496
Slick, Grace *(Composer)* 3739
Slick, Grace *(Lyricist)* 3739
Sloan, Estelle *(Cast)* 4428
Sloan, Lenwood *(Choreographer)* 4697
Sloan, Mimi *(Cast)* 1158

Sloan, W.H. *(Cast)* 2157
Sloan, W.H. *(Composer)* 2343
Sloan, Will H. *(Cast)* 1640, 2316
Sloan, William *(Cast)* 357
Sloane, A. Baldwin *(Author)* 3436
Sloane, A. Baldwin *(Composer)* 29, 76, 77, 235, 336, 354, 559, 735, 737, 830, 938, 939, 1005, 1031, 1213, 1244, 1246, 1505, 1515, 1535, 1573, 1685, 1686, 1728, 1738, 1752, 1835, 1845, 1927, 2181, 2324, 2373, 2399, 2465, 2485, 2559, 2675, 2711, 2865, 2868, 2917, 3090, 3096, 3575, 3673, 3753, 3755, 3867, 3883, 3989, 4165, 4203, 4206, 4382, 4552, 4608, 4648, 4721, 4723
Sloane, A. Baldwin *(Lyricist)* 1927, 4206
Sloane, Everett *(Cast)* 1893
Sloane, Everett *(Composer)* 1408
Sloane, Everett *(Lyricist)* 1408
Sloane, Frank *(Lyricist)* 559
Sloane, Mae Anwerda *(Composer)* 1728, 2324, 2465
Sloane, Mae Anwerda *(Lyricist)* 2324
Sloane, Mike *(Producer)* 657, 2496, 3801, 4423
Sloat, John *(Lighting Designer)* 4408
Sloate, Maynard *(Librettist)* 1326
Sloate, Maynard *(Producer)* 1326
Slocum, John P. *(Director)* 2722
Sloman, John *(Cast)* 2305, 4517
Sloman, Larry *(Composer)* 3076
Sloman, Larry *(Librettist)* 3076
Sloman, Larry *(Lyricist)* 3076
Slosberg, Bertha *(Choreographer)* 4207
Slovick, Sam *(Cast)* 119
Slutsker, Peter *(Cast)* 595, 2241, 3992
Slyde, Jimmy *(Cast)* 432
Small, Allan *(Orchestrations)* 2705, 4123, 4428
Small, Jack *(Director)* 84
Small, Larry *(Cast)* 1068, 4689
Small, Mary *(Cast)* 861, 3902
Small, Marya *(Cast)* 1664
Small, Neva *(Cast)* 278, 1222, 1380, 1609, 1739, 1846, 2477, 2775, 3577, 3956, 4060, 4062
Small, Ralph *(Cast)* 1120
Smalle, Ed *(Lyricist)* 3973
Smallens, Alexander *(Musical Director)* 1366, 3541
Smalley, Victor H. *(Librettist)* 2840
Smalley, Victor H. *(Lyricist)* 2840
Smalls, Charlie *(Composer)* 4722
Smalls, Charlie *(Lyricist)* 4722
Smalls Jr., Arthur *(Cast)* 4003
Smalls Jr., Arthur *(Composer)* 4003
Smallwood, Mildred *(Cast)* 739
Smallwood, Richard *(Composer)* 3987, 3991
Smallwood, Richard *(Lyricist)* 3987, 3991
Smallwood Singers, The, Richard *(Cast)* 3991
Smart, Dick *(Cast)* 817
Smart, Jack *(Cast)* 3104
Smartt, Suzanne *(Cast)* 2784
Smedberg, John *(Cast)* 1973
Smicoeve Prod. *(Producer)* 563
Smidt, Burr *(Producer)* 2553
Smiley, Joseph *(Cast)* 2233
Smit, Edward J. *(Cast)* 4732
Smith *(Composer)* 1925
Smith *(Librettist)* 950
Smith *(Lyricist)* 1246, 1925, 4697
Smith, Ada *(Cast)* 2044
Smith, Adrian *(Composer)* 3901
Smith, Adrian *(Lyricist)* 3901
Smith, Alexis *(Cast)* 1329, 3515
Smith, Alma *(Cast)* 567, 725, 877, 3707
Smith, Art *(Cast)* 2228, 3947, 4625
Smith, Baker S. *(Costumes)* 4740
Smith, Bert *(Cast)* 1593
Smith, Bessie *(Cast)* 3361
Smith, Bessie *(Composer)* 478, 3297
Smith, Bessie *(Lyricist)* 478, 3297
Smith, Betty *(Author)* 4446
Smith, Betty *(Librettist)* 4446
Smith, Betty Jane *(Cast)* 849, 4702
Smith, Bruce *(Cast)* 4014
Smith, Bruce *(Set Design)* 2964, 2974
Smith, Buddy *(Cast)* 4676
Smith, C. Aubrey *(Cast)* 2952
Smith, Carl *(Composer)* 146, 1638, 3739
Smith, Carl *(Lyricist)* 146, 1638, 3739
Smith, Carolyn *(Costumes)* 580
Smith, Carrie *(Cast)* 432
Smith, Chris *(Composer)* 146, 295, 434, 545, 1544, 2254, 2765, 3297, 3308, 4390, 4833
Smith, Chris *(Lyricist)* 146, 500, 545, 1909, 2254, 3297, 3308, 4804, 4833
Smith, Christopher *(Cast)* 2661
Smith, Clay *(Cast)* 1531
Smith, Cyrena *(Cast)* 1342
Smith, Cyril *(Cast)* 3605
Smith, Darrel H. *(Lyricist)* 750
Smith, Darrell H. *(Lyricist)* 18
Smith, David Rae *(Cast)* 2839
Smith, Dick *(Composer)* 4824
Smith, Dick *(Lyricist)* 4824
Smith, Don *(Musical Director)* 4035
Smith, Don *(Orchestrations)* 3638
Smith, Don *(Vocal Arranger)* 3638
Smith, Doug *(Librettist)* 4786
Smith, Duncan *(Cast)* 846
Smith, Edgar *(Author)* 3436
Smith, Edgar *(Librettist)* 93, 182, 301, 473, 551, 677, 687, 833, 940, 950, 1095, 1188, 1217, 1240, 1264, 1526, 1530, 1607, 1661, 1735, 1738, 1799, 1823, 1836, 1844, 1881, 1900, 1926, 1927, 1994, 2041, 2262, 2334, 2358, 2469, 2471, 2515, 2816, 2826, 2842, 2869, 2963, 2978, 3051, 3258, 3265, 3303, 3424, 3525, 3550, 3573, 3632, 3701, 3737, 3755, 3962, 4148, 4170, 4206, 4382, 4473, 4478, 4521, 4654, 4658, 4681, 4721, 4797
Smith, Edgar *(Lyricist)* 77, 182, 301, 687, 940, 1095, 1188, 1217, 1264, 1881, 1900, 1926, 2469, 2938, 3258, 3303, 3632, 3976, 3989, 4236, 4382, 4473, 4478, 4654, 4681, 4723, 4797, 4804
Smith, Edgar A. *(Lyricist)* 1188, 2471
Smith, Edith *(Cast)* 1157
Smith, Ella *(Cast)* 4113
Smith, Emily *(Composer)* 2871

Smith, Emily *(Lyricist)* 2871
Smith, Ernest Allen *(Set Design)* 729, 3019, 3858
Smith, Ethel *(Cast)* 1157
Smith, Eugene *(Cast)* 159
Smith, F.E. *(Librettist)* 4047
Smith, F.E. *(Lyricist)* 4047
Smith, Felton *(Choreographer)* 1785, 3211
Smith, Frank *(Choreographer)* 2489
Smith, Fred T. *(Composer)* 92
Smith, Fred T. *(Librettist)* 92
Smith, Fred T. *(Lyricist)* 92
Smith, Gary *(Producer)* 3454
Smith, Gary *(Set Design)* 3366
Smith, George Malcolm *(Author)* 180
Smith, George T. *(Lyricist)* 688
Smith, George Totten *(Librettist)* 591, 1003, 1547, 2107, 2343, 2485
Smith, George Totten *(Lyricist)* 939, 1003, 2341, 2343, 2485, 2964, 3129, 3820
Smith, Gerald Oliver *(Cast)* 3243, 3379
Smith, Gladys
See also Miss Pickford.
Smith, Gladys *(Cast)* 1157
Smith, Gordon *(Cast)* 125, 4179
Smith, Grace *(Cast)* 14
Smith, Greg *(Orchestrations)* 2674
Smith, Greg *(Producer)* 580
Smith, H. Jess *(Cast)* 2340
Smith, Harry *(Cast)* 340
Smith, Harry B. *(Composer)* 4258
Smith, Harry B. *(Librettist)* 41, 49, 136, 184, 252, 256, 350, 361, 380, 405, 457, 613, 618, 659, 666, 718, 734, 771, 905, 1016, 1066, 1260, 1355, 1375, 1388, 1444, 1465, 1535, 1538, 1555, 1602, 1712, 1720, 1722, 1896, 2041, 2101, 2213, 2345, 2373, 2465, 2486, 2502, 2506, 2528, 2534, 2574, 2622, 2671, 2697, 2716, 2733, 2747, 2774, 2885, 2892, 2923, 2931, 3053, 3078, 3084, 3085, 3087, 3229, 3352, 3362, 3363, 3372, 3387, 3566, 3586, 3658, 3680, 3681, 3710, 3732, 3736, 3771, 3784, 3881, 3977, 3996, 4094, 4119, 4158, 4181, 4249, 4250, 4258, 4293, 4348, 4500, 4559, 4603, 4662, 4669, 4691, 4724, 4801, 4802, 4803, 4804, 4806
Smith, Harry B. *(Lyricist)* 41, 49, 75, 126, 184, 252, 256, 350, 361, 380, 405, 457, 613, 618, 627, 659, 666, 677, 687, 718, 734, 771, 905, 934, 947, 1027, 1066, 1111, 1183, 1228, 1250, 1260, 1313, 1327, 1355, 1375, 1388, 1444, 1465, 1535, 1538, 1544, 1555, 1711, 1712, 1720, 1722, 1774, 1844, 1896, 2101, 2149, 2213, 2345, 2373, 2385, 2424, 2465, 2502, 2506, 2534, 2602, 2620, 2622, 2671, 2697, 2706, 2716, 2747, 2761, 2885, 2892, 2922, 2923, 2931, 3020, 3053, 3078, 3084, 3177, 3193, 3229, 3237, 3304, 3362, 3363, 3372, 3387, 3398, 3420, 3566, 3573, 3586, 3591, 3627, 3658, 3680, 3681, 3710, 3732, 3736, 3751, 3784, 3881, 3977, 3994, 3996, 4094, 4119, 4121, 4181, 4249, 4250, 4258, 4293, 4348, 4352, 4390, 4418, 4430, 4500, 4555, 4559, 4616, 4644, 4658, 4662, 4691, 4724, 4799, 4802, 4803, 4804, 4806
Smith, Helen *(Librettist)* 4786
Smith, Henry Clapp *(Librettist)* 2475
Smith, Howard *(Director)* 1251
Smith, Howard *(Lyricist)* 208
Smith, Howlett *(Musical Director)* 2796
Smith, Jabbo *(Cast)* 2302
Smith, Jabbo *(Composer)* 3297
Smith, Jabbo *(Lyricist)* 3297
Smith, James *(Cast)* 4735
Smith, Jay *(Choreographer)* 3318
Smith, Jennifer *(Cast)* 690
Smith, Jo Jo *(Choreographer)* 1637
Smith, Joe
See Smith & Dale
Smith, Joe *(Cast)* 17, 532, 1132, 3264, 3968, 4204, 4654, 4686
Smith, Joe C. *(Choreographer)* 2826
Smith, John *(Cast)* 434
Smith, Joseph *(Choreographer)* 4650
Smith, Joseph C. *(Choreographer)* 68, 687, 1026, 1295, 1578, 2209, 3053, 3205, 3304, 3626, 3951, 4098
Smith, Joseph C. *(Director)* 1307, 4269
Smith, Joseph H. *(Cast)* 4119
Smith, Joy *(Cast)* 4406
Smith, Kate *(Cast)* 1323, 1965, 3153, 3287
Smith, Kenneth *(Cast)* 1085
Smith, Kenneth *(Composer)* 3172
Smith, Kent *(Cast)* 2202
Smith, Kirby *(Cast)* 4486
Smith, Lee Orean *(Composer)* 185, 4201
Smith, Lee Orean *(Musical Director)* 4687
Smith, Lew *(Costumes)* 4750
Smith, Loring *(Cast)* 536, 1456, 4314, 4323, 4702
Smith, Lotte *(Cast)* 1157
Smith, Madame *(Costumes)* 331
Smith, Maggie *(Cast)* 3108
Smith, Mamie *(Cast)* 1288, 2672
Smith, Mark *(Cast)* 2344, 2569
Smith, Martin *(Cast)* 730, 3429
Smith, Maybelle *(Composer)* 432
Smith, Maybelle *(Lyricist)* 432
Smith, Michael C. *(Set Design)* 1171
Smith, Michael R. *(Set Design)* 3306
Smith, Milburn *(Librettist)* 1306
Smith, Mildred *(Cast)* 341
Smith, Muriel *(Cast)* 653, 1887, 3321
Smith, Norwood *(Cast)* 1884, 3151, 3752
Smith, Oliver *(Costumes)* 3815
Smith, Oliver *(Lighting Designer)* 2894
Smith, Oliver *(Producer)* 404, 454, 490, 1064, 1475, 2268, 3278, 3954
Smith, Oliver *(Set Design)* 95, 98, 269, 270, 341, 367, 404, 454, 521, 530, 623, 630, 649, 652, 657, 820, 823, 989, 1012, 1029, 1119, 1315, 1369, 1456, 1475, 1511, 1564, 1828, 1886, 1990, 2014, 2050, 2106, 2190, 2217, 2268, 2304, 2582, 2626, 2775, 2894, 2987, 3038, 3164, 3274, 3278, 3294, 3347, 3564, 3703, 3767, 3787, 3815, 3845, 3954, 4095, 4270, 4323, 4386, 4450, 4516, 4625
Smith, Paul Gerard *(Director)* 2032, 3966
Smith, Paul Gerard *(Librettist)* 1134, 1419, 1800, 1859, 2032, 2298, 2700, 3007, 3172, 3342, 3966, 4668
Smith, Paul Gerard *(Lyricist)* 2032, 2298
Smith, Paul Gerard *(Producer)* 2032

Smith, Pete Kite *(Lyricist)* 924
Smith, Polly P. *(Costumes)* 729
Smith, Queenie *(Cast)* 317, 765, 1551, 1819, 2253, 2276, 2540, 2855, 3312, 3754, 4001, 4170, 4392
Smith, Rebecca *(Cast)* 3507
Smith, Reginald *(Cast)* 703
Smith, Rex *(Cast)* 572, 2033
Smith, Robert *(Cast)* 3292
Smith, Robert B. *(Librettist)* 136, 522, 734, 1016, 1243, 1525, 1538, 1552, 1712, 2347, 2774, 2848, 2923, 2931, 3053, 3087, 3372, 3681, 4119, 4209, 4650
Smith, Robert B. *(Lyricist)* 136, 246, 350, 522, 734, 737, 1016, 1243, 1327, 1334, 1523, 1525, 1538, 1547, 1552, 1712, 2347, 2486, 2493, 2574, 2848, 2923, 2931, 3020, 3053, 3087, 3319, 3352, 3420, 3681, 3771, 4119, 4209, 4250, 4478, 4650, 4712
Smith, Rollin *(Cast)* 897
Smith, Rufus *(Cast)* 3279, 3347
Smith, Russell *(Cast)* 2791
Smith, Russell *(Composer)* 4751
Smith, Sally *(Cast)* 3731
Smith, Sammy *(Cast)* 2014, 2019, 3509, 3526, 3577, 4718
Smith, Sheila *(Cast)* 1329, 4196, 4243, 4272, 4388
Smith, Sid *(Director)* 974, 3497, 3499
Smith, Speedy *(Cast)* 444, 691, 981, 2034
Smith, Speedy *(Choreographer)* 691, 981
Smith, Speedy *(Composer)* 981
Smith, Speedy *(Librettist)* 981
Smith, Speedy *(Lyricist)* 981
Smith, Stanley *(Cast)* 1932, 4778
Smith, Steven *(Dance Arranger)* 2969
Smith, Steven *(Musical Director)* 3641
Smith, Steven Scott *(Director)* 784
Smith, Suzanne *(Cast)* 1304
Smith, Sydney *(Choreographer)* 1201
Smith, Sydney *(Librettist)* 2620
Smith, Thorne *(Author)* 2584
Smith, Tom *(Lighting Designer)* 1900
Smith, Toni *(Cast)* 945
Smith, Trixie *(Cast)* 553, 2720
Smith, Tucker *(Cast)* 162, 658, 2742
Smith, Vincent D. *(Librettist)* 4697
Smith, Virginia *(Cast)* 1971, 2569
Smith, Vivian *(Choreographer)* 4273
Smith, W.H. *(Author)* 4606
Smith, W.H. *(Composer)* 3028
Smith, W.H. *(Lyricist)* 1824
Smith, Wallace *(Author)* 2786
Smith, Walt *(Composer)* 181
Smith, Walter *(Cast)* 3658
Smith, Ward *(Cast)* 159
Smith, Webb *(Author)* 4035
Smith, Will H. *(Choreographer)* 2056
Smith, Will H. *(Director)* 3754
Smith, Will H. *(Lyricist)* 1407
Smith, William C. *(Cast)* 2817
Smith, Winchell *(Author)* 577, 773, 4860
Smith, Winchell *(Cast)* 1537
Smith, Winchell *(Director)* 1009, 3535
Smith, Wonderful *(Cast)* 2259
Smith & Dale
See Joe Smith and Charles Dale.
Smith & Dale *(Cast)* 1395, 1397
Smith and DeForrest *(Cast)* 3512
Smithies, Richard *(Librettist)* 922
Smithies, Richard *(Lyricist)* 922
Smithson, Frank *(Cast)* 1540, 2938
Smithson, Frank *(Director)* 69, 203, 274, 336, 353, 470, 934, 1021, 1031, 1088, 1505, 1518, 1540, 1558, 1560, 1588, 1888, 1972, 2112, 2292, 2324, 2373, 2385, 2419, 2495, 2596, 2601, 2669, 2745, 2865, 2919, 2938, 2966, 3032, 3073, 3134, 3313, 3519, 3581, 3626, 3677, 3776, 3786, 3821, 4064, 4425, 4575, 4644
Smithson, Frank *(Librettist)* 2291
Smithson, Frank *(Producer)* 2373
Smits, Jimmy *(Cast)* 282
Smothers, Tom *(Cast)* 1389
Smothers Brothers *(Cast)* 58
Smuin, Michael *(Cast)* 2523
Smuin, Michael *(Choreographer)* 695, 3944, 4091
Smuin, Michael *(Director)* 695, 3944, 4091
Smyrl, David Langston *(Cast)* 3276, 4744
Smyrl, David Langston *(Composer)* 3276
Smyrl, David Langston *(Librettist)* 166, 3276
Smyrl, David Langston *(Lyricist)* 166, 3276
Smyth, Al *(Musical Director)* 3519
Sneed, Gary *(Cast)* 2630, 2913
Sneed Jr., Ray *(Cast)* 3528
Sneider, Vern J. *(Author)* 2626
Snell, Bruce *(Orchestrations)* 3818
Snider-Stein, Teresa *(Costumes)* 647
Snow, Clarence *(Cast)* 3987
Snow, Harry *(Cast)* 3288
Snow, Norman *(Cast)* 4796
Snow, Ross *(Cast)* 1515, 3750
Snow, Tom *(Composer)* 1804
Snow, Valaida *(Cast)* 445, 740
Snowden, Carolyn *(Cast)* 877
Snowden, Carolynne *(Cast)* 876
Snowden, Monica *(Cast)* 4601
Snowden, William *(Cast)* 4095
Snyder, Bozo *(Cast)* 2850
Snyder, Carrie *(Cast)* 1337
Snyder, Drew *(Cast)* 4151
Snyder, Gene *(Choreographer)* 216, 2161, 2162, 2458, 4772
Snyder, Gene *(Director)* 2161, 2162, 2458
Snyder, Jack *(Composer)* 3974
Snyder, Jack *(Lyricist)* 3974
Snyder, Nancy *(Cast)* 1268
Snyder, Ted *(Cast)* 4521
Snyder, Ted *(Composer)* 149, 179, 511, 830, 1126, 1250, 1327, 1343, 1501, 1523, 1550, 1793, 2149, 2232, 2706, 2978, 2996, 3293, 3401, 3827, 3917, 3985, 4257, 4493, 4521, 4603, 4604, 4655, 4813
Snyder, Ted *(Lyricist)* 149, 1327, 1417, 1519, 1793, 2261, 3665, 3695, 3737, 3917, 4714
Sobol, Edward *(Director)* 1889
Sobol, Louis *(Cast)* 3153
Soboloff, Arnold *(Cast)* 16, 162, 946, 1596, 3018, 3956, 4238

Society of Illustrators *(Producer)* 2105, 4047
Sodero, Domenic *(Orchestrations)* 1266
Soeder, Fran *(Director)* 809, 1496
Sogata *(Costumes)* 2032
Soglow, Otto *(Cast)* 2105
Soglow, Otto *(Librettist)* 2105, 3810
Sohlke, Augustus *(Choreographer)* 284
Sohlke, Gus *(Choreographer)* 506, 639, 2155, 2159, 2334, 3488, 3701, 4589, 4805
Sohlke, Gus *(Director)* 561, 822, 1738, 1927, 2155, 2159, 2347, 3755, 4333, 4364, 4506
Sohlke, Gus *(Musical Director)* 3033
Sohlke, Gustave *(Director)* 2262
Sokol, Lawrence E. *(Producer)* 3902
Sokol, Marilyn *(Cast)* 3937, 4454, 4619
Sokoloff, Vladimir *(Cast)* 223, 979
Sokolov, Lydia *(Choreographer)* 4207
Sokolow, Anna *(Choreographer)* 868, 1748, 2940, 3691, 4015, 4169
Sokolow, Peter *(Orchestrations)* 1609
Solar, Willie *(Cast)* 4465
Solen, Paul *(Cast)* 723
Solis, Bernabe Roxas *(Orchestrations)* 364
Sollar, Fabien *(Author)* 3466
Solley, Marvin *(Cast)* 1770
Solley, Marvin *(Librettist)* 1770
Solly, Bill *(Composer)* 508, 1665
Solly, Bill *(Librettist)* 508, 1665
Solly, Bill *(Lyricist)* 508, 1665
Solman, Alfred *(Composer)* 246, 675, 1504, 2387, 2415, 2671, 3384, 3857, 4054, 4801
Solman, Alfred *(Producer)* 1504
Solms, Kenny *(Composer)* 3112
Solms, Kenny *(Librettist)* 2590, 3111, 3112, 3444
Solms, Kenny *(Lyricist)* 3112
Solomon, Edward *(Composer)* 402
Solomon, Frederic *(Cast)* 1594, 2507, 3652, 4500
Solomon, Frederic *(Composer)* 2029, 2035, 2493, 2964, 2974, 4014, 4662
Solomon, Frederic *(Lyricist)* 2493
Solomon, Frederic *(Musical Director)* 1356, 2481, 3251, 4662, 4802, 4803
Solomon, Renee *(Musical Director)* 1269, 2866, 3670, 4773
Solomon, Renee *(Orchestrations)* 3781
Solomons Jr., Gus *(Choreographer)* 2220
Solotaroff, Mischa *(Set Design)* 3130
Solov, Zachary *(Choreographer)* 2322, 2838
Soloway, Leonard *(Producer)* 1762, 4279, 4396
Solt, Andrew *(Author)* 1506
Solt, Andrew *(Director)* 1506
Somerville, Phyllis *(Cast)* 2243
Sommer, J.W. *(Set Design)* 571
Sommer, Josef *(Cast)* 3175, 4109
Sommer, Kathy *(Dance Arranger)* 3760
Sommer, Kathy *(Musical Director)* 3760
Sommer, Kathy *(Vocal Arranger)* 3760
Sommers, Avery *(Cast)* 3515
Sommers, Bryon *(Composer)* 2171, 4799
Sommers, Joanie *(Cast)* 3275
Somner, Pearl *(Costumes)* 135, 259, 415, 2074, 3928
Sondergaard, Hester *(Cast)* 3180
Sonderskov, Robert *(Narrator)* 2977
Sonderson, Lora *(Cast)* 2602
Sondheim, Stephen *(Composer)* 80, 162, 212, 779, 832, 1060, 1200, 1329, 1406, 1422, 1571, 2143, 2205, 2417, 2536, 2764, 2769, 2822, 2860, 3340, 3411, 3471, 3843, 3967, 4067, 4210, 4233, 4268, 4399, 4474, 4700, 4746
Sondheim, Stephen *(Incidental Music)* 1184, 2144
Sondheim, Stephen *(Librettist)* 80, 3471
Sondheim, Stephen *(Lyricist)* 80, 162, 212, 599, 630, 779, 832, 1060, 1200, 1214, 1329, 1406, 1422, 1571, 1709, 1991, 2076, 2143, 2205, 2417, 2536, 2663, 2677, 2764, 2769, 2822, 2860, 3018, 3340, 3411, 3471, 3843, 3967, 4067, 4210, 4233, 4268, 4399, 4625, 4700, 4746
Song Spinners, The *(Cast)* 4409
Soo, Jack *(Cast)* 1315
Sophocles *(Author)* 1636
Soreanu, Mary *(Cast)* 3670, 3781
Sorel, Dian *(Cast)* 3167
Sorel, Felicia *(Cast)* 3822
Sorel, Felicia *(Choreographer)* 2115, 2202, 2595, 3036, 4479
Sorg, John C. *(Musical Director)* 2996
Soriero, Patrice *(Choreographer)* 595, 4137
Sorin, Louis *(Cast)* 1343, 3767, 4365, 4620
Sorin, Louis *(Librettist)* 1446
Sorkin, Herbert *(Composer)* 226
Soroka, Heather Lee *(Cast)* 2229
Sorvino, Paul *(Cast)* 273
Sosa, Astrid *(Costumes)* 4729
Sosnik, Harry *(Musical Director)* 2313
Sosnowski, Janusz *(Set Design)* 2846
Sotager, Mme. *(Costumes)* 1712
Sothern, Ann *(Cast)* 1207, 1674
Sothern, Jean *(Lyricist)* 3104
Sottile, Michael *(Arrangements)* 1700
Sottile, Michael *(Musical Director)* 1700
Sottile, Michael S. *(Musical Director)* 2237
Soudeikine, Sergei *(Costumes)* 3103
Soudeikine, Sergei *(Set Design)* 710, 1352, 3103, 3541
Soul Stirrers, The *(Cast)* 1636
Soule, Frank *(Cast)* 2156
Soule, Robert *(Costumes)* 1319, 3725
Soule, Robert *(Set Design)* 722, 1319, 1697, 3725, 4292, 4380
Soules, Dale *(Cast)* 3666
Sour, Robert *(Composer)* 3104
Sour, Robert *(Lyricist)* 432, 2985, 3103, 3905, 3986, 4367, 4534
Sour, Robert B. *(Lyricist)* 2751
Sousa, John Philip *(Additional Music)* 1208
Sousa, John Philip *(Cast)* 1396, 1901, 2403
Sousa, John Philip *(Composer)* 118, 527, 698, 749, 964, 1165, 1388, 1901, 3261, 4100, 4297, 4390
Sousa, John Philip *(Incidental Music)* 1208
Sousa, John Philip *(Librettist)* 527
Sousa, John Philip *(Music Based On)* 4297
Sousa, Leone *(Cast)* 4677
Sousa, Pamela *(Cast)* 723, 4196

Sousa, Pamela *(Choreographer)* 3272, 3760
Soutar, Farren *(Cast)* 675, 1153
Souter, Farren *(Cast)* 1543
Southerland, Evelyn Greenleaf *(Author)* 1096
Southern, Jean *(Lyricist)* 3103
Southern Enchantment Co. *(Producer)* 1909
Souvaine, Henry *(Composer)* 123, 124, 125, 827, 2827
Sove, Staci *(Cast)* 1496
Sovey, Raymond *(Costumes)* 1453, 3861, 3924, 4335
Sovey, Raymond *(Lighting Designer)* 3983
Sovey, Raymond *(Set Design)* 142, 247, 1011, 1476, 1850, 1874, 2060, 2187, 2348, 2786, 3659, 3823, 3919, 3924, 3983, 4179, 4345, 4426, 4550
Soyfer, Jura *(Librettist)* 1413
Soyfer, Jura *(Lyricist)* 3698
Spaak, Charles *(Author)* 657
Spaeth, Sigmund *(Composer)* 4137
Spaeth, Sigmund *(Lyricist)* 4817
Spahr, Scott *(Cast)* 3637
Spalding, Charles *(Librettist)* 4018
Spangler, David *(Additional Lyrics)* 4244
Spangler, David *(Composer)* 3088, 4244
Spangler, David *(Dance Arranger)* 2687
Spangler, David Sheridan *(Cast)* 3507
Sparer, Paul *(Cast)* 3309
Sparkman, SuSu *(Cast)* 3004
Sparkman, SuSu *(Choreographer)* 3004
Sparks, Don *(Cast)* 2027
Sparks, Grace *(Cast)* 1606
Sparks, John *(Cast)* 1627
Sparks, John G. *(Cast)* 118, 2990, 3093, 3504, 3750, 4130
Sparks, Joseph *(Cast)* 559, 2428, 2493
Sparks, Joseph M. *(Cast)* 2675, 3999
Sparks, Louise *(Musical Director)* 2511
Sparks, Ned *(Cast)* 78, 1794, 2214, 3043
Sparling, Herbert *(Cast)* 1682
Spaulding, George *(Cast)* 2175
Spaulding, George L. *(Cast)* 117
Speaks, Lee *(Cast)* 1201
Speaks, Margaret *(Cast)* 293
Spear, David *(Musical Director)* 1262, 2820
Spear, David *(Vocal Arranger)* 2820
Spearman, Rawn *(Cast)* 2000
Spears, Sally *(Producer)* 3787
Specht, Bobby *(Cast)* 2078
Specht, Don *(Orchestrations)* 2084
Specter, Edward *(Producer)* 1290, 1846
Specter Prods., Edward *(Producer)* 160
Spector, Arnold *(Director)* 190
Spector, Joel *(Producer)* 309, 2449, 4155
Spector, Phil *(Composer)* 2427, 3739, 4031, 4193, 4534
Spector, Phil *(Lyricist)* 2427, 3739, 4031, 4193, 4534
Spectorsky, Auguste *(Lyricist)* 3698
Spektor, Charline *(Lyricist)* 2007
Spektor, Eryk *(Producer)* 2007
Spektor, Mira J. *(Composer)* 2007
Spektor, Mira J. *(Vocal Arranger)* 2007
Speller, Robert *(Cast)* 4611
Spellman, Larry *(Producer)* 4347
Spelly, Robert *(Choreographer)* 4611
Spelly, Robert *(Director)* 4611
Spence, Chenault *(Lighting Designer)* 1770
Spence, Chenault *(Set Design)* 1770
Spence, Lew *(Composer)* 2079
Spence, Ralph *(Librettist)* 1136, 4815, 4816
Spencer *(Composer)* 1132
Spencer, Alexander *(Musical Director)* 639, 4201
Spencer, Anna *(Costumes)* 2276, 3538
Spencer, Beth *(Cast)* 4732
Spencer, Bob *(Cast)* 3988
Spencer, Christine *(Cast)* 279
Spencer, David *(Librettist)* 2359
Spencer, David *(Lyricist)* 171, 2359
Spencer, Frank *(Costumes)* 2689, 2737, 3126, 3637, 4035
Spencer, Herbert *(Composer)* 1482, 1802
Spencer, Herbert W. *(Orchestrations)* 1619
Spencer, Lillian *(Cast)* 1111, 1565
Spencer, Otis *(Composer)* 2574, 4586
Spencer, Peter *(Librettist)* 4335
Spencer, Richard S. *(Composer)* 1866
Spencer, Robert *(Cast)* 3902
Spencer, Ron *(Choreographer)* 3539
Spencer, Ron *(Lyricist)* 3539
Spencer, Vernon *(Cast)* 4168
Spencer, Willard *(Composer)* 2880, 3582, 3765
Spencer, Willard *(Director)* 2880
Spencer, Willard *(Librettist)* 3582, 3765
Spencer, Willard *(Lyricist)* 2880, 3582, 3765
Sperling, Milton *(Librettist)* 4577
Sperling, Milton *(Producer)* 4386
Sperling, Ted *(Musical Director)* 3039
Spero, Arete *(Producer)* 1761
Speros, Jo *(Cast)* 2472
Speros, Tia *(Cast)* 4264, 4288
Sperry, Steve *(Composer)* 1298
Sperry, Steve *(Lyricist)* 1298
Spewack, Bella *(Author)* 2432, 3066
Spewack, Bella *(Librettist)* 2331, 2432, 2975
Spewack, Sam *(Author)* 3066, 3526
Spewack, Sam *(Librettist)* 2331, 3526
Spewack, Samuel *(Author)* 2432
Spewack, Samuel *(Director)* 2432
Spewack, Samuel *(Librettist)* 2432, 2975
Spialek, Hans *(Composer)* 3035
Spialek, Hans *(Orchestrations)* 2, 82, 117, 123, 124, 163, 173, 180, 216, 247, 289, 372, 512, 514, 622, 637, 680, 901, 971, 1109, 1145, 1275, 1322, 1342, 1440, 1453, 1494, 1670, 1827, 1879, 1894, 1930, 1931, 1948, 2061, 2068, 2103, 2187, 2258, 2382, 2423, 2453, 2475, 2479, 2595, 2712, 3002, 3035, 3036, 3103, 3104, 3117, 3131, 3157, 3170, 3254, 3283, 3292, 3353, 3359, 3885, 3990, 4015, 4058, 4142, 4174, 4249, 4357, 4362, 4374, 4420, 4483, 4550, 4569, 4586, 4652, 4667, 4777, 4825
Spiegel, Max *(Producer)* 3623
Spiegel, Terry *(Producer)* 583
Spiegel's Productions *(Producer)* 2587
Spielman, Fred *(Composer)* 2397, 4155
Spier, Larry *(Composer)* 4828

Spier, Larry *(Lyricist)* 4828
Spiering Jr., Frank *(Lyricist)* 3527
Spigelgass, Leonard *(Librettist)* 2583
Spillane, Sherri *(Cast)* 2584
Spiller, Marshal S. *(Lighting Designer)* 2007
Spina, Harold *(Composer)* 1937, 2165, 4163, 4255, 4825
Spina, Harold *(Director)* 4163
Spina, Harold *(Librettist)* 4163
Spina, Harold *(Lyricist)* 4163
Spinelli, Larry *(Cast)* 4089
Spiner, Brent *(Cast)* 2429
Spinetti, Victor *(Cast)* 2362, 3259
Spink, George *(Composer)* 2383, 3642
Spink, George *(Lyricist)* 2383, 3642, 4723
Spink, George A. *(Composer)* 470, 2982, 4044, 4642
Spink, George A. *(Lyricist)* 470, 4044, 4642
Spink, George F. *(Composer)* 688
Spink, George F. *(Lyricist)* 688
Spink, William *(Composer)* 2906, 4311
Spinola, Marina *(Producer)* 562
Spiroff, Tom *(Cast)* 3178
Spisak, Neil *(Costumes)* 655
Spitalny, H. Leopold *(Composer)* 1414
Spitz, Arthur *(Producer)* 4792
Spivak, Allen *(Producer)* 4534
Spivakowsky, Michael *(Musical Director)* 4863
Spohn, Leslie *(Lighting Designer)* 564
Spoliansky, Mischa *(Composer)* 4235
Spolidoro, A. *(Puppeteer)* 55
Spong, Hilda *(Cast)* 1894
Spooner, Cecil *(Cast)* 3050
Spooner, Cecil *(Producer)* 3050
Spottswood, James C. *(Cast)* 929
Sprague, George R. *(Cast)* 1537
Sprague, Sidney *(Choreographer)* 439
Sprecher, Ben *(Producer)* 155
Spreckels, Geraldine *(Cast)* 1109
Spring, Helen *(Cast)* 1013
Springer, Ashton *(Producer)* 74, 166, 576, 952, 1198
Springer, Phil *(Composer)* 3940, 4435
Springer, Phil *(Lyricist)* 4435
Springer, Philip *(Composer)* 747, 1993, 2294, 3940, 4268, 4828
Sproat, Ron *(Librettist)* 260
Spross, Charles Gilbert *(Composer)* 4590
Sprosty, Paul *(Orchestrations)* 3314
Spyri, Johanna *(Author)* 1815
Squadron, Anne Strickland *(Producer)* 2654
Squibb, June *(Cast)* 669, 1418, 3186
Squire, Jack
See also Jack Squires.
Squire, Jack *(Cast)* 1033, 1923, 2780, 2972, 3655
Squire, Katherine *(Cast)* 3984
Squires, Gil *(Cast)* 1603, 4118
Squires, Harry D. *(Composer)* 4137
Squires, Jack
See also Jack Squire.
Squires, Jack *(Cast)* 202, 1756, 2757, 3508, 3980, 4741, 4793
Sroka, Jerry *(Cast)* 843, 4707
St. Albin, Bisson *(Author)* 1663
St. Clair, Stewart *(Librettist)* 2371
St. Claire, Dorothy *(Cast)* 4836
St. Claire, Minnie *(Cast)* 3068
St. Cyr, Lily *(Cast)* 4260
St. Cyr, Val *(Costumes)* 4661
St. Germain, Mark *(Composer)* 2241
St. Germain, Mark *(Librettist)* 1509, 2185, 2229, 2283
St. Germain, Mark *(Lyricist)* 1509, 2185, 2229, 2241
St. John, Betta *(Cast)* 4096
St. John, Howard *(Cast)* 458, 1507, 2484, 3584
St. John, Jai Oscar *(Cast)* 166, 593
St. John, Jill *(Cast)* 2267
St. John, Orford *(Librettist)* 2168
St. Leo, Leonard *(Cast)* 4077
St. Louis, Louis *(Arrangements)* 4031
St. Louis, Louis *(Cast)* 2775, 4459
St. Louis, Louis *(Composer)* 4459
St. Louis, Louis *(Dance Arranger)* 535, 1164, 1664, 3330, 3643, 3792
St. Louis, Louis *(Musical Director)* 535, 1664, 2658, 3792, 4031, 4089
St. Louis, Louis *(Vocal Arranger)* 535, 1164, 1664, 3330, 3792, 4089
St. Matthew *(Author)* 1595
Staats, Phil *(Composer)* 3205
Staats, Phil *(Lyricist)* 3205
Stabile, Bill *(Set Design)* 2877, 2970, 2992, 3169, 3873
Stacklin, Andy *(Set Design)* 2468
Stadlen, Lewis J. *(Cast)* 2874, 2945, 3272
Staff, Frank *(Choreographer)* 4579
Stafford, Adam *(Cast)* 3454
Stafford, Bill *(Composer)* 2080
Stafford, Bill *(Lyricist)* 2080
Stafford, Bill *(Orchestrations)* 2080, 4796
Stafford, Jim *(Composer)* 914
Stafford, Jim *(Lyricist)* 914
Stafford, Joseph *(Cast)* 3453
Stafford-Clark, Max *(Director)* 3884
Stage Managers Club *(Producer)* 4273
Stage Promotions Ltd. & Co. *(Producer)* 2798
Stages Theatrical Prod. *(Producer)* 2177
Stahl, Cordell *(Cast)* 4136
Stahl, Mary Leigh *(Cast)* 695
Stahl, Richard *(Composer)* 436, 998, 4165
Stahl, Richard *(Lyricist)* 436
Stahl, Rose *(Cast)* 3341
Stahlberg, Frederic *(Musical Director)* 4547
Stahlberg, Fritz *(Musical Director)* 1851
Staiger, Libi *(Cast)* 603, 1029, 4090
Stainbrook, Richard D. *(Producer)* 2288
Stair, E.D. *(Producer)* 1641, 1798, 2642
Stall, Karl *(Cast)* 3372
Stallings, Laurence *(Librettist)* 3650, 4569
Stallings, Laurence *(Lyricist)* 1020, 4569
Stamer, Fred *(Composer)* 596
Stamford, Wybert *(Director)* 1626
Stammers, Frank *(Choreographer)* 628
Stammers, Frank *(Director)* 1911, 2056, 2174, 3045, 3207, 3531, 4381

Stammers, Frank *(Librettist)* 258, 3045, 3207
Stammers, Frank *(Lyricist)* 258, 3045, 3207
Stammers, Frank M. *(Librettist)* 3425
Stammers, Frank M. *(Lyricist)* 3087
Stamp, Terence *(Cast)* 4685
Stamper, Dave *(Cast)* 4834
Stamper, Dave *(Composer)* 335, 543, 1124, 1215, 2126, 2528, 2570, 2628, 3314, 3605, 3796, 4206, 4271, 4642, 4806, 4807, 4808, 4809, 4810, 4811, 4812, 4813, 4814, 4815, 4816, 4817, 4818, 4819, 4823, 4831, 4832, 4833, 4834, 4835, 4836, 4837, 4838, 4839, 4840, 4841, 4842, 4843, 4844, 4849, 4851, 4852, 4853, 4858
Stamper, Dave *(Librettist)* 4813
Stamper, Dave *(Lyricist)* 4809, 4817
Stamper, George *(Cast)* 1514, 1960, 3808
Stamper, George *(Choreographer)* 1514, 2021
Stampfel, Peter *(Composer)* 3309
Stampfel, Peter *(Lyricist)* 3309
Stan, Walter *(Cast)* 985
Stan, Walter *(Set Design)* 985
Stander, Arthur *(Librettist)* 924
Stander, Lionel *(Cast)* 297, 837
Standing, Guy *(Cast)* 2361
Standing Jr., Guy *(Cast)* 4524
Standish, Burt L. *(Author)* 1380
Stanfield, J. Samuel *(Producer)* 3904
Stanford, Arthur *(Cast)* 2025, 2254, 4453
Stanford, C. Villiers *(Composer)* 3912
Stanford, Jack *(Cast)* 1693
Stanford, Paul *(Librettist)* 1539
Stanford, Ralph *(Cast)* 289
Stang, Arnold *(Cast)* 2182, 4782
Stange, Stanislaus *(Author)* 743, 1831
Stange, Stanislaus *(Director)* 742, 2335
Stange, Stanislaus *(Librettist)* 355, 523, 742, 1071, 1401, 1553, 1570, 1594, 2233, 2335, 2632, 2673, 3488, 3994, 4187, 4497, 4614, 4646
Stange, Stanislaus *(Lyricist)* 355, 523, 742, 1071, 1401, 1570, 2233, 2632, 2673, 3488, 4187, 4497, 4614, 4646
Stanger, Robert *(Set Design)* 4416
Stanhope, Frederick *(Director)* 1502, 4208
Stanislawczyk, Valerie *(Cast)* 1004
Stanley, Aileen *(Cast)* 203, 3149, 3523, 3973
Stanley, Charles *(Cast)* 2029
Stanley, Edmund *(Cast)* 698, 3360, 4161
Stanley, Fred *(Author)* 831
Stanley, Gertrude *(Cast)* 1163
Stanley, Gordon *(Cast)* 330, 1171, 1509, 2142, 2242, 2805, 3305, 4297
Stanley, Hal *(Composer)* 2588
Stanley, Hal *(Lyricist)* 3487
Stanley, Harry *(Cast)* 995
Stanley, Helene *(Cast)* 3381
Stanley, Henry A. *(Cast)* 2673
Stanley, Jack *(Composer)* 879
Stanley, Jack *(Librettist)* 3405
Stanley, Jack *(Lyricist)* 879, 4104
Stanley, Jessie *(Cast)* 4161
Stanley, Jim *(Producer)* 974
Stanley, Marion *(Cast)* 2119, 3748
Stanley, Pamela *(Composer)* 2171
Stanley, Pat *(Cast)* 657, 1280, 1614, 4585
Stanley, Paul *(Composer)* 3739
Stanley, Paul *(Lyricist)* 3739
Stanley, Ralph *(Cast)* 4633
Stanley, Truman *(Cast)* 3218
Stanton, Anthony *(Cast)* 760
Stanton, Frank *(Cast)* 3050
Stanton, Frank H. *(Lyricist)* 2584
Stanton, Frank L. *(Lyricist)* 1704
Stanton, George *(Producer)* 651
Stanton, Harriet *(Cast)* 1523
Stanton, Jack *(Cast)* 1109
Stanton, Jane *(Producer)* 3249
Stanton, Joyce *(Composer)* 459
Stanton, Olive *(Cast)* 919
Stanton, Paul *(Cast)* 3980
Stanwood *(Composer)* 4093
Stanwood *(Lyricist)* 4093
Stanwood, Rita *(Cast)* 3031
Stanwyck, Barbara *(Cast)* 587, 4291
Stanwyck, Jay *(Producer)* 4318
Stapleton, Christopher *(Set Design)* 3272
Stapleton, Jean *(Cast)* 363, 957, 1420, 2268
Stapleton, John *(Director)* 104
Stapley, Richard *(Composer)* 4232
Starbuck, Betty *(Cast)* 82, 711, 1446, 1447, 1453, 1800, 1827, 3436
Starbuck, James *(Cast)* 3013, 4015
Starbuck, James *(Choreographer)* 23, 1815, 2850, 3234, 4180
Starbuck, Jo Jo *(Cast)* 2080
Starbuck, Josh *(Lighting Designer)* 3960
Starbuck, Joshua *(Lighting Designer)* 1236
Starbuck Productions, Ltd. *(Producer)* 4515
Starer, Robert *(Dance Arranger)* 1456
Starger, Martin *(Producer)* 2822, 3682, 4138
Stark, Bruce W. *(Producer)* 406, 4089
Stark, Fred *(Composer)* 3708
Stark, Graham *(Cast)* 194
Stark, Karl *(Composer)* 4374
Stark, Karl *(Lyricist)* 4374
Stark, Molly *(Cast)* 159
Stark, Ray *(Producer)* 1420
Stark, Sally *(Cast)* 956
Starkie, Ben *(Cast)* 1871
Starkie, Martin *(Director)* 634
Starkie, Martin *(Librettist)* 634
Starner, Marie *(Cast)* 1836
Starobin, Michael *(Arrangements)* 1234
Starobin, Michael *(Dance Arranger)* 1082
Starobin, Michael *(Musical Director)* 109, 1234, 2132, 3070
Starobin, Michael *(Orchestrations)* 109, 143, 154, 424, 661, 754, 1015, 1082, 1822, 2132, 2359, 2437, 2746, 3039, 3285, 3644, 3760, 4210, 4349
Starobin, Michael *(Vocal Arranger)* 1015, 1082
Starr, Bill *(Cast)* 134, 3159
Starr, Jean *(Cast)* 1983, 2302, 2561, 3657
Starr, Kay *(Cast)* 2588

Starr, Lita *(Producer)* 4176
Starr, Wayne *(Producer)* 2633
Starrett, Ken *(Costumes)* 1924
Stauch, Bonnie *(Costumes)* 450
Stauder, Al *(Cast)* 2791
Staudt, Chris *(Composer)* 1282, 4168
Staudt, Christian *(Composer)* 1282
Stauffer, Aubrey *(Composer)* 2358, 3877
Stauffer, Aubrey *(Lyricist)* 2358
Stauffer, Blaine *(Cast)* 1354
Staunton, Virginia *(Cast)* 2765
Steadman, Hugh *(Librettist)* 1887
Steadman, Hugh *(Lyricist)* 1887
Stearns, Roger *(Cast)* 1342, 1448, 3103, 4142, 4777
Stearns, Roger V. *(Cast)* 3325
Stearns, Theodore *(Musical Director)* 1308, 1794
Steck, Hazel Weber *(Cast)* 2925
Steck, Olga *(Cast)* 735, 1378, 2780, 4121, 4194
Steck, Ray *(Musical Director)* 420
Stecko, Bob *(Dance Arranger)* 251
Stecko, Joe *(Musical Director)* 3863
Stecko, Joseph *(Musical Director)* 302, 825, 1878, 2339, 3725
Steel, John *(Cast)* 2698, 3007, 3008, 4813, 4814
Steele, Bernard *(Director)* 966
Steele, Bill *(Cast)* 3802, 4444
Steele, Brian *(Cast)* 643
Steele, Brooks *(Musical Director)* 2458
Steele, David *(Cast)* 2626
Steele, Jevetta *(Cast)* 1636
Steele, Porter *(Composer)* 1235
Steele, Robert L. *(Lighting Designer)* 3439
Steele, Robert L. *(Producer)* 3196, 4124
Steele, Tommy *(Cast)* 1721, 1741
Steele, Vernon *(Cast)* 4730
Steeley, Guy F. *(Librettist)* 1351, 1646, 4161
Steeley, Guy F. *(Lyricist)* 1351, 4161
Steen, Jan *(Director)* 1500
Steen, Jan *(Librettist)* 1500
Steere, Clifton *(Cast)* 1347
Stefanni, Prima
See also Prima Stephen.
Stefanni, Prima *(Cast)* 4157
Steffan, Ernest *(Composer)* 379
Steffe, Edwin *(Cast)* 347, 1766, 2928
Steffe, William *(Composer)* 3020
Steffen, Paul *(Choreographer)* 943
Steger, Julius *(Cast)* 405, 1375, 1905, 2160, 3834
Steger, Julius *(Composer)* 3753
Stegman, Richard *(Cast)* 2022
Stegmeyer, Bill *(Orchestrations)* 3696, 4828
Stegmeyer, William *(Dance Arranger)* 31
Stegmeyer, William *(Orchestrations)* 2248, 3280
Stegmeyer, William *(Vocal Arranger)* 31
Stehli, Edgar *(Cast)* 4548
Steig, William *(Author)* 99
Steiger, Jimmie *(Composer)* 4668
Stein, Ben *(Producer)* 225
Stein, Debra *(Costumes)* 1353, 2704
Stein, Douglas *(Set Design)* 1234, 2746
Stein, Gertrude *(Librettist)* 1498, 2110
Stein, Gertrude *(Lyricist)* 1366, 1498, 2110
Stein, Harry *(Librettist)* 1038
Stein, Joseph *(Author)* 951, 1190, 4038
Stein, Joseph *(Librettist)* 59, 273, 483, 652, 951, 1265, 1892, 2267, 2268, 2318, 2439, 2987, 3509, 3644, 4038, 4270, 4862
Stein, Julian *(Composer)* 722, 1436
Stein, Julian *(Dance Arranger)* 1369, 1727, 3835
Stein, Julian *(Musical Director)* 1158, 1245, 1369, 1727, 2016, 3920, 4028, 4541, 4764
Stein, Julian *(Orchestrations)* 461, 1245, 1354, 1727, 2016, 3491, 3835, 4541
Stein, Julian *(Vocal Arranger)* 1158, 1369, 1727, 3835, 4028, 4764
Stein, Leo *(Author)* 132, 473, 1066, 1121, 2262, 2509, 2603, 2701, 2836, 2837, 2838, 3053, 3727, 3996, 4553, 4563, 4726
Stein, Meridee *(Director)* 3164
Stein, Walter *(Author)* 475
Steinbeck, John *(Author)* 1864, 3224, 3505
Steinberg, Ben *(Musical Director)* 3452, 3831
Steinberg, Harry A. *(Lyricist)* 2628
Steinberg, Maurice *(Composer)* 4723
Steinberg, Maurice *(Lyricist)* 4723
Steinberg, Neil *(Lyricist)* 2356
Steinberg, Samuel *(Composer)* 4342
Steinbrenner III, George M. *(Producer)* 2437, 3869
Steindorff, Paul *(Musical Director)* 698, 1594, 2156, 2507, 3994, 4500
Steiner, Howard *(Composer)* 898
Steiner, Irwin *(Producer)* 3167
Steiner, Max *(Composer)* 1631, 3420
Steiner, Max *(Musical Director)* 21, 1485, 1643, 1827, 1935, 2336, 2602, 3319, 3472, 3650, 3652, 3770, 3868, 4001, 4283, 4300, 4476
Steiner, Max *(Orchestrations)* 3650
Steiner, Oscar *(Composer)* 710
Steiner, Oscar *(Lyricist)* 710
Steiner, Rick *(Producer)* 394, 2143, 3862, 4031
Steiner, Steve *(Arrangements)* 1969
Steiner, Steve *(Cast)* 3695
Steiner, Steve *(Musical Director)* 1969
Steiner, Steve *(Orchestrations)* 1969
Steininger, Franz *(Composer)* 1415, 3013
Steininger, Franz *(Musical Director)* 3013
Steinman, Harold *(Producer)* 4006
Steinman, Jim *(Composer)* 2953
Steinman, Jim *(Lyricist)* 2953
Stell, John *(Cast)* 3297
Stell, Joseph *(Lighting Designer)* 1370
Stell, Joseph *(Set Design)* 1370
Stempfel, Theo. *(Cast)* 96
Stempfel, Theo. *(Librettist)* 96
Stempfel, Theo. *(Lyricist)* 96
Stempfel Jr., Theodore *(Librettist)* 1405, 2740
Stempfel Jr., Theodore *(Lyricist)* 1405
Stenborg, Helen *(Cast)* 1268
Stenborg, James *(Musical Director)* 3306
Stenborg, James *(Orchestrations)* 4790

Stenhammer *(Composer)* 2803
Stenhammer *(Lyricist)* 2803
Stenod Prods. Inc. *(Producer)* 157
Stephen, Joe *(Costumes)* 4035
Stephen, Prima
See also Prima Stefanni.
Stephen, Prima *(Cast)* 2776
Stephens, Claudia *(Costumes)* 2229
Stephens, Dick *(Choreographer)* 1581
Stephens, Garn *(Cast)* 1664
Stephens, Greg *(Composer)* 1736
Stephens, Greg *(Lyricist)* 1736
Stephens, Hal *(Author)* 3068
Stephens, Hal *(Librettist)* 561
Stephens, Henry Pottinger *(Librettist)* 402
Stephens, Henry Pottinger *(Lyricist)* 402
Stephens, Kelley *(Cast)* 2928
Stephens, Lannyl *(Cast)* 1161, 3039, 3227
Stephens, Lillian *(Cast)* 939
Stephens, Linda *(Cast)* 4708
Stephens, Norman *(Producer)* 4379
Stephens, Ray *(Cast)* 3279, 3724
Stephens, Stephanie *(Cast)* 3649
Stephens, Ty *(Cast)* 3905
Stephens, Ty *(Choreographer)* 3905
Stephens, Ty *(Composer)* 3905
Stephens, Ty *(Lyricist)* 3905
Stephens, William *(Cast)* 311, 4581
Stephens, William *(Composer)* 700
Stephens, William *(Lyricist)* 700
Stephens, Willie *(Cast)* 30
Stephenson, Albert *(Cast)* 1000
Stephenson, Albert *(Choreographer)* 826
Stephenson, B.C. *(Librettist)* 1080
Stephenson, Laurie *(Cast)* 2737
Steppe, Harry *(Cast)* 806
Steppe, Harry *(Librettist)* 806
Steppenwolf Theatre Co. *(Producer)* 4074
Steppers, Whitey *(Cast)* 1840
Stept, Sam *(Composer)* 850, 1481
Stept, Sam H. *(Composer)* 321, 1481, 1689, 2141, 2587, 3373, 3907, 4772, 4842
Stept, Sammy *(Composer)* 2850
Sterck, Wilhelm *(Author)* 1219
Steriopoulos, Alkiviades "Alki" *(Musical Director)* 3667
Sterk, Wilhelm *(Author)* 12, 2914
Sterling, Andrew B. *(Composer)* 1404, 2805, 4842
Sterling, Andrew B. *(Lyricist)* 662, 1404, 1526, 1685, 1897, 1963, 2254, 2299, 2349, 2415, 2805, 3396, 3962, 4390, 4842
Sterling, Clarence A. *(Cast)* 4756
Sterling, Ford *(Cast)* 522, 2314
Sterling, Lee *(Composer)* 3079
Sterling, Lee *(Lyricist)* 3079
Sterling, Oliver *(Cast)* 1523
Sterling, Richard *(Cast)* 715, 1221
Sterling, Robert *(Composer)* 1036
Sterling, Robert *(Lyricist)* 1036
Sterling, Warren *(Cast)* 4275
Stern, Alan *(Composer)* 4660
Stern, Alan *(Librettist)* 4660
Stern, Alan *(Lyricist)* 4660
Stern, Eric *(Composer)* 3221
Stern, Eric *(Librettist)* 3221
Stern, Eric *(Musical Director)* 171, 747, 809, 2437, 3221, 3299, 3485, 3644, 4412, 4695
Stern, Eric *(Vocal Arranger)* 2437
Stern, Ernest *(Costumes)* 429
Stern, Ernest *(Set Design)* 1202, 1763, 4667
Stern, Harold *(Composer)* 203, 4352
Stern, Harold *(Lyricist)* 203
Stern, Harold *(Musical Director)* 1840, 3310, 3523, 4086, 4621
Stern, J.W. *(Composer)* 2892
Stern, J.W. *(Lyricist)* 2892
Stern, Jack *(Lyricist)* 2601
Stern, James D. *(Producer)* 4690
Stern, Reva *(Producer)* 1079
Sternbach, Gerald *(Composer)* 1804
Sternbach, Gerald *(Vocal Arranger)* 1804
Sternberg, Ann *(Composer)* 1498
Sternberg, Ann *(Dance Arranger)* 71
Sternberg, Ann *(Music Adaptation)* 1498
Sternberg, Ann *(Musical Director)* 1498
Sterner, Steve *(Cast)* 2354, 4769
Sterner, Steve *(Composer)* 2630
Sternhagen, Frances *(Cast)* 135, 1620
Sternroyd, Eva *(Cast)* 1534
Stetson, Dale *(Set Design)* 1856, 3131
Stetson, Evie *(Cast)* 4681
Stettheimer, Florine *(Set Design)* 1366
Stettler, Steve *(Director)* 143
Stevens *(Composer)* 4823
Stevens *(Lyricist)* 4823
Stevens, Allan *(Cast)* 2177
Stevens, Augusta *(Cast)* 3979
Stevens, B.D. *(Director)* 3828
Stevens, B.D. *(Producer)* 527, 749
Stevens, Cat *(Composer)* 964
Stevens, Cat *(Lyricist)* 964
Stevens, Connie *(Cast)* 1898, 2553
Stevens, Craig *(Cast)* 1860, 2496
Stevens, D.K. *(Additional Music)* 761
Stevens, D.K. *(Composer)* 306, 3047, 3882
Stevens, D.K. *(Lyricist)* 306, 761, 2934, 3882, 3951
Stevens, David *(Librettist)* 2670
Stevens, David *(Lyricist)* 2670
Stevens, Donna *(Cast)* 914
Stevens, Donna *(Composer)* 914
Stevens, Donna *(Librettist)* 914
Stevens, Donna *(Lyricist)* 914
Stevens, Edward *(Cast)* 3073
Stevens, Edwin *(Cast)* 2179, 2824, 4103
Stevens, Ellis *(Cast)* 4339
Stevens, Fisher *(Cast)* 3852
Stevens, Fran *(Cast)* 2014
Stevens, Gary Keith *(Cast)* 1380
Stevens, Geoffe *(Cast)* 1782
Stevens, Gilbert C. *(Musical Director)* 2080
Stevens, Gilbert C. *(Orchestrations)* 2080

Stevens, James *(Cast)* 1210
Stevens, Jodi *(Cast)* 484
Stevens, Josephine *(Cast)* 1587
Stevens, June K. *(Costumes)* 3217
Stevens, Kenneth *(Cast)* 4316
Stevens, Leonard *(Composer)* 4683
Stevens, Leonard *(Lyricist)* 4683
Stevens, Leslie *(Cast)* 2360
Stevens, Leslie *(Librettist)* 912, 3493, 3914
Stevens, Leslie *(Lyricist)* 912
Stevens, Marti *(Cast)* 808, 4153
Stevens, Morton *(Musical Director)* 2987
Stevens, Morton *(Orchestrations)* 2987
Stevens, Morton L. *(Cast)* 2061
Stevens, Rise *(Cast)* 743, 2550
Stevens, Roger L. *(Producer)* 652, 837, 1294, 1600, 1897, 2260, 3452, 3577, 3787, 3984, 4004
Stevens, Ronald "Smokey" *(Cast)* 166, 2133
Stevens, Tony *(Choreographer)* 251, 484, 3018, 3444, 3636, 4114
Stevens, Tony *(Director)* 4701
Stevens, Will H. *(Cast)* 1185
Stevens Productions *(Producer)* 1721
Stevens Studio *(Set Design)* 1984
Stevensen, Scott *(Cast)* 319, 4480
Stevenson *(Set Design)* 1880
Stevenson, Bob *(Cast)* 3259
Stevenson, Bob *(Choreographer)* 3259
Stevenson, Charles *(Cast)* 1434
Stevenson, Charles A. *(Cast)* 2778
Stevenson, Douglas *(Cast)* 736, 4208
Stevenson, Katherine *(Cast)* 4453
Stevenson, Katheryn *(Cast)* 2495
Stevenson, McLean *(Cast)* 1648
Stevenson, Robert *(Costumes)* 2300, 3342, 3379, 3965, 3968, 4545
Stevenson, Robert *(Set Design)* 2330
Stevenson, Robert Louis *(Author)* 31, 1089, 2197, 2198, 2199, 3485, 4444
Stevenson, Robert Louis *(Lyricist)* 3450, 3999
Stevenson, Robert T. *(Costumes)* 1880
Stevenson, William *(Composer)* 4534
Stevenson, William *(Lyricist)* 4534
Steward, Johnny *(Cast)* 2615
Steward, Ron *(Cast)* 344, 3825
Steward, Ron *(Composer)* 3825
Steward, Ron *(Librettist)* 3825
Steward, Ron *(Lyricist)* 3825
Stewardson, Jerome *(Musical Director)* 4429
Stewart, Anita *(Author)* 575
Stewart, Anita *(Cast)* 575
Stewart, Anita *(Set Design)* 3853
Stewart, Athole *(Cast)* 841
Stewart, D.A. *(Lyricist)* 1713
Stewart, Daniel *(Choreographer)* 1510
Stewart, Dink *(Cast)* 254, 984, 2690, 4339
Stewart, Don *(Cast)* 249, 2219, 4186
Stewart, Donald *(Cast)* 289, 1448
Stewart, Donald Ogden *(Librettist)* 1275
Stewart, Fred *(Cast)* 837, 933
Stewart, Grant *(Author)* 531, 3508
Stewart, Grant *(Cast)* 1806
Stewart, Grant *(Librettist)* 2886
Stewart, Grant *(Lyricist)* 219, 377, 617, 1455, 2117, 2126, 2404, 2495, 2855, 2886, 2982, 3753, 3790
Stewart, Gwen *(Cast)* 4460
Stewart, Harrison *(Cast)* 645, 2044, 3358
Stewart, James H. *(Cast)* 4439
Stewart, Jim *(Set Design)* 4488
Stewart, John *(Cast)* 937, 1990, 4292
Stewart, Johnny *(Cast)* 2312
Stewart, Joseph *(Cast)* 4095
Stewart, Katherine *(Cast)* 2614, 3481
Stewart, Larry *(Cast)* 2173
Stewart, Leon *(Cast)* 1262
Stewart, Melville *(Cast)* 618, 767, 906, 1305, 2826, 2885, 3828
Stewart, Michael *(Librettist)* 534, 607, 656, 1171, 1359, 1478, 1660, 1776, 1828, 2011, 2058, 2288, 2554, 2660, 3485, 3664, 3941
Stewart, Michael *(Lyricist)* 305, 1892, 2058, 2246, 2804, 3664, 3940, 3941, 3942
Stewart, Nellie *(Cast)* 205
Stewart, Paul *(Director)* 524
Stewart, Paul Anthony *(Cast)* 949
Stewart, Paula *(Cast)* 1408, 2449, 4693
Stewart, Ray *(Cast)* 491
Stewart, Red *(Composer)* 4264
Stewart, Red *(Lyricist)* 4264
Stewart, Ronni *(Choreographer)* 3661
Stewart, Rosalie *(Producer)* 2
Stewart, Scot *(Cast)* 4197
Stewart, Sylvester *(Composer)* 3739
Stewart, Sylvester *(Lyricist)* 3739
Stewart, W.G. *(Cast)* 1375
Stewart, William G. *(Cast)* 4646
Stewart & Morrison *(Producer)* 380
Stiasny, Walter *(Musical Director)* 346
Sticco, Dan *(Composer)* 690
Sticco, Dan *(Librettist)* 690
Stickney, Dorothy *(Cast)* 759, 1200
Stiebel, Victor *(Costumes)* 3139
Stieger, Charles *(Musical Director)* 3323
Stiers, David Ogden *(Cast)* 2687
Stiers, David Ogden *(Narrator)* 330
Stigwood, Robert *(Producer)* 1211, 2212, 3636, 3903
Stiles, Leslie *(Lyricist)* 356
Stilgoe, Richard *(Cast)* 2240
Stilgoe, Richard *(Librettist)* 3464
Stilgoe, Richard *(Lyricist)* 678, 3464, 4138
Still, Frank *(Composer)* 2388
Still, Frank *(Dance Arranger)* 2388
Still, Frank *(Musical Director)* 2388
Still, Frank *(Orchestrations)* 2388
Still, Frank *(Vocal Arranger)* 2388
Still, William *(Orchestrations)* 26
Stiller, Jerry *(Cast)* 1600, 2804
Stillman, Al *(Composer)* 3287
Stillman, Al *(Lyricist)* 1138, 1941, 2099, 2161, 3287, 3640, 4131, 4143, 4569, 4677

Stillman, Albert *(Lyricist)* 2023, 2024
Stillman, Bob *(Cast)* 3181
Stillman, Henry *(Director)* 1235
Stillman, Robert *(Cast)* 2565
Stilwell, Frank *(Composer)* 1963
Stilwell, Gene *(Cast)* 3202
Stimac, Anthony *(Director)* 840, 1249
Stimac, Anthony *(Librettist)* 669, 840, 1249, 3875
Stine, Chas. J. *(Cast)* 1513
Sting
See also Sting Sumner.
Sting *(Cast)* 4371
Stirling, J.R. *(Producer)* 3998
Stites, Kevin *(Arrangements)* 4703
Stites, Kevin *(Incidental Music)* 1236
Stites, Kevin *(Musical Director)* 1701
Stites, Kevin *(Vocal Arranger)* 1701
Stitt, Milan *(Producer)* 2332
Stix, John *(Director)* 3389
Stobitzer, Heinrich *(Author)* 2619, 2914
Stock, Larry *(Composer)* 4534
Stock, Larry *(Lyricist)* 3739, 4534
Stockdale, Joseph *(Librettist)* 2992
Stockdale, Muriel *(Costumes)* 1589
Stocken, Jasmine *(Cast)* 4016
Stockler, Michael Lee *(Musical Director)* 1082, 2746
Stockton, Frank *(Author)* 170
Stockwell, Harry *(Cast)* 207, 1135, 1494, 2755
Stockwell, Jeremy *(Cast)* 3654
Stockwell, Jock *(Lighting Designer)* 2977
Stockwell, Jock *(Set Design)* 2977
Stockwell, Rick *(Cast)* 1159
Stoddard, Brandon *(Cast)* 4041
Stoddard, George E. *(Librettist)* 735, 1173, 1587, 2214, 2270, 2446, 2491, 2564, 2888, 2944, 3252, 3915, 4437
Stoddard, George E. *(Lyricist)* 735, 1971, 2159, 2214, 2270, 2491, 2888, 2944, 3786, 4437
Stoddard, Haila *(Producer)* 2375, 2418, 2598
Stokkermans, Joop *(Composer)* 1865
Stoklosa, Janusz *(Arrangements)* 2846
Stoklosa, Janusz *(Musical Director)* 2846
Stoklosa, Janusz *(Vocal Arranger)* 2846
Stokowski, Leopold *(Cast)* 3153
Stolber, Dean *(Cast)* 1585, 3714
Stolberg, Ferdinand *(Librettist)* 517
Stolberg, Ferdinand *(Lyricist)* 517
Stoll, Bambi *(Costumes)* 1435
Stoll, Louis *(Musical Director)* 2623
Stoll, Sylvia *(Cast)* 2896
Stoller, Mike *(Composer)* 964, 3428, 3739, 4031
Stoller, Mike *(Lyricist)* 964, 3428, 3739, 4031
Stolz, Robert *(Author)* 475, 967, 4010
Stolz, Robert *(Composer)* 95, 475, 967, 1603, 2985, 3152, 3680, 3946, 4010, 4486, 4550, 4667
Stolz, Robert *(Musical Director)* 340, 2985
Stolz, Robert *(Orchestrations)* 4550
Stone, Agnes *(Cast)* 1080
Stone, Allene *(Cast)* 4150
Stone, Amelia *(Cast)* 132, 830, 1458, 1469, 1900, 2262, 2335, 3313, 3786, 4080, 4165, 4563
Stone, Carol *(Cast)* 4667
Stone, Danton *(Cast)* 1268
Stone, Dorothy *(Cast)* 930, 2479, 3415, 3721, 3860, 4025, 4150, 4345
Stone, Ed *(Lighting Designer)* 3004
Stone, Edward *(Director)* 705, 2993
Stone, Elly *(Cast)* 793, 2188, 3215, 4541
Stone, Ezra *(Cast)* 3365, 4340
Stone, Ezra *(Director)* 2910, 3698, 4340, 4582
Stone, Florence *(Cast)* 3133
Stone, Fred *(Cast)* 17, 736, 930, 1543, 2184, 2394, 3268, 3675, 3721, 4025, 4150, 4393, 4723
Stone, Gene *(Composer)* 1337
Stone, Gene *(Director)* 1337
Stone, Gene *(Librettist)* 1337
Stone, Gene *(Lyricist)* 1337, 4128
Stone, George *(Cast)* 513
Stone, Harold *(Director)* 1194
Stone, Harry *(Cast)* 1433, 3883
Stone, Harry *(Composer)* 708
Stone, Harry *(Librettist)* 708
Stone, Harry *(Lyricist)* 708
Stone, Jerald B. *(Musical Director)* 1500
Stone, Jeremy *(Musical Director)* 314
Stone, Jeremy *(Orchestrations)* 2242
Stone, Jeremy *(Vocal Arranger)* 305
Stone, Jon *(Cast)* 2935
Stone, June *(Cast)* 1465
Stone, Leonard *(Cast)* 3687
Stone, Mark *(Cast)* 766
Stone, Mimi *(Composer)* 3491
Stone, Mrs. Fred *(Cast)* 3721
Stone, Paddy *(Choreographer)* 2682, 3302, 4469
Stone, Paula *(Cast)* 3721, 3916
Stone, Paula *(Producer)* 657, 2496, 3801, 4423
Stone, Peter *(Librettist)* 134, 3060, 3897, 4013, 4167, 4196, 4481, 4695, 4727
Stone, Sid *(Cast)* 84, 1898, 4197
Stone, William *(Author)* 21
Stone, Wilson *(Composer)* 1837
Stone, Wilson *(Lyricist)* 1837
Stone Jr., Melville E. *(Composer)* 2508
Stonebeck, Ric *(Cast)* 695
Stoneburner, Sam *(Cast)* 2945
Stonehill, Maurice *(Lyricist)* 2317
Stonehill, Maurice J. *(Composer)* 1537
Stonehill, Maurice J. *(Lyricist)* 1537, 4544
Stoner, Joyce *(Choreographer)* 2069
Stoner, Joyce *(Composer)* 2069
Stoner, Joyce *(Director)* 2069
Stoner, Joyce *(Lyricist)* 2069
Stoner Arts, Inc. *(Producer)* 2069
Stoppard, Tom *(Author)* 2260
Stoppard, Tom *(Lyricist)* 2260
Storage, Jo *(Cast)* 202
Storch, Arthur *(Cast)* 1571
Storch, Arthur *(Director)* 1611
Storch, Larry *(Cast)* 943, 2554, 3683
Stordahl, Axel *(Composer)* 4743
Storey, Belle *(Cast)* 1901

Storey, David *(Choreographer)* 2283
Storey, Jack *(Cast)* 3693, 4351
Stork, Clifford *(Director)* 2281
Story, Belle *(Cast)* 736, 1208, 1631, 1753
Story, O.E. *(Composer)* 4206
Stoska, Polyna *(Cast)* 4169
Stothart, Herbert *(Composer)* 96, 97, 548, 953, 1405, 1560, 1603, 1617, 1733, 1788, 2216, 2740, 2757, 2768, 3020, 3532, 3772, 3783, 4056, 4077, 4197, 4378, 4575, 4694
Stothart, Herbert *(Director)* 96
Stothart, Herbert *(Musical Director)* 97, 468, 953, 1603, 1617, 2216, 2768, 3532, 3772, 4063, 4077, 4378, 4464, 4692, 4694
Stouse, Jake *(Producer)* 981
Stout, Kate *(Cast)* 1308
Stout, Mary *(Cast)* 754, 3364
Stout, Stephen *(Cast)* 2646
Stovall, Count *(Cast)* 2133, 3468
Stovall, James *(Cast)* 1099
Stover, Fred *(Set Design)* 2809
Stover, Frederick *(Set Design)* 1337, 3914, 4331
Stowe, Harriet Beecher *(Author)* 4429
Stowitts *(Choreographer)* 3007
Strachey, Jack *(Composer)* 346, 478, 702, 703, 1813, 2389, 4153
Strachey, Jack *(Lyricist)* 478, 702, 4153
Straeter, Ted *(Arrangements)* 848
Straeter, Ted *(Musical Director)* 848
Straeter's Orchestra, Ted *(Cast)* 847
Strahlendorff, P. *(Set Design)* 2939
Straiges, Roy *(Arrangements)* 4679, 4774
Straiges, Roy *(Composer)* 4679, 4774
Straiges, Tony *(Set Design)* 869, 975, 1038, 1775, 1914, 2143, 3277, 4210, 4383
Straight, Beatrice *(Cast)* 499, 933
Straight, Willard *(Composer)* 227
Straight, Willard *(Orchestrations)* 227
Strain, Ralph *(Composer)* 3286, 3889, 4585, 4829
Straine, Doc *(Cast)* 926
Stram, Henry *(Musical Director)* 693
Strand, Chuck *(Composer)* 2472
Strand, Chuck *(Costumes)* 2472
Strand, Chuck *(Librettist)* 2472
Strand, Chuck *(Lyricist)* 2472
Strand, Chuck *(Musical Director)* 2472
Strand, Chuck *(Vocal Arranger)* 2472
Strang, Hilary *(Cast)* 3901
Strang, Hilary *(Librettist)* 3901
Strange, James *(Cast)* 3660
Strange, Robert *(Cast)* 2059, 2121
Strasberg, Lee *(Cast)* 1446
Strasberg, Lee *(Director)* 2228
Strasberg, Susan *(Cast)* 4386
Strasfogel, Ignace *(Musical Director)* 3536
Stratas, Teresa *(Cast)* 3644
Stratford, Bert *(Producer)* 3019, 4171
Strathairn, David *(Cast)* 474
Stratton, Clare *(Cast)* 4424
Stratton, Frank *(Composer)* 3134
Stratton, Gil *(Cast)* 372
Stratton, Mike *(Lyricist)* 3226, 4394
Stratton Jr., Gil *(Cast)* 2401
Strauder, Alfred *(Cast)* 2792, 4751
Straus, Oscar *(Author)* 517, 743, 3053, 3084, 4590
Straus, Oscar *(Composer)* 517, 742, 743, 2419, 3051, 3053, 3084, 4365, 4590
Strauss *(Composer)* 710
Strauss *(Lyricist)* 710
Strauss, Barnard S. *(Producer)* 4558
Strauss, Edward *(Musical Director)* 2801
Strauss, Haila *(Choreographer)* 2354
Strauss, Haila *(Librettist)* 3557
Strauss, Johann *(Author)* 2825, 3150, 3151, 3767, 4563
Strauss, Johann *(Composer)* 3020, 3151, 4563, 4733
Strauss, Johann *(Music Based On)* 1933, 2825, 2985, 3767
Strauss, John *(Composer)* 2554
Strauss, John *(Musical Director)* 2958
Strauss, John *(Orchestrations)* 2554
Strauss, Josef *(Composer)* 2089
Strauss, Marilyn *(Producer)* 3608
Strauss, Oscar *(Composer)* 2837
Strauss, Robert *(Cast)* 3543
Strauss, Ron *(Librettist)* 3507
Strauss, Sara Mildred *(Choreographer)* 110, 622
Strauss Jr., Johann *(Composer)* 689, 1680
Strauss Jr., Johann *(Music Based On)* 1681, 4365
Strauss Sr., Johann *(Composer)* 1680
Strauss Sr., Johann *(Music Based On)* 1681, 4365
Stravo, George *(Orchestrations)* 2994
Strawbridge, Edwin *(Choreographer)* 1244, 1342
Strawbridge, Edwin *(Director)* 1244
Strawbridge, Edwin S. *(Choreographer)* 720
Strawbridge, Stephen *(Lighting Designer)* 3853
Strayhorn, Billy *(Composer)* 146, 1713, 2259, 3905, 4091
Strayhorn, Billy *(Lyricist)* 1713, 2259, 3905, 4091
Strayhorn, Billy *(Orchestrations)* 341
Strayhorn, Dan *(Cast)* 952, 1063, 2173, 3830
Strayhorn, Danny *(Cast)* 166, 1649, 1970
Strayhorn, William *(Orchestrations)* 2259
Strech, Dave *(Orchestrations)* 2083, 2089, 2092, 2094
Streep, Meryl *(Cast)* 54, 1755, 4736
Street, Anthony *(Set Design)* 2140
Streeter, Edward *(Librettist)* 1026, 1863
Streeter, Edward *(Lyricist)* 1026
Streets, Laura *(Cast)* 2416
Streger, Paul *(Librettist)* 4180
Streisand, Barbra *(Cast)* 157, 1420, 2048
Streitz, Paul *(Librettist)* 2676, 3239
Streitz, Paul *(Lyricist)* 2676, 3239
Streitz, Paul *(Producer)* 3239
Strelitzer, Dr. Hugo *(Librettist)* 2841
Strelitzer, Dr. Hugo *(Lyricist)* 2841
Strelitzer, Dr. Hugo *(Musical Director)* 2841
Stremel, Henry *(Cast)* 1152
Stretch, Dave *(Orchestrations)* 2090
Strickland, Bruce *(Cast)* 2133
Strickland, Dan *(Musical Director)* 128, 4790
Strickland, Daniel *(Pianist)* 1436
Strickland, Mabel *(Cast)* 1470
Strickler, Dan *(Cast)* 753, 829

Stricklin, Debra *(Cast)* 1291
Stringer, Marcie *(Cast)* 1329
Stringer, Robert *(Composer)* 3108
Stripling, Byron *(Cast)* 3840
Stritch, Elaine *(Cast)* 137, 832, 1614, 3815, 3914, 3984
Strohmeier, Robert *(Lighting Designer)* 3076, 3905
Strohmeier, Robert F. *(Lighting Designer)* 729, 3858, 4175
Strollers, The *(Producer)* 934
Strom, A. William *(Lighting Designer)* 1056
Strom, A. William *(Set Design)* 1056
Strom, William *(Lighting Designer)* 597
Stroman, Guy *(Cast)* 1353, 4398
Stroman, Messeret *(Cast)* 2272
Stroman, Susan *(Choreographer)* 131, 754, 921, 3708, 3851
Stromberg, John *(Composer)* 182, 195, 301, 677, 833, 940, 950, 976, 1217, 1264, 1844, 1926, 1927, 2041, 3303, 3550, 3632, 4478, 4511, 4658, 4797, 4804
Strong, Austin *(Author)* 3899
Strong, Austin *(Librettist)* 3486
Strong, Barrett *(Composer)* 166, 3695
Strong, Barrett *(Lyricist)* 166, 3695
Strong, Harry *(Librettist)* 4477
Strong, Michael *(Cast)* 973, 1294, 4294
Strong, Rod *(Cast)* 2772
Strong, Tao *(Choreographer)* 3920
Stroud, Samuel S. *(Producer)* 1604
Strouse, Barbara *(Cast)* 2988
Strouse, Charles *(Composer)* 57, 64, 150, 154, 155, 167, 486, 534, 550, 602, 607, 699, 958, 1393, 1601, 1828, 1873, 2047, 2163, 2246, 2294, 2554, 2658, 2758, 2790, 2804, 3142, 3164, 3355, 3549, 3644, 3930, 3940, 3941, 3942, 4002, 4005, 4135, 4461, 4533, 4639, 4827
Strouse, Charles *(Librettist)* 2658, 3164, 4002
Strouse, Charles *(Lyricist)* 602, 1601, 2294, 2554, 2658, 2790, 3164, 3355, 4002, 4533
Strouse, Charles *(Musical Director)* 3941
Strouse, Charles *(Orchestrations)* 534
Strouse, Charles *(Vocal Arranger)* 3941
Strouse, Irving *(Director)* 265
Strudwick, Kate *(Cast)* 792
Strudwick, Shepperd *(Cast)* 1235, 1670
Struthers, Philip *(Lyricist)* 4303
Struthers, Thomas P. *(Set Design)* 1781
Stryker, Muriel *(Cast)* 2691, 4211, 4844
Stuart, Charles *(Cast)* 4470
Stuart, Eddie *(Composer)* 3264
Stuart, Frank *(Composer)* 242
Stuart, Frank *(Producer)* 242
Stuart, Harvey *(Director)* 1233
Stuart, Harvey *(Producer)* 1233
Stuart, James *(Cast)* 2095
Stuart, Jay *(Cast)* 62
Stuart, Jesse *(Author)* 4107
Stuart, John *(Director)* 2436
Stuart, John *(Producer)* 2436
Stuart, Leslie *(Author)* 3976
Stuart, Leslie *(Composer)* 356, 604, 1313, 1783, 2334, 2388, 2825, 3433, 3627, 3857, 3976, 4017, 4837
Stuart, Leslie *(Lyricist)* 356, 1313, 1783, 2388, 3433, 3857, 3976, 4837
Stuart, Mark *(Choreographer)* 1386
Stuart, Mary Ellen *(Cast)* 2205
Stuart, Melvin *(Cast)* 3983
Stuart, Michel *(Cast)* 746
Stuart, Michel *(Choreographer)* 2100
Stuart, Michel *(Costumes)* 785, 1000
Stuart, Michel *(Producer)* 785, 3171, 4286
Stuart, Mike *(Librettist)* 59
Stuart, Mike *(Lyricist)* 59
Stuart, Patricia Quinn *(Costumes)* 766, 2618, 2801
Stuart, Ralph *(Cast)* 4557
Stuart, Sebastian *(Cast)* 2435
Stuart, Vicki *(Cast)* 4027
Stuart & Kent *(Producer)* 2552
Stuarti, Enzo
See also Larry Laurence.
Stuarti, Enzo *(Cast)* 3151, 3696
Stubbs, George *(Musical Director)* 3276
Studdiford, Grace *(Cast)* 178, 2358, 3313
Studio Productions *(Producer)* 4314
Studley, Kate *(Producer)* 3608
Studley, S.L. *(Musical Director)* 3570, 4598
Studley, Samuel L. *(Musical Director)* 2345, 2697, 3881, 4559
Studwell, David *(Cast)* 494
Stump and Stumpy *(Cast)* 889
Sturchio, Malcolm *(Lighting Designer)* 556
Sturge, Tom *(Lighting Designer)* 139, 3306, 4342
Sturges, Arthur *(Librettist)* 1994, 2365
Sturges, Charles *(Cast)* 2316
Sturges, Ida *(Cast)* 1332
Sturges, Preston *(Director)* 657
Sturges, Preston *(Librettist)* 657, 2705, 4620
Sturges, Preston *(Lyricist)* 4620
Sturges, Preston *(Screenwriter)* 837
Sturgis, Frank *(Lyricist)* 822
Sturgis, Julian *(Lyricist)* 2348
Sturiale, Grant *(Composer)* 1120, 3272
Sturiale, Grant *(Dance Arranger)* 1120, 2539
Sturiale, Grant *(Musical Director)* 1120
Sturiale, Grant *(Vocal Arranger)* 1120
Sturm, Jason *(Lighting Designer)* 757
Sturm, Murray *(Composer)* 3926
Sturm, Murray *(Lyricist)* 3926
Sturn, Justin *(Producer)* 4319
Sturn, Katherine *(Producer)* 4319
Sturtevant, Roger *(Librettist)* 2076
Stutler, Bill *(Producer)* 2231
Stutz, Richard *(Composer)* 95
Styles, Edwin *(Cast)* 1137, 4159
Styne, Jule *(Composer)* 299, 363, 974, 989, 1061, 1227, 1390, 1420, 1475, 1503, 1577, 1709, 1729, 1791, 1842, 1886, 2073, 2076, 2077, 2078, 2205, 2583, 2590, 2677, 2850, 2980, 3160, 3299, 3444, 3453, 3485, 3564, 3682, 3800, 3844, 3845, 3878, 3879, 3961, 3967, 4060, 4190, 4196, 4399, 4496, 4582, 4737, 4743
Styne, Jule *(Director)* 4060
Styne, Jule *(Producer)* 1227, 1791, 2705, 2987, 3845
Styne, Stanley *(Lyricist)* 1503, 4737
Styne Organization, Jule *(Producer)* 1290

Styx, Carl *(Musical Director)* 4735
Suarez, Ilka *(Costumes)* 2188
Suarez, Olga *(Cast)* 3013
Subin, Eli *(Cast)* 4543
Sucke, Greer *(Librettist)* 2703
Sucke, Greer *(Lyricist)* 2703
Sues, Alan *(Cast)* 4703
Suesse, Dana *(Cast)* 3153
Suesse, Dana *(Composer)* 173, 397, 417, 420, 662, 924, 1813, 2413, 2460, 3894, 3975, 4235, 4777, 4824
Suesse, Dana *(Lyricist)* 924, 3894, 4777
Suffin, Herb *(Director)* 679
Suffin, Jordan *(Cast)* 2969, 3928
Sugarman, Dave *(Cast)* 4141
Sukman, Harry *(Composer)* 3381
Sukman, Harry *(Musical Director)* 3, 3381
Sullavan, Margaret *(Cast)* 1831
Sullivan, Alex *(Librettist)* 4562
Sullivan, Alex *(Lyricist)* 1065, 1154, 2662, 3614, 4393
Sullivan, Arthur *(Author)* 1948, 2817, 2861
Sullivan, Arthur *(Composer)* 727, 1178, 1913, 1948, 1987, 2348, 2977, 3259, 3280, 3777, 4254
Sullivan, Arthur *(Librettist)* 1446
Sullivan, Arthur *(Music Based On)* 2861
Sullivan, Barry *(Cast)* 347, 1476
Sullivan, Brad *(Cast)* 4124
Sullivan, Brian *(Cast)* 2837, 4169
Sullivan, Charles *(Cast)* 516
Sullivan, Charles *(Composer)* 516
Sullivan, Charles *(Lyricist)* 516
Sullivan, D.J. *(Additional Music)* 761
Sullivan, Dan *(Composer)* 2902, 2934
Sullivan, Dan *(Lyricist)* 2902, 2934
Sullivan, Dan J. *(Composer)* 2662
Sullivan, Dan J. *(Lyricist)* 2662
Sullivan, Daniel J. *(Composer)* 3220, 3642
Sullivan, Daniel J. *(Lyricist)* 3220, 3642
Sullivan, Ed *(Cast)* 3153
Sullivan, Frank *(Director)* 4660
Sullivan, Frank *(Librettist)* 1874
Sullivan, Frank *(Lyricist)* 3409
Sullivan, Frank *(Puppeteer)* 997, 2726, 4710
Sullivan, Henry *(Cast)* 750
Sullivan, Henry *(Composer)* 2227, 2300, 2540, 2545, 3005, 4335, 4374, 4583
Sullivan, Ian *(Cast)* 1959
Sullivan, J.P. *(Cast)* 2310
Sullivan, James E. *(Cast)* 2929
Sullivan, Jerry *(Cast)* 3024
Sullivan, Jo *(Cast)* 2961, 3224, 3444, 4369, 4399
Sullivan, Joe J. *(Cast)* 1758
Sullivan, John Carver *(Costumes)* 1997
Sullivan, Joseph *(Cast)* 2085
Sullivan, Joseph L. *(Cast)* 1759
Sullivan, K.T. *(Cast)* 112, 4371
Sullivan, Lee *(Cast)* 530, 2447
Sullivan, Maxine *(Cast)* 889, 3059, 4256
Sullivan, Niel *(Composer)* 1964
Sullivan, Niel *(Lyricist)* 1964
Sullivan, Patrick *(Cast)* 1612
Sullivan, Paul *(Lighting Designer)* 1412, 1809, 1816, 2630, 2962, 3112, 4192
Sullivan, Sheila *(Cast)* 842, 3516
Sullivan, Terry *(Lyricist)* 336
Sully, William *(Cast)* 3185
Sumac, Yma *(Cast)* 1300
Sumbay, Dormeshia *(Cast)* 432
Summer, Donna *(Composer)* 3636, 3739
Summer, Donna *(Lyricist)* 3636, 3739
Summerhays, Jane *(Cast)* 2798
Summers, Beatrice *(Cast)* 4063
Summers, Bryon *(Composer)* 2171
Summers, Caley *(Costumes)* 2418
Summers, Cecil *(Cast)* 1562
Summers, Sam *(Librettist)* 4741
Summerville, Ada *(Cast)* 3677
Summerville, Amelia *(Cast)* 354, 523, 1123, 1505, 1728, 1793, 2324, 4644
Sumner, George *(Lyricist)* 297
Sumner, Sting
See also Sting.
Sumner, Sting *(Composer)* 3739
Sumner, Sting *(Lyricist)* 3739
Sumter, Gwen *(Cast)* 1282
Sunbar Productions *(Producer)* 2245
Sundberg, Clinton *(Cast)* 4142
Sunderland, Nan *(Cast)* 1368
Sundgaard, Arnold *(Librettist)* 1085, 2339, 3195, 3703
Sundgaard, Arnold *(Lyricist)* 1085, 2339, 4785
Sundquist, Edward *(Set Design)* 567, 1852
Sunshine, Marion *(Cast)* 335, 468, 558, 642, 953, 1536, 1598, 3207, 4158, 4801
Suntory International Corp. *(Producer)* 775, 2205, 3285
Suppon, Charles *(Librettist)* 2437
Suratt, Valeska *(Cast)* 356, 433, 501, 1900, 3681, 4104
Suratt, Valeska *(Costumes)* 3681
Suratt, Valeska *(Set Design)* 3681
Surovy, Nicolas *(Cast)* 785
Surtees, R.S. *(Author)* 2240
Susann, Jackie *(Cast)* 1546
Susann, Jacqueline *(Author)* 2629
Susann, Jacqueline *(Cast)* 297, 2187, 2397
Susskind, David *(Producer)* 695, 2304, 4279
Susskind, Milton *(Composer)* 1312
Sussman, Bruce *(Composer)* 2022, 2677
Sussman, Bruce *(Librettist)* 846
Sussman, Bruce *(Lyricist)* 829, 845, 846, 2022, 2677
Sussman, Don *(Lighting Designer)* 4401
Suszon *(Orchestrations)* 1134
Sutcliffe, Berkeley *(Costumes)* 1467
Sutcliffe, Berkeley *(Lighting Designer)* 2608
Sutcliffe, Berkeley *(Set Design)* 2608
Suter, William P. *(Producer)* 3724
Sutherland, Claudette *(Cast)* 2019
Sutherland, Evelyn Greenleaf *(Author)* 3730
Sutherland, Lillie *(Choreographer)* 509
Sutherland, Marie *(Composer)* 4098
Sutherland, Marie *(Lyricist)* 4098
Suttell, Jane *(Costumes)* 4229

Sutton, Harry O. *(Composer)* 246, 1148, 1246, 4762, 4803
Sutton, Harry O. *(Lyricist)* 4390
Sutton, Julia *(Cast)* 3429
Sutton, Kay *(Cast)* 1109
Suzette Producing Company *(Producer)* 4227
Suzuki, Pat *(Cast)* 1315
Svar, John *(Cast)* 3479
Svigals, Phil *(Composer)* 551, 3012
Svoboda, Josef *(Set Design)* 2260
Swados, Elizabeth *(Additional Lyrics)* 3661
Swados, Elizabeth *(Cast)* 3162
Swados, Elizabeth *(Composer)* 54, 1053, 1077, 1700, 1715, 1740, 2237, 2648, 3162, 3661, 3806, 4736
Swados, Elizabeth *(Director)* 1053, 1700, 1715, 2237, 2648, 3162, 3806, 4736
Swados, Elizabeth *(Librettist)* 1053, 1700, 1715, 2237, 2648, 3806, 4736
Swados, Elizabeth *(Lyricist)* 54, 1053, 1700, 1715, 2237, 2648, 3162, 3806, 4736
Swados, Elizabeth *(Musical Director)* 54
Swados, Elizabeth *(Orchestrations)* 1077
Swados, Kim *(Set Design)* 298, 4155
Swaebe, Philip *(Producer)* 74
Swain, Lillian *(Cast)* 195, 2116
Swan, Boots *(Cast)* 1514
Swan, E.A. *(Composer)* 4534
Swan, E.A. *(Lyricist)* 4534
Swan, Mark *(Author)* 2253, 2378
Swan, Mark *(Librettist)* 60, 1793, 2253, 2519, 2642, 2893, 3560, 3574, 4425
Swan, Mark *(Lyricist)* 2893
Swan, Rima *(Cast)* 3130
Swan & Lee *(Cast)* 876, 877, 896, 3709
Swanlee *(Producer)* 615
Swann, Donald *(Cast)* 220, 221
Swann, Donald *(Composer)* 220, 221
Swann, Donald *(Lyricist)* 221
Swann, Francis *(Director)* 3371
Swann, Francis *(Librettist)* 3371
Swanset Productions *(Producer)* 4232
Swanson, Britt *(Cast)* 3927
Swanstrom, Arthur *(Composer)* 1063, 1176, 3973, 4374, 4393, 4824
Swanstrom, Arthur *(Librettist)* 1687, 3860
Swanstrom, Arthur *(Lyricist)* 667, 1063, 1685, 1686, 1687, 1932, 2700, 3584, 3860, 3973, 4087, 4374, 4824
Swanstrom, Arthur *(Producer)* 3584, 4087
Swarbrick, Carol *(Cast)* 1093, 1581
Sward, Anne *(Cast)* 337
Swarthart, G. *(Lyricist)* 4387
Swartz, Frederick *(Librettist)* 4679
Sweatnam, Willis *(Cast)* 1259, 1480
Sweatnam, Willis P. *(Cast)* 4203
Sweeney, Bob *(Cast)* 752
Sweeney, Chuck *(Lyricist)* 2313, 4827
Sweet, Blanche *(Cast)* 3267
Sweet, Dolph *(Cast)* 406
Sweet, E. Tracy *(Lyricist)* 938
Sweet, Jeffrey *(Author)* 114
Sweet, Jeffrey *(Composer)* 114, 3557
Sweet, Jeffrey *(Librettist)* 2065, 2598, 3557
Sweet, Jeffrey *(Lyricist)* 114, 2065, 3557
Sweet, Marjorie *(Cast)* 3030
Sweet Olive, Inc. *(Producer)* 908
Sweetser, Norman *(Cast)* 1513
Sweningston, P. *(Composer)* 1562
Swenson, Dean *(Orchestrations)* 2074
Swenson, Inga *(Cast)* 134, 270, 817, 3108, 3294, 4715
Swenson, Karl *(Cast)* 1342, 3104
Swenson, Linda *(Composer)* 459
Swenson, Rod *(Composer)* 3739
Swenson, Rod *(Lyricist)* 3739
Swenson, Swen *(Cast)* 454, 496, 2248, 2523, 2925, 4273, 4693
Swerd, Lester *(Choreographer)* 77
Swerdlow, Elizabeth *(Choreographer)* 2618
Swerdlow, Robert *(Composer)* 2618
Swerdlow, Robert *(Librettist)* 2618
Swerdlow, Robert *(Lyricist)* 2618
Swerling, Jo *(Librettist)* 1706, 3130
Swete, E. Lyall *(Director)* 165, 758, 2802
Swete, E. Lyall *(Lyricist)* 165
Swibard *(Lyricist)* 1550
Swift, Allen *(Cast)* 3059, 4186
Swift, Judith *(Director)* 2132
Swift, Kay *(Composer)* 1275, 1448, 2545, 3172, 3386, 3849
Swift, Kay *(Lyricist)* 3386
Swift, Thomas *(Librettist)* 537, 538
Swift, Thomas *(Lyricist)* 538
Swift, Thos F. *(Cast)* 1513
Swinburne, Ann *(Cast)* 902, 2670
Swor, Irene *(Cast)* 2238
Sydenham, George *(Cast)* 310
Sydney, Basil *(Cast)* 715, 2211
Sydney, Robert *(Choreographer)* 4340
Sydow, Jack *(Director)* 127, 4090
Syers, Mark *(Cast)* 1211
Syers, Mark Hsu *(Cast)* 3340
Sykes, Dick *(Cast)* 4432
Sykes, Jerome *(Cast)* 113, 405, 749, 1260, 1375, 1896
Sykes, Jerome *(Director)* 3570
Sylber, Charley *(Cast)* 2669
Sylva, Marguerita *(Cast)* 1355, 1392, 1603, 1712, 2636, 2714, 2938, 4365
Sylvester, Joyce *(Cast)* 2133
Sylvon, Jerry *(Director)* 4110
Sylvon, Jerry *(Librettist)* 4110
Sylvon, Jerry *(Producer)* 4110
Symes, Marty *(Lyricist)* 1951
Symon, Burk *(Director)* 3002
Syms, Sylvia *(Cast)* 4337, 4682
Synge, John Millington *(Author)* 259
Syrjala, Sointu *(Set Design)* 1734, 3501, 4548
Szabo-Cohen, Laura *(Lyricist)* 4107
Szarabajka, Keith *(Cast)* 1077
Sze, Julia *(Costumes)* 137, 1930
Szell, Lajos *(Author)* 3537
Szilasi, A.F. *(Librettist)* 340
Szirmay, Albert *(Author)* 3583

Szirmay, Albert *(Composer)* 3583
Szony, Francois *(Cast)* 1326

T

TV Asahi *(Producer)* 589, 3862
Tabbert, William *(Cast)* 404, 1242, 3893, 4096
Tabor, Desiree *(Cast)* 771, 1130, 2747
Tabor, Eithne *(Lyricist)* 932
Tabor, Richard *(Cast)* 75
Tabori, George *(Lyricist)* 369
Taffner, Don *(Producer)* 3695
Tagliarino, Salvatore *(Set Design)* 1418
Tahse, Martin *(Producer)* 2958
Taintor, Melinda *(Choreographer)* 4536
Taiz, Lillian *(Cast)* 1113, 4118
Taj Mahal *(Composer)* 3001
Takazauckas, Albert *(Director)* 3476
Take, Marilyn Ruth *(Cast)* 2090
Talbert, George *(Cast)* 689
Talbert, Wen *(Composer)* 2720
Talbot, Arthur *(Cast)* 1087, 3945
Talbot, Howard *(Author)* 1526
Talbot, Howard *(Composer)* 178, 353, 470, 737, 1526, 1537, 1538, 1626, 2341, 2714, 2938, 3856, 3857, 3996, 4354, 4663
Talbot, Howard *(Musical Director)* 2524, 4663
Talbot, Sharon *(Cast)* 2007
Talbot Productions *(Producer)* 584
Talbott Choir, Wen *(Cast)* 435
Taliaferro, Edith *(Cast)* 1250
Taliaferro, Hugh *(Composer)* 4433
Taliaferro, Hugh *(Librettist)* 4433
Taliaferro, Hugh *(Lyricist)* 4433
Taliaferro, John *(Cast)* 72
Taliaferro, Mabel *(Cast)* 462, 2336
Tallchief, Maria *(Cast)* 4075
Tallman, Bill *(Cast)* 1858
Tallon, Ninon *(Producer)* 1062
Tally, May *(Lyricist)* 1780
Tally, Ted *(Author)* 829
Tally, Ted *(Librettist)* 4535
Talman, Ann *(Cast)* 4790
Talman, George *(Cast)* 1388
Talsky, Ron *(Costumes)* 2058
Talva, Galina *(Cast)* 619
Tamaino, Anita *(Cast)* 4168
Tamanya, Hesla *(Cast)* 27
Tamara *(Cast)* 418, 1387, 2432, 3009, 3130, 3153, 3713
Tamara, Florenz *(Cast)* 2569
Tamaris, Helen *(Choreographer)* 153
Tamber, Selma *(Producer)* 1017
Tambin, David *(Orchestrations)* 1415
Tambornino, Jeff *(Librettist)* 1086, 2142
Tamir, Moshe *(Librettist)* 2866
Tamiris, Helen *(Cast)* 2167, 2175, 2653
Tamiris, Helen *(Choreographer)* 454, 603, 657, 1242, 1300, 1679, 2137, 2167, 2751, 3390, 3509, 4524
Tamiroff, Akim *(Cast)* 743
Tamm, Peter *(Cast)* 81
Tananis, Robert *(Cast)* 2114
Tandet, A. Joseph *(Producer)* 2539
Tandy *(Cast)* 3451
Tandy, Jessica *(Cast)* 1372
Tandy, Spencer *(Producer)* 1813, 4454
Tanguay, Eva *(Cast)* 694, 3229, 4223, 4803
Tannassy, Cornell *(Orchestrations)* 1336, 3234, 3280
Tannehill, Bessie *(Cast)* 1295, 3154
Tannehill Jr., Frank *(Director)* 537, 1469, 3021, 3024, 3028, 3437, 3877
Tannehill Jr., Frank *(Librettist)* 3021
Tannen, Julius *(Cast)* 1131, 1132, 1403, 1847, 2481
Tannen, William *(Cast)* 1448
Tanner, Chris *(Cast)* 2488
Tanner, Florence *(Cast)* 3033
Tanner, James T. *(Author)* 3322
Tanner, James T. *(Director)* 284
Tanner, James T. *(Librettist)* 284, 767, 770, 906, 1544, 1561, 2131, 2844, 3098, 3313, 3322, 3618, 4430
Tanner, James T. *(Lyricist)* 3020
Tanner, Tony *(Choreographer)* 2242, 3555, 3576, 4062
Tanner, Tony *(Director)* 669, 1635, 1761, 2242, 3555, 3576, 3600, 4062
Tapla, Jose *(Lyricist)* 4343
Tapper, Lester *(Lighting Designer)* 1837, 3427, 4577
Tapping, Simon *(Lighting Designer)* 3429
Tapps, George *(Cast)* 125, 1112, 1898
Tapps, George *(Choreographer)* 1112, 1898
Tapps, Georgie *(Cast)* 2068, 3036, 4631
Tapps, Herman *(Cast)* 715
Tarasoff, I. *(Choreographer)* 3006
Tarbox, Russell *(Composer)* 1836, 3402
Tarbox, Russell *(Musical Director)* 2569
Tarchetti, I.U. *(Author)* 3411
Tarica, Laurence *(Cast)* 4679
Tarica, Laurence *(Composer)* 4679
Tarica, Laurence *(Lyricist)* 4679
Tarkington, Booth *(Author)* 1501, 1831, 2937, 3768, 3895
Tarkington, Booth *(Lyricist)* 3768
Taros, George *(Musical Director)* 2278
Taros, George *(Orchestrations)* 2278
Tarr, William *(Lyricist)* 1017
Tarr, Yvonne *(Librettist)* 1017
Tarr, Yvonne *(Lyricist)* 1017
Tarrasch, William *(Musical Director)* 1299
Tarrent, Robert T. *(Librettist)* 1134
Tarrytown Music Hall *(Producer)* 2388
Tartaglia, Bob *(Dance Arranger)* 4022
Tartel, Michael *(Cast)* 2674
Tarver, Ben *(Librettist)* 2731
Tarver, Ben *(Lyricist)* 2731
Tarver, Bernard J. *(Cast)* 114
Tashamira *(Cast)* 3861
Tashman, Lilyan *(Cast)* 683, 2900, 4810, 4811
Tatanacho *(Composer)* 1446
Tatch, Eric *(Librettist)* 4565
Tate, Beth *(Cast)* 179

Tate, Charles *(Director)* 1676
Tate, Harry *(Cast)* 2571
Tate, I. *(Composer)* 246
Tate, James W. *(Composer)* 248, 954, 1208, 1588, 2698, 3827, 3882
Tate, Neal *(Composer)* 3825
Tate, Neal *(Musical Director)* 3599, 3825, 4192
Tate, Neal *(Orchestrations)* 1198, 2173
Tate, Neal *(Vocal Arranger)* 4192
Tate, Robert *(Cast)* 4309
Tatum, Marianne *(Cast)* 305
Taub, Allen *(Lyricist)* 715
Taub, Theodore *(Author)* 3625
Taub, William L. *(Producer)* 1834
Taube, Sven-Bertil *(Cast)* 2047
Tauber, Chaim *(Composer)* 1609
Tauber, Chaim *(Lyricist)* 1609, 2356
Tauber, Doris *(Composer)* 4131
Tauber, Richard *(Cast)* 4792
Taubman, Alfred *(Producer)* 3299
Taupin, Bernie *(Composer)* 3739
Taupin, Bernie *(Lyricist)* 3739
Tavel, Harvey *(Director)* 1304
Taverne, Joost *(Producer)* 1865
Tavor, Edward M. *(Cast)* 1570
Tax, Yan *(Costumes)* 949
Taylor *(Composer)* 432, 830
Taylor *(Lyricist)* 432
Taylor, Alice *(Cast)* 3267
Taylor, Ann *(Cast)* 455
Taylor, Bert Leston *(Librettist)* 1220
Taylor, Bert Leston *(Lyricist)* 1220
Taylor, Billie *(Cast)* 2209, 2232, 2722, 4553, 4655
Taylor, Billie *(Composer)* 246, 830, 2358
Taylor, Billie *(Lyricist)* 830
Taylor, Billy *(Cast)* 1667, 2300
Taylor, Billy *(Composer)* 2300
Taylor, Charles A. *(Librettist)* 3786
Taylor, Charles A. *(Lyricist)* 3786
Taylor, Charles H. *(Lyricist)* 100, 333, 675, 1043, 2803, 3857, 3976, 4404
Taylor, Charles M. *(Lyricist)* 246
Taylor, Charles W. *(Lyricist)* 2261
Taylor, Charlotte *(Cast)* 4596
Taylor, Chris *(Lyricist)* 4824
Taylor, Clarice *(Cast)* 166, 1592, 2932, 4722
Taylor, Clifton *(Lighting Designer)* 3561
Taylor, Cornelia Osgood *(Librettist)* 4549
Taylor, David *(Librettist)* 3555
Taylor, Deems *(Cast)* 4565
Taylor, Deems *(Composer)* 584, 1151, 2487
Taylor, Deems *(Librettist)* 1151
Taylor, Deems *(Lyricist)* 1151
Taylor, Deems *(Orchestrations)* 2487, 4372
Taylor, Dwight *(Librettist)* 3326
Taylor, Edwin *(Cast)* 1502
Taylor, Elizabeth *(Cast)* 3361, 4625
Taylor, Eva *(Cast)* 500, 3623
Taylor, Evelyn *(Cast)* 85
Taylor, Gina *(Cast)* 338, 2427
Taylor, Henry *(Cast)* 396
Taylor, Henry *(Librettist)* 3683
Taylor, Hiram *(Author)* 2968
Taylor, Hiram *(Composer)* 2968
Taylor, Hiram *(Director)* 2968
Taylor, Hiram *(Lyricist)* 2968
Taylor, Holland *(Cast)* 1249
Taylor, Irving *(Composer)* 1120
Taylor, Irving *(Lyricist)* 447, 524, 839, 1120, 2588, 3487, 4006
Taylor, James *(Composer)* 4744
Taylor, James *(Lyricist)* 4744
Taylor, James A. *(Set Design)* 679
Taylor, Jane *(Cast)* 2490, 3042, 3069, 4240, 4276
Taylor, Jeannine *(Cast)* 1897, 1955
Taylor, Jeremy *(Composer)* 4579
Taylor, Jeremy *(Lyricist)* 4579
Taylor, Jonathan *(Choreographer)* 1619
Taylor, June *(Cast)* 1799
Taylor, June *(Choreographer)* 190, 2750, 3371
Taylor, June *(Director)* 2750
Taylor, Kenneth *(Composer)* 2239
Taylor, Laura *(Composer)* 4171
Taylor, Laura *(Lyricist)* 4171
Taylor, Laurette *(Cast)* 2855, 3328, 3432
Taylor, Mary K. *(Cast)* 2996
Taylor, Matt *(Librettist)* 971
Taylor, Morris *(Set Design)* 778
Taylor, Nellie *(Cast)* 2788
Taylor, Noel *(Costumes)* 483, 1742, 3188, 4278, 4633
Taylor, Philip *(Director)* 3522
Taylor, Ray *(Composer)* 90
Taylor, Ray *(Lyricist)* 90
Taylor, Raymond *(Composer)* 722
Taylor, Raymond *(Lyricist)* 722
Taylor, Renee *(Cast)* 32
Taylor, Renee *(Librettist)* 2016
Taylor, Robert Lewis *(Author)* 4577
Taylor, Robert U. *(Set Design)* 482, 1249, 1755, 2579, 3656, 4431
Taylor, Ron *(Cast)* 2544
Taylor, Ronald *(Producer)* 227
Taylor, Rose Mary *(Cast)* 2618
Taylor, Russ *(Composer)* 1412
Taylor, Samuel *(Author)* 1764, 2435
Taylor, Samuel *(Librettist)* 3187
Taylor, Stephen *(Cast)* 2682
Taylor, Telford *(Composer)* 2122
Taylor, Theda *(Lighting Designer)* *1676*
Taylor, Todd *(Cast)* 3249
Taylor, Tom *(Cast)* 4410
Taylor, Tom *(Librettist)* 3249, 4410
Taylor, Valerie *(Cast)* 1618
Taylor & Johnson *(Cast)* 26
Taylor-Corbett, Lynne *(Choreographer)* 721, 1149, 2199, 3306, 3909
Taylor-Corbett, Lynne *(Director)* 3306, 4325
Taymor, Julie *(Choreographer)* 4442
Taymor, Julie *(Costumes)* 1715
Taymor, Julie *(Director)* 4442

Taymor, Julie *(Librettist)* 4442
Taymor, Julie *(Set Design)* 1715
Taynton, David *(Producer)* 1233
Tayte, Maggie *(Cast)* 2509
Tazewell, Charles *(Librettist)* 4198
Tazwell, Charles *(Author)* 2553
Tchaikowsky, Peter *(Composer)* 2162
Tchaikowsky, Peter Illitch *(Music Based On)* 3013, 3078, 3212
Tchakirides, Bill *(Producer)* 3711
TeWiata, Inia *(Cast)* 1119
Teagarden, Jack *(Cast)* 1528
Teague, Anthony *(Cast)* 1257
Teague, Scooter *(Cast)* 3294
Teal, Ben *(Director)* 20, 543, 571, 675, 749, 1188, 1318, 1375, 1565, 2025, 2117, 2145, 2181, 2498, 2592, 2723, 2854, 3268, 3672, 3710, 3744, 3745, 3748, 3751, 3753, 4012, 4130, 4681
Teal, Ben *(Librettist)* 2145
Teal, Ben *(Lyricist)* 2145
Teal, Ben *(Set Design)* 527
Teasdale, Verree *(Cast)* 1219
Tebelak, John-Michael *(Director)* 1581, 1595, 2285
Tebelak, John-Michael *(Librettist)* 1595
Tebesli, Ilsebet Anna *(Cast)* 169
Tedesco, John *(Lighting Designer)* 1999
Tedro, Henrietta *(Cast)* 331
Teer, Barbara Ann *(Director)* 344
Tees, Levin C. *(Librettist)* 215
Teeter, Lara *(Cast)* 1762, 3888
Teich, Lois *(Producer)* 4027
Teichner, Charles *(Set Design)* 242
Teichner Studios *(Set Design)* 4299
Teifer, Jerry *(Composer)* 4278
Teifer, Jerry *(Lyricist)* 4278
Teijelo, Gerald *(Choreographer)* 2043, 2219
Teijelo, Gerald R. *(Cast)* 3702
Teisch, Steve *(Lyricist)* 4
Teitlebaum, Maurice *(Librettist)* 1974
Teitlebaum, Maurice *(Lyricist)* 1974
Telbin, W. *(Set Design)* 1470
Tell, Olive *(Cast)* 913
Teller, Frank L. *(Producer)* 2380
Telson, Bob *(Composer)* 756, 1636
Telson, Bob *(Lyricist)* 756
Temchin, Jack *(Producer)* 1166, 4480
Temme, Leonard A. *(Choreographer)* 2393
Tempest, Florence *(Cast)* 2534, 4158, 4801
Tempest, Marie *(Cast)* 1260
Temple, Dick *(Cast)* 4713
Temple, Dick *(Composer)* 4713
Temple, Dick *(Lyricist)* 4713
Temple, Edgar *(Cast)* 2500, 3384, 3585
Temple, Edward *(Director)* 236, 2623, 2929
Temple, Edward *(Librettist)* 236
Temple, Edward P. *(Cast)* 727, 1401, 1720
Temple, Edward P. *(Director)* 228, 1557, 2546, 2671, 2794, 3093, 3504, 3613, 4046, 4133, 4753
Temple, Edward P. *(Librettist)* 3093
Temple, Edward P. *(Lyricist)* 3093
Temple, Elaine *(Cast)* 3481
Temple, Nancy *(Cast)* 3802
Temple, Renny *(Cast)* 4468
Temple, Richard *(Composer)* 906
Temple, Richard *(Lyricist)* 906
Templeton, Fay *(Cast)* 559, 677, 1213, 1264, 1356, 1926, 1927, 2041, 2123, 2481, 2493, 3735, 4478
Templeton, Jan *(Cast)* 272
Templeton, Lester *(Choreographer)* 2299
Templeton, Mercer *(Cast)* 4010
Templeton, Olive *(Cast)* 1760
Templeton Brothers *(Cast)* 4673
Tennant, H.M. *(Composer)* 605, 1780
Tennant, H.M. *(Producer)* 4361
Tennen, Julius *(Cast)* 3783
Tenney, Del *(Producer)* 3181
Tennis, Eleanor *(Cast)* 689
Tennyson, Alfred Lord *(Lyricist)* 2819
Tennyson, Jean *(Cast)* 1134, 4290
Teppe, Herman Patrick *(Costumes)* 1625
Ter-Arutunian, Rouben *(Costumes)* 1076, 1991, 3113, 3687
Ter-Arutunian, Rouben *(Lighting Designer)* 3113
Ter-Arutunian, Rouben *(Set Design)* 223, 1076, 1634, 1991, 2075, 2838, 3113, 3602
Terhune, Alice *(Composer)* 326
Terhune, Alice *(Lyricist)* 326
Terjeson, Arthur *(Lighting Designer)* 239
Terjeson, Arthur *(Set Design)* 239
Terkel, Studs *(Author)* 4744
Terrel II, Elwin Charles *(Set Design)* 3297
Terrell, John Canada *(Cast)* 2239
Terrell, Sarah Laine *(Cast)* 2676
Terrell, Stephen *(Choreographer)* 992
Terris, Dorothy *(Lyricist)* 1687
Terris, Norma *(Cast)* 317, 1670, 3148, 3149, 3623, 3949, 4620
Terriss, Ellaline *(Cast)* 333, 719, 1454, 1905
Terriss, Thomas *(Director)* 2500
Terriss, Tom *(Choreographer)* 2803
Terry, Charlotte *(Cast)* 1462
Terry, David *(Orchestrations)* 3110, 3899
Terry, Ethelind *(Cast)* 796, 1962, 2308, 2947, 3006, 3170, 3719
Terry, John S. *(Cast)* 222
Terry, Megan *(Lyricist)* 4343
Terry, Michael *(Composer)* 3987
Terry, Michael *(Lyricist)* 3987
Terry, Mike *(Dance Arranger)* 578
Terry, Mike *(Orchestrations)* 578
Terry, Mike *(Vocal Arranger)* 578
Terry, Muriel *(Cast)* 1455
Terry, Ruth *(Cast)* 2059
Terry, Sonny *(Cast)* 1278
Terry, Susan *(Cast)* 2643
Tesori, Jeanine *(Composer)* 4136
Testa, Mary *(Cast)* 789, 1832, 2346, 2477, 2646, 3853
Tester, Hans *(Cast)* 4830
Tester, Ruth *(Cast)* 3861
Tetley, Glen *(Cast)* 2268

Tetley, Glen *(Choreographer)* 1354
Teuber, Max *(Lighting Designer)* 1126
Teuber, Max *(Set Design)* 3002
Tewkesbury, Joan *(Cast)* 3453
Texas, Temple *(Cast)* 1204, 3505
Thacker, Cheryl *(Lighting Designer)* 788, 3162
Thacker, Russ *(Cast)* 1010, 1059, 1662, 1809, 1959, 3018, 4789
Thacker, Russ *(Producer)* 4731
Thaler, Fred *(Dance Arranger)* 3515
Thaler, Fred *(Musical Director)* 3515
Thaler, Fred *(Orchestrations)* 3515
Thaler, Fred *(Vocal Arranger)* 3515
Thalheimer, Norman *(Composer)* 2754
Thalheimer, Norman *(Lyricist)* 2754
Tharp, Twyla *(Choreographer)* 3992
Tharp, Twyla *(Director)* 3992
Tharpe, Sister Rosetta *(Cast)* 888
Thatcher, Heather *(Cast)* 334, 3569
Thatcher, Torin *(Cast)* 1294
Thawl, Evelyn *(Cast)* 3955
Thayer, Bert *(Cast)* 2675
Thayer, Edith *(Cast)* 37
Thayer, Pat *(Composer)* 702, 792, 2789, 2843
Theard, Sam *(Composer)* 1296, 3840
Theard, Sam *(Lyricist)* 1296, 3840
Theater Opera Music Inst. *(Producer)* 871
Theater-in-Limbo *(Producer)* 3606
Theatre 1972 *(Producer)* 1093, 1662
Theatre Atlanta *(Producer)* 3684
Theatre Collective *(Producer)* 99
Theatre Corp. of America *(Producer)* 3234
Theatre Guild, The *(Producer)* 85, 183, 363, 660, 989, 1446, 1447, 1448, 2144, 2487, 3020, 3263, 3365, 3541, 4146, 4516
Theatre Now *(Producer)* 482, 786
Theatre Projects *(Producer)* 2047
Theatre Royal Drury Lane *(Producer)* 972, 4207
Theatre Workshop *(Producer)* 874, 2572
Theatreworks USA *(Producer)* 2197
Theatrical Art Studios *(Set Design)* 3069
Theatrical Operating Co. *(Producer)* 1964
Thebaud, Estelle *(Cast)* 909
Theise, Mortimer M. *(Librettist)* 1409
Theise, Mortimer M. *(Producer)* 2694
Theodore, Donna *(Cast)* 962, 3928
Theodore, Laura *(Cast)* 338
Theodore, Lee *(Cast)* 3286, 4312
Theodore, Lee *(Choreographer)* 170, 270, 974, 989, 1310, 1648, 1769, 3196, 3286, 3389, 3577
Theodore, Lee *(Director)* 997, 3196, 3498, 4660, 4710
Theodore, Ralph *(Cast)* 1749
Thery, Jacques *(Author)* 2669
Thesiger, Ernest *(Cast)* 792, 4154
Thesiger, Ernest *(Director)* 4154
Theyard, Harry *(Cast)* 3612
Thiele, Bob *(Lyricist)* 4091
Thigpen, Lynne *(Cast)* 593, 3159, 4390, 4744
Thimar, David *(Choreographer)* 3108
Thimar, David *(Director)* 817, 3380, 3524
Thomas *(Composer)* 77
Thomas *(Lyricist)* 77, 560
Thomas, A.E. *(Author)* 1391, 2277, 2691
Thomas, A.E. *(Librettist)* 2495, 2532, 3323
Thomas, A.E. *(Lyricist)* 2495, 2532
Thomas, Augustus *(Author)* 2602
Thomas, Augustus *(Librettist)* 688
Thomas, Beverly Jane *(Costumes)* 2027
Thomas, Brandon *(Author)* 4652
Thomas, Danny *(Cast)* 928
Thomas, Dave *(Cast)* 3347
Thomas, Edward *(Arrangements)* 4278
Thomas, Edward *(Composer)* 278, 2777, 3018
Thomas, Edward *(Producer)* 278
Thomas, Freyda-Ann *(Cast)* 164
Thomas, Frozine *(Cast)* 1425
Thomas, George W. *(Composer)* 478, 3297
Thomas, George W. *(Lyricist)* 478, 3297
Thomas, Henry *(Director)* 4299
Thomas, Hilda *(Cast)* 3952
Thomas, Hugh *(Cast)* 1245
Thomas, Hugh *(Librettist)* 2680
Thomas, James *(Cast)* 676
Thomas, John Byron *(Cast)* 1304
Thomas, John Charles *(Cast)* 17, 93, 168, 1681, 1852, 2614, 3396, 3399, 3424, 4133, 4148
Thomas, Joseph *(Costumes)* 4343
Thomas, Joyce Carol *(Author)* 10
Thomas, Lewis T. *(Composer)* 4751
Thomas, Lewis T. *(Lyricist)* 4751
Thomas, Maceo *(Cast)* 4730
Thomas, Margaret Ward *(Cast)* 4183
Thomas, Marie *(Cast)* 1072
Thomas, Marlo *(Cast)* 928, 1389
Thomas, Martha *(Cast)* 444
Thomas, Maude *(Cast)* 4563
Thomas, Millard *(Lyricist)* 567
Thomas, Milton *(Composer)* 243
Thomas, Olive *(Cast)* 4809
Thomas, Paul *(Cast)* 1347
Thomas, Philip Michael *(Cast)* 3690
Thomas, Queenie *(Cast)* 704
Thomas, Rhys *(Cast)* 727, 1030, 4242
Thomas, Richard *(Cast)* 404
Thomas, Ross *(Lyricist)* 3410
Thomas, Rudolph *(Musical Director)* 689
Thomas, Tasha *(Vocal Arranger)* 2173
Thomas, Trina *(Cast)* 4645
Thomas, William *(Lighting Designer)* 2397
Thomas, Wynn P. *(Set Design)* 2239
Thomas II, T. Gaillard *(Cast)* 870
Thomas II, T. Gaillard *(Director)* 130, 870
Thomas II, T. Gaillard *(Librettist)* 130, 870
Thomas Jr., Augustus *(Librettist)* 2620
Thomas Jr., William *(Cast)* 2360
Thomas Sisters *(Cast)* 3388
Thomashefsky, Boris *(Cast)* 3995
Thomashefsky, Boris *(Librettist)* 3995
Thomashefsky, Boris *(Lyricist)* 1609
Thomashefsky, Harry *(Librettist)* 3995

Thomashefsky, Harry *(Producer)* 3995
Thomason, Brian *(Set Design)* 2006
Thome, David *(Cast)* 1103
Thompson, A.M. *(Librettist)* 246, 954, 4404
Thompson, Aaron *(Dance Arranger)* 1876
Thompson, Aaron *(Orchestrations)* 1876
Thompson, Aaron *(Vocal Arranger)* 1876
Thompson, Alexander M. *(Librettist)* 178
Thompson, Alfred *(Costumes)* 3360, 3887
Thompson, Alfred *(Set Design)* 3887
Thompson, Allistair *(Composer)* 4153
Thompson, Allistair *(Lyricist)* 4153
Thompson, Blanche *(Cast)* 554, 987, 1479
Thompson, Charlotte *(Author)* 2264
Thompson, Donald V. *(Producer)* 3724
Thompson, Elsie *(Composer)* 924
Thompson, Evan *(Cast)* 775, 3802, 4444
Thompson, Evan *(Director)* 3802, 4444
Thompson, Evan *(Lyricist)* 3802
Thompson, Frank *(Costumes)* 369, 943, 1017, 1380, 2595, 2775, 4689, 4863
Thompson, Fred *(Author)* 1539
Thompson, Fred *(Director)* 1336
Thompson, Fred *(Librettist)* 25, 1153, 1297, 1336, 1419, 1577, 1610, 1859, 2376, 2379, 2757, 3467, 3719, 4087, 4300, 4392, 4418, 4419, 4575
Thompson, Fred *(Lyricist)* 4443
Thompson, Frederick *(Librettist)* 1626
Thompson, Frederick W. *(Producer)* 1566, 4046, 4753
Thompson, Hal *(Cast)* 4021, 4235
Thompson, Harlan *(Author)* 1814
Thompson, Harlan *(Director)* 2833
Thompson, Harlan *(Librettist)* 1814, 2516, 2833, 3042, 4476
Thompson, Harlan *(Lyricist)* 1814, 2516, 2833, 3042, 4476
Thompson, Helen *(Cast)* 3005
Thompson, Hilda *(Cast)* 1499
Thompson, Jack *(Cast)* 834, 1272
Thompson, James *(Lyricist)* 3450
Thompson, Jay *(Composer)* 1023, 1081, 1408, 2482, 2804, 3615, 3788, 4388
Thompson, Jay *(Dance Arranger)* 2590
Thompson, Jay *(Librettist)* 1081, 3288, 3788
Thompson, Jay *(Lyricist)* 1023, 1081, 1408, 2804, 3615, 3788
Thompson, Jay *(Musical Director)* 1081
Thompson, Jay *(Orchestrations)* 1081
Thompson, Jeffrey V. *(Cast)* 4534
Thompson, Jeffrey V. *(Librettist)* 4534
Thompson, John *(Set Design)* 2326, 2543
Thompson, John A. *(Set Design)* 1627
Thompson, Julian F. *(Author)* 601
Thompson, Kay *(Composer)* 1760
Thompson, Kay *(Lyricist)* 1760
Thompson, Kay *(Vocal Arranger)* 1973
Thompson, Keith *(Musical Director)* 778, 4731
Thompson, Keith *(Orchestrations)* 778
Thompson, L.S. *(Composer)* 306, 3951
Thompson, Lewis S. *(Composer)* 306, 4103
Thompson, Lottie *(Cast)* 4088
Thompson, Madame *(Costumes)* 4704
Thompson, Mary *(Cast)* 2521
Thompson, Maudie *(Cast)* 571
Thompson, May *(Cast)* 4784
Thompson, Myrtle *(Cast)* 4756
Thompson, Neil *(Cast)* 2521
Thompson, Paul *(Choreographer)* 99
Thompson, Randall *(Composer)* 266, 1654
Thompson, Randall *(Orchestrations)* 1654
Thompson, Rosewell G. *(Cast)* 4507
Thompson, Rosewell G. *(Librettist)* 4507
Thompson, Sada *(Cast)* 2268, 4474
Thompson, Tazewell *(Director)* 10
Thompson, Tommy *(Cast)* 1037
Thompson, Toni Nanette *(Costumes)* 2488
Thompson, U.S. *(Cast)* 3513
Thompson, Virgil *(Composer)* 1366
Thompson, Vivian *(Composer)* 914
Thompson, Vivian *(Lyricist)* 914
Thompson, W. *(Composer)* 4193
Thompson, W. *(Lyricist)* 4193
Thompson, Woodman *(Costumes)* 1283
Thompson, Woodman *(Set Design)* 799, 1020, 1027, 1283, 4565
Thomson, Brian *(Set Design)* 3742
Thomson, Carolyn *(Cast)* 4539
Thomson, Henry *(Cast)* 4520
Thomson, Herbert *(Lyricist)* 3996
Thorburn, Don *(Composer)* 924
Thorburn, Don *(Lyricist)* 924
Thorne, Eric *(Cast)* 3213
Thorne, Francis *(Composer)* 1354
Thorne, Raymond *(Cast)* 150, 154, 155, 2731, 4297
Thornhill, Alan *(Librettist)* 1887
Thornhill, Alan *(Lyricist)* 1887
Thornhill, Chester *(Cast)* 3802, 4444
Thornton, Arthur *(Cast)* 3982
Thornton, Clarke *(Lighting Designer)* 4172
Thornton, Clarke W. *(Lighting Designer)* 10, 1638, 3181
Thornton, Evans *(Cast)* 2615
Thornton, James *(Cast)* 3153
Thornton, Jim *(Cast)* 3968
Thornton, Sandra *(Cast)* 1249, 1498
Thrall, Bernie *(Orchestrations)* 1834
Thrasher, Ethelyn R. *(Producer)* 413
Thrasher, H.E. *(Lighting Designer)* 1435
Thrasher, H.E. *(Set Design)* 1435
Three Berry Brothers *(Cast)* 897
Three Eddies, The *(Cast)* 2366
3 Knights, Ltd. *(Producer)* 721
350 Soldiers *(Cast)* 4770
Three Midnight Steppers *(Cast)* 1980
Three Poms, The *(Cast)* 467
Three Sailors *(Cast)* 1126
Three Stooges, The *(Cast)* 1494
3W Productions *(Producer)* 2017, 2188
Thress, Frances *(Cast)* 3314
Thripp, George B. *(Cast)* 1549

Throckmorton, Cleon *(Director)* 691
Throckmorton, Cleon *(Producer)* 691
Throckmorton, Cleon *(Set Design)* 587, 691, 4267, 4368
Thronson, Ron *(Composer)* 2962
Thronson, Ron *(Librettist)* 2962
Thronson, Ron *(Lyricist)* 2962
Thun, Nancy *(Set Design)* 4731
Thuna, Lee *(Librettist)* 31, 3956
Thuna, Lenora *(Librettist)* 2199
Thunder, Rino *(Cast)* 3908
Thurber, J. Kent *(Cast)* 1343
Thurber, James *(Author)* 322, 3630, 3863, 4336
Thurber, James *(Librettist)* 2611
Thurber, James *(Lyricist)* 2611
Thurn, Jane *(Set Design)* 2764
Thurston, Barbara *(Costumes)* 92
Thurston, Ted *(Cast)* 681, 1300, 1441, 1585, 1841, 2012, 2053, 2449, 3305, 4029, 4272, 4689
Tibbett, Laurence *(Cast)* 309
Tichacek, Jan *(Set Design)* 979
Tice, David *(Pianist)* 4768
Tichenor, James *(Set Design)* 26
Ticketts, Bob *(Additional Music)* 552
Tidwell, Brian W. *(Musical Director)* 2651
Tierce, Pattie *(Cast)* 778
Tierney, Frank *(Cast)* 3308
Tierney, Harry *(Composer)* 25, 324, 379, 560, 627, 684, 685, 931, 1208, 1334, 1582, 1784, 1823, 1919, 2148, 2308, 2946, 3400, 3401, 3719, 3791, 3958, 3985, 4529, 4634, 4813, 4814, 4817, 4818
Tierney, Harry *(Lyricist)* 3958
Tierney, Thomas *(Composer)* 1099
Tierney, Tom *(Composer)* 2100
Tietjens, Eunice *(Librettist)* 174
Tietjens, Eunice *(Lyricist)* 174
Tietjens, Paul *(Composer)* 2329, 4723
Tietjens, Paul *(Orchestrations)* 2329
Tiffany, Patty *(Cast)* 450
Tighe, Harry *(Cast)* 815, 1334, 1900, 1911, 2619, 4023
Tilden, Fred *(Cast)* 4664
Tilford, Joseph P. *(Set Design)* 3987
Tiller, John *(Choreographer)* 2569, 4212, 4816
Tiller, Ted *(Cast)* 127
Tiller Girls *(Cast)* 4816, 4818
Tiller Girls, The *(Cast)* 1113, 4357, 4793, 4819
Tiller Sunshine Girls *(Cast)* 4150
Tilley, John 1877
Tilley, Martin *(Set Design)* 1256
Tilley, Vesta *(Cast)* 3049
Tillinger, John *(Director)* 4535
Tillotson, W.W. *(Director)* 4161
Tilton, Edwin *(Cast)* 3267
Tilton, James *(Lighting Designer)* 278, 1662, 1985, 3651
Tilton, James *(Set Design)* 278, 1075, 1662, 1985, 3233, 3651
Tilton, Jim *(Set Design)* 753
Timberg, Herman *(Cast)* 1065, 3400, 3855, 4375
Timberg, Herman *(Composer)* 726, 1065, 3333, 3958, 4375
Timberg, Herman *(Director)* 4782
Timberg, Herman *(Librettist)* 418, 4375, 4782
Timberg, Herman *(Lyricist)* 726, 4375, 4782
Timberg, Herman *(Producer)* 4375
Timberg, Sam *(Lyricist)* 551
Timberg, Sammy *(Composer)* 1113, 2843, 4170, 4545, 4669
Times Producing Co. *(Producer)* 1565
Timmens, Jim *(Orchestrations)* 3638
Timony, Jim *(Producer)* 831
Tincher, Fay *(Cast)* 1900
Tine, Hal *(Lighting Designer)* 3522
Tine, Hal *(Set Design)* 2208, 3522
Tinney, Frank *(Cast)* 231, 683, 953, 1065, 1399, 3008, 3701, 4378, 4603, 4712, 4807
Tinsley, Jordan *(Cast)* 4830
Tinsley, Jordan *(Choreographer)* 4830
Tinsley, Jordan *(Director)* 4830
Tinsley, Jordan *(Librettist)* 4830
Tinsley, Jordan *(Lyricist)* 4830
Tinturin, Peter *(Composer)* 567, 1137
Tiomkin, Dimitri *(Composer)* 2540, 4193, 4823
Tippett, Tom *(Librettist)* 4444
Tipton, Jennifer *(Lighting Designer)* 52, 273, 282, 414, 952, 1053, 1344, 1755, 1977, 2205, 2766, 3702, 3806, 3992, 4091, 4736
Tira Productions *(Producer)* 4380
Tiraco, Joseph *(Producer)* 1508
Tirrell, Don *(Set Design)* 1590
Titheradge, Dion *(Author)* 203
Titheradge, Dion *(Librettist)* 133, 216, 475, 702, 1333
Titheradge, Dion *(Lyricist)* 475, 582, 702, 3020
Titheradge, Dion *(Producer)* 704
Titterton, W.R. *(Lyricist)* 377
Titunik, Gail *(Cast)* 319
Titus, Alan *(Cast)* 2775, 2839
Titus, David *(Cast)* 2046
Titus, W.I. *(Lyricist)* 1518
Titzell, Josiah *(Lyricist)* 1448
Tizol, Juan *(Composer)* 3905, 4091
Tizol, Juan *(Lyricist)* 4091
Toback, Hannah *(Cast)* 2802
Tobani, Theo M. *(Composer)* 1535
Tobey, Kenneth *(Cast)* 1601
Tobias, Charles *(Composer)* 1126
Tobias, Charles *(Lyricist)* 24, 297, 1126, 1127, 1 137, 1840, 2296, 2857, 3523, 4583, 4607, 4772, 4821
Tobias, Fred *(Lyricist)* 272, 427, 602, 1441, 2689, 3479, 3551, 4273
Tobias, George *(Cast)* 2432, 3972
Tobias, Harry *(Composer)* 1215, 3375
Tobias, Harry *(Lyricist)* 831, 1126, 2857
Tobias, Henry *(Composer)* 1127, 1137, 1873, 3342, 3375, 4683
Tobias, Henry *(Lyricist)* 4683
Tobin, Genevieve *(Cast)* 17, 1011, 1272, 2537, 3246, 3529, 3535
Tobin, Margaret *(Costumes)* 922
Tobin, Tom Matthew *(Cast)* 2284
Tod, Kenneth *(Composer)* 703

Tod, Quentin *(Cast)* 700, 703
Tod, Quentin *(Choreographer)* 703
Tod, Quentin *(Director)* 700
Tod, Quentin *(Librettist)* 700
Todd, Beverly *(Cast)* 3788
Todd, Bob *(Cast)* 1741
Todd, Clarence *(Cast)* 1980
Todd, Clarence *(Composer)* 443, 2302, 3297, 3709
Todd, Clarence *(Lyricist)* 443, 3297, 3709
Todd, Henry *(Composer)* 3297
Todd, Henry *(Lyricist)* 3297
Todd, Ivan *(Choreographer)* 1978
Todd, Michael
See also Michael Todd Midnight Players.
Todd, Michael *(Producer)* 206, 1987, 2847, 2850, 3151, 4058, 4131, 4524
Todd, Mildred *(Cast)* 3103, 4677
Todd, Miriam *(Cast)* 1342
Todd, Paris *(Cast)* 4332
Todd Midnight Players, Michael
See also Michael Todd.
Todd Midnight Players, Michael *(Producer)* 4110
Toddings, Ann *(Cast)* 2870
Tofel, Tom *(Cast)* 2472
Toguri, David *(Choreographer)* 682
Toibin, Niall *(Cast)* 1256
Toigo, Alfred *(Cast)* 139, 4541, 4543
Tokio, Prince *(Cast)* 4801
Tolbert, Skeets *(Composer)* 4091
Tolbert, Skeets *(Lyricist)* 4091
Toler, Sidney *(Cast)* 1357, 2008, 2309, 3229
Toler, Sidney *(Composer)* 2008
Toler, Sidney *(Librettist)* 606
Toler, Sidney *(Lyricist)* 2008
Toles, Bill *(Additional Music)* 2239
Toles, Bill *(Composer)* 2239
Toles, Bill *(Lyricist)* 2239
Tolin, Mel *(Lyricist)* 4377
Tolka, Mary Ann *(Costumes)* 3654
Tolkien, J.R.R. *(Lyricist)* 221
Tolkin, Mel *(Composer)* 4342
Tolkin, Mel *(Librettist)* 3226
Tolkin, Mel *(Lyricist)* 4342, 4377
Toller, Ernst *(Librettist)* 3441
Toller, Ernst *(Lyricist)* 3441
Tolliver, Edward *(Cast)* 731, 2792, 4184
Tolsatyan, Leon *(Librettist)* 4337
Tolsch, Adrianne *(Cast)* 4347
Tolstoy, Leo *(Author)* 147, 3686, 4176
Tom, Lauren *(Cast)* 1077
Tomasson, Verna *(Librettist)* 3571
Tomasson, Verna *(Lyricist)* 3571
Tombes, Andrew *(Cast)* 82, 465, 1225, 3011, 3207, 3538, 3721, 4170, 4276, 4299, 4300, 4392
Tomei, Concetta *(Cast)* 785, 3198
Tomkins, Don *(Cast)* 288, 4693
Tomlin, Blanche *(Cast)* 2937
Tomlin, Lily *(Cast)* 366, 2138, 3474, 4494
Tomlin, Pinky *(Composer)* 1813, 4799
Tomlin, Pinky *(Lyricist)* 1813, 4799
Tomlinson, Tomm *(Lighting Designer)* 1155, 3165, 3329
Tompkins, Georgia *(Cast)* 4674
Tomson, Bob *(Director)* 460
Tomson, Jack *(Cast)* 4491
Tomson, Tommy *(Cast)* 4491
Tone, Franchot *(Cast)* 1416
Tone, Richard *(Cast)* 2928, 3366, 3551, 4337
Tone, Richard *(Choreographer)* 3366
Toner, Joseph *(Cast)* 184
Toner, Thomas *(Cast)* 1418
Toner, Tom *(Cast)* 3862, 4450
Topall, Lawrence *(Producer)* 3926
Topol *(Producer)* 2147
Toppall, Lawrence *(Producer)* 4769
Toran, Peter *(Cast)* 2177
Torgerson, Elizabeth *(Cast)* 3764
Torme, Mel *(Composer)* 520
Torme, Mel *(Lyricist)* 520
Torn, Rip *(Cast)* 477
Torns, Jamie-Chandler *(Cast)* 3682
Toro, Jeannette *(Cast)* 696
Torre, Janice *(Lyricist)* 4155
Torren, Frank *(Cast)* 2372
Torrence, David *(Cast)* 1731, 2549, 2863, 2886, 3049, 3943
Torrence, Ernest *(Cast)* 1083, 1424, 1794, 2923, 3146, 3304, 3866, 4148, 4547
Torrens, Grace *(Composer)* 758
Torres, Carmen *(Cast)* 63
Torres, Gina *(Cast)* 373
Torres, Liz *(Cast)* 3499
Torti, Robert *(Cast)* 4138
Toser, David *(Costumes)* 31, 583, 915, 1665, 2026, 2578, 3196, 3671, 3851, 4124, 4454, 4796
Tost, Bill *(Puppeteer)* 3449, 4660
Tost, Bill *(Voice)* 56, 3498
Tost, William *(Puppeteer)* 997, 4710
Tost, William *(Voice)* 3449
Tosti, Kenneth *(Choreographer)* 3125
Toto *(Cast)* 396, 1901
Toumanova, Tamara *(Cast)* 4142
Tourag, Vincent *(Producer)* 3490
Tours, Frank *(Composer)* 465, 466, 954, 1067, 1088, 1334, 1454, 1557, 1780, 2358, 2498, 2891
Tours, Frank *(Lyricist)* 906, 954
Tours, Frank *(Musical Director)* 207, 685, 1225, 1334, 1557, 1680, 2252, 2334, 2385, 2620, 2794, 2802, 2960, 3006, 3007, 3008, 3009, 3740, 4023, 4341, 4418, 4814, 4815, 4821
Tours, Frank *(Orchestrations)* 207, 799, 1225, 1534, 1680, 3006, 3007, 3008, 3009, 3403, 4821
Tours, Frank E. *(Composer)* 954, 1454, 2867, 3098, 3213
Tours, Frank E. *(Lyricist)* 1470
Tours, Frank E. *(Musical Director)* 1454, 3674, 4354
Toussaint, Allen *(Arrangements)* 1890
Toussaint, Allen *(Cast)* 1890
Toussaint, Allen *(Composer)* 1890, 4127
Toussaint, Allen *(Conductor)* 4127

Toussaint, Allen *(Lyricist)* 1890, 4127
Toussaint, Allen *(Musical Director)* 1890
Toussaint, Allen *(Orchestrations)* 1890
Tovar, Candice *(Cast)* 3517
Tovatt, Ellen *(Cast)* 2607
Towb, Harry *(Cast)* 299
Towers, Constance *(Cast)* 63, 161, 181, 1119
Towers, Leo *(Composer)* 3820
Towers, Leo *(Lyricist)* 3820
Towle, George P. *(Musical Director)* 1021
Town Hall *(Producer)* 3802
Townly, Barry *(Producer)* 3580
Townsend, "Babe" *(Librettist)* 4183
Townsend, "Babe" *(Lyricist)* 4183
Townsend, E.W. *(Author)* 2795
Townsend, Florence *(Cast)* 1469
Townsend, Margaret *(Cast)* 236, 3093, 4113
Townsend, William "Babe" *(Cast)* 1906
Townshend, Peter *(Author)* 4676
Townshend, Peter *(Composer)* 3739, 4676
Townshend, Peter *(Librettist)* 4676
Townshend, Peter *(Lyricist)* 3739, 4676
Toy, Christine *(Cast)* 275, 3239
Toy, Malcolm *(Cast)* 382
Toye, Wendy *(Choreographer)* 129, 453, 4009
Toye, Wendy *(Director)* 129, 453
Tozere, Frederic *(Cast)* 1871
Trabert, George *(Cast)* 1384, 1710, 2519
Tracey, Andrew *(Cast)* 4579
Tracey, Andrew *(Musical Director)* 4579
Tracey, Paul *(Cast)* 4579
Tracey, William *(Composer)* 3989
Tracey, William *(Lyricist)* 1531, 3958, 3989, 4804, 4840
Tracy, Arthur *(Cast)* 1395, 3153
Tracy, Cora *(Cast)* 3765
Tracy, George Lowell *(Composer)* 1213
Tracy, George Lowell *(Musical Director)* 761, 1274, 2543
Tracy, Teresa *(Cast)* 2420
Tracy, William *(Librettist)* 1987
Traditional *(Composer)* 39, 114, 143, 166, 306, 466, 642, 662, 887, 906, 964, 979, 1073, 1609, 1713, 1736, 1897, 2180, 2200, 2203, 2356, 2388, 2415, 2464, 2805, 3018, 3020, 3261, 3450, 3598, 3631, 3704, 3739, 3793, 3836, 3840, 3949, 3987, 4111, 4342, 4390, 4438, 4460, 4479, 4534
Traditional *(Lyricist)* 39, 114, 143, 166, 466, 642, 662, 887, 906, 964, 1073, 1609, 1713, 1736, 1897, 2180, 2200, 2203, 2356, 2388, 2415, 2464, 2805, 3018, 3020, 3261, 3631, 3793, 3836, 3840, 3949, 3987, 4111, 4342, 4390, 4438, 4460, 4534
Traditional *(Music Based On)* 422
Trahan, Al *(Cast)* 3861
Trainor, William *(Cast)* 3357
Tramp Band, The *(Cast)* 884
Tramutola, Franklin C. *(Librettist)* 1604
Trantman, Edward *(Musical Director)* 222
Trapp, Maria Augusta *(Author)* 4095
Trappert, Harry *(Composer)* 1459
Traube, Shepard *(Director)* 1548
Traube, Shepard *(Producer)* 1548
Traubel, Helen *(Cast)* 3505
Traver, John *(Lyricist)* 3535
Traver, Sharry *(Cast)* 283
Travers, Alma *(Cast)* 2640
Travers, Ben *(Author)* 3216
Travers, Jean *(Cast)* 3365
Travis, J. Michael *(Costumes)* 820, 1766
Travis, Michael *(Costumes)* 2016, 3543
Travizo, Mary *(Cast)* 2968
Travolta, John *(Cast)* 3330
Traxler, Mark *(Cast)* 3601
Traylor, Gene *(Librettist)* 2100
Traylor, Gene *(Lyricist)* 2100
Traynor, Blair *(Lyricist)* 545
Treacher, Arthur *(Cast)* 1113, 2669, 3359, 3371, 3467, 4235, 4730, 4826
Treadwell, Tom *(Cast)* 4136
Treas, Terri *(Cast)* 3299
Trebitsch, Paul M. *(Producer)* 398, 3069
Trednick, H.W. *(Cast)* 3228
Tree, Dolly *(Costumes)* 611, 2140
Tree, Lady *(Cast)* 2788
Trelfall, David *(Cast)* 2474
Tremaine, Bobby *(Cast)* 3168
Trenet, Charles *(Lyricist)* 1834
Trenholme, Helen *(Cast)* 814
Trenk, William *(Director)* 3046
Trenk, William *(Producer)* 3046
Trenkler, Freddie *(Cast)* 1941
Trent, Ivy *(Costumes)* 2650
Trent, Jackie *(Composer)* 4193
Trent, Jackie *(Lyricist)* 4193
Trent, Jo *(Composer)* 1960, 1983
Trent, Jo *(Librettist)* 1983
Trent, Jo *(Lyricist)* 124, 500, 587, 741, 1134, 1281, 1411, 1960, 1983, 3297, 3660, 3808, 4198, 4766
Trentini, Emma *(Cast)* 1285, 3081, 3424
Tresmand, Ivy *(Cast)* 2547, 4795
Tressler, I. *(Lyricist)* 4387
Trevelyan, Arthur *(Composer)* 4130
Trevillion, Florence *(Cast)* 574
Trevor, Austin *(Cast)* 3214
Trevor, Huntley *(Composer)* 605, 3755, 4206
Trevor, Huntley *(Lyricist)* 605, 3755, 4206
Treyz, Russell *(Director)* 900
Treyz, Russell *(Librettist)* 900
Triaco, Joseph *(Producer)* 1695
Tribble, Andrew *(Cast)* 739, 1909, 2721, 3241
Tribble, Bessie *(Cast)* 646
Tribune, Dean *(Cast)* 2571
Trigg, Helen M. *(Composer)* 4735
Trikonis, Gus *(Cast)* 269
Trinder, Marsia *(Costumes)* 2728
Trini *(Cast)* 200, 969, 4271, 4730
Trinity Square Repertory *(Producer)* 35
Trinkaus, George *(Musical Director)* 4269
Triplett, Sally Ann *(Cast)* 661
Tripolino, Joseph *(Cast)* 3654

Tripp, Paul *(Cast)* 2202
Trisler, Joyce *(Choreographer)* 101, 1676, 2583, 3615
Trivers, Barry *(Librettist)* 1811, 3683
Trivers, Barry *(Lyricist)* 1811, 3683, 4799, 4823
Trix, Helen *(Composer)* 1334
Trix, Helen *(Lyricist)* 1334
Troika Organization, The *(Producer)* 4799
Tronto, Rudy *(Cast)* 287, 2150, 3863, 4022, 4577
Tronto, Rudy *(Choreographer)* 3019, 4627
Tronto, Rudy *(Director)* 3019, 4197
Troob, Daniel *(Dance Arranger)* 273, 534, 1634, 3340
Troob, Daniel *(Orchestrations)* 534, 1591, 1762, 3838
Troob, Danny *(Orchestrations)* 171, 330, 394
Troob, Danny *(Vocal Arranger)* 1161
Troobnick, Eugene *(Cast)* 4397
Trost, Victoria *(Cast)* 4830
Trott, Karen *(Cast)* 4358
Trouille, Clovis *(Librettist)* 3233
Troup, Bobby *(Cast)* 1885
Troup, Bobby *(Composer)* 4093
Troutman, Ron *(Director)* 508, 1371
Trovaioli, Armando *(Composer)* 3798
Trowbridge, Charles *(Cast)* 2276
Troxler, Gus *(Cast)* 4507
Troy, Henry *(Cast)* 1087
Troy, Louise *(Cast)* 1891, 3505, 4435, 4588
Troy, William *(Costumes)* 3662
Truax, Harry *(Cast)* 537, 4509
Trudeau, Garry *(Author)* 1077
Trudeau, Garry *(Librettist)* 1077
Trudeau, Garry *(Lyricist)* 1077, 3661
Trueblood, Paul *(Cast)* 272
Trueblood, Paul *(Composer)* 871, 4533
Trueblood, Paul *(Musical Director)* 2230
Trueblood, Paul *(Pianist)* 1363
Trueblood, Paul *(Vocal Arranger)* 2230
Truehart *(Lyricist)* 1833
Trueman, Paula *(Cast)* 1237, 1651, 1654, 1657, 1990, 4235, 4582
Truesdale, Tad *(Cast)* 3814
Truesdell, Frederick *(Librettist)* 3147
Truex, Ernest *(Cast)* 17, 152, 1088, 1384, 1566, 1817, 2262, 2403, 2751, 3324, 4335, 4555
Truex, Philip *(Cast)* 2729, 4340
Trullinger, George *(Cast)* 2436
Trunz, Barbara *(Cast)* 319
Tryon, Tom *(Cast)* 4718
Tschudin, Michael *(Arrangements)* 3714
Tschudin, Michael *(Composer)* 3714
Tshabalala, Linda *(Cast)* 1719
Tsu, Susan *(Costumes)* 1595
Tubb, Dan *(Cast)* 4518
Tucci, Louis *(Cast)* 3695
Tucci, Maria *(Cast)* 1977, 4109
Tucci, Stanley *(Cast)* 2945, 3853
Tucholsky, Kurt *(Composer)* 4379
Tucholsky, Kurt *(Librettist)* 4379
Tucholsky, Kurt *(Lyricist)* 4379
Tucker, Al *(Cast)* 3264
Tucker, Bob *(Choreographer)* 3059
Tucker, Bobby *(Vocal Arranger)* 1336, 4640
Tucker, Carl *(Composer)* 2227
Tucker, Don *(Composer)* 4, 3684
Tucker, Don *(Director)* 3684
Tucker, Don *(Librettist)* 3684
Tucker, Don *(Lyricist)* 4, 3684
Tucker, Earl "Snake Hips" *(Cast)* 1772
Tucker, Earl "Snakehips" *(Cast)* 892
Tucker, Henry *(Composer)* 3259
Tucker, Ian *(Cast)* 2590
Tucker, Robert *(Choreographer)* 135, 273, 915, 3020, 3928
Tucker, Robert *(Director)* 915
Tucker, Shona *(Cast)* 4055
Tucker, Sophie *(Cast)* 1130, 1333, 1416, 1889, 2432, 2596, 2649, 2831, 3796, 4803
Tucker, Stan *(Vocal Arranger)* 4055
Tuckfield, Ellen *(Composer)* 2486
Tudor, Anthony *(Choreographer)* 650, 999, 1948
Tudor, Martin *(Lighting Designer)* 337, 2074, 4480
Tudor, Rowan *(Cast)* 1300, 4524
Tuerk, John *(Producer)* 814
Tuesart, Helene *(Cast)* 2938
Tufts, Sonny *(Cast)* 3986, 4677
Tulin, Alan *(Cast)* 2022
Tully, Richard Walton *(Author)* 2636
Tully, Richard Walton *(Lyricist)* 3033
Tumeo, Vincent *(Cast)* 4217
Tun Tun *(Cast)* 3837
Tunbridge, Joseph *(Author)* 203
Tunbridge, Joseph *(Composer)* 2833, 4299
Tune, Tommy *(Cast)* 270, 589, 2100, 2248, 3060, 3869
Tune, Tommy *(Choreographer)* 373, 374, 1000, 1649, 3060, 3171, 3624, 4695
Tune, Tommy *(Director)* 373, 374, 785, 788, 1000, 1649, 3060, 3171, 4695
Tune Twisters, The *(Cast)* 383
Tunezi, Gene *(Lighting Designer)* 3615, 3970, 4433
Tunick, Jonathan *(Composer)* 4268
Tunick, Jonathan *(Orchestrations)* 71, 253, 287, 746, 832, 958, 1329, 1406, 1408, 1634, 1662, 1864, 2143, 2536, 2822, 3171, 3340, 3411, 3456, 3603, 3871, 4029, 4233
Tunie, Tamara *(Cast)* 4398
Tunkeler, J. *(Lyricist)* 2421
Tunsill, Johnnie *(Cast)* 4677
Tunstall, Fred *(Musical Director)* 2645
Tuotti, Joseph Dolan *(Author)* 578
Turbitt, Ben *(Cast)* 1562
Turgend, Harry *(Librettist)* 4824
Turgeon, Peter *(Cast)* 2523
Turk, Robert *(Choreographer)* 2080, 2482
Turk, Robert *(Director)* 2080, 2482
Turk, Robert *(Producer)* 2482
Turk, Roy *(Composer)* 3149, 4193
Turk, Roy *(Lyricist)* 39, 481, 1058, 1129, 1763, 2308, 2462, 2706, 3149, 3513, 4458, 4838
Turley, Richard *(Producer)* 2728
Turnbough, Zedrick *(Composer)* 1713
Turnbough, Zedrick *(Lyricist)* 1713

Turnbull, Laura *(Cast)* 1279
Turnbull Jr., William J. *(Lighting Designer)* 528
Turner *(Composer)* 2754
Turner *(Lyricist)* 2754
Turner, Elma *(Cast)* 3709
Turner, Elmer *(Cast)* 877, 3709
Turner, Glenn *(Cast)* 1296
Turner, Holly *(Cast)* 1471
Turner, Janet *(Cast)* 1757
Turner, Jayne *(Cast)* 649, 1329
Turner, Jim *(Composer)* 459
Turner, John *(Composer)* 4264
Turner, John *(Lyricist)* 4264
Turner, John Hastings *(Librettist)* 1338, 2392, 2788, 4581
Turner, Kay *(Costumes)* 4637
Turner, Lenny *(Cast)* 2521
Turner, Lily *(Producer)* 3215
Turner, Maidel *(Cast)* 831
Turner, Richard *(Librettist)* 2272
Turner, Roland *(Set Design)* 2110
Turner, Susan *(Librettist)* 2272
Turoff, Robert *(Director)* 1474, 2664
Turoff, Robert Ennis *(Librettist)* 1837
Turque, Mimi *(Cast)* 2727, 3612
Turrin, Joseph *(Composer)* 1382
Turturice, Robert *(Costumes)* 556
Tuschl, Karl *(Librettist)* 1043
Tuschl, Karl *(Lyricist)* 1043
Tushar, James *(Cast)* 72
Tuskegee Institute Choir *(Cast)* 3639
Tuthill, Bob *(Composer)* 1282
Tutt, J. Homer *(Cast)* 291, 449, 731, 816, 980, 987, 1019, 1028, 1479, 1514, 2013, 2791, 2792, 3040, 3062, 3200, 3241, 4520, 4751
Tutt, J. Homer *(Composer)* 449, 987, 1479, 1906, 2013, 2791, 2792, 3040, 3241, 4520
Tutt, J. Homer *(Director)* 1514, 2013
Tutt, J. Homer *(Librettist)* 291, 449, 731, 816, 980, 987, 1019, 1479, 1514, 1906, 2013, 2791, 2792, 3040, 3062, 3200, 3241, 4520, 4751
Tutt, J. Homer *(Lyricist)* 449, 816, 980, 987, 1019, 1479, 1906, 2013, 2791, 2792, 3040, 3062, 3241, 3958, 4520, 4751
Tutt, J. Homer *(Producer)* 291, 731, 816, 980, 1479, 1514, 1906, 2013, 3040, 3062, 3200, 4520, 4751
Tuttle, Howard *(Set Design)* 1801
Tuvim, Abe *(Additional Lyrics)* 27
Tuvim, Abe *(Lyricist)* 2736
Twain, Mark *(Author)* 170, 394, 834, 1086, 2027, 2028, 2029, 2030, 2556, 3571, 4409
Twain, Mark *(Librettist)* 2029
Twain, Norman *(Producer)* 269, 1846, 2568
Tweebeke, Reiner *(Lighting Designer)* 949
Twiggy *(Cast)* 3060
Twine, Linda *(Conductor)* 789
Twine, Linda *(Musical Director)* 394, 789, 2200
Twine, Linda *(Vocal Arranger)* 394
Two Arts Playhouse *(Producer)* 4431
Twomey, John *(Cast)* 1769
Twomey, Kay *(Lyricist)* 1539
Twomey, Neil *(Director)* 3434
Ty Bell Sisters, The *(Cast)* 4753
Tyers, John *(Cast)* 72, 2137, 4479
Tyers, William H. *(Composer)* 295
Tygett, Nanon *(Choreographer)* 1940
Tyler, Bernice *(Cast)* 3647
Tyler, Beverly *(Cast)* 1284, 2234
Tyler, Cornelia *(Librettist)* 1518
Tyler, Cornelia *(Lyricist)* 1518
Tyler, Ed *(Composer)* 4243
Tyler, Ed *(Lyricist)* 4243
Tyler, Edward Lee *(Cast)* 653
Tyler, George C. *(Producer)* 3328
Tyler, Jeanne *(Cast)* 4174
Tyler, Jim *(Orchestrations)* 534, 681, 1146, 1441, 1699, 1721, 1955, 1970, 2208, 2360, 2551, 3231, 3330, 3743, 4297
Tyler, Jim *(Vocal Arranger)* 2728
Tyler, Judy *(Cast)* 3505
Tyler, Marie *(Cast)* 4113
Tyler, Royall *(Author)* 840
Tyler, Steve *(Incidental Music)* 2185
Tyler, Steve *(Musical Director)* 2185
Tyler, Steve *(Vocal Arranger)* 2185
Tynan, Kenneth *(Librettist)* 3233
Tynan, Nicholas J. *(Cast)* 4507
Tyne, George *(Cast)* 4369
Tyrell, Pha *(Cast)* 890
Tyrrel, Henry *(Lyricist)* 1675
Tyrrell, Tara *(Cast)* 198
Tyson, Grace *(Cast)* 2710, 2869, 4804
Tzigane Orchestra *(Cast)* 125

U

U.S. 8th Air Force *(Producer)* 4009
U.S. Ambulance Service *(Producer)* 1632
U.S. Army *(Producer)* 4141
U.S. Army Air Forces *(Producer)* 4706
U.S. Coast Guard *(Producer)* 4287
U.S. Dept. of Agriculture *(Producer)* 2175
Uart, Lottie *(Cast)* 4382
Udall, Lyn *(Composer)* 1038
Udell, Chas. W. *(Cast)* 2642
Udell, Peter *(Librettist)* 105, 135, 828, 3610, 3928
Udell, Peter *(Lyricist)* 105, 135, 828, 3610, 3928
Uffer, Charles *(Cast)* 782
Uggams, Eloise *(Cast)* 441, 444, 3704
Uggams, Leslie *(Cast)* 478, 1729, 1848, 2208
Uhl, Constance *(Composer)* 2363
Uhr, Ira *(Cast)* 1357
Uhry, Alfred *(Librettist)* 112, 693, 3733
Uhry, Alfred *(Lyricist)* 112, 693, 1864, 3733, 4252
Uke, Paul *(Cast)* 23
Ukena, Paul *(Cast)* 4523
Ukena, Paul *(Musical Director)* 23
Ukena Jr., Paul *(Cast)* 4695
Ullett, Nick *(Cast)* 2798

Ullman, Furth *(Set Design)* 1681
Ullman, Jeffrey *(Costumes)* 4515
Ullmann, Liv *(Cast)* 2064
Ulric, Lenore *(Cast)* 2255, 2309, 4043, 4066, 4521
Ulrich, Olive *(Cast)* 1743, 2893
Ulvaeus, Bjorn *(Composer)* 721
Umeki, Miyoshi *(Cast)* 1315
Uncle Sam *(Producer)* 4340
Underdown, Edward *(Cast)* 1238, 3678, 3906, 4610
Underhill, John Garrett *(Author)* 3412
Underwood, Frank *(Composer)* 1436
Underwood, Frank *(Lyricist)* 1436
Underwood, Franklin *(Composer)* 2626, 2913
Underwood, Franklin *(Lyricist)* 2626, 2913
Underwood, Franklyn *(Cast)* 3812
Underwood, Robert *(Cast)* 2034
Unger, Gladys *(Author)* 1219, 2624
Unger, Gladys *(Librettist)* 324, 379, 2628, 2669, 2761, 2825, 4424
Unger, Gladys *(Lyricist)* 839
Unger, Stella *(Lyricist)* 1135, 3899, 4352
Unicorn Productions *(Producer)* 3224
United Producing Corp. *(Producer)* 4320
Unitt, E.G.
See also Emens & Unitt and Unitt & Wickes.
Unitt, E.G. *(Set Design)* 205, 1905, 3581, 4735
Unitt, Edward G. *(Set Design)* 3488, 3774, 3820
Unitt & Wickes
See also E.G. Unitt and Joseph Wickes.
Unitt & Wickes *(Set Design)* 335, 742, 1961, 2698, 2830, 2889, 3218, 3220, 4805
Universal, Pictures *(Producer)* 1077
Universal City Studios *(Producer)* 1674
Universal Pictures *(Producer)* 374
Unknown *(Composer)* 8, 90, 117, 125, 128, 152, 165, 166, 168, 178, 191, 200, 201, 224, 231, 295, 326, 437, 444, 447, 452, 476, 542, 545, 638, 642, 662, 671, 684, 791, 805, 827, 875, 879, 885, 913, 924, 965, 1036, 1107, 1120, 1126, 1213, 1224, 1327, 1334, 1357, 1395, 1535, 1544, 1609, 1690, 1713, 1726, 1740, 1880, 1897, 1910, 1986, 2160, 2215, 2282, 2315, 2402, 2483, 2653, 2677, 2754, 2778, 2821, 2900, 2938, 3005, 3110, 3144, 3254, 3268, 3322, 3342, 3400, 3404, 3424, 3440, 3460, 3538, 3605, 3709, 3747, 3766, 3782, 3791, 3796, 3840, 3905, 3926, 3981, 4010, 4083, 4104, 4131, 4264, 4291, 4300, 4430, 4465, 4478, 4567, 4683, 4723, 4804, 4814
Unknown *(Lyricist)* 18, 90, 128, 152, 166, 191, 224, 231, 295, 326, 437, 444, 447, 452, 476, 512, 541, 542, 545, 576, 630, 638, 662, 671, 684, 738, 791, 875, 879, 885, 913, 924, 954, 965, 1036, 1107, 1120, 1126, 1224, 1327, 1334, 1357, 1395, 1417, 1454, 1491, 1537, 1544, 1609, 1690, 1713, 1726, 1806, 1880, 2122, 2160, 2215, 2282, 2315, 2464, 2549, 2633, 2653, 2677, 2698, 2754, 2778, 2821, 2839, 2925, 2938, 3005, 3025, 3110, 3144, 3184, 3254, 3268, 3322, 3400, 3401, 3440, 3460, 3538, 3605, 3709, 3745, 3747, 3791, 3827, 3840, 3905, 3926, 4010, 4083, 4104, 4131, 4132, 4247, 4264, 4291, 4300, 4438, 4465, 4478, 4567, 4683, 4723, 4798, 4804, 4814
Up Front Productions *(Producer)* 778
Upbin, Shari *(Choreographer)* 2784
Upbin, Shari *(Director)* 2784
Upbin, Shari *(Producer)* 3297
Upstairs at the Downstairs *(Producer)* 2935, 3186, 3890
Upton, Florence *(Cast)* 4476
Upton, Frances *(Cast)* 1932, 2380, 2516, 3042, 4276, 4683, 4821
Upton, Richard Everett *(Producer)* 4433
Urban, Frederick *(Cast)* 3784
Urban, Joseph *(Set Design)* 168, 186, 376, 627, 683, 1309, 1323, 1492, 1580, 1603, 1979, 2184, 2813, 2900, 2907, 2960, 3014, 3179, 3532, 3537, 3584, 3652, 3719, 3721, 3727, 3768, 3775, 3819, 3949, 3953, 3980, 4023, 4077, 4357, 4683, 4692, 4793, 4809, 4810, 4811, 4812, 4813, 4814, 4815, 4816, 4817, 4818, 4821, 4823, 4831, 4833, 4834, 4836, 4838, 4844, 4846, 4847, 4849, 4851, 4852
Urban, Ruth *(Cast)* 1689
Urban Arts Th. *(Producer)* 593
Urbont, Jack *(Composer)* 1107, 2993, 3889
Urbont, Jack *(Lyricist)* 1107
Urbont, Jacques *(Arrangements)* 2993
Urbont, Jacques *(Composer)* 71, 2556, 3889, 4124, 4643
Urbont, Jacques *(Dance Arranger)* 4124
Urbont, Jacques *(Lyricist)* 3889
Urbont, Jacques *(Musical Director)* 71, 4124
Urbont, Jacques *(Producer)* 71
Urbont, Jacques *(Vocal Arranger)* 71, 4124
Urich, Tom *(Cast)* 3939
Uris, Leon *(Author)* 181
Uris, Leon *(Librettist)* 181
Uris, Leon *(Lyricist)* 181
Urmston, Ken *(Cast)* 1697
Ustinov, Peter *(Author)* 3761
Ustinov, Peter *(Cast)* 3761
Ustinov, Peter *(Composer)* 3761
Ustinov, Peter *(Lyricist)* 3761
Utley, Byron *(Cast)* 4442
Utterson, Gabriel John *(Cast)* 2198
Uttry, Arthur *(Cast)* 3623

Vacarra, Vilma *(Cast)* 4536
Vaccaro, Brenda *(Cast)* 2014
Vaccaro, James Adams *(Producer)* 3858
Vaccaro, John A. *(Producer)* 729, 1166
Vacek, Karl *(Composer)* 3457
Vadimova, Dora *(Cast)* 703
Vail, Olive *(Cast)* 2155, 2335, 4387, 4506
Val, Jack *(Composer)* 4827
Valadin, Brigitte *(Cast)* 2362
Valaida *(Cast)* 3704
Valchera, Master *(Cast)* 333, 719
Valcourt, Gaston *(Author)* 3596
Valdez, Daniel *(Cast)* 4861
Valdez, Daniel *(Composer)* 4861
Valdez, Daniel *(Vocal Arranger)* 4861
Valdez, Luis *(Author)* 4861
Valdez, Luis *(Director)* 4861

Valdo, Pat *(Director)* 3715
Vale, Michael *(Cast)* 1406
Valency, Maurice *(Librettist)* 3694
Valency, Maurice *(Lyricist)* 961, 3694
Valente, Richard *(Composer)* 1069
Valente, Richard *(Librettist)* 1069
Valente, Richard *(Lyricist)* 1069
Valenti, Michael *(Cast)* 4789
Valenti, Michael *(Composer)* 461, 1970, 2278, 2633, 2674, 3231
Valenti, Michael *(Librettist)* 2674
Valenti, Michael *(Lyricist)* 2278, 2633
Valenti, Michael *(Orchestrations)* 2633
Valenti, Michael *(Vocal Arranger)* 2633
Valentina *(Costumes)* 818, 1891
Valentine, Arthur *(Lyricist)* 2698
Valentine, C. Walsh *(Set Design)* 1640
Valentine, C.W. *(Set Design)* 1459
Valentine, Eric *(Lyricist)* 1780
Valentine, Grace *(Cast)* 1749
Valentine, James *(Cast)* 2020
Valentine, P.H. *(Lyricist)* 1208
Valentine, Paul *(Cast)* 1918, 3234, 4718
Valentine, S.B. *(Librettist)* 4047
Valentine, William *(Cast)* 1733
Valentini, Vincent *(Composer)* 3388
Valentini, Vincent *(Director)* 3388
Valentini, Vincent *(Librettist)* 3388
Valentini, Vincent *(Lyricist)* 3388
Valentinoff, Valia *(Cast)* 4569
Valerie & Jenna *(Cast)* 2087
Valerio, Frederico *(Composer)* 1918
Valery, Dana *(Cast)* 4579
Vall, Seymour *(Producer)* 13, 461, 2016, 2018, 2278
Valle, Ernie *(Musical Director)* 3069
Vallee, Rudy *(Cast)* 1492, 1493, 1744, 1949, 1950, 2019, 2406, 3153
Vallee and His Orchestra, Rudy *(Cast)* 1396
Vallely, Helen *(Cast)* 1907
Valli Valli *(Cast)* 804, 1067, 2341, 2385, 2897, 3529, 3613, 3627, 4554
Vallon, Una *(Cast)* 3002
Valor, Henrietta *(Cast)* 426, 1249, 3195
Valori, Bice *(Cast)* 3798
Valsy, Lucette *(Cast)* 672
Valverde, Joaquin *(Composer)* 60, 2407
Van, Billy B. *(Cast)* 21, 201, 1460, 1784, 2209, 2534, 3417, 3604, 3652, 4213, 4637
Van, Billy B. *(Composer)* 2644
Van, Billy B. *(Lyricist)* 2644
Van, Bobby *(Cast)* 59, 1063, 3683
Van, Gus *(Cast)* 683, 959, 2900, 3144, 3264, 4428, 4813, 4814
Van, Gus *(Composer)* 3144, 4813, 4814, 4842
Van, Gus *(Lyricist)* 4813, 4814, 4842
Van, Kitty *(Cast)* 3158
Van, Sammy *(Cast)* 691
Van, Willa *(Costumes)* 2077, 2162
Van Aken, Gretchen *(Cast)* 4588
Van Alstyne, Egbert *(Composer)* 349, 561, 954, 1026,1247, 1566, 1626, 1629, 1806, 2025, 2232, 2274, 2889, 2892, 3073, 3085, 3205, 3268, 3332, 3400, 3675, 3996, 4840
Van Antwerp, John *(Librettist)* 1286, 1546, 3082
Van Antwerp, John *(Producer)* 1286, 1546
Van Antwerp, Ted *(Producer)* 556
Van Biene, Eileen *(Cast)* 2056
Van Bridge, Tony *(Cast)* 3066
Van Buren, A.H. *(Director)* 2351, 4050
Van Cleave, Carroll *(Cast)* 2573
Van Cleve *(Orchestrations)* 1336
Van Cleve, N. Lang *(Orchestrations)* 2597
Van Cleve, Nathan *(Orchestrations)* 612
Van Dame, Corinne *(Costumes)* 4416
Van Den Ende, Joop *(Producer)* 949
van der Horst, Ellen *(Costumes)* 1865
van der Wurff, Erik *(Composer)* 1865
van der Wurff, Erik *(Musical Director)* 1865
Van Dijk, Ad *(Composer)* 949
Van Dijk, Bill *(Cast)* 949
Van Dijk, Koen *(Librettist)* 949
Van Dijk, Koen *(Lyricist)* 949
Van Dresser, Marcia *(Cast)* 4559
van Druten, John *(Author)* 610, 2064
van Druten, John *(Director)* 2312
von Seyffertitz, Gustave *(Cast)* 4187
von Seyffertitz, Gustave *(Director)* 2528
von Tilzer, Albert *(Composer)* 1038, 4026
Van Dyke, Dick *(Cast)* 607, 1040, 1567, 2072
Van Dyke, Leroy *(Composer)* 4197
Van Dyke, Leroy *(Lyricist)* 4197
Van Dyke, Marcia *(Cast)* 4446
van Eeden, Ron *(Producer)* 1865
Van Epps, Fred *(Orchestrations)* 341, 4586
Van Epps, Jack *(Cast)* 1573
Van Every, Dale *(Author)* 647
Van Fleet, Jo *(Cast)* 1815
Van Fossen, Harry *(Cast)* 801
Van Goetz, Eyck *(Composer)* 4498
Van Griethuysen, Ted *(Cast)* 3215
Van Griethuysen, Ted *(Costumes)* 937
Van Grona, Eugene *(Choreographer)* 447, 1275, 2444
Van Grove, Isaac *(Arrangements)* 4149
Van Grove, Isaac *(Musical Director)* 3647
Van Grove, Isaac *(Orchestrations)* 1299
Van Heusen, James *(Composer)* 879, 2183, 3091, 3100, 3324, 3832, 4255, 4743
Van Heusen, James *(Lyricist)* 879
Van Heusen, Jimmy *(Composer)* 657, 820, 1296, 2443, 3178, 4013, 4256, 4588
Van Heusen, Jimmy *(Lyricist)* 4256
Van Horne, Randy *(Vocal Arranger)* 1326
Van Keyser, William *(Choreographer)* 4244
van Laast, Anthony *(Choreographer)* 1159
van Laast, Anthony *(Director)* 1159
Van Loan, Paul *(Dance Arranger)* 2023, 2024, 2098, 2099
Van Loan, Paul *(Musical Director)* 1941
Van Loan, Paul *(Orchestrations)* 2023, 2024, 2098, 2099, 4143
Van Loan, Paul F. *(Musical Director)* 587

Van Patten, Dick *(Cast)* 1196
Van Patten, Joyce *(Cast)* 4111
Van Peebles, Mario *(Cast)* 4591
Van Peebles, Melvin *(Cast)* 4591
Van Peebles, Melvin *(Composer)* 40, 1074, 4591
Van Peebles, Melvin *(Director)* 1074, 4591
Van Peebles, Melvin *(Librettist)* 40, 1074, 3690, 4591
Van Peebles, Melvin *(Lyricist)* 40, 1074, 4591
Van Peebles, Melvin *(Producer)* 1074, 4591
Van Rensellaer, Hal *(Cast)* 545, 4528
Van Rensselaer, E.E. *(Cast)* 1910
Van Sant, A. *(Cast)* 1526
Van Scott, Glory *(Cast)* 415, 1319, 2616, 2785, 2908
Van Scott, Glory *(Composer)* 2908
Van Scott, Glory *(Librettist)* 2908
Van Scott, Glory *(Lyricist)* 2908
Van Scoyk, Bob *(Librettist)* 2554
Van Studdiford, Grace *(Cast)* 1602, 2697, 3372, 3673
Van Valkenburgh, Deborah *(Cast)* 2555, 3752
Van Vechten, Carl *(Author)* 4292
van Veen, Herman *(Cast)* 1865
van Veen, Herman *(Composer)* 1865
van Veen, Herman *(Lyricist)* 1865
Van Vooren, Monique *(Cast)* 2227, 2728
Van Voorhis, Gail *(Lighting Designer)* 164
Van Voorhis, Gail *(Set Design)* 164
Van Way, Nolan *(Cast)* 616, 2928
Van Winkle, Dorothy *(Costumes)* 4021
Van Witsen, Leo *(Costumes)* 322
Van Zandt, Julie *(Cast)* 1884
Van Zandt, Philip *(Cast)* 4316
Vanarelli, Mario *(Set Design)* 1878
Vanbery, Robert *(Author)* 2323
Vance *(Producer)* 1259
Vance, Dana *(Cast)* 262, 528, 1155, 3329, 4295
Vance, Dick *(Cast)* 2415
Vance, Dick *(Orchestrations)* 279
Vance, Joseph *(Composer)* 4779
Vance, Joseph *(Lyricist)* 4779
Vance, Vivian *(Cast)* 163, 1973, 2453, 3674
Vance & Sullivan *(Producer)* 2008
Vandair, Maurice *(Lyricist)* 924
Vandenberg, Jose *(Musical Director)* 2865, 4624
Vanderbilt, Gertrude *(Cast)* 115, 1270, 1588, 1746, 2232, 2385, 2491, 3252, 3322, 3685, 4012, 4277, 4802, 4803, 4808
Vanderbilt Producing Co. *(Producer)* 1582
Vanderneers, Gerda *(Costumes)* 2809, 4316
Vandernoot, Edwin *(Set Design)* 4484
Vandis, Titos *(Cast)* 2106, 3274
Vandross, Luther *(Composer)* 4722
Vandross, Luther *(Lyricist)* 4722
Vane, Sybil *(Cast)* 1726
Vanessi *(Cast)* 2135
Vanloo, Albert *(Author)* 1576, 2524, 4554
Vanna, Della *(Cast)* 1691
Vannessi *(Cast)* 4010
Vanni, Vannio *(Lighting Designer)* 3798
Vanoff, Nick *(Producer)* 775
Vanoni, Ornelia *(Cast)* 3798
Vanstone, Hugh *(Lighting Designer)* 846
Varady *(Costumes)* 207
Varden, Venita *(Cast)* 2813
Varese, Edgard *(Composer)* 964
Varga, Joseph *(Set Design)* 3960
Vargas, Angel *(Cast)* 4138
Vargas, Robert *(Cast)* 3227
Varley *(Composer)* 3981
Varnel, Marcel *(Director)* 184
Varnell, M.H. *(Director)* 771
Varney, Almon C. *(Lyricist)* 3631
Varney, Louis *(Author)* 613
Varney, Louis *(Composer)* 2361
Varona, Jose *(Costumes)* 2568
Varrato, Eddie *(Cast)* 283
Varrone, Gene *(Cast)* 519, 1012, 1094, 1614, 1660, 2354, 2536, 4038, 4190, 4270, 4435
Vartanian, Evelyn *(Cast)* 3025
Vaselle, Renata *(Cast)* 278
Vassar, Queenie *(Cast)* 2374, 3999, 4017, 4430
Vassiliev, Vladimir *(Choreographer)* 2269
Vassilkova *(Cast)* 710
Vaszary, Janos *(Author)* 2061
Vaucaire, Maurice *(Author)* 1743, 3362
Vaucaire, Maurice *(Librettist)* 1743
Vaughan, David *(Cast)* 755, 3418
Vaughan, David *(Choreographer)* 755
Vaughan, Melanie *(Cast)* 4138, 4210
Vaughn, Aida *(Cast)* 2159
Vaughn, David *(Choreographer)* 1229, 2220
Vaughn, Dona D. *(Cast)* 832
Vaughn, Frances *(Cast)* 1206
Vaughn, James *(Composer)* 291, 1479, 2111
Vaughn, James *(Lyricist)* 291
Vaughn, James *(Musical Director)* 1479
Vaughn, James J. *(Composer)* 9
Vaughn, James J. *(Musical Director)* 9, 295, 2979
Vaughn, Jim *(Additional Lyrics)* 1821
Vaughn, Jim *(Additional Music)* 1821
Vaughn, Mark *(Cast)* 2239
Vaughn, Olive *(Cast)* 1484, 1486
Vaughn, Robert *(Cast)* 938
Vaughn, Theresa *(Cast)* 1213
Vaux, Lyn *(Cast)* 1509
Vavra, Velma *(Cast)* 1448
Vawter, Tom *(Set Design)* 4416
Veasey, William *(Cast)* 3321
Veber, Pierre *(Author)* 1527, 3254, 3866, 4213
Vecsey, Armand *(Composer)* 1992, 3163, 3775
Vedder, Charles Nicholas *(Additional Music)* 819
Veiller, Anthony *(Librettist)* 3536
Vejvoda, Jaromir *(Composer)* 4772
Vel Johnson, Reginald *(Cast)* 2133
Velasco, Eulogio *(Author)* 2407
Velasco, Eulogio *(Director)* 2407
Velasco, Javier *(Choreographer)* 261, 4193
Velasco, Vi *(Cast)* 2306
Velasco Brothers *(Producer)* 2407
Velazquez, Russell *(Cast)* 3739
Velden, Kaj *(Set Design)* 1984, 4265

Velez, Lupe *(Cast)* 1979, 4177, 4777
Velie, Janet *(Cast)* 606, 799, 1800, 2328, 2363, 2767, 3245, 3344, 3443, 3783
Velie, Jay *(Cast)* 2, 619, 1643, 2516, 3783, 3900
Velie, Jay *(Composer)* 3783
Veljohnson, Reginald *(Cast)* 1099, 1970, 4127
Velona, Tony *(Composer)* 4193, 4828
Velona, Tony *(Lyricist)* 4193, 4828
Venable, Percy *(Lyricist)* 432
Venable, Sara *(Cast)* 449
Venneri, Darwin *(Composer)* 991
Venneri, Darwin *(Lyricist)* 991
Vennum, Tom *(Composer)* 4041
Venora, Lee *(Cast)* 1766, 2295
Ventre, Frank *(Orchestrations)* 2083
Ventriss, Jennie *(Cast)* 2049
Ventry, Frank *(Composer)* 4006
Ventura, Frank *(Choreographer)* 3181
Venuta, Benay *(Cast)* 601, 868, 1791, 2653, 3091, 3314, 3619
Venuti and His Orcheatra, Joe *(Cast)* 662
Venza, Jac *(Costumes)* 4260
Ver Planck, J. "Billy" *(Orchestrations)* 1099, 1662
Vera, Irene *(Cast)* 284
Vera-Ellen *(Cast)* 601, 4557
Verady *(Costumes)* 423
Verdi, Giuseppe *(Author)* 3035
Verdi, Giuseppe *(Composer)* 1897, 2809, 4579
Verdi, Giuseppe *(Music Based On)* 3035
Verdon, Gwen *(Cast)* 59, 490, 629, 723, 957, 3113, 3687, 4238
Vereen, Ben *(Cast)* 1699, 2212, 3506
Verhoeven, Pauline *(Choreographer)* 1743, 3081
Vermer, James *(Producer)* 2153
Vermont, Ted *(Director)* 3490
Verne, Jules *(Author)* 189, 190, 1161
Verneuil, Louis *(Author)* 495, 2808, 3248
Verneuil, Louis *(Librettist)* 627
Vernon, Charles *(Cast)* 3345
Vernon, Doris *(Cast)* 3045
Vernon, Dorothy *(Cast)* 3674
Vernon, Gilbert *(Cast)* 920
Vernon, H.M. *(Librettist)* 292
Vernon, Michael *(Choreographer)* 1256
Vernon, Nina *(Cast)* 185
Vernon, Olga *(Cast)* 1342
Vernon, Paul *(Cast)* 526
Vernon, Walter *(Cast)* 538, 542
Veronica *(Costumes)* 1840, 4777
Veronica, Betty *(Cast)* 1135
Vertes, Marcel *(Costumes)* 2364, 3899
Vertes, Marcel *(Set Design)* 3899
Verwayen, Percy *(Cast)* 2720
Vessella, Oreste *(Composer)* 3729
Vestoff, Floria *(Cast)* 288
Vestoff, Floria *(Lyricist)* 3810
Vestoff, Virginia *(Cast)* 482, 937, 1233, 1408, 2599, 2731, 2877, 3075, 3897, 4109, 4558
Vetkin, S. *(Composer)* 4176
Vetman, Charlotte M. *(Costumes)* 1630
Vicars, Harold *(Composer)* 1626, 4258
Vicars, Harold *(Lyricist)* 1626, 4258
Vicars, Harold *(Musical Director)* 136, 1538, 1723, 2761, 3658, 3996, 4258
Vici, Berni *(Musical Director)* 2271
Vici & His Symphonic Girls, Count Berni *(Cast)* 2271
Vickers *(Composer)* 627
Vickers, Larry *(Cast)* 3936
Vickers, Larry *(Choreographer)* 4460
Vickery, John *(Cast)* 1015
Vicks, Walker *(Choreographer)* 2306
Victor, Eric *(Cast)* 4782
Victor, Eric *(Choreographer)* 67, 4782
Victor, Lucia *(Director)* 415, 1809, 1816, 4192
Victor, Lucia *(Librettist)* 1816
Video Techniques Inc *(Producer)* 159
Vidnovic, Martin *(Cast)* 253, 808, 1597, 1959, 2470, 3272
Vieha, Mark *(Composer)* 107, 3126
Vieha, Mark *(Lyricist)* 107, 3126
Viele, S.K. *(Costumes)* 452
Viele, S.K. *(Set Design)* 452
Viele, Sheldon K. *(Set Design)* 1357, 2569, 4345
Viera, Sandra *(Cast)* 2611
Viertel, Jack *(Producer)* 992
Viertel, Thomas *(Producer)* 992, 4031, 4076
Vieth, Bradley *(Musical Director)* 158, 4708
Vig, Joel *(Cast)* 3811
Vigal, John *(Cast)* 2302
Vigard, Kristen *(Cast)* 2064
Vigel, Al *(Cast)* 1989
Vigialante, Jeanne *(Cast)* 2658
Viglione, Carolyn *(Cast)* 2027
Vigoda, Bob *(Composer)* 3530
Vilan, Demetrios *(Cast)* 3822
Vilanch, Bruce *(Librettist)* 1159, 1298, 3515
Vilanch, Bruce *(Lyricist)* 1262
Villa-Lobos, Heitor *(Composer)* 2395, 2679
Villani, Paul *(Cast)* 114
Villard, Jean *(Composer)* 4264
Villard, Jean *(Lyricist)* 4264
Villars, Jessie *(Lyricist)* 4094
Villella, Edward *(Cast)* 2556
Villon, Francois *(Composer)* 1736
Vimnera, August *(Set Design)* 1132, 1343, 2330, 3157, 4275
Vinal, Edgar A. *(Composer)* 2455
Vinal, Edgar A. *(Lyricist)* 2455
Vinal, Edgar A. *(Musical Director)* 2455
Vinaver, Chemjo *(Composer)* 2202
Vinaver, Chemjo *(Orchestrations)* 2202
Vinaver, Steven *(Director)* 1056, 2663
Vinaver, Steven *(Librettist)* 1056, 4268
Vinaver, Steven *(Lyricist)* 1056, 2663, 4268
Vinay, Ramon *(Cast)* 4174
Vincent, A.J. *(Cast)* 2654
Vincent, Nat *(Composer)* 1065, 2974, 3770, 3958, 4813
Vincent, Nat *(Lyricist)* 2557, 3402, 4813
Vincent, Nathaniel *(Composer)* 1404
Vincent, Ruth *(Cast)* 3777, 4554
Vincent, Stephen *(Librettist)* 2653

Vine, Billy *(Cast)* 1889
Vineyard Theatre, The *(Producer)* 1739
Vinocur, Burt *(Librettist)* 3688
Vinovich, Stephen *(Cast)* 112, 1082, 1660, 2598, 3733
Vinovich, Steve *(Cast)* 3764
Vinton, Arthur *(Cast)* 814, 1352, 1384
Vinton, Doris *(Cast)* 1448
Viola, Albert T. *(Composer)* 1797
Viola, Albert T. *(Librettist)* 1796
Violett, Ellen *(Librettist)* 868
Violette, Helene *(Cast)* 909
Violette, Yvette *(Cast)* 3803
Violinsky, Sol *(Composer)* 1922
Virag, Oscar *(Composer)* 710
Virag, Oscar *(Lyricist)* 710
Virgo, Hilary *(Costumes)* 1386
Vitacco, Lou *(Composer)* 1940
Vitacco, Lou *(Librettist)* 1940
Vitacco, Lou *(Lyricist)* 1940
Vitacco, Lou *(Pianist)* 1940
Vitale, Bill *(Composer)* 1450, 2776
Vitale, Bill *(Director)* 1450, 2776
Vitale, Bill *(Lyricist)* 164, 1450, 2776
Vitale, Bill *(Producer)* 164
Vitale, Joseph *(Cast)* 2504
Vitali, Michael *(Arrangements)* 114
Vitali, Michael *(Composer)* 114
Vitali, Michael *(Incidental Music)* 114
Vitella, Sel *(Cast)* 4062
Vitkin, Shlomo *(Set Design)* 2811
Vivanco, Moises *(Composer)* 1300
Vivanco, Moises *(Lyricist)* 1300
Viverito, Sam *(Choreographer)* 944
Vivian, Ann *(Cast)* 2657
Vivian, George *(Director)* 2264, 4673
Viviano, Sal *(Cast)* 549, 674
Vivino, Jimmy *(Musical Director)* 2427
Vivino, Jimmy *(Orchestrations)* 3873
Vizard, Harold *(Cast)* 2760
Vleugel, Guus *(Lyricist)* 1865
Vodery, Henry *(Choreographer)* 2009
Vodery, Will *(Arrangements)* 4661
Vodery, Will *(Composer)* 513, 545, 1087, 2009, 2302, 4487, 4809
Vodery, Will *(Musical Director)* 875, 1058, 2009, 3007, 3513
Vodery, Will *(Orchestrations)* 441, 444, 545, 883, 2009, 2020, 2302, 3007, 3179, 3963, 3965, 4360, 4569, 4823
Vodery, Will *(Vocal Arranger)* 3949
Vodery, Will H. *(Composer)* 2721, 3337
Vodery, Will H. *(Musical Director)* 3337
Vodery Singers, Will *(Cast)* 4177
Voe, Madge *(Cast)* 77, 561
Voegtlin, Arthur *(Set Design)* 106, 188, 228, 331, 436, 998, 1464, 1526, 1783, 1866, 1925, 2139, 2232, 2317, 2358, 2858, 2869, 2978, 3085, 3093, 3504, 3856, 4046, 4113, 4165, 4203, 4452, 4509, 4599, 4753
Voegtlin, William *(Set Design)* 476
Voelpel, Fred *(Costumes)* 534, 658, 1094, 1233, 1408, 1736, 3187, 3233, 4090, 4481, 4566, 4785
Voelpel, Fred *(Lighting Designer)* 1233, 1408, 1736, 4785
Voelpel, Fred *(Set Design)* 658, 915, 1233, 1408, 1736, 2043, 4029, 4566, 4785
Vogel, Ed *(Composer)* 1282
Vogel, Ed *(Musical Director)* 1282, 4168
Vogeley, Mark *(Lighting Designer)* 4462
Vogelle, Sheila *(Cast)* 283
Voget, Frederic B. *(Producer)* 2654
Voha, Frank *(Cast)* 825
Voices Inc. *(Composer)* 344
Voices Inc. *(Lyricist)* 344
Vokes, Harry *(Cast)* 1641, 1798, 3350
Vokes, Harry *(Composer)* 1641
Vokes, Harry *(Librettist)* 1641
Vokes, Harry *(Lyricist)* 3350
Vokes, Margaret Daly *(Cast)* 1641, 1798, 3350
Vokes, May *(Cast)* 1935, 2291, 2347, 4293, 4644
Volavkova *(Costumes)* 2731
Vollmoeller, Karl *(Author)* 795
Volpe, Frederick *(Cast)* 30
Volpin, Iza *(Musical Director)* 839
Volpin Orchestra, Iza *(Cast)* 839
Voltaire *(Author)* 630
Volterra, Leon *(Producer)* 2753
Von Bakony, Karl *(Author)* 1455
Von Brandenstein, Rizis *(Costumes)* 1082
Von Busing, Fritzi *(Cast)* 351
Von Fossen, Harry *(Cast)* 803, 4453
Von Gatti, Emmerich *(Author)* 2486, 3776
Von Hatzfeldt, Countess Olga *(Cast)* 4242
Von Kleist, Heinrich *(Author)* 3272
von Mayhof, Grete *(Cast)* 4492
von Mayrhauser, Jennifer *(Costumes)* 253, 682, 1581, 1787, 2429
von Mendelssohn, Frencesco *(Director)* 4368
Von Ottenfeld, Eddison *(Composer)* 3495
Von Ottenfeld, Eddison *(Lyricist)* 3495
Von Tilzer *(Composer)* 1520, 1686, 3981, 4804
Von Tilzer *(Lyricist)* 1520
Von Tilzer, Albert *(Composer)* 8, 21, 573, 581, 587, 608, 830, 1120, 1332, 1516, 1746, 1919, 1961, 2122, 2232, 2261, 2286, 2489, 2667, 2857, 3737, 3856, 3857, 3973, 4050, 4757, 4766, 4802, 4813
Von Tilzer, Harry *(Cast)* 3153
Von Tilzer, Harry *(Composer)* 685, 688, 954, 1063, 1138, 1295, 1526, 1569, 1613, 1897, 1963, 2111, 2299, 2335, 2349, 2415, 2465, 2481, 2724, 3298, 3396, 3820, 3926, 3962, 4197, 4390, 4655, 4757, 4804, 4808, 4815
Von Tilzer, Harry *(Director)* 1295
Von Tilzer, Harry *(Lyricist)* 3926
Von Tilzer, Harry *(Producer)* 1295
Von Tilzer, Jules *(Composer)* 3973
Von Tilzer, Jules *(Lyricist)* 3973
Von Waldberg, H. *(Author)* 3308
Von Waldren, Ethel *(Cast)* 2186
Vonn Busing, Fritzi *(Cast)* 2825
Vonnegut, Edith *(Producer)* 1591
Vonnegut, Kurt *(Author)* 1591
Voohees, Bettye *(Cast)* 2580
Vool, Ruth *(Cast)* 4773

Vorhees, Don *(Musical Director)* 117, 383, 1131, 1132, 4256
Vorhees, Donald *(Musical Director)* 2225, 3172
Vornaholt, John *(Librettist)* 4389
Vos, David *(Composer)* 4062
Vos, David *(Librettist)* 4062
Vos, David *(Lyricist)* 4062
Vos, Richard *(Producer)* 4295
Vosburgh, David *(Cast)* 1068, 3722, 4029
Vosburgh, Dick *(Librettist)* 1000, 2204, 4703
Vosburgh, Dick *(Lyricist)* 392, 1000, 4703
Voskovec, George *(Cast)* 1062
Votos, Christopher *(Cast)* 1060
Vousden, Ernest *(Composer)* 737
Vousden, Ernest *(Lyricist)* 737
Voynow, Dick *(Composer)* 4137
Voytek *(Set Design)* 194
Voznesensky, Andrey *(Librettist)* 2269
Voznesensky, Andrey *(Lyricist)* 2269
Vroom, Lodewick *(Producer)* 3767
Vye, Murvyn *(Cast)* 660

W

WPA *(Producer)* 3495
WPA Federal Theatre *(Producer)* 1871
WPA Theatre *(Producer)* 2038, 2544, 3986
WPA Variety Theatre *(Producer)* 4253
Waara, Scott *(Cast)* 775, 2643, 4619, 4701
Waas, Cinthia *(Costumes)* 2171
Waas & Son *(Costumes)* 4093
Waaser, Carol M. *(Lighting Designer)* 1406
Wachtel, Mussina *(Musical Director)* 2981
Waddell, Geoffrey *(Choreographer)* 945
Waddington, Patrick *(Cast)* 703
Wade, Adam *(Cast)* 4127
Wade, Herman Avery *(Composer)* 1526, 3387, 3693
Wade, Uel *(Arrangements)* 1496
Wade, Uel *(Dance Arranger)* 2598
Wade, Uel *(Musical Director)* 626, 1496, 2598, 3544
Wade, Uel *(Vocal Arranger)* 2598, 3544
Wade, Warren *(Cast)* 4028
Wadsworth, F. Wheeler *(Musical Director)* 4651
Waelder, Fred *(Cast)* 1560
Wager, Michael *(Cast)* 1294, 3439
Waggoner, George *(Lyricist)* 2747, 4291
Wagman, Benny *(Composer)* 2580
Wagner, Brent *(Director)* 4732
Wagner, Charles L. *(Producer)* 2967
Wagner, Chuck *(Cast)* 2143, 4229
Wagner, Daryl *(Cast)* 2436
Wagner, F. *(Composer)* 1538
Wagner, Frank *(Cast)* 2737
Wagner, Frank *(Choreographer)* 107, 272, 382, 427, 1107, 2018, 2052, 3112, 3479, 3889, 4035, 4828
Wagner, Frank *(Director)* 107, 272, 427, 1049, 2737, 3112, 4035
Wagner, Jack *(Cast)* 595
Wagner, John H. *(Librettist)* 2986
Wagner, John H. *(Lyricist)* 1188, 2986
Wagner, Nathaniel *(Cast)* 780, 3056, 3168, 3580
Wagner, Richard *(Composer)* 992
Wagner, Robin *(Librettist)* 3903
Wagner, Robin *(Set Design)* 287, 721, 746, 775, 828, 921, 1103, 1359, 1441, 1717, 2134, 2200, 2212, 2307, 2617, 2659, 2660, 2820, 3279, 3299, 3603, 3636, 3869, 3903, 4067, 4068, 4196, 4252, 4297, 4338, 4560
Wagner, Ruth *(Costumes)* 157
Wagner, Thomas *(Composer)* 3890
Wagoner, Dan *(Choreographer)* 755, 2478, 2579
Wagoner, Dan *(Director)* 2124
Wagstaff, Joe *(Cast)* 1275
Wagstaff, Joseph *(Cast)* 403
Wahl, Walter Dare *(Cast)* 662, 2475
Wahler, David *(Dance Arranger)* 4470
Wailes, Benjamin *(Cast)* 3990
Wain, John *(Lighting Designer)* 2147
Wainer, Lee *(Composer)* 2540, 3105, 3986
Wainer, Lee *(Lyricist)* 875
Wainer, Lee *(Musical Director)* 3105
Wainwright, Bert *(Cast)* 2139
Wainwright, Lee *(Producer)* 1971
Wainwright III, Loudon *(Composer)* 908
Wainwright III, Loudon *(Lyricist)* 908
Waissman, Kenneth *(Producer)* 209, 1164, 1664, 3330
Waite, Bruce *(Cast)* 4205
Waite, Eric *(Cast)* 2077, 2097
Waite, Genevieve *(Cast)* 2728
Waite, Ralph *(Cast)* 477
Waites, Thomas G. *(Cast)* 4295
Waiwaiole, Lloyd K. *(Costumes)* 3463
Wakefield, Ann *(Cast)* 507
Wakefield, Frank L. *(Librettist)* 1824
Wakefield, Oliver *(Cast)* 4824
Wakula, Frank *(Set Design)* 4611
Walberg, Betty *(Dance Arranger)* 162, 1265, 1709, 2163, 2304, 3274, 4625
Walberg, Paul *(Musical Director)* 2084, 2095, 2096
Walberg, Paul *(Orchestrations)* 2084, 2096
Walburn, Raymond *(Cast)* 1422, 4299, 4352
Walcott, Derek *(Director)* 4147
Walcott, Derek *(Librettist)* 4147
Walcott, Derek *(Lyricist)* 4147
Walden, Robert *(Composer)* 2250
Walden, Stanley *(Composer)* 259
Walden, Stanley *(Musical Director)* 259, 1977
Walden, Stanley *(Orchestrations)* 1977
Walden, Stanley *(Vocal Arranger)* 259
Walden, Walter *(Set Design)* 4253
Waldman, Robert *(Composer)* 112, 693, 1864, 3733, 4252
Waldman, Robert *(Dance Arranger)* 3733
Waldman, Robert *(Vocal Arranger)* 3733
Waldock, Dennis *(Librettist)* 4153
Waldon, James T. *(Lyricist)* 3673
Waldron, Jack *(Author)* 4629
Waldron, Jack *(Cast)* 3351, 4542
Waldron, James A. *(Librettist)* 938

Waldrop, Mark *(Cast)* 2968
Waldrop, Mark *(Librettist)* 2022
Waldrop, Mark *(Lyricist)* 2022
Waldrop, Uda *(Composer)* 3921
Waldteufel, Emile *(Composer)* 2772
Waliter, William *(Composer)* 4583
Walke, Gillian *(Cast)* 1412
Walken, Christopher *(Cast)* 270
Walker, Aida Overton *(Cast)* 9, 295, 633, 1909, 2111, 4088
Walker, Aida Overton *(Choreographer)* 9, 295
Walker, Anna *(Choreographer)* 2560
Walker, Bert *(Vocal Arranger)* 2150
Walker, Berta *(Producer)* 3711
Walker, Bill *(Costumes)* 951, 3198, 4109, 4175, 4601
Walker, Billy B. *(Lighting Designer)* 1146, 3126
Walker, Charlotte *(Cast)* 2904
Walker, Chinese *(Cast)* 1821
Walker, Chris *(Arrangements)* 4067
Walker, Chris *(Dance Arranger)* 2798
Walker, Chris *(Orchestrations)* 2798
Walker, Cindy *(Composer)* 4030
Walker, Cindy *(Lyricist)* 4030
Walker, Dan *(Cast)* 1654
Walker, Dan *(Composer)* 1653
Walker, Dan *(Lyricist)* 1652, 1653
Walker, David *(Composer)* 1873
Walker, Dianne *(Cast)* 432
Walker, Don *(Composer)* 84, 454, 911, 2817, 2910
Walker, Don *(Dance Arranger)* 454, 563
Walker, Don *(Music Adaptation)* 1548
Walker, Don *(Musical Director)* 3138
Walker, Don *(Orchestrations)* 84, 135, 145, 161, 162, 180, 216, 270, 273, 323, 372, 454, 512, 596, 601, 610, 619, 649, 657, 660, 680, 901, 911, 943, 957, 1112, 1140, 1265, 1278, 1290, 1310, 1352, 1456, 1475, 1494, 1507, 1548, 1679, 1698, 1764, 1791, 1841, 1848, 1860, 1879, 1918, 1931, 1973, 2432, 2453, 2475, 2539, 2550, 2582, 2590, 2680, 2786, 2797, 2817, 2894, 2961, 3016, 3064, 3278, 3351, 3359, 3390, 3536, 3780, 3900, 3918, 3928, 3972, 4058, 4142, 4214, 4365, 4384, 4423, 4483, 4499, 4516, 4524, 4586, 4633, 4702, 4718, 4734, 4777, 4825, 4826, 4862
Walker, Don *(Vocal Arranger)* 84, 145, 911, 1848, 2797, 3138
Walker, Douglas *(Cast)* 2305
Walker, Edward *(Musical Director)* 349
Walker, George *(Cast)* 1599, 4088
Walker, George *(Composer)* 3820
Walker, George *(Librettist)* 4088
Walker, George *(Lyricist)* 2111, 3820, 4390
Walker, George *(Producer)* 4088
Walker, George W. *(Cast)* 9, 295, 2111
Walker, Hughie *(Composer)* 1876
Walker, Hughie *(Lyricist)* 1876
Walker, James J. *(Lyricist)* 1118, 1897, 3849
Walker, Jerry Jeff *(Composer)* 964
Walker, Jerry Jeff *(Lyricist)* 964
Walker, John *(Librettist)* 3169
Walker, Joseph A. *(Cast)* 344
Walker, Joseph A. *(Librettist)* 344
Walker, Joseph A. *(Set Design)* 344
Walker, June *(Cast)* 1546, 1567, 3048
Walker, Kary M. *(Producer)* 1701
Walker, Mabel *(Cast)* 4254
Walker, Margaret *(Cast)* 3003, 3655
Walker, Marshall *(Composer)* 4840
Walker, Mildred *(Cast)* 165
Walker, Nancy *(Cast)* 95, 304, 372, 868, 1061, 1567, 2582, 2940, 3278, 3473
Walker, Natalie *(Costumes)* 2759
Walker, Peter *(Cast)* 3059
Walker, Peter *(Lyricist)* 1776
Walker, Phil *(Musical Director)* 1562
Walker, Polly *(Cast)* 403, 1836, 2829, 3179
Walker, Ray *(Composer)* 3989
Walker, Ray *(Lyricist)* 3989
Walker, Raymond *(Composer)* 965, 1531, 4195
Walker, Sid *(Librettist)* 3933
Walker, Suzanne *(Cast)* 2231
Walker, Sydney *(Cast)* 461
Walker, Tippy *(Cast)* 635
Walker, W. Raymond *(Composer)* 4806
Walker, William *(Composer)* 703
Walker and Thompson *(Cast)* 2271
Wall, Bill *(Cast)* 2092
Wall, Harry *(Librettist)* 4335
Wall, Max *(Cast)* 1137, 3291
Wall, Phil *(Orchestrations)* 4256, 4569
Wall, Phil *(Pianist)* 1494
Wallace, Art *(Cast)* 2248, 3209
Wallace, Ben *(Costumes)* 4265
Wallace, Beryl *(Cast)* 1127, 1136, 1137, 1138, 3002, 4443
Wallace, Chester *(Lyricist)* 4153
Wallace, Edgar *(Author)* 4207
Wallace, Edgar *(Librettist)* 3500, 3649
Wallace, Edna *(Cast)* 1165
Wallace, Emmett "Babe" *(Cast)* 497
Wallace, Frederick *(Librettist)* 2456
Wallace, G.D. *(Cast)* 3505
Wallace, George *(Cast)* 2201, 3113
Wallace, George D. *(Cast)* 3925
Wallace, Helen *(Lyricist)* 3849
Wallace, Lee *(Cast)* 1699, 2422, 2925
Wallace, Lizzie *(Cast)* 646
Wallace, Oliver *(Composer)* 69
Wallace, Oliver G. *(Composer)* 3297, 3973
Wallace, Oliver G. *(Lyricist)* 3297
Wallace, Pat *(Author)* 4207
Wallace, Paul *(Cast)* 1709
Wallace, Ronald *(Lighting Designer)* 951, 4601
Wallace, Royce *(Cast)* 3286
Wallace, Slappy *(Cast)* 444, 1876
Wallace, W.V. *(Composer)* 1897
Wallace, W.V. *(Lyricist)* 1897
Wallach, Ira *(Additional Lyrics)* 4244
Wallach, Ira *(Librettist)* 1047, 1435, 2284, 2910, 3286, 3473, 3524, 4028, 4244, 4829
Wallach, Ira *(Lyricist)* 1047, 2284, 2910, 3286, 4153

Wallbye, Kay *(Cast)* 2704
Waller, Frank *(Composer)* 710
Waller, Frank *(Lyricist)* 710
Waller, Henry *(Composer)* 1226, 2833
Waller, Jack *(Author)* 203
Waller, Jack *(Composer)* 4299
Waller, Jack *(Lyricist)* 2833
Waller, Kenneth H. *(Cast)* 456
Waller, Lewis *(Librettist)* 1692
Waller, Thomas "Fats" *(Cast)* 2302
Waller, Thomas "Fats" *(Composer)* 39, 432, 1140, 1980, 1986, 2266, 2302, 2561, 3020, 3782, 4282
Walling, Stratton *(Cast)* 3544
Wallis, Bertram *(Cast)* 466, 2671
Wallis, Shani *(Cast)* 4384
Wallman, Jan *(Producer)* 3124
Wallop, Douglass *(Author)* 957
Wallop, Douglass *(Librettist)* 957
Walls, Mary *(Costumes)* 3596
Walmsley, Andy *(Costumes)* 460
Walmsley, Andy *(Set Design)* 460, 580
Walnut Street Theatre *(Producer)* 1236
Wals, Christopher *(Cast)* 3461
Walsh, Barbara *(Cast)* 460
Walsh, Ellis *(Composer)* 1296
Walsh, Ellis *(Lyricist)* 1296
Walsh, Frank *(Cast)* 3357
Walsh, Helen *(Cast)* 3980
Walsh, James *(Producer)* 1077, 3285
Walsh, Ken *(Choreographer)* 3066
Walsh, Lionel *(Cast)* 4688
Walsh, Mary Jane *(Cast)* 84, 849, 2068, 2453, 2751, 3990, 4420
Walsh, Maurice *(Screenwriter)* 1076
Walsh, Michael *(Cast)* 4830
Walsh, Phil *(Orchestrations)* 216
Walsh, Thomas *(Cast)* 3636
Walsh, Thomas A. *(Set Design)* 4861
Walsh, Thommie *(Cast)* 746
Walsh, Thommie *(Choreographer)* 544, 1000, 1059, 3039, 3060, 3175
Walsh, Thommie *(Director)* 13, 544, 2646
Walsh, Tim *(Cast)* 1159
Walsh, Townsend *(Author)* 516
Walsh, Townsend *(Cast)* 516
Walsh, Townsend *(Librettist)* 516
Walsh, Townsend *(Set Design)* 516
Walsh, Valerie *(Cast)* 874
Walsh, William *(Lyricist)* 4291
Walston, Ray *(Cast)* 32, 957, 2000, 2797
Walstrum, Judy A. *(Cast)* 4799
Walt Disney Theatrical Productions *(Producer)* 330
Walter, Cy *(Composer)* 1370
Walter, Edwin *(Cast)* 1014
Walter, Eugene *(Librettist)* 4215
Walter, Max *(Cast)* 1608
Walter, Serge *(Composer)* 364, 1656, 1657, 3409, 3907
Walters, Ashley *(Cast)* 730
Walters, Charles *(Cast)* 383, 1109, 1342, 2061, 2252, 3103, 3365, 3916, 3955
Walters, Charles *(Choreographer)* 297, 2453, 3916, 3 990, 4123
Walters, Dorothy *(Cast)* 3369
Walters, Homer *(Musical Director)* 1867
Walters, Lou *(Librettist)* 204
Walters, Lou *(Producer)* 204, 4265
Walters, Polly *(Cast)* 3674, 3919
Walters, Susan *(Cast)* 2811
Walters, Teddy *(Cast)* 4545
Walters, Thorley *(Cast)* 1467
Walthall, Alfred G. *(Composer)* 4201
Waltinger, Bertha *(Cast)* 3176
Walton, Bob *(Cast)* 3555
Walton, Florence *(Cast)* 558, 1735, 2892, 3433, 3494, 4094, 4802
Walton, Fred *(Cast)* 902, 1565, 1910, 2424, 2723, 3053, 3362, 3400, 4761
Walton, George *(Director)* 2500
Walton, Gladys *(Cast)* 2419, 2816, 2856, 2857, 3962
Walton, Grace *(Cast)* 20, 336, 2316, 2917
Walton, Jim *(Cast)* 131, 158, 2822, 3444, 4137
Walton, Maurice *(Cast)* 558, 1735
Walton, Richard *(Author)* 422
Walton, Tony *(Costumes)* 170, 1422, 1601, 1620, 3927, 4541
Walton, Tony *(Set Design)* 16, 170, 589, 723, 754, 1000, 1422, 1601, 1620, 1649, 2427, 3506, 3927, 4091, 4541, 4695, 4727
Waltzer, Bernard *(Producer)* 279
Waltzinger, Bertha *(Cast)* 2233
Walz, Christopher *(Cast)* 4740
Walz, Fred *(Musical Director)* 473
Walzer, W. *(Author)* 1935
Wanamaker, C.C. *(Producer)* 2888
Wanda, Gustav *(Musical Director)* 30
Wandersman, Walt *(Cast)* 1190
Waner, Anne *(Author)* 3693
Wanger, John H. *(Lyricist)* 2986
Wank, Jesse *(Producer)* 4763
Wann, Jim *(Cast)* 1037, 3608
Wann, Jim *(Composer)* 1037, 1038, 1915, 1985, 3608
Wann, Jim *(Librettist)* 1037, 1985
Wann, Jim *(Lyricist)* 1037, 1038, 1402, 1915, 1985, 3608
Wantuck, Michael *(Producer)* 2022
Waram, Percy *(Cast)* 1110
Warburg, Gerald *(Composer)* 2193, 3847
Ward *(Composer)* 792
Ward *(Costumes)* 675
Ward *(Lyricist)* 792
Ward, Aida *(Cast)* 441, 876, 877, 879, 886, 896, 1984, 2462, 2739, 3709
Ward, Ann Hould *(Costumes)* 3306
Ward, Charles *(Cast)* 964
Ward, Donald *(Librettist)* 508, 1665
Ward, Dorothy *(Cast)* 3472
Ward, Douglas Turner *(Director)* 1671, 2719
Ward, Eddie *(Composer)* 2088, 4212
Ward, Eddie *(Lyricist)* 2628
Ward, Edward *(Composer)* 4291
Ward, Edward *(Lyricist)* 2628

Ward, Edward *(Orchestrations)* 4291
Ward, Elsa *(Costumes)* 573
Ward, Hap *(Cast)* 1646, 4817
Ward, Happy *(Cast)* 1641, 1798
Ward, Happy *(Composer)* 1641
Ward, Happy *(Librettist)* 1641
Ward, Harrison *(Lyricist)* 2543
Ward, Herbert
See also Ward & Harvey.
Ward, Herbert *(Set Design)* 21, 208, 545, 1391, 1484, 1485, 2927, 3144, 3623, 4104
Ward, Joe Patrick *(Composer)* 2046
Ward, Joe Patrick *(Lyricist)* 2046
Ward, Joe Patrick *(Musical Director)* 2046
Ward, Joe Patrick *(Vocal Arranger)* 2046
Ward, John *(Set Design)* 3273
Ward, Jonathan *(Cast)* 2027
Ward, Joseph P. *(Cast)* 1647
Ward, Kelly *(Cast)* 4459
Ward, Ken *(Cast)* 2285
Ward, MacKenzie *(Cast)* 3481
Ward, Mackenzie *(Cast)* 4207
Ward, Michael *(Musical Director)* 4246
Ward, Paula *(Cast)* 3202
Ward, Penelope Dudley *(Cast)* 3885
Ward, Phylis *(Cast)* 164
Ward, Sam *(Cast)* 4421
Ward, Sam *(Librettist)* 1397
Ward, Samuel *(Composer)* 4390
Ward, Solly *(Cast)* 184, 1680, 2747, 3008, 3012, 4733
Ward, Ted D. *(Composer)* 913
Ward, Theara J. *(Cast)* 754
Ward, Theodore *(Author)* 3321
Ward, Theodore *(Lyricist)* 3321
Ward, Toni *(Costumes)* 3831
Ward, William J. *(Cast)* 3327
Ward & Harvey
See also Herbert Ward and Walter H. Harvey.
Ward & Harvey *(Set Design)* 82, 443, 1916, 2382, 3556, 4372, 4545
Ward-Stephens *(Composer)* 1009
Warde, Willie *(Choreographer)* 719, 2131, 2524, 3828
Warde, Willie *(Musical Director)* 2509
Wardell, Carter *(Cast)* 2366
Wardell, Harry *(Producer)* 3043
Warden, George *(Cast)* 2791
Warden, Jack *(Cast)* 483
Wardewell, Edward R. *(Cast)* 3325
Ware, Eric *(Cast)* 3001
Ware, Helen *(Cast)* 3730
Ware, N. Harris *(Composer)* 1568, 1573
Ware, N. Harris *(Lyricist)* 1573
Ware, N. Harris *(Musical Director)* 1573
Warfield, Charles *(Composer)* 1425
Warfield, Charles *(Lyricist)* 146, 1425
Warfield, David *(Cast)* 357, 1264, 2041, 2116, 2842, 3750, 4658
Warfield, Joel *(Cast)* 3217
Warfield, Joseph *(Cast)* 3
Warfield, Ruth White *(Composer)* 174
Warfield, William *(Cast)* 3691
Wargo, Dan *(Director)* 2511
Wargo, Richard *(Composer)* 3864
Wargo, Richard *(Librettist)* 3864
Wargo, Richard *(Lyricist)* 3864
Warhol, Andy *(Costumes)* 322
Warhol, Andy *(Producer)* 2728
Waring, Fred
See also Fred Waring & His Pennsylvanians, Fred Waring Glee Club, Orchestra, Pennsylvanians, World's Fair Glee Club.
Waring, Fred *(Cast)* 3153
Waring, Fred *(Composer)* 3131
Waring, Fred *(Musical Director)* 2401
Waring, Fred *(Producer)* 3645
Waring, J. *(Set Design)* 932
Waring, J.D. *(Set Design)* 345
Waring, James D. *(Set Design)* 821, 2028, 2641
Waring, Richard *(Cast)* 55, 814, 2859
Waring, Richard *(Lyricist)* 392
Waring, Tom *(Composer)* 3645, 4170
Waring, Tom *(Lyricist)* 3645, 4170
Fred Waring & His Pennsylvanians/Glee Club/Orchestra/Pennsylvanians/World's Fair Glee Club
See also Fred Waring.
Waring & His Pennsylvanians, Fred *(Cast)* 1839, 2402, 2405, 3131, 3645
Waring Glee Club, Fred *(Cast)* 2400, 3100
Waring's Orchestra, Fred *(Cast)* 2366
Waring's Pennsylvanians, Fred *(Cast)* 2401
Waring's World's Fair Glee Club, Fred *(Cast)* 173
Warneke, Marleta *(Cast)* 1940
Warner, Edyth *(Cast)* 399
Warner, Jack L. *(Producer)* 2217
Warner, Neil *(Musical Director)* 2727, 3612
Warner, Neil *(Vocal Arranger)* 36
Warner, Russell *(Dance Arranger)* 1665, 2578, 3671, 3928, 4796
Warner, Russell *(Orchestrations)* 1665, 4537
Warner Theatre Productions *(Producer)* 1068, 3608, 4727
Warnick, Clay *(Composer)* 23, 1101, 1815, 1933, 4377
Warnick, Clay *(Dance Arranger)* 3390
Warnick, Clay *(Lyricist)* 2817
Warnick, Clay *(Musical Director)* 67, 1076, 1811, 1930, 2187, 2850
Warnick, Clay *(Orchestrations)* 4586
Warnick, Clay *(Vocal Arranger)* 180, 204, 297, 601, 834, 901, 971, 1076, 1112, 1577, 1604, 1815, 1930, 2523, 2817, 3036, 3390, 4543, 4702
Warnick, Steven *(Producer)* 4139
Warnow, Mark *(Producer)* 4640
Warrack, David *(Composer)* 3066
Warrack, David *(Librettist)* 3066
Warrack, David *(Lyricist)* 3066
Warrack Prods. *(Producer)* 3066
Warren, Bob *(Cast)* 863, 864
Warren, Brett *(Director)* 1416
Warren, C. Dernier *(Cast)* 4302
Warren, Chandler *(Lyricist)* 916
Warren, David *(Director)* 647

Warren, Frances *(Cast)* 1550
Warren, Harry *(Composer)* 173, 397, 418, 964, 1359, 1638, 1813, 2423, 2772, 2808, 3018, 3020, 3175, 3382, 3796, 3840, 3913, 4235, 4730, 4799, 4815, 4817
Warren, Harvey *(Set Design)* 2742
Warren, Jennifer Leigh *(Cast)* 10, 394, 2544
Warren, Julie *(Cast)* 189
Warren, Lesley Ann *(Cast)* 1094, 1616, 3294
Warren, Mary Mease *(Costumes)* 1671
Warren, Richard Henry *(Composer)* 934
Warren, Richard Henry *(Musical Director)* 934
Warren, Rod *(Composer)* 128, 272, 366, 1049, 1107, 1436, 1437, 1438, 1770, 2279, 2913, 3186, 3484, 3889, 4433
Warren, Rod *(Librettist)* 1436, 2279, 4433
Warren, Rod *(Lyricist)* 128, 272, 366, 1049, 1107, 1436, 1437, 1438, 2279, 2913, 3186, 3484, 3889, 4433
Warren, Rod *(Musical Director)* 62
Warren, Rod *(Producer)* 128, 366, 1436, 1438, 2138, 2279, 2913
Warren, Ruth *(Cast)* 4241
Warren, Tom *(Set Design)* 962
Warrender, Scott *(Composer)* 992
Warshavsky, M. *(Composer)* 4342
Warshavsky, M. *(Lyricist)* 4342
Wartski, Sheila *(Choreographer)* 2147
Warwick, Robert *(Cast)* 276, 2903
Washburn, Jack *(Cast)* 3371
Washburne, Elizabeth *(Cast)* 4313
Washington, Fredi *(Cast)* 2712, 3993
Washington, Geneva *(Cast)* 435, 3704
Washington, George Dewey *(Cast)* 875, 878, 885, 1288, 4177
Washington, Isabell *(Cast)* 290
Washington, Lamont *(Cast)* 1717
Washington, Mildred *(Cast)* 2640, 4184
Washington, Ned *(Lyricist)* 444, 878, 1134, 3002, 3373, 4193, 4545
Washington Square Players *(Set Design)* 1919
Wassall, Edward *(Costumes)* 2443
Wassall, Edward *(Set Design)* 2443
Wassau, Hinda *(Cast)* 420
Wasserman, Allan *(Cast)* 829
Wasserman, Dale *(Director)* 1892
Wasserman, Dale *(Librettist)* 2556, 2727, 3908, 3961
Wasserman, Dale *(Lighting Designer)* 1892
Wasserstein, Wendy *(Librettist)* 4535
Wasson, David *(Cast)* 1291
Watanabe, Gedde *(Cast)* 1053
Watanabe, Trich *(Lyricist)* 1053
Waterbury, Laura *(Cast)* 3015, 3305
Waterbury, Marsha *(Cast)* 4020
Waterhouse, Jane *(Librettist)* 2861
Waterman, Willard *(Cast)* 2713
Waterous, Herbert *(Cast)* 4293
Waterous, Jack *(Cast)* 4621
Waters, Daryl *(Vocal Arranger)* 10
Waters, Ethel *(Cast)* 26, 207, 216, 443, 467, 612, 875, 878, 885, 1499, 2712, 2881, 3241, 3704
Waters, Ethel *(Composer)* 3709
Waters, Ethel *(Lyricist)* 3709
Waters, Fred *(Cast)* 2986
Waters, Marianne Brown *(Librettist)* 3713
Waters, Marianne Brown *(Lyricist)* 3713
Waters, Mr. *(Composer)* 998
Waters, Roger *(Composer)* 3739
Waters, Safford *(Composer)* 934, 1226, 1417, 4414
Waters, Safford *(Librettist)* 1226
Waters, Safford *(Lyricist)* 934, 1226, 1417, 4414
Waters, Tom *(Cast)* 1430
Waterston, Sam *(Cast)* 3000
Watkin, Fen *(Musical Director)* 1255
Watkins, Linda *(Cast)* 2265, 3850
Watkins, Maurine Dallas *(Author)* 723
Watkins, Perry *(Producer)* 315, 341
Watkins, Perry *(Set Design)* 315, 467, 2712, 3495, 4782
Watling, Dilys *(Cast)* 1497
Watson, Betty Jane *(Cast)* 206, 4015, 4428
Watson, Billy *(Cast)* 1032, 1457
Watson, Billy *(Director)* 1032
Watson, Billy *(Librettist)* 1032
Watson, Billy W. *(Librettist)* 1457
Watson, Bobby *(Cast)* 86, 152, 931, 1693, 2148, 3310, 3723
Watson, Brian *(Cast)* 3527, 3697
Watson, Douglass *(Cast)* 3000, 3330, 3468
Watson, Edith *(Orchestrations)* 2034
Watson, Edna *(Costumes)* 1072
Watson, Eric *(Composer)* 1638
Watson, Ernie *(Orchestrations)* 1336
Watson, Frank *(Cast)* 3468
Watson, Frederic *(Composer)* 815
Watson, Harry *(Cast)* 2800, 3404, 4392, 4802, 4804, 4805, 4806
Watson, Harry B. *(Cast)* 671, 2868
Watson, Janet *(Choreographer)* 394, 809, 2229
Watson, Jim *(Cast)* 1037
Watson, John *(Cast)* 169
Watson, Lee *(Lighting Designer)* 1062, 1571, 2664, 2772, 3543, 3619, 3938
Watson, Lisa *(Set Design)* 2272
Watson, Lucile *(Cast)* 1904
Watson, M.G. *(Composer)* 1535
Watson, M.G. *(Lyricist)* 1535
Watson, Milton *(Cast)* 1136, 3822, 4177
Watson, Minor *(Cast)* 2691
Watson, Rita *(Costumes)* 708
Watson, Sam *(Cast)* 1845
Watson, Susan *(Cast)* 367, 491, 607, 681, 2248
Watson, Virginia *(Cast)* 1533, 3752
Watson, Walter *(Costumes)* 4062
Watson, Whitford *(Lyricist)* 1900
Watson II, Harry *(Cast)* 3977
Watson Jr., Harry *(Cast)* 3222, 4801
Watt, Robert *(Cast)* 3910
Watters, Bill *(Producer)* 407, 408
Watters, George Manker *(Author)* 587
Watters, Hal *(Cast)* 369, 4002
Watters, Safford *(Composer)* 4348
Watterston, Henry *(Composer)* 2792
Watts, Al *(Cast)* 2013
Watts, Al F. *(Cast)* 980, 2127

Watts, Al F. *(Librettist)* 2127
Watts, Elizabeth *(Cast)* 1029
Watts, George *(Cast)* 2344
Watts, William E. *(Director)* 3180
Waxman, A.P. *(Producer)* 1112, 3813
Waxman, Franz *(Composer)* 2611
Waxman, Jeff *(Musical Director)* 1077, 1985, 2289
Waxman, Jeff *(Orchestrations)* 4740
Waxman, Jeff *(Vocal Arranger)* 1077, 4740
Waxman, Jeffrey *(Arrangements)* 3752
Waxman, Jeffrey *(Musical Director)* 3752
Waxman, Percy *(Librettist)* 584
Waxman, Percy *(Lyricist)* 584, 1309
Wayburn, Ned *(Cast)* 604
Wayburn, Ned *(Choreographer)* 405, 558, 1801, 1826, 1967, 2519, 2869, 2914, 3146, 3395, 3768, 4023, 4130, 4203, 4491, 4687, 4813, 4816
Wayburn, Ned *(Composer)* 1835
Wayburn, Ned *(Costumes)* 604
Wayburn, Ned *(Director)* 354, 604, 638, 683, 1154, 1403, 1523, 1606, 1640, 1728, 1731, 1783, 1801, 1835, 1922, 1963, 2035, 2123, 2232, 2378, 2481, 2485, 2493, 2519, 2600, 2700, 2858, 2900, 2906, 2964, 2974, 2978, 3086, 3087, 3096, 3265, 3395, 3396, 3422, 3433, 3538, 3575, 3746, 3747, 3749, 3773, 3855, 4203, 4206, 4382, 4387, 4437, 4491, 4662, 4687, 4757, 4810, 4811, 4812, 4813, 4816, 4817, 4831, 4833, 4836, 4837, 4838, 4849, 4851
Wayburn, Ned *(Librettist)* 4437
Wayburn, Ned *(Lighting Designer)* 2378, 3538
Wayburn, Ned *(Lyricist)* 638, 1523, 1920, 2978, 4437
Wayburn, Ned *(Producer)* 1593, 2700, 3086, 3087, 4437
Wayburn, Ned *(Set Design)* 2378, 2519
Wayland, Newton *(Musical Director)* 369
Wayland, Newton *(Orchestrations)* 369
Wayne, Bernie *(Composer)* 673, 4484, 4828
Wayne, Bernie *(Lyricist)* 673, 4828
Wayne, Charles *(Cast)* 4223
Wayne, David *(Cast)* 1278, 1730, 1764, 2267, 3390, 3800, 3845, 3874, 4764
Wayne, Jerry *(Cast)* 2751
Wayne, Paula *(Cast)* 1601
Wayne, Rollo *(Set Design)* 200, 787, 1618, 3405, 3409, 4121, 4669
Wayne, Shirley *(Cast)* 1840
Wayne, Sid *(Lyricist)* 4337
Wayne, William *(Cast)* 4241
Wearing, Michael *(Director)* 2153
Weatherly, Fred E. *(Lyricist)* 2891
Weatherly, Frederick E. *(Lyricist)* 3259
Weatherly, Joe *(Cast)* 2721
Weatherly, Michael M. *(Producer)* 4619
Weatherly, Tom *(Director)* 2105
Weatherly, Tom *(Producer)* 1453, 2105, 2545, 3861, 3919, 4335
Weathersbee, Gary *(Lighting Designer)* 1229
Weathersby, Jennie *(Cast)* 1193
Weaver, Carl Earl *(Cast)* 166, 3739, 4722
Weaver, Carl Earl *(Composer)* 2541
Weaver, Carl Earl *(Librettist)* 2541
Weaver, Carl Earl *(Lyricist)* 2541
Weaver, Dennis *(Cast)* 1674
Weaver, Doodles *(Cast)* 2809
Weaver, Fritz *(Cast)* 64, 270
Weaver, William *(Costumes)* 606, 1384, 3573, 3580
Weaver, William *(Set Design)* 728, 3404, 3580, 3770
Webb, Alan *(Cast)* 1238, 3678, 3906, 4610
Webb, Alice *(Cast)* 2071
Webb, Barbara *(Cast)* 2075
Webb, Charles *(Author)* 1645
Webb, Chick *(Composer)* 146, 432, 4534
Webb, Chloe *(Cast)* 1348
Webb, Clifton *(Cast)* 207, 208, 1322, 2180, 2491, 2545, 2620, 3087, 3467, 3478, 3613, 3865, 3924, 4212, 4367, 4443, 4777
Webb, Dorothy *(Cast)* 628
Webb, Elida *(Choreographer)* 876
Webb, Elmon *(Set Design)* 2776
Webb, Janet *(Cast)* 2682
Webb, Jimmy *(Composer)* 3852
Webb, Jimmy *(Lyricist)* 3852
Webb, Kenneth *(Director)* 1956, 1957
Webb, Kenneth *(Librettist)* 1453, 2005, 2105, 4673
Webb, Kenneth *(Lyricist)* 423, 1780
Webb, Kenneth S. *(Director)* 3284, 3419
Webb, Kenneth S. *(Librettist)* 3284
Webb, Kenneth S. *(Lyricist)* 3284
Webb, Laura *(Composer)* 4264
Webb, Laura *(Lyricist)* 4264
Webb, Lizbeth *(Cast)* 453, 1467
Webb, Lyda *(Choreographer)* 3808
Webb, M. Tello *(Cast)* 2154
Webb, Marti *(Cast)* 1619, 4301
Webb, Nella *(Cast)* 1910
Webb, Robert *(Dance Arranger)* 3888
Webb, Roy *(Composer)* 17, 1502, 1780, 3148, 3419, 4644
Webb, Roy *(Lyricist)* 17
Webb, Roy *(Musical Director)* 711, 834, 1447, 2382, 3436, 3556
Webb, Roy *(Orchestrations)* 711, 834, 2382, 3007, 3436, 4328, 4821
Webb, Roy S. *(Composer)* 3284
Webb, Roy S. *(Musical Director)* 3284, 4308
Webber, Florence *(Cast)* 2569, 3538
Webber, James Plaisted *(Author)* 1235
Weber, Bernard *(Author)* 2657, 2658
Weber, Edwin *(Composer)* 1944
Weber, Edwin J. *(Composer)* 3405
Weber, Florence *(Costumes)* 1126
Weber, Fredricka *(Cast)* 1049, 2418
Weber, Harry *(Cast)* 77
Weber, Joe *(Cast)* 3639, 3755, 4681
Weber, Joe *(Producer)* 2262, 2494
Weber, Joseph *(Cast)* 182, 258, 301, 510, 677, 940, 1095, 1217, 1264, 1881, 1900, 1926, 1927, 2041, 2835, 3303, 3632, 4473, 4478, 4511, 4658, 4797
Weber, Joseph *(Director)* 88, 1881
Weber, Joseph *(Producer)* 88, 182, 301, 677, 940, 1095, 1162, 1188, 1217, 1264, 1851, 1881, 1926, 1927, 1962, 2835, 3303, 3304, 3632, 4473, 4478, 4658, 4681, 4797
Weber, Joseph A. *(Cast)* 1806

Weber, L. Lawrence *(Producer)* 1911, 2516, 2818, 2950
Weber, Lawrence *(Cast)* 3427, 3920
Weber, Rex *(Cast)* 125, 1932, 3264, 4368
Weber, Shirley *(Cast)* 2098
Weber, Steve *(Composer)* 3309
Weber, Steve *(Lyricist)* 3309
Weber & Fields
See Joseph Weber and Lew Fields.
Weber & Rush *(Producer)* 3384
Webster, A.S. *(Producer)* 1206
Webster, Byron *(Cast)* 367, 3274, 3931
Webster, H.T. *(Librettist)* 199
Webster, Howard *(Composer)* 1206, 3021
Webster, Howard *(Lyricist)* 1206
Webster, Howard *(Musical Director)* 1206
Webster, J.P. *(Composer)* 3020
Webster, Jack *(Cast)* 1968
Webster, Jean *(Author)* 2608
Webster, Paul Francis *(Author)* 616
Webster, Paul Francis *(Lyricist)* 59, 616, 673, 751, 1034, 2246, 2259, 2311, 3002, 3046, 3175, 3739, 3905, 4091, 4702
Webster, Rev. H.D.L. *(Lyricist)* 3020
Wedgeworth, Ann *(Cast)* 477
Wedgworth, Ann *(Cast)* 2468
Weede, Robert *(Cast)* 935, 2864, 2961, 4155
Weeden, Bill *(Composer)* 2043, 2075, 2279, 2913, 3181, 3479
Weeden, Bill *(Lyricist)* 3181
Weedon, William C. *(Cast)* 2524, 2836
Weedon, Willliam C. *(Cast)* 4187
Weeks, Ada Mae *(Cast)* 824, 2214, 2491, 2569, 3218, 3420
Weeks, Al *(Librettist)* 1847
Weeks, Alan *(Cast)* 393, 406, 415, 550, 1729, 3231, 3276, 3741, 4286
Weeks, Alan *(Choreographer)* 1890, 3239
Weeks, Alan *(Director)* 1890, 3239
Weeks, Bonnie *(Producer)* 908
Weeks, Harold *(Composer)* 3297
Weeks, Harold *(Lyricist)* 3297
Weeks, Mabel *(Cast)* 2317
Weeks, Sarah *(Cast)* 4533
Weeks, Sarah *(Composer)* 3181, 4533
Weeks, Sarah *(Librettist)* 3181
Weeks, Sarah *(Lyricist)* 3181, 4533
Wehlen, Emmy *(Cast)* 1561
Wehner, George B. *(Lyricist)* 2857
Wehrle, Helen *(Cast)* 1461
Weick, Richard *(Lighting Designer)* 3080
Weidhaus, G.A. *(Set Design)* 1490
Weidhaus, Gustave *(Set Design)* 1489
Weidhaus, Ted *(Set Design)* 1491, 3086, 4374
Weidlin, Jane *(Composer)* 3739
Weidlin, Jane *(Lyricist)* 3739
Weidman, Charles *(Cast)* 1933
Weidman, Charles *(Choreographer)* 125, 207, 309, 2068, 2103, 2187, 2475, 2554, 2748, 3105, 3543, 3989
Weidman, Jerome *(Author)* 2048
Weidman, Jerome *(Librettist)* 842, 1280, 2048, 3551, 4312
Weidman, John *(Librettist)* 112, 212, 1038, 3340
Weigall, Arthur *(Lyricist)* 702, 1733
Weigert, Rene *(Dance Arranger)* 4828
Weigert, Rene *(Musical Director)* 678
Weil, Cynthia *(Composer)* 964
Weil, Cynthia *(Lyricist)* 146, 964
Weil, David *(Producer)* 942
Weil, Oscar *(Composer)* 4598
Weil, Oscar *(Librettist)* 4598
Weil, Raymonde *(Producer)* 4689
Weil, Richard *(Librettist)* 2259
Weil, Robert *(Cast)* 3059, 3288
Weil, Tim *(Musical Director)* 838
Weiler, Norman *(Cast)* 2055
Weill, Harry *(Cast)* 1267
Weill, Harry *(Composer)* 1267
Weill, Harry *(Lyricist)* 1267
Weill, Irving *(Lyricist)* 4010
Weill, Kurt *(Author)* 4368, 4369, 4370
Weill, Kurt *(Composer)* 369, 996, 1085, 1120, 1196, 1284, 1299, 1755, 2030, 2228, 2323, 2344, 2386, 2591, 2615, 2653, 2753, 3301, 3647, 3840, 4169, 4368, 4369, 4370, 4371, 4399, 4504
Weill, Kurt *(Dance Arranger)* 1284, 2591, 2615, 3301, 4169
Weill, Kurt *(Incidental Music)* 1416, 4495
Weill, Kurt *(Orchestrations)* 1284, 2228, 2344, 2386, 2591, 2615, 3301, 4169, 4368, 4369, 4371
Weill, Kurt *(Producer)* 2653
Weill, Kurt *(Vocal Arranger)* 1284, 2386, 2591, 2615, 3301, 4169
Weill, Stephen *(Producer)* 4707
Weille, Blair *(Composer)* 1436, 2876, 4433
Weille, Blair *(Librettist)* 4433
Weille, Blair *(Lyricist)* 4433
Weimar, Lorraine *(Cast)* 2540
Weinberg, Arthur *(Lyricist)* 4642
Weinberg, Charles *(Composer)* 123, 4763
Weinberg, Charles *(Lyricist)* 4763
Weinberg, Charles *(Musical Director)* 4218
Weinberg, Charles A. *(Cast)* 3751
Weinberg, Edwin *(Composer)* 4433
Weinberg, Edwin *(Librettist)* 4433
Weinberg, Edwin *(Lyricist)* 4433
Weinberg, Gus *(Cast)* 47, 1351, 1515, 2868, 4161
Weinberg, Gus *(Librettist)* 3086
Weinberg, Gus C. *(Lyricist)* 47
Weinberg, Tom Wilson *(Composer)* 4309
Weinberg, Tom Wilson *(Lyricist)* 4309
Weiner, Ellis *(Librettist)* 251
Weiner, John *(Cast)* 2360
Weiner, Lazar *(Composer)* 1609
Weiner, Lee *(Composer)* 885
Weiner, Lee *(Lyricist)* 885
Weiner, Mark *(Dance Arranger)* 1978
Weiner, Mark *(Musical Director)* 1978
Weiner, Mark *(Vocal Arranger)* 1978
Weiner, Meri *(Cast)* 4168
Weiner, Robert *(Producer)* 2804, 4278
Weiner, Stephen A. *(Composer)* 4107

Weinrib, Len *(Cast)* 411
Weinstein, Arnold *(Director)* 1122
Weinstein, Arnold *(Librettist)* 1122, 1354
Weinstein, Arnold *(Lyricist)* 369, 1122, 1354, 3937
Weinstein, Edward A. *(Composer)* 1626, 3552
Weinstein, Edward A. *(Lyricist)* 1626, 3552
Weinstein, Robert S. *(Producer)* 4431
Weinstein, Sol *(Librettist)* 427
Weinstock, Jack *(Librettist)* 1991, 2019
Weintraub, Fred *(Director)* 1596
Weir, Helen *(Cast)* 4322
Weisgal, Meyer W. *(Producer)* 1196
Weishar, Joseph *(Set Design)* 2887
Weisman, Sam *(Director)* 2470
Weisman, Sari *(Lighting Designer)* 4540
Weismar, Lorraine *(Cast)* 4352
Weiss, Elliot *(Composer)* 430, 1079
Weiss, Elliot *(Musical Director)* 430
Weiss, Elliot *(Orchestrations)* 2477
Weiss, George David *(Composer)* 825, 2230, 2681, 2987, 3343, 4022
Weiss, George David *(Librettist)* 825, 2230, 2681
Weiss, George David *(Lyricist)* 1290, 1390, 2230, 2681, 2987, 3628, 3874, 4022
Weiss, Gordon J. *(Cast)* 2318
Weiss, Jonathan *(Producer)* 3076
Weiss, Joseph *(Librettist)* 3587
Weiss, Joseph *(Lyricist)* 3587
Weiss, Juliellen *(Costumes)* 1730
Weiss, L. *(Composer)* 4193
Weiss, L. *(Lyricist)* 4193
Weiss, Marc B. *(Lighting Designer)* 262, 599, 1268, 1289, 1713, 2231, 3517, 3643, 3718, 3902, 3909, 4534, 4743
Weiss, Noel *(Producer)* 73
Weiss, Peter *(Author)* 3445
Weiss, Peter *(Lyricist)* 3445
Weiss, Peter Eliot *(Librettist)* 3901
Weiss, Peter Howard *(Composer)* 67
Weiss, Peter Howard *(Lyricist)* 67
Weiss, Stanley G. *(Producer)* 2887
Weiss, Stephen *(Composer)* 1840, 4264
Weiss, Stephen *(Lyricist)* 4264
Weissberger, Felix *(Producer)* 2327
Weissler, Barry *(Producer)* 589, 753, 1713
Weissler, Fran *(Producer)* 589, 753, 1713
Weissman, Bernard *(Dance Arranger)* 4782
Weissman, Bernard *(Orchestrations)* 4782
Weissman, Bernard *(Vocal Arranger)* 4782
Weissmuller, Johnny *(Cast)* 173, 417
Weist, George D. *(Composer)* 1302
Weist, George David *(Composer)* 4748
Weitz, Eric *(Cast)* 1914
Weitz, Millie *(Cast)* 3501
Weitzenhoffer, Max *(Producer)* 1149, 1775, 3608, 4349, 4695
Weitzman, Ira *(Director)* 3221
Weixelbaum, Karl *(Incidental Music)* 4859
Welch, Ben *(Cast)* 3384
Welch, Charles *(Cast)* 3696
Welch, Eddie *(Librettist)* 1126, 1135, 1136
Welch, Edgar *(Composer)* 1722
Welch, Edgar *(Lyricist)* 1722
Welch, Elisabeth *(Cast)* 441, 740, 2204, 3214, 3808
Welch, Joe *(Cast)* 2506
Welch, Ken *(Composer)* 3941, 4047
Welch, Ken *(Lyricist)* 3941
Welch, Kenneth *(Composer)* 2288
Welch, Kenneth *(Lyricist)* 2288
Welch, Loren *(Cast)* 2582
Welch, Melba *(Cast)* 2099
Welch, Patrick *(Composer)* 4264
Welch, Patrick *(Lyricist)* 4264
Welchman, Harry *(Cast)* 325
Welchman, Henry *(Cast)* 3586
Weld *(Costumes)* 1225, 2423
Weld *(Set Design)* 2423
Weld, Arthur *(Composer)* 246, 2495, 3129, 3976, 4590
Weld, Arthur *(Lyricist)* 246, 4590
Weld, Arthur *(Musical Director)* 20, 350, 1313, 2495, 2803, 3494, 3805, 3976, 4187, 4293
Weld, Bill *(Cast)* 3714
Weldon, Bunny *(Choreographer)* 796, 3069
Weldon, Bunny *(Director)* 1343
Weldon, Charles *(Cast)* 1671
Weldon, Joan *(Cast)* 2295, 2838
Weldon, M. Francis *(Choreographer)* 717, 910, 1033, 4427
Weldon, M. Francis *(Costumes)* 717
Weldon, M. Francis *(Director)* 199
Weldon, Martin *(Librettist)* 1880
Weldon, Mortimer *(Cast)* 3776
Weldy, Frederick *(Musical Director)* 424
Weldy, Max *(Costumes)* 202, 1490, 1491, 2293, 2843, 2900, 4154, 4188
Welford, Dallas *(Cast)* 2768
Welford, Nancy *(Cast)* 2112, 2380, 3072, 3648
Welgel, Hans *(Librettist)* 1413
Welisch, Ernst *(Author)* 2384, 2469, 2666, 3084
Welisch, Ernst *(Librettist)* 1044
Welisch, Ernst *(Lyricist)* 1044
Welk, Lawrence *(Composer)* 3444
Well Jr., Edward *(Cast)* 3978
Welleminsky, J.M. *(Author)* 4486
Weller, Michael *(Author)* 282
Weller, Michael *(Composer)* 282
Weller, Michael *(Librettist)* 2953
Weller, Michael *(Lyricist)* 282, 2953
Welles, Halsted *(Author)* 4191
Welles, Halsted *(Director)* 3947
Welles, Halsted *(Librettist)* 3947
Welles, Orson *(Cast)* 189, 979, 1899, 2257
Welles, Orson *(Director)* 189, 919, 979, 2257
Welles, Orson *(Librettist)* 189
Welles, Orson *(Producer)* 189, 979, 2257
Welles II, Benjamin *(Composer)* 4039
Welles II, Benjamin *(Librettist)* 4039
Wellesley, Charles *(Cast)* 2662
Wellington, Amanda *(Cast)* 4313
Wells *(Composer)* 2376
Wells *(Lyricist)* 1132, 2376

Wells, Caroline *(Lyricist)* 2495
Wells, Carolyn *(Librettist)* 2701, 3611
Wells, Carolyn *(Lyricist)* 1417, 2701
Wells, Christopher *(Cast)* 198, 1092, 4297
Wells, Craig *(Cast)* 275
Wells, Deanna *(Cast)* 1701
Wells, Dickie *(Cast)* 899
Wells, Eleanor *(Librettist)* 4572
Wells, H.G. *(Author)* 1721
Wells, Jack *(Composer)* 965, 1334, 3189
Wells, Jack *(Lyricist)* 3189
Wells, John *(Librettist)* 1251
Wells, Matthew *(Librettist)* 1732
Wells, Matthew *(Lyricist)* 1732
Wells, Pauline *(Costumes)* 1244
Wells, Rhea *(Costumes)* 720
Wells, Rhea *(Set Design)* 720
Wells, Robert *(Composer)* 520
Wells, Robert *(Lyricist)* 520, 4346
Wells, Stephen *(Producer)* 2702, 4349
Wells, Tico *(Cast)* 2283, 4171
Wells, Tony *(Cast)* 3927
Wells, William K. *(Director)* 1494, 4572
Wells, William K. *(Librettist)* 67, 1481, 1486, 1487, 1488, 1489, 1490, 1491, 1493, 1549, 1690, 1779, 2227, 2734, 2850, 4296, 4300, 4572
Wells, William K. *(Lyricist)* 1549, 2912
Welsh, Harry *(Cast)* 203, 2808
Welsh, Jack *(Producer)* 709
Welsh, Jane *(Cast)* 2547
Welsh, Kenneth *(Cast)* 4129
Welsh, Scott *(Cast)* 2730
Welty, Eudora *(Author)* 3733
Welty, Eudora *(Librettist)* 2554, 2560
Welty, Max *(Cast)* 4528
Welzer, Irving *(Producer)* 3600
Wendall, Beth *(Librettist)* 3103
Wendel, Elmarie *(Cast)* 249, 392, 1018, 1924, 2522, 3217, 4319
Wendling, Pete *(Composer)* 3737
Wendt, George *(Cast)* 4690
Wenger, John *(Set Design)* 1419, 1485, 1617, 1643, 1859, 3179, 3379, 3489, 4118, 4532, 4818, 4819
Wenger, Wally *(Director)* 4265
Wenrich, Percy *(Cast)* 3153
Wenrich, Percy *(Composer)* 132, 371, 529, 670, 913, 929, 1208, 1248, 1687, 1920, 2402, 2403, 2405, 3259, 3425, 3662, 3712, 4054, 4673
Wenrich, Percy *(Lyricist)* 1687, 3662
Wenter, John *(Set Design)* 3243
Wentworth, Edward S. *(Cast)* 1392
Wentworth, Estelle *(Cast)* 1521
Wentworth, Scott *(Cast)* 147, 1702, 2354, 4619
Wentworth, Scott *(Librettist)* 1702
Wenz, Carol *(Costumes)* 2968, 3688
Wenzel, Leopold *(Musical Director)* 205
Wenzelberg, L. *(Costumes)* 1424
Weppner, Christina *(Costumes)* 2049
Weppner, Christina *(Set Design)* 3908
Werau, A. *(Composer)* 2419
Werba, Louis F. *(Producer)* 21, 966, 1003, 2528, 2886, 4119, 4476
Werber & Luescher
See also Louis A. Werber and Mark A. Luescher.
Werba & Luescher *(Producer)* 1849, 3771, 4250
Werfel, Franz *(Author)* 1196, 1660
Werkheiser, John *(Choreographer)* 4168
Werner, Fred *(Dance Arranger)* 837, 2523, 3196, 4238
Werner, Fred *(Musical Director)* 1891, 3526, 4238
Werner, Fred *(Orchestrations)* 4013
Werner, Fred *(Vocal Arranger)* 3815
Werner, Howard *(Lighting Designer)* 1832
Werner, Ken *(Musical Director)* 2426
Werner, Ken *(Orchestrations)* 2426
Werner, Mort *(Vocal Arranger)* 4331
Wernher, Hilda *(Author)* 751
Wernick, Richard *(Composer)* 3186
Wertheim Studios *(Set Design)* 1989
Wertimer, Edward *(Cast)* 750
Wertimer, Ned *(Cast)* 3497
Wertimer Jr., Sidney *(Cast)* 1885
Wescott, Marcy *(Cast)* 514, 3916, 4420, 4479
Wesley, James K. *(Cast)* 2303
Wesley, Richard *(Librettist)* 1099, 4535
Wesley, Ward *(Lyricist)* 4809
Weslyn, Louis *(Lyricist)* 2154, 2291, 2662, 3973, 4723
Wessell, Vivian *(Cast)* 94
Wessels, Henri *(Cast)* 877, 883, 892, 3709
West, Alvy *(Composer)* 3440
West, Alvy *(Musical Director)* 3449, 3498, 4660, 4710
West, Alvy *(Orchestrations)* 2726
West, Alvy *(Vocal Arranger)* 3449, 3498, 4710
West, Arthur *(Cast)* 3842
West, Augusta *(Cast)* 938
West, Bernie *(Cast)* 363
West, Blanche *(Cast)* 1707
West, Bob *(Composer)* 3739
West, Bob *(Lyricist)* 3739
West, Buster *(Cast)* 1336, 2366, 4667
West, Clarence *(Musical Director)* 132, 3052, 3679, 3865
West, Clarence *(Orchestrations)* 2931
West, Con *(Composer)* 792
West, Con *(Lyricist)* 792
West, Dennis *(Arrangements)* 4055
West, Dennis *(Musical Director)* 4055
West, Edwin *(Producer)* 3920
West, Eugene *(Lyricist)* 4197
West, Everett *(Cast)* 420, 3767
West, Fay *(Cast)* 1154
West, Harry *(Cast)* 4762
West, Helen Stevenson *(Costumes)* 750, 4303
West, Helen Stevenson *(Set Design)* 750
West, John *(Cast)* 1332, 2366
West, Mae *(Author)* 1036
West, Mae *(Cast)* 638, 1036, 2870, 4063, 4553, 4656, 4712
West, Mae *(Director)* 1036
West, Matt *(Choreographer)* 330
West, Moritz *(Lyricist)* 205
West, Paul *(Librettist)* 2722, 3134, 3422, 4414
West, Paul *(Lyricist)* 591, 719, 737, 1226, 1246, 1417,

1464, 1504, 1526, 2448, 2722, 2826, 2906, 2990, 3052, 3134, 3229, 3313, 3422, 3450, 3451, 3679, 3710, 3753, 3856, 3857, 3882, 4663, 4666, 4723, 4801
West, Will *(Cast)* 3350
West, Will *(Lyricist)* 3350
West, William Herman *(Cast)* 2959
West and McGinty, Willie *(Cast)* 420
Westbrook, Frank *(Choreographer)* 616
Westbrooke, Evelyn *(Cast)* 574
Westby-Gibson, Richard *(Costumes)* 4540
Westenberg, Robert *(Cast)* 754, 1015, 2065, 2143, 3862, 4210
Westendorf, Thomas P. *(Composer)* 4390
Westerfield, James *(Director)* 4486
Westergaard, Louise *(Producer)* 4091, 4137
Westerly, Pauline *(Cast)* 1647
Western Producing Co. *(Producer)* 1560
Westerton, Frank *(Cast)* 2340
Westford, Owen *(Cast)* 3625
Westley, Helen *(Cast)* 3686
Westley, John *(Cast)* 1904, 2059
Westminster Productions *(Producer)* 1887
Westmoreland, Lillian *(Cast)* 3660
Weston, Charles H. *(Cast)* 3450
Weston, Ellen *(Librettist)* 1997
Weston, Ellen *(Lyricist)* 1997
Weston, Jack *(Cast)* 3299
Weston, Jim *(Cast)* 280
Weston, Lucy *(Cast)* 965, 1524, 4802
Weston, Paul *(Composer)* 3449, 4743
Weston, Paul *(Musical Director)* 192, 193
Weston, R.P. *(Composer)* 336, 1208, 3084, 3117, 3259
Weston, R.P. *(Librettist)* 133, 702, 1855, 2547, 4299
Weston, R.P. *(Lyricist)* 133, 336, 1208, 1784, 1916, 1963, 2833, 2858, 3222, 3259, 4299, 4757
Weston, Ruth *(Cast)* 121, 1352
Westport County Playhouse *(Producer)* 689
Westport Productions *(Producer)* 1609
Wetmore, Joan *(Cast)* 4479
Wever, Edward L. *(Lyricist)* 720
Wever, Ned *(Cast)* 3861
Wever, Ned *(Composer)* 3728
Wever, Ned *(Lyricist)* 418, 3728, 3783
Wexler, Connie *(Set Design)* 602
Wexler, George
See also George Wexter Presents Inc.
Wexler, Irving *(Librettist)* 3914
Wexler, Jerry *(Producer)* 3297
Wexler, Peter *(Lighting Designer)* 550, 2248
Wexler, Peter *(Set Design)* 550, 602, 1764, 2248, 2874
Weygandt, Gene *(Cast)* 3461
Weyman, Stanley *(Author)* 3680
Whalen, Harold *(Cast)* 1494, 2140
Whalen, Michael *(Cast)* 831
Whaley, Thomas *(Orchestrations)* 1984
Wharton, Carly *(Producer)* 2940
Wharton, Diana *(Composer)* 1344
Wheat, Lawrence *(Cast)* 1271, 1543, 1826, 2714, 2745, 2906, 2923, 3229, 3882
Wheatley, Clifford *(Director)* 4159
Wheatley, Joanne *(Cast)* 863
Wheaton, Anna *(Cast)* 340, 2668, 2884, 3230, 3395, 3478, 3773, 4360, 4521, 4644, 4853
Wheaton, Gladys *(Cast)* 202
Whedon, John *(Librettist)* 4314
Whedon, Tom *(Librettist)* 73, 2935
Whedon, Tom *(Lyricist)* 73, 427, 1049, 2935
Wheelan, Albertine Randall *(Costumes)* 1484, 3443, 3839, 4066
Wheelan, Alfred *(Cast)* 1305
Wheeler, Bert *(Cast)* 67, 568, 1396, 3121, 3138, 3719, 4366, 4817
Wheeler, Betty *(Cast)* 568, 4817
Wheeler, Billy Edd *(Librettist)* 1781
Wheeler, Billy Edd *(Lyricist)* 1781
Wheeler, Francis *(Cast)* 694
Wheeler, Francis *(Lyricist)* 1343, 2706
Wheeler, Harold *(Dance Arranger)* 798, 3603
Wheeler, Harold *(Musical Director)* 40, 1074, 3603, 4485
Wheeler, Harold *(Orchestrations)* 146, 572, 661, 1103, 1236, 1699, 4286, 4722
Wheeler, Harold *(Vocal Arranger)* 4286
Wheeler, Harris *(Composer)* 474
Wheeler, Hugh *(Librettist)* 2536, 2539, 2805, 4233, 4459
Wheeler, Hugh *(Lyricist)* 2607
Wheeler, John *(Cast)* 4238
Wheeler, Josh *(Cast)* 3841
Wheeler, Margaret *(Cast)* 934
Wheeler, Ruth *(Cast)* 1343
Wheeler, Sandra *(Cast)* 705
Wheeler, Van Rensselaer *(Cast)* 356, 737, 1071, 1470, 1912, 2233, 2399, 2668, 2936, 3805, 3839, 4404
Wheeler, Virginia *(Cast)* 731, 980
Whelan, Alf C. *(Cast)* 618, 1543, 2101, 2548
Whelan, Harold
See also Jan & Whelan.
Whelan, Harold *(Cast)* 2636
Whelp, William C. *(Cast)* 3981
Whetsol, Arthur *(Composer)* 895
Whidden, Jay *(Composer)* 4806
Whiffen, Thomas *(Cast)* 3422
Whipper, Leigh *(Cast)* 552, 691, 2792, 3807, 4763
Whipper, Leigh *(Director)* 2645
Whipper, Leigh *(Librettist)* 3807, 4763
Whipper, Leigh *(Lyricist)* 552
Whipple, Waldo *(Cast)* 3030
Whistler, Edna *(Cast)* 929, 3184
Whistler, Rex *(Set Design)* 791
Whitaker, Grenna *(Cast)* 3814
Whitaker, Johnnie *(Cast)* 2553
Whitaker, Mical *(Director)* 3905
Whitaker, Rodgers E.M. *(Author)* 1402
Whitcup, Leonard *(Composer)* 3926
Whitcup, Leonard *(Lyricist)* 3926
White, Alexander *(Cast)* 291
White, Alton Fitzgerald *(Cast)* 789
White, B. *(Composer)* 4193
White, B. *(Lyricist)* 4193
White, D. *(Composer)* 4193
White, D. *(Lyricist)* 4193

White, Dan *(Composer)* 4826
White, David A. *(Cast)* 1822
White, Diz *(Cast)* 1166
White, E.B. *(Librettist)* 1874, 3946
White, Elmore *(Composer)* 2942
White, Elmore *(Lyricist)* 2942
White, Elsie *(Composer)* 4815
White, Frances *(Cast)* 1919, 1992, 2216, 2456, 3466, 4810, 4836, 4840
White, George *(Cast)* 645, 1151, 1482, 1483, 1484, 1485, 1491, 1824, 2734, 2900, 4655, 4805, 4809
White, George *(Choreographer)* 1482, 1489, 1494
White, George *(Composer)* 1491, 3685
White, George *(Director)* 1323, 1481, 1483, 1484, 1485, 1486, 1487, 1488, 1489, 1490, 1491, 1492, 1493, 1494, 2734, 2813
White, George *(Librettist)* 1481, 1483, 1484, 1485, 1486, 1487, 1488, 1489, 1490, 1491, 1492, 1493, 1494, 2734
White, George *(Lyricist)* 1481, 1482, 3685
White, George *(Producer)* 1323, 1481, 1482, 1483, 1484, 1485, 1486, 1487, 1488, 1489, 1490, 1491, 1492, 1493, 1494, 2734, 2813, 3808, 3883
White, Georgie *(Cast)* 1640
White, Harry *(Composer)* 4137
White, Harry Sheldon *(Librettist)* 1562
White, Henry
See Roland Oliver.
White, Herbert *(Choreographer)* 4256
White, Jack *(Cast)* 1491
White, Jane *(Cast)* 33, 52, 2565, 3088, 3288, 3456, 3664
White, Jane *(Composer)* 2876
White, Jane Douglass *(Musical Director)* 2219
White, Jesse *(Cast)* 2304, 3036
White, Josh *(Cast)* 467
White, Josh *(Composer)* 467
White, Joshua *(Cast)* 2225
White, Kenneth *(Librettist)* 2751
White, Lillias *(Cast)* 261, 3628, 3739, 3757
White, Lilyan *(Cast)* 4150
White, Marjorie *(Cast)* 1831, 1979, 2382
White, Michael *(Producer)* 682, 2006
White, Miles *(Costumes)* 84, 145, 172, 372, 454, 462, 607, 649, 660, 692, 999, 1002, 1101, 1140, 1369, 1475, 1548, 1711, 1791, 1886, 2190, 2864, 3234, 3263, 3619, 3954, 4180, 4270, 4323, 4366, 4386, 4402, 4450, 4499, 4516, 4798, 4826
White, Miles *(Set Design)* 3715
White, Olive *(Cast)* 3759
White, Onna *(Cast)* 183, 1706, 3563
White, Onna *(Choreographer)* 1441, 1511, 1634, 1721, 1744, 1955, 2053, 2058, 2106, 2150, 2449, 2713, 2965, 3016, 3897, 3900, 4270, 4682, 4744
White, Onna *(Director)* 1441
White, Paul *(Cast)* 856, 2259
White, Richard *(Cast)* 1155, 1171
White, Rita *(Cast)* 1950
White, Robert *(Cast)* 1657
White, Roxanna *(Cast)* 3688
White, Ruth *(Cast)* 586, 1220, 4150
White, Sam *(Cast)* 3402, 3958
White, Sammy *(Cast)* 1529, 1577, 1689, 1823, 2814, 3949, 4792
White, Stanley *(Producer)* 4286
White, Susan *(Lighting Designer)* 2250
White, Susan A. *(Lighting Designer)* 3211
White, T.H. *(Author)* 623
White, Terri *(Cast)* 305, 788, 2250, 4619
White, Terri *(Choreographer)* 2100
White, Thelma *(Cast)* 1135, 3713, 3822, 4118, 4299
White, Willard *(Cast)* 4447
White, William *(Composer)* 1919
White, William C. *(Librettist)* 4152
White, Willy *(Composer)* 1919, 1920, 4742
White, Willy *(Lyricist)* 1919
White Heather Producing Co. *(Producer)* 2056
White Horse Tavern Prod. *(Producer)* 2300
White Jr., Al *(Choreographer)* 1476, 2817, 3138, 3823, 4131, 4314
White's Jazz Rabbits, Gonzell *(Cast)* 986
Whitechurch, Missy *(Choreographer)* 564
Whitehead *(Composer)* 2133
Whitehead *(Lyricist)* 2133
Whitehead, Allen *(Producer)* 3526
Whitehead, Fannie *(Cast)* 2285
Whitehead, Joe *(Cast)* 3255
Whitehead, Joseph *(Cast)* 4381
Whitehead, Mary *(Costumes)* 1769
Whitehead, O.Z. *(Cast)* 1342, 2105, 3103
Whitehead, Ralph *(Cast)* 376, 391, 1580
Whitehead, Robert *(Producer)* 837, 3577, 4004
Whitehead, Ron *(Costumes)* 3167
Whitehill, B.T. *(Set Design)* 4462, 4518
Whitehouse, Fred *(Composer)* 3926
Whitehouse, Fred *(Lyricist)* 3926
Whitelaw, Arthur *(Director)* 456, 4034
Whitelaw, Arthur *(Librettist)* 456, 4034
Whitelaw, Arthur *(Producer)* 594, 2874, 3900, 4176, 4264, 4343, 4537, 4783
Whiteman, Paul *(Cast)* 2406, 2638, 3153, 4847
Whiteman, Paul *(Composer)* 1643
Whiteman and His Orchestra, Paul *(Cast)* 662, 1485, 2258, 4817, 4845, 4846
Whitey's Jitterbugs *(Cast)* 497
Whitfield, Alice *(Cast)* 2188
Whitfield, Hugh *(Costumes)* 4629
Whitfield, June *(Cast)* 2608
Whitfield, Norman *(Composer)* 166, 3695, 4534
Whitfield, Norman *(Lyricist)* 166, 3695, 4534
Whitford, Annabelle *(Cast)* 4803
Whitham, Charles W. *(Set Design)* 4103
Whiting, Byron *(Puppeteer)* 997, 4660, 4710
Whiting, Byron *(Voice)* 3498
Whiting, George *(Cast)* 3396
Whiting, George *(Lyricist)* 879, 1134, 2978, 3989, 4808, 4821
Whiting, Jack *(Cast)* 111, 152, 323, 622, 1600, 1791, 1800, 1929, 1931, 1973, 2402, 3312, 3335, 3655, 3659, 3924, 4150, 4180, 4267, 4557, 4651, 4766
Whiting, Mack *(Director)* 2619

Whiting, Margaret *(Cast)* 4272
Whiting, Ralph *(Cast)* 2836
Whiting, Richard A. *(Composer)* 393, 709, 1387, 1482, 1638, 1689, 2574, 3018, 3139, 3297, 3404, 3737, 3783, 3842, 3985, 4267, 4393, 4421, 4654, 4799
Whiting, Richard A. *(Lyricist)* 1638, 3297, 4654
Whitman, Bill *(Cast)* 1155
Whitman, Stuart C. *(Lighting Designer)* 3002
Whitman, Walt *(Author)* 2433
Whitman, Walt *(Lyricist)* 1416, 2433, 4744
Whitmore, D. *(Cast)* 2293
Whitmore, Dean *(Director)* 1257
Whitmore, Maude *(Cast)* 148
Whitney, B.C. *(Producer)* 561, 639, 740, 1154, 2155, 2159, 2347, 3078, 3443, 4333
Whitney, Doris *(Cast)* 3174
Whitney, F.C. *(Producer)* 1071, 2408, 2632, 3078, 3488, 4200
Whitney, Fred C. *(Lyricist)* 3199
Whitney, Fred C. *(Producer)* 742, 1682, 2179, 3199, 3732
Whitney, Howard *(Composer)* 1308
Whitney, Joan *(Composer)* 1296
Whitney, Joan *(Lyricist)* 1296
Whitney, Nina *(Cast)* 216, 3011
Whitney, Salem *(Cast)* 1019
Whitney, Salem *(Librettist)* 1019
Whitney, Salem Tutt *(Cast)* 291, 449, 731, 816, 980, 987, 1479, 1906, 2013, 2791, 2792, 3040, 3062, 3200, 3241, 4520, 4751
Whitney, Salem Tutt *(Composer)* 449, 987, 1479, 1906, 2013, 2791, 3040, 3241, 4520
Whitney, Salem Tutt *(Director)* 2013
Whitney, Salem Tutt *(Librettist)* 291, 449, 731, 816, 980, 987, 1479, 1906, 2013, 2791, 2792, 3040, 3062, 3200, 3241, 4520, 4751
Whitney, Salem Tutt *(Lyricist)* 449, 816, 980, 987, 1479, 1906, 2013, 2791, 2792, 3040, 3062, 3241, 4520, 4751
Whitney, Salem Tutt *(Producer)* 291, 731, 816, 980, 987, 1479, 1514, 1906, 2013, 2791, 2792, 3040, 3062, 3200, 4520, 4751
Whitney Opera Company *(Producer)* 307, 3053, 4646
Whitredge, Jack *(Cast)* 3314
Whitridge, Arnold *(Cast)* 2287
Whitson, Beth Slater *(Lyricist)* 4799
Whittaker *(Composer)* 1963
Whittaker *(Lyricist)* 1963
Whittell, Josephine *(Cast)* 380, 3184
Whittlesey, White *(Cast)* 3730
Whorf, Richard *(Cast)* 1342
Whorf, Richard *(Director)* 3895
Whorf, Richard *(Librettist)* 1342
Whytal, Russ *(Cast)* 1187
Whyte, Ron *(Author)* 669, 1418
Whyte, Ronny *(Cast)* 62, 3124
Wicheler *(Author)* 94
Wichmann, Scott *(Cast)* 533
Wickand, Lyons *(Cast)* 1795
Wickersham, Robert *(Director)* 4543
Wickersham, Robert *(Producer)* 4303, 4543
Wickes, Joseph
See also Unitt & Wickes.
Wickes, Joseph *(Set Design)* 2756, 2829, 3723
Wickes, Mary *(Cast)* 979, 1948, 2187, 2729, 3390, 4142
Wickland, Lyons *(Cast)* 2981
Wickwire, Nancy *(Cast)* 1864, 4715
Widdoes, James *(Cast)* 2152
Widdoes, Kathleen *(Cast)* 669, 1294, 3000, 4609, 4749
Wideman, Beverly *(Cast)* 755, 3697
Widerman, Steven *(Puppeteer)* 56
Widney, Stone *(Director)* 101, 2941
Wiegert, Rene *(Musical Director)* 1045, 1211, 2248, 3235
Wiegert, Rene *(Vocal Arranger)* 1045, 3235
Wiener, H. *(Composer)* 4193
Wiener, H. *(Lyricist)* 4193
Wiener, Stuart *(Producer)* 766
Wierzel, Robert *(Lighting Designer)* 655, 2185, 2932
Wierzel, Robert M. *(Lighting Designer)* 4515
Wiest, Dianne *(Cast)* 2429
Wiest, Stan *(Cast)* 4124
Wietrzychowski, Stanley *(Musical Director)* 4175
Wietrzychowski, Stanley *(Orchestrations)* 4175
Wiffen, Mrs. Thomas *(Cast)* 2277
Wiggenton, Eliot *(Author)* 1372
Wiggin, Tom *(Cast)* 2555
Wiggins, Fred *(Cast)* 1421
Wightman, Robert *(Lighting Designer)* 4629
Wightman, Robert *(Set Design)* 4629
Wilberg, John *(Producer)* 2817
Wilbur, A.L. *(Producer)* 3676
Wilbur, Crane *(Author)* 4083
Wilbur, Crane *(Lyricist)* 1666
Wilbur, Mabel *(Cast)* 2944
Wilbur, Richard *(Librettist)* 2877
Wilbur, Richard *(Lyricist)* 630
Wilcher, James "Red" *(Cast)* 1093, 1425
Wilcox, Carol *(Cast)* 643
Wilcox, Ed *(Lighting Designer)* 4729
Wilcox, Ed *(Set Design)* 4729
Wilcox, Frank *(Cast)* 1308
Wilcox, Larry *(Orchestrations)* 154, 278, 808, 842, 1158, 1585, 2230, 2583, 2820, 3126, 3428, 3429, 3551, 3788, 3931, 3992, 4588, 4764
Wilcox, Ralph *(Cast)* 40, 4722
Wilcox, Ruth *(Librettist)* 3172
Wildberg, John *(Producer)* 3301
Wilde, Cornel *(Cast)* 2202, 2946, 4670
Wilde, Oscar *(Author)* 1194, 3195, 3236
Wilde, R. *(Author)* 2540
Wilde, R. *(Librettist)* 2540
Wilder, Alec *(Composer)* 1049, 1744, 2339, 3175, 3195, 3286, 3496, 3941, 4256, 4367
Wilder, Alec *(Lyricist)* 3175
Wilder, Amy *(Cast)* 3682
Wilder, Anne *(Producer)* 4
Wilder, Billy *(Author)* 3603, 3972, 4196
Wilder, Billy *(Director)* 4217
Wilder, Billy *(Screenwriter)* 4217
Wilder, Carrie *(Cast)* 3305
Wilder, Clinton *(Producer)* 1184, 2678, 3691
Wilder, Duane *(Producer)* 2418
Wilder, Gene *(Cast)* 1122

Wilder, Jim *(Cast)* 1155
Wilder, Laura Ingalls *(Author)* 3553
Wilder, Thornton *(Author)* 1701, 1828, 2703, 3324, 4008
Wilderman, Steve *(Puppeteer)* 3449
Wilderman, William *(Cast)* 3035, 3691
Wildhack, Robert *(Cast)* 2475
Wildhorn, Frank *(Composer)* 2198, 4229, 4560
Wildhorn, Frank *(Lyricist)* 4229
Wildhorn, Frank *(Vocal Arranger)* 2198
Wile, Everett *(Director)* 2259
Wile, Joan *(Lyricist)* 1023
Wiles, Anthony *(Director)* 732
Wiley, Dennis *(Composer)* 2483
Wiley, Dennis *(Musical Director)* 2483
Wilhelm *(Costumes)* 178, 256, 333, 719, 736, 1454, 1555, 2394, 2666, 3098, 3228, 3268, 3675, 3948, 4393, 4760
Wilhelm, Carl *(Composer)* 3450
Wilhelm, Carl *(Lyricist)* 3450
Wilhelm, Julius *(Author)* 2249, 2594, 3839, 4119, 4490
Wilk, Max *(Librettist)* 63, 943, 3020, 4018
Wilke, Hubert *(Cast)* 1260, 2963, 4500
Wilke, James *(Costumes)* 1940
Wilke, Ray *(Set Design)* 1769
Wilkerson, Arnold *(Cast)* 1072
Wilkerson, Guy *(Cast)* 831
Wilkes, Anna *(Cast)* 1707, 2291
Wilkes, Patricia *(Cast)* 3286
Wilkes, Thomas *(Producer)* 69, 3072
Wilkes, Tom *(Producer)* 4429
Wilkins, Anita *(Cast)* 43
Wilkins, Jeffrey *(Cast)* 4020
Wilkinson, Colm *(Cast)* 2442
Wilkinson, Dudley *(Cast)* 3623
Wilkinson, Dudley *(Composer)* 3623
Wilkinson, Kate *(Cast)* 2965
Wilkinson, Marc *(Composer)* 2260
Wilkinson, Michael *(Cast)* 4830
Wilkinson, Ralph Norman *(Musical Director)* 4409
Wilkof, Lee *(Cast)* 140, 212, 2544, 3557
Wilkof, Lee S. *(Composer)* 3557
Wilkof, Lee S. *(Lyricist)* 3557
Will, Ethyl *(Dance Arranger)* 1146
Will You Remember Prods. *(Producer)* 4251
Willard, Dorothy *(Producer)* 2464
Willard, Harold *(Cast)* 1493
Willard, John *(Cast)* 3147
Willcock, Dave *(Cast)* 4316
Wille, Frank *(Composer)* 2580
Willemetz, Albert *(Author)* 3466
Willemetz, Albert *(Lyricist)* 1176, 3769, 3905
Willeminsky, Ignaz M. *(Author)* 1110
Willemote, Albert *(Lyricist)* 2356
Willens, Doris *(Librettist)* 3476
Willens, Doris *(Lyricist)* 3476
Willenz, Maria *(Costumes)* 2
Willes, Christine *(Cast)* 3901
Willes, Christine *(Librettist)* 3901
Willett, John *(English Lyrics)* 4370
Willett, John *(Librettist)* 4370
Willey, Robert A. *(Producer)* 1698
William, W.R. *(Composer)* 631
William, Warren *(Cast)* 1221
William Patterson College *(Producer)* 1435
Williams *(Lyricist)* 736
Williams, Alexander *(Composer)* 3946
Williams, Alexander *(Lyricist)* 3946
Williams, Alfred *(Set Design)* 284
Williams, Ann *(Cast)* 167
Williams, Barbara *(Cast)* 4173
Williams, Ben *(Cast)* 3022
Williams, Bert *(Cast)* 9, 295, 545, 1599, 2111, 2979, 4088, 4804, 4805, 4806, 4808, 4809, 4810, 4811, 4813, 4838, 4851
Williams, Bert *(Composer)* 9, 295, 2111, 2979, 3820, 4390, 4697, 4804, 4805, 4806, 4808
Williams, Bert *(Librettist)* 4088
Williams, Bert *(Lyricist)* 295, 3820, 4806
Williams, Bert *(Producer)* 4088
Williams, Betty *(Cast)* 3819
Williams, Bob *(Cast)* 1326, 1842
Williams, Charles *(Cast)* 2888
Williams, Charles LaVont *(Cast)* 2908
Williams, Clarence *(Cast)* 500
Williams, Clarence *(Composer)* 146, 432, 443, 500, 1425, 3297, 3709, 3840, 4282
Williams, Clarence *(Librettist)* 500
Williams, Clarence *(Lyricist)* 39, 432, 443, 500, 1425, 3297, 3709, 3840
Williams, Clarence *(Producer)* 500
Williams, Debbie *(Cast)* 2092
Williams, Derek *(Cast)* 2252
Williams, Diane *(Lighting Designer)* 1701
Williams, Diane *(Set Design)* 1701
Williams, Diane Ferry *(Lighting Designer)* 3461
Williams, Dick *(Cast)* 868
Williams, Dick Anthony *(Cast)* 40
Williams, Dorian *(Cast)* 3814
Williams, Edgerton B. *(Cast)* 1867
Williams, Edna *(Composer)* 1212
Williams, Elizabeth *(Cast)* 3676
Williams, Elizabeth *(Producer)* 921, 3862
Williams, Ellis E. *(Cast)* 3285
Williams, Emlyn *(Author)* 2898
Williams, Emlyn *(Librettist)* 2898
Williams, Emlyn *(Lyricist)* 2898
Williams, F.H. *(Composer)* 295, 2111
Williams, F.H. *(Lyricist)* 295
Williams, Florence *(Cast)* 2394
Williams, Frances *(Cast)* 201, 532, 799, 1207, 1489, 1490, 1491, 2135, 2453, 2475, 3131, 4586, 4702
Williams, Frank *(Lyricist)* 3797
Williams, Fred *(Choreographer)* 762
Williams, Freida *(Cast)* 1713
Williams, Fritz *(Cast)* 824, 1926, 2858, 4203, 4359
Williams, George H. *(Set Design)* 4434
Williams, Grace *(Costumes)* 3276
Williams, Grafton *(Cast)* 1561
Williams, Gus *(Cast)* 644
Williams, Gus *(Composer)* 644
Williams, Gus *(Lyricist)* 644

Williams, Hannah *(Cast)* 4235
Williams, Harry *(Composer)* 3020
Williams, Harry *(Lyricist)* 349, 561, 685, 736, 822, 954, 965, 1247, 1566, 2025, 2232, 2889, 2892, 2960, 2990, 3020, 3085, 3205, 3268, 3332, 3675, 3996, 4570, 4753, 4787
Williams, Harry H. *(Composer)* 3259
Williams, Harry H. *(Lyricist)* 3073, 3259
Williams, Hattie *(Cast)* 1066, 1537, 1538, 2498, 2548, 3745, 3751, 3753
Williams, Henry *(Lyricist)* 3525
Williams, Henry "Rubber Legs" *(Cast)* 878
Williams, Herb *(Cast)* 216, 1135, 4637
Williams, Hope *(Cast)* 1972, 3131, 4177
Williams, Hugh *(Composer)* 3605
Williams, Irene *(Cast)* 1385
Williams, Ivan *(Composer)* 1736
Williams, Ivan *(Lyricist)* 1736
Williams, Jack *(Cast)* 1494, 2103, 2453, 2809, 3713
Williams, Jack Eric *(Cast)* 4233
Williams, Jack Eric *(Composer)* 2992
Williams, Jack Eric *(Librettist)* 2992
Williams, Jack Eric *(Lyricist)* 2992
Williams, Jack Eric *(Musical Director)* 2992
Williams, Jesse *(Composer)* 45, 175
Williams, Jesse *(Musical Director)* 1193
Williams, Jill *(Composer)* 2650, 3653
Williams, Jill *(Librettist)* 3653
Williams, Jill *(Lyricist)* 2650, 3653
Williams, Jill *(Musical Director)* 2650
Williams, Jodi *(Cast)* 3788
Williams, John *(Composer)* 4399
Williams, John *(Lighting Designer)* 1701
Williams, John *(Set Design)* 1701
Williams, John H. *(Producer)* 4127
Williams, John R. *(Musical Director)* 1229
Williams, Lotte *(Cast)* 9
Williams, Lottie *(Cast)* 295, 2111
Williams, Malcolm *(Composer)* 2819
Williams, Malcolm *(Lyricist)* 2819
Williams, Marian *(Cast)* 1013
Williams, Marie *(Cast)* 3887
Williams, Marshall *(Lighting Designer)* 1592
Williams, Mary Lou *(Cast)* 467
Williams, Mathew J. *(Lighting Designer)* 2197, 4107
Williams, Maud K. *(Producer)* 2062
Williams, Maude *(Cast)* 904
Williams, Maurice *(Composer)* 4264
Williams, Maurice *(Lyricist)* 4264
Williams, Midge *(Cast)* 889
Williams, Mr. *(Costumes)* 2935
Williams, Musa *(Cast)* 1749, 3541
Williams, Olena *(Cast)* 4253
Williams, Pat *(Orchestrations)* 1611
Williams, PeeWee *(Cast)* 739
Williams, Percy G. *(Director)* 522
Williams, Queenie *(Cast)* 2762
Williams, Ralph *(Cast)* 3918
Williams, Richard *(Set Design)* 2692
Williams, Robert *(Cast)* 4495
Williams, Robert T. *(Lighting Designer)* 227
Williams, Robert T. *(Set Design)* 227, 766, 2941, 3527
Williams, Sammy *(Cast)* 746
Williams, Sarah McCord *(Cast)* 3853
Williams, Spencer *(Composer)* 393, 432, 443, 739, 740, 1813, 1986, 3018, 3297, 3614, 3709, 3840
Williams, Spencer *(Lyricist)* 393, 432, 443, 500, 739, 740, 1813, 2266, 3297, 3614, 3709, 3840, 4282
Williams, Sylvia "Kuumba" *(Cast)* 3297
Williams, Taylor *(Cast)* 1088
Williams, Tennessee *(Author)* 3878, 3879
Williams, Timothy *(Cast)* 4309
Williams, Tom *(Cast)* 1766
Williams, Treat *(Cast)* 2787, 3330, 3852
Williams, Vanessa *(Cast)* 3001
Williams, W.R. *(Composer)* 917
Williams, Wade *(Cast)* 4055
Williams, Walter *(Cast)* 3467
Williams, William *(Cast)* 711, 1145, 1391
Williams Sisters, The *(Cast)* 1487
Williamson, Bruce *(Composer)* 1363, 4433
Williamson, Bruce *(Librettist)* 1049, 4433
Williamson, Bruce *(Lyricist)* 1049, 1363, 1436, 3484, 4433
Williamson, Nicol *(Cast)* 3702
Williamson, Ruth *(Cast)* 3708, 4020
Williamstown Th. Festival *(Producer)* 3195
Williford, Steven *(Cast)* 2737
Willis, Herbert Florence *(Cast)* 1594
Willis, Michael *(Cast)* 1004
Willis, Sally *(Cast)* 1166
Willis, Tom *(Composer)* 459
Willis, Walter *(Choreographer)* 2944
Willison, Walter *(Cast)* 556, 1649, 3311, 4481, 4689
Willison, Walter *(Director)* 556
Willison, Walter *(Librettist)* 556, 3311
Willison, Walter *(Lyricist)* 556, 3311
Willison, Walter *(Producer)* 556
Willman, Noel *(Director)* 989, 2568
Willmetz, Alfred *(Author)* 3295
Willner, A.M. *(Author)* 93, 307, 463, 902, 1066, 1067, 1199, 1680, 1712, 2947, 4119, 4490
Willoughby, Hugh *(Costumes)* 670, 740, 2253, 3489, 4296
Willoughby, Hugh *(Set Design)* 670, 1134, 1135, 1136, 3822, 4296
Willoughby, Joe *(Composer)* 1296
Willoughby, Joe *(Lyricist)* 1296
Willoughby & Jones *(Set Design)* 1529
Wills, Lee *(Composer)* 4264
Wills, Lee *(Lyricist)* 4264
Wills, Lou *(Cast)* 2626
Wills, Mary *(Costumes)* 2092, 3629
Wills, Nat *(Cast)* 712, 1543, 1901, 2865, 4807
Wills, Nat M. *(Cast)* 1118, 2642
Wills, Walter S. *(Cast)* 1975
Wills Jr., Lou *(Cast)* 372, 616, 4629
Willson, Meredith *(Author)* 3016
Willson, Meredith *(Composer)* 1369, 1860, 2510, 3016, 4516

Willson, Meredith *(Librettist)* 1369, 1860, 3016
Willson, Meredith *(Lyricist)* 1369, 1860, 2510, 3016, 4516
Willson, Michael *(Cast)* 2346
Willson, Millicent *(Cast)* 4298
Wilma *(Costumes)* 4777
Wilmer & Vincent *(Producer)* 317
Wilmink, W. Gebe *(Lyricist)* 1865
Wilmink, Willem *(Lyricist)* 1865
Wilmore, Carl *(Composer)* 2902
Wilmot, Gary *(Cast)* 846
Wilner, A.M. *(Author)* 3053, 3996
Wilner, Lori *(Cast)* 1739, 1740, 4342
Wilner, Max *(Producer)* 2601, 2684
Wilner, Sis *(Lyricist)* 4131
Wilshire, George *(Cast)* 1057
Wilson *(Composer)* 3297
Wilson *(Lyricist)* 3297
Wilson, Al *(Composer)* 487, 4763
Wilson, Al *(Lyricist)* 123, 487, 1065, 3443, 4763
Wilson, Andrea *(Lighting Designer)* 2006
Wilson, Art *(Dance Arranger)* 2809
Wilson, Billy *(Choreographer)* 576, 958, 1198, 2539, 2820
Wilson, Billy *(Director)* 3714
Wilson, Brian *(Composer)* 3695, 3739
Wilson, Brian *(Lyricist)* 3695, 3739
Wilson, Clarence *(Composer)* 3958
Wilson, Clarence G. *(Composer)* 2013
Wilson, Clarence G. *(Musical Director)* 4751
Wilson, Dolores *(Cast)* 935, 2064, 4764
Wilson, Don *(Librettist)* 340
Wilson, Dooley *(Cast)* 462, 612
Wilson, Edith *(Cast)* 444, 445, 892, 925, 926, 1980, 1984, 1989, 2034, 2462, 2817, 3513, 3705, 3965
Wilson, Edwin *(Cast)* 2919
Wilson, Edwin *(Producer)* 32
Wilson, Eileen *(Cast)* 587
Wilson, Elizabeth *(Cast)* 3479, 4151, 4370
Wilson, Ethel *(Cast)* 77, 1836
Wilson, Flip *(Cast)* 3264, 3499
Wilson, Frances *(Cast)* 947, 3951
Wilson, Francis *(Cast)* 727, 1030, 1193, 1720, 2502, 2936, 4181, 4430
Wilson, Frank *(Cast)* 2817, 3993
Wilson, Frank *(Librettist)* 2977
Wilson, Gerald *(Composer)* 4091
Wilson, Gerald *(Lyricist)* 4091
Wilson, Hansford *(Cast)* 1182, 3986
Wilson, Harry Leon *(Author)* 1501, 3800
Wilson, Imogene *(Cast)* 4817
Wilson, Jack *(Cast)* 1343
Wilson, Jack *(Composer)* 4566, 4828
Wilson, Jack *(Librettist)* 4566
Wilson, Jack *(Lyricist)* 4566, 4747, 4828
Wilson, Jay *(Cast)* 294, 1322
Wilson, Joe *(Lighting Designer)* 4738
Wilson, John C. *(Director)* 454, 999, 1475, 2331, 2705, 3899
Wilson, John C. *(Producer)* 462, 999, 1238, 3678, 3885, 3906, 4610
Wilson, John P. *(Cast)* 4599
Wilson, John P. *(Librettist)* 106, 1014, 1274, 3560, 4599
Wilson, John P. *(Lyricist)* 1014, 1274, 3560
Wilson, Joseph *(Lighting Designer)* 1455, 2603, 2686, 4064, 4404, 4422
Wilson, Joseph P. *(Lighting Designer)* 3868
Wilson, Julie *(Cast)* 1739, 2217, 2437, 3389
Wilson, K.C. *(Cast)* 1377, 4020, 4288, 4370
Wilson, Knox *(Cast)* 586, 1220, 2408
Wilson, Knox G. *(Cast)* 509
Wilson, Lanford *(Author)* 1268
Wilson, Leola *(Composer)* 478
Wilson, Leola *(Lyricist)* 478
Wilson, Lester *(Cast)* 162, 2796, 4003
Wilson, Lester *(Choreographer)* 1699, 2796, 4003
Wilson, Lester *(Director)* 4003
Wilson, Lester *(Librettist)* 4003
Wilson, Lester *(Lyricist)* 4003
Wilson, Lloyd *(Cast)* 4165
Wilson, Lohr *(Costumes)* 2284
Wilson, Lucille *(Cast)* 876
Wilson, Margaret *(Cast)* 1460
Wilson, Marie *(Cast)* 242
Wilson, Mary Louise *(Cast)* 1049, 1107, 1310, 1364, 1585, 1991, 2072, 3468, 3787, 3889, 4659
Wilson, Nina *(Cast)* 4278
Wilson, Pasean *(Cast)* 484
Wilson, Patricia *(Cast)* 1280
Wilson, Randal *(Cast)* 3741
Wilson, Robert *(Cast)* 2559
Wilson, Robert *(Choreographer)* 4774
Wilson, Robert *(Composer)* 3695
Wilson, Robert *(Lyricist)* 3695, 4774
Wilson, Robert H. *(Cast)* 1532, 3028
Wilson, Robin *(Cast)* 1846
Wilson, Rowland *(Composer)* 418
Wilson, Ruth *(Choreographer)* 55
Wilson, Sandy *(Composer)* 507, 4541
Wilson, Sandy *(Librettist)* 507, 4541
Wilson, Sandy *(Lyricist)* 507, 4541
Wilson, Scat *(Musical Director)* 3814
Wilson, Scott *(Costumes)* 1670
Wilson, Snoo *(Librettist)* 1161
Wilson, Speedy *(Cast)* 435
Wilson, Stuart *(Cast)* 2446
Wilson, Teddy *(Cast)* 3893
Wilson, Thomas *(Composer)* 4679
Wilson, Thomas *(Lyricist)* 4679
Wilson, Trey *(Cast)* 1289, 1372, 3448, 4390
Wilson, Walter *(Cast)* 1098, 4360
Wilson, Walter *(Director)* 2927, 3179, 3655, 3712, 4296, 4648
Wilson, Walter C. *(Cast)* 2836
Wilson, Wesley *(Composer)* 478
Wilson, Wesley *(Lyricist)* 478
Wilson, William E. *(Cast)* 3856
Wilson, William J. *(Choreographer)* 60, 188, 1613, 2334, 2358, 3701, 4509, 4655
Wilson, William J. *(Director)* 60, 106, 276, 340, 2358, 2732, 2789, 3096, 3236, 3342, 3525, 3663, 3729, 4490, 4493, 4521, 4599, 4616, 4657, 4692

Wilson Jr., Earl *(Cast)* 1002
Wilson Jr., Earl *(Composer)* 1002, 2451
Wilson Jr., Earl *(Librettist)* 1002
Wilson Jr., Earl *(Lyricist)* 1002, 2451
Wilton, Joe *(Cast)* 395, 3158
Wilton, Joe *(Choreographer)* 395, 3158
Wilton, Joe *(Composer)* 61, 395, 3158
Wilton, Joe *(Director)* 61, 3158
Wilton, Joe *(Librettist)* 61, 395, 3158
Wilton, Joe *(Lyricist)* 61, 395, 3158
Wilton, Joe *(Producer)* 61, 3158
Wilzak, Crissy *(Cast)* 746, 3175
Wiman, Dwight Deere *(Director)* 2545, 3861
Wiman, Dwight Deere *(Producer)* 247, 601, 689, 961, 1453, 1670, 1894, 2061, 2545, 3283, 3861, 3919, 4142, 4169, 4331, 4335
Wiman, Nancy *(Cast)* 4142
Wimperis, Arthur *(Author)* 3584
Wimperis, Arthur *(Librettist)* 1554, 2424, 2594, 3398, 3583
Wimperis, Arthur *(Lyricist)* 152, 178, 208, 276, 702, 954, 1454, 1538, 1544, 1763, 2293, 2317, 2424,2594, 2891, 3020, 3397, 3398, 3583, 4154, 4219
Winans, Marvin *(Composer)* 1073, 3987
Winans, Marvin *(Lyricist)* 1073, 3987
Winans, Ronald *(Vocal Arranger)* 1073
Winant, Forrest *(Cast)* 4053
Winberg, Paul *(Cast)* 4732
Winchell, Paul *(Cast)* 1615
Winchell, Walter *(Cast)* 3153
Wincott, Michael *(Cast)* 3884
Wind, Lee S. *(Cast)* 4729
Window, Muriel *(Lyricist)* 3397
Windsor, Barbara *(Cast)* 1277, 3259, 4469
Windsor, John *(Cast)* 1262
Windust, Bretaigne *(Director)* 1278, 1670
Wing, Charles A. *(Producer)* 668
Wing, Ted *(Lyricist)* 724
Wing, Toby *(Cast)* 4777
Wingate, Phillip *(Lyricist)* 1301
Wingert, Melanie *(Cast)* 760
Winkler, Carlton *(Lighting Designer)* 620, 1112, 2078, 2413, 3105
Winkler, Peter *(Composer)* 3600
Winkler, Peter *(Lyricist)* 3600
Winkler, Richard *(Lighting Designer)* 119, 669, 1108, 1804, 1813, 2790, 3555, 4062, 4788
Winlocke, Isabelle *(Cast)* 4322
Winn, Darrell F. *(Lighting Designer)* 973
Winne, Max *(Musical Director)* 3765
Winner, J.E. *(Composer)* 3175
Winner, J.E. *(Lyricist)* 3175
Winner, Septimus *(Composer)* 1897
Winner, Septimus *(Lyricist)* 1897
Winninger, Charles *(Cast)* 17, 560, 804, 805, 3065, 3184, 3254, 3403, 3699, 3949, 4372, 4589, 4634, 4642, 4757, 4766, 4814
Winninger, Charles *(Director)* 4589, 4642
Winona *(Cast)* 2105
Winslow, Eddie *(Cast)* 4092
Winslow, Herbert Hall *(Author)* 1795, 2274, 2818
Winslow, Herbert Hall *(Librettist)* 1532, 2518
Winslow, Horatio G. *(Lyricist)* 96, 1405
Winslow, Pamela *(Cast)* 2143
Winson, Suzi *(Cast)* 3211
Winsten, Brooke *(Cast)* 3111
Winston, Bruce *(Cast)* 3481
Winston, Hattie *(Cast)* 415, 1671, 2719, 2801, 3825, 4286
Winston, Jennie *(Cast)* 2938
Winston, Tarik *(Cast)* 1890
Winter, Bob *(Composer)* 1181
Winter, Bob *(Lyricist)* 1181
Winter, Edward *(Cast)* 610, 3603
Winter, Winona *(Cast)* 560, 1247, 1793, 2498
Winter Garden Company *(Producer)* 965, 1963, 2538, 2696, 2706, 3395, 3396, 3397, 3399, 3400, 3401, 3701, 3737, 3958, 4553, 4655, 4657, 4747
Winterberg, Richard *(Composer)* 2385
Winterberg, Robert *(Author)* 3051
Winterberg, Robert *(Composer)* 1530
Winters, David *(Cast)* 1709, 4625
Winters, David *(Director)* 1089
Winters, Janet *(Cast)* 2020
Winters, Lawrence *(Cast)* 620
Winters, Marian *(Cast)* 3280, 4278
Winters, Marian *(Director)* 3123
Winters, Marian *(Librettist)* 3123
Winters, Marian *(Lyricist)* 3123
Winters, Nancy *(Set Design)* 2132, 2441, 2783
Winters, Pauline *(Cast)* 531
Winters, Percy *(Cast)* 488
Winters, Roland *(Cast)* 2550
Winters, Shelley *(Cast)* 1571, 2874, 3767
Winters, Shelly *(Voice)* 3793
Wintersteller, Lynne *(Cast)* 784, 2065, 3722
Winther, Michael *(Cast)* 3561
Winthrop, Maurice *(Cast)* 2841
Winwood, Estelle *(Cast)* 1584
Wipf, Alex *(Cast)* 1256, 1364, 2704
Wirges, William *(Composer)* 3175
Wirges, William *(Lyricist)* 3175
Wirtz, Arthur *(Producer)* 1423
Wirtz, Arthur M. *(Librettist)* 2024
Wirtz, Arthur M. *(Producer)* 1782, 1941, 2023, 2098, 2099, 2161, 2162, 4143
Wisdom, Norman *(Cast)* 134, 4588
Wise, Ben *(Cast)* 633
Wise, Fanny *(Cast)* 2520
Wise, Henri *(Cast)* 3979
Wise, Henri *(Composer)* 3979
Wise, Henri *(Lyricist)* 3979
Wise, James *(Composer)* 3615
Wise, Jim *(Composer)* 956
Wise, Joseph *(Cast)* 3279
Wise, Laura *(Cast)* 947
Wise, Mike *(Producer)* 1262
Wise, Scott *(Cast)* 1633, 2205, 4068, 4146
Wise, Sybil *(Cast)* 700, 704
Wise, Thomas *(Cast)* 2383

Wise, Thomas *(Director)* 2383
Wise, Tom *(Cast)* 2498, 2889, 3163
Wiseman, George *(Musical Director)* 4671
Wiseman, George *(Vocal Arranger)* 3154
Wiseman, Joseph *(Cast)* 2411
Wishy, Joe *(Producer)* 635
Wisinski, Ron *(Cast)* 4288
Wisner, James J. *(Musical Director)* 729
Wisner, James J. *(Producer)* 729, 793
Wisner, James J. *(Vocal Arranger)* 729
Wisner, Jimmy *(Arrangements)* 793
Wisner, Jimmy *(Musical Director)* 3858
Wisner, Jimmy *(Orchestrations)* 2235, 3858
Wisner, Jimmy *(Producer)* 3858
Wisner, Jimmy *(Vocal Arranger)* 3858
Wisner, John *(Set Design)* 63
Wissman, Gary *(Set Design)* 3641
Wiswell, L.C. *(Producer)* 2919
Witchie, Katherine *(Cast)* 3137
Witcover, Walt *(Director)* 3970
Witham, John *(Cast)* 2568
Withee, Mabel *(Cast)* 200, 1033, 2270, 2546, 2888, 3770, 4085
Withers, Charles *(Cast)* 543
Withers, Jane *(Cast)* 1577
Witherspoon, Cora *(Cast)* 3850
Witherspoon, Marc *(Composer)* 1713
Witherspoon, Marc *(Lyricist)* 1713
Witke, Robert *(Cast)* 3625
Witkin, Stephen *(Librettist)* 3601
Witler, Ben Zion *(Composer)* 2356
Witler, Ben Zion *(Lyricist)* 2356
Witmark, Isadore *(Composer)* 694
Witmark, Julius P. *(Cast)* 1627
Wits' End *(Producer)* 597
Witt, Max *(Composer)* 1535, 2518
Witt, Max *(Director)* 1118
Witt, Max *(Lyricist)* 2518
Witt, Max *(Musical Director)* 1118
Witt, Max S. *(Composer)* 909, 1118, 2879, 3073
Witt, Max S. *(Producer)* 909
Wittlinger, Karl *(Librettist)* 1062
Wittman, Scott *(Choreographer)* 2555
Wittman, Scott *(Composer)* 2555
Wittman, Scott *(Librettist)* 2555
Wittman, Scott *(Lyricist)* 2555
Wittop, Freddy *(Costumes)* 269, 323, 521, 656, 1012, 1119, 1478, 1764, 1828, 2050, 2078, 2304, 2626, 3274, 3526, 3731, 4190, 4395, 4482, 4701
Wittstein, Ed *(Costumes)* 519, 681, 1190, 1245, 2295, 4764
Wittstein, Ed *(Lighting Designer)* 681, 1190, 2357
Wittstein, Ed *(Set Design)* 461, 681, 1049, 1091, 1190, 1245, 2051, 2295, 2357, 2418, 4288, 4764
Wizoreck, Barry *(Cast)* 2735
Wodehouse, P.G. *(Author)* 3819, 4678
Wodehouse, P.G. *(Librettist)* 163, 334, 611, 1527, 1610, 1784, 1805, 2340, 2430, 2900, 3163, 3213, 3230, 3243, 3245, 3250, 3727, 3866
Wodehouse, P.G. *(Lyricist)* 333, 334, 611, 627, 773, 1454, 1527, 1610, 1784, 2204, 2340, 2372, 2430, 2900, 2907, 3018, 3163, 3177, 3213, 3230, 3243, 3245, 3250, 3727, 3766, 3775, 3819, 3866, 3949, 4001, 4357
Woess, Carl *(Composer)* 2931
Wohl *(Composer)* 907
Wohl, David *(Cast)* 3544
Wohl, Herman *(Composer)* 1609
Wohl, Herman *(Lyricist)* 1609
Wohl, Jack *(Lyricist)* 757
Wohl, Jack *(Producer)* 3499
Wohlman, Al *(Cast)* 3842
Wojak, Regina *(Librettist)* 2178
Woldin, Judd *(Cast)* 322
Woldin, Judd *(Composer)* 2320, 2513, 3656, 4288
Woldin, Judd *(Dance Arranger)* 3656
Woldin, Judd *(Librettist)* 2320, 4288
Woldin, Judd *(Lyricist)* 2320, 2513, 4288
Woldin, Judd *(Orchestrations)* 4288
Wolever, Harry *(Choreographer)* 4401
Wolf, Don *(Composer)* 1296
Wolf, Don *(Lyricist)* 1296
Wolf, Edward E. *(Costumes)* 1880
Wolf, Edward E. *(Set Design)* 1880
Wolf, Leo *(Vocal Arranger)* 4331
Wolf, Peter *(Set Design)* 4395
Wolf, Rennold *(Composer)* 4799
Wolf, Rennold *(Librettist)* 1327, 1663, 1849, 3652, 3685, 4809, 4812, 4813
Wolf, Rennold *(Lyricist)* 335, 1663, 1849, 3031, 3652, 3685, 4799, 4805, 4809, 4811, 4813, 4831
Wolf, Richard R. *(Composer)* 3527
Wolf, Tommy *(Composer)* 2928, 3094
Wolf, Tommy *(Musical Director)* 3094
Wolf, Tommy *(Vocal Arranger)* 3094
Wolf, Walter *(Cast)* 201
Wolfe, Burton *(Director)* 2177
Wolfe, Burton *(Librettist)* 2177
Wolfe, Burton *(Lyricist)* 2177
Wolfe, Carol *(Cast)* 1597
Wolfe, Edwin R. *(Director)* 1632
Wolfe, George C. *(Director)* 2200
Wolfe, George C. *(Librettist)* 2200, 3368, 3628, 4535
Wolfe, George C. *(Lyricist)* 3368
Wolfe, Jacques *(Composer)* 2225
Wolfe, John Leslie *(Cast)* 564, 1804, 3411
Wolfe, Karin *(Cast)* 239, 1511, 2219
Wolfe, Mindy *(Costumes)* 4740
Wolfe, Sharon *(Lyricist)* 2039
Wolfe, Thomas *(Author)* 135
Wolfe, Tom *(Librettist)* 4690
Wolfe, Wendy *(Cast)* 793
Wolff, Alexander *(Cast)* 99
Wolff, Art *(Director)* 474
Wolff, David M. *(Librettist)* 1556
Wolff, David M. *(Lyricist)* 1556
Wolff, Reuben *(Musical Director)* 3842, 4211
Wolfington, Iggie *(Cast)* 759, 3016
Wolfson, D.S. *(Producer)* 4204
Wolfson, David *(Conductor)* 4251
Wolfson, David *(Musical Director)* 696, 3568

Wolfson, David *(Vocal Arranger)* 3568
Wolfson, Martin *(Cast)* 3180, 4369
Wolfson, Ted *(Author)* 2940
Wolfson, Victor *(Librettist)* 3899
Wolheim, Louis *(Cast)* 2403
Wolk, James *(Set Design)* 139, 2372
Wolk, Jesse *(Cast)* 4021
Wolpe, Lenny *(Cast)* 869, 2142, 2578, 2703, 2790, 3305, 3641, 4731
Wolper, David *(Producer)* 1336, 1577
Wolpert, Harold *(Producer)* 4729
Wolshonak, Derek *(Director)* 2704
Wolsk, Eugene V. *(Producer)* 40, 259, 1620, 2898, 3838
Wolsk, Gene *(Producer)* 1353
Wolsky, Albert *(Costumes)* 146, 1471, 3551, 4789
Wolviston Ltd. *(Producer)* 299
Womack, Norman *(Costumes)* 3571
Womack, Norman *(Set Design)* 3571
Women's Project & Prods. *(Producer)* 4775
Wonder, Betty *(Cast)* 2540
Wonder, Stevie *(Composer)* 4534
Wonder, Stevie *(Lyricist)* 4534
Wonder, Tommy *(Cast)* 2540, 4377, 4826
Wonder, Tommy *(Choreographer)* 1834
Wong, Janet *(Cast)* 3239
Wonsek, Paul *(Set Design)* 3734
Wonsel, Paul *(Costumes)* 2012
Wonsel, Paul *(Set Design)* 2012
Woo, Jenny *(Cast)* 3944
Wood, Arthur *(Composer)* 4795
Wood, Arthur *(Musical Director)* 4795
Wood, Bill *(Set Design)* 2022
Wood, Cy *(Lyricist)* 2288
Wood, Cyrus *(Librettist)* 199, 480, 2263, 2384, 2628, 3821, 4121, 4170, 4741
Wood, Cyrus *(Lyricist)* 199, 480, 1033, 2263, 2384, 2628, 2794, 2816, 3406, 4121
Wood, Cyrus D. *(Director)* 1799
Wood, Cyrus D. *(Lyricist)* 25, 199
Wood, David *(Librettist)* 3930
Wood, Deedee *(Cast)* 2484
Wood, Deedee *(Choreographer)* 1061
Wood, Douglas *(Cast)* 4267, 4331
Wood, Ellie *(Cast)* 4401
Wood, Frank *(Lyricist)* 1544
Wood, G. *(Cast)* 83, 392, 2339, 3696, 3942
Wood, G. *(Composer)* 83, 272, 1107, 1222, 1363, 2288, 3615, 3889, 3940, 3941, 4310
Wood, G. *(Librettist)* 1222
Wood, G. *(Lyricist)* 83, 272, 1107, 1222, 1363, 3615, 3889, 3940, 4310
Wood, Haydn *(Author)* 203
Wood, Haydn *(Composer)* 3259
Wood, J. Hickory *(Author)* 2035, 2964, 2974, 3882, 4014, 4662
Wood, J. Hickory *(Lyricist)* 1537, 3882
Wood, Leo *(Composer)* 4697
Wood, Leo *(Lyricist)* 200, 1998, 2446, 2461, 4697, 4815
Wood, Lillian *(Cast)* 1154
Wood, Natalie *(Cast)* 1815
Wood, Norma Jean *(Cast)* 2001
Wood, Otis F. *(Lyricist)* 3981
Wood, Peggy *(Cast)* 17, 579, 780, 1826, 2394, 2620, 2670, 2756, 2794, 3268, 3332, 4359
Wood, Peter *(Director)* 2260
Wood, Randy *(Lighting Designer)* 2742
Wood, Susan *(Cast)* 1149
Woodard, Charlaine *(Cast)* 4, 39, 1737, 3368
Woodbridge, Patricia *(Set Design)* 1053, 3162
Woodbury, Al *(Orchestrations)* 223, 3046, 3381
Woodbury, Al *(Vocal Arranger)* 3381
Woodeson, Nicholas *(Cast)* 262
Woodford, Jack *(Librettist)* 4482
Wooding, Russell *(Orchestrations)* 207, 216, 1980
Wooding, Sam *(Musical Director)* 439
Wooding and His Orchestra, Sam *(Cast)* 927
Woodjetts, Stephen *(Musical Director)* 3066
Woodruff, Helen S. *(Librettist)* 1972, 2276
Woodruff, Helen S. *(Lyricist)* 2276
Woodruff, Henry *(Cast)* 1472, 3363, 3579
Woods, A.H. *(Producer)* 349, 913, 929, 1144, 1247, 1553, 1712, 1904, 2070, 2667, 2923, 3866, 4285, 4526, 4686, 4726
Woods, Aubrey *(Cast)* 2047
Woods, Carol *(Cast)* 789, 1291, 1633, 1699
Woods, Duane *(Cast)* 1255
Woods, Edward *(Producer)* 596
Woods, F.B. *(Composer)* 1421
Woods, Frank *(Cast)* 3033
Woods, Franker *(Cast)* 1916, 3556, 3623, 4545
Woods, Harry *(Composer)* 487, 4027, 4212
Woods, Harry *(Lyricist)* 487, 4027, 4212
Woods, Johnny *(Cast)* 1138
Woods, Richard *(Cast)* 3815, 4020
Woods, Walter *(Author)* 421
Woodson, Paul *(Cast)* 4016
Woodson, Sally *(Cast)* 3249
Woodthorpe, Peter *(Cast)* 989
Woodvine, John *(Cast)* 2474
Woodward, Charles *(Producer)* 1662, 4233
Woodward, Edward *(Cast)* 194, 1891
Woodward, Fred *(Cast)* 4381
Woodward, Matt *(Cast)* 1301
Woodward, Matt *(Librettist)* 2471
Woodward, Matt *(Lyricist)* 2471, 4094, 4801
Woodward, Matt C. *(Composer)* 2974
Woodward, Matt C. *(Librettist)* 1576
Woodward, Matthew *(Composer)* 2964, 4130
Woodward, Matthew *(Lyricist)* 93, 1530, 2029, 2334, 2964, 3592, 3745, 3996, 4130
Woodward, Matthew C. *(Librettist)* 2851, 4121
Woodward, Matthew C. *(Lyricist)* 93, 1900, 2851, 3333, 4133
Woody, Charles *(Cast)* 984
Woody, Charley *(Cast)* 4339
Woolard, David *(Costumes)* 1740, 3661
Woolard, David C. *(Costumes)* 1915, 3368, 4676
Wooley, Arthur *(Cast)* 2986

Wooley, Monty *(Director)* 3861
Wooley, Reginald *(Costumes)* 507
Woolf, Edgar Allen *(Director)* 3446, 3717, 3911, 4422
Woolf, Edgar Allen *(Librettist)* 529, 994, 1796, 2601, 2717, 3446, 3740, 3754, 3796, 3911, 4422, 4687
Woolf, Edgar Allen *(Lyricist)* 529, 1796, 2601, 2717, 3446, 3717, 3754, 4080, 4422
Woolf, Walter *(Cast)* 684, 787, 905, 1113, 1219, 2419, 2813, 2856, 3403, 3406, 3680
Woolf, Walter *(Composer)* 2506
Woolf, Walter *(Incidental Music)* 1218
Woolfolk, Boyle *(Composer)* 4215
Woolfolk, Boyle *(Lyricist)* 4215
Woolfolk, Boyle *(Producer)* 1966
Woolford, Hughie *(Composer)* 2223
Woolley, Monty *(Cast)* 130, 2348, 2729, 3283, 4622
Woolley, Monty *(Director)* 111, 423, 689, 1272, 2252, 3131, 3325, 3378, 4583
Woolley, Scot *(Dance Arranger)* 36, 4146
Woolsey, Robert *(Cast)* 78, 468, 1026, 2789, 3207, 3466, 3540, 3712, 3719
Woolverton, Linda *(Librettist)* 330
Wopat, Tom *(Cast)* 426
Worde, Phil *(Composer)* 3022
Worde, Phil *(Lyricist)* 3022
Worde, Phil *(Musical Director)* 3022
Work, Henry Clay *(Composer)* 1897
Work, Henry Clay *(Lyricist)* 1897, 3923
Work, Julian *(Orchestrations)* 620, 1336, 3813
Workman, Jason *(Cast)* 2805
Workmen's Circle, The *(Producer)* 4172
Worley, Jo Anne *(Cast)* 410, 1993, 2663, 3576
Worrall, Tom *(Composer)* 2082, 2482
Worrall, Tom *(Lyricist)* 2082, 2482
Worrall, Tom *(Orchestrations)* 2482
Worsley, Pat *(Cast)* 841
Worth, Adelaide *(Cast)* 1473
Worth, Billie *(Cast)* 649, 911, 1894, 3893, 4374, 4557
Worth, Bobby *(Composer)* 2085, 2086, 2087
Worth, Bobby *(Lyricist)* 2085, 2086, 2087, 2162
Worth, Caroline *(Cast)* 2339
Worth, Gracie *(Cast)* 2444, 3011
Wortheim, Louis *(Set Design)* 2845
Worthley, Abbott *(Cast)* 2448
Worthley, Minthorne *(Cast)* 2448
Worthy & Thompson *(Cast)* 444
Wouk, Herman *(Librettist)* 1957
Wray, Fay *(Cast)* 3168
Wray, John *(Choreographer)* 620, 3105
Wray, John *(Director)* 1858
Wray, Josephine *(Cast)* 1467
Wreford, Reynell *(Composer)* 1187
Wren, Jane *(Cast)* 3450, 3451
Wright *(Composer)* 1460
Wright, Amy *(Cast)* 1268
Wright, Andrea *(Cast)* 2285
Wright, Ann-Marie *(Costumes)* 2197
Wright, Ben *(Cast)* 2143, 3368, 4146
Wright, Bob *(Cast)* 2838
Wright, Charles Randolph *(Cast)* 2784
Wright, Daniel *(Cast)* 3682
Wright, David *(Composer)* 1736
Wright, David *(Librettist)* 1736
Wright, David *(Lyricist)* 1736
Wright, David C. *(Choreographer)* 2676
Wright, David C. *(Director)* 2676
Wright, E.H. *(Cast)* 4343
Wright, Ellen *(Lyricist)* 2506
Wright, Fred E. *(Producer)* 331
Wright, Frederic Colt *(Composer)* 4549
Wright, G.G. *(Cast)* 3270
Wright, G.M. *(Librettist)* 3319
Wright, Garland *(Director)* 3010
Wright, George *(Cast)* 489
Wright, Helena-Joyce *(Cast)* 105
Wright, Hugh *(Composer)* 1391
Wright, Hugh *(Lyricist)* 1391
Wright, Hugh E. *(Lyricist)* 702
Wright, Margaret *(Cast)* 23, 755, 2243, 3418, 4684
Wright, Margaret *(Librettist)* 4209
Wright, Margaret *(Lyricist)* 4209
Wright, Mark *(Producer)* 2418
Wright, Martha *(Cast)* 3013
Wright, Mary Catherine *(Cast)* 1914, 4252, 4390
Wright, Mason *(Cast)* 1882
Wright, Mason *(Lyricist)* 1882
Wright, Michael *(Cast)* 1797
Wright, Michael *(Choreographer)* 2580
Wright, Michael *(Director)* 2580
Wright, Ned *(Cast)* 2415
Wright, Peter *(Choreographer)* 455
Wright, Ray *(Orchestrations)* 3126
Wright, Rebecca *(Cast)* 2820
Wright, Richard *(Author)* 952
Wright, Rick *(Composer)* 3739
Wright, Robert *(Author)* 4383
Wright, Robert *(Cast)* 1918, 4155, 4278
Wright, Robert *(Composer)* 161, 223, 649, 848, 849, 1119, 1415, 1649, 2295, 2327, 3683, 4073, 4075, 4117, 4316, 4383
Wright, Robert *(Director)* 1711
Wright, Robert *(Librettist)* 649
Wright, Robert *(Lyricist)* 161, 223, 649, 848, 849, 1119, 1415, 1649, 1680, 1681, 1711, 2295, 2327, 2679, 3683, 4073, 4075, 4117, 4316, 4383
Wright, Russell *(Costumes)* 1653
Wright, Russell *(Lighting Designer)* 1653
Wright, Russell *(Set Design)* 1653
Wright, Samuel E. *(Cast)* 1086, 3001, 3330, 3548, 4286, 4619
Wright Jr., Fred *(Cast)* 675
Wrightson, Ann *(Lighting Designer)* 4
Wrightson, Ann G. *(Lighting Designer)* 2658
Wrightson, Earl *(Cast)* 1284
Wrigley, Ben *(Cast)* 302
Wroderick Productions *(Producer)* 3235
Wromley, Dan *(Cast)* 645
Wrubel, Allie *(Composer)* 1251
Wuerz, Charles N. *(Director)* 421
Wulff, Derick *(Librettist)* 2330

Wulff, Derick *(Lyricist)* 2330
Wulp, John *(Director)* 1354
Wulp, John *(Lyricist)* 1354
Wulp, John *(Producer)* 1354, 1635
Wurtzebach, Edward *(Musical Director)* 4254
Wurtzel, Stuart *(Set Design)* 1082, 1581, 3565, 4343
Wyche, Ron *(Cast)* 3202
Wycherley, William *(Author)* 2654
Wycherly, Margaret *(Cast)* 1871, 2981
Wycherly, William *(Author)* 3920
Wyckham, John *(Lighting Designer)* 3271
Wyckoff, Evelyn *(Cast)* 1710, 2379
Wyckoff, Fred *(Cast)* 2694, 3205
Wyeth, Howard *(Orchestrations)* 4089
Wykoff, Evelyn *(Cast)* 2386
Wyler, Gretchen *(Cast)* 3801, 3972, 4737
Wyler Productions *(Producer)* 280
Wylie, Edward *(Librettist)* 4765
Wylie, John *(Cast)* 1649
Wylie, Julian *(Director)* 1855
Wylie, Julian *(Producer)* 1618, 1855, 2976, 4765
Wylie, Laurie *(Author)* 203, 3584
Wylie, Laurie *(Librettist)* 1805, 2227, 3583
Wyman *(Composer)* 560
Wyman, Douglas *(Librettist)* 1714
Wyman, Nicholas *(Cast)* 140, 915, 3464
Wyman, Nick *(Cast)* 158, 533
Wymore, Patricia *(Cast)* 67, 1930
Wynburn, Ray *(Composer)* 1131, 1132
Wynburn, Ray *(Lyricist)* 1131, 1132
Wyncoop, Paul *(Choreographer)* 1957
Wyndham, John *(Producer)* 4302
Wyndham, Olive *(Cast)* 1524
Wyndham, Victoria *(Cast)* 3764
Wynn *(Costumes)* 2258, 2475, 3005
Wynn *(Librettist)* 3005
Wynn, Bessie *(Cast)* 250, 613, 2506, 2901, 4206, 4222, 4298, 4723, 4735
Wynn, Bob *(Producer)* 58
Wynn, Ed *(Cast)* 17, 78, 512, 685, 1003, 1065, 1154, 1240, 1643, 1973, 2423, 2734, 2872, 3153, 3400, 3443, 3962, 3980, 4063, 4808, 4809
Wynn, Ed *(Composer)* 1154, 1643, 3443
Wynn, Ed *(Director)* 512, 2423
Wynn, Ed *(Librettist)* 512, 1154, 1643, 2423, 3443, 3980
Wynn, Ed *(Lyricist)* 1154, 1643, 3443, 4063
Wynn, Ed *(Producer)* 512, 1643, 2423
Wynn, H. *(Composer)* 4193
Wynn, H. *(Lyricist)* 4193
Wynn, Keenan *(Cast)* 3292, 3833, 4483
Wynn, Larry *(Composer)* 1296
Wynn, Larry *(Lyricist)* 1296
Wynn, Nan *(Cast)* 3893
Wynne, Maud *(Cast)* 3384
Wynne, Tonya *(Lyricist)* 2239
Wynne Jr., Angus *(Producer)* 4395
Wynyard, John *(Cast)* 1467
Wyse Jr., Ross *(Cast)* 1494
Wyss, Patti *(Arrangements)* 944
Wyss, Patti *(Orchestrations)* 944

X

Xanroff *(Author)* 3433
Xantho, Peter *(Lighting Designer)* 242, 4463
Xifo, Ray *(Cast)* 1630
Xulu, Michael *(Cast)* 1719

Y

Yablokoff, Herman *(Composer)* 1609, 2356, 4342
Yablokoff, Herman *(Lyricist)* 1609, 2356, 4342
Yacht Club Boys *(Cast)* 3153
Yaeckel, Louis *(Cast)* 4548
Yahya, Easter *(Librettist)* 1677
Yahya, Easter *(Lyricist)* 1677
Yai, N. Tong *(Composer)* 2850
Yai, N. Tong *(Lyricist)* 2850
Yakim, Moni *(Director)* 2188, 4379
Yakovieff, Alex *(Choreographer)* 3011
Yakovieff, Alexander *(Choreographer)* 1688
Yakus, Milt *(Composer)* 4264
Yakus, Milt *(Lyricist)* 4264
Yale, Chas. H. *(Producer)* 3348
Yale Repertory Theatre *(Producer)* 1406
Yale University Dramatic Assn.
See also Members Yale Drama Assn.
Yale University Dramatic Assn. *(Producer)* 130, 945, 2287, 3325, 3378, 4041
Yama, Conrad *(Cast)* 1315, 3340
Yamaguchi, Shirley *(Cast)* 3913
Yanconelli, Frank *(Cast)* 347
Yancy, Emily *(Cast)* 4004
Yankee, Luke *(Director)* 4232
Yankowitz, Susan *(Author)* 253
Yanthe, Paul *(Author)* 1193
Yantis, Fannie *(Cast)* 4634
Yap, Donald *(Orchestrations)* 92
Yarbo, Billie *(Cast)* 2271
Yarbo, Vivian *(Cast)* 4316
Yardley, Peter *(Cast)* 346
Yarnell, Bruce *(Cast)* 623, 1745
Yarnell, Lorene *(Cast)* 547
Yartin, Paul *(Musical Director)* 1839, 2972
Yates, Ken *(Producer)* 2470
Yde, Bob *(Director)* 1769
Yde, Bob *(Librettist)* 1769
Yeager, Barbara *(Cast)* 2427
Yeager, Fabian *(Lighting Designer)* 3272
Yeamans, Annie *(Cast)* 737, 1627, 2040, 2428, 2695
Yeargan, Lisa *(Musical Director)* 4690
Yeargan, Michael *(Set Design)* 2766
Yeargan, Michael H. *(Costumes)* 599
Yeargan, Michael H. *(Set Design)* 54, 599, 1406, 1787, 3544, 4505
Yeats, William Butler *(Author)* 1977
Yellen, Jack *(Composer)* 4813
Yellen, Jack *(Librettist)* 4778

Yellen, Jack *(Lyricist)* 79, 393, 487, 512, 1333, 1404, 1493, 1494, 1888, 2135, 2696, 2706, 2856, 2857, 3005, 3140, 3175, 3428, 3648, 3985, 4086, 4197, 4296, 4342, 4460, 4637, 4683, 4778, 4813, 4821, 4825, 4826, 4858
Yellen, Jack *(Producer)* 4778
Yellen, Sherman *(Librettist)* 1089, 3233, 3702, 3780
Yellenti, Nicholas *(Set Design)* 1314, 3352
Yellin, Gleb *(Musical Director)* 3894
Yellin, Gleb *(Orchestrations)* 4567
Yellman, Duke *(Composer)* 4501
Yeo, Mary Jane *(Cast)* 4143
Yerxa, Alison *(Set Design)* 1636
Yeston, Maury *(Composer)* 785, 1638, 1649, 3171, 3465, 3624
Yeston, Maury *(Lyricist)* 785, 1638, 1649, 3171, 3465, 3624
Yeston, Maury *(Vocal Arranger)* 3171
Yetman, Charlotte M. *(Costumes)* 838, 1804, 4055
Yo-Hay-Tong *(Cast)* 3170
Yockey, Denton *(Cast)* 2573
Yockey, Denton *(Director)* 2573
Yoder, Jerry *(Choreographer)* 1732
Yohe, May *(Cast)* 822, 1505
Yokel, Alexander *(Producer)* 4083
Yolanda Mero-Irion *(Producer)* 1817
Yomen, Ben *(Composer)* 4342
Yopp, Don *(Lighting Designer)* 4643
Yopp, Lee R. *(Director)* 2169
Yordan, Philip *(Librettist)* 4702
York, Alva *(Cast)* 3433
York, Chick *(Cast)* 2, 1889
York, Don *(Dance Arranger)* 753
York, Donald *(Dance Arranger)* 1298
York, Donald *(Musical Director)* 4216
York, Michael *(Cast)* 2539
York, Rachel *(Cast)* 775, 4067, 4560
York, Rebecca *(Cast)* 3743
York Players *(Producer)* 809
York Theatre Company *(Producer)* 2565
Yorke, Alice *(Cast)* 20, 561, 1083, 2159, 2732, 3237, 4247, 4333
Yorke, Gus *(Cast)* 3047, 3519
Yorke, Letty *(Cast)* 1014
Yoshimura, Akira *(Set Design)* 1512, 4127
Yossiffon, Raquel *(Cast)* 1269, 2866
Yost Varsity Eight, Ben *(Cast)* 4825
Yost's Catalina Eight, Ben *(Cast)* 3860
Youlin, Alma *(Cast)* 1351, 4161
Youmans, James *(Set Design)* 647, 1169, 3456, 4255
Youmans, Vincent *(Composer)* 146, 704, 1667, 1733, 1873, 1916, 2489, 2569, 2768, 3018, 3020, 3150, 3157, 3172, 3184, 3249, 3254, 3478, 3650, 3953, 4023, 4267, 4372, 4491, 4565, 4694
Youmans, Vincent *(Producer)* 1667, 1916, 4372
Youmans, William *(Cast)* 394
Young *(Composer)* 3926
Young *(Lyricist)* 3926
Young, Arthur *(Composer)* 703
Young, Aston *(Cast)* 2719
Young, Billie *(Cast)* 552
Young, Cy *(Cast)* 1056, 1363, 1567, 3890, 4190
Young, Cy *(Composer)* 1581, 4319
Young, Cy *(Librettist)* 1581, 4319
Young, Cy *(Lyricist)* 1581, 4319
Young, Donna Jean *(Cast)* 382, 3275
Young, Eleanor *(Composer)* 4137
Young, Emily *(Librettist)* 3677
Young, Emily M. *(Librettist)* 1823
Young, Ernest F. *(Cast)* 598, 2893
Young, Ernest F. *(Choreographer)* 598
Young, George *(Cast)* 3703
Young, Gig *(Cast)* 4329
Young, Halfred *(Cast)* 184, 203, 1722
Young, James K. *(Cast)* 4779
Young, Joe *(Composer)* 1735, 3926
Young, Joe *(Lyricist)* 26, 39, 123, 391, 428, 444, 505, 567, 965, 1044, 1626, 1813, 1904, 2045, 2308, 2380, 2382, 2423, 2939, 3018, 3120, 3401, 3402, 3525, 3709, 3726, 3737, 3827, 3985, 4148, 4235, 4255, 4257, 4604, 4806, 4813, 4817, 4821
Young, John *(Cast)* 2895
Young, John *(Set Design)* 250, 252, 767, 1065, 1243, 1356, 1520, 1926, 1927, 2041, 2160, 2517, 2534, 2835, 3737, 4392, 4478, 4723, 4735
Young, John E. *(Cast)* 136, 1527, 2497, 2559, 2931, 3494
Young, John H. *(Set Design)* 215, 1071, 1188, 1563, 1896, 2117, 2824, 4382, 4681, 4801, 4802, 4803, 4804, 4807
Young, Joseph *(Composer)* 1215
Young, Joseph *(Lyricist)* 393, 2194, 4534
Young, Karen *(Cast)* 2468
Young, Marie *(Cast)* 3807
Young, Ralph *(Cast)* 4682
Young, Rida Johnson *(Author)* 515, 2154, 2537, 2662, 3642, 3679, 3910
Young, Rida Johnson *(Librettist)* 310, 640, 1096, 1852, 1911, 2282, 2390, 2546, 2794, 3081, 3679, 3892, 4063, 4647, 4716
Young, Rida Johnson *(Lyricist)* 310, 719, 1096, 1274, 1535, 1852, 1911, 2154, 2282, 2390, 2537, 2546, 2715, 2794, 3081, 3892, 4063, 4716
Young, Roland *(Cast)* 579, 1357, 1517, 1623, 1850, 2070
Young, Ronald *(Cast)* 1108, 3249
Young, Tammany *(Cast)* 3131, 4668
Young, Thomas *(Cast)* 4129
Young, Thomas *(Vocal Arranger)* 4129
Young, Victor *(Composer)* 3, 190, 444, 878, 3002, 3381, 3683, 3899, 4264
Young, William B. *(Producer)* 2764
Young, Willie Fong *(Composer)* 119
Young, Willie Fong *(Lyricist)* 119
Youngman, Henny *(Cast)* 3121
Youngman, Henry *(Cast)* 1899
Younin, M. *(Composer)* 4342
Younin, M. *(Lyricist)* 4342
Younin, Wolf *(Lyricist)* 400
Yount, Kenneth M. *(Costumes)* 757, 1785, 3858
Yourgrau, Tug *(Author)* 4074
Yourgrau, Tug *(Lyricist)* 4074
Youth Theatre *(Producer)* 2447

Yuen, Lily *(Cast)* 4763
Yulin, Harris *(Cast)* 4601
Yunker, Ken *(Lighting Designer)* 4732
Yurka, Blanche *(Cast)* 17
Yurman, Lawrence *(Arrangements)* 2945, 4515
Yurman, Lawrence *(Incidental Music)* 2945
Yurman, Lawrence *(Musical Director)* 1589, 2945
Yuskis, Antoinette *(Cast)* 3936
Yvain, Maurice *(Author)* 2637
Yvain, Maurice *(Composer)* 25, 1176, 1425, 2637, 3148, 3295, 3500, 3905, 4815, 4816, 4817, 4831, 4847, 4852
Yvain, Maurice *(Lyricist)* 2637
Yves *(Costumes)* 2599
Yvette *(Cast)* 2696

Z

Zabelle, Flora *(Cast)* 17, 1536, 2730, 2844, 3423, 3828, 4422, 4754, 4762
Zacharias, Emily *(Cast)* 757, 3272
Zagaeski, Mark *(Cast)* 3162
Zagnit, Stuart *(Cast)* 2354, 2646, 2704, 4288
Zakharov, Mark *(Director)* 2269
Zakrzewski, Paul *(Librettist)* 3876
Zakrzewski, Paul *(Lyricist)* 3876
Zaks, Jerry *(Cast)* 4390
Zaks, Jerry *(Director)* 212, 4031
Zakutansky, Peter J. *(Costumes)* 1004, 1155
Zalon, Paul *(Set Design)* 4595
Zalotoff, Max *(Librettist)* 4463
Zaltzberg, Charlotte *(Librettist)* 3656
Zalud, S. *(Costumes)* 764, 1626, 2546, 2939, 3985, 4269
Zalud, Samuel *(Costumes)* 2665
Zamecnik, John S. *(Composer)* 1866, 1868
Zangwill, Israel *(Author)* 2319, 2320, 2321, 2819, 4288
Zanini, Ester *(Cast)* 4113
Zany, King *(Composer)* 4814
Zany, King *(Lyricist)* 487, 4814
Zaremba, Kathryn *(Cast)* 155
Zaret, Hy *(Lyricist)* 7, 146, 1880, 2175, 2447
Zarro, Ron *(Cast)* 1978
Zarrow, Happy *(Cast)* 4859
Zaslow, Michael *(Cast)* 482, 3305
Zavin, Benjamin Bernard *(Librettist)* 1158
Zazarus, Emma *(Lyricist)* 1609
Zbornak, Kent *(Cast)* 544
Zeb, Jolly *(Cast)* 4859
Zehavi, D. *(Composer)* 1740
Zeibarth, Frances *(Costumes)* 396, 1901
Zeitz, Johnny *(Cast)* 562
Zelby, Lottie *(Costumes)* 2321
Zelenko, Michael *(Composer)* 3426
Zelenko, Michael *(Lyricist)* 3426
Zelinka, Sidney *(Librettist)* 924, 1898
Zell, F. *(Author)* 3150, 3151
Zell, Gladys *(Cast)* 2394, 2566, 2835, 2892, 3791
Zell, Violet *(Cast)* 2184, 2902, 4393
Zeller, Gary *(Lighting Designer)* 4536
Zeller, Gary *(Set Design)* 4536
Zeller, Kathy *(Cast)* 1781
Zeller, Mark *(Cast)* 181, 757, 2354
Zeller, Robert *(Musical Director)* 911
Zeller-Alexis, Dana *(Cast)* 1169, 4790
Zemach, Benjamin *(Choreographer)* 1196, 3501
Zender, Marguerite *(Cast)* 136, 1174, 3192, 3420, 3533, 4378
Zeno, Norman *(Librettist)* 1342
Zeno, Norman *(Lyricist)* 532, 1127, 1191, 1342, 3955, 4667
Zentner, Morris *(Musical Director)* 1215
Zentner & His Orchestra, Si *(Cast)* 1326
Zera, Lanie *(Cast)* 81
Zhurbin, Alexander *(Author)* 2012
Zhurbin, Alexander *(Composer)* 2012
Ziebarth, Frances *(Costumes)* 3093
Ziebarth, Frances M. *(Costumes)* 4599
Ziebarth, Mme. *(Costumes)* 2139
Ziegfeld, Florenz *(Librettist)* 4817
Ziegfeld, Florenz *(Producer)* 152, 376, 429, 683, 827, 1175, 1881, 1979, 2308, 2506, 2594, 2715, 2872, 2892, 2900, 3179, 3332, 3387, 3392, 3673, 3719, 3766, 3768, 3819, 3949, 3953, 3980, 4023, 4094, 4357, 4453, 4683, 4712, 4801, 4802, 4803, 4804, 4805, 4806, 4807, 4808, 4809, 4810, 4811, 4812, 4813, 4814, 4815, 4816, 4818, 4819, 4821, 4823, 4831, 4832, 4833, 4834, 4835, 4836, 4837, 4838, 4839, 4840, 4841, 4842, 4843, 4844, 4845, 4846, 4847, 4848, 4849, 4851, 4852, 4853
Ziegfeld, Mignon *(Composer)* 3085
Ziegfeld, Mignon *(Lyricist)* 3085
Ziegfeld, William *(Producer)* 1550
Ziehrer, Carl M. *(Author)* 2334, 2914
Ziehrer, Carl M. *(Composer)* 2334, 2914
Zielinski, Scott *(Lighting Designer)* 1702, 2945
Ziemba, Karen *(Cast)* 131, 4297
Zien, Chip *(Cast)* 1038, 1234, 2143, 2746, 3666, 3711, 4022, 4540
Ziering, Ian *(Cast)* 2064
Ziff, Stuart *(Composer)* 3076
Zimbalist Sr., Efrem *(Composer)* 1962
Zimmer, Bernard *(Author)* 657
Zimmerman, Charles *(Cast)* 998
Zimmerman, Charles *(Composer)* 998
Zimmerman, Charles *(Musical Director)* 3268, 4723
Zimmerman, Charles *(Orchestrations)* 3626
Zimmerman, Harry *(Orchestrations)* 1891
Zimmerman, Mme. *(Costumes)* 2836
Zinberg, Arthur D. *(Producer)* 4595
Zink, Adolph *(Cast)* 1375
Zinkeisen, Doris *(Cast)* 4341
Zinkeisen, Doris *(Costumes)* 791, 792, 1680, 1763, 3214, 3291, 3756, 4154
Zinkeisen, Doris *(Set Design)* 791, 3214, 3756, 4154
Zinn, Randolyn *(Choreographer)* 3010
Zippel, David *(Librettist)* 1597
Zippel, David *(Lyricist)* 4, 146, 775, 1038, 1298, 1597, 1633, 2171, 2283, 2754, 4799
Zippel, Joanne L. *(Producer)* 2283
Zipper, Herbert *(Musical Director)* 309

Zipprodt, Patricia *(Costumes)* 161, 393, 610, 723, 975, 1265, 1497, 2318, 2660, 2664, 2958, 3039, 3299, 3506, 3551, 3897, 3918, 3944, 4019, 4210, 4216, 4252, 4338, 4862
Zipser, Arthur *(Lyricist)* 3226
Ziskin, Victor *(Composer)* 4785
Ziskin, Victor *(Musical Director)* 4785
Zito, Ron *(Arrangements)* 944
Zito, Ron *(Orchestrations)* 944
Zito, Torrie *(Orchestrations)* 1633, 3428, 4020
Zittel, C.F. *(Composer)* 4757
Zittel, C.F. *(Lyricist)* 4757
Zmed, Adrian *(Cast)* 1149
Zodrow, John *(Librettist)* 1637
Zoellner, Peter Lee *(Producer)* 92
Zogott, Seymour *(Lyricist)* 1049, 2611
Zoob, Dave *(Composer)* 4283
Zook, Elizabeth *(Costumes)* 4291
Zoran *(Costumes)* 4533
Zorich, Louis *(Cast)* 1634
Zorina, Vera *(Cast)* 1101, 2061, 2597
Zoritch, George *(Cast)* 3, 1140
Zuber, Catherine *(Costumes)* 158, 2185, 3682, 3937, 4147
Zucca, Mana *(Cast)* 1888
Zucker, Stan *(Producer)* 1898
Zuckerberg, Regina *(Cast)* 3995
Zulu, Mamthandi *(Cast)* 4438
Zur, Menachem *(Composer)* 4514
Zur, Menachem *(Musical Director)* 4514
Zuro, Josiah *(Musical Director)* 1743, 3308
Zwar, Charles *(Composer)* 1408, 2168, 2227, 4153
Zweibel, Alan *(Librettist)* 1038, 1512
Zwerling, Ruby *(Musical Director)* 1898
Zwick, Joel *(Cast)* 963
Zwick, Joel *(Choreographer)* 963
Zwick, Joel *(Director)* 963
Zwroh, Stefan *(Librettist)* 2202

Song Index

A

A + B = C 3490
A-B-C 2014
A.B.C. 3828
A.B.C. Song, The 4160
A.B.C.'s 3110
A-B-C's of the U.S.A., The 4759
A Caroling We Go 4391
A-Choo 1962
I'm a Cuban Girl 1783
A-Hunting We Will Go 4443
A Is For 2069
A.J. 1191
A Kis Grof 4228
A Kisassonyi Ferje 2526
A-L-E 2119
A-L-E-X-A-N-D-R-I-A 2671
A la Gastronome 2691
A La Girl, The 737
A la Hockey 3403
A La Lenox Avenue 876
A La Minute 1962
A la Mode Girl, The 2715
A La Parisienne 68
A La Pimpernel 3491
A la Viennese 3978
A...My Name Is Ellie 2427
A Nier Tzeit 4463
A-1 March 162
A.P.I.S. Parade, The 98
A Razz a Ma Tazz 1120
A-Stage 1116
A-Tangle, A-Dangle 1698
A-Tisket A-Tasket 4534, 887
A-Weaving 705
Aba Daba Honeymoon 3589
Ababu (dance) 2327
Abadaba Club, The 3532
Abandon 1182
Abandoned 2565
Abbe's Appearance 3456
Abbondanza 2961
Abby's Lament 10
ABC of Traffic Sketch, The (inst.) 1657
ABC to XYZ 2784
ABC's of Success, The 4028
Abdication 3766
Abduction 1700
Abduction, The 2727
Abduction Ballet 1245
Abductions, (and so forth) 1245
Abdullah 1079
Abdullah's Farewell 2686
Abe and Me and the Baby 3926
Abe Lincoln 1840
Abe Lincoln Has Just One Country 1476
Aber Nit 2800
Abi Tsu Zein Mit Dir
(As Long As I'm with You) 1279
Abide with Me 1073
Abiding with You 1037
Abie Baby 1717
Abie's Irish Rose 1250
Abou Ben Adhem 59
About a Quarter to Nine 1359
About Face 1930
About the Ompire 654
About Time 1234
Above! Above! 2551
Above the Law 155
Abracadabra 2847, 4517
Abraham, Martin and John 3018
Absent-Minded Maid 2101
Absent Minded Me 1420
Absinthe 1834, 2287
Absinthe Drip 2287
Absinthe Frappe 2160, 4818
Absolute Don of a Juan 2336
Absolutely Certain 2336
Absolutely Nothing Tonight 3203
Absolution 3944
Absurd As a Chuck-a-Walla Bird 863
Abundance and Charity 754
Abuse 4447
Abyssinia 10
AC/DC 4138
Academic Fugue 1846
Academy Award 338
Academy Award Highlights 407
Academy Awards Theme 3636
Academy Rag, The 1531
Acapulco Polka 865
Accent Makes No Difference in the
Language of Love, The 1088
Accident!, An 3675
Accidents Will Happen 3068
Accompaniment 1450

According How You Take 'Em 1783
According to Dr. Holt 3740
According to Mr. Grimes 4443
According to Plotnik 2887
Accusation 2338
Ace in the Hole 2453
Ace of Spades 290
Ace's Revelation (Inst.) 2046
Aces Up 4328
Ache in Acorn 2346
Aches, Pains an' Strains 4163
Aching 158
Achoo Cha-Cha (Gesundheit) 4264
Acid Queen 4676
ACLU 1700
Acorn in the Meadow 2227
Acrobatic Dance 3573
Acrobatic Rag, The 4851
Acrobatie 2364
Acrobats 1419
Across the Border 451
Across the Garden Wall 265
Across the Great Divide 264
Across the River from Queens 608
Act, The 2874
Act I Finale 3081, 2938
Act II Finale 2348
Act II Grand Finale —
The New York Herald Topical Song 2938
Act II Prologue 2759
Act Like a Lady 1864
Act Like a Villager 3654
Act One Finale 2839, 3853
Act Three Finale 2839
Act Two Finale 2839, 2185
Act Two Opening 808
Acting 2982
Action 1706
Action in the Auction 1119
Actions Speak Louder Than Words 4249
Actor, The 1010
Actor's Purgatory 528
Actors in Society 934
Actress, An 2352
Actress Hasn't Learned, The 1211
Acts of God
(Births, Deaths and the Weather) 3136
Acushla 2454
Ad Astra 1879
Ad Ripae Mildewensis Fluminis 4331
Ad, The 2451
Ad-dressing of Cats, The 678
Ada with the Golden Hair 1776
Ada, My Sweet Potater 3676
Adam 1309
Adam and Eve 537, 1404, 3486
Adam and Eve Had a Wonderful Time 257
Adam & Yvette 194
Adam Clayton Powell 1436
Adam Was the Only Lover 1334
Adamant Eve 18
Adaptations 2279
Add a Little Wiggle 3648
Addie's At It Again 2053
Addio, Bambino 3456
Adelaid 616
Adelaide Caprice 1148
Adelaide's Lament 1706, 3444
Adele 20
Adele's Soliloquy 98
Adeline 3951
Adios 4022, 4311
Adios Barrio 1164
Administration 2364
Admirable Admiral, An 3786
Admiral, The 1392
Ado About Kean 2295
Adolescents 3162
Adopt a Pretty Baby 1065
Adorable 1131, 1132, 4523
Adorable Julie 1440
Adorable Toreador, The 3748
Adorable You 4669
Adored One 3170, 3953
Adoring You 4818
Adrift 920
Adrift on a Star 1745
Ads Infinitum 128
Adulteress 2766
Adultery Waltz 2007
Adunde 3814
Advancement 1131
Advantage of a College Education, The 4650
Advantages of Floating in the Middle
of the Sea, The 3340
Adventure 1061
Adventures of Huckleberry Finn, The
394, 1086, 2027, 2029, 2030, 2556, 2028
Advertise 4477, 4530
Advertising 1819
Advertising Blues 2403
Advertising Song, The 4826
Advice 3951, 4292
Advice to Husbands 1817
Advice to Producers 3858
Advice to the Lovelorn 2934
Advice to the Young 3424
Aerobicantata 4535
Aeroplane Duet 2495
Aeroplane Joy Ride, The
(The Air Ship Joy Ride) 2232
Aeroplane Rag, That 1835
Aesop Was a Very Moral Man 2931
Aesthetic Dancing 2667
Affable Balding Me 4314
Affair of the Heart, An 863
Afferdytie 2664
Affinity 2779
Affluent Society, The 2053
Afgar, ou Les Loisirs Andalous 25

Afraid of Love 4566
Afraid of the Dark 4139
Afraid of You 3409
Afraid to Fall in Love 2219
Afraid to Go Home at All 2892
Africa 2346, 1538, 1603, 2135, 240
Africa Burning in the Sun 3836
Africa Shrieks 4335
Africa Speaks 2043
African Dance 3656
African Dip 3963
African Golf 1014
African Sequence 344
African Whoopie 290
Africana Stomp 26
Afro Blue 2245
After 3227
After All 4425
After All, I'm Only a Schoolgirl 4581
After All, It's Spring 3895
After All These Years 3718
After All, You're All I'm After 3919
After Burton, Who? 3890
After Business Hours 3229
After Commencement (inst.) 1628
After Dark 1041
After Dinner 4478
After Dinner Drinks 583
After Forty 2294
After Forty It's Patch, Patch, Patch 1168
After Graduation Day 304
After High School 4019
After Hours 2439
After I've Spent My Best Years on You 1495
After Looking for Love 1073
After Love 2106
After Office Hours 3085
After Opening Night 424
After Rehearsal 2674
After School Special 3448
After the Ball 3949
After the Clouds Roll By 3821
After the Curfew Rings 3185
After the End 655
After the First of July 4851
After the Flickers 1004
After the Gold Is Gone 992
After the Holidays 4643
After the Rain 496
After the Rain-Sunshine 3424
After the Show 4130
After the Wedding 1342
After This 2249
After Today 742
After Tonight 4394
After Vespers 1531
After We're Happily Married 4437
After You Feed the Little Chickens
They Want a Little Chicken Feed 910
After You Say I Love You 1241
After You, Who? 1453, 1762, 4517
After You're Married a While 1014
After You've Gone 3840, 432, 2796, 3297, 4037
After Your Lover Has Gone 3004
Aftermath 3873
Afternoon 1888
Afternoon Delight 1035
Afternoon of a Black Faun 924
Afternoon of a Phony, The 323
Afternoon Tea 204
Afternoon Tea, An 965
Afterthought, An 2927
Afterward 3763
Afunani Amaphoyisa eSoweto?
(What Is That Army Doing in Soweto?) 3836
Ag Pleez Deddy 4579
Agaba-Saba Dance (inst.) 1251
Again 1000
Against the Storm 4479
Against the Tide 1161
Agatha Sue 32
Age Is a State of Mind 2616
Age of Brass, The 3305
Age of Innocence 780
Age of Innocence Sketch, The (inst.) 1657
Age of Miracles 4696
Age of Rock-Rock of Ages 4737
Aged Aged Man, An 54
Agent 3858
Agent's Blood 227
Agent's Lot Is Not a Happy One, An 1948
Ages Ago 4386
Aggie 3863
Aggie, Oh Aggie 935
Aggie Song (1) 374
Aggie Song (2) 374
Aggie's Sewing Machine Song 2228
Agnes and Me 937
Agnus Dei 2346, 2775
Agony 2143
Agony Round 900
Agreer, The 1846
Agua Sincopada Tango (inst.) 4581
Ah! Ah! Ah! 3500
Ah, At Last 4616
Ah Bon Ben Ala 1573
Ah, but Underneath 1329
Ah, but Underneath...! 4067
Ah! Camminare 519
Ah! Che Vedo 1561
Ah! Cupid, Meddlesome Boy! 3570
Ah! Eh! Oh! 1526
Ah Fong Low 1921, 1923
Ah! He's a Prince 3570
Ah! Heaven's Height Has Cracked! 1636
Ah, How Capricious 4479
Ah, Hum, Oh, Hum 3938
Ah, I Laugh 1743
Ah! List to Me 3570
Ah Lovely Art, We Worship at Thy Shrine 1388

Ah, Maien Zeit! 1822
Ah, May the Red Rose Live Alway 4149
Ah Men 3666
Ah, Miss 4233
Ah Oui 1175
Ah, Oui! 3618
Ah, Our Germans 1739
Ah, Paris! 1329, 3967
Ah! Sweet Mystery of Life (Dream Melody) 3081
Ah, Sweet Revenge 3197
Ah, Sweet Youth! 4106
Ah, There 3392
Ah, There You Are 919
Ah, To Be Home Again 3526
Ah, Well, We'll Try to Be Precise 4554
Ah! Wilderness 34
Ah, Wilderness! 4270
Ah! Woe Is Me 104
Ah, Yes, I Am in Love 2701
Ah! Yon Is No Song of Triumph 3732
Ah, Men 33
Ahoy for a Sailor 4357
Ai Yi Yi 4510
Aida 3035
Aida McCluskie 1318
Aimee Is No Angel 35
Ain't Broadway Grand 36
Ain't Cha Coming Back, Mary Ann to Maryland 3963
Ain't Everything Grand! 1387
Ain't Got No 1717
Ain't Got No Tears Left 599, 3278
Ain't Got No Worry Long As Your're My Baby 740
Ain't Gwine to Work No More 352
Ain't Had No Lovin' in a Long Time 3676
Ain't He a Joy? 4764
Ain't I Something? 2437
Ain't It a Grand and Glorious Feeling 3230
Ain't It a Joy 3210
Ain't It a Shame 2556
Ain't It Awful 1271
Ain't It Awful the Heat 4169
Ain't It Awful the Heat? 369
Ain't It de Truth 2190
Ain't It Funny 2067
Ain't It Funny What a Difference a
Few Drinks Make 4810
Ain't It Funny What a Difference
Just a Few Hours Make 4754
Ain't It Good 730
Ain't It Romantic 3243
Ain't It Sad 4693
Ain't Love Easy 4398
Ain't Love Grand 487, 942, 1074, 2277
Ain't Love Grand? 1690
Ain't Love Wonderful 642
Ain't Marryin' Nobody 3599
Ain't Misbehavin' 39, 1980, 3020
Ain't Nature Grand 4718
Ain't Nature Grand? 4815
Ain't Never Gonna Find Another Love Song 916
Ain't No Party 1103
Ain't No Place Like Home 1201
Ain't No Women There 564
Ain't Nobody Got a Bed of Roses 4398
Ain't Nobody Here but Us Chickens 1296
Ain't Puttin' Out Nothin' 691
Ain't She Sweet 393, 3175
Ain't She Sweet? 3754
Ain't That Always the Way 2696
Ain't That Delicious 1707
Ain't That Langwidge Though 3908
Ain't That Something 4343
Ain't Too Proud to Beg 4534
Ain't We Got Fun 393, 3842
Ain't We Got Love 4253
Ain't Worth a Dime 562
Ain't You Ashamed? 3210
Ain't You Heard? 2028
Ain't You Never Been Afraid? 2726
Ain'tcha Glad You Got Music? 2034
Aintcha Got Music 1772
Air 1717
Air Conditioning 924
Air Guitar 119
Air Male 1116
Air Minded 1323
Air Strip 1841
Airy Mary 4497
Ajade Papa 4579
Akiwawa 3814
Al Fleagle Arrangement, An 3955
Al Fresco 3837
Al Smith for President 1837
Al the Chemist 42
Alabam 822
Alabam' 561
Alabam' Banjo Man 1223
Alabama 4762
Alabama Barbecue 883
Alabama Bound Blues 43
Alabama Cadets, The 2721
Alabama Coon 45
Alabama Family 3364
Alabama Sam 4801
Alabama Song 369
Alabama Stomp 1128, 1132
Alabamy 1989
Alabamy Bound 1425
Aladdin 44, 2547, 3712, 3958
Aladdin's Daughter 3091
Alaiyo 3656
Alamo Widows' Lament 2573
Alarm 255
Alas for a Man without Brains 4723
Alas for You 1595
Alas, Lorraine 3931
Alas, the Time Is Past 429
Alaura's Theme 775
Alba 533
Albany 2481

Albany or Dat's de Only Town Looks Good to Me 2990
Albert Porter 4479
Albertina's Beautiful Hair 2000
Alborada 2783
Album Song 2475
Alcalde Mayor 2830
Alcatraz 1736
Alcazar 3084
Alcron 408
Alderberan 229
Aldonza 2727
Ale, Ale, Ale 1013
Ale House Song 3215
Alessandro the Wise 1284
Alexander's Back from France 3158
Alexander's Bagpipe Band 1927
Alexander's Band Is Back in Dixieland 3985
Alexander's Discount Rag 427
Alexander's Ragtime Band 789, 1398, 1327
Alexander's Ragtime Wedding Day 2645
Alexandra 3583
Alexandria 165
Alexius the Heroic 742
Alfa Romeo 4737
Alfie 261
Algae 922
Algeria 3773
Algerian Girl 3333
Algerian Serenade 49
Algerian Slave Song and Chorus 2974
Algy 3265
Algy's Simply Awfully Good at Algebra 4354
Alhambra Nights 3544
Ali Baba 1829, 4477, 4530
Ali Baba Babies, The 930
Ali-Up 1027
Alibi Baby 3540
Alibi Blues 3973
Alice 52, 2173, 3196, 3235
Alice Again 2876
Alice Alone 2876
Alice Back Home 2876
Alice Blue Gown 2148
Alice in Boogyland 304
Alice in Italy 2876
Alice in Spain 2876
Alice in Wonderland 683
(I'd Like to Wander with) Alice in Wonderland 1544
Alice in Wonderland 55
Alice in Wonderland (Come Along with Alice) 3009
Alice in Wonderland Ball 2482
Alice Is Coming to Tea 58
Alice O'Grady 3746
Alice Sat By the Fire 4115
Alice Through the Looking Glass 58
Alice's Adventures in Wonderland 52, 54, 56, 593, 57, 4736
Alien Song 3309
Alike, Alike 2737
Alimony Alley 1228
Alimony Blues 3652
Alison Dear 1500
Alive! 2198
Alive Again 559
Alive and Kicking 59
Alive at Last 4798
All a Dream 1503
All a Lie! 178
All a Matter of Strategy 2676
All Aboard 60, 395, 2382, 2800, 2887, 3348, 4657, 15
All Aboard for Broadway 1478, 1480
All Aboard for Dixie Land 2984
All Aboard for Dixieland 1888
All Aboard for Gay Paree 3298
All Aboard for Kankakee 15
All Aboard for Paris 2622
All Aboard for Sunny Kansas 4723
All Aboard for Times Square 4271
All Aboard, Step Lively Do 15
All Aboard with E.M. Frimbo 1402
All About Eve 167
All About Evelyn 348
All About He 127
All About Him 127
All About Me 127
All about the Plum 1581
All, All Alone 4757
All Alone 1469, 1488, 3009, 3045, 3209, 2766, 3427, 3431, 4053
All Alone in a City Full of Girls 1852
All Alone in a Crowd 3032
All Alone Monday 1944, 3659
All American 1158, 4160, 4566
All American Boy, The 2496
All American Male 474
All-American Man 4428
All American Rainbow 3683
All-American Two-Step, The 4318
All Around the Town 589
All Around the World 3091, 3473
All Ashore 1536
All at Once 247
All at Once You Love Her 3505
All at Sea 3352
All Because of You 692
All Bless the Genius of Man 2047
All By Yourself 3741
All Choked Up 1664
All Clear 1664, 4252
All Dark People 247
All Days Are Gay Days in Paris 2869
All Decked Out 3489
All Dolled Up 154, 155
All Down Piccadilly (Willie from Piccadilly) 178
All Dressed Up 3801
All Dressed Up in a Tailor Made 805
All er Nothin' 3263

All Fall Down 109, 3757
All for a Green Ribbon 4404
All for Charity 2768
All for Him 3347
All for Love 67, 1955
All for One and One for All 4357
All for the Best 1595
All for the Sake of a Girl 1016
All for You 69, 2642, 2723, 2262, 3590, 3843, 4435
All for You, Louis 3840
All Full of Ginger 3087
All Full of Talk 2907
All Fwoo 112
All Gall 221
All Girl Band 4
All Girl Band, The 4483
All Girls Are Like a Rainbow 560
All Glory to the Young 1770, 3280
All God's Chillun Got Movie Shows 1000
All Goes Badly 996
All Goin' Out an' Nothin' Comin' In 2111
All Good Gifts 1595
All Good Things 1770
All Greece 4615
All Hail, Great Judge 2977
All Hail the Bride 4032
All Hail the Empress 161
All Hail the King 3337, 4615
All Hail the Political Honeymoon 2344
All Hail the Queen 3628
All Hail to the General 1027
All Hallowe'en 2394
All Hearts with a Keen Curiosity Burn (Opening Chorus) 4258
All I Ask Is to Forget You 4751
All I Ask of You 3464
All I Can Do Is Cry 4533
All I Care About 723
All I Crave Is More of Life 3081
All I Do Is Dream of You 544
All I Got Is You 314
All I Need 1072, 1637
All I Need Is Me (I Need Me Babe) 2172
All I Need Is One Good Break 1310
All I Need Is Someone Like You 2296
All I Need Is the Girl 1709
All I Owe Ioway 4146
All I Remember Is You 1171
All I Want 1308
All I Want from You Is You 3057
All I Want in the Wide, Wide World Is You 1525
All I Want in the Wide, Wide, World Is You, Just You 1900
All I Want Is a Home 277
All I Want Is a Little Bit of Fun 3828
All I Want Is a Lullaby 4271
All I Want Is Love 2263
All I Want Is My Black Baby Back 1063
All I Want Is Not to Want 3355
All I Want Is Plenty of Loving 2013
All I Want Is You 3052
All I Want to Do 528
All I Wanted Was a Cup of Tea 1015
All I Wanted Was the Dream 2437
All I've Got Is Me 3576, 154
All I've Got to Get Now Is My Man 3359
All in a Little Dance 2732
All in a Short Half Hour 2214
All in Fun 1611, 4557
All in Love 71
All in the Cause of Economy 1721
All in the Line of Duty 3882
All in the Name of Love 3167
All in the Point of View 2513
All in the Wearing 1478, 2533
All Is Fair 1682
All Is Fair in Love and War 3736
All Is Vanity 1128, 1132
All Is Well 1351
All Is Well in Larchmont 1273
All Is Well in the City 3602
All Kinds of Giants 73
All Kinds of People 3505
All Lanes Much Reach a Turning 1011
All Life Is Full of Pleasure 4687
All Long Island Gossips 2352
All Love, All Love 4523
All Men 3558
All Men Are the Same 4795
All Men Have Their Troubles 4559
All Mucked Up 1619
(They're) All My Boys 2533
All My Days Till End of Life 758
All My Girls 470, 4364
All My Good Mornings 4558
All My Heart's Desire 1636
All My Life 1215, 1345, 2248, 2373, 1750, 3741
All My Life I Lost It for Him 4108
All My Worldly Belongings 2368
All My Yesterdays 3697
All Nature Is at Peace and Rest (Forest Song) 3736
All Night Long 3723
All of 'Em Say 2556
All Of a Sudden It's Spring 692
All of It All 3080
All of My Dreams 3517
All of My Laughter 1273
All of My Life 101, 1061, 789
All of Them Was Friends of Mine 317
All of These and More 483
All of Us Are Brothers 109
All of Us Are Niggers 109
All of You 3972
All on Account of Eliza 402
All Our Friends 1478
All Our Tomorrows 4027
All Out Bugle Call 901
All Over My Mind 1216
All Over Town 3649

All Paris 4073
All Pepped Up 4818
All Pleasures in Life 4032
All Pull Together 2571, 3500
All Right 1232
All Roads Lead to Church 353
All Roads Lead to Hollywood 2754
All She Can Do Is Say No 1634
All She Could Say Was 'Oui' 2951
All She Did Was This 2569
All She'd Say Was 'Um Hum' 4814
All-Talking, All-Singing, All-Dancing 2968
All That and Heaven Too 4498
All That Glitters 3909
All That Has Happened 2626
All That He'd Want Me to Be 652
All That I Know 564
All That I Need Is A Hallway 1685
All That I Want 2216
All That Jazz 723, 131
All the Boys Love Mary 4842
All the Children in a Row 3718
All the Comforts of Home 135, 1270, 2494, 4037
All the Dark Is Changed to Sunshine 3418
All the Dearly Beloved 2050
All the Elks and Masons 2475
All the Flowers Turn to Snow 2177
All the Girls Are Lovely at the Seaside 537
All the Girls Have Got a Friend in Me 1663
All the Girls Look Wonderful to Me 1961
All the Girls Love Me 4115
All the Girls Were Pretty 4541
All the Ifs and Maybes 4330
All the King's Horses 4367
All the King's Horses and Men 3774
All the Little Birds in Nests Agree 792
All the Little Glooms Start Dancing 764
All the Little Things in the World Are Waiting 3389
All the Livelong Day (I Hear America Singing) 4744
All the Lovely 778
All the Luck in the World 3493
All the Magic Ladies 1873
All the Men in My Life 259
All the People on the Levee 2225
All the Pretty Little Horses 2958
All the Same for Me 593
All the Stars and Stripes Belong to Me 2869
All the Things You Are 2204, 2372, 3175, 4557
All the Time 1506, 3234, 4142
All the Time in Dixie 1421
All the Time in the World 1377
All the Time Is Loving Time 4276
All the Way 4743
All the Way Down 2918
All the Way Home 2072
All the Way to Here 166
All the While 2363
All the World Is Dancing Mad 1731, 4001
All the World Is Madly Prancing 3395
All the World Is Swaying 1796
All the World Is Wonderful 1176
All the World Loves a Lover 1693, 2293, 2923, 2966, 2771
All the World Loves a Winner 3770
All the World Wants Ragtime 2349
All the World's a Clock Shop 782
All the World's a Hold 669
All the World's in Love 917
All the Wrongs You Done to Me 740
All the Years 708
All the Young Men 1081
All These People I Have Wronged 4212
All These Things 1890
All Things Bright and Beautiful 1329, 2764
All Things to One Man 1699
All This Time 1804
All Those Years 615
All Through the Day 2372
All Through the Love of You 3786
All Through the Night 163
All to Myself 1345
All Together 281
All Together Now 83
All Washed Up 3754
All We Need to Know 227
All WIse Chickens Follow Me 1995
All Woman 607, 614
All Work and No Play 4651
(I'm) All Wrapped Up in You 1207
All Ya Have to Do Is Wait 775
All Year 'Round 1096
All Year Long 779
All You Can Do Is Tell Me You Love Me 2568
All You Gotta Do Is Tell Me 4196
All You Have to Do Is Stand There 4782
All You Need Is a Fife and Drum 3351
All You Need Is a Girl 4001
All You Need Is a Little Love 4536
All You Need Is a Quarter 1061
All You Need Is a Song 4346
All You Need to Be a Star 3538
All You Want Is Always 2185
All Your Own Am I 1183
Allaballa Goo-Goo 3251
Allah Be Praised 84
Allah Guard Thee 2802
Allah Jazz 3404
Allah! Strike for Thee 4201
Allah's Holiday 2292
Allay Up 4815
Allegheny Moon 4264
Allegorical Blues, The 1357
Allegro 85
Alleh Villn 2356
Alleluia 630, 2775, 1258, 755
Allez Oop 1764
Allez-Up 1447
Allez-Vous-En (Go Away) 629
Allied High Command, The 2228
Allies 3590

Allies Forever 1824
Alligator Meat 1684
Alligators All Around 3668
Allons 3780
All's Fair in Love and War 184, 1551, 2747
All's Right with the World 1862
All's Well 1322, 2563, 4316
Alluring Gypsy Girl, The 710
Alma 88
Alma Mater 661, 1664, 1770
Alma What's the Matter 3889
Alma, Wo Wohnst Du? 88
Almanac Covers, The 3005
Almighty American 3873
Almighty Dollar, The 1351
Almighty Father 2775
Almiro 2366, 4517
Almond Tarts 946
Almost 2805, 1230, 2053
Almost a Love Song 4560, 3479
Almost, But Not Quite 3725
Almost Everybody Suffers More Than Us 2017
Almost Like Being in Love 530
Almost Nearly Friend, An 2027
Almost Real 3527
Almost There 572
Almost Too Good to Be True 1761
Almost Working 2784
Almosts, Maybes and Perhapses 2049
Aloha 1809, 2636
Aloha (I Love You) 1650
Aloha Lord 1809
Alomo 3238
Alone 2188, 3035, 3276, 198, 4015, 544, 647
Alone at a Drive-In Movie 1664
Alone at Last 804, 3237, 4555
Alone at Last, Alone 3653
Alone at Night 4798
Alone in a Crowd 2479
Alone in a Great Big World 4053
Alone in a World of Men 2910
Alone in the Light 3682
Alone in the World 2980
Alone (My Lover) 4664
Alone on Life's Highway 3586
Alone on My Honeymoon 4181
Alone (the Whaling Widows) 3074
Alone Together 1322
Alone Too Long 603
Alone with Love 3966
Alone with You 1281, 3057
Alone with You (All Alone) 4555
Along Broadway 4359
Along Came Another Little Girl 2184
Along Came Love 1137
Along Came Lyle 2657
Along Came Ruth 94
Along Life's Highway 4387
Along the Old Canal 4704
Along the Rio Grande 381
Along the Road to Love 3511, 3238
Along the South American Coastline 3410
Along the Way 974
Along the Way Where Lovers Go 2938
Along the Winding Road 4214
Along with Me 620
Alpha, Beta, Pi 3735
Alphabet 54
Alphabet Song, The 249, 181
Alphabet Song 4337
Alphagenesis 4431
Alpine Girl, The 3525
Alpine Horn, The 1213
Alpine Horn, The (Tyrolean Song) 3994
Alpine Rose 2366
Alpine Symphony (inst.) 4667
Alt Wein 216
Altdeutscher Leibersreim 2566
Alternate Parking 2657
Althea 3110
Although I Am a Soldier I Prefer a Private Life 3976
Although I'm So Demure 457
Altogether Too Fond of You 579, 4302
Altogether Too Outrageous 2877
Alumnae Report 1049
Always 3197, 1073, 789
Always Alone 223
Always, Always You 1873
Always, Always You (It Was Always You) 656
Always Another Girl 2330
Always Autumn 1648
Always Be a Gentleman 2786
Always Come Back to You 1569
Always Do As People Say You Should 1355
Always for Science 1785
Always Goodbye 2751
Always in My Heart 2808
Always Late 4201
Always Leave 'Em Laughing (When You Say Good-Bye) 2964
Always Leave 'Em Wanting More 2657
Always Leave Them Laughing (When You Say Goodbye) 3809
Always Leave Them Laughing When You Say Good-Bye 2517
Always Left Them Laughing 2415
Always Look for a Rainbow 3369
Always Mademoiselle 798
Always Make Allowances for Love 350
Always Me 299
Always on the Job 2645
Always One Day More (Death of a Ballad) 3940
Always or More 1857
Always Something Doing in Paris 1868
(There's) Always Something There to Remind Me 4193
Always Something There to Remind Me 261
Always Take Mother's Advice 1424
Always Tell the Truth 90

Always the Fault of the Men 4360
Always the Same 200
Always Together 3395
Always True to You in My Fashion 2331
Always Wear a Smile 3921
Always You 97, 1930
Am I? 1191
Am I a Man or a Mouse? 2103
Am I a Wife, Widow or Maid? 2892
Am I a Wizard 4724
Am I Blue 478, 432
Am I Enchanted? 3013
Am I in Love? 629
Am I Late? 2876
Am I Ready for This 944
Am I Right 561
Am I To Blame? 2340
Am I to Wish Her Love 3682
Am Yisroel Khay!
(The Jewish People Live) 1609
Amapu 3310
Amaryllis 3570
Amasalela 4579
Amasendenduna (chant) 4438
Amateur Entertainer, The 350
Amateur Night 166
Amazing 3551
Amazing Adele, The 98, 98
Amazing Bone, The 99, 99
Amazing Grace 4534
Amazing Journey 4676
Amazing What Love Can Do 4586
Amazon Land 646
Ambassador of Peace 1417
Ambassadors, The 101
Ambassador's March 2869
Ambassador's Polka, The 4516
Amber Club, The 4657
Ambition 1061
Ambitious Animals, The 2159
Ambivalent Rag 2702
Ambulance 2111
Amedee 2017
Amedee, Amedee, It Isn't Too Late 2017
Ameer, The 104
Amelia's Theme 4459
Amen Corner 105
Amen Corner, The 105
America 3873, 1722, 3489, 3871, 4625, 4644, 4782
America, Be Seated 108
America Don't Know How Any More 1955
America Dreaming 4744
(You'd Better See) America First 3399
America I Love You 538
America, I Love You 3705
America Is Bathed in Sunlight 1955
America, Kick Up Your Heels 109
America, Look Out 1067
America Loves a Band 323
America Marches On 1879
America the Beautiful 2279, 3418, 4390
America, We're in New York 169
America, You're Looking Good 4635
Americadenya 1885
American Beauties 4794
American Beauty, The 3747
American Beauty (inst.) 4390
American Beauty Rose, An 1285
American Beauty Rose 1447
American Bolero (inst.) 1138
American Business 2478
American Cannes 206
American Courtship 2761
American Dancers 4427
American Dollars 2590
American Dream, The 695, 2905, 2173
American Dreaming (1) 4004
American Dreaming (2) 4004
American Eagle 2026
American Eagles 4340
American Express, The 1272
American Family Plan 3725
American Girl, The 118, 2485
American Girl, The (Song of the Cities) 3578
American Girl in Paris, The 3387
American Girls 3856
American Girls
(Chickoo We're Only Just Sixteen) 3857
American Heiress, An 1535, 2885
American Heiress, The 3771
American Heiresses 3784
American Idea, The 4759
American in Paris 1358
American in Paris Blues Ballet, An (inst.) 3953
American Invasion, The 2934
American Jazz 2135, 3405
American Man on the Moon 2728
American Maxixe, The 4657
American Millionaire, An 4247
American Minstrels in Paris, The 3749
American Monte Carlo, The 2119
American Music
('Tis Better Than Old Parsifal to Me) 2885
American, Oh Girls? 3073
American Opera in Three Acts:
Cavalier Americana, An 123
American Pie 3739
American Plan 2809
American Prelude 827
American Primitive 4432
American Punch (It's the Punches), The 1923
American Ragtime, The 1478
American Ragtime Tune, The 115
American Revue Girls 123, 124
American Serenade, The 1851
American Tourists — We'll Go to the Cabaret 335
(A Real) American Tune 1490
American Way, The 1415, 2542
American Women 964
Ameri-can-can, The 124

Americans All Drink Coffee 3359
Americans Are Coming, The 1145
Americans Are Here, The 4345
America's Answer 4421
America's Fighting Back 3401
America's Popular Tune 3403
America's Sweetheart 112
Amerike, Hurrah for Onkl Sem
(America, What a Name!) 1609
Amigos 1034
Amina 2858
Amishman, An 600
Amo 2145
Amo, Amas 129
Amoeba's Lament, The (inst.) 1657
Among My Yesterdays 1764, 4480
Amorous Arrow, The 1761
Amorous Esquimeaux, The 2722
Amorous Flea, The 127
Amorous Goldfish, The 1470
Amorous Morons 946
Amorous Pigeon, The 1521
Amorous Rose 3051
Amorous Star 4098
Amos Gonna Give You Hell 1769
Amour a la Militaire (inst.) 125
Amphitryon 3272
Ample Fronts 3908
'Amstead 'Eath and Amsterdam 30
Amsterdam 1852, 2188, 2295, 2889
Amusing Myself 606
Amy 3148
An Invitation 4372
An Old Spanish Custom 1979
Anabella Jerome 4359
Anarchist, The 426
Anastasia 161
Anastasia Reilly 3911
Anatevka 1265
Anatol's Last Night 1439
Anatole of Paris 4166
Anatomy 649
Ancestors Bold 3996
Ancestry 3236
Ancient Days 4001
Ancient Minstrel, The 2538
Ancient Oriental Custom 3239
Ancient Rules of Observing Etiquette 1849
And... 746
And a Drop of Lavender Oil 2664
And a Host of Others Too
Numerous to Mention 3845
And a Little Child Shall Lead
Them to the Promised Land 496
And a Messenger Appeared 2913
And Dreams Come True 3424
And Eve Was Weak 661
And Father Wanted Me to Learn a Trade 4158
And Freedom 1978
And Furthermore 1164, 3382
And He Flipped 3108
And Her Mother Came Too 582, 3020
And I Am All Alone 1784
And I Am Telling You I'm Not Going 1103
And I Believe Him 4012
And I Have You 1528
And I in My Chair 2558
And I Laughed 2716
And I Love You 4591
And I Was Beautiful 1012
And I Was Fired 1055
And I'm So Glad 797
And If I Told You That I Wanted You 2674
And In That Region There Were Shepherds 755
And It Rained, Rained, Rained 904
And Love Was Born 3014
And Mrs. Grundy Winked 1466
And Now 4615
And Now It's Spring 1496
And Other Things 2914
And Points Beyond 1619
And She Loved Me 2451
And She Went Home in a Barrel 4851
And She Would Smile 1497
And So He Died 1748
And So to Bed 129
And So Will You 1670
And Still His Whiskers Grew 3228
And That Is All 2145
And That Little Girl Is You 1183
And That's Nice 451
And the Band Began to Play 2324, 3129
And the Gods Heard Her Prayer 3285
And the Manager Said...? 1640
And the Money Kept Rolling In 1211
And the Moonlight's Calling You 3072
And the Mountains Sing Back 4384
And the Supremes 4309
And the Weeping Willow Wept 356
And the World Goes On 1148
And the World Goes On Just the Same 4762
And the World Goes 'Round 131
And Then Came a Carriage
Filled with Flowers 1551
And Then He Kissed Me 2427
And Then I Saw Him 2742
And Then I Wrote 3484
And Then She Winked Her Eye 4439
And Then That Cigar Went Out 1783
And Then They Dream of Love 3876
And Thereby Hangs a Tail 1446
And They All Call the Hatter Mad 593
And They Came with Haste 755
And They Held High Carnival 1154
And They Lived Happily Ever Afterward 2394
And They Say He Went to College 3313
And This Is My Beloved 2327, 4383
And Very Nice Too 132
And What If We Had Loved Like That 253
And Why Not I 4362

And You Were Shy Eighteen 2906
And Your Mother Said 4013
Andalusia Bolero 1711
Andrews's Fantasy ('Yes' Ballet) (inst.) 1698
Androcles and the Lion 134
Andy Jackson 3558
Andy Mack 1264
Andy You Are de Candy 2485
Anema E Corre 2227
Angel! 307
Angel 1138
Angel Angelica 693
Angel Child 231, 4104
Angel Face 136, 3763
Angel Mom 3811
Angel Mother, Angel Father 3306
Angel of Love 610
Angel of Mercy 1822
Angel of Music 3464
Angel Recordings Is Offering a Job 128
Angel Theme 135
Angel Town 2527
Angel Voices 331
Angel Without Wings, An 539
Angel without Wings 2061
Angel's Ballet 2236
Angel's Rink and Social Center 3718
Angelette March 374
Angelica 1354
Angelina 276, 382, 139, 4693
Angeline 352, 484
Angeline from the Opera Comique 4553
Angelo 2261
Angels (We Call Them Mother Down Here) 2857
Angels 2513, 3958, 4003
Angels on Your Pillow 3428
Angelus, The 531, 4250
Angie Blossom's Party 476
Angie's Patriotic Rally 4634
Angle Worm Wriggle 2261
Angling 4228
Angling By a Babbling Brook 2986
Anglo-Saxons of Today 1021
Angry Boogie 4403
Angry Guy 4349
Angry Young Man, The 722
Angus, Are You There? 2934
Angus Gordon Donald Douglas Ewart John McKee 2495
Animal Attraction 64
Animal Band 786
Animal King, The 4753
Animal Song, The 3456
Animal Stomp 4162
Animal Trainer, The 1123
Animals 2584
Animals Are Better Off Than Humans to Day 20
Animals Are Nice 3105
Animals Came in Two By Two 702
Animal's Convention 2029
Ankle Up the Altar 3172
Ankle Up the Altar with Me 1448
Anna 290
Anna and Son Klin 2312
Anna and the King of Siam 2312
Anna Christie 3113
Anna Karenina 147
Anna Lee 1978
Anna Lilla 3113
Anna Louisa 4379
Anna Louise of Louisiana 1127
Anna of Havana 2931
Anna, What's Wrong with You? 2469
Annabel 118
Annabelle Lee 1689
Anna's Entrance 2839
Anne Frank: The Diary of a Young Girl 4790
Anne of Green Gables 148, 148
Annette 4352
Annexation 1650
Annie 150, 152
Annie 2 154
Annie Ain't Just Annie Anymore 155
Annie Laurie 2111, 3973
Annie Laurie Rag 1643
Annie McGinnis Pavlova 1956
Annie's Thing 4089
Annina 3011
Anniversary Song (Rememberance) 1189
Announcement, The 2307
Announcement of Inheritance 4058
Announcement/Rehearsal (inst.) 4798
Annual Ball 1259
Annunciation, The 2241
Another April 1119
Another Autumn 3347
Another Backers' Audition 262
Another Big Strike 4516
Another Bumper Crop 2876
Another Candle 3366
Another Case of the Blues 4291
Another Cold Day 4172
Another Crummy Day 1990
Another Cry 535
Another Day 2229, 1222, 1729, 4286
Another Day, Another Buck 1048
Another Find Day 912
Another Free Translation 3088
Another Girl 3853
Another Girl and Boy Thing 2742
Another Good Man Gone Wrong 231
Another Hot Day 3294
Another Hundred People 832, 3967
Another Kind of Man 4004
Another Law 2344
Another Life 4106, 958, 3305
Another Little Girl 3193
Another Love 599, 3278

Another Lovely April Day 3823
Another Mad Scene 2193
Another Melody in F 1321, 2193
Another Memorable Meal 1077
Another Mile 662, 2413
Another Miracle of Judaism 1234
Another Morning 455
Another Mr. Right 146, 2171, 1597
Another National Anthem 212
Another New Day 117
Another New York Day 262
Another Night 261
Another One Gone Wrong 3163
Another Op'nin, Another Show 2331
Another Openin' Another Show 4399
Another Princely Scheme (Tarantella) 3453
Another Road, Another Destiny 2970
Another Sad Penny 4172
Another Sentimental Song 1921
Another Shout 104
Another Sleepless Night 2132
Another Soiree 2565
Another Suitcase in Another Hall 1211
Another Summer 2542
Another Time, Another Place 2355
Another Wedding Song 784
Answer 800, 43
Answer Is No, The 439
Answer Me 1327
Answer My Heart 2034
Answer Song, The 2283
Answer That 3025
Answering Machine 3858
Answers That You Don't Expect to Get 9
Ante-Bellum Days 3425
Anthem 721, 1216, 533
Anthem for Presentation 619
Anthem Song of the Common Wheel, The 4109
Anti-Cigarette Society, The 357
Anticipation 119
An-ti-ci-pa-tion 3051
Anticipation Is Much More Fun, The 3320
Antidote 579
Antidotes 1801
Antigone 1636
Antioch Prison 3469
Antique Man, The 3366
Antiques 25, 159, 600, 2180
Antiquity 2173
Antoinette 3304
Antonio 4662
Antonio's Telegram 3461
Anuska 710
Anvil Chorus 1492
Anxious 1518
Any Afternoon about Five 2680
Any Day Now 239
Any Day-Now Day 273
Any Dream Will Do 2242
Any Fool Can Fall in Love 1577
Any Girl 1796, 2614
Any How, I'm Pleased to Meet You 1308
Any Kind of Man 4063
Any Little Fish 4335
Any Little Girl Will Fall 969
Any Little Melody 764
Any Little Thing 1297
Any Little Tune 3649, 3659
Any Man but Thomas T 453
Any Man Is Easy (If You Just Know How) 3611
Any Moment 2143
Any Moment Now 4019
Any Night on Broadway 3400
Any Night on Old Broadway 2870, 4656
Any Old Alley Is Paradise Alley 3369
Any Old Girl 2318
Any Old Nag 2869
Any Old Night 2107, 4419
Any Old Night (Is a Wonderful Night) 4418
Any Old Night Is a Wonderful Night 3193
Any Old Place I Can Hang My Hat Is Home, Sweet Home for Me 3298
Any Old Place in the World with You 4094
Any Old Place in Yankee Land Is Good Enough for Me 295
Any Old Place with You 2574
Any Old Port in a Storm 801
Any Old Thing 457
Any Old Time at All 1587, 1902, 3710, 4812
Any Old Time of the Day 261
Any Old Time with You 3399
Any Old Tree 2160
Any Old Where 4327
Any Other Day Will Do 675
Any Other Way 2731
Any Place I Hang My Hat Is Home 4123
Any Place Is Home Sweet Home with You 2387
Any Place the Old Flag Flies 2525
Any Place Will Do with You 487
Any Place Would Be Paradise 4779
Any Place Would Be Wonderful with You 4814
Any Pretty Little Thing 2174
Any Sort of Girl 2803
Any Spare Change? 2051
Any Step 1678
Any Time 500
Any Time, Any Place, Any Way 830
Any Time Is Dancing Time 3866
Any Time Is Love Time 2605
Any Time New York Goes Dry 4547
Any Time's Kissing Time 758
Any Way the Wind Blows 3907
Any Wednesday 160
Any Woman Who Is Willing Will Do 3813
Anya 161
Anybody Round Here Looking for a Scrap 4453
Anybody Wanna Buy a Little Love 2776
Anybody Want a Baby 2749
Anybody's Man Will Be My Man 2645
Anyone 869

Anyone Can Do the Heartbreak 1804
Anyone Can Make a Mistake 249
Anyone Can Move a Mountain 281
Anyone Can Whistle 162, 3967
Anyone Else but You 2698
Anyone! Who Does That Can't Be So Dumb 608
Anyone Who Had a Heart 4193, 261
Anyone Who Loves 958
Anyone Who's Anyone 2279
Anyone Would Love You 1029
Anything 292
Anything but Lonely 211
Anything But the Truth 1804
Anything Can Happen 1493, 1811, 3221
Anything Can Happen Any Day 3721
Anything Can Happen in New York 2707
Anything for a Quiet Life 2820
Anything for Him 2333
Anything for You 977, 1237
Anything Goes 163, 146
Anything Is Possible 1158, 4450
Anything That's Near to Where You Are 1503
Anything to Declare 194
Anything You Can Do 153
Anything You Liked 1961
Anything You Want to Do, Dear 2767
Anything Your Heart Desires 2271
Anytime 130, 3344
Anytime, Anywhere, Anyhow 2263
Anytime at All 4012
Anytime New York Goes Dry 3921
Anytime of Day 1884
Anyway, We've Had Fun 4023
Anyway You Bless 3987
Anywhere 738
Anywhere but Here 3234
Anywhere I Wander 4399, 1741, 3444
Anywhere the Wind Blows 1063
Anywhere You Are 1605, 2558
Apache 2426, 4560, 4380
Apache Argentine 381
Apache Dance 2135, 4527
Apaches, The (dance) 629
Apartheid Lover 3076
Apartment, The 3603
Apartment House 2134
Apartment Lament 2007
Apartmento 4389
Apassionette 680
Ape Can Save the World, An 164
Ape Over Broadway 164
Aphrodite 181
Aphrodite Waltz 165
Apocalypse Fugue 4789
Apocalyptic Horses 264
Apologia 2597
Apologize 3057
Apology, The 430
Apology? 2295
Apology, The 4319
Appearance of Lady Volumnia with Court 4046
Appearances 1079
Appearances Are Deceitful 4497
Appearances Were Against Her 195
Appendectomy 3806
Appendectomy II 3806
Appian Way, The 3484
Applause 167, 602, 2437
Apple and the Bough, The 2238
Apple Blossom Victory 1914
Apple Doesn't Fall, The 3718
Apple Jack 1811, 2030, 4199
Apple Mary Maguire 734
Apple Sketching, The 4591
Apple Tree (Forbidden Fruit), The 170
Apple's the Cause of It All, An 4381
Apples 150, 3485
Apples and Raisins 4659
Apples, Bananas and You 2972
Apples in the Garden 482
Apples in the Lilac Tree 3094
Apples on the Lilac Tree 2928
Apples! Oranges! Crackerjack! 96
Applicant, The 3162
Appointments 2925
Appreciation 197
Apprentice Seaman 4287
Apprenticeship of Duddy Kravitz, The 171
Approach the Lady Gently 1837
'Appy 'Oliday, A 102
Apres la Guerre 1175
Apres Vous I 3602
April Blossoms 4694
April Can't Do This to Me 850
April Child 2633
April Face 4366
April Fool 817, 1446
April Fool Ditty 2408
April Fooled Me 1928
April Fools, The 261
April in Fairbanks 3108
April in Harrisburg (1) 70
April in Harrisburg (2) 70
April in Paris 4583
April in Siberia 4536
April in Wisconsin 2949
April Showers 487
April Snow 4524
April Song 634
April Song, An 172
April Twenty One 1015
Aqua Vitae 1797
Aquarius 1717
Arab Death 4325
Arab Maid with Midnight Eyes 2330
Arab of Ararat 3191
Arabas 'n' Elephants 2028
Arabella's Wedding Day 2462
Arabia My Land of Sweet Romance 4809

Arabian for 'Get Happy' 1300
Arabian Lover 895
Arabian Moon 3965
Arabian Nights 551
Araby 1404, 2107, 3982
Araminta to Herself 911
Arbiter's Song 721
Arbor Day 1966
Arcadia 496
Arcadians, The 906
Arcady 487
Arcadya Is Ever Young 178
Archie 4430
Architect, The 4332
archy and mehitabel 3934
Arctic Ballet (Storm Ballet), The 2150
Ardent Admirer 3484
Are There Any More Rosie O'Grady's? 941
Are We Downhearted? 266
Are We Downhearted? No 3259
Are We Feeling Any Better 1614
Are We Late? 2307
Are We Ready? 900
Are We Strong? 2659
Are We Talking About the Same Thing? 190
Are We Widows, Wives or What? 4490
Are You a Man 3711
Are You a Single or a Married Man? 1912
Are You Asking Me to Forget? 4013
Are You Engaged 248
Are You Going to Dance 902
Are You Havin' Any Fun 4825
Are You Havin' Any Fun? 1494
Are You Here Maggie Mooney Are You Here? 3144
Are You in Love? 2
Are You Kiddin' Bud? 847
Are You Lonesome Tonight 4193
Are You Love? 1145
Are You My Darlin' 3683
Are You Now 2810
Are You Ready, Gyp Watson? 1029
Are You Satisfied 1489
Are You Smiling? 2933
Are You Steppin' Out Tonight 2939
Are You Stepping Out Tonight 2494
Are You Sure That They Are All in Bed? 1080
Are You Sure? 4516
Are You the Man Whose Name Is on the Paper 2017
Are You the One 3561
Are You There with Another Girl 261
Are You There? 3719
Are You Thrilling 3442
Are You Washed in the Blood of the Lamb 3631
Are You With It? 180
Are You with Me? 3162
Aren't We All? 2950
Aren't You Glad? 2961
Aren't You the Girl I Met at Sherry's 1464
Aren't You Warm? 4173
Arena Pantomime, The (inst.) 134
Arethusa and the Snoozer 306
Argentina 1485, 4182
Argentine 659, 3149
Argentine, The 4219
Argentine 4437
Argentine Arango, The 765
Argentine Tango 868
Argentine Tango (inst.) 4063
Argument, The 519
Argument 721, 2630
Argument, The 4830
Argument 1276
Argument, The 4652
Ari's Promise 181
Ari's Soliloquy 181
Aria 949
Aria, An 2216
Aria 3064, 4579
Aria for a Cow 2038
Ariella 1570, 4646
Arieni (Let's Dance) 2147
Aries 3825
Aristocracy 375
Aristocracy, The 586
Aristocratic Servants 2519
Aristotle 649
Arithmetic 3855
Arizona 4540, 2602
Arkansas 394
Arlee 47
Arm in Arm 1860, 4287
Arm in Arm in Harmony 2283
Arm with a Bow in Its Hand 857
Armadillo Idyll 221
Armageddon 3568
Armful of Trouble 3735
Armful of You, An 1916
Armies of the Right 2001
Armorer's Song, The 3736
Armoured Knight, The 104
Arms 2458
Arms and the Girl 742
Arms for the Love of America 1416
Arms for the Love of Me 4173
Arms of the China Wall 1378
Army, The 3873, 1852
Army Air Corps Song 4706
Army and Navy, The 4761
Army and the Shuberts Depend on You, The (Opening) 4340
Army Blue 1476
Army Club, The 965
Army Corps, The 2914
Army Directory, The 1455
Army Life, The 1972
Army Mule Song, The 4366
Army of Oogaboo, The 4381
Army of the Just, The 4312
Army Service Forces, The 4141
Army So Grand, The 476

Army Song, The 4109
Army Song 4369
Army's Made a Man Out of Me, The 4340
Around in a Whirl 1193
Around the Clock 185
Around the Town 3400, 187, 3973
Around the World 190, 4264
Around the World in Eighty Days
190, 189, 1161
Arrest, The 2212
Arrest Ballet, The (inst.) 2777
Arrival 1068
Arrival, The 3830
Arrival 1159
Arrival of Guests 531, 931, 3170
Arrival of Gypsies 4046
Arrival of Madeline 1573
Arrival of Robert E. Lee 3426
Arrival of Society, The 3723
Arrival of Steamboat 4667
Arrival of the Amber Express, The 102
Arrival of the Boom 3729
Arrival of the Plot, The 3723
Arrival of the Princess Pat 3590
Arrival of Tourists 4667
Arrivederci My Little Iron 3165
Arriverderci Roma 4264
'Arry and 'Arriet 188
Art 1112, 3437, 3972
Art Film Premiere 408
Art for Art's Sake 919
Art Is Calling Me
(I Want to Be a Prima Donna) 1183
Art of Conversation, The 483
Art of Deceiving, The 2654
Art of Exercising, The 1798
Art of Fascination, The 4209
Art of Knowing How, The 248
Art of Making Love, The 2543
Art of Pleasing Me, The 2877
Art of Stimulation, The 2715
Art of the Possible, The 1211
Art Song 1229, 1851
Art with a Capital "A" 41
Arthur 198
Arthur in the Afternoon 16, 131
Arthur, Son of Martha 920
Article 213 2936
Artie 3578
Artificial Flowers 4312
Artists 4798
Artists and Models 200, 1646, 3387
Arts, The 2804, 3940, 3942
Arty 3615
Arverne Rose 332
Aryans Under the Skin 4340
As a Boy 259
As a Butterfly Sips the Roses 4133
As a Friend 2498
As a Girl 259
As a Troubador 1312
As Adam 2433
As Advertised in Life 62
As All the Maids 4404
As Along the Street We Wander 4554
As Befits My Rank and Station 3786
As Birds Greet Morning Skies 4064
As Busy As Anyone Can Be 1766
As Calm As the Ocean 414
As Far As I'm Concerned 4481
As Far As Thought Can Reach 1651
As for the Future 3161
As Good As a Man 305
As Good As Gold 2162
As Good As Paradise 4523
As Happy As a King 2317
As I Came Up the Aisle 351
As I Choose 2659
As I Grow Older 3159
As I Love You 355, 2287
As I Say Goodbye 4515
As I Was Going Along 3989
As I Was Remarking 4099
As I Went Over 2134
As I'd Like to Be 1258
As I'm Growing Older 4595
As If 1797
As If for the First Time 945
As If I Weren't There 3491
As If We Never Said Goodbye 4217
As It Should Be 1649
As Kipling Says: 'I Learned About
Women from Her' 606
As Life Is Short, Let Life Be Gay 3736
As Long As He Loves Me 4817
As Long As He Needs Me 3271
As Long As I Have You 628
As Long As I Live 880, 4788
As Long As I Love 2323
As Long As I've Got My Mammy 391
As Long As It's Not about Love 2432
As Long As Man Loves Woman 1083
As Long As the Wife Don't Know 21
As Long As the World Goes Round
(Tra-La-La) 2336
As Long As the World Goes Round 3676
As Long As There's a Mother 1290
As Long As There's Love 797
As Long As They Keep On Making Them 3369
As Long As This Is England 455
As Long As We Have Bromo Seltzer in
Our Love Nest Baby, We're Through 289
As Long as We're in Love 1827
As Long As We're Together 2039
As Long as You're Along 4498
As Long As You're Happy 3142
As Much As That 1265
As Much to Me 260
As of Today 4142
As on Moonlit Waves We Ride 1926

As On Through the Seasons We Sail 3972
As Once I Loved You 3702
As Plain as Daylight 2617
As Plain As the Nose on My Face 2022
As Simple As That 2864
As the Agent 698
As the Case May Be 4617
As the Flitting Swallows Fly 1266
As the Girls Go 206
As the Prince Waked the Princess 3951
As the Years Roll By 1851
As the Years Roll On 3061
As Things Go Bump 1757
As Though You Were There 1800
As Time Goes By 1207
As Was and As Is 4483
As We Go Along 3671
As We Go Out Walking 4248
As We Leave the Years Behind 2972
As We Lie in Langour Lazy 3777
As We Pass By 2299
As We Sow 1847
As We Swing Sweetheart 3753
As We Told You 90, 3914
As Wonderful As I 3714
As Ye Sow—Shall Ye Reap 750
As You Are 1171
As You Make Your Bed 369
As You Rest in His Arms 3627
As You Walk Down the Strand 4802
As You Would Love Paree 3465
Asbury Park 4283
Ascot Gavotte 3038
Ashes and Fire 1020
Ashley 3355
Ashley's Departure 1616
Asia 60
Asiatic Angels 4477
Asiatic Angles 4530
Ask and You Shall Receive 3825
Ask Dad 3250
Ask Dad-He Knows 2619
Ask Dodge 1573
Ask Her While the Band Is Playing 48, 3773
Ask Me Again 4015
Ask Me Beauty 717
Ask Me No Question 109
Ask Mr. Jorrocks 2240
Ask Papa 2844
Ask the Cabby 1307
Ask the Flowers to Tell You 4381
Ask the Man 2155
Ask the Stars 3207
Asking for You 1061
Asp, An 1757
Aspects of Love 211
Aspirations 2844, 2100
Assassination 3944
Assembling of the Two Courts 1388
Assembly Dance, The 1290
Asses Song, The 1195
Assistant Undersecretary of
State for Human Rights, The 3661
Associated Press 2276
Association Word Game 1857
Assyrians, The 2033
Astor Hotel, The 3867
Astoria Gloria 135
Astrociggy 2918
Astrology 3825, 4468
Astronomy 2724
Asylum Chorus 2228
At 0700 Tomorrow 2472
At a Georgia Camp Meetin' 3905
At a Grand Hotel 4258
At a Reception 4364
At a Time Like This 2511
At an Early Stage of Life 1178
At Any Age at All 4461
At Arrowhead Inn 4787
At Christmastime 4075
At Court 1522
At Dommayer's 1680
At Gay Raatenbad 3755
At Half Past Seven 3144
At Happy Hollow 1866
At Home with My Range 2338
At Jolly Coon-ey Island 217
At Last 1068, 1127, 1388, 3175, 3195, 3319
At Last I Find You 307
At Last I Hold You 1458
At Last It's Love 4483
At Last United 1565
At Last We're Alone, Dear 4666
At Least 2012
At Least I Tried 305
At Least That Is My Supposition 1274
At Least There Are Parties 2346
At Least We Can Say 2876
At Least You Can Say You Have Seen It 2006
At Liberty in Thebes 3272
At Long Last 3986
At Long Last Love 1762, 4777
At Longchamps Today 1272
At Lovetime 4620
At Madame Regay's 3723
At Mammy's Fireside 1963
At Maxims 2837
At Midnight on My Pillow Lying
(The Dream Song) 1193
At Mrs. Simpkin's Finishing School 3953
At My Age 4, 842
At My Lady's Feet 3049
At My Side 4619
At Night, At Night 4738
At Night She Comes Home to Me 253
At Our Tango Tea Last Week 1544
At Peace Wid de World 295
At Sea 787
At Siesta Time 758

At Stony Brook 3014
At Such a Tender Age 1815
At Such a Time as This 325
At Sundown 3989
At That Bully Wooly Wild West Show 3525
At that San Francisco Fair 3193
At the 'Alls 2938
At the Annual Vice-Regal Ball 2055
At the Automat 4206
At the Ball 611, 2887, 2976, 4808
At the Ball, That's All 983, 3041
At the Ballet 746
At the Barbecue 2628, 4763
At the Barber's Ball 800
At the Bed-D-Bye Motel 2568
At the Block Party 1876
At the Bottom Lookin' Up 474
At the Bottom of Brixton Hill 1544
At the Bottom of It—Love! 649
At the Bottom of Your Heart 4343
At the Brookside Inn 1868
At the Camp Meeting 1876
At the Casino 4774
At the Check Apron Ball 3113
At the Circus 2004
At the Cocktail Bar 796
At the Court Around the Corner 3006
At the Crossroads of Life (We'll Meet Again) 2039
At the Dansant 1796
At the Dawn Tea 2287
At the Drive In 4467
At the End of a Period of Time 2017
At the End of the Day 415, 2442
At the End of the Road 2564
At the Fair 3949
At the Field of Cloth of Gold 3702
At the Flower Garden Ball 1963
At the Folies Bergere 511
At the Fountain 4528
At the Fox Trot Ball 2696
At the Game 2224
At the Garbage Gentlemen's Ball 2415
At the Gate of Roses 1131
At the Grand 223
At the Grand Hotel 1649
At the Hockey Game 2072
At the Hotel 69
At the Hotel Amerique 1868
At the Jazz Town Novelty Ball 3402
At the Krazy Kat's Ball 1686
At the Mardi Gras 2137
At the Matinee 2780
At the Movies 426, 3296
At the Moving Picture Ball 3020
At the Music Hall 705, 1188, 3542, 187
At the Opera 2474
At the Pan-American 3751
At the Party 642, 3867, 4249
At the Piano 2856
At the Picture Show 3525, 4206
At the Play 3819
At the Playland Jamboree 941
At the Prohibition Ball 815
At the Prom 1822, 4249
At the Rag-Time Ball 2107
At the Rail 3698
At the Rainbow 3547
At the Rainbow's End 1096
At the Red Rose Cotillion 4652
At the Reefer Smoker's Ball 4501
At the Round Table (Knight's Opening) 834
At the Roxy Music Hall 2061
At the Saskatchewan 376
At the Seaside 3588, 3348
At the Shore 3207
At the Spotlight Canteen 1336
At the Stage Door 910
At the Toy Shop 4747
At the Wheel of an Auto 3258
At the Widder Sadie Simpkins Buildin' Bee 2090
At Twenty-Two 3940
At Weddings as a General Rule 4554
At Ye Olde Coffee Shoppe in Cheyenne 3674
At Your Age 260
At Your Service 3054
At Ze Naughty Folies Bergere 357
Atheism 624
Athena 4798
Athena's Dance (inst.) 4798
Athletic 1224
Athletic Boy 381
Athletic Girl, The 75
Athletic Prancing 2667
Atlanta 3368, 2137
Atlanta Burning 1616
Atlantic Blues 2467
Atlantic City 1332, 1407, 229
Atlantic City Girl, The 1678
Atlantic City Welcomes You 98
Atta-Boy, Atta-Girl 423
Attack of the Banshees 4139
Attends! 839
Attention 4403
Attention Pray! 1470
Attuck's March, The 2111
Atwater College Songs (Good Old Atwater) 2430
Au Revoir 2238, 3931, 4011
Au Revoir, but Not Goodbye 2762
Au Revoir, Cher Baron 4777
Au Revoir My Little Hyacinth 3710
Au Revoir Poland—Hello New York! 615
Au Revoir, Soldier 3536
Aucassin & Nicolette 1262
Auckland, New Zealand 108
Auction Day 1758
Auction Pinochle Song 233
Auction Rag 2494
Auction Sell (What a Grand Day for an Auction Sell), The 1086
Auction Song, The 2399

Auctioneer's Song 3736
Auctions 4004
Audition, The 3682
Audition 1359
Audition, The 3366
Audition 4557
Audley Family Honour, The 2375
Auf Den Berg Es Is Schon 188
Auf Wiedersehen 392, 511, 958, 4132, 3763, 3890
Auf Wiedersehn! 473
Augie Masters 2304
August Moon, The 2627
Auld Lang Syne 1897
Aunt Dinah 61
Aunt Dinah Has Blowed de Horn 4447
Aunt Jemima (I'm Comin' Home) 2645
Aunt Jemima (I'm Going Home) 14
Aunt Jessie 3235
Aunt Polly's Prayer 4409
Aunt Sophie (inst.) 499
Auntie Mame 2713, 2713
Aunties 1809
Aural Misunderstanding
(I'm Whirling, Twirling), An 1071
Aurora 2209
Aurora (from Aurora, Illinois) 4425
Aurora Blushing Rosily 2670
Aurora Borealis 4753
Aurory Bory Alice 1654
Austrian Patrol (inst.) 3613
Author, The 3822
Auto Da Fe (What a Day) 630
Auto Galop 1148
Auto Girls Song 4811
Auto Show Girl 3296
Auto-Mo-Biling 4130
Autograph Chant
(An Autograph of Hazel Flagg) 1791
Autograph Gals' Song 3437
Autograph Girls 3531
Autographs of You 364
Automobile Horn Song 4683
Automobiling 2631
Automobilla 1228
Automotivation 364
Autumn 945, 4145, 4292
Autumn Afternoon 807
Autumn Afternoon, The 808, 3542
Autumn Carol 946
Autumn Courting, The (inst.) 1698
Autumn Day 2168
Autumn Flowers 3978
Autumn in New York 4374
Autumn Love 809
Autumn Moon 1558
Autumn Songs 3536
Autumn Sun 3472
Autumn's Here 239
Autumn's in the Red Again 4415
Aux Armes 3406
Available Me 1884
Avalon 487, 3985
Avalon Ballroom, The 339
Ave Maria 3890
Ave Nelson 2284
Avenue F 3668
Avenue, Fifth Avenue 3126
Avenue of Americas, The 3410
Avenue of Trees 3374
Average Man, The 2784
Aviation 1550
Aviation Ballet 4271
Aviator 1419
Aviator, The 1598
Aviatrix Love Song 3641
Avon Garde 272
Avonlea, We Love You 148
Avos 2269
Avrum and Sore's Duet 4082
Aw C'mon Evie 2578
Awake and a Dream 535
Awake, Children, Awake 2872
Awake Dearest One 4094
Awake, Ma Chile 457
Awakened Love 4616
Award, The 3568
Awarding the Prize Sketch 1657
Awards 4019
Away 3035
Away! 3691
Away, Away, Away 2940
Away Down Souf 4149
Away for a Lovely Ocean Cruise 1285
Away from Home 2682, 3683
Away from It All 3326
Away from Thee 2424
Away from You 3702
Away to Jail 1469
Away to Moscow 1602
Away to the Dungeon Cell 1758
Away to the Links 1925
Away to the Mountains 3786
Away We'll Float 2534
Away with Him 104
Away with Them 2944
Awefull Battle of the
Pekes and Pollicles, The 678
Awf'lly Nice 242
Awful Truth, The 3668
Awkward Age, The 3401
Awkward Little Boy 227
Awkward Questions 194
Ay Caramba 846
Ay, Lye, Luy, Lye 4390
Ay Mi Do 3830
Ay, Michael, Oh, Michael 2055
Ay-Oomps 2903
Ay! Que Rico 2407
Ay Vant to Go Back to Sveden 1351
Ayama 4579

Aye-Caramba 845
Aye, Lad 1619
Ayes of Texas, The 3615
Ayre and Fa-La 129
Az Obsitos 1852
Azure Te 1296
Azuri's Dance of Triumph (inst.) 1027
Azusa 1928

B

B & O, The 1663
B-a-b-e-e 4064
B Apostrophe, K Apostrophe, L-Y-N 1577
B.G. Bigelow, Inc 2234
B.G. Bigelow, Inc. 1300
B'Gosh! 4014
B Is the Note 4360
B-R-O-A-D-W-A-Y 4836
B Valse 2491
B.Y.O.B. 1713
Ba-Be 1964
Ba-Boom! 1665
Baa, Baa, Black Sheep 2481
Babbette 3279
Babbitt and the Bromide, The 1419
Babbitts in Love 1725
Babbling Babette 4150
Babes in Arms 247
Babes in the Wood 249, 4555
Babes in Toyland 251
Babette 2906
Babette of Beaujolais 2670
Babette's Military Dance 1722
Babette's Wedding Day 1722
Babies on the Brain 572
Baby! 441
Baby 670
Baby, A 1497
Baby 2615, 132
Baby! [1] 4300
Baby! [2] 4300
Baby 4840
Baby Ain't a Baby No More 1862
Baby and Nursie 4115
Baby, Baby 3901, 2147, 3210
Baby! Baby! (Somethin's Happ'nin') 4789
Baby, Baby, Baby 253
Baby Be Good 381
Baby Blue 4716
Baby Blues 702, 3478, 4033, 254
Baby Bond for Baby, A 2068
Baby Boom Babies 4731
Baby Boom Boogie Boy 1077
Baby Breath 1116
Baby Buntin' 1174
Baby Couldn't Dance 4499
Baby Doll 478, 4063
Baby-Doll Dance 551
Baby Dollie Walk 4033
Baby Dolls 560, 2960, 3619
Baby, Don't You Count on Me 1101
Baby, Dream Your Dream 4238
Baby Dreams 2216
Baby Duet 1712
Baby Eyes 4599
Baby Face O'Flynn 255
Baby Games 2453
Baby, I Could Do It for You 4763
Baby I Love You 2427, 4016
Baby, I Love Your Biscuits 1969
Baby in Love, A 2419
Baby in the House 8
Baby, It's Cold Outside 3261, 3444
Baby It's You 4193
Baby Johann 2290
Baby John 4433
Baby June and Her Newsboys 1709
Baby Lamb 4360
Baby, Let's Dance 2366
Baby Let's Face It 4428
Baby Lonesome 2286
Baby Lou 1316
Baby Love 4808
Baby Me 589
Baby Mine 443, 1565, 3054, 3740
Baby Moon 1378
Baby Number, The 2307
Baby Nurse 3322
Baby on the Shore 3998
Baby, Play with Me 4550
Baby, Please Thaw Out 2083
Baby Rose 2127
Baby Rue 459
Baby San 4048
Baby Talk 1566
Baby, Talk to Me 607
Baby, That's Love 1222
Baby Vampire, The 2620
Baby Vampire 2870, 4421
Baby Vampire Land 3962
Baby, Wait till It Happens to You 277
Baby Walk 465
'Baby Wampus' Stars, The 4772
Baby Wanna Go Bye-Bye With You 1440
Baby Wants 3054
Baby Wants to Dance 4709
Baby, What Else Can I Do 1658
Baby! What? 1628
Baby When I Find You 4151
Baby with the Dimple and the Smile, The 3976
Baby, Won't You Please Come Home 1425
Baby, You Can Count on Me 534
Baby You Love, The 2797
Babying You 3583
Babykins 3721
Babylon Is Falling 3705
Baby's Awake Now 4118

Baby's Baby 868
Baby's Baby Grand 1460
Baby's Best Friend, A 3521, 3924
Baby's Blue 2
Baby's Born, A 1385
Baby's Eyes 166
Baby's Gone 3134
Baccanale Dance 4283
Bacchanal Rag, The 3395
Bacchanale 322, 1342, 2802
Bacchanale (Ballet) 3301
Bacchanale 3543
Bacchus 3573
Bachanol 1461
Bachelor, The 521, 3230
Bachelor Bear 1560
Bachelor Belles, The 256
Bachelor Days 1558
Bachelor Gal 4633
Bachelor Gay, A 2698
Bachelor Girl and Boy, A 1530
Bachelor Girls 3981
Bachelor Hoedown 673
Bachelor Song, The 2344
Bachelorhood 1048
Bachelors 4619
Bachelor's Button, A 4133
Bachelor's Dance 2188
Bachelor's Dream, The 4849, 4832
Bachelor's Lament 4093
Back Again 258
Back Again, Back Again 402
Back at the Palace 4377
Back Back Back to Akron 1357
Back, Back, Back to the Land! 3092
Back Bay Beat 532
Back from Hollywood 1492
Back from the Great Beyond 3564
Back from Thirty-Six to Twenty-Nine 2710
Back Home 1026, 3841, 4296
Back Home Again in Indiana 3840
Back in Business 4067
Back in Circulation 435, 3329
Back in Circulation Again 3946
Back in My Hometown 1532
Back in My Tumble Down Shack 728
Back in Old Dubuque 538
Back in Show Biz Again 534
Back in the Days of Long Ago 2005
Back in the Dear Old Days 4453
Back in the Kitchen 1729
Back in the Kitchen Again 3410
Back in the Quaint Little School in Caroline 3246
Back in the Street 3548
Back in the World Now 1053
Back in Town 2905
Back o' Town 4162
Back of Life, The 1865
Back on Base 784
Back Out While the Backing Is Good 2665
Back Seat of a Taxi 364
Back So Soon? 3272
Back to American Furniture 520
Back to Broadway 3031
Back to Bundling 3105
Back to Genesis 3824
Back to Him 1842
Back to Killarney 2180
Back to London 3828
Back to My Heart 2293
Back to My Shack 70
Back to Nature 2145, 3763, 3958
Back to Nature with You 3214
Back to New York 4758
Back to Normal 3558
Back to Old Broadway 3417, 3562
Back to Old Montana 2286
Back to Paris 3729
Back to School Again 64
Back to School Ballet 148
Back to Sioux Sioux City 228
Back to the Boulevards 3578
Back to the Dear Old Trenches 1527
Back to the Farm 4826
Back to the Heather 466
Back to the Palace 2143
Back to the Play 3272
Back to the U.S.A. 632, 646
Back to Work 3501
Back to You 4147
Back Together Again 1999
Back with a Beat 3515
Back Your Fancy 178
Backbiting Me 4520
Backlot Blues, The 1048
Backstage 595
Backstage at the Vic 1757
Backstage Babble 167
Backstage Girls 119
Backwards 4468
Backwards Alphabet, The 58
Bacon and the Egg, The 4765
Bad, Bad Men, The 2376
Bad-Bad-Bad 4416
Bad Bill Jones 4199
Bad Boy 1713
Bad Boy and a Good Girl, A 3618
Bad Breath 3653
Bad But Good 4168
Bad Chinaman from Shanghai, A 805
Bad Companions 1614
Bad Girl 1612, 2637
Bad Girl in Paree 3382
Bad Girl of West Seattle, The 2992
Bad Glad Good and Had 1637
Bad Habits 1298
Bad If He Does, Worse If He Don't 4623
Bad Karma 3309
Bad Little Apple and the Wise Old Tree, The 2909

Bad Little Boy and Good Little Girl 480
Bad Little Boy with Dancing Legs 1461
Bad Luck, I'll Laugh at You 2628
Bad Man Number 4664
Bad Man Walk 1992
Bad Man Walk, The 2378
Bad News 1451
Bad News Report 2084
Bad Timing 404
Bad Trip 1450
Bad Whitey 4343
Bad, Bad Stacker Lee 2225
Badaroma 4018
Badchen 4773
Badchen's Verses 4769
Baddest Mammyjammy 3825
Badmen 3865
Bag of Luck, The 4447
Bag with Which You Shop, The 272
Bag-pipe Serenade 3710
Bagdad 2394, 3985, 4227
Bagdad on the Subway 3508
Bagels and Yox 268
Bagpipes on Parade 1138
Bah 2978
Bah, Bah Black Sheep 47
Bah! Bah! 1165
Bah! Humbug! 753
Bahia 850
Bailar 1164
Bajour 269
Bake a Cake 455
Baker's Boy and the Chimney Sweep, The 1016
Baker's Dozen 272
Bakerloo, The 791
Baking, The 273
Baksheesh 1079
Bal Bullier 284
Bal Masque 2394
Bal Masque, The 3154
Bal Petit Bal 3107
Bal Tabarin, The 2135
Balalaika Serenade, The 3013
Balance the Plate 4515
Balancing 944
Balancing the Books 753
Balcony of the Faithful 119
Balcony Scene 949
Balcony Trio 945
Bali Ha'i 4096
Balinasia 4029
Balinda's Triumph 355
Balkan Dance 2293
Ball, The 2805, 3285, 1959
Ball and Chain 338
Ball Begins, The 3406
Ball Im Savoy 277
Ball Is in Your Court, The 775
Ball of All Nations 4723
Ballad (1) 2790
Ballad (2) 2790
Ballad for a Firing Squad 278
Ballad for a Park 427
Ballad for a Pencil 4060
Ballad for a Summer Evening 3000
Ballad for Americans (Ballad of Uncle Sam) 3986
Ballad for Billionaires 4018
Ballad for Bimshire 279
Ballad for Christmas 1736
Ballad in Which Macheath Begs All Men for Forgiveness 4370
Ballad Maker 2248
Ballad of a Bus 3110
Ballad of a Redneck 3684
Ballad of Adam and Eve 2285
Ballad of Baby Face McGinty (Who Bit Off More Than He Could Chew), The 4825
Ballad of Beauregard Green 3186
Ballad of Beauregard Green, The 392
Ballad of Bedford Gaol 3490
Ballad of Belle Boyd, The 1474
Ballad of Billy McCaw, The 678
Ballad of Booth, The 212
Ballad of Castle Maiden 1978
Ballad of Cy and Beatrice, The 4533
Ballad of Czolgosz, The 212
Ballad of Dependency 4369
Ballad of Dry Dock Country 2051
Ballad of Federal City, The 3530
Ballad of Frimbo 1402
Ballad of Gracious Living 4370
Ballad of Guiteau, The 212
Ballad of Harry Lewis, The 1832
Ballad of Herman Schlepps, The 4827
Ballad of Immoral Earnings 4370
Ballad of Jack and the Beanstalk, The 2182
Ballad of Johnny Pot, The 280
Ballad of Mac the Knife 4370
Ballad of Mack the Knife, The 4369
Ballad of Marcia LaRue, The 4323
Ballad of Nellie Gwynne, The 346
Ballad of Norman, The 871
Ballad of Oh and For the Love 1262
Ballad of Phoebe Cousins 2928
Ballad of Progress, The (1) 451
Ballad of Progress, The (2) 451
Ballad of Sexual Obsession 4370
Ballad of Sheriff Dunlap 4543
Ballad of Sir Topaz 1500
Ballad of Sloppy Joe, The 2653
Ballad of Smokey the Bear 281
Ballad of Stonewall Jackson, The 1474
Ballad of Sweeney Todd, The 4233
Ballad of Tancred 1017
Ballad of the Billow, The 402
Ballad of the Dauntless Courier 842
Ballad of the Easy Life 4369
Ballad of the Garment Trade 2048
Ballad of the Gun 1029

Ballad of the Lily of Hell 1755
Ballad of the Liver Bird 2682
Ballad of the Prisoner of Sex 4371
Ballad of the Robber Esteban 2323
Ballad of the Robbers 2344
Ballad of the Sad Cafe, The 3162
Ballad of the Sad Young Men 3094
Ballad of the Seigneur 4285
Ballad of the Shape of Things 2554
Ballad of the Southern Suburbs 4579
Ballad of the Tree 157
Ballad of the Triangle Fire 1609
Ballad of '39 3688
Ballad of Utopia, The 4536
Ballad Singer, The 702
Ballad to a Brute 2304
Ballad to the International Business
Machines Building 157
Ballade 2439
Ballade of the Duel 4670
Balled of Lovers 2611
Balled of the Easy Life, The 4368
Ballerina, The 336
Ballerina 3233
Ballerina's Story, The 3013
Ballet 157
Ballet (inst.) 559
Ballet (dance) 4486
Ballet 842, 1183, 1864, 1878
Ballet (inst.) 2608, 2915, 2950
Ballet 3151, 3201, 1884
Ballet (inst.) 3977
Ballet at the Village Vortex (dance) 4734
Ballet Classique 2364
Ballet Dance 2135
Ballet Divertissement (dance) 1711
Ballet Eccentrique 559
Ballet Erotique 1695
Ballet Girl, The 284
Ballet Modern 2569
Ballet Moderne 2364
Ballet Music (inst.) 294
Ballet Music 3569, 1213
Ballet of Jewels, The 4452
Ballet of Siam, A 3405
Ballet of the Book According to Gerald 999
Ballet of the Butterflies 188
Ballet of the North Wind 1643
Ballet of the Pyramids (inst.) 2857
Ballet of the Warsaw Ghetto (dance) 181
Ballet of Wealth 4528
Ballet Oriental 3778
Ballet-Pantomime 3466
Ballet Peculaire (inst.) 4557
Ballet Rehearsal 4365
Ballet Romantique (inst.) 4357
Ballet San Damiano 1377
Ballet Suite, The (inst.) 2394
Ballet Suite 3590
Ballet-Youth 2394
Ballhouse Krazy Bar 194
Ballin' 3824
Ballin' the Jack 146, 1544, 4390
Ballinasloe 3049
Ballo Moderno 3822
Balloon 786
Balloon Girls, The 804
Balloon Is Ascending, A 367
Balloon Underplay (inst.) 190
Ballooning 1246
Balloons 392, 1408
Ballroom for Two 2458
Bally-Burlesk 4816
Bally Hoo Bay 3158
Ballyhoo 153, 2540
Ballyhooey Lassies (Opening Act II) 289
Ballyhujah 289
Balnesmoor Lane 1216
Baloon, Baloona 519
Baltimo' 3396
Baltimore 2852, 3067
Baltimore Bombashay, The 1501
Baltimore Buzz 1198, 3963
Baltimore Sun 1420
Bambalina 3249, 4694
Bambalina Maid 2462
Bambazoola 3149
Bambino 3478
Bamboo Babies 1460
Bamboo Isle 3241
Bamboo Lane 2119
Bamboula 3840
Bamboula, The (El Relicario) 4033
Ban Joe 4191
Ban the Book! 1035
Banana, Banana, Banana 3690
Banana Oil 682
Bananas 2470
Banco Number, The 4768
Band, The 4788
Band Box Girl, The 4801
Band Came Back, The 2448
Band of the Ne'er Do Wells, The 2102
Band Plays Home Sweet Home, The 1129
Band Started Swinging a Song, The 3893
Bandana Babies 3709
Bandana Ball 3009
Bandana Days 3512, 3963
Bandana Girls 489
Bandana Ways 3965
Bandanna Anna 2009
Bandanna Babies 441
Bandanna Land 2160
Bandar-Logs, The 2970
Bandbox Girl, The 1526
Bandit Am I, A 1518
Bandit Band, The 1923, 2788
Bandit Raffles I, A 538
Bane of Man, The 1384
Bane of My Life 649

Bang! 157, 4067, 992, 2536, 2764
Bang! Bang! Bang! 1687
Bang, Bang, Bang 4014
Bang, Bang, Bang, You're Dead 2496
Bang, Bang, the Most Harmonious Sound 4724
Bang, the Bell Rang! 2105
Bang! There Goes My Heart 1855
Bang Up Time 2135
Bang Your Way to the Top 1940
Banga Boo 317
Bangaway Isle 202
Banishment, The 1027
Banjo Dance 1374
Banjo Eyes 297
Banjo Land 3808
Banjo that Man Joe Plays, The 4581
Banjo, Banjo 496
Banjos 2805
Bankrupt Blues 1064
Banks of Wye, The 2891
Banquet, The 1655, 1714
Banshee Man 2853
Bantu Baby 2337
Bar, The 4635
Bar Mitzvah, The 299
Bar Mitzvah Boy 299
Bar Mitzvah of Eliot Green 299
Bar on the Piccola Marina, A 3196
Bar on the Piccolo Marina, A 3235
Barabanchik 3526
Barbara 4145
Barbara Fritchie 3056
Barbara Song 369, 4369, 4370
Barbarian Dance 4735
Barbary Coast 190, 302, 1528
Barbecue, The 2534
Barbecue for Two 992
Barbeque 897
Barber, The 2317
Barber and His Wife, The 4233
Barbering Wop of Seville, The 4010
Barber's Society of Philosophical Research 2111
Barber's Song, The 2727
Barbershop, The 2229
Barbershop Opera 3705
Barbizon 3618
Barcarole 559, 1530
Barcarole, The 1689
Barcarole 3087
Barcarolla 336
Barcarolle 2222, 2622
Barcarolle from 'Anthony and Cleopatra' 2115
Barcelona 130, 832, 3967
Barcelona Girls 2938
Barcometer Love 720
Bard, The 2339
Bard and the Beard, The 3107
Bare Facts 251
Bare Necessities, The 223
Barefoot Boy with Cheek 304
Barefoot Gal 2248
Barefoot Girl 3721
Bargain Day 3981
Bargaining 1060
Barking Baby Never Bites, A 1894
Barley Mow, The 4404
Barn Dance, The 1374
Barn Dance 3049, 3265
Barn Dance Schottische 1230
Barnabo 1017
Barnaby Beach 4362
Barney (A Song Full of Blarney) 2991
Barney Donohue 3488
Barney McGuire 2885
Barney O'Flynn 250
Barnum and Bailey Rag 1478
Barnum & Bailey Rag 1826
Barnum Had the Right Idea 2525
Barnyard, The 547
Barnyard Blues 2992
Baron de Ragotin 3769
Baron Papouche 4115
Baron Samedi 3814
Baron Trenck 307, 307
Baron's 100th Birthday, The 2673
Baron's Entrance 2745
Baron's Star Act, The 4165
Baron, the Duchess, and the Count, The 138
Baroness Bazooka 3036
Barrel of Beads 3813
Barrelhouse Beguine 1928
Barretts of Wimpole Street, The 3734
Barry's Boys 272, 1049
Bartender's Song, The 2496
Bartholomew Fair 129
Baseball 1823, 1862
Baseball Cards 119
Baseball Game, The 1234
Baseball Girl, The 3096
Basement Blues 3989
Bashful Bill 496
Bashful Boy, A 255
Bashful Chappie, The 522
Bashful Lover 4479
Bashful Moon, The 2722
Basic 722, 3920
Basic Black 4584
Basilica 2407
Basin Street Blues 3840, 3018
Basket—Make a Basket 651
Basket Trio 2159
Basketball 1149, 2072
Basketball Song, The 3806
Basse Dance 3702
Bastard for the Lord 3817
Batata 2626
Bathing 2122, 4834
Bathing Beauty Ballet (inst.) 1886
Bathing Girl 542
Bathing Girl, The 1532

Bathing Girls, The 586, 4803
Bathing Lesson, The 1374
Bathroom 3651
Bathtub, the Lodge, and the Rafter, The 1435
Bats About You 2386
Battalion of France 613
Battersea Butterfly, The 1540
Battle, The 1092, 949
Battle 1769
Battle, The (inst.) 2228
Battle, The 2318, 330
Battle at Eagle Rock (inst.) 3059
Battle Ballet (inst.) 3536
Battle Cry 1809
Battle Cry of Freedom, The 1314
Battle for the Western Name 4405
Battle Hymn of Groundhog 1700
Battle Hymn of the Republic 4460, 2203, 3020
Battle Hymn of the Rialto 1049
Battle of Armageddon 655
Battle of B Flat, The 3122
Battle of Chicago, The 2616
Battle of Old Jim Crow, The 2203
Battle of Roses, The 96
Battle of San Juan Hill, The 2228
Battle of the Alamo (inst.) 996
Battle of the Genie 1101
Battle on the Tiles, The 4497
Battle Song 657
Battle Was Over, It Was Quiet Now, The 4163
Battleground Bummer 3159
Battlelines 4297
Battling Butler 2972
Baubles, Bangles and Beads 2327, 4383
Baxter & Company 496
Baxter Avenue 2428
Baxter's Party 1831
Bay of Botany 971
Bayakhala (They Mourn) 1719
Bayakhala (Zulu-The Child) 2147
Bazaar Hymn 1616
Bazaar of the Caravans 2327
Bazaar Opening Chorus 2915
Bazoom 1596
Bazoom! 1730
BBIWY Blues 932
Be a Jolly Molly 938
Be a Lady All the Time 3433
Be a Lion 4722
Be a Little Lackadaisical 1874
Be a Little Sunbeam 3230
Be a Lover 3215
Be a Man 3551
Be a Mess 4432
Be a Mother 2523
Be a Mountain Man 3908
Be a Party at the Party Tonight 1753
Be a Performer! 2523
Be a Phony 2053
Be a Pussycat 3934
Be a Santa 4190
Be a Spy for Love's Sake 2722
Be a Vamp 4543
Be Aesthetic 2387
Be-Angeled 649
Be Anything But a Girl 2805
Be Back Soon 3271
Be Be Beatrice 2490
Be-Bee 4382
Be Black 3825
Be Bop Lullaby 4829
Be Calm 2447
Be Careful 2264
Be Careful, It's My Heart 789
Be Careful What You Do 702, 4808
Be Careful Whom You Kiss 4788
Be Clever 350
Be Courageous 4062
Be Demure 3710
Be-Deviled 649
Be Flexible 3722
Be Fruitful and Multiply 2354
Be Gentle 4789
Be Glad 3846
Be Glad You're Alive 1101
Be Good 4802
Be Good, Be Good, Be Good 2994
Be Good or Be Gone 3608
Be Good to Her 4643
Be Good to Me 4023
Be Grateful for What You've Got 941
Be Happy 1121, 2462, 2874
Be Happy Boys Tonight 3304
Be Happy, Too 3949
Be Italian 3171
Be Joyful 4588
Be Joyful To-day 3024
Be Joyful Today 3028
Be Kind to People Week 314
Be Kind to Poor Pierrot 252
Be Kind to the Young 3764
Be Kind to Your Parents 1242
Be Like a Basketball and Bounce Right Back 550
Be Like the Bluebird 163
Be More Aggressive 4488
Be My Baby 2427, 4534, 4193
Be My Guest 1837, 4423
Be My Guiding Star of Love 822
Be My Host 3187
Be My Lady 808, 809
Be My Little Apple Dumplin' Do 3951
Be My Little Baby Bumble Bee 4712
Be My Love 4743
Be My Only Love 757
Be My War Bride 525
Be Naughty 4240
Be Not Afraid 3651
Be Oh So Careful Ann 4620
Be On Your Own 3171

Be Our Guest 330
Be Our Mother 3453
Be Our Parents 3453
Be Prepared 4412
Be Prepared to Pay 3833
Be Rational 1161
Be Rich 42
Be Somewhere 3682
Be Sure and Kiss the Blarney Stone 1907
Be Sure and See Them All 3068
Be Sure It's Light 4784
Be Sweet to Me Kid 1563
Be That Way 495
Be the Life of the Crowd 4241
Be the Secret of My Life 3532
Be There 2142
Be Very Careful 1498
Be What You Wanna Be 455
Be Wise in Time 1080
Be with Me 3696
Be Witness to My Madness 2877
Be Young Again 2087
Be Young, Young Man 3066
Be Yourself 73, 318
Beach Ballet 2190
Beach House, The 674
Beach Scene 2252
Beaded Bag, The 3407
Beadle with a Dreydl 3937
Beale Street Blues 1823, 3962
Bean of the Coffee, The 4117
Beans, Beans, Beans 758
Bear, The 2766
Bear Away the Bride 767
Bear Down 1658
Bear Hunt 4764
Bear Likes Honey, A 4710
Bear, the Tiger, the Hamster and the Mole, The 784
Bearded Stranger 1145
Beardsley Ballet (dance) 4270
Beardsley School for Girls 2568
Bearing Silver Platters 138
Bears in the Mud 143
Beast in You, The 1614
Beat Begins, The (Overture) 3330
Beat Behind, A 1633
Beat Goes On, The 338
Beat, Little Pulse 4401
Beat Me Daddy Eight to the Bar 393
Beat of a Heart, The 1766
Beat of the City, The 3370
Beat of the Feet in the Street, The 3354
Beat Out Dat Rhythm on a Drum 653
Beat the World 2664
Beata Biax 1262
Beatin' the Blues 4778
Beating the Groom Bay 3442
Beatitudes 4788
Beatnik Love Affair 3815
Beatrice 482
Beatrice Barefacts 250, 2160
Beatrice Lillie Ballad 1654
Beau Brummel 324, 3569, 325
Beau James 2217
Beau of Georgian Days, The 1896
Beauteous Is the Bride 4157
Beauteous Widow Bohea 45
Beautiful 154, 922, 1237, 2617, 2664
Beautiful (1) 4145
Beautiful (2) 4145
Beautiful 4210
Beautiful Allelujah Days 578
Beautiful and Damned 3406
Beautiful Arizona 1264
Beautiful Baby 2818, 2289, 3622
Beautiful Band 4487
Beautiful, Beautiful Girl 4806
Beautiful, Beautiful World 170
Beautiful Bed 2642
Beautiful Bicycle Belle 993
Beautiful Birds 4842, 4852
Beautiful Booby Prize 4393
Beautiful Bounding Sea 4644
Beautiful Bouquet 3921
Beautiful Buddies 1837
Beautiful Candy 656
Beautiful Charms 1125
Beautiful Children, The 1508
Beautiful Day 2935
Beautiful Dolls 2406
Beautiful Dreamer 1897, 4149
Beautiful Dreams I'm Dreaming 3877
Beautiful Dreamtown 1095
Beautiful Eyes 2978
Beautiful Face—Have a Heart 419
Beautiful Faces (Need Beautiful Clothes) 545
Beautiful Faces 3404
Beautiful Fairy Tales 2465
Beautiful Fan, A 1461
Beautiful Feathers Make Beautiful Birds 4033
Beautiful for Once 1053
Beautiful Garden Girl 1313
Beautiful Garden of Day Dreams 4626
Beautiful Garden of Girls 4811
Beautiful, Gay Paree 1627
Beautiful Girl 537, 3992, 2222, 2306, 544, 4839
Beautiful Girl, Goodbye 4811
Beautiful Girls 1329, 1460, 1688, 2238, 3967
Beautiful Girls Are Like Opium 2857, 3404
Beautiful Girls You Have the World at Your Feet 4296
Beautiful Golden Land 1753
Beautiful Gypsy 3766
Beautiful Has Come 3088
Beautiful Heaven 2719
Beautiful Island of Girls 4810
Beautiful Isle of Dreams 3675
Beautiful Isle of Love 513
Beautiful Ladies of the Night 1131

Beautiful Lady 4395
Beautiful Lady in Red 2385
Beautiful Lady Tell Me 3652
Beautiful Land of Bon Bon 1515
Beautiful Land, The 3731
Beautiful Legs 3782
Beautiful Little Mama 4438
Beautiful Love 2378
Beautiful Man 2918
Beautiful Monte Carlo 1926
Beautiful Music 2033
Beautiful Night 4063, 4374
Beautiful People 3136, 1612, 327, 4408, 4609
Beautiful People of Denver 4516
Beautiful, Primitive Indian Girls 3865
Beautiful Queen of the Nile 712
Beautiful Roses 2912
Beautiful Sea 1312
Beautiful Ship from Toy-Land The 1285
Beautiful Shore, The 4149
Beautiful Shoulders 2856
Beautiful Show Girls 4668
Beautiful Shubert Poses of My Dreams 303
Beautiful Soup 54
Beautiful Spring, The 4115
Beautiful Sunshine Makes a Beautiful Day 857
Beautiful Through and Through 4196
Beautiful Venice 3803
Beautiful You 1694
Beauty 1110, 1448
Beauty Adorned 2843
Beauty and the Beast 330, 330, 3013, 3985
Beauty Brigade, The 2286
Beauty Contest (Miss Hampstead Heath) (Opening the Beauty Contest) (Opening Act I) 1202
Beauty Doctor, The 2900
Beauty Doctors 332
Beauty in the Movies 1859
Beauty Is Like a Rose 2856
Beauty Is Vanity 1678
Beauty of Another Day, The 2467
Beauty of Bath, The 333, 605
Beauty Part, The 392
Beauty Retire 129
Beauty School Dropout 1664
Beauty Secrets 2565
Beauty That Drives Men Mad, The 4196
Beauty, the Brawn and the Brain, The 520
Beauty Treatment 1370
Beauty Within 4139
Beauty's Candy Shop 3770
Beaux and Belles of Bath, The 2937
Beaver Ball at the Bug Club 3261
Bebe 4767, 4817
Bebe of Gay Paree 3972
Because 2150, 3903
Because, Because 3225
Because I Am a Duke 2986
Because I Am Not Understood 1243
Because I Can't Tango 4808
Because I Love Her 2603
Because I Love Nice Things 4848
Because I Love You 4189
Because I Love You Dear 3976
Because I Love You So 3312
Because I'm a Woman 2759
Because I'm Married Now 4756
Because It Can't Sit Down 1746
Because of Her 944
Because of Them All 1276
Because of You 830
Because There's You 1616
Because They All Love You 3953
Because You Do Not Know 2328
Because You Love the Singer 4150
Because You Might Say Yes 1342
Because You're Different 2270
Because You're Mine 3703
Because You're You 2112, 3675
Beckie, Stay in Your Own Back Yard 3926
Becky from Babylon 3404
Becky Is Back at the Ballet 4838
Becoming Is a Lot Like Dying 2243
Bed 220, 944
Bed, The 1717
Bed Was Not My Own, The 1822
Bed, Wonderful Bed 3193
Bedalumbo, The 3985
Bedelia 2209, 2991, 3313
Bedouin Chief 4293
Bedroom Scene 139
Bedroom, The 4635
Bedsheets 2478
Bedsprings 4796
Bedtime at the Zoo 3322
Bedtime on the Prairie 1931
Bedtime Story, A 1655
Bee, The 4652
Bee, Be My Honey Bee 2851
Bee Song 2880
Beecher's Defense 3305
Beecher's Processional 3305
Beedle 'Em Boo 3614
Beedle-Um-Bee 1780
Beehive Dance, The 338
Beehive Polka 3261
Been a Hell of an Evening 4048
Been a Long Day 2019
Beer 2152
Beer and Flowers 4512
Beer Barrel Polka 4772
Beer, Beautiful Beer 350
Beer Girl, The 1569
Beer Is Best (Beer, Beer, Beer) 634
Beer that Made Milwaukee Famous, The 2974
Bees 'n' Flowers 1385
Bees Ain't to Blame 3332
Bees Are Buzzin' 1467

Beetle Race, The 3913
Before and After 250, 410, 3890
Before and After Taking 1374
Before Breakfast 3763
Before I Fall 3201
Before I Gaze at You Again 623
Before I Go 1667
Before I Kiss the World Goodbye 2201
Before I Met You 3245
Before I Was Born 2319
Before I'll Settle for Him 4408
Before It's Too Late 3764
Before Me Lies the World 1026
Before Our Eyes 1470
Before Stonewall 4309
Before the Dawn 3042
Before the Miracle 1435
Before the Parade Passes By 2208
Before the Parade Passes By (2) 1828
Before the Parade Passes By (1) 1828
Before the Parade Passes By (3) 1828
Before the Twilight Shadows 698
Before the World Began 676
Before the World Was Made 1977
Before We Leave 18
Before We Were Married 4320
Before You Knew I Loved You 459
Before You Love 3320, 3880
Before You Take a Man 1513
Before Your Very Eyes 2687
Beg, Borrow or Steal 339
Begat, The 1278
Beggar and Poet 1358
Beggar on Horseback 80
Beggar Waltz, The (inst.) 294
Beggars at the Feast 2442
Beggars' Chorus 2213
Beggar's Dream 4159
Beggar's Music 2655
Beggar's Opera, The 341, 4368, 4369, 4370, 4371
Begging 1088
(Just) Begging for Love 3946
Begging Milady's Pardon 3507
Begin the Beguine 2252
Beginner's Guide to Cruising 2114
Beginnin' of Sinnin' 898
Beginning, The 3876, 4002
Beginning of Love, The 1492
Beginning of the End 3159
Beguile, Beguile, with Music Sweet 4404
Beguine, The 956
Behave Yourself 3687
Behind Milady's Fan 2135
Behind My Lady's Fan 200
Behind the Fan 1308, 3006
Behind the Mask 2829
Behind the Scenes 3537
Behold 758
Behold a Prima Donna 1774
Behold El Capitan 1165
Behold Our Lady Great 2632
Behold the Coming of the Sun 4011
Behold the Governor 1640
Behold the King 1768
Bei Kerzenlicht 4777
Bei Mir Bist Du Schoen (To Me, You're Beautiful) 4342
Bei Mir Bistu Schoen 343
Bei Mir Bistu Shayn 2356
Bein' a Kid 3389
(It's Not Easy) Bein' Green 2677
Being a Pal 4577
Being a Parent 1094
Being Alive 4067, 832, 1764
Being Bad 3752
Being for the Benefit of Mr. Kite 3903
Being Good Isn't Good Enough 1729
Being Left Out 4515
Being Made Love To 1665
Being Quiet with You 3788
Being Too Good Has Its Bad Points 2069
Being with Me 3181
Being with You 4038
Belgian Rose 1833
Belgium Put the Kibosh on the Kaiser 3259
Believe 1862, 3900
Believe in Me 3680
Believe in Me, Baby 2742
Believe in Me, or I'll Be Leavin' You 778
Believe in You 337
Believe in Yourself 1269
Believe It or Not 817, 4673
Believe It or Not Tango 3111
Believe Me 2979, 3476, 4450, 4804
Believe Me, Beloved 1962
Believe Me I'm Blue 1989
Believe Us Receive Us 2285
Believer's Chant 344
Believers' Laments 344
Belinda! 345
Belinda 2240
Belinda on the Telephone 3856, 3857
Belinda's Love Song 4617
Bell Boys Brigade 2349
Bell Chorus 604
Bell for Adano, A 347, 347
Bell Hop Blues 2587
Bell of Doom Is Clanging, The (Song of the Hangman) 1284
Bella 2278
Bella Donna 3064
Bella Mia 3740
Bella Signora 3, 3381
Bella Stella New York 528
Bellboys 3547
Belle 362, 4138, 330
Belle, a Beau and a Boutonniere, A 4213
Belle Boyd's Back in Town 1474
Belle Boyd, Where Have You Been? 1474

Belle of Avenue A, The 349, 1226, 4414
Belle of Bald Head Row, The 2408
Belle of Bohemia, The 350
Belle of New York, The 357
Belle of New York 2122
Belle of New York, The 4654, 4654, 641
Belle of the Ball 4137
Belle of the Ball, The 4575
Belle of the Barber's Ball, The 1478
Belle of the Beach, The 697
Belle of the Boulevard 3384
Belle of the Dairy Lunch, The 2966
Belle of the Ring, The 1602
Belle of the Silvery Nile 3749
Belle of the Stage 2341
Belle of Today, The 4575
Belle of Vienne!, The 2334
Belle Plain 279
Belles of Basin Street 2115
Belles of Belle Harbor, The 2352
Belles of the Bronx, The 765
Belles of Zig-Zag Alley 4859
Bellevue and the Judge 1700
Bellhops, The 799
Bells 3387, 3555, 4814
Bells (Sousta) (dance) 4862
Bells and Bells 3025
Bells Are Ringing 363
Bells in the Morning 356
Bells of Hell, The 3259
Bells of Monterey 3373
Bells of St. Marks 3151
Bells of St. Sebastian, The 3171
Bells of St. Swithin's, The 3736
Bells of the Sea 4054
Belly Up to the Bar, Boys 4516
Belonging 2368
Beloved Mine 325
Below the Equator 3813
Below the Macy-Gimbel Line 2216
Belt and Leather 2630
Belz (Wonderful Girl of Mine) 1279
Belz, Mayn Shtetle Belz 1609
Bench in the Park 1811
Bend of the Road, The 4862
Bend Your Knee and Tie My Shoe 4665
Beneath the Eastern Moon 3649
Beneath the Moon 2566
Beneath the Skies 1429
Beneath the Stars 3511
Beneath the Window of My Love 4792
Beneath Those Sunny Skies 2512
Benedicite 3211
Benedictine 3286
Benediction, The 2551
Benediction 2579
Benedictus 2411
Benjamin B. O'Dell 67
Benjamin Calypso 2242
Benjamin Did It 367
Benjamin Franklin, in God We Trust 2846
Benjamin Partridge a Person of Parts 4404
Benny and the Jets 3739
Benny, Dear 402
Bensinger's Poem 4703
Bensonhurst Gavotte, The 3562
Benvenuta 2961
Berenike Motif 165
Bergerac 946
Berkeley Square and Kew 3569
Berlin on the Spree 1569
Berlin Stories, The 610
Bermuda 2446
Bernice 4182
Berry and the Brook 1518
Bert, Betty & Co. 568
Bertha 3970
Berthena (inst.) 4390
Bertie 152, 4819
Bertie and Gertie 3674
Bertie the Bounder 3322
Beside a Bridge (Along the River Tiber) 519
Beside Me 4055
Beside the Country Stile 954
Beside the Zuyder Zee 284
Beside Your Window 1235
Bess, You Is My Woman Now 3018, 3541
Bessie Smith 4003
Bessie's Blues 521
Bessie's Bossa Nova 842
Best Ain't Good Enough, The 3549
Best Brittany, The 353
Best Dance I've Had Tonight, The 4694
Best Dance of All, The 1871
Best Game 2947
Best Gold 1408
Best I Ever Get Is the Worst of It, The 468, 495
Best in the Business, The 2420
Best in the Trade, The 3185
Best in the World 2303
Best in the World, The 1000
Best Is Yet to Be, The 4162
Best Kept Secret 535
Best Little Lover in Town, The 3719
Best Little Sweetheart of All, The 1735
Best Loved Girls 3940
Best Man, The 2195, 3608
Best Man Never Gets the Worst of It, The 1580
Best Night of My Life, The 167
Best of All Possible Worlds, The (1) 630
Best of All Possible Worlds, The (2) 630
Best of Everything, The 2363
Best of Friends Must Part, The 116
Best of Friends, The 1158
Best of Good Friends 4121
Best of Me, The 2754
Best of Times, The 482, 2208, 2360
Best of What This Country's Got 4682
Best Part College Days 4778
Best Part-Time Job in Town, The 3600

Best Queen of All 2497
Best Song of All, The 4010
Best Sort of Mother, Best Sort of Child 3779
Best That I Can Do Is Try to Do the Best I Can, The 4453
Best Thing a Waiter Does Is Wait, The 3579
Best Thing for You, The 619
Best Things in Life Are Free, The 1215, 1628, 3020
Best Things of All, The 3691
Best Time of Day, The 95
Best Toast of All, The (Kiss Her and Look in Her Eyes) 4228
Best Undressed Girl in Town 2449
Best Waltz of All, The 3424
Best Wishes 2913
Best Years of His Life, The 2386
Best Years of My Life 4309
Bestiario 3162
Bestowal of the Yellow Jacket 3573
Bet on the Jockey 4194
Betamax Blues, The 871
Betcha I Make Good 4782
Betrayed 3215
Betrothal, The 2673
Betsy Moberly 140
Betsy Ross 4528
Betsy's the Belle of the Bathers, The 2770
Better 262, 2677, 1258
Better All the Time 4060
Better Be Good to Me 711
Better Bein' Loved 556
Better Day, A 4168
Better Days 4396
Better Far 578
Better Far Than Sitting This Life Out 3598
Better Get Out of Here 4652
Better Idea, A 1940
Better Keep Your Promise 1732
Better Late Than Never 2162, 2213
Better Leave Segregation Alone 2203
Better Luck Next Time 789, 2137
Better Man, A 31
Better Not Try It 4545
Better Off Bad 112
Better Off Dead 2970
Better or Worse 3409
Better Place to Be 2470, 3159
Better Safe Than Sorry 2876
Better Than a Dream 363
Better Than Broadway 3019
Better Than Nothing 4862
Better Things to Do 3273
Better Times 378
Better Times Are Coming 4668
Better to Be Loved 1681
Better Together 521
Better Word Than Love, A 1507
Better World, A 109
Better World 4740
Bettin' Calls 1385
Betting Song, The 2511
Betty Lee 381
Betty Lou 567
Betty Simpson 157
Betty Song, The 1575
Betty's Advice (inst.) 3322
Betty, the One Best Bet 2826
Between Me and Myself 1358
Between Romances 3916
Between the Devil and the Deep Blue Sea 3709
Between the Sheets 2346
Between You and Me 4359
Between You and Me and the Lamppost 2161
Beulah 224
Bevo 4770, 4813
Beware 3207
Beware As You Ride Through the Hollow 239
Beware, Brother, Beware 1296
Beware of Lips That Say "Cherie" 2595
Beware of Love 3543
Beware of Me 1096
Beware of Pink Pajamas 1904
Beware of the Bomb 1783
Beware of the Boy with His Mind Made Up 3453
Beware of the Chickens 4182
Beware of the Girl with the Fan 1488
Beware of the Sirens 3996
Beware of the Sophomore 2287
Beware the Dragon 2504
Bewitched, Bothered and Bewildered 3353
Beyond My Reach 2260
Beyond My Wildest Dreams 2820, 3485
Beyond the Binge I Want to Get Off 3124
Beyond the Blue Horizon 4251
Beyond the Clouds 3371
Beyond the Horizon 194
Beyond the Moonbeam Trail 4296
Beyond the Sunset 23
Beyond Words 3142
Bharatha Natyan 751
Biarritz and Bali 4540
Bible Stories 2990
Biblical story of Joseph 2948
Bicentennial March 1695
Bichloride of Mercury 3865
Bicycle Built for Two 3989
Bicycle Song, The 1891
Bid Him a Fond Goodbye 1644
Bid Me Forget 2701
Bid Me Love 2633
Bidding the World Farewell 1377
Biddle-De-Boo 3754
Bide-a-Wee in Soho, The 4369
Bidin' My Time 921, 1528
Biff! Bang! 3578
Big 1997
Big Al 2643
Big Apple 2243
Big Baby 251
Big Back Yard, The 4524

Big Banshee, The 1316, 4506
Big Battle, The 3453
Big Beat, The 3330
Big Best Shoes 4541
Big Betty's Song 1319
Big, Big 348
Big, Big Contest 4470
Big Bill 3934
Big Bill Murphy 1737
Big Bird 1498
Big Black Giant, The 2797
Big Blond, The 1861
Big Bottom Betty 3015
Big Bow-Wow, The 4034
Big Boy, I Gotta Belong to You 1514
Big Brass Band from Brazil 137
Big Broad Smile 4143
Big Brother 514
Big Brown Boo Loo Eyes 800
Big Business 952
Big Ca-lown Balloons, The 1860
Big Chief 4127
Big Chief Smoke 2576
Big City, The 708
Big City 2024, 3517
Big City Blues 845
Big City Dance 3599
Big 'D' 2961
Big D 3444
Big Day 1306
Big Day Tomorrow 1770
Big Deal on Madonna Street 393
Big Drum, Little Drum 815
Big Fat Heart 3869
Big Fish, Little Fish 3610
Big Four, The 67
Big Future 1074
Big Glass Cage, A 4818
Big Guitar, The 2248
Big Hats, The (Hat Song) 4802
Big-Hearted Ned 3842
Big Idea 2513
Big Indian and Little Maid 1881
Big Indian Chief 1188, 4681
Big Job, A 36
Big Lucy 240
Big Man 4193
Big Meeting Tonight 1991
Big Missouri, The 4409
Big Mole 2591, 4504
Big Movie Show in the Sky, The 4314
Big Night of the Year, The 4461
Big Noise from Winnetka (inst.) 964
Big Offense 815
Big Old River 2817
Big One, A 2362
Big Papoose Is on the Loose 2140
Big Parade, The 62, 3893
Big People 1955
Big Pound Cake 4478
Big Red Shawl, The 3676
Big Rich 3691
Big Rock Candy Mountain 3989
Big Show, The 1796
Big Spender 3428, 4238
Big Spring Drive, The 3740
Big Talk 1729
Big Tim 3644
Big Time, The 4695
Big Time 1277, 2304, 2660, 2987
Big Time Buck White 578
Big Time Buck White Chant 578
Big Top Parade 4273
Big Town 3893, 3004
Big Town Blues 898
Big Towns and the Small Towns, The 664
Big Trouble 2014
Big Walk, The 62, 3124
Big White Horse 4796
Big White House 4107
Big Winner, The 400
Bigger and Better Than Ever 1491
Bigger Isn't Better 305
Biggest Ain't the Best, The 3211
Biggest Pair of 38's in Town 362
Biggest Thing in My Life, The 2780
Bikini Dance 1760
Bilbao Song 369
Bilbao Song, The 1755
Bilbo's Song 221
Bill 2204, 3018, 3245, 3949, 4860
Bill and Coo 2261, 2336
Bill and Willa 1700
Bill Bailey 1120
Bill Bailey, Won't You Please Come Home 4390
Bill of Fare 2928, 4535, 4687
Bill of Rights, The
(Congress Shall Make No Law) 2809
Bill Poster's Song 2062
Bill Robinson Stomp 877
Bill Robinson Walk, The 884
Bill Simmons 1926, 3399
Bill Simmons (I've Got to Dance Till
the Band Gits Through) 4044
Bill, the Bill Poster 3820
Bill's a Liar 4663
Bill's Lament 54
Billet Doux 2364
Billet-Doux, A 2465
Billiard and Baccarat Ballet (inst.) 2938
Billie 403, 1478
Billiken Man 1224
Billiken Man, The 2858
Billing and Cooing 4795
Bills 2816
Billy 406, 2056
Billy Ballou 4655
Billy Baxter's Swing Song 2008
Billy Budd 406
Billy Grey, U.S.A., O.K. 2974

Billy Joe Ju 3684
Billy Noname 415
Billy Phibbs Is Married 1866
Billy Shakespeare
(The Shakespearian Rag) 3399
Billy Sol Estes 3186
Billy the Bubbler 186
Billy the Kid 4679
Billy's Blues 1107
Billy's Melody 4655
Billy's Very Good to Me 694
Biminy 4818
Bingo Blast 3165
Binnie 624
Birch Bark Boat 823
Bird, a Bottle and a Cigarette, A 998
Bird Americana 2992
Bird and the Bottle, The 4738
Bird Ballet, The 1131
Bird Chorus 3162
Bird Dance 4429
Bird in a Cage, A 143
Bird in a Gilded Cage, A 4390
Bird Lament 3162
Bird of a Chicken, The (dance) 4809
Bird of Gay Bohemia, The 1334
Bird of Love, The 2100
Bird of Paradise 558
Bird of Paradise, The 2636
Bird of Passage, A 2591
Bird on the Wing 3249
Bird Song, The 54
Bird Song 3673
Bird Talk 1975
Bird That Never Learned to Fly, A 4798
Bird Upon the Tree 2268
Bird Watcher's Song
(We're the Ladies' Walking Society) 1886
Birdcage Walk 792
Birdie 959
Birdie, A 2308
Birdie and Ferdie 4719
Birdie Follies 4011
Birdies 1958, 2669
Birdies in the Trees, The 1557
Birds 1300
Birds, The 4707
Birds and the Bees, The 4524
Birds Are Winging 4188
Birds in the Sky, The 2033
Birds in the Spring 2808
Birds in the Trees, The 1569, 2033
Birds' Nests 325
Birds of a Feather 1481, 3258
Birds of Paradise 424
Birds of Plumage 3406
Birds on High (Birds Up High) 376
Birmingham 2787
Birth of a Beatnik 1697
Birth of a New Revue, The 1129
Birth of American Fantasy Dance 4528
Birth of Dixie 1514
Birth of Passion, The 2667
Birth of the Blues 1489
Birth of the Butterfly (inst.) 250
Birth of the Century Girl, The 683
Birthday... 1369
Birthday, A 2278, 2633
Birthday Ensemble 2390
Birthday Girl 1701
Birthday of the Dauphin, The (scene) 4815
Birthday of the Infantata, The 1689
Birthday Party 4193, 1419
Birthday Party (Rich Kids Rag) 2523
Birthday Party of the King 4155
Birthday Serenade 3151
Birthday Song 337
Birthday Song, The 3496
Birthday Song 1242
Birthday Toast 3339
Birthdays 1497
Birthdays Are Fun 4710
Bis Bolo 3958
Bish Ne Ara 4325
Bismark Is a Herring, Napoleon
Is a Cake 1667
Bist Mein Krein, Mein Welt 907
Bistro 1358
Bit o' Breeze 1536
Bit O' Dancin', A 994
Bit o' Pink and White, A 452
Bit o' the Brogue, A 4120
Bit of a Ballad, A 4073
Bit of Character, A 3482
Bit of Earth, A 3862
Bit of Foolishness, A 3384
Bit of Gingham, A 1799
Bit of Harmony, A 3877
Bit of Home, A 3485
Bit of Nonsense, A 1340
Bit of Nonsense 2122
Bit of Opera, A 3404, 3958
Bit of Ribbon, a Bit of Love, A 4148
Bit of the Band, A 30
Bit of Villainy, A 2687
Bit Player Polka 3046
Bit Too Far, A 1392
Bitch, Bitch, Bitch 2198
Bite Your Tongue 1816
Bits and Pieces 1634
Bits & Pieces XIV Finale 427
Bits & Pieces XIV Opening 427
Bitten By Love 3966
Bitter Harvest 2655
Bitter Tears 4696
Bitter Twitter 96
Bittersuite, The 430
Bittersweet 3722
Bivouac Song 4616
Bivouac, The 118

Bixley Girl, The 116
Bizabara's Wedding 4139
Black 2801
Black and Blue 39, 432, 3873, 1980
Black and Blue Pumps 3370
Black and Tan Fantasy (inst.) 432, 875, 885
Black and White 305, 1446, 3953
Black Balloons 578
Black-Black Song, The 1592
Black Bogie Man, The 3384
Black Bottom, The 1489, 1491
Black Bottom 3297
Black Bottom (dance) 14
Black Bottom 2881
Black Bottom Dance (dance) 554
Black Boy 415
Black Boys/White Boys 1717
Black Butterfly, The 1523
Black Cargo 26
Black Coffee 3905
Black Dog Rum 461
Black Four Hundred Ball 217
Black Hills of Dakota 616
Black Horse Tavern 3822
Black Horsemen, The 2751
Black Is Beautiful 314
Black Laugh, The 1685
Black Magic 883, 886, 1385
Black Man 3825
Black Mask (Temptation), The 3148
Black Pearls 4243
Black Rape 3814
Black Rhapsody 4565
Black Rhythm 435
Black Sheep, The 1768
Black Silence 2580
Black Slacks 3178
Black Velvet 3598
Black-White Calypso 4579
Black Widow 4153
Black Widow Spider 1890
Blackberries 439
Blackberry Vine, The 1498
Blackberry Wine 1737, 10
Blackberryin' To-day 4806
Blackbird Knows 3004
Blackbirds on Parade 443
Blackest of Tresses 3490
Blackout! Hold Me Tight 3870
Blackouts 2304
Blacksheep 1747
Blade of Mine 1281
Blah, Blah, Blah 3060
(I May Feel) Blah! But Not Too Blue 2380
Blair Rose 3844
Blame It All on Me 1201
Blame It All on the Girls 4037
Blame It on Chichita 1231
Blame It on the Danube 3444
Blame It on the Depression 98
Blame It on the Night 1352
Blame It on the Summer Night 3644
Blame It on the Wine (Zu Jeder Liebe Gehort ein Glaschen Wein) 1044
Blame It on These Times 3757
Blame the Weather Man 2408
Blamen Is Our Birthright 1162
Blanche Ring's Doll Song 2213
Blank Piece of Paper, A 2702
Blarney 4803
Blarney Castle Walk 2696
Blarney of Killarney 188
Blarney of Killarney, The 2632
Blarney Stone, The 2340, 3746
Blase 4484
Blaze of Glory 533
Blazing Like Fire 4438
Bleecker Street 1924
Bleed and Purge 649
Bleeding Heart 2984
Bleeding Moon 3676
Bleinelech Tzvey 3781
Bless Our Home 1886
Bless the Bride 1762, 453
Bless the Lord 1595
Bless the Sea 453
Bless This Day 1698
Bless This House (Save the Village) 3366
Bless This Land 4312
Bless This School 1049
Bless Us Everyone 752
Bless You All 454
Bless Your Beautiful Hide 3888
Bless Your Ever Loving Little Heart 4017
Bless Your Everyloving Little Heart 2113
Blessed Art Man Among Women 755
Blessed Be God 4398
Blessed Is the Match 1740
Blessing, A 1715
Blessing Your Counts 3587
Blessings 3899
Blessings of the Havdoloh 343
Blest? 223
Blew, Blew, Blew 2062
Bli-Blip 2259, 4091
Blightly Bound 4421
Blind Alleys 364
Blind Date 2187
Blind Junkie 1282
Blind Man 1385
Blind Man's Bluff 1314
Blind Man's Buff 1746, 3920, 3996
Blindman's Bluff 3015
Blinky Winky Chinatown 806
Bliss 3602
Bliss Forever Past 1710
Blissful Christmas 1616
Blissful Pleasure, I Profess, The 1193
Blithe Spirit 1891
Blitz 3698

Bloat (Fat Don't Finish First) 1289
Blob, The 2822
Blockheads 456
Blocks 411, 413
Blond Haired Little Girl 2648
Blond Louise 233
Blonde Blues 483, 3404
Blonde Haired Babies 4515
Blonde Song, The 1702
Blondes 2969
Blondes Intro 2969
Blondes Song, The 3970
Blood Lines 4288
Blood Red Roses 461, 2633
Bloody Mary 4096
Bloom Is Off the Rose, The 1456
Bloom of the Apple Tree, The 4554
Blossom of My Own 1309
Blossom Time 2706
Blow a Balloon Up to the Moon 1840
Blow, Blow, Blow 545
Blow de Whistle 1385
Blow, Gabriel 2540
Blow, Gabriel, Blow 163
Blow High, Blow Low 660
Blow Hot and Heavy 86
Blow Hot-Blow Cold 288
Blow It Out Your Barracks Bag 4141
Blow Me Down 3138
Blow on Your Piccolo 4655
Blow Slow Kisses 2346
Blow the Blues Away 495
Blow the Man Down 3493
Blow the Smoke Away 1593, 4387
Blow the Whistle 2108
Blow Upon Your Bugles 2534
Blow Us a Kiss 589
Blow Your Horn 4158
Blow Your Own Horn 2090
Blowin' in the Wind 3739
Blowing Bubbles All Day Long 378
Blowing Bubbles in the Bathtub 556
Blowing Soap Bubbles 4439
Blowing the Blues Away 123, 4765
Blowing the Top 204
BLT Baby, You Bore Me 1697
Bluddle-Uddle-Um-Dum
(The Washing Song) 4035
Blue 3643, 920
Blue (inst.) 845
Blue Again 4545
Blue and Troubled 2661
Blue Baby 3649
Blue Beard 1687
Blue Bell & the Hyacinth, The 639
Blue Bird 2349, 4226
Blue Bird Blues 2461
Blue Blondes 2857
Blue Blood 2976
Blue, Blue 3710
Blue, Blue, Blue 2444
Blue Book 4162
Blue Book of Girls, A 3778
Blue Bowery 4023
Blue Boy Blues, The 2788
Blue Bulgarian Band 2317
Blue Classique (inst.) 4253
Blue Crystal 3718
Blue Danube Ballet 1207
Blue Danube Blues 1625
Blue Danube Waltz 1680
Blue Day 1679
Blue Days, Black Nights 580
Blue Devils of France 4812
Blue Diamonds 3552
Blue Eyed Sue 2493, 2964
Blue Eyes 465, 466, 4667
Blue Flame 2022, 4136
Blue Grass 1490, 2137
Blue-Grass Dreamers 3671
Blue Holiday 467
Blue Hours 2366, 3382
Blue Hullaballoo 1419
Blue Jean Blues 2643
Blue Kitten Blues 468
Blue Manhattan Nights 262
Blue Monday Blues 1485
Blue Moon 3175
Blue Mouse, The 2494
Blue Night 2850
Blue Norther 264
Blue Notes 1982
Blue Ocean Blues 3556
Blue Pipes of Pan 2389
Blue Plate Special 474
Blue Prelude 3992
Blue Print Blues 2888
Blue Ribbon Girls, The 350
Blue Room, The 1529
Blue Shadows 1134
Blue Sierras 1918
Blue Skies 376, 789
Blue Skies, Gray Skies 2829
Blue Step 1778
Blue-Tail Fly 3989
Blue Train, The 475
Blue Zulu 2457
Bluebeard's Beard (inst.) 3980
Blueberry Eyes
(Kokemomo No Hitomi) 1616
Blueberry Hill 4534, 3739
Bluebird 937
Bluebird, The 2516
Bluebloods 2333
Bluer Than You 4
Blues, The 108
Blues 916, 3158, 3691, 4484
Blues, The 2611
Blues Blues 478
Blues for Mr. Charlie 477

Blues for Two Young Women, A 3628
Blues Have Got Me, The 1058
Blues in the Night 478, 1385, 3175, 4131
Blues My Naughty Sweetie Gve to Me 1063
Blues Was a Pastime 4343
Bluestep 293
Bluezwis 2846
Bluff 403, 2040, 2986
Blunderland 4816
Blushing Bride, The 480
Blushing Bride, A 989
Blushing Bride and Groom, The 712
Blushing, Gushing Widow, The 3754
Bo Koo 2569
Bo-Peep 591, 606
Bo Peep 1613
Bo's Theme (inst.) 485
Board Meeting 2992
Board of Directors of
Continental Steel, The 3756
Board of Governors 2198
Boarder, The 3722
Boarding House Love Call 4373
Boardwalk Blues 481
Boardwalk Crawl, The 3701
Boasting Song 1958
Boat Race Chorus 3977
Boat Sails on Wednesday, A 1067
Boat Song, The 1121
Boating Song 1301
Boat's In, The 1386
Bob About a Bit 4529
Bob and Me 1537
Bob White 3146
Bobbed Haired Baby 3148
Bobbi McGee 914
Bobbing-Bobbing 453
Bobby 1264
Bobby and Jackie and Jack 2822
Bobby and Me 4345
Bobby the K 2913
Bobby Watson and Family 2146
Bobby's Nightmare 1839
Bobo's 16
Bob-o-Link 978
Bobolink, The 1707
Bob-o-link 4304
Bob's Song 4020
Bodoni Country 3370
Body and Soul 3905, 4534, 432, 4367
Body Beautiful, The 483
Body in the Trunk 4415
Body Language 1298
Boffola 673
Bogie Man 2543
Bogie Man, The 4753
Bogie Ogie Man, The 4439
Bohemia 902, 1538, 2155, 3229, 2552
Bohemia, Good Bye 48
Bohemia Good-Bye 3773
Bohemia Is the Life for Me 3348
Bohemian Girl, The 1710
Bois D'Amour, The (Opening Chorus) 353
Bois D'Boulogne, The 694
Bojangles 486
Bojangles of Harlem 2204
Bold Gendarmes, The 115
Bold Hussars, The 4181
Bold Logger, The 4579
Bold Pierre 1720
Bold, Bad, Bandits 307
Bolero 1056
Bolero (inst.) 2772
Bolero 2830
Bolero, The 2848
Bolero d'Amour (dance) 1329
Bolero de Amor 846
Bolero on Rye 4038
Bolo, Bolo Man 2853
Bolshevik Love 3157
Bolsheviki Glide 684
Bolt of Love 4325
Bom Bouche 357
Bom-Bom Day 2107
Bom-Bom-Beedle-Um-Bo 1690
Bombashay 4247
Bombay Bombashay, The 3538
Bombo 487
Bombo-Shay, The 1334
Bon Appetit 3837
Bon-Bon-Buddie 295
Bon Bon Buddy 4697
Bon-Bon-Buddy the Chocolate Man 3134
Bon Bon Buddy, Jr. 489
Bon Jour 1720
Bon Jour! 4830
Bon Jour (The Language Song) 4516
(Madammuzzelle) Bon Nuit 1026
Bon Nuit 2057
Bon Nuit, Papa 695
Bon Soir 4260
Bon Soir, Paris 2679
Bon Vivant 1373, 4075
Bon Voyage 163, 630, 3365
Bon Voyeur 2913
Bonanza 490
Bonbonera 364
Bond Sequence 3277
Bonds 3780
Bones 4378
Bongo-Boola 3966
Bongo on the Congo 4001
Bonita 2602
Bonjour 3178, 4401
Bonjour Amour 1649
Bonjour Finis 3756
Bonjour Goodbye 4670, 4665
Bonne Nuit, Merci 429
Bonnet Shop 1537
Bonnie 3369

Bonnie Banks 3986
Bonnie Blue Flag 1476, 1616, 3020
Bonnie Blue Flag, The 3056
Bonnie Briar Bush 2408
Bonnie Gone (Boni No Shi) 1616
Bonnie Sue Sunshine 2996
Bonnie's Song 4459
Bonny, My Highland Lassie 2835
Bonsoir 2443
Bonus Blues, The 1176
Boo! Boo! Boo-oo! 3092
Boo-Gee-Boo, The 1469
Boo-Hoo 2412
Boo-Hoo Blues, The 4041
Boo Hoo Hoo, Ha Ha Ha! (I'm Between a Laugh and a Cry) 4235
Boo-Hoo Tee-Hee Ta Ha 4364
Boo-Hoo-Who 88
Boo-Ra-Boo 1417
Boogey Boo Lady, The 1550
Boogey Man 583
Boogie Boo 88
Boogie-Boo, The 3134
Boogie Bug 3239
Boogie Woogie 1425
Boogie-Woogie, The 887
Boogie Woogie Ball 4192
Boogie Woogie Bugle Boy 3175, 3739
Boogie Woogie Bunga Boo 4503
Boogie Woogie GI Joe 2026
Boogie-Woogie-Katie 1415
Boogie Woogie Man 4459
Boogy-Woogy 612
Book Agent, The 3392
Book Burning 3873
Book in the Cave, The 1092
Book of Dori, The 1079
Book of Life, The 1074
Book Report 4783
Boola Boo 4784
Boola Boola 1593, 1738
Boom! 757
Boom, A 284
Boom a Rang 2546
Boom-Boom (Le Grand Boom-Boom) 2523
Boom Chicka Boom 4619, 3142
Boom, Crunch! 2143
Boom Ditty Boom 3900
Boom Whee! 1847
Boomerang 1251
Boomerang, The 3538, 4780
Boomps-a-Daisy 1840
Boop-Boop-a-Doop 2140
Boost the Morale 3239
Boosters' Song of the Far North, The 1654
Boot-It Boy 1425
Bootblack Blues 4025
Booth! Is Back in Town 496
Bootlegger's Chanty (We're an English Ship) 1800
Bootlegging Blues 1867
Boots 1056
Boots and Shoes 4419
Booze 3656
Booze of Auld Lang Syne, The 2378
Booze Tree, The 2286
Boozin' & Barfin' 3873
Bop-A-Bye 3286
Bop Will Never Die, The 843
Bored 681, 2327, 2580, 3753
Borgia Orgy 2168, 4153
Born Again 828, 2201
(You'll Be) Born All Over Again 3813
Born and Bred in Brooklyn, Over the Bridge 3723
Born and Bred in Old Kentucky 391
Born at Last 4798
Born Happy 497
Born in America 1878
Born Lover 1634
Born Reporter 4703
Born to Be Bored 1951
Born to Be Happy 898
Born to Be Together 3944
Born to Be Wild 3695
Born to Entertain 3811
Born to Hand-Jive 1664
Born to Lose 3276
Born to Rock and Roll 843
Born to Sing 2195
Born to Swing 498
Born Too Late 602, 2554
Borneo 1824, 2481
Borrow from Me 4806
Borrowers, The (inst.) 499
Borrowers, The 499
Bosky Countrie (Sic), The 3612
Bosom Buddies 2208, 2713
Bosphorus 2358
Boss Is Bringing Home a Bride, The 2386
Boss Tweed 4524
Bossa Nova, The 3522
Boston 4198
Boston Beguine 3107
Boston Beguine, The 2611
Boston in the Spring 1546
Boston Merger, The 1649
Boston Post Road 1859
Boston Tea Party (inst.) 4303
Boston Tourist Girls 917
Botany Babies 792
Both Ends Against the Middle 298
Both Sides Now 3739
Both Sides of the Coin 3070
Bottle and a Bird, A 1481, 3744
Bottle Dance, The 1265
Bottle Imp, The 1602
Bottle of Canada Dry, A 1131
Bottle Song 869
Bottle Up a Pretty Girl 684

Bottleneck 1029
Bottles 2889
Bottom End of Bleecker Street 1612
Bottomland 500
Bottoms Up 601, 1491
Bottom's Up 1500
Bouboulina 4862
Boudoir Dolls 3172
Bougainvillea 1053
Bought and Paid For 2424
Bouilloux Girls, The 807
Boukra Fill Mish Mish 1539
Boule Miche, The 48
Boule Miche 3773
Boulevard 326
Boulevard Break 2366
Boulevard Guide, The 336
Boulevard Street 3796
Boulevardiers, The 3384
Boulloux Girls, The 3542
Bounce 4798
Bounce Me 2342
Bouncin' Back for More 1842
Bouncing All Over Town 4844
(We Keep) Bouncing Back for More 4693
Bound Away 1086, 1985
Bound for Glory 4740
Bound for the Opera 1095
Bound Me in My Mammy's Arms 489
Bound No'th Blues 3001
Bouquet of Fond Memories, A 3361
Bouquet of Girls 2706
Bourbon Street Parade 1890
Bow Belles 466
Bow Bow 2348
Bow Down 45
Bow Down Sinners 435
Bow-Legged Sal 4214
Bow-Wow 3310
Bowery of Today, The 969
Bowl of Gold, A 1119
Bowl of Roses, A 3220
Bowler Hat, A 3340
Bowling 4809
Bows 4034, 4124
Box Office Tells the Story, The 1458
Boxing at Shadows 637
Boy, a Girl and the Moon, A 3238
Boy and Girl 906
Boy and Man (E L'omo Mio) 3798
Boy Blue 3825
Boy, Do I Hate Horse Races 239
Boy, Do I Need You Now 916
Boy, Do We Need It Now 4533
Boy for Sale 3271
Boy Friend, The 507
Boy Friend Back Home, The 1272
Boy Friends 2628
Boy From..., The 2663, 3967
Boy, Girl, Moon 3314
Boy Guessed Right, The 3803
Boy I Left Behind Me, The 601
Boy in Blue 2495
Boy in the Blue Uniform 2371
Boy Is Perfect, The 2354
Boy Like That, A 101, 3967, 4625
Boy Like You, A 4169
Boy Meets Boy 508
Boy Meets Girl 3442, 2641, 4029, 4416
Boy Most Likely to Succeed 817, 3108
Boy Named Lem, A 4772
Boy Needs Love, A 2992
Boy Next Door, The 2805, 3184
Boy of Mine, I Wait for You 3045
Boy of My Dreams, The 4016
Boy Oh Boy 4038
Boy, Oh, Boy 1762
Boy Scouts, The 4064
Boy Talk 4764
Boy, the Woodshed and the Strap, The 591
Boy Wanted 977, 3060, 3569
Boy What a Perfect Waste of Time Is Love 1004
Boy! What Love Has Done to Me! 1528
Boy with a Drum 1476
Boy with Magic in His Eyes, A 973
Boy with the Fiddle, The 4396
Boy with the Violin, The 4644
Boy without a Sweetheart, A 1988
Boychild 415
Boyola 2235
Boys 902, 2761
Boys All Fall for Me, The 4642
Boys and Girls Come Out to Play 2134
Boys and Girls Like You and Me 3263, 4146
Boys Are Like Wonderful Toys 4604
Boys, Be Proud that You're a USAAC 1632
Boys Before the Mast, The 1021
Boy's Best Friend Is His Mother, A 1897
Boys! Boys! Boys! 4247
Boys, Boys, Boys 971, 2053, 3677, 4642
Boys from the South 2728
Boys in Blue 1573, 3365
Boys in Gray 3056
Boys in the Back Room, The 3444
Boys of Summer, The 1038
Boys, The 394
Boys Who Fight the Flames, The 1271
Boys Will Be Boys 336, 3714, 2982
Boys Will Be Boys
(and Girls Will Be Girls) 4293
Boys Will Be Girls 778
Bozo Allegro 4389
Bracelets 202, 1462
Brack Weaver, My True Love 1085
Bradshaw's Guide 2844
Brag and Bluster Song, The 1083
Braggart Song, The 3215
Braggin' in Brass (inst.) 886
Bragging Song 3842, 4211
Braid the Raven Hair 1987

Brainwash 194
(Got a) Bran' New Daddy 971
Brand New Day, A 2318
Brand New Dress, A 798
Brand New Friends 1616
Brand New Hammer, A 3181
Brand New Soldier Tune, A 1531
Brand New Start 373
Brand New World 3644
Brandy in Your Champagne 1676
Brava! Brava! 2715
Brave and the Free, The 2072
Brave Deserve the Fair, The 3978
Brave Gendarmes 1392
Brave Girl 1092
Brave Hussar, The 3744, 4228
Brave Old City of New York, The 2134
Brave Soldier Boy, The 2715
Brave You 1508
Brave's Lament, The 412
Bravo! 2150
Bravo, Antonio! 3222
Bravo Bravo 3792
Bravo, Bravo 3464, 771
Bravo! Bravo! 340
Bravo, Bravo, Novelisto 4060
Bravo, Giovanni 519
Brazil 1662, 2897
Brazilian Boogie Woogie 847
Brazilian Can-Can 4571
Brazilian Interlude 4303
Brazilian Max-Cheese 3397
Brazilian Nut 3087
Brazilian Nuts 4131
Brazilian Samba 1414
Brazilian Suite 2540
Breachy's Law 519
Bread 273
Bread and Butter 930
Bread and Butter and Sugar 1831
Bread and Freedom 3644
Bread and Jam 2816
Bread and Kisses 4025
Bread and Love 2106
Bread and Roses 1609
Breadline Dance 1729
Break Into Your Heart 2071
Break It Now, Buck Private 213
Break It Up 323
Break It Up Cinderella 4586
Break Me Out 1985
Break-Me-Down, The 2271
Break-Neck Quadrille, The (inst.) 3613
Break That Party 1074
Break-up Rag 169
Breakfast 322
Breakfast at Thebes 3088
Breakfast at Tiffany's 521, 521
Breakfast Ball 880
Breakfast Ball, The 1014
Breakfast Dance 3172, 3709
Breakfast for Two 4798
Breakfast in Bed 2628, 3163, 4237
Breakfast Over Sugar 2132
Breakfast with Hazel 3036
Breakfast with You 3648
Breakin' 'Em Down 740
Breakin' 'Em In 3965
Breakin' a Leg 4182
Breakin' th' Rhythm 3361
Breakin' the Ice 1941, 2099
Breakin' the Spell 825, 4022
Breaking Camp 4046
Breaking Into the Movies 3842, 4211
Breaking Up a Rhythm 4291
Breath from Bohemia, A 1565
Breath of a Rose 2387
Breath of Spring 2193, 3900
Breath of Spring, A 4780
Breathing In 1053
Breathing the Air 3711
Breeze in the Trees 3258
Breeze Kissed Your Hair, The 672
Breezin' Along 577
Breezy 137
Bremen Town Musician, The 3844
Brendan's Dream 1412
Brent's Credo 3429
Breton Boat Song 49
Brewing the Love Potion 4623
Brewster the Millionaire 1464
Brewster's Millions 577, 4860, 4860
Brian 3493
Brickerty-Brackety—Tootsies 4742
Bridal Bevy, The 351
Bridal Chorus 3028, 526
Bridal Fete 177
Bridal Finale (Bridal Procession) 3772
Bridal Hour, The 1121, 2509
Bridal March 3051
Bridal Song 2793
Bridal Song, The 2673
Bride, The 1250, 2292
Bride and Groom 3243
Bride Bells 4345
Bride of Sirocco 528
Bride Shop 3045
Bride Was Dressed in White, The 3650
Bride Wore Something Old, The 4446
Bride's Song 1537
Bridegroom Trio 2947
Briderlekh Tayere (Dear Brothers, Help) 1609
Brides and Grooms 1071
Brides in Love 729
Brides' Lullaby 1911
Bridesmaids 1537, 2816
Bridesmaids Ballet 3850
Bridesmaids' Sextette (Chorus of Bridesmaids) 3322

Bridge 333, 3085
Bridge of Caulaincourt, The 2150
Bridge of Lovers, The 650
Bridge Song (The Bubbe Rag), The 573
Bridge to Nowhere, The 406
Bridge to the Future 564
Bridges 159
Bridget McShane 2870
Bridget Salome 4801
Brief Dissertation on the Relevancy of a Liberal Education in a Contemporary Society, A 1002
Brief Encounter 4701, 1346, 2913
Briefcase, The 3873
Brigadoon 530
Brigand Chief 2803
Brigand's Chorus, The 2701
Bright and Black 4004
Bright and Early 4047, 4778
Bright Blue Sea 2348
Bright College Days 4412, 4718
Bright Day Dawning 3729
Bright Eyes 545
Bright Lights 1784, 2173
Bright Moon Above 4405
Bright Morning Star 93, 1037
Bright New Day 460
Bright Side Somewhere 3987
Bright Spring Morn 760
Bright Was the Day 3339
Bright Young People 3235
Brighten Up and Be a Little Sunbeam 206
Brighter Days Are Coming 1121
Brighton 4219
Brighton Beach Rag 1531
Brindle's Farm 2757
Bring All the Boys Back Home 4485
Bring Along the Camera 3494
Bring Along Your Dancing Shoes 965
Bring Along Your Lovin' Ways 3737
Bring Back Birdie 534
Bring Back My Blushing Rose 4815
Bring Back My Lena to Me 1793
Bring Back Nelson Mandela 3836
Bring Back Swing 426
Bring Back that Yama Dance to Me 4776
Bring Back the Days of Yea and Nay 1073
Bring Back the Good Old Days 3204
Bring Back the Roxy to Me 1107
Bring Back Those Good Old Days 18
Bring Back Those Minstrel Days 3796
Bring Back Those Wonderful Days 4813
Bring Back Tomorrow 2949
Bring Back Your Heart to Me 728
Bring Back Your Love 1963
Bring 'Em Back 1922
Bring 'Em Back Alive 3409
Bring Him Home 2442
Bring Him My Love Thoughts 2419
Bring in the Morning 535
Bring It on Home 1816
Bring It to the Bar 3846
Bring Me a Blonde 1632
Bring Me a Radio 1690
Bring Me a Rose 178
Bring Me Back My Butterfly 1921
Bring Me My Bride 1422
Bring on the Booze 4577
Bring on the Bride to Be 177
Bring on the Concubines 1817
Bring on the Ding Dong Dell 3243
Bring on the Follies' Girls 4823
Bring on the Girls 1250, 1329, 3402, 4816, 4828
Bring on the Heavenly Host 1809
Bring on the Loot 3555
Bring on the Men 2198
Bring on the Pepper 3007
Bring on Tomorrow 1236
Bring Out the Beast in Me 3890
Bring Your Darling Daughter 1456
Bring Your Kisses to Me 3958
Bringing Up Badger 778
Bringing Up Daughter 868
Bringing Up Father 537, 538, 539, 541, 540, 542
Briny Blues, The 1656
Britain's Own Ambassadors 834
Britannia Rules 2913
Britannia Rules the Waves 4341
Britannia's Song 1392
British Justice 3482
British Maidens 1657
British Subject, A 3070
Brittania Waives the Rules 3501
Brittany 1066, 1690
Brivele Der Mamen (A Letter to Mother), A 1609
Broad Highway 1096
Broad, Majestic Hudson, The 1568
Broadcast a Jazz 1690
Broadminded 1112
Broads Ain't People 2449
Broads of Broadway 3137
Broadway 164, 1176, 2195
Broadway (The Heart of the World) 2734
Broadway 4673
Broadway Baby 956, 1329, 3967
Broadway Battle Cry, The 2298
Broadway Beauty Show, The 4165
Broadway Belles 1482, 2349
Broadway Blossom 404
Broadway Blues, The 1847
Broadway Boudoir 1780
Broadway, Broadway 546, 550
Broadway Cabaret, The 3332
Broadway Down in Dixieland 3614
Broadway Favorites 4735
Broadway Follies 547
Broadway for Mine 2056
Broadway Girls 1573

Broadway I Love You 3636
Broadway in Dahomey 2111
Broadway in Paree, A 4657
Broadway in Sahara 3404
Broadway Indians 4817
Broadway Jones 403
Broadway Lady 2141
Broadway Lament 4012
Broadway Lights 4226
Broadway Love 2912
Broadway Love Song 4432
Broadway Mammy 2296
Broadway Mammy Blues 1653
Broadway Means Home to Me 4762
Broadway Melody 544
Broadway Musical, A 550, 602
Broadway, My Street 3900
Broadway My Street 3953
Broadway, My Street 4480
Broadway New York 4011
Broadway of My Heart, The 1380
Broadway Pirates 2870
Broadway Reverie 4823
Broadway Rhythm 3992, 1298, 3636
Broadway Rose 3915
Broadway Sam 3399
Broadway School Days 3400
Broadway Show, The 1464
Broadway Strut 208
Broadway Strut, The 481
Broadway Swell and Bowery Bum 4378
Broadway Tipperary 1826
Broadway to Madrid 1132
Broadway Walk, The 545
Broadway Wedding 556
Broadway Whirl, The 560
Broken 2947
Broken & Bent 562
Broken Blossoms 542, 3775
Broken Bus, The 2679
Broken Doll, A 3827
Broken Guitar, A 4152
Broken Heart, or the Wages of Sin, The 935
Broken Hearted Romeo 4572
Broken Hearts 2686
Broken Idol, A 561
Broken Kimono, The 3108
Broken Pianolita, The 2679
Broken Rhythm 1461
Broken Romance 796
Broken String Blues 3983
Brom and Katrina 239
Brom Bones 2100
Brom's Compaint 2344
Bronco Busters 1528
Bronx Express 563
Bronxville Darby and Joan 3815
Brook, The 2055
Brooklyn 564
Brooklyn Belle 1303
Brooklyn Cantata 3226, 4394
Brooklyn Dodger Strike, The 1289
Brooklyn Heights 1693
Brooklyn U.S.A. 2397
Broth of a Boy, A 1803
Brother 4003
Brother and Sister 4795
Brother Against Brother 3558
Brother Can You Spare a Dime? 125
Brother, Can You Spare a Dime? 1609
Brother Can You Spare a Dime? 3018
Brother Dear 689
Brother Department, The 4481
Brother, Give Yourself a Shove 1755
Brother Masons 4650
Brother Men 1736
Brother of Mine 3084
Brother to Brother 1684
Brother Trucker 4744
Brother, Where Are You? 2245
Brotherhood of Man 2019, 3444
Brothers 168, 2302, 3088
Brothers and Sisters 115
Brothers Came to Egypt, The 2242
Brothers Vendetto, The 1970
Brown 3660
Brown Baby 2245
Brown Buddies 567
Brown-Eyed Girl 905
Brown Eyes 4692
Brown October Ale 3736
Brown Paper Bag 2051
Brown Penny 341, 1977
Brown Skin Baby Mine 2111
Brown-Skin Gal in the Calico Gown, The 2259
Brown Sugar 439
Brownies 2155
Brownie's Picnic, The 528
Brownstone 1697
Bruderlein Fein 2249
Brunhilde's 1714
Brunnhilde Rides Again 4467
Brunnhilde Steps Out 70
Brush Off, The 4048
Brush Up Your Shakespeare 2331
Brushing Stone, The 4292
Brussels 2188
Bub Oder Madel? 3771
Bubbe Meises Bubbe Stories 573
Bubbie 3910
Bubble, The 1888
Bubble and the Butterfly, The 3134
Bubble, Bubble 1638
Bubble Bubble 4405
Bubble-Land 719
Bubbles 575, 1096, 1535
(I'll Make) Bubbles 2587
Bubbles 3921, 4547
Bubbles in Me Bonnet 705

Bubbles in the Wine 3444
Bubbles of Bliss 773
Bubbling 2532
Bubbling Brown Sugar 576
Bubbling Over 577
Bubbling Over with Joy 2833
Bubbling Wine 1549
Bucharest 1352
Buck 2135
Buck in the Bank 1930
Buck Up 4784
Buckin' Barley 3224
Buckin' for Beardsley 2568
Buckle Down Winsocki 372, 4332
Budapest 203
Buddies 579
Buddies Ensemble 579
Buddy Beware 163
Buddy Buddy 112
Buddy on the Nightshift 2653
Buddy Rose 2380
Buddy System, The 775
Buddy's Blues 3967
Buds Won't Bud 1973
Budweiser's a Friend of Mine 4801
Buena Senorita Am I, A 4478
Buenos Aires 1211
Buffalo Belle 270
Bug on the Windshield of Life 3515
Bugaboo 3677
Bugaboo Man, The 4478
Buggy Riding 1922
Bugle, The 1860
Bugle Blow 376
Bugle Blues (dance) 26
Bugle Blues 2302
Bugle Call Blues 3513
Bui-Doi 2905
Build a Little Fence Around Today 1316
Build a Nest for Birdie 9
Builders of Dreams 3005
Building a Bridge to Ireland 3028
Building Bee, The 2089
Building Up to a Let-Down 1342
Built Up Area 220
Bulgaria Victorious 742
Bull and Bear 764
Bull Blood and Brandy 1046
Bull Frog and the Coon 2795
Bull Frog and the Coon, The 3981
Bull Frog and the Dove, The 1566
Bull Frog and the Governor, The 1521
Bull-Frog Ben 2675
Bulldog Breed, The 2392
Bullfrog & Coon 1758
Bullfrog Ben 352
Bullfrog Patrol 3923
Bulls, The 2188
Bulls and Bears 1246, 3950
Bully Song 3949
Bum Luck 1509
Bum Won, The 1280
Bumble Bee 4805
Bumble Bee and the Butterfly, The 968
Bumble Bee, The 531, 3923
Bump and Grind for God 2285
Bump Bump Bump 2195
Bumpity-Bump 2949
Bumpty-Bump 437
Bums 1289, 1490
Bums' Opera 3505
Bunch of Cows, A 2504
Bundle of Love 138
Bundle of Love, A 487
Bundle of Nerves 583, 3658
Bundling 4214
Bungalow for Two, A 3754
(A Little) Bungalow in Quogue 3727
Bunk 584
Bunker Hill to Yorktown 3558
Bunny, Bunny, Bunny 4131
Bunny Dear 3775
Bunny's Lament, The 3124
Buon Giorno, Signore 4169
Buona Sera, Mrs. Campbell 652
Burger Beguine 2294
Burglar Dance (inst.) 627
Burglar Inn 4104
Burglars 2854
Burglar's Lament (Like Butterflies That FLith from Flower to Flower) 2174
Burglar's Serenade 2408
Buried Alive 989
Buried Alive in the Mud 414
Burlesque 90
Burlesque Ballet 4437
Burlesque Trio 1259
Burma Moon 3137
Burmah Girl 470
Burmese Babies 1986
Burmese Ballet, A 3958
Burn 'Em Up 3130
Burn This Town 344
Burn Up 376
Burn, Baby, Burn 415
Burnin' Up 3724
Burning Bush 1715
Burning Desire 4139
Burning Flower 2970
Burning Love (Ahi Wela) 422
Burning of the Henrietta (inst.) 190
Burning to Sing (sketch) 4054
Burning Up the Boulevard 4277
Burt and I 4041
Bury Him Here 4107
Bus from Amarillo 374
Bus Ride 3261
Bus Stop 716, 4433
Busby Berkeley Girl 2969
Bushel and a Peck, A 4399, 1706, 3444

Busiest Week, The 4037
Business As Usual 3239
Business for a Good Girl Is Bad 2894
Business Is an Art 674
Business Is Bad 1516, 3988
Business Is Booming 3482
Business Is Business 1182, 1308
Business Is Fundamentally Sound 1280
Business Man, A 4648
Business of Our Own, A 4860
Business or Pleasure 4798
Busker, The 1857
Busker Alley 589
Buster Brown 591, 591
Buster Brown's Bobby Burns Brigade 591
Buster, He's a Hot Dog Now 3641
Buster's Chums 591
Bustle 1689
Bustopher Jones 678
Busy Bee 2276, 3730
Busy Bees of DeVere's, The 2533
Busy Body 4199
Busy, Busy 253
Busy, Busy, Business Man, The 96
Busy, Busy, Busy 804
Busy, Busy Day 3067
Busy Day 3925
Busy Evening, A 2263
Busy Lady 2284
Busy Little Broadway 4277
Busy Little Center, A 2829
Busy Mr. Bee 4425
Busy Night at Lorraine's, A 3142
But 2150
But After the Ball Was Over! (Then He Made Up for Lost Time) 4812
But Alive 167, 602
But He Never Says He Loves Me 3131, 4132
But He Said It So Politely 2906
But I Do Say So 2833
But I Kissed Her on the Shoulder 340
But I Love New York 4635
But, I Love You 4470
But I Rode Some 3001
But I Was There 2388
But I Will Never Say 1369
But I'm Always Sensitive to You (Hot and Cold) 363
But in Brazil 4121
But in the Morning 628
But in the Morning, No 1018, 1109
But It Ain't 4046
But It's Love 90
But It's Wrong 1435
But Mary Kept All Those Things in Her Heart 755
But Mr. Adams 3897
But Never Jam Today 593
But No 70
But Not for Me 921, 1528
But Not for You 3658
But Not Me 2846
But Not Right Now 4297
But Not Today 2467
But Now 4643
But Our Charms Do Not Stop Quite There 4549
But That's the Way You Are 798
But They Didn't 4646
But Wasn't It an Odd Place to Do It 1466
But Where 545
But Where Is Love 924
But Yesterday 737
But You Alone 4133
But You Can't Believe Them 815
But You Do It 518
But You Go On 154, 155
But Yours 4270
Butcher Baker 2032
Butcher, Baker, Candle-Stick Maker 1446
Butcher, the Baker, the Candlestick Maker, The 2462, 4830
Butler, The 4219
Butler and the Cook Desire 2338
Butler and the Handy Man 2338
Butler in the Abbey 989
Butler Is a Butler, A 1604
Butler's Fox-Trot, The 2494
Butler's Song, The 4038
Butter and Egg Baby 3252
Butter Fingers 157
Butter Milk Soldier (Johnny Soldier) 4579
Buttercup 825, 4022
Buttercups and Daisies 604
Butterflies (Dance) 2836
Butterflies 3325, 4037
Butterflies and the Bees, The 4214
Butterflies Are Free 594
Butterflies of Fashion 934, 1796
Butterflies of Fashion, The 4473
Butterfly, The 3631
Butterfly 1424
Butterfly, The (Birth of the Butterfly) 2667
Butterfly 3396, 3677
Butterfly, The 3828
Butterfly 4133
Butterfly, The 4862
Butterfly and the Clover 1602
Butterfly and the Clover, The 734
Butterfly and the Flower, The 4663
Butterfly and the Rose, The 1417
Butterfly Ballet (inst.) 3819
Butterfly, Butterfly 1522
Butterfly Child 3167
Butterfly Life, The 4215
Butterfly Love 2460, 4477, 4530
Butterfly on the Wheel 2706
Butterfly Waltz 252
Butterfly's Lament 3619
Button Me Up the Back 560, 685

Button Up with Esmond 1475, 2590
Button Up Your Heart 4545
Button Up Your Overcoat 393, 1339
Buttonhole Bouquet, A 668
Buxom Mrs. Bascom, The 1493
Buy a Bond 1632
Buy a Bond for Baby 498
Buy a Kiss 1743
Buy a Little Button from Us 2376
Buy a Slave 1769
Buy a Song 3036
Buy a Victory Bond 3330
Buy an Extra 4651
Buy, Baby 2981
Buy Bonds, Buster 597
Buy Bonds, Buster, Buy Bonds 3217
Buy Buy Baby 3681
Buy Her a Box at the Opera 3865
Buy My Pardons 1500
Buy My Passamentaries 4172
Buy Your Way 2669
Buy Yourself a Balloon 1763, 3955
Buyers, The 4247
Buying and Selling 2284
Buying Little Things for Me 965
Buzz!!! 4389
Buzz-A-Buzz 273
Buzz Mirandy 4182
Buzz on Little Busy Bees! 4490
Buzza Buzza Buzz 1680
Buzzard Song, The 3541
Buzzin' Around 598
Buzzin the Bee 3189
Bwee Dah 1233
Bwis Jolem Tanz 4773
By a Piccadilly Cab Stand 3588
By a River in Spain 1950
By Air 221
By and By 1650, 3323
By Bacchus 1682
By Candlelight (1) 4777
By Candlelight (2) 4777
By Candlelight (Bei Kerzenlicht) 3756
By Chance We're Both Willy's 2880
By Dawn's Early Light 4619
By Gentle Means 333
By Hook or By Crook 3454
By Jove, It Is a Pretty Slipper 1090
By Love Undying Crowned 4014
By Moonlight, on the Odyllic Influence of the Moon 654
By My Mien (Greta's Waltz) 3994
By My Side 1595
By Myself 383, 690
By Our Bearing So Sedate 4188
By Our Majesty's Monarch Command 3828
By Pigeon Post 4840
By Proxy 1388
By Radiophone 4194
By Rule of Three 402
By Special Permission of the Copyright Owners I Love You 1440
By Strauss 1763, 3955
By the Blue Lagoon 1523
By the Blue Summer Sea 4037
By the Candlelight 1125
By the Country Stile 2761
By the Garden Wall 2378
By the Glenside 3831
By the Grace of the Land 2766
By the Honeysuckle Vine 3985
By the Light of the Honeymoon or Kiss Me and Say You'll Be Mine 246
By the Light of the Moon 2666
By the Light of the Silvery Moon 2892, 4803
By the Mississinewah 1018, 4058
By the O-Hi-O (O-My-O) 2856
By the Old Oak Tree 1090, 3749
By the Palmest Tree 1536
By the People 117
By the Pyramids 2642
By the Sad Luana Shore 4148
By the Same Old Light Above 4439
By the Saskatchewan 3494
By the Sea 1922, 3112, 4233, 3111
By the Side of the Mill 3675
By the Side of the Road 827
By the Side of the Zuyder Zee 4762
By the Silver Sea 1121, 2509
By the Silvery Nile 3749
By the Susquehanna 538
By the Sweat of Your Brow 4253
By the Sycamore Tree 3747
By the Waters of Babylon 1715
By the Waters of Minnetonka 3840
By the Way 605
By This Sweet Token 4559
By This Token 3586
By Threes 2058
By Tumna's Rolling Waters 2665
By Welawela 2636
By Wireless 632
By-and-By 3951
Bye and Bye 632, 1013, 1093, 2919, 3134, 552
Bye and Bye You Will Miss Me 4807
Bye Bye 3788
Bye-Bye Babe 458
Bye Bye Baby 1475
Bye, Bye, Baby 2590
Bye-Bye Baby 4738
Bye, Bye Barbara 606
Bye Bye Birdie 602
Bye, Bye, Bonnie 608
Bye-Bye Butterfly Lover 383
Bye, Bye, Conrack! 838
Bye, Bye Dear Old Broadway 4801
Bye, Bye, Drowsy Eyes 631
Bye Bye for Baby 3953
Bye-Bye My Caroline 1902

Bye-Bye My Little Wife 2549
Bye Bye Osiris 3004
Bye Lo 1032
Bye Room 2224
Bygone Days 3529
Bygone Days Are Best 2990
Bygone Days in Dixie 2979
Bylo Bay, The 487
Byrd Influence, The 3103
Byzantine Things 1714

C

C.C. Rider 3297
C.D.Q. 1663
C-H-A-R-L-E-S-T-O-N 1131
C.I.A. Man 3309
C.O.D. 1849
C-o-n-s-t-a-n-t-i-n-o-p-l-e 4264
C.Q.D. (Help! I'm in Love) 1550
C'est Cheesecake 1940
C'est Comme Ca 3551
C'est Defendu 2362
C'est La Vie 2475
C'est la Vie 3899
C'est Magnifique 629
C'est Moi 623, 1470
C'est Paree 2813
C'est Si Bon 2356
C'Est Si Bon 4264
C'est Toi 1154
C'mon Folks (Queenie's Ballyhoo) 3949
C'mon Up to Jive Time 576
Ca, C'est Sixth Avenue 1342
Ca Ira 979
Cab-arabian Nights 4037
Cab Song 2755
Caballero 3170, 4341
Cabaret 610, 131, 4480
Cabaret Dancer, The 1901
Cabaret Girl 2216
Cabareting in Pumpkinville 1560
Cabarets 1529
Cabby's Serenade, The 2301
(Down at the Ole) Cabin Door 443
Cabin in the Cotton 1481
Cabin in the Sky 612
Cabinet Music 2252
Cable Car 4643
Cablegram 870
Caboceer's Choral 2111
Cachita (inst.) 3440
Cacophony 729, 3651
Cactus Flower 1867
Cadava 1699
Cadenza 3864
Cadet's March 945
Cadets of St. Cry, The 613
Cadillac Car 1103
Caesar and Cloepatra 1848
Caesar Comes 614
Caesar Is Wrong 1848
Cafe 'Round the Corner, A 1550
Cafe Au Lait 3628
Cafe Boheme, The 728
Cafe Chantant 734
Cafe Crown 615
Cafe Girl (I Met Her at the Metropole, but I Lost Her at Jacks) 2826
Cafe Royale Rag 3956
Cafe Scene 672
Cafe Society 3124
Cafe Society Set, The 4777
Cafe Society Still Carries On 3893
Cafeteria Chow 827
Cafeteria March 827
Cahoots 2925
Cairo 1307
Cajun Dance, The 1917
Cake-Eaters' Ball, The 2308
Cake Song 1385
Cake-Walk, The 3999
Cake Walk 3955
Cake Walk Ball 3134
Cake Walk Parade 822
Cake Walk Promenade 1560
Cake Walkin' Babies from Home 3297
Cakewalk 1616, 3814
Cakewalk (inst.) 4805
Cakewalk into Kansas City 1037
Cakewalk Turns: Blues (inst.) 1385
Cakewalk Turns: Boogie (inst.) 1385
Cakewalk Turns: Genteel Bastard (inst.) 1385
Cakewalk Turns: Minuet (inst.) 1385
Cakewalk Turns: Pandemonium (inst.) 1385
Cakewalk Turns: Soft-Shoe, Sword Dance (inst.) 1385
Cakewalk Turns: Tambourine (inst.) 1385
Cakewalk Turns: Tangissimo (inst.) 1385
Cakewalk Turns: Waltz (inst.) 1385
Cakewalk Your Lady 1385, 4123
Cal Gets By 1864
Calabash Cousins 4337
Calamity Jane 616
Calcium Moon, The 4203
Calcutta 4021
Caldonia 1296
Calendar of Love, The 3855
Calico Days 878, 3144
California (Follow the Setting Sun) 496
California 1182, 3397, 1604, 4152, 4173
California Belle 3357
California, Claremont 1316
California Cousins 496
California Dance Scene 189
California, Here I Come 391
California Here I Come 487
California, Here We Go 1777

California Skies 3659
California Suite 275
California Summer Sports 1938
California Sunrise 2576
California Sunshine 3133
Californ-i-ay 2204
Calinda, The 2
Caliph I, The 1908
Calisthenic Song 604
Call, The 1698, 3463
Call Around Again 1016
Call Around on Sunday 1910
Call Around Some Other Day 2724
Call Back in the Morning 2544
Call Back the Times 669
Call from the Grave 4369, 4370
Call from the Vatican, A 3171
Call Him Papa 1354
Call in the Cops 2660
Call in the Tax Collector 112
Call in to Her 935
Call It a Day 136
Call It a Dream 4214
Call It Applefritters 95
Call It Love 1679
Call Me 373
Call Me Babylove 1662
Call Me Back 2626
Call Me Bill 2858
Call Me Flo 4712
Call Me Irresponsible 4743
Call Me Lucky 766
Call Me Madam 619
Call Me Mister 620, 3018
Call Me Mr. Lucky 845
Call Me Rusty 4138
Call Me Savage 1227
Call Me Uncle 1285
Call Me Whate'er You Will 3225
Call of Broadway, The 202
Call of Home, The 3117
Call of Life, The 429
(Come at the) Call of Love 905
Call of Love, The 3672
Call of Love 3712
Call of Spring, The 2464
Call of the Birds 4707
Call of the City 2306
Call of the Clans, The 1503
Call of the Cozy Little Home, The 4269
Call of the Great White Way, The 1381
Call of the Sea, The 3184
Call of the South, The 3009
Call of the Wild 4433, 4484
Call of the Wild Women, The 2070
Call On Rag Doll 4742
Call on Your Neighbor 4446
Call Right Here 1544
Call 'Round Again 3856, 3857
Call the Doc 3538
Call the Police 868
Call to Arms, The 2126
Call to the Colors, The 965
Call to Wander, The 1698
Calla Lily Lady 4485
Callarer's Toast, The 2697
Callin' the Children Home 3840
Calling All Men 621
Calling All Stars 622
Calling Me Home 2392
Calling of the Sea, The 2154
Calling Romance 318
Calling You My Own 735
Calling Your Loved Ones 194
Calliope 3386
Calloway for President 877
Calypso 1600, 932
Calypso Island 1693
Calypso Joe 4483
Calypso Kitty 322
Calypso Pete 3954
Camaraderie 1619
Came from Germany 2538
Came the Dawn 4039
Camel Song, The 2171
Camel's Blues 2283
Camelot 623
Camelot Samba, The 834
Camera Doesn't Lie, The 417, 420
Camera Shoot 2467, 3924
Camille, Colette, Fifi 3899
Camouflage 572, 2713, 4269
Camouflage Clutch, The 126
Camouflaging 4742
Camp 366, 1438
Camp Headstrong 1047
Camp Karefree 4718
Camp Let-Yourself-Go 4397
Camp Meeting Time 830
Camp's Daily Dozen 3405
Campaign, The 837
Campaign Song 4318
Campanile 684
Campbell Soup Kids 3855
Campfire Songs 3209
Campmeetin' Time 3205
Camptown Races 2415, 4149, 3989
Campus Walk 3361
Can Anyone See? 2985
Can Can 971, 3091
Can I? 690
Can I Build My Home in You 1073
Can I Do It All 564
Can I Find a Toreador? 1961
Can I Forget 2697
Can I Forget You? 2204
Can I Leave Off Wearin' My Shoes 2000
Can I Let Her Go? 4297
Can I Live Without the Man 198
Can I Survive This Overbearing 1948

Can I Touch You 1612
Can It 4477, 4530
Can It Be Love 3579
Can It Be Love at Last? 1266
Can It Be Possible? 2053
Can It Be That I'm in Love? 4760
Can Macy Do without Me? 2601
Can My Son Be President? 4003
Can Song 2979
Can That Boy Fox Trot 1329, 2764, 3967
Can the Can-Can 1138
Can This Be a Toe Print? 2339
Can This Be Hell? 3937
Can This Be Love? 1275
Can This Be Why We Came Here? 842
Can We Do Anything? 3569
Can We Forget? 3251
Can Ye Fancy That? 962
Can You Can-Can 4316
Can You Do This? 4064
Can You Find Me a House 4732
Can You Forget? 998
Can You Hear Me Calling 2546
Can You Hear My Voice? 4396
Can You Hear the Morning? 2703
Can You Read My Mind 4399
Can You See 4403
Can You See a Girl Like Me in the Role? 3940
Can You Sing? 4214
Can You Tell 1154
Can You Type? 3548
Can You Use Any Money Today? 619
Can't Be Bothered Now 691
Can't Can't 3239
Can't Get Out of This Mood 3444
Can't Get Rid of Me 4025
Can't Help Lovin' Dat Man 2204, 2372, 3949
Can't Help Singing 2372
Can't Keep My Heart from Racing 2754
Can't Leave Now 2759
Can't Make Love Without You 3202
Can't No Grave Hold My Body Down 4788
Can't Nobody Do Me Like Jesus 3987
Can't Stand in the Way of My Country 4615
Can't Stop Now 1415
Can't Stop Talking 3444
Can't Stop the Sea 651
Can't We Be Friends 2545
Can't We Get Together 1980
Can't We Have a Rally? 2615
Can't You Do a Friend a Favor? 834
Can't You Hear Me Callin', Caroline 2415
Can't You Hear Me Calling? 3024
Can't You Hear Your Country Calling: The Spirit Calling 4811
Can't You Just See Yourself 4399, 1886
Can't You Read Between the Lines 1577
Can't You See? 4053
Can't You See I Love You? 3134
Can't You See I Mean You 3177
Can't You See I'm in Love 317
Can't You See It? 1601
Can't You Take My Word? 2844
Can't You Tell? 799
Can-Can 629, 3386
Can-Can vs. Cake-Walk 1243
Can-Can, The 4365
Can-Canola, The 4087
Canada at War 414
Canajoharie 1922
Canard, The 2357
Canarsie Diner, The 3178
Canary 4627
Canary Cottage 628
Canceling the Bar Mitzvah 1234
Cancun 4533
Candidates' March 4201
Candide 630
Candle Light 4777
Candy Cane Rock 'n' Roll 2083
Candy Choo-Choo 2089
Candy Girls, The 4327
Candy Jag 2574
Candy Kid 1340
Candy Shop, The 632
Candy Soldiers on Parade 2089
Candygram Song, The 1362
Candyland 2184
Candy's Lament 3224
Candystick 2083
Cane Dance, The 3721
Cane Dance 4025
Cane Dance (inst.) 4150
Cane Dance 4817
Cane Song 4839
Canis Minor Bolero Waltz 2728
Cannibal Barbecue 2534
Cannibal Island, The 2534
Cannibal Maid, The 1071
Cannon Song 4370
Cannonading Eyes 102
Cannot Wait 3876
Canny Canner, The 3422
Canon's Song 3612
Cantata 4627
Cantcha Kinda Go for Me 885
Canteen Girl 1026
Canteen Serenade 597, 3217
Canter Banter 1500
Canterbury Day 634
Canterbury Tales, The 634
Canterbury Tales 1500
Canterville Ghost, The 635
Canterville Hall 635
Cantible (A Song without Words) (inst.) 1476
Canticle Charon 1450
Canticle of Pleasure 1377
Canticle to the Wind 4243
Cantineer of the Regiment 613

Canzonetta 2614, 2670
Capdedious 946
Cape Cod Chanty 637
Caper, The 3900
Capering Coopers 69
Capital H 2710
Capital of the World 3490
Capital Punishment 4181
Capone 112
Capone's Day in Court 112
Capped Teeth and Caesar Salad 4068, 4301
Caprice Viennois 3703
Capricious and Fickle 3602
Capt. Kidd 60
Captain 2108
Captain Andy's Entrance and Ballyhoo 3949
Captain Bold, The 2500
Captain Cholly Chumley of the Guards 2101
Captain Cupid 1570
Captain Dinklepop 2760
Captain Flo 2119
Captain Henry St. James 3234
Captain Hook's Soliloquy 599, 3452
Captain Hook's Waltz 3453
Captain Jinks 3989
Captain Jinks of the Horse Marines 642, 643, 1897, 1897
Captain Jones 4405
Captain Kidd (Was a Private Man) 1518
Captain Kidd (Spread the News) 2111
Captain Kiddo 1703
Captain Kidd's Kids 953
Captain Lincoln March, The 4785
Captain, Mate and Crew 4253
Captain Mutt of the Lemonade Brigade 3033
Captain of a Ten-Day Boat 2517
Captain of the Mineola Guards, The 2826
Captain of the Pinafores 3889
Captain Pott (They Are All After Pott) 2844
Captain Reginald D'Arcy of the Guards 688
Captain Schumaker 408
Captain Terror 3871
Captain Valentine's Tango 2228
Captain Walker 4676
Captain Willie Brown 1246
Captains Courageous 647, 647
Captain's Jig, The 2654
Captain's Paradise, The 3234
Captain's Song, The 2225
Capture of the Yaraboo, The 9
Capturing the Boys and Wendy 3453
Car of Love 35
Caramba 1313, 2559
Caravan 4091
Caravan Land 2774
Caravan on a Country Road 1971
Cardinal's Guard Are We, The 1548
Career Girls 3714
Career Guidance 868
Career Malice 2804
Carefree Cairo Town 560
Carefree Heart, The 649
Carefree Miner, The 1387
Careful with My Heart 4824
Carefully on Tiptoe Stealing 1948
Careless Love 2225
Careless Rhapsody 601
Careless with the Truth 616
Caress Me, Possess Me Perfume 4682
Caresses 25
Caribbeana 4021
Carinito 4572
Carino Mio 3347
Carioca, The 3249
Carissima 1281, 3673
Carlo Rocco 82
Carlos, Juan and Miguel 4635
Carlotta 2847
Carlotti's 2216
Carlsbad Legend, The 4119
Carmela 4271
Carmelina 652
Carmen 653, 653, 3698, 4839
Carmen Girl, The 3701
Carmen Has Nothing on Me 4271, 4837
Carmen Jones Is Goin' to Jail 653
Carmen the Second 2858
Carmen Vincenzo 4659
Carmena 4201
Carmencita 199
Carmencita Shea 3627
Carmenita 256
Carmina 2984
Carne Asada 42
Carnegie Hall Pavanne (inst.) 3278
Carnival 3724
Carnival! 902
Carnival 1281
Carnival, The 1518
Carnival 2115
Carnival (Al Fresco), The 2160
Carnival 2827, 3157, 3970, 3977
Carnival Ballet (inst.) 657
Carnival Ballet 3011, 3509
Carnival for Life, A 902
Carnival in Capri 157
Carnival in Caroline 886
Carnival in Court 673
Carnival in Rio 4117, 859
Carnival Night 2601
Carnival of Dance, The 1868
Carnival of Springtime 4188
Carnival Ride 2598
Carnival Scene 4187
Carnival Song, The 3845
Carnival Tango 507
Carnival Theme (Love Makes the World Go Round) 656
Carnival Time 2376, 2666, 2939
Carol, A 280

Carolin' 108
Carolina 2631, 4328, 4421
Carolina in the Morning 3405
Carolina Lou 1963
Carolina Mammy 487
Carolina Rolling Stone 4137
Carolina Sue 3022
Carolina Sunshine 1032
Carolina's Lament 2354
Caroline 2373, 2787, 813, 3904
Carousel 1878, 2188
Carousel in the Park 4524
Carousel Waltz (inst.) 660
Carriage for Alida, A 298
Carrie 702, 661, 661
Carrie Barry 4723
Carried Away 991, 3278, 198
Carried Off 2917
Carrier Pigeon, The 1388
Carrion Train 1216
Carry On 190, 567, 3643, 3674
Carry On, Chums 4062
Carry On Keep Smiling 4023
Carry That Weight 3903
Carryin' On 2682
Carter Song, The 3557
Cartoon Town 4858
Carve Up! 1277
Cary: Who? 407
Caryl Ann 2580
Casablanca 663
Casamagordo 2583
Casanova 3214, 3955
Casanova, Romeo, and Don Juan 3953
Case of Rape, A 1373
Case of the Hum-drum Killer, The 3615
Casey 2682, 1173
Casey Is a Wonderful Name 4317
Casey Jones 3989, 4687
Cash for Your Trash 39
Cash Politics 564
Casino Girl, The 666
Casino Music Hall, The 4327
Cassie 1637
Cassie's Not a Bit Like Mother 2760
Cast Call 4268
Cast of Thousands 4358
Casting Call, A 275
Castle in India, A 3763
Castle of Dreams 2148
Castle on a Cloud 2442
Castle on the Nile 982
Castle Walk, The (dance) 1886
Castles in Spain 3774, 4037, 49
Castles in the Air 2219, 2696, 1392
Castles in the Sand 1797
Castles of the Loire, The (ballet) 1634
Castro Tango!, The 1363
Cat and Fox Song 3495
Cat and Mice 1309
Cat and Mouse 139
Cat and the Custard Pot, The 2240
Cat Came Back, The 3860
Cat Can Look at a Queen, A 111
Cat Duet 541
Catalina 3860
Catalog Woman 4467
Catamaran 3031
Catamarang 2317
Catch 129
Catch a Butterfly 2384
Catch a Star! 673
Catch As Catch Can 4437
Catch 'em Young, Treat 'em Rough, Tell 'em Nothing 1552
Catch Hatch 3301
Catch Me 3309
Catch Me If I Fall 674
Catch Me If You Can 3664, 4169
Catch My Garter 1764
Catch of the Season, The 675, 1043
Catch Our Act at the Met (Vaudeville Ain't Dead) 4496
Catch That on the Corner 40
Catchy Coo 3828
Caterpillar's Advice 54
Catfish 1985, 3608
Catfish Song 2030
Cathedral of Clemenza, The 4541
Catherine the Great 4374, 4772
Catland 4662
Cat's Away, The 614
Cat's in the Cradle 2470, 3159
Cat's Quartet, The 2315
Catskills, Hello 3146
Caught 4102, 4199
Caught in the Rain 2545, 3508
Caught Ole Blue 2225
Cause I'm Happy 784
Cause of Civilization, The 762
Cause of the Situation, The 403
Cause Uncle Mord'che Is So Smart 2811
'Cause We Got Cake 4420
'Cause You Won't Play House 3103
Caution: Men Cooking 3608
Cautionary Tale, A 533
Cautiously Optimistic 3557
Cavachok 680
Cavalcade of Curtain Calls 2477
Cavalier, The 2836
Cavalier Cat, The 4143
Cavalier Song 2671
Cavaliers 3011
Cavalier's Lament, The 4244
Cavalier's Waltz 2910
Cavalry Captain, A 2659
Cave Girl 4226
Cave Man, The 4553
Cave of the Patriachs 2421
Caveat Emptor 3788

Caveman and the Cavewoman, The 1083
Caveman, The 1580
Cavorting 249
Cazzaza 480
CB 4138
Cecelia 2710
Cecil in London Town, The 2517
Cecilia and Amelia 4242
Cecily 3195, 3236
Ceilin's Comin' Dahn, The 1277
Celebrate 2354
Celebration 681, 1322, 3542, 3599, 3909
Celebration Dance (Serfs Up) 3587
Celebration of St. Joan the Good 2594
Celebration! 1766
Celeste Aida 4579
Celestine 968
Celia's First Essay 1373
Celina Couldn't Say 'No' 383
Cell Block Tango 723
Cellini's Dream 201
Cellini's Plate 3150
Cello Fellow, The 1405
Cendrillon, ou la Petite Pantoufle de Vair 759
Censorship 1035
Central Intelligence 4397
Central Park 1841
Central Park on a Sunday Afternoon 4468
Century Girl, The 683
Century of Progress, A 1699
Century Promenade, The 2856
Century Toddle 2857
Ceremonial Beheading 3280
Ceremonial Chant 3371
Ceremonial March 3371
Ceremonial to the Wedding 3573
Ceremony, The 2905, 1262, 4378
Ceremony of Veils 25
Certain Girl, A 1605, 1764
Certain Individuals 4718
Certain Something About You, A 2854
Certain Sort of Father, A 4017
Certainly Is the Truth 2009
Cesar 1242
Ceylon 3070, 1518
Cha-No-Yu 3944
Chaconne (inst.) 964
Chaguanas 4147
Chain Dance 4654
Chain of Love 1662
Chain Store Daisy 3501
Chained 753
Chair Ballet 764
Chair Bottom Dance, The 202
Chair Dance 187
Chair Dance, The 3830
Chairman's Song, The 1077
Chalhatchee 1969
Challenge Dance 1890
Challenge to Love 2229
Chamber of Commerce Convention 408
Chambermaids 1392
Champagne 1343, 1910, 198, 3580, 3618, 3763
Champagne and Kisses 2728
Champagne and Laughter 2931
Champagne and Terrapin 3952
Champagne and Terrapin, Vision Divine! 3951
Champagne Charlie 1897
Champagne Charlie March (inst.) 688
Champagne fo' de Lady 1385
Champagne Song 697, 1183, 4011
Champagne Waltz 350
Champion 4147
Championship of the World, The 4815
Chan Ballet 3688
Chance He'll Never Stray, A 1614
Chance of a Lifetime, The 3555
Chance of You 2065
Chance to Dream 4039
Chances 4689
Chandelier Waltz, The 2928
Chang, the Lover (inst.) 4699
Change If to Is 2286
Change in Direction 1985
Change in Me 373
Change in Raquel 3636
Change Is Gonna Come, A 166
Change of Climate, A 336
Change of Heart, A 3108
Change of Scene 2584
Change of Watch 750
Change Partners 2317, 3043
Change Your Immigrant Ways 3926
Change Your Living 11
Change Your Luck 691
Change Your Mind 2896
Change Your Mind About Me 2034
Change Your Nature 1073
Change Your Step 4296
Change, The 2993
Changeable Girls 3246
Changes 692, 154, 155, 3305
Changing 1737, 3927
Changing All These Changes 580
Changing Channels 494
Changing My Tune 846, 845
Changing of the Guard 3159
Changing of the Guards 3683, 4823
Changing Partners 4635
Changing Styles 1557
Chanson 273, 1621, 2856, 49
Chanson Apache 3962
Chanson d'Enfance 211
Chanson de Paree (The "Oo-La-La, Ca C'est Paree" Song) 3587
Chanson on the Prater, A 2786
Chansonette 3732, 4817
Chant 56, 279, 1275, 1281, 2583, 2686
Chant d'Amour 95
Chant, Dance and Prayer to Venus 3466

Chant des Galleriens 3769
Chant of the Dead Pilot 3913
Chanticleer and Pertelote Duet 634
Chanticleer, Pertelote, Fox Trio 634
Chantilly Lace 580
Chanty 406
Chanty, A 3117
Chaparone Song 934
Chapeau 693
Chapel of Love 2427, 4193
Chaperon, The 694, 1173
Chaperone 674
Chaperons 2287
Chaplin Walk, The 3193
Chaplin Walked Here 2969
Chappies Song 3437
Chaps from Annapolis 4180
Chapter 54, Number 1909 3869
Chapter One 1786
Character in Search of a Character, A 3698
Characteristic Waltz 2525
Characters 3142
Charade of the Marionettes 3473
Charge 4297
Charge! 4108
Charge 1168, 2072
Charge, Boys, Charge 1768
Charge It to A.R. 2437
Charge of the Song Brigade 4421
Chariot 336
Charisma 3873, 2018
Charismatic 1732
Charity 130, 697, 722, 2399, 2906, 2478, 3881, 4267, 4405
Charity Ball, The 1533
Charity Bazaar, The 1796, 2915, 3051
Charity Begins at Home 2650
Charity Class, The 4001
Charity Quartet 3757
Charity's Soliloquy 4238
Charity's Theme (dance) 4238
Charity's Useful Disguise 1392
Charles Atlas Song 3742
Charleston 201
Charleston (inst.) 404
Charleston 2205, 3670, 3808
Charleston (South Carolina) 720
Charleston Cut Out 2009
Charleston Dancy, The 2557
Charleston Finale 2009
Charleston Hound 4282
Charleston Mad 2818
Charleston Rag (inst.) 1063
Charleston Rag 1198
Charleston Time 1777
Charleston Under the Moon 556
Charley Does the Charleston 2896
Charley from That Charleston Dancin' School 2645
Charley My Boy 393
Charley the Busker 589
Charley's Aunt 4652
Charlie 699, 915, 1188, 1408
Charlie and Algernon 699
Charlie Brown 4031
Charlie Chan 1363
Charlie Chaplin 3026
Charlie Chaplin Dance (inst.) 4543
Charlie Is the Darling of My Heart 466
Charlie, My Back Door Man 2302
Charlie on the M.T.A. 2246
Charlie Welch 2987
Charlie's Place 3330
Charlie's Plant 2918
Charlie's Songs 3610
Charlotte Sweet 705
Charlotte's Letter 2568
Charm 200, 1506, 2680, 797
Charm School, The 2263, 3404
Charmed Life 3835
Charmin' Son-of-a-Bitch, The 2217
Charmin's Lament 2687
Charming 82, 101, 1138, 2829, 3164, 3791
Charming, Charming 841
Charming, Charming (Store Opening) 3436
Charming Ladies 2419
Charming Senoritas 3170
Charming Waltz (inst.) 4798
Charming Weather 178
Charming Weather (Opening) 4795
Charming Women 2263
Charming Young Man 621
Charms Are Fairest When They're Hidden 2292
Charro Dance, The 3719
Chart, The 2598
Charwoman's Song 2115
Chase, The 99, 177, 239, 341, 530, 669
Chase 4138
Chase, The 1093, 1985, 2378, 3231, 2542
Chase (dance) 3687
Chase, The 3702, 4212
Chase Me Charlie 3235
Chase of the Fox, The 3184
Chase the Cat 570
Chase the Devil 3690
Chasing Butterflies 2108
Chasing Henry 3860
Chasing Little Rainbows 1129
Chasing the Squirrel 4634
Chasing the Talkies Away 791
Chassene 3670
Chassene Habn Iz Doch Zeyer Git 3781
Chat-Chat-Chatter 2774
Chat-Chat-Chatter on the Telephone 4453
Chat Noire 90
Chattanooga 1964
Chattanooga Choo Choo 3175
Chatter 584
Chatter Chatter 4603
Chatterbox, The 4204

Chatterbox Girl 709
Chauffeur 2338
Chauffeur, The 4787
Chauffeur's Song, The 1866
Chauve Souris 710
Chauve-Souris of Our Own, A 1688
Chavaleh 1265
Chaya 2626
Che Mai T'Ho Fall' Amor 2464
Cheap Exit, The 1872
Cheating Peddler, The 1375
Check Your Troubles 1747
Checkers 1961, 4813
Checkhov 424
Checking the Facts 1354
Chee Chee Girl, The 497
Cheek to Cheek 789
Cheeky Kiki 2706
Cheer Boys, Cheer 4738
Cheer for Simplicitas! 178
Cheer for the Kibosh, A 4724
Cheer, Girls, Cheer 381
Cheer Up 21, 118, 1650, 2884
(Be Happy, Too) Cheer Up 3949
Cheer Up 3949
Cheer Up! 4785
Cheer Up, Eat and Grow Thin 913
Cheer Up Everybody 2793
Cheer Up Father, Cheer Up Mother 61
Cheer Up! Girls 954
Cheer Up Hamlet 3644
Cheer Up, Liza! 712
Cheer Up, Madame 1427
Cheer Up, My Honey 531
Cheerful Little Earful 4235
Cheerio 1013, 3849
Cheerio! 4424
Cheerio, Old Boys 4380
Cheerleader 2677
Cheers 1171
Cheers for the Hero 1745
Cheese 3661
Cheese Nips 1591
Cheeta's Aria 528
Chemicals 2962
Cherchez la Femme 385
Cherchez la Femme
(Get Your Woman) 2818
Cheri-Beri 2467
Cherokee Rose 1020
Cherries Are Ripe 715, 2884
Cherries Ripe 4662
Cherry Blossom Lane 3962
Cherry Blossom Time 3173
Cherry Blossoms 1758
Cherry Hill 3384
Cherry in the Glass, The 1526
Cherry Pies Ought to Be You 3326
Cherry Trees Are Blue, The 1427
Cherry's Soliloquy 716
Chesapeake Bay 1964
Cheshire Puss 54
Chess 52
Chess and Checkers 3113
Chess Duet 2886
Chess Game, The 2746
Chess Hymn 721
Chestnutty Language of Lovers, The 2906
Chevalier of the Highway, The 1678
Chew Chewy Chow 275
Chew Your Bitter Nails 2478
Chewska 1067
Chi-Chi 1888, 3104
Chi-ni-qui-chi 4117
Chi-Ri-Bin 268
Chi-Town Strut 2692
Chianti 1580, 1644
Chibi 2669
Chic 722
Chic, Chic, Chic, Chic, Chicken 1124
Chic, Chic, Chic 1745, 1327
Chic Talk 3493
Chic Technique 703
Chic to Cheap 1637
Chicago 723, 393, 2870
Chicago (A Great Big Town) 3353
Chicago 4635
Chicago After Midnight (inst.) 723
Chicago Fire, The 1390
Chicago Jazz 3840
Chicago Stomp, The 2200
Chicago Style 112
Chicago That I Knew, The 4629
Chicago Trot 1560
Chicago, Illinois 4560
Chick-a-pen 4516
Chick! Chick! Chick! 1922, 3146
Chick, Chick, Chick 336
Chickabees 4619
Chickadee Girls, The 4577
Chickady Chay 2089
Chicken 2119
Chicken and the Frog, The 1872, 4012
Chicken Bone 981
Chicken Is He 3602
Chicken Pie 4589
Chicken Shack Boogie 1890
Chicken Song, The 1786
Chicken Soup with Rice 3668
Chicken Thief Man, The 4804
Chicken Today and Feathers Tomorrow 3793
Chicken's a Popular Bird 279
Chickens 3677
Chickens Come Home to Roost 3965
Chicklet 3606
Chicks 2603
Chicky 2643
Chico Chico 597
Chico-Chico Chico-Layo Tico-Tico Pay Pa
Payo Bueno Vista de Banana By-the-Sea 3217

Chico's Reverie 3899
Chief Cook and Bottle Washer 3718
Chief of Love 3845
Chief of the Aggrivation 646
Chief Rocky Boy 4682
Chiffon 2637
Chiffon Fantasie 4814
Chihuahua Choo-Choo 3841, 4321
Child Is a Horse's Best Friend, A 2084
Child Is Born, A 198, 1716
Child of Erin 3219
Child of My Heart 533
Child of Pure Unclouded Brow 54
Child of Sympathy 4089
Child of the Devil 259
Child of the Shade 1581
Child of the West, A 1373
Child Within, The 871
Child You Are, Man You'll Be 2016
Childhood 3697
Childhood Days 88, 1702, 1530, 2384, 2944, 4761
Childhood Lesson 3424
Childhood Lullaby 3938
Childhood's Happiest Moments 3855
Children, The 2679
Children and Art 4210
Children Are 52
Children Are for Loving 2908
Children Have It Easy 3835
Children in the Dark 1887
Children of Adam 729
Children of Eden 730
Children of the Drama 4486
Children of the Ritz 3885
Children of the Sun 4558
Children of the Wind 3644
Children Will Listen 2143
Children, You Seem Rather Distant to Me 1555
Children's Game 4169
Children's Games 344, 4659
Children's Lament 181
Children's Play Song 732
Children's Sake, The 4659
Children's Song 3441
Children's Song (Recess with Mrs. Grimm) 2001
Children's Taunt 4107
Child's Song, The 1062
Chile 875, 885
Chili Bean 3973
Chili Bom Bom 4573
Chill Out! 2283
Chilli Con-Can (Chili Glide) 1560
Chillun, Be Yourself 1876
Chime In! 2295
Chime of the Liberty Bell 2534
Chimes Number 2668
Chimes of Long Ago 3581
Chimes of the Chapel 1935
Chimneys Are Black, The 3630
Chin-Che 3947
Chin-Chin (Open Your Heart and Let Me In) 736
Chin Chin 2111
Chin-Chin 3028, 3799
Chin-Chin-Chinaman 1470
Chin Chin Chinaman 4184
Chin Chin Chow 2215
Chin Chin Open Your Heart and Let Me In 1901
Chin Up, Ladies 2864
China 606, 2654
China Bogie Man 735
China Doll 1921
China Girl 2872
China Loo 717
China Rose 735
Chinatown, My Chinatown 4521
Chinchilla 202
Chine of Beef, A 129
Chinese-American Rag 4375
Chinese Ballet 2397
Chinese Ballet (inst.) 4765
Chinese Billikens 710
Chinese Celebration 1826
Chinese Ceremony 4792
Chinese Dragon Blues 2385
Chinese Fireworks 4814
Chinese Flower 1144
Chinese Fox Trot, The 102
Chinese Honeymoon, A 736, 737
Chinese Idol, The 1132
Chinese Interlude 2802
Chinese Lantern Man 735
Chinese Letter Song 1919
Chinese Love Boat, The 1462
Chinese Love Song, A 3573
Chinese Lullaby 1142
Chinese March (inst.) 4765
Chinese Market Place 2655
Chinese Melody 4792
Chinese New Year's Ballet 4654
Chinese Number 632
Chinese Phantasy 1962
Chinese Porcelain Ballet (dance) 3703
Chinese Potentate 735
Chinese Soje Man 3828
Chinese Song, The 3765
Ching-A-Ling Fling 598
Ching-a-ring-a-ree 1470
Ching Chong 1833
Ching Ling Foo 2159
Chingo-Pingo 4792
Chink! Chink! 666
Chink-Chink, Chink-Chink, Chinyman 2979
Chink, Chink, Don't Talk to Me of Marriage 3994
Chinky China Charleston 1312
Chinky Chink 953
Chinkypin 3691
Chinquapin Bush 4123
Chip Along 2869
Chipper China Chaps 736
Chiquette 2135

Chiquita 3783, 3022
Chiquita Banana 3175
Chiquita Bonita 1164
Chiquitin Trio 3152
Chiribim 2811
Chiribin 2356
Chiromancy 920
Chiropractic Papa 123
Chirp Along 3258
Chirp, Chirp 3946
Chirp-Chirp 4320
Chivalry 1470
Chivalry Reel 4323
Chivaree 4199
Chivor Dance (dance) 2679
Chloe 2506, 3985
Choc'late Bar 2302
Chocolate Brown 3614
Chocolate Covered Cherries 573
Chocolate Covered Future 4830
Chocolate Dandies 740
Chocolate Drop (inst.) 4697
Chocolate Drops 2111
Chocolate Pas de Trois 4075
Chocolate Shake 2259
Chocolate Soldier 395
Chocolate Soldier, The 742
Chocolate Soldier 4521
Chocolate Soldier, The 743
Chocolate Soldier 743
Chocolate Turkey 1958
Chocolates and Chiclets 639
Choice Is Yours, The 278, 2777
Choices 337, 2289
Choir Boy, The 4165
Choir Practice 2451
Cholesterol Love Song 1049
Chon Kina 1470
Choo Choo Cars 1759
Choo, Choo, Ch'boogie 1296
Choo-Choo Honeymoon 956
Choo Choo Love 2342
Choo Choo Rap 562
Choose! Choose! Choose! 2551
Choose Her in the Morning 336
Choose Your Flowers 1756
Choose Your Partner 911
Choosing a Husband's a Delicate Thing 2928, 1970
Chop Stick Rag, The 3332
Chop Sticks 1777, 2276
Chop Sticks and Room 202 1032
Chop Stix 2096
Chop Suey 1315
Chopin 4669
Chopin Ad-Lib (Opening Chorus) 611
Choral Prelude 3673
Choral Russe 3091
Chorale 3277
Chords Like These 1521
Chorus and Entrance of Marquis 353
Chorus and Entrance of Regent 1183
Chorus Girl, The 3401
Chorus Girl Blues 266, 3847, 3848, 4781
Chorus Girl's Longing 331
Chorus Girl's Song, A 1643
Chorus of Assistants 1114
Chorus of Citizens 341
Chorus of Constant Lunchers, Constant Diners, Constant Dancers and Constant Kissers 186
Chorus of Courtiers 1114
Chorus of Footmen (Servants' Chorus) (Charge of the Footmen) 2915
Chorus of Guests 1537
Chorus of Lamentation 1470
Chorus of Laundresses 1114
Chorus of Models 3466
Chorus of Nurses 186
Chorus of Perambulator Girls 3887
Chorus of Poets 947
Chorus of Snobs 2964
Chorus of Soldiers 3586
Chorus of Villagers 2035, 1896
Chorus of Villagers and Policemen 2964
Chorus of Welcome 4121, 4219
Chorus of Welcome to Gilfain 1313
Chorus Picking Time on Broadway 1965
Chosen, The 747, 747
Chosen Doime le Meilech & Rikodle 4773
Chow-Chow's Honeymoon 737
Chow Mein Girls 1131
Chowder Ball 4408
Chris Crosses 750
Christ Is Alive 1716
Christening, The 2979
Christening of the Boat, The 1525
Christian Cowboy 4030
Christianity 1809
Christina Swanson 1316
Christina's Room 3463
Christine 751
Christine Swanson 399
Christmas 4676, 2224
Christmas at Hampton Court 3702
Christmas — Baby Please Come Home 2427
Christmas Buche, A 705
Christmas Carol, A 753, 828, 752, 4155, 4155, 754
Christmas Carol 2474, 4173
Christmas Carol, A 2980
Christmas Child 2150
Christmas Chimes 4471
Christmas Dances (inst.) 3977
Christmas Day 3603
Christmas Day in the Cookhouse 3259
Christmas Eve 3066, 753, 750, 3918, 3931
Christmas Fair Waltz 250
Christmas Gifts 4732
Christmas in July 3793
Christmas in Laurel Canyon 2992

Christmas in New York 2689, 3637
Christmas in Your Heart 1507
Christmas Is Comin' Uptown 828
Christmas Is Coming 2134
Christmas Is Over 3066
Christmas Long Ago 3889
Christmas Night in Harlem 445
Christmas Prayer 1418
Christmas Puppies 3806
Christmas Shopping 943, 4379
Christmas Song 1300
Christmas Spirit, The 4155
Christmas Stockings 260
Christmas Tidings 939
Christmas to Blame 1509
Christmas Together 754
Christmas Trees 1370
Christmas Waltz, The 4743
Christmastide Love 4742
Christopher 2759
Christopher Street 4734
Christy Girl, The 4803
Chromolume #7 4210
Chronicle of a Death Foretold 756
Chrysanthemum Tea (1) 3340
Chrysanthemum Tea (2) 3340
Chu Cha Chacha Olay 853
Chu Chem 757
Chu, Chin, Chow 4811
Chuck It! 3436
Chum Highball 1550
Chummy 260
Church 652
Church and State 4635
Church Around the Corner 69
Church Around the Corner, The 3086
Church Ballet 1809
Church Box Social 255
Church Doors 2754
Church of Birch, The 3530
Church of My Choice 4060
Church Parade, The 675
Church Social, The 1600
Churinga 2246
Churning Song 2880
Churning, Churning 3736
Chutzpah 4288, 2320
Ciao, Ciao, Bambino 4137
Ciao, Compare 521
Cigarette 1493, 3978, 4801
Cigarette Land 133
Cigarette Song, The 3602
Cigarette Song, A 3092
Cigarettes 1358, 1889
Cigarettes, Cigars 4823
Cincinnati 2209, 4622
Cindelia 3539
(Little) Cinderelatives 1485
Cinderella 379, 760, 1199, 1693, 1756, 2642, 3294, 4748
Cinderella and Prince Charming 2454
Cinderella at the Grave 2143
Cinderella at the Shoe Store 2858
Cinderella Backwards 2071
Cinderella Blues 1688
Cinderella Brown 2140
Cinderella, Darling 2019
Cinderella Girl 930
Cinderella Lost Her Slipper 959
Cinderella Meets the Prince 953
Cinderella of Our Block 266
Cinderella on Broadway 764
Cinderella Song 1090
Cinderella Waltz 4655
Cinderella! You Have Won 675
Cinderella's Dream 2394
Cinderella's Dreams 709
Cinderella's Ride 930
Cinders 765
Cindy 764, 766, 1924, 1925
Cindy with the Two Left Feet 2259
Cindy's Birthday 4193
Cinema Blues 3898
Cinema Girl 3405
Cinema I and Cinema II 3186
Cinema Lorelei 4335
Cinema Queen, The 1972
Cinematograph, The 336
Cingalese Village (Cingalese Girls) 2638
Cingoma Chakabaruka 4579
Circassian Dance 2292
Circe, Circe 1600
Circle 2470, 3724
Circle, The 2558
Circle This Day on the Calendar 4588
Circle Waltz, The 869
Circles 4147
Circles 'Round Us 4703
Circumstances 3276
Circus Ballet, The (inst.) 4813
Circus Band, The 1360
Circus Day 2089, 2090
Circus Day in Dixie 2107
Circus Days 2845, 3405, 3648
Circus in the Moon, The 3537
Circus Is Coming to Town, The 1208
Circus Is on Parade, The 2258, 420
Circus Is Over, The 2772
Circus of Jade 300
Circus of Voices, The 705
Circus Parade 2062
Circus Queen, The 4215
Circus Queen 4361
Circus Sort of Day 2804
Circus, the Circus, The 2443
Ciribiribi 3024
Ciribiribin 4251
Cirque-O-Pade 2146
Citation, The 2075
Cities I Love 4713

Cities of Light 962
Citizen of the United States 2422
Citizen of the World 595
Citizens' Assault 3227
City, The 1478
City Blues 344
City Called Heaven 3966
City Chap, The 773
City Flat, A 1267
City Girls 716
City Hall 1225
City Junket 774
City Life 2134, 3684
City Lights 16, 838
City Mouse, Country Mouse 3509
City of Angels Theme (inst.) 775
City of Dreams 2185
City of the Angels 411, 413
City of the Angels, The 412
City on Fire! 4233
City Song 4197, 4431
City Street Scene 827
Ciumachella (Ciumachella de Trastevere) 3798
Civic Improvement 3046
Civil War Ballet (inst.) 462
Civilian 4287
Civilization (Bongo, Bongo, Bongo) 137
Civilization 1714, 4283
Civilized 2375
Civilized People 2295
Civilized People, The 2679
Civilized Society 730
Claim Thou Thine Own 2315
Clancy 830
Clandestine 1233, 3484
Clang Dang the Bell 1698
Clansman March and Fling 582
Clap Hands 4757
Clap Yo' Hands 3243
Clap Your Hands 4131
Clap Your Hands All Ye People 912
Clara 339, 1920
Clara, Don't You Be Downhearted 3541
Clara Jenkins' Socialistic Tea 1776
Clara the Divine 3
Clara's Dancing School 2420
Claremont 4277
Clarence and Mildred 3233
Clarence Duffy 3039
Clarence's Turn 508
Claribel the Great 4467
Clarinet and the Coronet 3827
Clarinet Marmalade 1425
Class 723, 131, 3142, 36, 883, 2764, 897, 3843, 3976, 4480, 1771
Class Act 484, 4286
Class of 1984, The 3661
Class of Summer '32 2925
Class with a Capital K 3714
Classic Ingredients 413
Classical Music 4019, 3565
Classics, The 1938
Classification Blues 1880
Classifieds/Personals 3136
Classy Clothes 2749
Claudine 808, 809
Clay and Frelinghuysen 2018
Clean Out the Corner 3069
Clean Up Your Own Backyard 4584
Cleanin' Women 4744
Clear All Wires 2432
Clear! Clear! 284
Clear Day 1884
Clear Out of This World 2301
Clear the Way 4738
Cleavage 778
Clem's Drill (Dance Drill) 1729
Clementina 3735
Clementine 1569, 2259
Cleo from the Congo 2640
Cleo's Theme 4645
Cleonice 2464
Cleopatra 1823, 3252, 3818, 3985, 4634
Cleopatra Had a Jazz Band 1063
Cleopatra Had a Little Song 1966
Cleopatra, We've Found You 2005
Cleopatra's a Strawb'ry Blonde 118
Cleopatra's Aria 4724
Cleopatra's Dance 758
Cleopatra's Nile 758
Cleopatterer 2430
Clever Detective, The 2701
Clever, These Chinese 4023
Cliche Waltz, The 430
Click, Click 737
Click of Her Little Brogans, The 3642
Clickety-Clack 2344
Client Service 2676
Climax 1717
Climb 1055
Climb a Rose 306
Climb Ev'ry Mountain 4095
Climb High 779
Climb-Out 2093
Climb Up the Mountain 3326
Climb Up the Social Ladder (The New Blue D.A.R.) 2444
Climbin' 2949
Climbing the Ladder of Love 1464, 2489
Climbing Up the Ladder of Love 1128, 1132
Climbing Up the Scale 3008
Clinching the Sale 4823
Cling a Little Closer 1735
Cling, Clang 2262
Cling Cling 1096
Cling! Cling! 1631
Clinging Vine, The 780
Clinging Vine 1247
Clink Clank Clunk 4321
Clink, Clink 2041

Clip the Coupons 4208
Clippity Clop and Clementine 781
Clock, The 255
Clock in the Tower, The 4761
Clock Is Striking Ten, The 20
Clock on the Mantel, The 4014
Clock Song 2856, 3626
Clocking in the Stocking 1613
Clockmaker's Song 252
Clockwork Man, The 4381
Clog and Grog (dance) 4588
Clog Dance 2248, 4478
Cloistered from the Noisy City (The Union League) 2444
Clop, Clop, Clop 1742
Clorinda 26, 2722, 3134
Clorinda Jackson 4506
Close As Pages in a Book 4524
Close Every Door 2242
Close Harmony 1227
Close in Your Arms 1182
Close the Door Norma 2754
Close to Home 730
Close to My Heart 2107
Close to You 261
Close to Your Heart 1961
Close-Up 2969
Close Upon the Hour 2318
Close Were We 753
Close Your Eyes 20, 2201, 2564, 2739, 4173, 1276
Closed for Renovations 2544
Closeness Begets Closeness 127
Closer 3763
Closer Than Ever 784
Closing 3476
Closing, The 3527
Closing Arguments 1700
Closing Chorus 554
Closing Time 3608
Clothes 2216, 3806
Clothes and the Flapper 4104
Clothes Make the Man, The 3602
Clothing 1824
Cloud Nine 785
Cloud of Joy 1099
Cloudburst 3178
Cloudland 3423
Clouds 4034
Clouds of Love 1174
Clouds Roll By Dance 3821
Cloudy Morning 4153
Clown, The 710, 4767, 4496
Clown Alley 786
Clown and the Bareback Riders, The 1360
Clown of London 2295
Clown Song 4011
Clown Song, The 3280
Clowns 202, 786
Clowns in Clover 787
Clowns in Color 886
Clowns Say Goodnight 786
Club A Go-Go 4016
Club Song 2005
Club, The 2542
Clump! Clump! Swish! 2344
Clutching at Shadows 637
CNR 426
Coaching 4001
Coaching Chorus 1647
Coachman's Heart, A 953
Coachmen and Maids 1646
Coal Black Lady 3949
Coal Oil 2645, 14
Coax Me 2159, 3801
Coaxing 2724
Coaxing the Ivories (inst.) 3261
Cobbler and the Flies, The 2697
Cobbler's Ghost, The 2502
Cobbler's Song, The 758
Cobblers We 175
Cobra Ritual Dance (inst.) 751
Cobra Woman 3636
Cobweb Man, The 349
Coca-Cola Girl 2478
Cocaine 3076
Cochran Will Return 1277
Cock-a-doodle 1540
Cock-a-Doodle-Doo 1462
Cock-a-Doodle Doo 1689
Cock-a-doodle-doo 2408
Cock of the Walk, The 4804
Cock Robin 2055
Cockatoo and the Chimpanzee, The 2715
Cockeyed John, Give Me a Dream 3159
Cockeyed Optimist 3936
Cockeyed Optimist, A 4096
Cockroach Song, The 3565
Cocktail 795
Cocktail and a Cherry, A 2481
Cocktail Counterpoint 2360
Cocktail Hour 3712
Cocktail Melody 4249
Cocktail of Flowers, A 1240
Cocktail Party 3873
Cocktail Party Types 3530
Cocktail Song Energy 4109
Cocktail Time 2788, 4302
Cocktail, The 383
Cocktails at the Copa 865
Cocktails with Conservatives 4679
Coco 798
Coco Palm Tree Island 4737
Cocoa Bean Song, The 2355
Cocoanut Cream Pie 2033
Cocoanut Dance (inst.) 2638
Cocoanut Girl, The 1564
Cocoanut Sweet 2190
Cocoanut Tree, The 863
Coconut Wireless, The 3371

Cocotte, The 3214
Coda di Guido 3171
Code, The 145
Code of the Licensed Pilot 4243
Coeds 203
Coffee 1203
Coffee and Cheese 2966
Coffee and Tea 4303
Coffee Beans 1940
Coffee, Beer and Whiskey 3517
Coffee Break 2019
Coffee Coolers Tea 61
Coffee in a Cardboard Cup 131, 3900
Coffee Morning 1770
Coffee Mother Used to Make, The 4806
Coffee on the Stove 139
Coffee Pot 1131
Cognac 4000
Cohan's Pet Names (That's the Pet Name for Me) 115
Cohan's Rag Babe 4759
Cohen Owes Me $97 3926
Cohen Owes Me Ninety-Seven Dollars 789
Cohens Are Coming, The 299
Cohen's Yiddisha Band 3395
Cokey Joe 3409
Cold 3441
Cold and Dead 2961
Cold Cash 4468
Cold Clear World of the Intellect 270
Cold, Cold Room 4863
Cold, Cold World 270
Cold Comfort 920
Cold Cream Jar Song 1242
Cold Cruel Dark 140
Cold Hands-Warm Heart 2458
Cold Hard Cash 2754
Cold in the Morning 229
Cold of Nichette, The 1119
Cold Steel 459
Cold War 3873
Cold's the Wind 3939
Colder By the Hour 4643
Colie Gone 2719
Collaboration 262
Collecting of the Plaid 1049
Collective Beauty 3110
Collector's Item (Moose Murders) 871
Colleen Machree 2186
College Baby 265, 978, 4780
College Boy, A 4657
(I'll Be a) College Boy's Dear 3401
College Boy's Dream 1900
College Boys 3701
College Chaperone, The 1881
College Chums 2724
College Days 331, 1461, 1556, 1563, 1738, 3026, 3342, 3981
College Education, A 2232
College Girls 3745
College Glees 939
College Inn Rag, The 4720
College Life 187, 3480
College Man, The 698
College Medley 1230
College of L'Amour 1596
College on Broadway, A 1321
College Pals 1343
College Spirit 3775
College Trot, The 1248
College Widow, The 2430
Collegians, The 1312
Collette 2610
Colombo 4169
Colonel and the Major, The 4357
Colonel Buffalo Bill 153
Colonel of the Crimson Hussars, The 4258
Colonel's Lady 3551
Colonial Ballet 1065
Colonial Chorus 1480
Colonial Days 1181, 1693, 4842
Color and Light 4210
Color Ballet, The 1131
Color Blind 4374
Color Me White 415
Color Music 1774
Color My World 4193
Color of Her Eyes, The 1800, 2032, 4118
Color Organ, The 1651
Color Red, The 2674
Colorado 3077
Colorado Love Call 2522
Colorado, My Home 4516
Colored Gentlemen's Ball 1532
Colored Lights 131, 3718
Colored Spade 1717
Colorful 602, 1601
Coloring Book 3124
Colorland 1631
Colors of My Life, The 305
Colossal, Tremendous, Terrific 3975
Colour of Her Eyes, The 1202
Columbia 2385, 3357
Columbia Pictures 2969
Columbia Won the Race Today 762
Columbian Exposition, The 114
Columbia's Colleen 522
Columbina's Song 2464
Columbine (The Timid Humming Bird) 2722
Columbine's Courtship 2858
Columbus' Blues 2452
Columbus Was a Famous Man 2500
Columbus Wouldn't Know Columbus Circle As It Is Today 1378
Columnists 3409
Comb Is Hot, The 2306
Combat 1871
Combat Chorus 175
Combat Pay 4619
Come 2333
Come a Little Closer 4689

Come A-Wandering with Me 1456
Come Across 1552, 4378
Come Along (It's a Trifling Affair) 1458
Come Along 3543, 4814, 4816, 4834
Come-Along-a-Me, Babe 4678
Come Along and Tell Me 1849
Come Along, Boys 1600
Come Along Down 2750
Come Along, Honey! 1524
Come Along, Let's Gamble (Finale Act I) 1419
Come Along, Little Girl, Come Along 335
Come Along Little Girls 1588
Come Along, Ma Cherie 3681
Come Along Mandy 437
Come Along, Mandy 2232
Come Along Mandy 4804
Come Along My Boys 2724
Come Along, Pretty Girl 1519, 2317
Come Along, Sunshine 931
Come Along to the Carnival 1154
Come Along to the Movies 4644
Come Along to the Show 213
Come Along to Toy Town
(Come Along to Toyland) 1208
Come Along to Toy Town 1598
Come Along with Me 387, 629, 1123, 3313
Come and Be Married 3831
Come and Be My Butterfly 1828
Come and Bring Your Instruments 2103
Come and Cuddle Me 3537
Come and Dance 4553
Come and Dance with Me 2684
Come and Float Me Freddie Dear 4801
Come and Get Cozy with Me 90
Come and Go with Me 2203
Come and Have a Smile with Me 4762
Come and Have a Swing with Me 2184
Come and Play with Me 3392
Come and See Our Island 1313
Come and Spend Your Life with Me 181
Come and Take a Walk with Me 2481
Come and Take Me Out of Lonely Land 909
Come and Tell Me 376, 3436
Come and Watch the Moon with Me 1975
Come, Answer to Our Call 4188
Come Around on Our Veranda 3313
Come As a Carrier Dove 1712
Come As You Are 817
Come Avec! 4379
Come Away 4690, 1456, 4789
Come Away Death 3909
Come Away with Me 3429
Come Back, Baby 2173
Come Back Home Baby 2426
Come Back Little Genie 1300, 2234
Come Back Little Girl 1544
Come Back, Little Sheba 3925
Come Back My Honey Boy to Me 1264
Come Back, Sweet Dream! 1530
Come Back to Bohemia 1793
Come Back to Erin 77, 2853
Come Back to God (Me) 989
Come Back to Me 2939
Come Back to Me (2) 3274
Come Back to Me (1) 3274
Come Back to Me 4553, 4655
Come Back to Me Daddy 43
Come Back to Our Alley Sally 4815
Come Back to the Island 3339
Come Back to the Old Cabaret 2854
Come Back with the Same Look in Your Eyes
4068, 4301
Come Be My True Love 1564
Come Be My Wife 4547
Come Birdie Come 3998
Come Blow Your Horn 2543
Come Boys 4188
Come Buy a Trinket 1439
Come Buy Our Luscious Fruit 2974
Come Buy, Come Boy 1589
Come By Sunday 4153
Come Closer (Come a Little Closer) 2291
Come! Come! 697
Come, Come 4032
Come, Come, Come 3065
Come, Come, Come/Convent Maids 3081
Come, Dance, My Dear 453
Come Dance with Me 1920
Come Dancing, John (inst.) 499
Come Down 3831
Come Down from the Tree 3285
Come Down Ma Evening Star 4478
Come Down Mister Man in the Moon 3951
Come Down, Mr. Man in the Moon 331
Come Down Salomy Jane 4801
Come Down Susie 591
Come Down to Argentine 3369
Come Down to Devonshire 906
Come Down to Earth, My Dearie 4521
Come Down to Me Love 2519
Come Dream, So Bright 3736
Come Drink a Toast to Man and Wife 4554
Come Elijah, Come 3167
Come Farballe 3064
Come Fly with Me 2454, 4743
Come Follow the Band 305
Come from the Dyin' 3612
Come Gather 'Round 4769
Come, Gentle Stanger 613
Come Help Yourself to America, or
Frank in the Melting Pot 1256
Come Hit Your Baby 551
Come Hither Eyes 1888
Come Home 85, 3682
Come Home and Get Cozy with Me 3914
Come Home My Little Honeycomb 457
Come Home, Runaway 1086
Come In and Browse 1107
Come in from the Rain 2677
Come In My Mouth 2451

Come in Out of the Wet 4762
Come In, Mornin' 2030
Come Into My Jungle 535
Come Join in the Waltz 4590
Come Join the Party 1648
Come Let Us Dance 4615
Come Little Children 2046
Come Little Dearie 2040
Come Little Fishes (Gold Fish Song) 1183
Come Little Girl and Dance with Me 2335
Come Little Girl, and Tell Me Truly 3976
Come Live with Me 2278
Come Live with Me and Be My Love 3909
Come Love, Go Love 3585
Come, My Dear 1388
Come My Lad and Be a Soldier 1502
Come My Love to Araby 830
Come My Pretty Maiden 762
Come My Sweetheart 2903
Come My True Love 3422
Come Nestle in My Arms 2761
Come O Come (to Pittsburgh) 2137
Come of Age 4388
Come On 2516
Come-on-a-good Life 3871
Come on a Whistle 4440
Come On, All Together 4644
Come on Along 2818
Come On Along 3294
Come On Along to Honeymoon Town 1966
Come on and Dance 1816
Come On and Let's Make Whoopee 2637
Come On and Marry Me Honey 634
Come on and Pet Me 2768
Come On and Pet Me 3249
Come On and Play 391
Come On and Play Ball with Me 4803
Come on Children, Let's Sing 4460
Come On! Come On! 1577
Come On, Daisy 4635
Come On — Dance 2896
Come on Down 4788
Come On Down to Ragtime Town 396
Come on Down to the Sea 1985
Come On Down to Venezuala 1061
Come on Down Town 4759
Come on Feet, Do Your Thing 40
Come on Feet, Let's Go 3511
Come On, Feets, Let's Go 792
Come On Home 500, 2307, 3825
Come On Honey 3460
Come On In 1425
Come on In 1018
Come On In 1109, 2616, 4107
Come On In the Dancing's Fine 4657
Come On, Jim 126
Come on Joan 2220
Come on Kittens 3580
Come On, Let's Go 2569, 4844
Come On, Let's Two Step 2408
Come On, Li'l Augie 4123
Come On Mabel 2305
Come On, Men (FInaletto Act I Scene 5) 3980
Come On, Midnight 3181
Come On Outside and Get Some Air 4401
Come on Over 1884
Come On Over and Dance 3410
Come On Over Here 1066, 3134, 4726
Come on Papa 4812
Come On Strong 820, 1990
Come on Train 1216
Come One and All, Haste to the Ball 4554
Come One Come All 4382
Come One, Come All and See the Sights 1264
Come Out 4751
Come Out and Play 1969
Come Out, Come Out, Wherever You Are 58
Come Out Dinah on the Green 4014
Come Out of the Kitchen 1784, 2691
Come Out Sue 591
Come Over Here 822
Come Over to Deauville 2843
Come Play Wiz Me 162
Come Rain or Come Shine 1385, 4123
Come Raise Your Cup 1194
Come Raising Your Leg on Me 40
Come Said My Soul 2433
Come Save Me 2437
Come See About Me 338
Come Seven 2640
Come Sir, Will You Join Our Noble Saxton Corps 4188
Come Skate with Me 2097
Come Spirit, Come Charm 3862
Come Sta 4060
Come Summer 823
Come Sunday 432
Come, Sweet Love 1017
Come Take a Dance with Me 3031
Come Take a Dip in the Sea with Me 4203
Come Take a Skate with Me 1910
Come Take a Stroll with Me 3820
Come Take a Trip 3719
Come Take a Trip in My Airship 4390
Come Take a Trip in My Automobile 3891
Come the Bowmen in Lincoln Green 3736
Come, the Night Descends 1176
Come Tiny Goldfish to Me 3322
Come to Africa 3660
Come to Arcady 178, 2377
Come to Blackpool 603
Come to Bohemia 130, 1686
Come to Colombia 2679
Come to Court 3702
Come to Cuba 3557
Come to Florence (Civic Song) 1284
Come to Friville 3433
Come to Harlem 4763
Come to Life 808, 809
Come to Lower Falls 4276

Come to Me 2442, 1614, 327, 3815, 4798
Come to Me, Bend to Me 530
Come to Me Chimpanzee 558
Come to Mee-ow 3934
Come to My Garden 3862
Come to My Heart 1266
Come to My Heart (1) 2159
Come to My Heart (2) 2159
Come to My Land of Love Dreams 1430
Come to My Party 152
Come to Paris 1284
Come to Portofino 3543
Come to St. George's 356
Come to St. Georges 1313
Come to St. Thomas's 403
Come to Sunny Spain 1183
Come to the Ball 3618
Come to the Land of Bohemia 2996
Come to the Land of the Argentine 4603
Come to the Masquerade 2731
Come to the Moon 638
Come to the Pavillion 2837
Come to the Road 4431
Come to the Sacrifice 1817
Come to the Supermarket in Old Peking 1638, 44
Come to These Holy Arms 1730
Come, Toddle Along 2119
Come Together 3903
Come Tom 1162
Come Tomorrow 3227, 2654
Come Unto These Yellow Sands 3909
Come Up and Have a Cup of Coffee 4826
Come Up to My Place 3278
Come West, Little Girl, Come West 4683
Come What May 4701, 1734
Come with Me 514, 1075, 1101, 1817, 1834, 3167, 3469, 3507, 4408
Come with Me to My Bungalow (Cohan's Bungalow Song) 2525
Come with Me to Paree 4489
Come with Me to Rio 2026
Come with Me to San Torino 652
Come with Me...We Know Love 2953
Come with the Gypsy Bride 1710
Come with Welcome 2937
Come Ye Heroes All (The Emperor's War Song) 1388
Come You Men 4384
Comedy 825, 1148
Comedy Dance 3011
Comedy Fantasie, A 152
Comedy of Errors, The 514, 3231
Comedy Tonight 2205, 1422, 3967
Comedy Version for Frankie 3974
Comes a Time 2375
Comes a Train of Little Ladies 1987
Comes an Exquisite Situation 2145
Comes Love 4772
Comes Once in a Lifetime 4190
Comes the Dawn 4696
Comes the Revolution 2290, 2444
Comes the Right Man 2018
Comeuppance 1757
Comfort for the Taking 4707
Comfort Me 4709
Comforts of Boston, The 1809
Comforts of Home, The 971
Comforts of Home Sweet Home 4000
Comic, The 2776
Comic Book Hero 4139
Comic Opera, The 1264
Comic Opera Bandits 694
Comic Opera Capsule, A 2793
Comic Strip 2322
Comin' at Ya 1664
Coming and Going 1232
Coming Attractions 2968, 4002
Coming Home to Harlem 2032
Coming Out of the Garden 2271
Coming-Out Party, The 4297
Coming Through the Rye 3650
Coming True 424
Coming U.S.A. 2286
Command Me 240
Command Performance 4798
Command to Love 1656, 2300
Commander Robot and the Squiggles 2094
Commandress-in-Chief 2160
Comme Blonde Dumbellina 528
Comme Ci, Comme Ca 2264, 3532
Comme Tu Es Different 4600
Commencement Day Ode 3998
Commerce, The 4843
Commercials, Commercials 4389
Commitment 2935
Common Little Girl, A 1569
Common Sense 4428
Commont Allez-Vous 3178
Commonwealth Fair 220
Communicate 2941
Communism 3873
Commuters' Song, The 4018
Como Camel Corps, The 4694
Como le Gusta Me? 2493
Compact, The 3304
Companeros 3875
Companions, I Have Summoned You 2670
Companions of the Blade 4735
Companionship 1727
Company 832, 3967
Company Manners 3533
Company of Men 2584
Company of Men, The 4270
Company Picnic 4408
Company Way, The 2019
Complements 2761, 3573
Complicated Man 1077
Complications 1371
Compliments 2650
Composer Tango 3858

Composers' Song, The 3018
Composing 375
Compromise 3389
Compromise Soft Shoe 4379
Computer Love Song, The 2069
Comrade Alonzo 2432
Comrade, You Have a Chance Here 3078
Comrade Your Hand 1710
Comrades 3591
Comrades Fill No Glass for Me 4149
Con-Con-Con 4754
Con Edison 1107
Concentrate 2180
Concentrate a Little on Love 444
Concentration 870
Concert, The (dance) 3869
Concert Encore 4627
Concert Tonight 119
Concert Waltz 2115
Concerted Number 334, 2516
Concerto in E-Flat Major 3916
Concerto Inferno (inst.) 4155
Conchita 1689, 1979
Conclusion 654, 1701
Concrete Shoes 3739
Conductor of the Stationary Express, The 15
Coney by the Sea 3082
Coney Island, The 1590
Coney Island 154, 2299, 198, 3479
Coney Island (Opening Act I) 3980
Coney Island 4172
Coney Island Ballet 2379
Coney Island Boat 603
Coney Island, U.S.A. 2053
Confessin' (That I Love You) 432
Confession 294, 871, 4579
Confession #2 2646
Confession to a Park Avenue Mother 3161
Confession to a Park Avenue Mother (I'm in Love with a West Side Girl) 3366
Confessional, The 935
Confessional 1346, 1634
Confessional (Dear Abbe) 3587
Confidence 2923, 3863
Confidences 2448
Confidential 1682
Confidential Source 3996
Confidentially 1341, 412
Confirmation 3968
Confiteor 2775
Conflict at Council Rock 2970
Conformity 3440
Confrontation, The 721, 2905
Confrontation 949, 2198
Confrontation, The 1993
Confrontation Song 4431
Confused 1757
Confusion 3067, 4447
Confusion to the Perruquiers 325
Conga! 4734
Conga Tap, The 4503
Congai 1145
Congo-Conga 887
Congo Ivory 1477
Congo Love Song 3073
Congratualtions 2293
Congratulations 1015, 1855, 3476, 4709
Conjure Man 1385
Conjure Man, The 2951
Conjuror's Forgiven 4447
Connecticut Yankee in King Arthur's Court, A 834
Connemara Christening 4723
Connie 583
Connubial Bliss 3304
Conquering New York (dance) 4734
Conscience Is a Coward 3522
Conscience of a Nation, The 2472
Conscience's Song No. 1 1210
Conscience's Song No. 2 1210
Consciousness of Innocence, The 2399
Consecutive Fifths 3196
Consenting Adults 2616
Consequence Is Awful, The 2344
Consequences 1793, 2803
Consider 52
Consider Yourself 3271
Consider Yourself Unmarried 693
Consolation 1603, 1977
Consolation Lane 1909
Consoler of Women 495
Conspiracy, The 4046
Conspirators 1912
Conspirators, The 3673
Conspirators Are We 2793
Conspirators' Chorus 2035
Constancy 1629, 3256
Constant Lover 2891
Constant's Entrance 2563
Constantina Number 4063
Constantly 4697, 4804
Consternation 1300
Contagious Rhythm 1135
Contempery 1277
Contented Caterpillar, The 3753
Contented Man 3925
Contentment I Give You 1080
Contest, The 3136, 1959, 3839, 4233
Continental Honeymoon 4374
Continuous Performances 104
Continuous Show 1213
Contortion Dance 4437
Contraband Ball, The 1474
Contract, The 1511, 2861
Contrary Mary 2927
Contrast, The 840
Contribution Box 3337
Conumdrums 357
Convent 2728
Convent Bell, The 3803
Convent Bells Are Ringing 3586

Convent Song 1720
Convention Bound 3107
Conventional Opening, A 720
Conversation 4639
Conversation Piece 1770
Conversation Piece
(Nice Talk, Nice People) 4734
Conversation Song 1568
Conversation Step, The 3218
Conversational Song 2481
Conversations 159
Coo! 906
Coo-Coo 2277
Coo Coo 2522
Coo Coo (The Fable of the Dove) 2765
Coo Coo Jug Jug 2168
Coo-Coo Song 487
Coo-ee 336
Coo-ee, Coo-ee 1295
Coo-ee-doo 2446
Coo-Ee-Doo 2461
Coo-oo, Coo-oo 2317
Cook House Door, The 4302
Cook's Tour 1107
Cookie Chase (waltzes), The 162
Cookie Cutters 1059
Cookies 2333
Cookies and Bookies 391
Cookin' Breakfast for the One I Love 1873
Cookin' with Steam 2702
Cooks, The 591
Cool 4579, 4625
Cool Combo Mambo 868
Cool, Cool, Considerate Men 3897
Cool Cool Elbow 1662
Cool Credo 868
Cool 'Em Off 1128, 1132
Cool Off 142, 842
Coolest Cat in Town, The 843
Coolest Place in Town 40
Coolie Dance (inst.) 1625
Coolie's Dilemma, The 599, 1214
Coolie's Prayer 1214
Coon Banshee, The 2160
Coon College 1900
Coon, the Moon and the Octaroon, The 1188
Coon Will Follow a Band, A 4508
Cooney Country Fair, The 3323
Cooney-Spooney Dance, The
(That Spooney Dance) 3977
Coonjine 2225
Coonjine (inst.) 3753
Coonland 2481
Coonskin Cap 1216
Coontown Bank 2349
Coontown Quartet 3332
Cooper Square 1700
Cooperatin' Nature 716
Co-Operation 817
Cooperation 4433
Co-operation 2093
Co-op-hooray-shun 4602
Cop a Bit of Pride 1277
Cop and the Nurse, The 827
Copacabana 846
Copacabana (At the Copa) 845
Copacabana 2677
Copenhagen 478
Copenhagen, Denmark 2876
Copper Colored Gal 883, 897
Copper's Creed 2001
Copperfield 869
Cop's Lament 2615, 3696
Cop's Serenade 2615
Copulation Round 3445
Coquette 1475, 2590
Coquin de Printemps! 4115
Coquin de Printemps 4115
Cora Angelique 357
Cora Angelique (Musical Comedy Queen)
(The Queen of Musical Comedy) 4654
Cora, the Fair Chorine 870
Coral Isle 3423
Coralee 1613
Cord on the Hat, The 3154
Corday Waltz 3445
Cordelia Malone 1579, 3488
Corduroy Road 4693
Coreggio Ben Mio 2464
Corey's Coming 2470
Corn-Huskers, The 4447
Corn Is Green, The 2898
Corn on the Macabre 2962
Corn Shucking Time 1909
Corn Song 295
Cornelia 3631
Cornelia-Emily Letters (Opening) 3320
(I've a) Corner in My Heart (For You) 387
Corner of My Heart, A 1550
Corner of the Sky 3506
Cornet Man 1420
Cornshucking 1372
Coronation 1281, 1634
Coronation, The 1793
Coronation 1908
Coronation, The 4692
Coronation Chorale
(Westminster Abbey) 1564
Coronation Parade 2617
Coronation Rehearsal (inst.) 3791
Coronation Song 3571, 3586
Coroner Said Oh!, The 1518
Coronet Dance 336
Corps de Ballet 3682
Corraline 758
Corrandoli Song 2486
Correct 3322
Correspondence 1561, 3575
Correspondence School, The 2383, 3679
Corruption 4438, 4168

Corsage 3601
Corsica 2347
Corsican, The 4490
Cortez 154
Coryphee, The 1111
Cosi Fan Tutte 4522
Cossack Love Song, The
(Don't Forget Me) 4077
Coster's 'Oliday, The 3747
Costumes for 1950 1922
Cosy Corner 3962
Cosy Little Cottage By the Sea, A 3519
Cotillion, The 4337, 4655
Cottage I Call Je T'Aime 4373
Cottage in Kent, A 334
Cottage in the Country 4352
Cottage in the Country
(That's the Thing), A 3980
Cottleston Pie 4710
Cotton 882
Cotton Blossom 3949
Cotton Blossom Lane 883
Cotton Cloth Ghost, A 762
Cotton Club Express (inst.) 875
Cotton Club Express 885
Cotton Club Revue 3814
Cotton Club Stomp 437
Cotton Club Stomp (inst.) 4534, 895
Cotton Moon 357
Cotton Patch Version of Matthew and John 900
Cotton Pickers Ball 1833
Cotton Pickin Time in Tennessee 548
Cotton Song 3321
Cotton Tail 4091
Cotton Time 4429
Cotton-Blossom Serenade 3087
Could Be 348, 4718, 2933
Could Have Been 3858
Could He Be You? 1797
Could I But Tell You 737
Could I Ever Have It All? 1940
Could I Fascinate You 2717
Could I Forget 1182
Could I Leave You? 4067, 1329
Could I Leave You 3967
Could It Be You? 4058
Could She Be the One 2953
Could Such a Face Be False 669
Could We Start Again, Please 2212
Could You But Read My Heart 3952
Could You Get Along with Me 1690
Could You Love a Dreamer 1475
Could You Love a Girl Like Me? 4712
Could You Love a Man Like Me? 1557
Could You Love Me? 1570
Could You Please Inform Us 3598
Could You Teach Me? 3258
Could You Use a New Friend? 3410, 4484
Could You Use Me 921
Could You Use Me? 1528
Could'st Thou But Know 1090
Could've Been a Ring 1698
Couldn't Be More in Love 1112
Couldn't Happen Now 2303
Couldn't Hear Nobody Pray 3987
Couldn't We 1319
Couldn't We Be Like That? 3172
Couleur de Rose 3618
Count of Luxembourg, The 902
Count of Ten, The 302
Count on Me 98
Count the Stars 4798
Count Your Blessings 3261, 2847, 4018
Count Your Money 2009
Counter Melody 1408, 4388
Counterman, The 169
Counterpoint 1346, 1438
Countess Dubinsky 4824
Countin' Cobblestones 3908
Countin' Our Chickens 3837
Counting Sheep, Counting the Hours 4291
Counting the Hours 1130
Countrary Mary Clary 2310
Country Belles 457
Country Club, The 1374
Country Cousin 1411
Country Cousins 3322
Country Dance (inst.) 353
Country Dance 3056
Country Dancing 1857
Country Fair 992
Country Gentleman, A 3094
Country Girl, The 1071, 1071
Country Girl 932
Country House 4067, 1329
Country of the Mind, A 2220
Country Quadrille 1374
Country Song 2294
Country Spell 962
Country Store Living 4089
Country that Is Missing 1715
Country Wife, The 3920, 2654
Country's in the Very Best of Hands,
The 2484
Countryside (This Is the Life for a Man),
The 3569
Couple of Clowns, A 3210
Couple of Senseless Censors, A 3009
Couple of Years from Now, A 2783
Couplet 3670
Couplets 49
Courage Makes a Man 949
'Course I Will 4694
Course in Your Mother, A 2965
Course of True Love, The 767, 3771
Courses of Nature, The 4479
Court Dance 2504, 3011
Court Etiquette 1518
Court House Sequence 3528
Court Is Like a Chessboard, A 4662

Court of Louis XIV, The 4291
Court Office Song 3887
Court Song 2859, 2411
Courting (dance), The 1076
Courting 2029
Courting in the Moonlight 762
Courting Time 2364
Courtly Etiquette 2102
Courtly Lovers 2611
Courtship Ballet (inst.) 1120
Courtship Dance 3177
Cousin Kevin 4676
Cousins 693
Cousins of the Czar 902
Covenant, The 4481
Cover a Clover with Kisses 4235
Cover Girls 4533
Cover Me with Kisses 69
Covered Wagon Days 3133
Covina 408
Cow and a Plough and a Frau, A 183
Cow Boy 1185
Cow Jumped Over the Moon, The 2134
Cow Patty 914
Cow's Divertissement 4620
Cowboy 915, 916
Cowboy Girl, The 917
Cowboy Girl 1182
Cowboy Hoedown 2961
Cowboy Song 4109
Cowboy Songs 381
Cowboy's Burning Desire 3239
Cowshed Rhapsody 4667
Coy Young Maid, A 3981
Cozy Corner 1565
Crabbed Age and Youth 3909
Cracked Her Shell 264
Cradle of Jazz 2023
Cradle of Rhythm 4503
Cradle of the Deep 376
Cradle Song 303
Cradle Song and Aria 2623
Cradle Will Rock, The 919
Cradled in Thy Arms 1522
Craftsmen 426
Cranberry Pickin' 637
Cranes 1865
Crap Game Dance, The (inst.) 1706
Crap Game Fugue 3541
Crashing the Golden Gate 1126
Crashing Through 4166
Cravin' for the Avon 1644
Crazy 280, 1053, 2993
Crazy About Some Boy 2113
Crazy 'Appy Tears 589
Crazy As a Loon 2301
Crazy Downtown 1832
Crazy Elbows 3556
Crazy House Suite 1337
Crazy Idea of Love 4763
Crazy Jane on the Day of Judgment 1977
Crazy New Words 3178
Crazy Night Ballet 2014
Crazy Now 922
Crazy Over You 2518
Crazy People 1813
Crazy Place, The 1699
Crazy Pops 4041
Crazy Quilt 418
Crazy Quilt Sextette, The 418
Crazy Rhythm 1859
Crazy Street 3993
Crazy Walk 1514
Crazy with the Heat (1) 924
Crazy with the Heat (2) 924
Crazy World 2702, 4560
Crazyisms 1912
Cream in My Coffee 4627
Cream of English Youth, The 461
Cream of Mississippi 4388
Cream of Mush 3931
Cream of Mush Song 3501
Cream of the Sky 2889
Creation of Eve, The 4523
Creation of the World and Other Business, The 4523
Creation Scene (inst.) 4814
Creative Block 871
Creatures Go to Sleep in Peace 2243
Credit Card 1575
Credit Face 3722
Credit's Due to Me, The 1313
Credo (Rich Is Better) 2014
Creep, Creep, the World's Asleep 1309
Creme de la Creme 95
Creole Blues 2200
Creole Crawl 2371
Creole Crooning Song 1529
Creole Days 336
Creole Gal 3614
Creole Girls from the Follies 489
Creole Love Call 3628
Creole Love Call (inst.) 3709
Creole Love Song, The 3949
Creole Way, The 2200
Creoles 2595
Creon 2918
Crepe Suzette 2751
Crescendo 223
Crescent Moon 3086
Cretonne 3740
Cretonne Girl 1129
Cricket on the Hearth 928, 4250
Crickets Are Calling, The 2430
Cries in the Common Marketplace 272
Crime 4476
Crime des Femmes 68
Crime Doesn't Pay 112
Crime in the Streets 4635
Crime of Giovanni Venturi, The 519

Crinoline Days 3007
Crinoline Girl 2527
Crinoline Girl, The 3397
Crispus Attucks 2748
Crispy and Crunchy 4237
Crispy, Crunch Crackers 1931
Criss Cross 930
Cristobel 779
Critic, The 3235, 4002
Critical List 3667
Critics 2618
Critics' Blues, The 1685
Critters 2027
Cro-Ack 3463
Crockfield 3931
(Oh, Be Careful of the) Crocodile 470
Crocodile, The 767
Crocodile, a Crocodile, A 2658
Crocodile Wife 4863
Crocodiles Cry 2657
Crooked Path, The 1649
Croon-Spoon 919
Crooning 4182
Croquet 3970
Croquet Game, The 2040
Croquet, Croquet 453
Cross On Over 4558
Cross Word Puzzles 3523
Cross Your Fingers 932, 4087
Cross Your Heart 3622, 4506
Crossbridge Dance 1903
Crossing 3001
Crossing Boundaries 4515
Crossing Over 394
Crossing the Red Sea 1715
Crossover 2998
Crosstown 4286
Crossword Puzzle 1648, 2594, 4145
Crossword Puzzle Song 1725
Croupier 4677
Crow 434
Crow, The 4579, 4862
Crowd of Girls 2373
Crown Me 3602
Crown Us with the Truth 4615
Crucifixion, The 2212
Cruel and Brutal 545
Cruel Chief 2293
Cruel One 1119
Cruel Youth, The 4579
Cruelty Man, The 935
Cruelty Stomp, The 4139
Cruikshank March 490
Cruise of the Boozemobile, The 3423
Crumbs in My Bed 1665
Crunch Granola Suite 964
Crusaders March, The 2697
Crush on You 3654
Cry 4264, 10
Cry Baby 1819, 3739
Cry, Baby 4323
Cry, Baby, Cry 59, 3563
Cry for Us All 935
Cry from the Dungeon 4368
Cry Like a Baby 432
Cry Like the Wind 1061
Cry Loud (Lift Your Voice Like a Trumpet) 1073
Cry of the Peacock 4541
Cry the Beloved Country 369
Cry, the Beloved Country 2591, 2591
Crying Jane 804
Crystal Ball 2342
Crystal Ball, The 2495
Crystal Candelabra 672
Crystal Lute, The 118
Crystal Temple, The 2460
Crystal Wedding Day 1780
Csardas 689, 2615
Csibeszkiraly 3537
Cuba Si, Yanqui No 3530
Cuban Glide, The 4804
Cuban Love Song 4251, 4197
Cuban Song 2101
Cubana 2162
Cubes and Abstracts 1878
Cubist Opera, The 1016
Cubs 143
Cuckold's Delight 1017
Cuckoo 2354, 815, 1852
Cuckoo-Cheena, The 2595
Cuckoo Clock, The 1777
Cuckoo Clock 1173
Cuckoo Song 4433
Cuckoo Town 2494
Cuckoo Trio 1518
Cuddle 3951
Cuddle Me As We Dance 969
Cuddle Me Up 728
Cuddle-Uddle, The 1404
Cuddle Up 584, 969, 2098, 3665, 4661
Cuddle Up a Little Closer, Lovey Mine 4364
Cuddle Up Together (My Old Brown Coat) 2756
Cuh-Razy for Love 667
Cuisine! 4139
Cultural Pursuits 2754
Cultural Sunday 2483
Culture Drill 331
Culture Twist, The 3530
Cumbia/Wedding Party 4459
Cunnilingus Champion of Co. C, The 2451
Cup of China Tea, A 4792
Cup of Coffee, A 941
Cup of Coffee, a Sandwich and You, A 702
Cup of Tea, A 1458, 1748, 1962
Cup of Tea, A (Lido Lady, Opening) 2467
Cup of Tea, A 3573, 3882
Cup of Tea, The 4258
Cupid 780, 1532, 1726
Cupid and You and I 4425
Cupid at the Plaza 3193

Cupid Does Not Marry 586
Cupid Has Found My Heart 4754
Cupid Holds the Key 2944
Cupid Is a Cruel Master 307
Cupid Is the Captain of the Army 591, 675
Cupid Is the Postman 2534
Cupid Keeps the Love Light Burning 2486
Cupid Might Have Been a Little Coon 1220
Cupid Reigns King 2035
Cupid-Sly Little Rascal 2745
Cupid Tell Me Why (Love That's Sincere) 1111
Cupid the Conqueror 3996
Cupid, the Cunnin' Pandeen 1162
Cupid, the Winner 1922
Cupid Will Guide 104
Cupid's a Lad 2632
Cupid's Alphabet 2385
Cupid's Auctioneer 3710
Cupid's Car 4285
Cupid's College 3236
Cupid's Dart 3481, 4807
Cupid's Entrance 4064
Cupid's Garden 2986
Cupid's Grammar 1768
Cupid's Ladder 2623
Cupid's March 2603
Cupid's Mistakes 1123
Cupid's Private Code 1650
Cupid's Ramble 3073
Cupid's Rifle Range 2498
Cupid's Soldiers 2732
Cupid's Telephone 1783
Cupid's Wedding Bells 3519
Cupid's Wireless Telegraph 3575
Cure, The 3837, 4119
Cure for the Blues, A 306
Cure or Kill 4014
Cured 561
Curfew Bell Has Sounded, The 4616
Curfew Shall Not Ring Tonight, The 2253
Curfew Walk, The 3149
Curio Song (Old King Solly) 1923
Curiosity 606, 808, 2880, 3218, 281, 3305
Curiouser and Curiouser 593
Curley McDimple 941
Curley's the Girlie for Me 941
Curley's Wife 3224
Current Events 3806
Currier and Ives 4524
Curse 1385
Curse, The 1104
Curse of Cinderella, The 1691
Curt, Clear and Concise 1564
Curtain 723
Curtain Going Up 943
Curtsey, The 466
Custody of the Child, The 3323
Custom-Made Maids 2336
Customary 639
Customer Is Always Right 4629
Customer's Always Right 3815
Customer's Always Right, The 3916
Customer's Nightmare, The 1412
Customers at Kay's 1537
Cut Down the Tree 2967
Cut In 4545
Cut Movie Songs 3615
Cut of the Cards 2437
Cut the Ribbons 944
Cute an' Cunnin' (inst.) 2574
Cute Little Beaut from Butte, Montana 1177
Cute Little Dance, A 1647
Cute Little Quaker Maids Are We 2880
Cute Little Summery Time 1735
Cute Little Two by Four 2216
Cute Peekin' Knees 1136, 4373
Cutest Little House 2897
Cutey 4837
Cutie 468, 3627
Cutie Come and Tie My Tie 4094
Cuttin' the Persian Rug 2453
Cutting Hair 109
Cuyahoga 2935
Cymbal Sockin' Sam 2259
Cymbals and Tambourines 3112
Cynical Owl, The 2858
Cynthia Jones 457
Cyrano 948, 4670
Cyrano de Bergerac 946, 948, 945, 949, 4073, 947
Cyrano De Bergerac 4670
Cyrano's Nose 946
Cyrano's Story 949
Czar, The (Czar of Dixie) 2111
Czardas 1849, 2755, 2947, 3602, 4187, 4550
Czardus 3261

D

D. and D. Rag 4433
D.F.C. and Bar 194
I'd Like to Call You Mine 3052
D-O-G 937
D.W. Washburn 4031
Da Da Da 4661
Da Da Da Da 1511
Da, Da, Daddy Dear 4194
Da Doo Ron Ron 2427, 3739
Daarlin' Man 2268
Dab-Derro 4033
Dachau 3698
Dachshund in a Dusenberg, A 3444
Dad 3136, 3539
Dad Got Girls 3067
Dad Gum Your Hide Boy 1296
Dad's a Millionaire 1897
Dad's Old Violin 516
Daddy 468, 545, 1198, 3175, 3581
Daddy and Me 109

Daddy Blues 33
Daddy Buy Me a Bow Wow 2870
Daddy, Daddy 1045
Daddy Dear 1335
Daddy Doesn't Care 3561
Daddy Goodness 952
Daddy Has a Sweetheart and Mother Is Her Name 4806
Daddy Long-Legs 2608
Daddy Long Legs 2608
Daddy Mine 1833
Daddy Oh! 793
Daddy Says, Mama Says 4286
Daddy Was a Railroad Man 3428
Daddy Will Not Come Walking Through the Door 2033
Daddy Won't You Buy Him for Me 2912
Daddy Won't You Please Come Home 3963
Daddy, You've Been a Mother to Me 393
Daddy's Decision 952
Daddy's Sweetheart 3580
Daedalus 3824
Daffodil, The 487
Daffodil Time 353
Daffodils and Mud 2579
Daffydill, The 2950
Dago 591
Dago and Monk, The 2506
Dahomian Queen 2111
Daily Buzz 344
Daily Dozen 1839
Daily Dozen, The 381
Daily Echo 1386
Daintily and Lightly 1458
Dainty Cavalier 1570
Dainty Cupid 1469
Dainty Flo from Idaho 2062
Dainty Housemaids We 2631
Dainty June and Her Farmboys 1709
Dainty Lingerie 2749
Dainty Little Girl Like You 3258
Dainty Little Ingenue 4738
Dainty Little Maid 1926
Dainty Little Maid, The 3348
Dainty Little Milliner, The 2399
Dainty Mignon 1459
Dainty Milliners, The 1910
Dainty Music Maid, The 2724
Dainty Nosegay, A 3431
Dainty Quainty Me 3893
Dainty Wisp of Thistledown 3117
Daisies 1958
Daisy 1123, 4310, 1784, 3615
Daisy and the Lark, The 3538
Daisy Bell 4109, 4390
Daisy Chain 2724
Daisy, Daisy 662
Daisy Days 2870
Daisy Goes Out with Bert 4153
Daisy Hill 4034
Daisy Tell Me Truly 2276
Daisy's Blues 3840
Daisyland 1469
Dallas Last Night 528
Damages 3482
Dame Crazy 4180
Dame Rumor 2695
Dames 1359
Dames at Sea 956
Damn 3780
Damn-Alot 410
Damn Clever, These Chinese 2135
Damn Connecticut Yankees 4047
Damn Police (Thieves March) 2487
Damn the Torpedoes (Full Speed Ahead) 2748
Damn the Woman 367
Damn You, Tony Lumpkin! 2650
Damned for All Time 2212
Damned No Matter How He Turned 2472
Damned Old Jeeter 532
D'Amour en Amour 839
Damsel Who Done All the Dirt, The 1529
Damsel, Damsel (Prithee Come Crusading with Me) 3865
Dan 632, 2996
Dan, My Darlin Dan 4605
Dance (His Invitation to Love) 364
Dance 2275, 2420, 1298, 1962, 2011, 4232
Dance, The 2399
Dance 2684, 2830, 3035
Dance, The 3162
Dance 4823, 1804
Dance a Bomba at Funeral Time 696
Dance a la Russe 582
Dance a Little Closer 958
(Go Ahead and) Dance a Little More 3737
Dance Alone with You (Why Does Everybody Have to Cut In) 1419
Dance-American Impromptu 2028
Dance and Grow Thin 959
Dance Arabe 3013
Dance Around the World with Me 3239
Dance at the Ball Tonight 760
Dance at the Gym, The (dance) 4625
Dance at the Salon 278
Dance Away the Night 3949
Dance Band on the Titanic 2470
Dance Characteurtique 3011
Dance Class 1236
Dance Classiceccentrique 4807
Dance Climatique 2390
Dance Conceptions 965
Dance Contests, The 2513
Dance Coquette 1613
Dance d'Amour 4064
Dance, Dance, Dance 203, 1065, 3679, 4654, 4664
Dance! Dance! Dance! 4192
Dance de Maitre de Ballet 4803
Dance de Nautica Americaine 4421

Dance Divertissement 1513
Dance Drama 2830
Dance du Fragonard 1625
Dance Eccentric (inst.) 152
Dance Eccentric 2684, 4657
Dance Eccentrique 250, 965
Dance Eccentrique (inst.) 1625
Dance Eccentrique (dance) 2907, 4250
Dance Espagnol 2628
Dance Excentrique (inst.) 136
Dance Extraordinaire 4657
Dance Fantastique 3265
Dance Fever 1637
Dance Finale 145
Dance for Jack, A 906
Dance for Six 3015
Dance for the Gentlemen 1110
Dance from Down Yonder, The 391
Dance Gypsy 1710
Dance Hall 943
Dance Hall Hostess 3704
Dance Hall Saturday Night 3294, 3542
Dance Hilda 1458
Dance If It Makes You Happy 4286
Dance in the Snow 490
Dance Into His Heart 3771
Dance It Again with Me 69
Dance, Let's Waltz 554
Dance Little Lady 3196, 3235, 4341
Dance Me a Song 961
Dance Me Around 2527
Dance Me Darling Dance Me 4194
Dance Me Goodbye 1565
Dance, Milonga, Dance! (inst.) 2356
Dance Montage, The 287
Dance, My Darlings 2786
Dance Noveau 4662
Dance-O-Mania 1922
Dance of Beauty 2135
Dance of Bewilderment 3087
Dance of Danger, The 2667
Dance of Distraction 280
Dance of Isis, The (dance) 2907
Dance of Joy 3087
Dance of Life 1619
Dance of Love 4719
Dance of Moderate Chastity (dance) 3913
Dance of Pleasures and Pulchritude 4139
Dance of Procreation (dance) 1817
Dance of Resignation (dance) 4537
Dance of Sacrifice (inst.) 190
Dance of Scheherezade (inst.) 3440
Dance of Sing Ling Foo 4007
Dance of Spousal Arousal, The 4139
Dance of the Aborigines 2344
Dance of the Aboriginies 336
Dance of the Apple 2005
Dance of the Camel Boys 930
Dance of the Candle Killers 3798
Dance of the Crinoline Ladies 4581
Dance of the Dinosaur (inst.) 1136
Dance of the Dolls 1513, 4742
Dance of the Falasha Maids (inst.) 9
Dance of the Fan 4673
Dance of the Fates 1748
Dance of the Fortune Wheel, The 4657
Dance of the Four Leaf Clovers 930
Dance of the Frogs 2111
Dance of the Golden Apple 1816
Dance of the Golden Calf 1196
Dance of the Golden Sprite 930
Dance of the Green Eyes 2330
Dance of the Grizzly Bear, The 4804
Dance of the Jewels (inst.) 50
Dance of the Ladies in Waiting 1817
Dance of the Levants 1580
Dance of the Lunatics, The 671
Dance of the Marionettes 3081
Dance of the Matador (dance) 1112
Dance of the Midnight Sons, The (inst.) 4747
Dance of the Mirrors 1207
Dance of the Moods (inst.) 1251
Dance of the Nile 2749
Dance of the Nymphs 545
Dance of the Orchid 3313
Dance of the Parisian Twist, The 4803
Dance of the Porters 1312, 1580
Dance of the Ragamuffins 4581
Dance of the Rose, The 671, 4784
Dance of the School Girls 4393
Dance of the Squareheads (inst.) 4747
Dance of the Tumblers (inst.) 2386
Dance of the Valentines 4393
Dance of the Waitresses 4670, 4665
Dance of the Whirling Dervishes (inst.) 50
Dance of the Whirling Wimpus (inst.) 3543
Dance of the Widow Mexetexa 4803
Dance of Time 1556
Dance of Time (dance) 3913
Dance of Times 3011
Dance of Welcome (dance) 3913
Dance, Oh, Lonely Gypsy Maid 4550
Dance on a Country Grave 962
Dance on Friday Night 352, 2675
Dance Only with Me 3845
Dance Orientale 2684
Dance Poem 2802
Dance Polka 362
Dance Porto Rico 981
Dance Tangerine 4283
Dance: Ten, Looks: Three 746
Dance, Tenderfoot, Dance 2516
Dance the Dark Away! 4558
Dance the Night 1890
Dance the Polka 4726
Dance Through Life with Me 2620
Dance to the Sun God 3813
Dance Vampire 2684
Dance Venitian 3150
Dance We All Do for Al, The 4730

Dance, Why Not? 2550
Dance with Me 21, 379, 1298, 1544, 1663, 2426
Dance with Me (Tonight at the Mardi Gras) 2597
Dance with Me 132, 4031, 3586, 3688, 4119
Dance with You 2293
Dance Your Troubles Away 1836, 3007
Dance Your Way to Paradise 4424
Dancemania 892
Dancer, The 2467
Dancers in Love (inst.) 4091
Dances All Turned Around 4037
Dances and Vilia 2839
Dances of the Tabarin, The 4094
Dancin' (inst.) 964
Dancin' 'Way Your Sin 567
Dancin' Fool 846, 4763
Dancin' Free and Easy 157
Dancin' in the Middle 451
Dancin' in the Streets 4534
(I Always Wanted to Be a) Dancin' Man 486
Dancin' My Blues Away 3055
Dancin' Off Third (dance) 1289
Dancin' on a Dime 3032
Dancin' Shoes 2195
Dancin' to a Jungle Drum 4517
Dancin' to a Jungle Drum
(Let's End the Beguine) 3893
Dancing 130, 550, 910, 1828, 2950, 284, 4311, 14
Dancing Alone 791, 4484
Dancing Around the Course 4209
Dancing Around the Town 3958
Dancing Around the U.S.A. 2696
Dancing at the Wedding 4547
Dancing Band, The 1723
Dancing Bear 4398
Dancing Blues 1780
Dancing Blues, The 3404
Dancing By Moonlight 3796
Dancing Ceremony, The 4759
Dancing Colors 200
Dancing Courtship, A 2900
Dancing Dan 4192
Dancing Dean, The 2938
Dancing Detective, The 2533
Dancing Devil Dolls, The 2303
Dancing Doctor, The 1691
Dancing Dollies 1374
Dancing Duet 30
Dancing Family 3401
Dancing Festival, The 4747
Dancing Fools 4654
Dancing Girl 500
Dancing Girl, A 2465
Dancing Honeymoon 2972, 3007
Dancing in the Dark 294, 2180
Dancing in the Moonlight 1667, 4621
Dancing in the Rain 941
Dancing in the Sky 3409
Dancing in the Streets 971, 3379
Dancing in the Temple 1079
Dancing Is Delightful 2978
Dancing Is Everything 4286
Dancing Is not What It Used to Be 1080
Dancing Jim 2843
Dancing Jubilee, The 3827
Dancing Kangaroo, The 2986
Dancing Lesson, The 1016, 1580
Dancing Lesson 2897
Dancing Lesson, The 3540
Dancing Lesson, A 3618
Dancing Lesson, The 2500
Dancing M.D., A 2900
Dancing Mad 2457, 4419, 4817
Dancing Man 1405
Dancing My Dinner Down 2736
Dancing My Worries Away 2533
Dancing on a Dime 3444
Dancing on a Rainbow 4782
Dancing On and On 1099
Dancing on Saturday Night 1496
Dancing on the Ceiling 1202, 1763, 3980
Dancing on the Levee 1799
Dancing on the Old Plantation 4184
Dancing on Your Grave 754
Dancing Our Worries Away 1478
Dancing Pirates, The 804
Dancing Politely 3813
Dancing Princess, The 4735
Dancing Rogue, The 2599
Dancing Romeo, A 4657
Dancing 'Round 1096
Dancing Sal 4761
Dancing School 2816
Dancing School-Her First Lesson,
The (scene) 4814
Dancing Shoes 977, 1923, 2494, 4844
Dancing Spanish 4063
Dancing Step Child 1689
Dancing Sue 2111
Dancing the Blues Away 965
Dancing the Cotillion 3977
Dancing the Devil Away 2638
Dancing the Numbers 2108
Dancing the Razz-Ma-Tazz 1551
Dancing the Seasons Away 3006
Dancing Through Lifetime 1216
Dancing Through the Ages 2056
Dancing Time 611, 1011, 4001
Dancing to the Rhythm of Love 4571
Dancing to the Rhythm of the Raindrops 3810
Dancing to the Score 4825
Dancing Toes 2351
Dancing Town 1678, 844
Dancing Tumble-Down 4360
Dancing Turk, The 1627
Dancing Wedding, The 2525
Dancing Wedding 4023
Dancing Will Keep You Young 2794
Dancing with Alice 1094
Dancing with My Darling 839

Dancing with My Shadow 4027
Dancing with Tears in Their Eyes 4235
Dancing with the Fools 3644
Dancing, and I Mean Dancing 2034
Dandelion 3631
Dandelion Coon 2879
Dandelion Time 2298
Dandelion Wine 973, 973
Dandies on Parade
(The Sports of Gay Chicago) 3949
Dandy 2557
Dandy Colored Coon 1301
Dandy Dan 2645, 14
Dandy Night Clerk or How to
Get On in the Hotel Trade 1256
Dandy Soldier Coon 352
Dandy Sparrow Cops, The 1466
Dandy Waiters of the Golden Light 1259
Dandy's Polka 3703
Danger Ahead 465
Danger If I Love You 2540
Danger in the Dark 4174
Danger Men Working 4171
Danger of Peace Is Over, The 4514
Dangerous 451
Dangerous Age, The 1227, 1848
Dangerous Game 3491
Dangerous Girl 2299
Dangerous You 1338
Dangle Him Lightly 4201
Daniel Boone 4635
Danilo's Rap 1700
Danke Schoen 3598
Danny Cupid at the Bat 1247
Danny the Dragon 1390
Danny's Plea 747
Dans des Hottentots 1230
Dansa de la Arana 2565
Danse Blanche et Noir 2793
Danse Bohemienne (inst.) 4357
Danse d'Abandon 2222
Danse D'Une Coquette (inst.) 1458
Danse de Volstead 2135
Danse Diversement 2888
Danse Erotique 1109
Danse Excentrique (inst.) 4747
Danse Modern 3011
Danse Poetic 3424
Danse Poetique 736
Danse Tzigane 1109
Danse Victoire 1109
Dante, Petrarch and Poe 2568
Danube, The 30
Danube So Blue 968, 1680
Danza and Danzon 3830
Daphne 1312, 4196
Daphne Sue 1123
Dapper Dan 2857
Darby and Joan 1243, 3043
Dardanella 25
Dardanella Blues, The 4375
Dare I 2388
Dare to Do 1842
(You've Got to) Dare to Take a Chance 1741
Daring Gibson Girl, The 1339
Dark Eyes 106, 710, 2623
Dark Lady of the Senates 392, 3186
Dark New England Night 239
Dark Side of My Love, The 962
Dark Song 2000
Dark Stranger, A 3860
Darkest Before the Dawn 1619
Darkest the Hour 1193
Darkie's Serenade 3134, 4487
Darkies Have Music in Their Souls 1982
Darkies Song, The 1592
Darkness 705
Darkness Fades 2970
Darkness Here Is Only Darkness 2243
Darkness Song 1958
Darktime Dancing School 4183
Darktown Band, The 434
Darktown Barbeque 3744
Darktown Dancing School 3985
Darktown Is Out Tonight 783, 2415
Darktown Poker Club 4808
Darktown Strutter's Ball 1813
Darktown Strutters' Ball, The 3297
Darky Rhythm 567
Darlin' Darla 2541
Darlin' of New York, The 2217
Darling 579, 4279, 1212, 2506, 2816
Darling! 2822
Darling, I Am Growing Young 2933
Darling, I Love You So! 1530
Darling, It's Been Fun, Hasn't It? 1792
Darling, Let Me Teach You How to Kiss 634
Darling of the Day 989
Darling They're Playing Our Song 794
Darling Will Not Grow Older 265, 4709
Darn Clever These Chinese 4586
Darn It Baby, That's Love 4377
Darn Nice Campus, A 85
Darn That Dream 4256
Dartmoor Days 1610
Das Bissele Erd 907
Das Chicago Song 2913, 3112
Das Drei Maedelhaus 463
Das Hollandweibechen 1121, 2509
Das Land des Lachelns 3573, 4792
Das Lied Ist Aus 3946
Das Madel von Montmartre 1538
Das Musikantenmadel 1522
Das Telefunken 4774
Dashing Matador 4218
Dashing Militaire 175
Dastardly Attack on W. Epigram 3236
Dat Friend of Mine 954
Dat Gal of Mine 2111
Dat Lovin' Touch 2358

Dat Ol' Boy 653
Dat's All, Ragtime Girl 3129
Dat's de Way I Lubs You, Honey Mine 1532
Dat's Love 653
Dat's Our Man 653
Dat's Sufficiency 3040
Data, The 2142
Data! 3131
Date, The 2783
Date Tree, The 1975
Dathydill 2919
Daughter 1684
Daughter, A 1750
Daughter of Annie Rooney, The 3422
Daughter of Heaven 4765
Daughter of Rosie O'Grady 3717
Daughter of Satan 3405
Daughter of Senator Fish, The 1867
Daughter of the Devil 1306
Daughter of the Moon Am I, A 1295
Daughter of the Regiment, The 522
Daughter of the Regiment 3051
Daughter of Valentine's Day, A 705
Daughter or Dowry 4337
Daughter's Lullaby 2007
Daughters 3157
Daughters of a Minister, The 3790
Daughters of Satan 1923
Daughters of the Guard 3856
Daughters of the Guard, The 3857
Daughters of the Trusts 1568
Dauntless 3714
Daveyton 4438
David and Bathsheba 2075
David and Lenore 1489
David Copperfield 869
David Crockett (Davy Crockett) (Who Kept the Wolves Away from the Door When Davy Crockett Went to War) 1447
David Kolowitz, the Actor 4038
David's Psalm 1196
Davy Crockett 996
Davy Jones 3423
Davy the Fat Boy 2852, 2787
Dawn, A 1116
Dawn 1603, 2734, 3207
Dawn Chorus 143
Dawn in Florida 3562
Dawn Music (inst.) 3865
Dawn of a New Day 1528, 3127
Dawn of Dreams 4793
Dawn of Love, The 353
Dawn of Love, The (Kiss Me and 'Tis Day) 1285
Dawn of Love, The 1738, 2340
Dawn Turns to Morning 3472
Dawn Will Come 2298
Dawning Day, The 4201
Day After Day 1322, 1508, 2236, 1701, 4320
Day After That, The 2333
Day After Tomorrow, The 455
Day and Age 3667
Day Around Town Dance, A 2646
Day at the Club, A 2308
Day Before Spring, The 999
Day Before the Morning After, The 375
Day Before Yesterday (1) 924
Day Before Yesterday (2) 924
Day Born of Love 1470
Day Borrowed from Heaven, A 1698
Day by Day 1595
Day By Day 4743, 43
Day Dream Bay 2276
Day Dreams 71, 902, 1163, 2135, 2716, 3185, 4795, 4014, 4119, 4476
Day I Do, The 4693
Day I Left Her Last, The 496
Day I Meet My Friend, The 2065
Day I Met You, The 1947, 3173
Day I Met Your Father, The 1158
Day I Quit This Rag, The 4703
Day I Rode Half Fare 391
Day I Say I Do, The 1257
Day in Falsettoland, A 1234
Day in New York, A 2805
Day in Our Life, A 2318
Day in Sec-Moxena Mambo 3988
Day in the Life, A 3903
Day in the Life of a Fat Kid in Philly 2038
Day Late and a Dollar Short 1300
Day of Atonement, The 2194
Day of Judgement 1500
Day of the Fair 4357
Day of the Game, The 1230
Day of the People Is Coming, The 624
Day Off, The 4210
Day Oh Day 4343
Day Sven Gundersen Died, The 2064
Day the Peace Action Broke Out, The 1438
Day the Snow Is Meltin', The 1076
Day We Celebrate Edna May, The 3332
Day We Longed For, The 1469
Day Will Come, The 3407
Day Will Never Be the Same, A 2539
Day You Came Into My Life, The 4701
Day You Leave Me, The 229
Daybreak 2379
Daybreak Express (inst.) 4534, 432
Daydreaming 2204
Daydreams 4028
Dayenu Chant 1715
Daylight Is Dawning 2974
Days Gone By 3918, 4001
Days Like This 1234
Days of Chivalry, The 2430
Days of Forty-Nine, The 1881, 4473
Days of Long Ago, The 1014
Days of Long Ago 1301
Days of My Boyhood 4473
Days of My Youth, The 3763
Days of Pharaoh 3405

Days of Romance 3443, 3856
Days of the Dancing Are Gone 2114
Days of the Waltz 3338
Days of This Life, The 1116
Days of Youth 2546
Days That Used to Be 1723
Dayton Ohio 1903 2787
De Bode o' Edicashun 3945
De Cakewalk Queen 1264
De Cards Don't Lie 653
De Chimney Man 2200
De Dum Dum 3149
De Ebony Spook 2978
De Goblin's Glide 2358
De Land O' Good Times 1476
De Old Clay Road 1020
De Pullman Porter's Ball 1926
De Right Answer 1385
De Trop 1285, 2465
Deacon Pettigue 2893
Dead 4288, 2320
Dead End 1717
Dead End Street 3178
Dead Men Tell No Tales 2375, 4443
Deadwood Stage, The 616
Deal, The 721, 2918
Dealer, The 2134
Dealing in Wheeling 3873
Dear Abbey 128
Dear Algerian Land 930
Dear Bath 2340
Dear Boy 630
Dear Brother 2033
Dear Curracloe 2340
Dear Dad 3227
Dear Daisy Chain 939
Dear Dear 300
Dear! Dear! 1202
Dear, Dear Departed 2371
Dear Delightful Women 276
Dear Desperate 1004
Dear Diary 3368
Dear Doctor 130
Dear Editor 3136
Dear Eyes That Haunt Me 771
Dear Eyes that Shine 1610
Dear Felicia 3136
Dear Francois 1114
Dear Friend 3764, 3918, 4312
Dear Girls, Goodbye 3063
Dear God 2224
Dear Golden Days 3392
Dear Home of Mine, Goodbye 905
Dear Horse 1546, 4498
Dear Icarus 1015
Dear Jane 3702
Dear Joe 2653
Dear Kitty: I Am a Woman 4790
Dear Kitty: I Am Longing 4790
Dear Kitty: I Am Thirteen Years Old 4790
Dear Kitty: I Have a Nicer Side 4790
Dear Kitty: I Still Believe 4790
Dear Kitty: In the Night 4790
Dear Kitty: It's a Dangerous Adventure 4790
Dear Kitty: It's a New Year 4790
Dear Kitty: My Sweet Secret 4790
Dear Kitty: We Live with Fear 4790
Dear Liar 1007
Dear Little Cafe 429
Dear Little Cottage 2187
Dear Little Daisy 3581
Dear Little French Grisette, The 2936
Dear Little Gad-About 2927
Dear Little Game of Guessing 4364
Dear Little Games of Guessing 1558
Dear Little Ghost of Your Smile, The 2901
Dear Little Girl (I Hope You've Missed Me) 3243
Dear Little Girl Who Is Good, The 2915
Dear Little Girlie 3623
Dear Little Girls 2498
Dear Little Girly Girly 4717
Dear Little Jappy-Jap-Jappy, The 1470
Dear Little Maid 906
Dear Little Pages 3613
Dear Little Peter Pan 4150
Dear Little Rose Girl 3770
Dear Little Soldiers 841
Dear Little Wise Old Bowery, The 1403
Dear Lonely Lover 25
Dear Lord 1372, 1605
Dear Lord Chesterfield 840
Dear Love 203, 1310, 696
Dear Love, My Love 2264
Dear Luzon 2111
Dear Madame Salvador (Letter Song) 3339
Dear Madame Scarlatina 1081
Dear Me 1009, 1013
Dear Miss Streisand 3636
Dear Mom 3210
Dear Mother, in Dreams I See Her
(The Lullaby) 1193
Dear Mother Mine 2310
Dear Motherland (Victory) 4113
Dear Mr. Gershwin 3641
Dear Mr. Santa Claus
(If Santa Claus Were Crazy) 1860
Dear Mr. Schubert 2106
Dear Mrs. Brown 1004
Dear Nightingale 710
Dear, Oh Dear 711
Dear Old Boston 4434
Dear Old Broadway 3384, 1327, 4434
Dear Old Bronx 3222
Dear Old College Days 586, 4273, 3745
Dear Old Crinoline Days 1225
Dear Old Dad 4028
Dear Old Dinah 4642
Dear Old Dixie 3041
Dear Old Dixie Home 731
Dear Old Dixieland 2481

Dear Old Dublin 2340
Dear Old Fairyland 4649
Dear Old Farm, The 1403
Dear Old Farm 4544
Dear Old Fashioned Prison of Mine (Tulip Time in Sing Sing) 4001
Dear Old Father 4803
Dear Old Fighting Boys, The 186
Dear Old Friend 2887
Dear Old Gown 2816
Dear Old Hank 4381
Dear Old Heidelberg 3755
Dear Old London Town 30, 2399
Dear Old Manhattan Isle 3488
Dear Old Moulin Rouge 2135
Dear Old Pals 3981
Dear Old Prison Days 3245
Dear Old Southland 4182
Dear Old Story, The 1417
Dear Old Syracuse 514
Dear Old White House, The 4509
Dear Old Wisconsin Days 1405
Dear One 2333
Dear Ophelia 1591
Dear Sing Sing 4014
Dear Sir 2654
Dear Sweet Eyes 3593
Dear Sweet Sewing Machine 1265
Dear Tom 1737, 2074
Dear Waters of the Danube Blue 306
Dear World 1012, 4644
Dear Yankee Maid 2559
Dearer to Me 4696
Dearest, Best, Divine 1458
Dearest Darling 1846
Dearest Enemy 1013
Dearest Heart of My Heart 3732
Dearest Man 1064
Dearest Mary 194
Dearest Miss Bell 4479
Dearest Miss Flo 4479
Dearie 2715, 3882, 4063, 4477, 4530
Dearie, My Dearie 1014
Dearie, Won't You Snuggle Close to Me? 2261
Dearie, You and I 2635
Dearly Beloved 2204
Death 4789
Death and Reality 2001
Death Beware 1500
Death Comes Like a Thief 3817
Death Dance 2332
Death Duet 3164
Death in the Afternoon 216
Death Message 4369
Death of Me, The 4481
Death of Moses 1715
Death of the Firstborn 1715
Death of Tinker Bell 3453
Death or Victory 1118
Death Walk 3944
Debbie's Pastry Order 2093
Debil, The 1876
Debonairs, The 2402
Debt I Owe, The 2898
Debtors Lament 3482
Debutante 3064
Debutante's Ball, The 2787
Debutantes 3080
Debutantes, The 3313
Deca Dance 2618
Decadence 3365
Decameron, The 482
Deceive Me 1017
Deceiving Blue Bird 4668
December Nights 414
Decent Thing to Do, The 317
Deception Is the Better Part of Valor 1424
Decisions 4330
Declaration 4431
Declaration Day 3850
Decorating Eliza 3038
Decorations 2854
Decoys 2628
Dedicated Teacher, A 1158
Dedicated to the One I Love 4193, 4264
Dee Deedle De Dum Dey 2174
Dee-Lightful 1255
Dee-lightful Is the Word 1076
Deed I Do Do Blues 3528
Deedle Doodle 3691
Deedle, Deedle Dumpling 4233
Deedle-Dee-Dum, The 4589
Deep Blue Sea 2302
Deep Down Inside 2523
Deep Down Inside You 3813
Deep End 318
Deep Harlem 1019
Deep in Alaska 369
Deep in Me 1761
Deep in My Heart 279, 2569, 3249
Deep in My Heart, Dear 4188
Deep in My Mind 3201
Deep in Someone's Heart 2686
Deep in the Bosom of the Family 2219
Deep in the Dark 3651
Deep in the Night 2134
Deep in Your Eyes 1723
Deep in Your Heart 1094
Deep Paradise 1836
Deep Purple 4137
Deep Sea 4765
Deep Sea Divin' Papa 876
Deeper 2767
Deeper in the Woods 3733
Deepest Shelter in Town, The 4027
Deer and the Park Avenue Lady, The 4557
Defense 2072
Definitely Not for Debs 621
Defying the Storm 1712

Degas Ballet (inst.) 364
Degenerations 730
Deja Vu 2318
(My Most) Delectable Dream 2057
Delia 4201
Delicatessen 4468
Delighted 3643
Delighted, I'm Sure 3843
Delighted You Invited Me 760
Delightful, Delicious, Delovely 497
Delights of London 4115
Delilah Done Me Wrong
(The No Haircut Song) 2362
Delilah's Dilemma 4542
Deliliah 281
Deliver 1019
Deliver My Soul 535
Delivery Boys' Lament 3636
Della and Ella 2493
Della's Desire 1508
Della's Entrance
(Whatcha Sayin' Della?) 1385
Dem Peddlers Brivele
(The Peddler's Letter) 1609
Demagogue 3441
Demetrios Motif 165
Democracy 3791
Democracy Is Lunacy 3654
Democracy's Call 2228
Democratic Club Dance 3644
Demon in the Compass 732
Demon of the Deep, The 613
Demonstrate 4209
Demonstration Number 2710
Den of Iniquity 3353
Denied Stone 1073
Denishawn 2489
Denmark Is Still 3741
Denny Grady's Hack 2428
Dentist! 2544
Denver Police, The 4516
Departure 1068
Departure, The 1959
Departure for Rhododendron, The 1600
Depends on Beautiful Clothes 2960
Deportee (Plane Wreck at Los Gatos) 4740
Deportment 2282
Depression Is Over, The 109
Deprogramming Song 2648
Der Ayznban (The Train) 4342
Der Graf von Luxemburg 902
Der Hochtourist 4532
Der Kleine Freundin 3053
Der Lachende Ebemann 2424
Der Lieber Augustin 2469
Der Lila Domino 2486
Der Mann Mit Den Drei Frauen 2732
Der Opernball 3308
Der Orlov 1805
Der Shimmy 3020
Der Tanz Ins Gluck 4010
Der Tapfere Soldat 742
Der Verlorene Waltzer 4486
Der Vetter Aus Dingsda 659
Der Zigeunerprimas 3839
Derby Day 1014, 2088
Derby Day in Dixie 61
Dere's a Cafe on de Corner 653
Dervish Dance (inst.) 2844
Des Brillanten-Konigin 3625
Descending 654
Descriptive Song 666
Desdie, My Desdemona 1731
Desert Dessert 2283
Desert Flame, The 454
Desert Incident 2876
Desert Isle 3042
Desert Love 1177
Desert Moon 1611
Desert of Dreams 3415
Desert Rose 2706
Desert Song, The 1027
Desire 484, 2850, 3064, 1028
Desire Under the Alps 4532
Desmond's Dilemma 4689
Despair 2220
Desperate 937
Desperate Ones, The 2188
Desperation 1229
Desperation Quintet! 1093
Dessert 3763
Destination Broadway 4799
Destiny 3515
Destruction 459
Destruction, The 661
Detective 2495
Detective Story 1056
Detectiveland 3142
Detectives, The 1177
Detectives Bold 175
Determination 2784
Determined Woman, A 4323
Detrimental Man, The 3976
Deuce Young Man!, The 2670
Deuteronomy XVII Verse 2 3824
Deutschland 8, 2314, 1647
Devil and the Deep Blue Sea, The 1851
Devil and the Farmer's Wife, The 3989
Devil in My Angel's Eyes, The 2087
Devil in My Feet 2168
Devil in You Is Strong, The 3813
Devil in Your Eyes, The 2785
Devil Is a Man You Know, The 4750
Devil Is Responsible 2275
Devil Man 4011
Devil May Care, The 2808
Devil to Pay, The 3568
Devil's Disguise 4127
Devil's Dream, The (ballet) 1505
Devil's in Your Toes, The 2567

Devil's Serenade, The 2408
Devilish Blues, The 2492
Devotion 1857
Dew Lies on the Heather, The 2697
Dew on the Heather, The 734
Dew Was on the Rose, The 3390
Dewey and Sal 426
Dewey Blues, The 3528
Dey Don't Do Dat T'day 2682
Di Demerung (The Twilight) 4082
Di Dinst (The Maid) 4342
Di Fon Fun Frayhayt
(The Flag of Freedom) 1609
Di Greene Kuzeene (My Little Cousin) 1279
Di Rod (The Circle) 4342
Diabolo 3958
Diagnosis 3643
Diagnostician, The 3439
Dialect Soubrette, The 2844
Dialogue on Dalliance 127
Diamond for Carla, A 1034
Diamond in the Rough 3650
Diamond Jim Brady 259
Diamond King, The 3392
Diamond Lil 1036
Diamonds Are a Girl's Best Friend 1475, 2590
Diamonds Are Forever 1038
Diamonds in the Starlight 2805
Diana 2033, 2315, 2696, 3202
Diana (The Lady of the Moon) 4012
Diana 4237
Diana's Arrival in Athens (dance) 1745
Diana's Transformation (dance) 1745
Diane Is 367
Dianna Lee 443
Diaries and poems 1740
Diary of a Dying Princess, The 3088
Diary of a Homecoming Queen 2152
Diary of Adam and Eve, The 170
Diary of Anne Frank, The 4790
Diaspora 1079
Diatribe 533
Diavalo 2258
Dibarti 3162
Dice Are Rolling 1211
Dickey Birds 1829
Dickie 1012
Dickie and the Birdie 2673
Dickie the King of the Dudes 4130
Dictation 2888
Dictator, The 1536
Did He, No He Didn't 4646
Did He Really Think 1959
Did He? Yes, He Did! 1866
Did I Ever Really Live? 1832, 1273
Did I Just Fall in Love 2535
Did I Make a Good Impression? 1222
Did It Really Happen? 260
Did Not 2278, 2633
Did You Close Your Eyes? 3113
Did You Come Back? 728
Did You Ever, Etc. 2760
Did You Ever Get Stung? 2061
Did You Ever Get the Feeling 1120
Did You Ever Hear Such Topics? 762
Did You Ever Hear That in Turkey? 4787
Did You Ever Hear the Blues? 3983
Did You Ever Look at You 3869, 4238
Did You Hear? 148
Did You Hear That? 2355
Did You Know 2511
Did You Mean It? 3149
Did You Send Me these Beautiful Flowers? 3663
Did You Think You Would Break My Heart? 1940
Did You Want to Hear a Country Tune? 3461
Did You, My Boy, Did You? 2489
Diddle-daddle 3074
Diddle Diddle Dumpling 2134
Didja Ever See the Like? 4378
Didja See That 2163
Didn't I Tell You 4788
Didn't It? 3489
Didn't It Rain 3987, 3724, 4460, 166, 4055
Didn't Know Exactly What to Do 3578
Didn't My Lord Deliver Daniel? 3989
Didn't She Do It for Love 3741
Didn't You? 4248
Didn't You Believe? 1625
Didn't You Used to Be Him? 4114
Didn't Your Mother Tell You? 423
Didoes 3236
Die Bajadere 4760
Die Csardasfurstin 3727
Die, Die, Die Like a Soldier 1162
Die Dollarprinzessin 1067
Die Dreigroschenoper 4368, 4369, 4370
Die Flabbergast 1621
Die Fledermaus 689, 2825, 3767
Die Frau Im Hermelin 2384
Die Fraulein Fressen 4726
Die Geschiedene Frau 1555
Die Herzogin von Chicago 1113
Die Ideale Gattin 2701
Die Keusche Susanne 2923
Die Keusche Suzanne 1554
Die Kino Koenigin 3627
Die Kubbandel 2323
Die Landstreicher 4181
Die Lustige Witwe 2836, 2838, 2837
Die Meistertrinker (Deutsches Weinlied...
Watschplattltanz) 4579
Die Mitternachtsmadel 2854
Die Moderne Eva 2922
Die Neue Art 3755
Die Schone Schwedin 1530, 3051
Die Sirene 3996
Die Sprudelfee 4119
Die Susse Pariserin 1043
Die Tanzgrafin 967
Die Tolle Lola 2567

Die Vogelein Singen In Dem Wald 188
Die Zirkusprinzessin 771
Die Zusammenfugung 3112
Died & Died & Died 871
Diet 4645
Diet of Wein 194
Diet Song 2590
Diff'rence of Drink, The 1550
Difference Is Me, The 1985
Different 4558, 4107
Different Days 480
Different Days-Different Ways 1551
Different Drummer, A 415
Different Girls 4434
Different Girls on Broadway 3867
Different Kind of World, A 4689
Different Kinds of Weather 2534
Different Stage, A 1770
Different Times 1045
Different Ways of Making Love, The 4723
Different Ways of Proposing 1573
Difficult Transition, A 3211
Dig, Dig, Dig 3602
Dig, Sister, Dig 2216
Dig Ye Dagos Dig 559
Diga Diga Doo 441, 3905, 4534
Diggin' Up Dirt 4543
Diggywig Two-Step 1561
Dilly 1048
Dime a Dozen 1049, 4034
Dime Ain't Worth a Nickle, A 135
Diminuendo in Blue (inst.) 4091
Dimple on My Knee, The 3225
Dimples 2523, 3180
Din't Cha Mother Tell You Nothin'? 1889
Dinah 26, 295, 4534, 1813, 2009, 3709, 3120
Dinah Lee 116
Dinah Lou 882
Dinah's in a Jam (inst.) 886
Ding-a-ling, Ding-a-ling 974
Ding a Long Dong 3068
Ding Dong 627, 2538
Ding, Dong 2665
Ding-Dong 1540
Ding Dong 4770
Ding Dong Bell 2134, 2457
Ding, Dong Dell (Spells I Love You) 3489
Ding Dong Ding 3623
Ding, Dong It's Kissing Time 1922
Ding Dong School 412
Ding Dong Song, The 4749
Dingere Dingale 4579
Dinghy 4062
Dingle Dangle 4064
Dingle, Dingle, Dingle 4806
Dining Out 1318
Dinky Doodle Dicky 1626
Dinner 3865
Dinner at the Mirklines 3476
Dinner at Thebes 3088
Dinner Bells 2990
Dinner Gong Jazz, The 1972
Dinner Is Served 2201, 2579
Dinner Minuet (dance) 2731
Dinner Pail, The 118
Dinner Party, The 2041
Dinner Song 3390
Dinner Time 8
Dinner with W.R. 695
Dinny Maginnity 2232
Dinny's Serenade 1162
Dino Repetti 1878
Dino's in Love 1878
Dionne Quintuplets 1337
Dior, Dior 2052
Dip, Dip, Dip 4806
Dip in the Ocean, A 2506
Dip Me in the Golden Sea 1776
Diplomacee 639
Diplomacy 1816, 2155, 3613, 947, 3751
Diplomats 1417
Dippermouth Blues 3840
Dipping in the Moonlight 2112
Dipsey's Coming Over 4286
Dipsey's Vaudeville (inst.) 4286
Direct from Vienna 656
Dirge 920, 2243, 3986
Dirge for a Soldier 2344
Dirge for Two Veterans 2433
Dirge Song 2655
Dirt Between My Fingers 3873
Dirty 3752, 4403
Dirty Dig 1693
Dirty Dish Rag 2007
Dirty Dog, The 1748
Dirty Face 2535
Dirty Hands, Dirty Face 487
Dirty Is the Funniest Thing I Know 4449
Dirty Mind 922
Dirty No Gooder Blues 478
Dirty Old Town 4579
Dirty Pitchers, Dirty Books 2705
Dirty, Rotten, Vicious, Nasty Guys 362
Dirty Up the Alley 568
Dirty Words 2451, 2998
Dirty Work 2698
Dis-donc, Dis-donc 2150
Dis Flower 653
Dis Is de Day 1020, 1385
Dis Little While 1385
Disappear 3862
Disappointed in Love 725
Disappointed Suitors 1617
Discarded Blues 280
Disco 52, 2426, 2908
Disco Baby 2426
Disco Destiny 3515
Disco for Margo 167
Disco Rag 843
Disco Shuffle 1637

Disco Toyland 251
Disconnected 2702
Discontent 1176
Discontented Bandits, The 1654
Discontented Blues 4127
Discovering Talent 3982
Discovery of Queenie Pie on the Beach 3628
Discussion 3970
Discussions 143
Disguises 2317
Disgustingly Rich 1894
Dismissal Whistle 1859
Disneyland 4020
Disorder and Genius 2295
Disposition 1458
Disraeli 1832, 4332
Dissatisfied Blues 443
Dissatisfied Women 2579
Dissertation on Transportation, A 413
Dissipated Kitten, The 1535
Dissipation 2044
Dissolves (inst.) 1385
Distant Lands 2766
Distant Melody 3453
Dites-moi 4096
Ditto Ditto 2938
Ditty of the Drill 1165
Diva 424
Diva Supreme 3568
Divali Festival, The 751
Diversion 4623
Divertissement 102, 3091, 3397
Dividing the Spoils 2698
Divine Decree, A 4107
Divorce 1575
Divorce Has Brought Us Together 3666
Divorce Lament 2007
Divorce of Course 3654
Dixiana Rise, The 1888
Dixie 441, 964, 2415, 3025, 2113
Dixie After Dark 4137, 881
Dixie Ann in Afghanistan 4281
Dixie Ballet, The 9
Dixie Cinderella 1980
Dixie Dan 1464
Dixie Doodle (You're the Land for Me) 3877
Dixie Dreams 1058, 1763
Dixie Girls 489
Dixie, I Love You 2749, 4387
Dixie Is Dixie Now 395
Dixie Isn't Dixie Any More 446, 3705
Dixie Isn't Dixie Anymore 447
Dixie Jubilee 3426
Dixie Land 1535
Dixie Land Is Calling Me 2013
Dixie Love 4206
Dixie Love Song 1738
Dixie Moon 740, 1198
Dixie Prelude (Civil War) 2001
Dixie Rose 3985
Dixie Roses 1972
Dixie Vagabond 290
Dixie Wildflowers 1058
Dixieland 4673
Dizzily, Busily 1284
Dizzy Baby 3382
Dizzy Feet 4426
Dizzy Fingers (inst.) 3261
Djibuti 2876
Djinn of Algazam 2691
Do a Duet 4373
Do a Little Exercise 4319
Do a Little Favor 139
Do a Little This, Do a Little That 1690
Do a Revue 411
Do As You Please 2334
Do As You Would Be Done By 3482
Do Black Patent Leather Shoes Really Reflect Up? 1059
Do Buy Some Candy, Sir 3051
Do, Do, Do 3243, 1325
Do-Do-Re-Do 3278
Do Horses Talk to Horses? 2354
Do I Dear?, I Do 2780
Do I Do 4534
Do I Do Wrong? 466
Do I Have to Say? 919
Do I Hear a Waltz? (1) 1060
Do I Hear a Waltz? (2) 1060
Do I Hear You Saying 'I Love You'? 3556
Do I Like Love! 4354
Do I Love Him? 2598
Do I Love You Because You're Beautiful? 759
Do I Love You? 1109, 3079, 2909
Do I Make You Happy? 3577
Do I Take Him Back? 916
Do It 300, 2071
Do It Again! 1391
Do It for Charity 3489
Do It for Me 1598
Do It for Willy 808, 809
Do It Girl 3309
Do It in Two 4566
Do It Now 317, 466, 3245
Do It Properly 2012
Do It the Hard Way 3353
Do It Yourself 4011
Do Listen, Please 2839
Do Look at Him 3245
Do Lord 2415
Do Me a Favor 661, 1222, 3551
Do My Eyes Deceive Me? 1286
Do Not Be Afraid of Love 2000
Do Not Bruise the Fruit 1958
Do Not Hesitate to Shoot 2317
Do Not Hold On 808, 1701
Do Not Jump at Your Conclusions 1392
Do Not Wed at All 904
Do Nothing 'Til You Hear from Me 4091
Do-Nuts 3104

Do Puppies Go to Heaven? 1420
Do Re Mi 1061
Do, Re, Mi 2216
Do-Re-Mi 4095
Do Re Mi 4740
Do-Re-Mi 4429
Do Re Mi Fa Sol La Si Do 1759
Do, Re, Mi, Fa, Sol, La, Si, Do 2765
Do Right Woman 338
Do Say You Do 4025
Do Something 1563, 1276
Do Something Different 2808, 4025
Do Svedanya 3682
Do Tell 1448
Do That Doo-Da 1461
Do That Thing 202
Do the Funny Fox Trot 351
Do the Heavenental 4527
Do the Least You Can 2618
Do the New York 4799
Do the Truck 1982
Do This, Do That 3571
Do Unto Others 3653
Do Us a Favor 1816
Do Wah Diddy 2427, 4193
Do Watcha Gotta Do 1737
Do We? 3900
Do We Understand Each Other 1667
Do What the Good Book Says 4764
Do What You Can Do 2643
Do What You Do 2565
Do What You Do! 3953
Do What You Like 3946
Do What You Must 1816
Do What You Wanna Do 612
Do What You Want to Do 4038
Do What Your Mother Did 2853
Do You? 1932, 3080
Do You Believe in Flirting 1550
Do You Believe in Santa Claus 1515
Do You Believe Me 4037
Do You Belong to Anyone Particular? 4017
Do You Call That Dancing? 2497
Do You Care Too Much? 3825
Do You Do the Charleston? 584
Do You, Don't You, Will You, Won't You 3405
Do You Ever? 2478
Do You Ever Dream of Vienna? 2522
Do You Ever Go to Boston? 1846
Do You Follow Me? 1424, 3994
Do You Hear Me Calling? 2537
Do You Hear the People Sing? 2442
Do You Know? 2670
Do You Know a Better Way to Make a Living 454
Do You Know Jesus 4788
Do You Know Mr. Schneider? 1569
Do You Know the Milky Way? 1062
Do You Know the Way to San Jose 261
Do You Know What It Means to Miss New Orleans 3840
Do You Know What the Children Are Doing Today? 1079
Do You Know What This Could Do to Me? 615
Do You Like Me 968
Do You Love As I Love 1923, 2112
Do You Love As I Love? 4766
Do You Love Me? 1265, 1446
Do You Not Remember Jeanie 1589
Do You Notice Anything? 1267
Do You Really Mean to Go? (Finale Act II) 2467
Do You Recall? 2178, 4365
Do You Recall the House of Leather? 2001
Do You Remember 62
Do You Remember? 1865, 3821, 4272
Do You Remember Love 1896
Do You Suppose Enough 2433
Do You Take This Woman for Your Lawful Wife (I Do, I Do) 3396
Do You Think I'm Pretty? 239
Do You Think It's Alright 4676
Do You Think That You Have Known Me Long Enought? 4354
Do You Want to Go 692
Do You Want to Go to Heaven 394
Do You Want to Know a Secret 4193
Do You Want to See Paris 1272
Do You Want Us to Lose? 3222
Do You Wear Glasses? 3227
Do You Wonder What Became of Romanoff? 3110
Do Your Daily Dozen 2004
Do Your Duty 2796
Do Your Own Thing 3846, 4789
Do Your Thing Miss Truth 2908
Doatsey Mae 374
Doctor, The 169
Doctor 953
Doctor and Ella 919
Doctor and the Scribe, The 2673
Doctor Byrne 954
Doctor Cupid 2492
Doctor In Spite of Himself, The 649
Doctor in Spite of Himself, The 1091
Doctor Jekyll and Mr. Hyde 31
Doctor Scholl 943
Doctor Tinkle Tinker 1558
Doctor Will Fix You, The 1091
Doctor's Canon 1700
Doctor's Dance, The 1748
Doctor's Orders 3441
Doctor's Out Today, The 3600
Doctor's Prayer, A 3600
Doctor's Soliloquy, A 751
Doctor's, Doctor's 2723
Doctors, The 413
Dodo 407, 2330
Does a Duck Love Water? 4825
Does Anybody Here Love Me? 408, 2969
Does Anybody Love You? 508
Does God Ever Make Mistakes? 624

Does He Know 1242
(I Ask You) Does It Pay to Be a Lady? 1667
Does It Really Matter? 2583
Does Polly Want Wally? 1424
Does Your Heart Beat for Me? 4137
Doesn't Anybody Love Anymore 2451
Doesn't Anybody Want Me? 1588
Doesn't It Bug You 1064
Dog, A 1498
Dog 3614
Dog, The 43, 489
Dog and Cat Ballet 3934
Dog Eat Dog 3837
Dog Eats Dog 2442
Dog Face 7
Dog Is a Man's Best Friend, A 4423
Dog Walker 3548
Dogalo 3337
Doge's Dilemma, The 4467
Dogface Jive 3217
Doggie in Our Yard, The 2498
Doggies and the Bone, The 353
Doggone 2271
Doggone That Chili Man 4805
Doggone Whippoorwill 1587
Dogs Versus You 2646
Dogtown 2470
Doh-Doh-Dohdy-O 2004
Doin' All I've Dreamed Of 2993
Doin' It and Sayin' It Are Two
Different Things 374
Doin' It by the Book 3814
Doin' the Chamberlain 4174
Doin' the Consumer 1047
Doin' the Crazy Walk 437
Doin' the Dishes 3587
Doin' the Ethnic Reach 2998
Doin' the Freedom Ride 2306
Doin' the Frog 892
Doin' the Gorilla 86
Doin' the Hot-Cha-Cha 2296
Doin' the Mozambique 443
Doin' the Neighborhood Rag 3926
Doin' the New Low Down 441
Doin' the New York 4823
Doin' the Old Yahoo Step 2439
Doin' the Production Code 1000
Doin' the Reactionary 3501
Doin' the Shim Sham 444
Doin' the Susi-Q 883
Doin' the Toledo 435
Doin' the Town 898
Doin' the Truck 4021
Doin' the Waltz 1286
Doin' What Comes Natur'lly 153
Doing a Dance 1281
Doing a Little Clog Dance
(Doing a Little Waltz Clog) 1202
Doing Good 2163
Doing My Bit 1065
Doing My Job 1732
Doing the Apache 910, 4427
Doing the Charlie Chaplin 695
Doing the Dumbbell 1251
Doing the Eddie Cantor 2706
Doing the High 4089
Doing the Light Fantastic Alley Style 3369
Doing the Psycho-Neurotique 4268
Doing the Ritz 3915
Doing the Saboo 4256
Doing the Town 3185
Doing Time 2523
Doings at Dommayer's, The 1680, 1681
Dolce Far Niente 4516
Doll and the Jumping Jack, The 4725
Doll Dance, The 1127
Doll Dance (What a Peculiar Tune),
The (inst.) 1943
Doll Dance, The (inst.) 4747
Doll Fantasy, A 2786
Doll House, A 3443
Doll Song, The 1436
Doll Song 4352
Doll's House 2378
Doll's House, A 3108
Dollar, The 1568
Dollar Bill's the Flag That Rules
the World, The 1738
Dollar for a Dime 4281
Dollar Princess, The 1067
Dollar Princesses, The 1067
Dollar Sign, The 4094
Dollar Song, A 2248
Dollars and Debutantes 3575
Dolls 410, 413, 4150
Dolly 2854, 3249, 4491
Dolly Dear 186, 830
Dolly Dimple 4014
Dolly Dimple Song 3951
Dolly Dimple's Holiday 1949
Dolly Dimples 2505
Dolly Dollars 2885
Dolly from the Folies Bergere 3381
'Dolly' Sisters, The 2279
Dolly Twinkle, The 3246
Dolly Varden 1071
Dolly with a Dimple on Her Chin
(Daisy with a Dimple on Her Chin) 737
Dolly's Seduction 3274
Dollys and Their Collies, The 1690
Dolores 3362, 3444
Dombaye 3814
Domestic Champagne Waltz, The 3274
Domesticity 2295
Dominus Vobiscum 2775
Domus Sur Pampas 2935
Don Brandeiro, We Await You 4032
Don Jose O'Brien 4572
Don Jose of Far Rockaway 4718
Don Juan 1427, 4031

Don Medigua, All for Thy Coming Wait 1165
Don Medigua, Here's Your Wife 1165
Don Pasquale 3197
Don Pasquale De Mesquita 1521
Don Quixote 2727, 3829
Don's Chorus (The Things That Are Done By a Don), The 3818
Don't Advertise Your Man 1425, 3705
Don't Ask! 3243
Don't Ask a Lady 2523
Don't Ask Her Mother 1655
Don't Ask Me 71, 3718
Don't Ask Me Not to Sing 672, 2204, 3735
Don't Ask the Lady What the Lady Did Before 2294
Don't Ask Too Much of Love 3385
Don't Bait for Fish You Can't Find 90
Don't Be a Geografoof 1477
Don't Be a Miracle 2618
Don't Be a Sailor 3737
Don't Be a Woman If You Can 3390
Don't Be Afraid 1755, 4196, 4446
Don't Be Afraid of an Animal 134
Don't Be Afraid of Romance 2983
Don't Be Afraid of the Dark 3908
Don't Be Afraid to Love 181
Don't Be Anybody's Moon but Mine 4185
Don't Be Anything Less Than Everything You Can Be 4034
Don't Be Ashamed of a Teardrop 1061
Don't Be Blue 2557
Don't Be Cross with Me 1833, 4185
Don't Be Like an Eskimo 1342
Don't Be Like That 1617
Don't Be Like Your Old Man 821
Don't Be Rash 2538, 2668
Don't Be So Cruel, Ducky Dear! 1090
Don't Be Subtle, Don't Be Coy 1577
Don't Be That Way 4137
Don't Be What You Ain't 2951
Don't Believe 376
Don't Believe a Tale Like That 2714
Don't Bet Your Money on de Shanghai 4149
Don't Betray His Love 2630
Don't Bite the Hand That Feeds You 843
Don't Blame It All on Broadway 357, 3525
Don't Blame Me 787, 4197
Don't Blow That Horn, Gabriel 2161
Don't Bother 410
Don't Bother Me, I Can't Cope 1072
Don't Break the Spell 2115
Don't Breathe a Word 68
Don't Bring Her Flowers 3272
Don't Call Me 255
Don't Call Them Dearie 2264
Don't Call Us 459
Don't Change the Way You Love Me 3671
Don't Cheat on the Meat 1917
Don't Choose a Gibson Girl 1593
Don't Come Near Me 2304
Don't Come to Court 3702
Don't Count on It 2702
Don't Count Your Chickens 187
Don't Cry 2961
Don't Cry Anymore 3227
Don't Cry Bo-Peep 251
Don't Cry for Me 2477
Don't Cry for Me Argentina 1211
Don't Cry Swanee 487
Don't Cry When He's Gone 2462
Don't Destroy the World 4396
Don't Dilly Dally on the Way 4027
Don't Do Anything Till You Hear from Me 2574
Don't Do It 1657
Don't Do It Mr. Hermes 3418
Don't Do the Charleston 3179
Don't Don't Stop Loving Me Now 2706
Don't-Don't-Don't 2756
Don't Drop the Bomb 3076
Don't Eat It 3602
Don't Even Start 1630
Don't Even Think About It 2333
Don't Ever Be a Poor Relation 3295
Don't Ever Book a Trip on the IRT 4279
Don't Ever Leave Me 2372, 4234
Don't Ever Run Away from Love 4702
Don't Fall Asleep 3107
Don't Fall for the Lights 4535
Don't Fall in Love with Me 2843
Don't Fall Until You've Seen Them All 2767
Don't Feed the Animals 1426
Don't Forget 1513
Don't Forget (Your Auntie) 3622
Don't Forget 3863
Don't Forget 127th Street 602, 1601
Don't Forget Bandanna Days 2645, 14
Don't Forget Me 1602, 2299, 3024, 3028
Don't Forget the Beau You Left at Home 1845
Don't Forget the Girl from Punxsutawney 532
Don't Forget the Girl You Left Behind 1606
Don't Forget the Lilac Bush 4169
Don't Forget the Number 1593, 4247
Don't Forget the Waiter 4795
Don't Forget to Dream 1811
Don't Forget You're Talking to a Lady 2906, 4311
Don't Forget Your Etiquette 138
Don't Forget Your Old Pal, Al 3982
Don't Get Around Much Anymore 4091
Don't Get Your Hopes Up 3165
Don't Give Up the Hunt, Dr. Puffin 2339
Don't Give Up the Ship 2772
Don't Give Your Love Away 928
Don't Go Away 3051
Don't Go Away Monsieur 383
Don't Go for to Leave Us, Richard Carr 402
Don't Go in the Water 1248
Don't Go in the Water Daughter 1247
Don't Go Into the Lion's Cage Tonight 470
Don't Go Sally 610
Don't Go To Dangerously Nigh 2123

Don't Go Too Far Girls 4669
Don't Go Too Fast Little Dearie 4453
Don't Grow Old Gracefully 159
Don't Hang Up the Telephone 2754
Don't Hang Your Dreams on a Rainbow 1126
Don't Have a Song to Sing 3233
Don't Have the Baby 4485
Don't Have to Take It Any More 4584
Don't Hesitate with Me 3397
Don't Hold Everything, Let Everything Go 1929
Don't I Know You From Somewhere 181
Don't Introduce Me to That Angel 4652
Don't It Feel Good 3724
Don't It Go to Show Ya Never Know 2544
Don't It Sometimes 4055
Don't Join the Navy to See the World 4180
Don't Judge a Girl by Her Name 1513
Don't Kick My Dreams Around 3299
Don't Kiki Me 3469
Don't Knock It 4827
Don't Know If I'm Comin' or Goin' 875, 885
Don't Know What I Expected 1702
Don't Laugh 1991, 2677
Don't Laugh at Me 157
Don't Laugh at Trina 2064
Don't Leave Me 4789
Don't Leave Me Dangling in the Dust 3309
Don't Leave Your Little Blackbird Blue 567
Don't Let a Good Thing Get Away 2014
Don't Let a Good Thing Go 1099
Don't Let Anybody Vamp Your Man 2594
Don't Let Him Know You 920
Don't Let It Be Today 1997
Don't Let It Get You Down 4399, 1931, 4777
Don't Let It Happen Again 297
Don't Let Me Be Misunderstood 3695
Don't Let Me Bother You 2785
Don't Let Me Catch You Falling in Love 2214
Don't Let Me Down 392, 3186
Don't Let the Girlies Get You 88
Don't Let the Parade Pass You By 3793
Don't Let the Rhythm Go to Your Head 1659
Don't Let the Sun Catch You Crying 1296
Don't Let the World Go By 496
Don't Let Them Take the Paramount Away 427
Don't Let's Meet Again 276
Don't Like Goodbyes 2000
Don't Listen to Your Heart 3713
Don't Look at Me 1329
Don't Look at Me That Way 1018, 3382
Don't Look Back 4090
Don't Look Now 868
Don't Lose Your Head (And Lose Your Gal) 2807
Don't Lose Your Head, Then Lose Your Girl 4199
Don't Lose Your Sense of Humor 1120
Don't Lose Your Way 1335
Don't Lose Your Way, Little Boy 102
Don't Love Me Like Othello 1321, 3847, 4780
Don't Make a Move 4060
Don't Make a Plaything Out of My Heart 1765
Don't Make Me Cry 916
Don't Make Me Dance 4527
Don't Make Me Laugh 3792
Don't Make Me Nervous 615
Don't Make Me Over 4193, 261
Don't Marry Me 1315
Don't Mess with Bill 4534
Don't Mind Me 2906, 4311
Don't Open the Door 1785
Don't Overdo It 457
Don't P-P-Point Them Guns at Me 4785
Don't Play That Lovesong Anymore 2949
Don't Play with Me 1334
Don't Pour the Thames Into the Rhine 989
Don't Pull the Wool Over My Eyes 2115
Don't Pull Up the Flowers 518
Don't Put It Down 1717
Don't Put Me 'On' 2551
Don't Put Me Out of Your Heart 2950
Don't Put Out the Light 1613
Don't Put Your Daughter on the Stage Mrs. Worthington 3196
Don't Quit While You're Ahead 3070
Don't Rain on My Parade 1420
Don't Say F-A-T in Front of Conrad 534
Don't Say Goodbye 2897
Don't Say I Didn't Give You Anything 255
Don't Say 'Love'-I've Been There and Back 4048
Don't Say Paris, Say Paree 2443
Don't Say Shoo-Be-Do-Bop 843
Don't Say Yes If You Want to Say No 2049
Don't Say You Like Tchaikowsky 3940
Don't Scold 3236
Don't Sell the Night Short 372
Don't Send Me Back to Petrograd 3009
Don't Send Your Wife to the Country (Keep Her Home and Love Her Yourself) 487
Don't Settle for Less (Than the Best) 1615
Don't Shake My Tree 4793
Don't Shoot the Hooey to Me, Louie 3330
Don't Sing Solo 3226
Don't Sleep in the Subway 338
Don't Speak of Love to Me 3151
Don't Stand Too Close to the Picture 339
Don't Stop 1831
Don't Stop Mr. Jenkinson 1327
Don't Tag Along 2927
Don't Take a Girl Down to Coney 4804
Don't Take Him Away 434
Don't Take Our Charlie for the Army 1564
Don't Take Sides 1761
Don't Take Your Beau to the Seashore 1247
Don't Take Your Troubles to Bed 3511
Don't Talk 183
Don't Talk, Don't Think 518
Don't Talk to Me About Those Happy Days 1741
Don't Talk to Me of Love 2727
Don't Tamper with My Sister 3274
Don't Teach Me to Swim Alone 4185
Don't Tear Up the Horse Slips 2322

Don't Tell a Soul 4828
Don't Tell Mama 610
Don't Tell Me 550, 1760, 2033, 2556, 595
Don't Tell Me Everything 572
Don't Tell Me I'm Flying 3844
Don't Tell Me It's Bad 3850
Don't Tell Me It's Forever 3927
Don't Tell Me Too Many Lies 1978
Don't Tell Momma 1864
Don't Tell the Old Home Town 2378
Don't Tell Your Folks 3980
Don't Tempt Me 75, 905, 2620
Don't Thank Me 363
Don't Think That We're the Chorus of the Show 4781
Don't Throw Me Down 4668
Don't Touch Him 2452
Don't Touch That Dial 952
Don't Trust Anyone 4289
Don't Trust Them 1308
Don't Turn Away from Love 3815
Don't Turn His Picture to the Wall 1380
Don't Turn My Picture to the Wall 1538
Don't Turn Us Out of Your House 3003
Don't Turn Your Back 1073
Don't Turn Your Back on Me 3297
Don't Twist Her Mind 2618
Don't Twist My Mind 2618
Don't Unmask Your Beauty to the Moon 3741
Don't Wait 281
Don't Wait Till It's Too Late to See Paris 3108
Don't Wake Them Up Too Soon 2397
Don't Wanna B N Luv 4786
Don't Wanna Be No Superstar 4349
Don't Wanna Write about the South 454
Don't Want to Be a Lady 3952, 3951
Don't Waste the Moon 661
Don't Wear Your Heart on Your Sleeve 1333
Don't Whistle So Loud 3049
Don't Wish 2677
Don't Worry 'Bout Me 888
Don't Worry, Don't Worry (I Don't Worry) 4013
Don't Yo' Want to See de Moon? 2216
Don't You Believe It 4602
Don't You Care 3052
Don't You Cheat 458
Don't You Ever Cross Me Path 3493
Don't You Ever Give It All Away 2648
Don't You Ever Tell I Told You 3085
Don't You Ever Think About Me, Dearie? 2448
Don't You Feel Me Leg 1890
Don't You Find the Weather Charming? 4404
Don't You Hate It? 1004
Don't You Know or Don't You Care 3356
Don't You Love the Dream of Dear Old Ireland? 4120
Don't You Make a Noise 1247
Don't You Really Think I'll Do? 2390
Don't You Remember Those School Days 1753
Don't You Remember? 97
Don't You Start Me Talking 2692
Don't You Tell 4387
Don't You Think It's Time to Marry? 470
Don't You Think It's Very Nice? 2681
Don't You Think You'll Miss Me 1266
Don't You Want a Paper Dearie 3710
Don't You Want to Take Me? 3146
Don't You Wish You Were a Kid Again 4835
Don't! 1993
Don'tcha Hate It 1048
Dona Flor and Her Two Husbands 3838
Donald Brian Polka, The 1544
Doncha Feel Proud? 1099
Donkey and the Hay, The 3996
Donna 1717
Donna Clara 203
Donny Didn't, Donny Did 3494
Donnybrook 1076
Dont Talk About God 2583
Donuts for Defense 597
Doo-Dab, The 3617
Doo, Dah, Deh 1667
Doo-Waa, Doo-Wee 1059
Doodlin' Song, A 1648
Doolittle Hop, The 2400
Doom Is Due at Dawn 3368
Doomed 3080
Doomed, Doomed, Doomed 1600
Doonesbury 1077
Doop-De-Doop 3940
Door Is Closed, The 944
Door Mats 3431
Door of Her Dreams 3772
Doors 784
Doors Are Closed, The 4232
Doowah Diddy Blues, The 4252
Dope 2776, 3738
Dope Double Time 2776
Dope Fiend, The 4521
Dope Rag 2776
Dope Song 2461
Dora 2724
Dora Lane 1573
Dorcas 1080
Dorine und der Zufall 12
Doris 1437
Doris' Nightmare 484
Dormez-Vous 3456
Dorothy 1131
Dorothy Flop 45
Dorothy's Opener 3178
Dorrie's Wish 1698
Dorris, the Moon, and the Dart, The 2928
Dost Thou 4323
Dost Thou Know that Fair Land 2159
Dot and Carry One 2546, 4758
Dot, Dot, Dot 2163
Dou, Dou 2540
Double 2877
Double Dummy Drill, The (inst.) 2444
Double Feature 1082

Double Murder 1748
Double Order of Chicken, A 4375
Double Soliloquy 989
Double Standard 3234
Double Standard, The 1657
Double Step Drag, The 3080
Double Talk 775
Double Trouble 383
Dougal 3322
Doughnuts 2960, 4561
Doughnuts and Coffee 3713
Doughnuts for Defense 3217
Doughnuts for Doughboys 815
Dov's Nightmare 181
Dove Dance, The (inst.) 3222
Dove of Peace 1083
Dove Song, The 2384, 730
Dover 705
Dow Jones 4635
Dow Jones Disco, The (inst.) 4774
Dowager Fairy Queen, The 2004
Dowdling 1076
Down 1699
Down a Down Down Derry 3939
Down a Shady Lane 1095
Down Along the Vineyards 2164
Down Among the Grass Roots 2018
Down and Out Blues 1763
Down at Madeleines 2318
Down at Mammy Jinny's 4687
Down at the Bottom of the Sea 2035
Down at the Gaiety Burlesque 4197
Down at the Village 1693
Down By the Blue Rio Grande 361
Down By the Countryside 1561
Down By the Erie Canal 1478
Down by the Erie Canal 1826
Down by the Kongaloo 2385
Down By the Mill 3802
Down By the Ocean 2153
Down By the Ocean Strand 4681
Down By the Old Southern River 1984
Down By the Railroad Track 4281
Down By the Sea 3191
Down by the Sea (Whoopie) 3556
Down De Lover's Lane 666
Down Down Down 54
Down-Down-Down 610
Down East Flapper, The 1516
Down Goes the Price of Eggs 1593
Down Home 1876, 3610
Down Home Stomp 2881
Down in a Dungeon Deep 3378
Down in Arkansas 1617, 1686
Down in Catty Corner 4747
Down in Dear Old New Orleans 4806
Down in Fraternity Row 1879
Down in Honeymoon Alley 2934
Down in Honky Tonk Town 3297
Down in Mulberry Bend 2035
Down in My Heart 2525
Down in the Depths 1018, 1873, 3674, 4517
Down in the Old Rathskeller 4206
Down in the Philippines 3945
Down in the Sand 2555
Down in the Streets 4566
Down in the Valley 1085
Down in the Valley of Dreams 1631
Down in Waterloo 965
Down Lovers' Lane 2056, 3378
Down Manila Bay 434
Down Old Harmony Way 1963
Down on a Country Farm 2789
Down on a South Sea Isle 1295
Down on de Ole Yazoo 1568
Down on MacConnachy Square 530
Down on Me 1282, 4168
Down on the Bangway Isle 1462
Down on the Banks of Subway 3775
Down on the Delta 2739
Down on the Dude Ranch 1931
Down on the Farm 1306
Down on the Gipsy Trail 1517
Down on the Nile 2684
Down on the Old Kansas Farm (That Farm Out in Kansas) 2767
Down on the Old-Time Farm 536
Down on the River 4149
Down Once More 3464
Down Red Rose Lane 3134
Down Round the 19th Hole 2308
Down South 487
Down the Bridle Path of Love 2619
Down the Drain 1832, 1273
Down the Fields 4659
Down the Hall 3601
Down the Lane 455
Down the Line 1926
Down the Line with Arabella 4662
Down the Mississippi 4544
Down the Road 3998
Down the Strand 954, 1327
Down the Well 1930
Down Through History 3209
Down Through the Agents 323
Down Through the Ages 21, 3352
Down to Cooney Island 217
Down to Eartha 90
Down to the Cellar 1312
Down to the Folies Bergere 1327
Down to the Sea 3473
Down to the Sea in Other People's Ships 621
Down Town East of Broadway 2148
Down Under 2565
Down! Up! Left! Right! 1598
Down Virginia Way 3958
Down Where the Bluebells Grow 4209
Down Where the East River Flows 4023
Down Where the Jack O' Lanterns Grow 805
Down where the Mortgages Grow 2768

Down Where the Mortgages Grow 3770
Down Where the Suwannee River Flows 3737
Down Where the Tennessee Flows 1963
Down Where the Watermelon Grows 2415, 2978
Down Where the Watermelons Grow 801
Down with Everybody but Us 1272
Down with Everything That's Up 2444
Down with Love 1973
Down with Sin 2985
Down with Whiskey 2750
Down Your Tea 4075
Downcast Eye, The 1188, 3976
Downriver 1086
Downstream 1047
Downtown 338, 2804, 4827
Downtown Rag 1420
Dozen Husbands 1878
Dozens, The 40
Dr. Baltimore M.D. 2696
Dr. Blotz 2160
Dr. Brock 4312
Dr. Chumley 3846
Dr. Clambake's Ballet 4316
Dr. Crippen 3301
Dr. Freud 2053
Dr. Grouch Is Going Away 1888
Dr. Iatro 4401
Dr. Jazz 2200, 1063, 1876
Dr. Lucy (The Doctor Is In) 4783
Dr. Rosalyn Green 157
Dr. Willy Nilly 1091
Draggin' the Chain 1799
Dragon Dance 2504
Dragon Flight 4485
Dragon Strikes Back 4459
Dragon's Challenge 1092
Dragons 1092
Drama of Love 3745
Drama Quartet 4332
Dramatic Ring, The 2448
Dramatic Situation 1388
Dramatico Musical Scene 4692
Dramatis Personnae 1347
Dramatized Message, A 1233
Drat! 1093
Drat! The Cat! 1094
Draw Me a Circle 4319
Draw the Blinds 2047
Drawing Lesson, The 3085
Drawing the Line 233
Drawn to You 161
Dream, The 415, 1118
Dream 932
Dream, The 4002
Dream 4085
Dream, A (scene) 4812
Dream a Dream 4212
Dream Ago, A 842
Dream Babies 2801
Dream Ballet 1046
Dream Boat 1281, 3434
Dream Dance 1414, 3687
Dream Days of Seville 1925
Dream! Dream! 3658
Dream Drumming 3330
Dream Duet, The 1763
Dream Ends, The (inst.) 752
Dream Fantasies 3404
Dream for Angela, A 3543
Dream for Sale 4316
Dream Girl 42, 2174, 3925, 4013, 1097
Dream Girl O' Mine 3910
Dream Girl, Give Back My Dream to Me 2684
Dream Girls 1103
Dream House 157
Dream Kingdom 680
Dream Love 375
Dream Love ('Twas Only Dreaming) 3567
Dream Lovers, The 1689
Dream Melody 2756
Dream Minute (Finale Act II) 4185
Dream O'Day Jill 4404
Dream of Demetrios, The 165
Dream of Joy 3472
Dream of Orange Blossoms, A 3312
Dream of the Philippines, A 2111
Dream of You, The 3098
Dream On 661, 2160, 4352
Dream on Little Soldier Boy 4770
Dream On, My Princess 2390
Dream One Dream of Me 4478
Dream Safe with Me 699
Dream Shadows 1939
Dream Song 1109, 2508, 4382
Dream Street Station 563
Dream Sweetheart 931
Dream Team 1099
Dream Time 4252
Dream Toyland 251
Dream Waltz 4644
Dream with Me 599, 3278, 3452
Dreamboat from Dreamland 597, 3217
Dreamchild 4469
Dreamer with a Penny 67
Dreamers 2196
Dreamin' Suits Me Just Fine 781
Dreaming 123, 276, 827, 1593, 2062, 2990, 3562
Dreaming Alone 3623
Dreaming, Dreaming (The Moon Song) 2209
Dreaming in Paradise
(Love's Dear Yearning) 1027
Dreaming of Allah 930
Dreaming of Love 1455
Dreaming on the Ohio 4859
Dreaming Princess, The 1183
Dreaming True 1321, 3847
Dreamland 954, 1518, 3520, 3716
Dreamland Lover, The 1121, 2509
Dreams 287
Dreams (Follow Your Dreams) 2239

Dreams 2239, 729, 1003, 1500, 1650, 2919, 3655, 1972, 1867, 4207, 494
Dreams Ago 1679
Dreams Come True 404, 490, 2205
Dreams Don't Die 2846
Dreams Don't Mean a Thing 4527
Dreams for Sale 1965, 4104, 4816
Dreams Go By 2470
Dreams Have I 4408
'Dreams' Melody 1103
Dreams Never Die 577
Dreams of 1897 3463
Dreams of Egypt 808, 809
Dreams of Heaven 4349
Dreams of the Past 3397
Dreams of Tomorrow 4227
Dreams! Oh Dreams! 2884
Dreams to Do 1258
Dreamy Araby 3032
Dreamy Day 813
Dreamy Days 3310
Dreamy Egypt 1833
Dreamy Eyes 3580
Dreamy Florence 3403
Dreamy Hollow 3677
Dreamy Montmartre 2380
Dreamy Parisian Coon, The 1919
Dreary 270
Dreary, Dreary, Rainy Days 2645
Drei Arme Kleine Madels 4352
Drei Walzer 4365
Dreidel 4172
Dresden China Belle, The 4248
Dresden China Love Affair, A 2733
Dresden China Plate, The 3486
Dresden China Soldiers 3378
Dresden Northwest Mounted, The 3379
Dress, Dress, Dress 3402
Dress! Dress! Dress! 1868
Dressed to Kill 3178
Dressed to the Nines 1107
Dressed Up for Your Sunday Beau 2277
Dresses 3827
Dressing 4575
Dressing Room, A 4830
Dressing Room Echoes 3348
Dressing Room Scene 4020
Dressing Them Up 2333
Dressing Up 3453
Dressing Up Sequence (Riding on the Moon) (inst.) 1385
Drift with Me 2620
Drifting 135, 1845, 1510
Drifting Along with the Tide 1484
Drifting On 97
Drigo's Polka 545
Drill, The 1131
Drill 3485
Drill of the Coquette Corps 3626
Drill of the Seventh 2525
Drink 3893
Drink and Be Jolly To Day' 2745
Drink and Be Merry 1849
Drink Drink, Drink 1469
Drink Me 54
Drink Out the Old Drink 2373
Drink Some Tea 4133
Drink the Waters 1456
Drink the Wine 3543, 3626
Drink to the Glorious Night 1908
Drink to the Health of This Great Man 3265
Drink Up 3348
Drink with Me 4277
Drink with Me the Night Away 355
Drink with Me to Days Gone By 2442
Drinkin' Shoes 3608
Drinking 1087
Drinking Fool 1985
Drinking Song 520, 586, 1225, 2464, 3131
Drinking Song, The 4186
Drinking Song 4188, 4539
Drinking Song and Dance 1817
Drinking Song, Um Pa Pa Pa 2811
Drinking Trio 3626
Drinks of the Day 2131
Drip, Drip, Drip, Went the Waterfall 4720
Drip, Drop, Tapoketa 3863
Drive In, The 3211
Driving Home with Angeline 1919
Drop In on Me at Luncheon 1243
Drop In on Me, At Luncheon 1243
Drop Me a Line 1962
Drop Me Off in Harlem 4091
Drop That Name 363
Drop Your Kerchief 1491
Dropsy Cure Weather 1662
Drowsily, Dreamily 4014
Drucilla 3562
Drug Addicts 194
Drug Free 1282
Drug Store Song, The 620
Drugstore Scene 919
Drum Brigade, The 1982
Drum in My Heart — Gun in My Hand 3485
Drummed Out 3626
Drummerboy at Shiloh, The 973
Drums, The 4646
Drums 4678
Drums in My Heart 3249, 4372
Drums of All Nations 2394
Drums of Kane 2636
Drums of the Fore and Aft 4506
Drunkard, The 4606
Drunken Man's Praise of Sobriety, A 1977
Drunken Sisters, The 1867
Drunkenness 2866
Dry Mouth with No Water 3276
Du Barry Was a Lady 1109
Du Iz Mein Hartz 2356
Du Zelbege Zah 4463

Dubarry, The 1110
Dubbing (Knight of the Woeful Countenance), The 2727
Dublin Night Ballet 2268
Dublin Rag, The 2667
Dublin Town 4566
Dublinola 3407
Ducal Cousin, Give You Greeting 1388
Duchess of Central Park, The 3744
Duchess of Devonshire, The 3402
Duchess of Dreams, The 379
Duchess of Killarney, The 1464
Duchess of Table D'Hote 4802
Duchess of the Long Ago, The 3402
Duchess Song, The 3197
Duchess's Entrance 1284
Duck, The 3444
Ducks and Geese 2756
Ducks Call It Luck, The 1343
Ducky 453, 4550
Ducky Daddies 371
Dude All Dude 1116
Dudin' Up 3224
Duel 73
Duel, The 949, 1281, 2358, 3015, 3494
Duel! A Duel!, A 1000
Duello, The 4214
Duet 8, 690, 1624, 3171, 3976, 3549, 4252, 4537, 526
Duet and Dance 473
Duet for 5 People 1047
Duet for One (The First Lady of the Land) 4004
Duet of the Robin and the Nightingale 526
Duke of Berkshire 1080
Duke's Place 4091
Duke, the Dauphin, The 2028
Dulcinea 2727
Dull and Gay (The Gay and the Dull) 3980
Dullest Couple in Scarsdale 2231
Dumb Bell, The 228
Dumb Girl 1440
Dumb Luck 740
Dumb-Dumb-Dumb-Dumbbell 993
Dumbbells May Be Foolish 3580
Dumber They Come the Better I Like 'Em, The 2308
Dummy Juggler 4577
Dumplings 669
D'Une Coquette 1458
Dunerwetter 2667
Dungeons and Dragons 430
Duo Thoughts 3201
Duodecimalogue 2287
During Life 3887
Dus Yiddishe Leid 2356
Dusky Debutante 4677
Dusky Dream 934
Dusky Love 2302
Dusky Salome, The 2978
Dusky Shadows 1064
Dust Bowl Refugee 4740
Dust Chasers 728
Dust in Your Eyes 3002
Dust Storm Disaster 4740
Dustbane: The Ballad of Minka 3601
Dusters, Goggles and Hats 4292
Dusting Around 3965
Dusty Roads 3167
Dutch Cadets, The 586
Dutch Comedians 998
Dutch Country Table 239
Dutch's Song 576
Dutchman's Pants, The 915
Dutiful Wife, A 2836
Duty Calls! 455
Dvoyreh 3781
Dvoyreh Fan Rumeynie 3781
Dwarf's Song 941
Dwarf's Yodel Song (The Silly Song) 4035
Dwight D. Eisenhower 3558
D'Ye Folly Me 1544
D'Ye Love Me? 4212
Dying Business, A 1770
Dying Child 2290
Dying Cowboy, The 1546
Dying Flamingo, The 4730
Dying Is 1450
Dying Schwann, The 128
Dying Swan, The 3314, 4810
Dying to Meet You 924
Dynamic 1918

E

E Didn't Know Just W'at to Say 1925
E-Gypsy-Ann 2009
Each Little Jack 4208
Each Night Is a New Day 2580
Each of Us 4288, 2320
Each Pearl a Thought 3237
Each Tomorrow Morning 1012
Eadie Was a Lady 4267
Eager Beaver 3187
Eagle and Me, The 462
Eagle Rock, The 3397
Eagle Soliloquy 4863
Earl Is Crazy 1139
Earl of Stole 1123
Earl Was Ahead 1139
Early Bird Eddy 1093
Early Hours of the Morn 4657
Early in the Morning 1296, 2342
Early Monday Morning 2748
Early Morning Rain 2007
Early One Morning Blues 344
Early Sunday 1770
Early to Bed 1140
Earth, The 1116

Earth and Other Minor Things, The 1511
Earth and the Sky, The 2227
Earth Dance 2918
Earthly Paradise 807, 807, 809, 3542
Earthquake 3628
Earthworms 2918
Ease on Down the Road 4722
Easier Said Than Done 4193
Easier to Love 253
Easier to Sing Than Say 1969
Easin' Along 1687
East Brooklyn Blues 3636
East Indian Mambo 268
East Is West 1142, 2872
East of Eden 1864
East River Rhasody 2949
East Side Glide 2422
East Side Lil 1403
East Side Moon 3926
East Side Story, The 722
East Side Walk 1403
East St. Louis Toodle-oo (inst.) 432, 4235
East Wind 1145
Easter in Waikiki 197
Easter Parade 207, 4159
Easter Sunday Parade 2829
Eastern and Western Love 1027
Eastern Moon 2952
Easy 90, 964, 2775, 3763
Easy Come, Easy Go 1257, 1335, 2064, 2382
Easy Dawson March 1148
Easy Does It 518, 4432
Easy for Me 1732
Easy for Them to Say 3901
Easy for You 3644
Easy Goin' Man 3610, 3808
Easy Life, The 3456
Easy Money 3520
Easy Pickin's 1625
Easy Ridin' Papa 888
Easy Street 150, 1385, 1758
Easy Terms 460
Easy to Be Happy 3507
Easy to Be Hard 1717
Easy to Be Lonely 1139
Easy to Love 163, 1762, 4799
Easy to Take 3551
Eat a Little Something 2048
Eat and the World Eats with You 2816
Eat, Eat, Eat 2283
Eat It 1116
Eat the Bubbles in Your Soup 2091
Eat the Lunch 3601
Eat Your @*!#&*!@#! Cornflakes 140
Eat Your Nice Lily, Unicorn 322
Eating Mushrooms 54
Eating Raoul 1149, 1149
Eave's Song 3811
Ebb and Flow 2936
Ebony Rag 4182
Eccentric Dance 1308, 1867, 3772, 4735
Eccentricities 1532
Eccentricity 3704
Ecch 2663
Ecclesiasticus I Can Spell 1741
Echo 2278, 2412, 2633
Echo (dance) 3390
Echo 3581
Echo of a Song, The 3314
Echo of My Heart 1318
Echo Song 1404
Echo Song, The 1422
Echo Song 1761, 3453
Echo Song, The 4724
Echo Waltz, The 956
Echoes of Harlem (inst.) 4091
Echoes of Jazzland 3022
Echoes of Swannee 3025
Echoes of the Past 2050
Ecology 314
Ecology Waltz, The 2962
Economic Situation, The (Aren't You Wonderful) 4825
Economics 2615, 3501
Eddie, Be Good 4819
Eddie's Catchy Tunes 1155
Eddie's Fifth Encore 1420
Eddie's Teddy 3742
Eddy-Mac 3314
Edelweiss 2594, 3362, 4095, 4666
Eden, Eden 170
Edgar Allan Poe 4034
Edge of the World, The 3788
Edinboro Wriggle, The 2358
Editorial 3136
Edna, the Elephant Girl 3641
Educate Your Feet 3005
Educated Feet 4, 1630
Educated Fool, An (It Keeps Me Guessing All the Time) 2885
Educated Whisk Broom, An 2927
Education 2686, 2100
Education of H*Y*M*A*N K*A*P*L*A*N, The 1158
Education of Peg Ballet, The 3427
Eee! 1757
Eels Are a Girl's Best Friend 2659
Eenie, Meenie, Minee, Mo 2379
Eenie Meenie Miney Moe (The Counting Song) 1744
Eenie-Weenie, Lovey Dovey 1629
Eenie, Weenie, Lovey Dovey 3256
Eeny Meeny Miny Mo 1555
Efficiency 1887
EFX 1159
Egano D'Galluzzi 482
Egg, The 3897
Egg Has Fallen Down, The 2035
Egg Song 2880
Eggs 1970, 1412

Eglamour 4485
Egon Edgon Band, The 962
Egypt 737, 1537, 4148
Egypt Is Egypt Again 3088
Egypt Land 694
Egypt's No Place for a Lady 69
Egyptian 4811, 4838
Egyptian Ballet 612
Egyptian Dance 1154
Egyptian Dance, The 2264
Egyptian Dance 1867
Egyptian Eyes 3409
Egyptian Melange 4104
Egyptian Night 978
Egyptian Rag 1065
Egyptianna (inst.) 662
Eibig Dein 4463
8 1/2 3171
Eight Bells 3799
8 Days a Week 1074
8:14 to Nooma City, The 3318
Eight Little Daughters 3434
Eight Little Debutantes Are We 356
Eight Little Girls 3322
Eight Little Gringitos 3719
Eight Little Nobodies 3137
Eight Weight Lifters 837
Eight Years 533
Eight-horse Parlay 1590
18 Days Ago 1491
1845 496
1898 3064
1861 4521
Eighteen-Wheelin' Baby 3517
Eighteen Years Ago 1258
18th Century Garden (inst.) 2088
Eighth Avenue 1842
8th Avenue 4684
Eighth Day 1809
Eighth Wonder, The 2250
80 Days 1161
88 Rag, The 4395
Eileen 515
Eileen, Allana Asthore 1162
Eileen Asthore 1163
Eileen Avourneen 4374
Eily Riley 2858
Ein Herbstmanoever 1455
Ein Koloheinu 4773
Ein Nacht in Venedig 3150
Ein Tag Im Paradies 473
Ein Tolles Madel 2914
Ein Walzerlraum 4590
Eine Kleine Nachtmusic Cha Cha Cha 220
Eine Nacht in Venedig 3151
Einstein 2478
Eisenhower-Grandfather Hero to the World 2579
Either You Do or You Don't 587
Ekufikeni 4438
El Bravo 1164, 845
El Bravo! 846
El Bruta 2108
El Capitan (inst.) 4390
El Choclo Tango 822
'El Cuando' 1046
El Gaucho 3356
El Matador Terrifico 4572
El Presidente 1536
El Rancho 2479
El Sombrero 4693
Elaine (Girl of My Heart) 3581
Elbow Room 2941
Elderly Actress, The 3235
Eldorado 630, 4575
Eleanor 1169, 3405
Eleanor, I Adore You 3100
Eleanor Roosevelt (A Discussion of Soup) 109
Eleanor Roosevelt: A Discussion of Soap 3757
Elect Me President 242
Election 1971
Election Day 3531, 3963
Election Ensemble 4187
Election Eve 4297
Election Returns 1409
Election Spectacular 3484
Election Time 434
Election, The 3291
Electric Blues 1717
Electric Light Cadets, The 3751
Electric Prophet 1116
Electric Signs 3268
Electric Windows 1497
Electricity 3821, 4390
Elegance 1828, 3113
Elegant Lovers 2611
Elegy (inst.) 1385
Eleleu! 227
Element of Doubt 2246
(That) Element of Doubt 4828
Elements, The 2820, 4412
Elena 2295
Elephant Joke 128
Elephant Skid 231
Elephant Song, The 3900
Elephant Walk 143
Elevation (What I Seen I Done) 2334
Elevator Papa—Switchboard Mama 2337
Eleven Commandments, The 1769
Eleven Levee Street 4214
Eleven O'Clock Number 426
Eleven O'Clock Song 145
Eleventh Commandment, The 3551
Elf King, The 1602
Eli, Eli 1740
Eli Eli 3704
Elijah 1715
Elijah Rock 4645
Eliot Rosewater 1591
Eliot, Sylvia 1591

Elisha's Vision 3908
Elite Syncopation 4390
Elixir Motive (inst.) 136
Elizabeth 407, 3389, 2022, 3702, 4730
Elizabeth the Queen 1171
Elizabeth Vanities, The 2969
Elizabeth's Song 1653, 4537
Ella 2851
Ella the Elephant 971
Ellen, Ellen 3820
Ellen Roe 1076
Elliot Garfield Grant 1633
Ellis Island (Ellis Island,
So Awesome and Cold!) 1609
'Ello England 'Ello 2231
Elmer Gantry 1441, 1172
Elopement, The 284, 3809
Elopement in Elsinore, An (ballet) 325
Eloping 2276
Elsie (1) 1174
Elsie (2) 1174
Elsie in Her Pride 392
Elsie, There Isn't Anybody Else-Y but You 1209
Elusive Mr. Rassendyl, The 4798
Elwood P. Dowd 3846
Emaline 435
Emancipation Day 2111, 4831
Embassy Burglarious, An (The Burglars) 3229
Embassy Waltz (dance) 3038
Embrace Me 1145
Embraceable You 921, 1528, 2872, 1325
Emdudeni (Street Sweepers) 2147
Emelia 2759
Emerald, The 2679
Emerald City Ballet (inst.) 4722
Emerald Isle 687
Emigrants, The 1272, 3348
Emigrants Chorus 3887
Emigrants' Song 3489
Emily, the M.B.A. 4
Eminent Doctor Fizz, The 2315
Emmy Lou 3615
Emmy-Lou, Lafayette and the Football Team 3600
Emperor, The 1605
Emperor and the Nightingale, The 3164
Emperor Hang Chow, The 737
Emperor Is a Man, The 3164
Emperor Jones 3103
Emperor Me, The 3711
Emperor's Bones, The 2259
Emperor's Lot, An 45
Emperor's Own, The 3828
Emperor's Thumb, The 134
Empire Days 2939
Empire Soiree, The 414
Empire Song, The 1161
Empire State Opening 1492
Empire Strikes First, The 3661
Employment Agency, The 4747
Employment Office Dance 3599
Empty 2874
Empty Bed 1149
Empty Bed Blues 2796
Empty Chairs at Empty Tables 2442
Empty Pockets Filled with Love 789, 2983
Empty Space 2616
Empty Wigwam Blues 4316
Empty World of Power 3654
Empty Yourself 757
En Angleterre, Les Demoiselles 453
En Douce 2135
En Locacion 194
Enchanted 2843
Enchanted Castle 1182
Enchanted Isle 1182
Enchanted Train 4001
Enchanting Girls 4798
Enchantment 1300
Encounters (dance) 2368
End, The 1233, 413, 1665
End of a Perfect Night 4583
End of a String, The 2376
End of Aria (from LA SARACENA) 223
End of My Line 4740
End of My Race, The 935
End of Summer 139
End of the Line 3667
End of the News, The 3235
End of the Road, The 2229, 2368
End of the World, The 3261, 4193
Endangered Species, An 4774
Endgame 721
Ending, The 4537
Endless Delights 273
Ends Justify the Means, The 2759
Enduch Allein 93
Enemy of the West 451
Enemy Overture, The 1187
'Enery the Eighth I Am 2388
Engaged 345, 4617, 4617
Engaged in a Sort of Way 4201
Engagement Party, The 2198
Engagement Ring 2371
Engine of Love 4138
England 2027
England Every Time for Me 4158
England Remember 3663
England-The U.K. 1015
English Are Barbarians, The 346
English Bow, The 246
English Breakfast 1857
English Coon Song, An 4181
English Country Life, The 2375
English Daisy, An 1188, 2991
English Favorite, An 1652
English Gentleman, An
(Domestic Discussion, A) 2798
English Gentleman, An 3322
English Girl, An 3856
English Girls 4068

English Language, The 2893
English Lesson 841
English Lido 4341
English Maids 2937
English Rose, The 461, 508
English Sparrow Told Me So, An 2880
English Summer Day, An 1891
English Teacher, An 607
English Way to Die, The 1736
Englishman, The 4713, 453
Englishman in Love, An 1467
Englishman's Head, The 4015
Englishman's Idea of Ragtime, An 3751
Enid 1526
Enough! 2047, 4108
Enough 3337
Enough of Work 3675
Ensemble (1) 168
Ensemble (2) 168
Ensemble 426, 805
Ensemble (1) 1555
Ensemble 1712, 2923, 3525, 4753, 1274
Ensemble Entrance 3915
Ensemble Finale 4816
Ensemble Song 3064
Ensenanza 1327
Enter Hyacinthe 4450
Enter Juliet 1189
Enter Laughing 1190, 1190, 4038, 4038
Enterprise 3806
Enterprising Frenchman, The 1526
Enterprising People 1341
Entire History of the World in Two Minutes and
Thirty-Two Seconds 3941
Entirely Surrounded By Girls 1270
Entr'acte (inst.) 1442
Entr'acte 696
Entrance 3578, 4201
Entrance and Song of Czardas 3078
Entrance Chorus of the Khedive 666
Entrance Lisa 2334
Entrance of American Girls 1246
Entrance of Babette 252
Entrance of Brahmins 2101
Entrance of Bridesmaids 1962
Entrance of Colonel Budd 4201
Entrance of Contrary Mary (inst.) 250
Entrance of Czarinia 3078
Entrance of Dancers 3170, 3218
Entrance of Dolly 2885
Entrance of Duke 582
Entrance of Duke Rodolph 3994
Entrance of Emigrants 4581
Entrance of English Visitors 3828
Entrance of Eric 2252
Entrance of Fascinating Flora 1246
Entrance of Flower Girls 336
Entrance of General Hard Tack 3805
Entrance of Gibson Girls 675
Entrance of Girls 3423
Entrance of Governor 1521
Entrance of Grand Duke 276
Entrance of Hanki-Pank 3943
Entrance of Hans 1743
Entrance of Herr Bangkeyski and the
Piano King 1183
Entrance of Hilda 3673
Entrance of Ilsa 4187
Entrance of Immigrants 2917
Entrance of Johnny Rocks 2848
Entrance of Kafoozelum 2286
Entrance of Kow Tow 2793
Entrance of Lew Fields with Children 3265
Entrance of Lisa 3573
Entrance of Lucky 2638
Entrance of Major Domo and His Shadow 4046
Entrance of Meorema 1417
Entrance of Messenger from Mars 4753
Entrance of Montana 2847
Entrance of Napoleon 1114
Entrance of Orange and Flower Girls 466
Entrance of Prince Ivan 1183
Entrance of Queen Berenike 165
Entrance of Regent 4761
Entrance of Rose (Auction Song) 1111
Entrance of Shah 4293
Entrance of Soubrette 4753
Entrance of Sultan 4201
Entrance of Supreme Court Judges 3225
Entrance of Sylvia 4250
Entrance of the Bath Buns 333
Entrance of the Courtesans 1745
Entrance of the Emperor and the Empress 2622
Entrance of the Forty Thieves (inst.) 50
Entrance of the French Ambassador 3225
Entrance of the Friendly Rival's Club 2885
Entrance of the Hussars 3766
Entrance of the King 2666, 3581
Entrance of the Kings 1817
Entrance of the Rajah 4434
Entrance of the Sailors
(When the Guns Are Booming) 1625
Entrance of the School Children 2534
Entrance of Vivien 1183
Entrance of Widows 3943
Entrance of Yankee Circus 4753
Entrance of Yeomanry 3052
Entrance Picture Buyers 719
Entrance Polonaise (dance) 2731
Entrance Scena 611
Entrance Scene 334
Entrance Song 3774
Entre Act 1148
Entre-Nous 1191
Entre Nous 2605, 3064
Entre-Nous 3990
Entropy 4518
Entry of the Council 2344
Envoy's Duty, An 3585
Ephraham Played Upon the Piano 4805

Epilogue 31, 3628, 23
Epilogue (The Answer) 2229
Epilogue 1265, 1652, 1770, 2650, 3544, 3864, 3955, 4379, 2224
Epilogue in Suede 2001
Epiphany 2775, 4233
Episode in Victor's Play 'The Passionate Pilgrim' 672
Episode of the Swing 3014
Episodes, The 2992
Epistle of Love 2599
Epitaph 2228, 2278
Epitaph, An 2633
Epitaph 3619, 4371
Epitaph for Marina 3909
Equal Rights 3304
Equilib 729
Equine Paradox 4725
Equipment Song 1958
Equitable Distribution Waltz 3600
Erase Him 3201
Erbie Fitch's Twitch 3687
Ere I Wed You 2936
Eric's Gonna Keep Doing 4016
Eric's Hokey Cokey 4016
Erin Slanthogal Go Bragh 1162
Erminie 1193
Ernest Beware 3195
Ernest in Love 1194
Ernestina 1828
Eros, Eros 165
Escamillo 4037
Escape 3944
Escape, The 1262, 2027
Escape 1159
Escape Me Never 3734
Escorte-Moi (Take Me Out to the Ball Game) 1038
Eskimo 47
Eskimo Bacchante 4237
Eskimo Blues 1654
Esmeralda 1735
Espagnola 3567
Espana 4430
Espanita 2122
Espanola Prance 3545
Espanole 2384
Especially for Mr. Winterbottom 3441
Especially in the Dark 2992
Espresso House 1697
Essence 2557
Estelle 4298
Estellita 3590
Esther 4499
Esther, Sonja and Carmen 2969
Et Maintenant 1427
Eternal Sleep 1636
Eternal Stars 3702
Eternal Virgin, The 3825
Eternal Youth Is Worth a Little Suffering 4217
Eternity 1087
Ethel, Baby 2987
Ethel Levey's Smile Song 1584
Ethel Levey's Virginia Song 1480
Ethel's Waltz 3429
Ethics Waltz, The 3549
Ethiopia Ballet (inst.) 295
Ethiopian Essence, An 2465
Ethiopian Pageant 3690
Etiquette 152, 364, 1568, 1746, 1829, 3580, 4478
Etiquette Quintette 3063
Eugene O'Neill's Hairy Ape 3405
Eugenia (inst.) 4390
Eugenic Girls 3397
Eugenic Kiss 1560
Eulalie 2341
Eulogy 2472
Eunuch Scene 2655
Euphemism 1914
Euphoria 2584, 3309
Euranian Anthem 2293
Eureka 1745
Ev'ry Boy in Town's My Sweetheart 403
Ev'ry Day (Comes Something Beautiful) 2064
Ev'ry Day a Holiday 1109
Ev'ry Day Can't Be a Sunday 4730
Ev'ry Day Is Mother's Day 4317
Ev'ry Guest Is in the Room 4212
Ev'ry Hour Brings Its Flower 2914
Ev'ry Little Girl Can Teach Me Something New 4327
Ev'ry One of Us 1035
Ev'ry Other Heartbeat 323
Ev'ry Road Is the Right Road 1173
Ev'ry Sunday Afternoon 1894
Ev'ry Time 372, 4399
Ev'ry Time I See You, Dear 2174
Ev'ry Woman 2839
Ev'rybod-ee Who's Anybod-ee 2252
Ev'rybody Gets Hot 725
Ev'rybody Knows I Love Somebody 3766
Ev'rybody Likes You 656
Ev'rybody Loves a Soldier 106
Ev'rybody Loves My Girl 4821
Ev'rybody Loves You 2068
Ev'rybody Needs Somebody to Love 3571
Ev'rybody's Boppin' 3178
Ev'rybody's Got a Home but Me 3505
Ev'rybody's Gotta Be Somewhere 775
Ev'rything I Love 2453
Ev'rything I've Got 601
Ev'rything That's Gonna Be Has Been 4481
Ev'rytime We Say Goodbye 3893
Eva (Das Fabriksmadel) 1199
Eva Beware of the City 1211
Eva Tanguay's Love Song 457
Eva's Final Broadcast 1211
Eve 170
Eve Cost Adam Just One Bone 545
Evelina 462

Evelyn 3032, 3537
Evelyn, What Do You Say? 834
Evelyn Woods Hoedown 871
Even a Doctor Can Make a Mistake 4401
Even a Miracle Needs a Hand 4471
Even As You and I 1207, 1488
Even for a Horse 693
Even If I Say It Myself 4586
Even Me 4460
Even Then 949
Evenin' 290, 4137
Evening 3277, 1701
Evening Made for Lovers, An 949
Evening News-A Song of Success 1256
Evening Prayers 661
Evening Primrose 1200
Evening Song (Soft Through the Woodland) 1744
Evening Star 82, 638, 2376, 3294
Evening, The 949
Evensong 3070
Ever and Ever Yours 3865
Ever By Your Side 1335
Ever Lovin' Bee 4818, 4819
Ever Since the Movies Learned to Talk 4683
Ever So 2004
Ever-Ready Freddie 2467
Everlasting 2033, 4496
Everlovin' Bee 4817
Evermore and a Day 429
Every After 2143
Every Animal Has Its Mate 2739
Every Baby Is a Sweet Bouquet 3134
Every Bee Has a Bud All His Own 1796
Every Bit of You 1836
Every Blossom I See Reminds Me of You (scene) 4814
Every Body Hands Me a Lemon 3357
Every Body Must Love Someone 2107
Every Cloud Is Silver-Lined 1557
Every Coon 2710
Every Darkey Is a King 2111
Every Day 2333, 1345, 4589
Every Day a Little Death 4067, 2536
Every Day Another Tune 4197
Every Day, Every Night 949
Every Day for Four Years 564
Every Day in Every Way 582
Every Day Is a Challenge Sweet 3880
Every Day Is a Holiday 596
Every Day Is Christmas When You're Married 2922
Every Day Is Ladies' Day with Me 3675
Every Day Is Night 424
Every Day Will Be a Happy Day 2896
Every Days 3711
Every Dog Must Have His Day and Every Puss Her Afternoon 4414
Every Eve 2103
Every Father 459
Every Fellow Loves a Pretty Girl 697
Every Fellow Wants Someone to Love 2282
Every Fellow Wants to Love Me 2025
Every Flower Has a Melody 2619, 4206
Every Girl 1625
Every Girl Has a Way (Every Girl Has a Method of Her Own) 977
Every Girl I Meet 2317
Every Girl in All America 4422
Every Girl Is Doing Her Bit 4837
Every Girl Is Doing Her Bit Today 1208
Every Girl Is Fishing 4835
Every Girl Is Like a Weather Glass 3312
Every Girl Loves a Uniform 4452
Every Girl Must Have a Little Bull 1460
Every Girl Wants to Get Married 1237
Every Girl's a Soldier in the Army of Love 1183
Every Girlie Loves Me but the Girl I Love 1558
Every Girlie Wants to Be a Sally 2193, 4033
Every Goodbye Is Hello 2224
Every Heart Has a Dream 3420
Every Hour Away from You Is Sixty Minutes Lost 3319
Every Inch a Lady 4130
Every Little Dog Must Have His Day 3267
Every Little Girl Has a Way of Her Own 1270
Every Little Miss 2461
Every Little Moment 2976
Every Little Movement 2667
Every Little Note 2833
Every Little Nothing 2522
Every Little Object Has a History 2716
Every Little Something 1515
Every Little Thing You Do 3179
Every Little While (1) 1588
Every Little While (2) 1588
Every Little While 4357
Every Log in My House 3631
Every Lover Must Meet His Fate 4250
Every Man for Himself 483
Every Man Is a Stupid Man 629
Every Month Is May 3012
Every Mother's Lullaby 4079
Every Movie's a Circus 4217
Every Nation Has a Broadway of Its Own 598
Every Nation Has a Flower 4509
Every National Hymn Is Just a Rag-Time Tune 4453
Every New Beginning 1064
Every Night 1242, 3913
Every Now and Then 3806
Every Once in a While 1029
Every One Is Beautiful in Someone's Eyes 4208
Every Other Saturday Night 1086
Every Pretty Girl 4382
Every Road 2984
Every Saturday Afternoon 3882
Every Shade of Blue 2490
Every Silken Lady 4424
Every Silver Lining 3623
Every Star Falls in Love with Its Mate 3220
Every Street's a Boulevard in Old New York 1791
Every Telephone (Telephone Song) 4831
Every Thing Happens to Me 2458

Every Thursday Night 3666
Every Time I Hear a Band Play 4815
Every Time I Look at You 3921
Every Time I Meet a Lady 2767
Every Time I'm with You 382
Every Time the Clock Ticks 4424
Every Time the Music Starts 3019
Every Time You Dance with Me 3913
Every Woman Brings Something with Her 2243
Every Woman Is a Queen 1369
Every Woman's Got a Man but Me 552
Every Year Is a Leap Year 1707
Everybody Calls Me By My Name 3231
Everybody Dance 3407
Every-body Dance 4809
Everybody Else's Girl but Mine 61
Everybody Else's Girl Looks Better to Me Than Mine 3567
Everybody Gets It in the End 1500
Everybody Has a Tip 2299
Everybody Has His Own Way 4788
Everybody Has the Right to Be Wrong 4013, 4743
Everybody Hum with Me 3799
Everybody in the Town Is Sober Since My Cellar Went Dry 4626
Everybody Is a Star 3739
Everybody Is Bagpipe Crazy 4521
Everybody Knows It but Her Husband 68
Everybody Knows Madame Moselle 2665
Everybody Knows What Jazz Is 4819
Everybody Leaves You 1063
Everybody Likes a College Girl 1247
Everybody Loves 390
Everybody Loves a Chicken 558, 822
Everybody Loves a Hero 211
Everybody Loves a Single Girl 1002
Everybody Loves a Tree 2661
Everybody Loves a Winner 302, 1227
Everybody Loves Everybody 4718, 3383
Everybody Loves Leona 1060
Everybody Loves Louis 4210
Everybody Loves Me Up in London 1454
Everybody Loves My Baby 393, 432, 1813, 3297
Everybody Loves My Girl 1215
Everybody Loves to Take a Bow 1791
Everybody Means It When They Say Good-Bye 4657
Everybody Must Be Happy 4046
Everybody Needs Someone to Hold Them Tight 2728
Everybody Ought to Have a Gun 4635
Everybody Ought to Have a Maid 4067, 1422
Everybody Ought to Know 3987
Everybody Ought to Know How to Do the Tickle Toe 1598
Everybody Out the Castle Is Sinking 1205
Everybody Rag with Me 965
Everybody Rejoice (Brand New Day) 4722
Everybody Says Don't 162, 3967
Everybody Shimmies Now 395
Everybody Shout 3660
Everybody Sometime Must Love Somebody 4807
Everybody Sometime Must Love Someone 4642
Everybody Sometimes Must Love Someone 2730
Everybody Step 789, 3006
Everybody Swat the Profiteer 1483
Everybody Tells It to Sweeney 4814
Everybody Today Is Turning On 2058
Everybody Two-Step 2644
Everybody Wants a Key to My Cellar 4813
Everybody Wants to Be a Movie Star 2969
Everybody Wants to Be in Show Business 673, 2742
Everybody Wants to Be Loved 3484
Everybody Wants to be Remembered 2657
Everybody Wants to Do a Musical 3142
Everybody Wants to Get into the Act 4602
Everybody Wants to See the Baby 4697, 2213
Everybody Who's Anybody 2541
Everybody Wondered Why He Knew 2714
Everybody Wonders Why They Married 1606
Everybody's Awfully Good to Me 4430
Everybody's Crazy Half of the Time 136
Everybody's Crazy Over Dixie 1032
Everybody's Doin' the Charleston Now 2942
Everybody's Doing It 1649, 4108
Everybody's Doing the Disco 4192
Everybody's Favorite City 1605
Everybody's Gone to California 1770
Everybody's Got a Guy but I 2439
Everybody's Got a Pitch 2173
Everybody's Got Somebody but Me (Ev'rybody but Me) 2214
Everybody's Got Something 4162
Everybody's Got the Right 212
Everybody's Happy in Jimtown 2302
Everybody's Happy in Vienna 968
Everybody's Happy When the Sun Shines 2964
Everybody's Loved by Someone 2964
Everybody's Mad 52
Everybody's Making It Now 4816
Everybody's Rag Time Crazy 2119
Everybody's Running 4089
Everybody's Struttin' Now 1174
Everybody's Talking 3739
Everybody's Tango Crazy 3877
Everyday 580
Everyday Blues 2026
Everyday I Do a Little Something for the Lord 3305
Everyday Will Be Sunday When the Town Goes Dry 1580
Everyone Celebrate 577
Everyone Complains About the Weather 616
Everyone Has a Right to Love 3670
Everyone Has Something to Hide 278, 2777
Everyone Hates His Parents 1234
Everyone He Swear at the Waiter 1794
Everyone Here Loves Kelly 2304
Everyone in the World Is Doing the Charleston 799
Everyone Is in Slumberland but You and Me 3068
Everyone Knows 2097
Everyone Looks Lonely 3542
Everyone Should Play a Musical Instrument 1581
Everyone Starts to Dance 796

Everyone Tells Jason to See a Psychiatrist 2746
Everyone Who's 'Who's Who' 1760
Everyone's a Good American 3026
Everyone's Moving Up Town (Everyone's Moving Up on Broadway) 2696
Everyone's Wrong but Me 1658
Everythin' Is Tinglin' 3939
Everything 2542, 3780, 4114
Everything Beautiful 2449, 4764
Everything Beautiful Happens at Night 3294
Everything but My Man 3907
Everything Changes but Love 3011
Everything Comes to Those Who Wait 1319, 2897
Everything Depends on Money 2978
Everything Finds Its Way to Paris 2715
Everything for Roz 3124
Everything Happens for the Best 708, 1974
Everything Happens to Me 4586
Everything Has a Time 3631
Everything Has Been Done 2794
Everything Has Stung Me But a Bee 1552
Everything I Do Goes Wrong 1992
Everything I Do Is News 3667
Everything I Said Was True 595
Everything I Want 2053
Everything I've Always Wanted 3793
Everything I've Got 4399
Everything in America Is Ragtime 4158
Everything in the World Has a Place 1045
Everything in the World I Love 4764
Everything Is All Right 2723, 4694
Everything Is Alright, Uptight 166
Everything Is Big in Chicago 4713
Everything Is Changed 2033
Everything Is Coming Rosie's Way 2519
Everything Is Going Higher 4053
Everything Is High Yellow Now 3137
Everything Is Higher Nowadays 4666
Everything Is Hunky Dory Down in Honky Tonk Town 1208
Everything Is Lovely in the Morning 1601
Everything Is Only for a Little While 2243
Everything Is Possible 3088
Everything Is Possible in Life 3559
Everything Is Rosy Now 1335
Everything Is Wonderful 4623
Everything Leads Right Back to Love 304
Everything Looks Rosy and Bright 4742
Everything Needs a Something 2368
Everything Reminds Me of You 1467, 3963
Everything Seems Funny to Me 830
Everything Serves Its Purpose 3463
Everything That Father Did Was Right 3579
Everything That Goes Around Comes Around 4108
Everything that Happens to You 518
Everything That He Does 1887
Everything That Touches You 3690
Everything That's Yours Is Mine 197
Everything Under the Sun 2283
Everything Was Perfect 699
Everything Will Be All Right 3508
Everything Will Happen for the Best 3622
Everything You Are 4244
Everything You Hate Is Right Here 4468
Everything You Wrote 949
Everything's All Right 3925
Everything's Alright 2212
Everything's at Home Except Your Wife 3251
Everything's Changed 158
Everything's Coming Up Roses 1709
Everything's Easy When You Know How 2163
Everything's Fair When You're in Love 3026
Everything's Fine 147
Everything's Going to Be All Right 2818
Everything's Gonna Be Much Worse Next Year 90
Everything's Great 602, 1601
Everything's Just Divine 3491
Everything's Like a Picnic 2641
Everything's New in Old New York 2094
Everytime 1689
Everytime I Dance the Polka 3064
Everytime I Look I See a Stranger 2243
Everytime I Think of You 2193
Everytime We Call It Quits 105
Everywhere 4510
Everywhere I Go 3476
Evil 1636, 3112
Evil Bumble Bee 4127
Evil Eye 1515
Evil Weasel 4701
Eviva 3063
Evocation 2236
Evoe! (Hymn to Dionysos) 1406
Evoe for the Dead 1406
Evolution 632, 1318
Evolution of a Rag 1735
Evolution of Rag Time, The 2493
Evolution of Ragtime 2964
Evolution Papa 1063
Ex-Foreman 919
Ex-Gigolo 4545
Exactly Like a Man 1360
Exactly Like Me 2558
Exactly Like You 2140, 4197
Exactly the Same as It Was 690
Examination, The 54
Examination Song, or Get Me on That Boat, The 1256
Exanaplanatooch 1717
Excelsior 2433, 1213
Except of Course Men 1201
Exception and the Rule, The 1214
Exchange for Lovers 3536
Exchanges of Information 3233
Excursion 2940
Excuse Me 4422
Excuse Me Baby, Please If You Don't Mind Baby, Thank You 3836
Excuse Me? Certainly! 2922
Excuse Me Mr. Moon 2528

Excuse My Dust 567, 1132
Excuse My Laughter 1745
Excuse of Song and Dance 2423
Execution of Prince Eagle 4738
Exercise 1992, 2467, 3547
Exhibit "A" 3843
Exhibition Dance (inst.) 2187
Exhortation 295, 2302
Existential 2284
Exit 526
Exit of Lady Volumnia 4046
Exits 3039
Exits and Entrances 669
Exodus, The 181
Exodus 181
Exodus of Children 3487
Exodus Song, The (inst.) 3261
Exorcism, The (dance) 1891
Exorcism Revisited, The 1891
Expect a Miracle 3568
Expect Things to Happen 1860
Expectant Father Dance (inst.) 4366
Experience 383, 2498, 1549
Experience Fox-Trot, The 1218
Experience One-Step, The 1218
Experiment, The 31
Experiment 3214
Experts 1700
Explanations 4269
Explorers and Angels 3463
Expose, The 1695
Exposition 4319
Express 4534
Express Yo-self 1221
Express Yourself 1310
Expulsion, The 730
Exquisite 3415
Exquisite Moment 3011
Exquisite Moments 2947
Exquisite Passions 2177
Extenuatin' Circumstances 664
Extra! 1588
Extra! Extra! 1817
Extra, Extra! 2894
Extra! Extra! 3266, 4516
Extra Man, The 3131, 4581
Extracurrickeler Girl 1862
Extraordinary 3506, 3823
Extraordinary Girl 1341
Extravaganza 1619
Eye of the Storm 496
Eye That Never Sleeps, The 558
Eyeful of You 4668
Eyes 3158, 1549
Eyes, Eyes 558
Eyes, Eyes, Eyes 2869
Eyes Have a Language of Their Own 379
Eyes Like a Stranger 2961
Eyes Look Your Last 1717
Eyes of Black and Eyes of Blue 4559
Eyes of Blue 25
Eyes of Egypt, The 1684
Eyes of Love 293
Eyes of the Army 4421
Eyes of the Girl I Love 3057
Eyes of the Girl I Love, The 1962
Eyes of the Girl You Love, The 2385
Eyes of Youth 2527
Eyes of Youth See the Truth, The 805
Eyes Right! Here's a Girlie 2854
Eyes So Dark and Luring 4760
Eyes So Tender 2293
Eyes That Are Smiling 4550
Eyes that Come from Ireland 1163
Eyes That Come from Ireland 3642
Eyes That Haunt Me 3078
Eyes That Love 2602
Eyesight to the Blind 4676
Ezekiel Saw the Wheel 2203

F

F-A-M-E 115
F-A-S-H-I-O-N 2774
F.F. (Forbidden Fruit) 1227, 2073
F. Jasmine Addams 1222
F.P.A. 1357
F.U.N.E.X. 700
Fa La 1171
Fa La La, Fa, Fa La La 1860
Fable for Two, A 453
Fable of the Cable Car, The 1884
Fables (Don't Believe Their Fables) 1378
Fables for Our Time 322
Fabric of Dreams 3144
Fabulous 2234
Fabulous Feet 4286
Fabulous You 4415
Facade 2198
Face, The 2535
Face Behind the Mask, The 1016
Face in the Crowd, The 3
Face in the Crowd, A 3381
Face Lifting 3591
Face of Love, The 1761
Face of the Girl I Love 47
Face of the Girl You Love, The 2159
Face on the Dime, The 620
Face the Fact 4462
Face the Facts 4629
Face the Music 4147
Face to Face 623, 2618, 4853
Face to Face Meeting, A 2421
Faces 2969, 3400
Faces in a Crowd 4192
Faces, Names and Places 4089
Faces Without Names 1002
Fact Can Be a Beautiful Thing, A 3603

Factory Ballet (dance) 4237
Facts, The 148
Facts 1702, 3661
Facts and Figures 1648
Facts of Life 2637
Facts of Life Backstage, The 1711
Fade Away 1903
Fade Out-Fade In 1227
Faded Flowers 1692
Faded Rose, A 3650
Faded Rose 1209
Fading Girl 965
Fads 1264
Failure 3763
Faint Heart Ne'er Won Fair Lady 4687
Fainting Ensemble 3921
Fair and Warmer Cocktail, The 804
Fair Colonus 1636
Fair Dissenter Lass, The 2633
Fair Enough 953
Fair Flower of Japan 4452
Fair Honeymoon Shine On 4547
Fair India 2571
Fair Is Fair 3128
Fair Lady 466
Fair Land of Dreaming 2622
Fair Men, Square Men 451
Fair Moon 1948
Fair One 870, 1426
Fair Plymouth Maiden 912
Fair Rosita 3117
Fair Senorita of the Argentine 792
Fair Sex, The 4323
Fair Trade 2064
Fair Warning 483, 1029
Fair Weather 4741
Fair Weather Friends 1112, 2950
Fair Women of England 333
Fairest Maiden 762
Fairest of Roses 4497
Fairest of the Fair 470
Fairfield Country 167
Fairies Chorus 1912
Fairies, Fairies, Come Forth 3588
Fairies in My Mother's Flower Garden 3641
Fairies Rule the World 3765
Fairies We 4014
Fairies' Lullaby 350
Fairies' Meeting, The 3422
Fairies' Revel 4649
Fairlight Glen 1262
Fairly Fresh 413
Fairy Beauty's Queen 355
Fairy Bells 4285
Fairy Boat, A 1095
Fairy Dance 764
Fairy Music 2394
Fairy Prince 1610
Fairy Song 1852
Fairy Tale, A 690
Fairy Tale 1935
Fairy Tale, A 2453
Fairy Tales 263
Fairy Tales (Cinderella Tale) 579
Fairy Tales 1164, 2101, 2298, 3555
Fairy Tales Are All Untrue 2504
Fairy Whispers 2412
Fairyland 656, 2035, 3163, 4646, 158
Fairylands (scene) 4816
Faith 1878, 2053
Faith, Hope and Charity 3923, 4467
Faith in Myself 1103
Faith Is Such a Simple Thing 2220
Faithful Crew, The 402
Faithless 404
Fake It 2026
Fake Your Way to the Top 1103
Fakir Man, The 1469
Falcon, The 3774
Falena 2235
Fall In! 3578
Fall of Babylon, The 1611
Fall of Man, The 3727
Fall of the Leaves, The 2843
Fall of Valor, The 4696
Fall River Folly 943
Fallen Angel 1232
Fallen Angels 4689
Fallin' 4334
Fallin'-Out-of-Love Rag, The 1380
Falling 211, 4031, 3966
Falling for You 2275
Falling in Love 742, 796, 1232, 3965, 4335
Falling in Love with Love 514, 4519
Falling Leaves Ballet (inst.) 2900
Falling Off the Wagon 289
Falling Out of Love 4025
Falling Out of Love Can Be Fun 2894
Falling Rain-Dream of You 2850
Falling Star 1450, 3648, 1337
Falling Stars 4803
Falling Through Life 2305
Falling Too Far 181
Fallout Shelter 4433
Falsettoland 1234
Fam'ly We Will Be, A 2064
Fame 3764
Fame! 3988
Fame, Fame, Fame 4634
Fame Is a Phony 82
Family 4399, 690, 1103, 198, 3835
Family Affair, A 871, 1237, 3124
Family Brawl, The 1088
Family Council, The 4616
Family Cycle Car 2454
Family Faces 2385
Family Fallout Shelter 1363
Family Fan, The 717
Family Farewell 1358
Family Fugue 4160

Family Ghost, The 3951
Family Grace 3339
Family Jewels 4437
Family Moulton-Barrett, The 3734
Family of Man 2728
Family Plan, The 2876
Family Solicitor, The 2798
Family Ties 2702
Family Tree 1257
Family Tree, The 2148
Family Tree 3067
Family Tree, The 3519
Family Trouble 3940
Family Way, The 2048
Family's Ancient Tree, The 4590
Famine 1769
Famous Falls 2686
Famous Feet 1000
Famous People of the Week 3441
Famous Rabbi, The 4514
Famous You and Simple Me 4378
Fan Club Chant 4542
Fan Intro 2969
Fan Me with a Movement Slow 2334
Fan Number 2135
Fan Tan Fannie 1315
Fan the Flame 3863
Fancies, Only Fancies 104
Fancy Dress 3313
Fancy, Fancy 213
Fancy Forgetting 507
Fancy Me Just Meeting You 1916, 3117
Fancy Meeting You Here 2646
Fancy Our Meeting 4320, 4581
Fancy You Fancying Me 3222
Fandango 784
Fandango Dance 4823
Fandango Rag 4804
Fannette 2188
Fanny 1242, 1242
Fans 3150
Fantana Song 1243
Fantasie 2216
Fantastic Dance 3265
Fantasy 1371, 2993, 3434, 4679
Far Above You Is My Throne 1682
Far Apart, You're Still in My Heart 3246
Far Away 455, 2432, 4077
Far Away and Long Ago 4669
Far Away Island 4243
Far, Far Away 870
Far Far Away 2728
Far, Far Away (Memories, Fond and True) 2745
Far Far Better Way, A 1991
Far, Far, Far Away 3526
Far, Far from Wipers 3259
Far From Home 4384
Far from the Home I Love 1265
Far Mir Alayn 2356
Far Off Lights 1969
Far Off Village 3630
Far, Oh Far Is the Mango Island 1083
Far Rockaway 2322
Far Up the Hill 2670
Faraway Boy 1698
Faraway Love 4199
Fare Thee Well 130, 1002
Fare-Thee-Well, The 1086
Fare Thee Well 2796, 4620, 813
Fare You Well 1474
Farewell (Aloha Oe) 422
Farewell 1027, 1098, 1422
Farewell (Letter Song) 1663
Farewell 2286, 2698, 3484, 762, 3835, 4635
Farewell, Dear 4188
Farewell, Dear Toys (March of the Toys) (inst.) 246
Farewell, Dear Toys (inst.) 248
Farewell Duet 4169
Farewell, Farewell 1729
Farewell First Amendment 4635
Farewell, Fond Dreams of Love 1521
Farewell, Fondest and Dearest 45
Farewell for a While 971, 4287
Farewell, Goodbye 2228
Farewell, I Go, It Must Be So 4554
Farewell Letter 3411, 2610
Farewell, Little Dream, Goodbye 2568
Farewell Love 3765
Farewell, Me Butty 2268
Farewell Music 530
Farewell, My Belle 1518
Farewell, My Life's True Love 4617
Farewell, My Lovely 216
Farewell My Lovely 320
Farewell My Own 1948, 2817
Farewell Prosperity 41, 2716
Farewell Song, The 4082
Farewell Song 1903
Farewell Tango 4368
Farewell, Time to Go 3907
Farewell to Adrian 2384
Farewell to Auld Lang Syne 705
Farewell to Dreams 4251
Farewell to Love 4218
Farewell to New York 1048
Farewell to Rudolph 3595
Farewell to the Flag 2126
Farewell to the Forest 2697
Farewell to the King's Highway 1896
Farewell Waltz, The 1243
Farewell Waltz 205
Farewell with Love 3966
Farewells, The 2067
Farijandis (scene) 4816
Farmer 3690
Farmer and the Cowman, The 3263
Farmer and the Scarecrow, The 1896
Farmer Jacob 4188
Farmer Tan 3608
Farmerettes, The 1404

Farmer's Daughter 462, 858
Farmer's Daughters 2897
Farmer's Life, A 1095, 2622
Farmers Market Hoe Down 3046
Farmer's Wife, The 911
Farming 1018, 2453, 4517
Farming Life-Country Life 3996
Farrell Girl, The 67
Fas' Fas' World 295
Fascinating Females 3865
Fascinating Girl 4712
Fascinating Lady 3148
Fascinating Rhythm 2376, 3020
Fascinating Venus 4311
Fascinating Widow, The 1247
Fascinating You 1126
Fascination 1177, 4747
Fascination Waltz 1835
Fashion 1900
Fashion Girl, A 1973
Fashion Parade, The 765
Fashion Parade 2813
Fashion Plates, The 108
Fashion Show, The 1065, 2477, 4555
Fashion Waltz 3958
Fashions 3215
Fashion's Slave, A 965
Fast and Furious 1251
Fast Cars and Fightin' Women 4090
Fast Colors (inst.) 2161
Fast Food 3548
Fast Step Creation, A 1962
Fast Steppers 2939, 3737
Fasten Your Seat Belts 167
Faster and Faster 4325, 3401
Faster Than Sound 1891, 4827
Fastest Man in New York 4704
Fastrigossa's Lament 2811
Fat and Forte 4091
Fat and Greasy 39
Fat City 2618
Fat-Fat-Fatima 2601
Fat, Fat, the Water Rat 4169
Fat Luigi 1108
Fat Song, The 2913
Fat Tuesday Parade 4162
Fatal Blonde 4373
Fatal Curse of Beauty 4544
Fatal Fascination 1322
Fatal Step 1557
Fatality Hop, The 583
Fate 1016, 1453
Fate (It Was Fate when I First Met You) 1687
Fate 2327
Fate, The 3951
Fate 4383
Fate Is Such a Mystic Puzzle 3592
Fate of the Sailor, The 2711
Fate of the Veiled Mugs 2979
Father 3088, 4064
Father and Son 1418, 2923, 4337
Father, Dear Father, Stop Testing 3530
Father Divine 447
Father, Father 459
Father Is a Business Man 1743
Father Keeps on Doing It 3134
Father Knickerbocker Fox Trot 3401
Father Never Raised Any Foolish Children 1565
Father Nile, Keep Us in Thy Care 4724
Father Now, A 4349
Father of Claudine, The 808, 809
Father of Fathers 784
Father of the Bride, The 2050
Father Penn 185
Father Said 3507
Father Speaks, A 4401
Father Thames 1467
Father to Son 2746
Father Wants the Cradle Back 3068
Father Will Be with Us Soon 231
Father William 52
Father, Won't You Speak to Sister Mary? 4165
Father's Always Talking in His Sleep 2159
Father's Argument/Aucassin's Reply 1262
Father's Daughter 298
Father's Day 206, 2289
Father's Pride and Joy, A 1080
Father's Song 2478
Father's Waltz 169
Father's Whiskers 3729
Fatherhood Blues 253
Fatherland Is Free, The 742
Fatherland, Mother of the Band (Drink, Drink, Drink) 3379
Fathers and Mothers (And You and Me) 2033
Fathers and Sons 430, 4744
Fathers of the World 1490
Fathers that Wear Rags 3909
Fatima the Fair 3348
Fattening Frogs for Snakes 3657
Fatty 116, 135
Faucett Falls Fancy 823
Faust Finale 3463
Faust Up to Date 3525
Favorite at Maxim's, A 116
Favorite Son 4695, 2783
Favorite Song 595
Favorite Sons 1038
Fear 1227
Fear! 2591
Fear in My Heart 3365
Fear No More 1406
Fear No More the Heat of the Sun 3909
Fearfully, Frightful Love 4793
Fearless Frank 1256
Fearless Waltz, The 3395
Feast of the Lanterns 718
Feast on Me 1074
Feather in a Breeze 1207
Feather in My Shoe 823

Feather Your Nest 2491, 2721
Feathered Friends 427
Feathers 4830
Feathertop 1257, 1258
Feats of Piper 3487
February 2379
Fede, Fede 2142
Fee Fi Fo Fum 2182
Fee, Fi, Fo, Fum 1975
Fee Fi Fo Fum 2134
Fee-Fie-Fo-Fum 4569
Feed Me with Love 3613
Feeding the Chickens 2888
Feeding Time 223
Feel at Home 3619
Feel Free 2483
Feel Like Waltzing 1435
Feel That Jazz 4162
Feel the Beat 1732
Feel the Love 2074
Feelin' Good 3648
Feelin' Loved 135
Feeling Good 3731
Feeling I'm Falling 4443
Feeling in My Chest, A 1169
Feeling in the Air 108
Feeling in Your Heart, A 2829
Feeling Rich 3757
Feeling Sentimental 3953
Feeling We Once Had, The 4722
Feeling Wonderful 3236
Feelings 170
Fees and Dues 3344
Feet 3439
Feet, The 4533
Feet Do Yo' Stuff 1729
Feet Don't Fail Me Now 1890
Feet, Get Movin' 42
Feet on the Sidewalk (Head in the Sky) 3036
Feign a Faint, Ladies 3920
Felicita 139
Feline Wisdom 1871
Fellas Kiss Their Dads 2965
Fellatio 101 2451
Feller from Indiana 2137
(It Seems There Was a) Fellow and a Girl, A 2809
Fellow and a Girl, A 2809
Fellow Like Me Likes a Girl Like You, A 3042
Fellow Needs a Girl, A 85
Fellow Who Might Be Galloping, The 1313
Fellowship 1047
Female Chorus of Muleteers 4032
Female Drummer, A 1259
Feminine Companionship 273
Feminine-inity 4678
Femininity 3234
Femme du Monde 807
Femme Du Monde 3542
Femme Fatale 2201, 2318
Femmes Fatales 2364
Fence, The 1865
Fencing 4817
Fencing Girl, The 2506, 2893
Fencing Girls, The 4801
Fender Mender 3275
Fenwick 1261
Ferban Waltz 1544
Fergus' Dilemma 2820
Ferhuddled and Ferhexed 600
Fernando's Suicide 3456
Fertility Dance 4623
Festa (dance) 3543
Festina Lente 4404
Festival of Mourning 2793
Festival of Roses, The 2673
Festivals 392
Festive Continong, The 1540
Festive March (inst.) 4798
Festive Nights 2939
Festudo 1386
Fetch Yo' Baby Home 1264
Fetish (dance) 2355
Feudin' and Fightin' 2400
Fever 3428
Few Fast Steppers, A 2135
Few Get Through, A 2285
Few Small Tasks, A 3549
Fiasco 798
Fickle Finger of Fate, The 2053
Fickle Fortune 178
Fickle Weather Vane, The 2848
Fiction Writer 572
Fiction Writer Duet 572
Fiddle About 4676
Fiddle and I 3154, 604
Fiddle Dee Dee 1871
Fiddle-Dee-Dee March 1264
Fiddler and the Fighter, The 1227
Fiddler Must Be Paid, The 1746
Fiddler on the Roof 1265
"Fiddler on the Roof medley" 3018
Fiddler on the Roof selections 2205
Fiddler's Tune, The 259
Fiddlers Three 1266
Fiddlers' Green, The 406
Fidelity 2837
Fidgety Feet 69, 3243
Fie, Fie, Fie 632
Fie On Goodness 623
Field and Forest, The 3578
Field By Field 4055
Field Hollers and Work Songs 344
Fiesta 1065, 1979, 2602, 3716, 4796
Fiesta in Madrid, The 4021
Fiesta in Spain 190
Fifi 2083
Fifteen Glorious Years 3445
Fifteen Minutes 3348
Fifteen Minutes a Day 2034, 3042
Fifth Army's Where My Heart Is, The 4340

Fifth Avenue 95, 4747
Fifth Avenue Brigade, The 4364
Fifth from the Right, The 275
Fifth Season, The 1269, 1269
50's, The 3873
Fifty Cents 3577
Fifty, Fifty 1609
Fifty-Fifty 573, 4390
55 Cities in 62 Days 3752
Fifty Great Places All in One Place 107
Fifty Million Years Ago 681, 3542
Fifty Percent 287
Fifty-Seven Ways to Win a Man 4553
Fifty Years Ago 3203
Fifty Years of Making People Laugh 4577
Fig Leaf Number 684
Fig Leaves Are Falling, The 1273
Figaro's Aria 4342
Fight, The 302, 1601
Fight Duet, The 3355
Fight Fiercely, Harvard 4412
Fight for the Man 4090
Fight Over Me 3184, 664
Fight Sequence 3576
Fight Song, The 64
Fight to the Death 3197
Fighting for Pharoah 1072
Fighting for U.S.A. 2711
Fighting Kid, The 3855
Fighting Regiment, The 2139
Fights, The 411, 1341, 413, 412
Fights and Assignations 1750
Fiji 830, 2939
Fiji Fanny 4467
Fiji Island Ballet (inst.) 467
Filibuster 3530
Filibuster Brown 1783
Fill 'Er Up 490, 4635
Fill, Fill, Fill Our Little Basket 2681
Fill High! Drink Deep! 45
Fill in the Words 4334
Fill It to the Top 1903
Fill the Cup 1056
Fill Up the Cup 1439
Fill Up Your Life with Sunshine 3835
Filling Station, The 4030
Filmzauber 1561
Fils a Papa 1553
Filth 534
Filthy Rich 42
Fin de Sickle 4292
Fin de Siecle 4234
Final Choral Blessing 1977
Final Judgement 169
Final Report 2472
Final Selection 4138
Final Sequence 3272, 4233
Final Storm 3862
Finally 2754, 4312
Financial Status 2944
Financial Viking, The 1530
Find a Girl 4476
Find a Good Time 4010
Find a Way 1108
Find Him and Bring Him Home 2643
Find Me 426
Find Me a Body 838
Find Me a Hero 3806
Find Me a Primitive Man 1018, 1272, 1762, 3020, 4799
Find My Way Alone 280
Find My Way Home 4459
Find Out What They Like 39
Find Someone to Love 2616
Find the Foot 4461
Find the Map 3485
Find Your Own Cricket 2626, 2627
Find Yourself a Man 1420
Find Yourself Something to Do 3818
Finder Please Return 1467
Finders Is Keepers (and I Found You) 4393
Finding a Place 1997
Finding the Door 3463
Finding Words for Spring 270
Fine 823
Fine and Dandy 1275
Fine and Private Place, A 1276
Fine Art of Schnorring, The 2320
Fine Art of Treachery, The 2933
Fine Feathers 1065, 1129, 1461, 2870
Fine Feathers Make Fine Birds 4818
Fine for the Shape I'm In 4272
Fine Guy, A 3258
Fine Romance, A 2204, 2372
Fine, Thank You, Fine 823
Fine White Horse, A 3862
Fine Words and Fancy Phrases 239
Fine Young Man, A 134
Finer Things of Life, The 4750
Finery 2747
Finesse 2966
Finest Ever Is the Military Beau, The 306
Finest of the Finest, The 1419
Finest Thing in the Country, The 3866
Finger Song, The 3602
Fingers and Toes 135
Fings Ain't Wot They Used T'Be 1277
Fini 2227
Finishing School 4180
Finishing the Hat 4210
Finishing with an Affair 1439
Finnegan 4589
Finnegan and His Flute 191
Finnegan's Wake 790
Fioretta 1281
Fire 2146
Fire and Brimstone 1809
Fire and Ice 1649
Fire Belles 3096
Fire Belles' Gallop 1286

Fire Cracker 3404
Fire-Fly Dance 49
Fire Ladies' Ball, The 3096
Fireflies 3944, 937, 973
Firefly, The 1174
Firefly 2174, 3729
Firefly, The 4738
Firefly 1708
Firefly and the Rose, The 246
Firefly Ballet (inst.) 559
Fireman's Ball 1604
Fireman's Bride, The 4524
Fireman's Flame, The 1286
Fireman's Parade, The 1148
Fireman's Song 1064
Firemen's Quartet 2375
Fireside, a Pipe and a Pet, A 3641
Fireside Dreams 3344
Firestorm Consuming Indianapolis, A 1591
Fireworks 1061, 3016, 4426
Fireworks, The 4479
Fireworks Gallop 3151
First, The 1289
First Act Crisis 2918
First Act Finale 621, 4173
First and Only 4387
First Blossom, The (ballet) 4077
First Born 3599
First Bouquet 3064
First Campaign Song 3684
First Chanukah Night, The 4790
First Christmas, The 928
First Class All the Way 4732
First Class Number One Bum 2583
First Class Private Mary Brown 7, 3460
First Dance, The 3618
First Day of May, The 3230
First Final 4138
First Finale 4368
First Gray Hair 375
First I Propose 4707
First Impression 3453
First Impressions 2539, 3501
First Is Last, The 1314
First Jam Session, The 3830
First Kid on the Block 140
First Kiss, The 1521, 3763
First Kiss of Love, The 670
First Lady, The 2983
First Lady and First Gent 2444
First Lady of the Land, The 3946
First, Last and Always 3405
First, Last, and Only 3655
First Lesson, The 910
First Let's Kill All the Lawyers 3600
First Letter 3411
First Letter Home 4068
First Love 4731, 1292, 2610, 2614
First Love (Is the Best Love of All) 3399
First Love 3848, 2611
First Love Days 3096
First Man I Kiss, The 3117
First Man You Remember, The 211
First March (inst.) 1385
First Mate Martin 4234
First Midnight 2143
First Night 2187
First Nighters 4742
First Nighters, The 3369
First Ones There 2876
First Prize at the Fair 2137
First Quarter 3619
First Rose of Summer 611
First Rose of Summer, The 3923
First Snow of Winter, The 197
First Snow of Winter 858
First Spring Day, The 4291
First Step, The 4200
First Submarine Boat, The 1374
First Sunbeam 3584
First There Was a Fletcher 4179
First Thing About You, The 4643
First Thing in the Morning 439
First Thing Monday Mornin' 3610
First Things First 4312
First 3 Penny Finale 4371
First Threepenny Finale 4370
First Time I Heard a Bluebird, The 518
First Time I Saw You 2195
First Time I Spoke of You, The 3801
First Time, The 4862
First to Know Ireland, The 1171
First to Walk Away 2783
First Touch of Autumn, The 1082
First Toymaker to the King 3833
First Up Is the Best Dressed, The 4154
First We Throw Moe Out (Finaletto Act II) 376
First Weekend in July, The 1333
Fish 347, 2366
Fish, The 453
Fish Chorus 3337
Fish Go Higher than Tigers 4048
Fish 'n' Chips 928
Fish Scales 3498
Fish Song 3938
Fish Soup Song 3764
Fisher and the Mermaid, The 4161
Fisherman's Prayer 3608
Fisherman's Wharf 3813
Fishing 632, 1458, 2334, 2493, 2756, 3399, 1562, 4509, 4666
Fishing Fleet, The 3429
Fishing Fleet Is Homeward Bound 335
Fishing Is an Art 1525
Fishing Scene 2323
Fishing Yarns 335
Fit As a Fiddle 3992, 544
Five A.M. 4825
Five A.M. Ballet 4602
Five Cent Piece 4498

Five Daughters 1290
Five Foot-Two 1831
Five Growing Boys 2874
Five Guys Named Moe 1296
Five Hundred Garments 3722
Five Hundred Million 3674
Five Hundred Pages 3722
Five Lovely Ladies 2217
Five-Minute Opera, The 1229
Five Minutes 2650
Five Minutes Ago 4470
Five Minutes More 4743
Five Minutes of Spring 125, 1745, 12
Five More Hours 2703
Five More Minutes in Bed 180
Five O'Clock 383, 4484
Five O'Clock Tea 799, 3710
Five Plus One 1056
Five Profiteers, The 2270
Five Senses, The 270
Five Shots of Whiskey 837
Five, Six, Seven, Eight...DANCE! 1298
Five Thousand Francs 2808
Five to One 2017
Five Zeros 3279
Five-Step, The 2734
Fix Yo'self Up 1385
Fixed for Life 1654
Fixin' for a Long Cold Winter 911
Fixing a Hole 3903
Fiyou on the Bayou 1890
Fizkin and Pickwick 3482
Flacton-On-The-Sea 351
Flag, The (dance) 294
Flag of My Country 4646
Flag of Our Land 4836
Flag That Flies, The 4188
Flags of Allies 1527
Flahooley 1300, 2234
Flame, The 1310
Flame Indigo 2259
Flame of Life 4168
Flame of Love 765, 1643
Flame of Love, The 3424
Flame of Love 4550
Flame Water 4289
Flamenco 3699, 4374
Flamenco Dancer 1358
Flaming Agnes 2050, 3542
Flaming Youth 1628, 4018
Flamingo 2259
Flamingo Fuss 164
Flannel Petticoat Gal, The 1733, 2768, 3249
Flannigan 4688
Flap-a-Doodle 930
Flapper, The 2706
Flapper and the Vamp, The 2264
Flapper Club, The 1516
Flappers 3407, 4816
Flappers Are We (Opening Chorus) 3184
Flash, Bang, Wallop 1721
Flash in the Pan 2969
Flash of the Skipper's Eye, A 2917
Flashback 3873, 3411
Flat Broke 3429
Flat in Montmartre, A 2637
Flat Tire Papa 877
Flatfoot's Theme (inst.) 612
Flattery 722, 1629, 3256, 4682, 4718
Flattery Will Get You Everywhere 520
Flatulent Ballad, The 1748
Flaunting It 4309
Flavia (inst.) 4798
Flea Hop, The 1953
Fleet's In 2106
Fleeting Honeymoon 2180
Flesh Failures (Let the Sun Shine In) 1717
Flesh for Sale 4003
Fletcher's American Cheese Choral Society 4178
Fletcher's American Chocolate Choral Society 4179
Fleugel Street Rag 3551
Flex-a-tone 201
Fliberty Jibits 3294, 3542
Flickers, The 4542
Flight of the Air Ship 4382
Flight of the Phoenix 430
Flight to Health 1700
Flights of Fancy 4747
Flim-Flam 1306
Flim Flam Floo 3487
Flim Flam Flooey 3217
Flim Flam Floosie 597
Flings 3113
Flip Religion 1053
Flippity Flop 2984
Flirt 2495
Flirtation 728, 1417, 2603, 2851, 4616, 688
Flirtation Dance 905, 2767, 3599
Flirtation Duet 1466
Flirtation Fantasies 2574
Flirtation on the Beach 2506, 3809
Flirtation Quartette 3770
Flirtation Sextette 331
Flirtation Waltz 2829
Flirtatious Frascita 2452
Flirtie Little Gertie 4161
Flirting 1707, 2412, 2446, 3590
Flirting at St. Moritz Ballet (inst.) 1901
Flirting with the Bus 3350
Flit Drill, The 3131
Flo 2695
Float Me 116
Float Me Charlie 3560
Float Me Down Your Pipeline 3309
Floating Along 3254
Floating Away 595
Floating Down a Moonlight Stream 2816
Floating Down the Nile 3945
Floating Down the Old Green River 2800
Floating Isle of Bong Bong, The 2155

Floating Through the Air 3130
Floating with Your Summer Girl 1541
Flood, The 1667
Floogie Walk 888
Floozies (1) 1662
Floozies (2) 1662
Floppy Disk, The 2861
Flora Bella 1309, 1309
Flora Dora Girls 2541
Flora I Am Your Adorer 4014
Flora Offering 1309
Floral Flirtation, A 2041
Floral Wedding, The 4293
Florence Quits 721
Floretta 250
Florida 2111, 112
Florida By the Sea 799
Florida Mammy 1460
Florida, the Moon and You 3179
Florist Shop, The 4688
Florrie 3856, 3857
Florrie the Flapper 1544
Flossie 1314
Flotsam and Jetsam 3934
Flow'r of Kildaire, The 141
Flower, A 3602
Flower Ball (on a Summer Afternoon) 106
Flower Child 4584
Flower Drum Song 1315
Flower Fete (Our Floral Queen) 3578
Flower Garden Ball, The 1901, 4642
Flower Garden of My Heart, The 3353
Flower, I Don't Need You Anymore 2941
Flower Maidens 2287
Flower of My Heart 580
Flower of My Heart, My Rose 3399
Flower of Spain 4661
Flower of the Woodland 199
Flower of Their Days 112
Flower Shop 2674
Flower Song, The 1216
Flower Song 1910
Flower Song, The 3
Flower Song 3378
Flower Song, The 3381
Flower Song 3711
Flower Song (Introduction) 2233
Flower Vendor 1385
Flower Waltz 3013
Flowering Peach, The 4481
Flowers 694, 1891, 3690
Flowers, The 4789
Flowers A-Blooming So Gay 1313
Flowers and Bees 685
Flowers and Flowers 3428
Flowers and the Rainbow, The 729
Flowers for Algernon 699
Flowers from the Sixties 4731
Flowers in Bloom 2447
Flowers of Dixieland, The 4681
Flowers of Evil (Garden of Evil), The 4427
Flowers of Springtime, Sweetly Scented (Opening Chorus) 4554
Flowers of the Harem 1627
Flowers of the Nations Ballet 4509
Flowers That Bloom in the Spring 1987
Flowers That Bloom in the Spring, The 2348
Flowers, Who'll Buy? 1009
Flowing to the Sea 2245
Flubby Dub the Cave Man 3230
Fluffy Ruffles 1318, 1318
Flutter and Sway 56
Flutter Little Bird 3943
Flutter on By, My Broadway Butterfly 2939
Flutterby Baby 1134
Fluttermill Song 4764
Fly 854
Fly Away 1786, 4011
Fly Away (The Kite Song) 4383
Fly Away 4401
Fly Away Kite 2889
Fly Away Rose 4076
Fly Bird 4346
Fly Blackbird 1319
Fly, Butterfly 1488
Fly By Night 383
Fly Eagle Fly 3688
Fly Forth O Gentle Dove 4479
Fly Little Bird 2811
Fly, Little Heart 673
Fly Now, Pay Later 2554
Fly Song 516
Fly Song, The (Olcott's Fly Song) 4239
Fly Up to Heaven 1799
Fly with Me 1108
Fly! 3454
Flying 583, 2146
Flying Down to Rio 3249
Flying Dutchman 2889
Flying High 4203
Flying Home 4256
Flying Kaganovich, The 1159
Flying Machine, The 333
Flying Milk and Runaway Plates 2801
Flying Somehow 1216
Flying the Blimp 4780
Fog and the Grog, The 2295
Fogarty 687
Fogarty and Mandolin Girls 3091
Fogarty and Nellie Bly Parade 3091
Fogarty the Great 3091
Foggy Day, A 1325
Foggy, Foggy, Dew 3989
Fol-De-Iddledy-Ido 3422
Fol-De-Rol-Dol-Doi 4655
Fol-De-Rol-Lol 968
Fol-de-rol-rol 341
Folette 4687
Folies Bergere 1638
Folies Bergeres 2674, 3171

Folk Dance 1214
Folk Lore 1857
Folk Song 2294, 4775, 3900
Folk Song and Yodle 473
Folk Song Army, The 4412
Folk Song 1950 3
Folks Makin' Money 2643
Folks Who Live on the Hill, The 2204, 2372
Foller It Through 4693
Follies Chorale Ensemble 4824
Follies Minstrel, The 4813
Follies Nocturne 4828
Follies Salad, The 4813
Follow a Star 1333
Follow Along with Me 1245, 3542, 2244
Follow Daddy 4488
Follow, Follow, Follow 4666
Follow Handy Andy 1011
Follow Him 2958
Follow in Our Footsteps 134
Follow Mama's Advice 2619
Follow Master 2382
Follow Me 623, 1334, 1555, 1692, 1759, 1824, 240, 3839, 4056, 158
Follow Me Around 1067, 3031
Follow Me 'Round 3996
Follow Me Up the Stairs 3551
Follow Mister Cook 702
Follow Mr. Watteau 208
Follow On 357, 376, 4654
Follow Schmidt 4379
Follow the Boys 2546
Follow the Cook 628
Follow the Crowd 2888, 3627
Follow the Drinking Gourd 2203
Follow the Drum 3766
Follow the Fiddler 821
Follow the Flag 1208, 2632, 4802
Follow the Flag We Love 2622
Follow the Fold 1706
Follow the Girl 2547
Follow the Girls 1336
Follow the Girls Around 2184
Follow the Guide 4793
Follow the Lamb 2583
Follow the Leader 3576
Follow the Leader Jig 2894
Follow the Leader Septet 3210
Follow the Man that Leads the Band 2465
Follow the Midnight Girl 3525
Follow the Midnight Sun 910
Follow the Minstrel Band 3953
Follow the Music Man 1732
Follow the Parade 1337
Follow the Rainbow 4485
Follow the Rainbow's Trail 3579
Follow the Rajah 2594
Follow the Star 2855
Follow the Sun 1338
Follow the Sun to the South 3063
Follow the Swallow 4818
Follow the Way of the Lord 486
Follow Through 3489
Follow Thru 1339
Follow You All Over the World 2384
Follow Your Heart 4830, 3509, 3956
Follow Your Heart to Fairyland 4719
Follow Your Instinct 4701
Follow Your Leader 737, 4469
Follow Your Star 200, 201
Follow Your Uncle Dudley 4277
Following in Father's Footsteps 1297
Following the Drum 4258
Following the Hounds 1014
Following the Sun Around 3719
Folly 3308
Folly! 4381
Fond Love 4616
Fond Love, True Love 104
Fond of the Ladies 2394
Fond of You 642
Fonye Ganev (Ivan the Czar, The Rogue) 1609
Food for Thought 221, 2679, 3064
Food Is Love 2918
Food, Glorious Food 3271
Foof to Old Geography 1477
Foofaraw 3908
Fool, The 4817
Fool for Luck 4483
Fool House, The 1340
Fool in Love, A 338
Fool Me 1334
Fool Meets Fool 601
Fool That I Am 533
Fool That I Was 3813
Fool There Was, A 2802, 346
Foolin' Ourselves 411, 1341, 412
Fooling Around with Love 4198
Foolish 2951, 2552
Foolish Cinderella Girl 3396
Foolish Face 3861
Foolish Gardener, The 48, 3773
Foolish Geese 4076
Foolish Heart 3301
Foolish Little Maiden I 3051
Foolish Questions 336
Foolish Song, A 4801
Foolish the Heart 255
Foolish Wedding Bells 4201
Foolish Wives 2789
Foolishment 4194
Foolishness 1066, 2793, 3177, 3395, 981
Fools Come and Fools Go 4629
Fools Fall in Love 2597, 4031
Fool's Gold 3487, 2248
Football Boys and Girls, The 3809
Football Girls, The 2800
Football Girls at Vassar, The 185
Football Song (Opening Act II) 2430
Football Song 2800

Footlight Walk 1343
Footloose 1619, 3947
Footloose Youth and Fancy Free 3824
Footman and the Maid, The 4489
Footprints 2783
Footprints in the Sand 4750
Footstep 3806
Footsteps 1633
Footwork 1929
For a Girl Can Love a Sailor 1417
For a Girl Has Her Living to Make 1975
For a Girl Like You 2491, 3137
For a Little While 3430
For a Moment of Your Love 657
For a Quarter 4131
For an Autograph 957
For Anne Gregory 1977
For Aye, My Love 4404
For Better or for Worse 1874, 3590
For Better or Worse 2588, 2201
For Certain 1887
For Charity's Sake 3710
For Critics Only 3940
For Days and Days (I Love You, I Do) 4766
For de Lawd's Sake, Play a Waltz 3332
For Ever 3824
For Every Boy That's Lonely, There's a Girl Who's Lonely Too 1088
For Every Fish There's a Little Bigger Fish 2190
For Every Lover 4250
For Everyone, Everywhere 1887
For Example 1974
For Glory and for Love 2722
For God, Home, Mother and Country 3788
For Goodness' Sake 503
For Hans Tonight 1741
For He's the One, the Only Baby 3134
For Honor 3040
For I Am a Married Man 2722
For I Am Blithe 2348
For I Dream of You 47
For I Love Only You 4017
For I'm in Love 3898
For I'm in Love Again 4235
For I'm Just I 2760
For I'm O'Hoolegan 2500
For in the Fields 357
For Instance 3021
For Jupiter and Greece 601
For Love 1266, 2268
For Love I Live Alone 2315
For Love of Cleopatra 559
For Love of Thee (Olcott's Love Song) 1163
For Love or Money 348, 1760, 860
For Many a Year 2698
For Me and My Gal 3175
For Men 840
For Months and Months 2528
For My Glory Land 1369
For My Mary 3644
For My Own 1076
For My Sweetheart 123
For Myself Alone 1916
For No Good Reason at All 393
For No Reason at All 2189
For No Reason Whatsoever 3842
For No Rhyme or Reason 4777
For Old Times' Sake 1215
For Once in My Life 2958
For Once in Your Life 1611
For One Sweet Day 4634
For Our Country, Our U.S.A. 3350
For Our Sake 1273
For Poland 1660
For Publicity's Sake 2511
For Sale 1421
For Someone I Love 1126
For Sweet Charity's Sake 1466, 1929
For the Benefit of Man 1071
For the Children 4790
For the Common Good of Mankind 4798
For the First Time 1456, 4408
For the First Time in My Life 1989
For the Good of Brotherhood 1377
For the Good Times 4168
For the Harvest Safely Gathered 239
For the Knot There's No Untying 1071
For the Last Time, Call Me Sweeheart 813
For the Life of Me 842, 3390
For the Love of Suzanne 1347
For the Love of You 1034
For the Man I Love 334
For the Papa 3012
For the People 117
For the Rest of My Life 1273
For the Right Guy 3683
For the Sake of Art 2985
For the Sake of Auld Lang Syne 1308
For the Sake of Humanity 1065
For the Sake of Lexington 4772
For the Twentieth Time We'll Drink 357
For Thee, My Love 1466
For Them 2152
For Those in Love 3145
For to Tie Up My Shoe 3612
For Two Minutes 3059
For Universal Peace 4509
For We Love You Still 1680
For We Turn the Bull's Eye On 2715
For You 273, 1979, 2362, 2747, 3273, 3299, 3488
For You a Rose 2490
For You and For Me 4620
For You Baby 3343
For You Bright Eyes 531
For You Brother 1809
For You Dear Heart 4064
For You, Honey, for You 1881
For You I Will Live 1497
For Your Child Will Be Called the Prophet 755
For Your Country and My Country 789

Forbidden Broadway 1348
Forbidden Broadway 1991 1/2 1350
Forbidden Broadway 90 1349
Forbidden Fruit 2424, 4760
Forbidden Love (In Gaul) 170
Forbidden Orchard, The 2679
Forbidden Planet 3695
Forbidden Tropics 3889
Fordyce 1275
Fore Day Noon in the Mornin' 279
Foreign Cars 673
Foreign Eyes 2239
Foresight 1441
Forest Air, The 2982
Forest Bird, The 1975
Forest in the Sky 390
Forest Legend, A 4227
Forest of Silver 4470
Forest Rangers, The 2522
Forethought! 4053
Forever 705, 1846, 2944, 2950, 3551, 4240
Forever and a Day 1891, 3805, 4100
Forever and Always 4243
Forever and Ever 2077, 3648
Forever Delighting in Fighting 1388
Forever Fantasticks 871
Forever Is a Long, Long Time 541
Forever Nearer to Me 1891
Forever Spring 2115
Forever Yours 3285
Forevermore 3088
Forget! 2731
Forget All Your Books 4367
Forget All Your Troubles (and Smile) 489
Forget It 2171, 2745
Forget Me 4566
Forget Me Not (Mai Poina Oe) 422
Forget Me Not 2603, 3670, 4064
Forget-Me-Not 4860
Forget Yesterday 2260
Forget Your Troubles 2557
Forgetful Maid, A 1340
Forgive 1682, 743
Forgive and Forget 3372, 3627
Forgive Her, Forgive Her 2375
Forgiveness 624
Forgotten Dreams 4137
Forgotten Man, The 1957
Forgotten Words 1436
Forlane 1110
Formation of Camp 4046
Formula, Formulae, Formulorum 649
Forsa del Destino 1867
Forsaken Again 1137
Forties, The 408
Fortuna Con 'F' Maiscula 1354
Fortuna with a Capital 'F' 1354
Fortunate Father, A 2421
Fortunate Woman 139
Fortune, The 1081
Fortune Hunter, The 773
Fortune Teller's Song 2602
Fortune Telling 3540
Fortune Telling Man, The 3045
Forty Acres and a Mule 4004
Forty Days 2236, 3411
Forty-Eight States 2023, 3683
Forty-Five Minutes from Broadway 1356
Forty-five Minutes from Broadway 1478
Forty Gallant Thieves Are We 175
Forty Minutes for Lunch (Ballet) 3301
Forty Nights 4481
Forty-Niner and His Clementine 3650
42nd Street 1359, 1359, 2776
42nd Street Blues 3276
Forty-Second Street Man 2757
42nd Street Strut 1516
40 Thieves 51
42-32-42 3561
Forty Winks 2137
Forward into Tomorrow 1045
Forward, Joe Soap's Army 3259
Forward March 4177
Forward March into My Arms 184, 2747
Fossil Man, The 47
Foster Beach 1664
Fountain Fay, The 4119
Fountain Fay Protective Institution, The 4119
Fountain of Dreams 1034
Fountain of Forgiveness 451
Fountain of Youth, The 773, 2005
Fountain of Youth 2135
Fountain of Youth, The 2308
Fountain of Youth 2366
Four 3602
Four and Twenty Little Men 3976
Four Bad Men from Arizona 917
Four Black Dragons 3340
4-11-44 217
Four Eyes 1978
Four Fo' Me 4182
Four for the Road 1408
Four Freedoms 323
Four Freedoms, The 2748
Four Hours Away from Paradise 1510
Four Hundred Girls Ago 4558
Four Infant Prodigies 1448
Four Jews in a Room Bitching 2746
Four-Leaved Clover, The 2623
Four Little Angels of Peace 3501
Four Little Flirty Girls 2040
Four Little Girls with a Future and Four Little Girls with a Past 4815
Four Little Misfits 4542
Four Little Sirens 3569
Four Little Song Pluggers 1447
Four Lunatics, The 2631
Four More Shopping Days 3970
Four Nightingales 2874
Four O'Clock 2591

Four O'Clock Girls 3978
Four O'Clock on Broadway 2711
Four O'Clock Tea 4655
Four of Us, The 2550
Four Part Harmony 1371
Four Part Invention 426
Four Questions 1715
Four Rivers, The 2748
Four Seasons, The 236
Four Seasons 1107, 1363
Four Strikes Against Me 4286
4001 871
Four Thousand Years 459
Four-Two-Two 944
Four Walls 3149
Four Walls (and One Dirty Window) Blues 478
Four Well Known Dames and a Guy (Song Scene) 4816
Four White Horses 1015
Four Would Be Angels 2164
Four Young People 4166
Fourflushers 1624
Four-score and Seven Years Ago 1982
Fourteen Hours and Thirty-Seven Minutes 272
Fourth Avenue North 1370
Fourth Letter 3411
Fourth Light Dragoons 461
Fourth of July, The 4297, 1469
Fourth of July 2542
4th of July Parade 1255
4th of July Parade, The 3795
Fourth Telegram, The 2033
Fourtune 1371
Fox Has Left His Lair, The 702, 4212
Fox Hunt, The 2713
Fox Trot 3985, 2567
Fox's Pitch, The 3496
Fox's Song 99
Foxfire 1372
Foxy 1373
Foxy Grandpa 1374
Foxy Little Bee 2944
Foxy Quiller's Entrance Chorus 1375
Foyo 4579
Fra Francisco's Flirtation 3881
Fracas at Old Drury 2295
Fragrant Flower 1290
Frahngee-Pahnee 3893
'Fraid Cat 1314
Fran and Janie 2152
France, Glorious France 2917
France Is Free 2909
France Will Not Forget 1722
Frances' Ballad 1575
Frances Dances with Me 3025
Frances Discovers Nietzsche 2992
Franchise, A 83
Francie 2850, 3180
Francis' Feast 4470
Franco American Rag 4804
Franco-American Ragtime 3977
Franco-American Step, The 2135
Frank and Johnnies 4332
Frank, Frank, Frank 1380
Frank Loesser medley 4399
Frank Merriwell's School Days 1380
Frank Mills 1717
Frankenstein 1382
Frankie and Johnnie 662
Frankie and Johnny 3989
Franklin D. Roosevelt Jones 3990
Franklin Shepard, Inc. 2822
Frantically Romantic 1846
Frantzi Frankenstein 1523
Fraternal Fiesta 4019
Fraternization Ballet 596
Frauen-Rechte 907
Fraught 2447, 3180
Fraulein Katrina (inst.) 1569
Fraytik Oyf Der Nakht (Friday Night) 1609
Fred and Ginger 3688
Fred Astaire 2713
Fred Astaire Affair, The 3931
Fred Karno's Army 3259
Freddy and His Fiddle 4075
Freddy Chant 521
Freddy Liked to Fugue 2114
Freddy, My Love 1664
Frederica 1384
Fred's Farewell 1624
Free 619, 789, 1422, 3654
Free and Easy 1063
Free and Easy (Any Place I Hang My Hat Is Home) 1385
Free and Easy 3653
Free and Equal Blues 467
Free As a Breeze 1604
Free as Air 4489
Free As the Air 3493, 4792
Free at Last 394
Free, Cute and Size Fourteen 323
Free Etiquette 1522
Free for All 1387
Free! Free! 4489
Free, Free, Free 1756
Free Speech, Free Thought, Free Love 1256
Free Thought in Action Class Song 4238
Free Time 2784
Free to Be - You and Me 1389
Free to Sing 1386
Free Trade and a Misty Moon 1162
Free Translation, A 3088
Free, White and Twenty-One 1836
Freedom 3884, 1436
Freedom! 2679
Freedom 3928, 4111, 1682
Freedom and Rain 4055
Freedom Anthem 169
Freedom Can Be a Most Uncomfortable Thing 751

Freedom Charter 4438
Freedom Choo-Choo, The 597
Freedom Choo Choo Is Leaving Today, The 3217
Freedom Diet 2908
Freedom Is Coming Tomorrow 3836
Freedom Land 2203
Freedom March (dance) 1729
Freedom of the C's 3962
Freedom of the Press, The 919
Freedom of the Seas, The 2150
Freedom Road 3226
Freedom Train, The 1474
Freedomland 3110
Freer Love 337
Freeway Song, The 407
Freeze and Melt 895
Freeze Music 3233
Freezing and Burning 1053
Freight 4138
Freight Train 1496
French 1955
French Auction, The 3780
French Colonial Exposition Scene 3214
French Fling 4000
French Flip Flop 2299
French Flirt 1647
French Have a Word for It, The 4174
French Lesson, The 2691
French Maids, The 591
French Marine Ashore, A 1220
French Militaire 115
French Military Marching Song 1027
French Pastry Walk, The 1345
French Soldiers on Leave Dance 4421
French Song, The 4
French Thing Tango 2332
French Wench 367
French with Tears 59, 3178, 3563
French You Hear on Broadway 3475
Frenchman's Paree, The 3234
Frenetica 4117
Frere Jacques 2364
Fresh Air and Exercise 3301
Fresh and Young 3941
Fresh As a Daisy 3359
Fresh, Bloomin' Health 2240
Freshie, O Freshie 2232
Freshman Song, A 3542
Fresno Beauties 2961
Freud 2478
Freud and Jung and Adler 3379
Freud Is a Fraud 314
Friar's Life, A 1213
Friars' Parade 1399
Friar's Song, The 1394
Friar's Song 1397
Friar's Tune 3876
Frickered Fling 1497
Friday Dancing Class 2439
Friday, Friday 1093
Friday Night 1269
Frieda 1569
Friederike 1384
Friend 4034
Friend Is a Friend, A 825
Friend Like You, A 2731
Friend of a Friend of Mine 1707
Friend of Mine, A 2504
Friend of Mine Gave This to Me, A 2966
Friend of the Family 4586, 2044
Friendliest Thing, The 4633
Friendly Bar, A 971
Friendly Country 3947
Friendly Enemy 1930
Friendly Ghosts 702
Friendly Liberal Neighborhood 2913
Friendly Neighborhood Dump 1750
Friendly Polka 2219
Friends 73, 170, 403, 3539, 1206, 2233, 4022, 4168, 4528
Friends Ain't S'posed to Die 414
Friends and Lovers 2637
Friends, Dear Friends 698
Friends for Life 2702
Friends Have to Part 2698
Friends That Are Good and True 1926, 3753
Friends, the Best Of 1059
Friends to the End 999
Friends Who Understand 4694
Friendship 1109, 2808, 2951, 1867, 1549, 4517
Friendship Ain't No One Way Street 4750
Friendship and Love 2698
Friendship Leads Us to Love 3369
Friendship's Sacred Touch 1388
Friggin New Orleans Interlude (inst.) 3564
Frightened Fawn, The 2722
Frightened of the Dark 1093
Frills Upon Their Petticoats 2803
Frimbo Special 1402
Fringe of Society, The 4508
Frisa Linda 1374
Frisco, The 4712
Frisco Fanny 4583
Frisco Flo 883
Frisco Frizz, The 1835
Frisco Frizz 2600
Fritzie 278
Frivolette 3769
Frivolity 1526
Frivolity Frolics 3664
Frocks and Frills 1580, 3333
Frog, The 2717
Frog and the Owl, The 361
Frog He Lived in a Pond, A 1682
Frogs, The 1406, 1406
Frolic of a Breeze, The 333
Frolic of a Breeze 675
Frolic of the Bears 4447
Frolic of the Fairies 4649
Frolics of Pierrot, The 1900

Frolics of the Nite 1407
From a Different Point of View 2917
From a Prison Cell 2150
From A to Z 4018
From a Window on the Seine 3386
From Afar 3702
From Africa 666
From Alpha to Omega 4777
From Another World 1894
From Atlanta to the Sea 1474
From Bagdad We Come 2802
From Barcelona I Come 4032
From Broadway to Main Street 2516
From Cairo, Bagdad, Khorasan 758
From Cottage to Subway 1780
From Far Cohoes 4654
From Far Kohoes 357
From Far Peru 3313
From Here to Shanghai 1556
From Hunger 4518
From Maine to Oregon 118
From Me to You 1231
From Morning Prayer the Sultan 3777
From Morning Till Night 1539
From Now On 337, 2363, 2432, 4170
From Now Onward 3064
From Now Till Forever 946
From Out the Convent Walls 2623
From Saturday to Monday 2986
From Seventh Avenue to Seventh Heaven 1269
From Skowhegan, Maine, B'Gosh 1466
From Stopchut to Kolomay 2811
From Tango to Taps 1656, 1657
From the Ankles Down 1699
From the Bottom of the Sea 3764
From the Bottom to the Top 2461
From the Chimney to the Cellar 4640
From the Circle to the Square 3374
From the Convent 3197
From the Cradle to the Grave 3813
From the Land of Dreams 4759
From the Lips 1910
From the Meadow's Fairest Flower 2538
From the Moment 1924
From the Plaza to Madison Square 560
From the Red 1991
From the U.S.A. to the U.S.S.R. 2432
From Then and Now 4269
From This Day 2674
From This Day On 530, 1679
From This Moment On 3326
From This Out 2268
From Where I Stand 4643
From Where the Scotch Mountains 3588
From You I'll Never Part 4735
From Your Heart to Mine 2214
Fromage 3756
Front Page, The 4703
Front Page Expose 3136
Front Page News 383
Front Porch in Flatbush 3843
Frontier Politics 4785
Frontier Rabbi 4325
Frosty the Snowman 3793
Frowns 1251
Frug 1990
Fruhling Im Herbst 1935
Fruit of My Heart 345
Fruits and Vegetables 3651
Frustration 3103, 3734, 4089
Frutti Di Mare 3011
Frying Pan, The 4515
Ft. Lauderdale 1107
Fu-Ji 69
Fuddle-Dee-Duddle (Funny Little Tune) 1840
Fudge, Fudge, Fudge 939
Fughetta 3386
Fugitive from Esquire, A 2301
Fugitive from Fifth Avenue, The 95
Fugue 612, 2106
Fugue for a Menage a Trois 4468
Fugue for Four Girls 2801
Fugue for Thought 4774
Fugue for Tinhorns 1706, 3444
Fugue Furioso 1757
Fugue on a Hot Afternoon in a Small Flat 3831
Fulfilling Requests 194
Full Circle 4171
Full Fathom Five 1104
Full House, A 3921, 4547
Full Moon, The 2992
Full Moon Street 3630
Full of Pep 1462
Full-Blown Roses 1013
Fumfumbolo 3339
Fun 2887, 198
Fun and Games 52, 3186
Fun Band, The 2084
Fun Downtown-Uptown (From Downtown, We Move Uptown) 1609
Fun in the Country 2680
Fun Life 3094
Fun on a Motor 3976
Fun Time 1890
Fun to Be Fooled 2475
Function Bound 981
Fundamental Character 1930
Funeral Dirge 1422
Funeral Dirge, The 2759
Funeral March 2464, 2464
Funeral Music (inst.) 3493
Funeral of Charleston 266
Funeral Passed By, A 654
Funeral Procession 3202
Funeral Tango 2188
Funky 3515
Funky Bessie 2195
Funky Eyes 535
Funky Girl on Motherless Broadway 40
Funky Love 1371

Funky Monkeys 4722
Funky People 4192
Funky World 2245
Funnies, The 207
Funny 775
Funny Bunny Hug 3989
Funny Face 1419, 3060
Funny Family, The 1374
Funny Feathers 1425
Funny Feelin' 2245
Funny Funeral, A 3731
Funny Girl 1420
Funny Heart, A 3473
Funny Honey 723
Funny Little Old World 4432
Funny Little Sailor Men 3117
Funny Little Something 1796
Funny Little Tracks in the Snow 3378
Funny Man 695
Funny Old House 4361
Funny Papers 137
Funny: The Duck Joke 3039
Funny Thing Happened
(On My Way to Love), A 2048
Funny Wind-Up Toy 562
Funnybone 589
Funzapoppin 1423
Furnished Bed 4362
Furnished for Monty 4860
Furnishing a House for Two 4045
Furs and Feathers, Buckles and Bows
(Opening Chorus) 2915
Furs and Frills 1424
Furs, Fortune, Fame, Glamor 3561
Further Comments 2243
Further It Is from Tipperary, The 3222
Future for Sale 1064
Future in Fish, A 2218
Future Is Here, The 2307
Future Looks Promising, The 1581
Future Mrs. Coleman, The 3390
Future Stars 4782
Future, The 1959
Futures 3884
Futurist Girl, The 4808
Futurist Rag, The 2377
Futurist Whirl, The 2761
Futuristic Melody 4033
Futuristic Rhythm 1827

G

G.A. 456
G.I. Joe 2555
G.O.P. 1118
G.O.T.O. 4325
Ga-Ga 1110, 2382
Gabey's Comin' 599, 3278
Gabie 1991
Gabriel Is Blowing His Horn 2827
Gabriel's Letter 2333
Gabrielle 2420, 798, 1427
Gabrielle's Dream 3463
Gaby 804
Gaby Glide, The 2538, 4553, 4655
Gaby Waltz, The 2934
Gaggle of Celebrities, A 3757
Gaggle of Geese, The 1422
Gaiety Chorus Girls, The 4361
Gaiety Glad 1467
Gaiety of the Gaiety, The 3880
Gaiety, The (Delicatessen) (A Way of Life) 4013
Gainesboro Glide, The 539
Gal from Baton Rouge, The 1917
Gal from Joe's, A (inst.) 886
Gal Named Cinderella, A 2234
Gal Who Took the Minutes, The 3124
Gal with a Past 3605
Galatea! 3333
Gallant Girl 1991
Gallant Thunderbomb, The 402
Gallantry 3691
Galli Curci Rag 3402
Gallop 2178
Gallop, Gallop 531
(You'll Have To) Gallop Some 3737
Galloper, The 4762
Gallopin' Dominoes 3054
Galloping Major 4794
Galloping Through the Park 1932
Gallows Pole 1736
Gallus Old Goddess of Greece, The 4012
Galop 3691
Galloping Cavalree, The 2903
Gal's Got to Do What a Gal's Got to Do 3641
Gamble on Me! 3399
Gambler of the West, The 1528
Gamblers, The (dance) 3837
Gambler's Lullaby 4702
Gamblin' Hand, The 962
Gambling 3081
Gambling Man 1616
Gamboling on the Green 2222
Game, The 957, 407
Game Goes On, The 2289
Game I Lost, A 482
Game I've Been Teaching You, The
(Same Old Love) 2922
Game Is Over!, The 427
Game Is Up, The 1436
Game of Basket Ball, The 939
Game of Cards, A 3424
Game of Dance 3942
Game of Eyes 929
Game of Golf, The 2576
Game of Hearts, A 4434
Game of Love, The 1760
Game of Love, A 1881

Game of Love, The 3567
Game of Love 3677, 1549
Game of Love, The 3751
Game of Love 4250
Game of Make Believe 2454
Game of Morra, The (La Morra) 3798
Game of Poker, A 3837
Game of War, The 2681
Game that Ends with a Kiss, A 1626
Games 83, 4003
Games I Play, The 2746
Games of Childhood 3045
Games We Used to Play, The 3943
Gamester, The 639
Gangland Chase 2437
Gang's All Here, The 1440
Gangster Influence, The 3103
Gangster of the Puppet Show, The 3441
Gantry's Reaction 1441
Gant's Waltz 135
Gap in the Hedge, The 3431
Garbage 1012, 2804, 3941, 3055
Garbage Court Round 3571
Garbage-Ella 1695, 4470
Garbo Bit, The 2992
Garcon, S'il Vous Plait 3225
Garden, The 4002
Garden Ballet 3369
Garden for Two, A 1116, 3651
Garden Gate 1544
Garden Guaracha 2626
Garden in the Sky 3813
Garden in the Sun, A 461
Garden of Dreams 2347
Garden of Dreams, The 3673
Garden of Eden 4104
Garden of Eden Ballet, The (dance) 629
Garden of Eden Sketch 1657
Garden of Evil 4139
Garden of Flowers 4206
Garden of Girls, The 336, 558
Garden of Girls 965
Garden of Imagining, The 23
Garden of Love 1486
Garden of Love, A 1306
Garden of Love 2135
Garden of Love, The 1439
Garden of Love 3951
Garden of Love, The 4554
Garden of Love for Two 4776
Garden of Love's Desire, The 1562
Garden of Make Believe 25
Garden of Memories, A 1678
Garden of Memory 733
Garden of My Dreams, The 4812
Garden of Paradise 2696
Garden of Used to Be, The 1690
Garden of Yesterday, The 1927
Garden Party, The 2394
Garden Path to Hell, The 3070
Garden Scene 1476
Garden Sequence 3411
Garden Song 4431
Garden — The Beauty Contest, A 4818
Gardeners' Chorus 4381
Garibaldi Band 2385
Garland of Roses 4022
Garlands Bright 4188
Garment Trade, The 3722
Garrison Ball, The 1316
Garrotin Sarrano 2407
Garrotin Song and Dance 2407
Garside the Great 2053
Garter Song 3688
Gary, Indiana 3016
Gary Owen 964
Gas 815
Gas Can 459
Gas Man Cometh, The 221
Gascon Flute Song 946
Gascon Marching Song 946
Gascony 4357
Gasoline Can-Can, The 4701
Gassed Last Night 3259
Gaston 330
Gastrointestinal Rag 3600
Gate in the Road, The 3671
Gate of Dreams, The 2686
Gate Tender 4615
Gates of Cairo, The 2802
Gates of Hell, The 2027
Gateway of the Temple of Minerva, The 601
Gather Roses While You May 605
Gather the Rose 4664
Gather to the Water 4645
Gather Ye Autographs While Ye May 2252
Gather Ye Rose Buds 3939
Gather Ye Rosebuds 2603, 4392
Gathering 3723
Gathering Nuts in May 1610
Gathering of the Clan, The 427
Gathering of the Clans 2495
Gathering of the Slaves, The (inst.) 805
Gatsby Bridge March, The 4028
Gaucho Love Song, A 3170
Gaucho March 3170
Gaucho with the Black Mustache, The 321
Gave Me One Day 2567
Gavotte (inst.) 250
Gavotte 630, 1013, 1021, 1109
Gavotte (inst.) 759
Gavotte 3011, 3472, 3730, 4188
Gavotte and Solo Dance 1213
Gay and Merry Play, The 185
Gay Bar Cantata, The 1229
Gay Brazilian 2870
Gay Butterfly (on the Wheel) 2706
Gay Divorcee, The 2399
Gay Dragoon 346
Gay Excursion, A 106

Gay Fleurette 3437
Gay Fusilier, The 1570
Gay Gendarme, The 1392
Gay Golf Girl, The 1925
Gay Hussars, The 1455
Gay Lieutenant, The 4187
Gay Life, The 1016, 1456
Gay Little Ladies of Drury Lane 346
Gay Little Wives (Six Little Wives) 2252
Gay Lothario, The 4590
Gay Manhattan Rag 3041
Gay Name Game 4309
Gay New York 1459
Gay Nineties, The 1840
Gay Old Seville 4478
Gay Rap, The 2346
Gay Soldier Boy 20
Gay Young Students 2919
Gayest Manhattan 1466
Gayest Old Sport, The 4165
Gaze Not on Swans 129
Gaze on This Face 4724
Gazelles 1358
Gazette, The 4073
Gazooka, The 4825
G'bye 4029
Gebentsht Iz Amerike 1609
Gee, Ain't I Glad I'm Home! 4277
Gee, Ain't I Glad I'm Single 2835
Gee! Ain't It H— to Be Rich 4762
Gee! But I Hate to Go Home Alone 1391
Gee, But I'd Like to Be Bad 1965
Gee But I'd Like to Furnish a Flat for You, Dear 4203
Gee, But It's Cold in Russia 2653
Gee, But It's Good to Be Here 1760
Gee But It's Good to Be in the Army! 7
Gee, But It's Great to Be Free 525
Gee But It's Great to Meet a Girl from Home 1175
Gee, But This Is a Lonesome Town 246
Gee! But This Is a Lonesome Town 2576
Gee! But You Look Awful Good to Me 511
Gee Chee 3054
Gee I Only Wish I Could Make My Dreams Come True 4833
Gee, I Wish I Had a Girl 4654
Gee, I Wish I Had Someone to Rock Me i n the Cradle of Love 1198
Gee, I Wish I Was a Caveman's Kid 1688
Gee, I'm Glad I'm from Dixie 2415
Gee, I'm Glad I'm No One Else but Me 148
Gee I'm Glad that I'm from Dixie So I Can Get a Dixie Welcome Home 1052
Gee It's Gonna Be Wonderful 2057
Gee! It's Great to Be a Sailor! 1524
Gee, It's Great to Be Alive 4345
Gee It's So Good, It's Too Bad 3172
Gee, Officer Krupke 4625
Gee, We Get Along 4651
Gee! What a Wonderful Mate You'll Be 712
Gee Whiz! Those Eyes 2108, 4071
Gee, You Must Be in Love 606
Gee, You're Pretty 362
Gee, How I Hate You 2448
Geendikt Iz Der Tog 3781
Geezer 4478
Geisha 2626
Geisha Are We 1470
Geisha Girl 266
Geisha's Life, A 1470
Gelato Song 139
Gelber Meets the Wolfgang 1648
Gemini 3619
Gems of the Night 1707
Gemutlichkeit 1097
Gendarme, The 383
Gendarmes 4777
Gendarme's Dance, The 115
Genealogy 1929
Genealogy of Daisy Belle, The 4316
Geneology 755
General Bingham's Brigade 3867
General Boomerang 2938
General Consensus of Opinion 3801
General Effect 2168
General Election 1857
General! General! 4379
General Orders, The 1880
General Sir Hugh M. Trenchard 414
General Store 148
Generalonely 3309
Generals' Pandemonium 3272
General's Song, The 612, 3684
Generation 1471
Generation Gap 2657
Generations 730
Generic Woman 140
Genesis 3724
Genie's Music 2655
Genius 1369, 1498
Genius Burns 2219
Genteel 298
Gentle Afternoon 1739
Gentle Annie 4149
Gentle Art of Seduction, The 2563
Gentle As Dew 4147
Gentle Buffoon, The 3711
Gentle Jane 1866
Gentle Lover 3741
Gentle Moon 2884
Gentle River 3575
Gentle Sufficiency of Abundance, A 1662
Gentleman Friend 2707
Gentleman Is a Dope, The 85
Gentleman Jim 302
Gentleman Jimmy 1280
Gentleman Never Falls Wildly in Love, A 1290
Gentleman of Leisure 2648
Gentlemanly Brigand, The 4616
Gentleman's Gentleman, A 989, 2341, 3482

Gentlemen 3295
Gentlemen of Breeding 1257
Gentlemen of Japan 444
Gentlemen of the Leased Wire Press 1884
Gentlemen of the Press 1356, 3721, 3801, 4373
Gentlemen Prefer Blondes 799, 1475, 1475, 3179, 3622
Gentlemen Unafraid 1476
Gentlemen's Duel 1358
Gentlemen's Understanding 298
Gently 3494
Gents for Rent 2275
Genuine Feminine Girl, A 766
Genuine Grade A Canadian Superstar 426
Genuine Hall-Marked Alpha-Plus Little Brick, A 3429
Genuine Plastic 1045
Geographically Undesirable 2477
Geography 1346, 2261, 3026, 3855
Geography Song (Rumania, Rumania) 3937
George 1699, 1770, 1872
George and Mary 1448
George L. 170
George Washington, Jr. 2517
George's Love Affair 333
Georgette 1688
Georgia Avenue 1496
Georgia Camp Meeting, A 2415
Georgia Land 4589
Georgia Rose 3614, 3241
Georgia Sand 3214
Georgia Shows 'Em How 1063
Georgianna Dunn 2631
Georgie 2180, 4154
Georgie and I 2674
Georgy 1497
Georgy Girl 1497, 1497
Geraldine 1386
Geraniums in the Winder 660
Germ in the German, The 2751
German Country Dance 4620
German Evening 4379
German Philosophy 591
German Prince May Wed Me Since, A 3588
German Specialty 3357
Germans at the Spa, The 3171
"Gershwin Medley" 3018
Gershwin Specialty Introduction 2366
Gertie 3235, 1882
Gertie the Stool Pigeon's Daughter 3226
Gertrude Hoffman Glide, The 558
Gertrude Hoffman March, The 558
Gertrude Stein's Song 3320
Gertrude, You and Me 3914
Gesticulate 2327, 4383
Get a Girl to Lead the Army 4634
Get a Girlie 3958
Get a Horse 4753
Get a Horse for Your Horseless Carriage 2608
Get a Horse, Get a Mule 3650
Get a Load of That 4169
Get a Load of This 4476
Get a Map 1369
Get a Move On! 4219
Get a Personality 2305
Get a Wife 3888
Get an Education 3825
Get Away, Boy 2200
Get Away for a Day in the Country 1886
Get Away from It All 216, 3683
Get Away from My Window 2845
Get Away, Young Man 1140
Get Back 3903
Get Black Crow 3736
Get Busy 830
Get Down 578, 1104
Get Down Brother Get Down 828
Get Happy 1876, 3172
Get Her Away from Me 167
Get Him Up 3258
Get Hot Foot 3907
Get in a Bathing Suit 1129
Get in Line 4124
Get in Touch with Me 3622
Get It Together 3814
Get Married Shirley 2940, 4018
Get Married Shyrlee 4585
Get Me Out 596
Get Me Out of Here 4332
Get Me Right 3033
Get Me to the Church on Time 3038
Get Naked 922
Get Next to the Man with a Pull 3751
Get Off My Lawn 3366
Get Off on Somebody Else 3830
Get on Out of Here 3297
Get on the Merry-Go-Round 3855
Get on the Raft with Taft 2018
Get on to the Bride and Groom 15
Get on with It 2470
Get Out of Here 4635
Get Out of My Way 2640
Get Out of Town 2432
Get Out the Vote 2018
Get Pissed 4690
Get Ready 166
Get Ready, Eddie 1059
Get Rhythm in Your Feet 4502
Get Rich Quick Wallingford 1531
Get That Sun Into You 125
Get That Will 4405
Get the Answer Now 2049
Get the Hook 687
Get the Money 4662
Get the News 3264
Get the Point, Mrs. Brown? 2175
Get Thee Behind Me, Satan! 10
Get Thee Out 1265
Get Thee to a Nunnery 3741
Get Thee to Bed 2177
Get Thee to Canterbury 1500

Get Them All Over at Once 1130
Get Together 765, 1077
Get Up 4540
Get Up and Go, Lad 1903
Get Up, Get Out, Get Under the Sun 3709
Get Up Jack, John Sit Down 3266
Get Up on a New Routine 2545
Get Your Act Together 828
Get Your Man 1693, 2490, 2909
Get Your Partner for the Barn Dance 1318
Get Your Program for de Big Fight 653
Get Your Rocks Off Rock 4124
Get Your Show Rolling 3636
Get Your Slice of Cake 415
Get Yourself a Geisha 216, 1763
Get Yourself a Girl 2453
Get Yourself a New Broom 878
Get Yourself Some Lovin' 2513
Getaway 1108
Getaway Quintet, The 1786
Gethsemane 2212
Gettin' a Man 3837
Gettin' Back to Me 1497
Gettin' Off 567
Gettin' Some 3299
Gettin' to the Top 1637
Gettin' Together 3361
Getting Around 871
Getting Better 3903
Getting Dressed 1706
Getting From Day to Day 2648
Getting Into the Talkies 3005
Getting Married 4190
Getting Married (Living As One) 2073
Getting Married to a Person 4481
Getting Married Today 4067, 832, 3967
Getting Oriental Over You 84
Getting Out 1940
Getting Out of Town 1359
Getting Ready for the Ball 760
Getting Tall 3171
Getting the Beautiful Girls 1134
Getting to Know You (inst.) 3261
Getting to Know You 2312
Getting to Wilson 112
Getting Younger Every Day 1764
Gevald Aria, The 2811
Ghetto Glide 697
Ghetto of My Mind 535
Ghost, The 2886
Ghost from the Past 2307
Ghost Music (inst.) 3493
Ghost of a Hoodoo Man 1340
Ghost of Deacon Brown, The 3945
Ghost of Kelly, The 4521
Ghost of Little Egypt, The 3168
Ghost of Old Black Joe 1823
Ghost of Old Black Joe, The 3388
Ghost of Smokie Joe, The 888
Ghost of Sorority Days 4092
Ghost of the Violin 513, 4655
Ghost Quintette 1538
Ghost Recitative 3808
Ghost That Never Walked, The 3488
Ghost Town 1342, 3461
Ghost's Turn, The 2100
Ghosties and Ghoulies and Things That Go Bump in the Night 2805
Ghosts 3770
Ghosts of the Ukulele, The 3958
Gianina 2684
Giannina Mia 4251, 1285
Giant 3548
Giants in the Sky 2143
Gibson Bathing Girl, The 1504
Gibson Bathing Girls, The 4801
Gibson Coon, The 800
Gibson Girl, The 8, 3387
Gibson Girls' Entrance 1690
Gibson Sailor, The 1504
Gibson School Marm, The 1316
Gibson Widow, The 1504
Giddy, Gay Lothario, The 3581
Giddy Up, Giddy Up, Dearie 4644
Giddybug Gallop, The (inst.) 2259
Giddyup 4011
Gideon Briggs, I Love You 1698
Gideon's Charm 1698
Gift, The 1508, 2250
Gift for Each Day of the Week, A 4798
Gift Number 1811
Gift of a Second Chance, The 2523
Gift of Christmas, The 1509
Gift of Love, A 4798
Gift of Maggie, The 2663
Gift of the Magi, The 1509, 1507, 1508
Gift of Time, A 4798
Gift Today, A (The Bar Mitzvah Song) 2048
Gifts of Love 273
Gifts of the Magi, The 1509
Gifts to You 1262
Gig, The 1510
Gigi 1511, 1511, 1511
Gigolette 702
Gigolo 1018, 1447, 3063, 3291
Gigolos 1492
Gilbert and Sullivan Blues, The 2817
Gilbert Becaud 1427
Gilbert the Filbert 1544, 3020, 3398, 3397
Gilding the Guild 1446
Gilfriends for Life 1785
Gimme 3258
Gimme a 'G' 2285
Gimme a Pigfoot 2796
Gimme a Raincheck 4238
Gimme Get Me I Want It 4731
Gimme Love 2333
Gimme Mick 1512
Gimme Some (Beer and Whiskey) 1601
Gimme the Shimmy 2850

Gimme This — Gimme This — Gimme That 1065
Gimmie, Gimmie, Gimmie 3210
Gin Game, The 2230, 2230
Gin Rummy 4143
Gin Rummy Rhapsody 4323
Gina 3180, 3824
Ginette 4213
Ginger 1513, 2020, 3677, 4206, 4742
Ginger Girl 1735
Ginger Town 3923
Gingerbread Boy, The 2209
Gingerbread Cadets, The 1515
Gingerbread Doll, The 1994
Gingerbread Girl 2618
Gingerbread Train, The 2093
Gingerbrown 3808
Gingerena 2009
Gingham and Orchid 1597
Gingham and Yarn 3643
Gingham Girl, The 1516
Gingham Girl 43
Ginny Ginny Shore 487
Gip-Gip 2829
Gipsy Melody 3339
Gipsy of Poughkeepsie 4758
Gipsy Song 1896
Giraffe's Reprise 2283
Girl, A 1865
Girl, a Man, a Night, a Dance, A 168
Girl at the Helm, The 1243
Girl Becomes a Woman, A 2766
Girl Behind the Counter, The 1316, 1526
Girl Behind the Man Behind the Gun, The 1417, 1527
Girl Belongs to You 764
Girl Brought Up with the Utmost Care, A 3195
Girl Can Go Wacky, A 4252
Girl Crazy 921
Girl Don't Cry 4722
Girl for Each Day of the Week 1796
Girl for Each Month in the Year, A 4809
Girl for Each Month of the Year A 4799
Girl for Me, The 3333
Girl Friend, The 1529, 3018
Girl Friend of a Boy Friend of Mine, A 4683
Girl from Broadway, The 1532
Girl from Casimo 4694
Girl from Childs, The 2853
Girl from Home Sweet Home, The 558
Girl from Kay's, The 351, 1537
Girl from London, The 1386
Girl from Mars, The 2316
Girl from My Home Town, The 4833
Girl from My Own Town, The 3753
Girl from Paree, A 1565
Girl from Paris, The 1540
Girl from Rector's 3866
Girl from the Golden West, A 4104
Girl from Utah 1544
Girl Has a Sailor in Every Port, A 487
Girl He Adores 1878
Girl He Couldn't Kiss, The 2701
Girl He Left Behnid Him, The 3883
Girl I Can't Forget, The 2328
Girl I Knew, The 1230
Girl I Know, A 2517
Girl I Left in Boston Town, The 1926, 3753
Girl I Love, The 4178
Girl I Marry, The 4528
Girl I Mean to Be, The 3862
Girl I Might Have Been, The 1657
Girl I Used to Know, The 41, 4313
Girl I Want to Call My Wife, The 2270
Girl I'll Call My Sweetheart Must Look Like You, The 2662
Girl I've Never Met, The 3540, 4393
Girl in Blue, The 3609
Girl in Every Port 2939
Girl in His Arms, The 4682
Girl in My Soup 4329
Girl in Pink, The 4805
Girl in Short Supply, The 1665
Girl in the Clogs and the Shawl 1544
Girl in the Coffee 2719
Girl in the Front Porch Swing, The 320
Girl in the Gingham Gown, The 106
Girl in the Mirror, The 3112
Girl in the Moon, The 2457
Girl in the Show, The 3954
Girl in the Spotlight 1552
Girl in the Valley, A 3862
Girl in the Window, The 2949
Girl in the Window 4415
Girl in Your Arms, A 3712, 4249
Girl Is Gone, The 2766
Girl is Like a Book, A 4640
Girl Is Like Sunshine, A 1129
Girl Is Nobody, A 2112, 3721
Girl Is You and the Boy Is Me, The 1489
Girl Land 1389
Girl Like Grandma 2601
Girl Like I, A 2590
Girl Like Nina, A 277
Girl Like That, A 1456
Girl Like You, A 4741
Girl May As Well Marry Well, A 1033
Girl Meets Boy 4217
Girl My Heart Beats For, The 3998
Girl Next Door, The 1387
Girl o' Mine 1557
Girl O' My Heart 2310
Girl of Greater New York, The 3751
Girl of Mine 1556
Girl of My Dreams, The 1558
Girl of My Dreams 4635
Girl of My Heart 4056
Girl of Pearl I Love You 1308
Girl of the Golden West 1562
Girl of the Great Divide, The 2347
Girl of the Minute, The 3112
Girl of the Moment 2386

Girl of the Mystic Star 1776
Girl of the Pi Beta Phi, A 1628
Girl of To-Day, The 3397
Girl of Tomorrow, The 1488
Girl on the Magazine Cover, The 4158, 4799
Girl on the Persian Rug, The 3446
Girl on the Police Gazette, The 4131
Girl on the Prow, The 3117
Girl on the Square 3958
Girl Power 3346
Girl Really Needs a Woman, A 2243
Girl She Can't Remain, A 651
Girl That I Adore, The 2371
Girl That I Court in My Mind, The 4366
Girl That I Marry, The 153
Girl That I'd Call Mine, The 2505
Girl That I'll Adore, The 4170
Girl That Leads the Band, The 187
Girl That You Leave Behind, The 639
Girl That's Most Chased After, The 2020
Girl to Remember, A 1227
Girl Wanted 2209
Girl Who Can Love, A 3319
Girl who Comes from the West, The 3437
Girl Who Doesn't Ripple When She Bends 1140
Girl Who Drinks Champagne, The 3401
Girl Who Gets Her Man, The 1986
Girl Who Is Up-To-Date 350
Girl Who Keeps Me Guessing 4393
Girl Who Keeps You Waiting, The 3319
Girl Who Lives in Montparnasse, The 3954
Girl Who Works in the Laundry, The 3916
Girl Who Wouldn't Spoon, The 1558
Girl with a Brogue, The 178
Girl with a Flame, A 183
Girl with a Ribbon, A 937
Girl with Talent, A 3165
Girl with the Baby-Blue Tights, The 8
Girl with the Banjo Eyes, The 4859
Girl with the Changeable Eyes, The 3384
Girl with the Clocking on Her Stocking, The 353
Girl with the Come Hither Eyes 1285
Girl with the Curls, The 1695
Girl with the Green Eye, The 2187
Girl with the Major General, The 1885
Girl with the Naughty Wink, The 509
Girl with the Orange Hair, The 1496
Girl with the Paint on Her Face, The 4677
Girl with the Prettiest Legs in Town, The 664
Girl with the Yellow Roses, The 1783
Girl without a Name, The 3894
Girl Worth the While 4007
Girl You Dream About, The 1563, 2408
Girl You Left Behind 4636
Girl You Love, The 1071, 3976, 4354
Girl You Never Have Kissed, The 3770
Girl You Take Out to Supper, The 2498
Girl You're a Woman 374
Girl's Song 1977
Girlie 4422
Girlie from the Cabaret, The 2696
Girlie Girl 694
Girlie-Land, A 1111
Girlie of All the Year 2879
Girlie with a Bustle 293
Girlie with the Baby Stare, The 2906, 3820
Girlie with the Winsome Smile, The 248
Girlies 88
Girlies Are Out of My Life 4747
Girlies You've Kissed in Dreams, The 1247
Girlish Laughter 3395
Girls 326
Girls, The 1889
Girls 2835, 2555, 2728, 2847
Girls! 3024
Girls 4798
Girls Against the Boys, The 1567
Girls Ahoy! 36
Girls All Around Me 3712
Girls Along Fifth Avenue, The 1723
Girls and Boys 1567, 4662
Girls and Dogs 2188
Girls and French Chauffeurs 3701
Girls and Rassendyl 4798
Girls and the Gimmies 670
Girls Are Getting Wiser (Every Day), The 1334
Girls Are Like a Rainbow 3146
Girls Are Like the Weather to Me 1482
Girls at Maxim's (Girls, Girls, Girls), The 2836
Girls at Maxims 2838
Girls at Maxims, The 2835
Girls Can't Lie 4409
Girls Do Not Tempt Me 1013
Girls Dream of One Thing 2263
Girls from the Folies Bergeres, The 1868
Girls from the Follies 806
Girls from Yankee Land 3771
Girls! Girls! 837
Girls, Girls 1707
Girls! Girls! Girls! 511
Girls, Girls, Girls 513, 1584
Girls, Girls, Girls (What's a Maiden?) 1768
Girls, Girls, Girls 2869, 4375, 2837
Girls, Girls, Keep Your Figure 4687
Girls Grow More Wonderful Day by Day 2180
Girls I Am Leaving in England Today, The 702
Girls, I Am True to You All
(I'm True to Everyone) 771
Girls I Have Met 2378
Girls I Left Behind, The 4802
Girls, If I Ever Get Married 543
Girls If You Ever Get Married 1588
Girls in the Band 4196
(There Are Plenty of) Girls in the Sea 1922
Girls in the Sea 3146
Girls in Their Summer Dresses 3110
Girls I've Met, The 2184
Girls Just Girls 2724
Girls Like Me 4190
Girls 'n' Girls 'n' Girls 3108

Girls of DeVere's 2533
Girls of Every Land, The 1417
Girls of Gottenburg, The 1569
Girls of Long Ago 3721
Girls of My Dreams 4814
Girls of New York, The 539
Girls of Summer 1571
Girls of Summer, The 2764
Girls of the Midnight Matinee 4704
Girls of the Night, The 2198
Girls of the Old Brigade, The 3254
Girls of the U.S.A. 2517
Girls Prepare 3958
Girls Pretty Girls 3443
Girls Quartette 2013
Girls Run Along 3627
Girls That Boys Dream About, The 3734
Girls That Can Never Be Mine, The 3579
Girls Want a Hero 341
Girls Were Made for Dancing 1129
Girls Who Go Upon the Stage 3134
Girls Who Sell Orangeade, The 3490
Girls Who Sit and Wait, The 2664
Girls Will Be Girls and Boys Will Be Boys 2964
Girls Would Have Me Blushing, The 1240
Girls You Are Such Wonderful Things 4258
Girly Girly 1926
Girofle-Girofla 2843, 1576
Git on de Boat, Chillun 4479
Gitka's Song, The 4481
Give a Cheer 197, 2935
Give a Girl a Break! 556
Give a Girl a Chance 2768
Give a Little, Get a Little 4496
Give a Little, Get a Little Kiss 2594
Give a Little Thought to Me 4860
Give a Little Whistle (and I'll Be There) 4693
Give a Man Enough Rope 4695
Give a Viva! 2447
Give All Your Love Away 519
Give and Take 3763
Give, Baby, Give 4586
Give 'Em a Kiss 3615
Give 'Em a Lollipop 1727
Give 'Em Hell 1201, 4679
Give 'Em What They Want 1597
Give England Strength 3780
Give, Give 3218
Give Him a Great Big Kiss 338
Give Him a Welcome Quite Spanish 3774
Give Him Back His Job 4421
Give Him the Oo-La-La 1109
Give Him Your Sympathy 381
Give It 1836
Give It All You Got 3234
Give It All You've Got 2057
Give It Back to the Indians 4420
Give It Love 3966
Give It to Me 2451
Give Me 2433
Give Me a Cause 1273, 3159
Give Me a Cozy Corner 2587
Give Me a Good Cigar 515
Give Me a Good Havana 2261
Give Me a Good Old Mammy Song 2235
Give Me a Man Like That 567
Give Me a Martial Air 3442
Give Me a Night 3849
Give Me a Pinch 4319
Give Me a Pink Coat 2240
Give Me a Road 3159
Give Me a Roll on a Drum 2813
Give Me a Share in America 3564
Give Me a Ship 4408
Give Me a Sock with Your Shoes 4041
Give Me a Song I Can Whistle 3104
Give Me a Star 4396
Give Me a Thought Now and Then 1610
Give Me a Thrill 2071
Give Me a Wall 3159
Give Me a Word 2864
Give Me All of You 1309, 2762
Give Me All the Flowers (Flower Song) 2254
Give Me All the Money 2033
Give Me an And 778
Give Me an Old-Fashioned Girlie 3222
Give Me Back My Liza 2675, 4130
Give Me Excess of It 4449
Give Me Four Beats 943
Give Me Love 3697
Give Me Love, Love, Love 2903
Give Me More 2195
Give Me My Mammy 487, 3649
Give Me Old Broadway and I'll Be Satisfied 1332
Give Me One Good Reason 181
Give Me One Hour 4664
Give Me Someone 3236
Give Me Something in a Uniform 1561
Give Me Something in a Uniform of Blue 3525
Give Me That Key 4537
Give Me That Letter 4393
Give Me That Rose 3768
Give Me the Girls 994
Give Me the Land 3972, 4517
Give Me the Love 3830
Give Me the Moonlight 1240
Give Me the Open Air 1214
Give Me the Rain 1460
Give Me the Simple Life 2953
Give Me the South All the Time 1823
Give Me the Sunshine 2302
Give Me Thy Heart Love 1768
Give Me Thy Heart, Love 4187
Give Me Your Heart and Give Me Your Hand 4429
Give Me Your Love 4283, 4763
Give Me Your Tired, Your Poor
(The New Colossus) 1609
Give Me Your Tired, Your Poor 2894
Give My Regards to Broadway 1478, 2517, 2975
Give Shalom and Sabbath to Jerusalem 4396

Give, Sinbad, Give 1101
Give the Devil His Due 25
Give the Devil His Dues 1754
Give the Doctor the Best in the House 1748
Give the Little Girl a Great Big Hand 2057
Give the Little Kids a Chance 3617
Give the Little Lady a Great Big Hand 1614
Give the Public What It Wants 2742
Give Them Girls 2460
Give This Little Girl a Hand
(Give That Little Girl a Hand) 3436
Give Trouble the Air 2
Give Us a Drink 4453
Give Us a Fleet 2534
Give Us a Kiss 942
Give Us a Ragtime Tune 256
Give Us a Tune 4532
Give Us Barabbas 4788
Give Us Dames 1577
Give Us Power 3836
Give Us This Day 1002
Give Us Your Kind Applause 335
Give Your Bride a Kiss 4486
Give Your Heart a Chance to Sing 2439
Give Your Heart a Try 4471
Give Your Heart in June-Time 4010
Give Your Heart to Jesus 3651
Give Your Love 3601
Givers and Getters 3684
Givers and Takers 4196
Giving It Up for Love 508
Giving Life 2451
Giza-on-the-Nile 3490
Glad 2547
Glad Feet 2833
Glad I Have a Boy 2636
Glad That You Were Born 3888
Glad Tidings 3648
Glad to Be Back 2707
Glad to Be Home 2983
Glad to Be Unhappy 3283
Glad to Have a Friend Like You 1389
Glad to Know Ya 4089
Glad, Triumphant Hour 1162
Gladiators 1154, 1358
Gladiators' Ballet 134
Gladys O'Flynn 591
Glamorous Life, The 4399
Glamorous Life, The (1) 2536
Glamorous Life, The (2) 2536
Glamour Girl 3975
Glass Glass 1537
Glass of Beer, A 1569
Glenda's Place 4682
Glendy Burk 4149
Glengall 3912
Glide DeLuxe 487
Gliding Through My Memoree 1315
Glimpse-Impse-Impse, A 3976
Glimpse of Eden, A 2632
Glimpse of Love 4718
Glimpses of the Moon 2071
Glitter and Be Gay 630
Glittering Gold 47
Gloaming 726
Global Glamor Girls 3561
Globe Trot, The 487
Globe-Trotter, The 3672
Globe Trotters, The 2004
Globligated 3651
Gloom and Joy 378
Gloom Heaven 3103
Gloria 483, 3695, 2411, 240
Gloria in Excelsis 2775
Gloria in Excelsis Deo 3211
Gloria Tibi 2775
Gloriana 1171
Glorianna 1580, 1799, 2717
Glorias, The 764
Glorified at Last 888
Glorifying the Girls 4817
Glorioius Chase, The 3063
Glorious Age 1581
Glorious Cheese 322
Glorious Highball 2159
Glorious Land of Hope 1534
Glorious Russian 4160
Glory (Glory and Liberty) 405
Glory 1535, 1582, 3506, 3965
Glory Be 1809
Glory, Glory, Glory
(I Want to Be Glorified) 1653
Glory Hallelujah 4460
Glory-Land Intro 1369
Glory of Each Morning, The 535
Glory of France, The 2715
Glory of Sleepy Hollow, The 2100
Glory of Spring 3523
Glory of Spring, The 3012
Glory of the Corps 2806
Glory of the Morning Sunshine, The 1460
Glory That is Greece, The 1745
Glory to the Dragon 1092
Glory to the Dragon Slayer 1092
Gloss of Fashion 4404
Glove Dance 3899
Glow of the Cigarette, The 4248
Glow Worm 1174
Glow Worm, The 1526
Glow-Worm, The 3951
Glow Worm and the Moth, The 3073
G'Night Dearie 1277
Gnu, A 220
Go and Get Your Old Banjo 2608
Go and Get Yourself a Yo-Yo 98
Go and Search Diligently for the Child 755
Go As Far As You Like 4803
Go Away 4388
Go Away Devil 98
Go Away, Girls 2794

Go Away Girls Go Away 2757
Go Away, Little Girl — Go Back to School 3433
Go Back 561, 2220
Go Back to the Hills 530
Go Back Where You Stayed Last Night 3709
Go Bravely On 4827
Go, Don't Want to Love You No More 302
Go Down to Boston Harbor 2400
Go Down to the River (Washer Woman Song) 651
Go Down, Moses 2203
Go Easy, Mabel 1584
Go Easy with Rosa 3879
Go for Broke 2742
Go for It 3901
Go Forth 1716
Go Gar Sig Gong-Jue 736
Go Get 'Em Harry 3558
Go Get 'Im 4683
Go-Getter, The 773
Go-Go Bug 1587
Go, Go, Go 322
Go! Go! Go! 2876
Go, Go, Go Guerrillas 2953
Go, Go, Go, Joseph 2242
Go, Go, Morgan 2898
Go Happy Bride 3773
Go Harlem 2337
Go Holy Ghost 1116
Go Home 194
Go Home Ev'ry Once in a While (Ev'rybody Ought to Take a Day Back Home) 403
Go Home Train 1227
Go In the Best of Health 2925
Go Into Your Dance 1359, 3131, 3406
Go Into Your Trance 1891
Go Little Boat 2372, 2900, 3250
Go Now 3695
Go on and Marry! 2936
Go On Your Mission 4521
Go Out Big 3299
Go Places and Do Things 142
Go Sit By the Body 651
Go Slow, Johnny 3815
Go Slow Saturday 3111
Go South 1691
Go South, Young Man 884
Go There 240
Go to Church on Sunday 651
Go to It 1588
Go to It, Old Girl! 2047
Go to Naxos 1817
Go to Paris or Vienna 2424
Go to Sleep 3274
Go to Sleep Slumber Deep! 250
Go to Sleep Whatever You Are 170
Go to the Mirror 4676
Go to the Mountains 2357
Go to the Movies 2454
Go to the Wall 1195
Go Up to the Mountain 2661
Go Visit 3900
Go 'Way Blues, Ya Bother Me! 1879
Go 'Way Mistah Moon 3575
Go West Young Girl 3402
Go Where Fate Will Lead 3943
Go Where You Go 2392
Go While the Goin' Is Good 3675
Goal in My Life, The 722
Goblin Man 1518
Goblin Market 1589
Goblin's Bride, The 1602
God Bless! 167
God Bless All the Misfits 1590
God Bless America 789, 4770
God Bless Coney 1590
God Bless Rockefeller 1755
God Bless the Buskers 589
God Bless the Child 3905
God Bless the Family 453
God Bless the Fig Tree 825, 4022
God Bless the Human Elbow 367
God Bless the Ladies 61
God Bless the Women 3359
God Bless Us Everyone 754
God Bless You All the Day 1255
God Bless You, Mr. Rosewater 1591
God Could Give Me Anything 593
God Damn Everythang 374
God Fearing Wife 1347
God Gave Me Eyes 111
God Help Us 2173
God Is an American 3684
God Is Black 2001
God Is Good 482
God Is in the People 1282
God Is Smiling on You 2284
God Loves the Baptist 2046
God Never Closes a Door 2065
God of Faithful 1715
God of Mercy 1715
God Said 1872, 2775
God Save Our Glorious Queen 3461
God Save the King 3450
God Save Us 4449
God Sends Sunday 4123
God Shall Wipe All the Tears Away 2796
God, That's Good! 4233
God-Why-Don't-You-Love-Me Blues, The 1329
God Will Take Care 1592
Goddess of Liberty, The 1593
Goddess of Mine (Star of Love) 2670
Goddess of Rain 1980
Goddess of Rector's, The 4650
Goddesses of Love 2611
Godmother's Song 170
God's Country 1973
God's Curse 4523
God's Garden 3564
God's Gift 2171
God's Gonna Cut You Down 2203

God's Good to the Irish 2829
God's Green World 999
Gods Have Gone Away, The 3418
God's in the People 4168
Gods on Tap, The 3272
God's Peculiar Care 2992
God's Song (That Why I Love Mankind) 2787
Godsons and Godmothers 1527
Gogo 1596
Goin' Back in Time 576
Goin' Back to New Orleans 4197
Goin' Back to School 2608
Goin' Back to That Feelin' 337
Goin' Courting 3888
Goin' Downtown 1103
Goin' East 915
Goin' Gone 828
Goin' Home 1002, 1813, 4167
Goin' Home Blues 339
Goin' Home Train 620
Goin' Home with My Children 1737
Goin' on a Hayride 4366
Goin' to Broadway 550
Goin' to Chicago 3814
Goin' to the Moon 90
Goin' to Town (inst.) 895
Goin' Where the River Goes 2027
Going All the Way 3601
Going Back Home 2985
Going Back to Dixieland 1479
Going Down 1717
Going Down Slowly 4127
Going, Going, Gone 2568
Going, Going, Gone! 4335
Going Home 1402, 1618, 2147, 3747, 4447
Going Home on New Year's Morning 4077
Going Home to Lulu 1405
Going Home Tomorrow 2318
Going Home with My Children 3927
Going Native 4243
Going on the War Path 3357
Going Out, The 3830
Going Over the Bumps 3655
Going Places 695, 1665
Going Rowing 2569
Going Some 381
Going South 554
Going-Staying 3902
Going There 4807
Going to Fight the Indians 3855
Going to Make It Better All the Time 3925
Going to Miss Me 981
Going to the Ball 2937
Going to the Devil with Me 1548
Going to the Theatre 3858
Going to Town with Me 1136
Going to Work 568
Going Up 924, 1135
Going Up (in My Aeroplane) 1566
Going Up 1598
Gol-Durn! 3323
Gold 1732
Gold! 2591
Gold 4444
Gold and Blue and White 2937
Gold Bug March (inst.) 1599
Gold Cannot Buy 1918
Gold Digger, The 1486
Gold-Diggers, The 1847
Gold Digger's Blues, The 200
Gold Fish 2857
Gold, Gold 4106
Gold! Gold! Gold! 1926
Gold Rush in the Sky 3204
Gold, Silver and Green 3407
Gold to Make You a Queen 4364
Gold, Women and Laughter 2595
Goldbergs, The 2925
Golden Age, The 1016
Golden Anniversary 4828
Golden Boy 1601, 1601
Golden Butterfly, The 1602
Golden Calf 1715
Golden Crown 1890
Golden Crowns of Greece, The 2357
Golden Days 2363, 2993, 3697, 4188
Golden Days of Good Queen Anne 346
Golden, Delicious Fish 656
Golden Dream, The 2754
Golden Dreams 905, 4155, 2644
Golden Eagle 3204
Golden Evenings of Autumn Time 4437
Golden Gang, The 4611
Golden Gate 1605, 1693, 3149
Golden Gates of Happiness 2843
Golden Girl, The 1606
Golden Girl 3796
Golden Goblet 1017
Golden Helmet 2727
Golden Indian, The 4437
Golden Isle, The 1682
Golden Key, The 3777
Golden Land 2106, 2422
Golden Land, Golden Life 4383
Golden Light, The 1259
Golden Long Ago, The 4649
Golden Love 823
Golden Memories of Perfume 1779
Golden Moment 911, 1990
Golden Net, The 4662
Golden Oldie 2949
Golden Perbanou, The 818
Golden Pheasant, The 3333
Golden Rainbow 1611
Golden Ram, The 4481
Golden Rule Song, The 1592
Golden Rules 2982
Golden Sails 4762
Golden Slumbers 3450, 3903
Golden Stairs of Love, The 3396

Golden Sunshine 1852
Golden Trail 1689
Golden Wedding Waltz, The 1311
Golden West, The 1967, 3401
Goldfarb! That's I'm! 1528
Goldfarb Variations, The 2687
Goldfish Glide 3968
Goldstein, Swank & Gordon 573
Goldwyn & Warner & May'r & Zanuck & Cohn 1000
Golf 4354
Golfing 4424
Golfing Blues 199, 3406
Golliwog 3388
Gona Get Right Some Day 3202
Gonda Waltzes 1555
Gondola and the Girl, The 2526
Gondola Duet 3151
Gondola Song 3151
Gondolier 3478, 4843, 4853
Gondolier Song 3011
Gone 3643
Gone Are the Days 1321, 1886
Gone Away Blues 266
Gone Everywhere but Home 1402
Gone, Gone, Gone! 3541
Gone in Sorrow 4384
Gone Is the Smile 1179
Gone So Long 2702
Gone to Texas 2573
Gone with the Dawn 662
Gone with the Wind 1616, 1616
Gong Song, The 1319
Gonna Be Another Hot Day 3542
Gonna Be Rich 3940
Gonna Build a Mountain 4160
Gonna Get a Woman 4318
Gonna Get Hot 3515
Gonna Go Along with Lincoln 2806
Gonna Run 3555
Gonna Take My Time 108
Goo-Goo 336
Goo-Goo Da Da (Goo Goo G'Da) 4824
Goo Goo Goo 827
Goo-Goo Land 2858
Goo-Goo Man, The 2159
Gooch's Song 2713
Good-a-Bye John 349
Good Advice 1832, 4258, 4447
Good Afternoon 4363
Good and Lucky 4569
Good As Anybody 1222, 2958
Good, Bad, Beautiful Broadway 4269
Good, Better, Best 47
Good Book and Lyrics 3186
Good Book, The 2588
Good Boy 1617, 1864
Good Boy Wedding March 1617
Good-By, Little Girl Good-By 2493
Good By Mr. Ragtime 2485
Good Bye 480, 3346
Good-Bye 3403
Good Bye 4452, 4200
Good-Bye and Good Luck 4422
Good-Bye, Au Revoir, Auf Wiedersehen 4667
Good-Bye Bargravia 3791
Good Bye Becky Cohen 4804
Good-Bye Bill 1632, 2490
Good Bye Boys 357
Good-Bye Boys 1407
Good Bye Boys 1963
Good-Bye Broadway 2900
Good-Bye Broadway, Hello France 3401
Good Bye Christina Swenson 3268
Good-Bye Ethiopia 9
Good-bye Everybody 2922
Good Bye Everybody 3237
Good-Bye Flo 2517
Good-Bye Forever 4453
Good Bye France 1920
Good-Bye Happy Days 1308
Good Bye Helen of Troy 208
Good-Bye! Hello! 3868
Good Bye, Honey Falls 1587
Good Bye, Jennie Jones 2505
Good-bye, Little Dream, Good-bye 1762
Good-Bye, Little Dream, Good-Bye 3216
Good Bye, Little Dream, Goodbye 3674
Good Bye Little Girl 2665
Good-Bye, Little Girl 2893
Good-Bye Little Girl, Good-Bye 4181
Good-Bye, Little Girls, Good-Bye 3996
Good-Bye, Little Rose-Bud 4694
Good-Bye, London Town 4657
Good-Bye Main Street 2706
Good Bye, Miss Liberty 2119
Good Bye, Mr. Ragtime 800
Good-Bye My Emerald Land 2662
Good Bye My Sailor Boy 591
Good-bye, My Sailor Good-bye 1972
Good-Bye My Tango 4807
Good-Bye My True Love 2287
Good-Bye New Amsterdam 586
Good Bye, Old Home 2505
Good Bye School Days 4437
Good-Bye Sweet Marie 3350
Good-Bye, Sweet Old Manhattan Isle 1731
Good Bye Sweet Old Manhattan Isle 3480
Good-Bye, Take Care of Yourself 1551
Good-Bye to All That 3390
Good-Bye to Dear Old Alaska 1688
Good-bye to Sadness 3125
Good-bye World 1857
Good Clean Fight 2333
Good Clean Fun 4312
Good Clean Sport 3861
Good Companions, The 1618
Good Companions 1619
Good Connections 3858
Good Day, Good Night 1309

Good Day, Yankees! 4646
Good Days and Bad Days 931
Good Deed for Today 4237
Good Doctor, The 3864
Good Evening 3576
Good Evening (A Dream of the Dance) 2745
Good Evening, Caroline 2044
Good Evening, Friends 3068, 4730
Good Evening, Mr. Man in the Moon 1932
Good Evening, Princesse 4777
Good Fairy, The (A Jo Tunder) 2705
Good Fellow, Mine 1529
Good Fellows Club, The 4747
Good Folks of Lubbock, The 264
Good for Nothin' 2337
Good for Nothin' Joe 882
Good for You-Bad for Me 1323
Good Friends 167, 602
Good Friends Surround Me 2813
Good from Any Angle 4252
Good Girl 555
Good Girl in the Country 1992
Good Golly Miss Molly 3695
Good-Good-Good 1993
Good, Good Times 1010
Good Guy Always Gets the Girl, The 2235
Good Hand Organ and a Sidewalk's All We Need 317
Good Impression, A 1168
Good Impression 4238
Good in Black 1757
Good, Kind, Jolly Man, The 4046
Good King James, The 466
Good King Phillip 732
Good Little Boy 3876
Good Little Girls 2554, 4499
Good Little Kiddies 4382
Good Little Sunday School Boy, The 2906
Good Little Things We Do, The 3246
Good Luck 1015, 2352
Good Luck, Mr. Flyin' Man 653
Good Luck Sam! 1624
Good Luck to You 4272
Good Madam Geneva 346
Good Man Is Hard to Find, A 2796
Good Mornin' 3992
Good Mornin' Brother 3541
Good Mornin' Mornin' 2027
Good Morning 685, 2017, 698, 3835, 4206, 4453, 4766, 544
Good Morning All 2549
Good Morning Dearie 1625
Good Morning, Dr. Puffin 2339
Good Morning, Good Day 3918
Good Morning, Good Morning 3903
Good Morning Judge 2254, 3096
Good Morning, Miss Standing 2252
Good Morning, Mr. Sun 4003
Good Morning Starshine 1717
Good Morning Sunshine 2640
Good Morning Teacher 1573
Good Morning World 2962
Good News 3987, 1628, 2415
Good News, The 4168
Good News, Bad News 1633
Good Night 47, 200, 4732, 954, 1021, 2050, 1193, 4015, 4808, 4817
Good Night, and Au Revoir 333
Good Night Angeline 3963
Good Night Boat 3146
Good Night Dear 598, 2624
Good Night, Evangeline 2800
Good Night Hymn 634
Good Night Ladies 2789
Good Night, Love 2854
Good Night, Lucindy 2029
Good Night, Marie 2792
Good Night, Mr. Organ Grinder Man 228
Good Night, My Beautiful 1494
Good Night, My Dear 3649
Good Night My Dear 43
Good-night My Own Love 3488
Good Night Number 3022
Good Night Nurse 4806
Good Night Paul 3256
Good Night, Sweetheart, Good Night 4364
Good Night Weirdy 2029
Good Nite, Germany 1407
Good Ol' Mammy Song, A 556
Good Old American Way, The 1249
Good Old Burlesque Show, A 4197
Good Old California 2517
Good Old Cambria 4113
Good Old Circus Band 4806
Good Old College Days 4215
Good Old Days, The 2707
Good Old Days 4433
Good Old Days, The 3479, 3551
Good Old Days 3831
Good Old Days of Burlesque 4180
Good Old Days of Yore, The 531
Good Old Egg, A 2637
Good Old Fashioned Get Together 4737
Good Old-Fashioned Revolutionary, A 4022
Good Old Fashioned Way, The 1415
Good Old-Fashioned Way, The 1650
Good Old Fashioned Western Smile, A 1562
Good Old German Beer 2335
Good Old Girl 374
Good Old Glory 357
Good Old Harry (Finale Act I) 2467
Good Old Levee Days 3397
Good Old Mammy Song, A 4197
Good Old Mill, The 1561
Good Old Palmy Days, The 1466
Good Old Pickwick 3482
Good Old Porfirio Diaz 4609
Good Old Times, The 2940
Good Old U.S.A., The 4681
Good Old Ways, The 71

Good or Bad 1816
Good Pals 2602
Good People Gather Round 2698
Good Queen Bess 4427
Good Ship Caledonia, The 414
Good Ship Honeymoon, The 396, 1901
Good Ship Whip-poor-will 2800
Good Sports 1630
Good Thing Going 16, 2822
Good Thing I Learned to Dance 4
Good Things and Bad Things 2757
Good Things Come 705
Good Time Charlie 603, 823
Good-Time Flat Blues 1063
Good-Time Girl, The (V.D. Polka) 3330
Good Time Ladies Rag 3506
Good Times 2790, 2333, 793, 3318
Good Times Are Here to Stay 956
Good Times Are Here, The 3757
Good To Be Alive 2646
Good Triumphs Over Evil 4102
Good Vibrations 3695, 1072, 3739
Good Way to Be Bad, A 2542
Good-Will Movement, The 2847
Gooda-Bye John 3675
Goodby 2043
Goodby, Dixieland 3041
Goodby Forever 984
Goodby My Old Kentucky Home 1479
Goodby Ragtime 984
Goodbye 3757, 1269, 1555, 1619, 2243
Goodbye (Crossover) 166
Goodbye 1714
Goodbye America 2373
Goodbye Bachelor Days 2749
Goodbye Boys 870
Goodbye, Canavaro 4862
Goodbye, Charlie 3551
Goodbye Chickasaw County 3564
Goodbye, Darlin' 2961
Goodbye, Dear Friend, Goodbye 911
Goodbye, Dear Old Bachelor Days 4810
Goodbye, Dinah 4425
Goodbye—ee 3259
Goodbye, Emil 3760
Goodbye, Failure, Goodbye
(Gawk, Tousle and Shucks) 2014
Goodbye Feet 54
Goodbye Forever 1033
Goodbye Fred 3000
Goodbye, George 3918
Goodbye Girl 2282
Goodbye Girl, The 1633
Goodbye Girls 1990
Goodbye Girls, Hello Yale 3082
Goodbye Girls, I'm Through 736
Goodbye Girls I'm Through 1176
Goodbye, Good Luck 994
Goodbye, Goodbye 2377
Goodbye, Hiram 106
Goodbye Hives 1590
Goodbye Ike 392
Goodbye Is Hard to Say 4337
Goodbye Johnny 2229
Goodbye, Kind Sir, Goodbye 1290
Goodbye, Lennie! 1529
Goodbye Little Dream, Goodbye 4517
Goodbye Little Rascals 2541
Goodbye Love 4718
Goodbye, Mae 456
Goodbye, Maggie Doyle 4662
Goodbye Magic 1104
Goodbye, Molly Brown 2978
Goodbye, My Bachelor 823
Goodbye, My City 3938
Goodbye, My Fancy 2433
Goodbye My Honey 1616
Goodbye, My Lady Love 1897, 3949
Goodbye My Love 2323
Goodbye, My Sweet 2731
Goodbye, Old Girl 957
Goodbye, Once Again 496
Goodbye Pal 1532
Goodbye, Paree 4792
Goodbye Poor Old Manhattan 60
Goodbye Saccharine 1512
Goodbye Salome 3733
Goodbye Song, The 1828
Goodbye Sunshine Hello Moon 4813
Goodbye Sunshine, Hello Moon 1154
Goodbye Sweetheart 3575
Goodbye to Flirtation 4219
Goodbye to the Old Love, Hello to the New 4443
Goodbye, World 1701
Goodbye Yankee Doodle 4012
Goodbye, Yesterday 3507
Goodbyes 1116, 4431
Goodfellow Days 1935
Goodly Little Things We Do, The 1582
Goodness, Ain't You Glad? 186
Goodness Don't Come Easy When You're Bad 952
Goodness Gracious 4426
Goodnight 920, 1056, 2132, 2292, 4192
Goodnight and Thank You 1211
Goodnight Angeline 1198
Goodnight Brother Green 2009
Goodnight, Goodnight 1120
Goodnight Is Not Goodbye 287
Goodnight Mirster Hurdy-Gurdy Man 4808
Goodnight My Lady Love 3252
Goodnight, My Love, Good Night 191
Goodnight My Someone 3016
Goodnight Sweetheart 1135, 1136
Goodtime Charley 610, 1634
Goodtime While I Can 3041
Goody, Goody 3178
Goody Goody 3428
Goody, Goody Girls 1537
Googly, Googly, Goos 4793
Googy Oo 632

Googy-oo 2986
Googy-Oogy-Oo 830
Goona-Goona 364, 1600
Goona Goona 4021
Goose Girl, The 1388
Goose Never Be a Peacock 3837
Goozy Woozy 1568
Gordie 1736
Gordita Es Bonita 2478
Gorgeous 170, 2896
Gorgeous Alexander 3117
Gorgeous Lily 3636
Gorgeous to Gaze At 1414
Gospel 612
Gospel According to King, The 3039
Gospel According to Lillian 2992
Gospel According to St. Matthew, The 1595, 4788
Gospel According to the Leopard 2283
Gospel News 4147
Gospel of Gabriel Finn 4558
Gossip 101, 102, 1171, 2532, 2754, 3013, 4303, 4169, 4210, 4292
Gossip Song, The 249
Gossip Song 3129
Gossip's Chorus 3675
Gossiping 4010
Gossiping Grapevine 4268
Gossips 4357
Gossips, The 4652
Gossips' Chorus 4754
Got a Bran' New Suit 216
Got a Head Like a Rock 2225
Got a Match 2388
Got a Need for You 879
Got a New Boy Friend 1414
Got a Notion 1985
Got a Rainbow 4443
Got It Again 1448
Got Myself a New Love 3605
Got Myself Another Jockey Now 2302
Got No Time 888
Got That Good Time Feelin' 2400
Got the Lady Dressed 3792
Got the World in the Palm of My Hand 766
Got to Be a Woman Now 1002
Got to Be Bad to Be Good 3278
Got to Be Good Times 1103
Got to Find My Way 4292
Got to Get Away from Here 2551
Got to Go to Town 2423
Got to Have More 2308
Got to Sing Me a Song 3697
Got Tu Go Disco 1637
Got Un Zayn Mishpet Iz Gerekht (God and His Judgment Are Right) 1609
Got what It Takes 2850
Got You Right Where I Want You 18
Gott Is Gut 2583
Gotta Be a Dream 2664
Gotta Dance 2582
Gotta Do My Duty 2238
Gotta Find a Way to Do It 3172
Gotta Get a Partner 2196
Gotta Get Back to You 2426
Gotta Get de Boat Loaded 4763
Gotta Get Joy 2400
Gotta Get Out 1164
Gotta Getaway 1638
Gotta Go West 1597
Gotta Hang My Wash Out to Dry 825
Gotta Have a Man Around the House 2516
Gotta Have a Man, Sometime 4180
Gotta Have Hips Now 1836
Gotta Hurry 2307
Gotta Live Free 3035
Gotta Move 2084
Gotta New Song 3173
Gotta Pay 2661
Gotta Pretend 2784
Gotta Take a Chance 3690
Gottet Got 613
Gout, The (The Spasms) (dance) 3274
Governor of the State 2698
Governor of the State, The 1640
Governor of Villaya, The 4430
Governor's Entrance 3081
Governor's Lady 2112
Governor's Son, The 1640
Governor's Song, The 2917
Gown for Each Hour of the Day, A 3387
Gown Is Mightier Than the Sword, The 3538
Gowns 1629
Gowns By Roberta 3735
Gowns Soft and Clingy 4464
Gozinto 4837
Gra Ma Chree 1445
Grab a Girl 1011, 4001
Grab Bag, The 1485, 1643
Grab Me a Gondola 1644
Grab Them While You Can 2048
Grace 3908
Graceful and Fair 3978
Graceful Exit, A 2231
Grade 'A' Treatment 521
Graduate, The 1645
Graduates of Mrs. Grimm's Learning 2001
Graduation 1077, 2224
Grafin Mariza 905
Grafitti 4468
Graft 2848, 4662
Grain of Sand 2539, 3167
Grand and Glorious Fourth, The 2985
Grand Army of Crooks 3537
Grand Banks Sequence 647
Grand Cafe, The 1068
Grand Canal 965
Grand Canal, The 3171
Grand Central Station 3279
Grand Coulee Dam 4740
Grand Diversion, The 2617

Grand Ensemble of Martians 4753
Grand Finale 2035, 3041
Grand Hotel 223, 1649
Grand Imperial Cirque de Paris 656
Grand Jury Jump 1408
Grand Knowing You 3918
Grand Manner, The 1035
Grand March 1474, 3887
Grand Old Ivy 2019
Grand Old Life 4642
Grand Old Party, The 4004
Grand Old Rag 1759
Grand Old Veterans in the U.S.A. 2013
Grand Opening 1023
Grand Opera Up-to-Date 1964
Grand Operatic Finale Act II 3348
Grand Panjandrum 1119
Grand Parade, The 1649
Grand Parade 2947
Grand Parade, The 3439
Grand Polonaise (dance) 4435
Grand Prix, The 1881
Grand Prix of Portofino, The 3543
Grand Processional March (inst.) 2974
Grand Review and Finale 4439
Grand Street 3722
Grand Street Presentation, A 3577
Grand Street Tivoli Presentation, A 3577
Grand Tango, The 223
Grand Tour, The 1933
Grand Vizier's Lament 177
Grand Waltz, The 1649
Grande Ensemble 2455
Grandfather's Clock 2270
Grandfathers 1727
Grandioso 1046
Grandma 780
Grandma Dear Grandma 2816
Grandma Small 1055
Grandma's a Flapper Too 317
Grandma's Day 765
Grandma's Diary 159
Grandpa Guerrilla 2447
Grandpa's Hat 1213
Grandpa's Spells 1120
Grandpapa 4862
Grangeford Prayer 2027
Granny 974
Granny's Gulch 974
Grant 2018
Grant Avenue 1315
Grape Dance, The 3397
Grapes of Roth (dance) 3603
Grapevine, The 4416
Grass Between My Toes 2065
Grass Grows Green (in No Man's Land), The 3330
Grass Harp, The 1662, 1662
Grass Is Always Greener, The 131, 4727
Grass Widow, The 1663
Grass Widows 200
Grasshopper Song 2322
Grasshoppers Chorus 476
Gratitude 2982
Grau Brae Nicht 1831
Grave Digger's Song, The 3909
Gravy Train 4107
Gray 1164
Gray Goose, The 4015
Grazie Dio 139
Grazie Per Niente 4060
Grease 1664
Greased Lightnin' 1664
Great-All-American-Power-Driven-Engine 2616
Great Am I with a Capital I, The 645
Great American Opera 2168
Great American Roof, The 924
Great Balls of Fire 3695, 3739
Great Big Baby 4281
Great Big Bear 4077
Great Big Blue Eyed Baby 3134
Great Big Girl Like Me, A 77, 1881
Great Big Judge, A 2122
Great Big Sky, The 4169
Great Chandler, The 4166
Great Cleopatra Comes 2041
Great Connection 922
Great Day 612, 1667, 3018, 3020, 3249
Great Dictator and Me, The 3822
Great Divide 3159
Great Easter Sunday Parade, The 1478
Great Forever Wagon, The 4558
Great Game 451
Great Gatsby, The 1451
Great Gettin' Up Mornin' 444
Great Git-Away, The 2941
Great God Boogie, The 4117
Great, Great Lover, The 2387
Great Guy 1862
Great If, The 2134
Great Immortals, The 4707
Great Indoors, The 4517
Great Little Guy 4532
Great Lover Tango, The 2148
Great Magician, The 825
Great Man Says, The 4163
Great Man's Whiskers, The 1674
Great Men, Great Days, or the King of the Cafe Royal 1256
Great Musicians 1602
Great New York Police, The 2533
Great News 3760
Great North Road 1619
Great Professor, The 2771
Great Purple Butterfly, The 1977
Great Ram-Jam, The 3348
Great Scot! 1676
Great Society Waltz, The 366, 1437
Great Unknown, The 3439
Great Waltz, The 1681

Great White Easiest Way, The 48, 3773
Great White Father 3610
Great White Way 1464
Great White Way in China 735
Great White Way, The 2069
Great Wide Open Spaces, The 4818
Great Wind, The 3697
Great Wisconsin 390
Great Workers for the Cause 148
Great Zampano, The 2368
Greatest Battle-Song of All, The 4747
Greatest Comic of Them All, The 4577
Greatest Gift, The 1059
Greatest Invention, The 3108
Greatest Man in the World, The 2289
Greatest Man of All, The 1256
Greatest Navy in the World, The 4803
Greatest of These, The 3469
Greatest Show in France, The 1347
Greatest Show on Earth, The 397, 2386
Greatest Show on Earth 4611
Greatest Showman in the Universe, The 1159
Greatest Star of All, The 4217
Greatest Team of All 1345
Greathead Shield 3831
Grecian Bend, The 2789
Grecian Frieze 1817
Grecian Skies 3466
Greed 42, 1509
Greedy Girl 3691
Greek Dance 1214, 3214
Greek Marine Hymn, The 1745
Greek Scene 2252
Greek to You 1683
Greeks Have Got the Girdle, The (Finaletto) 601
Green 1259, 1099
Green and Blue 4253
Green and Gray 243
Green Are the Waving Branches 762
Green As Grass 2928
Green Bird, The 3788
Green Carnations 429
Green Eyes 4824
Green Finch and Linnet Bird 4233
Green Gravel 962
Green, Green, Green 3631
Green Grow the Lilacs 716, 3263
Green Pants 3233
Green Pastures 443, 1328
Green Place, A 3544
Green Pond 1684
Green Ring, The 1651
Green River Glide 1625
Green-Up Time 2615
Greenbaum 2461
Greenhorn 4172
Greenhorns 3644
Greenspons 3476
Greenwich Village
(Down Greenwich Village Way) 1516
Greenwich Village 2377, 3245
Greenwich Village Belle 3333
Greenwich Village Follies 1695
Greenwich Village Green, The 1692
Greenwich Village Ladies Barber Shop 1690
Greenwich Village Nights 1688
Greenwich Village U.S.A. 1697
Greenwich Village Violet 293
Greenwillow 1698
Greenwillow Christmas 1698
Greenwillow Walk (inst.) 1698
Greeting 2679
Greeting Cards, The 297
Greetings 3691, 4186
Greetings, Gates 4586
Greetings Gentlemen 3865
Greetings to the King 2020
Greetings to You, Sabbath Angels 747
Grenadier's Song 3732
Grenadiers 1123
Grenadiers' Marching Song, The 4186
Gretchen Maedchen Mine 782
Grey Dove, The 736
Grey Eyes 1222
Greyhound 3254
Grief 710
Grieving for You 542, 2856
Grin-Tin-Tugger 528
Grind, The 1699
Grinding Out a Revue 3144
Gringola 1127
Gripe of the Group, The 272
Griselda, the Goose-Girl in Me
You Behold 1388
Griselda, the Inn Keeper's Daughter 4041
Grisette Song 2839
Gristedes 4268
Grizabella, the Glamour Cat 678
Grocery Boy 4124
Groovy Green Man Groovy 3651
Grouchy 716
Ground and Lofty Dancing 1259
Ground Was Always in Play, The 1053
Groundhog Has Won 1700
Groundhog Is Becoming Important 1700
Groundhog Is Going to Trial 1700
Grove of Eucalyptus, The 4396
Grovel, Grovel 2242
Grover 2018
Grow for Me 2544
Grow Mrs. Goldfarb 1832
Growin' Boy 245
Growing Man, The 4150
Growing Older 807, 808, 809, 3542
Growing Pains 2817, 4446
Growing Up 2822, 3454
Growing Up Catholic 3211
Growing Up Is Learning How to
Say Goodbye 4764
Growltiger's Last Stand 678

Grown Up Children 1544
Grown Ups 732
Grown-Ups Are the Stupidest People 1577
Grownups Song 99
Grub Time 2282
Gruntled 673
Gruntles 2246
Guadalajara 3600
Guantanamo 62
Guarantees 269
Guarded 771
Guardians of the Gate, The 4723
Guardians of the House 355
Guardians of the Nation 3195
Guards of Fantasy, The 1678
Guards of the Parade 1467
Guenevere 623
Guess 3581
Guess Again 1646
Guess, Guess, Guess 2990
Guess I'm Seasick 228
Guess My Name 3802
Guess We're Gonna Get Along 725
Guess We've Fallen in Love 4092
Guess What 1846
Guess What Charlie 2014
Guess What from Guess Who? 3539
Guess Who 1614, 3243
Guess Who I Am 1521
Guess Who I Saw Today? 3107
Guess Who Was There 1023, 2804
Guess-Yes 4373
Guests, The 799
Guide Me Mystic Moon to Dixieland 4184
Guided By Love 2320
Guides Stuff 4192
Guido's Song 3171
Guido's Tango (inst.) 3543
Guild Guilded, The 1446
Guileless Orphan, A 402
Guilt 871, 4461
Guilt Inside Your Head, The 2905
Guilty 4619, 1077
Guilty! 3938
Guilty Party 1857
Guinea Pig 3651
Guiness, Woman 4431
Guinevere Among the Grapefruit Peels 2007
Guitar Song 1139
Guitarist 426
Gum Boot Dance 2147
Gum Shoe Man 1963
Gum Shoe Man, The 2448
Gun Moll 2969
Gun Scene 169
Gun Song 212, 4067
Gunfighter, The 3688
Gunfighter's Ballad, The 362
Gunga Din 1321
Gunman, The 4793
Gunmetal Blues 1702
Gunner in the Navy, A 2465
Guns Are Fun 4595
Guru 3858
Gus and Sadie Love Song 919
Gus the Bus 3032
Gus: The Theatre Cat 678
Gussie Giles 1213
Gussy and the Beautiful People 3370
Gustave 1110
Gusto 3763
Gut Rocks 4011
Guten Abend 610
Guten Morgen, Buon Giorna, Bon Jour 1355
Gutte Nacht 1639
Gutter Song, The 3103
Guv'ment 394
Guy, a Guy, a Guy, A 3224
Guy I Love, The 3448
Guy Like Me, A 1990
Guy Who Brought Me, The 372
Guy with the Polka Dotted Tie 2078
Guys and Dolls 1706, 3444
Guys Like You 3752
Gvald Ich Vil Es 3781
Gwendolyn 2765
Gwendolyn of Grosvenor Square 4115
Gymnasium Chorus 954
Gypsy 680
Gypsy Blues 3513, 3512, 3963
Gypsy Born and Bred Am I 1712
Gypsy Bride 152
Gypsy Bring Your Fiddle 3727
Gypsy Caravan 1011
Gypsy Dance 1121, 2385, 2262, 3424
Gypsy Dance, A 4186
Gypsy Days 3086
Gypsy Girl 1096, 4450
Gypsy in Me, The 163
Gypsy Jan 1355
Gypsy Joe 4683
Gypsy Land 351
Gypsy Life 1096
Gypsy Life, The 4186
Gypsy Love 1712, 2140, 3020, 4450
Gypsy Love Song 1711, 4818
Gypsy Madness 3165
Gypsy Man, The 1065
Gypsy Melodies 4056
Gypsy of Love 4186
Gypsy Rose 1440, 2020, 3025, 4227
Gypsy Rover, The 1707
Gypsy Saraband 4050
Gypsy Song 1203, 2794
Gypsy Song, The 3853
Gypsy Song 3372
Gypsy Song (Come to Gypsy Land) 3658
Gypsy Trail, The 4491
Gypsy Warned Me, The 3500
Gypsy Wedding Ceremony and Festivities 4046

H

H.G. Wells' Laboratory 1159
H.M.S. Goldilocks or the Lass That Loved a Mailman 4679
H.M.S. Pinafore 1948, 2817
H.N.I.C. 578
Ha! Cha! Cha! 672
Ha Ha Family, The 45
Ha, Ha, Ha 2696
Ha! Ha! Ha! 4649
Ha, Ha, Ha 4777
Ha-Ha-Ha (Gang Song) 4778
Ha, Ha, Ha! Millionaires! 2880
Ha, Ha, They Must Sail for Siberia 3547
Ha-Za-Za 3839
Ha'am Haze 4396
Habanera 2830
Habit As We Go Along, The 1562
Hacienda Garden 1182
Hack 'em 1985
Had to Give Up Gym 1425
Had You But Wit 945
Hagar the Horrible 1714
Haggadah, The 1715
Haggle, The 269
Hah 2153
Hail and Reign 3591
Hail Angele, Our Nightingale 902
Hail! Antonia, Hail! 1682
Hail Bibinski 3972
Hail Bompopka 2159
Hail Britannia 279
Hail Celestial Potentate 1243
Hail David 1769
Hail, Franz of Zilania 4250
Hail Gentle Eros 1768
Hail, Gracious Owner of This Spot 2722
Hail, Hail 4168
Hail, Hail, Hail 3326
Hail Hio 3539
Hail Majesty (1) 3526
Hail Mary! 755
Hail Mary 1716
Hail! Mr. Beverly 333
Hail Number One 2504
Hail Poetry 2977
Hail Sphinx 1848
Hail Stonewall Jackson 3056
Hail the Bridegroom 735
Hail the Conquering Hero 837
Hail, the Conquering Hero! 837
Hail, the Falcon 4550
Hail the Grand Wazir 758
Hail the Groom and Hail the Bride 2936
Hail, the Happy Couple 3379
Hail, the Hero of the Day 1540
Hail the Hero of Today 2139
Hail the King 4620
Hail, the Mythic Smew 2339
Hail the Rajah 3786
Hail the Son of David 2075
Hail the Wedding Pair 4616
Hail to Aurora 4425
Hail to Christmas 250
Hail to Cyril 3378
Hail to MacCracken's 4423
Hail to Monty 4860
Hail to Our General 2419
Hail to Our Noble Guest 3578
Hail to Our Queen 3422
Hail to the Baronet 1021
Hail to the Bey 2500
Hail to the Blood 459
Hail to the Bride 1121
Hail to the Caliph 175
Hail to the Golden Calf 1309
Hail to the Judge 3887
Hail to the King 2317, 2320
Hail to the Magistrate 3882
Hail to the Piccadilly Hero 3882
Hail to the Precarious Isles! 1887
Hail to the Queen of Beauty 331
Hail! To the Queen of Beauty 1458
Hail to the School 4169
Hail to the Sultan 177
Hail U.S.A. 969
Hail, We Hope It's a Male 4590
Hail, Ye Indian Maidens 3865
Hair 1388, 1717
Hair of the Dog that Bit You, The 2335
Hair of the Heir, The 82
Hair Pulling Ballet 1108
Hairdo Hop, The 3628
Hairdresser Sequence 2992
Hairpin Harmony 1718
Hairpin Turn 2032
Halala Song, The 1719
Halevay Volt Ikh Singl Geven (I Wish I Were Single Again) 4342
Half a Dozen Little Bits of Lace 3882
Half a Dream to Go 4602
Half a Kiss 4765
Half a Married Man 3727
Half a Moon Is Better Than No Moon 1965
Half a Sixpence 1721
Half Alive 2134
Half and Half 417
Half As Big As Life 3603
Half Caste Woman 4823
Half Moon! 1723
Half of a Couple 534
Half of It, Dearie, Blues, The 2376
Half of Life 602
Half of Me 1497, 3
Half of the World Laughs 1518
Half Past April, and a Quarter to May 2183
Half Past Eight 1726
Half-Past Kissing Time 2209

Half Past Two 178
Half-Past Two 1538
Half the Battle 367
Half the World 2775
Half Time 2072
Half Way Chalet 2610
Half Way to Heaven 4545
Halfway to Heaven 474, 2470
Hall of Fame, The 4430
Hall of Mirrors Ballet 52
Hallapalooza 3452
Hallelujah 322, 1916, 3020
Hallelujah! 3249
Hallelujah 4523, 4635
Hallelujah, Baby! 1729
Hallelujah Basketball 2579
Hallelujah, He's on His Way 1086
Hallelujah, I'm a Bum 3989
Hallelujah to Love 2269
Hallo! Little Miss U.S.A. 4657
Hallowe'en 1965
Halloween Ballet (dance) 4446
Halloween Hayride 3209
Halloween Party 1757
Hallow'eve (dance) 1698
Hallucination 1418
Hallucination of Love 4283
Hallucinations 3814
Halo-Halo-Halo 3736
Halted at the Very Gates of Paradise-
A Song of Frustration 1256
Ham and Eggs 443
Ham and Eggs in the Morning 4271
Ham That I Am 4237
Ham Tree Barbecue, The 1731
Hamakom 299
Hamba Bheklie (
Let the Drinks Be Served) 2147
Hamburg Waltz 2362
Hamil's Birthday 3792
Hamlet 3741
Hamlet Comes Home 412
Hamlet of Fancy, The 3570
Hamlet Was a Melancholy Dane 2974
Hamlets of the Ages 2406
Hammacher Schlemmer, I Love You 2545
Hammer Ring 3989
Hammer Song 4579
Hammers Will Go Rap, Rap, Rap, The 4754
Hammershine 3122
Hammerstein's Music Hall 3544
Hammock Built for Two 1090
Hammock in the Blue 1539
Hammock Song (Then You
Swing, Swing, Swing) 3681
Han 1214
Hand for the Hog 394
Hand in Hand 161, 348, 382, 2761, 3511, 4361
Hand in Hand in Heaven 3374
Hand Is Quicker Than the Eye, The 996
Hand It to the Glands 4232
Hand-Me-Down Blues, The 2569
Hand Me Down My Dancin' Shoes 4389
Hand Me Down That Can o' Beans 3347
Hand Me Down, The 2479
Hand Me Out a Laugh 4425
Hand Me the Wine and the Dice 211
Hand of Fate, The 2290
Hand Organ, The 2686
Handbag Is Not a Proper Mother, A 1194
Handful of Keys 39
Handicap, The 509
Handkerchief Song 871
Handle Me with Care 1902, 4801
Handle to My Name, A 2986
Handle with Care 2229
Handlebar Moustache, The 2460
Hands Across the Sea 1113
Hands Across the Table 4137, 839
Hands Around 3631
Hands Off 903
Hands Up 694, 1631, 4555, 4757
(All I Need Is a) Handshake 486
Handsome Cabin Boy 1985
Handsome Husbands 937
Handsome Stranger 2114
Handsomest Man, The 1116
Handy Andy 3395
Handy Man 2338
(You're a) Handy Thing to Have
Around the House 1029
Hang a Little Moolah on the Washline 1662
Hang By Your Heels in a Cave 2728
Hang Down Your Head and Die 1736
Hang March (inst.) 250
Hang on to Me 2376
Hang on to the Good Times 1737
Hang Together 1212
Hang Together (We'll Hang Together) 3422
Hang Tough 3576
Hang Up! 603
Hang Up Your Hat on Broadway 4291
Hang Your Hat on the Moon 4213
Hang Your Sorrows in the Sun 3540
Hangin' Around with You 4179
Hanging Around Yo' Door 4198
Hanging Gardens of Babylon, The 1132
Hanging Johnny 1736
Hanging Over and Out 1637
Hanging Throttlebottom in the Morning 2444
Hangman's Plea, The 1046
Hanky Panky 2427
Hanky-Panky Glide, The 1738
Hannah 1095
Hannah Dooley 3746
Hannah Jackson Greene 1259
Hannah Will Take Care of You 1739
Hannah's a Hummer 1478, 4717
Hannibal's Comin' 4522
Hans 2047, 2366

Hans Christian Andersen 1741
Hans, Le Jouer de Flute 1743
Hans Rap 2345
Hans' the Man 4135
Happenings 3657
Happier Side 3201
Happiest Day of My Life, The 1734
Happiest Day of Your Life 3318
Happiest Girl in the World, The 1745, 4719
Happiest House on the Block, The 3505
Happiest Man Alive, The 2240
Happiest Millionaires, The 4829
Happiest Moment I've Ever Known, The 3868
Happiest Moment of My Life 109
Happiest Night of His Life, The 1746
Happiest People, The 708
Happily Ever After 832, 2504, 2764, 3307, 3288, 3453
Happily Ever After, After All 690
Happily Married Wolf, A 3844
Happily the Days Are Running By 1258
Happiness 3792, 1971, 3411, 3110, 3921, 4528, 4783, 3369, 2044
Happiness Calling 1414
Happiness Hill 3454
Happiness Is... 128
Happiness Is a Bird 3479, 3484
Happiness Is Going on a Picnic 2092
Happiness Machine, The 973
Happy 403, 567, 1649, 1747, 1974, 2389, 2645
Happy Again 3813
Happy Alienist, The 2786
Happy Anniversary 2033
Happy Any Day 4048
Happy As the Day Is Long 878
Happy Because I'm in Love 1667, 3249
Happy Birthday 1737, 1918, 2033, 2074, 1750, 3953, 4862
Happy Birthday, Erwin 2449
Happy Birthday Harry 1149
Happy Birthday, Mrs. J.J. Brown 4516
Happy Birthday Sweet Sixteen 4193
Happy Birthday to Love 417
Happy Birthday to Vegas 362
Happy Bride 735
Happy Cavalier Overture, The (inst.) 1751
Happy Cigarettes 4137
Happy Day! Happy Day! (Country Dance) 3736
Happy Days 349, 561, 1628, 1753, 2373, 2827, 3020
Happy Days (inst.) 4094
Happy Days 4203, 4737
Happy Days and Lonely Nights 3980
Happy Days Are Here Again 4460
Happy Days in Dixie 1535
Happy Days in Dixieland 2415
Happy Daze Saloon, The 4318
Happy End, The 1755
Happy End 1755
Happy Ending 369, 760
Happy Ending, A (inst.) 752
Happy Ending 1245, 1435, 3703, 3763, 4491
Happy Endings 2757
Happy Enough 2241
Happy Factory 2084
Happy Family 1527
Happy Family, A 3157
Happy Family 3218
Happy Family, The 3771
Happy Family 3858
Happy Feet 4041
Happy Go Lucky 1297, 1756
Happy Go Lucky Days 4429
Happy Guy 1697
Happy Habit 603
Happy, Happy Day 2178
Happy, Happy, Happy 3760
Happy Happy Illinois 3437
Happy, Happy New Year 958
Happy Heart 2267
Happy Heaven of Harlem, The 1272
Happy Hickory 2949
Happy Hindu Waltz 4617
Happy Hoboes 4345
Happy Hollywood 4639
(In a) Happy Home for Two 69
Happy Hooligan 1758, 1759
Happy Horns and Merry Bells 4798
Happy Hottentots 3737
Happy Hukilau, A 3371
Happy Hunting 1300, 1760
Happy Hunting Horn 3353
Happy Hypocrite, The 1761
Happy in Love 4086
Happy in the Morning 4727
Happy Is the Boy 3453
Happy Is the Cricket 2355
Happy Is the Summer's Day 1768
Happy Is the Word 751
Happy Japan 1470
Happy Jest Bein' with Me 556
Happy Jim 2111
Happy Land of Once-Upon-a-Time 2534
Happy Landing 1323
Happy, Laughing Girls! 2455
Happy Life, A 2866
Happy Little Country Girl, A 1964
Happy Little Crook 3899
Happy Little Jeanne 1110
Happy Little Weekend 1932
Happy Love Affair 1596
Happy Man 101
Happy Married Life, A 2334
Happy Melody 1690, 1756
Happy Mother's Day 2962
Happy New Year 692, 1605, 1676
Happy New Year Blues, The 3009
Happy New Year - Every Day 2097
Happy New Year to You 4586
Happy News 3496
Happy Noble Outlaw Band, The 1975

Happy Place Is in My Heart, A 2657
Happy Prince 1691
Happy Rickshaw Man (Jinrikisha Song) 718
Happy Song, A 220
Happy Song 2362
Happy Talk 4096
Happy Thanksgiving 3055
Happy the Day 3949, 4299
Happy Time (inst.) 4127
Happy Time, The 131, 1764, 1764, 1764
Happy Time 3041
Happy Time Al 112
Happy Time Rag 302
Happy Times 3639
Happy to Keep His Dinner Warm 2019, 3444
Happy to Make You Acquantance 3444
Happy to Make Your Acquaintance 2961
Happy Tramp, The 187
Happy Wanderer, The (Val-De Ri, Val-De Ra) 4264
Happy Wedding Day, A 3923
Happy When We Eat 694
Happy with Winged Feet 2348
Happy Years, The 722
Happyland 1334
Harbor Deep Down in My Heart, The 1923
Harbor Haven Heaven on the Sound 3576
Harbor of Dreams 4392
Harbor of Home 1558
Harbor of Lost Dreams, The 2979
Harbor of My Heart 1916
Harbour of Love 4076
Hard, Ain't It Hard 4740
Hard As a Nail 4769
Hard-Boiled Herman 3772
Hard Candy Christmas 374
Hard Day's Night, A 3739
Hard Hat Stetsons 280
Hard Hearted Hannah 2135
Hard Job Being God 1769
Hard Life, A 276
Hard Luck in Society 4655
Hard-On 4684
Hard Time Blues 467
Hard Time War Time 459
Hard Times 3722, 919, 922, 3054
Hard Times-Good Times 1612
Hard to Be a Lady 3258
Hard to Be a Pauper 2866
Hard to Be a Prince 3644
Hard to Be Diva 4139
Hard to Get Along With 2253
Hard to Love 1684
Hard to Say Goodbye, My Love 1103
Hard to Understand the Ladies 3052
Hard Travelin' 4740
Harder They Fall, The 3610
Hardest Part of Love, The 730
Hardest Thing in the World to Do, The 3630
Hardly Think I Will 3989
Hare Krishna 1717
Harem, The 3914, 4131
Harem Dance 3214
Harem Life 4813
Harem Scarem 531
Hari Krishna 1229
Hark! 1770
Hark For'ard! (Away) 1080
Hark the Extra Marital Lark 3107
Hark the Hour 2977
Hark! The Merry Marriage Bells 4404
Hark the Merry Marriage Bells 402
Hark to the Chimes 185
Hark to the Lark 2222
Hark to the Scream of the Eagle 631
Hark to the Song of the Night 3326
Hark to the Sound of the Horn 4719
Hark to the Sound of the Hunter's Horn 1866
Hark to the Voice of Your Lover 2848
Hark, While I Sing to Thee! 4754
Harlem 443, 3905, 3660
Harlem Barcarolle 1342
Harlem Blues 2672
Harlem Bolero 884
Harlem Dan 2034
Harlem Fan Tan 879
Harlem Follies 2195
Harlem Holiday 3709, 877
Harlem Hop 3905
Harlem Hospitality 879
Harlem Hotcha 1772
Harlem Lullaby 4291
Harlem Makes Me Feel! 576
Harlem Mania 439
Harlem Moon 3704, 3965
Harlem Nocturne 1713
Harlem Number Man 3528
Harlem on My Mind 207
Harlem on the Sand 1800
Harlem Prince 295
Harlem Rhumbola 3704
Harlem River Chanty 4392
Harlem River Quiver (Brown Berries) 892
Harlem Rose 2302
Harlem Scat 3628
Harlem Serenade 3953
Harlem '70 576
Harlem, Sweet Harlem 576
Harlem Time 576
Harlem Town 2845
Harlem Waltz, The 4799
Harlem Woogie 3528
Harlem's a Garden 4503
Harlem's Hot As Hades 570
Harlemania 1202, 894
Harlequin Hoops, The 2858
Harlequinade 2227
Harlequinade (inst.) 2394
Harlequinade 3103
Harlequin's Doll 4817

Harmonica Dance 1182
Harmonica Man 1700
Harmony 606, 1237, 3091, 3712, 3280, 3370
Harmony Boys, The 3501
Harmony, Mass. 2219
Harmony on High 264
Harmony, Sweet Harmony 227
Harold and Maude 1775
Harolds of This World, The 299
Harriet Sedley 3931
Harriet's Pavan (dance) 3931
Harrigan 1271, 1478, 2975
Harry, Harry 2800
Harry Is Only Physical 4702
Harry Masters, Jack Craft and Company 4858
Harry's Rag 169
Harry's Resolution 2598
Hartman Ballet (inst.) 4212
Harum Scarem, The 1088
Harvard Beet Song, The 2039
Harvest Days 3424
Harvest Moon, The 2264
Harvester's Song 3754
Harvey 3757, 3846, 4332
Harvey and Sheila 1832
Harvey Bloom 1832
Harvey Promised to Change the World 3757
Harvey's Theme (inst.) 3493
Has Anybody Here Seen Kelly 2232
Has Anybody Seen Jim Jackson? 3041
Has Anybody Seen My Bennie 1027
Has Anybody Seen My Cat? 2844
Has Anybody Seen Our Ship? 3235, 3678
Has Anyone Here Seen My Daddy 1093
Has Anyone Seen My Joe 1485
Has Cupid Laid in Wait for You 4649
Has I Let You Down? 2000
Hash House Habit 4459
Hashish 1717
Hasidic Medley 4396
Hassan, the Sultan with His Court Approaches 3777
Hast Thou Been to Mecca? 2802
Hasta Manana (So This Is Havana) 4291
Haste to Thy Window 1518
Hat, The 1194, 4810
Hat Attack, The 2993
Hat Check Dance 1551
Hat Crossover 597, 3217
Hat Like That, A 1494
Hat My Father Wore, The 801
Hat Song, The 4799
Hate Me 949
Hate Me Please 3734
Hate Song, The 1107
Hate Song 2663
Hate to Say Goodbye to You 3015
Hathor 3309
Hats 3322, 4153, 4473
Hats Make the Woman 2915
Hats Off 1546
Hats Off to Ice 1782
Hattie 4165
Hattie's Time 3671
Haughtiest Naughtiest Girls, The 3298
Haunted Cask, The 1602
Haunted Heart 2137
Haunted Hot Spot 4499
Haunted Pool, The 1593
Haunted Television 3873
Haunted Violin, The 1687
Haunting Honeymoon, The 627
Haunting Me 1808
Haunting Melody 3395
Haunting Refrain 4328
Haute Couture 4013
Haute Ecole 336
Havana 1783, 2174
Havana (Havana Opening) 3436
Havana 194
Havana Bay 2834
Havana Bound 2303
Havana Dance (inst.) 1706
Havana for a Night 1840
Havana Nights 1688
Havanola Jazz 3677
Havanola Roll 2780
Have a Cup of Tea 1477
Have a Dream 64
Have a Good Day 708
Have a Good Time Everybody 740
Have a Good Time, Jonica 2238
Have a Happy 3795
Have a Happy Holiday 4409
Have a Heart 1136, 1784, 4810
Have a Little Bit on Me 178
Have a Little Dance with Me 385
Have a Little Drinkee 418
Have a Little Faith in Me 3795
Have a Little Fun 1075, 3167
Have a Little Pity 1012
Have a Little Regiment of Your Own 377
Have a Little Sip with Me 1560
Have a Little Sooth on Me 227
Have a Memory on Me 374
Have a Nice Day 2208, 2360
Have a Restaurant of Your Own 2696
Have a Smile (dance) 1823
Have a Smile with Momus 4521
Have an Old Waltz with Me 3237
Have an Umbrella 1891
Have Feet Will Dance 2267
Have Gun, Get Gold 4482
Have I Finally Found My Heart? 828
Have I Got a Girl for You 692, 1785, 4067, 832, 1786, 3741
Have I Got a Guy for You 692
Have I Stayed Away Too Long 1741
Have I the Right 699
Have I Told You Lately? 2048

Have More Than Thou Showest 3909
Have Patience, Don't Worry 4751
Have Pity, Sheriff 4621
Have Some Pot 280
Have We Still Got It? 456
Have You Any Little Thing 1587
Have You Anything On for Tonight 1031
Have You Been to Arndyk? 2889
Have You Ever Been Alone with a King Before? 2075
Have You Ever Been on Stage? 3858
Have You Ever Been to China? 1245
Have You Ever Heard It Told That Way Before? 1521
Have You Ever Seen a Prettier Little Congress? 3780
Have You Forgotten? 2371
'Have You Forgotten Me' Blues, The 582
Have You Got Another Girl Like Mary 2341
Have You Got Charm? 279
Have You Got What You Came With? 2568
Have You Heard? 2075, 2925
Have You Heard? (Gossip Song) 3837
Have You Heard 4300
Have You Heard About Philias Fogg? 190
Have You Heard the Brave News 1178
Have You Heard the News? 1290
Have You Heard the Scandal 1565
Have You Met Delilah? 4542
Have You Met Miss Jones? 66, 2068
Have You No Shame 3873
Have You Seen Him, Did He Pass This Way? 1474
Have You Seen My Baby 2826
Have You Seen My Girl 1613
Have You Seen My Henry Brown 2122
Have You Seen the Countess Cindy? 2103
Have You Seen the Ducks 1919
Have You Seen the Ducks Go By 2456
Have You Seen the Princess? 4470
Have You Used Soft Soap? 608
Have Your Bumps Read 1313
Have Yourself a Merry Little Christmas 2805, 3175
Have Yourself a Night 3696
Haven't I Seen You Somewhere Before? 4022
Haven't We Met? 3858
Haven't We Met Before? 532, 3431, 3664
Haven't You Wondered 4522
Havin' a Ball 4423
Havin' a Blues 3528
Havin' a Time 404
Havin' a Wonderful Time 2645, 14
Having a Ball 2940
Having My Own Sweet Way 1113
Having Someone 2420
Having Someone There 1660
Having Wonderful Time 4718
Hawaii 2362
Hawaii (Coralline) 3556
Hawaii's Shore 2636
Hawaiian Moon 2636
Hawaiian Moonlight 1823
Hawaiian Night in Dixie 1829
Hawaiian Night in Dixieland 3513
Hawaiian Skies 3404
Hawk, The 3628
Hawks! 4561
Hay Foot, Straw Foot 1777
Hay, Hay, Hay 3536
Hay-Long 3404
Hay Pitchin' 259
Hay Ride, The 954
Hay! Straw! 3650
Hayfoot, Strawfoot 1722, 2653
Haying Chorus 3998
Hayseed 2896
Hayti 1985
Hayward's Harlem Hellions 97
Haywire 680
Hazards of the Profession 4828
Hazel's Ballet 2306
Hazel's Hips 2306
He 1420
He Ain't Scared of Nothing 682
He Always Comes Home to Me 958
He and I 4372
He and She 514
He Came Down This Morning 3656
He Can Cure You of Love 804
He Can Dance 3713
He Can Do It 3610
He Can, I Can 1596
He Cannot, Must Not, Shall Not, Dare Not Wed You 1165
He Certainly Has a Soft Spot for Me 3999
He Certainly Kills the Women 2847
He Comes Home in the Evening 624
He Could Show Me 3209
He Dangled Me on His Knee 1295
He Did 822
He Did It, She Did It! 1508
He Didn't Leave It Here 572
He Didn't Like the Look of It at All 1313
He Died Good 1698
He Disappeared 4161
He Does Me So Much Good 3962
He Doesn't Know 150, 3163
He Doesn't Know I'm Alive 154
He Eats 2290
He Failed to Underwrite a Happy Home 1513
He Follows Me Around 1056
'He' for Me, The 4357
He Gets Away with Murder 112
He Goes to Church on Sunday 3313
He Gon' Stay 838
He Got His 2653
He Got It in the Ear 3741
He Had Refinement 4446
He Had the Callin' 2195
He Had to Pay the Piper 1777
He Has a Way 589
He Hasn't a Thing Except Me 4825

He Is a Movie Man 1948
He Is an Animal 1978
He Is Gone 3613
He Is My Bag 2043
He Is Sweet, He Is Good 965
He Is the Bridegroom 737
He Is the Type 773
He Isn't My Style at All 1774
He Just Beats a Tom-Tom 622
He Knows Milk 4179
He Knows Where to Find Me 1676
He Let Me Live 3944
He Lights Another Mecca 243
He Looked at Her, She Looked at Him 1207
He Looked at Me 1590
He Lost 4163
He Loved Her Tender 336
He Loves and She Loves 1419, 3060
He Loves Her 751
He Loves Me 3103, 4208
He Loves Me, He Loves Me Not 1532, 2328
He Loves Me-He Loves Me Not 1313
He Loves My Dreamy Eyes 1307
He Loves the Flag 3951
He Loves to Make a Fuss 2877
He Loves to Make Us Laugh 949
He Made Me Feel I'm Lovely 1255
He Makes Me Feel I'm Lovely 1076
He Man 1839
He-Man, The 4300
He May Be Your Man (But He Comes to See Me Once in a While) 3963
He May Not Come When You Want Him 4460
He May Say 'Yes' Today 3084
He Must Be Nice to Mother 3529
He Must Be Punished 1071
He Needs Me Now 1611
He Needs Somebody 1991
He Needs You 2449
He Never Looks My Way 2182
He Only Comes to See Me Once in a While 1058
He Only Comes to See Me Once in a While (but Oh That Once in a While) 2462
He Paid His Debt to LaFayette, but He Never Settled Up with Me! 1966
He Plays the Violin 3897
He Pleasures Me 1848
He Put the "Uh" in Mambo 372
He Reminds Me of Someone I Want to Forget 1327
He Said 664
He Sang Songs 1959
He Says 1164
He Says Yes, She Says No! 1285
He She We 3527
He Smiles 1045
He Stole the Heart of a Vamp 3296
He Sympathized with Me 1501
He Takes Me Off His Income Tax 3107
He Talks to Me 3389
He Talks with His Fingers 2857
He Threw Out the Ball 1038
He Took It in a Good-Natured Way 1540
He Tossed a Coin 3780
He Treated Me White 917
He Tried to Make a Dollar 1886
He Walked Right In 1340
He Walked Right In, Turned Around and Walked Right Out Again 1573
He Walks Across the Sky 4163
He Wanted to Go and He Went 3319
He Wants to Put the Army in Jail 2472
He Was a Married Man 350
He Was a Sailor 513
He Was a Soldier Too 48
He Was a Soldier, Too 3773
He Was a Wonderful Man 1480
He Was All Right Here (He'll Be All Right There) 2748
He Was the Only Man I Ever Loved 2706
He Was There 1441
He Was Too Good to Me 3980
He Wasn't a Bad Boy 4409
He Wasn't Born in Araby 3514
He Went in Like a Lion 541
He Went In Like a Lion 3973
He Went in Like a Lion and Came Out Like a Lamb 3962
He Went to the East 2225
He Whistled at Me 4138
He Who Gets Slapped 3130
He Who Knows the Way 2820
He Who Laughs Last 2368
He Who'd Thrive Must Rise at Five 252
He Will Come Home Again 1959
He Will Take Me to His Heart 4726
He Will Tonight 183
He Will Understand 4784
He Will Walk with Thee 732
He Winked at Me 694
He Won't Be Happy Till He Gets It 250
He Works at Night 4136
He Would Smile 139
He Wouldn't Dare 4798
He Writes a Song 2622
He'd Have to Get Under, Get Out and Get Under (To Fix His Automobile) 3525
He'll Be Here 154
He'll Come to Me Crawling 4173
He'll Follow in His Father's Footsteps 496
He'll Get It 2304
He'll Make It Alright 1073
He'll Make Me Believe That He's Mine 3428
He'll Make Some Girl a Wonderful Husband 3947
He'll Never Be Mine 181
He'll Never Know 2651
He'll Understand 166
He's a Bold Rogue 1748
He's a Comic 1974
He's a Company Man 1507

He's a Cousin of Mine 2765
He's a Dear Old Pet 4642
He's a Fallen Angel 4289
He's a Fan, Fan, Fan! 531
He's a Guy 1189
He's a Jolly Good Fellow 3348
He's a Ladies Man 1628
He's a Man 3871
He's a Man's Man 1339
He's a Peculiar Guy 2478
He's a Right Guy 4058
He's a Winner (Sporting Life)
(Reporters' Opening) 1529
He's a Wonder 4788
He's All That We Need 2133
He's an American 3158
He's Back 1764
He's Back in Town 1048
He's Beginning to Look a Lot Like Me 1002
He's Coming 3469
He's Coming Home 1852
He's Crazy 4359
He's Dead 3066
He's Goin' Home 4142
He's Going to Call on Baby Grand 4327
He's Going to Die 3937
He's Gone 2974, 143, 4434
He's Gone Away 4111
He's Gonna Keep His Eye on Us 1289
He's Good for Me 3869
He's Good for Nothing but Me 2187
He's Got a Bungalow 2853
He's Got Larceny in His Heart 1420
He's Got the Whole World in
His Hands 344, 4460
He's Got to Go 4297
He's Here! 2014
He's in Love! 2327
He's Just My Ideal 495
He's Ma Romeo 2631
He's Mah Dancing Man 548
He's Mine 124, 607
He's My B-B-B-Baby 2541
He's My Guy 36
He's My Kiddo 806
He's My Pal 3952
He's Never Too Busy 1441
He's Not for Me 1676
He's Not Himself 3379
He's Not the Prince 1868
He's Not Worth Your Tears 4235
He's on the Police Force Now 476
He's Only Wonderful 1300
He's Our Boy 483
He's Out of His Mind 1864
He's Oversexed! 3379
He's Ravin', Let Him Rave 2964
He's Reliable 702
He's So Good 4807
He's the Hottest Man in Town 2308
He's the Man 2680
He's the Wizard 4722
He's the Wonder of Them All 1845
He's with My Johnny 1748
He's Wonderful 3956
Head Down the Road 280
Head in the Stars 298
Head on Her Shoulders, A 1698
Head Over Heels 792, 1796, 1714
Head Over Heels in Love 1965
Head Song, The 1985
Headache and a Heartache, A 3895
Headin' for a Weddin' 1679
Headin' for a Weddin' in the Sky 2806
Headin' for Harlem 3968
Headin' for Heaven (Down South) 885
Headin' for the Bottom 145
Headin' South 3054
Headin' West 1782
Headless Horseman Ballet 4015
Headlines 3938
Heads I Win 3918
Heads or Tails 1713
Heads Up 3683
Headsman and I, The 3798
Healer Am I of All Sorrow, The 4719
Healing 624
Healing Chant, The (1) 2565
Healing Chant, The (2) 2565
Health Food Man, The 250
Health to Dear Mama, A 4479
Health to Noah 2340
Health, Wealth and the Girl You Love 3028
Healthy Relationship 871
Heap Big Suffragette 3087
Heap Love (An Indian Serenade) 2155
Hear Me, Amelia (Finale Act I) 4430
Hear My Prayer 4438
Hear My Song of Love (Serenade) 4293
Hear O Israel 3995
Hear the Bell 2184
Hear the Coachman Crack His Whip 252
Hear the Guns 459
Hear the Gypsies Playing 1352
Hear the Hunter's Horn 1646
Hear the Trumpet Call 2602
Hear Ye! Hear Ye! 1284
Hear Your Voice 1903
Heard It Through the Grapevine 166
Hearing Voices 1700
Hearings, The 3873
Heart 4399
Heart, The 3703
Heart Ache 2303
Heart and Soul 3444
Heart Beats 3915
Heart Bow'd Down, The 1710
Heart Breaker, The 4801
Heart-Breakers 3962
Heart Breakin' Joe 3808

Heart Dance, The 2830
Heart Foolish Heart 2673
Heart for Sale, A 3146
Heart Full of Love, A 2442
Heart Has Won the Game, The 1290
Heart in Hand 911
Heart Is Free, The 2371
Heart Is Quicker Than the Eye, The 3283
Heart, My Heart! 3736
Heart o' Me 1177
Heart o' Mine 1802
Heart of a Girl, The 4639
Heart of a Rose 551, 1460, 3424
Heart of a Sailor Is True, The 1521
Heart of Gold 3714
Heart of Mine 1602, 4357
Heart of My Heart 1424, 3729
Heart of My Heart, I'm Here 47
Heart of My Rose, The 1643
Heart of Paddy Whack, The 1803
Heart of Stone 1614
Heart of the Bowery 1036
Heart of the Rose, The 191
Heart that Broke Was Mine, The 2928
Heart That Is Still the Same, A 2131
Heart That's Free, A 3065
Heart to Heart 1455, 1530
Heart to Let, A 1054, 2408
Heart Will Fall, A 2424
Heart's Desire 1235, 1907
Heartbeat 4379
Heartbreak Hall of Fame 1969
Heartbreak Hotel 3739
Heartbreaker 3561, 4016
Heartbreakers 2856
Hearts and Flowers 1238
Hearts Are Trumps 1806, 4649
Hearts in Tune 1174
Hearts to Be Young 3667
Hearty Breakfast, A 1701
Heat, The 139
Heat Is On 4019
Heat Is on in Saigon, The 2905
Heat Sensation 105
Heat Wave 207
Heatbeat 580
Heathen 1809, 3813
Heather on the Hill, The 530
Heaven 661, 791, 4429
Heaven Bless Our Home 3703
Heaven Help My Heart 721
Heaven Help the Sailors on a
Night Like This 2106
Heaven Help You
(When You Fall in Love) 3046
Heaven Hop 3382
Heaven in My Arms (Music in My Heart) 4557
Heaven Measured You for Me 4228
Heaven Must Have Been Smiling 1985
Heaven of Harlem, The 1272
Heaven on Earth 3272, 1811, 3243
Heaven on My Mind 259
Heaven on Their Minds 2212
Heaven Protect Me! 1766
Heaven Sent 1930
Heaven Smiles on Tepancingo 3875
Heaven Will Protect the
Working Girl 3989, 4382
Heavenly Bodies 3186
Heavenly Chorus, A 3643
Heavenly Day 3390
Heavenly Ever After, The 2553
Heavenly Ladies 2701
Heavenly Party 3568
Heaven's Blessed Me 255
Heavens Declare 2115
Heaven's Gift to the Girls 4212
Heavens to Betsy 3427
Heavy 1103
Heavyweight Champ of the World 2304
Hebrew Benediction 1715
Hector 3222
Hector's Dream 535
Hector's Song 1600
Hee-Bee Jee-Bees 4575
Hee Haw 2693
Heebie Jeebie Blues 1058
Heebie Jeebie Dance 1890
Heebie-Jeebie Furies 459
Heebie Jeebies 3840
Heebie Jeebies, The 1813
Heed the Signs 647
Heel and Toe 3532
Heel Beat 1929
Heel Toe and Away We Go 695
Heh Heh (Chuckle) Good Mornin' Sunshine 40
Heidelberg (Stein Song) 3578
Heidi 1815, 1815
Heigh-Ho 4035
Heigh-Ho Cheerio 2271
Heigh Ho for Mother
(Heigh Ho for a Husband) 4289
Heigh-Ho, Lackaday 1013
Heigh Ho, the Gang's All Here 1136
Heights of a Pillow, The 3612
Heimweh 1849
Heint Viel eich Vu Tzi Zingen 4463
Heir to My Fortune, The 3853
Heiresses, The 3771
Heisses Blut 976
Heist, The 2993
Hela! See the Horseman Come 2839
Heldites, The 4673
Helen 1816
Helen Is Always Willing 1600
Helen Lynd and the Girls 2105
Helen Manicure Girl, The 1240
Helen of Troy 208, 4558
Helen of Troy, New York 1819
Helen Quit Your Yellin' 3988

Helena 249
Helena's Solution 249
Helene's Hat 2448
Helicopter, Helicopter 1053
Heliopolis 3651
Hell Hath No Fury 1761
Hell in Paradise 3125
Hell of a Hole, A 2444
Hell of an Election, A 3482
Hell's Finest 2005
Hellahahana 1341, 413, 412
Hello! 693
Hello 1056, 1865
Hello (Herro) 4048
Hello! 3436
Hello 554
Hello Again 1822
Hello, Aloha, Hello 2762
Hello America 1824
Hello America Minstrels 1824
Hello Beautiful 1638
Hello, Broadway 1826
Hello, Broadway, Hello 2541
Hello Central, Give Me No Man's Land 3985
Hello Chicago 1560
Hello! Come Along, Girls! 356
Hello, Cousin Lola 1831
Hello, Cupid Send me a Fellow 904
Hello Cupid, Send Me a Fellow 558
Hello Doc 2033
Hello, Dolly 2208, 3840
Hello, Dolly! 1828
"Hello, Dolly! medley" 3018
Hello, Dorothy May 3045
Hello Dorothy May (There She Goes) 3045
Hello, Everybody 2494
Hello Fellas 4349
Hello, Friends 2455
Hello, Frisco! (I Called You Up to Say Hello) 4809
Hello Girl 1780
Hello, Girlie 2108
Hello Girlie 4634
Hello, Good Morning 3225
Hello! Good-Bye 2180
Hello, Goodby 3203
Hello, Hannah 2222
Hello Hawaii 3399
Hello, Hazel 1791
Hello, Hello 659, 2290, 2732, 132
Hello-Hello 3741
Hello, Hello, Hello 1120, 2705, 4770, 4816
Hello, Hello, Sandy 3349
Hello, Hello, Telephone Girlie 3184
Hello, Hello There 363
Hello, Honey 4807
Hello, I Love You, Goodbye 3863
Hello, I've Been Looking for You 396
Hello Imagination 1631
Hello Is the Way Things Begin 3389
Hello Jeremy 2346
Hello, Little Girl 2143
Hello Little Girl 4067
Hello Little Miss U.S.A. 357, 2984
Hello, Lizzie 2519
Hello Love 3918
Hello, Ma 2105
Hello Ma Baby 3949
Hello, Ma Baby 4390
Hello, Ma Lulu 2123
Hello, Miss Chapel Street 870
Hello Miss Knickerbocker 3404
Hello, Miss Tango! 1065
Hello Mom 1842
Hello, Mr. Love 398
Hello, Mr. Moon Man 1550
Hello Muddah, Hello Fadduh 1832
Hello!, Must Do a Show, Goodbye! 4798
Hello, My Dearie! 4811
Hello, My Love, Hello 1614
Hello, My Lover, Goodbye 1856
Hello, My Old Friend 533
Hello, New York 1695
Hello, Paree 1834
Hello Paris 1835
Hello People 1313
Hello, People! 1783
Hello Peter We're Going Out 2346
Hello Springtime 1742
Hello Stranger! 4106
Hello, Sucker 1837
Hello Sunshine 4459
Hello Sweetheart 2922
Hello, the Little Birds Have Flown 4010
Hello There 1717
Hello to France 1837
Hello Tom 2783
Hello 'Tucky 391
Hello Twelve, Hello Thirteen, Hello Love 746
Hello, Waves 1310
Hello World 415
Hello Yank 278
Hello, Yank! 2777
Hello, Young Lovers 2312, 2611
Hello, Yourself 1839
Hellrakers', The (dance) 3274
Helluva Big Job 2513
Helluva Day, A 2132
Helluva Group, A 1420
Helluva Hullabaloo 42
Hellzapoppin' 1840, 1841
Hellzapoppin 1842
Hellzapoppin Polka, The 2400
Help 1072
Help!! And the Villain Goes to Jail 632
Help Cometh from Above 2013
Help, Help, Help 152
Help, I Implore 2334
Help Is on the Way! 4769
Help Me Girl 4193

Help the Drive 3063
Help the Seamen 3822
Help Us Tonight 1667
Help Yourself 434, 1650
Help Yourself to Happiness 4823
Helping 1389
Helping Hand and a Willing Heart, A 2580
Helplessness at Midnight 2702
Hemlines 4679
Hen and the Cow, The 541
Hen and the Weather Vane, The 2534
Hence It Don't Make Sense 3893
Hennie Soup 3757
Henny 3437
Henny Klein 4662
Henrietta 2231
Henry 466, 4099
Henry Dinkenspiel 2800
Henry Is Where It's At 4089
Henry Leek 989
Henry Street 1420
Henry, Sweet Henry 1846
Hep Cat, The 4281
Hep Cats Done Gone High Hat 1917
Hep, Hep, Hep 2108
Hep, Hot and Solid Sweet 4826
Her Anxiety 1977
Her Baggage Was Checked for Troy 1417
Her Bright Shawl 3431
Her Career 944
Her Dream Man 2098
Her Eyes Are Blue for Dear Old Yale 3579
Her Eyes, Her Eyes 2106
Her Eyes Kept Saying
'Kiss Me!' All the Time 1524
Her Face 656
Her Father's Daughter 4297
Her Faults 2733
Her First Can Can 2986
Her First Kiss 2519
Her First Roman 1848
Her Gentleman Friend 1988
Her Glove 902
Her Heart Was in Her Work 629
Her Is 3351
Her Jazz Drummer 1882
Her Laughter in My Life 2011
Her Lilywhite Hand 4479
Her Love Is Always the Same 468
Her Majesty 3903
Her Mummy Doesn't Like Me
Any More 1386
Her Name Is Aurora 2333
Her Name Is Leona 3653
Her or Me 2905
Her Pop's a Cop 3986
Her Portrait 2716
Her Song 3539
Her's a Fool 3927
Herb Song, The 3764
Herbert 2168
Here! 1161
Here 'Tis 435, 3966, 3965
Here Am I 1132, 4234
Here Am I-Broken Hearted 202
Here and Now 3576, 1564, 4015, 2250
Here and There 4021, 4798
Here and There and Everywhere 2605
Here Are Your Children 786
Here at Baiae on the Bay 1682
Here at Monte Carlo 2938
Here Be Oysters Stewed in Honey
(Opening Chorus) 758
Here Beside Me 3286
Here Busted a Captive Heart 2028
Here Come the Blues 90
Here Come the Dreamers 2535
Here Come the Married Men 4037
Here Come the Rah Rah Boys 2490
Here Come the Soldiers 3791
Here Come the Yanks 4838
Here Come the Yanks with Their Tanks 1920
Here Come Your Men 4384
Here Comes Another Song About Texas (Pass the
Cotton, Pass the Cotton) 3832
Here Comes My Blackbird 441
Here Comes My Show Boat 26
Here Comes Never 3299
Here Comes the Ballad 1056
Here Comes the Big Brass Band 3173
Here Comes the Bride 1626, 2373, 2888, 4655
Here Comes the Groom 379
Here Comes the Hot Tamale Man 1425
Here Comes the Kid 1250
Here Comes the Prince of Wales 3130
Here Comes the Rabbi 1590
Here Comes the Showboat! 2204
Here Comes the Spring 1792
Here Comes the Sun 599, 4008
Here Comes Tootsi 186
Here for the Hearing 373
Here Goes 880
Here Goes Nothing 3837
Here He Is 2068
Here I Am 519, 690, 1489, 1846, 2001,
3210, 1258, 3342, 1940
Here I Am Again 426
Here I Come 3543, 4629
Here I Go Again 180, 932
Here I Go Bananas! 3539
Here I'll Stay 2615
Here in Cadiz 2500
Here in Eden 170
Here in Minipoora 1638
Here in My Arms 1013
Here In My Arms 2467
Here in My Hands 4055
Here in My Heart 2238
Here in the Dark 1603
Here in the Inn 4244

Here in the Moonlight on the Fence 1900
Here in the Playbill 550
Here in the South 2898
Here in the Starlight 1230
Here in the Womb 4729
Here Is a Sword 3584
Here Is the Tunic of a Soldier 4616
Here It Comes 4361
Here It Comes Again 9, 1567
Here It Is 1492
Here on Lord and Lady Waiting 1193
Here on Sunlit Sands 1429
Here on the Fence at Doolittle College 1900
Here She Comes (Musical Entrance—Tilly) (All Set! Let's Go) 3924
Here on the Lot 1948
Here On The Lot 1948
Here She Comes Now (East River Hoedown) 4496
Here, Steward 4491
Here They Are 3766
Here They Come 1589, 1470, 4434
Here They Come in Glittering Glory 4430
Here They Come Now 1958
Here Tonight, Tomorrow Where? 161
Here We Are 73, 1590, 1015, 2608
Here We Are, a Gypsy Troupe Quite Famous 1355
Here We Are Again 1060, 2231, 3113
Here We Are Dance 3258
Here We Are in Love 2747, 4823
Here We Are Scrubbing 3096
Here We Are Together 4291
Here We Are Together Again (Opening Act I) 4212
Here We Go Again 4006
Here with You 2200
Here You Are 3551
Here You Come Again 964
Here You See Eight Ladies of Quality 1975
Here's a Bale of Cotton for You 2696
Here's a Book 869
Here's a Chance for Visitors 2938
Here's a Cheer for Dear Old Ciro's 2847
Here's a Day to Be Happy 4023
Here's a Hand 601
Here's a How-de-do 1987
Here's a Kiss 1013
Here's a Kiss for One and Twenty 453
Here's a Lady (Opening Chorus) 3494
Here's a Little Clue 2861
Here's a Love Song 3688
Here's a Lucky Find 2944
Here's a Paradox for Lovers 4404
Here's a Toast 1238
Here's How 3063, 3304
Here's Howe 1859
Here's Lookin' at You 4019
Here's Looking at You 4761
Here's Love 1860
Here's Momma 1045
Here's My Ticket 3887
Here's One Who Wouldn't 1929
Here's That Rainy Day 657
Here's the Happy Ending 4035
Here's the Latest Thing 4382
Here's to a Bashful Girl of Fifteen 2399
Here's to a Lady 112
Here's to Dear Old Us 145
Here's to Health, Here's to Wealth (Here Is Health) 3304
Here's to Love 4219
Here's to Luck 1782
Here's to My Comrades and You 3567
Here's to Night 2540
Here's to Panama Hattie 3359
Here's to Surprises 693
Here's to the Bride 351, 2276
Here's to the Crabgrass 1832
Here's to the Girl 1569
Here's to the Girl of My Heart 4683
Here's to the Land We Love, Boys! 3304
Here's to the Two of You 1598
Here's to Us 2523, 4492
Here's to You 680, 2282
Here's to You, Jack 1747
Here's to You, Mrs. Rodriguez 1770
Here's to You My Sparkling Wine 473
Here's to Your Illusions 1300
Here's to Your Last Girl 1593
Here's What a Mistress Ought to Be 3920
Here's When I Belong 3576
Here's Where I Belong 1864
Here's Where the Action Is 2010
Hereabouts 4015
Hereafter 2847
Heredity 4415
Heredity-Environment 4028
Herein Lies the Seeds of Revolution 2418
Herman 262
Herman, Let's Dance That Beautiful Waltz 1519, 4493
Herman, My German 610
Hermits, The 978
Hermits, The (What Do All the Hermits Do in Springtime) 1013
Hermits, The 4304
Hermits, The (What Do All the Hermits Do in Springtime?) 4709
Hernando's Hideaway 3351
Hero, A 2504
Hero Ballet 1973
Hero Hill 1754
Hero Is Coming, A 162
Hero of All My Dreams 177
Hero Sandwiches 3280
Hero Song 1154
Hero Time 3688
Hero's Love, A 3835
Herod 2241
Heroes 1865, 2579, 4713, 3539

Heroes Come Home, The 1600
Heroes in the Fall 4420
Heroes Just the Same 1568
Heroes of Yesterday 2843
Heroism 4696
Heron, The 143
Herringbone 1872
Herzen im Schnee 2610
Hesitation 3304
Hesitation Waltz (inst.) 2772
Hesitation Waltz 4751, 2984
Hester Street 4172
Hey 1729
Hey! 3741
Hey, Boy! 486
Hey Boy 3825
Hey, Butterfly 716
Hey, Chicago 2246
Hey Chico 1164
Hey, Delilah 1990
Hey Derry Down 4404
Hey-diddle-diddle! When Man Is in Love 1470
Hey Dreamboat! (inst.) 2483
Hey Fellas Let's Talk 4190
Hey, Feller! 3949
Hey for the Merry Greenwood 3736
Hey Gal 4498
Hey, Gal! 3105
Hey Gimme, Jimmy 2551
Hey Girlie 4481
Hey Good Lookin' 4058
Hey, Granny 486
Hey Groundhog 1700
Hey! Hey! 1529
Hey, Hey 2628
Hey Hey Blues 3001
Hey, Hey, Fever 1302
Hey! Hey! Hey! 2232
Hey! Hey! Let 'Er Go! 4241
Hey! Ho! 3882
Hey, I Don't Need Nobody Now 3628
Hey, I'm Talkin' to You, Beethoven! 838
Hey Jimmy, Joe, John, Jack 2449
Hey, Joe 1601
Hey Joe 3831
Hey, Kid! 915
Hey Kiddo, You Through Again 1108
Hey Lady 1232
Hey Listen, Johnny Johnny 973
Hey, Little Star 4093
Hey Look at Me 699
Hey, Look at Me, Mrs. Draba 2318
Hey, Look Me Over 4693
Hey, Love (See What You Can Do for Me) 1991
Hey, Ma 1873
'Hey Ma, You Were Right' Cantata, The 159
Hey, Madame 3234
Hey Mama 1890
Hey Man 3690
Hey, Mister Conductor 2305
Hey Mr. Bossman 3989
Hey, Nonny, Hey 1656
Hey Nonny No 973
Hey Nonny Nonny 1874
Hey, Rube 3648
Hey! Rube! 4753
Hey Rube (inst.) 4091
Hey, Say Anything 4450
Hey, Star 2703
Hey Star 1099
Hey, Sweet Columbine 3498
Hey, Sweet Mamma 2663
Hey There 3351
Hey There Good Times 2058
Hey There! Hey There! 2964
Hey, What's This? 2236
Hey, Why Not! 4196
Hey Young Fella Close Your Old Umbrella 787
Hey Young Fella! 3639
Hey Yvette! 3330
Heyday 4761
Hezekiah Doo 434
Hi 119
Hi! 2783
Hi 3902
Hi! Allez! Hoopla! (Finale Act I) 1458
Hi Boys, Ho Boys 2938
Hi De Hi De Hi, Hi De Hi De Ho 941
Hi-De-Ho 1876
Hi-De-Ho-High 1140
Hi-De-Ho Miracle Man, The 883
Hi-De-Ho Romeo 884, 886
Hi-Diddle-I-Dee 2028
Hi! For the Thames on a Summer's Day 1540
Hi! Hi! Hi! 47
Hi-Ho 2490, 1258
Hi, Ho the Hoe-Down Way 4086
Hi-Ko, Hi-Ko 3943
Hi Low Downs, The 3173
Hi, Paisano 1878
Hi There! 2243
Hi There, Buddy 2390
Hi There, Joan 572
Hi Ya Kid 2033
Hi Ya, Gentlemen 1879
Hi Yah 1417
Hiaka 4337
Hiawatha 3805
Hiawatha's Melody of Love 3677
Hic Haec Hoc 367
Hickety, Pickety 2134
Hickory, Dickory 4696
Hickory Dickory Dock 2289
Hickory Stick 2259
Hicky Do 3958
Hidden in My Heart 483
Hidden Princess, The 1258
Hide and Seek 1088, 2803
Hide Your Sister 190
Hifalutin' Music 3437

High Air 3831
High and Dry 1884, 1883
High and Dry Let Her Lie 3588
High and Low 108, 294, 1855
High As a Kite 1885
High Ballin' 2225
High Class Ladies and
Elegant Gentlemen 2925
High Cotton 4055
High Diplomacy 1887
High Flyin' Man 876
High Flying Adored 1211
High Hat 1191, 1419, 3060
High-Hat, Low-Down 1771
High Hats 1267, 1533
High! High! High! 2858
High, High, High 3012
High, High Up in the Clouds 1693
High-Ho, At Last 2450
High Hopes 4743
High in the Hills 317
High Is Better Than Low 2201
High Jinks 1888
High Jinks Tangle 1888
High Life Down Stairs 379
High Lonesome 459
High, Low, Jack and the Game 1385, 4123
High Old Time 1537
High on a Hill 1027
High Pressure 3823
High Risk for Afraids 4309
High School 1575
High School All Over Again 2152
High School Diploma 2284
High School Ladies at Five O'Clock 2132
High Seas, The 2876
High Shoes 1932
High Society 2538
High Steppin' Days 1198
High Street, Africa 605
High Summer 1985
High Tide, Low Tide 717
High Time 1892, 2590
High Toned Trot 1831
High Tor 1893
High Up 4292
High Up in Harlem 4557
High Up in the Hills 4667
High, Wide and Handsome 2640
High Yaller 4793
Highbrow, Lowbrow 4432
Higher and Higher 1638, 146, 3739
Higher den de Moon 1385
Higher Education, The 1881
Higher Ground 4534
Higher than a Hawk 616
Higher Than High 2759
Highest Judge of All, The 660
Highland Kiltie Rag, The 1424
Highland Mary 4662
Highland Swing 1763
Highland Swing, The 887
Highly Important Fly, The 1295
Highway 57 3608
Highway Narrows 922
Highway Toes 3077
Highway's Call, The 1935
Highwayman, The 2186, 1896
Highwayman 104
Hike! 4201
Hiking to a No Woman's Land 2276
Hill of Dreams 4075
Hill, The Hill, The 4147
Hills of Amalfi, The 3696
Hills of Ixopo, The 2591
Hills of Tomorrow, The 2822
Him, Them, It, Her 2646
Himmlisher Vater 2583
Hindoo Honey 3693, 4803
Hindoo-Hop 21
Hindoo Moon 3847
Hindoo Paradise 355
Hindoo Serenade 4826
Hindu Dance Tag (inst.) 190
Hindustan 3297
Hinkee Dee 1459, 3480
Hinkey Dee 3028
Hinky Dee 2851
Hinky Dinky Parlay Voo 3018
Hip 971
Hip Chick (inst.) 886
Hip-di-di-o-tee 3947
Hip-Hip-Hooray 1901
Hip, Hip, Hurrah! 1067
Hip-Hip-Hip 3626
Hip Hooray 1436
Hip Hooray for America 1770
Hip-Hooray for Washington 3684
Hip, Hop, Hoorah! 1721
Hippity Hop, The 1131
Hippodrome Folks 1826
Hippodrome Street Parade, The 396
Hippodrome Tango 106
Hippopotamus 220
Hiram 2897
Hiram Green 3350
Hiram Greene 2286
Hiram Skinner's Comb 4194
Hiram's Band 4206
Hire a Guy 1408
Hired Man, The 1903
His and Hers 145, 4540
His Chances Are Not Worth a Penny
(Finaletto) 2068
His End Is Near 2970
His Excellency Regrets 3339
His Eye Is on the Sparrow 4534
His Family Tree 3456
His Father's Son 649
His Gift to Me 4460

His Highness 760, 3570
His Honor, the Mayor 1657
His Little Sister 1243
His Little World 190
His Love 807, 3542
His Love Makes Me Beautiful 1420
His Majesty 1912
His Majesty Advances 4187
His Majesty Orders 1114
His Majesty's Dragoons 466
His Name Is Charlie Gordon 699
His Name Is Love 426
His Old Man 620
His Own Little Island 2449
His Own Peculiar Charm 2268
His Pipe 2377
His Room 4643
His Royal Highness 2047
His Spanish Guitar 2780
His Work—and Nothing More 2198
Hispanola Crawl 4218
Hiss, Hiss, Hiss 2493
Historic Huzzies 2377
Historic Kisses 4437
Historical Spots 15
History 1634, 1852
History Eight to the Bar 2447
History Is Made at Night 4174
History of a Rock Star, The 3667
History of New York, A 2344
History of Stand-Up Comedy, The 4349
History of Three Generations of Chorus Girls, The 4365
History Repeats Itself 2458
Hit 'Em on the Head 2660
Hit Enormous 2715
Hit It, Lorraine 3900
Hit Me with a Hot Note 146
Hit Me with a Hot Note and Watch Me Bounce 4091
Hit the Ground Running 2702
Hit the Ladies 3019
Hit the Ramp 2379
Hit the Road Jack 1713
Hit the Stride 1917
Hitch Hiker 1804
Hitch-Hiker, The 2421
Hitch Your Wagon to a Star 557
Hitchy-Koo 1919
Hitchy Koo 3259
Hitchy-Koo 4655
Hitchy Koo Girl 1920
Hitchy's Garden of Roses 1921
Hither Bring the Bold Intruder 1388
Hitler und Goering und Goebbels und Schacht 4152
Hittin' the Bottle 1135
Hitting on High 1747
Hitting the New High 364
Hive Full of Honey 616
Hiya Sucker 3907
Hm, Hm, I Love Harmony 525
Hm! She Is the One Girl 3996
HMJFC 181
Ho! (The Riff Song) 1027
Ho, Billy, O! 2615
Ho Christina 979
Ho for the Greenwood 2697
Ho! Ye Townsmen 1355
Hoax and Coax 2632
Hobbies 2148, 3043
Hobble on the Cobbles 1917
Hobby Horses 4515
Hobgoblins 4725
Hobo Man 1532
Hobo's Song 2784
Hobohemia 2253
Hobson's Choice 4588
Hoch, Caroline! 4299
Hocus Pocus 1460
Hodge Podge 2979
Hoe, Boy, Hoe 3321
Hoe-Down 1085
Hoe Down 3684
Hoe Ry Die Boere 4579
Hoedown 3631
Hoedown Hanging 451
Hoedown! 1766
Hoffa Love Is Better Than None 3186
Hoffmann Belles 1829
Hog Beneath the Skin, The 220
Hog-Tie Your Man 992
Hogan's Alley 2827
Hogan's Goat 935
Hoger and the Turks 4082
Hoger's Lament 4082
Hoggenheimer of Park Lane 351
Hogwash 3000
Hohihlahla Mandela 4438
Hoku Loa 2636
Hokum 2296
Hokus Pokus 70
Hola 4713
Hola! 4754
Hola, Follow, Follow Me (Song of Greeting) 905
Hola! Hola! 1066
Hold Back 2388
Hold Down the Fort 2224
Hold 'Em Cowboy 1462
Hold 'Em, Joe 2227
Hold I Command (Septette) 3585
Hold It! 1930
Hold Me 684, 764, 1370, 2303, 2783, 2950, 1750, 4814, 4183
Hold Me Closer 1481
Hold Me Gently 482
Hold Me In Your Arms 231
Hold Me in Your Arms 1944
Hold Me in Your Arms Again 69, 1942

Hold Me in Your Loving Arms 4809, 4834
Hold Me-Hold Me-Hold Me 4496
Hold My Baby Back 3757
Hold My Hand 2798
Hold On 4171, 3862
Hold On Abraham 3020
Hold on Tight 1816
Hold On to Your Hats 1931, 4090
Hold That Crown 690
Hold That Smile 4826
Hold That Thought 198
Hold the Lanterns High 1243
Hold Tight, Hold Tight 393
Hold-Up Ensemble 3865
Hold Your Hand Out Naughty Boy 3259
Hold Your Head Up High (Opening Hymn) 3014
Hold Your Horses 1932, 4753
Hold Your Man 2637
Holden and Phoebe 2913
Holding Hands 361, 2101, 2780, 3613, 3981
Holding the Bag 1108
Holding to the Ground 1234
Hole in My Sidewalk 4330
Hole in the Wall 4114
Hole-in-One 1865
Holiday 1762, 2028, 750
Holiday for Nuns 3997
Holiday in Court 2246
Holiday in Hades Today 3904
Holiday in Hollywood 1048
Holiday in the Country 206
Holiday in the Market 9
Holiday Island 1386
Holiday Joys 2632
Holidays 276, 4619, 3407
Holier Than Thou 3211
Holka-Polka 1935
Holler Blue Murder 137
Hollow 2918
Hollow Faces 3539
Hollow of My Hand 3500
Holly Golightly 521
Holly Gollucci 521
Holly Jolly Christmas, A 3793, 3794
Holly Pine and Mistletoe 752
Hollyhocks of Hollywood, The 4709
Hollywood 4790, 1785, 1777, 2757, 3670, 4635
Hollywood and Vine 4474, 4772
Hollywood Baby 2305
Hollywood Be Thy Name 1937
Hollywood, California 16
Hollywood Folk Song 4433
Hollywood Holiday 1939
Hollywood! Hollywood! 3636
Hollywood Hollywood! 1940
Hollywood Is Dying 3636
Hollywood Lullaby 1201
Hollywood Money Makers 407
Hollywood Museum 407
Hollywood 'n' Vinyl 275
Hollywood, Park Avenue and Broadway 4177
Hollywood Party (Party Parlando) 2386
Hollywood Rag 2992
Hollywood Relief, A 1944, 1946
Hollywood Rhythm 1597
Hollywood Scene 3987
Hollywood Story 372
Hollywood West 408
Hollywood's a Funny Place 1948
Holmes and Watson 1094
Holy and Innocent 3197
Holy Frygga 1714
Holy God 4398
Holy Little World 747
Holy Man and the New Yorker 1023, 3484, 3542
Holy Mary, Mother of God 755
Holy Mystery 2290
Holy of Holies (Prayer) 711
Holy Smoke 42
Holy Week 2407
Homage to Marat 3445
Home 4309, 735, 1420, 1427, 2887, 330, 3243, 3465, 1258, 3900, 4252, 4480, 4558, 4722
Home Again 632, 954, 3682, 1231, 1280, 1852, 1955, 2304, 2388, 2462, 4094, 4218, 4819, 43
Home Again Blue 986
Home Away from Home 31
Home Blues 3953
Home Brew 981
Home Companion, A 834
Home Folks Theme 2692
Home for Wayward Girls 521
Home for You, A 4664
Home Free All 935
Home from Algeria 2622
Home from Home 1506
Home Is Home 1054
Home Is Where the Heart Is 1811
Home Is Where the Heart Is (Home Sweet Home) 4509
Home Is Where You Hang Your Hat 4484
Home Lights I Long to See 1486
Home Lovin' Gal 3953
Home Lovin' Man 3953
Home Made Heaven 1231
Home Movie, A 3211
Home Never Leaves You 674
Home o' Mine 3680
Home of My Heart 1935
Home of Our Own, A 620, 2615
Home on the Range 2413
Home Pals 2194
Home Sweet Heaven 1891
Home Sweet Home 4279
Home, Sweet Home 3840
Home Sweet Home 1425, 275, 1897
Home, Sweet Home 2716
Home Sweet Home 3923, 4811, 4462, 2127
Home Sweet Homer 1959
Home to Harlem 4177

Home to You 1212
Home Town 4276
Home Town Girl 4292
Home with the Milk in the Morning 2481
Homecoming 3035
Homecoming Game, The 4278
Homeland (Dear Old Homeland) 2291
Homeland 2594, 3163
Homeless 2658
Homeless Children 2681
Homeless Girl in Harlem, The 3809
Homely, But Clean 3254
Homely Woman 2776
Homemade Happiness 780
Homer's Pitch 2583
Homes They Hold So Dear 579
Homesick 958, 2590, 4522
Homesick Blues 1475
Homesick for Hell 3568
Homesick in Our Hearts 4243
Homesick Yankee or You're Thinking of Home Sweet Home, The 3710
Homestead Must Be Sold, The 1667
Homeward 161
Homeward Bound 994, 3710, 4178, 4603
Homework 1158, 2894, 2703
Hommage Musical 2364
Homo Haven Fight Song 4309
Homogeneous Cabinet, A 2068
Honduran Mahongany 1477
Honduras 3185
Honest Abe 4163, 3558
Honest Confession Is Good for the Soul 3824
Honest Honore 4401
Honest Injun!-I Love You! 4247
Honest John's Game 1164
Honest Man 269
Honest Man, An 3066, 175
Honest Sailors 4444
Honest Work 2449
Honest, You're the Only One for Me 1332
Honestly 1745
Honestly Sincere 607
Honesty 691, 1108, 1992
Honey (Touch Me with My Clothes On) 1512
Honey 1535, 1587, 1601, 2822
Honey and Lemon 10
Honey Babe 1968
Honey, Be Mine 3179
Honey, Be My Honey Bee 2669
Honey, Be My Little Honey Bee 2095
Honey Boy 4756
Honey-Bun 2569
Honey Bun 4096
Honey Bunch 632, 1270
Honey-Bunch 4844
Honey, Come and Shimmie with Me 2349
Honey, Come Hurry Along 2108
Honey Gal O' Mine 653
Honey, I Love You 1584
Honey I'm in Love with You 2818
Honey in the Honeycomb 612
Honey Is Sweet 4723
Honey Love 4649
Honey, Love Me All the Time 1731
Honey-Love-Moon 4227
Honey Man Song 578
Honey Moon Land 3134, 4422
Honey to Love, A 4243
Honey Trust Me 2810
Honey, Won't You Please Come Down? 3531
Honey You Were Made for Me 60
Honeydew Waltz 1962
Honeyland 4687
Honeymoon 145, 2761
Honeymoon (When Will You Shine for Me?) 4491
Honeymoon Ballet (inst.) 2061
Honeymoon Bells 3134
Honeymoon Blues 2950
Honeymoon Choo-Choo 4696
Honeymoon Cruise, A 2700
Honeymoon Days 1531
Honeymoon Express 965
Honeymoon for Four, A 2976
Honeymoon Girl, A 3856, 3857
Honeymoon Hall 2854, 3422
Honeymoon Home 1174
Honeymoon Hop 3238
Honeymoon in May, A 1565
Honeymoon Inn 1784
Honeymoon Is Over, The 483, 4619, 1112, 2050, 3542
Honeymoon Island 3866
Honeymoon Isle 334
Honeymoon Land 1335, 2684
Honeymoon Lane 1965, 4219
Honeymoon of Pancho Pincus, The 3036
Honeymoon Row 3915
Honeymoon Trail 1593, 1967
Honeymoon Trip All Alone, A 351
Honeymoon with You, A 20
Honeymoon, The 2632
Honeymooning Blues 2669
Honeymooning Honey in Bombay 2261
Honeypot 4
Honeysuckle 465
Honeysuckle and the Bee, The 3566
Honeysuckle Rose 39, 2561, 927
Honeysuckle Vine 4380
Hong Kong 190, 868, 1726
Hong Kong Gong 2067
Hong Kong to Hoboken 3091
Honky Tonk Nights 1970
Honky Tonk Nights Rag (Professor Walker and His Solo Symphony), The 1970
Honky Tonk Queen 474
Honky Tonk Toodle 3349
Honolulu 919
Hon-o-lulu 1308
Honolulu 1650

Honolulu Blues 2299
Honolulu Lady 604
Honolulu-lu 1908
Honolulu Lulu 3129
Honolulu Rag 1566
Honor 3763, 595
Honor and Glory 3078
Honor Code, The 693
Honor Me with This Dance 664
Honor of Altenstein, The 2966
Honor of the Family, The 2829
Honor of Your Presence, The 4004
Honor System, The 2900
Honor the Brave 3265
Honora Doolin 2996
Honorable Mambo 4829, 4828
Honorable Profession of the Fourth Estate, The 2894
Honour 71
Honour and Love 2937
Honours of War, The 2937
Honto 3944
Hoo-doo-doo-doo-man 175
Hoodlums and Whores 3840
Hoodoo Blues 2446
Hoof, Hoof 86
Hooked! 2565
Hooker, The 2134
Hook's Entrance Song 3453
Hook's Hook 3453
Hoola-Boola Love Song 984
Hoola from Coney Isle 4182
Hoolah Goolah Stone 3348
Hooligan's Hop 4536
Hoomalimali 4337
Hoop-de-Dingle 1029
Hoop-Dee-Doo 3444
Hoop La 1532
Hoop-La-La Papa! (Hoop-la Father Doesn't Care) 1538
Hoop-Ti-Do 2939
Hoopla 1971
Hoops 294
Hoorah for Jones 3526
Hooray for Anywhere 2400
Hooray for Captain Spaulding! 142
Hooray for Friday 2306
Hooray for George the Third 603
Hooray for Hollywood 3018
Hooray for Nicoletti 1539
Hooray for the Bridgroom 1866
Hooray for the Girls 1972
Hooray for the Judge 2784
Hooray for the U.S.A.! 4241
Hooray for the Yankee Dollar (Workin' for the Yankee Dollar) 2190
Hooray for Us! 213
Hooray for What? 1973
Hoosier Way 3895
Hoot Man 2620
Hootch Rhythm 2706
Hootenanny with Peter, Paul, Irving 3530
Hootin' Owl Trail 4314
Hootsatsa 4342
Hootspa 2790
Hop, a Skip, a Jump, a Look, A 2397
Hop, Hop, Hop 1975
Hop o' My Thumb 1975
Hop Scotch 1308, 2056
Hop Up, My Ladies 1085
Hope for the Best 3390
Hope On 2040
Hope On, Dear Heart 2944
Hopes An' Dreams 838
Hoping 2180
Hoping That Some Day You'd Care 4178
Hoppin' the Buck 2371, 3342
Hoppy Poppy Queen 4375
Hora 343, 1265
Hora-Galilee 181
Horace's Entrance 3691
Horehound Compound 3641
Horicon Hop 243
Hornpipe Rag, The 2978
Horoscope 221, 3136
Horrible, Horrible Love! 2582
Horrortorio 4299
Hors d'Oeuvres 2
Horse 915
Horse, The 2801
Horse-Car Days 3409
Horse Trot, The 487
Horse with the Hansom Behind, The 2301
Horsin' Around 2171
Horticultural College, The 3313
Hosanna 2212, 3796, 3838
Hose Boys 1286
Hospitality 3869
Hostess with the Mostes' on the Ball 619
Hot 1855, 4532
Hot and Bothered 1970, 4426
Hot and Cold 2439, 3117
Hot as Hades 4011
Hot August Night 964
Hot Blues (inst.) 1202
Hot Canary, The 4264
Hot-Cha 682
Hot-Cha Cha 4038
Hot-Cha Chaquita 2300
Hot China 3573
Hot Choc'late 1799
Hot Chocolate and Marshmallow 2177
Hot Chocolate Days 367
Hot Dog 582
Hot-Dog Waltz 4169
Hot Dog, Mustard and You 3415
Hot Enough for You? 16
Hot Feet 1198, 1251, 895
Hot Flashes 3136
Hot Food 3603

Hot Foot Dance 981
Hot-Foot'n 3120
Hot Gavotte 2479
Hot Grog 1985
Hot Harlem 4198
Hot Heels 3342
Hot Hindoo 1689
Hot, Hot Honey 3149
Hot, Hot Mama 1251
Hot Jello 3782
Hot Lover 4485
Hot Monkey Love 1149
Hot Moonlight 3946
Hot Music 1938
Hot Number 4825
Hot Off the Oven 1131
Hot Pants 124
Hot Pants Dance 3599
Hot Patata, The 3131
Hot Patootie Land 2700
Hot Patootie Wedding Night 290
Hot Rhythm 1989, 4198
Hot Rod 932
Hot Sands 931
Hot September Dance 1990
Hot Shot 3568
Hot Spell 1125
Hot Spot 3735
Hot Stuff 2513
Hot Tamale Alley 509
Hot Tamale Sam 2792
Hot Time in the Old Town 662
Hot Time in the Old Town, A 3297
Hot Time in the Old Town Tonight 1425, 2796
Hot Time in the Old Town Tonight, A 4390
Hot Voo-Doo 1638
Hot Water 194, 4240
Hot Water Bottles 1993
Hotcha Ma Chotch 4023
Hotel Clerk's Song 934
Hotel Life 2363
Hotel Lobby Scene 919
Hotel Never Tell 3157
Hotel Paradiso 1993
Hotel Passionato 1993
Hotel Stadt-Lemberg 184, 2747
Hotsy Totsy Hats 551
Hotsy Totsy Nazi 1739
Hotten Trot, The 2462
Hottentot Love Song, A 2765
Hottentot Potentate 216
Hottest Knishe 4172
Hound Dog 4031, 3739
Hounds of John Jorrock's, The 2240
Houp-La 1021, 1796
Hour Ago, An 2187
Hour for Lunch 924
Hour for Thee and Me, The 1897, 4149
Hour Is Ripe, The 3527
Hours Creep on Apace, The 2977
Hours I Spent with You, The 1215
House, The 4297, 1750
House and Garden 2961
House Full of People, A 840
House I Live In, The 467, 2447
House in Algiers 3792
House in the Country 4415
House in the Woods, A 1997
House in Town, A 1290
House Is Haunted, The (By the Echo of Your Last Goodbye) 4824
House Is Not a Home, A 261
House Is Not the Same Without a Woman, A (E Bello Ave 'Na Donna Dentro Casa) 3798
House of Blue Lights 2772
House of Don Pasquale, The 3197
House of Flowers 2000
House of Flowers Waltz (inst.) 2000
House of Grass 1809
House of Leather Theme 2001
House of Marcus Lycus, The (1) 1422
House of Marcus Lycus, The (2) 1422
House on a Cloud 2115
House on East 88th Street 2657
House on East 88th Street, The 2658
House on Rittenhouse Square, A 1475
House on the Hill 4337
House that Hook Built, The 2889
House That Jack Built, The 764, 2123
House that Jazz Built, The 1533
House that Monty's 'Jack' Built, The 577
House Upon the Hill, The 3862
House We'd Build, The 2004
House Where I Was Born, The 3386
House with a Little Red Barn, A 4483
Houseboat on the Styx 2005
Houseboat on the Styx, The 2005
Household Brigade, The 4725
Housekeeping 69
How a Monocle Helps the Mind 2123
How About a Ball? 2681
How About a Boy? 4179
How About a Cheer for the Navy? 4340
How About a Date? 3091
How About a Little Date for Breakfast? 289
How About a Man? 4178
How About It? 111, 3849
How About Me 1146
How About Me? 789, 981
How About Us Last Nite 1697
How About You 3175
How About You and Me 1222
How Actresses Are Made 666
How Am I Doin', Dad? 1770
How America Got Its Name 2132
How Are Things in Glocca Morra? 1278
How Are You Feeling? 2578
How Are You Going to Start the American Revolution? 4488
How Are You, Lady Love? 1756

How Are You Since? 935
How Awful 147
How Beautiful 3225
How Beautiful It Was 4029
How Beautiful the Days 2961
How Blest We Are 394
How Can a Lady Be Certain? 2950
How Can Anyone So Sweet 1697
How Can Harry Marry 2938
How Can I Be Alone Again 3182
How Can I Be Sure 4193
How Can I Continue On? 2198
How Can I Ever Be Alone? 117
How Can I Get Rid of Those Blues? 1440
How Can I Hold You Close Enough 4159
How Can I Leave Here? 1276
How Can I Tell? 2935
How Can I Tell Her 287, 1649
How Can I Tell Him She Loves Me 400
How Can I Tell My Joy? 4615
How Can I Tell You 3487
How Can I Tell You That It's Over? 2069
How Can I Wait? 3347
How Can I Win? 1633
How Can I Win You Now? 3312, 4300
How Can Love Survive? 4095
How Can the Cat Cross the Water? 4769
How Can They Tell I'm Irish 4206
How Can Those Things Be 755
How Can We Bring the Folks Round 4479
How Can We Swing It? 3986
How Can You Describe a Face? 4190
How Can You Forget 4749
How Can You Keep Your Mind on Business? 4692
How Can You Kiss Those Times Good Bye 3931
How Can You Say You Feel Rich Anymore 1955
How Can You Tell? 638, 1920, 4620
How Can You Tell an American? 369, 2344
How Can You Tell Till You Try 2159
How Can You Toot? 1523
How Cold, Cold, Cold (An Empty Room) 4863
How Come I'm Born Wid a Hook in My Hand 2225
How Could a Fellow Want More 1352
How Could I Be So Wrong 1611
How Could I Dare to Dream 1959
How Could I Ever Know 3862
How Could I Ever Say No 154
How Could I Forget 3953, 4527
How Could I Know What Was Goin' On? 3564
How Could I Let You Leave Me 4515
How Could Little Red Riding Hood 3179
How Could She Love Me Like That? 598
How Could We Be Wrong? 3214
How Could You Do This to Someone Who Robbed for You? (Prison Music) 3757
How Dare He 1010
How Dare You? 2877
How Dear Is Our Day 758
How Deep Is the Ocean 789
How Did Freud Know? 2579
How Did He Look? 2772
How Did I End Up Here? 3760
How Did I Lose a Friend? 2657
How Did It Get So Late So Early 70
How Did It Happen to Me? 2516
How Did the Bird Know That? 1783
How Did They Know I Was American 2180
How Did This Happen to Me 1269
How Different Things Would Be 4249
How Do I Feel? 3956
How Do I Feel 4289
How Do I Get Out of This 4540
How Do I Grow a Rose? 4163
How Do I Know? 3471
How Do I Know He Loves Me? 2950
How Do I Know You're Not Mad, Sir? 2599
How Do I Look? 2805
How Do They Ever Grow Up? 2322
How Do You Account for That? 2848
How Do You Bring Up Children? 2064
How Do You Do? 383
How Do You Do 1692
How Do You Do? 2496, 2522
How Do You Do 2866
How Do You Do? 3202
How Do You Do 1972, 4064
How Do You Do? 1327, 4490
How Do You Do-Good Bye 4657
How Do You Do? How Do You Do? 2789
How Do You Do I Love You 2011, 2010
How Do You Do It? 289
How Do You Do, Katinka? 582
How Do You Do, Middle Age 1564
How Do You Do, Miss Pratt 3895
How Do You Do, Miss Ragtime 4655
How Do You Doodle? 4208
How Do You Doodle Do? 2263
How Do You Find the Words? 1194
How Do You Get That Way? 136
How Do You Go About It 1884
How Do You Keep Out of Love? 1797
How Do You Know 3908
How Do You Know? 4655
How Do You Like It? 3515
How Do You Like the Army 214
How Do You Like Your Love? 3094
How Do You Like Your Men 3561
How Do You Love a City? 4684
How Do You Make Magic? 2993
How Do You Raise a Barn? 3509
How Do You Say Goodbye 135
How Do You Say Goodbye? 3801
How Do You Speak to an Angel? 1791
How Do You Spell Ambassador? 2432
How Do You Spot a Geishanette? 2861
How Do You Stop Loving Someone? 4678
How Do You Want Me? 3231
How Do You Write a Book? 2550
How Does It Start? 3902
How Does the Wine Taste? 4609

How Dot Man Played the Flute 2454
How Doth the Apple Butterfly 3439
How Dreamlike 3651
How Dry I Am 4528
How D'Ya Talk to a Girl 4588
How D'Ye Do? 246
How D'Ye Do 3489, 3562
How D'Ye Do Fifth Avenue 1901
How D'You Do 133, 702
How Far a Girl Should Go 3578
How Far Away Is Far Away? 823
How Far Can a Lady Go? 657
How Far Can You Follow 2941
How Far Is It to Broadway? 924
How Far Is It to the Next Town? 2568
How Far Is Too Far 1059
How Far Will You Go with Me 2344
How Fear Came 2970
How Fiercely You Dance 2384
How Fine It Is to Name Things 4523
How Fly Times 4640
How Free I Feel 3469
How Fucked Up Things Are 461
How Good It Is 3670
How Great It Is to Be a Bird 4707
How Green Was My Valley 4384, 4384
How Happy Could This Chappie Be 2951
How Happy Is the Bride 4372
How High Can a Little Bird Fly 1338
How High the Moon 4483
How I Could Go for You 288
How I Feel 2801
How I Grieve 3612
How I Love a Pretty Face 4119
How I Love Flowers 1768, 4094
How I Love You 391
How I Love Your Thingamajig 2033
How I Missed You, Mary 3821
How I Put Down the War 1274
How I React to You 1387
How I Saved Roosevelt 212
How I Thought I Looked 2722
How Is Your Technique? 3916
How It All Ends 1347
How Jazz Was Born 2302, 3020
How Jolly Our Folly 3204
How Laughable It Is 367
How Like Her Papa! 1530
How Little We've Learned 430
How Long? 423, 3505
How Long 3022
How Long Ago 4147
How Long Can a Heart Go on Loving 302
How Long Can Love Keep Laughing? 3990
How Long Has It Been 177
How Long Has This Been Going On 1419
How Long Has This Been Going On? 3060, 3766
How Long Have I Loved Libby? 589
How Long Is from Now On? 3227
How Long Must This Go On? 330
How Long Will It Be? 3410
How Lovely, How Lovely 1727
How Lovely to Be a Woman 602, 607
How Lucky 1616
How Lucky Can You Get 131
How Lucky Can You Get? 2234
How Many Daddies 407
How Many Men? 147
How Many Stars Are There in the Sky? 3630
How Many Women 721
How Marvin Eats His Breakfast 2132
How Much Am I Bid 2596
How Much Do You Want Me to Bear? 2203
How Much I Love You 3301
How Much Is That Doggy in the Window 4264
How Much Richer Could One Man Be 1265
How Much to Buy My Dream 1509
How Nice for Me 4586
How Nice to See You 3944
How Now Dow Jones 2014
How Often, How Often 1616
How Peaceful Is the Evening 4323
How Proud Indeed I Ought to Feel 526
How Sad 3187
How Shall I E'er Forget 68
How Shall I See You Through My Tears? 1636
How She Glows 4292
How Should I Your True Love Know? 3909
How Solemn 2433
How Soon, Oh Moon? 1745
How Strange the Silence 937
How Strangely Sweet 1090
How Sweet Is Peach Ice Cream 1222
How Sweet Is the Taste of Revenge 158
How Sweet to Be a Cloud 4710
How Sweetly Friendship Binds 2228
How Sweetly Simple 4450
How the Body Falls Apart 2132
How the Fairies Came to Ireland 1907
How the First Song Was Born 2034
How the Money Changes Hands 4312
How the Winds Blow 954
How They Changed the Day 202
How They Do, Do 1498
How Things Change 3960
How Things Have Changed 3827
How To 2019
How to Be a Bandit 1867
How to Be a Jewish Mother 2016
How to Be a Muse 1155
How to Be Happy Though Married 734
How to Behave Like a Lady (How to Dress Like a Lady) (How to Faint Like a Lady) 2805
How to Get in Central Park 2481
How to Get Rich 4379
How to Handle a Woman 623
How to Kill a Man 100 Ways Ballet (inst.) 607
How to Make a Pretty Face 3400
How to Pick a Man a Wife 751
How to Play an Ole Banjo 443

How to Prevent a Nuclear Explosion 2421
How to Sell a Fall-Out Shelter 4397
How to Steal an Election 2018
How to Succeed in Business Without Really Trying 2019
How to Succeed in Business without Really Trying 3890
How to Survive 369, 4369
How to Tell a Fairy Tale 1183, 4735
How to Welcome Home Your Hubby 3130
How to Win a Man 3650
How to Win Friends and Influence People 2061
How to Write a Comic Opera 3805
How Very Long Ago It Seems 584
How Was I to Know 2408
How Was I to Know? 2620, 3924
How We Get Down 1684
How We Miss You Georgie Cohan 1224
How We Would Like Our Man 2661
How? What? Why? 2375
How Will He Know? 4496
How Will I Know? 2357
How Wonderful Blue Your Eyes 3195
How Wonderful It Is 280
How Wonderful You Are 4360
How Wonderfully Fortunate 1284
How Would a City Girl Know? 3172
How Would I Know? (I Wish Dat Dere Wasn't No War) 1476
How Would You Like Me? 3429
How Would You Like to Be My Pony? 4805
How Would You Like to Bounce a Baby on Your Knee 1334
How Would You Like to Have Me for a Model? 2919
How Ya' Baby 39
How Ya Gonna Keep 'Em Down on the Farm? 3018
How Ya' Gonna Keep 'Em Down on the Farm (After They've Seen Paree)? 4813
How Ya Gonna Keep Your Mind on Dancing When You're Dancing with Someone You Love 1486
How You Gonna Keep Kool? 2298
How Young You Were Tonight 278, 2777
How'd You Like To? 4766
How'd You Like to Be a Kid? 487
How'd You Like to Be My Bow-Wow-Wow? 4425
How'd You Like to Be My Daddy? 61
How'd You Like to Be My Daddy 3985
How'd You Like to Be the Shoe Store Man 1327
How'd You Like to Flirt with Me 187
How'd You Like to Kiss a Girl Like Me 1340
How'd You Like to Like a Girl Like Me 1520
How'd You Like to Like a Girl Like Me? 4723
How'd You Like to Put Your Head Upon My Pillow 4656
How'd You Like to Spoon with Me? 2372
How'd You Like to Spoon with Me 1123
How'd You Like to Spoon with Me? 3710
How'd You Like to Take Me Home with You 1900
How'dja Like to Love Me 3444
Howdjadoo 1497
How'dy Do 1573
Howdy-Do 3031
Howdy-Do? 3867
Howdy-Do, Goodbye 1735
Howdy! How D'Ye Do? 1613
Howdy, London 3436
Howdy, Mr. Sunshine 1380
Howdy to Broadway 3436
How'ja Like to Take Me Home 204
Howl 4485
How'm I Doin'? 2790
How'm I Doing? 4635
How's Chances? 207
How's It Gonna End? 1082
How's the King 2020
How's Your Health? 1894
How's Your Romance 1018
How's Your Romance? 1453
How's Your Uncle? 3946
(On the Beach at) How've You Been? 1486
Hub Bub 3992
Hubba Hubba 2026
Hubble Bubble 2282
Hubby 1345
Hubby, the Wifey, the Sweetie and the Vamp, The 3466
Hudl Mitn Shtrudl (Hudl with the Shtrudl) 4342
Hudson Duster 2734
Huggin' and Muggin' 4253
Hugh! Hugh! 2519
Hughie 3322
Hugs and Kisses 1128, 1132
Huguette Waltz 4539
Hula Dance 2135
Hula Hoop 843
Hula, Hula, Sailor Man 2135
Hula Lou 200
Hula Love Song 589
Huliet Huliet Kinderlech 3781
Hulla-Baloo-Balay 2731
Hullabaloo at Thebes 3112
Hullo and Goodbye 2368
Hullo Hullo 4320
Hullo! Little Stranger! 954
Hum a Little Tune 605
Hum Along 4262
Hum Da Di Di 3173
Hum Drum Life 1116
Hum To 1529
Human Again 330
Human Band, The 2722
Human Beings 3846
Human Comedy, The 2033
Human Heart, The 3285
Human Nature 3177
Human Pin-Wheel, The 2858
Human Race, The 1615
Human Species, The 4707
Human Voice, A 1770
Humanity 2784

Humble Hollywood Executive, A 2847
Humble Pie 148
Humbug 4155
Humbug! 752
Humility 4774
Humming 656, 4393
Humming a Tune 3405
Hummingbird 108
Humoresquimos 2706
Humorous Ghost, The 3673
Humphrey Bogart Rhumba, The 67
Humpty Dumpty 54, 683, 2035, 2903, 4440
Humpty-Dumpty 2277, 4267
Humpty Dumpty Drag 4833
Hunca Munca 4789
Hunchback of Notre Dame, The 2037
Hundavieh 169
Hunder Runs Off to the Sea (inst.) 3630
Hundred Million Miracles, A 1315
Hundred Song, The 220
Hundred Thousand Ways, A 840
Hundred Women in One, A 3493
Hundred Years Ago, A 1481
Hundred Years from Now, A 2070, 2951
Hundred Years from Today, A 444
Hundreds of Girls 2660
Hundreds of Hats 1038
Hungarian Dance 2122
Hungarian Folk Song 721
Hungarian Rhythmic Air 1522
Hungaria's Hussars (Chorus of Huzzars) 1355
Hunger Song 2880
Hungry 952, 3112, 3111
Hungry Blues 3315
Hungry for Love 1989
Hungry Men 3294
Hungry Women 4683
Hunker Down Cowboy 915
Hunky Dory 602
Hunnie's Rag, The 2200
Huns/British Improv/EDT 3858
Hunt, The (Opening Act II) 1111
Hunt, The 4673
Hunt Ball Rehearsal 3431
Hunt Dance, The (inst.) 4212
Hunted, The 341
Hunted Stag, The 4420
Hunter's Chorus, The 2155
Hunter's Dance 1710
Hunter's Fox Trot Ball 3737
Hunter's Holiday 2335
Hunting 3025, 4539
Hunting Ballet (dance) 3980
Hunting Chorus 2880, 4094
Hunting Dance, The 3063
Hunting Days 3721
Hunting for a Happy Little Home in Harlem 559
Hunting of the Cook, The 4735
Hunting Song 627
Hunting Song (The Chase) 1111
Hunting Song 4412
Hunting the Fox 3980
Huntsman's Song of Love, The 464
Hup! Tup! Thrup! Four! (Jack the Sleepy Jeep) 4141
Hup-Two-Three 1745
Hurdi Gurdi Verdi 2809
Hurdy Gurdy 3813
Hurdy-Gurdy 3823
Hurdy-Gurdy Girl, The 2040
Hurdy Gurdy Man, The 349, 3855
Hurly-Burly 2041
Hurrah for Baffin's Bay 4723
Hurrah for the Bars and Stripes 4185
Hurrah for the Shassa Gail 1351
Hurrah! They Come 762
Hurray Back 167
Hurray for Life 1871
Hurray for the Field 3049
Hurricane 1684
Hurroo, Hurray and Hurrah for That 2347, 2716
Hurry 2775, 3108
Hurry, Boys 1746
Hurry, Bustle! 4404
Hurry, Harry 2043
Hurry Home 1296, 2219
Hurry, Little Children 4806
Hurry Now 3740
Hurry Up 2135
Hurry Up and Telephone 919
Hurry! It's Lovely Up Here! 3274
Hurt Somebody Blues 1804
Hurt They Write About, The 4270
Husband, a Love, a Wife, A 1842
Husband and Wife 632
Husband Cage 2000
Husband in Love with His Wife, A 2424
Husband, Lover and Wife 1440
Husband of Mine 3490
Husbands and Wives 2698
Husbands and Wives Dance 4744
Husbands Beware! 2364
Husbands Beware 2654
Husband's Clock, The 4467
Husband's Love, A 4590
Husband's Only a Husband, A 4760
Hush 4558
Hush a Baby Bye 668
Hush Here Comes a Whizzbang 3259
Hush Hush 2344
Hush! Hush! 2546
Hush-Hush 3818
Hush! Hush! Hush! 3251
Hush, Hush, Hush 3326
Hush! Hush! She's Meditating 4554
Hush, I Think I Hear Him 1593
Hush Little Baby 4579
Hush Little Girl Don't Cry 3887
Hush! Little Lion 1220
Hush, Look Away 4575
Hush, Not a Word 2323

Hush, Silence 1213
Hush You Now 1496
Hushabye Baby 2134
Hush-a-Bye Land 297
Hush-a-Bye My Baby 1823
Huskin' Bee, The 2902
Husking Bee 1031
Husking Bee, The 3845
Husky, Dusky Annabelle 1656
Hussar March 3766
Hussar's Quadrille 1455
Hussars' Song, The 771
Hustle and Bustle 2897
Hustle Back to Old New York 11
Hustle Bustle 4382
Hustle, Bustle 4476
Hustler, The 1229
Hut in Hoboken 2545
Huxley 2386
Huzzar March 1121
Hydrophobia Blues 930
Hygiene 4014
Hymen, Hymen 634
Hymn, The 2239
Hymn 823, 933
Hymn, The 2248
Hymn 2268, 2630, 4237
Hymn by the Royal Roosters 3040
Hymn for a Sunday Evening 607
Hymn of Betrothal 4075
Hymn of Shame, The 2046
Hymn of Temperance 451
Hymn to Her, A 1842
Hymn to Him, A 3038
Hymn to Hymen 3674
Hymn to Hymie 2864
Hymn to Jongo 4117
Hymn to Peace 369, 2228
Hymn to Spring 1700
Hymn to the Moon 3847
Hymn to the Sun 3504, 3775, 4664
Hypnotic Kiss, The 4364
Hypnotic Waltz, The
(Hyp-Hyp-Hypnotism) (inst.) 2782
Hypnotism Song, The 1439
Hypnotizing 1309
Hypnotizing Man 4655
Hypocrite, The 2399
Hyrcynian Wood, The 1962
Hysteria 3873
Hysterical Ensemble 1312
Hysterical Tune 2710

I

I Accuse 2949
I Actually Am 3172
I Admire You Very Much, Mr. Schmidt 2583
I Adore a Certain Party 1188
I Adore the American Girl 2884
I Adore Thee 2315, 4724
I Adore You 44, 1343, 4240
I Ain't Afraid 1385
I Ain't Afraid of Scarecrows
(I Ain't Scared of Crows) 1667
I Ain't Down Yet 4516
I Ain't Gonna Marry 2608
I Ain't Gonna Work No More 2675
I Ain't Got It for the One That's Got It for Me 2014
I Ain't Got No Shame 3541
I Ain't Had No Lovin' in a Long Time 3676
I Ain't Looking Back 474
I Ain't Married No More 4811
I Ain't No Fool 4806
I Ain't to Blame 1360
I Ain't to Blame for Lovin' You 3332
I Almost Asked You to Marry Me 932
I Always Believe Me 2568
I Always Come Back to You 3996
I Always Give the Wrong Impression 2387
I Always Keep My Girl Out Late 277
I Always Knew 155
I Always See Them Safely Home 1334
I Always Stay at the Ritz 3931
I Always Think I'm Up in Heaven when
I'm Down in Dixieland 2939
I Always Think of Sally 297
I Am 2876
I Am a Camera 610
I Am a Cloud 3651
I Am a Court Coquette 947
I Am a Handsome Prince 2243
I Am a Happy Man 170
I Am a Hundred Years Ahead of All the Rest 2619
I Am a Judge 2348
I Am a Little Jazz 986
I Am a Little Worm 2236
I Am a Lone-Star Girl 4453
I Am a Military Man 356
I Am a Noble Grandee, Ha! Ha! 4032
I Am a One Girl Boy 3770
I Am a Pirate 513
I Am a Piratical Brigand 104
I Am a Poor Unfortunate 2261
I Am a Potentate 1388
I Am a Prince 711, 760
I Am a Regular Romeo 4650
I Am a Tailor's Daughter 400
I Am a Tiny Mermaid in the Sea 1155
I Am a Tom-Boy 4285
I Am a Travelling Poet 3988
I Am a Vietnam Veteran 2017
I Am a Witch 3505
I Am All A-Blaze 634
I Am All Alone 3613
I Am an Absence 2243
I Am an Actor, All the Rage (Matinee Idol) 2603
I Am an Indian 2603

I Am Angling for You 2700
I Am Ashamed That Women Are So Simple 2331
I Am Captured 2602
I Am Child 3825
I Am Chu Chin Chow of China 758
I Am Cleopatra 208
I Am Craving for That Kind of Love (Kiss Me) 3963
I Am Daguerre 1922
I Am Free 4862
I Am Frosine! 81
I Am Gaston 4777
I Am Going to Be One of the Boys 525
I Am Going to Dance 3439
I Am Going to Like It Here 1315
I Am Going to Love the Man You're Going to Be 1634
I Am Happy Here 1284
I Am Here 2784
I Am Here at the Place Where Time Began 2017
I Am Human After All 2620
I Am, I Am 4111
I Am in Love 629
I Am It 3015
I Am Lonely for You (Story of the Pearl) 3423
I Am Longing, My Dearie, for You 4596
I Am Loved 1762, 3326
I Am Me 143
I Am Melpomene 4521
I Am More Than Young, I Am Childish 2233
I Am Movin' 4403
I Am Moving 1079
I Am No Good at Love 3235, 3815
I Am No Queen 3570
I Am Not Afraid 1418
I Am Not Free 3651
I Am Not Interested in Love 4485
I Am Not Old 4272
I Am Only Human After All 1448
I Am Real 52
I Am Royal 3764
I Am Sick of Love 2648
I Am Simply Irresistible 3613
I Am Small 916
I Am So Eager 3014
I Am So Easily Assimilated 630
I Am So Fair 1521
I Am So Shy 2505
I Am St. Jacques' Pilgrim 3909
I Am the Angel Gabriel 755
I Am the Author of Divorce 476
I Am the Boss 2861, 2012
I Am the Boy (and I Am the Girl) 1626
I Am the "Dernier Cri" 1197
I Am the English Daisy 1188
I Am the Herr Professor 2282
I Am the King 2035
I Am the Light 3515
I Am the Lord Lieutenant 1178
I Am the Luckiest Boy 255
I Am the Man 4595
I Am the Man They Talk So Much About 3387
I Am the Monarch of the Joint 1948
I Am the News 3136
I Am the Next 2785
I Am the Pasha 2213, 2684
I Am the Royal Chancellor 3805
I Am the Ruler 4724
I Am the Seventh Son of a Seventh Son 698
I Am the Sheriff of Nottingham 3736
I Am the Sherrif's Faithful Man 1080
I Am the Sign 3817
I Am the Singer, You Are the Song 2813
I Am the Starlight 4138
I Am the Wizard of Wall Street 2848
I Am Thinking of You 381, 1689
I Am True to All 1334
I Am Wearing a Hat 2132
I Am What I Am 2208
I Am What I Am! 1766
I Am What I Am 2075, 2360, 2583
I Am Who I Am 2910
I Am Writing a Love Song for You 3299
I Am You 2616
I Am Your Man 649
I Am Your Master 2012
I Am Yours 275
I Am "Yours Truly" 3943
I Am Yours, You Are Mine 2886
I and Albert 2047
I and I 3690
I and Myself and Me 4735
I and the King 2168
I Annex It 613
I Ask Myself 3227
I Ask Not Who You Are 4550
I Ask You Why Dear 233
I Asked My Heart 1384
I Been 'Buked and I Been Scorned 2203
I Been Up in Hell 3599
'I' Before 'E' 1496
I Beg Your Pardon 1013, 1327
I Believe 1075, 3167
I Believe in Babylove 1662
I Believe in God 4398, 2775
I Believe in Love 1717
I Believe in Marriage 2598
I Believe in Me 2172, 3630
I Believe in Music 3018, 3469
I Believe in Signs 3923
I Believe in Survival 3817
I Believe in Takin' a Chance 2201
I Believe in You 383, 2019, 2541, 3444
I Believe My Body 2451
I Believe My Own Eyes 4676
I Believe You 1310, 2558, 4818
I Believed All They Said 3740
I Belong 2657
I Belong Here 695, 1660
I Belong to the World 916
I Blame God 264

I Blew It 1990
I Blush 834
I Bought a Bicycle 31, 3059
I Bow a Glad Good Day (Tavern Opening) 711
I Bring Him Seashells 3927
I Bring My Boys Along 3086
I Bring You Good Tidings 2553
I Brought Red Roses in December to You 1334
I Brought Them Home to Mother 2160
I Brought You a Gift 3702
I Built a Dream One Day 2786
I Built a Fairy Palace in the Sky 758
I Cain't Say No 3263
I Call Him 'Al' 4415
I Call Upon You Gentlemen (Finale Act II) 1447
I Call You Back to Me 2486
I Call You Sunshine 487
I Came Here 317
I Came Here to Dance 4153
I Came Home 4579
I Came! I Saw! I Fell! 3405
I Came to Life When I Found You 1135
I Came to Tan 1077
I Came to Your Room 818
I Can 269
I Can Always Find a Little Sunshine
in the Y.M.C.A. 4770
I Can Always Find Another Partner 4694
I Can Carry a Tune 2033
I Can Cook Too 3278
I Can Count on Me 2785
I Can Count on You 2049
I Can Dance 3294, 3542
I Can Dance with Everybody but My Wife 4258
I Can Do It to Myself 4343
I Can Do No Wrong 154
I Can Do That 746
I Can Do Without Broadway 1120
I Can Do without Broadway 3953
I Can Do Wonders with You 1800, 3980
I Can Dream, Can't I? 3713
I Can Drink 4589
I Can Feel 729
I Can Get It For You Wholesale 2048
I Can Give You Music 2785
I Can Give You the Starlight 972
I Can Have It All 1077
I Can Hear It Now 454
I Can Hear Music 2427
I Can Laugh, I Can Love 906
I Can Learn 600
I Can Live Without It 90
I Can Live without You 4807
I Can Make It 729, 1216
I Can Make It Happen 2820
I Can Never Go Home Again 338
I Can Play This Part 1633
I Can Say Truly Rural 1067
I Can See 3389
I Can See Him Clearly 4279
I Can See It 1245
I Can See It All 302
I Can See It All Now 4060
I Can See the Lord in the Garden Now 4523
I Can Sew a Button 431
I Can Speak Espagnol 3719
I Can Stand for Your Color, but
Your Hair Won't Do 4451
I Can Still Remember 850
I Can Take It 1876, 4292
I Can Take It or Leave It 664
I Can Talk Now 2898
I Can Talk to You 4703
I Can Teach Them 64
I Can Tell By the Way You Dance, Dear 2292
I Can Trust Myself with a Lot of Girls 3740
I Can't Afford to Dream 4772
I Can't Argue with You 3312
I Can't Be Bothered Now 921, 3060
I Can't Be Happy 3254
I Can't Be in Love 1614
I Can't Be True So Far Away 3579
I Can't Believe It 2230
I Can't Believe It's Real 2657
I Can't Believe It's True 138, 4532
I Can't Believe It's You 135
I Can't Believe My Arms 2496
I Can't Believe That You're in Love with Me 1460
I Can't Believe You Really Love Me 4440
I Can't Complain 4481
I Can't Dance 1832
I Can't Do It Alone 723
I Can't Do the Sum 250, 4818
I Can't Do This and I Can't Do That 3345
I Can't Do Without Girls 4809
I Can't Do Without Love 497
I Can't Do Without the Men 3031
I Can't Explain (1) 139
I Can't Explain (2) 139
I Can't Find a Girl Like You! 1524
I Can't Find Another Girl Like You 2122
I Can't Find My Wife 3151
I Can't Forget the Dear Old Folks at Home 3614
I Can't Forget Your Eyes 75, 2385, 3237
I Can't Get 'Em Up 118
I Can't Get Enough 3372
I Can't Get Into the Quota 3130
I Can't Get Over a Girl Like You 3796
I Can't Get Started 4825
I Can't Give You Anything But Love 39, 441
I Can't Give You Anything but Love 432, 4197
I Can't Help Thinking of You 4544
I Can't Hide My Grief No More 2172
I Can't Keep My Eyes from Looking at You 2538
I Can't Keep Running in Place 2049
I Can't Let You Down 4238
I Can't Let You Go 1168
I Can't Live in Solitary 2418
I Can't Love Everybody 1606
I Can't Make It Anymore 1612

I (Really) Can't Make My Feet Behave 3402
I Can't Make My Heart Behave 1667
I Can't Make My Husband Behave 3254
I Can't Make This Movie 3171
I Can't Make Up My Mind 1883
I Can't Pretend 4536
I Can't Refrain from Laughing 1470
I Can't Remember 4076, 1262, 1474, 1612
I Can't Remember Living without Loving You 2171
I Can't Remember the Words 3005
I Can't Resist Them When They're Beautiful 4815
I Can't Say No to You 3004
I Can't Say You're the Only One 1569
I Can't See You All 1335
I Can't See You at All 3891
I Can't Sleep 2132, 1393
I Can't Stand Dragons 1092
I Can't Stop Talking in Time 339
I Can't Tell Where They're From When They Dance 1485
I Can't Tell You 699
I Can't Think 4341
I Can't Turn You Loose 146, 3695
I Can't Wait 1757, 2368, 4848
I Can't Wait to Get Married 1750
I Can't Wait to Take You Home to Mother 2443
I Can't Walk on Water 3817
I Cannot Be Faithful 3011
I Cannot Drink the Old Drinks 3755
I Cannot Leave You 2546
I Cannot Let You Go 3875
I Cannot Live Without Love 2950
I Cannot Live Without Your Love 4667
I Cannot Love 1682
I Cannot Make Him Jealous 1848
I Cannot Marry You All 1532
I Cannot Sleep Without Dreaming of You 1552
I Cannot Speak 4719
I Cannot Take a Step Too Far 75
I Cannot Tell Her So 3725
I Cannot Turn to Love 3741
I Cannot Understand 2587
I Cannot Wait Till Monday 355
I Care Not If the Cup I Hold 3777
I Char 276
I Chose Right 253
I Click the Heel and I Kiss the Hand 1973
I Cling to You 4670, 4665
I Come As a Cavalier 3736
I Come from Afar 1743
I Come from Gascony 947
I Come Out of a Dream 818
I Come Riding 3643
I Come to You 1940
I Confess 2877
I Could Always Go to You 3448
I Could Be Good for You 4048
I Could Be Happy with Either One 3073
I Could Be Happy with One Little Boy If There Were No Others Around 1482
I Could Be Happy with You 507
I Could Dig You 3825
I Could Do a Lot for You 468
I Could Drive a Person Crazy 4067
I Could Fall in Love 1665
I Could Get Married Today 3895
I Could Get Used to Him 4286
I Could Get Used to This 154
I Could Give My Heart to You 3519
I Could Give Up Anything but You 1339
I Could Go for You 2140
I Could Go Home to a Girlie Like You 4747
I Could Go Places with You 2458
I Could Go with the Wind 4157
I Could Learn to Love a Boy Like You 2792
I Could Love a Man Like That 1323
I Could Love a Million Girls 2717
I Could Love Him 3108
I Could Love You If I Tried 4419, 4418
I Could Never Get Enough 273
I Could Say Goodnight to a Thousand Girls (But Only Dream of One) 326
I Could Still Try 4262
I Could Teach Her 1169
I Could Use Five 1646
I Could Waltz on Forever 4646
I Could Write a Book 3353
I Could've Gone to Nashville 3211
I Couldn't Be Happier 4416
I Couldn't Be with Anyone but You 4732
I Couldn't Have Done It Alone 64
I Couldn't Hold My Man 2475
I Couldn't Make a Hit with Molly 1902
I Couldn't Make a Hit with Susie 591
I Couldn't Say 556
I Cover the Waterfront 2772
I Cried 4264
I Cried a Tear 4127
I Cried for My Troubles 2236
I Cried for You 544
I Crowed What I Knowed 4330
I Dance Alone 4677
I Danced with a Major 3594
I Dare Not Love You 3586
I Dare to Dream 2227
I Dare to Speak of Love to You 771
I Dare You 4200
I Dare You Not to Dance 944
I Dearly Adore a Saloon 2187
I Delight in the Sight of My Lydia 2339
I Depend on Myself 42
I Depend on You 3305
I Did It 900, 3227
I Did It for Defense 2447
I Did It for the Missus 3091
I Did It for the Red, White and Blue 447
I Did It on Roller Skates 1420
I Did Not Intend To 20
I Did Not Sleep Last Night 278
I Didn't Grieve Over Daniel 2009

I Didn't Hesitate 'Cause I Knew that I Was Lost 1632
I Didn't Know It Was That Good 18
I Didn't Know That It Was Loaded 1874
I Didn't Know What Time It Was 4420
I Didn't Know Where to Look 4467
I Didn't Make the World 99
I Didn't Mean No Harm 246
I Didn't Raise My Boy to Be a Soldier 3018, 3020
I Didn't Think She'd Do It 45
I Die for Love of You 1521
I Dig 1717
I Dig Myself 4468
I Discover New Worlds 4316
I Disremember Quite Well 3309
I Do 629, 642, 3922
I Do All the Dirty Work 3313
I Do Business in My Hat 2344
I Do! He Doesn't! 911
I Do! I Do! (1) 2050
I Do! I Do! (2) 2050
I Do, I Do, I Do! 3313
I Do, I Do, I Do 3933
I Do! I Do! Waltz 3542
I Do It All By Proxy 1388, 3591
I Do Like You 1422, 2764
I Do Like Your Eyes 3031
I Do Miracles 2333
I Do Not Know 2937
I Do Not Know a Day I Did Not Love You 4481
I Do, So There 357
I Do So There! 4654
I Do the Best I Can 4595
I Do, You Don't 4765
I Do, You Don't 4765
I Don't Ask About Tomorrow 1015
I Don't Believe a Word of It 1721
I Don't Believe I'll Ever Be a Lady 1095
I Don't Believe in Fairies Now 2761
I Don't Believe in Heroes Anymore 4349
I Don't Believe It 2617, 4145
I Don't Belong on a Farm 4393
I Don't Blame 'Em 670
I Don't Care 1537, 2698, 3543, 4390, 4431, 4803
I Don't Care Much 610
I Don't Care to Be Yo' Lady Fren' No Mo' 3999
I Don't Care What They Say about Me 2397
I Don't Care Where They Buried My Body 2225
I Don't Feel at Home on the Bowery No More 4740
I Don't Get It 3960, 4131
I Don't Have the Time 3880
I Don't Hope for Great Things 3651
I Don't Know 133, 702, 2333, 958, 2570, 2775
I Don't Know (The Letter) 2961, 3444
I Don't Know 3691
I Don't Know, But I Guess 4115
I Don't Know Enough about You 3428
I Don't Know Her Name 2707
I Don't Know Her Name Yet 186
I Don't Know His Name 3918
I Don't Know How 834, 2064
I Don't Know How I Can Do Without You 46
I Don't Know How I Do It but I Do 4250
I Don't Know How to Be My Daddy's Father 3671
I Don't Know How to Have Sex 583
I Don't Know How to Love Him 2212
I Don't Know How to Pick the Proper Girl 3652
I Don't Know How to Talk to a Lady 4609
I Don't Know How You Do It 2947, 3466
I Don't Know Nothin' 3921
I Don't Know What I'd Do Without You 4816
I Don't Know What to Do 4201
I Don't Know What You See in Me 1308
I Don't Know Where I'm Going 1848
I Don't Know Where I'm Going, but
I'm on My Way 1995
I Don't Know Where She Got It 1729
I Don't Know Why (When I Dance with You) 1026
I Don't Know Why I Trust You But I Do 4062
I Don't Laugh at Love Any More 4378
I Don't Like School (School Days) 434
I Don't Like the Sea 3399
I Don't Like Them Too 4249
I Don't Like This Dame 2961
I Don't Like You 2368
I Don't Like Your Family 4387
I Don't Live Anywhere Anymore 426
I Don't Love Nobody 2845
I Don't Love You No More, No More 1577
I Don't Love You — Not Much 665
I Don't Love You Well Enough for That 1525
I Don't Mind 2664
I Don't Mind Walkin' in the Rain 2415
I Don't Need a Man to Know I'm Good 1037
I Don't Need Anything but You 150
I Don't Need No Wimmin' 1754
I Don't Need the Moonlight 924
I Don't Owe You a Thing 3507
I Don't Play with Humans 562
I Don't Really Mind 3880
I Don't Regret a Thing 2539
I Don't Remember Christmas 4145
I Don't Remember That 4713
I Don't Remember You 131, 1764, 4480
I Don't Repent 1414
I Don't See Him Very Much Anymore 278, 2777
I Don't Smoke 4330
I Don't Suppose You Have 45
I Don't Think I Like This Game 562
I Don't Think I Love You, I Know I Do 1247
I Don't Think I'll End It All Today 2190
I Don't Think I'll Ever Love You 300
I Don't Think I'll Fall in Love Today 4443
I Don't Think I'm in Love 4588
I Don't Wanna Be a Loser 4193
I Don't Wanna Do It Alone No More 952
I Don't Wanna Rock 4828
I Don't Wanna Talk About Her 1372
I Don't Wanna Work 3227
I Don't Want a Boy 869
I Don't Want a Girlie 3184

I Don't Want a Little Canoe 1403
I Don't Want a Million Dollars 1967
I Don't Want an Auto 4801
I Don't Want Any Help 1865
I Don't Want Any in Mine 1532
I Don't Want Any Labor in My Job 4199
I Don't Want Any Wurzburger 3488
I Don't Want Him 2342
I Don't Want the Dark 3313
I Don't Want To (Oh, Come On) 257
I Don't Want to Be a Fly 2550
I Don't Want to Be a Gentleman 3800
I Don't Want to be a Lady 2964
I Don't Want to Be a Mirror Anymore 2243
I Don't Want to Be a Sailor 830, 2286
I Don't Want to Be a Soldier 1151, 1722, 3259
I Don't Want to Be Fired Again 109
I Don't Want to Be Hurt Again 4830
I Don't Want to Be in Buttons 2016
I Don't Want to Be in Dixie 4816
I Don't Want to Be Married (I Just Wanna Be Friends) 1225
I Don't Want to Be President (If It Means Losing You) 622
I Don't Want to Behave Like a Lady 2240
I Don't Want to Feel What I Feel 3757
I Don't Want to Go Home 136, 4240
I Don't Want to Go Over to Vietnam 2472
I Don't Want to Grow Old 602, 3355
I Don't Want to Hear No But, But, But 3830
I Don't Want to Know 2208, 1012
I Don't Want to Marry You 3085
I Don't Want to Marry Your Family 3579
I Don't Want to Play in Your Back Yard 1301
I Don't Want to Say Goodnight 2240
I Don't Want to Walk Without You 3444
I Don't Want to Watch TV 2630
I Don't Want You 3035
I Don't Want You to Be a Sister to Me 3322
I Done Good (1) 451
I Done Good (2) 451
I Draw the Line 2333
I Dream 1108
I Dream About Frankie 338
I Dream of a Girl in a Shawl 4581
I Dream of You 1231
I Dream of Your Eyes 771
I Dream Too Much 2204
I Dreamed a Dream 2442
I Dreamed About Roses 1045
I Dreamed I Was at Home Again 346
I Dreamt about My Home 459
I Dreamt I Dwelt in Bloomingdale's 2051
I Dreamt I Dwelt in Marble Halls 1710
I Dreamt that I Went to the Grand Opera Ball 378
I Drink from My Heart to You 586
I Dun-No-Wat, The 3842
I Dunno What, The 4211
I Eat 583
I Enjoy Being a Girl 1315
I Enter the Shrine 3573
I Envy the Bird 4724
I Envy You Rio 4117
I Fall in Love Too Easily 4743
I Fancy You 4016
I Faw Down and Go Boom 4683
I Feel a Bump Inside 2334
I Feel a Real Bad Lad Tonight 2293
I Feel a Song Comin' On 4197
I Feel at Home with You 834
I Feel Fine 2940
I Feel Good 2796
I Feel Grand 1045
I Feel Him Slipping Away 2132
I Feel Humble 4633
I Feel It in My Bones 1293
I Feel Like a Brother to You 1766
I Feel Like I'm Gonna Die Rag 3739
I Feel Like I'm Gonna Live Forever 1791
I Feel Like I'm Not Out of Bed Yet (Sleep in Your Baby's Arms) 3278
I Feel Like New Year's Eve 4060
I Feel Like They Feel in Castile 657
I Feel Love 716
I Feel My Luck Comin' Down 4123
I Feel Pretty 4625
I Feel So Happy 379
I Feel So Jazzy 1475
I Feel Sorry for the Girl 1290
I Feel Sorta— 680
I Feel the Earth Move 3739
I Feel Wonderful 2052
I Fell for You 703
I Fell Head Over Heels in Love 2293, 2843
I Fell in Love All By Myself 1307
I Fell in Love on Monday 3579
I Fell in Love with Polly 2695
I Fell in Love with You 2707, 4375
I Fell In with Evil Companions 1848
I Felt Like Smashing My Face in a Clear Glass Window 3125
I Flew to Havana Last Wednesday 3889
I Fly By Night 3576
I Follow the Ponies 293
I Forget What I Started to Say 3766
I Forgot the Number of the House 1565
I Fought Every Step of the Way 4423
I Found a Baby on My Doorstep 4814
I Found a Bit of Paris in Old New York 839
I Found a Bud Among the Roses 468
I Found a Four Leaf Clover 1485
I Found a Friend 3012
I Found a Hobby 2544
I Found a Horseshoe 3016
I Found a Million Dollar Baby 418
I Found a Rainbow 1938
I Found a Song 82
I Found a Way (I Lost Another Chance to Be a Hero) 2213
I Found God in Myself 1344

I Found Him 71, 3889
I Found Love 2949
I Found My Twin 2599
I Found the Answer 4460
I Found the Girl of My Dreams on Broadway 4635
I Found the Heart of You 2215
I Found the Sweetest Rose That Grows in Dixie 3552
I Found You at Last 2568
I Found Youse 3329
I Furnished My One Room Apartment 4533
I Gave Her That 3985
I Gave My Love a Cherry 4579
I Gave You Me 2238
I Get a Kick Out of You 163, 4132
I Get a Lonesome Feeling 3085
I Get Along with the Aussies 4340
I Get Around 3273
I Get Embarrassed 4270
I Get Myself Out 1699
I Get Tired 4619
I Give My Heart 1110
I Give My Soul Into Your Keeping 25
I Give Myself Away 3172, 4545
I Give Up 2357
I Give You the Ladies 324
I Go My Way 1815
I Go On 2775
I Go to Bed 4435
I Go to Rio 1298
I Got a Cookie Jar but No Cookies 2271
I Got a Dream to Sleep On 135
I Got a Friend 699
I Got a Gal in Californy 2089
I Got a Marble and a Star 4169
I Got a New Girl 958
I Got a Right to Know 1310
I Got a Song 462
I Got a Song in Me 2235
I Got Another One 3357
I Got Beauty 3326
I Got Feelings 2307
I Got It 4796
I Got It Bad and That Ain't Good 3905, 2259, 3175, 4091
I Got It from Agnes 4412
I Got It Made 1990
I Got Life 1717
I Got Lost in His Arms 153, 4399
I Got Love 3610
I Got Lucky 3286
I Got Me 155
I Got My Man 4693
I Got Plans for You Baby 1155
I Got Plenty o' Nuthin' 3541
I Got Religion 952, 2640, 4267
I Got Rhythm 3905, 921, 3989
I Got Rhythm Too 2776
I Got Statistics 973
I Got That Other Lady's with My Baby Feeling 562
I Got the Bird on the Canary Island 226
I Got the Blood 40
I Got the Sun in the Morning 153
I Got the What? 1665
I Got to Have a Somebody 3875
I Got to See de Minstrel Show 1526
I Got You (I Feel Good) 4193
I Got You 4695, 1613
I Got You Babe 3739
I Gotta 1955
I Gotta Be 3934
I Gotta Go 2224
I Gotta Have Music 2305
I Gotta Have My Moments 2808
I Gotta Have You 1567
I Gotta Hear a Song 556
I Gotta Keep Movin' 1072
I Gotta Keep My Eye on You 184
I Gotta Little Time 1822
I Gotta Make My Own Music 2294, 943
I Gotta Perform 2231
I Gotta Right to Sing the Blues 478, 432, 1137, 1385
I Gotta Whitewash 4409
I Grovel to the Earth (Chee-Chee's First Entrance) 711
I Grovel to Your Cloth (Chee-Chee's Third Entrance) 711
I Guess Everything Will Turn Out All Right 4459
I Guess I Love You 1932
I Guess I Talk Too Much 2534
I Guess I'll Go Back to Home and Mother 421
I Guess I'll Hang My Tears Out to Dry 1577, 4743
I Guess I'll Have to Change My Plan 2545, 3020
I Guess I'll Have to Count Some Sheep 924
I Guess I'll Have to Telegraph My Baby 1988
I Guess I'll Miss the Man 3506
I Guess I'll Take a Ride 2155
I Guess I'll Take the Train Back Home 830
I Guess I'm More Like Mother Than Like Father 2574
I Guess This Is Goodbye 2143
I Guess We Should Be Satisfied (Finale Act I) 376
I Guess We're Gonna Get Along 4502
I Had a Ball 2053
I Had a Dog 473
I Had a Little Teevee 2134
I Had a Love Once 781
I Had a Night 2925
I Had a Son 459, 2766
I Had Big Plans 837
I Had Just Been Pardoned 1284
I Had My Pitcher Tooken 4104
I Had Myself a True Love 1385, 4123
I Had to Go 3806
I Had Twins (He Had Twins) 514
I Had Two Dregs 1991
I Hail from Cairo 3985
I Happen to Like New York 1018, 3131, 4517
I Happen to Love You 2805, 1742

I Happened to Be There 1994
I Hate a Fly 3258
I Hate a Parade 2850
I Hate Being Me 2243
I Hate Football 2069
I Hate Her 4617
I Hate Him 656, 1029
I Hate It 3600
I Hate Little Boys 1255
I Hate Men 2331
I Hate Musicals 3811
I Hate Myself (For Falling in Love with You) 567
I Hate Myself in the Morning 1112
I Hate Spring 2294, 3292
I Hate the Avant Garde 2935
I Hate the Lovely Women 25
I Hate to Love You So 3591
I Hate to Talk About Myself 4476, 4780
I Hate to Think That You'll Grow Old Baby 4177
I Hate to Travel 190
I Hate to Wake Up 2493
I Hate to Work on Monday 1563
I Hate Trains 1402
I Hate You 1924, 2637, 4603
I Hate You, Darling 2453
I Hate Your Struttin' Style 3541
I Have a Charge to Fulfill 2243
I Have a Date 2549
I Have a Family 2132
I Have a Friend 4862
I Have a Friend at the Chase Manhattan Bank 314
I Have a Heart 3051
I Have a Little Secret 4106
I Have a Longing for Long Acre Square 4277
I Have a Love 3967, 4625
I Have a Noble Cock 634
I Have a Run in My Stocking 2540
I Have a Single Track Mind 2178
I Have a Song 2504, 2977
I Have a Swain in the Army 2345
I Have a Terrible Secret 2965
I Have Acted Like a Fool 1245
I Have Been a Good Boy 3989
I Have Been A-Maying 4724
I Have Born So Much Pain 2172
I Have Changed 2283
I Have Courted in Vain 2538
I Have Dreamed 2312
I Have Forgotten You Almost 3137
I Have Found Them All 3372
I Have Grown to Love New York 971
I Have Just One Heart for Just One Boy 627
I Have Lived 600
I Have Lost My Little Brown Bear 2892
I Have Loved and I've Learned 3505
I Have My Fingers Crossed, Why Don't You 1580
I Have My Moments 1617
I Have My Own Way 1076
I Have My Own Way of Loving Him 1255
I Have No Words 949, 2547
I Have Not Lived in Vain 4288, 2320
I Have Room in My Heart 1670
I Have Saved 2553
I Have Seen the Wind 10
I Have Somebody's Heart 764
I Have Something Nice 4437
I Have the Room Above Her 2204
I Have to Get Used to Being in Love 3880
I Have to Laugh 1095
I Have to Tell You 1242
I Have Waited for You 1552
I Have What You Want! 3559
I Have Written a Play 3279
I Have You to Thank 3800
I Haven't a Bean in My Jeans 3383
I Haven't Got a Worry in the World 1749
I Haven't Got You 3342
I Haven't Told Him 2498
I Hear (Oil) 4693
I Hear a Song 1075, 3167
I Hear a Symphony 338
I Hear a Woodpecker Knocking at My Family Tree 1606
I Hear America Singing 2077, 2433, 3683, 1416, 4316
I Hear Bells 2617, 3526, 4145
I Hear Hawaii 1809
I Hear Music 3444
I Hear the Music When I'm Dancin' with You 1940
I Hear the Quarter Chime 1080
I Hear They Want Some More 737
I Heard 3182
I Heard a Bugle Blowing 2806
I Heard It Through the Grapevine 3695
I Heard My Mother Crying 1612
I Heard So Much About You 2848
I Heard Someone Crying 3862
I Heard That Tale Before 1561
I Heard the Bells on Christmas Day 3793, 3794, 4391
I Heard You Were Lovely 1879
I Held a Hope 3201
I Hold Her Hand and She Holds Mine 4815
I Hold Your Hand in Mine 4412
I Hope He's Not Ashamed of Me 1974
I Hope I Don't Love Him 1306
I Hope I Get It 746
I Hope That My Hope Comes True 1521
I Hope You'll Forgive These Tears 4473
I Hope You're Happy 3615
I, Huckleberry, Me 394
I Hunder 3630
I Hurry Home to You 550
I Idolize Ida 2770
I Intend to End It All 4617
I Introduced 1018, 1921
I Invented Myself 367
I, John, Take Thee Matilda 2291
I Jot It Down (Stenographers Song) 3073

I Jupiter, I Rex 3326
I Just Can't Help It 3418
I Just Can't Keep My Eyes Off You 3337
I Just Can't Make My Eyes Behave 3387
I Just Can't Move in Her Shadow 944
I Just Can't Wait 4012, 4190
I Just Couldn't Do Without You 4663
I Just Couldn't Take It, Baby 444
I Just Dropped In 2101
I Just Dropped in to Say Goodbye 3756
I Just Fell in Love 2422
I Just Found Out 2294
I Just Found Out about Love 4180
I Just Got in the City 344
I Just Gotta Make Love 1231
I Just Have to Breathe 261
I Just Heard 1265
I Just Kissed My Nose Goodnight 2294
I Just Looked at You 3953
I Just Pressed Button A 4635
I Just Slipped Away from My Wedding 3940, 4047
I Just Want Jazz 3868
I Just Want Somebody to Love Me 4064
I Just Want to Be a Song and Dance Man 4180, 4197
I Just Want to Be a Star 3211
I Just Want to Know 572
I Just Want to Know That You're All Right 708
I Just Want to Make Friends 2516
I Keep Forgettin' 4031
I Keep Telling Myself 596
I Kiss My Hand to Thee 762
I Kiss Your Hand Madame 2382
I Kissed My Girl Goodbye 2187
I Knew 446
I Knew a Girl in Barcelona 2178
I Knew a Man 3873
I Knew at First Sight That I Loved Her 737
I Knew Her When 4203
I Knew Him Before He Was Spanish 4235
I Knew Him When 1552, 2475
I Knew I'd Know 304
I Knew It 2861
I Knew It All the Time 4577
I Knew the Music 275
I Knew 'Twould Be So 4121
I Knew You Well 3074
I Know 170, 270, 1146, 3246
I Know a Fella 599
I Know a Foul Ball 2444
I Know a Girl 356, 723
I Know a Girl Like You 830
I Know a Lot About You 1837
I Know a Man 4163
I Know a Place 4193
I Know a Town (1) 451
I Know a Town (2) 451
I Know about Love 1061
I Know and She Knows 3237
I Know and You Know 2587
I Know He'll Understand 4627
I Know Him So Well 721
I Know How It Is 2961
I Know How You Wonder 991
I Know I Could 1513
I Know I Have to Leave Here 4788
I Know I Ought to Say No 1836
I Know I Shall Meet Her Someday 1552
I Know I'm Nobody 4772
I Know It Can Happen Again 85
I Know Loneliness Quite Well 3542
I Know My Love 600
I Know My Wife 3272
I Know Now 1359, 3734, 4034
I Know Someone Loves Me 605
I Know Something 1831
I Know That I Love You 3185
I Know That I'm in Love 4654
I Know That I'm in Love with You 2897
I Know That This Must Be Love 1961
I Know That You Know 3249, 3254
I Know That You Love Me 4249
I Know the Feeling 674, 4435
I Know the Kind of a Girl for You 2485
I Know the Kind of Girl (A Girl Like You) 3139
I Know the Man 101
I Know Things Now 2143
I Know What He's Up To 1878
I Know What I Am 1721
I Know What I've Got 1296
I Know What It Is to Be Alone 3577
I Know What You Need 451
I Know Where I'm Going 4579
I Know Where the Bodies Are Buried 3181
I Know Where There's a Cozy Nook (The Nozy Cook) 1284
I Know You 3658, 3970
I Know You Are There 518
I Know You By Heart 372
I Know You Sell It 1958
I Know You're Too Wonderful for Me 4709
I Know Your Heart 1891
I Know Your Husband Very Well 1888
I Know Your Kind 1029
I Know, I Know 1017
I Knows What I Knows 2375
I Laughed at Spring 4273
I Lay Alone All Winter 2565
I Learned About Women (from Her) 1552
I Learned About Women from Her 2706
I Leave the World 1634
I Left a Dream Somewhere 1676
I Left Her on the Beach at Honolulu 4810
I Left My Door Open and My Daddy Walked Out 789
I Left My Heart at the Stage Door Canteen 4340
I Left My Heart in Bala Cynwyd 4093
I Left My Heart in Dixie 3437
I Left You There 275
I Lerve You 289

I Let a Song Go Out of My Heart 886, 4091
I Light a Light 119
I Like 2219, 4623
I Like a Big Town, I Like a Small Town 1819
I Like a Man Around the House 4018
I Like All Girls 4490
I Like America 3196
I Like 'Em All 2919
I Like 'Em Fat Like That 1296
I Like 'Em Plump 4017
I Like Everybody 2961, 3444
I Like Him 1094
I Like His Ass 119
I Like It 1273, 1527, 3494, 4272, 4741
I Like It Here 183
I Like It Like That 1890
I Like It with Music 1493
I Like London 178
I Like Love 4586
I Like Me 871, 1012, 4635
I Like My Misfortunes to Be Taken Seriously 2539
I Like New York 1208, 4635
I Like Nonsense 56
I Like the Boys 771, 1335, 4258
I Like the Company of Men 3482
I Like the Girls 735
I Like the Job 1438
I Like the Ladies 629, 4693
I Like the Likes of You 4824
I Like the Look 3233
I Like the Looks of You 3172
I Like the Military Man 3978
I Like the Nose of Your Face 1286
I Like Them Wild 387
I Like to Go to Strange Places 2105
I Like to Have a Flock of Men Around Me 2261
I Like to Linger in the Lingerie 4269
I Like to Look 1804
I Like to Look Around a Little 4218
I Like to Look My Best 2248
I Like to Make It Cozy 608
I Like to Play with the Boys 1557
I Like to Recognize the Tune 4420
I Like to See It 2122
I Like to Walk with a Pal Like You 1174
I Like to Win 593
I Like Trains 1341
I Like What I Do 534
I Like What I See 4093
I Like What You Like 1667
I Like You 184, 410, 968, 1045, 1242, 1629, 413, 2793, 2808
I LIke You 3256
I Like You 3515, 3663, 1647, 4025
I Like You All 276
I Like You As You Are 3650
I Like You Lil, for Fair 3437
I Like You, Too 2155
I Like You Too 3205
I Like You Very Much 2951
I Like Your Face 3861
I Like Your Style 305
I Like Your Way 1118, 1995
I Live a Little 2220
I Live Alone 1684, 2049
I Live By My Wits 1064
I Live By Myself (and I Like It) 3294
I Live for Love 277, 2654
I Live for That Day 4169
I Live for You Alone 3771
I Live, I Die for You 2602
I Live in Turkey 4814
I Live My Life in Color 1075
I Live to Love 3920
I Lived in a House with a Piano 3813
I, Living I 1987
I Long for the Sun 758
I Long to Be Simple 1655
I Long to Belong 1780
I Long to Linger Longer Dearie 4840
I Look for Love 3650
I Lost Everything Losing You 567
I Lost It 935
I Lost My Beat 1577
I Lost My Head All Over You 740
I Lost the Love of Anatol 1456
I Lost the Rhythm 2554
I Lost You 2705, 4332
I Love a Cop 1280
I Love a Fat Man 3844
I Love a Fight 3511
I Love a Film Cliche 1000
I Love a Fool 71
I Love a Girl in a Shawl 1690
I Love a Lark 2135
I Love a Man 2682, 4319
I Love a Man in a Uniform 1779
I Love a Man with a Uniform On Polka 3239
I Love a Musical Comedy Show 3250
I Love a Parade 1856, 3709
I Love a Piano 789, 3024, 4158
I Love a Polka So 2105
I Love a Romance 198
I Love a Wedding 1456
I Love a Yankee Doodle Girl 2834
I Love a Yankee Girl 1003
I Love All the Boys 258
I Love All the Boys in the World 335
I Love America 2180
I Love and the World Is Mine 4590
I Love Being Here with You 3428
I Love But You 1580
I Love Central Park 3576
I Love 'Em All 534
I Love 'Em All from A to Z 4247
I Love Everyone in the Wide Wide World 1640
I Love Everything That's Old 3215
I Love Harlem 3905
I Love Her and She Loves Me 231

I Love Her Oh! Oh! Oh! 1963
I Love Her-She Loves Me 2706
I Love Him 3875, 751, 1743, 2961, 3772
I Love Him for He Loved the Love That I Loved 2619
I Love Him, the Rat 1387
I Love His Face 3469
I Love, I Adore Her 2500
I Love It 1063
I Love It Rag 4804
I Love Louisa 294
I Love Love 3584, 4669
I Love Love (I Love You Dear) 3685
I Love Love in New York 95
I Love Lydia 2057
I Love MacIntosh 3322
I Love Me 1785
I Love Me (I'm Wild About Myself) 3405
I Love My Art 1551, 3031
I Love My Boo Boo 1116
I Love My Father 4485
I Love My Little Susie (Camel Song) 930
I Love My Love 2936
I Love My Love with an "A" (J'Aime Mon Amour) 1569
I Love My Movie Picture Man 75
I Love My Wife 2050, 2058, 4004
I Love Myself in Two 2243
I Love Nashville 2248
I Love New York 4068
I Love Not but You 3392
I Love Not One but All 3304
I Love Only One Girl in the Wide, Wide World 4723
I Love Only You 1453
I Love Order 3469
I Love Paris 629
I Love Petite Belle 2719
I Love Power 1092
I Love Rosie Casey 4317
I Love Someone 945
I Love That Boy 1539
I Love the Boys 2135
I Love the Charleston 4795
I Love the Girls 379
I Love the Ground You Walk On 1552
I Love the Heart of Dixie 3985
I Love the Ladies 367, 2091
I Love the Land of Old Black Joe 1154
I Love the Lassies (I Love Them All) 3146
I Love the Last One Best of All 2765
I Love the Love That's New 3770
I Love the Misses 1972
I Love the Moon 3079
I Love the Name of Mary 310
I Love the Rain 2988
I Love the River and You 4840
I Love the Sun 1282
I Love the Way We Fell in Love 3713
I Love Them All 1759, 2950, 3026, 3586
I Love Them Just a Little Bit 1175
I Love This Child 4764
I Love This Land 4004
I Love, Thou Lovest 2180
I Love to Be in Love 1439
I Love to Be Loved 4809, 4834
I Love to Be Unhappy 1512
I Love to Cry at Weddings 4238
I Love to Dance 287, 545, 1298, 2342, 2446, 2461, 4158
I Love to Dance When I Hear a March 200
I Love to Flirt with the Ladies 3920
I Love to Flutter 4021
I Love to Follow a Band 1776
I Love to Fox Trot 1961
I Love to Go Shopping 511
I Love to Go Swimmin' with Wimmin' 2601
I Love to Have the Boys Around Me 4603
I Love to Hear a Yankee Doodle Tune 2493
I Love to Linger with You 4851
I Love to Look Again 3921
I Love to Love a Mason 1550
I Love to Quarrel with You 1964, 4440
I Love to Raise the Dickens 4849, 4832
I Love to Ramble 1815
I Love to Read the Papers in the Morning 4649
I Love to Say Hello to the Girls (I Hate to Say Goodbye) 3538
I Love to Sing-A 4399
I Love to Sing the Words (While We're Dancing) 3036
I Love to Sit and Look at You 1318
I Love to Two Step with My Man 2990
I Love What I'm Doing 1475, 2590
I Love What the Girls Have 2801
I Love Ya, Love Ya, Love Ya 1120
I Love You 1321, 1484, 1847, 2059, 2481, 2516
I Love You (As Much As I Am Able) 2523
I Love You 2847, 3021, 3117, 3544, 4075, 4143, 4403, 4719, 4764
I Love You All the Time 3856, 3902
I Love You and I Adore You 4669
I Love You and I Like You (Love You but I Like You Even More) 1855
I Love You As You Are 1707
I Love You Babe, and You Love Me 1925
I Love You Because You Are You 830
I Love You Best of All 2126
I Love You but Good 4602
I Love You but I Like You Even More (I Love You and I Like You) 1657
I Love You Dear 195
I Love You Dear and Only You 586
I Love You, Dear, I Love but You 2884
I Love You, 'Deed I Do' 3998
I Love You Dolly 2213
I Love You Etcetera 80
I Love You, Evaline 1213
I Love You for That 3210
I Love You, Honey 4198
I Love You, I Adore You 1711, 3978

I Love You, I Love You, I Love You 943
I Love You in Velvet 3052
I Love You Just the Same 335
I Love You Lady Deed I Do 3384
I Love You Ma Cherie 3387
I Love You Madly 4091
I Love You, Mommy 2307
I Love You, Mon Cherie 1188
I Love You More 2877
I Love You More Than Yesterday 3556
I Love You More Today Than Yesterday 2382
I Love You, My Darling 1487, 2747
I Love You No More Than... 4073
I Love You Oh! Oh! Oh! 3134
I Love You Only 4713
I Love You So 758, 2384, 2637, 2673
I Love You So (The Merry Widow Waltz) 2836, 2838
I Love You So 4765, 3547
I Love You So I Keep Dreaming 1999
I Love You So Much Jesus 4788
I Love You Sweetheart 1248
I Love You This Morning 999
I Love You to Distraction 3765
I Love You Today 4090
I Love You Whoever You Are 51
I Love You, You Love Me 4792
I Love Your Brains 3666
I Love Your Laughing Face 3725
I Love Your Sunny Teeth 363
I Love Your Vibrato 4289
I Love Ze American Ragtime 457
I Love Ze Parisienne 3265
I Loved 2188
I Loved a Man 4541
I Loved Her Best of All 2135
I Loved Her Too 4169
I Loved Him But He Didn't Love Me 1018
I Loved Him but He Didn't Love Me 4581
I Loved You Once in Silence 623
I Loved You Wednesday 2060
I Loves You Porgy 3018
I Loves You, Porgy 3541
I-M-4-U 4264
I Made a Deal 3844
I Made a Fist! 2961
I Made It 1073
I Made the Day Shorter 3227
I Made Them Jump 4115
I Made Them Step 3310
I Make Hay While the Moon Shines 3569
I Make Up for That in Other Ways 1979
I Makes Mine Myself 545
I Married an Angel 2061
I Married Seven Brothers 3888
I Marry You 4609
I May 3084
I May Be Crazy but I Ain't No Fool 4697
I May Be Crazy But I Ain't No Fool 2111
I May Be Gone for a Long, Long Time 1919
I May Be Small, But I Have Big Ideas 1065
I May Be Wrong (But I Think You're Wonderful) 3005
I May Be Wrong 4170
I May Believe Half-That's All 1530
I May Blush from Anger 4173
I May Look Strong but I'm Far from Healthy 2619
I May Never Fall in Love with You 4516
I May Never Get Well Again 1035
I May Say Maybe 664
I May Stay Away a Little Longer 4742
I May Want to Remember Today 2617
I Mean No-One-Else-but-You 2567
I Mean to Be a Good Girl Now 3049
I Mean to Be Married as Soon as I Can 3051
I Mean to Introduce It into China 3828
I Mean to Marry a Man 1526
I Mean to Say 4179
I Mean What I Say 4741
I Meant You No Harm 1103
I Met a Girl 363
I Met a Girl on Monday 1176
I Met a Man 3564
I Met My Love 2114, 3280, 4262
I Met My Love in a Restaurant 2383, 2952
I Might 133
I Might Be Your Once-in-a-While 136
I Might Be Your Once-In-a-While 4250
I Might Fall Back on You 3949
I Might Grow Fond of You 4212
I Might Say 'Yes' To You 3658
I, Miles Gloriosus 1422
I Miss a Place Called Home 1536
I Miss Him (Her) 3576
I Miss Him 1045
I Miss My Home in Harlem 4076
I Miss My Mammy's Kissin' 542
I Miss My Swiss, My Swiss Miss Misses Me 710
I Miss the Mississippi Miss 676
I Miss You 808, 809
I Miss You Old Friend 1103
I Miss You So 2532
I Murdered Them in Chicago 1577
I Must Away 45
I Must Be Dreaming 80
I Must Be Going 2467
I Must Be Home By Twelve O'Clock 3953
I Must Be in Love 1059
I Must Be Loved By Someone
(and That Someone Must Be You) 4079
I Must Be Missing Something 1884
I Must Be One of Those Roses 3584
I Must Devise a Plan 1249
I Must Find Out About Love 2439
I Must Go Now 729
I Must Go to Moscow 4817
I Must Have a Dinner Coat 4677
I Must Have a Lot of Little Girls
All Around Me 954
I Must Have Been Mistaken 1515
I Must Have Her 652
I Must Have That Man 441

I Must Love Some One 1313
I Must Love You 711
I Must Marry a Handsome Man 947
I Must Paint 937
I Must Propose to You 3313
I Must Smile 1761
I Must Waltz 621, 4677
I Need a Friend 4764
I Need a Garden 1487
I Need a Little Bit, You Need a Little Bit (A Little Bit of Love) 3489
I Need a Ship 786
I Need Affection 3590
I Need All the Help I Can Get 868
I Need Love 80
I Need Music 486
I Need New Words 839
I Need One Man 2177
I Need Some Cooling Off 3291, 3924
I Need Someone's Love 1911
I Need the Morning Air 1316
I Need This One Chance 1776
I Need Time 2307
I Need to Know 1282, 2198
I Need You 314, 2352, 2845
I Need You So 1657
I Never 840
I Never Can Think of the Words 1333
I Never Danced with You 2651
I Never Did Imagine 3564
I Never Do a Thing Like That 4507
I Never Do Anything Twice 3967
I Never Do It Now 2383
I Never Dream When I'm Asleep 2608
I Never Dreamed 3351
I Never Felt Better in My Life 1158
I Never Felt This Way for Anyone Before 2163
I Never Guessed 158
I Never Had a Chance 1456
I Never Had a Date Before 4316
I Never Had a Mammy 4429
I Never Had to Work 3229
I Never Has Seen Snow 2000
I Never Imagined Goodbye 1959
I Never Knew 628, 1116
I Never Knew (I Could Love Anybody Like I'm Loving You) 2856
I Never Knew 3339
I Never Knew! 3866
I Never Knew 4589
I Never Knew My Husband 1496
I Never Knew What Eyes Could Do Till Yours Looked Into Mine 4712
I Never Knew What Love Could Do 1292
I Never Know How to Behave When I'm with Girls, Girls, Girls 4203
I Never Know When 1614
I Never Laughed in My Life 2680
I Never Let Anyone Beat Me but You 2426
I Never Loved a Man As Much As That 4478
I Never Loved You 946
I Never Made Money from Music 4272
I Never Meant to Fall in Love 751
I Never Met a Girl Like You 3723
I Never Met a Russian I Didn't Like 518
I Never Met Before a Girl Like You 3910
I Never Miss 97
I Never Realized 579, 1153
I Never Said I Didn't Love You 3757
I Never Saw a Better Day 2588
I Never Saw a Girl Like That 284
I Never Saw a King Before 1670
I Never Thought 3740
I Never Thought of That 834
I Never Took a Lesson in My Life 734
I Never Want to Go Home Again 1511
I Never Want to See You Again 958
I Never Wanted to Love You 2746
I Never Was Born 462
I Never Was Right in My Life 1388
I Never Would Believe It 331
I Never Would Do It in Society 4206
I Nominate You to Dominate Me 18
I Notice You 1701
I Now Believe in Love 757
I Nver Lose My Head 4364
I Once Believed 757
I Once Was a Very Abandoned Person 2977
I Only Have Eyes for You 4799
I Only Know 3292
I Only Know I Love Thee 2938
I Only Meant 2705
I Only Miss Him When I Think of Him 4743
I Only Miss the Feeling (Not the Man) 4398
I Only Wanna Laugh 2217
I Only Want a Little House 1721
I Only Want Someone to Love Me 1701
I Only Want the Band to Play a Waltz for Me 939
I Only Wish I Knew 2023
I Ought to Know More About You 3, 3381
I Owe It All 4062
I Owe Ohio 322
I Paused, I Looked, I Fell 364
I Pity the Poor Poor Parisians 2539
I Play On My Old Bassoon 4187
I Played My Concertina 4747
I Plead, Dear Heart 3680
I Prefer the Cat 4489
I Professionisti 3600
I Promise I'll Be Practically True to You 3310
I Promise You a Happy Ending 2660
I Promised Their Mothers 1548
I Put It Right Back Where I Found It 924
I Put My Hand In 1828
I Question Not 1088
I Quite Forgot Arcadia 178
I Reach for a Star 2171
I Read 3411
I Really Don't Have Time to Be Thinking about Romance 1940

I Really Like Him 2727
I Really Love You 3067
I Really Loved You 699
I Rejoice That It's Decided 2977
I Remember 4790, 3644, 3464, 4076, 1200, 2633, 3967
I Remember a Feeling Called Love 2243
I Remember Efficiency Rag 1426
I Remember Her 1748
I Remember How It Was 4286
I Remember How Those Boys Could Dance 661
I Remember It Well 1511, 2615
I Remember Love 533
I Remember Mama 2064, 2064
I Remember Nothing After That 1469
I Remember That 3843
I Remember You 1569
I Represent the Evening Blow 3765
I Resign 4062
I Resolve 3918
I Rise Again 3279
I Said It and I'm Glad 4190
I Said Love 3734
I Said My Last Farewell 1759
I Said to Love 1408
I Said, Oh No 2033
I Sail the Airy Blue 4704
I Saved a Waltz for You 3508
I Saw a Man 3602
I Saw from the Beach 3612
I Saw No Shadow 3339
I Saw the Roses and Remembered You 4150
I Saw Your Eyes 1145
I Say a Little Prayer 4193
I Say a Little Prayer for You 261
I Say, Flo 4759
I Say Hello 1029
I Say It's Spinach
(— and the Hell with It) 1225
I Say What I Mean and I Mean
What I Say 4293
I Say Yes 2248
I Says to Him 4237
I See... 1306
I See a Man 2925
I See a Road 1053
I See All of It 3227
I See By Your Smile 4559
I See Everything Beautiful 3028
I See Him Over There 1342
I See My Picture in Your Eyes 1351
I See Rainbows 3793
I See Something 4633
I See the Light/Gentle Sighs 4089
I See the People 1770
I See What I Choose to See 181
I See You but What Do You See in Me? 2296
I See You Everywhere 4403
I See Your Face 2071, 4528
I See Your Face Before Me 383
I Seek not for Rank 526
I Seen It with My Own Eyes 2958
I Sell Nothing but the Best 1884
I Send a Suit to the Tailor 4147
I Sent a Letter to My Love 2065
I Set My Heart on One Love 4750
I Shall Be All Right Now 3250
I Shall Be Happy 4617
I Shall Experience It Again 2898
I Shall Love You 1019
I Shall Miss You, Holmes 270
I Shall Never Look at a Pretty Girl Again 3685
I Shall Not Let Money Get in My Way 4617
I Shall Not Mind 2131
I Shall Positively Pay You Next Monday 629
I Shall Scream 3271
I Shiver and Shake with Fear 758
I Shot the Works 1207
I Should Care 4743
I Should Have Been Born a Boy 4589
I Should Have Been Offended If My Waist
You Hadn't Squeezed 355
I Should Have Quit When I Was Ahead 2057
I Should Have Waited for You 2069
I Should Like to Know the Reason 3486
I Should Live So 3669
I Should Rather Like to Try 1682
I Should So Love to Be a Boy 2498
I Should Stay 1786
I Should Think That You Could Guess 2915
I Should Worry 4806
I Should've Said 4588
I Should've Stood in Bed 3138
I Shouldn't Love You 4323
I Showed That I Know Something When
I Fell in Love with You 4037
I Shut the Door 451
I Sigh for a Change 1264
I Simply Can't Resist You 3746
I Sing a Little Tenor 4691
I Sing of Love 2331
I Sing the Rainbow 2908
I Sit in the Sun 3818
I Sits Down 4152
I Sleep Easier Now 3326
I Smile and That's All Right 255
I Sold My Heart to the Junkman 338
I Sometimes Wonder 4365
I Spy 1474, 4689
I Stand Outside Myself 595
I Start Sneezing 2473
I Started on a Shoestring 3861
I Still Believe 2905
I Still Believe in Love 4334
I Still Believe in You 4765, 3980
I Still Can Dream 4760
I Still Can Hear Your Sighs! 398
I Still Get Jealous 2205, 1886
I Still Have Plenty to Learn 4015
I Still Look at You That Way 2201
I Still Love the Red, White and Blue 1453, 4132

I Still Love You 399
I Still See Eliza 3347
I Still Suits Me 2204
I Struck Out 1168
I Stumbled Over You 1836, 4025
I Stumbled Over You and Fell in Love 2808
I Suddenly Find It Agreeable 1290
I Sure Have Been in Love 1048
I Sure Like the Boys 4
I Surrender 3538
I Surrender! 3848
I Swear I Won't Ever Again 2132
I Take After Dad 4712
I Take After Rip 3721
I Talk to the Trees 3347
I Talk, You Talk 1699
I Thank Heaven 3126
I Thank You for Your Welcome 4554
I Think an Awful Lot of You 3945, 4381
I Think I Like His Eyes 119
I Think I May Want to Remember Today 4145
I Think I Oughtn't Auto Any More 4801
I Think I Shall Learn, Don't You? 2041
I Think I Think 1660
I Think I'd Better Go 4136
I Think I'd Better Go Home 1549
I Think I'd Like to Fall in Love 1233
I Think I'll Go Back to Bed 4719
I Think I'm Going to Like It Over Here 2201
I Think I'm Gonna Like It Here 150
I Think I'm in Love with My Wife 277
I Think It's Going to Rain Today 2852
I Think Myself Out 4790
I Think of You the Whole Year Round 2566
I Think She Needs Me 2106
I Think So Much of All the Boys 1014
I Think So, Too 2527
I Think Such a Lot of You 1041
I Think the Kid Will Do 2033
I Think the World of You 1991
I Think You Should Know 3448
I Think You Think to Much about Too Many 2596
I Think You'd Better Hurry Home 2292
I Think You're Absolutely Wonderful (What Do You Think of Me) 3246
I Think You're Pretty Too 4499
I Think You're Wonderful 61
I Thought About You 3178
I Thought He Was a Business Man 4804
I Thought I Knew You 101
I Thought I Wanted Opera 4787
I Thought They'd Never Go Home 817
I Thought Wrong 3229
I Tied the Knot 340
I to the World 3231
I Told a Friend of Mine 470
I Told Them We Were Lovers 2965
I Told You So 2682, 4727
I Took a Little Walk 4363
I Took Another Look 2103
I Took My Time 1970
I Took Them All 4187
I Travel the Road 792
I Tried 1420
I Tried and I Tried and I Tried 690
I Trust the Wrong People 1662
I Try 941
I Turn to Jesus 344
I Understand 3278
I Understood 2698
I Used to Be Above Love 4825
I Used to Believe in Fairies 3642
I Used to Go to School with Annie Laurie 2056
I Used to Love Them All 243
I Used to Love You, but It's All Over Now 542
I Used to Sigh for the Silvery Moon 1430
I Wait for a Ship 369
I Wait for Him 2375
I Wake at Morning 711
I Walk a Little Dog 4190
I Walk with Music 4586
I Walked Around 1417
I Waltz Alone 223, 1649
I Wan' to Be a Real Lady 2111
I Wanna Be a Dancin' Man 964
I Wanna Be Bad 341
I Wanna Be Gay (And Have a Good Time) 3587
I Wanna Be Good 'n' Bad 2705
I Wanna Be Loved 418
I Wanna Be Loved by You 1617, 3020
I Wanna Be Yours 2523
I Wanna Bivouac with a WAC 4141
I Wanna Come Home 1055
I Wanna Get Married 1336
I Wanna Get to You 4645
I Wanna Go Back 2187
I Wanna Go Back to Bali 397
I Wanna Go Back to Dixie 4412
I Wanna Go to City College 4428
I Wanna Go Voom Voom 3489
I Wanna Make the World Laugh 2660
I Want 3204
I Want a Big Butter and Egg Man 432
I Want a Boy 625, 687
I Want a Boy Who's Determined to Do As I Say 1598
I Want a Bungalow 2174
I Want a Daddy 542
I Want a Daddy Who Will Rock Me to Sleep 1685
I Want a Doll 1833
I Want a Girl 4197
I Want a Girl Like Mother Was 3911
I Want a Girl Like You 3958, 4506
I Want a Girl to Call My Own 3179
I Want a Good Girl (and I Want Her Bad) 4634
I Want a Good Time 2628, 2004
I Want a Home 1643, 2174
I Want a Kiss 1027
I Want a Lily 4393
I Want a Little Lovin' 1212
I Want a Little Lovin', Sometimes 2254

I Want a Little Loving Sometimes 3308
I Want a Lonely Romeo 2574
I Want a Lot of Girlies, Girlies (I Want a Whole Lot of Girls) 4521
I Want a Loveable Baby 1488
I Want a Man 111, 2467, 3650, 3754, 4247, 4709
I Want a Man to Love Me 3265
I Want a Man Who Can Cook 2069
I Want a Pal 4793
I Want a Picture of You 1687
I Want a Pretty Girl 2180
I Want a Real Man 4171
I Want a Regular Man 1584, 4589
I Want a Steam Yacht 3085
I Want a Surprise 3725
I Want a Toy Soldier Man 1963
I Want a Wife that Can Cook 1774
I Want a Yes Man 3157
I Want a Yes-Man 3249
I Want All the Boys 4794
I Want All the World to Know 2292
I Want Another Portion of That 1979
I Want Another Situation Just Like That 687
I Want 'em Wild, Weak, Warm and Willing 4817
I Want Gas 1736
I Want Him Saved 3332
I Want It 3233
I Want It All 253, 3581
I Want It Just to Happen 3389
I Want Jesus to Walk with Me 2225
I Want Love 25
I Want More 4153
I Want More Out of Life Than This 4124
I Want My Country Back 533
I Want My Husband When I Wed 2816
I Want My Little Gob 3923
I Want My Mama 1138
I Want My Mammy 2857
I Want My Ragtime 1640
I Want Plenty of You 1827
I Want Romance 2504
I Want Somebody 2385
I Want Someone 2238
I Want Someone to Call Me Papa 1964
I Want Someone to Love 4453
I Want Someone to Love Me 2485, 3791
I Want Someone to Make a Fuss Over Me 4833
I Want Someone Who's Lonesome 3087
I Want Something Lovely 1750
I Want Something New to Play With 4553, 4655
I Want That Man 3980
I Want That Star 4810
I Want the Boys Around Me 4776
I Want the Kind of a Fella 4090
I Want the Strolling Good 1963
I Want the World to Know 1839, 2976
I Want the World to Know I Love You 4277
I Want Them All 1911
I Want to Be a Bachelor 2869
I Want to Be a Bad Little Boy 1935
I Want to Be a Ballet Dancer 3009
I Want to Be a Blooming Bride 4248
I Want to Be a Bride 3670
I Want to Be a Chaste Woman 2818
I Want to Be a Drummer Boy 4801
I Want to Be a Drummer in the Band 2029
I Want to Be a Gambling Man 2882
I Want to Be a Grocer 738
I Want to Be a Laidy 737
I Want to Be a Liberty Belle 2888
I Want to Be a Little Frog in a Little Pond 4785
I Want to Be a Military Man 1313
I Want to Be a Naughty Little Girl 2534
I Want to Be a Popular Millionaire 1356
I Want to Be a Rockette 2307
I Want to Be a Romeo 1530
I Want to Be a Santa Claus 1314
I Want to Be a Soldier Boy in Blue 4439
I Want to Be a Soldier Lady 3820
I Want to Be a Somebody 3688
I Want to Be a Vampire 2056
I Want to Be a War Bride 4179
I Want to Be a Wild, WIld Rose (The Wild Rose) 4649
I Want to Be Bad 1339
I Want to Be First to the Moon 2928
I Want to Be Glorified 4821
I Want to Be Good but My Eyes Won't Let Me 1334
I Want to Be Happy 3184, 3249
I Want to Be in Dixie 4655
I Want to Be in Texas for the Round-Up in the Spring 2413
I Want to Be Like Cleo 2385
I Want to Be Loved 152
I Want to Be Loved By an Expert 4620
I Want to Be Loved Like a Leading Lady 1526
I Want to Be Married (to a Delta Kappa Epsilon Man) 3547
I Want to Be Merry 3472
I Want to Be Naughty Too 2892
I Want to Be Popular 1682
I Want to Be Raided By You 4581
I Want to Be Rich 4160
I Want to Be Seen with You Tonight 1420
I Want to Be Somebody's Baby 3973
I Want to Be Somebody's Girlie 4381
I Want to Be the Captain 1544
I Want to Be the Last to Kiss You 2903
I Want to Be the Mayor 2790
I Want to Be the One to Show Her That 3529
I Want to Be There 718, 1011
I Want to Be Vamped in Georgia 3513
I Want to Be Wanted by You 1026
I Want to Be with You 1601, 4267
I Want to Be Your Baby Boy 1458
I Want to Be Your Congressman 2173
I Want to Be Your Mother 1730
I Want to Be Your Wife 2889
I Want to Blow Up the World 4595
I Want to Bring You a Ring 4382

I Want to Chisel in on Your Heart 3946
I Want to Dance 1342, 3429
I Want to Dance My Way In 3258
I Want to Dance with You 2351
I Want to Do a Number with the Boys 418
I Want to Fight for Uncle Sam 11
I Want to Get Arrested 1729
I Want to Get Offa This Island 4076
I Want to Go Back to New York 1531
I Want to Go Back to the Bottom of the Garden 2103
I Want to Go Back to the Boulevard 2951
I Want to Go Back to the War 126
I Want to Go Bye-Bye 1626
I Want to Go Dancing 2307
I Want to Go Home 56, 1096, 4409, 1502, 2432, 3259, 3328, 3409, 1867
I Want to Go Home Now 2724
I Want to Go Home to God 624
I Want to Go to Hollywood 1649
I Want to Go to Paree, Papa 3809
I Want to Go to Paris 511
I Want to Go To-Morrow 357
I Want to Hear a Yankee Doodle Tune 1478, 2964
I Want to Join the Army 2978
I Want to Know Where Tosti Went 545
I Want to Learn to Dance 2328
I Want to Learn to Jazz Dance 4812
I Want to Live 415
I Want to Live (As Long As You Love Me) 512
I Want to Live 2519
I Want to Live Each Night 1660
I Want to Live-I Want to Love 2595
I Want to Look Like Lillian Russell 335
I Want to Love Him So Bad 2427
I Want to Make You Cry 3651
I Want to Marry 1922, 2897, 3246
I Want to Marry a Male Quartette 2292
I Want to Marry a Man, I Do 1313
I Want to Marry a Marionette 4443
I Want to Meet You Some Day in California 3842, 4211
I Want to Play House with You 2667
I Want to Play with the Girls 2105
I Want to Pray 3035
I Want to Report a Fire 3728
I Want to Ride with You 4595
I Want to Row on the Crew 3378
I Want to See More of You 1539
I Want to See My Child 4447
I Want to See My Ida Hoe in Idaho 4393
I Want to See Peace Again 3418
I Want to Share It with You 2925
I Want to Sing in Opera 3996
I Want to Spread a Little Sunshine 3048
I Want to Step 1829
I Want to Take 'Em Off for Norman Rockwell 3810
I Want to Tell a Story 2669
I Want to Tell You Something 3618
I Want to the World to Know I Love You 3026
I Want to Walk in a Garden 535
I Want to Walk to San Francisco 2418
I Want to Wed a Soldier Boy 2765
I Want to Whisper Something 455
I Want Twins 1690
I Want Two Husbands 4077
I Want What I Want When I Want It 2915, 4390
I Want You 538, 2067, 2700, 2756, 3043, 3903, 4277
I Want You All to Myself 2382
I Want You Baby 1103
I Want You for My All Time Girl 1570
I Want You Ma' Honey 3387
I Want You Morning, Noon and Night 4079
I Want You to Be 674
I Want You to Be the One First to Know 3110
I Want You to Love Me 203
I Want You to Marry Me 3675
I Want You to See My Girl 1613
I Want You to Want Me with You 4634
I Wanted to Change Him 1729
I Wanted to Come to Broadway 1826
I Wanted to Do Something Dirty 3280
I Wanted to See the World 937
I Wants to Be a Actor Lady 2111
I Was a Florodora Baby 4814
I Was a Gyp in Egypt 3104
I Was a Hero 3085
I Was a Hollywood Baby 3280
I Was a Pale Young Curate Then 2348
I Was a Shoo-In 4190
I Was a Very Good Baby (in the Daytime) 2491
I Was Afraid of That 3138
I Was Beautiful 3110
I Was Blue 2833
I Was Born in Virginia 1478
I Was Born on a Friday 3882
I Was Born on the Day Before Yesterday 4722
I Was Born on the Isle of Man 965
I Was Born This way 2022
I Was Born to Rule 355
I Was Born Where You Were Born 2970
I Was Born with Blues in My Heart 389
I Was Down Texas Way 3262
I Was First to Call You Father 4615
I Was Gonna Be Big 2230
I Was in the Closet 840
I Was Just Going to Ask You About That 1798
I Was Just Supposing 2848
I Was Lonely 1796
I Was Lost 3164
I Was Mad for You 552
I Was Made for Champagne 2437
I Was Meant for Someone 391, 1460
I Was Never Kissed Before 453
I Was Never Meant for You 3021, 3155
I Was Quite Upset 4646

I Was So Weak, Love Was So Strong 1772
I Was So Young (and You Were So Beautiful) 1626
I Was the Most Beautiful Blossom 3225
I Was the Slave 935
I Was There 2925
I Was Thinking of You 1004
I Was Wrong 1959
I Wash My Hands 4682
I Wasn't Home for Christmas 572
I Wasn't Meant to Be a Queen 58
I Watch the Love Parade (Crystal Candalabra) 672
I Wear a Chain 4155
I Went Back Home 3806
I Went to a Marvelous Party 3885
I Went to Paris with Papa 2842
I Went to the Animal Fair 143
I Whispered It to the Roses 1565
I Whistle a Happy Tune 2312
I (Who Have Nothing) 4031
I Whoever I Am 1300
I Will 4048
I Will Always Love You, Dear 2782
I Will Be Good 2691
I Will Be Waiting for You 1569
I Will Bow 3780
I Will Capture the Cat 1094
I Will Follow Him 4193
I Will Follow You 2864
I Will Give Him Love 314
I Will Give You All for Love 1712
I Will Have Him 2599
I Will, I Won't 2174
I Will Knit a Suit of Dreams (Teepee) 4422
I Will Love You Always 3545
I Will Love You Forever, My Dear 2724
I Will Make My Way Alone 2928
I Will Make Things Happen 2472
I Will Marry Him to Make a Home for Mother 470
I Will Miss You 4541
I Will Never See You Again, I Will Never Forget You 2269
I Will Not Tell a Soul 3806
I Will Recall the Day 2240
I Will Survive 3739
I Will Wait 3057
I Wish 2103, 2012
I Wish He Knew 869
I Wish I Could Forget You 3411
I Wish I Could Laugh at Love 2423
I Wish I Could Say 3161
I Wish I Didn't Love Him 1045
I Wish I Didn't Love You So 3444
I Wish I Had a Darling House 3450
I Wish I Knew 1974
I Wish I Knew Now 1372
I Wish I Was 2307
I Wish I Was a Big Sky Rocket 1919
I Wish I Was a Boy and I Wish I Was a Girl 4803
I Wish I Was a Bumble Bee 2994
I Wish I Was a Hero Too 3085
I Wish I Was a Queen 2216
I Wish I Was an Island in an Ocean of Girls 3590
I Wish I Was in Blighty 377
I Wish I Was in Texas 4479
I Wish I Wasn't Quite Such a Big Girl 3339
I Wish I Were a Man 2033
I Wish I Were a Star 2307
I Wish I Were Back in My Cradle 495
I Wish I Were in Love Again 247
I Wish I Were Rich 1707
I Wish It So 4399, 2268
I Wish It Was Over 3669
I Wish It Would Rain Down 4786
I Wish Leola Here 1496
I Wish My Honeymoon Would Shine! 1524
I Wish That I'd Been Born in Borneo 3973
I Wish You a Waltz 287
I Wish You Needed Me 1255
I Wish You Success 2650
I Wish You'd Never Grow Up at All 1667
I Woke Up Today 459
I Won't Be Home for a Long, Long Time 1079
I Won't Be Home to Dinner 2826
I Won't Dance 2204, 2372, 4361
I Won't Give You the Bucket 423
I Won't Go 1764
I Won't Go Way Back Home Again 939
I Won't Grow Up 3453
I Won't Let It Happen Again 2681
I Won't Let That Happen to Him 1865
I Won't Let You Get Away 2590
I Won't Love a Soldier Boy 669
I Won't Play Games with You Anymore 4041
I Won't Say I Will, but I Won't Say I Won't 2526
I Won't Send Roses 2208, 2660
I Won't Sleep a Wink Tonight 2617
I Won't Stand in Your Way 4798
I Won't Take No for an Answer 1046
I Won't Worry 2941
I Wonder 98, 3652, 3679, 947, 3902, 4404, 4615
I Wonder As I Wander 3536
I Wonder How I Ever Passed You By 3218
I Wonder How It Is (To Dance with a Boy) 1846
I Wonder How She Is Tonight 226
I Wonder How They Get That Way 4817
I Wonder If 4384
I Wonder If It's True 4553
I Wonder If It's You 2491
I Wonder If Love Is a Dream 3898
I Wonder If She Cares 1722
I Wonder If She Will Remember 1722
I Wonder If That's the Answer 830
I Wonder If the Thing's Worthwhile 2779
I Wonder If They're All True to Me 4802
I Wonder If You Could Be Happy with Anyone Else but Me 4085
I Wonder If You're Lonely 1523
I Wonder What Became of Me? 1385, 4123
I Wonder What Happened to Miss O'Brien 2130

I Wonder What He Meant By That 4798
I Wonder What It's Like 821, 4312
I Wonder What She's Thinking of Now 2587
I Wonder What the Audience Would Say 2603
I Wonder What the King Is Doing Tonight 623
I Wonder What's the Matter with My Eyes 2892
I Wonder Where I Met You 1531
I Wonder Where My Girl Is Now 3547
I Wonder Where They'll Go 4094
I Wonder Whether I've Loved You All My Life 3250
I Wonder Who She Spoons with Now 3087
I Wonder Who's Keeping Him Now 4235
I Wonder Who's Kissing Her Now 1593, 3579
I Wonder Whom I'll Marry 2497
I Wonder Why 2643, 2145, 2222, 2620, 2661, 3063, 3821, 4148
I Wonder Why Jane Is a Suffragette 1318
I Wonder Why She Kept on Saying Si-Si-Si-Si Senor! 3985
I Wonder Why the Glow-worm Winks His Eye at Me 1733
I Wonder Why the Glow-Worm Winks His Eye 3783
I Wonder Why They Stare at Me 4630
I Wonder Why You Wander 2397
I Wonder Will You Forget 4453
I Wore a Tunic 3259
I Work Eight Hours, Sleep Eight Hours, That Leaves Eight Hours for Love 3827
I Work for Pravda 4536
I Work with Wood 3059
I Worry 635
I Worry About You 2019
I Worship the Lily 3195
I Worship You 1018, 1272, 4132
I Would Be Your Romeo 3805
I Would Die 4270
I Would Do Anything in the World for You 2642
I Would Have Told Thee Long Ago 2673
I Would If I Could 2798
I Would If I Could but I Can't 4137
I Would Like a Frank Opinion 1521
I Would Like to Be Your Pal 246
I Would Like to Correspond with You 2119
I Would Like to Flirt with You 3519
I Would Like to Fondle You 670
I Would Like to Have a Phonograph of You 349
I Would Like to Marry You 246, 1123
I Would Like to Paint a Picture of You All 1532
I Would Like to Play a Lover's Part 3949
I Would Like to Say 3456
I Would Like to See the Peaches 2923
I Would Love to Have You Love Me 4667
I Would Love You Still 649
I Would Rather Be 4498
I Would Rather Dance a Waltz 3185
I Would Rather Fight Like Ma 1606
I Would Rather Look at You Than Kiss Any Other Girl 1307
I Wouldn't Be the First 1903
I Wouldn't Bet One Penny 1076
I Wouldn't Care 2367
I Wouldn't Change a Thing 2417
I Wouldn't Do That, Would You? 2793
I Wouldn't Give That for the Man Who Couldn't Dance 627
I Wouldn't Go Back 253, 784
I Wouldn't Have Had To 2449
I Wouldn't Have It Any Other Way 520
I Wouldn't Have You Any Other Way 2681
I Wouldn't Know 3816
I Wouldn't Marry You 1456
I Wouldn't Mind a Job Like That 4130
I Wouldn't Say No 3070
I Wouldn't Take a Case Like That 2534
I Wouldn't Take Nothing for My Journey Now 4030
I Wrote a Play 3893
I Wrote a Song for You 4204
I Wrote the Book 4727
I, Yes Me, That's Who 2583
I'm Better with You Than without You 3454
I've Lost My Head Over You 4648
Icarus 1770
Ice 2805, 1742
Ice-Box 3409
Ice Cream 148, 430, 3918, 4169
Ice Cream Girl, The 3663
Ice House Fire, The 1354
Ice Mazurka 1654
Ich Bin Gerecht 3781
Ich Hob Dich Tzufil Lieb (I Love You Too Much) 1279
Ich Lib Dich 3781
Ich Vel Dir Kayn Mol Nisht Fabeytn 2356
Ichabod 4015
Ick 262
Icky Wicky Woo 1381
Icy Ebenezer 753
Icy Switzerland 4853
I'd Always Be There 2692
I'd Be a Fool 1145
I'd Be a Wild Man 21
I'd Be Attracted 4701
I'd Be Crazy to Be Crazy Over You 1380
I'd Be Happy 3361
I'd Be Happy Anywhere with You 1852
I'd Be Happy If That Was Mine 811
I'd Be Satisfied with Life 3976
I'd Be Surprisingly Good for You 1211
I'd Do Almost Anything to Get Out of Here and Go Home 3469
I'd Do Anything 3271
I'd Do It Again 270, 2578
I'd Do It All Over Again 3485
I'd Do the Same 2340
I'd Forgotten How Beautiful She Could Be 3725
I'd Give My Life for You 2905
I'd Give the Whole Show By Myself 47
I'd Give to Her the World of Diamonds 2001

I'd Gladly Trade 372
I'd Gladly Walk to Alaska 2339
I'd Guess You 1417
I'd Kick Up My Heels 4764
I'd Know It 4090
I'd Know That Smile 2750
I'd Leave My Honeymoon for You 1801
I'd Like a Honeymoon with You 3043
I'd Like a Lighthouse 3146
I'd Like Another Situation Just Like That 2347
I'd Like It 104
I'd Like My Picture Took 2894
I'd Like to Be 4309
I'd Like to Be a Gardener in a Garden of Girls 4819
I'd Like to Be a Monkey in the Zoo 1919
I'd Like to Be a Quitter, but I Find It Hard to Quit 3590
I'd Like to Be a Rose 4485
I'd Like to Be a Sitter for a Baby Like You 1423
I'd Like to Be a Soldier 4754
I'd Like to Be a Soldier Gay 307
I'd Like to Be Like You 1386
I'd Like to Be Liked 4426
I'd Like to Be Shot from a Cannon with You 2597
I'd Like to Borrow a Kiss 2538
I'd Like to Bring My Mother 4419
I'd Like to Call You Mine 3357
I'd Like to Corral a Gal 4819
I'd Like to Dunk You in My Coffee 622
I'd Like to Get Close to You 4062
I'd Like to Give a Nice Sweet Kiss 3258
I'd Like to Go on a Honeymoon with You 3681
I'd Like to Go Up in an Airship 41
I'd Like to Have a Girl Like You, Like Me 2934
I'd Like to Have a Little Girl Like You Like Me 68
I'd Like to Have a Million in the Bank 4555
I'd Like to Have a Sweetheart 2771
I'd Like to Have You Around 68, 3590
I'd Like to Have You Call Me Honey 1563
I'd Like to Hide It 1013
I'd Like to Know You Better 3653
I'd Like to Know Your Address and Your Name 4756
I'd Like to Love Them All 3012
I'd Like to Make a Date with You 3891
I'd Like to Marry them All 1212
I'd Like to Meet Your Father 954
I'd Like to Plant a Smile 4200
I'd Like to Poison Ivy 2814
I'd Like to Rent a Flat for You 538
I'd Like to Run Away with You 3358
I'd Like to See a Little More of You 3387
I'd Like to See More of You! 1549
I'd Like to See the Kaiser With a Lily in His Hand 1065
I'd Like to Take You Away (Sam and Marion) 380
I'd Like to Take You Home 1529
I'd Like to Take You Home to Meet My Mother 265, 1932
I'd Like to Talk About the Weather 2379
I'd Like to Teach you the ABC of Love 4248
I'd Like You to Love Me 2734
I'd Love To 2491
I'd Love to Be a Lady 1162
I'd Love to Be in Ireland the Day They Set Old Ireland Free 2857
I'd Love to Be in Love with You 3239
I'd Love to Dance Through Life with You 2922
I'd Love to Hate Her 4244
I'd Love to Waltz Through Life with You 4817
I'd Marry You Again 3389
I'd Much Rather Stay at Home 4590
I'd Place a Bet 1961
I'd Rather Be a Billy Goat 4215
I'd Rather Be a Chippie Than a Charity Bum 697
I'd Rather Be a Fairy than a Troll 1371
I'd Rather Be a Friend of Yours Than Someone Else's Dear 3033
I'd Rather Be a Lobster Than a Wise Guy 3519
I'd Rather Be Right 1478
I'd Rather Be Right (1) 2068
I'd Rather Be Right (2) 2068
I'd Rather Be with You 665
I'd Rather Charleston 2376
I'd Rather Cry Over You 700
I'd Rather Dance Alone 3448
I'd Rather Dance Here Than Hereafter 1859
I'd Rather Dance Here than Hereafter 2385
I'd Rather Go to Jail 2448
I'd Rather Have a Memory of You 3719
I'd Rather Have Nothin' All de Time than Somethin' fo' a Little While 295
I'd Rather Have Nothin' All the Time Than Somethin' for a Little While 4697
I'd Rather Look at You 3846
I'd Rather Love What I Can't Have 2901
I'd Rather Paint Than Fight 513
I'd Rather See a Minstrel Show 4813
I'd Rather Two-Step 1246
I'd Rather Two-Step than Waltz 1902
I'd Rather Wake Up by Myself 603
I'd Sooner Be a Has Been Than a Never Was at All 2566
I'd Steal a Star 3254
I'd Sure Like to Give It a Shot 2583
I'd Write a Song 2813
Ida 3395
Ida Bell 2851
Ida Ho the Cowboy Girl 1759
Ida, Sweet As Apple Cider 3754
Idaho 185, 3952, 3951
Iddle-Iddle-Iddle-E 4247
Ideal Deal, The 692
Ideal Girl 3024
Ideal Girls, The 509
Idiot's Delight 958
Idle Dreams 1483
Idle House 4283
Idles of the King 1447, 3291
Idol of Eyes, The 3087
Idol of the Ring, The 4218
Idyll 3378

Idyll of Miss Sarah Brown, The 1706
Idylle 526
If 95, 687, 2485, 2188, 2377, 4015
If (There's Anything You Want) 4422
If a Bachelor in Love Should Fall 4133
If a Bee Can't Behave in a Beehive when Can a Bee Behave? 68
If a Girl Isn't Pretty 1420
If a Sudden Stroke of Fate 3777
If a Table at Rector's Could Talk 4807
If a Table at Romano's Could Talk 822
If a Wish Could Make It So 4378
If Adam Hadn't Seen the Apple Tree 3945
If All Is As You Say 1905
If All Moons Were Honey Moons 1593
If All My Thoughts Were Stars 103
If All the Stars Were Mine 3588
If, and and But 4360
If Anyone Had Told Me 287
If Bill Gillette Could Only See Me Now 1640
If By Sea 4488
If Cabby Told Half what He Knows 3744
If Dreams Are True 3804
If Dreams Come True 2145, 3709
If Eve Had Left the Apple on the Bough 1162
If Ever I Get in the White House Chair 1332
If Ever I Loved Him 135
If Ever I Marry 4430
If Ever I Would Leave You 623, 2611
If Ever Married I'm 2331
If Ever Married I'm 4517
If Ever We Discover the North Pole 11
If Ever We Get Out of Jail 3972
If Every Day Was Sunday 2972
If Every Month Were June 2227
If Everyone Got What They Wanted 2925
If Flowers Could Speak 3511
If Flutterby Wins 2449
If France 2628
If Girls Had Wings 2803
If God Had Call Waiting 2488
If Harry Weren't Here 2598
If He Hollers 2115
If He Only Knew 2148
If He Really Knew Me 4334
If He Really Loves Me 4778
If He Should Come 2756
If He Walked Into My Life 2208, 2713
If He'd Only Be Gentle 2114
If He'll Come Back to Me 1916
If Helen Only Knew 1817
If Her Mother Only Knew 2368
If I Again Would Be a Baby 3609
If I Am Dreaming 1110
If I Am Released 1700
If I Am to Marry You 3920
If I Be Your Best Chance 4588
If I Became His Bride 3318
If I Became the President 4179
If I But Dared 246
If I But Knew 4201
If I Came Back to You and Said I'm Sorry 1434
If I Can Take You from Someone 1263
If I Can't Get the Sweetie I Want I Pity the Sweetie I Get 4817
If I Can't Love Her 330
If I Can't Sell It, I'll Keep Sittin' on It 432
If I Can't Take It with Me 1614
If I Could 1903, 1010
If I Could Be Beautiful 3019
If I Could Buy a Dream 2551
If I Could Choose One Day 1427
If I Could Dance with You 1597
If I Could Find Another Place Like That 4382
If I Could Live My Life Again 1002
If I Could Live My Life All Over Again 244
If I Could Love a Girl Like You 2628
If I Could Make a Difference 1169
If I Could Make the Sun Stand Still 2013
If I Could Only Get a Decent Sleep 1627
If I Could Put You in a Song 3094
If I Could Read the Kisses Others Printed on Your Lips 4037
If I Could Teach My Teddy Bear to Dance 2534
If I Could Trust Me 1776
If I Could've Been 4744
If I Didn't Have You 2034
If I Die Young 1092
If I Don't, Nobody Else Will 1887
If I Ever Get Back to Cincinnati 434
If I Ever Get My Dander Up 1513
If I Feel This Way Tomorrow (Then It's Love) 4177
If I Feel This Way Tomorrow 4772
If I Felt Any Younger Today 4028
If I Find the Girl 4555
If I Gave You 1891
If I Gave You a Rose 3310
If I Give in to You 1202
If I Had a ... 1222
If I Had a Hammer 3280, 3280
If I Had a Hundred Hearts 1801
If I Had a Little Boy to Love Me 2324
If I Had a Lover 3342
If I Had a Million Dollars 2801
If I Had a Sweetie Like You 525
If I Had a Wish 4732
If I Had an Igloo 2805
If I Had Any Sense 1296
If I Had My Druthers 2484
If I Had Only Met You, Dear 2587
If I Had the Answers 1216
If I Had Wings 669
If I Had You for a Father 2319
If I Had You in My Canoe 1041
If I Hadn't a Husband 3893
If I Have the Will 1015
If I Have to Be Alone 4518
If I Have to Live Alone 273
If I Just Think of Her 256

If I Knew 3847, 4516
If I Knew Now 3551
If I Knew Then 2196
If I Knock the 'L' Out of Kelly
(It Would Still Be Kelly to Me) 4148
If I Lost You 1610
If I Love Again 124, 1932
If I Loved You 660
If I Marry the King of France 2671
If I May 4173
If I Met a Nice Little Girl 1868
If I Never See You Again 1819
If I Never Waltz Again 2755
If I Only a Laugh Could Hear 3592
If I Only Had 2245
If I Only Had a Mustache Like the Kaiser 3673
If I Only Had a Theatre on Broadway 734
If I Only Knew the Way 2938
If I Only Said My Name Was Flannigan 3855
If I Only Were a Boy 1321
If I Possessed Aladdin's Lamp 2880
If I Ruled the World 3482
If I Saw Much of You 3319
If I Should Dream of You
(When Out on the Desert) 1111
If I Should Lose My Only Girl 2665
If I Should Say Goodbye 3129
If I Sing 784
If I Thought I Could Live
without You I'd Die 1492
If I Told You 4694
If I Was a Boy 2994
If I Was a Different Man 3888
If I Was a Dove 4004
If I Was a Man 716
If I Wasn't Around 154
If I Were 4309
If I Were a Bandit 4550
If I Were a Bell 1706, 3444
If I Were a Bright Little Star 3805
If I Were a Football Man 3547
If I Were a Girl Instead 3976
If I Were a Hypnotist 586
If I Were a King 4724
If I Were a Man 4560, 3339
If I Were a Man Like That 250
If I Were a Rich Man 1265
If I Were a Sailor 671
If I Were a Woman 1265
If I Were an Actress 4681
If I Were Anybody Else but Me 3081
If I Were 80 Years Younger 3880
If I Were King 265, 466, 978, 2102, 4539, 4709
If I Were King of Babylon 675
If I Were of the Hoi Polloi 2950
If I Were on the Stage (Kiss Me Again)
2915, 4390, 4818
If I Were Only a Man 68, 1578
If I Were Only Mr. Morgan 3809
If I Were Only Someone 73
If I Were Only Taller 2518
If I Were Really a King 1720
If I Were Sure of You 888
If I Were the Bride of a Soldier 3229
If I Were the Governor of Guam 2160
If I Were the Man 519
If I Were the Man in the Moon 2155
If I Were You 64, 288, 376, 2389, 3924, 3928, 4200
If I Were You, Love 4023
If I Weren't King 759
If I Weren't Me 2898
If I'd Known You 2563
If I'm Going to Die I'm Goin' to
Have Some Fun 1968
If-If-If-If 1727
If in Spite of Our Attempts 3865
If It Ain't Fun 2568
If It Comes from Dixieland 3158
If It Feels Good, Let It Ride 964
If It Hadn't Been for Me 148
If It Hadn't Been for You 1456
If It Isn't Everything 1076
If It Makes You Happy
(The Syndicate Song) 410
If It Pleases You 1917
If It Should Be You 1911
If It Was Up to Me 2650
If It Wasn't for My Wife and Family 1308
If It Wasn't for People 410
If It Wasn't for the Fairies 1051
If It Wasn't for the Irish and the Jews 1927
If It Wasn't for the Wife 1270
If It Wasn't for You 273, 2235
If It Wasn't for Your Father 197
If It Were Easy to Do 137
If It Were Mine 717
If It Were True 379
If It's a Dream 3899
If It's Any News to You 3965
If It's Good Enough for Gentlemen 277
If It's Good Enough for Lady Astor 2626
If It's Good Enough for Rector It's
Good Enough for Me 1123
If It's Love 622, 766, 4362
If Jesus Don't Love You 4270
If Jesus Walked 1282
If Jesus Walked the Earth Today 4168
If Jesus Was a Cowboy 914
If Life Were All Peaches and Cream 2259
If Love Ever Comes My Way 2483
If Love in a Cottage Be All that They Tell 3588
If Love Is Love 2861
If Love Is Madness 2596
If Love Is There 2698
If Love Never Comes 2542
If Love Should Come to Me 2827
If Love Were All 429, 146, 3196, 3235
If Love's Content 4404
If Love's Like a Lark 2339
If Ma Says No 3856, 3857

If Mama Could See Us 1837
If Me No If—But Me No But 4588
If Menelaus Only Knew It 1817
If Momma Was Married 1709, 3967
If Mr. Boston Lawson Has His Way 2517
If Music and Sweet Poetry Agree 3909
If Music Be the Food of Love 3909
If My Dreams Come True 1058
If My Friends Could See Me Now 4238
If My Man Could Do It for Me 1118
If My Morning Begins 3741
If Not Fer You 992
If Not for the Ale 533
If Not to You 3741
If Number 1 Met Number 2 2770
If One Little Girl Loves Me 3423
If One of Us Was You Dear 3783
If Only 3197, 1616, 2953, 3064
If Only a Little Bit Sticks 299
If Only He Were a Woman 4279
If Only He'd Looked My Way 1467
If Only I Could Be a Kid Again 3559
If Only I Were Santa Claus 3977
If Only Mrs. Applejohn Were Here 1564
If Only Someone Like You 3066
If Only Someone Would Teach Me 1247
If Only Things Was Different 2074
If Only You 1414
If Only You Could Love Me 629
If Only You Had a Moustache 4149
If Only You Had Cared for Me 2798
If Only You Were Here 695
If Only You Were Mine 3994
If Only You Would Take a Tip from Me 531
If Plymouth Rock Had Landed on the Pilgrims Instead of the Pilgrims Landing on the Rock 4815
If She Could Only Feel the Same 2599
If She Has Never Loved Before 634
If She Means What I Think She Means 4812
If She Walked Home with Me 1630
If She Were Only Mine 2928
If Somebody Only Would Find Me 1096
If Someone Should Ask You 1886
If Something Leads to Good, Can It Be Bad? 4523
If That Didn't Do It It Can't Be Done 1637
If That Was Love 3113
If That's Not Love What Do You Call It? 3319
If That's Not Love—What Is 1470
If That's What You Want 2602
If the Blues Don't Get You 3361
If the Col'nel Wasn't Coming (Opening Chorus) 3251
If the Folks Down Home Could See Me Now 1910
If the Girl Has Charm 1255
If the Girl Wants You (Never Mind the Color of Her Eyes) 2341
If the Girlies Could Be Soldiers 4809
If the Good Die Young (You'll Live to Be a Hundred!) 4037
If the Man in the Moon Were a Coon 917, 2795
If the Man in the Moon Would Only Speak 2710
If the Man in the World Were a Coon 1759
If the Managers Only Thought the Same As Mother 2232
If the Moon Was a Great Big Banjo 1124
If the Morning After Were the Night Before 3031
If the Old Folks Could See Us Now 4208
If the Rain's Got to Fall 1721
If the Sergeant Steals Your Rum 3259
If the Shoe Fits 2103, 3844
If the Sun Didn't Shine Each Day 2784
If the Telephone Could Tell 4226
If the World Were Like the Movies 3039
If the World Were Upside Down 3791
If There Is Someone Lovelier Than You 3699
If There Were More People Like You 3869
If There's Love Enough 1662
If They Ever Parted Me from You 3250
If They Ever Take the Sun Out of Sunday 685
If They Must Tear Me from Thy Heart 476
If They'd Only Left Poor Adam's Rib Alone 4185
If They'd Only Move Old Ireland Over Here 4642
If Things Were What They Seem 1851
If This Is Glamour! 95
If This Is Goodbye 161
If This Is Love 1804
If This Is Paradise 3667
If This Isn't Love 1278
If This Were My World 2785
If War Is What Sherman Said It Was 1532
If Washington Should Come to Life 1480
If We Could Only Stop the Old Town Clock 3895
If We Didn't Get 'Em Back 1997
If We Give It Time 4334
If We Had a Little More Time 2137
If We Had Met Before 3043
If We Knew What the Milkman Knows 4801
If We Only Have Love 2188
If We Open Our Eyes 373
If We Part 2632
If We Pass Beyond the Portals 3588
If We Were on Our Honeymoon (Railway Duet) 1066
If Wishes Were Horses 2134
If Wives Were Put on Sale 2567
If Women Had Their Way 522
If Yankee Doodle Hadn't Come to Town 405
If You and I Incorporate 3069
If You and I Should Meet 2345
If You Are As Good As You Look 773
If You Are in Love with a Girl 670
If You Are Looking for a Sweetheart 3065
If You Ask 912
If You Ask Me to Advise You 3777
If You Believe (Believe in Yourself) 4722
If You But Dreamed 1972
If You But Knew What I Know 4489
If You Can Find a True Love 2219
If You Can Love Like You Can Dance 136
If You Can't Be Good, Be Careful 3466
If You Can't Be Happy as You Want to Be (Just Be as Happy as You Can) 1183

If You Can't Bring It, You've Got to Send It 2645
If You Can't Get Five Take Two 3707
If You Can't Get in the Corners 4467
If You Can't Get the Love You Want 3813
If You Can't Join 'Em, Beat 'Em 4449
If You Can't Sing, Dance 3681
If You Care 2293
If You Care for Me 1763
If You Could Care for Me 208
If You Could Fancy Me 2893
If You Could Learn to Love Me 1868
If You Could Love Me 2992
If You Could Only Come with Me 429
If You Could Read My Mind 3866
If You Could See Her 610
If You Couldn't Change Your Mind 2917
If You Dance Dear, I Know a Cabaret 4808
If You Dare 2947
If You Did It Once 1727
If You Didn't Love Me, Who Else Would 2105
If You Do What You Do 2308
If You Don't Love Me 59
If You Don't Mind 3517
If You Don't Mind My Saying So 3016
If You Don't Think So You're Crazy 481
If You Don't Want Me 4440
If You Ever Come Down to Virginia There'll Be Nothing too Good for You 2696
If You Ever want a Favor Mention Me 2851
If You Ever Want to Do Some Lovin' 4596
If You Examine Human Kind 1165
If You Give Me Your Attention 2977
If You Go I'll Die 2549
If You Got Music 4828
If You Grow Tired Little Girl 2408
If You Had Seen 482
If You Hadn't Answered No 4742
If You Hadn't but You Did 4496
If You Have Troubles Laugh Them Away (Laff 'em Away) 1779
If You Haven't Got a Sweetheart 4446
If You Haven't Got 'It' 1655
If You Keep Them Wondering 3770
If You Knew 2857
If You Knew Now (What I Knew Then) 3551
If You Knew Susie 391, 3020, 4799
If You Knew Time 54
If You Know What I Mean 1654
If You Know What I Think 718
If You Know What's Good for You 3599
If You Leave Me Now 1764
If You Let Me Make Love to You Then Why Can't I Touch You 3824
If You Like People 3871
If You Listen to My Song 1216
If You Look Close 1512
If You Look in Her Eyes 1598
If You Love but Me 3675
If You Love Her (Tell Her So) 69
If You Love Me As I Love You 4439
If You Love Me, Lindy 4738
If You Love Me, Marry Me 68
If You Loved Me Truly 629
If You Must Make Eyes at Someone 1464
If You Never Try 635
If You Only Knew 4133
If You Only Knew How Much I Loved You 470
If You Only Knew Love 81
If You Only Knew the Ways to Pull the Wires 734
If You Only Know the Way 3250
If You Only Will 4589
If You or I Should Tell the Truth 3777
If You Peek in My Gazebo 4467
If You Please 3592
If You Propose to Propose 2884
If You Said What I Thought 458
If You Should Ever Leave 1658
If You Should Meet Me 2323
If You Smile at Me 189
If You Think It's Love, You're Right 1011
If You Think of Speculating 2389
If You Wanna Dance 4769
If You Wanna Have Fun 4016
If You Wanna Keep Your Man 3905
If You Want a Kiss 4677
If You Want a Receipt 2977
If You Want the Old Battalion 3259
If You Want to Be Successful in the Cinema 2808, 4025
If You Want to Break Your Father's Heart 4038
If You Want to Die in Bed 2905
If You Want to Get Ahead 4584
If You Want to Know Who We Are 2861
If You Want to Make a Deal with Russia 3036
If You Were a Rose 1707
If You Were a Tree 2028
If You Were Here 1919
If You Were I and I Were You 2697, 3567, 4544
If You Were in My Place 886
If You Were Lost to Me 4544
If You Were Mine Alone 2671
If You Were My Son 3485
If You Were Someone Else 3655, 4569
If You Were There with Me 1793
If You Were You 1321
If You Will Come to Tea 1470
If You Will Marry Us We'll Stroll Beneath the Babbling Brook 3144
If You Will Spare the Time 3588
If You Will Spend Your Life with Me 259
If You Win, You Lose 3351
If You Wind Me Up 2874
If You Wish To Appear As an Irish Type 1178
If You Won't Marry Me, Then I'll Marry You 2901
If You Would Only Come Away 653
If You Would Only Love Me 2871
If You'd Be Happy, Don't Fall in Love 2637
If You'd Only Let Me 4303
If You'll Always Say Yes 2330
If You'll Be a Soldier, I'll Be a Red Cross Nurse 4634
If You'll Be Good, Like My Own Mother Dear 2973

If You'll Be Mine 2582
If You'll Be My Eve I'll Build an Eden for You 2528
If You'll Just Come Back to Me 2640
If You'll Just Wait a Little While 2897
If You'll Let Me Be Your Husband, I'll Let You Be My Wife 3327
If You'll Only Lead the Way 1247
If You'll Only Say It with Flowers 208
If You'll Only Say My Honey You'll Be Mine 1032
If You'll Only Say You'll Be a Friend of Mine 3575
If You'll Put Up with Me 1747
If You'll Remember Me 3642
If You'll Walk with Me 1526
If You're a Friend of Mine 2392
If You're a Woman 2478
If You're Crazy About the Women 1240
If You're in Love, You'll Waltz 3719
If You're Single 978
If You've Got It, You've Got It 766
If You've Never Been Vamped by a Brownskin 1198
If You've Never Been Vamped By a Brown Skin (You've Never Been Vamped at All) 3963
If You've Only Got a Moustache 1897
If Your Heart's in the Game 2308
If Your Kisses Can't Hold the Man You Love Your Tears Won't Bring Him Back 1333
If Your Name Had Been LaRocca 4694
If'n 1760
Ifs 1910
Ifs and Ans 402
Iggie's Nightmare 2322
Ignoble Theft of the Idol's Eyes 1094
Ikh Bin a Border Bay Mayn Vayb (I Am a Border at My Wife's House) 1609
Ikh Breng Aykh a Grus Fun Di Trenches (I Bring You Greetings from the Trenches) 1609
Iko Iko 4127
Il est de Beaux Reves 3769
Il Lago de Innamoratti (dance) 4060
Il Pleurait 924
Iliad 1816
I'll Admit 1836
I'll Agree If You'll Agree 1655
I'll Always Be an Optimist 4709
I'll Always Be in Love 1662
I'll Always Be with You 3125
I'll Always Believe in You 2174, 1882
I'll Always Love Old Dixie 3945
I'll Always Love You 2033
I'll Always Need Someone Like You 2567
I'll Always Remember 1855, 4621
I'll Always Remember the Song 3760
I'll Applaud You with My Feet 2301
I'll Ask No More 3250
I'll Ballyhoo You 2540
I'll Be a Buoyant Girl 1027
I'll Be a Good Little Girl 675
I'll Be a Hero Too! 2504
I'll Be a Santa Claus to You 4809
I'll Be a Sister to You 178, 1957, 1327
I'll Be a Star 111
I'll Be Around 3175
I'll Be Coming Home to You 1031
I'll Be Coming Home with a Skate On (Skating Song) 4158
I'll Be Dictator 1536
I'll Be Different 1171
I'll Be Glad When You're Dead You Rascal You 3840
I'll Be Hanged 4469
I'll Be Happy Too 4787
I'll Be Hard to Handle 2204, 3735
I'll Be Here 3221
I'll Be Here Tomorrow 1660
I'll Be Home 2787
I'll Be in My Dixie Home Again Tomorrow 2706
I'll Be Just the Same 598
I'll Be Married to the Music of a Military Band 3567
I'll Be Respectable 3837
I'll Be Seeing You 2772, 3713
I'll Be Sittin' in de Lap o' de Lord 4569
I'll Be Smiling 4213
I'll Be Someone Today 1412
I'll Be Somewhere in France 4811
I'll Be There 430, 1482, 1552, 2563, 2665, 3319, 3584, 3739, 1969
I'll Be There in a Public Square 3809
I'll Be There in the Public Square 1968
I'll Be There with Bells On 1480
I'll Be There with You 2834
I'll Be True, But I'll Be Blue 2034
I'll Be True, I Love You 2880
I'll Be True to My Honey Boy 800
I'll Be True to You 168, 1538, 2439, 2483
I'll Be Waitin' 3688
I'll Be Waiting for You 2457, 4053
I'll Be Waiting for Your Coming 2508
I'll Be Waiting 'Neath Your Window 1538
I'll Be Your Artist and You Be My Model 202
I'll Be Your Chanticleer 531
I'll Be Your Honey 591
I'll Be Your Honey in the Springtime 4723
I'll Be Your Honey When It's Moonlight 2901
I'll Be Your Jujube 3855
I'll Be Your Rainbow 1021
I'll Be Your Soldier 2666
I'll Be Your Valentine 1686
I'll Bet on Anything but Girls 480
I'll Bet Two Dollars 1605
I'll Bet You 1593, 1598
I'll Bet You're a Cat Girl 3370
I'll Betcha That I'll Getcha 3907
I'll Black His Eyes 4777
I'll Break the Bank at Monte Carlo 1177
I'll Bribe the Stars 252
I'll Bring the Roses 4102
I'll Build a Bungalow 953
I'll Build a Bungalow for Two 3425

I'll Build a House for You 3663
I'll Build a Palace for My Girl 1721
I'll Build a Stairway to Paradise 1485
I'll Build a Statue 1591
I'll Build for You a Little Nest 531, 2667
I'll Buy Everybody a Beer 2961
I'll Buy It 2267
I'll Buy Me a Ship 4444
I'll Buy You a Star 4446
I'll Call It Love 389
I'll Can-Can All Day 4365
I'll Capture Her Heart 789
I'll Carry You an Inch 2236
I'll Cling to You 3024, 4720
I'll Collaborate with You 4694
I'll Come Back to You 4372, 4657
I'll Come By 3067
I'll Cuddle Up to You 2351
I'll Dance 3161
I'll Dance My Way Into Your Heart 4760
I'll Dance You 3286, 4585
I'll Die If I Can't Live Forever 2069
I'll Do All My Dancing with One Girl 1533
I'll Do Anything for Love 1514
I'll Do As Much for You 2834
I'll Do It for You 1360
I'll Do or Die 2315
I'll Do the Strutaway 1120
I'll Do What the Rest Do 75
I'll Dream of That Sweet Co-ed 1230
I'll Dream of Thee 48, 3773
I'll Dream of You 1992, 4354
I'll Dream Your Dream 915
I'll Fall in Love Again 2357
I'll Fascinate You 3880
I'll Find a Boy (Girl) 558
I'll Find a Dream Somewhere 1676
I'll Find Her There 3227
I'll Find My Love in D-I-X-I-E 740
I'll Find the Key to Your Heart 1174
I'll Fly Away 4030
I'll Follow My Secret Heart 841, 3235
I'll Follow My Star 4577
I'll Follow You 632, 994
I'll Get Another Place 4725
I'll Get Even 1373
I'll Get Even with You 1989
I'll Get My Man 1323
I'll Get You Killed 2306
I'll Get You Out of My Life 3757
I'll Get You Yet 4804
I'll Get You Yet Cigarette 3087
I'll Give My Love a Ring 634
I'll Give the World to You 3252
I'll Give You One Guess 1886
I'll Go Along with You 2182
I'll Go Home with Bonnie Jean 530
I'll Go On 4244
I'll Grow a Garden for You 2626
I'll Hate Myself in the Morning 1577
I'll Hate to Leave the Boys 3051
I'll Have My Way 4360
I'll Have the Law, I'll Have My Right 2982
I'll Hit a New High 1275
I'll Just Pretend 3371
I'll Keep a Warm Spot in My Heart for You 9
I'll Keep Loving You 1883
I'll Keep on Dreaming 905
I'll Keep on Dreaming of You 4668
I'll Keep the Roses Blooming for You 3087
I'll Keep You Here All Night 4053
I'll Know 1706
I'll Know and She'll Know 4426
I'll Know Him 1323
I'll Learn Ya 2449
I'll Lend You Anything 2415
I'll Lend You Everything I've Got Except My Wife 4804
I'll Live a Million Years 4030
I'll Live for You 3943
I'll Love Them All to Death 3680
I'll Love You Just the Same 2066
I'll Love You Marina 4228
I'll Love You Then as Now 2715
I'll Make a Man of One of You 3398
I'll Make a Man of the Man 4588
I'll Make a Man of You 965, 3259
I'll Make a Ring Around Rosie 4757
I'll Make a Space 430
I'll Make Bubbles 2587
I'll Make You Like the Town 4747
I'll Marry a Soldier 4798
I'll Marry Him for Love 68, 1578
I'll Marry No Explorer 628
I'll Meet You 1726
Ill Met (dance) 4153
I'll Miss You 3702
I'll Miss You, Old Ireland 2662
I'll Name My Dolly for You 2276
I'll Never Be a Lady 31
I'll Never Be Jealous Again 3351
I'll Never Be Lonely Again 3482
I'll Never Complain 4620
I'll Never Die (I'll Just Change My Address) 4030
I'll Never Fall in Love Again 261, 3603
I'll Never Forget 1657
I'll Never Get Over the Guy 1004
I'll Never Know 3682
I'll Never Lay Down Any More 2106
I'll Never Learn 183
I'll Never Leave You 3584
I'll Never Make a Frenchman Out of You 2705
I'll Never Say I Love You 1369
I'll Never Say No 4516
I'll Never See You Again 183
I'll Never Share You (If You Were My Concubine) 711
I'll Never Sing a Song 3671
I'll Never Smile Again 3175
I'll Never Stop Loving You 4743

I'll Never Want for More 139
I'll Not Let Love Disparage Marriage 4228
I'll Not Marry 31, 3274
I'll Only Miss Her When I Think of Her 4013
I'll Pay the Check 4142
I'll Peek-a-boo You 718
I'll Produce for You 3822
I'll Put a Tax 666
I'll Put You Through 2017
I'll Putcha Pitcha in the Papers 4335
I'll Read You Such a Dance 1392
I'll Remember 1732
I'll Remember Her 1564
I'll Remember You 3207
I'll Return for You 2614
I'll Ring the Bell 3675
I'll Run in from Troy 2964
I'll Save All My Evenings for You 2020
I'll Say I Love You 2614, 4393
I'll Say I Will 2270
I'll Say She Does 3985
I'll Say She Is 2874
I'll Say So 97
I'll Scratch Your Back 4192
I'll See You Again 429, 3018, 3235
I'll See You Home 1191
I'll See You in C-U-B-A 1685, 1686, 4840, 4842
I'll Sell You a Girl 1685
I'll Send You Roses 2754
I'll Set My True Love Free 2974
I'll Share It All with You 153
I'll Shoot My Way 3663
I'll Show Him 148
I'll Show Him! 3509
I'll Show Them All 4090
I'll Show You a Wonderful World 2960
I'll Show You Off 277
I'll Show You the Ropes 956
I'll Show You the World Tonight 3763
I'll Sing 4769
I'll Sing and Dance 758
I'll Sing of a Golden Age 2344
I'll Sing of a Lady 1606
I'll Sing You a Song 4366
I'll Sing You a Song about Dear Old Dixie Land 3985
I'll Sing Your Praises 1885
I'll Smile 2599
I'll Stay, I'll Go 3876
I'll Stay There 796
I'll Still Be Here 2478, 4577
I'll Still Belong to You 4683
I'll Still Love Jean 1676
I'll Suffer with You 324
I'll Take a Little of You on Toast 2459
I'll Take a Ragtime Tune 1738
I'll Take an Option on You 4291
I'll Take Any Man 4238
I'll Take Care of Him 3868
I'll Take Care of You 4741
I'll Take Down My Etchings 1885
I'll Take My Fantasy 1229
I'll Take the City 297
I'll Take the High Note 1879
I'll Take the Solo 1101
I'll Take You All 2390
I'll Take You All Over the World 750
I'll Take You Back to Italy 2184
I'll Take You Home Again, Kathleen 4390
I'll Take You Home Tomorrow If You'll Take Me Home Tonight 2635
I'll Take You to the Country 2637
I'll Take You to Your Home Town 3045
I'll Talk to Her 757
I'll Tell Papa 4479
I'll Tell the Man in the Street 2061
I'll Tell the World 596, 1619, 2174, 2373, 2479, 3985
I'll Tell You 4352
I'll Tell You a Truth 170
I'll Tell You All Someday 4275
I'll Tell You to Your Face 98
Ill-Tempered Clavichord, The 4640
I'll Think of You 4264, 3652
I'll Travel the Links with You 1910
I'll Treat You Just Like a Sister 3218
I'll Try 3687
I'll Try It Your Way 1371
I'll Try to Smile 3067
I'll Turn a Little Cog 304
I'll Wait 2458
I'll Wait for Joe 1665
I'll Wait for You, Little Girlie (Round at the Sweet Shop) 356
I'll Walk Alone 4696, 4743
I'll Walk Every Step of the Way 4030
I'll Whistle and Wait for You 4439
Ill Wind 221, 4534, 880, 1385
Illegitimate Daughter, The 3225
Illinois 4111, 2806
Illinois Republican, An 4163
Illusion in White 4823
Illya Darling 2106
Ilmar's Tomb 4558
Ilona 3918
Ilona's Rampage 1439
Iloveyouiloveyouiloveyou 3249, 4694
Ilsa's Song 1203
I'm a Bachelor 3508
I'm a Bad Character 1074
I'm a Bad, Bad Man 153
I'm a Big Time Director at Piñafore 1948
I'm a Brass Band 4238
I'm a Broken Hearted Blackbird 893
I'm a Bundle from Britain 924
I'm a Butter Hoarder 1718
I'm a Butterfly 413
I'm a Collector of Moonbeams 2475
I'm a Crazy Daffydill 4805
I'm a Crazy Jay on Circus Day 4439

I'm a Dancing Fool 545
I'm a Dancing Teacher Now 4603
I'm a Dandy 279
I'm a Daughter of Peru 3170
I'm a Devil with the Ladies 969
I'm a Duchess 356
I'm a Dumb-Bell 3006
I'm a Fairy 42
I'm a Fan 2754, 2969, 2072
I'm a Fickle Maid 8
I'm a Flapper Lady 1033
I'm a Fool, Little One 3556
I'm a Funny Dame 1760
I'm a Genius Too 4061
I'm a Gigolo 4581
I'm a Girl with Too Much Heart 3577
I'm a Girl You Should Know 4145
I'm a Good Old Girl 3983
I'm a Great Big Baby 1198
I'm a Gypsy Blonde 1710
I'm a Harem Scarum Boy 3887
I'm a Hermit 3581
I'm a Hieland Lassie 4815
I'm a Highway Gentleman 2277
I'm a Human Pousse Cafe (Cocktail Song) 126
I'm a Hundred Percent for You 881
I'm A-Hunting Jaguar 2497
I'm a Jonah Man 4697, 2111
I'm a King 2504
I'm a Lady 362, 884, 886
I'm a Lady! 4830
I'm a Lady 3745
I'm a Lawyer 2347, 2716
I'm a Little Bit Fonder of You 3721, 4766
I'm a Little Bit Fonder of
You than of Myself 2818
I'm a Little Blackbird 1763
I'm a Little Blackbird Looking
for a Bluebird 1058, 2462
I'm a Little Butterfly 1944
I'm a Little Jail Bird Looking for a
Love Bird Like You 1302
I'm a Little Lady 175
I'm a Little Movie Queen 4373
I'm a Little Too Old to Dance 2342
I'm a Lonely Man 1564
I'm a Lonesome Little Raindrop 1686
I'm a Lonesome Melody 538, 3827
I'm a Lonesome Romeo 3755
I'm a' Looking for My Ten 2951
I'm a Man 1257
I'm a Manicurist 4817
I'm a Marvelous Musician 1246
I'm a Merry Maiden 767
I'm a Millionaire 4419, 4418
I'm a Mischievous Girl 2040
I'm a Native 4232
I'm a Natural Born Hoodoo 3357
I'm a Naughty Girl 1682
I'm a Nurse for Aching Hearts 4809
I'm a One Girl Man 403
I'm a One-Man Girl 577
I'm a Peaceable Party 4311
I'm a Pickford that Nobody Picked 1777
I'm a Pinkerton Man 1474
I'm a Poor Unhappy Maid 2974
I'm a Popular Man 1968
I'm a Positive Guy 4629
I'm a Potentate 1351
I'm a Practical Politician 1466
I'm a Prize 334
I'm a R-U-L-E-R 9
I'm a Real American Girl 1824
I'm a Real Carnegie Hero 263
I'm a Red Hot Cradle Snatcher 577
I'm a Respectable Working Girl 1264
I'm a Rolling Stone 996
I'm a Rough Man 3051
I'm a Sailor 1414
I'm a Scion of the House of Highball 1925
I'm a Sergeant of Police 3882
I'm a Shy Little Innocent Thing 3258
I'm a Simple Author-Manager 3951
I'm a Sleuth 190
I'm a Star 3577
I'm a Statesman 4808
I'm a Stew 1131
I'm a Stranger Here Myself 2010, 3301
I'm A'Tingle, I'm A'Glow 1475
I'm a Trout 3021
I'm a Two Way Woman 4577
I'm a Vamp from East Broadway 4814
I'm a Vampire 3296
I'm a Very Different Girl 1335
I'm a Very Fly Conductor 1213
I'm a Very Good Sailor on Land 2035
I'm a Very Lucky Boy 1742
I'm a Woman 652, 432, 4031, 3428
I'm a Woman of Importance 1403
I'm a Wonderfully Wicked Woman 3159
I'm a Wow 4171
I'm About to Be a Mother
(Who Could Ask for Anything More?) 3225
I'm About to Become a Lover 1048
I'm Abu-el-Hassan 3777
I'm Afire 1282
I'm Afraid 583, 1894, 3721
I'm Afraid I Love You 2847
I'm Afraid I'm in Love 1101
I'm Afraid It's Love 599, 3278
I'm Afraid of the Dark 818
I'm Afraid, Sweetheart, I Love You 2331
I'm Afraid to Be Alone 1606
I'm Afraid to Come Home in the Dark 399
I'm Afraid to Go Home in the Dark 2347
I'm After Madame Tetrazzini's Job 4803
I'm Against Rhythm 383
I'm Alive 576, 4396
I'm All Alone 735
I'm All for You 3096

I'm All I've Got 519
I'm All In 667
I'm All It Takes to Make You Happy 3697
I'm All O.K. with K&E 2730
I'm All Right 2910, 2667, 2041
I'm All Smiles 4764
I'm All the Way from Gay Paree 1540
I'm All Yours 59, 1892, 4643
I'm Alone 181, 3014
I'm Already Gone 105
I'm Always Chasing Rainbows 3246
I'm Always Doing Something I Don't Want to Do 3675
I'm Always Happy When I'm in Your Arms 4763
I'm Always Happy when I'm Sad 4521
I'm Always in Love with Someone 1751
I'm Always in the Mood for You 884
I'm Always Misunderstood 2915
I'm Always Wrong 4384
I'm an Actor 11, 3233
I'm an American Billionaire 1926
I'm an Anaesthetic Dancer 1921
I'm an Honorary Member of the G.A.R. 3425
I'm an Indian 4686, 4814
I'm an Indian Assassin 4290
I'm an Indian Too 153
I'm an International Orphan 3365
I'm an International Sweetheart 1333
I'm an Ordinary Man 3038
I'm an Upper East Side Neurotic 2478
I'm as Good as I Ought to Be 2974
I'm at the Mercy of Love 883
I'm at Your Service Girls 913
I'm Available 2987
I'm Awfully Afraid of Girls 2261
I'm Awfully Strong for You 4759
I'm Back in Circulation 3687, 4777
I'm Back in Circulation Again 1136
I'm Bad 4686
I'm Beautiful 837
I'm Beginning to See the Light 4091
I'm Bettin' You 2195
I'm Betting on You 4011
I'm Betwixt and Between 1886
I'm Blue 3278
I'm Blue Too 1846
I'm Bluff King Hal 2671
I'm Born in the Country 2225
I'm Breaking Down 2132
I'm Bringing a Red, Red Rose 4683
I'm Broke 4781
I'm Bugs Over You 4817
I'm Built for Speed 1565
I'm Called the King 2357, 1818
I'm Calm 4067, 1422
I'm Checkin' Home Now 919
I'm Checkin' Out Goombye 4091
I'm Clay in Your Hands 3442
I'm Coming 'Round to Your Point of View 2759
I'm Coming at Your Call 4188
I'm Coming Home 2307
I'm Coming Home (Letter Song) 3014
I'm Coming Virginia 26
I'm Countin' on You 1769
I'm Craving for that Kind of Love 1198
I'm Crazy About Somebody 4831
I'm Crazy About the Charleston 792
I'm Crazy About the Way You Dance with Me 1911
I'm Crazy 'Bout Somebody 4206
I'm Crazy for That Kind of Love 3512
I'm Crazy Over You 3134, 3951
I'm Crazy to Go on the Stage 3951
I'm Crazy to Marry Again 2261
I'm Crazy when the Band Begins to Play 2892
I'm Cured 4808
I'm Cuttin' Out: Goodbye 2513
I'm Cynical 2504
I'm Dancing with the Mamas with the Moolah 4086
I'm Descended from Brian Boru 1178
I'm Desperate For Your Love 2172
I'm Different 2852
I'm Doin' Okay in My Own Way 3564
I'm Dreaming 4234
I'm Dreaming of a Wonderful Night 473
I'm Dreaming While We're Dancing 4021
I'm Dying for You 256
I'm Dying to Dance with Oscar 1794
I'm Eighteen To-Day 1964
I'm Everybody's Baby 4542
I'm Excelsior 1213
I'm Falling in Love 4730
I'm Falling in Love with Someone 3081
I'm Falling in Love with You Dear 2763
I'm Fancy Free 1555
I'm Fascinating 64
I'm Feelin' Blue 3704
I'm Feelin' Blue 'Cause I've Got Nobody 2140
I'm Feelin' Like a Million 544
I'm Feeling Better All the Time 3490
I'm Feeling Lucky Today 2379
I'm Fine 1804
I'm Flyin' High 1134
I'm Flying 2205, 1298, 3453
I'm Flying High 1323
I'm Fond of the Girls 1794
I'm Fond of You 246
I'm Fond of You-You're Fond of Me 4492
I'm for You 457
I'm for You, You're for Me 3150
I'm Forever Blowing Bubbles 3402
I'm Forty 4108, 2998
I'm Free 4676
I'm Fresh from the Country 953
I'm from Chicago 473
I'm from Granada 4545
I'm from the Court of the Empress Queen 307
I'm from the Middle West 3683
I'm Full of the Devil 787

I'm Gay 2451
I'm Getting Myself Ready for You 3131, 4517
I'm Getting Quite American You Know 3745
I'm Getting Such a Big Girl Now 4327
I'm Getting Tired So I Can Sleep 4340
I'm Glad He's Irish 4626
I'm Glad I Met You 2446
I'm Glad I Waited 4023
I'm Glad I'm from Dixie 1823
I'm Glad I'm Here 2049
I'm Glad I'm Leaving 1791
I'm Glad I'm not a Man 2554
I'm Glad I'm Not Methusalem 3073
I'm Glad I'm Not Young Anymore 1511
I'm Glad I'm Single 1456, 3134
I'm Glad I'm Spanish 487
I'm Glad My Wife's in Europe 965
I'm Glad that I Came Home 326
I'm Glad to Be Back Again 3973
I'm Glad to Get Back to New York 4094
I'm Glad to See You've Got What You Want 681
I'm Glad You Didn't Know Me 2152
I'm Goin' Places 664
I'm Goin' South 487
I'm Goin' to Live Anyhow, 'Til I Die 4390
I'm Goin' to Sea 4452
I'm Going Arla 2307
I'm Going Away 1066
I'm Going Back 363, 1487
I'm Going Back to Dixie 3917, 4655
I'm Going Back to Mobile, Alabam' 4776
I'm Going Crazy with Strauss 3698
I'm Going Down the River and Have Myself a Darn Good Cry 4611
I'm Going Home 2472, 801, 3742
I'm Going Home to Dixie Land 3805
I'm Going in for Love 4777
I'm Going Moroccan for Jimmy 849
I'm Going on a Long Vacation 179
I'm Going Through a Change 4645
I'm Going to Be a Boy 2097
I'm Going to Be a Marquis 2803
I'm Going to Be Lonesome 2270
I'm Going to Be Married Today 1360
I'm Going to Dance at Your Wedding 381
I'm Going to Exit 2984
I'm Going to Find a Girl Someday 2430
I'm Going to Follow the Boys 632, 4037
I'm Going to Leave You 1908
I'm Going to Let the Whole World Know I Love You 2781
I'm Going to Live Forever 430
I'm Going to Marry a Nobleman 4759
I'm Going to Meet Minnie Tonight 4209
I'm Going to Settle Down 3866
I'm Going to Steal the Moon 1967
I'm Gonna 2043
I'm Gonna Be a Movie Star 1940
I'm Gonna Be a Pop 596
I'm Gonna Be a Star 4684
I'm Gonna Be John Henry 3983
I'm Gonna Change the World 3695
I'm Gonna Cry 1813
I'm Gonna Do It If I Like It 4843, 4853
I'm Gonna Do My Things 344
I'm Gonna Fall in Love 1293
I'm Gonna Get Him 2983
I'm Gonna Get Lit Up 4027
I'm Gonna Git Down on My Knees 2225
I'm Gonna Hang My Hat 1336
I'm Gonna Have a Baby 1676
I'm Gonna Hit the Numbers Today 3528
I'm Gonna Make a Fool Out of April 3, 3381
I'm Gonna Make It 2284, 3697
I'm Gonna Miss Him So 4117
I'm Gonna Miss Those Tennessee Nights 474
I'm Gonna Move 615
I'm Gonna Pin My Medal on the Girl I Left Behind 4812
I'm Gonna See My Mother 1485
I'm Gonna Sit Right Down and Write Myself a Letter 39
I'm Gonna Take Her Home to Momma 2949
I'm Gonna Walk Right Up to Her 2304
I'm Gonna Wash That Man Right Outa My Hair 4096
I'm Good for Nothing but Love 4823
I'm Great 4543
I'm Grover 1448
I'm Growing 2518
I'm Growing Fond of You 2025
I'm Growing Wary 4761
I'm Gwine Lie Down 1958
I'm Gwine to Marry Angeline 2675
I'm Gwine to Talk 2557
I'm Hans Christian Andersen 1741
I'm Happy 348
I'm Happy (Tira e Campa) 3798
I'm Happy Darling, Dancing with You 3726
I'm Harold, I'm Harold 2594
I'm Harvey Ellesworth Cheyne 647
I'm Head and Heels in Love 773
I'm Head and Heels in Love with You 2952, 3065
I'm Headed for Big Things 3837
I'm Here 2200, 1200, 2388
I'm Here Again 75
I'm Here and You're Here 2243
I'm Here Little Girls, I'm Here 1784
I'm Here with Bells On 1999
I'm Hi, I'm Lo 735
I'm His Loving Wife 2869
I'm Home 57, 2033, 260, 647
I'm Honest 691
I'm Hook 3453
I'm Hung 1717
I'm Hungry for Beautiful Girls 2706
I'm in a Highly Emotional State 3869
I'm in a Position to Know 506
I'm in a Tree 3564
I'm in Favor of Friendship 861

I'm in League with the Devil 3543
I'm in Like with You 164, 314
I'm in London Again 270
I'm in Love 168, 717, 1125, 1272, 1797, 2069, 2342, 3012, 3669, 821
I'm in Love Again 197, 1690
I'm in Love at Last 1762
I'm in Love Dear 4085
I'm in Love! I'm in Love! 3780
I'm in Love, It's a Wonderful Feeling 1534
I'm in Love Vienna (1) 1680
I'm in Love With... 4635
I'm in Love with a Dame 971
I'm in Love with a Girl Named Dora May 2641
I'm in Love with a Soldier Boy 1018, 4058
I'm in Love with All the Girls I Know 4185
I'm in Love with Miss Logan 3107
I'm in Love with One of the Stars 2730
I'm in Love with the Beautiful Bugs 1295
I'm in Love with the Girl on the Car 942
I'm in Love with Vienna (2) 1680
I'm in Love with Vienna 3020
I'm in Love with Walter Cronkite 2069
I'm in Love with You 4104, 4804, 4604
I'm in My Glory 2308
I'm in Pursuit of Happiness 3800
I'm in Search of a Novelty 2717
I'm in Showbiz 708
I'm in That Mood 1492
I'm in the Market for a Dream 4768
I'm in the Mood 3645
I'm in the Mood for Love 4197
I'm in Trouble 2940
I'm in Wonderland 1314
I'm Into Music 871
I'm Jotte, the Dressmaker 379
I'm Jumpin' In 3888
I'm Just a Bundle of Sunshine 3953
I'm Just a Doorstep Baby 3946
I'm Just a Good Man 3246
I'm Just a Jungle Jidjolo 3174
I'm Just a Little Bit Confused 3913
I'm Just a Little Sparrow 751
I'm Just a Lone Vampire 1685
I'm Just a Lucky So-and-So 4091
I'm Just a Memory 1496
I'm Just a Sentimental Fool 3117
I'm Just a Simple Girl 2151
I'm Just a Slave to Your Crave 1982
I'm Just a Statistic 4584
I'm Just a Toy 2478
I'm Just A-Wearyin' for You 1985
I'm Just from 'Bam 2721
I'm Just Holdin' On 3987
I'm Just Nuts About You 3501
I'm Just One of My Teens 1746
I'm Just Simply Full of Jazz 3905, 1198, 3963
I'm Just Taking My Time 4190
I'm Just Wild About Harry 393, 1198, 3020, 3963
I'm Keeping Myself Available for You 4197
I'm Laying Away a Buck 1577
I'm Lazy 4011
I'm Learning Something Every Day 2892
I'm Learning to Live All Alone 2275
I'm Leavin' Texas 373
I'm Leaving the Bad Girls for Good 3314
I'm Like a New Broom 4446
I'm Like a Sailor (Home from the Sea) 1855
I'm Like the Bluebird 162
I'm Lise 169
I'm Little Bo Peep 4382
I'm Living in the Past with a Love That Cannot Last 991
I'm Lonely 4523
I'm Lonely for Only One 1228
I'm Lonely When I'm Alone 2549
I'm Lonesome, Dear 1824
I'm Lonesome for You 2155
I'm Longing for You 326
I'm Longing My Dearie for You 335
I'm Looking All Over for You 4001
I'm Looking for a Certain Little Boy 4688
I'm Looking for a Daddy Long Legs 3007
I'm Looking for a Financier 2667
I'm Looking for a Girl 1866
I'm Looking for a Girl Like Venus 968
I'm Looking for a Husband 2782
I'm Looking for a Little Girl Who's Looking for a Man 4012
I'm Looking for a Lonely Soldier 214
I'm Looking for a Man 423, 3838
I'm Looking for a Sweetheart and I Think You'll Do 3486
I'm Looking for an Irish Husband 2761
I'm Looking for Another Handy Man 878
I'm Looking for Hubby Dear 3791
I'm Looking for My Sweetheart 2914
I'm Looking for Old Broadway 4839
I'm Looking for Someone's Heart 2696
I'm Looking for Something 1103
I'm Looking for the Great White Way (I'm Looking for Old Broadway) 4837
I'm 'Lord Knows Who' 2696
I'm Losing My Heart to Someone 1961
I'm Lost 170, 147, 4015
I'm Luckier than Dorian Gray 255
I'm Mad 1342
I'm Mad About You 4341
I'm Madame Kapinski 186
I'm Madame Margaret the Therapist 2220
I'm Madly in Love with a Dream Girl 3051
I'm Madly in Love with You 887
I'm Marching Home to You 1491
I'm Married, I'm Single, I'm Divorced, I'm in Love 126, 1335
I'm Married Now 3480, 4666
I'm Mathew P. Brady, the Camera Man 1474
I'm Me 1290, 2682, 4523
I'm Me! (I'm Not Afraid) 4789
I'm Me and You're You 2516

I'm Mighty Glad I'm Living and That's All 2517
I'm Mother Nature of You All 4011
I'm Moving Away 4212
I'm My Mama's Baby Boy 4458
I'm My Own Encounter Group 83
I'm My Own Woman 935
I'm Myself 1255
I'm Naive 974, 4196
I'm Neutral 4809
I'm Ninety-Eight Pounds of Sweetness 2271
I'm No Angel 2651
I'm No Butterfly 735
I'm No Stingy Romeo 2869
I'm Nobody's Girl 4182
I'm Not a Bit Like Other Girls 3998
I'm Not a Bit Superstitious 4649
I'm Not a Jew 4790
I'm Not a Lady's Maid 353
I'm Not a Silly Billy 2761
I'm Not a Well Man 2048
I'm Not Alone 661
I'm Not at All in Love 3351
I'm Not Blue, I'm Mauve 1655
I'm Not Finished Yet 2163
I'm Not for You 249
I'm Not Getting Any Younger 3956
I'm Not Going Gently 1276
I'm Not His Sister Anymore 1035
I'm Not in Love 2439
I'm Not in Love with You 2264
I'm Not in Philadelphia 64, 602
I'm Not Jealous 1626
I'm Not Just Another Mother 2785
I'm Not Mercenary 345
I'm Not Myself 2475
I'm Not Myself Anymore 4635
I'm Not Myself Tonight 2103
I'm Not Particular 3867
I'm Not Queer 871
I'm Not Saying a Word 460
I'm Not So Bright 2582
I'm Not Taking a Chance on Love 4635
I'm Not Talking to You 1721
I'm Not That Kind of Girl 2892
I'm Not That Sort of Picture 353
I'm Not the Girl 521
I'm Not Through 1045
I'm Nuts on You 2636
I'm Off to School 3498
I'm Off You 289
I'm Old Enough to Do a Little Thinking 2966
I'm Old Enough to Know 2027
I'm Old Enough to Know Better (And Young Enough Not to Care) 1760
I'm Old Fashioned 2204
I'm on My Own 2049, 2318
I'm on My Way 3880, 2203, 3347, 3541, 535, 4682
I'm on My Way to Mandalay 1457
I'm on My Way to Paradise 1414
I'm on My Way to the Top 4789
I'm on the Crest of a Wave 1490
I'm on the Inside 589
I'm on the Lookout 2439
I'm on the Water Wagon Now 3229
I'm One Little Party 1297
I'm One of God's Children (Who Hasn't Got Wings) 288
I'm One of God's Children 289
I'm One of the Smart Ones 2558
I'm One of Your Admirers 657
I'm Only a Girl from the City 1794
I'm Only a Pilgrim 659
I'm Only a Poor Little Kid 2456
I'm Only a Woman 4288, 2320
I'm Only Dreaming 4784
I'm Only Thinking of Him 2727
I'm Oriental 3404
I'm Out 4379
I'm Out for No Good Reason Tonight 3953
I'm Out on Strike for a Beautiful Girl 4290
I'm Outta Here 1633
I'm Over Here All Alone 3045
I'm Part of You 347, 3699
I'm Past My Prime 2484
I'm Payin' You 3947
I'm Percy Pinchill of Harlem 4503
I'm Physical, You're Cultured 323
I'm Plenty That Way Too 4545
I'm Props 3952, 3951
I'm Proud I'm Irish 2512
I'm Proud to Be a Yankee 537
I'm Ready 2248
I'm Ready Now! 1377
I'm Ready to Quit and Be Good 1558
I'm Really Disappointed with America 1124
I'm Really Not That Way 1874
I'm Repressed 18
I'm Romantic (I've Always Had a Passion) 4430
I'm Rosie O'Grady Herself 3717
I'm Rotten I'm Rotten 3844
I'm Running After Nancy 2576
I'm Satisfied 4816
I'm Saving My Kisses 4655
I'm Saving Myself for a Soldier 278, 2777
I'm Scared 183, 939
I'm Scared of You 1587
I'm Seeing Rainbows 2355
I'm Seeing Things 3491
I'm Seeking for Siegfried 965
I'm Setting My Cap for a Throne 2397
I'm Sharing My Wealth 4825
I'm Shooting High 4197
I'm Sick of the Whole Damn Problem 1319
I'm Sick of You (Horace's Last) 3691
I'm Simply Crazy Over You 1735
I'm Simply Mad About the Men 765
I'm Simply Wild About You 21
I'm Singing About a Man 2225
I'm Single for Six Weeks More (I'm Going to Be Married in June) 3494

I'm Sitting on Top of the World 393
I'm Sixteen Years Old Today 4014
I'm Slappin' Seventh Avenue (with the Sole of My Shoe) (inst.) 886
I'm Small 1116
I'm Smiling at de Moon Dat Smiles at You 3031
I'm Snow White—A Human Woman 2243
I'm So Bored 2069
I'm So Busy 1784
I'm So Dizzy 2695
I'm So Excited 3218
I'm So Fat 2477
I'm So Fond of a Little Bit of Fun 3828
I'm So Glad 344, 1414
I'm So Glahd to Meet You 2847
I'm So Happy 1424, 2430, 3488, 4811
I'm So Humble (Inferiority Complex) 3436
I'm So in Love 1342
I'm So Lonesome 1881
I'm So Particular 3085
I'm So Shy 4477, 4530
I'm So Sympathetic 2494
I'm So Upset 4646
I'm So Weary of It All 3885
I'm Sober 4833
I'm Somebody 1103
I'm Someone Now 3277
I'm Somethin' on Avenue A 4300
I'm Sorry 8, 338, 4264, 1764
I'm Sorry Dat I Left My Happy Home 2714
I'm Sorry I Ain't Got It If I Had It You Could Have It Blues 4813
I'm Sorry Says the Machine 2134
I'm Standing in This Room 4358
I'm Stepping Out of the Picture 622
I'm Still Here 1329, 3967
I'm Still Me 167
I'm Still Your Single 1228
I'm Stuck with Love 1766
I'm Subtle, I'm Doll and I'm Ace 42
I'm Such a Nervous Man 1530
I'm Such a Romantic Girl 1111
I'm Sure of Your Love 404
I'm Sure to Astonish You All 762
I'm Takin' a Chance on You 3907
I'm Taking a Flight 4030
I'm Taking the Steppes to Russia 2432
I'm Talking to My Pal 3353
I'm Tall 327
I'm Telling You, Louie 3365
I'm That Way Over You 4087
I'm the Boom Boom Boomer 186
I'm the Boy 522
I'm the Boy (You Should Say 'Yes' To) 920
I'm the Boy 509
I'm the Bravest Individual 4238
I'm the Bravest of the Brave 3765
I'm the Broadway Kid 806
I'm the Brother of the Lily of the Valley 1065
I'm the Captain of the Ship 796
I'm the Cockalorum 825, 4022
I'm the College President 2724
I'm the Doctor 1570
I'm the Emperor of Japan 1987
I'm the Extra Man 4692
I'm the Fellow 1961
I'm the Fellow Who Loves You 1493
I'm the First Girl in the Second Row in the Third Scene of the Fourth Number 2582
I'm the Girl 961, 1436, 3914
I'm the Greatest Individual 4238
I'm the Greatest Star 1420
I'm the Greenwich Village Chambermaid 4208
I'm the Guy 1632
I'm the Guy Who Guards the Harem 4813
I'm the Hostess of a Bum Cabaret 1685
I'm the Human Brush (That Paints the Crimson of Paree) 2358
I'm the Human Night Key of New York 4094
I'm the Last of the Red Hot Mamas 4197
I'm the Leader of Society 4559
I'm the Leading Lady 3205
I'm the Lily 4521
I'm the Little Girl 1837
I'm the Major Bozo 1131
I'm the Man In Washington 3387
I'm the Manager 3952, 3951
I'm the Master Here 3734
I'm the Mayor of Newtown 2792
I'm the Mistress of a Bum Cabaret 1685
I'm the Most Forgetful Man 1443
I'm the New Clerk 4050
I'm the Old Man in the Moon, The 2900
I'm the One That Got Away 1702
I'm the Only One 2969
I'm the Only One of My Kind 1650
I'm the Original Devil 2835
I'm the Potentate 1388
I'm the Queen Thamar 3972
I'm the Sheriff 2557, 3026, 1185
I'm the Sultan's Vigilant Vizier 3777
I'm the Villain 130
I'm the Woman You Wanted 4279
I'm Thinking About You Honey All the While 3998
I'm Thinking of Love 3152
I'm Through with Men 4577
I'm Through with Roaming Romeos 1888
I'm Through with the Blues 4240
I'm Through with You 4303
I'm Throwing a Ball Tonight 1638, 3359
I'm Thru' with War 1722
I'm Tickled Pink 1718
I'm Tickled Silly (Slapstick) 4491
I'm Tight 4382
I'm Tillie of Longacre Square 2214
I'm Tired 4181
I'm Tired of Everything but You 4154
I'm Tired of Me 518
I'm Tired of Texas 2582

I'm to Be a Blushing Bride 1247
I'm to Be Married Today 3245
I'm to Blame 3988
I'm Toein' the Line 4281
I'm Too Young to Die 2163
I'm Trying 1961
I'm Twirling 2046
I'm Unlucky 3537
I'm Unlucky at Gambling 1272
I'm Up Early 1386
I'm Up in the Air Over You 1687
I'm Using My Bible for a Roadmap 4030
I'm Very Fond of Jokes 295
I'm Very Glad to Meet You 2623
I'm Very You, You're Very Me 4068, 4301
I'm Waiting for a Wonderful Girl 3254
I'm Waiting for You 3184
I'm Walkin' the Chalk Line 444
I'm Way Ahead 3869, 4238
I'm Way Ahead of the Game 1373, 4267
Im Weissen Rossl 4667
I'm Well Known 3313
I'm Wide Awake When I Dream 3995
I'm Wild About Wild Men 2706
I'm Wise 3205
I'm Wishing 4035
I'm with You 1227, 4823
I'm Wonderful 4765
I'm Wonderin' Who 587
I'm Wondering 1911
I'm Worried to Death About That 2990
I'm Worse than Anybody 1237
I'm You 2105
I'm Your Girl 2797
I'm Your Guy 1955
I'm Your Man 2615
I'm Your Space Angel 2172
I'm Your Valentine 2887
I'm Yours 3980, 4777
Image of His Papa, The 1306
Image of Me, The 652
Image of Our Retina Has Gone, The 2243
Image of You, The 3726
Imaginary Coney Island Ballet (dance) 3278
Imaginary Invalid, The 3956
Imaginary Man, The 4801
Imagination 1859, 3578, 3729
Imaginative Opera 2686
Imagine 247, 3739, 3936
Imagine Me 1786
Imagine Me without My You (and You without Your Me) 4424
Imagine My Finding You Here 3986
Imagine My Frustration 4091
Imagine My Surprise 3448
Imagine That 3931
Imagine You're Alive 2001
Imagining You 424
Imitation 1520
Imitation of Life 1496
Imitation Rag, The 4805
Immigration Rose 4197
Immolation 4139
Immortal Gods 3909
Immortality 973
Imp of Montmartre, The 1199
Impatient Years, The 3324, 3324
Impeachment Waltz, The 3684
Imperial Conference, An 3536
Imperial Guards' March 4201
Imperial March 2655
Importance of Being Earnest, The 1194
Importance of Being Ernest, The 3195, 3236
Important Man, The 2986
Important Things 1809
Imported Yes We Are 3437
Impossibility 4470
Impossible 4067, 759, 1422
Impossible Dream (The Quest), The 2727
Impossible Eyes 3944
Impossible Men 1855
Impossible She, The 4542
Impresario 3682
Impression of the Derby, An 4361
Impressions 3397
Imprisoned 4704
Impromptu Review 3158
Improvements 1095
Improvisation, The 2069
In 661
In a Backyard in Belmont 4147
In a Beauty Shop 335
In a Brownstone Mansion 298
In a Bungalo 1731
In a Bungalow 2950, 2635
In a Bungalow for Two 2448
In a Cape Cod Garden 637
In a Cozy Kitchenette Apartment 3006
In a Curio Shop 487
In a Doll's House 545
In a Dory 2902
In a Far Off Corner of My Mind 31
In a Gadda de Vida (inst.) 3261
In a Garden 1498
In a Garden One Day 1518
In a General Sort of Way 3805
In a Gondola with You 3388
In a Great Big Way 711, 1827
In a Hammock (Hammock Love Song) (Swinging the Summer Night Long) 336
In a Hundred Years 1770
In a Hundred Years from Now 2115
In a Hurry 2292
In a Jewelled Grotto 2902
In a Kingdom of Our Own 3791
In a Little Canoe 2490
In a Little Canoe with You 1998
In a Little French Cafe 710
In a Little Stucco in the Sticks 4025
In a Little Swiss Chalet 4667

In a Little Town in California 2033
In a Little While 1935, 3288
In a Little World for Two 3590
In a Love Boat with You 3403
In a Month or Two 3652
In a Moorish Garden 2366
In a One-Night Stand 1968, 3809
In a Pagoda 2722
In a Pretty Little Cottage 4806
In a Pretty Little White House of Our Own 4806
In a Room 147
In a Sentimental Mood (inst.) 432
In a Sentimental Mood 4091
In a Simple Way 3734
In a Simple Way I Love 2074
In a Simple Way I Love You 1737
In a Small Cafe 2364
In a State 4732
In a Story Book 3571
In a Summer Hotel 2978
In a Taxi Cab 3349
In a Town 1862
In a Venetian Theatre 791
In a World of Our Own 4322
In Again 2107
In America 3644, 3722, 284
In Amsterdam 8
In an Indian Temple 2364
In an Orem Shtibele (In a Poor Little House) 4342
In an Oriental Garden 2919
In an Oriental Way 736
In an Unconventional Way 2500
In and Out 1637
In Another Life 2153, 3463
In April 4272
In Arabia 4747
In Araby with You 930
In Arcady 3193
In Arizona 638
In Armenia 3084
In Athens 3466
In Bad Man's Land 1403
In Bamville 740
In Barcelona 954, 1404, 3717
In Beautiful Italiano 2424
In Beauty's Garden 1518
In Bed 1430
In Berlin 3877
In Between 341, 3347, 3824
In Black and White 3856, 3857
In Bohemia 2040, 4187, 306
In Bohemia with You 2826
In Bokhara, Miss O'Hara 2601
In Bond Street 1561
In Bright Array 4046
In Buddy's Eyes 1329
In Cabaret-Land 1911
In Cahoots 4454
In Califor-n-i-a 111
In Catalina 1961
In Central Park 3744, 4276
In Chelsea Somewhere 1153
In Cherry Blossom Time with You 545
In Chi-chi-castinango 2809
In Chicago 1113
In Chinatown in Frisco 3148
In Cinema Land 1726
In Cloudland 4364
In College 349
In Constantinople 2665
In Corsica 335
In Dahomey 3949
In Darkest Russia 2462
In Day Dreams 3590
In Days Gone By 402
In Days of Long Ago 1250
In Dear Old Fatherland 2800
In Dear Old Grandma's Day 1646
In Dear Old Grandma's Days 2399
In Dear Old Kankakee 1908
In Dear Old London 604
In Disguise 2754
In Dreamland 4724, 4681
(I Live But) In Dreams Alone 68
In Dreams Alone 126
In Dreams Begin Responsibilities 3162
In Dutch 1432
In Egern on the Tegern See 3014
In English 1809
In Erin's Isle 1162
In Every Dancing Show 3407
In Fair Japan 4637
In Fairyland 4649
In Far Off Mandalay 2979
In Farsovia 2835
In Fashion's Ring 3887
In Flagrante Delicto 2992
In Florida 2465
In Florida Among the Palms 4148, 4810
In Gay Ballyhoo 3073
In Gay Ceylon 767
In Gay Japan 3951
In Gay Mayfair 356
In Gay New York 3747
In Gay Paree 115, 1457, 1526, 1881, 2936, 3384, 1473
In Gay Paris 586
In Gay Philopolis 1026
In Gingham 265
In Grandma's Day They Never Did the Fox Trot 4834
In Gypsy Land 1793
In Happy Slumberland 2534
In Havana 4025
In Hennequeville 3312
In Her Little Blue Bonnet with the Red Ribbon on It 815
In His Arms 3436

In His Eyes 2198
In His Own Good Time 1764
In Hitchy's Bouquet 1923
In Holy Divorce 83
In Honeysuckle Time 1198
In Honeysuckle Time (When Emmaline Said She'd Be Mine) 3963
In Housekeeping I Am a Martinet 2623
In Italy 3405
In Izzenschnooken on the Lovely Essenzook Zee 2522
In Jail 48, 1966, 2293, 3773
In January You May Love Mary 736
In Khorossan 4815
In-Laws 400
In Little Old New York 3404
In Louisiana 4197
In Love 466
In Love Again 152
In Love Am I 2944
In Love in Vain 2372
In Love with a Fool 2075
In Love with All the Girls 1833
In Love with Love 2121, 4150
In Love with Romance 3064
In Love with You 2947
In Lovers Lane 982
In Loving Memory 1373
In Loving Time 1
In Madrid 2777
In Marsovia 2836
In May and June 3466
In Merry, Merry May 307
In Michigan 4723
In Missouria 567
In Monkey Land 3480
In Monte Carlo Town 2869
In Montezuma 356
In Monticello's Kingdom Grand 3591
In My Birch Bark Canoe (With Emmy Lou) 3755
In My Birch Bark Canoe 4206
In My Canoe 830
In My Castle in Sorrento 2380
In My Country Oriental 3573
In My Curriculum 2803
In My Day 2200, 1664, 3295
In My Dixie Dreamland Jazz 2009
In My Dream of You 929
In My Dreams 971
In My Dreams of You 1555
In My Garden 2813
In My Garden of Eden for Two 60
In My Hat 1354
In My Heart 3042
In My Heart of Hearts I've Always Known 3777
In My Heart, on My Mind 184
In My Home Town 2363
In My Life 2442
In My Little Blue Bonnet 69
In My Little Red Book 4104
In My Little Runabout 1525
In My Love Boat 3849
In My Merry Oldsmobile 4390
In My Museum Now 613
In My Official Capacity 694
In My Old Home 295
In My Own Irresistible Way 1097
In My Own Lifetime 3780
In My Own Little Corner 759
In My Riksha of Bamboo 1243
In My Silent Universe 2220
In My Submarine 2951
In My Tippy Canoe 4815
In New York the Only Sin Is Being Timid 3305
In 1999 4757
In No Man's Land (inst.) 2228
In No Time at All 4060
In Nomine Dei 3876
In Nomine Patris 2775
In Old Granada 487
In Old Havana Town 203
In Old Japan 1154, 1417
In Old Kentucky 391, 2034
In Old Mexico 4412
In Old New York 1403, 4754
In Old Versailles 4812
In Old Villanelle 49
In Old Wall Street 4589
In One Cell 253
In Orcania 3626
In Other Words, Seventeen 4557
In Our Chateau in Brooklyn 1048
In Our Childhood's Bright Endeavor 1755
In Our Cozy Little Cottage of Tomorrow 180
In Our Hands 4020
In Our Hide-Away 2983
In Our Little Castle in the Air 2174
In Our Little Home Sweet Home 2794
In Our Little Paradise 3866
In Our Little Salon 3988
In Our Little School 4201
In Our Mountain Bower 4283
In Our Orange Grove 196
In Our Own Orange Grove 1777
In Our Parlor on the Third Floor Back 376
In Our Set 2951
In Our Teeny Little Weeny Little Nest for Two 3954
In Our Teeny Little Weeny Nest 2439
In Panama 1524, 3748
In Paradise 1570
In Paree 3877, 4382
In Paris 1246, 1602
In Paris and in Love 1548
In Peacock Alley 1404
In Philadelphia 1900, 2966
In Pity Spare Them 2724

In Poster Land 824
In Praise of Love 972
In Praise of the Jolly Tar 4012
In Praise of Women 2536
In Rang a Pang 4434
In Real Life 1380
In Romany 4275
In Rose Time 4054
In Rotterdam 4115
In Ruritania 3586
In Salem 3403
In Sapphire Seas 1285
In Sardinia (Where the Delicatessen Flows) 4300
In Search of a Sinner 2264
In Search of a Thrill 1228
In Seville 4115
In Sherwood Forest 3736
In Siam 4599
In Silence 2917
In Slumberland 443
In Snowman's Land 2085
In So-So Society 4649
In Society 902, 1573
In Society (dance) (High Society) 2484
In Society It's Always Dress Parade 3685
In Some Little World 1846
In Some Other Life 1822
In Someone Else's Sandals 2075
In Someone's Eyes 1329
In Spain 326, 1308
In Spirit Land 1538
In Spotless Town 3951
In Stage Land 4478
In Sunny Spain 68, 4032
In Sweet Loveland 3384
In Sweetheart Time 4249
In Swell Society 3805
In Tammany Hall 1403
In That Clearing 4764
In That Little Irish Home Sweet Home 4815
In the Afternoon of Our Years (Afternoon of Your Years) 2925
In the Air 1989
In the Arms of a Stranger 406
In the Autumn 4429
In the Autumn in the Night 1730
In the Back of a Hack 1811
In the Ballet 284
In the Bamboo Tree 4066
In the Bath 220
In the Bathroom 1448
In the Bathroom Tra La 2827
In the Beginning 1651, 730
In the Beginning Was the Word 755
In the Beginning, Woman 4383
In the Big Money 1109
In the Bois 1110
In the Broken Promise Land of Fifteen 2568
In the Canoe 545
In the Cards 1038
In the Carefree Realm of Fancy 1670
In the Cellar 2146
In the Center of Your Mind Keep the Lord 4523
In the Champs de Mars 1475
In the Chest 353
In the Chorus 1881
In the Clear 3180
In the Clear Light of Dawn 657
In the Clouds 2636
In the Convent They Never Taught Me That 4250
In the Cool of the Evening 1202
In the Corner of My Mind 3185
In the Cottage of My Heart 910, 4427
In the Country Where I Come From 461
In the Courtroom (dance) 3390
In the Cradle of Love 4807
In the Dark 1831, 3537
In the Dark of an Arkansas Moon 3940
In the Days Gone By 905, 3086
In the Days of '49 1316
In the Days of Old 4754
In the Days of Wild Romance 1345
In the Days When Grandma Dear Was Young 939
In the Department Store 1259
In the Desert 221
In the Evening 4804, 4809
In the Eyes of a Child (1) 451
In the Eyes of a Child (2) 451
In the Garden 4012
In the Garden of Romance 2907
In the Gardens of Noor-Ed-Deen 931
In the Golden Dawn 2978
In the Golden Long Ago 4649
In the Good Old Days 4713, 2262
In the Good Old Summer Time, The 662
In the Good Old Summertime 1021
In the Gypsy's Life 1710
In the Hallway 119
In the Harem 2802
In the Hay 4015
In the Heart of Spain 86
In the Heart of the Dark 4557
In the Heart of the Golden Wine 2495
In the Hollow of His Hand 3913
In the House 3258, 4272
In the Interval Between Dusk and Dawn 3352
In the Isle of Our Dreams 3675
In the Japanese Gardens 3564
In the King's Name — Stand! 906
In the Land of Go to Bed Early 4604
In the Land of Lorraine 4489
In the Land of Romance 248
In the Land of Spain 252
In the Land of Sunny Sunflowers 3965
In the Land of the Buffalo 4756
In the Land of Yesterday 3538

In the Land Where My Heart Was Born 2287
In the Latin Quarter 1175
In the Life 2648
In the Lobby 95
In the Lobby of the Ritz 1862
In the Long Run (You'll Run After Me) 2380
In the Mandarin's Orchid Garden 2872
In the Meantime 1628
In the Mediaeval Ages 2938
In the Merry Month of Maybe 418
In the Middle of the Night 3699
In the Mind's Eye 4659
In the Mirror's Reflection 4398
In the Mood 3018
In the Morning 679, 2103, 3110, 1896, 3786, 4208
In the Mountains 1513
(Soon You'll See Me) In the Movies 486
In the Movies 1066, 1544, 3843, 3936
In the Music Hall Bar when the Curtain Is Down 2041
In the Name of Art 1267
In the Name of Love 4619, 1282, 4168
In the Name of the King 1162
In the Night 4111
In the Noonday Sun 3699
In the Old Fashioned Way 4056
In the Old Town Hall 4815
In the Orange Blossom Land 1908
In the Oven 353
In the Palace Gardens 2802
In the Papers 1513
In the Park 1004, 2756, 4188
In the Pink 1440, 2023
In the Prison 2433
In the Rain 3649
In the Rattle of the Battle 4179
In the Real World 105
In the Red 3046
In the Reign of Chaim 4514
In the Right Kind of Light 3603
In the Sack 3161
In the Same Way I Love You 605
In the Sea 4393
In the Shacks that Little Flower Built 1316
In the Shade of a Sheltering Tree 3009
In the Shade of My Bungalow 2408
In the Shade of the Alamo 4819
In the Shade of the Lemon Tree 3525
In the Shade of the New Apple Tree 1973
In the Shadow of the Pyramids 2990
In the Shadows 1845, 3096, 2806
In the Silence of the Night 876
In the Silent Deep 2552
In the Sky 414
In the Sleeping Line 3806
In the Slums of the Town 3723
In the Snow-Covered Mountains of Switzerland 545
In the South of France 1130
In the Spring 2972, 4409, 2509
In the Spring It's Nice to Have Someone to Love 4359
In the Starlight 3677, 4760
In the Starlit Skies 1910
In the State of Matrimony 2619
In the Stretch 2034
In the Summer 4426
In the Summertime 2222
In the Sunny Old South 1474
In the Sunshine of Your Love 310
In the Surf 4801
In the Sweet By and By 3817
In the Sweet Bye and Bye 3261
In the Swim 637
In the Swim (If You Will Take Our Tip) 1419
In the Swim 2291, 2308, 2317, 3060
In the Swim (inst.) 700
In the Swim 3751
In the Theatre Mirror 2421
In the Toymaker's Workshop (inst.) 250
In the Toyshop 1261
In the Tuileries Gardens 2364
In the Twilight 1128
In the U.S.A. 4201
In the Very Next Moment 3931
In the Village By the Sea 3005
In the Waldorf Halls 2730
In the War Against Men 4747
In the Way Off There 487
In the Year of Fifty-Fifty 4637
In There 599, 1214
In They Go, Out They Come 2298
In This Abode of Madame la Mode (Opening Chorus Act II) 3618
In This Automatical World 3369
In This Delicious World 3195
In This Heaven 528
In This Superior Establishment 1750
In This Wide, Wide World 1511
In Those Boyhood Days 4756
In Those Days a Decree Went Out 755
In Those Good Old Horsecar Days 1874
In Three-Quarter Time 3379
In Timbuktu 1518
In Time 298, 3702
In Time of Peace Prepare for War 3087
In Times Like These 1300, 3801
In Times of War and Tumults 2228
In Trinidad 1414
In Tune 3869
In 2010 3395
In Twos 4276
In Vanity Fair 256
In Variety 376
In Vaudeville 632, 1095, 1316, 1756
In Venice 3043
In Vienna 2292, 1439
In Vino Veritas 1848
In Voodoo 466
In Waikiki 1494

In Walked Bill 1525
In Washington Square 584
In Watermelon Time 4290
In Whatever Time We Have 730
In Which to Marry Me 4167
In Yama 4182
In Yama Yama Land 4054
In Ylang-Ylang 737
In Yorkshire 3322
In Your Arms 4687
In Your Cradle of Love 2636
In Your Defence 4219
In Your Eyes 1741, 2925, 3526
In Your Hands 4089
In Youth 2633
In Youth's Fair Springtime 184
In Yucatan 506, 2559
In Zanzibar 2803, 3951
In ze Park 465
Incantation 559, 1515, 2918, 4724
Incantation Ballet (inst.) 1257
Incantations, The 1258
Incest and Apples 3619
Inch Worm 1741
Inchworm 4399
Inchworm, The 3444
Incident in Arch Street 4467
Incidents in the Lives of Famous Men 405
Incognito 307, 2341
Incompatibility 2190
Incomplete 3619
Inconsistency 3363
Incoq 4364
Indecision 3162
Indefinable Charm 971
Independance 2888
Independence Day 591, 1646
Independence Day Hora 2864
Independence Day Parade 4737
Independent 363
Indestructible Kate 4234
India 632
India Rubber 4378
Indian Benefit Ball, The 4595
Indian Blues 1662
Indian Ceremonial Music 4664
Indian Chant 3130
Indian Dance 750
Indian Fox Trot 4422
Indian Fox Trot Ball 4835
Indian Girls Chant 3865
Indian Giver 943
Indian Love Call 3772
Indian Love Song 1606
Indian Lullaby 4664
Indian Maiden's Chorus 3865
Indian Maiden's Lament, The 3279
Indian Moon 1587
Indian Nuts 157
Indian Prance 3218
Indian Prayer 3086
Indian Rag, The 4589
Indian Raid (inst.) 190
Indian Scene (inst.) 190
Indian Summer (inst.) 638
Indian Summer 2633
Indian Talk 3908
Indian War Song 3504
Indiana Anna 349
Indians 3453
Indians Along Broadway 3753
Indians Are About 3453
Indictment, The 2472
Indigent Aristocrat, An 4761
Indignation Meeting 930
Individual Thing 1420
Individual Thing, An 3564
Individuals 1233
Indoor Girl 2000
Indoor Sports 2939
Inebriated Acrobation 684
Inevitable 2295
Inevitably Me 3941
Inexpensive Tango 4076
Infamy 4405
Infant Marriage 284
Infatuation 3860
Infelice 45
Influenza 2477
Influenza Blues 2574
Information Please 2432
Ingenue, The 2171
Initials 1717
Initiation of Daphne, The 256
Injun Love 3332
Injuns Here We Come 1890
Inka Dinka Doo 1120
Inky's Pastry Shop 2093
Inner City Mother Goose, The 2134
Inner Office Scene 1300
Inner Peace 534
Inner Thoughts 167
Innocence 2579, 3467
Innocent Chorus Girls of Yesterday 111
Innocent Debutante, The 2779
Innocent Eyes 274, 2135
Innocent Games of Childhood, The 3422
Innocent Girls 1723
Innocent Ingenue Baby 3323
Innocent, Innocent Maids 3378
Innocent Lonesome Baby 3649
Innocent Man Is Never Hanged, An 1736
Innocent Stander-By 1577
Innocent Stander-By, The 1886
Inquest of Love 1664
Ins and the Outs, The 3530
Insane Poontang 1139
Insanity 4756
Inside 3368
Inside Looking Out 2540

Inside Story, The 1856
Inside U.S.A. 2137
Insignificant Me 3420
Insolent Breed, The 2248
Inspection 1067
Inspector Barnes 363
Inspiration 490, 1321, 2097, 2135, 2535, 2666
Inspirational Song 1974
Instant Hate 1282
Instant Magic 4102
Instead-of Song 4369
Instinct 944
Institute for Psychodrama 1370
Instructional Rag, The 4197
Instrumental Man, The 2465
Insufficient Sweetie 2376
Insurance 2304
Insurgents 1908
Intellectual's Rag, The 1023
Interesting Questions 2143
Interfering Parrot, The 1470
Intergalatic Circus Finale 1159
Interlude (inst.) 1408
Interlude 1711, 2610, 3014, 3525, 750, 4319, 4664
Interlude After Scene III (inst.) 2228
Interlude and Gallop 4537
Interlude in the Dark (We Are a Band of Brothers) 1476
Interlude: Rhythms of a Summer Night 494
Intermezzo 1095
Intermezzo, The 2667
Intermezzo 2802, 3056, 3081, 3586, 4010, 4620
Inter-mish-un 1637
Intermission Rag 1590
Intermission Talk 2797
Intermission's Great, The 599, 3278
International, The 1951
International Merry Widow, The 4802
International Monopoly 366
International Rag, The 60
International Rhythm 2140
International Vamp 3149
Interrogation Ballet (inst.) 2777
Interrogative Child (Mrs. Wimple's Party), The 2906
Interrogative Child, The 4311
Interrupted Allegory 4119
Interrupted Love Song, An 3117
Interrupted Love Song, The 4616
Interrupted Tete-a-Tete, The 639
Interruptions 2884
Interview, The 413, 1865
Interviews 3561, 4019
Intimate Friends 1257
Into a Green and Smiling Age 3280
Into Society 1312
Into the Bright of Loving 4330
Into the Dream (Act I Finale) 2919
Into the Kitchen Boys 1624
Into the Light 2142
Into the Night 2985
Into the Woods 2143
Intombenjani 4438
Intoxication 4828
Intoxication Dance (inst.) 4677
Intrigue 1079
Intriguers, The 3494
Intro 1978, 3476
Introduce Me 1928
Introducin' Mr. Paris 1600
Introducing Mr. Rassendyl (inst.) 4798
Introducing the Futurity Debutante Chorus 2601
Introduction, The 1086
Introduction 1695
Introduction (inst.) 2228
Introduction 2368, 2668, 3104, 4119, 526
Introduction Act II 307
Introduction, Chorus and Melodrama 307
Introduction of the Kings 1817
Introduction Tango (dance) 4435
Introduction to Neverland 3453
Introductions 2243
Introductory Chorus 1710
Intruder, The 4751
Intruder Dance, The 2308
Intuition 363
Inventory 2992
Investigate 717
Investigation 4718
Invisible Man, The 4002
Invisible Man 4332
Invitation, The 999
Invitation, An 4372
Invitation, Carmilla Stays, An 654
Invitation to the Basketball 157
Invitation to the Jellicle Ball, The 678
Invitation to the Waltz 3339
Invocation 1422
Invocation and Instructions 4067
Invocation and Instructions to the Audience 1406
Invocation of Venus 3976
Invocation to Pie 3951
Invocation to Venus 1818
Inza 1380
Io Sono Cosi Stanco 240
Iole 2145, 2145
Ionisation (inst.) 964
Iowa Stubborn 3016
Iphigenia 4615
Ipi-Tombi (Where Are the Girls?) 2147
Ira, My Dope Fiend 2220
Irate Pirate Am I, An 2005
Ireland a Gra Ma Chree 1445
Ireland Is Ireland to Me 2310
Ireland, Land of My Dreams 4576
Ireland Must Be Heaven 2853
Ireland My Sireland 1162
Ireland Was Never Like This 751
Ireland, You're the Motherland 2662

Ireland's Eye (dance) 2268
Ireland's Native Green 668
Irena's Aria 3864
Irene 2148
Irene O'Dare 2148
Iris 3261
Iris the Fleet 4707
Irish American 2517
Irish and Proud of It, Too 965
Irish Ballad 4412
Irish Cakewalk 1988
Irish Eyes of Blue 1803
Irish Girl, An 2148
Irish Girl I Love, The 3746
Irish Have a Great Day Tonight, The 1162
Irish Heart, An 4720
Irish Ireland, An 2055
Irish Jig (The Singing Blacksmith of Curriclough) (inst.) 2900
Irish Lads 4762
Irish Moon 994, 3911
Irish Reel 1162
Irish Romeo 3396
Irish Rose for Me, An 3580
Irish Sheik, The 2298
Irish Sidewalk Conversationalists, The 2041
Irish Stew 4285
Irish Suffragette, The 537
Irish Swell, The 3759
Irish Washerwoman's Lament 4380
Irish Were Egyptians Long Ago, The 1154
Irma La Douce 2150, 2150
Iron Horse 4390
Iron! Iron! Iron! (Opening Chorus) 4250
Irrepressible Yank, The 3943
Irresistible You 971, 1779
Irrisistible Tune, The 2724
Irving Berlin Medley 2294
Is a Kiss 246
It's All Right to Cry 1389
Is Anybody There? 3897
Is Everybody Happy 2795
Is Everybody Happy Now? 202
Is He Nisnardi? 2178
Is He the Only Man in the World? 2983
Is It a Crime? 363
Is It a Dream? 1817
Is It Any Wonder? 3252
Is It Any Wonder 4424
Is It Anybody's Business 2289
Is It Art? 3666
Is It Hard to Guess? 2601
Is It Him or Is It Me? 2615
Is It Love? 1155, 2622, 3721, 4859
Is It Love or Fascination 302
Is It Madness, Is It? 1730
Is It Possible? 4174
Is It Really Me? 3294
Is It Safe to Depend on the Irish 3472
Is It So? 284
Is It the Girl or Is It the Gown? 1270
Is It the Girl? (Or Is It the Gown) 3893
Is It the Singer Or Is It the Song? 839
Is It the Uniform? 3556
Is It Too Late? 1119
Is It Too Late 2284
Is It Worth While? 20
Is It Yes or Is It No? 3744
Is It You 23
Is It You or the Cocktail? 3914
Is It Your Smile? 4056
Is Izzy Azzy Woz? 1491
Is Marriage a Failure? 2793
Is Massa Gwine to Sell Us Tomorrow? 2203
Is Me 3792
Is My Face on Straight 2534
Is No Succor Near? 1710
'Is Old Man's 'At Won't Fit 'Im 3129
Is Rhythm Necessary? 1207
Is She on Our Side? 1887
It's Spring 2737
Is That All There Is? 2294, 3428
Is That All? 2665
Is That Good? 4013
Is That Love 4515
Is That My Prince? 4446
Is the Girl You Marry Still the Girl You Love 2922
Is There a City? 4659
Is There a Maid? 1220
Is There Any Little Thing I Can Do for You? 4248
Is There Anybody There Tango 1891
Is There Anyone Here By the Name of Smith? 2765
Is There Anything Better Than Dancing? 3142
Is There Some Place for Me? 3224
Is There Something to What He Said? 766
Is This Any Way to Fight a War? 2472
Is This Fact? 278, 2777
Is This Gonna Be a Wedding? 455
Is This Love at Last 1888
Is This My Town 4689
Is This Not a Lovely Spot? 4001
Is This the End? 4021
Is This the Happy Ending? 2563
Is This the Way 692
Is This the Way? 3938
Is This What You Call Love? 3411
Is This Where the Rainbow Ends? 456
Is This Year Next Year? 1289
Is What's It's All About 781
Is You Happy-Go-Lucky? 2115
Is You Is or Is You Ain't My Baby? 1296
Isaac's Equation 4558
Isabel 944, 1587, 1912
Isabel's a Jezebel 2153
Isabella 3162
Isabella Catholica 1369
I'se Found Yo', Honey, Found Yo', Now Be Mine 604

I'se Juliet 2631
Ish-Ga-Bibble (I Should Worry) 3926
Isidudla 4438
Isizwe (The Nation Is Dying) 3836
Island, An 3944
Island, The 1959
Island in the Sun 1435
Island in the West Indies 4825
Island of Bolamazoo 3235
Island of By-and-By 9
Island of Do As You Please 1026
Island of Happiness 4678
Island of Love, The 1313, 1417
Island of Never-Mind-Where, The 1610
Island of Roses and Love, The 1927, 4351, 4613
Island of Sweet Sixteen 4649
Island Ritual 4029
Island Update 1 3628
Island Update 2 3628
Isle d'Amour 3399
Isle D'Amour 4807
Isle O' Dreams 2154
Isle of Lost Romance, The 1919
Isle of Man, The 3028
Isle of Meinisooris 204
Isle of Tangerine 4283
Isle of the Midnight Rainbow 1782
Isle of the Philippines, An 1230
Isle of Youth 3985
Isle of Zanzibar 498
Isles of Love, The 1909
Ism #1 3873
Isms 2804, 4566
Isn't He a Terrific Guy 1885
Isn't It a Funny Thing? 2300
Isn't It a Lovely View? 1539
Isn't It a Pity? 3379
Isn't It Creepy 1757
Isn't It Exasperating, Sadie? 115
Isn't It Fun to Be in the Movies 1914
Isn't It Great to Be Married 4555
Isn't It June? 3850
Isn't It Kinda Fun? 4146
Isn't It Nasty of Papa? 1111
Isn't It Remarkable 3907
Isn't It Romantic 146
Isn't It Something 499
Isn't It Strange 674, 3349
Isn't It Swell to Dream 3907
Isn't It Terrible What They Did to Mary
Queen of Scots 3569
Isn't It Time for the People 2790
Isn't It Wonderful? 3250, 3543
Isn't It Wonderful 3569, 1540
Isn't It Wonderful! 3866
Isn't It? 3843
Isn't Love a Rainbow? 226
Isn't She 669
Isn't She Lovely? 3108
Isn't She Lovely 1169
Isn't She Marvelous! 270
Isn't That a Wonderful Way to Die?
3542, 491
Isn't That Always the Way 2516
Isn't That Clear? 3602
Isn't That Like a Man! 2931
Isn't That What Makes Life Worthwhile 1002
Isn't There a Crowd Everywhere? 4327
Isn't This a Fine Kettle of Fish 1155
Isn't This Better 16
Isn't This Better? 131
Isn't This Better 4480
Isn't This Fun 692
Isn't This the Way to Go? 154
Isola 223
Israel Shall Live 2352
It 723
It Ain't Easy 729
It Ain't Etiquette 1109
It Ain't fer Me 4409
It Ain't Gonna Be Easy 339
It Ain't Gonna Work! 1289
It Ain't Necessarily So 3541
It Ain't Nice Not to Play on
Your Own Turf 2579
It Ain't No Fault of His 105
It Ain't Us Who Makes the Wars 406
It All Belongs to Me 2388, 4821
It All Comes Out of the Piano 1000
It All Depends 3486
It All Depends on You 391, 1489, 2467
It All Goes Up in Smoke 2261
It All Seems So Long Ago 1203
It Always Happens for the Best 4208
It Always Takes Two 1440
It Better Be Good 294
It Can All Be Explained 2142
It Can Happen to Anyone 4214
It Can't Be Did 2261
It Can't Be Done 2620
It Can't Be True 4440
It Can't Be Wrong 2549
It Can't Happen Here 417, 4152
It Can't Keep Raining All the Time 3203
It Could Be Calais 3264
It Could Be Worse 3788
It Could Happen, It's Possible 4782
It Could Have Been Him 1161
It Could Only Happen in the Movies 297
It Could Only Happen in the Theatre 705
It Couldn't Please Me More 610
It Depends on How You Look at Things 679, 3110
It Depends on the Hair 1388
It Depends on What You Pay 1245
It Depends on What You're At 634
It Does Amuse Me So! 4430
It Does Not 4798
It Doesn't Cost You Anything to Dream 4524
It Doesn't Have to Be That Way 3925
It Doesn't Look Deserted 2339

It Doesn't Matter 3866
It Doesn't Matter Anymore 580, 3275
It Doesn't Matter Now 1616
It Doesn't Seem a Lot Like Christmas 3066
It Doesn't Take a Minute 3687
It Don't Add Up 2513
It Don't Mean a Thing 3905
It Don't Meen a Thing 4091
It Feels Good 2797
It Feels Like a Party 3576
It Feels Like Forever 1706
It Feels So Good to Be Alive Today 337
It Fills Me with Distress 4704
It Gets Lonely in the White House 2983
It Gets Them All 4056
It Goes Like This 4019
It Got to Be a Habit 4061
It Had to Happen Sometime 2420
It Happened 3011
It Happened in 1600 1777
It Happened in Chicago 662
It Happened in Miami 173, 417
It Happened in the Dark 2909
It Happens Every Day 1878, 4723
It Happens to the Best of Friends 4137
It Happens Very Softly 3088
It Happens When I See You 3463
It Has All Begun 2047
It Has Reached Me a Lady
Named Hubbard 3777
It Hasn't Been Easy 3181
It Hasn't Got a Chance 486
It Hurts to Be Strong 661
"It" in Italy, The 3150
It Is a Dear Old World After All 3579
It Is All for You 2696
It Is Done 3741
It Is I 1066
It Is Not the End of the World 2064
It Is Past My Comprehension 1178
It Is Really to Good to Be True 4614
It Is the English 3422
It Is the Fourteenth of July 3569
It Is the Girl and Not the Horse That
Wins the Prize 1243
It Is Their Nature To 1392
It Is Time for the King to Behold the
Fair Princess 2317
It Is Very Hard to Bring Up Father 1309
It Is Wonderful 1521
It Is Writ 2319
It Isn't Done 1272
It Isn't Easy 900, 1766
It Isn't Enough 3731
It Isn't Fair 1092
It Isn't Hard to Do 2216
It Isn't Hard to Get Married 1701
It Isn't Much 1308
It Isn't the End of the World 572
It Isn't the Moonlight 3258
It Isn't the Same 348
It Isn't the Same in the Daylight 4767
It Isn't the Way You Play the Game 2357
It Isn't What You Have 2201
It Isn't Working 4727
It Isn't Your Fault 1888, 3177
It Just Had to Happen 3489
It Just Occurred to Me 4499
It Kinda Makes You Wonder 2304
It Looked Good to Me 1307
It Looks Like Liza 2386
It Looks Like More People Were
Agin' Him 4163
It Makes a Fellow Sort of Stop and Think 3250
It Makes My Love Come Down 478
It Makes No Difference 1074
It May Be a Good Idea for Joe 85
It May Be Life 4467
It Means So Little to You 1856
It Might As Well Be Her 4588
It Might As Well Be Spring 4146
It Might Be an Oomps Sight Worse 2761
It Might Be Love 3543, 1857
It Might Have Been 4155, 2903
It Might Have Been Worse 2334
It Might Have Been You 2747
It Must Be Ernie 3301
It Must be Fun to Be You 2847
It Must Be Good for Me 757
It Must Be Great to Be a General but
I'd Rather Lead the Band 2901
It Must Be Heaven 1800
It Must Be Love 830, 2569, 2833, 4029, 4360
It Must Be Now 1424
It Must Be So 630
It Must Be Spring 4366
It Must Be True 2563
It Must Be You 1154, 3677
It Must Have Been the Night 3850
It Needs No Poet 3570
It Needs Work 775
It Never Entered My Head 1683
It Never Entered My Mind 1894
It Never, Never Can Be Love 3081
It Never Was You 2344
It Never Will Get You a Thing 3042
It Never Would Have Worked 958
It Only Happens in Dreams 3131
It Only Happens when I Dance with You 1298
It Only Takes a Moment 2208, 1828
It Pays to Advertise 1697, 1826, 3622
It Pays to Have Friends 2925
It Rained 30 and 10 2164
It Rains All the Time 1876
It Really Doesn't Pay to Be Too Good 1707
It Really Was a Very Pretty Story 3486
It Requires a Man 3004
It Ruined Marc Antony 628
It Says Here 3473
It Seems Like Yesterday 694

It Seems Somehow, They Want Me Now 2495
It Seems to Me 1429
It Should Happen to Me 924
It Shouldn't Happen to a Dog 1609
It Showered Again 2428
It Simply Happened So 1220
It Sort of Makes a Fellow Stop and Think 2363
It Still Isn't Over 4272
It Stinks 1155
It Take a Long Pull to Get There 3541
It Takes a Drum to Make a Band 3065
It Takes a Lot of Do-Re-Mi 1892
It Takes a Lot of Trouble to Be Bad 2641
It Takes a Man 1171
It Takes a Whole Lot of Human Feeling 1072
It Takes a Woman 2208, 1828
It Takes a Woman to Catch a Man 2383
It Takes a Woman to Get a Man 206
It Takes an Idea Man 1884
It Takes an Irishman to Make Love 683
It Takes Nine Tailors to Make a Man 3736
It Takes One to Know One 362
It Takes the Cop to Cop the Girls 3855
It Takes Three to Make Music 4363
It Takes Time 600
It Takes Two 2143
It...That... 4013
It Thrills! It Thrills! 4228
It Took a Long Time 3427
It Took Me a While 2224
It Took Them 937
It Used to Be 4435
It Was a Dark and Stormy Night
(The Great Writer) 4034
It was a Glad Adventure 1600
It Was All on Account of Nipper 1266
It Was Alone 4788
It Was Always You 167, 695
It Was Destiny 1918
It Was Fate 4692
It Was for Fashion's Sake (1) 1249
It Was for Fashion's Sake (2) 1249
It Was Fun 109
It Was Good Enough for Grandma 462
It Was Good Enough for Grandpa 3209
It Was Great Fun the First Time 2331
It Was Great When It All Began 3742
It Was Just Like Magic 166
It Was Just One of Those Things 2677
It Was Long Ago 2475
It Was Love 1169
It Was Marie 4726
It Was Me 3272, 4805
It Was Meant to Be (1) 1819
It Was Meant to Be (2) 1819
It Was My Father's Fashion 3940
It Was Never Like This 1322, 2475
It Was Nice Knowing You 2187
It Was So Nice Having You 1930
It Was Worth It 1075, 3167
It Was Written in the Stars 1109
It Was You 2539, 327
It Was You Again 3055
It Wasn't a Dream 4139
It Wasn't Me 3004
It Wasn't Meant to Happen 1329, 2764
It Wasn't My Fault 2620
It Will All Come Right 906
It Will All End Up with the Right End Up 1920
It Will Be My Day 2785
It Will Keep You Guessing 3068
It Will Stand 1890
It Won't Be Long 828, 4089, 4659
It Won't Be Long Now 2734
It Won't Mean a Thing 4212
It Won't Work 1637
It Wonders Me 3509
It Works! 2681
It Would Be Nice 4630
It Would Be No Holiday 4163
It Would Have Been Something 1092
It Would Have Been Wonderful 155, 2536
It Wouldn't Be a Saturday Night
Without a Fight 4016
It Wouldn't Be You 4619
It Wouldn't Work Out 2196
It's Lovely When Your Love Loves You 3052
It's My Temperament (My Artistic
Temperament) 1175
Italia 3822
Italian Ballet Miniature 3958
Italian Straw Hat, The 693, 2178
Italian Straw Hat 4319
Italian Straw Hat, The 4319
Italian Street Song 4251, 3081
Italian Whirlwind, The 3723
Italianesque Scene 1477
Italie 579
Italy 2, 145, 3518
Italy in Technicolor 4169
Itch to Be a Witch 3654
Itch to Be Rich 2726
It'd Be Nice 3902
It'll All Blow Over 610
It'll Be All Right in a Hundred Years 4432
It'll Be Good for Me 167
It'll Be Green Again 1730
It'll Come to You 2597
It's a Bad, Bad World (1) 451
It's a Bad, Bad World (2) 451
It's a Bad, Bad World 2568
It's a Beautiful Day Today 4683
It's a Beginning 1289
It's a Big Night 2847
It's a Big, Wide, Wonderful World 70
It's a Bomb 2317
It's a Bore 1511
It's a Boy! 4695
It's a Boy 4676, 3928
It's a Boy's Life 508

It's a Brand New World 2164
It's a Bubbe Meise 573
It's a Busy Day 3777
It's a Chemical Reaction, That's All 3972
It's a Clue 1735
It's a Cold, Cruel World 3947
It's a Cute Little Way of My Own 1334
It's a Dangerous Game 2198
It's a Deal 3656
It's a Different World 4825
It's a Dolly 508
It's a Doris Day Morning 2477
It's a Dream That Never Comes True 4014
It's a Duck 2230
It's a Fact It's Easy 1155
It's a Fairy Tale 3682
It's a Far Far Better Thing 133
It's a Fine Life 3271
It's a Fine Night for Romance 2083
It's a Fine Old Institution 657
It's a Fish 170
It's a Funny Thing 572
It's a Gentlemen's World 3091
It's a Ghost! 3463
It's a Glorious Day 1974
It's a Glorious Fourth 3800
It's a Good Day 3428
It's a Good Good Mornin' 2089
It's a Good Good Morning 2090
It's a Good Thing to Have 1540
It's a Good World After All 3857
It's a Good World for All 3856
It's a Great Big Land 2430
It's a Great Country 2163
It's a Great Day for Hawaii 3371
It's a Great Idea 2235
It's a Great Life 3674
It's a Great Life If You Don't Weaken 4528
It's a Great Life If You Weaken 4602
It's a Great Little World 392, 3186
It's a Great Little World! 4392
It's a Great Sport 1339
It's a Hard, Hard, World (for a Man) 3245
It's a Hard Life Bein' a Bum 1086
It's a Helluva Way to Run a Love Affair 3509
It's a Hit 4279
It's a Hit! 2822
It's a Hit, It's a Flop 167
It's a Jolly Good Thing to Be Alive 246
It's a Law 2344
It's a Lie 2958
It's a List 194
It's a Living 67, 2320, 2443, 4061
It's a Long Day at Our Hotel 3157
It's a Long Lane That Has No Turning 188
It's a Long, Long, Day 334
It's a Long, Long March to Kansas City 793
It's a Long, Long Time 1458
It's a Long, Long Way to Tipperary 3020
It's a Long Road Home 239
It's a Long, Slow Climb Going Up but a
Short Fast Slide Coming Down 2163
It's a Long Time Till Tomorrow 1679
It's a Long Way from Broadway to
Edinboro Town 804
It's a Long Way to Berlin, but
We'll Get There 3401
It's a Long Way to Tiffany's 3246
It's a Long Way to Tipperary 736, 965, 3259
It's a Lot of Idle Gossip 1951
It's a Lovely Day Today 619
It's a Lovely Day Tomorrow 2597
It's a Lovely Night on the Hudson River 1286
(You Can Have Your "Oh, You Kids" but)
It's a Loving Wife for Mine 3977
It's a Man's World 3695, 3231
It's a Matter of Military Tactics 657
It's a Maze 3862
It's a Mighty Fine Country We Have Here
(dance) 4086
It's a Mighty Fine Country We Have Here 4086
It's a Monochrome World 1426
It's a Most Disagreeable Thing to Do 3073
It's a New Kind of Thing 4086
It's a Nice Night for It 4362
It's a Nice Place to Visit 1697, 2217
It's a Noel Coward Custom 4152
It's a Nuisance Having You Around 2484
It's a Party 944
It's a Perfect Day 2022
It's a Perfect Relationship 363
It's a Pleasure 1799
It's a Political-Satirical Revue 4635
It's a Pop, Pop, Popular Song 1378
It's a Premiere Night 2754
It's a Pressing Invitation That I Bring 3588
It's a Quaint Little Custom 4798
It's a Queer Old World 3026
It's a Scandal! It's an Outrage! 3263
It's a Secret 1212
It's a Serious Situation! 3630
It's a Simple Little System 363
It's a Sin to Tell a Lie 39
It's a Small, Small World 1962
It's a Stretchy Day 127
It's a Sunbeam 4283
It's a Sure Sign 1784
It's a Thrill! 659
It's a Thrill All Over Again 839
It's a Topsy Turvy World 3549
It's a Trust 114
It's a Typical Day 2484
It's a Very Fine World 186
(Follow Me) It's a Very Simple Matter 1961
It's a Walk-In with Walker 789
It's a Waste of Time to Worry 1148
It's a Way That They Have in Chicago 3786
It's a Way the Old Thing Has 2532
It's a Way We Have in Spain 252
It's a Widow for Mine 2767

It's a Windy Day at the Battery 2794
It's a Wishing World 4366
It's a Woman 101
It's a Wonderful Day to Be Seventeen 1363
It's a Wonderful Day to Do Nothing 4186
It's a Wonderful Land! 2509
It's a Wonderful Life 4732
It's a Wonderful Spot 1536
It's a Wonderful World 1145, 2774
It's About Magic 2820
It's About Power 2820
It's About Time 2168, 1395
It's All Done By Kindness 675
It's All for the Good of the People 4022
It's All Gotta Go Through Me 1997
It's All in Fun 70
It's All in the Book You Know (Ollendorf Duet) 2885
It's All in the Family 1911
It's All in the Game 423
It's All in Your Mind 339
It's All Mine 603
It's All O.K. 3069
It's All Off 4319
It's All Over Now 3395
It's All Right for God 1015
It's All Right If You Love (One Another) 4742
It's All Right with Me 629, 3236
It's All Right with Me If It's All Right with You 577
It's All Such a Horrible Bore 4161
It's All the Same 2727
It's All the Same to Me 3581
It's All Yours 4142
It's Allus de Same in Dixie 4098
It's Almost Time Now 4512
It's Alright Now 1073
It's Always Going to Be that Way 4649
It's Always Like the First Time 3682
It's Always Love 4196
It's Always Nice Weather Indoors or Oh! Oh! Oh! Says Rosie 4762
It's Always Orange Day in California 628
It's Always Summertime at the Winter Garden 3403
It's Always the Way 1603
It's Amazing What God Can Do 4460
It's an Art 4744
It's An Awful Thing to Not Know Where You Are 75
It's an Old Spanish Custom 657, 4345
It's Autumn Again 197
It's Awfully Hard to Shop 3747
It's Awfully Hard when Mother's Not Along 3547
It's Awfully Nice to Love One Girl 4293
It's Bad for Me 3214
It's Beautiful 1104
It's Been a Long, Long Time 4743
It's Been a While 373
It's Been Done 1048
It's Been Nice 2183
It's Been Pleasant, Pleasant 3383
It's Best Not to Say too Much About It 3350
It's Better Rich 2608
It's Better to Give 2320
It's Better to Have Loved and Lost Than Never to Have Loved at All 3765
It's Better with a Band 1298, 2171
It's Better with a Union Man (Bertha the Sewing Machine Girl) 3501
It's Bound to Be Right on the Night 1467
It's Charming 1004
It's Christmas Today 2052
It's Comin' True 1786
It's Coming Back to Me 3476
It's Coming Off Today 1470
It's Commencement Day 3361
It's Crazy, It's Mad 1887
It's Delicious 400
It's Delightful Down in Chile 1475, 2590
It's Delightful to Be Married 3387, 4390
It's Delovely 3674
It's Different Now 4269
It's Different with Me 4778
It's Distinctly Nice 4064
It's Doom 3845
It's Easier to Kiss than Talk 1919
It's Easy for Her 3305
It's Easy-Let-Go 1450
It's Easy to Lie to Your Husband 1424
It's Easy to Love 3955
It's Easy to Say Hello (But So Hard to Say Goodbye) 3489
It's Easy to Sing 3818
It's Easy When You Know How 1373
It's Enough to Make a Lady Fall in Love 989
It's Even My Endeavor 1392
It's Every Girl's Ambition 4372
It's Feminine 2010
It's for the Young 1439
It's Fun for the Money Tonight 1415
It's Fun to Be Free 2447
It's Fun to Be in London 3913
It's Fun to Think 64
It's Funny about Love 1770
It's Gayer Whistling as You Go (Gaily I Whistle a Song) 1476
It's Getting Better 4635
It's Getting Dark on Old Broadway 4816
It's Getting Harder to Love You 2702
It's Getting Hotter in the North 3949
It's Going to Be a Pretty Wedding 1246
It's Going to Be a Very Busy Day 3486
It's Going to Be Good to Be Gone 2064
It's Gone Eight Bells 1392
It's Gonna Be Fun 140
It's Good 4237
It's Good-Bye Pal 1563
It's Good for a Woman's Morale 4060
It's Good for You to Exercise Your Mind 3783
It's Good to Be Alive 3113, 4863
It's Good to Be Back Home 1227
It's Good to Have God on Your Side 4679

It's Got to Be Bad to Be Good 599
It's Got to Be Done 2844
It's Got to Be Love 3283
It's Gotta Be Venus 3346
It's Great 1227
It's Great Sport Just the Same 4630
It's Great to Be a Doughboy 1722
It's Great to Be a Soldier Man 3480
It's Great to Be a Wonderful Detective 4644
It's Great to Be Alive 177, 1979, 4177, 4314
It's Great to Be an Actor 2408
It's Great to Be an Animal in America 2657
It's Great to Be an Orphan 2608
It's Great to Be Back on Broadway 2980
It's Great to Be Crazy 2695
It's Great to Be Gay 2069
It's Great to Be Home Again 3713
It's Great to Be in Love 1136, 2363
It's Great to Be Married 2549
It's Great to Be Married
(and Lead a Single Life) 4283
It's Great to Communicate 3160
It's Great to Hate Yourself 2580
It's Greek to Me 4422
It's Hard I Know 3817
It's Hard to Be a Hero 4735
It's Hard to Be a Lady 2276
It's Hard to Be a Lady All Night Long 2275
It's Hard to Care 3927
It's Hard to Find a King Like Me 9
It's Hard to Love Just One Girl All the Time 4382
It's Hard to Love Somebody (When
That Somebody Don't Love You) 1917
It's Hard to Love Somebody When
Your Somebody Don't Love You 295
It's Hard to Tell 2363
It's Hard to Understand the Men 1868
It's Heaven to Boheme 1228
It's Heaven to Me 3489
It's High Time 1475
It's High Time I Got the Low Down on You 3103
It's High Time I Got the Low-Down 3104
It's His Kiss (The Shoop Shoop Song) 3695
It's Home 1420
It's Hopper 2519
It's Hot in Chile 226
It's Hot Up Here 4210
It's How You Deal with It 2578
It's in the Air 418
It's in the Cards 4279, 3696
It's in the Stars 3946
It's In, It's Out 1756
It's Italy 223
It's Just a Little Love Song 1656
It's Just a Question of Technique 2702
It's Just an Old Spanish Custom 4025
It's Just Like I Was You 4523
It's Just Like the Good Old Days 2847
It's Just that Feeling for Home 2308
It's Just What I Wanted 2267
It's Just Yours 2847
It's Legitimate 1061
It's Like 4038
It's Like a Beautiful Woman 1760
It's Like a Movie 4325
It's Lonely 52
It's Lonesome Tonight 4387
It's Love! 20
It's Love 519, 3381, 1883, 4050, 4595, 4734
It's Love, I Think 255
It's Love—I Think 158
It's Love! It's Love! 4619
It's Love That Makes the World Go 'Round 2485
It's Lovely to Love a Lovely Girl 4723
It's Magic 4743
It's Making Me Love You All the More 1334
It's Mardi Gras 2595
It's Mardi Gras Time 4127
It's Matrimonial Weather 2178
It's Me 2797
It's Me Again 4772
It's Me They Talk About 2290
It's Men Like You 2388
It's Merely a Matter of Time 1866
It's Money-It's Fame-It's Love 2808
It's Money That I Love 2852, 2787
It's More Fun Than a Picnic 206
It's Much Too Nice to Cut 1507
It's My Belief 2134
It's My Body 2473
It's My Day 3159
It's My Nature 1856
It's My Party 338, 4193
It's My Turn Now 4192, 889
It's Naughty to Be Kissed 954
It's Naughty-But It's Nice 2070
It's Never Been Done Before 339
It's Never Quite the Same 3234
It's Never That Easy 784
It's Never Too Late to Fall in Love 507
It's Never Too Late to Mendelssohn 2386
It's New York Town for Mine 2122
It's Nice 1412
It's Nice to Be a Boy Sometimes 3828
It's Nice to Be a Girl 2779
It's Nice to Be a Widow 625
It's Nice to Be Nasty 3318
It's Nice to Get Money from Home 1624
It's Nice to Have a Sweetheart 4434
It's Nice to Have Some Money 2641
It's Nice to Know 3329
It's Nice Weather for Ducks 3094
It's Nicer in Nice 507
It's Nicer to Be Naughty 4795
It's No Fun Eating Alone 4331
It's No Laughing Matter 4777
It's No Use Crying for the Moon! 2524
It's Nobody's Business but My Own 4840
It's None of My Business 2702, 1276
It's Not a Commerical, It's Art 2676

It's Not a Real Wedding 674
It's Not Christmas Yet 2224
It's Not Easy 410
It's Not Easy Being Next 2785
It's Not Easy to Change Your Life 337
It's Not for Me 2596
It's Not Irish 2268
It's Not My Dish of Tea 2928
It's Not So Bad to Be Good 612
It's Not Such a Brave New World, Mr. Huxley 4167
It's Not the End of the World (If He's Younger) 4301
It's Not the End of the World (If He's Married) 4301
It's Not the End of the World (If I Lose Him) 4301
It's Not the Principle, It's Just the Money 2020
It's Not the Proper Thing 2745
It's Not the Trick Itself, but It's the Tricky Way It's Done 1845
It's Not the Truth 757
It's Not the Weather Cock that Changes, It's the Wind 1994
It's Not the World, It's You 2716
It's Not Their Mother 1342
It's Not Too Late 3760
It's Not What You Say 3207
It's Not What You Weigh 1298
It's Not Where You Start 603, 3869
It's Not Wrong to Have Fun 1917
It's Nothing but a Bubble 4803
It's Oh So Nice in Your Arms 853
It's Only a Game 2230
It's Only a Paper Moon (If You Believed in Me) 1672
It's Only a Paper Moon 4799
It's Only a Piece of Advice 1417
It's Only a Play 424, 1406
It's Only a Show 2949
It's Only Been Done on the Stage 1557
It's Only Business (1) 451
It's Only Business (2) 451
It's Only Or-ee-vwor (Au Revoir) 3558
It's Only the Best Yet 1258
It's Only Thirty Years 2680
It's Only Your Carriage That Counts 4283
It's Our Time Now 415
It's Out of My Hands 2941
It's Over 4288, 2320
It's Paris Everywhere 4767
It's Perfectly All Right 1538
It's Permissible 68
It's Pleasant and Delightful 1748
It's Positively You 2887
It's Possible 757, 759, 3051
It's Pouring 3067
It's Pretty in the City 1894
It's Pretty Soft for Simon 3081
It's Probably Just As Well 1203
It's Queer What a Little Love Will Do 1003
It's Quick and Easy ('No Botta E Via) 3798
It's Quiet on the Potomac Tonight 1474
It's Rainin' 3814
It's Rainin' on Prom Night 1664
It's Raining Sunshine 3795
It's Rather a Lark 1726
(Hooray, Hooray) It's Ray-Ray-Raining 4821
It's Really Very Singular 2619
It's Really You 729
It's Sad to Be Lonesome 2661
It's She and It's Me 946
It's Silk, Feel It 3286, 4829
It's Simply My Smile 4492
It's So Clear 3066
It's So Different in London 361
It's So Easy to Fall in Love 580
It's So Easy to Say 2339
It's So Easy to Sing (About Things in the Southland) 903
It's So Frightening Out There 4108
It's So Good 4124
It's So Heartwarming 298
It's So Nice 2220, 3653
It's So Nice to Be Civilized 2173
It's So Nice to Have a Man Around the House 2165
It's So Simple 270
It's Spring 2439
It's Spring I Guess 4041
It's Style That Makes the Girl 256
It's Such a Different World 2420
It's Super Nice 2163
It's Superman 2163
It's Teen Time 2579
It's Terrible 1094
It's Terribly, Horribly, Frightfully Nice 3800
It's That Kind of a Neighborhood 3843
It's That Time of the Year 3638
It's the Better Me 4702
It's the Bump 1111
It's the Clothes that Make the Man 2774
It's the Company 1255
It's the Cook Who Saves the Day 3184
It's the Dancer You Love Who Makes You Love to Dance 3185
It's the Darndest Thing 3993
It's the Dress That Makes the Girl 4382
It's the End of the Party 610
It's the Girl Everytime, It's the Girl 2397
It's the Girls 2498
It's the Going Home Together 1600
It's the Gown That Makes the Gal That Makes the Guy 3966
It's the Gown that Makes the Girl 3087
It's the Hard-Knock Life 150
It's the Hat and Not the Girl 351
It's the Hat That Makes the Lady 2580
It's the Irish 2534, 4169
It's the Irish in Me 197
It's the Jay Town 1031
It's the Least We Could Do 2196
It's the Little Bit of Irish 627
It's the Little Things That Count 2559
It's the Little Things That Count in Life 3486

It's the Little Things That Count Most Ev'ry Way 1334
It's the Little Things That Irritate the Most 4093
It's the Nicest Sort of Feeling (Ting-a-ling-a-ling) 2336
It's the Nuns 1059
It's the Only One for Me 102, 1335
It's the Perfect Time to Get Married 2307
It's the Right Time to Be Rich 1077
It's the Same Old Chow 1624
It's the Same Old South, The 2809
It's the Same the Whole World Over 750
It's the Scotch 1794
It's the Second Time You Meet that Matters 3845
It's the Shirt 1845
It's the Smart Little Feller Who Stocked Up His Cellar, That's Getting the Beautiful Girls 4814
It's the Smile That Gets 'Em 3726
It's the Strangest Thing 16
It's the Thing to Do 1290
It's the Things You Do with Your Feet 1658
It's the Unexpected Happens 1458
It's the Uniform that Makes the Man 4453
It's the Weather 961
It's the Witching Hour By the Old Water Tower 1474
It's the Woman Who Pays 1557
It's the Women 2619
It's the Youth in Me 4253
It's Three O'Clock 3011
It's Time for a Cheer-Up Song 550
It's Time for a Love Song 652
It's Time for an Improvisation 3997
It's Time for Something New 3628
It's Time I Had a Break 4702
It's Time to Go 36
It's Time to Say 'Aloha' 1840
It's Time to Say Goodnight 3186
It's Today 2208, 2713
It's Too Late 4788
It's Too Late Now 353
It's Too Much 840
It's Tough to Be a Flower Girl in Uric 2020
It's Tough to Be a Hostess 3342
It's Tough to Be a Man 3493
It's Tough to Be a Working Girl 3493
It's Tough to Love a Girl Who Doesn't Love You 2485
It's Traditional 2511
It's Twelve O'Clock 42
It's Up to a Cop to Cop a Pretty Maid 1378
It's Up to Me 64, 2163, 2307, 3998
It's Up to the Band 4821
It's Up to Us 3888
It's Up to You 603, 2175
It's Up to You to Do the Rest 1532
It's Up with the Cup and Down with the Ale 4161
It's Very Clear 4032
It's Very Hard to Be a Boy 2879
It's Wasn't a Real One 3073
It's What Eve Said to Adam 350
It's What You Believe In 3453
It's What You Do (That Makes Your Wishes Come True) 760
It's Wilde! 2177
It's Wonderful 1756, 3775, 3985
It's Wonderful Being a Genius 1091
It's Worth While Waiting for Someone Worth While 2546
It's You 487, 4690, 956, 3016
It's You Again 3468
It's You Again, Kid 1611
It's You for Me 3801
It's You I Love 4087
It's You I Want 4677
It's You I Want to Love Tonight 3011
It's You Who Makes Me Young 681
It's Your Fault 1094
It's Your Life 2702, 3091
It's Your Turn 4379
It's Yourself 2682
Itsche 343
Ivan Valensky 4041
I've a Garden in Sweden 2528
I've a Little Favor 3710
I've a Million Reasons Why I Love You 954
I've a Most Decided Notion 1165
I've a Parasol for You Dear 3203
I've a Shooting Box in Scotland 3378
I've a Sweetheart in Each Star 1685
I've a Very Nasty Temper So Beware 1521
I've Already Started In 4516
I've Always Been a Good Old Sport 2730
I've Always Been a Lucky Little Guy 4453
I've Always Been Brought Up Polite 1473
I've Always Been Fond of Babies (That's Why I'm in Love with You) 2214
I've Always Been the Patsy 543
I've Always Loved You 1605, 4542
I've an Inkling 1313
I've Been 'Buked 4460
I've Been a-Bragging 3571
I've Been About a Bit 3177
I've Been Around the Horn 708
I've Been Decorated 48, 3773
I've Been Discharged by Them All 1417
I've Been Floating Down the Old Green River 2696
I've Been Fooling Around 1774
I've Been Here Before 784
I've Been Here Before with Love 70
I've Been in Love 1695
I've Been in Those Shoes 550
I've Been Invited to a Party 1564
I've Been Kissed in San Francisco 1307
I've Been Looking for a Perfect Man 1183
I've Been Looking for You 968, 3051
I've Been Married 3055
I've Been Married Once 632
I've Been Sent Back to the First Grade 1139

I've Been Starting Tomorrow 518
I've Been There and I'm Back 3234
I've Been to America 4219
I've Been to the Durbar 4219
I've Been to the Moon 4416
I've Been Too Busy 2987
I've Been True to Myself 3186
I've Been Waiting 1176
I've Been Waiting All My Life 287
I've Been Waiting for You 969
I've Been Waiting for You All the Time 3923
I've Been Waiting for Your Phone Call 2611
I've Been Wanting You 969
I've Been Watching You 4358
I've Booked the Date 45
I've Changed My Mind 4303
I've Come Along to Paris 4115
I've Come Home to Stay 1776
I've Come to Wive It Wealthily in Padua 2331
I've Confessed to the Breeze 3249
I've Confessed to the Breeze I Love You 3184
I've Conquered My Fears of Younger Boys 3280
I've Danced to Beat the Band 4547
I've 'Eard the Bloody 'Indoos 'As It Worse 2047
I've Even Been in Love 4512
I've Fallen in Love 2004
I've Fallen Out of Love 2808, 4025
I've Found a New Baby 4282
I've Found the Bluebird 605
I've Found the Girl I've Been Looking For 1753
I've Given My Heart to You Dear 1629
I've Given My Heart to You, Dear 3256
I've Gone Off the Deep End 3138
I've Gone Romantic on You 1973
I've Got a Baby 4532
I've Got a Bug in My Head 2140
I've Got a Crush on You 4399, 4179, 4443, 4581
I've Got a Date with a Dream 478
I've Got a Day Off Today 3157
I've Got a Feelin' You're Foolin' 3992, 393
I've Got a Feeling for Somebody 2392
I've Got a Feeling I'm Falling 39
I've Got a Friend 1750
I've Got a Girl 1015, 4609
I've Got a Goose 1727
I've Got a Great Idea 1536
I've Got a Heart Full of Rhythm 887
I've Got a Letter from My Jack 762
I've Got a Little Chalet in the Valley 3525
I've Got a Little Hubby Now 4554
I've Got a Little List 1987
I've Got a Little Secret 941
I've Got a Lot to Learn About Life 3094
I've Got a Man on the Moon 3204
I've Got a Mind of My Own 1734
I've Got a Molly 2925
I've Got a New Idea 4234
I've Got a New Rhythm for Old Shoes 1415
I've Got a One Track Mind 2187
I've Got a Pain 2599
I've Got a Pair of Swinging Doors that Lead Right Into My Heart 1626
I've Got a Passport from Georgia (and I'm Going to the U.S.A. 2259
I've Got a Penny 521
I've Got a Pocketful of Dreams 2850
I've Got a Problem 3067
I've Got a Rainbow Working for Me Now 989
I've Got a Sentry 3973
I've Got a Shooting Box in Scotland 3865
I've Got a Smile 357
I've Got a Song to Sing 2388
I've Got a Surprise for You 3763
I've Got a Sweet Tooth Bothering Me 4148
I've Got a Vegetable Garden (Garden of Liberty) (Vegetable Song) 4634
I've Got a Wonderful Future 4028
I've Got a Wonderful Girl 4661
I've Got a 'Yes' Girl 2827
I've Got an Awful Lot to Learn 3865
I've Got Another Baby 1259
I've Got Ants in My Pants 1136
I've Got Elgin Watch Movements in My Hips 1063
I've Got 'Em Standing In Line 4090
I've Got Enough to Marry You 4037
I've Got Everybody's Number 3982
I've Got Everything I Want but You 4642
I've Got Feelings 3273
I've Got Five Dollars 111
I've Got Good Common Sense 645, 2044
I've Got Him Dead 4165
I've Got Him Now! 4808
I've Got It 3076, 3680
I've Got It Again 1448
I've Got It All 3279
I've Got Me 283, 341
I've Got Money in the Bank 2761
I've Got My Captain Working for Me Now 4813
I've Got My Eyes on Tomorrow 2928
I've Got My Feet on the Ground 1386
I've Got My Fingers Crossed 39
I've Got My Man Where I Want Him 3950
I've Got My Orders 593
I've Got No Use for Opera when There's Ragtime Around 1332
I've Got No Use for Opera When There's Ragtime 4630
I've Got Nothin' to Do 4060
I've Got Nothing to Give 4384
I've Got Quelque Chose 1690
I've Got Rings on My Fingers or Mumbo-Jumbo-Jijjiboo-J. O'Shay 2858, 4757
I've Got Some Unfinished Business with You 2453, 4517
I've Got Somebody Waiting 1921
I've Got Somethin' 1889
I've Got Something 3020
I've Got Something Better 1508
I've Got the Blues 2140
I've Got the Man 1722

I've Got the Nerve to Be in Love 3501
I've Got the Nicest Little Home in Dixie 4037
I've Got the President's Ear 206
I've Got the Red White and Blues 1176
I've Got the Right to Moan 3822
I've Got the Sweetest Girl in Maryland 4037
I've Got the World on a String 877
I've Got Them Feelin' Too Good Today Blues 964
I've Got Those One Foot Blues 4334
I've Got to Be a Rug Cutter 4091
I've Got to Be Around 2983
I've Got to Be Famous 430
I've Got to Be Lovely for Harry 2807, 4199
I've Got to Be Me 1611
I've Got to Be There 3379
I've Got to Dance 4555
I've Got to Do What I Want Today 2172
I've Got to Find a Reason 656
I've Got to Get a Drink 2455
I've Got to Get Hot 1493
I've Got to Get Somewhere with You 3091
I've Got to Give Her Her Own Way 3372
I've Got to Hand It to You 297
I've Got to Know 2283
I've Got to Leave You 2549
I've Got to Pass Your House to Get to My House 3376
I've Got to Trust You 3871
I've Got to Try Everything Once 4279
I've Got Troubles of My Own 2675
I've Got What It Takes 3297, 4763
I've Got What It Takes and It Breaks My Heart to Give It Away 166
I've Got What You Want 170
I've Got You 2976
I've Got You and You've Got Me 1534
I've Got You on My Mind 1018, 1453
I've Got You On My Mind 1657
I've Got You on My Mind 4132
I've Got You to Lean On 162
I've Got You to Thank for All This 2539
I've Got Your Number 2523
I've Gotta Crow 3453
I've Gotta Go Back to Texas 4603
I've Gotta Keep My Eye on You 2747
I've Gotta See a Man About His Daughter 4374
I've Grown Accustomed to Her Face 3038
I've Grown Up (Reprise) 70
I've Grown Up 70
I've Had a Lovely Time, Good Night 1845
I've Had Enough 3841
I've Had Everything but a Man 164
I've Had It 1970
I've Had It with Men 1155
I've Had My Share 2430
I've Hardly Known You Long Enough 3154
I've Heard It All Before 3928
I've Heard That Before 4553
I've Heard That Song Before 4743
I've Her Portrait Nex' My Heart 1392
I've Just Been to a Wedding 2114
I've Just Been Waiting for You 2922
I've Just Begun 299
I've Just Lost My Teddy Bear 3676
I've Just Seen Her 64
I've Known a Lot of Guys 2033
I've Known You All My Life 2417
I've Laid Him on the Shelf 2675
I've Learnt a Lot 2389
I've Looked for Trouble 4212
I've Lost My Bow 4381
I've Lost My Gal 2232
I've Lost My Heart 4335
I've Lost My Heart but I Don't Care 4185
I've Loved Only Once 913
I've Made a Habit of You 2545
I've Made Up My Mind 383
I've Made Up My Mind to Mind a Maid Made Up Like You 3962
I've Missed You 3312
I've Never Attended at All 408
I've Never Been a Woman Before 716
I've Never Been in Love Before 1706, 3444
I've Never Been Introduced to You 671
I've Never Been Over There 1480
I've Never Been So Happy 150
I've Never Found a Girl Like You 2430
I've Never Had a Manifestation 1891
I've Never Had a Sweetheart 1801
I've Never Said I Love You 1012
I've Never Seen Anything Like It in My Life 64
I've No Idea Where I'm Going (The Victoria Variations) 4560
I've No Patience with a Soldier 3052
I've Nothing to Offer 622
I've Planned a Rendezvous 2293
I've Played for You 2430
I've Said Goodbye to Broadway 4810
I've Saved All My Lovin' for You 4810
I've Seen No Indians Yet 15
I've Shaken Everything I've Got 3973
I've Spent All My Life Preserving Things 3280
I've Still Got My Bite 2173
I've Still Got My Health 1018, 3359
I've Taken Such a Fancy to You 1538
I've Told Every Little Star 2204, 2204, 2372, 3020
I've Told Ev'ry Little Star 3014
I've Told My Love 4464
I've Trampled All Over 2225
I've Tried Everything 4238
I've Waited for You 718
I've Waited Long for Thee 3626
I've Walked in the Moonlight 2105
Ivy and Oak 1530
Ivy and the Oak, The 4250
Ivy League, The 1341, 412
Ixed Mup 2026
Izicatulo Gumboot Dance 4579
Izintombi Zomjolo 4438

J

J. J. Flynn 3312
J.B. Pictures, Inc. 4623
Ja-Da 395
Jabberwock Song 58
Jabberwocky 54, 2843
Jack and Jill 1271, 1313, 2180, 3233, 3307, 3848, 1724
Jack Be Nimble 2134
Jack in the Box 4497
Jack-in-the-Box, The 306
Jack in the Country 3195
Jack Ketch 1736
Jack-O-Lantern Boogieman, The 2008
Jack-o'-Lantern 1757
Jack O'Lantern 2465
Jack O'Lantern Girl, The 2160
Jack O'Lantern Joe 3422
Jack O'Lantern Love 2394
Jack O'Lantern Man 1021, 2215
Jack O'Lantern Moon 3425
Jack Roosevelt Robinson 1289
Jack Rose 1340
Jack the Ripper 345
Jackdaw of Rhiems, The (sketch) 4545
Jackie 2188
Jackie, The 3943
Jackie Coogan 199, 3406
Jackie Look, The 3889
Jackies 2853
Jackpot 2187
Jack's the Boy 1470
Jackson Island 2027
Jacob and Sons 2242
Jacob in Egypt 2242
Jacob Is Dead 1865
Jacob's Ladder 1251, 2992
Jacobowsky and the Colonel 1660
Jacqueline 1091
Jacques D'Iraq 2987
Jade 4793
Jaded, Degraded Am I 4060
Jag 1047
Jag, a Drone and a Tank of Air, A 4094
Jaggy-Jazz, The 3043
J'Ai 322
J'ai Deux Amants 3079
J'ai Deux Amours 166
Jail Bird and the Tiger, The 2155
Jail-Birds of a Feather 1193
Jail Birds, The 2825
Jail Life Walk 2801
Jailer, Jailer 1068
Jailhouse Blues 2052, 2177, 4595
Jailhouse Rock 4031
Jake the Ball Player 3926
Jalopy Song, The 1390
Jamaica Is Waiting 3690
Jamais D'La Vie 2770
Jambalaya 1890
Jamboree 3035
James the Chauffer 2739
Jamie 3389
Jamie's Responsibilities 4366
Jane 250, 1290, 1746
Jane, Jane, Jane 2711
Jane's Song 3565
Janet Get Up 4272
Janette 2705
Janho 9
Janitor's Boy, The 4467
Janitor, The (King Janitoro) 3437
Janken and Meken 284
Jap-German Sextette 4340
Japanese Baby 604
Japanese Ballet 4747
Japanese Box, The 710
Japanese Dream 894
Japanese Elopement, A 2733
Japanese Flirtation Dance 2944
Japanese Jazz 4477, 4530
Japanese Moon 4271
Japanese Sandman, The 986
Japanese Serenade 718
Japanese Toyland 1778
Japanese Umbrella, A 2159
Japanese Willow 1829
Jarge, We've Such a Tale to Tell (Opening Chorus) 3618
Jasbo Brown 3541
Jason's Bar Mitzvah 1234
Jason's Therapy 2746
Jasper's Vision 3070
Jassamine Lane 740
J'Attends Un Navire 2753
Javanese Dance 758
Jaw Bone of a Donkey 2164
Jaybird 2225
Jazz 1182, 2582, 3146
Jazz All Your Troubles Away 2816
Jazz Babies Ball 3962
Jazz Band All My Own 1867
Jazz Band Am the Firstest Aid for Me, A 1632
Jazz Band Man, The 986
Jazz Blues 4182
Jazz City 124
Jazz Fugue (inst.) 612
Jazz-How I Love It 2816
Jazz Jubilee 1342
Jazz-Ma-Tazz 1920
Jazz Marimba 627
Jazz Marimba (Jazzamarimba Dance) 2939
Jazz Reception (Kindly Nullify Your Fears) (Opening Act I — Me for You) 1800
Jazz Time Came from the South 1058, 2462
Jazz Time City 1753
Jazz Town Jazz 2489
Jazz Up Jasper 1404
Jazz Wedding 4427

Jazz with Me 1549
Jazz Your Troubles Away 3808
Jazza-Da-Dadda (Jazzadadadoo) 487
Jazza Painted Jazza Ma Renos 2706
Jazzanova 2870
Jazzbo Brown 2195, 2796
Jazzbo the Jazz King 4382
Jazzin' the Alphabet 4604
Jazzing the Alphabet 764
Jazzing Thunder Storming Dance (Thunderstorm Dance) 1174
Jazzing Toes 2276
Jazzmania 892, 1129
Jazztime Baby 740
Jazztown Features 2992
Jazzy Scene 3717
Je Cousse 4062
Je M'em Fiche 4292
Je M'em Fiche du Sex Appeal! 1202
Je Ne Ai Rien 3551
Je Ne Comprends Pas 2856
Je Ne la Comprend Pas 1264
Je ne le Comprends Pas 1392
Je Ne Parle Pas Anglais 1632
Je Ne Sais Pas 4421
Je Ne Savais Pas 839
Je Sais Que Vous Etes Gentil (It's Our Wedding Day) 377
Je Suis le Tenebreux 220
Je T'Aime 4367
Je T'Aime—I Love You 3074
'Je T'Aime' Means I Love You 1461
Je T'Aime Vous Paris 716
Je Vous Aime 200, 3617
Je Vous Aime Milady 2949
Jealous 3655
Jealous Moon 4811
Jealous of Me 395
(War Is Hell But Oh You) Jealousy 1088
Jealousy (War Is Hell, But Oh, You Green-Eyed Monster, Jealousy!) 1088
Jealousy 2334, 2408
Jealousy Begins at Home 1384
Jealousy Duet 369, 4368, 4370, 4371
Jean 4528
Jean's Magic Song 2909
Jeanne—Marie 1764
Jeannette and Her Little Wooden Shoes (Sabot Dance) (Clip Clop Clop) (Wooden Shoes Dance) 4250
Jeannie 3873
Jeannie with the Light Brown Hair 4149
Jeannie's Packin' Up 530
Jeepers Creepers 3840
Jeff's Plaints 2918
Jeff's Song 1804
Jefferson Davis Tyler's General Store 1363, 1892, 4416
Jehoshaphat Makes Up His Mind 4157
Jekyll and Hyde 1687
Jellicle Ball, The 678
Jellicle Songs for Jellicle Cats 678
Jelly Beans at Walgreens 4782
Jelly Donuts and Chocolate Cake 699
Jelly Roll 1890, 2800
Jelly Roll Party 2093
Jelly's Jam 2200
Jemima Green 1912
Jennie 2201
Jennie Jones 3357
Jennifer's Song 1804
Jenny 1702, 1370, 1498, 2426, 4713, 4689
Jenny Is Like an Angel 2290
Jenny, Jenny (Save Your Dreams) 3383
Jenny Kiss'd Me 2633
Jenny Kissed Me 1741, 2278
Jenny Lind 117, 1688
Jenny Rebecca 4398
Jenny von Westphalen 2290
Jenny's Ball 3297
Jeremiah 2653
Jeremiah Obadiah 2134
Jerezanos 2407
Jericho 1839, 3705
Jerome the Bogie Man 2481
Jerome's Song 3517
Jerry 3158
Jerry, My Soldier Boy 2453
Jerry's Dream 1412
Jerry's Ecstasy 4196
Jersey 157
Jersey City Rhapsody 4415
Jersey Heart 2861
Jersey Plunk, The 3301
Jersey Walk (Shake 'Em Up Kid) 1965
Jerusalem 1075, 2075, 732
Jess and Jamie 2711
Jesse James Glide, The 1826
Jesse James Robbed This Train 1037
Jest Her Way 2498
Jester's Tale, The 4157
Jesus 4609
Jesus Come Down 1612
Jesus Hi 1116
Jesus Is Mine 4030
Jesus Is My Main Man 4343, 4459
Jesus Remembers When Others Forget 4460
Jesus Sweetest Name I Know 2992
Jesus the Light of the World 344
Jet Song 4625
Jew Do Your Duty 3780
Jewel Ballet 2939
Jewel of a Duel, A 2464
Jewel of Asia, The 1470
Jewel Song, The 3406
Jewel Song 4153
Jewelry 270
Jewels of Pandora, The 4637
Jibin' 966
Jig (inst.) 1162

Jig 2111
Jig, The (dance) 2201
Jig (dance) 2268
Jig Hop, The 1275
Jig Is Up, The 4498
Jig Saw Jamboree 4291
Jig Walk 741
Jigaboo Jig, The 1779
Jigaree, The 4747
Jiggle Your Feet 2380
Jiggs and His Pipe 542
Jigi Hoo 1499
Jijibo, The 4241
Jikel Emaweni 4579
Jill 2976
Jilted 3225
Jim 1888
Jim and Della 1509
Jim, Consider What You Are Doing! 4178
Jim Dandy 741, 1342
Jim Jam Jems 1919, 2214
Jim Jam Jumpin' 4534
Jim-Jam Man 2215
Jim's Lament 2556
Jimmie 2216, 3000, 3821
Jimmy 2217, 4821
Jimmy and Me 203
Jimmy Jimmy 2754
Jimmy on the Chute 1429
Jimmy the Well-Dressed Man 1120
Jimmy the Well Dressed Man 3953
Jimmy Valentine and Sherlock Holmes 487
Jimmy's Bar 1644
Jimsy 2636
Jimtown's Fisticuffs 3963
Jingle, The 846
Jingle Bells 3175, 4858
Jingle Dance, The 3719
Jingle Feet 1731
(I Got Spurs That) Jingle Jangle Jingle 3444
Jingle Jingle Jingle 3794
Jingle of the Jungle 881
Jingle Step 1174
Jitterbug (inst.), The 3905
Jitterbug Jamboree 888
Jitterbug Waltz 39
Jitterbugging with the Young Folks 512
Jitters 2034
Jiu Jitsu Waltz 4801
Jive 2085
Jive (A Lesson in Jive) 887
Jive Drill 3966
Jive Guy 1885
Jivette Boogie Beat 2427
Jo-Jo the Cannible Kid 446
Joan 407
Joan of Arc 1248
Joan of Arc (You Can't Keep a Good Girl Down) 3819
Joanne 746
Job Application, The 287
Job for Me, A 1742
Job Hunter 408
Job I Highly Recommend, A 198
Job Interview 407
Jo'burg Talking Blues 4579
Jockey Song 1124
Jockey's Life for Mine 740
Jocko Homo 3739
Jockomo 1890
Joe 4744
Joe and Paul's 1609
Joe Crowell 2703
Joe Dynamite's Dentistry Song 4693
Joe Porter's Car Is Seen 1948
Joe Simon 3982
Joe Worker 919
Joe's Liver 3873
Joey, Joey, Joey 2961, 3444
Joey Looks into the Future Ballet (inst.) 3353
Jogging Along Thru the Park 4374
Jografree 4735
Johann Der Zweite 2262
Johanna (1) 4233
Johanna (2) 4233
Johanna (3) 4233
Johannesburg 4635
John Anderson, My Jo John 3450
John Barleycorn 1893
John Birch Society 3889
John Brown's Body 2203
John Chinamen 3025
John Dough 1515
John Held, Jr. 3407
John 19:41 2212
John Paul Jones 1336
John Singing About a Man 2225
John Sweet Ballet, The (dance) 3564
John's Song 430
Johnnie 199
Johnnies of Long Acre Square, The 559
Johnny 1195
Johnny (dance) 2268
Johnny Angel 4193, 4264
Johnny B. Goode 4534, 580, 3739
Johnny Cake 183
Johnny Come Follow Me 1911
Johnny Come Lately 1049, 2611
Johnny Freedom 1390
Johnny from London Town 1014
Johnny, Get Off the Corner 3809
Johnny Is a Hoarder 2447
Johnny Is My Darling 1616
Johnny Is the Man for Me 3239
Johnny Mishuga 3110
Johnny O 3831
Johnny One Note 247
Johnny Pye and the Foolkiller 2229
Johnny Ride the Sky 911
Johnny Space 562

Johnny Strong 1535
Johnny Too Bad 3814
Johnny Wanamaker 1448
Johnny's Arrest and Homecoming 2228
Johnny's Back in Town 395
Johnny's Creed 280
Johnny's Cursing Song 3831
Johnny's Song 369
Johnny's Song (Listen to My Song) 2228
Johnny's Speech 2228
Johny Wise 1274
Join in Pleasure 1193
Join It Right Away 3359
Join Our Jubilee 68
Join Our Ranks 3365
Join the Army, Kill 2472
Join the Circus 305
Join the Dance 593
Join the Families 1565
Join the Marines 3813
Join the Movies 2969
Join the Navy 1916
Join the Navy? 3868
Join Us in a Cup of Tea 2439, 2483, 3954
Joint Is Jumpin', The 39
Jojo the Cannibal Kid 447
Joke, The 1310
Joke a Cola 3651
Joke's on Us, The 4086
Joker, The 3731
Jokers 2230
Jokes 550, 2771
Jolie's Back in Town 2235
Jolly British Tar 1392
Jolly Coachman, The 3496
Jolly Coppers on Parade 2787
Jolly Good Fellow 1640, 3177, 3771
Jolly Good Uncle 2919
Jolly Jazz Joy Man 980
Jolly Jungle Boys 9
Jolly Life Is the Sailors, A 3951
Jolly Little Japs 3856, 3857
Jolly Me 2574
Jolly Miller, The 3732, 4187
Jolly Old Owl, The 3266
Jolly Old Pirates 1340
Jolly Old Potentate, A 2315
Jolly Old Tar 998
Jolly, Rich and Fat 754
Jolly Theatrical Season, A 3161
Jolly Theatrical Season 3366
Jolly Troubador Sketch, The (inst.) 1657
Jolly Young Jacks Are We 1470
Jolly Yourself Along 522
Jollyanna 2234
Jonah 647
Jonah and the Whale 2237
Jonah Man 4390
Jonah's Melodrama 2236
Jonah's Wail 1924
Jones' Family Friends, The 403
Jones Is a Jones, A 2323
Jorrocks 2240
Jose, Can't You See! 1979
Joseph 1716
Joseph All the Time 2242
Joseph, James and John 2936
Joseph, Son of David, Do Not Fear to Take Mary for Your Wife 755
Joseph Taylor, Jr. 85
Joseph's Coat 2242
Joseph's Dream 2242
Josephine 2856, 3163, 3350, 3527, 3972, 4003, 4219
Josephine Waters 3955
Josette 2146
Joshua 4640
Joshua Fit de Battle 3965
Joshua Noveck 3960
Journey, The 1500
Journey Home 2618
Journey into Christmas Past, The (inst.) 752
Journey of a Lifetime, The 211
Journey to Portsmouth 2474
Journey to the Heaviside Layer, The 678
Journey Underground 3463
Journey's End 611, 773, 3639, 4529, 4373
Joustin' Time (I Found You) 3587
Jousts, The 623
(Jouyeux Noel, Buon Natale, Feliz Navidad) A Merry Merry Christmas to You 4391
Joy 808, 809
Joy and Glass 1199
Joy and Gloom 3407
Joy Attend on Erminie 1193
Joy Bells 334, 771
Joy Dance 764
Joy Duet, The 2914
Joy in the Earth 624
Joy Is Mine 711
Joy of a Kiss, The 1570
Joy of Life, The 178
Joy of Living, The 4208
Joy of That Kiss, The 3679
Joy or Strife 3680
Joy Out of Life 4200
Joy Ride, A 1746
Joy Ride 2246, 2780
Joy Spreader (A Jazz Opera), The 1446
Joy to the World 3739
Joy Town 712
Joy, Joy, Joy 35
Joyeux Noel 695
Joyful Noise, A 2248
Joyful Thing, A 4588
Joyous Christmas 4391
Joyous Love 806
Joyride 4602
Joys and the Glooms, The 2596
Joys from Children 343

Joys of an Irish Dance 191
Joys of Love, The 3372
Joys of Manhattan Life 2069
Joys of Yiddish, The 2422
Ju, Ju, Jupiter 3653
Juanita 2376
Juanita's Place Montage 3275
Jub Jub 2173
Juba 1125, 2250
Juba Dance 1063, 3808
Jubalay 426
Jubi-lie, Jubi-lo 3234
Jubilation 900
Jubilation T. Cornpone 2484
Jubilee (inst.) 3001
Jubilee 1340, 2034
Jubilee Joe 3684
Jubilee Presentation 2252
Jubilo 3923
Judas Dance (inst.) 4788
Judas' Death 2212
Jude's Holler 823
Judge Decision, The 1700
Judgement Day 2285, 4764
Judgement of Paris 220
Judgement of Paris, The 1600, 1817, 2252, 1818
Judges Comic Opera, The 3887
Judging Song 2661
Judy 4332
Judy Forgot 2253
Judy Garland National Anthem, The 128
Judy Two-Step, The (inst.) 2254
Judy Waltz, The (inst.) 2254
Judy, Who D'Ya Love? 2253
Judy's Turn to Cry 338
Jug Band and Dance 3146
Jug of Wine, A 999
Jugglar 470
Juggling 1273
Juke Box 3226
Juke Box Hop, The 1061
Juke Box Saturday Night 4143
Jule 3952
Julia 1459
Julia Dear 1066
Julia, Donald and Joe 804
Julianne 1182
Julie 25, 1924, 2974, 3787, 3951
Julie and Her Johnnies 627
Julie Dooley 1908
Julie Is Mine 722
Julie's Song 4729
Julie's Tango (inst.) 3787
Julienne 509
Juliet and Romeo 3433
Juliet of the Spirits 1189
Julius Baum 2797
Julius Caesar 1158
Jump Back, Honey 783
Jump, Chillun, Jump 2234
Jump de Broom 2000
Jump Down, Spin Around 1832
Jump for Joy 1633, 2259
Jump In! (Connubiality) 519
Jump Jim Crow 2794
Jump, Little Chillun 1300
Jump, Shout, Boogie 846
Jump Steady 740
Jumpety Jump Family 4439
Jumpin' at the Woodside (inst.) 4534
Jumpin' at the Woodside 4256
Jumpin' Frog 1035
Jumpin' Jehosephat 1727
Jumping Bean, The 3719
Jumping from Rock to Rock 593
Jumping Jack 2780, 2596
Jumping Jimminy 4170
Jumping to the Juke Box 4009
Jumping to the Jukebox 4141
June 1799, 1845, 2645, 3073, 4651
June Bells 773, 4248
June Bride 3888
June Bug, The 1962
June Days 2263
June Is Bustin' Out All Over 660
June Is in the Air 2761
June Love 2264, 3614
June Moon 2265
June, Moon, Spoon 4498
June Night 3056
June Taylor, The 2332
Jungle 897
Jungle Ball 4833
Jungle Book, The 2970
Jungle Bungalow (I'll Build a Home in the Jungle) 3500
Jungle Dance 3813
Jungle Hip Hop 1713
Jungle in Manhattan 877
Jungle Jamboree 1980
Jungle Jingle 883, 4821
Jungle Joy 827
Jungle Jump 3657
Jungle Man, The 336
Jungle Nights in Dixie Land (Jungle Town Has Moved to Dixieland) 2462
Jungle Nights in Dixieland (Jungle Town Has Moved to Dixieland) 1058
Jungle Number, The 2307
Jungle of Lies 3873
Jungle Rhythm Roundup 4503
Jungle Rose 1923, 3660
Jungle Shadows 1603
Jungly Tune 3796
Junior Miss 2267, 2267, 4387
Junk Food Boogie 2477
Junk Mail 2702
Junk Man 3444
Juno and the Paycock 2268
Juno, My Honeymoon Girl 1823

Jupiter Forbid 601
Jupiter Slept Here 3272
Just a Barber Shop Chord 2557
Just a Barefoot Boy (A'Whistlin' to His Dog) 4824
Just a Big-Hearted Man 495
Just a Bunch of Wild Flowers 3072
Just a Closer Walk with Thee 4534
Just a Commission 742
Just a Coupla Sisters 3211
Just a Cozy Hideaway 2734
Just a Fan 378
Just a Feeling 729
Just a Flower from an Old Bouquet 3617
Just a Friend of Mine 3584
Just a Gigolo 393
Just a Girl, Just a Boy 3754
Just a House 1077
Just a Housewife 4744
Just a Kiss 735, 2494, 2917
Just a Kiss and Then Goodbye 4453
Just a Kiss Apart 1475
Just a Kiss from Someone 2282
Just a Kiss from You 2490
Just a Little After Taps 1175, 1632
Just a Little Bit 459
Just a Little Bit Behind the Times 2214
Just a Little Bit More 4142
Just a Little Bit of Blarney 3575
Just a Little Bit of Jesus Goes a Long Way 4788
Just a Little Bit of Lingerie 3096
Just a Little Bit of Love 1250
Just a Little Blue for You 2296
Just a Little Chinaman 3765
Just a Little Ever-Loving Girl 2493
Just a Little Extra 4373
Just a Little Gossip 2424
Just a Little Joint with a Juke Box 372
Just a Little Laughter 1580
Just a Little Lie 3847, 4304, 4781
Just a Little Line 3923
Just a Little Love 3658
Just a Little Love Song (Mais le Son de Ta Voix) 505
Just a Little Penthouse and You 4328
Just a Little Quaker Girl 2644
Just a Little Smile 2600, 3021
Just a Little Smile from You 3968
Just a Little Space Can Be a Growing Place 518
Just a Little Stranger 3236
Just a Little Sunshine 2546
Just a Little Sunshine Makes a Rainbow 3552
Just a Little Thing 711
Just a Little Thing Called Rhythm 4212
Just a Little Touch of Paris 1175
Just a Little White House 454
Just a Little Widow 2518
Just a Map 3780
Just a Minute 2271
Just a Moment 2100
Just a Moment Ago 1760
Just a Paper Doll 2408
Just a Piece of Ass 2478
Just a Plain American Girl 2771
Just a Play 2603
Just a Pretty Little Home 21
Just a Promise 27
Just a Regular Girl 480
Just a Sentimental Tune 4291
Just a-Settin' and a-Rockin' 2259
Just a Simple Girl from the Prairie 4723
Just a Sister 1448
Just a Slip of the Tongue 1266
Just a Smile 2216
Just a Song and Dance 444
Just a Tiny Cup of Tea 1485, 3466
Just a Touch 3623
Just a Voice to Call Me Dear 3727
Just a Whistle 164
Just a Wonderful Time 1918
Just Across the River 2011, 4145
Just Act Natural 3723
Just an Honest Mistake 2449
Just an Hour of Love 587
Just an Ordinary Guy 3501, 3990, 4018
Just Another Guest 4244
Just Another Guy 1760
Just Another New Step 1314
Just Another Page in Your Diary 2432, 4498, 4517
Just Another Rumba 3060
Just Another Silly Day 2722
Just Another Song 778
Just Around the Corner 1322, 2274
Just Around the Corner from Broadway 1704
Just Around the Corner from Easy Street 4421
Just Arrived 846
Just Arrived from New York 2771
Just As a Rosebud Blossoms 2839
Just as Father Used to Do 3618
Just As It Should Be 1082
Just as Long as I Have You 1862
Just As Long As You Have Me 1516
Just As You Are 2723
Just Be Available 821
Just Because 2276
Just Because I'm Me 4012
Just Because It's You 2497
Just Because We're Kids 1842
Just Because You Love 4590
Just Because You're You (Because You Are Just You) 4811
Just Before I Go to Sleep 4750
Just Between the Two of Us 3506
Just Between You and Me 1887
Just Beyond the Rainbow 180
Just Cause the Moon Was Shinin' 405
Just Dissatisfied 4645
Just Don't Know What to Do with Myself 261
Just Don't Make No Sense 40
Just Eighteen 1387
Just for a Day 3350

Just for a Kiss 1540
Just for a Little While 4429
Just for a Night 2293
Just for a While 2419
Just for Auld Lang Syne 3545
Just for Fun 4381
Just for Love 2278
Just for Me 2320
Just for Me (An Awful Bore) 3073
Just for Me and Mary 638
Just for Once 3687
Just for Openers 2279
Just for the Ride 1497
Just for To-Night 689
Just for Today 1848, 4559
Just for Tonight 2105, 3536, 4334
Just for What You Are 1757
Just for You 1577, 2600, 2944, 4550
Just Friends 1883
Just Get Out and Walk 2885
Just Girls 4836
Just Give Me the World 83
Just Go to the Movies 2208, 1000
Just Good Friends 2341
Just Hello 1352
Just Him 3473
Just Home from College 2566
Just How Much I Love You 3945
Just Imagine 1628, 1734, 2270
Just Imagine It 4703
Just in Case (We're Soldiers of a Duchy) 1284
Just in Time 363
Just Keep A-Dreaming 2635
Just Keep Cool 586
Just Keep the Dear Boys Guessing 1088
Just Kids 2542, 4044
Just Lean on Me 381
Just Leave Everything to Me 2208
Just Let Me Get Away with This One 154
Just Let Me Get My Hands on Peace 3418
Just Let Me Look at You 2204
Just Like a Diamond 4427
Just Like a Doll 4121
Just Like a Gypsy 542, 2373
Just Like a Man 4237, 4499
Just Like a Wild, Wild, Rose 4271
Just Like a Woman 3082
Just Like a Young Man 3197
Just Like an Old Time Movie 1841
Just Like Children 3493
Just Like Eva 2385
Just Like Jane 2642
Just Like Love 1086
Just...Like...Me 3722
Just Like Me 2262
Just Like That 1000, 139, 3165, 3312
Just Like the Movies 4147
Just Like the Sunshine 4437
Just Like This 2966, 4063
Just Like You 307, 1262, 4285, 4491, 2224
Just Listen to Me 3653
Just Look! (Anvedi Si Che Paciocca) 3798
Just Look Around 2768
Just Look at Me Now 829
Just Love Me All the Time 2394
Just Lovin' 123
Just Lucky, I Guess 1048
Just Mahalia Baby 2692
Just Married 2281
Just Marry the Man and Be Merry 4646
Just Mention Joe 622
Just Missed the Opening Chorus 1487
Just My Luck 483, 508, 3091
Just My Style 1243
Just My Type (They're All My Type) 2939
Just Once 146
Just Once Around the Clock 2786
Just Once More 4541
Just One Country, Just One Flag 1206
Just One Good Time 4654
Just One Kiss 3248, 3659, 3740
Just One Little Kiss 1964
Just One More Kiss 4794
Just One More Time 4584
Just One More Waltz with You 2700
Just One Night 1077
Just One of Those Things 2252, 3131
Just One Person 4034
Just One Rose 728
Just One Way to Say I Love You 2894
Just Our Way of Doing Business 1108
Just Passing Through 1161
Just People 1564
Just Plain Folks 3366
Just Plain Will 4388
Just Plant a Kiss 2377
Just Reach Out and Touch Me 3788
Just Remember Coq d'Or 3847
Just Say Goodbye 1536
Just Say That You Will Miss Me 1405
Just Say the Word 2628, 3822
Just Say Yes 494
Just Say You Care 1316
Just Sisters 632
Just Sit Around 3418
Just Sit Back 3548
Just Sit Back and Relax 4243
Just Snap Your Fingers at Care 1686
Just So Stories 2283
Just Someone 2576
Just Someone to Talk To 3224
Just Squeeze Me 2259, 4091
Just Stay Alive (Sempre Boia E) 3798
Just Strollin' 70
Just Suppose 465, 2277, 2633, 3523
Just Suppose You Loved Me 2966
Just Supposing 4241
Just Sweet Sixteen 1686
Just Take Things As They Come 3883
Just Tell Me with Your Eyes 1845

Just that You Are You 2825
Just the Crust 4013
Just the Facts 2784
Just the One I'm Looking For 4044
Just the Same 295, 3489
Just the Same Old Situation 511
Just the Two of Us 2373
Just the Way We're Bred 2046
Just the Way You Are 3217
Just This Once 2627
Just Thought I'd Call 3517
Just Three Words 4497
Just to Be a Little Boy Again 231
Just to Keep Expenses Down 4634
Just to Keep Peace in the Family 4453
Just To Know That He's Around 2551
Just to Know What's Going On in New York Town 2465
Just to Know You Are Mine 977
Just to Look at Him 2783
Just to Make the World a Little Brighter 3921
Just to Pass the Time Away 2233
Just to Please You, Sue 719
Just to Say That I Love You 2115
Just to You 796
Just Trust Me 1700
Just Us 1047
Just Use a Bit of Blarney 2155
Just Wait 150, 4001
Just Walking Through Mocking Bird Lane 3705
Just Want You 4240
Just We Two 632, 2340, 4148, 4188
Just We Two Dear 697
Just What I Wanted 1456, 2794
Just When I Thought I Had You All to Myself 1343
Just When You Least Expect It 16
Just Win a Pretty Widow 473
Just You 2455
Just You Alone 3652
Just You and I 1206
Just You and I and the Baby 2818
Just You and I and the Moon 4807
Just You and I in Dreamland 2394
Just You and Me 1663, 2047, 4811
Just You Wait 3038
Just You Watch My Step 2430
Just Your Old Friend 1139
Justice Game, The 4449
Justice Triumphant 1094
Justine Johnstone Rag, The 3333
Juvenile Deliquency 4047
Juvenile Fiction 4454

K

K.C. Line 1037
K.P. 815
K-ra-zy for You 921, 4443
Ka-lu-a 611
Ka-Lu-A 1625
Ka-razy 1038
Ka Wahine Akamai 4337
Kaa's Rescue 2970
Kabuki Rock 2332
Kaddish 3644
Kadoola, Kadoola 3540
Kaiser Bill 3259
Kalamazoo 2745
Kaleidoscope 300, 4388
Kalialani 1809
Kalidah Battle 4722
Kalimera 2659
Kalodner and Marks Revisited 262
Kaltenborn Blues 2379
Kalua Bay 1237
Kama's Garden 1689
Kamikaze Kabaret 4349
Kan the Kaiser 4422
Kandahar Isle 1461
Kangaroo 2
Kangaroo, The 519
Kangaroo Court 562
Kangaroo Hop, The 3395
Kangaroo Ragout, The 2519
Kansas City 4031, 3263
Kansas City Blues 4192
Karabitz! 2163
Karate 3196
Karen's Lullaby 181
Karenin's List 147
Karma 3944
Kate O'Donoghue 4239
Kate the Great 163, 4517
Kathakali 751
Katherine Receives Advice 999
Kathleen 2149
Kathleen Aroon 2154
Kathleen, Mine 4372
Katie and Her Kodak 2803
Katie Carney, Stop Your Blarney! 2902
Katie Clancy 186
Katie Come and Kiss Me 506
Katie Did 2291
Katie Did in Madrid 1112
Katie Gray 3855
Katie Jonas 1441
Katie, My Love 1699
Katie, My Southern Rose 4646
Katie O'Sullivan 3831
Katie Rooney 4807
Katie Strauss 3531
Katie Went to Haiti 1109
Katinka 705, 710, 1486, 2292, 4575
Katinka to Eva to Francis 84
Katja, Die Tanzerin 2293
Katrina 591, 3951
Katrina Waltz, The 2100

Katy Bill 4149
Katy Did 3209
Katy-Did 3237
Katy Was a Business Girl 1246
Katydid, the Cricket and the Frog, The 3073
Katzenjammer Kinda Song, A 4454
Kava Ceremony 1809
Kayo Tortoni 4817
Keb, Sir, Want a Keb? 3129
Kee-Kee-Koo 487
Keep A-Countin' Eight 3723
Keep A-Diggin' 2645
Keep a Fox Trot for Me 2336
Keep a Goin' 1819
Keep-a-Hoppin' 4516
Keep a Kiss for Me 3252
Keep-A-Stepping Along 3200
Keep a Taxi Waiting, Dear 1327
Keep a Twinkle in Your Eye 446
Keep Alookin' Straight Ahead 3683
Keep Away 408
Keep Away from a Married Man (I'm a Married Man) 3618
Keep Away from Broadway 2990
Keep Away from Emmaline 2041
Keep Away from the Fellow Who Owns an Automobile 1531
Keep Building Your Castles 4651
Keep Cool 4666
Keep 'Em Busy 3209
Keep 'Em Guessin' 4198
Keep 'Em Guessing 4199
Keep 'Em Quiet 3209
Keep Going 913
Keep Hope Alive 1282
Keep in Shape 821
Keep in Touch 1596
Keep It Casual 323
Keep It Confidential 2427
Keep It Dark 463, 3578
Keep It Gay 2797
Keep It Hot (dance) 723
Keep It in the Family 2297, 1168, 4238
Keep It Low 705
Keep It Simple 3234
Keep It Under Your Hat 3388
Keep It Under Your Sombrero 1415
Keep It Up 1831
Keep Laughing 3698
Keep Love Away 692
Keep Me Close to You 3485
Keep Me from Falling Asleep 1588, 2919
Keep Me Out of the Caisson 564
Keep Moving 2366, 2922, 3193, 3808, 3933
Keep Off the Grass 4430, 4784
Keep on A'Shining, Silv'ry Moon 248
Keep on Building Castles in the Air 4054
Keep on Croonin' a Tune 4010
Keep on Dancing 3388, 3902
Keep On Doing 4434
Keep On Rollin' 4031
Keep on Running 4534
Keep on Smiling 4756, 4063, 4738
Keep on the Grass 58
Keep on the Right Hand Side of Father 4634
Keep On Walking 30
Keep Our Love on an Even Keel 1503
Keep Out of the Moon 3866
Keep Out of the Water 1407
Keep Repeating It 3051
Keep Running (inst.) 499
Keep Sakes 709
Keep Shufflin' 2302
Keep Smilin' Through 2046
Keep Smiling 4361
Keep Smiling and Carry On 4023
Keep Smiling at Trouble (Trouble's a Bubble) 391
Keep Tempo 879
Keep that Beat 3427
Keep That Schoolgirl Complexion 69
Keep the Castle Warm 760
Keep the Conversation Going 2641
Keep the Home Fires Burning 3259
Keep the Love Lamps Burning in the Windows of Your Eyes 380
Keep the Man You've Got 2009
Keep the Party Going 3185
Keep Them Guessing 4651
Keep Them in a Golden Cage 2857
Keep Thy Faith, Children 1261
Keep Working 2648
Keep Your Amateur Standing 971
Keep Your Chin Up 3972, 3965
Keep Your Distance 2496
Keep Your Eye on Little Mary Brown 4634
Keep Your Eye on Pretty Sarah 4298
Keep Your Eye on the Ball 2264, 2308, 2380
Keep Your Eye on the Girl 3489
Keep Your Eye on the Girl Just Out 3943
Keep Your Eye on the Red 2173
Keep Your Foot on the Soft Pedal 1613
Keep Your Hand on My Heart 1670
Keep Your Head Down Fritzi Boy 1502
Keep Your Little Eye Upon the Main Chance, Mary 840
Keep Your Love for Me (Save Your Love for Me) 4808
Keep Your Nose to the Grindstone 4542
Keep Your Shirt On 266
Keep Your Undershirt On 4426
Keep Your Weight Down 684
Keep Your Whip in Your Hand 3268
Keepin' Books 374
Keepin' It Hot 1310
Keepin' Myself for You 3249
Keepin' Out of Mischief Now 39
Keeping Cool with Coolidge 1475, 2590
Keeping Out of Trouble 69
Keeping Prigio Company 1871

Keeping Score with Myself 4515
Keeping the Peace 4635
Keeping Up with the Joneses 2303
Keepsakes 2686
Keewa-Tak-A-Yaka-Holo 4393
Keith's, Pantages and Loews 3264
Kellerman Girlie, The 4521
Kelly's Gone to Kingdom Come 2858
Kenosha Canoe Ballet 4362
Kensington Stories, The 2805
Kentucky 1019
Kentucky Babe 4390
Kentucky Jubilee 4037
Kentucky Sue 3963
Keokuk Culture Club, The 2915
Kept in Suspense 418
Ker-choo! 3056
Kermess Dance and Song 1555
Kermess Day 252
Kermesse Dance 3586
Kettle Is Singing (The Kettle Song), A 3740
Kevin 4366
Kewpie Dolly 542
Key to Lorayne 4194
Key to My Heart, The 443, 4043
Key to the Gates, The 3813
Key to Your Heart, The 782
Keys of Heaven, The 2180
Keys of My Heart, The 2180
Keys to Heaven 1447
Keys to My Heart 2140
Keystone Glide, The 3087
Keystone Strut 2305
Khave and the Apple Tree 4082
Khazndl Oyf Shabes (A Cantor for the Sabbath), A 4342
Khonghouse Song 711
Khosn—Kale Mazl Tov (Congratulations to the Bride and Groom) 4342
Khrushchev-Kennedy Press Conference 4397
Khulem, A 1609
Ki Ram's Wedding March 4201
Ki-Yo 248
Kick in the Pants 1191
Kick in the Pants, The 4340
Kick It Around 1093
Kick Me Again 944
Kick the Door 2583
Kickapoo Kick, The 3800
Kickin' a Hole in the Sky 1693
Kickin' the Clouds Away 3060, 4300
Kickin' the Gong Around 3709
Kickin' Up a Storm 4180
Kicking Polka, The 3626
Kicking the Mule 981
Kicks 2307
Kid Brother 791
Kid Days 1968, 3809, 3821
Kid Days Again 1556
Kid Herself, The 1310
Kid, I Love You 4780
Kid Inside, The 2152
Kid Is Clever, The 4209
Kid Stuff 3947
Kid's Gonna Make It, The 275
Kidder's Reception 2793
Kiddie Medley 2096
Kidland 4804
Kidnapped 4485
Kidnapper, The 2184
Kids 607
Kids Ain't (Like Everybody Else) 599, 4625
Kids Are Out 1508
Kids Game 460
Kids in School, The 4169
Kikerikee 2336
Kiki 642, 2309, 2309
Kilimanjaro 3836
Kill, The 3876
Kill It Now 1418
Kill Johnny One Note Dead 3667
Kill the Beast 494
Killarney 1902, 3746
Killer Cheer 1055
Killer on the Loose 3004
Killer-Diller Miller 3802
Killing 4609
Killing Sequence 1385
Killing Time 3277
Kin of Nur Al-Din, The 2802
Kind Fate 2563
Kind Fortune Smiles Today 2632
Kind Gentle Looking Person, A 1620
Kind of a Girl 2750
Kind of a Man 2751
Kind of a Man a Woman Needs, The 4764
Kind of Girl I 2763
Kind of Girl I'd Like to Be, The 4289
Kind of Guy, The 3619
Kind of Man, The 3215
Kind of Woman 3506
Kind Old Gentleman 1848
Kind Sir 669
Kind to Animals 2608
Kinda Cute 1126
Kinda Dukish (inst.) 4091
Kinda Like You 3249, 4372
Kinda Sorta Doin' Nothing 1081
Kinder, The 2925
Kinder Yohrn 3781
Kinder Yurn 2356
Kindergarten Blues 953
Kindly Pass the Chloroform Along 4650
Kindly Pay Us 2363
Kindness 2134, 3749
Kindred Spirits 148
King 1216
King, The 4016

King Becomes a Clown, The 4171
King Called Cotton 3035
King Can Do No Wrong, The 3766
King Carnival 102, 2830
King Cole 1037
King Edward's Subjects 3747
King Foo-Foo the First 3571
King Hal's Gals 2341
King Herod's Song 2212
King Joe 415
King Kazoo of Kacaroo 1926
King Lear 3539
King Lear Ballet 615
King Louis Is Havin' a Dream (The King of Swing Is Havin' a Dream) 1982
King Neptune 4404
King of a South Sea Isle 3423
King of Baby Land, The 3134
King of Broadway 805
King of Fools 1119
King of France, The 2917
King of Hearts 2318, 2318
King of London 2295
King of My Heart 3051
King of Old 3573
King of Schnorrers, The 4288, 2320, 2319
King of Schnorrers 2321
King of Swing 3640
King of the Boulevards 2495
King of the Delta, Queen of the River 4055
King of the Imps Am I 4439
King of the Mound 4619
King of the Sword 3680
King of the World 2322
King Solomon 21, 126
King Tut's Birthday 978
King Who Is Pestered with Cares, A 1905
Kingdom of a Woman's Heart, The 353
Kingdom of Dreams 3766
Kingdom of Love, The 2992
Kingly Duties 2243
Kings and Cabbages 4798
Kings and Queens 3941
King's Baracarolle, The 630
King's Dilemma 4560
King's Favorite, The 3403
King's Musketeers, The 947
King's New Clothes, The 1741
King's Own, The 2906
King's Regiment 4379
Kinkajou, The 3719
Kinky 295
Kip 2705
Kipps 1721
Kismet 2327, 4383, 4383
Kismet Quick 4388
Kiss, The 2549
Kiss, A 2771
Kiss, The 4269
Kiss a Four Leaf Clover 930
Kiss Affects Me Most of All, A 102
Kiss and Be Friends 3308
Kiss and Make Up 2454
Kiss Before I Go, A (One Kiss) 4357
Kiss Before the Dawn, The 4105
Kiss Burglar, The 3096
Kiss Burglar 3403
Kiss Ensemble 1513
Kiss for Cinderella 1703
Kiss for Cinderella, A 2329, 3225, 3246, 3439, 3556
Kiss for Each Day in the Week, A 3805
Kiss from a Red-Headed Miss, A 1688
Kiss from You, A 733
Kiss Her Now 2208, 1012
Kiss I Must Refuse You, A 3170
Kiss in a Cab, A 318
Kiss in the Dark, A 3312, 4816
Kiss in the Moonlight, A 1131
Kiss Invention 606
Kiss It 1664
Kiss, Kiss 4440
Kiss, Kiss, Kiss 1911
Kiss Me 348, 429, 1598, 2261
Kiss Me! 2330
Kiss Me 4186, 4233, 4429
Kiss Me Again, Bebe 4490
Kiss Me and Kill Me with Love 145
Kiss Me and We'll Both Go Home 3292
Kiss Me, Dearest, Kiss Me Do 2495
Kiss Me Good-Night Dear 2819
Kiss Me Honey 4092
Kiss Me Honey Do 2041
Kiss Me, Honey, Do 976
Kiss Me, Kate 2331
Kiss Me Like This 557
Kiss Me, My Love 88
Kiss Me No Kisses 4633
Kiss Me Once More 2390
Kiss Me Once More Goodnight 1998
Kiss Me Sweet 3297
Kiss Now 2332
Kiss of Myer 1832
Kiss of the Spider Woman 131, 2333, 2333
Kiss of Yore, The 2519
Kiss or Two, A 1916
Kiss the Boys Goodbye 3444
Kiss the Bride 3063
Kiss the Bride Now 1694
Kiss Time 2378
Kiss to Remind You, A 1384
Kiss Trot 3434
Kiss Waltz, The 1852, 2334, 3494
Kiss with a Kick, A 86
Kiss You Gave, The 2667
Kiss You Never Get, The 3203
Kiss Your Baby Goodbye 971
Kiss Your Minstrel Boy Goodbye 800
Kiss Your Soldier Boy Au Revoir 1588
Kissable Lips 3406

Kissed on the Eyes 1739
Kisses 1515, 4662
Kisses and Hugs 3811
Kisses at Auction 256
Kisses from My Violin to You 1951
Kisses That I Have Missed 2732
Kissimee 2336
Kissing 827, 2884, 2947, 3157, 4479
Kissing Duet 1470
Kissing Eyes 1788
Kissing Forest Ballet (dance) 3980
Kissing Me 18
Kissing Rock, The 1476, 2231
Kissing Song, The 1048
Kissing Time 1544, 2336, 3268, 4590
Kissing Trust, The 1925
Kissinger und Kleindienst und Klein 4635
Kissland 2519
Kit 4478
Kitchen Cabaret, The 2710
Kitchen Man 478, 2796, 3297
Kitchen Mechanic's Parade 2337
Kitchen Range, The 4219
Kitchen Sink 1865
Kite, The 4388, 4272
Kite 4783
Kitten That Couldn't Be Good 4293
Kittens in the Snow 3641
Kittiwake Island 2339
Kitty 452, 2996
Kitty and the Owl, The 1908
Kitty Car Ballet 3543
Kitty Darlin' 2340
Kitty Kat Song 4011
Kitty Kitty 4859
Kitty MacKay 3397
Kitty Malone 141
Kitty McKay 2412
Kitty More 1259
Kitty O'Brien 1896
Kitty of Juniper Green 2412
Kitty Please Give Me a Kiss 1455
Kitty's Kisses 2342
Kitty's Not Built That Way 2341
Kitzel Engagement, The 376
Kiyomori 2851
Kleine Soft Shoe, A 1279
Kleptomania 1896
Kling-Kling Bird on the Divi-Divi Tree, The 2252
Knave of Hearts, The 4735
Knee Dance 2870
Knee Deep in June 1135
Knees 1800
Kneipe, The 4187
Knickerbocker Grey's March 1846
Knife, The 2346, 2669
Knife Dance 4623
Knife-Grinder's Daughter, The 710
Knife-Thrower's Wife, The 4825
Knight of Noble Mien 1095
Knight of the Chafing Dish, A 1220
Knights of the Mystic Star 1776
Knights of the Table 2605
Knights of the White Cross 3035
Knights on White Horses 4270
Knit, Knit 2184
Knit, Knit, Knit 4283
Knitting Chorus 1624
Knitting Sextet 2889
Knitting Song 4000
Knock at the Window 644
Knock, Knock 1310
Knock-Knock Nobody Home 3424
Knock on Wood 2496
Knock Wood 246, 2168
Knockers 2437
Knockin' on Wood 3172
Knocking Bookworms, The 2516
Knocking in Vain 2992
Knocking Myself Out 4127
Knocking on Wood 4170
Knocking the 'K' Out of Kaiser 1919
Knocks 2146
Knot of Blue, The 2160
Knothole Scene 1628
Know What I Mean? 31
Know When to Smile 4669
Know You 2993
Know Your Business 1074
Knowing When to Leave 261, 3603
Knowledge 624
Ko-Ko 4091
Kodak Girl 3129
Kohala Welcome 3556
Kokoraki 220
Kolossal 1569
Kongo Kate 1487
Kongshee, the Mandarin's Daughter (inst.) 4699
Koo-La-Loo 3230
Kook Spooks 2443
Kooka-Rooki Bongo 4196
Kosher Kitty Kelly 2351
Kosher Kleagle 123
Kow Tow 2159
Koze Kubenini (Until When) 1719
Kranko Waltz 2732
Kravitz to Snyder to Smith 4172
Kreolenblut 3776
Ku Klux Klan 1556
Kuckoo Kapers 2174
Kuensler-Blut 2603
Kukla Katusha 4435
Kukuska (dance) (inst.) 902
Kuli Kuli 4337
Kulturny 3970
Kwai Sonata, The 1621
Kyrie 4398, 3507
Kyrie Eleison 101, 2775

L

L.A. Blues 775
L.A. Freeway 2676
L.A. Incident 1216
L.A. Is 408
L-O-V-E 203, 4264, 3051
L.Z. in Quest of His Youth (ballet) 1227
La Bamba 580
La Belle Francaise 2834
La Belle Helene 2357
La Belle Lulu 4489
La Belle Paree 1927
La Belle Parisienne 357, 1523, 4654
La Belle Province 426
La Boheme 2359
La Cabeza... 1306
La Cage Aux Folles 2208
La Cage aux Folles 2360
La Cage Aux Folles 2360, 3624
La Calinda 3810
La Carmagnole 979
La Chanson de Craonne 3259
La Chanteuse 1834
La Clare de la Lune 1927
La Corrada 2364
La Cumparcita 1638
La-da-diddle-de-dum 3350
La Danse Parisienne 2716
La Danse Parisienne et La Americaine 1243
La-De-Da 2319
La-de-da-da 2375
La Demoiselle du Telephone 4298
La Femme 101
La Femme a Toujours Vingt Ans! (Lovely Woman's Ever Young) 1202
La Femme de Chambre 1392
La Femme Du Boulanger 273
La Festa 145
La France, La France 946
La Gardeuse d'Oies 3199
La Goulue 3386
La Grosse Valise 2362
La Java 2135, 2362
La Kermesse Heroique 657
La Koquette 470
La, La, La 1581
La La La 3187
La-La-La-La 2368, 3117
La-La-La-La-La—Love Is Our Epistemology! 2243
La La Land 1149
La, Lil, In Two International Cameos 703
La Loge 2168
La Malade Imaginaire 4401
La Marseillaise 4023
La Mattchiche 3387
La Morale 3197
La Nuit d'Amour 101
La Orchidea (Orchid Lady) 851
La Papilion 511
La-Par Micado (Rag-Time Opera) 604
La Parisian Peacock 1334
La Parisienne 1374
La Passerelle 3312
La Petite Chocolatiere 4285
La Petite Oiseau 760
La Pintada 850
La Poupee 2365
La Presidente 3254
La Princess Zenobia Ballet (inst.) 3283
La Prisonniere 1655
La Promenade Anglais 3313
La Rhumba 570
La Ronde 3108, 1822, 3763
La Sarancena 223
La Seine 1834
La Soeur 2025
La Sorella Dance 116
La Strada 2368
La Tickero 1396
La Tiddle De Um 3981
La Tra Ma La (Latramalay) 732
La Traviata Waltzes (inst.) 1897
La Vagabonde 808
La Veda 2856
La Vie Boheme 868
La Vie Devant Soi 3792
La Vie en Rose 2356, 166
La Vie Parisienne 2857
La Vita 3822
Label on the Bottle, The 1456
Labor Agitator, The 764
Labor Day Parade 2062, 2302, 3965
Labor Is the Thing 2068
Lac-Des-Scenes 392
Lac des Scenes 3186
Lace Land (scene) 4816
Lace Makers Song 2180
Laces and Graces 591
Lack-a-Day 2464
Lackadaisical 3409
Lackawanna 391
Lad for Ev'ry Lass, A 1048
Lad Who Leads, The 2315
Ladder of Roses, The 1901
Ladder to the Lord 747
Laddie 3941
Laddie Boy 1703
Laddie Daddy 2376
Laddy Buck of Mine 1751
Ladies, The 178
(We're) Ladies 1029
Ladies, The 1849
Ladies 4219
Ladies, The 4742, 4373
Ladies and Babies a la Mode 4209
Ladies and Gentlemen, Good Evening 3518
Ladies and Gentlemen, That's Love 1492

Ladies and Gentlemen, We're Here Again (Opening Act II) 3291
Ladies and Mateys of Hades, The 4325
Ladies Are Present 4001
Ladies Auxilliary Picnic Community, The 1380
Ladies Beware 2914
Ladies, Beware 3011
Ladies, Beware (When the Lights Are Low) 3433
Ladies' Choice 2419
Ladies Come from Baltimore, The 3817
Ladies' Day 126
Ladies Day 1588, 2383, 2486
Ladies Don't Have Fun 1577
Ladies Fair 1285
Ladies from the Cultured West, The 3778
Ladies Have a Care 1796
Ladies' Home Companion 376
Ladies in Society 3313
Ladies in Their Sensitivities 4233
Ladies in Waiting 1727
Ladies! Ladies! 2947, 3996
Ladies' Lament 3517
Ladies Like Us 664
Ladies Look at Yourselves 2648
Ladies Maid 1123
Ladies' Maid, The 2938
Ladies 'n' Gentlemen 1385
Ladies of Fiction 2288
Ladies of London and Paris, The 1632
Ladies of My Day, The 3320
Ladies of Portugal 1663
Ladies of Quality 2654
Ladies of the Ballet 2750
Ladies of the Box Office 1446
Ladies of the Chorus 4340
Ladies of the Evening 418, 514
Ladies of the House 1697
Ladies of the Night 1161
Ladies of the Town 429
Ladies of Wealth 1342
Ladies' Opinion, The 2464
Ladies Room 4777
Ladies Should Be Beautiful 3669
Ladies Singin' Their Song, The 253
Ladies Who Lunch, The 832
Ladies Who Sing with the Band, The 39, 1140
Lads and Lasses 1080
Lady 1033, 1369, 2379, 2598
Lady (Bless Your Heart I Loves You Lady) 2996
Lady, The 1857, 4394
Lady Alice 989
Lady and Bird 408
Lady and Gentleman 276
Lady and the Kick, The 2101
Lady Audley's Secret 2375
Lady Be Dainty 3714
Lady Be Good 4534
Lady Bird 2412, 1438, 4181
Lady Bred in the Purple, A 539
Lady Bug Song, The 3934
Lady Butterfly 2378, 2519
Lady By Choice 1402
Lady Can Love, The 70, 621
Lady Clara 703
Lady Do 2380
Lady Don't Do, A 362
Lady Fair 1489, 4817
Lady Fair, Lady Fair 3865
Lady Fortune 1067
Lady Godiva (Go Bob Your Hair) 266
Lady Has Oomph, The 1138
Lady I Love, The 4581
Lady I've Vowed to Wed, The 3865
Lady in Ermine 2384
Lady in the Moon, The 350
Lady in the Window 1352
Lady in Waiting 1614, 1874
Lady Is a Tramp, The 247, 3175
Lady Is a WAAC, The 2447
Lady Is Indisposed, The 4827
Lady Isn't Looking 4558
Lady Known As Lulu 4465
Lady Known As Lulu, The 420
Lady Lady 426
Lady Lies, The 1171
Lady Likes to Dance, The 2083
Lady Lindy 434
Lady Lizzie of Milan 2933
Lady Love 3855
Lady Luck 780, 3680
Lady Luck (Smile on Me) 4345
Lady Luck 4392
Lady Luck Is Grinning 4118
Lady Luck Smile on Me 4529
Lady Luxury 2390
Lady Madcap 3052
Lady Marmalade 1890
Lady Mary's Song to Taberie 4539
Lady Must Live, A 111
Lady Needs a Change, The 4142
Lady Needs a Rest, A 2453, 4517
Lady of Leisure, A 227
Lady of Mars 764
Lady of My Heart 1312
Lady of Society, The 355
Lady of the Castle in the Air, The 2317
Lady of the Evening 3007
Lady of the Fan 4545
Lady of the House, The 154
Lady of the Lantern 4817
Lady of the Manor 4541
Lady of the Moon 2872, 4154
Lady of the Rose 4692
Lady of the Roses, The 1716
Lady of the Sea 1919
Lady of the Slipper, The 2394
Lady of the Snow, The 1691
Lady of the Snow 1692
Lady of the Veil 1132
Lady of the Year 3879

Lady of Tomorrow 397
Lady or the Tiger, The 170
Lady Osteopath, The 3617
Lady Precious Stream 2396
Lady Raffles-Behave 3538
Lady Ride with Me 562
Lady Romance 4742
Lady Secretary, The 3313
Lady Seeks Gentleman 2065
Lady Sleeps, The 3773
Lady St. Heller 414
Lady, the Lover and the Jealous Husband, The 758
Lady-Ushers Ball, The 4203
Lady Vagabond 3167
Lady Was Made to Be Loved, The 71, 3756
Lady Whippoorwill 931
Lady Who Loved to Sing, The 426
Lady with Money, A 734
Lady with the Fan, The 879
Lady with the Tap, The 216
Lady, You Don't Know Me 2020, 2888
Lady, You Drop Yo Feminine Wiles 4504
Ladylike Lady Like Me 362
Lady's Choice 3015
Lady's Got Potential, The 1211
Lady's in Love with You, The 3444
Lady's Maid 3828
Lady's on the Job (on Time), The 2653
Lady's Paying, The 4217
Laendler (dance) 4095
Laertes Coercion 3741
Lafayette 2523
Lagoon Scene 3450
Lak Jeem 3772
Lalage Potts That's Me 1473
Lallapalooza 4734
Lama Su Apapi 3088
Lambert's Quandary 101
Lambeth Walk, The 2798
Lambshine Pudding (Madrigal) 2401
Lame, the Halt and the Blind, The 162
Lament 2143, 1211, 1300, 2053, 2114, 2268, 2477, 2979, 3386
Lament for Ten Men 521
Lament Mauricette 364
Lament of Shakespeare 1132
Lament of the Crusty Dames, The 4544
Lament on Fifth Avenue 3940
Lamentation 2028, 4523
L'America Ha Fato per Te 1282, 4168
L'Ami Fritz 1401
L'Amorcage 3433
L'Amour 2723
L'Amour de L'Apache 3626
L'Amour Qui ne Finit Pas 3338
L'Amour-Toujours-L'Amour (Love Everlasting) 102
L'Amour-Toujours-L'Amour 385
L'Amoureuse 2506
Lamp, The 3098
Lamp of Love 3962
Lamp Post in New York Town 3982
Lamp Post of Old Broadway, The 1901
Lamplight 3103
Lamplight Land 2706
Lampoon for Louis 2168
Lana Turner 260
Lancashire Lassies 4010
Lancers 250
Lancers, The 2789
Lancers 3049, 4724
Lancers, The 3856, 3857
Lancers 3882
Lancers' Waltz 1095
Land, The 2766
Land and Water 4419
Land Beyond the Candle Light, The 764
Land I Love 568
Land I Love, The 1631, 3805
Land O' Mine 2384
Land of a Thousand Dances 3739
Land of Beautiful Dreams, The 88
Land of Betrayal 4485
Land of Broken Dreams 3796
(Down in the) Land of Dancing Pickaninnies 740
Land of Dreams, The 4293
Land of Enchantment (Land of Romance) 659
Land of God 655
Land of Going to Be, The 3382
Land of Golden Dreams 2717
Land of Heart's Desire 1482, 2938
Land of Honor 1313
Land of Hope and Glory 1534
Land of Jass 395
Land of Let's Pretend, The 1544
Land of Long Ago, The 4429
Land of Love, The 1523, 2500
Land of Love and Roses, The 1901
Land of Make Believe 902
Land of Make Believe, The 1433
Land of Make-Believe 4218
Land of Mine 3035
Land of My Own Romance 4250
Land of Nod, The 1908, 2408
Land of Opportunitee, The 3390
Land of Promises, The 2682
Land of Provence 3680
Land of Rockefellera 3105
Land of Rocky Boo 2112
Land of Romance 361, 670
(Come to) The Land of Romance 1208
Land of Sky Blue Waters 3677
Land of Sultan's Dreams, The 1111
Land of the Brave and Home of the Free, The 1521
Land of the Free, The 4017
Land of the Gay Caballero 1528
Land of the Midnight Sun 586
Land of the Midnight Sun, The 3362, 3658
Land of the Sky, The (Adios Senorita) 4185

Land of the Whisp'ring Sea 306
Land of the Wiener and the Wurst, The 4761
Land of Used-to-Be, The 1606
Land of Wot, The 1118
Land of Yesteryear, The 2456
Land Where Dreams Come True, The 2340
Land Where Journeys End, The 3250
Land Where the Best Man Wins, The 1526
Land Where the Good Songs Go, The 2900, 3230
Land Where There Is No Death, The 2229
Land Where We'll Never Grow Old 3631
Land which My Heart Calls Home, The 1650
Land You Left Behind, The 1910
Landlord at My Door! 4025
Land's End to John O'Groats 3663
Landslide, The 4185
Langenstein in Spring 82
Language of Cauli-Flowers, The 1534
Language of Flowers, The 3865
Language of Love, The 906, 2387
Language of Love 4094, 4860
Language of Love, The 3383
Language of Lover's Smiles, The 3031
Language of Signs 2232
Language of the Fan, The 3401
Language of the Flowers, The 4430
Languanay 1588
Languid Man, The 4165
Languid Man 998
Lanky Yankee Boys in Blue, The 2576
Lantern Dance 3509
Lantern Fete 1243
Lantern Night 3798
Lantern of Love, The 4393
Lanterns 4488
Lanterns of Love 670
L'Apres Midi d'un Boeuf 1109
L'Apres Midi d'un Papillon (inst.) 1447
Lapse of Time, A 1584
Larceny and Love 1373
Large Cold Bottle and a Small
Hot Bird, A 2041
Larger Than Life 3039
Lark, The 2602
Lark in the Park 382
Larry 3205
Lars, Lars 2064
Larue's Blues 2993
Las Siete Potencias and Despoho 3830
Las Vegas 411, 673
Lash the Wheel 1369
Lass I Love, The 1445
Lass of Richmond Hill 3450
Lass Who Loved a Sailor, The 1800
Lass with the Delicate Air 7
Lass with the Lasso, The 3433
Lassie 2412
Lasso Queen 3677
Last 3970
Last Affairs of Anatol, The 1439
Last Blues, The 3741
Last Chance Blues, The 2200
Last Chance Revue, The 2477
Last Chance Series 2477
Last Confession 1977
Last Dance, The 429, 3218
Last Dance, That's Out, The 487
Last Day on the Job 1737
Last Dream Ballet, The 2416
Last Eleven O'Clock Number, The 2416
Last Elf Aria, The 4106
Last Finale, The 2416
Last Flight, The 3168
Last Girl Is the Best Girl, The 4528
Last Hate Duet, The 2416
Last Home Town Song, The 2416
Last 'I Love New York' Song, The 2790
Last Incantation, The 1258
Last Jazz Specialty, The 2416
Last Leaf, The 3221
Last Little Girl Is You, The 1183
Last Long Mile, The 2187, 4422
Last Love Duet, The 2416
Last Man on Earth 2542
Last Midnight 2143
Last Minute Waltz, The 33
Last Night 2143, 2065
Last Night in a Dream 4615
Last Night of the World, The 2905
Last of the Cabbies, The 4825
Last One, The 1857
Last One of the Boys, The 4635
Last One Picked 2022
Last Opening, The 2416
Last Overture, The 2416
Last Paradise, The 3368
Last Part of Any Party, The 2148
Last Production Number, The 2416
Last Quarter 3619
Last Resort, The 2992
Last Rose of Summer 1897
Last Roundup, The 4824
Last Saturday Night 4016
Last Seduction Song, The 2416
Last Shake o' the Bag, The 2055
Last Show, The 4467
Last Soft Shoe, The 2416
Last Soliloquy, The 2416
Last Soubrette Song, The 2416
Last Supper, The 2212
Last Sweet Days of Isaac, The 2418
Last Tap Dance, The 2416
Last Ten Years, The 112
Last Thing That I Want to Do Is
Fall in Love, The 2477
Last Time I Saw Paris, The 2204, 2372
Last Torch Song, The 2416
Last Waltz, The 1687, 2416, 2419
Last Waltz I Had with You, The 764
Last Will and Testament 3036

Last Word, The 1871
Last Words of Divine Devore, The 1415
Latavia 670
Latavian Chant, The 670
Late Bloomer 4619
Late Bloomer and Prom Montage 1059
Late Bloomers 496
Late Hours 295, 4804
Late Love 2556
Late Nite Comic 2420
Late, Late Show, The 1061, 2017
Lately I've Been Feeling So Strange 279
Later 722, 2163, 2536
Later Than Spring 3815
Latest Creation in Girls, The 3134
Latest Cure for Ennui, The 1264
Latest Fad, The 116
Latest News, The 4663
Latest Society Pet, The 1111
Latest Thing from Paris, The 1285
Latigo 3170
Latin American Way, The 3598
Latin in Me, The 512
Latin Quarter, The 4094
Latin Tune, a Manhattan Moon and You, A 2301
Latins Know How 2597
Latirana 2407
L'Auberge Tohu-Bohu 1994
Lauder Melodies 4094
Laugh 2258
Laugh, The 4464
Laugh After Laugh 4173
Laugh and Grow Fat 2601
Laugh and Play 4575
Laugh and the World Laughs Too 3748
Laugh and the World Laughs with You 2798
Laugh at Life 3064, 3680
Laugh at Love 4373
Laugh, I Thought I'd Die 3094
Laugh It Off 2768, 3036
Laugh It Up 766, 2983
Laugh Parade, The 2423
Laugh Song 786
Laugh the Clouds Away 2637
Laugh with a Tear in It, A (Laugh and the World Will Laugh with You, Weep and You'll Weep Alone) 3642
Laugh Your Blues Away 3054
Laugh Your Cares Away 1486
Laughing Americans 3667
Laughing and Happy Am I 1522
Laughing Bells 3536
Laughing Daffodil 4527
Laughing Eyes 1902
Laughing Generals (inst.) 2228
Laughing Ha Ha 1521
Laughing Little Almond Eyes 1243
Laughing Low, on Tip-Toe 3777
Laughing Out Loud 4629
Laughing Powders 47
Laughing School, The 4046
Laughing Song 1295, 1593, 2334, 3028
Laughing Song, The 3602
Laughing Song 2454
Laughing Stock 4138
Laughing Waltz 2985
Laughing Water 2964
Laughing Water Ripple 4644
Laughing Waters 638
Laughs 456, 4649
Laughter Ain't There Anymore 2305
Laughter and Love 375
Laughter Is Queen Tonight 737
Launching, The 3110
Laundry Duet 3146
Laundry Scene 629
Laundry Trio 45
Laura De Maupassant 1791
Laurey Makes Up Her Mind Ballet (inst.) 3263
Lavender and Lace 2461
Law, The 629
Law and Order 2018, 2134, 2616
Law Breakers 4488
Law Is, The 3227
Law Is Law 3823
Law Must Be Obeyed, The 4158
Law of Barataria, The 2500
Law of the Jungle 2970
Lawn As White As Driven Snow 3909
Lawyer's Lament 1700
Lawyer's Out Today, The 3600
Lawyerman 3600
Lawyers 550
Lay of the Cavalier 3732
Lay of the Jay, The 1071
Lay of the Lute, The 3774
Lay of the Merry Ha! Ha!, The 2982
Lay Your Bets 4741
Layers of Underwear 705
Laying Abaht 1277
Laying the Foundations 2004
Lazar's Heroes 3806
Lazily, Drowsily 2500
Lazy 4219
Lazy Afternoon 1600, 1873
Lazy Boy 70
Lazy Land 954
Lazy Levee Loungers 1448
Lazy Lulu 186
Lazy Moon 1614
Lazy Step 612
Le Bal Chez Madame de Mortemouille 2364
Le Beau Sabreur 4616
Le Bon Mot 3491
Le Can Can 3100
Le Chasseur de Chez Maxim's 468
Le Cochon Qui Voulait Maigrir 1253
Le Coeur de Ninon 2914
Le Controlleur des Wagon-Lits 3146
Le Croissant 3491

Le Cygne 2976
Le Dernier Pierrot 1638
Le Fils Surnatural 3362
Le Five O'Clock 4335
Le Folly Bergere 2876
Le Grand Cirque de Provence 2318
Le Grand Lustucru 2753
Le Grand Mogul 1650
Le Grand Rape 1695
Le Grisbi Is le Root of le Evil in Man 2150
Le Hot Spot 1049
Le Jazz Hot 4560
Le Jockey Malgre Lui 3229
Le Kic-King 1464
Le Lion et La Souris (The Lion and the Mouse) 2715
Le Maitre de la Conte, or Maupassant Tells All 1256
Le Marquis de Faublas 277
Le Minet Bleu (The Blue Kitten) (Meow) 468
Le Monsieur de Cinq Heures 4213
Le Nouveau Regiment 4624
Le Paradis de Mahomet 3372
Le Peril Jaune 1663
Le Petit Cafe 2497
Le Petit Duc 2507
Le Petit Prince 2539
Le Reflection 3910
Le Reve d'Absinthe 870
Le Reveillon 4733
Le Rigodon 2715
Le Roi D'Aquitaine 2753
Le Roi de Carreau 1720
Le Satyr 3494
Le Sport American 1625
Le Train du Ciel 2753
Lead 'Em Around By the Nose 778
Lead 'Em On 391
Lead Me Now 4615
Lead Me to Laughter 4290
Lead Me to Love 4603
Lead Me to That Beautiful Band 802, 4655
Lead Me to the Water 3724
Leader of a Big Time Band 1018
Leader of a Big-Time Band, The 4058
Leader of Fashion Am I 1900
Leader of Frocks and Frills, The 737
Leader of the Ball, The 4088
Leader of the Colored Aristocracy 2111
Leader of the German Band, The 246
Leader of the Labour Party, The 4551
Leader of the Pack 2427
Leader of Vanity Fair, The 4478
Leaders of Society 130
Leaders of the Modern Regime 930
Leading Girl, The 512
Leading Lady 211
Leading Man 2757
Leadville Johnny Brown 4516
Leaf in the Wind 84
Leaflets 919
League of Nations, The 1404, 2960
Lean on Me 1093
Leander 2293
Leanin' on the Lord 105
Leaning on a Lamppost 2798
Leaning on a Shovel 3986
Leanyvasar 2761
Leap of Faith 3568
Leaping Leopards 3915
Learn a Little Something 3482
Learn About Life 1739
Learn Everything 148
Learn How to Laugh 2681
Learn to Be Lonely 1068
Learn to Croon 4778
Learn to Do the Strut 3008
Learn to Love 344
Learn to Sing a Love Song 4821
Learn to Skate 2086
Learn to Smile 3218
Learn Your Lessons Well 1595
Learning Hebrew 181
Learning Love 127
Learning to Love 2546
Lease on My Heart 1207
Least That's My Opinion 1385, 4123
Leave a Light 114
Leave a Message 2234
Leave Her, Johnny, Leave Her 2682
Leave It Alone 2047
Leave It to Jane 2430
Leave It to Katrina 4667
Leave It to Levy 376
Leave It to Love 184, 2376, 2747
Leave It to the Boys in the Navy 1230
Leave It to the Girls 155
Leave It to the Ladies 455
Leave It to Us, Gov 270
Leave It to Your Milliner 2574
Leave My Pulse Alone 2137
Leave My Women Alone 297
Leave the Atom Alone 2190
Leave the Thinking to Me 4288
Leave the World Behind 2618
Leave Them Wanting More 943
Leave Us Let Things Alone Like They Was 2397
Leave Well Enough Alone 483
Leave Your Mind Alone 1363
Leaves of Grass 2433
Leavin' fo' de Promis' Lan' 3541
Leavin' Time 1385, 4123
Leaving Town While We May 3569
Leaving's Not the Only Way to Go 394
Leben Sie Wohl 161
Lebn Zol Kolumbus (Long Live Columbus!) 1609
Lechaim 2811
Leche Bella 3718
Lecon le Danse 2057
Lees of Old Virginia, The 3897

Leetle Bit Too Much, A 3717
Left All Alone Again Blues 3146
Left Alone to Be 562
Left by the Wayside 2965
Left, Right, Left 2674
Leg It 2302
Leg o' Mutton 4297
Leg of Nations, The 4814
Leg of the Duck, The 935
Legacy, The 3279
Legacy Blues 2200
Legal Heir 4062
Legal Writ a Day, A 42
Legalize My Name 1385, 4123
Legend, The 2377
Legend 2435
Legend, The 1560, 4075
Legend Fulfilled, The 2673
Legend of a Stocking, The 2286
Legend of Black-Eyed Susan Grey, The 1766
Legend of Grimm, The 2673
Legend of King Arthur, The 1377
Legend of La La Lu, The 47
Legend of Leda, The 3150
Legend of Mackie Messer 4368
Legend of Old Rufino, The 1377
Legend of Sleepy Hollow 239
Legend of Sleepy Hollow, The 2100, 4015
Legend of the Castle 250
Legend of the Chimes, The 3736
Legend of the Cyclamen Tree, The (The Legend of the Golden Tree) 4815
Legend of the Djin, The 4293
Legend of the Drums 4817
Legend of the Glowworm 3312
Legend of the Islands 4243, 4823
Legend of the Maguires, The 4605
Legend of the Mill, The 3675
Legend of the Mission Bells 4328
Legend of the Mojaves, The 8
Legend of the Pearls, The 3006
Legend of the Rose 735
Legend of the Sea 3352
Legend of the Shirt, The 4575
Legend of the Sleeping Beauty, The (Scene) 2809
Legend of the Sons of Samson, The 1388
Legend of the Stork, The 2543
Legend of the Tea Tree, The 3775
Legend of the Wishing Well, The 4719
Legend of the Woodland, The 4427
Legend of Villa 2837
Legend Olden, The 1114
Legend Song 718
Legendary Eino Fflliikkiinneenn, The 304
Legends of the Munkacs 306
Legionnaires 1132
Legions 3088
Legions of the Night 3088
Legislature Sat in Poland, The 340
Legitimate 3986
Legomania 2645
Legs 2007
Legs, Legs, Legs 1126
Lei of Memories 1809, 4337
Lekho Dodi, Ko Riboyn Olam, Sholem Aleykhem, Gut Vokh 1609
L'Elefant Skeed 4421
Lemme Tell Ya 3224
Lemmings Lament 3077
Lemon in the Garden of Love, A 121, 4115
Lemon Peels 1588
Lemons 3945
Lena, Lena 2317
Lend Me a Bob Till Monday 3386
Lend Me a Kiss Until To-morrow 4079
Lend Us a Daddy 2446
Lennie 4629
Lenore 1798
Lenox Avenue 1950, 4730
L'Envers Du Music Hall 3010
Leocadia 172
Leola and Me 1496
Leonara 4687
Leonard Stokes and Hal LeRoy (scene) 4823
Leonardo's Lemonade (Lennie's Lemonade) (Leonard's Lemonade) 2676
Les Demoiselles de Saint-Cyriens 613
Les Deux Temps Parisienne 1307
Les Dominos Roses 4418
Les Fetards 2341, 3784
Les Filles de Bordeaux 2753
Les Finale de Paris 2364
Les Fourberies De Scapin 4450
Les Girls 3598
Les Halles 2949
Les Miserables 2442
Les Parapluies de Cherbourg 4505
Les Poulettes 1347
Les Poupees de Paris 2443
Les P'tites Michu 2524
Les Romanesques 1245
Les Sylphides avec La Bumpe 4131
Less Is More 2022
Less Is More and More 2069
Less Than Eighty Days 3091
Lesson, The 2106
Lesson Book Song 2465
Lesson Five 3463
Lesson in C, A (inst.) 886
Lesson in Dancing, A 1458
Lesson in Etiquette, A 1243
Lesson in French 3150
Lesson in Kissing, A (Kiss, Kiss, Kiss) 3387
Lesson in Love, A 2135
Lesson in Love, A (Kiss Song) 2745
Lesson in Love, A 4590, 4616
Lesson in Terpsichore, A 2397
Lesson in Yiddish, A 3559
Lesson #8 4210
Lesson One 3463

Lesson with a Fan, A 2465
Lessons in Love 1712, 3837
Lessons in Verse 3673
Lessons on Life 127
Lest We Forget 392, 3296
Let 'Em Eat Cake 2444
Let 'Em Eat Caviar 2444
Let 'Em Rot 4619
Let 'Er Go Letty 2446
Let-a-Go Your Heart 4337
Let a Satirist Enumerate a Catalogue of Crimes 3777
Let Antipholus In 514
Let Bygones Be Bygones 3562
Let Cupid In 3400
Let Cutie Cut Your Cuticle 560, 2960
Let De Sun Sink Down 2225
Let Down Your Hair with a Bang 4677
Let Every Day Be a Holiday 1690
Let Fate Decide 2747
Let George Do It 2448
Let Georgie Do It 3977
Let Gloomy Thoughts Go Hang 1521
Let Her Down 3952
Let Her Drown 1148, 3951
Let Her Go 944, 1065
Let Her Not Be Beautiful 4798
Let Him Kick Up His Heels 4764
Let Him Love You 1262
Let It All Hang Out 871
Let It Alone 9
Let It Be 4789
Let It Be Gay 847
Let It Be Him (1) 451
Let It Be Him (2) 451
Let It Be Soon 2549
Let It Be Today 337
Let It Be Written 1161
Let It Come Down 4734
Let It Fall 3817
Let It Rain 535, 4010
Let It Ride 2449
Let It Snow! Let It Snow! Let It Snow! 4743
Let Love Go 1027
Let Me Awake 463
Let Me Be 823
Let Me Be a Friend to You (The Kind of Friend) 3766
Let Me Be a Kid 3806
Let Me Be Born Again 444
Let Me Be Free 1111, 3011
Let Me Be Lonely 261
Let Me Be Myself 266
Let Me Be Your House Boat Beau 4544
Let Me Be Your Last Sweetheart 2901
Let Me Be Your Mirror 518
Let Me Be Your Sugar Baby 4197
Let Me Believe in Me 2285
Let Me Build a Little Fence Around Your Heart 2108
Let Me Come In 2801
Let Me Dance 201
Let Me Down 2618
Let Me Draw You a Picture 839
Let Me Drink in Your Eyes 3538
Let Me Drown 1878
Let Me Entertain You 1709
Let Me Explain 1276
Let Me Finish 4068, 4301
Let Me Give All My Love to Thee 3650
Let Me Go Back 3786
Let Me Go to Him 261
Let Me Have a Little Corner of Your Heart 4776
Let Me Have a Son 3702
Let Me Hear You Love Me (Everbody Love Me) 3299
Let Me Hold You in My Arms 2296
Let Me Introduce You to My Rosie 2308
Let Me Lead the Way 1848
Let Me Live Today 4214
Let Me Look Deep into Your Eyes 324
Let Me Love You 943, 4384
Let Me Make Love to You 2426
Let Me Match My Private Life with Yours 125
Let Me Put It This Way 2057
Let Me Put My Arms Around You 1902
Let Me Remember 1751
Let Me Ride the Wind 2196
Let Me Run to You 4153
Let Me Shimmy and I'm Satisfied 4851
Let Me Show You Paris 558
Let Me Show You the World 4522
Let Me Sing! 1695
Let Me Sing 3882
Let Me Sing and I'm Happy 789
Let Me Sing My Song 550
Let Me Take You Away from All This 2511
Let Me Take You for a Ride 3983
Let Me Teach You How to Swim 149
Let Me Tell You a Little Story 2659
Let Me Tell You About My House 4408
Let Me Think for You 518
Let Me Weep on Your Shoulder 2382
Let Me Whirl to an Old Refrain 4844
Let Me Whisper in Your Ear 684
Let My People Come 2451
Let Others Boast 104
Let the Band Play 1295
Let the Canakin Clink 3909
Let the Circus Now Appear 4046
Let the Day Perish When I Was Born 2648
Let the Devil Take Us 373
Let the Good Book Lead the Way 181
Let the Good Times Roll 1296, 1890, 166
Let the Grass Grow 1386
Let the Healing Begin 1073
Let the Juice Ooze Through 2127
Let the Little Joy Bells Ring 487
Let the Lower Lights Be Burning 3845
Let the Man Who Makes the Gun 1127

Let the Moment Slip By 3824
Let the Music Play 2486
Let the Play Begin 945, 3527
Let the Show Go On! 2285
Let the Soul Kiss Be Mine Today 4094
Let the Toast Pass 2633
Let the Trumpets Sound 4662
Let the World Begin Again 4089
Let Them Go 4014
Let Them See a Star 2658
Let There Be 730
Let There Be Light 2142
Let There Be Time 753
Let Things Be Like They Always Was 4169
Let Those Who'd Wed 104
Let Us Be Jolly as Long as We Can 2974
Let Us Be Married 1555
Let Us Build a Little Nest 3529
Let Us Charm Each Other 3764
Let Us Dance 1565
Let Us Dance the Boston 4642
Let Us Dance Till the Dawn 903
Let Us Find a Cosey Little Nook (Let Us Find a Charming Rendezvous) 3308
Let Us Gather at the Goal Line 4428
Let Us Gossip of the Latest Court Flirtation 355
Let Us Greet With Joy Pretended 1388
Let Us Keep the Shimmie 3962
Let Us Part Good Friends 3573
Let Us Put Him in the Stocks (Finale Act II) 3736
Let Us Romance Together 296
Let Us Sing 2559
Let Us Sing Praise 10
Let Us Stay Where the Crowd Is 186
Let Us Swear It By the Pale Moonlight 2974
Let Well Enough Alone 2771
Let Your Body Have Its Way 482
Let Your Hair Down 621
Let Yourself Go 789, 1813
Let Yourself Go! 4320
Let's 508, 3551
Let's All Be Exactly and Precisely What We Are 3215
Let's All Go Raving Mad 702
Let's All Go to the Lobby 2776
Let's All Sing 4611
Let's All Sing the Lard Song 4345
Let's Away 175
Let's Ball Awhile 3983
Let's Be Buddies 1762, 3359
Let's Be Dreamers in Love 46
Let's Be Elegant or Die! 2219
Let's Be Frank, Mr. Frankenstein 2443
Let's Be Friends 4444
Let's Be Happy 904
Let's Be Happy Now 2827
Let's Be Lonesome Together 1486
Let's Be Merry 346, 4404
Let's Be Sentimental 2547
Let's Be Strangers Again 339
Let's Be Young 4237
Let's Begin 2204, 2372, 3735
Let's Believe in the Captain 2472
Let's Bring Back Show Business 3264
Let's Build a Little Nest 1796
Let's Bungalow 2696
Let's Call It a Day 4177
Let's Comb Beaches 323
Let's Dance a Frailichs 268
Let's Dance and Make Up 4651
Let's Dance Till the Dawn 2806
Let's Do a Ballet 2582
Let's Do and Say We Didn't 1539, 2308
Let's Do It 1018, 3196, 3235
Let's Do It All Over Again 4611
Let's Do It for Granny 2541
Let's Do It, Let's Fall in Love 4581
Let's Do Something 919
Let's Dream Again 4465
Let's Dream Together 2806
Let's Drink 1734
Let's Drink to That 2681
Let's Evolve 4028
Let's Face It 2453
Let's Face the Music and Dance 789
(Let's Do It) Let's Fall in Love 3382
Let's Fetch the Carriage 1290
Let's Fly Away 1018, 3131, 1393, 4639
Let's Forget Bandana Days 1499
Let's Forget We Ever Had a Care 306
Let's Get a Move On 4719
Let's Get Acquainted 1520
Let's Get Back to Bach 1885
Let's Get Back to Glamour 4510
Let's Get Drunk 410, 4041
Let's Get Lost in Now 3824
Let's Get Married 1524
Let's Get Married or Something 1191
Let's Get Married Right Away 792
Let's Get Started 337
Let's Get the Umpire's Goat 4802, 4803
Let's Get Together 4534
Let's Give a Cheer 1617
Let's Go 632, 1094, 1175, 1191
Let's Go! 2574
Let's Go 4422
Let's Go A-Roaming 1560
Let's Go Around the Town 4603
Let's Go Back to the Waltz 2983
Let's Go Boating 556
Let's Go Broadway 1953
Let's Go Down 3825
Let's Go Down to the Shop 3652
Let's Go Eat Worms in the Garden 1275
Let's Go Flying 4695
Let's Go Home 3142, 798
Let's Go Lovin' 1874
Let's Go Native 4561
Let's Go Out and Ring Doorbells 2748
Let's Go South 320

Let's Go Steppin' 845
Let's Go to Fairyland 1753
Let's Go to the Dogs 4011
Let's Go to the Ritz 1496
Let's Go to Town 2302
Let's Go Too Far 84
Let's Go What Do You Say? Let's Go! 2336
Let's Have a Fling 1540
Let's Have a Good Time 2135, 4651
Let's Have a Love Affair 1027
Let's Have a Party 1679
Let's Have a Rattling Good Time 3404
Let's Have a Simple Wedding 956
Let's Have Another Cup of Coffee 789, 1225
Let's Have Lunch 4217
Let's Hear It for Daddy Moola 1064
Let's Hear It for Me 708, 4402
Let's Hit the Road 4041
Let's Hold Hands 1342
Let's Improvise 2295
Let's K'nock K'nees 4823
Let's Keep It That Way 204
Let's Kiss and Make Up 1419, 4529
Let's Kiss Goodbye 381
Let's Laugh and Be Merry 1722
Let's Listen to the Ladies 2928
Let's Live in Sin 2590
Let's Live It Over Again 843
Let's Live It Up 4127
Let's Make a Night of It 3230, 848
Let's Make Believe 1971, 2888
Let's Make Hey, Hey, Hey (While the Sun Is Shinin') 1514
Let's Make It a Night 1762, 3972
Let's Make It Christmas All Year 'Round 2267
Let's Make It Forever 596
Let's Make Love Among the Roses 4757
Let's Make Memories Tonight 4772
Let's Make Up 2421, 3472
Let's Make Whoopie 3342
Let's Marry 97
Let's Merge 4087
Let's Misbehave 3382
Let's Mop Up These Yankees and Go Home 669
Let's Not Behave Like People 3160
Let's Not Fall in Love 80
Let's Not Get Married 3312, 3810
Let's Not Go Away This Summer 1370
Let's Not Have a Kissless Day 4037
Let's Not Say Goodbye 1347
Let's Not Talk About It 3760
Let's Not Talk About Love 2453
Let's Not Waste a Moment 2864
Let's Paint the Town Red 1867
Let's Play a Tune on the Music Box 1238
Let's Play at Love 1079
Let's Play Ball 1038
Let's Play Hookey 953
Let's Play Hookie 1920
Let's Play Let's Say 562
Let's Play the Game 1079
Let's Pretend 606, 766, 1552, 2489, 2601, 3236, 4094, 4626
Let's Pretend We're Grown Up 3603
Let's Pretend You Love Me 1593
Let's Put a Man on the Sun 1842
Let's Put It to Music 4777
Let's Put on the Ritz 876
Let's Raise Hell 1251
Let's Reminisce 4062
Let's Rub Noses 47
Let's Run Away and Get Married 3655
Let's Say Goodbye 3235
Let's Say Goodnight 'Til It's Morning 4212
Let's Say Goodnight with a Dance 4086
Let's See What Happens 989
Let's Sing, Sing, Sing 806
Let's Sit and Talk about You 1827
Let's Steal a Tune from Offenbach 2809
Let's Step Out 1272
Let's Stroll Along and Sing a Song of Love 3489
Let's Suppose 3352
Let's Swing It 1127
Let's Take a Look Into the Future 2275
Let's Take a Stroll through London 3818
Let's Take a Trolley Ride 4506
Let's Take a Walk Around the Block 2475
Let's Take Advantage of Now 3850
Let's Take an Old-Fashioned Walk 1968, 2894
Let's Take Him Home in Triumph 4687
Let's Talk About a Woman 1029, 1242
Let's Talk About the Weather 1136, 2105
Let's Talk About You 4301
Let's Talk Dirty to the Animals 1512
Let's Turn on the Love Interest 1272
Let's Turn Out the Lights and Go to Bed 1481
Let's Walk Home the Long Way 'Round 4163
Let's Waltz and Whistle 2479
Let's Wander Off Nowhere 1900
Let's Work Together 721
Let's Wreck the Joint 2151
Let's You and I Just Say Good-Bye 3723
Letter, The 280
Letter (Me Charlotte Dear), The 705
Letter, The 4193
Letter (My Little Women), The 2550
Letter, The 949, 4073, 1811, 2713, 3671, 1940, 3938, 4233, 4537
Letter Boxes 959
Letter Chansonette 2671
Letter Comes, A 945
Letter Duet 2101, 3035
Letter Duet (My Dearest Paul) 4258
Letter Duet 4670
Letter for Roxane, A 949
Letter from a Friend 2333
Letter from Klemnacht 1068
Letter Home to England 4301
Letter #3 2185

Letter of Farewell, A 3084
Letter of the Law 3204
Letter of the Law, The 1373
Letter Song 168, 3862
Letter Song, The 742
Letter Song 996, 2825
Letter Song, The 132, 4010
Letter Song 4352, 743
Letter Song-Goodbye 2897
Letter to J.D. Salinger, A 392
Letter to the Children 1068
Letter Trio 3308, 4037
Letters 270, 2492, 2695, 2770, 4433, 3918, 2224
Letters from America 1265
Letters from Home 3773
Letters I Write All the Day 252
Letters That Lighten Broadway 4079
Letting Go 2198, 838
L'Evasion 3910
Levee Gang 2462
Levee Land 3677
Levee Lou 2247
Levee Nights 554
Levi Is a Grand Old Name 3525
Leviathan 2236
L'Exposition Universalle 3091
Lezione 139
L'Heure Bleu Ballet 3431
L'Heure D'Or (One Golden Hour) 4692
L'Histoire de Madame de la Tour 4557
Liable to Catch On 512
Liaisons 2536
Liar, The 2464
Liar 3117
Liar's Song, The 2464
Lib & Let Live 4679
Libby 1516, 589
Liberal's Lament 4635
Liberate 674
Liberated Woman 413
Liberation Tango 4635
Liberia 2918
Liberty 1208, 2573
Liberty, Equality, Fraternity 3491
Liberty Girl, The 586
Liberty Glide, The 2108
Liberty Hall 3771
Liberty Statue 3341
(Welcome to) Lichtenburg 619
Lick, and a Riff, and a Slow Bounce, A 532
Lickin's 4429
Lickpenny Lover, A 3221
Lida Rose 3016
Lido Beach, The 4341
Lido Lady 2467
Lie a Little 4019
Liebchen, Liebchen 3351
Lieben Dich 1158
Lieber Augustin 2469
Liebeslied 4370
Liebeswalzer 2334
Lies 2032, 4016
Lies, Lies, Lies 2648
Lieutenants of the Lord 1755
Life 729, 2043, 2717, 1771
Life All Free from Care, A 3943
Life Among the Roses 4382
Life and Adventures of Nicholas Nickle by, The 2474
Life and Love 4547
Life As a Twosome 124, 1859
Life as Rumor 2992
Life Begins (At Exactly 8:40 or Thereabouts) 2475
Life Begins at City Hall (Beautifying the City) 2475
Life Begins at Sweet Sixteen 1493
Life Begins Today 496
Life Belongs to You 972
Life By Love Unlighted 2603
Life Can Be a Fairy Tale 3844
Life Can Be Beautiful 2304, 2629
Life Can Be Funny 4450
Life Could Be a Cakewalk with You 4259
Life Could Be So Beautiful 3365
Life Does a Man a Favor (When It Gives Him Simple Joys) 3234
Life Full of Surprises, A 2011
Life Goes On 3714
Life Has Just Begun 1565
Life I Wanted, The 31
Life in a Harem 3298
Life in America 2196
Life in Kansas 4723
Life in the Morning 429
Life in the Old Girl Yet 3663
Life in the Theatre 4389
Life in Town 317
Life in Venetia 4700
Life Is 4862
Life Is a Balancing Act 275
Life Is a Carousel 4248
Life Is a Dance 1298
Life Is a Dirty Business 1711
Life Is a Drag 4518
Life Is a Gamble 487
Life Is a Game of Bluff 2907
Life Is a Game of Chance 1534
Life Is a Game of Checkers 3676
Life Is a Garden 4228
Life Is a Masquerade 1199
Life Is a Merry-Go-Round 1566
Life Is a One-Way Street 2217
Life Is a Riddle 1111
Life Is a See-Saw 2716, 2347
Life Is a Toy Shop 666
Life Is a Toyshop 3784
Life Is a Woman 4160
Life Is Ahead of Me 3792
Life Is All Sunshine with You 3593

Life Is Happiness Indeed 630
Life Is Just a Bowl of Cherries 393, 1492, 1813, 3936
Life Is Just What You Make It 1526
Life Is Like a Dance 1866
Life Is Like a Toy Balloon 1691
Life Is Like a Train (Entr'acte) 3279
Life Is Lonely 2701
Life Is Love 3532
Life Is Love and Laughter 4590
Life Is Lovely 1596
Life Is Not a Fairy Tale 3844
Life Is One Thing After Another 1335
Life Is Only What You Make It, After All 4382
Life Is Short, My Dear Friends 4554
Life Is Simple As Water 1426
Life Is So Peculiar 1296
Life Is Such a Funny Proposition 3068
Life Is Too Sad 2323
Life Is Too Short 2011, 4060
Life Is Too Short to be Wasting Your Time 2722
Life Is Tough 3823
Life Is What We Make It 1466
Life Like That, A 4405
(There'll Be) Life, Love, and Laughter 1284
Life of a Bold Free Lance, The 252
Life of a Buckaroo 3329
Life of a Nurse, The 2382
Life of a Rose, The 1486
Life of a Rose, The (Rose of the Morning) 3406
Life of a Rover, The 1260
Life of a Sailor, The 1690
Life of a Woman, The 1045
Life of Love, The 3753
Life of Sin 1342
Life of the Party, The 1691, 1764
Life of the Party 2479, 3914
Life of the Party, The 4267
Life on a Farm 3258
Life on the Inside 1064
Life on the Mississippi 2028
Life on the Rocks 708
Life on the Stage (inst.) 2481
Life Oriental 3372
Life-Saver's Song, The 3139
Life Story 4535, 784
Life That I Planned for Him, The 766
Life That Jack Built, The 430
Life That You Own, A 4055
Life Upon the Wicked Stage 2372, 3949
Life Was Monotonous 601
Life Was Pie for the Pioneer 1931
Life Was Worth While 3973
Life Wins 4558
Life with Father 601, 924
Life with Rocky, A 404
Life Without a Cigarette 4290
Life without Her, A 1249
Life Without Him, A 840
Life without Love 1888
Life's Too Short to Be Blue 4392
Lifeguards, The 266
Lifeline 828
Life's a Circus 1546
Life's a Dance 1973, 2620
Life's a Dress Parade 4657
Life's a Funny Present from Someone 3813
Life's a Funny Proposition After All 2517
Life's a Gamble 1611
Life's a Game 57
Life's a Game at Best 1162
Life's a Game of Polo 75
Life's a Holiday 1497
Life's a Masquerade 2885
Life's a Race 1753
Life's a Tale 3727
Life's Ambition 2171
Life's Darkest Moment 1373
Life's No Blooming Airy Bubble 2715
Life's Not That Simple 1061
Lifesaver 2555
Lifetime of Love, A 615
Liffey Waltz, The 2268
Lift 'Em Up and Put 'Em Down 653
Lift Every Voice and Sing 2908
Lift Him Up 1636
Lift Me Up 1636
Lift the Cup 1021
Lift Up Your Voice! 10
Lift Your Eyes to Mine 4258
Lift Your Skirt (A Little Bit Higher) 2547
Lifted 3666
Light, The 3643
Light Around the Corner, The 2285
Light at the End of the Tunnel 4138
Light Fantastic, The 3664
Light in Girlish Eyes, The 4544
Light in the Heart 649
Light Is My Heart 178
Light of Love 3000
Light of the World 1595
Light of Your Love (La Luz de Tu Amor), The 535
Light on the Other Side 3125
Light One Candle 1273
Light Romance 460
Light Sings 2801
Light Soprano 2364
Light That Lies in Women's Eyes, The 355, 1316
Light the Candles 81
Light Travelin' Man 1567
Light Up 2747
Light Will Shine 3088
Lighted Candles 4003
Lighthouse and the Boat 1021
Lighting Me a Candle 4127
Lightly, Lightly 2937
Lightnin' Bug 10
Lightning Bug Song, The 3934

Lightning Rod Interlude 367
Lights Come Up, The 3039
Lights of London, The 869
Lights of Long Ago, The 754
Lights Up 1395
Like a Bird on the Wing 3157
Like a Bolt from the Blue 881
Like a God 1315
Like a King 4226, 4276
Like a Lady 2173
Like a Leaf Falling in the Breeze 4143
Like a Lily 1589
Like a Little Ladylike Lady Like You 2829
Like-a-Me, Like-a-You 2780
Like a Newborn Child 2306
Like a Park on Sunday 729
Like a Rock 4537
Like a Rolling Stone 3739
Like a Sherpherdess 2145
Like a Wandering Minstrel 2829
Like a Woman Loves a Man 2961, 3444
Like a Young Man 2864
Like Clouds Up in the Sky 1385
Like Everyone Else (Soliloquy) 2053
Like Her 287
Like Him 4286
Like It 280
Like It Was 4067, 2822
Like June Skies 476
Like Me Less-Love Me More 1126
Like She Loves Me 3254
Like Swallow Flying 20
Like the Breeze Blows 4863
Like the Eagles Fly 135
Like the Fjords of Scandinavia 1530
Like the Nymphs of Spring 773
Like the Rose (Paris Song) 1680
Like Wow 1435
Like You 771
Like You Do 3659
Like Yours 1832, 1273
Likin' Ain't Like Lovin' 434, 2025
Liking and Loving 1588
Li'l Abner 2484
Li'l Augie Is a Natural Man 4123
Li'l Gal 3945
Li'l Ol' You and Li'l Ol' Me 4582
Lil Old Bitty Pissant Country Place, A 374
Lil Ole Letter 4273
Lila Tremaine 1227
Lilac Time 4341
Lilac Tree 1319
Lilac Tree, The 4120, 346
Lilac Wine 961
Lilacs Bring Back Memories 3211
Lilas 101
Lili 656
Lili Is a Lady with a Suitcase Up Her Sleeve 3688
Lilies in the Pond Are not for Me, The 4761
Lilies of the Field 2583, 3184, 4104
Lilies of Your Love May Die, The 698
Liliom 660
Lilith 462
Lillian 1273
Lillian, Lillian, Lillian 1273
Lillie, Lawrence and Jack 1267
Lilly, The 645
Lilly 1126
Lilly's Address 4518
Lilt of a Gypsy Strain, The 3727
Lilt That's Lazy and Dreamy and Hazy (Waltz-Song) 1554
Lily 3796
Lily and the Dew, The 3951
Lily and the Moon, The 1768
Lily and the Nightingale, The 1355
Lily and the Rose, The 4359
Lily Bell Polka 3431
Lily Belle May June 4374
Lily Garland 3279
Lily Has Done the Zampoughi Every Time I Pulled Her Coattail 40
Lily of Laguna 2388
Lily of Longacre Square, The 1920
Lily of the Alley 1970
Lily of the Valley 3254
Lily, Oscar 3279
Lily Pad Tango 1872
Lily Pool, The 200
Lily White 3422
Lily's Eyes 3862
Lily's Promenade, The 2209
Lima 3865
Lima Bean 2834
Limbo 4147
Limbo Dance (Under the Ropes) 1729
Limbo-Land 4464
Lime House Nights 560
Limehouse Blues 133
Limehouse Night, A 2570
Limehouse Nights 2960
Limerick Girls 3267
Limerick's Running Yet 4508
Limo to the Plaza 119
L'Important C'est La Rose 1427
Lim'ricks 4123
Lina, Mah Lady 3744
Lincoln and Juarez 2748
Lincoln and Liberty 2018
Lincoln and Soda 2018
Lincoln Center 1049, 1107
Lincoln Soliloquy 4163
Lincoln Stroll 3614
Linda 570
Linda and Her Londonderry Air 4467
Linda, Georgina, Marilyn and Me 2451
Linda, Look Out De Windah 3745
Lindy Lou 2338
Lindy's 36
Line, The 1699

Line Is Busy, The 2276
Line Is Unbroken, The 4615
Line It Out, Mr. Maginnity 2481
Line of Duty 3882
Lines in Mollie's Hands, The 531
Linger in the Lobby 2376
Linger Longer, Letty 2489
Linger Longer, Lingerie 4803
Lingerie 1308, 2628, 3203, 3770
Linguine 4732
Link By Link 754
Linnet in the Tree, The 762
Lion and the Lamb, The 1101, 2695
Lion and the Monk, The (Die Trying) 9
Lion and the Mouse, The 2917
Lion and the Unicorn, The 54
Lion Dance 2655, 3340
Lion King, The 1202
Lion Tamer 70, 2687
Lion's Dream 4722
Lion's Queen 1067
Lionet 3691
Lippy Song, The 3811
Lips 458
Lips, Lips, Lips 2684
Lips that Laugh at Love 3012
Lipstick Traces 1890
Liquid Air 2724
Liquid Air Police 2724
Liquor Dealer's Dream, The 1755
L'Irlandesa Rosa Dell' Abie 1653, 1657
Lisa Carew 2198
Lisbon Sequence 630
Lise Dear 169
Lise Loves Everybody 945
Lisette 948, 4670, 4665
List and Learn 2977
List Song 2677
List to Our Matin Serenade 4724
List to the Pleading 3348
List'ning on Some Radio 4816
Listen, Cosette 3931
Listen, Fellas! 919
Listen Fool 2200
Listen for the Rooster 4337
Listen, I Feel 3602
Listen Little Boy 708
Listen Mr. Verdi 3420
Listen to Me 580, 2492, 3308, 4283
Listen to My Little Song 696
Listen to My Prayer 1743
Listen to the Band 2749
Listen to the Beat! 411
Listen to the Music 1822
Listen to the Rain 1439
Listen to the Raindrops 4283
Listen to Your Heart 3496
Listen with Your Heart 3227
Listen World 708
Listenin' to the Grand Ol' Opry 3671
Listening 1056, 3009
Listening to the Radio 2757
Listening to You 4676
Literary Cocktail Party 3615
Lites-Camera-Platitude 4633
Lithograph Land 2858
Litt'ry and Artistic Scene, 1930, The 3180
Little Angel Cake 4150
Little Babes That Sleep All Night 3631
Little Baby 4654
Little Backyard Band, The 4860
Little Bag of Tricks 4491
Little Baggie Maggy 2570
Little Band of Gold, A 2335
Little Bandbox Girl 4148
Little Bas Bleu 1388
Little Bid for Sympathy, A 2907
Little Big Man 462, 462
Little Bird, A 284
Little Bird, Little Bird 2727
Little Bird of Paradise 48
Little Bird's Story 1157
Little Birdie Told Me, The 3073
Little Birdie Told Me So, A 3436
Little Birds 1924
Little Birds of Paradise 3773
Little Biscuit 2190
Little Bit Delighted with the Weather, A 3292
Little Bit Furter On, A 2844
Little Bit in Love, A 4734
Little Bit Individual, A 2240
Little Bit More, A 2064
Little Bit o' Country 4314
Little Bit O' Glitter 2285
Little Bit of Blarney, A 2232, 2493
Little Bit of Cheese, A 2889
Little Bit of Constitutional Fun, A 2068
Little Bit of Dinner with a Friend 675
Little Bit of Every Nationality, A 3985
Little Bit of Everything, A 4756, 4806
Little Bit of Fixin', A 374
Little Bit of Good, A 723
Little Bit of Heaven, A 538, 1532
Little Bit of Heaven (Shure They Call It Ireland), A 1803
Little Bit of Jazz, A 1270, 1819
Little Bit of Lace, A 3295
Little Bit of Love Won't Hurt You 1604
Little Bit of Love, A 3508
Little Bit of Magic 1300, 2234
Little Bit of Me in You, A 3653
Little Bit of Nonsense, A 1334
Little Bit of Now and Then 4756
Little Bit of Paint, A 780
Little Bit of Power and Powder and Paint, A 695
Little Bit of Quicksilver, A 2034
Little Bit of Ribbon, A 3230
Little Bit of Scotch, A 2385
(I've a) Little Bit of Scotch (in Me), A 3401

Little Bit of Silk, A 2761
Little Bit of Soup, A 4193
Little Bit of Spain in California, A 1944
Little Bit of Spanish, A 2780
Little Bit of This, A 317, 1265
Little Bit of This Morning, A 1082
Little Bit of Trouble on the Side, A 4450
Little Bit Off, A 4145
Little Black Baby 3814
Little Black Cat, The 1780
Little Black Sheep, The 2328
Little Black Sheep 4735
Little Black Train, The 1085
Little Blanche Marie 3313
Little Blue Moon 470
Little Blue Pig, The 2594
Little Blue Star 3654
Little Bo-Peep 235
Little Bo Peep 2214
Little Bo-Peep 3532
Little Book, The 1723
Little Boy 2384
Little Boy Blue 639, 1831, 2055, 2543, 3543
Little Boy Blue Jeans 4209
Little Boy Blues, The 2582
Little Boy, Little Girl 2013
Little Boy's Blue 1693
Little Brains-a Little Talent, A 957
Little Bride 3775
Little Bride, A 4616
Little Brown Hen 4425
Little Brown Jug 3144, 3175
Little Brown Suit My Uncle Bought Me, The 4009, 4141
Little Bull, A 3962
Little Bum 3968
Little Bunch of Daisies, A 4473
Little Bungalow, A 799
Little Butter-Up 1948
Little Butterfly 3008
Little By Little and Bit By Bit 1588
Little Cabaret at Home, The 1963
Little Cafe, A 353
Little Champagne for Papa, A 4479
Little Change, A 3322
Little Change of Atmosphere, A 3489
Little Chat, A 1817
Little Chauffeur, The 4544
Little Chicken Fit for Old Broadway, A 4464
Little Child Like Me, A 2465
Little Chimney Sweep 3313
Little China Doll, A 561
Little China Maid, The 3828
Little Choo Choo Gee-Gee, The 3945
Little Church Around the Corner, The 1246, 1746, 2684
Little Church Around the Corner 3819
Little Class of One, A 2160, 2328
Little Comedy, The 3760, 3760
Little Continental, A 796
Little Coronas, The 3344
Little Corporal, The 1670
Little Country Mice 353
Little Country Mouse, A 2907
Little Crinolira 3592
Little Dancing Jumping Jigger 4687
Little Dark Bird 1970
Little Darlin' 4264
Little Dash of Love, A 796
Little Dental Music, A 2544, 2038
Little Devil 3402
Little Devils 728
Little Did I Know 3722
Little Did We Know 3722
Little Difference at Breakfast, A 1565
Little Do They Know 16
Little Dog Blue 2322
Little Dream that Lost Its Way, A 2601
Little Dream That's Coming True 3086
Little Drops of Water 3915
Little Dutch Girl, The 1121
Little Dutch Girls 2509
Little Eden 1518
Little Egypt 4031
Little Emmaline 3064
Little Eva 954
Little Fairies 1093
Little Fairy in the Home 4393
Little Fall of Rain, A 2442
Little Farm in Normandy, A 1851
Little Fat Girls 1059
Little Feet that Lightly Beat 466
Little Fish 490, 647
Little Fish in a Big Pond, A 2894
Little Flapjack 98
Little Flat in a Great Big Town, A 3268
Little Fly 1021
Little Follies Theatre-During Intermission (sketch) 4814
Little Fool 3602
Little Ford Rambled Right Along 2454
Little Foxes, The 3691
Little Fred 4467
Little Further, A 511
Little Game of Tennis 2439
Little Game of Tennis, A 2483
Little Gamins 3036
Little Gardenhouse, The (inst.) 4699
Little Geezer 4335
Little George Washington 178
Little Girl, The 1427
Little Girl 2833, 1426, 4092, 4764
Little Girl Again 259
Little Girl and Boy 4547
Little Girl at Home 2394
Little Girl at the Sweet Shop, The 356
Little Girl-Big Voice 2477
Little Girl Blue 2258, 3186
Little Girl Come Back to Me 4726
Little Girl from Illinois, The 1910

Little Girl from Little Rock, A 1475
Little Girl, I Love You 2261
Little Girl in Blue, The 2347
Little Girl Like Me, A 1910
Little Girl Like You, A 4382
Little Girl, Little Boy 4780
Little Girl, Mind How You Go! 4219
Little Girl That's Wise, A 1230
Little Girl Up There, The 4364
Little Girl, What Have You Done to Me? 2884
Little Girl Who Couldn't Care 4206
Little Girl You'll Do 675, 3856, 3857
Little Girlie You Have Caught My Eye 917
Little Girls 150, 2573
Little Girls Beware 3996
Little Girls, Goodbye 168
Little Girls Should Be Seen 1614
Little God of My Heart 2905
Little Golden Maid 3679
Little Goose, A 4554
Little Gossip, A 2727
Little Grand Opera 750
Little Gray House, The 2591
Little Green Isle 2511
Little Green Snake 4270
(I Wore a) Little Grey Bonnet 3618
Little Gypsy Lady 4150
Little Gypsy Sweetheart
(Gypsy Love Song) 1355
Little H and Little G 4533
Little Ham 2513
Little Happiness, A 3448
Little Harlequin, The 379
Little Hero 4139
Little Hindoo Man 4378
Little Home for Two (Somewhere that
Little Home Is Waiting) 3317
Little Horse Sense 3688
Little House for Me, A 992
Little House in Soho, A 3924
Little House on the Prairie series 3553
Little Houston Street 8
Little Igloo for Two 1654, 1657
Little Investigation, A 2014
Little Italy 413, 1845
Little Jack Frost 4143
Little Jack Horner 2134
Little Japan Lady, A 1417
Little Jazz Bird 2376
Little Jesse James 1814, 2516
Little Jesus/Little Light 3454
Little Johnny Jones 2517
Little Joker, The 2518
Little Kangaroo, The 2519
Little Kleptomaniac, The 2739
Little Known Facts 4783
Little Lace Petticoat 2371
Little Lad 1502
Little Lady in Distress 1123
Little Lady in the Moon 2782
Little Lady Opportunity 1911
Little Lady/Little Man 2012
Little Ladybird 1862
Little Lamb 1709, 3306
Little Laquer Lady 3310
Little Leaguers 408
Little Learning, A 2354
Little Like Magic, A 2521
Little Lipstick Line, A 716
Little Liqueurs 2889
Little Little 1108
Little Log Cabin 11
Little Lord Fauntleroy 476, 1255
Little Lost Dream 1619
Little Lotte 3464
Little Love, A (But Not for Me) 2891
Little Love, A 3295
Little Love, a Little Kiss, A 4807
Little Love, a Little Money, A 1792, 2554
Little Love, a Little While, A 1893
Little Love Mill, The 4853
Little Macho Me 1940
Little Maid of Nicobar 2159
Little Maid Who Couldn't Say No, The 694
Little Maiden 2947
Little Man 1751
Little Marie 3179
Little Marriage Is a Dangerous Thing, A 2187
Little Mary 1579, 3313
Little Mary Gardeners, The 2858
Little Mary Sue 3684
Little Mary Sunshine 2522
Little Mary Waited for the Pie 4094
Little Mary Wise 1646
Little Maud Isn't Meant for You 186
Little Me 2523, 2523
Little Milliner, The 3673
Little Millionaire, The 2525
Little Miquette 1783
Little Miss Brown 2342
Little Miss Charity 2527
Little Miss Dracula 4542
Little Miss Fix It 2528
Little Miss Killarney 3327
Little Miss Melody 1626
Little Miss Nobody 1533
Little Miss Small Town 2380
Little Miss Understood 2424
Little Miss Up-to-Date 4364
Little Miss Victory Jones 2447
Little Miss Vogue 1703
Little Miss Wooden Shoes 2889
Little Mister Tippy Toes 1872
Little Mohee 3989
Little Moon 3871
Little Moozoo-May 3943
Little More, A 2937
Little More Champagne, A 3463
Little More Heart, A 1791
Little More Like You, A 4522

Little More Mascara, A 2360
Little Mother 1992
Little Music, A 3643
Little Music in Your Life, A 1435
Little Musketeer 948, 4670
Little Naked Boy, The 1284
Little Nell 3842
Little Nemo in Slumberland 2534
Little Nest for Two, A 3043
Little Neutral Dog 1852
Little Night Music, A 2535
Little of Everything, A 4801
Little Ol' Boy 4117
Little Old America for Me 3710
Little Old Cabin Door 183
Little Old Dream Waltz 2261
Little Old Dreamy New York (Any Side Street of New York) 3150
Little Old Gehenna 1745
Little Old Lady 3955
Little Old Lady in Black 2565
Little Old Main Street for Mine 2559
Little Old New Hampshire 1965
Little Old New York 1390, 1979, 2545, 3626, 4312, 4817
Little Old New York Is Good Enough for Me 2041
Little One 2649, 4226
Little One's ABC, The 3815
Little Orchestra, The 4363
Little Orphan Annie 150, 154, 155
Little Part of Me That's Mine, The 2617
Little Partner of Mine 4079
Little Peach 2594
Little People 339
Little Persian Rug, The 3446
Little Pie, The 476
Little Pip, A 3923
Little Pitchers Have Big Ears 1886
Little Place of Your Own, A 3042
Little Plastic Man 4398
Little Plate of Soup, A 2216
Little Pony of Mine 381
Little Poppa Satan 612
Little Poster Maid, The 104
Little Pot of Tea, A 2723, 4017
Little Priest, A 4233
Little Prince 2539
Little Princess 4275
Little Privacy, A 1448
Little Quonset in Neponset, A 1892
Little Rag Doll 2731
Little Raindrop 69
Little Rascals, The 2542, 2541
Little Red Book 4853
Little Red Book and a Five Cent Bag, A 2903
Little Red Hat 3294
Little Red Lacquer Cage, The 3007
(Everybody Calls Me) Little Red Riding Hood 4150
Little Red Riding Hood 974, 3593
Little Red Roof Tops 1880
Little Red School 1532
Little Revolutionary, The 3441
Little Rhumba Numba, A 2453
Little Rock 2590
Little Rock Roll 3841
Little Rover (Don't Forget to Come Back Home) 2706
Little Sambo 4416
Little Sammy 2235
Little Scandal Dolls 1486
Little Ships 732
Little Shop of Horrors 2544
Little Side Street in Paree, A 4104
Little Sir Hugh 4579
Little Sister Kissie 357
Little Skipper from Heaven Above, A 3674
Little Slut of Six, A 702
Little Smile, a Little Sigh, A 1965
Little Smith Minor 3092
Little Snowflake 3855
Little Song in My Heart, The 4249
Little Soubrette, The 586
Little Souvenir, A 1447, 2446
Little Sparrow 2584
Little Sparrows 280
Little Starch Left, A 3059
Little Stick of Candy and a Jumping Jack, A 2771
Little Street in Heaven They Call Broadway, A 737
Little Streptococcus, The 2187
Little Sunbeam 1726
Little Swing for Swinging, A 4169
Little Tango Maid, A 351
Little Taste of Heaven, A 273
Little Tea, A 4136
Little Tear 249
Little Theatre 2376
Little Thing, The 3819
(Just) a Little Thing Called Rhythm 792
Little Thing Like a Kiss, A 1066
Little Things 2232
Little Things About You 621
Little Things Meant So Much to Me 454
Little Things We Like, The 2447
Little Things We Used to Do, The 3598
Little Things You Do Together, The 832, 3967
Little Tin Box 1280
Little Tin God, The 2591, 4504
Little Tin Pail 2062
Little Tin Soldier 2723
Little Tin Soldier and the Little Rag Doll, The 3500
Little Tittle Tattle Tale 3855
Little Town Gal 879
Little Travelin' Music Please, A 3299
Little Traveling Music, A 673
Little Travelling Music, A 1619
Little Trouble, A 1991
Little Tune Go Away 3740

Little Two By Four 827
Little Usher, A 3400
Little Villages 3323
Little Wallflowers 3472
Little Washerwoman (Down in Rio), The 320
Little Weather Vane, The 355
Little What-If, Little Could-Be 4693
Little White Dog 1612
Little White House 1329, 2764
Little White House at the End of Honeymooon Lane 1965
Little White House with Green Blinds, A 1582
Little White Lie, The 4004
Little White Lies (1) 3849
Little White Lies (2) 3849
Little Widow Brown 4478
Little Wigwam for Two, A 3345
Little Wild Rose 954
Little Willie Brown 2498
Little Witch, The 2551
Little Woman 868
Little Woman, The 2217
Little Women 2550, 2007, 2219, 2931, 4341
Little Wonders (Kawaii Odoroki) 1616
Little Wooden Boy 3498
Little World for Two 2723
Little World, Good Morning 732
Little World of Our Own, A 396, 1588
Little World of Two 75
Little World, Hello 2551
Little World, Hello! 2551
Little Yellow Bird 1148
Little Yetta's Gonna Get a Man 304
Little Zouave 1476
Littleflea Hop, The 793
Littlest Angel, The 2553
Littlest Revue, The 2554
Liturgy of the Roman Mass 2775
Litvak/Galitsyaner 4342
Live 1990
Live a Little 3792, 2014, 3210
Live a Little, Love a Little 3756
Live a Long, Long Time 154
Live Alone and Like It 4067
Live and Let Live 629
Live and Love 1799
Live and Love a Lot 1035
Live for a Moment 1754
Live for All You're Worth 208
Live for Love 25
Live for the Moment 2759
Live for Today 606, 2419, 2698, 3081, 4148
Live Hard, Work Hard, Love Hard 1385
Live I Mean 2550
Live It Up 1611
Live, Laugh and Love 3907
Live, Laugh, Love 1329
Live Today 2380
Live Where You Can 1636
Live While You're Here 21
Live Wire, The 3569
Liverpool Sunset 705
Livin' Doll, A 2555
Livin' in a Hole 1786
Livin' Lovin' Doll 4321
Livin' the Life 2556
Living Alone 602
Living in a Brand New Day 3410
Living in Dreamland (Tan-Tan-Ta-Ra! Farewell) 2368
Living in Sin 778, 1387
Living in the Shadows 4560
Living It Up 612
Living Love 1346
Living Next Door to the Sun 4102
Living One Day at a Time 1893
Living Simply 269
Living with a Stranger 4786
Liza 2557, 3020, 981
Liza (All the Clouds'll Roll Away) 3953
Liza Ann (A Yorkshire Idyll) 3313
Liza Crossing the Ice 462
Liza Jane 2691, 3783, 4645
Liza Quit Vamping Me 3963
Liza with a 'Z' 2558
Lizette 2424
Lizzie Borden 2294, 3107
Lizzie, Lizzie, Have You Tasted 1589
Lizzie's Coming Home 3294
Llamala 4104
Llewellyn 130
Lloyd's of London 190
Lo! Hear the Gentle Lark 3842
Lo Hear the Gentle Lark 4211
Lo-La-Lo 1486
Loadin' Time 216
Loading Up the Mandy Lee 2667
Loads of Love 3187
Loafin' 2028
Lobby of the Roxy, The 2925
Lobster and the Lady 2209
Lobster Crawl, The 202
Lobster Quadrille 54
Lobster Quadrille, The 56
Lobster Rock 52
Local 403 (The Socially Conscious Civic Minded Iron Workers Union) 4013
Lock Me in Your Harem and Throw Away the Key 4603
Lock-Step, Two-Step Slide 3332
Lock Up Your Daughters 2563
Lock Your Heart 2025
Locked and Secluded 4106
Locker of Love 3539
Locker Room, The 2579, 2615
Locket in My Heart 324
Locks 2134
Loco Finale, A 696
(The) Loco-Motion 4193
Lodger 2816

Log Cabin Days 3808
Log of the Ship, The 4378
Loggers' Song, The 823
Logic! 73
Logic 3921, 4547
Loidy Wot Is Studyin' for the Stoige, A 2041
Loie and Chlodo 3547
Loki and Baldur 1068
Lola 106
Lola (White Witch of Jamaica) 817
Lola 845, 2567
Lola Cornero from the Trocadero 2567
Lola Delaney 3925
Lola in Bavaria 2565
Lola Montez 1363
Lola Waltz (Close in Your Arms) 2564
Lola's Ceremony 3792
Lola's Saucepan 4467
Lola's Theme (Lola Pretty Lola) 3925
Lola-Marie (She Isn't Lola) 3925
Lolaland 2565
Lolita 434, 1567, 2135, 2568, 2568
Lolita, My Love 3953
Lollipop 4264, 4388
Lollipop Lane 3186
Lollipops and Roses 4193
Lolly-Papa 1587
Lollypop Polka, The 2089
Lombardy Hunting Breakfast 621
Lomir Loybn (Let Us Praise) 4342
Lomir Trachtn Nor Fin Haynt 2356
Lona, Partner, Lona 1530
London Bank Clerk Blues, The 605
London Cries 324
London, Dear Old London 611
London Empire Girls 4818
London Is a Little Bit of All Right 1564
London Johnnies 4010
London Pastoral 3235
London Pride 3235
London Talking Blues 4579
London Taps (The Broken Doll) 1588
London Town 3295, 3310
London Underworld (Baker Street Mystery) (dance) 270
Lone Star Girl, The 4808
Lonegan 2710
(Manhattan's the) Loneliest Isle 4583
Loneliest Man in Town 167
Loneliness 2551
Loneliness of Evening 759, 4096
Loneliness Song, The 4523
Loneliness Trio 4684
Lonely 1564, 1593
Lonely at the Bottom 3077
Lonely at the Top 2852
Lonely Boy 3541
Lonely Boy Blues 2200
Lonely Canary 705
Lonely Children 3876
Lonely Clearing 4764
Lonely Feet 4361
Lonely for My New York 943
Lonely Girl, A 4276
Lonely Girl 4584
Lonely Goatherd, The 4095
Lonely Heart 207, 789, 4159
Lonely Heartache 1370
Lonely Hearts 463
Lonely House 369, 4169
Lonely in a Crowd 1644
Lonely in Paris 3383
Lonely in Town 3177
Lonely Is the Life 280
Lonely Lady 1737, 2074
Lonely Lamp, The 2162
Lonely Little Extras 2808, 4025
Lonely Little Melody 4818
Lonely M.P. 3460
Lonely Man 1370
Lonely Man, Lonely Woman 430
Lonely Me 599, 3278
Lonely Men (inst.) 3347
Lonely Nest, The 3312
Lonely Nights 2201
Lonely Ones 3863
Lonely Princess, The (The Sleeping Princess) 1852
Lonely Road, The 3978
Lonely Room 3263
Lonely Soldier 1610
Lonely Sparrows of Essex, The 962
Lonely Star 3674
Lonely Straggler 2115
Lonely Stranger (Passing Through) (Sabishii Tabibito) 1616
Lonely Stranger 4099
Lonely Times 337
Lonely Town 3278
Lonely Voice 2661
Lonely Woman 1857
Lonely Women 2511
Loner, The 916
Lonesome 1131, 2914, 4648, 3856, 3857
Lonesome Alimony Blues 4840
Lonesome Boy 2605
Lonesome Cinderella 4817
Lonesome Cowboy, The 1528
Lonesome Dove, The 1085
Lonesome for You 2155
Lonesome in New York 2052
Lonesome Is As Lonesome Does 4829
Lonesome Little Maid 2671
Lonesome Longing Blues 4182
Lonesome Man 3965
Lonesome of the Road 3806
Lonesome Polecat 3888
Lonesome Romeos 1297
Lonesome Valley 61, 4740
Lonesome Walls 2712

Long Ago 1721, 2161, 3171, 1213, 3913
Long Ago and Far Away 2204, 2372
Long Ago I Loved You 3734
Long Ago Love, A 177
Long Ago, or Yesterday? 1695
Long and Beautiful Life, A 4337
Long and Weary Wait 2680
Long and Winding Road, The 3903
Long As You've Got Your Health 3955
Long Before I Die 3667
Long Before I Knew You 363
Long Goodbye, The 3178
Long Green Blues 137
Long Green, The 4478
Long Is a Wonderful Thing 2888
Long Island Low Down, The 142
Long, Lean, Lanky Letty 3562
Long, Lean, Lanky, Letty Pepper 2461
Long Live Folly 2715
Long Live Free Enterprise 1064
Long Live He 2319
Long Live Nancy 466
Long Live the English Scene 190
Long Live the Greedy 4157
Long Live the King! 3774
Long Live the King (Vive le Roi) 3839
Long Live the King-If He Can 1564
Long Live the Queen 593, 2160
Long, Long Ago 4837
Long, Long Green, The 1525
Long, Long Time 815
Long, Long War, A 275
Long Long Way to Heaven 2046
Long Lost Blues 2984
Long Night Again Tonight 4703
Long Overdue 2970
Long Past Sunset 2033
Long Sunday Afternoon 460
Long Time Ago, A 2961, 3623
Long Time Coming, A 973
Long Time Dead, A 3879
Long Time No Song 1140
Long Walk Back, The 4016
Long Way, A 2250
Long Way from Home, A 1736
Long Way from Home 3299
Long Way to Boston, A 2578
Long Way to Jerusalem 2319
Longest Running Unproduced Production 2742
Longest Way 'Round Is the Sweetest Way Home, The 3238
Longing 2866, 3011
Longing for Dear Old Broadway 3547
Longing for You 1722, 2390, 2446
Longing to Be Elsewhere 83
Longshoreman's Chanty 4762
Longtime Travelin' 2248
Lonliness 3125
Lontananza 364
Loo-Loo 1916
Loo-Low 4163
Look, The 2676
Look 1233
Look! 3227
Look-a-Look 4528
Look Ahead 197
Look All Around You 2616
Look Aloft 2341
Look and Love Is Here 2808
Look Around 4695, 3156
Look Around You 4172
Look Around Your Little World 2681
Look at 'Er 3113
Look at Him 2630
Look at Me 83, 690, 3811, 1475, 1695, 2657, 3427, 3577, 3599, 2026, 1048
Look at Me, I'm Sandra Dee (1) 1664
Look at Me, I'm Sandra Dee (2) 1664
Look at Me, Joan 2220
Look at Me Now 1722
Look at Me Please 3103
Look at Me with Love 3879
Look at My Sister 3370
Look at That Face 3731
Look at the Children 1715
Look at the Damn Thing Now 1419
Look at the Package They Handed to Me 3423
Look at the World and Smile 4793
Look at Them 578
Look at Them Doing It! 4603
Look at Those Faces 2965
Look at Us 2173, 4459
Look at What It's Done 4629
Look at You 1318
Look Away 227
Look Before You Leap 1680, 3051, 3677, 4039, 4053
Look Closer, Love 3456
Look Down 2442
Look for a Sky of Blue 2522
Look for Small Pleasures 367
Look for the Girl 3712
Look for the Happiness Ahead 1380
Look for the Happy Ending 1819
Look for the Men with Potential 2472
Look for the Morning Star 3983
Look for the Rainbow 1551
Look for the Silver Lining 2204, 3018, 3819, 4860
Look for the Sunshine 3318
Look for the Woman 273
Look Homeward Angel 135
Look Homeward, Angel 135
Look in Her Eyes 2469
Look In Her Heart and See 333
Look in His Eyes 1784
Look in My Eyes 1113
Look in the Book 2620
Look in the Book and See 2315
Look in the Looking Glass 1486
Look in Your Engagement Book 608
Look Inside 337

Look Into My Eyes 3712
Look Into Your Heart 3482
Look, Little Girl 1860
Look Ma, I'm Dancin'! 2582
Look Me Over 1835
Look Me Over Carefully and Tell Me Will I Do 4804
Look Me Over Dearie 2358
Look No Further 3187
Look of Love 2427
Look of Love, The 4193, 261
Look on the Bright Side 2658
Look Out 4420
Look Out for Her 591
Look Out for Lil 1063
Look Out for Mr. Wu 1826
Look Out for My Heart 2301
Look Out for the Bolsheviki Man 4813
Look Out for the Strange Young Man 4064
Look Out for Us, Broadway 3185
Look Out I'm Falling in Love 3787
Look Out! Look Out! Look Out! 3372
Look Out, Sister 1296
Look Over There 2360
Look Pleasant 4345
Look Through the Moongate 4157
Look Through the Window 415
Look to the Lilies 2583
Look to the Rainbow 1278
Look to the Rainbow Dance (inst.) 1278
Look to Your Heart 3324
Look Underneath 159
Look Up 4127, 3956
Look What a Hole You're In 1385
Look What Happened to Mabel 2208, 2660
Look What Hovers There (Chorus of Fear) 178
Look What I Found 189
Look What Love Done Done 1984
Look What's Happened to Me 2483
Look Where I Am 2726
Look Where I'm At! 2584
Look Who I Am, Surprise! Surprise! 1474
Look Who's Alone Now 3142
Look Who's Dancing 4446
Look! Who's Here 1340
Look Who's Here 1591, 2587
Look Who's in Love 3687
Look Who's Throwing a Party 3956
Look Your Partner Straight in the Eye 996
Looka Me 2182
Lookin' fo' Somebody 1385
Lookin' for a Gentleman 2083
Lookin' for Me 916
Lookin' Good 944
Lookin' Good! 838
Lookin' Good but Feelin' Bad 39
Lookin' Out for Mame After Dark 2578
Lookin' Over from Your Side 1072
Looking All Over for You 611
Looking at Life Through a Rainbow 637
Looking at the Sun 4124
Looking at Us 3167
Looking at You 2366, 4581
Looking Back 2590
Looking for a Bluebird 2940
Looking for a Boy 4392
Looking for a Candidate 4323
Looking for a Girl Like You 4359
Looking for a Girl My Size 3729
Looking for a Happy Man 4544
Looking for a Man 2518
Looking for a Needle in a Haystack 3857
Looking for a Thrill 2253
Looking for Another Job 2519
Looking for Love 871, 4847
Looking for Myself 656
Looking for Someone 2663, 3548
Looking for Someone to Love 580
Looking for Something 4403
Looking for the Action 4397
Looking for the Lovelight in the Dark 4426
Lookit Those Stars 4690
Looks Are No Matter If— 333
Looks Like Candy to Me 187
Looks Like I'm Off O' Ya 1931
Looks Like Love Is Here to Stay 3860
Looks Like They Need Old Mame Again 166
Looney Mooney Man 2667
Looney Park 4681
Loopin' the Loop 723
Loose Ankles 1944, 2490, 3150, 1946
Loose Diamond 264
Loose Ends (1) 451
Loose Ends (2) 451
Loose in the Foot 649
Loose Woman, A 1865
Loosen Up 3152
Lopsided Bus, A 3505
Lord and I, The 2028
Lord Don't Rain Down Manna, The 3631
Lord Done Fixed Up My Soul, The 2597
Lord, Hear Your Child A-Callin' 4645
Lord Helps Those Who Help Themselves, The 181
Lord, I Am but a Little Child 2075
Lord, I'm Determined 4460
Lord Is My Light, The 4595
Lord Is My Shepherd 4438
Lord Jesus 1496
Lord, Keep Me Wicked 451
Lord Lawntennys and Pupils 762
Lord, Now Let Thy Servant Depart in Peace 755
Lord of All Creation 4312
Lord Only Knows, The 3538
Lord Piccolo 2495
Lord, You Sure Know How to Make a Sunday 2248
Lord's Bright Blessing, The 2980
Lord's Prayer, The 3836, 2992
Lords of Creation 4283
Lordy 337, 4214
Lorelei 1747, 2590

Lorelei, The 2848, 3379, 3441
Lorelei 972
Lorelei, The 3819
Lorelei 4341
Lorelei on the Rocks 3501
Lorena 3020
Loretta 2657
Lorna's Here 1601
Los Angeles Is Just Like Any Other Town 408
Los Chuchos Suaves 4861
Losers 4480
Losing My Mind 1329, 3967
Lost 1112, 1194, 2679, 4537
Lost a Heart 3771
Lost and Found 775
Lost Highway 655
Lost Horizon 3913, 3913
Lost in a Cloud of Blue 3460
Lost in Loveliness 1548
Lost in Space 2555
Lost in the Catacombs 3824
Lost in the Crowd 1322
Lost in the Stars 369, 2591, 4504
Lost in the Wilderness 730, 4645
Lost Liberty Blues, The 2366
Lost Liberty Blues 4517, 4799
Lost My Cool 843
Lost My Rhythm, Lost My Music, Lost My Man 665
Lost New York 3548
Lost Paradise, The 3344
Lost Pleiad, The 1682
Lost Sheep 732
Lost Step, The 2628
Lost Word 4167
Lot of Livin' to Do, A 602, 607
Lot of Lovin' 943
Lot of Men, A 2033
Lots of Little Things Can Happen 1247
Lots of Little Things Can Happen (In a Very Little While) 531
Lots of Time for Sue 3532
Lotta Locomotion, A 4138
Lottery Blues 1231
Lottery Celebration 400
Lottery Drawing, The 307
Lottie Gibson Specialty (Please Send Me Down a Baby Brother) 603
Lottie of the Literati 3104
Lottie's Purification 952
Lotus, The 1650
Lotus Blossom 3788
Lotus Flower 4427, 4760
Lotus Flower, The 4793
(Love Has Come from) Lotus Land 3828
Lotus Land 4489
Lou 1047
Lou and Sue 4165
Lou My Lou 984
Loud and Funny Song, A 3231
Loud and Tacky 915
Loud Enough 119
Loud Is Good 2171
Loud Let the Bugle Sound 4713
Loudly We Shout 4201
Louie 1713
Louis Is All Right 1409
Louis Says 4560
Louis XIII Gavotte 2569
Louis XIV 3730
Louise 233
Louisiana 152, 3148, 3958, 4806
Louisiana 1927 2852
Louisiana Belle 4149
Louisiana Gals 3989
Louisiana Hayride 1322
Louisiana Lize 3999
Louisiana Lou 2596
Louisiana Purchase 2597
Louisiana's Holiday 2595
Lounging at the Waldorf 39
Lousiana Lizabeth 4757
Lousy Life, A 3846
Loute 3866
Louwanna 152
Lovable Moon 3403
Love 695, 961, 155, 2489, 2587, 2598, 2982, 3297, 2338, 3883
Love a Gypsy Knows, The 3842, 4211
Love a la Mode 1926
Love Affair, A 4774
Love Affair 4627
Love Ahoy! 3985
Love All 1342
Love Among the Daisies 954
Love Among the Freabs 45
Love Among the Freaks 4044
Love Among the Lions 1360
Love and a Legacy 161
Love and Beauty 3681
Love and Devotion 4093
Love and Duty 2293, 3734
Love and Gingerbread 1680
Love and I 70
Love and I Are Playing 2670, 2670
Love and I Went Waltzing 1577
Love and Joy 3305
Love and Kindness 2961
Love and Kisses 1516, 3149
Love and Kisses 'n' Everything 3254
Love and Laughter 3064
Love and Logic 1168
Love and Marriage 3324, 4743
Love and No Dinero 696
Love and Rhythm 4177
Love and the Automobile 3031
Love and the Moon 3768
Love and Victory 2854
Love and War 1680
Love and Wine (Drinking Song) 2603

Love and You 2761
Love, Are You Raising Your Head? 3105
Love Aria 1426
Love at an Auction 1370
Love at First Sight 1351, 4064
Love at Golden Years 3559
Love at Last 1817
Love at My Door 3899
Love at Second Sight 1101
Love at Sundown 2850
Love at the Door 1537
Love at the First Word 3696
Love Baby 3796
Love Before Breakfast 652
Love Behind Bars 4619
Love Birds 1491, 1678, 4276
Love Boat 3849
Love Boat, The 4814
Love Boats 1135
Love Breaks Every Bond 902
Love Bug 3808
Love Bug Sting, The 1562
Love but You 3675
Love By Proxy 2399
Love By Telephone 1095
Love C.O.D. 2112
Love Calls Me (I Hear Love Call Me) 3078
Love Calls Us, Dear 2907
Love Came and Crowned Me 3865
Love Came By 2115
Love Came First when I Saw You 1626
Love Came Into My Heart 1136
Love Came to Me 423, 459
Love Came to Me One Day 3585
Love Can 2043
Love Can Be 382
Love Can Get You Crazy 3355
Love Can Get Your Down 4577
Love Can Settle Everything 4331
Love Can Sometimes Make You Cry 155
Love Can't 3159
Love Can't Happen 1649
Love Can't Say No 586
Love Cannot Be Bought 4590
Love Cannot Die 4372
Love Changes Everything 211
Love Child 2426
Love Clock, The 3580
Love Come A-Callin' 2555
Love Come Back to Me 3532
Love, Come Take Me 1342
Love, Come Take Me Again (ballet) 1860
Love Comes a Stealing 1240
Love Comes and Goes 1282
Love Comes First 167
Love Comes in the Strangest Ways 4684
Love Comes Like a Butterfly 2377
Love Comes Once in a Lifetime 4352
Love Comes without a Call 3203
Love Conquers All 1439
Love Contagious 2408
Love Dance, The 2667
Love Days 800
Love Design 3713
Love Dies Hard 105
Love Doesn't Ask Any Questions 2511
Love Doesn't Grow on Trees 348
Love Don't Need a Referee 4199
Love, Don't Turn Away 3294
Love Dreams 2605, 3203, 3723
Love Duet 262, 369, 4139, 2846
Love Duet, The 3830
Love Duet 4368
Love Duet II 2846
Love Elixir, The 1319
Love Eyes 4682
Love Finds a Way 4121
Love Finds the Lonely 101
Love Flies Everywhere 102
Love Flower, The 2606
Love for a Day 1405
Love for a Year, Love for a Day 1712
Love for an Hour 2233
Love for Sale 3131, 4517, 4539
Love for Sure 3493
Love Forgotten 2632
Love from a Heart of Gold 2019
Love from Judy 2608
Love Game, The 96
Love, Good-Bye 902
Love Has Come to Live in Our House 3562
Love Has Come to Me 3921
Love Has Come to Me at Last 3573
Love Has Driven Me Sane 4485
Love Has Found My Heart 905
Love Has Nothing to Do with Looks 4366
Love Has Wings 3839
Love Held Lightly 3837
Love Her All the Time 355
Love Her Like a Blind Man 482
Love, Here I Am 1363, 3479
Love Holds Sway 4794
Love, Honor and O Baby 545
Love, Honor and Obey 2919
Love, I Give You My All 2636
Love, I Hear 1422
Love I Long For, The 3813
Love, I Never Knew 4300
Love, I'd Give My Life for You 1953
Love in a Barbershop 1730
Love in a Changing World 2748, 4331
Love in a Cottage 1121, 2569, 2509
Love in a Haystack 910, 4427
Love in a Home 2484
Love in a Mist 3301
Love in a New Tempo 3112
Love in a Palace Is Better 694
Love in a Persian Garden 387
Love in an Orchard 1535
Love in Bergdorf Goodman 198

Love in Disguise 4518
Love in Mine Eyes 1682
Love in My Breast 2802
Love in My Heart 2836
Love in My Life, The 2255
Love in Outer Space 1061
Love in the Barnyard 90
Love in the Morning 1713
Love in the Ranks 710
Love in the Shadows 1131
Love in the Smoking Car 4830
Love in the Snow 2610
Love in the Springtime 4803
Love in the Springtime Is Not What It Used to Be 1176
Love in the Wings 3858
Love in Transit (I'm Leaving Home Papa) 2922
Love Is 757, 1233
Love Is... 3539
Love Is 18
Love Is (Very) Wonderful 1753
Love Is a Ball! 2611
Love Is a Battle 1016
Love Is a Bore 2443
Love Is a Bubble 717, 2830
Love Is a Business 4283
Love Is a Chance 269
Love Is a Curious Feeling 3486
Love Is a Dance 1309
Love Is a Dancer 3103, 3104
Love Is a Dancing Thing 216
Love Is a Fable 43
Love Is a Feeling 1412, 3940
Love Is a Fragile Thing 4022
Love Is a Game 2213
Love Is a Game for Soldiers 3013
Love Is a Garden of Roses 4209
Love Is a Gift 537, 538
Love Is a Lie 2594
Love Is a Many Splendored Thing 3739
Love Is a Mixture 4032
Love Is a Pain 4022
Love Is a Peculiarity 4589
Love Is a Race 1088
Love Is a Random Thing 4428
Love Is a Riddle 463
Love Is a Ripple on the Water 3354
Love Is a Sandman 4424
Love Is a Shovel 157
Love Is a Simple Thing 2294, 3107
Love Is a Story That's Old 2670
Love Is a Summer's Morning 968
Love Is a Tingling Tune 1121
Love Is a Torment 1235
Love Is a Traitor 1455
Love Is a Two-Edged Sword 1027
Love Is a Two-Way Street 4264
Love Is a Very Light Thing 1242
Love Is a Whole Other Scene 692
Love Is a Will-O-the-Wisp 4387
Love Is a Wonderful Thing 1334, 1971
Love Is All 21
Love Is All That Matters 2559
Love Is an Ailment 3805
Love Is an Art 2931
Love Is an Idle Dream 771
Love Is an Infant 2543
Love Is an Intrusion 3051
Love Is an Old-Fashioned Feeling 3345
Love Is Around the Corner 4830
Love Is Beautiful 4168
Love Is Blind 2746
Love Is Come to Me 1847
Love Is Coming Back 2728
Love Is Elusive 2770, 4311
Love Is Everything 159, 302
Love Is Faded Away 2808
Love Is for the Birds 181
Love Is for Youth (Prudence Has Fled) 3051
Love Is Good for You 679, 3110
Love Is Hate 172
Love Is Hell 3234
Love Is in the Air 1422, 3967, 4300
Love Is International 3669
Love Is Just a Fairy Tale 1557
Love Is Just Around the Corner 393, 1310
Love Is Just the Same 3951
Love Is Just the Same Old Game in Every Land 60
Love Is King 538, 1584, 2986, 3626, 4113
Love Is Like a Blushing Rose 608
Love Is Like a Bubble 3958
Love Is Like a Butterfly 3424
Love Is Like a Cigarette 48, 3773
Love Is Like a Firefly 1285, 3431
Love Is Like a Little Rubber Band (Hoop Song) 2334
Love is Like a Mushroom 4843
Love Is Like a Pinwheel 2135
Love Is Like a Rainbow 2139
Love Is Like a Rose 2282, 2335
Love Is Like a Violin 2424
Love Is Like an Elephant 3074
Love Is Like an Itching in My Heart 166
Love Is Like That 138, 1448
Love Is Like the Rose 1712
Love Is Like This Little Wheel of Mine 4218
Love Is Love 3823, 4723
Love Is Lovely 249
Love Is Making a Sport of Me 2334
Love Is Merest Folly 3994
Love Is My Enemy 1284
Love Is My Friend 3353
Love Is Mystery 3978
Love Is New 3064
Love Is No Laughing Matter 339
Love Is Not a Sentiment 807, 3542
Love Is Not a Sentiment Worthy of Respect 808, 809

Love Is Not All That It Seems to Be 1534
Love Is Not for a Day 2622
Love Is Not for Children 1899
Love Is Not in Vain 4477, 4530
Love Is Not Love 946
Love Is on Its Knees 4279
Love Is Only Love 2713
Love Is Only What You Make It 3011
Love Is Our Umbrella 2073
Love Is Paradise 1017
Love Is Queen of the Sea 1021
Love Is Quite a Simple Thing 3117
Love Is Sickness 3954
Love Is Simply Heavenly 3983
Love Is Spring 3570
Love Is Still in Town 2554
Love Is Strange 991
Love Is Such a Cheat 3036
Love Is Such a Fragile Thing 825
Love Is Such a Funny Little Feeling 4644
Love Is Sweeping the Country 3225
Love, Is That You? 4485
Love Is the Best of All 3590
Love Is the Bunk 3915
Love Is the Funniest Thing 1548
Love Is the Greatest 2449
Love Is the Leaven 2126
Love Is the Loveliest Love Song 941
Love Is the Prize 1959
Love Is the Reason 3424, 4446
Love Is the Same Everywhere 4439
Love Is the Same Old Game 3771
Love Is the Same the Whole World Over 2884
Love Is the Sovereign of My Heart 3013
Love Is the Springtime of Life 3592
Love Is the Sun 4357
Love Is the Thing 878
Love Is the Worst Possible Thing 4798
Love Is Trouble 3035
Love Is Tyrant 3994
Love Is Victor 1417
Love Is What I Never Knew 3913
Love Is Where You Find It 3992, 544
Love Isn't Born It's Made 3178
Love Isn't Everything 2050
Love, It Hurts So Good 59
Love, It's Not Easy 3840
Love Jitters, The 4252
Love Knots 1171
Love Knows No Season 2153
Love Land 3732
Love-Land 4784
Love Lasts a Day 1020
Love Laughs 2613
Love Laughs at Locksmiths 3883
Love Leads On 2532
Love Lesson 2599
Love, Let Me Know 2449
Love Letter to Manhattan 454
Love Letter Words 1923
Love Letters 3978
Love Letters in the Sand 4264
Love Letters Written to My Mother 427
Love Life 1590
Love Life of a Gondolier, The 4579
Love Life of a Sailor 3683
Love Light in Your Eyes 2762
Love Light in Your Eyes, The 3585
Love Like Mine, A 2027
Love Like Ours 692
Love Like That 703
Love Like Yours Is Rare Indeed 3163
Love-Line 269
Love Lives in Dreams 3466
Love Lives On 4328
Love Look Away 1315
Love, Look in My Window 1828
Love-Lorn Maid, A 1871
Love! Love! 1470
Love, Love Alone 3424
Love, Love, Love 302, 387, 537, 538
Love! Love! Love! 1067
Love, Love, Love 1340
Love! Love! Love! 1580, 1663
Love, Love, Love 2106, 2587
Love! Love! Love! 2616
Love-Love-Love 3488
Love, Love, Love 3519, 187
Love! Love! Love! 346
Love, Love, Love 3899
Love, Love, Sweetest Love 3266
Love Love You Baby 1103
Love Loves the Difficult Things 2648
Love Made a Fool of Me 214
Love Made the Song 650
Love Makes Such Fools of Us All 305
Love Makes the World Go 3187
Love Makes the World Go Round 2798
Love Makes the World Go 'Round 2684
Love Makes the World Go Round 3082
Love Makes the World Go 'Round 3344, 3996
Love Makes the World Go Round, Boys! 1720
Love Maketh the Heart a Garden Fair 4404
Love Match, A 3802
Love May Be a Mystery 4258
Love May Come and Love May Go 2697
Love May Not Hide 3796
Love Me (The Tom Cat Song) 88
Love Me 343, 4191, 2174, 2261, 2557, 3254, 4485, 4512
Love Me a Little 991
Love Me and the World Is Mine 591, 1926, 3981, 1995
Love Me Anywhere 1479
Love Me As Though There Was No Tomorrow 4180
Love Me As You Used to Do 1532
Love Me at Twilight 4148
Love Me, Baby! 3654
Love Me Baby Mine 3676

Love Me Best of All 1911
Love Me By Parcel Post 4477, 4530
Love Me Dear 1523
Love Me, Don't You? 4692
Love Me Enough to Remember 4762
Love Me for What I Am 2132
Love Me Forever 2423
Love Me in the Candlelight 684
Love Me in the Morning Early 3045
Love Me in the Spring 627
Love Me in the Winter 2779
Love Me Just a Little Bit 1588
Love Me Just Because 4185
Love Me Just Like Romeo Loved His Juliet 2119
Love Me Lightly 337
Love Me Like a Real, Real Man 2394
Love Me Little, Love Me Long 2906, 129
Love Me Lize 3154
Love Me, Love Me Not 2276
Love Me, Love Me, Dorothy Lamour, La Sarong 3651
Love Me, Love Me, Won't You? 1975
Love Me, Love My Children 2618
Love Me, Love My Dog 2915, 4314
Love Me More-Love Me Less 439
Love Me or Leave Me 3020, 3557, 3980, 4683
Love Me or Leave Me Alone 806
Love Me Some Mo 293
Love Me Sweetheart in Sweet Song 2906
Love Me, Sweetheart Mine 4360
Love Me Tender 3739
Love Me to a Viennese Melody 3525
Love Me to That Beautiful Tune 3996
Love Me Tomorrow (But Leave Me Alone To-Day) 612
Love Me Tonight 3508, 4539
Love Me Too 2661
Love Me While the Loving Is Good 3396
Love Me While the Snowflakes Fall 545
Love Me While You're Gone 2645
Love Me/Don't 4031
Love Means 564
Love Mill, The 2619
Love Monopoly, The 2907
Love Moon 736
Love Must Be Delicate 3197
Love Ne'er Came Night 3570
Love Needs No Single Words 780
Love Nest 4462
Love Nest, The 2767
Love Nests in France 4853
Love Never Changes 2587
Love Never Dies 2495
Love Never Goes Away 3888
Love Never Went to College 4420
Love, Nuts and Noodles (Bring 'Em Back Alive) 289
Love-O-Love 1343
Love-O-Meter 140
Love of a Day 1266
Love of a Maid of a Man, The 4663
Love of a Wife, The 2363
Love of Long Ago 3405, 3491, 3951
Love of Mine 3791, 4719
Love of My Life, The 530
Love of My Life 1846
Love of the Lorelei, The 1016
Love of Your Life, The 3835
Love on a Summer's Day 1570
Love on Our Side 4016
Love on the American Plan 1228
Love on the Street 4388
Love or Money 2542, 4450
Love Pirates 3137
Love Please Stay 2177
Love Potion, The 4328
Love Potion #9 4031
Love Power 1072, 2658
Love, Put on Your Bridal Veil 2428
Love Put on Your Orange Blossoms 1776
Love Racketeer 1836
Love Ranger Rides Again, The 1940
Love Remains the Same 620, 2875
Love Revolution 2058
Love Rules the World 670
Love Runs Deeper Than Pride 3724
Love Scene 169
Love Set, The 1533
Love Ship, The 4194
Love Sick 3042
Love Sign 3575
Love Sneaks Up on You 3899
Love Sometimes Has to Wait 4141
Love Song 369, 392, 400, 550, 681, 1108
Love Song, A 1648
Love Song 2615
Love Song, The 2686
Love Song 2804, 3013, 3506, 4002, 4369
Love Song (Sara Lee) 4480
Love Song 4586, 4371
Love Song of a Thief, The 4539
Love Song of Renaldo 3789
Love Song to Order, A 2519
Love Songs 16
Love Songs Are Made in the Night 4826
Love Spans the World 2571, 3500
Love Spats 902
Love Spell, The 3613
Love Stolen 3733
Love Story 2787, 4635
Love Swept Like a Storm 596
Love Tales, The 1017
Love Test, The 3778
Love That Came Before, The 674
Love That Cannot Be 4539
Love That Game 4099
Love That Is True 1392
Love That Lasts, A 3117
Love that Man 454
Love That's Gone 1266

Love That's New, The 3770
Love the Magician 2745
Love the Minstrel 2419
Love the Wife of Your Neighbor 4760
Love the World Over Is Much the Same 3053
Love Theme 4330
Love They Assure Us Is Blind 3051
Love Thought Garden 1182
Love Thoughts 1756
Love Through the Ages 1250
Love Time 3134
Love-Time 112
Love Tiptoed Through My Heart 3457
Love to Love You Baby 3739
Love to Your Heart's Desire 942
Love To-day 3915
Love Turned the Light Out 612
Love Up a Tree 1316
Love Wager, The 2623
Love Was 2248
Love Was a Stranger to Me 1974
Love Was Dancing Beside Me 4416
Love Was Just a Game 482
Love Was Young As an April Leaf 4163
Love Watches (inst.) 2624
Love Waves 4687
Love, What Has Given You This Magic Power? 4792
Love While You May 4121
Love Will Always Be the Same 1782
Love Will Always Find a Way 2601
Love Will Bring You Happiness 2009
Love Will Call 3538
Love Will Come Your Way 2661
Love Will Conquer All 634
Love Will Do the Rest 132
Love Will Find a Way 2698, 3963
Love Will Find a Way — They Say 4588
Love Will Find Out the Way 1290
Love Will Find You 1313, 1680
Love Will Find You Some Day 2622
Love Will Keep Us Young 3252
Love Will Make or Break a Man 2730
Love Will See Us Through 1329
Love Will Win 178, 1538
Love Wins Again 4173
Love with a Capital L 4644
Love You 189
Love You 1616
Love You Are My Inspiration 1137
Love, You Are So Difficult 227
Love You Came to Me 2418
Love You Dearly 616
Love, You Must Be Blind 3943
Love You That Is 520
Love, You're a Wonderful Game 4354
Love Your Neighbor 2240
(Tell Me What's the Matter) Loveable Eyes 2706
Loveable Fellow, A 3151
Loveable Irish, The 1076
Loveable Love 1071
Loveable You 2098, 2490
Loved One, So Pure and Tender 331
Loveland 1329
Loveland Express, The 558
Loveless You and Hateful Me 4798
Lovelier Than Ever 4652
Loveliest Child in the World, The 2993
Lovelight 1098, 4843, 4844
Lovelight Beaming from Your Eyes, The 1458
Lovelight in Your Eyes, The 96
Loveliness of You, The 850
Lovelit Eyes 3406
Lovelorn Lily, The 559
Lovelost 194
Lovely 4067, 1422, 1883
Lovely Autumn Day, A 2496
Lovely Bridesmaids 937
Lovely Budapest 30
Lovely Child 2289
Lovely Corals 2412
Lovely Day 4349
Lovely Day for a Murder 1894
Lovely Girl, A 404
Lovely Girls of Akbarabad, The 751
Lovely Heroine, The 130
Lovely Island 937
Lovely Ladies 2442
Lovely Ladies, Kind Gentlemen 2626
Lovely Lady 796, 1488, 1720, 2628, 2768, 3219, 4163, 4692
Lovely Lady Nicotine 4437
Lovely Lassie 582
Lovely Laurie 4312
Lovely Lazy Kind of Day, A 4362
Lovely Light 1648
Lovely Little Diamond 3880
Lovely Little Sister 4486
Lovely Liza Lee 1981
Lovely, Lovely Day 2300
Lovely Lover 2563
Lovely Me 2629
Lovely Morning 919
Lovely Night, A 759
Lovely Party 3549
Lovely Rita 3903
Lovely Sunday Mornin' 2949
Lovely to Look At 2204, 2372
Lovely Trip, A 4657
Lovely Vienna 771
Lovely Woman 3562
Lover 3428
Lover, Come Back to Me 3117
Lover in Me, The 4828
Lover Lost 2731
Lover Man 478
Lover of Love 4127
Lover Waits, A 249
Lover, Where Are You Now? 364
Lover's A-B-C, The 1535

Lovers 1575, 2630, 4379
Lover's Dream, A 1282
Lover's Holiday 4328
Lovers in Love 1149
Lover's Lane 2717, 3951
Lover's Lane with You 4194
Lover's Luck 1207
Lovers Manage 2877
Lovers of Art 1487
Lovers of the Lamplight 3763
Lovers on Christmas Eve 2058
Lover's Prayer 2852
Lover's Quarrel 2532
Lover's Quarrel, The 2631
Lover's Quarrels 3765
Lovers' Roost 1226
Lovers' Springtime 3998
Lovers Waltz, The 1940
Love's a Bond 3843
Love's a Dreamy Tune 2600
Love's a Race 1067
Love's a Riddle 4256
Love's a Very Funny Thing 3866
Love's Art 1513
Love's Awakening 3424
Love's Bouquet 1318, 4626
Love's Call 2843
Love's Charming Art (The Dove Duet) 2334
Love's Conquests 375
Love's Corporation 4194
Love's Crystal 4000
Love's Dream Is O'er 2715, 3626
Love's Eternal Song 3774
Love's Ever New 3652
Love's Fairy Tales 2732
Love's Flower Is Always Blooming 2732
Love's Funny Propsition 43
Love's Golden Day 4735
Love's Got Me Down Again 889
Love's Happy Dream 4352
Love's Hesitation 335
Love's Highway 480, 1220
Love's in Full Bloom 696
Loves in My Life, The 1436
Love's in the Air 2293
Love's Intense in Tents 3538
Love's Labor's Lost 128
Love's Labour Lost 366
Love's Language 1532
Love's Last Day 659
Love's Last Word 2498
Love's Lesson 4017
Love's Little Journey 3712
Love's Longing 2454
Love's Lottery 702
Love's Lucky Emblem 668
Love's Melody 1697
Love's Menu 1424
Love's Merry-Go-Round 1464
Love's Misgivings 4497
Love's Mystery 3626
Love's Nest 49
Love's Never Lost 1680
Love's Night 4646
Love's No Stranger to Me 2000
Loves of New Orleans 3081
Love's Old Sweet Song 1897, 2739
Love's Own Flower 493
Love's Own Kiss 1888
Love's Own Sweet Song 3839
Love's Paradise 1308
Love's Prescription 2025
Love's Refrain 670
Love's Revenge 4485
Love's Roulette 2869
Love's Roundelay 4590
Love's Sad Glance 1713
Love's Secret 355
Love's Serenade 4165, 4794
Love's Sextette, A 1624
Love's Sorcery 1712
Love's Still Growing, The 4449
Love's Sweet Mystery 2303
Love's Tale Is Told 325
Love's Telephone 2336
Love's the Same, the Same Old Game 3573
Love's Thoughts 4590
Love's Vow 526
Love's Wireless Telephone 687, 1524, 4544
Love's Young Dream 224, 1556, 3431, 4691
Love-Sick Serenade 1745
Lovesongs and Lullabies 2354
Lovey 1689
Lovey Dove 3778
Lovey Dovey 1629, 3256
Lovey-Dovey 3011
Lovie 1908
Lovie Joe 4804
Lovin' 2616
Lovin' Ain't My Aim 4199
Lovin' Al 4744
Lovin' Chile 1174
Lovin' Is a Lowdown Blues 2200
Lovin' Off My Mind 608
Lovin' Sam the Sheik of Alabam' 2706
Lovin' You 827
Loving 2139, 3235
Loving a la Spain 4218
Loving Cup, The 4119
Loving Cup 4477
Loving Daddy, A 1065
Loving Eyes 1224
Loving Friends 981
Loving Her 949
Loving Is a Habit 3915
Loving Moon 1835, 2644
Loving Time 4226
Loving Ways 1613, 2782
Loving You 1158, 3411, 3072, 4031, 3711
Loving You Is My Career 2483

Loving You the Way I Do 1328, 1989
Lovingly Yours 3712
Low 478
Low and Lazy 4237
Low Bottom Woman 518
Low Down Blues 1198, 3963
Low Down Dance 691
Low Down, The 2402
Low Fidelity 3124
Low Moon 4357
Lowen-Green Country Club, I Love You 4204
Lower Deck Diplomacy 2876
Lower the Boom 1958
Lowlands 147
Loyal American 2067
Loyal, Resourceful and Cooperative 3603
Loyalist Wife, The 1748
Loyalty 4303
Lozt Arayan (Let Us In) 1609
Lu-Lu 545
Lu Lu Babe 1316
Luana 2636
Luana Lou 4835
Luana Waltz 422
Luau Chant 3371
Lucia My Italian Maid 3504
Lucie 998
Lucio's Victorian Family 2909
Lucita 201
Luck Be a Lady 1706, 3444
Luckiest Man in the World, The 273
Luckiest Man in the World 3379
Lucky 2646, 1730, 2263, 2638, 4795, 3986
Lucky Anichino 482
Lucky Baby 2783
Lucky Bird 1916
Lucky Boy 799, 1963, 2944
Lucky Break, A 3655
Lucky By Lucky Girl 3165
(Gee! But This Sure Is My) Lucky Day 1424
(This Is My) Lucky Day 1489
Lucky Day 3020, 2641
Lucky Day That I Found You, The 4079
Lucky Dog! 30
Lucky Duck 4702
Lucky Guy 2643, 2306
Lucky in Love 969, 1628
Lucky in the Rain 206
Lucky Jim 357
Lucky Lily 3279
Lucky Lindy 3018
Lucky Little Lucy 4115
Lucky Little Me and You 1836
Lucky Louie 4171
Lucky Love 2783
Lucky Pierre 3107
Lucky Seven 3861
Lucky to Be Alive 663
Lucky to Be Me 3278
Lucre, Love or Liquor 1048
Lucy 1640, 2148
Lucy at Cards 3978
Lucy in the Sky with Diamonds 3903
Lucy Lindy Lady 1537
Lucy Locket 2134
Lucy Meets Hyde 2198
Lucy Meets Jekyll 2198
Lucy's Song 4368
Lud's Wedding (1) 4004
Ludwig XIV 2594
Lulamae 521
Lullaby 93, 109, 158, 369, 459, 593, 703, 764, 933, 1193, 1385, 1770, 1831, 2064, 2171, 2225, 2283, 2579, 2582, 2682, 2732, 2940, 3197, 3202, 3288, 3495, 3761, 3934, 4032, 4123, 4379
Lullaby (Bye Bye Baby) 136
Lullaby (Satin Gown and Silver Shoe) 462
Lullaby (Apukad Eros Kezen) 721
Lullaby (The Spotted Snakes with Double Tongues) 2859
Lullaby (Sleep Baby Dear) 4169
Lullaby for a Princess 4435
Lullaby for Junior 341
Lullaby for Luis 3806
Lullaby from Baby to Baby 3806
Lullaby Lane 1923
Lullaby of Broadway 1359, 3018, 3020
Lullaby of the Plain 1546
Lullaby to Grow On 83
Lullaby Wind 4623
Lullabye 99, 426, 3496, 1872, 4286, 2478
Lullabye to Myself 1797
Lullabyland 3134
Lulu 4325, 2620, 3036, 3384, 2044
Lulu, Come into the Zoo 2286
Lulu Lavinia 2385
Lulu's Honeymoon 4508
Lumbered 4160
Lump of Sugar 1833
Lumpin' 1385
Luna 3357
Luna Park 1004, 228
Lunch 2651
Lunch Is Ready 2724
Luncheon Ballad 3112
Luncheon Line, The 2232
Lunching at the Automat 1225
Lupe 4394
Lure of the Cape, The 637
Lure of the Waltz, The 4489
Lush Life 1713
Lust 2654
Lustspiel 3799
Lusty Month of May, The 623
Lute Song, The 2655
Lutie 3488
Luv 2598
Luxembourg Valse 902
Luxury Lane 3485
Lydia Waltz Song, The 307

Lydia's Entrance Song 307
Lying Here 3876
Lying in State 989
Lyle 2657
Lyle and Valenti 2658
Lyle's Turn 2657
Lyle's Wedding 4433
Lynch-Him Song, The 1592
Lyncher's Prayer, The 1592
Lynn's Dream 1412
Lyre Bird and the Jay, The 1738
Lysistrata 227, 1745, 2659
Lysistrata's Serenade 1745

M

M-10 3493
M-11 3493
M.a.c.a.r.o.n.i. 3488
M-A-Y-B-E 2373
M.C.P. 2007
M-i-s-s-i-s-s-i-p-p-i 1919
M'Lady Chatterley 3484
M'lle Pirouette 2341
M'Lord and M'Lady 324
M-O-N-E-Y 126, 1866, 4759
M-O-N-E-Y Spells Money 3154
M.P., The 1175
M.R.S. for Me 2010
M'sieur Jimmy, Come and Shake Z Shimmy 231
M Word 914
Ma 2857
Ma! 3770
Ma Angelina 2812
Ma Belle 3372, 4357
Ma Belle Marguerite 453
Ma Belle Petronilla 3769
Ma Blossom 4507
Ma Blushin' Rosie 4804
Ma Blushing Rosie, My Posey Sweet 1264
Ma Ebony Belle 3751
Ma Honey Babe 1640
Ma Ma Ho Ne 1340
Ma, Ma, Where's My Dad? 3831
Ma Mere 4235, 4730
Ma Petite Cherie (The Land of Smiles) 4792
Ma Petite Ninette 870
Ma Poppy Belle 1926
Ma Soeur et Moi 2808
Ma Southern Oriole 3981
Ma Starlight Queen 3745
Ma Temme 2870
Ma Tiger Lily 235
Mabel 2168, 2439
Mabel Moore 352
Mabel What's-Her-Name 2305
Mabel's Prayer 1236
Mac, Mac, Macs, The 2886
Macaronis We 2399
Macavity 678
Mach Es Motkeh Noch Amol 3781
Machine Age 70
Machinery 1981
Macht a Lehaim 4463
Mack Sennett Where Are You 708
Mack the Knife 369, 3840, 4399
Mackey of Appalachia 2661
MacSavage MacSpleen 528
Macula Non Est In Te 935
Macumba 70, 2346
Macushla 2662
Macushla Asthore 2662
Macy's Parade 1860
Mad 2910, 958
Mad About 3548
Mad About the Boy 3196, 3235
Mad about the Boy 3885
Mad About You 1747
Mad About You, Manhattan 314
Mad as the Mist and Snow 1977
Mad Ballet, The 4319
Mad Bombers and Prom Queens 1059
Mad-Cap Dance 1549
Mad Dogs and Englishmen 3196, 3235, 4335
Mad for Art 989
Mad Madrid, The 2667
Mad Moments 3639
Mad Opera House 4803
Mad Rum Below 3944
Mad Waltz, The 3741
Madagascar Guards, The 2863
Madam, I Beg You! 937
Madam Is Mad 649
Madam of the Manor 3427
Madamazelle 3325
Madame 2877
Madame Arthur 3386
Madame Butterfingers 695
Madame Butterfly 595
Madame Colette 808, 809
Madame et son Filleul (Madame and Her Godson) 1527
Madame from Paree 348
Madame Is at Home 1670
Madame La Chanson 426
Madame la Duchesse 2115
Madame Marie 3045
Madame Pompadour 910, 2666, 2666
Madame Rose's Toreadorables 1709
Madame Sans Gene 1114
Madame Sherry 2667
Madame Tango's Particular Tango 2000
Madame Tango's Tango 2000
Madame Troubador 2668
Madame Troubadour 2538

Madame Venus (Take a Tip from Venus) 4803
Madame Zuzu 2615
Madcap Princess, A 2671
Madcap, the Vamp and the Sweet Young Thing, The 2969
Madchenlied 2566
Made by Dirks 2385
Made for Each Other 871, 2539
Made for the Movies 1597
Made in Nantucket 3074
Made in the U.S.A. 4019, 2696
Madeira, M'Dear? 220
Madel Mine 1569
Madeleine 468, 2146, 2188
Madeleine's First Kiss 2673
Madeline 3602
Madelon 3258, 4023, 4421
Mademoiselle 2869
Mademoiselle Clichè de Paris 798
Mademoiselle Colombe 2674
Mademoiselle from Armentieres 3020
Mademoiselle in New Rochelle 4179
Mademoiselle Marie (Mlle. Scandale Ballet) (inst.) 2582
Madi 475
Madison Avenue 2676, 3548
Madiwa-Madiwa (Calling for Rain) 2147
Madly for Adlai 932
Madly in Love 2554
Madly in Love with You Am I 4401
Madman 460
Madness Murder 459
Madonna Isabella 482
Madrigal 1183, 1621, 2236, 3323
Madrigal, The 3543
Madrigal, A 3673
Madrigal 3280, 2933
Madrigal Blues, The 2759
Madrigal of May 2211
Madrigal, A 1216
Madwoman of Chaillot, The 1012, 2678
Mafia 4635
Magdelena 2679
Maggie Flynn 2681
Maggie Got Another Situation 2695
Maggie, Maggie May 2682
Maggie Murphy 114
Maggie Murphy's Home 1776
Maggie O'Connor 1259
Maggie's Date 3931
Magi Waltz, The 1508
Magic and Charms 2766
Magic Carpet 1848
Magic Falute 1745
Magic Fan 595
Magic Fingers 4541
Magic Garden of Love, The 201
Magic Gifts 1871
Magic Hour, The 2691
Magic in Your Big Blue Eyes, The 231
Magic Kiss, The 697, 2214
Magic Licorice 4470
Magic, Magic 656
Magic Melody 2637
Magic Melody, The 3193
Magic Moment 1456, 3064
Magic Moments 2666, 327
Magic Music 3980
Magic Music (inst.) 4798
Magic Nights 4196
Magic Number, The 1736
Magic of Me, The 829, 2022
Magic of Springtime, The 4188
Magic of the Moon, The 4795
Magic Place, The 1270
Magic Spell of Love, The 2636
Magic That Surrounds You, The 1159
Magic Time 3788
Magic to Do 3506
Magic Toy Shop 1337
Magic Tree 4366
Magical Garden of Dreams, The 2092
Magical Isle 3611
Magical Lasso 3464
Magical Night 198
Magical Spell 2026
Magical Things in Life 615
Magician Does His Stuff, The 4150
Magician Love 355
Magician of High Degree, A 45
Magnet of Love, The 4381
Magnetic 825, 4022
Magnetic Healing 3305
Magnetic Rag (inst.) 4697
Magnetism 3770
Magnificent Failure 1539
Magnolia in the Woods 4212
Magnolia's Wedding Day 441
Magpie, The 2697
Mah Honey Love 4649
(You'll Find Me Playing) Mah-Jong 334
Mah Jong 2308
Mah-Jongg 1487, 4241
Mah-Jongg Maid 265
Maha Roger 4377
Maharajah, The 1392
Maharanee 4825
Mahbuba 758
Mahoneyphone, The 1136
Mai Mai 4147
Maid and the Miller, The 4713
Maid and the Valet, The 2340
Maid from Boston Town, The 1912
Maid from Gay Paree 2505
Maid from Montbijou (In the Valley of Montbijou) 3996
Maid-o-the-Mist 3663
Maid of Arcadie, The 1912
Maid of Gold 4817
Maid of Mesh 3008

Maid of My Dreams 2485, 2159
Maid of Pekin, The 737
Maid of Santiago 2287
Maid of Sevilla 4757
Maid of the Milky Way 201
Maid of Timbuctoo 4681
Maid to Order Maid 2489
Maid with a Wink in Her Eye, The 2131
Maid's Sextette 3146
Maiden and the Jay, The 3805
Maiden and the Kissing Bug, The 3786
Maiden Fair 735, 2944, 3326
Maiden Let Me In 1096
Maiden of Caprice, The 3613
Maiden of the Wild and Woolly West 4650
Maiden Often Seen, A 1948
Maiden with the Dreamy Eyes 2506
Maiden with the Dreamy Eyes, The 4390
Maiden's Heart, A 3229
Maiden's Prayer (Anorexia) 871
Maiden's Thought, A 3736
Maiden's Voyage 2876
Maidens Aquatic 4704
Maidens Typical of France 629
Maids of Forest 1518
Maids of Killarney 3746
Mail Man, The 2261
Mail Order Annie 2470
Mailman Bring Me No More Blues 580
Mailman Must Be Mad at Me, The 1587
Mailu 4823
Main Event, The 1450
Main Floor, The 1412
Main Street Ballet (inst.) 3683
Maine 3187
Maine Will Remember the Maine 911
Maisie 2844
Maison des Lunes 330
Maja de Goya 2407
Maja Moderna 2407
Majestic Sails at Midnight 207
Major Domo, The 2594
Major General Pumpernickel 2335
Major Margery 2848
Major's Song 470
Majority, The 3661
Make a Date with a Great Psychoanalyst 2453
Make a Friend 4435
Make a Fuss of Me 767
Make a Joyful Noise 4398
Make a Little Sunshine 135
Make a Lot of Noise 1968
Make a Miracle 3444
Make a Quiet Day 3691
Make a Wish 2705
Make Allowance for Love 2506
Make an Honest Woman of Me 4469
Make Believe 25, 2204, 3643, 2722, 2230, 3949
Make Believe World 2580
Make Believe You're Happy 2628
Make Believe You're Mine 3084
Make-Believing 2091
Make 'Em Laugh 3992, 1944, 544
Make Every Day a Holiday 1690
Make Friends (inst.) 2772
Make Hay, Hay, Hay 208
Make Hay Little Girl 1626
Make Hey! Hey! Hey! (While the Moon Shines) 3291
Make Him Guess 3590
Make Him Think I'm Still Pretty 1508
Make It 2630
Make It Another 871
Make It Another Old Fashioned 1018
Make It Another Old-Fashioned, Please 3359
Make It Happen Now 1497
Make It Hot 203
Make It New 942
Make It Nice 143
Make It Night 2012
Make It Snappy 3828
Make It Up 1537
Make Love in the Morning 1096
Make Love to Me 3562
Make Me 4828
Make Me a Star 2171
Make Me Over 4611
Make Mine Latin 867
Make Mine the Same 1884
Make My Bed Down in Dixieland 4673
Make Our Garden Grow 630
Make Someone Happy 1061
Make the Best of It 4491
Make the Heart Be Stone 3180
Make the Man Love Me 4446
Make the Most of Carnival! 902
Make the Most of Spring 615
Make the Most of Your Music 1329
Make the People Cry 1791
Make Them Hate 1282, 4168
Make Them Pay 2012
Make Up 3873, 1240
Make Up My Heart 4138
Make Up Your Mind 787, 905, 2140, 2610, 4748
Make Way 170, 612, 44, 1985, 3595
Make Way for My Lady 2731
Make Way for the Law 2452
Make Way for Their Excellencies 3339
Make Way for Tomorrow 2204, 1298, 4316
Make with the Feet 297
Make Your Mate Miserable 345
Make Your Own Kind of Music 338
Make Your Own Sunshine 1054
Make Yourself at Home 2708
Make Yourselves at Home 1424
Makes No Difference Now 2897
Makin' Believe 2051
Makin' Guacamole 992
Makin' It (Seeing a Chance and Taking It) 486

Makin' It 4162
Makin' Movies 456
Makin' the Rounds 3858
Makin' Whoopee 4683
Making a Home 2746
Making a Venus 1096
Making Conversation 4214
Making Every Minute Count 2539
Making Eyes 2481, 2869
Making It 1371
Making Light of Day 1651
Making of a Girl, The 3400
Making of a Man, The 1049
Making of a Woman, The 4497
Making Them Beautiful 2927
Makulele 3838
Malaguena 1710
Malaiya 2686
Male and Twenty-One 4518
Male Animal, The 924
Male Chauvinist Pig of Myself 4635
Male Is an Animal, A 2267
Male Vamps 4520
Malkele's Song 4773
Malpractice 3600
Maluan Moon 4243
Malumbo 1046
Mam'selle 666, 3772
Mam'selle Fauchette 2517
Mam'selle Frappe 141
Mam'selle Sallie 2716
Mama 101, 337, 3836, 2231, 3236, 3428, 3741
Mama, a Rainbow 2874
Mama Always Makes It Better 2064
Mama Always Said 3825
Mama at the Bat 3914
Mama, Do Not Leave Your Pappoose 2902
Mama Don't Cry 430
Mama Don't Get Married 869
Mama Don't 'Low 2796
Mama Don't Want No Baby 2153
Mama, Earl Done Ate the Tooth Paste Again 1139
Mama Fantastic 1037
Mama Frimbo 1402
Mama Goddess 1426
Mama Is Here 900
Mama, It's Me 2333
Mama Lazarus 3817
Mama Loves You 3651
Mama, Mama 1265, 2961
Mama, Mama, Mama 1139
Mama! Mama! Papa's Got a Lot of Lovin' (All Saved Up for You) 2857
Mama the Balabusta 2422
Mama, What's Love 3914
Mama Will Be Waiting with the Dawn 3368
Mama Will Provide 3285
Mama You Better Watch Out for Daughter 2953
Mama's Bank Account 2064
Mama's Boarding House 1881
Mama's Boys 3448
Mama's China Twins 141
Mama's Gotta Get Her Rent 1989
Mama's Little Girl 2523
Mamam 3018
Maman 278, 2777
Mamaw 3608
Mamba's Daughters 2712
Mambo '52 3059
Mambo-Java 3954
Mame 2208, 2713
Mamenyu Tayere (Dear Mama) 4342
Mamenyu, Elegy of the Triangle Fire Victims 1609
Mamie and Bess Bicker 3873
Mamie in the Afternoon 1237
Mamie Is Mimi 1475, 2590
Mamie McGee 1209
Mamma, It's Saturday Night 2748
Mamma Taught Me 4162
Mamma's Cooking 1346
Mamma's Little Pet 1088
Mammie's Day in Dixie Land 2462
Mammie's Going to Kiss Your Tears Away 1824
Mammy 2739, 4817
Mammy Jinny 4687
Mammy Land 2337
Mammy Sue 1799
Mammy Traders 2355
Mammy's Black Baby 3657
Mammy's Chocolate Soldier 1833
Mammy's Jubilee 443, 3134
Mammy's Knee 1267
Mammy's Lit'l Choc'late Cullud Chile 740
Mammy's Little Baby 2595
Mammy's Little Pumpkin-Colored Coons 1627
Mammy's Pickaninny 4663
Mamselle 948, 4670
Mamzelle Fifi 3134
Mamzelle Papazelle 82
Man 170, 2056
Man, A 3231, 2262
Man, The 3651
Man, A 4388
Man a Maid, A 3508
Man About Town, The 692, 1602
Man About Town 2545, 3314
Man About Town, The 2131
Man About Town 4727
Man About Yonkers 289
Man Among Men, A 1809
Man and a Maid, A 3567
Man and a Woman, A 3294
Man and His Message, The 3814
Man and Shadow 2295
Man and Wife 1590
Man Around the House, A 4860
Man at the Piano, The 556
Man Behind, The 2803
Man Behind the Club, The 1403
Man Behind the Hammer and Saw, The 2853

Man Behind the Scenes, The 694
Man Better Man 2719
Man Can Have No Choice, A 2355
Man Could Go Quite Mad, A 3070
Man Doesn't Know, A 957
Man Eating Ape Waltz, The 164
Man for Sale 462
Man for You, The 2928
Man from 'Bam, The 2721
Man from Conjure Land, The 295
Man from Glad 1978
Man from Mexico 25
Man from the Mainland, A 1386
Man Has Got to Wear the Pants, The 4588
Man Has Other Things to Do 1518
Man, His Pipe and His Dog, A 4064
Man I Am with Her, The 1435
Man I Love, The 1793
Man I Love 2376
Man I Love, The 3766, 4178
Man I Love Is Here, The 3219
Man I Married, The 36
Man I Marry, The 2317
Man I Marry Must Be a Man, The 1525
Man I Never Met, The 3913
Man I Used to Be, The 3505, 4146
Man in My Life, The 3837
Man in the Dark 3913
Man in the Doorway 2134
Man in the Mirror, The 610
Man in the Moon 382
Man in the Moon, The 659, 2208
Man In the Moon 1518
Man in the Moon, The 2713
Man in the Moon 4286, 3952
Man in the White House 70
Man in the Window, The 564
Man Is a Man's Best Friend 127
Man Is a Mistake 458
Man Is As Old As He Feels, A 2174
Man Is Faithful till He's Caught 2732
Man Is for Woman Made 2278
Man Is for Woman Made (A Rondelay) 2633
Man Is Good for Something After All, A 4611
Man Is Made for Woman 2599
Man Is Not Meant to Reason, A 2320
Man Is Only a Man, A 805, 4666
Man Is the Lord of It All 4283
Man Isn't Old, A 4611
Man Like Me, A 2651
Man Like You, A 3171
Man Loves Me, The 4798
Man, Man, Man 2035, 3727
Man Meant Well, The 2160
Man Must Have Something to Live For, A 615
Man Must His Honor Defend, A 629
Man My Mother Married, The 664
Man Nobody Could Love, The 2437
Man Not a Mouse 1644
Man o' My Dreams 4010
Man of High Degree, A (Entrance of Colonel Homes) 4179
Man of La Mancha (I, Don Quixote) 2727
Man of Many Parts 1970
Man of Rank, A 2126
Man of Spirit, A 4450
Man of the Family 2550
Man of the Hour, The 3041
Man of the People 4619
Man of the World, A 1088
Man of the Year This Week, The 4423
Man of Vision, A 4190
Man, Oh Man 1770
Man on a Subway 3557
Man on the Box, The 531
Man Overboard 2333
Man Overboard! 2378
Man Say 3656
Man She Has Found, A 340
Man She'll Never Meet, The 3943
Man Should Have a Double When He's Single, A 136
Man Tan 1363
Man That Broke the Bank at Monte Carlo, The 1301
Man That Is Born of a Woman 2648
Man That Leads the Band Leads the Army, The 4650
Man That Rules the Town, The 3040
Man, the Master 745
Man They Meant, The 3280
Man to Man 4769, 2998
Man to Man Talk 3288
Man Up My Sleeve, A 722
Man Upon My Mind 4153
Man Upstairs, The 612
Man Wanted 846, 845
Man, We're Beat 3094
Man Who Broke the Bank at Monte Carlo, The 2646
Man Who Built the Subway, The 4801
Man Who Built the Summer Hotel, The 2978
Man Who Came to Dinner, The 3931
Man Who Came to Win 'Er 3916
Man Who Feels the Dart, A 1197
Man Who Has Everything, The 3187
Man Who Hypnotized McCarthy, The 1021
Man Who Invented Ragtime, The 604
Man Who Isn't, A 2477
Man Who Leads the Band, The 1415
Man Who Made His Life into a Work of Art, The 1256
Man Who Owns Broadway, The 2730
Man Who Plays the Alto Flute, The 3522
Man Who Speaks for Himself, A 4157
Man Who Was My Boy, The 3485
Man Who Wrote "The Vampire" Must Have Known My Wife 4808
Man Who Wrote the 'Merry Widow Waltz', The 954
Man Who's Got a Mortgage on the Mist, The 263
Man with a Dream 3899
Man with a Load of Mischief 2731

Man with a Plan, A 4190
Man with a Problem, A 2935
Man with an Axe to Grind, A 4544
Man with the Ginger Mustache, The 4062
Man with the Money, The 2834
Man with the Tamborine, The 2506
Man Without Words, A 946
Man Worth Fightin' For, A 534
Man You Are, The 1035
Man You Can Set Your Watch By, A 101
Man You Love, The 4479
Man's a Man, A 276
Man's a Man for A' That, A 4649
Man's Alright, The 2796
Man's Forever, A 4767
Man's Gotta Fight, A 4123
Man's Home, A 4499
Man's Inhumanity 3941
Man's Inhumanity to Man 2246, 2804
Man/Woman 1575
Managed 4435
Manager of Personnel, The 2861
Manana 934, 1536, 1992, 3428, 3774
Manana Land 2056
Manchester 1717, 2004
Manchild 415
Manda 740
Mandala 1031
Mandalay 4654
Mandalay Song, The 1755
Mandarin, The 3828
Mandarin Palace on the Grand Concourse, The 2925
Mandarin's Garden, The (inst.) 4699
Mandie 3384
Mandie from Ohio 737
Mandolin and the Man, The 4860
Mandolin Serenade 1375
Mandy 106, 934, 1900, 2098, 822, 2506, 2642, 3513, 4182, 4340, 4770, 4813
Mandy Make Up Your Mind 1058, 2462
Mandy's Blessing 2338
Mango Tango, The 693
Mangoes 4828
Manhattan 1638, 3039, 1446, 2032, 2992, 3018, 214, 4709
Manhattan Beggar 1717
Manhattan Hometown 3429
Manhattan Isle 3480
Manhattan Lullaby 1874, 4192
Manhattan Mad 2696
Manhattan Madness 789, 1225
Manhattan Mary 2734
Manhattan Moves 2735
Manhattan Nights 1688
Manhattan Serenade (inst.) 703
Manhattan Shines 696
Manhattan Showboat 2737
Manhattan Transfer 266
Manhattan Walk 1617
Manhattan's Automatons 4316
Mania, A 1958
Manic Depressives (Don't Do Rewrites) 3564
Manicure Girl, The 1845
Manicure Song (Profession of a Manicure, The) 4044
(Come Back to) Manistee 4201
Manita Wanna Eat, Wanna Eat 3406
Mankind Should Be My Business 4155
Manly Art or Self Defense, The 483
Manly Art, The 1601
Mannequin's Ball 632
Manners and Motions 200
Mannikin Dolls 3523
Mansion 4485
Mansion Hill 1702
Mansion of Roses, The 2856
Mantelpiece Tragedy, The 2328
Manuel Your Friend 1380
Manuelo 1546, 4086
Manuelo (dance) 4086
Manufacture and Sell 4168
Many a Fairer Face 2633
Many a Lofty Mountain 1476
Many a New Day 3263
Many a Time 3652
Many Happy Returns 2742, 2565, 2743
Many Kinds of Love 1385
Many, Many Men 1734
Many Men Like You 4343
Many Moons Ago 3288
Many People Live Inside My Mind 518
Many the Beasts 2659
Many Trades 2866
Many Ways to Skin a Cat 1373
Many Years Ago 1178, 3759
Many Young Men from Now 1848
Maori 295
Map Sellers 4232
Maple Leaf Rag 4196
Mapleton High Chorale 2386
Marabi Dance Song (Chuzi Mama/ Gwabi Gwabi) 4579
Maracas Make Me Nervous 3004
Marat We're Poor 3445
Marat's Nightmare 3445
Marathon, The 1224
Marathon 2188
Marathon Dance, The (dance) 404
Marathon Step, The 3723
Marathon Street 2071
Marbella Maid 4218
Marc Antony 2696
Marcel Mousse 621
Marceline's Meat Sauce 2347
Marcella 3000, 4507
Marcelle 684
March 1095, 1459, 2546
March 3531, 3570, 1355
March Ahead 1755
March Along to the Sound of the Band 1041

March Chorus and Entrance of the Regent 1183
March for Brotherhood 1155
March Gypsys 3086
March Louis XI (inst.) 2102
March, March, March 2318
March of Old Glory 1505
March of Rhyme 4467
March of the Allies 2865
March of the Beauties of the Nation (inst.) 1327
March of the Beaver Patrol 2496
March of the Bridegrooms 3613
March of the Dejected 2511
March of the Delegations from All Parts of the World (inst.) 1327
March of the Dos 4012
March of the Dragon 4509
March of the Enchantress 4742
March of the Falsettos 2746
March of the Flags 3488
March of the Foreign Commissioners 3322
March of the Frisco Chinks 2517
March of the Gladiators 1154
March of the Grenadiers (inst.) 190
March of the Guards 2464
March of the Ill-Assorted Guards, The 2182
March of the Infernal Guards 1327
March of the King's Amazons 2730
March of the Militant Suffragettes, Ochone! 1083
March of the Musketeers 4357
March of the New York Clubs 1327
March of the New York Dailies 1466
March of the Prince's Regiment 1183
March of the Rice and Old Shoes 2238
March of the Royal Siamese Children (inst.) 2312
March of the States, The (inst.) 1901
March of the Toreadors (inst.) 1327
March of the Toys (inst.) 250, 3704
March of the Toys 4818
March of the Trollgers 4075
March of the Valentines (inst.) 2534
March of the Vigilant Vassals 127
March of the Watch 49
March of the White and Gold Imps 4381
March of the Wooden Soldiers (inst.) 251
March of the Yuppies 2790
March of Time, The 784, 1135
March On 1580, 3078
March On for Tennessee 3035
March On Oh Soldier 1515
March on September Morn 1964
March Out of My Life 2568
March Song 3424, 4165
March to Zion, The 1196
March with Me 133, 702, 2570, 3924
Marche de L'Armee Panemeenne (Panamanian Army March) (inst.) 2753
Marches (inst.) 4816
Marching 2770, 4115
Marching Along with Time 789
Marching By 2747
Marching Down This Road 3989
Marching for Peace 1049
Marching Home in the Rain 3626
Marching Song, A 4320
Marching Songs of the Pollicle Dogs, The 678
Marching to the Flight 743
Marching with Johnny 2748
Marching with the Circus Band 1650
Marconigram 3799
Marcus, My Friend 2033
Mardi Gras 1667, 2000, 2608
Mardi Gras, The 3773
Mardi Gras Day in New Orleans 1127
Mardi Gras Time 4127
Mardi Gras Waltz, The 2750
Maressi 2106
Margaret 3557, 2578
Margie 542
Margie's Lament 3576
Marginal People 922
Margineers 787
Margineers, The 2140
Margo's Theme 167
Margot 1027
Marguerite 141
Maria 223, 2333
Maria (Annina) 3011
Maria 3699, 4095, 4625, 4777
Maria in Spats 3366
Marian 4249
Marian the Librarian 3016
Mariana of the Moated Grange 2819
Marianna 2384
Marianne 1045, 1660, 2751, 3117
Marie 561, 2852, 2787, 4616
Marie Cahill's Arab Love Song 511
Marie from Paree 1409
Marie Galante 2753
Marie Leveau 1890
Marie-Louise 3308
Marie, Marie 2892
Marie Odile 4809
Marie's Law 1280
Marieke 2188
Marietta 1281, 2262
Mariette 4429
Marihuana 2032
Marilyn 4252
Marilyn Monroe 460
Marilyn's Theme 2426
Marimba 1536, 1686
Marina 4228
Marine's Hymn, The 189
Mariner's Tale, The 2519
Marintch at Coney Island 1647
Marionettes 2931, 3087, 3586
Marital Infidelity 410
Marital Malignity 2424
Maritza Darling 307
Marius 1242

Marjolaine 2756
Marjorie 2757
Marjorie Morningstar 602, 2758
Marjorie's Dream 1412
Mark Anthony 4747
Mark of a Man, The 4004
Mark Twain 2227
Marked By Fire 10
Marked Millions 1656
Market 3690
Market Day 30, 600, 23, 2594
Market Day in the Village 4667
Market Song 651
Market Today 1744
Marketing, Marketing 4089
Marlene 3276
Marley's Ghost 752
Marlon Mood, The 363
Marooned Messin' 1985
Marquis of Jolifontaine, The 1067
Marriage, The 2673
Marriage 2944, 4617
Marriage (Wedding) Song 1955
Marriage a La Mode 3274
Marriage C.O.D. 3623
Marriage Counsel 3970
Marriage Game 522
Marriage Is a Game of Blind Man's Bluff 3591
Marriage Is a Lottery 4311
Marriage Is for Old Folks 3863
Marriage Is Sublime 2974
Marriage Knot, The 168
Marriage License 827
Marriage Market, The 2761
Marriage Music 2655
Marriage of Convenience, A 1962
Marriage of the Daffodil and Daisy, The 2851
Marriage of the Lily and the Rose, The 1753
Marriage Type Love 2797
Married 610
Married Couple Seeks Married Couple 2058
Married I Can Always Get 2677
Married Life 3142, 1016, 4437, 4784
Married Life Blues 2180
Married Man, A 270
Married Man 4068
Married Man, A 3722
Married Man 3619
Married Man Makes the Best Soldier 1852
Married Men and Single Men 1339
Married Via Wireless 2762
Married with Children 2229
Marry a Girl in June 2262
Marry a Sunshine Girl 4206
Marry an American 508
Marry Me 131, 1993, 412, 3718, 3839
Marry Me a Little 4067, 832, 2764, 3967
Marry Me and See 1552, 2931
Marry Me Now 4695
Marry Me to the Music of a Big Brass Band 1430
Marry the Family 3365
Marry the Girl Myself 3931
Marry the Man Today 1706, 3444
Marry the One You Love 177
Marry with Me 1662
Marrying for Fun 1616
Marrying for Love 619
Marseilles 2939
Marshall's Blues 169
Marshall's Reply 169
Marshosito 2407
Marsovia 4251
Marsovian Dance (inst.) 2838
Martha Spanks the Grand Pianner 737
Martial Music of the Fife and Drum, The 1798
Martin Luther Drinking Song 3586
Martina 1739
Martini Rock, The 4774
Marvelous, Curious and Strange 1258
Marvelous Fire Machine 4270
Marvelous Party, A 3235
Marvelous Weekend, A 4062
Marvin at the Psychiatrist 2746
Marvin Hits Trina 2746
Marvin Takes a Victory Shower 2132
Marvin's Giddy Seizures 2132
Marx 2478
Mary 96, 791, 1032, 1149, 1478, 1533, 1866, 2767, 2897, 2975, 3322
Mary Alice, Don't Say Shit 1978
Mary and Doug 4814
Mary Ann 1849, 2278, 2600, 2633, 2724, 4359, 4521
Mary Ann McManus 934
Mary Ann O'San 1228
Mary Ann O'Shea 1629
Mary Black 1926
Mary Brown 959
Mary Carey 2869
Mary Cary 3746
Mary Come Down 3191
Mary Dear! I Miss You Most of All 1965
Mary from Maryland 1535
Mary from Tipperary 2035
Mary, Get Up 3580
Mary Had a Little Lamb 2673
Mary Has a Little Fair 4793
Mary in the Dairy 954
Mary Jane 4761
Mary Jane and Her Little Playmates 591
Mary Jane McKane 2768
Mary Jape 1798
Mary Lee 1502
Mary Mack 1713
Mary Make Believe 4341
Mary Margaret's House in the Country 1737, 3927
Mary, Mary 250, 2098, 2134
Mary! Mary! 4247
Mary, Mary, Quite Contrary 2844
Mary McGee 954
Mary My Hearther Queen 3085

Mary My Prairie Fairy 830
Mary Pistologlione 4099
Mary, Queen of Scots 2193
Mary Queen of Scots 3538
Mary, Queen of Scots 4780
Mary Rose 4817
Mary Smith 625
Mary the Wary 3745
Mary to the Market Went 1935
Mary Was a Housemaid 3999
Mary Was a Manicure 2123
Mary Wise 3205
Maryanna 1479
Maryland 4037
Maryland Scene 1923
Mary's a Grand Old Name 1356
Mary's Lamb 4434
Mary's Lament 1785
Mary's Prayer 1716
Mascot of the Troop, The (Mascot of the Moon) 2915
Masculine Man, A 2910
Masculinity 911, 2360
Masetto's Song 482
Mash 'Em Up 3690
Mash Ethiopia 3690
Mash Notes 2780
Masha's Song 3686
Mask of Evil 2727
Mask Waltz, The 3683
Masked Ball 3463
Masked Ball, The 1347
Masks 1978, 4844
Masochism Tango 4412
Mason, The 4744
Mason Cares 3871
Mason Dixon Blues 2870
Masque, The 3702
Masquerade 708, 3464
Masquerade, The 1427
Masquerade 3763, 4484
Masquerade Ball 4449
Mass 2198
Massa Marries Tonight (Nuptual Celebration), The (dance) 4383
Massachusetts Mermaid 2137
Massacre 2472
Massacre, The 4196
Massage a Trois 4635
Masses Are Asses, The 4536
Masses of Masses 2177
Masseuse 2168
Master and Slave 3035
Master Class, The 2654
Master of All I Survey, The 2553
Master of His Fate 255
Master of the Greatest Art of All, The 4060
Master of the House 2442
Master Race Polka 597
Master Race Polka, The 3217
Mata Hari 2522
Mata Hari in Spain 2777
Mata Hari Mine 4395
Mata Hari's Dance at the Salon 2777
Matador Dance 4572
Matador Song 1979
Match Makers, The 4228
Match Race, The 3752
Matchmaker, The 1828
Matchmaker, Matchmaker 1265
Matchmaker's Daughter, The 2354
Matelot 3196
Mater Terra 2962
Mater's Song 2778
Mates 589
Mathematical Quartet 3600
Mathilde 2188
Matilda 961
Matilda and the Builder 1537
Matinee, The 410
Matinee 2783
Matinee Girl 3926
Matinee Girls 350
Matinee Maid, The 2160
Mating Dance, The 169
Mating Time 1513
Matrimonial Agent, The 3744
Matrimonial Handicap, The 4241
Matrimonial Mart, The 118
Matrimonial Stomp, The 2484
Matrimony 1712, 2996
Matron and the Maid, The 356
Matron's Good Night Sleep, A 3754
Matter of Experience, A 4359
Matter of Minutes, A 3429, 1467
Matter of Opinion 20, 2784
Matter of Time, A 1991, 484, 2785
Matter Very Serious, The 1962
Matter We Can Easily Arrange, A 1868
Matters Culinary 1871
Matters of the Heart 3937
Matthew 3227
Mattress House, The 1651
Maude Adams of the Screen, The 3397
Maude, the Bawd 3920
Maudlin Maiden 2896
Mauricette 1992
Mauve Decade 4240
Max Jacobs 3279
Max the Millionaire 3094
Max's Visit 3792
Maxford House 3039
Maxie 3159
Maxim Girl, The 3251
Maxim's 2836, 2838
Maxine! 4431
Maxixe, The 3877
Maxixe-Habanera 101
Maxwell's Silver Hammer 3903
May All Our Children Have Rhythm 3036

May and January 2344
May and September 3770
May Day March (inst.) 2534
May I? 2518
May I Dance with You? 2968
May I Have My Gloves? 1493
May I Present 4363
May I Return to the Beginning 2242
May I Say I Love You? 4087
May I Suggest Romance 1670
May in Manhattan 3810
May It Bring Him Pleasure 2553
May Moon 3163
May 7th, 1901 2703
May Tells All 4557
May the Best Man Win 3142, 3091
May We Come A'Wooing 2880
May We Entertain You 1709
May Wine Polka 3703
May Your Heart Stay Young (L'Chayim) 4863
Maybe 150, 250, 3243, 1701
Maybe Baby 580
Maybe for Instance 2285
Maybe He's Some Kinda of Crazy 2961
Maybe I Could If I Tried 1911
Maybe I Know 2427, 2427
Maybe I Ought to Stay 2925
Maybe I Should Change My Ways 341
Maybe I Will 4226, 4276
Maybe I'll Baby You 1215, 4271
Maybe I'm Better Off 4518
Maybe I'm Doing It Wrong 2852, 2787
Maybe Is a Woman's Word 4366
May-be It's a Bear 3855
Maybe It's Because 95
Maybe It's Love 720
Maybe It's Me 1267, 3436
Maybe It's Not Too Late 484
Maybe It's Time for Me 3931
Maybe Land 965
Maybe Leola Call Today 1496
Maybe, Maybe, Maybe 2064
Maybe, Maybe Not 36
Maybe Means Yes 1827
Maybe Monday I'll Conquer 3165
Maybe My Baby Loves Me 1649
Maybe Now a Little House 2992
Maybe So 138
Maybe the World Has a Chance 2998
Maybe There's a Place 1581
Maybe There's an Angle 4232
Maybe There's More 327
Maybe They're Magic 2143
Maybe This Is Love 4345
Maybe This Time 131, 4480
Maybe Tomorrow 1216
Maybe Yes or No 728
Maybe You Can See Yourself 729
Maybe You Think I Did 4704
Maybe You'll Look Good to Me 2546
Maybe You're My Man 1754
Maybells 2135
Maydee (Pretty Little South Sea Island Lady) 1295
Mayer's Fine Coins 3780
Mayfair 4583, 4793
Mayfair Affair 2295
Mayflower I Love You 2789
Mayflower Will Sail, The 912
Mayn Alte Heym 4342
Mayn Rochele 3781
Mayn Ruchele 2356
Mayn Yidishe Meydele 1609
Mayonnaise Marines, The 1220
Mayor 2790
Mayor Doesn't Care, The 1732
Mayor of Harlem, The (Meet the Mayor) 888
Mayor of Kankakee, The (Entrance of Todd) 1910
Mayor of Tango Town! 1971
Mayor of Tokio, The 2793
Mayor's Chair, The 935
Mayor's Invocation 1092
Maypole Dance (inst.) 4524
Maze, The 699
Mazel Tov 2866
Mazeltov 1660
Mazie 556, 1515
Mazourka 4620
Mazuma (The Plaint of the Prima Donna) 4070
Mazuma 3122, 3778
Mazurka (inst.) 630
Mazurka 147, 2623, 3536, 3994
Mazurka, The (inst.) 4798
Mazzini and Mankind 4244
McCoy 1041
McDougal's Cave 4409
McInerney's Farm 4428
McNabb (Who Drives the Cab) 3749
McNally's Row of Flats 1776
McNamara's Band 3479
McSorley's Trip to Paris 1264
Me 508, 1796, 330, 3084, 4004, 4678
Me, a Big Heap Indian 2522
Me Alone 2719
Me an' My Bundle 2894
Me and Bobby McGee 338
Me and Columbus 1658
Me and de Minstrel Band 2111
Me and Delilah 1496
Me and Dorothea 4028
Me and Him 3844
Me and Jesus 2173
Me and Juliet 2797
Me and Lee 3035
Me and Love 868
Me and Marie 2252
Me and My Baby 723, 131, 4480

Me and My Boss 3949
Me and My Dog 1270
Me and My Girl 2798
Me and My Heart Went A-Gadding 2089
Me and My Horse 239
Me and My Old World Charm 1140
Me and My Perch 3636
Me and My Shadow 393, 3020
Me and My Town 162
Me and Pollyanna 603
Me and the Bombers 3752
Me and the Boy Friend 4322
Me and the Elements 2304
Me and the Mule 3001
Me and the Role and You 4557
Me & Thee 3485
Me and You 695, 2373, 2587, 2906, 4424
Me Atahualpa 4623
Me for You 1800
Me for You Forever 3002
Me Go Soldier! No, No, No! 306
Me God, Please God 2785
Me, Him and I 2800
Me I Want to Be, The 2584
Me Man — You Mansfield 412
Me, Me, Me 2657
Me Myself and I 1497
Me 'n You 4621
Me Nobody Knows, The 2801, 2801
Me Oh Me Oh Man Do I Miss Milwaukee 2658
Me, the Moonlight and Me 2669
Me Welly Poor Old Chinaman 2802
Me, Who Am I 2797
Meadow Serenade 4178
Meadowlark 273, 3536
Mean 269, 1766
Mean Man 1667
Mean Moon Man 3579
Mean Mr. Mustard 3903
Mean Old Lion 4722
Mean Old Man's World, A 4127
Mean to Me 39
Meanest Man in the World, The 3614
Meanest Man in Town, The 941
Meaning Me, Meaning You 568
Meaningful Life, A 2617
Meanwhile 2163, 1347
Meanwhile Back in Yonkers 3476
Measure the Valleys 3656
Meat and Potatoes 2797, 2983, 1168
Meatface 1277
Mecca 3404
Mechanical Ballet 1275
Mechanical Bird, The 3164
Mechanical Doll Dance, The 4439
Mechanical Man 3069
Mechanical Soldiers 4747
Meddler, The 4325
Medea in Disneyland 2804, 3941
Medea Tango 2106
Medicare Rock, The 3530
Medicine Marches On 412
Medicos 4575
Mediocrity 722
Meditation 3928
Mediterranean 4701
Mediterranean Blue 1123
Mediterranean Nights 200
Mediterrania 4079
Medley 2177
Medley of College Songs 4589
Medley of Negro Spirituals 4645
Mee-rah-lah 189
Meek Shall Inherit, The 2544
Meeskite 610
Meet Her with a Taximeter 1318
Meet Me at Eight in the Hall
(The Letter Song) 4490
Meet Me at the Barber Shop 3337
Meet Me at the Fair 4569
Meet Me at the Front Door 1407
Meet Me at the Masquerade 4094
Meet Me at the Stage Door, Johnnie 4215
Meet Me at the Stage Door Tonight 1738
Meet Me at the Station 4094
Meet Me at the Station Dearie 3401
Meet Me at the Tabarin 4094
Meet Me at Twilight 2498
Meet Me Beside the River 2287
Meet Me By the Candy Pole 813
Meet Me Down on Main Street 334
Meet Me Down on the Corner 632
Meet Me Girlie 1557
Meet Me in Bubble Land 3402
Meet Me in Panama 2912
Meet Me in Peacock Alley 4655
Meet Me in Rose Time Rosie 115, 800
Meet Me in Rose Time, Rosie 3134
Meet Me in St. Louis 2805, 2805
Meet Me in St. Louis, Louis 662, 4390
Meet Me on the Fence Tonight 4662
Meet Me Tonight 1249
Meet Me Tonight at 9 2261
Meet Me Tonight in Dreamland 4799
Meet Me Under the Wysteria 4650
Meet Me Where the Lanterns Glow 4452
Meet Me, Dear, on Saturday, a Little After Two 306
Meet Mesalia (dance) 3931
Meet Miss Blendo 4423
Meet My Girl 2011, 2010
Meet My Seester 2583
Meet My Sister 2641
Meet-Su-No 595
Meet the Blands 1149
Meet the Boy Friend—Don't Laugh 1667
Meet the Elite 3916
Meet the People 2809
Meet the Press 4737
Meet You 'Hind the Barn 3000
Meet Your True Love Half Way 3508

Meeting, The 3215
Meeting 4303
Meeting Here Tonight, A 2203
Meeting of the Minds, A 2354
Meeting Tonight 3836
Meg 2949
Meg's New York 2965
Megadeath 3077
Megalopolis 272
Megatron (dance) 3869
Mei Lan-Fang 1448
Meilinki Meilchick 4160
Mein Herr 4480
Mein Hertz 4467
Mein Junger Herr 517
Meine Kleine Akrobat 1322, 1338
Meine Schwester Und Ich 2808
Melancholy 2511
Melancholy Blues 3500
Melancholy Lady 4620
Melancholy Marshmallow, The 3073
Melancholy Melody 4073
Melancholy Sunbeam and the Rose, The 3488
Melanie's Aria 841
Meleko 4438
Melican Man, A 376
'Melican Papa (Chink Song) 1625
Melinda 3274
Melinda Schecker 843
Melisande 3294, 3542
Melissa's Refrain 4041
Mellow Moon 2927
Mellow Sax 1890
Melodies of May 3014
Melodies Within My Heart 4669
Melodrama (inst.) 136
Melodrama 334, 2884, 3590
Melodrama and Polly's Song 4371
Melodrama Known as Married Life 3396
Melodramatic Captain, The 2938
Melodramatic Music (inst.) 250
Melody 2270, 2813, 4029
Melody Dreams 2927
Melody in Four F 2453
Melody Land 712, 3405
Melody Makers 1132
Melody Man 1531
Melody of Dance 2684
Melody of Love, The 1712
Melody of Love 2947
Melody of Manhattan 1695
Melody of the Century 3087
Melody Rises, A 4147
Melody Triste 463
Melody Will Keep You Young 102
Melons 2231
Melos, That Lovely Smiling Isle 1683
Melt It Down 4488
Melt Us! (Old Immigration and Naturalization Rag, The) 64
Melt Us (Immigration Rag) 602
Melting of Molly, The 2816
Melting Pot, The 4289, 4747
Melvin 3286
Member of the Wedding, The 1222
Member of the Yale Elizabethan Club 2287
'Member When 4209
Members of the Club 1161
Memoirs 1709
Memorabilia 1648
Memories 1176, 1889, 2277, 2734, 17, 3799, 4033
Memories Fond and True (Far Away) 2745
Memories of Buffalo Bill 2413
Memories of Madison Square Garden 2258
Memories of My Swedish Home 3270
Memories of You 443, 432, 1198
Memory 678, 1012
Memory, A 1235
Memory Ballet (inst.) 589
Memory of a Happy Moment, A 211
Memory of Tonight 198
Memory Song 374
Mem'ry's Garden 1602
Mem'rys of Childhood Day 3998
Men, The 250
Men 323, 616, 716, 3142
(If There Were Not Any) Men 1033
Men 1112
Men! 1306
Men 2590, 4038, 4354, 4682
Men About Town 2595, 3196, 3235, 3678
Men and Women Are Awful 1387
Men Are a Pain in the Neck 1918
Men Are Ambitious 457
Men Are Only Boys Grown Tall 3913
Men at Work 2364
Men Awake 3501
Men Behind the Man Behind the Gun 2653
Men Come with Guns 169
Men from Milwaukee, The 2061
Men Grow Older 2384
Men in My Life, The 3983
Men! Men! Men! 3681
Men, Men, Men 4194
Men, Men, You Are Foolish Men 1213
Men of Business 4219
Men of China 4792
Men of Hades 2005
Men of Jaloux 4670
Men of Spain, The 1570
Men of Stone 1903
Men of the Watermark 4432
Men Run the World 1744
Men Who Have Loved Me, The 482
Men Who Run the Country, The 3837
Menaechmi 514
Menage-a-Trois 1439
Menagerie Song 2506
Mendelssohn and Liszt 3958
Mender of Broken Dreams, The 702

Mendocino Stroll, The 2761
Mene, Mene, Tekel 3501
Menehune, The 3371
Menelik's Tribute to Queen Tai Tu 9
Men's Dance 3813
Men's Eyes 2346
Mental Hygiene 2992
Menu, The 1169
Menu Dance, The 3663
Menu Song 1227, 3608
Meow! Meow! Meow! 2394
Meow Meow Meow 4437
Merano 721
Meraviglioso! 2551
Mercenary Mary 2818
Mercenary Mary Ann 2159
Merchandise 4750
Merchandisers' Song 721
Merchant's March (1) 1214
Merchant's March (2) 1214
Merci 3792
Merci Beaucoup 385
Merci, Bon Dieu 1634
Merci, Madame 273
Mercy! 83
Merely a Matter of Form 586
Merely Marvelous 3687
Mermaid and Merman, The 3891
Mermaid and the Lobster, The 4754
Mermaid and the Rainbow, The
(Song of the Mermaid) 1908
Mermaid and the Whale, The 4614
Mermaid Song 211, 934
Mermaids 2779
Mermaids' Chorus 3337
Mermaid's Evening Song, The 1897
Mermaid's Tail, The 3450
Mermaid's Tale, The 846
Merrie Merrie, The 265
Merrill, Lynch, Pierce,
Fenner and Clyde 1002
Merrily, Mary Lee 3068
Merrily on My Way 3916
Merrily! Verily! Oh! 526
Merrily We Roll Along 4067,
2821, 2822, 2822
Merrily We Waltz Along 4374
Merry and Bright 1335
Merry-Andrew (inst.) 3766
Merry Cavalier, The 3673
Merry Christmas 3054
Merry Christmas Bells 3918
Merry Christmas to Me 692
Merry Doll, The (inst.) 396
Merry Gallows, The 4539
Merry-Go, Merry-Go-Round 1363
Merry-Go-Round 272, 1695, 3978
Merry Go Round, The 539
Merry Little Birds Are We 4149
Merry Little Chop! Chop! Chop! 106
Merry Little Minuet 2227, 2246
Merry Little Widows, The 1378
Merry Maiden and the Jerk, The 1948
Merry Marriage Market of the East 2844
Merry May 4186
Merry Medieval Maid 3049
Merry Merry Christmas, A 3794
Merry Merry Maids of the
Old Front Row, The 558
Merry Miller, The 3732
Merry Minstrel Band, The 1731
Merry Minuet 4499
Merry Month of May, The 188
Merry Mummers 934
Merry Mystic Man (I Did It), The 4161
Merry Old King 2408
Merry Partners, The 1776
Merry Wedding Bells 1248, 1793, 4547
Merry Widow Brown 1909
Merry Widow Music without Words, The 4374
Merry Widow Waltz, The 3018
Merry Wives of Windsor, The 2841, 2841
Merry Young Heart 2348
Mescaline Hat Dance 272
Mesdames and Messieurs 1109
Meshugah 3937
Mesmerized 654
Mess Call, The 4141
Mess o' Dirt 1717
Message from Mars 1459
Message from Roxanne, A 949
Message from the Sea, A 3765
Message in a Bottle 3739
Message of Spring, The 4738
Message of the Cameo, The 1685
Message of the Moonbeam 246
Message of the Red, Red Rose, The 2745
Message of the Rose 45
Message of the Violet 3578
Message to Michael 261
Messages I 2949
Messages II 2949
Messenger Boy, The 2844
Messenger Number and Dance 3791
Messieurs, Mesdames 2909
Messin' Around 2845
Messin' Round 495
Messing About in Boats 4701
Messing Around 1425
Messy Bessy 1296
Metamorphosis 920
Metaphor 1245
Metaphorically Speaking 1194
Metro 2846
Metropolis (scene) 3005
Metropolitan Handicap, The 4843
Metropolitan Ladies 4831, 4852
Metropolitan Nights 4603
Metropolitan Squak-tette, The 3395
Mexican Bean 3203

Mexican Blues 1019
Mexican Hat Dance 1832
Mexican Magic 3444
Mexican Rose 1867
Mexico (To Hell with Mexico) 1447
Mexico 2035, 2387, 2642, 3056, 3332, 1185, 3796
Mexico City 3875, 4796
Mexico Querido 2573
Mexiconga, The 1494
Meyer Chickerman 4619
Mfoka Ngema 4438
Mgeniso WaMgodo WaShambini 4579
MGM 2969
Mi Amigo 4796
Mi Chiquita 2277
Mi-Komash Melon (What Is the Meaning?) 1279
Mi! Mi! 3822
Mi Mi, Tu Li 3573
Mia Cara 728
Mia Luna 3079
(Lead 'Em On) Miami 391
Miami 2987, 4243
Miami Beach 4619
Michael 3448
Michael McGinnity 3220
Michele 3960
Michelemma 2464
Michigan Bound 4252
Michigan Water 2200
Mickey 4204
Mickey O'Toole 2902
Micritza Violetta Doanne 4684
Micro-Chip Jingle 2861
Microbes 1226
Microbes in a Kiss, The 3820
Microfilm 3873
Micromaniac 4826
Midas Touch, The 363
Middle Age Blues 534
Middle Aged 2007
Middle C 4004
Middle-Class-Liberal-Blues 2616
Middle Class Revolution 3876
Middle Class, The 2188
Middle Ground, The 595
Middle of the Night, The 4363
Middle of the Sea 4243
Middle Years, The 4789
Middy, The 2761
Midnight at the Onyx 4137
Midnight Ballet (dance) 3703
Midnight Bells 4077
Midnight Blue 4825
Midnight Blues 3649
Midnight Cabaret 1626, 2645
Midnight Cabaret, The 2854
Midnight Cabaret 14
Midnight Daddy 3533
Midnight Deadline Blastoff 2728
Midnight Flirtation 3011
Midnight Frolic Glide 4809
Midnight Frolic Rag, The 4810
Midnight Girl, The 2854
Midnight Girl, The (One Midnight Supper at Home) 3538
Midnight Girl at the Midnight Cabaret, The 3397
Midnight-Hot Blood 3741
Midnight Lullabye 2953
Midnight Masquerade 822
Midnight Mass 3741
Midnight Matinee 3885
Midnight Mooch 2800
Midnight Riding 699
Midnight Rounders 2870
Midnight Serenade, The 3999
Midnight Show Trio, A 1652
Midnight Swim Ballet, The 98
Midnight Waltz 2985
Midnight Waltz, The 1347
Midnight Zeppo, The 4836
Midsummer Fox 2240
Midsummer Maiden 3973
Midsummer Night 249, 2064, 3326
Midsummer Night's Dream, A 249, 1780, 4256
Midsummer Night's Dream 4748
Midsummer Waltz 3087
Midsummer's Eve 4075
Midtown 2300
Midwestern Summer 4659
Mighty Big Dream 3947
Mighty Dollar Greets You, The 3771
Mighty Fortress, A 1592
Mighty Like a Rosenbloom 2870
Mighty Race, A 1092
Mighty Svengali Legree, The 4507
Mighty Whitey 578
Mignonette 250, 3675
Migration 143
Migration Song 2573
Mikado, The 2861
Mikado Anthem 2861
Mike 1267, 3180
Milady 4139, 3384
Milady's Perfume 685
Milady's Toilette Set 1334
Mile After Mile 3647
Mileage Millionaire, The 1402
Miles Gloriosus 1422
Miliaria Rubra 4252
Milindy 981
Milindy Blues 981
Militant Suffragette, The 96
Military, The 4761
Military Ball, The (inst.) 250
Military Band, The 3073
Military Charleston 2843
Military Charley 1374
Military Dance (inst.) 3193

Military Dancing Drill 4178, 4179
Military Decoration Dance 3962
Military Fox Trot Tune, A 2546
Military Glide, The 2939, 4521
Military Irresistibles, The 639
Military Life 620
Military Maid, The 185
Military Maid 3799
Military Maids 2366, 2986
Military Man, The 830, 1188, 1650, 2323
Military Man 4480
Military March 822
Military Marches 1404
Military Mary Ann 1523
Military Model 604
Military Review 1602
Military Song 3887
Military Stamp 1852
Military Touch, The 3092
Military Wedding March 639
Military Wedding of the Nations 1404
Military Willie 1910
Milk and Crackers 203
Milk and Honey 2208, 2864
Milk Bottle Parade, The 2090
Milk, Milk, Milk 2453
Milkmaid 4485
Milkmaid Known As Joan 2026
Milkmaids' Chorus 2880, 4753
Milkmaids from Broadway 3069
Milkmaid's Song 3736
Milky Way, The 584
Millefleurs 3064
Millennium, The 2135, 3092
Miller's Daughter, The 4354
Miller's Son, The 4067, 2536
Millinery Mannequin, The 1922
Millinery Mary 694
Million, A 2716
Million, The 4806
Million Dollar Ball, The 1738
Million Dollar Ball 2834
Million Dollar Pier 1886
Million Dollar Smile 404
Million Dollars, A 3314
Million Eyes, A 3149
(There's a) Million Girls Around Me 685
Million Goes to Million 1354
Million Good Reasons, A 2238
Million Miles from You, A 589
Million Songs 2195
Million Windows and I, A 3941
Millionaire, The 1313
Millionaire's Daughters 1532
Millionaires Don't Whistle 1415
Millions 1073
Millions of Tunes 684
Millwork 4744
Milo (You're Just My Style-O) 246
Milo 984
Milonga 1046
Milord Sir Smith 2131
Milwaukee 1237
Mimette 1768
Mimette Doll, The 3867
Mimi 293, 2336, 2336
Mimi Jazz 2336
Mina 3337
Mind of My Own 1734
Mind Over Matter 3835
Mind Reader, The 2232
Mind the Paint 2871
Mind Where You Are Going 1726
Mind Your Business 2017
Mind Your Own Business 2601
Mind Your Own Heart 2319
Mind Your P's and Q's 1800
Mindin' the Baby 2101
Mine 4399, 2444, 2617, 3279
Mine Celebration (dance) 4862
Mine for Aye 3680
Mine Forever More 1522
Mine 'til Monday 4446
Mine Was a Marriage of Convenience 4812
Mineola 4060
Ming Poo 2216
Ming Ting Hai 4110
Miniature Girl, The 3098
Miniatures 764
Mink, Mink, Mink 2804, 3941, 4047
Minnesota 157, 3268
Minnesota Strip 3806
Minnie 1145
Minnie, Ha Ha 4644
Minnie the Moocher 896, 883
Minnie the Moocher's Wedding Day 876, 1813
Minnie's Boys 2874
Minnowillen 4218
Minnows and the Sharks, The 1049
Minny Belle's Song 2228
Minor Prophets, The 1750
Minorities Is No Damn Good 3530
Minsky 3314
Minsky's Metropolitan Grand Opera 1874
Minstrel Band, The 3701
Minstrel Days 799, 3737, 4054
Minstrel Man 444
Minstrel Parade, The 1731
Minstrel Parade 1926
Minstrel Parade, The 1927
Minstrel Parade 2615
Minstrel Parade, The 4603
Minstrel Serenade 3754
Minstrel Show 1604, 3953
Minstrel Show, The 1926
Minstrel Song 1914
Minstrel Tune 1531
Minstrel's Advice 1262
Minstrel's Prayer, The 452

Minstrel's Prayer 2415
Minstrel, the Jester and I, The 3288
Minstrels on Parade, The 1469
Minstrels on Parade 3134, 3513
Minuet 295, 582
Minuet, The 710
Minuet 764, 1046, 1885, 3011, 4735
Minuet for Clarinet 4391
Minuet of the Minute, The 3772
Minuet Waltz (inst.) 2102
Minuette, A 4427
Minuette 4670
Minute, A 4358
Minute By Minute 459
Minute Maid 3091
Minute Minuet 367
Mio Fratello 3938
Mir Forn Kayn Amerike (We're Going to America, Goodbye Mother Russia) 1609
Mira (Can You Imagine That) 656
Miracle 2626
Miracle Cure 4676
Miracle Happened, A 1842
Miracle of Judaism 1234
Miracle of Miracles 1265
Miracle on 34th Street 1860, 1860
Miracle Song 162, 3696
Miracle Town 1377
Miracles 4398
Miraculous Cure, The 4616
Mirage, The 200
Mirage 1589
Mirage Dance, The (inst.) 4818
Mirages 3463
Miranda 519, 3753
Mirandolina's Dander 2910
Mirele 4463
Mirror 2451
Mirror Ball 3718
Mirror Finale, The 202
Mirror Graphic News, The 720
Mirror Mine 3406
Mirror, Mirror 3136, 3865
Mirror, Mirror on the Wall 40
Mirror Song, The 1114
Mirrors and Shadows 2565
Mis-Handel-ed Tribute (To the Nixon Administration), A 1770
Misalliance 220
Misanthrope, The 2877
Misbehavin' Hips 570
Mischief in Your Eyes 3403
Miser's Serenade, The 4827
Miserable with You 294
Miserere 2346, 2236
Misery Is 2663
Misfit Family, The 2711, 3867
Misfit Soldier, A (Orders but Confuse Me) 1455
Mis'ry's Comin' 'Round 3949
Miss Addie Loggins 3364
Miss America 2074, 4011
Miss America Now (The Fairest of the Fair) 829
Miss America Teen 3714
Miss Annabelle Lee 3020
Miss Bell of the Telephone 3327
Miss Blush! 4219
Miss Bubbles 2754
Miss Byrd 4535, 784
Miss Cadwallader 4659
Miss Daisy's Gown 3867
Miss Dennett 4203
Miss Dorothea Dix 1474
Miss Dudelsack 2886
Miss Emily Fleetwood 3371
Miss Euclid Avenue 2664
Miss Fairfax Ever Since I Met You 3195
Miss Fiddle-Dee-Dee 1616
Miss Follies 4829, 4828
Miss Follies of 192... 4828
Miss Ginger of Jamaica 4801
Miss Glamouresse 3346
Miss Got Rocks 1662
Miss Greenwich Village 157
Miss Hallelujah Brown 887
Miss Hazelton 4029
Miss Heinshlinger 157
Miss Helen of Troy 2261
Miss Hi-Fie 1697
Miss Hickok Was in Love 1169
Miss Hilary Bacon of Beacon Hill 3055
Miss Hook 2889
Miss Hook of Holland 2869
Miss Innocent 719
Miss Innovation 4747
Miss Langley's School for Girls 4640
Miss Liberty 2894
Miss Lorelei Lee 2590
Miss Lucy Long 1081
Miss Marmelstein 2048
Miss Mary 1157
Miss May 4830
Miss Me 1536
Miss Mere 1761
Miss Moonshine 317
Miss New York 1647
Miss Otis Regrets 875, 1877, 885
Miss Page 3682
Miss Pinchin's Boarding School 4478
Miss Pinhead 1222
Miss Platt Selects Mate 4432
Miss Rhinestone 943
Miss Susanna from Urbana 3805
Miss Truth 2908
Miss Turnstiles (dance) 3278
Miss Unruly 3403
Miss Venus 2519
Miss Walker of Kalamazoo 4713
Miss Watermelon Sweet 1881
Miss Whoozis and Mr. Whatchaname 1250
Miss Williams 3484

Miss Yankee Doodle 1417
'Miss You' Kiss, A 3899
Missa Solemnis 3066
Missed America 3112
Missed the Toilet Last Night 2945
Missing Person 535
Mission, The 3239
Mission Bells 1777, 2576
Mission Control 2728
Missionary Maids 3031
Missis and the Guv'nor 30
Mississippi 3024, 3530, 4836
Mississippi Cabaret 332
Mississippi Cradle 3677
Mississippi Day 3953
Mississippi Honeymoon 2151
Mississippi Joys 4763
Mississippi Miss 61
Mississippi Moan 2845
Mississippi Mud 1425
Mississippi Steamboat 363
Missouri 567
Missouri Meadowlark 4409
Missouri Mule 2958
Missouri Polka 18
Missus Aouda 189
Mistah Jim 2942
Mistaken in Love 4235
Mistakes Are Apt to Happen 734
Mistakes Will Happen 531
Mister and Mrs. Fitch 4132
Mister Bonaparte 2951
Mister Boy 1319
Mister Brown, Miss Dupree 4432
Mister Cellophane 723
Mister Destiny 2949
Mister Drummer Man 3652
Mister Earth and His Comet Love (The Comet and the Earth) 4804
Mister Harvey Pruitt 664
Mister Izzy Always Busy Rosenstein 2119
Mister Jones 2563
Mister Love 3537
Mister Madero and Friend 4609
Mister Man 1476
Mister Mississippi 1799
Mister Moon Man, Turn Off Your Light 2528
Mister Off-Broadway 1023, 3542
Mister Othello 632
Mister Producer 1770
Mister Rag and I 1065
Mister Snow 660
Mister Soldier Man 106
Mister Spaceman 3695
Mister Sun 1866
Mister Washington! 183
Misterioso 97
Mistletoe Bough, The 2697
Mistreated Gypsy 2379
Mistress Mullen and Master Alden 912
Mistress of the Inn 4244, 2910
Misty Mornin' (inst.) 895
Misty Mountain 2168
Misunderstood 490
Mit Zaltz un Fefer 3781
Mittel-Europa 2447, 4331
Mitzi 1763
Mix, The 1053
Mix! 4625
Mix and Mingle 4718
Mix-up Rag, The 2891
Mixed Doubles 2913
Mixed Marriages 2913
Mixed-Up Media 164
Mixing of the Ads, The 639
Mlle. DeLeon 2858
Mlle. Loose Heels 1687
Mlle. Ma Mere 495
Mme. Mangdolin 2770
Mngani Wamina 4438
Mo Ticht-tit! 3673
Mo'lasses 1587
Moan You Moaners 2796
Moana, I Love You So 141
Moana Loa (dance) 3827
Moanin' and Groanin' 1983
Moanin' in the Mornin' 1973
Moanin' Low 2545
Mob Song, The 330
Mobile Squad 2364
Mocambo Mambo 1048
Mock Battle 2556
Mock Turtle Lament 54
Mockin' Bird Hill 4264
Mocking Bird 1474
Mocking Bird, The 3056
Mockowitz, Gogeloch, Babblekroit and Svonk (The Lawyer Song) 2827
Mod Man of Manhattan 4611
Model, The 2665
Model Girl, A 2919
Model Happy Fair, A 3591
Model Hasn't Changed, The 2850
Model Maid, A 2454
Model Married Pair 2923
Model of Decorum & Tranquility, A 721
Model of Fashion Am I, A 2834
Model Toddle 200
Model's Complaint 1459
Models, The 200
Models 1493
Moderation 3913
Modern Banditti, The 4616
Modern Bride 765
Modern Butterfly 3057
Modern Century Girls, The 509
Modern Crusaders 3404
Modern Diplomat, A 4227
Modern Duel, The 75
Modern Eve, The 2457

Modern Girls 1240
Modern Gladiator, The 586
Modern Housing 3970
Modern Japanese, The 3268
Modern Love 3395
Modern Madrigal 3103
Modern Maiden's Prayer, The 4811
Modern Melody, A 4794
Modern Pirate, The 3578
Modern Song, The 1218
Modern Wedding Day, The 525
Modernistic 1251
Modernistic Moe 4825
Modes Made in Manhattan 2379
Modest Little Model, The 2770
Modest Little Thing, A 584
Modest Maidens We 1925
Modest Man, The 102
Modest Manicure, The 2040
Modiste, The 2061
Modiste, A 4115
Moi 3920
Moi, Je Crache Dans l'Eau 839
Mojo 2513
Mokhibo (The Sotho Girls' Dance) 2147
Molasses to Rum 3897
Moldova, Country of My Birth 810
Molecules 4089
Moliere 649
Moll's Song 919
Mollie from Mayo 591
Mollie Green 2111
Mollie Has Her Say 4703
Mollie Mine 1907
Mollie O'Donahue 4234
Mollie Shannon 2506
Molly 406, 1770, 2925, 3185
Molly and I 2926
Molly By Golly 2496
Molly Darling 2927
Molly Dear, It's You I'm After 1544
Molly Maguire 4359
Molly Malone 2286, 2829, 3403
Molly, Me Own 2930
Molly Mine 1470
Molly, Molly 4654
Molly O 1758
Molly O'Hallerhan (Edna May's Irish Song) 675
Molly O'Reilly 2439
Molly on the Trolley 4654
Molly the Marchioness 906
Mom 363, 3274
Mom and Dad 1418
Mom, I Want to Be in Yiddish Vaudeville 1279
Mom Will Be There 944
Mom! You Don't Understand 1269
Moment, a Minute, A 3204
Moment Ago, A 2304
Moment Has Passed, The 3602
Moment I Looked in Your Eyes, The 4377
Moment I Saw You, The 844, 4367, 4510
Moment in the Dark 4073
Moment Is Mine, This 3561
Moment Is Now 4689
Moment Musical 463
Moment of Love 3696
Moment of Truth, A 3110
Moment to Scheme, A 1521
Moment with You, A 2764, 3843
Moments 3254, 3515
Moments by the Sea 3167
Moments from Shakespeare 603
Moments in the Woods 2143
Moments of Happiness, The 678
Moments of the Dance, The 1796
Momma, Come Stay with Me 3780
Momma Know Best 4048
Momma Look Sharp 3897
Momma, Momma 2048
Momma Said 1149
Momma Tembu's Wedding 2147
Momma's Talkin' Soft 1709
Mommas' Turn 4533
Mommy Cat 1846
Mommy Dear Has Dropped Dead in Her Sleep 2132
Mommy Number Four 944
Mommy We Love You 2478
Moms and Dads 3476
Mon Ami 1007
Mon Ami, My Friend 2228
Mon Desir 3537
Mon General 4614
Mon Homme 1176
Mon Pauvre Petit Pierre 453
Mona 3608
Mona and Her Kitties 3131
Mona from Arizona 603
Mona Lisa Crouch 194
Mona When She Taps on Her Corona 702
Monarch Notes 4731
Monastary Opening 711
Monastery 2757
Monday 3039
Monday and Tuesday 1259
Monday Morning Blues 3696
Monday Through Sunday 2000
Monday You Love Me 3683
Monday's Mail (Mail # 1) 1804
Money 30, 943, 1094, 3131, 3780
Money and Family 3853
Money and Insanity 3667
Money Burner 405
Money Burns a Hole in My Pocket 1791
Money in the Bank 1064, 1310
Money Is Better Than Men 345
Money Is Honey 430
Money Isn't Everything 1373
Money Isn't Everything, But... 2584
Money Isn't Ev'rything 85

Money Makes the World Go 'Round 4492
Money Means Nothing to me 1306
Money Men and More 2754
Money Minuet, The 81
Money, Money 131
Money, Money, Money 578, 630, 989
Money, Money, Money! 2363
Money, Money, Money 2767
Money Quartet 1536
Money Rings Out Like Freedom, The 798
Money Runs Through My Fingers 1604
Money Song, The 610, 1012, 4323
Money Song 4480
Money Talks 2928, 3771
Money to Burn 1721
Money Tree, The 16
Money Tree 3498
Money, Wealth, Gold 400
Mongolia Song 1161
Mongst the Magnolias 4098
Monica 2058
Monkey Dance 302
Monkey Doodle Dandy 938
Monkey Doodle Doo 60
Monkey Doodle-Doo 799
Monkey in a Tree 459
Monkey in My Mind, The 2910
Monkey in the Mango Tree 2190
Monkey Land 3660
Monkey on a String 1119
Monkey See, Monkey Do 2655
Monkey When He Loves, A 937
Monkeys, The 767
Monks Merrie Minstrel Show 1023
Monks of Malabar, The 2936
Monks' Quartette, The 4250
Monolithic Madness 2702
Monologue 3565
Monopoly 194
Monotonous 3107
Mons. France and Miss America 4836
Monsieur 3853
Monsieur Beaucaire 1780, 2937
Monsieur Scapin 4450
Monsignor Prom, The 128
Monsoon (dance) 4633
Monster Mash 3695
Monster Medley 3688
Monster's Song, The 1785
Mont Martre 3007
Montage 1211, 1822
Montage Poster (inst.) 4798
Montana 716, 915, 4682
Montana Moon 2265
Monte Carlo 2646
Monte Carlo Moon 2358
Monte Cristo 2939
Monte, the Model 584
Montebanks, The (inst.) 4767
Montenegrin Patrol 4713
Monterey 381, 4487
Montevideo 1450
Montezuma 577, 3332
Montgomery Moon 2579
Montgomery School Song 2579
Month of Sundays 2941
Month of Sundays, A 4314
Montmart' 629
Montmarte Fair and the Magic Dolls, The 1244
Montmartre 1176, 4818
Montparnasse 1834
Montreal 1841
Moo Cow 2620
Mooche, The (inst.) 3709, 4091, 893
Mooching Along 3407
Mood Indigo 4091
Mood Music 4416
Mood of the Moment 4572
Mood You Are In, The 531
Moods 2219
Moody and Blue 431
Moody Moorland Moon 1757
Moola Makes the Hula Feel Much Cooler 4750
Moolbari 830
Moon, The 3828
Moon About Town 4824
Moon Am Shinin' 4429
Moon and You, The (Moonlight and You) 1321
Moon and You, The 3847
Moon and You and I, The 293
Moon Beams 3519
Moon Bird 938, 3855
Moon Dear 470, 591, 2674, 4046
Moon Eyes 1573
Moon-Faced, Starry-Eyed 369, 4169
Moon-Fairies 3322
Moon Fell in the River, The 2161
Moon Flower 2594
Moon in My Pocket, The 3734
Moon in My Window 1060
Moon Is on the Sea, The 3243
Moon Like a Silver Window 3792
Moon Love 334
Moon, Lovely Moon! 3771
Moon Madness 249
Moon Maiden, The 2944
Moon Man 2287, 2691
Moon Men 371
Moon, Moon 4430
Moon, Moon, Moon 1515, 2232
Moon of Love 1922
Moon of Manakoora, The 3444
Moon of May, The 4115
Moon of My Delight 711
Moon Over Miami 2945
Moon Over Mulberry Street 2946
Moon Shines Down, The 3385
Moon Shines on the Moonshine, The 545
Moon Should Be Rising Soon, The 2153
Moon Song, The 1101, 2917

Moon Song 3245
Moon, the Coon, and the Octoroon, The 1188
Moon Was Good Enough for Dad and Mother, The 1582
Moon Will Help You Out Maybe, The 250
Moon Will Ride Away, The 277
Moon, Wind, and Sun 1440
Moonbeams 632, 2387
Moonbeams, The 2934
Moonbeams 3024, 3207, 3675
Mooney Time 1520, 187
Moonfall 3070
Moonglade 823
Moonglow 445
Mooning 1664
Moonland 4256
Moonlight 539, 1075, 1758, 2062, 3021, 4033, 4359
Moonlight and Lace 3078
Moonlight and Love and All 4189
Moonlight and Violins 1352
Moonlight and You 2193
Moonlight Ballet 3719
Moonlight Ballet (inst.) 4817
Moonlight Buggy Ride, A 2481
Moonlight Fancies (inst.) 2500
Moonlight Gavotte 3729
Moonlight in Versailles 3649
Moonlight Kisses 1689
Moonlight Legion 1518
Moonlight Mama 2814
Moonlight on Notre Dame 3386
Moonlight on the Ganges 4153
Moonlight on the Waters 765
Moonlight Passing Through a Window 3760
Moonlight Serenade 4137
Moonlight Soliloquy 3536
Moonlight Waltz 1033
Moonlight, You and I 2717
Moon's Shining Cool, The 4620
Moonshine 2996
Moonshine (inst.) 3312
Moonshine 3719, 4764
Moonshine Lullaby 153
Moonshine of Kentucky (Give Me the Moonshine of My Old Kentucky Home) 1270
Moonsong 949, 949
Moonstruck 3020, 3322
Moontime 2174
Moosh, Moosh 3651
Mophams, The 3569
Mopperty Mo 129
Moral Rearmament 3110
Morality 3215, 4303
Morality's a Matter of Geography 405
Morals of a Sailor-Man, The 1962
More and More 596, 3901, 4328
More and More/Less and Less 1660
More Better Go Easy 1809
More Fish 90
More I Cannot Wish You 1706, 3444
More I See of Men the More I Love My Dog, The 628
More I See of Other Girls, The (Elephant Song) 2258
More I See of Others the Better I Love You, The 3304
More I See People, The 593
More Incredible Happenings 4581
More Love than Your Love 603
More Mittel-Europa 4331
More of Everything 3482
More of Me to Love 2049
More of the Same 287, 2018
More Precious Far 2874
More Racquetball 1234
More than Earth 2153
More Than Enough 1132
More Than Ever 1440, 4023
More Than Ever Now 4028
More Than Friends 2219
More Than Just a Pretty Flower 2539
More Than Love 1282, 3858
More Than Music 2319
More Than One Man in Her Life 2674
More Than One More Day 298
More Than One Way 4013
More Than Ordinary Glorious Vocabulary, A 71
More Than These 3989
More Than You Deserve 2953
More Than You Know 1667, 3249, 1232
More the Merrier, The (The More We Are the Merrier We Be) 1742
More We Dance, The 1461
More You Get, The 1064
More You See of It, The 4048
Morgan Le Fay 834
Morgana's Entrance 1159
Morgiana's Dagger Dance (inst.) 50
Moriva 2147
Morlock Exterior 1159
Mormon Life, A 1011
Morning 1680, 3277, 4169, 4537
Morning After, The 2056, 2070, 2918
Morning Anthem 369, 4369
Morning Breaking 1213
Morning Cy 2642
Morning Exercises 1556
Morning Glory 582, 1962
Morning Glory Mountain 474
Morning Glow 3506
Morning in Madrid 1112
Morning in Manhattan 1539
Morning in the Gypsy Camp 4046
Morning Is Midnight 2467, 3924
Morning Lark 668
Morning Light 2426
Morning Mist Spread O'er the Mead, The 762
Morning, Morning, Morning 4147
Morning Music of Montmartre, The 3234
Morning of the Dragon, The 2905
Morning Prayer 3543
Morning Song (inst.) 3487

Morning Song 1744
Morning Star 916, 2535
Morning Sun 2958, 3876
Morning Will Break 496
Morning Will Come 487
Morning You Were Born, The 4798
Mornings at Seven 1761
Morning's at Seven 1894
Morocco Dance of Marriage (inst.) 1027
Morphine Tango 2333
Morris Brodkin Loves Me 2422
Morris Dance and Sword Dance 3702
Morris Kaplan of Hampstead Gardens 299
Mort's Telegram 3461
Mos Scoscious 1890
Moscow Belles 3431
Moscow Blues, The 722
Moses Andrew Jackson, Goodbye 2996
Moses Supposes 3992
Moses' Song 1769
Moshi, Moshi 595
Mosquito 1840
Mosquito and the Midge, The 4754
Mosquito Ballet (inst.) 3312
Mosquito Queen 1155
Mosquito Song, The (inst.) 2900
Mosquito Song 4802
Most Beautiful Girl in the World, The 2258
Most Beautiful Girls in the World, The 1137
Most Confused Prince 3654
Most Disagreeable Man (1), A 2064
Most Disagreeable Man (2), A 2064
Most Every Town Has a Broadway 4215
Most Expensive Statue in the World, The 2894
Most Folks Are Dopes 2306
Most Gentlemen Don't Like Love 1018, 2432, 4799
Most Girls 4588
Most Happy Fella, The 2961
Most Important Job, The 1880
Most Important Thing, The 3195
Most Likely 3601
Most Omniscient Maid 118
Most People 2580
Most Popular and Most Likely to Succeed 4454
Most Unpopular Potentate, A 2974
Most Unusual Pair 1695
Most Unusual Weather (For This
Time of Year) 1577
Most Wonderful Day of the Year, The 3794
Mostes' to Say the Least, The 4543
Motele 4342
Moth and the Bumble Bee, The 47
Moth and the Flame 1286
Moth and the Flame, The 2648
Moth and the Flame 2870
Moth and the Moon, The 2885
Moth For My Flame, The 1485
Moth for My Flame, The 1643
Moth Song, The 3934
Mother's March 169
Mother 249, 1732, 1077
Mother (1) 1852
Mother (2) 1852
Mother 2056, 3056
Mother Africa's Day 2245
Mother and Father 2317
Mother Angel Darling 2148
Mother Come and Fight with Me 483
Mother Darling 2284
Mother Dear 815
Mother Did 47
Mother, Dixie and You 1824
Mother, Dixie, the Flag and You 4033
Mother Doesn't Know 4806
Mother Earth 415, 2962
Mother Eve 1484
Mother Goose 2315, 2964, 4250
Mother Goose and Baby Dolls 671
Mother Goose's School 4382
Mother Grows Younger 1800
Mother Hare's Seance 1600
Mother in Ireland 452
Mother-in-Law 4619, 1890
Mother Isn't Getting Any Younger 1286, 3082
Mother, Look, I'm an Acrobat 2909
Mother Love 1581
Mother Machree 310, 2154
Mother, May I Be Forgiven? 2046
Mother, Me and the Flag 3133
Mother Mississippi 2400
Mother Nature 4623
Mother Needs a Boyfriend 2568
Mother of Exiles 3667
Mother of Mankind, The 4523
Mother of Spring 259
Mother of the Bridegroom 3696
Mother of the Regiment, The 2340
Mother Peep 2146
Mother Phi 870
Mother Pin a Rose on Me 830
Mother Shouldn't Have Daughters 4013
Mother Son 2866
Mother Told Me So 1322
Mother Who's Really a Mother, A 2201
Mother Will Be Pleased 1544
Motherhood 1828
Motherload 3901
Motherlove 2992
Motherly Love 3215
Mothers 3454
Mothers and Sons 841
Mother's Blues 3564
Mother's Complaint 4341
Mother's Day 90, 2616, 4034, 4153
Mother's Getting Nervous 2615
Mother's Heart, A 615
Mother's Kisses, A 2965
Mother's Lament 3487, 3339
Mother's Love, A 3602
Mothers O' Men 3086

Mothers of the World 201, 1462
Mother's Prayer, A 4163
Mother's Prayer 4591
Mother's Smile, A 1897
Mother's Tears, A 2811
Mother's Wedding Dress 1582
Mother's Wish Is a Daughter's Duty, A 2375
Motl Der Opereyter (Motl the Operator) 1609
Motley Assemblage, A 2062
Motor Boat, The 717
Motor Car Is Treacherous, The 1644
Motor Girl, The 4838
Motor Girls 1550
Motor Perpetuo 221
Motoring Along the Old Post Road 3740
Motto 1597
Moulin Rouge Girls, The 3063
Moulin Rouge Roulette 558
Mountain Greenery 85, 1447
Mountain High, Valley Low 2655
Mountain Maids 4666
Mountain Moon 1513
Mountain Top Duet 721
Mountains, The 1116
Mountains of Gold 3485
Mountains of Nebraska Ballet, The 3813
Mountbank, the Amulet, A 654
Mounted Messenger, The 4369
Mounties, The 3772
Mouse, The 722
Mouse and the Trap, The 143
Mouse Meets Girl 1101
Mouse! Mouse! 702
Mousetrap, The 3828
Mouth Full of Kisses, A 2856, 3962
Mouth So Charmful 1589
Move (You're Steppin' on My Heart) 1103
Move 3456
Move Along 4191, 729
Move into My Heart 1270
Move On 4210, 4415
Move on Up a Little Higher 4460
Move Over 3968, 4603
Move Over, New York 269
Move Over You Guys 1412
Movements 2489
Mover's Life, A 2058
Movie 1358
Movie Ball, The 3659
Movie Buff 2968
Movie Cowboy, The 2968
Movie Fan's Love Song 1000
Movie Game of Make Believe, The 3688
Movie House in Manhattan 2707
Movie in My Mind, The 2905
Movie Lesson, The 4528
Movie Melodrama, A (inst.) 584
Movie Montage 400
Movie Music 4269
Movie Queen 2171
Movie Show 2196
Movie Star 2969
Movie Star Mansion 3515
Movie Stars 2968
Movie to End Them All, The 3598
Movies, The 3258
Movies Are Your Best Entertainment 1000
Movies in Flight 407
Movies Ruined My Life, The 2969
Movies Were Movies 2208, 2660
Movietown 2968
Movin' 415, 3347
Movin' Day 2657, 4198
Movin' On 496
Movin' Out 534
Moving Day in Jungle Town 4803
Moving Finger Writes, The 3795
Moving in With Linda 3448
Moving Into a New House 2658
Moving Man, The 1963
Moving On 3555
Moving Picture Baby 3009
Moving Picture Glide, The 3397
Moving Picture Mary 537, 538, 541
Moving Pictures 4064, 4589
Moving Up in the World 4701
Moving Uptown 576
Mowla, The 4522
Mozambamba 4572
Mozart Lincoln 2851
Mr Berger 1717
Mr. and Missus Fitch 1453
Mr. and Mrs. 1312, 2342
(Now That We're) Mr. and Mrs. 3478
Mr. and Mrs. 4491
Mr. & Mrs. & Company 1971
Mr. and Mrs. and Company 2888
Mr. & Mrs. Brown 906
Mr. and Mrs. Dick Dickerson 4454
Mr. & Mrs. Myth 729
Mr. and Mrs. Ordinary People 520
Mr. and Mrs. Patter 480
Mr. and Mrs. Rover 4001
Mr. and Mrs. Sipkin (Monty! Their Only Child) 4300
Mr. and Mrs. Smith 2252
Mr. and Mrs. Wrong 1101
Mr. Banjo Man 4197
Mr. Bingham 1968
Mr. Bluebeard 2974, 932
Mr. Bojangles 964
Mr. Brady Takes a Photograph 1474
Mr. Breezy 3747
Mr. Broadway U.S.A. 60
Mr. Bunbury 1194
Mr. Burns of New Rochelle 4277
Mr. Cellophane 131, 4480
Mr. Chamberlain 333
Mr. Chigger 2958
Mr. Clown 2681
Mr. Corbett 1370

Mr. Cosy Corner Man 69
Mr. Cupid 2765, 3056
Mr. Director 4781
Mr. Dolan Is Passing Through 111
Mr. Dooley 737
Mr. Dumbbell and Mr. Tough 4199
Mr. Fezziwig's Annual Christmas Ball 754
Mr. Fixer 2007
Mr. Flynn 1076
Mr. Fox, I'm Sorry for You 2286
Mr. Gallagher and Mr. Shean 4816
Mr. Goldstone, I Love You 1709
Mr. Graffiti 3806
Mr. Gravvins-Mr. Gripps 611
Mr. Grogan, Wake Up 2033
Mr. H.M. Woggle-Bug, T.E. 4725
Mr. Hamlet of Broadway 2978
Mr. Harris It's All Over Now! 1256
Mr. Henderson 3186
Mr. Henry Jones 4090
Mr. Hoggenheimer of Park Lane 1537
Mr. Hot Stuff 1836
Mr. James Dillingham Young 1508
Mr. Jeremiah Esquire 3618
Mr. Jessel 4235
Mr. Jiggers 3134
Mr. Johnson, Good Night 2667
Mr. Kicks 2306
Mr. Know It All 843
Mr. Know-It-All 2279
Mr. Lawson the Man from Boston 1731
Mr. Lawson, the Man from Boston 228
Mr. Lee 4264
Mr. Livingstone 1760
Mr. Love 1588
Mr. Love Will Catch You Yet 2385
Mr. Mammy Man 691
Mr. Mardi Gras 1890
Mr. Maybe 484
Mr. Might've Been 2018
Mr. Mistoffelees 678
Mr. Monkey 3387
Mr. Monotony 619, 2205, 2894
Mr. Moon 1526, 2540
Mr. Moon and Lady Fire 259
Mr. Mosenstein, Mrs. Hoggenheimer 1537
Mr. Mouse 1864
Mr. Pagliacci 3395
Mr. Pat O'Hare 1553
Mr. Patrick Henry Must Have Been a Married Man 4037
Mr. Phelps 3602
Mr. Popple (of Ippleton) 3193
Mr. Potato Head 3448
Mr. President 2852, 2983
Mr. Right 1918, 2615, 4542
Mr. Right and Mrs. Dream 2615
Mr. Roosevelt and Mr. Churchill 2748
Mr. Rubber Ball Professor 1573
Mr. Sandman 4264
Mr. Schnoodle 3031
Mr. Soldier 2341
Mr. Strauss Goes to Boston 2985
Mr. Tanner 2470, 3159
Mr. Tannhauser 1003
Mr. Tosti Goodbye 2696
Mr. Used-To's Gone Forever 1426
Mr. Voodoo 3081
Mr. Wagner's Wedding March 1129
Mr. Wanamaker's Home 128
Mr. What's-His-Name 4540
Mr. Witherspoon's Friday Night 2646
Mr. Wonderful 2987
Mr. Yankee Doodle 558
Mrs. A 3718
Mrs. Arris Goes to Paris 2989
Mrs. Badger-Butts 4467
Mrs. Black Is Back 2710
Mrs. Bodie 3439
Mrs. Brown 3690
Mrs. Casey 531
Mrs. Cockatoo 1318
Mrs. Finished Lament 2784
Mrs. Grimm 2001
Mrs. Grudden's Goodbye 2474
Mrs. Grundy 3265
Mrs. Kraus's Boarding House 423
Mrs. Krause's Blue-Eyed Baby Boy 1323
Mrs. Larry, Tell Me This 1748
Mrs. Maloney 2481
Mrs. McThing 2993, 2993
Mrs. Meltzer Wants the Money Now! 4619
Mrs. Mister and Reverend Salvation 919
Mrs. Oho 2347
Mrs. Patterson 2994
Mrs. Pettibone's Chandelier 4467
Mrs. Robinson 3739
Mrs. S.L. Jacobowsky 1660
Mrs. Sally Adams 619
Mrs. Shlemiel's Lament 3937
Mrs. Sippi You're a Grand Old Belle 3562
Mrs. Ulysses 2231
Mrs. Worthington 3235
My, It's Been Grand 4319
Mu-Cha-Cha 363
Much As I Love You 2245
Much More 1245
Much More Alive 1276
Much Obliged to You 1526, 3417, 1647
Much Too Happy Dancing (The Hansel and Gretel Song) 1744
Much Too Soon 3233
Muchacha 3946
Mucho Macho Trip 1149
Muddling Through 3908
Muddy Shoes 1658
Muddy Water 394, 3297
Muezzin Call 188
Muezzins and Bayaderres 4293
Muffin Song, The 1194

Muffy and the Topsiders 1077
Mug Dance 634
Mugger's Work Is Never Done, A 4635
Muggin' Lightly 878
Mugging Sequence 2998
Muito Bom 3838
Mulberry Street 3313
Mulberry Tree, The 736
Mulhaney's Song 1697
Mulligan Guards 1776
Multi-Colored Bush 4433
Multi-Millionaires 4014
Multiplied by Eight 4283
Multiplied by Six 4283
Multitudes of Amys 832
Mulunghu Thabu 1603
Mum's the Word 2990, 3052
Mum's the Word, Mr. Moon 2979
Mumble Nothing 1216
Mumblin' Fool 1426
Mumbo Jumbo 2750, 4160
Mummies 2844
Mummified Giant 11
Mummy That Was, The 1848
Mums and Dads 455
Mungojerrie and Rumpleteaser 678
Murder 4288, 2320, 3218
Murder, He Says 3444
Murder in My Heart 1686
Murder in Parkwold 2591
Murder Isn't Proper 2069
Murder, Murder! 2198
Murderous Monty
(And Light-Fingered Jane) 4300
Murmuring Water 2919
Murphy's Law 3718
Murrayisms 2601
Muscovite 4203
Muse, Darling 3418
Museum Piece (Naked Lady) 157
Museum Song 305
Mushari's Waltz 1591
Mushnik and Son 2544
Mushroom Ride 2092
Mushrooms Are Coming in Here, The 2017
Music 1404, 1680, 1680, 1768
Music and the Emotions 3518
Music and the Mirror, The 746
Music at Night 2115
Music Box 2756
Music Call, The 4669
Music Caresssing of Violins
(Waltz Caprice) 3996
Music for Madame 4828
Music Goes 'Round and 'Round, The 393
Music Goes Round and Round, The 1813
Music Hall 807, 808
Music Hall Medley 1590
Music Hall Scandal 808
Music Hall, The 809
Music Hath Charms (My Heart Is Yours) 3011
Music in May 650
Music in My Fingers 1856
Music in My Heart 3103
Music in the Air 1871, 4343
Music in the City 3167
Music in the House 2268
Music in the Sky 3409
Music Is 3015
Music Is a Woman 4091
Music, It's a Necessity 4769
Music Lesson, The 683
Music Lessons, The 3465
Music Makes Me 3249
Music Makin' Man, The 885
Music, Music 4089
Music! Music! Music! 4264
Music, Music, Music 3691
Music of a Little Rippling Stream, The 3489
Music of Bavaria, The 1439
Music of Forest Fires 188
Music of Love 199
Music of Love, The 1544, 158
Music of Moonlight and Love 3078
Music of the Band, The 246
Music of the Night, The 3464
Music of the Stricken Redeemer (inst.) 2228
Music of Viol 1522
Music Scene 2276
Music That Makes Me Dance, The 1420
Music Thrills Me, The 905
Music to a Dancing Bird 3947
Music to Their Ears 2014
Music Went Out of My Life, The 2437
Music with Her Silver Sound 3909
Music with Meals 1228
Musical Bullfrogs, The 1521
Musical Calisthenics 2972
Musical Chairs 255, 957, 2776, 3019, 2458, 4374
Musical Comedy Maid, The 1968
Musical Comedy Man 1478
Musical Cooks 591
Musical Culture 1774
Musical Gypsy, The 2951
Musical Interlude 2813
Musical Lesson, A 4015
Musical Lover I'd Be, A 1521
Musical Me 4527
Musical Moon 1478
Musical Moon, The 2525
Musical Moon 2113
Musical Opening 2972
Musical Poker Game 3258
Musical Rass 43
Musical Scene 4550
Musical Shoes 2135
Musical Snore, The 4784
Musical Tour of the City 1811
Musicale, The 1086
Musicians 1056

Musketeer Sketch, The 3039
Musketeer Sketch Finale, The 3039
Musketeer Sketch Rehearsal, The 3039
Musketeers, The 2041
Muskrat Ramble (inst.) 3297
Musky and Whiskey 3696
Must Be a Witch in Town 1581
Must Be Given to You 837
Must Have a Chorus 1763
Must It Be Love? 269
Must We Say Goodbye? 2825
Must You 4723
Must You Go 4588
Mustapha 4541
Mustapha Abdullah Abu Ben Al Raajid 3108
Muted 4623
Mutt and Jeff 3021, 3024, 3025, 3026, 3028
Mutt and Jeff in Chinatown 3025
Mutual Admiration Society 1760
My Advice 2897
My Aeroplane Maid 1868
My Affair 2641
My Affection Knows No Bounds 345
My Affinity 4094
My All 745
My Almond Eyes of Eastern Skies 3573
My Alsatian Maid 2505
My American Beauty Girl (The Melting Pot) 4835
My Angeline 4724
My Arab Complex 4374
My Arabian Maid 4811
My Arms Are Open 1134
My Aunt Minnie 1273
My Auto Girl 1798
My Autumn Leaf Girl 3877
My Averne Rose 3525
My Babe from Boston Town 4717
My Baby and Me 705
My Baby Elephant 3422
My Baby Just Cares for Me 4683, 4799
My Baby Talk Lady 1831
My Baby Talking Girl
(My Baby Talk Lady) 3402
My Baby's Arms 4813
My Baby's Bored 67
My Bajadere 4760
My Bandana Land 295
My Banjo Girl 1332
My Beautiful American Rose 1753
My Beautiful Circus Girl 4361
My Beautiful Fragonard Girl 2706
My Beautiful Lady 3494, 4805
My Beautiful Rhinestone Girl 1225
My Beautiful Tiger Girl 3962
My Beauty 1698
My Bed Is Like a Little Boat 3999
My Bedouin Girl 3401
My Belle Zabelle 1998
My Ben Ali Haggin Girl 3006
My Best Girl 2713, 3031
My Best Love 1315
My Best Pal 2669
My Better Half 3352
My Bibliophile 1240
My Bicycle Girl 117
My Big Break 1155
My Big Mistake 4695
My Big Moment 2737, 453
My Billy Boy 932
My Bio Is a Blank 275
My Biography 1644
My Bird of Paradise 2636, 3827
My Bird of Paradise (My Honolulu Girl) 1042
My Birthday Party 1537
My Black Cloud 2722
My Blackbirds Are Bluebirds Now 4683
My Blanket and Me 4783
My Blue Bird's Home Again 2734
My Blue Heaven 4127, 3989, 4821
My Blue Melody 567
My Blushing Rose 2711
My Blushing Rosie 3867
My Boardwalk Girl 3065
My Bod Is for God 3076
My Bohemian Fashion Girl 1334
My Bonita Conchita 2800
My Bonny Heeland Lassie 2912
My Boy 1502, 3740
My Boy and I 2768
My Boy Friend 953
My Boy, You're in Society 1720
My Boyfriend 264
My Boyfriend's Back 338
My Bridal Gown 4569
My Bridal Rose 712
My Bridal Veil 4637
My British Buddy 4340
My Broadway Butterfly 4742
My Broadway Chorus Girl 545
My Broker Told Me So 4237
My Broncho Boy 830
My Brother Bill 3399
My Brother Willie 1831
My Brother's Keeper 181
My Brown Eyed Daisy 1573
My Brown Paper Bag 2598
My Brudder and Me 2707
My Bumble Bee 986
My Bunco Queen 3751
My Bungalow Babe 1646
My Bus and I 2679
My Business Man 2103
My Busy Day 2040, 3623
My Bwana 1603
My Cabin Door 3753
My Calicoquette 2298
My Camera Man 3296
My Captain 406
My Caravan 648, 2546, 4248
My Card 348

My Carolina Hide-Away 667
My Castilian Girl 2706
My Castle in Spain 250, 605
My Castle in the Air 2907
My Castle on the Nile 2111, 4088
My Catamaran 2160
My Cavalier 1689
My Cave Man 4437
My Caveman-My Venus 3915
My Celia 3976
My Charcoal Charmer 1925
My Cherokee Rose 2180
My Chicago 3262
My Chiffon Girl 728
My Child 460
My Children Searching 3814
My Chin Toy 733
My China Rose 3775
My Choc'late Soldier Sammy Boy 1823
My Cigarette 3045, 3748
My Cigarette Maid 2576
My Cinderella 2408
My Cinnamon Tree 767
My City 2790, 2294, 3544, 3869
My Clementine 1374
My Cleopatra 978
My Cleopatra Girl 4657
My Coal Black Mammy 3405
My Coca-Cola Belle 1963
My Coloring Book 131
My Combination Girl 3422
My Conviction 1717
My Cornfield Queen 3877
My Cosey Corner Girl 3857
My Cosy Corner Girl 3856
My Cottage in Sunshine Lane 2378
My Country 'Tis of Thee 3830
My Cousin Beauregard 2072
My Cousin Carus 4803
My Cousin Caruso 2892
My Cousin Christian 3780
My Cousin in Milwaukee 3379
My Cozy Little Corner in the Ritz 1921
My Crazy Sister Rose 2246
My Creole Girl 2557
My Crinoline 906
My Crinoline Girl 1174
My Crooning Melody 2912
My Cubist Girl 60
My Cup Runneth Over 2050, 3542
My Cupie Doll 1173
My Curley Headed Baby 1823
My Daddy 154
My Daddy Always Taught Me to Share 1699
My Daddy Is a Dandy 2994
My Daddy Was Right 2067
My Dahomian Queen 2111
My Dainty Dresden Shepherdess 1118
My Dainty Mermaid 4382
My Darlin' Aida 3035
My Darling 1137
My Darling I Love You March 1116
My Darling Wife 4492
My Darling, My Darling 3444, 4652
My Daughter 3702
My Daughter Fanny the Star 1420
My Daughter Is Wed to a Friend of Mine 2730
My Daughter the Countess 1249
My Daughter, My Angel 3490
My Day 3966
My Day Has Come 109, 3319
My Dear Benvenuto 1284
My Dear Old Chum 4085
My Dear Old Daddie 4716
My Dear Old New Jersey Home 2209
My Dear Public 3036
My Dear Young Ladies 762
My Dearest Dear 972
My Dearest Pal Is Albert, Prince of Wales 3998
My Death 2188
My DeeTees 3916
My Defenses Are Down 153
My Desert Flower 758
My Diabalo Beau 4094
My Diamond Girls 3405
My Diamond Horseshoe of Girls 3007
My Dickey Say Nodings at All 284
My Dixie 4104
My Dixie Girl 2314
My Doctor 3184
My Dog 108
My Dolls 4425
My Dream Book of Memories 4706
My Dream for Tomorrow 3330
My Dream Girl (I Loved You Long Ago) 1096
My Dream Is Through 1786
My Dream of Dreams 3562, 4620
My Dream of Love 1067
My Dream of Love Is You 2363, 2605
My Dream of You 1473
My Dream, Dream Man 2254
My Dreamland 2127
My Dreams 3670, 4357
My Drug Store 3918
My Dusky Baby 632
My Dusky Dago Boy 2485
My Dutch Lady 3406
My Dynamo 1657
My Easy Ridin' Man 1014
My Edelweiss 96
My Egyptian Queen 2695
My Emmaleen 3437
My Empty Arms 709
My Eternal Devotion 1194
My Evaline 2324
My Eyes Speak Love 2880
My Faces of 1958 4153
My Fair Lady (Lady Fair) 4300
"My Fair Lady medley" 3018
My Fair Unknown 2885

My Fairy Prince 1849
My Fairy Tale 2846
My Faithful Stradivari 3839
My Family Tree 1564
My Fannie 2363
My Fatal Charm 1918
My Fate Is in Your Hands 2561
My Father Said 3699
My Father Took Me Dancing 4540
My Father Was a Peculiar Man 4380
My Father's a Homo 2746
My Father's Island 3628
My Father's Wooden Leg 2025
My Favorite Person 787
My Favorite Things 4095
My Favorite Year 3039, 3039
My Feet Are Firmly Planted on the Ground 3365
My Feet Took T'Walkin' 1372
My Filipino Belle 2711
My Filipino Pet 2465
My Fire-Fly Lady 2858
My First Girl 2941
My First Long Pants 1703
My First Love 2551, 3810
My First Love Letter 2594
My First Love Song 3731
My First Love, My Last Love 3170
My First Mistake 2283
My First Moment 4689
My First Promise 372
My First Real Christmas 2689
My First Smoke 2481
My First Solo Flight 414
My First True Love 2632
My First Woman 2333
My Flag 1826
My Flower of the South 331
My Fortune Is My Face 1227
My Fox Trot Wedding Day 1901
My Friend 164, 460, 2452
My Friend from India 2291
My Friend Huckleberry Finn 4409
My Friend John 4327
My Friend Lebel 1455
My Friend Yama 371
My Friend, My Father 4690
My Friends 4233
My Friends, the Celebrities 3124
My Frivolity Girl 1404
My Funny Valentine 247, 3175
My Furry Castle in the Air 758
My G.I. Joey 597, 3217
My Gaby Doll 3406
My Gal 1885
My Gal and I 1880
My Gal Is Mine Once More 2137
My Gal! My Gal! 2465
My Galilee 181
My Gang 3723
My Garden 681
My Garden of Perfumes 3443
My Garden That Blooms for You 115
My Gasoline Automobile 2695
My Gasoline Maid 2724
My Generation 3739
My Gentle Young Johnny 4312
My Georgia Gal 2287
My Georgiana 2122
My Geranium 1093
My Gink 797
My Girl 1610, 3949
My Girl and I 4214
My Girl Back Home 4096
My Girl Is Just Enough Woman for Me 3687
My Girl of Chance 2723
My Girl of Dreams 2262
My Girl Takes Another Beau 2334
My Girl's Gone Screwy Over Huey 4374
My God When I Think 2153
My God, Why Hast Thou Forsaken Me? 2236
My Golden Dream Ship 378
My Golden Girl 3043
My Gondolier Queen Good Night 141
My Goo-Goo Queen 4681
My Good Friends of Erin's Isle 1162
My Grammar Book 4687
My Grandfather's Girl 543
My Greatest Day! 4625
My Guiding Star 363
My Gypsy Maid 1908
My Gypsy Sweetheart 3265
My Hairt Is in the Highlands 3732
My Handsome 3813
My Handy Man Ain't Handy Any More 1198
My Handy Man Ain't Handy No More 443
My Hannah 3780
My Hannah Lady 4130
My Harlem Wench 1272
My Havana Maid 4687
My Hawaii 4337
My Haytian Queen 2119
My Head Is Like a Whirring Top 1518
My Head, My Head 758
My Headache 1772
My Heart 3592
My Heart Beats to You 2614
My Heart Begins to Thump! Thump! 3861
My Heart Belongs to Daddy 2432
My Heart Belongs to the U.S.A. 4776
My Heart Belongs to You 1281
My Heart Controls My Head 4365
My Heart Decided 3074
My Heart Flies Blind 2087
My Heart Flies Homing 178
My Heart for You Pines Away 4751
My Heart Goes Out to Dixieland 1332
My Heart Has Come a Tumbling Down 4798
My Heart I Cannot Give You 3996
My Heart Is a Drum 1415

My Heart Is a Stranger 3551
My Heart Is At Your Feet 767
My Heart Is Calling 3168, 3778
My Heart Is Dancing 4569
My Heart Is in Thrall 3912
My Heart Is Like a Bird 2751
My Heart Is Like a Bird in May 4133
My Heart Is Like a Violin 1227
My Heart Is On a Binge 204
My Heart Is Part of You 1322
My Heart Is Saying 2004
My Heart Is Sheba Bound 2467
My Heart Is So Full of You 2961, 3444
My Heart Is True 355
My Heart Is Unemployed 3990
My Heart Is Waking 2419
My Heart Is Weary 77
My Heart Is Young 4372
My Heart Leaps Up 2660
My Heart Says Yes 3756
My Heart Stood Still 834, 1763, 3291
My Heart Told Me 343
My Heart Will Be True to You (Too-Whoo) 2715
My Heart Will Sail Across the Sea 1485
My Heart Won't Learn 937
My Heart Won't Say Goodbye 1548
My Heart's a Banjo 3946
My Heart's a Marionette 3204
My Heart's a Roomy Hotel 2587
My Heart's Achin' for Macon 1560
My Heart's an Open Book 680
My Heart's an Open Door 2754
My Heart's Darlin' 4366
My Heart's in the Middle of July 67
My Heart's in the Sunny South 2691
My Heart's Mine Own 307
My Heather Belle 1927
My Heaven with You 4664
My Hero 742, 1096
My Hero (Parody) 1738
My Hero's Grenades 3619
My High School Sweetheart 2132
My Highbrow Fling 3623
My Hills of Home 2636
My Hindoo Love 434
My Hindoo Man 2160
My Holiday 3209
My Holiday Girls 3402
My Holy Prayer 482
My Home 284
My Home Is in My Shoes 4423
My Home Is Where the Heather Blooms 3732
My Home Town 3045, 4192, 4412
My Home Town Girl 870
My Home Town in Kansas 2516
My Home Town Is a One-Horse Town 4814
My Home's a Highway
(Sunday Night Supper) 4366
My Hometown 4633
My Honey Bunch 2213
My Honeysuckle Girl 4646
My Honolulu Honey Lou 1801
My Honor and My Sword (Borrow Trouble) 252
My Horse Has Cast a Shoe 3339
My Hortense 4393
My House 3452
My Houseboat on the Harlem 1011
My Houseboat on the Thames 3547
My Hula Maid 3399
My Hula-Hula Girl 1650
My Human Mermaid 1768
My Hungarian Girl 3710
My Husband 1783, 4319
My Husband Makes Movies 3171
My Husband Taught Me to Be
One of the Boys 1466
My Husband the Pig 4067
My Husband's Dearest Friend 1962
My Husband's First Wife 4234
My Husband, the Pig 2536
My IBM and I 2130
My Icy Floe 1654
My Idea About the Boys 351
My Idea of a Girl 3327
My Idea of a Wife (My Idea of a Man) 3170
My Idea of Love 1568
My Idea of Paradise 3372
My Idea of Something to Go Home To 136
My Ideal 457, 1819
My Illinois 2155
My Indian Family 751, 751
My Indian Summer Moon 1646
My Indiana Anna 228
My Indispensable Girl 579
My International Girl 431
My Intimate Friend 4478
My Intuition 3861
My Irish Daisy 1403
My Irish Gibson Girl 1464
My Irish Girl 1566, 3205, 4589
My Irish Maid 3746
My Irish Molly-O 3882
My Irish Romeo 3396
My Irish Rosie 2498, 2552
My Irish Senorita 3332
My Isle of Golden Dreams 1823, 3246
My Isle of Sweethearts 1689
My Jack O'Lantern 1307
My Japanese 3268
My Japanese Baby 2851
My Japanese Cherry Blossom 1926
My Japanese World 595
My Java Lady 3951
My Jewels 1489
My Joe 653
My Joe Louis of Love 3782
My Josephine 2041
My Jug 1842
My Jungle Home 1514
My Kiki Girl 2927

My Kind of Batid 2027
My Kind of Guy 4041
My Kind of Love 3954
My Kind of Night 2615
My Kind of People 3683
My Kind of Person 1846
My Kind of Town 4743
My Kinda Love 124
My King Can Do No Wrong 1849, 3595
My King of Love 2802
My Kingdom for a Queen Like You 2020
My Knees Are Weak 2290
My Lady 1483, 3622, 4766
My Lady 'Tis for Thee 252
My Lady Bug 4130
My Lady Busy 3882
My Lady Fair 335, 356, 4048
My Lady Friends 3184
My Lady Frog 2111
My Lady Hottentot 3298
My Lady Molly Waltz 3049
My Lady Moon 307
My Lady Nicotine 3579
My Lady of Japan 4662
My Lady of the Cameo 684, 2856
My Lady of the Fan 3662
My Lady of the Lake 4720
My Lady of the Lamp 3404
My Lady of the Manor 252
My Lady of the Nile (1) 4810
My Lady of the Nile (2) 4810
My Lady of the Telephone 965
My Lady Silhouette 4104
My Lady Wine 2869
My Lady's Clothes 3222
My Lady's Coach Has Been Attacked 4404
My Lady's Dress 1625, 2939, 3177
My Lady's Fan 539
My Lady's Hand 3314
My Lady's Maid 3052
My Ladye Faire 1570
My Land 310, 1075, 1378, 2662, 3167
My Land of Nod 4185
My Land, My Flag 1901
My Landlady 4806
My Last Affair 3103
My Last Farewell 20
My Last Love 4640
My Last Strike 3485
My Late, Late Lady 4828
My Life Is Love 2698
My Life's a Musical Comedy 2069
My Lips Are Sealed 2196
My Lips, My Love, My Soul 670
My Little Address Book 1482
My Little Baby 357
My Little Belgian Maid 4836, 4839
My Little Blarney Stone 2869
My Little Book of Poetry 3880, 3006
My Little Buckaroo 714
My Little Bugaboo 1919
My Little Buttercup 675
My Little Canoe 3218, 3856, 3857
My Little Castagnette 1027
My Little China Doll 734
My Little Dancing Heart 3345
My Little Deutcher Girl 1783
My Little Dog Has Ego 961
(You're Mighty Lucky) My Little Ducky 4241
My Little Dudeen 3910
My Little Friend 3053
My Little Full-Blown Rose 4194
My Little Girl 2661, 4487
My Little Girl Is a Shy Little Girl 356
My Little Girlie 906, 4354
My Little Grass Shack 4264
My Little Gypsy Maid 4691
My Little Highland Highball 2489
My Little Hong Kong Baby 737
My Little Irish Girl 2763
My Little Irish Rose 1051, 1162
My Little Jail-Bird 4208
My Little Javanese 1685
My Little Kodak Girl 1562
My Little Lady Bug 4806
My Little Lamb 2745
My Little Laplander 246, 248
My Little Lassoo 361
My Little Lost Girl 751
My Little Lotus Flower 3406
My Little Love Bird 1537
My Little Loving Baby Mine 4776
My Little Madamoiselle 115
My Little Mimi San 331
My Little Pansy 405
My Little Pet Chicken 4808
My Little Piano Man 4170
My Little Prayer 12
My Little Queen Bee 2884
My Little Red Book 261
My Little Redskin 953
My Little Room 593
My Little Sea Shell 2446
My Little Sea Shell Told Me So 2564
My Little Submarine 4809
My Little Sunbeam Sue 3753
My Little Sunday Girl 1213
My Little Tailor Maid 2826
My Little Yellow Dress 3845
My Log Fire Girl 1154
My Log-Cabin Home 3443
My Lola 2565
My Lolo Maid 1316
My Long Ago Girl 1690
My Long Lost Love Lenore 20
My Lord and Ladies 1284
My Lord and Master 2312
My Lotus Flower 2254
My Lotus Lady 4324
My Lou 4553

My Louisa 3131, 3214, 4581
My Loulou 2252
My Love 630, 669
My Love Awaits 4724
My Love Belongs to You 4591
My Love Bouquet 969
My Love Carries On 4204
My Love Does No Know 4073
My Love for Her 3760
My Love Goes Down 2055
My Love Has Gone Away 4409
My Love I Dare Not Tell Thee 2803
My Love Is a Blower 118
My Love Is a Flower 2623
My Love Is a Married Man 999
My Love Is a Secret 1911
My Love Is a Wanderer 2227
My Love Is Fair 1213
My Love Is for Thee 3652
My Love Is Greater than the World 3545
My Love Is Like a Butterfly 945
My Love Is Like the River 4207
My Love Is on the Way 1600
My Love Is Young 3103, 3104
My Love Is Yours 4186
My Love of Long Ago 4407
My Love Song 1418
My Love Will Come By 279
My Love Works in a Greenhouse 123
My Love, My Love 3285, 2661
My Loved One 3152
My Lovely Lad 3939
My Lover 3249, 4267
My Lover Is a Scoundrel 3526
My Luck Has Changed 98
My Luck Is Changing 4286
My Lucky Fly 42
My Lucky Lover 4015
My Lucky Star 734, 1339, 3291, 3924
My Lulu 2546
My Lungs 3651
My Madagascar Maid 2770
My Magic Lamp 2327, 4383
My Magnolia 3054
My Maid from Hindoostan 2959
My Maid in the Moon 671
My Mammy 986, 3985
My Man 3905, 1425, 3619, 4815, 4831, 4847, 4852
My Man Blues 3297
My Man Godfrey 3055
My Man Is Good for Nothing but Love 1980
My Man Is on the Make 1800
My Man Must Dance 570
My Man's Gone Now 3541
My Manicure Maids 4375
My Maori Maid 2062
My Marionette 1685
My Master Plan 279
My Matilda 3820
My Matrimonial Bon Bon 1417
My Meadow 708
My Melody 4816
My Melody Man 3523
My Memories Started with You 70
My Merry Go Round 4248
My Merry Oldsmobile 3350
My Mexican Rose 434
My Middy 1726
My Midnight Frolic Girl 4814
My Midnight Girl 4833
My Midnight Sweetheart 3057
My Might-Have-Been 1270
My Military Man 876
My Mimosa 3063
My Mind on Freedom 2203
My Mind Says No 1745
My Mind's on You 2680
My Mindanao Chocolate Soldier 3177
My Miracle Man 1826
My Miss Mary 4312
My Mississippi Miss 4092
My Mississippi Missus Misses Me 2879
My Missus 376
My Mobile Gal 350
My Mocking Bird 3350
My Model Girl 473
My Moment Supreme 890
My Money 81
My Moonlight Lou 1798
My Morning Glory 1798
My Most Embarrasing Moment 3916
My Most Important Moments Go By 2418
My Most Intimate Friend 2252
My Mother Bore Me 3465
My Mother Said 2134
My Mother Told Me Not to Trust a Soldier 3650
My Mother Was a Fortune Teller 2677
My Mother Would Love You 3359
My Mother's Wedding Day 530
My Motter 178
My Moustache Is Twitchin' 4102
My Movie Is Going to Trial 1700
My Movie of the Week 1700
My Moving Picture Man 75
My Musical Comedy Maiden 804
My Name 3271
My Name Is Can 2728
My Name Is Leda Pearl 1139
My Name Is Man 1072
My Name Is Rumpelstiltskin 3844
My Name Is Samuel Cooper 2615
My Name's Abundance 3418
My Name's Marie, Who Wants to Be My Peanut Vendor 1492
My New Friends 2677
My New Kentucky Home 1014
My New York 666, 4821
My New York Slip 4467
My Nice Ways 521, 4196
My Night in Venice 2587

My Ninette 4148
My Nose 948, 4073, 4670
My Number Is Eleven 1958
My Object All Sublime 1987
My Official Wife 3685
My Old Banjo 2302
My Old Boy 2631
My Old Brass Band 3423
My Old Brass Bed 4516
My Old Fashioned Garden Flower 531
My Old Flame 4799
My Old Friend 2643
My Old Friends 3059
My Old Girl Is My New Girl Now 4821
My Old Hoss 622
My Old Kentucky Home 2415, 2787, 4149, 1995
My Old Kentucky Rock and Roll Home 3261
My Old Lady 3855
My Old Love Is My New Love 1483
My Old Man 2557, 2979
My Old New Jersey Home 1551, 3770
My Old Times 4055
My Old Town 188, 1316
My Old Virginia Home (On the River Nile) 612
My One and Only 3060
My One and Only (What Am I Gonna Do) 1419
My One and Only Shlemiel 3937
My One Girl 3849
My Only One 545, 1759
My Only Romance 1112
My Operatic Samson 4521
My Orchard of Girls 4813
My Oriental Symphony 69
My Otaheitee Lady 100
My Own 1912, 2833
My Own Best Friend 723, 4480
My Own Best Love 1259
My Own California 2385
My Own Dear Irish Queen 4313
My Own Dear Sue 516
My Own Individual Star 51
My Own Light Infantry
(Nursery Fanfare) 3740
My Own Little Girl 906
My Own Morning 1729
My Own Paree 2745
My Own Place 3925
My Own Space 16
My Own United States 4251, 4646
My Own Vienna 2914
My Own Way 1104
My Own Willow Tree 718
My Own, or True Love at Last 1256
My Pa 4764
My Palace of Dreams 3011
My Papa from Panama 4180
My Paradise 2292
My Paramount-Publix-Roxy Rose 2475
My Part of Somewhere 3485
My Partners 906
My Party 3422
My Passion Flower 3063
My Peaches and Cream 3679
My Personal Rainbow 4374
My Picture in the Papers 1600
My Picture of You 1646
My Pin-Up Girl 4009, 4141
My Pipe of Peace 3238
My Pirate Lady 3737
My Place or Yours? 2069
My Pleasure 4337
My Plume (My Life) 4073
My Polly Is a Peach 509
My Pony Boy 2892
My Pony Pony Girl 1798
My Poor Wee Lassie-A Scottish Lament 1256
My Post Card Girl 2892
My Potential 3577
My Pousse-Cafe 97
My Prayers Have Come True 4764
My Pretty Little Family 2497
My Prince 73
My Prince (What a Prince!) 4420
My Prince Came Riding 2755
My Prince o' Dreams 2232
My Prince of Wales 2193
My Princess Zulu Lulu 4014
My Private Life 695
My Propensities Are All the Other Way 2131
My Queen of Ping Pong 3820
My Radiant Fire Fly 3805
My Radium Girl 4809
My Rag Doll Girl 250
My Raggedy Doll 1524
My Raggydore 1963
My Rainbow 1779, 3406
My Rainbow Beau 965
My Rainbow Girl 3333, 3652
My Rambler Rose 4816
My Real Ideal 203
My Red Riding Hood 974
My Red-Letter Day 4825
My Regular Man 691
My Religion 2908
My Reuben Girlie 3395
My Reunion Prayer 3181
My Rhapsody 3703
My Riviera Rose 200
My Road 317
My Roly Poly Oly Tulip Maid 2485
My Romance 2031, 2258
My Room and Me 4540
My Rosary of Melodies 4831, 4852
My Rose 274, 2135, 3998
My Rose of Memory 3973
My Rose of Spain 3149
My Rosemarie 1113
My Royal Majesty 4798
My Rules 1633
My Runaway Girl 3400

My Sabots 1114
My Sahara Girl 3085
My Sahara Rose 1154
My Sailor Boy 2324
My Salvation Army Queen 3547
My Sambo 694
My San Domingo Maid 4754
My Sawdust Queen 4324
My Screen Maid 2870
My Secret Dream 3469
My Seminole 2800
My Senorita 522, 1530
My Sergeant and I Are Buddies 4340
My Sergeant Doesn't Look Like Big John Wayne 3688
My Service Flag 1557
My Shaggy Old Polar Bear 4425
My Shassa Maid 1351
My Ship 369, 2386
My Ship of Dreams 1606
My Ship's the Girl for Me 1071
My Silver Tree 4345
My Sing Song Girl 1753
My Sist' Tetrazin' 2858
My Sister Bess 2033
My Sister Eileen 4734, 4734
My Sister-in-Law 2958
My Skating Girl (1) (inst.) 396
My Skating Girl (2) 396
My Sky without a Star 3493
My Soldier (Home Again) (Watashi No Heishi) 1616
My Soldier Boy 2254, 2335
My Son 2294, 139, 3507, 1716
My Son Charles 2650
My Son-In-Law 3390
My Son in Law the King 4798
My Son, the Doctor 1269
My Son the Druggist 4038
My Son, the Lawyer 1237
My Son, Uphold the Law 1094
My Song 242, 1492
My Song Without Words 297
My Sonny Boy 4313
My Sort of Ex-Boyfriend 4398
My Soul Magnifies the Lord 755
My Southern Belle 1123, 1656, 1657
My Southern Queen 806
My Spanish Love 2570
My Spanish Maid 3040
My Spanish Shawl 1923
My Special Friend Is Back in Town 26
My Spies Tell Me (You Love Nobody But Me) 3036
My Spooky Girl 4833
My Springtime Thou Art 463
My Stagecoach Is A-Comin' in Real Soon 451
My Star 73, 4135
My State 1860
My Story Ends that Way 2238
My Sugar Is the Salt of the Earth 1507
My Sulu Lulu Lou 4201
My Sumuran Girl 4655
My Sumurun Girl 822
My Sunday Fella 3953
My Sunday Girl 2934
My Sunflower Sue 1925
My Sunny South 1126
My Sunny Tennessee 2857
My Sunshine 3915
My Sweeheart's a Soldier in the Army 3945
My Sweet 111, 1403
My Sweet Crow 3384
My Sweet Hunk O' Trash 4198
My Sweet Hunk of Trash 4199
My Sweet Queen 1445
My Sweet Sunflower 2122
My Sweet Tomorrow 1809
My Sweet Wild Rose 1118
My Sweet Woman 3517
My Sweetheart 1534
My Sweetheart Mamie 1889
My Sweetheart 'Tis of Thee 1856
My Sweetie's Smile 3842, 4211
My Switzer Bride 3134
My Sword and I 4357
My Swwet Hawaiian Home 2013
My Syncopated Gypsy Maid 4473
My Syndi-Kate (Cindy Kate) 2481
My Talking Day 4541
My Tambourine Girl 4813
My Tango Girl 4833
My Tango Queen 335
My Texas Man 1028
My Thoughts Would Still Be with Thee 1466
My Three Angels 3066
My Tiger Rose 4837
My Time 3019
My Time of Day 1706, 3444
My Tina Dear 3065
My Title Song 1249
My Toast to You 2882, 4649
My Tokio Queen 4007
My Tom 4408
My Tonita 728
(I'm in Love with) My Top Sergeant 2187
My Toreador 256, 2254, 4430
My Totem Pole 47
My Town 1478
My Town Is Just As Good As Your Town 11
My Treasure 1711
My Treasure Island 709, 3485
My Trilby Maid 3399
My True Heart 2268
My True Love 2608, 3465
My True Love Is a Shepherdess 3732
My Turkish Opal 1212

My Turn 484
My Turn to Fall 2368
My Turn to Shine 2022
My Twilight Rose 2757
My Two Feet Polka 753
My Type 2208, 3161
My Uncle Sam 2155
My Uncle's Mistress 1596
My Unkissed Man 3488
My Unknown Someone 4695
My Venetian Maid 1351
My Venetian Rose (Sweet Venetian Rose, A) 1518
My Very Best New Friend 3752
My Very First Impression 1194
My Very Own 2347, 3191
My Violin 3538
My Vision Girl 2856, 3963
My Vision in Vermillion 2706
My Volo Maid 4762
My Voodoo Maiden 3737
My Waltz Divine 2223
My Waltz Queen 186
My Way 2356, 3731
My Wedded Life 1905
My Wedding 2382
My Wedding Day 3372
My Wedding Morning 353
My Weight in Gold 1373
My White Knight 3016
My Wife 85, 4790, 3404
My Wife and I 3067
My Wife Bridget 1501
My Wife-My Man 1784
My Wife! My Wife! 1558
My Wife Will Be My Lady 2498
My Wife's Family 3068
My Wife's Gone 106
My Wild Imagination 1791
My Wild Irish Rose 3759
My Window Full of Stars 4561
My Wish 1768, 1860
My Wonderful Dream Girl 4381
My Wonderful Love for Thee 3024
My Word 1243
My Word! (It Surely Was a Treat) 2885
My Word! Ain't We Carrying On 377
My World 31, 747
My World and Your World 3371
My World Is Beginning Today 3833
My World of Romance 4780
My Yankee Doodle Girl 4017
My Yankee Rose 625
My Yellow Flower 283
My Yellow Jacket Girl 1963
My Yesterday Shop 2232
My Yiddish Colleen 2299, 4804
My Yiddisha Colleen 3926
My Yiddishe Butterfly 3958
My Yiddishe Mame 4342
My Yiddishe Mammy 2706
My Yokohoma Girl 3401
My Yorkshire Lassie 3322
My Young and Foolish Heart 24
My Young Man 195
My Yukon Belle 2800
My Zebra Lady Fair 4809
My Ziegfeld Midnight Girl 4833
My Zingara Maid 68
My Zoo 4430
Mygar Maid 1910
Myltyl and Tyltyl (The Bluebird Song) 1961
Myrella 1538
Myron Brown, Farewell 331
Myrtle Gets an Idea 1004
Myrtle Is a Sensation 1004
Myrtle's March 1451
Mysterious Kiss, The 3613
Mysterious Lady 3453
Mysterious Maid 1968
Mysterious Maid, The 1640
Mysterious Melody 3081
Mysterious Moon 3681
Mysteriously 4132
Mystery, A 4732
Mystery Date 4193
Mystery Moon 3069
Mystery of Edwin Drood, The 3070
Mystery of History, The 1388
Mystery of Love 2880
Mystery of the Flesh 3696
Mystery of the Moon, The 4454
Mystery Play, The 2533
Mystery Song 432
Mystery Song, The (inst.) 437
Mystic Hussars, The 4150
Mystic Sorcerers 4161
Mystical Maidens Are We 3777

N

N.E.T. and This Is Remote 1978
'N Everything 3985
'N That's Nice 451
N.Y.C. 150, 602, 3664
N.Y.U. 1697
Naches Fin Kinder 2356
Nadia (Song of Hope) 2147
Nag! Nag! Nag! 4160
Naga Saki 1779
Nagasaki's Butterfly 3796
Najala's Lament 1300
Najala's Song of Joy 1300
Naji's Nuptial Dance 2355
Naked Foot 344
Naked in the Bethesda Fountain 3039
Naked Love 2611
Naked Truth, The 1686

Name a Day, Love! 2902
Name: Cockian 3469
Name Dropping 1978
Name: Emily Adams 2887
Name Game, The 338
Name It and It's Yours 447
Name of Kelly, The 2533
Name of Love, The 3070
Name of Our Own, A 3484
Name of the State Is Texas!, The 1341
Name Song, The 3844
Name the Day 3043
Name the Lady 4617
Namely You 2484
Names 392, 1107, 4147
Names I Love to Hear 3323
Name's LaGuardia, The 1280
Names of Trains 1402
Name's the Same, The 1507
Naming of Cats, The 678
Naming, The 730
Nana 1873
Nancy 3072, 932
Nancy Brown 4691
Nancy Clancy 1881
Nancy, I Fancy You 1095
Nancy Lee 2490
Nancy: The Unauthorized Musical 2022
Nancy's Farewell 168
Nanette 294, 1270
Nanette and Rin Tin Tin 2939
Nanking Blues 3973
Nanny 1107
Nanny Fling, The 1757
Nantucket, The 3605
Nanty Puts Her Hair Up 3107
Naomi 2051
Naomi the Salesrat 528
Napanee 3786
Napoleon 1342, 1784, 2190, 3134
Napoleon and the Miller's Daughter 1561
Napoleon und die Frauen 3613
Napoleon's a Pastry 1973
Napoleon's Nightmare 3456
Narcissism Rag 430
Narcissus 1358
Narcissus (inst.) 4390
Nargileh 203
Narrentanz 2830
Nasality 1974
Nashville Nightingale 3144
Nashville U.S.A. 2248
Natacha 1132
Natalie 4703
Natasha 1000
Natchez Trace 3551
Natchitoches, Louisiana 1319
Natchul Man 1385
Nathan, Nathan, What Are You Waitin' For? 3926
Nation of Nations, A 4169
Nation that Wasn't There, The 4004
National Air's Medley 2546
National Anthem 4798
National Anthem of Utopia, The 4536
National Anthem of Zoolakia 1177
National Brotherhood Week 4412
National Dish, The 4150
National Italian Sport 194
National Pastime (This Year's Nigger), The 1289
National Service Corps 272
National Theatre, The 4115
Native Son 3046
Native Son, A 4503
Native Women 3424
Natives 4434
Natives Are Restless, The 162
Natural Born Females 3346
Natural High 2074
Natural History Class, The 3134
Natural Man 2248
Natural Woman, A 338
Nature 2757
Nature and I 1982
Nature Class, The 4735
Nature Divine 93
Nature Hunt Ballet 148
Nature Played a Dirty Trick on You 1207
Nature's Serenade 4696
Nature's Song Is But a Dream 4724
Natuscha 3013
Naughty 61
Naughty Baby 921, 3569
Naughty Bird Tarantella 3938
Naughty Boy 2277, 4234
Naughty Continong, The 1301
Naughty Eyes 764, 4651
Naughty Forty-Second Street 3161, 3366
Naughty Girl 3080
Naughty Kid Song 2505
Naughty Little Clock 666
Naughty Little Lady, O 47
Naughty Little Raindrop 69
Naughty Little Step 2263
Naughty Marietta 3081
Naughty Marietta selections 4251
Naughty-Naught 3082
Naughty, Naughty 3378
Naughty, Naughty Nancy 2522
Naughty, Naughty, Naughty 3958
Naughty Nineties, The 1655
Naughty Nobleman 582
Naughty Riquette 3084
Naughty Widow Wise 1430
Nausea Before the Game 2132
Nausikaa's Theme 1959
Nautch Girls' Dance 2974
Nautical Domesticity 1155
Navajo 3073

Naval Manoeuvres 2761
Navy, The 1071
Navy Foxtrot Man, The 3923
Nay, Nay Pauline 968
Nazi Party Pooper 2949
Ndinosara Nani?
(With Whom Shall I Stay?) 4579
Nduna Ngibolekinduku
(The Zulu Warriors) 4438
Neapoli 1374
Neapolitan Jazz 3403
Neapolitan Love Song
(Sweet One How My Heart Is Yearning)
(T'Amo) 3590
Neapolitan Nostalgia 194
Near but Never Too Near 1369
Near Future, The 4813
Near to You 957
Nearing the Day 4529
Nearly True to You 1992
Nearsighted Gambler 1757
Neat Cafe, A 2286
Neat Little Cat, A 1972
Neat Ned Nuff Sed 2792
Neat/Not Neat 2142
Neat to Be a Newsboy 4744
'Neath a New Moon 3117
'Neath Egyptian Skies 208
'Neath Italian Skies 487
'Neath My Lattice 3777
'Neath the Blue Neapolitan Sky 4559
'Neath the Cherry Blossom Moon 718
'Neath the Greenwood Tree 3736
'Neath the Old Cherry Tree 2314
'Neath the Pale Cuban Moon 3709
'Neath the South Sea Moon 4816
'Neath the Southern Moon 3081
'Neath Thy Casement 25
'Neath Thy Window 947
'Neath Thy Window, Senorita 2209
Neauville-Sur-Mer 3214
Nebraska 1991
Necessarily Evil 3568
Necessity 1278
Neckin' Time in Great Neck 1533
Necrology 4076
Nectar for the Gods 1746
Nectar, Sweet Nectar 2650
Needle in a Haystack 2643, 3856
Needle's Eye, The 3631
Needles 2342
Negotiation 2692
Neighbor, Neighbor 4147
Neighborhood 4031
Neighborhood Song, The 2053
Neighbors 4659
Neighbors Above, Neighbors Below 572
Neighbors Song, The 2925
Neither the Time Nor the Place 3526
Nel Blue di Pinto di Blue (Volare) 4137, 4264
Nell Brinkley Girl, The 4802
Nell Gwynne 3730
Nellie Bly 3091
Nellie Kellie 3951
Nellie Kelly 2298
Nellie Kelly I Love You 1478, 2533
Nellie the Manicure 2543
Nellie's Entrance 2533
Nelly Bly 4149
Nelson 2208, 1000
Nemo's Dream of Fourth of July (inst.) 2534
Nenette and Rin-Tin-Tin (Rintintin) 1580
Neptune's Daughter 4808
Neptune's Son 3173
Nero, Caesar, Napoleon 298
Nerves 611, 4020, 1270, 1851, 3866
Nervous 407, 3902
Nervous Set, The 3094
Nervous Wreck, The 4683
Nervous Wrecks 3819
Nesting in a New York Tree
(Nesting Time in New York Town) 2517
Nesting Time in Flatbush 3230
Nestle By My Side 1650
Network 3548
Neurotic You and Psychopathic Me 2439
Nevada Hoe Down 1918
Nevada Moonlight 1387
Never 3802
Never a Dull Moment 1879, 4142
Never Again 2, 98, 350, 1228, 2617,
2717, 3308, 3885
Never Any Time to Play 3371
Never Been the Petted Party 2490
Never Borrow Trouble 2770
Never Breathe a Word of This to Mother 1640
Never Can Tell 3456
Never Choose a Girl from Her Photograph 1307
Never Count Your Chicks before They're Hatched 2761
Never Do A Bad Thing 3224
Never Ever Land 1216
Never Feel Sorry for Anybody 957
Never Feel Too Weary to Pray 2510
Never Felt Better in My Life 2229
Never for You 3117
Never Forget Your Parents 2559
Never Get Lost 3696
Never Give a Sucker an Even Break 4577
Never Give Anything Away 629
(I'll) Never Go There Anymore 2304
Never Go Walking without Your Hat Pin 4467
Never Had a Dream 2640
Never Had an Education 2813
Never Had It So Good 898
Never Had This Feeling Before 362
Never in Paris 610
Never in the Wide, Wide World 2697
Never Is Now 494
Never Land 3452, 3453
Never Let Her Go 4015

Never Let the Same Bee Sting You Twice 2127
Never Let Them Know What's Going On 4798
Never Let Your Dander Down 2910
Never Lose Your Heart in the Bright Moonlight 1801
Never Lose Your Sense of Humor 3636
Never Marry a Dancer 3699
Never Marry a Girl with Cold Cold Feet 954
Never Marry a Girl with Cold Feet! 954
Never Mention Love When We're Alone 1016
Never Met a Man I Didn't Like 4106, 4695
Never Mind Bo-Peep We Will Find Your Sheep 250
Never Mind How 3584
Never Mind Ma'mselle 3173
Never Mind the Weather 3882
Never Mind the Why and Wherefore 1948
Never More 88
Never, Never Be an Artist 629
Never Never Land 3453
Never, Never Land 4293
Never Never Land 3454
Never, Never Leave Me 2584
Never on Sunday 2106
Never or Now 674
Never Pay Musicians What They're Worth 4076
Never Play Croquet 54
Never Put It in Writing 1699
Never Raise a Razor 'Less You Want to Raise a Row 2996
Never Saw Myself 3227
Never Say a Butcher Has No Soul 1265
Never Say Die 4249
Never Say Diet 2780
Never Say Good-bye 3125
Never Say Never 474, 4373
Never Say No 1245, 1453
Never Say the World Was Made to Cry 1678
Never Speak Directly to an Emperor 3164
Never Stop Believing 535
Never Take No for an Answer 3916
Never Too Late Cha-Cha-Cha 3097
Never Too Late for Love 1242
Never Too Old to Love 1457
Never Trouble Trouble 3236
Never Trust a Man 1862
Never Trust a Soldier Man 965
Never Trust a Virgin 1745
Never Trust Anyone Under Three 4577
Never Try Too Hard 2339
Never Underestimate the Power of a Woman 18
Never Wait for Love 3473
Never Was There a Girl So Fair 3225
Never Was There Such a Lover 742
Never Whirl 968
Never Will I Marry 1698, 3444
Never Without Your Love 4337
Never You 2333
Neverland 1298
Nevermore 118, 841, 1930
Nevertheless 572
Neville 4627
New Amsterdam 545
New Argentina, A 1211
New Art Is True Art 3301
New Ashmolean Marching Society and Students Conservatory Band, The 3444, 4652
New Belle of New York, The 998
New Boy, A 4633
New Boy in Town 2958
New Cook, The 2209
New Coon, A 3065
New Day 4062
New Deal for Christmas, A 150, 155
New Dreams for Old 3543
New Evaline 1612
New Faces 3103, 3104
New Fangled Preacher Man 3610
New-Fangled Tango, A 1760
New Game, The 642
New Generation, A 2245
New Girl on the Town 3752
New Hampshire Nights 4515
New Haven 4041
New Hollywood Plots 673
New Ice Age, The 2095
New Ideas 938
New Italian Folk Song, A 272
New Jerusalem 4558
New Kind of Blues, A 2496
New Kind of Girl 4461
New Kind of Husband, A 1412
New Kind of Rhythm 876, 3533
New Lady Bantok, The 3652
New Leaf (New Life, New Me) 3576
New Life Coming, A 3835, 4145
New Life, A 2198, 2565
New Look Feeling 1918
New Look, The 2582
New Love 642
New Love, A 1859
New Love Is Old, A 672
New Loves for Old 1797
New Man 1699
New Math 4412
New Me, The 2680
New Menace, The 3479
New Moon 2698, 4010
New Moon selections 4251
New Musketeers 273
New Nantucket 1539
New New York 3861
New Number Two 1928
New Orleans 2115
New Orleans Hop Scop Blues 3297
New Orleans Hop Scotch Blues 2796
New Orleans Hop-Scop Blues 478
New Orleans Jeunesse Doree 3081
New Orleans Mardi Gras and You, The 3715
New Orleans Poon 3564

New Orleans Saga 2115
New Oysters 1985
New Pair of Shoes, A 4633
New Pas 1798
New Pilgrim's Prayer, The 1035
New Place, A 1997
New Prisoner's Song 1037
New Rhythm 4769
(There Are) New Roses Every Summer 4826
New Sensation 1342
New Snow 459
New Soft Shoe, The 871
New Song, A 2007
New Sounds 2772
New Style Bonnet 3460
New Sun in the Sky 294
New to Me 1644, 3941
New Town Is a Blue Town, A 3351
New Waltz, A 3112
New War Situation 213
New Ways to Dream 4217
New Words for an Old Love Song 3605
New World 3987, 1265, 1498
New World, The 3088, 1258
New Worlds 4117
New Year Filled with Love, A 1035
New Year's Eve 1068
New Year's in New Orleans 3840
New Years in Beirut, 1983 3661
New York 4289
New York '69 4468
New York (New York Confidential) 3094
New York (You're the Best Town in Europe) 4805
New York and Chicago 1746
New York at Night 3126
New York Cliche 3476
New York for Five Dollars a Day 427
New York Forever 2851
New York from the Air 4468
New York Has a New Hotel 3889
New York Hippodrome March, The (inst.) 1901
New York Is a Festival of Fun 2913
New York Is a Party 1713
New York Is a Summer Festival 3479
New York Is Going Up 2307
New York Is My Home 4684
New York Is Not a Town 4273
New York Is the Same Old Place 3312
New York Isn't Such a Bad Old Town 3332, 4521
New York Life 728
New York Love Is So Hard 4684
New York Lullaby 3126
New York, New York 2205, 3278, 4480
New York Number 2909
New York on Parade 2460
New York Serenade 3766
New York Summer, A 3126
New York Town 1587
New York Town (Is Wearing Its Bandannas
on Broadway) 2827
New York Town 3025, 4740
New York Town for Mine 2122
New York Way 2986
New York, What's Become of You? 4742
New York, What's the Matter with You? 4807
New York without Bob 2279
New York Women 139
New York's Good Morning Song 4289
New Yorker, The 3005
"New Yorker" stories 3353
New Yorkers 2525
New Zealand Maori Dance 2062
Newlywed Express 3252
Newlyweds 1516
Newlyweds, The 3134
Newlyweds' Song, The 1616
Newport By the Sea 1459
Newport Dip, The 2123
Newport Glide, The 1151, 3148
Newport Is Waiting for Me 41
News 142
News, The 583, 1737
News Chant 1385
News Item 3970
News News 3528
News, News 4488
News of You 1665
Newspaper Girl, The 2456
Newspaper Song (Read the
Papers Every Day) 2534
Newsreel, The 4323
Newsy Bluesies 4586
Next 2188, 3340, 3679
Next Dance with You, The 2419
Next Dream, The 595
Next Horse I Ride On, The 2795
Next King, The 3507
Next May Be the Right, The 4119
Next Morning Tells Another Tale 1562
Next Stop, New York City 275
Next Summer in Dear Old New York 1881
Next Summer in Old New York 4473
Next Sunday 355
Next Time 784
Next Time I Care, The 3536
Next Time I Love, The 3366
Next Time It Happens, The 3505, 4146
Next Time We Love 1884
Next Time We Meet 2250
Next to Lovin' I Like Fightin' 3928
Next to Texas, I Love You 1886
Next Tuesday 1777
Next Year Gonna Be Pink 4019
Nexus 1159
Ngatheth Amacala 4438
Ngobammakhosi 4438
Ni-nana Duet 3151
Niagara Falls 1625
Nicaragua 4635
Niccolo's Piccolo 4723

Nice 2646
Nice As Any Man Can Be 2219
Nice Baby 3926
Nice Baby! (Come to Papa!) 4392
Nice Fella 3224
Nice Girl 303
Nice Girl Like You, A 1786
Nice Girls 4796
Nice Goin' 3138
Nice Goings On 3139
Nice House We Got Here 3224
Nice Little Day 4415
Nice Little Girl on the Side, A 3770, 3791
Nice Little Girls and Boys 1246
Nice Little Home Is What I Sigh For, A 233
Nice Little Plot for a Play 2730
Nice Running in to You 3161
Nice Running Into You 3366
Nice She Ain't 1709
Nice Small Town Girls 2888
Nice to Know 2422
Nice to See You 3140
Nice Town 779
(My) Nice Ways 4196
Nice Work If You Can Get It 921, 3060
Nice Young Man, A 357
Nicer Girl than You, A 2892
Nicest Girl I Know, The 1863
Nicest Man I Ever Saw, The 830
Nicest Sort of Feeling 2112
Nicest Thing, The 2449
Nicest Time of the Year 3278
Nicest Time to Say Goodnight, The 2583
'Nichevo' Means Yes 464
Nicholas Nickleby 3143
Nicholini 2155
Nick 3180
Nickel for a Dime, A 4281
Nickel to My Name, A 297
Nickel Under the Foot 919
Nickel Worth of Dreams 1665
Nicodemus 1118, 3254
Nicol in the Picolo 498
Nicole You Is My Woman Now 2452
Nicolini 1123
Nicotina 1338
Nigger Heaven Blues 2739
Night 1680, 3822
Night After Night 2103, 4367, 3255
Night Alone, A 3448
Night and Day 1453, 1762
Night and the Sea, The 406
Night at Luna, A 632
Night Before Christmas Song, The 3794
Night Before the Morning After, The 383
Night Bird Is Calling, The 3348
Night Birds 2293
Night Boat to Albany 1833
Night Brigade, The 4206
Night Club Nights 2490, 2540
Night Club Opening 4581
Night Flies By 3014
Night Gondolfi Got Married, The 2322
Night Has a Thousand Eyes, The 126
Night! Healing Darkness! 2243
Night, Hold Back the Dawn 4267
Night Idyll 710
Night in June, A 4818
Night in Paris, A 787
Night in the Orient, A 3985
Night in the Ukraine, A 1000
Night Is a Weapon 3817
Night Is Filled with Wonderful Sounds, The 4798
Night Is Young, The 277
Night Is Young and You're So Beautiful, The 662
Night It Had to End, The 3760
Night It Happened, The 2238
Night Lady 2426
Night Letter 4485
Night Life 4621
Night Life in Old Manhattan 4808
Night Life in Santa Rosa 4019
Night May Be Dark, The 2201
Night May Have Its Sadness 133
Night Music 2357
Night of Love 2684
Night of Masquerade, A 2829
Night of My Nights 2327, 4383
Night of Nights 4110
Night of Screams 3944
Night of Shooting Stars 3306
Night of St. Leandre 1119
Night of Stars 3153
Night of Terror 3461
Night of the Ball, The 1203
Night on the Town 846, 3277
Night Out, A 2707, 3157
Night People 4127, 3094
Night Pulse 3576
Night Remembers 3094
Night School for Revue, The 703
Night Song 602, 1601
Night That Made America Famous, The 3159
Night the Hurricane Hit, The 3942
Night the Hurricane Struck, The 3484
Night the Lion Broke Loose, The 4827
Night the Old Cow Died, The 4206
Night They Drove Old Dixie Down, The 3739
Night They Invented Champagne, The 1511
Night Time 1340
Night Time, The 1552
Night Time 1640, 2291
Night Time, The 3319
(It's) The Night Time 3819
Night Time in Araby 1487
Night Time's the Right Time to Spoon with the Girl You Love 2448
Night Waltz (1) 2536
Night Waltz (2) 2536
Night Waltzes 4067

Night Was All to Blame, The 2595
Night Was Made for Love 25
Night Was Made for Love, The 672, 2372
Night Wind 680, 2032
Nightfall in Louisiana 884
Nightie Parade 1248
Nightie-Night 4392
Nightingale 1017
Nightingale, The (Turk's Song) (Samarkand) 1784
Nightingale, The 3164, 641
Nightingale and the Rose, The 3774, 1260
Nightingale and the Star, The 2915
Nightingale, Bring Me a Rose 1688, 2227
Nightingale Sang in Berkeley Square, A 4027
Nightingale Song, The 3005
Nightingale Song, A 2464
Nightingale, the Moon and I, The 2817
Nightingale's Song, The 3318
Nightlife 64
Nightly My Love 4110
Nightmare 4790
Nightmare, The 1112
Nightmare 1358
Nightmare, The 3469
Nightmare 1347
Nightmare and Goblin March, The 2408
Nightmare Ballet 2556
Nightmare Quartet, The 3938
Nightmare Was Me, The 2648
Nights of Cabiria 4238
Nights When I Am Lonely 1813
Nightskate 4744
Nightsong 3167
Nightsong in the Jungle 2970
Nighttime Is No Time for Thinking, The 1284
Nighty Girl 1247
Nihilists, The 3685
Nijigo Novgo Glide 1819
Nijinksy 4810
Nikita Marlena 3997
Nikki 261
Nikki and Her War Birds 3168
Nile, The 3148
Nimble Symbaline 2978
Nina 495, 1617, 3235
Nina Rosa 3170
Nina, the Pinta, and the Santa Maria, The 750
Ninas 3960
Nine 3171, 4754
Nine Hundred Miles 4740
Nine Little Missionaries 1536
Nine O'Clock 4270
Nine Supreme Chords, The 3181
Nine to Five 2011
Nine to Twelve 3661
1918 1015
1950's Singing Group 3814
1945 3515
1919 1038
1999 4534, 973
1908 728
1908 Life, The 1339
1960's Twist 3814
1934 154
1934 Hot Chocolate Jazz Babies Revue, The 550
Nineteen Twenty-Seven 4276
Ninety Again! 4481
'98 998
99% Pure 3130
Niniche 2824
Ninja Raid 3944
Nino and Dino and Gino 2551
Ninon Was a Naughty Girl 208
Ninon's Father Doesn't Seem to Mind 3883
Ninotchka 3972
Nipper, The 3626
Nippy 605
Niri-Esther 4541
Nirvana 4171
Nita 487, 3753
Nitchevo 4435
Nite Club 3178
Nix on the Glow-Worm, Lena! 4804
Niyayibona Lento Engiyibonayo
(Do You See What I See?) 3836
Nize Baby 3179
Nkosi Sikeleli'Afrika 3836
No 723, 823
No (You Can't Have My Heart) 4777
No, a Million Times, No! 1828
No Bad News 4722
No Bed of Roses 3793
No Big Deal 3555
No Bird Ever Flew So High He Didn't
Have to Light 4738
No Birdie Ever Flew So High 2270
No Boom Boom 4862
No Bottom 2225
No Champagne 3988
No Chance, No Dice, No Deal 1611
No Choir of Angels 1903
No Comprenez, No Capish, No Versteh! 2444
No Contest 721
No Croissants 4619
No Damaged Goods 1975
No Dessert 1978
No Doubt I Ought to Try 2760
No Doubt You'd Like to Cuddle Up to Baby 2695
No Encore 1649
No Faceless People 518
No-Fault Waltz, The 4108
No Foolin' 2457, 3179
No for an Answer 3180
No-Frills Revue, The 3181
No Garlic Tonight 227
No Give, No Take 1739
No Good at Bein' Bad 451
No Good Can Come from Bad 3070
No Good Man (Will Make a Good Good
Woman Bad), A 1917

No Goodbyes 3330
(There's) No Greater Sound (Than Da, Da, Da, Da) 486
No Happy Ending 3788
No Hard Feelings 2132, 847
No Hearts for Sale 3252
No Holds Barred 3608
No Home, No Job 2961
No Hope for the Human Race 2201
No, I Won't 3252
No Ifs! No Ands! No Buts! 4798
No Irish Need Apply 2250
No, Joe 4147
No Journey's Too Far for a Lover 3053
No Ketchup 3224
No Lies 374
No Life 4210
No Light in Your Eyes 3667
No Lookin' Back 2809
No Love, No Heartbreak 346
No Lover 3326
No Man 3944
No Man Better 'n His Pa 2028
No Man Is Worth It 958
No Man Left for Me 4695
No Man of Your Own 490
No Man's Land 25
No Matter What 330
No Matter What or Where 1335
No Matter Where 3015
No Matter Who or What You Are It's Great to Be in Love 1666
No More 2143, 1633, 1601, 2751, 2640
No More at Evening 3686
No More Candy 3918
No More Dancing 1461
No More Edens 4522
No More Enchantment 1104
No More Flahooleys! 1300
No More Games 729
No More Girls for Me 3051
No More Love 4798
No More Mornings 1068
No More Rainbows 3428
No More Staying Out Late 2528
No More Swing 2439
No More than a Moment 2777
No More Thrills 3707
No More to Roam 496
No More Waiting 134
(If There Were) No More You 1339
No, Mother, No 601
No, My Heart 1787
No Never 1636
No News Today 3091
No Night to Fear 3913
No No! 4227
No, No, Mamselle 2595
No, No, Nanette 3184, 3249
No! No! No! 1918, 3013, 4435
No Offence 2937
No Olive in My Martini, Please 2479
No-One 1116
No One Believes 4027
No One But You 2303
No One but You 4063, 4110
No One but You! 1088
No One Can Take That Away 1997
No One Cares for Dreams 2595
No One Could Love You More Than I Do 3352
No One Dreams About Me 2505
No One Else But that Girl of Mine 3443
No One Else But You 466
No One Ever Died of Love 306
No One Ever Knows 1276
No One Ever Leaves Our Island 3371
No One Ever Loved Like Me 3866
No One Ever Told Me Love Would Be So Hard 1371
No One Has Ever Loved Me 3411
No One Has Gotten to Georgy 1497
No One in the World Like You 3803
No One Is Alone 2143
No One Is Perfect 2357, 1818
No One Knows (How Much I'm in Love) 773
No One Knows Me 339
No One Knows Who I Am 2198
No One Like You 3022
No One Listens 3539
No One Loves a Clown 487
No One Must Ever Know 2198
No One Thanks the Go-Between 2837
No One to Blame but You 1855
No One to Call Me Victoria 2047
No One Will Steal Him 2885
No One Would Steal You from Me 3921
No One'll Ever Love You 1614
No One's Ever Kissed Me 605
No One's Heart 3064
No One's Perfect 1832
No One's Perfect, Dear 4789
No One's to Blame but You 75
No One's Toy 2677
No-one's Tried to Kiss Me 4510
No Ordinary Day 31
No Other Eyes 2180
No Other Gal 1847
No Other Girl 3185
No Other Love 2797, 3012
No Peace in My Soul 27
No Peach Hangs Too High for Him 1090
No Peach Hangs too High for Him 1118
No Place but Home (If We're in China) 1202
No Place for Me 3876
No Place Like Home 124
No Place Like London 4233
No Place Like the Country 596
No Place to Go 4623
No Profit in That 1092
No Questions 4060

No Questions Asked 2555
No Regret 1169
No Regrets 4114
No Room in My Heart 3849
No Room in the Inn 755
No Room No Room 54
No Ross Dixon 3947
No Sacrifice 4696
No Sad Songs for Me 2357
No Show Tonight 4735
No Sign of the Times 3124
No Sinners in Jah Yard 3690
No Sir, Yes Sir 42
No Small Roles 3858
No Song 4191
No Song More Pleasing 3702
No Stamp Attached 1887
No Strings 3187
No Substitute for a Man 916
No Surprises 699, 1161
No Talent 2248
No Tears in Heaven 4030
No-Tell Motel, The 3564
No Telling 2275
No Thank You 364
No, Thank You 946
No Thank You from a Mocking Sun 2784
"No They Can't" Song 4370
No Tickee, No Washee 3379
No Time 1864, 4018
No Time at All 3506
No Time for Nothin' but Love 67
No Time for Sergeants 3188, 3188
No Time Has Come When I Must Yield 1080
No Touch Mine 2332
No True Love 3920
No Two People 1741, 3444
No Understand 1060
No Use Pretending 1352
No Used Actin' Coy with a Boy from Illinois 903
No Ve Vouldn't Gonto Do It 2344
No Way in Hell 1809
No Way to Stop It 4095
No Ways Tired 3987
No Wedding Bells for Me 2996, 3313, 3543
No Where 4191
No Wonder I'm Blue 288
No Wonder Man Won't Wed 1910
No Wonder Taxes Are High 44
No Word for Love 3944
No You Didn't, Yes I Did 3337
Noah 4167
Noah and Jeff 262
Noah Knew a Thing or Two 2765
Noah's Ark 694, 3382, 4396, 3191
Nobility 483
Noble 451
Noble Cause of Art, The 4657
Noble Ladies 4161
Nobles of Castilian Birth 1165
Nobody 331, 4697, 1935, 4390, 4804
Nobody Breaks My Heart 1275
Nobody but Fanny 391
Nobody but Tess 3493
Nobody But You 1873, 2123
Nobody but You 2363, 2481, 4816
Nobody Cares 3841, 4312, 4453
Nobody Cheats Big Mike 4629
Nobody Do Me Like My Daddy Do Me 2235
Nobody Does It Like Me 3869, 3936
Nobody Does My Thing 578
Nobody Does That to Me 1155
Nobody Else but Me 3949
Nobody Else But You 486
Nobody Else but You 1567, 3080
Nobody Ever Asked Me 4153
Nobody Ever Died for Dear Old Rutgers 1886
Nobody Ever Pins Me Up 2187
Nobody Goes Out Anymore 4744
Nobody Holds My Hand 821
Nobody Home Cakewalk (inst.) 3193
Nobody Knows 541, 4528
No-body Knows the Answer 2765
Nobody Knows You When You're
Down and Out 478, 2796
Nobody Looks at the Man 1202
Nobody Looks at the Moon 595
Nobody Loves a Fairy 4027
Nobody Loves a Fat Man 1556
Nobody Loves Me 2291, 4293
Nobody Loves You Like I Do 2658
Nobody Makes a Pass at Me 3501
Nobody Needs a Man As Bad As That! 556
Nobody New 3626
Nobody Nobody Knows 1837
Nobody Really Do 828
Nobody Rings the Telephone 3063
Nobody Said 3908
Nobody Seems to Know 4808
Nobody Shoots No-One in Canada 414
Nobody Steps on Kafritz 1846
Nobody Tells Me How 4744
Nobody Throw Those Bull 4682
Nobody to Cry To 4678
Nobody Told Me 3187, 4018
Nobody Understands Me 4423
Nobody Wants Me 123, 3532
Nobody Was in Love with Me 4657
Nobody Will Remember Him 2820
Nobody's Chasing Me 3326, 4517
Nobody's Doin' It 3941
Nobody's Ever Gonna Love You 2961
Nobody's Ever Gonna Step on Me 109
Nobody's Family Is Going to Change 4286
Nobody's Fault 459
Nobody's Heart 601
Nobody's Heart but Mine 206
Nobody's Listening 2018
Nobody's Lookin' Out for Me But Me 3752
Nobody's on Nobody's Side 721

Nobody's Perfect 2050, 2289, 3476
Nobody's Valentine 2555
Noches Espanolas 584
Nocturne 426
Nocturne, The 3149
Nocturne 4539
Nodding Away 1462
Nodding Roses 4555
Noe Noe 4117
Noi 2513
Noises in the Street 2707, 4394, 4498
Noises in the Theatre 4827
Noisy Illinois 1613
Noisy Neighbors 4198
Nomad 2876
Non Credo 2775
Non-Stop Dancing 334
None but the Brave Deserve the Fair 4185
None but the Brave Deserves the Fair 2145
None of My Dreams 4244
None of Them's Got Anything on Me 2978
None Shall Part Us 2348, 2977
Nonsense 2408, 2782, 4742
Nonsensical Nonsense 3134
Nookie Time 1229
Noo-vo Riche, The 3268
Nora 2981
Nora Malone Call Me By Phone 4757
Nora, My Irish Rose 3882
Nora Ryan 3820
Nora the Nursemaid's Door 1256
Norah McNamara 1051
Nordland 2160
Nordraak's Farewell 4075
Noreen Mavourneen 3267
Normal, Normal, Normal 4470
Normal Thing to Do, The 3274
Normandy 3288
North American Shmear 2618
North and South 1823
North Atlantic 3201
North Dakota, South Dakota, Minnesota Moon 1397
North of 53 3222
North of the Popo 4579
North Road 2655
North, South, East or West 1243
Northchester 3654
Northfield, Minnesota 1037
Northward Ho! 1220
Northwest Mounted Police, The 1131
Norway 4487
Nose Ahead 3491
Nose with a Mind of It's Own, A 3498
Noses 2033
Nostalgia 2949
Not a Bit Like Other Girls 3998
Not a Care in the World 297, 612
Not a Day Goes By 2822
Not a Dull Moment 817
Not a Little Bit Like You 2317
Not a Proper Way to Treat a Lady 770
Not a Song at Twilight 2739
Not a Thing in the Papers Anymore! 4262
Not All but Nearly 1525
Not Allowed 4309
Not Alone 2766
Not Another Day Like This 699
Not Anymore 3656
Not As Good As Last Year 1490
Not As Simple As I Look 1458
Not at Home 140
Not Available in Stores! 1702
Not Because Your Hair Is Curly 1908
Not Cricket to Picket 3501
Not Dancing This Evening 3424
Not Enough Magic 3718
Not Even You 4621
Not Every Day Can Be a Day of Shine 2784
Not Every Day of the Week 1310
Not Fade Away 580
(Love Is) Not for a Day 1650
Not for All the Rice in China 207
Not for Him 1027
Not Getting Any Younger 1993
Not Getting Murdered Today 871
Not Guilty 1029
Not Here! Not Here! 1067
Not in Business Hours 2768
Not in the Market 273
Not in the Mood for Blues 4645
Not Like Me 1290
Not Like Other Girls 2986, 306
Not Long Ago 945
Not Love 4297
Not Me 3142, 2248
Not Me, Not Much 1342
Not Meg 957
Not Mine 1729
Not Mister Right 2477
Not Much of a Dog 2542
Not My Day 1358
Not My Problem 681, 3542
Not Now 1171, 1928
Not Now but By the Moon 93
Not Now, but Later 1888
Not Now, Not Here 278, 2777
Not of Her World 562
Not of This World 4262
Not on the Top 1279
Not on Your Nellie 989
Not on Your Tintype 3003
Not Peace but a Sword 4312
Not President, Please 1872
Not Quite Night 2536
Not Really 3085
Not Right 143
Not Since Chaplin 3171
Not Since Nineveh 2327
Not So Bad 647

Not So Fast 1557
Not So Long Ago 1885, 2645, 2789, 14
Not So Very Old 4115
Not So Young Love 3763
Not Tabu 4243
Not That I Care 1387
Not that She Was Prettier 75
Not That Sort of Person 3322
Not the Back 1407
Not the Little Boy She Knew 906
Not the Proper Way to Treat a Lady 3999
Not Today (Soliloquy) 2275
Not Today 572
Not Tomorrow 101
Not Tonight 1273
Not Too Fast and Not Too Slowly 2249
Not Too Young (To Get Married) 2427
Not What I Expected 4732
Not While I'm Around 4233
Not While I'm Eating 3204
Not with Me 1497
Not Yet 3245
Not You 3740
Not Your Cup of Tea 535
Notes 3464
Nothin' 2259, 3149, 3947
Nothin' for Nothin' 183
Nothin' Like a Picture Show 373
Nothin' Personal 456
Nothin' to No One 3004
Nothin' Up 3733
Nothing 746, 2153, 2261, 2368
Nothing As Sweet As a Sweetheart 3318
Nothing at All 145, 757, 1544, 1569
Nothing But 3515
Nothing but a Fool 2245
Nothing But a Slight Recession 2275
Nothing but Love 2734
Nothing but Nerves 1682
Nothing but Sea and Sky 1386
Nothing but Talk 2990
Nothing but the Best 4019
Nothing but the Truth 4299, 4299
Nothing But the Truth 4766
Nothing but You 1894
Nothing Can Ever Happen in New York 3968
Nothing Can Get to Me Now 167
Nothing Can Replace a Man 145, 3178
Nothing Can Stop Me Now 3731
Nothing Could Be Sweeter 1916
Nothing Counts but Love 2354
Nothing Ever Dies 3088
Nothing Ever Ever Ever Hardly Ever Troubles Me 4802
Nothing Ever Happens 1792, 2554
Nothing Ever Happens in Angels' Roost 1600
Nothing Ever Happens in Greece 1816
Nothing Ever Happens in London 1891
Nothing Ever Happens Till 2 A.M. 4522
Nothing from Nothing 3739
Nothing Happens Anymore 324
Nothing Has Changed 147
Nothing in Common 1766, 1860
Nothing Is Forever 1189
Nothing Is New in New York 521
Nothing Is Sweeter Than You 1813
Nothing Is Too Good 3074
Nothing Is Working Quite Right 2339
Nothing I've Ever Read 1730
Nothing Left but Dreams 3130
Nothing Like a Darned Good Cry 3723
Nothing Like a Friend 3427
Nothing Like a Spot of Tea 31
Nothing Like Home 1075
Nothing Like Ragtime After All 968
Nothing Like You've Ever Known 4068, 4301
Nothing Man Cannot Do 4337
Nothing Matters 1539
Nothing More 4764
Nothing More Than This 630
Nothing More to Look Forward To 2355
Nothing More—Excepting You 4666
Nothing Much to Do 3913
Nothing Naughtie in a Nightie 3407
Nothing New Beneath the Sun 1340, 1640, 1968, 2517, 3538, 4759
Nothing On To-Day 1065
Nothing Personal 4727
Nothing Really Happened 2152
Nothing Sacred 1791
Nothing Seems Right 3256
Nothing Seems Right, Oh! The World Is All Wrong 1629
Nothing So Soft Ever Happened to Me 3423
Nothing to Do (Ballaia De Rugantino) 3798
Nothing to Do but Dance 2490
Nothing to Do but Nothing 1967
Nothing to Do But Relax 601
Nothing to Do but Work 629
Nothing to Do with Love 3448
Nothing to Do with Me 754
Nothing to Lose 4297
Nothing to Wear 4808
Nothing Too Good for You, Dear 4247
Nothing Up Our Sleeve 844
Nothing Was Ever Like This 680
Nothing Will Hurt Us Again 3644
Nothing's All Good and Nothing's All Bad 2925
Nothing's Good Enough for a Good Little Girl 3400
Nothing's Left but Hollywood 2992
Nothing's Left of God 4523
Nothing's Missing 3838
Nothing's Wrong 834, 1997
Nothing, Only Love 2318
Nothin's Gonna Change 4678
Notice Me 1227, 4114
Notoriety 2122
Notre Dame de Paris 3208
Nova 755
Novellette 1928

Novels 2240
Novelty Dance 2569
November in Kenya 2288
November Song 4196
Now 699, 3760, 4067, 1319
Now (1) 2536
Now (2) 2536
Now (It's Just the Gas) 2544
Now! 2918
Now 3909, 3936, 3955, 4075
Now and Always Yours 4073
Now and Evermore 2115
Now and Then 597, 1066, 3217, 3793, 4684
Now and Then But Not All the Time 3250
'Now' Dance, The (inst.) 3299
Now, Darling, We Must Part 1540
Now Fades My Golden Love Dream 2419
Now for the First Time 1903
Now Gaily Gather for Good Cheer 526
Now Generation, The 4789
Now Give Three Cheers 2348
Now Go to Your Cabin (Finale Act I) 1800
Now He's Got a Beautiful Girl 3737
Now Here's to the 'Prentices 3588
Now His Choice We See 3771
Now Hush! 1757
Now I Am a Man 4690
Now I Believe 111
Now I Have Everything 1265
Now I Have Someone 4190
Now I Know 3168, 4815
Now I Know Your Face by Heart 3536
Now I Lay Me 1966, 2134
Now I Lay Me Down to Sleep 828, 2856, 3202, 248
Now I See It 3690
Now I'm Back in New York City 3542
Now I'm Ready for a Frau 1456
Now I'm Satisfied 3738
Now Is Here 3201
Now Is My Moment 161
Now Is the South Wind Blowing 2670
Now Is the Time 98, 1713, 1314, 2300, 4096
Now Is the Time for All Good Men 1048
Now I'se Got Some Money I'm Comin' 'Round 559
Now Isn't That Lovely? 2876
Now It's Fall 1380
Now It's Gone, Gone, Gone 2001
Now It's Hook or Me 3453
Now I've Married a Millionaire 1526
Now Let the Weeping Cease 1636
Now Listen 4477, 4530
Now, Morris 1237
Now My Season's Here 482
Now, Now, Now 3092
Now or Never 3125
Now, She Is Rich 2551
Now Take Your Seats 1080
Now That I Am Forty 3863
Now That I Have Got Them, I Don't Want Them 357
Now That I Have Springtime 4361
Now That I Know 3080
Now That I Know You 4498
(Where Are You) Now That I Need You 3444
Now That I'm Free 3036
Now That I've Got It, I Don't Want It 632
Now That I've Got My Strength 601
Now That I've Seen Her 2905
Now that My Ship Has Come In 1454
Now That We Are Alone 3151
Now That We're Married 2108, 3876
Now That Winter's Here 2097
Now the Carriages All Are Waiting 4554
Now the Day Is Done 3151
Now the Time Has Come 3371
Now the Wedding Day Is Here 1774
Now the World Begins Again 4798
Now We Are Glorified 4821
Now We Need to Cry 2318
Now We Pray 2285
Now What Would I Do If You Proved Untrue 1905
Now You Are One of the Family 2648
Now You Know 2822
Now You Leave 2312
Now You See Him, Now You Don't (inst.) 499
Now You See It Now You Don't 305
Now You See Me, Now You Don't 2437
Now You Talks Might Big in the Country 2225
Now You've Been to the Big Time 2478
Nowadays 723
Nowhere 1797
Nowhere Man 3903
Nowhere to Go but Up 3210
Nowhere to Run 146
Now's the Moment 3171
Now's the Time 1729
Now's the Time to Fall in Love 393
Ntaba Zenyuka (The Mountains Are High) 2147
Nub of the Nation, The 2134
Nubian Dance (inst.) 49
Nubian of Lemon, The 194
Nuclear Winter 4635
Nude Descending a Staircase 2145
Nude-Lewd 164
Nude Ranch 3409
Nude with Violin 1695
Nudel, Nudel, Nup, Nup! 4187
Nuevo Laredo 4318
Nuf Sed 1192
Nuggets 3415
Number 1 on Your Hit Parade 3161
Number 10 1032
Number One 682
#X9RL220 3112
Numberless Are the World's Wonders 1636
Numbers 408, 2134, 2801
Numbers (Gonna Hit Today) 2513
Nuns Song 482
Nunsense Is Habit-Forming 3211
Nurse Girls and Doctors 3205

Nurse Me 3652
Nurse, Nurse, Nurse 2701
Nursery, The (inst.) 499
Nursery 4484
Nursery Clock, The (inst.) 4150
Nursery Rhyme Dances 3981
Nursery Rhymes 737, 1515, 3486, 4014
Nurses Are We 3308, 4440
Nursey Won't You Go A-Fishing 2485
Nursie 2770
Nursie, Nursie 4178
Nut Sundae, A 4808
Nuthin' 1176
Nutmeg Insurance 180
Nuts 1112, 4219
Nuts about Nuns 3997
Nuts, He Travels with Us Nuts 3556
(I've Gone) Nuts Over You 82
Nuts to You 2163
Nymph Errant 3214
Nymphs and the Satyr 2715

O

O' Barrin'-o'-the-Door 2412
O Come My Love 3205
O, Granada 3661
O, Heart of Love 2228
O Heart of My Country 3536
O-I-L Spells Oil 598
O.K. for T.V. (You're O.K. for T.V.) 4423
O.K. Goodbye 3651
O-K-L-A-H-O-M-A 1836
O-K-M-N-X 565
O.K. Two Step 4644
O, Kaiser, My Kaiser 1522
O, Katharina! 710
O, Leo! 216
O Maid Divine 1518
O Marry Me! 3215
O! Mia Speranza 3567
O Miserere 630
O, Miss Walkaround, Come Walking
Out with Me 1474
O Mistress Mine 2290
O My Soul 3817
O Need I Speak 1624
O Negros Bahianos 3814
O.P.E.C. Maiden 3231
O Pallas Athene 3988
O Pretty Maids of France 1027
O, Promise Me 3736
O Rubber at the Swizzle Sisters 1318
O Sacrilege 4707
O, Salty Sea 2551
O Say Can You See 597
O Say Can You See! 3217
O, See the Lambkins Play 3736
O, Shed Not Blood 2910
O, Silver Moon! (Forgive! Forgive!) 1455
O Sole Mi-Whose Soul Are You? 2380
O, Spare a Daughter's Aching Heart 1165
O Stomach of Mine, We Eat! 1354
O, Time, Time! 3618
O Tixo, Tixo, Help Me 2591
O Wandering Breeze 4663
O, Warrior Grim 1165
O, Weary Wives 2977
O! Weather-Man! 4247
O, What a War 2953
O What a Wonderful World 216
O You Heavenly Body 2856
Oak and the Ash, The 1721
Oak Leaf Memorial Park 2925
Oasis of Delightful Imagining, The 2327
Oath, The 1745
Obbligato 2535
Obedian March 2887
Obedience 3651, 4408
Obey, Abide 4470
Obeying Father 343
Obituary 4309
Object Matrimony 3784
Object of My Affection, The 1813, 4799
Oblivia 3801
O'Brien Is Tryin' to Learn to Talk Hawaiian 2930
Ocarina, The 619
Occasional Flight of Fancy, An 4013
Occupations 2229
Ocean Blues 1536
Ocean of Dreams 3729
Ocean Will Never Run Dry, The 680
Ocean, the Ocean, The 4228
Oceanography and Old Astronomy 2339
Oceans of Love 4555
Ochone, When I Used to Be Young 3912
Ochos Rios 3636
O'Conner 2201
Octet 2847
Octette 1224, 3129
Octette to Bacchus 3073
Octopus Song 1242
Odalie 2580
Odd Lots, Job Lots (Opening Chorus Act III) 2794
Odds 71
Odds and Ends 649
Odds and Ends of Love, The 3210
Ode to a Friend 4609
Ode to a Key 4060
Ode to Allah 2013
Ode to an Eminent Daily 1049
Ode to Aphrodite 336
Ode to Electricity 2069
Ode to Lola 3895
Ode to Love 1358
Ode to Marcello 1786
Ode to Menelik 9
Ode to Reason 979

Ode to Steam 1402
Ode to Suicide 1865
Ode to the Bridge 2304
Ode to the One I Love 2654
Ode to the Styx 2005
Ode to the Sun 9
Ode to Victrola 3045
Ode to Willie 1978
Ode, The 2341
Odem and Khave Duet 4082
Odenemya 1279
Odle-De-O Do, 'I Do' 2669
O'Dooley's First Five O'Clock Tea 1627
Odyssey, The 1959
Oedipus at Colonus 1636
Oedipus Rex 1636, 4412
Oedipus Rex a la Jazz 4427
O'er Moonlit Waves 1926
O'er Our Love Forever Blessing 4032
O'er the Blue Waters 2334
O'er the Snow 4425
Of All Her Sex a Paragon 2760
Of Men and Violins 1680, 1681
Of Mice and Men 3224
Of the People 117
Of the People Stomp 2447, 2504
Of the Stars and Stripes I Am Dreaming 4646
Of Thee I Sing (Baby) 3225
Of V We Sing 3226
Of Viceroys Tho' We've Had 1178
Of When Stars Fall Down 2992
Off Again, On Again 4583
Off Broadway Broads 1697
Off for a Sail 2667
Off for Atlantic City 4859
Off for San Francisco Town 1524
Off Her Rocker and Roll 3741
Off Limits 4488
Off on a Weekend Cruise 3860
Off on the Great Adventure (inst.) 499
Off the Record 2068
Off Time 1980
Off to Cairo 2844
Off to Fight the Hun 414
Off to Gluckstein 1871
Off to Gottenburg 1569
Off to Greenwich Village 200
Off to Italy 2723
Off to Jail 1573
Off to Maxim's 904
Off to New York 1246
Off to Russia 1602, 3685
Off to Spain 2407
Off to the Deacon 3104
Off to the Derby 2517
Off to the Heelands 2056
Off to the Hunt 2631
Off to the Low Countree 346
Off to the Matinee 4359
Off to the Races 3070, 2641
Off to the Wedding 4359
Off to Turkey 2213
Off to Washington! 4453
Off to Wimblemere 152
Off We Go 2571, 3500, 3887
Off with the Old 2532
Off-Time 39
Offenbach 2622
Offer Yourself to Him 1441
Offering Ballet (inst.) 3630
Offerings du Jour 2651
Office Blues, The 2494
Office Hours 4153, 4603
Office Romance 2676
Office Under the Sky 1878
Officers of the 125th 3051
Official Adviser and Reminder, The 3486
Official Looney Gooney Bird Patrol Hand Clapping and Marching Song, The 2094
Official Resume 4179
Oh, Alice 4427
Oh, Allah 4657
Oh! Argentine 4063
Oh Auntie 4086
Oh Babe 560, 1418
Oh, Baby! (I Know That You Wouldn't but Gosh How I Wish That You Would) 3489
Oh, Baby! 3648
Oh, Baby, Glide 2749
Oh Baby, Won't You Please Come Home 146
Oh! Be Careful 4490
Oh Be Jolly 2603
Oh, Beautiful Land of Spain 1165
Oh, Beautiful Star (Falling Star) 3051
Oh, Bess, Oh Where's My Bess? 3541
Oh, Better Far to Live 2977
Oh Boy 580
Oh, Boy 1273
Oh, Boy! 1570
Oh Boy, Can We Deduct 3986
Oh! Boy!, What a Girl 1460
Oh Boy! What Joy We Had in Barefoot Days 487
Oh, Bright, Fair Dream 3865
Oh, Brother! 1377
Oh Brother 3231
Oh, Buddha! 1351
Oh By Jingo! (Oh By Gee You're the Only Girl for Me) 2489
Oh! Calcutta! 3233
Oh, Captain! My Captain! 2433
Oh, Catch Me Mr. Harris, 'Cause I'm Falling for You! 1256
Oh, Cecelia 3627
Oh, Charles 2388
Oh, Cheerily Soundeth the Huntsman's Horn 3736
Oh Come to the Ball 3038
Oh, Comrades 3586
Oh Dad 2276

Oh Daddy! 3137
Oh Daddy Dear 3418
Oh, Daddy, Please 3230
Oh! Darling 3903
Oh Day in June! 3043
Oh, De Lawd Shake De Heaven 3541
Oh, Dear! 1262
Oh Dear! 3595
Oh Dearie 560
Oh Dem Golden Slippers 2415
Oh, Diogenes 514
Oh Do Step the Two-Step 3996
Oh, Doctor 627, 1538
Oh Doctor, Doctor 2816
Oh, Doctor Koo-ay 1513
Oh, Donna Clara 4730
Oh Dr. Sternroyd 2756
Oh, Fabulous One in Your Ivory Tower 2386
Oh Fascinating Night 4228
Oh, Father Don't Sell 3592
Oh, Fatherland (Maxim's) 2839
Oh, Fifth Avenue 4359
Oh Fish in the Sea 2153
Oh, Foot 3657
Oh, For That Country Air 345
Oh, For the Life of a Bootlegger's Wife 4209
Oh, For the Life of a Chorus Girl 1824
Oh, for the Life of a Cowboy 3968
Oh, Freedom! 2203
Oh, Fudge 3129
Oh, Gala Day, Red-Letter Day 711
Oh Gee 3628
Oh, Gee! 2217
Oh, Gee, It's Great to Be Great 3350
Oh Gee! Oh Gosh! 1345
Oh! Gee, Oh! Gosh, Oh! Golly, I'm in Love 4817
Oh Gee! Oh Gosh! Oh Golly! I'm in Love 4816
Oh Gee! Oh Joy! 3766
Oh, Give Me the Good Old Days 3501
Oh Glorious Sun 3786
Oh, Go Away 4285
Oh God 3418
Oh God, I'm Thirty 426
Oh, Goddess 1768
Oh, Gosh 1929
Oh Grand Riviera 2334
Oh Great God of Power 1717
Oh, Gustave! 2854
Oh Happy Day 3987
Oh, Happy Day 2484, 2233
Oh, Happy We 630
Oh, Harold 3847
Oh, Heart of Mine 1852
Oh, Heavenly Salvation 369
Oh, Heigh-Ho! 4473
Oh, Help! 3882
Oh, Henry 4226
Oh, Ho, in the Morning 2113
Oh, Honey, My Honey 2500
Oh How Easy to Be Scornful 3469
Oh, How Happy We'll Be 4532
Oh How He Plays His Ukulele 495
Oh, How I Adore Your Name 4384
Oh, How I Could Go for You 4058
Oh! How I Hate to Get Up in the Morning 789, 4340, 4770
Oh How I Hate to Get Up in the Morning 4812
Oh! How I Hate Women 642
Oh, How I Long for Someone! 1962
Oh How I Long to Belong to You 4267
Oh How I Love Her Family 968
Oh, How I Love My Teacher 2498
Oh, How I Love You 4629
Oh How I Loved Him 4767
Oh-How-I-Miss-You Blues 4532
Oh, How I've Waited for You 605
Oh How Near and Yet So Far 2761
Oh, How She Can Dance 487, 3962
Oh, How She Can Sing 4813
Oh, How She Could Yacki, Hacki, Wicki, Wacki, Woo 2853
Oh, How that Baby Could Baby Me 2888
Oh, How That German Could Love 1523
Oh, How That Man Can Love 1134
Oh How That Taxi Got on My Nerves 2538, 2668
Oh, How the Girls Adore Me 3680
Oh, How Unfortunate You Mortals Be 67
Oh! How Warm It Is Today 1527
Oh! How We Love our Alma Mater 3659
Oh, How We Love You, Mrs. Cornwall 3764
Oh! Hugh Ho! 1687
Oh I Am a Fork 3651
Oh I Can't Sit Down 3541
Oh I Love Everything Dream Ballet 99
Oh, I Love the Jolly Rattle 2977
Oh! I Must Go Home Tonight 353
Oh, I Say! 4302
Oh I Want to Be Good but My Eyes Won't Let Me 1334
Oh, I Want to Be the Mayor 2790
Oh! If You Were a Girl 1561
Oh! I'll Be Good 4596
Oh! I'll Greet Him 3049
Oh Innocent Young Thing 2261
Oh, Is There Not One Maiden Breast 2348
Oh, Isn't It Fine to Be Robbers 2029
Oh, It Looks Like Rain 418
Oh, It Must Be Fun 3326
Oh, It Used to Be 1864
Oh, It's Rah, Rah, Rah 2724
Oh, Joe! 1250
Oh Joe, with Your Fiddle and Bow 1532
Oh, John 132
Oh, Johnny 3239
Oh Johnny, Oh Johnny, Oh! 1334
Oh! Joseph 2666
Oh, Joy 2493
Oh Joy 4716
Oh, Joy! Oh, Bliss! (A Sickening Sadness Sits on Me) 1768

Oh! K-Y Chorale (or, Beyond the Labia Majora) 3901
Oh, Kay! 3243
Oh, Kitty 3883
Oh La La 395
Oh, La! La! 3024
Oh, La La 3028
Oh La La Boom Boom 3756
Oh, Lady 202, 1481, 327
Oh, Lady, Be Good! 3709
Oh, Lady! Lady! 3245
Oh Lady, Be Good! 2376
Oh Lars! 194
Oh! Leonard! 4149
Oh, Lonely One 651
Oh, Look! 3246
Oh, Look at Me! 3818
Oh Lord 2285
Oh, Lord Could She Go 647
Oh, Love, Airy Like, Fairy Like 694
Oh! Mabel Behave 2857
Oh Maiden 4713
Oh, Mama 3248
Oh Mama, Am I in Love 4769
Oh Man 2478
Oh, Marie! 2481
Oh! Marie 346
Oh Marie 4801
Oh, Marjorie 1295
Oh Married Life 1555
Oh, Mary 1923
Oh Mary Don't You Weep 3987
Oh Me! Oh My! 3249
Oh Me! Oh My! (Oh You) 4491
Oh, Mein Liebchen 1456
Oh Mio Snow White! 2243
Oh, Mister Dream Man 4655
Oh, Mister Sun 4434
Oh, Mr. Brown 954
Oh, Mr. Chamberlain 675
Oh Mr. Harris You're a Naughty, Naughty Man! 1256
Oh! Mr. Hays 1415
Oh, Mr. Jupiter 4012
Oh! Mr. Moon 1640
Oh Mr. Moon You're Full Tonight 4215
Oh, Mr. Postman 4248
Oh, Mr. Registrar! 3313
Oh, Mrs. Lynde! 148
Oh Mummy Darling 2153
Oh, My! 1851
Oh, My Age 3876
Oh My Darling 2407
Oh My Darling Tillie 93
Oh, My Dear 3250, 555
Oh My Goodness, Here's the Nobility! 1905
Oh, My Rose 3059
Oh, My Yes 1136
Oh! Nina 3649
Oh, No 1834
Oh! No Regular Wits 762
Oh, Oh, Baby 283
Oh, Oh Columbus 487
Oh Oh Could It Be That I'm an Oh No Tango, The 2477
Oh! Oh! Delphine 3251
Oh-Oh-Lady 4257
Oh! Oh! Oh! 1561
Oh, Oh, Oh 3651
Oh, Oh, Oh, O'Sullivan 3831
Oh, Papa 1584, 2184
Oh Pauline 1565
Oh, Peggy 202
Oh! Pity Me! 1351
Oh Pity Poor Old Solomon 904
Oh, Pity the Man 3571
Oh Please 4270
Oh, Please My Dear Miss Tropics 762
Oh Pom-Pom-Pom-Pompadour! 2666
Oh Precious Thought 2145
Oh, Pretty Woman 3695
Oh, Professor! 4208
Oh Promise Me You'll Write to Him Today 627
Oh Rash Muezzin 49
Oh, Romeo! 4359
Oh, Rosalie 2760
Oh! Sam 2789
Oh Say, Can You See? 1233
Oh, Say No More 2836
Oh Say, Oh Sue! 3662
Oh, Senor, Pray 4430
Oh Setting Sun 1178
Oh Shrine of Psyche 3951
Oh! Silvery Moon 1243
Oh, Sky, Goodbye 3035
Oh So Bad 4016
Oh, So Gently 4115
Oh So Lovely 3980
Oh, So Nice 4443
Oh So Soon 1921
Oh Sonny 357
Oh, Star of Hope 3883
Oh, Strange Situation 4554
Oh, Sun 4537
Oh Sunlight of No Light 1636
Oh, Susanna 4149
Oh, Susannah 3989
Oh! Teach Me How to Kiss, Dear 357
Oh, Tell Me If with Your Heart 4188
Oh, Tender Remembrance 1540
Oh, That Beautiful Rag 1550, 2232, 4521
Oh That Shimmy! 3258
Oh That We Two Were Maying 1626
Oh! That Yankiana Rag 2892
Oh the Deuce, What's the Use 2155
Oh, the Heat and the Skeet! 1095
Oh! The Last Rose of Summer 4813
Oh, the Men 1307
Oh, the Music Is Sublime 3592

Oh, The Paying Guests 4713
Oh, the Picnic at Manassas 1474
Oh, the Regatta 4479
Oh, the Rio Grande (Cowboy Song) 2228
Oh, the Shame 2887
Oh, the Things They Put in the Papers Now-a-Days 4649
Oh, the Women 3020
Oh! the World Is All Wrong 3256
Oh, the World of Peace 1083
Oh, Theobold, Oh, Elmer 4170
Oh, This Is a Happy Day 1496
Oh, This Is Such a Lovely War 4178
Oh, This Love! 3362
Oh, Those Americans 3800
Oh, Those Boys! 4649
Oh, Those Days 2696
Oh, Those Eyes 1469
Oh Those Thirties 1227
Oh! Thou Art Fair, My Love 2213
Oh, to Be a Movie Star 170
Oh to Be Home Again 4340
Oh, Uncle 3258
Oh, Up! It's Up! 2670
Oh, Waiter 4227
Oh Wasn't It Lovely? 2833
Oh, We Know 4012
Oh! What a Ball! 2357
Oh, What a Beautiful Mornin' 3263
Oh, What a Beautiful Morning 1746
Oh, What a Bump! 4201
Oh What a Circus 1211
Oh What a Delight to Be Dancing 2906
Oh, What a Dream 2465
Oh, What a Filthy Night Court 919
Oh What a Fund of Joy 1905
Oh, What a Girl! 3258
Oh, What a Girl 4651
Oh, What a Happy Day 1378
Oh What a Happy Fisherman Am I 1155
Oh, What a Knight! (The Best Knight of My Life) 3587
Oh! What a Little Whopper 2549
Oh, What a Lovely Day 3622
Oh, What a Lovely Dream 671
Oh, What a Lovely Princess 3378
Oh What a Lovely War (Oh It's a Lovely War) 3259
Oh, What a Man 1617
Oh What a Man 4621
Oh What a Moanin' Man 638
Oh, What a Night for a Party 1423
Oh, What a Night to Spoon 2795
Oh, What a Performance! 3760
Oh! What a Pity! 30
Oh, What a Playmate You Could Make 458
Oh, What a Pretty Pair of Lovers 2287
Oh! What a Siege That Was 2659
Oh, What a Time We Had 159
Oh, What a Wedding 3197
Oh, What a Wonderful Plan 2785
Oh What an Island 3788
Oh, What Bridal Song 4615
Oh What Fools We Mortals Be 2534
Oh, What Is a Woman's Duty? 3588
Oh! What Is the Matter? 104
Oh, What She Hangs Out She Hangs Out in Our Alley 1485
Oh, What Will Be the End of It? 1682
Oh, What Will Mother Say? 453
Oh, What You Can Do to Me 2976
Oh What's the Use? 2145
Oh, What's the Use? 2213
Oh, What's the Use 4508
Oh, Why Am I So Happy? 4149
Oh Why, Oh Why, Oh Why 277
Oh, William Morris 2477
Oh Woe Is Me-oh 2293
Oh Woman in Days of Romance 3857
Oh, Won't You Shed a Little Tear for Me? 3774
Oh, World 2785
Oh, Yes! Oh, Yes! 2500
Oh You! 1312
Oh! You 3877
Oh You Bear Cut Rag 3545
Oh! You Beautiful Doll 662, 2231
Oh, You Beautiful Doll 3681, 4799
Oh, You Beautiful Person! 3923
Oh, You Beautiful Spring 3679
Oh! You Bold Bad Men 1455
Oh You Chicago, Oh You New York 2261
Oh, You Circus Days 1738
Oh! You Coon 800
Oh! You Dream 3395
Oh, You Girls! 1911
Oh! You Girls! 2334
Oh, You John 965
Oh You John 2854
Oh! You Kewpie Kandy Doll 2492
Oh, You Lady! 3323
Oh You Lovely Ladies 1530
Oh, You Major Scales 2549
Oh, You Men 3738
Oh, You Silv'ry Bells (Jingle Bells) 1531
Oh, You Summertime Romeo! 4203
Oh! You Sweet Sweet Day 822
Oh, You Sweeties 1065
Oh You Vampire Girls 3402
Oh, You Wonderful Boy 1478
Oh, You Wonderful Girl 2525
Oh You, You Darling! 2886
Oh You're a Wonderful Person 4362
O'Hara 1616
O'Hara See Saw 1051
Ohh! That Kiss 2423
Ohhh! Ahhh! 1856
Ohio 4734
Ohio Afternoon 3261
O'Houlihan 1588
Ohrbach's, Bloomingdale's, Best and Saks 798
Oisgetzaychnet (Out of This World) 4863

Oka Saka Circus 189
Okay for Sound 4142
Okay, I'll Marry You 83
Okay, Mister Major 347
Okey-Doke 3165
Oklahoma 3263
Oklahoma Hills 4740
"Oklahoma medley" 3018
Ol Pease Puddin' 1497
Ol' Man River 2204, 2372, 1984, 3949
Ola in Her Little Gondola 293
Olaf, You Ought-a-Hear Olaf Laff 710
Olayithi (It's All Right) 3836
Olcott's Home Song 2875
Olcott's Lullaby 3759
Old Are Getting Younger Every Day, The 3087
Old Army Game, The 3166
Old Ballet Days, The 3681
Old Barn Dance, The 2576, 3531
Old Barn Floor, The 1776
Old Bill Baker (Undertaker) 4555
Old Black Crow, The 1758, 2795
Old Black Joe 3513
Old Black Joe and Uncle Tom (Old Black Joe and Uncle Tom) 3963
Old Blue Paradise 473
Old Board Walk, The 591
Old Book Cooker, The 3066
Old Boy Neutral 4555
Old Brudder Gum 4149
Old Buck and Wing, The 1563
Old Camp Chef, The 1632
Old Cape Cod 4264
Old Chateau, The 353
Old City Boy at Heart, A 2064
Old Clarinet, The 3237
Old Clothes Little League 2224
Old College Avenue 2470
Old Days, The 2776, 4577
Old Deuteronomy 678
Old Devil Moon 1278
Old Doctor Budd 335
Old Dog Trey 4149
Old Dope Peddler, The 4412
Old Eight Ten, The 272
Old English Cake Walk, The 3856
Old English Cake Walk 3857
Old Enough to Know Better 583
Old Enough to Love 603, 1013, 4709
Old Enough to Marry 2669
Old Established Firm 3617
Old Fashioned 389
Old Fashioned Ballet 3130
Old Fashioned Boy 700
Old Fashioned Buggy Ride, An 4756
Old Fashioned Cake Walk 4104
Old-Fashioned Chase, An 4102
Old Fashioned Christmas, An 4155
Old Fashioned Dances 1922
Old Fashioned Drama, The 2907
Old Fashioned Flowers 3754
Old-Fashioned Garden 1921
Old Fashioned Girl 249, 487, 1567
Old-Fashioned Girl (Boy), An 2366
Old-Fashioned Girl, An 1446
Old Fashioned Girl, An 1490, 3246
Old-Fashioned Girls 1065
Old-Fashioned Glimmer in Your Eye, An 911
Old Fashioned Gown 3821
Old-Fashioned Groom and an Up-To-Date Bride, An 3087
Old Fashioned Husband 1158
Old Fashioned Irish Stew 2691
Old-Fashioned Love 3808
Old Fashioned Man Is Hard to Find, An 1584
Old Fashioned Melody 2800
Old Fashioned Mother, The 4239
Old Fashioned Mothers 145
Old Fashioned Rag 1823
Old-Fashioned Rose 554
Old Fashioned Rose, An 250
Old Fashioned Song 3960, 1273
Old Fashioned Songs 3437
Old Fashioned Sweetheart 2870
Old Fashioned Theatre 2032
Old Fashioned Tin Types 200
Old Fashioned Tune 4237
Old-Fashioned Waltz 2259
Old Fashioned Waltz 1426
Old-Fashioned Waltz, The 1923
Old Fashioned Wedding 153, 289
Old-Fashioned Wife, An 3230
Old Father Time 2315
Old Flag Never Touched the Ground, The 3945
Old Flame Never Dies, An 4569
Old Flames 3712
Old Folks, The 2188
Old Folks 3900
Old Folks at Home, The 1689, 3671
Old Folks at Home 4149
Old Friend 1737, 2074, 4798, 3221
Old Friends 4067, 1900, 2822
Old Gals 3641
Old Gavotte, The 3453
Old Gentlemen's Jazz 4382
Old Ghosts for Ancient Castles, Extended Ltd. 924
Old Glory 669, 2209, 1562, 1647
Old Gray Owl, The 3144
Old Gumbie Cat, The 678
Old Habits Die Hard 1804
Old Heidelberg 4188
Old Home Town 4148
Old Home Week 3443
Old Home Week in Alabama 1731
Old Is In 2230
Old Is Not in Years 1770
Old Jay Bird, The 4201
Old Jitterbug 2301

Old Job Man 2470
Old John Barleycorn 3056
Old John Henry 2225
Old Kentucky Blues 1499
Old Kentucky Home 2852
Old King Cole 764
Old King Lear 496
Old Kitchen Sink, The 1168
Old Lady in the Shoe 203
Old Lake Trail, The 2308
Old Landmark 4534
Old Landmark, The 166
Old Long John 4384
Old Love and Brand New Love 2817
Old Love Is the True Love, The 4360
Old Maid, An 2375
Old Maid 3294
Old Maids Are Willing to Please 104
Old Man 259, 2852, 2787
Old Man, An 4481
Old Man Blues 4091
Old Man Danube 2755
Old Man in the Moon 2950
Old Man Manhattan 4044
Old Man Methuselah 628
Old Man Says to the Old Woman, The 2017
Old Man Shea 3882
Old Man Shouldn't Be Born, An 3559
Old Man Subway 1932
Old Man's Darling, An 1587
Old Man's Darling, Young Man's Slave 2597
Old Masters' Fox Trot 4037
Old McGinty Place, The 2439
Old Melodies 4283
Old Men Should Say Goodbye 496
Old Military Canal, The 1721
Old Miss 3124
Old Mister Fate 962
Old Mother Goose 3786
Old Mother Nature 4177
Old Movies 1082, 407
Old Music Masters 764
Old New England Home 3323
Old New York 1922
Old Noblesse, The 1111, 4115
Old Oak Tree, The 671
Old Oaken Bucket with Love 1823
Old Operas in a New Way
(Opera Medley) 4603
Old Pal of Mine 1502
Old Park Bench, The 2301
Old People 2961
Old Pete Is in the City 2344
Old Pied Piper, The 1745
Old Plantation 875, 885
Old Plantation Ball 3982
Old Possum's Book of Practical Cats 678
Old Prayer, An 2992
Old Rabbit Hole, The 3817
Old Rameses 1515
Old Rat Mort, The 870
Old Red Gate, The 2691
Old Reliable Jokes 2765
Old Rhineland, The 141
Old Rip Was a Flip 4704
Old Sayin's 2268
Old Ship of Zion 4460
Old Soft Shoe, The 2294, 4362
Old Soldiers Never Die 3259
Old Song, The 3445
Old Songs 1096
Old Testament, The 1769
Old Things 2173
Old-Time Ball, The 1738
Old Time Blues 3614
Old Time Swing 4253
Old-Time Tune, An 3144
Old Timer 1931
Old Timer, An 2155
Old Times, Good Times 3515
Old Town Band, The 4818
Old Town Hall, The 3025
Old Tunes 1873
Old Veterans Jubilee 2013
Old Vienna 4486
Old Virginia Reel, The 659
Old Waltz, The 639
Old War Horse, The 2502
Old Ways 4172
Old Ways Are the Best Ways 2998
Old White Tom 1319
Old Woman Who Lived in a Shoe, The 2974
Old World Charm 3551
Old World Melody, An 2571
Old Wound, An 949
Old Yahoo Step, The 2483
Old Yankee Land for Me 1246
Olde Books 2650
Olden Days, The 4365
Older and Wiser 550, 607
Older They Are the Harder They Fall, The 2373
Oldest Au Pairs in the Business, The 1887
Oldest Established, The 1706
Oldest Trick in the World, The 1081
Ole King Cole 2098
Ole Man River Is Lonely Now 2151
Ole Ole 1112
Ole Soft Core 1695
Olga 4517
Olga (Come Back to the Volga) 2788
Olga from the Volga 4553
Olive, An 1267
Olive Oil 758
Olive Tree, The 2327
Oliver 2495
Oliver! 3271
Oliver Tambo 4438
Oliver Twist 3271
Olly, Cholly, Wally (I'm Dolly) 621
Olympian Dance, The 2534

Olympian Glide, The 2696
Olympian Octet 2498
Olympics, The (The Greeks Had a Word for It) (dance) 1745
Olympics 3858
Olympics '36 2949
Olympus Is a Lonely Town 3272
Olympus 7-000 3273
Om Mane Padme 1717
Om Mani Padme Hum 3913
Omar Khayyam 1557, 2494, 3397
Omar Khayyam Was Right 780
Ombo 1710
Omen Bird (Teru, Teru), The 2679
Omi Omai 2851
Omnibus 2366
On a Beautiful Beach 4037
On a Beautiful Distant Island 1295
On a Beautiful Evening 4427
On a Chinese Honeymoon 2209
On a Christmas Night 1130
On a Clear Day You Can See Forever 3274
On a Day Like This 2268
On a Day Such As This 615
On a Desert Island with the One You Love 3422
On a Desert Island with Thee 834
On a Desert Island with You 4001
On a Holiday 1337, 3723
On a Hundred Different Ships 2730
On a January Morning (in Zummersetscheer) 4404
On a Little Farm in Normandie 231, 2274
On a Little Journey in Springtime with You 464
On a Modern Wedding Day 3397
On a Moonlight Night 541, 1404, 4208
On a Paper and a Comb 331
On a Pay Night Evening 4723
On a Pony for Two 4271
On a Pullman Honeymoon 2869
On a Roof in Manhattan 1225
On a Saturday Afternoon 379
On a Scale of One to Ten 4635
On a Ship with Fifty Oars 4615
On a Shoestring 3940
On a Side Street 4240
On a Slow Boat to China 3444
On a South Sea Isle 4182
On a Starlight Night 3747
On a Steamer Coming Over 879
On a Sunday By the Sea 2205
On a Sunday by the Sea 1886
On a Train 147
On a Train at Night 1402
On a Wonderful Day Like Today 1711
On Account of Because 1415
On Account of I Love You 3168
On an Automobile Honeymoon 1731
On an Island Surrounded by Girls 2853
On an Island with You 2070
On and Off the Stage 1613
On and On and On 2444
On Any Street 4177
On Atlantic Beach 1208
On Broadway 1964, 4031
On Broadway and in Dahomey 2111
On Broadway at Night 4382
On Chestnut Street 830
On Cleopatra's Wedding Day 4724
On Cupid's Green 3985
On Double Fifth Avenue 2380
On Dreamy Bay 1524
On Fifth Avenue 3434
On Fifth Avenue-The Ziegfeld Follies Sextette 4814
On Guard 4579
On Hawaiian Shores 765
On Her Own 2284
On It Goes 705
On Lalawana's Shore 2035
On Leave for Love 901
On Living 3162
On Love Alone 1680
On Mahaneyheya 3368
On Monday Wear a Blue One 1629, 3256
On My Mind the Whole Night Long 1483
On My Nude Ranch with You 1874
On My Nuptial Day 4559
On My Own 363, 2442, 3124, 3209, 4798
On My Private Telephone 3962
On My Way 1619
On My Wedding Day 912
On My Yacht 2287
On, On, On 2659
On One Summer Night 1192
On Our Honeymoon 3540
On Our Little Merry-Go-Round 1335
On Our Own 3320
On Our Way to Spain 539
On Parade 904, 3365, 4250, 3200
On Parchment This with Grey Goose Quill 1388
On Patrol in No Man's Land 3963
On Revient de Chantilly 3618
On Robinson Crusoe Isle 3782
On Stage 4480
On Such a Beautiful Night 292
On Such a Night 2950
On Such a Night As This 2535, 1467
On Sunday Morning 632, 1558
On Ten Square Miles by the Potomac River 4004
On That Day 161
On That Day of Days 2583
On That Matter, No One Budges 3225
On That Old Production Line 2653
On the Amazon 2976
On the Avenue 1665, 4687
On the Balcony of the Casa Rosada 1211
On the Banks of the Bronx 168
On the Banks of the Old Raritan 1886
On the Battlefield for My Lord 4460
On the Beach 2364, 3236
On the Beach at Narragansett 357

On the Beaches 827
On the Beat 389
On the Blue Danube's Bank 3592
On the Boardwalk 2270, 4203
On the Border Line 4426
On the Bosom of the Sleepy Nile 208
On the Bosphorus 277
On the Boulevard 172, 969, 1602
(On the B, on the Bou) On the Boulevard 2335
On the Boulevard 4681
On the Brim of Her Old Fashioned Bonnet 3478
On the Brim of Her Old-Fashioned Bonnet 4033
On the Campus 1628
On the Charts 4089
On the Checkerboard of Time 2243
On the Choo Choo Cars 2711
On the Congo 3701
On the Corner of the Rue Cambon 798
On the Day I Lost My Novel 3195
On the Day I Marry 1199
On the Day When the World Goes Boom 1924
On the Dial 1682
On the Edge 533
On the Farm 3113, 3996
On the Fourth Day of July 3644
On the Gay Luneta 3945
On the Go 2964
On the Golden Trail 3650
On the Good Ship Whipoorwill 1084
On the Grand Old Sands 4801
On the Great White Way 2122
On the Ground at Last 1684
On the Heights of Glentann 1178
On the Honeymoon Express (On That Spoony, Spoony Honeymoon Express) 1963
On the Lake (The New Year Festival) 767
On the Levee 2302
On the Levee Along Broadway 1735
On the Level with You 2337
On the Level You're a Little Devil, but I'll Soon Make an Angel of You 3402
On the Lighter Side 2483
On the Links 1459
On the Lovely Lagoon 2854
On the Map 1161
On the Mississippi 1738, 3562, 4655
On the Moon 4073
On the Moonlit Swanee 2557
On the Mountain 396
On the Music 3463
On the Old See Saw 3855
On the Other Hand 2201, 3103
On the Other Side of the Counter 3221
On the Other Side of the Wall 252
On the Phone 1095
On the Quiet 4589
On the Radio 827
On the Relative Merits of Education and Experience 1500
On the Rialto 3882
On the Right Track 3506
On the River 2417
On the River Nile 1308
On the Riviera 577, 3312
On the Road 1371, 2657
On the Road that Leads to You 2934
On the Road to Calais 1823, 3985
On the Road to Monterey 3676
On the Road Together 496
On the Road with the Roadrunners 1099
On the Rue Macabre 1119
On the Run (inst.) 3739
On the S.S. Bernard Cohn 3274
On the Sands By the Sea 2153
On the Sands of Wah-ki-ki 2891
On the Screen 1829
On the Seashore By the Sea 348
On the Seventh Day He Rested 3046
On the Shimmering Glimmering Nile 824
On the Shore at Le Lei Wi 4555
On the Shores of Sheepshead Bay 1783
On the Showboat 1390
On the Side 2563, 2982
On the Side of the Angels 1280
On the Stage 252, 1110, 1927
On the Steps of the Palace 2143
On the Street 36
On the Street Where You Live 3038
On the Sunny Side of the Street 3905, 2140, 4197
On the Thomas J. Muldoon 2201
On the Track 1896, 4119
On the Trail of Her Wedding Gown 683
On the 20th Century 3279
On the Up and Up 1113
On the Via Veneto 2551
On the Washington Train 2691
On the Weekend 3479
On the Willows 1595
On the Wings of Romance 2443
On the Winning Side 3871
On the Z-R-3 391
On This Night of a Thousand Stars 1211
On This Rock 2134
On This Wedding Day 615
On Through the Night 2747
On Time 2653
On to Africa 2813
On to Chicago 2500
On to Conquer 3424
On to Glory 4014
On to Hollywood 1965
On to Paris 2715
On to Petrograd 1309
On to Pittsburgh 4732
On to the Buffet 1757
On to Victory 1388, 2373, 3591
On Top 495
On Top of the World 958
On Trial for My Life 2472
On Wings of Doubt 4056

On with the Dance 968, 1446, 2976, 3532, 3819
On with the Dance (inst.) 3980
On with the Game 2308
On with the New 4232
On with the Rehearsal 531
On with the Show 3561, 1918
On Your Mark 1140
On Your Toes 3283
Once 1419, 3914, 4300
Once a Fisherman Went to Sea 4509
Once a Year Day 3351
Once and Future King, The 623
Once Day We Dance 4693
Once Every Four Years 2983
Once Excess Baggage 4165
Once He's In 2240
Once I Fall 664
Once I Wondered 190
Once I Wore Ribbons Here 4048
Once I've Got My Cane 1842
Once in a Blue Moon 2522, 3258, 4150
Once in a Glade 2861
Once in a Lifetime 520, 1134, 2387, 2610, 1597, 4160
Once in a While 431, 3032, 2745
Once-in-a-While 3699
Once in a While 3742, 4010
Once in Love with Amy 3444, 4332, 4652
Once in September 3163
Once in the Highlands 530
Once in 2.7 Years 2075
Once Is Enough 821
Once Is Not Enough 2439
Once It Was Different 3670
Once Knew a Fella 1029
Once More 1509
Once More to Dream 2408
Once, Only Once 1761
Once the Man You Laughed At 2016
Once There Was a Russian 3526
Once There Were Two of Us 1928
Once Too Often 3049
Once Upon a Dream 2198
Once Upon a Long Ago 1893
Once Upon a Morning (sketch) 4498
Once Upon a Time 64, 307, 602, 766, 780, 1203
Once Upon a Time (Your Eyes Are Blue) 1422
Once Upon a Time 1762, 4108
Once Upon a Time (The Magic Melody) 2684
Once Upon a Time 2887, 2907, 3013, 3292, 3371, 1426, 3806, 4053, 3454
Once Upon a Time Is Always 3844
Once Upon a Time Today 619
Once Upon Another Time 2553
Once Upon My Life 3576
Once Upon No Particular Time (Opening) 3880
Once Upon the Natchez Trace 3733
Once You Lose Your Heart 2798
Once You've Had a Little Taste 2731
Once You've Seen a Rainbow 1638
Once You've Seen Everything 1958
One 746, 1384
One a Day 4709
One Alone 1027
One and All 1023
One and One 626
One and One Are Two 3682
One and Only 3424
One and Only Person in the World, The 1662
One and Twenty 2278
One at a Time 757
One Baby 2253
One Beating a Day 3428
One Big Happy Family 3653, 3956
One Big Union for Two 3501
One Blink of an Eye 2651
One Boy 602
One Boy (One Girl) 607
One Boy's Enough for Me 4276
One Brick at a Time 305
One Brief Moment 4142
One By One 287
One Candle 3944
One Cell 4011
One Chance 2305
One Cuff Link 456
One Dam Thing After Another 3291
One Day 2328, 3117
One Day at a Time 916, 4192, 4516
One Day in May 1174
One Day It Will Come to Pass 3445
One Day More 2442
One Day, 'Neath an Apple Tree Laden 4554
One Day, One Day, Congotay 2719
One Day the Synic of This Town 1905
One Does Not Smile 1369
One Drop Alone 3724
One Extraordinary Thing 1660
One Family 753
One Fellow's Joy Is Another Fellow's Woe 4559
One Fine Day 338
One Finger, Keep Moving 520
One Flag 181
One Flower Grows Alone in Your Garden 1027
One Flower That Blooms for You 953
One Foot In 1857
One Foot, Other Foot 85
One for All 3584
One for Another 1599
One for the Road 1385
One Fragment of a Moment 949
One Friend 4073
One Giant Step 607
One Girl 1837, 3008
One Girl, The 3150, 3650, 4425
One Girl Too Many 3857
One Glourie 1503
One Good Friend 1747
One Good Friend's Enough 4289
One Good Man Gone Wrong 1027
One Good Time 765

One Hallowe'en 167
One Hand, One Heart 4625
One Hand Tied Behind My Back 3182
One Heart 3907
One Helluva Party 1169
One Hippopotami 1832
One Hour Ahead of the Posse 673, 1892
One Hour Mama 1425
One Hour Sweetheart, with You 1266
One Hundred and Fifteen 4591
110 in the Shade 3294
One Hundred Easy Ways 4734
One Hundred Percent Cockeyed 4252
One Hundred Virgins 3763
One Hundred Women in One 3493
One I Love, The 2761, 1822
One I Love the Best Gave that to Me 3883
One I Love the Other I Abhor 2917
One I Love, Two I Love 2574
One I Need, The 2705
One-I-Want-Doesn't-Want-Me Blues, The 3080
One I'm Looking For, The 632, 905, 4320
One in a Million 117, 680, 1207, 2217
One in a Million to Me 199
One in My Position 1046
One in the Game of Love 93
One in the World, The 3828
One in the World for Me 606
One Indispensable Man, The 2344
One Is a Lonely Number 596, 961
One Kind of Man 2478
One Kind Word 2268
One Kiss 843
One Kiss (Is Waiting for One Man) 3117
One Kiss 3295
One Kiss Is Waiting for One Man 3117
One Last Bop 1149
One Last Fling 2057, 3846
One Last Kiss 602, 607
One Last Love Song 2755
One Last Waltz (One More Waltz) 1250
One Leg Is Better Than Two 3485
One Less Bell to Answer 261
One Life to Live 2386
One Little Baby 2973
One Little Boy 4155
One Little Boy Had Money 764, 1967
One Little Brick at a Time 2583
One Little Girl 1849, 2387, 3258, 4651
One Little Girl I Prize, The 1026
One Little Smile 568
One Little, Sweet Little Girl 3220
One Little Taste 3456
One Little WAC 7, 3444
One Little Wink 3562
One Little World Apart 519
One Little Year 1634
One Long Last Look 4060
One Look, One Word 3658
One Lost Weekend 2702
One Love 1135, 1667
One Loves at Sight 184
One Man 2134, 3389, 3636, 3888, 3953
One Man Ain't Quite Enough 2000
One Man Band 695
One Man Girl 2976
One Man I Need, The 3152
One Man Is Like Another 152
One Man Woman 3772
One Man's Death Is Another Man's Living 1284
One Misty, Moisty Morning 2134
One Moment Alone 672
One Moment of Paradise 3369
One Monkey Don't Stop No Show 4127
One More Angel in Heaven 2242
One More Chance 753, 2692
One More Dance 3014
One More Day 298, 1700, 198
One More for the Last One 2626
One More Kiss 4399, 1329
One More Lullabye 1104
One More Picture Please 1103
One More Romance 4403
One More Samba 4829
One More Step 952
One More Study 3661
One More Time 430, 1045, 2230, 4089
One More Walk Around the Garden 652
One Mother Each 837
One Never Knows 3622
One Nice Little Million 2722
One Night 1427, 3555, 4620
One Night Ago 4798
One Night in Bangkok 721
One Night in the Rain 3069
One Night of Love 3150
One Night, One Waltz, One Girl 1626
One Night Only 1103, 1123
One Night Stands, The 3348
One Note 2950
One O' Clock 2485
One O'Clock in the Morning 3665
One of a Great Big Family 2307
One of a Kind 167, 602, 3576
One of My Own Hussars 2126
One of the Boys 1538, 2282, 3856, 3857, 4343, 4360, 4727
One of the Crowd 3221
One of the Good Guys 784
One of the Lucky Ones 4732
One of the Ruins of France 4421
One of the Smart Ones 1605
One of the Things I Don't Profess to Know 4795
One of Them 572
One of These Fine Days 3990
One of Those Days 411
One of Those Moments (Just for the Moment) 2014
One of Those Windows 3489
One of Us 1282, 1985, 4168

One of Us Is a Thief 51
One of Us Lucky Listeners Out Here 119
One of Us Should Be Two 376
One of You 2654
One on the Drum 3827
One on the Left, The 4210
One Only-Al Dame, The 2880
One or Another 2701
One Perfect Moment 3108
One Person 1012
One-Piece Blues 3580
One Rich Brother 51
One Robin Doesn't Make a Spring 2479, 3823
One Rock & Roll Too Many 4138
One Room 3780
One Room Home 1120
One Second of Sex 1856
One Side of the World 2626
One Small Girl 3285
One Small Umbrella, Dear 1882
One Smile from Polly 3622
One Song 4191, 4035
One Starry Moment 2183
One Step (inst.) 136
One Step 1298, 2011, 3170, 4145
One Step Ahead of Love 4777
One Step at a Time 699, 2702, 2651, 1082
One Step Away 3555
One Step Further 1262
One Step Into Love 473
One Step Nearer the Moon 2238
One Step to Heaven 2628, 3849
One-Step Two-Step 4147
One Step, Two Step 3837
One Summer's Day 538
One Sunny Day 4213
One Sweet Moment 3920
One Tender Smile 3011
One That He Loves Best 3952, 3951
One That's Run Away 1721
One Thing Different 2986
One Thing in Particular 1662
One Third Princess 170
1001 3824
One Thousand Year Old Man 1717
One to a Customer 1842
One Touch of Alchemy 2344
One Touch of Loving 1992
One Touch of Venus 3301
One Track Mind 404
One, Two 2134
One, Two and One, Two, Three 2666
One, Two, Button Your Shoe 4255
One! Two! Three! 59
One, Two, Three 712, 1740, 2719, 1258
One, Two, Three (Dance with Me) 2262
One Two Three 3339, 3352, 3476
One, Two, Three 3740, 3900
One, Two, Three-Down and Out 1417
One Two Three Four 202
One, Two, Three, Four 1131
One Umbrella Would Be Big Enough for Two 734
One Waltz-Only One Waltz 3771
One Was Johnny 3668
One Way of Doing It 2931
One Way or Another 1435
One Way Street 3172, 4249
One Way Ticket to Hell 828
One Way to Love 1876
One-Way Walk, The 700
One Who Will Understand 2292
One Who Yells the Loudest Is the Captain, The 2909
One Wife 2355
One-Woman Man 190
One Woman Man 2580
One Wonderful Day 568, 3843
One Wonderful Night 2020
One Word from You 1183, 2371
One Word Led to Another 59
One Would Have to Be Blind 957
One You Care For, The 2392
One You Love, The 2780
Ongsay and Anceday 1800
Onh-Honh-Honh! 4029
Only a Clover Blossom 1650
Only a Day Dream 2661
Only a Dream 2622
Only a Dream of You 1443
Only a Fool 3517
Only a Gypsy 1522
Only a Kiss 1550, 3772, 4311
Only a Little Moss Rose 1009
Only a Man 600, 2261
Only a Paper Rose 1533
Only a Passing Phase 4541
Only a Rose 4539
Only a Rose in the Strand 3663
Only a Slave 758
Only a Smile 3680
Only a Story from Fairy Tales 263
Only a Tear 516
Only a Voice 375
Only a Woman 1985
Only an Older Woman 2437
Only Another Boy and Girl 3893
Only at Night 147
Only Beautiful 945
Only Boy 4226
Only Boy, The 4276
Only Dance I Know (Song for Belly Dancer), The 2983
Only Dreamin' 4325
Only Fancy 1473
Only Fool 3527
Only for a Moment 4769
Only for Americans 2894
Only for Men 3091
Only for You 1922

(It Is All for You) Only for You 2696
Only Game in Town, The 16
Only Game That I Would Play, The 3978
Only Girl, The 152, 1569, 2506, 2614, 4609
Only Girl Alive 178
Only Her Ankles 233
Only Home I Know, The 3928
Only Human 2241
Only If You're in Love 4423
Only in Dreams 627, 2112
Only in My Song 482
Only in the Movies 2333, 3718
Only in the Play 1355
Only Love 466, 131, 778, 1075, 2664, 4480, 4862
Only Man for the Job, The 3653
Only More! 2368
Only Myself to Blame 299
Only One 2780, 3025, 3586, 3611
Only One, The 4365, 4435, 4735
Only One Dance 3858
Only One for Me, The 202, 642
Only One Girl for Me 2794
Only One Hour 3537
Only One Love Ever Fills the Heart 463
Only One of Anything 48, 3773
Only, Only, Only in My Dreams 1492
Only Our Love 1380
Only Pebble on the Beach, The 4663
Only Place for Me, The 3059
Only Rainbows 837
Only Right Here in New York City 4468
Only So Much I Can Give 2674
Only Steal from Thieves 2437
Only Stone 4615
Only the Beginning 1103
Only the Lonely 3695
Only Thing Green About the Girl of Today Is the Green Upon Her Hat, The 3179
Only Thing I Missed, The 194
Only Time Is Now, The 2318
Only Time of Day, The 3698
Only Time Will Tell 1029
Only Time You're Out of Luck, The 1981
Only to Love Her 4239
Only to You 1544
Only Two Allowed 3527
Only Way, The 4419
Only Way to Go Is Up, The 3844
Only Way to Love, The (Love's Lesson) 2724
Only with You 1850, 3171
Only Wonderful 842
Only Yesterday 1380
Only You 83, 4138, 1552, 2071
Only Your Heart Can Tell 3995
Ontario 2671
Onward 4014
Onward, Christian Soldiers 2348
Oo, How I Love to Be Loved By You 1154
Oo, How I Love to Be Loved by You 2363
Oo, How I Love You 4276
Oo La La 200
Oo-La-La 808, 809
Oo La La 1552
Oo-La-La 2419
Oo-La-La, Wee Wee 1032
Oo-Le-Le 2147
Oo-oo-oo 3679
Oof Dah Man, The 3054
Oogie-Woogie-Shoogie 363
Ooh! (Maybe It's a Robber) 1558
Ooh, Do You Love You! 2163
Ooh, I'm Thinking 4177
Ooh-La-La 1018
Ooh! La! La! 2546
Ooh, Maybe It's You 4821
Ooh, Merci Beaucoup 483
Ooh, My Feet 2961, 3444
Ooh, Ooh, Ooh, What You Do to Me 3895
Ooh Poo Pa Doo 1890
Ooh, That's Hot 4690
Ooh! What You Said 4586
Oom-Pah-Pah 3271, 2611
Oom, Ta-ra-ra 4795
Oompa, Oompa 1774
Ooo, Ooo Lena 1538
OOOO-EEEE 1158
Oop Shoop 4264
Ootsey Tootsey 4646
Oozey-Woozey 1992
Oozums 4158
'Op in My 'Ansom 2517
Opeless Ze State of Me 3049
Open a New Window 2713
Open All Night 2633
Open and Shut Idea 3012
Open Book, An 2382
Open Bright 3890
Open Door Club 4793
Open Letter 3136
Open Sea, The 2346
Open Secret, An 1901
Open Sesame 50
Open Sesame! 51
Open Sesame 175
Open That Door 691
Open the Door 1700
Open the Gates of Madrid 1128, 1132
Open the Lattice, Love 4149
Open the Window 4727
Open the Windows 595
Open Up 1890
Open Up Your Heart 1667
Open Your Arms 1971
Open Your Arms (And Close Your Eyes) 2888
Open Your Eyes 3644, 1387, 3307
Open Your Heart 661, 825, 624, 3808, 4022, 4360
Open Your Heart to Love 102
Open Your Mouth 1597

Open Your Window 3012
Opened Up Again 3342
Opener 62
Opening Chorus and Dance Act III 1896
Opening Chorus and Entrance of Irish Girls 3322
Opening Chorus and Tarantelle 1518
Opening Chorus of Cooks 2035
Opening Chorus of King's Guards 2035
Opening Chorus of Schoolgirls 1355
Opening Chorus Part One 2834
Opening Dance 3719
Opening Day at the Five-and-Ten 2988
Opening Doors 2822
Opening Dream 3862
Opening Ensemble 165, 231, 375, 598, 1033, 1532, 1602, 1851, 2330, 2587, 3084, 3157, 3819, 3915, 4427, 4616
Opening for a Princess, An 3288
Opening for Everybody, An 4432
Opening Goulash 1832
Opening Knight 4579
Opening March 2528
Opening Music 3590
Opening Night 550, 1155, 3986
Opening Number 2798, 674, 871, 1183, 1448, 1598, 1665, 1758, 1965
Opening Number, The 2069
Opening Number 2451, 2602, 3229, 3914, 3866, 4064, 4194, 4240, 4673, 4827
Opening of Act II 4194
Opening of Atlantic City 1735
Opening of Hat Shop 2574
Opening of Second Act 4340
Opening of the Ball 3081
Opening Scene III 4524
Opening Scene V 4524
Opening Second Act 2797
Opening Song 2771
Opening Song and Chorus Act I 3727
Opening Song and Dance 385
Opening, Act II 111
Opening: Prayer 4732
Opera, The 1785
Opera 3440
Opera Ain't Over, The 1289
Opera and Rag Time 541
Opera Ball, The 276
Opera, Comic Opera 3791
Opera Comique 1523
Opera in 1860, The 1460
Opera, Opera 949
Opera Parody 1817
Opera, Pyramus, and Thisbe, The 4256
Opera Star 3325, 3763
Operatic Ensemble 604
Operatic Maiden, An 1095
Operatic, Most Emphatic 604
Operatic Mountebanks 175
Operatic Pills 4581
Operatic Solution, An 3134
Operator 4349
Operator, The 1887
Opium Song 4011
Opportunity! 1766
Opportunity 3821, 4435
Opportunity Knocks but Once 44
Opportunity, Please Knock 2306
Opposite Sex, The 3860
Opposite the Ducks 379
Opposites 455, 4013
Opposites Are We 4187
Or Know the Reason Why 1183
Or More 3448
Or Thereabouts 3618
Or What Have You? 2545
Orange Blossom Home 4345
Orange Blossom Time in San Jose 1735
Orange Blossoms 1065, 3312, 4213
Orange Girl 1735
Orange Grove 554
Orange Grove in California, An 3008
Oranges 1312
Oranges and Lemons 4449
Oranges from Seville 2565
Oratorio 3814
Oratorium Salzburgiensis 3698
Orb Divine 175
Orchard of Girls 4831
Orchids 435
Orchids in the Moonlight 3249
Orchids of the Opera 2826
Order of the Garter 2057
Order Wedding Bells for Two 115
Ordinary Couple, An 4095
Ordinary Couples 589
Ordinary Day, An 4790, 2289
Ordinary, Extraordinary Day 3136
Ordinary Family, An 690
Ordinary Life 3463
Ordinary Man, An 4288
Ordinary People 2355
Ordinary Things 1229
Ordinary Woman 4684
Ordinary Women 3901
Ore from a Gold Mine 341
O'Reilly 3786, 4815
Organ Grinder's Swing 4137
Organ, The 202
Organdie Days 2135
Organization 4798
Organization Man 2019
Organized Sex 1730
Orgy 3401
Orgy Burlesque, The 4312
Orgy the Temptress 2147
Orient, The 542
Orient 3403
Orient Yourself 757
Orienta 4491
Oriental 1233, 3484

Oriental Atmosphere 2389
Oriental Bacchanale, The (inst.) 1963
Oriental Blues 1198, 3963
Oriental Dance 2605, 3729, 4735
Oriental Divertissement 21
Oriental Dreams 611
Oriental Eyes 3701
Oriental Guards 2041
Oriental Love 4809
Oriental Magic 1953
Oriental March 509
Oriental March (Entrance of Omar) 4293
Oriental Memories 201
Oriental Moon 4234
Oriental Nights 1461
Oriental Pearl 1777
Oriental Plan 4337
Oriental Prelude 4742
Oriental Rag, The 3891
Oriental Rose 4655
Oriental Serenade 3712
Oriental Slaves Are We 2974
Oriental Song 1580
Oriental Swell, An 476
Oriental Yogi 2460, 420
Orientale 303
Orientale Moderne 1874
Orientation 4020
Original Jimmy Shine, An 2218
Original libretto 2467
Original Rag (inst.) 4697
Original Sin 1676
Original story 2597
Originality 1602
Orphan Girl (An Orphan Is the Girl for Me) 2569
Orphan I Am 2033
Orphan in the Storm 681
Orphan's Drill 2276
Orphans of the Storm 3405
Orpheus 2257, 2611
Orpheus with His Lute 3909
Orthodox Fool, An 3187
Osage County Line 2643
Oscar 4388, 4332
Oscar Wilde Has Said It 1010
Osculation 69
Oshi Dori 2851
Oshkosh 1246
Oskaloosa Pets, The 3087
Oskee Wow Wow 1593
Ossified Man, The 4735
Ostend 2506
Ostende Nobis Tosca 1914
Osteopathy Rag, The 3286
Osvaldo's Song 2945
Othello (inst.) 2061
Other Alternatives 1346
Other Day I Went to an Affair 2877
Other Days and Now 1031
Other Eyes 1623
Other Fellow, The 2667
Other Fellow's Girl, The 670
Other Generation, The 1315
Other Girls 2940
Other Half of Me, The 2053
Other Hands, Other Hearts 1242
Other One, The 3110
Other One (Darling), The 3178
Other Part of Me, The 3428
Other People 3019
Other People's Houses 426
Other People's Waltzes 4262
Other Pleasures 211
Other Side, The 4148
Other Side of the Sky, The 4558
Other Side of the Tracks, The 2523
Other Side of the Wall 127
Other Side of the Wall, The 682
Other Than That 649
Other Woman, The 155
Other You, The 4073
Otherwise 2484
O'Toole 3472
Otter Song, The 1496
Otto and the Elephants 2909
Otto of Roses 1569
Otto's Patter Song 2909
Ouch 82
(Oui) Oui Madame 3319
Oui-Oui!! 138
Oui, Oui, Madame 4209
Oui! Oui! Mademoiselle 2675
Oui Oui Marie 1833
Oui Oui Marie (Wee Wee Marie) 2336
Oui, Oui, Monsieur 4296
Ouija Board 1847
Ouija, Ouija 1882
Ounce of Cavendish Cut Plug 2055
Our Acrobatic Melodramatic Home 805
Our American Colleges 4804
Our Ancestors 3985
Our Ancient Liberties 2344
Our Boy Charlie 699
Our Bridal Night 3063
Our Bungalow in Winter Time 2492
Our Business Is News 3264
Our Busy Needles Fly 4121
Our Cabinet 3673
Our Castle of Love 4669
Our Cause Is the Cause 3805
Our Cheerleader 243
Our Child 3054
Our Children 64
Our Chinese Bungalow 3775
Our City of Dreams 3250
Our College Gowns 3976
Our Country Is Free 340
Our Crown 2252

Our Day 4117
Our Day of Independence 619
Our Day Will Come 4193
Our Doctor Comes 1570
Our Dollies 2276
Our Emblem Is the Lily 2135
Our Emporium 3882
Our Family Tree 4314
Our Farm 3322
Our Father... 2775
Our Favorite Restaurant 430
Our First Kiss 1494
Our Gang 2541
Our Girls 2282
Our Glorious Stripes and Stars 2701
Our Goose Has a Mint in Her Little Insides 2964
Our Goose Is Cooked 4707
Our Health Farm 3426
Our Hearts Were Young and Gay 3320, 3320
Our Hero 3332
Our Home 1546
Our Home, Sweet Home 3821
Our Home Town 4815
Our Honeymoon 2871, 1774
Our Hotel 455, 3156
Our Household, a Dream 654
Our Jimmy 2217
Our Just Portion 3653
Our Kind of War 757
Our Land of Dreams 2714
Our Language of Love 2150
Our Last Dance 1476
Our Last Dance Together 1082
Our Last Waltz Together 4365
Our Lips Are Sealed 3739
Our Little Captain 4392
Our Little Desert Island 3866
Our Little Family 3527
Our Little Gray Home (in the Red) 3046
Our Little Kitchenette 2363
Our Little Lady Upstairs 2813
Our Little Nest 3245
Our Little Secret 3603
Our Little World 2143
Our Lives Have Just Begun 732
Our Love Has Flown Away 4186
Our Love Is Here to Stay 3175
Our Lovely Rose 4150
Our Marriage Lines 3313
Our Master Is Free Again 1284
Our Memoirs 3916
Our Miss Gibbs 3322
Our Morals Are Most Refined 3423
Our Native Land 1852, 3994
Our Navy's the Best in the World 4452
Our New Best Friends 128
Our New Jerusalem 747
Our Own Broadway 676
Our Own Way of Going Along 2829
Our Presidents 1536
Our Private Love Song 3036
Our Private World 3279
Our Red Knight 1015
Our Rendezvous 324
Our Secret 324
Our Song 1262, 4572
Our Special Love 2177
Our State Fair 4146
Our Tale Is Told 3777
Our Time 2822
Our Time Together 31, 3059
Our Town 451, 3324, 3324, 1701, 2703, 4166
Our Usual Place 4798
Our Wedding Day 207, 1911
Our Wives 3304
Ours 4288, 1762, 3674, 4517
Ours Is a Happy Little Home 1301
Ourselves Alone (Tiocfaedh Ar La) 533
'Ousing Cha-Cha, The 1319
Out-a-Town 550
Out Comes Oom-Pa-Pa 1815
Out for Blood 661
Out for No Good 1336
Out in Frisco Town 3397
Out in the Barnyard 2966
Out in the Breezy Morning Air 4554
Out in the Cold 3498
Out in the Open Air 3946, 4367
Out in the Sun 1384
Out of a Clear Blue Sky 1135, 1778
Out of a Dream 2458
Out of a Job 4477, 4530
Out of Breath 1448, 3818
Out of Focus 4579
Out of Here 3757
Out of His Heart He Builds a Home 763
Out of Love 708
Out of Luck with Luck 4629
Out of My Dreams 3263
Out of My Mind 4602
Out of My Sight 2224
Out of Sight, Out of Mind 2464, 3210
Out of the Blue 2547, 4234
Out of the Clear Blue Sky 4499
Out of the Dark 2751
Out of the Way 1548
Out of Town 1002
Out of Town Buyers 608
Out on a Limb 3576, 4702
Out on the Loose 3719
Out on the Street 2173, 3806
Out There 305
Out There in an Orchard 3949
Out to Launch 3988
Out to Lunch 3329
Out to Set the World on Fire 3752
Out Town 1701
Out Where the Blues Begin 1827

Out Where the Pavement Ends 2298
Out with the Boys! 2715
Out with the Owl 2667
Outcasts 1426
Outdoor Man (for My Indoor Sports) 1929
Outlaw Bold, An 246
Outlaw Man 4595
Outracing Light 3876
Outside Agitator 3180
Outside Looking In 4273, 4235
Outside O' That You're Doin' Fine 952
Outside of That I Love You 2597
Outsider 2766
Outstanding Member, The 1770
Outta Your Mind 2643
Over 1991
Over a Garden Wall 2818
Over and Over 2052, 2705, 4408
Over and Over Again 2258, 2270
Over at the Frankenstein Place 3742
Over Forty 1878
Over Here! 3330
Over Here 4087
Over in Europe 2228
Over-Night 4555
Over on the Jersey Side 4802
Over Sunday 2481
Over the Coals 1857
Over the Edge 3724
Over the Garden Wall 266, 3236, 3319
Over the Hill 3600, 3928
Over the Hills 3923, 4579
Over the Hills in Monterey 2761
Over the Lowlands 3848
Over the Moonlit Sea 2800
Over the Mountain 947
Over the Ocean 60
Over the Phone (Telephone Song) 2533
Over the Radio 1130
Over the River 1032
Over the River and Into the Woods 679, 3110
Over the Sea, Boys 149
Over the Tiles 719
Over the Top 262, 3714
Over the Trenches 4379
Over the Wall 2333
Over There 1478, 3018, 3020, 4364
Over There and Over Here 2698
Overdose 3636
Overflow 3541
Overhead 635, 3294
Overland Mail, The 3531
Overnight 4235
Overrated 2317
Overseas Girl 126
Overspend 1567
Overture 372, 1142, 1927
Overture Delle Donne 3171
Overture — His Heart's Desire (inst.) 1907
Overture to Love 867
Owen Roe 4366
Owl and the Moon, The 4014
Owl and the Thrush, The 1599
Owl and the Turtle Doves, The 2494
Oxford Bags 702
Oxford Days 4010
Oy Der Pesach Pesach 3669
Oy, How I Hate That Fellow Nathan 573
Oy, I Like Him (Oy, I Like She) 1609
Oy, I Like Him 573
Oy Mama 1279
Oy Ses Git 4463
Oyaneetah (Seminole Love Song) 2160
Oyez, Oyez, Oyez 2444
Oyfa Pripetshik (At the Fireplace) 4342
Oyster 924
Oyster Waltz, The 1439
Oysterman, The 3337
Oysters 4558
Oysters in July 4446
Oysters, Cockles and Mussels (Fish Market) 1242
Ozarks Are Callin' Me Home, The 3674
Ozymandias 2962

P

P.S. I Love You 4687
P. Stone's Prayer 451
P.T. Barnum 2794
P.T. Playwrighting Kit 3858
P'r'aps a Puss 306
P** P* B**** B** D****** 221
Pablo 3170
Pacific 4048
Pack My Bag 143
Pack of Cards, A 3949
Pack Up Your Blues and Smile 4766
Pack Up Your Heart 1558
Pack Up Your Sins 4399
Pack Up Your Sins and Go to the Devil 3007
Pack Up Your Troubles 3259
Pack Up Your Troubles in Your Old Kit Bag and Smile, Smile, Smile 964
Pack Up Your Troubles in Your Old Kit Bag 1852
Package of Seeds 3177
Package of Seeds, A 3230
Packing Song 2617
Packing Up 2132
Pact with the Devil, A 2230
Paddlin' Madelin' Home 4212
Paddy Boy 4512
Paddy MacNeil and His Automobile 1564
Paddy's Cat 1445
Padlock Your Blues 1693
Padre, I Have Sinned 3875
Padre's Theme, The 3543
Paducah 3941
Pagan Death March 1155

Page a Man for Me 3580
Page Jingle #1, 2, 3, 4 and 5 1597
Page Miss Venus 3344
Page Mr. Cupid 3345
Page Mr. Jackson 981
Page Nine 3005
Pageant of Los Angeles, The 408
Pageant Song 148
Pages 4357
Pages of My Diary 2702
Paging Mr. Sousa 2805
Pagliacci 1703, 1921
Pain 131
Pain and Sorrow 1092
Pain de Menage 3760
Pain in the Heart 3140
Pain of Love's First Kiss, The 4486
Paint a Rainbow 4633
Paint Me a Rainbow 73
Paint My Dreams 595
Painted Butterfly 4853
Painted Rose 2298
Painted Women 3508
Painted, Tainted Doll 3318
Painting a Mural of Muriel 1539
Painting a Vanities Girl 1134
Painting Chicago Red 586
Painting My Picture of You 4053
Painting Paris 3626
Painting the Town 3348
Paintings for Sale 3409
Pair of Ordinary Coons, A 4158
Pair of Sixes, A 3622
Pair of Trousers, A 3068
Paira Litefoot Tennis Sneakers 973
Pairs of One 1282
Paisan 2227
Paisley Shawl 4296
Pajama and the Nightie, The 1316
Pajama Dance 2582
Pajama Game, The 3351
Pajama Girlies 3958
Pal Is a Pal, A 4619
Pal Joey (What Do I Care for a Dame?) 3353
Pal Like You, A 3230
Palace Dance (inst) 4150
Palace of Dreams 3584
Palace of Pleasure, The 2565
Palace of the Czar, The 4342
Palace or Cot 102
Pale Golden Star 1307
Pale Hands I Loved 758
Pale Venetian Moon 582
Palesteena 2856
Paletas 2755
Palm Beach 4287, 3355
Palm Beach Baby 2
Palm Beach Girl, The 2900
Palm Beach Walk, The 3086
Palm Branches Waving 4201
Palmy Days, The 1154
Palmy Days 2934
Paloma Blanca 2573
Palomino Pal 1310
Pals 42, 642, 3821, 1630
Pals of the Pentagon 59
Pamplona 3527
Pan Americana 3730
Pan for le Pain, A 273
Pan Pan Pan 3875
Panache 946, 989
Panama 1945, 4807
Panama-Pacific Drag 3399
Panassociative 2918
Pancho and Pepita 1530
Pancho de Panther from Brazil 653
Pancho Villa 1037
Pancito, She Would Call Me 3875
Pandora 1695
Pandour Does His Duty, A 307
Pango Moon 2700
Pango Pango 969
Pango Pango Maid 1131
Panic 2014
Panic at the Building and Loan 4732
Panic Ballet 1974
Panic in Panama 1889
Panic's On, The 3584
Panisse and Son 1242
Panouche 946
Pansies on Parade 1251
Pansy 2844, 3361, 1206
Pansy and the Poppy 2944
Pansy Day 1626
Pansy Eyes 723
Pansy Faces 2964
Pansy of the Dell 4014
Pantalettes 1110
Pantomime 1711
Pantomime (inst.) 2446
Pantomime Baseball 1823
Pantomime Bouffe Fantastique 2035
Pantry Scene 3949
Pants, Angela 2065
Papa 1066, 4648
Papa, At Last I Met You 1774
Papa Bird 159
Papa, Come Home 3875
Papa-De-Da-Da 443, 3709
Papa Do Da Da 3297
Papa Don't Go Out Tonight 4197
Papa Don't Love Mama Any More 3501
Papa Got Hot 1617
Papa Is a Traveler 1079
Papa, Let's Do It Again 766
Papa Lewis, Mama Green 3501
Papa Likes a Hot Papoose 1126
Papa Says 109
Papa Was a Running Dog Lackey of the Bourgeoisie 3077

Papa, Won't You Dance with Me? 1886
Papa, Won't You Dance with Me 4743
Papa Wouldn't Care for That 4681
Papa, You Won 109
Papa's Gonna Make It Alright 3928
Papa's Got a Job 3986
Papa's Return 901
Paper Bag Rag, The 547
Paper Ballet 961
Paper Fan, A 737
Paper Hat Brigade, The 3855
Paper Matches 4696
Paper of Gold 4337
Paper Picker's Polka 18
Paper Tiger 1002
Papers, The 4426
Papers! Papers! 3592
Papirosn (Buy Cigarettes) 1609
Papirosn 2356
Papirosn (Cigarettes) 4342
Pappagalli 194
Paprica 3087
Paprika 1415
Par Avion 2539
Parable 1857, 3160
Parable of the Monkey, The 1848
Parade (inst.) 623
Parade (dance) 1860
Parade 2178
Parade, The 3453, 4270
Parade Is Passing Me By, The 4829
Parade Is Town, A 162
Parade Night 3955
Parade of Clowns 1865
Parade of the Chocolate Dolls 884
Parade of the Christmas Dinner 3054
Parade of the Toys (inst.) 928
Parade of the Wooden Soldiers 710
Paradiddle 3940
Paradise 1732, 1809, 2598, 4022
Paradise Alley 487
Paradise Bound 2976
Paradise for Two, A 2698
Paradise Island 3371
Paradise Lost 4332
Paradise Quintet 2236
Paradise Stolen 3064
Paradise Waltz 2141
Paragraphs 1067
Paraguay 3520
Parahara, The 767
Parallel Lines 4518
Paramilitary Dance 533
Paramount, Capitol and the Strand 2294
Paranoia 3378
Paraphrase of St. Louis Blues 1337
Paraphrase on Upidee 1213
Parasol Dance 2858
Parasol Lady 4595
Parasols on Parade 1136
Pardon Me a Minute 3088
Pardon Me If I Stutter 3627
Pardon Me Porter 2231
Pardon Me, Sir 279
Pardon Me While I Dance 3725
Pardon My English 3379
Pardon Our French 3381
Pardon, Ma'am 1474
Paree 216, 1224, 3117, 4365
Paree, Gay Paree 4553
Paree Has the Fever Now 3388
Paree, I Love but Thee 3437
Paree Is a Lark 3465
Paree, What Did You Do to Me? 1272
Paree's a Branch of Broadway 558
Parent/Kid Dance 3806
Parents Are People 1389
Parents' Farewell, The 3555
Parfum d'Amour 1686
Parfum du Passe 3248
Parfumerie 3918
Paris 220, 1763, 1836, 2590, 2877, 2923, 3382, 3544
Paris? (Oh My! Yes Dear) 3839
Paris 3849
Paris After Dark 3383
Paris By Night 4560
Paris Carnival 3387
Paris Cuisine 946
Paris, France 2705
Paris, Goodbye! 20
Paris Gown (ballet) 1791
Paris Green 3388
Paris, I'm Prepared 3366
Paris in New York 3493
Paris in Spring 797
Paris Is a Paradise for Coons 1461, 2358
Paris Is a Spot So Fair 3308
Paris Is a Tomb 3465
Paris Is Paris Again 1511
Paris Is Really Divine 3291, 3436
Paris Loves Lovers 3972
Paris Makes Me Horny 4560
Paris, Oh Festive Land 2732
Paris on a Moonlight Night 4681
Paris Original 2019
Paris, Paris 68
Paris Police 797
Paris Push, The 2834
Paris Rose 4322
Paris Sings Again 4792
Paris Taught Me 'Zis 2380
Paris Today 4247
Paris Wakes Up and Smiles 2894
Parisian Dance 1647
Parisian Flip, The 904
Parisian Glide 1457, 4787
Parisian Model, A 3387
Parisian Nights 1688
Parisian Pierrot 133, 2570

Parisian Rag 75
Parisian Tango 203
Parisian Two-Step, The 3494
Parisian Two-Step 3626
Parisiana Roses 3388
Parisianna Anna 1464
Parisians, The 1511
Parisienne 2716
Parisienne Mechanical Marvels 2489
Parisienne Passionettes 3404
Park 3389
Park Avenue 364, 2827
Park Avenue Strut 3523
Park Avenue's Going to Town 2105
Parking Meter Like Me, A 4514
Parks of Paris, The 3837
Parlez Moi d'Amour 839
Parlez-Vous Francais? 211
Parlor Match, A 3392, 3392
Parlor Songs 4109, 4233
Parnasse 1596
Parodies 349
Parody Man, The 2631
Part of Me 4388
Part of the Crowd 2941
Part of the Plan 729, 3908
Part of the Plan Finale 3908
Part of Us, A 3285
Particular Marguerite 1455
Parties 664
Parting 2033
Parting Time 4320
Partners 738, 753, 2584, 3218
Party 4543
Party Dance 1497
Party Dance (dance) 3947
Party Doll 3858
Party Dress 2610
Party Gets Going, The 3505
Party in Room 203 508
Party Is Where I Am, The 4279
Party Line 1827
Party of the Second Part 47
Party, Party 1103
Party Scene 2584
Party Shoes 2550
Party Sickness 3636
Party Song 3094
Party Talk 4060
Party That We're Gonna Have Tomorrow Night, The 3505
Party with Me 2239
Party with Our Memories, A 3698
Party's Getting Wild, The 703
Party's Going with a Swing 3339
Party's Gonna End 1064
Party's on Me, The 3869
Party's on the House, The 1721
Party's Over, The 363, 1342
Party's Over Now, The 3885, 4332
Pas D'Equestrienne (inst.) 4212
Pas de Deux (inst.) 1548
Pas de Deux 1625, 2375
Pas de Deux (Choreography) (dance) 3094
Pas de Nuit 1095
Pas de Seul 4687
Pas Seul 336, 606
Pas Seul (inst.) 2446
Pas Seul 2493
Pas Seul (inst.) 3828
Paseo, The 3875
Pass a Little Love Around 2173
Pass Around the Apples Once Again 4037
Pass the Biscuits 3741
Pass the Bread and Butter 915
Pass the Contribution Box 1560
Pass the Cross to Me 3928
Pass the Eau de Cologne 3734
Pass the Football 4734
Pass the Soap 630
Passacaglia, A 3871
Passacaglia for Three Severed Heads 1092
Passatella 3798
Passe 324
Passe-Pied 1685
Passenger's Always Right, The 3235, 3815
Passers Bye 2896
Passes By 3420
Passin' Through 4522
Passing Away 1589
Passing By 426, 1526
Passing Centuries, The 3466
Passing Days 654
Passing Fancies 1250
Passing of Six Months 4528
Passing of the Night, The 2950
Passing of Time, The 3602
Passing Regiment 710
Passing Show, The 3401, 3405
Passing Show 3410
Passing Show Cakewalk 3396
Passing the Buck 4141
Passing Through 97
Passing Through Exotic Places 1450
Passion Flower, The 3412
Passion's Song 1210
Passione di Amore 3411
Passionella 170
Passionettes 2857
Passover 1769
Past and Future 1193
Past the Age of Innocence 837
Past, the Present and Future, The 631
Pastime Rag (inst.) 4390
Pastrami Brothers 3162
Pastry Cooks, The 4654
Pastures of Plenty 4740
Pat 3590
Pat Your Feet 1587
Patchland 764

Patchwork Quilt, A 1992
Patent Leather City (dance) 2032
Path to Honeymoon Land, The 2854
Pathway of Love, The 3676
Pathway to Paradise, The 780
Patience 239
Patience and Gentleness 1046
Patience of a Saint 4270
Patient's Lament 3600
Patiently Smiling 4792
Patisserie, The 2705
Patrick J. O'Hara 3545
Patrick Would Be Proud of Me Now 3880
Patriotic Coon 1988
Patriotic Fantasy (inst.) 3261
Patriotic Rally 4178
Patriotic Song 2474
Patrol Mysterioso 712
Patron Saints 1059
Patroness of Art 4798
Patrons of the Play 3685
Patsy 4090
Patsy Bolivar 1632, 2209
Patter Song — Through the Years 576
Patterns 253, 784, 2970
Patti-Cake Waltz, The 2093
Pattison Valse Song 4165
Patty Cake, Baker Man 4725
Patty Dear, Oh, Stop Your Teasin' 3472
'Paul Jones', The (dance) 2148
Paul Poirot Number 2461
Paul Revere 4488
Paula (An Improvised Love Song) 1633
Pauline 3396
Pause for Prayer 2477
Pause Oriental 2919
Pavanne 252, 948
Pavanne (inst.) 2161
Pavanne 4670
Pavilion of Love, The 613
Pavlova Gavotte, The 4657
Pawn for Wernher Von Braun, A 3186
Pay As You Go 3113
Pay Attention to the Girls 867
Pay Day 3054, 3170
Pay Day on Levee 3808
Pay Day Pauline 3184
Pay Heed 612
Pay, Pay, Pay 3067
Pay Phone 1700
Pay the Lawyer 4619
Pay Them No Mind 4
Payador 3170
Payday 4446
Paying Off 3314
Payola 1363
Pazzo 3197
PE 4016
Peace 635, 3366, 3418, 4403
Peace and the Diplomat Ballet 3990
Peace Anthem 3418
Peace, Brother! 4256
Peace Celebration 3764
Peace Come to Every Heart 4384
Peace Love and Good Damn 3825
Peace of Mind 4619
Peace! Peace! 906
Peace, Sister, Peace 4198, 4199
Peace Teachers 3159
Peace to My Lonely Heart 463
Peace Will Come 3276
Peaceful Place, A 2357
Peaceful Warriors 4061
Peach Blossom Time 378
Peach Girl 582
Peach King, The 2722
Peach of a Life, A 2430
Peach on the Beach 3184
(Papa Would Persist in Picking) Peaches 2900
Peaches 4648, 4085
Peachie 1404, 3962
Peachum's Morning Hymn 4370
Peachy Teacher, The 4201
Peacock Alley 1617, 3821
Peacock and I, The 3880
Peacock Dance (inst.) 149
Peacock Parade, The 1482
Peacock Strut 2135
Peanut Butter Affair, The 427
Peanut Butter Affair 3112
Peanut Butter Sandwiches and Hard Boiled Eggs 1886
Peanut Song 1958
Peanuts 4034, 4783
Peanuts and Kisses 1932
Pear Tree Quintet 634
Pearl 597, 3217, 4684
Pearl Maiden, The 3423
Pearl of Broadway 2638
Pearl of Ceylon Ballet, The (inst.) 2638
Pearl of Ceylon, The (1) 2638
Pearl of Sweet Ceylon 767
Pearl of the East (scene) 4818, 4819
Pearl We Called Prague, The 1739
Pearls 1012, 4485
Pearl's a Singer 4031
Pearl's Walking Song 99
Pears and Peaches 1116
Pears of Anjou, The 3702
Peasant Girl, The 3399
Peasant Girl 3424
Peasant Wedding Party, The 93
Peasants' Idyll 147
Peasants' Song, The 1785
Pebble Waltz 2958
Peckin' 875
Peckin' (inst.) 885
Peculiar Julia 2695
Peculiar State of Affairs 3801
Peculiar That Way 2579

Peddler's Song 252
Pedestrian Song 2734
Pedro 4015
Peek-a-Boo! 170, 2603
Peek-a-boodle Man 1613
Peek-in Peking 1321
Peekaboo, Jehovah 2898
Peep-Peep 3868
Peepin' Tommy 3388
Peeping Tom of Coventry 4719
Peg and Jerry 3429
Peg O' My Dreams 3431
Peg O' My Heart 3427
Peg o' My Heart 3429, 3429, 3431, 3432
Peg O' My Heart 4807
Peg of My Heart 822
Peggy 685, 767, 2960, 3433
Peggy Brady 2159
Peggy Is a New Yorker Now 2123
Peggy McVey 2763
Peggy O' Mine 3434
Peggy Sue 580
Peggy Sue Got Married 580
Peggy's a Creature of Moods 1016
Peggy's Leg 2340
Peking (ballet) 1638
Penalty of Love, The 1989
Penang-Ourang-Outang, The 4662
Pendulum of Time, The 700
Penelope 737
Penelope's Hand 1959
Penguins 3415
Penguins Must Sing 424
Penis Envoy 3901
Penis Envy 2049
Penitentiary Blues 1249
Penmut's Apology 3088
Pennies from Heaven 4255
Penniless Bums 4196
Pennsylvania 1600 3530
Penny a Tune 3644
Penny By Penny 753
Penny Candy 3107, 3180
Penny for Your Thoughts, A 1321, 4269, 4304, 4583
Penny Friend, The 3439
Penny in My Pocket 1828
Penny Plain, Twopence Colored 2295
Penny Saved, A 1508
Pensacola Mooch, The 4804
Pension Elite, The 2262
Penthouse of Your Mind 2728
Penthouse Serenade (When We're Alone) 3173
Pents-un-Wreckum 1958
People 871, 1420, 3440, 412
People and Pastry 1680
People Are Like Porcupines 4635
People Are No Damn Good 932
People Collecting Things 3666
People Don't Do That 4029
People Get Hurt 3142
People Got to Be Free 3739
People Have to Change 4540
People in Love 2680
People in My Head 4786
People in My Life, The 4196
People in the Street, The 1002
People Like Us 2275, 2289, 3555
People Make Me Cry 952
People of Passionate Nature 2965
People of Taste 3103
People Should Listen to Me 2182
People Shouldn't Change 4540
People Stink 3651
People Watchers 1846
People Were Nice 4153
People Who Are Nice (No More Mr. Nice) 4588
People Who Live on Islands 4488
People Will Say We're in Love 3263
People Will Talk, You Know 4649
People Would Laugh 1120
People You Know, The 708
People You Like to Talk To 62
People's Choice, The 3615, 3558
People's Reaction 3445
Pep 2594
Pep It Up 4816
Pep Up, Step Up 4621
Pep! Zip! and Punch! 3569
Pepe Hillo 2407
Pepita 1128, 1132, 4241
Pepper and Salt 3069
Pepperpot 1885
Peppersauce Woman 3468
Percolatin' 691
Percussion 322
Percy 1118, 4359
Percy with Perseverance 4291
Perdido 3905, 4091
Perennial Debutantes 3674
Perfect 1864, 2674
Perfect Casting 4703
Perfect Chaperone, The 1035
Perfect Day, A 1780
Perfect Evening, A 1290
Perfect Every Time 273
Perfect Family, The 3601
Perfect for Each Other 4297
Perfect Gentleman, A 3184
Perfect Gentlemen, A 998
Perfect Harmony 3164
Perfect Jewels 1065
Perfect Kid, The 154
Perfect Lady, A 3313
Perfect Lover, The 4378
Perfect Man 2067
Perfect Married Life, A 3324
Perfect Model for Your Arms, A 2567
Perfect Models 203
Perfect Person, The 3846

Perfect Place, A 4136
Perfect Stranger 4268
Perfect Strangers 3070, 1257
Perfect Timing 2065
Perfect Understanding, The 1010
Perfect Year, The 4217
Perfect Young Ladies 507
Perfection 1194, 1797, 3764
Perfection's Palace 1426
Perfectly Alone 2651
Perfectly Charming Visit, A 1993
Perfectly Lovely Couple 1060
Perfectly Marvelous 610
Perfectly Peaceful Person, A 2844
Perfectly Terrible 4425
Perfectly Terrible, Dear 2892
Performance Art 871
Perfume 1130
Perfume and Passion 2857
Perfume Counter on the Rue de la Paix, A (At a Perfume Counter) 2460
Perfume Number 3770
Perfume of Love 3045
Perfume of Love, The 3972
Perfume of Paradise, The 2387
Perfume Waltz 2135
Pergola Patrol, The 611
Perhaps 385, 737, 1060, 2723
Perhaps Love's Dream Will Last Forever 1798
Perhaps You May Not Like It 2041
Perils of Paulette, The 4543
Period Piece, A 944
Perish the Baubles 3215
Permissible 1578
Permission 3197
Pernambuco 4652
Peron's Latest Flame 1211
Perpetual Anticipation 2536
Persevere 1568
Persian Fantasy (Persiana) 2601
Persian Love Song 387
Persian Room-Ba 3493
Persian Skies 2700
Persian Way of Life, The 84
Persian Women 1745
Person of Parts, A 4404
Personal Appearance 1342
Personal Heaven 4484
Personal President 3873
Personal Touch, The 62
Personality 403, 1651, 3466, 3304, 2454, 4255
Personally Yours 1874
Personals 4309, 3476
Perspective 3918
Perspiration 3986
Persuasion, The 623
Perusing in Peru 3170
Pervenche 1305
Pesach Has Come to the Ghetto 1715
Pessimistic Voices 2046
Pet of the Family 2261
Petals of the Plum Tree, The 3828
Peteca! 2679
Peter 3827
Peter Pan 418, 1784, 2494, 2717, 3177, 3286, 3453, 3980, 3454
Peter, Peter 3452
Peter Piper 1921
Peter's Denial 2212
Peter's Journey Ballet (inst.) 247
Petite Belle Lily 2719
Petite Mama 1834
Pets 2453
Petticoat High 3837
Petticoat Lane 4288
Petticoat Lane (On a Saturday Ain't So Nice) 455
Petticoat Lane 2320
Pettin' and Pokin' 1296
Pettin' on the Old Porch Swing 2231
Petting Party Baby 2490
Petty Crime 4689
Pffft! 483
Phantom Loves 764
Phantom of the Musical, The 1349, 1350
Phantom of the Opera, The 3464, 3464
Phantom of the Opera 2114
Phantom of the Opera, The 3465, 3462, 3463
Phantom of Your Smile, The 1065
Phantom Patrol 4723
Phantom Rival, The 2614
Phantom Ship, The 3422
Phantom Waltz, The (dance) (inst.) 3538
Phantoms of the Ballroom 2691
Phantoms of the Night 203
Pharoah's Chant 1715
Pharoah's Daughter 4849, 4832
Pharoah's Dream Explained 2242
Pharoah's Story 2242
Phata Phata (Touch, Touch) 2147
Pheira 1308
Phi Phi 3466
Phil the Fiddler 2707
Phil's Entrance 4226
Phil's Medley 1832
Philadelphia 1060, 4004
Philadelphia Drag 1
Philadelphia Drag, The 3395
Philadelphia 1890 4577
Philadelphia Feeling 4428
Philadelphia Maid, The 3784
Philadelphia Press, The 1849
Philanthropist's Progress, The 2935
Philological Waltz 220
Philomel 2937
Philosophic Tale Is Told, The 698
Philosophy 3112
Phinney's Rainbow 3471
Phoebe Snow 2869, 3250, 1866
Phoebus Apollo 4073

Phoenix and the Turtle, The 3909
Phoenix Dance 2655
Phoey, Phoey 166
Phone Call, The 2646
Phone Calls 3603
Phony Game, The 1074
Phooey 3684
Photograph of You 3958
Phrenology 1313
Phyllis Frog 4470
Phyllis Tango 1544
Physical Fitness 64
Physical Society, The 3626
Physician, The 3214
Pi in the Sky 3110
PI-PA-KI 2655
Piano in the Parlor 2422
Piano Lesson 3016
Piano Talk 1477
Pianologue 1963, 2135, 2891
Picaninny Days 3676
Picasso 2168
Picasso's Theme (inst.) 4171
Piccadilly 547, 791
Piccadilly, The 1763
Piccadilly Band, The 1327
Piccadilly Crawl, The 8
Piccadilly, 1830 (inst.) 791
Piccadilly Walk, The 3500
Piccolo 4590
Piciyumi Gazette 3564
Pick 'Em Up and Lay 'Em Down 495
Pick a Husband 3839
Pick-a-Little, Talk-a-Little 3016
Pick a Number XV 3479
Pick a Partner 855
Pick a Pickaninny 1799
Pick-A-Pickaninny 2390
Pick a Rib 4256
Pick a Star 2028
Pick Me Up 1337
Pick Me Up and Lay Me Down 4132, 4517
Pick-Me-Up! 1766
Pick More Daisies 4272
Pick-Pocket Tango (dance) 3687
Pick Up the Pieces 3869
Pick Yo' Partner! (Get Ready for the Raggy Blues) 3478
Pick Yourself a Flower 1662
Pick Yourself Up 2204, 393, 2372
Pickaninnies, The 3803
Pickaninny All Dressed Up 3200
Pickaninny Mose 3981
Pickaninny Pie 1718
Pickaninny Sam 4626
Pickaninny Shoes 3963
Pickaninny Vamp 2009
Pickaninny's Lullaby, The 2543
Pickaninny's Paradise, The 1824
Pickaninny's Paradise 2415
Pickers Are Comin', The 3928
Picket Fence 2857
Picketing the Old Plantation 887
Pickin' 'Em Up and Layin' 'Em Down 543
Pickin' Cotton 1490
Pickin' Up the Pieces 10
Picking Peaches 4063
Picking Up the Pieces 3448
Pickpocket, The 2134
Pickwick Club, The 2982
Pickwick Papers, The 2982, 3481, 3482
Pickwick's Horse Brigade 2982
Pickwickians, The 3482
Picnic, The 148
Picnic 1990
Picnic, The 1169
Picnic Club, The 4687
Picnic for Two, A 2286
Picnic in the Sky 93
Picnic Song, The 4161
Picture 914
Picture Any Girl Can Paint, A 4437
Picture Bride, The (scene) 4823
Picture I Want to See, The 2900, 3245
Picture in the Hall, The 4358
Picture Me with You 556
Picture No Artist Can Paint, A 1925
Picture of Happiness, The 4312
Picture of Me without You, A 2252
Picture of Real Life, The 904
Picture Show, The 822
Pictures 175
Pictures and an Exhibition 2776
Pictures in the Smoke 3578
Piddle, Twiddle and Resolve 3897
Pidgee Woo 977
Pidgie Widgie 4194
Pie 4150
Pie and Coffee 1665
Pie Eyed Piper 1207
Pie-Eyed Piper of Heidsieck, The 1892
Pie in the Sky 3946
Piece de Resistance 2679
Piece of a Girl, A 2187
Piece of Cake, A 4619, 4252
Piece of Ground, A 4579
Piece of My Heart 338
Piece of the Pie 373
Piece of the Rainbow, A 2925
Pieces 4330
Pieces of Eight 3484
Pieces of Lives 3631
Pied Piper 1216
Pied Piper's Can-Can, The (dance) 1745
Pieniadze 2846
Pierre 2213, 3252, 3668
Pierrette and Pierrot 902
Pierrot 356, 3401, 4575
Pierrot and Pierrette 1281, 2498, 2623, 2919, 3433, 3648

Pierrot et Pierette 3738
Pierrot Land 764
Pierrot Patrole and Dance 2892
Pierrot's Ball 2884
Pierrot's Moonlight Serenade 710
Pierrotland 351
Piff Paff 1711
Pigeon and the Weathercock, The 1521
Pigeon-Hole Time 3476
Pigeon Run 3159
Pigeon Walk, The 1588
Pigeons of San Marco, The 3151
Piggy Back 668
Piggy Bank Song, The 2091
Pigtails and Freckles 2983
Pilate and Christ 2212
Pilate's Dream 2212
Pilgrim Fathers, The 1657
Pilgrim of Love, The 3774
Pilgrim Riding Music 634
Pilgrim's Chorus 4316
Pilgrims of Love 4250
Pilgrim's Prayer, The 2802
Pilgrim's Procession 630
Pill, The 159, 1770
Pill a Day, A 773
Pill Box Revue, The 1919
Pill Parade 1408
Pillar to Post 1846
Pillow for His Royal Head, A 2397
Pillow Magic 2685
Pillow Song, The 3227
Pillowing 3944
Pills 2962
Pilot Me 2366
Pimp Like That, A 4127
Pin a Bluebonnet on Your New Bonnet 3356
Pin Cushion, A 1678
Pinball Wizard 4676
Pinching Myself 2034
Pincus et Cie 3074
Pine Cones and Holly Berries 1860
Pine Country 1390
Pineapple Swing 1773
Pineapples 24
Ping Pong 522, 4478
Ping Pong Duet 3976
Ping Pong, Ping 3820
Pining 2302
Pink and the Butterfly, The 1568
Pink and White 4419, 4418
Pink Cherry Blossoms 717
Pink Hungarian Band, The 906
Pink Jungle, The 3493
Pink Lady 2776
Pink Lady Waltz (inst.) 4823
Pink Lemonade 4191
Pink Petty from Peter, A 2889
Pink Police Gazette, The 302
Pink Poodle, The 904
Pink Pussycat School 408
Pink Taffeta Sample, Size 10 4238
Pinkerton Detective Moon 3755, 4206
Pinkey, My Darling 1259
Pinky Panki 1693
Pinky Panky Poo 1021, 4859
Pinocchio 3496, 3495, 3498, 3499, 3497
Pinocchio's Song 3496
Pinpipi's Sob of Love 4541
Pioneers 2433
Pip Pip? 598
Pipe Dreaming 189
Piper o' Dundee 2412
Piper You Must Pay, The (Pay the Piper) 659
Pipers of Pan Dance (dance) 805
Pipes of Pan Americana 3036
Pipes of Pan Are Calling, The 178
Pipes of Pansy, The 1013, 1529, 3436, 3924
Pippin, Pippin 3507
Piraeus, My Love 2106
Pirate Dance (Huckleberry Island Ballet) 1614
Pirate Dance 2005
Pirate Jenny 369, 4368, 4369, 4370, 4371
Pirate Song 3453
Pirate Song, The 3452
Pirates (Yo Ho and a Bottle of Rum), The 3719
Pirates and Quaker Girl 3395
Pirates Are We 3422
Pirate's Gold 953
Pirate's Lament 2750
Pirates Life, The 1985
Pirate's Polka 2750
Pirate's Rag 1735
Pirate's Song, The 1017
Pirates Song 1262
Pirelli's Miracle Elixir 4233
Piscean, The 3825
Pistachio 4018
Pit-a-Pat 470
Pit Solo 718
Pitch for Pot 3094
Pitkin's Song 3278
Pitter-Patter 1923
Pitter, Patter 2681
Pitter Patter 3508
(I Met You In) Pittsburgh, Pa. 3701
Pity de Sunset 2190
Pity Me 2605, 3256
Pity Me Please 3865
Pity My Pitiful Plight 2793
Pity Poor Old Solomon 904
Pity the Child 721
Pity the Poor 4004
Pixie's Holiday 3329
Pixies 906
Pixies Entrance 3488
Pizarro Was a Very Narrow Man 3170
Pizza Man 3077

Place Called Alimony Jail, A 4619
Place Called Home, A 754
Place in Space 2728
Place in the Country 4443
Place in the Sun 3139
Place in the World, A 3577
Place in Your Heart, A 1161
Place Like This, A 3160
Place of My Own, A 3764
Place of Your Own, A 451
Place to Hide, A 2970
Place Where You Belong, A 3364
Places I Fainted from Hunger 3757
Places, Everybody 4142
Plagues, The 1715
Plain and Simple 273
Plain Clean Average Americans 1591
Plain Girls 1750
Plain in Love 1644
Plain Jane 2768, 589, 3511
Plain Mamie O'Hooley 3229
Plain Men in Dirty Overalls 2175
Plain Ol' Name of Smith, The 3562
Plain, Old Room 3925
Plain Rustic Ride ('Neath the Silv'ry Moon) 2498
Plain We Live 3509
Plan (Tom and Huck's Argument), The 1086
Plan B 2627
Plan It by the Planets 2679
Planet of No Thigh Bulge 1575
Planet Shmanet Janet 3742
Plank, The 3452
Planning 2557, 554
Planning the Bar Mitzvah 1234
Plans A & B 3760
Plant a Radish 1245
Plant Roses in Memory's Garden 3084
Plant You Now, Dig You Later 3353
Plantation Days 1799
Plantation in Philadelphia 183
Plantation Melodies 4429
Planting Fever 4764
Plastic Alligator, The 1860
Plastic Surgery 1747
Plate Dance 3403
Platinum 4216
Platinum Dreams 3515
Play a Half a Chorus 787
Play Away the Blues 275
Play Ball with the Lord 1441
Play-Fair Man!, A 2308
Play-Ground in the Sky 3968
Play Gypsies, Dance Gypsies 905
Play in Native Fashion 4550
Play Is the Bunk, The 2300
Play It Again 2617
Play It Again, Sam 3516
Play It As It Lays 4591
Play Me a Bagpipe Tune 539
Play Me a Country Song 3517
Play Me a New Tune 2789
Play Me a Tune 969, 1923
Play Me a Ukulele 4037
Play Me an Old Time Two-Step 4204
Play Me Something I Can Dance To 3319
Play Me That Tune 4418
Play Me That Tune (Ya-Da-De-Dum-Dum) 2385
Play, Mr. Bailey 4829
Play My Melody 3400
Play Nice 2357, 1510
Play Orchestra Play 3235
Play, Orchestra, Play! 3906
Play, Play, Play 796, 2834
Play Street 4153
Play That Barbershop Chord 4804
Play That Fandango Rag 4803
Play That Wedding March Backwards 1566
Play the Game 356, 1111, 1667
Play the Game and Smile 2686
Play the Music for Me 2200
Play the Queen 3838
Play the Star-Spangled Banner 2902
Play to Win 747
Play Us a Polka Dot 4234
Play Us a Tune 3291
Play with Fire 2384
Play with Me 562
Play Without a Bedroom, A 3006
Play's the Thing, The 4670
Playboy 1800
Playboy of the Western World 259
Playboy's Work Is Never Done, A 4522
Player, The 496
Players' Plaint 3908
Playground of the Planets 2539
Playground Songs 1601
Playhouse Planned for You, A 3511
Playin' the Halls 456
Playing Croquet 2522
Playing Field, The 1289
Playing for Position 3517
Playing Golf 3998
Playing Second Fiddle 3211
Playing the Game 2004
Playland 185
Plays 1422
Playthings of Love 2371
Plaza 6-9423 3990
Plaza Music 3493
Plaza Song, The 253
Plaza, the Barclay and the Old Waldorf, The 4093
Plaza Waltz Waltz, The 1049
Plaza's Going Native, The 3479
Plea for Understanding, A 4388
Plea to the Duchess 325
Pleadle-Eadle 4609
Pleasant Company 1684
Pleasant Day 3357
Pleasant Greeting, A 3185

Pleasant Little Kingdom 1329
Pleasantly Plump 3666
Please 2905
Please Be a Poppa to Us 1206
Please Be Human 3015
Please Be Kind 4403, 4743
Please Be Patient with Me 1035
Please Buy My Flowers 2546
Please Come Again 4317
Please Come to My House 2746
Please Continue 3088
Please Don't Cry 2854
Please Don't Despise Me 4609
Please Don't Flirt with Me 4418
Please Don't Keep Me Waiting 1230
Please Don't Make Me Be Good 1272
Please Don't Make Me Hear That Song Again 3164
Please Don't Move 2213
Please Don't Ration Love 2026
Please Don't Take Away the Girls 3962
Please Don't Take My Boop-a-Doop Away 4545
Please Don't Tell Me 4016
Please Find Me (I Really Need You to See Me Through) 2172
Please Go Find My Billy Boy 2528
Please God 3067
Please Hello 3340
Please Keep Me Young in Your Heart 1593
Please Learn to Love 579
Please Let Me Read 3988
Please Let Me Tell You 2961
Please Make Up 4409
Please Mr. Banjo 108
Please, Mr. Cinders 2976
Please Mr. Postman 4193
Please Mr. President 3714
Please Not Me 3227
Please, Oh, Please 2232
Please, Please 2282, 2668
Please Please Please 1430
Please Sell No More Drink to My Father 4467
Please Send My Daddy Back Home 4825
Please, Sir 16
Please, Sir, We Want If We May 4554
Please Stay 1764
Please, Teacher 2263
Please Tell Me What They Mean 2892
(We Are the Girls in the Chorus) Please Tell Me Who Looks Good to You 4858
Please the Ladies 998
Please to Put That Down 3266
Please Turn Your Backs 3251
Pleased with Myself 2011, 4145
Pleasing Land, A 2100
Pleasure 2557
Pleasure and Privilege 3780
Pleasure Brigade, The 3626
Pleasure Capsules 1426
Pleasure Him 1848
Pleasure of Doubt, The 526
Pleasure of Your Company 1619
Pleasure Pusher 1637
Pleasures 3711
Pleasure's About to Be Mine, The 2014, 2010
Pleasures and Palaces 3526
Pledge, The 2565
Plenty Bambini 2961
Plenty Little Chinee 3828
Plenty More Fish in the Sea 2023
Plenty of Pennsylvania 3509
Plenty of Zip 842
Pliney, Come Out in the Moonlight 3676
Plodding Along 2736
Plot, The (scene) 4818
Plot Again, The 3723
Plot and Counterplot 2618
Plot to Catch a Man In, A 2464
Plow It All Under 2962
Plum Blossom 4248
Plumbing 3214, 3418
Plumed Knight, The 2018
Plundering of the Town (inst.), The 657
Plunger, The 2579
Plunk (Plunk, Plunk, Plunk) 1516
Plus Ca Change 208
Po' Li'l Frenchie 2225
Po' Little Lamb 3200
Po, Po, Po 2106
Po' Li'l Black Chile 1020
Poaching 954
Pocahontas 1998, 4801
Pocapdedious 946
Pocket Full of Miracles 4743
Pocket Telephone, The 4758
Pocketful of Dreams 3563
Pockets 1509
Poco Loco 850
Poem by William Blake, A 1591
Poems 4082, 3340
Poet Aster Is Cornered, The 3889
Poetry 949, 3221
Poetry and All That Jazz 339
Poetry Competition 3944
Poetry of Motion, The 4300
Pogrom Ballet 4172
Poindexter's Lament 2555
Point of No Return, The 3464
Point of View, The 2917
Point to Bear in Mind, The 4283
Pointy's Lament 3456
Poison Ivy 4031
Poisoning Peter's Medicine 3453
Poisoning Pigeons 4412
Pokenhatchit Public Protest Committee, The 2949
Poker 870
Poker Game 2602
Poker Game, The 4727
Poker Love (Card Duet) 3710

Poker Polka, The 3
Poker Polka 3294
Poker-Polka, The 3381
Polar Bear in a Zoo 143
Polar Bear Strut, The 1654
Police 1354
Police, The 3157
Police Song 4029
Police Trouble 2992
Policeman's Ball, The 2894
Policeman's Lot Is a Happy One, A 3395
Policeman's Song 2348
Policeman's Whistle, A 4588
Policemen's Chorus, The 2500
Policemen's Hymn 3564
Policeology 3921, 4547
Politenss Pays 4258
Political Lady 4323
Political Science 2852, 2787
Politicians' Song 3548
Politics 996, 1745, 2293, 4314
Politics and Poker 1280
Polka 1962, 3011, 3064
Polka, The (dance) 3837
Polka Contest, The 1828
Polka Dot, The 3005
Polka Dot 3344
Polka Dot, The 4001
Polka Dot Polka 2088
Polka Dots 1277
Polka Duet 132
Polka Is Good Fun, The 3996
Polka Mazurka, The 1203
Polla 1183
Pollution 4412
Polly 1374, 3532
Polly and the Polka 1538
Polly Believed in Prepardness 1784
Polly of Hollywood 3009, 3533
Polly of the Circus 2869, 3534
Polly, Pretty Polly (Polly with a Past) 805
Polly Put the Kettle On 2308
Polly Wants a Cracker 1375
Polly With a Past 3532
Polly Wolly Doodle 2415, 3989
Pollyanna 1971, 3236
(They Call Me) Pollyanna 3842
Polly's Lied 4370
Polly's Song 4369
Polnische Wirtschaft 3529
Polo 2803
Polo Dance 4437
Polo Rag (inst.) 4747
Polo Song 934
Polonaise 3536
Polyandry 1435
Polyarts U. 2598
Polyphonic 919
Polythene Pam 3903
Pom-Pom 3537
Pom Pom on Your Hat, The 2751
Pomander Walk 2756
Pompadour 2700, 2813
Pompanola 4345
Poncho's Thoughts (Little Man) 4609
Ponies on Parade 1131
Pony Ballet 1224
Pony Ballet (inst.) 2974
Pony Trot, The 3663
Poodle & Canary, also Tom & Jerry Menage a Culinary Croak, The 1450
Poogie-Woo 1314
Pool of Love 2330
Pool Room Papa 876
Pools, The 1619
Poontang 2451
Poopsie Woopsie 2993
Poor 71, 4468
Poor Are Rich, The 3131
Poor As a Church Mouse 3813
Poor Baby 832
Poor Bosie 1010
Poor Bouchette 3251
Poor Boy 1064
Poor but Honest Working Girl, A 2389
Poor Butterfly 396, 4799
Poor Cinderella 2253, 762
Poor Dear Mabel 2519
Poor Don Pasquale 3197
Poor Everybody Else 3869, 4238
Poor Fellow 4824
Poor Fish 4780
Poor Fool, He Makes Me Laugh 3464
Poor Grandma 3329
Poor Horse 451
Poor Isabel 1046
Poor J'en-Ai-Marie 3405
Poor Jerusalem 2212
Poor Joe 85, 2983
Poor Johnny Brown 485
Poor Kitty Popcorn (The Soldier's Pet) 1897
Poor Little Boy 2322
Poor Little Fluttering Moths 1926
Poor Little Foolish Man 2566
Poor Little Girl Like Me, A 2978
Poor Little Hollywood Star 2523
Poor Little Marie 3179
Poor Little Me 180, 4812, 3022
Poor Little Me, I'm on K.P. 4770
Poor Little Me-I'm on KP 4340
Poor Little Model 3848
Poor Little Model Girl 2919
Poor Little Orphans (Sixteen of 'Em) 1667
Poor Little Person 1846
Poor Little Pierette 507
Poor Little Red Papoose 1881, 4473
Poor Little Rich Girl 702, 3020, 3235
Poor Little Rich Girl's Dog 3658
Poor Little Rich Little Me 2214
Poor Little Ritz Girl (1) 3538

Poor Little Ritz Girl (2) 3538
Poor Little Trigger 4710
Poor Little Wall Flower 2180
Poor Little, Shy Little, Demure Little Me 4025
Poor Man, A 3602
Poor Man 4015
Poor Man at Parting, A 3939
Poor Marat in Your Bathtub Seat 3445
Poor Mary Ann O'Shea 1629
Poor Mary Anne O'Shea 3256
Poor Me, Oh My 3318
Poor Michael! Poor Golo! 3379
Poor Mortals 3418
Poor Mouse 974
Poor Mr. Keeley 1966
Poor Mrs. Peachum 4368
Poor Old Dad in New York for the Summer 561
Poor Old Florodora Girl 2214
Poor Old Fluff 1318
Poor Old Man 1118
Poor Old Marat 3445
Poor Old World 3723
Poor Pierrot 672, 2833
Poor, Poor Joseph 2242
Poor, Poor Pharoah 2242
Poor Porgy 3605
Poor Prune 2430
Poor Relations 2686
Poor Rose 3672
Poor Sam 1911
Poor Sweet Baby 4034
Poor Teddy Bear 2177
Poor Thing 4233
Poor Tied Up Darlin' 3733
Poor Uncle Gasazus 335
Poor Unfortunate Sister Anne 2974
Poor Wandering One 2348
Poor Wicked Man, The 402
Poor Winter Garden Girl 598
Poor Working Girl 506
Poor Workingman 2527
Poor Young Millionaire 4517
Pop! Fizz! Happy! 3039
Pop, Pop, Pop 4704
Pop Song 3479
Popcorn and Piss 2776
Pophams, The 3243
Poplar and the Rainbow, The 470
Poppa 1601
Poppa Help Me 1265
Poppa Isn't Poppa Anymore 4481
Poppa Knows Best 4481
Poppa's Blues 4138
Poppa's Popular Boy 3626
Poppin' 3202
Poppy 4154
Poppy and the Pink, The 939
Poppy Chorus 4723
Poppy Dear 3540
Poppy Fields 1282
Poppy Land 560
Poppy the Dream Girl 539
Poppyland 2960
Popsey Wopsey 1538
Popsicles in Paris 4395
Popular Girl, A 256
Popular March 1968
Popular Pauline 4735
Popular Pests, The 4813
Popular Rag 1735
Popular Song, A 3268
Popular Songs 2498
Popular Tune, A 2697
Popularity 1478, 1582, 2730, 2757, 2041
Population 23
Population Explosion 3440
Porcelain Maid 3007
Porcelaine De Saxe 710
Pore Jud Is Daid 3263
Porgy (Blues for Porgy) 441
Porgy 3541
Pork, Pork, Pork 11
Port Authority 2648
Port of Debarkation 2876
Porter! Porter! 1033
Porterhouse Lucy 2175
Porterology 2645
Porter's Love Song to a Chambermaid, A 2337, 3964
Porters on a Pullman Train 114
Portia's Plan 3600
Portion of Caviar, A 1777
Porto Banos 1536
Porto Rico (inst.) 1909
Portofino 3543, 4060, 4268
Portofino P.T.A. 4060
Portrait, The 4, 2317
Portrait for Posterity 2610
Portrait of Jennie 3544, 3544
Portrait of Marie, A 1119
Portrait Parade, The 930
Posey from Over the Sea, A 3828
Posin' (inst.) 886
Posin' 1658
Posing for Venus 3251
Posing Scene 3681
Positively Love You 787
Positively No (Construction Gang) 1425
Positively Wall Street 3077
Posse Im Himmelshof 1925
Possessed 2198
Possibilities 1086
Possum Pie 3557
Post Card Beau, A 3096
Post Cards 96
Post Office 1582
Postage Stamp Principality 1760
Postcard #1 4020
Postcards 3718

Poster Dance 2390
Poster Girl, The 2193
Poster Specialty 2695
Posterity Is Just Around the Corner 3225
Posterland 3333
Postillion, The 3996
Postlude (Inst.) 2046
Postman's March (Hurray for the Postman) 2823
Posty and a Maid, A 2870
Pot of Myrtle, A 4319
Pot, Pan and Skillet 2259
Pot Pourri 1131, 1424, 3258
Potash and Perlmutter Ball, The 805
Potato Bug, The 4811
Potato Song, The 2982
Potion, A 4470
Potiphar 2242
Potpourri 3670
Pots and Pans 2276, 4805
Pottawatomie 4420
Pouche 3079
Pound in Your Pocket, A 3549
Pound the Drum 2315
Pour Faire le Tournedos 3769
Pour Le Sport 2764, 2417, 4268
Pour Out Your Soul 4459
Pour Se Faire Adorer 3769
Pour Vivre Aupres Vous 3769
Pourquoi 3265
Pourquoi? 4649
Pousse Cafe 4712
Poverty Program 2134
Poverty Row or Luxury Lane 557
Poverty's Tears Ebb and Flow 3266
Pow! Bam! Zonk! 2163
Pow Wow, The 3453
Pow-Wow Polka, The (dance) 3453
Powder Puff 2455, 3148
Powder Your Nose 2135
Power 4171, 1068, 3876, 4383
Power Comes, Power Goes 2539
Power Lies Within, The 4171
Power of Light 1357
Power of Love, The 4139, 1373
Power of Negative Thinking, The 2554
Power of the Human Eye, The 1355
Power of the Press, The 2399
Power Stronger Than Will, A 1958
Pox on Love and on Wenching, A 2654
Pox Upon the Traitor's Brow, A 1094
Practical 2680
Practical Patriots 1849
Practically in Love with You 4476
Practically Speaking 1258
Practice in Love 3382
Practice on Me 2547
Practice Scherzo, The 1475
Practising Up on You 3861, 4367
Prairie Belle 2379
Prairie Blues 1836
Prairie Mary 2314
Praise 2970
Praise the Day 466
Praise the Lord 2220
Praise the Lord and Pass the Ammunition 3444
Praised Be Moses 4498
Praises Be to David Ogilvy 4093
Praises to the Sun! 1377
Prapsis, The 1313
Prast Chi-Prast Chi 642
Prater, The 4590
Pray 3285
Pray Don't Talk about the Weather 3195
Pray Excuse 1743
Pray for Sunshine 1833
Pray for the Snow 2898
Pray Go Gently 1570
Pray Pretty Maid 4187
Pray What Would I Do 1521
Prayer 1056, 1769, 2583
Prayer (Our Journey May Be Long) 3014
Prayer 3064, 755, 3814
Prayer for Mama, A 2046
Prayer in the Desert, The 758
Prayer of Guidence 451
Prayer Song 562
Prayers 3340
Prayers in the Delta 1053
Prayers of Tears and Laughter 3980
Prayin' in Rhythm 3373
Preach Them Blues 2796
Preacher Man 2616
Preacher, The 887
Precious Jewels 764
Precious Little 4732
Precious Little Darkness 300
Precious Lord 4460
Precious Patterns 2195
Precious to Me 4106
Precious Twins 2046
'Precision' 2364
Prefatory Prayers 2775
Prehistoric Complaint 221
Pre-Historic Man 1083
Preliminary Skirmish 4421
Prelude 461, 4073, 1715
Prelude (inst.) 2450
Prelude 2411, 3493
Prelude (Inst.) 2046
Prelude 4004
Prelude to a Kiss 3175
Prelude to Live for Today 3081
Prelude to Puppet Scene (inst.) 4150
Prelude to War and War 1262
Prelude with Fanfares (inst.) 1092
Preludium 4095
Premeditated Luck 1354
Prenez Mes Roses 839

Prep School Widow, The 3378
Preparation, The 798
Preparation Fugue 2798
Preparations 3507
Prepare the Dolls 1743
Prepare Ye Now for the World to Come 2055
Prepare Ye the Way of the Lord 1595
Prepossessing Maid 1188
Preposterous 2075
Presentation, The 1786
Presentation 3703
Presentation of Albert 2617
Presenting Clara Spencer 339
Presents for Mr. Rogers 4695
President, The 3558
President Jefferson Sunday Luncheon Party March, The 4004
President's Daughter, The 3559
President's Dream, The 3076
Press Conference 721, 1103
Press Conference (Blest!) 223
Pressroom Pasa Doble 4703
Prestige 3487
Pretend You're Living 482
Pretending 3265
Prettiest Place in Greece 70
Pretty Ankle 1033, 2135
Pretty As a Picture 462, 4020, 4250
Pretty Babies 3080
(Pretty Up, Pretty Up) Pretty Baby 1823
Pretty Baby 3400
Pretty Baby Doll from Paree 1240
Pretty Betsy Brown 2506
Pretty Boy 3021
Pretty Butterfly 902
Pretty City Girl 2180
Pretty Dance Is Like a Violin, A 3842, 4211
Pretty Dark Blue Eyes 644
Pretty Daughter of Mine 1948
Pretty Doll 1425
Pretty Dresses 3429
Pretty Edelweiss 93
Pretty Eskimo 1469
Pretty Face 2949
Pretty Faces 3561, 4843
Pretty Flower 3825
Pretty Girl 1134, 1369, 1513, 2071, 3925
Pretty Girl in Gray 1220
Pretty Girl Is Like a Melody, A 789, 4829, 4813, 4799
Pretty Is 3294
Pretty Isabella and Her Umbrella 2101
Pretty Jack 1770
Pretty Kitty 3934
Pretty Lady 1508, 3340, 3967
Pretty Like Your Mama 3364
Pretty Lips of Velvet 4784
Pretty Little Bridesmaids 3339
Pretty Little Chichis 3613
Pretty Little China Girl 357
Pretty Little China Maid 688
Pretty Little Chinee 3828
Pretty Little Cinderella 1404
Pretty Little Flowers, How I Envy You 2944
Pretty Little Girl Inside, The 4521
Pretty Little Girls Like You 2385
Pretty Little Japanese Lady 4007
Pretty Little Lady 3291
Pretty Little Leader of the Band, The 2358
Pretty Little Maiden on the Screen 4509
Pretty Little Mayflower Girl 3737
Pretty Little Missus Bell 3893
Pretty Little Picture 1422
Pretty Little Pirate 2086
Pretty Little Rainbow 2455
Pretty Little Rose, A 516
Pretty Little Shoe 762
Pretty Little So-and-So 3130
Pretty Little Squaw from Utah, The 2493
Pretty Little Stranger 2253
Pretty Little Sunshade 188
Pretty Little You, Homely Little Me 3573
Pretty Maid Adelaide 3805
Pretty Maiden 1768
Pretty Malinda 2009
Pretty Melody 3022
Pretty Milliners, The 2358
Pretty Ming Toy 3538
Pretty Molly Shannon 2506
Pretty Mrs. Smith 3562
Pretty Part for Me to Play, A 2603
Pretty Patty Moss 4479
Pretty Peggy 1129, 3745
Pretty, Petite and Sweet 2271
Pretty Phrosia of the Sparkling Spa 306
Pretty Piggy 54
Pretty Pin-Up 1914
Pretty Polly 1404, 3749, 4121
Pretty Punchinello 336
Pretty Soft, Pretty Soft 2302
Pretty Suzette 1392
Pretty Thing 1846, 1739
Pretty Things 3772
Pretty to Walk With 2190
Pretty Woman 2290
Pretty Women 4067, 4233
Pretty Words 1795
Pretty Young Men 4
Prettybelle 3564, 3564
Pretzels 3565
Prevalent Condition of the Mind, The 2601
Preview of Heaven 242
Priam's Little Congai 1657
Priceless Relics 1684
Pricklepear Bloom, The 3733
Pride and Freedom 2195
Pride and Prejudice 1290, 1290
Pride in My Work 4629

Pride of Company B 3040
Prigio Didn't Know 1871
Prima Donna 3464, 1596
Prima Donna, The 4666
Prima Donnas, The 3755
Primary Tango 4635
Primitive Ebony, The 364
Primitive Island 1771
Primitive Prima Donna 880
Primping 3650
Primrose 3052, 972
Primrose Path, The 1033
Primrose Way 764
Primrose Way, The 3399
Prince and Me, The 747
Prince and the Pauper, The 3571
Prince Charming 680, 953, 3063, 3258, 4352
Prince Do and Dare 466
Prince Eagle's Entrance 4738
Prince Edward Island 148
Prince Edward Skool 128
Prince from Borneo, A 336
Prince Is Giving a Ball, The 759
Prince Is Mad, The 3571
Prince of Bohemia 3575
Prince of Borneo 2631
Prince of Central Park 3576
Prince of Central Park, The 3576
Prince of Good Fellows, The 3673
Prince of Grand Street, The 3577
Prince of Humbug, The 305
Prince of My Maiden Fancies 1121, 2509
Prince of Peace, The 3598
Prince of Wales 3405
Prince Rupert's Cavaliers 3732
Prince's Chorus 276
Prince's Farewell (Goodbye), The 2523
Princely Scheme (Hook's Tango), A 3453
Princes' Street 1676
Princess, The 16, 3619
Princess April 3580
Princess Charming 3466, 3584
Princess Jimmy Sure Has Big Balls 3587
Princess Nicotine 3915
Princess of Dreams 4012
Princess of Far-Away 2394
Princess of Herzogovinia, The 2565
Princess of My Dreams, The 4815
Princess of Pure Delight, The 2386
Princess of the Willow Tree 4780
Princess Virtue 3593
Princess We Adore, The 4014
Princeton Pastorale 3970
Principle of the Thing, The 3067
Printemps 4666
Priorities 3226
Pripoz Diva Se 64
Priscilla 3848, 4478
Prisms 3112
Prisms, Plums and Prunes 4477, 4530
Prison Glide 2020
Prisoner of Love, A 3679
Prisoner of Zenda, The 3586, 3586, 3595, 4798
Prisoner, Prisoner, Run Along 1624
Prisoners Chorus 1624
Prisoners in Niggertown
(Three Five Zero Zero) 1717
Prisoner's Lullaby 3490
Prisoners Stand Up! 1083
Prisoners Up to Date 1058
Prisoners' Patrol 3332
Prithee Gentle Echo 2715
Privacy 3181
Private Hunting Ground 239
Private Parts 1059
Private Thoughts 4297
Private Tommy Atkins 3828
Privates on Parade 3598
Prize for That, A 2803
Prizen Ivy, The 78
Pro Musica Antiqua, The 4268
Probably 1139
Probably in Love 2556
Problem 1233
Problem After Problem 3806
Problem, Solution, Conclusion 2627
Problematical Solution 4062
Proceeding in a Westerly Direction 1277
Procession 2719, 4623
Procession and Ballet 2802
Procession of Peasants 1309
Processional 747, 4139, 1435, 3011
Processional (inst.) 4095
Processional March (inst.) 1682
Prodigal Daughter 67
Prodigal Has Returned, The 3599
Prodigal Papa 1119
Producer Didn't Hire Me, The 3161
Producers 4860
Producer's Office 4828
Production Number 1056
Productivity 62
Professional Showbizness Comedy 3039
Professor and His Pupils, The 2800
Professor Cupid 1016
Professor Hossenpfeffer's
Saucer-Sighters 932
Professor Unrath 3551
Program Your Return 166
Progress 369, 1306, 1864, 2615
Progress Is the Root of All Evil 2484
Progress Will Ruin Us Yet 2928
Progressive Poker Game, The 2041
Prohibition 4813
Prohibition Blues 2108, 2373
Prohibition Song 1549
Project Heal 1700
Prologue 150, 374, 444, 3528, 4790, 2442, 690,
787, 840, 1068, 1244, 1310, 1358, 1373, 4217
Prologue, The 1500

Prologue 2198, 1277, 1959, 2103, 2228, 2306, 2323, 2648, 2728, 2759, 3159, 2542, 3326, 3406, 3543, 3544, 3656, 3670, 3691, 4173, 1276, 4470
Prologue (dance) 4625
Prologue 2224, 2065
Prologue (Little Shop of Horrors) 2544
Prologue March 1214
Prologue of Dutch Girls 586
Prologue of the Magi 2241
Prologue Shakespearean Opening 3955
Prologue to the Second Act 1817
Prologue/Overture 3864
Promenade, A 1670
Promenade 2318
Promenade, The 2360
Promenade 3091
Promenade (Street Cries) 3837
Promenade 4537
Promenade the Esplanade 3149
Promenade Theme 3602
Promise 1196
Promise, The 1079
Promise in Your Eyes 123
Promise Me a Rose (A Slight Detail) 4270
Promise Me Not to Love Me 462
Promise Me Tomorrow You Will Again Love Me 1083
Promise Not to Stand Me Up Again 608
Promise of Greatness 4349
Promise of What I Could Be, The 1441
Promise Your Kisses 2342
Promised 649
Promised Land 1970, 3690
Promises and Love 2866
Promises, Promises 261, 3603
Propaganda 3526
Proper Air, The 1540
Proper Due 3215
Proper Gentleman, A 1721
Proper Man, A 2563
Proper Way to Kiss, The 3229
Property Boy, The 3951
Property Man 1176
Prophecy 1079
Propinquity 59
Proposal, The 4761
Proposal Duet 3931, 1041
Proposals 3775, 4787
Propose 1526
Prosit 2966
Prosperity 3424
Prosperity Song, The 3757
Protect Me 2137
Protections 2100
Proteges, The 3770
Protest 4077
Proud 4004
Proud, Erstwhile, Upright, Fair 4537
Proud Inside 1119
Proud Lady 273
Proud Lady Have Your Way 1948
Proud Little Pages 1266
Proud Mary 4534, 338, 3739
Proud of You 323
Proud Pelican and the Priceless Gem, The 717
Prove I'm Really Here 4659
Prove It 4162
Proverbs 3511
Proverbs Up-to-Date 1568
Providing 3827
Proving Ground 4003
Prudence, Have Faith 4696
Prunella 351
Prunella Mine 4808
Prunes 4063
Prunes, Prisms, Potatoes 1774
Przeaprodensky 2619
Psalm 2727
Psalm of Jehoshaphat, The 4157
Psyche 3952, 3951
Psychiatry Song, The 2228
Psychoanalyse Me 1387
Psychological Moment 495
Psychology 2806
Ptolemy 1848
Pub Pianist 194
Puberty 778
Public Enemy No. 1 3501
Public Enemy Number 1 992
Public Enemy Number One 163
Public Service Message 2477
Publicity 2803, 4602
Publish Your Book 2702
Puddles 1216
Puff-Puff 1627
Puff, Puff, Puff 2711, 4843
Puffed Up Proud 2685
Puka Puka Pants 4337
Pulitzer Prize, The 2894
Pull 2724
Pull a Rabbit Out of the Hat 4798
Pull Away 1926
Pull It Together 109
Pull Me Up, O'Reilly 306
Pull the Boat for Eli 3082
Pull Your String 200
Pull Yourself Together 86
Pullman Dining Car 1496
Pullman Strike, The 114
Pulse of My Heart 2662
Pulverize the Kaiser 1864
Pump Boys 3608
Pumping Iron 4138
Punch and Judy 1091, 2756, 4430
Punch and Judy Divorce (Ballet) 2615
Punch and Judy Man 2423
Punch Bowl Glide (inst.) 2394
Punchinello (inst.) 763
Punk 1575

Puns 4627
Punting on the Thames 3997
Puppet Dream 2236
Puppet Rebbe 1715
Puppy Love 4264, 2623
Pure America 451
Pure and White As the Lotus 4724
Pure Gold Is My Security 3592
Pure in Heart, The 1380
Purefoy's Lament 1094
Purest Kind of a Guy 3180
Purgatory 3004
Purgatory U 2785
Purification, The 3830
Purim Song 2354
Puritan Damsel, A 2345
Puritan Prance, The 2596
Purity 1629, 3256, 3258
Purity Brigade, The 357
Purity Brigade March 4712
Purity Brigadiers, The 4654
Purity Is Power 621
Purity League, The 2532
Purlie 3610
Purlie Victorious 3610
Purple Dust 3612
Purple Hearted Soldiers 3561
Purple Rose 4499
Purpose in Life 3345
Pursuit 270
Pursuit of Excellence, The 730
Purty Little Thing, A 3172
Push a Button in a Hutton 1811
Push and Pull 109
Push Around 376
Push Cart Man 2275
Push de Button 2190
Push Ka Pi Shi Pi 1296
Push Me Along in My Pushcart 1478, 1640
Pusher, The 4679
Pushful 3313
Pussy 374
Pussy and the Bow-Wow 2035
Pussy Cat Song 1958
Pussy Cats Three 719
Pussy Foot, The 1614
Pussy Foot 4360
Pussyfoot Detective, The 4218
Pussyfootin' 3873
Pussy's in the Well 2543
Pusuit of Happiness, The 183
Put a Curse on You 40
Put a Little Bet Down for Me 4277
Put a Little Magic in Your Life 2820
Put a Little Spring in Your Step 1146
Put a Nickel in the Slot 476
Put a Sack Over Their Heads 2847
Put and Take 3614
Put and Take Top, The 4437
Put Another Nail in Hitler's Coffin 2653
Put 'Em Back 2484
Put 'Em in a Box 4743
Put Him Away 4481
Put 'Im in the Box 3731
Put in a Package and Sold 1737, 2074
Put It Away Till Spring 1448
Put It in the Book 3731
Put It in the Scrap Book 306
Put It in Writing 3615
Put It on My Tab 1702
Put It Over 3087
Put It Right Here 2796
Put It Right in My Hand 3358
Put It Together 109
Put It Where the Moon Don't Shine 1037
Put Me Among the Girls 470, 1900
Put Me in My Little Bed 1776, 3998
Put Me in My Little Cell 3882
Put Me to Sleep with an Old Fashioned Lullaby 1532
Put Music in the Barn 4586
Put on a Happy Face 602, 607
Put on the Ritz 3369
Put on Your Sunday Clothes 2208, 1828
Put One Foot in Front of the Other 3833
Put the Ball Over the Pan, McCann 3033
Put the Blame on Mamie 3178
Put the Devil in Hell 482
Put the Fire Out 3724
Put the Ribbons On 1262
Put Your Arms Around Me Honey 1120, 1247, 2667
Put Your Best Foot Forward Little Girl 2394
Put Your Hand on My Hand 2075
Put Your Hand on the Radio 3364
Put Your Heart in a Song 3850
Put Your Lovin' Arms Around Me, Dearie 4808
Put Your Loving Arms Around Me 2771
Put Your Mind Right on It 2845
Put Your Old Bandana On 1058
Put Your Shoulder to the Wheel 2004
Put Your Troubles in a Candy Box 2789
Putnams of Westport, The 1047
Putney on the Thames 989
Puttin' It On 1637
Puttin' on the Ritz 789, 3511
Putting It Together 4067, 4210
Putting on the Ritz 4345
Putting Things Away 1804
Putty in Your Hands 3931
Puzzlement, A 2312
PX Parade 7
Pygmalion 3038
Pygmalion Roses 1826
Pyjama Jazz 4154
Pyjama Song 3626
Pynka Pong 3828
Pyramid Land 3136
Pyramus Arise 3909

Q

Q.T.U.C.I.M.4.U. (Cutey, You See I Am for You) 2619
Qhobosha (The Unfaithful One Will Die) 2147
Quack, Quack 1942, 1944
Quack! Said the Duck 306
Quadrille 324
Quadrille (dance) 629
Quadrille 1616
Quadrille, The 1035
Quaint Little House for Two 606
Quaint Old Bird 675
Quaint Toys 736
Quaker Girl, A 3618
Quaker Maids, The 2465
Quaker Song 4200
Quaker Talk 1558
Quakers' Meeting 3618
Quakertown Cadets, The 1640
Quakin' and Shakin' 1053
Qualifications 4763
Quality Street 3472
Quand les Soldats Vont au Pas 3769
Quarrel, The 1199, 2254, 3251, 3626
Quarrel and Part 4422
Quarrel Duet 954, 1513
Quarrel for Three 341
Quarrel Song 2268
Quarrel Trio 3308
Quarreling 906
Quarreling Coachmen 3749
Quarrelling Song (You're a Cad, You're a Bounder) 3756
Quarrel-tet 4682
Quarterback, The 4506
Quartet 3862, 4233, 1276
Quartet Agonistes 705
Quartet Erotica 2475
Quartet Finale 630
Quartet for Losers 1695
Quartette 1513, 2710
Quat-Z Arts 3626
Que Pasa, My Love 1164
Queen Alice 54
Queen and the Sailor, The 1369
Queen Cobra 4011
Queen Elizabeth 1447
Queen Elizabeth's Tea 2005
Queen Esther 3226
Queen Is Always on Display, A 1818
Queen Isabella 1483
Queen Mab 3876
Queen McButterfly's Lament 3587
Queen Mother's Crossover (inst.) 4798
Queen of Beauty Am I, The 331
Queen of Belle Paree, The 3085
Queen of Comic Opera 357
Queen of Country Music 2643
Queen of My Dreams 1515, 4017, 4094
Queen of My Heart 1080, 4357
Queen of Queens 670
Queen of Sheba 2610
Queen of Song 4153
Queen of Spain 3940
Queen of Terre Haute, The 1272, 4517
Queen of the Alley 4859
Queen of the Boulevards 3520
Queen of the Bungaloo 3747
Queen of the Burlesque Wheel 4090
Queen of the Jungle Show 1793
Queen of the Land of Snow (inst.) 396
Queen of the Mermaids 396
Queen of the One Ring Show 3268
Queen of the Opera, The 2379
Queen of the Philippine Islands 1313
Queen of the Ring 2885
Queen of the Ring, The 1602
Queen of the South Sea Isles, The 4302
Queen of the Stardust Ballroom 287
Queen of the Striptease 2364
Queen of the Track 3805
Queen of the Yale Dramat 870
Queen of Vanity Fair, The 3681
Queen Thou Art, A 2903
Queenie Pie 3628
Queenie, Take Me Home with You 3641
Queenie with Her Hair in a Braid 1569
Queenly Comments 705
Queens 3157
Queen's Aria 4357
Queen's Entrance 4064
Queens of Long Ago 4427
Queens of Society 1021
Queens of Terpsichore 130
Queen's Presentation 4035
Queer Fish 260
Queer Little Insect 3934
Queer Little Ostrich, The 4201
Quelle Heure Est-il? 1596
Quelque-Chose 3382
Querida 1678
Question, The 2235
Question Is, The 3987
Question of Gait, A 1871
Question of Lighting, A 3235
Questions 1004, 1072, 2913
Questions Questions 3651
Queue at Drury Lane 2295
Quick Henry, the Flit! 4025
Quickly 71
Quiet 630, 3288
Quiet Afternoon 2516
Quiet Cafe, The 3951
Quiet Country 4431
Quiet Evening at Home, A 2922
Quiet Girl, A 2653, 4734
Quiet Land, A 161

Quiet Life, A 1076
Quiet Life at Child's, A 1533
Quiet Little Game, A 2771
Quiet Little Royal Household 4750
Quiet Man, A 1076
Quiet Morning 1508
Quiet Night 3283
Quiet, Pod's Thinking (inst.) 499
Quiet Road to Sundown 2703
Quiet Street 3934
Quiet Sunday in 1920, A 4094
Quiet Thing 131
Quiet Thing, A 1310, 4480
Quiet Town 2248
Quiller Has the Brain 1375
Quillow and the Giant 3630
Quillow Plants the Blue Men 3630
Quilters: Women and Domestic Art, The 3631
Quiltin' and Dreamin' 3631
Quintet 3151, 49
Quintette 78, 1103, 1992
Quintette and Phillip's Story 168
Quit Kiddin' 4793
Quite a Party 4241
Quite and Nifty and Effective Detective Am I 3312
Quite Like Him 31, 1435
Quite Suddenly 1222
Quite the Thing 1916
Quittin' Time 70, 1074, 3209

R

R-E-M-O-R-S-E 4201
R.S.V.P. (dance) 723
R. Strenuous Brown and Summer Girls 1912
Raah-Too-Tee-Too 1415
Rabbi's Daughter, A 3926
Rabbit Song 3163
Rabbit's Excuse, The 54
Rabbit's Foot 998
Rabbit's House, The 54
Race 1385
Race, The 4629
Race Is Over, The 391
Race of Life, The 2884
Race of the Lexington Avenue Express, The 1023, 1364
Race of the Year, The 1922
Race One 4138
Race Sequence 3080
Race Through the Desert (I Have Got to Get There in Seven Days Flat) 1214
Race You to the Top of the Morning 3862
Races, Races 434
Racin' Form 4123
Racin' Forms 1385
Racing 3021
Racing Blues 1961
Racing Form Lullaby 1420
Racing Game, The 4113
Racing Scene 4044
Racing with the Clock 3351
Rackety Boys, The 45
Rackety-Coo! 2292
Radetsky March 1680
Radetzky March 4365
Radiance 3405
Radiant Diamonds 910
Radio City, I Love You 3105
Radio City Music Hall 1437, 3484
Radio City Overture 3639
Radio Dance (dance) 1739
Radio Voices 152
Radium Dance (inst.) 3488
Radium Numbers (inst.) 3528
Radziwill 2808
Rafesville, U.S.A. 339
Rafferty 2964
Raffi: The Concert Movie 3960
Raffles 2301
Raft Song, The 2227
Raft, The 2168
Rag, The 3682
Rag, a Bone, a Hank of Hair, A 4629
Rag Bag Man 185
Rag Dance 3045
Rag Doll, The 2856
Rag Doll Rag 562
Rag Dolly 3643
Rag from Home, The 2571
Rag Lad of Bagdad, The 3985
Rag Man, The 1340
Rag Man, Music Man 2869
Rag Me Around 4206
Rag Me That Mendlessohn March 2860
Rag Mop 4264
Rag Offen the Bush 2484
Rag Picker's Dance, The 3157
Rag, Rag, Rag 4487
Rag-Time Banjo Serenade, The 1464
Rag Time Land 1613
Rag Time Lil 3480
Rag Time Quadrille (dance) 800
Rag Time Wedding Bells 1557
Rag with Me 332
Raga 3162
Rage, The 157
Raggedy Ann 2214, 4150
Raggedy Blues 489
Raggedy Rag 4815
Raggety Man, The 3332
Ragging Along 4487
Ragging the Apache 3400
Ragging the Nursery Rhymes 3396
Rags 3644, 4684, 4401
Rags and Tatters 3980

Rags Is Royal Raiments 765
Ragtime (inst.) 157
Ragtime 4090
Ragtime Alphabet 1919
Ragtime Arabian Nights 4657
Ragtime Base Ball 3891
Ragtime Boxing Match, The 558
Ragtime Calisthenics 3400
Ragtime Carnival 4747
Ragtime Chimes 2984
Ragtime College Girl, The 1247
Ragtime Dance, The (inst.) 4390
Ragtime Dance (inst.) 3041
Ragtime Dinner Order, The 2696
Ragtime Drummer 2111
Ragtime Express 1963
Ragtime Fight 1852
Ragtime Goblin Man, The 1541
Ragtime in Europe 4681
Ragtime in the Air 106
Ragtime Jockey Man 3395
Ragtime Love 2127
Ragtime Marriage 2455
Ragtime Melodrama 4158
Ragtime Mixes My Brain 604
Ragtime Mocking Bird, The 3917
Ragtime Nightingale (inst.) 4390
Ragtime Opera (Ragtime Sextette) 1738
Ragtime Pinafore 4657
Ragtime Pipes of Pan 3467
Ragtime Pipes of Pan, The 4747
Ragtime Promenade 10
Ragtime Razor Brigade 4770
Ragtime Restaurant, The 3679
Ragtime Romeo 4542
Ragtime Sextette 4655
Ragtime Soldier Man 2834, 4655
Ragtime Suffragette, The 4807
Ragtime Temple Bells 736
Ragtime Terpsichore 3043
Ragtime Wedding, The 231
Ragtime Whirl, The 968
Ragtime Will Be My Finish 2324
Ragtime Yodeling Man 60
Ragueneau's Cafe 947
Ragueneau's Patisserie 949
Rah, Rah, Rah 1481
Rah! Rah! Rah! (Those College Yells) 4094
Rah-Rah-Rah 4704
Rah Tah Tah Tio Beep Doo Doo 4707
Rahadlakum 2327, 4383
Raid on the Sunday School Picnic, The (dance) 2028
Railbird 135
Railroad 1758
Railroad Fight (dance) 3837
Railroad Number 2892
Railroad Woman, A 664
Rain 317, 3285, 4575
Rain Ballet 4572
Rain Chorus 4479
Rain Drops and the Rose 728
Rain Finale 4667
Rain in My Heart 4824
Rain in Spain, The 3038
Rain in the Doorway 2584
Rain-in-the-Face 1464
Rain of Summer, The 3522
Rain on the Roof 1329
Rain on the Sea 3036
Rain or Shine 2803, 3648
Rain Over Manhattan 3605
Rain, Rain 2588
Rain, Rain Go Away 4439
Rain! Rain! Rain! 2700
Rain Song, The 170, 3294
Rain Your Love on Me 3209
Rainbow 675, 1385, 2614, 3655, 4011, 4762
Rainbow and Thistle 47
Rainbow Ball 3962
Rainbow Bride 4381
Rainbow from the U.S.A., A 1208
Rainbow Gold 659
Rainbow High 1211
Rainbow Hook and Ladder, The 2222
Rainbow in the Sky 4039
Rainbow Logic 2142
Rainbow of Flowers, The 2571
Rainbow of Girls 4821
Rainbow of Jazz 3042
Rainbow of Your Smile, The 670
Rainbow on the Road 823
Rainbow Shines 4403
Rainbow Song, The 1740
Rainbow Sue 1909
Rainbow Tour 1211
Rainbow Woman 451
Rainbow's End 2705
Rainbows 716, 2222
Rainbows End 3485
Raindrops 2986
Raining 675
Raining in My Heart 580, 956
Raining Memories 3107
Rainmaker of Syria, The 4728
Rainy Afternoon 545, 2516
Rainy Afternoon Girls 2376
Rainy Daisies, The 586
Rainy Day, A 60, 1322
Rainy Day 2168, 2071
Rainy Day! 4044
Rainy Day Pal 3149
Rainy Day Sadie 886
Rainy Days 2457
Raise the Flag of Dixie 3928
Raisin and You 2780
Raisin' Hades in Green Pastures 877
Raisin in the Sun, A 3656
Raisin' the Dust 994
Raisin' the Rent 878

Raisin' the Roof 1689, 4848
Raising an Igloo 3201
Raising Cain 1864
Rajah Glide, The 1731
Rajah of Bhong, The 906
Rajah of Broadway, The 4802
Rake, The (Ballet) 4154
Rakish Young Man with the Whiskers 462
Raksha's Lullabye 2970
Rally, The 1717, 1837
Rally Around 3866
Rally Chant 1862
Rally 'Round Me 4023
Rally Round the Flag 964
Ram Jam 3348
Rambler Rose 3658
Ramona's Lament 474
Ran Tin Tin 4427
Rancho Mexicano 1446
Rang-Tang 3660
Ranger's Song, The 2602
Rangers' Song, The 3719
Rangoon Wedding 3137
Rank & File 430
Rann's Message 2970
Ransom of Red Chief, The 1306
Raoul, I've Been There 3464
Rap, The 1103
Rap 240
Rap Master Ronnie 3661
Rap, Rap, Rap 1266
Rap-Tap-a-Tap 4637
Rap-Up, The (Alimony Rap) 4619
Rape 1978
Rape and Resurrection 3564
Rape Ballet 1245
Rape Me 2177
Rape of Liberty 3873
Rape of Miss Goldberg, The 2132
Rape Upon Rape 2563
Rapid Reading Rachel 4433
Raptures of the Deep 1857
Raquel 1134
Raquel Gives the Dish 3636
Rare Wines 1068
Rascals 2542
Rascal's Song 3937
Rasmussin's Law 3016
Raspberries 2798
Rasta Roll Call 3690
Rastafari 3690
Rastus Johnson, U.S.A. 9
Rat Catcher's Daughter 4467
Rat Exodus (inst.) 3487
Rat Killing 4041
Rat-Tat-A-Tat 1240
Rat-Tat-Tat-Tat (Private Schwartz) 1420
Rat Trap 1732
Rather Stay Home with You 621
Rather Than See You Once in a While 1154
Rathskeller Trio, The 2696
Rational Love Song, A 2289
Rats and Mice and Fish 1068
Ratta Tat Tat 3688
Rattle Rattle 2856
Rattletrap 635
Raunchy 3294
Rave On 580
Raven Tresses or Golden Locks 2262
Ravenous Rooster, The 1095
Raving 2974
Raving Beauty, A 372
Raving Beauty 2805
Ray of Sunshine 2461
Ray, Ray 1581
Raymond's Song 3636
Raz-Ma-Taz 3985
Razz-Me-Tazz-Jazz 4380
Razzle Dazzle 723, 4480
Re-Incarnation 4801
Re-Orient Yourself 757
Re-7, The 414
Reach 4527
Reach for the Sky 2177
Reach Out 1662, 2616
Reach Out and Touch Her 3527
Reach Out for Me 261
Reach Out in the Darkness 4193
Reach Right Down 4139
Reaching for the Cake 586
Reaching for the Moon 4426
Reaching, Touching 4431
Read All About It 695, 4323
Read Between the Lines 385
Read It in the Weekly 3305
Read My Sighs 1743
Read the Answers in the Stars 2974
Read the Label (Don't Take My Word for It Neighbor) (Get Away You Bother Me) 4516
Read What the Papers Say 1488
Readin', Writin' and 'Rhythmatic 4782
Reading 699
Reading People 1887
Reading the News 3837
Reading the Writing 1717
Reading, Writing and a Little Bit of Rhythm 4174
Reading, Writing, Arithmetic 767
Ready Cash 145
Ready for the Woods 2143
Ready Made Sandwich, The 3401
Ready Maids, The 333
Ready Money 3246
Ready or Not 426, 2318
Ready, Steady Sailor Man, The 2938
Ready Teddy 580
Real American Folk Song Is a Rag, The 921, 2373
Real American Girl, The 1230
Real American Girls 1407
Real Coney Island, The (dance) 3278
Real Estate 1077

Real Girls, The 1640
Real Good Cry Together, A 1114
Real Life 3667
Real Life Funnies 3666, 3666
Real Life Lullaby, A 593
Real Live Girl 2523
Real Live Man 1407
Real Me, The 64
Real Mike Fink 3733
Real Nice Clambake, A 660
Real Nice Trip, A 1510
Real Old Mountain Dew, The 516
Real Rich Ladies 1081
Real Slow Drag, A 4447
Real Smart Set, The 906
Real Thing, The 2663, 3734, 4252
Real Town Lady 3856, 3857
Reality 1711
Reality! 2615
Really and Truly 4213
Really Great Mood 198
Really Quite Armless 924
Really Rosie 3668
Really, Would You Believe It? 3157
Reap the Harvest 1385
Reason to Marry 1878
Reason Why, The 3887, 4200
Reasons of State 2317
Reba 4373
Rebbitzen from Israel, The 3669
Rebecca of Sunnybook Farm 4807
Rebel Girl 1609
Recall Goodhue 2432
Reception 931
Reception of the Court 3584
Recipe, The 430
Recipe 10
Recipe, The 3313
Recipe, A 3710
Recipe for a Husband 2012
Recipe for Husbandry, The 3939
Recipe for Love 300
Recipe of Love, The 2869
Reciprocity 3895
Recital 1262
Recitative 4401, 4687
Recitativo 3197
Reckless Blues 478
Reckless Rooster March 1846
Reckoning, The 705
Recognized Man of the Hour 1602
Reconciliation 2385
Recruiting Doll, The 2184
Rector Rhythm 1989, 498
Red 3576
Red, A 4503
Red and Black 2442
Red Ball Express, The 620
Red Bandanna Rag, The 3396
Red Beans and Rice 3840
Red-Blooded American Boy 2053
Red, Blue and White 1717
Red Blues, The 3972
Red Blues 4152
Red Cap Cappers 3808
Red Collar Job 3543
Red Faces at the Kremlin 109
Red Fox Trot, The 3087
Red Head 4203
Red Head Blues 3489
Red-Headed Woman, A 3541
Red Heads 2504
Red Hot and Blue 1018
Red, Hot and Blue 1762, 3674
Red, Hot and Blue! 4517
Red Hot and Blue Rhythm 4087
Red Hot Band 892
Red Hot Chicago 1323
Red Hot Mama 3942, 4090
Red Hot Tomatoes 1168
Red Hot Trumpet 4118
Red Hots 217
Red Kimono, The 159
Red Ladies, The 1780
Red Leather Wrist Watch 2290
Red Letter Day 3801
Red Light Annie 4817
Red Light Ballet, The (inst.) 3113
Red Man 1185
Red Mikado 3501
Red Moon 3535, 3676
Red Queen 54
Red, Red As the Rose 1685
Red, Red, Beautiful Red 248
Red, Red Rose 295
Red Red Rose 4579
Red Riding Hood 2494, 4630
Red Riding Hood Improvisation (inst.) 974
Red Riding Hood on Broadway 1829
Red River 2005
Red Rose 2937
Red Sails in the Sunset 3605
Red Shoes, The 3682, 3682
Red Shoes 1408
Red Shoes Ballet (dance) 3682
Red Sky 3504
Red Tape Blues 4061
Red, the White and the Blue, The 1914
Red Visitors, The 3530
Red, White & Blue 639
Red, White and Blue 1067
Red, White & Blue, The 2854
Red, White and Blue 4833
Red, White and Blue Girl 3073
Red, White and Blues, The 4004
Red, White and Maddox Kazoo March 3684
Red Wine and a Wench 2563
Redecorate 1679
Rediscovery of the Eunuch, The 1426
Rednecks 2852

Redskinland 1980
Refer them to Me 1255
Reflection 4537
Reflections 2198, 2618, 3763
Reform 4312
Reform Song, The 1970
Refrain, Audacious Scribe 1948
Refugees on Parade 3705
Regal Romp, The 138
Regal Sadness Sits on Me 3570
Regardez-Moi 1145
Regency Rakes 841
Regent Street 4115
Reggae Music Got Soul 3690
Reggie's Family Tree 3951
(What Would You Do Without) Reggy 2722
Regiment Loves the Girls, The 2789
Regimental Band 2594
Regimental Review 2978
Regimental Roly Poly Girl, The 3755
Regimental Song 4664
Regina's Aria 3691
Regretful Blues 805
Regular Army Man 3031
Regular Family, A 838
Regular Fellas 647
Regular Guy, A 262, 1174, 3177
Regular Limited Train, The 3437
Regular William Gillette, A
(Regular Mr. Gillette) 1640
Regulation Purple 922
Rehearsal 4019, 1824
Rehearsal, The 2123
Rehearsal Hall 4374
Rehearsal Tap 1063
Rehearse! 4004
Reidhof's 3763
Reified Expression 169
Reindeer Dance 1654
Reindeer Moss 3201
Rejection 3094
Rejoice 2801
Rejuvenation 2028
Relations 1537
Relatively Simple Affair, A 483
Relax 4718
Relax and Enjoy It 1101
Relax with Me, Baby 2420
Release That Man 1388
Release Yourself 1713
Relic Seller Theme 1581
Religion in My Feet 691
Religious Establishment, The 2220
Reluctant Cannibal, The 220
Remarkable 2067
Remarkable Doctor, A 4497
Remarkable Fellow 3899
Remarkable People We 1856
Rememb'ring 4429
Remember (Walking in the Sand) 338
Remember 789
Remember? 2536
Remember 3599, 3838, 4154
Remember Always to Give 2033
Remember Caesar 3599
Remember Cameo 3796
Remember Him 3913, 4696
Remember Love 3817
Remember Me 69, 695
Remember Me (Love Song) 2622
Remember Me 3453
Remember Me Smiling 4522
Remember Radio 4395
Remember, Remember 3938
Remember Someone 4192
Remember That Day 3711
Remember That I Care 4169
Remember the Alamo 3558
Remember the Dancing 868
Remember the Dream 1108
Remember the Good Times 2305
Remember the Night 1918
Remember the Ocean 4515
Remember the Old Continentals 2534
Remember the Rose 1847
Remember the Time 4106
Remember There Was Me 3600
Remember to Forget 4136
Remember Today 3544
Remember When I Hated You? 1958
Remember You 1569
Remembering 2541, 1347
Remembering You 2263
Remembrance 1189
Remembrances 2114
Remind Me 2204, 2372, 2294, 902, 2772
Reminds Me of Home Sweet Home 2481
Remington Rainger 4141
Reminiscence 1067, 1961, 2419
Reminiscence, A 2546
Reminiscence 2666, 2794, 2816, 3078
Reminiscences (inst.) 1784
Reminiscing 4846
Reminiscing of Dixie 3040
Reminiscing Saturday Afternoon 3965
Rendezvous 324, 2813, 4033
Rendezvous of Love, The 710
Rendezvous Time in Paree 4174
Rendezvous Waltz, The 387
Renew My Mind 1073
Renita Reinette 2371
Renoir, Degas & Toulouse Lautrec 3942
Renoir, Degas and Toulouse 3940
Rent-a-Grandma 159
Rent a Robot 2962
Rental Cruelty 3960
Rep Up Your Step 2276
Repent 3279
Repent! Repent! 3318
Repent St. Louis 2928

Report from the Caribbean 1880
Report on Status 2477
Repose 2375
Reprise Me 778
Reputation 2363, 2605
Requiem 406, 1064, 2411, 3913
Requiem Blues 2200
Requiem for a Lightweight 2651
Requiem for Everyone 1049
Requiem for Evita 1211
Rescue, The 2731, 4447, 4634
Rescue Me 146
Residuals 2676
Resist 3318
Resolutions 3944
Resolved 591
Respect 338, 4193, 3739
Respectability 1029, 1373
Respectable 3305
Respectable Wife, A 2838
Responsible 2998
Rest of the Week She's Mine, The (Caroline) 2261
Rest Rest 2519
Rest Room Rose 418
Rest Stop 4459
Restaurant, The 1509
Reste La 1540
Rested Body Is a Rested Mind, A 4722
Restless 4177, 4377
Restless Heart 1242
Restless River 3605
Restless Rover 2910
Restoration Piece 3107
Result of Miss Brice's Going to Dancing School, The 1944
Resurrection 3667
Resurrection Rag 1920
Retiring from the Stage 1356
Retreat 3515
Return, The 2923
Return of Little Neil 1938
Return of the Animals, The (inst.) 730
Return of the Children (inst.) 3487
Return to Africa 3814
Return to Warm My Heart Again 93
Reuben 4476
Reuben Talks 3696
Reuben Tell Your Mandy 4753
Reubens on Parade, The 3809
Reunion 2152
Reunion, The 3565
Reunion 3697
Reveille 1523, 3078
Reveille, The 49
Revelation 3724
Revelation Ensemble 3865
Revels of the Jewels 1881
Revenge 1237, 2163, 2453, 2527
Revenge! 81
Revenge Is Sweet 2233
Revenge! Revenge!! and Retribution 402
Revenge Song 2648, 3806
Reverie in Blue 3940
Reverie in Rhythm 2458
Reveries 1162
Review of Athletes 2534
Reviewing the Situation 3271
Revival, The 1139
Revival Day 4235
Revival of the Fittest 1857
Revolt in Cuba 207
Revolution 3231
Revolution Festival 4692
Revolution Now 3539
Revolutionary Man, The 2119
Revolutionary Song 2811
Revue Hoedown 4388
Rewrite Your Own Story 1700
Rex 3702
Reykjavik 720
Reynosa 1804
Rhapsodie Table d'Hote 1392
Rhapsody 3292
Rhapsody for Pinochle Players 615
Rhapsody in Black 3705
Rhapsody in Blue (inst.) 445, 447, 1489, 3704, 3705
Rhapsody of Love 4620
Rhapsody of Sounds and Motion 2084
Rheims Cathedral, The 202
Rhett, Scarlett, Ashley 2301
Rhinegold 1569
Rhinestones 3342
Rhoda and Her Pagoda 3828
Rhode Island Is Famous for You 2137
Rhode Island Tango 1591
Rhodopa's Tavern 1745
Rhumba, The 796
Rhumba 3823, 4380
Rhumba Jake 3036
Rhumba Jumps!, The 4586
Rhumba on the Right 3990
Rhumbop 3628
Rhyme for Angela, A 1284
Rhymes Have I 2327, 4383
Rhyming 1992
Rhyming for a Dance 4133
Rhyming Menu 949
Rhythm 1763, 3521, 3955
Rhythm Feet 691
Rhythm Holiday 1982
Rhythm in My Hair 1342
Rhythm in Waltztime (inst.) 886
Rhythm Is a Racket 4253
Rhythm Is Our Business 432, 4743
Rhythm Is Red an' White an' Blue 4394
Rhythm Lullaby 725
Rhythm Makes the World Go Round 1982
Rhythm of America 3966
Rhythm of Joy 1462

Rhythm of Life, The 4238
Rhythm of the Day 1131, 4823
Rhythm of the Line, The 3830
Rhythm of the Waves 1126
Rhythm River 882
Rhythmic Rhapsodies on the Piano 4437
Rhythms of a Summer Night 494
Rib of Adam 2992
Ribbons and Bows 4821
Ribbons Down My Back 1828
Ribbons I Will Give Thee 3939
Riblah's Lament 4157
Ricardo's Lament 4459
Rice and Shoes 4491
Rich, The 656, 919
Rich and Famous 1371
Rich and Happy 4067, 2822
Rich Butterfly 1567
Rich Coon's Babe, A 2111
Rich Enough to Be Rude 2580
Rich Girls 154
Rich Is 2874
Rich Man, Poor Man 649, 3177
Rich Man, Poor Man (Beggar Man, Thief) 3265
Rich Man! Poor Man! 4118
Rich Man's Frug (dance) 4238
Rich or Poor 1275
Rich People of Texas 413
Rich People of Texas, The 412
Rich, Rich, Rich 1991
Rich Woman 943
Richard Crudnut's Charm School 3105
Richard Interred 1633
Riches 3733
Richest Man in the World, The 2678
Rick-Chick-a-Chick 2287
Rickety Crickety 2216
Rickety-Rackety-Shack 1215
Ricochet 4264
Riddle, The 2164, 1679
Riddle Diddle Me This 4058
Riddle-Ma-Ree 4425
Riddle Me This 289
Riddle of Life 593
Riddle of You, The 2322
Riddle Song, The 2096
Riddles 1388
Riddleweed 1698
Ride, The 2100
Ride, Baby, Ride 3515
Ride, Cowboy, Ride 1546
Ride 'Em Cowboy 4314
Ride 'Em Cowboys 3086
Ride in the Puff-Puff, A 4430
Ride Me Around with You, Dearie 558
Ride on a Rainbow, A 3800
Ride on to Highest Destiny 4615
Ride Out the Storm 3869
Ride, Ride, Ride 302
Ride the Winds 3711
Ride Through the Night 4190
Ride to the Castle, The (inst.) 2394
Ride to the Course, The 4544
Rider in the Rain 2787
Rider to the Sea 2364
Ridin' High 1018, 1762, 3674, 881
Ridin' on the Breeze 283
Ridin' on the Moon 4123
Ridin' the Rails 4825
Riding 4437
Riding for a Fall 593
Riding Habit 1322
Riding High 3639
Riding in a Motor Car 236
Riding in the Choo-Choos 3092
Riding Lesson, The 1067
Riding Lesson 1498
Riding on a Carousel 2838
Riding on a High Horse 3080
Riding the Range-A Song of the Old West 1256
Riff-Raff-Rafferty 3087
Rig O' the Day, The (Mink) 1644
Rigadoon, The 2917
Rigauden 129
Right 4334
Right About Here 3112
Right Across from Brooklyn (Oh, Yes, New York) 2934
Right As the Rain 462
Right at the Start of It 4367
Right Boy Comes Along 3821
Right Brazilian Girl, The 1530
(You're in) The Right Church but the Wrong Pew 295
Right Finger of My Left Hand, The 3687
Right Girl, The 1329, 2931, 3712
Right Girls 1237
Right Hand Man 2626
Right Here 2737
Right Image, The 2477
Right Key but the Wrong Key Hole, The 3297
Right Key, Wrong Keyhole 3905
Right Kind of People, The 3427
Right Man, The 551
Right Now 3987, 1246
Right-O 3431
Right of Way 2682
Right Off the Board 1667
Right Out of Heaven Into My Arms 931
Right Place at the Right Time, The 4635
Right Place, Right Time 4138
Right, Right, Right 3788
Right This Way 3713
Right Time, the Right Place, The 101
Right Up Your Alley 3714
Right Way 1319
Rigoletto 1332
Rigo's Last Lullaby 4275
Rilly Great Shew, A 3530
Rin-Tin-Tin 2135, 2594

Rin-tin-tin and Ninette 4302
Ring-a-Ding-a-Ding Dong Dell 4179
Ring-A-Ting-A-Ling on the Telephone 3332
Ring Cycle 992
Ring for Rose 3420
Ring in the Joys 2298
Ring Iron 3831
Ring Master's Song 2062
Ring Me Up in the Morning 1566
Ring of Gold in Texas, A 992
Ring of Roses (Hansel and Gretel) 1067
Ring on the Finger 1029
Ring Out Glad Bells 335
Ring Out the Bells 3274
Ring Out the Blues 1135
Ring Out the Liberty Bell 3401
Ring, Ring de Banjo 4149
Ring the Bell 657
Ring the Bells and Bang the Brasses! 1905
Ring the Merry Bells 2348
Ring the Praises Merrily 1466
Ring the Wedding Bells 2834
Ring Them Bells 131, 2558, 4480
Ring to the Name of Rosie 1478
Ring to the Name of Rosie, The 3723
Ring Up the Curtain 2447
Ring, Ring, Ring 4648
Ringa Zinga 1279
Ringalevio 2707
Ringaroundarosy 599, 630
Ringle, Ringle 2980
Ringmaster Song 4011
Rings of Smoke 3717
Rings of the Sea 2671
Ringside Madison Square Garden (inst.} 125
Ringside Table for Two 1125
Rink, The 131, 3718
Rinka Tinka Man 4677
Rio 4619
Rio Bamba, The 599
Rio de Janeiro 2540
Rio Grande 292
Rio Rhapsody 3409
Rio Rita 3719
Riot 1282
Riot, The (dance) 2681
Riot 4168
Rip Van Winkle 395, 3720, 4524
Rip Van Winkle and His Little Men 3146
Rip Van Winkle Was a Lucky Man 4014
Ripening Heart 2100
Riquette 3084
Riquette et Sa Mere 1066
Rise and Fall of Legs Diamond, The 2437
Rise and Fall of the American Empire
Waltz, The 4635
Rise and Fall of the City of Movieville, The 3970
Rise and Fly 10
Rise and Meet the Sun Half Way 2275
Rise and Shine 3249
Rise 'n' Love 729
Rise 'N' Shine 4267
Rise of David Levinsky, The 3722
Rise Tafari 3690
Rise Up! 2565
Rise Up and Stand Again 105
Rise Up Jah-Jah Children 3690
Rising Expectations 4379
Rising Star 1384
Rising Surf, The 1809
Risk a Little Bit 1992
Rit Tit Tat 2132
Rita 1568
Rita Cheeta 4089
Rita from Argentina 4454
Rita, My Marguerita 2922
Rita's Confession 2646
Rita's Request (Kill Me) 299
Ritual 2284
Ritual Dance 4572
Ritual of Ruku 4243
Ritual, The 2785
Rivals, The 71, 2057
River, The 3724, 757
River and Me, The 4235
River Ballad 2556
River Bank, The 837
River Chanty 2030
River Deep Mountain High 338
River Deep, Mountain High 2427
River God 4207
River in the Rain 394
River Man 3605
River of Change 2172
River of Dreams 2756
River of Faces, The 3332
River of Fire 992
River Rats 1086
River Song, The 818, 1369
River Song 1667, 2679, 3719
River to Dora Flora 4331
River Will Sweep You Away, The 364
Riverboat Shuffle 4137
Rivers Cannot Flow Upwards 3164
River's in Me, The 3724
Rivers of Roses 2220
Rivers of Tears 4863
Rivers to the South 1319
Riverside Bus 123
Riverside Drive 2217, 4194
Riverside Sailors 2405
Riverwind 3725
Riviera, The (2) 507
Riviera, The (1) 507
Riviera 2057
Riviera, The 2227
Riviera 4692
Riviera Nights 808, 809
Riviera Rage (dance), The 2148
Rivkele 2356

Rivkele Dem Rebns 3670
Ro-Ro-Rollin' Along 203
Road, The (inst.) 2368
Road Ends Here, The 2224
Road House Rag 1031
Road I'm Taking, The 573
Road that Leads Back Home 1502
Road that Lies Before, The 1784
Road to Anywhere, The 1240
Road to Destiny, The 3403
Road to Dreams, The 2789
Road to Hampton 823
Road to Happiness, The 1110, 1534
Road to Hell, The 3788
Road to Home, The 4372
Road to Mandelay 3729
Road to Paradise, The 1377, 2794
Road to the Girl You Love, The 2774
Road to Yesterday, The 1096, 3730
Road Tour, The 1601
Road You Didn't Take, The 1329
Roam On, My Little Gypsy Sweetheart 1343
Roaming Around the Town 2123
Roaring Twenties Strike Back, The 454
Robbed 2650
Robber-Baron Minstrel Parade, The 4004
Robber Bridegroom, The 3733
Robbers Everywhere 4492
Robbery, The 3938
Robert, Alvin, Wendall and Jo Jo 2801
Robert E. Lee 3513
Robert E. Lee Cakewalk 2231
Robert the Roue 4131
Robert the Roue (from Reading, Pa.) 4174
Robin and the Rose, The 4559
Robin Hood's Arrest 246
Robin Hood's Entrance 3736
Robinson Crusoe 2339, 3737
Robinson Crusoe's Island 4010
Robinson Crusoe's Isle 2951, 2552
Robinson Hotel, The 2376
Robot Man 3695
Robot Will Never Say No, A 2861
Rocco's Dream 1412
Rochelle Hudson Tango, The 3940
Rock, The 2470
Rock-a-Bye Baby 250
Rock-a-Bye-Baby 1823
Rock-A-Bye Baby 3009
Rock-a-Bye Baby Dear (Lullaby) 3740
Rock a Bye Ma Baby 395
Rock-a-Bye River 3950
Rock-a-Bye Your Baby with a Dixie Melody 3985
Rock & Roll All Night 3739
Rock and Roll Bump 4180
Rock and Roll Critic 1978
Rock and Roll Music 3739
Rock Around the Clock 3739
Rock Back the Clock 843
Rock Garden Rock 2092
Rock Is My Way of Life 3515
Rock Island 3016
Rock, Little Children 1300
Rock Me 887
Rock Me in the Cradle of Love 4808
Rock Me in the Cradle of the Deep 3041
Rock Me in Your Loving Arms 764
Rock 'n Horse 2084
Rock 'N' Roll 1813
Rock 'n' Roll Party Party Queen 1664
Rock 'n' Roll Star 1695
Rock 1975 3814
Rock of Rages 2427
Rock, Rock 3531
Rock, Rock, Rock 206, 591
Rock-Rock-Rock Let Me Rock in My Old Rocking Chair 2383
Rock with Rock 1822
Rockabye Hamlet 3741
Rockaway Beach 197
Rockaway Mary 4842
Rocket to the Moon 3716
Rockette's Dance 4629
Rockin' 823
Rockin' and Rollin' in Loch Lomond 1771
Rockin' Around the Christmas Tree 338, 3793, 3794
Rockin' at the Cannon Ball 1644
Rockin' in Rhythm 875, 1137
Rockin' in Rhythm (inst.) 885
Rockin' in Rhythm 4091
Rockin' Pneumonia 1890
Rocking Chair Fleet 3712
Rocking Chair Interlude 367
Rocking the Boat 2759
Rocks in My Bed 2259
Rocky on the Rocks 62, 3124
Rocky Road 3631
Rocky Road to Dublin 1532
Rocky Road to the White House, The 3530
Rococo Rag 1249
Rodeo 2332
Rodeo Dreams 3517
Rodeo Rider 3517
Rodeo Romeo 992
Rodgers and Hammerstein 779
Roebling Plan, The 564
Roger De Coverly 2399
Roger the Ox 1262
Roger the Ugly 4469
Rogue Song, The 4251
Role-Playing 2630
Roll a Little Pill for Me 2127
Roll Along 1208
Roll Along, Covered Wagon 1836
Roll Along, Sadie 4499
Roll Call 3630
Roll Call in the Morning, The 2005
Roll 'Em 1930
Roll Jordan 1198
Roll Me 2270

Roll Me Out on the Boardwalk 1332
Roll of the Drums 3680
Roll On 2779
Roll On, Mighty Wave 3337
Roll on Missouri 1738
Roll On, Rolling Road 4361
Roll On Silver Moon 2631
Roll On, Silvery Moon 538
Roll Out the Hose, Boys 1548
Roll Out the Morning 4089
Roll Pony, Roll 3415
Roll The Cotton Bales 822
Roll Up the Ribbons 2050
Roll with the Punches 1970
Roll Yer Socks Up 3113
Roll Your Hoop 3958
Roll, Jordan, Roll 443
Rolland from Holland 3369
Rolled Into One 3230
Roller Rinkers 558
Roller Skates for Mine 2383
Roller Skating on a Rainbow 173
Roller Skating Waltz 3962
Rollerskating Granny 2541
Rollicking Blarney O 2973
Rollin' 2787
Rollin' de Bones a Coblenz on de Rhine 815
Rollin' in Gold 1373
Rollin' Up the River 4162
Rolling Exercise 2816
Rolling Stock 4138
Rolling Stone 4292
Rolling Stones 3310
Rolling Up the Barcarolle 764
Rolling, Rolling 870
Roly Poly 737
Roma (Roma Nun Fa La Stupida Stasera) 3798
Romance 253, 273, 718, 969, 1027, 1863, 1992
Romance! 2731
Romance 2838, 3011, 3064, 3064, 3322, 284, 4186
Romance and Musketeer 2344
Romance and Reality 1246
Romance and Rondeau 526
Romance in a Dance, The 293
Romance in Candlelight 3756
Romance in the Dark 2796
Romance Is Calling 82, 1610
Romance Land 3396
Romance of a Bachelor Bird, The 4738
Romance of the Laundry 2715
Romance! Romance! 3760
Romance with Music 3064
Romancing the Mardi Gras 2087
Romantic Atmosphere, A 3918
Romantic Blues 764
Romantic Girl 4806
Romantic Knight, A 1847
Romantic Notions 3760
Romantically Inclined 2439
Romany 3028, 3130
Romany Life 1711
Romany Life (Czardas) 1355
Romany Rover 4668
Romanza 1849, 3864
Rome 519, 1848
Rome Is Burning 1657
Romeo 1923, 4478
Romeo and Juliet 466, 3400, 2244, 2131, 3775, 3876, 3934
Romeo, Juliet, Johnny and Jane 3783
Romp in the Hay 1414
Romper Room 916
Romping Red Heads, The 683
Ron and Bobby 3873
Rona, Mona and Me 3636
Ronald Liebowitz, My Hero 3227
Ronald Reagan 2913
Rondelay 3763
Roof Space 270
Roof Tree 4529
Roofs 4343
Rook and the Robin, The 3581
Rookie in the Ring 3039
Room Enough for Me 1488
Room for Improvement 2513
Room for One 3501
Room for Two 3149
Room in Bloomsbury, A 507
Room in My Heart 751
Room Is Filled with You, The 808
Room-Mates 610
Room 317 2905
Room to Be Free 2962
Room with a Bath, A 1657
Room with a View, A 3196
Room with a View 3235
Room with a View, A 4341
Room Without Windows, A 4633
Roommate Beguine, The 2069
Rooneyisms 2601
Roosevelt, Bryan and Hughes 3400
Roosevelt of Germany 4803
Roosevelt, Wilson and Hughes 3400
Rooster and the Hen, The 4514
Rooster and the Lark, The 1570
Rooster Man 341
Root for Riley 3809
Root, Petite and Gone 1296
Rootless 339
Roots 2073
Roots of the Tree 3690
Rootsie-Pootsie 902
Rope Dance (inst.) 3347
Rope Song 2970
Ropin' Dogies 3548
Rosa 3764, 3764
Rosa Rosana 2261
Rosa Rosetta 1332, 2232
Rosabella 2961, 3444
Rosabella Clancy 4201

Rosalie 2906, 3765, 3766, 4115, 4723, 4804
Rosalilla of Sevilla 1066
(There's None So Sweet As) Rosalind 4649
Rosalynde 3909
Rosamund's Dream 3733
Rosario 3879
Rose, The 521, 1959, 2328, 1804
Rose, a Child, a Butterfly, A 1270
Rose and a Lily, A 3951
Rose and I, The 2142
Rose and the Breeze, The 3673
Rose Aria, The 2371
Rose Briar 3768
Rose Colored Glasses 723
Rose de France 3769
Rose Girl Blues, The 3770
Rose Girl Waltz 3770
Rose in Bloom 3236
Rose in My Hair, A (A Rose in Your Hair) 1855
Rose in the Heather 1384
Rose in the Snow 3431
Rose Is a Rose, A 454
Rose Lovejoy of Paradise Alley 1029
Rose, Lucky Rose 1183
Rose Marie 1625
Rose-Marie 3772
Rose Marie 4497
Rose-Marie selections 4251
Rose Minuet 2937
Rose of Argentine 2107
Rose of Arizona 1448, 1944
Rose of Delight 930
Rose of Iran 2330
Rose of Kenmare, The 4605
Rose of Killarney, The 801
Rose of Madrid 1487
Rose of My Heart 4818, 4843
Rose of Old Derry, A 3220
Rose of Old Seville 545
Rose of Pyramid Land 1738
Rose of Rangoon, The 4076
Rose of Roses, A 149
Rose of San Antone 1938
Rose of Seville 25
Rose of Spain 487, 1154
Rose of Stamboul 3778
Rose of Tenement Row 709
Rose of the Rio Grande 3175
Rose of the Riviera, The 2964
Rose of the Rotisserie 2870, 4290
Rose of the Studios 3796
Rose of the World 48, 1134
Rose of the World (My Life I Love Thee) 3773
Rose of Verdun 4421
Rose of Washington Square 4824, 4840, 4842
Rose of Yesterday 2732
Rose of Yesternight 2884
Rose, Rose, Rose 4713
Rose Rosetta 2122
Rose Ruby 1625
Rose Song 3696
Rose Tattoo, The 3878, 3879
Rose-Time 1488
Roseanna 3444
Roseanne 2896
Rosebud 870, 3191
Rosebud Queen 4161
Rosebuds, The 591
Roseland 3902
Rosemarin 3703
Rosemary 293, 683, 2019, 2907, 4815
Rosemary and the Planet 2887
Rosemary's Soliloquy 1990
Rosencrantz and Guildenstern Boogie 3741
Rosenthal Ain't Rosenthal No More 3926
Roses 1065
Roses and Butterflies 256
Roses and Thorns 1466
Roses Are Nodding 4001
Roses Are Sweetest 2603
Roses at the Station 1649
Roses Begin with R, Love 2906
Roses Bloom for Lovers 3771
Roses for the Girl I Love 1295
Rose's Goodbye to Easter 4169
Roses Have Made Me Remember, The 702
Roses in the Garden 4815
Roses in the Rain 1048
Roses, Lovely Roses 4760
Roses of France 3569
Roses of Picardy 1823, 3259
Roses of Red 1281
Roses Out of Reach 2419
Roses Red and White 737
Roses Say You Will, The 4716
Rose's Turn 1709
Roses Understand 2829
Rosetime and You 1587
Rosewater Foundation, The 1591
Rosey-Posey 4747
Rosey Posey 4804
Rosh Hashono 4773
Rosie 607, 1640, 1927, 4099
Rosie from Palermo 2665
Rosie Lee 2209
Rosie O'Grady's a Charleston Lady Now 994
Rosie Petals 675
Rosie Posies 1777
Rosie Road 1836
Rosie Rosenblatt, Stop the Turkey Trot! 3926
Rosie Rosenblott 3399
Rosie the Riveter 2026
Rosita 1118
Rosita Rodriguez 3602
Rosy 2481
Rosy and John 1427
Rosy Dreams 671

Rosy Morn, The 3681
Rosy, Posy 480
Rosy Red 2065
Rothschild and Sons 3780
Rothschilds, The 3780
Rotisserie, The 201
Rottenest Job 4063
Rouge 3108
Rough and Ready Man 478
Rough Riders 3558
Rough, Rugged and Robust 4117
Rough Stuff 2439
Rough Times 837
Roulette 415, 1182
Roulette Dance 764
Roulette Game, The 3703
Roumania 780
Roumania, Roumania 2356
Roumeynische Libe 3781
Round, A 1162
'Round About Midnight 2555
Round and Round 1245, 4114
Round by Red Mountain 451
Round Every Corner 4193
Round in Circles 4703
Round on the End and High in the Middle 1992
Round-Shouldered Man 3862
Round the Clock 4603
'Round the Corner 2549
Round the Corner 4419
Round the Ray Wain 710
'Round the Town 3745
Round the World 1613
Round Up, The 3661
Round-Up, The 1316
Roundabout 4237, 4499
Roundelay 3736
Rounders' Serenade, The 2232
Roundhouse O'Leary 821
Roust-abouts 2845
Roustabouts 3808
Roustabouts' Song (We Follow the Trail) 3648
Routine Exercise, The 4634
Roving Gambler, The 3989
Row, Row 2387
Row, Row, Boatman 1518
Row Row Row 3259
Row, Row, Row 4655, 4806
Row 10 Aisle 6 Bench 114 3277
Rowing 4113
Rowing, Rowing 2711
Rowing Song, The 1566
Roxana 946
Roxane's Confession 949
Roxie 723
Royal Anthem 3445
Royal Bangkok Academy, The 2312
Royal Barge 1281
Royal Blood 3944
Royal Confession, A 4798
Royal Court Dance 3814
Royal Crocodile, The 3073
Royal Damn Fango, The 1651
Royal Dressing Room Scene 759
Royal Family, A 138
Royal Garden Blues (inst.) 3840, 432
Royal Hessian Auction 3780
Royal Honeymoon, A 737
Royal Hussars Are We 1768
Royal March 1110
Royal March, The 1871
Royal Nonesuch, The 394
Royal Pair Are Off Today, The 4014
Royal Radio 3641
Royal Rounds, The 1605
Royal Wedding 3406
Royalty 3791
Rozinkes Mit Mandlen (Raisins and Olives) 1279
Rozita 385
Rub a Dub 2986
Rub-A-Dub-Dub (1) 451
Rub-A-Dub-Dub (2) 451
Rub a Dub Dub 2134
Rub-a-Dub Your Rabbit's Foot 290
Rub the Lamp 3098
Rub Your Lamp 2453
Rubadub Dub 324
Rubaiyats from the Rubaiyat 3404
Rubber Man, The 104
Rubber Plant Song, The 3368
Rube Jazz Dance (inst). 1026
Rube Song 2964
Rube Wedding 3426
Ruben's Holiday 2642
Rubenstein Rag, The 1863
Rubies for a Queen 1857
Ruby 4137, 2231
Ruby Baby 4031
Rudolph the Red-Nosed Reindeer 3793, 3794, 3795
Rue Broadway 1
Rue de la Paix 4249
Ruffian Ballet, The 1965
Rug, Snug 1557
Rugantino in the Stocks (La Berlina) 3798
Ruggles of Red Gap 3800
Ruined 3427
Ruined Maid, The 4467
Ruins 3214
Ruisenor 1414
Rule Britannia 3450
Ruler of Central Park, The 1466
Ruler of My Heart 4127
Rulers of the Earth 4803
Rules and Regulations 3551
Rules of Asylum 1865
Rum Below 3944
Rum-Dum-Dum-Dum 3072

Rum, Tum, Fidele 3395
Rum-Tum-Tiddle 4528
Rum Tum Tiddle 4553
Rum Tum Tugger 678
Rumania, Rumania 1609, 4342
Rumba, The 203
Rumba Rhythm 1135
Rumbatism 1251
Rumble, The (dance) 4625
Rumble of the Subway, The (Subway Chant) 2768
Rumble, Rumble, Rumble 3444, 4692
Rumbola 4198
Rumors 147
Rumors from Rome 456
Rumpelstiltskin 1727
Rumplestiltskin 4106
Rumson 3347
Run Along Mr. Ogre Man 1975
Run and Hide 2224
Run Away 2307, 3866
Run Away, Naughty Man 4044
Run Away with Me 1730
Run Between the Raindrops 2754
Run, Brudder Possum, Run 3744
Run, Brudder Rabbit, Run! 3945
Run for Your Life 3576, 4013
Run, Indian, Run 4785
Run Into Your Arms 3507
Run, Musashi, Run 3711
Run on the Bank 740
Run River Run 3724
Run, Run, Run 2449
Run, Run, Run Cinderella 1373
Run Something 4147
Run to Me, My Love 67
Runaway 4827
Runaway Colts 4422
Runaway Little Girl 2264
Runaway Match, A 3618
Runaways 4635
Runnin' 2645, 14
Runnin' for Jesus 3987
Runnin' to Meet the Man 3656
Runnin' Wild Blues 2557, 554
Running 1764
Running Around with Chorus Girls 804
Running Down the Sun 2618
Running for Office 1968
Running Out of Time 692
Running Wild 2044
Rupert Bear Song 4449
Ruritania 1467
Rushing the Growler 4362
Russia the Fatherland 3129
Russian Art 4817
Russian Barcarolle, A 710
Russian Blues 702, 2570
Russian Dance (Opening Act Two) 1066
Russian Dance 2292, 2358
Russian Dance at the Yabacabana 1993
Russian Duo and Dance 3265
Russian Love 2567
Russian Lullaby 789
Russian Maidens, The 1758
Russian Movie 2333
Russian Song 1387
Russian Toys, The 710
Russian Wedding March 2292
Rustic Ann 4054
Rustic Anna 132
Rustic Country Inn, A 3760
Rustic Patrol 1095
Rustle of Your Bustle, The 1127
Rusty Bell 4460
Rusty's Dream Ballet 2949
Rusty's Up in the Air 1323
Ruth 4732, 1769
Ruth St. Denis 3401
Ruthless! 3811
Ruthless 1435
Rutland Bounce, The (Dance) 1791

S

S & M Polka, The 2426
S.A.D.U.S.E.A. 3598
S-E-X 3124
S Eureka Presents (sketch) 3954
S.I.P. 3960
'S Over but the Shoutin' 1929
S.S. Commodore Ebenezer McAffee the Third 1373
S-S-Something Comes Over Me 4701
'S Wonderful 1419, 3020, 3060
S'a Mechaye 2811
Sabbath Blessing 4172
Sabbath Prayer 1265
Sabbath Queen 1609
Sabbath Song 2422
Sabot Dance 1570
Sabot Dance (inst.) 4357
Sabra, The 4514
Sabre Song, The 1027
Sabre Song 1745
Sacred Bodies 327
Sacred Tree, The 4447
Sacrifice, The 4139
Sacrifice 825, 2016, 2918
Sacrifice, The 4396
Sacrifice Your Body 4171
Sad Affair, A 2642
Sad at Heart Am I 4792
Sad Bad Man 1458
Sad Experience 2695
Sad Happy, Peek a Boo 456
Sad Is the Life of the Sailor's Wife 1893
Sad Is the Whippoorwill 4161

Sad Tale of the Beauxhommes, The 3285
Sad Was the Day 1076
Sadder-but-Wiser Girl, The 3016
Saddest Moon, The 2153
Saddle Up the Horse 3279
Sade 3111
Sadie 2506, 1627
Sadie Fats 2443
Sadie Hawkins Ballet (inst.) 2484
Sadie, Sadie (Married Lady) 1420
Sadie Salome Go Home 4804
Sadie's Song 2573
Safe 1002, 1822
Safe Home 1665
Safe in His Arms 3987
Safe in the Arms of Bill Hart 4378
Safe in Your Arms 4328
Safe in Your Heart 4424
Safe Little World 1035
Safe, Sane and Single 1296
Safe Sex Slut 4309
Safety First Love 1735
Safety in Numbers 507, 2263
SAG Card Blues 4389
Saga of Billy the Kid 3947
Saga of Carmen, The (Carmen Was) 4826
Saga of Jenny, The 2386
Saga of Killer Joe, The 3479
Saga of Men and Marriage 164
Saga of the Haganah, The 181
Saga of the Presidents, The 3558
Saga of the Sack 1880
Saga of the Sea 1539
Sage 3814
Sahara 1032
Sahara (Now We're As Dry As You) 2939
Sahara Moon 1343
Sahara Sarah 4215
Sahara Twins, The 4203
Said I to Myself 356
Said the Governor 1521
Sail Away 2852, 2787, 3235, 3517, 3729, 3815
Sail Home 88, 3944
Sail On 1369
Sail on Sweet Universe 2962
Sail on the Tail of a Whale, A 1295
Sailin' Away on the Henry Clay 1629
Sailing, The 1959
Sailing 2800, 4243, 4478, 96
Sailing at Midnight 3813
Sailing Away 4662
Sailing In a Sea-Going Hack 4425
Sailing on the Henry Clay 3256
Sailor 426
Sailor Ballet, The (inst.) 2938
Sailor Beware 3138
Sailor Man, The 906
Sailor of My Dreams, The 956
Sailor Song 3952, 4158
Sailor Talk 3485
Sailor Tango 369
Sailor with the Tap-Tap-Tap, The 213
Sailors, The 4572
Sailor's Bride, A 4121
Sailors 'Fake' Walk, The 1083
Sailor's Fling 3737
Sailor's Fox Trot Wedding 387
Sailor's Life, The 906
Sailor's Life, A 4559
Sailor's Life for Me, A 108
Sailor's Number 2559
Sailors of the Sea 4090
Sailors of the St. Hurrah 2517
Sailors on Leave (inst.) 2205
Sailor's Round 2236
Sailors Sail Away 2378
Sailor's Song, A 1896
Sailor's Tango, The 1755
Saint Genesius 3763
Saint Lazare 3386
Saints 3817
Saints Go Marching In 1890
Saints of the Latter Day 1911
Sal 1754
Salaam 336
Salaam Salaam 3348
Salaaming the Rajah 931
Salamaggis Birthday 40
Sale, The (ballet) 2705
Sale Is On, The 1119
Sales Lady, The 2695
Sales Reproach 2664
Salesladies' Annual Ball, The 1259
Salesmanship 4828
Salley Gardens 1977
Sally 1093, 1111, 1573, 2478, 3744, 3819, 3820, 4197
Sally Ann 981
Sally Ann Revival 981
Sally Bright Self-Risin' Flour Song, The 3671
Sally Dog 1425
Sally Down Our Alley 1065
Sally Ensalada 518
Sally in Our Alley 3820, 4859
Sally in the Alley 3450
Sally, Irene and Mary 392
Sally Simpson 4676
Sally Slide, The 4844
Sally, Won't You Come Back (Come Back to Our Alley, Sally?) 4815
Sally's Blues 2415
Salome 1318, 4217
Salome Dance 2869
Salomee (with Her Seven Veils) 1791
Saloon Piano 1037
Salt Air 1453
Salt and Pepper 2470
Salt Lake City 1911
Salt of the Sea 2493
Salt Water Pirate from Sugar Loaf Hill Brazil 854
Saltarello, The (La Saltarello) 3798

Saltpeter in the Rhubarb 1730, 1730
Salute 3526, 4201
Salute to Spring 3823
Salute to the King 1975
Salute to the Toreador 188
Salvation 3423, 3824
Salvation Army Girl 2749
Salvation Glide, The 548
Salvation Hymn 559
Salvation Sal 4421
Salvation Tess 4630
Salve Madonna 2220
Salzburg 363
Sam and Delilah 1528
Sam Hill 1736
Sam Johnson's Colored Cakewalk 1776
Sam, You Made the Pants Too Long 3926
Samandoza-we! 4579
Samaris Dance (dance) 2327
Samba at Daybreak 4117
Sambo 3676
Sambo and Dinah 2035
Sambo Was a Bad Boy 3825
Sambo's Banjo 3660
Sambo's Syncopated Russian Dance 2337
Same, The 139
Same As a Man 664
Same As Love, The 214
Same Girl, The 1509
Same Little Girl 4720
Same Mistakes 521
Same Old Clown, The 1514
Same Old Color Scheme 3656
Same Old Crowd The 2213
Same Old Game!, The 4187
Same Old Game, The 4555
Same Old Girl, The 8
Same Old Love 3493
Same Old Love Songs 771
Same Old Me, The 4785
Same Old Moon 3005
Same Old Moon, The 2408, 2638
Same Old Moon 4811
Same Old Places 97
Same Old Silv'ry Moon Is Shining, The 3676
Same Old Song, The 2568
Same Old Song 3401
Same Old Stars, Same Old Moon
(but Which Is the Girl?) 380
Same Old Story 1054
Same Old Story, The 1316, 1582, 4241
Same Old Story, Nothing New 3784
Same Old Summer 1081
Same Old Sun, The 1469
Same Old Sweethearts, The 538
Same Old Thing Turned Around, The 4037
Same Old Tune, The 2195
Same Old Two, The 48, 3773
Same Old Way, The 2308
Same Old Way 2546
Same One They Picked for Me, The 1963
Same Silver Moon, The 3056
Same Sort of Girl 1544
Same Sweet Baby, The 3663
Same Thing 2008
Same Thing Over Again, The 509
Same Time, Same Place 3301
Same Way Home 2055
Samee Gamee 3828
Sammy 4723
Sammy and Topsy 3660
Samoa Sam 293
Samoan Song (Ka Tahua) 3339
Samovar the Lawyer 1000
Sampson Beauties, The 1970
Samson and Delilah 4542
Samson's Epiphany 3456
Samson's Gonna Be Born 2164
Samson's Thoughts 3456
Samurai Stomp, The 2861
San Antonio 3205
San Fernando 2935
San Francisco 4251, 4635
San Francisco Bay 3387
San Francisco Fair 4630
San Francisco Fran 1390
San Francisco Sadie 4717
San Francisco Waltz 1604
San Gennaro 3696
San Salvatore 2323
San Pasquale 3798
San Slavatore 2323
San Sebastian's Shores 1920
San Simeon 2969
San Toy 2071
Sancocho 3830
Sanctus 2775, 2411
Sand 2153
Sand Flowers 1174
Sand in My Eyes 3818
Sand in My Shoes 3444
Sand Man, The 830, 3981
Sand Witches 2857
Sanders of the River 4207
Sandhog Song 3831
Sandman, The 2784, 3419
Sandow Girl, The 954
Sandpaper 4540
Sands Hotel Song 3832
Sands of Time 2327, 4383
Sandwich for Two 2362
Sandwich Man, The 1891
Sandwich Men, The 834
Sandy 4398
Sandy Mahatma Gandy 1136
Sandy McDougal 2495
Sandy's Bags 1857
Sans-Gene 1114
Sans Souci 4423
Santa Barbara 1216

Santa Claus 668, 752, 3163, 3184
Santa Claus Is Comin' to Town 3833
Santa Evita 1211
Santa Fe 639
Santa Land 1261
Santa Rosa Rose 3134
Santa's Lullaby 363
Santiago 1992
Santo Dinero 95
Saposhkelekh (The Boots) 4342
Sapsea's Song 3070
Sara Jane 2001
Sara Lee 131
Sarabande 1865, 129
Saracen Patrol, The 2697
Saracen Song March 4762
Sarafina 3836, 3879
Sarah 1015
Sarah from Sahara 1308
Sarah Jackman 1832
Sarah of Sahara 185
Sarah, the Sunshine Girl 4824
Sarasa 1327
Saratoga 3837
Saratoga Trunk 3837
Sarava 3838
Sari 568
Sari Dance, The 3397
Saroot 4252
Saroyan 3940
Sartor Sartoris 2913
Sascha's Got a Girl 924
Saskatchewan 280
Sas'parilla 3250
Satan 624
Satan Rules 2820
Satanic Strut 4741
Satan's Li'l Lamb 125
Satellite City 1390
Satellite Moon 220
Satin and Silk 3972
Satin, Cigarettes and Warm Brandy 4830
Satin Doll 3905, 146, 4091
Satins and Spurs 3841
Satisfaction 3739
Satisfaction Guaranteed 474
Saturday 2568, 4703, 4033
Saturday After Two 3882
Saturday Afternoon on Broadway 335
Saturday Afternoon Till Monday Morning 208
Saturday Chat 4016
Saturday Evening Post 3434, 4227
Saturday Morning 3835
Saturday Night 98, 870, 1074, 1557, 1648, 2764
Saturday Night (A Very Good Girl on Sunday) 2907
Saturday Night 2028, 3843
Saturday Night (Is the Loneliest Night in the Week) 4743
Saturday Night 4373, 3844
Saturday Night at the Rose and Crown 1564, 3235
Saturday Night Fish Fry 1296
Saturday Night in Central Park 2707
Saturday Night in Napoleon (dance) 2028
Saturday Night Polka 3453
Saturday Night's Our Night to Be Alone 494
Saturday Till Monday 1188
Saturday's Child 3178, 4018
Saturnalia 681
Sauce Diable (dance) 2201
Sauce for the Gander Is Sauce for the Goose 1558
Saucer Song, The 3818
Saucy Little Sadie 295
Saucy Moon 2934
Saucy Sparrow, The 1458
Saunter Away 4652
Saunter, Twilight, A 654
Sausage King, The 2040
Savage I Remain, A 1552
Savage Rhythm 884
Savage Serenade 3002
Savannah 612, 2190, 2232, 554
Savannah Stomp 3086
Savannah Sue 1776
Savannah's Wedding Day 2190
Save a Kiss 1614
Save a Kiss for Rainy Weather 3783
Save a Little Daylight for Me 2574
Save a Little Money for a Rainy Day 2996, 3480
Save It for Me! 3073
Save It for Me 3057
Save Me from Caesar 1848
Save the Last Dance 1015
Save the Men 3332
Save the Mission 617
Save the People 1595
Save the Village 1697
Save the World for Children 2962
Save Up Your Kisses for a Rainy Day 2291
Save Us 2698
Save Your Money John 4697
Save Your Money, John 4812, 4813
Save Your Yesses 4825
Saved 4031
Saved! 3568
Saved By Grace 4127
Saved By the One She Loves 3887
Savin' Souls 2776
(I've Been) Saving Myself for You 1659
Savoir Faire 1596
Savoire Faire 2610
Saw Mill River Road 1582
Sawbuck, a Fin or a Dime, A 2401
Sawing a Couple in Half 778
Sawing a Woman in Half 4768
Sawney Pott, the Idiot 4719
Saxon Stranger, A 1178
Saxophone, The 904
Saxophone Baby 2039
Saxophone Man 1096
Say (What I Wanna Hear You Say) 1979

Say a Prayer for Me Tonight 1511, 3038
Say, Darling 3845
Say! Have You Seen a Daughter? 30
Say Hello to Harvey 3846
Say Hello to the Folks Back Home 4281
Say Hello to Your Feet 2513
Say Hitchy-Koo, That's All 1920
Say It Again 1713, 2950
Say It Isn't So 2437, 789
Say It Loud I'm Black and Proud 3739
Say It Once Again 2387
Say It with a Red Red Rose 3342
Say It with a Sable 1488
Say It with a Solitaire 1779
Say It with a Uke 577
Say It with a Ukelele 199
Say It with Flowers 2222
Say It with Gin 3131
Say It with Girls 1134
Say It with Music 3006
Say It with Toes 1655
Say It with Your Feet 1980
Say Mama 2318
Say No More 298, 2937
Say Not Love Is a Dream (Valse-Song) 902
Say So! 3766
Say That You Love Me 1839
Say the Word 4335
Say the Word That Will Make You Mine 1989
Say the Words 4038
Say to Him 2830
Say 'Uncle' 2522
Say What You Want to Say 1116
Say When 136, 599, 3278, 3849, 3850, 448
Say When-Stand Up-Drink Down 3980
Say Yes, Look No 3215
Say Yes, Sweetheart, Say Yes 905
Say You'll Be a Friend of Mine 3747
Say You'll Be My Own, Dear 2944
Say You'll Stay 4435
Say Young Man of Manhattan 4023
Sayonara 126, 3851
Scaddle-de-Mooch 4833
Scandal 1556, 2123, 2897, 3547, 3580, 4365, 4547
Scandal, and a Cup of Tea 1780
Scandal Club, The 2399
Scandal in the Synagogue 2012
Scandal Number 3011
Scandal! Scandal! 4453
Scandal Town 2614
Scandal Walk 1483
Scandalizing Fashion 3796
Scandals! 556
Scandals Finale 556
Scandals in the Air 93
Scandinavia (Sing Dose Song and Make Dose Music) 2857
Scapin 3853, 3853, 4450
Scare Crow Maidie 2635
Scarecrow Dance, The 3024
Scared 280
Scarlet Coat, A 4404
Scarlet Pimpernel, The 3491
Scarlet Trimmings 3920
Scarlett (Skarettu) 1616
Scarlett O'Hara from Seventh Avenue 887
Scars, The (1) 2344
Scars, The (2) 2344
Scat 240
Scat Song, The 4137
Scena (Tingle Tangle) 3014
Scene 3864
Scene and Aria 3864
Scene and Pas de Seul 3735
Scene Au Dancing (inst.) 2753
Scene Changes, The 3596
Scene Dansant 138
Scene with the Grapes, The 4325
Scenes de la Vie de Boheme 2359
Scenes from Some Marriages 3476
Scheherazade 2234
Scheherazade Interlude 1300
Scheherazade Serenade 931
Scheherzade 1448
Schemes 3943
Scherzo 3703, 3864
Schickelgruber 2653
Schlaf Mein Kind 3844
Schlal 4790
Schneeglockchen 4490
Schnitza Komisski, The 3819
Schoe Plattler Tanz 2594
School Bells Ringin' Out 2090
School Days 1902, 2096, 4756
School Days (When We Were a Couple of Kids) 3855
School Days Are Over 4209
School Daze 3889
School Don't Mean a Damn Thing 344
School for Scandal, The 2399
School for Waiters 2137
School for Wives, The 127
School Mates 3855
School of Acting 1464
School of Bop 2168
School of Hard Knocks 779
School of Love, The 1274
School Song, The 2152
School Spirit 1418
Schoolboy Blues 4449
Schoolhouse Blues, The 3006
Schoolma'm's Song 4201
School's Out 3739
Schottische 3056
Schottische Scena 4557
Schrafft's 2707
Schrafft's University 3005
Schroeder 4783
Schuetzen Corps, The 2335
Schwabs 1940

Schwartz 3824
Schwindle Corps, The 2745
Science Fiction 3742
Scientific Classes 2724
Scoobi-doo 2243
Scooby Do 2579
Scotch Archer's Song 4539
Scotch Lassie 4815
Scotch on the Rocks 3107
Scotch Quadrille 2056
Scotch Twins 1923
Scotland for Ever! 3663
Scotland Forever 4509
Scourge of the Sea, The 1962
Scratch 1754
Scratch a Wife and Find a Doll 1745
Scratch My Back 3108
Scream 2058
Screaming and Yelling 3668
Screaming Clocks (The Dummies Song) 4349
Screams 1318
Screen Song, The 3937
Screen Test (inst.) 4543
Screening the Cast 1857
Screw May Twist, The 2348
Screwing My Way to the Top 4389
Screwy Little Tune 3168
Scrimmage of Life, The 341
Scrooge Rejoins the Human Race 752
Scrubwoman's Ballet (inst.) 123
Scrubwoman's Ballet (Dance) 827
Scrynatchkieloosaw 3806
Scum-Dee-Dum 521
Scylla and Charybdis 1600
Scythe and the Sickle, The 2766
Sea, The 3724
Sea, The 3485
Sea Breeze 1985
Sea Chanty 189, 2014, 2827, 3989
Sea Cruise 1890
Sea Fever 220
Sea-Gull and the Ea-gull 4237
Sea Is All Around Us, The 2227, 3941
Sea Is Calling, The 1921
Sea Legs 642
Sea of the Tropics Dance 4283
Sea Shell 4312
Sea Shell Telephone, The 4616
Sea Siren, The 4758
Sea Song (By the Beautiful Sea), The 603
Sea Song 920
Seagulls 1590
Seal, The 3527
Sealed Feet 702
Sealed Orders 2101
Seamy Side of Heaven 1450
Seance, The 1159
Search, The (inst.) 759
Search, The 2591, 4366
Search for Diana 3202
Search for Roger Evans, The 345
Search for Wisdom 1914
Search Your Heart 64, 935
Searchin' 4031
Searching 302
Searching for Love 2616
Searching for Yesterdays 2616
Sears and Roebuck Wedding Band 3306
Sears Roebuck 204
Sea's Too Salty for Me, The 2657
Seashell Game 2368
Seasick Blues 1411
Seasick Buccaneer, A 2619
Seaside Frolics 2139
Seaside Sultan, The 3049
Season, The 906, 1891
Season at the Shore, A 3578
Season Ended, The 1874
Season in the Sun 3094
Seasonal Pleasure 3918
Seasonal Sonata, A 1023, 3542
Seasons 1439
Season's Ended, The 3409
Season's Greetings 3484
Seaweed 675
Sechaba 3836
Second Act Beginning 2918
Second Avenue and 12th Street Rag 2554
Second Best 410, 2877
Second Campaign Song 3684
Second Childhood 1490
Second City Theme Song 4397
Second Deck Diplomacy 2876
Second Finale 4368
Second Glances 3970
Second Grade 3448
Second-Hand Rose 4815
Second Honeymoon, The 2918
Second Jam Session, The 3830
Second Journey, The 3463
Second Kiss, The 2673
Second Letter 3411
Second Letter Home 4068, 4301
Second March (inst.) 1385
Second Thoughts 2152, 3970
Second Threepenny Finale 4370
Second Time Around, The 4743
Second Time in Love 3913
Second to None 4073
Second Violin, The 168
Second Wind 1385
Seconds 3970
Secrecy 3051
Secret, The (Gossip Song) 1243
Secret 3485
Secret Agent Man 4193
Secret Dan 264
Secret Garden, The 3862
Secret Life, The 3863
Secret Life of Walter Mitty, The 3863

Secret Love 616, 1713, 871
Secret of Love, The 4110
Secret of My Life, The 3170
Secret of Success, The 1871
Secret of the Tapping Shoes, The 4454
Secret Service, The 2983
Secret Service Club, The 2494
Secret Singing 3180
Secret Snow 4498
Secret Society 1295
Secret Song 84
Secret Songs 2775
Secretary Bird 4061
Secretary Is Not a Toy, A 2019
Secretary Opening 621
Secrets 916, 2196, 2230, 3544, 4228
Secrets of the Household 2730
Security 1412
Seduction 415
Seduction, The 2667
Seduction 624
Seduction Is a Holy Thing 1730
Seduction Samba 3636
Seduction Second Degree 2918
Seductive 506
See 2618
See a Rainbow Arch 3588
See America First 3729, 3865
See Everything New 3209
See for Yourself 1762
See Her First 2491
See Here, My Lads, What Would You Do? 402
See How She Runs 2578
See How the Sun Shines 4358
See How They Done My Lord 4788
See How They Run 1879
See It Now 3873
See Me, Feel Me 4676
See! My Cloak! 1285
See No Evil 935
See-No-Evil Eye 4296
See Rome and Live 223
See-Saw 3868
See Seattle 2201
See That Lady There 572
See That You're Born in Texas 4058
See the Blue 4537
See the Light 3539, 3900
See the River Flow 3817
See the Royal Parade 188
See the U.S.A. in Your Chevrolet 4264
See This Golden Rooster 3847
See What It Gets You 162
See, What You've Done to Me 2892
See You Around 4196
See You in San Diego 4643
See You in the Funny Papers 4727
See You in the Morning 1506
See You Later Girls! 3866
See You Later Shimmy 3866
See Yourselves in the Mirror 1691
Seed of God, The 2679
Seeing Dickie Home 2376
Seeing Is Believing 211
Seeing Red 3601
Seeing Stars 1689
Seeing the Sights 1045
Seeing the Town in a Yap Wagon 8
Seeing Things 1764, 4480
Seek the Spy 742, 743
Seems Like a Good Idea 1099
Seems Like Yesterday 2850
Seems to Me 915
Seems to Me I've Heard of That Before 1562
Seen One, You've Seen 'Em All 614
Seena (1) 4004
Seena (2) 4004
Seesaw (1) 3869
Seesaw (2) 3869
Segue 708
Segue to Palace (inst.) 4798
Segue to Story 2726
Seizure to Roam 1985
Self-Expression 2686, 3130, 4734
Self-Made Family (She's a Lady with Money), The 2885
Self-Made Knight, The 402
Self Made Maiden, A 1067
Self Made Man 3661
Self Made Man, A 1849
Self-Made Man, The 2800
Self Made Man 328, 4142
Self-Made Woman 2908
Self-Portrait 4535
Self-Sacrificing Woman 962
Selling a Song 3314
Selling Gowns 2794
Selling of the President, The 3871
Selling Sex 3365
Selling the Business 2012
Semi-Detached 1537
Semi-Tropical Isle, A 2940
Seminary Girl, The 4634
Seminary Song 1958
Seminole 3951
Semiramis 808, 3923
Semper Fidelis 1165
Senate in Session 2809
Senatorial Roll Call, The 3225
Senators' Song, The 620
Send a Boy 3292
Send for Me 3508, 3980
Send for Nielsen 978
Send for the Militia 3365, 4152
Send in the Clowns 2536, 3967
Send Me a Girl 4053
Send Me a Man 1957, 498
Send Me Back My Husband, You've Had Him Long Enough 4634
Send Me No Flowers 3874

Send-Off, The 1864
Send One Angel Down 4569
Send Out for Food (Take-Out) 871
Send the Marines 4412
Send Us Back to the Kitchen 180
Sender 4199
Senegambian Moon 3657
Senior Citizens 408, 4463
Senior Citizen's Ball 1770
Seniorita 1414
Senor Discretion Himself 3875
Senora 3677, 2552
Senoras de la Noche 3806
Senorita 1927
Senorita Diaz 4423
Senorita Mine 4282
Senorita-Senorita 3868
Sensation 4676
Sensational Stomp 1799
Sensations 3876
Sense of Love and Humor, A 161
Sense of Motherly Pride, A 1258
Sensemaya 2395
Sensible Decisions 1169
Sensible Thing to Do, The 911
Sensible Woman, A 1012
Sensitivity 3288
Sentimental Ending 1717
Sentimental Eyes 4016
Sentimental Gentleman from Georgia 4137, 1813
Sentimental Knights 2939
Sentimental Me 1446, 3634
Sentimental Melody 4087
Sentimental Moon, The 1793
Sentimental Oriental Blues 3657
Sentimental Sally 1131
Sentimental Sarah 3486
Sentimental Silly 2827
Sentimental Tommy 1835, 3575
Sentimental Turk 2919
Sentimental Weather 4825
Separate but Equal 4343
Separate Tables 4262, 4262
Separate Thoughts 81
Separation Blues 3614
Sephardic Lullaby 2320
Sepia Fashion Plate 4199
September in Boston 2578
September Night 608
September Song 369, 1120, 2344
Sequel to a Tale from Mother Goose 248
Sequel to the Legend, The 2673
Sera Sera Jim 40
Serafina 60, 2407
Seraphica 2670
Serena 157, 3880
Serena Blandish 3880
Serenade, The 102
Serenade 273, 463, 3197, 758, 780, 1066, 1377, 1538, 1629, 1720, 1723, 1912, 2407, 2464, 2610, 2666, 2673, 2825, 3020, 3256, 3402, 3602, 3736, 3774, 3865, 3978, 4056, 4188, 4539, 4577, 4620, 1260
Serenade Creole 1020
Serenade D'Amour (Song of Love) 1570
Serenade for You 3152
Serenade Me Sadie with a Ragtime Tune 3926
Serenade of Love Tango 3170
Serenade of the Trees 281
Serenade to a Chambermaid 3916
Serenade to the Emperor 4667
Serenade with Asides 4652
Serenades of All Nations 1355
Sergeant Brue 3882, 3882
Sergeant Philip of the Dancers 3308
Sergeant Wix 2986
Sergeant's Chant 2228
Sermon, The 4325
Sermon: The Life of Peter 344
Sermon, the Sword, and the Song, The 732
Serpent of the Nile 559
Serpent of the Nile, The 2893
Serpentine, The 1747
Serpentine Dance, The 3525
Servant of Two Masters, A 225
Servants' Frolic Dance, The 3723
Serve 'Em Right 1804
Serve It Up 4076
Serve the Caviar 2497
Serve the Dog Right 2654
Serve Yourself 3608
Serves You Right 240
Service, The 1412
Service for Service 2295
Service Star and Hooverize, The 1972
Service with a Smile 3103
Serving the People 1732
Sesiyahamba (We Are Going About Our Labors) 2147
Sesquicentennial 3137
Sesquicentennial Baby, The 1678
Set 'em Sadie 3808
Set It Right 3741
Set Me Free 1918
Set the Table 1743
Set Those Sails 2132
Set Us Free 1092
Settee, Stereoscope and You 2168
Setting Up Exercise 3766
Setting Up the Score 3070
Settle Down 3880
Settle Down in a Little Town 4819
Settle Down in a One-Horse Town 4603
Settle Down, Travel Round 4529
Settle for Less 3551
Settling Down 2070
Seul sur Son Etoile 1427
Seven Ages of Society 256
Seven Ages of Women 3403
71/2 Cents 3351

7 1/2 Cents 3351
Seven Brides for Seven Brothers 3888
Seven Chances 126
Seven Come Eleven 3889
Seven Days 1011, 2789
Seven Deadly Virtues, The 623
Seven Hours in New York 3891
Seven Little Crows 1518
Seven Lucky Ways 2542
Seven Miles 4163
Seven Million Crumbs 2961
Seven O'Clock in the Morning 3588
Seven O'Clock in the Evening 3588
Seven or Eleven, My Dixie Pair o' Dice 2706
Seven Reasons Why, The 1570
Seven Seas, The 348
Seven Sheep, Four Red Shirts and a Bottle of Gin 2355
Seven Sisters 2623
Seven Songs 4191
Seven Souls of Clement O'Reilly, The 656
Seven Syncopating Sirens 4437
Seventeen 1831, 1831, 3895, 4016
17 and 21 (Seventeen and Twenty-One) 4178
Seventeen Gun Salute, A 657
Seventeen on Mars 494
1776 995
1776 to 1901 3751
Seventeen Summers 2958
Seventeenth Century Rag, The (18th Century Drag) 2976
Seventh Daughter 649
Seventh Heaven 3899
Seventh Heaven Waltz 4186
Seventh Sacrament, The 1450
70, Girls, 70 3900
72nd Street 3960
76 Foolish Things 1436
Seventy Six Trombones 3016
Sevilla 1489, 4335
Sevillian Serenade 2830
Sew a Button 1739, 3577
Sew the Buttons On 3725
Sew-Up, The (dance) 269
Sewash Today 3033
Sewing Bee, The 1600
Sewing Circle on the Seine, The 2989
Sewing Department Dance (inst.) 3735
Sewing Rainbows 1262
Sex 2007
Sex Appeal 203, 2389, 4240, 4276, 4476
Sex Delicious 1455
Sex Is a Spectator Sport 2785
Sex Is Animal 729
Sex Marches On 2597
Sex, Sex, Sex 2284
Sex Talk 3235
Sexperts 1149
Sextette 278, 1016, 1334, 1518, 2102, 2135, 2777, 4365, 4802, 4803
Sextette Number 1686
Sexually Free 2058
Sez I 1076
Sez You? Sez I! 3622
Sganarelle 649
Sgt. Pepper's Lonely Hearts Club Band 3903, 3903
Sh! 3347
Sh-Boom 4264
Sh-Boom (Life Could Be a Dream) 3739
Sh-Sh Is the Word 116
Sh! Sh! Shirley! 293
Sha Shtil (The Rabbi's Coming) 4342
Shabbos 2356
Shabes, Shabes, Shabes (Welcome to the Sabbath) 4342
Shack Town 1917
Shades of Harlem 3905
Shadow, The 4106
Shadow 3227
Shadow Man 1733
Shadow March, The 3450
Shadow of a Kiss 948
Shadow of Love 4670, 4665
Shadow of the Moon 4001
Shadow of the Sun 2134
Shadow Play 2295
Shadow Song 2776
Shadow Waltz 1359
Shadowgraph Chase 3531
Shadowland 1130, 1704
Shadowland Ballet (inst.) 1631
Shadowplay 1702
Shadows 1500, 1796, 2305, 2884, 3729
Shadows Dance Behind You 2346
Shadows on the Wall 1251, 1694
Shadows That Walk in the Night 1352
Shadowy Forest of Garandufi Dance 2283
Shadowy Glass, The 2591
Shady Dan 4763
Shady Lady Bird 372
Shady Side of Broadway 1573
Shady Side of Broadway, The 3867
Shaftway Danger 922
Shaganola 1840
Shaggy Man, The 4381
Shah! Raise the Dust! 2382
Shak Graa's Tirade 4139
Shake a Leg 3361
Shake a Little Shoe 3236
Shake, Brother! 2277
Shake 'Em Off 2089, 2090
Shake Hands with Your Uncle Max 1832
Shake High, Shake Low 495
Shake It and Bake It 1425
Shake Me and Wake Me 577
Shake, Rattle and Roll 3695
Shake, Shake, Shake 4076
Shake That Thing 26, 3297, 3709
Shake Well Before Using 1856

Shake Your Bluesies with Dancing Shoesies 447
Shake Your Duster 3054, 2337
Shake Your Feet 2570, 4817
Shake Your Furnace 1876
Shake Your Head from Side to Side 4743
Shake Your Little Shoulder 2503
Shake Your Music 4763
Shake Yourself Out of Here 1131
Shakespeare Lied (You'll Get Over It) 2014
Shakespearean Opening 213
Shakespeare's Epitaph 3909
Shakespeare's Garden of Love 2870, 3404
Shakin' All Over 3695
Shakin' at the High School Hop 1664
Shakin' the African 389
Shakin' the Shakespeare 4025
Shakin' Up the Folks Below 4281
Shaking Hands with the Wind 406
Shaking of the Sheets, The 3939
Shaking the Blues Away 789, 1461, 4821, 4799
Shalimar 2298
Shall Be All Right Now 3250
Shall I Compare Thee to a Summer's Day 3909
Shall I Sing It Now 2298
Shall I Take My Heart and Go? 1614
Shall I Tell Him? 3078
Shall I Tell You What I Think of You? 2312
Shall We Dance? 921, 2312
Shall We Dance 3741
Shall We Friend 4558
Shall We Join the Ladies 605
Shall We Plant a Tree? 114
Shall We Say Farewell? 1745
Shall We Take a Cruise 696
Shalom 2208, 2864
Shalom L'Chaim 1769
Sham Dancing 3858
Shamanile 2147
Shame 2908
Shame on You 757
Shame, Shame, Shame 4453
Shameen 3910
Shameen Dhu 3910
Shamrock 3911
Shamrock Flirtation 452
Shamrock of Ireland, The 3746
Shan Shan-O' Han 2511
Shandu Misboo Ganash 2876
Shangaan (A Dance of Happiness) 2147
Shanghai 4840
Shango 1706
Shango Ritual 651
Shangri La 2772
Shangri-La 3913
Shangri La 420
Shanley Girl, The 1541
Shannon Belles 3575
Shanty Town Romance 1914
Shantyland Pool Hall Lunchroom Crowd, The 2993
Shape I'm In, The 2346
Shape Up 534
Sharazad's Theme 2802
Share and Share Alike 1373
Share with You 426
Sharlee 3915
Sharp 3722
Sharp Easter 2259
Shauny O'Shay 2582
Shave and a Haircut 3696
Shavian Shivers 1448
Shayn Vi Di Levune 2356
She 172, 1262, 407, 2426
She! 3355
She Alone Could Understand 2216
She Always Told the Truth 4434
She Believes in Brooklyn Tonight 4206
She Called Me Fellow 2599
She Came in Through the Bathroom Window 3903
She Came, She Saw, She Can Canned 1931
She Can Do Little Who Can't Do This 1243
She Can't Make Coffee 1414
She Can't Really Be 840
She Can't Resist Me 669
She Could Do a Lot Worse 2100
She Could Have Been My Girl 3752
She Could Shake the Maracas 4420
She Deserves Me 3763
She Did the Fandango 4479
She Didn't Know Enough About the Game 3976
She Didn't Say 'Yes' 672
She Didn't Say Yes 2204, 2372
She Didn't Seem to Care 4359
She Didn't Understand 3784
She Doctor 482
She Doesn't Exist at All 824
She Doesn't Have a Chance 2998
She Doesn't Understand Me 4790, 1061
She Don't Wanna 4821
She Gonna Come Home with Me 2961
She Got Him 4214
She Hadda Go Back 1860
She Has a Way 589
She Has to Be the Right Girl 1035
She Has Trouble with Her Eyes 1563
She Hasn't a Thing Except Me 213
She Is a Diamond 1211
She Is Fast Asleep 2944
She Is Making Norman Antsy 871
She Is My Ideal 2808
She Is the Right Girl, Right for Your Money, O! 2632
She Just Loves Las Vegas! 1298
She Just Suits Me 4605
She Just Walked In 2935
She Knew a Thing or Two 2914
She Knows It 4393
She Likes Basketball 3603
She Lives with Me 2001

She Loves Me 1885, 3918, 4651
She Loves Me Not 784, 3835, 3919
She Loves Me, She Loves Me Not 3443
She Loves Thee 4479
She Loves You 944
She Makes You Think of Home 3439
She May Not Be That Sort of Girl
(A Legend of the Laundry) 3857
She Needs a Good Cry 3522
She Never Loved a Man as Much as That 350
She Never Spent a Cent on Me 1831
She Never Told Her Love 4789
She or Her 4682
She Passed My Way 101
She Pushed Me Into the Parlour 1430
She Really Didn't Mind the Thing at All 4723
She-Ro 914
She Said I Was So Lonely 1355
She Sells Sea Shells 336
She Shall Have Music 3920
She Shook Him in Chicago 2667
She Should Have Me 4689
She Showed Me 2992
She Sighs in Vain 1521
She Smiled at Me 583
She Stoops to Conquer 3215, 3302, 2650, 2650, 4497
She Stopped It 3280
She Thinks Nothing of It Now 1573
She Told Him Emphatically NO 750
She Touched Me 1094
She Touches My Heart 3427
She Trimmed Them All So Nicely 256
She Used to Be the Slowest Girl in Town 965
She Walks Like This 457, 2209
She Was a Dear Girl 511
She Was a Fair Young Mermaid 3547
She Was a Maid 4405
She Was a Maid of Sweet Simplicitee 698
She Was a Woman 1441
She Was a Wonderful Queen 3254
She Was K.C. 4358
She Was Poor but Honest 4467
She Was So Blue, He Was So Lonely 3079
She Was Very Dear to Me 4283
She Wasn't You 3274
She Will Come Around 4408
She Won't Charleston 1944
She Would Be a Soldier 669, 669
She Would Rather Light a Candle 1169
She Wrapped Him in Swaddling Clothes 755
Sheath Gown in Darktown, The 295
She'd Be Far Better Off with You 211
Sheep's Song 630
Sheik of Alabam' Wed a Brown Skin Vamp, The 3808
Sheik of Araby, The 2706
Sheik of Avenue B, The 3926
Sheik Song 4011
Sheik with New Ideas, A 2669
Sheila Franklin 1717
Sheldon Bloom 4301
She'll Be Coming 'Round the Catskill Mountains 289
'Shell' Game, A (dance) 2522
She'll Get the Business in the End 4011
She'll Say Bye Bye to You 2151
Sheltered from the Noonday Glare 2844
Shem, Ham and Japheth 2164
Shenandoah 4251, 3928
Shepherd Ballet, The 1384
Shepherd Gavotte, The 965
Shepherd Song 1715
Shepherd Song, The 1817
Shepherd's Duet 1375
Shepherd's Song 2864, 3909
Shepherd's Song (When Daffodils Begin to Peer) 4715
Shere Khan Sniffs Out Mowgli Blues, The 2970
Shere Khan's Dream of the Dance of Death 2970
Sheriffs 1613
Sherlock Holmes 4260
Sherman's March to the Sea 2001
Sherman's Mom 922
Sherrif's Song 2697
Sherry 3931
Sherry's Theme 3601
She's a Big Girl Now 2988
She's a Fool 338
She's a Good Kid 1886
She's a Lady 2218
She's a Nice Jewish Girl (She's a Perfectly Marvelous Girl from the Bronx) 2016
She's a Nut 3279
She's a Queen 821
She's a Virgin 3197
She's a Woman 2333, 1171
She's Acting 906
She's All My Own (Mary Ann) 1910
She's All Right 767
She's an Actress 2674
She's an English Girl 3857
She's Appealing, She's Alluring 649
She's Artistic 4248
She's but a Woman, He's but a Man 3585
She's Different Now 2854
She's Exciting 183
She's for Me 3158
(I Got a Woman Crazy for Me) She's Funny That Way 3297
She's Gettin' Mo' Like the White Folks Every Day 2415
She's Getting More Like the White Folks Every Day 4390
She's Gone 3537
She's Gonna Love Me! 3355
She's Got Everything 3108
She's Got to Go 4297
She's in Love with Death 1426
She's Innocent 4491

She's Irish 2662
She's Just a Baby 1484
She's Just a Little Different from the Others That I Know 3943
She's Just Another Girl 1760
She's Leaving Home 3903
She's Like a Big Bouquet 231
She's My Daisy 2835
She's My Girl 1737, 3927, 4412
She's My Love 656
She's My Lovely 2976
She's My Native Land 4723
She's No Longer a Gypsy 167
She's Not Enough Woman for Me 3687
She's Not in a Class with You 2705
She's Not There 3695
She's Not Thinking of Me (Waltz at Maxim's) 1511
She's Nuts About Me 4267
She's on File 3136
She's on Her Way 930
She's Our Gretel 1776
She's Out There 424
She's Right (Security) 1886
She's Roses 1094
She's Salvations Sal 815
She's So Different Now 1689
She's Spanish 3146
She's Such a Comfort to Me 2004, 4581
She's Sweet 3788
She's Talking Out 3863
She's Tall, She's Tan, She's Terrific (Tall, Tan and Terrific) 884
She's the Apple of My Eye 2040
She's the Girl 257
She's the Girl I Love 284
She's the One 2754
She's the Same Old Girl 2715
She's the Same Old Sunbonnet Sue 4209
She's Too Far Above Me 1721
She's Venus De Milo to Me 377
Shew! Fly, Don't Bother Me 1897
Shewing Up of Blanco Posnet, The 451
Shh! 4741
Shhhhh! He's on the Beat! 2259
Shika Shika 1242
Shillelagh Dance (dance) 2268
Shiloh 1474
Shim Sham 4824
Shimmering, Glimmering Nile, The 2328
Shimmy a La Egyptian 3403
Shimmy Nods 684
Shimmy Nods from Chaminade 2856
Shimmy on Your Own Side 4209
Shimmy-Shaking Love 2494
Shimmy Town 4813
Shimmy Valentine 684
Shimmy with Me 611
Shimmying Everywhere 1823
Shinbone Alley 3934
Shine 4020, 2111, 4253
Shine Down Lord 1086
Shine 'Em Up! 26
Shine It On 16
Shine On Harvest Moon 2892
Shine on Harvest Moon 4390, 4802, 4823
Shine On, Little Son 684
Shine On Southern Moon 1479
Shine On Your Shoes, A 1322
Shine Out, All You Little Stars 1455
Shine! Shine! Shine! 1926
Shine, Shine, Shine 2415, 3981
Shine You Shine 2682
Shining Shoes 1799
Ship-a-Hoy 2080
Ship Ahoy (Opening Chorus) 2917
Ship Ahoy 1206
Ship Comin' In 4408
Ship Concert 2490
Ship Has Sailed, The 4772
Ship in a Bottle 1804
Ship of Love 3086
Ship of Zion 2225
Ship Without a Sail, A 1800
Ship's Concert, The 4374
Shipboard Frolics 4382
Shipoopi 3016
Ships in the Night 3537
Ships That Pass in the Night 2385
Shipshape 730
Shir Hamaylesn (Song of Blessings) 4082
Shirts 119
Shirts by Millions 2444
Shivaree 1373
Shlemiel the First 3937
Shloymele-Malkele 4342
Shnel Loyfn Di Reder (The Wheels Turn Quickly) 1609
Sho-Gun of Kachoo, The 3943
Sho' Nuff 900
Shocking, Uncouth, Middleclass 1884
Shoe-Clap-Platter 3978
Shoe Shine Boy 1982
Shoein' the Mare 2475
Shoeless Joe from Hannibal Mo. 957
Shoemaker's Holiday, The 3939
Shoes 1164, 1342, 3105
Shoes of Husband No. 1 Are Worn by Number Two, The 3590
Shoes Upon the Table 460
Shoeshine 4750
Shogun 3944, 3944
Sholom Aleichem 2356, 3995
Shoo-Fly Crow 2095
Shoom-Shi-Baasha 194
Shoot the Pig 4764
Shooters 1540
Shootin' 2754
Shootin' the Pistol 500
Shooting Gallery 1604, 3698

Shooting Show 3701
Shooting Star 2470
Shooting Star, The 3643
Shooting Star 3043, 3294
Shooting Stars 3136, 3252
Shop 1784
Shop Girls and Mannikins 4300
Shopkeepers Trio 1697
Shopper's Fugue 1804
Shoppers' Dance 4393
Shoppin' for Clothes 4031
Shopping 1123, 1412, 1526, 1961, 3399, 3747, 4382
Shopping Around 4718
Shopping at a Woolworth Store 2988
Shopping Bag Lady 2784
Shopping Chorus 2465
Shopping Glide, The 4382
Shopping in the Orient 736
Shopping Is Torture (Even Off the Rack) 3587
Shore Leave 1916, 1916, 2636
Short and Sweet 4602
Short Farewell Is Best, A 1424
Short People 2852, 2787
Short Piano Roll 2200
Shortest Day of the Year, The 514
Shortnin' Bread 4390
Shorty George 889
Shosholaza (A Work Song) 2147
Shotgun Papa 1986
Shotgun Wedding 4118
Should I? (My Land) 2998
Should I 544
Should I Be Sweet? 3249
Should I Be Sweet 4267
Should I Speak of Loving You 3015
Should I Tell You 189
Shoulder Arms 659
Shoulders 3946
Shoulders to Lean On 4591
Shout 4193
Shout On! 2845
Shout, Sister, Shout 1813
Shoutin' Sinners 290
Shove It 2152
Show a Little Pep 3252
Show a Little Something New 2491
Show Boat 3949
Show Business Is My Life 695
Show Business Nobody Knows, The 2451
Show Girl 3953, 4332
Show Girls 534
Show Him the Way 1441, 3848
Show Is On!, The 1119
Show Is On, The 3955
Show Me 1958, 3038
Show Me a Suitcase 4732
Show Me How to Make Love 376, 3762
Show Me Round and Around 88
Show Me 'Round the Town 3045
Show Me the Key 3862
Show Me the Sun 1959
Show Me the Town 2214, 3243, 3766
Show Me the Way 805
Show Me Where the Good Times Are 1990, 3956
Show Me Your Qualifications 3707
Show Must Go On, The 2204
Show Off 4018
Show That Card 696
Show Train 4496
Show Us How to Do the Fox Trot 4603
Show You Care 1609
Show Your Love 3111
Showbiz 1412
Showbiz Finale 4389
Shower 4360
Shower Chorus 178
Shower of Rice, A 4422
Shower of Sparks 2229
Shower of Stars, A 496
Showgirl Victim 2307
Showing a Little Ankle 2069
Showing Off 3960
Showing the Yankees London Town 4759
Show's the Thing, The 1736
Showstopper 4627
Showtune in 2/4 3161
Shpil Gitar (Play Guitar) 4342
Shrimp and a Crab, A 2286
Shrug Your Shoulders 1557
Shtil Di Nacht 1740
Shuffle 376
Shuffle Along 1198, 3963
Shuffle Off to Buffalo 1359
Shuffle the Cards 2565
Shuffle Yo' Black Feet 2640
Shuffle Your Feet (And Just Roll Along) 441
Shuffle Your Troubles Away 2757
Shufflin' Home 2462
Shufflin' Sam 4001
Shuffling Bill 4793
Shuffling Shiveree, The 965
Shunned 600
Shunning, The 3509
Shush Katy 1831
Shut de Do' 3987
Shut Up and Dance 690, 3039
Shut Up Gerald 4727
Shy 3288
Shy Little Irish Smile 3431
Shy Little Violet Blue 3626
Shy Little, My Little Girl 3057
Shy Strephon 1768
Shy Suburban Maid, A 1095
Si Petite 839
Si, Si, Senor 1667
Si, Si, Senorita 4121
Si, Signora 3197
Si Vous Aimez Les Poitrines 3214

Siberia 1402, 3972
Siberian Whirl, The 1835
Sibling Rivalry 3600
Siciliana 710
Sick 3889
Sick, Sick, Sick 1745
Sickness 2478
Sid, Ol' Kid 4270
Side By Side 4425
Side By Side By Side 832, 3967
Side of Fries 474
Side-Street Off Broadway, A 3130
Sidestep, The 374
Sidewalk 2870
Sidewalk in Paris, A 4824
Sidewalk Tree 3656
Sidewalks of Cuba 4137, 881
Sidewalks of New York 3968
Sidewalks of Paris 190
Sidonie 3237
Siegal-Nathan's Marching Songs 1237
Siege at Loha 1369
Siegfried! 992
Siesta 1046
Siesta Time 3719
Sigh by Night 2755
Sighin' 4429
Sighing Swain, The 1193
Sighs 4469
Sight Seeing 194
Sight-Seeing Tour, A 2847
Sights of London 1096
Sigmund Freud's Impersonation 2852
Sign Here 1310, 3664, 4480
Sign, Lily, Sign 3279
Sign of the Rose, The 3969
Sign of the Times 4153
Sign Off 3641
Sign on Rosie's Door, The 3668
Sign on the Dotted Line 1497, 4798
Sign Song 3201
Signal, The 4077
Signature Tune 1665
Signed, Peeled, Delivered 4533
Signor Gazanna 1264
Signor Monsieur Muldoni 1355
Signora 3973
Signora Campbell 652
Signora Pandolfi 519
Signorina Adelina 3740
Signs 1273, 2566, 3229, 3970
Signs of the Season 3479
Silas 2506, 2715
Silence 747, 1710, 1857
Silence Is Golden 456, 4332
Silence of Love 1270
Silent Cal 2018
Silent E 4412
Silent Heart 1047
Silent Heart, The 453
Silent Movie 1822
Silent Music, The 4232
Silent Night (Heilige Nacht) 3259
Silent Screen, The 407
Silent Spring 3124
Silenzio 582
Silhouette 771, 786
Silhouette Ballet 965
Silhouette Duet 2384
Silhouettes Under the Stars 1127
Silk Stocking Trail, The 764
Silk Stockings 2843
Silk Stockings (I Will Follow Her) 3399
Silk Stockings 3972
Silken Screen 2424
Silken Song, The 1369
Silks and Satins 3404
Silly Ass 4794
Silly Boy 1776
Silly Brats and Rum 1290
Silly Cock-a-Doodle-Doo 2760
Silly Little Dance of Life 945
Silly Little Hill 702
Silly People 2536, 2764
Silly Sailors 2159
Silly Season, The 4491
Silly Simon 3690
Silly Thoughts 2446
Silo 1232
Silver and Gold 3794
Silver Apron Strings 1655
Silver Bells 23, 1206
Silver Diamond Rhinestone Glasses 3636
Silver Dollar 4138
Silver Earring 279
Silver Moon 130, 3998
Silver Path, The 2232
Silver Ring, The 77
Silver Rose 2462
Silver Sails 680
Silver Screen, The 3320
Silver Sea of Love, The 2793
Silver Shield 4287
Silver Skates (inst.) 1742
Silver Slipper, The 3976
Silver Star, The 3977
Silver Star of Love 1313
Silver Stars 3662
Silver Threads Among the Gold 1897
Silver Vision 3688
Silver Wedding, The 480
Silver Wedding Day 1551
Silver Wing 4664
Silver Wings 4271
Silvers Theme 1139
Silvery Days 4243
Silvery Moon, The 632
Silvery Moon 4782
Silvery Moon, Keep on a Shining 2851
Simchas (Joyous Occasions) 299

Simon Legree 462
Simon Smith 2852
Simon Smith and the Amazing Dancing Bear 2787
Simon Zealotes 2212
Simpatico 2910
Simple 162, 3171, 4136
Simple Ain't Easy 2304
Simple Country Wedding, A 809
Simple Dance, A 3507
Simple Dimple, A 4497
Simple Girl, A 3549
Simple Home 1992
Simple Humble Neighborhood 3668
Simple Joys 3506
Simple Joys of Maidenhood, The 623
Simple Life, The 977, 1529
Simple Life, A 3209
Simple Life 3737
Simple Little Girl, A 357
Simple Little Ingenue 1824
Simple Little Sister Mary Green 3047
Simple Little Things 3294, 3542
Simple Little Tune, A 2620
Simple Love Song 3822
Simple Man, A 3838
Simple Melody 4603
Simple Movie Folk 1948
Simple People 1991
Simple Raga 4147
Simple Serenade 1745
Simple Simon 2134, 4719
Simple Simon Instep 3980
Simple Song, A 2775
Simple Spanish Maid 3149
Simple Tune, A 3890
Simple Wife, A 1500
Simple Word 2626
Simpler 3856, 3857
Simplified Language 4167
Simply Love 2276
Simpson Sisters, The 3687
Sin of Pat Muldoon, The 3984
Since Arrawana Married Barney Carney 399
Since Dolly Dimple's Made a Hit (Dolly Dimples) 3488
Since Eros Went Away 791
Since Eve 2052
Since First I Left My Home 2323
Since Grandpa Learned to Tango 2424
Since Henry Ford Apologized to Me 3926, 3796
Since Hiram Went to Yale 1566
Since I Am Queen of the Carnival 4559
Since I Am Your Auntie to Be 2854
Since I First Met You 4201
Since I Met Wonderful You 2328
Since I Met You 4794
Since I Remember You 4709
Since I Sang E Flat 2869
Since Last We Talked Alone 367
Since Little Baby Brother Became a Movie Star 1921
Since Ma Got the Craze Espagnole 1921
Since Memphis 4416
Since Mother Was a Girl 4802
Since Mrs. McNott Learned to Do the Turkey Trot 1963
Since My Linda's in the Syn-de-cate 1925
Since My Mariutch Learned the Merry Widow Waltz 4094
Since My Wife Got Fat 2587
Since Nora Brought Her Angora Around 3388
Since Sister Nell Heard Paderewski Play 2506
Since That Time We Met 2016
Since the Ballet Came to Shubert Alley 2187
Since the Days of Grandmama 3679
Since Today Our Colonel's Mating 3051
Since We Met 4244
Since We Met in Paris 4110
Since We've Met 3547
Since When 3752
Since You Came Into My Life 3508
Since You Came My Way 1883
Since You Came to This Town 1591
Since You Said You Loved Me 1531
Since You Said You're Mine 4543
Since You Went Away 1989
Since You're Alone 4620
Since You're Not Around 3330
Sincere 3016
Sincere Replies 3233
Sincerely 4264
Sincerely, Harold Berlin 2598
Sincerest Form of Flattery 1692
Sinful 898
Sinful Music 2640
Sing 376
Sing! 746
Sing 2382, 2389
Sing a Christmas Song 828
Sing a Little Jingle 418, 1813
Sing a Little Love Song 4661
Sing a Little Song 1756, 3409, 4188
Sing a Little Song of Christmas 3637
Sing-A-Long 3517
Sing a New Song 496
Sing a Song in the Rain 3532, 292
Sing a Song of Sambo 3825
Sing a Song of Sing Sing 2894
Sing a Song of Sixpence 3173
Sing a Song of Sunshine 4816
Sing a Swanee Song 4816
Sing a Tropical Song 3444
Sing, All Ye Women of the Lord 2046
Sing Alone 3741
Sing American Tunes (1) 4291
Sing American Tunes (2) 4291
Sing and Dance 3565
Sing and Dance Your Troubles Away 3965
Sing, Brothers! 4299

Sing, Dance and Smile 4766
Sing for Your Supper 514, 4519
Sing Hallelujah! 3987
Sing Happy 1310, 4480
Sing Hey, For a Gallant Baroque 3298
Sing Hey! For a Smuggler Bold 4032
Sing Hi 3015
Sing Ho for the Life of a Bear 4710
Sing Home Sweet Home for Me 2303
Sing Hubbard 3691
Sing, Jacques, Sing 3491
Sing "Jubilee" 2252
Sing Me a Come All Ye (Like My Daddy Sang to Me) 4802
Sing Me a Sensible Song 1000
Sing Me a Song 1777
Sing Me a Song of Love 3799
Sing Me a Song of the South 4083
Sing Me a Song with Social Significance 3501
Sing Me No April Songs 172
Sing Me No Love Songs 2641
Sing Me Not a Ballad 1284
Sing Me Sunshine 3427
Sing Me to Sleep Dear Mammy (with a Hushabye Pickaninny Tune) 3963
Sing Me to Sleep with an Old-Fashioned Melody 3399
Sing Muse 3988
Sing Out in the Streets 3490
Sing Sing 21
Sing, Sing, Darkies, Sing 4646
Sing Sing for Sing Sing 3131
Sing Sing Sammy Sen 1054
Sing, Sing, Sing 146
Sing, Sing, Sing (inst.) 964
Sing, Sing, Sing 4047
Sing Sing Tango Tea 1735, 1735
Sing, Sing, You Tetrazzini 3679
Sing Something Simple 203, 4399, 3861
Sing-Song Girl 1625, 2872
Sing Song Girl 3403
Sing Song Lee 4713
Sing Sorrow 3831
Sing! South! Sing! 3035
Sing the Merry 1300
Sing to Andy Jackson 496
Sing to Me Guitar 2847, 4517
Sing to Me Gypsy 1355
Sing to Your Dear One 353
Sing Trovatore 2358
Sing Us a Good Ragtime Song 938
Sing You Sinners 2987
Sing Your Merriest Lays 2345
Singapore Sue 956
Singer and the Song, The 227, 1927
Singer Must Be Free, A 3164
Singer Sang a Song, A 3085
Singer Who Moves Well 2477
Singer's Career, Ha! Ha!, The 670
Singers Protest 1298
Singin' in the Rain 3992, 3992, 1944, 1946
Singin' Pete 2376
Singin' the Blues 3993
Singin' the Red Hot Blues 4830
Singin' to 'Em 915
Singing a Love Song 711
Singing and Dancing 2936
Singing Commercial 4237
Singing Drums 3814
Singing Lesson 650
Singing Lessons 1602, 3463
Singing Mermaids 4011
Singing Models, The 1259
Singing Nurses 2645
Singing Sweet Melodies 2640
Singing to You 1932
Singing Tree, The 2679
Singing Wheels 3810
Single 4619
Single Bird, The 2232
Single Day, A 2914
Single Dream, A 2754
Single Girl 4579
Single Lady, A 3168
Single Life, A 3838
Singspielia 4186
Sinking of the Reuben James, The 4740
Sins of Sura, The 3526
'Sippi 2302
Sir Archie 4430
Sir Frog and Mistress Toad 4646
Sir Galahad 2430
Sir Greenbaum's Madrigal 1832
Sir Joseph's Barge is Seen 2348
Sir or Ma'am 1564
Sir Oswald Sodde 4579
Sir Pumphrey Mildew 4331
Sir Walter Raleigh 1526
Siren of the Ballet, The 3994
Siren of the Tropics 3813
Siren's Honeymoon, The 3996
Siren's Song, The 2430
Siren's Song 3463
Sirens, The 977
Sirens of the Sea 200
Sis, Boom, Ah 1833
Sisseretta 3998
Sissiphus 4002
Sissy Wishing Well 374
Sister 3480, 595
Sister Aimee 408
Sister and Brother, A 4470
Sister Love 3599
Sister Mary Has the Measles 2863
Sister Mary Jane's Top Note 1540
Sister Mine 905
Sister Paradise 3276
Sister Sue 1240
Sister Susie Glide 3222
Sister Susie's Sewing Shirts 3259

Sister Susie's Sewing Shirts for Soldiers 1963
Sister Susie's Started Syncopation 2696
Sisters 4
Sisters, The 1589
Sisters 3608
Sisters and Brothers 1389
Sisters Galatine 2938
Sisters Giggle, The 2500
Sisters Liked Them Handsome, The 1886
Sisters of Healing 10
Sisters Under the Skin 1670, 3226
Sit Down, John 3897
Sit Down Song, The 1592
Sit Down, You're Rockin' the Boat 1706
Sit Down You're Rockin' the Boat 3444
Sit Down, You're Rockin' the Boat (Stop Rocking the Boat) 3525
Sit In-Wade In 415
Sit Up! Lie Down! Roll Over! Play Dead! 4034
Sittin' in Clover 606
Sittin' in Ya Ya 1890
Sittin' Pretty 2461, 4000
Sitting Around 1195, 1857
Sitting at Home Eating Bon Bons and Doing My Nails 1940
Sitting in a Corner 487, 4816
Sitting in Gaol 2344
Sitting in the Garden 1015
Sitting in the Park 4431
Sitting in the Sun 4668
Sitting in the Sun (Just Wearing a Smile) 1491
Sitting on the Back Porch 3505
Sitting on the Porch in the Moonlight 85
Sitting on the Starboard Tack 3422
Sitting on Your Status Quo 3501
Sitting Over There 1342
Sitting Pretty 4001
Sitting the Lute A-Striking 49
Situation 2347
Situations 2317
Sitwells, The 1363
Six 4002
Six Bells 3485
Six Blocks from the Bridge 2304
Six Fucking Shades of Green 1053
6 Gun Joe from Cicero 1423
Six Impossible Things 593
Six Lilies of the Valley 1564
Six Little Cinderellas 2253
Six Little Kids 1770
Six Little Kitzels 376
Six Little Lonely Hearts 2389
Six Little Love-Birds 1911
Six Little Plays (Requiescat in Pace) 1447
Six Little Sinners 2545
Six Little Wives 3828
Six Little Wives of the King 4810
Six Months Out of Every Year 957
Six O'Clock 4433, 4766
6 O'Clock News 4019
Six Palaces 161
Six Prayers, The (Oh, Heav'nly Father) 3541
Six String Orchestra 3159
Six Times Six Is Thirty Six 1919
Sixteen Going on Seventeen 4095
1600 Pennsylvania Avenue 3186, 4433
1617 Broadway 2987
Sixteen, Sweet Sixteen 3009
Sixteen to One (Gold and Silver Ballet) 2865
Sixteenth Summer 1233
Sixth Finger Tune (inst.) 4005
Sixty Percent of the Accidents 1168
Sixty Second Romance 621, 1342
Sixty Seconds Every Minute I Think of You 1688
Size Places 3814
Sizilietta 2952
Sizing Up the Girls 3623
Skadatin-Dee 4813
Skalo-Zwi 4579
Skate Boy, The 4712
Skateboard Acrobats 4398
Skating 3882
Skating Ballet 1654
Skating Dance 387
Skating Shoes 703
Skeleton Dance 2541
Skeleton Ghost 2371
Skeleton Janitor, The 4150
Skeletons 1702, 2412
Skeltons in the Closet 1088
Sketch Book 1126
Ski-ing 1530
Ski Teacher, The 3441
Skid Row (Downtown) 2544
Skid Row Downtown 2038
Skidaddle 1108
Skiddle-de-Scow 2302, 2845
Skidiskischatch 2292
Skidmore Fancy Ball 1776
Skies Have Gone Dry, The 1015
Skiing at Saks 4677
Skimbleshanks 678
Skin and Bones 823
Skin of Our Teeth, The 4008
Skinnin' a Cat 3610
Skip the Build-Up 145
Skip the Opening Number 3366
Skip to My Lou 2805, 3020
Skipper 1312
Skipping Rope Chorus 3887
Skipping Rope Hornpipe 2608
Skipping the Skips 2308
Skirt Dancer, The 2101
Skirts 4009
Sklip, Dat, Doobee 3557
Skrontch (Doin' the Skrontch) 886
Skull and Bones 4443
Sky and Sea 2245
Sky City 1800, 4235

Sky Girl, The 3149
Sky High 3091, 4010
Sky High Bungalow 4033
Sky of Stars 2115
Sky Ran Out of Stars, The 850
Sky Symphony 190
Skye Boat Song 1985
Skyhook 3410
Skylark, The 2893
Skylark 533
Skyline 2651
Skyrocket 2148
Skyscraper Blues 95
Skyscrapers 303
Slacking 1549
Slap My Face 3104
Slap on the Greasepaint 4484
Slap That Bass 921
Slapstick 4491
Slapstick and Laughter 2305
Slatey Fork 2661
Slaughter on Tenth Avenue (ballet) 3283
Slave Auction 189, 3814
Slave Chant 1715
Slave Dealers' Song 666
Slave Market, The 2802
Slave Market 3409
Slave of Love, The 740
Slave Scene, The 3830
Slave Song and Dance 4550
Slavery 1852
Slavery Chain Done Broke at Last 2203
Slaves of Broadway 1693
Slaves of the Demon 1962
Slavlova 3958
Sleep 3696
Sleep, Baby, Don't Cry 651
Sleep, Laura, Sleep 1589
Sleep Little Mouse 2236
Sleep, My Baby, Sleep 3927
Sleep My Child 729
Sleep My Darling 3256
Sleep Now, Baby Bunting 1420
Sleep, O Sleep 298
Sleep On, Santa Maria 2323
Sleep Peaceful Mr. Used-to-Be 1385
Sleep Peaceful, Mr. Used-to-Be 4123
Sleep, Sleep, Sleep 4073
Sleep Sublime and Perfect Poet 4293
Sleep Time Lullaby 467
Sleep Time, My Honey 4807
Sleep-Tite 3351
Sleep Walkers Lament 3561
Sleepin' Around 729
Sleepin' Bee, A 2000
Sleeping 2330
Sleeping Beauty and the Beast 4014
Sleeping Beauty's Dream 2330
Sleeping Chair, The 1538
Sleeping Dreams, Waking Dreams 3549
Sleeping Prince, The 1564
Sleepless Night 3125
Sleepy Canal, The 2889
Sleepy Hollow 239
Sleepy Little Valley 2100
Sleepy Man 3733
Sleepy Time 3891
Sleepy Time Down South 1037
Sleepy Village 487
Sleepyhead 1447, 1529
Sleepyland 3134
Sleigh Bells 1338
Sleigh Bells May Be Wedding Bells 3977
Sleigh Ride 4137
Sleigh with the Cream Colored Team 3201
Slewfoot 4764
Slewfoot Shuffle 4380
Slice, The 1729
Slice of Life 583
Slice of Saturday Night, A 4016
Slide a Little Closer 992
Slide, Boy, Slide 2000
Slide Some Oil to Me 4722
Sliding Down a Silver Cloud 3150
Slight Case of Ecstasy, A 4428
Slight Case of Murder 871
Slightly Less than Wonderful 1140
Slightly Perfect 180, 180
Slightly Slightly 180
Slim Princess, The 4017
Slip Away 3599
Slip Jig (dance) 2268
Slip of a Girl, A 4696
Slippery Hips 2337
Slippery James 2160
Slippin' Around the Corner 1619
Slipping Around the Corner 1618
Slipping Away from You 1073
Slipping By 496
Slippy Sloppy Shoes 2362
Slither 152
Slogan Song (You Gotta Have a Slogan) 4423
Slopes of Denmark Hill, The 1783
Sloping Path, The 3397
Sloth 221
Slow and Easy Goin' Man 3808
Slow As the Moon 3873
Slow Dancing 2992
Slow Down 2382, 2637
Slow Down Moses 1049
Slow Motion 3150
Slow Movies 3500
Slow Rhythms of Long Ago 650
Slow River 3130
Slow Rockin' Blues 2580
Slow Sinks the Sun 3378, 3865
Slow Town Is Jazz Town Now 2489
Slow Train 221
Slumber 1206
Slumber Music 2574

Slumber On 4201
Slumber On, My Little Gypsy Sweetheart (The Fortune Teller) 1355
Slumber Song (Goodnight) 1387
Slumberland 2534
Slumbertown 2893
Slumming 2776, 2993
Sly Musette 2917
Sly Old Fox 2631
Small Apartment 4401
Small Cartel, A 4435
Small Circle of Friends 1770
Small Craft Warnings 3760
Small Fry 3444
Small House of Uncle Thomas, The 2205
Small House of Uncle Thomas Ballet, The 2312
Small Mama—Big Mama 3782
Small Restaurant, A 1149
Small Talk 3351
Small Talk (Marshall) 3691
Small Talk 1048, 4262
Small Things, The 657
Small-Time Crook, The 821
Small Town 4028
Small Town Girl, A 1271
Small Town Girl 407, 1961, 4433
Small Town Girlie (Every Small Town Girlie Has a Big Town Way) 3399
Small World 1709, 1048
Smalltown, U.S.A. 3846
Smart 2051
Smart Bootery Scene, The 545
Smart Girls Day, A 333
Smart Little Girls 1494
Smart People 1770, 3924
Smart People Stay Single 2523
Smart Set, The 2399
Smart Set 3365, 4025
Smart Set, The 3098
Smart Set Carbineers, The 434
(It's) Smart to Be Smart 4824
Smarty 2408
Smash Him 1074
Smash the Mirror 4676
Smashing New York Times 167
Smashing, New York Times 550
Smell of Christmas, The 2874
Smell of Money, The 4518
Smellin' of Vanilla (Bamboo Cage) 2000
Smew Song, The 2339
Smile 26, 4020, 4020, 4264, 4019, 2074, 2285, 4023, 4403, 4666
Smile, a Kiss, A 3011
Smile a Little Smile for Me 3658
Smile and Be Merry 4497
Smile and Forget 4194
Smile As You Go By 3628
Smile at Me 4021
Smile Awhile 911
Smile, Darn You, Smile 4664
Smile for Me 2680
Smile for the Press 4586
Smile, Girls 1709
Smile Is Up, A 314
Smile of Your Dreams 2224
Smile On 1312
Smile On, Sue 3040
Smile She Means for You, The 2667
Smile, Smile 1729
Smile, Smile, Smile 825
Smile, Smile, Smile! 2760
(I Could Learn to Love You When You) Smile! Smile! Smile! 3748
Smile, Smile, Smile 4022
Smile with Me 2749
Smiles 61, 1991, 3402, 4063, 4250, 4390
Smiles Go with Tears 928
Smiles of a Summer Night 2536
Smiles, Smiles, Smiles 2959
Smilin' Joe 2462
Smilin' Through 4372
Smilin' Through My Tears 4199
Smiling at the Sea 1342
Smiling Isle 4201
Smiling Rainbows 1597
Smiling Sam 3404
Smiling Sambo 1537
Smiling Through My Tears 4429
Smoke 4422
Smoke and Fire 550
Smoke Dreams 2174
Smoke Dreams IThe Cigarette Song) 4000
Smoke 'Em Up, Smoke 'Em Up! 4561
Smoke Gets in Your Eyes 2204
Smoke Gets In Your Eyes 2372
(When Your Heart's on Fire) Smoke Gets in Your Eyes 3735
Smoke Gets in Your Eyes 497
Smoke on the Mountain 4030
Smoke Rings 468, 3593
Smokey Joe's Cafe 4031
Smokey-Mokey Elf, The 3717
Smokin' Reefers 1322
Smooth Sailin' 2089
Smother Me with Kisses 1457
Smut Song, The 373
Snagtooth Gertie 189
Snake 2785
Snake Charmer's Dance 4293
Snake Charmer's Song 2697
Snake Dance 4623
Snake Eyes 1385
Snake Hip Dance 1980
Snake in the Grass Ballet, The (inst.) 1272
Snake in the Grass, A 725
Snap a Wishbone with Me 2857, 3404
Snap Back 430
Snap Decision 1346
Snap 'Em Blues 3614
Snap in My Heart 568

Snap Into It 2380
Snap of the Whip, The 4053
Snap Out of It 202
Snap Out of the Blues 577
Snap Your Fingers 2549, 4655, 1302
Snappy Answers 2663
Snappy Show in Town 3254
Snapshots 2559
Snapshots, Photographs 1701
Snatched from the Cradle 4784
Sneaky, Creepy Fellows 4470
Sneaky Steps 1826
Sniff Me, Snort Me, Steal Away 4003
Snip, Snip, Snip 3923
Sniper 2470, 3159
'Sno Use Talking I've Got to Be Good 4213
Snookey Ookums 789
Snoop Snoop 375
Snoopy 4783
Snoopy's Song 4034
Snooty, The 4503
Snow Ball Rolling 1733
Snow Flake 1687
Snow White and the Seven Dwarfs 4035
Snow White My Daughter 3688
Snowballing 47
Snowdrops and the Spring 4490
Snowflakes and Sweethearts (The Snowbird Song) 161
Snowman's Dream, The 1570
Snowtime 3808
Snubbed 974
Snug As a Bug in a Rug 2180, 3444
Snuggle and Dream 4464
Snuggle, Snuggle, Snuggle 1966
Snuggle Up Closer to Me 4439
So 1054
So Am I 1757, 2376
So Are You! 3953
So Away with Sorrow 4490
So Beats My Heart for You 3645, 4170
So Beautiful 322, 3643, 4162
So Close to Heaven 398
So Different 3746
So Do I (Ode to Virginity) 2759
So Do I 4213, 4267
So Do I! 4381
So Does You Old Mandarin 1267
So Ends Our Night 2153
So Far 85, 840, 4146
So Far, So Good 4496
So Glad I Married Her 3760
So Good to See You 1739
So Happy 2143
So Hard to Keep When They're Beautiful 4814
So Help Me God 3568
So Here We Are Again 521
So I Bid You Beware 3994
So I Didn't Marry Him 4191
So I Give You 2290
(And) So I Married the Girl 1481
So I Smile 2497
So I Ups to Him 3953
So I'll Never Be a Millionaire 884
So I'll Tell Him 2925
So in Love 2331
So It Goes 1786
So It's Over Then 3718
So I've Been Told 3877, 4544
So Laugh a Little 2016
So Let Us Hail 3547
So Little Time 1072
So Lonesome 1251
So Long 607
So Long, 174th Street 4038
So Long As He Loves You 1370
So Long As It Isn't Shakespeare 615
So Long, Baby 3278
So Long, Big Guy 2163
So Long Bill (Take Care O' Yourself) 4762
So Long Dearie 2208
So Long, Dearie 1828
So Long Dude 1116
So Long, Farewell 4095
So Long for Ever So Long 3850
So Long for Now 597, 3217
So Long-Goodbye 1270
So Long Herbert 2275
So Long Jazz 465
So Long Letty 4037
So Long Ma (I'm Headin' for New Orleans) 1390
So Long, Mary 1090
So Long Mary 1356
So Long, Mary 1478
So Long Mom 4412
So Long-No Longer 3415
So Long! Oo-Long 4799
So Long Pa 4695
So Long Sammy 1072
So Long, San Antonio 4058
So Long, Sing Song 2517
So Long, So Long (No More Sunshine, Nothing but Rain) 515
So Long, Yesterday 2067
So Low 3103
So Many Nights 424
So Many People 2764, 3843
So Much Better 1630
So Much for Me 692
So Much That I Know 4089
So Much to Be Thankful For 4696
So Much to Do in New York 4068
So Much World 823
So Much You Loved Me 3702
So Near and Yet So Far 912, 4063
So Near Yet So Far 4249
So Nonchalant 4583
So Proud 161

So Raise the Banner High 2339
So Right 2940
So Sing the Children on the Avenue 1717
So Small 56
So, So, Sophie 3264
So Stand Back, All You Bullies 2225
So Take You a Warning 1540
So Tell Me 455
So That's the Way 919
So They Call It New York 840
So They Say 4559
So This Is Broadway 545
So This Is How It Is 1290
So This Is How You'd Have Us Sue You 1905
So This Is Italy 1577
So This Is Kissing 3157, 3249
So This Is Love 2526
So This Is Mexico 1979
So This Is Paris! 3400
So This Is the States 642
So This Is Venice 3489, 4815, 4817
So Undulating, So Fascinating 1580
So Unreal Does This Seem 1199
So Very, Very Dry 325
So We'll Go No More a-Roving 2278
So We'll Go No More A-Roving 2633
So Well So Soon 1862
So What? 610, 843, 1497, 3379
So What Else Is New? 4727
So What Goes? 2161
So What Now? 1168
So What? Why Not! 1354
So What's the Use 4762
So Will I Love My Love 1119
So Would I 3648
So Ya Wanna Be a Toy 562
So You Got What You Want 721
So You Want to Be a Nun 3211
So You Want to Go into the Theatre, Baby 621
So You Wanted to Meet the Wizard 4722
Soap Bubble Days 2261
Soap Opera 430
Soap Operettas 4533
Soapbox Sillies 3713
Sobbin' Women 3888
Sobbin' Women, The 3888
Sobs 2108
Sociable Amoeba 1107
Social, The 1029
Social Coach of All the Fashionable Future Debutantes, The 3865
Social Dance (inst.) 3888
Social Dancing (inst.) 1329
Social Director 4718
Social Director's Song, The 3970
Social Drum, The 333
Social Eclat 2964
Social Function Stomp 981
Social Game, The 3819
Social Laws 698
Social Notes 3440
Social Observer, The 2308
Social Security 343
Social Whirl, The 2295
Social Work 376
Societies Magnificat: An Oratorio 3479
Society 349, 434, 913, 2111, 2880, 3580, 1972, 3803, 3749, 4104, 4738, 4802
Society Bells 1541
Society Blues 3407
Society Buds 4473
Society Circus, The 2254, 1866
Society Circus Parade 4806
Society Farmerettes, The 2900
Society Ladder 1297
Society Means Propriety 2177
Society Queen, The 1926
Society Snobs 1533
Society's Child 338
Society's Shimmying Now 685
Society, The 1891
Sock-It-Rock-It to Your Heart 1497
Sock Life in the Eye 1045
Sockin' the Cymbal 1953
Socrates Jackson (An Educated Coon) 1881
Sodomanager 556
Sodomy 1717
Soft and Low 3049
Soft in de Moonlight 1020
Soft Is the Sparrow 1864
Soft Lights and Sweet Music 1225
Soft Music 3330
Soft Shoe Freak 682
Soft Shoes 3031
Soft Spot, The 2285
Soft to Sensuous Music Swaying 104
Soft Zephyr 2715
Softly, As in A Morning Sunrise 3117
Softly, Softly in the Garden 3197
Softly Stealing, Lanterns Gleaming 4478
Softly Through the Summer Night 3839
Soil, Seed, Sun, and Rain 2095
Solace (inst.) 4390
Sold 931
Soldier 3088
Soldier and the Washerwoman, The 4533
Soldier Bold, The 2543
Soldier Boy 1722
Soldier Boy, The 2745
Soldier Boy 3239, 3749
Soldier Is the Idol of the Nation, The 3073
Soldier Like You, A 2806
Soldier Men 1851
Soldier Needs No Truer Friend, A 104
Soldier of Bohemia, A 3771
Soldier of Fortune, A 3680, 4311
Soldier of Love, A 1768
Soldier of Love 4374
Soldier of Love Am I, A 1925
Soldier of My Own, A 3052

Soldier Song 1518
Soldier Stole Her Heart, A 4590
Soldier Takes Pride in Saluting His Captain, A 1977
Soldier's Dream, A 4340
Soldier's Goodbye, A 1616
Soldier's Life, A 1455
Soldier's Life 1193
Soldier's Life, A 1193
Soldier's Life Is Grand, A 4521
Soldier's Life Is Never Long 3567
Soldier's Life Is One of Strife, A 4032
Soldier's Love 3567
Soldier's March 3035
Soldier's March (Unofficial March of General Holmes) 4179
Soldier's Musical, A 2022
Soldier's Prayer (O Rock Eternal) 461
Soldier's Song 2411
Soldier's Song, The 4368
Soldier's Song 4601, 4616
Soldier's Story, The 4691
Soldiers 4725
Soldiers All 104
Soldiers and Girls 4210
Soldiers' Chorus 526
Soldiers' Gossip 3411
Soldiers in Love's War 604
Soldiers in the Park, The 4390
Soldiers of the Army 3976
Soldiers of the Czar 3685
Soldiers of the King 4759
Soldiers of the Netherlands 2889
Soldiers of the Queen 1857
Soldiers of the Stage, The 1640
Soldiers' Song 4371
Soldiers to the King 4161
Soldiers True 735
Soldiery, The 4311
Soliciting Subscriptions 1446
Solicitor's Song 3274
Solid Silver Platform Shoes 2687
Soliloquy 277, 660, 4191, 3628, 2442, 1281, 2591, 1750, 3507, 3650, 3734
Soliloquy and Song 3453
Soliloquy on a Sunny Wedding Morn 2055
Solitaire Land 2328
Solitary Finish, A 2025
Solitude 4091
Solo Dance 1213
Solo for the Telephone 3561
Solo on the Drum, A 3042
Solo Thoughts 3201
Solomon 3214, 3403
Solomon Song 4369, 4370
Solution 2338
Solutions 159
Sombrero 2481
Sombrero Land 4714, 3701
Some Are Born Great 2599
Some Baby 720
Some Beautiful Day 2209
Some Beautiful Morning I'll Find You in My Arms 487
Some Beer, Some Bowlin' 3564
Some Big Something 97
Some Boy 4806
Some Bright Morning 602, 699
Some Call It Love 634
Some Cats Know 4031
Some Crummy Season 2053
Some Day 466, 659, 718, 924, 1031, 1530, 1851, 3660, 1647, 4539
Some Day I'll Find You 2309
Some Day I'll Wander 796
Some Day I'm Gonna Fly 4764
Some Day Soon 3299, 4488
Some Day the Sun Will Shine 4815
Some Day Waiting Will End 1527
Some Day When Dreams Come True 3205
Some Day when Dreams Come True 3480
Some Day When My Dreams Come True 4738
Some Days Everything Goes Wrong 4633
Some Days It Seems That It Just Don't Even Pay to Get Out of Bed 1074
Some Do! Some Don't! 2906
Some Dough for the Army Relief (Opening) 4340
Some Enchanted Evening 4096
Some Far-Away Someone 3569
Some Fine Day 3146, 3623
Some Folks Do 4149
Some Girl Has Got to Darn His Socks 186
Some Girl Is on Your Mind 4234
Some Girls 3285, 4794
Some Girls Can Bake a Pie 3225
Some Girls Pick Their Sweethearts from the Infantry 513
Some Golden Day 1801
Some Have, Some Have Not 1649
Some How 199
Some Incredible Guy 3722
Some Kind of Man 2583
Some Kind'a Woman 2969
Some Like It Hot 3444, 4196
Some Like to Hunt 4694
Some Little Bug Is Going to Find You 75
Some Little Bug Is Going to Find You Some Day 93
Some Little Bug Will Get You 3028
Some Little Girl 1911
Some Little People 339
Some Little Someone 2927
Some Night 4053
Some Nonsense 684
Some of These Days 4197
Some of These Men 3989
Some of These Nights 1560
Some One 2907, 2927
Some One Loves You After All 2308
Some Other Day 4668

Some Other Girl 2270
Some Other Time 2205, 3207, 3278
Some Party 3923
Some People 1709, 2677, 3055
Some People Make Me Sick 2216
Some Pretty Day 428
Some Quiet Afternoon 1626
Some Ragtime Opera 632
Some Rain Must Fall 977
Some Said They Were Crazy 3831
Some Sort of Somebody 2891
Some Sort of Somebody (All the Time) 4555
Some Sort of Something 4765
Some Special Place for Me 4408
Some Summer Day 58
Some Sunday 4318
Some Sunday Morning 2762
Some Sunny Day 2363, 4182
Some Sweet Day 4018, 4201, 4816
Some Sweet Someone 1617
Some There Are Who Never Venture 1589
Some Things (1) 4863
Some Things (2) 4863
Some Things a Man Must Have 2504
Some Things Cannot Be Explained 1551
Some Things Don't End 3448
Some Things You Can't Learn in College 1879
Some Time 379, 4063
Some Time Ago 4041
Some Times You Get a Good One 632
Some Wonderful Sort of Someone 2373, 2385, 2587
Somebody 681, 424, 814, 1313, 2598, 3392, 1540, 3828, 4813, 1804
Somebody Did All Right By Herself 287
Somebody Died Today 2418
Somebody Else 4272, 4793
Somebody Else, Not Me 545
Somebody Lied 295
Somebody Like You Somebody Like Me 1819
Somebody Likes Me 290
Somebody Loves Me 1487
Somebody Loves You 257, 3507
Somebody New 699
Somebody Ought to Be Told 2786
Somebody Said 1447
Somebody Should Have Told Me 382
Somebody, Somebody Hold Me 2630
Somebody, Someplace 1846
Somebody, Somewhere 2961
Somebody Somewhere 3444
Somebody Stole de Wedding Bell 862
Somebody Stole My Gal 4697
Somebody Stole My Heart Away 3953
Somebody Stole My Kazoo 3299
Somebody Thinks I'm Wonderful 3880
Somebody Told Me 1560, 2133
Somebody Touched Me 1816
Somebody Wants to Go to Sleep 4361
Somebody Write Me a Love Song 426
Somebody Wrote the Wrong Words to My Song 3741
Somebody's Been Around Here Since I've Been Gone 1464
Somebody's Coming to My House 60
Somebody's Crazy About You 1131
Somebody's Dancing with My Girl 965
Somebody's Doin' Somebody All the Time 4450
Somebody's Eyes 4064
Somebody's Going to Throw a Big Party 1272
Somebody's Got To 4416
Somebody's Gotta Do Somethin' 155
Somebody's Keeping Score 4829
Somebody's Stepping on My Olive Branch 1075
Somebody's Sunday 4491
Somebody's Sweetheart 4056
Somebody's Waiting for Me 3508
Someday 1739, 1258, 4286, 3666
Someday, Baby 3364
Someday I'll Find You 3235, 3597
Someday I'll Walk 3711
Someday, If We Grow Up 4584
Someday, Maybe 3920
Someday My Grandson 2422
Someday My Prince Will Come 4035
Someday Soon 1496
Someday Today Will Be the Good Old Times 3715
Someday We'll All Be Free 4786
Somehow 2479, 3823
Somehow I Never Could Believe 4169
Somehow I'd Rather Be Good 3084
Somehow I'm Taller 2630
Somehow It Made Me Think of Home 694
Somehow It Seldom Comes True 2363
Somehow It's Not the Same 20
Somehow I've Always Known 1918
Somehow, Sometime, Somewhere 4490
Someone 466, 1345, 2556, 3084, 3664
Someone a Lot Like You 3217
Someone Else 4560
Someone Else's Dream 494
Someone Else's Story 721
Someone Has Your Number 1240
Someone I Could Love 2750
Someone I Used to Know 4490
Someone I've Already Found 1441
Someone in a Chair 2065
Someone in a Tree 3340
Someone in April 652
Someone in the Know 901
Someone Is Calling Me Home 3461
Someone Is Coming from Dixie 1738
Someone Is Discovering Something 1700
Someone Is Sending Me Flowers 3941
Someone Is Waiting 832
Someone Just Like You 4794
Someone Like Me 2075
Someone Like You 136, 1060, 2198, 2005, 2264
Someone Must Try 4384
Someone Needs Me 2050

Someone Nice Like You 4160
Someone on Your Side 798
Someone Should Tell Them 834
Someone, Someday, Somewhere 152
Someone Special 1873
Someone Such as Me 1354
Someone to Admire, Someone to Adore 1656, 1657
Someone to Care For 3551
Someone to Come Home with Me Tonight 3666
Someone to Console Me 2174, 1882
Someone to Count On 4401
Someone to Love 2296, 3902
Someone to Talk To 2535
Someone to Watch Over Me 921, 3243, 1325
Someone Waiting 1233
Someone Was Here 3088
Someone Who Believes in You 4241
Someone Who Cares 3549
Someone Who Touches Me 2346
Someone Will Make You Smile (Vienna Dreams) 3540
Someone Woke Up 1060
Someone Wonderful I Missed 2058
Someone You Know 4785
Someone You Thought You Could Trust 4147
Someone's Always Calling a Rehearsal 3953
Someone's Calling Me 965
Someone's Got to Do It 3181
Someone's Moving In 572
Someone's Moving Out 572
Someone's Waiting 615
Somethin' Cold to Drink 2000
Somethin' More 2200, 1990
Somethin' Ya Gotta Find Out Yo'self 1385
Somethin' You Gotta Find Out for Yourself 4123
Somethin' You Gotta Find Out Yourself 3815
Somethin's Brewin' 900
Somethin's Doin' 1816
Something 1785, 1285, 1593, 4533
Something the Air of May 2786
Something About a Uniform 2730
Something About a War 1422
Something About Love 2376, 2385
Something About Me 1420
Something About Palaces 2820
Something Bad Is Happening 1234
Something Beautiful 2801
Something Better Than Being in Love 657
Something Better, Something More 4286
Something Big 2355, 3112
Something Devilish Wrong 767
Something Different 1258
Something Doesn't Happen 4481
Something Doing Around My Heart 1054
Something Extra 3346
Something for a Rainy Day 98
Something for Me 2676
Something for Nothing 391, 4540, 1662
Something for Nothing (with appreciation to Mayfair Music Hall) 3661
Something for the Books 3046
Something for the Boys 4058
Something for the Summer 809
Something for the Summer (Something for the Winter) 808
Something Funny's Going On 2646
Something Good Like You 1049
Something Greater 167
Something Happened 1532
Something Has Happened 2050
Something Holy 3871
Something I Dreamed Last Night 1494
Something in Here 3821
Something in His Eyes 2075
Something in My Eye 2439
Something in the Air 3643
Something in the City 3777
Something in the Wind 1791
Something Indescribable 2910
Something Is Coming to Tea 1891
Something Is Wrong in Jerusalem 4788
Something Is Wrong with Everyone Today 535
Something Just Broke (November 22, 1963) 212
Something Like Me 3847, 4781
Something Like Someone 1435
Something Like This 1538
Something More 101, 2820, 4060
Something Must Be Done 251
Something New 600, 424, 3460, 3672, 3770, 4798
Something New and It's You 364
Something New for a Change 4039
Something New Is in My Heart 2786
Something New, Something Different 1776
Something Nice in Lingerie 4218
Something Nice Is Going to Happen 941
Something Old, Something New 3056
Something Peculiar 1528
Something Seems Tingle-Ingleing 1888
Something Seems Tingle Ingleing 3020
Something Seems to Say You Love Me 3520
Something Seems to Tell Me 4730
Something Should Be Done 3578
Something So Delightful 2837
Something, Somewhere 4481
Something Sort of Grandish 1278
Something Special 1497, 1766, 2368, 2555, 3201
Something Tells Me 1891, 2827, 2230, 4332
Something Tells Me I Am Going to Love You 1845
Something Tells Me I'm in Love 3655
Something That Money Can't Buy 4053
Something There 330
Something to Believe In 716, 2968
Something to Call Our Own 1617
Something to Dance About 619
Something to Do 413
Something to Do Tonight 3277
Something to Do with My Hands 922
Something to Do with Spring 3235
Something to Get Up For 4790
Something to Live For 2382, 4091, 4633
Something to Point To 4744

Something to Remember 3457
Something to Remember You By 4367
Something to Sing About 4023
Something to Tell 2669
Something to Think About 4025
Something Very Mysterious 1558
Something Very Strange 3815
Something Very, Very Good 31
Something Was Missing 150
Something We Keep Q.T. 1562
Something Will Turn Up 869
Something Wonderful 2312
Something Wonderful Can Happen 4689
Something Wrong with Me 2263
Something You Lack 3103
Something You Never Had Before 1456
Something's Afoot 4062
Something's Always Going Wrong 2745
Something's Always Happening on the River 3845
Something's Coming 4625
Something's Going to Happen to You 4198
Something's Gone Wrong 2472
Something's Gonna Happen Really Strange Tonight 3368
Something's Got to Be Done 273, 2533, 3865
Something's Got to Happen 3735
Something's Gotta Give 3178
Something's Happened to Rosie 3723
Something's Rotten in Denmark 3741
Sometime-Perhaps 3951
Sometime Tomorrow 3947
Sometimes 3469, 3806
Sometimes a Day Goes By 131, 4727
Sometimes at Night 674
Sometimes I Feel Just Like Grandma 3727
Sometimes I Feel Like a Motherless Child 4390
Sometimes I Wonder 3938
Sometimes I'm Happy 1916, 3020, 3157, 3249
Sometimes It Rains 1809
Sometimes You're Up 3428
Somewhere 178, 191, 295, 3643, 809, 1837, 2077, 2717, 3913
Somewhere! 4053
Somewhere 4186, 4625
Somewhere a Girl Is Waiting 258
Somewhere a Voice Is Calling 3028
Somewhere Along the Road 2616
Somewhere Between a Laugh and a Cry 496
Somewhere Close By 105
Somewhere I Know There's a Girl for Me 1552
Somewhere in Africa 888
Somewhere in America 1175
Somewhere in Love's Garden 4121
Somewhere in Lovers' Land 4010
Somewhere in the Past 2043
Somewhere in the World (There's a Little Girl for Me) 4544
Somewhere in Your Eyes 1924
Somewhere Is Here 2318
Somewhere Out There 2654
Somewhere She's Flirting with Someone 1801
Somewhere, Someone 2033
Somewhere Sometime 1536
Somewhere That's Green 2544
Somewhere There's a Little Bluebird 3954
Somewhere There's Some Girl 1753
Somewhere There's Someone for Me 1663
Somewhere Under the Rainbow 3651
Somnambulistic Tune 4810
Son of a Billionaire 2829
Son of Africa 3825
Son of France, A 2937
Son of Man 4396
Son of the Grand Eunuch, The 711
Son of the Hill and Plain, The 1220
Son of the Sun, A 2636
Sonatina (1) 4004
Sondheim Song 2294
Song 2633
Song, The 4285
Song and Dance 1722, 2388
Song and Mime of Corday's Arrival in Paris 3445
Song Bird Singing in a Bamboo Tree 2089
Song Birds Quartette 3808
Song Cycle 693
Song for a Banjo Dance 3001
Song for a Crowded Cabaret 3557
Song for a Hunter College Graduate 1038
Song for a Pinch Hitter 1038
Song for Dancing, A 287
Song for Jesus 3561
Song for Myself, A 2171
Song for the Dead 2852
Song from Somewhere, A 161
Song from the Fountain 3081
Song Games 4407
Song Is Born, A 3410
Song Is You, The 2204, 3014, 3020
Song of a Child Prostitute 3806
Song of a Sailor 2756
Song of a Summer Night 2961, 2028
Song of a Veteran, The 2502
Song of Advice 1660
Song of Ali Baba and Zsa Zsa 50
Song of Assisi, The 732
Song of Cyrano 4073
Song of Defiance 3703
Song of Expense, A 1071
Song of Freedom 789
Song of Futility 4371
Song of Greater Britain 461
Song of Hareford 2798
Song of Harlem 290
Song of Home 1852
Song of Indifference, The 4379
Song of Joy 4773
Song of Love 463
Song of Love, The 1663
Song of Love 2757
Song of Love, A 3130

Song of Love 3288
Song of Love, A 1682
Song of Me 4145
Song of Miriam 1196
Song of Mother Samuels 10
Song of Mourning 2027
Song of My Heart 3219
Song of Myself 2433
Song of Norway, The 4075
Song of Our Love 3074
Song of Patriotic Prejudice, A 221
Song of Plays 2711
Song of Prigio, The 1871
Song of Reproduction 220
Song of Russia 3595
Song of Ruth 1196
Song of Sallah Shabeti, The 4514
Song of Singapore 4076
Song of Songs, The 968
Song of Songs 1715
Song of Songs, The 4094
Song of Sorrow 3814
Song of Spring 1342
Song of Summer Time, The 1798
Song of Symbols 1126
Song of the Ads (The Pluto Boys, We're the Ads) 3501
Song of the Aimlessness of Life 4368
Song of the Arrow 3696
Song of the Auctioneer 4197
Song of the Balcony 948, 4670
Song of the Banshee, The 3912
Song of the Barricade 2830
Song of the Bat, The 3180
Song of the Bathers 217
Song of the Bends 3831
Song of the Big Shot 1755
Song of the Black Hussars 710
Song of the Bloomers 217
Song of the Bourgeois 2007
Song of the Brass Key 1027
Song of the Butterfly 1307
Song of the Chimes (Bim Bam) 2486
Song of the City of Hope 2953
Song of the Claque 3013
Song of the Cocktail 4206
Song of the Colonization Society 2111
Song of the Cotton Fields 1980
Song of the Cow 2323
Song of the Crowing Hens 1083
Song of the Crusader 2697
Song of the Danube, The 3994
Song of the Dawn 457
Song of the Devonshire Man 1178
Song of the Dice 1388
Song of the Dolls 1743
Song of the Drum Major 666
Song of the Enchanted Rope 1300
Song of the Fair Dissenter Lass 461
Song of the Fashions 256
Song of the Field 10
Song of the Flame 4077
Song of the Flowers (ballet) 4046
Song of the Flute 1743
Song of the Foreign Legion (Foreign Legion Number) 1492
Song of the Forty Thieves 175
Song of the Free, The 2653
Song of the Free Lance (I Am a Salaried Warrior) 1388
Song of the Frog 4029
Song of the Gascon Cadets 4670
Song of the Gaston Cadets 948
Song of the Gigolo 570
Song of the Glove 4715
Song of the Goddess 2228
Song of the Golden Egg 2953
Song of the Golden Peacock 2811
Song of the Grenadier 2715
Song of the Guard 3673
Song of the Guns 369, 2228
Song of the Harp 2182
Song of the Heart 1523
Song of the Hired Man 1903
Song of the Honeymoon, The (Honeymoon) 2254
Song of the Husbands 2673
Song of the Immigrant Mothers 2231
Song of the Insufficiency of Human Endeavor 4370
Song of the King 2242, 2312
Song of the King, A 4759
Song of the Jolly Coachman 3495
Song of the Little Mouse, The 2854
Song of the LURP 1053
Song of the Ma 2268
Song of the Malcontents 3684
Song of the Mask, The 1761
Song of the Millers 3774
Song of the Moonbeams 1126
Song of the Mormon 976
Song of the Napkin Rings 2806
Song of the Navy 4802
Song of the Night 4161
Song of the Nose 947
Song of the Open Road 2007, 2433
Song of the Optimist 4724
Song of the Orient 3239
Song of the Pictures 1624
Song of the Pipe 1243
Song of the Pirates (Avast Belay!), The 3450
Song of the Pregnant Women 2478
Song of the Priestess 2101
Song of the Reapers, The 3613
Song of the Riffles 47
Song of the Riveter 2545
Song of the Rosebuds 4064
Song of the Roustabouts, The 2258
Song of the Samovar 1686
Song of the Sarong, The 1138

Song of the Saved, The 917
Song of the Scimitar, The 758
Song of the Sea, A 336
Song of the Setting Sun 4683
Song of the Shepherds, The 2241
Song of the Sheriffs 4507
Song of the Silver Blades 2098
Song of the Sirens, The 2922
Song of the Sirens 3996
Song of the Southern Seas, The 1524
Song of the Spokesong (Spokesong) 4109
Song of the Swing 2364
Song of the Sword, The 1071, 1375
Song of the Tenement 423
Song of the Thirteen Colonies 239
Song of the Trees 996
Song of the Troika 3013
Song of the Tub 2632
Song of the Vagabonds 3020, 4539
Song of the Waiters 561
Song of the Walnut Tree 2811
Song of the Weather, A 220
Song of the Witch 4157
Song of the Witches 645
Song of the Woodman 3955
Song of the World, The 1794
Song of the Wounded Frenchman 2228
Song of the Zodiac 2386
Song of Troubles 3814
Song of Two Islands 323
Song of U.S.A. 1573
Song of Victory 3056
Song of Vienna 1113
Song of Welcome 634
Song of Yesterday 2968
Song of Yesterday, A 4201
Song on the Sand 2208, 2360
Song Song 729
Song to Forget, A 2137
Song to Sing, A 1116
Song to Sing 3651
Song with a Chorus, A 3827
Song without (Many) Words, A 3043
Song Without Words 780
Song without Words 2850
Songbird of Melody Lane 2974
Songbook 2949
Song's for Free, The 1494
Songs I Can't Forget 4816
Songs My Mother Used to Sing to Who, The 2189
Songs of Long Ago 1483
Songs of Long Ago, The 2261
Songs of Nations 2800
Songs of Peace and War 369
Songs of Yesterday 4712
Songs Tell You What to Do 2490
Songs We Sang 1175
Songs You Used to Sing to the Girls You Used to Love, The 1801
Sonnet 2877
Sonny 4085
Sonny-Boy Slave Song, The 1592
Sonoba (We Shall Conquer) 1719
Sons 3780
Sons and Daughters of the Sea 4253
Sons Of 2188
Sons of Eli 224
Sons of Every Nation Are American Today, The 2139
Sons of France 2150
Sons of Greentree 4028
Sons of Old Black Joe, The 740
Sons of the Sea 1539
Sons Say 3285
Soon 269, 1740, 2536, 3060, 4089, 4179
Soon As I Get Home 4722
Soon I Will Be Done 4460
Soon I'll Be Done 3814
Soon It's Gonna Rain 1245
Soon We'll Be Home 2993
Soon We'll Be Seen Upon the Screen 3652
Soon You Gonna Leave Me, Joe 2961
Sooner or Later 4067, 2368, 1451
Soothing Serenade 61
Soothing Symphony 1532
Sophia 223, 2633
Sophie 1831, 2706
Sophie in New York 4090
Sophisticated Lady 4137, 3020, 4091
Sophisticated Songs 817
Sophisticated Swing 4137
Sorceress, The 1959
Sore Foot Blues 3965
Sore's Lullaby 4082
Sorority Girls 1557
Sorrow Is Mine 4161
Sorry 2845
Sorry Charlie Your Time Is Up 4093
Sorry for Myself 4682
Sorry-Grateful 4067, 832
Sorry We Won 4396
Sorry Wrong Valley 4332
Sort O' Lonesome 2
Sort of Courting Song, A 840
Sortie a La Guerre 3111
So's Your Old Lady 2896
So's Your Old Man 4212
Soubrette's Secret, The 2858
Soul 3428
Soul Kiss, The (Just for You from Above) 4094
Soul Mates 2005
Soul of a Harp, The 1129
Soul Saving Sadie 4824
Soulless a Faery Dies 1977
Sound and Light 3548
Sound of a Ragtime Band, The 10
Sound of Laughter, The 2580
Sound of Love, The 3644

Sound of Money, The 2048
Sound of Music, The 4095
Sound of Muzak, The 784, 1648
Sound of Poets, The 1406
Sound of Schmaltz, The 1408
Sound of the Night 4319
Sound of the Sound, The 1962
Sound the Call 2573
Sounds 2801, 3876
Sounds of a World 1809
Sounds of Silence 1878
Sounds of the Day 4319
Sounds of the Drum, The 4328
Sounds We Love to Hear, The 2632
Sounds While Selling 3918
Soup 1663
Soup's On (The Dying Nun Ballet) 3211
Sour Apple Serenade 857
Sour Grape Theme 2084
Souris d'Hotel 1992
Sousa's Marches, The 3701
South America, Take It Away 620
South American Way 1408, 4011, 4174
South Grape High 1734
South of the Rio Grande 1657
South Sea Blues 4154
South Sea Island Blues 4283
South Sea Island Real Estate Association of Mariposa, The 1435
South Sea Island Rhapsody 4561
South Sea Islands According to Broadway, The 1652
South Sea Isle 3024
South Sea Isles 1923
South Sea Sweethearts 3500
South Wind 446
Southbound Train 1232
Southend-on-Sea 792
Southern Belles Ballet 2540
Southern Charm 4830
Southern Comfort 4619
Southern Discomfort 4153
Southern Heart of Mine 1963
Southern Hobby 3513
Southern Hospitality 1289
Southern Lady, A 1616
Southern Nightingale, The 4859
Southern Nights 1014, 1985
Southern Queen 352
Southland 295, 3677, 3513, 3945
Southwind Is Calling 2371
Souvenir 3064, 3538
Souvenirs 2168, 2227, 3124, 3500, 3921
Sow the Seed and Reap the Harvest 4123
Sow Your Wild Oats Early 136
Spa Music 3171
Space Oddity 3739
Spacious and Gracious 3551
Spade Ballet 4667
Spades Is Trumps 884
Spaghetti Jamboree 3165
Spaghetti Song 3151
Spain 2140, 3953, 4056, 4780
Spanglish 3869
Spaniard that Blighted My Life, The 1963
Spanish 42, 805, 1248, 2373
Spanish Aria, A 1404
Spanish Ballet 3737
Spanish Basque Carol 250
Spanish Bolero 4723
Spanish Dance 969, 1188, 2135, 2362, 2489, 2794, 2892
Spanish Fado 3523
Spanish Fandango, The 3399
Spanish Fandango Rag, The (Dreamy Fandango Tune) 4521
Spanish Fantasie 3392
Spanish Grandee 1570
Spanish Grandee, A 2632
Spanish Harlem 4031
Spanish Jazz, The 1536
Spanish Juanita 200
Spanish Love 545, 1689, 1722, 2602, 1327
Spanish Maid (Nina Espagnola) 4063
Spanish Mazurka 2565
Spanish Melody 2490
Spanish Mick, The 2833
Spanish Moon 3021, 4651
Spanish Panic (dance) 3288
Spanish Rose 607
Spanish Senorita, The 3770
Spanish Serenade, The 2882
Spanish Shawl, A 3149, 3605
Spanish Shawl, The 3719
Spanish Song 1962, 3681
Spanish Sweetheart 3392
Spanish Villa (inst.) 190
Spanky's Clubhouse Show 2541
Spare a Little Love 3310
Spare Me Your Kindness 1097
Spare Rib from the Butcher Shop of Life, A 3877
Spare Some Change 1702
Spare That Building 4013
Spark of Creation, The 730
Spark of Life Dance, The 3395
Spark Plug Blues March 2084
Sparkling Champagne 364
Sparkling Eyes 2977
Sparkling Moselle, The 3362
Sparkling Wine 3298
Sparks 4676
Sparrow and Hippopotamus 2317
Sparrow and the Bullfinch, The 2938
Sparrows Can't Sing 2572
Sparrows in the Rain 46
Spats-s-s Palazzo 4196
Speak-Easy 1440
Speak for Yourself John 1580
Speak for Yourself, John 621

Speak in Silence 1354
Speak Irma, I Implore Thee 1355
Speak Low 369, 2982, 3301
Speak No Love 1363
Speak Roughly to Your Little Boy 56
Speak to Me of Love 945
Speak to Me with Your Eyes 839
Speak Without Compunction 4208
Speakeasy 2437
Speakeasy, The 4196
Speakeasy Christmas 2437
Speakerine 2364
Speaking French 2646
Speaking of Love 4583
Speaking of Pals 404
Speaking of You 1440
Spear Games 1809
Special Announcement, A 4160
Special Boy, A 2114
Special Bulletin 2918
Special Day 1262
Special Delivery!
(I Seen Her at the Station) 2961
Special Envoy 1569
Special Man 4168
Special Man, A 1282, 2754
Special Summer 973
Special Train, The 613
Specialist Am I 4364
Specially for You 133
Specially Made for You 2238
Specialty 3258
Specialty Dance 3434
Speech 1354
Speed 1015, 2768
Speed of Light 2728
Speed Won't Get Me 4102
Speedy Gonzales 2772
Spell Me a Riddle 1503
Spell of Those Harlem Nights 4763
Spend an Evening in Caroline 1813
Spend It 3054
Spend Your Vacation on Broadway 3916
Sphinx, The 684
Sphinx of the Desert 1154
Spic and Span (1) 42
Spic and Span (2) 42
Spic and Spanish 4420
Spider and the Fly, The (1) 3551
Spider Woman 382
Spider's Den, The (inst.) 250
Spider's Web, The 1678, 2264
Spiel, The 4542
Spielman, The 4575
Spies 3441
Spiked Fist of War, The 4163
Spin-Off Blues, The 3844
Spin! Spin! Spin! 4106
Spinner Learned the Conga 1879
Spinning a Yarn 3737
Spinning Song 1727, 4109, 4316
Spirit, Not the Letter 355
Spirit Is Moving, The 1045
Spirit of America, The 107
Spirit of Capsulanti 1300
Spirit of Christmas 753
Spirit of Education, The 2134
Spirit of Jasmine 3192
Spirit of Java 2857
Spirit of Mischief, The 4497
Spirit of the Carnival, The 1794
Spirit of the Chinese Vase, The 4654
Spirit of the Drum, The 3775
Spirit of the Garden (scene) 4811
Spirit of the Manager, The 78
Spirit of the Radio 2927
Spirit of the Tom Tom, The 1982
Spirit Theme 4155
Spirits of Banality and Hate! 2243
Spirits of the Midnight Bell 4014
Spiritual 1656
Spiritual Ballet 3035
Spit 'n Whittle 1662
Spitball 900
Spittin' Image 4107
Splash! Dash! Bang! 3774
Splash Me 1246
Splendor in the Grass 4124
Splendor of Her Gaze, The 935
Spoken Aria 2220
Spoleto 2913, 3124
Sponge, The 1923, 2788
Spoofing 830
Spook Dance 4382
Spooks of Reichtenstein, The 96
Spooky Girl 3045
Spooky Nights 1270
Spooky-ookum 3921
Spooky-Ookum 4547
Spoon River 4111
Spoon River Anthology 4111
Spoon Time 830
Spooney Sam 434
Spooning 185, 1206
Spooning on Sunday Night 625
Spoons 3806
Spoony Croony Tune 2135
Spoony Land 4589
Spoony Words 2448
Sport 93
Sport, The 387
Sport a Sport 4025
Sport of Kings, The 2240, 4665, 3022
Sport, Joke and Two Spot 3820
Sporting Girls 3745
Sporting King of Nicobar, The 2159
Sporting Man, A 4450
Sporting Song 1123
Sporting Times 822
Sporty Boys 1626

Sposalizio 2961, 3444
Spot, The 3696
Spotlight 4114
Spread a Little Happiness 2976
Spread a Little Sunshine 3506
Spread Joy 952
Spread Some Joy Around 4543
Spread the News 2340
Spread Your Knees 1514
Spreadin' Rhythm Around 39
Sprechen Sie Deutsch, Mein Herr? 1569
Sprig of Rosemarie, A 3588
Sprig of Shamrock, A 1051
Spring 490, 1424
(Today Is) Spring 1796
Spring 1971, 2464, 932, 3754, 292
Spring Ballet (inst.) 3409
Spring Beauties 3602
Spring Can Really Hang You Up the Most 3094
Spring Chicken, The 4115
Spring Cleaning 572, 2050, 2338
Spring Dance 545, 3888
Spring Day 1258
Spring Doth Let Her Colours Fly 2554
Spring Drive, The 4838
Spring Fever 780, 2475
Spring Has Me Out on a Limb 4048
Spring Hat 2465
Spring in Autumn 1935, 1944
Spring in Brazil 4117
Spring in the City 1158
Spring in Vienna 2068
Spring Is a New Beginning 4764
Spring Is Blue 2736
Spring Is Here 2061, 2638, 4234, 4694
Spring Is Here in Person 4118
Spring Is In the Air 557
Spring Is in the Air 2827
Spring Is Spring 4710
Spring of Next Year, The 1012
Spring Returns 2483
Spring Song 3103, 2411, 4256
Spring, Spring, Spring 942, 3888
Spring, Sweet Spring 4646
Spring Theme, The (inst.) 96
Spring Time 904
Spring Time of the Year 2248
Spring Tra La 2540
Spring Will Be a Little Late this Year 3444
Spring Will Come Again 599, 4008
Springfield Mountain 3989
Springtide 1711
Springtime 1154, 1515, 1534, 1780, 3622, 1867, 4817, 4839
Springtime Ballet 3977
Springtime Cometh, The 1300, 2234
Springtime Dance 1552
Springtime in Mayo 4120
Springtime in the Country 3399
Springtime Is in the Air 4365
Springtime Is the Time for Loving 480
Springtime of Long Ago 3968
Springtime on the Avenue 3063
Sprinkle Me with Diamonds 2857, 3404
Sprite Dance, The 1159
Sprites of Earth and Air 2977
Spunk 3902
Spy on Time 830
Squab Farm, The 3402
Squabble Song, The 2217
Square Dance 2958
Square Dance (dance) 4314
Squash the Blues Away 3329
Squaw Man, The 4664
Squaw Man Travesty 830
Squeaky Shoes 4847
Squeeze Me 39
Squeeze Me in the Rain 3601
Squeeze Me Tight 3855
Squeeze, Squeeze, Squeeze 2676
Squidgulums 1404
Ssh! Dumas at Work! 1119
Ssh! Ssh! Ssh! 2489
Ssh! You'll Waken Mr. Doyle 4642
St. Agnes Eve 2992
St. Anthony 3066
St. Bridget 2713
St. Columba and the River 3831
St. Cyr March 4794
St. George for England 1235
St. James Infirmary 445
St. Louis Blues 441
St. Louis Blues, The 662
St. Louis Blues 691, 3840, 432, 4460, 1813, 3704, 4390
St. Martin's Lane (Sidewalks of London) 589
St. Patrick's Day 3746
St. Patrick's Day Parade 3548
St. Pierre 1764
Stability 3780
Stag Movie 4124
Stage and Fashion Hand in Hand, The 2715
Stage Door John 1619
Stage Door Johnnies 457, 3821
Stage Door Johnny 2093
Stage Door Number 4806
Stage Managers' Chorus (Walk Upon Your Toes) 1446
Stage Society 3723
Stage Struck 1619
Stage, Stage 1469
Stagedoor Johnny 2874
Staggerlee 4127
Stain on the Name, A 2318
Stairway Leading Nowhere 2754
Stairway Lullaby 390
Stairway of Dreams 4128
Stairway to Paradise 1638
Stairway to the Stars 4137, 4799

Stale World and a Pale World, A 2917
Stalling for Time 140
Stamboul 2292
Stamp Act 4488
Stamp Enclosed, A 4489
Stamp! Stamp! Stamp! 4703
Stan' Up and Fight 653
Stand Around the Bend 2817
Stand Back 2906, 3831
Stand By Me 4031, 3817, 4796
Stand Together 2133
Stand-Up 2420
Stand Up and Cheer 3264
Stand Up and Fight Like Hell 1356
Stand Up and Flex 427
Stand Up and Sing for Your Father 560
Stand Up on Your Feet and Dance 303
Stand Up the Fatherland 1015
Stand Your Ground 533
Standin' on the Corner 2961
Standing 1139
Standing in Line 3757
Standing in Need of Your Love 3515
Standing in this Phonebooth 4459
Standing on the Corner 3444
Standing Ovulation, A 4774
Standing Pat 522
Stanislaw 3858
Stanley Irritability 2153
Star, The 3051, 3235
Star and Garter Girls 4131
Star Babies, The (The "Boogie Boo" Man) 248
Star Dust 4137
Star Eyes 4290
Star Factory, The 2254
Star Gazer 4133
Star in Heaven's Firmament, A 4830
Star in the Sky, A 1680
Star in the Twilight 4669
Star Is Born, A 3272
Star Isn't Born, A 4117
Star Light, Star Bright (Starlight Waltz) 4724
Star? No a Bomb, A 2421
Star Number, The 164
Star of Destiny 4575
Star of Fate 2159
Star of Glory, The 3078
Star of Hitchy-Koo, The 1922
Star of Love 168, 2039
Star of Love, The 2387
Star of Love 2870
Star of Mine (Aeroplane Song) 2922
Star of My Native Land 4723
Star of My Soul 1470
Star of Stars 86, 1829
Star of the Monument, A 3209
Star of the Night 1509
Star of the North Star State 304
Star of the Show, The 1665
Star of This War, The 2472
Star of Zion 3690
Star Quality 456, 1644
Star Song, The 1770
Star Song 3651
Star Spangled Banner 1897, 3739
Star Spangled Banner, The 117
Star Spangled Susan Brown 498
Star Stepping Stranger 2728
Star Tar 956
Star That Warms My Heart, The 3592
Star Wars 4135
Star without a Job 4415
Starburst 2728
Stardust 4424
Stardust Waltz, The 287
Stares that Lead to Love 4373
Starfish, Seagull, Pebble 2368
Stargazer 945
Staring 2565
Staring at the Moon 1055
Starlight 75, 2465, 4812
Starlight Express 4138
Starlight Guards, The 1199
Starlight Maid 236
Starlight of Hope 4121
Starlight, Starbright 2134
Starlit Hour, The 1138
Starmites 4139
Starry Night 2766
Starry Old Night 3651
Starry Sky 2540
Stars 2442, 4419, 4418
Stars Alone Can Tell, The 45
Stars and Bars 3651
Stars and Lovers 941
Stars and Pool 3409
Stars and Rosebuds 1162
Stars and Stripes (inst.) 3261
Stars and Stripes Forever, The 964
Stars and Stripes Forever (inst.) 4390
Stars Are Shining 3422
Stars Fell on Alabama 4137
Stars Have Blown My Way 3094
Stars in the Service Flag, The 231
Stars in Your Eyes 3698
Stars in Your Wine 1681
Stars of Broadway 560
Stars of Glory 3871
Stars of the Stage 4760
Stars of the Vaudeville 3154
Stars of Your Eyes 2756
Stars on Ice 4143
Stars Remain, The 2809
Stars Seem So Low Tonight, The 991
Stars, Stars Shining Bright You May See Future Stars Tonight 1490
Stars We Know 764
Stars Will Be Laughing 2539
Stars with Stripes 1655
Start, The 2979

Start All Over Again 1605
Start Dancing 3091
Start Stompin' 2253
Start the Ball Rollin' 2103
Start the Band 202, 1462
Startin' Over 4764
Starting at the Bottom 1275
Starting from Now 456
Starting Here, Starting Now 4145
Starting Out Again 54
Starved 3548
State of the Dance, The 1681
State of the Kingdom 73
Statehood Hula 1023
Stately American Rose, The 1753
Stately Homes of England 3235
Stately Homes of England, The 4093, 3885
Staten Island Barcarole 4684
Station 1865
Station L-O-V-E 266
Station Rush (dance) 4190
Statistics 2134
Statue, The 2188
Statue of Liberty 2717
Statue Song 2559
Statues 4170, 4240
Status 2019
Status Quo 2014
Stay 1060, 2307, 3456
Stay a While 4031
Stay and Rest Awhile in California 496
Stay As We Are 3390
Stay at Home 69
Stay Away from Louisville Lou 3428
Stay Away, Joe 4682
Stay Awhile 4279, 1723
Stay Close 4232
Stay East Young Man 1546
Stay Home Here with Me 4769
Stay in My Arms 1119
Stay in the Field 2203
Stay in Your Own Backyard 1038
Stay on the Path 1581
Stay on the Subject 4828
Stay Out, Sammy 3501
Stay, Stay for I Am No Man 402
Stay Well 2591, 4504
Stay with Me 521, 2143, 775
Stay with Me! 949
Stay with Me 407, 3577, 3654
Stay With Me, Nora 1068
Stay with the Happy People 2850
Stayin' Alive 3739
Staying Alive 3956
Staying In 2565
Staying Young 4270
Steady Eddie 4817
Steady Freddy 1561
Steady Job 2001
Steady, Steady 519
Steal Away 258
Steal with Style 3733
Stealin' Apples 1986
Stealin' My Thunder 3782
Stealing 276
Steam Heat 3351
Steam Is on the Beam, The 323
Steamboat 2556
Steamboat Days 500
Steamboat Whistle, The 216, 1338
Steamers Go By, The 3429
Steel Guitars and Barking Seals 3484
Steeple 762
Steeplejack 844
Stein Song 2122
Steinland 3755
Steins 4177
Stella 1534
Stenka Razin 710
Step Across That Line 578
Step Along with Me 3973
Step by Step 114
Step Inside 2527
Step into My World 2173
Step Into the Light 3568
Step-Mama 4459
Step on a Stone 1319
Step on It 3406, 4249
Step on the Gasoline 1831
Step Out and Dance 2168
Step Out in Front 251
Step, Step Sisters 2833
Step, Step, Step 1722
Step This Way 1482, 1544, 4148
Step to Paris Blues 2669
Step to the Rear 2014, 2010
Step Up and Pep Up the Party 931
Step Up and Shake 664
Step We Grandly 3865
Stephanie 157
Steppe Sisters, The 3063
Steppin' 1421
Steppin' Along 2034
Steppin' Baby 3655
Steppin' on It 1989
Steppin' on the Blues 2342
Steppin' Out with My Baby 789
Steppin' School 4858
Steppin' to the Bad Side 1103
Stepping 1250
Stepping All the Way Home 577
Stepping Around 3540
Stepping on Butterflies (inst.) 2148
Stepping Out of the Picture 622
Stepping Out with Lulu 2
Stepping Some 2927
Stepping Stones, The 353, 1657
Stepping Stones 4150
Stepping to the Stars 2728
Stepping with Baby 3243

Steps 389
Steps of the Capitol, The 2400
Stepsisters' Lament 759
Stepsons of the Revolution 3154
Stereophonic Sound 3972
Sterling Silver Boy 2713
Sterne, die Wieder Leuchtat 4121
Stetson 4683
Steward's Song 4762
Stick Around 602, 1601
Stick to Your Arithmetic 3138
Stick to Your Dancing, Mabel 2545
Stick to Your Knitting 2768
Sticks and Stones 427, 4153
Sticky Feet 1411
Stiff Upper Lip 921
Stiffen Up That Upper Lip 2183
Still a Debutante 791
Still Dancing 4154
Still Dreaming 346
Still Got My Heart 3471
Still I'd Love You 1339
Still in Love with You 1073
Still in the Old Front Line 2964
Still Single 2011
Still Small Voice, A 3724
Still the Heart Hopes On 1568
Still the Same Sky 4136
Still the World Rolls On 355
Still We Smile 2486
Stimela Sasezola 3836
Stingaree Song 2225
Stingaree, The (dance) 1564
Stingiest Man in Town, The 4155
Stingo-Stungo 1486
Stingy 4439
Stiochket 3559
Stitch in Time, A 284
Stitch in Time (ballet) 3940
Stitch, Stitch 3085
Stitching, Stitching 3740
Stix 3628
Stock on the Rocks 3889
Stock Report 3615
Stockboy Blues, The 169
Stockings 2123, 2532
Stolen Kisses 1530, 3013
Stolen Melody, The 1685, 2696
Stolen Opera, The 1602
Stolen Sweets 545, 4283
Stomachs and Stomachs 2464
Stomp the Blues Away 1970
Stompin' at the Savoy 146, 432
Stompin' 'Em Down 2034
Stone Age, The (scene) 683
Stone Bridge at Eight, The 1965
Stone the Crows 2242
Stonecutters' Song (Work Away with a Song, My Boys) 4724
Stoned in Saigon 1053
Stones in the Furrow 4055
Stones of Jehoshaphat, The 4157
Stonewall Moskowitz March 376
Stools 3181, 4533
Stoopid 3159
Stop 2645, 14
Stop and Go 4810
Stop Beating Those Drums 27
Stop Dance (inst.) 4557
Stop, Do Not Go On 1636
Stop! Go! 2669
Stop Holding Me Back 2464
Stop in the Name of Love 4534
Stop It 1388
Stop It, Stop It 3839
Stop Kidding Yourself 1276
Stop, Look and Kiss 'Em 3623
Stop, Look and Listen 1096
Stop, Look, Listen 2927
Stop! Look! Listen! 4158
Stop Pretending 1495
Stop, Rest Awhile 3614
Stop that Clock 4824
Stop That Dancing 2400
Stop That Dog 1772
Stop That Rag (Keep on Playing Honey) 2232
Stop the Flahooleys 1300
Stop, Thief 331
Stop Tickling Me 1334
Stop, Wait, Please 211
Stop Waltz, The 3207
Stop Your Camouflaging with Me 4742
Stop Your Teasin' 3717
Storebought Suit 1600
Stories 2040
Stories Adam Told to Eve, The 2964
Stories Adam Told to Eve 2974
Stories of a Summer Night 1908
Stories of the Stage 4473
Stork Don't Come Around Anymore, The 3150
Stork, Stork 3771
Storm at Sea, A 4381
Storm Ballet 2887
Storm Come A' Risin' 4409
Storm I 3862
Storm II 3862
Storm in My Heart, A 2949
Storm, The 3453
Stormy Love 1384
Stormy Weather 4534, 878, 3018, 885
Story Book, The 3585
Story Book Ball, The 638
Story Book Days 2383
Story Book Land 1831, 4039
Story Conference, The 1048
Story Goes On, The 253
Story Medley 1212
Story of a Bird, The 1568

Story of a Butterfly, The 969
Story of a Horn, The 3986
Story of a Life 2470
Story of a Marionette 1558
Story of a Sparrow, The 1565
Story of Alice, The 673, 2246
Story of Alice 3186
Story of Alice, The 3890
Story of an Inventory 2653
Story of Buster, The 1342
Story of Carrot, The 304
Story of Chess, The 721
Story of Fung Toy 969
Story of Kitty, The 1679
Story of Lou, A 262
Story of Lucy and Jessie, The 1329
Story of Marie, The 3954
Story of My Life, The 599
Story of My Life 1822
Story of My Life, The 4734
Story of the Dance 559
Story of the Rainbow, The 2982
Story of the Wedding March, The 1640, 1968
Story of Two Bad Boys, The 1374
Story Song 362
Story Teller, The 194
Stout 2650
Stout Hearted Men 3018
Stouthearted Men (Liberty Song) 3117
Stowaway 3905
Straight 4089
Straight and Narrow Trail, The (1) 451
Straight and Narrow Trail, The (2) 451
Straight Soda with a Lemon Twist 494
Strait and Narrow 2692
Stranded Again 3279
Strange Agony, A 654
Strange Amusing People, A 194
Strange and Wonderful (Fushigisa to Subarashisa de Ippai) 1616
Strange Case of Adam Standish, The 4557
Strange Case of Dr. Jekyll and Mr. Hyde, The 2197, 2198, 2199, 1089
Strange Duet (When You Help a Friend Out) 4190
Strange Fruit 4343
Strange Music 4075
Strange New Look 961
Strange New World 1158
Strange, Odd, Queer 3073
Strange Thing Mystifying 2212
Strange Things Time Will Do 1867
Strange Variation of Love, A 1730
Strange Weather 991
Strange What Love Will Do 2151, 1917
Strangely 3224
Stranger 3536
Stranger & a Scandal, A 1347
Stranger in Paradise 2327, 4383
Stranger in the Glass, The 4114
Stranger in the Mirror 3916
Stranger in the Rain 730
Stranger Interlude, A 3361
Stranger Than You Dreamt It 3464
Strangers 134
Strangers in the Dark 417
Strangers on a Train 157
Strangest Dream, The 4579
Strangest Show on Earth, The 4611
Strategy 1745
Straw Hat in the Rain 622
Straw Into Gold 4106
Straw into Gold 3802
Straw That Broke the Camel's Back, The 4060
Strawberries 2528, 3270, 4659
Strawberries and Cream 20
Strawberries, Pickles and Ice Cream 1282, 4168
Strawberry Day 2332
Strawberry Festival 2489
Strawberry Fields Forever 3903
Strawberry Jam 3056
Strawberry-Blueberry 1064
Strays 589
Streak o' Lightnin' 1385
Streak of Madness 2198
Stream, The 3724
Streamlined Pompadour 3152
Street, The 2067
Street Cries 279, 3541
Street Jesus 1282, 4168
Street Lady 1575
Street Light Is My Moonlight 4169
Street Moves 2578
Street Music 426
Street People 1700, 4635
Street Scene (L'Abandonnement) 2200
Street Sermon 2134
Street Song 1761
Street Songs 2804
Streets of Antioch Stink, The 3469
Streets of Bed-Stuy, The 2616
Streets of Gold 4172
Streets of New York, The 298
Streets of New York (In Old New York), The 3675
Streets of New York, The 4173, 4390
Streets of Paris, The 4174
Strength Is My Weakness 134
Strenuous 1118
Stretchers 2027
Stretto 4623
Strew the Way with Flor'rets Blooming 4724
Strictly Business 642, 1306
Strictly Confidential 3314
Strike 2263
Strike! 3347
Strike, The 4529
Strike 4637
Strike for the Rent 717
Strike Me Pink 4177
Strike Out McCracken 4478

Strike, Strike, Strike 4241
Strike Up a Bagpipe Tune 2834
Strike Up the Band 3060, 3175, 4179, 4179, 4390
Strike Up the Band! 4178
String 'Em Along 3580
String a Ring of Roses 'Round Your Rosie 4712
String Along with Texas 3342
String of Girls, A 97
String of Pearls, A 3422
String Quartet 1233
Strings Are Sighing 2839
Strip for Action 4180, 4180
Stroll in the Moonlight 2493
Stroll On 2682
Stroll on the Plaza Sant'ana, A 3359
Stroller in Dreamland, A 2494
Strollers, The 736, 1375
Strollin' 576
Strollin' Along 3683
Strolling 130, 1318, 2645, 3805, 14, 1499, 2721
Strolling and Patrolling 1569
Strolling Down Broadway 4192
Strolling Down the Avenue 685
Strolling Eyes 3737
Strolling in Society 3129
Strolling in the Gloaming 2341
Strolling on the Lido (Lido Shores) 3150
Strolling, or What Have You? 4212
Strolling Quite Fancy Free 3865
Strolling 'Round the Camp with Mary 231
Strolling Thru the Park 1840
Strolling Thru the River 350
Strolling with the One I Love the Best 3056
Strong for Girls 3677
Strong Heart 3396
Strong Woman Number 1737, 2074
Stronger Sex, The 657
Strongest Man in the World, The 2163
Struggles 3782
Strut 1587
Strut Lady with Me 3649
Strut Miss Lizzie 2415
Strut Miss Lizzy 4815
Strut Your Stuff 3677
Strutter's Ball, The 1556
Struttin' Hound 1799
Struttin' School 4296
Struttin' the Blues Away 1587
Struttin' Time 3054
Struttin' to Sutton Place 1952
Struttin' with Some Barbecue (inst.) 3840
Struttinest Strutter, The 1033
Strutting Sam 3040
Stub Me Out I'm a Cigarette 2992
Stuck for an Answer 4013
Stuck Like a Sandwich 919
Stuck on You 2022
Stuck-Up 3209
Stuck with Each Other 4435
Stud Shows Us 4611
Student Arch Duke, The 3688
Student Days 96
Student King, A 4187
Student Ponce, The 1277
Student Robin Hood of Pilsen, The 266
Students Ball (We're Havin' a Ball) 2705
Student's Ball, The 3749
Students' Chorus 2892
Students' Glide (Turkey Wing) (inst.) 3681
Students' Life 4188
Students of Art Are We 2665
Students on a Lark 1459
Students' Serenade 2254
Student's Serenade, The 30
Studio Stamp 4373
Studs 583
Study in Black 3025
Study in Black and White, A 3405, 3958
Study in Color 3352
Study in Legs, A 1460
Study in Pink 3384
Study in Porcelain, A 3407
Stuff to Give the Troops, The 844
Stump Caprice 2259
Stupid Mr. Cupid 3951
Stupidina 2551
Stupidity Talks 3441
Stupidly in Love 3600
Stuttering Song 1958
Stygian Shore, The 345
Style 3628, 2040, 2687, 887
Style Show Ballet (inst.) 462
Style, Style, Style 4012
Su L'Boul'vard 2135
Suannee River 3337
Sub-Babylon 2648
Sub-Debs' First Fling 3314
Subito (Nearer to the Lord) 3197
Submarine 130
Submarine Attack 2762
Submarine Fire Bridgade, The (Fighters of Flame Are We) 3422
Substitute 2877
Subtle Slough 2259
Subuhi Sana 4579
Suburban Lullaby 3186
Suburban Retreat 3473
Suburbia 842
Suburbia Square Dance 366, 1770, 1438
Subway 1978
Subway (Funky R.T.D.) 4003
Subway Directions 4190
Subway Dream 2134
Subway Express, The 1246
Subway Incident (dance) 4190
Subway Love 3087
Subway Rag 1056
Subway Rider 2173
Subway Song 2707
Subway Squeeze, The 2448

Subway Sun, The 1693
Subway to Coney 1590
Subways Are for Skiing 128
Subways Are for Sleeping 4190, 4190
Success 1061, 3763, 3369
Success Story 1948
Successame Street 2452
Such a Baby 3258
Such a Beautiful World 298
Such a Bore 2760, 3092
Such a Business 4114
Such a Chauffeur 628
Such a Funny Feeling 3307
Such a Happy Family 3319
Such a Little King 2203
Such a Little Queen 1685, 1849
Such a Little While 3696
Such a Lonesome Place 1206
Such a Merry Party 2522
Such a Night 1890
Such a Noble Lover 743
Such a Sociable Sort 4588
Such a Sudden Spring 4191
Such an Education Has My Mary Ann 1776
Such Good Fun (1) 2064
Such Good Fun (2) 2064
Such Is Fame 931
Such Is Life in a Love Song 2516
Such Is Love (How to Woo) 4187
Such Stuff as Dreams Are Made Of 512
Such Sufferin' 3668
Suck Up 4784
Sucker's Soliloquy, A 2426
Sudden Death Overtime 426
Sudden Lilac 3015
Sudden Thrill, The 657
Suddenly 1092, 2560, 4824
Suddenly I'm Real 3876
Suddenly Last Tuesday 3889
Suddenly Love 3019
Suddenly Now 2626
Suddenly, Seymour 2544
Suddenly Seymour 2038
Suddenly She Was There 3548
Suddenly Stop and Think 73
Suddenly the Music Starts 4192
Suddenly the Sunrise 4048
Suddenly There Was You 4108
Suddenly You 1611
Suddenly You're a Stranger 2657
Sue 3846
Sue Me 1706
Sue Ryan 4826
Sue! Sue! 363
Sue, Sue I Love You 591
Suez Dance 189
Suffer 1809, 484
Sufficiency 1537
Suffragettes 2869
Sugar (Doin' It for Sugar) 4196
Sugar Babe 3965
Sugar Baby 2939
Sugar Baby Bounce, The 4197
Sugar Cane 108, 567, 320
Sugar City 3551
Sugar Daddy Blues 3688
(My) Sugar Plum 1460
Sugarfoot 2187
Suicide Song 3934
Suite for a Growing Corpse 2017
Suite for Five Letters 3233
Suite of Dances (inst.) 2205
Suits Me Fine 2705
Sullivan 115
Sullivan Street Flat 1508
Sullivan's Got a Job 2925
Sultana 4056
Summer 2227, 453
Summer Afternoon 4718
Summer Ain't So Hot 692
Summer Day (Two Old Drybones) 3691
Summer Days 4317
Summer Dresses 454
Summer Girl, The 256, 586
Summer Girl 934
Summer Girl, The 2938
Summer Girls 3520
Summer Has Gone 2080
Summer in New York 1648
Summer in the City 3739
Summer in the Snow 490
Summer Incident 1886
Summer Is 483, 2804
Summer Is A-Comin' In 2379, 2554
Summer Is Over 1237
Summer Is Over, The 139
Summer Love 2941, 863
Summer Morn 2107
Summer Night 4794
Summer Nights 1664, 2134, 3660
Summer of Love 1518
Summer Pastimes 4364
Summer Rain 4381
Summer Romance, A 722
Summer Share 3760
Summer Sports 3399
Summer Stock 3970
Summer, Summer 4485
Summer Time 3979
Summer Was Made for Lovers 1772
Summer Weather 919
Summer's Nice 3418
Summer's Symphony 197
Summertime 378
Summertime, The 1831
Summertime 3342, 3541, 3555, 4357, 4491, 4843
Summertime Is Summertime 3895
Summertime Love 1698
Summertime Moon 4037

Sun About to Rise, The 4234
Sun and Moon 2905
Sun and Rain 3133
Sun at My Window 3899
Sun Down 1770
Sun Girl 1780
Sun Gold 4758
Sun Has Got Its Hat On, The 2798
Sun Is Aslant, The 2670
Sun Is Beginning to Crow, The 2355
Sun Is Down and Over the Town, The 1783
Sun Is Nigh, The 4378
Sun Kist Rose 3808
Sun Never Sets, The 4207
(With the) Sun on My Face 4196
Sun on My Face 4196
Sun Queen 3903
Sun Rises, The 298
Sun-Shade Girl, The 3877
Sun Shines Brighter, The 2430
Sun Shines Out of Your Eyes 299
Sun Showers 4208, 544
Sun Starts to Shine Again, The 3245
Sun-Tanned Tenth of the Nation 2259
Sun That Shines on Dixieland, The 4506
Sun Up 4673
Sun Will Shine, The 3086
Sun Won't Set, The 2536
Sun Worship 735
Sun Worshippers 2749
Sunbeam of My Heart 2973
Sunbeams, Snowflakes, Raindrops 2534
Sunbonnet Sue 3855, 4209
Sunday 692, 1315, 2843, 2940, 4210
Sunday Afternoon 844, 4115, 4476
Sunday Brunch 1697
Sunday Dress 498
Sunday Dress Parade, The 68
Sunday-Go-to-Meeting 2085
Sunday in Cicero Falls 462
Sunday in London Town 3649
Sunday in New York 1023
Sunday in the Park 1763, 3501
Sunday in the Park with George 4210
Sunday Morning 1076, 3850
Sunday Morning Breakfast Time 2252
Sunday Morning Churchman 1191
Sunday Morning in Harlem 888
Sunday Morning in June 4677
Sunday Morning Social Call 962
Sunday Morning Sunshine 3159
Sunday Night in New York 1127
Sunday Poipers 827
Sunday Promenade 2556
Sunday Tan 4825
Sunday Television 1436
Sunday's Child 3973
Sundown Brings Back Memories of You 1687
Sundown in My Soul 2225
Sundown Serenade 3054
Sunflower 1520
Sunflower and the Sun, The 1535
Sunflower and the Violet, The 2029
Sunflower Seed 649
Sunflower Sue 3782
Sung-Fu 2776
Sunkissed Land 3246
Sunlight 4405
Sunlight of My Heart 2830
Sun'll Be Up in the Morning, The 512
Sunny 2372, 4212
Sunny California 2400
Sunny Day 786, 2479
Sunny Disposish 123, 124
Sunny May Afternoon, A 2070
Sunny Moon 2728
Sunny River 4214
Sunny Riviera Bay, The 2486
Sunny Side of You 1747
Sunny Side to Every Situation 1359
Sunny South, The 2286
Sunny South 4816
Sunny South Sea Isles 1484
Sunny Spain 2
Sunny Sunbeam 3500
Sunny Sunday Morning 2563
Sunnyside Lane 3598
Sunrise 4076, 2907, 3650, 3927
Sunrise at the Zoo 3748
Sunrise Dance, The 3721
Sunrise Intermezzo 3775
Sunrise Letter 3411
Sunrise Melody 3641
Sunrise on Sunset 84
Sunrise, Sunset 1265
Suns that Daily Rise, The 2236
Sunset 3515, 3871, 2012
Sunset Boulevard 4217, 4217, 4332
Sunset in Samolo 3196
Sunset Song 2539
Sunset Sue 2206
Sunshine 1475, 1498, 4212, 4343, 1087
Sunshine Alley 1208
Sunshine and Shadows 4814
Sunshine Face 4090
Sunshine Girl, The 2543
Sunshine Girl 3113
Sunshine Is Bright 4094
Sunshine Lane 2978
Sunshine Maxixe, The 335
Sunshine of Berkeley Square 324
Sunshine of Love 1962, 175
Sunshine of Springtime, The 276
Sunshine of Virginia 3028
Sunshine of Your Love, The 3739
Sunshine of Your Smile 632
Sunshine of Your Song, The 3238
Sunshine Returns Again
(Tell Me You Love Me) 68
Sunshine Tomorrow 1222

Sunshine Valley 25
Sunshine Will Come Again 668
Super Bad 4192
Super Heroes 3742
Super Note, The 2163
Super-Sheik 2757
Super Singo 3136
Super Wasp 2477
Superhero Girl 4139
Superior Soap Jingle, The 3004
Superland 1955
Superlative Love 1851
Superman 2163
Superman March, The (inst.) 2163
Supermarket 2284
Supersational Day 2556
Superstar 843, 2212
Superstition 4534, 2300
Superwoman 3599
Supper Chorus 2465
Supper Club 1873
Supper Girl, The 2498
Supper Out of Doors 3134
Supper Time 789
Supper Trio 2464
Suppertime 207, 2544, 4783
Supple Couple 1140
Suppose 675, 4761, 3057
Suppose I Came Home at Nine 2189
Suppose I Had Never Met You 2516
Suppose-I Say, Suppose 3777
Supreme Court Saved from Fire, The 3757
Sur la Mer Immense 3769
Sur La Plage 507
Sur Les Quais 2568
Surabaya Johnny 369, 1755
Surburban Rose 2007
Sure Sign You Really Love Me 1343
Sure Thing 2372
Sure Thing Baby 2437
Sure to Go to Heaven 3541
Surfing Ballet 1809
Surplus Blues (Little Surplus Me) 620
Surplus Women 3622
Surprise 101
Surprise! 3272
Surprise 3234, 4447
Surprise Me 778
Surprise! Surprise! 705
Surprising People 2146
Surrender 4217, 1768
Surrender, Surrender 104
Surrey with the Fringe on Top, The 3263
Surrounded by the Girls 2135
Survey, The 382
Survey of Western Culture 1426
Survival of the Fittest 3722
Survival Song 169
Survive 681, 4645
Susan 709, 2986
Susan Belle, The 4253
Susan Brown from a Country Town 2358
Susan Dear Sue 1798
Susanna 2044
Susannah's Squeaking Shoes 702, 1733
Susan's Dream 2615
Susan's Soliloquy 2028
Susan's Song 4431
(I Love My Little) Susie 930
Susie 1267, 998
Susie Blair 1568
Susie for Everybody 1619
Susie from Sioux City 3921
Susie Had a Song 382
Susie Mah Sue 559
Susie Smith from Troy 1466
Susie Woosie 4478
Susie's Back in Town 3914
Suspended Animation 843
Suspicion 4200
Suspicion Song 1214
Suspicious 4062
Susquehanna! 2028
Suttee Procession 189
Suwanee River 434
Suwannee River 1482
Suzanne 1524, 4226
Suzanne, Suzanne 2923
Suzanne, Suzanne, We Love You to a Man 1554
Suzanne's Entrance 4226
Suzette 4227
Suzette and Her Pet 1523
Suzi Ann 2696
Suzie Moon 1116
Suzy Is a Good Thing 3505
Swagger Swedish Swell 3270
Swain and Swain 2319
Swallow and the Lark, The 3592
Swallows, The 3924
Swamp Boy 943
Swamps of Home, The 3288
Swan and Edgar's 1010
Swanee 638, 2415, 3985
Swanee Fashion Plate 2337
Swanee Glide 1823
Swanee Melody 2
Swanee Moon 3966
Swanee River 3513
Swanee River Blues 4817
Swanee River Melody 123
Swanee River Overture 2001
Swanee River Rhapsody 437
Swanee River, The 4646
Swanee Rose 487
Swanee Sway, The 4104
Swanislavsky 4332
Swannee River 3028, 3808
Swannee Strut 1063
Swap Her for a Mule 1029

Swapping Sweet Nothings with You 1932
Swattin' the Fly 971
Sway Brittania 3955
Swearing Skipper, The 1375
Sweat Song 3831
Sweatheart of Mine 3580
Sweehearts Waltzes 2670
Sweeney Todd 4233
Sweep 1081
Sweep No More My Lady 4503
Sweepin' Up 888
Sweeping Change 1864
Sweepstakes 2702
Sweet Alice 3144, 4817
Sweet Anastasia Brady 1910
Sweet and Hot 4778
Sweet and Low-Down 3060, 4392
Sweet and Pretty 395, 3400
Sweet Angeline 4182
Sweet Annie Moore 666
Sweet Arabian Dreams 381
Sweet as a Rose 1476
Sweet As Sugar Cane 1667
Sweet As You Can Be 468
Sweet Babette (She Always Did the Minuet) 2299
Sweet Beginning 3731
Sweet Belinda 2227, 3940, 3942
Sweet Bells of Spring 1925
Sweet Betsy from Pike 3020
Sweet Bitter Candy 1700
Sweet Blossoms 4479
Sweet By and By 3081
Sweet Bye and Bye 4237
Sweet Cactus Rose 381
Sweet Charity 3810, 4238
Sweet Clarissa (Darky Love Song) 104
Sweet Cookies 1516
Sweet Danger 2295
Sweet Dreams (Are Made of This) 1713
Sweet Dreams 1116, 2549, 4393
Sweet Ecstasy 2906
Sweet Emmaline, My Gal 1824
Sweet Emmy Lou 1667
Sweet Eternity 1015
Sweet Evening Breeze 3660
Sweet Fantasy 3167
Sweet Fool 3011
Sweet Georgia Brown 3905
Sweet Geraldine 111
Sweet Girl Graduate, The 2347, 2716
Sweet Girl of My Dreams 3642
Sweet Heaven 846
Sweet Heaven (I'm in Love Again) 845
Sweet Helen 1817
Sweet Henry Loves You 4089
Sweet Inniscarra 4239
Sweet Is the Perfume of Summer Flowers 236
Sweet Is the Rose 2859
Sweet Italian Love 4521
Sweet Jesus, Blessed Savior 3817
Sweet Kentucky Lady 538
Sweet Kisses 4813
Sweet Kitty 2341
Sweet Kitty Bellairs 2340, 4804
Sweet Kitty Kellairs 4650
Sweet Lady 4240, 4283
Sweet Land of Dreams 3021
Sweet Liar 1481, 3532
Sweet Life 251
Sweet Lips 1514
Sweet Lisette, So People Say 4554
Sweet Little Baby O' Mine 691
Sweet Little Buttercup 1824
Sweet Little Devil 4241
Sweet Little Mary Ann 733
Sweet Little Rosey Posey 509
Sweet Little Stranger 2214, 4025
Sweet Longings 4272
Sweet Lorraine 4137
Sweet Love 580
Sweet Madness 3002
Sweet Magnolia Rose 4281
Sweet Mamie 1995
Sweet Man 1425, 2449
Sweet Man o' Mine 3513
Sweet Marie, Make a Rag-a-Time Dance with Me 2232
Sweet Matilda 4725
Sweet Memories 3264
Sweet Memory 1497
Sweet Mistress 4244
Sweet Mistress of My Heart 2910
Sweet Music 294
Sweet Nevada (waltz version) 3390
Sweet Nevada (western version) 3390
Sweet Nothings 2927
Sweet Nudity 3214
Sweet Old Fashioned Waltz 3086
Sweet One 487, 3139, 4532
Sweet Onion in Bermuda 4429
Sweet Penelope 4161
Sweet Peter 1013
Sweet Pickings 1777
Sweet Polly Plunkett 4067
Sweet Popopper 3054
Sweet Popularity 3809
Sweet Rhythm 3103
Sweet River 3294
Sweet Rosa Pompetta 3626
Sweet San-oo 3857
Sweet Sans-oo 3856
Sweet Savannah Sue 1980
Sweet Senorita 188
Sweet Seventeen 246, 3792, 1240, 248
Sweet Shirren 2919
Sweet Simplicatas 178
Sweet Simplicity 1687, 3865
Sweet Sixteen 1667, 3545, 4616, 4813
Sweet Sixty-Five 2068

(You) Sweet So-and-So 4235
Sweet So-and-So 4320
Sweet Song of India 4264
Sweet Spirit of '76 (inst.) 3683
Sweet Stuff 2491
Sweet Sue's 3476
Sweet, Sweet, Sweet 2687
Sweet Sweetheart of Mine 2490
Sweet Talker 1372
Sweet Talkin' Guy 338
Sweet Temptation 703
Sweet Thames 1467
Sweet Thing Like Me, A 1699
Sweet Thoughts of Home 2632
Sweet Thursday 3505, 3505
Sweet Time 3656, 4318
Sweet to See Two Hearts So True 630
Sweet Tokay 1910
Sweet Transvestite 3742
Sweet Ukulele 3925
Sweet Virginia Blues 1028
(Oh You) Sweet Whatch-May-Call-It 3382
Sweet William 868, 1670, 175
Sweet Wind Blowin' My Way 2190
Sweet Words 2648
Sweet World 2182
Sweet Yesterday 4437
Sweetenheart 3980
Sweeter Den a Sugar Cane 2964
Sweeter Than Sugar 2349
Sweeter Than Sweet 898
Sweeter Than You 4426, 4476
Sweetest Girl in Paris, The 4247
Sweetest Girl, Silly Boy I Love You (Reckless Boy, I Love You) 1318
Sweetest Little Girl 2490
Sweetest Little Girl in Tennessee 2762
Sweetest Little Prison in the World, The 1031
Sweetest Love 1776
Sweetest Maid of All 4590
Sweetest Melody 3404
Sweetest of the Roses 4532
Sweetest Part of Loving Is to Dream, The 1118
Sweetest Songs Remain to Be Sung, The 729
Sweetest Sounds, The 3187
Sweetest Thing in Life 3451
Sweetest Words That E'er Were Said, The 2383
Sweetheart 118, 255, 659, 742, 913, 1864, 2914, 3258
Sweetheart (I'm So Glad That I Met You) 3649
Sweetheart 4227
Sweetheart, Answer Yes 3443
Sweetheart, Farewell 2009
Sweetheart from the Emerald Isle 1550
Sweetheart, I'm Waiting 1165
Sweetheart Lane 1688
Sweetheart Let's Go a Walking 4509
Sweetheart Mine 2209
Sweetheart, My Own Sweetheart 3736
Sweetheart o' Mine 2056
Sweetheart of Boyhood Days 1908
Sweetheart of Mine 2594
Sweetheart of My Own, A 2184
Sweetheart of Mystery 21
Sweetheart of Our Student Corps 3012
Sweetheart of the Nation 486
Sweetheart of Your Dreams, The 670
Sweetheart on the Rhine (Du Blonde Lindenwirtin Vom Rhein) 1044
Sweetheart Semicolon 3, 3381
Sweetheart Shop, The 4248
Sweetheart Shop Wedding, A 4248
Sweetheart Special (On the Lovey-Dove Line), The 2939
Sweetheart Sue 591
Sweetheart Ties 1316
Sweetheart Time 4249
Sweethearts 4251, 806, 3719
Sweethearts (If You Ask Where Love Is Found) 4250
Sweetheart's Cotillion, The 4163
Sweethearts in Every Town 3480
Sweethearts in the Sky 1264
Sweethearts of Every Town (Drummer Song) 1731
Sweethearts of the Team, The 4420
Sweethearts, Wives and Good Fellows 3771
Sweetie 1922, 2349, 4633
Sweetie Dear 9, 1425
Sweetie Mine 4836, 4839
Sweetie Pie 924
Sweeties 3962
Sweetly I Spoke 4550
Sweetness 1924
Sweetness of It All, The 3933
Sweetnin' Water 1385
Sweets for Sweet 3844
Sweets to the Sweet 948, 2574, 4670
Sweety Mine 567
Swell 3142
Swellest Thing in Town, The 1627
Swellest Thing, The 1259
Swept Away 2295
Swimmers (dance), The 323
Swimming Master, The 2506
Swing, The 2856
Swing 4252
Swing! 4734
Swing-a-Ding-a-Ling 941
Swing Along 2111
Swing Is the Thing, The 446
Swing Left, Sweet Chariot 4152
Swing Low Sweet Chariot 887
Swing Low, Sweet Harriet 204
Swing Me High, Swing Me Low 4804
Swing, My Pretty One, Swing 1071
Swing on the Corner 1423
Swing Shift (Miss Parachute) 2754
Swing Song 1564, 2340, 2880
Swing Song, The (You Are Laughing) 4554
Swing Struck 447, 3705
Swing, Swing, Swing 1149
Swing That Music 4534
Swing That Swing 2252

Swing Waltz, The 2089
Swing Your Bag 935
Swing Your Calico 1931
Swing Your Lady Mister Hemingway 4826
Swing Your Projects 4190
Swing Your Tails 3861
Swingaroo Trio, The 4166
Swingin' a Dream 4256
Swingin' Along 1137
Swingin' the Jinx Away 4517
Swingin' the Nursery Rhymes 1953
Swingin' with the Swing Shift 1311
Swingin' with the Wind 3375
Swinging 1573, 2522
Swinging a Dance 2248
Swinging Along 4838
Swinging on the Gate 1831
Swinging the Bhumba 4782
Swinging Uptown 4003
Swinging with Someone 4687
Swing's Gonna Rock Your Bones 2275
Swingtime in Honolulu 886
Swingtime on the Swanee 883
Swingy Little Thingy 3907
Swiss Miss 2376
Swiss Warble 1264
Switch It Miss Mitchell 3782
Switchblade Bess 3954
Switzerland 3525
Swivel, The 3551
Swoop of the Moopem 1958
Sword Dance 3573
Sword for Mine, The 1606
Sword Is My Sweetheart True, The 4787
Sword of Damocles, The 3742
Sword of My Father, The 2340
Sword, Rose and Cape 656
Swordfight 3741
Swordfight, The 1985
Sydney's Hymn 695
Sylvia 306
Sylvia the Gibson Girl 675
Sympathetic Someone 773
Sympathy 742, 1285, 1924, 2837
Sympathy-Tenderness 2198
Symphonic Pantomime (inst.) 4214
Symphonic Poem (inst.) 1174
Symphonie 2877
Symphony 4485
Symphony for Today (inst.) 3683
Symphony in Dress (inst.) 684
Symphony Rap 1713
Syncojassologists 3580
Syncopate 2927
Syncopated City 2389
Syncopated Clock, The 4137
Syncopated Cocktail, A 4813
Syncopated Frolic, A 4838
Syncopated Heart 97
Syncopated Minuet, The 3500
Syncopated Pipes of Pan 1690
Syncopated Strain 2009
Syncopated Vamp, The 4814
Syncopated Walk, The 4603
Syncopated Whisk Brooms, The 2927
Syncopatia Land 1963
Syncopatin' 4192, 4678
Syncopating Baby (Syncopating Sadie) 4819
Syncopation 4747
Syncopation Stenos 3963
Synergy 3309
Syringa Tree 2756
Syringa Tree, The 4248
System 3623, 4241
System of My Own 1173
Szibill 4258

T

T'Ain't Nobody's Bizness If I Do 432
T.E.A.M. (The Baseball Game) 4783
T.L.C. (Tender Loving Care) 2095
T'morra', T'morra' 462
T.N.D.P.W.A.M. 3608
T-W-I-N-S 3831
Ta, Ta, My Dainty Little Darling 1095
Ta Bouche 3295
Ta, Luv 1619
Ta Ra Ra Boom De Ay 429
Ta-Ra-Ra-Boom-Dee-Ay! 4390
Ta-Ra-Ta 1852
Ta Rah Ta Rah 1774
Ta-Ta, Little Girl 2334
Ta Ta, Ol' Bean 3172
Ta Ta, Old Bean 1207
Ta Voo 3404
Table Bay 4579
Table D'Hote Cabaret, The 3319
Table for Two, A 1551, 3401
Table for Two 3968
Table Manners 1815
Table Talk 4727
Table Tango 1878
Table with a View, A 223
Table with a View 1649
Tableland 4147
Tabloid Papers 123
Taboo 3423
Taboo or Not Taboo 1346
Tackin' 'Em Down 4812, 4838
Tact 468, 1313
Taffy 2134
Taffy Finally 3979
Tag 3453
Tag Day 2557
Tahiti 398, 740, 792, 1244
Tahiti Sweetie 4249
T'ai Chi 944

Tail of a Kite, The 3348
Tail of the Honey Bee, A 1707
Tailor and the Crow, The 3736
Tailor Made Babies 290
Tailor Man, A 1522
Tailor, Motel Kamzoil, The 1265
Tailor's Drinking Song, The 2811
Tailor's Dummy 246
Tailors of Hong Kong, The 194
Tails Up 2293
Tain't Gwine to Be No Rain 295
Tain't Kosher 343
Tain't No Sin 2415
'Tain't No Use in Lovin' That Way 2990
'Tain't Nobody's Bizness If I Do 39
Tain't Nobody's Bizness If I Do 2796
Tainted Gold 4046
Taisez-Vous 3081
Tait Song 1628
Take a Bow 2195, 4265
Take a Break 1702
Take a Broken Heart 3275
Take a Chance 348, 1513
Take a Chance (Little Girl and Learn to Dance) 627
Take a Chance on Me 2876
Take a Chance with Me 2857
Take a Crank Letter 4314
Take a Good Look Around 2664
Take a Job 1061
Take a Knife 2918
Take a Letter to the King 3584
Take a Little Baby Home with You 201
Take a Little Dip 1312
Take a Little Drink of Ouzo 2106
Take a Little Kiss 3045
Take a Little One Step 2569, 3184
Take a Little Perfume 1975
Take a Little Shine to Me 3618
Take a Little Sip 1662
Take a Little Stroll with Me 2789
Take a Little Tip from Me 1014
Take a Little Walk (inst.) 700
Take a Little Wife 3007
Take a Longer Look 1615
Take a Look 1770, 4303
Take a Look at Life 716
Take a Look at Me Now 2318
Take a Look at That 690
Take a Maid 2383
Take a Pair of Sparkling Eyes 2348
Take a Pick 1500
Take a Poem 3226
Take a Professor 3873
Take a Raisin 3508
Take a Ride! 2876
Take a Ride with Me 1926
Take a Step 3618
Take a Step with Me 2424
Take a Stroll 2505
Take-a-Tour, Congressman 2134
Take a Trip 821
Take a Trip in My Auto 1118
Take a Trip to Harlem 443
Take a Trip to the Seaside 2139
Take a Trippie with a Hippie 1364
Take a Vacation 1201
Take a Walk on the Wild Side 3739
Take a Walk with Me 2622
Take and Take and Take 2068
Take Back Your Mink 1706, 3444
Take Break Blues 1214
Take Care 842, 1318
Take Care, Little Girl, Take Care 4805
Take Care of Him 4073
Take Care of One Another 1092
Take Care of This House 4004
Take Care of Yourself 943
Take Care-Senor 2848
Take Comfort 4366
Take Courage Heart 2478
Take Courage, Daughter 2220
Take de Picture 3960
Take Down Dis Letter 740
Take 'Em Away (He's Breakin' My Heart) 799
Take 'Em to the Door Blues 1831
Take 'em to the Door Blues 2263
Take Every Opportunity 2067
Take Good Care of that Lady 1638
Take Her Away 4014
Take Her Down to Coney and Give Her the Air 4654
Take Her Lord 1496
Take Her My Boy 4331
Take Her, My Boy, She's Yours 1768
Take Her to Pigeon Walk 2385
Take Him 3353
Take Him Away, the Law Commands It 434
Take Him Away to the Mountains 2760
Take Him to Evaline 1213
Take Him to Jail 2645
Take Hold the Crutch 2801
Take It All Off 2208
Take It Away 596
Take It Back, We're Through 2707
Take It from a Happy Married Man 4437
Take It from a Lady 1373
Take It from a Pal 4102
Take It from Me 1228, 2145, 3087, 2547, 4269
Take It from the Top 4769
Take It in Your Stride 153
Take It Mr. Gladstone 1857
Take It on the Chin 2798
Take It Right Back 478
Take It Slow, Joe 2190
Take Kids 2556
Take Love 3703, 3838
Take Love Easy 341, 3551
Take Love While You May 797
Take Me 1249

Take Me (Back Again) 1626
Take Me! 2069
Take Me 2135, 1439, 3552
Take Me a Drink of Whiskey 2225
Take Me Along 1360, 4270
Take Me Along with You Dearie 3096
Take Me As I Am 2198
Take Me Away 3368, 1137
Take Me Away to Jail 3041
Take Me Back 60, 3210, 3565
Take Me Back to Dixie Blues 14
Take Me Back to Herald Square 3129
Take Me Back to Manhattan 3131, 4517
Take Me Back to Old Broadway 4094
Take Me Back to Philadelphia, Pa. 4375
Take Me Back to Samoa Some More 199
Take Me Back to Texas 3217
Take Me Back to Texas with You 2705
Take Me Back to Town 2538
Take Me Dear 4119
Take Me Down to Coney Island 357
Take Me Down to Luna 625
Take Me For—- 4219
Take Me for a Buggy Ride 478
Take Me for a Honeymoon Ride 4234
Take Me Home 2159
Take Me Home with You 2451
Take Me in Your Arms 4137, 822
Take Me on a Ride of Joy 186
Take Me on the Merry-Go-Round 675, 248
Take Me 'Round in a Taxicab 4802
Take Me Savage 3636
Take Me There 2014
Take Me to Heaven 465
Take Me to That Swanee Shore 558
Take Me to That Tango Tea 3134
Take Me to the Masquerade 1566
Take Me to the Midnight Cakewalk Ball 3399
Take Me to the World 1200
Take Me Up 3724
Take Me with You, Mary 1541
Take More Out of Life 573
Take My Advice 1817
Take My Hand 935, 3871
Take My Hand in Friendship 3490
Take My Heart with You 2397
Take My Place 614
Take-Off 2364
Take Off a Little Bit 4158
Take Off the Coat 454, 4323
Take Off the Mask 3107
Take Off the Sandal 3088
Take Plenty of Shoes 511
Take That 1458
Take That Look Off Your Face 4068, 4301
Take That Off, Too 3626
Take That Smile Off Your Face 3661
Take the "A" Train 4091
Take the 'A' Train 3905, 2259
Take the Air 4271
Take the Book 3180
Take the Eyes of Mabel 2620
Take the Glamour Out of War 1053
Take the Moment 1060
Take the Money 1048
Take the Picture First! 3204
Take the Road 3092
Take the Steamer to Nantucket 1539
Take the Time to Fall in Love 1227
Take the Wheels Off the Wagon 3347
Take the Word of a Gentleman 657
Take Them All Away 702
Take Them Away They'll Drive Me Crazy 1897
Take Things Easy 4293
Take This Little Rosebud 3133
Take Those Lips Away 4817
Take Thy Way to Earth 4014
Take to the Air 4707
Take Up with an Older Woman 367
Take Us Back King George 4635
Take Us 'Round the Island 3423
Take Us to Our Leader 1047
Take Us to the Forest 3164
Take What Comes 3221
Take What You Can 1015
Take What You Will 693
Take Your Hat Off 4558
Take Your Pretty Partner 906
Take Your Time 1918, 2469
Take Your Time and Take Your Pick 3509
Take Yourself a Trip 4777
Taken at Her Word 392
Taken by Surprise 3236
Taken for a Ride 3946
Takes a Heap of Love 4529
Takin' Miss Mary to the Ball 3992
Takin' My Time 3608
Takin' the Light 1637
Takin' the Long Way Home 1103
Taking a Chance on Love 612, 4799
Taking a Wife 2594
Taking Care of You 1611
Taking Chances 3561, 1867
Taking Inventory 1046
Taking It Slow 3608
Taking No Chances 2615
Taking Off 3168
Taking Off the Robe 3233
Taking Our Turn 4272
Taking the Cure 2219
Taking the Easy Way Out 2962
Taking Ways 2455
Tale of a Bumblebee, The 2315
Tale of a Coat, The 1424
Tale of a Decent Married Hen 4704
Tale of a Fan 378
Tale of a Mermaid, The 335
Tale of a Monkey 2793
Tale of a Music Box Shop
(Tale of a Song Box Shop) 4735

Tale of a Shirt, The 799
Tale of a Stroll 2795
Tale of a Turtle Dove, The 4738
Tale of an Oyster, The 1272, 4517
Tale of an Oyster 4581
Tale of Bro' Crow, The 2541
Tale of the Bachelor and the Maid, The 1550
Tale of the Calamari 3587
Tale of the Chamois, The 96
Tale of the Highborn Rooster, The 3673
Tale of the Jealous Cat 2732
Tale of the Kangaroo, The 586
Tale of the Mermaid 3021
Tale of the Mermaid, The 3022
Tale of the Monkey and the Snake, The 645
Tale of the Oyster 2294, 1018
Tale of the Scungilli 3587
Tale of the Sea Shell, The 3578
Tale of the Tadpole 2717
Tale of the Tailless Frog, The 3786
Tale of the Wedding Bell, The 734
Tale of Woe, A 3173
Talent 3811, 4019, 3108
Talent Is What the Public Wants 1489
Tales, The 1959
Tales 2100
Tales of Hoffman, The 376
Tales of the South Pacific 4096
Talk 1017, 3482
Talk About a Busy Little Housewife 2829
Talk About Girls 4276
Talk About the Men 3619
Talk About This-Talk About That 4250
Talk About Time, A 2142
Talk About Yo' Luck 2101
Talk It Over 2516
Talk of the Town, The 2148
Talk Sunshine 2771
Talk, Talk, Talk 75, 694, 4232, 3599
Talk to Him 2987
Talk to Me 722, 3136, 2707, 2887, 3619
Talk to Me About Love 1116
Talk to Me Baby 1373
Talk to Me Tomorrow 1475
Talk with My Heel and Your Toe 3721
Talk with One's Conscience, A 4157
Talk Your Feelings 4192
Talkative Toes 4367
Talkin' 'bout You 1766
Talkin' About Reggae 3690
Talkin' Blues 3276
Talkin' Glory 4123
Talkin' in Tongues 1662
Talkin' Morosco Blues 4533
Talkin' Subway 4740
Talkin' with Your Feet 3913
Talking About Love 3836
Talking Picture Show 2949
Talking to Myself Again 2032
Talking to People 2173
Talking to You 1891
Talking to Yourself 1729
Tall Dames and Low Comedy 36
Tall Hope 4693
Tall Pines, The 3262
Tallahassee 487, 971, 2843
Tallahassee Lassie 722
Tallulah 4279
Tally Ho 37
Tally-Ho 138, 1532
Tally Ho!!! (We'll Blow the Jolly Horn) 4044
Talons of Time 2962
Talullahbaloo 4279
Tam, Tam, Tam Tam Tam 1686
Tamara, Queen of the Nile 3600
Tamboree 82
Tambourin Chinois 168
Tambourine 137
Tambourine Dance, The 3719
Tambourine Jamboree 3374
Tambourine Song 49
Tame Me 528, 1393
Tammany 1243, 4172
Tammany Ball, The 1403
Tampa 2827
Tampa Bay 1823
Tampico Tap 608
Tampico Tune 290
Tan 'n' Hot 597, 3217
Tan Manhattan 4281
Tan-Tivy 2910
Tandem, A 4285
Tangiers 2014
Tangle Up Puppet 2470
Tangled Tangents 3651
Tanglefoot, The 4269
Tangles 3236
Tangletoes 4284
Tango, The (dance) 98
Tango 326
Tango, The 400
Tango 556
Tango (dance) 1886
Tango 2379
Tango, The 4560
Tango 3112, 3117, 2753, 3476, 4380
Tango Ballad 369, 4368
Tango-Ballad 4369
Tango Band, The 1173
Tango Brazilian Dreams 4808
Tango Breakfast, The 968
Tango Contest, The 287
Tango Dip 351
Tango Edward 2424
Tango Espagnol 4271
Tango Glide 2390
Tango Melody 799
Tango Moon, The 537
Tango Moon 538
Tango Rehearsal 400

Tango Rhythm 4374
Tango Tea 4440
Tango Tragique 3918
Tangolango Tap 2923
Tangorilla 4808
Tanguera (inst.) 2356
Tankhum 1279
Tantalizing April 3580
Tantalizing Ida 2528
Tanz Mit Mir (Blue Bird Girls) 656
Tap Along with Me (inst.) 4534
Tap 'Appy Feet 589
Tap Combination, The 746
Tap Dance (dance) 723
(Origin of the) Tap Dance 1490
Tap Dance 1974
Tap Dance Drill 1474
Tap Is Tops 885
Tap Mathematician 875, 885
Tap Tap 4286
Tap-Tap-Tapnotized 3955
Tap, Tap, The 3342
Tap the Plate 578
Tap the Toe 391
Tap Your Troubles Away 2208, 2660
Tapaholics 1970
Tape and Chain, The 617
Tapestry Piece 2168
Tappin-G-Minor 2235
Tappin' the Barrel 444
Tappin' the Toe 4668
Taps 567, 4290, 4683
Taps for Private Tussie 4107
Taps Is Tops 875
Tar's Farewell, The 2013
Tara 1616
Tarantella 825
Tarantella (inst.) 2844
Tarantella 3151, 4187
Tarantella Rhythm 3822
Tarantula 596
Tarentella 3011
Tartar 953, 4077
Tartar Song, The 711, 23
Tartarin Now Comes This Day 49
Tartarin the Terrible 49
Tarts 1757
Tarts and Flowers 680
Taste 1611
Taste of Forever, A 3305
Taste of the Sea, A 4374
Tasy Freeze 3564
Tattered Tom 4289, 4289
Tattle Tales 4290
Tattoo Dance 1809
Tattoo Song 1664
Tattooed Countess, The 4292
Tattooed Man, The 2101
Tattooed Woman 4292
Tavern Chorus 526
Tavern Song (Red Wine) 3117
Tax Collector's Soliloquy, The 4536
Tax the Bachelors 2232
Taxi 2470, 3159, 4294
Taxi Cab 1613
Taxi Dancer's Tango 2437
Taxi Drivers' Lament 1654
Taxi, Taxi 1593
Taxi to Dreamland 528, 3997
Tchaikowsky 512
Tchaikowsky (and Other Russians) 2386
Te Deum 3702
Te Deum Laudamus! 4539
Tea 3236
Tea Chanty 3940
Tea Dance 4488
Tea for Two 146, 3184, 3249
Tea in Chicago 2994
Tea Leaves 2884
Tea Leaves Say Good-Bye, The 2255
Tea Number 2813
Tea Party, The 2208
Tea Party 937, 1697
Tea Party, The 2373
Tea Song, The 2228
Tea! Tea! 1926
Tea, Tea, Tea 767
Tea-Tea-Tea 1993
Tea Time 303
Tea Time in Timbuctoo 1227
Tea Time Tango Tune 433
Tea Time Tap 1297
Tea, Toast and Kisses 1560
Teach It How to Dance 2022
Teach Me 4200
Teach Me a Dance Like Grandma 3196
Teach Me Everything You Know 4712
Teach Me How 1513
Teach Me How to Dance 4764
Teach Me How to Fast Dance 4731
Teach Me How to Kiss 4654
Teach Me How to Love 357, 4158
Teach Me How to Shimmy 4031
Teach Me to Dance 2516, 4795
Teach Me to Dance Like Grandma 4341
Teach Me to Forget 1111
Teach Me to Love in Mexico 1911
Teach Me to Smile 1565
Teach Me Tonight 4743
Teach the Children 1581
Teach the Young Idea How to Shoot 3943
Teach Us the Subtle Art of Kissing 3805
Teacher Teacher 3923
Teachers 2261
Teacher's Out Today, The 3600
Teaching Me Fadder to Waltz 1501
Teaching the Baby to Walk 4437
Teacup and a Spoon, A 2412
Teahouse, The 2627
Teahouse of the August Moon 2626

Teahouse of the August Moon, The 2626
Teahouse of the Sliding Screens, The 2861
Team Spirit 3752
Tear Down the Wall 747
Tear Drops from Her Eyes Are Pearls 2004
Tear It Up 1155
Tear Out Your Heart 526
Tear the Town Apart (dance) 4196
Tears 922, 2433
Tears and Tears Ago 3561
Tears of Ice 300
Tears of Joy 3526
Tears of Love 4378
Tease, Tease, Tease 513
Teasing 2358
Teasing Mama (Teasing Baby) 2302
Technique 2535
Tecla's Mood 3536
Teddy Bear and Dresden Doll 1532
Teddy Bear and the Bee, The 263
Teddy Bird, The 3855
Teddy De Roose 4390
Teddy Girl, The 4762
Teddy the Jungle Boogie Man 3134
Teddy Toddle, The 1625
Tee-Oodle-Um-Bum-Bo 2363
Tee Ta Tee 243
Tee-dle-oo 1499
Teenage Love 722
Teenage Tenderness 1418
Teenie-Eenie-Weenie 4228
Teeny Bopper 4584
Teeny Little Nest 2483
Teeny Tiny 1873
Teeny Weeny Genie 177
Teeter-Totter 3065
Teeter Totter Tessie 3292, 4483
Tel-Aviv 3669
Tel-Aviv Construction Worker 2421
Telegram 1155
Telegram, The 4107
Telegraph Girl 2448
Telegraph Me 3626
Telepathetique, The 1276
Telepathic Eye, The 2830
Telephone, The 3873, 2905, 1511
Telephone Duet 2424
Telephone Girl, The 3401, 4298
Telephone Girls 4860
Telephone Hour, The 607
Telephone Jazz, The 1972
Telephone Me Dearie 3520
Telephone Me, Baby 4717
Telephone Song 610, 2303, 3771
Telephone Switchboard Scene 1300
Telephone Tango 920
Telephone to the Moon 719
Telephone Your Riffky Issey 4804
Tell a Little Lie or Two 2968
Tell Her 101, 3695, 946, 1990, 3108, 4384
Tell Her in the Golden Summer 1307
Tell Her in the Springtime 3009
Tell Her Now 949
Tell Her the Truth 4299
Tell Her While the Waltz Is Playing 1516
Tell Him 4193
Tell Him, Tell Her 1161
Tell Him-Tell Her! 455
Tell It All 2160
Tell It All Over Again 3304
Tell It Like It Is 1890
Tell It to a Turtle 4391, 281
Tell It to Bart 3696
Tell It to Me Dad 1955
Tell It to Sweeney 4757
Tell It to the Marines (A Bunch o' Nuts) 3556
Tell It with a Melody 3006
Tell Me 4288, 1823, 2320, 2373, 3402, 3702, 4754
Tell Me a Bedtime Story 3008
Tell Me About Your Eden 1864
Tell Me Again 263, 1722
Tell Me Again, Sweetheart 2697
Tell Me All Your Troubles, Cutie 2900
Tell Me Am I Shooting at the Moon 2950
Tell Me Cigarette (Cigarette Song) 718
Tell Me, Crystal Ball 1580
Tell Me, Daisy 380
Tell Me Daisy 463
Tell Me, Do You Love Me As of Old? 3998
Tell Me Dusky Maiden 2041, 4014
Tell Me Goodbye 2958
Tell Me How 1918
Tell Me I Look Nice 3918
Tell Me Lies 3094
Tell Me Lilac Domino 2486
Tell Me Little Gypsy 4814
Tell Me More! 4300
Tell Me Not That You Are Forgetting 2622
Tell Me of Love 948
Tell Me on a Sunday 4068, 4301
Tell Me Once Again 1602
Tell Me Pray 104
Tell Me Pretty Maiden 1313
Tell Me Shooting Star (Money! Money! Money!) 4201
Tell Me Some More 2107
Tell Me Something About Yourself 1874
Tell Me, Tell Me 2568
Tell Me That You Love Me 3349, 4492
Tell Me That You Miss Me 20
Tell Me the French Word for Squeeze Me 2665
Tell Me the Story 4362
Tell Me the Story of Your Life 1596
Tell Me the Truth 1990
Tell Me Tonight 126
Tell Me Truly 3369
Tell Me What Can This Be 2808
Tell Me, What Is Love? 429
Tell Me What You Want 1804
Tell Me what Your Eyes Were Made For 2666

Tell Me When I Shall Find Him 350
Tell Me Where Is Fancy Bred? 3909
Tell Me Who I Was 1865
Tell Me Who You Are 4532
Tell Me Why 490, 4137, 3246, 4320
Tell Me Why the World 2620
Tell Me Why You Love Me! 306
Tell Me with a Love Song 4778
Tell Me with Smiles 487
Tell Me You Are Happy 1462
Tell Me You Love Me 3197
Tell Some Pretty Lies to Me 593
Tell Sweet Saroyana 3231
Tell That to the Marines 3985
Tell the Band to Play an Irish Tune 2795, 3867
Tell the Blushing Bridegroom 2947
Tell the Doc 1419
Tell the Town, Hello, Tonite 473
Tell the World I'm Through 1297
Tell Tony and Rosabella Good-bye for Me 2961
Tell Us, Handsome Man 4194
Tell Us Pretty Ladies 1264
Tell Us the Story of Love 3344
Tell Us What's the Row? 2978
Tell Your Friends 167
Telling Fortunes (Your Fortune) 659
Telstar 3695
Temperament 1538, 2328, 2334, 4795
Temperamental Dances 2903
Temperamental Honeymoon 2570
Temperance Polka 4028
Temperance Song, The 562
Tempest, The 1104
Tempest 1104
Temple, The 2212
Temple Bells 717, 4509
Temples 4048
Tempo di Gavotte 2732
Tempo of the Times 2804
Temporarily Unemployed 1280
Temporary Arrangement, A 1420
Temporary Widow, The 2732
Temporary Wives 2336
Tempt Me Not 4420
Temptation 3992, 1513
Temptation, The 2632
Temptation 4378, 544
Temptation Strut, The 1678
Temptations 4094
Tempting Salome 2290
Tempus Fugit 3688
Ten Cents a Dance 2772, 3980
Ten Commandments 1715
Ten Commandments of Love, The 1726, 2363
Ten Days Ago 3651
Ten Little Bridesmaids 3663
Ten Little Children 10
Ten Little Chorus Girls 1866
Ten Minutes Ago 759
Ten Minutes in Bed 4235
Ten O'Clock 2854
Ten O'Clock Town 3860
Ten Percent 723, 4480
Ten Percent Banlon 1049
Ten Percenters 3105
Ten Plagues, The 1769
Ten Seconds 647
Ten Strokes Under Par 2072
Ten Thousand Feet in the Air 3239
Ten to One 2489
Ten Year 1872
Ten Years from Now 4703
Tender Shepherd 3453
Tender Spot, A 4633
(Love Is) The Tender Trap 4743
Tender Understanding 4591
Tenderloin 4312
Tenderloin Celebration, The 4312
Tendin' to My Knittin' 1539
Tenement Lullaby, The 154, 155
Tengu 3711
Tennessee 317, 806, 4415, 4487
Tennessee Dan 111
Tennessee Fish Fry 117
Tennessee, I Hear You Calling Me 3397
Tennessee, That's the Place for Me 2990
Tennessee Waltz 4264
Tennessee Williams Note, A 413
Tennessee, I Hear You Calling 965
Tennis 1067, 1738, 2976, 4673
Tennis Champs (Helen! Susanne! and Bill!) 1447
Tennis Song 775, 3015
Tennis Terpsichorean 2870
Tennis Tournament 1963
Tenth and Greenwich 40
10th Avenue Waltz 867
Tequila 2847
Terence 4313
Teresa 1878
Terhou 1386
Termanix 3871
Terpsichorean Trifle, A 1259
Terrace Duet 721
Terre Haute 3970
Terre Haute High 4558
Terrible Feeling, A 4523
Terrible Puppy Dog 4161
Terrible Tuesday 2173
Terribly Attractive 4142
Terrific Band and a Real Nice Crowd, A 287
Terrorist Trio 4635
Terzetto 3014
Terzetto Buffo 2667
Tessie You Are the Only, Only, Only 3976
Test, The 3956
Test of Love, The 3791
Test Tube Baby 4635
Testament 4368
Testimony 1700
Testing, The 2142

Tete-A-Tete with You, A 1334
Tetrazzini Family, The 511
Tette-a-Tette at 8 2830
Tevye and His Daughters 1265
Tevye's Dream 1265
Texas 3342
Texas Aristocracy 992
Texas Dan 2481
Texas Guinan's Playground 1837
Texas Has a Whorehouse in It 374
Texas Li'l Darlin' 4314
Texas Lullabye 914
Texas Rangers 4311
Texas Rose 580
Texas Steer, A 4453
Texas Stomp 3533
Texas Tommy Swing 4805
Texas Will Make You a Man 4058
Texas, Brooklyn and Love 4237
Texatina 3356
Textile Troops, The 1657
Thad's Journey 2958
Thank God 1059
Thank God for the Homeland 4719
Thank God for the Volunteer Fire Brigade 1591, 2038
Thank God I'm Not Old 3059
Thank God I'm Old 305
Thank Heaven for Christmas 753
Thank Heaven for Little Girls 1511
Thank Heaven for the Heathen 1809
Thank Heaven for You 1072
Thank My Stars 289
Thank the Lord 4405
Thank the Lord the War Is Over 742
Thank Them for Your Love 3542
Thank You 846, 2432, 2775, 3602, 3696
Thank You for Coming 2822
Thank You for the Change in My Life 4460
Thank You in Advance 711
'Thank You, Kind Sir!' Said She 2261
Thank You Kindly Sir 2691
Thank You Lord 3599
Thank You, Ma'am 3551
Thank You, Madam 3918
Thank You, Mr. Chaplin 695
Thank You, Mrs. Butterfield 1679
Thank You, No 101
Thank You So Much 1060
Thank You So Much Mrs. Lowsborough-Goodby 4517
Thank You Song, The 2681
Thank You, South America 4086
Thank You, South America (dance) 4086
Thank You, You're Welcome, Don't Mention It 4025
Thank Your Father (Thank Your Mother) 1323
Thank Your Lucky Stars and Stripes 4255
Thanks a Lot 572, 1045
Thanks Awful 123
Thanks! Don't Mention It 2523
Thanks for a Darn Nice Time 931
Thanks for a Lousy Evening 1336
Thanks for Nothing 695
Thanks for the Francs 4174
Thanks in Old Age 2433
Thanks Just the Same 4093
Thanks, Sweet Jesus! 1441
Thanks to Love 4798
Thanks to the Banks 2275
Thanks to You (I'm a Brand New Woman) 1107
Thanks to You 2163, 3409, 2540
Thanks to You Mr. Handy 887
Thanksgiving Day 48, 3773
That Aero-Naughty Girl 4803
That Ain't Right 39
That Airship of Mine 3333
That American Boy of Mine 969
That Awful Bogie Man 1515
That Baboon Baby Dance 1738, 4589
That Barber in Seville 487
That Beautiful Isle of the Sea 2671
That Big-Bellied Bottle 1676
That Black and White Baby of Mine 1921
That Bohemian Rag 3397
That Boy of Mine 4780
That Bran' New Gal O' Mine 3144
That Broadway Chicken Walk 683
That Brother of Mine 3846
That Brownskin Flapper 2557
That Certain Feeling 4392
That Certain Look 4433
That Certain Party 1831
That Certain Something 2527
That Certain Thing 4741
That Champagne Glide 1212
That Charleston Dance 740
That Chop Stick Rag 3134
That Colored Jassboray 3973
That Come "Hither" Look 4327
That Creepy Weepy Feeling 1911
That Creole Flower Garden of Mine 980
That Dance of Mine 3877
That Dancing Big Banshee 2782
That Day Will Come 3264
That Deviling Tune (Rag) 2358
That Dirty Old Man 1422
That Does It 4602
That Does the Trick for Me 2230
That Dream-Waltz Melody 2108
That Extra Bit 4512
That Face! 2705
That Face 4435
That Faraway Look 4060
That Feels Good 2992
That Fellow Manuelo 3699
That Forgotten Melody 704
That Frank 2822
That Frisco Melody 804
That Funny Fellow 1215
That Funny Little Movement 2214

That Gal Is a High Born Lady 1897
That Gal of Mine 1963
That Girl Belongs to Me 764
That Girl of Mine 513
That Good Old Fashioned Cake Walk 3396
That Grand Terrace Trot 725
That Great Come and Get It Day 1278
That Guilty Feeling 2075
That Guy 460
That Gypsy Rag 387
That Happy American Dream 1955
That Happy Face 345
That Happy Land 737
That Happy Melody 1346
That Has Nothing to Do with You 1626
That Haunting Melody 632, 4553
That Horrible Hobble Skirt 4804
That Horrid Mosquito 3384
That House/This Time 4004
That Hula-Hula 4158
That Hypnotizing Rag 4757
That International Rag 789
That Is Art 2670
That Is Love 3265, 4723
That Is Normal 3197
That Is Rock and Roll 4031
That Isn't Done 3186
That It Should Come to This 3741
That Ivy League Look 2483
That Kind of Guy 520
That Ladies Cannot Bathe 1429
That Lady in Eng-a-land 2375
That Latin Lure 1164
That Lindy Hop 443
That Linger Longer Look 1014
That Little German Band 627, 1963
That Little Girl Is You 1573
That Little Lamb Was Me (Mary's Li'l Lamb) 3424
That Little Monosyllable 840
That Little Something 930, 2638
That Little Spanish Hacienda 557
That Little Thatched Cottage All Covered with Vine 310
That Lost Barbershop Chord 123
That Lovin' Traumerei 2358
That Lucky Boy Is Me 4409
That Lucky Fellow 4557
That Lucky Lady 4557
That Man 734
That Man and Woman Thing 70
That Man Is Doing His Worst to Make Good 657
That Man Loves Me 4798
That Man Over There 1860
That Man Up There 456
That Man's Wife 4270
That Means Nothing to Me 3079, 4154
That Melodious Melody 1560
That Melody 1458
That Might Have Satisfied Grandma 2767
That Minor Strain 4804
That Minstrel Man 3754
That Mister Man of Mine 956
That Mittel-Europa Europe Man 2748
That Mittle-Europa Mine 2810
That Moment Is Now 3697
That Moment of Moments 4825
That Mysterious Lady Called Love 1300
That Mysterious Rag 3665
That Naughty Show from Gay Paree 1548
That New-Fangled Mother of Mine 3569
That New-Time Religion 1364
That Nifty Song Show 4215
That Night of the Embassy Ball 1973
That O'Brien Girl 3218
That Ol' Black Magic 3905
That Old Black Magic 3175, 3178
That Old Church Bell 3866
That Old Familiar Ring 2217
That Old Fashioned Cake Walk 1826
That Old Fashioned Garden of Mine 4817
That Old Feather Bed 1776
That Old Hooked Rug 637
That Old Piano 3428
That Old Piano Roll 1329, 2764
That Old Time Crowd 2304
That One Sweet Hour with You 3770
That Opera Rag 1501
That Oriental Blues 2174
That Ought to Count for Something 1513
That Parisian Trot 75
That Pathetique Melody 2193
That Peach-A-Reeno, Phil-I-Peeno Dance 3401
That Peculiar Tune 3193
That Prelude! 161
That Pretty Little Song 1183
That Rag-Tag Dance 2390
That Ragtime Dinner Band 1066
That Rainbow Rag 3547
That Really Was a Lovely Place for Me 2383
That Reminiscent Melody 4637
That Revolutionary Rag 3791
That Revue 3161
That Rhythm Man 432, 1980
That Rhythm Parade 1981
That Romance of Mine 969
That Rushin' Rag 4037
That Russian Winter 4340
That Samson and Delilah Melody 4194
That Shakespearian Rag 4806
That Slavery Is Love 935
That Small Still Voice 3945
That Society Bear 4655
That Society Budd (I'm a Society Bud) 4817
That Something Extra Special 989
That Something Special 1279
That Soul Inspiring Sneeze 1558
That Sound 583
That Special Day 1676
That Special Night 3601

That Spooky Tune 3096
That Strictly Neutral Jag 1560
That Stupid Melody 3342
That Summer — That Fall 139
That Swanee River Melody 1378
That Sweet Oblivion-Drink 2233
That Syncopated Bogie Boo, The 3031
That Syncopated Harp 628
That Tantalizing Nod 4247
That Tempting Tango 929
That Terrible Tune 4483
That Terrific Rainbow 3353
That Tinkling Tango Tune 257
(Try This for) That Tired Feeling 288
That Toledo Tune 1501
That Touch 3711
That Tumble Down Shack in Athlone 4576
That Typical, Topical, Tropical Tune 3423
That was Jerry 260
That Was My Way 2224
That Was the Last That I Remembered 4161
That Was Then 4199
That Was Then, Mr. Rassendyl 4798
That Was Wonderful 1270
That Was Yesterday 928, 2864
That Was Your Life 3264
That Wasn't All 4094
That We're Soldiers 1178
That Will Keep Him True to You 1088
That Will Serve Her Right 147
That Winter Was a Spring 4830
That Woman Can't Play No Piano 105
That Woman in the Mirror 944
That Wonderful Girl 1031
That Wonderful Melody 429
That Wonderful 'One' Girl 4258
That Wonderful Rhythm 2168
That Wonderful Thing Called Love 1516
That Would Be Lovely 742
That Zip Cornwall Cooch 130
That'll Be the Day 580, 1745, 4678
That'll Show Him 1422
That's a Beginning 4862
That's a Clue 306
That's a Crime 2150
That's a Man Everytime 1679
That's a Plenty 2979
That's a Ridiculous Statement! 2230
That's a Thing That's Really Wanted 1318
That's a Very Different Thing 4354
That's a Very Interesting Question 4485
That's a Woman 4619
That's a Woman's Way 2937
That's About the Size of It 1264
That's All 4802
That's All Charming 2907
That's All He Wants 2377
That's All Right 580
That's All Right for McGilligan 2358
That's All There Is 2308
That's Amusement 3997
That's an Egg Cream! 3926
That's Art 1243
That's As Far As I Can Go 2216
That's As Far As It Goes 3179
That's As Far As You Can Go 2978
That's Atmosphere 2717
That's Boys Your Boys 4649
That's Broadway 532
That's Called Walking the Dog 3400
That's Class 3091
That's Easy for a Little Girl to Do 1532
That's Enough for Me 3757
That's Enough for Me Duet 3757
That's Fine 4299
That's for Me 1892, 4146
That's for Sure 4423
That's Good 1566
That's Good Enough for Me 2014
That's Good, That's Bad 1207
That's Good-That's Bad 1991
That's Gratitude 3480
That's Happiness 1971, 2888
That's Harmony 4805
That's Her Life 4292
That's Him 369, 3231, 3301
That's How a Woman Gets Her Man 108
That's How Calisthenics Go 4161
That's How Darkies Keep Warm 877
That's How I Get Treated 1458
That's How I Know that I'm in Love 1539
That's How I Learned to Sing the Blues 3428
That's How I Love the Blues 372
That's How I Love You 939
That's How Imitations Look to Me 4247
That's How It Goes 4446
That's How It Starts 4270
That's How Rhythm Is Born 1813
That's How the Cakewalk's Done 2111
That's How the Shannon Flows 2662
That's How We Met the Girl 4801
That's How You Get Your Kicks 1697
That's How You Jazz 2200
That's How Young I Feel 2208, 2713
That's in My Line 1314
That's Life 4583
That's Love 3914, 3543
That's Love with a Capital L 1066
That's Me 1306, 3770
That's Music 2014
That's My Approach to Love 1718
That's My Daisy 4278
That's My Father 3429
That's My Fella 183
That's My Idea of Love 4559
That's My Idea of Paradise 4045
That's My L.A. 3046
That's My Man 4276
That's My Partner 1776
That's My Pop 2653

That's Not Cricket 216
That's One Thing a Wizard Can Do 4724
That's Our Annie 150
That's Peculiar Isn't It? Very 2893
That's Politics 561
That's Religion 4763
That's Right! 2958
That's Right, Dear 233
That's RIght, Mr. Syph 3370
That's So Papa 1537
That's Some Love 115, 4277
That's That 2798, 3623
That's the Doctor Bill 511
That's the Girl 591
That's the Irish in Her 539
That's the Kind of a Boy for Me 1308
That's the Kind of a Man You Ought to Marry 968
That's the Kind of a Wifie to Be 1911
That's the Kind of Baby for Me, The 4811
That's the Kind of Noble Savage That I Am 1521
That's the Kind of Woman 154, 155
That's the Law 3482
That's the Lesson I'm Teaching to You 2922
That's the Life 1784
That's the Life for Me 615, 4409
That's the Life for Me (This Is the Life for Me) 1963
That's the Life of a Stable Boy 531
That's the News I'm Waiting to Hear 3674
That's the Only Place Where Our Flag Shall Fly 4784
That's the Reason 1224
That's the Sign of a Honeymoon 561
That's the Time 4434
That's the Time When I Miss You 637
That's the Trouble with Women 3482
That's the Tune 1733
That's the Way a Woman Wants to Love a Man 335
That's the Way I Am 4408
That's the Way It Goes 150, 480, 4798
That's the Way It Happens 2797
That's the Way It Is 4108, 4727
That's the Way of a Sailor 3951
That's the Way to Make It Move 1402
That's the Way to Treat a Little Doggie 1088
That's the Way to Win a Girl 968
That's the Way We Do Things in New York 2200
That's What a Fellow Does When He's in Love 1316
That's What a Fellow Does When He's In Love 4387
That's What a Woman Sees 4408
That's What Friends Are For 4701, 2590
That's What He Did 2444
That's What I Get for Wearing My Heart on My Sleeve 3373
That's What I Got Not Listening to My Mother 3810
That's What I Hate About Love 876, 877
That's What I Like in a Man 1957
That's What I Need Tonight 101
That's What I Told Him Last Night 183
That's What I Want for Janie 4693
That's What I Would Do 4444
That's What I'd Like for Christmas 3482
That's What It Is to Be Young 3731
That's What Made Those Happy Old Indians Dance 750
That's What Men Are For 627
That's What the Little Girl Said 3026
That's What the Papers Say 522
That's What the Poor Woman Is 305
That's What the Public Wants 2067
That's What the Rose Said to Me 830
That's What the Well Dressed Man in Harlem Will Wear 4340
That's What They Like About Me 1026
That's What You Mean to Me 883, 2847
That's What Young Ladies Do 4384
That's What's Happening, Baby 4678
That's When a Fellow Needs a Friend 2818
That's Where a Man Fits In 4542
That's Where My Heart Will Be 467
That's Where Our Horoscopes Lie (She's a Gemini Girl) 4169
That's Where She Sits All Day 3951, 4723
That's Where the South Begins 1333
That's Where We Come In 4824
That's Why Darkies Were Born 1492
That's Why I Love You 1272, 4517, 4692
That's Why I Never Married 2025
That's Why I Want to Go Home 2595
That's Why I'm Here Tonight 3810
That's Why Lots of People Marry 1555
That's Why the Danube Was Blue 4666
That's Why They Call Me the Shanley Girl 1541
That's Why They Call Us Johns 3369
That's Why They Say I'm Crazy 4735
That's Why We Misbehave 637
That's Why We're Dancing 2140
That's You 364
That's Your Funeral 3271
That's Your Thing, Baby 1612
The End? 410
The End 4830
The Tick, Tick, Tick of the Ticker 480
Theater, the Theater, The 36
Theatre! 1119
Theatre Comes to L.A. 408
Theatre Is a Lady, The 4499
Theatre Marquis 4177
Theatre Party Ladies 3858
Theatre Quadrille 3920
Theatre/Theatre 1116
Theatres 4433
Theatre's in the Dining Room, The 1107
Theatrical Blues, The 4637
Theda Bara 764
Thee Loves Me and I Love Thee 3618
Their Fathers Fought 1178
Their Hearts Are Over Here 805
Theirs 3025
Them and They 2583
Them As Has Gets 1662

There's a Lot of Things That Noah Never Knew 3191
There's a Lovely Crop of Girls This Year 3222
There's a Lump of Sugar Down in Dixie 3985
There's a Maid 335
There's a Man in a Motor-Car 3092
There's a Man in My Life 1140
There's a Mate in This Big World for You 4381
There's a Message of Love in Your Eyes 3590
There's a Million Little Cupids in the Sky 740, 1198
There's a Muddle 3236
There's a New Deal on the Way 2925
There's a New Gang on the Way 3100
There's a New Girl in Town 4409
There's a Party Going On 1601
There's a Plot Afoot 2563
There's a Popular Impression 1521
There's a Rainbow at the End 3201
There's a Rainbow in America 4037
There's a Rainbow on the Way 4087
There's a Rainbow Shining 1966
There's a Rainbow Waiting for You 3431
There's a Resting Place for Every Girl (Sun Chair Song) 2334
There's a Room 1439
There's a Room for Me 2172
There's a Room in My House 1237
There's a Room to Rent in My Heart for You 917
There's a Small Hotel 2258, 3283
There's a Song Up There 1155
There's a Strange Fascination About the Stage 1226, 4414
There's a Stranger in Town 4788
There's a Sucker Born Every Minute 305
There's a Sunbeam for Every Drop of Rain 4283
There's a Sunny Side to Everything 887
There's a Tender Look in Your Eyes 1552
There's a Trace of the War in Everyone's Home 1624
There's a War Going On 3277
There's a Way Out 4360
There's a Woman at the Bottom of It All 4050
There's a World of Beauty in You 2939
There's a Yacht Come In 4713
There's Always a Girl Who Is Waiting 2732
There's Always a Way 3045
There's Always a Woman 162
There's Always One You Can't Forget 102, 958, 1335
There's Always Room for a Smile 4424
There's Always Room for One More 1321, 2193, 4477, 4530
There's Always Someone Who'll Tell You No 2069
There's Always Something Doing in Paree 1868
There's Always Something Fishy About the French 841
There's Always Something Wrong 3945
There's Always the Blues 4255
There's Always Tomorrow 3794
There's an Aeroplane Air About You 1793
There's an Eve in Ev'ry Garden 2927
There's an Old Flame Burning 3712
There's Another Auction Today 520
There's Another Seed 143
There's Another Woman in Your Mind 3880
There's Another World 808, 809
There's But One New York 3609
There's Everything Waiting for You 1966
There's Going to Be a Wedding 3209
There's Gold on the Trees 2925
There's Gonna Be a Commission 1736
There's Got to Be Love 2661
There's Gotta Be a Villain 2322
There's Gotta Be a Wedding 4256
There's Gotta Be Something Better Than This 4238
There's History to Be Made 4015
There's Just a Little Bit of Monkey Still Left in You and Me 1334
There's Just One Girl I'd Like to Marry 4293
There's Life in the Old Dog Yet 1527, 4010
There's Life in the Old Folks Yet 4186
There's Life in the Old Girl Yet 133, 2570
There's Lots of Room for You 1011
There's Lots of Things You Can Do with Two (But Not with Three) 304
There's Love in My Heart for You 883
There's Love in the Country 2001
There's Love in the Heart I Hold 3012
There's Magic in a Cup of Tea (Cup of Tea, A) 4118
There's Magic in the Air 1726
There's Me 4138
There's Money in Graft (There's a Raft of Money in Graft! Graft! Graft!) 4649
There's More to a Man than His Head 2898
There's More to Life Than Love 147
There's More to the Kiss than the X X X 1626, 2363
There's Music in a Kiss 1127
There's Music in an Irish Song 4424
There's Music in That Boy 1601
There's Music in the Metro 2705
There's Never Been Anything Like Us 958
There's No Better Use for Time than Kissing 3740
There's No Business Like Show Business 153
There's No Cure Like Travel 163
There's No Fool Like an Old Fool 917, 1962
There's No Getting Away from You 206
There's No Holding Me (If I Can Keep on Holding You) 3390
There's No Hotel Like the Algonquin 2658
There's No Love Like 4588
There's No Man Like a Snowman 3, 3381
There's No More Regular Kids 1703
There's No One As Sweet As Trilby 4189
There's No Other Solution 2472
There's No Place as Grand as Bandana Land 740
There's No Place Like Home Boys When Your Wife Has Gone Away 4203
There's No Place Like Home with You 3839
There's No Reason in the World 2864
There's No Room for People Any More 722
There's No School Like Our School 1380
There's No Such Girl As Mine 4149
There's No Such Word As "Can't" 3630
There's No Time Like Now Time 3921

There's No Wolf Around My Door 814
There's Not a Girl, In All This World That Won't Have Me 2826
There's Not a Thing I Wouldn't Do 4497
There's Not Another Girlie in the World Like You 2566
There's Nothin' So Bad for a Woman (Stonecutters Cut It on Stone) 660
There's Nothing Doing in the Old, Old Town 2481
There's Nothing Fair About It 2928
There's Nothing Left for Daddy (But the Rhumba) 2615
There's Nothing Left to Give Away 3527
There's Nothing Like a Model T 1886
There's Nothing Like a Wife 3857
There's Nothing Like It 784, 1679
There's Nothing Like Marriage for People 3390
There's Nothing Like Music 4459
There's Nothing Like Swimming 2252
There's Nothing Like the Life We Sailors Lead 2974
There's Nothing Like This Old Fasioned 1048
There's Nothing Like Travel 3091
There's Nothing Much More to Say 767
There's Nothing New in Old New York 202
There's Nothing New Under the Sun 605, 2236
There's Nothing Nicer Than People 4718
There's Nothing on the Level Any More 1793
There's Nothing So Uncertain As a Dead Sure Thing 102
There's Nothing Stranger Than Love 302
There's Nothing the Matter with Me 1979
There's Nothing the Matter with You 2534
There's Nothing Too Fine for the Finest 4547
There's Nothing Wrong in a Kiss 3721
There's Nothing Wrong with Marriage 4798
There's Nothing Wrong with Our Values 410
There's Nowhere to Go but Up 2344
There's One Born Every Minute 1746
There's One in a Million Like You 4806
There's One Little Girl 1308
There's One Sweetheart I'll Never Forget 1118
There's One Thing a Wizard Can Do 4724
There's Only Moon Beams 4756
There's Only One Little Girl 1308
There's Only One Little Old New York 228
There's Only One Rose in the Garden of Love (Opening Chorus) 3567
There's Only One Thing a Coon Can Do 186
There's Only One Thing to Do 2549
There's Only One Union 2682
There's Only One Who Rules My House 473
There's Plenty of Love in the World 906
There's Ragtime in the Air 4810
There's Room Enough for Us 2484
There's Room for Her 4798
There's So Much More 111
There's Somethin' Might Peculiar Goin' On 2484
There's Something About a Horse 2449
There's Something About Me They Like 4491
There's Something About Sympathy 4249
There's Something About You 771, 956, 965, 1335, 3482, 3921
There's Something About You Dear That Appeals to Me 1588
There's Something About You Makes Me Love You 1334
There's Something About You That Appeals to Me 3372
There's Something in That 2382
There's Something in the Air 2148
There's Something in the Air in Springtime 4808
There's Something Missing in the Movies 3399
There's Something Nice About the South 959
There's Something Rather Odd About Augustus 1318
There's Something Spanish in Your Eyes 1491, 3532
There's the Moon 634
There's Trouble 3236
There's Trouble Brewin' 4163
There's 'Yes' in the Air (Martinique) 1140
Thermodynamic Duo 221
Thernadier Waltz 2442
These Acres 4292
These Are Not the Merriest of Days 2820
These Are the Brave 4796
These Are the Good Old Days 3551
These Are the Good Times 2307
These Are the Jokes 1279
These Are the Things 2153
These Are the Words 2907
These Are Worth Fighting For 597, 3217
These Boots Are Made for Walking 4193
These Charming People 4392
These Colors Will Not Run 3246
These Eyes Have Seen Too Much 4196
These Foolish Things 1813
These Foolish Things Remind Me of You 478
These Four Walls 1441
These Sorry Men 1099
These Southern States That I Love 1037
These Things I Know Are True 4627
These Three 4316
These Tropics 1145
These Two Hands 2617
These Were the Faces 1053
Thessaly 2716
They 593
They Ain't Done Right by Our Nell 3359
They All Follow Me 357
They All Know Better Now 998
They All Lived Happily Ever After 51
They All Look Alike 1784
They All Look Alike to Mary 1902, 4801
They All Look Good to Me 4148
They All Look Good when They're Far Away 1183
They All Love Me 4328
They All Need a Little Hot-Cha 1979, 4799
They Always Blame the Caddy 4209
They Always Follow Me 115
They Always Follow Me Around 4603

They Always Run a Little Faster 381
They Are Angels Without Wings 457
They Are Hypnotized 3809
They Are Nothing but Girls 613
They Are Waiting for Me 830
They Aren't There 4635
They Blame It All on Me 806
They Call It Dancing 3006
They Call It Dixie Land 3877
They Call Me a Dudelsack 2886
They Call Me Pollyanna 4211
They Call Me the Belle of New York 357
They Call Me the Virgin Mary 2220
They Call the Wind Maria 3347
They Can't Fool Me 3985
They Can't Get You Down 4331
They Can't Prohibit Love 1914
They Can't Run Off the Reels Too Fast for Me 102
They Can't Start Christmas Without Us 2689
They Can't Take That Away from Me 921, 1325
They Cannot Smoke with Me 4094
They Come, They Come 2827
They Couldn't Compare to You 3326
They Didn't Believe Me 2204, 2372, 1544, 3020, 3259, 4419, 4418
They Do You Much Better at Home 1228
They Don't Give Medals (To Yesterday's Heroes) 3275
They Don't Give You Life at Sixteen 3576
They Don't Have To 4790
They Don't Like Me 2106
They Don't Look the Same in the Morning 69
They Don't Make 'Em Like That Any More 317
They Don't Make 'Em Like That Anymore 1891, 2014, 4332, 3454
They Don't Make Them Like That Any More 2010
They Don't Write Songs Like That Anymore 159
They Fall in Love, Those Wonderful Friends 403
They Finished Me in the East 1604
They Follow Me Around 1774
They Follow Me Everywhere 4649
They Found Me 2497
They Gave Me a Medal for That 2315
They Give Me Love 2874
They Got This Little Secret 1214
They Had to Change 1258
They Had to Get the Rhythm Out of Their Souls 1765
They Handed Me a Lemon 3052
They Handed Me You 2452
They Have Carried the Bridegroom Off 4046
They Just Got Married 2852
They Keep Coming 1072
They Kiss 2793
They Knew What They Wanted 2961
They Laugh and March Away 3051
They Laughed for 120 Years 2164
They Learn About Women from Me 4777, 4778
They Led Me to Believe 4090
They Left Me 2069
They Like Ike 619
They Lived to Be Loved in Vain 4434
They Lost the Revolution 3076
They Love Me 2983
They Mean More 4712
They Never Do That in Our Set 2951
They Never Hear What I Say 4286
They Never Proved a Thing 2217
They Never Told Me 3074
They Pass By Singing 3541
They Pictured Me Like This 355
They Say 1871, 3780
They Say I Oughta Dance 1659
They Say I'm Frivolous 351
They Say It's Wonderful 153
They Sent for Me 1646
They Sing My Marriage Song at Home 4615
They Sing! They Dance! They Speak! 1800
They Still Look Good to Me 2818
They Struck Her Name from the Blue Book Set 'Cause She Made Headlines in the Pink Police Gazette 302
They Talk a Different Language (The Yodel Blues) 4314
They Were All Doing the Same 4691
They Were Irish 1
They Were Only Playing Leapfrog 3259
They Were You 1245
They Weren't Any Better in the Good Old Days 4296
They Will Listen to You 3507
They Will Send Ye a Sign 3306
They Won't 1499
They Won't Have Me 1726
They Won't Know Me 4718
They Won't Regret It 2965
They Write the News 3136
They'll Be Whistling It All Over Town 4742
They'll Do It Everytime 520
They'll Have to Go 4738
They'll Know We're Over 61
They'll Never Split Us Apart 57
They'll Never Take Us Alive 36
They'll Say I've Been Dreaming 2599
They're All My Friends 2517
They're All Sweeties 2349
They're All the Same 3703
They're Always Entertaining 3214
They're Always Taking Me for Someone Else 4165
They're at the Post 1227
They're Either Too Young or Too Old 3444
They're Getting Away with Murder 627
They're Getting Shorter All the Time 4836, 4839
They're Gonna Love It 3275
They're Hot Now Up in Iceland 3388
They're in the Junk Pile Now 4809
They're Jazzing It Up in Havana 3508
They're Looking for Me 4713
They're Making Them Wonderful 2214
They're Never Gonna Make Me Fight 2681
They're Not Doing That This Season 1961, 3977
They're Off 2034, 4382

They're on Their Honeymoon 3525
They're Playing Our Song 4334
They're Yours 3960
They've All Got Tails but Me 4710
They've Courage High 1178
They've Got a Lot to Learn 4090
They've Got Me Doing It Too 683
They've Got Nothing on Us 'Over There' 3296
They've Got to Complain 3067
They've Gotcha on the Hutska 2352
Thief (dance), The 722
Thief in the Night 216
Thieves Carnival 3355
Thimbleful 2680
Thin Man, The 3142
Thine Alone 1162
Thine Eyes Are Like Twin Stars 3882
Thing About Willie, The 4827
Thing I Can't Seem to Forget 1275
Thing Like This, A 4750
Thing that Johnny Did!, The 3186
Thing to Do, The 1916
Thingamajig 786
Things 1763
Things! 2475
Things 3636, 4018
Things a Girl Should Be, The 3879
Things Ain't As Nice 2661
Things Ain't Just Right 3358
Things Are Getting Better Every Day 108
Things Are Going Nicely 4659
Things Are Going Well Today 3941
Things Are Gonna Hum This Summer 3895
Things Are Looking Up 921
Things Are Most Mysterious 2877
Things Are Very, Very Bad 42
Things Are Very, Very Good 42
Things Get Broken 2775
Things Go Bump in the Night 1674
Things Have Changed from Then to Now 4507
Things Have Never Been Better 556
Things I Can't Forget 424
Things I Didn't Know I Loved 3162
Things I Learned in Dear Old Jersey 3712
Things I Learned in High School 2152
Things I Never Had, The 2588
Things I Used to Know 4635
Things I've Heard, The 1868
Things Left Unsaid 1746
Things Starting to Grow Again 3418
Things That Cannot Be Explained 765
Things That Go Bump in the NIght 494
Things That Happen Every Day 3205
Things That I Know I Could Do 2317
Things that Lovers Say, The 4015
Things That They Must Not Do 4784
Things That We Don't Learn at School 4723
Things That Were Made for Love, The 3523
Things They Do in Hollywood, The 3375
Things They Told Us Not to Do, The 817
Things to Remember 3731
Things Unfeminine 697
Things We Are Not Supposed to Know 4293
Things We Did Last Summer, The 4743
Things We Leave Unspoken, The 1169
Things We Pay Money to See 387
Things We Think We Are, The 1848
Things We've Collected 4515
Things Were Much Better in the Past 2657
Things Were Out 4468
Things Which Are Equal to the Same Thing 717
Things You Never Learn at School, The 333
Think 339
Think About That 1146
Think About Tomorrow 1149
Think Beautiful 2053
Think Beautiful Thoughts 2940
Think Big 2420, 2224
Think Big Rich 1662
Think Ginger Rogers 2010
Think How It's Gonna Be 167
Think How Many People Never Find Love 1791
Think, Inc. 1047
Think It Over 246, 580, 1319, 3043, 3699
Think It Over Carefully 4759
Think Mink 766
Think of All the Starving Orphans 1664
Think of It 4244
Think of Me 3464, 2477
Think of Meryl Streep 1236
Think of My Reputation 4025
Think of Something Else 4588
Think of That 2145
Think of the Odds 3760
Think of the Time I Save 3351
Think of Where You Might Be Instead of Where You Are 3740
Think Positive 140
Think Spring 823
Think Up! 3788
Thinkability 4693
Thinkin' 3505
Thinkin' of You 2342
Thinkin' Things 4270
Thinking 1060, 3531
Thinking About You 3757
Thinking Always Thinking 2241
Thinking of Home Sweet Home 434
Thinking of Me 740
Thinking of No-One but Me 2798
Thinking of Our Childhood Days 3998
Thinking of You 1131, 1297, 1873, 2478
Thinking Out Loud 622
Thinking the Unthinkable 3661
Thinky Thanky Thunk 2254
3rd Avenue El 1023
Third Avenue El 2554
Third Degree of Love, The 1321
Third Finale 4368
Third from the End, The 303

Third Grade 3811
Third Kiss, The 2673
Third Letter 3411
Third Letter Home 4068
Third March (inst.) 1385
Third Party, The 1551
Third Threepenny Finale 4370
Thirteen Clocks, The 4336
13 Daughters 4337
1348 1017
13 Old Maids 4337
Thirteen-Passenger Airport Limousine 83
Thirteenth Orphan, The 3287
Thirties, The 1341, 413, 412
30 Miles from the Banks of the Ohio 1591
Thirty Seconds 2676
Thirty Weeks of Heaven 603
Thirty-Five Summers Ago 4826
This Amazing London Town 3780
This and That and the Other 4248, 4285
This Bright Morning 2674
This Can't Be Love 514, 4519
This Can't Be Real 846
This Can't Go On 147
This City Is a Kisser 2332
This Coat 757
This Cornucopian Land 935
This Could Be My Lucky Day 4389
This Could Be the End 3368
This Could Go on for Years 4179
This Darkness 3817
This Darling Industry 1597
This Dawn 669
This Dear Lady 2148
This Dear Little Fellow Was Cupid 604
This Decadent Age 4696
This Diamond Is Real 264
This Dream 3731
This Empty Place 261
This Funny World 376
This Gay Paree 2497
This Gentle Land 2047
This Goes Up (Smile) (Keep Your Eye on Me) 3924
This Gumshoe's Gonna Stick Around 3004
This Guy's in Love with You 261
This Had Better Be Love 4432
This Had Better Come to a Stop 2746
This Handsome Soldier Is Too Bold 307
This Has Never Been Done Before 2052
This Heart of Mine 1638
This Heat 2958
This House 2050
This Is a Changing World 3235, 3339, 3815
This Is a Darned Fine Funeral 3954
This Is a Dollar Bill 2067
This Is a Great Country 2983
This Is a Man I Could Love 4108, 2998
This Is a Night Club 1131
This Is a Night for Lovers 3339, 3815
This Is a Serious Matter 284
This Is a Situation 3595
This Is a Statement Most Untoward 402
This Is a Tough Neighborhood 2304
This Is a Very Special Day 2908
This Is All I Ask 3724
This Is All Very New to Me 3509
This Is As Far As I Go 2400
This Is As Good As It Gets 1633
This Is Different, Dear 1874
This Is England 3491
This Is Finale 4273
This Is Gonna Be My Time 1103
This Is Heaven 3914
This Is His First Love 2599
This Is How I Do 3943
This Is Indeed My Lucky Day 4454
This Is It 4142, 4826
This Is Miami 867
This Is Most Exciting 2233
This Is My Beloved 180
This Is My Busy Day 118
This Is My Dance 1935
This Is My Holiday 999
This Is My Kind of Love 161
This Is My Last Spring 1614
This Is My Lovely Day 453
This Is My Night to Howl 834, 1373
This Is My Night with Trixie 1400
This Is My Song 4272
This Is My Wedding Day 2380
This Is New 2386
This Is New York 3889, 3890, 847
This Is No Place for a Good Little Girl 2893
This Is No Place for Me 4094
This Is Not a Song 4824
This Is Not a Very Nice War 2777
This Is Not Going to Change My Life 4560
This Is Not Long Island (Opening Act II) 4118
This Is Not the End 3368
This Is Our House 499
This Is Our Private Love Song 3036
This Is Our World 3202
This Is Quite a Perfect Night 3108
This Is Right Where It Happened 3320
This Is Samurai 3944
This Is So Nice 39, 1140
This Is Someone I Could Love 1809
This Is South Africa 4579
This Is Spring 2301
This Is the Army, Mister Jones 789
This Is the Army, Mr. Jones 4340
This Is the Best We Ever Struck 1911
This Is the Day 943, 1046, 1573, 2011, 3279, 3962
This Is the End of the Story 2103
This Is the Existence 2907
This Is the Girl for Me 239
This Is the Kiss of Romance 839
This Is the Land 4579
This Is the Life 602, 1457, 1601, 2615, 3868
This Is the Life for Me 4750

This Is the Love 412
This Is the Missus 1492
This Is the Moment 2198
This Is the Night 2357, 3339
This Is the One 2182
This Is the Perfect Time to Be in Love 1245
This Is the Place to Be 4462
This Is the Show 2356
This Is the Time 627
This Is the Way We Go to School 2134
This Is War 1997
This Is What I Call Love 1760
This Is What I Do When I'm Angry 3806
This Is What I Give to You 3427
This Is What I Want 327
This Is What You Want 2224
This Is Where I Belong 3752
This Is Where I Came In 2379
This Is Where the Bus Stops 716
This Is Winter 2301
This Is Worth Fighting For 4579
This Is Wrong 158
This Is Your Life! 838
This Is Your Year 1976 2785
This Isn't a Gentlemen's War Anymore 1474
This Isn't How I Imagined a Trial to Be 1700
This Jesus Must Die 2212
This Kind of a Girl 1456
This Lady Isn't Right for Me 2420
This Land Is Your Land 4740
This Land We Now Forsake 335
This Life Is Fantasy 1730
This Life Will Roll Along 4550
This Life's the Right One for Me 562
This Little Doll 1617
This Little Girl 3819
This Little Light 3814
This Little Yankee 1991
This Lovely Night 277
This Lovely Night in June 4719
This Lovely Place 757
This Man Could Never Be a Spy 453
This Means War 4796
This Merry Christmas 4483
This Modern Age 2458
This Moment 2785
This Much I Know 1760
This Must Be the End 3368
This Must Be the Place 1699
This Nearly Was Mine 1040, 4096
This New Land 4615
This Noble Land 2047
This Old Ship 344
This One Day 1662
This Other Eden 2364
This Particular Party 971, 4443
This Place Is Mine 3465
This Plum Is Too Ripe 1245
This Rescue Is a Calamity (Finaletto, Act II, Scene 3) 3556
This State of Affairs 249
This Time 2172, 2231, 2626, 4172
This Time (Is the Last Time) 4340
This Time It's Hook or Me 3453
This Time It's Love 3312
This Time It's True Love 1564
This Time Next Year 4217, 2030, 4433
This Time No Bananas 2458
This Time of the Year 1278
This Time Tomorrow 299, 1497
This Too Shall Pass 83
This Town 1741, 1990
This Town I Now Must Shake 1948
This Train Is Bound for Glory 3840
This Turf Is Ours 4625
This Tuxedo Is Mine! 3473
This Utterly Ridiculous Affair 101
This War Gets Old 1053
This Was Just Another Day 3895
This Was Meant to Be 490
This Was the War, What Did It Do for Me and You?...Didn't It, Did It? 1474
This Way or No Way at All 781
This Way Out 924, 4388
This Week Americans 1060
This Will Be The First Time for Me 1323
This Woman 651
This World (2) 630
This World (1) 630
This World 2801
This World Is a Toy Shop 3710
This World of Confusion 4319
This Year of Disgrace 3186
Thistledown 2768
Thistledown Girl 3791
Thither, Thother, Thide of the The 946
Tho We've No Authentic Reason (Finale Act I) 1013
Tho' Delight, Dany and Night 3308
Tho' I Had Never Meant to Tell You 2178
Thomas Alva Edison 2092
Thomas Jefferson Witherspoon 1955
Thor 1049, 4310
Thoroughly Modern Millie 4743
Thorsping 942
Those ABC's 2285
Those Awful Tattle-Tales 2390
Those Beautiful Chimes 3369
Those Beautiful Girls 1482
Those Canaan Days 2242
Those Come Hither Eyes 913
Those Days Are Gone Forever 611
Those Days Gone By 236
Those Days of Long Ago 1975
Those Dear Old Wedding Bells 4787
Those Dixie Melodies 1823
Those Eyes 3372
Those Eyes of Mine 1699
Those Fat Monkeys 3445
Those Good Old Days Can Never Come Again (They Were the Happy Days) 256

Those Great Big Eyes 2506
Those Irving Berlin Melodies 1826
Those Knowing Nurses 1692
Those Magic Changes (Rock Progression) 1664
Those Mammy Boys 584
Those Mason-Dixon Blues 4290
Those Ragtime Melodies 697
Those Royal Princesses 4019
Those Seven League Boots 1975
Those Sheik-of-Araby Blues 1063
Those Since-I-Met-You Days 136
Those Tassels on Her Boots 1897
Those Two Girls and That Boy 1215
Those Were Happy Days 361
Those Were the Days 602, 702, 4342, 4318
Those Were the Good Old Days 957, 1492, 1513
Those Were the Good Old Times 947
Those Were the Happy Days 4203
Those Who Dance 880
Those Who Speak 3711
Those Wonderful Eyes 1593, 1405
Those Wonderful People Out There in the Dark 4232
Thou Art Mine 4720
Thou Shalt Not 299
Thou Shalt Not Be Afraid 1053
Thou Shalt Not Dance 4316
Thou Swell 834
Thou Wilt Surely Know 2508
Thou, Julia, Thou Has Metamorphosed Me 4485
Thou, Proteus, Thou Has Metamorphosed Me 4485
Though Born a Man of High Degree 1080
Though Hearts We May Secure 106
Though I Said No to You Yesterday 1048
Though I'm a Little Angel 2728
Though It Was Within This Hour We Met 3736
Though of Staying Too Long You're Accusing Us 1470
Though Tongues May Wag 1670
Thought Never Entered My Head, The 2004
Thought Occurs, A 1149
Thought of You, The 1242
Thoughtless 532
Thoughts 815, 1012, 4343
Thoughts By a River 3527
Thoughts I Wrote on the Leaves of My Heart, The 4464
Thoughts Will Come to Me 4188
Thousand and One Arabian Nights, A 3985
Thousand and One Nights, A 177
Thousand Islands Song, The 137
Thousand Summer Nights, A 240
Thousand Times, A 1722
Thousand, Thousand 2719
Thousands of Flowers 2050
Thousands of Girlies (The Reason of Love) 3045
Thousands of Miles 2591
Thousands of Trumpets 2152
Thousands of Years Ago 627
Thread the Needle 3631
Threads of Life 4055
Three 826
Three B's, The 372
Three B's, The (Questions and Answers) 3283
Three Bears, The 1617
Three Beats Too Late 692
Three Bells, The 4264
Three Blind Mice 924
Three Boxes of Longs, Please 40
Three Cans of Film 1056
Three Cheers 4093
Three Cheers for Education 4201
Three Cheers for the Red, White and Blue 3007
Three Cheers for the Union! 4179
Three Coins in the Fountain 4743
Three-Cornered Hat, The 3699
Three Cornered Tune 1706, 3444
Three Cowards Craven 4696
3-D Adventure 1159
Three Dames Ziegfeld Failed to Glorify, The 1251
Three Disguises 392
Three Doctor's Wives 3600
Three Dog Knights 2969
Three Favorite Airs 2670
Three Feet Two of Rhythm 1982
Three Fierce Men 3654
Three First Ladies 3873
Three Foolish Monkeys 3683
Three Friends 784
Three Girls in a Boat 4640
Three Good Deeds, The 4773
Three Guesses 3352
Three Guys Naked from the Waist Down 4349
Three Horsemen of the Metropolis, The 3527
Three Hot Tamales, The 4196
Three Hundred Days 1959
300 Foxes 2164
Three Hundred Letters a Day 2496
365 Days 4327
Three Huntsmen 710
Three Kings 4147
Three Letters 3918
Three Little Bears 1597
Three Little Columnists 1874
Three Little Debutantes 3885
Three Little Girls 2691
Three Little Hollywood Wolves 2593
Three Little Maids 463, 560, 924, 1655, 4174, 4575
Three Little Maids from School 1827, 2348
Three Little Marys 2856
Three Little Pebbles 3433
Three Little Piggies 2982
Three Little Pigs 3314
Three Little Queens of the Silver Screen 2439
Three Little School-Girls 3310
Three Little Temps 2861
Three Little Topical Debutantes 2301
Three Little Vampires 487
Three Little Words 1228
Three Love Stories 1388
Three Loves 3941

Three Maids and a Man 1351
Three Men in a Boat 2765
Three Men on a Date 372
Three Men on a Horse 297, 2449
Three Menu Songs 1064
Three Midrash 1715
Three Mile Limit Cafe 1482
Three Million Buck-a-roos 1997
Three Musketeers, The 1446, 1448, 3047, 4357, 4709
Three Musketeers of Broadway 764
Three O'Clock in the Morning 1687
Three of a Kind 3429
Three of Us, The 2142, 3273
Three Old Ladies from Hades 1748
Three Paradises 3234
Three Postcards 4358
Three Pullman Porters 2462
3/4 Drag 1786
3/4 for Three 1872
3/4 Moon 528
Three Questions 2103
Three R's, The 3314
Three Riddles, The 2075
Three Rousing Cheers 2379
Three Seconds 2132
Three Ships 4384
Three Sisters Opening (Act Two) 4361
Three Sisters Who Are Not Sisters, The 1498
Three Smart Girls 924
Three Smarter Girls 924
Three Songs to the One Burden 1977
Three Square Meals a Day 3165
Three Stones to Stand On 3035
Three Sunny Rooms 3644
3:33 in the Morning 4130
Three Thousand Years Ago 765
Three Times a Day 4300
Three to the Bar 392
Three Trees, The 2684
Three Twins 4364
Three Waltzes, The 4365
Three Weeks with You 2892
Three White Feathers 3196, 3235, 3885
(If I Had) Three Wishes for Christmas 1709
Three Wishes for Jamie 4366
Three Women to Every Man 3129
Three's a Crowd 3013
Threesome 4309, 4635
Threnody 624
Threshing Song 2880
Thrifty Little Mabel 2760
Thrill in Spain 2151
Thrill Is Gone, The 1492, 2992
Thrill Me 289
Thrill of a Kiss, The 3680
Thrill of First Love, The 2746
Thrill of the Chase, The 778
Thro' the Forest 1355
Throckmorton's Permanent Pleasure 4061
Throttle Throttlebottom 2444
Through All Eternity 1118, 2518
Through All the World 2967
Through Curs May Quail 2698
Through Excessive Concern 3418
Through Glass 426
Through Life We Go Dancing Together 2293
Through My Eyes 928
Through the Bamboo 735
Through the Bottom of the Glass 1012
Through the Door 4729
Through the Eyes of Your Imagination 2096
Through the Looking Glass 54, 58, 4736, 55
Through the Mist 487
Through the Night 1747
Through the Shadows 259
Through the Years 3249, 4372
Through These Portals Pass the Most Beautiful Girls in the World 1127
Through Twilight Lane 1031
Throw a Little Party 2460
Throw a Petal 4337
Throw 'Em In 685
Throw 'Er in High! 1486
Throw It Out the Window 288
Throw Me a Kiss 4816
Throw Me a Rose 2907
Throw Out the Lifeline 1590
Throw the Anchor Away 603
Throw the Egg 4488
Throw the House Out of the Window 1046
Throw Your Arms Around Me Honey 11
Throw Your Cares Overboard 3320
Throwin' a Ball Tonight 1018
Throwing a Party 2540
Throwing the Bull 3921, 4547
Thrown Together 1047
Thrush, The 954
Thrush and the Star, The 4666
Thumbelina 4399, 1741
Thumbs Down 1154
Thumbs Up 4373
Thump Thump 4325
Thunder and Bells 3526
Thunder and Lightning 3526
Thunder Dance 4664
Thunder Drumming 2970
Thunderer, The (inst.) 4297
Thurio's Samba 4485
Thursday 447, 3705
Thursday Is My Jonah Day 4387
Thus You May Detect 2944
Thy Heart Is My Prize 93
Thy Mouth Is a Rose 2497
Thy Neighbor and Thy Shelter 3530
Thy Subjects Are We 4559
Ti Monte 3285
Ti Voglio Bene 3171
Tia-Da-Tia-Da-Dee 2587
Tibetan Dance 1351

Tick-a-Tock (Suzi I'm Ticking Love Taps) 4228
Tick, Tack, Toe 4313
Tick-Tick 4794
Tick, Tick, Tick 1961, 2340
Tick, Tock (Dance) 832
Tick Tock (The Dresden Clock) 4296
Tick Tock Goes the Clock 3603
Ticker Tape Caper (inst.) 4774
Ticket, The 3076
Ticket for the Promised Land, A 1970
Ticket Speculator, The 4521
Tickets 119
Tickets Please 4377
Tickets' Song 3548
Ticketyboo 901
Tickle Me 2852, 2457, 2787, 4378
Tickled Pink 4267
Tickles 4379
Tickling the Ivories 4821
Tid Bits from the Plays 737
Tiddelee Tot 1130
Tiddle Om Pom 1464
Tiddledum 2056
Tiddley Pom 1613, 4710
Tide Pool, The 3505
Tie a String Around Your Finger 2569, 3249
Tie Your Cares to a Melody 2238
Tiffany Girl 1735, 2094
Tiffin, Tiffin 4654
Tiger 1358
Tiger Lady 1053
Tiger Lily Ballet (dance) 2137
Tiger Lily Lou 2691
Tiger Love 1003
Tiger Rag 3297
Tiger Rag Blues 4380
Tiger, Tiger 170
Tiger! Tiger! 2962
Tight 3173
Tight-knit Family, A 2746
Tight Rope Walker, The 1374
Tightrope 4515
Tik Tok Man of Oz, The 4381
'Til Our Good Luck Comes Along 1086
'Til the Big Fat Moon Falls Down 4682
'Til Then 1347
'Till Doomsday 431
Till Dreams Come True 659
'Till Good Luck Comes My Way 3949
Till I Come Home to You 1632
Till I Met You 3978
Till I'm Gone 1232
Till It Goes Outta Style 1373
Till the Birds Sing 3970
Till the Blossoms Fall 2861
Till the Bootlegger Comes 1280
Till the Clouds Roll By 2204, 2372
'Till the Clouds Roll By 3230
Till the Day of My Majority 3588
Till the End of Time 728
Till the Liberty Bells Ring Out 1502
Till the Real Thing Comes Along 3704
Till the Volunteers Return 4201
Till Then 3897
Till There Was You 3016
Till Tomorrow 1280, 1508
'Till We All Belong 462
Till You Belong to Me 3045
Till You Try 3729
Tiller, Foster, Hoffman, Hale and Albertina Rasch 3005
Tiller Girls at Home Sketch, The (inst.) 2545
Tiller Girls Dance (inst.) 4818
Tiller Routine 3214
Tillich's Nightmare 2954
Tillie of Longacre Square 1460
Tillie Tit Willow 3737
Tillie's Nightmare 3436, 4382
Timbuctoo 1658
Time 348
Time (Love Must Have Time) 519
Time 2064, 2245
Time After Time 4743
Time Ain't Very Long 26
Time and a Half for Overtime 2569
Time and the Place and the Girl, The 2915
Time and Tide 3215, 4374, 4583
Time and Time Again 3124, 3835
Time and Time Again (Oh, Doctor Jesus) 3541
Time Brings About a Change 1072
Time-Clock Slaves 2768
Time Drags 942
Time Flies 1426
Time for a Quickie 2940
Time for Another Affair 3890
Time for Dreams, A 4719
Time for Jukin' 4772
Time for Love, A (Imakoso Koi No Toki) 1616
Time for Love 4249
Time for Singing, A 4384
Time for Tea 3107
Time for the King 2317
Time for You 3318
Time Goes By 1701, 3879
Time Goes Faster 3764
Time Has Changed So Many Customs in the Last Decade 2710
Time Has Come to Say Goodbye, The 4409
Time Has Come, The 1080
Time Heals All Wounds 3873
Time Heals Everything 2208, 2660
Time Is a Gypsy 4824
Time Is a Travellin' Show 2785
Time Is Come, The 1262
Time Is Flying 2145, 4738
Time Is Now, The 1611, 4566
Time Is Ripe for Loving, The 3015
Time Is Standing Still 996, 4214
Time Magazine 4828
Time Marches On 2001, 213

Time Marches On! 4825
Time of Dolls Is Past, The 1743
Time of My Life, The 3818
Time of Night, The 30
Time of Our Life, The 2962
Time of the Cuckold, The 1648
Time of the Cuckoo, The 1060
Time of Your Life 924
Time of Your Life, The 2992
Time Off for Love 3823
Time, Oh Time You Tyrant King 3839
Time on My Hands 3249
Time on My Hands, You in My Arms 4023
Time on Our Side 2171
Time, Only Time Deary 3778
Time Passed Her By 1865
Time Passes 3757, 2229
Time Remembered 4386
Time Stand Still 1496
Time Stands Still 2651, 4015
Time Stands Still in Truro 3544
Time Stop 1408
Time Step, The 2705
Time to Call It Quits 1697
Time to Change My Earl 3587
Time to Find Something to Do 4707
Time to Get Movin' 916
Time to Go 482
Time to Go Home 2776
Time to Kiss a Girl, The 3531
Time to Let Go 2075
Time to Love, A 181
Time to Love, The 2964, 4014
Time to Love Is Now, The 1771
Time to Put the Toys Away 1510
Time to Say Good Night Again 1415
Time to Say Goodnight 392
Time to Sing 1889
Time to Take a Drink 1962
Time to Think of Yourself 2692
Time to Wake Up 2132
Time Warp 3742
Time We Talked 1878
Time We Were Dancing 3439
Time Will Be 2219
Time Will Come, A 3736
Time Will Tell 1564, 3821
Time You Old Gypsy Man 2294
Timeline 2224
Time's A-Flyin' 2898
Times Are Getting Hard 4111
Times Divine 2177
Times Like This 2646
Times May Change 797
Times Square 582, 2231
Times Square Arguments, The 2696
Times Square Dance 512
Times Square Dance (dance) 3278
Times That Linger, The 2304
Times We Had, The 4703
Timid Frieda 2188
Timing 1699, 456
Timing and Lightning 674
Tin Can Incantation 3970
Tin Cup 1736
Tin Gee-Gee, The 2714, 2863
Tin Pan Alley 2227
Tin Whistle Tune 589
Tina and Nina 871
Tina, My Daughter 3811
Tina Seeks Solace 3568
Tina's Final Hour 3568
Tina's Mother 3811
Ting-a-Ling (The Bells'll Ring) 799
Ting-A-Ling 1735, 3778
Ting-a-Ling-a-Ling Ping Pong 522
Ting-a-ling Dearie 4186
Ting, Tang, Kee (If You Understood Chinese) 2722
Tinker, Tailor 954, 1756
Tinker Tom 3026
Tinker's Song 3736
Tinkle-Inkle-Inkle 1240
Tinkle Ting Ting 2089
Tinkle! Tinkle! 3005
Tinkle Tune 2972
Tinsel 1436
Tinted Venus, The 3301
Tiny Bit of Faith, A 2183
Tiny Feet (The Princess of the Disco Rio Bamba) 2677
Tiny Flat, A 1240
Tiny Flat Near Soho Square, A 2467
Tiny International Empire 1108
Tiny Light 4470
Tiny Room 2582
Tiny Touch, A 4219
Tiny Tours 4093
Tiny Town 1107
Tiny, the Champion 2719
Tinymite 4425
Tio Paco 1369
Tip-Tip Tippy Canoe 4290
Tip Toe 1966
Tip-toe 3618
Tip Toe 4269
Tip-Toe Tap-Tap 1126
Tip-Toes 4392
Tip Top 4393
Tip Top Tipperary Mary 351
Tip Top Toreador 3404
Tip Your Hat 3713
Tip Your Hat to a Carrot 2095
Tip Your Hat to Hattie 136
Tippecanoe 3951
Tippecanoe and Tyler Too 2018, 3558
Tipperary Mary 4840, 4851
Tipperary Nora 8
Tipperary Twinkle, The 2952
Tippery 541

Tippin' Out Tonight 3782
Tippity Top 1108
Tippy-Tappy 3181
Tippy Tippy Toes 4693
Tips 1537, 1537, 3608
Tips from Tina 3568
Tips of Gay Paree, The 1264
Tips! Tips! Tips! 1868
Tiptoe March 1092
Tirade, The 1600
Tiralala (Romance) 742
Tired 1121, 2509
Tired Business Man 97
Tired Heroes 1075
Tired of It All 1839
Tired of Living Alone 1921
Tired of Love 3861
Tired of the South 4021
Tirrallallera (Tirollallero) 3798
Tis a Glorious Day 659
'Tis a Merry, Merry World 355
'Tis a Wonderful Thing in Nature 4366
'Tis an Irish Girl I Love and She's Just Like You 2662
'Tis Dreadful! 'Tis Astonishing 4473
'Tis Hard By Fate Thus to Be Parted 402
'Tis Hard to Be a Lady in a Case Like That 4473
Tis Incredible As Love 367
'Tis Love 2602
'Tis Love Has Caused All Trouble 762
'Tis Love That Most Enriches 1071
Tis Noon of Tropic Day 1783
Tis of Thee 3654, 4394
Tis Pity, Tis True 3741
'Tis Plain to See 2563
'Tis Sad to Leave 1710
'Tis Sad to Love in Vain 2673
'Tis Summer 4509
'Tis the End of Time 240
'Tis the End, So Farewell 2292
'Tis the Hour (Opening Chorus) 4497
'Tis the Morning of the Fair (Opening Chorus) 3736
Tis Thy Beauty 4312
'Tis You I Love 1798
Tit Street 1010
Tit Willow 2977
Titania 3617
Titania's Philosophy 249
Titina 200, 4819
Titipu 2861
Titles 4802
Titsy-Bitsy Girl 1569
Tittle-Tattle 2844, 2399
Titwillow 1987
Tiy's Song: Fear Is a Faraway Country 3088
Tkambuza (Zulu Hunting Song) 4863
TNT 341
To a Small Degree 3564
To Adjust Is a Must 3801
To an Isle in the Water 1977
To and Fro 45
To Arms (Dear One, Divine) 4503
To Arms 4187
To Bath Derry-O 71
To Be a King 73, 3507
To Be a Performer 2368, 1708
To Be Alone with You 367
To Be Artistic 1846
To Be at Sea 2346
To Be or Not to Be 207, 708, 2246
To Be or Not to Be Blues 703
To Be or Not to Be in Love 673, 1892, 2593
To Be Together Is the Thing 579
To Be Truly Refined 405
To Be Wanted 139
To Be with Thee 1071
To Be Young 4602
To Become a Man 3485
To Bed 1080
To Belong 157
To Blazassus 3337
To Boston on Business 4717
To Bring Up a Girl 3977
To Broadway with Love 4395
To Call Thee Mine 3673
To Cook My Gander's Goose 649
To Dance Is To Fly 4171
To-Day Is the Day 1557
To Do a Little Good 2583
To Do What We Like 3528
To Dream or Not to Dream 4696
To Drink We Have No Fear 355
To Each His Dulcinea (To Every Man His Dream) 2727
To Educate These Young Ladies 762
To Feel So Needed 2953
To Find True Love 4022
To Follow Ever Fancy 3865
To France 453
To Get Away 2252
To Get Out of This World Alive 989
To Get Us All Together 1393, 4639
To Go Shopping 340
To Go Upon the Stage 1948
To Greece I Gave This Body of Mine 4615
To Have and to Hold 85, 4269
To Have, to Hold, to Love 184
To Health 2352
To Hear Your Voice 4037
To Heaven on the Bronx Express 2829
To Hell with Everybody but Us 1762
To Hell with Everyone but Us 3326
To Horse 3703
To Japan 1243
To Keep My Love Alive 834
To Keep the Chill Off the Bones 4588
To Keep Up My Spirits 2657
To Keep You in Your Seats 3218
To Know You Is to Like You 3415

To Know You Is to Love You 1929
To Life 1265
To Like to Love One Girl 2387
To Live Again 4619
To Live and Die a Soldier Bold (Battle Song) 2745
To Live Another Summer to Pass Another Winter 4396
To Live Is to Love 4365
To Live, to Love Again 2387
To London 2732
To Look Upon My Love 2295
To Love Again 159
To Love and Be Loved 4391
To Love and to Lose 663
To Love Is to Live 314
To Love with a Lovely Life 2910
To Love You 2148
To Make a Hit in Par-ee 3613
To Make the Boy a Man 1634
To Make Them Beautiful Ladies 2706
To Make Them Fall 2270
To Make You Love Me 4240
To Marry 3526
To Marry a Millionaire 2465
To Marry for Love 1265
To Measure the Darkness 2142
To-morrow 3337
To My Dear and Loving Husband (If Ever Two Were One) 2633
To My Judicial Mind 1429
To My Wife 1242
To-night at Ten 3045
To-night's the Night 3976, 4418
To Our Charity Bazaar 2844
To Our Homes We'll Go 1758
To Overcome Passion and Acquire Perfection 2437
To Paradise We'll Gaily Trip 473
To Paris! 2670
To Play This Part 3811
To Please My King 3702
To Prove My Love 4572
To Rent, to Let 2145
To See Her 3875
To Sir with Love 338
To Stop a Marriage 694
To Tell the Truth 4769
To the Barracks We Have Come 1429
To the Beat of My Heart 4824
To the Cave Away 175
To the Clinic 649
To the Dance 1839
To the Dead of Family Wars 3806
To the End of the World Together 1188
To the Ends of the Earth 4029
To the Fair 1011
To the Girl You Dance With 2614
To the Guard House 3883
To the Harbormaster 3162
To the Inn We're Marching 4188
To the Island 3805
To the Land of My Own Romance 1183
To the Paris Exposition 2844
To the Pyramid 4724
To the Races 3310
To the Regiment We'll Go 2914
To the Sound of the Pipe and the Roll of the Drum 252
To the Strains of That Wedding March 2261
To the Top 2248
To the Victor Belongs the Spoils 2747
To the Victor Belongs the Spoils (Chewing Gum Song) 4725
To the Woods 4469
To Think He Remembered Me 4212
To Think That Once We Were Sweethearts (And Now We're Not Even Friends) 418
To Think That This Could Happen to Me 629
To Touch the Sky 2659, 4089
(I've Already Started In) To Try to Figure Out a Way to Go to Work to Try to Get You 3016
To What I Say, Attention Pay 1199
To Whom It May Concern 4398, 1670
To Whom It May Concern Me 4485
To Win a Prince 4470
To You 1825
To You I Gave My All 4379
To You Sir Miles 3049
To Your Health 3526
Toad's Lament, The 1786
Toast, The 1518
Toast, A 2603
Toast, The 2705
Toast, A 4303
Toast 'To Sally' 1515
Toast of the Boys at the Post, The 297
Toast of the Town 4011
Toast of Volstead, A 1272
Toast Song 405, 2897
Toast to Alpha Cholera, A 304
Toast to the Bride, A 1076
Toast to the King of War, A 4113
Toast to the Moon (Round Red Moon) 2793
Toast to Women's Eyes, A 473
Toast We'll Give You To-Night, A 1197
Toastin' Sequence 1385
Toasts of the Town 2240
Tobacco Blues, The 1748
Tobacco Road 194
Toccata 3864
Today 1110, 390, 3476, 3697
Today at Your House, Tomorrow at Mine 911
Today I Am a Glamour Girl 4586
Today I Found Me 4171
Today I Is So Happy 651
Today I Met the Boy I'm Gonna Marry 2427, 4193
Today I Saw a Rose 1273
Today I Went Adventuring 3453
Today I'm Gonna Think About Me 2660

Today I'm Smiling Rainbows Upside Down 1597
Today Is a Day for a Band to Play 1094
Today Is the Day 2250
Today Is the First Day of the Rest of My Life 2617, 4145
Today My Spinet 4404
Today Will Be 1282, 4168
Today Will Be Yesterday Tomorrow 1336
Today's a Wonderful Day 57
Today's the Day 227, 1628, 1189
Today's the Day (He Loves Me) 1616
Today, Today, Is Holiday 402
Toddle All Over the Town 1588
Toddle All Over Town 75
Toddle Along 4819
Toddle-Dee-Doo 1687
Toddle Go the Girls 2760
Toddle Quartette 1625
Toddle Top Whirl, The 2605
Toddle Trot 1460
Toddler's Ball 1557
Toddlin' Along 3172
Toddling the Todalo 1845
Toddy's the Drink for Me 4479
Toe, Head, Tap, Tap 4003
Toe Tangling Tune 2180
Together 550, 1628, 3202, 3279
Together As One 4106
Together at Last 3379
Together Forever 2050
Together in Central Park 3493
Together, Wherever We Go 1709
Togetherness 1408, 3110
Toilet Chorus 526
'Toinette 649
Tokay 429
Tokay! (Hungarian Song) 2830
Tokio 2793
Tokio Blues 3009
Tokio Rag 60
Tokyo, Mon Amour 128, 1436
Told Me Yo' Had Money in the Bank 604
Toll Basket 922
Toller's Theme (inst.) 4402
Tom 1822
Tom and Huck's Argument 1086
Tom and Jack 2101
Tom Boy, Tom Boy 531
Tom, Dick or Harry 2331
Tom Jones 4404, 4406
Tom Sawyer 4409
Tom, Tom 2134
Tom-Tom 3342, 3623
Tom-Tom Dance 4823
Tom-Tom-Toddle 2767
Tommy 377, 4676
Tommy Atkins 1301, 3973
Tommy Atkins on a Dress-Parade (I Want to Be a Jolly Soldier) 1285
Tommy Atkins, You're All Right 4759
Tommy Can You Hear Me 4676
Tommy Robbins 1340
Tommy Rot 1558
Tommy, Tommy 4312
Tommy Won't You Teach Me How to Tango 1561
Tommy's Holiday Camp 4676
Tomorrow 150, 200, 602, 735, 1959, 2432, 2706, 2818, 2898, 2968, 2992, 3016, 4269, 4394, 4516, 4539
Tomorrow All Day 973
Tomorrow and Tomorrow 1258
Tomorrow Belongs to Me 610
Tomorrow I'm Gonna Be Old 135
Tomorrow Is Another Day 1616
Tomorrow Is Christmas 2224
Tomorrow Is Here 3473
Tomorrow Is Only a Moment 2925
Tomorrow Is St. Valentine's Day 3909
Tomorrow Is the First Day of the Rest of My Life 3824
Tomorrow Is the Time 3390
Tomorrow Morning 1029, 1764
Tomorrow Mountain 341
Tomorrow Night 3476
Tomorrow Waltz, The 3490
Tomorrow When the World Comes Crashing Down Around Our Ears 1993
Tomorrow Will Be the Same 3389
Tomorrow's Another Day (1) 200
Tomorrow's Another Day (2) 200
Tomorrow's Good Old Days 1634
Tondelayo 1130, 3150, 4819
Tong War, The 302
Tongue Tied Tune 1971
Toni Caponi 3701
Tonight 1387, 3379, 4625, 1159
Tonight at Eight 3918
Tonight I Love You More 3326
Tonight in San Francisco 3262
Tonight Is Opening Night 4267
Tonight, Love 644
Tonight May Never Come Again 2813
Tonight or Never 111, 1136, 2238, 3152, 3152
Tonight We Love 2162
Tonight Will Never Come Again 3579
Tonight with You 4486
Tonight You Are in Paree 2705
Tonight You Belong to Me 4264
Tonight You Dance with Me 3763
Tonight's the Fight 3988
Tonight's the Night 921, 766, 3019, 3096, 3103, 3104, 3626, 3953, 4419, 4547
Tonsils 4212
Tony 3434
Tony from America 3618
Tony Pastor's 4289
Tony the Peddler 252
Tony, Tony, Tony 2602
Tony's Thoughts 2961
Too! 871
Too a Roi-oor a Loi-a 399
Too Bad 1770, 2739, 2992, 3972, 1630

Too Beautiful Tonight 4798
Too Charming 367
Too Close for Comfort 2987
Too Darn Hot 2331
Too Early or Too Late 3235
Too Fast 143
Too Good for the Average Man 3283
Too Good to Be Bad (2 Good 2 B Bad) 1633
2 Good 2 B Bad 1633
Too Good to Be True 1929, 453
Too Hot for Paris 1837
Too Late, Daddy 2200
Too Late for Yesterday 255
Too Little Time for Love (1) 3543
Too Little Time for Love (2) 3543
Too Long at the Fair 411, 1341, 413, 412
Too Long from Longacre Square 115
Too Many Boys 3007
Too Many Cookers 220
Too Many Cooks 351, 4529
Too Many Girls 4420
Too Many Men 4416
Too Many Miles from Broadway 1640
Too Many Mirrors 3515
Too Many Mornings 1329
Too Many Old Ideas 2962
Too Many People 327
Too Many People Alone 3294
Too Many Questions 1233
Too Many Rings Around Rosie 3184, 3249
Too Many Sweethearts 799, 3008
Too Many Tomorrows 4238
Too Many Women in My Life 1737, 3927
Too Marvelous for Words 1638, 4799
Too Much Bowden 2148
Too Much in Love to Care 4217
Too Much Money Blues 1201
Too Much Motet, The 169
Too Much Pain 259
Too Much to Forgive 101
Too Much Trouble 911
Too Much Work 818
Too Much World 3159
Too Nice a Day to Go to School 304
Too Old 4623
Too Old for Love 4292
Too Old to Be So Young 3299
Too Particular 4419
Too Plump for Prom Night 3561
Too-ra-loo-ra-loo-ra That's an Irish Lullaby 3910
Too-Re-Loo-Re (A French Pavanne) 1162
Too Soon 1886, 2048, 3301
Too Soon the Day 127
Too Tall 1780
Too Tired 554
Too Tired to Love 2332
Too, Too Divine 1448, 3307
Too Too Too 3104
Too Young 4292
Too Young to Go Steady 4180
Too Young to Live 1567
Too Young to Love 1176
Toodle-oo 608
Toodle-Oo! 1580
Toodle-oo 2768, 3249
Toodle-Oo 3915
Toodle-oodle-oodle on Your Piccolo 4712
Toodle Oodle Um 2216
Toodles Is the Elephant's Name 3251
Took Me a Little Time 1420
Tool for You 1149
Toons 2305
Toot Toot 598
Toot-Toot! 4422
Toot, Toot, Tootsie (Goodbye) 487
Tooth and Claw 341
Toothache Blues 570
Tootle, Tootle 1540
Tootsie Tripper 1900
Tootsie-Wootsie 2732
Tootsie Wootsie 4161
Top Banana 4423
Top Hat, White Tie and Tails 789, 3175
Top Hole 4424
Top o' the Mornin' 452
Top o' the Morning 4120
Top of the Climb 1837
Top of the Hill, The 4862
Top of the List 3615
Top of the Morning, The 4757
Top of the Sky 3682
Top of the Train 1864
Top Spot 4527
Top Stories 62
Top That If You Can 1842
Topic of the Tropics, The 1951
Topical Song 185
Topics of the Day 764, 3623
Topple Down 4741
Topsy Turvy 1682
Topsy Turvy Oskaloosa Lou 228
Torch Parade 3850
Torch Singer (What Do You Think My Heart Is Made Of?) 4374
Torch Song 1225
Torch Song, The 2423
Torch Songs 4177
Toreador 141
Toreador Song 3952
Toreador's Song (I'm the Glory and Pride of the Land of Spain) 4430
Torelore 1262
Tormented 1046
Tornado Ballet 4722
Torpedo Till 1902
Torrito, Torerazo 2407
Torture 1164
Tortured Thomas Cat 4311
Tosca 1304
Toscanini, Stokowski and Me 2301

Tosy and Cosh 3274
Totem Dance 490
Totem Tom Tom 3020
Totem Tom-Tom 3772
Touch a Hair of His Head 4588
Touch a Touch Me 3742
Touch and Go 1056, 2014
Touch Kiss 2332
Touch Me 3830, 4003
Touch of a Woman's Hand, The 1598
Touch of a Woman, The 2027
Touch of Class, A 4743
Touch of Paris 3491
Touch of Sweetness, A 945
Touch of the Irish, A 2805
Touch of Voodoo, A 2608
Touch of You, A 851
Touch of Your Hand, The 3735
Touched in the Head 3860
Touching Your Hand Is Like Touching Your Mind 2418
Tough Cookie 3165
Tough Guy 3004
Tough to Be a Fairy 2022
Tough Town, A 275
Toujour la Politesse 1868
Toujours Gai 3934
Toujours L'Amour on the Cote D'Azur 3756
Toujours La Politesse 336
Tour de Force 4798
Tour de Four 4433
Tour de France 4579
Tour Must Go On, The 2705
Touring 'Round 1351
Tourist Madrigal 4173
Tourists, The 2056
Tourists 3729
Tourists, The 3746
Tourists 96
Tout le Monde 962
Tout Suite 4421
Tovarich 4435
Tower of Babble 1595
Tower of Babel 2846
Town & Country Suite 1657
Town and Country 1561, 1896
Town and Country Mouse, The 4354
Town Called Might-Have-Been 3057
Town Crier's Song 3732
Town Folks Will Be Pleased, The 1925
Town Gossip 4437
Town Hall Tonight 1529
Town House Maxixe Dance, The 1614
Town Meeting 2095
Town That Grows Where the Hudson Flows, The 4644
Town Topics 3087
Town Without Pity 4193
Townsfolk's Lament, The 3888
Township Fever 4438
Toy Balloon 1497
Toy Boat 3125
Toy Broadway, The 4544
Toy Clog Dance (inst.) 2900
Toy Dance 764, 2939
Toy Duet 1470
Toy Monkey, The 1470
Toy of Destiny 1690
Toy Soldier Number, The 2307
Toy Soldiers, The (inst.) 683
Toy Song 4439
Toy Store 1068
Toy Town 632
Toy Trumpet, The 4799
Toyland 250, 3112, 4390, 4818
Toymakers Shop, The 250
Toys, Toys, Toys 1703
Tra Gog Vo In Dien Whole 3806
Tra-La-La 1345
Tra La La 1871
Tra-La-La 2889
Tra-la-la, Etcetera 2668
Tra-la-la-la 3617
Tra La, La, La, La, La 3805
Tra-La-Li 3701
Track Down This Murderer 3464
Tract, The 2341
Trade a Minute 2289
Tradesmen Ensemble 1746
Trading Fours 3840
Trading Fours — Prelude 3840
Trading Solos 2142
Tradition 1265
Traditional Seder 3669
Tragedian Ballet (inst.) 3955
Tragedy and Comedy 4378
Tragedy of an Elderly Gentleman, The 1651
Tragedy of the Hats 3673
Tragedy Waltz 2478
Trail, The 3035, 2766
Trail of No's, A 3173
Trailer Park Romance 2643
Trailing a Shooting Star 3584
Trailing Along in a Trailer 70
Train, The 1402, 2894
Train Music (inst.) 4798
Train of Adolescence 3461
Train That Brought You to Town, The 4652
Train That Leaves for Town, The 3866
Train Time 4677
Train to Johannesburg 369, 2591
Train Walking 1402
Train with the Cushioned Seats, The 2680
Trainers and Pugilists 568
Training Rap, The 3752
Trains and Boats and Planes 261
Trains or Me 1402
Tramp Has Ups and Downs, A 2880
Tramp! Tramp! Tramp! 3081

Trampin' Along 3436
Trample Your Troubles 4213
Tramps and Scamps 3777
Tramps of the Desert 3660
Tranquil Boxwood, The 3641
Tranquilizers 3942
Transform-ed 158
Transformation, The 3722
Transformation 2198, 2357, 330
Transformation Lullaby 3579
Transition (Bonds) 3691
Transition 1 3411
Transition 2 3411
Transition 3 3411
Transition 4 3411
Transition 5 3411
Transkei Xha Xha 4579
Transparent Crystal Moment, A 2418
Transplant 2876
Transport of Delight, A 220
Transposed Heads, The 4442
Trapp Family Singers, The 4095
'Trapped' 2364
Trapped 2918
Trash 4
Trashy Effeminate Hoodlum, The 2046
Trastmara Rose, The 1369
Travel 4145
Travel Music (chant) 1406
Travel Now 194
Travel On 1031
Travel the Road of Love 3094
Travel, Travel, Travel 1312, 2679
Travel, Travel, Travel, Little Star 3268
Traveler and the Pie, The 4723
Travelin' 731
Travelin' Light 1706
Travelin' Man 2332, 4387
Travelin' On 1222
Travelin' Show, A 2028
Traveling 521
Traveling Memories 4540
Traveling Together 1955
Traveling Troubador 3802
Travellin' 4645
Travellin' Light 4399
Travellin' Man 108
Travellin' 691
Travelling Englishman 346
Travelling First Class Style 4769
Travelling Song 4380
Travelogue 930
Travesty 1033, 1466
Travesty Opera 3258
Treasure Hunt, The (inst.) 2638
Treasure Island 1922, 3485, 4443, 4444, 4444
Treasure Island Trio Dance (inst.) 4744
Treasure of a Girl, A 3031
Treasure to Burn 1985
Treat a Woman Like a Drum 2755
Treat 'Em Rough 98, 303, 1312, 4218
Treat Me Nice 4031
Treat Me Rough 1528
Treaty, My Sweety with You, A 2068
Treble 1648
Tree, The 203, 2801
Tree and the Sun, The 3571
Tree Grows in Brooklyn, A 4446
Tree in the Park, A 3436
Tree Loves 4075
Tree of Life Ballet, The 1310
Tree of Love, The 1462
Tree of Truth 1992
Tree-Top of Love 3238
Tree Without Sun, A 2319
Treeless Leaflets of Times Square, The 1450
Treemonisha in Peril 4447
Treemonisha's Bringing Up 4447
Treemonisha's Return 4447
Trelawney 2041
Tremont Avenue Cruisewear Fashion Show, The 2925
Trench Fantasy, A 1502
Trench Girl 371
Trenck Is My Name 307
Trenck March Song 307
Trenck's Entrance 307
Trepak 3013
Tres Bien, Monsieur 4115
Tres Parisien 2839
Trial, The 169, 1214
Trial, The (Ladies of the Jury) 3117
Trial, The 4312
Trial 4788
Trial Before Pilate 2212
Trial By Jury 3204
Trial in Trinidad 1892
Trial of Minnie the Moocher, The 877
Trial of Shimmy Mae, The 4656
Trial of the Century 4635
Trial Song, The 3978
Trials and Tribulations 3515
Trials of a Simple Maid, The 3229
Triangle 3130
Triangle, The 3177
Triangle (sketch) 4496
Triangle, The (scene) 4555
Triangle Blues 303
Triangle Song 164
Tribes 1769
Tribute 2477
Trickeration 3709
Tricks 3753, 4450
Tricks of the Trade 3511, 4114, 2185
Tried Jumpin' You Once 2304
Trieste 1280
Trilby 4809, 4229, 4230
Trim Little Phoebe 402
Trim Them All but the One You Love 4010
Trim Up the Tree 2015

Trina's Song 2746
Trini 965, 969
Trinity 2918
Trink's Narration 4139
Trinka Brinker 1742
Trinket Vendor 932
Trio 3944, 3411, 2642, 3347, 3418, 3813, 4773, 526
Trio Con Brio 1436, 4433
Triology 3615
Trip 535, 4002
Trip Doesn't Care at All, A 95
Trip Round the U.S.A., A 3262
Trip Through My Mind, A 2043
Trip Tick Talking Blues 1612
Trip to Bermuda, A 1285
Trip to Chinatown, A 4712
Trip to Paris, A 4830
Trip to the Library, A 3918
Tripe Seller's Lament 1736
Triple Flank Maneuver 919
Triple Sec 1448
Triple Tango 4388
Triplets 383, 1322
Tripping 4431
Tripping the Light Fantastic 4718
Tripping, Tripping 4148
Tripping Your Troubles Away 568
Tristan and Isolated 128
Triumphant Entry of Hans 1743
Triumphant Youth 3839
Trixie True Teen Detective! 4454
Trixie's on the Case! 4454
Trocadero Opening: Happy New Year 3949
Trojan Horse, The (inst.) 3980
Trolley Line, The 1118
Trolley Song, The 2805
Trombone Cholly 2796
Trombone Jazz 3402
Trombone Man (My Trombone Man) 3399
Trombone Man 984
Trombone Symphony 4437
Tropic Love 4283
Tropic Vamps 4283
Tropicabana Rhumba 2437
Tropical Moon 1328, 1902, 1989
Tropicana 1414
Tropics 1027
Trot Here and There, Take Care, Take Care 4554
Trot-I-Ty Trot 2966
Trottin' to the Fair 4366
Trottin' to the Land of Cotton Melodies 1058
Trou-Trou-Ba-Ba-Troubadour 2668
Troubador 1370, 1518
Troubadour Sang to His Love, A 3736
Troubadours 2315
Trouble 1312, 2796, 4031
Trouble About the Drama, The 466
Trouble in Mind 1425
Trouble Man 369, 2591, 4504
Trouble Tree, The 47
Trouble, Trouble 3989
Trouble with Marriage, The 2368
Trouble with Me 600, 140
Trouble with Women, The 3301
Trouble with Women Is Men, The 3046
Trouble with You, The 4619
Troubled Lady 4629
Troubled Lullaby 3780
Trouble's a Ruler 4450
Troubles of My Own 352, 4172
Troubles of the Reuben and the Maid 3745
Trousseau Ball, The 4464
Trousseau Incomplete, The 2601
Trousseau Song 1034
Trousseau Waltz 4464
Trowl the Bowl 3939
Troyerik Zayn Darf Men Nit (Why Be Sad...?) 1609
Truce, The 2318
Truckers Ball 435
Truckin' 882
Truckin' in Hollywood 1940
Truckin' in My Tails 1493
Truckload 4459
Trucks, The 2630
True 2227
True Barbaric Soldier, A 2315
True Blue 1839, 2282, 2631, 2858
True Blue American Boy 4758
True Blue Pals 2053
True Confession 2114
True Hearts 2594
True Irish Girl, The 1409
True Love 391, 977, 3765
True Love Is a Star 948
True Love Is Not for a Day 2697
True Love Is the Mother of Us All 952
True Love Lives but in Our Dreams 3883
True Love Ways 580
True Love Will Find a Way 2486
True Love Will Never Grow Cold 4694
True Music 3515
True Romance 3934
True to Me 1527
True to Them All 3766
True to Two 577, 2976, 3236
True Value 4690
Truly a Queen 3628
Truly Blessed 4460
Truly Content 4746
Truly Loved 1741, 3526
Truly My Soul 4398
Trumpet Rag (inst.) 3840
Trumpet Solo 323
Trumpeter and the Lover, The 4372
Trumpeter, Blow Your Golden Horn 3225
Trunk Packing Song 4405
Trust In Me 4798
Trust Me 299, 1637, 2449, 4560

Trust Me, Love Me 1518
Trust Me Tango 4106
Trust Your Destiny to a Star 44
Trustee's Decision, The 1997
Trustee's Song 1997
Truth 837, 2464
Truth, The 2523
Truth About a Big Fish Story, The 4397
Truth About Cinderella, The 4461
Truth About Ruth 4462
Truth and Lies 2766
Truth Cannot Be Treason 2728
Truth Is So Beautiful 178
Truth Is Spoken with Your Eyes, The 2970
Try (Just a Little Bit Harder) 338
Try a Little 3788
Try a Little Harder 430
Try a Little Kiss 2293
Try a Ring, Dear! 4838
Try a Trio 4124
Try Again 3250
Try Again, Johnny 906
Try Again Tomorrow 2467, 3924
Try Dancing 4426
Try Her Out at Dances 3117
Try It on the Day 591
Try It, You'll Like It 4463
Try Me 2216, 2320, 3918
Try Not to Need Her 944
Try the Sky 2332
Try This on Your Pianna Anna 1845
Try to Forget 672
Try to Forget Me 172
Try to Learn to Love 4341
Try to Love Me Just As I Am 3845
Try to Make the Best of It 2657
Try to Remember 1245, 3542
Try to Remember It All 198
Try to See It My Way 3275
Try, Try Again 1226, 2876, 4102
Try, Try, Try 1536
Trying Hard 4343
Trying It On 256
Trying on Dresses 3387
Trysting Tree, The 353
Tsin 1686
Tsing-la-la 1817
Tsivye's Song 4773
Tu Carrisimo 2216
Tu Sais 364, 1656
Tu Way Pocky Way 1890
Tuamani 2085
Tubal Cain 2286
Tubular Bells (inst.) 3739
Tuck Me in a Taxi Cab 4012
Tuesday's Mail (Mail # 2) 1804
Tulip Print Waltz 1872
Tulip Time 60, 4813
Tulips (Two Lips) 675
Tulips and Pansies 3799
Tulips with Your Color So Bright 4509
Tum On and Tiss Me 1483
Tum-Tiddly-Tum-Tum 2216
Tumble El Toro 2385
Tumble Inn 3403
Tumblin Down 914
Tumbrel Song, The 3445
Tummy-Tummy-Tum 1593
Tune for Humming, A 1706, 1741
Tune In (to Station J.O.Y.) 1487
Tune in My Heart 747
Tune in Tomorrow 838
Tune Like You, A 1177
Tune They Croon in the U.S.A., The 473
Tune They Play, The 2377
Tune to Take Away 3890
Tune You Can't Forget, The 4063
Tup'ny Show, The 3976
Turk Has the Right Idea, The 2587
Turkey and the Turk, The 2675
Turkey Baster Baby 4309
Turkey in the Straw 1529, 2415
Turkey Lurkey Time 3603
Turkey Trot 687
Turkey Trot, The 1531
Turkey Trot (inst.) 2528
Turkey Trotting Boy (Oh! You Turkey Trotter), The 351
Turkish Corner 2664
Turkish Delight (dance) 3526
Turkish Drill 2013
Turkish Love Song 2254
Turkish Oomph 4131
Turkish Trotteshness 4807
Turlututu 4798
Turn Around 2318, 3619
Turn Back, O Man 1595
Turn Back the Years 3795
Turn Her Out 2648
Turn It Around 900
Turn Me Loose on Broadway 4499
Turn My Life Is Taking, The 1581
Turn My Little Millwheel 3386
Turn My Tears to Smiles 1972
Turn of the Year 2458
Turn on the Charm 2755
Turn on the Lights 798
Turn on the Popular Moon 2950
Turn on the Radio 3931
Turn Out the Light 4267
Turn Over 2481
Turn the Other Cheek 2306
Turn the Tide 992
Turn Those Eyes Away 3384
Turn to Me 2382
Turn Up the Spotlight 3211
Turn Us Again 1073
Turn Your Thoughts and Faces 2389
Turnabout 4467
Turning (Shaker Hymn) 16

Turning 2442
Turnip Time 3663
Turnkey's Song 3732
Turoola 4243
Turtle Song 2000
Tuscaloosa 603, 4446
Tuscaloosa's Calling Me but I'm Not Going 4468
Tuskegee 984
Tutti Frutti 4534, 3739
Tutu and Tights 3869
TV Quiz Show 407
Twang of My Trusty Bow 2902
Twang!! 4469
Twanger! 4470
'Twas a Kiss in the Moonlight 2302
'Twas Brillig 58
'Twas but a Dream 2673
'Twas Different Years Ago 3567
'Twas Down in the Garden of Eden 4646
'Twas in a Garden 4228
'Twas in September 335
Twas in the Month of June 1552
'Twas in the Month of May 710
T'was Love All the Day (Artist and Model) 457
'Twas Not So Long Ago 4234
'Twas Only an Irishman's Dream 543, 2930
T'was the Night Before Christmas 2689
'Twas the Rose 1768
Twas Twenty-Seven Bells by the Waterbury Watch 1392
Tweedle Dee 4264
Tweedledee for President 2444
Tweedledum and Tweedledee 54, 2670, 1540
Tweet-Tweet 1489
Tweet, Tweet, Tweet 1407
Twelfth Night 2599, 3015, 4789
Twelve Days to Christmas 3918
Twelve Feet Tall 2182
Twelve Little Heels 1130
Twelve Miles Out from the Coast 720
Twelve O'Clock and All Is Well 1336
Twelve O'Clock Girl in a Nine O'Clock Town, A 468
Twelve O'Clock Song 3920
Twelve Pretty Wives from Turkey 2213
Twelve Rooftops Leaping 2134
Twenties Are Here to Stay, The 3243
Twentieth Century 3279
20th Century Fox 2969
20th Century Girl, The 1213
Twentieth Century Is Almost Here, The 2928
Twentieth Century Love 1478
Twentieth Century Lullaby, A 2489
Twentieth Century Rag 4657
Twentieth Reunion 430
Twenty-Eight 2472
Twenty-Eight Men 2433
28 Men 3831
20 Fans 374
Twenty-Five Bucks a Week 4331
25 Miles 426
Twenty Five Words or Less 3460
Twenty-five Years Ago 1796
Twenty-Four Hours a Day 1127
24 Hours a Day 1611
24 Hours from This Moment 2069
24 Hours from Tulsa 261
Twenty-Four Hours of Love 1746
24 Hours of Lovin' 374
Twenty Happy Years 534
Twenty Million People 3039
Twenty-Nine Years Ago 2702
Twenty-One 4676
Twenty-One Bucks a Week 4331
Twenty-One Candles 453
Twenty One Chateaux 3015
Twenty Questions 753
26 Market Mix 62
Twenty Thousand Pounds 902
Twenty Tons of TNT 221
Twenty-Two Years 1649
Twenty Years 2433, 2630
Twenty Years Ago 1489, 3701, 4809
Twenty Years of Treason 3873
Twice a Year 880
Twice as Nice 474
Twice Shy 221
Twice Told Tale, A 1312
Twiddley Bits, The 737
Twilight 130, 1132, 1345, 2020, 2610, 725, 1173
Twilight at Home Sweet Home 9
Twilight Double Header 1630
Twilight in Barakeesh 48, 3773
Twilight Night 1920
Twilight Rhythms 797
Twilight Serenade 2112
Twilight Song 579, 1319
Twilight Voices 1462, 3586
'Twill Never Be the Same 2464
Twilly of Fifth Avenue 152
Twin Butterflies That Fitfully Fall 3588
Twin Sisters 1923
Twin Soliloquies 2511
Twin Soliloquies (Wonder How It Feels) 4096
Twinkle 4056
Twinkle in Your Eye, The 1516
Twinkle in Your Eye, A 2061
Twinkle, Little Broadway Star 1911
Twinkle Little Star 2549
Twinkle Little Stars 1617
Twinkle, Twinkle 3955, 4133
Twinkle Twinkle 4476
Twinkle Twinkle Little Star 593
Twinkle, Twinkle Little Star 4064, 4296
Twinkling Eyes 1321, 4477, 4530
Twinkling Toes 2858
Twist, The 3739
Twist Her Mind 3741
Twist My Arm 673, 3046

Twist of Fate, A 275
Twist of the Wrist 924
Twisted Every Way 3464
Twitter 1533
'Twixt Love and Duty 1851
Twixt the Devil and the Deep Blue Sea 3139
Twizzle, The 1040
Two 2305
Two (Little) Bits of Greece 208
Two a Day 204
Two-a-Day 2208
Two a Day, The 3366
Two-a-Day for Keith (Twice a Night) 3283
Two a Day on the Milky Way 4828
Two Against the World 2674
Two Are Company 3084
Two Are One (You Need Two Souls but One Thought) 1378
Two Bags 2876
Two Best Girls I Love You 994
Two Best Girls I Love, The 3911
Two Big Eyes 2891
Two Blocks from the Capitol Building 374
Two Boys 4345
Two By Two 300, 1060, 1681
Two by Two 4028
Two By Two 4249, 4481
Two Can Live As Cheaply As One 345
Two Cat Scat Fight 3628
Two Cigarettes in the Dark 2311
Two Claudines 808, 809
Two Clocks, The 2774
Two Cockatoos 2495
Two Dandy Darkies 1826
Two-Dollar Ring 2305
Two Doves 1589
Two Dummies, The 4758
Two Eyes 3073
Two Eyes Of Blue 3976
Two-Faced Woman 1322
Two Faces in the Dark 3687
Two Fairy Tales 2536, 2764
Two Falls to a Finish 1958
Two Feet in Two-Four Time 1481
Two Fellows and a Girl 2342
Two for the Seesaw 3869
Two Gat Gertie 2, 3172
Two Gentlemen of Verona 4485, 4485
Two Get Together 1342
Two Giddy Goats 353
Two Girls from the Chorus 3723
Two Graces, The 4388
Two Grown-Up People at Play 1002
Two Guitars 710
Two Handsome Men 3022
Two Happy Tadpoles 1334
Two Heads 3733
Two Heads Are Better Than One 913, 4206
Two Hearts 2323
Two Hearts Beat as One 2869, 3357
Two Hearts in Danger 3335
Two Hearts in Gypsy Time 3664
Two Hearts in Tune 1174
Two Hearts in Waltz Time 4486
Two Hearts in Waltz Time (Zwei Herzen im Dreivierteltakt) 4486
Two Hearts Made One 2315
Two Horse Fellow in a One Horse Town 2826
Two If By Sea, I Think! 4488
Two in a Taxi 2301
Two Is Company 2330, 2491
2 Is Company 4289
Two Is Company 4489
Two Is Plenty 4590
Two Key Rag 2299
Two Key Rag, The 2853
Two Keys 1377
Two Kinsmen 3070
Two Ladies 610
Two Ladies and a Man 1352
Two Ladies in de Shade of de Banana Tree 2000
Two Lands, Two Ladies 595
Two Laughing Irish Eyes 3590
Two Left Feet 2259
Two Lips Are Roses 1174
Two Lips Are Waiting in Tulip Town 2448
Two Lips from Georgia 1823
Two Little Angels 3602
Two Little Applekins 246
Two Little Babes in the Wood 1690, 3382
Two Little Bits of Greece 3466
Two Little Bluebirds 4212
Two Little Cannibal Ladies 1083
Two Little Chicks 906
Two Little Doves 4713, 4046
Two Little Girls in Blue 4491
Two Little Girls Loved One Little Boy 3350
Two Little Kids 2224
Two Little Kittens 2347, 4617
Two Little Losses 4212
Two Little Love Bees 4119
Two Little Love Birds 2601
Two Little Pals 2972
Two Little Pussycats 3863
Two Little Ruby Rings 953
Two Little Sausages 1569
Two Little Ships 3163
Two Little Stars 1020
Two Little Wooden Shoes 4104
Two Lost Souls 957
2 Lots in the Bronx 4492
Two Lovely Lying Eyes 4815
Two Lovers 2759
Two Loving Arms 2277
Two Make a Home 3540
Two Miss Browns, The 392
Two Mrs. Browns, The 3186
Two Musketeers 949
Two of a Kind 3722, 1529
Two of a Kind (Nitamono Doshi) 1616

Two of a Kind 2161
Two of Me 4272
Two of Us, The 251, 403
Two of Us 2275
Two of Us, The 4619, 2582, 3967, 4727, 4766
Two on an Island 2400
Two People in Love 253
Two People Who Love 1068
2% Income Tax, The 1094
Two Perfect Lovers 203
Two Playhouses, The 1826
Two Possibilities 1660
Two Queens 3104
Two Quick Quackers 4853
Two Rivers, The (Yesterday and Tomorrow) 402
Two Roads Meet 3461
Two Robertas, The 2146
Two Rooms 3221
Two Rubes 4814
Two Short Years 85
Two Should Be Harmonious 2177
Two Sides to a Story 2711
Two Sleepy People 39, 3444
Two Souls without a Single Thought 187
Two-Step (inst.) 1197
Two-Step 2101, 3570
Two Strangers 2114
Two Strings to a Bow 2278
2000 Miles 1612
Two Time Dan 1129
Two Times Young and Twice in Love 4486
Two to Duluth 1801
Two to Eleven 2467
Two-Two-Four 944
Two Unfortunate Orphans 111
Two Waltzes in C 3379
Two Wise Cops 2455
Two Wishes 494
Two Years in the Making 1614
Twobly's Thingamajig 4061
Twos 3937
Two's Company 2687, 4289
Two's Company, Three's a Crowd 2605, 2684
Two's Company — Three's None 1178
Tyger, Tyger 793
Tyler M'Boy 1341
Tyler My Boy 411
Typewriter Song, The 3443
Typewriting 1067
Typical American Consumer 2676
Typical New Yorkers 3548
Typical Opening Chorus, The 2696
Typical People 62
Typical Self-Made American 4178
Typical Self-Made American, A 4179
Typical Topical Tunes 3246
Typical Tune of Zanzibar, A 1165
Typically English 4160
Typische Deutsche 4160
Tyrolean Maid 4187
Tyup 4529
Tzi Vus Darf Ich Zein Du? (Why Do I Have to Be Here?) 1279
Tzotskele (My Darling) 898

U

U Dearie 3265
U Mandela Uthayihlome 4438
U.N. 3716
U.N.C.O.U.P.L.E.D. 4138
U.S.A. Limited, The 106
U.S. Grant 3558
U.S. Versus U.S.S.R. 721
Uber'n Grossen Teich 1409
Uciekali 2846
Ufil Ubotha (chant) 4438
Ugg-a-Wugg 3453
Ugga-Da-Bugga-Da-Boo 1435
Ugly Duckling, The 1741
Ugly, Ugly Gal 1729
Uh-Huh 2754
Uh-huh, Oh, Yeah! 483
Uh-Oh! 157, 4435
Uh-Uh! 317
Uking the Uke 1780
Ukulele Blues 3512
Ukulele Lady 4429
Ukulele Lorelei 4300
Ulterior Motive 1046
Ultivac 2887
Ultra Peacock Strut, The 3133
Ulysses Africanus 4504
Ulysses Soliloquy 1600
Um-Um-Da-Da 4429
Umble 869
Umbrella Man, The 194
Ump-Pom Man, The 2209
Umpire Is a Most Unhappy Man, The 4506
Umpty Umpty Aye 205
Un Bon Garcon 2637
Un Consomme 453
Un, Deux, Trois 4401
Un Mariage Sous Louis XV 168
Un Mazzo di Fiori 2464
Un Mejor Dia Vendra 4744
Un Oncore 2111
Un Peu D'Amour 2363
'Un' Song, The 4690
Un Sourire 3218
Un Voyage Cook 2723
Una 1544
Una a Dieci 3879
Unaccustomed As I Am 657, 1448, 1655, 1836, 4583
Unafraid 1310
Unbirthday Song 56
"Unborn" Sequence 4732

Unchained Melody 146
Uncle Bill 4756
Uncle Billy 1872
Uncle Chris 2064
Uncle Dan Song, The 3368
Uncle George 183
Uncle Harry 3235, 3339
Uncle John Tappit 4404
Uncle Martin 2954
Uncle Sam Is Santa Claus to the World 4837
Uncle Sam Land 2314
Uncle Sam Needs a "Man Who Can Take It" 125
Uncle Sam Rag, The 3687
Uncle Sam Wants Who? 1436
Uncle Sam's Best Girl 4387
Uncle Sam's Boys in Blue 1264
Uncle Sam's Children (inst.) 683
Uncle Sam's Lullaby 4772
Uncle Sam's Marines 2159
Uncle Says I Mustn't, So I Won't 2667
Uncle Tom 4004
Uncle Tom's Cabin 1654, 4429
Uncle Tom's Cabin Blues 4429
Uncrowned Queen of Californiay 2565
Undaunted 3667
Under-Takers' Frolic, The 604
Undecided Blues, The 3617
Undeniably Mine 1841
Under a Blanket in a Folding Bed 2517
Under a Gay Sombrero 4599
Under a One-Man Top 4241
Under a Parasol 200
Under a Pretty Hat 1923
Under a Spell 3288, 3543, 3734
Under a Tree 2339
Under and Over Forty 4115
Under Any Old Flag at All 4277
'Under Fire' Dance, The 804
Under Grecian Skies 208
Under My Skin 1191
Under My Umbrella 971, 3252, 4826
Under Secretary 3530
Under the Allworthy Road 4405
Under the Bamboo Tree 2805, 1537, 3820
Under the Boardwalk Ballet (dance) 98
Under the Cinnamon Tree 2872
Under the Clock at the Astor 418
Under the Clover Moon 3149
Under the Deodar 906
Under the Double Eagle 964
Under the Dream Tree 3455
Under the Dress 3972
Under the Eastern Moon 60
Under the Elms at New Haven 1926
Under the Goo-Goo Tree 3488
Under the Honeymoon 1335, 2978
Under the Jessamine 2412
Under the Jungle Moon 443, 3748
Under the Linden 1613
Under the Linden Tree 2498
Under the Love Tree 4589
Under the Midsummer Moon 1722
Under the Mistletoe 3848
Under the Mistletoe Bough 2964
Under the Moon 2937, 981
Under the Mulberry Tree 1295
Under the Oriental Moon 4787
Under the Pump 1080
Under the Ragtime Flag 1738
Under the Red Robe 3680
Under the Roller Coaster 3718
Under the Sea 671, 683, 2749, 4809
Under the Shade of Our Lovely Umbrellas 3488
Under the Shade of the Sheltering Palms 1313
Under the Sky 4212
Under the Sleeping Volcano 4432
Under the Spell 4106
Under the Sun 2245, 3088
Under the Sunset Tree 989
Under the Tree 681
Under the Willow Tree 3401
Under the Wisteria 2834
Under the Yum Yum Tree 1526
Under Thy Rose Wreathed Window 1188
Under Wicket 1768
(Let Me Walk) Under Your Umbrella 1393
Underneath a Big Umbrella 2574
Underneath a Parasol 1920
Underneath a Parasol with You 4762
Underneath a Pretty Hat 3405
Underneath It All 2874
Underneath the Arches 4027
Underneath the Honey Moon 638
Underneath the Japanese Moon 4808
Underneath the Marquee 1601
Underneath the Palms 3405
Underneath the Wabash Moon 3796
Undersea Ballet 1779
Understand Don't You See, Don't You Know 3887
Understand It 1216
Understudies 1690
Understudy, The 1892
Understudy Dance Specialty, The 1965
Undertow 635
Underworld, The (Apache Dance) (inst.) 3626
Undiscovered Son, The 3806
Undo 1116
Undressing Dance, The 1809
Undressing Girls with My Eyes 4038
Une Nuit de Noces 3237
Une Nuit Paris 3525
Uneasy Lies the Head 23
Unemployed, The 3313
Unemployment 1412
Unemployment Line 407
Unescorted Women 3305
Unexpected Love 962
Unexpected Song 4068
Unexpectedly 298
Unfair 1280

Unfinished Song, An 4515
Unfinished Song 1262
Unfinished Symphony 3409
Unfortunate Rose 3388
Ungrateful 1046
Unhappiness Remembering 4615
Unhappy 4811
Unhappy Bella 2633
UNICEF Marching Song 751
Uniform, The (dance) 383
Uniform 2032
Uniform, The 213
Uniform 972
Union Label 2809
Union Maid 4740
Union Square 1054, 2444
United Nation's Rag, The 108
United We Stand 2848
Universal Good 630
Universal Lullaby 1587
Unknown 21, 94, 165, 253, 269, 339, 374, 423, 563, 596, 736, 904, 1046, 1066, 1075, 1219, 1391, 1506, 1534, 1539, 1565, 831, 1620, 1827, 1871, 2058, 2061, 2146, 3456, 2348, 2378, 2407, 2527, 2619, 2624, 2698, 2931, 2958, 3012, 3048, 3063, 3131, 4608, 3689, 3219, 3248, 3580, 3357, 4439, 2401, 3147, 3703, 1193, 3363, 1105, 3919, 3974, 4075, 4176, 4275, 4283, 4313, 4586, 4629, 4667, 4696, 4796, 2540
Unlearnable Lesson, The 2830
Unlikely Lovers 1234
Unlucky in Love 1971, 3009
Unlucky Pierre 3074
Unmistakable Sign 868
Unnecessary Town 2484
Uno 1587
Unofficial Spokesman, The 4178, 4179
unproduced screenplay 1699
Unpromised 649
Unreconstructed Rebel, The 1037
Unrepentant Butterfly, The 1199
Unrequited Love 1962, 3602
Unrequited Love March 4627
Unrequited Love or the Storm 3013
Unseen Buds 2433
Unseen Hands 4469
Unsuspecting Hearts 661
Untalented Relative, The 3110
Unter Den Linden, in Germany 2566
Until Eternity 4163
Until I Fell in Love with You 4158
Until My Luck Comes Rolling Along 2533
Until the Real Thing Comes Along 1813, 4743
Until Then 295
Until Today 2248
Until Tomorrow Night 4020
Until Tonight 3
Until We Kiss 3385
Until We Meet Again 4735
Until You Are Caught 4199
Until You Get Somebody Else 4683
Until You Say Goodbye 4378
Until You Say Yes 3821
Until You're Recognized 367
Untitled 3016
Untitled Love Story 4232
Untitled Waltz 1690
Unto Your Heart 3012
Untogether Cinderella 3825
Untrue Pigeon, The 3806
Unusual Way 3171
Unveil My Eyes 1232
Unveiled Threat, The 101
Unveiling of a Broadway Girl, The 1584
Unveiling of the Statue, The 1570
Unworthy of Your Love 212
Unzer Amerika 4331
Up 223, 4558
Up Above the Stars 1482
Up Against It 4518, 4518
Up Among the Chimney Pots 3172
Up and At 'Em!, on to Vict'ry 2444
Up and Down 277, 3876, 4630
Up and Down the Boardwalk 522, 4650
Up and Down, Over the Town (Opening Chorus Act II) 3313
Up Chickamauga Hill 2228
Up from the Gutter 4524
Up Front Behind 2173
Up in a Balloon 561, 1650
Up in Heaven 3418
Up in Jessica's Room 1879
Up in Mabel's Room 4526
Up in My Room 4262
Up in Smoke 490, 2014
Up in the Air 1823
Up in the Air, Boys 4527
Up in the Clouds 1297, 4528
Up in the Elevated Railway 1548
Up in the Sky 1989
Up Is a Long, Long Climb 2216
"Up" Number, The 2535
Up on the Roof 3744
Up on Your Toes 1819
Up Pops the Devil 1207
Up She Goes 4529
Up the Creek 216
Up the Hill There 871
Up the Ladder 869
Up the Line John Henry 69
Up the Line, John Henry 2176
Up the Revolution 4796
Up There 1873, 3295
Up-to-Date Policeman, The 509
Up-To-Date Troubador, The 1199
Up-To-Date Tune, An 378
Up to His Old Tricks 2687
Up to His Old Tricks Again 2453
Up to My Elbows 4289
Up to My Tits in Water 3901
Up to the Moon 4625

Up-Town Down-Town 568
Up, Up, Up 2677
Up! Up! Up! in My Aeroplane 4803
Up Where the Joke's Goin' On 4516
Up Where the People Are (dance) 4516
Up with the Stars 4529
Up Your Ante 3551
Update 4635
Upon a Moonlight Night in May 4792
Upon Our Little Farm 2345
Upon the Hudson Shore (Give Me the Hudson Shore) 1963
Upon the Stage 1540
Upper Broadway After Dark 3745
Upper Crust, The 1582
Upper East Side Blues 2676
Ups-a-Daisy 4532
Ups and Downs 203, 3078
Upsala 2379
Upsi-Daisy 1111
Upside Down 258, 2614
Upside Down Song, The 2089
Upside Down Thief, The 1094
Upstairs 3603
Upstairs at O'Neal's 4533
Upstairs at the Downstairs 157
Upstairs at the Downstairs Waltz 4268
Upstairs-Downstairs 4659
Upstairsy 3696
Uptown 3644
Uptown Downtown 1329
Uptown Dreamer's Express 4171
Uptown, Downtown 2764
Urban Renewal 2134
Urga 1214
Uriti 519
Uriti Kitchen (dance) 519
Us on a Bus 4204
Us Two 597, 3217
Uschi 4795
Use My Name 2153
Use of French, Red Is the Wine, The 2938
Use Your Imagination 1638, 3326
Use Your Noggin 4588
Use Your Own Judgment 3842, 4211
Used to Me 1496
Useful 170
Useful Phrases 3815
Useless Song 369, 4369
Usher 2827
Usher from the Mezzanine, The 1227
Us-ness of We, The 2742
Usual Opening Chorus, The 545
Uthando Luphelile (Love Is Lost, Love Is Gone) 2147
Utopia 1916, 4491
Utopia Ballet 4536
Utterly Delicious 3439
Utterly Lovely 318
Uyamemeza Ungoma 3836

V

V.I.P. 1061
V.I.P's: Very Influential Politicos 3530
Va Bene 223
Va-Va-Va-Vee (for Victory) 4561
Vacancy 1857
Vacant Lot Ballet 3934
Vacation 3608
Vacation Days 591, 904
Vacation in the Store 95
Vadinho Is Gone 3838
Vagabond King 4539
Vagabond Song, The 1062
Vagabond Student 3186
Vaginal Angel 264
Vagrant Fancies 1455
Vagrant Stream, The 3774
Vagrants of Erin, The 516
Vale of Dreaming, The 2732
Valencia 1678
Valentine 2356
Valentine for Beecher, A 3305
Valentine Song 337
Valentines (inst.) 2534
Valentine's Day 4540
Valley of Beautiful Dreams, The 3613
Valley of Dreams, The 4637
Valley of Hokus-Po, The 4738
Valley of Jewels 177
Valley of the Nile 3241
Valmouth 4541, 4541
Valparaiso 3962
Val's Ballad 1575
Vals de Espana 2679
Valse 101, 336
Valse (Billet Doux) 1230
Valse 1537
Valse Anglaise 920
Valse au L'Air 4464
Valse Ballet 1312
Valse du Salon 4378
Valse Duet 3170
Valse Julian 1247
Valse Lente 3976
Valse Mauve 1912 (inst.) 3432
Valse Milieu 2150
Value 157
Vamos a Bailar 4861
Vamp a Little Lady (The Vamp) 3246
Vamp Your Man 2594
Vampire Dance 1307, 2939
Vampire Dance (inst.) 4269
Vampire Maid, The 3222
Vamps, The 4542
Van Buren 2018
Vanderbilt Cup Gallop 4544
Vanessa 220
Vaniteaser 1134

Vanities 3426
Vanity 1536, 2340
Vanity Box, The 3500
Vanity of Human Wishes 284
Variations on a Theme By Bird 269
Variety 666, 3036, 3043, 2896
Variety Is the Spice of Life 4283
Variety Is the Spice of Life, Life, Life 858
Various Sherlock Holmes stories 270
Varsity Bug, The 3500
Varsity Drag, The 1628
Varsovienne 4479
Vase of Flowers, A 143
Vasectomy 4635
Vashti's Farewell 2811
Vatican Rag, The 4412
Vaudeville 485, 2224
Vaudeville Is Back 3594
Vaudeville King, The 4478
Vaudeville, Kosher Style 1279
Vaudeville Pets from the West, The 688
Ve Don't Like It 4340
I've Got Money in the Bank 2761
Ve Vas Germans 613
Veasy Drew 47
Vedi la Vita 3938
Vee Zenen Meine Zibn Gute Yor (Where Are My Seven Good Years) 1279
Vegas Revisited 1341
Vegetable Party, The 2041
Vegetable Reggie 705
Vein of Gold, The 490
Velasquez 4341
Velcome to Shul 4325
Velvet Foot 3134
Velvet Lady 4547
Velvet Paws 134
Velvet's Vest 2284
Velvoota Cheese Jingle 1155
Ven I Valse 3113
Ven Sis Du Lieve 4463
Vendors 1038
Vendors' Calls 530
Vendor's Song 279
Vendor's Song (Lawn as White as Driven Snow) 4715
Vendor's Song 2909
Venedig, Fair Venedig 4473
Venetia 965, 3981
Venetian 969
Venetian Carnival, The 965
Venetian Glass 720
Venetian Nights 1131, 1460
Venetian Serenade 188
Venetian Skies 1312
Venetian Wedding Moon 1460
Venezia 2073
Venezia and Her Three Lovers (ballet) 3, 3381
Vengeance 635
Vengeance (Ballet) 2357
Vengeance 2732, 4696, 2654
Vengeance of Valdez 3318
Venice 3131
Venice Sings to One and All 2397
Ventriloquism 1824
Ventriloquist, The 2364
Ventriloquist 3955
Ventriloquist and Dummy 3162
Venulia, The 3601
Venus and Adonis Suite 3909
Venus and I Are Pals 4228
Venus Calls and I'll Obey 4228
Venus de Milo 2222
Venus, Goddess of Love 698
Venus in Ozone Heights (Ballet) 3301
Venus In Seide 4550
Venus Waltz, The 3251
Venus Was a Modest Goddess 3301
Ver Der Ershter Vet Lakhn (Who Will Laugh First?) 4342
Vera Violetta 4553, 4553
Veranda, The (inst.) 3691
Veranda's Toe 2551
Verandah Waltz, The 935
Verb to Love, A 2546
Verb to Love (I Love You), The 2934
Verbal Abuse 533
Verdi Duo (inst.) 4798
Verdict, The 451, 2472
Verdict Finale, The 1652
Verily, Merrily 2914
Verily, Verily 1282
Veritable Work of Art, A 270
Vermicelli - Minestrone 2464
Vernon 2776
Vernon Duccini (inst.) 4798
Veronica Takes Over 3217
Veronique 3279, 4554
Verrazano Narrows Bridge 157
Versailles 969, 1923, 2843
Versatile DaVincis, The 490
Vertigo 90
Very 3482
Very Best Week of Our Lives, The 4020
Very Careful, If You Please 2938
Very Charming Spot, A 3823
Very Close to Wonderful 4588
Very Far Away 3668
Very First Girl, The 4659
Very First Time, The 4115
Very Fortunate Man, A 2551
Very Full and Productive Day, A 3439
Very Good Friends of Mine 1556
Very Little Thing, A 30
Very Little Time for Loving Nowadays 2761
Very Lonely King, A 1769
Very Merry Christmas, A 752
Very Much in Love 4186
Very Necessary You, The 657
Very Next Girl I See, The 487

Very Next Man, The 1280
Very Nice Man, A 656
Very Nice Prince, A 2143
Very Nice Sermon, Parson Potter, A 255
Very Proper Town, A 3234
Very Silly Story, A 3091
Very Simple 2626
Very Soft Shoes 3288
Very Special Day, A 2797
Very Truly Yours 2065
Very, Very 3301
Very, Very Lucky Lady 2626
Very, Very, Very 1132
Very Well Then 4094, 4666
Very Young Man, A 3671
Vesper Bell 4357
Vesper Bells 1021
Vespers 4710
Vet 4019
Veterinarian 674
Vi Shver S'iz Tsu Sheydn (How Hard to Leave Old Homes) 1609
Vi, Vi! 4044
Via Galactica 4558
Vicious Circle 1892
Vicki Lawrence 1575
Victim Dream 169
Victim of Normality 3901
Victim of the Talkies 4823
Victims of the Darkness 4127
Victims of the Past 159
Victims of Voodoo Drums 444
Victor/Victoria 4560, 4560
Victoria 1768, 2047, 4332
Victoria and Albert Waltz, The (inst.) 2047
Victoria Trio, The 1233
Victoria Variations 4560
Victoria's Banner 3305
Victorious 3507
Victor's Announcement 139
Victor's Request 299
Victory 808, 2949, 4838
Victory Begins at Home 2175
Victory Garden 2026, 4467
Victory Kicks 2307
Victory March, The 4539
Victory Song 231
Victory Symphony, Eight to the Bar 2653
Victory to the Bold 93
Vidi Na Croce 139
Vienna 4590
Vienna Girls 2292
Vienna Gossip 4365
Vienna, How D'Ye Do? 473
Vienna Roll 1538
View from My Window, The 1002
View from the Top, A 3722
Vigil 4034
Vigilantes, The 3679
Vignettes 1456, 2027
Vile Thing 3853
Vilia 2836, 2838
Villa on a Hill 1649
Villa Primrose 3251
Village Band, The 3426
Village Called Hollywood, A 1048
Village Gossip, The 3103
Village Maid, The 3749
Village of Chelm 2422
Village Recruits, The 2632
Villain Always Gets It, The 145
Villain Dance (inst.) 3949
Villain Still Pursued Her, The 357, 4655
Villains Aren't Bad Anymore 4611
Villain's Credo Tango, The 2541
Villains in the Play 4759
Villainy 4696
Villainy Is the Matter 869
Vineyards of Manhattan, The (inst.) 1657
Vintage, The 1602
Vintage Chorus 2622
Violent Crime 3136
Violet 736
Violet in Broadway's Garden, A 1250
Violet Ray 4844
Violets 2506, 2622, 3154
Violets and Silverbells 3928
Violetta Mia 1518
Violin and Cello 1177
Violin in the Graveyard 3463
Violin Song, The 1334
Violincello, The 2889
Violins from Nowhere 2850
Violins Over Broadway 4567
Viper's Drag, The (The Reefer Song) 39
Virgin of Velez-Jermano, The 4522
Virgin Polka, The 1924
Virginia 3650
Virginia (Don't Go too Far) 4241
Virginia 4569, 1087
Virginia Clay 4648
Virginia Hoe Down 1476
Virginia Rag 4487
Virginia Reel 1616
Virginia Rose 4630
Virginia Skedaddle 175
Virginia Town 4050
Virgins of the Sun 1244
Virgins Wrapped in Cellophane 3002
Virtual Sexuality 484
Virtue Is Its Own Reward 2306, 2923
Virtue Wins the Day 4781
Virtue, Arrivederci 519
Virtuoso, The 1702
Virtuosos Great Are We 1266
Virtuous Gardener, The 402
Vis-a-vis 3910
Vision, A (The Girl I Can't Forget) 2377
Vision, The 3064
Vision 3690

Vision Ballet (inst.) 612
Vision of Hassan, A 1460
Vision of the Future, A 3995
Vision Scene 2813
Vision Song, The (Love Is a Pilgrim) 1199
Vision Song 2655
Visions and Voices 1634
Visions of Love 2893
Visions of the Fireside 2385
Visions on Your Television Screen 4273
Visions That Pass in the Night 3443
Visit, A 2333
Visit, The 4657
Visit from De Guiche 949
Visit Looney Park 3701
Visit Panama 3359
Visiting Hours 1002
Visiting Rights 3902
Visitors, The 4529
Visitors Ashore 3103
Vitabelle 2523
Vitality 1467
Vite, Vite, Vite 2432
Viva a Vida 3838
Viva Amigos 4571
Viva Italia 376
Viva la Buck 2057
Viva la Duel 2057
Viva la Liberte 4014
Viva la Toreador 4056
Viva the Gay Fiesta 4754
Viva the Women! 2615
Viva Villa 4609
Viva Villa! 4609
Viva Vitamins 2397
Vivaldi 4272
Vivandiere, The 1177
Vivat! Vivat Regina! 2047
Vive for Geneva 1973
Vive la Boheme! (The Latin Quarter) 4115
Vive La Bohemia 694
Vive La Canadienne 3772
Vive La Difference 3301, 4579
Vive la Difference 4862
Vive la France! 1851
Vive la Virtue 1745
"Vive Le Demimonde" 2992
Vive le Marquis 1193
Vive Paulette 4543
Vive Pichon 2751
Vive the USA 2705
Vivian Beaumont Song 3440
Vivianne the Vivandiere 252
Vivian's Reverie 180
Vivienne 3382
Vo-De-O-Do-Do 3342
Vodka (Don't Give Me Vodka) 4077
Vodka, Vodka! 161
Voice at the End of the Line, The 4283
Voice Calling Me, A 2546
Voice for It, The 4735
Voice Foretold, A 1636
Voice I Can't Forget, The 1121
Voice in My Heart, The 2533
Voice in the Dark, A 3117
Voice of Bagdad, The 97
Voice of God, The 3490
Voice of Love, The 2931
Voice of Love, The (Cellini's Love Song) 1283
Voice of Nature, The 2286
Voice of Paris, The 1199
Voice of the City 1617
Voice of the High Sierras 1182
Voice of the Violet, The 3267
Voice of the World, The 202
Voice of Tomorrow, The 4316
Voice Was Heard Wailing, A 755
Voice with a Smile Wins, The 3222
Voices 1012, 139
Voices from Home 3575
Voices of the Children 778
Voila 273
Volcano Song, The 2539
Volga Boat Song 710
Volpone 1373
Volunteer Fireman Picnic (For Sweet Charity) (The Only Pair I've Got) 4270
Volunteer Fireman, The 1095
Volunteers, The 2745, 2844
Volunteers 2986
Voo Doo Pageant (inst.) 444
Voodoo 888, 3814, 4678
Voodoo Hagamin & Hamid 4648
Voodoo Man 2180
Voodoo Night in Hotchkiss Corners 4527
Voodoo of the Zulu Isle 3148
Vote for Crane 2100
Vote for Lincoln 4785
Votes for Women 3024
Voting Blues 454
Voulez-Vous 598
Voulez Vous, May I Have the Next Waltz, Mrs. Yiffnif 2809
Vous Etes Jolie 2538
Voyageur's Song 2937
Voyeur As Conscience 1358
Vu Nemt Men Parnose? (How Do I Make a Living?) 1609

W.C. Fields, His Follies and Fortunes 4577
W*O*L*D 2470
Wabash 4-7473 3941
Wabash Cannonball (inst.) 4390
WAC Hymn, The 3460, 4578
Wad-D'ya-Say We Steal Away? 1965
Wade in the Water 612, 4460

Wading 336
Wading We Go 2506
Wages of Sin, The 3070, 3664
Wagon Wheels 4824
Wah-Wah 3796
Wah Wah Wah 1116
Wahoo! 4595
Waika Kiki Blues 2462
Waikiki 3752
Waikiki, I Hear You Calling Me 2706
Wail of a Debutante 4104
Wail of the Reefer Man, The 877
Wail of the Tale of the Long, Long Trail, The 579
Wailing Wall 426
Wait 4089, 4233
Wait a Bit 3084
Wait a Bit, Susie 3569
Wait a Little While 3653
Wait and See 718, 1282, 4168, 2654
Wait, Baby, Wait 2965
Wait for Me 2574, 650, 4689
Wait for Me Marlene 3330
Wait for the Big Gate of Lover's Lane 2457
Wait for the Happy Ending 3005
Wait for the Moon 1690
Wait for the Wagon 4390
Wait for Tomorrow 3536
Wait 'Til It Dawns 3272
Wait 'Til My Bobby Gets Home 2427
Wait 'Til We're Sixty-Five 3274
Wait 'til You See My Baby do the Charleston 3297
Wait Till After the Wedding 2551
Wait Till I Get You on Your Own 4703
Wait Till the Cows Come Home 2184
Wait Till the Silver Moon Rolls By 4742
Wait 'Till the Sun Shines Nellie 1897
Wait Till the Sun Shines Nellie 2415
Wait Till To-morrow 2430
Wait Till You See Her 601, 2677
Wait Till You See Me in the Morning 213, 4586
Wait Till You See New York 664
Wait Until It's Bedtime 4581
Wait Until My Ship Comes In 487
Wait Until You See My Madeline 1686
Waiter Girl, The 185
Waiters 771
Waiters, The 3348, 4777
Waiter's Dance 2870
Waiters V. Waitresses 1453
Waitin' 2000
Waitin' at the Station 2165
Waitin' for Ann 589
Waitin' for My Dearie 530
Waitin' for the Evening Train 2201
Waitin' for the Robert E. Lee 2415
Waitin' on the Women 760
Waitin' Tables 3517
Waiting 142, 583, 2846, 1086, 1427, 2193, 2312, 2590, 2767, 3162, 755, 3717, 4379, 4405, 4016
Waiting All the Time for You 2780
Waiting and the Wedding 1972
Waiting Around the Corner 3245
Waiting at the Church 3952
Waiting for a Certain Girl 4115
Waiting for Life 3285
Waiting for Me 2938, 4490
Waiting for Something 3157
Waiting for the Bride 4250
Waiting for the Bus of Life 2477
Waiting for the Curtain 3561
Waiting for the Girls Upstairs 1329
Waiting for the Leaves to Fall (She Was Poor) 1202
Waiting for the Light to Shine 394
Waiting for the Men 3831
Waiting for the Moon to Shine 30
Waiting for the Ride 4666
Waiting for the Robert E. Lee 1531
Waiting for the Sun to Come Out 4248
Waiting for the Train (Florida) 4392
Waiting for the Whistle to Blow 3965
Waiting for This 2373
Waiting for Trolley Cars to Pass 1342
Waiting for You 147, 1244
(I Was) Waiting for You 2057
Waiting for You 2491, 2698, 2986
Waiting in a Garden 595
Waiting in a Queue 4341
Waiting in the Garden 882
Waiting in the Wings 36, 1597, 3080
Waiting Is Over, The 2766
Waiting Song 3814
Waiting, Waiting 1061
Wait'll My Ship Comes In 3950
Wake, The 4366
Wake, Love, Wake 3865
Wake Me Up a Star 3860
Wake Me Up with a Rag 4487
Wake Up 158, 732, 1319, 3848, 4795
Wake Up and Dream 1018, 4581
Wake Up! It's Cake-Walk Day 3087
Wake Up Little Dream Girl 2092
Wake Up Little Hepzibah 4064
Wake Up Little Susie 3739
Wake Up Little Theatre 2797
Wake Up Miss Aida 978
Wake Up, Sleepy Moon 2300
Wake Up Song 3937
Wake Up Song, A 3091
Wake-Up Sun 2173
Wake Up Your Feet 3343
Wake Us with Your Song 747
Wakin' Up the Folks Down Stairs 443
Waking This Morning 3162
Waking Up Sun 1864
Wal, I Swan! (Ebenezer Frye) 4762
Waldo's Song 2542
Waldorf Suite 3039
Walk 3154
Walk Away 2014
Walk Down My Street 4584

Walk Down the Avenue with Me 4742
Walk Him Up the Stairs 3610
Walk in Love 4398
Walk Into Heaven 1662
Walk Into My Heart 149
Walk Like a Sailor 145
Walk, Lordy, Walk 4584
Walk Me Around Through the Village 2275
Walk, Mister, Walk 3578
Walk-on 4186
Walk on Air 614
Walk on By 4193, 261
Walk on Gilded Splinters 1890
Walk On Home 459
Walk Sweet 3913
Walk the Plank 1694
Walk This Way 2232, 4589
Walk Through the Night 973
Walk Thru That Golden Gate 4011
Walk to de Grave 2000
Walk Together 981
Walk Together, Children 691
Walk, Walk, Walk 3679
Walked Right In 3951
Walked Right Out Again 187
Walker Walk, The 2217
Walker's Dancing School 4165
Walkin' 729
Walkin' Along Mindin' My Business 1931
Walkin' in the Rain 1093
Walkin' My Dog on Christopher Street 2681
Walkin' on Air 1251
Walkin' the Dog 2173
Walkin' the Track 2342
Walkin' with Mariah 2089, 2090
Walking 1731
Walking All the Way to Rome 1377
Walking Delegate, The 687
Walking Dogs Around 1489
Walking Down Broadway 1897
Walking Down the Road 3615
Walking Family, The 3348
Walking Happy 4588, 4743
Walking Home with Angeline 2341, 3323
Walking Home with Josie 773
Walking in Space 1717
Walking in Strange New Places 4343
Walking in the Sunshine 4019
Walking in the World 2618
Walking Music Store, The 2292
Walking My Baby Back Home 3528
Walking on a Wire 2760
Walking on Air 4765
Walking on the Lake 3087
Walking Papers 16
Walking the Deck 3822
Walking the Dog 4810
Walking Tour, The 3085
Walking with Miss Harkness 924
Walking with Peninnah 3863
Walking with You 300, 3409
Walks 2885
Wall Song, The 4707
Wall Street 956
Wall Street Blues 2071
Wall Street Hoedown 2014
Wall Street Reel 3110
Wall Street Zoo 1756, 3434
Walla Walla 1314
Walla Walla Boola, The 1564
Wallflow'r Sweet 3996
Wallflower 862, 3718, 3783
Wallowing in the Mire 3724
Wallpaper 1082
Walpole Band, The 3425
Walrus and the Carpenter, The 54, 56
Walt's Truth 3476
Walter Kerr 2913
Walter Mitty March, The 3863
Waltz, The 361
Waltz 1121, 1679, 2835
Waltz (inst.) 2102
Waltz 2877, 3515, 2509, 3570, 3712, 3729, 4090, 4823
Waltz and Can-Can (dance) 1817
Waltz and Polka 3864
Waltz and Two-Step 3085
Waltz Aviation 4644
Waltz Away the Night 324
Waltz Ballet 1275
Waltz Continental 4550
Waltz Divine 1980
Waltz Down the Aisle 163, 2252
Waltz-Duet 3778
Waltz Duet, The 1243
Waltz Ensemble 4188
Waltz Entrancing 93
Waltz Eternal 4075
Waltz Fantasies 1352
Waltz Fantasy (inst.) 4798
Waltz for a Ball (inst.) 759
Waltz for Christmas, A (inst.) 928
Waltz for Eva and Che 1211
Waltz for Mollie—Never Even Touched Me 4703
Waltz for Two Balloons, A 1002
Waltz from Nine (inst.) 3171
Waltz I Heard in a Dream, The 3386
Waltz in Blue 1658
Waltz Interlude 3064
Waltz It Should Be, A 3778
Waltz Lesson, The (That's the Waltz for Me) 2334
Waltz Me Around Again Willie 1910, 2885
Waltz Me Around Again, Willie 4390
Waltz Me Around and Around in the Old Ball Room 1405
Waltz Me Away with You Dearie 2978
Waltz Me to the Altar, Walter 2448
Waltz of Lise's Childhood 169
Waltz of Long Ago, The 3008
Waltz of Love, The 4667

Waltz of Memory, The 2162
Waltz of My Heart 972
Waltz of My Heart's Desire 2385
Waltz of the Cameleopard, The 1086
Waltz of the Mazy 1627
Waltz of the Season 473
Waltz of the Toreadors, The 4592, 3377
Waltz of the Wild, The 4687
Waltz Refrain, The 2131
Waltz Reve d'Amour 2209
Waltz Scream, The 4381
Waltz Serenade 1213
Waltz Song 186, 3772, 3778
Waltz Specialty 387
Waltz that Brought You Back to Me, The 1481
Waltz That Is Fashioned for Love, A 4550
Waltz Time 2378
Waltz Time Girl, The 3679
Waltz, Waltz, Waltz 3384
Waltz Was Born in Vienna, A 2105, 3823
Waltz Was Made for Lovers, The 4760
Waltz with Me 1271, 4352
Waltz with Me, Lady 1770
Waltz without a Kiss, A 4490
Waltz, You Siren of Melody 2701
Waltzes from Vienna 1680
Waltzing 2335, 3313
Waltzing in the Moonlight 1889
Waltzing in the Shadow 1474
Waltzing in Venice with You 3107
Waltzing Is Passing from Land to Land 3472
Waltzing Lieutenant, The 4804
Waltzing on a Moonbeam 2086
Waltzing Tonight Together 4107
Waltzing Wedding Night 3425
Walzer aus Wien 1680
Wanapoo Bay 2636
Wanda 709, 3424, 3673
Wander Away 4077
Wander Off Nowhere 1900
Wanderer, The 1780, 2784, 3545
Wanderin' 3989
Wanderin' in the Wilderness 3724
Wanderin' Man 992
Wandering Child 3464
Wandering in Dreamland 3796
Wandering Minstrel's Song 1602
Wandering Minstrel, A 1987
Wandering, Walking Every Day 2243
Wanderlust 137, 3714
Wandrin' Child 3542
Wand'rin Star 3347
Wand'ring Heart 3699
Wand'ring Lover 383
Wand'ring Man Am I, A 2861
Wang-Wang Blues 4815
Waning Honeymoon, The 4387
Wanna Buy a Duke? 622
Wanna Get Married 4470
Wanna Lotta Love 642
Wanna Make a Bet? 3110
Wanna Trade 4060
Want a Little More 1532
Want to Be Well 3734
Want to Get Retarded? 4584
Wanta, Hope to Feel at Home 3224
Wanted 4469
Wanted: A Fly (Spider and Fly) 2213
Wanting 3644
Wanting Things 3603
Wanting to Be Wanted 2961
Wanting You 465, 3117, 3533
War 3883
War, The 4537
War Against War 4379
War and Rebellion 2719
War Babies 2801, 3737
War Doll, The 371
War Is a Beautiful Jade 3585
War Is a Science 3506
War Is Bully 1169
War Is Good Business 3876
War Is War 1013
War of 1812 3558
War Ritual 3908
War Song 3455
War Song: So Tell Your Children 1903
War That Ended War, The 4178
War-Time Railroad Ride, A 525
War! War! 919
Warm All Over 2961, 3444
Warm and Willing 4197
Warm Breezes at Twilight 4243
Warm Spot in My Heart, A 4633
Warm Up 842, 2578
Warner Brothers 2969
Warrior's Husband, The 601
Warrior's Song, The 559
Wars' Child 1092
Warsaw! 4769
Wart Song, The 3741
Wartime Wedding 3330
Was Always 269
Was Dog a Doughnut 964
Was Ever a Daintier Infant Seen? 4014
Was I? 4823
Was I Blind 3066
Was I Wazir? 2327
Was Mrs. MacBeth Really Sleeping When She Took That Famous Walk? 3973
Was She Prettier Than I? 1891
Was That Me Talking? 4522
Was There Love 3873
Was Tut Man Nicht Alles Aus Liebe 1334
Wash Me in the Water 3259
Wash, Wash, Wash! (In the Wash) 2844
Washboard Ballet (inst.) 2302
Washed Away 3209
Washing My Memories Away 2305
Washing Song 4311

Washing the World 1717
Washington 1824
Washington D.C. 1556
Washington, D.C. 4058
Washington Is Your Home 3530
Washington Square 201, 208, 1508, 1694, 3161, 4377, 4600
Washington Square Dance 619
Washington Square Long Ago 3133
Washington Squeeze, The 4453
Washington Summers 1169
Washington Twist, The 2983
Washingtons Are Doin' Okay 3108
Washtub Rubsudy 3704
Wasiqoqela Ndawonye 4438
Wasn't He a Terrific Guy 1885
Wasn't I Loved By You 916
Wasn't It a Simply Lovely Wedding? 1290
Wasn't It Beautiful While It Lasted? 1323
Wasn't It Fun 2805
Wasn't It Grand 4486
Wasn't It Great? (It's All Over Now) 3924
Wasn't It Nice? 3179
Wasn't It Romantic? 2535
Wasn't That a Miracle? 1079
Wasp Nest 4447
Wassail 3542
Waste of Rice, A 915
Waste of Time to Plan, A 20
Wasted Life Blues 478
Wasteland 730
Wastin' Our Talents 3782
Wastin' Time 2513
Wasting Away 691
Wasting Time 2490
Watch Dog Theme 374
Watch Me Close 4381
Watch Me Tonight in the Torchlight Parade 2851
Watch My Baby Walk 1134
Watch My Dust 1729
Watch on the Rhine 3450
Watch Out, Angel! 4602
Watch Out for Claggart/Work 406
Watch Out for Me 996
Watch Out for the Baobabs 2539
Watch That First Step 18
Watch the Birdies 2371
Watch the Professor 4293
Watch the Things You Eat 2619
Watch Your Heart 3351
Watch Your Step 1609, 4603
Watch Yourself 3848, 4781
Watching 4431
Watching Her Sleep 494
Watching the Big Parade Go By 3835, 4145
Watching the Blue Smoke Curl 1316
Watching the Clock 3808
Watching the Clouds Roll By 142
Watching the Parade Go By 1337
Watching the Stars Go By 1885
Watching the Wildlife 1770
Watching the World Go By 1272
Watchmen's Chorus 2745
Water and the Flame, The 1195
Water Front Pastime Dance 3723
Water Is Wide, The 4111, 838, 838
Water Lily 3403
Water Movin' Slow 651
Water on the Brain 157
Water Pollution 272
Water Sprite, A 306
Water Through the Trees, The 572
Water Under the Bridge 4703, 4824
Water, Water, Wildflowers 1831
Water Wears Down the Stone, The 4863
Waterfall, The 3724
Waterfaucet Blues 1713
Waterfront Saloon Scene 3949
Watergate Suite 4635
Waterhole, The 143
Watermelon, The 2880
Watermelon and a Pair O' Dice 1624
Watermelon Cry 3989
Watermelon Party 3751
Watermelon Time 2870
Waters of Minnetonka 3677
Waterworks Madrigal, The 4292
Wave a Hand 1441
Wave Crest Waltz, The 4687
Wave the Flag 4297
Wax Works 4802
Way, The 3988
Way Back in 1939 A.D. 4586
Way Back in Dixie Land 3040
Way Back in Old Dubuque 537
Way Back When 4537
Way Down Blues 3934
Way Down East 3397, 3819
Way Down in Barbizon 4189
Way Down in C-U-B-A 3755, 4206
Way Down in Colon Town 3748
Way Down in Jersey 1054, 2897
Way Down in Lil' Old Texas 348
Way Down in Pago Pago 969
Way Down in Pensacola 1783
Way Down in Yucatan 4547
Way Down on Honolulu Bay 1735
Way Down on the Farm 3205
Way Down South 659, 959, 1535, 1986, 3805
Way Down the Ohio 3989
Way Down Town 1625, 3968
Way Down Yonder in New Orleans 4104, 4182
Way for the Ambassador 2937
Way He Arranges His Face, The 45
Way I Got, The 3853
Way I See It, The 1955
Way My Ancestors Went, The 901
Way of a Woman, The 4416
Way of My Father, The 3666

Way of the Heart, The 1804
Way of Trade, The 1526
Way Out in Rainbowland 3252
Way Out West 190, 247
Way Out West in Jersey 3301, 3312
Way Out West Where the East Begins 1931
Way That I Want You, The 851
Way that Walker Walked Away, The 2465
Way Things Are, The 2048
Way Things Are 2941
Way to a Family's Heart, The 3800
Way to a Girlie's Heart, The 1523
Way to a Man's Heart, The 2484
Way to Do Bamboola, The 290
Way to Do It, The 4258
Way to Kiss, The 904, 1292
Way to Win a Girl, The 4604
Way to Your Heart, The 584
Way Up North in Dixie 204
Way Up North in Southland 879
Way We Have in the Army, A 3052
Way You Look Tonight, The 2204, 2372
Way You Manoeuvre, The 1916
Wayfaring Stranger 4390
Ways to Catch a Man 2906
Wayside Flower 2594
Wayside Inn 2731
We 1273, 4108, 4392, 4798
We Ain't Got No Luck 4053
We All Agree on a Pretty Girl 2903
We All Need Love 1890, 3653
We All Play the Grand Piano 3310
We Always Disagree 4795
We Always Get Our Man 1953, 1867
We Always Got Our Man 3151
We Always Work the Public 586
We Are a Band of Gentlemen 3786
We Are a Gallant Regiment 3883
We Are All Dead Men 1715
We Are Alone 3573
We Are Americans Too 4281
We Are China 3164
We Are Cut in Twain 2344
We Are Engaged 4201
We Are Four Actors 4859
We Are Free 2732
We Are Friends 2661
We Are Gay Young American Tars 2500
We Are Going on Our Honeymoon 4837
We Are Going to the Ball All in White 3313
We Are Guerrillas 3836
We Are Here to Sing a Chorus 2837
We Are Laughing Widows 1746
We Are Looking at You 3341
We Are Marching Through the Night 742
We Are Not Married to Each Other 1966
We Are Not Speaking Now 2937
We Are Not Strangers 3806
We Are Nuts 3024
We Are of One Blood 2970
We Are One 2790, 4558
We Are Only Poor Weak Mortals 2667
We Are Only Poor Weak Mortals After All 531
We Are Prom Girls 2287
We Are Puritans 2135
We Are Santa's Elves 3794
We Are So Aesthetic 3547
We Are Starting Off for England 2519
We Are Strolling Peddlers 4161
We Are the Band 175
We Are the Boys in Blue 42
We Are the Bright Lights of Broadway 4837, 4838
We Are the Chorus of the Show 130
We Are the Clerks 1313
We Are the Clouds 3651
We Are the Fixers 2684
We Are the Follies 4812
We Are the Girls in the Chorus 4668
We Are the Heiresses 613
We Are the Horrors of Deadliest Woe (Chorus of Torments) 711
We Are the Laddies (Entrance of College Students) 2724
We Are the Maids of the Merry Merry 4831
We Are the Missionaries 1536
We Are the Modern Musketeers 1911
We Are the Ones 2754
We Are the Priests and Elders 4788
We Are the Principals 3437
We Are the Robbers of the Woods 758
We Are the Royal Canadian Mounties 2452
We Are the Show Girls 1128, 1132
We Are the Waiters 1131
We Are the Way We Are 1426
We Are the Whores 2918
We Are Theodore & Company 4327
We Are Trying to Support Our Only Mother 3951
We Are Very Highly Polished at the Court Don't You Know 252
We Are Visitors Here 2872
We Are Waiting 3821
We Are What We Are 1864, 2360
We Are Women 630
We Bachelor Blades (A Bachelor's Song) 2623
We Beg to Announce 3617
We Beg Your Kind Consideration 1165
We Believe 4398, 1871, 2241
We Belong 2657
We Belong to Old Broadway 4364
We Belong to You (Watashi Mo Kokoro Mo Anatano Monoyo) 1616
We Belong Together 3014
We Belong Up There 1099
We Beseech Thee 1595
We Both Reached for the Gun 723
We Bring Ye Fruits 758
We Came Along Too Late 572
We Came in Chains 578
We Came Together 4124
We Came, We Saw, We Made 'Em! 4709

We Can All Give Love 1441
We Can Be Proud 2268
We Can Do Without the Men 3685
We Can Live on Love (We Haven't Got a Pot to Cook In) 4174
We Can Make It 131, 3718
We Can Take It 2175
We Can Talk to Each Other 4145
We Can Work It Out 4193
We Can't Be As Good As Last Year 1447
We Can't Do without Men 2723
We Can't Get Along without Money 2853
We Can't Go on This Way 3987
We Cannot Let You Go 613
We Chant a Song of Labor 118
We Clearly Requested 148
We Come from Dalmatia 2974
We Come from Maison de la Vere 4453
We Come from Proud Castilian Blood 4754
We Come This Way 357
We Come to the Lively Market Square 4559
We Come to the Theatre 943
We Compare Notes 654
We Could Be Close 4196
We Couldn't We Mustn't We Won't 2539
We Dance 3285, 1739
We Dance at a Wedding 1521
We Deserve Each Other 2797
We Detest a Fiesta 3359
We Did It Before (We'll Do It Again) 4607
We Did It Before, We'll Do It Again 297
We Didn't Ask to Be Born 2051
We Do Not Belong Together 4210
We Do the Best That We Can 4634
We Do the Dirty Work 2525
We Don't All Wear D'Same Size Boots 2682
We Don't Believe It 1307
We Don't Know When-But 1946
We Don't Know Why We Love 93
We Don't Know Why-But 1944
We Don't Matter at All 2163
We Don't Talk Anymore 1597
We Don't Understand Our Children 3818
We Don't Want to Lose You (Your King and Country Want You) 3259
We Doubt You, Papa 2290
We Drink to You J.H. Brody 2432
We Dwell in Our Hearts 757
We Fear You Will Not Do, Lady Wetherell 3652
We Feel Our Man Is Definitely You 304
We Float 3340
We Forgot the Number of the House 4657
We Gave It a Shot 595
We Get the Fee 4108
We Get Up at 8 A.M. 1313
We Give Her Up 4244
We Give Him Time 336
We Go On 4055
We Go to Church on Sunday 3323
We Go to Find the Ring 2035
We Go to Work 1609
We Go Together 1664
We Gon' Jump Up 279
We Got a Deal 2304
We Got a Future 3224
We Got a Good Thing Goin' 105
We Got a Job to Do 3277
We Got Annie 150
We Got Caught 3066
We Got It 3330
We Got Love 1697
We Got Married 159
We Got Optimism 2627
We Got to Get Organized 900
We Got Troubles 2661
We Got Us 1611
We Gotta 3752
We Gotta Find a New Kentucky Home 2446
We Gotta Get Hitched Baby 1917
We Gotta Have More 496
We Gotta Make It Through the Winter 3888
We Gotta Pack 3696
We Gotta Put the Sun Back in the Sky 1813
We Had a Show 3036
We Had to Rehearse 4569
We Have a Date 2447, 3226
We Have a Lot in Common 3004
We Have Come to Invade 3777
We Have Come to See 3828
We Have Dined 3882
We Have Never Met 4319
We Have Nothing to Fear 3558
We Have Only One Life to Live 3308
We Have So Much in Common 4693
We Have Thrown Our Dolls Away 1342
We Have to Die? 3806
We Have to Give You More 4145
We Have to Sing This Song 3181
We Haven't Begun to Live 2097
We Haven't Fought a Battle in Years 2820
We Head for Little Old New York Tomorrow 126
We Hope to Make a Hit 539
We Incorporated 3822
We Is Wonderful 2876
We Just Might 4798
We Just Sing and Dance 2068
We Kiss 1822
We Kiss in a Shadow 2312
We Know a Secret 1727
We Know It's Wrong to Flirt 3578
We Know Reno 1856
We Know, Sweetheart, We Know 1707
We Know What You Want and We Got It 3810
We Know Where We've Been 2941
We Learned a Trade 821
We Like It Over Here 117
We Like the Very Same Things 3846
We Like Things the Way They Are 1010
We Like to Play Numbers 3528
We Like to Whirl 4489

We Live for Another Day 3389
We Live on Park 1860
We Lived Our Lives in the Gap 3280
We Lobby for a Hobby 18
We Love a Conference 1075
We Love an Old Story 3231
We Love Thee, Krispy Krackles 2496
We Love to Go to Work 3523
We Love to Live 1640
We Love Us 4237
We Love You, Conrad! 607
We Loved and We Lost, Goodbye 4133
We Loves Ya, Jimey 3687
We Made a Promise 415
We Made the Doughnuts Over There 4813
We Make a Beautiful Pair 3928
We Make the Show 4010
We Makin' Cash with Sour Mash: No Rickie Tickie No Licq-ie Rag, The 3210
We March You Off in Style 2322
We Marched Away 2964
We May Be Happy Yet 256
We May Not Get Another Chance 398
We Men Ought to Combine 379
We Met in Lover's Lane 1071
We Might Play Tiddle De Winks 1839
We Mind Our Own Business 2388
We Miss Ike 3890
We Must Have a Ball 4004
We Must Hooverize 2619
We Must Not Look 1589
We Must Talk 3197
We Need a Few More Servants 3197
We Need a Little Christmas 2208, 2713
We Need a Man 2228
We Need Him 2163
We Never Sleep 3721
We Never Thought of That 2174
We of Me, The 1222
We Only Remember 1828
We Open in Venice 2331
We Owe Our Life to Duncan Phyfe 520
We Paint Life 4171
We Pirates from Weehawken 3436
We Prize Most the Things We Miss 4667
We Ran Away from School 4424
We Really Ought to Be Married 3488
We Redcoat Soldiers Serve the King 4404
We Rule the Waves 417
We Said We Wouldn't Look Back 3818
We Sail the Seas 367
We Saw a Movie Together 1082
We Saw Everybody There 1993
We Say We'll Do a Thing 2213
We Shall Meet in the Great Hereafter 3209
We Shall Meet to Part, No Never 4123
We Shall Never Be Younger 2331
We Shall Not Be Moved 4390
We Shall Overcome 2203
We Shall Release You 3539
We Shall See What We Shall See 325
We Should Care (Let the Lazy Sun Refuse to Care) 799
We Should Care (Let the Sky Start to Cry) 799
We Should Care 2774
We Should Talk 572
We Sing a Jubilee 1570
We Sing America 3501
We Somehow Feel That You Enjoyed Our Show 213
We Speak the Same Language 64
We Stand for Moderation 4488
We Start Today 253
We Stick to Our Letters 402
We Still Like Ike 619
We Stopped Them on the Marne 1502
We Take It Just Take It from You 2684
We Take Only the Bets 4781
We Take the Town 4609
We Tell Him Just What to Do 3486
We Think You Ought to Stay 2243
We Two 1033, 1603
We Two (Someday) 4561
We Two 3559
We Two in an Aeroplane 2892
We Two Shall Meet Again 771
We Used to Talk Once 3299
We Wanna Be His Paw 3908
We Wanna Star 1695
We Want a Mighty Navy 3982
We Want Our Breakfast 3655
We Want Our Pay 1360
We Want Our Wages 904
We Want the Charleston (Give Us the Charleston) 1488
We Want to Be Simpler 3857
We Want to Laugh 2900
We Want to Make the Laws 2344
We Want You 1297, 4426
We Want You to Be the First Ones to Know 3890
We Welcome Thee 4751
We Were a Wow 2833
We Were Always to Be Married 4048
We Were Born By Chance 4380
We Were Dancing 3576, 147, 3235, 4610
We Were Friends 4398
We Were Here 4515
We Were Here First 4316
We Were in Love 2614
We Were Made to Love 3712
We Were Taught to Walk Demurely 4754
We Were Waltzing 1219
We Who Are About to Die 4416
We Will All Go Together 4412
We Will Be Quick and Do Our Shopping (Opening Chorus) 3322
We Will Fight for Our Land 3836
We Will Gladly Live in a Bungalow 4017
We Will Go, Go to Go-Go 3685
We Will Love and Love Alone 3246

We Will Ramble, You & I, Dear 2854
We Will Rest Awhile 4447
We Will Sail Back Home 335
We Will Survive 2766
We Will Take the Road Together (Finale Act III) 334
We Will Trust You as Our Leader 4447
We Win in Love 2841
We Wish the World a Happy Yule 974
We Wish We Could Turn Back the Clock 4196
We Wish You a Pleasant Journey 473
We Women 2877
We Won't Charleston 3659
We Won't Discuss It 519
We Won't Do a Thing to His Opera 1458
We Won't Forget to Write 2248
We Won't Let It Happen Here 1840
We Won't Take It Back 2137
We Work Away 3591
We'd Imagined a Man 2240
We'd Just Die 2988
We'd Like to Go Back 1412
We'd Like to Thank You 150
We'd Rather Be Right 3501
We'd Rather Dance than Eat 4271
We'd Rather Switch 4611
We'll All Be in Heaven When the Dollar Goes to Hell 207
We'll All Shout Together in the Mornin' 4409
We'll Always Be in Love 2087
We'll Always Stay in Love 991
We'll Barricade Her 1285
We'll Be Right Back After This Message 4533
We'll Be the Same 111
We'll Be There 1776, 3636, 4087
We'll Build a Brand New Bamboo Bungalow 735
We'll Build a Bungalow 1519
We'll Build a Cute Little Nest 2549
We'll Build a Little Home in the U.S.A. 4809
We'll Catch You at Last, Tivolini! 4559
We'll Dance in the Moonlight 357
We'll Dance through Life Together 4429
We'll Dance Till Dawn of Day 1309
We'll Do the Riviera 4529
We'll Drift Along (Opening Chorus Act II) 4784
We'll Drown It in the Bowl 3759
We'll Find a Way 3988
We'll Get Along 3523, 4621
We'll Get Through This 198
We'll Give Him a Home 3908
We'll Go Away Together 4169
We'll Go to the Minstrel Show 4203
We'll Greet Each Tomorrow Together 2567
We'll Have a Birthday Party for You 2657
We'll Have a Kingdom 4692
We'll Have a New Home in the Morning 4271
We'll Have a Party 1010
We'll Have a Wonderful Party 2767
We'll Have Our Good Days 931
We'll Have Tomorrow 2544
We'll Help You Through the Night 2754
We'll Impeach Him 3225
We'll Just Be Two Commuters 2271
We'll Keep 'Em Rolling 4006
We'll Keep the Feast in Pynka Pong 3828
We'll Let the People Decide 952
We'll Live All Over Again 612
We'll Make a Bet 1922
We'll Make a Plot 2464
We'll Make Hay While the Sun Shines 544
We'll March to Victory Under the Stars and Stripes 371
We'll Meet Again 4027
We'll Never Grow Old 4283
We'll Never Make a Lady Out of You 1532
We'll Put Him to Work 1351
We'll See 2422, 2620
We'll See the World Together 1169
We'll Settle Down in Washington Square 579
We'll Sing 4769
We'll Sleep with the Radio On 119
We'll Snoop It Out 1957
We'll Stand and Cheer 2014
We'll Stand By Our Country 396
We'll Stick Together 2085
We'll Still Be Friends 2541
We'll Suffer Together 1993
We'll Swing It Through 3105
We'll Take a Glass Together 223, 1649
We'll Take Care of You All (Refugee Song) 1228
We'll Take Care of You All (The Little Refugees) 1544
We'll the New Master Greet 1199
We're a Comic Opera Company 559
We're a Couple of Misfits 3793, 3794
We're a Couple of Salesmen 3965
We're a Family 1092
We're a Group of Nonentities 2287
We're a Home 1864
We're a Little Family 2033
We're About to Start Big Rehearsin' 3674
We're Alive 2268
We're All A-Worry, All Agog 1419
We're All at Sea 1536
We're All Going on a Honeymoon 1035
We're All Good Fellows 694
We're All in the Bread Line Together 3591
We're All in the Same Boat 1548
We're All in the Swim 3580
We're All of Us Excited (Finale Act II) 3184
We're All of Us Lovely and Young (Chorus of Bridesmaids) 4430
We're All Water 3125
We're Almost There 1660
We're Alone in the World 664
We're Always Glad to See You, But You'd Better Call Again 2623
We're an Able Bodied Crew 2938
We're Back 2177, 33
We're Banking on You Now 2728

We're Betting on You 1233
We're Blase 3020
We're Bold, Bad Bandits All 307
We're Busy Building Boats (Ship Building Song) 4812
We're Butchers and Bakers and Candlestick Makers 3588
We're Calling on Mr. Brooks 1929
We're Civilized 586, 4623
We're Cleaning Up Broadway 3179
We're Clowns 1426
We're Crooks 2900
We're Despicable (Plunderer's March) 2980
We're Dying to Die 722
We're Everywhere 4309
We're for Love 4366
We're Four Jolly Sailor Men 3588
We're Gathered Here 2698
We're Gentlemen 324
We're Getting Away with It 2148
We're Getting on Very Well 1544
We're Goin' Around 4447
We're Going Across 387
We're Going Away 584
We're Going Back 4323
We're Going to Atlanta 900
We're Going to Balance the Budget (Tune Up Bluebird) 2068
We're Going to Be Dramatic 3002
We're Going to Blitz the Blitz 4199
We're Going to Call on the Marquis 1470
We're Going to Fight the Indians 3855
We're Going to Make a Man of You 1285
We're Going to Make Boom-Boom 495
We're Going to Rush the Russians 1187
We're Going to the Country 455
We're Gonna Be All Right (2) 1060
We're Gonna Be All Right (1) 1060
We're Gonna Be All Right 3967
We're Gonna Do It Good 4127
We're Gonna Have a Baby 2307
We're Gonna Have a Good Time 4788
We're Gonna Have a Wedding 1676
We're Gonna Have Fun 3120
We're Gonna Howl Tonight 974
We're Gonna Live It Together 3871
We're Gonna Love It 900
We're Gonna Make History 362
We're Gonna Make It (After All) 2427
We're Gonna Raise Hell (Finaletto Scene 1) 4118
We're Gonna See the Voodoo Queen 2750
We're Gonna Turn Off Your Juice 2702
We're Gonna Turn On Freedom 415
We're Gonna Win 3273, 2018
We're Gonna Work It Out 4727
We're Gymnastic 4212
We're Having a Baby, My Baby and Me 297
We're Having a Party 2661
We're Having Our Fling 532
We're Heading for a Wedding 4695
We're Here 691, 4790
We're Here Because 2376
We're Holding Hands 1386
We're Hollandaise 2770
We're Home 4270
We're Identical 831, 524
We're in a Race 3371
We're in a Salad 1914
We're in the Money 1359
We're Jumping Into Something 3617
We're Living in Wartime 3198
We're Looking for a Piano 3818
We're Looking for Marie 1565
We're Looking for Something in Peaches 4203
We're Love 3838
We're Men of Brains 711
We're Needed Here 3368
We're Never Too Particular 2944
We're Not as Bad as We're Painted 4296
We're Not Children 3234
We're Not Going to Take It 4676
We're #1 708
We're Off 870, 1286
We're Off for a Hayride in Mexico 2847
We're Off for Budapest 968
We're Off on a Wonderful Trip 4491
We're Off the Wagon 4586
We're Off to a Wonderful Start 3374
We're Off to Feathermore 2252
We're Off to India 4491
We're Off to Paris 4188
We're Off to the Races 850, 1745
We're on a Shelf in Your Attic 562
We're on Our Way 4555
We're on Our Way to France 4770
We're on Our Way to Hell 2747
We're on the Highway to Heaven 1813
We're on the Map 4476
We're on the Road to Athens 3326
We're Only Here for a Day 2235
We're Only Lovers 1010
We're Only Marking Time 3506
We're Pals 1026
We're Photogenic 1415
We're Rats 1732
We're Recrootin' 1632
We're Regular Army Soldiers 3765
We're Rich 4076
We're Saving Ourselves for Marriage 1059
We're Secret Society Members 1295
We're Selling Sunshine 2615
We're Sharin' Sharon 1441
We're So Happy 1424, 4110
We're Soldiers of the Queen 2977
We're Sorry to Delay You 1080
We're Staying Here 2064
We're Still Friends 2058
We're Still Here 1426
We're Still on the Map 901
We're Strangers Who Sleep Side By Side 2069

We're Supposed to Be 115
We're Sweethearts 728
We're Taking a Trip 3098
We're Taking Over Now 2615
We're Talkin' About Bout Blanco 451
We're Talking Chelm 3937
We're the Berries 443
We're the Cream of Courtly Creatures 3828
We're the Doormen of New York 2024
We're the Famous Impresarios 4630
We're the Gentlemen of the Harem 25
We're the Girls You Can't Forget 3968
We're the Gnomes 4434
We're the Handy Dandy Cops 3357
We're the Jolly Chain Gang 1351
We're the Men 1120
We're the Merry, Merry Chorus O 47
We're the Noble Army 4382
We're the People 400, 2998
We're the Statesmen Great 3591
We're Three of the Four Musketeers 142
We're Today 4584
We're Together 793
We're Tramps Upon Our Way 1351
We're Trarvelin' 731
We're True to the College Days 3437
We're Twenty Million Strong 565
We're Waiting on the Weather 1929
We're Wanted 2750
We're Wild Men 4690
We're Woolly Westerners 917
We'uns from Dixie 2232
We've Been Married Today 1922
We've Been Sent by the President 1868
We've Been Spending the Summer with Our Families 3131
We've Been Taken In 2978
We've Been Through the Mill Together 971
We've Been to Boston Town 3945
We've Been to Europe 3395
We've Chosen You, Lieutenant 2472
We've Come from Court 356
We've Come to Woo the Ladies 351
We've Decided to Stay 3913
We've Done All Right 299
We've Got a Date with Spring 4273
We've Got a Feeling in Our Bones 4536
We've Got a Great Feeling 4303
We've Got a Little Dirty Work to Do 2928
We've Got a Lot to Learn 2848
We've Got an Evening with Jimmy 860
We've Got Connections 1063
We've Got Each Other 3555
We've Got Five Legs Among Us 42
We've Got Him 2829
We've Got It 3869
We've Got Meg 2965
We've Got Something 4378
We've Got Talent 4273
We've Got the British Lion By the Tail 367
We've Got the Song 3990
We've Got the Stage Door Blues 545
We've Got to Build 1582
We've Got to Clean Out the Freezer 3211
We've Got to Find William 4320
We've Got to Get On 3139
We've Got to Put Up with It 3222
We've Got to Win 957
We've Had a Busy Day 1610
We've Had a Grand Old Time 2829
We've Had a Lovely Time, So Long, Good-Bye 513, 4440
We've Had a Stormy Trip 3578
We've Hunted the Wolf in the Forest 3081
We've Just Begun 1600, 3501
We've Never Discovered Him Yet 586
We've Never Missed a Sabbath Yet 1265
We've Never Seen the Sun or Stars 2286
We've Painted All the Morning 2448
We've Travelled Far 2496
We've Won 4676
Weak As a Woman 3585
Weak Little Women (Suffragette) 3268
Weaker Is the Stronger After All, The 2567
Weaker Sex, The 138, 3622
Weakest Point, The 3873
Weaknesses 1321, 3847, 4477, 4530
Wealth 170
Wealth, Beauty and Power 2886
Wealthiest Girl in the Country 2452
Wealthy, Shmelthy, as Long as You're Healthy 4137
Wear a Little Grin (inst.) 1739
Wear Your Sunday Smile 2253
Wearers of the Green 1163
Wearin' the Grin 2479
Wearing of the Blue 868
Wearing of the Green 116
Wearing of the Green, The 191
Weary 1198
Weary Feet 26
Weary Near to Dyin' 1846
Weary Soul 2476
Weather Dance (inst.) 616
Weather Factory in Cloudland 2534
Weather Man 2376
Weather Report 408
Weather Report #1 1700
Weather Song, The 3227
Weather Song 3641
Weather-Vane, The 49
Weather's in Your Eyes, The 2705
Weatherbee's Drug Store 3895
Weave From Your Loom 2884
Weaver of Dreams 579
Weaving My Dreams 4816
Web of Dreams 2180
Wedded Man, A 4609
Wedding, The 169, 3643, 3873, 729, 1092, 1237

Wedding 1281, 1616, 2692
Wedding, The 2864, 2941, 2766
Wedding 3409
Wedding, The 3551, 1470, 3741
Wedding! A Wedding!, A 2219
Wedding Anthem 2474
Wedding Anvils 132
Wedding Ball 3202
Wedding Ballet (dance) 341
Wedding Bed Lies Waiting, The 693
Wedding Bells 20, 765, 1275, 3614
Wedding Bells (Wedding Chorus) 3675
Wedding Bells 3677, 3681
Wedding Bells, The 801
Wedding Bells 284, 2896
Wedding Bells, The 175
Wedding Bells 3958, 4012, 4393, 4547
Wedding Bells Are Calling Me 3193, 4555
Wedding Bells Ring On 1667
Wedding Bells Were Ringing, The 1777
Wedding Bells Won't Ring Tonight 4704
Wedding Blues 3508
Wedding Blues, The 4464
Wedding Bulgar Dance (inst.) 4769
Wedding By Proxy 2816
Wedding By the Sea 3958
Wedding Celebration, The 4157
Wedding Ceremony, The 3197, 3652
Wedding Ceremony 4792
Wedding Chimes 539
Wedding Chorale 2442
Wedding Chorus 2623, 1774
Wedding Conversation 1660
Wedding Dance 400
Wedding Dance, The 693
Wedding Dance 1242, 1265
Wedding Dance (inst.) 2368
Wedding Dance 3781
Wedding Dance (inst.) 3888
Wedding Dance 4773
Wedding Day 792
Wedding Day, The 1570
Wedding Day 981, 3677
Wedding Day in Georgia 3614
Wedding Ensemble 3063, 3883
Wedding Fete, The 1523
Wedding Gifts of Silver 736
Wedding Glide 357
Wedding Glide, The 3395
Wedding Guests 1712
Wedding in the Park 1811
Wedding Is Off, The 832
Wedding Knell, The 4212
Wedding March 767
Wedding March, The 902
Wedding March 1360
Wedding March, The 3778
Wedding March 4354
Wedding March, The 4366
Wedding March (inst.) 4798
Wedding March and Hymn 4590
Wedding Medley 3426
Wedding Night 1966
Wedding Night, The 2766
Wedding Night 4408
Wedding of a Solid Sender, The (dance) 4826
Wedding of Jack and Jill, The 1901
Wedding of Minnie Chimmie and Mr. Jazz, The 1032
Wedding of Mr. and Mrs. Jazz!, The 897
Wedding of Mr. and Mrs. Swing, The 883
Wedding of the Blue and Grey 3205
Wedding of the Blue and the Gray, The 1480
Wedding of the Chafing Dish and the Alcohol Lamp, The 2408
Wedding of the Dancing Doll, The 1631
Wedding of the Flower and the Bee, The 2013
Wedding of the Flowers 3641
Wedding of the Lily and the Rose 4293
Wedding of the Painted Doll 3992
Wedding of the Reuben and the Maid, The 3751
Wedding-of-the-Year Blues 1760
Wedding of the Year, The 4633
Wedding of Words and Music, The 805
Wedding Pantomime 1761
Wedding Parade, The 2238
Wedding Procession (Finale Act I) 3436
Wedding Procession 4429, 4434
Wedding Procession, A (inst.) 4699
Wedding Procession 4773
Wedding Processional 4337
Wedding Reception, The 2198
Wedding Rehearsal, The 2789, 4382, 4437
Wedding Rehearsal 4644
Wedding Ring 4648
Wedding Ring Don't Mean a Thing When You're Married, The 2706
Wedding Scene 1145, 2323, 3719, 4817
Wedding Song 4309, 784
Wedding Song, The 2016
Wedding Song 2132
Wedding Song, A 2407
Wedding Song, The 2484, 3539
Wedding Song 3742, 4368, 4369, 4371
Wedding Song for the Less Well-Off 4370
Wedding Time 3821
Wedding Toast 3339
Wedding Waltz 1694
Wedding Waltz, The 345
Wedding, Wedding 155
Weddings and Funerals 4591
Wedgewood Maid 1460
Wednesday Forum, The 3846
Wednesday Night Hop (inst.) 432
Wee Bit o' Scotch, A 4617
Wee Bit of Lace, A 3791
Wee Bit of Scotch, A 3025
Wee China Rose 738
Wee Copper o' Fife, The 4579
Wee Golden Warrior, The 3702

Wee Highland Mon 4723
Wee Toy 1312
Weeds in the Wind, The 2153
Week End 4320
Week-End in July, A 3254
Weekend, The 690
Weekend 3970
Weekend Affair, A 1453
Weekend at Hareford, A 2798
Weekend Cruise, A (Will You Love Me Monday Morning as You Did on Friday Night?) 2475
Weekend in the Country, A 2536
Weekend Shopping 1697
Weekly Wedding, The 2292
Weenie and Widgee 1613
Weep and You Dance Alone 1763
Weep No More 95
Weep No More, My Baby 3002
Weep No More, My Mammy 2870
Weeping 1116
Weeping Sky, The 3813
Weeping Widow, The 1640
Weeping Willow Tree 1011
Weight of Love, The 4786
Wein, Wein, You're Calling Me 3020
Weird Fun 562
Welcome 599, 757, 4676, 2114, 2201, 3548, 3970, 4737
Welcome a Hero 4732
Welcome America 910
Welcome and Au Revoir 2262
Welcome Banana 3651
Welcome, Bienvenue 275
Welcome Chorus 3437
Welcome Christmas 2015
Welcome Dance 1991
Welcome Fatima 2974
Welcome, Happy Groom 4550
Welcome Hinges 462
Welcome Home 391, 3800, 3487, 1242, 2330, 2355, 533, 1604, 4186, 4623
Welcome Home Again 4785
Welcome Home Miz Adams 4004
Welcome Home with You 3506
Welcome, Honey, to Your Old Plantation Home 2853
Welcome, Jellie Canvas 1021
Welcome, Little One 4659
Welcome Mr. Anderson 2173
Welcome, Mr. Brue 3882
Welcome, Mr. Golden! 3559
Welcome, Official Mother-in-Law 737
Welcome Oloto 2793
Welcome, Otto, Welcome Home 2745
Welcome Song 279
Welcome Song (You're Indian Family) 751
Welcome Song 2511
Welcome the Boys Back to Meadowbridge, Cal. 255
Welcome the Bridegroom 3887
Welcome the Brides 2209
Welcome to a New World 3927
Welcome to a Small Town 916
Welcome to Broadway 2478
Welcome to Brooklyn 3039
Welcome to Concorde 273
Welcome to Greece 3272
Welcome to Havana! 846
Welcome to Hell 2785
Welcome to His Majesty 2341
Welcome to Holiday Inn 3869
Welcome to India 1161
Welcome to Jerry 3359
Welcome to Kafeteria 3587
Welcome to Kanagawa 3340
Welcome to Kindergarten 4
Welcome to L.A. 3643
Welcome to Looneyland 2094
Welcome to Milan 2933
Welcome to My Heart 1792
Welcome to Our Country 1991
Welcome to Paradise 3368
Welcome to Pootzie Van Doyle 1564
Welcome to Prince 4188
Welcome to Princess 356
Welcome to Sherwood 4469
Welcome to Sludgepool 4160
Welcome to Sunvale 4160
Welcome to the Army (Brotherhood of Light) 3088
Welcome to the Bride 4361
Welcome to the Club 4619
Welcome to the Fold 496
Welcome to the Kingdom 4035
Welcome to the Landing Stage 4667
Welcome to the Lovely Bride to Be 1783
Welcome to the Moon 2728
Welcome to the Queen 4357
Welcome to the Theatre 167, 602
Welcome to the World 2224
Welcome to This Window 1702
Welcome to Union City 4180
Welcome to Wonderland 56
Welfare Rag 3159
Well All Right 580
Well Beloved, The 3994
Well-Bred Englishman 1161
Well-Bred Girl, A 2803
Well, Did You Evah! 1109
Well Done, Da Costa 4288
Well Fellows, I Guess We're Here 4064
Well, I Just Wouldn't Know 4058
Well I'm Not! 534
Well It Ain't 2663
Well Known Fact, A 2050, 3542
Well Laid Plans 3900
Well Met (dance) 4153
Well of Romance, The 4620
Well, This Is Jolly 3237
Well-to-Do Waltz, The 1702

Well, to Speak with Perfect Candor 3195
Well, Well! 3105
Well Wishers, The 167
Well, Yes, He's a Friend 2017
Well, You See 1856
Wells Fargo Wagon, The 3016
Wendy 3453
Wenn Zwei Sich Lieben 2471
Were I Happily Married 2399
Were I Thy Bride 2977
Were Thine That Special Face 2331
Were This to Prove a Feather in My Heart 2339
Were You Not to Ko Ko Plighted 2977
Were You Saying Something? 840
Were You There? 4147
Wernher von Braun 4412
West Country Lad 4404
West End Avenue 2687
West Indies Blues 1425
West Is Best, The 2479
West Is Best 932
West Point Bugle 3766
West Point March 3766
West Point Song 3766
West Pointers, The 2228
"West Side Story medley" 3018
West Virginia's Home to Me 4775
West Wind 3301
Western Approaches Ballet (inst.) 3598
Western People Funny 2312
Western Slope, The 259
Westminster Funeral 989
Westphalia Chorale 630
Westport! 4268
Westward Ho! 1138
Wetona 487
Whaddaya Say, Kid 280
Whaddaye Do Sundays, Whaddaye Do Mondays, Mary? 3540
Whale of a Story, A 177
Whaler's Life, A 3074
Whaler's Return, The 3074
Wham 372
What a Ball 3972
What a Beautiful Baby You Are 3087
What a Beautiful Face Will Do 200
What a Blessing 1698
What a Bore 1786
What a Break 2641
What a Case I've Got on You 3861
What a Change 68, 1578
What a Charming Afternoon 3547
What a Charming Couple 1456
What a Country! 64
What a Country 602
What a Crazy Way to Spend Sunday 2847
What a Curious Girl 1993
What a Day 1732, 1120
What a Day! 1679
What a Day 1865
What a Day for a Miracle 732
What a Day for Me 3491
What a Day It Would Be 2303
What a Delightful Day 59, 1892
What a Difference a Day Makes 166
What a Difference a Uniform Will Make 4770
What a Difference When You're Married 1746
What a Dry World This Would Be 1458
What a Fair Thing Is a Woman 629
What a Fool I'd Be 1963
What a Fool I've Been 1903
What a Friend We Have in Jesus 2046
What a Funny Story 1925
What a Girl! 495, 4118
What a Girl Can Do 2373
What a Good Day Is Saturday 4384
What a Great Pair We'll Be 3674
What a Guy 2427, 1633
What a Handsome Little Fellow 2654
What a Happy Day 4764
What a Jamboree 1182
What a Joy to Be Young 163
What a Killing 4629
What a Language 2422
What a Life 1046, 1265
What a Life! 2598
What a Life 2833, 3939
What a Long Cold Winter! 2219
What a Lot of Loving 2636
What a Lovely Day for a Wedding 85, 2386
What a Lovely Dream 1354
What a Lovely Night 1747
What a Lovely Wife 912
What a Man! 3731
What a Man Won't Do for a Woman 2000
What a Mess 158
What a Nice Idea 4485
What a Nice Municipal Park 2252
What a Night! 1993
What a Night This Is Going to Be 270
What a Notion 2988
What a Party 4384
What a Piece of Work Is Man 1717
What a Pity 177
What a Position for Me 2446, 4547
What a Pretty Baby Are You 4782
What a Pretty Girl 1092
What a Priceless Pleasure 4777
What a Privilege 324
What a Reward 949
What a Ride 4349
What a Sense of Beauty Glorious 4113
What a Shame 1676
What a Song Can Do 673
What a Team 1169
What a Village Girl Should Know 200
What a Waste 2905, 4734
What a Wedding 766
What a Whale of a Difference a Woman Can Make 2253

What a Whalen of a Difference Just a Few Lights Make 4847
What a Woman 1306
What a Wonderful World 3795
What a World This Would Be 1488, 2457, 4815
What a Wretched Way to Run St. Anne's 2318
What-a-Ya-Say 1718
What a Young Girl Ought to Know 3139
What About It? 4490
What About Me 280
What About Me? 2392, 3752, 2578
What About Today 4145
What About Today? 4389
What Abraham Lincoln Once Said 4514
What Am I? 413, 4617
What Am I Bio 4114
What Am I Doing? 784
What Am I Doing Here 198, 3603
What Am I Doing Wrong? 614
What Am I Going to Do 1240
What Am I Going to Do to Make You Love Me? 2232
What Am I Going to Say 4648
What Am I Gonna Do 2305
What Am I Hangin' Around For? 4536
What Am I Living For? 4127
What Am I Supposed to Do? 2033
What Am I to Do 2729
What Am I with You 1660
What America Means to Me 3684
What an Awful Hullabaloo 3547
What an Evening 2017
What Are Little Girls Made Of 1744
What Are Little Husbands Made Of? 2453
What Are Names? 2937
What Are the Basic Things? 4396
What Are the Facts 1644
What Are They Doing to Us Now? 2048
What Are They Trying to Tell Us? 260
What Are We Coming To? 3308
What Are We Doing in Egypt? 1848
What Are We Going to Do? 3962, 4218
What Are We Going to Do About It? 2665
What Are We Going to Do with All the Jeeps? 4340
What Are We Gonna Do Tonight? 339
What Are We Here For 3060
What Are We Here For? 4443
What Are You Doing in Here? 3546
What Are You Doing New Year's Eve 3444
What Are You Going to Do About It? 958
What Are You Going to Do About Love? 3314
What Are You Gonig to Do with Me? 965
What Are You Proposing 1064
What Are You Running from, Mister? 2584
What Art Thou? 2632
What Beautiful Is 1189
What Became of Me? 1601
What Became of the People We Were? 2953
What Becomes of the Broken Hearted 1713
What Better Time for Love 828
What Better Way to Tell You 3833
What Can a Fellow Do? 2966
What Can a Girl Do 3236
What Can Be Sweeter 3532
What Can I Do? 4479, 2224
What Can I Do for You 3651
What Can I Give You? 1191
What Can I Name Him 4764
What Can I Say 466
What Can I Say? 4023
What Can I Tell Her? 2050
What Can It Be? 71
What Can One Man Do? 1186
What Can They See in Dancing? 605
What Can We Do without a Man 742
What Can You Do with a General 4144
What Can You Do with a Man? 514
What Can You Do with a Nude? 101
What Can You Say in a Love Song? (That Hasn't Been Said Before?) 2475
What Care We? (Song of Destiny) 4275
What Causes That? 921, 4443
What Chance Have I with Love 2597
What Color Eyes Do You Love Best? 3786
What Color Is the Sky? 2962
What Could Be Better? 253
What Could Be Fairer Than That 2373
What Could Be Fairer Than That? 2898
What Could Be More Romantic 3371
What Could Be Sweeter 2461, 2516
What Could I Do? 495
What Could I Do, but Fall in Love with You 3069
What Could I Have Done? 1700
What D'Ya Say? 771, 1490
What D'Ya Say 2827
What D'Ya Wanna Be? 1770
What Did Della Wear (When Georgie Came Across)? 1657
What Did Dey Do to My Goil? 3428
What Did Eve Give Adam for Christmas 1334
What Did I Do? 1577
What Did I Ever See in Him? 607
What Did I Have That I Don't Have 3274
What Did I Lose 3643
What Did Noah Do (When the Big Wind Came?) 2190
What Did the Butler See? 4219
What Did the Woggle Bug Say? 2711
What Did We Do Wrong? 2616
What Did William Tell? 86
What Did You Do? 1842
What Did You Expect? 1276
What Did You Put in That Look? 3204
What Difference Does It Make 2780
What Do I Believe In 2177
What Do I Care? 508
What Do I Care 1778, 3586, 4838
What Do I Do? 1168
What Do I Do Now? 1002, 1371, 1662, 3577, 4016

What Do I Do Now, Mom? 3925
What Do I Have to Do? 1769
What Do I Have to Do 2751
What Do I Have to Do? 3947
What Do I Have to Do to Get My Picture in the Paper? 2894
What Do I Have to Say 1120
What Do I Know? 4366, 4789
What Do I See in You? 2608
What Do I Tell People This Time 3231
What Do I Want with Love? 4253, 4541
What Do People Do? 572
What Do the Neighbors Say? 1718
What Do the Simple Folk Do? 623
What Do They Care? 3490
What Do They Want 262
What Do We Care? 3934, 4778
What Do We Care If It Rains 3939
What Do We Do About This 1604
What Do We Do? We Fly! 1060
What Do We Have to Hold on To? 410
What Do Women Want 634
What Do You Do? 583
What Do You Do 2553
What Do You Do? 1990
What Do You Do 2320, 3913
What Do You Do? 4016
What Do You Do in the Infantry 3444
What Do You Do When I'm Gone? 4226
What Do You Give to a Man Who's Had Everything? 4196
What Do You Have to Do? 4063
What Do You Hear from the Mob in Scotland 1659
What Do You Kiss For? 4409
What Do You Mean? 1650
What Do You Say? 322, 2757
What Do You Say, Dolly Dear? 1066
What Do You Think 1868
What Do You Think About Men? 3326
What Do You Think I Am? 372
What Do You Think of That? 3486
What Do You Think She'll Do 1213
What Do You Wanna Get Married For? 1035
What Do You Want for Christmas 3637
What Do You Want of Me? 2727
What Do You Want to Make Those Eyes at Me For (When They Don't Mean What They Say!) 1334
What Does a Little Boy Know? 2016
What Does a Lover Pack? 4485
What Does a Queen Have? 1369
What Does Atlanta Mean to Me 900
What Does He Look Like? 4340
(Tell Me) What Does He See in Me? 486
What Does He Think? 2681
What Does It Mean? 86, 3777
What Does My Heart Keep Saying 4486
What Does One Do? 4798
What Does That Dream Mean? 3108
What Does the Public Want 204
What Does the Public Want? 4630
What Does Your Servant Dream About 2331
What Ever? 413
What Ever Happened? 413
What Ever Happened to #'s 1, 2, 3 411
What Ever Happened to Saturday Night 3742
What Ever Happened to the Good Old Days 314
What Ever Happened to You? 4684
What Every Little Girl Should Know 2545
What Every Old Girl Should Know 3913
What Every Woman Knows 178
What Every Woman Knows (Frocks and Frills) 2486
What Every Woman Knows 2680, 2680, 4803
What Every Young Man Should Know 297, 2379
What Foolish Creatures We Are 4330
What Fools They Be 158
What Fools We Mortals Be 2347
What Gets Into Me? 83
What Goes Up, Must Come Down (and Baby, You've Been Flyin' too High) 888
What Good Are Words? 4361
What Good Are You? 3204
What Good Does It Do? 2190
What Good Is Love? 3501
What Good Is Money? 577
What Good Is the Lane, If You Can't Have the Girl of Your Dreams 4235
What Good Would the Moon Be? 4169
What Great Men Cannot Do 3084
What Happened? 1155, 2187
What Happened Here? 1079
What Happened Nobody Knows 3538
What Happened to Him 3235
What Happened to Jones 1519
What Happened to Mary 4206
What Happened to Me Tonight? 2355
What Happened to Paris? 101
What Happened to the Old Days? 3718
What Happened to the Original Six Floradora Boys 545
What Happened, What? 757
What Happens to Life 2801
What Harlem Is to Me 1981
What Harm Can It Do? 299
What Has Become of the English Language 2261
What Has Become of the Girl I Used to Know 256
What Has Become of the Girls I Used to Know 4804
What Has Become to Beauty? 1474
What Has Happened? 2522
What Has He Got? 3955
What Has Made the Movies? 2669
What Has the Night Time to Do with the Girl 2481
What Has Your Tongue to Tell? 4615
What Have I? 1109
What Have I Done? 691, 4068, 4198
What Have We Done 3814
What Have You Been Doing for the Past Ten Years 2702

What Have You Done to Me? 1440
What Have You Got to Have? 289
What Have You to Declare? 969
What He Needs I Got 3873
What He'd Done for Me 2415
What Ho, Mrs. Brisket 1564
What Ho Mrs. Brisket! 3235
What Homage of Human Lovers 1682
What I Almost Said 2185
What I Am 2065
What I Could Do on the Stage 4382
What I Could Have Done Tonight 3019
What I Did for Love 746
What I Had in Mind 992
What I Know I Knows 3358
What I Like Is You 2171
What I Mean 3273
What I Mean to Say 4682
What I Need the Most 871
What I Never Knew 198
What I Say Goes 1237
What I Want to Be 4433
What I Was Warned About 2705
What I Wonder 2220
What If? 2651
What If 2289
What If I Asked You for a Dance? 1082
What If She's Awfully Pretty? 1004
What If We... 2049
What If You're Not 1048
What I'll Do for You 3658
What I'm Longing to Say 2430
What in the World 3136
What in the World Did You Want? 1891
What Is a Friend? 2245
What Is a Friend For? 2000
What Is a Kiss? 4073
What Is a Letter 54
What Is a Maid to Do? 4354
What Is a Melodrama? 4102
What Is a Poor Girl to Do 3883
What Is a Queen 1229
What Is a Street Man 1306
What Is a Woman 227, 2050
What Is a Woman Like? 2633
What Is All This Excitement About 1868
What Is Done You Can Never Undo 2486
What Is Good for Depression 4380
What Is Her Name? 1809
What Is It? 518, 1529, 1569
What Is Life? 3526
What Is Life-What Is Love? 2779
What Is Love? (Canzonetta) 252
What Is Love? 600, 1404
What Is Love 1616, 2633, 3567
What Is Love? 4724, 762, 3777, 4603, 2224
What Is Missing in My Life 3561
What Is My Status 345
What Is That Tune? 4777
What Is the Difference? 1768
What Is the Good? 3086
What Is the Matter with Me? 3320
What Is the Secret of Your Success 2313
What Is the Stars? 2268
What Is There to Say? 4399, 2616, 4824
What Is There to Sing About? 4002
What Is This Called Love? 4581
What Is This Feeling in the Air 4190
What Is This Sensation? 1993
What Is This Thing I've Got 1227
What Is Wrong with Me 318
What Is Your Love to Me? 639
What Is Your Name? 1878
What It Takes to Bring You Back 3297
What It Takes to Make Me Love You-
You've Got It 4390
What It Was Was Love 4827
What I've Always Wanted 2163
What Joy Untold 1080
What Kind of a Grandma Are You? 98
What Kind of a Place Is This? 2358
What Kind of a Wife to Choose 2892
What Kind of a Woman Does a Man Expect? 3200
What Kind of Animal Is That? 2096
What Kind of Audience Are You? 4363
What Kind of Baby 4514
What Kind of Boy 4766
What Kind of Fool Am I? 4160
What Kind of Life Is That? 3615
What Kind of Man? 2064
What Kind of Man Is He? 1249
What Kind of Noise Annoys an Oyster? 2115
What Kind of Parents 3876
What Kind of Soldier Are You? 1476
What Kind of Tune Did Nero Play 4199
What Lips Are Made For 1083
What Love Is 3378
What Love Means 1071, 2570
What Makes a Business Man Tired? 1819
What Makes a Marriage Merry 989
What Makes a Star 4469
What Makes It Happen 4588
What Makes Me Love Him 170, 2677
What Makes Me Love You? 4821
What Makes My Baby Blue 1971
What Makes Sammy Run? 4633
What Makes the Tired Businessman So Tired 4269
What Makes the Wild Waves Wild 4393
What Makes the World Go Round 561
What Makes You So Wonderful? 1617
What Makes You the Woman? 356
What! Marry? 4161
What May a Lovesick Maiden Do 4497
What Means Home to Me 545
What Memories 4188
What Men and Women Will Wear 1462
What Men Can Do 2373
What Might Have Been 278
What More Can a General Do?
(I've Brushed My Teeth) 2444

What More Can I Say? 1234
What More Do I Need? 3559, 3843
What More Do I Want? 2615
What Mother Used to Say to Me 1794
What Must I Be to Be Yours 1734
What My Lips Can Never Say 948, 4670
What-No Dixie? 444
What Noise Was That? 1080
What Now? 1068
What Occurence! 284
What on Earth Is Going on Tango, The 3197
What Price Have I Paid? 3600
What Price Love 3556
What Ragtime Did to Business 2193
What Real True Friends Are For 4102
What Shadows We Are 4584
What Shall I Believe in Now? 344
What Shall I Do? 1018, 4777
What Shall I Do with the Rest? 1783
What Shall I Give My Lad for Christmas? 752
What Shall We Do If the Moon Goes Out 3043
What Shall We Sing? 4056
What She Needs 1649
What She Wanted and What She Got 4250
What Should I Do? 1276
What Sort of Wedding Is This? 3379
What Stuart Has Planted 4690
What Style! 2731
What Takes My Fancy 4693
What the Butler Sang 2319
What the Critics Said 3842
What the Dicky Birds Say 1193
What the Doctor Ordered 2070
What the Fortune Teller Said 1961
What the Girls Will Wear 1819
What the Hell 3934, 4635
What the Hell Am I Doing Here? 3902
What the Men Will Wear 1780
What the Prince Is Saying 3456
What the Red, White and Blue Did for You 1938
What the Song Should Say 4358
What the World Calls Love 3734
What the World Needs Now 261
What Then? 278, 1977
What Then Can Make Him Come So Slow? 4541
What There Is 54
What They Say and What They're Meaning 1887
What This Country Needs 2742, 2511
What This Party Needs 3501
What Thou See'st When Thou Doest Awake 3909
What Thrills Can There Be 4817
What to Do? 1507, 2322
What to Do with 'Er 589
What Turns You On 2861
What Was 4399
What Was Adam Doing 1966
What Was That 170
What We Need Around Here 3059
What We Want and What We Get 1088
What Wealth Is Here 1523
What? What? What? 3853
What! What! What! 3775
What Will Become of Me? 3777
What Will Become of Our England? 1453
What Will Daddy Say 3817
What Will Happen Then? 1246
What Will I Tell Her To-night 1963
What Will It Be? 3691
What Will the Future Say? 1817
What Will the Marquis Do? 1470
What Will the Neighbors Say 1513
What Will the World Say 356
What Will We Do on a Saturday Night when the Town Goes Dry 2373
What Will You Give Me? 3802
What Women and Men Will Wear 202
What Would Happen? 4060
What Would I Care? 4426
What Would I Do If I Could Feel 4722
What Would I Do? 1234
What Would Mrs. Grundy Say 1243
What Would Society Say? 2844
What Would We Do Without You? 832
What Would You Do? 610, 2115, 3559
What Would You Do for $50,000 1784
What Would You Do in a Case Like That? 1794
What Would You Do in My Place? 2346
What Would You Say? 139
What Would You Say to Your Son? 1903
What You Are 3763
What You Are and What You Want to Be 3087
What You Don't Know About Women 775
What You Don't Know Won't Hurt You 3611, 3791
What You Go Through 550
What You Mean to Me 2346
What You Need 223
What You Need Is A Woman 1776
What You Need Is Ginger Springs 4751
What You See Is What You Get 2790
What You Told Me to Do 264
What You Want and What I Get 2481
What You Want Wid Bess? 3541
What You Will 3015
What You'd Call a Dream 1038
What You're Gonna Do for Me 4830
What'd We Come to College For? 4778
What'd Yo' Do Wid de Letter, Mr. Johnson? 2506
What'll 4657
What'll I Do? 789
What'll I Do 3008, 4799
What'll It Be 3427
What'll It Take 1955
What'll They Think of Next? 4586
What's a Barber Shop Quartet 2641
What's a Body to Do? 1872
What's a Gang without a Guy Named Muggsy? 1974
What's a Girl Supposed to Do? 2985
What's a Guy Like You Doin' in a Place Like This? 3209

What's a Kiss 4497
What's a Kiss Among Friends? 1916
What's a Mama For? 2322
What's a Man to Do? 273
What's a Nice Country Like You 4635
What's a Nice Girl Like Her 4485
What's a Nice Kid Like You Doing in a Place Like This 57
What's a Sailor Got? 1539
What's a Show 3664
What's a Show? 3940
What's a Witch? 2993
What's Become of the Bowery? 3388
What's Become of the Night 1476
What's Cooking? 3615
What's Destined to Be 2352
What's for Real 4162
What's Goin' On Here? 3347
What's Going On 1997
What's Going on Around Here? 1884
What's Going On Inside? 2368
What's Gone Wrong 3688
What's Gonna Be 2940
What's Gonna Be Tomorrow 615
What's Gonna Happen? 2234
What's Gonna Happen to Me? 4089
What's Good About Good Morning 3082
What's Happened? 577
What's He Like? 1539
What's His Name 177
What's-His-Name 2805
What's His Name 4289, 4332
What's in a Name? 4106, 991, 1436, 2464
What's in a Name? (Love Is Always Love) 4637
What's in a Name 4646
What's in It for Me? 2048, 2306
What's in It for You? 4312
What's in Store for You 2351
What's in the Air 3209
What's in the Air Tonight? 4361
What's It All About 2068
What's It to Be a Legend 1201
What's Keeping My Prince Charming 3704
What's Left 2368
What's Mine Is Thine 4394
What's Mine Is Yours 2187
What's Missing in My Life 3561
What's My Lie 3873
What's My Man Gonna Be Like? 4545
What's My Name 2354
What's Natural 3734
What's New? 3511
What's New at the Zoo? 1061
What's New in New York 4602
What's New in New York? 84
What's Next 4399
What's on the Penny? 2161
What's on Your Mind 1982
What's Out There for Me? 2217
What's Possible 451
What's Sauce for the Goose Is Sauce for the Gander 3073
What's That? 583
What's the Angle 3136
What's the Answer? It's Love! 4232
What's the Big To-do? 2993
What's the Buzz? 2212
What's the Difference 1856
What's the Fun of Being King 1727
What's the Idea 4218
What's the Latest News from Town? 2982
What's the Mail? 2674
What's the Matter? 2982
What's the Matter with a Nice Beef Stew 1564
What's the Matter with Buffalo? 615
What's the Matter with Hannah 235
What's the Matter with Letty? 2489
What's the Matter with Me? 31
What's the Matter with My Man in the Moon 3786
What's the Matter with Our City? 1811
What's the Matter with Our Team 2724
What's the Matter with the Moon Tonight? 2917
What's the Matter with Women? 1723
What's the Matter with You? 3400
What's the Name of That Tune 1735
What's the Name of What's-His-Name? 1727
What's the Reason 1693
What's the Rush 4639
What's the Use 531, 1011, 2467, 4185, 4364, 3591
What's the Use of Being Lonesome 4784
What's the Use of Dreaming? 1054
What's the Use of Dreaming 1316
What's the Use of Getting Sober 1296
What's the Use of Going to Bed 2760
What's the Use of Love 457
What's the Use of Lovin' (If I Can't Have You) 3645
What's the Use of Loving Only One Girl 1663
What's the Use of Moonlight? 1111
What's the Use of Saying No 1088
What's the Use of Talking? 1447
What's the Use of Wond'rin' 660
What's the Use? 630, 1900, 2869, 3243, 1866, 4762, 3241
What's the Younger Generation Coming To? 2103
What's There About Me (Why Am I a Hit with the Ladies?) 799
What's This? A Kiss 821
What's 3000 Miles? 4389
What's to Become of the Children 4661
What's to Lose 3094
What's Up for You 3873
What's Weak About the Weaker Sex 2070
What's Wrong with Me? 1017, 2355
What's Wrong with Our Love 1073
What's Wrong with That? 3644
What's Your Husband Doing? 2878
What's Your Name? 729
What's Your Sign 1770
What's Your Wife Doing? 2818
Whatcha Sayin? 1385
Whatever Became of Jenny? 3485

Whatever Became of Old Temple 367
Whatever Goes Swoop Lilting Lofting 2810
Whatever Happened 4433
Whatever Happened to Me 3088
Whatever Happened to Spring 2580
Whatever Happened to the Communist Menace 4635
Whatever Happened to Tomorrow? 4102
Whatever Happened To? 413
Whatever I Say 269
Whatever It Happens to Be 3276
Whatever Lola Wants (Lola Gets) 957
Whatever That May Be 1745
Whatever Time There Is 699
Whatever Turns You On 2451
Whatever You Do 3139
Whatever You Want Me to Be 2011
Whatja Do to Me 1813
Whatshisname 3619
Wheatless Days 3245
Wheel 'em and Deal 'em 1385
Wheel of Fate 764
Wheels 1134, 3752
Wheels of Progress 4006
Wheels of Steel 1275
Wheels Through the Night 3647
When 266, 454
When? 2294
When 690
When? 1200, 2064
When 3489, 1028, 321
When a Band That Is Jazz 1026
When a Black Man's Blue 567
When a Body's in Love 3865
When a Boy from New Hampshire Loves a Girl from Tennessee 3545
When a Boy Gets Siviled 2028
When a Brother Is a Mother to His Sister 2949
When a Carnation Meets a Red Red Rose 2151
When a Fella Needs a Friend 3210
When a Fellow Gets to Thinking 3091
When a Fellow Loves a Girl 2317
When a Fellow Meets a Flapper on Broadway 3532
When a Fellow's on the Level with a Girl That's on the Square 4277
When a Fellow's Twenty-One 1556
When a Girl 1580
When a Girl Doesn't Know Where She Is 613
When a Girl Forgets to Scream 1352
When a Girl Is Born to Be a Lady 4762
When a Girl's About to Marry 3590
When a Girl's in Love 3192
When a Good Man Takes to Drink 180
When a Hick Chick Meets a City Slicker 1539
When a Jew Sings 3670
When a Lady Has a Piazza 4467
When a Little Boy Loves a Little Girl 3877
When a Little Girl's in Love 333
When a Maid Comes Knocking at Your Heart 1285
When a Maid Wears Purple Stockings 3939
When a Maiden Comes to School 3026
When a Maiden Weds 3736
When a Maiden Won't 1521
When a Man Cries 2043
When a Man Is Middle Aged 758
When a Man Is Single 1334
When a Man Is Twenty-One 357
When a Man Loves a Woman 81
When a New Star 1476
When a Pansy Was a Flower 4235
When a Peer Makes Love to a Damsel Fair 3736
When a Pimp Meets a Whore 2648
When a Pretty Girls Gets Married 307
When a Pretty Peeping Ankle Peeps at You 4634
When a Pullet Is Plump It's Tender 758
When a Regular Girl Loves a Regular Boy 3821
When a Robin Leaves Chicago 2339
When a Rolls Rolls In 4226
When a Small Town Girl Meets a Small Town Boy 1308
When a Woman Exits Laughing 2767
When a Woman Has a Baby 4169
When a Woman Has Her Way 2869
When a Woman Has to Choose 3429
When a Woman Loves a Man 478
When a Woman Makes Up Her Mind 4786
When a Youth and a Maid Pine and Love 1213
When Alexander Takes His Ragtime Band 61
(They Love It) When All Your Castles Come Tumbling Down 2927
When All's Said and Done 2432
When Am I Going to Meet Your Mother? 2227
When an Englishman Marries a Parisian 965
When an Interfering Person 1313
When Any Woman Makes a Running Issue Out of Her Flesh 2648
When April Comes Again 1951
When Athena Dances (inst.) 4798
When Autumn Comes 4391
When Black Sallie Sings Pagliacci 1921
When Britain Really Ruled 2977
When Broadway Was a Pasture 501
When Buffalo Bill and His Wild West Show First Came to Baltimore 3337
When Butterfly Does the Shimmy 2455
When Cadets Parade 3766
When Claudia Smiles 4642
When Cupid Calls (The Rat-Tat-Tat-Song) 4258
When Cupid Flys Away 1847
When Dad Was Twenty-One 539
When Daddy Came Home 521
When Daddy Goes A-Hunting 3254
When Dancing's a Profession 3754
When Did I Fall in Love? 1280
When Did You Know 1168
When Did You Know? 4238
When Did You Leave Me 1010
When Do I Get Mine? 589
When Do the Word Come True 4643
When Do We Dance? 4392

When Does the Bus Come By? 2032
When Does the Ravishing Begin? 2563
When Does This Feeling Go Away? 2705
When Dreams Come True 1687, 4644
When Duty Calls 4738
When Each Day 2698
When Eve Is Alone 4523
When Evening Shadows Fall 1690
When Everything Human Has Failed You 2243
When Everything Is Hunky-Dory 4170
When Eyes Meet Eyes (When Lips Meet Lips) 1391
When First I Saw My Lady's Face 3015
When First My Old, Old Love 2977
When Foreign Princes Come to Visit Us 1564
When Fortune Smiles 355, 2931
When Gaby Did the Gaby Glide 1963
When Gemini Meets Capricorn 2048
When Gentlemen Disagree 465
When Gentlemen Grew Whiskers and Ladies Grew Old 2253
When Girls Command the Army 3567
When Gramercy Square Was Uptown 465
When Grandma Was a Girl 2696
When Grandpa Was a Boy 4831
When Greek Meets Greek 2569
When Greek Meets Greek of Liza-Strata 364
When He Calls Half-Hour 4011
When He Comes Back to Me 4835
When He Comes Home 3262, 7
When He Goey La-di-da 3828
When He Is Broken 181
When He Looks at Me 4384
When He Marries Me 2011
When He's Away 3222
When He's Near 4621
When He's Not Near 3437
When Hearts Are Broken 3765
When Hearts Are Young (In Springtime) 2384
When His Eyes Look into Mine 3372
When I Am Chief of Police 2123
When I Am Free to Love 1548
When I Am Lost 2033
When I Am Movin' 2420
When I Am Yours Dear 3820
When I Bestow My Bosom's Store 1905
When I Bounce Off to Bed 4273
When I Build a Home 2373
When I Came to America 1240
When I Close My Eyes 3117
When I Come Around Again 3274
When I Consider the Heavens 4398
When I Count Three 3519
When I Crack My Whip 1603
When I Dance Alone 2174
When I Dance with the Person I Love 367
When I Die 2195
When I Discover My Man 706
When I Discovered You 4603
When I Do a Dance for You 4279
When I Do the Highland Fling 2964
When I Drank with My Love 937
When I Dream 3343
When I Dream My Dream 2437
When I Dream of Annie Laurie 1532
When I Dream of You 3021
When I Enter Paree 2933
When I Fall in Love 4018
When I Feel Like Loving 1967
When I Feel Like Moving 1072
When I Fell in Love with You 773
When I Find My Romeo 3319
When I Find That Girl 1644
When I First Saw You 1103
When I Found You 3045, 3382, 3538
When I Get Back to Boston Town 2795
When I Get Back to the U.S.A. 4158
When I Get Home 2978
When I Get in the Movies 4317
When I Get Married 307
When I Get My Name in Lights 2437
When I Get the Call 1037
When I Go on the Stage 3924
When I Go Out Walkin' with My Baby 3263, 4146
When I, Good Friends 2348, 2977
When I Grow Up (The G-Man Song) 3501
When I Grow Up I'm Going to Be a Soldier 1703
When I Had a Uniform On 1921
When I Happen By 4093
When I Have Become a Social Butterfly 3144
When I Hear a Syncopated Strain 132
When I Hear a Syncopated Tune 4812
When I Hear an Old Fashioned Waltz 3179
When I Hear My Country Calling 1332
When I Hear That Jazz Band Play 4836
When I Hit Broadway 1617
When I Join the Circus 4289
When I Lead the Band 306
When I Leave the World Behind 965, 3827
When I Leave Town 1313
When I Led the Amazon Army 1962
When I Look at You 910
When I Look Into Those Lovey Dovey Eyes 1535
When I Look Into Your Eyes Mavourneen 4576
When I Look Up 900, 3159
When I Lost You 1538
When I Love Again 2052
When I Love, I Love 1929
When I Make a Million for You (I Want a Million for You, Dear) 1756
When I Make the Grade with O'Grady 3369
When I March with April in May 500
When I Marry 3246
When I Marry Alice 989
When I Marry Mary in Maryland 1430
When I Marry Mr. Pilbeam 466
When I Marry My Mary in Maryland 632
When I Met Her 1082
When I Met Love 3593
When I Played Carmen 1016
When I Plot a Plan 3549

When I Propose 2903
When I Reach Old London Town 822
When I Rise 2173
When I Rode on the Choo Choo Cars 3746
When I Rule the Town 434
When I Sang My Low C 694
When I Sang Toreador 1523
When I Say It's So, It's So 659
When I Say My Say 148
When I See You 80
When I Sing in Grand Opera 2390
When I Struck New York 4382
When I Take My Lady 2750
When I Take My Sugar to Tea 1813
When I Take You All to London 2602
When I Talk about You 1420
When I Teach You How to Swim 1735
When I Think about the Girls I Fell For 3796
When I Think of the Sweethearts That I Might Have Had 3246
When I Think of You 3133
When I Took My Jazz Band to The Fatherland 1175
When I Used to Lead the Ballet 3547, 3865
When I Walk Out with You 3207
When I Walk with Minnie 2686
When I Walk with You 341
When I Walked in the Land of Oaks 340
When I Waltz with You 468, 2834, 4712
When I Was a Boy 634
When I Was a Child 1002
When I Was a Country Girl 906
When I Was a Cowboy 1037
When I Was a Girl 906, 3856
When I Was a Girl Like You 3063, 3857
When I Was a Kid Like You 2978
When I Was a Lad 1948, 2348, 2977
When I Was a Little Boy 1035
When I Was a Little Cuckoo 1018, 3893
When I Was a Man 2346
When I Was a Pickaninny 4504
When I Was Born the Stars Stood Still 357
When I Was but a Bounding Boy 4479
When I Was in the Chorus at the Gaiety 1526
When I Was King of Bath 2937
When I Was Learning to Read 128
When I Was One and Twenty 2633
When I Was Single 3989
When I Was Small 1154
When I Was Sweet Sixteen 295
When I Was the Dandy and You Were the Belle 1643
When I Was Twenty-One 537
When I Was Twenty One 538
When I Was Twenty-One 2966, 3028
When I Was Young 2583, 3053
When I Was Your Age Young Man 2275
When I Wave My Flag 3222
When I Went Home 3453
When I Went to School 4150
When I Went to School with You 1919
When I Went to the Bar 2977
When I Would Think of You 3268
When I Write 949
When I'm 64 3903
When I'm a Duchess 2966
When I'm Alone 322
When I'm Alone, I'm Lonesome 2834
When I'm Alone with You 3626
When I'm an Alderman 4859
When I'm an American Citizen 3855
When I'm Being Born Again 3274
When I'm Blue 2009
When I'm By Her Side 2675
When I'm Dancing 2685
When I'm Dancing with Peg o' My Heart 4630
When I'm Drunk I'm Beautiful 3564
When I'm High 1757
When I'm in a Quiet Mood 3983
When I'm in Congress 996
When I'm in Love 4090
When I'm in Paree 2637
When I'm Looking at You 4812
When I'm Not Near the Girl I Love 4399, 1278
When I'm on Duty 644
When I'm Out with You 4158
When I'm Sad 2896
When I'm Traveling on the Road 559
When I'm Waltzing 3755
When I'm Waltzing with You 1712
When I'm with the Girls 4491
When I'm with You 568
When in France 2838
When in Love 1469
When In Rome 2988
When in Trouble Come to Papa 4381
When in Vienna a Waltz Is Played 3592
When Ireland Stands Among the Nations of the World 1162
When Irish Eyes Are Smiling 2154
When Islam First Arose 3777
When It Comes to Loving 1955
When It Dries 4481
When It Gets Dark 539
When It Happens to You (1) 3682
When It Happens to You (2) 3682
When It's All Goin' Out and Nothin' Comin' In 3820, 4390
When It's Apple Blossom Time in Normandy 3755, 4206
When It's Cactus Time in Arizona 1528
When It's Cotton Blossom Time, Sweet Rosalie 1963
When It's Love 3074
When It's Moonlight in Mayo 2310
When It's Moonlight on the Mississippi 3982
When It's Night Time in Dixie Land 4603
When It's Raining 3581
When It's Sleepy Time Down South 3840
When It's Snowing in Hawaii 3144
When It's Spring in Vienna 972

When It's Summer 1076
When It's Sweetpea Time in Georgia 3641
When It's Young and It's Spring 2089
When I've Made Up My Mind to a Thing 1417
When Johnny Comes Marching Home 964
When Johnny Comes Marching Home from College Again 2869
When June Comes Along with a Song 3723
When Knighthood Was in Flower 2671, 3407
When Knights Were Bold 3580
When Knott's Not Tying Knots 2888
When Labor Comes into Its Own 1565
When Life Seems Made of Pains and Pangs 3736
When Little Tommy Sawyer Saw the Circus 2029
When Love Awakes (Love's Awakening) 1162
When Love Beckoned 1109
When Love Begins 3753
When Love Calls You 1212
When Love Comes Finaletto 2478
When Love Comes Knocking at Your Heart 257, 1026
When Love Comes Stealing In 2922
When Love Comes Swinging Along 3850
When Love Comes to Call 629
When Love Comes to Your Heart 2527
When Love Comes Your Way 1203, 2252, 3214
When Love Dies 4434
When Love Goes A-Straying 3494
When Love Grows Up 1804
When Love Has Gone 3573
When Love Is Free 1555
When Love Is Near 1935
When Love Is There 4012
When Love Is True Love 717
When Love Is Waiting 'Round the Corner 3579
When Love Is Young 1193
When Love Knocked Upon the Door 2802
When Love Was Born 1466
When Lovers Are Alone 1071
When Lovers Fall in Love 3763
When Mabel Comes in the Room 2660
When Madame Reaches Her High C 680
When Mamie Sweet Mamie's a Bride 4508
When Marie Antoinette Learned to Pet 4527
When Martha Was a Girl 929
When Maudey Wants a Man 3159
When McGregor Sings Off Key 1840
When Me, Mowgli, Love 2252
When Men Are Alone 3540
When Men Are Free 3703
When Men Are in Love 3595
When Miss Park Avenue Does the Bumps 302
When Moses Spake to Goldstein 4514
When Mother Was a Girl 994
When Mr. Shakespeare Comes to Town 1926
When My Baby Goes to Town 4058
When My Baby Smiles at Me 1032
When My Back Is to the Wall 1848
When My Brother Beats the Big Bass Drum 1351
When My Buddy Steps with Me 1516
When My Caravan Comes Home 1923
When My Eyes Meet Yours 3898
When My Man Comes Home 3657
When My Man Returns 4396
When My Man Sails Home 2750
When My Name Is Writ in History 1351
When My Ship Comes In 2716, 2780
When My Sweetie Comes Back to Me 4849, 4851
When My Violin Is Calling 2622
When My Wife Returns 1424
When Nancy Brown Kissed Hirem Green Good Bye 2635
When Nathan Was Married to Rose of Washington Square 4819
When Not Engaged in Fighting 4554
When O'Donahue Presided at the Grip 559
When Old Glory Floats from Everywhere 3786
When Old New York Goes Dry 712
When Old New York Was Young 4079
When Once I Get Hold of a Good-Looking He? 1429
When One Deems a Lady Sweet 2339
When One Marries an Exceptional Woman 1169
When One You Love 3424
When Opportunity Knocks 1191
When Orient Roses Bloom 3372
When our Hearts Go Waltzing Along (Mein Herz Hat Leise Dein Herz Gegrusst) 1044
When Our Lips In Kisses Met 4646
When Our Ship Comes Sailing In 3243
When Our Sundays Are Blue 3770
When Papa Would Waltz 4829, 4827
When Pavlova Starts Buck and Winging 3958
When Perrico Plays 4735
When Reuben Comes to Town 3744
When Rogers Come to Town 4507
When Rosie Lived on Essex Street 1609
When Sammy Sang the Marseillaise 1888
When Santa Claus Gets Your Letter 3794
When Shakespeare Comes to Town 3154
When Shall I Again See Ireland 1162
When Shall We Meet Again 3404, 4393
When She Gets Home Tomorrow 273
When She Gets Up in the Morning 2222
When She Gives Him a Shamrock Bloom 2340
When She Walks in the Room 4524
When She Was Bad 4830
When Sist' Tetrazin' Met Cousin Carus 4521
When Skies Are Bright 2603
When Some Serious Affliction 1165
When Somebody Cares 1345
When Somebody Isn't There 824
When Someone Marries Me 3613
When Someone You Love Loves You 2439
When Songs Were Sung 1688
When Sousa Comes to Coontown 2111
When Sousa Leads the Band 4130
When Springtime Comes to My River 4701
When Summer Comes 4648, 4648
When Summer Goes 139
When Sunday Comes Around 4853

When Swallows Return in the Spring 4094
When Tender Love You Are Confessing 1088
When Tetrazzini Sings High F 2869
When Texas Tommy Did the Turkey Trot 697
When That Band Plays 2540
When That Dixie Sun Goes Down 3782
When That Somebody Comes 3770
When the Animals Are Gone 1911
When the Antonellis Were Here 3718
When the Autumn Leaves Are Falling 4858
When the Baby Comes 4384
When the Band Begins to Play 2854
When the Band of Reubenville Turns Out 349
When the Band Plays 'Home Sweet Home' 3085
When the Band Plays Killarney 2349
When the Band Plays Ragtime 3229
When the Band Plays Yankee Doodle 1902
When the Banners Lead 3680
When the Bell Goes Ting-A-Ling-Ling 2691
When the Bell in the Lighthouse Rings Ding Dong 2415
When the Berry Blossoms Bloom 4772
When the Birds Begin to Sing 906
When the Bloom Is on the Bottle 4012
When the Bluebirds Fly All Over the World 597, 3217
When the Bo-Tree Blossoms Again 2638
When the Boys Come Home 462
When the Boys Come Home to Tea 4419
When the Bugles Are Calling 4724
When the Bus Stops 3227
When the Cat Comes Back 3372
When the Cat's Away 1731, 2601, 3617
When the Cat's Away the Mice Will Play 235, 476, 2915, 2974
When the Cherry Blossoms Fall (Love Is Love) 3791
When the Children Are Asleep 660
When the Circus Comes to Town 4113, 4723, 306
When the Clock in the Tower Strikes Twelve 3266
When the Clock Strikes One 4644
When the Cocoanuts Call 2308
When the Colored Band Comes Marching Down the Street 2974
When the Colored Regiment Goes Off to War 3799
When the Creditor Comes to Call 335
When the Crime Wave Rolls 3848
When the Cuckoo Met the Pussy Cat 4161
When the Curfew Rings at Nine 1582
When the Curtain Falls 1598
When the Day Is Ended 69
When the Debbies Go By 4300
When the Devil Played the Fiddle 3074
When the Dreamer Awakes 737
When the Duchess Is Away 1284
When the Eenie Meenies Do the Minie Mo 3796
When the Elves Hold Masquerade 307
When the Fiddle Bows Begin to Fly 1266
When the Girl You Love Is Loving You 4802
When the Girl You Love Says "Yes" 1573
When the Girls Get Wise 1920
When the Girls Grow Older They Grow a Little Bolder 1334
When the Goblins Are at Play 4754
When the Going Gets Tough 1955
When the Grown Up Ladies Act Like Babies 965
When the Hansom Cabs Were Lined Up on the Ranks 1128
When the Heart Is Light 4738
When the Heart Is Young 2701
When the Hen Stops Laying 2432, 4517
When the Henry Clay Comes Steaming into Mobile Bay 3031
When the Honeymoon Stops Shining 1963
When the Hurdy Gurdy Plays 3655
When the Idle Poor Become the Idle Rich 1278
When the Jiggs Do the Juba 2640
When the Kids Get Married 2050
When the Ladies Have Their Way 4219
When the Lady Passes 1262
When the Landlord Comes Knocking at the Door 1849
When the Lights Are Low 4810
When the Lights Turn Green 3849
When the Little Birds Are Sleeping 20
When the Love You Love Loves You 548
When the Madame Goes Away 2922
When the Messiah Comes 1265
When the Minstrels Come to Town 263, 800, 801
When the Mists of the Night 2495
When the Mites Go By 1324
When the Money Comes In 1665
When the Moon Comes Over the Hill 1535
When the Moon Is in the Sky (Shadow Song) 3422
When the Moon Looks Down 2122
When the Moon Plays Peek a Boo 434
When the Moon Plays Peek-a-boo 2576
When the Moon Plays Peek-a-Boo 2552
When the Moon Plays Peek-a-Boo with You 3480
When the Moon Plays Peekaboo with You 1647
When the Moon Shines Down 1240
When the Moon Shines on the Moonshine 2111, 4813
When the Moon Slyly Winks in the Night 3627
When the Moonbeams Shine in Dear Old Alabama 1972
When the Moonlight's Bright in Brighton 589
When the Nylons Bloom Again 39, 1140
When the Ocean Breezes Blow 2793
When the Old Top Hummed (The Humming Top) 1088
When the One You Care For 2253
When the One You Love Loves You 1643
When the Orchestra Plays 4181
When the Orchestra's Playing Your Favorite Waltz 2430
When the Orchestra's Playing Your Favorite Dance 3230
When the Organ Plays 2686
When the Parisian Goes for a Ride 1199
When the Party Gives a Party 4524
When the Piper Plays 4575
When the Plumber Goes A'Plumbing 3592
When the Power Comes 4788
When the Preacher Makes You Mine 3426

When the Queen Wakes Up in the Morning 1849
When the Ragtime Army Goes Away to War 4808
When the Rain Goes Pitter Patter (inst.) 294
When the Record Player's On 3671
When the Right Boy Comes Along 984
When the Right Boy Meets the Right Girl (That's the Right Time to Love) 2020
When the Right Girl Comes Along 186, 1541
When the Right Little Girl Comes Along 2214
When the Right Man Sings Tra-La-La 1183
When the Right One Comes Along 3766, 4814
When the Saints Go Marching In 3840, 3018
When the Sandman's on His Way 910
When the Saxophone Is Playing 1663
When the Shadows Fall 2071, 2491
When the Shaker Plays a Cocktail Tune 3179
When the Sheets Come Back from the Laundry 1679
When the Ships Come Home 3245
When the Snowflakes Fall 1129
When the Song of Love Is Heard 4590
When the Spirit Moves Me 3100
When the Spring Is in the Air 3014
When the Statues Come to Life 2870, 4290
When the Sun Goes Down 728
When the Sun Goes Down in Chinatown 2349
When the Sun Goes Down in Romany 2853, 4148
When the Sun Goes Down in the South 394
When the Sun Kissed the Rose Goodnight 3137
When the Sun Meets the Moon in Finale-Land 1448
When the Sunflower Turns to the Sun 4098
When the Tall Man Talks 4682
When the Teddy Bears Come to Life 263
When the Tenor Married the Soprano (and the Alto Married the Bass) 1582
When the Time Comes 3619
When the Time Is Right 1766
When the Troupe Comes Back to Town 3820
When the Village Goes to Sleep 1697
When the Weather's Better 1729
When the Weddin' March Is Ended 2115
When the Wedding Bells Are Ringing 168
When the Wedding Bells Ring Out 2378
When the Wedding Chimes Are Ringing 2706
When the Weekend Comes Round 2112
When the Whistle Blows 3511
When the Whole World Has Gone Back on You 3327
When the Wind Blows 1426
When the Wind Is Still 1204
When the Wings of the Wind Take Me Home 3810
When the Wintry Moon Is Bright 698
When the Young Men Are Away 1824
When There Isn't a Girl About 1417, 3348
When There's No Light at All 3332
When There's No One 661
When There's No One to Love 3404
When They Call the Roll at West Point 2806
When They Do the Dippy Doodlums 3754
When They Grow Up 3888
When They Play Your Favorite Melody 525
When They Rub Noses in Alaska 3296
When They Saw the Star 755
When They Start Again 1045
When They Start to Yodel Ragtime Songs in Tennessee 4037
When They're Beautiful 815
When They're Old Enough to Know Better It's Better to Leave Them Alone 4813
When They're Petite 3466
When Things Are Bright and Rosy 142
When Things Come Your Way 2491
When Things Go Wrong You Will Be Mine 1314
When This Lousy War Is Over 3259
When This You See 3437
When Those Mason-Dixon Minstrels Hit Town 1823
When Three Is Company (Cupid Song) 1066
When Time Takes Your Hand 127
When Toby Is Out of Town 3569
When Tommy Atkins Marries Dolly Gray 8
When Tommy Atkins Smiles at All the Girls 965
When Tomorrow Comes 3277, 3956
When True Love Is True 796
When Tu-lips Are True 1121
When Two Hearts Are One 1090
When Two Hearts Are True Hearts 4087
When Two Hearts Beat in Time 2774
When Two Hearts Discover 3868
When Two Little Hearts Are One 1926
When Two Little Hearts Beat Together 3771
When Two Love Dearly 1550
When Uncle Sam Rules the Wave 683
When Uncle Sammy Leads the Band 2853
When Velma Takes the Stand 723
When Villains Ramble Far and Near 4447
When Was There Ever a Night Like This 3395
When We Are Born Again 3913
When We Are Free 4790
When We Are M-A-Double-R-I-E-D 4277
When We Are Married 357, 2293, 2569, 3295, 4053, 4148, 4654, 4780
When We Are Married to You and Me 1793
When We Are Together 1282
When We Chance to Meet 3887
When We Get Our Divorce 4212
When We Get What's Coming to Us 4723
When We Grow Up 1389
When We Hear the Call for Battle 1165
When We Made the Gallant Charge Up Bunker Hill 2978
When We Meet Again 620
When We Meet the Mormon 1544
When We See a Pretty Girl We Whistle 314
When We Strike Broadway 187
When We Waltz Down the Aisle 1203
When We Were Girls 2570
When We Were Twenty-One 4148
When We Were Young 1862
When We're Alone 1947
When We're Bride and Groom 4476
When We're Dancing 4273
When We're Home on the Range 4058

When We're in Love 3082
When We're Married 2633, 3387
When We're on the Stage 1313
When We're Running a Little Hotel of Our Own 799
When We're Together 2610
When Whiteman Starts to Play 2691
When Will Grown-Ups Grow Up? 534
When Will I Be Loved 3739
When Will I Learn 1158
When Will I Plant the Tree 2113
When Will My Dreams Come True, Love 2906
When Will the Music Be Gone 3619
When Will They Finish New York? 3124
When Willie Waltzes with Me 4588
When Woman Is the Question 3685
When Woman, Lovely Woman, Gets Her Rights 4364
When Worlds Collide 4518
When Ya Get Yourself Married 2235
When You and I Were Dancing 1780
When You and I Were Tadpoles 3319
When You and I Were Young, Maggie Blues 4197
When You Are Close to Me 2595
When You Are Eighteen 304
When You Are Happy 815
When You Are in China 3775
When You Are in My Arms 3540
When You Are Mine 168
When You Are Mine All Mine 4133
When You Are Near 2506
When You Are Old and Grey 4412
When You Are Seventeen 2079
When You Are Wed to Me 3828
When You Are Young 1145
When You at Last Are Mine 3578
When You Carry Your Own Suitcase 4090
When You Change Your Name to Mine 118
When You Choose to Love Somebody 3576
When You Come Back 37
When You Come Back to Me 132
When You Come Home Again, Johnny 4599
When You Come Near I Feel All of a Ooh! 3868
When You Come to the End of Your Rainbow 556
When You Come to Town 1469
When You Dance 3868
When You Dance for a King 3682
When You Dance in Paris, France 3800
When You Dance with a Certain Girl 2270
When You Dance with a Wonderful Girl 1587
When You Dance with the Girl You Love 1584
When You Dance with the One You Love 302
When You Do the Hinky Dee 2533
When You Done Gone Broke 4762
When You Drop Off at Cairo, Illinois 4148
When You Feel a Little Longing 2619
When You Find the Girl Who Loves but You 421
When You First Kiss the Last Girl You Love 4185
When You Get to Congress 608
When You Go Down By Miss Jenny's 341
When You Go Down to London Town 1295
When You Go Out to Dine 1054
When You Gonna Learn (To Put Your Money on This Baby) 2965
When You Grow Tired Just Let Me Know 2408
When You Grow to Be Twenty-One (When I Was Twenty-One) 379
When You Grow Up 3035, 4639
When You Have a Son 2925
When You Have Forgotten My Kisses (and I Have Forgotten Your Name) 732
When You Hear Jackson Moan on His Saxophone 4037
When You Hear Love's Hello 4553
When You Hear That Humming 1476
When You Hear the Old Kentucky Blues 1479
When You Hear the Umpah-Umpah in the Band 335
When You Hear the Wind 4337
When You Hold Your Husband's Hand 4107
When You Kiss the Blarney Stone 452
When You Kiss the One You Love 2335
When You Know Me Better 3319
When You Live in a Furnished Flat 2363
When You Live in New York 674
When You Live on an Island 3813
When You Lock a Weary Warlock from His Room 1757
When You Look in Her Eyes 1183
When You Look in the Eyes of a Mule 4182
When You Look in the Heart of a Rose 377
When You Look in Your Looking Glass 1840
When You Looked at Me for the First Time 2243
When You Lose a Friend 451
When You Love 910, 4427
When You Love a Girl 1866
When You Love Me with All My Heart 1680
When You Love Only One 3699
When You Love, Love, Love 4723
When You Marry 2262
When You Meet a Man in Chicago 4196
When You Meet Her in the Summertime 256
When You Meet Them on Broadway 4806
When You Mention It Don't Mention That I Mentioned It to You 2498
When You Plow Through the Fields 3997
When You Run the Show 2754
When You Said How Do You Do 4206
When You Sail for Paris in the Spring 3129
When You Sang the Rosary to Me 2984
When You See Miss Load of Coal 2640
When You Skate with a Wonderful Girl 913
When You Smile 154, 155, 1723, 4651
When You Smile at Me 3951
When You Speak with a Lady 2047
When You Steal a Kiss or Two (Making Love) 1526
When You Stop and Think 4798
When You Take a Trip 4434
When You Take That Trip Across the Rhine 377

When You Take the Road with Me (Opening Number) 334
When You Touch Me 4191
When You Visit Paris 1868
When You Wake Up Dancing 4422
When You Walked Out Somebody Else Walked Right In 3008
When You Waltz with Me 1911
When You Want Me 3815
When You Wear a 13 Collar 4555
When You Weren't Lookin' 1418
When You Write a Greek Comedy 227
When You're a Millionaire 1313
When You're Above the Crowd 4232
When You're All Dressed Up and No Place to Go 335
When You're an Alrightnick 2422
When You're Asleep in Your Bed at Night 1177
When You're Away 216, 3304
When You're Away from Me 2519
When You're Crazy Over Daddy 4520
When You're Dancing in a Nightie on the Lawn 208
When You're Driving Through the Moonlight 759
When You're Far Away from New York Town 2201
When You're Good to Mama 723
When You're Home Again 496
When You're In 2240
When You're in Love 1893, 2698, 1868, 3888
When You're in Love with Somebody 2986
When You're in Love You'll Know 1588
When You're in My Arms 4334
When You're in Right with the Right Little Girl 2684
When You're in Rome 1345
When You're in Town 3665
When You're on the Stage 1066
When You're Only Seventeen 3623
When You're Pretty and the World Is Fair 3675
When You're Sad 3184
When You're Shot in the Movies 2776
When You're Single 1419
When You're Smiling (What a Smile Can Do) 4860
When You're Starring in the Movies 3737
When You're Sweet Sixteen 1849
When You're the Only One 564
When You're Traveling 2732
When You're Young and In Love 4789
When You've Loved Your Man 2195
When You've Pampered Your Adipose Tissue 4473
When You've Picked Your Basket of Peaches (The Girls of Home Sweet Home) 1919
When Your Ankle Wears the Ball and Chain 3304
When Your Boy Becomes a Man 1387
When Your Heart Is Too Young 1745
When Your Heart's in the Ring 3511
When Your Love Is Away 3921
When Your Lover Has Gone 4534
When Your Lover Says Goodbye 798
When Your Sweet Lips Meet Mine 132
When Your Troubles Have Started 1762, 3674
When Yuba Plays the Rumba on His Tuba 4335
When Ziegfeld's Follies Hit the Town 805
When Zim Zim Got the Cymbals 2760
Whenever I Dream 2342
Whenever I Think of You 3658
Whenever I Visit the Town 2695
Whenever I'm with You 4289
Whenever Night Falls (1) 3772
Whenever Night Falls (2) 3772
Whenever You Want Me 708
Wher'er in the Thick of the Fight 1355
Where? 2268, 3674
Where 3989
Where Am I 2553
Where Am I? 4093, 3777
Where Am I Going? 4238
Where Am I Now? 4701
Where Are All the Good Times Gone 935
Where Are the Blossoms? 1500
Where Are the Days 3466
Where Are the Faces? 589
Where Are the Girls of Yesterday 634
Where Are the Men? 163
Where Are the Old Pals of Yesterday 3144
Where Are the Plays of Yesterday 4831
Where Are the Rich Little Poor Little Children? 4679
Where Are the Snows 2050
Where Are the Songs We Sung? 3235
Where Are the White Birds Flying? 2182
Where Are They? 483
Where Are They Now 1593
Where Are Those People Who Did 'Hair'? 3806
Where Are You Going, My Pretty Maid? 3298
Where Are You/Where Am I? 2702
Where Are Your Children 411
Where Are Your Children? 1341
Where Are Your Children 412
Where Art Thou, Romeo? 25
Where Be My Daughter 4404
Where Broadway Meets Fifth Avenue 4662
Where Can He Be? 294
Where Can I Find a Cherry 725
Where Can I Go from You? 70
Where Can One Go to Powder Her Nose? 3131
Where Can That Someone Be 2275
Where Can the Baby Be? 3924
Where Can the Rich and Poor Be Friends 4173
Where Can You Take a Girl? 3603
Where Did I Go Wrong 2542
Where Did It Go? 681, 2953
Where Did Our Love Go? 338
Where Did Robinson Crusoe Go with Friday on Saturday Night 3737
Where Did That Little Dog Go? 4034
Where Did the Bird Hear That? 3679
Where Did the Dreams Go 2616
Where Did the Good Times Go? 3330
Where Did the Night Go? 4718
Where Did the Summer Go 2965
Where Did the Summer Go To? 148
Where Did We Go Wrong? 2279, 2360

Where Did You Get Dem High Heeled Shoes? 2225
Where Did You Get Those Irish Eyes? 3222
Where Did You Learn to Dance 1298
Where Do I Belong? 2615
Where Do I Go? 1717
Where Do I Go from Here? 344, 1280, 2630
Where Do I Stand 3427
Where Do Little Birds Go? 1277
Where Do Mosquitos Go? 4814
Where Do People Go 3806
Where Do They Come From? 1920
Where Do They Come From 2774
Where Do They Get Those Guys? 3985
Where Do We Go From Here? 842
Where Do We Go from Here? 3893
Where Do We Go from Here 4702
Where Do You Buy Your Chapeau 3191
Where Do You Come From, My Pretty Maid 333
Where Do You Get Your Greens? 4483
Where Do You Go When You Arrive? 3493
Where Do You Go When You're on Top? 3493
Where Do You Hang Your Heart? 1885
Where Do You Travel? 372
Where Does a Man Begin? 1676
Where Does Love Go? 3577
Where Does One Begin? 3066
Where E'er I Go 2848
Where East Meets West 1484
Where Fate Shall Guide 4425
Where Has My Hubby Gone Blues 3249
Where Has the Rainbow Gone? 1300
Where Has Tom Gone? 920
Where Has Una Gone? 1544
Where Have I Been? 1864
Where Have I Been All My Life? 1346, 1730
Where Have I Heard That Song Before? 1745
Where Have We Met Before? 4583
Where Have You Been 3131
Where Have You Been All My Life? 86
Where Have You Been Hiding 1833
Where Have You Been Up to Now? 4595
Where He Goes We Go Too 2936
Where I Belong 3908
Where I Come From 3544
Where I Want to Be 721
Where in the World 3862, 916, 2877, 3465
Where Is Away 3427
Where Is Blue 2553
Where Is Bundy? 4237
Where Is Cinderella? (inst.) 759
Where Is Everybody 4114
Where Is Love? 1817, 3271
Where Is Matthew Going? 148
Where Is Me? 3112
Where Is Me 3111
Where Is My Boy 1689
Where Is My Handsome Knight? 3165
Where Is My Homeland 3698
Where Is My Little Old New York? 3009
Where Is My Love 825
Where Is My Soldier Boy? 1616
Where Is My Son? 3702
Where Is My Wife? 693
Where Is Respect 4450
Where Is She? 1486, 3754
Where Is She When We Need Her? 2578
Where Is That Lucky Star? 1837
Where Is That Rainbow? 1676
Where Is That Someone for Me? 3899
Where is the Angel Now 2241
Where Is the Boss 4602
Where Is the Bride? 345
Where Is the Clown? 410, 413
Where Is the Devil in Evelyn? 1999
Where Is the Girl? 90
Where Is the Handy Man 2338
Where Is the Knight for Me? 3939
Where Is the Language to Tell? 3333
Where Is the Life That Late I Led? 2331
Where Is the Love? 4360
Where Is the Magic? 407
Where Is the Man 2968
Where Is the Man? 3912
Where Is the Man for Me? 1093
Where Is the Man I Married? 1891
Where Is the Man of My Dreams 1485
Where Is the News? 3530
Where Is the One Who Will Mourn Me When I'm Gone? 1085
Where Is the Pleasure in Wine and Song-If the Woman Is Not There 3877
Where Is the Rainbow 275
Where Is the Reason 3741
Where Is the She for Me? 2439
Where Is the She for Me 2483
Where Is the Sun? 875, 885
Where Is the Times? 453
Where Is the Tribe for Me? 269
Where Is the Waltz 3112
Where Is the Warmth? 273
Where Is the Wind? 2196
Where Is This Man? 4577
Where It Goes When It's GOne 494
Where It's Day 306
Where It's Hot 1277
Where Jasmine Flowers Are Twining 3951
Where Jazz was Born 2302
Where Lanterns Gleam 1992
Where Love Grows 3680
Where Love Is Waiting 2486
Where My Caravan Rests 2696
Where My Forefathers Died 9
Where, Oh Where? 3326
Where Oh Where 3733
Where, Oh Where Can I Find Love? 3907
Where or When 247, 3020
Where Shall I Find Him? 3815
Where Shall I Go? 344
Where Shall We Go for Our Honeymoon 3362

Where Smoke Rings Go 2605
Where the Bamboo Babies Grow 2706
Where the Bee Sucks 1104
Where the Black Eyed Susan Grows 3737
Where the Boys Are 4193, 4264
Where the Bulls Are 128
Where the East Meets the West 382
Where the Edelweiss Is Blooming 1738
Where the 'Ell Is 'Ome? 589
Where the Fairest Flow'rs Are Blooming (Butterfly Waltz Song) 252
Where the Fairest Flowers Blooming 3567
Where the Flag Is Waving 361
Where the Ganges Flows 21
Where the Gigantic Ocean Atlantic (Opening Chorus) 4430
Where the Green Pines Shadow the Ground 996
Where the Hell Is Annie? 3201
Where the Honeymoon Alone Can See 468
Where the Hudson River Flows 1013
Where the Millionaires Live 563
Where the Morning Glories Twine 3796
Where the River Shannon Flows 1902
Where the Sun God Walks 3813
Where the Sunset Meets the Sea (Gypsy Song) 4683
Where the Trees Are Green with Parrots 4541
Where the War Left Us 3873
Where the Wild Thyme Grows 1655
Where the Wild Vine Clings 1910
Where There's a Will 4303
Where There's Smoke 2114
Where Those Cotton Blossoms Grow 2619
Where Tina Gets It From 3811
Where Tomorrows Begin 1847
Where Was I 4588
Where Was I When They Passed Out Luck 2874
Where Was the Music 408
Where We Came From 2064
Where We Can Be in Love 2351
Where Were You 1552
Where Were You? 3319, 3669
Where Were You-Where Was I? 403
Where Will I Be Next Wednesday Night? 2049
Where Will I Lie Down? 2203
Where Will We Be Tomorrow 2368
Where Would We Be without Perverts? 2069
Where Would You Be Without Me? 3731
Where Would You Get Your Coat? 1272
Where You Are 203, 2333, 1336, 2014, 2010, 2201, 2655
Where You Been Hiding Till Now 1064
(I Love to Be 'Neath the Old Apple Tree) Where You r Name Is Carved with Mine 1490
Where You Go, I Go 3379
Where You Go, Will I Go 356
Where You Lead 2636
Where'd Marilla Come From? 148
Where's All This Anger Coming From 949
Where's Charley? 4652
Where's Jim? 2976
Where's Louis? 1109
Where's Mama? 4757
Where's My Happy Ending? 1251
Where's My Love A'Wanderin' 3764
Where's My Picture? 944
Where's My Shoe? 3918
Where's My Sister 1662
Where's My Wife? 999
Where's North? 4485
Where's That Little Girl (with the Little Green Hat)? 1267
Where's That Rainbow? 3436
Where's the Boy? Here's the Girl! 4443
Where's the Boy I Saved for a Rainy Day? 70
Where's the Bridegroom? 4359
Where's the Funeral 912
Where's the Girl for Me 2385, 2492
Where's the Girl for Me? 3177
Where's the Little Boy for Me? 1588
Where's the Mate for Me? 3949
Where's the Music Coming From? 299
Whereas 1846, 1879
Wherefore and the Why, The 2399
Wherefore Art Thou, Juliet 2105
Wherefore Art Thou, Romeo 272
Wherever He Ain't 2208, 2660
Wherever I May Go 1918
Wherever There's Music and Beautiful Girls 3246
Wherever They Fly the Flag of Old England 189
Wherever You Are 1959, 3968
Wherever You Go 994, 1769
Which? 3382
Which 4581
Which Did You Say Was Number One? 62
Which Do You Prefer? 200
Which Door 170
Which Hat Shall I Wear? 1770
Which One Shall We Marry? 4434
Which Shall I Choose 4655
Which Shall It Be? 1747
Which Way Do I Go? 3838
Which Way Is Home? (Ie Wa Doko) 1616
Which Way? 64
Which Witch? 2227, 4153
Which Witch 4722
Whichaway'd They Go 4314
Whichness of the Whatness, The 1345
Whiffer's Song 2225
Whiffin' the Weed 1773
Whiffle Walk, The 4037
While All Are Asleep 4133
While Drinking and Eating 340
While I Am Still Young 2306
While I Am Waiting 4554
While I'm Swinging 1829
While I'm Waiting 3221
While in My Submarine 1118
While My Baby's Gone 2026

While My Lady Sleeps 4251
While Strolling Through the Forest 2559
While Strolling Through the Park One Day 3989
While the Big Old World Rolls Round 4649
While the City Sleeps 1601, 2070
While There's a Song to Sing 3013
While They Were Dancing Around 1963, 3737
While They Were Sleeping 2284
While We Go Waltzing Around 1831
While We Tell them About It All (Opening Act II) 3949
While We're Waltzing 3787
While You Are Young 4778
While You Were Away 3507
While You're Thinking 4646
Whiling My Time Away 2540
Whimsical Peddler, The 702
Whip, The 4827
Whip Dance, The 2565, 3723
Whip Hand, The 2419
Whip-o-Will 552
Whip-Poor-Will 3819, 4860
Whip-poor-wills 4704
Whippoorwill 669, 2190
Whippoorwill (Never Again for Me) 4805
Whippoorwill in a Willow Tree, A 3726
Whirl of the Opera, The 4657
Whirl of the World, The 4657
Whirled Into Happiness 4010, 4010
Whirligig 1682
Whirling 2571
Whirlwind, The 4381
Whirlwind Circle 825
Whirlwind Dance 3154
Whirlwind Trot 1784
Whirlwind Whirl, The 1663
Whiskers 2, 1689
Whiskers' Dance 406
Whiskey Bug 2556
Whisper in My Ear 2856
Whisper on the Wind 1168
Whisper to Me 152
Whispering 1120
Whispering Hope 1897
Whispering Pines 1152, 3641
Whispering Shade 2902
Whispering Song, The 458
Whispering to You 4595
Whispering Trees 2843
Whispering Whispers 3203
Whispers 3296
Whispers on the Wind 4659
(If You Want a Little Doggie) Whistle and I'll Come to You 2696
Whistle 3627, 3659, 4476
Whistle a Song 733
Whistle and I'll Come to Meet You 764
Whistle and I'll Wait for You 3868
Whistle and the Girls Come Round 3433
Whistle Away Your Blues 1691
Whistle If You Want Me Dear 4801
Whistle in the Rain 4424
Whistle It 3675, 1173, 4589
Whistle of a Train 1990
Whistle When You Walk Out 2347, 2716
Whistle When You Want Me 2390
Whistle When You're Lonely 2576
Whistle While You Work 4035
Whistle While You Work, Boys 4352
Whistle While You're Lonely 1151
Whistle Works, A 4186
Whistles 459
Whistling 4654
Whistling Bill 3820
Whistling Cowboy Joe 3396
Whistling Dan 3177
Whistling for a Kiss 125
Whistling Wizard, The 4660
Whistling Yankee Girl, The 3387
White and Brown Girl 767
White and Gold Ballet 3899
White and Gray Cadets, The 1925
White and the Pink, The 4479
White and the Red!, The 3732
White Bum 2055
White Cat, The 4662
White Cavaliers, The 4150
White City, The 3322
White Cliffs of Dover, The 3018, 4027
White Fete, The (inst.) 3685
White Flags 3879
White Folks 4504
White Heat 294, 3709
White Horse Inn 4667
White House Resident 2007
White Is the Dove 1056
White Knight, The 54
White Liberal to the Rescue 838
White Lies 3578
White Lies, Black Lies 2710
White Light Alley 1845
White Light Lane 4382
White Lights 4668
White Lights Were Coming 551
White Like Me 2954
White Lilacs 4669
White Man's Hope, The 2710
White Moon 2766
White Queen, The 54
White Rabbit 3739
White Rhapsody 3410
White Rose, Red Rose 1678, 2843
White Roses Red 54
White Russian New York 1370
White Sails 4667
White Sash, A 949
White Sheeting 2290
White Sister, The 4671, 4672
White Slavery Fandango, The 1081
White Trash Motel 1737

White Wash 3337
White Witch of Jamaica, The 3108
Whiter Shade of Pale 3739
Whitewash Man, The 632
Whitewings Marimba, The 1632
Whither Thou Goest 2248
Whiting 1824
Whittling 917
Whizzer Brown 2132
Whizzer Gong Down 2132
Whizzin' Away Along de Track 653
Who? 2204, 2372
Who 3009
Who? 4212, 4799
Who Am I? 83, 550, 2442, 766, 905
Who Am I 2705
Who Am I? 3167
Who Am I 3249, 3301
Who Am I? 3452
Who Am I Kidding? 846
Who Am I That You Should Care for Me? 3650
Who Am I Thinking Of? 735
Who Am I, Who Are You, Who Are We? 3439
Who Are Those People? 3164
Who Are We 3651
Who Are We Kidding 4090
Who Are You? 58, 2876
Who Are You 3453
Who Are You? 3920
Who Are You Anabel 1997
Who Are You Beautiful Unknown? 3051
Who Are You Now? 1420
Who Are You with Tonight? 1566
Who Ate Napoleons with Josephine When Napoleon Was Away? 208
Who Bites the Holes in Schweitzer Cheese? 3252
Who, but You 3674
Who Can Control the Human Heart 3202
Who Can I Turn To (When Nobody Needs Me) 3731
Who Can Say? 1282
Who Can Say 4168
Who Can Tell? 168
Who Can? You Can! 1456
Who Cares? 487, 703
(But) Who Cares? 771
Who Cares? 2620
Who Cares 2856
Who Cares? 3225
Who Cares! 3362
Who Cares? 4673
Who Cares for a Name 659
Who Cares If the World Is Round? 2962
Who Carries the Gun 1502
Who Comes in My Garden 4066
Who Committed the Murder? 3002
Who Could Be Blue? 1329, 2764
Who Could Eat Now 4718
Who Could Ever Have Dreamed Up You 3465
Who Couldn't Dance with You 1649
Who Dat Say Chicken in Dis Crowd? 783
Who Dealt? 3301
Who Did? You Did 1297
Who Do They Know? 1349, 1350
Who Do We Thank! 2069
Who Do We Thank 2804
Who Do You Love? 805
Who Do You Love 1128
Who Do You Love? 3945
Who Do You Love, I Hope 153
Who Do You Think We Are? 2020
Who Do You Think You Are? 304, 4722
Who Does She Think She Is? 2584
Who Done It? 426, 1679
Who Fills the Bill 4060
Who, Gal 1182
Who Gave You Permission? 287
Who Gives a Hey 3939
Who Gives a Sou 2705
Who Hit Me? 2439
Who in the Name of Pete Is R.M.B.? 2496
Who Is General Staff? 901
Who Is Hannah? 1739
Who Is He? 1699
Who Is It Always There? 920
Who Is Like Unto Thee 1715
Who Is Samuel Cooper? 2615
(Who, Who, Who, Who) Who Is She? 170
Who Is Sylvia? 4485
Who Is the Bravest? 1791
Who Is the Lucky Girl to Be? 3225
Who Is the Man? 3989
Who Is the Phony? 2993
Who Is There Among Us Who Knows 3274
Who Is This Man 1161
Who Is This Man? 3722, 1636, 2766
Who Is This One? 2
Who Is This Woman 3908
Who Is This? 2970
Who Is to Know? 3627
Who Is? You Are! 649
Who Killed Nobody 2134
Who Knew My Father 3280
Who Knows 1803, 2439
Who Knows Better Than I 2941
Who Knows the Way to My Heart? 2838
Who Knows What Might Have Been? 4190
Who Knows? 2048, 2662, 2985, 4646
Who Loves to Ride on a Slide Trombone? 854
Who Loves You As I Do 4249
Who Made Bluebeard Blue? 725
Who Makes Much of a Miracle? 2433
Who Makes the Finest Ginger Bread? 3422
Who, Me? 23
Who Needed You 1189
Who Needs 'Em? 3429
Who Needs a Woman? 1745
Who Needs Baseball 957
Who Needs Her? 521
Who Needs Him? 1709

Who Needs It 98
Who Needs It? 1990, 3920
Who Needs Love 2235
Who Needs Love? 4542
Who Needs the Birds and Bees 153
Who Needs the Love of a Woman 3653
Who Needs the Vote? 2928
Who Needs to Dream? 846
Who Needs to Dream 845
Who Paid the Rent for Mrs. Rip Van Winkle When Rip Van Winkle Was Away 351
Who Paid the Rent for Mrs. Rip Van Winkle (When Rip Van Winkle Went Away) 965
Who Paid the Rent for Mrs. Rip Van Winkle When Rip Van Winkle Went Away 4823
Who Played Poker with Pocahontas when John Smith Went Away? 2939
Who Put Out the Light That Lit the Candle That Started the Flame Deep Down in My Heart? 1924
Who Said Blackbirds Are Blue 443
Who Said Gay Paree 629
Who Said He Couldn't Dance? 3068
Who Said There Ain't No Santa Claus? (1) 1300
Who Said There Ain't No Santa Claus? (2) 1300
Who Says a Coon Can't Love 4717
Who Says You Always Have to Be Happy? 550
Who Sent Those Persian Plums 3446
Who Shall Be Bold When Love Arrives? 526
Who Started the Rhumba (Who Made the Rhumba) 297
Who Swore to Be Good and True? (You Swear to Be Good and True) 1080
Who Taught Her Everything? 1420
Who That Knows How I Love You, Love 3588
Who the Hell Do These Wise Guys Think They Are? 3600
Who to Love If Not a Stranger 935
Who Walked Across the Water 4147
Who Walks Like a Scarecrow 239
Who Wants to Love Spanish Ladies? 3650
Who Wants to Settle Down? 455
Who Wants to Work? 2935
Who Was Chasing Paul Revere? 391
Who Was I? 4450
Who Was the Last Girl (You Called By Her First Name)? 2491
Who? Where? What? 1727
Who-Who-Who-Hoolahan 1188
Who Will Be the Children 1116
Who Will Be There 3901
Who Will Be with You When I'm Far Away 1120, 3953
Who Will Buy 3271
Who Will Count the Stitches? 3631
Who Will Dance with the Blind Dancing Bear 4398
Who Will I Be? 2051
Who Will It Be? 1700
Who Will Lay Hands? 4615
Who Will the Next Fool Be 3608
Who Will Walk with Me? 732
Who Will You Marry Then? 1903
Who Would a Bachelor Be? 1521
Who Would Have Dreamed? 3359
Who Would Have Dreamed 4727
Who Would Have Thought? 962
Who Would Refuse? 2312
Who Would've Thought? 1633
Who Wouldn't 3388
Who? You! 3622
Who'd Be Seventeen? 4016
Who'd Believe 3956
Who'd Ever Guess It? 721
Who'd Have Guessed It? 3201
Who'll Buy? 2591
Who'll Buy My Flowers 2803
Who'll Buy My Violets? 2526
Who'll Help Me Spend My Money? 2041
Who'll Mend a Broken Heart? 3622
Who'll Prop Me Up in the Rain 774
Who's Been List'ning to My Heart? 142
Who's Been Sitting in My Chair? 1614
Who's Boss in Boston 4303
Who's Doing What to Erwin? 2449
Who's Excited 1048
Who's Going to Teach the Children? 2173
Who's Gonna Be the Winner? 404
Who's Gonna Get You? 3648
Who's Got a Match? 850
Who's Got the Pain? 957
Who's It? 1116
Who's Next 4412
Who's on Our Side? 4595
Who's Perfect? 2322
Who's Perfect for You? 2322
Who's Sorry Now 3695
Who's That? 2097
Who's That Girl? 167
Who's That Woman? 1329
Who's the Boss? 4219
Who's the Boy? 1693
Who's the Boy 3849
Who's the Fool? 1319
Who's the Greatest? 2444
Who's the Little Girl? 4644
Who's the Lucky Fellow? 200
Who's the Thief 2242
Who's the Who (Where Has My Hubby Gone Blues) 3184
Who's This Chick? 2243
Who's This Geezer Hitler 455
Who's to Blame 924
Who's to Blame? 2516
Who's Who 920, 3019
Who's Who? 4249
Who's Who 4677, 4678
Who's Who Are You? 3249
Who's Who with You 1942, 1944
Who's Who with You? 3478

Who's Who with You 4491
Who's Whom? 4679
Who's Your Gen'man Frien'? 2779
Who's Your Little Who-zis? 393
Who's Zoo in Girl Land 2900
Whoa! 4648
Whoa, Bill 830
Whoa Bill 3298
Whoa Boy 2477
Whoa, Emma! 2789
Whoa-Haw 3020
Whoa Pagliacci 1129
Whoa San 2851
Whoever You Are (I Love You) 3603
Whoever You Are 4038
Whoever You Are, I Love You 261
Whole Hot or Nothin' 3294
Whole Long Year from Today, A 3453
Whole Lot of Happy, A 4798
Whole Lotta Love 3739
Whole Lotta Real Good Feeling 4192
Whole Lotta Sunlight, A 3656
Whole New Ballgame, A 1099
Whole New Board Game, A 721
Whole Story, The 3828
Whole Town's Talking, The 3349
Whole World Loves, The 2813
Whole World Revolves Around You, The 2283
Whole World's Doing It Now Charleston 2700
Whole World's Waitin' to Sing Your Song 2200
Whole Year Round, The 4113
Wholesome Honeys Here at Home 864
Whoop Daddy Ooden Dooden Day 4757
Whoop De Doo 1581
Whoop-de-oodle-do! 611
Whoop-Dee-Doo 2022
Whoop-Diddy-Ay 3841
Whoop 'er Up (with a Whoop-La-La) 2254
Whoop Her Up with a Whoop-La-La! 511
Whoop-La-La 115
Whoop-Ti-Ay 3347
Whoopee! 2004
Whoopee 4320
Whoopem Up 2302
Whoopin' and a-Hollerin' 4314
Whoops-a-Daisy 4719
Whoops My Dear 797
Whoopsie 3924
Whoopsie Daisy Day 4255
Whoopsy Daisy 30
Whoosh, Bang 2542
Whooshin' Through My Flesh 1662
Whoppers 178
Whores Behind the Doors, The 2565
Whose Baby Are You? 3146
Whose Baby Blues 456
Whose Izzy Is He? 3926
Whose Little Angry Man 3656
Whose Little Bird Are You 4537
Whose Little Girl Are You? 4469, 1967, 3486
Whosis-Whatsis, The 1488
Why 109, 299
Why? 322
Why 773
Why? 969, 2430, 2880, 2958
Why 3064
Why? 3165, 3702
Why 4087
Why? 4497, 3221
Why Adam Sinned 2111
Why Ain't I Home? 4023
Why Ain't We Free? 3035
Why Ain't We Got a Dome? 1474
Why All This Fuss About Spain 1176
Why Am I Afraid to Love 3239
Why Am I Blue 4824
Why Am I in Love 4321
Why Am I Me 3928
Why Am I So Happy? 3164
Why Am I So Sad? 969
Why Am I So Sad Today? 762
Why Am I So Wonderful 1297
Why and Because 4659
Why Are Chickens So High? 1823
Why Are They Following Me? 4010
Why Are We Here? 4536
Why Are We Invited Here? 473
Why Be Afraid to Dance? 1242
Why Be Good? 4320
Why Can't a Girl Be a Soldier 1759
Why Can't He See? 2583
Why Can't I? 4118
Why Can't I 4172
Why Can't I Be Happy Too? 2235
Why Can't I Forget You? 2432
Why Can't I Speak 4480
Why Can't I Speak? 4862
Why Can't I Walk Away? 2681
Why Can't I Walk Through That Door? 808, 809
Why Can't It All Be a Dream? 2619
Why Can't It Be Me? 446
Why Can't It Happen Again? 67
Why Can't It Happen to Me? 1784, 2669
Why Can't Me and You? 2173
Why Can't the English? 3038
Why Can't the World Go and Leave Us Alone? 958
Why Can't They Hand It to Me? 3230
Why Can't They Leave Me Alone 3294
Why Can't They Song 4371
Why Can't This Night Last Forever? 1670
Why Can't We All Be Nice 1634
Why Can't We Be Unhappy? 1697
Why Can't You Behave 2331
Why Did Daddy Tell Me Those Lies? 3165
Why Did He Have to Die? 3741
Why Did He Kiss My Heart Awake? 1384
Why Did I Choose You? 4764
Why Did I Do It? 299
Why Did I Forget? 1700
Why Did It Have to Be You 2674

Why Did They Die? 1616
Why Did We Marry Soldiers? 1027
Why Did You Do It? 383
Why Did You Have to Come Into My Life 2654
Why Did You Make Me Love You? 3641
Why Didn't I Meet You Long Ago 3345
Why Didn't We Meet Before 3156
Why Do Fools Fall in Love 4534, 580, 166, 3739
Why Do I? 1529
Why Do I Care for You? 2857
Why Do I Dream? 214
Why Do I Keep Going to the Theatre? 4635
Why Do I Like You? 3091
Why Do I Love Bennie? 3202
Why Do I Love You? 2204, 3949, 4300
Why Do I See Good 3306
Why Do Lovers Break Each Others' Hearts 2427
Why Do the Girls 1992
Why Do the Wrong People Travel? 3235, 3815
Why Do They All Take the Night Boat to Albany 3985
Why Do They Call a Private a Private? 7, 3444
Why Do They Call Me a Gibson Girl? 356
Why Do They Call Me a Gibson Girl 662
Why Do They Die at the End of Classical Dance? 3778
Why Do They Make 'Em So Beautiful? 735
Why Do They Make Them So Beautiful 136
Why Do They Say They're the Fair Sex? 901
Why Do We Love Them? 3312
Why Do Women Always Choose the Wrong Man? 4577
Why Do Women Have to Call It Love 101
Why Do Ya Roll Those Eyes? 123
Why Do You Betray Me 1079
Why Do You Keep Us Guessing? 3623
Why Do You Love Me? 720
Why Do You Make Me Like You 4048
Why Do You Suppose? 1800
Why Do You Tease Me? 3523
Why Do You Think I Love You So? 2145
Why Do You Think You're Fooling with That Million Dollar Talk 3985
Why Do You Want to Hurt Me So? 3326
Why Do You Want to Know Why? 799
Why Does a Woman Leave Her Man 3517
Why Does Everybody in the City Put You Down 4684
Why Does It Always Happen to Me? 2541
Why Does It Have to Be Funny? 550
Why Does It Have to Be You? 4542
Why Does Love Get in the Way? 3196
Why Does the Whole Damn World Adore Me? 3931
Why Don't I Leave Him 3619
Why Don't My Baby Write? 3999
Why Don't Some Baby Pick Me 525
Why Don't the Band Play? 352, 2675
Why Don't They Believe Me 3161
Why Don't They Dance the Polka Anymore 1544
Why Don't They Give Us a Chance 4158
Why Don't They Leave the Sheik Alone? 606
Why Don't We? 551
Why Don't We Move to Philadelphia 4830
Why Don't We Run Away 2171
Why Don't We Save Our Love for Marriage? 3165
Why Don't We Switch? 3571
Why Don't We Try Staying Home 1272, 4517
Why Don't Ya Waltz with Me? 914
Why Don't You? 25, 4425
Why Don't You Be Nice to Some Nice Fellow? 256
Why Don't You Believe Me? 1216
Why Don't You Do Right? 3428
Why Don't You Get a Girl Like Me 4657
Why Don't You Get a Sweetie? 764
Why Don't You Hand It to Me? 3727
Why Don't You Say So? 2308
Why Don't You Take One, Little Boy? 470
Why Don't You Try? 349, 1758
Why Fall at All? 2651
Why Fight This? 3837
Why Go Anywhere at All? 1456
Why God Why? 2905
Why Grow Old? 3067
Why Hast Thou Done Evil to These People? 1715
Why Have You Brought Me Here 3464
Why Her? 868
Why Him? 652
Why I Love You 2518
Why Is a Girl? Do You Know? 2723
Why Is It? 1570
Why Is It Love Makes Us Feel Queer? 742
Why Is Love? 2263
Why Is Love 3466
Why Is the Ocean So Near the Shore? 4642
Why Is the World So Changed Today? 905
Why Is There Ever Good-Bye? 650
Why Johnny? 4635
Why, Mama, Why 1699
Why Marry Them? 1453
Why Me? 4481
Why Moses Never Saw the Promised Land 813
Why Must I Be a Teenager in Love? 3695
Why Must the Show Go On 520
Why Must We Always Be Dreaming? 3766
Why Must We Part? 2552
Why Must We Say Good-Bye 1026
Why No One to Love? 4149
Why Not? (Manhattan Carnival) 146
Why Not 3643, 1369
Why Not? 3602, 4798
Why Not for Marriage 3543
Why Not Have a Little Party? 1855
Why Not Katie? 3509
Why Not Me? 90
Why Not Surrender 347
Why Oh Why 1916
Why Oh Why? 3249
Why Oh Why 3263
Why Save for That Rainy Day? 4825
Why Should a Little Girl Be Lonely? 2351

Why Should I Feel Lonely 2392
Why Should I Let You? 910
Why Should I Trust You? 3972
Why Should I Wake Up? 610
Why Should She Be Happy? 3227
Why Should the Young Men Fight 3280
Why Should the Young Men Fight the Wars? 1770
Why Should They Know About Paris? 1249
Why Should This a Desert Be? 3909
Why Should We Be Wasting Time? 1693
Why Should We Be Wasting Time 3148
Why Should We Stay Home and Sew 3304
Why Shouldn't I Have You? 1272
Why Shouldn't I? 2252, 4401
Why Shouldn't We? 3772
Why Shouldn't You Tell Me That? 3251
Why Sing a Love Song 390
Why So Late 1459
Why So Silent 3464
Why Speak of Love When There's Work to Be Done? 1524
Why Speak of Money? 2444
Why Take a Sandwich to a Banquet (You Don't Take a Sandwich to a Banquet) 3193
Why Talk About Sex 3131
Why the Chicken? 4685
Why They Made Him King 2730
Why Try Hard to Be Good? 3224
Why Was I Born? 2204
Why Was I Born 2372
Why Was I Born? 3020, 4234
Why Was I Born on a Farm? 4015
Why We Do It 2648
Why We Tell the Story 3285
Why? Why? Why? 2312
Why Wives 71
Why Work and Slave All Day 905
Why Worry? 1847, 1961
Why Would Anyone Want to Get Married 4384
Why Would You Want to Kiss Me? 4409
Why Wouldn't I Do? 4581
Wick 3862
Wicked Little Pair of Eyes 720
Wicked Man, A 1194
Wicked Man 2233
Wicked Old Willage of Wenice 1281
Wicked, Unwholesome, Expensive 1342
Wicky Wacky Hula Hula Honka Wonka Honolulu Hawaiian Honey of Mine, The 3641
Wide-Awake Morning 3938
Wide Open Spaces 1918
Wide Pants Willie 1460
Wide Smile, High Style, That's Me 4138
Widow, The 3578
Widow at Windsor, The 2047
Widow Douglas' House, The 2027
Widow Fascinating, The 1248
Widow from Amarillo 859
Widow Has Ways, A 3675
Widow Kiddo 3022
Widow Wood, The 4805
Widows 2358
Widows Blues 2276
Widow's Song, The 2027
Widows Song, The 3805
Widow's Wile, A 1640
Wie Einst Im Mai 2794
Wiener Blut 4563
Wife Beating Song 2648
Wife for Each Day in the Week, A 1911
Wifie of Your Own, A 3237
Wiggle Waggle 4200
Wiggley Walk 1953
Wiggly-Woggly-Walk, The 3442
Wigmaker's Sequence 4233
Wild About Music 2637
Wild About You 2597
Wild and Reckless 1094
Wild and Wonderful 4689
Wild and Wooly West, The 4271
Wild Bird, The 2947
Wild Birds Calling 823
Wild-Flower 4694
Wild Flowers 2934
Wild Indians 3453
Wild Irish Rose 537, 538
Wild Justice, The 2591
Wild Oat Joe 124
Wild Pen 1498
Wild Romantic Blues 2856
Wild Rose 310, 2947
Wild Rose, The 3819, 4649
Wild Rose 4692
Wild Trumpets and Crazy Piano (Got a Guy to Forget) 2105
Wild Wedding Bells 1683, 2432
Wild White Rose, The 2269
Wild, Wild Women, The 1065
Wild Women 146, 1425, 3158
Wild Women Don't Have the Blues 478
Wild Women's Wiles 4477, 4530
Wildcat 4693
Wildcat Smathers 3841
Wildcats 85, 3009
Wilderness and Thou, A 3618
Wilderness Man 1674
Wildest Dream, The 1079
Wildfire 1014
Wildflower 3249
Wildflowers 1498
Wilful Girl, A 402
Wilhelm Der Grosser 3134
Wilhelmina 3998
Wilkes-Barre, Pa. 4435
Wilkommen 610, 4480
Will, The 4522
Will-a-Mania 4695
Will All My Dreams Come True 3033
Will He Ever Know? 2599

Will He Ever Smile Again? 2035
Will He Like Me? 3918
Will I Ever See Her Again 4035
Will I Ever Tell You 3016
Will It All End in Smoke? 1066
Will Lipton Lift the Cup 2851
Will Make It to the Moon Tonight 2094
Will My Love Come Home to Me 4096
Will My Real Love Please Stand Up 3124
Will-O-the-Wisp 2534
Will O' the Wisp 2574
Will o' the Wisp 4094
Will-O-the Wisp, The 1016
Will-of-the-Wisp 4835
Will She Come from the East (North, West, or South)? 3007
Will She or Won't She? 621
Will Somebody Tell Me Why? 1466
Will There Be a Street in the Future 1887
Will They Remember 1412
Will Thou Be Gone, Love? 1897
Will We Ever Know Each Other 1289
Will We Meet Again? 2
Will You Be Hating Me Tomorrow 1989
Will You Be My Hero, Noble Sir? 3229
Will You Be My Little Bride 4738
Will You Be My Teddy Bear 3387
Will You Buy Any Tape? 3909
Will You Come to the Bow'r 2573
Will You Forget? 3727
Will You Forgive Me? 978, 3538, 4781
Will You Forgive Us? 598
Will You Have a Gin Rickey? 331
Will You Love Me in December As You Do in May? 1897
Will You Love Me on Monday Morning 4498
Will You Love Me When My Flivver Is a Wreck? 3865
Will You Marry Me? 2972
Will You Marry Me 496
Will You Marry Me? 3505
Will You Promise 4240
Will You Remember 4251, 1176
Will You Remember (Sweetheart) 2794
Will You Remember Me? 2344, 2376
Will You Remember? Will You Forget? 4532
Will You Sing This Glee with Me? 3322
Will You Still Love Me Tomorrow 4534, 338, 3739
Will You Think of Me Tomorrow? 2217
Will You, Won't You? 1972
Will-O-the-Wisp 659
Willa 3863
Willard Scott 1700
Willful Woman 2233
William McKinley High 4018
William Tell It to Me (William Tell Me) 2856
William's Doll 1389
William's Fine Troops 3780
William's Song 4286
Willie Off the Yacht 1469
Willie or Will He Not 4813
Willie Was a Gay Boy 1313
Willie's Got Another Girl Now 1318
Willie's Little Whistle 1342
Willing to Learn 2642
Willing to Try 306
Willow Pattern Plate, The 604
Willow Song, The 3909
Willow Tree, The 718
Willow Tree 2302, 2655
Willow Weep for Me 478
Willow, Willow, Willow 2295
Willy Will Grow Cold 807, 809
Wilt Thou Be Gone, Love? 4149
Wily Gazzoo, The 2282
Wimmen's Ways 2245
Wimmens 4794
Wimmin (I Got to Have 'Em That's All) 2857
Wimmins 4690
Wimpole Street Song, The (Here on the Corner of Wimpole Street) 3734
Win and Lose 430
Win for Me 2308
Win for Us, Guys 2579
Win Some Winsome Girl 4491
Win the War for Lili 3239
Wind (dance) 490
Wind at My Window, The 3138
Wind Bloweth, The 2319
Wind Blows in My Window, The 4399
Wind from the Bayou 2115
Wind in the Night, The 1189
Wind in the Willows, The 4701, 4701, 791
Wind of Love, The 2317
Wind Quillow Up (inst.) 3630
Wind, Sand & Stars 2539
Wind-Up in New York City 562
Wind Yourself Around Me, Dearie 3519
Windchild 4431
Windflowers (When We Were Young) 1600
Winding, Winding 1375
Windmill Song, The 3631
Window Across the Way 1422
Window Cleaners 1944
Window Cleaners, The 1297, 1691
Window on the Avenue, A 95
Windows 2846, 4484
Windy City 4703
Windy City Marmelade 4196
Wine and Peaches 3718
Wine Ballet 3403
Wine Divine 1640
Wine Is Mine, The 4798
Wine Maid Divine 1845
Wine of France 1114
Wine of Malaga, The 4032
Wine Song 2424
Wine Song, The 750
Wine, Wine! (Champagne Song) 1188
Wine, Wine, Wine 1565, 2947

Wine, Woman and Song 3400
Wine Women and Song 357
Wine, Women and Song 695, 1534, 1570
Wine Women and Song 3923
Wine, Women and Song 4544
Winged Love 2670
Winged Victory 4706
Wings 4732, 4708, 4707
Wings in the Morning 3584, 4328
Wings of Romance 3680
Wings of Sleep, The 972
Wink of His Eye, The 1473
Winner 2785
Winners 1601
Winners, Losers 400
Winnie the Pooh 4710
Winning Is Half the Fun 2579
Winning Race, The 1557
Winning the Prize 3511
Wino Will 2134
Winona 4664
Winsome Winnie 4713
Wint's Song (Pleasant Beach House) 4270
Winter and Spring 3172
Winter and Summer 681
Winter Battle 3944
Winter Beaches, The 4831
Winter Comes in Summer 2565
Winter Garden Girl 3396
Winter Garden Hop 3958
Winter in New York 1038
Winter in California 867
Winter in Central Park 4234
Winter Nights 2134, 3827
Winter of the Mind 3544
Winter Rain 1955
Winter Rose, The 2375
Winter Wonderland 4824
Wintergreen for President 3225
Winters Go By 85
Winter's on the Wind 3862
Wipeout 3695
Wipeout at Panic Point 2555
Wireless Heart, The 1536, 4393
Wireless Telephone, The 2724
Wisdom 3937, 2134
Wisdom of Eve, The 167
Wisdom of the Heart, The 3875
Wisdom Says "Festina Lente" 4404
Wise Men, The 755
Wise Old Owl 1515
Wise Old Owl, A 3073
Wise Old Saws 4404
Wish 1216, 3544, 3801
Wish for a Wish 1270
Wish I May 372
Wish Me Good Luck on My Journey 2552
Wish Me Luck 4027
Wish Them Well 85
Wish You Were Fanny 817
Wish You Were Here 4718
Wisha Wurra 1076
Wishbone Song, The 911
Wisherman's Song, The 194
Wishes 2142
Wishful Thinking 1713
Wishin' and Hopin' 338
Wishing 2147, 4493
Wishing and Hoping 4193
Wishing Cup, The 350
Wishing Song 3725
Wishing Tree of Harlem 4825
Wishing Well, The 2233
Wishing You Were Somehow Here Again 3464
Wishy-Washy 4034
Wishy Washy Woman 4522
Wisteria, My Bride 3943
Witch Behind the Man, The 4723
Witch Dance 4439
Witch Hazel 842
Witch Song 4623
Witch Woman 1342
Witchcraft 4268
Witches 685
Witches, The 2159
Witches and Jack O'Lanterns (inst.) 525
Witches Ballet (inst.) 2394
Witches Brew 1729
Witches' Incantation, The 671
Witches' Sabbath, The 2993
With a Boo 767
With a Dollar in Your Pocket 3442
With a Dream 4281
With a Family Reputation 799
With a Feather in Your Cap 3639
With a Glance Demure 1522
With a Little Bit of Cider Inside of Ida, Ida Was Full of Ideas 4604
With a Little Bit of Luck 3038
With a Little Help from My Friends 3903
With a Little Help from Your Mother 2965
With a Man 2368
With a Man on First 664
With a Pick and a Shovel 3741
With a Smile and a Song 4035
With a Snap of My Finger 2626
With a Song in My Heart 791, 4118
With a Song in Your Hair 2089
With a Sword in My Buckle 3571
With a Wave of My Wand 2103
With a Woman to Be 3696
With a Woman You Can Never Tell 2264
With a World to Conquer 2285
With a Yo Ho Heave Ho 3371
With Alice 3318
With All Due Respect 3731
With All My Heart 1681
With All Proprietee 2906
With All the Town in Bright Array (Opening Chorus Act II) 4430

With All These Worldly Possesions 2368
With Anger Stern 1905
With Anne on My Arm 2360
With Apparent Ebullition 1388
With Bells On 4469
With Cat Like Tread 2977
With Caution Tread 3887
With Downcast Eye 250
With Downcast Eye (Wedding Song) 1247
With Drum and Fife 3051
With Every Breath I Take 775
With Every Star 1782
With Fear I Tremble 4032
With Fife and Drum 402
With Frame, Two Forty Nine 4735
With Joy That Is Ecstatical 968
With Keen Anticipation 2936
...ance in Rest 1355
...e 1369
...red Head 3839
... Stride 102
...omp 4559
...2318
... Clouds 4340
... Moustache 3433
...3778
...162
...62
...50
...231
...t? 2486
...667
...e 1922
...3344
Withered Irish Rose 1970
Within the Land of Geishas 718
Within this Empty Space 3469
Without a Caress 2397
Without a Chaperon 2906
Without a Girl Like You 465
Without a Mother 3559
Without a Shadow of a Doubt 203
Without a Song 1667, 1873, 3249
Without a Sponsor 1718
Without a Stitch 1748
Without Him 1189
Without Kissing Love Isn't Love 4637
Without Love 1323, 3595, 3972
Without Me 1306, 1764, 3456
Without My Love 1680
Without My Money 4481
Without Rhythm 3709
Without Rules 2579
Without That Man 3933
Without the Girl — Inside! 1464
Without the One You Love 3137
Without Thinking of You 2638
Without You 123, 4695, 2373, 3038, 3152, 4807
Without You I'm Nothing 2987
Without You There Is No Me 302
Without Your Love 1110
Without Your Music 3465
Witty Invention 2464
Wizard of Magic Town 4019
Wizard of Oz Medley 2294
Wizard's Dual, The 1159
Wizards of Wizards 973
Wm. Desmond Taylor Murder Mystery 407
Wob-a-ly Walk 3382
Woe and Misery 4139
Woe Betide 2334
Woe Is Me 1871, 4766
Woggle-Bird Song, The 2183
Woggle Bug Book, The 4725
Woke Up Today 3927
Wolf Dance 2496
Wolf of Gubbio, The 732
Wolf Time 4428
Wololo! 3836
Woman 97, 465, 3628, 1369, 2789
(Am I a) Woman 2998
Woman, A 3491
Woman 4862
Woman Alone, A 1068, 2163
Woman Always Pays, The 132
Woman and Man 3734
Woman and the Bottle, The 1792
Woman and the Man, The 2317
Woman at Home, A 2676
Woman at the Altar, The 2386
Woman Child 3599
Woman, Delightful Woman 1868
Woman for the Man (Who Has Everything), The 2163

Woman Haters, The 132
Woman, How Dare You! 1083
Woman I Am, The 1630
Woman I Love, The 2220
Woman I Was Before, The 751
Woman in His Room, A 4652
(You Look Like a) Woman in Love (to Me) 1846
Woman in Me, The 484
Woman in My Bathroom, A 2646
Woman in Search of Happiness, A 3456
Woman in the Case, The 2160
Woman in the Palace, A 3802
Woman Is a Rascal 651
Woman Is a Sometime Thing, A 3541
Woman Is a Woman Is a Woman, A 4186
Woman Is How She Loves, A 798
Woman Is Just a Female, A 1002
Woman Is Only a Woman but a Good Cigar Is a Smoke (Puff, Puff, Puff), A 2885
Woman Like Beth, A 3305
Woman Looking for Love, A 2617
Woman, Lovely Woman 2383, 2869
Woman Makes the Man 1596
Woman Must Never Grow Old, A 3725
Woman Must Think of These Things, A 3725
Woman Needs Approval, A 4684
Woman Never Understan' (Wife Never Understan') 2000
Woman of Importance, A 830
Woman of the Century, The 275
Woman of the World 808, 809
Woman of the Year, The 901
Woman of the Year (1) 4727
Woman of the Year (2) 4727
Woman of the Year, The 4727
Woman of Valor, A 747
Woman on the Run 3927
Woman Ought to Know Her Place, A 3888
Woman Porters 703
Woman Power 3619
Woman Rarely Ever, A 840
Woman Rules the King 2671
Woman, Source of All Our Bliss 2233
Woman Talk 649
Woman That I Am 3561
Woman to Lady 3541
Woman to Woman 1684
Woman Waits for Me, A 2433
Woman Was Meant to Be Woman 2998
Woman Who Lived Up There, The 4169
Woman Who Rules the Kitchen Is the Woman Who Rules the World, The 2039
Woman Who Thinks I'm Wonderful, A 958
Woman-Woman 2756
Woman, Woman 2233
Woman Wouldn't Be a Woman, A 3934
Woman's "No" Means "Yes", A 2213
Woman's a Wonderful Thing 3486
Woman's Career, A 2331
Woman's Day, A 4153
Woman's Dream, A 4804
Woman's Dress 1193
Woman's First Thought Is a Man, A 4735
Woman's Hands, A 2659
Woman's Heart, A 3237
Woman's Much Better Off Alone, A 4292
Woman's No, A 2384
Woman's Place 4737
Woman's Prerogative, A 1385, 4123
Woman's Said to Be the Fickle Sex 3051
Woman's Smile, A 1285
Woman's Touch, A 616, 2527
Woman's Touch, The 3243
Woman's Work 2464, 3888
Woman's Work Is Never Done, A 2723
Womb Chant 2478
Women 466, 823
Women! 1017
Women 1534, 2123, 2258, 2546, 2836, 2838
Women Against the World 1101
Women Always Get Their Way 1121, 2509
Women and Light 2939
Women and Men 346, 3902
Women and Song 3250
Women Are All Perfect Pearls 1388
Women Are Here to Stay 3151, 4289
Women Get the Best of Us, The 1555
Women Haven't Any Mercy on a Man 1527
Women in Love 1371
Women in Room Thirteen 3158
Women in Uniform, The 4141
Women of Equity 2855
Women of Temperament 2732
Women of Vienna 3760
Women on the Move 2676
Women Simple 71
Women Weaving 2679
Women, Wine and Jazz 1335
Women, Wine and Song 45
Women with Women-Men with Men 1229
Women Without Men 2064
Women, Women! 68
Women, Women, Women 341, 3117
Women's Club Blues 2615
Women's Eyes 2576
Women's Liberation 3559
Women's Work Is Never Done 4077
Wompom, The 220
Won't Dat Be de Blessed Day 1385
Won't I Do? 4741
Won't It Be a Lark (We're Dear Little Girls) 4430
Won't Someone Find Me a Sweethea
Won't Someone Marry Me? 3652
Won't Someone Take Me Home?
Won't They Be Surprised 367
Won't You All Fall in Love with M
Won't You Be My Daddy 3401
Won't You Be My Girlie? 1054
Won't You Be My Little Kewpie

Won't You Be My Lovey Dovey 3753
Won't You Be My Playmate? 2534
Won't You Be My Teddy Bear 3480
Won't You Be My Valentine? 2534
Won't You Buy? 1526
Won't You Buy a Flower? 2706
Won't You Buy a Little Canoe 4551
Won't You Buy a Little Flag 1726
Won't You Buy a War Stamp (War Stamps) 3402
Won't You Charleston with Me? 507
Won't You Come Across? 4692
Won't You Come and Waltz with Me? 1561
Won't You Come Crusading with Me 3378
Won't You Come Home Judge Crater 427
Won't You Come Into My Boudoir 3628
Won't You Come Over 2919
Won't You Come to Margate 1473
Won't You Come to the Party 3439
Won't You Come Under My Merry Widow Hat 2826
Won't You Come Up to the Table? 4133
Won't You Cuddle Up a Little Closer? 1270
Won't You Dance? 2884
Won't You Follow Me There? 712
Won't You Go with Us to Monte Carlo 694
Won't You Harmonize with Me 1318
Won't You Harmonize with Me? 2978
Won't You Have a Little Feather 3451
Won't You Have a Little Feather? 3450
Won't You Help Me Out? 4464
Won't You Keep Me Company 2454
Won't You Kiss Me Once Before I Go? 675
Won't You Let Me Build a Nest for You (The Robin and the Wren) 2782
Won't You Let Me Carry Your Parcel 1318
Won't You Let Me Creep Into Your Heart 3033
Won't You Let Me Put My Arms Around You 830
Won't You Let Me Put My Arms Around You? 2122
Won't You Let Me Take a Picture of You? 545
Won't You Marry Me? 837, 3056
Won't You Play the Game? 4851
Won't You Smile? 2922
Won't You Take Me Home with You 2215
Won't You Take Me There? 3626
Won't You Take Me to Paris 4121
Won't You Tell Me? 303
Won't You Tell Me Why? 4299
Won't You Waltz? 2498
Won't You Write to Me (Won't You Send a Letter to Me) 3401
Won't You Write Your Autograph in My Album 2782
Won't Your Momma Let You Come Out and Play 2879
Wond'ring Night and Day 2788
Wonder, A 2731
Wonder Hat 1797
Wonder of the Age 4041
Wonder of the Kingdom 3939
Wonder Where My Heart Is 3920
Wonder Why 3168, 4743
Wonderful 3272, 2516, 3409, 3618
Wonderful! 4450
Wonderful Bad, Wonderful Good 600
Wonderful Cape Cod Girl 637
Wonderful Copenhagen 4399, 1741, 3444
Wonderful Creature, A 1308
Wonderful Dad 4150
Wonderful Dance 1587
Wonderful Day Like Today, A 3731
Wonderful Days 3177
Wonderful Dream 3192
Wonderful Dreams 4540
Wonderful Eyes 30
Wonderful Game, A 2898
Wonderful Game, The 1099
Wonderful Garden of Love 4808
Wonderful Girl 1460, 2270, 4148, 4831
Wonderful Girl-Wonderful Boy 4393
Wonderful Girls 2455
Wonderful Guy, A 4096
Wonderful Hindoo 3434
Wonderful Kiss 4794
Wonderful Land of Romance 904
Wonderful Life, A 4732
Wonderful Love 1549
Wonderful Machine, The 4028
Wonderful Magician, The (Love, the Marvelous Magician) 3994
Wonderful Man, A 2422
Wonderful Man 3207
Wonderful, Marvelous You 837
Wonderful Me 1776
Wonderful Mother 4322
Wonderful Music 3294
Wonderful Night with You 1966
Wonderful Nile, The 2071
Wonderful Party 1237
Wonderful Party, A 2376
Wonderful Plan, The 1369
Wonderful Rhythm 4651
Wonderful Something 4528
Wonderful Sun in the Sky, A 1681
Wonderful Sunday 255
Wonderful Thing, A 744
Wonderful Time Up There 4030
Wonderful Time Was Had By All 2446
Wonderful U.S.A. (Your Wonderful U.S.A.) 4491
Wonderful Underworld 3204
Wonderful War, A 97
Wonderful Way of Life, A 3810
Wonderful Wizard of Oz, The 4722, 4723
Wonderful Wonderful 4193
Wonderful, Wonderful Day 3888
Wonderful, Wonderful Tulip Land 2262
Wonderful, Wonderful, Wonderful 427
Wonderful World 276, 3329

Wonderful World-Wide Fair 272
Wonderful Yesterday 4651
Wonderful You 2378, 2833, 4303
Wondering 1216
Wondering When 1028
Wondering Who 637, 2057
Wonderland 2756, 3205
Wonderman 3136
(The Wonder of It All) Wonderworld 4737
Wondrin' 148
Wondrous Midnight Eyes 3770
Wondrous Spell of Love 355
Woo Me 948
Wood 3131
Wood Alcohol Blues 560
Wood Nymphs, The 4150
Woodcutters, The 3581
Wooden People, The 729
Wooden Shoe Dance 3952
Wooden Wedding 3301
Woodland Dance 3865
Woodman, Woodman, Spare That Tree 4805
Woods Are Full of Birds, The 1518
Woodsman's Serenade 974
Woodstock's Theme 4034
Woof 3955
Woofus Bird 568
Woogie Boogie, The 597, 3217
Wooing 152
Wooing of the Violin, The 3319
Woolworth Country 2988
Woolworth Manager's Work Song, The 2988
Woolworth of Japan, The 718
Wop Cabaret, The 4747
Word, The 4488
Word a Day, A (Ambiguous Means I Love You) 4423
Word from an Irishman's Tongue, The 2662
Word in Edgeways, A 4118
Word Is Love, The 732, 3835, 4145
Word of Love, A 1334
Word of the Lord, The 1809, 2775
Word to Mr. Jones, A 1415
Word to Remind You, A 1384
Wordless Dentistry 4397
Words, The 148
Words 270, 747
Words and Music 3130
Words Are Not Needed 3230
Words He Doesn't Say 3760
Words I Never Said, The 1045
Words, Music, Cash 4669
Words of Love 580
Words Unspoken, The 2898
Words Will Pay My Way 2941
Words Without Music 4825
Words, Words, Words 269, 630
Words, Words, Words! 4798
Work Alive 2545
Work Chant 4360
Work It Girl! 1155
Work, Lads, Work! 4381
Work Song 3487
Work Song, The 3227
Work Song 3831
Work Song: It's All Right for You 1903
Work Songs 3837
Work, Work, Work 830
Worker and the Shirker, The 2918
Workin' for the Man 52
Workin' It Out 4334
Workin' on de Railroad 2225
Working for Stella 3636
Working for the Government 1321
Working for the Institute 3847
Working for the Pictures 3397
Working Girl, The 2140
Working Girl's Apache (dance) 4744
Working in a Coal Mine 1890
Working with a Scarf (inst.) 1446
Workout 1601, 1630
World 1216
World According to Snoopy, The 4034
World and I, The 1711
World and You 2617
World Around Us, The 3351
World Belongs to the Young, The 798
World Full of Girls, A 3868
World Full of Grey 2306
World Goes Bobbing Up and Down 4843
World Goes Round, The 4480
World Has Gone Insane, The 2198
World Has Gone Shimmy Mad, The 4813
World I'll Make for Me, A 3697
World in a Jug, The 4750
World Is a Jungle, The 2318
World Is Beautiful Today, The 1791
World Is Comin' to a Start, The 3610
World Is Full of Loneliness, The 2033
World Is Full of Love, The 2140
World Is Full of Villains, The 1284
World Is Full of Women's Eyes, The 2254
World Is Getting Better, The 2354
World Is Going Shimmy Mad, The 4842
World Is in My Arms, The 1931
World Is Mean, The 4369
World Is Mine, The 733, 1419
World Is My Oyster, The 2068
World Is Round, The 3651
World Is Round-O, The 750
World Is Upside Down, The 2224
World Is Waiting for Me, The 4701
World Is Young Again, The 3703
World Is Young, The 4670
World Is Your Balloon, The 1300, 2234
World Keeps Going Round 2173
World Keeps Turnin' 3814
World Must Be Bigger Than an Avenue, The 2148
World of Beautiful Girls, The 589

World of Black and White, The 3688
World of Creation 2290
World of Dreams 3172
World of Henry Orient, The 1846
World of Love, A 2617
World of Melody, A 2636
World of Our Own, A 1957
World of Strangers 2246
World of Suzie Wong, The 4749
World Outside, The (inst.) 499
World Outside, The 3734, 3913, 4643
World Owes You This My Dear, The 2605
World Peace 3875
World Set on Fire By a Black and a Jew, The 2702
World, Take Me Back 1828
World to Win, A 4028
World Today, The 3439
World Weary 3196, 3235, 4341
World-Wide Romeo, A 2538
World Without End 2775
World Without Us, A 1079
World Without You 730
World's a Lovely Place, The 2682
World's a Stage for Every Girl, The 965
World's All Wrong Again, The 1524
World's Full of Boys, The 1329
World's Greatest Magical Act, The 1075
World's Greatest Show 2023
World's Oldest Boy Violinist, The 4415
World's Worst Woman, The 4694
Worlds 23
Worlds Apart 394, 2726, 3555
Worm Gene, The 4558
Worm's Revenge, The 2377
Worried 1316
Worried Man 4740
Worries 4001
Worry 4281
Worry Not a Whit Not I 1255
Worst Is Yet to Come, The 231
Worst of Friends, The 3595
Worst Pies in London, The 4233
Worst Thing That Happened to Me, The 1644
Worst Woman in London, The 906
Worst Woman on the Stage, The 2800
Worth Waiting For 4208
Worthy of You 2148
Wotch-Ma-Callit, The 3354
Wot's 'Is Name 1010
Wotta Night! 661
Would I Lie to You 716
Would I Not Love You 3702
Would I Were 649
Would That I 3939
Would You? 3992, 147
Would You 2399
Would You Ask? 1720
Would You Be So Kindly 1931
Would You Believe 327
Would You Do It? 2631
Would You If You Were I? 3786
Would You Know the Kind of Maid 2977
Would You Leave Your Happy Home for Me? 3951
Would You Let Me 2805, 3630
Would You Let Me Know? 920
Would You Like a Little Girl Like Me 4187
Would You Like to Learn to Like Me? 1332
Would You Like to Make a Fuss Over Me? 3222
Would You Like to Motor with Mater? 1783
Would You Like to Sleep Upon My Pillow 2857
Would You Like to Take a Walk? 418
Would You Like to Take a Walk? (Sump'n Good'll Come from That) 4235
Would You Love Me 1308
Would You Love Me More? 4403
Would You Marry a Nut Like Me? 1730
Would You Rather Be a Soldier with a Eagle on Your Shoulder or a Private with a Chicken on Your Knee? 4812
Would You Say No? 1308
Would-ja? 266
Would'ja for a Big Red Apple? 125
Wouldja Like It If—? 2496
Wouldn't Fool Me, Would You? 1339
Wouldn't I 840
Wouldn't It Be Crazy 4058
Wouldn't It Be Fun 44
Wouldn't It Be Loverly? 3038
Wouldn't It Be Nice 2275
Wouldn't It Break Your Heart? 4588
Wouldn't It Puzzle You? 1521
Wouldn't That Be a Stroke of Luck 3603
Wouldn't That Be Wonderful 1874
Wouldn't You? 1691
Wouldn't You Like to Be on Broadway? 4169
Wouldn't You Like to Flirt with Me? 917
Wouldn't You Like to Have Me for a Sweetheart? 4762
Wouldn't You Like to Have Me Tell Your Fortune 684
Wouldn't You Like to Know 4434
Wouldn't You Like to Learn to Love Me? 3581
Wouldn't You Like to Taste My Pear? 4197
Wouldn't You Think? 693
Wow 170
Wow-ooh-wolf! 3893
Wow Wow Wow 54
Wow-Yip-Po 2779
Wrangler 914
Wrap Me in Your Serape 4572
Wrapped in a Ribbon (and Tied in a Bow) 4169
Wrapped Up in a Blanket 3238
(I'm) Wrapped Up in You 4823
Wrath of Achilles, The 3988
Wreath, The 4447
Wreath of Fragrant Orange Blossoms, A 3573
Wreath the Golden Flower (Opening Act II) 353
Wreck of a Mec, The 2150

Wrenboy 533
Wriggly Rag 60
Write a Letter 4309
Write About What You Know 2535
Write Him a Challenge 2599
Write to Marian the Maid 4650
Writer, A 4790
Writer Fills the Lowest Niche, A 1948
Writer Writes at Night, A 2064
Writings 1977
Written in the Book of Destiny 2390
Written in Your Hand 3064
Wrong! 1757, 4013
Wrong Is Never Right 4447
Wrong Kind of Man 3161
Wrong Man, The 1848
Wrong Note Rag 4734
Wrong Plan, The 157
Wrong Side of the Railroad Tracks, The 341
Wrong Song, A 550
Wrong Thing at the Right Time 317
Wunderbar 2331, 4730
Wyoming Lullaby 4182

X

X Marks the Spot 1887
Xanadu 23
Xanadu (Les Elephants Roses) (La Marijuana) 2362
Xanadu 2962
Xolisinhlizyo 4438

Y

A.M. Survival Manual, The 4019
Y' Can't Win 1766
Y-La 506
Y.M.D. 3372
Y.O.U. 1116
Y-O-U, Dear, Y-O-U 4644
Ya Chara 2106
Ya Got Me 2205, 3278
Ya Got the Time 98
Ya Got Trouble 3016
Ya Gotta Be Versatile 2337
Ya Gotta Bend Down 2225
Ya Gotta Fit, Boy 1997
Ya Gotta Have a Car 4389
Ya Gotta Look Out for Yourself 775
Ya Pushin' Ya Luck 1385
Ya Ta Ta 2290
Ya Won't Complain 3201
Ya' Won 'Em All for Cherry 716
Ya've Got What It Takes 2993
Yacht, The 1783
Yacht Club Swing 39
Yacht Song 924
Yachting 2139
Yachting Song 934
Yacki Hula Hicki Doola 3737
Yaddie Caddie 3028
Yahoo Step, The 3954
Yakety Yak 4031
Yakiana Rag 1224
Yale 3775
Yale and Harvard Days 2107
Y'All Got It! 4722
Yaller 4367
Yama Yama Man, The (Pajama Song) 4364
Yamboo 27
Yank, Yank, Yank 1880
Yankee Banners 604
Yankee Bohemia 3575
Yankee Boy 3644
Yankee Doodle 1272, 3274
Yankee Doodle Blues 4104
Yankee Doodle Boodle 1403
Yankee Doodle Boy 1478, 2517
Yankee Doodle Boy, The 4390
Yankee Doodle Coon 3337
Yankee Doodle Dandy 964, 3018, 2975
Yankee Doodle Guards, The 1151
Yankee Doodle on the Line 4422
Yankee Doodle Oo-La-La, The 910
Yankee Doodle Oo-la-la, The 4427
Yankee Doodle Patriotic Tune 4834
Yankee Doodle Polka, The 2077
Yankee Doodle Rhythm 3766, 4178
Yankee Doodle Tune 3020
Yankee Doodle Up-To-Date 3981
Yankee Doodle Yarns 4425
Yankee Doodles Are Coming to Town 652
Yankee Doodle's Come to Town 4759
Yankee Doodle's Gonna Go to Town Again 173
Yankee Father in a Yankee Home, The 2829
Yankee Girl 2912
Yankee Girl, The 457, 4757
Yankee, Go Home 3187
Yankee Honeymoon 2858
Yankee Land 561, 815, 4070, 3749
Yankee Man 3557
Yankee Millionaire 4762
Yankee Millionairess, A 3771
Yankee Prince March & Two-Step, The (inst.) 4759
Yankee Prince Waltz 2869
Yankee Prince Waltz (inst.) 4759
Yankee Romeo 2782
Yankee Son of a Gun 4094
Yankee Stay 4623
Yankee Strut 2135
Yankee Tar, A 2465
Yankee Tourist Girl, The 2974
Yankev and Rokhl Duet 4082

Yankiana Rag 4804
Yanks Are at It Again, The 1833
Yanks Are On the March Again, The 297
Yanks Aren't Coming! The 3501
Yankyula 2636
Yarns 3588
Yashmack Song, The 4467
Yasni Kozkolai 1564
Y'assou 4862
Yatata, Yatata, Yatata 85
Yazoo Rag 1823
Ye Ho, for the Sailor's Life 4478
Ye Lunchtime Follies 834
Year After Year (We're Together) 1487
Year and a Day, A 4662
Year from Today, A 2496, 4001
Year In, Year Out 51
Year Is a Day, A 937
Year Is a Long Long Time, A 4784
Year of Jubilo, The 1037
Year of the Child 1234
Year the Yankees Lost the Pennant, The 957
Yearling, The 4764
Yearning, Burning 3268
Years Ago 4014
Years Are Burning, The 3817
Years Are Passing By, The 754
Years Before Us, The 4652
Years from Now 2674
Years Later 1342
Years Touch Not the Heart 4646
Yee-Eeucchh 1664
Yeemy Yeemy 4542
Yehi Rutzoin 3669
Yellow Blues 2872
Yellow Drum 1662
Yellow Flower 2294
Yellow Man 2852, 2787
Yellow Mask 4765
Yellow Rain 4048
Yenki Doodl Fort Uptown
(Yankee Doodle Rides Uptown) 1609
Yenta Power 550
Yer Baby's a Comin' to Town 2116
Yer My Friend, Aintcha? 3113
Yerushaliam 181
Yes 131, 1556, 1698, 3900, 4480
Yes Alexandra, No Alexandra 2674
Yes and No 364
Yes, Aunt 937
Yes I Can 1601
Yes I Know It Was Long Ago 4163
Yes, I Know That I'm Alive 2418
Yes, I Love You Honey 532
Yes, I'm Your Angel 3125
Yes, It's Love 3760
Yes, Ma'am 1699
Yes Ma'am (You're from the Show Boat) 3949
Yes! Mistress It's a Pity 3836
Yes, Mr. Baiello 3210
Yes My Darling Daughter 924
Yes, My Heart 656
Yes/No 1700
Yes or No 1131, 2622
Yes or No? 3586
Yes or No 4479
Yes, Sir, I've Made a Date 3105
Yes Sir, That's My Baby 393, 3018, 3989
Yes Sir, Very Good Sir! 1440
Yes Sirree 1023
Yes, There Is a Santa Claus 4155
Yes! We Have No Bananas (Parody) 3008
Yes, Yes 2461, 3297, 4237
Yes, Yes, I Love You 2598
Yes, Yes, Yes 4777
Yes, Yes, Yvette 4766
Yesterday 20, 2757, 3718, 3775
Yesterday an Egg 1342
Yesterday and Today 2668
Yesterday I Left the Earth 2728
Yesterday I Loved You 3288, 4585
Yesterday I Was You 716
Yesterday Is Over 169, 4768
Yesterday Is Today Is Tomorrow 3320
Yesterday Is Where I'll Stay 1497
Yesterday Is Yesterday 1605
Yesterday It Rained 2069
Yesterday, Tomorrow and Today 754
Yesterday Was Such a Lovely Day 279
Yesterday's Lover 426
Yesterdays 2204, 2372, 166, 3735
Yesterday's Forgotten 4798
Yesterthoughts (inst.) 763
Yet I'm the Same Little Girl 3805
Yeth, Yeth 3696
Yetta's Blintzes 3937
Yeverechecha 3669
Yi, Yi, Yi (Aye, Aye, Aye) 4863
Yiddish 2356
Yiddish Cowboy, The 2485
Yiddish International Radio Hour 4342
Yiddish Vaudeville Tonight 1279
Yiddish Wedding Jubilee 4094
Yiddisha Charleston 3926
Yiddisha Luck and Irisha Love (Kelly and
Rosenbaum, That's Mazel- Toff) 3926
Yiddisha Nightingale 3926, 789
Yiddishe Wampire, A 4851
Yiddisher Wedding 806
Yiddle with a Fiddle 4769
Yidl Mitn Fidl (Yiddle with His Fiddle) 1609
Yip Ahoy (Adrift on the
Lo-one Prairie!) 3990
Yip-I-Addy-I-Ay! 2858
Yip-I-Addy-I-Ay 3322
Yip-I-Adee-I-Ay! 2835
Yip! Yip! 1823
Yip Yip 3258
Yitl Midn Fidl 4769
Yo' a Little Lady 2643

Yo Ho 2490
Yo-Ho 4444
Yo Ho! For a Jolly Good Sail 586
Yo Ho Ho, The (dance) 2019
Yo Ho, Little Girls, Yo Ho! 906
Yo Ho, My Lads, Heave Ho 2851
Yo! Ho! When You're in the Chorus 4507
Yo, Ho! Yo, Ho! 2500
Yodel 3614
Yodel O 2363
Yodel Song 1213, 4806
Yodeler, The 3441
Yodelin' Dixieland 3178
Yodeling Yan 1041
Yodle Song 43
Yoga and Yoghurt 3548
Yokohama 1758
Yokohama Little Charmer 1759
Yokohama Lullaby 4033
Yoo-Hoo 487
Yoo-Hoo! 4210
Yoo-Hoo Blues, The 3292
Yoo Hoo, Hi There! 779
Yoofry 1662
Yorkshire 3322
Yosef's Tango 4082
Yoshe Kalb 4773
Yoshke Fort Avek (Yoshke's Going Away) 4342
Yosl Ber 4342
Yosl, Yosl 4342
Yossel, Yossel (Joseph, Joseph) 1279
You 1990, 3584
You (Tu) 535
You 4038, 4192, 4481, 3041
You After All These Years 3074
You Ain't Gonna Pick Up Where You Left Off 105
You Ain't Gonna Shake Them Feathers No More 1729
You Ain't Got No Savoir-Faire 111
You Ain't Got Time for Love 1763
You Ain't Heard Nothin' Yet 3985
You Ain't Hurtin' Your Ole Lady None 3564
You Ain't No Astronaut 40
You Ain't Nothin' Yet 646
You Ain't One, Two, Three 1259
You Ain't Seen Ball 1099
You Ain't Seen Nuthin' Yet 2231
You Ain't Seen the Last of Me 154
You Ain't So Hot 3365
You All Remember Jack 494
You Alone 1134
You Alone Would Do 4001
You Always Love the Same Girl 834
You Always Talk of Friendship 3069
You and I 357, 721, 765, 767, 1047, 1090, 1093
You and I (In Old Versailles) 1486
You and I 2159, 2186, 2723
You & I 2854
You and I 3042, 4219
You and I and Cupid 2158
You And I Are Changing Too 2677
You and I Are Passersby 3680
You and I Atta Baby 4283, 230
You and I Could Be Just Like That 2540
You and I Know 4569
You and I Love 934
You and I, Love 3900
You and I Love You and Me 608
You and Me 146, 1729, 1921, 2366, 2446, 3976
You and Only You 20, 345
You and the Girl You Love 4473
You and the Night and the Music 4159, 3699
You and You and Me 4077
You and Your Broken Heart 2748
You Appeal to Me 1679, 2602, 1883
You Are 3112
You Are All I've Wanted 1352
You Are All That's Beautiful 4798
You Are All the World to Me 1525, 3765
You Are an Orphan 762
You Are Beautiful 1315
You Are Doing Very Well 4361
You Are for Loving 372, 2805, 3630
You Are Free 168, 2614
You Are Love 3020, 3949
You Are Me, I Am Thee 1262
You Are Mine Evermore 771
You Are Music 3465
You Are My Darlin' Bride 3035
You Are My Day Dreams 1491
You Are My Downfall 4428
You Are My Fiancee 3820
You Are My Gold 2177
You Are My Heart's Delight 4792
You Are My Heaven 4083
You Are My Hope, Dear 214
You Are My Ideal 2022
You Are My Little Cupid 1565
You Are My Lucky Star 3992, 544
You Are My Melody 1763
You Are My Rain Beau 1688
You Are My Solace 3670
You Are My Songs 1680, 1681
You Are My Woman 1145
You Are Never Away 85
You Are Not Real 170
You Are Not the One for Me 263
You Are Romance 204
You Are So Beyond 2754
You Are So Fair 247
You Are So Lovely and I Am So Lonely 4059
You Are Something Very Special 2968
You Are Standing on My Bed 1717
You Are Still My Boy 900
You Are the One 4550
You Are the Only One 2307
You Are the Only Song 2470
You Are the Someone 1963
You Are the Tree 4617

You Are There 466
You Are Tomorrow 4048
You Are Unforgettable 2386
You Are Woman 1420
You Are You 1310, 2285, 4077, 4114
You Are Youth 1035
You, Babe, Only You 2792
You Be the Rock I'll Be the Roll 1315
You Beautiful So and So 1126
You Become Me 2680
You Belong 98
You Belong to Me 683, 4264
You Belong to the Night 1792
You Bet Your Assets 4774
You Better Get Outta Town 2702
You Better Go Now 2772, 3103
You Better Mind 3989
You Break My Heart 1636
You Bring Out the Worst in Me 1792
You Bring the Scotch and I'll Bring the Soda 4571
You Broke It Up (When You Said Dixie) 4501
You Brought Me Through It 4108
You Burn Me Up When You Turn Me Down 2747
You Came Along 2277, 2392, 3517
You Came from Outer Space 4433
You Came to Me as a Young Man 2630
You Can Always Count on Me 775
You Can Always Count on Us 1991
You Can Always Find Another Partner 3249
You Can Always Find Someone to Love You 687
You Can Be a New Yorker Too 2294
You Can Be a New Yorker Too! 2790
You Can Be Like Grandpa 1718
You Can Dance 4785
You Can Dance with Any Girl 3249
You Can Dance with Any Girl at All 3184
You Can Dance Your Way Into Her Heart 2387
You Can Depend on Me 2240
You Can Do It 3427
You Can Do Nothing About It 1116
You Can Find It in the Papers Every Day 1566
You Can Flirt in All Kinds of Languages 1524
You Can Fly 2553
You Can Go As Far As You Like with Me 3681
You Can Hang Your Hat Here 4623
You Can Have Broadway 1480
You Can Have Him 789, 2894
You Can Have My Husband 1890
You Can Kill Love 1737
You Can Leave Your Hat On 2852, 2787
You Can Make My Life a Bed of Roses (Marry Me) 1979
You Can Never Blame a Girl for Dreaming 4694
You Can Never Go Back 534
You Can Never Know My Mind 1737
You Can Never Tell Until You Try 3423
You Can Play with My Dolly 2122
You Can Reach the Sun 4689
You Can Read It in My Eyes 1392
You Can Sail in My Boat 1157
You Can Stay 821
You Can Tell a Lady By Her Hat 101
You Can Tell That I'm Irish 804
You Can Trust Me 3712, 4633
You Can Wait Too Long 2941
You Can't Argue 2667
You Can't Be a Friend to Everybody 1967
You Can't Be a Husband Today 1663
You Can't Beat My Bill 2453
You Can't Beat the Luck of the Irish 1631
You Can't Beat the System 3830
You Can't Blame Your Uncle Sammy 4197
You Can't Brush Me Off 2597
You Can't Cash in On an Alibi 1917
You Can't Catch Me 4469
You Can't Deny You're Irish 4576
You Can't Do That to an Irishman 1824
You Can't Do What My Last Man Did 26
You Can't Experiment on Me 1033
You Can't Eye a Shy Baby 2380
You Can't Fool a New York Kid 1735
You Can't Fool All the People All the Time 3073
You Can't Fool the People 3226
You Can't Fool Your Dreams 3538
You Can't Get a Man with a Gun 153
You Can't Get Ahead 3517
You Can't Get Away from Tipperary 2696
You Can't Get By Me 4645
You Can't Get Over the Wall 4524
You Can't Get the Merchandise 2379
You Can't Get Up Before Noon without Being a Square 40
You Can't Go Home Again 3094
You Can't Go Wrong with Us 3397
You Can't Have Everything 198
You Can't Have My Sugar for Tea 2392
You Can't Hurry Love 4193
You Can't Keep a Good Man Down 2408
You Can't Keep Me Away from You 3591
You Can't Let Romance Die 3757
You Can't Lose a Broken Heart 4198, 4199
You Can't Lose 'Em All 4238
You Can't Lose Me 953
You Can't Make It Anywhere 2443
You Can't Make Love 1194
You Can't Make Love By Wireless 334
You Can't Miss It 3509
You Can't Overdo a Good Thing 3966
You Can't Pay the Landlord with Love 3685
You Can't Play Every Instrument in the Band 4219
You Can't Please Everybody Always 4663
You Can't Put Catsup on the Moon 512
You Can't Say You Feel Rich Anymore 1955
You Can't Stop Me from Loving You 1549, 3704
You Can't Stop Me from Thinking 2884
You Can't Stop the Sun from Shining 293
You Can't Take It with You 4377
You Can't Take It with You When You Die 1424
You Can't Teach an Old Dog New Tricks 4409

You Can't Unscramble Scrambled Eggs 1528
You Can't Walk Back from an Aeroplane 1343
You Can't Win 4722
You Cannot Drown the Dreamer 3305
You Cannot Make Your Shimmy Shake on Tea 4813, 4799
You Cannot Roll Ze Eyes No More 2349
You Cannot Shake That Shimmie 395
You Cheated Me 2754
You Click with Me 3713
You Come and Float Me 2506
You Come and Stay with Me 3322
You Come First After Me 4577
You Could 4577
You Could Drive a Person Crazy 832, 3967
You Could Have the Richest Man in Town 1265
You Could Hurt Me 808, 809
You Could Learn to Love Me, Rosie 1630
You Could Never Shame Me 2333
You Could Not Please Me More 2064
You Could Say I Miss Him 1092
You Couldn't Be Cuter 2372
You Couldn't Blame Me for That 4426
You Couldn't Get On without Me, Girls 1188
You Couldn't Please Me More 4481
You Cut Up the Clothes in the Closet of My Dreams 1074
You Dear 202, 2044
You Deserve Me 2053
You Devil You 2067
You Did It 3038
You Didn't Live to Love 1492
You Didn't Want Me 3158
You Do 3838, 2250
You Do-Do-Do-It Good! 1289
You Do Not Understand 1743
You Do Something to Me 1272, 1762
You Do This 4595
You Don't Dance 1336
You Don't Have to Be a Toreador 4780
You Don't Have to Do It for Me 2874
You Don't Have to Kiss Me Goodnight 3016
You Don't Have to Prove It If You Sing It 1860
You Don't Have to Say You Love Me 338, 4193
You Don't Know 1860, 2546, 4285
You Don't Know Him 3234
You Don't Know Paree 1272
You Don't Know What I Know About You 684
You Don't Look for Love 3965
You Don't Love As Good As I Do 1391
You Don't Love Right 4825
You Don't Need a Nailfile in a Cornfield 2898
You Don't Need It 1873
You Don't Need the Wine to Have a Wonderful Time 1032, 4813
You Don't Own Me 338, 4193
You Don't Remind Me 3326
You Don't See Anything but It Hurts (Oh How It Hurts) 363
You Don't See It but It's There 1561
You Don't Tell Me 3187
You Don't Understand 3806
You-Don't-Want-To-Play-With-Me Blues 507
You Done Right 3656
You Excite Me 2400, 3950
You Fascinate Me So 1023, 4337
You Feel Too Much 1310
You Fell Out of the Sky 4062
You Flew Away from the Nest 3185
You for Me 47, 2942, 3837, 3916
You Forgot Your Gloves 4335
You Found Me and I Found You 3245
You Gave Me Ev'rything But Love 876
You Gave Me Love 2648
You Gay Dog You! 1993
You Get a Lot of Help when You're in Love 1293
You Get in My Way 4099
You Get What You Give 4106
You Go to My Head 3020, 3175
You Go with Me 423
You Go Your Way 1306
You Go Your Way and I'll Go Mine 552
You Gonna Miss Me 4786
You Got Me Grinding My Teeth 3757
You Got Something I Want 1407
You Got to Be Clever 3651
You Got to Do Better Than That 4291
You Got to Get the Gittin While the Gittin's Good 1198
You Got to Git the Gittin' (While the Gittin' Is Good) 1917
You Got What Gets 'Em 765
You Gotta Be Holdin' Out Five Dollars on Me 40
You Gotta Depend on Luck 2641
You Gotta Die Sometime 1234
You Gotta Do What You Gotta Do 4076
You Gotta Fight Harder 3576
You Gotta Get a Gimmick 1709
You Gotta Go East to Go West 850
You Gotta Go Out with a Bang! 829
You Gotta Have a Destination 4536
You Gotta Have a Gimmick 2205, 3967
You Gotta Have Dancing 550
You Gotta Have 'IT' 4821
You Gotta Have Light Entertainment 496
You Gotta Keep Movin' and Dance (You Gotta Keep A' Going) 4806
You Gotta Keep Saying 'No' 180
You Gotta Please All the People 2998
You Gotta Take All the Fruit 4060
You Gotta Take Pains 1149
You Gotta Yes 'Em to Know Them 4817
You Have ... 4433
You Have a Pretty Wit 4404
You Have a Straight and Shapely Back 3256
You Have a Way with You 3756
You Have Cast Your Shadow on the Sea 514
You Have Everything 383
You Have Got the Style 3087
You Have Got to Have a Rudder on the Ark 4481

You Have Made a Fool of Me 4330
You Have Made Me Love 946
You Have Me 3855
You Have-Me-I-Have-You 1691
You Have My Heart 3822
You Have No Heart 3806
You Have No Idea 2777
You Have to Choose Sides 2998
You Have to Do What You Do Do 1284
You Have to Get It Out to Get Away 3517
You Have to Go with Me 1441
You Have to Hand It to Them 1
You Have to Have a Party to Make a Hit 3304
You Have to Have Love 2940
You Have Touched Me 2766
You Haven't Changed at All 999
You Haven't Got Time for Love 4454
You Haven't Lived Until You Die in L.A. 3046
You Haven't Lived Until You've Played the Palace 3954
You Heard It Here 2196
You Heard It Here First 275
You Help Me 4633
You Hoo 3404
You I Like 1660, 2664
You in Your Room, I in Mine 2330
You Inspire a Mad Desire 3735
You Interest Me 1068
You Irritate Me So 2453
You Just Can't Copa with a Copacabana Baby 847
You, Just You 2383
You-Just-You 1173
You Just You 851
You Keep Coming Back Like a Song 789
You Keep Me Hanging On 3739
You Kept Me in Touch with Mama 3718
You Kill Me 1475
You Kind O' Look Good to Me 1031
You Kissed Me 183
You Knew I Was No Good 4127
You Knew What I Needed 3227
You Know 3803
You Know and I Know (and We Both Understand) 1559
You Know and I Know 2684
You Know and I Know (and We Both Understand) 3193
You Know and I Know the Way 3238
You Know How It Is 3766
You Know I Know 4476
You Know Me, Al 2112
You Know, Oh Lord 651
You Know What I Mean 1276, 4831
You Know Who 1597
You Like Me 484
You Little Blue Devil 2494
You Little Cafe, Good Day 2497
You Little Monkey, You 941
You Live in Flowers 3651
You Look Awful Good to Father 4506
You Look Just Like Margie 1883
You Look Like Me 1958
You Look Like My Valley 915
You Look Like Someone I Used to Know 2165
You Lost Your Opportunity 1448
You Love a Child 1104
You Love Me 3002, 4435
You Loved Me Then 4489
You Made It Possible, Dear 3264
You Made Me Love You 1873, 4823
You Made Me Love You I Didn't Want to Do It 3396
You Made Me Love You, I Didn't Want to Do It 1963
You Made Me Think You Were in Love 4068, 4301
You Make It Seem Like Halloween 255
You Make Me Dance 382
You Make Me Feel So Foolish, When I'm Making Love to You 1065
You Make Me Feel Younger 343
You Make Me Oh, So Glad to Be Me 916
You Marry a Marionette 3081
You Matthew Dear 2794
You May Always Be My Sweetheart 2559
You May Be a Bad Man 3404
You May Be a Whale in Georgia 2302
You May Be Far Away from Me 216
You May Be the Someone 239
You May Be the World to Your Mother 4360
You May Have Planted Many a Lily 3252
You May Kiss Me Good-Night, Dear 1
You May Not Love Me 3091
You, Me and London Town 1497
You Might As Well Pretend 4335
You Might As Well Stay on Broadway 4806
You Might Get to Like Me 1846
You Might Have Known I Loved You 4170
You Musn't Blame the Copper Blame the Cook 694
You Must Be Born with It 1225
You Must Be Good Girls 380
You Must Be Mine Dear 1555
You Must Come Over 4815
You Must Come Over Blues 317, 642, 3622
You Must Come Over Eyes 4424
You Must Have a Kick and Punch 545
You Must Have Experience 4807
You Must Keep a Little Actress in Your Life 3880
You Must Meet My Wife 2536, 3967
You Must Not Flirt with Me 4419
You Must Walk Like This 2532
You Must Whistle Like This 1407
You Mustn't Be Discouraged 1227
You Mustn't Do That in High Society 2399
You Mustn't Eat People 3688
You Mustn't Kick It Around 1298, 3353
You My Sweetheart Will Have to Be 4133
You, My You 224
You Need a Hobby 2983
You Need a Lift! 4279
You Need a Little Magic 1300
You Need a Man, Suzanne 642

You Need a Song 4029
You Need Me 2196
You Need No Crown of Gold to Make You a Queen 4364
You Need Someone 3623, 4114
You Needn't Come at All 1909
You Never Can Tell 1544, 2574, 2663, 3352, 3508, 4170
You Never Can Tell About a Woman 3675
You Never Can Tell About Love 3721
You Never Can Tell How a Marriage Will Take 1851
You Never Can Tell Till You Try 4738
You Never Can Tell What a Kiss Will Do 1925
You Never Change 4527
You Never Could Tell We Were Married 3395
You Never Give Me Your Money 3903
You Never Had It So Good 2797, 4146
You Never Knew About Me 3230
You Never Know 344, 3250, 4777
You Never Know the Mind of a Woman 1816
You Never Know What a Kiss Can Mean 4378
You Never Know What Comes Next 2985
You Never Know What Hit You (When It's Love) 3563
You Never Know What Hit You When It's Love 454
You Never Know What Hit You-When It's Love 4323
You Never Know What's Going to Happen Next 3883
You Never Know Who's Behind You 2185
You Never Looked Better 3564
You Never Met a Feller Like Me (I Never Met a Feller Like Me) 3482
You Never Miss the Water 239
You Never Need Latin or Greek 2813
You Never Saw 647
You Never Saw That Before 3091
You Never Say Yes 4118
You Never See the Sun 1903
You Never Told Me That Before We Married 2347, 2716
You Only Get One Chance 550
You Only to Love Me 3734
You-oo Just You 1920
You or No One 3837
You or Nobody! 4766
You Ought to Be Here with Me 394
You Ought to Be in Pictures 1813
You Ought to Go to Paris 4148
You Ought to Know! 740
You Ought to See the Women Swimming 1032
You Oughta Be in Pictures 4824
You Out There 2659
You Pat Me 737
You Poor Thing 2268
You Puzzle Me 1068
You Remember Me 2816
You Remind Me of My Mother 2533
You Remind Me of My Old Dad 4381
You Remind Me of Someone 765
You Remind Me of You 2874
You Rule the Kingdom of My Heart 520
You Said It 3359, 4778
You Said Something 1784
You Satisfy 289
You Say the Nicest Things, Baby 206
You Say You Care 1475
You Say You Love Me 4330
You See Before You What Fashions Can Do 1249
You See in Me 1165
You See in Me a Bobby 705
You Send Me 4534, 580
You Set My Heart to Music 4337
You Shall Not Go 3537
You Should Be Made Love To 1665
You Should Be Set to Music 924
You Should Have Most Everything 4806
You Should Know 691
You Should Oughta Be for Me 1883
You Should See Yourself 4238
You Show Me Yours 1695
You Smiled at Me 1944, 3659
You Spoke, I Never Heard a Word 318
You Started Something 12
You Started Something (When You Came Along) 4491
You Started Something When You Came Along 3249
You Stepped Out of a Dream 3992, 544, 4799
You Still Don't Know 572
You Still Have a Long Way to Go 1634
You Still Love Me 1139
You Sure Don't Know How to Shake That Thing 880
You Take Paris 4292
You Talk Just Like My Maw 653
You Teach Me 2461
You Tell 'Em 4860
You Tell Him 1534
You There in the Back Row 4338
You Think I Got Rhythm? 1072
You Think It's Easy? 4108
You Think of Everything 3100
You Tickle Me 2857
You Told Me That You Loved Me But You Never Told Me Why 584
You Told Me Yo' Had Money in the Bank 604
You Too Can Be a Puppet 1300, 2234
You Took Advantage of Me 3556
You Took Me By Surprise 2379
You Took My Breath Away 364, 4798
You Took Possession of Me 1930
You Touched Her 4038
You Treacherous Men 2726
You U.S.A. 3813
You Understand Me 3875, 4399
You Understand Me So 2615
You Used to Be Good to Me 4037
You Wait and Wait and Wait 2786
You Wake Up in the Morning in Chicago 4720
You Walked By 4357
You Walked Out 868
You Walked Out of the Picture 3375
You Wanna Be My Friend 784
You Wanna Bet 4238
You Want the Best Seats, We Have 'Em 611
You Want to Be an Idler 4147

You Want to Lose Your Only Friend? 721
You Want to Mourn 3831
You Want to Ruin Everything 42
You Wanted Me, I Wanted You 3172
You Was 2024
You Wash and I'll Dry 4640
You Were a Hell of a Crowd Tonight 793
You Were Dead, You Know 630
You Were Made for Love 2884
You Were Meant for Me 133, 1279, 2570, 544
You Were There 3235, 3906
You Will Have to Sing an Irish Song 4802
You Will Know When the Time Has Come 4537
You Will Need Them at Home Some Day 2715
You Will Never Be at Home 496
You Will Never Be Lonely 1456
You Will Never Know 3172
You Will Not Touch Him 2905
You Will-Won't You? 930
You Win 2816
You Women! 3042
You Won't Be an Orphan for Long 150
You Won't Be Happy 2043
You Won't Believe Me 157
You Won't Do Any Business If You Haven't Got a Band 2493
You Won't Find Any Gold in Scotland 345
You Won't Say No 1612
You Would Like Him 339
You Would Say 4537
You Wouldn't Be You 299
You Wouldn't Fool Me 1339
You, You 2760
You, You, You 385
You, You, You! 3528
You, You, You 4264, 1454, 1535
You, You, You! 4133
You! You! You! 154
You'd Be Amazed 2731
You'd Be Surprised 25, 4560, 3258, 3567, 3962, 4813
You'd Better Dance 532
You'd Better Go Now 3104
You'd Better Love Me 1891
You'd Better Take It Back 2906
You'd Better Tell Her! 1508
You'd Do for Me-I'd Do for You 3307
You'd Think You Were in Paris 2730
You'd Too 552
You'll Always Be the Same Sweet Girl 1532
You'll Always Remember the First Time 3320
You'll Be Returning Again 1503
You'll Be Seeing Me 23
You'll Be Something 3788
You'll Be Sorry 2477
You'll Be the Prettiest Girl at the Party 4060
You'll Call the Next Love the First 1963
You'll Come Back 938
You'll Do 4778
You'll Do It All Over Again 4464
You'll Dream and I'll Dream — Then Wake to Find Your Dreams Come True 2549
You'll Feel Better Then 48, 3773
You'll Find a Beautiful Face Behind a Love Song 3796
You'll Find It in the Almanac 671
You'll Find It on the Bill 3301
You'll Find Mice 2134
You'll Find Nothing Better Than Beer 2632
You'll Find Old Dixieland in France 4838
You'll Find the End of the Rainbow in Your Own Back Yard 3796
You'll Find the Party Isn't There 3729
You'll Find the Rainbow 3472
You'll Get a Cold in Your Toes 3726
You'll Get Nothing from Me 3712
You'll Get Over It 2010
You'll Get Yours 112
You'll Give In 4822
You'll Have to Change 757
You'll Have to Do the Turkey Trot 2126
You'll Have to Find Out 3868
You'll Have to Guess 3078
You'll Have Your Moment 4167
You'll Kill 'Em 2271
You'll Know that It's Me 204
You'll Learn How, Bye and Bye 3796
You'll Love It 3643
You'll Love It in Jail 4701
You'll Love Me in Paris 2837
You'll Make an Elegant Butler 4435
You'll Never Get a Whimper Out of Me 4421
You'll Never Get Away from Me 1709
You'll Never Get to Heaven 261
You'll Never Know 3622, 4781
You'll Never Know What Love Is Till I Say I Love You 1900
You'll Never Know Where You're Going Till You Get There 4743
You'll Never Make Heaven That Way 3543
You'll Never See Me Run 2171
You'll Never Walk Alone 660
You'll Regret It! 4707
You'll Regret Your Stand 4488
You'll Remember Love 4136
You'll Remember Me 1710
You'll See 2340
You'll See the Day 3962
You'll Still Be There 3243
You'll Thank Me in the End 4518
You'll Think of Someone 3603
You're a Bad Influence on Me 3674
You're a Big Boy Now 2279
You're a Builder-Upper 2475
You're a Character 1879
You're a Charming Little Maiden 4554
You're a Clever Kid 1549
You're a Clown 786
You're a Damned Exasperating Woman 1828
You're a Dangerous Girl 3737
You're a Good Man, Charlie Brown 4783

You're a Grand Old Flag 1478, 1480, 4390
You're a Great Big, Blue-Eyed Baby Boy 4806
You're a Hero 102
You're a Liar 4693
You're a Little Young for the Job 2033
You're a Long, Long Way from America 3815
You're a Lovable Lunatic 3869
You're a Lucky Guy 889
You're a Magician 4021
You're a Man 4186
You're a Mean One, Mr. Grinch 2015
You're a Perfect Jewel to Me 4841
You're a Perfect Little Lady 1533
You're a Queer One, Julie Jordan 660
You're a Regular Girl 4712
You're a Rock 2583
You're a Standout 3442
You're a Stranger in This Neighborhood 615
You're a Sweet Patootie 1886
You're a Wonderful Girl 1722
You're About to Be Beautiful 2535
You're All That I Need 2070
You're All That Queed 2070
You're All the World to Me 3387, 3655, 4741
You're Altogether Model Girls 1925
You're an Eyeful 398
You're an Indian 830
You're an Old Smoothie 3139, 4267
You're As English As 2355
You're As Young As You Feel 2535
You're Asking Me 82
You're at the Music Hall 2737
You're Awfully Smart 4143
You're Bad for Me 817
You're Beautiful 508
You're Colossal 4542
You're Dancing Inside Me 573
You're Dead! 657
You're Delicious 322
You're Devastating 3735
You're Divine 314
You're Dreaming 2618
You're Dreamlike 3813, 4826
You're Driving Me Crazy 3175, 4023
You're Drunk, By Gosh, You're Drunk 1910
You're Dull Johnny 4635
You're Everything in the World I Love 4764
You're Everywhere 4372
You're Exactly My Style of Girl 4589
You're Falling in Love After All 1911
You're False 3035
You're Far Away from Home 4693
You're Far from Wonderful 2554
You're Far Too Near Me 1284
You're Getting to Be a Habit with Me 1359
You're Getting Younger Every Day 2874
You're Going Somewhere, We're Going Nowhere 426
You're Going to Lose Your Husband If You Do 687
You're Gone 4083
You're Gonna Dance with Me, Willie 1791
You're Gonna Love Tomorrow 1329
You're Good for My Morale 2748
You're Gorgeous, You're Fantastic 1974
You're Gwine to Get Something What You Don't Have 4804
You're Here and I'm Here 2424, 2761, 3398, 3627, 4644
You're Home 952
You're in Heidelberg 4188
You're in Kentucky 487
You're in Love 1453, 3988, 4372, 4784
You're in New York Now 4029
You're in Paree 662
You're in Paris 367
You're Invited to Attend a Dream 4006
You're Just a Little Better (Than the One I Thought Was Best) 3397
You're Just a No Account 889
You're Just a Perfect Peach Beyond My Reach 2358, 3996
You're Just in Love 619, 4264, 789
You're Just Like a Rose 1631
You're Just Made to Order for Me 2299
You're Just the Boy for Me 3855
You're Just the Girlie 3738
You're Just the Girlie that I Adore 1151
You're Just the One I've Waited For 1557, 4599
You're Just the Same to Me 2155
You're Just the Sort of Boy for a Girl Like Me 1332
You're Like 4623
You're Like a Red, Red Rose 2856
You're Like a Toy Balloon 662
You're Living Right Next Door to Heaven When You Live in Dixieland 1823
You're Lonely and I'm Lonely 2597
You're Looking Very Good, Marie 1440
You're Lovely Love 2705
You're Loving Me 3711
You're Lucky to Me 443
You're Married Under False Pretenses 3591
You're Mine 424, 2614
You're Mine, All Mine 596
You're Momma's 1864
You're More than a Name and Address 2397
You're Musical 2368
You're My Baby 4206
You're My Boy 4642
You're My Everything 2423
You're My Family Now 1099
You're My Favorite Lullabye 2648
You're My Girl 632, 1457
You're My Girl (Boy) 1886
You're My Girl 4743
You're My Happiness 3956
You're My Happy Ending 4818
You're My Honey 1798
You're My Kind of Ugly 3410
You're My Last Chance 843
You're My Man 1233
You're My Relaxation 3103
You're My Rose 2807, 4199

You're My Silvery Symphony 318
You're My Star 36
You're My Temptation 3922
You're Near and Yet So Far 3064
You're Nearer 4420
You're Never Fully Dressed Without a Smile 150, 602
You're Never Fully Dressed without aSmile 4048
You're Never Too Old 2768
You're Never Too Old to Love 4807
(T' Me Baby) You're News 4152
You're No Brother, No Brother of Mine 1601
You're No Good 4633
You're Not 3863
You're Not Alone 2188
You're Not at All Like You 4798
You're Not Foolin' Me 3294
You're Not Getting Older 430
You're Not Old Enough 4798
You're Not Pretty but You're Mine 125
You're Not Ready 3661
You're Not Real 2553
You're Not the Mayor 2790
You're Not the One 3907
You're Not the Only Cinder in the Grate 2317
You're Not the Only Oyster in the Stew 4255
You're Not the Type 1456
You're Not Unique 2346
You're Nothing 1056
You're Nothing Without Me 775
You're Oh So 4016
You're OK, U.S.A.! 3262
You're on My Mind 1889
You're on the Barbary Coast 302
You're on the Lido Now 2467
You're on the Right Road 4806
You're on Your Own 1769
You're One in a Million 680
You're One of a Kind 1201
You're Only a Barefoot Boy 4331
You're Only Young Once or Twice 3664
You're Out of Fashion 1249
You're Perf 1336
You're Perfect 1045, 2382
You're Probably in Love 172
You're Right, You're Right 4588
You're Right You're Right 4727
You're So Beautiful 627
You're So Beautiful That — 4423
You're So Cute Soldier Boy 4422
You're So Different from the Rest 3372
You're So Fascinating 1066
You're So Indiff'rent 4137
You're So Indifferent 447
You're So Much a Part of Me 2227
You're So Near (So Near and Yet So Far) 1811
You're So Nice to Me 4766
You're So Nice to Remember 4706
You're So Right 4321
You're So Right for Me 3841, 3234
You're So Sweet 2972
You're Some Girl 4589, 4807
You're Something More Than I Bargained For 427
You're Something to Write Home About 1514
You're Such a Lonesome Moon Tonight 2922
You're Super 635
You're the Better Half of Me 4545
You're the Boss 4031
You're the Candy 349
You're the Cream in My Coffee 1929
You're the Fairest Flower 2522
You're the Fellow the Fortune Teller Told Me All About 1756
You're the Finest of Them All 638, 3652
You're the First 4244
You're the First Cup of Coffee 1811
You're the First Thing I Pray for Each Morning (Du Bist Mein Morgen — Und Mein Nachtgebetchen) 1044
You're the Girl 558, 1309
You're the Girl (That Sets Me Stuttering) 1588
You're the Girl 2268, 1867, 1866
You're the Girl I'm Looking For 3191
You're the Kind of a Girl I Like 2631
You're the Little Girl I've Looked So Long For 2900
You're the Lord of Any Manor 2397
You're the Most Impossible Person 4401
You're the Mother Type 376
You're the Nicest Girl I Ever Knew 1536
You're the Nicest Little Girl I Ever Knew 1835
You're the One 1890, 1617, 2833, 4476
You're the One Best Bet 811
You're the One for Me 2869
You're the One Girl for Me 3304
You're the One I'm For 3112, 3111
You're the Only Girl He Loves 3529
You're the Only Girl I Want to Marry 2282
You're the Only One 500, 1676
You're the Only One for Me 1794, 3581
You're the Only One for Me, Dear! 4453
You're the Reason 1718
You're the Reason I Fell in Love 437
You're the Sunrise 3861
You're the Sweet Beginning 1727
You're the Sweetest Girl I Know 1054
You're the Top 163
You're the Type 4378
You're the Very Girl I've Looked For 1208
You're Thrilling 2849
You're Too Far Away 3131
You're Too Far Away (I Look at You) 3214
You're Too Good to Be True 173
You're Too Smart 2661
You're Underrated 3587
You're Very Like Your Sister, Dear 2495
You're Waltzing on My Heart 665
You're Welcome 1729
You're Welcome Back to California 4037
You're What I Need 834, 3924
You're Wonderful 1056, 4415
You're Working for Me Now 3355

You're You 4279, 3997
You're Your Highness 2504
You've Been a Good Old Wagon but You've Done Broke Down 2796
You've Been Bitten 3066
You've Been Kissing the Blarney Stone 256
You've Brightened Up My Day 1086
You've Broken a Fine Woman's Heart 2626
You've Built a Fire Down in My Heart 1247, 4805
You've Come Home 4693
You've Got a Friend 3739
You've Got a Good Thing Going 2011
You've Got a Hold on Me 4640
You've Got a Way with You 1839
You've Got It 1816
You've Got It All 901
You've Got Me Out on a Limb 2148
You've Got Possibilities 2163
You've Got Something 3674
You've Got Something to Say 339
You've Got Something to Sing About 4394
You've Got That 2459
You've Got that Kind of Face 4015
You've Got That Thing 1272
You've Got the Devil in Your Eyes 4536
You've Got to Appease with a Strip Tease 3226
You've Got to Be a Lady 4090
You've Got to Be a Little Crazy 1548
You've Got to Be a Tiger, Tiger 793
You've Got to Be American to Feel That Way 2552
You've Got to Be an Acrobat 3084
You've Got to Be an American to Feel That Way 1759
You've Got to Be Carefully Taught 4096
You've Got to Be Fast 1414
You've Got to Be Hard Boiled 3131
You've Got to Be in Love to Do That 700
You've Got to Be Way Out to Be In 619
You've Got to Dance to Win the Prince of Wales 69
You've Got to Die to Be Born Again 729
You've Got to Do It 363
You've Got to Do That Salome Dance 1464
You've Got to Get Rid of It 2017
You've Got to Give Them What They Want 1518
You've Got to Go In or Go Under 1502
You've Got to Have a Sense of Humor 42
You've Got to Have Heart 957
You've Got to Have Koo Wah 3965
You've Got to Keep Building 3059
You've Got to Keep on Moving 4290
You've Got to Know How to Make Love 2005
You've Got to Let Go 3368
You've Got to Pay 1414
You've Got to Pay for What You Get 1360
You've Got to Pick a Pocket or Two 3271
You've Got to Surrender 1800
You've Got What I Need 2163
You've Got What It Takes 1782
You've Got Yourself a Bunch of Women 3418
You've Gotta Have a Passion 708
You've Gotta Leave Them Laughing 4577
You've Just the Boy for Me 1961
You've Lied to Me 2399
You've Made a Hit with Me 263
You've Made Me Happy Today! 4170
You've Married a Man (Who's Been Married Before) 614
You've Never Been Loved 2850
You've Never Kissed Her 521
You've Outstayed Your Welcome 1732
You've Still Got a Lot to Learn 1360
You've Stolen My Heart 2464
Young 534
Young America 804, 2232
Young and American 4020
Young and Foolish 3509
Young and Fresh and Willing 3107
Young and Healthy 1359
Young Black Joe 124
Young Blood 4031
Young Days 1075, 3167
Young Dreams 3697
Young Enough to Dream 3825
Young Folks and Old Folks 1626
Young Girl 3695
Young Girl and Young Man 4479
Young Ideas 1127, 2313
Young King, The (scene) 3005
Young Lady a la Mode 1711
Young Man 3866
Young Man About Paris 1119
Young Man in a Shop 3882
Young Man in Love 1145
Young Man with a Horn 3986
Young Man with a Reefer 70
Young Man's Fancy, A (Music Box Song) 4637
Young Man's Rescue League 357
Young Man, Older Woman 4786
Young Men Take a Tip from Me 1309
Young People 2961
Young People Think about Love 2344
Young Pretty Girl Like You, A 3603
Young Was I 2633
Young with Him 101
Younger Generation, The 1747
Younger Man, A 154, 155
Younger Men Grow Older 3814
Younger Set, The 3968, 4087
Younger Sons of Peers 3865
Younger Than Springtime 4096
Younger with the Years 1119
Youngest Person I Know, The 3577
Youngest President, The 3615
Youngsters of the Navy 4509
Your Arms Too Short to Box with God 4788
Your Auto Ought to Get Girls 3400
Your Baby Is Comin' to Town 3392
Your Broadway and Mine 551
Your Broadway and My Broadway 544
Your Cavalcade of Hits 4137
Your Cigarette 126

Your Country Needs You 2622
Your Daddy's Gone Away 3741
Your Darling Daughter 2422
Your Disposition Is Mine 1827
Your Dream (Is the Same As My Dream) 1476
Your Eyes 4357
Your Eyes Are Blue 2764
Your Eyes Have Told Me So 1026
Your Eyes Have Told Me That You Love Me 4817
Your Eyes Shall Speak to Me 2567
Your Eyes, Your Smile (Those Eyes) 1419
Your Face Is So Familiar 3103, 3104
Your Face Is Your Fortune 532
Your Fatal Fascination 1539
Your Fault 2143
Your Feet's Too Big 39
Your Flag 1972
Your Good Morning 3161, 3366
Your Hand in Mine 3366, 2685
Your Hat and My Hat 3008
Your Heart Alone Must Tell 1157
Your Heart and Mine 446
Your Heart, If You Please 4735
Your Heart Is Palpitating 2519
Your High Note! 705
Your Home Away from Home 2114
Your Honeymoon Will Last 3943
Your Isle 4737
Your Kind of Man 1729
Your Kiss Is Champagne 2328
Your Kiss Told Me 292
Your Land and My Land 3056
Your Last Love Is Your First 2931
Your Life 2478
Your Life Is My Life 18
Your Lips 3295
Your Lips Are No-Man's-Land but Mine 3341
Your Lips Say No, but Your Eyes Say Yes 2869
Your Love I Crave 2845
Your Love Is My Love 4192
Your Loving Eyes 1268
Your Lullaby 3847, 4781
Your Momma Is Your Number One Friend 3714
Your Most Exciting Set of Bones 1884
Your Mother's Son-in-Law 444
Your Name May Be Paris 3988
Your Night to Howl 838
Your Other Side 3406
Your Own 2844
Your Own College Band 4652
Your Own Two Feet 2578
Your Photo 2292
Your Picture 1565
Your Place in the Sunshine 166
Your Prayers Are Answered 2012
Your Prince 2065
Your Prince Was Not So Charming 680
Your Rose 3170
Your Second Wife 1962
Your Sins Will Find You Out 981
Your Smiles, Your Tears 3170
Your Sticks, Your Hat, Your Hand 760
Your Sunny Southern Smile 4823
Your Time Is Different to Mine 2949
Your Turn 1714
Your Turn Has Come 4615
Your Type Is Coming Back 3907
Your Voice I Hear 3754
Your Way of Loving 1229
Your Way or My Way 3369
Yours 1203, 2252
Yours, All Yours 837
Yours All Yours 1772
Yours and Mine 1734
Yours for a Song 173, 397, 3893
Yours for Me, and Mine for You 20
Yours Is My Heart Alone 3573, 4792
Yours Sincerely 4118
Yours Sincerely U.S.A. 3400
Yours Truly 4208, 4793
Yours with a Song 2458
Yours, Yours, Yours 3897
Youth 2884, 1867
Youth in Spring 4121
Youth Is Gay 2249
Youth, Joy and Freedom 3453
Youth of the Heart, The 220
Youth Remembers 81
Youth Who Sows, The 4479
Youth's the Time of Fun and Folly (Youth Must Have Its Fling) 1388
Yrs. Truly 1004
Yuca Tango, The 1228
Yucatana 4572
Yuletide Spirit, The 1424
Yuletide, Park Avenue 620
Yum Ticky-Ticky 656
Yum Yum Time 697
Yum-Yum's Vision 2861
Yup and Away 47
Yuppie Love 3076
Yusef's Visit 3792
Yvonne 1131, 4795

Z

Zabelle 1900
Zabelle Waltz 1148
Zal Shain Shulem Zine 4463
Zambaloo 18
Zamboanga 2578
Zamona 2315
Zanzibar 2230
Zap! 3576
Zara 1783
Zarape (Antoinette's Dance) (inst.) 4798
Zaru Zaru Zee 2736
Zaza 2041

Zbuyile Emasisweni (It's Finally
| | Happening) 3836
Ze American Millionaire Barcarolle 3298
Ze English Language 2915
Ze Patent Love Perfume 3765
Zebekiko (Youao's Dance) 2106
Zebra Girl 4809
Zei Gezent 1822
Zeigeunerliebe 1712
Zel, Zel 2123
Zen is When 339
Zenda 4798
Zenedee 1118
Zeroing in on You 2011
Ziegeuner 429, 3235
Ziegfeld Dollies, The 4843
Ziegfeld Follies Rag 4811
Ziegfeld Girl, The 1308, 4830
Ziegfeld Paper Dollies 4853
Ziegfeld Rag 804
Ziegfeld Show, A 4829
Ziegfeld, Where Are You Now? 4093
Zig Zag 4858
Zig, Zig, Zig 4792
Zigeunerliebe 2947
Zim Boom Ta-ra 1627
Zim Zam Zee 3082
Zim-Zim 3537
Zimbaba 2147
Zina 3192
Zing Boom Bah 2373
Zing! Went the Strings of My Heart 4374
Zinga-Zula Man, The 1793
Zingara 2947
Zingara Dance 2407
Zingaras, The 3755
Zingra 4550
Zip 1756, 3353
Zip Code I Love You 4093
Zip Community 3654
Zis Lettle Girl 2070
Zita 4275
Zizi 4285
Zog Nit Keyn Mol 1740
Zonky 2561
Zoo Step, The 3958
Zoo, The 2013
Zoological Party 3882
Zoological Rag 1360
Zoot Suit Theme (inst.) 4861
Zorba the Greek 4862
Zsuzsi Kisasszony 2907
Zubbediya 2327, 4383
Zulu and the Zayda, The 4863
Zulu Lou 1690
Zulu Love Song (Wait for Me) 4863
Zuyder Zee 1246
Zwanzinette 1199

Chronological Index

When looking through the dates in this index note dates such as 00/00/1934. The zeros indicate that the exact opening date is not known; available records indicate only the year a particular show opened.

1877

Old Lavender 09/03/1877

1879

His-Mud-Scow-Pinafore 02/21/1879

1881

Cinderella at School 00/00/1881
Billee Taylor 02/19/1881

1884

1776 02/26/1884
Little Duke,The 08/04/1884

1886

Leather Patch, The 02/15/1886
Erminie 05/10/1886
Bridal Trap, The 05/31/1886

1887

Dorothy 11/05/1887

1889

Bluebeard Jr. or Fatima and the Fairy 01/13/1889
Seven Ages, The 10/14/1889

1891

Robin Hood 09/28/1891

1892

Fencing Master, The 11/14/1892
Isle of Champagne, The 12/31/1892

1893

La Vivandiere 00/00/1893
Woman-King, The 00/00/1893
Friend Fritz 04/17/1893
Panjandrum 05/01/1893
Girofle-Girofla 05/08/1893
Up to Date 05/15/1893
Knickerbockers, The 06/03/1893
Algerian, The 10/23/1893

1894

Passing Show, The 05/12/1894
Dr. Syntax 06/23/1894
Little Trooper, The 08/30/1894
Devil's Deputy, The 09/10/1894
Gaiety Girl, A 09/18/1894
Little Christopher Columbus 10/15/1894
Rob Roy 10/21/1894
Queen of Brilliants 11/07/1894
Brownies, The 11/12/1894
Prince Ananias 11/20/1894
Jacinta or the Maid of Manzarillo 11/26/1894
Flams, The 11/26/1894

1895

Twentieth Century Girl, The 00/00/1895
Off the Earth 01/21/1895
Madeleine, or the Magic Kiss 02/25/1895
Grand Vizier, The 03/04/1895
Aladdin, Jr. 04/08/1895
Tzigane, The 05/16/1895
Daughter of the Revolution, The 05/27/1895
Merry World, The (1895) 06/08/1895
Sphinx, The 07/08/1895
Kismet 08/12/1895
Fleur-De-Lis 08/29/1895

Day and a Night in New York, A 08/30/1895
Bathing Girl, The 09/02/1895
Princess Bonnie 09/02/1895
Chieftain, The 09/09/1895
His Excellency 10/14/1895
Shop Girl, The 10/28/1895
Merry Countess, The 11/02/1895
Wizard of the Nile, The 11/21/1895
Excelsior, Jr. 11/25/1895
Stag Party, or a Hero in Spite of Himself, A 12/17/1895
Artists' Model, An 12/17/1895
School Girl, The 12/30/1895

1896

At Jolly 'Coon'-ey Island 00/00/1896
Minstrel of Clare 00/00/1896
War-Time Wedding or, In Mexico in 1847, A 00/00/1896
Black Sheep and How It Came to Washington, A 01/06/1896
Gentleman Joe, the Hansom Cabby 01/06/1896
Lady Slavey, The 02/03/1896
Goddess of Truth, The 02/26/1896
El Capitan 04/20/1896
In Gay New York 05/25/1896
Caliph, The 09/03/1896
Geisha, The 09/09/1896
Half a King 09/14/1896
Gold Bug, The 09/14/1896
Lost, Strayed or Stolen 09/16/1896
Parlor Match, A 09/21/1896
Santa Maria 09/24/1896
Brian Boru 10/19/1896
Jack and the Beanstalk 11/02/1896
Mandarin, The 11/02/1896
Girl from Paris, The 12/08/1896
Dorcas 12/21/1896

1897

Shamus O'Brien 01/05/1897
Boy Wanted, A 01/18/1897
At Gay Coney Island 02/01/1897
Under the Red Globe 02/18/1897
La Falote 03/01/1897
Boys of Kilkenny, The 03/15/1897
Serenade, The 03/16/1897
Gayest Manhattan or Around New York in Ninety Minutes 03/22/1897
Mrs. Radley Barton's Ball or In Greater New York 03/26/1897
Miss Manhattan 03/30/1897
Wedding Day, The 04/08/1897
Circus Girl, The 04/23/1897
Isle of Gold, The 04/26/1897
At the French Ball 04/26/1897
Sweet Inniscarra 04/26/1897
Good Mr. Best, The 08/30/1897
Very Little Faust and Much Marguerite 08/30/1897
In Town 09/06/1897
Stranger in New York 09/13/1897
French Maid, The 09/27/1897
Belle of New York, The 09/28/1897
La Poupee 10/21/1897
Idol's Eye, The 10/25/1897
1999 11/15/1897
Pousse-Cafe, or the Worst Born 12/02/1897
Highwayman, The 12/13/1897
Ballet Girl, The 12/21/1897
Telephone Girl, The 12/27/1897

1898

Gayest Manhattan 00/00/1898
Hot Old Time 00/00/1898
Hotel Topsy-Turvy 00/00/1898
Governors, The 01/03/1898
Who Is Who 02/07/1898
Normandy Wedding, A 02/21/1898
Monte Carlo 03/21/1898
Trip to Coontown, A 04/04/1898
Bride Elect, The 04/11/1898
Koreans, The 05/03/1898
War Bubbles 05/16/1898
Con-Curers, The 05/17/1898
Clorindy, the Origin of the Cakewalk 07/05/1898
Kings of Koondom 08/00/1898
Runaway Girl, A 08/25/1898
Charlatan, The 09/05/1898
Hurly Burly 09/08/1898
Golden Horseshoe, The 09/15/1898
Wine, Women and Song 09/19/1898
Little Corporal, The 09/19/1898
Fortune Teller, The 09/26/1898
Sure Cure, A 09/26/1898
Cyranose de Bricabrac 11/03/1898
Dangerous Maid, A 11/12/1898
Jolly Musketeer, The 11/14/1898
Little Host, The 12/26/1898
American Beauty, An 12/28/1898

1899

Jes' Lak White Fo'ks 00/00/1899
Man in the Moon, The 00/00/1899
Onions 00/00/1899
Smugglers of Badayez, The 00/00/1899
Wise Guy, The 00/00/1899
Zaza 00/00/1899
Catherine 01/19/1899

Female Drummer, A 01/23/1899
In Gay Paree 03/20/1899
Helter Skelter 04/06/1899
Arabian Girl and 40 Thieves, An 04/29/1899
Mother Goose 05/01/1899
Rounders, The 07/12/1899
Cyrano de Bergerac 09/18/1899
Rogers Brothers in Wall Street, The 09/18/1899
Whirl-i-gig 09/21/1899
Singing Girl, The 10/23/1899
Sister Mary 10/27/1899
Papa's Wife 11/13/1899
Greek Slave, A 11/28/1899
Ameer, The 12/04/1899
Barbara Fidgety 12/07/1899
Three Little Lambs 12/25/1899

1900

Sons of Ham 00/00/1900
Chris and the Wonderful Lamp 01/01/1900
Little Red Riding Hood 01/08/1900
Broadway to Tokio 01/23/1900
Princess Chic, The 02/17/1900
Hearts Are Trumps 02/21/1900
Aunt Hannah 02/22/1900
Mam'selle 'Awkins 02/26/1900
By the Sad Sea Waves 03/05/1900
Regatta Girl, The 03/14/1900
Casino Girl, The 03/19/1900
Viceroy, The 04/09/1900
Knickerbocker Girl, The 06/15/1900
Cadet Girl, The 07/25/1900
Quo Vass Is! 09/06/1900
Rose of Persia 09/06/1900
Fiddle-Dee-Dee 09/06/1900
Monks of Malabar, The 09/14/1900
Rogers Brothers in Central Park, The 09/17/1900
Belle of Bohemia, The 09/24/1900
Million Dollars, A 09/27/1900
San Toy, or the Emperor's Own 10/01/1900
Military Maid, The 10/05/1900
Arizona 10/18/1900
Hodge, Podge & Co. 10/23/1900
Belle of Bridgeport, The 10/29/1900
Nell Go In 10/31/1900
Foxy Quiller 11/05/1900
Florodora 11/10/1900
Star and Garter 11/26/1900
Sweet Anne Page 12/03/1900
Madge Smith, Attorney 12/10/1900
After Office Hours 12/24/1900
Giddy Throng, The 12/24/1900
Royal Rogue, A 12/24/1900
Miss Prinnt 12/25/1900
Burgomaster, The 12/31/1900

1901

Cannibal King, The 00/00/1901
Champagne Charlie 00/00/1901
Curl and the Judge, The 00/00/1901
Little Dutch Girl, A 00/00/1901
Little Miss Modesty 00/00/1901
Miss Bob White 00/00/1901
My Antoinette 00/00/1901
Girl from Up There, The 01/07/1901
Garrett O'Magh 01/07/1901
Night of the Fourth, The 01/21/1901
Vienna Life 01/23/1901
Little Joker, The 01/27/1901
My Lady 02/11/1901
Governor's Son, The 02/25/1901
Exhibit II 03/10/1901
Romance of Athlone, A 03/18/1901
Prima Donna, The 04/17/1901
King's Carnival, The 05/13/1901
Strollers, The 06/24/1901
Melodius Menu, The 08/01/1901
Tom Moore 08/31/1901
Rogers Brothers in Washington, The 09/02/1901
Hoity Toity 09/05/1901
Messenger Boy, The 09/16/1901
Ladies' Paradise, The 09/16/1901
Circus Day 09/30/1901
Liberty Belles, The 09/30/1901
New Yorkers, The 10/07/1901
Sweet Marie 10/10/1901
Little Duchess, The 10/14/1901
Sleeping Beauty and the Beast, The 11/04/1901
Supper Club, The 12/23/1901

1902

Explorers, The 00/00/1902
Huckleberry Finn 00/00/1902
Zig Zag Alley 00/00/1902
Toreador, The 01/06/1902
Dolly Varden 01/27/1902
Maid Marian 01/27/1902
Uncle Tom's Cabin 01/27/1902
Hall of Fame, The 01/30/1902
Miss Simplicity 02/10/1902
Foxy Grandpa 02/17/1902
Belle of Broadway, The 03/17/1902
Show Girl or the Magic Cap, The 05/05/1902
Wild Rose, The 05/05/1902
King Dodo 05/12/1902
Storks, The 05/18/1902

Chinese Honeymoon, A 06/02/1902
Chaperons, The 06/05/1902
Defender, The 07/03/1902
Sally in Our Alley 08/29/1902
Emerald Isle, The 09/01/1902
Rogers Brothers in Harvard, The 09/01/1902
King Highball 09/06/1902
Twirly Whirly 09/11/1902
Old Limerick Town 09/14/1902
Country Girl, A 09/22/1902
Tommy Rot 10/20/1902
Silver Slipper, The 10/27/1902
Mocking Bird, The 11/10/1902
Fad and Folly 11/27/1902
Hungry Women of 1903 12/05/1902
When Johnny Comes Marching Home 12/16/1902
Paraders, The 12/21/1902
Sultan of Sulu, The 12/29/1902
Billionaire, The 12/29/1902

1903

Babes in the Wood 00/00/1903
Baron Humbug 00/00/1903
Darktown Circus Day 00/00/1903
Sis Hopkins 00/00/1903
Tom Tom 00/00/1903
Mr. Pickwick 01/19/1903
Mr. Bluebeard 01/21/1903
Wizard of Oz, The 01/21/1903
Jewel of Asia, The 02/16/1903
Nancy Brown 02/16/1903
In Dahomey 02/18/1903
Prince of Pilsen, The 03/17/1903
Running for Office 04/27/1903
My Lady Peggy Goes to Town 05/04/1903
Runaways, The 05/11/1903
Punch, Judy & Co. 06/01/1903
Auf Japan 06/07/1903
Blonde in Black, The 06/08/1903
Mid Summer Night's Fancies 06/22/1903
Princess of Kensington, A 08/31/1903
Three Little Maids 09/01/1903
Arrah-Na-Pogue 09/07/1903
Rogers Brothers in London, The 09/07/1903
Peggy from Paris 09/10/1903
Jersey Lily, The 09/14/1903
Under Cover 09/14/1903
Whoop-de-doo 09/24/1903
Fisher Maiden, The 10/05/1903
Babes in Toyland 10/13/1903
Girl from Kay's, The 11/02/1903
Office Boy, The 11/02/1903
Mrs. Delany of Newport 11/03/1903
Red Feather 11/09/1903
Babette 11/16/1903
Winsome Winnie 12/01/1903
Mother Goose 12/02/1903
Mam'selle Napoleon 12/08/1903
Girl from Dixie, The 12/14/1903
Cherry Girl, The 12/21/1903
Little Hans Andersen 12/23/1903
Merely Mary Ann 12/28/1903

1904

Anheuser Push, The 00/00/1904
Elopers, The 00/00/1904
Filibuster, The 00/00/1904
Lambs Frolic 00/00/1904
My Lady Molly 01/05/1904
Terence 01/05/1904
Medal and the Maid, The 01/11/1904
English Daisy, An 01/18/1904
Sergeant Kitty 01/18/1904
Cinderella and the Prince or Castle of Heart's Desire 02/01/1904
Glittering Gloria 02/15/1904
Tenderfoot, The 02/22/1904
Yankee Consul, The 02/22/1904
Piff! Paff!! Pouf!!! 04/02/1904
Man from China, The 05/02/1904
Venetian Romance, A 05/02/1904
Southerners, The 05/23/1904
Little Bit of Everything, A 06/06/1904
Paris by Night 07/02/1904
Maid and the Mummy, The 07/25/1904
Isle of Spice, The 08/23/1904
School Girl, The 09/01/1904
Royal Chef, The 09/01/1904
Madcap Princess, A 09/05/1904
Mr. Wix of Wickham 09/19/1904
West Point Cadet, The 09/30/1904
Love's Lottery 10/03/1904
Burning to Sing or Singing to Burn 10/07/1904
Sho-Gun, The 10/10/1904
Easy Angel, An 10/17/1904
Higgledy-Piggledy 10/20/1904
Cingalee, The 10/24/1904
Little Johnny Jones 11/07/1904
Mrs. Black Is Back 11/07/1904
Cupid and Co 11/14/1904
Humpty Dumpty 11/14/1904
China Doll, A 11/19/1904
Baroness Fiddlesticks, The 11/21/1904
His Highness the Bey 11/21/1904
Two Roses, The 11/21/1904
Woodland 11/21/1904
It Happened in Nordland 12/05/1904
Smiling Island, The 12/15/1904
Lady Teazle 12/24/1904
In Newport 12/26/1904

1905

All Around Chicago 00/00/1905
All Round Chicago 00/00/1905
Grafter, The 00/00/1905
Pair of Pinks, A 00/00/1905
Girl and the Bandit, The 01/09/1905
Fantana 01/14/1905
Duchess of Dantzic, The 01/16/1905
Forbidden Land, The 01/16/1905
Buster Brown 01/24/1905
Mama's Papa 02/01/1905
Athletic Girl, The 02/15/1905
Me, Him, and I 03/13/1905
Isle of Bong Bong, The 03/14/1905
Yankee Circus on Mars, A 04/12/1905
Sergeant Brue 04/25/1905
Rollicking Girl, The 05/01/1905
Kafoozelum 05/21/1905
Lifting the Lid 06/05/1905
When We Were Forty-One 06/12/1905
Woggle Bug, The 06/20/1905
Geezer of Geck, The 07/24/1905
Pearl and the Pumpkin, The 08/21/1905
Easy Dawson 08/22/1905
Catch of the Season, The 08/28/1905
Ham Tree, The 08/28/1905
White Chrysanthemum, The 08/31/1905
Rogers Brothers in Ireland, The 09/04/1905
Miss Dolly Dollars 09/04/1905
Rogers Brothers in Paris, The 09/05/1905
Breaking Into Society 10/02/1905
Edmund Burke 10/02/1905
Happyland or the King of Elysia 10/02/1905
Fritz in Tammany Hall 10/16/1905
It's Up to You, John Henry 10/23/1905
Wonderland 10/24/1905
Belle of the West, The 10/29/1905
Moonshine 10/30/1905
Veronique 10/30/1905
White Cat, The 11/02/1905
Earl and the Girl, The 11/04/1905
Peter Pan 11/06/1905
How Baxter Butted In 11/13/1905
Press Agent, The 11/27/1905
Umpire, The 12/02/1905
Mayor of Tokio, The 12/04/1905
Society Circus, A 12/13/1905
Mlle. Modiste 12/25/1905
Gingerbread Man, The 12/25/1905
Babes and the Baron, The 12/25/1905

1906

Garden Matinee 00/00/1906
Rosalie 00/00/1906
Man from 'Bam, The 00/00/1906
Maid and Mule 00/00/1906
Lovers and Lunatics 00/00/1906
I.O.U. 00/00/1906
Hottest Coon in Dixie 00/00/1906
Happy Hooligan's Trip Around the World 00/00/1906
Girls Will Be Girls 00/00/1906
Girl from Broadway, The 00/00/1906
Rufus Rastus 00/00/1906
Fool House, The 00/00/1906
Cowboy Girl, The 00/00/1906
College Days 00/00/1906
Captain Careless 00/00/1906
At Yale 00/00/1906
Around the Town 00/00/1906
Thebe 00/00/1906
Forty-Five Minutes from Broadway 01/01/1906
Blue Moon, The 01/03/1906
Coming Thro' the Rye 01/09/1906
Twiddle-Twaddle 01/11/1906
Way to Kenmare, The 01/13/1906
Vanderbilt Cup, The 01/16/1906
Galloper, The 01/22/1906
Mexicana 01/29/1906
Gay New York 02/01/1906
Abyssinia 02/20/1906
Belle of Avenue A, The 03/05/1906
Beauty of Bath, The 03/19/1906
His Majesty 03/19/1906
Three Graces, The 04/02/1906
Social Whirl, The 04/09/1906
Free Lance, The 04/16/1906
Venus, 1906 04/17/1906
District Leader, The 04/30/1906
His Honor the Mayor 05/28/1906
Seeing New York 06/05/1906
Mam'zelle Champagne 06/25/1906
Little Cherub, The 08/06/1906
Tourists, The 08/25/1906
Marrying Mary 08/27/1906
About Town 08/30/1906
New Aladdin, The 09/00/1906
Man from Now, The 09/03/1906
My Lady's Maid or Lady Madcap 09/20/1906
Red Mill, The 09/24/1906
Around the Clock 10/00/1906
Genius, The 10/03/1906
Spring Chicken, The 10/08/1906
Rich Mr. Hoggenheimer, The 10/22/1906
Eileen Asthore 10/22/1906
Girl and the Gambler, The 11/05/1906
Mrs. Wilson, That's All 11/05/1906
My Wife's Family 11/05/1906
Mam'selle Sallie 11/26/1906
Parisian Model, The 11/27/1906
Neptune's Daughter 11/28/1906
Pioneer Days 11/28/1906

Everybody Works but Father 11/30/1906
Belle of Mayfair, The 12/03/1906
Show Girl, The 12/04/1906
George Washington, Jr. 12/12/1906
Dream City 12/25/1906
Student King, The 12/25/1906
Road to Yesterday, The 12/31/1906
Matilda 12/31/1906

1907

Girls of America 00/00/1907
Not Yet but Soon 00/00/1907
Noah's Ark 00/00/1907
Merry Widower, The 00/00/1907
Lucky Dog, A 00/00/1907
In New York Town 00/00/1907
House Melodious, The 00/00/1907
Happy Hooligan's Trip Around the World 00/00/1907
Simple Simon Simple 00/00/1907
Dion O'Dare 00/00/1907
Captain Jasper 00/00/1907
Candy Kid, The 00/00/1907
Across the Continent in the Stationary Express 00/00/1907
Painting the Town 01/02/1907
Princess Beggar 01/07/1907
Nelly Neil 01/10/1907
Mimic and the Maid, The 01/11/1907
Belle of London Town, The 01/28/1907
Little Michus, The 01/31/1907
Girl and the Governor, The 02/04/1907
Rose of Alhambra, The 02/04/1907
White Hen, The 02/16/1907
Tattooed Man, The 02/18/1907
Beauty Doctor, The 02/21/1907
McFadden's Flats 02/28/1907
Grand Mogul, The 03/25/1907
Land of Nod, The 04/01/1907
Song Birds, The 04/01/1907
Orchid, The 04/08/1907
Boys of Company 'B', The 04/08/1907
Miss Camille 04/14/1907
Fascinating Flora 05/20/1907
Honeymooners, The 06/03/1907
Maid and the Millionaire, The 06/22/1907
Ziegfeld Follies of 1907 07/08/1907
Time, the Place and the Girl, The 08/05/1907
Shoo-Fly Regiment, The 08/06/1907
Happy Days 08/08/1907
Captain Rufus 08/12/1907
Hired Girl's Millions 08/12/1907
Yankee Tourist, A 08/12/1907
Alaskan, The 08/12/1907
Lady from Lanes, The 08/19/1907
Cupid at Vassar 08/23/1907
Dairymaids, The 08/26/1907
Patsy in Politics 09/02/1907
Rogers Brothers in Panama, The 09/02/1907
From Across the Big Pond 09/07/1907
Bubbles 09/09/1907
Gay Gordons, The 09/11/1907
Black Politician 09/14/1907
Boy with the Boodle, The 09/16/1907
Lola from Berlin 09/16/1907
Yankee Regent, The 09/17/1907
Pan Handle Pete 09/19/1907
Hurdy Gurdy Girl, The 09/23/1907
Little Yennie Yensen 09/30/1907
Girl Behind the Counter, The 10/01/1907
Girl Over There, The 10/02/1907
Gay White Way, The 10/07/1907
Hip! Hip! Hooray! 10/10/1907
Hoyden, The 10/19/1907
Top o' the World, The 10/19/1907
Ma's New Husband 10/20/1907
Merry Widow, The 10/21/1907
Miss Pocahontas 10/28/1907
Girl from Yama, The 11/04/1907
End of the Trail, The 11/05/1907
Tom Jones 11/11/1907
Rejuvenation of Aunt Mary, The 11/12/1907
Girls of Holland, The 11/18/1907
King Casey 11/18/1907
Morals of Marcus, The 11/18/1907
Auto Race, The 11/25/1907
O'Neill of Derry 11/25/1907
Talk of New York, The 12/03/1907
Knight for a Day, A 12/16/1907
Original Cohen, The 12/16/1907
Playing the Ponies 12/23/1907
Bad Boy and His Teddy Bears, The 12/30/1907
Miss Hook of Holland 12/31/1907

1908

Simple Molly 00/00/1908
Accidental Discovery of the North Pole, An 00/00/1908
Blackville Strollers 00/00/1908
Ephraham Johnson from Norfolk 00/00/1908
Happy Youngsters 00/00/1908
Little Dolly Dimples 00/00/1908
My Sweetheart 00/00/1908
Oysterman, The 00/00/1908
Panama 00/00/1908
Playing the Ponies 00/00/1908
Merry Widow and the Devil, The 01/02/1908

Funabashi 01/06/1908
Toyland 01/08/1908
Billy the Kid 01/11/1908
Yankee Drummers, The 01/19/1908
Lonesome Town 01/20/1908
Waltz Dream, A 01/27/1908
Soul Kiss, The 01/28/1908
Grafters, The 02/02/1908
Fifty Miles from Boston 02/03/1908
Bandanna Land 02/03/1908
Pickings from Puck 02/09/1908
Nearly a Hero 02/24/1908
Big Stick, The 03/16/1908
Honeymoon Trail 03/23/1908
Busy Izzy's Boodle 04/06/1908
Ole Olson 04/19/1908
Flower of the Ranch, The 04/20/1908
Li'l Mose 04/20/1908
Yankee Prince, The 04/20/1908
Merry-Go-Round, The 04/25/1908
Friar's Festival, The 05/14/1908
Gay Musician, The 05/18/1908
Mary's Lamb 05/25/1908
Naked Truth, The 06/00/1908
Ski-Hi 06/02/1908
Three Twins 06/15/1908
Ziegfeld Follies of 1908 06/15/1908
Mimic World, The 07/09/1908
Cohan and Harris Minstrels 08/03/1908
Girl Question, The 08/03/1908
Love Watches 08/29/1908
Prince Humbug 08/31/1908
Algeria 08/31/1908
Girls of Gottenburg, The 09/02/1908
Girl at the Helm, A 09/05/1908
Sporting Days 09/05/1908
Fluffy Ruffles 09/07/1908
Duke of Duluth, The 09/11/1908
School Days 09/14/1908
Mater 09/23/1908
Mlle. Mischief 09/28/1908
Marcelle 10/01/1908
American Idea, The 10/05/1908
Morning, Noon and Night 10/05/1908
Golden Butterfly, The 10/12/1908
Little Nemo 10/20/1908
Boys and Betty, The 11/02/1908
Winning Miss, A 11/21/1908
Blue Mouse, The 11/30/1908
Miss Innocence 11/30/1908
Prima Donna, The 11/30/1908
Pied Piper, The 12/03/1908
Queen of the Moulin Rouge, The 12/07/1908
Mr. Hamlet of Broadway 12/23/1908

1909

My Friend from Kentucky 00/00/1909
Yankee Mandarin, The 00/00/1909
Politicians, The 00/00/1909
Colored Aristocrats, The 00/00/1909
Dick Whittington 00/00/1909
Follies of the Day 00/00/1909
Gaiety Jubilee, The 00/00/1909
Golden Widow, The 00/00/1909
Husband, The 00/00/1909
Mayor of Newtown, The 00/00/1909
Miss Molly May 00/00/1909
Kitty Grey 01/25/1909
Stubborn Cinderella, A 01/25/1909
Fair Co-Ed, The 02/01/1909
Havana 02/11/1909
Prince of Tonight, The 03/09/1909
Golden Girl, The 03/16/1909
Newlyweds and Their Baby, The 03/22/1909
Beauty Spot, The 04/10/1909
Candy Shop, The 04/27/1909
Red Moon, The 05/03/1909
Midnight Sons, The 05/22/1909
Boy and the Girl, The 05/31/1909
Ziegfeld Follies of 1909 06/14/1909
Motor Girl, The 06/15/1909
Gay Hussars, The 07/29/1909
Broken Idol, A 08/16/1909
Cohan and Harris Minstrels 08/16/1909
Lo 08/29/1909
In Hayti 08/30/1909
Love Cure, The 09/01/1909
Trip to Japan, A 09/04/1909
Dollar Princess, The 09/06/1909
Chocolate Soldier, The 09/13/1909
Rose of Algeria, The 09/20/1909
Girl and the Wizard, The 09/27/1909
White Sister, The (1909) 09/27/1909
Man Who Owns Broadway, The 10/11/1909
Kissing Girl, The 10/25/1909
They Loved a Lassie 10/31/1909
Flirting Princess, The 11/01/1909
Mr. Lode of Koal 11/01/1909
Silver Star, The 11/01/1909
Belle of Brittany, The 11/08/1909
Old Dutch 11/22/1909
Air King, The 12/00/1909
Goddess of Liberty, The 12/22/1909

1910

Cat and the Fiddle, The 00/00/1910
City Chap, The 00/00/1910
Face That Wins, The 00/00/1910
Girl and the Drummer, The 00/00/1910
Gotts Schtroff 00/00/1910
Isle of Love, The 00/00/1910
Photo Shop, The 00/00/1910
Possum Hunt Club Revue, The 00/00/1910

Jolly Bachelors, The 01/06/1910
Old Town, The 01/10/1910
King of Cadonia, The 01/10/1910
American in Paris, The 01/10/1910
Prince of Bohemia, The 01/13/1910
Arcadians, The 01/17/1910
Barry of Ballymore 01/30/1910
Miss Nobody from Starland 01/31/1910
Young Turk, The 01/31/1910
Katie Did 02/18/1910
Bright Eyes 02/28/1910
Just One of the Boys 03/07/1910
Skylark, A 04/04/1910
Alpsburg 04/08/1910
Molly May 04/08/1910
Lulu's Husbands 04/14/1910
Matinee Idol, A 04/28/1910
Tillie's Nightmare 05/05/1910
Hermits at Happy Hollow, The 05/30/1910
Merry Whirl, The 05/30/1910
Girlies 06/03/1910
Summer Widowers, The 06/04/1910
Ziegfeld Follies of 1910 06/20/1910
Up and Down Broadway 07/18/1910
Wife Tamers, The 08/08/1910
Echo, The 08/17/1910
Our Miss Gibbs 08/29/1910
Sweetest Girl in Paris, The 08/29/1910
Madame Sherry 08/30/1910
International Cup, The 09/03/1910
Ballet of Niagara, The 09/03/1910
He Came from Milwaukee 09/10/1910
Hans, the Flute Player 09/20/1910
Alma, Where Do You Live? 09/26/1910
Girl in the Train, The 10/03/1910
Deacon and the Lady, The 10/04/1910
Judy Forgot 10/06/1910
Madame Troubadour 10/10/1910
Lower Birth Thirteen 10/16/1910
Girl in the Taxi (1910) 10/24/1910
Gamblers, The 10/31/1910
Bachelor Belles, The 11/07/1910
Getting a Polish 11/07/1910
Naughty Marietta 11/07/1910
Girl in the Kimono, The 11/11/1910
Girl and the Kaiser, The 11/22/1910
Yankee Girl, The 12/10/1910
Spring Maid, The 12/26/1910

1911

Spoony Sam 00/00/1911
Winter Garden Vaudeville Show 00/00/1911
Country Girl, The 00/00/1911
Friar's Frolic of 1911 00/00/1911
In the Jungles 00/00/1911
Little Kiln Club, The 00/00/1911
My Cinderella Girl 00/00/1911
My Pearl Maiden 00/00/1911
Real Girl 00/00/1911
Runaway Slave 00/00/1911
Slim Princess, The 01/02/1911
Marriage a la Carte 01/02/1911
Paradise of Mahomet, The 01/17/1911
Hen-Pecks, The 02/04/1911
Balkan Princess, The 02/09/1911
Two Men and a Girl 02/13/1911
Happiest Night of His Life, The 02/20/1911
Everywoman 02/27/1911
Jumping Jupiter 03/06/1911
Pink Lady, The 03/13/1911
La Belle Paree 03/20/1911
Little Miss Fix-It 04/03/1911
Love and Politics 04/03/1911
Merry Mary 04/16/1911
Dr. Deluxe 04/17/1911
Certain Party, A 04/24/1911
Folies Bergere Company 04/27/1911
His Honor the Barber 05/08/1911
Heart Breakers, The 05/30/1911
Red Rose, The 06/22/1911
Ziegfeld Follies of 1911 06/26/1911
Girl of My Dreams, The 08/07/1911
Hello Paris 08/19/1911
Siren, The 08/21/1911
Around the World 09/02/1911
Louisiana Lou 09/03/1911
Miss Jack 09/04/1911
Widow, The 09/11/1911
When Sweet Sixteen 09/14/1911
Kiss Waltz, The 09/18/1911
A La Broadway 09/22/1911
Little Millionaire, The 09/25/1911
Revue of Revues, The 09/27/1911
Never Homes, The 10/05/1911
Duchess, The 10/16/1911
Miss Dudelsack 10/16/1911
Gypsy Love 10/17/1911
Enchantress, The 10/19/1911
Quaker Girl, The 10/23/1911
Three Lights, The 10/31/1911
Wife Hunters,The 11/02/1911
Red Widow, The 11/05/1911
Three Romeos, The 11/13/1911
California 11/20/1911
Undine 11/20/1911
Vera Violetta 11/20/1911
Little Boy Blue 11/27/1911
Cora 11/28/1911
Peggy 12/07/1911
Betsy 12/11/1911
Wedding Trip, The 12/25/1911

1912

Rock and Fulton Act 00/00/1912
Auction Pinochle 00/00/1912
Cohan and Harris Minstrels 00/00/1912
Dr. Beans from Boston 00/00/1912
First Love 00/00/1912
In the Barracks 00/00/1912
Love Wager, The 00/00/1912
Mayor of Newtown, The 00/00/1912
Peck o' Pickles 00/00/1912
Persian Garden, A 00/00/1912
Modest Suzanne 01/01/1912
Over the River 01/08/1912
Bird of Paradise, The 01/08/1912
She Knows Better Now 01/15/1912
Rose of Panama 01/22/1912
Pearl Maiden, The 01/22/1912
Macushla 02/05/1912
Hokey-Pokey 02/08/1912
Opera Ball, The 02/12/1912
Whirl of Society, The 03/05/1912
Baron Trenck, The 03/11/1912
Man from Cook's, The 03/25/1912
Winsome Widow, A 04/11/1912
Wall Street Girl, The 04/15/1912
Rose Maid, The 04/22/1912
Let George Do It 04/22/1912
Two Little Brides 04/23/1912
And the Villain Still Pursued Her 05/10/1912
Mama's Baby Boy 05/25/1912
Hermits in Paris, The 05/27/1912
Under Many Flags 05/31/1912
Passing Show of 1912, The 07/22/1912
Girl from Montmartre, The 08/05/1912
Hanky-Panky 08/05/1912
Merry Countess, The 08/20/1912
Girl from Brighton, The 08/31/1912
Polish Wedding, A 08/31/1912
Girl at the Gate, The 09/01/1912
Girl in the Taxi, The 09/05/1912
'Mind the Paint' Girl, The 09/09/1912
My Best Girl 09/12/1912
Count of Luxembourg, The 09/16/1912
June Bride, The 09/23/1912
Oh! Oh! Delphine 09/30/1912
Tantalizing Tommy 10/01/1912
Charity Girl, The 10/02/1912
Woman Haters, The 10/07/1912
At the Barracks 10/09/1912
Ziegfeld Follies of 1912 10/21/1912
Lady of the Slipper, The 10/28/1912
Red Petticoat, The 11/13/1912
Dove of Peace, The 11/14/1912
Gypsy, The 11/14/1912
Broadway to Paris 11/20/1912
Roly Poly 11/21/1912
Without the Law 11/21/1912
Pot of Gold, The 11/26/1912
Sun Dodgers, The 11/30/1912
Firefly, The 12/02/1912
Peg o' My Heart 12/20/1912
Frivolous Geraldine 12/22/1912
Exceeding the Speed Limit 12/23/1912
Miss Princess 12/23/1912
Village Blacksmith, The 12/29/1912
Eva 12/30/1912
All for the Ladies 12/30/1912

1913

Earl and the Girls, The 00/00/1913
Out on Broadway 00/00/1913
My Friend from Kentucky 00/00/1913
Mutt and Jeff 00/00/1913
Merry Martyr 00/00/1913
Little Parisienne, The 00/00/1913
In Ethiopiaville 00/00/1913
Girl of Today, A 00/00/1913
Girl from Shanley's, The 00/00/1913
Eternal Waltz, The 00/00/1913
Wrong Mr. President, The 00/00/1913
Die Ballkonigin 00/00/1913
Darktown Politician, The 00/00/1913
Darktown Follies 00/00/1913
Court By Girls 00/00/1913
Boys from Home, The 00/00/1913
Bachelor's Dinner 00/00/1913
Sorority Days 01/16/1913
Somewhere Else 01/20/1913
Man with Three Wives, The 01/23/1913
Isle o' Dreams 01/27/1913
Sunshine Girl, The 02/03/1913
Honeymoon Express, The 02/06/1913
Countess Coquette 02/28/1913
Traitors, The 03/00/1913
All Star Gambols 03/10/1913
American Maid, The 03/13/1913
Dance Dream 03/17/1913
Beggar Student, The 03/22/1913
Purple Road, The 04/07/1913
When Claudia Smiles 04/13/1913
Come Over Here 04/19/1913
Amazons, The 04/28/1913
Kaleidoscope, The 04/30/1913
My Little Friend 05/19/1913
All Aboard 06/05/1913
Ziegfeld Follies of 1913 06/16/1913
Tik Tok Man of Oz, The 06/23/1913
Passing Show of 1913, The 07/24/1913
Trip to Washington, A 08/18/1913
When Dreams Come True 08/18/1913
Doll Girl, The 08/25/1913
Adele 08/28/1913
America 08/30/1913
Lieber Augustin 09/03/1913
Sweethearts 09/08/1913

Marriage Market, The 09/22/1913
Broadway Honeymoon, A 10/03/1913
Her Little Highness 10/13/1913
Glimpse of the Great White Way, A 10/27/1913
When Love Is Young 10/28/1913
Oh, I Say! 10/30/1913
Two Lots in the Bronx 11/00/1913
Pleasure Seekers, The 11/03/1913
Little Cafe, The 11/10/1913
Madcap Duchess, The 11/11/1913
Hop o' My Thumb 11/26/1913
September Morn 12/00/1913
High Jinks 12/10/1913
Iole 12/29/1913
Girl on the Film, The 12/29/1913

1914

Choir Rehearsal, The 00/00/1914
Props 00/00/1914
Princess of Ragtime 00/00/1914
New Song Birds, The 00/00/1914
Mr. Ragtime 00/00/1914
Matinee Girls 00/00/1914
Hermits in Vienna, The 00/00/1914
Heart of Paddy Whack, The 00/00/1914
Gus Edwards's New Song Revue of 1914 00/00/1914
Society Buds, The 00/00/1914
Captain Rufus 00/00/1914
Bringing Up Father 00/00/1914
Black Crepe and Diamonds 00/00/1914
Alma's Return 00/00/1914
After the Girl 00/00/1914
Trained Nurses, The 00/00/1914
Nuts and Wine 01/04/1914
Whirl of the World, The 01/10/1914
Queen of the Movies, The 01/12/1914
Sari 01/13/1914
Laughing Husband, The 02/02/1914
Shameen Dhu 02/02/1914
When Claudia Smiles 02/02/1914
Maids of Athens 02/19/1914
Midnight Girl, The 02/23/1914
Along Came Ruth 02/23/1914
Crinoline Girl 03/16/1914
Jerry 03/18/1914
Belle of Bond Street, The 03/30/1914
Forward March (1914) 04/13/1914
Red Canary, The 04/13/1914
Beauty Shop, The 04/13/1914
Gay Modiste, The 04/17/1914
Honeymoon Girls, The 04/17/1914
Passing Show, The (London) 04/20/1914
Paranoia 04/24/1914
We're All Dressed Up and We Don't Know Huerto Go 05/22/1914
Madame Moselle 05/23/1914
Ziegfeld Follies of 1914 06/01/1914
Passing Show of 1914, The (New York) 06/10/1914
Manicure Girl, The 06/29/1914
Dancing Duchess 08/19/1914
Girl from Utah, The 08/24/1914
Wars of the World 09/05/1914
One Girl in a Million 09/06/1914
Miss Daisy 09/09/1914
Let's Get Married 09/21/1914
Pretty Mrs. Smith 09/21/1914
Dancing Around 10/10/1914
Chin-Chin 10/20/1914
Experience 10/27/1914
Lilac Domino, The 10/28/1914
Papa's Darling 11/02/1914
Only Girl, The 11/02/1914
Suzi 11/03/1914
Jack's Romance 11/26/1914
Debutante, The 12/07/1914
Watch Your Step 12/08/1914
Tonight's the Night 12/24/1914
Lady Luxury 12/25/1914
Hello, Broadway! 12/25/1914

1915

Did You Ever? 00/00/1915
Samples 00/00/1915
On Your Way 00/00/1915
Mutt and Jeff in College 00/00/1915
Little Half Breed, The 00/00/1915
In and Out 00/00/1915
His Excellency, the President 00/00/1915
George Washington Bullion Abroad 00/00/1915
Down in Bom-Bom Bay 00/00/1915
What's Going On 00/00/1915
Cohen on the East Side 00/00/1915
Clock Shop, The 00/00/1915
Broadway Rastus 00/00/1915
Bringing Up Father 00/00/1915
Beauty Doctors, The 00/00/1915
Within the Loop 00/00/1915
Lonesome Lasses 01/18/1915
90 in the Shade 01/25/1915
Model Girl, The 01/26/1915
Maid in America 02/18/1915
Ziegfeld Midnight Frolic 03/00/1915
Peasant Girl, The 03/02/1915
Fads and Fancies 03/08/1915
Rosy Rapture, the Pride of the Beauty Chorus 03/22/1915
Nobody Home 04/20/1915
All Over Town 05/00/1915
Modern Eve, A 05/03/1915
One of the Boys 05/24/1915

Passing Show of 1915, The 05/29/1915
Ziegfeld Follies of 1915 06/21/1915
Hands Up 07/22/1915
Blue Paradise, The 08/05/1915
Girl Who Smiles, The 08/09/1915
No. 13 Washington Square 08/23/1915
Cousin Lucy 08/27/1915
Molly and I 08/31/1915
Ziegfeld Midnight Frolic 09/00/1915
Two Is Company 09/22/1915
Ned Wayburn's Town Topics 09/23/1915
Princess "Pat," The 09/29/1915
Hip-Hip-Hooray 09/30/1915
Miss Information 10/05/1915
Alone at Last 10/14/1915
World of Pleasure, A 10/14/1915
Girl of Tomorrow, The 10/18/1915
Darkydom 10/23/1915
Around the Map 11/01/1915
Sadie Love 11/29/1915
Katinka 12/23/1915
Very Good Eddie 12/23/1915
Stop! Look! Listen! 12/25/1915
Ruggles of Red Gap 12/25/1915

1916

Darktown Follies 00/00/1916
Dear Dorothy 00/00/1916
Garden of Eden, The 00/00/1916
How Newton Prepared 00/00/1916
Lieutenant Gus 00/00/1916
Peace Pirates, The 00/00/1916
Two Husbands and One Wife 00/00/1916
Ziegfeld Midnight Frolic 00/00/1916
Sybil 01/10/1916
Cinderella Man, The 01/17/1916
Cohan Revue of 1916, The 02/09/1916
Kilkenny 02/14/1916
Robinson Crusoe, Jr. 02/17/1916
Pom-Pom 02/28/1916
Road to Mandalay, The 03/01/1916
See America First 03/28/1916
Tickets Please 04/03/1916
Simplex Marriage Parlors 04/24/1916
Come to Bohemia 04/27/1916
Molly O' 05/17/1916
Friar's Frolic of 1916 05/28/1916
Step This Way 05/29/1916
Bride Tamer, The 06/12/1916
Ziegfeld Follies of 1916 06/12/1916
Razzle Dazzle 06/19/1916
Passing Show of 1916, The 06/22/1916
His Heart's Desire 08/00/1916
Yvette 08/10/1916
Broadway and Buttermilk 08/15/1916
His Bridal Night 08/16/1916
Keep Moving 08/27/1916
Girl from Brazil, The 08/30/1916
Big Show, The 08/31/1916
Flora Bella 09/11/1916
Regular Girl, A 09/18/1916
Amber Empress, The 09/19/1916
Theodore and Co. 09/19/1916
Miss Springtime 09/25/1916
Betty 10/03/1916
So Long, Letty 10/23/1916
Show of Wonders, The 10/26/1916
Good Gracious Annabelle 10/31/1916
Century Girl, The 11/06/1916
Follow Me 11/29/1916
Her Soldier Boy 12/06/1916
Go To It 12/24/1916
Kiss for Cinderella, A 12/25/1916

1917

My People 00/00/1917
Ziegfeld Midnight Frolic 00/00/1917
Wanted—A Wife 00/00/1917
Switzerland Sam 00/00/1917
Boys Will Be Boys 00/00/1917
Bringing Up Father Abroad 00/00/1917
Dance and Grow Thin 00/00/1917
Dew Drop Inn 00/00/1917
Fascinating Widow, The 00/00/1917
Girl of Mine 00/00/1917
Gus Edwards's Bandbox Revue 00/00/1917
Jim-Jam Revue 00/00/1917
Mutt and Jeff Divorced 00/00/1917
Mutt and Jeff's Wedding 00/00/1917
My Aunt from Utah 00/00/1917
My Home Town Girl 00/00/1917
Have a Heart 01/11/1917
Love O' Mike 01/15/1917
Canary Cottage 02/05/1917
You're in Love 02/06/1917
Oh, Boy! 02/20/1917
Up Stage and Down 03/08/1917
Eileen 03/19/1917
Out There 03/27/1917
Home, James 03/28/1917
Masked Model, The 04/17/1917
Little Missus, The 04/23/1917
Passing Show of 1917, The 04/26/1917
His Little Widows 04/30/1917
Captain Cupid 05/15/1917
Hitchy-Koo 06/07/1917
Ziegfeld Follies of 1917 06/12/1917
My Lady's Glove 06/18/1917
What Next? 06/24/1917
What Is Love? 07/02/1917
Oh! So Happy 07/19/1917
Ziegfeld Midnight Frolic 07/27/1917
Maytime 08/16/1917
Cheer Up 08/23/1917
Leave It to Jane 08/28/1917
Good Night, Paul 09/03/1917

Rambler Rose 09/10/1917
Riviera Girl, The 09/24/1917
Naughty Princess, The 09/25/1917
Venus on Broadway 10/01/1917
Furs and Frills 10/09/1917
Make Yourself at Home 10/09/1917
Jack O'Lantern 10/16/1917
Doing Our Bit 10/18/1917
Chu Chin Chow 10/22/1917
We Should Worry 10/26/1917
Land of Joy, The 10/31/1917
Miss 1917 11/05/1917
Kitty Darlin' 11/07/1917
Her Regiment 11/12/1917
Odds and Ends of 1917 11/19/1917
Words and Music 11/24/1917
Star Gazer, The 11/26/1917
Over the Top 11/28/1917
Golden Goose, The 11/29/1917
Grass Widow, The 12/03/1917
Gipsy Trail, The 12/04/1917
Flo-Flo 12/20/1917
Going Up 12/25/1917
One Minute Please 12/29/1917
Cohan Revue of 1918, The 12/31/1917

1918

Darkest Americans 00/00/1918
Ten for Five 00/00/1918
Song Birds 00/00/1918
Pack Up Your Troubles 00/00/1918
Married by Wireless 00/00/1918
House That Jack Built, The 00/00/1918
Hooray for the Girls 00/00/1918
Hello America 00/00/1918
Frolics of the Night 00/00/1918
Ziegfeld 9 O'Clock Frolic of 1918 00/00/1918
Century Midnight Whirl 00/00/1918
Catching the Burglar 00/00/1918
Bridal Not, The 00/00/1918
Bessie McCoy Davis' Period Dance Review 00/00/1918
Annette Kellerman's Big Show 00/00/1918
All Aboard 00/00/1918
Ziegfeld Midnight Frolic of 1918 00/00/1918
Ziegfeld Midnight Frolic 00/00/1918
In and Out 01/22/1918
Girl o' Mine 01/28/1918
Oh, Lady! Lady!! 02/01/1918
Love Mill, The 02/07/1918
Sinbad 02/14/1918
Follow the Girl 03/02/1918
Let's Go 03/09/1918
Toot-Toot! 03/11/1918
Oh, Look! 03/17/1918
Getting Together 03/18/1918
Rainbow Girl, The 04/01/1918
Fancy Free 04/11/1918
See You Later 04/15/1918
Good-Bye Bill 04/22/1918
Back Again 04/29/1918
Kiss Burglar, The 05/09/1918
Rock-a-Bye Baby 05/22/1918
She Took a Chance 06/00/1918
Made in Harlem 06/00/1918
Hitchy-Koo of 1918 06/06/1918
Ziegfeld Follies of 1918 06/18/1918
Passing Show of 1918, The 07/25/1918
Marry in Haste 08/05/1918
Yip! Yip! Yaphank! 08/19/1918
He Didn't Want to Do It 08/20/1918
Everything 08/22/1918
Why Worry? 08/23/1918
Head Over Heels 08/29/1918
Telling the Tale 08/31/1918
Fiddlers Three 09/03/1918
Maid of the Mountains, The 09/11/1918
Girl Behind the Gun, The 09/16/1918
Some Night 09/23/1918
Miss Blue Eyes 10/03/1918
Redemption (The Living Corpse) 10/03/1918
Sometime 10/04/1918
Ladies First 10/24/1918
Glorianna 10/28/1918
Canary, The 11/04/1918
Little Simplicity 11/04/1918
Victory Girl, The 11/16/1918
Oh, My Dear! 11/27/1918
Half Past Eight 12/09/1918
Good Luck, Sam! 12/09/1918
Better 'Ole or the Romance of Old Bill, The 12/19/1918
Atta Boy 12/23/1918
Listen Lester 12/23/1918
Somebody's Sweetheart 12/23/1918
Voice of McConnell, The 12/25/1918
East Is West 12/25/1918
Melting of Molly, The 12/30/1918

1919

Diri 00/00/1919
Suite Sixteen 00/00/1919
Song Romance, A 00/00/1919
Night Owls, The 00/00/1919
My Midnight Sweetheart 00/00/1919
Midnight Elopers, The 00/00/1919
Merry Mary Brown 00/00/1919
Knockers of 1919 00/00/1919
Hi and Dri 00/00/1919
Hello Paree 00/00/1919

This and That 00/00/1919
Children of the Sun, The 00/00/1919
Bugland 00/00/1919
Big Sensation, The 00/00/1919
Bessie Clayton Vaudeville Act 00/00/1919
Baby Blues 00/00/1919
B-R-A 00/00/1919
Visions of 1969 00/00/1919
Water's Fine, The 00/00/1919
Ziegfeld Midnight Frolic 00/00/1919
Up in Mabel's Room 01/15/1919
Velvet Lady, The 02/03/1919
Good Morning, Judge 02/06/1919
Monte Cristo, Jr. 02/12/1919
Just Around the Corner 02/15/1919
Royal Vagabond, The 02/17/1919
Girl in State Room "B" 02/27/1919
Yesterday 03/10/1919
Tumble Inn 03/24/1919
Take It From Me 03/31/1919
Come Along 04/08/1919
I Love You 04/28/1919
She's a Good Fellow 05/05/1919
Toot Sweet 05/07/1919
Lady in Red, The 05/12/1919
I Love a Lassie 05/15/1919
Twinkling Eyes 05/18/1919
Love Laughs 05/20/1919
La-La-Lucille 05/26/1919
Biff! Bang! 05/30/1919
George White's Scandals 06/02/1919
Daly Dreams 06/08/1919
Lonely Romeo, A 06/10/1919
Ziegfeld Follies of 1919 06/16/1919
Honeymoon Town 06/17/1919
Greenwich Village Follies, The 07/15/1919
Shubert Gaieties of 1919 07/17/1919
Oh, What a Girl! 07/28/1919
Cohan and Harris Minstrels 08/16/1919
Happy Days 08/23/1919
See-Saw 09/23/1919
Roly Boly Eyes 09/25/1919
Ziegfeld Midnight Frolic 10/02/1919
Hitchy-Koo of 1919 10/06/1919
Apple Blossoms 10/07/1919
Hello Alexander 10/07/1919
Little Whopper, The 10/13/1919
Nothing but Love 10/14/1919
Dream Song, The 10/23/1919
Passing Show of 1919, The 10/23/1919
Capitol Revue ('Demi-Tasse') 10/24/1919
Fifty-Fifty Ltd. 10/27/1919
Buddies 10/27/1919
Just a Minute 10/29/1919
Among the Girls 11/00/1919
Eclipse, The 11/00/1919
Little Blue Devil, The 11/03/1919
Magic Melody, The 11/11/1919
Irene 11/18/1919
Son-Daughter, The 11/19/1919
Linger Longer Letty 11/20/1919
Aphrodite 11/24/1919
Rose of China, The 11/25/1919
Elsie Janis and Her Gang 12/01/1919
My Lady Friends 12/03/1919
Miss Millions 12/09/1919
Monsieur Beaucaire 12/11/1919
Morris Gest's Midnight Whirl 12/27/1919
Angel Face 12/29/1919

1920

I'll Say She Does 00/00/1920
Sunshine 00/00/1920
Strut Your Stuff 00/00/1920
Satires of 1920 00/00/1920
Rings of Smoke 00/00/1920
Oh, By Jingo 00/00/1920
Mutt and Jeff in Chinatown 00/00/1920
Love Flower, The 00/00/1920
Little Dutch Girl, A 00/00/1920
Keeping Up with the Joneses 00/00/1920
Tattle Tales (1920) 00/00/1920
Girl in the Private Room, The 00/00/1920
Emerald Isle, The (1920) 00/00/1920
Dew Drop Inn (1920) 00/00/1920
Dere Mable 00/00/1920
Chin Toy 00/00/1920
Bits and Pieces 00/00/1920
Wet and Dry 00/00/1920
You'd Be Surprised 00/00/1920
Zip Goes a Million 00/00/1920
Always You 01/05/1920
Frivolities of 1920 01/08/1920
Passion Flower, The 01/13/1920
As You Were 01/27/1920
My Golden Girl 02/02/1920
Night Boat, The 02/02/1920
Rose Girl, The 02/11/1920
Lady Kitty, Inc. 02/16/1920
Tick-Tack-Toe 02/23/1920
Look Who's Here 03/02/1920
Ziegfeld Girls of 1920 03/08/1920
Mimi 03/13/1920
Ziegfeld Midnight Frolic of 1920 03/15/1920
What's in a Name? 03/19/1920
Oui Madame 03/22/1920
Fly with Me 03/24/1920
Three Showers 04/05/1920
Ed Wynn Carnival 04/05/1920
Lassie 04/06/1920
Girl from Home, The 05/03/1920
Honey Girl 05/03/1920

Betty Be Good 05/04/1920
Actors' Equity Benefit 05/09/1920
Page Mr. Cupid 05/17/1920
George White's Scandals 06/07/1920
Ziegfeld Follies of 1920 06/22/1920
Cinderella on Broadway 06/24/1920
Buzzin' Around 07/06/1920
Century Grove Revue 07/12/1920
Girl in the Spotlight 07/12/1920
Midnight Rounders of 1920, The 07/12/1920
Silks and Satins 07/15/1920
Poor Little Ritz Girl 07/27/1920
Ziegfeld 9 O'Clock Frolic 08/02/1920
Good Times 08/09/1920
Tickle Me 08/17/1920
Charm School, The 08/21/1920
Greenwich Village Follies, The 08/30/1920
Sweetheart Shop, The 08/31/1920
Little Miss Charity 09/02/1920
Dearie 09/05/1920
Honeydew 09/06/1920
Little Old New York 09/08/1920
Night Out, A 09/18/1920
Piccadilly to Broadway 09/27/1920
Pitter Patter 09/28/1920
Broadway Brevities of 1920 09/29/1920
Jim Jam Jems 10/04/1920
Mecca 10/04/1920
Tip Top 10/05/1920
Kissing Time 10/11/1920
Jimmie 10/17/1920
Mary 10/18/1920
Hitchy-Koo of 1920 10/19/1920
Half Moon, The 11/01/1920
Afgar 11/08/1920
Lady Billy 12/14/1920
Sally 12/21/1920
Her Family Tree 12/27/1920
Passing Show of 1921, The 12/29/1920

1921

Song Revue of 1921 00/00/1921
Whirl of the Town, The 00/00/1921
Troubles of 1920 00/00/1921
Town Gossip 00/00/1921
Alabama Bound 00/00/1921
Bamboula 00/00/1921
Chocolate Brown 00/00/1921
Happy Cavalier, The 00/00/1921
Hello 1921 00/00/1921
Irish Eyes 00/00/1921
Let 'Er Go Letty 00/00/1921
Marcus Show of 1920 00/00/1921
Peacock Alley 00/00/1921
Peggy 00/00/1921
Ragged Robin 00/00/1921
Three Kisses, The 01/00/1921
Springtime in Mayo 01/17/1921
Dear Me 01/17/1921
Midnight Rounders of 1921, The 02/07/1921
Ziegfeld 9 O'Clock Frolic of 1921 (3rd Edition) 02/08/1921
Ziegfeld Midnight Frolic (11th Edition) 02/09/1921
Say Mama 02/12/1921
Blue Eyes 02/21/1921
Love Birds 03/15/1921
Right Girl, The 03/15/1921
Dangerous Maid, A 03/21/1921
It's Up to You 03/28/1921
Liliom 04/20/1921
You'll Never Know 04/20/1921
Bringing Up Father at the Seashore 04/21/1921
June Love 04/25/1921
Just Married 04/26/1921
Two Little Girls in Blue 05/03/1921
Princess Virtue 05/04/1921
Biff! Bing! Bang! 05/09/1921
Phoebe of Quality Street 05/09/1921
Last Waltz, The 05/10/1921
Hermits on Main Street, The 05/23/1921
Shuffle Along 05/23/1921
Sunkist 05/23/1921
Say It with Jazz 06/01/1921
Snapshots of 1921 06/02/1921
Broadway Whirl, The 06/08/1921
Whirl of New York, The 06/13/1921
Ziegfeld Follies of 1921 06/21/1921
George White's Scandals 07/11/1921
All Star Jamboree 07/13/1921
All Star Idlers of 1921 07/14/1921
Tangerine 08/09/1921
Mimic World of 1921, The 08/15/1921
Sonny Boy 08/16/1921
Put and Take 08/23/1921
Greenwich Village Follies, The 08/31/1921
Silver Fox, The 09/05/1921
Music Box Revue 09/22/1921
Blossom Time 09/28/1921
Phi Phi 10/00/1921
O'Brien Girl, The 10/03/1921
Love Letter, The 10/04/1921
Golden Moth, The 10/05/1921
Bombo 10/06/1921
Love Dreams 10/10/1921
Darktown Frolics of 1921 10/11/1921
Good Morning, Dearie 11/01/1921
Perfect Fool, The 11/07/1921
Ziegfeld Midnight Frolic 11/17/1921
Suzette 11/24/1921
Kiki 11/29/1921
Mountain Man, The 12/12/1921
Ain't It the Truth 12/19/1921

1922

Listen to Me 00/00/1922
Shades of Hades 00/00/1922
Plantation Days 00/00/1922
Oh Joy! 00/00/1922
Mutt and Jeff 00/00/1922
Lola in Love 00/00/1922
Lola 00/00/1922
Little Kangaroo, The 00/00/1922
Up and Down 00/00/1922
Hello, Sue 00/00/1922
Flying Island 00/00/1922
Elusive Lady, The 00/00/1922
Bon Bon Buddy, Jr. 00/00/1922
Boardwark, The 00/00/1922
Winkle Town 00/00/1922
Up in the Clouds 01/02/1922
Blue Kitten, The 01/13/1922
Elsie Janis and Her Gang 01/16/1922
Marjolaine 01/24/1922
Chauve Souris 02/01/1922
Pins and Needles 02/01/1922
Bibi of the Boulevards 02/06/1922
Blushing Bride, The 02/06/1922
Frank Fay's Fables 02/06/1922
For Goodness Sake 02/20/1922
French Doll, The 02/20/1922
London Follies 03/06/1922
Rose of Stamboul, The 03/07/1922
Mayfair and Montmartre 03/09/1922
Hotel Mouse, The 03/13/1922
Just Because 03/22/1922
Chinese Lantern, The 04/07/1922
Letty Pepper 04/10/1922
Make It Snappy 04/13/1922
Some Party 04/15/1922
Go Easy Mabel 05/08/1922
And Very Nice Too 05/09/1922
Red Pepper 05/29/1922
Plantation Revue 06/00/1922
Jazz a la Carte 06/02/1922
Strut Miss Lizzy 06/03/1922
Ziegfeld Follies of 1922 06/05/1922
Raymond Hitchcock's Pinwheel 06/15/1922
Sue, Dear 07/02/1922
Spice of 1922 07/06/1922
Phi-Phi 08/16/1922
Daffy Dill 08/22/1922
Gingham Girl, The 08/28/1922
George White's Scandals 08/28/1922
Zig Zag 09/00/1922
Molly Darling 09/01/1922
Better Times 09/02/1922
Sally, Irene and Mary 09/04/1922
Joe Hurtig's Social Maids 09/05/1922
Fantastic Fricassee, A 09/11/1922
Greenwich Village Follies, The 09/12/1922
Cabaret Girl, The 09/14/1922
Orange Blossoms 09/19/1922
Passing Show of 1922, The 09/20/1922
East of Suez 09/21/1922
Lady in Ermine, The 10/02/1922
Yankee Princess, The 10/02/1922
Queen o' Hearts 10/10/1922
Hitchy-Koo of 1922 10/10/1922
Music Box Revue 10/23/1922
Springtime of Youth 10/26/1922
Up She Goes 11/06/1922
'49ers, The 11/07/1922
Little Nellie Kelly 11/13/1922
Midnight Jollies, The 11/18/1922
Liza 11/27/1922
Bunch and Judy, The 11/28/1922
Our Nell 12/04/1922
Rose Briar 12/25/1922
Glory 12/25/1922
Clinging Vine, The 12/25/1922

1923

Dinah 00/00/1923
Swanee River Home 00/00/1923
Sunbonnet Sue 00/00/1923
Sign of the Rose, The 00/00/1923
Plantation Revue 00/00/1923
Peaches 00/00/1923
North Ain't South 00/00/1923
Hot Chops 00/00/1923
Hello Everybody 00/00/1923
Get Set 00/00/1923
Ted Lewis Frolic 00/00/1923
Courtesan, The 00/00/1923
Chopin project 00/00/1923
Broadway Rastus of 1923 00/00/1923
Box Party 00/00/1923
Bal-Tabarin, The 00/00/1923
Atta Baby 00/00/1923
Arabian Nights 00/00/1923
Polly Preferred 01/11/1923
Stepping Stones, The 01/16/1923
Lady Butterfly 01/22/1923
Dancing Girl, The 01/24/1923
Caroline 01/31/1923
Sun Showers 02/05/1923
Wildflower 02/07/1923
Just Apples 03/09/1923
Go-Go 03/12/1923
Half Moon Inn 03/19/1923
Jack and Jill 03/22/1923
If I Were King 03/25/1923
Elsie 04/02/1923
Cinders 04/03/1923
Rainbow, The 04/03/1923
How Come? 04/16/1923
Dew Drop Inn 05/17/1923
Adrienne 05/28/1923

Hermits in Mexico, The 05/28/1923
Danish Yankee in King Tut's Court, A 05/31/1923
Passing Show of 1923, The 06/14/1923
Grand Street Follies, The 06/16/1923
George White's Scandals 06/18/1923
Helen of Troy, New York 06/19/1923
Earl Carroll's Vanities of 1923 07/05/1923
Raisin' Cain 07/09/1923
Fashions of 1924 07/18/1923
In Love with Love 08/06/1923
Newcomers, The 08/08/1923
Little Jessie James 08/15/1923
Artists and Models 08/20/1923
Little Miss Bluebeard 08/28/1923
London Calling 09/04/1923
Beauty Prize, The 09/05/1923
Poppy 09/13/1923
Greenwich Village Follies, The 09/20/1923
Music Box Revue 09/22/1923
Nifties of 1923 09/25/1923
Magic Ring, The 10/01/1923
Hammerstein's Nine O'Clock Revue 10/04/1923
Mr. Battling Buttler 10/08/1923
Ginger 10/16/1923
Ziegfeld Follies of 1923 10/20/1923
That Casey Girl 10/22/1923
Runnin' Wild 10/29/1923
Topics of 1923 11/20/1923
Sharlee 11/22/1923
Sancho Panza 11/26/1923
One Kiss 11/27/1923
Kid Boots 12/13/1923
Rise of Rosie O'Reilly, The 12/25/1923
Mary Jane McKane 12/25/1923

1924

Trial Honeymoon, A 00/00/1924
Willow Plate, The 00/00/1924
Vive la Femme 00/00/1924
Amber Fluid, The 00/00/1924
Come Along Mandy 00/00/1924
Cotton Land 00/00/1924
Creole Follies, The 00/00/1924
Everything Will Be All Right 00/00/1924
Gallagher and Shean Vaudeville Act 00/00/1924
Girl from Child's, The 00/00/1924
Honey 00/00/1924
Joy Shop, The 00/00/1924
Moon Maiden, The 00/00/1924
Negro Nuances 00/00/1924
Sittin' Pretty 00/00/1924
Creole Follies, The 01/00/1924
Town Clown, The 01/06/1924
Andre Charlot Revue of 1924 01/09/1924
Lollipop 01/21/1924
Sweet Little Devil 01/21/1924
Moonlight 01/30/1924
Chiffon Girl, The 02/19/1924
Creole Follies, The 03/00/1924
Paradise Alley 03/03/1924
Temple Belles 03/20/1924
Prisoner of Zenda, The 03/23/1924
Vogues of 1924 03/27/1924
Sitting Pretty 04/08/1924
Peg-o-My-Dreams 05/05/1924
Plain Jane 05/12/1924
Melody Man, The 05/13/1924
I'll Say She Is 05/19/1924
Innocent Eyes 05/20/1924
Grand Street Follies, The 05/20/1924
Round the Town 05/21/1924
Keep Kool 05/22/1924
Flossie 06/23/1924
Ziegfeld Follies of 1924 06/24/1924
George White's Scandals 06/30/1924
Belle of Quaker Town, The 07/00/1924
Marjorie 08/11/1924
No Other Girl 08/13/1924
Dream Girl, The 08/20/1924
Keep Moving 08/23/1924
Bye, Bye, Barbara 08/25/1924
Chocolate Dandies, The 09/01/1924
Top-Hole 09/01/1924
Rose-Marie 09/02/1924
Be Yourself 09/03/1924
Passing Show of 1924, The 09/03/1924
Earl Carroll's Vanities of 1924 09/10/1924
Primrose 09/11/1924
Greenwich Village Follies, The 09/16/1924
Hassard Short's Ritz Revue 09/17/1924
In Dutch 09/22/1924
Charlot's Revue 09/23/1924
Dear Sir 09/23/1924
Grab Bag, The 10/06/1924
Artists and Models 10/15/1924
Firebrand, The 10/15/1924
Expressing Willie 10/16/1924
Polly of the Circus 10/20/1924
Dixie to Broadway 10/29/1924
That's My Boy 11/00/1924
Annie Dear 11/04/1924
Peter Pan 11/06/1924
Madame Pompadour 11/11/1924
My Girl 11/24/1924
Magnolia Lady, The 11/25/1924
Lady, Be Good! 12/01/1924
Music Box Revue 12/01/1924
My Boy Friend 12/01/1924
Princess April 12/01/1924

Student Prince, The 12/02/1924
Topsy and Eva 12/23/1924
Betty Lee 12/25/1924

1925

Dixie Brevities 00/00/1925
Out o' Luck 00/00/1925
New Plantation Revue 00/00/1925
How've You Been? 00/00/1925
How's the King 00/00/1925
Hollywood Music Box Revue 00/00/1925
Frank Silvers Revue 00/00/1925
Flashes of the Gay White Way 00/00/1925
Dutch Girl, The 00/00/1925
Romany Love 00/00/1925
Daughter of Rosie O'Grady, The 00/00/1925
Chocolate Kiddies 00/00/1925
Chatter Box Revue 00/00/1925
Broadway Rastus 00/00/1925
Aces and Queens 00/00/1925
World of Pleasure 00/00/1925
Big Boy 01/07/1925
Comic Supplement (Of American Life), The 01/09/1925
Love Song, The 01/13/1925
China Rose 01/19/1925
Harry Carroll's Pickings 02/02/1925
Puzzles of 1925 02/02/1925
Bad Habits of 1925 02/08/1925
When Summer Comes 02/15/1925
Natja 02/16/1925
Tangletoes 02/17/1925
Sky High 03/02/1925
Louie the 14th 03/03/1925
Louisiana Lady 03/03/1925
Half Moon Inn 03/09/1925
Ziegfeld Follies of 1925 03/09/1925
Bamboula, The 03/24/1925
Bringing Up Father 03/30/1925
Mercenary Mary 04/13/1925
Tell Me More 04/13/1925
Fourflusher, The 04/13/1925
Birds of the Evening 04/26/1925
Dashing Belles of Yesterday and the Dumbbelles of Today, The 04/26/1925
Lambs Annual Public Spring Gambol, The 04/26/1925
Night in Old Paris, A 04/26/1925
Garrick Gaieties, The 05/17/1925
Brown Derby, The 05/18/1925
Lucky Sambo 06/06/1925
Kosher Kitty Kelly 06/15/1925
Grand Street Follies, The 06/18/1925
George White's Scandals 06/22/1925
Artists and Models 06/24/1925
Earl Carroll's Vanities of 1925 07/06/1925
June Days 08/06/1925
Lucky Break, A 08/11/1925
Gay Paree 08/18/1925
Oh! Mama 08/19/1925
Night Out, A 09/07/1925
Captain Jinks 09/08/1925
Still Dancing 09/11/1925
Jazz Singer, The 09/14/1925
No! No! Nanette! 09/16/1925
Dearest Enemy 09/18/1925
Vagabond King, The 09/21/1925
Sunny 09/23/1925
All for You 09/24/1925
Merry, Merry 09/24/1925
Some Day 10/06/1925
Arabesque 10/10/1925
Holka-Polka 10/14/1925
Enemy, The 10/20/1925
When You Smile 10/25/1925
City Chap, The 10/26/1925
Florida Girl 11/02/1925
Princess Flavia 11/02/1925
Naughty Cinderella 11/09/1925
Charlot Revue of 1926 11/10/1925
Mayflowers 11/24/1925
Moochin' Along 12/07/1925
Oh! Oh! Nurse 12/07/1925
Cocoanuts, The 12/08/1925
Greenwich Village Follies, The 12/24/1925
Tip-Toes 12/28/1925
By the Way 12/28/1925
Song of the Flame 12/30/1925

1926

Hollywood Music Box Revue 00/00/1926
Tan Town Topics Revue 00/00/1926
Sweet Lady 00/00/1926
Miss Happiness 00/00/1926
Miss Calico 00/00/1926
Maiden Voyage 00/00/1926
Magnolia 00/00/1926
Junior Blackbirds 00/00/1926
Thumbs Up! 00/00/1926
Geechie 00/00/1926
Chicago Loop 00/00/1926
Caravan 00/00/1926
Bubbling Over 00/00/1926
Blue Moon 00/00/1926
Fifth Avenue Follies, The 01/00/1926
Night in Paris, A 01/05/1926
Hello, Lola 01/12/1926
Cherry Blossom 01/18/1926
Sweetheart Time 01/19/1926
Suzanne 01/25/1926
Pair o' Fools 01/25/1926

Matinee Girl, The 02/01/1926
Jest, The 02/04/1926
Bunk of 1926 02/16/1926
Patsy 03/08/1926
Greenwich Village Follies, The 03/15/1926
Rainbow Rose 03/16/1926
Girl Friend, The 03/17/1926
Cherry Pie Revue 04/14/1926
Cochran's Revue of 1926 04/29/1926
Bad Habits of 1926 04/30/1926
Kitty's Kisses 05/06/1926
Garrick Gaieties, The 05/10/1926
High and Dry 05/10/1926
Nancy 05/16/1926
Great Temptations, The 05/18/1926
Yvonne 05/22/1926
Hearts and Diamonds 06/01/1926
Merry World, The 06/08/1926
George White's Scandals 06/14/1926
Grand Street Follies, The 06/15/1926
No Foolin' 06/24/1926
My Magnolia 07/12/1926
Blonde Sinner, The 07/14/1926
Bare Facts of 1926 07/16/1926
Americana 07/26/1926
Nic-Nax of 1926 08/02/1926
Miss Manhattan 08/09/1926
Earl Carroll's Vanities of 08/24/1926
Queen High! 09/05/1926
Castles in the Air 09/06/1926
Lew Leslie's Blackbirds 09/11/1926
Naughty Riquette 09/13/1926
Countess Maritza 09/18/1926
Ramblers, The 09/20/1926
Honeymoon Lane 09/20/1926
Happy Go Lucky 09/30/1926
Desires of 1927 10/00/1926
Deep River 10/04/1926
Criss Cross 10/12/1926
Katja 10/18/1926
Wild Rose, The 10/20/1926
Princess Charming 10/21/1926
Oh, Kay! 11/08/1926
R.S.V.P. 11/09/1926
Gay Paree 11/09/1926
Twinkle Twinkle 11/16/1926
Desert Song, The 11/30/1926
Lido Lady 12/10/1926
Oh, Please! 12/17/1926
Peggy-Ann 12/27/1926
Listen Dearie 12/27/1926
Betsy 12/28/1926

1927

Arthur Freed's Orange Grove Theatre Revue 00/00/1927
Hayfoot Strawfoot (1927) 00/00/1927
Hollywood Music Box Revue 00/00/1927
I Told You So 00/00/1927
Jake the Plumber 00/00/1927
Let's Go 00/00/1927
On with the Show 00/00/1927
Peg O' Mine 00/00/1927
Struttin' Sam from Alabam' 00/00/1927
Studio Girl, The 00/00/1927
Earl Carroll's Vanities 01/03/1927
Featuring the New Charlot Revue
Nightingale, The 01/03/1927
Lace Petticoat, The 01/04/1927
Piggy 01/11/1927
Bye Bye, Bonnie 01/13/1927
Yours Truly 01/25/1927
Hollywood Music Box Revue 02/02/1927
Rio Rita 02/02/1927
Judy 02/08/1927
Polly of Hollywood 02/21/1927
New Yorkers, The 03/10/1927
Spider, The 03/22/1927
Lucky 03/23/1927
Cherry Blossoms 03/28/1927
Rufus Lemaire's Affairs 03/28/1927
Lady Do 04/18/1927
Circus Princess, The 04/25/1927
Hit the Deck! 04/25/1927
Hoop-La! 04/25/1927
Seventh Heart, The 05/02/1927
Night in Spain, A 05/03/1927
Oh, Ernest! 05/09/1927
He Loved the Ladies 05/10/1927
White Sister, The 05/17/1927
One Dam Thing After Another 05/19/1927
Grand Street Follies, The 05/19/1927
Tales of Rigo 05/30/1927
Merry-Go-Round (1927) 05/31/1927
White Birds 05/31/1927
Talk about Girls 06/14/1927
Bottomland 06/27/1927
Padlocks of 1927 07/05/1927
Africana 07/11/1927
Rang-Tang 07/12/1927
Kiss Me 07/21/1927
Allez-Oop 08/02/1927
Manhatters, The 08/03/1927
Ziegfeld Follies of 1927 08/16/1927
A La Carte 08/17/1927
Footlights 08/19/1927
Strike Up the Band 08/29/1927
Band Box Follies, The 09/05/1927
Pickwick 09/05/1927
Good News 09/06/1927
Burlesque 09/12/1927
Half a Widow 09/12/1927
My Maryland 09/12/1927
Enchanted Isle 09/19/1927
Manhattan Mary 09/26/1927
Merry Malones, The 09/26/1927
Speak Easy 09/26/1927

Joan of Arkansaw 10/00/1927
Sidewalks of New York 10/03/1927
Yes, Yes, Yvette 10/03/1927
Blue Train, The 10/05/1927
My Princess 10/06/1927
5 O'Clock Girl, The 10/10/1927
Just Fancy 10/11/1927
White Lights 10/11/1927
Bow-Wows 10/12/1927
Love Call, The 10/24/1927
Girl from Cook's, The 11/01/1927
Connecticut Yankee, A 11/03/1927
Artists and Models 11/15/1927
Funny Face 11/22/1927
Take the Air 11/22/1927
Harry Delmar's Revels 11/28/1927
Golden Dawn 11/30/1927
Cotton Club Revue 12/04/1927
Happy 12/05/1927
Morning After, The 12/16/1927
Excess Baggage 12/26/1927
White Eagle, The 12/26/1927
Show Boat 12/27/1927
Lovely Lady 12/29/1927

1928

Bringing Up Father at the Seashore 00/00/1928
Charlot 1928 00/00/1928
Cotton Club Revue 00/00/1928
Festivities of 1927 00/00/1928
Headin' South 00/00/1928
Oh Johnny 00/00/1928
She's My Baby 01/03/1928
Rosalie 01/10/1928
Optimists, The 01/30/1928
Madcap, The 01/31/1928
Sunny Days 02/08/1928
Yellow Mask, The 02/08/1928
Rain or Shine 02/09/1928
Parisiana 02/09/1928
Mr. Moneypenny 02/16/1928
Lady Mary 02/23/1928
Keep Shufflin' 02/27/1928
Veils 03/13/1928
Three Musketeers, The 03/13/1928
Diamond Lil 04/09/1928
Greenwich Village Follies, 04/09/1928
Present Arms 04/26/1928
Lady Luck 04/27/1928
Blue Eyes 04/27/1928
Here's Howe! 05/01/1928
Blackbirds of 1928 05/09/1928
La Revue des Ambassadeurs 05/10/1928
Grand Street Follies, The 05/28/1928
That's a Good Girl 06/05/1928
Say When 06/26/1928
George White's Scandals 07/02/1928
Earl Carroll's Vanities of 1928 08/06/1928
Songwriter, The 08/13/1928
Good Boy 09/05/1928
White Lilacs 09/10/1928
Luckee Girl 09/15/1928
Cross My Heart 09/17/1928
New Moon, The 09/19/1928
Chee-Chee 09/25/1928
Billie 10/01/1928
Just a Minute 10/08/1928
Paris 10/08/1928
Ups-a-Daisy 10/08/1928
Hold Everything! 10/10/1928
Three Cheers 10/15/1928
Animal Crackers 10/23/1928
Hello, Yourself!!!! 10/30/1928
Americana 10/30/1928
This Year of Grace! 11/07/1928
Treasure Girl 11/08/1928
Rainbow 11/21/1928
Well, Well, Well 12/00/1928
Angela 12/03/1928
Whoopee 12/04/1928
Falstaff 12/25/1928
Red Robe, The 12/25/1928
Houseboat on the Styx, The 12/25/1928
Hello Daddy! 12/26/1928
Ziegfeld Midnight Frolic 12/28/1928

1929

Ziegfeld Midnight Frolic 00/00/1929
Blackbirds of 1929 00/00/1929
Cotton Club Revue 00/00/1929
Duchess of Chicago, The 00/00/1929
Gay Paree (1929) 00/00/1929
Harry Carroll's Revue 00/00/1929
Load of Coal 00/00/1929
Ming Toy 00/00/1929
Open Your Eyes 00/00/1929
Padlocks of 1929 00/00/1929
Wishing Well, The 00/00/1929
Ziegfeld Midnight Frolic 01/07/1929
Deep Harlem 01/07/1929
Polly 01/08/1929
Follow Thru 01/09/1929
Ned Wayburn's Gambols 01/15/1929
Boom-Boom 01/28/1929
Lady Fingers 01/31/1929
Fioretta 02/05/1929
Ziegfeld Midnight Frolic 02/06/1929
Pleasure Bound 02/18/1929
Spring Is Here 03/11/1929
Music in May 04/01/1929
Darktown Affairs 04/22/1929
Messin' 'Round 04/22/1929
Little Show, The 04/30/1929

Grand Street Follies, The 05/01/1929
Pansy 05/14/1929
Friars Frolic for Mayor J. J. Walker 05/19/1929
Night in Venice, A 05/21/1929
Hot Chocolates 06/20/1929
Keep It Clean 06/24/1929
Bamboola 06/26/1929
Earl Carroll's Sketch Book 07/01/1929
Show Girl 07/02/1929
Broadway Nights 07/15/1929
Noble Rogue, A 07/19/1929
Murray Anderson's Almanac 08/04/1929
Jerry for Short 08/12/1929
Sweet Adeline 09/03/1929
Street Singer, The 09/17/1929
Cape Cod Follies 09/18/1929
George White's Scandals 09/23/1929
Moon Madness 09/30/1929
June Moon 10/09/1929
Great Day! 10/17/1929
Wonderful Night, A 10/31/1929
Mr. Cinders 11/02/1929
Bitter Sweet 11/05/1929
House That Jack Built, The 11/08/1929
Heads Up! 11/11/1929
Sons o' Guns 11/26/1929
Fifty Million Frenchmen 11/27/1929
Silver Swan, The 11/27/1929
Top Speed 12/25/1929
Woof, Woof 12/25/1929
Great Day in N' Orleans 12/30/1929
Wake Up and Dream 12/30/1929
Ginger Snaps 12/31/1929

1930

Biff-Boom-Bang 00/00/1930
Blackberries of 1930 00/00/1930
Brown Sugar 00/00/1930
Funny Money 00/00/1930
Kitchen Mechanic's Revue 00/00/1930
Runnin' de Town 00/00/1930
Three Little Maids 00/00/1930
Ziegfeld Follies of 1930 00/00/1930
Strike Up the Band 01/14/1930
Ripples 02/11/1930
Nine-Fifteen Revue 02/11/1930
Simple Simon 02/18/1930
Here Comes the Bride 02/20/1930
International Revue, The 02/25/1930
Flying High 03/03/1930
Cochran's 1930 Revue 03/27/1930
Shuffle Along of 1930 04/00/1930
Co-optimists of 1930, The 04/04/1930
Jonica 04/07/1930
Three Little Girls 04/14/1930
Folies Bergere Review, The 04/15/1930
Garrick Gaieties, The 06/04/1930
Change Your Luck 06/06/1930
Artists and Models (1930) 06/10/1930
Mystery Moon 06/23/1930
Fireworks of 1930 06/26/1930
Earl Carroll's Vanities of 1930 07/01/1930
Who Cares? 07/08/1930
Hot Rhythm 08/21/1930
Second Little Show, The 09/02/1930
Charlot's Masquerade 09/04/1930
Follow a Star 09/17/1930
Luana 09/17/1930
Nina Rosa 09/20/1930
Fine and Dandy 09/29/1930
Prince Chu Chang 10/06/1930
Pajama Lady, The 10/06/1930
Brown Buddies 10/07/1930
Princess Charming 10/13/1930
Girl Crazy 10/14/1930
Three's a Crowd 10/15/1930
Blackbirds of 1930 10/22/1930
Arms and the Maid 11/00/1930
Vanderbilt Revue, The 11/03/1930
Well of Romance, The 11/07/1930
Hello, Paris 11/15/1930
Sweet and Low 11/17/1930
Smiles 11/18/1930
Little Tommy Tucker 11/19/1930
Ever Green 12/03/1930
New Yorkers, The 12/08/1930
Ballyhoo 12/22/1930
Life Is Like That 12/23/1930
Meet My Sister 12/30/1930

1931

Accidentally Yours 00/00/1931
B.S. Moss Varieties 00/00/1931
Blue Bird Revue, The 00/00/1931
Cotton Club Revue 00/00/1931
Hollywood Nine O'Clock Revue, The 00/00/1931
Star Dust 00/00/1931
You Said It 01/19/1931
Private Lives 01/27/1931
Through the Years 01/28/1931
America's Sweetheart 02/10/1931
Gang's All Here, The 02/18/1931
Venetian Glass Nephew, The 02/23/1931
Paris in Spring 02/26/1931
Rhythmania 03/00/1931
Making Mary 03/01/1931
Wonder Bar, The 03/17/1931
Rhapsody in Black 05/04/1931
Billy Rose's Crazy Quilt 05/19/1931
Third Little Show, The 06/01/1931
Band Wagon, The 06/03/1931
Ziegfeld Follies of 1931 07/01/1931
Box of Tricks 07/13/1931

Shoot the Works 07/21/1931
Nine O'Clock Revue, The 07/27/1931
Earl Carroll's Vanities of 1931 08/27/1931
Free for All 09/08/1931
Singing Rabbi, The 09/10/1931
George White's Scandals 09/14/1931
Fast and Furious 09/15/1931
Singin' the Blues 09/16/1931
Cherries Are Ripe 09/21/1931
Nikki 09/29/1931
Good Companions, The 10/01/1931
Everybody's Welcome 10/13/1931
Cat and the Fiddle 10/15/1931
The
East Wind 10/27/1931
Laugh Parade, The 11/02/1931
Here Goes the Bride 11/03/1931
Social Register, The 11/09/1931
Sugar Hill 12/25/1931
Of Thee I Sing 12/26/1931
Experience Unnecessary 12/30/1931

1932

Alarm Clock, The 00/00/1932
Forward March 00/00/1932
Hot Harlem 00/00/1932
Hushabye Lane 00/00/1932
La Ronde des Heures 00/00/1932
Little Racketeer, A 01/18/1932
Lucky Day 02/01/1932
Face the Music 02/17/1932
Marching By 03/03/1932
Hot-Cha! 03/08/1932
Blackberries of 1932 04/04/1932
Friars Frolic 05/08/1932
There You Are 05/16/1932
Yeah Man 05/26/1932
Hey Nonny Nonny! 06/06/1932
Hullabaloo 06/09/1932
Smiling Faces 08/30/1932
Passing Show of 1932, The 09/05/1932
Ballyhoo of 1932 09/06/1932
Flying Colors 09/15/1932
Belmont Varieties 09/26/1932
Earl Carroll's Vanities of 09/27/1932
1932
Americana 10/05/1932
I Loved You Wednesday 10/11/1932
Cotton Club Parade 10/23/1932
Cotton Club Parade 10/23/1932
Tell Her the Truth 10/28/1932
Harlem Hotcha 11/00/1932
Cyrano de Bergerac 11/04/1932
Music in the Air 11/08/1932
George White's Music Hall 11/22/1932
Varieties
Dubarry, The 11/22/1932
Take a Chance 11/26/1932
Gay Divorce 11/29/1932
Great Magoo, The 12/02/1932
Walk a Little Faster 12/07/1932
Alice in Wonderland 12/12/1932
Shuffle Along of 1933 12/26/1932
Radio City Music Hall 12/27/1932
Opening

1933

Show Boat Revue of 1933 00/00/1933
Birdie 00/00/1933
Clowns in Clover 00/00/1933
Cotton Club Parade 00/00/1933
Ever Yours 00/00/1933
Hollywood Be Thy Name 00/00/1933
Hollywood Revels of 1933 00/00/1933
International Revue, The 00/00/1933
Nine O'Clock Revue, The 00/00/1933
Paradise Revue 00/00/1933
Pardon My English 01/20/1933
Melody 02/14/1933
Strike Me Pink 03/04/1933
Home, James 03/10/1933
Die Lindenwirtin 03/30/1933
Cotton Club Parade 04/06/1933
Hummin' Sam 04/08/1933
Threepenny Opera, The 04/13/1933
Hi-De-Ho 05/06/1933
Tattle Tales 06/01/1933
Shady Lady 07/05/1933
Beau Brummel 08/07/1933
Ball at the Savoy 09/08/1933
Murder at the Vanities 09/12/1933
Nice Goings On 09/13/1933
Hold Your Horses 09/25/1933
As Thousands Cheer 09/30/1933
Hollywood Revels of 1934 10/02/1933
Nymph Errant 10/06/1933
Champagne, Sec 10/14/1933
Let 'Em Eat Cake 10/21/1933
Her Master's Voice 10/23/1933
Rose de France 10/23/1933
Please! 11/16/1933
Roberta 11/18/1933
She Loves Me Not 11/20/1933
Blackbirds of 1934 (First Edition) 12/02/1933
Beau Brummell 12/22/1933

1934

Manhattan Music Hall Revue 00/00/1934
Rhythm for Sale 00/00/1934
Billy Rose's Music Hall 00/00/1934
Revue
Bizarrities 00/00/1934
Casino Varieties 00/00/1934
Chicago Rhythm 00/00/1934

Cotton Club Parade 00/00/1934
Greenwich Village Follies, The 00/00/1934
Harmony Hill 00/00/1934
Hearts on Parade 00/00/1934
Hollywood Music Box Revue 00/00/1934
Ice Follies of 1934 00/00/1934
Julie 00/00/1934
Man from Baltimore, The 00/00/1934
Ziegfeld Follies of 1934 01/04/1934
All the King's Horses 01/30/1934
Four Saints in Three Acts 02/20/1934
New Faces 03/15/1934
Cotton Club Parade 03/23/1934
Three Sisters 04/09/1934
Moon Rises, The 04/23/1934
Caviar 06/07/1934
Gypsy Blonde 06/25/1934
Life Begins at 8:40 08/27/1934
Saluta 08/28/1934
Kill That Story 08/29/1934
Blackbirds of 1934 (Second Edition) 09/00/1934
Night of Stars 09/20/1934
Great Waltz, The 09/22/1934
Merrily We Roll Along 09/29/1934
Continental Varieties 10/03/1934
Hi Diddle Diddle 10/03/1934
America Sings 10/09/1934
Bring on the Girls 10/22/1934
Conversation Piece 10/23/1934
Say When 11/08/1934
Anything Goes 11/21/1934
Africana 11/26/1934
Revenge with Music 11/28/1934
Calling All Stars 12/13/1934
Marie Galante 12/22/1934
Fools Rush In 12/25/1934
Thumbs Up! 12/27/1934
O'Flynn, The 12/27/1934
Music Hath Charms 12/29/1934

1935

Casino de Paris Revue 00/00/1935
Cocktails 5 to 7 00/00/1935
Cotton Club Parade 00/00/1935
First Manhattan Music Hall Revue 00/00/1935
Hot Chocolates 00/00/1935
Paradise Parade of 1935 00/00/1935
Princess Slips Away, The 00/00/1935
Riviera Revue 00/00/1935
Ubangi Club Follies 00/00/1935
Come of Age 01/12/1935
Hollywood Holiday 02/15/1935
Stop Press 02/21/1935
Post Depression Gaieties, The 02/24/1935
Petticoat Fever 03/04/1935
Something Gay 04/29/1935
Parade 05/20/1935
Earl Carroll's Sketch Book 06/04/1935
Kingdom for a Cow, A 06/28/1935
Common Flesh 08/12/1935
Smile at Me 08/23/1935
Moon Over Mulberry Street 09/04/1935
At Home Abroad 09/19/1935
Venus in Silk 10/01/1935
Porgy and Bess 10/10/1935
Jubilee 10/12/1935
Let's Have Fun 10/22/1935
Provincetown Follies 11/03/1935
Jumbo 11/16/1935
May Wine 12/05/1935
George White's Scandals 12/25/1935
Entre-Nous 12/30/1935

1936

Earl Carroll's Palm Island Revue 00/00/1936
Hollywood Revels of 1936 00/00/1936
Hot Chocolates 00/00/1936
Palladium Frolics 00/00/1936
Paradise Parade 00/00/1936
Perfect 00/00/1936
Radio City Music Hall production 00/00/1936
Illustrators' Show, The 01/22/1936
Lady Precious Stream 01/27/1936
Ziegfeld Follies of 1936 01/30/1936
Murder in the Old Red Barn 02/01/1936
Follow the Sun 02/04/1936
On Your Toes 04/11/1936
Follow the Parade 04/12/1936
Broadway Sho-Window 04/12/1936
Summer Wives 04/13/1936
Lambs Spring Gambol, The 04/25/1936
Waltz Was Born in Vienna 04/25/1936
Private Affair, A 05/14/1936
New Faces of 1936 05/19/1936
Billy Rose's Show of Shows 06/08/1936
Casa Manana 06/08/1936
Last Frontier, The 06/08/1936
Blackbirds of 1936 07/09/1936
Careless Rapture 09/11/1936
Cotton Club Parade 09/24/1936
White Horse Inn 10/01/1936
Red, Hot and Blue! 10/29/1936
Forbidden Melody 11/02/1936
Johnny Johnson 11/19/1936
Family Album 11/24/1936
Red Peppers 11/24/1936
Shadow Play 11/24/1936
O Mistress Mine 12/03/1936
Lambs Winter Gambol, The 12/05/1936
One April Day 12/05/1936
Oh Say Can You Sing 12/11/1936

Black Rhythm 12/19/1936
We Were Dancing 12/24/1936
Show Is On, The 12/25/1936
Dancing Coed, The 12/29/1936

1937

Calling All Men 00/00/1937
Cotton Club Express 00/00/1937
Cotton Club Parade 00/00/1937
Cotton Club Revue, The 00/00/1937
Grand Terrace Revue, The 00/00/1937
Greek to You 00/00/1937
Hollywood Revels of 1937 00/00/1937
Pan-American Casino Revue 00/00/1937
Riviera Follies of 1937 00/00/1937
Pepper Mill 01/05/1937
Eternal Road, The 01/07/1937
Cocktail Bar 01/13/1937
Naughty-Naught '00 01/23/1937
Frederika 02/04/1937
Babes in Arms 04/14/1937
Orchids Preferred 05/11/1937
Sea Legs 05/18/1937
Salute to Spring 07/12/1937
Swing It 07/22/1937
Harlem Uproar House 09/00/1937
Virginia 09/02/1937
Hero Is Born, A 10/01/1937
Fireman's Flame, The 10/09/1937
Bric-a-Brac 10/20/1937
I'd Rather Be Right 11/02/1937
Julius Caesar 11/11/1937
Pins and Needles 11/27/1937
Hooray for What! 12/01/1937
Between the Devil 12/23/1937
Three Waltzes 12/25/1937

1938

Davy Crockett 00/00/1938
Grand Terrace Revue, The 00/00/1938
Hollywood Revue Production 00/00/1938
Paradise Restaurant and Revue 00/00/1938
So Proudly We Hail 00/00/1938
Cradle Will Rock, The 01/03/1938
Right This Way 01/04/1938
Let's Play Fair 01/18/1938
Who's Who 03/01/1938
Cotton Club Parade 03/09/1938
Happy Returns 04/19/1938
I Married an Angel 05/11/1938
Two Bouquets, The 05/31/1938
Gentlemen Unafraid 06/03/1938
Sun Never Sets, The 06/09/1938
Come Across 09/14/1938
You Never Know 09/21/1938
Hellzapoppin 09/22/1938
Sing Out the News 09/24/1938
Cotton Club Parade 09/28/1938
Knights of Song 10/17/1938
Knickerbocker Holiday 10/19/1938
Girl from Wyoming, The 10/29/1938
Danton's Death 11/02/1938
Leave It to Me! 11/09/1938
Boys from Syracuse, The 11/23/1938
Great Lady 12/01/1938
Lambs Annual Gambol, The 12/03/1938
Pinocchio 12/23/1938
Policy Kings, The 12/30/1938

1939

Aquacade Revue 00/00/1939
Big Show 00/00/1939
Fair Enough 00/00/1939
Hello Beautiful 00/00/1939
New York World's Fair 00/00/1939
Peter Penny Under the Dream Tree 00/00/1939
Turn of the Century, The 00/00/1939
White Flame, The 00/00/1939
Mamba's Daughters 01/03/1939
Set to Music 01/18/1939
American Way, The 01/21/1939
Jeremiah 02/03/1939
One for the Money 02/04/1939
Stars in Your Eyes 02/09/1939
Blackbirds of 1939 02/11/1939
Little Foxes, The 02/15/1939
Swing Mikado, The 03/01/1939
Dancing Years 03/23/1939
Hot Mikado, The 03/23/1939
Cotton Club Parade (World's Fair Edition) 03/24/1939
Big Show, The (1) 04/09/1939
Sing for Your Supper 04/24/1939
Railroads on Parade 04/30/1939
Streets of Paris, The 06/19/1939
From Vienna 06/20/1939
Yokel Boy 07/06/1939
Sticks and Stones 08/14/1939
George White's Scandals 08/28/1939
Nice Goin' 09/00/1939
Straw Hat Revue, The 09/29/1939
Man Who Came to Dinner, The 10/16/1939
Too Many Girls 10/18/1939
Cotton Club Parade 11/01/1939
Very Warm for May 11/17/1939
Swingin' the Dream 11/29/1939
Du Barry Was a Lady 12/06/1939
All Clear 12/20/1939
White Plume, The 12/26/1939
Two for Tonight 12/28/1939

1940

At Your Service 00/00/1940
Billy Rose's Aquacade Revue 00/00/1940
Cotton Club Parade 00/00/1940
Georgia 00/00/1940
Ice Follies of 1941 00/00/1940
Let's Go 00/00/1940
New Aquacade Revue, The 00/00/1940
Nights of Gladness 00/00/1940
Organizer, The 00/00/1940
Royal Palm Revue (Fifth Edition) 00/00/1940
John Henry 01/10/1940
Earl Carroll's Vanities of 1940 01/13/1940
Two on an Island 01/25/1940
Two for the Show 02/08/1940
Reunion in New York 02/21/1940
Higher and Higher 04/04/1940
Up and Doing 04/17/1940
American Jubilee 05/12/1940
Keep Off the Grass 05/23/1940
Louisiana Purchase 05/28/1940
Walk with Music 06/04/1940
Merry Wives Swing It!, The 06/14/1940
Two Weeks with Pay 06/24/1940
Little Dog Laughed, The 08/13/1940
Hold on To Your Hats 09/11/1940
Boys and Girls Together 10/01/1940
Cabin in the Sky 10/25/1940
'Tis of Thee 10/26/1940
Panama Hattie 10/30/1940
Thank You, Columbus! 11/15/1940
High As a Kite 11/25/1940
Hi Ya, Gentlemen 11/29/1940
Pal Joey 12/25/1940
Meet the People 12/25/1940
All in Fun 12/27/1940
She Had to Say Yes 12/30/1940

1941

We Did It Before 00/00/1941
Beachcomber Nites Revue 00/00/1941
Florentine Garden Revue 00/00/1941
Hulbert's Follies 00/00/1941
Ice-Capades of 1941 00/00/1941
Joys of Youth 00/00/1941
Silver Screen, The 00/00/1941
Tan Manhattan 00/00/1941
Ubangi Club Follies 00/00/1941
No for an Answer 01/05/1941
Night of Love, A 01/07/1941
Crazy with the Heat 01/14/1941
Rhapsody in Black (1941) 01/20/1941
Lady in the Dark 01/23/1941
Hot from Harlem 05/13/1941
Turnabout! Revues 07/00/1941
Jump for Joy 07/10/1941
It Happens on Ice 07/15/1941
Marinka 07/18/1941
Fun for the Money 08/00/1941
Best Foot Forward 10/01/1941
Fun to Be Free 10/05/1941
Viva O'Brien 10/09/1941
Let's Face It! 10/29/1941
High Kickers 10/31/1941
It Happens on Ice 11/09/1941
They Can't Get You Down 12/00/1941
Sons o' Fun 12/01/1941
Sunny River 12/04/1941
Lambs Annual Dinner, Gambol and Ball, The 12/06/1941
Here We Are Again 12/06/1941
Banjo Eyes 12/25/1941

1942

Blackouts of 1942 00/00/1942
Dreamy Kid, The 00/00/1942
Ice Follies of 1942 00/00/1942
Symphony in Brown 00/00/1942
Lady Comes Across, The 01/09/1942
Of V We Sing 02/11/1942
Priorities of 1942 03/12/1942
It's About Time (1942) 03/28/1942
By Jupiter 06/03/1942
Star and Garter 06/24/1942
Stars on Ice 07/02/1942
This Is the Army 07/04/1942
Heels Together 09/15/1942
New Priorities of 1943 09/15/1942
Let Freedom Sing 10/05/1942
Count Me In 10/08/1942
Life of the Party 10/08/1942
Oy Is Das a Leben! 10/12/1942
Beat the Band 10/14/1942
Copacabana Revue 10/17/1942
Rosalinda 10/28/1942
High and Dry 12/05/1942
At Ease 12/11/1942
New Faces of 1943 12/22/1942
Full Speed Ahead 12/25/1942
You'll See Stars 12/29/1942

1943

At Your Service 00/00/1943
Born Happy 00/00/1943
Dancing in the Streets 00/00/1943
Ice-Capades of 1943 00/00/1943
Lunchtime Follies 00/00/1943
Miss Underground 00/00/1943
Nutcracker Jive 00/00/1943
Something for the Boys 01/07/1943

Marching with Johnny 01/22/1943
Copacabana Revue 03/10/1943
Oklahoma! 03/31/1943
Ziegfeld Follies of 1943 04/01/1943
Copacabana Revue 06/02/1943
Early to Bed 06/17/1943
Stars and Gripes 07/13/1943
My Dear Public 09/09/1943
Bright Lights of 1944 09/16/1943
Hairpin Harmony 10/01/1943
One Touch of Venus 10/07/1943
Artists and Models 11/05/1943
What's Up? 11/11/1943
Winged Victory 11/20/1943
Carmen Jones 12/02/1943

1944

Broadway Rhythm 00/00/1944
Copacabana Revue 00/00/1944
Glad to See You 00/00/1944
Ice Follies of 1944 00/00/1944
PFC Mary Brown 00/00/1944
Stovepipe Hat 00/00/1944
Viva Amigos 00/00/1944
WAC Musical 00/00/1944
Marianne 01/10/1944
Jackpot 01/13/1944
Skirts 01/25/1944
Vincent Youmans' Ballet Revue 01/27/1944
Mexican Hayride 01/28/1944
Follow the Girls 04/08/1944
Allah Be Praised! 04/20/1944
Helen Goes to Troy 04/24/1944
Tars and Spars 05/05/1944
Dream with Music 05/18/1944
About Face! 05/26/1944
Take a Bow 06/15/1944
Hats Off to Ice 06/22/1944
Hi, Yank! 08/07/1944
Song of Norway 08/21/1944
Copacabana Revue 09/20/1944
Bloomer Girl 10/05/1944
Sadie Thompson 11/16/1944
Rhapsody 11/22/1944
Seven Lively Arts 12/07/1944
Spook Scandals 12/08/1944
Laffing Room Only 12/23/1944
Sing Out, Sweet Land! 12/27/1944
On the Town 12/28/1944

1945

OK, USA! 00/00/1945
Ulysses Africanus 00/00/1945
Lady Says Yes, A 01/10/1945
Up in Central Park 01/27/1945
Overtons, The 02/06/1945
Firebrand of Florence, The 03/22/1945
It's Up to You 03/31/1945
Watch Out Angel 04/03/1945
Carousel 04/19/1945
Blue Holiday 05/21/1945
Memphis Bound! 05/24/1945
Hollywood Pinafore (Or the Lad Who Loved a Salary) 05/31/1945
Mr. Strauss Goes to Boston 09/06/1945
Carib Song 09/27/1945
Spring in Brazil 10/01/1945
Polonaise 10/06/1945
Girl from Nantucket, The 11/08/1945
Passing Show of 1945, The 11/09/1945
Are You With It? 11/10/1945
Day Before Spring, The 11/22/1945
Gift for the Bride, A 12/01/1945
Billion Dollar Baby 12/21/1945
Tonight's the Night 12/24/1945

1946

Beachcomber Club Revue of 1946 00/00/1946
Copacabana Show in Miami 00/00/1946
Holiday on Ice 00/00/1946
Night at the Copa, A 00/00/1946
Nellie Bly 01/21/1946
Lute Song 02/06/1946
Duchess Misbehaves, The 02/13/1946
Three to Make Ready 03/07/1946
Love in the Snow 03/15/1946
St. Louis Woman 03/30/1946
Shootin' Star 04/04/1946
Windy City 04/18/1946
Call Me Mister 04/18/1946
Annie Get Your Gun 05/16/1946
Around the World in Eighty Days 05/31/1946
Icetime 06/20/1946
Two Hearts in Three-Quarter Time 07/08/1946
Yours Is My Heart 09/05/1946
Flag Is Born, A 09/05/1946
Gypsy Lady 09/17/1946
Sweet Bye and Bye 10/10/1946
Happy Birthday 10/31/1946
Park Avenue 11/04/1946
Chris Crosses 11/22/1946
If the Shoe Fits 12/05/1946
Friars Frolic in honor of Ted Lewis 12/15/1946
Pacific 1860 12/19/1946
In Gay New Orleans 12/25/1946
Lovely Me 12/25/1946
Toplitzky of Notre Dame 12/26/1946
Beggar's Holiday 12/26/1946
Affairs of Vanity Fair 00/00/1947

1947

Kitchen Opera 00/00/1947
Meet Miss April 00/00/1947
Meet Miss Jones 00/00/1947
Lady Passing Fair, A 01/03/1947
Street Scene 01/09/1947
Finian's Rainbow 01/10/1947
Washington Square 01/23/1947
Brigadoon 03/13/1947
Barefoot Boy with Cheek 04/03/1947
Our Lan' 04/18/1947
Bless the Bride 04/26/1947
Icetime of 1947-48 05/28/1947
Reluctant Lady 07/00/1947
Shape of Things, The 07/26/1947
Music in My Heart 10/02/1947
Under the Counter 10/03/1947
High Button Shoes 10/09/1947
Allegro 10/10/1947
Here's the Pitch 12/09/1947
Angel in the Wings 12/11/1947
Bonanza Bound 12/26/1947

1948

Big As Life 00/00/1948
Counter Melody 00/00/1948
New Faces of 1948 00/00/1948
Phinney's Rainbow 00/00/1948
Stars on My Shoulders 00/00/1948
Make Mine Manhattan 01/15/1948
Look Ma, I'm Dancin'! 01/29/1948
Copacabana Revue 04/14/1948
Inside U.S.A. 04/30/1948
Hold It! 05/05/1948
Ballet Ballads 05/09/1948
Sleepy Hollow 06/03/1948
Howdy Mr. Ice! 06/24/1948
Hand in Hand 07/06/1948
Hilarities 09/09/1948
Small Wonder 09/15/1948
Heaven on Earth 09/16/1948
Magdalena 09/20/1948
That's the Ticket 09/27/1948
Love Life 10/07/1948
Where's Charley? 10/11/1948
My Romance 10/29/1948
As the Girls Go 11/13/1948
Lend an Ear 12/16/1948
Kiss Me, Kate 12/30/1948

1949

Patricia 00/00/1949
Tambourita 00/00/1949
Sugar Hill 00/00/1949
Flatbush Follies 00/00/1949
Friars Frolic of 1949 00/00/1949
He and She 00/00/1949
Hellzapoppin of 1949 00/00/1949
Ice Follies of 1949 00/00/1949
Lo and Behold 00/00/1949
Mooncalf 00/00/1949
Mr. Ambassador 00/00/1949
Along Fifth Avenue 01/13/1949
All for Love 01/22/1949
All That Glitters 03/19/1949
Belinda Fair 03/25/1949
Tongue in Cheek 03/28/1949
South Pacific 04/07/1949
Howdy Mr. Ice of 1950 05/26/1949
Pretty Penny 06/20/1949
Miss Liberty 07/15/1949
Touch and Go 10/13/1949
Lost in the Stars 10/30/1949
Regina 10/31/1949
A La Carte 11/16/1949
Adamant Eve 11/17/1949
Texas, Li'l Darlin' 11/25/1949
Gentlemen Prefer Blondes 12/08/1949

1950

Break It Up 00/00/1950
Fresh Airs 00/00/1950
Huckleberry Finn 00/00/1950
Ice Follies of 1950 00/00/1950
It's a Small World 00/00/1950
Nantucket 00/00/1950
Happy As Larry 01/06/1950
Copacabana Revue 01/11/1950
Down in the Valley 01/14/1950
Alive and Kicking 01/17/1950
Dance Me a Song 01/20/1950
Arms and the Girl 02/02/1950
Copacabana Revue 02/12/1950
Copacabana Revue 02/22/1950
Great to Be Alive! 03/23/1950
Peter Pan 04/24/1950
Tickets Please! 04/27/1950
Lucky Day 04/28/1950
Talent 50 04/28/1950
Copacabana Revue 05/10/1950
Liar, The 05/18/1950
Personalities, The 06/00/1950
Michael Todd's Peep Show 06/28/1950
Just Around the Corner 07/31/1950
High & Dry 09/11/1950
Little Boy Blue 09/11/1950
Pardon Our French 10/05/1950
Red, White and Blue 10/07/1950
Call Me Madam 10/12/1950
Barrier, The 11/02/1950
Guys and Dolls 11/24/1950
If You Please 11/28/1950
Bless You All 12/14/1950
I Love Lydia 12/18/1950
Out of This World 12/21/1950

1951

Adamses, The 00/00/1951
Bagel Scandals 00/00/1951
Be Yourself 00/00/1951
Lou Holtz' Merry-Go-Round 00/00/1951
My L.A. 00/00/1951
Gay's the Word 02/16/1951
Razzle Dazzle 02/19/1951
Let Me Hear the Melody 03/09/1951
It's About Time 03/14/1951
King and I, The 03/29/1951
Bagels and Yox of 1951 03/30/1951 (Bagel Scandals)
Copacabana Revue 04/04/1951
Make a Wish 04/18/1951
Tree Grows in Brooklyn, A 04/19/1951
Come Out Swinging 04/27/1951
Flahooley 05/14/1951
Courtin' Time 06/13/1951
Seventeen 06/21/1951
Two on the Aisle 07/19/1951
All About Love 10/17/1951
And So To Bed 10/17/1951
Top Banana 11/01/1951
Paint Your Wagon 11/12/1951
Month of Sundays, A 12/25/1951

1952

Ringling Brothers-Barnum and Bailey Circus 00/00/1952
Syn-cyr-ities of 1952 00/00/1952
Curtain Going Up 02/15/1952
Paris '90 03/04/1952
Three Wishes for Jamie 03/21/1952
Shuffle Along of 1952 05/08/1952
New Faces of 1952 05/16/1952
Night in Venice, A 06/00/1952
Wish You Were Here 06/25/1952
Jollyanna 08/11/1952
Baby Face O'Flynn 08/13/1952
Love from Judy 09/25/1952
Copacabana Revue 10/08/1952
Buttrio Square 10/14/1952
My Darlin' Aida 10/27/1952
Seven Year Itch, The 11/20/1952
Two's Company 12/15/1952

1953

Cockles and Champagne 00/00/1953
Great Waltz, The 00/00/1953
Ice Follies of 1954 00/00/1953
Nice to See You 00/00/1953
Ringling Brothers-Barnum and Bailey Circus 00/00/1953
Crucible, The 01/22/1953
Arthur Godfrey's TV Calendar Show 01/28/1953
Hazel Flagg 02/11/1953
Maggie 02/18/1953
Wonderful Town 02/25/1953
Copacabana Revue 04/22/1953
Can-Can 05/07/1953
Me and Juliet 05/28/1953
Stock in Trade 07/10/1953
Rip Van Winkle 07/13/1953
Hurly-Burly 08/05/1953
Great Scott 08/11/1953
Thirteen Clocks 08/17/1953
High Time 08/17/1953
Little Green Isle 08/28/1953
Wayward Way, The 09/03/1953
Carnival in Flanders 09/08/1953
Himberana 11/13/1953
Golden Fleece, The 11/18/1953
Kismet 12/03/1953
John Murray Anderson's Almanac 12/10/1953

1954

Hollywood Ice Revue, The 00/00/1954
Saturday Night 00/00/1954
That's Life 00/00/1954
What's the Rush 00/00/1954
Come On and Play 02/15/1954
Girl in Pink Tights, The 03/05/1954
Threepenny Opera, The 03/10/1954
Golden Apple, The 03/11/1954
Copacabana Revue 04/07/1954
By the Beautiful Sea 04/08/1954
Dolly 04/20/1954
Between Friends 05/01/1954
Huck Finn 05/07/1954
Happy Dollar, The 05/09/1954
Pajama Game, The 05/13/1954
Copacabana Revue 05/26/1954
Melody of Love 05/27/1954
Copacabana Revue 06/10/1954
Arabian Nights 06/25/1954
Walk Tall 07/12/1954
Up in Lights 08/01/1954
Satins and Spurs 09/12/1954
Boy Friend, The 09/30/1954
Pardon Our Antenna 10/16/1954
I Feel Wonderful 10/18/1954
Peter Pan 10/20/1954
Fanny 11/04/1954
Tempest in a Teapot 11/17/1954
Sailor's Delight 11/22/1954
Hello, Paree 11/24/1954
Sandhog 11/29/1954
Mrs. Patterson 12/01/1954
Hit the Trail 12/02/1954
Christmas Carol, A 12/23/1954
House of Flowers 12/30/1954

1955

Dilly 00/00/1955
In the Pink 00/00/1955
Irvin C. Miller's Brown Skin Models 00/00/1955
Meet the People of 1955 00/00/1955
Mighty Man Is He, A 00/00/1955
Once Over Lightly 00/00/1955
Society of Illustrators Show 1955 00/00/1955
Plain and Fancy 01/27/1955
Silk Stockings 02/24/1955
Shoestring Revue 02/28/1955
Come As You Are 03/00/1955
3 for Tonight 04/06/1955
Merry Widow, The 04/09/1955
Lighter Side, The 04/14/1955
Ankles Aweigh 04/18/1955
All in One 04/19/1955
Phoenix '55 04/23/1955
So What! 04/28/1955
Damn Yankees 05/05/1955
Seventh Heaven 05/26/1955
Chocolate Soldier, The 06/04/1955
Almost Crazy 06/20/1955
Svengali and the Blonde 07/30/1955
King and Mrs. Candle, The 08/22/1955
Catch a Star! 09/06/1955
Romance in Candlelight 09/15/1955
Our Town 09/19/1955
Heidi 10/01/1955
Reuben, Reuben 10/10/1955
No Time for Sergeants 10/20/1955
Vamp, The 11/10/1955
Lark, The 11/17/1955
Vamp Till Ready 11/22/1955
Pipe Dream 11/30/1955
Ali Baba and the Forty Thieves 12/26/1955

1956

Ah! Wilderness 00/00/1956
Last Resorts, The 00/00/1956
Four Below 03/04/1956
High Tor 03/10/1956
My Fair Lady 03/15/1956
Strip for Action 03/17/1956
Mr. Wonderful 03/22/1956
Adventures of Marco Polo, The 04/14/1956
Ziegfeld Follies of 1956 04/16/1956
Wake Up, Darling 05/02/1956
Most Happy Fella, The 05/03/1956
Cross Your Fingers 05/04/1956
Littlest Revue, The 05/22/1956
Bell for Adano, A 06/02/1956
Holiday 06/09/1956
Shangri-La 06/13/1956
New Faces of 1956 06/14/1956
By Hex 06/18/1956
World's My Oyster, The 07/31/1956
Sudden Spring, A 09/04/1956
Lord Don't Play Favorites, The 09/17/1956
Son of Four Below, The 09/27/1956
Sixth Finger in a Five Finger Glove, The 10/08/1956
Shoestring '57 11/05/1956
Everybody Loves Me 11/08/1956
Jack and the Beanstalk 11/12/1956
Li'l Abner 11/15/1956
Girls of Summer 11/19/1956
Tom Sawyer 11/21/1956
Cranks 11/26/1956
Grab Me a Gondola 11/27/1956
Bells Are Ringing 11/29/1956
Candide 12/01/1956
Happy Hunting 12/06/1956
Pleasure Dome 12/13/1956
Stingiest Man in Town, The 12/23/1956
Amazing Adele, The 12/26/1956

1957

Ali Baba and the Forty Thieves 00/00/1957
Courtship of Miles Standish, The 00/00/1957
Ice Capades 00/00/1957
Ice Follies 00/00/1957
Mistress of the Inn, The 00/00/1957
New Faces 00/00/1957
Pound in Your Pocket, A 00/00/1957
Foolin' Ourselves 01/16/1957
Something Cool 02/00/1957
Ruggles of Red Gap 02/03/1957
Ziegfeld Follies of 1957 03/01/1957
Sin of Pat Muldoon, The 03/13/1957
Cinderella 03/31/1957
Shinbone Alley 04/13/1957
Livin' the Life 04/27/1957
Belinda! 05/03/1957
Mr. Broadway 05/11/1957
New Girl in Town 05/14/1957
Simply Heavenly 05/21/1957
Be My Guest 06/00/1957
Free As Air 06/06/1957
Kaleidoscope 06/13/1957
Sticks and Stones 06/30/1957
Cotton Club Revue 07/09/1957
Mask and Gown 09/10/1957
West Side Story 09/26/1957
Italian Straw Hat, The 09/30/1957
Ziegfeld Follies 09/30/1957
Carefree Heart, The 09/30/1957
Romanoff and Juliet 10/10/1957

Take Five 10/10/1957
Pinocchio 10/13/1957
Copper and Brass 10/17/1957
Jamaica 10/31/1957
Rumple 11/06/1957
Time Remembered 11/12/1957
Pied Piper of Hamlin, The 11/26/1957
Music Man, The 12/19/1957
Junior Miss 12/20/1957

1958

Geografoof, The 00/00/1958
Happy Times 00/00/1958
Hit the Stride 00/00/1958
Sands Hotel Copa Room Show 00/00/1958
Body Beautiful, The 01/23/1958
Oh Captain! 02/04/1958
Hans Brinker or the Silver Skates 02/09/1958
Aladdin 02/21/1958
Portofino 02/21/1958
Say, Darling 04/03/1958
Tongue in Cheek 04/05/1958
Hansel and Gretel 04/27/1958
Firstborn, The 04/30/1958
Joy Ride 05/12/1958
Nightcap 05/18/1958
Midsummer Night's Dream, A 06/20/1958
At the Grand 07/07/1958
Winter's Tale, The 07/20/1958
Shoestring Revue in Fort Worth 09/00/1958
Copacabana Revue 09/17/1958
Demi-Dozen 10/11/1958
Goldilocks (1958) 10/11/1958
World of Suzie Wong, The 10/14/1958
Little Women 10/16/1958
Diversions 11/07/1958
Salad Days 11/10/1958
La Plume de Ma Tante 11/11/1958
Whoop-Up 11/22/1958
Flower Drum Song 12/01/1958
Of Mice and Men 12/04/1958
Gift of the Magi, The (1958) 12/09/1958

1959

Diamond for Carla, A 00/00/1959
Merry Christmas 00/00/1959
Timothy Gray's Taboo Revue 00/00/1959
She Shall Have Music 01/22/1959
Tall Story 01/29/1959
No Man Can Tame Me 02/01/1959
Redhead 02/05/1959
Juno 03/09/1959
First Impressions 03/19/1959
Three to Make Ready (Magic with Mary Martin) 03/29/1959
Art Carney Meets the Sorcerer's Apprentice 04/05/1959
Once Upon a Mattress 04/11/1959
Destry Rides Again 04/23/1959
Art Carney Meets Peter and the Wolf 05/03/1959
Nervous Set, The 05/12/1959
Chic 05/19/1959
Fallout 05/20/1959
Gypsy 05/21/1959
Dr. Willy Nilly 06/04/1959
Billy Barnes Revue, The 06/09/1959
Dig We Must 07/04/1959
Pieces of Eight 09/17/1959
Happy Town 10/07/1959
At the Drop of a Hat 10/08/1959
Mis-Guided Tour 10/12/1959
Pink Jungle, The 10/14/1959
Take Me Along 10/22/1959
Kosher Widow, The 10/31/1959
Girls Against the Boys, The 11/02/1959
Sound of Music, The 11/16/1959
Little Mary Sunshine 11/18/1959
Fiorello! 11/23/1959
Saratoga 12/07/1959
Once Upon a Christmas Tree 12/09/1959
Free and Easy 12/17/1959

1960

Dream Girl 00/00/1960
Four Below Strikes Back 00/00/1960
Freedomland 00/00/1960
Hail Mary 00/00/1960
Harlem Heatwave 00/00/1960
President, The 00/00/1960
Underworld 00/00/1960
Parade 01/20/1960
Do Re Mi 01/26/1960
Russell Patterson's Sketch Book 02/06/1960
Beg, Borrow or Steal 02/10/1960
Fings Ain't Wot They Used t'Be 02/11/1960
Crystal Heart, The 02/15/1960
Copacabana Revue (1960) 03/02/1960
Greenwillow 03/08/1960
Dear Liar 03/17/1960
41 in a Sack 03/25/1960
Miss Emily Adam 03/29/1960
Bye Bye Birdie 04/14/1960
From A to Z 04/20/1960
Lock Up Your Daughters 04/27/1960
Fantasticks, The 05/03/1960
Ernest in Love 05/04/1960
Christine 05/07/1960

Medium Rare 07/06/1960
Art of Living, The 07/25/1960
Here Is the News 08/15/1960
Vintage '60 09/12/1960
Dressed to the Nines 09/22/1960
Greenwich Village U.S.A. 09/28/1960
Irma La Douce 09/29/1960
Valmouth 10/06/1960
Kittiwake Island 10/12/1960
Shoemaker and the Peddler, The 10/14/1960
Tenderloin 10/17/1960
Darwin's Theories 10/18/1960
Invitation to a March 10/29/1960
Unsinkable Molly Brown, The 11/03/1960
Camelot 12/03/1960
Send Me No Flowers 12/05/1960
Wildcat 12/16/1960

1961

Magic Nutcracker, The 00/00/1961
Quillow and the Giant 00/00/1961
Show Girl 01/12/1961
Conquering Hero, The 01/16/1961
Two for Fun 02/13/1961
Tiger Rag, The 02/16/1961
Double Entry 02/20/1961
13 Daughters 03/02/1961
What a Killing 03/27/1961
Tattooed Countess, The 04/03/1961
Happiest Girl in the World, The 04/03/1961
Hobo 04/10/1961
Decameron, The 04/12/1961
Carnival! 04/13/1961
Smiling, the Boy Fell Dead 04/19/1961
Young Abe Lincoln 04/25/1961
Donnybrook! 05/18/1961
Calamity Jane 06/05/1961
Billy Barnes People, The 06/13/1961
Paradise Island 06/22/1961
Billy Barnes Party 09/00/1961
I Want You 09/14/1961
Fourth Avenue North 09/27/1961
Hi, Paisano! 09/30/1961
Sap of Life, The 10/02/1961
Sail Away 10/03/1961
Milk and Honey 10/10/1961
Kicks and Co. 10/11/1961
Seven Come Eleven 10/11/1961
Let It Ride! 10/12/1961
How to Succeed in Business Without Really Trying 10/14/1961
Do You Know the Milky Way? 10/16/1961
Feathertop 10/19/1961
Another Evening with Harry Stoones 10/21/1961
Bei Mir Bistu Schoen 10/21/1961
Kwamina 10/23/1961
O Marry Me! 10/27/1961
Kean 11/02/1961
All in Love 11/10/1961
Automobile Graveyard, The 11/13/1961
Bella 11/16/1961
Gay Life, The 11/18/1961
'Toinette (1961) 11/20/1961
Sing Muse! 12/06/1961
Signs Along the Cynic Route 12/14/1961
All Kinds of Giants 12/18/1961
Not While I'm Eating 12/19/1961
Subways Are for Sleeping 12/27/1961
Madame Aphrodite 12/29/1961

1962

Dick Van Dyke Show, The 00/00/1962
Molly Darling 00/00/1962
Mr. Magoo's Christmas Carol 00/00/1962
Fortuna 01/03/1962
Banker's Daughter, The 01/22/1962
Family Affair, A 01/27/1962
New Faces of 1962 02/01/1962
Fly Blackbird 02/05/1962
We Take the Town 02/17/1962
All American 02/19/1962
No Strings 03/15/1962
Pilgrim's Progress 03/20/1962
I Can Get It for You Wholesale 03/22/1962
Half-Past Wednesday 04/06/1962
Difficult Woman, The 04/25/1962
Blitz! 05/08/1962
Funny Thing Happened on the Way to the Forum, A 05/08/1962
Bravo Giovanni 05/19/1962
Billy Barnes Summer Revue 05/28/1962
Cat's Pajamas, The 05/31/1962
Look at Us 06/05/1962
World of Jules Feiffer, The 07/02/1962
La Belle 08/13/1962
Sweet Miani 09/25/1962
Stop the World - I Want to Get Off 10/03/1962
Come On Strong 10/04/1962
O Say Can You See! 10/08/1962
Billy Barnes' L.A. 10/10/1962
Dime a Dozen 10/18/1962
Lady of Mexico 10/19/1962
Mr. President 10/20/1962
Beyond the Fringe 10/27/1962
Old Bucks and New Wings 11/05/1962
We're Civilized? 11/08/1962
Nowhere to Go but Up 11/10/1962
Little Me 11/17/1962
Coach with the Six Insides, The 11/26/1962
Never Too Late 11/27/1962
Big Broadcast of 1963 12/00/1962
Riverwind 12/11/1962

1963

All About Life 00/00/1963
Little Night Music, A 00/00/1963
Oliver! 01/06/1963
Establishment, The 01/23/1963
Graham Crackers 01/23/1963
Enter Laughing 03/13/1963
Tovarich 03/18/1963
To the Water Tower 04/03/1963
Sophie 04/15/1963
Hot Spot 04/19/1963
New York Coloring Book 04/22/1963
She Loves Me 04/23/1963
Utopia! 05/06/1963
Put It in Writing 05/13/1963
Beast in Me, The 05/16/1963
Tour de Four 06/18/1963
Around the World in Eighty Days 06/22/1963
Money 07/12/1963
Seven Come Eleven 08/00/1963
Zenda 08/05/1963
No Shoestrings 09/16/1963
Political Party, A 09/26/1963
Spoon River Anthology 09/29/1963
Student Gypsy or the Prince of Liederkrantz, The 09/30/1963
Here's Love 10/03/1963
Morning Sun 10/06/1963
Gentlemen Be Seated! 10/10/1963
Prince and the Pauper, The 10/12/1963
Ballad for Bimshire 10/15/1963
Jennie 10/17/1963
110 in the Shade 10/24/1963
Streets of New York, The 10/29/1963
Man in the Moon 11/22/1963
Plot Against the Chase Manhattan Bank, The 11/26/1963
Girl Who Came to Supper, The 12/08/1963
Stones of Jehoshaphat, The 12/17/1963

1964

...And In This Corner 00/00/1964
Golden Gate 00/00/1964
Ice-Travaganza 00/00/1964
Skin of Our Teeth, The 00/00/1964
Jericho-Jim Crow 01/05/1964
Pimpernel! 01/06/1964
Baker's Dozen 01/09/1964
Will the Milk Train Run Tonight? 01/09/1964
Athenian Touch, The 01/14/1964
Hello, Dolly! 01/16/1964
Rugantino 02/06/1964
Jo 02/12/1964
Foxy 02/16/1964
Amorous Flea, The 02/17/1964
Any Wednesday 02/18/1964
Sorry, Charlie, Your Time Is Up 02/24/1964
What Makes Sammy Run? 02/27/1964
Dynamite Tonight! 03/15/1964
Cindy 03/19/1964
Funny Girl 03/26/1964
Cool Off! 03/31/1964
Anyone Can Whistle 04/04/1964
High Spirits 04/07/1964
Wonderworld 04/07/1964
King of the Whole Damn World! 04/12/1964
Cafe Crown 04/17/1964
To Broadway with Love 04/21/1964
America, Be Seated! 04/22/1964
Les Poupees de Paris 04/22/1964
New York World's Fair 04/22/1964
Blues for Mr. Charlie 04/23/1964
Home Movies 05/11/1964
Billy Barnes' Hollywood 05/26/1964
Fade Out-Fade In 05/26/1964
Merry Widow, The 08/17/1964
Awf'lly Nice 09/07/1964
Maggie May 09/22/1964
Fiddler on the Roof 09/22/1964
That Hat! 09/23/1964
Game Is Up, The 09/29/1964
Bits & Pieces XIV 10/07/1964
Gogo Loves You 10/09/1964
Hang Down Your Head and Die 10/15/1964
That 5 A.M. Jazz 10/19/1964
Golden Boy 10/20/1964
Secret Life of Walter Mitty, The 10/26/1964
Ben Franklin in Paris 10/27/1964
Something More! 11/10/1964
P.S. I Love You 11/19/1964
Bajour 11/23/1964
Rudolph the Red-Nosed Reindeer 12/00/1964
I Had a Ball 12/15/1964
Babes in the Wood 12/28/1964
Oh, What a Lovely War 12/30/1964
Royal Flush 12/31/1964

1965

How Do You Do, I Love You 00/00/1965
Kelly 02/06/1965
Pleasures and Palaces 02/11/1965
Baker Street 02/16/1965
Game Is Up, The 03/11/1965
Do I Hear a Waltz? 03/18/1965
Decline and Fall of the Entire World as Seen Through the Eyes of Cole Porter, The 03/30/1965
Wet Paint 04/12/1965

Half a Sixpence 04/25/1965
Flora, the Red Menace 05/11/1965
Roar of the Greasepaint-the 05/16/1965
Smell of the Crowd, The
Game Is Up, The 06/15/1965
Mr. Woolworth Had a Notion 06/16/1965
Mardi Gras 06/26/1965
Hot September 09/14/1965
Love Is a Ball! 09/27/1965
Pickwick (1965) 10/04/1965
Generation 10/06/1965
Mackey of Appalachia 10/06/1965
Drat! The Cat! 10/10/1965
On a Clear Day You Can See Forever 10/17/1965
Hotel Passionato 10/22/1965
Just for Openers 11/03/1965
Great Scot! (1965) 11/10/1965
Zulu and the Zayda, The 11/10/1965
Skyscraper 11/13/1965
Man of La Mancha 11/22/1965
Dangerous Christmas of Red 11/28/1965
Riding Hood, The
Anya 11/29/1965
Yearling, The 12/10/1965
La Grosse Valise 12/14/1965
Twang! 12/20/1965
Persecution and Assassination of Jean-Paul Marat as Performed by the Inmates of the Asylum of Charenton Under the Direction of the Marquis de Sade, The 12/27/1965

1966

Ballad of Smokey the Bear 00/00/1966
Go Fly a Kite 00/00/1966
Little World, Hello! 00/00/1966
New Faces of 1966 00/00/1966
Mad Show, The 01/09/1966
Jacques Brel Is Alive and Well and Living in Paris 01/22/1966
Sweet Charity 01/29/1966
Jonah (1966) 02/15/1966
Wait a Minim! 03/07/1966
Hooray! It's a Glorious Day... and All That 03/09/1966
Pousse-Cafe (1966) 03/18/1966
It's a Bird... It's a Plane... It's Superman 03/29/1966
Alice in Wonderland or What's a Nice Kid Like You Doing in a Place Like This? 03/30/1966
Time for Singing, A 05/21/1966
Mame 05/24/1966
Below the Belt 06/21/1966
Ice Follies of 1967 09/08/1966
Olympus 7-0000 09/28/1966
My Wife and I 10/10/1966
Apple Tree, The 10/18/1966
How the Grinch Stole Christmas 10/18/1966
Mixed Doubles 10/19/1966
Autumn's Here 10/25/1966
Canterville Ghost, The 11/02/1966
Alice Through the Looking Glass 11/06/1966
Man with a Load of Mischief 11/06/1966
Evening Primrose 11/16/1966
Cabaret 11/20/1966
Walking Happy 11/26/1966
I Do! I Do! 12/05/1966
On the Flip Side 12/07/1966
Agatha Sue I Love You 12/14/1966
Breakfast at Tiffany's 12/14/1966
Joyful Noise, A 12/15/1966
Jorrocks 12/22/1966
Penny Friend, The 12/26/1966
At the Drop of Another Hat 12/27/1966

1967

Ghost Goes West, The 00/00/1967
Softly 00/00/1967
Two Much 00/00/1967
Golden Screw, The 01/27/1967
Jack and the Beanstalk 02/26/1967
Shoemaker's Holiday 03/02/1967
You're a Good Man, Charlie Brown 03/07/1967
I'm Getting Married 03/16/1967
Sherry! 03/28/1967
Hellza-poppin 04/00/1967
Illya Darling 04/11/1967
Hallelujah, Baby! 04/26/1967
Pippin, Pippin 05/01/1967
Dumas and Son 08/01/1967
Peg 08/01/1967
Ice Follies of 1968 09/07/1967
Now Is the Time for All Good Men 09/26/1967
Keep It in the Family 09/27/1967
Hair 10/17/1967
There's a Girl in My Soup 10/18/1967
Henry, Sweet Henry 10/23/1967
Freaking Out of Stephanie Blake, The 10/30/1967
How Do You Do, I Love You 10/31/1967
Androcles and the Lion 11/15/1967
Mata Hari 11/18/1967
Curley McDimple 11/22/1967
How Now, Dow Jones 12/07/1967
Cricket on the Hearth 12/18/1967
How to Be a Jewish Mother 12/28/1967

1968

Diamond in the Rough 00/00/1968
Exception and the Rule, The 00/00/1968
Four in Hand 00/00/1968
Instant Replay 00/00/1968
Tattered Tom 00/00/1968
Love and Let Love 01/03/1968
Have I Got One for You 01/07/1968
Your Own Thing 01/13/1968
Happy Time, The 01/19/1968
Darling of the Day 01/27/1968
Who's Who, Baby? 01/29/1968
Golden Rainbow 02/04/1968
Here's Where I Belong 03/03/1968
Photo Finish 03/08/1968
Education of H*Y*M*A*N K*A*P*L*A*N, The 04/04/1968
George M! 04/10/1968
I'm Solomon 04/23/1968
New Faces of 1968 05/02/1968
Believers, The 05/09/1968
Walk Down Mah Street! 06/12/1968
After You, Mr. Hyde 06/24/1968
In Circles 06/25/1968
Happy Hypocrite, The 09/05/1968
Month of Sundays, A 09/16/1968
Mother's Kisses, A 09/23/1968
Noel Coward's Sweet Potato 09/29/1968
Megillah of Itzak Manger, The 10/09/1968
How to Steal an Election 10/13/1968
Just for Love 10/17/1968
Her First Roman 10/20/1968
Maggie Flynn 10/23/1968
Peace 11/01/1968
Love Match 11/03/1968
Zorba 11/17/1968
Up Eden 11/27/1968
Morning 11/28/1968
Promises, Promises 12/01/1968
Jimmy Shine 12/05/1968
Fenwick 12/08/1968
Pinocchio 12/08/1968
Ballad for a Firing Squad 12/11/1968
God Is a (Guess What?) 12/17/1968
Dames at Sea 12/20/1968

1969

Eleanor 00/00/1969
Folies Bergere 00/00/1969
Goldilocks 00/00/1969
Ice Follies of 1969 00/00/1969
Mona and Lisa 00/00/1969
Senor Discretion 00/00/1969
Southpaw, The 00/00/1969
Fig Leaves Are Falling, The 01/02/1969
Horseman, Pass By 01/15/1969
Many Happy Returns 01/16/1969
Oh! Calcutta! 01/17/1969
Celebration 01/22/1969
Get Thee to Canterbury 01/25/1969
Red, White and Maddox 01/26/1969
Canterbury Tales 02/03/1969
Dear World 02/06/1969
Play It Again, Sam 02/12/1969
Come Summer 02/18/1969
Paradise Gardens East 03/10/1969
1776 03/16/1969
Billy 03/22/1969
Tom Jones 04/00/1969
Man Better Man 04/02/1969
Belle Starr 04/30/1969
We'd Rather Switch 05/02/1969
Promenade 06/04/1969
High Diplomacy 06/06/1969
Hello, Sucker 07/08/1969
Tom Piper 07/14/1969
Salvation 09/24/1969
Butterflies Are Free 10/21/1969
Jimmy 10/23/1969
1491 10/28/1969
Rondelay 11/05/1969
Buck White 12/02/1969
Littlest Angel, The 12/06/1969
Sambo 12/12/1969
La Strada 12/14/1969
Gertrude Stein's First Reader 12/15/1969
Coco 12/18/1969

1970

Carol Channing with Ten Stouthearted Men 00/00/1970
King of Schnorrers, The 00/00/1970
Lovely Ladies, Kind Gentlemen 00/00/1970
Serafina 00/00/1970
Wee Bit o' Scotch, A 00/00/1970
Unfair to Goliath 01/25/1970
Last Sweet Days of Isaac, The 01/26/1970
Joy 01/27/1970
Exchange 02/08/1970
I Dreamt I Dwelt in Bloomingdale's 02/12/1970
Gantry 02/14/1970
Georgy 02/26/1970
Billy Noname 03/02/1970
Show Me Where the Good Times Are 03/05/1970
Operation Sidewinder 03/12/1970
Purlie 03/15/1970
House of Leather, The 03/18/1970
Lyle 03/20/1970
Blood Red Roses 03/22/1970

Minnie's Boys 03/26/1970
Look to the Lilies 03/29/1970
Applause 03/30/1970
Cry for Us All 04/08/1970
It's About Time 04/18/1970
Park 04/22/1970
Mod Donna 04/24/1970
Company 04/26/1970
Colette 05/06/1970
Whispers on the Wind 06/03/1970
Hatfields & McCoys 06/20/1970
Rothschilds, The 10/19/1970
Sensations 10/25/1970
President's Daughter, The 11/03/1970
Touch 11/08/1970
Two by Two 11/10/1970
Santa Claus Is Comin' to Town 12/13/1970
Isabel's a Jezebel 12/15/1970
Lovely Ladies, Kind Gentlemen 12/28/1970

1971

Ice Follies of 1971 00/00/1971
King of the Schnorrers, The 00/00/1971
Night the Animals Talked, The 00/00/1971
Victory Canteen 00/00/1971
W.C. 00/00/1971
When Do the Words Come True 00/00/1971
Stag Movie 01/03/1971
Soon 01/12/1971
Ari 01/15/1971
Prettybelle 02/01/1971
Who's Whom? 02/04/1971
House of Blue Leaves 02/10/1971
Lolita, My Love 02/15/1971
Look Where I'm At! 03/05/1971
Blood 03/07/1971
Day in the Life of Just About Everyone, A 03/09/1971
Follies 04/04/1971
Six 04/12/1971
70, Girls, 70 04/15/1971
Kiss Now 04/20/1971
Frank Merriwell, or Honor Challenged 04/24/1971
Ballad of Johnny Pot, The 04/26/1971
Children's Crusade, The 04/29/1971
Cyrano 05/02/1971
Earl of Ruston 05/05/1971
Godspell 05/17/1971
Me Nobody Knows, The 05/18/1971
Two If by Sea!? 06/18/1971
Two Gentlemen of Verona 07/27/1971
Leaves of Grass 09/12/1971
Jesus Christ Superstar 10/12/1971
Drat! 10/18/1971
Ain't Supposed to Die a Natural Death 10/20/1971
To Live Another Summer/ To Pass Another Winter 10/21/1971
F. Jasmine Addams 10/27/1971
Grass Harp, The 11/02/1971
Love Me, Love My Children 11/03/1971
Sticks and Bones 11/07/1971
Twigs 11/14/1971
Wild and Wonderful 12/07/1971
Wedding of Iphigenia, The 12/16/1971
Inner City 12/19/1971
Anne of Green Gables 12/21/1971

1972

Ice Follies of 1972 00/00/1972
Let's Celebrate 00/00/1972
Carmilla 01/16/1972
Wanted 01/19/1972
I'm a Fan 01/25/1972
Grease 02/14/1972
Dandelion Wine 03/10/1972
Selling of the President, The 03/22/1972
Londoners, The 03/27/1972
Sugar 04/09/1972
Don't Bother Me, I Can't Cope 04/19/1972
Clownaround 04/27/1972
Different Times 05/01/1972
God Bless Coney 05/03/1972
Hard Job Being God 05/15/1972
Don't Play Us Cheap! 05/16/1972
Heathen! 05/21/1972
Hark! 05/22/1972
Buy Bonds, Buster 06/04/1972
They Don't Make 'Em Like That Anymore 06/06/1972
Sunshine Train, The 06/15/1972
Joan 06/19/1972
Mass 06/28/1972
Safari 300 07/12/1972
Speed Gets the Poppys 07/25/1972
Much Ado About Nothing 08/19/1972
Song for Cyrano, A 09/04/1972
Crazy Now 09/10/1972
Halloween 09/20/1972
Life of a Man, The 10/00/1972
Berlin to Broadway with Kurt Weill 10/01/1972
Lady Audley's Secret 10/03/1972
Oh Coward! 10/04/1972
Costa Packet 10/05/1972
Dude (The Highway Life) 10/09/1972
Rebbitzen from Israel, The 10/10/1972
Hurry, Harry 10/12/1972
Mother Earth 10/19/1972
Yoshe Kalb 10/22/1972

Pippin 10/23/1972
Winnie the Pooh 10/29/1972
Comedy 11/06/1972
I and Albert 11/06/1972
Quarter for the Ladies Room, A 11/12/1972
Lysistrata 11/13/1972
Twanger 11/15/1972
Dear Oscar 11/16/1972
Ambassador 11/19/1972
Doctor Selavy's Magic Theatre 11/23/1972
Contrast, The 11/27/1972
Via Galactica 11/28/1972
Bar That Never Closes, The 12/03/1972
Please Don't Cry and Say No 12/06/1972
Rainbow 12/18/1972
Trials of Oz, The 12/19/1972
Davy Jones' Locker 12/24/1972

1973

Caesar's Wife 00/00/1973
Clippity Clop and Clementine 00/00/1973
Ice Capades 00/00/1973
Ice Follies 00/00/1973
Stephen Foster Story, The 00/00/1973
Tricks 01/08/1973
National Lampoon's Lemmings 01/25/1973
Look at the Fifties, A 02/00/1973
Shelter 02/06/1973
Great Man's Whiskus, The 02/13/1973
El Coca-Cola Grande 02/13/1973
Little Night Music, A 02/25/1973
Dr. Jekyll and Mr. Hyde 03/07/1973
Try It, You'll Like It 03/14/1973
Karl Marx Play, The 03/16/1973
Seesaw 03/18/1973
Thoughts 03/19/1973
Smile, Smile, Smile 04/04/1973
What's a Nice Country Like You Doing in a State Like This? 04/19/1973
Hot and Cold Heros 05/09/1973
Cyrano 05/13/1973
Nash at Nine 05/17/1973
Smith 05/19/1973
Rumplestiltskin 05/23/1973
All Together Now 06/08/1973
Faggot, The 06/18/1973
Antiques 06/19/1973
Treasure Island 08/21/1973
Gone with the Wind 08/28/1973
$600 and a Mule 08/28/1973
Whistling Wizard and the Sultan of Tuffet, The 10/17/1973
Raisin 10/18/1973
Molly 11/01/1973
Gigi 11/13/1973
Good Evening 11/14/1973
Enclave, The 11/15/1973
More Than You Deserve 11/21/1973
Rachael Lily Rosenbloom and Don't You Ever Forget It 11/26/1973
Good Doctor, The 11/27/1973
Aimee 12/02/1973
Borrowers, The 12/14/1973
Pinocchio (1973) 12/15/1973

1974

Many Happy Returns 00/00/1974
Liza 01/06/1974
Let My People Come 01/08/1974
Lorelei 01/27/1974
Great MacDaddy, The 02/12/1974
Rainbow Jones 02/13/1974
Fashion 02/18/1974
Sextet 03/03/1974
Over Here! 03/06/1974
Free to Be - You and Me 03/11/1974
Future, The 03/22/1974
Brainchild 03/25/1974
Pop 04/03/1974
Music! Music! 04/11/1974
Ride the Winds 04/16/1974
Words and Music 04/16/1974
Jumpers 04/22/1974
Ionescopade 04/25/1974
Kaboom! 05/01/1974
Funeral March for a One Man Band 05/04/1974
Frogs, The 05/20/1974
Magic Show, The 05/28/1974
Nobody's Perfect 06/00/1974
Laugh a Little, Cry a Little 06/06/1974
Good Companions, The 07/11/1974
Sheba 07/24/1974
Mack and Mabel 10/06/1974
Miss Moffat 10/07/1974
For the Love of Suzanne 10/29/1974
In Gay Company 10/29/1974
I'll Die If I Can't Live Forever 10/31/1974
Love for Love 11/11/1974
Street Jesus 11/16/1974
How to Get Rid of It 11/17/1974
Sgt. Pepper's Lonely Hearts Club Band on the Road 11/17/1974
Prodigal Sister, The 11/25/1974
Up in the Air, Boys 11/29/1974
Peter and the Wolf 12/06/1974
Portfolio Revue 12/06/1974
'Twas the Night Before Christmas 12/08/1974

Pretzels 12/16/1974
Hans Andersen 12/17/1974
Big Winner, The 12/20/1974

1975

Gambler's Paradise 00/00/1975
Happy Birthday 00/00/1975
Truth About Cinderella, The 00/00/1975
Gabrielle 01/00/1975
Philemon 01/03/1975
Wiz, The 01/05/1975
Shenandoah 01/07/1975
Downriver 01/10/1975
Diamond Studs 01/14/1975
Dance with Me 01/23/1975
Lovers 01/27/1975
Man on the Moon 01/29/1975
Alice in Wonderland 02/19/1975
Straws in the Wind 02/21/1975
Night That Made America Famous, The 02/26/1975
Bone Room, The 02/28/1975
Goodtime Charley 03/03/1975
Lieutenant, The 03/09/1975
Rocky Horror Show, The 03/10/1975
Ape Over Broadway 03/12/1975
Wings 03/16/1975
Doctor Jazz 03/19/1975
Be Kind to People Week 03/23/1975
Rainbow Rape Trick, The 04/13/1975
Matter of Time, A 04/27/1975
Glorious Age, The 05/11/1975
Rodgers and Hart 05/13/1975
Flatbush Tosca 05/22/1975
Journey of Snow White, The 05/29/1975
Chicago 06/01/1975
Cowboy 08/19/1975
Truckload 09/06/1975
Boy Meets Boy 09/17/1975
Captain Jinks of the Horse Marines 09/20/1975
Why I Love New York 10/10/1975
5th Season, The 10/12/1975
Chorus Line, A 10/19/1975
Treemonisha 10/21/1975
Me and Bessie 10/22/1975
Musical Jubilee, A 11/13/1975
Mass Murder in the Balcony of the Old Ritz-Rialto, A 11/14/1975
By Bernstein 11/23/1975
Boccaccio 11/24/1975
Christmas Rappings 12/00/1975
Rudolph and Frosty 12/00/1975
Rudolph's Shiny New Year 12/00/1975
Tiny Tree, The 12/00/1975
Gift of the Magi 12/01/1975
Tuscaloosa's Calling Me... But I'm Not Going! 12/01/1975
Tom Eyen's Dirtiest Musical 12/09/1975
Royal Family, The 12/30/1975

1976

Bojangles 00/00/1976
It's a Brand New World 00/00/1976
Tom Jones 00/00/1976
Home Sweet Homer 01/04/1976
Pacific Overtures 01/17/1976
Fire of Flowers 01/29/1976
Apple Pie 02/13/1976
Rockabye Hamlet 02/17/1976
Bubbling Brown Sugar 03/02/1976
Pinocchio 03/27/1976
Dreamstuff 04/02/1976
Le Bellybutton 04/02/1976
I Knock at the Door 04/12/1976
Rex 04/25/1976
Tickles by Tucholsky 04/26/1976
So Long, 174th Street 04/27/1976
Can You Smell Gas? 04/29/1976
Camp Meeting 1840 05/00/1976
Threepenny Opera, The 05/01/1976
1600 Pennsylvania Avenue 05/04/1976
Baker's Wife, The 05/11/1976
Legend 05/13/1976
Daarlin' Juno 05/14/1976
Something's Afoot 05/27/1976
Greenwich Village Follies, The 06/10/1976
Becoming 06/15/1976
Saints 06/30/1976
Sirocco 08/13/1976
Something to Do — A Salute to the American Worker 09/00/1976
Sweet Mistress 09/08/1976
For Colored Girls Who Have Considered Suicide/When the Rainbow Is Enuf 09/15/1976
Lovesong 10/05/1976
Robber Bridegroom, The 10/09/1976
Club, The 10/14/1976
2 by 5 10/18/1976
Don't Step on My Olive Branch 11/01/1976
Hellzapoppin 11/22/1976
Peter Pan 12/12/1976
Music Is 12/20/1976
Your Arms too Short to Box with God 12/22/1976
Bride of Sirocco, The 12/31/1976

1977

Enter Juliet 00/00/1977
Saturday Night (1977) 00/00/1977

T*ts D*amond 01/00/1977
Nightclub Cantata 01/09/1977
Ichabod 01/12/1977
Ipi-Tombi 01/12/1977
Cockeyed Tiger, The 01/13/1977
North Atlantic 01/16/1977
Castaways, The 02/07/1977
Happy End 03/08/1977
Movie Buff, The 03/14/1977
For Love or Money 03/29/1977
I Love My Wife 04/17/1977
Side by Side by Sondheim 04/18/1977
Dance on a Country Grave 04/21/1977
Annie 04/21/1977
On the Lock-In 04/27/1977
New World!, A 05/09/1977
Toller Cranston's The Ice Show 05/19/1977
Up from Paradise 06/14/1977
Love! Love! Love! 06/15/1977
Starting Here, Starting Now 06/19/1977
Chapeau 07/24/1977
Red Blue-Grass Western Flyer Show, The 08/16/1977
Children of Adam 08/17/1977
Unsung Cole 09/04/1977
Nefertiti 09/20/1977
Misanthrope, The 10/04/1977
Hot Grog 10/06/1977
Housewife! Superstar!! 10/29/1977
Act, The 10/29/1977
Nightsong 11/01/1977
Radio City Music Hall 11/03/1977
Christmas 1977
Present Tense, The 11/04/1977
Green Pond 11/22/1977
Streets of Gold, The 11/25/1977
Gates of Paradise, The 11/25/1977
Nightmare!! 12/14/1977

1978

Merry Widow, The 00/00/1978
Spotlight 01/08/1978
By Strouse 02/01/1978
Ain't Misbehavin' 02/08/1978
On the Twentieth Century 02/19/1978
Barbary Coast 02/28/1978
Timbuktu! 03/01/1978
Prince of Grand Street, The 03/07/1978
Runaways 03/09/1978
In Praise of Death 03/11/1978
Last Minstrel Show, The 03/20/1978
Dancin' 03/27/1978
History of the American Film, A 03/30/1978
Best Little Whorehouse in Texas, The 04/17/1978
Bistro Car on the CNR, A 04/23/1978
5th of July 04/27/1978
Angel 05/10/1978
Rosa 05/10/1978
Reunion 05/12/1978
Working 05/14/1978
Alice 05/31/1978
Mahalia 05/31/1978
My Cup Runneth Over 06/08/1978
Piano Bar 06/08/1978
I'm Getting My Act Together and Taking It on the Road 06/14/1978
Coolest Cat in Town, The 06/22/1978
Out to Lunch 07/07/1978
Broadway, Broadway 07/31/1978
Back Country 08/15/1978
Eubie! 09/20/1978
King of Hearts 10/22/1978
Laugh a Lifetime 10/22/1978
Music-Hall Sidelights 10/26/1978
Gorey Stories 10/30/1978
Bar Mitzvah Boy 10/31/1978
Jolson 11/08/1978
Platinum 11/12/1978
Helen 11/22/1978
Lady Lily 11/28/1978
Ballroom 12/14/1978
Broadway Musical, A 12/21/1978
Wonderland in Concert 12/27/1978
Taxi Tales 12/28/1978

1979

City Junket 00/00/1979
Magnificent Christmas Spectacular, The 00/00/1979
Ms. Pres 00/00/1979
Umbrellas of Cherbourg, The 01/02/1979
Grand Tour, The 01/11/1979
My Old Friends 01/12/1979
You Bet Your Assets 01/25/1979
Storyville 01/27/1979
They're Playing Our Song 02/11/1979
Sarava 02/23/1979
Sweeney Todd, the Demon Barber of Fleet Street 03/01/1979
Joley 03/08/1979
Home Again, Home Again 03/10/1979
Spokesong, or the Common Wheel 03/15/1979
Zoot Suit 03/25/1979
Sancocho 03/28/1979
Leave It to Beaver Is Dead 03/29/1979
Carmelina 04/08/1979
Dispatches 04/19/1979
Eddie's Catchy Tunes 04/25/1979
Suddenly the Music Starts 05/03/1979
Bea's Place 05/09/1979
Utter Glory of Morrissey Hall, The 05/13/1979

Festival 05/16/1979
Strider 05/31/1979
I Remember Mama 05/31/1979
New York Summer, A 06/01/1979
Miss Truth 06/05/1979
Not Tonight, Benvenuto! 06/05/1979
Scrambled Feet 06/11/1979
Madwoman of Central Park West, The 06/13/1979
Got Tu Go Disco 06/25/1979
Sky High 06/28/1979
But Never Jam Today 07/31/1979
Gilda Radner, Live from New York 08/02/1979
Daddy Goodness 08/19/1979
Long Way to Boston, A 09/00/1979
Evita 09/25/1979
Sun Always Shines for the Cool, The 09/27/1979
King of Schnorrers 10/04/1979
All Night Strut!, The 10/04/1979
1940's Radio Hour, The 10/07/1979
Potholes 10/09/1979
Sugar Babies 10/09/1979
God Bless You, Mr. Rosewater 10/14/1979
Snow White and the Seven Dwarfs 10/18/1979
One Mo' Time 10/22/1979
Rebecca, the Rabbi's Daughter 11/04/1979
Amazing Bone, The 11/25/1979
Tom Taylor As Woody Guthrie 11/26/1979
Comin' Uptown 12/20/1979
Babes in Toyland 12/21/1979

1980

Bojangles 00/00/1980
One Night Stand 00/00/1980
Tell Me on a Sunday 01/00/1980
Watch on the Rhine 01/03/1980
Millionaire in Trouble, A 01/16/1980
Elizabeth and Essex 01/31/1980
Shakespeare's Cabaret 02/01/1980
Harold and Maude 02/07/1980
Housewives' Cantata, The 02/17/1980
Changes 02/19/1980
Censored Scenes from King Kong 03/06/1980
Haggadah, The 03/31/1980
Al Chemist Show, The 04/05/1980
Tintypes 04/17/1980
Coupla White Chicks Sitting Around Talking, A 04/20/1980
O. Henry Duet 04/21/1980
Fourtune 04/27/1980
Reggae 04/27/1980
Barnum 04/30/1980
Day in Hollywood/A Night in the Ukraine, A 05/01/1980
Happy New Year 05/10/1980
Musical Chairs 05/18/1980
It's Wilde! 05/25/1980
Billy Bishop Goes to War 05/29/1980
It's So Nice to Be Civilized 06/03/1980
Chase a Rainbow 06/12/1980
Fearless Frank 06/15/1980
Jazzbo Brown 06/24/1980
Manhattan Showboat 06/30/1980
What Ever Happened to Georgie Tapps? 08/12/1980
42nd Street 08/25/1980
April Song, An 08/25/1980
Charlie and Algernon 09/14/1980
Cowboy and the Legend, The 09/16/1980
Zapata 09/17/1980
Girls, Girls, Girls 09/25/1980
Really Rosie 09/30/1980
Matter of Opinion, A 09/30/1980
Streetsongs 10/14/1980
All That Glitters 10/28/1980
Quick Change 10/30/1980
Frimbo 11/09/1980
Philadelphia Story, The 11/14/1980
Ka-boom 11/20/1980
Perfectly Frank 11/30/1980
Trixie True Teen Detective 12/07/1980
Alice in Concert 12/09/1980
Onward Victoria 12/14/1980
Hijinks! 12/18/1980
Swing 12/25/1980

1981

Light Up the Ice 00/00/1981
Keystone 01/13/1981
Oh Me, Oh My, Oh Youmans 01/14/1981
Evening with Joan Crawford, An 01/20/1981
Ice-Capades (Light Up the Ice) 01/21/1981
Dear Desperate 01/23/1981
Real Life Funnies 02/11/1981
Apollo... It Was Just Like Magic, The 02/19/1981
In Trousers 02/22/1981
Sophisticated Ladies 03/01/1981
Bring Back Birdie 03/05/1981
America 03/06/1981
Matinee Kids, The 03/10/1981
Marry Me a Little 03/12/1981
Broadway Follies 03/15/1981
Tinseltown 03/20/1981
Reel American Hero, A 03/25/1981

Woman of the Year 03/29/1981
March of the Falsettos 04/01/1981
It's Me, Sylvia 04/13/1981
Copperfield 04/13/1981
Mooney Shapiro Songbook, The 05/03/1981
Inacent Black 05/06/1981
Ah, Men 05/11/1981
I Can't Keep Running in Place 05/14/1981
Cloud Nine 05/18/1981
Heebie Jeebies 06/03/1981
El Bravo! 06/16/1981
Cleavage 06/23/1981
Fauntleroy 07/02/1981
Pump Boys and Dinettes 07/10/1981
Turn to the Right 08/08/1981
Say Hello to Harvey! 09/14/1981
Life and Adventures of Nicholas Nickleby, The 10/04/1981
Double Feature 10/08/1981
Cotton Patch Gospel 10/10/1981
Marlowe 10/12/1981
Roumanian Wedding, The 10/25/1981
Christmas Carol, A 10/30/1981
Oh, Brother! 11/10/1981
Merrily We Roll Along 11/16/1981
First, The 11/17/1981
Joseph and the Amazing Technicolor Dreamcoat 11/18/1981
Coming Attractions 11/22/1981
Tomfoolery 12/03/1981
Head Over Heels 12/05/1981
Francis 12/15/1981
Dreamgirls 12/20/1981

1982

Little Prince and the Aviator, The 00/00/1982
Movie Star 00/00/1982
Queen of Basin Street 00/00/1982
Waltz of the Stork 01/05/1982
Oh, Johnny 01/10/1982
Curse of an Aching Heart, The 01/25/1982
Lullaby and Goodnight 02/07/1982
Colette 02/09/1982
Orphan's Revenge, The 02/20/1982
Livin' Dolls 03/09/1982
Nightingale 03/12/1982
Maybe I'm Doing It Wrong 03/14/1982
Great Grandson of Jedediah Kohler, The 03/22/1982
Lola 03/24/1982
Is There Life After High School? 05/03/1982
Nine 05/09/1982
Forbidden Broadway 05/15/1982
Do Black Patent Leather Shoes Really Reflect Up? 05/27/1982
Blues in the Night 06/02/1982
Life Is Not a Doris Day Movie 06/08/1982
Herringbone 06/16/1982
Drifter, the Grifter and Heather McBride, A 06/17/1982
Play Me a Country Song 06/27/1982
Broadway Scandals of 1928 07/07/1982
Seven Brides for Seven Brothers 07/08/1982
Broken Toys 07/16/1982
Little Shop of Horrors 07/27/1982
Death of Baron Von Richthofen As Witnessed from Earth, The 07/29/1982
Charlotte Sweet 08/22/1982
Great American Backstage Musical, The 09/15/1982
Doll's Life, A 09/23/1982
Lennon 10/05/1982
Corkscrews 10/06/1982
Cats 10/07/1982
Rock and Roll! The First 5,000 Years 10/24/1982
Upstairs at O'Neal's 10/28/1982
Robert and Elizabeth 11/03/1982
Foxfire 11/11/1982
Herman Van Veen: All of Him 12/12/1982
Snoopy!!! 12/20/1982

1983

America Kicks Up Its Heels 00/00/1983
Flim-Flam 00/00/1983
One Wonderful Night 00/00/1983
Prairie 00/00/1983
Shubert Alley 00/00/1983
Shim Sham 01/03/1983
Merlin 02/13/1983
Bundle of Nerves, A 03/13/1983
It's Better with a Band 03/28/1983
From Brooks with Love 03/30/1983
Colette Collage 03/31/1983
Teaneck Tanzi: The Venus Flytrap 04/20/1983
My One and Only 05/01/1983
Dance a Little Closer 05/11/1983
On the Swing Shift 05/20/1983
Shakespeare and the Indians 05/27/1983
Taking My Turn 06/09/1983
Five-Six-Seven-Eight... Dance! 06/15/1983
Booth Is Back in Town 07/07/1983
American Passion 07/10/1983
Mrs. Farmer's Daughter 07/20/1983

When Hell Freezes Over I'll Skate 07/22/1983
Non Pasquale 08/09/1983
Chaplin 08/12/1983
Brooklyn Bridge, The 08/17/1983
Preppies 08/18/1983
La Cage Aux Folles 08/21/1983
Blue Plate Special 10/18/1983
Weekend 10/24/1983
Tallulah 10/30/1983
Sunset 11/07/1983
Amen Corner 11/10/1983
Huck and Jim on the Mississippi 11/11/1983
Jean Seberg 11/15/1983
Doonesbury 11/21/1983
Baby 12/04/1983
Marilyn: An American Fable 12/04/1983
Peg 12/14/1983
Backers' Audition, A 12/20/1983
Tap Dance Kid, The 12/21/1983
Lenny and the Heartbreakers 12/22/1983
Human Comedy, The 12/28/1983

1984

Ace of Diamonds 00/00/1984
Hollywood Hollywood! 00/00/1984
Kicks: The Showgirl Musical 00/00/1984
Phantom of the Opera, The 00/00/1984
Portrait of Jennie 00/00/1984
Scandal 00/00/1984
A...My Name Is Alice 02/24/1984
Hey, Ma...Kaye Ballard 02/27/1984
Rink, The 03/09/1984
Peg 04/12/1984
Love 04/15/1984
Shirley MacLaine on Broadway 04/19/1984
Sunday in the Park with George 05/02/1984
End of the World 05/06/1984
Seduction of a Lady, The 05/11/1984
Blanco 05/11/1984
Dragons 05/12/1984
Nite Club Confidential 05/14/1984
Gotta Getaway! 06/16/1984
Shades of Harlem 08/21/1984
Quilters 09/25/1984
Rap Master Ronnie 10/03/1984
Kuni-Leml 10/09/1984
Mrs. McThing 10/12/1984
Feathertop 10/17/1984
Blockheads 10/17/1984
Ballad of Soapy Smith, The 11/12/1984
Haarlem Nocturne 11/18/1984
La Boheme 11/29/1984
Broadway Baby, A 12/04/1984
Diamonds 12/16/1984
Ann Reinking...Music Moves Me 12/23/1984
Everybody Out the Castle Is Sinking 12/26/1984

1985

13 Days to Broadway 00/00/1985
My Man Godfrey 00/00/1985
Princess Jimmy 00/00/1985
Sherlock Holmes and the Case of the Missing Santa Claus 00/00/1985
Smile 00/00/1985
Hang on to the Good Times 01/22/1985
Streetheat 01/27/1985
Harrigan 'n Hart 01/31/1985
3 Guys Naked from the Waist Down 02/05/1985
America's Sweetheart 03/08/1985
Sing, Mahalia, Sing 03/26/1985
Leader of the Pack 04/08/1985
Hannah Senesh 04/10/1985
Grind 04/16/1985
Normal Heart, The 04/21/1985
Dream Team, The 04/23/1985
Lies and Legends: The Musical Stories of Harry Chapin 04/24/1985
Big River: The Adventures of Huckleberry Finn 04/25/1985
Mayor 05/13/1985
Ladies and Gentlemen, Jerome Kern 06/10/1985
Singin' in the Rain 07/02/1985
Options 07/11/1985
Hit Parade, The 07/12/1985
Georgia Avenue 07/30/1985
Game of Love, The 09/00/1985
Roller Derby! The Musical 09/11/1985
Windy City 09/18/1985
Song & Dance 09/18/1985
Mowgli 09/26/1985
Paradise! 09/28/1985
Yours, Anne 10/13/1985
Dori 10/17/1985
Tatterdemalion 10/27/1985
News, The 11/07/1985
Hamelin: A Musical Tale from Rats to Riches 11/10/1985
Golden Land, The 11/11/1985
Magnificent Christmas Spectacular, The 11/15/1985
Personals 11/24/1985
Pieces of Eight 11/27/1985
My Three Angels 12/02/1985
Mystery of Edwin Drood, The 12/02/1985
Just So 12/03/1985
Copacabana 12/03/1985
Lie of the Mind, A 12/05/1985
Hay Fever 12/12/1985

Nunsense 12/12/1985
To Whom It May Concern 12/16/1985
Jonin' 12/17/1985
Jerry's Girls 12/18/1985
Wind in the Willows 12/19/1985

1986

Little Rascals, The 00/00/1986
Sweet Will 01/05/1986
Jerome Kern Goes to Hollywood 01/23/1986
Uptown...It's Hot! 01/29/1986
Halala! 03/09/1986
Williams & Walker 03/09/1986
Beehive 03/30/1986
Big Deal 04/10/1986
Goblin Market 04/13/1986
Phantom of the Opera, The 04/19/1986
National Lampoon's Class of '86 05/22/1986
Professionally Speaking 05/22/1986
Tropicana 05/29/1986
Olympus on My Mind 07/15/1986
Honky Tonk Nights 08/07/1986
Me and My Girl 08/10/1986
Eleanor (Don't Frighten the Horses!) 08/15/1986
Rags 08/21/1986
Angry Housewives 09/07/1986
Brownstone 10/08/1986
Queenie Pie 10/09/1986
Jokers 10/14/1986
Raggedy Ann 10/16/1986
Into the Light 10/22/1986
Little Like Magic, A 10/26/1986
Have I Got a Girl for You 10/29/1986
Transposed Heads, The 10/31/1986
L'Chaim to Life 11/05/1986
Womb, The 11/22/1986
House in the Woods, A 12/09/1986
Sex Tips for Modern Girls 12/19/1986

1987

Abyssinia 00/00/1987
Foggy Day, A 00/00/1987
Graduate, The 00/00/1987
Hagar the Horrible 00/00/1987
Lone Star, The 00/00/1987
Lyle 00/00/1987
Smile 01/03/1987
Rise of David Levinsky, The 01/12/1987
Stardust 02/19/1987
Knife, The 03/10/1987
Les Miserables 03/12/1987
Starlight Express 03/17/1987
Staggerlee 03/18/1987
Standup Shakespeare 04/04/1987
Asinamali! (We Have No Money) 04/23/1987
Kaleidoscope 05/12/1987
Three Postcards 05/14/1987
Satchmo: America's Musical Legend 07/14/1987
Psycho Beach Party 07/20/1987
Grover's Corners 07/29/1987
Moms 08/04/1987
Little Ham 08/31/1987
Sayonara 09/16/1987
Apprenticeship of Duddy Kravitz 09/30/1987
Roza 10/01/1987
Bittersuite 10/05/1987
Little Rascals, The 10/07/1987
Butterfly 10/10/1987
Late Nite Comic 10/15/1987
Birds of Paradise 10/26/1987
Don't Get God Started 10/29/1987
Sing Hallelujah! 11/03/1987
Into the Woods 11/05/1987
Oil City Symphony 11/05/1987
Teddy & Alice 11/12/1987
Fat Pig 11/20/1987
No-Frills Revue, The 11/25/1987
Mademoiselle Colombe 12/09/1987

1988

80 Days 00/00/1988
Elmer Gantry 00/00/1988
Chosen, The 01/06/1988
River, The 01/13/1988
Phantom of the Opera, The 01/26/1988
Sarafina! 01/28/1988
Serious Money 02/09/1988
Last Musical Comedy, The 02/12/1988
Gospel at Colonus, The 03/24/1988
Ten Percent Revue 04/13/1988
Mail 04/14/1988
Lucky Stiff 04/25/1988
Chess 04/28/1988
Romance, Romance 05/01/1988
Carrie 05/12/1988
Kaye Ballard: Working 42nd Street at Last 05/16/1988
Wonder Years, The 05/25/1988
Urban Blight 06/19/1988
Suds 09/25/1988
Hired Man, The 11/10/1988
Middle of Nowhere, The 11/20/1988
Majestic Kid, The 12/01/1988
Sweethearts 12/07/1988
Legs Diamond 12/26/1988

1989

Nimrod and the Tower of Babel 00/00/1989
Senator Joe 01/05/1989
Songs of Paradise 01/23/1989
Ziegfeld Girl, The 01/23/1989
Black and Blue 01/26/1989
Moon Over Miami 02/14/1989
Jerome Robbins' Broadway 02/26/1989
Together Again for the First Time 02/27/1989
Chu Chem 03/17/1989
Fame 03/25/1989
Taffetas, The 04/09/1989
Welcome to the Club 04/13/1989
Starmites 04/27/1989
Legends in Concert 05/10/1989
Blame It on the Movies! 05/16/1989
Showing Off 05/18/1989
Fine and Private Place, A 08/03/1989
Durante 08/12/1989
Privates on Parade 08/23/1989
Carnage, A Comedy 09/17/1989
Frankie 10/06/1989
Dangerous Games 10/19/1989
Angelina 10/25/1989
Rhythm Ranch 11/01/1989
Meet Me in St. Louis 11/02/1989
3 Penny Opera, The 11/05/1989
Closer Than Ever 1i/06/1989
Real Life Story of Johnny de Facto, The 11/08/1989
Prince of Central Park 11/09/1989
Grand Hotel 11/12/1989
Up Against It 12/04/1989
City of Angels 12/11/1989
Romance in Hard Times 12/28/1989

1990

Annie 2: Miss Hannigan's Revenge 01/04/1990
Junon and Avos: The Hope 01/07/1990
Forbidden Broadway 1990 01/23/1990
Spinning Tale, A 02/20/1990
Jekyll and Hyde 03/14/1990
Jonah 03/20/1990
Aspects of Love 04/08/1990
Animal Fair 04/18/1990
Truly Blessed 04/22/1990
Change in the Heir, A 04/29/1990
Smoke on the Mountain 05/12/1990
Mikado, Inc. 05/16/1990
Further Mo' 05/17/1990
Forever Plaid 05/20/1990
Jekyll and Hyde 05/25/1990
Hannah...1939 05/31/1990
Jekyll and Hyde 06/25/1990
Falsettoland 06/28/1990
Broadway Jukebox 07/19/1990
Once on This Island 10/18/1990
Pretty Faces 10/21/1990
Yiddle with a Fiddle 10/28/1990
Arthur, the Musical 11/01/1990
Buddy: The Buddy Holly Story 11/04/1990
Those Were the Days 11/07/1990
Catch Me If I Fall 11/12/1990
Shogun: The Musical 11/20/1990
Gifts of the Magi, The 12/04/1990
Township Fever 12/19/1990

1991

Phantom of the Opera, The 00/00/1991
Ziegfeld a Night at the Follies 00/00/1991
Children of Eden 01/08/1991
Assassins 01/27/1991
Unfinished Song, An 02/10/1991
Juba 02/12/1991
Mule Bone 02/14/1991
And the World Goes 'Round 03/18/1991
Murder on Broadway 03/18/1991
Svengali 04/03/1991
How It Was Done in Odessa 04/10/1991
Miss Saigon 04/11/1991
Steel 04/14/1991
Secret Garden, The 04/25/1991
Will Rogers Follies, The 05/01/1991
Pageant 05/02/1991
Hunchback of Notre Dame 05/16/1991
Charge It, Please! 05/23/1991
Song of Singapore 05/23/1991
Forbidden Broadway 1991 1/2 06/20/1991
Book of the Night 06/24/1991
Notre Dame 06/25/1991
Prom Queens Unchained 06/30/1991
Woody Guthrie's American Song 07/31/1991
Return to the Forbidden Planet 10/13/1991
Conrack 11/07/1991
Nick & Nora 12/08/1991
Finkel's Follies 12/15/1991
Cinderella 12/19/1991

1992

Just a Night Out 02/16/1992
Crazy for You 02/19/1992
Gunmetal Blues 04/04/1992
Five Guys Named Moe 04/08/1992
Groundhog 04/14/1992
Metro 04/16/1992
High Rollers Social and Pleasure Club, The 04/21/1992
Jelly's Last Jam 04/26/1992
Ruthless! 05/06/1992

Eating Raoul 05/13/1992
Anna Karenina 05/26/1992
Balancing Act 06/15/1992
Some Sweet Day 08/06/1992
Cut the Ribbons 09/20/1992
You Could Be Home Now 10/11/1992
Bubbe Meises Bubbe Stories 10/29/1992
Good Sports 11/05/1992
Happy Haunting 11/07/1992
Radio City Christmas Spectacular 11/13/1992
3 From Brooklyn 11/19/1992
Sheik of Avenue B, The 11/22/1992
Hello Muddah, Hello Fadduh 12/05/1992
My Favorite Year 12/10/1992
Madison Avenue 12/29/1992

1993

Theda Bara and the Frontier Rabbi 01/09/1993
Scapin 01/20/1993
Martin Guerre 01/22/1993
Manhattan Moves 01/24/1993
Goodbye Girl, The 03/04/1993
Wings 03/09/1993
Song of Jacob Zulu, The 03/24/1993
Back to Bacharach and David 03/25/1993
Sondheim—Putting It Together 04/01/1993
Easter Show 04/02/1993
Ain't Broadway Grand 04/18/1993
Who's Tommy, The 04/22/1993
Blood Brothers 04/25/1993
Linda 05/02/1993
Kiss of the Spider Woman 05/03/1993
Wild Men 05/06/1993
Prime Time Prophet 06/10/1993
Howard Crabtree's Whoop-Dee-Doo! 06/29/1993
Heartbeats 07/07/1993
Annie Warbucks 08/09/1993
Paper Moon 09/08/1993
Johnny Pye and the Foolkiller 10/31/1993
Cyrano the Musical 11/21/1993
First Lady Suite 12/15/1993
Red Shoes, The 12/16/1993

1994

Hello Again 01/30/1994
Smiling Through 02/02/1994
Avenue X 02/21/1994
C'mon & Hear 03/22/1994
New York Rock 03/30/1994
Spittin' Image 04/01/1994
American Enterprise 04/13/1994
Fallen Angel 04/14/1994
Beauty and the Beast 04/18/1994
Bring in the Morning 04/23/1994
Passion 05/09/1994
Best Little Whorehouse Goes Public, The 05/10/1994
Captains Courageous 05/12/1994
Shlemiel the First 05/13/1994
Hysterical Blindness 05/19/1994
Phantom of the Country Palace, The 06/22/1994
Copacabana 06/23/1994
Lunch 06/28/1994
Brimstone 06/29/1994
Truth About Ruth, The 07/00/1994
Das Barbecu 10/10/1994
Diva Is Dismissed, The 10/30/1994
Starcrossed the Trial of Galileo 11/03/1994
Sunset Boulevard 11/17/1994
Christmas Carol, A 12/01/1994
Swanson on Sunset 12/07/1994
Petrified Prince, The 12/18/1994
Comedy Tonight 12/18/1994

1995

Busker Alley 00/00/1995
Young Man, Older Woman 00/00/1995
Body Shop 00/00/1995
Cow Pattys, The 00/00/1995
Joseph and Mary 00/00/1995
Lust 00/00/1995
Paramour 00/00/1995
Radio Gals 00/00/1995
Star Wars 00/00/1995
State Fair 00/00/1995
I Sent a Letter to My Love 02/08/1995
Opal 02/18/1995
Slice of Saturday Night, A 03/00/1995
Smokey Joe's Cafe 03/02/1995
Jack's Holiday 03/05/1995
EFX 03/22/1995
Swingin' on a Star 04/05/1995
Off-Key 04/07/1995
Honky-Tonk Highway 04/27/1995
john & jen 06/01/1995
Bad Girls Upset By the Truth 06/04/1995
Hundreds of Hats 06/13/1995
Chronicle of a Death Foretold 06/15/1995
Another Midsummer Night 06/26/1995
I've Heard That Song Before 07/14/1995
Gig, The 08/10/1995
Victor/Victoria 10/25/1995